PEARCE & STEVENS'
TRUSTS AND EQUITABLE OBLIGATIONS

Pearce & Stevens' Trusts and Equitable Obligations

Sixth Edition

PROFESSOR ROBERT PEARCE, BCL, MA, Hon LLD, FRSA

Professor in Law at the University of Buckingham; Visiting Professor at the University of Gloucestershire; Emeritus Professor, University of Wales Trinity Saint David; Former Vice-Chancellor, University of Wales Lampeter

WARREN BARR, LLB, LLM (Th)

Senior Lecturer, University of Liverpool; Ex-Director & Current Member, Charity Law and Policy Unit (Liverpool Law School); Academic Lead for Student Experience (Humanities and Social Sciences); Principal Fellow of the Higher Education Academy; National Law Teacher of the Year 2006

OXFORD

UNIVERSITY PRESS

OXFORD

UNIVERSITY PRESS

Great Clarendon Street, Oxford, OX2 6DP,
United Kingdom

Oxford University Press is a department of the University of Oxford.
It furthers the University's objective of excellence in research, scholarship,
and education by publishing worldwide. Oxford is a registered trade mark of
Oxford University Press in the UK and in certain other countries

Third edition published 2002
Fourth edition published 2006
Fifth edition published 2010

Impression: 6

Published in the United States of America by Oxford University Press
198 Madison Avenue, New York, NY 10016, United States of America

British Library Cataloguing in Publication Data

Data available

Library of Congress Control Number: 2014943843

ISBN 978–0–19–964445–2

Printed and bound in Great Britain by
Bell and Bain Ltd, Glasgow

This edition is dedicated to our students, past, present, and future
for teaching us as much as we have ever taught them.

New to this edition

- Fully revised structure and content throughout, including new chapters on equitable remedies
- Expanded coverage of succession, injunctions, and privacy, including discussion of proposed reforms affecting the law in these areas
- Coverage of *Jones v Kernott* and developments relating to trusts of the family home
- Coverage of *FHR European Ventures LLP v Cedar Capital Partners LLC* and the Supreme Court's decision in relation to breach of fiduciary duties and proprietary remedies
- Updates to legislation surrounding the law of perpetuities, intestacy, trustees' powers, and charitable trusts

Preface

Like a good home, every now and then it is worth reorganizing the content of a textbook. This edition has been streamlined in the number of chapters (down two from the last edition), and has seen a growth in the number of parts (from five to seven). These changes are designed to group topics more clearly together. New chapters have been introduced on equitable remedies, and coverage now includes more on both succession and the use of injunctions and superinjunctions to enforce the emerging law of privacy. Treatment of the law of pensions has been reduced because the statutory regulation of this area of the law makes it less illustrative of general principles of equity than used to be the case.

In this digital information age, it is worth saying something that would have seemed trite to generations past. This book is designed to be read from cover to cover, and the treatment of issues is presented in a logical structure, which allows it to flow from one topic to the next. However, as a textbook it is also designed to be read in parts, so that readers can navigate through the index to a particular chapter or topic, and follow the treatment clearly and easily. The interrelationship between topics means that on occasion the reader will need to refer to more than one chapter, but those links can be followed through cross-references. For example, a reader wishing to consider the rules applicable to the creation and the operation of express trusts and powers will find that the different themes within this topic are explained in Chapter 7 of Part II Creating the Relationship and Chapter 16 of Part IV Allocation of Benefit, respectively.

So, what of the law? It was predicted in the preface to the last edition that there would 'be further turbulence in the aftermath of *Stack v Dowden*' in relation to trusts of the family home. Just a few short weeks after the fifth edition went to print, the Court of Appeal delivered what was soon to become the first Supreme Court judgment on the family home; *Jones v Kernott*. Clearing up some of the unintended confusion caused by *Stack*, this key decision, and those that have followed in its wake, move common intention constructive trusts of the family home even closer to an entirely new form of jurisprudence which gives effect to the fact that the 'family home' enjoys a particular status in people's lives which is not captured well by treating it as just another type of property. While this approach has its detractors, the law in this area may well be reaching a period where it is more settled than in the past. Time will tell, as the area remains emotive for those concerned in disputes over ownership of the home, and the impact of this new jurisprudence on claims to a share in property outside the context of the family home has yet to be fully explored.

There have been some significant changes in legislation in the time between editions. The law of perpetuities, intestacy, trustees' powers of advancement and maintenance and a consolidation of the various statutes regulating trusts for charitable purposes into one have all been enacted, and various other amendments and commencement orders have impacted on the law. The Property, Family and Trusts law team in the Law Commission is more active than ever. The Commission agreed a new Protocol in relation to their work, which seeks to make sure they are working in areas that are of concern to the government of the day, and not 'law for lawyers' sake'. While many would rightly lament the loss of the ability to clear up areas of technicality that might not inflame political fervour (the perpetuity periods themselves are doubtless a good example, work having finished on those proposals some years past), there are too many good suggestions for law reform gathering dust on the shelves for even the most fervent advocate of the old system to suggest that it worked without issue. Early successes suggest the approach is working, though the Commission still do not always get their way. Their wish for extended rights for cohabitants, especially those with children, were not accepted by the current government and do not form part of the new Inheritance and Trustees' Powers Act 2014. The 11th and 12th Programmes of law reform suggest many weighty issues are up for consideration, not least key elements of the law relating to charities.

Staying with charities, another Commission, this time the Charity Commission, is going through a challenging period. At a time of major funding cuts, the independent regulatory body is in the process of changing its approach to regulation, in the wake of perceived and actual scandals that have suggested damage may have been done to public trust and confidence in charities and their regulator. Australia, which just a few short years ago introduced a version of the Charity Commission, is now waving good-bye to it—it is hoped no similar fate awaits the Commission in England and Wales, and that the restructuring which is ongoing will silence its critics and allow it to continue as an effective check and balance on the charity sector.

The law continues to develop in other areas. The use of injunctions to protect the new right to privacy very nearly caused a constitutional crisis between Parliament and the courts, although a more measured judicial approach seems to have stilled that area of controversy. Shortly before the manuscript was finalized, the Supreme Court in *Lawrence v Fen Tigers Ltd* questioned some of the settled principles which had been used to decide when an injunction rather than damages was the most appropriate remedy for a wrong such as a nuisance caused by noise. By the court's own admission, new principles will need to be developed through future decisions. In *Marley v Rawlings*, the Supreme Court upheld the validity of a will even though the testator had erroneously signed the wrong document (by mistake, the husband and the wife signed each other's will rather than their own). The Supreme Court in *Futter v Revenue Commissioners* has confirmed the Court of Appeal's view that the circumstances in which the decisions of trustees can be set aside as improperly made are relatively limited, but has suggested a much wider jurisdiction to overturn decisions based on mistake. Litigation prompted by the global recession and the collapse of international banks has had an impact on some areas of the text, and days before the book went into its proof stage the Supreme Court delivered the landmark decision in *FHR European Ventures LLP v Cedar Capital Partners LLC* clarifying when proprietary remedies will be available for breach of fiduciary duty.

We are grateful to the members of the editorial team at Oxford University Press who have given us support and advice throughout the preparation of this latest edition. We would particularly like to thank them for their help in accommodating last minute changes to statute and case law, particularly those coming at an inconvenient stage of the production process. We are also grateful for their forbearance in dealing with the inevitable delays that bedevil the production of a new edition like this. Thanks are also due to Dr Karen Atkinson, Research Associate to the Charity Law and Policy Unit, University of Liverpool, in supporting the updating of the law in this edition. Most especially, we owe a debt of gratitude to our wives and families. For too many weekends our families have had to take solace in their own company as work on the book continued apace. John Stevens has not been involved in the production of this new edition, but the editors continue to owe him a considerable debt of gratitude.

We have attempted to state the law in this text as at 1 August 2014.

Robert Pearce
Warren Barr
August 2014

Contents

Part VI Administration of Trusts

Part VII Checks, Controls, and Remedies

List of figures

Table of statutes

Page references in **bold** indicate where a statute has been set out in part or in full

Table of cases

Glossary of common terms

Acquiescence   assent to a set of events that can be express, or inferred from the conduct of a party.

Ad valorem   proportionate to the value of the property.

Administrator   a person appointed by the court to deal with the estate of a deceased person (a female administrator is known as an 'administratrix'); an administrator can also be appointed to wind up an insolvent company.

Advancement, power of   enables the trustees to advance (make an immediate payment of) part of the capital to beneficiaries who are contingently interested in the trust fund, but who have not yet satisfied all the conditions for immediate payment.

After-acquired property   property acquired after a trust or settlement is created. To be distinguished from future property.

Agency   an arrangement where one person (the agent) acts for another (the principal), and where the acts of the agent can bind the principal.

Annuity   an annual payment made in return for the payment of a lump sum (unless the contract otherwise specifies, there is no right to the repayment of all or any part of the capital).

Assignment   where one person transfers the whole of his/her entitlement to property to another, so that he/she retains no rights in the property whatsoever.

Attorney, power of   a form of agency under which one person (the attorney) is empowered to act for another (the principal) in executing deeds or (in the case of a lasting power of attorney) making defined decisions on behalf of the principal; also the instrument conferring this authority.

Bankruptcy   a legal process started by or against an individual (a 'bankrupt') who is no longer able to meet outstanding debts owed to creditors.

Bare trust   a trust in which the trustees are only effectively nominees and must act according to the beneficiaries' instructions.

Beneficiary   a person entitled to the benefit or enjoyment of the trust property held by the trustees.

Beneficial interest   the nature of the equitable interest the beneficiary has in a trust.

Bequest   a gift of personal property made under a will.

Bona fide   in good faith.

Bona vacantia   property which vests in the Crown, because no other owner can be established.

Capacity   to be of the age of legal majority (18) and not to be suffering from a disability that prevents the person from understanding the transaction in question. Capacity is required for making binding legal arrangements such as entering into legally binding agreements or making a will. Also known as being 'sui juris' (in charge of one's own affairs).

Capital   the property (or fund) held under a trust.

Cestui que trust   a beneficiary under a trust.

Charge   a security for the payment of a debt or the fulfilment of an obligation that operates over identified property (*see* mortgage).

Charity   an organization or purpose which is recognized by law as being of such public benefit as to merit special treatment.

Chattel   an item of personal property (*see* personal property).

Chose in action   property (such as copyright or the right to payment of a debt) which has no physical existence but is enforceable through legal proceedings.

Civil partners   partners in a registered same-sex relationship, which gives similar property entitlements as conferred on married couples.

Claimant   a person initiating an action in court (formerly known as a 'plaintiff').

Cohabitant   a person living with another, in a close personal relationship, who is neither a registered civil partner nor a spouse. A cohabitant is sometimes referred to as a 'cohabitee'.

Consideration   the concept of value given in return for a promise or the transfer of property, which is a prerequisite to transform a promise into a binding contractual obligation at law. In equity, consideration has a slightly wider meaning and can include the reason why a transfer is made (such as love and affection), even if no value is provided.

Constructive trust   a trust that is implied or imposed by operation of law, in defined circumstances relating to unconscionable conduct by the parties.

Contempt of court   conduct which impedes the court process. In the context of equity, this would usually consist of a failure to follow an order of the court, which may lead to a fine or a custodial sentence.

Conveyance   the transfer and vesting of title to, or the creation of an interest in, property (usually land).

Conditional gift   a gift which is dependent on a specified event occurring or thing being done (eg, a gift to Charlie if she graduates with a degree in law).

Contingent interest   a right which is provisional because it is dependent on the happening of an event which has not yet taken place (eg, a gift to Clarissa if she survives her mother who is still alive).

Covenant   a contractual promise contained in a deed.

Debt   a sum of money due from one person (the debtor) to another (the creditor).

Deed   a specialized form of document, which must declare on its face that it is a deed and must be signed by the parties in the presence of a witness.

Dehors the will   literally, outside the will.

Devise   a gift of real property made under a will.

Determinable interest   an interest that ends on the happening of an event, although the event may never occur (eg, a gift of an annual sum to Davina until she qualifies as a solicitor).

Discretionary trust   a trust in which the trustees elect how to distribute property among a class of potential beneficiaries (the objects of the discretionary trust), as they in their discretion think fit.

Disclaimer   a refusal to accept either an office (such as the office of trustee) or a gift.

Disposition   a transfer of title to property.

Distributive power   power to allocate property either generally or to the members of a defined class (objects).

Donee   a person who receives either property or a distributive power.

Donor   a person who gives property by way of a gift or creates a distributive power in favour of the donee.

Election   a choice, eg, to rescind a contract or keep it in existence, or to choose a particular remedy.

Endowment   where property is given to provide a permanent fund or source of income.

Equitable title   title to property that is only enforceable in equity, and is vested in the beneficiaries under a trust.

Equitable interest   an interest that can only be enforced in equity.

Estate   either describes the property assets of a deceased person, or describes the ownership rights a person enjoys over land.

Executor   a person who acts as personal representative of a deceased person in carrying out the terms of a will and who was named in the will. (A person acting as a personal representative who is not named in the will is known as an administrator.)

Exemption clause   a contractual term designed to exclude or reduce the liability of one or other parties.

Express trust   a trust that is intentionally created.

Fiduciary   a person who has undertaken an obligation of loyalty to another and is compelled to put that other person's interests before his/her own (eg, director of a company is a fiduciary for the company shareholders).

Fiduciary obligations   the duties imposed by equity on a fiduciary to make sure that they act in the best interests of the person to whom they stand as a fiduciary.

Future property   rights to property that have not yet been acquired, but may be acquired in the future.

Gift   a gratuitous transfer of all title in property.

Gratuitous   without receiving a legally recognized benefit in return.

Holding trust   specific type of trust in which the trustees simply obey the orders of the principal, often used to conceal the true identity of the principal.

Implied trust   the label given to a trust that has not been formally declared by the parties, but is found to exist by the courts because the evidence indicates that the parties meant to create this kind of obligation (either through a resulting or constructive trust).

Inalienable   unable to transfer eg, inalienable property is property that may not be transferred.

Intangible   without physical form, eg, intangible property, such as shares in a company.

Inter alia   among other things.

Inter vivos   during one's lifetime.

Intestacy   the process relating to the distribution of an individual's property after death where an individual dies without leaving a will.

Insolvency   a legal process started by or against a company that is no longer able to meet outstanding debts owed to creditors.

Instrument   the legal document that creates an obligation or transfers an interest (eg, a trust instrument is the document creating a trust).

Judicial trustee   a person appointed by the court to replace a trustee or fiduciary who has acted improperly (eg, personal representatives under a will).

Knowledge   the state of mind or awareness of facts necessary to the imposition of liability.

Lease   an estate in land of limited duration (held by a tenant), which is created out of a large estate of another (the landlord).

Lien a right to claim or hold another's property as security for a debt.

Life interest an interest in property that lasts for the duration of the holder's life.

Maintenance, power of enables the trustees to apply the income generated by a trust fund for the maintenance of the beneficiaries, even where they are not as yet entitled to the capital of the fund.

Mortgage the creation of a specific form of charge (usually of land) to provide security for a loan.

Mortgagee the person or company that advances the loan, and receives the mortgage charge as security.

Mortgagor the person or company that receives the loan, and creates the mortgage charge over their property in favour of the mortgagee.

Nominee a person or company who holds the legal title to property and ostensibly the control of the property, but who must exercise it in accordance with the directions of their principal (person who appointed the nominee or persons to whom the nominees owe their duty).

Notice, doctrine of an equitable doctrine that affects the durability of equitable property rights. Notice can be either actual (being aware of rights) or constructive (the rights would have been revealed if reasonable enquiries had been made).

Objects the persons who may benefit from property on the exercise of a distributive power or discretionary trust.

Option a right to elect to create a binding contract to purchase property, when exercised.

Overreaching a process by which the asset value of beneficial interests in land

is transferred to the proceeds of sale, so that a purchaser takes free from the beneficial interests.

Pari passu a right to share in property equally and without preference.

Parol oral (eg, a parol evidence lease is one created without writing).

Personal property rights or interests relating to property other than land.

Personal rights *see* Rights in personam.

Possession, interest in an immediate entitlement to rights or income in property (compare with an interest in remainder).

Power an authority to do something (eg, allocate property to beneficiaries).

Principal person to whom obligations are owed under a relationship (eg, agency, or fiduciary).

Priority to enforce a claim to property in preference to others.

Privity a rule of common law that provides that obligations can only be enforced by and against the parties to a transaction.

Probandum something which has to be proved. The plural is probanda, so that if there are three probanda, there are three things to be proved.

Probate court authority approving a will given to an executor to begin the administration of a deceased person's estate.

Proprietary rights *see* Rights in rem.

Protective trust a specialized form of trust, which allows beneficiaries to receive income on the property, but preventing them from transferring the right to income to someone else (sometimes called a 'spendthrift trust').

Real property rights or interests relating to land.

Receiver a person appointed (usually by court order) to receive income payments from property (eg, on the bankruptcy of an individual).

Remainder, interest in an interest granted to take effect on the expiry of an interest in possession (eg, to Lucy for life, remainder to Raoul). The person entitled to a remainder is known as a remainderman.

Residuary estate the final property of a deceased person, once all debts have been paid and any specific gifts by will have been made.

Restitution the body of law designed to prevent unjust enrichment of the defendant by the claimant.

Resulting trust an implied trust in which the beneficial interest in property results (comes back) to the person who transferred the property.

Rights in personam rights that are enforceable only against the person granting them (also known as personal rights).

Rights in rem rights that are enforceable against the whole world, not just the person granting them (also known as proprietary rights).

Secret trust a specialized form of trust used to provide for someone on death, which is secret because it does not appear in the will (fully secret) or does not disclose the beneficiaries (half-secret).

Senior courts the new title of the High Court and Court of Appeal. Until the creation of the United Kingdom Supreme Court, these courts were known as the Supreme Court of Judicature.

Settlor the person who creates a trust by putting (settling) his property on trust.

Spouse a married partner.

Stranger to a trust a third party who is neither the trustee nor beneficiary under a trust, but who deals with trust property (eg, a bank facilitating the deposit of trust funds in a trust account).

Sui juris to be of full legal capacity. *See* Capacity.

Supreme Court the court which in October 2009 replaced the House of Lords as the highest court in the United Kingdom.

Testamentary property transfers on death made by will (wills are also known as testaments).

Testator a male person who executes (creates) a will (a female person is known as a 'testatrix').

Title a right to ownership of property.

Transferee person who receives a transfer of property.

Transferor person who transfers property to another.

Trust although impossible to define accurately, it describes a form of property ownership in which the control and benefit to property are separated, with legal title and control vested in trustees who are compelled by equity to exercise such control for the benefit of the beneficiaries, who hold the equitable title.

Ultra vires in excess of authority (beyond the powers of a body or person with limited authority).

Value payment, usually in money or money's worth.

Vesting the satisfaction of all the requirements necessary for a right to property to become unconditional; the completion of the transfer of property to a person, so that they can begin to enjoy the rights in that property.

Void (ab initio) of no legal effect (from the outset).

Voidable a transaction which can be set aside at the election of one party, but which is otherwise effective until set aside.

Volunteer   a person who has not given consideration for a promise to have property settled on them on trust.

Will   the instrument by which a person declares what their wishes are concerning their property after their death. The terms of the will do not take effect automatically, but have to be implemented by an executor or administrator.

The idea of 'equity' has always been particularly associated with judicial decisions, and emphasizes that cases should be decided in a way which is fair and right, so that justice is achieved between the parties. However, although the branch of English law known as 'equity' may have its origins in such concepts of fairness and justice, it carries a specific and technical meaning.

(2) **A legal definition**

Legally, the term 'equity' describes a particular body of law, consisting of rights and remedies, which evolved historically through the Courts of Chancery. Until the late nineteenth century there were two parallel systems of law operating in England, each recognizing, upholding, and applying its own distinct rights and remedies. The common law courts applied the common law and the Courts of Chancery applied equity. Although this division between courts was removed by the Judicature Acts of 1873 and 1875, those rights and remedies which are today described as 'equitable' were either originally developed by and enforced through the Chancery courts, or have evolved by extension from such rights and remedies.

2 **The origins of the equitable jurisdiction**

(1) **The common law**

(a) **History and emergence**

Prior to the Norman Conquest of 1066 there was no developed legislature or judicature operating throughout England.[3] Instead, a system of 'custom' was applied by a variety of decision-making bodies, ranging from the King's Council to village meetings. Custom inevitably varied with geographical location. However, the notion had already begun to evolve that justice was the prerogative of the Crown. This laid the jurisprudential foundation for the emergence of the common law in the twelfth century. The focus of the common law was the *Curia Regis*, the King's Court. By 1234 the two common law courts, the Court of Common Pleas and the King's Bench, had developed.

(b) **Writs, actions, and remedies**

A plaintiff (now a claimant) who wished to start an action in the Court of Common Pleas or the King's Bench needed to obtain a royal writ authorizing the commencement of proceedings. These writs were purchased from the King's Chancery. As plaintiffs sought redress for novel legal problems new writs were developed to meet their needs until the Provisions of Oxford in 1258 prevented the issue of new writs without the permission of the King's Council. This closed the categories of writ which were available, severely limiting the ability of the common law to develop effective redress

---

[3] See Holdsworth, *A History of English Law* (7th edn, 1956), Vol 1, Ch V; Baker, *An Introduction to English Legal History* (2nd edn, 1979), Ch 6.

1

What is equity?

This chapter answers the fundamental question posed by the title. Equity[1] is understood as at one and the same time both a different system of law which recognizes rights and obligations that the common law does not, and a system which seeks to address the inherent gaps which can exist in following any set of rules. It is important to understand its historical origins to appreciate how the system operates today. The greatest creation of equity, the trust, will also be considered, and the significance of the separation of control and ownership of property that the concept allows. The impact of equity on the rules of property and the durability of equitable rights will be addressed before considering briefly the contribution of equity to the law more widely (which most of this first part of the book is about) and the creativity of equity in the future. We conclude this first chapter with a discussion of the maxims of equity, which are principles that underlie the whole operation of the equitable jurisdiction.

1 Equity: moral and legal conceptions

Equity is understood as at one and the same time both a different system of law which recognizes rights and obligations that the common law does not, and a system which seeks to address the inherent which can exist in following any set of rules.

(1) A layperson's understanding

To the layperson the term 'equity' connotes justice and fairness, so that to act 'equitably' is synonymous with acting 'fairly'. For example, Psalm 96 speaks of God's justice in such terms:

> The LORD reigns.
>   The world is firmly established, it
>   cannot be moved;
>   he will judge the peoples with equity.[2]

---

[1] For a succinct and engaging account of the development and contribution of Equity, see Hayton, 'The development of equity and the "good person" philosophy in common law systems' [2012] Conv 263.

[2] Psalm 96 v 10: New International Version.

PART I

The Importance of Equity

for new types of case. The common law therefore became stultified and inflexible. Furthermore, the common law also offered only a limited range of remedies, predominantly monetary damages, to redress the wrong suffered by a successful plaintiff. This straitjacketing of the common law was the predominant motive for the emergence of 'equity' as administered by the Courts of Chancery.

(2) **The Courts of Chancery**

(a) **The Chancery and the Chancellor**

The Chancery was essentially a department of State. The Chancellor was the Keeper of the Great Seal, a Minister of the Crown who sometimes acted in a Prime Ministerial capacity to the King.

(b) **Emergence of the judicial role of the Chancellor**

Despite the development of the common law, justice remained a royal prerogative, and therefore the King retained a residuum of justice which enabled aggrieved parties to appeal directly to him for redress. These appeals were initially heard by the King in Council, but by the fourteenth century they were delegated to the Chancellor, who acted on behalf of the King. By 1473 the Chancellor had begun to issue decrees by his own authority in his own name.

(c) **Motivation for the emergence of the Courts of Chancery**

The Chancery courts and their equity jurisdiction emerged because of the defects and rigidity of the common law, typified by the limited range of writs and the tendency to apply the strict rules of the common law even when this caused hardship, or seemed to do injustice, on the particular facts. For example, a debtor who had paid his debt but who had not ensured that his sealed bond was cancelled could be compelled by the common law to pay his creditor a second time because the bond was incontrovertible evidence of the debt.

In contrast, the Court of Chancery developed as a court of 'conscience' to remedy these defects of the common law system. In the *Earl of Oxford's Case*,[4] heard in 1615, Lord Ellesmere explained why there was a Chancery:

> [M]en's actions are so diverse and infinite that it is impossible to make any general law which may aptly meet with every particular and not fail in some circumstances. The office of the Chancellor is to correct men's consciences for frauds, breaches of trust, wrongs and oppression of what nature so ever they be, and to soften and mollify the extremity of the law.

This corresponds with the conception of equity in classical writings, where Aristotle had defined 'equity' as 'a correction of law where it is defective owing to its universality'.

(d) **Commencing an action in the Chancery Court**

Unlike the common law courts, where an action could only be commenced by means of a writ, actions in the Chancery Court were commenced by an informal bill of

---

[4] (1615) 1 Rep Ch 1, at 6.

complaint, and the process was begun by means of a *subpoena*. Proceedings were characterized by informality, and the court could sit outside of the legal terms which determined when the common law courts sat. It could sit anywhere, including the Chancellor's house.

(3) Character of the equity jurisdiction

(a) A court of conscience

The Chancery Courts initially functioned as courts of conscience. In 1452 Fortescue CJ responded to a legal argument presented in the Court of Chancery: 'We are to argue conscience here, not the law.'[5] The Chancellor decided cases on the basis of his own sense of justice. Inevitably, different Chancellors had different conceptions of justice so that, in Selden's well-known phrase, equity varied with the length of the Chancellor's foot.[6]

(b) Court of Equity

By the seventeenth century the Chancellor[7] tended to be a lawyer rather than a churchman. Decisions were reported, leading to a system of precedent and the development of a settled body of law, with distinct rights and remedies, that was almost as rigid as the common law. The Court of Chancery was no longer a simple court of conscience, but a court of 'equity' in the technical sense. At the beginning of the nineteenth century the process was complete. Lord Eldon, Chancellor (1801–06 and 1807–27), reflected in *Gee v Pritchard* that:

> The doctrines of [the Court of Chancery] ought to be well settled, and made as uniform, almost, as those of the common law, laying down fixed principles, but taking care that they are to be applied according to the circumstances of each case. I cannot agree that the doctrines of this court are to be changed by every succeeding judge. Nothing would inflict on me greater pain in quitting this place than the recollection that I had done anything to justify the reproach that the equity of this court varies like the Chancellor's foot.[8]

(4) The relationship between equity and the common law

(a) Equity challenges the law

Initially equity avoided conflict with the common law and the common law courts. However, with two parallel systems of law administered by separate courts it was inevitable that there would be conflict as each struggled for dominance over the other. It had become frequent practice for the Court of Chancery to issue so-called 'common injunctions', either ordering a party to a dispute to restrain his action at common law, or, if judgment had already been given in his favour by the common law court, to prevent him enforcing it. Refusal to obey these injunctions would be a contempt

---

[5] Mich 31 Hen VI, Fitz Abr Subpoena, pl 23.
[6] Table Talk of John Selden (F Pollock edn, 1927), p 43.
[7] The last non-legal chancellor was Lord Shaftesbury (1673–82).   [8] (1818) 2 Swan 402, at 414.

of court, deterred by the threat of imprisonment. These 'common injunctions' were a direct threat to the jurisdiction of the common law courts, which saw their supremacy being at stake.

(b) Equity prevails

The threat, and with it the struggle between law and equity, came to a head in the early seventeenth century. Sir Edward Coke, the Chief Justice of the King's Bench, held that imprisonment for disobedience of the Chancery injunctions was unlawful, and ordered the release of those affected under the writ of *habeas corpus*.[9] The Chancery Court argued that the injunctions did not interfere with the common law, as any judgment still stood, but rather, concerned only the conduct of the parties. This jurisdictional civil war was finally ended in 1616, when James I issued an order in favour of the Chancery Court and the common injunctions. Despite some subsequent attempts to reverse this resolution,[10] the primacy of the Chancery Courts was well established by the end of the century.

(5) Equity in the eighteenth and nineteenth centuries

(a) Defects

Although the supremacy of equity was firmly established by the end of the seventeenth century, its administration was affected by severe procedural defects causing extreme delay. The Chancellor was the sole judge and the court officers abused their positions. The Chancery offices, in particular that of the Master, were lucrative for the holders. The offices were sold and the purchasers appointed by the Chancellor.[11] A fee system operated for tasks performed by the officers, leading to inefficiency. In 1824 these difficulties led to the establishment of a Commission headed by Lord Eldon, who was himself notorious for delay. At that time some £39 million derived from cases awaiting decision was held by the court.

The development and administration of equity and the common law in different courts also added confusion and great expense, since neither had full power to grant complete relief. A case could be started in the common law courts when it should have been started in Chancery, or may have had to be referred between courts during proceedings. The duration and expense of suit soon became intolerable 'equity had become a byword for delay and injustice'. Lord Denning, echoing the historic reputation of equity in more recent times, said: '[e]ven a court of equity would not allow him to do anything so inequitable and unjust.'[12]

---

[9] See *Heath v Rydley* (1614) Cro Jac 335.
[10] For example, in 1690 a bill was introduced in the House of Lords enacting that no Court of Equity should entertain any suit for which the proper remedy was at common law. However, the bill was dropped when it was shown that it would make equity unworkable, which would lead to injustice.
[11] For up to £5,000 each; roughly equivalent to £350,000 in contemporary currency.
[12] *Re Vandervell's Trusts No.2* [1974] Ch 269.

(b) Reforms

In order to improve the administration of the equity jurisdiction a number of reforms were introduced.

(i) Reform of the personnel of the Chancery Courts

The number of persons competent to exercise the equity jurisdiction was increased. In 1813, a Vice Chancellor was appointed to assist the Chancellor, followed by a further two in 1843. In 1833, the Master of the Rolls was granted jurisdiction to sit concurrently with the Chancellor. In 1851, a Court of Appeals in Chancery was created. The other court offices were also reformed. In 1833, the office of Master became a Crown appointment with a fixed salary. In 1842, the six Clerks were abolished, as were the Masters in 1852.

(ii) Limited reform of the jurisdiction of the Chancery Courts

The Common Law Procedure Act 1854 introduced changes marking a step towards the fusion of the common law and equity jurisdictions. True fusion was only effected by the dramatic reform of the English legal system.

(6) The Judicature Acts 1873 and 1875

(a) Restructuring the system of the courts

The Judicature Acts effected a radical restructuring of the English court system. The Courts of Chancery, King's Bench, Common Pleas, Exchequer, Admiralty, Probate, and the London Court of Bankruptcy were consolidated and merged to form a single Supreme Court of Judicature,[13] now known as the Senior Courts of England and Wales,[14] divided into the High Court and the Court of Appeal. As a matter of convenience, rather than of jurisdiction, the High Court was organized into divisions, comprising the Chancery Division; King's Bench Division; Common Pleas Division; Exchequer Division; and the Probate, Divorce, and Admiralty Division.

(b) Uniform jurisdiction given to judges of the Senior Courts

The central feature of the reform was that all the judges of the Supreme Court of Judicature (now the Senior Courts)[15] irrespective of the division in which they sat, were to have both common law and equitable jurisdiction. This was achieved by the 1873 Act, s 24, which provided that all judges were to give effect to such equitable estates, rights, relief, defences, duties, and liabilities as would have been given effect by the Court of Chancery, and also to recognize and give effect to all estates, titles, rights, duties, obligations, and liabilities existing by the common law.[16]

---

[13] To be distinguished from the Supreme Court of the United Kingdom, established by the Constitutional Reform Act 2005, s 23, to replace the Judicial Committee of the House of Lords as the highest appellate court in the UK.   [14] Constitutional Reform Act 2005, s 59.

[15] Constitutional Reform Act 2005, s 59.

[16] Judicature Act 1925, ss 36–44; Senior Courts Act 1981, s 49.

(c) Procedural implications of the reforms

The concurrent common law and equity jurisdiction conferred on the Senior Courts by the Judicature Acts revolutionized the process of litigation. It was no longer necessary to commence a separate action in the Chancery Court to gain recognition of an equitable right or to obtain an equitable remedy.

(d) Supremacy of equity enshrined

(i) Supreme Court of Judicature Act 1873, s 25

Common injunctions were abolished by the Supreme Court of Judicature Act 1873, s 24(5), since the concurrent jurisdiction granted to judges under s 24 rendered them unnecessary. The supremacy of equity was itself placed on a statutory footing by s 25, which provided that in a number of specific instances[17] the existing equitable rule was to supersede the common law rule. Section 25(11) provided somewhat more generally that:

> in all matters not herein-before particularly mentioned, in which there is any conflict, or variance, between the Rules of Equity and the Rules of the Common Law with reference to the same matter, the Rules of Equity will apply.[18]

(ii) Operation of s 25(11)

Section 25(11) only operates if there is a genuine conflict between the rules of equity and the rules of common law. A good example is provided in in the context of contractual terms as to the time when performance is expected. Whereas at common law requirements as to time were regarded as of the essence of the contract, in equity they were not, so that a party in breach of a requirement of time was not entitled to repudiate the contract for breach. Outside of commercial contracts, where stipulations as to time are regarded as crucial, the equitable rule has been held to prevail over the common law rule where there is no express agreement that time is to be of the essence.[19]

(e) The fusion of law and equity

(i) The effect of the Judicature Acts

One question arising from the reforms instituted by the Judicature Acts is whether there has been a 'fusion' of law and equity. Jurisprudential debate has questioned whether there is now one single body of 'English law', which has its heritage in the rules, rights, and remedies of the previously distinct bodies of 'common law' and 'equity', or whether there has been a mere fusion of the administration of these two

---

[17] S 25(1)–(10).

[18] This provision is retained by the Senior Courts Act 1981, s 49(1), which provides that: 'wherever there is any conflict or variance between the rule of equity and the rules of the common law with reference to the same matter, the rules of equity shall prevail'.

[19] *United Scientific Holdings Ltd v Burnley Borough Council* [1978] AC 904. Another good example is *Walsh v Lonsdale* (1882) 21 Ch D 9, where the creation of an equitable lease where formalities for a legal lease were wanting allowed a remedy of distress for rent to be brought which would not have been applicable in a legal lease—see Stevens and Pearce, *Land Law* (5th edn, 2013), Chapter 9.

distinct bodies of law so that 'common law' and 'equity' are now administered by a single court replacing the pre-existing duality of courts.

(ii) Fusion of administration

Traditionalists hold that the Judicature Acts merely fused the administration of equity and the common law.[20] In the famous words of Ashburner the result is that:

> the two streams of jurisprudence, though they run in the same channel, run side by side, and do not mingle their waters.[21]

This view enjoys the support of judicial dicta contemporaneous with the passing of the Acts. For example, in *Salt v Cooper* Jessel MR commented:

> the main object of the Act was to assimilate the transaction of Equity business and Common Law business by different Courts of Judicature. It has been sometimes inaccurately called 'the fusion of Law and Equity'; but it was not any fusion, or anything of the kind; it was the vesting in one tribunal of the administration of Law and Equity in every cause, action or dispute which should come before that tribunal.[22]

The Attorney-General at the time that the Acts were passed disavowed the object of fusion when explaining their effect to the House of Commons during the second reading of the Judicature Bill:

> Law and Equity therefore, would remain if the Bill passed, but they would be administered concurrently, and no one would be sent to get in one court the relief which another court had refused to give…[23]

More recent statutory language also implies that law and equity remain distinct bodies of law.

(iii) Fusion in substance

As time passed and the separate administration of law and equity became little more than a distant memory, an increasing number of judges advocated practical realism and declared that law and equity had been fused. In the middle years of the twentieth century Lord Denning regarded law and equity as unified, and manipulated this as a justification for law reform. In *Errington v Errington and Woods*,[24] for example, he stated that 'law and equity have been fused for nearly eighty years'. Some twenty years later, members of the House of Lords expressed similar sentiments in *United Scientific Holdings Ltd v Burnley Borough Council*.[25] Lord Diplock specifically commented on Ashburner's metaphor:

> by 1977 this metaphor has in my view become both mischievous and deceptive. The innate conservatism of English lawyers made them slow to recognise that by the Supreme Court of Judicature Act 1873 the two systems of substantive and adjectival law formerly

---

[20] See (1954) 70 LQR 326 (Lord Evershed); (1961) 24 MLR 116 (V T H Delaney); (1977) 93 LQR 529 (P V Baker); (1977) 6 AALR 119 (T G Watkin); (1994) 14 LS 313 (David Capper), pp 315–317.
[21] Snell, *Principles of Equity* (2nd edn), p 18.   [22] (1880–81) 16 Ch D 544, at 549.
[23] Hansard 3rd Series, Vol 216, pp 644–645.   [24] [1952] 1 KB 290, at 298.
[25] [1978] AC 904.

administered by the Courts of Law and Courts of Chancery...were fused. As at the confluence of the Rhone and Saone, it may be possible for a short distance to discern the source from which each part of the combined stream came, but there comes a point at which this ceases to be possible. If Professor Ashburner's fluvial metaphor is to be retained at all, the waters of the confluent streams of law and equity have surely mingled now.

Lord Simon also held that the Judicature Acts had 'truly...brought about a fusion of common law and equity'[26] but considered that there were institutional reasons why English lawyers had been slow to accept this conclusion. First, there had been some dovetailing of the systems before the Acts themselves. Second, the High Court had continued to sit in administrative divisions. Third, the conservatism of lawyers and their training tended to minimize the change that had been made.

(iv) A single coherent body of law

While the debate has not been settled clearly in favour of either view, it seems that the central problem is often the meaning invested in the term 'fusion'. If 'fusion' means that any distinction between equity and common law, and especially between equitable and legal rights and remedies, has been completely removed so that adjectivally the term 'equitable' has no continuing relevance, then it has not occurred. The law still distinguishes between legal and equitable ownership, the foundation of the trust concept which is the main subject of this book. However, it is also clear that English law no longer preserves the strict distinction between equitable and legal rules that was maintained before the Judicature Acts. The law has developed as a whole, so that there has been some synthesis of legal and equitable rights and remedies and cross-fertilization between them, and some of the old distinctions between rights and remedies historically equitable in origin and those historically of common law origin have ceased to be significant. The adjectives 'equitable' and 'common law' are useful to distinguish the different rights and remedies that make up English law but, as Lord Diplock observed in *United Scientific Holdings Ltd v Burnley Borough Council*:

> [To] perpetuate a dichotomy between rules of equity and rules of common law which it was a major purpose of the Supreme Court of Judicature Act 1873 to do away with, is, in my view, conducive to erroneous conclusions as to the ways in which the law of England has developed in the last hundred years.[27]

The approach which best represents the prevailing judicial attitude is that the long fusion of the administration of law and equity has produced a single, coherent, body of rules which operate harmoniously together, even though some historically have their origin in equity and others in the common law.[28] Those historical roots can often still be discerned, and in some cases may still remain significant. In other cases it may indeed be accurate to describe the rules as having merged or melded. There are different types of ownership, different rights and remedies in English law which by historical origin are equitable and legal, and although they form one coherent body of

---

[26] [1978] AC 904, at 944.   [27] [1978] AC 904, at 924.
[28] See also Duggan 'Is Equity Efficient?' (1997) 113 LQR 601.

law they must still be distinguished or identified as such because of the different 'incidents' that accompany them. In *Napier and Ettrick v Hunter*, Lord Goff considered the relationship between equitable proprietary rights and personal rights and obligations deriving from a contract of insurance:

> No doubt our task nowadays is to see the two strands of authority, at law and in equity, moulded into a coherent whole; but for my part I cannot see why this amalgamation should lead to the rejection of the equitable proprietary right...[29]

Examples of situations where there is a need to draw a distinction between legal and equitable rights and remedies are abundant in English law, but a few will suffice here. In relation to land, the entire scheme of the Law of Property Act 1925 is predicated upon the distinction between legal and equitable estates and interests in land,[30] and the character of an interest determines its ability to endure through transfers of the legal title. This is something to which we return in this Chapter, and in Chapter 3. Specific performance, an equitable remedy, is only available where a contract has been entered in return for valuable consideration and not of a promise made by deed, which would be enforced by the common law. This significant remedy is considered in Chapter 5. Many other examples will unfold themselves in the pages of this book, but none more important than the concept of the trust, which, as we shall see emerged because, through the parallel systems of law and equity, English law developed the abstract concept of the double-ownership of property. Thus, legal and equitable title can exist simultaneously in the same item of property, enjoyed by different persons as owners. It is to that we turn next.

3 Equity and the trust

The majority of this book will be devoted to an examination of the modern trust, and in particular to the means by which such a relationship can be brought into existence and the nature of the rights and duties of trustees and beneficiaries. What follows here is a description of the trust and its origins.

(1) The trust

The trust is the most important creation of equity, and is a form of ownership of things (property) which allows someone to manage property for someone else's benefit. Where property is subject to a trust, equity treats the persons for whose benefit the trust exists as the owners of the property, even though they are not the owners of it at law. Where property is subject to a trust, there is a duality of ownership, or 'double dominium', and a distinction must be drawn between the legal ownership and the equitable ownership. This capacity for dual ownership at law and in equity is the most distinctive feature of English property law. It emerged as a product of the historical divide between equity

---

[29] [1978] AC 904, at 401.   [30] Law of Property Act 1925, s 1.

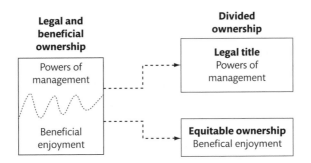

Figure 1.1 Separation of ownership

and the common law. Duality of ownership of property is the essential characteristic of a trust. A person enjoying the legal ownership of the trust property is referred to as a 'trustee', and a person enjoying the equitable ownership is a 'beneficiary'.

(2) The importance of separation of ownership

What is important about separating the rights to property into legal and equitable ownership (strictly legal title and equitable ownership) is that it enables the powers of management to be split from the beneficial enjoyment (see Figure 1.1). In addition, it allows much greater complexity in the division of beneficial enjoyment. The relationship between the legal owner and the equitable owner does, of course, have to be regulated, and equity does this through the trust.

(3) Creation of the trust concept

(a) The feudal system of land holding

An understanding of the origins of the trust[31] requires an elementary grasp of the feudal system of landowning operative during the medieval period.[32] All land was technically owned by the King, while others enjoyed the right to use it as tenants. Individuals were granted 'tenure' of land by their 'over-lord', who would himself enjoy tenure from his 'over-lord'. These levels of tenure formed a feudal pyramid of landholdings stretching from the King (who was at its pinnacle because he had no 'over-lord') downwards. The terms of 'tenure' defined the conditions under which the tenant was entitled to enjoy the land, generally requiring the performance of services on behalf of his lord. These might include the provision of military forces,[33] religious functions,[34] or agricultural services.[35] On the death of a tenant, the person

---

[31] See Holdsworth, *History of English Law* (7th edn, 1956), pp 407–480; Baker, *Introduction to English Legal History* (2nd edn, 1979), pp 210–219 and 242–244. See also (1998) 61 MLR 162 (Pottage).

[32] See Gray and Gray, *Elements of Land Law* (5th edn, 2009), pp 64–68.

[33] The tenure of 'Knight's service', for example, which required the provision of armed horsemen for battle.

[34] 'Spiritual tenure'.   [35] Tenures in socage.

who succeeded to his tenure and thereby inherited his position on the feudal ladder
was required to make a payment to his over-lord. These medieval inheritance taxes,
termed 'feudal incidents', provided the Crown with a significant source of revenue.
While the doctrine of tenure defined the terms under which land was held, the parallel doctrine of 'estates' determined the duration for which a grant of tenure was
to last.[36] An estate in fee simple[37] was a grant of tenure for ever, and within the feudal structure the right to tenure of land in fee simple was tantamount to absolute
ownership.

(b) Development of the 'use'

In the context of this feudal structure, the 'use', the ancestor of the modern trust, was
developed by the Chancery courts. If land was conveyed to X 'to the use of Y' this had
the effect that, while X became the owner of the land, X was obliged to apply it for the
benefit of Y and was prevented from treating it as his own. X was termed the 'feoffee'
and Y the 'cestui que use'. The common law did not recognize, and would not enforce,
a 'use' of land, but rather, regarded the feoffee, in whom the legal estate was vested, as
the absolute owner. From the perspective of equity, however, the feoffee was bound in
conscience to apply the property for the benefit of the cestui que use, because of the
undertaking he had given. The Court of Chancery was therefore prepared to enforce
the use in personam, requiring the feoffee to apply the property vested in him to the
benefit of the cestui que use. Equity did not deny the reality of the ownership of the
feoffee at common law, but instead prevented him from exercising the entitlements
concomitant with his legal ownership in a manner inconsistent with the interests of
the cestui que use. Thus, the use shared a central characteristic of the modern trust,
namely that the formal ownership of the property subject to it was separated from
the right to enjoy the benefit derived from such ownership (see Figure 1.2). The use
evolved as a popular mechanism for landholding because of the positive advantages it
offered. It provided a means of making gifts to charities that were technically unable
to own property. For example, the monastic order of St Francis was forbidden to own
property by its rule, but land could be given to feoffees for its use. Though technically
it would not 'own' the property, it would be entitled to derive the benefits flowing
from such ownership. A landowner could avoid the strict legal rules of inheritance
by directing feoffees in his will to hold the land as he wished. The use also offered
a mechanism for primitive tax-planning through the avoidance of feudal dues. If
land was vested in a group of feoffees, who would never die as a group because each
individual feoffee would be replaced on death, the legal title would never have to be
passed by way of succession. The feudal incidents payable on inheritance would thus
be avoided altogether.

---

[36] See *Walsingham's Case* (1579) 2 Plowd 547, at 555: 'the land itself is one thing, and an estate in the land
is another thing, for an estate in the land is a time in the land, or land for a time, and there are diversities of
estates, which are no more than diversities of time...'

[37] To be distinguished from a 'fee tail' (or 'entailed interest'), which was only to last for so long as the
grantee had lineal descendants, and the life interest, which was only to last for the length of the grantee's
life.

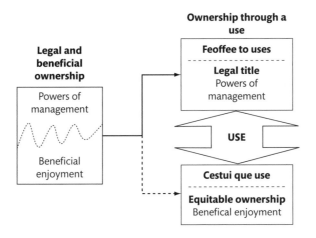

Figure 1.2 Separation of ownership and the use

(c) The development of the trust

The financial advantages attendant upon a use were so attractive to landowners that by 1500 the majority of land in England was held in use.[38] This inevitably led to a serious diminution in the King's feudal revenue. In order to close this tax-avoidance loophole, legislation (the Statute of Uses 1535) was introduced to abolish uses by 'executing' them, which means vesting the legal estate in the cestui que use. It did not take the ingenuity of lawyers long to find ways around the Statute of Uses and, indeed, to turn it to their advantage. The statute did not apply to uses where the feoffee had active duties to perform, for example the collection and distribution of profits and the management of an estate.[39] A further means to avoiding 'execution' of a use under the statute was to create a double use, termed a 'use upon a use', whereby the legal estate in land would be conveyed 'to X, to the use of Y, to the use of Z'. Although the first use would be executed by the Statute of Uses, so that Y would be treated as the legal owner, the second use remained unexecuted. The Court of Chancery would then enforce the second use, requiring Y to hold the land for the benefit of Z. This second use was termed a 'trust', providing the modern terminology.[40] The 'use upon a use' was accepted as valid by the latter part of the sixteenth century,[41] by which time it had come to serve different social functions than the mere avoidance of feudal dues. Common objectives were to protect estates from spendthrift sons, and to enable married women to enjoy property independently of their husbands. The effect of the trust to avoid the execution of uses was so successful that in 1739 Lord Hardwicke was able to observe that the Statute of Uses 'has had no other effect than to add at most, three words to a conveyance'.[42] Although the trust had emerged as a recognized legal instrument by the end of the sixteenth

---

[38] YB Mich 15 Hen VII, 13, p 1, per Frowyk Sjt.

[39] A use of leasehold land, a term of years, was also not executed.

[40] In fact, the term was also used for a single 'use' prior to the development of the 'use upon a use'.

[41] See (1966) 82 LQR 215 (Barton); (1977) 93 LQR 33 (Baker).

[42] *Hopkins v Hopkins* (1739) 1 Atk 581. Lord Hardwicke was a better lawyer than a mathematician.

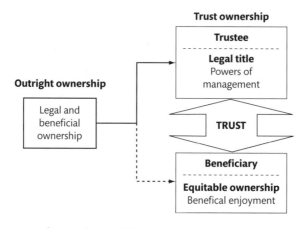

Figure 1.3 Separation of ownership and the trust

century, it flourished in the nineteenth century, when it served as the foundation for property holding by families and as a device to preserve family estates.

(4) The modern trust

The cardinal features of a modern trust are very much the same as those of the early use from which it has developed. Under a trust, the legal and equitable ownership of the trust property are separated and held by different persons.[43] A trust arises where property is conveyed to or vested in the trustee by a settlor in such circumstances that equity will compel the trustee to administer the property for the benefit of the beneficiary.

(a) Separation of title under a trust

The legal title is vested in the trustee, who must apply the property for the benefit of someone else, the cestui que trust, more commonly termed the 'beneficiary', who is regarded as the equitable owner (see Figure 1.3). It follows from this separation of the legal and equitable ownership of the trust property that there is also a separation between the management responsibilities arising in connection with the property and the enjoyment thereof.

(b) Trustee as legal owner

The trustee looks like the outright owner of the property. He has legal title vested in him, and as legal owner, the trustee controls the property.[44] He is usually entitled to decide whether it should be retained or sold, and how it should be invested. In some types of trust the trustee even has the right to determine how the property should be

---

[43] *Selby v Alston* (1797) 3 Ves 339.

[44] It is possible that the trustee may have an equitable title only, which occurs where the property settled on the trust is equitable (technically, this is usually referred to as a sub-trust). In this case, the key points about control and separation of the benefit are exactly the same as where a trustee has legal title.

distributed among a class of defined beneficiaries. However, he is compelled by equity to exercise this control over the property strictly for the benefit of the beneficiaries. Thus, he must not exercise his rights to deal with the trust property for his own personal advantage, and equity will prevent him applying the trust property inconsistently with the terms of the trust, which define the entitlement of the beneficiary or beneficiaries. Similarly, he must consider the interests of all the beneficiaries collectively, and not favour any one of them, sometimes referred to as his duty to consider the trust as a whole. This is particularly important where persons are entitled to the beneficial interest in succession, so that someone entitled for life does not get all the benefits of ownership to the exclusion of those beneficiaries entitled after the death of the currently entitled beneficiary.

(c) Beneficiary as equitable owner

The beneficiary has equitable ownership of the property, which identifies him as being entitled to the benefits of the property held under the trust.[45] The fact that the beneficiary has equitable ownership of the trust property differentiates the trust from a contract for the benefit of a third party. The beneficiary, as a property holder, has additional rights against other parties in addition to those against the trustee. The beneficiary's rights can be enforced not only against the trustee, but also against any new trustees (as the trust property will be vested in them) or against third parties who receive the trust property in breach of trust. A beneficiary does not have control of the property, so although the beneficiary has rights against the trustee to make sure he performs his duties throughout the duration of the trust, he does not have the right to instruct the trustee in performing those duties.

(5) Impact of the trust

This capacity of the trust to separate the management of property from its enjoyment renders it a perfect vehicle to facilitate complex arrangements involving property. Its tremendous flexibility has enabled it to adapt through the centuries and into new social and commercial contexts. Maitland was of the opinion that the trust was 'the greatest and most distinctive achievement performed by Englishmen in the field of jurisprudence'. Trusts now underpin many aspects of modern life. The contribution of trusts to the management of property is considered in Chapter 3, and Part III of this book considers the application of trusts in a variety of contexts, from creating rights for cohabitants in the family home through to allowing people to plan their financial affairs to provide for others after death. Equity has also added significant depth and sophistication to our conception of property ownership beyond the trust, and it is to that that our attention now turns.

---

[45] It is possible for a person to be both trustee and one of the beneficiaries of the same property, in which case the person is compelled by equity to control the property for the benefit of all those sharing the beneficial ownership.

4 Equity and property

To understand the contribution of equity, it is first necessary to outline the salient features of our property system, including the different types of right the system regulates and the distinction between proprietary and personal rights.

(1) What is property?

At its most basic, the term 'property' is simply a more technical expression describing 'things'. Things can readily be distinguished from 'persons'. Persons are either individual human beings or abstract entities, such as companies or corporations, which are treated as separate legal persons for the purposes of the law. In general, persons are capable of owning things, whereas things have no capacity to own other things. Since the abolition of slavery, human persons are incapable of being owned as such. Body parts are also incapable of ownership.[46] Companies are owned by their shareholders, but the separate identity of the company is maintained so that it is not treated as synonymous with its shareholders. Animals are regarded as things and are capable of being owned, whereas they are not capable of owning.

Lawson and Rudden have commented that 'the law of property deals with the legal relations between people with regard to things'.[47] It addresses such questions as the following: Who owns the thing? What is the owner entitled to do with the thing he owns? How can the owner of the thing transfer it to someone else so that they become the owner in his place? Can the owner continue to assert his ownership of the thing even when a third person has taken it from him without permission, or against a person who has acquired the thing from such a third person? [48]

(2) Proprietary rights

Proprietary rights are those rights and entitlements which exist in reference to things.[49] The most important and absolute right is that of ownership, but there are many lesser interests that may be enjoyed in respect of an item of property. It has been said that the law of property is about the relationship persons enjoy with things:

> For serious students of property, the beginning of truth is the recognition that property is not a thing but a *power relationship*—a relationship of social and legal legitimacy existing between a person and a valued resource (whether tangible or intangible).

---

[46] See Skene, 'Proprietary rights in human bodies, body parts and tissue: regulatory contexts and proposals for new laws' (2002) 22 LS 102.   [47] Lawson and Rudden, *The Law of Property* (1982), p 1.
[48] See further Lawson and Rudden, *The Law of Property* (1982), pp 1–38; (1998) 18 LS 41 (Rotherham); McFarlane, *The Structure of Property Law* (2008).
[49] See Eleftheriadis 'The Analysis of Property Rights' (1996) 16 OJLS 31; Chambers 'Proprietary Interests in Commercial Transactions' (1998) 18 OJLS 363.

To claim 'property' in a resource is, in effect, to assert a significant degree of control over that resource.[50]

More accurately, the law of property is about the relationship which one person has with other persons in regard to things.

(a) Ownership

A person who owns a thing in which nobody else has any interests is the absolute owner thereof. Such ownership is the 'greatest possible interest in a thing which a mature system of law recognises'.[51] The rights of an owner are best understood in terms of the legal powers which are conferred in relation to the thing. Lawson and Rudden identify three main elements of ownership:

(a) the right to make physical use of a thing;

(b) the right to the income from it, in money, in kind, or in services; and

(c) the power of management, including that of alienation.[52]

By virtue of ownership a person is entitled to do as he wishes with his property. He can possess, use, enjoy, and exploit it as he pleases. He is even free to destroy it. He can give it away, or sell it to a third person. The person who owns property is said to have 'title' to it, a term derived from the fact that he is 'entitled' to it. Of course, that owner-ship may be constrained by other rules of law, so, for example, a landowner may not lawfully build on his land without applying for planning permission. In many cases the ownership of property will be more complex. For example, there may be multiple owners of the thing, termed co-owners, who enjoy concurrent ownership, or there may be multiple owners with successive interests.

(b) Other rights in property

Although the most important right in property is ownership, there is a large range of other proprietary rights that a person may enjoy over a thing. The complexity of property law follows from the fact that, often, a number of persons may have dif-ferent, sometimes competing, rights in the same thing. Such subsidiary rights may qualify or limit the absolute entitlement of the owner to do as he chooses with the thing. This multiplicity of proprietary rights in the same thing is most clearly illus-trated in the context of land. Assume that Norman is the owner of a piece of house, Blackacre, which he purchased with the help of a Building Society loan secured by a mortgage. He has leased the house to Owen for twenty-five years. He has granted his next-door neighbour, Penelope, the right to walk to her garage across his back garden, and reached an agreement with his other next-door neighbour, Quentin, that he will not use the land for business purposes. In this simple scenario Norman,

---

[50] Gray and Gray, *Elements of Land Law* (5th edn, 2009), p 88.
[51] Honoré, 'Ownership', in Guest (ed), *Oxford Essays in Jurisprudence* (1961).
[52] Lawson and Rudden, *The Law of Property* (1982), p 8.

Owen, Penelope, Quentin, and the Building Society all have different proprietary interests in the same land.[53]

(c) The need to distinguish proprietary and personal rights

While noting that there is a wide range of rights that might be enjoyed in relation to an item of property, it is important to draw a more fundamental distinction between those rights and interests recognized and enforced by the law which are proprietary in nature and those which are personal. The essence of a proprietary interest is that it is a right subsisting in relation to a thing, and not as against a particular individual or small group of individuals. For example, if Kevin owns a car, his ownership is a right which subsists in relation to the car itself. In the event that his car is stolen, and sold by the thief to Michael, his entitlement to that particular car persists. He can demand that it be returned to him. It has remained his throughout, irrespective of the fact that his possession was interrupted.

In contrast, a personal right is a right which is only enforceable against a specific individual.[54] For example, a contract creates a purely personal right enforceable only against the person who made the relevant promise. If Kevin contracted to buy a specific car from a garage, and before the sale was completed the garage sold the car to Michael, Kevin would have no rights in that car itself which he could enforce against Michael. The car would not be his but Michael's and his only right would lie against the garage for breach of contract. Proprietary rights are described as rights in rem,[55] whereas personal rights are rights in personam.

(b) The defining characteristic of proprietary rights

In *National Provincial Bank Ltd v Ainsworth*[56] Lord Wilberforce identified the essential characteristics of a property right:

> Before a right or an interest can be admitted into the category of property, or of a right affecting property, it must be definable, identifiable by third parties, capable in its nature of assumption by third parties, and have some degree of permanence or stability.[57]

The central characteristic of a proprietary right is therefore that it is capable of enduring through changes in the ownership of the property to which it relates.

---

[53] The nature of these rights is considered in detail in the relevant land law texts, but the salient features are outlined here. The mortgage to the Building Society gives it ultimately a right to sell the house if the loan is not repaid. Owen as a tenant can claim the exclusive right to the use of the house for the twenty-five-year duration of his lease. Penelope's right of way may be an easement, which is a binding entitlement which Norman, his tenants, and any future owners cannot interfere with. Finally, Quentin and Norman may have entered into a restrictive covenant, which is a right attaching to Quentin's land, controlling the use of Norman's land, as detailed in the agreement.

[54] For a detailed treatment of the law relating to personal property, see Bridge, *Personal Property Law* (3rd edn, 2002).   [55] Meaning 'in the thing', from the Latin word 'res', meaning 'thing'.

[56] [1965] AC 1175.   [57] [1965] AC 1175, at 1248.

(3) **Equitable rights and property**

We have already seen that the trust allows a separation of control and benefit, and through it a separation of ownership. Equity has also created or recognized other rights in property.

(a) **Equitable rights corresponding to legal rights**

The common law only recognized the creation of proprietary rights if appropriate formalities were satisfied. This generally required the grant of the right using the special formality of a deed.[58] For example, under the Real Property Act 1845, a legal lease would not be created unless made by deed.[59] However, equity, which looks to the substance rather than the form of transactions, was prepared to recognize and enforce proprietary interests even if the requisite formalities for creation at law had not been observed. Equity regards a mere contract for a lease as creating an equitable lease despite the absence of a deed.[60] The difference between the legal and equitable form of these rights affects the quality of the right, not the nature of it. Thus, a legal and equitable mortgage, for example, give the mortgage holder the same rights and obligations. However, while both are proprietary interests capable of binding third parties, the circumstances in which they may bind third parties are different.

(b) **Equitable proprietary rights without a legal equivalent**

The creativity of equity also allowed it to develop proprietary interests that were not parasitic equivalents of corresponding common law rights. For example, in law the burden of a covenant affecting the use of freehold land is enforceable only against the original covenantor because of the doctrine of privity of contract.[61] However, following *Tulk v Moxhay*,[62] equity elevated freehold covenants restrictive of the owner's use of his land to the status of proprietary interests, with the consequence that they are capable of passing with the title of the land so as to bind subsequent purchasers.[63] Other contracts concerning rights over land have also been given the status of proprietary interests rather than merely personal rights. A contract to purchase an interest in land is an equitable proprietary interest known as an 'estate contract', which will be binding against subsequent purchasers of the land, subject to any legislative requirements of registration.[64]

---

[58] This originally required the document to be 'signed, sealed, and delivered'. Because of this, the grant was sometimes said to be made 'under seal'. See now Law of Property (Miscellaneous Provisions) Act 1989, s 1.

[59] See now Law of Property Act 1925, s 2(1). By s 52(2)(d) and s 54(2) there is no need for a deed for the creation of a legal lease for less than three years at the best rent which can reasonably be obtained.

[60] *Parker v Taswell* (1858) 2 De G & J 559; *Walsh v Lonsdale* (1882) 21 LR Ch D 9.

[61] *Austerberry v Oldham Corpn* (1885) 29 Ch D 750, CA; *Rhone v Stephens* [1994] 2 AC 310.

[62] (1848) 2 Ph 774.

[63] For some reason, English law has failed to recognize restrictions on the use of land as capable of existing as easements, the nearest equivalent right recognized by the common law.

[64] See *Midland Bank Trust Co Ltd (No 1) v Green* [1981] AC 513, HL.

(c) Mere equities

Equity further recognizes a category of entitlements described as 'equities' or 'mere equities'. This terminology is intended to distinguish them from complete equitable proprietary interests. They have been held to include the right to have a transaction set aside for fraud[65] or undue influence,[66] the right to have a document rectified,[67] and the deserted wife's right to occupy the matrimonial home.[68] When mere equities relate to property, they have a limited capacity to affect third parties who acquire ownership of it, but they are not true interests in the property itself.

(4) Equity and the durability of proprietary rights

As has been noted earlier, one of the defining characteristics of a proprietary right is that it is capable of enduring through changes in the ownership the thing to which it relates.[69] However, the durability of a specific proprietary right will depend upon its character. Different rules developed in equity and the common law to govern the durability of their respective proprietary rights. In general, legal rights are more durable than their equitable equivalents. A statutory scheme has been introduced which determines issues of priority between legal and equitable rights and interests in land, so their durability is statutory rather than based on their intrinsic character. The details of this registered title system which is governed by the Land Registration Act 2006 are beyond the scope of this text,[70] but the traditional rules developed by equity and the common law remain operative in relation to personal property.[71]

(a) Legal proprietary rights

Of all types of ownership and rights, legal ownership is the most durable, subject to a few exceptions at common law and to rather more which have been introduced by statute. The basic rule is that the ownership or rights of a legal owner will continue indefinitely until the owner has transferred them to someone else. In relation to some forms of property, such as land or shares, legal ownership is determined by means of a register. Apart from those situations where a special rule applies,[72] the rule relating to legal ownership or rights is therefore that 'legal rights bind the world'. In consequence, where two people can assert a claim with a lawful origin, 'the first in time prevails'.

---

[65] *Ernest v Vivian* (1863) 33 LJ Ch 513.

[66] *Bainbrigge v Browne* (1881) 18 Ch D 188; *Barclays Bank v O'Brien* [1994] 1 AC 180.

[67] *Shiloh Spinners Ltd v Harding (No 1)* [1973] AC 691, at 721, per Lord Wilberforce.

[68] *National Provincial Bank Ltd v Ainsworth* [1965] AC 1175.

[69] For personal property, see Worthington, *Personal Property Law* (2000), pp 457–473. In relation to real property, see Jackson, Stevens, and Pearce, *Land Law* (5th edn, 2013).

[70] See Stevens and Pearce, *Land Law* (5th edn, 2013), Chapter 4.

[71] For personal property, see Worthington, *Personal Property Law* (2000), pp 457–473. In relation to real property, see Jackson, Stevens, and Pearce, *Land Law* (4th edn, 2008).

[72] When a chattel has been lost, a finder will not acquire a right to it superior to that of the legal owner—see *Parker v British Airways Board* [1982] QB 1004.

So, for example, if Alf steals a car belonging to Mary and sells it to Peter, neither Alf nor Peter become the owner of the car. It continues to belong to Mary. If Peter still has the car in his hands, Mary can demand that it be returned to her, vindicating her continuing legal ownership. Only if the car is destroyed will Mary's legal ownership be terminated, as there will no longer be any subject matter in which the right can continue to subsist.

(b) Equitable proprietary rights

(i) Priority between equitable interests

Equity followed the law when it was dealing with the relative status of claims based in equity. It therefore accepted the principle that competing claims should be judged on the footing that where they all had a lawful origin 'the first in time prevails'.

(ii) The doctrine of notice

When it came to dealing with the relative status of rights, some of which were legal and some equitable, equity again adopted the root philosophy that they should be judged in accordance with the time order of their creation. However, this philosophy is applied with one very important qualification. A pre-existing equitable interest will not subsist in property which is acquired by a bona fide purchaser of a legal interest who was not aware at the time of its acquisition of the earlier equitable interest. This principle is known as the 'doctrine of notice'.

The operation of the doctrine of notice to destroy equitable proprietary interests is rooted in concepts of good conscience, which lies at the heart of the equitable jurisdiction. In the view of equity, a person who was aware of a pre-existing interest subsisting in a property cannot acquire it free from such interest. He has no grounds for complaint when equity requires him to continue to give effect to it because he knew what he was getting. Only if he purchased the property without knowing of its existence is his conscience unaffected so as to justify the conclusion that he should not be bound by it. As Lord Browne-Wilkinson explained in *Barclays Bank plc v O'Brien*:[73]

> The doctrine of notice lies at the heart of equity. Given that there are two innocent parties, each enjoying rights, the earlier right prevails against the later right if the acquirer of the later right knows of the earlier right (actual notice) or would have discovered it had he taken proper steps (constructive notice). In particular, if the party asserting that he takes free of the earlier rights of another knows of certain facts which put him on enquiry as to the possible existence of the rights of that other and he fails to make such enquiry or take such other steps as are reasonable to verify whether such earlier right does or does not exist, he will have constructive notice of the earlier right and take subject to it.

(iii) Requirements of the equitable doctrine of notice

The equitable doctrine of notice only operates in favour of a person who can demonstrate that he was the bona fide purchaser of the legal ownership of the property for

---

[73] [1994] 1 AC 180.

value without notice. Because a purchaser who meets this test takes free of any equitable interests in the property acquired, such a person is also referred to as 'equity's darling'. Each component element of this formula must be satisfied.

(iv) Bona fides

The doctrine of notice only operates in favour of a person who acted in good faith. However, this requirement adds little to the element that he must not have notice of the equitable interests in the property.

(v) Purchase for value

The doctrine of notice will only operate in favour of a person who purchased the property in which there was a pre-existing equitable interest for valuable consideration. The concept of consideration in equity is different to that at common law. In equity, nominal consideration, which would be sufficient to establish an enforceable contractual obligation at common law,[74] is insufficient. It follows from this requirement of valuable consideration that the doctrine of notice will never operate in favour of a volunteer. Thus, a person who receives property by way of gift or succession will always acquire the legal ownership subject to any pre-existing equitable interests.

(vi) Of the legal title

The doctrine of notice only protects a purchaser of the legal title to the property. In the case of land, the purchase must be of a legal estate or interest.[75] A person who purchases an equitable interest in property will therefore take subject to all other pre-existing equitable interests, since between competing equitable entitlements 'the first in time prevails'.

(vii) Without notice

Without notice[76] is the most important of the requirements. It concerns the extent to which the purchaser was aware or ignorant of the existence of any pre-existing equitable interests subsisting in the property acquired. Clearly, he will have 'notice' of such interests if he consciously knew of their existence, for example if the seller had informed him. Such awareness is termed 'actual notice'. However, the concept of notice has been given a wider ambit in equity, so that a person is treated as if he was actually aware of all pre-existing equitable interests that he would have discovered if he had taken all reasonable steps to investigate the property concerned by making 'such inquiries and 'inspections' as ought reasonably to have been made'.[77] This prevents a person claiming the benefit of the doctrine of notice simply

---

[74] For example, a peppercorn.

[75] Under the Law of Property Act 1925, s 1 this means a fee simple absolute in possession (freehold) or a terms of years absolute (leasehold) or one of the subsidiary legal interests listed in the section.

[76] See Law of Property Act 1925, s 199.

[77] Law of Property Act 1925, s 199(1)(ii)(a). See *Jones v Smith* (1841) 1 Hare 43; *Northern Bank Ltd v Henry* [1981] IR 1.

by seeking to avoid receiving actual notice of such rights. Such deemed notice is termed 'constructive notice'. A person will also be treated as having notice if the purchase was conducted by an agent acting on his behalf if the agent had actual or constructive notice of the existence of the equitable interest. Such notice is termed 'imputed notice'.

(viii) Destruction of equitable proprietary interests by the doctrine of notice

Where all the requisite elements of the doctrine of notice are satisfied, it operates so as to completely destroy any subsisting equitable interests in the property concerned. Even if the property is subsequently transferred to a person with notice of the relevant interest, it will not revive. This can be seen from the facts of *Wilkes v Spooner*.[78] Spooner was the tenant of a pork butcher's shop. Wilkes was the beneficiary of an equitable restrictive covenant, affecting the shop, preventing its use as a general butcher's. Spooner surrendered his lease of the shop to the landlord.[79] As the landlord was unaware of the restrictive covenant, he was protected by the doctrine of notice, with the consequence that his legal ownership was not encumbered by it. Subsequently, the landlord granted a new lease of the shop to Spooner's son, who had actual notice of the restriction. Since the doctrine of notice had operated so as to destroy the right altogether, he too acquired the shop free from the restriction. The operation of the doctrine of notice in relation to the enforceability of the beneficial interest behind a trust is considered in Chapter 3, alongside the other management of property.

(c) Mere equities

Mere equities relating to property are incapable of binding a person who purchases an interest in it, whether legal or equitable, irrespective of whether they have notice. As Lord Upjohn stated in *National Provincial Bank Ltd v Ainsworth*:

> I myself cannot see how it is possible for a 'mere equity' to bind a purchaser unless such an equity is ancillary to or dependent upon an equitable estate or interest in the land…a 'mere equity' naked and alone is, in my opinion, incapable of binding successors in title even with notice; it is personal to the parties.[80]

5 The continued creativity of equity

(1) The historical impact of equity

The remaining chapters in Part I of the textbook will describe the extent of the creativity of equity in providing new rights and remedies in English law. One of the outstanding characteristics of equity has been its capacity to develop new rights and remedies

---

[78] [1911] 2 KB 473.
[79] The surrender of the lease satisfied the requirement that the landlord be a purchaser of a legal estate for value.   [80] [1965] AC 1175, at 1238.

for the benefit of plaintiffs. The need for such creativity within English law was the very reason for equity's genesis, and it led in particular to the evolution of the trust. Today, despite its undisputed and revered pedigree, the question has arisen whether equity retains such dynamic creative capacity. Or, to borrow a favourite metaphor of Lord Denning, is equity 'past the age of childbearing'?

(2) Constraints on the development of new rights by Equity

Some judges have stated extra-judicially their feeling that equity has lost its creative power altogether. For example, in 1953 Lord Evershed expressed his opinion that:

> the passing of the Judicature Act, and section 25(11) in particular, put a stop to, or at least a very severe limitation on, the inventive faculties of future Chancery judges.[81]

Two main fears seem to have influenced the courts against a creative role for equity.

(a) Reluctance to countenance judicial law making

Some judges fear that a willingness to create new equitable rights and remedies threatens the delicate constitutional balance between the legislative and judicial arms of government because it usurps the proper function of Parliament. This fear is not unique to equity, but affects English law as a whole. This reluctance to undermine Parliament was evident in *Westdeutsche Landesbank Girozentrale v Islington London Borough Council*.[82] The unwillingness of the majority to extend the jurisdiction of equity to award compound damages was grounded in the concern that such an extension would be an unjustifiable usurpation of the functions properly belonging to Parliament, because Parliament had twice legislated to grant the common law the power to award simple interest but had not felt it necessary to go further. As Lord Lloyd explained:

> To extend the equitable jurisdiction for the first time to cover a residual injustice at common law, which Parliament chose not to remedy, would, I think, be as great a usurpation of the role of the legislature, and as clear an example of judicial lawmaking as it would have been in *President of India*.[83] If it is thought desirable that the courts should have a power to award compound interest in common law claims for actions for money had and received, then such a result can now only be brought about by Parliament.[84]

(b) Danger of uncertainty

Some judges have equally expressed their concern that radical creativity by equity, generating new rights and remedies to do justice in individual cases, would result in uncertainty. The courts are reluctant to allow the situation to develop where equity

---

[81] (1953) 6 CLP 1, at 12.
[82] [1996] 2 All ER 961. See also [1996] RLR 3 (Birks); [1996] LMCLQ 441 (Stevens).
[83] *President of India v La Pintada Cia Navigacion SA* [1985] AC 104.
[84] [1996] 2 All ER 961, at 1021.

could again appear subjective and attract the criticism of varying with the length of the Chancellor's foot. As Bagnall J stated in *Cowcher v Cowcher*:

> I am convinced that in determining rights, particularly property rights, the only justice that can be attained by mortals, who are fallible and are not omniscient, is justice according to law; the justice that flows from the application of sure and settled principles to proved or admitted facts. So in the field of equity the length of the Chancellor's foot has been measured or is capable of measurement…[85]

(3) **Evolution of new rights and remedies from existing principles**

Despite the reluctance of the court to 'invent' new rights and remedies, this does not mean that equity is stagnant and incapable of flexible development to meet new circumstances. The law is a coherent and dynamic whole, subject to constant re-evaluation and adjustment, sometimes culminating in the birth of new principles and doctrines. The emergence of new rights and remedies labelled 'equitable' must be viewed within the framework of judicial development of the law as a whole. Equity does not enjoy any special ability to be more creative than other branches of law, but equity has made a tremendous contribution to the law and the continuous process of remoulding equitable rights and remedies should be seen as an essential part of this overall process of legal development. Rights and remedies which are in practice 'new' can be developed from existing principles and precedents. The operation of the constructive trust, which will be considered in Chapter 9, provides a striking example of how rights can be developed, as the operation of this type of trust in protecting cohabitants who have no express proprietary rights ably demonstrates, as we shall see in Chapter 10. This development parallels past common law achievements, such as the acceptance of a general law of negligence in *Donoghue v Stevenson*.[86]

The fears which have been expressed in relation to the ability of equity to create new rights and remedies have also curtailed the willingness of the court to introduce changes to traditional common law doctrines. For example, in *Prudential Assurance Co Ltd v London Residuary Body*[87] the House of Lords refused to overrule the ancient common law rule that a lease is void if it is not created with an ascertainable maximum duration, despite the fact that it served no useful purpose and they could find no satisfactory rationale for its existence, because of fear that so doing might 'upset long-established titles'.

So, is equity 'past the age of childbearing?' The answer it appears is no, but to continue Lord Denning's metaphor, progeny will not happen by accident but as a result of careful planning.

---

[85] [1972] 1 WLR 425, at 430.   [86] [1932] AC 562.   [87] [1992] 3 All ER 504.

6 The maxims of equity

Finally, attention turns to the key principles underlying the operation of the whole of the equitable jurisdiction, which the maxims of equity are an attempt to formulate in short, pithy phrases.[88] They are not binding rules, nor do they provide guidance for every situation in which equity operates. Nevertheless, they provide useful illustrations of some of the principal recurrent themes which can be identified within the corpus of the rules of equity.

(1) Equity will not suffer a wrong to be without a remedy

This maxim provides the philosophical foundation of equity, namely, that wrongs should be redressed by the courts if possible. Equity developed as a response to defects of the common law to provide relief where none was available. For example, equity intervened to allow a person to escape from a contract which they had entered having been misled by a mistake of fact, even though the contract was enforceable at common law.[89] Similarly, through a trust equity enabled a beneficiary to enforce an obligation to use property in a particular way where there was no remedy at common law.

(2) Equity follows the law

This is arguably the most important maxim, as it underpins the operation of the equitable jurisdiction. The Court of Chancery did not override the courts of common law except to remedy an injustice, and could not depart from statute.[90] Equity does not unnecessarily depart from legal principles.[91] The fact that equity follows the law is well illustrated in the context of land by the fact that the equitable estates and interests largely correspond to those at law.

(3) Where the equities are equal the law prevails

This maxim means that where there are two persons with competing rights to the same item of property, one with a legal right and the other an equitable right, the legal right will take priority over the equitable right, even if the equitable right had pre-existed it. In *Wortley v Birkhead*,[92] Lord Hardwicke LC explained that this was 'by reason of that force [the Court of Chancery] necessarily and rightly gives to the legal title'.[93] In the context of land, issues of priority between competing rights, whether

---

[88] See Snell's *Principles of Equity* (30th edn, 2000), pp 27–44.
[89] See eg *Cooper v Joel* (1859) 1 De G F & J 240; *Torrance v Bolton* (1872) 8 Ch App 118.
[90] See Gardner 'Two Maxims of Equity' [1995] CLJ 60.
[91] *Burgess v Wheate* (1759) 1 Eden 177, at 195, per Clarke MR; *Sinclair v Brougham* [1914] AC 398, at 414–415, per Lord Haldane LC.   [92] (1754) 2 Ves Sen 571, at 574.
[93] Compare also *Marsh v Lee* (1670) 2 Vent 337; *Pfeiffer (E) Weinkellerei-Weineinkauf GmbH & Co v Arbuthnot Factors Ltd* [1988] 1 WLR 150.

legal or equitable, are governed by statutory rules which have displaced the operation of this maxim and the next.[94]

(4) **Where the equities are equal the first in time prevails**

This maxim means that if two parties have competing equitable rights in the same item of property, and neither has the legal estate, the right which was created first enjoys priority.[95] This maxim mirrors the common law rule as to priority between competing legal rights.

(5) **He who seeks equity must do equity**

This maxim looks to a claimant's future conduct. If a claimant seeks equitable relief, he must be prepared to act fairly towards the person against whom it is sought.[96] For example, if a purchase is set aside in equity, the purchase money must be repaid with interest.[97]

(6) **He who comes to equity must come with clean hands**

In contrast, this maxim looks to the past conduct of the claimant. If the claimant's conduct is tainted by illegal or inequitable conduct, he may be denied the relief to which he would otherwise be entitled. The maxim does not apply to conduct in general, but only that which has 'an immediate and necessary relation to the equity sued for'.[98] Therefore in *Argyle (Duchess) v Argyle (Duke)*[99] the plaintiff's adultery, which caused a divorce, was no bar to her claim for an injunction to restrain the defendant from publishing confidential material. The rationale for this maxim, as for the parallel common law rule against illegality, is to deter persons from entering into transactions which involve a dimension of illegality. However, since these rules may in practice allow one person who was party to an illegal purpose arbitrarily to retain the entire benefit of property transferred to him, because another equally guilty party is prevented from asserting any entitlement to it, the courts have systematically ameliorated their strictness through exceptions.

(7) **Delay defeats equity**

Equity will not assist a plaintiff who has failed to assert his rights within a reasonable time. This is the foundation of the equitable defence of laches, which was applied in *Nelson v Rye*,[100] where it was held that a musician could not claim an account of

---

[94] See Chapter 3.
[95] *Willoughby v Willoughby* (1756) 1 Term Rep 763; *Brace v Duchess of Marlborough* (1728) 2 P Wms 491; *Rice v Rice* (1854) 2 Drew 73; *Phillips v Phillips* (1861) 4 De GF & J 208.
[96] See eg *Lodge v National Union Investment Co Ltd* [1907] 1 Ch 300; *Solle v Butcher* [1950] 1 KB 671; *Chappell v Times Newspapers Ltd* [1975] 1 WLR 482.   [97] *Peacock v Evans* (1809–10) 16 Ves 512.
[98] *Dering v Earl of Winchelsea* (1787) 2 White & Tud LC 488 at 489.   [99] [1967] Ch 302.
[100] [1996] 2 All ER 186; Stevens 'Too Late to Face the Music? Limitation and Laches as Defences to an Action for Breach of Fiduciary Duty' [1997] Conv 225.

earnings wrongfully retained by his manager in breach of fiduciary duty because he had waited for more than six years before commencing an action. The operation of this defence must today be considered in conjunction with the statutory rules concerning limitation of actions under the Limitation Act 1980, considered in Chapter 27.

(8) **Equality is equity**

Where persons enjoy concurrent entitlement to identical interests in property, and there is no express provision, agreement, or other basis as to how it should be divided among them, equity prescribes that equal division should occur, so that each receives an equal share in the property.[101] This maxim is reflected in the preference of equity for a tenancy in common, which will sometimes be implied in equity even where the common law holds that there is a joint tenancy,[102] as, for example, where joint purchasers purchase land and there no express allocation of the equitable interest.[103]

(9) **Equity looks to the intent rather than the form**

The principle behind this maxim was well stated by Romilly MR in *Parkin v Thorold*:

> Courts of equity make a distinction between that which is matter of substance and that which is matter of form; and if it finds that by insisting on the form, the substance will be defeated, it holds it to be inequitable to allow a person to insist on such form, and thereby defeat the substance.[104]

Therefore, it is not necessary to use the precise word 'trust' to create a trust, provided that in substance the settlor intended to subject the legal owner of the property to a mandatory obligation regarding its use.[105] Similarly, equity will look to the substance, and not the wording used, to determine if a clause in a contract providing for the payment of a specific sum in the event of breach is a penalty or a genuine pre-estimate of damages.[106]

(10) **Equity regards as done that which ought to be done**

Where a contract is specifically enforceable, equity regards the promisor as having already done what he has promised to do, because he can be compelled to do it. Hence, a contract for the purchase of land,[107] or of unique personal property,[108] will give rise to

---

[101] *Petit v Smith* (1695) 1 P Wms 7; *Re Dickens* [1935] Ch 267; *Re Bradberry* [1943] Ch 35; *Hampton & Sons v Garrard Smith (Estate Agents) Ltd* [1985] 1 EGLR 23; see also *McPhail v Doulton* [1971] AC 424.

[102] See Stevens and Pearce, *Land Law* (5th edn 2013), 12.15–12.25.

[103] See *Jones v Kernott* [2011] UKSC 53.   [104] (1852) 16 Beav 59, at 66.

[105] *Re Kayford Ltd* [1975] 1 WLR 279.

[106] *Kembel v Farren* (1829) 6 Bing 141; *Pye v British Automobile Commercial Syndicate* [1906] 1 KB 425; *Diestal v Stevenson* [1906] 2 KB 345; *Cellulose Acetate Silk Co Ltd v Widnes Foundry (1925) Ltd* [1933] AC 20; *Robert Stewart & Sons Ltd v Carapanayoti & Co Ltd* [1962] 1 WLR 34.

[107] *Lloyds Bank plc v Carrick* [1996] 4 All ER 630.

[108] Eg in *Oughtred v IRC* [1960] AC 206, where there was a contract for the purchase of a beneficiary's equitable interest in shares in a private company.

an immediate constructive trust vesting the equitable ownership in the purchaser by way of a constructive trust at the very moment that the contract is entered.

(11) **Equity imputes an intention to fulfil an obligation**

Equity places the most favourable construction on a man's acts, so that if he does something which could be construed as fulfilling an obligation he owes, equity will regard it as having this effect. For example, if a debtor leaves a legacy to his creditor, this is presumed to be a repayment of the debt.[109] The doctrines of performance and satisfaction are founded on this maxim.

(12) **Equity acts in personam**

This maxim refers to the fact that equity enforces its decisions by means of a personal order against the defendant, for example by an order to perform a contract, observe a trust, or refrain from some behaviour by means of an injunction. If the defendant breaches the order, he will be in contempt of court.[110] The court may exercise jurisdiction over any person within the power of the court,[111] even though the order may relate to property which is situated abroad.[112]

---

[109] *Thynne v Glengall* (1848) 2 HL Cas 131; *Chichester v Coventry* (1867) LR 2 HL 71; *Re Horlock* [1895] 1 Ch 516.   [110] See *Co-operative Insurance v Argyll Stores* [1997] 3 All ER 297 at 302–303.
[111] Namely, someone who is within the jurisdiction or on whom the court order can be served outside of it.
[112] *Penn v Lord Baltimore* (1750) 1 Ves Sen 444; *Ewing v Orr Ewing* (1883–84) 9 App Cas 34, HL; *Richard West & Partners (Inverness) Ltd v Dick* [1969] 1 All ER 289; affd [1969] 2 Ch 424, CA.

2

Equitable obligations: trusts and powers

This chapter will examine the fundamental characteristics of the modern trust, and draw comparisons between it and other equitable obligations relating to property. Substantive treatment of both trusts and powers takes place later in the book, and this is clearly signposted throughout this chapter.

1 Fundamental characteristics of trusts

(1) The hybrid nature of trusts

It is difficult to categorize the essential nature of a trust.[1] As a legal concept a trust does not fit neatly into either the category of 'obligations' or of 'proprietary rights'. Rather, the trust shares some characteristics of obligations and some characteristics of proprietary rights. In this sense it is a hybrid, and can best be regarded as a sui generis 'proprietary obligation'. Despite difficulties of classification, three essential characteristics of trusts can be identified. First, a trust can only exist in relation to specific property. Second, this property must be held by trustees, who are subject to mandatory obligations governing how it should be used and applied. Third, the trustees must owe these mandatory obligations to legal persons who are entitled to enforce them. These persons are termed the beneficiaries of the trust, and they are entitled to the trust property in equity. These three elements all appear in the definition of a 'trust' in art 2 of the Hague Convention on the Law Applicable to Trusts and on their Recognition, incorporated into English law by the Recognition of Trusts Act 1987.

(2) Property subject to the trust

(a) A trust can only exist in relation to specific property

A trust can only exist in relation to specific property, whether land or personal property. As Lord Browne-Wilkinson stated in *Westdeutsche Landesbank Girozentrale*

---

[1] See Bartlett 'When is a "Trust" Not a Trust? The National Health Service Trust' [1996] Conv 186; Hayton 'Developing the Obligation Characteristics of the Trust' (2001) 117 LQR 96; Parkinson 'Reconceptualising the Express Trust' [2002] 61 CLJ 657.

v Islington London Borough Council: 'In order to establish a trust there must be identifiable trust property.'[2] This requirement is reflected in a number of principles limiting the circumstances in which there will be a valid trust. A trust cannot be effectively created over 'future property', which is property not yet in existence but merely expected as a possibility in the future. For example, a trust cannot be created over property that a person expects to receive under the will of a relative who has not yet died,[3] or over money that a person might win from the national lottery. In both cases it is uncertain whether the alleged property will ever materialize. It is possible to promise to create a trust of such future property in the event that it materializes, which may create a contractual obligation so to do, but this is essentially different from the creation of an immediate trust. Similarly, a trust cannot be created over unascertained property. There has to be definite property to which the trust can relate.[4] In *Re Goldcorp Exchange Ltd (In Receivership)*,[5] customers of a company were unable to establish a trust in relation to gold and other precious metals bought as investments with their money, on the basis that it was impossible to identify the specific metal derived from each customer's individual investment. The customers were therefore limited to a contractual claim against the company for the return of their investment. A trust will also cease to exist if all the property subject to it is destroyed or dissipated.[6]

(b) The concept of a 'trust fund'

Although a trust may exist in relation to a single, specific asset, such as a sum of money, a piece of land, or shares in a company, often the property to which the trust relates will comprise a wide range of different assets. In both cases, the trustees may be permitted to sell the assets and exchange them for new ones.[7] For this reason the property subject to the trust is generically identified as the trust 'fund'.[8] Often the precise content of the fund will be fluid, because the individual assets comprising the fund are frequently being substituted by means of sale and reinvestment. For example, if trustees hold capital under a trust requiring them to invest it and pay any income to the beneficiaries, the capital need not necessarily remain in the same investments throughout the life of the trust. Indeed, there will be some instances, such as with unit trusts and pension schemes, where the benefits of collective investment would largely be lost without a regular review of the investment portfolio. The trustees therefore have powers of disposition over the investments held and they will move or change those investments from time to time.[9] Provided that the proceeds from the realization of any investment are immediately reinvested, the value of the investment portfolio will remain unchanged, apart

---

[2] [1996] 2 All ER 961, at 988.   [3] See *Re Ellenborough* [1903] 1 Ch 697. See further Chapter 16.
[4] Certainty of property is one of the three requirements necessary to establish an express trust, and is explored in Chapter 7.   [5] [1994] 2 All ER 806.
[6] See *Re Diplock* [1948] Ch 465; *Bishopsgate Investment Management v Homan* [1995] 1 All ER 347.
[7] Trustees powers and duties to manage trust property are covered in Part V of this book.
[8] See Nolan 'Property in a Fund' (2004) 120 LQR 108.
[9] Investment of trust funds is covered in Chapter 21.

from any gains or losses that have been made on individual investments within the portfolio.[10]

This concept of trust assets forming a collective investment fund is a core principle in equity. It lies at the root of unit trusts and pension funds.[11] In more domestic contexts, it provides a means by which parents with sufficient money to invest can make provision for their children, preserving wealth within the family, but giving flexibility to the trustees as to how it will be managed and invested. The fund concept has also been employed in a corporate context, where equity has recognized that it is possible to create a floating charge over the assets of a company. This operates to use the assets of the company as security for an obligation, in a similar way to that in which a house can be mortgaged to secure the repayment of a loan. Instead of freezing any particular asset, a floating charge treats all the assets of the company as a fund, and applies to the fund as a whole. So long as it continues to trade in the ordinary course of business, so that assets disposed of are balanced by assets acquired, the company retains freedom of disposition over individual assets. Should the company cease to trade in the ordinary way, or if some other specified event occurs, then the charge settles and crystallizes by attaching to the specific assets then forming part of the fund.[12]

(c) Property that is the product of trust property will also be trust property

A feature of a fund is that it includes accretions as well as substitutions. Property produced by trust property itself becomes subject to the trust. For example, if the trust property includes shares in a company, any dividends paid on such shares will also comprise trust property. It has already been noted that property acquired by the sale and reinvestment of trust property will belong to the trust fund. As an extension of this principle, any unauthorized profits earned by the exploitation of opportunities arising from the trust property will also be trust property. Where, for example, the trust property comprises shares in a company, those shares inevitably carry voting rights in the company general meeting, which are controlled by the trustees by virtue of their legal title to the shares. If a trustee is then appointed director through the use of those voting rights any personal remuneration he receives in that capacity will *prima facie* constitute trust property.

(3) Trustees subject to the obligations of the trust

(a) The trust as a species of obligation

The essence of a trust is that the owner of specific property is subject to mandatory personal obligations governing how it should be used and applied. A trustee is someone who owns property subject to personal obligations to manage and apply it in

---

[10] See for example, *Re Earl of Strafford (Deceased)* [1980] Ch 28.

[11] Such schemes, known as 'collective investments', are covered in Chapter 22.

[12] *Governments Stock and Other Securities Co v Manila Railway Co* [1897] AC 81, at 86, per Lord MacNaghten; *George Barker (Transport) Ltd v Eynon* [1974] 1 All ER 900, at 905, per Edmund Davies LJ.

accordance with the terms of the trust to the advantage of the beneficiaries thereof. He does not enjoy the right to treat the property as if it were his own. The precise nature of the trustee's obligations and duties in relation to the trust property are dependent upon the terms of the particular trust. His rights and duties may be both positive and negative—there may be some things that a trustee should do in relation to the trust property, and others that he should not. The obligations imposed by a trust are not such as to limit the capacity of the trustee to deal with the property. His unencumbered capacity to deal with the trust property derives simply from the fact that he owns it. The trust obligations merely dictate what he should or should not do, and dealings with the trust property in contravention of these obligations are not *ultra vires* and void. A trustee who deals with the trust property inconsistently with the terms of the trust will instead become personally liable to the beneficiaries for 'breach of trust' and, in the absence of any defences, will be required to compensate them for any loss they suffer in consequence.[13]

(b) The source of the trust obligations

A trust arises when property is held by trustees subject to obligations owed in favour of beneficiaries. Such obligations will arise where the outright owner of property deliberately subjects it to a trust, is presumed to have subjected it to a trust, or if a trust is imposed by law.

(i) Express intention to impose trust obligations

Property may be subjected to a trust obligation by the deliberate act of its owner. An outright owner[14] of property may create a trust either by subjecting himself to trust obligations, by declaring that he holds it for specified beneficiaries, or by transferring the ownership to someone else, specifying that they are intended to hold it on trust.[15] For example, if Mike owns shares in a company and wishes to create a trust of them in favour of Norma, he can either declare himself a trustee of the shares or transfer them to Owen, directing him to hold them on trust for her. In either case the trust is said to be express, as it was created by the deliberate intention of the owner. The person creating an express trust is described as the 'settlor', as he is said to 'settle' the property on trust for the benefit of the beneficiaries.

(ii) Implied intention to impose trust obligations

While the paradigm source of trust obligations is the express intention of the settlor, there are some circumstances in which equity presumes that a person intended to subject property to a trust, even though in fact no such intention was expressed. If a presumption of a trust arises, and it is not rebutted by counter-evidence that no trust was intended, the property will be subject to what is known as a resulting

---

[13] See Chapter 27.

[14] This is where the owner has legal and equitable title to the property in his own right. If the owner only has equitable title, it is still possible to create a trust, normally referred to as a sub-trust.

[15] See Chapter 7.

trust.[16] Resulting trusts arise in two main circumstances, which were identified by Lord Browne-Wilkinson in *Westdeutsche Landesbank Girozentrale v Islington London Borough Council*:

> (a) where A makes a voluntary payment to B or pays (wholly or partly) for the purchase of property which is vested either in B alone or in the joint names of A and B, there is a presumption that A did not intend to make a gift to B; the money or property is held on trust for A (if he is the sole provider of the money) or in the case of a joint purchase by A and B in shares proportionate to their contributions…
>
> (b) where A transfers property to B on express trusts, but the trusts declared do not exhaust the whole beneficial interest.[17]

(iii) Imposed trust obligations

In some cases property will be regarded as subject to trust obligations despite the lack of either express or presumed intention on the part of the owner because his unconscionable conduct demands that he be required to hold the property for the benefit of others. In such circumstances, the law imposes a constructive trust.[18]

(c) The content of the trustees' obligations under the trust

The precise obligations imposed on any particular trustee will vary with the terms of the trust. In many cases the obligations of the trustees will be specified in the trust instrument by the settlor creating the trust. However, in the absence of any contradictory express terms, some powers and duties are granted and imposed by statute. Two main categories of obligation can be identified.

(i) The obligation to allocate the trust property

The most important obligation imposed by a trust is the obligation of the trustees to apply the trust property for the benefit of the beneficiaries in accordance with the terms of the trust. Under some trusts, the trustees have no part to play in deciding how the trust property should be allocated among the beneficiaries because the terms of the trust stipulate how the beneficial interest is to be shared. Such a trust is described as a 'fixed trust' because the settlor who created it has specified the respective entitlements of the beneficiaries in the terms of the trust, and the trustees' duty is merely to carry out his instructions. In other cases, the trustees have a role to play in determining how the beneficial interest is to be allocated. Rather than fixing the specific entitlements of the beneficiaries, the settlor may confer on the trustees the right to decide how the trust property should be allocated among a class of beneficiaries. Such a trust is called a 'discretionary trust' because the entitlement of any individual beneficiary to share in the trust fund is at the discretion of the

---

[16] See Chapter 8.   [17] [1996] 2 All ER 961, at 990.

[18] See Chapter 9. Constructive trusts have also been held to arise on the (implied) common intention of the parties owning a family home, which is discussed in Chapter 10.

trustees.[19] Where property is held on trust for children who have not yet reached the age of majority, so that they do not enjoy vested interests in the trust property or the income generated from it, the trustees may enjoy the power to apply such income to their benefit, or even to allow them to receive part of the trust property itself ahead of time. These powers are respectively termed the power of 'maintenance' and the power of 'advancement'. These powers may be granted expressly to the trustees by the settlor creating the trust, but in the absence of an express grant they are conferred by statute.[20]

(ii) The obligation to manage the trust property

The second category of trustees' obligations concerns their duties to manage the trust property and to maintain the integrity of the fund. The trustees enjoy complete control of the trust property by virtue of their legal ownership of the assets that comprise the fund.[21] Management functions include decisions on how the trust fund should be invested, and on whether assets held should be realized and the proceeds of sale reinvested. The precise scope of the trustees' management powers are determined by the terms of the particular trust. For example, the terms of the trust may expressly specify the investment powers that the trustees are to enjoy in relation to the trust property, perhaps limiting the type of investments that the trustees are entitled to pursue. In the absence of such express powers of investment, statute intervenes to grant the trustees standard investment powers.[22] The trust may also specify the means by which new or replacement trustees can be appointed,[23] and statute empowers the trustees to delegate some of their functions to an agent acting on their behalf.[24]

(d) The mandatory character of the trustees' obligations under the trust

The obligations of a trustee are mandatory in nature. This means that trustees are required to carry the terms of the trust into effect. In the event that they fail to carry out their obligations, especially the obligation to allocate the trust fund among the beneficiaries, the court will intervene to ensure that the trust is carried out, either by ordering them to act as required by the terms of the trust, or, if necessary, by finding an alternative means of enforcing the trust, for example by appointing new trustees. In this sense trust obligations can be distinguished from powers of appointment, which are discretionary rather than mandatory in character. The mandatory character of trust obligations is also seen in the operation of the maxim that 'equity will not allow a trust to fail for want of a trustee'. If a settlor transfers property to a person who refuses to accept the office of trustee, or if he leaves property by will to a trustee who predeceases him, equity will not allow the trust to fail but will instead find an alternative person to act as trustee.

---

[19] See further Chapter 16.   [20] See Chapter 15.   [21] See Chapter 20.
[22] Trustee Act 2000. See Chapter 21.   [23] See Chapter 24.   [24] See Chapter 23.

(e) The trustees' liability for breach of trust

Trustees do not lack capacity to deal with the trust property in a manner inconsistent with the terms of the trust. If they do act inconsistently with the terms of the trust, their breach of obligation will render them personally liable to compensate the beneficiaries for any loss caused by the breach.[25] The trustees may commit a breach of trust in three circumstances. First, they commit a breach of trust if they act in a manner inconsistent with the terms of the trust by doing something they were not authorized to do. Second, they commit a breach of trust by omission if they fail to do what the terms of the trust require them to do. Third, they commit a breach of trust if they fail to act with the requisite objective standard of care expected of them, namely, that of 'the ordinary prudent man of business'.

(f) The ability of the beneficiaries to override the terms of the trust

Although trustees are placed under personal obligations as to how the trust property should be allocated and managed, the terms of the trust stipulated by the settlor are not sacrosanct, and can be overridden by the wishes of the beneficiaries. If the trustees act in breach of trust with the authorization of the beneficiaries, they will not be liable to them for any losses that ensue from the breach. The trustees will only enjoy complete immunity from liability if all the beneficiaries authorize the breach, and they remain liable to any beneficiaries who do not give valid authorization.[26] Valid authorization can only be given by beneficiaries who are of age and legally competent. The power of the beneficiaries to override the terms of the trust is most vividly illustrated by the operation of the rule in *Saunders v Vautier*,[27] by which the beneficiaries are entitled to insist that the trust is brought to an end by requiring the trustees to transfer the legal title to the trust property to them. The erstwhile beneficiaries would become the outright owners of the trust property and it will be free from the control of the trustees. Similarly, the beneficiaries of a trust can countenance variations in its terms, again potentially undermining the wishes of the settlor embodied therein. The Variation of Trusts Act 1958 even permits the court to grant approval to variations on behalf of beneficiaries who are incapable of consenting for themselves, either because they lack the capacity to consent, are not yet in existence, or cannot be ascertained, provided that the proposed variations are for their 'benefit'.[28]

(g) The fiduciary obligations of trustees

While the trustees are subject to the specific obligations imposed by the terms of the trust, they are also subject to a general fiduciary duty imposed by

---

[25] The beneficiaries may also have a claim against someone who receives the trust property knowing of the breach, or who dishonestly assists in the breach. See Chapter 29.

[26] This helps to prevent any particular beneficiary dictating to the trustees how to exercise their powers in relation to the trust.   [27] (1841) 4 Beav 115. This is explored further in Chapter 14.

[28] See Chapter 17.

equity.[29] Equity recognizes that trustees may be tempted to take advantage of their position as the legal owners of the trust property and utilize it to their own advantage, rather than in the interests of their beneficiaries. It therefore imposes a strict duty of exclusive loyalty on trustees, obliging them to act solely in the interests of their beneficiaries, and assumes that any personal profit derived from their position as trustee was only obtained by allowing their own interests to prevail over those of their beneficiaries. Trustees are obliged to make restitution to the beneficiaries of any unauthorized profits that they received by virtue of their position, or in circumstances where there was a mere possibility of a conflict of interest between their duty and their personal interests. Trustees will be entitled to retain such profits received in breach of their fiduciary duty if they acted with the informed consent or authorization of the beneficiaries.

The fiduciary obligations are owed to *all* the beneficiaries of a trust, whether they are entitled immediately to an interest, or whether they are entitled in remainder.

(4) **Beneficiaries entitled to the benefit of the trust**

The third essential characteristic of a trust is that there must be persons for whose benefit the property is held, and to whom the obligations of the trustees are owed, often referred to as the 'objects' of the trust. With the exception of trusts for charitable purposes, and a very small number of other anomalous trusts for purposes, trusts must exist for the benefit of persons rather than purposes. The reason for this limitation is that only legal persons, whether human individuals, companies, or corporations, possess the necessary capacity to enjoy and enforce the obligation of the trustees. Therefore, a trust cannot be validly created for the abstract purpose of 'promoting good journalism' because there is no person to whom the obligation is owed, and no one who possesses sufficient *locus standi* to complain to the court if the trustees fail to apply the trust property to the specified purpose. In the case of charitable trusts, the trustees' obligations are supervised on behalf of the Crown by the Attorney-General and the Charity Commission.[30]

(a) **The beneficiaries have the right to enforce the trust obligations**

The prime entitlement of the beneficiaries of a trust is that the trustees carry out the terms of the trust. They are entitled to enforce the trust, either by preventing the trustees acting in breach or by requiring them to perform their obligations if they are refusing to do so. In effect, they are entitled to require full performance of the trust in their favour. Once property has been validly subjected to a trust in their favour, the beneficiaries are entitled to enforce it irrespective of whether or not they provided consideration in return for the creation of the trust.[31]

---

[29] See Chapter 28.   [30] See Chapter 26.
[31] See Chapter 7 for details in relation to express trusts.

(b) The beneficiaries have the right to override the terms of the trust

Beneficiaries of a trust enjoy the right to override the terms of the trust as stipulated by the settlor. They can authorize and require the trustees to act in a way which would otherwise be a breach of trust, or a breach of their fiduciary duty, and if they are all of age and legally competent they can demand that the trust be brought to an end in accordance with the rule in *Saunders v Vautier*.[32] They may not dictate to the trustees, however, as to the exercise of all or any of the trustees' powers under the terms of the trust.[33] Hence, the beneficiaries could not require a trustee to retire or a new trustee of their choice to be appointed, unless they did this by way of terminating the existing trust and creating a new one.

(c) The beneficiaries enjoy a proprietary entitlement to the trust fund

The beneficiaries of a trust enjoy more than merely personal rights to have the trust obligations carried out in their favour by the trustees. Despite some historical debate, the better view is that beneficiaries are also entitled to proprietary rights in the trust property.

(i) The beneficial interest as a mere interest in personam

Some have argued that the fact that the beneficial interest behind a trust is destroyed by the bona fide purchase of the trust property proves that it is a mere interest in personam. Maitland stated that equity had never regarded the beneficiary as 'owner' of the trust property, but only as entitled to enforce the personal obligation of the trustee to carry out the terms of the trust:

> [the trustee] is the owner, the full owner, of the thing, while the cestui que trust has no rights in the thing…[34]

More recent support for the view that beneficial interests behind a trust are mere rights in personam can be derived from the decision in *Webb v Webb*,[35] where the central issue was whether a father's assertion that his son held a holiday home in France on resulting trust for him, was a claim founded on a right in rem for the purposes of art 16(1) of the Convention on Jurisdiction and the Enforcement of Judgments in Civil and Commercial Matters 1968. Following the advice of Advocate-General Damon, the Court of Appeal held that the father's claim was not founded on a right in rem but merely on the existence of a personal fiduciary relationship. However, little weight should be placed upon this decision, as the classification of the nature of claims for the purposes of settling whether the English courts have jurisdiction when the property in dispute is situated abroad should not be determinative of the jurisprudential character of beneficial interests for domestic purposes.

---

[32] (1841) 4 Beav 115.   [33] *Re Brockbank* [1948] Ch 206.   [34] Maitland, *Equity* (1936), p 17.
[35] [1994] QB 696; MacMillian 'The European Court of Justice agrees with Maitland: Trusts and the Brussels Convention' [1996] Conv 125.

(ii) The beneficial interest as a proprietary interest in rem

In reality, it seems that the beneficial interest behind a trust is more than a mere personal interest enforceable against the trustee. A beneficiary's interest is enforceable against anyone acquiring the trust property except a bona fide purchaser for value, who is protected by the doctrine of notice. In this sense the beneficial interest shares the essential characteristic of proprietary rights identified by Lord Wilberforce in *National Provincial Bank Ltd v Ainsworth*,[36] namely, that they are capable of enduring through changes in ownership. Beneficial interests are certainly not as durable as legal ownership, but the mere fact that in some circumstances they are defeated by superior rights should not prevent the recognition that they are essentially proprietary in nature. Even Maitland later acknowledged that a beneficiary was entitled to more than a merely personal obligation:

> I believe that for the ordinary thought of Englishmen 'equitable ownership' is just ownership pure and simple, though it is subject to a peculiar, technical and not very intelligible rule in favour of bona fide purchasers ... so many people are bound to respect these rights that practically they are almost as valuable as if they were dominium.[37]

The proprietary nature of the beneficial interest under a trust is also supported by the fact that the beneficiary is entitled to deal with it in ways characteristic of property owners. He can transfer his equitable interest by assignment, either by way of sale or as a gift. He can dispose of it by will, or in the event of his dying intestate it passes to his heirs under the rules governing intestate succession. It can be used to provide security for a loan. He may be required to pay tax on its value. His rights, if he has a beneficial interest in land, are enforceable against third parties, subject to the limitations contained in the land registration rules. The proprietary character of the beneficial interest under a trust was clearly stated in *Westdeutsche Landesbank Girozentrale v Islington London Borough Council*,[38] where Lord Browne-Wilkinson said:

> Once a trust is established, as from the date of its establishment the beneficiary has, in equity, a proprietary interest in the trust property, which proprietary interest will be enforceable in equity against any subsequent holder of the property (whether the original property or substituted property into which it can be traced) other than a purchaser for value of the legal interest without notice.[39]

2 Powers of appointment

The trust is not the only mechanism that has been developed by equity to facilitate the management and allocation of property. A person may be granted a power of appointment in respect of specific property or a fund of property.[40] This enables him

---

[36] [1965] AC 1175. [37] Collected papers, Vol III, p 349. [38] [1996] AC 669.
[39] [1996] AC 669, at 705. [40] Thomas, *Powers* (1999).

to decide who should receive the property. The holder of the power (the donee) is able to allocate the property by exercising his power and making appointments thereof to the objects of the power. Unlike a trust, the donee of a power of appointment is under no obligation to exercise the power conferred upon him. It is discretionary rather than mandatory in character. A power of appointment may form part of a will, in which case it allows the donee to nominate beneficiaries to whom the personal representatives must give the property concerned. Alternatively, the power may be used to give similar instructions to trustees holding property on trust to give effect to the directions of the donee. Finally, a power may be given to the trustees themselves.[41]

3 Classification of equitable obligations

In the trust and the power, equity has developed two mechanisms which facilitate a separation between the three functions of the management and allocation of property and the right to the enjoyment of property. In the absence of either a trust or a power, these entitlements are enjoyed in a unitary manner by the owner of the property. With trusts and powers one or more of these functions is separated from the others. However, despite a degree of functional similarity between trusts and powers, it was historically important to draw a sharp distinction between them. Conceptually, a power is purely discretionary, imposing no obligations upon the donee and conferring no proprietary rights upon the objects. In contrast, a trust is mandatory in character, imposing an obligation to act upon the trustees and conferring a proprietary entitlement to the trust fund upon the beneficiaries. Equity at one time tended to differentiate between trusts and powers by examining any given situation and characterizing the mechanism created as either a trust or a power. The rights and duties of the parties were thus determined by that characterization. Traditionally, the two mechanisms were therefore clearly distinguishable from each other. However, over time such a simple bifurcation proved insufficiently flexible, and equity extended the boundaries of existing obligations and developed new obligations. As a result, the distinction between different categories of equitable mechanism may be extremely fine and very difficult to draw in practice. In the light of these developments, although convenient from the point of view of analysis, it is questionable whether it is still valid to regard the law as comprising a fixed group of categories of obligation into which each fact situation must be fitted, with the inevitable result that the categorization will determine the rights and duties. Instead, a 'scale' of equitable obligations has emerged, and the courts will be willing to construe any particular fact situation as falling somewhere along the scale, not necessarily within a fixed traditional category, and then finding the appropriate rights and duties. The shift has been from a 'black and white' categorization of equitable obligations as

---

[41] Powers of appointment are considered in Chapter 16.

either trusts or powers, to a recognition that there is a 'greyscale' with an almost infinite variation between the two extremes.

(1) **A traditional categorization**

(a) **Trust or power**

Originally, a trust and power were seen as being conceptually distinct, with only a limited scope for overlap. In construing a document, it was therefore simply a question of determining whether an obligation fell within the category of a trust or power. This would be determined by a consideration of the language used in the instrument creating it. In some circumstances the characterization of an arrangement as a trust or a power would determine whether the arrangement was valid or invalid.

For both trusts and powers it is necessary for the court to supervise the arrangement by ensuring that the fund is allocated only to those who fall within the terms of the original disposition. This requires that the beneficiaries of the trust, or the objects of the power, be defined with sufficient clarity and certainty. If this certainty of objects is lacking, then the whole arrangement will be void. Until the decision of the House of Lords in *McPhail v Doulton*,[42] the test of certainty of objects for powers was more generous than the test of certainty for trusts. Thus, it was often the case that an arrangement would be valid if characterized as a power but invalid if it was a trust.

(b) **Limitations of a traditional categorization**

One major limitation of the traditional categorization was the difficulty of determining whether a particular obligation was to be classed as a trust or a power, which could have such significant consequences for all the parties involved. The mere use of the words 'trust' or 'power' would not necessarily be conclusive, since what was important was the intention of the property owner creating the arrangement. If he intended to impose mandatory obligations, indicating that he expected the obligations to be carried out, a trust would be created, but if he intended to give discretion without imposing an obligation, then a power would be conferred. The difficulty lay in the fine distinction between these two alternatives. As Lord Wilberforce acknowledged in *McPhail v Doulton*, this is an area of 'delicate shading'.[43] No particular words were (or are) needed to create a trust or a power. There is therefore no easy way of telling whether a particular disposition (even if professionally drafted) creates a trust or a power, and the law reports are full of cases where even the courts have found it difficult to decide which is created in a given case. In *McPhail v Doulton* itself, the judge at first instance and the Court of Appeal found that the settlor had intended to create a power. These conclusions were influenced by the fact that the arrangement would be valid if characterized as a power, but void for want of certainty if it was a trust. The House of Lords ultimately held that the mandatory character of the language used indicated an

---

[42] [1971] AC 424.
[43] [1970] 2 All ER 228, at 240. See also Sir Richard Arden MR in *Brown v Higgs* (1800) 5 Ves 495, at 505, citing *Duke of Marlborough v Lord Godolphin* (1750) 2 Ves Sen 61.

intention to create a trust, but proceeded to revise the test of certainty applicable to trusts to ensure that it was not invalidated.

(c) Trusts combined with powers

The difficulty of making a distinction between trusts and powers is compounded by the fact that a power will always be associated with a trust. This is because a power of appointment is essentially the right to give directions to trustees as to how or for whom they are to hold trust property. This can happen in one of several ways. First, trustees could be directed to hold property for whomever the donee of the power selects. In the absence of the power being exercised, there may be a defined trust in default of appointment. Second, there might be a fixed trust, subject to the donee of a power being able to divest the beneficiaries of their interests by exercising the power. Finally, there might be an obligation to make a selection, so that the 'power' is really itself a trust. In each case, the power of selection could either be held by the trustees of the trust fund themselves, or by a separate donee.

(2) The evolution of intermediate obligations

The development of trusts and powers by equity was driven by the desire to enable property owners to deal with their property as they wish. The power enabled a property owner to delegate to another the control over the distribution of his property, within the limits he had specified. The trust enabled the owner of property to distribute his property to predetermined individuals by giving the legal title to a trustee and specifying the beneficial interests. However, as owners' intentions changed with time and they sought to distribute their property in more complex ways, a simple analysis of equitable obligations proved inadequate. Equity was able to develop new obligations which combined aspects of both the power and the trust. The prime example is the emergence of the discretionary trust. Despite its lengthy heritage the effect of the development was not fully felt until the decision of the House of Lords in *McPhail v Doulton*.[44]

(a) Early developments akin to discretionary trusts

The existence of hybrid obligations was recognized by Lord Eldon LC in the leading case of *Brown v Higgs*:[45]

> There are not only a mere trust and a mere power, but there is also known to the court a power which the party to whom it is given is entrusted and required to execute; and with regard to that species of power, the court considers it as partaking so much of the nature and qualities of a trust, that if the person who has that duty imposed on him does not discharge it, the court will to a certain extent discharge the duty in his room and place.

Such an arrangement was demonstrated in *Crockett v Crockett*,[46] which followed the case of *Hart v Tribe*.[47] Within just a few years the concept was sufficiently clearly

---

[44] [1971] AC 424.   [45] (1799) 4 Ves 708; reheard (1800) 5 Ves 495; affd (1803) 8 Ves 561.

[46] (1848) 2 Ph 553.

[47] (1854) 18 Beav 215. Sir John Romilly, who had been counsel in the *Crockett* case, was then Master of the Rolls.

established for Thomas Smith MR, in the Irish Court of Chancery, to describe it as a discretionary trust.[48]

However, as might be expected, the early development was uncertain. This is evident in the decision in *Burrough v Philcox*.[49] John Walton left property to his two children for life and granted them a power to dispose of it by will in favour of his nephews and nieces. His two children died without making any appointment and the question arose whether the nephews and nieces could claim the property or whether it would pass to the residuary legatees of John Walton's will. The arrangement was clearly a power, but the court found that there was a general intention in favour of the class by John Walton and since that intention had failed because a selection had not been made by his children, the court would carry into effect the general intention and divide the property equally between the nephews and nieces. The court chose to analyse this disposition as a power with a trust in favour of the class should the power fail to be exercised. It could equally well have been treated as a discretionary trust.

(b) The enforcement of hybrid obligations

While equity seemed willing to contemplate the emergence of mechanisms which were hybrid in nature, in that they were not exclusively mandatory or exclusively discretionary, there was uncertainty as to how the court could intervene if a trustee failed to exercise his discretion under a discretionary trust. For many years, judicial opinion was divided. In some cases, the courts had compelled a trustee to act,[50] or substituted its own judgment for that of a discretionary trustee who had failed to act.[51] In others, the court disclaimed the ability to substitute its own opinion for that of the trustee, [52] culminating in the condemnation of cases taking a flexible approach by the Court of Appeal in 1954 in *IRC v Broadway Cottages Trust*.[53] The orthodox view adopted in that case was that the court had no right to substitute its discretion for that of the designated trustees should they fail or refuse to act. The discretion being conferred on and exercisable by the trustees alone, the court could not do anything other than authorize a distribution in equal shares. To this there might have been a limited exception that where the testator or settlor had laid down pointers or guides to the exercise of the discretion, this could form a basis for the exercise of a more flexible order by the court.[54]

(3) *McPhail v Doulton*: a modern watershed

The decision in the House of Lords in *McPhail v Doulton* marks the major break from the traditional dichotomy between trust and powers. Mr Bertram Baden settled

---

[48] *Gray v Gray* (1862) 13 I Ch R 404.   [49] (1840) 5 My & Cr 72.

[50] See *Hart v Tribe* (1854) 18 Beav 215, at 217–218; *Gisborne v Gisborne* (1877) 2 App Cas 300, HL; *Tempest v Lord Camoys* (1882) 21 Ch D 571.

[51] *Moseley v Moseley* (1673) Cas temp Finch 53; *Clarke v Turner* (1694) Freem Ch 198; *Warburton v Warburton* (1702) 4 Bro Parl Cas 1; *Richardson v Chapman* (1760) 7 Bro Parl Cas 318.

[52] See, for example, *Gray v Gray* (1862) 13 I Ch R 404; *Kemp v Kemp* (1795) 5 Ves Jr 849.

[53] [1955] Ch 20, [1954] 3 All ER 120.

[54] See the dissenting judgment of Lord Hodson in *McPhail v Doulton* [1970] 2 All ER 228, at 234.

property on trust to enable the trustees to make grants in favour of the staff of Matthew Hall and Co Ltd and their relatives and dependants. It was obvious that Mr Baden did not intend each and every member of staff and their dependants and relatives to have a share in the property left on trust, as there would simply not be enough for them each to receive any meaningful sum. The trustees were to have discretion which of the members of staff and their relatives and dependants were to benefit. The House of Lords held by a majority that this was a trust and not a power. Most significantly, it held that if the trustees failed to exercise their discretion, the court could intervene to compel them, or to ensure by some other means that the trust was carried out. Lord Wilberforce stated that:

> The court, if called upon to execute the trust power, will do so in the manner best calcu-lated to give effect to the settlor's or testator's intentions. It may do so by appointing new trustees, or by authorising or directing representative persons of the classes of beneficiar-ies to prepare a scheme of distribution, or even, should the proper basis for distribution appear by itself directing the trustees so to distribute.

(4) The contemporary classification of equitable obligations

McPhail v Doulton[55] overturned the orthodox view that there were a limited number of categories of equitable obligation and that regard would be had to the wishes of the settlor by allocating the arrangement that he had created into the most appro-priate box or category. Some of the categories recognized before *McPhail v Doulton* did, of course, contain the potential for fine-tuning. The settlor could specify what discretions he was conferring upon his trustees, but the lack of anything but the crudest form of enforcement through equal division in the case of a failure by his trustees to exercise a discretion meant that the settlor's freedom of invention was comparatively limited. *McPhail v Doulton*[56] marked a watershed not merely because it changed the certainty requirement for discretionary trusts, but also because it altered the basis on which the courts would enforce fiduciary obligations. By recog-nizing that equal division was not the only remedy available where a trustee failed to act, the House of Lords opened the possibility of more varied and sophisticated obligations in equity. The possibilities opened up by the case have been confirmed and exploited since.

(a) Blurring distinctions

The historic categories of the mandatory fixed trust, discretionary trust, and mere power provided the beginnings of a broader scale of obligations developing as grey shades between the black and white of trusts and powers. *McPhail v Doulton* has led to the exploitation of more intermediate shades of grey. This has happened both by the evolution of new mechanisms filling the gaps between the old constructs, and also by expansion within the categories themselves (see Figure 2.1).

---

[55] [1971] AC 424.   [56] [1971] AC 424.

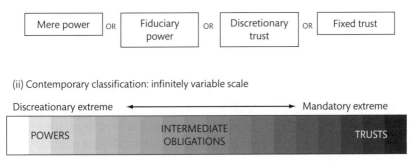

Figure 2.1 A scale of equitable obligations

(i) Exhaustive and non-exhaustive discretionary trusts

Within the category of discretionary trust, it is possible to distinguish between those under which the trustees are obliged to distribute the assets of the trust, and those where there is no such obligation. Since *McPhail v Doulton* the difference matters. The way in which the court is likely to intervene may differ markedly according to whether the trustees' obligation does or does not require the exhaustion of the trust fund.

(ii) Enforcing fiduciary powers

In a similar vein, it has long been recognized that some powers are fiduciary, in the sense that the donee is unable to agree voluntarily or by contract not to exercise the power. It is said, to use the technical term, that the power cannot be released. That was as far as the court was willing to intervene when the traditional dichotomy between mandatory trusts and permissive powers held sway. However, in *Mettoy Pension Trustees Ltd v Evans*[57] Warner J held that in some circumstances the courts might be willing to compel the donee of a fiduciary power to exercise it using the same methods of enforcement that were suggested by Lord Wilberforce as applicable to discretionary trusts in *McPhail v Doulton*.[58] The case, which has since been doubted, is fully discussed in a later chapter,[59] but at this stage it is sufficient to recognize that this runs against the tenor of previous cases, which had maintained the orthodox position that the exercise of fiduciary powers[60] cannot be enforced by the courts.[61]

(iii) Blurring of the traditional categories of trust and power

Discretionary trusts themselves represent a blurring between the distinct categories of the trust and power. The House of Lords in *McPhail v Doulton* described the arrangement which Bertram Baden had set up as a 'trust power'. That phrase encapsulates

---

[57] [1991] 2 All ER 513.
[58] [1971] AC 424.   [59] See Chapter 16.
[60] As opposed to the consideration of the exercise of the power.
[61] *Re Gulbenkian's Settlement Trusts (No 1)* [1968] Ch 126; *McPhail v Doulton* [1971] AC 424; *Re Hay's Settlement Trusts* [1981] 3 All ER 786.

the hybrid nature of the discretionary trust, which draws in elements both of trusts, in the obligation which is placed upon the trustees, and of power, in relation to the discretions which are conferred upon the trustees and the lack of defined rights, even in default, upon the part of the beneficiaries. The decision in the *Mettoy Pension* case, if correct on this point, suggests a further blurring. Rather than there being a sharp conceptual distinction between discretionary trusts and fiduciary powers, the case recognizes that there is a 'grey area' where obligations are neither distinctly one nor the other, but where they enjoy characteristics of both. The subsequent decision of the Privy Council in *Schmidt v Rosewood Trust Ltd*[62] further confirms the blurring of the traditional distinction between trusts and powers. In this case it was held that no distinction should be drawn between the rights of the object of a discretionary trust or of a fiduciary power in regard to the entitlement to the disclosure of trust documents. Thus, a right that was formerly predicated upon the proprietary right of the beneficiary to the trust property was extended to the objects of a power of appointment who have no proprietary interest. In reaching this conclusion Lord Walker referred to the way in which Lord Wilberforce had demonstrated in *McPhail v Doulton* that the differences between trusts and powers were 'a good deal less significant than the similarities'.[63]

(iv) Blurring in practice: pension schemes

The increasingly sophisticated use of trusts and powers further suggests the inevitability of a blending and melding between some of the old categories. Take, for instance, the pension scheme. The trustees of a pension fund will generally be under a binding obligation to pay pension benefits to the widow or dependent children of a contributing member if he dies in service, that is, while still in employment. A capital sum will usually also be available. With most pension schemes, the trustees hold any capital sum upon discretionary trusts to distribute it among a class of beneficiaries including the member's near family, any dependants and any person the member may have nominated. The trustees may also have powers to establish trusts containing discretions and powers where they are applying a lump sum on death in service. In considering what to do, the trustees may have received directions from the member. In one typical scheme, it is stated: 'In the exercise of their discretionary powers the Trustees may have regard to but shall not be bound by any wishes notified to them by the member.' In a single arrangement, therefore, one can find fixed trusts, discretionary trusts, powers, and directions with no express binding force alongside each other.

(b) Determining rights and duties

Given the blurring of the distinctions between the recognized equitable mechanisms and the difficulty of drawing conceptual distinctions between them, the traditional approach of categorizing obligations into a small number of well-defined categories seems inappropriate. In the past, there was a temptation to allow the classification of an arrangement to dictate the parties' rights and duties. However, this is a circular

---

[62] [2003] 3 All ER 76.   [63] [2003] 3 All ER 76, at [66].

activity and the fallacy of it is evident by examining an illustration. In *Re Gestetner Settlement*,[64] Harman J indicated that in addition to a discretionary trust where the trustees were under an obligation to distribute, there could also be a situation where trustees were simply under an obligation to consider whether a power to distribute should be exercised, without being obliged to part with any income or capital. This is sometimes described as a non-exhaustive discretionary trust, to distinguish it from the case where the trustees are under a duty to distribute and exhaust the fund (an exhaustive discretionary trust). In *McPhail v Doulton*, Lord Wilberforce drew a distinction between a discretionary trust (which he described as a trust power) and a mere power which was conferred on trustees. In the latter case he stated that 'although the trustees may, and normally will, be under a fiduciary duty to consider whether or in what way they should exercise their power, the court will not normally compel its exercise'. Lord Wilberforce did not consider this to be a discretionary trust (or a trust power, in the terminology which he used in the case), but it is difficult to see how it differs in any real respect from a non-exhaustive discretionary trust.[65]

The extent of the obligation to review the range of objects can also vary. Again, in *McPhail v Doulton* Lord Wilberforce said that:

> as to the trustees' duty of enquiry or ascertainment, in each case the trustees ought to make such a survey of the range of objects or possible beneficiaries as will enable them to carry out their fiduciary duty. A wider and more comprehensive range of enquiry is called for in the case of trust powers than in the case of powers.

Earlier in his opinion, he had indicated that the distinction was a functional one:

> Such distinction as there is would seem to lie in the extent of the survey which the trustee is required to carry out; if he has to distribute the whole of a fund's income, he must necessarily make a wider and more systematic survey than if his duty is expressed in terms of a power to make grants... The difference may be one of degree rather than of principle; in the well-known words of Sir George Farwell,[66] trusts and powers are often blended, and the mixture may vary in its ingredients.

(c) A scale of equitable obligations

The mix of trusts and powers, and the nature of the obligations that can be imposed on the donee of a fiduciary power, makes it undesirable to insist upon a rigid classification. There are, moreover, difficulties in locating some arrangements clearly under one category or another. As the litigation in *McPhail v Doulton* indicates, what one person sees as a trust in favour of a class with a power to accumulate may by another be seen as a trust to accumulate with a power to make grants in favour of a class. The House of Lords recognized that not only are the distinctions fine, but also that they

---

[64] [1953] Ch 672; [1953] 1 All ER 1150.

[65] See, however, Hayton's definition of a non-exhaustive discretionary trust as one in which 'the trustees must distribute the income amongst class "A" only if they fail to exercise a power to withhold the income for some purpose such as accumulating it or using it for class "B"': Hayton and Marshall, *Cases and Commentary on the Law of Trusts* (11th edn, 2001), p 152, n 90.

[66] *Farwell on Powers* (3rd edn, 1916), p 10.

are not determinative of the obligations of the donee or trustee. In the words of Lord Wilberforce:

> It is striking how narrow and in a sense artificial is the distinction...between trusts...and powers...And if one considers how in practice reasonable and competent trustees would act, and ought to act, in the two cases, surely a matter very relevant to the question of validity, the distinction appears even less significant. To say that there is no obligation to exercise a mere power and that no court will intervene to compel it, whereas a trust is mandatory and its execution may be compelled, may be legally correct enough, but the proposition does not contain an exhaustive comparison of the duties of persons who are trustees in the two cases.[67]

This marks a fundamental shift from a simple conceptual framework of equitable obligations, where characterization as either a trust or a power determines the rights and duties of the parties, to a functional analysis, where the courts will construe an arrangement in the way best capable of fulfilling the intention of the owner of the property. The absence of a rigid hierarchy of equitable obligations means that there is instead a wide spectrum of arrangements, the characteristics of which depend upon the terms and circumstances of their creation. Any classification can be adopted only as a matter of convenience as a way of describing, rather than prescribing, the incidents of any particular arrangement. It is possible to describe some of the principal kinds of equitable obligation which are found in practice, although it is impossible to draw up a definitive list. However, some features of the scale of equitable obligations can usefully be identified.

(i) The mandatory extreme

At one end of the spectrum of equitable mechanisms for property management and holding is the bare trust. The trustee may well have no independent powers of management or investment, and the shares in which the property is to be enjoyed are predetermined. The freedom of the trustee is constrained, and control is at its highest. Yet even here the position may be qualified. For instance, it is not unusual for a trust providing for fixed successive interests to contain a power enabling the trustee to draw down some of the capital and to pay it by way of an advancement to a beneficiary who has only a presumptive interest in the fund. There may also be a power to make applications of income (and sometimes capital) for the education and maintenance of an infant beneficiary who would otherwise have only a deferred right to those funds.

(ii) The discretionary extreme

At the other end of the spectrum is a mere power, the donee of which enjoys an unfettered discretion whether to exercise it and, if it is exercised, how to exercise it. Even here, however, the donee does not have complete freedom, for the court will ensure that the power is exercised only within its terms.

---

[67] [1970] 2 All ER 228, at 240.

(iii) Intermediate points on the scale

Between the black and white extremes of the bare fixed trust and the mere power there lies an almost infinite variety of intermediate arrangements. These include: trusts in favour of a fixed class, but with a power to make a selection between them in unequal shares;[68] a discretionary trust where the trustee is under an obligation to make a selection and which will be exercised by some means by the court if the trustee fails to exercise it;[69] a fiduciary power where the donee need not make a distribution but must at least consider periodically whether it should be exercised;[70] and a power or discretionary trust in favour of a class with a power to extend that class by appointing new members of the class.[71] Most of these possibilities can be combined in one form or another, creating a nearly infinite range of shades of grey.

---

[68]   *Wilson v Duguid* (1883) 24 Ch D 244 (where the gift to the class in equal shares was implied); *Burroughs v Philcox* (1840) 5 My & Cr. 72; *Re Llewellyn's Settlement* [1921] 2 Ch 281; *Re Arnold* [1947] Ch 131.

[69]   *Brown v Higgs* (1803) 8 Ves 561; *McPhail v Doulton* [1971] AC 424.

[70]   *Re Manisty's Settlement Trusts* [1974] Ch 17; *Re Hay's Settlement Trusts* [1982] 1 WLR 202.

[71]   *Re Hay's Settlement Trusts* [1982] 1 WLR 202.

3

Equity and the management of property

In the previous chapter the key characteristics of trusts and powers were examined. It is the purpose of this chapter to introduce some of the more important, practical usages of trusts in relation to the management of property. The concept of property and the separation of control and benefit that trust permits in relation to property, has already been outlined in Chapter 1. What follows demonstrates that, like Molière's character in *The Bourgeois Gentilhomme* who exclaimed 'Good Heavens! For more than forty years I have been speaking prose without knowing it', the way in which trusts underpin much of the modern law of property is often unnoticed or under-appreciated.

1 The facility of trusts

Trusts, and to a lesser extent powers, have evolved to enable property owners to accomplish objectives that they wish to achieve in respect of their property. While they first emerged in an entirely different social environment, where their primary use was as a means of ensuring that property remained within a family, they have proved extremely adaptable to modern family and commercial contexts. The majority of people enjoy some interaction with trusts, even though they may not be aware of it. Every person who is a co-owner of land is a beneficiary under a trust. Every person who has a pension fund, or who has investments in a unit trust or an ISA may find that the underlying assets behind their investment are held under a trust. Persons with considerable wealth may utilize trusts as a means of efficient tax planning. Every person who makes a donation to a charitable organization will in many cases unknowingly interact with the law of trusts.

2 Hiding the identity of the true owner of property

The fact that a trust enables the separation of the legal and beneficial ownership of property means that it can be used as an effective mechanism for hiding the identity of the true owner of property. If property is held on trust, it may appear to the world that the trustee is in fact the absolute legal owner, and others will have no knowledge of the existence of a trust. There is no obligation to publicly disclose the existence of a trust and therefore this mechanism will be particularly important where the legal ownership is made public, for example in the case of land where ownership is constituted by registration on a public register. For example, if a famous rock star wishes to purchase a cottage in a village without attracting attention, he may arrange for the house to be purchased on his behalf by a trustee, which would create what is known as a 'bare trust'.[1] Similarly, if a man wishes to make provision for his mistress on his death without members of his family discovering that she exists, he can leave the property he intends to give her in his will to a trusted friend who will take it as trustee on behalf of the mistress. There is no need for the identity of the mistress to appear in the will, which would become a public document as a consequence of the probate procedure, and nor is there any need for the will to make mention of the trust. Such trusts are known as secret trusts and are discussed in Chapter 13.

3 Transferring the ownership of property

One of the simplest dealings with real property is an outright transfer of ownership, whether by gift or sale. The requirements for effective transfer of ownership vary with the type of property involved. Some forms of property, including banknotes and ordinary goods like books and furniture (referred to as 'chattels'), can be transferred simply by handing over possession with the intention of transferring ownership. Other forms of property require more. The transfer of land, for instance, requires the transfer to be made in a prescribed form, and the transferee must then be registered as the new owner by the Land Registry.[2]

Equity normally has no role to play in outright transfers, except where the form of property concerned is recognized only in equity, for example a transfer of a beneficial share in a trust fund. In some cases equity will treat an attempted transfer as effective, even though some of the special formal requirements for the transfer of that form of property have not been used. Equity will, for instance, treat a transfer of land as being effective for some purposes after all the necessary documents have been completed and signed, even though the statutory rules require the transfer to be registered.[3] Conversely, in some special cases the principles of equity may become involved to deprive an apparent transfer of its full effect by imposing a resulting or constructive trust so that the original owner retains the equitable interest in the property transferred. For example, in *Bannister v Bannister*[4] Mrs Bannister sold

---

[1] Discussed in Chapters 15 and 19.
[2] See s 52(1)(b) Law of Property Act 1925. This is discussed in relation to the transfer of legal title to a trustee in Chapter 7, under Constitution of Trusts.
[3] *Mascall v Mascall* (1985) 50 P & CR 119 and further under Constitution of Trusts.
[4] [1948] 2 All ER 133.

two cottages to her brother-in-law for one-third less than their full market value. He promised orally to let Mrs Bannister stay on in one of the cottages rent-free for the rest of her life, but four years later he sought to evict her. The oral promise could not be enforced as a contract since it was not in writing, or proved in writing, as the statutory rules at the time required.[5] The Court of Appeal held, however, that in view of the promise that the brother-in-law had made, he acquired the cottage as trustee during the life of Mrs Bannister. He could not evict her so long as she desired to occupy the cottage.

4 Sharing ownership of property

(1) Concurrent ownership of property

Trusts also provide a mechanism by which the ownership of property can be shared between a number of persons. Their interests are said to be concurrent because they are enjoyed at the same time. Co-ownership can be effected by means of either a joint tenancy or a tenancy-in-common.

(a) Joint tenancy

Where the ownership of property is shared by means of a joint tenancy, all of the co-owners have identical rights to the property.[6] Taken together, they are entitled to the whole of the co-owned property, but they do not have specific shares in it. In the event of the death of one joint tenant, his interest passes automatically to the other remaining joint tenants under the principle of survivorship. A joint tenancy can be converted into a tenancy-in-common in equity by means of severance,[7] where the joint tenant severs his 'share', and the rules of survivorship no longer apply.

(b) Tenancy-in-common

Where the ownership of property is shared by means of a tenancy-in-common the co-owners enjoy 'undivided shares' in the co-owned property.[8] This means that they have specific notional shares in the property, which may be equal or unequal, and survivorship has no application. However, all the co-owners enjoy the right to use and enjoy the property, and no co-owner can regard part of it as representing his 'share' alone.

(c) Trusts and co-ownership

In relation to some property, the ownership can be shared concurrently by means of a joint tenancy or a tenancy-in-common without the need for a trust. For example, two students who purchase a car together may become the joint owners thereof and no trust

---

[5] Law of Property Act 1925, s 40.
[6] See Stevens & Pearce, *Land Law* (5th edn, 2013), 12.01–12.09.
[7] Stevens & Pearce, *Land Law* (5th edn, 2013), 12.26–12.63.
[8] Stevens & Pearce, *Land Law* (5th edn, 2013), 12.15–12.25, 370–72.

is involved. In the case of personal property, the legal title may be held by co-owners either as joint tenants or tenants-in-common. Where the chattels of two owners are commingled to form an indistinguishable whole (for instance because their oil has been mixed in the same tank), they share the whole as tenants-in-common in proportion to their contributions.[9] However, in general the common law preferred the mechanism of a joint tenancy, and thus a tenancy-in-common is relatively rare without a trust. Where the property concerned is land, any form of co-ownership will inevitably give rise to a trust of land.[10] By statute the legal title to land can only be held by individuals or joint tenants,[11] and therefore a tenancy in common can only exist in equity. The only situation in which land will not be held on trust is where there is a single outright owner. This means that the trust is the foundation of most land holding under English law.

(2) **Successive ownership of property**

It has been seen how the trust can provide a mechanism to facilitate the shared concurrent ownership of property. An owner of property may wish to divide the ownership of property so that it is enjoyed successively rather than concurrently. For example, imagine that Alice, an elderly lady with a significant shareholding, has one daughter, Claire, and three grandchildren. On her death she wants Claire to enjoy the benefit of the shares, but ultimately she wants to ensure that they pass to her grandchildren. Alice can grant Claire a life interest in the shares that will entitle her to receive the income they produce for the duration of her life, but without any right to their capital value. On her death the shares will become the property of the grandchildren (see Figure 3.1). Such an arrangement, sharing the enjoyment of the property successively, can only be achieved by means of a trust, irrespective of whether the property concerned is land or personal property.[12]

5 **Protecting equitable interests in property**

As has been noted in Chapter 1, an equitable interest behind trust is treated as a proprietary interest, which means it is incapable of enduring through changes in ownership of the property to which the beneficial interest behind a trust relates. The question of whether an equitable interest is binding on transfer of property depends, as we have seen, on the doctrine of notice.

---

[9] See *Spence v Union Marine Insurance Co* (1868) LR 3 CP 427; *Indian Oil Corpn Ltd v Greenstone Shipping SA* [1987] 3 All ER 893; cf *F S Sandeman & Sons v Tyzack and Branfoot Shipping Co* [1913] AC 680, HL.

[10] See Trusts of Land and Appointment of Trustees Act 1996, ss 1–5.

[11] Law of Property Act 1925, ss 1(6), 36(2).

[12] It was once possible to create limited interests in land without using a trust, but since the Law of Property Act 1925, a trust is now required whenever limited interests in land are created. It has always been the case that limited interests in property other than land can only be created by means of a trust. See Stevens & Pearce, *Land Law* (5th edn, 2013), 13.01–13.39; 14.01–14.26.

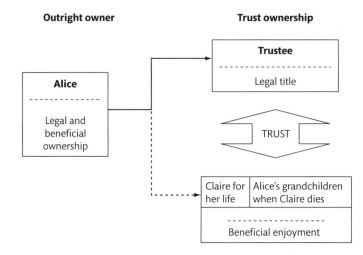

Figure 3.1 Creating successive interests using a trust

(1) **Trusts and the doctrine of notice**

The general rule is that if the trustee transfers the trust property to a bona fide purchaser who was unaware that it was subject to a trust, that person will acquire his legal title free from the entitlements of the beneficiaries. He will be the absolute and unencumbered legal owner of the property. The beneficiaries will be entitled to a personal remedy for breach of trust against the trustee if the trust property was wrongfully transferred, but they will have no continuing proprietary entitlements in the erstwhile trust property.

(a) **Trusts of personal property**

Where personal property is subject to a trust, the doctrine of notice operates, so that a bona fide purchase of the trust property will entirely destroy the proprietary interest of the beneficiaries. For example, if Robert holds shares on trust and sells and transfers them to Kevin, the equitable entitlement of the beneficiaries will be destroyed if Kevin had no knowledge, actual or constructive, that Robert was holding the shares as a trustee. The extension of the principles of constructive notice to commercial transactions involving personal property rather than land has sometimes been questioned. In *Manchester Trust v Furness* Lindley LJ stated:

> The equitable doctrines of constructive notice are common enough in dealing with land and estates with which the Court is familiar; but there has always been repeated protest against the introduction into commercial transactions of anything like an extension of those doctrines and the protest is founded on perfect good sense. In dealing with estates in land title is everything and it can be leisurely investigated; in commercial transactions possession is everything and there is no time to investigate title; and if we were to extend the doctrine of constructive notice to commercial transactions we should be doing infinite mischief and paralyzing the trade of the country.[13]

---

[13] [1895] 2 QB 539, at 545.

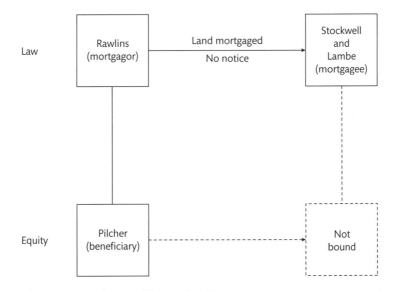

Figure 3.2 The doctrine of notice: *Pilcher v Rawlins*

However, the better view seems to be that the principle of constructive notice operates even where a commercial purchaser acquired legal title to personal property.
In *Macmillan Inc v Bishopsgate Investment Trust plc*[14] shares were held on trust for
Macmillan by Bishopsgate Investment Trust (BIT), an investment trust controlled
by Robert Maxwell. In breach of trust, and without the consent or knowledge of
Macmillan, BIT transferred legal title to the trust shares to various banks and financial institutions as security for the debts of other Maxwell companies. Millett J held
that, if English law applied,[15] the transferees of these shares would only have acquired
them free from the equitable interests of Macmillan if they had no constructive notice
that they were trust shares:

> It is true that many distinguished judges in the past have warned against the extension of
> the equitable doctrine of constructive notice to commercial transactions . . . but they were
> obviously referring to the doctrine in its strict conveyancing sense with its many refine-
> ments and its insistence on a proper investigation of title in every case. The relevance of
> constructive notice in its wider meaning cannot depend on whether the transaction is
> 'commercial': the provision of secured overdraft facilities to a corporate managing direc-
> tor is equally 'commercial' whether the security consists of the managing director's house
> or his private investments. The difference is that in one case there is, and in the other there
> is not, a recognized procedure for investigating the mortgagor's title which the creditor
> ignores at his peril.[16]

---

[14] [1995] 3 All ER 747.
[15] In the event, he concluded that the priority of proprietary rights to the shares was to be determined
by the law of New York. See: Stevens 'Restitution or Property? Priority and Title to Shares in the Conflict
of Laws' (1996) 59 MLR 741.   [16] Stevens (1996), at 769.

While this affirms the relevance of constructive notice to transactions involving personal property, it makes clear that the level of inquiry and investigation reasonably to be expected from a purchaser varies in relation to the nature and context of the transaction in issue. Where there is no recognized procedure for investigation into the title of the type of property offered for sale, a bona fide purchaser will satisfy the requirements of the doctrine of notice unless he had actual knowledge of the existence of the trust, was suspicious that the seller did not have the right to transfer, or had reason to know or be suspicious. If there is a recognized procedure, the purchaser will not be protected by the doctrine of notice if he has failed to follow it.

(b) Trusts of land

(i) Priority determined by the doctrine of notice

Historically, issues of priority between competing interests in land were also governed by application of the twin principle that the first in time prevailed, subject to the equitable doctrine of notice. A bona fide purchaser for value without notice of a legal estate in land would take free from any pre-existing equitable interests. For example, in *Pilcher v Rawlins*[17] trustees held £8,373 on trust for Jeremiah Pilcher, which they lent to Rawlins by way of a mortgage (see Figure 3.2). The mortgage was secured by the transfer of the legal title to the mortgaged land to the trustees. The trustees subsequently re-conveyed the legal title to Rawlins to enable him to fraudulently borrow a further £10,000 by granting a mortgage to Stockwell and Lambe. Jeremiah Pilcher, as beneficiary of the trust, claimed that Stockwell and Lambe were bound to observe the trust. However, the Court of Appeal held that they were bona fide purchasers without notice of the existence of the trust. They had therefore acquired their legal mortgage free from his equitable interest. James LJ explained:

> I propose simply to apply myself to the case of a purchaser for valuable consideration, without notice, obtaining, upon the occasion of his purchase, and by means of his purchase deed, some legal estate, some legal right, some legal advantage; and according to my view of the established law of this court, such a purchaser's plea of a purchase for valuable consideration without notice is an absolute, unqualified, unanswerable defence, and an unanswerable plea to the jurisdiction of this court.

In contrast, a purchaser with notice, whether actual or constructive, will be required to yield priority to a beneficiary of a pre-existing trust. In *Kingsnorth Trust v Tizard*[18] a husband held the legal title to his matrimonial home on trust for himself and his wife (see Figure 3.3). After they separated she no longer lived at the house, although she visited for part of each day. He mortgaged the house and absconded with the money raised. Prior to accepting a mortgage, the mortgage company had sent a surveyor to inspect the house. He visited on a Sunday afternoon, a time arranged by the husband when he knew that his wife would not be present. He told the surveyor that he and his wife had separated many months before and that she had no interest in the property. The

---

[17] (1871–72) LR 7 Ch App 259.
[18] [1986] 1 WLR 783; Thompson 'The Purchaser as Private Detective' [1986] Conv 283.

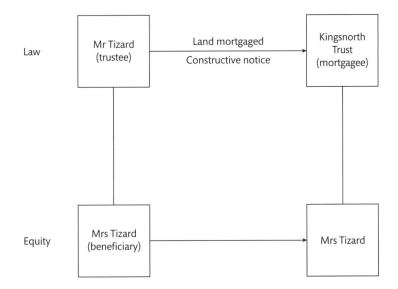

Figure 3.3 The doctrine of notice: *Kingsnorth Trust v Tizard*

court held that in these circumstances the mortgage company was bound by the wife's equitable interest under the trust. It had not made all the inquiries that were reasonably required from a potential mortgagee, and it was therefore affixed with constructive notice. Judge John Finlay, QC concluded that the inspection had been inadequate:

> What is such an inspection 'as ought reasonably to be made' must, I think, depend on all the circumstances. In the circumstances of the present case I am not satisfied that the pre-arranged inspection on a Sunday afternoon fell within the category of 'such inspections which ought reasonably to have been made', the words in s 199 of the Law of Property Act 1925 . . .[19]

(ii) Priority determined by statute

Statutory reform, starting in 1925 and culminating in the Land Registration Act 2002, has largely displaced the doctrine of notice as a means of determining whether a purchaser of land acquires his legal title free from pre-existing equitable trust interests. The Law of Property Act 1925 provides that where land is held on trust the interests of the beneficiaries are automatically eliminated if it is transferred to a purchaser who pays any purchase moneys arising to two or more trustees holding the legal title. This process is called 'overreaching', and it operates irrespective of whether the purchaser had knowledge, actual or constructive, of the existence of the trust. When overreaching occurs, the beneficiaries' equitable interests are not eliminated altogether, but they are displaced from the land and continue to subsist as rights in rem only in the purchase moneys paid to the trustees. Where overreaching occurs, a purchaser of land need not be concerned by the possible existence of any trusts affecting the land he acquires. He can be sure that, provided any purchase money arising from the

---

[19] [1986] 1 WLR 783, at 795.

transaction is paid to two trustees, no pre-existing trust interests will endure in the land to affect his legal ownership.

6 Delegating management functions

Many of the most significant uses of trusts arise because they enable an owner to delegate some of the management responsibilities attendant upon the ownership of property to a third person who will become the trustee. In some cases such delegation will be chosen for reasons of convenience, while in others it may be a matter of necessity because the owner of property is incapable of managing it for himself.

(1) **Delegation for reasons of convenience**

The owner of property may choose to create a trust of his property for reasons of convenience. Thus, a person owning a substantial share portfolio may transfer his shares to his stockbroker or a professional trustee to facilitate dealing transactions. In the case of such a bare trust, the trustee may not enjoy any active powers of management over the trust property but will act on the instructions of the beneficiary.

(2) **Delegation of allocation**

An owner may know that he wants to transfer the ownership of his property but not yet know who he wants to transfer it to. By means of a trust, combined with a power of appointment, the owner can effectively delegate the responsibility for choosing who should receive the ultimate benefit of his property to someone else,[20] the donee of the power.[21] Often, the donee of the power or the trustee of the discretionary trust will be in a better position than the original owner to determine how it should be distributed, either by reason of the time at which they can make the decision, or because of their superior knowledge. For example, imagine that Henry has no children of his own but has a large number of nieces and nephews. He only has a small estate and he wants to ensure that his property goes to those who really need it. In his will, he can leave his property to his sister Frances for life, giving her a power of appointment to choose which of his nephews and nieces are to receive the property on her death. By doing so, Henry is able to delegate the task of selecting who is to benefit, while at the same time stipulating the class of persons among whom allocations can be made. Alternatively, Henry could leave his estate to Frances on trust for such of his nephews and nieces in such shares as she determines. By means of this discretionary trust, Henry has imposed a mandatory obligation on Frances to allocate the property among the class of his nephews and nieces, but has left her the decision as to which specific members of that class should benefit and to what extent.

---

[20] These functions are considered in detail in Chapter 16.
[21] The distinction between trusts and powers, and the scale of equitable obligations on which they lie, was considered at the end of Chapter 2.

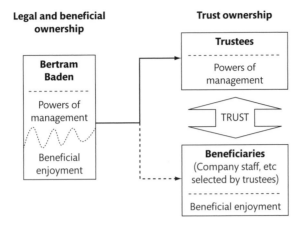

Figure 3.4 Delegating allocation using a trust: *McPhail v Doulton*

Again, a discretionary trust or a power of appointment can be used on a larger scale. For instance, William is the owner of a large business with some 10,000 employees. He wishes to establish a fund to provide for the education of the children of his employees. Obviously, he cannot provide for them all, so he is able to create a trust in which the fund is transferred to trustees who have the discretion to select which of his employees' children should receive this benefit. The result is that only some of the 10,000 will benefit, but William has delegated to others the task of deciding those who will benefit.[22]

McPhail v Doulton provides an example of such delegated allocation.[23] Bertram Baden wanted to give property for the benefit of the employees and ex-employees, and their relatives and dependants, of a company he owned. Rather than determining how the property should be allocated, he left the property to trustees, giving them the discretion as to which of the potential beneficiaries should actually receive a share of the property. In this way he delegated to them the task of allocating the property (see Figure 3.4). Similarly, in *Re Diplock*,[24] Caleb Diplock left his residuary estate to his executors to be applied to 'such…charitable or benevolent objects' as they shall 'in their absolute discretion select'. Again, this was an attempt to delegate the decision as to how the property should actually be allocated to others, namely the executors.[25]

(3) **Providing for vulnerable individuals**

An owner may want to take deliberate advantage of the possibility of separating the legal and equitable ownership of property through a trust to gain the advantage of ensuring that the beneficial owner does not have control of the management of the property. There are a number of reasons why this may be the case.

---

[22] For example, *Oppenheim v Tobacco Securities Trust Co Ltd* [1951] AC 297.
[23] [1971] AC 424.   [24] [1948] Ch 465.
[25] In fact, the gift failed because it was not exclusively charitable: see Chapter 11.

(a) The beneficiary cannot manage the property

An owner may wish someone to enjoy the benefit of property who is not capable of managing it adequately for himself. The device of the trust enables the owner to transfer the legal title, and therefore the management responsibility, to someone who is capable of looking after the interests of the beneficiary.

(i) Infancy

An owner may want to create a trust because the intended beneficiary is an infant, and is therefore incapable of managing the property for himself. This would be the case, for example, if parents die leaving their property to infant children. The trustee will have the control of the property, which will be invested and managed for their benefit until they reach the age of majority.

(ii) Incapacity

A trust may also be employed where the intended beneficiary lacks the capacity to conduct his own affairs for reasons other than infancy. Suppose that John has a disabled adult son for whom he wishes to make provision in his will. John knows that his son is unable to make decisions for himself. By means of a trust, John can nominate a trustee to hold the property for his son. The trustee will have the legal ownership of the money and will be able to decide how it should be invested and used. John's son will enjoy the equitable or beneficial ownership in the money.

(b) The beneficiary should not manage the property

An owner may also want to create a trust if he is concerned that it would be unwise to permit the beneficiary, although legally competent, to manage the property. In the Victorian period, the trust was often used to preserve the integrity of family estates from spendthrift heirs. A classic example can be found in Trollope's Victorian novel, *Dr Thorne*. There, a wealthy baronet, Sir Richard Scatcherd, dies leaving a vast estate of some £300,000. His son, Sir Louis, was 21, a drunkard and a spendthrift. In order to protect the estate Sir Richard left his property to his close and trusted friend, Dr Thorne, so that the son would not have control of it but rather that Dr Thorne would manage the estate until Sir Louis reached 25, with the hope that by such age he would be a reformed character. Somewhat fortunately for the story he died before reaching that age, leaving the heroine, Miss Thorne, to inherit the estate!

Similarly, if Alexander wanted to leave his property to a son whom he knew was a drug addict and therefore liable to waste the money in that way, he could leave it on some form of trust so that the son would be entitled to receive an income but not to rapidly dissipate the property.

(c) Protective trusts

A spendthrift may also be protected from the dangers of his own bankruptcy by a special type of trust, the protective trust. Under such a trust, property is held by the trustees with a direction that the beneficiary is to receive the income from the trust. In the case of a conventional trust, if the beneficiary becomes insolvent his trustee in bankruptcy will be entitled to receive the income from the trust. However, the terms of a protective trust provide that in the event of insolvency the beneficiary's entitlement to the income automatically fails or determines, so that he is no longer entitled to it as of right. Instead, the income is to be held by the trustees under a discretionary trust to be used for the support of a range of persons, including the original beneficiary. This means that the trustee in bankruptcy will only receive the income if the trustees of the settled fund make an appointment to the bankrupt beneficiary. By means of this device, the trust property and income are protected from the consequences of the beneficiary's bankruptcy.

It has been held that a settlor cannot create a trust to protect himself from his own bankruptcy.[26] However, a trust created by a third party that will protect the beneficiary from the consequences of his bankruptcy has been held to be valid.[27] Although a protective trust may be created expressly, a statutory form has been introduced. Section 33(1) of the Trustee Act 1925 provides that where any income is directed to be held on 'protective trusts' for the benefit of any person, then the property is to be held upon the terms set out in the section. These provide for a primary trust, and then a secondary trust that will only come into being if the primary trust fails.

(i) The terms of the primary trust

Section 33(1)(i) provides that the income will be held:

> Upon trust for the principal beneficiary during the trust period or until he...does or attempts to do anything, or until any event happens...whereby, if the said income were payable during the trust period to the principal beneficiary absolutely during that period, he would be deprived of the right to receive the same or any part thereof, in any of which cases...this trust of the said income shall fail or determine.

This primary trust entitles the principal beneficiary to receive the income from the trust, which entitlement determines automatically if he for any reason loses the right to retain it, for example if he becomes bankrupt, in which case his trustee in bankruptcy would be entitled to the income from the trust.[28] Other events have included the sequestration of the income[29] and the trustees impounding the income to repay capital wrongly advanced to the beneficiary.[30] In contrast, the fact that a beneficiary was resident in enemy-occupied territory, with the consequence that income could not be paid to her, was held not to be sufficient to determine the trust.[31]

(ii) The terms of the secondary trust

If the primary trust is determined, then the income is to be held on the terms of a secondary trust set out in s 33(1)(ii):

> If the trust aforesaid fails or determines during the subsistence of the trust period, then, during the residue of that period, the said income shall be held upon trust for the

---

[26] *Re Burroughs-Fowler* [1916] 2 Ch 251.

[27] *Billson v Crofts* (1873) LR 15 Eq 314; *Re Aylwin's Trusts* (1873) LR 16 Eq 585; *Re Ashby, ex p Wreford* [1892] 1 QB 872 QBD.

[28] *Trappes v Meredith* (1871) 7 Ch App 248; *Re Evans* [1920] 2 Ch 304; *Re Walker* [1939] Ch 974; *Re Forder* [1927] 2 Ch 291.   [29] *Re Baring's Settlement Trusts* [1940] Ch 737.

[30] *Re Balfour's Settlement* [1938] Ch 928.   [31] *Re Hall* [1944] Ch 46.

application thereof for the maintenance or support, or otherwise for the benefit, of all or any one or more exclusively of the other or others of the following persons—

   (a) the principal beneficiary and his or her wife or husband, if any, and his or her children or more remote issue, if any; or

   (b) if there is no wife or husband or issue of the principal beneficiary in existence, the principal beneficiary and the persons who would, if he were actually dead, be entitled to the trust property or the income thereof or to the annuity fund, if any, or arrears of the annuity, as the case may be;

as the trustees in their absolute discretion, without being liable to account for the exercise of such discretion, think fit.

This secondary trust takes the form of a discretionary trust, so that the principal beneficiary no longer has the right to the income of the trust, but the trustees may at their discretion give him some or even all of that income, or otherwise use it for the support of his family. At any event, it will be possible to ensure his family's support without the income being seized by his trustee in bankruptcy.[32]

7 Gifts to be applied for purposes

It is a general principle of property that only a legally recognized person[33] may be an owner. The owner of property might, however, wish to transfer it not to specified individuals, but for the carrying out of a specified purpose. Clearly, an owner can apply his own property in the furtherance of whatever purpose he chooses, but the problem arises when he wishes to oblige a transferee of the property so to apply it. While it might be thought that a trustee could be obliged to use trust property in furtherance of a specified purpose, equity has adopted the general rule that, subject to limited exceptions, a trust can only be validly created in favour of persons rather than purposes.[34] A trust for the benefit of a pure purpose will be void. For example, in *Re Astor's Settlement Trusts*[35] a trust was established for the purpose of the 'maintenance of...good understanding sympathy and co-operation between nations' and 'the preservation of the independence and integrity of newspapers'. This was held to be invalid, as it was a gift for a purpose and not persons.

The most important exception to this principle is that property can be transferred on trust for purposes that are regarded as charitable in law, and the facilitation of charitable giving is one of the most important functions of the trust today. For example, in *Re Delius*[36] the widow of the composer Frederick Delius left her residuary

---

[32] In some circumstance the trustee in bankruptcy will be entitled to income that is received by the bankrupt principal beneficiary as the assignee of his interests under the discretionary trust. See *Re Coleman* (1888) LR 39 Ch D 443; *Re Neil* (1890) 62 LT 649; *Re Ashby, ex p Wreford* [1892] 1 QB 872.

[33] This includes a company which is treated as having legal personality and therefore the capacity to hold property.

[34] See Chapter 14.   [35] [1952] Ch 534.   [36] [1957] Ch 299.

estate[37] to trustees to promote the musical works of her late husband. This was upheld as a charitable gift, even though there was no person who would directly benefit from this gift. Where the trust is charitable in status, it attracts certain privileges, both legal and financial. Charitable trusts are examined in detail in Chapter 11.

8 Collective investment

Trusts are an effective vehicle by which individuals can pool their resources for collective investment, because the trust both enables the responsibilities for the management of property to be severed from its ownership and enjoyment and enables the ownership of property to be shared concurrently.[38] One example of how trusts may be used in this way is the formation of a syndicate to enter the national lottery. Rather than entering as single individuals, a number of persons may come together to pool their resources and increase their chances of winning by financing the purchase of multiple combinations of numbers that they could not afford individually. Fundamental to the operation of such a syndicate would be the collection of the 'stakes' from the members, the purchase of the tickets and the distribution of any winnings. Since the ticket will be purchased in the name of only one member, that member will hold any winnings on trust for the members of the syndicate who have contributed, in proportion to the size of their stake.[39] More significantly, the ability of equity to facilitate collective investment lies at the heart of two important institutions, the unit trust and some pension schemes, both of which are explored in Chapter 22.

(1) Unit trusts

Unit trusts have grown in significance since the middle of the last century as a means of making modest investments on the stock exchange or in other securities. Suppose that Adrian has £1,000 to invest. He wishes to invest in stocks and shares, rather than to deposit his money with a bank or building society, because he believes that he will be better protected against the ravages of inflation. He knows the dangers of dealing on the stock market and wants to be able to spread the risk of his investment over a variety of securities, but his investment is too small to enable that. By buying units in a unit trust, Adrian is able to join together with other investors so that collectively they can spread their investments across the market. A management company, acting as a trustee, takes subscriptions from Adrian and other individual investors. They are allocated units in the trust assets in proportion to the sums that they have contributed. The subscriptions are pooled and used to purchase shares or to make other investments. The investors are thus able to share in a far wider portfolio than if they

---

[37] The residuary estate is the balance of a deceased person's assets after their debts have been paid and all specific gifts by will have been made.

[38] Collective investment vehicles are considered in detail in Chapter 22. Pension trusts are only considered in outline.   [39] See Wilkinson 'Running a Lottery Syndicate' (1995) NLJ 217.

were to invest alone. Although the management company is responsible for making investment decisions, it is the investors collectively who have beneficial entitlement. Sophisticated provisions enable Adrian or the other investors to withdraw from the trust by being paid back a sum that represents the proceeds of their initial investment. New investors may buy into the trust at a price that reflects the current value of units.

(2) **Pension schemes**

Pension schemes can work in a very similar way to unit trusts, enabling members of the scheme to pool their contributions for the purpose of making investments that will later pay the pensions. Individuals pay into a collective investment fund managed by trustees, knowing that they will receive better returns than if they each attempted to invest individually. It is the separation of ownership from the management of property that makes this possible. Not all pension schemes work in this way. Most state old-age pension and many public sector pension schemes are unfunded. This means that instead of the pensions being paid out of investments made by the pension scheme trustees, the pensions are paid directly by the government or the employer.

(3) **The interface with contract**

Although unit trusts and pension schemes are able to operate through mechanisms developed by the law of equity, the rights of individual investors and contributors may be dependent on the law of contract, not equity. For example, when a contributor to a pension scheme retires, he may have a contractual entitlement to receive a pension throughout his retirement based upon his final salary, rather than receiving back that proportion of the investments which represents his contributions. If he dies soon after retirement, he may draw less in pension than he has contributed. If he lives to a ripe old age, he may draw significantly more by way of pension than he has contributed. The contractual aspect of the arrangement is just as important as the trust or property aspects.[40]

9 Property holding by clubs and societies

Clubs and societies that are not incorporated as companies are not capable of owning property in their own right since they lack the necessary legal personality. This raises the question as to how the funds of the society are to be held. In most cases they can be treated as belonging to the whole membership of the club, subject to the rules of the club.[41] Where the assets are vested in the members of the committee or some

---

[40] For a detailed consideration of this interrelationship, and the law relating to pensions generally, see Pollard, *The Law of Pension Trusts* (2013).   [41] *Re Recher's Will Trusts* [1972] Ch 526.

other group of individuals on behalf of the members of the club, those holding the club assets will be trustees for the members.[42] The management of property by these groups, known as 'Unincorporated Associations', is explored in Chapter 12.

10 Trusts arising to protect legitimate expectations

Most of the situations examined concern the deliberate choice of a trust or power by an owner to achieve his objective. However, not every trust arises as a result of the owner's overt intention. For example, trusts commonly arise informally where a couple pool their resources in order to buy a home together, but the legal ownership of the home is put in the name of one of them alone. Often the couple will have given no thought as to how their arrangement would be characterized by the law. Provided that there is some common understanding that both of the couple were intended to have a share in the ownership of the property, the court will impose a trust to give effect to this intention. Even in cases where there is no clear agreement, a trust will be imposed if the contributions made by each of the couple are such that the only reasonable inference is that, if asked, the couple would have said they intended to be joint owners.[43] *Grant v Edwards*[44] is a clear example. Mrs Linda Grant left her husband and moved in with Mr George Edwards. A modest house was purchased with the aid of a mortgage to provide a home for the couple. The purchase was made in the name of George Edwards and his brother, Arthur. Mrs Grant's name was not included in the purchase, since Mr Edwards suggested that it might complicate her divorce proceedings. Mrs Grant helped with the purchase by contributing to the repayment of the mortgage and in other ways. The court imposed a trust on George and Arthur to give effect to the understanding that Mrs Grant would be entitled to a half-share in the net value of the house. Chapter 10 looks in detail at how equity supports the acquisition of rights in the family home in this and other ways.

11 Trusts that are remedial in effect

The examples above illustrate how equity enables a property owner to achieve more complicated objectives than making a simple outright transfer of his property. Those dealing with informal situations also show how equity sometimes acts to protect legitimate expectations. Equity also serves a powerful remedial function, however, by protecting the rights that it creates. In some situations equity protects an existing proprietary right, whereas in others it generates a new proprietary right. Although not universally accepted, some writers would characterize these proprietary rights as

---

[42] See further Chapter 12.
[43] *Lloyds Bank plc v Rosset* [1991] 1 AC 107.   [44] [1986] Ch 638.

remedial or restitutionary trusts.[45] The use of remedial trusts has proved especially significant in the context of commercial transactions.

(1) **Misappropriated property**

Where property is subject to a trust, the proprietary rights of the beneficiaries to the trust property will not be defeated unless the property is acquired by a bona fide purchaser for value. The trust property can be traced through mixtures and substitutions. However, where property is not subject to an express trust, the rights of the owner have traditionally been governed by the common law. These rights have proved less than adequate because the common law has not developed a sophisticated means of identifying the proceeds and substitute-products thereof. Thus, where property has been misappropriated, owners may instead seek relief in equity by the demonstration that a constructive trust relationship has come into being. Where, for example, money has been misappropriated from a company by one of its senior employees, the fiduciary relationship between the company and the employee fastens a constructive trust on the stolen funds in favour of the company, and thus the company can seek remedies in equity against the recipients of the money even though it has passed through a mixed bank account.[46] In *Westdeutsche Landesbank Girozentrale v Islington London Borough Council*,[47] Lord Browne-Wilkinson suggested that a constructive trust would arise whenever money was stolen, irrespective of whether there was a fiduciary relationship or not.

(2) **Avoiding the effects of insolvency**

Creditors have also sought to use trusts as a means of avoiding the consequences of the insolvency of their debtors. If a creditor can demonstrate that he enjoys an equitable proprietary interest in some property in the bankrupt's hands, in other words, that the bankrupt debtor was holding it on trust for him, then, as has been seen, it will not form part of the bankrupt's assets to be distributed among his general creditors and the beneficiary will gain priority in the insolvency as if he were a protected creditor. Thus, where one bank made a mistaken payment to another bank that became insolvent, it was held that the payee bank held the payment on trust for the bank making the payment.[48] Similarly, where a loan is made for a specific purpose, the money advanced may be held on trust for the creditor if the purpose has failed.[49] Where a customer has ordered goods from a supplier, they may be held on trust for him if they have been separated from the bulk so as to be identifiable as his property.[50]

---

[45] See Oakley, *Constructive Trusts* (3rd edn, 1996); Birks, *An Introduction to the Law of Restitution* (1985).

[46] *Agip (Africa) Ltd v Jackson* [1992] 4 All ER 451.   [47] [1996] AC 669.

[48] *Chase Manhattan Bank NA v Israel-British Bank (London) Ltd* [1981] Ch 105.

[49] *Barclays Bank Ltd v Quistclose Investments Ltd* [1970] AC 567.

[50] *Re Goldcorp Exchange* [1995] 1 AC 74.

12 Trusts and tax avoidance

Trusts have evolved to enable owners to deal with their property flexibly. However, one of the major motivations for the use of trusts is that they can be used effectively and creatively to reduce taxation. They are an essential aspect of tax planning, which aims to achieve legitimate tax avoidance.[51] As Lord Tomlin said in *IRC v Duke of Westminster*:

> Every man is entitled if he can to order his affairs so that the tax attaching under the appropriate Act is less than it otherwise would be. If he succeeds in ordering them so as to secure that result, then, however unappreciative the Commissioners of Inland Revenue or his fellow taxpayers may be of his ingenuity, he cannot be compelled to pay an increased tax.[52]

This general principle has been qualified by more recent House of Lords' decisions which have held that where steps are inserted into a pre-ordained series of transactions which have no commercial or business purpose but are inserted solely to avoid tax, the transaction will be treated as a single whole and taxed as such.[53] This limitation applies to trusts.[54]

A detailed consideration of taxation is outside the scope of this book,[55] but it is essential to have an elementary grasp of the tax structure. Trusts have historically been used to minimize liability to taxation. In consequence there has been an ongoing 'battle' with the government seeking to raise revenue. As a result, tax laws have become ever more complicated, and the scope to use trusts to reduce tax liabilities has diminished. There are still some instances where trusts can be used as part of tax planning, but expert advice or knowledge is required. There are three main types of taxation that will affect a trust: income tax, capital gains tax, and inheritance tax. Each will be briefly examined and their applicability to trusts considered.

(1) Income tax

(a) Definition of income tax

Income tax, as Lord Macnaghten somewhat unnecessarily pointed out,[56] 'is a tax on income'. However, income tax is not payable on a person's whole income, but only his 'taxable income'. There are a number of basic principles. Taxpayers can set some expenses against their income, and only the net figure is subject to tax. Most taxpayers are then given a personal allowance, which means that the first part of their income is not subject to any income tax. The rate of tax that is paid on the remainder of their

---

[51] Tax avoidance is to be distinguished from illegitimate tax evasion.

[52] [1936] AC 1. See also *IRC v Willoughby* [1997] 1 WLR 1071.

[53] *W T Ramsay Ltd v IRC* [1982] AC 300; *Furniss v Dawson* [1984] AC 474; *MacNiven (HM Inspector of Taxes) v Westmoreland Investments Ltd* [2003] 1 AC 311. See Lord Walker, 'Ramsay 25 Years on: Some Reflections on Tax Avoidance' (2004) 120 LQR 412.   [54] *Countess Fitzwilliam v IRC* [1992] STC 185.

[55] See, for example, Tiley, *Revenue Law* (7th edn, 2012).   [56] *LCC v A-G* [1901] AC 26, at 35.

income then increases, with higher rates of tax being paid on higher 'slices' of income. The levels of personal allowance, the percentage tax rate, and the levels at which these tax rates come into effect are varied frequently, often annually. Different types of income may be subject to different rates of tax, and some income is taxed before being received by the taxpayer. For instance, banks paying interest deduct a sum for income tax before paying the interest to the investor.

(b) Income tax and trusts

In order to prevent trusts being used to avoid the payment of income tax, trustees are liable to pay income tax on the income of the trust. There is no personal allowance. The rate of tax depends upon the type of trust and the type of income.

(c) The receipt of trust income by trust beneficiaries

Complicated provisions govern the payment of income tax by beneficiaries receiving trust income. In most cases the beneficiaries are able to set off any income tax paid by the trustees against their own liability for income tax. In some cases it is possible for a beneficiary to claim a refund of tax paid by the trustees where this exceeds the beneficiary's own liability for tax.

(d) Trusts as a means of avoiding income tax

Trusts have in the past been used as an effective means of avoiding income tax. The scope for doing this has been much reduced by changes to the tax regime, with measures such as the introduction of a high rate of tax for discretionary trusts, which had previously been used by some settlors to allow the trustees to distribute income to beneficiaries who the settlor might otherwise have wanted to support out of taxed income, but who had a lower rate of taxation than the settlor. To further limit tax avoidance, income under a trust is treated as the income of the settlor unless the income arises from property in which the settlor has no interest. A settlor is treated as having an interest in property if that property or any property derived from it can or might be payable to or for the benefit of the settlor or the settlor's spouse in any circumstances whatsoever.

(2) Capital gains tax

(a) Definition of capital gains tax

Capital gains tax is payable on the increase in value of 'chargeable assets' when they are realized. What is taxable is the difference in value of the asset between the date of acquisition and of disposal. Taxpayers are allowed an annual exemption, the amount of which is varied from time to time.

(b) Capital gains tax and trusts

Capital gains tax cannot be avoided by settling property on trust. A settlor will be liable to pay capital gains tax personally when he settles property on trust, as this is considered a disposal.[57] In addition, trustees pay capital gains tax on disposals by the trust. The trustees will be liable when they dispose of assets as part of the administration of the trust, and where the beneficiary becomes absolutely entitled to the property held on trust, other than by the death of the life tenant, which is a 'deemed disposal'.[58] This deemed disposal means that capital gains tax is payable whenever a settlement is brought to an end and the property resettled, which increases the costs of terminating or resettling property.[59]

(3) Inheritance tax

(a) Definition and history of inheritance tax

Inheritance tax is, in essence, a tax payable on capital that passes on death, but it also applies to inter vivos gifts that were made less than seven years before the death occurred. It is something of a combination of two earlier taxes: estate duty and capital transfer tax. Prior to 1974 there was just one tax, estate duty, which was payable on death.[60] Transfers inter vivos would be liable to estate duty if made seven years before the death.[61] Estate duty was payable on the whole trust fund on the death of a life tenant, but was easily avoided by the creation of a discretionary trust where the beneficiaries had no interest in the fund itself.[62] In 1974 estate duty was replaced by capital transfer tax, which was to be payable on any transfer of capital either inter vivos or on death, although higher rates applied to transfers on death. In 1986 capital transfer tax was replaced by inheritance tax.

(b) The operation of inheritance tax

Section 1 of the Inheritance Tax Act 1984 provides that 'Inheritance Tax shall be charged on the value transferred by a chargeable transfer.' The tax is charged on 'transfers of value', in other words, transfers which diminish the value of the transferor's estate. Some transfers are 'exempt transfers' that are not liable to tax. These include most transfers between spouses and relatively small gifts up to a specified annual limit. Where 'chargeable transfers' have been made, tax is payable on the cumulative total of all such transfers made within seven years of the taxpayer's death, but taper relief has the effect of reducing the rates of tax that apply to transactions made between three and seven years before death. Where a transfer has been made more than seven years before the taxpayer's death, the transfer is not subject to inheritance tax.

(c) Inheritance tax and trusts

The rules relating to inheritance tax and trusts are complicated. There are four main occasions when inheritance tax may apply to trusts: when assets are transferred into a trust; when a trust reaches a ten-year anniversary; when property is transferred out

---

[57] Taxation of Chargeable Gains Act 1992, s 53.   [58] Ss 54(1), 71.   [59] See Chapter 17.
[60] Finance Act 1894, ss 1, 2.   [61] Finance Act 1968, s 35.
[62] *Gartside v IRC* [1968] AC 553; see Chapter 16.

of a trust or the trust comes to an end; and when someone dies and a trust is involved when sorting out their estate. Inheritance tax rules were changed in 2006 and different rules may apply to existing trusts.

(i) Transfers into the trust

Where a settlor transfers funds into a trust, and that transfer, together with any other transfers he has made during the previous seven years exceed a specified threshold, a charge arises to inheritance tax. The rate of tax is lower than the rate payable on death, but if the settlor dies within seven years of making the gift, a further tax charge is made. Transfers into a trust for a disabled person do not carry an immediate tax charge, but are still subject to a tax charge on the death of the settlor.

(ii) Ten-year anniversary charge

Some trusts are subject to an inheritance tax 'periodic charge' on every tenth anniversary.

(iii) Charges on transfers out of the trust

An inheritance tax exit charge is levied on certain transactions when assets are distributed to beneficiaries, where a beneficiary becomes absolutely entitled, when the trust comes to an end, and in certain other situations.

(iv) Charges on a beneficiary's death

The value of assets within a trust can be treated as part of a beneficiary's estate, and therefore be subject to inheritance tax on the beneficiary's death. This is most obviously so where the beneficiary is a beneficiary under a bare trust. There are certain other instances where the value of a beneficiary's rights may be treated as part of the beneficiary's estate for inheritance tax purposes.

(v) Charges on the settlor's death

It has already been noted earlier that where a settlor dies within seven years of establishing a trust, and the inter vivos rate of inheritance tax has been paid, a further charge arises to bring the total inheritance tax rate up to the rate payable on death. Even if no inheritance tax were payable when the trust was first set up, the value of all transfers to trusts with seven years of the settlor's death have to be taken into account in valuing the deceased's estate for inheritance tax purposes.

13 Distinguishing other mechanisms that facilitate a separation between the management and ownership of property

Much of the practical usage of trusts derives from their ability to separate the management responsibilities from the ownership of property. However, this ability is not unique to trusts. This section will provide a brief examination of some situations where such a separation may be facilitated by other means.

(1) **Companies**

One means by which a separation between management and ownership of property can be made in practice is through public companies.[63] The capital for establishing a public company is provided by the shareholders who originally subscribed to the shares. They own the company. If it is wound up, any surplus funds remaining after the payment of the company's creditors will be distributed among them. Any profits that the company makes which are not capitalized by being retained to develop the business will also be distributed by way of a dividend to the shareholders. In a very real sense, therefore, the company belongs to the shareholders. It is they who benefit from its capital value and from the income that it produces. Yet the shareholders of a public company will very rarely be involved in its day-to-day management. Instead, they will appoint directors at a general meeting to whom they delegate the everyday management of the enterprise. The directors (unless they are also shareholders) will not themselves have a stake in the assets of the company, although within the limits of the authority given to them they will be able to decide how the assets of the company should be used. The directors will, of course, be under an obligation to exercise their powers of management honestly and properly. This is a duty that they owe, through the company, to the shareholders.

(2) **Agency**

(a) **The agency relationship**

The relationship of agency is the major means by which the common law enables the management and enjoyment of property to be separated. For example, Jake is the owner of a car he wishes to sell. Rather than arranging a contract of sale himself, he can delegate the task to another. He could authorize a garage to display the car on their forecourt and to sell the car to any purchaser prepared to pay more than a price arranged in advance. Here, Jake would be the principal and the garage would be acting as his agent. The relationship between the principal and the agent is contractual, and under this contract ownership in the car never passes to the agent. The agent is empowered to enter a contract with the purchaser on the principal's behalf, and property in the car will pass directly from the principal to the purchaser under that contract. Although he was not a party to the contract, the essence of agency is that it brings about a contract that is binding on the principal. For example, if the garage agreed to sell the car to Keith, this

---

[63] The analysis given here applies equally to private companies, although it is more likely with private companies that the same individuals will be both shareholders and directors.

would bring about a contract with Jake, and if he refused to deliver the car for personal reasons, Keith would be entitled to maintain an action against him for breach of contract. Again, subject to any special arrangement between them, the agent owes a duty to his principal to act honestly and properly. An agent will be liable to his principal under the tort of negligence even where the agent is acting gratuitously.[64]

Agency is most commonly found in commercial situations. All company directors are treated as agents of the company, authorized to make decisions and to enter into engagements on behalf of the company. The manager of a shop, and the sales staff in the shop, will be agents of the proprietor, whether that proprietor is an individual or a company. Agency is less commonly found in non-commercial contexts,[65] and where it is, it is most likely to be used to support a single transaction.

(b) Automatic termination of agency

In an agency relationship the agent represents his principal for the limited purposes for which the principal has granted him authority. However, the agent cannot enjoy a greater authority than the principal has given him, or than the principal himself enjoys. For this reason, if the principal loses his contractual capacity, the agent automatically loses his authority to enter into contracts with third parties that are binding on the principal. He cannot enjoy the capacity to enter into contracts that the principal could not have entered himself. Thus, if the principal dies, or loses mental capacity, the authority of the agent is automatically terminated, whether or not the agent is aware of the principal's situation.[66]

(c) Powers of attorney

Where a principal wishes an agent to be empowered to enter into a transaction requiring a deed, the authority must itself be conferred by way of deed termed a power of attorney. An agent so appointed is described as an attorney. The phrase 'power of attorney', as well as describing the deed and arrangement under which an agent is permitted to execute a deed on the principal's behalf, is also used to describe a general authority given by a principal permitting an agent to undertake any business concerning property on behalf of the principal. Such an authority could be given by a principal who was expecting to spend some time abroad, during which it would be impracticable for him to manage his own affairs.

(d) Lasting powers of attorney

(i) The need for lasting powers of attorney

Since a power of attorney is a form of agency, it will also terminate automatically if the principal loses his capacity. This poses particular difficulties for a society with an increasingly large elderly population, many of whom may go on to develop

---

[64] *Chaudhry v Prabhakar* [1988] 3 All ER 718, CA.

[65] Although see *Conservative & Unionist Central Office v Burrell* [1982] 1 WLR 522, discussed in Chapter 12.   [66] See *Drew v Nunn* (1879) 4 QBD 661; *Yonge v Toynbee* [1910] 1 KB 215.

senile dementia, or other types of mental incapacity. An older person may wish to grant someone she trusts, perhaps a child or other relative, a comprehensive power of attorney over her affairs because she may feel that she is no longer able to cope. However, although the power of attorney will be effective as long as she retains capacity, if she becomes mentally incapable, the authority will automatically terminate and the attorney will no longer be able to deal with her property. For this reason, the enduring power of attorney was introduced by the Enduring Powers of Attorney Act 1985. From 1 October 2007,[67] this mechanism was replaced by the lasting power of attorney under the Mental Capacity Act 2005, ss 9–14, which is more comprehensive, as it allows the donor to choose someone to not only manage their financial affairs and property, but also to make decisions concerning their health and welfare.[68]

(ii) Creation of lasting powers of attorney

A lasting power can only be created in accordance with the requirements set out in the Mental Capacity Act 2005, s 9(2); namely, that it must be created using the prescribed form and be registered with the Public Guardian,[69] the donees of the power must be properly appointed,[70] and the donor must have the capacity to execute the power.[71] The instrument creating the lasting power of attorney must be certified— this replaces the requirement to have the signature of the donor and donee witnessed as under the enduring power of attorney.[72] The certifier must confirm that, in his opinion, the donor understands the purpose and scope of the document they are signing.

(iii) Supervision by the court

Clearly, the lasting power of attorney gives the attorney tremendous power over the affairs of the person who created it, and there is a real danger of abuse, particularly after the creator has become incapable and is not able to supervise the exercise of the power. For this reason, the Court of Protection[73] exercises a supervisory function and this explains why the lasting power of attorney must be registered to be effective. By

---

[67] Enduring powers of attorney granted before that period may still be used (Mental Capacity Act 2005, s 66 and Sch 4), provided they have already been registered (Mental Capacity Act 2005, Sch 5, para 11), or they are registered under the 2005 Act (Mental Capacity Act 2005, Sch 4, Pt 4).

[68] Mental Capacity Act 2005, s 9(1). It is also possible for the donor to appoint different persons to look after their property and their personal welfare.

[69] S 9(2)(b). The requirements for registration are set out in Sch 1 of the Act. Part 1 of Sch 1 (paras 1–3) relates to the form of the power of attorney and include the requirement that the document creating the power contains explanatory information of the general effect of the power to make clear the effect to both the principal and to the attorney (see para 2(2)). Part 2 (paras 4–17) sets out the registration regime.

[70] Mental Capacity Act 2005, s 10.

[71] Capacity is presumed under the Act (s 1), but the court has power to act where the donor lacks capacity (see s 23). [72] Mental Capacity Act 2005, Sch 1, para 2(1)(e).

[73] The Court of Protection is an office of the Supreme Court of Justice responsible for administering the affairs of those who are incapable of doing so for themselves by virtue of mental incapacity. See Mental Capacity Act 2005, Pt 2.

ss 22 and 23, the court has powers in relation to the validity and operation of lasting powers of attorney, respectively.

(iv) Notice to named persons

When the attorney applies to the court for the power to be registered, he is under a duty to give notice to named persons in accordance with Sch 1 to the Act.[74] The Act allows the donor to nominate the 'named persons' he or she wishes to be notified,[75] and this will normally be used to allow relatives to be notified.[76] This would enable the relatives or other named persons (who will normally include those most likely to be affected by the way that the attorney deals with the donor's property), to object to the registration.[77]

(e) Agency and equity

Agency and powers of attorney are common law concepts, but both are supported by equity. The common law remedies for a failure by an agent or attorney to act in accordance with the terms of the authority conferred, or to break the duty of loyalty and care owed to the principal, are to deprive a purported but improper transaction of effect[78] and to impose on the agent or attorney an obligation to compensate the principal in damages for any loss. In some cases a third party suffering loss will have a right of redress against the agent by way of damages for breach of warranty of authority. Equity recognizes agency by treating agents or attorneys, and company directors, as fiduciaries,[79] standing in such a position of trust with regard to their principal that they can be held liable to account for any abuse of their position. Thus, if they make an unauthorized profit, they can be obliged to hand the benefit over to their principal. In this respect, there is a clear analogy between the position of an agent and the position of a trustee.

(f) Agency and ownership

Although agency provides a means by which powers of management can be divorced from the rights of enjoyment of property, it is generally considered to leave ownership in the principal unless the agent exercises his authority to pass ownership to himself or a third party. Even though the principal has conferred rights of disposal on the agent, this does not normally deprive him of his own rights of management and disposal. The agency is simply an authority which the principal gives to someone else to do some of those things which he can do himself. Moreover, apart from some limited exceptions, the principal retains the right to give instructions to the agent and to terminate the agency. The divorce between management and enjoyment is accordingly neither complete nor permanent.

---

[74] Sch 1, Pt 2, para 6.   [75] Sch 1, Pt 1, para (2)(1)(c)(i).

[76] The donor does not have to name any persons, and this is permissible under para (2)(1)(c)(ii) of Sch 1.

[77] Mental Capacity Act 2005, Sch 1, Pt 2, para 13.

[78] This will be the case both where the transaction lies outside the limits of the agent's authority and where there has been some procedural impropriety.   [79] See Chapter 28.

(g) Mandate

Agency is normally used to permit someone entrusted by the principal to enter into contracts on behalf of the principal. The common law recognizes, however, a form of agency in which an agent is permitted to dispose of property belonging to the principal. This form of agency is known as mandate. For instance, Howard might authorize his wife, Winnie, to sign cheques payable from his own bank account. Similarly, Elizabeth, wishing to distribute a sum of money to the poor, might give a sum in cash to Philip, authorizing him to choose the recipients. In each case, the agent may not be entering into contracts with third parties but is given authority to transfer title in the principal's property to a third party. Unless and until this authority is exercised, the title in the property remains with the principal.

4

Equitable remedies in modern English law

The previous chapters have charted the historical development of the Court of Chancery, of equity, and of equity's creation, the trust. The trust is not the only way in which equity has contributed to legal development. Equity also created remedies that were not available at common law. The following chapters will examine the most significant of these remedies and show how equitable remedies have continued to evolve and how they contribute to enforcing legal rights, on occasions creating new rights and obligations.

1 Introduction to equitable remedies

Equitable remedies apply in all fields of law, from disputes over property or entitlement in contract and intellectual property, to preventing harm, or to the proceeds of wrongdoing being dissipated before a claim can be made against them. Equity evolved these remedies in the Court of Chancery to ameliorate the common law. Sometimes the remedies (like rescission) modified the harshness of the common law rules. Sometimes the remedies (like specific performance and injunction) provide alternative relief to the common law remedy of damages. The remedies of specific performance and injunction are so important and pervasive that they are considered in chapters of their own. Other remedies, such as those depriving a fiduciary of the profits of his or her wrongdoing, and the processes of following and tracing misappropriated property, are best considered in the context in which they apply, and are therefore considered later. This chapter looks at the remedies of rescission, rectification and account, which have a general application.

2 Where equity intervenes

(1) Remedies supporting the common law

Equitable remedies are available in a range of circumstances. First, equity has intervened to support the common law. This is particularly evident in the law of contract, where the remedies of specific performance and injunction can be used respectively to compel the performance of a positive obligation or to prevent a party from doing something which he has contracted not to do. The remedy of account also supports the common law. This remedy could be used, for instance, to assist in quantifying damages where a defendant has failed to pay a contractual royalty on a musical recording by verifying the total receipts from sales. Equitable remedies are also available in other areas of the common law, for instance where injunctions are used to prevent the commission of a nuisance, to prevent interference with an easement, or to exclude an abusive spouse from the family home.

(2) Remedies ameliorating the common law

Equity's involvement has also been to ameliorate the common law. The common law would only rarely look at the circumstances which led to a contract being made, one exception being the doctrine of *non est factum* (it is not my act). The common law would not treat a signature as binding a person to a contract if they were only led to sign the document under the false impression that the document was something else (for instance where a person signed a contract thinking they were doing so only as a witness not as a contracting party). In equity other vitiating factors will be sufficient to justify not holding someone liable under a contract, for instance where the contract has been obtained as a result of a serious mistake, or through undue influence, or as a result of an unconscionable bargain.

(3) Remedies enforcing equitable obligations

Finally, equitable remedies are available in support of equitable obligations. By way of illustration, equitable compensation can be ordered where a trustee has caused loss to a trust or made an unauthorized profit. Where relevant, an equitable account can be ordered to verify the extent of the profit. A person in a fiduciary position, who owes duties of loyalty to another, can be prevented by injunction from acting in disregard of those duties.

3 Rescission

(1) Rescission for mistake

(a) Rescission of contracts

Rescission is the right of a party to a contract to have the contract set aside and to be restored to his former position as if the contract had never been made. There can be a number of reasons for rescission, including mistake, fraud, or lack of consent. The House of Lords held in *Johnson v Agnew*[1] that this type of rescission is to be

---

[1] [1980] AC 367, at 392.

distinguished from the situation (also called rescission) where a party is discharged from any obligation to perform the contract as a result of the breach of the other party. At common law a contract can be rescinded for *mistake* where the parties have made a mistake which negates agreement or which would make the performance of the contract as agreed impossible. The right of a party to rescind a contract for mistake was thought at one time to be wider in equity than at common law.[2] A number of cases accepted the existence of this more generous equitable jurisdiction.[3] The Court of Appeal has now, in *Great Peace Shipping v Tsavliris Salvage (International) Ltd*,[4] doubted the existence of any equitable jurisdiction to rescind a contract wider than that granted at common law. The Court of Appeal concluded that there was no authority for the proposition that there are two categories of mistake, one that renders a contract void at law and one that renders it voidable in equity.[5]

(b) Rescission of voluntary transactions

It is possible for voluntary transactions to be set aside for mistake.[6] A person who has transferred property to another, or who has created a trust, may sometimes be able to have that transfer or trust set aside. The doctrines of resulting and constructive trusts, considered later in this book, can have that effect. It has been held, for instance, that where a person transfers money to another in the mistaken belief that a debt is owing, when in fact it has been paid, then not only will there be a legal obligation on the recipient to repay, but also there may be an equitable obligation on the recipient which gives rise to a resulting or constructive trust.[7] It is also possible for a voluntary disposition to be rescinded or set aside as if it had never taken place. The leading authority is the decision of the Supreme Court in *Futter v Revenue Commissioners*.[8] The court made it clear that the test was not as onerous as that for contracts since equity had always looked differently upon voluntary dispositions, even if made by deed.[9] The court indicated that 'the true requirement is simply for there to be a causative mistake of sufficient gravity'.[10] Whilst that would normally be 'a mistake either as to the legal character or nature of a transaction, or as to some matter of fact or law which is basic to the transaction,'[11] it could also be a mistake as to the effects or consequences of the transaction, including the tax consequences. In assessing what constitutes a mistake of sufficient gravity, the court indicated that it would be inappropriate to apply strict rules, and the test was instead what would make it unconscionable or unjust to leave the mistaken

---

[2] *Solle v Butcher* [1950] 1 KB 671, CA. Denning LJ relied on *Cooper v Phibbs* (1867) LR 2 HL 149 and *Huddersfield Banking Co Ltd v Henry Lister & Sons Ltd* [1895] 2 Ch 273, CA.

[3] *Grist v Bailey* [1967] Ch 532; *Magee v Pennine Insurance Co Ltd* [1969] 2 QB 507; *Associated Japanese Bank (International) Ltd v Credit du Nord SA* [1988] 3 All ER 902; *West Sussex Properties Ltd v Chichester District Council* [2000] NPC 74.

[4] [2003] QB 679; [2002] 4 All ER 690; [2002] LMCLQ (McMeel); (2003) 119 LQR 177 (Reynolds); (2003) 62 CLJ 29 (Hare); [2003] Conv 247 (Phang); [2003] 1 RLR 93 (Cartwright).   [5] [2003] QB 679.

[6] *Gibbon v Mitchell* [1990] 1 WLR 1304; *Dent v Dent* [1996] 1 WLR 683; *Wolff v Wolff* [2004] STC 1633.

[7] See *Chase Manhattan Bank NA v Israel-British Bank (London) Ltd* ([1981] Ch 105 and the explanation of the case given by Lord Browne-Wilikinson in *Westdeutsche Landesbank Girozentrale v Islington LBC* [1996] AC 669.   [8] [2013] UKSC 26.

[9] [2013] UKSC 26 at [115].   [10] [2013] UKSC 26 at [122].   [11] [2013] UKSC 26 at [122].

disposition uncorrected. That judgement would depend, not upon an elaborate set of rules, but a consideration in the round of the centrality of the mistake to the transaction in question, and the seriousness of its consequences.[12]

The jurisdiction applies only to correcting mistakes, and not to decisions made through ignorance or inadvertence, even if this ignorance was causative (in other words directly influenced the decision). However, ignorance or inadvertence could lead to a conscious belief or tacit assumption which would be sufficient to constitute a mistake.[13] There is little doubt that the distinction between mistakes and ignorance will be a cause of difficulty in applying the new principles on rescission for mistake. Similarly, the vagueness of what makes it unconscionable not to rescind a transaction will make predicting the outcome of cases on mistake difficult.

Whether it is unconscionable not to set aside a voluntary disposition must be viewed objectively, doing so primarily from the perspective of the recipient of the bounty.[14] It is not necessary for the recipient to have contributed to the mistake or to have been aware of it, although these factors may affect the assessment of what is conscionable.[15] The fact that the recipients are volunteers will militate against a finding that they should in conscience be able to retain a benefit once they realise that it was the result of a serious mistake;[16] they may, however, receive protection through the defence that before they should have realised that it was unconscionable to retain the benefits of the disposition they have materially changed their position.[17]

(2) Rescission for misrepresentation

(a) Meaning of misrepresentation

In *Behn v Burness*,[18] Williams J defined a representation in the context of the formation of contracts as 'a statement or assertion, made by one party to the other before or at the time of the contract, of some matter or circumstance relating to it'.

(b) Rescission of contracts for misrepresentation

A misrepresentation does not render a contract void, but the other contracting party may be entitled to rescind it where the making of the contract was induced by misrepresentation. The representation must be of fact,[19] and not simply an expression of intention[20] or opinion.[21] Although there is no general duty on a contracting party to reveal all known relevant facts, in the case of some contracts, known as contracts *uberrimae fidei*, there is such a duty. These include contracts for insurance[22] and family settlements.[23] The right to rescind a contract applies both where the misrepresentation

---

[12] [2013] UKSC 26 at [124] to [128].   [13] [2013] UKSC 26, at [108].
[14] [2013] UKSC 26, at [124].   [15] [2013] UKSC 26, at [114].   [16] [2013] UKSC 26, at [124].
[17] [2013] UKSC 26, at [124]–[125].   [18] (1863) 3 B & S 751.
[19] *Ship v Crosskill* (1870) LR 10 Eq 73.   [20] *Edgington v Fitzmaurice* (1885) 29 Ch D 459, CA.
[21] *Bisset v Wilkinson* [1927] AC 177, PC.
[22] See *Lambert v Co-operative Insurance Society* [1975] 2 Lloyd's Rep 485, CA.
[23] *Gordon v Gordon* (1816) 3 Swan 400.

is fraudulent (which means a false statement made knowingly, or without belief in its truth, or reckless whether it is true or not[24]) and where the misrepresentation is innocent (where the party making the misrepresentation honestly believes it to be true).[25] By s 2(2) of the Misrepresentation Act 1967 the court has the discretion to award damages in lieu of rescission for innocent misrepresentation and declare the contract subsisting.

(c) Rescission of voluntary dispositions for misrepresentation

It cannot be assumed that the rules relating to the rescission of voluntary dispositions for misrepresentation are the same as those for contracts. By analogy with the position in relation to mistake, it is likely that the test will be whether it is unconscionable for the disposition to remain uncorrected. This viewpoint is reinforced because in most if not all cases a misrepresentation causing or inducing a voluntary disposition will have led the donor into making a mistake. Rescission for that mistake will be possible under the rules just described: the fact that the beneficiary has induced the mistake will make it more likely that it will be unconscionable for the mistake not to be redressed.

(3) Rescission for undue influence

(a) Meaning of undue influence

Contracts or voluntary dispositions, including wills,[26] can be set aside where they have been induced by undue influence. The rules in both instances are broadly the same. The essence of undue influence is that the party making the contract or disposition was dominated by the other so that he was not acting of his own free choice.

(b) Actual undue influence

Actual undue influence arises where one party has in fact applied improper pressure to the other, which falls short of that necessary to constitute duress (which at common law is also sufficient to avoid a contract or disposition).[27] This may be through the exercise of conscious deception, although there will also be cases where a trusted adviser has broken his fiduciary duty of loyalty by preferring his own interests.[28] Merely failing to reveal material facts is insufficient by itself to amount to undue influence because negligence is not the same as a breach of the duty of loyalty,[29] but it was held to be a

---

[24] *Derry v Peek* (1889) 14 App Cas 337.

[25] *Reese River Silver Mining Co v Smith* (1869) LR 4 HL 64; *Torrance v Bolton* (1872) 8 Ch App 118; *Redgrave v Hurd* (1881) 20 Ch D 1, CA; *Walker v Boyle* [1982] 1 All ER 634. By s 2(1) of the Misrepresentation Act 1967 he is also entitled to recover damages unless the defendant had reasonable grounds to believe that his statement was true: *Esso Petroleum v Mardon* [1976] QB 801; *Royscot Trust Ltd v Rogerson* [1991] 2 QB 297; *Smith New Court Securities Ltd v Scrimgeour Vickers (Asset Management) Ltd* [1997] AC 254.

[26] *Schrader v Schrader* [2013] EWHC 466 (Ch). For the principles applied to wills, see this case or *Edwards v Edwards* [2007] WTLR 1387.

[27] See eg *Re Craig* [1971] Ch 95; *Cheese v Thomas* [1994] 1 All ER 35.

[28] *Royal Bank of Scotland Plc v Chandra* [2011] EWCA Civ 192 at [26].

[29] *Royal Bank of Scotland v Chandra* [2010] EWHC 105 (Ch) at [140] *and Royal Bank of Scotland Plc v Chandra* [2011] EWCA Civ 192, at [24].

breach of duty where a husband had failed to inform his wife that he was engaged in a secret affair at the time of asking her to act as surety.[30]

In *Bank of Credit and Commerce International SA v Aboody*,[31] the court held that it was also necessary for the party alleging actual undue influence to demonstrate that they had suffered a 'manifest disadvantage' from the transaction, but this requirement was rejected by the House of Lords in *CIBC Mortgages plc v Pitt*.[32]

(c) Presumed undue influence

In some circumstances, the nature of the relationship between the parties itself gives rise to the presumption of undue influence, and the burden falls on the defendant to demonstrate that no such influence was exercised.[33] Examples of relationships where influence will be presumed include parent and child,[34] spiritual adviser and disciple,[35] doctor and patient,[36] married and cohabiting couples,[37] or couples in a close, stable, sexual, and emotional relationship,[38] or between solicitor and client.[39] In the case of other relationships, for example bank and customer[40] and pop artist and manager,[41] it may be possible to show that there was in fact a relationship of influence. Undue influence has increasingly been presumed where a relationship of confidence has been shown to have existed between family members or relations.[42] Similarly, the fact that a person agrees to act as surety of the debts of another will give rise to a presumption of a relationship of confidence if the surety gained no personal advantage from so acting.[43] In *Crédit Lyonnais Bank Nederland NV v Burch*,[44] the Court of Appeal held that an abuse of a relationship of confidence was presumed from the mere fact that a junior employee had executed an 'extravagantly improvident' unlimited guarantee of all her employer's debts, and that there was no need to show any sexual or emotional tie. In *National Westminster Bank Plc v Morgan*,[45] the House of Lords held that a party relying on presumed undue influence must also demonstrate that he had suffered a manifest disadvantage from the transaction. In the now leading case of *Royal Bank of*

---

[30] *Hewett v First Plus Financial Group plc* [2010] EWCA Civ 312. [31] [1990] 1 QB 923, CA.
[32] [1994] 1 AC 200. See also *Barclays Bank v O'Brien* [1994] 1 AC 180.
[33] See *Allcard v Skinner* (1887) 36 Ch D 145. See also *Hammond v Osborn* [2002] WTLR 1125; [2003] LMCLQ 145 (Scott); (2003) 119 LQR 34 (Birks). [34] [1934] 1 KB 380, CA.
[35] *Allcard v Skinner* (1887) 36 Ch D 145; *Tufton v Sperni* [1952] 2 TLR 516, CA; *Roche v Sherrington* [1982] 1 WLR 599. [36] *Dent v Bennett* (1839) 4 My & Cr 269.
[37] *Barclays Bank v O'Brien* [1994] 1 AC 180.
[38] *Massey v Midland Bank plc* [1995] 1 All ER 929. [39] *Wright v Carter* [1903] 1 Ch 27, CA.
[40] *Lloyds Bank v Bundy* [1975] QB 326, CA.
[41] *O'Sullivan v Management Agency and Music Ltd* [1985] QB 428.
[42] *Simpson v Simpson* [1992] 1 FLR 601; *Cheese v Thomas* [1994] 1 WLR 129; *Langton v Langton* [1995] 2 FLR 890; *Mahoney v Purnell* [1996] 3 All ER 61.
[43] *Barclays Bank v O'Brien* [1994] 1 AC 180; *CIBC v Pitt* [1994] 1 AC 200; *Massey v Midland Bank plc* [1995] 1 All ER 929; *Allied Irish Bank plc v Byrne* [1995] 2 FLR 325; *Banco Exterior Internacional SA v Thomas* [1997] 1 All ER 46; *Dunbar Bank plc v Nadeem* [1998] 3 All ER 876. But cf *Mumford v Bank of Scotland* 1996 SLT 392.
[44] [1997] 1 All ER 144; Hooley and O'Sullivan 'Undue Influence and Unconscionable Bargains' [1997] LMCLQ 17. [45] [1985] AC 686.

Scotland v Etridge (No 2),[46] the House of Lords held that the requirement of 'manifest disadvantage' was ambiguous and should be discarded.

Rebutting undue influence is normally done by ensuring that the party subject to the influence has received independent legal advice. The other contracting party must also ensure that they have been informed of any unusual aspects of the transaction.[47]

(d) Influence exercised by third parties

A transaction can be set aside where the circumstances are such that the person bene-fiting from the transaction was aware of circumstances in which the other party may have been acting under the undue influence of a third party. Most typically this has occurred where a wife has executed some kind of financial guarantee of her hus-band's debts in favour of a bank. For example, in *Barclays Bank v O'Brien*,[48] a hus-band whose business was in difficulties executed a second mortgage over the family home he jointly owned with his wife to provide additional security for the company's debts. The House of Lords held that the wife had signed the mortgage documents acting under the undue influence of her husband. Given that the bank had failed to take reasonable steps to satisfy itself that she had entered the transaction freely, it had constructive notice of the undue influence and she was therefore able to set the transaction aside.[49] A person will not be affixed with constructive notice of such undue influence if they ensure that the party they contract with received independent advice as to the effect of the transaction.[50] A creditor may also be put on notice where the undue influence has been exercised by a co-surety of the mortgagor, rather than the debtor.[51]

In *Royal Bank of Scotland v Etridge (No 2)*[52] the House of Lords clarified the circum-stances in which such surety transactions may be set aside. The Lords looked at eight cases in which a wife had agreed to a charge in favour of a bank to secure debts owed by her husband or a company that he controlled. In seven of these cases the wife claimed that the charge was unenforceable against her because it was tainted by undue influ-ence. In the eighth case, the wife who had agreed to a similar arrangement was suing a solicitor for breach of duty concerning the advice that he gave her. The House of Lords held that a bank would be put on inquiry whenever a wife offers to stand surety for her

---

[46] [2001] 4 All ER 449.

[47] *North Shore Ventures Ltd v Anstead Holdings Inc* [2011] EWCA Civ 230   [48] [1994] 1 AC 180.

[49] See also *Massey v Midland Bank plc* [1995] 1 All ER 929; *Banco Exterior Internacional SA v Mann* [1995] 1 All ER 936; *TSB Bank plc v Camfield* [1995] 1 All ER 951. In Scotland constructive notice is insuf-ficient and the transaction will only be set aside if the contracting party had actual notice of the undue influence: *Mumford v Bank of Scotland* 1996 SLT 392.

[50] *Barclays Bank plc v O'Brien* [1994] 1 AC 180; *Midland Bank plc v Kidwai* [1995] NPC 81; *Banco Exterior Internacional v Mann* [1995] 1 All ER 936; *Massey v Midland Bank plc* [1995] 1 All ER 929; *Bank of Baroda v Rayarel* [1995] 2 FLR 376; *Hemsley v Brown (No 2)* [1996] 2 FCR 107; *Banco Exterior Internacional SA v Thomas* [1997] 1 All ER 46; *Crédit Lyonnais Bank Nederland NV v Burch* [1997] 1 All ER 144.

[51] *First National Bank v Achampong* [2003] EWCA Civ 487; [2003] LMCLQ 307 (Enonchong).

[52] [2001] 4 All ER 449. See Capper 'Banks, Borrowers, Sureties and Undue Influence—A Half-Baked Solution to a Thoroughly Cooked Problem' [2002] RLR 100; Bigwood 'Undue Influence in the House of Lords: Principles and Proof' (2002) 65 MLR 435; Phang and Tijo 'The Uncertain Boundaries of Undue Influence' [2002] LMCLQ 231.

husband's debts. To avoid the transaction being impugned on the grounds of undue influence the bank must merely take reasonable steps to satisfy itself that the practical implications of the proposed transaction have been brought home to the wife, especially the risks involved, so that she is able to enter the transaction with her eyes open as to its basic elements. This does not require a meeting between the bank and the wife. The bank is entitled to rely upon confirmation from a solicitor acting for the wife that he has advised her appropriately. A solicitor who fails to give the advice correctly is likely to be held liable for negligence.[53] In *Padden v Bevan Ashford,*[54] a wife approved a mortgage of the family home in the erroneous belief that it would spare her husband from the prospect of criminal prosecution and possible imprisonment. Her husband was a financial adviser, who had embezzled substantial sums from a client and needed the money to repay the client debt. The firm, which had given inadequate advice was held liable (reversing the decision of the trial judge) as it could not prove that the wife would have signed regardless of the quality of the advice she received.

If a mortgage is executed to replace an earlier mortgage which could be set aside because the mortgagee had constructive notice that it was effected by undue influence, the subsequent mortgage could also be set aside, even if relates to another property. The two mortgages are inseparable, and the principle that a contract of insurance can be set aside for misrepresentation if it has been renewed, even though each renewal constitutes a fresh contract, can be applied by analogy.[55]

(4) **Setting aside unconscionable bargains**

Equity will set aside bargains and possibly gifts (although first instance decisions differ on this point[56]) that have been made in circumstances that can be regarded as 'unconscionable'. The scope of the doctrine is relatively narrow, and in *National Westminster Bank plc v Morgan,*[57] the House of Lords rejected the comprehensive principle of 'inequality of bargaining power' advocated by Lord Denning MR in *Lloyds Bank Ltd v Bundy.*[58] There are three requirements. The first is that the person seeking to avoid the disposition suffered from a significant disability.[59] A Victorian case suggested that the principle would apply to someone who was 'poor and ignorant';[60] in modern terms this refers to a person of limited means and limited education.[61] Other kinds of disability or disadvantage may be relevant in the particular circumstances of a case.[62] This may include a mental incapacity such as senile dementia,[63] illiteracy, or unfamiliarity with

---

[53] *Padden v Bevan Ashford Solicitors* [2011] EWCA Civ 1616.

[54] [2012] 2 All ER 718. The guidance is set out at [65].

[55] *Yorkshire Bank plc v Tinsley* [2004] 3 All ER 463; Gravells 'Undue Influence and Substitute Mortgages' [2005] 64 CLJ 42.

[56] *Evans v Lloyd* [2013] EWHC 1725 holds that the doctrine applies to gifts, differing from *Langton v Langton* [1995] 2 FLR 890.   [57] [1985] AC 686.

[58] [1975] QB 326, CA.   [59] [2013] EWHC 1725   [60] *Fry v Lane* (1888) 40 Ch.D. 312 at 322

[61] *Cresswell v Potter* [1978] 1 W.L.R. 255

[62] *Chagos Islanders v Attorney General* [2003] EWHC 2222 (QB) at [559].

[63] *Archer v Cutler* [1980] 1 NZLR 386; *Hart v O'Connor* [1985] AC 1000.

a language or culture,[64] age,[65] or youth and inexperience.[66] The second and third are closely related. The arrangement must be oppressive and must have been procured by the stronger party wrongly exploiting the weaker party. In *Boustany v Piggott*,[67] Lord Templeman stated that a bargain will not be held to be unconscionable merely because it was 'hard, unreasonable or foolish; it must be proved to be unconscionable, in the sense that "one of the parties to it has imposed the objectionable terms in a morally reprehensible manner,[68] that is to say, in a way which affects his conscience"'.[69] This requires an assessment not just of the terms of the bargain (which must be oppressive or unfair, for instance by conferring no personal advantage on the weaker party[70]), but also of the behaviour of the stronger party, ('which must be characterised by some moral culpability or impropriety').[71] The onus is on the person seeking relief to establish unconscionable conduct, namely that unconscientious advantage has been taken of his disabling condition or circumstances.[72] Such exploitation will not be demonstrated if the contracting party received independent legal advice before entering the bargain.[73]

Parliament has intervened with a regime of consumer protection, which extends to the regulation of terms in contracts,[74] and unconscionable terms in credit arrangements, such as hire purchase agreements, are now regulated by the Consumer Credit Act 1974, as amended by the Consumer Credit Act 2006.[75]

(5) Limitations on the availability of rescission

There are a number of circumstances where it will not be possible for a claimant to rescind a contract.

(a) Restitutio in integrum is impossible

When a contract is rescinded the parties must be returned to their former positions as far as is practically possible.[76] As Lord Blackburn said in *Erlanger v New Sombrero Phosphate Co*:

---

[64] *Commercial Bank of Australia Ltd v Amadio* (1983) 46 ALR 402.

[65] *Watkin v Watson-Smith* (1986) The Times, 3 July.

[66] *Crédit Lyonnais Bank Nederland NV v Burch* [1997] 1 All ER 144 (a junior employee).

[67] (1993) 69 P & CR 288. See Bamforth 'Unconscionability as a Vitiating Factor' [1995] LMCLQ 538.

[68] The requirement of moral turpitude does not apply in Ireland: *Prendergast v Joyce*[2009] 3 IR 519.

[69] (1993) 69 P & CR 288, at 303 drawing on *Multiservice Bookbinding Ltd v Marden* [1979] Ch 84 at 110.

[70] *Crédit Lyonnais Bank Nederland v Burch* [1997] 1 All ER 144.

[71] *Alec Lobb (Garages) Ltd v Total Oil (Great Britain) Ltd* [1983] 1 WLR 87, at 94; *Hart v O'Connor* [1985] AC 1000; *Nichols v Jessup* [1986] 1 NZLR 226.

[72] *Commercial Bank of Australia Ltd v Amadio* (1983) 46 ALR 402, at 413, per Mason J.

[73] *Fry v Lane* (1888) 40 Ch D 312; *Butlin-Sanders v Butlin* [1985] Fam Law 126.

[74] See, for example, the Unfair Terms in Consumer Contracts Regulations 1999.

[75] See further, Dobson and Stokes, *Commercial Law* (7th edn, 2008), Chs 10 (consumer contracts); 20 (credit arrangements).

[76] *Spence v Crawford* [1939] 3 All ER 271, HL; *Cheese v Thomas* [1994] 1 All ER 35, at 412, per Nicholls V-C. See also *Maguire v Makaronis* (1997) 71 ALJR 781; Moriarty 'Equitable Compensation for Undue Influence' (1997) 114 LQR 9.

It is…clear on principles of general justice, that as a condition to a rescission there must be *restitutio in integrum*. The parties must be put in *status quo ante*…[77]

For example, in *Clarke v Dickson*[78] the court held that a party could not rescind a contract to purchase shares in a partnership that had been converted into a limited liability company.[79] Equity approaches the question flexibly, and is particularly ready to grant rescission where there was fraud.[80] In granting rescission the court may impose terms,[81] for example to account for profits or allow for deterioration.[82] The overall objective is for the courts to do 'what is practically just'.[83] Thus, in *O'Sullivan v Management Agency and Music Ltd*[84] a contract for the management of a popular singer (Gilbert O'Sullivan) was rescinded on the grounds of undue influence. The managers were allowed to retain a reasonable remuneration for the work they had done which had contributed to his success. In *Cheese v Thomas*,[85] an uncle and his great-nephew had purchased a house for £83,000. The uncle had contributed £43,000 and the remainder had been borrowed by the nephew by way of a mortgage. The uncle was held entitled to set the transaction aside on the grounds of undue influence exercised by the nephew. However, when the house was sold its value had fallen considerably and only £55,000 was received. This was sufficient to discharge the mortgage but even if the balance was paid to the uncle he would remain £25,000 out of pocket. The Court of Appeal rejected the uncle's submission that his nephew should repay him the entire £43,000 he had contributed to the property. Nicholls V-C explained that, although the transaction was to be reversed on the grounds of undue influence, it was impossible to restore the parties to the precise position they were in before the contract had been entered. The court would thus 'do what is practically just' by restoring the uncle 'as near to his original position as is now possible'. It was thus held that the uncle was entitled to receive a share of the net proceeds of sale received from the property proportionate to his original contribution; 43/83 on the facts. Thus, he would bear a proportionate share of the loss caused by the fall in value thereof.

(b) Affirmation

A party cannot rescind a contract that he has subsequently affirmed. In *Long v Lloyd*,[86] a purchaser was taken to have affirmed a contract for the sale of a lorry when he used it a second time having discovered there were faults. He could not rescind on the grounds of the seller's misrepresentation. Similarly, a person cannot rescind a contract entered under undue influence if he affirms it after the influence has stopped.[87]

---

[77] (1878) 3 App Cas 1218, at 1278. See Halson 'Rescission for Misrepresentation' [1997] RLR 89.
[78] (1858) EB & E 148.
[79] See also *Thorpe v Fasey* [1949] Ch 649; *Butler v Croft* (1973) 27 P & CR 1.
[80] *Spence v Crawford* [1939] 3 All ER 271, HL.
[81] See Proksch 'Rescission on Terms' [1996] RLR 71.
[82] *Lagunas Nitrate Co v Lagunas Syndicate* [1899] 2 Ch 392; *Armstrong v Jackson* [1917] 2 KB 822; *Wiebe v Butchart's Motors Ltd* [1949] 4 DLR 838. See *TSB Bank plc v Camfield* [1995] 1 All ER 951.
[83] *Spence v Crawford* [1939] 3 All ER 271, at 288, per Lord Wright; *Cheese v Thomas* [1994] 1 All ER 35, at 412, per Nicholls V-C; *Vadasz v Pioneer Concrete* (SA) Pty Ltd (1995) 130 ALR 570.
[84] [1985] QB 428.   [85] [1994] 1 All ER 35.   [86] [1958] 2 All ER 402, CA.
[87] *Mitchell v Homfray* (1881) 8 QBD 587.

(c) Third-party rights

The right to rescind is lost once third parties have acquired rights in the property in good faith for value.[88]

(d) Delay

In *Allcard v Skinner*,[89] the plaintiff was held not to be entitled to rescind gifts of stock to a religious order five years after she left because of her delay. Lindley LJ stated that the victim must 'seek relief within a reasonable time after the removal of the influence'.[90] Similarly, in *Leaf v International Galleries*[91] a plaintiff was not entitled to rescind a contract for innocent misrepresentation after a delay of five years.

4 Rectification

Rectification is a discretionary[92] equitable remedy that allows for the correction of a document so that it reflects the real intention of the parties. It is an exception to the 'parol evidence rule' so that oral evidence may be admitted to demonstrate that a written instrument is incorrect. For example, in *Joscelyne v Nissen*[93] the Court of Appeal ordered the rectification of an agreement between a daughter and her father which they intended should include a provision that she was to pay the household expenses, which she had refused to pay, claiming that she was not required to do so on a true construction of the written agreement they had entered. A wide range of documents have been rectified, including a conveyance,[94] a bill of exchange,[95] a marriage settlement,[96] a transfer of shares[97] and, by statute, wills.[98]

(1) Requirements for rectification

(a) Mistake in written document

Rectification is only possible where a written document mistakenly fails to state what the parties had intended to agree. It is not necessary that the parties had actually entered a contract orally prior to the incorrect instrument. In *Joscelyne v Nissen*,[99] the Court of Appeal held that all that is necessary is a prior common intention as to what the written agreement was to be.[100] There are grounds for rectification if that common

---

[88] See *Oakes v Turquand* (1867) LR 2 HL 325; *Bainbrigge v Browne* (1881) 18 Ch D 188; *Re Scottish Petroleum Co (No 2)* (1883) 23 Ch D 413; *Coldunell Ltd v Gallon* [1986] 1 All ER 429.

[89] (1887) 36 Ch D 145.   [90] (1887) 36 Ch D 145, at 187.   [91] [1950] 2 KB 86.

[92] *Re Butlin's Settlement Trusts* [1976] Ch 251.   [93] [1970] 2 QB 86.

[94] *Beale v Kyte* [1907] 1 Ch 564.   [95] *Druiff v Lord Parker* (1867–68) LR 5 Eq 131.

[96] *Bold v Hutchinson* (1855) 5 De GM & G 558.

[97] *Re International Contract Co* (1872) 7 Ch App 485.

[98] Administration of Justice Act 1982, s 20(1). See *Wordingham v Royal Exchange Trust Co* [1992] Ch 412; *Re Segelman* [1996] Ch 171; [1995] 3 All ER 676.   [99] [1970] 2 QB 86.

[100] *Crane v Hegeman-Harris Co Inc* [1939] 1 All ER 662.

intention does not appear in the written document.[101] Rectification is only available for a mistake of the actual terms of the parties' agreement. Thus, in *Frederick E Rose (London) Ltd v William Pim Jnr & Co Ltd*[102] rectification was not possible where the parties had entered a written contract for the sale of 'horsebeans', which they had mistakenly believed were the same as 'feveroles'. The contract was a correct record of their agreement. Rectification was similarly refused in *Lloyds TSB Bank Plc v Crowborough Properties Ltd*[103] where a contract accurately recorded what the parties agreed, but did not have the effect either of them intended since they both shared a mistaken common assumption.

(b) Common mistake

Generally, an instrument will only be rectified if it records the agreement contrary to the intentions of both parties.[104]

(c) Unilateral mistake

Rectification is not normally available where a mistake is unilateral.[105] However, rectification will be available if the party who was not mistaken had acted fraudulently[106] or is estopped from resisting rectification. In *Thomas Bates & Son Ltd v Wyndham's (Lingerie) Ltd*,[107] Buckley LJ stated that a person would be estopped from resisting rectification if he knew that the other party was mistaken about the inclusion or omission of a provision and failed to draw it to the other party's attention. He also thought that the party estopped needed to derive some benefit from the mistake, although the reason for this requirement is not self-evident.[108]

A line of authorities which suggested that the party who was not mistaken has the option of accepting rectification or rescission of the contract has been disapproved by the Court of Appeal in *Riverlate Properties Ltd v Paul*.[109]

(d) Rectification of voluntary instruments

The requirement of a common intention, or estoppel does not apply where rectification is sought of a voluntary instrument. All that is necessary in such a case is that the settlor had executed the settlement in the mistaken belief that it implemented her or his intention. There is no need for any outward expression or objective communication of that intention as there was when it was sought to rectify a contract. In *Day v Day*[110] Mrs Day, who was staying with her daughter in Canada at the time, executed a power of attorney so that her solicitor could arrange a mortgage over her home to pay off her son's debts. The court found that it was never her intention to do this in the way actually adopted, which was to transfer her house into the names of

---

[101] *Earl v Hector Whaling Ltd* [1961] 1 Lloyd's Rep 459.   [102] [1953] 2 QB 450.
[103] [2012] EWHC 2264 (Ch).
[104] *Murray v Parker* (1854) 19 Beav 305; *Fowler v Fowler* (1859) 4 De G & J 250.
[105] *Sells v Sells* (1860) 1 Drew & Sm 42.
[106] *Ball v Storie* (1823) 1 Sim & St 210; *Lovesy v Smith* (1880) LR 15 Ch D 655.
[107] [1981] 1 All ER 1077, CA.   [108] [1981] 1 All ER 1077, CA, at 1086.   [109] [1975] Ch 133.
[110] [2013] 3 All ER 661

herself and her son with an express declaration that there was a beneficial joint tenancy. Because it would be unjust or unconscionable for the son to retain the benefit of this mistake, rectification to remove the declaration of trust was therefore ordered.

(e) Burden of proof

For rectification the mistake must be established with 'a high degree of conviction'.[111] In *Joscelyne v Nissen*,[112] Russel LJ said that there must be 'convincing proof' of the mistake. Thus, in *Re Segelman*[113] Chadwick J held that a testator's will should be rectified where extrinsic evidence of his intentions demonstrated convincingly that it had failed to carry out his intentions.

(2) Defences to rectification

Rectification will not be granted where it would affect the position of third parties who have acquired rights bona fides for value.[114] Delay may also bar a claim.[115]

5 Account

Where someone has obtained a benefit to which they are not entitled, or has incurred an expense which should be payable by another, an account in equity may be ordered, either on its own, or as an adjunct to another substantive remedy. An account may be ordered, for instance, where equitable co-owners are entitled to share the occupation of residential property, but only one of them has been paying the bills,[116] or where land held by co-owners has been let or exploited for profit.[117] Similarly, a fiduciary who has made improper use of information acquired as adviser to a trust may be obliged by means of an account to give up to the beneficiaries any profits which he has made.[118]

(1) Ancillary orders in support of legal rights

In some instances, the order for account will not be sought in its own right, but to make effective some other remedy of the plaintiff. The claimant owed a debt might seek an

---

[111] *Crane v Hegeman-Harris Co Inc* [1939] 4 All ER 68, CA. See also *Countess of Shelburne v Earl of Inchiquin* (1784) 1 Bro CC 338; *Fowler v Fowler* (1859) 4 De G & J 250.

[112] [1970] 2 QB 86, CA. See *Brimican Investments Ltd v Blue Circle Heating Ltd* [1995] EGCS 18; *Racal Group Services Ltd v Ashmore* [1995] STC 1151; *Re Segelman* [1995] 3 All ER 676.

[113] *Re Segelman* [1995] 3 All ER 676, at 684.

[114] *Garrard v Frankel* (1862) 30 Beav 445; *Smith v Jones* [1954] 1 WLR 1089; *Thames Guaranty Ltd v Campbell* [1985] QB 210.   [115] *Beale v Kyte* [1907] 1 Ch 564.

[116] *Leake v Bruzzi* [1974] 1 WLR 1528; *Leigh v Dickeson* (1884) 15 QBD 60. See also *Henderson v Eason* (1851) 17 QB 701, at 721, per Parke B.

[117] *Henderson v Eason* (1851) 17 QB 701; *Job v Potton* (1875) LR 20 Eq 84; *Jacobs v Seward* (1872) LR 5 HL 464.   [118] *Boardman v Phipps* [1967] 2 AC 46, HL. See Chapter 28.

account, for instance, to verify the amount owing. There were some instances where an account of this kind could be ordered at common law, but the superior procedures of equity[119] meant that the equitable order largely displaced the common law jurisdiction.[120] Following the amalgamation of the courts of law and the courts of equity, and the prevailing judicial view about the effect of that fusion, there is now probably no reason to distinguish between the legal and equitable jurisdictions.[121]

An order for account may be used as an adjunct to the obligation of an agent to answer to his principal under a contract of agency. The principal could, by means of account, obtain disclosure of any sums owing to him by his agent.[122] Equity was prepared to intervene because a principal places confidence in his agent, and without disclosure by the agent, may have no means of knowing what is owing.[123] For similar reasons, an inventor seeking by injunction to prevent the infringement of a patent[124] may use an account in order to discover what profits have been made from the unauthorized exploitation of the invention. Equity also offered aid through an action in account where the affairs of the parties were especially complicated[125] or where mutual accounts were involved.[126]

(2) Ancillary orders in support of equitable rights

Equity would, of course, order an account where this was necessary to support a purely equitable right, such as the right of a beneficiary against a trustee in respect of trust property, the right of a landlord against a tenant for equitable waste,[127] or the right of a mortgagor to obtain the best return reasonably possible from property of which the mortgagee has taken possession. In this last instance, the mortgagee is held accountable not only for what has in fact been received, but also for the sums that he ought to have received if he had fulfilled his duty. The mortgagee would thus be accountable for rents which could have been obtained if the property had been let as it ought[128] and for the full market rent which could have been obtained if the property had not been let subject to a disparaging condition.[129]

---

[119] *See A-G v Dublin Corpn* (1827) 1 Bli NS 312, at 337; *Beaumont v Boultbee* (1802) 7 Ves 599.

[120] *Sturton v Richardson* (1844) 13 M & W 17; *Shepard v Brown* (1862) 4 Giff 203.

[121] The distinction could, before the fusion of the courts of law and of equity, be of significance. For instance, equity would not order an account in favour of a customer against his banker, since the relationship between them was in the nature of a simple contract without any fiduciary character: *Foley v Hill* (1848) 2 HL Cas 28.

[122] *Beaumont v Boultbee* (1802) 7 Ves 599; *Mackenzie v Johnston* (1819) 4 Madd 373.

[123] That would not generally be the case where the agent brings an action against the principal: *Padwick v Stanley* (1852) 9 Hare 627.

[124] *Price's Patent Candle Co v Bauwen's Patent Candle Co Ltd* (1858) 4 K & J 727; *De Vitre v Betts* (1873) LR 6 HL 319. See Patents Act 1977, s 61.

[125] *O'Connor v Spaight* (1804) 1 Sch & Lef 305; *Taff Vale Rly Co v Nixon* (1847) 1 HL Cas 111; *North-Eastern Rly Co v Martin* (1848) 2 Ph 758.   [126] *Phillips v Phillips* (1852) 9 Hare 471.

[127] *Duke of Leeds v Earl of Amherst* (1846) 2 Ph 117. Equitable waste is deliberate and malicious injury to land or buildings affecting its permanent value.   [128] *Noyes v Pollock* (1886) 32 Ch D 53, at 61.

[129] *White v City of London Brewery Co* (1889) 42 Ch D 237.

Where a trustee's inaction amounts to a breach of duty[130] (for instance, where a trustee has taken inadequate steps to recover sums owing to the trust fund),[131] the trustee can be held liable, by means of account, for the losses which have arisen through this failure to act, or 'wilful default' as it has been described.[132] As with any action for breach of trust, at least one breach must be proved or admitted,[133] but if there is reason to believe that there may have been other instances of default, the court may order a general account, rather than limiting it to the particular instance proved.[134]

(3) **Substantive orders to account**

The order for account could be seen as merely a means of quantifying damages, but there are some instances in which the order to account appears to be used as or to be considered to be a substantive remedy: that is, as an alternative to an order for damages.[135] The order of account both quantifies the measure of profit or loss, and also imposes a liability to pay it.[136] Whether the payment of the sum owing should be described as 'damages' or 'compensation' or 'restitution' is a matter of debate, and for most purposes the description of the obligation is a matter of no significance. What is significant is that the order for account is being used in some situations as a remedy in its own right. It has long been a feature of English law that the availability of a remedy has been a key feature in the development of new rights. As account is used in novel situations, we are therefore observing the development of new rights, some of which in due course will be absorbed either into existing classifications of rights and obligations, or into the developing autonomous doctrine of restitution based on unjust enrichment.

Three principal examples can be given of the use of account in a substantive way. First, an obligation to account will be imposed on a fiduciary who has made a profit from a breach of confidence. Second, a formally appointed or constructive trustee will be obliged to account for any personal advantage gained through a position of trust. Finally, an agent may be obliged to account for an illicit bribe if the bribe is not held on a constructive trust. These cases can all be subsumed under the general rubric of unauthorized profits made by a fiduciary. These heads of liability are considered in detail in Chapter 28.

---

[130] *Re Stevens, Cooke v Stevens* [1898] 1 Ch 162, CA. See Chapter 27.

[131] See *Re Vickery* [1931] 1 Ch 572.   [132] See Stannard 'Wilful Default' [1979] Conv 345.

[133] *Sleight v Lawson* (1857) 3 K & J 292; *Re Youngs* (1885) 30 Ch D 421.

[134] *Re Tebbs* [1976] 2 All ER 858.

[135] For example, in *Mouat v Clark Boyce* [1992] 2 NZLR 559, at 566 Sir Robin Cooke included an account of profits in a list of remedies available to the court alongside other remedies such as damages. See also *Hollister Inc v Medik Ostomy Supplies Ltd* [2012] EWCA Civ 1419 at [55] where an account of profits is described as a remedy which is separate from an award of damages.

[136] For a discussion of the extent to which equity is able to award damages or compensation for the breach of purely equitable rights see Capper 'Damages for Breach of the Equitable Duty of Confidence' (1994) 14 LS 313–334, especially, at pp 313–328.

Whilst an account of profits is the usual remedy available for a breach of duty by a fiduciary who has made a profit, it is a discretionary remedy,[137] and it is for the court to decide upon the most appropriate remedy in any individual case: an award of damages has been held to be a more suitable remedy in the circumstances of one case.[138]

(4) **Settled accounts**

The essence of all the cases in which an account is sought is that the defendant owes a sum of money to the claimant, and the purpose of the taking of an account is to ascertain that sum. It is accordingly a defence to the request for an account either that nothing is due, or that the sum due has already been agreed between the parties. The agreement as to the sum owing does not need to be in any particular form,[139] but if the nature of the settlement of account involves the making of concessions, it will not be binding unless it has effect as a contract supported by consideration. That will usually be the case where there are mutual dealings.[140]

Where the agreement on a settled account has been reached as a result of fraud, then the agreement may be set aside and the accounts reviewed.[141] Similarly, the accounts may be reviewed where there has been a mistake or oversight.[142] In the case of fraud or serious error, the court will normally reopen the account and order that it be taken anew. Where the error or mistake is less substantial, the court may direct that the account stands, subject to 'surcharge and falsification',[143] that is, subject to the addition (surcharge) of items wrongly omitted and to the deletion (falsification) of items wrongly included. A settled account will not exclude the statutory jurisdiction to reopen extortionate credit bargains.[144]

(5) **Delay**

The right to an account lapses after the expiration of the statutory time limit applicable to the cause of action which it supports.[145] In other cases, no express limitation period applies, although it might be expected that the general six-year limitation period would apply by analogy with other claims, subject to the ordinary general exceptions.

---

[137] *Attorney General v Blake* [2001] 1 AC 268.   [138] *Walsh v Shanahan* [2013] EWCA Civ 411.

[139] *Yourell v Hibernian Bank* [1918] AC 372, HL; *Phillips-Higgins v Harper* [1954] 1 All ER 116; affd [1954] 2 All ER 51n, CA.

[140] *Anglo-American Asphalt Co v Crowley Russell & Co* [1945] 2 All ER 324, at 331.

[141] *Vernon v Vawdrey* (1740) 2 Atk 119; *Oldaker v Lavender* (1833) 6 Sim 239; *Millar v Craig* (1843) 6 Beav 433; *Gething v Keighley* (1878) 9 Ch D 547; *Allfrey v Allfrey* (1849) 1 Mac & G 87.

[142] *Pritt v Clay* (1843) 6 Beav 503; *Williamson v Barbour* (1877) 9 Ch D 529.

[143] *Pit v Cholmondeley* (1754) 2 Ves Sen 565.   [144] Consumer Credit Act 1974, ss 137–140.

[145] Limitation Act 1980, s 23.

5

Specific performance

The remedy of specific performance evolved to allow the courts to compel a defendant to perform a contractual obligation. At common law if a contracting party failed to do what was promised, the injured party had a remedy only in damages. But monetary compensation is not always sufficient. Suppose your parents are getting infirm and you plan to build a 'granny annexe' adjoining your house, and to do so you have contracted with your neighbour to be allowed to run utility services across her land. Compensation in damages may fail to put right your neighbour's failure to allow you the access for this purpose if no alternative route is available. The remedy of specific performance could be used to compel your neighbour to grant the necessary easements, just as she promised to do.

1 Introduction to specific performance

The remedy of specific performance is a remedy which applies only where someone has already engaged to do something, but has then failed to do so. The remedy provides an alternative to an award of damages, and may sometimes be awarded alongside damages. For instance, if Meredith has contracted to sell his house to Jamal, but then refuses to complete the sale and move out, Jamal may be able to obtain both an order for specific performance compelling Meredith to sell, and also an award of damages to compensate against the losses caused by the delay. A fundamental principle concerning the equitable remedies of specific performance and injunctions is that they are not available as of right, but are discretionary. Even if a strong prima facie case has been established, the judge may decide not to award a remedy. An equitable remedy of specific performance is a personal remedy against the defendant, as equity acts in personam,[1] and disobedience is classified as a contempt of court which can lead to imprisonment or other action.[2]

---

[1] See *Penn v Lord Baltimore* (1750) 1 Ves Sen 444; *Richard West & Partners (Inverness) Ltd v Dick* [1969] 1 All ER 289.

[2] See, for example, *Mid Suffolk DC v Clarke* [2007] 1 WLR 98, where it was confirmed that the failure of the defendant to comply with an order of specific performance is a contempt of court, not a breach of contract.

2 Specific performance

At common law the only remedy for breach of contract was damages. A defendant who had breached his contract could not be compelled to perform, but was liable to compensate the claimant for any loss he suffered as a consequence of the breach.[3] Depending on the circumstances this would be either his 'expectation loss' (the extent to which he expected to gain from performance) or his 'reliance loss' (the extent to which he had incurred costs in reliance on the contract). The claimant was expected, at common law, to use his compensation to purchase alternative performance. He could buy replacement goods on the open market, or find an alternative supplier of services. As Lord Diplock observed in *Photo Production Ltd v Securicor Transport Ltd*, this means the defendant has the option of either performing the contract, or breaching the contract and paying damages:

> Every failure to perform a primary obligation is a breach of contract. The secondary obligation on the part of the contract-breaker to which it gives rise by implication of the common law is to pay monetary compensation to the other party for the loss sustained by him in consequence of the breach...[4]

In effect, the defendant can buy his way out of performance of the contract. However, the payment of damages might not always be an adequate remedy. This is when equity intervenes.[5] By means of an order of specific performance the court can compel the defendant to perform his contractual obligations. The court is also willing to order specific performance of a contract to confer benefits on third parties,[6] although any action seeking specific performance must be brought by a party to the contract.[7] Like other equitable remedies, specific performance is an order made personally against the defendant.

3 When is specific performance available?

Specific performance is not generally available as a remedy for breach of contract. As Lord Selbourne LC said in *Wilson v Northampton and Banbury Junction Rly Co*:

> The court gives specific performance instead of damages, only when it can by that means do more and complete justice.[8]

---

[3] *Tai Hing Cotton Mills Ltd v Kanmsing Knitting Factory* [1979] AC 91.   [4] [1980] 1 All ER 556.
[5] *Hutton v Watling* [1948] Ch 26; affd [1948] Ch 398.
[6] *Beswick v Beswick* [1968] AC 58; *Gurtner v Circuit* [1968] 2 QB 587.
[7] *AK Investment CJSC v Kyrgyz Mobil Tel Ltd & Ors (Isle of Man)* (Rev 1) [2011] UKPC 7 at [22].
[8] (1874) 9 Ch App 279, at 284.

In *Co-operative Insurance v Argyll Stores*,[9] this perspective was reiterated by the House of Lords. Lord Hoffmann stated:

> Specific performance is traditionally regarded in English law as an exceptional remedy, as opposed to the common law damages to which a successful plaintiff is entitled as of right...by the nineteenth century it was orthodox doctrine that the power to decree specific performance was part of the discretionary jurisdiction of the Court of Chancery to do justice in cases in which the remedies available at common law were inadequate.[10]

There are a number of well-recognized circumstances in which it is known that damages would not provide an adequate remedy so that specific performance is ordinarily available.

(1) Contracts concerning land

Land is always deemed to be unique as it is assumed that there is no identical market alternative.[11] Therefore, as Lord Diplock observed in *Sudbrook Trading Estate Ltd v Eggleton*, damages would:

> constitute a wholly inadequate and unjust remedy for the breach. That is why the normal remedy is by a decree of specific performance...[12]

Specific performance is therefore available in respect of a contract for the sale of land, for the grant of an interest in land, or even for the grant of a licence to occupy land.[13] A contract for the sale of land, or the disposition of an interest in land, must be made in writing in accordance with the provisions of s 2 of the Law of Property (Miscellaneous Provisions) Act 1989. Specific performance will not therefore be available to enforce an oral contract in respect of an interest in land, although such an agreement might give rise to a remedy by way of proprietary estoppel.[14]

(2) Contracts for the sale of unique personal property

Specific performance will not normally be granted to enforce a contract for the sale of personal property because a market substitute can readily be obtained. However, if the item is unique and there is no available alternative the court may grant a decree of specific performance. For example, in *Falcke v Gray*,[15] Kindersley V-C would have granted specific performance of a contract for the sale of two oriental jars which were of 'unusual beauty, rarity and distinction' if he had not found that the consideration

---

[9] [1997] 3 All ER 297.   [10] [1997] 3 All ER 297, at 301.
[11] Equity treated land as unique before the practice developed in Georgian and later periods of building large estates of houses of identical or near-identical design.   [12] [1983] 1 AC 444, at 478.
[13] *Verrall v Great Yarmouth Borough Council* [1981] QB 202. This is so even though a contractual licence does not create an interest in the land capable of binding successors in title of the licensor: *Ashburn Anstalt v Arnold* [1989] Ch 1.
[14] *Yaxley v Gotts* [2000] Ch 162. See Chapter 10.   [15] (1859) 4 Drew 651.

was inadequate.[16] A contract to sell shares may also be specifically enforceable if they are not available in the general market.[17]

(3) **Practical unavailability of market substitutes**

Specific performance has also been granted of contracts for the sale of goods that are not unique and are normally readily available in the market where special circumstances have meant that substitutes are in fact unobtainable. In *Sky Petroleum Ltd v VIP Petroleum Ltd*,[18] the plaintiff sought an injunction to prevent the defendants from breaching their contract as the exclusive supplier of petrol and diesel for the plaintiff's garages. Goulding J granted the injunction,[19] which had the same practical effect as specific performance of the contract, because the market in petroleum had changed considerably since the contract had been entered and the plaintiff had no market alternative:

> the petroleum market is in an unusual state in which a would-be buyer cannot go out into the market and contract with another seller, possibly at some sacrifice as to price. Here, the defendant company appears for practical purposes to be the plaintiff company's sole means of keeping its business going... [20]

(4) **Contracts where the quantification of damages would be difficult**

Specific performance has been ordered of contracts to sell or pay annuities because the value of the rights is uncertain,[21] and of contracts to execute a mortgage for money already lent because the value of having security for the loan cannot be quantified.[22] Specific performance has also been awarded where the loss is difficult to prove,[23] or where the defendant is unlikely to be able to pay damages.[24]

(5) **Claimant entitled only to nominal damages**

Specific performance has been ordered where the claimant would only be entitled to recover nominal damages for his loss. In *Beswick v Beswick*,[25] Mr Beswick had made a

---

[16] See also *Pearne v Lisle* (1749) Amb 75 (slaves could be compelled to return to plantations by their master); *Thorn v Public Works Commissioners* (1863) 32 Beav 490 (removal of unspecified building materials under a tender for the whole); *Behnke v Bede Shipping Co Ltd* [1927] 1 KB 649 (contract for the sale of a steamship, which had unique and special value to the plaintiff); *Phillips v Lamdin* [1949] 2 KB 33. Contrast *Cohen v Roche* [1927] 1 KB 169 (eight 'Heppelwhite' chairs, which were not considered of any special value or interest by the court).

[17] *Duncuft v Albrecht* (1841) 12 Sim 189; *Oughtred v IRC* [1960] AC 206; *Neville v Wilson* [1997] Ch 144.

[18] [1974] 1 All ER 954. Compare also *Howard E Perry & Co Ltd v British Railways Board* [1980] 1 WLR 1375.

[19] An injunction is an order of the court prohibiting the person enjoined from a particular course of conduct. It is considered more fully later in the next chapter.   [20] [1974] 1 All ER 954, at 956.

[21] *Ball v Coggs* (1710) 1 Bro Parl Cas 140, HL; *Kenney v Wexham* (1822) 6 Madd 355; *Adderly v Dixon* (1824) 1 Sim & St 607; *Clifford v Turrell* (1841) 1 Y & C Ch Cas 138; *Beswick v Beswick* [1968] AC 58.

[22] *Ashton v Corrigan* (1871) LR 13 Eq 76; *Swiss Bank Corpn v Lloyds Bank Ltd* [1982] AC 584.

[23] *Decro-Wall International SA v Practitioners in Marketing Ltd* [1971] 1 WLR 361.

[24] *Evans Marshall & Co v Bertola SA* [1973] 1 All ER 992.   [25] [1968] AC 58.

contract with his nephew to pay a pension to his wife. On his death the nephew refused to pay. Although Mrs Beswick could not sue in her own right because she was not privy to the contract, she was entitled to sue in her capacity as Mr Beswick's personal representative. The court ordered the nephew to perform the contract because damages would be an inadequate remedy. Mr Beswick had not personally suffered any loss and would therefore have been entitled only to nominal damages. That would not have compensated his widow, who had suffered a substantial loss.

4 Contracts where specific performance is not available

(1) Types of contract which will not be specifically enforced

There are some types of contract that the courts will not enforce by means of a decree of specific performance.

(a) Contracts of personal service

Equity will not specifically enforce a contract of personal service requiring the defendant to work for the claimant for a variety or reasons,[26] one of them because this would infringe his liberty.[27] As Fry LJ observed in *De Francesco v Barnum*:

> The courts are bound to be jealous, lest they should turn contracts of service into contracts of slavery.[28]

The court will also normally refuse to grant an injunction to give effect to a contractual provision that the defendant is not to work for anyone else, as this would indirectly amount to specific performance of the contract.[29] However, the rule is not absolute. In *CH Giles & Co Ltd v Morris*,[30] Megarry J explained:

> Such a rule is plainly not absolute and without exception... The reasons why the court is reluctant to decree specific performance of a contract for personal services (and I would regard it as a strong reluctance rather than a rule) are, I think, more complex and more firmly bottomed in human nature. If a singer contracts to sing, there could no doubt be proceedings for committal if, ordered to sing, the singer remained obstinately dumb. But if instead the singer sang flat, or sharp, or too fast, or too slowly, or too loudly, or too quietly... the threat of committal would reveal itself as a most unsatisfactory weapon: for who could say whether such imperfections of performance were natural or self-induced.[31]

---

[26] *Societe Generale, London Branch v Geys* [2012] UKSC 63. For an account of the reasons see Lord Sumption (dissenting on the result) at 119.

[27] *Lumley v Wagner* (1852) 1 De GM & G 604; *Johnson v Shrewsbury and Birmingham Rly* (1853) 3 De GM & G 914; *Brett v East India and London Shipping Co Ltd* (1864) 2 Hem & M 404; *Britain v Rossiter* (1879) 11 QBD 123; *Rigby v Connol* (1880) 14 Ch D 482; *De Francesco v Barnum* (1890) 45 Ch D 430. See also Trade Union and Labour Relations Act 1974, s 16.   [28] (1890) 45 Ch D 430.

[29] *Page One Records Ltd v Britton* [1967] 3 All ER 822; *Scandinavian Trading Tanker Co AB v Flota Petrolera Ecuatoriana, The Scaptrade*, [1983] 2 AC 694.

[30] [1972] 1 WLR 307.   [31] [1972] 1 WLR 307, at 318.

He considered that 'not all contracts of personal service ... are as dependent as this on matters of opinion and judgment, nor do all such contracts involve the same degree of the daily impact of person upon person'. Therefore in some circumstances specific performance (or an injunction having similar effect[32]) might be available because 'the matter is one of the balance of advantage and disadvantage in relation to the particular obligations in question'.[33] In *Hill v C A Parsons & Co Ltd*,[34] the court prevented an employer from dismissing an employee shortly before the date at which he was due to retire. His dismissal would have had serious implications for his entitlement to a pension which could not adequately be compensated in damages.

(b) Contracts to carry on a business

In *Co-operative Insurance v Argyll Stores (Holdings) Ltd*,[35] the House of Lords held that specific performance should not be granted of a contract to carry on a business. The defendants operated a Safeway supermarket in a Sheffield shopping centre. In their lease they had covenanted to keep the premises open for 'retail trade'. Following a review of their national operations, the defendants decided to close the store, along with other loss-making supermarkets. The plaintiff landlords sought specific performance of the covenant for the remainder of the lease, which had over nineteen years left to run. The House of Lords held that specific performance should not be ordered, reiterating that there was a 'settled practice'[36] to this effect and also that such an order requiring the defendant to conduct an activity would require constant supervision by the court (see later). Lord Hoffmann also considered that the grant of an order might 'cause injustice by allowing the claimant to enrich himself at the defendant's expense' by requiring the defendant to run a business at a loss far greater than the claimant would suffer by reason of the breach of contract,[37] and that from the wider perspective of public policy it was not in the public interest 'to require someone to carry on business at a loss if there is any plausible alternative by which the other party can be given compensation'.[38]

(c) Contracts for partnership

Such contracts will not be specifically enforced unless the partners have begun to act upon their agreement.[39]

---

[32] See *Araci v Fallon* [2011] EWCA Civ 668 (where a jockey who had expressly contracted not to ride a competitor's horse in the Epsom Derby was prevented from doing so by means of an injunction).

[33] See also *Warner Bros Picture Inc v Nelson* [1937] 1 KB 209, where the film star Bette Davis was compelled to work for Warner Brothers for the remainder of her contractual period with the movie studio; *Powell v London Borough of Brent* [1987] IRLR 446; *Hughes v London Borough of Southwark* [1988] IRLR 55.

[34] [1972] Ch 305.   [35] [1997] 3 All ER 297.

[36] [1997] 3 All ER 297, at 301, citing *Braddon Towers Ltd v International Stores Ltd* [1987] 1 EGLR 209.

[37] [1997] 3 All ER 297, at 304, approving the comments of Millett LJ who dissented in the Court of Appeal [1996] Ch 286, at 303–305.   [38] [1997] 3 All ER 297, at 305.

[39] *England v Curling* (1844) 8 Beav 129; *Sichel v Mosenthal* (1862) 30 Beav 371; *Scott v Rayment* (1868) LR 7 Eq 112.

(d) Contracts to transfer goodwill

The court will not specifically enforce a contract to transfer merely the goodwill of a business,[40] unless annexed to an agreement to sell the premises or other assets of the business.

(e) Contracts to exercise a testamentary power of appointment

The court will not grant specific performance of a contract to exercise a testamentary power in favour of a specific person because this would undermine the intention of the person who had granted the power (the donor) that the donee should be able to exercise it until his death.[41]

(f) Contracts referring to arbitration

The court will not specifically enforce a contract to refer a matter to arbitration,[42] but it may stay proceedings under s 9 of the Arbitration Act 1996. This will indirectly enforce the agreement because the claimant will have no option other than to seek arbitration if he wishes to obtain a remedy. A decision made by an arbitrator can be enforced by means of specific performance.

(2) Other obstacles to ordering specific performance

Most of the instances just considered are contracts of types which the courts will normally decline specifically to enforce. There are some other reasons why specific performance may be refused.

(a) Agreements made without consideration

It is an established principle that equity will not assist a volunteer. A volunteer is someone who has not provided valuable consideration for the benefit they are seeking equity to enforce.[43] As specific performance is an equitable remedy, it may only be obtained by a person who has provided valuable consideration under the contract. Accordingly, specific performance may not be obtained by a volunteer who is a party to a covenant, even though a promise made by deed may be binding and enforceable at common law due to the presence of a deed.[44]

Although the Contracts (Rights of Third Parties Act) 1999 provides that a third party who is entitled to enforce a contract may obtain any remedy 'that would have been available to him in an action for breach of contract if he had been a party to the contract', it seems that a volunteer third party will still be unable to obtain specific performance. Section 1(5) provides that the 'rules relating to ... specific performance ... shall

---

[40] *Baxter v Conolly* (1820) 1 Jac & W 576; *Darbey v Whitaker* (1857) 4 Drew 134: the reason is because of the uncertainty of the subject matter.   [41] *Re Parkin* [1892] 3 Ch 510; *Re Coake* [1922] 1 Ch 292.
[42] *Re Smith and Service and Nelson & Sons* (1890) 25 QBD 545; *Doleman & Sons v Ossett Corpn* [1912] 3 KB 257.   [43] See Chapter 7.
[44] *Futter v Revenue and Customs* [2013] UKSC 26 at [115]. Equity does not consider the presence of the seal on a deed to provide valuable consideration for any of the promises contained therein—see *Jefferys v Jefferys* (1841) Cr & Ph 138; *Cannon v Hartley* [1949] Ch 213.

apply accordingly', thereby incorporating the long established rule that a volunteer may not obtain specific performance.[45]

(b) Contracts for transient interests

Traditionally, equity would not specifically enforce agreements for transient interests, such as tenancies at will or short tenancies.[46] In *Lavery v Pursell*,[47] the court would not grant specific performance of an agreement for a tenancy for one year because it was normally impossible to get the action heard within that period.[48] However, in the modern case of *Verrall v Great Yarmouth Borough Council*,[49] the Court of Appeal upheld an order for the specific performance of a contract to grant a licence for two days. Roskill LJ stated that, in his judgment:

> the old view...that courts of equity would not protect a so-called transient interest can no longer be supported, at any rate to its full extent.[50]

(c) Claimant in breach

If the claimant is in breach of an essential term of the contract (such as by not being ready to pay the full purchase price on completion of a contract for the sale of land after time has been made of the essence), then specific performance will not be available.[51]

(d) Contracts requiring constant supervision

In *Ryan v Mutual Tontine Westminster Chambers Association*,[52] the defendants, who were the lessors of a block of residential flats, covenanted to provide a resident porter who would be in constant attendance. The Court of Appeal held that this covenant could not be specifically enforced because 'the execution of it would require constant superintendence by the court, which the court in such cases has always declined to give'.[53] This rationale was questioned by the House of Lords in *Co-operative Insurance v Argyll Stores (Holdings) Ltd*.[54] Lord Hoffmann said such refusal was not because the court itself would have to supervise the execution of the order, but because the court might have to give an 'indefinite series of rulings' whether the order had been kept or broken.[55] He emphasized that the only means by which the court could enforce the order was through the 'quasi-criminal procedure of punishment for contempt', and

---

[45] See Hanbury & Martin, *Modern Equity* (18th edn, 2009), at pp 734, 762.

[46] *Glasse v Woolgar and Roberts (No 2)* (1897) 41 Sol Jo 573: tenancy for a day.

[47] (1888) 39 Ch D 508.

[48] See *Lever v Koffler* [1901] 1 Ch 543; *Manchester Brewery Co v Coombs* [1901] 2 Ch 608 (agreement for a tenancy from year to year is specifically enforceable).

[49] [1981] QB 202.   [50] [1981] QB 202, at 220.

[51] *Clarke Investments Ltd v Pacific Technologies* [2013] EWCA Civ 750.   [52] [1893] 1 Ch 116.

[53] [1893] 1 Ch 116, at 123, per Lord Esher MR.

[54] [1997] 3 All ER 297; Phang 'Specific Performance—Exploring the Roots of "Settled Practice"' (1998) 61 MLR 421; Jones 'Specific Performance: A Lessee's Covenant to Keep Open a Retail Store' [1997] CLJ 488.

[55] [1997] 3 All ER 297, at 302.

that given the seriousness of a finding of contempt litigation would be likely to be 'heavy and expensive'. Thus, he held that:

> The possibility of repeated applications over a period of time means that, in comparison with a once and for all inquiry as to damages, the enforcement of the remedy is likely to be expensive in terms of costs to the parties and the resources of the judicial system.[56]

The refusal to grant specific performance where constant supervision was required had been followed in many cases.[57] However, in *Tito v Waddell (No 2)*,[58] Megarry V-C considered that the prohibition was not absolute. He suggested that the real issue 'is whether there is a sufficient definition of what has to be done in order to comply with the order of the court'.[59]

In *Co-operative Insurance v Argyll Stores (Holdings) Ltd*,[60] the House of Lords held that Megarry V-C was wrong. Lord Hoffmann explained:

> This is a convenient point at which to distinguish between orders which require a defendant to carry on an activity, such as running a business over a more or less extended period of time, and orders which require him to achieve a result. The possibility of repeated applications for rulings on compliance with the order which arises in the former case does not exist to anything like the same extent in the latter. Even if the achievement of the result is a complicated matter which will take some time, the court, if called upon to rule, only has to examine the finished work and say whether it complies with the order.[61]

This distinction explains why the courts have decreed specific performance of building contracts[62] and repairing covenants,[63] since the performance of such obligations requires a result to be achieved. However, Lord Hoffmann held that even a contract requiring mutual supervision may be enforced by way of specific performance if a defendant had committed a gross breach of personal faith in breaching his obligation.[64] The need for the 'the full-hearted co-operation' of the respondent to achieve performance remains, however, a potent factor against ordering specific performance.[65]

---

[56] [1997] 3 All ER 297, at 303.

[57] *Rayner v Stone* (1762) 2 Eden 128; *Blackett v Bates* (1865) 1 Ch App 117; *Powell Duffryn Steam Coal Co v Taff Vale Rly Co* (1874) 9 Ch App 331; *Phipps v Jackson* (1887) 56 LJ Ch 550; *Dominion Coal Co v Dominion Iron & Steel Co Ltd and National Trust Co Ltd* [1909] AC 293; *Dowty Boulton Paul Ltd v Wolverhampton Corpn* [1971] 1 WLR 204; *Braddon Towers Ltd v International Stores Ltd* [1987] 1 EGLR 209.

[58] [1977] Ch 106.

[59] These principles were applied in *Posner v Scott-Lewis* 1987] Ch 25. See also *Wolverhampton Corpn v Emmons* [1901] 1 KB 515.

[60] [1997] 3 All ER 297.   [61] [1997] 3 All ER 297, at 303.

[62] *Wolverhampton Corpn v Emmons* [1901] 1 KB 515, where Romer LJ awarded specific performance of a building contract on the basis that the building work was clearly defined, damages would have been an inadequate remedy and the defendant had possession of the relevant land.

[63] *Jeune v Queens Cross Properties Ltd* [1974] Ch 97.

[64] [1997] 3 All ER 297, at 307–308. He held that the defendant had not in fact acted in such a way. See also *Greene v West Cheshire Rly Co* (1871) LR 13 Eq 44.

[65] *Kudos Catering (UK) Ltd v Manchester Central Convention Complex Ltd* [2013] EWCA Civ 38 at [18].

(e) Contractual terms are insufficiently precise

It goes without saying that an agreement which is too vague to be contractually enforceable cannot be specifically enforced[66] although, even absent a contractually enforceable obligation, it is possible for specific performance to be used to enforce a constructive trust.[67] Where specific performance is used in support of a binding contract, the terms must be sufficiently precise to enable an order to be drawn clearly defining what the defendant must do to comply.[68] The scope of this limitation was examined by Lord Hoffmann in *Co-operative Insurance v Argyll Stores (Holdings) Ltd*:

> If the terms of the court's order, reflecting the terms of the obligation, cannot be precisely drawn, the possibility of wasteful litigation over compliance is increased. So is the oppression caused by the defendant having to do things under threat of proceedings for contempt. The less precise the order, the fewer the signposts to the forensic minefield which he has to traverse. The fact that the terms of a contractual obligation are sufficiently definite to escape being void for uncertainty, or to found a claim for damages, or to permit compliance to be made a condition of relief against forfeiture, does not necessarily mean that they will be sufficiently precise to be capable of being specifically performed.[69]

The degree of certainty of the obligation in question is only a factor to be taken into account by the court in relation to the exercise of its discretion, and where the claimant's merits are strong the courts have 'shown themselves willing to cope with a certain degree of imprecision in cases of orders requiring a result'.[70]

(e) Indivisible contracts

The court will not specifically enforce only some of the obligations under a contract if they cannot be separated from other obligations in the contract that may not be specifically enforced. In *Ogden v Fossick*,[71] there was an agreement to grant the plaintiffs a lease of a wharf and to appoint the defendant as manager. The court would not specifically enforce the contract for the lease because it could not be separated from the agreement to appoint the defendant manager. The management agreement could not be specifically enforced because this was a contract for personal services. If the obligations under a contract can be separated, the court may enforce the relevant obligations, but not the remaining obligations.[72]

---

[66] *Frost v Wake Smith and Tofields Solicitors* [2013] EWCA Civ 772, at [9] and [17].

[67] *Banner Homes Group plc v Luff Developments Ltd* [2000] Ch 372, at 397 per Chadwick LJ.

[68] *Wolverhampton Corpn v Emmons* [1901] 1 KB 515, at 525, per Romer LJ; *Redland Bricks Ltd v Morris* [1970] AC 652, at 666, per Lord Upjohn; *Durham Tees Valley Airport Ltd v BMIBaby Ltd* [2010] EWCA Civ 485 at [90] per Toulson LJ.   [69] [1997] 3 All ER 297, at 303.

[70] [1997] 3 All ER 297, at 304.   [71] (1862) 4 De GF & J 426.

[72] See *Lewin v Guest* (1826) 1 Russ 325 (contract for the sale of two plots of land); *Wilkinson v Clements* (1872) LR 8 Ch App 96 (contracts to grant leases could be enforced without the plaintiff having to assume other contractual obligations under the original contract); *Odessa Tramways Co v Mendel* (1878) 8 Ch D 235 (allotment of shares could be enforced as it was divisible from other fraudulent elements of the contract).

(f) Illegal, unlawful or immoral contracts

The court will not grant specific performance if the contract is illegal, unlawful or contrary to public policy.[73] Specific performance will not be available where this would contravene a statutory provision.[74] Similarly, specific performance to transfer shares will not be ordered where this is contrary to the articles of association of the company concerned,[75] nor will a contract to assign a lease be enforced if this would be in breach of covenant.[76] In *Wroth v Tyler*,[77] specific performance was refused by Megarry J on the ground that it would offend public policy to compel the defendant husband to take legal proceedings against his own wife for an order terminating her statutory rights of occupation of the matrimonial home. An obligation which is not recognised by law, such as a contract to create a lease for an uncertain term, cannot be enforced by means of specific performance.[78]

5 Mutuality

Despite earlier cases suggesting that the court could not grant specific performance in favour of a claimant unless it could also have granted specific performance in favour of the defendant,[79] the current view is that lack of mutuality is not an absolute bar to specific performance. In *Price v Strange*,[80] Goff LJ stated the 'true principle':

> one judges the defence of want of mutuality on the facts and circumstances as they exist at the hearing, albeit in the light of the whole conduct of the parties in relation to the subject matter, and in the absence of any other disqualifying circumstances the court will grant specific performance if it can be done without injustice or unfairness to the defendant.[81]

The defendant had agreed to grant the plaintiff a new lease of premises he occupied if he carried out some internal and external repairs. At the time of trial, the plaintiff had completed the internal repairs and had only been prevented from completing the external repairs by the defendant, who had done them herself. In these

---

[73] *Ewing v Osbaldiston* (1837) 2 My & Cr 53 (a contract of partnership which concerned the enactment of plays without the proper licence from the King); *Sutton v Sutton* [1984] Ch 184 (an ante-nuptial agreement to settle property on divorce was not enforced as it would be against public policy to do so).

[74] *Hughes v La Baia Ltd (Anguilla)* [2011] UKPC 9. In this case the legislation (regulating land ownership by aliens) did not affect the enforceability of private rights.

[75] *McKillen v Misland (Cyprus) Investments Ltd* [2013] EWCA Civ 781.

[76] See *Clarence House Ltd v National Westminster Bank Plc* [2009] EWCA Civ 1311, at [45].

[77] [1974] Ch 30.

[78] See *Berrisford v Mexfield Housing Co-Operative Ltd* [2010] EWCA Civ 811 (this point was not considered on appeal).

[79] *Flight v Bolland* (1828) 4 Russ 298; *Lumley v Ravenscroft* [1895] 1 QB 683. The relevant date was when the agreement was made: Fry, *Specific Performance* (6th edn, 1921), p 219; See also *Clayton v Ashdown* (1714) 2 Eq Cas Abr 516; *Hoggart v Scott* (1830) 1 Russ & M 293; *Wilkinson v Clements* (1872) 8 Ch App 96.

[80] [1978] Ch 337; (1978) 128 NLJ 569 (Glover). See also *Sutton v Sutton* [1984] Ch 184.

[81] [1978] Ch 337, at 357.

circumstances, the Court of Appeal ordered specific performance, even though at the date of the agreement the defendant could not have compelled the plaintiff to carry out his promises to repair. There was no risk of hardship to the defendant in granting specific performance because the plaintiff's contractual undertakings had been performed.

6 Defences to specific performance

Even though the contract may be one where specific performance would be available, there are a number of defences available to a defendant.

(1) Absence of necessary formalities

Specific performance will not be available to a claimant where a contract was entered without the necessary formalities, for instance where a contract for the grant of an interest in land has not been made in writing as required by s 2 of the Law of Property (Miscellaneous Provisions) Act 1989.[82]

(2) Misrepresentation by the plaintiff

Any misrepresentation by the plaintiff to the defendant, whether innocent or fraudulent, which would entitle the defendant to rescind the contract, will be a defence to an action seeking specific performance.[83]

(3) Mistake

Where the defendant has made a mistake, which does not prevent the formation of a contract, this will generally be no defence to specific performance.[84] However, the court may refuse the order if it would cause the defendant 'a hardship amounting to injustice'.[85] In *Webster v Cecil*,[86] for example, the defendant vendor offered to sell land for £1,250 by mistake instead of £2,250. The plaintiff purchaser must have known that it was a mistake, because earlier the defendant had refused to sell for £2,000. The plaintiff accepted the offer of £1,250 by return of post. The defendant realized his mistake and immediately told the plaintiff. The plaintiff claimed specific performance of the contract, but the court refused specific performance.

---

[82] See, for example, *Keay & Anor v Morris Homes (West Midlands) Ltd* [2012] EWCA Civ 900; *Hardy & Anor v Haselden* [2011] EWCA Civ 1387.   [83] *Walker v Boyle* [1982] 1 WLR 495.
[84] See *Bashir v Ali* [2011] EWCA Civ 707.
[85] *Tamplin v James* (1880) LR 15 Ch D 215, at 221, per James LJ. Compare *Malins v Freeman* (1836) 2 Keen 25.   [86] (1861) 30 Beav 62.

(4) **Hardship**

Specific performance is a discretionary remedy,[87] and the courts may refuse to grant it if it would cause great hardship to the defendant[88] or a third party.[89] In *Patel v Ali*,[90] Mr and Mrs Ali had entered into a contract to sell their house to Mr and Mrs Patel. Mr Ali was then adjudicated bankrupt and spent a year in prison. Mrs Ali was diagnosed as having bone cancer, had a leg amputated just before the birth of her second child, and then subsequently had a third child. In these circumstances, Goulding J refused an order for specific performance on the grounds of the hardship to the plaintiffs. He stressed that:

> The important and true principle . . . is that only in extraordinary and persuasive circumstances can hardship supply an excuse for resisting performance of a contract for the sale of immoveable property . . .[91]

(5) **Misdescription of the property**

If the property has been misdescribed in a contract for sale, the defendant will be entitled to rescind the contract[92] and resist a claim for specific performance if the property he would be forced to buy was different in substance. For example, if the contract was for the grant of a lease, the purchaser would not be compelled to take an underlease.[93] Similarly, if the contract was for the sale of 'registered freehold property', the purchaser would not be compelled to take a merely possessory title.[94] The purchaser may, however, choose to take the interest under the contract subject to an abatement of the purchase price in compensation.[95] If the misdescription is slight, so that the purchaser receives substantially what he is entitled to under the contract, the court will order specific performance, subject to the vendor compensating the purchaser, as for example in *Scott v Hanson*,[96] where there was a contract for the sale of fourteen acres of water meadow, but only twelve could be so described.[97]

---

[87] *Co-operative Insurance v Argyll Stores* [1997] 3 All ER 297, at 299.

[88] *Denne v Light* (1857) 8 De GM & G 774; *Pegler v White* (1864) 33 Beav 403; *Tamplin v James* (1880) 15 Ch D 215; *Warmington v Miller* [1973] QB 877; *Mountford v Scott* [1975] Ch 258; *Francis v Cowcliff Ltd* (1977) 33 P & CR 368; *Shell UK Ltd v Lostock Garage Ltd* [1977] 1 All ER 481; *Cross v Cross* (1983) 12 Fam Law 182.

[89] *Earl of Sefton v Tophams Ltd* [1965] Ch 1140; *Sullivan v Henderson* [1973] 1 WLR 333; *Watts v Spence* [1976] Ch 165; *Cedar Holdings Ltd v Green* [1981] Ch 129.   [90] [1984] Ch 283.

[91] [1984] Ch 283, at 288. See also *Co-operative Insurance v Argyll Stores* [1997] 3 All ER 297, where one of the reasons the House of Lords refused to allow an order for specific performance was that to force the defendants to carry on business at a loss might well have caused greater hardship to them than it did to the plaintiffs, especially as the lease had a number of years left to run and may have led them to trading into insolvency. The court also seemed concerned that the general effect of such orders on the business community as a whole would be of similar detrimental effect.

[92] *Flight v Booth* (1834) 1 Bing NC 370; *Charles Hunt Ltd v Palmer* [1931] 2 Ch 287.

[93] *Madeley v Booth* (1848) 2 De G & Sm 718; *Re Russ and Brown's Contract* [1934] Ch 34.

[94] *Re Brine and Davies' Contract* [1935] Ch 388.

[95] *Mortlock v Buller* (1804) 10 Ves 292, at 315–316, per Lord Eldon LC; *Hill v Buckley* (1811) 17 Ves 394; *Barnes v Wood* (1869) LR 8 Eq 424; *Horrocks v Rigby* (1878) 9 Ch D 180; *Basma v Weekes* [1950] AC 441.

[96] (1829) 1 Russ & M 128.

[97] See also *M'Queen v Farquhar* (1805) 11 Ves 467; *Re Fawcett and Holmes Contract* (1889) 42 Ch D 150.

(6) **Delay**

Equity does not normally regard time as of the essence of a contract[98] and therefore specific performance may be granted after the due date for performance. Although there is no statutory time limit to a claim for specific performance,[99] the claimant must not delay unduly because specific performance will not be ordered if, in view of the delay, it would be unjust to either of the parties.[100] The length of the delay itself is not the decisive factor. Thus, in *Huxham v Llewellyn*[101] a delay of five months prevented specific performance,[102] but in *Williams v Greatrex*[103] specific performance was granted where there had been a delay of ten years because all that was involved was the completion of the formal transfer of land to a purchaser already in possession. A failure to perform a contract by its due date is a breach for which common law damages may be payable whether or not specific performance is available.[104]

7 Damages in lieu of specific performance

(1) **Jurisdiction to award damages**

The Court of Chancery was given the power to award damages in lieu of specific performance by s 2 of the Chancery Amendment Act 1858.[105] This had the procedural advantage that if a plaintiff was not awarded specific performance, he would not have to start a separate action for damages in the common law courts. After the Judicature Acts of 1873 and 1875 there was no need to rely on the earlier provision, except where damages would not have been available at common law. The Chancery Amendment Act 1858 has been repealed, but its provisions are preserved in the Supreme Court Act 1981, s 50.

(2) **Assessment of damages**

It is almost certainly the case that the measure of damages is the same, whether based on common law principles, or awarded in lieu of specific performance.[106] Megarry J in *Wroth v Tyler*,[107] sought, by holding that the measure of damages was different, to avoid the old rule that common law damages have to be assessed at the date of breach, but that old rule has now been discredited.[108] It is not a fixed rule that common law

---

[98] *United Scientific Holdings Ltd v Burnley Borough Council* [1978] AC 904.
[99] The normal six-year limitation period under the Limitation Act 1980 does not apply, even where the specific performance claim includes claims for damages for breach of contract—*P&O Nedlloyd BV v Arab Metals Co (No 2)* [2007] 1 WLR 2288.
[100] *Lazard Bros & Co Ltd v Fairfield Properties Co (Mayfair) Ltd* (1977) 121 Sol Jo 793; [1978] Conv 184.
[101] (1873) 21 WR 570.
[102] See also *Milward v Earl of Thanet* (1801) 5 Ves 720n; *Walker v Jeffreys* (1842) 1 Hare 341; *Mills v Haywood* (1877) 6 Ch D 196; *Cornwall v Henson* [1900] 2 Ch 298.   [103] [1957] 1 WLR 31.
[104] *United Scientific Holdings Ltd v Burnley Borough Council* [1978] AC 904.
[105] Lord Cairns' Act.   [106] *Johnson v Agnew* [1980] AC 367.   [107] [1974] Ch 30.
[108] *Hooper v Oates* [2013] EWCA Civ 91

damages must be assessed as at the date of breach.[109] In *AG v Blake*,[110] Lord Nicholls explained that the jurisdiction under Lord Cairns' Act enables a court to include in the assessment of damages any losses likely to follow from the anticipated future continuance of the wrong, in addition to losses already suffered.

8 Effect of order of specific performance

Once an order for specific performance has been granted, the supervision of the contract's performance is in the hands of the court, and the pursuit of alternative remedies such as rescission or cancellation is only possible with the approval of the court.[111]

---

[109] *Hooper v Oates* [2013] EWCA Civ 91; *Horsler v Zorro* [1975] Ch 302; *Radford v de Froberville* [1978] 1 All ER 33; *Malhotra v Choudhury* [1980] Ch 52; *Johnson v Agnew* [1980] AC 367; *Suleman v Shahsavari* [1989] 2 All ER 460.   [110] [2001] 1 AC 268.
[111] *Quest Advisors Limited Sharriba Ltd v McFeely* [2011] EWCA Civ 1517, at [41]; *Singh v Nazeer* [1979] Ch 474, at 480.

6

Injunctions

Whilst an order for specific performance is used to compel performance of a positive obligation, injunctions normally operate to prevent a person acting in a particular way (although they can also be used to require a person to act positively to put right a wrong). Injunctions can be used for a wide variety of purposes, and their scope has evolved considerably over the years. The late twentieth century saw the development of freezing and search orders. This century has seen the emergence of privacy orders and superinjunctions. More traditionally, injunctions have been used to prevent breaches of contract or breaches of restrictive covenants affecting land or to restrain the continuation of a public or private nuisance.[1] They have also been adopted by statute to restrain anti-social behaviour, [2] harassment,[3] and the activities of violent street gangs.[4]

1 Introduction to injunctions

Injunctions normally order a person[5] to refrain from doing something, such as preventing the sale of a non-alcoholic drink described as 'elderflower champagne'[6] because this would constitute passing off the product as genuine 'champagne'.[7] In some exceptional circumstances, an injunction can have a mandatory effect, operating like specific performance to compel the defendant to do something.

---

[1] *Watson v Croft Promo-Sport Ltd* [2009] EWCA Civ 15.   [2] See Housing Act 1996 s 152.

[3] See Protection from Harassment Act 1997 and Serious Organised Crime and Police Act 2005; *Astellas Pharma Ltd v Stop Huntingdon Animal Cruelty (SHAC)* [2011] EWCA Civ 752.

[4] See the Policing and Crime Act 2009 Part 4 and *Birmingham City Council v James* [2013] EWCA Civ 552.

[5] An injunction may also be granted against an unnamed person (*Bloomsbury Publishing Group plc v News Group Newspapers* [2003] 1 WLR 1633) or against the members of a class or organization (*M Michaels (Furriers) Ltd v Askew* (1983) *The Times*, 25 June).

[6] 'Elderflower champagne' is a traditional home-made country drink for which recipes are readily available on the Internet.

[7] *Taittinger SA v Allbev Ltd* [1994] 4 All ER 75. See also *Diageo North America Inc v Intercontinental Brands (ICB) Ltd* [2010] EWCA Civ 920 (prohibition on use of 'vodcat' to describe distilled alcohol-based drinks which might be confused with vodka).

Failure to comply with an injunction will constitute a contempt of court, which may lead to sanctions including imprisonment,[8] sequestration of property,[9] or a fine.[10] A third party who aids and abets a breach of an interlocutory injunction will also be guilty of contempt,[11] and third parties who nullify the effect of an injunction, for example by publishing information which others have been ordered not to publish, will be in contempt of court by virtue of their knowing interference with the administration of justice.[12] Gray J held in *Jockey Club v. Buffham*[13] that the same principle did not apply where a final injunction was granted, and that these injunctions bound only the parties named. Gray J thought that the contempt with which the court was concerned was an interference with pending proceedings, but it seems illogical to limit the jurisdiction of the court to control interference with its decisions in this way, and the *Jockey Club* decision on this point has been correctly questioned by the Court of Appeal in *Hutcheson v Popdog Ltd*.[14]

The power to grant injunctions, which was originally inherent in the judiciary, is now also conferred by a number of statutory provisions, the most important being s 37 of the Senior Courts Act 1981 which provides that the court can grant an injunction if 'just and convenient'. The discretion given to the judges by this provision must be exercised on settled principles, although the Supreme Court has recognized that some of the principles relating to the award of an injunction instead of damages are in need of review.[15]

2 Types of injunction

(1) Prohibitory and mandatory

A prohibitory injunction orders a person to refrain from, or to discontinue, a wrongful act. A mandatory injunction requires a person to perform some act, and is often given after the wrong has been done and orders its reversal. For example, if a defendant is about to build a structure in circumstances that would be wrongful, a prohibitory injunction would order him not to build. However, if the structure had already been built, a mandatory injunction would order the building to be pulled down.[16] Originally

---

[8] *JSC BTA Bank v Ablyazov* [2012] EWCA Civ 1411 (a case in which the court also made an order requiring the contemnor, who had become a fugitive, to surrender); *C (Children)* [2011] EWCA Civ 1230 (restraining order on mother of children in a foster home); *CJ v Flintshire Borough Council* [2010] EWCA Civ 393 (restraining order on father); *Doey v London Borough of Islington* [2012] EWCA Civ 1825 (breach of anti-social behaviour injunction).

[9] *Tombstone Ltd v Raja* [2008] EWCA Civ 1444; *Re Liddell's Settlement Trusts* [1936] Ch 365; *Phonographic Performance Limited v Amusement Caterers (Peckham) Limited* [1963] Ch 195.

[10] *Masri v Consolidated Contractors International Company SAL* [2011] EWHC 1024, at [349]; *Dublin City Council v McFeely* [2012] IESC 45 (fine of €1,000,000 for contempt lifted on appeal because no breach of the court order had taken place). [11] *Acro (Automation) Ltd v Rex Chainbelt Inc* [1971] 1 WLR 1676.

[12] *AG v Times Newspapers Ltd* [1992] 1 AC 191; *AG v Punch* [2003] 1 AC 1046.

[13] [2003] QB 462, at [23]-[27]. [14] [2011] EWCA Civ 1580.

[15] *Lawrence v Fen Tigers Ltd* [2014] UKSC 13.

[16] For an example, see *Broadland District Council v Brightwell* [2010] EWCA Civ 1516.

all injunctions had to be given in a prohibitory form, but for over a century an injunction which is mandatory in substance will be given in a mandatory form. [17]

(2) Perpetual and interlocutory

A perpetual injunction is granted to defend a claimant's rights after a full hearing. It is a final remedy, even if it does not last for ever as its name might suggest. An interlocutory injunction is granted in order to preserve the status quo pending a full trial and before the parties' rights have finally been established.

(3) Injunctions without notice

In urgent cases a claimant will be able to apply for an injunction without giving notice to the defendant (formerly called an ex parte injunction).[18] Where such an injunction is granted, the defendant will subsequently have the opportunity to have the order set aside or varied.[19]

(4) Quia timet injunction

A quia timet[20] injunction is an injunction to prevent a threatened infringement of the claimant's rights that has not yet taken place.[21]

(5) Superinjunction

A superinjunction is an order preventing the disclosure of information which also prohibits disclosure of the existence of the injunction. Most cases involve the protection of privacy, so superinjunctions are considered in that context later in the chapter, but they may also be used in other situations. In *W (Algeria) v Secretary of State for the Home Department*[22] it was suggested that in exceptional circumstances, which would be very rare indeed, a superinjunction may be justified to prevent disclosure of the identity of a witness who was otherwise likely to face recriminations.

(6) Undertakings to the court

The need for an injunction can sometimes be avoided by the party concerned giving an undertaking to the court that he will, or will not, do something. Such an undertaking is binding in a similar way to a court order, since a failure to comply will constitute a contempt of court.[23]

---

[17] Since *Jackson v Normanby Brick Co* [1899] 1 Ch 438.
[18] The change was introduced by the Civil Procedure Rules (CPR) 1998.
[19] CPR 23.9, 23.10, 25.3.   [20] The name comes from the Latin and means 'he who fears'.
[21] See *Redland Bricks Ltd v Morris* [1970] AC 652.   [22] [2012] UKSC 8.
[23] See *Edgerton v Edgerton* [2012] EWCA Civ 181 where a freezing order was discharged on the giving of an undertaking having similar effect.

3 General principles governing perpetual injunctions

(1) Damages would be an inadequate remedy

An injunction will only be awarded if damages would prove an inadequate remedy.[24] That will frequently be the case where there is a continuing infringement of the claimant's rights. An injunction is not available for a past infringement that will not be repeated. Damages may be inadequate simply because the defendant has no means of paying them.[25]

(2) An infringement of the claimant's rights

In *Paton v British Pregnancy Advisory Service Trustees,* Sir George Baker P stated:

> the first and basic principle is that there must be a legal right enforceable in law or in equity before the applicant can obtain an injunction from the court to restrain an infringement of that right.[26]

In that case, the court refused to grant a husband an injunction to prevent his pregnant wife having a lawful abortion because he had no right that was thereby infringed.[27] In *Day v Brownrigg,*[28] the Court of Appeal refused to grant an injunction restraining the defendant from giving his house the same name as that of the plaintiff, his next door neighbour, because this did not infringe any of the plaintiff's legal or equitable rights.

(3) Clarity of order

Just as with an order for specific performance, the terms of an injunction must be sufficiently clear to allow those affected to know when they have infringed the terms of the order. Clarity can be achieved by reference to objective standards, or to the opinion of an expert.[29]

(4) Grant of an injunction is discretionary

The award of an injunction is at the court's discretion, like any equitable remedy, although prima facie a party who establishes an infringement of his right should be granted an injunction unless there are special circumstances.[30]

---

[24] *London and Blackwall Rly Co v Cross* (1886) 31 Ch D 354.

[25] *Hodgson v Duce* (1856) 28 LTos 155.

[26] [1979] QB 76. See also *North London Rly Co v Great Northern Rly Co* (1883) 11 QBD 30, CA; *Re C* [1991] 2 FLR 168.   [27] See also *C v S* [1988] QB 135.

[28] (1878) 10 Ch D 294.

[29] *Morgan v Hinton Organics (Wessex) Ltd* [2009] EWCA Civ 107 approving *Environment Agency v Biffa Waste Services Ltd* [2006] EWHC 3495 (Admin).

[30] *HTC Corporation v Nokia Corporation* [2013] EWHC 3778 (Pat), at [8]; *Imperial Gas Light and Coke Co v Broadbent* (1859) 7 HL Cas 600; *Fullwood v Fullwood* (1878) LR 9 Ch D 176; *Pride of Derby and*

(a) Prohibitory injunctions

Some prohibitory injunctions are in practice available almost as of right. For example, with reference to an injunction to restrain a breach of a negative contract, Lord Cairns LC said in *Doherty v Allman*:

> it is not a question of the balance of convenience or inconvenience, or of the amount of damage or injury—it is the specific performance, by the Court, of that negative bargain which the parties have made, with their eyes open, between themselves.[31]

The fact that a claimant has only suffered nominal or very small damage from the infringement of his right does not prevent the court awarding an injunction,[32] although it is a factor to be taken into account. In *Society of Architects v Kendrick*,[33] the members of the Society placed the letters MSA after their name. Joyce J refused to grant them an injunction against the defendant, who placed the letters after his name even though he was not a member of the society, because he considered the matter 'too trivial for the granting of an injunction'. In *Behrens v Richards*,[34] Buckley J refused an injunction against the defendants who were trespassing on the plaintiff's land because their use of a path caused no damage. However, a more strict approach to trespass was taken in *Patel v WH Smith (Eziot) Ltd*,[35] where the Court of Appeal held that only in very rare cases would an injunction be refused to restrain a continuing trespass.[36]

(b) Mandatory injunctions

Lord Upjohn stated the principle in *Redland Bricks Ltd v Morris*:

> the grant of a mandatory injunction is…entirely discretionary and unlike a negative injunction can never be 'as of course'. Every case must depend essentially upon its own particular circumstances.[37]

He held that the question of the cost to the defendant to do the works necessary was an element to be taken into account in determining whether an injunction should be granted. For this reason, the House of Lords refused to grant a mandatory injunction requiring the defendants to perform remedial work costing some £35,000 to their land, to provide support for the plaintiff's land which was only worth £1,500. In *Wrotham Park Estate Co Ltd v Parkside Homes Ltd*,[38] Brightman J refused to grant a mandatory injunction requiring the demolition of houses which had been built in contravention

---

Derbyshire Angling Association Ltd v British Celanese Ltd [1953] Ch 149, at 181, per Evershed MR; *Harrow London Borough Council v Donohue* [1995] 1 EGLR 257.

[31] (1878) 3 App Cas 709, at 720.

[32] *Rochdale Canal Co v King* (1851) 2 Sim NS 78; *Wood v Sutcliffe* (1851) 2 Sim NS 163; *Marriott v East Grinstead Gas and Water Co* [1909] 1 Ch 70; *Woollerton & Wilson Ltd v Richard Costain Ltd* [1970] 1 WLR 411.

[33] (1910) 26 TLR 433. See also *Society of Accountants and Auditors v Goodway* [1907] 1 Ch 489.

[34] [1905] 2 Ch 614.

[35] [1987] 2 All ER 569. See also *Trenberth (John) Ltd v National Westminster Bank Ltd* (1980) 39 P & CR 104.

[36] Trespass to land is a tortious wrong—see further Rodgers, *Winfield & Jolowicz on Tort* (17th edn, 2006).

[37] [1970] AC 652, at 665.   [38] [1974] 1 WLR 798.

of a restrictive covenant because he felt that it would be 'an unpardonable waste of
much needed houses'.[39] Obviously, the defendant's conduct is a major factor that will
be taken into consideration in determining whether a mandatory injunction should
be awarded. As Lord Upjohn said in *Redland Bricks Ltd v Morris*:

> where the defendant has acted without regard to his neighbour's rights and has tried to
> steal a march on him or has tried to evade the jurisdiction of the court or…has acted
> wantonly and quite unreasonably in relation to his neighbour he may be ordered to
> repair his wanton and unreasonable acts by doing positive work to restore the status quo
> even if the expense to him is out of all proportion to the advantage thereby accruing to
> the plaintiff.[40]

(5) **Court order unlikely to be ineffective**

Since 'the court should not normally make orders which it does not intend, or will be
unable, to enforce',[41] there may be cases where an injunction should not be granted
because of the likelihood that it will be disregarded and the lack of practicable means
of enforcement (perhaps because the defendant has no means and is unlikely to be
committed to prison for contempt). However, the grant of an injunction may still
be merited if it has some deterrent effect and there is some prospect of enforcement,
for instance through a suspended order of imprisonment.[42] In *Secretary of State for
Environment, Food and Rural Affairs (Respondent) v Meier*[43] the Supreme Court
approved the grant of an injunction to prevent travellers trespassing on Forestry
Commission land even though it was unlikely that the injunction would be enforced
by imprisonment or sequestration of assets. Lord Rodgers adopted the observation
of Lord Bingham of Cornhill in *South Buckinghamshire DC v Porter*,[44] in connexion
with a possible injunction against gypsies living in caravans in breach of planning
controls:

> When granting an injunction the court does not contemplate that it will be dis-
> obeyed…Apprehension that a party may disobey an order should not deter the court
> from making an order otherwise appropriate: there is not one law for the law-abiding and
> another for the lawless and truculent.'

Lord Rodgers added that if 'the considered consensus of those with experience in the
field' was that only the intervention of a bailiff would be effective (the remedy for
enforcing an order to remove a trespasser), then 'consideration may have to be given to
changing the procedures for enforcing injunctions of this kind'. [45]

---

[39] [1974] 1 WLR 798, at 811.

[40] [1970] AC 652, at 666. See *Woodhouse v Newry Navigation Co* [1898] 1 IR 161, CA.

[41] *Secretary of State for Environment, Food, and Rural Affairs v Meier* [2009] UKSC 11, at [80] per Lord
Neuberger.

[42] See *South Bucks District Council v Porter* [2003] UKHL 26, [2003] 2 AC 558, at [32]; *Secretary of State
for Environment, Food, and Rural Affairs v Meier* [2009] UKSC 11, at [16], [39], and [81].

[43] [2009] UKSC 11.   [44] [2003] 2 AC 558, 580 at [32].   [45] [2003] 2 AC 558, 580, at [17].

(6) Delay and acquiescence

The court may refuse an injunction if the claimant has delayed for an inordinate time,[46] although where an injunction is refused for reasons of delay, a claimant may be entitled to damages in lieu.[47] His failure to seek interlocutory relief may also be relevant to a refusal to grant an injunction.[48] Equally, there will be no injunction if the claimant has acquiesced and waived his rights.[49] In *Shaw v Applegate*,[50] Goff LJ expressed the opinion that it was easier to establish acquiescence in the case of an equitable rather than a legal right. In *Fisher v Brooker*[51] one of the composers of Procol Harum's iconic song 'A Whiter Shade of Pale' (which was first released in 1967) sought to enforce his rights in 2005. His rights as a co-composer had never previously been acknowledged, and he had therefore received no royalties. The House of Lords held that he was not debarred by the significant length of time from bringing an action, although the delay would be relevant in deciding whether to grant an injunction against future exploitation of the work. The Lords' view was that in order for delay to justify a denial of equitable relief, some sort of detrimental reliance would usually be needed.[52]

(7) Claimant must come with 'clean hands'

A claimant will only be granted an injunction if he himself comes seeking the aid of equity with 'clean hands'. Breach of his own obligations or unfair conduct[53] will disentitle him to relief, as will his own refusal to carry out his future obligations.[54]

(8) Damages in lieu of an injunction

Under the Chancery Amendment Act 1858 (Lord Cairns' Act) the court has jurisdiction to award damages in substitution for the award of an injunction. The jurisdiction remains, despite the repeal of this Act.[55] In general, the courts will only award damages in substitution in exceptional circumstances.[56]

---

[46] *H P Bulmer Ltd and Showerings Ltd v J Bollinger SA* [1977] 2 CMLR 625, CA (where, technically, the opinions expressed were obiter). Cf *Newport Association Football Club Ltd v Football Association of Wales Ltd* [1995] 2 All ER 87, where, on the facts, there was not felt to be unreasonable delay.

[47] *Shelfer v City of London Electric Lighting Co (No 1)* [1895] 1 Ch 287; *Bracewell v Appleby* [1975] Ch 408; *Ketley v Gooden* [1996] EGCS 47.   [48] See *Shaw v Applegate* [1977] 1 WLR 970, CA.

[49] *Parrott v Palmer* (1834) 3 My & K 632; *Johnson v Wyatt* (1863) 2 De G J & Sm 18; *Blue Town Investments Ltd v Higgs and Hill plc* [1990] 1 WLR 696.   [50] [1977] 1 WLR 970, at 979.

[51] [2009] 1 WLR 1764.   [52] [2009] 1 WLR 1764, at [64] per Lord Neuberger.

[53] *Shell UK Ltd v Lostock Garage Bros Ltd* [1977] 1 All ER 481. The conduct must concern the subject matter of the dispute in relation to which the injunction is sought: *Argyll v Argyll* [1967] Ch 302.

[54] *Measures v Measures* [1910] 2 Ch 248; *Chappell v Times Newspapers Ltd* [1975] 1 WLR 482.

[55] Senior Courts Act (formerly the Supreme Court Act) 1981, s 50; *Leeds Industrial Co-operative Society Ltd v Slack* [1924] AC 851, HL.

[56] *Imperial Gas Light and Coke Co v Broadbent* (1859) 7 HL Cas 600; *Shelfer v City of London Electric Lighting Co (No 1)* [1895] 1 Ch 287, CA; *Leeds Industrial Co-operative Society v Slack* [1924] AC 851, HL; *Achilli v Tovell* [1927] 2 Ch 243; *Sefton v Tophams Ltd* [1965] Ch 1140.

(a) When damages will be awarded

For many years the generally adopted 'good working rule'[57] as to when damages should be awarded in substitution was that set out by AL Smith LJ in *Shelfer v City of London Electric Lighting Co (No 1)*:

(1) If the injury to the plaintiff's legal rights is small; and

(2) is one which is capable of being estimated in money; and

(3) is one which can be adequately compensated by a small money payment; and

(4) the case is one in which it would be oppressive[58] to the defendant to grant an injunction.[59]

It must be stressed that these guidelines were given in the context of the understanding that where the claimant's legal right has been invaded he is prima facie entitled to an injunction.[60] The rule was accepted by the Court of Appeal in *Kennaway v Thompson*,[61] where the court reversed the decision of the judge at first instance to award damages in substitution because the first three criteria of the rule had not been met. Similarly, it was applied by the Court of Appeal in *Jaggard v Sawyer*,[62] (a case involving trespass) although Millett LJ emphasized that it provided 'only a working rule and does not purport to be an exhaustive statement of the circumstances in which damages may be awarded instead of an injunction'.[63] Other factors may be taken into account: for example, delay in bringing an action,[64] or a willingness, expressed in pre-trial correspondence, to accept financial compensation.[65] In *Lawrence v Fen Tigers Ltd*[66] the Supreme Court considered that the guidelines set out in *Shelfer* were too prescriptive.[67] Lord Neuberger thought that while the starting point should be that an injunction should normally be available, 'the court's power to award damages in lieu of an injunction involves a classic exercise of discretion, which should not, as a matter of principle, be fettered'.[68] The *Shelfer* tests should be treated only as guidelines which should not be mechanically applied, and they did not exclude the importance of having regard to any other relevant factors.[69] A particularly important factor was the public interest. The court should have regard to such matters as how many people are adversely affected by the activity complained of, and also to the positive effects of the activity, such as providing employment or leisure activities. Lord Sumption (who was not supported on this point by the

---

[57] See *Watson v Croft Promosport Ltd* [2009] 3 All ER 249; *Regan Paul Properties DPF No 1 Ltd* [2007] Ch 125.

[58] It has been suggested that the test for this is whether the remedy is disproportionate to the wrong: *Navitaire Inc v EasyJet Airline Co Ltd (No. 2)* [2005] EWHC 282 (Ch), [2006] RPC 4.

[59] [1895] 1 Ch 287.

[60] See *Slack v Leeds Industrial Co-operative Society Ltd* [1924] 2 Ch 475, CA.

[61] [1981] QB 88. See also *Wakeham v Wood* (1982) 43 P & CR 40, CA.   [62] [1995] 2 All ER 189.

[63] [1995] 2 All ER 189, at 208.   [64] *Pilford v Greenmanor Ltd* [2012] EWCA Civ 756.

[65] *Gafford v Graham* [1999] 77 P & CR 73.   [66] [2014] UKSC 13.

[67] See [2014] UKSC 13 per Lord Neuberger at [119]-[123]; Lord Sumption at [161]; Lord Mance at [167]; Lord Clarke at [171]; Lord Carnwath at [239].   [68] [2014] UKSC 13 per Lord Neuberger, at [120].

[69] [2014] UKSC 13 per Lord Neuberger, at [123].

majority of the court) would have started from the proposition that damages should normally be treated as an adequate remedy for cases involving a nuisance where the activity had required and had received planning permission. The Supreme Court recognized that the new, less directive, principles would have to be developed on a case-by-case basis in future decisions.

(b) The measure of damages

The quantum of damages that may be awarded in lieu of an injunction has been a matter of some controversy. In *Johnson v Agnew*,[70] the House of Lords held that, where damages would have been available at common law, the court only possessed the jurisdiction to award damages on the same compensatory basis. However, in some cases the courts awarded damages in lieu of an injunction or specific performance even where there had been no obvious loss, suggesting that equity might adopt a measure of damages different from that at common law. In *Wrotham Park Estate Co Ltd v Parkside Homes Ltd*,[71] for example, Brightman J refused an injunction to demolish houses built in breach of covenant but granted the plaintiff damages in substitution. The plaintiff had suffered no loss in terms of a reduction in value of his land, so as the common law rule on damages was understood at the time, damages would have been purely nominal. Nevertheless, substantial damages were awarded, equivalent to the sum of money that might reasonably have been demanded by the plaintiffs for relaxing the restrictive covenant. (These are sometimes described as damages for loss of a bargaining opportunity or as 'negotiating damages'[72] or 'gain-based' damages.[73]) In *Surrey County Council v Bredero Homes Ltd*,[74] Dillon LJ questioned whether this measure of compensation was consistent with *Johnson v Agnew*. Subsequent decisions have resolved the conflict by holding that damages for loss of a bargaining opportunity are compensatory and can be awarded at common law.[75] The significant difference is that in equity, where damages are awarded in lieu of an injunction, they can compensate for future as well as for past losses.[76] Lord Nicholls explained in *A-G v Blake*[77] that although Lord Cairns' Act did not alter the measure to be employed in assessing damages, it did enable the court to award damages in respect of the future as well as the past, so that the damages awarded in lieu of an injunction could include losses likely to follow from the anticipated future continuance of the wrong as well as losses already suffered:

> The Court's refusal to grant an injunction means that in practice the defendant is thereby permitted to perpetuate the wrongful state of affairs he has brought about.[78]

---

[70] [1980] AC 367.   [71] [1974] 1 WLR 798.

[72] *Force India Formula One Team Ltd v 1 Malaysia Racing Team Sdn Bhd* [2012] EWHC 616 (Ch), [2012] RPC 29 at [383]–[386].   [73] *Lawrence v Fen Tigers Ltd* [2014] UKSC 13.

[74] [1993] 3 All ER 705.   [75] See *Jaggard v Sawyer* [1995] 2 All ER 189.

[76] *HTC Corporation v Nokia Corporation* [2013] EWHC 3778 (Pat); *Jaggard v Sawyer* [1995] 2 All ER 189, at 201–202, per Sir Thomas Bingham MR.

[77] [2000] 4 All ER 385.   [78] [2000] 4 All ER 385, at 394.

The House of Lords has therefore approved *Wrotham Park Estates* and doubted *Surrey County Council v Breredo Homes*.[79] The same general approach was approved by the Supreme Court in *Star Energy Weald Basin Ltd v Bocardo SA*,[80] although in that case damages were limited by the Petroleum (Production) Act 1934 to the current market value of the rights lost by the claimants. Some members of the Supreme Court referred to the question of gain-based damages in *Lawrence v Fen Tigers Ltd*, but whilst (with the exception of Lord Carnwath, who outlined a number of problems) inclining to the view that in appropriate cases they should be available, did not consider it necessary to reach any decision.

(9) **Suspension of injunctions**

In some circumstances the court will suspend an injunction so that it does not have immediate effect.[81] This may be because it may not be possible to immediately cease the infringing activity. In *Pride of Derby and Derbyshire Angling Association Ltd v British Celanese Ltd*,[82] for example, the Court of Appeal suspended an injunction made against the defendants who polluted a river with sewerage, giving them time to remedy the nuisance they were causing. In *Waverley Borough Council v Hilden*[83] Scott J suspended an injunction requiring gypsies to remove their caravans from an unauthorized site for three months to give them 'a reasonable time to comply with the order'. However, the courts have disapproved of the suspension granted in *Woollerton and Wilson Ltd v Richard Costain Ltd*,[84] which amounted to a licence for the defendants to continue trespassing in the plaintiff's airspace.[85]

(10) **Declarations**

In *Greenwich Healthcare National Health Service Trust v London and Quadrant*,[86] Lightman J held that the court has power to grant a declaration that a defendant will not be entitled to an injunction if the claimant engages in a particular course of conduct. The claimants wanted to redevelop their hospital, but this involved realigning a private right of way. The owners of the private right of way had been informed of the proposals and had raised no objection; but neither had they given any positive

---

[79] See *Tamares (Vincent Square) Ltd v Fairpoint Properties (Vincent Square Ltd)* [2007] 1 WLR 2148, where similar principles were applied in deciding the measure of damages to be awarded for interference with a right to light to a building.   [80] [2010] UKSC 35.

[81] *A-G v Birmingham Borough Council* (1858) 4 K & J 528; *A-G v Colney Hatch Lunatic Asylum* (1868) 4 Ch App 146; *Jones v Llanrwst UDC* [1911] 1 Ch 393; *Stollmeyer v Petroleum Development Co Ltd* [1918] AC 498n, PC; *Pride of Derby and Derbyshire Angling Association Ltd v British Celanese Ltd* [1953] Ch 149, CA; *Halsey v Esso Petroleum Co Ltd* [1961] 1 WLR 683; *Miller v Jackson* [1977] QB 966, CA; *Waverley Borough Council v Hilden* [1988] 1 WLR 246.

[82] [1953] Ch 149.   [83] [1988] 1 WLR 246.   [84] [1970] 1 WLR 411.

[85] Disapproved in *Charrington v Simons & Co Ltd* [1971] 1 WLR 598, CA; *Trenberth (John) Ltd v National Westminster Bank Ltd* (1980) 39 P & CR 104; *Jaggard v Sawyer* [1995] 2 All ER 189, at 199. Contrast *Kelsen v Imperial Tobacco Co of Great Britain and Ireland Ltd* [1957] 2 QB 334.   [86] [1998] 3 All ER 437.

consent.[87] The claimants were afraid that an injunction might be sought in the future. Lightman J was prepared to make the declaration that no future injunction would be granted, and that the defendants would in the future be limited to redress by means of damages. This was because the realignment was no less commodious than the original route (indeed, it constituted an improvement); the potential dominant owners had been informed and had raised no objection; and the realignment was necessary to achieve an object of substantial public and local importance and value. Lightman J observed:

> The jurisdiction of the court to grant declarations must extend to entitlement both to propri-
> etary rights and to particular remedies. Circumstances may exist when a declaration, e.g. that
> a defendant is not entitled to specific performance, rectification or an injunction, is necessary
> if a period of damaging (or indeed paralyzing) uncertainty is to be voided, and indeed the
> occasion for an unwarranted ransom demand is to be removed. The law is sufficiently adapt-
> able to grant declarations which are necessary to dispel uncertainties and remove obstacles to
> progress and legitimate activities.[88]

4 General principles governing interlocutory injunctions

Unlike permanent injunctions, which are granted to protect a claimant's established rights, an interlocutory injunction is granted to preserve the status quo between the claimant and the defendant before their respective rights can be determined at trial. As Lord Wilberforce said in *Hoffmann-La Roche (F) & Co AG v Secretary of State for Trade and Industry*:

> The object is to prevent a litigant, who must necessarily suffer the law's delay, from losing by
> that delay the fruit of his litigation.[89]

(1) When should an interlocutory injunction be granted?

The principles by which the court should determine whether to grant an interlocutory injunction were outlined by Lord Diplock in the leading case of *American Cyanamid Co v Ethicon Ltd*.[90] Subsequent cases have held that the principles are not 'rules', but rather, guidelines with room for flexibility.[91] It was initially considered that in *American Cyanamid* the House of Lords had rejected earlier authorities holding that a claimant

---

[87] This ownership was by means of an easement, which is an interest in land, enjoyed by one landowner (the dominant owner) over the land of another landowner (the servient owner). See further Stevens and Pearce, *Land Law* (5th edn, 2013), Chapter 15.   [88] [1998] 3 All ER 437, at 444.

[89] [1975] AC 295, at 355.

[90] [1975] AC 396, HL; (1975) 91 LQR 168 (Prescott); (1975) 38 MLR 672 (Gore); (1976) 35 CLJ 82 (Wallington); (1981) 40 CLJ 307 (Gray).

[91] See, for example. *Fellowes & Son v Fisher* [1976] QB 122, CA; *Cayne v Global Natural Resources plc* [1984] 1 All ER 225, CA; *Cambridge Nutrition Ltd v BBC* [1990] 3 All ER 523, CA; *Factortame Ltd v Secretary of State for Transport (No 2)* [1991] 1 All ER 70; *Kirklees MBC v Wickes Building Supplies Ltd* [1993] AC 227.

was required to demonstrate a prima facie case before an interlocutory injunction could be granted[92] in favour of a lower threshold which required the claimant merely to demonstrate that there was a 'serious question to be tried'. However, in *Series 5 Software Ltd v Clarke*,[93] Laddie J questioned this orthodoxy and provided a reinterpretation of *American Cyanamid* requiring the court to take into account the strength of the parties' respective cases on the evidence. He especially pointed to the decision of the House of Lords in *Hoffmann-La Roche (F) & Co AG v Secretary of State for Trade and Industry*,[94] which had been decided a few months before *American Cyanamid*, but which was not cited in the subsequent case. There, Lord Diplock had suggested that the award of an interlocutory injunction was conditional upon the claimant demonstrating a 'strong prima facie case that he will be entitled to a final order'.[95] Having concluded that the prospects of success at trial were relevant, Laddie J indicated the matters that he thought the court should take into account in deciding whether to grant an injunction:

(1) The grant of an interlocutory injunction is a matter of discretion and depends on all the facts of the case.

(2) There are no fixed rules as to when an injunction should or should not be granted. The relief must be kept flexible.

(3) Because of the practice adopted on the hearing of applications for interlocutory relief, the court should rarely attempt to resolve complex issues of disputed fact or law.

(4) Major factors the court can bear in mind are (a) the extent to which damages are likely to be an adequate remedy for each party and the ability of the other party to pay (b) the balance of convenience (c) the maintenance of the status quo, and (d) any clear view the court may reach as to the relative strengths of the parties' cases.[96]

He refused to award an interlocutory injunction despite the fact that the plaintiff's case was 'arguable in the sense that it is possible that the facts at the trial may support the allegation it makes' because he was 'not impressed with its strength'.[97] Laddie J's view has been praised as restoring judicial discretion to an area that was in danger of becoming 'so encrusted with expectations as to how that discretion should be exercised that it too had established a tyranny'.[98] Subsequent decisions have mostly taken *American Cyanamid* as the starting point, but some have recognized that there are circumstances where the strength of the parties' relative cases should also be a factor.[99]

---

[92] *Preston v Luck* (1884) 27 Ch D 497; *Smith v Grigg Ltd* [1924] 1 KB 655, CA; *JT Stratford & Son Ltd v Lindley* [1965] AC 269. Compare also *Fellowes & Son v Fisher* [1976] QB 122; *Hubbard v Pitt* [1976] QB 142.
[93] [1996] 1 All ER 853.   [94] [1975] AC 295.   [95] [1975] AC 295, at 360–361.
[96] [1996] 1 All ER 853, at 865.   [97] [1996] 1 All ER 853, at 867.
[98] Phillips [1997] JBL 486, at 487, reviewing the cases decided since *Series 5 Software*.
[99] The *Series 5 Software* principles were applied in *Quick Draw LLP v Global Live Events LLP* [2012] EWHC 233 (Ch).

(2) **The *American Cyanamid* guidelines**

Applying *American Cyanamid*, the following factors must be taken into account by the court to determine whether an interlocutory injunction should be granted.

(a) 'A serious question to be tried'

Although the claimant does not need to establish a prima facie case, Lord Diplock held that 'the court … must be satisfied that the claim is not frivolous or vexatious; in other words that there is a serious question to be tried'. Only if the plaintiff fails to show any real prospect of succeeding in his claim at trial should the court refuse the injunction without going on to consider the balance of convenience.

(b) The 'balance of convenience'

Once the claimant has shown that there is a serious issue, the court must weigh the balance of convenience between granting and refusing an injunction, and the effect that this would have on the respective parties if the issue was determined in favour of that party at trial. The court must assess the adequacy of damages as a remedy for any loss the parties may suffer in consequence of the grant or refusal of an injunction. Lord Diplock explained the issues to be considered:

> [T]he court should first consider whether, if the plaintiff were to succeed at the trial in establishing his right to a permanent injunction, he would be adequately compensated by an award of damages for the loss he would have sustained as a result of the defendant's continuing to do what was sought to be enjoined between the time of the application and the time of the trial. If damages in the measure recoverable at common law would be adequate remedy and the defendant would be in a financial position to pay them, no interlocutory injunction should normally be granted, however strong the plaintiff's claim appeared to be at that stage. If, on the other hand, damages would not provide an adequate remedy for the plaintiff in the event of his succeeding at the trial, the court should then consider whether, on the contrary hypothesis that the defendant were to succeed at the trial in establishing his right to do that which was sought to be enjoined, he would be adequately compensated under the plaintiff's undertaking as to damages for the loss he would have sustained by being prevented from doing so between the time of the application and the time of the trial. If damages in the measure recoverable under such an undertaking would be an adequate remedy and the plaintiff would be in a financial position to pay them, there would be no reason upon this ground to refuse an interlocutory injunction.[100]

He concluded that where the factors appear to be evenly balanced 'it is a counsel of prudence to take such measures as preserve the status quo'. This exercise of weighing the 'balance of convenience' has also been described as the 'balance of the risk of doing an injustice',[101] or, in other words, finding the balance of convenience requires that the balance of inconvenience between the parties be considered.

---

[100] [1975] AC 396, at 408.
[101] *Cayne v Global Natural Resources plc* [1984] 1 All ER 225, at 237, per May LJ.

(c) 'Other special factors to be taken into consideration'

Lord Diplock also recognized that there 'may be many other special factors to be taken into consideration in the particular circumstances of individual cases'.[102] For example, in *American Cyanamid*[103] itself, where the plaintiffs sought an interlocutory injunction to prevent the defendants launching a surgical product claimed to be in breach of the plaintiffs' patent, a number of additional factors were taken into account, including the fact that the defendants as yet had no business which would be brought to a stop by the injunction; that the launch of the defendants' product would prevent the plaintiffs' patented product becoming established in the market; and that if the defendants' product was allowed on the market before trial and patients and doctors became used to it, it might be impracticable for the plaintiffs to insist on a permanent injunction at trial. For these reasons the House of Lords held that an interlocutory injunction should be granted. The public interest, and the interests of the public in general may also be factors to be taken into account in determining whether an interlocutory injunction should be granted.[104] In *Themehelp Ltd v West*,[105] the Court of Appeal was asked to grant an interlocutory injunction preventing the enforcement of a performance bond pending a fraud trial. The court was prepared to grant the order, but recognized that the situations in which such orders should be granted had to be considered with care lest they disturb the mercantile practice that performance bonds should normally be treated as autonomous guarantees that could be enforced regardless of any problems extraneous to the guarantee itself.

(d) 'Real prospect of trial'

Although an interlocutory injunction is intended to preserve the status quo before the final determination of the issue at trial, it is inevitable that in many cases the matter will go no further. In some cases, this will be because the parties settle on the basis of the injunction granted.[106] In others it is because the injunction would no longer be relevant. The application of the *American Cyanamid* principles assumes the prospect of a full trial in which the 'arguable case' will be tested. One response is to apply the principles only where a future trial is likely to take place.[107] Another is to require a stronger case to be demonstrated where a future trial is unlikely. For example, where an injunction is sought to prevent a strike, the impetus for the strike may have disappeared by the time a trial could take place. This will affect the balance between the

---

[102] *Bryanston Finance Ltd v de Vries (No 2)* [1976] Ch 63; *Dunford and Elliot Ltd v Johnson and Firth Brown Ltd* [1977] 1 Lloyd's Rep 505, CA; *Roussel-Uclaf v G D Searle & Co Ltd* [1977] FSR 125; *A-G v Guardian Newspapers Ltd* [1987] 1 WLR 1248.   [103] [1975] AC 396.

[104] See *Smith v Inner London Education Authority* [1978] 1 All ER 411, CA; *Factortame Ltd v Secretary of State for Transport (No 2)* [1991] 1 All ER 70, at 118–119, per Lord Goff.   [105] [1995] 4 All ER 215.

[106] See *Fellowes & Son v Fisher* [1976] QB 122, at 133, per Lord Denning MR, who suggested that 99 cases out of 100 go no further than the grant of an interlocutory injunction. Reasons include the expense of litigation in both time and money.

[107] *Cayne v Global Natural Resources plc* [1984] 1 All ER 225 at 234. See also *Transfield Shipping Inc v Chiping Xinta Huaya Alumina Co Ltd* [2009] EWHC 3642 (Comm), at [51]–[52].

parties, and 'in disputes of this nature it is incumbent on them [the courts] to have regard to the underlying merits of the claim.[108]

(3) **Other considerations**

(a) **Breach of a negative covenant**

The balance of convenience does not normally need to be considered where an injunction is sought to enforce an express contractual undertaking not to do something.[109] As Jackson LJ said in *Araci v Fallon*:[110]

> Where the defendant is proposing to act in clear breach of a negative covenant, in other words to do something which he has promised not to do, there must be special circumstances (e.g. restraint of trade contrary to public policy) before the court will exercise its discretion to refuse an injunction.

(b) **Freedom of expression**

The principles by which it is determined whether an interlocutory injunction should be granted are different in cases involving a breach of confidence, privacy, or libel because of the effect of the Human Rights Act 1998, which incorporates into English Law art 10 of the European Convention on Human Rights protecting freedom of expression. Section 12(3) of the Human Rights Act provides that the court should not grant relief unless the court 'is satisfied that the applicant is likely to re-establish that the publication should not be allowed'. It follows that in such cases the courts must look at the strength of the claimant's case before granting an interlocutory injunction, and not simply apply the usual 'balance of convenience' test. An interlocutory injunction will therefore only be granted if the claimant can show that he would probably succeed at trail, unless the consequences of publication would be especially serious.[111] Even where the claimant can demonstrate the likelihood of success, the court may refuse an injunction and leave the claimant to a remedy in damages if the 'balance of convenience' favours refusing the award of an injunction.[112]

(c) **Approach on appeal**

An appellate court will be slow to overturn the decision of a trial judge unless there is some error of law, the judge was mistaken about the facts, or there are new circumstances.[113]

---

[108] *National Union of Rail, Maritime & Transport Workers v Serco Ltd (t/a Serco Docklands)* [2011] EWCA Civ 226, at [12].   [109] *Doherty v Allman* (1878) 3 App Cas 709, at 720 (Lord Cairns LC).
[110] [2011] EWCA Civ 668, at [39]. See also *Hampstead and Suburban Properties Limited v Diomedous* [1969] 1 Ch 248 and *Attorney General v Barton* [1990] 3 All ER 257.
[111] *Cream Holdings Ltd v Banerjee* [2004] 3 WLR 918.
[112] *Douglas v Hello! Ltd* [2001] QB 967. See Morgan 'Confidence and Horizontal Effect; "Hello" Trouble' [2003] 62 CLJ 444.
[113] *Hadmor Productions v Hamilton* [1983] 1 AC 191 at 220A (Lord Diplock); *Wright v Pyke* [2012] EWCA Civ 931; *Kinsley v The Commissioner of Police for the Metropolis* [2012] EWCA Civ 515.

(4) **Undertaking in damages**

On the grant of an interlocutory injunction the claimant is generally required to give an undertaking in damages to the defendant. By this undertaking, made to the court,[114] the claimant is liable to pay the defendant damages for any loss he has suffered as a result of the grant of the interlocutory injunction prior to the full hearing if at the subsequent trial it appears that the injunction should not have been granted.[115] There is no need for an undertaking in damages in matrimonial proceedings,[116] or where the Crown seeks an injunction to enforce the general law[117] rather than its own proprietary right.[118]

(5) **Mandatory interlocutory injunctions**

The courts are more reluctant to award mandatory interlocutory injunctions, and it seems that a higher test may have to be satisfied than that set out in *American Cyanamid*,[119] which involved a prohibitory injunction. In *De Falco v Crawley Borough Council*,[120] Lord Denning MR held that a mandatory interlocutory injunction should not be granted unless the plaintiffs made out a 'strong prima facie case',[121] and in *Shepherd Homes Ltd v Sandham*[122] Megarry J held that 'the case has to be unusually strong and clear before a mandatory injunction will be granted'. His suggestion that 'the court must...feel a high degree of assurance that at the trial it will appear that the injunction was rightly granted'[123] was approved and applied by the Court of Appeal in *Locabail International Finance Ltd v Agroexport & Atlanta (UK) Ltd*,[124] which felt that the statements of principle relating to mandatory interlocutory injunctions were not affected by *American Cyanamid*.[125] Where the requirements are met the court will grant such an injunction.[126]

(6) **Interlocutory injunctions in the context of trade disputes**

By s 221(2) of the Trade Union and Labour Relations Act 1992, in determining whether to grant an interlocutory injunction the court must have regard to the likelihood of the defendant establishing at trial that the action was in contemplation of

---

[114] Therefore, any breach is a contempt and not merely a breach of contract: *Hussain v Hussain* [1986] Fam 134, CA; *Mid Suffolk DV v Clarke* [2007] 1 WLR 980. Compare *Balkanbank v Taher* [1994] 4 All ER 239.
[115] See *Chappell v Davidson* (1856) 8 De G M & G 1; *Smith v Day* (1882) 21 Ch D 421; *Digital Equipment Corpn v Darkcrest* [1984] Ch 512.
[116] *Practice Direction (Injunction: Undertaking as to Damages)* [1974] 1 WLR 576.
[117] *Hoffman La Roche (F) & Co AG v Secretary of State for Trade and Industry* [1975] AC 295.
[118] See *A-G v Wright* [1988] 1 WLR 164.   [119] [1975] AC 396, HL.   [120] [1980] QB 460, CA.
[121] [1980] QB 460, CA, at 478.   [122] [1971] Ch 340, at 349.
[123] [1971] Ch 340, at 351.   [124] [1986] 1 WLR 657.
[125] See also *Films Rover International Ltd v Cannon Film Sales Ltd* [1987] 1 WLR 670, where Hoffmann J held that a mandatory interlocutory injunction could be granted where refusal carried a greater risk of injustice than granting it, even though the 'high degree of assurance' test was not met.
[126] *NWL Ltd v Woods* [1979] 1 WLR 1294, HL.

a trade dispute and therefore entitled to statutory immunity. The defendant must be able to show a high degree of probability that the statutory defence will succeed if the consequences of refusing the injunction will be severe damage to the claimant.[127]

(7) **Interlocutory injunctions in the context of libel**

The courts will generally refuse to award an interlocutory injunction in cases of alleged libel if the defendant intends to justify (ie to prove the truth of the defamatory statement).[128] This has not been altered by *American Cyanamid*.[129]

(8) **Impact on third parties**

As indicated earlier, a party who has notice on an interlocutory injunction 'is at risk of being in contempt of court if he does something which effectively flouts or undermines the injunction'.[130]

5 General principles governing quia timet injunctions

Quia timet injunctions are available where, although there has as yet been no infringement of the claimant's rights, such an infringement has been threatened or is apprehended. In *Redland Bricks Ltd v Morris*, Lord Upjohn distinguished two circumstances in which a quia timet injunction would be appropriate:

> first, where the defendant has as yet done no hurt to the plaintiff but is threatening and intending (so the plaintiff alleges) to do works which will render irreparable harm to him or his property if carried to completion...Secondly, the type of case where the plaintiff has been fully compensated both at law and in equity for the damage he has suffered but where he alleges that the earlier actions of the defendant may lead to further causes of action.[131]

In order for the court to grant a quia timet injunction the plaintiff must satisfy a relatively high burden of proof that the threatened or apprehended infringement will occur. As Lord Dunedin said in *A-G for the Dominion of Canada v Ritchie Contracting and*

---

[127] See *Smith v Peters* (1875) LR 20 Eq 511; *Esso Petroleum Co Ltd v Kingswood Motors (Addlestone) Ltd* [1974] QB 142; *Sky Petroleum v VIP Petroleum Ltd* [1974] 1 WLR 576; *Astro Exito Navegacion SA v Southland Enterprise Co Ltd (No 2)* [1982] QB 1248; *Parker v Camden London Borough Council* [1986] Ch 162; *Hemingway Securities Ltd v Dunraven Ltd* [1995] 1 EGLR 61.

[128] *Bonnard v Perryman* [1891] 2 Ch 269, CA.

[129] *Bestobell Paints Ltd v Bigg* (1975) 119 Sol Jo 678; *J Trevor & Sons v P R Solomon* [1978] 2 EGLR 120; *A-G v BBC* [1981] AC 303; *Gulf Oil (GB) Ltd v Page* [1987] Ch 327.

[130] *Hutcheson v Popdog Ltd* [2011] EWCA Civ 1580, at [5].   [131] [1970] AC 652, at 665.

Supply Co Ltd,[132] 'no one can obtain a quia timet order by merely saying "Timeo"'.[133] In *A-G v Manchester Corpn,* Chitty J stated:

> The principle which I think may be properly and safely extracted from the quia timet authorities is, that the plaintiff must show a strong case of probability that the apprehended mischief will, in fact, arise.[134]

In *Redland Bricks Ltd v Morris*,[135] Lord Upjohn said that 'a mandatory injunction can only be granted where the plaintiff shows a very strong probability upon the facts that grave damage will accrue to him in the future'.[136] Russell LJ suggested a different formulation in *Hooper v Rogers*:

> In different cases differing phrases have been used in describing circumstances in which…quia timet injunctions will be granted. In truth it seems to me that the degree of probability of future injury is not an absolute standard: what is to be aimed at is justice between the parties having regard to all the relevant circumstances.[137]

Where the defendant cannot demonstrate a strong probability of the threatened or apprehended infringement, the court will refuse to grant an injunction. In *London Borough of Islington v Elliott*,[138] an injunction was sought to remove ash trees which, if allowed to continue growing, would have undermined the foundations of the claimant's property. The injunction was refused because it would have involved expenditure by the defendant, it would be several years before the damage occurred, and the defendant had agreed to remove the trees before then.[139] In contrast, in *Goodhart v Hyett*,[140] the plaintiff owned, by virtue of an easement, a pipe running across the defendant's land. North J granted a quia timet injunction to prevent the defendant building a house above the pipe, because the plaintiff had shown that this would prevent him repairing the pipe.[141]

6 Rights which will be protected by the grant of an injunction

Having examined the general requirements governing the grant of perpetual, interlocutory, and quia timet injunctions, it is appropriate to consider the most important practical circumstances in which they are available as a remedy.

---

[132] [1919] AC 999, at 1005.

[133] 'Timeo' means 'I am afraid' and comes from the same Latin verb as quia timet.

[134] [1893] 2 Ch 87, at 92; *Caterpillar Logistics Services (UK) Ltd v de Crean* [2012] EWCA Civ 156, at [67].

[135] [1970] AC 652.

[136] See also *A-G v Manchester Corpn* [1893] 2 Ch 87; *A-G v Rathmines and Pembroke Joint Hospital Board* [1904] 1 IR 161. [137] [1974] 3 WLR 329, at 334.

[138] [2012] EWCA Civ 56. See also *Fletcher v Bealey* (1885) 28 Ch D 688, at 698.

[139] See also *A-G v Rathmines and Pembroke Joint Hospital Board* [1904] 1 IR 161; *A-G v Nottingham Corpn,* [1904] 1 Ch 673; *Worsley v Swann* (1882) 51 LJ Ch 576; *A-G v Manchester Corpn* [1893] 2 Ch 87; *Draper v British Optical Association* [1938] 1 All ER 115. [140] (1883) 25 Ch D 182.

[141] See also *Hooper v Rogers* [1973] 1 Ch 43; *Emperor of Austria v Day* (1861) 3 De G F & J 217; *Dicker v Popham, Radford & Co* (1890) 63 LT 379; *Torquay Hotel Co Ltd v Cousins* [1969] 2 Ch 106.

(1) **Trespass**

A landowner will normally[142] be entitled to a prohibitory injunction to prevent trespassers entering his land, and a mandatory injunction ordering trespassers to be removed. These remedies are available even though he has suffered no damage from the trespass.[143] Injunctions have been used to end occupations of public spaces by protest groups, such as the occupation of Parliament Square in 2010 by groups claiming to represent the Four Horsemen of the Apocalypse.[144]

(2) **Nuisance**

An injunction is an important remedy available to the occupier of land where the defendant is causing a private nuisance, or to a private individual who suffers particular damage from a public nuisance.[145]

(3) **Waste**

Waste is a tort committed when by any action or inaction, a tenant under a lease of land or a tenant of land with a life interest permanently alters the physical character of land in his possession.[146] An injunction will be granted to restrain voluntary[147] and equitable waste,[148] but not ameliorative[149] or permissive waste.[150]

(4) **Breach of contract**

An injunction is an appropriate remedy against a party who is in breach of a negative contractual term.[151] In *Nordenfelt v Maxim Nordenfelt Guns and Ammunition Co*

---

[142] *Jaggard v Sawyer* [1995] 2 All ER 189 is an example of an exception.

[143] See *Kelsen v Imperial Tobacco* [1957] 2 QB 334; *Patel v WH Smith (Eziot) Ltd* [1987] 1 WLR 853, CA; *Trenberth (John) Ltd v National Westminster Bank Ltd* (1980) 39 P & CR 104; *Harrow London Borough Council v Donohue* [1995] 1 EGLR 257.

[144] *Hall v Mayor of London (On Behalf of the Greater London Authority)* [2010] EWHC 1613; [2010] EWCA Civ 817. Injunctions have also been used to evict trespassers from St Paul's Cathedral churchyard in 2011–2012 by the 'Occupy Movement'. *The Mayor Commonalty and Citizens of London v Samede (St Paul's Churchyard Camp Representative)* [2012] EWCA Civ 160.

[145] *Lyon v Fishmongers' Co* (1875–76) 1 App Cas 662, HL; *Vanderpant v Mayfair Hotel Co Ltd* [1930] 1 Ch 138.   [146] See Gray and Gray, *Elements of Land Law* (5th edn, 2009), p 62.

[147] Any acts which positively diminish the value of the land, for example quarrying or cutting timber.

[148] Equitable waste is malicious or wanton destruction of the land or buildings exceeding the licence conferred by a clause exempting the tenant from liability for voluntary waste: *Vane v Lord Barnard* (1716) 2 Vern 738; *Weld-Blundell v Wolseley* [1903] 2 Ch 664.

[149] Where the land is improved: *Doherty v Allman* (1878) 3 App Cas 709.

[150] Defaults of maintenance and repair: *Powys v Blagrave* (1854) 4 De GM & G 448; *Re Cartwright* (1889) 41 Ch D 532.

[151] The term need not be expressed in a negative way as the court will look to the substance and not the form: *Wolverhampton and Walsall Rly Co Ltd v London and North Western Rly Ltd* (1873) LR 16 Eq 433. In exceptional circumstances breach of a negative term of a contract may give rise to the restitutionary remedy of an account of profits: *A-G v Blake* [2001] 1 AC 268; *Experience Hendrix LLC v PPX Enterprises Inc* [2003] 1 All ER (Comm) 830.

Ltd,[152] for example, the House of Lords granted an injunction to enforce a contractual stipulation that the defendant would not engage in the business of manufacturing guns or ammunition for 25 years after he had sold his patents and business to the plaintiffs.[153]

(5) **Arbitration**

An arbitration clause can be enforced by an order prohibiting, staying, or requiring the discontinuance of court proceedings in the UK or overseas.[154] Particular caution has to be exercised where proceedings in an overseas court are involved.[155]

(6) **Employment relationships**

The courts are reluctant to grant mandatory injunctions in the context of industrial disputes, as Geoffrey Lane J said in *Harold Stephen & Co Ltd v Post Office*:

> It can only be in very rare circumstances and in the most extreme circumstances that this court should interfere by way of mandatory injunction in the delicate mechanism of industrial disputes and industrial negotiations.[156]

The court will not normally grant an injunction to enforce a contractual term in a contract for personal services that would indirectly amount to specific performance of the contract because the employee will have no option but to perform the contract or remain idle.[157] There are, however, some circumstances where injunctions will be used in support of an individual employment contract, for instance to prevent a dismissal taking place until a required disciplinary procedure has been followed.[158] The court will also grant injunctions to enforce the terms of partnership agreements.[159]

The reluctance to award an injunction restricting a person's ability to work was a factor in holding that a 'barring-out' order was inappropriate in *Caterpillar Logistics v Huesca de Crean*.[160] The defendant had worked as a manager for a logistics

---

[152] [1894] AC 535.

[153] A worldwide prohibition would normally be invalid as being in restraint of trade, but it was upheld in this case because of the international scale and nature of the businesses concerned.

[154] *Ust-Kamenogorsk Hydropower Plant JSC v AES Ust-Kamenogorsk Hydropower Plant LLP* [2013] UKSC 35.   [155] *Ingosstrak-Investments v BNP Paribas SA* [2012] EWCA Civ 644.

[156] [1977] 1 WLR 1172, at 1180. See *Parker v Camden London Borough Council* [1986] Ch 162, CA, where the court was willing to grant a mandatory injunction for the defendants to turn on boilers where tenants had no heat or hot water, because of a boilermen's strike. There is thus a strong element of public policy to this decision.

[157] See *Lumley v Wagner* (1852) 1 De GM & G 604; *Rely-a-Bell Burglar and Fire Alarm Co v Eisler* [1926] Ch 609; *Warner Bros Pictures Inc v Nelson* [1937] 1 KB 209; *Page One Records Ltd v Britton* [1967] 3 All ER 822; *Evening Standard Co Ltd v Henderson* [1987] IRLR 64. See also Trade Union and Labour Relations (Consolidation) Act 1992, s 236.

[158] See *Societe Generale, London Branch v Geys* [2012] UKSC 63, at [73]–[74]; *Edwards v Chesterfield Royal Hospital NHS Foundation Trust* [2011] UKSC 58, [2012] 2 AC 22.

[159] *Hall v Hall* (1850) 12 Beav 414.   [160] [2012] 3 All ER 129.

company, but resigned to commence work for a client. Although there was no evidence that she was using confidential information she had acquired in her previous employment, her previous employers sought a barring-out order. This is an order normally used to prevent a professional adviser acting in litigation for a client with an adverse interest. The Court of Appeal unanimously held that such an order was not appropriate in the ordinary case of employer and employee since the restriction had not expressly been bargained for,[161] and the relationship was not generally a fiduciary one, although employees did owe certain fiduciary duties to their employer.[162]

(7) **Restrictive covenants**

The court may grant an injunction to enforce a restrictive covenant over land. In *Wakeham v Wood*,[163] for example, a mandatory injunction was granted requiring the defendant to demolish a building that obstructed the view of the sea from the plaintiff's house, contrary to a restrictive covenant.

(8) **Breach of trust**

The court will grant an injunction to restrain trustees from committing a breach of trust.[164]

(9) **Intellectual property rights**

An injunction can be granted to prevent a defendant using a description for a product which means that it is likely to be confused with another product,[165] from passing off a product so that it appears to have been produced by the plaintiff,[166] or from using his trade mark, or infringing his patent, his registered design or copyright.[167] This can also apply to foreign intellectual property rights.[168]

(10) **Expulsion from clubs and societies**

The court may grant an injunction to restrain the wrongful expulsion of a member from a club or professional association, for example where the rules of natural justice

---

[161] At [61] and [64].   [162] At [58].   [163] (1982) 43 P & CR 40, CA.

[164] *Fox v Fox* (1870) LR 11 Eq 142; *Dance v Goldingham* (1872–73) 8 Ch App 902; *Waller v Waller* [1967] 1 All ER 305.

[165] *Diageo North America Inc v Intercontinental Brands (ICB) Ltd* [2010] EWCA Civ 920; *Taittinger SA v Allbev Ltd* [1994] 4 All ER 75, CA.

[166] *GG Spalding & Bros v AW Gamage Ltd* (1915) 32 RPC 273, HL; *Erven Warnick BV v J Townend & Sons (Hull) Ltd* [1979] AC 731.

[167] See Trade Marks Act 1938; Patents Act 1949; Registered Designs Act 1949; Patents Act 1977; Copyright, Design and Patents Act 1988. *Prince Jefri Bolkiah v KPMG* [1999] 2 AC 222.

[168] *Lucasfilm Ltd v Ainsworth* [2011] UKSC 39 (27 July 2011), at [110].

have been breached.[169] The court will clearly act if the member has a proprietary interest in the club,[170] but even where there is no proprietary interest[171] an injunction is available to protect his right to work[172] or if a matter of public importance is involved.[173] One particular area where injunctions have been granted is to prevent wrongful expulsion from trade unions.[174]

(11) **Judicial review**

An injunction is one remedy[175] available where the decision of a public body is subject to 'judicial review', for instance because it has acted outside the scope of its powers. The House of Lords held in *O'Reilly v Mackman*[176] that an application for judicial review claiming a public body has infringed public rights must be brought under RSC Ord 53. However, where a private law right is infringed an injunction may be sought in the ordinary way.[177]

(12) **Family matters**

The court has statutory jurisdiction under the Family Law Act 1996[178] to grant injunctions excluding a spouse or partner from the matrimonial home, and to restrain one spouse molesting the other. Injunctions may also be used to protect minors. An injunction cannot, however, be obtained by a husband or partner to prevent a woman having an abortion.[179] A detailed consideration of these issues is outside the scope of this text.

(13) **Harrassment**

An injunction can be used to prevent harassment.[180]

---

[169] *Labouchere v Earl of Wharncliffe* (1879–80) 13 Ch D 346.

[170] *Rigby v Connol* (1880) 14 Ch D 482.

[171] See *Baird v Wells* (1890) 44 Ch D 661, CA; *Rowe v Hewitt* (1906) 12 OLR 13; *Lee v Showmen's Guild of Great Britain* [1952] 2 QB 329; *Gaiman v National Association for Mental Health* [1971] Ch 317.

[172] *Edwards v Society of Graphical and Allied Trades* [1971] Ch 354.

[173] *Woodford v Smith* [1970] 1 WLR 806.

[174] *Osborne v Amalgamated Society of Railway Servants* [1911] 1 Ch 540; *Edwards v Society of Graphical and Allied Trades* [1971] Ch 354; *Breen v Amalgamated Engineering Union* [1971] 2 QB 175; *Shotton v Hammond* (1976) 120 Sol Jo 780.   [175] Others are a declaration or prerogative order.

[176] [1983] 2 AC 237.

[177] *R v BBC, ex p Lavelle* [1983] 1 WLR 23; *Law v National Greyhound Racing Club Ltd* [1983] 1 WLR 1302; *R v East Berkshire Health Authority, ex p Walsh* [1985] QB 152; *R v Derbyshire County Council, ex p Noble* [1990] ICR 808.

[178] Extending and replacing earlier legislation, including the Matrimonial Causes Act 1973 and Matrimonial and Family Proceedings Act 1984.

[179] *Paton v Trustees of British Pregnancy Advisory Service* [1979] QB 76; *C v S* [1988] QB 135.

[180] *Hayes v Willoughby* [2013] UKSC 17.

(14) **Planning permission.**

Under s 187(B) of the Town and Country Planning Act 1990 an injunction can be used to support the planning laws, for example where land is used in contravention of planning permission.[181]

7 Injunctions to protect confidential information, privacy, and reputation

(1) Superinjunctions, anonymized injunctions, and privacy orders

Three types of injunction which have achieved prominence (indeed, notoriety) in the first part of the twenty-first century are the privacy order, the anonymized injunction, and the superinjunction. These forms of injunction are granted mainly to protect the privacy of individuals, although they have been used to prevent the disclosure of sensitive commercial information.[182] A privacy order prevents the disclosure of private or personal information, often preventing the naming of the individual obtaining the order (an anonymized injunction). In some cases, even the disclosure of the existence of the injunction is prohibited (a superinjunction). Some of the most infamous anonymized injunctions have involved prominent footballers such as Ryan Giggs[183] and John Terry,[184] but the disgraced former head of the Royal Bank of Scotland, Sir Fred Goodwin (later stripped of his knighthood) also successfully obtained an anonymized injunction preventing disclosure of an alleged extra-marital affair which took place during the period leading to the collapse of the bank.[185]

Disclosure of the existence of this injunction in Parliament almost led to a constitutional crisis involving a conflict between Parliament and the courts.[186] Less controversial instances where anonymity orders may be made involve 'clinical negligence, or other causes of action related to medical and other highly personal information'.[187]

---

[181] *South Bucks District Council v Porter* [2003] UKHL 26 [2003] 2 AC 558; *South Somerset District Council v Hughes* [2009] EWCA Civ 1245; *Davenport v The City of Westminster* [2011] EWCA Civ 458.

[182] The first known superinjunction, the *Trafigura* injunction, was not concerned with privacy, but prohibited disclosure of a legally privileged internal company report concerning alleged dumping of toxic waste. The case is discussed in the *Report of the Committee on Super-Injunctions: Super-Injunctions, Anonymised Injunctions and Open Justice,* May 2011 (the 'Neuberger Report') paras 6.1 to 6.4. There is no publicly available judgment.   [183] *CTB v News Group Newspapers Ltd* [2011] EWHC 1232.

[184] *TSE v News Group Newspapers Ltd* [2011] EWHC 1308.

[185] *Goodwin v News Group Newspapers Ltd* [2011] EWHC 1341.

[186] For an account of the use of these injunctions and the conflict between Parliament and the courts, see Pearce 'Privacy, Superinjunctions and Anonymity: "Selling My Story Will Sort My Life Out"' [2011] Denning LJ 92–130.

[187] *CVB v MGN Ltd* [2012] EWHC 1148 (QB) at [25] (Tugendhat J), giving citations of examples.

(2) Protection of confidential information

(a) Legal protection for confidential information.

It has long been recognized that injunctions can be granted to prevent the disclosure of confidential information even if the information is not protected by patent or copyright laws.[188] For example, in *Prince Albert v Strange*[189] the Prince obtained an injunction to prevent the publication of etchings that had been obtained in breach of confidence. In *Tchenguiz v Imerman*[190] the Court of Appeal held that a litigant whose confidential documents had been obtained for the purpose of litigation was entitled to an injunction requiring their return. The right to confidence can extend to preventing the publication of photographs[191] or of tape recordings of private conversations.[192]

(b) What is confidential?

In *Campbell v MGN Ltd*, the House of Lords held that a duty of confidence arises 'whenever a person receives information he knows or ought to know is fairly and reasonably to be regarded as confidential'.[193] The confidence may relate to a person's private life, or to business activities. In *Duchess of Argyll v Duke of Argyll*,[194] an injunction was granted to prevent the plaintiff publishing details of her marriage to the defendant. In the *Spycatcher* case, an interlocutory injunction was granted to prevent the publication of a book on the basis of the public interest of maintaining confidentiality in the work of the secret service.[195] In *Peter Pan Manufacturing Corpn v Corsets Silhouette Ltd*[196] the plaintiffs were granted an injunction to prevent the defendants manufacturing a brassiere to a design which they had been shown in confidence. The *Campbell* test for confidentiality does not require proof of a fiduciary relationship to justify the availability of a remedy,[197] although the disclosure of information in confidence may result in the recipient of that information becoming a fiduciary.

(c) Publication destroys confidentiality

Things can only be confidential if they are not already in the public domain. In *Mosley v News Group Newspapers Ltd*[198] Max Mosley, the son of Sir Oswald Mosley, and President of the FIA (which controls Formula 1 Grand Prix motor racing), had sought to prevent the *News of the World* showing video footage of him at a private party involving prostitutes and sado-masochistic activities. Although Eady J considered the publication to be in breach of confidence, the footage had been so widely accessible

---

[188] See *Lord Ashburton v Pape* [1913] 2 Ch 469, CA; *Foster v Mountford* [1978] FSR 582; *Woodward v Hutchins* [1977] 1 WLR 760, CA; *Lion Laboratories v Evans* [1985] QB 526, CA; *X (HA) v Y* [1988] 2 All ER 648; *W v Egdell* [1990] Ch 359.   [189] (1849) 1 Mac & G 25.

[190] [2010] EWCA Civ 908 [2011] Fam 116

[191] *Douglas v Hello* [2003] 3 All ER 996; *D v L* [2003] EWCA Civ 1169.

[192] *D v L* [2003] EWCA Civ 1169.   [193] [2004] 2 All ER 995, at [14], per Lord Nicholls.

[194] [1967] Ch 302.

[195] *A-G v Guardian Newspapers Ltd* [1987] 1 WLR 1248; *A-G v Guardian Newspapers Ltd (No 2)* [1990] 1 AC 109.   [196] [1964] 1 WLR 96.

[197] See *Douglas v Hello! Ltd (No.3)* [2008] AC 1.   [198] [2008] EWHC 687.

that it had entered the public domain, and granting an injunction 'would merely be a futile gesture'.[199] A different view would now be taken about the protection of privacy, since each repeated publication is seen as a new invasion of privacy.

(d) Balancing the right to confidence against other factors

The right to protection against breach of confidence may be balanced by other factors. For instance, where a breach of confidence is alleged against an employee or former employee, the court, when considering whether to grant an injunction will take into account the importance of the protection of freedom of employment.[200] By way of comparison, in *Douglas v Hello! Ltd (No.3)* the House of Lords held that there was no public policy reason not to protect an agreement giving a magazine exclusive photographic rights to a celebrity wedding ceremony (Michael Douglas and Catherine Zeta-Jones) by means of an injunction preventing publication of covertly taken photographs obtained by a rival.[201]

(3) Protection of privacy

(a) Development of a law of privacy

The incorporation of the European Convention on Human Rights into English law by the Human Rights Act 1998 has led to the very rapid development of a law protecting privacy, extending beyond the protection of confidence. [202] The development of the law in this area has been strongly influenced by the jurisprudence of the European Court of Human Rights (ECHR) expanding upon art 8 of the European Convention, although in some respects the newly created protection of privacy in English law goes further than the case law of the ECHR requires.[203]

(b) Protection through damages and injunctions

The English courts have held that the right to privacy can be protected not merely by an action for damages (the remedy on which Max Mosley was obliged to rely when he brought an action in respect of the publication of allegations that he had been involved in orgies with a Nazi theme, since he became aware of the breach of his right to privacy only after publication) but also by means of injunctions. If necessary, court proceedings will be held in private, although this will be exceptional. [204]

---

[199] [2008] EWHC 687, at [36].

[200] *Generics (UK) Ltd v Yeda Research & Development Co Ltd* [2012] EWCA Civ 726. See also *Caterpillar Logistics Services (UK) Ltd v de Crean* [2012] EWCA Civ 156 and *Standard Life Health Care Ltd v Gorman* [2009] EWCA Civ 1292 (employee working for commission).

[201] *Douglas v Hello! Ltd (No.3)* [2008] AC 1.

[202] See Phillipson 'Transforming Breach of Confidence? Towards a Common Law Right of Privacy under the Human Rights Act' (2003) 66 MLR 726; Caddick 'Show Me the Money!' (2007) 157 NLJ 805.

[203] See Pearce 'Privacy, Superinjunctions and Anonymity: "Selling My Story Will Sort My Life Out"' [2011] Denning LJ 92–130.

[204] *Giggs v News Group Newspapers Ltd* [2012] EWHC 431 at [107]; *CVB v MGN Ltd* [2012] EWHC 1148 (QB), at [22].

(c) What is private?

In principle, there is a right to prevent the disclosure of personal information or photographs where there is a reasonable expectation of privacy,[205] although this prima facie right to protection can give way where it is justified by competing considerations, and in particular the right to freedom of expression. The limits to the protection of privacy have not yet clearly been defined, but despite some inconsistency in the case law, it can be asserted with some degree of confidence that there is normally a right to prevent disclosure of intimate details about an individual's sexual activity.[206] Conversely, as the Master of the Rolls, speaking for the Court of Appeal, said in *Ambrosiadou v Coward*: [207]

> Just because information relates to a person's family and private life, it will not automatically be protected by the courts: for instance, the information may be of slight significance, generally expressed, or anodyne in nature. While respect for family and private life is of fundamental importance, it seems to me that the courts should, in the absence of special facts, generally expect people to adopt a reasonably robust and realistic approach to living in the 21st century.

A person is entitled to protection of their private life even when they are in a public place, particularly where the person concerned is a child.[208] However, a person who chooses to conduct a quarrel in public takes the risk that this will blur what would otherwise be the boundary between what is private and what is public. Partly for this reason, the Court of Appeal declined to grant an injunction preventing the disclosure that Christopher Hutcheson, the father-in-law of Gordon Ramsay, had a secret second family. Mr Hutcheson had chosen to contest publicly his dismissal for reasons of misconduct from the Gordon Ramsay Group.[209] It was also relevant that none of the other family members had expressly sought to keep the information private.

(4) **The right to publish**

Despite information having a private character, publication can still be justified where it is in the public interest. The right to privacy, protected by art 8 of the European Convention, needs to be balanced against the right to freedom of expression protected by art 10 of the Convention. The courts have held that neither provision outweighs the other, so that it is a question of balancing the competing rights. What interests the public is not necessarily in the public interest, but it may be in the public interest to expose hypocrisy by public figures, abuses of positions of authority, or conduct which may jeopardize national security or public safety. It was, for instance, considered justified to publish photographs of the model Naomi Campbell attending a drug

---

[205] *Campbell v Mirror Group Newspapers Ltd* [2004] 2 AC 457, at [21] per Lord Nicholls of Birkenhead, and *Murray v Big Pictures (UK) Ltd* [2008] EWCA Civ 446, at [24].

[206] *Mosley v News Group Newspapers Ltd* [2008] EWHC 1777.   [207] [2011] EWCA Civ 409.

[208] *Murray v Big Pictures (UK) Ltd* [2008] EWCA Civ 446.

[209] *Hutcheson (Formerly Known As "KGM") v News Group Newspapers Ltd* [2011] EWCA Civ 808.

rehabilitation clinic because this exposed as false her claims to have no drugs problem.[210] Conversely, it is not sufficient that a person about whom the press wish to publish an allegation of an extramarital affair is a well-known figure if there are no special factors taking the affair into the public domain.[211] The fact that premier league footballers serve as role models for the young has not, in itself, been considered to be such as to deprive them of the right to privacy, but the fact that Lord Browne of Madingley (at the time the Chief Executive of BP) was allegedly abusing his corporate position to provide favours for his male partner was held to be sufficient justification for publication.[212] The public interest would probably justify press reporting of a politician's sexual activity where it had the potential to jeopardize national security[213] and in one anonymously reported case was held to justify withholding an injunction to prevent publication of an allegation that a prominent politician had fathered a child as a result of an extra-marital affair because this might reflect upon the natural father's fitness for high public office.[214] However, even this would be unlikely to justify the publication of salacious details of the kinds of sexual activity involved, or the publication of intimate photographs, particularly if these were taken surreptitiously.[215]

(5) The principles applying to the grant of privacy orders

The grant of privacy orders, anonymised injunctions and superinjunctions is governed by the usual rules relating to interlocutory injunctions or perpetual injunctions, although there are some special features. It has been emphasized that where these injunctions are granted *ex parte*, as is often the case in order to prevent imminent publication, they should be limited in time until a full hearing can take place at the earliest opportunity. Since they often conflict with the principle of open justice and the European Convention right to freedom of expression, they should also be limited to the minimum necessary to protect the individuals concerned.[216] The Human Rights Act 1998, s 12(3) seems to indicate that a more stringent test is required for the grant of an interlocutory injunction inhibiting freedom of expression than for other injunctions, but in practice the provision has had limited impact in relation to privacy orders.[217]

---

[210] *Campbell v Mirror Group Newspapers Ltd* [2004] 2 AC 457.

[211] *ETK v News Group Newspapers Ltd.* [2011] EWCA Civ 439.

[212] *Browne v Associated Newspapers Ltd* [2007] EWCA Civ 295; [2008] 1 QB 103.

[213] The Profumo scandal (where the Minister for War shared a mistress with a Russian diplomat during the Cold War) might be an example: see *CC v AB* [2006] EWHC 3083, at [37].

[214] *AAA v Associated Newspapers Ltd* [2013] EWCA Civ 554. The case followed speculation in the *Daily Mail* and other publications that the father of the child was Boris Johnson, Mayor of London. The application for an injunction was made on behalf of the child, not the father, and damages were awarded by the judge at first instance for the breach of publicity involved through publishing photographs (*AAA v Associated Newspapers Ltd* [2012] EWHC 2103).

[215] *Campbell v Mirror Group Newspapers Ltd* [2004] 2 AC 457; *Theakston v Mirror Group Newspapers Ltd* [2002] EWHC 137; *Amanda Holden v Express Newspapers Ltd* (7 June 2001).

[216] *JIH v News Group Newspapers Ltd* [2011] EWCA Civ 42, at [29].

[217] See Pearce 'Privacy, Superinjunctions and Anonymity: "Selling My Story Will Sort My Life Out"' [2011] Denning LJ 92–130.

(6) **An inroad into the principle of open justice**

Whilst most commentators would agree that there are circumstances in which the protection of privacy is justified, it is generally seen as an intrusion into the principle of open justice, and some bounds upon the willingness of the courts to contemplate such injunctions were set by Lord Neuberger in his *Report of the Committee on Super-Injunctions: Super-Injunctions, Anonymised Injunctions and Open Justice*.[218] Tugendhat J in *CVB v MGN Ltd* [219] said quite emphatically that 'Derogations from open justice must only be ordered where that is necessary, and only to the extent that is necessary.'

(7) **Whither superinjunctions?**

The procedural measures proposed in the Neuberger Report have calmed some of the frenzy surrounding anonymized injunctions and superinjunctions. Moreover, there has been a recognition that the inability to control some of the social media such as Twitter can make anonymized injunctions valueless or even counterproductive: the fact that Ryan Giggs had obtained such an injunction very rapidly became public knowledge. The extent to which information is already in the public domain will also affect the willingness of a court to grant an injunction.[220] Despite this, there remains some concern that English law has gone too far in protecting privacy, and beyond the limits which would be required by our compliance with the judgments of the ECHR. In addition, the readiness of the courts to use injunctions to prevent publication of information which may be true appears to go further than used to be the case with the prevention of publication of untrue and defamatory information, where the claimant would often be left with only a claim in damages.

(7) **Libel**

Quite separately from the rules relating to breach of confidence and the protection of the right to a private life, the courts possess the jurisdiction to award an injunction to prevent the publication of defamatory material.[221] The relationship between this jurisdiction and the rules relating to confidences and privacy will in due course require exploration, since there are some differences in approach. An injunction to prevent a libel will only be granted if it is clear that the material to be published is false, since the court is concerned to protect the public interest in knowing the truth.[222] In *Holley v Smyth*,[223] for instance, the Court of Appeal held that an interlocutory

---

[218] May 2011.   [219] [2012] EWHC 1148, at [23].

[220] *AAA v Associated Newspapers Ltd* [2012] EWHC 2103 (decision affirmed on appeal).

[221] *Quartz Hill Consolidated Gold Mining Co v Beall* (1881–82) LR 20 Ch D 501; *Bonnard v Perryman* [1891] 2 Ch 269; *Hubbard v Pitt* [1976] QB 142; *Gulf Oil (Great Britain) Ltd v Page* [1987] Ch 327; *Femis-Bank (Anguilla) Ltd v Lazar* [1991] Ch 391.

[222] *Fraser v Evans* [1969] 1 QB 349; *Woodward v Hutchins* [1977] 1 WLR 760; *A-G v BBC* [1981] AC 303.

[223] [1998] 2 WLR 742. See also *British Data Management plc v Boxer Commercial Removals plc* [1996] 3 All ER 707.

injunction should not be granted to restrain the threatened publication of an allegedly libellous allegation that the plaintiff had caused a loss of £200,000 from a trust through a fraudulent misrepresentation, unless it could be shown that the allegation was 'plainly untrue'. In *Greene v Associated Newspapers*,[224] the Court of Appeal held that the Human Rights Act 1998 had not changed the rule in *Bonnard v Perryman*[225] that a court would not impose a prior restraint on publication unless it was clear that no defence would succeed at trial. Since the award of an injunction to prevent a libel may affect the right to freedom of expression, where an interlocutory injunction is sought the principles identified in *American Cyanamid* are inapplicable.[226] Where the untruthfulness of a statement has not been proved the law will allow publication. If it is subsequently proved that the allegation was libellous, then the claimant would be entitled to receive compensation. This could include an award of aggravated damages,[227] if warranted, to punish a malicious defendant for publishing.[228]

8 Freezing injunctions

(1) Definition

A freezing order or injunction[229] prevents a defendant (or a third party holding a defendant's assets)[230] from dissipating his assets or removing them from the jurisdiction so that there will be nothing remaining to satisfy a judgment that might be obtained against him at trial.[231] Originally freezing injunctions were known as 'Mareva' injunctions, taking their name from the case in which they were first exercised, *Mareva Compania Naviera SA v International Bulk Carriers SA*.[232] The new nomenclature was introduced in the Civil Procedure Rules.[233]

(2) Nature of the freezing injunction

The overriding purpose of a freezing order is 'to prevent the dissipation by a defendant of assets which would otherwise be available to satisfy a judgment in favour of the claimant'.[234] This has been described as the 'enforcement principle'[235] since 'the

---

[224] [2005] 1 All ER 30. The rationale of the decision has not been questioned in subsequent cases. See *LNS v Persons Unknown* [2010] EWHC 119 (QB); [2010] Fam. Law 453; *Vaughan v Lewisham LBC* [2013] EWHC 795 (QB). [225] [1891] 2 Ch 269.

[226] *Herbage v Pressdram Ltd* [1984] 1 WLR 1160; *Kaye v Robertson* [1991] FSR 62.

[227] *Rookes v Barnard* [1964] AC 1129.   [228] [1998] 2 WLR 742, at 758–759, per Auld LJ.

[229] For an approved specimen see *UL v BK* [2013] EWHC 1735 (Fam).

[230] See Devonshire 'Third Parties Holding Assets Subject to a Mareva' [1996] LMCLQ 268.

[231] It has been suggested that the jurisdiction extends to future assets of a defendant as well as those in existence at the date that the injunction is granted: *Soinco SACI v Novokuznetsk Aluminium Plant* [1998] QB 406, per Coleman J.

[232] [1975] 2 Lloyd's Rep 509.   [233] CPR 25.1(1)(f).

[234] *JSC BTA Bank v Solodchenko* [2010] EWCA Civ 1436, [2011] 1 WLR 888, at [32] (Patten LJ)

[235] *JSC BTA Bank v Ablyazov* [2013] EWCA Civ 928, at [34]

purpose of a freezing order is so that the court "can ensure the effective enforcement of its orders." '[236] A freezing injunction is granted in an interlocutory form and is usually obtained *ex parte* (ie on the application of the claimant without hearing the defendant).

(3) **When freezing injunctions will be granted**

Three conditions have to be satisfied for a freezing order to be granted. [237] First, there must be a 'good arguable case' that the claimant will obtain a judgment for damages in court proceedings.[238] A higher level of proof is required than is the case for ordinary interlocutory injunctions. In addition, the claimant must be frank about the strengths and weaknesses of the claim and any defence likely to be put forward by the defendant.[239] Secondly, there must be a real risk or danger that the defendant may take steps to ensure that the assets which would otherwise be available to meet the judgment 'are no longer available or traceable when judgment is given against him'.[240] Thirdly, there must be assets to preserve. A freezing injunction is available against both movable[241] and immovable property.[242] Originally, it was only available against assets within the jurisdiction, but today an order may be made with worldwide effect[243] and may probably also be made in respect of assets within the jurisdiction, even if the defendant is overseas and the order is made to support an overseas judgment.[244] Even where all the requirements for the grant of the order have been met, the grant of an injunction remains discretionary, and the judge must be satisfied that it would be just and convenient to grant the order.[245]

---

[236] *Parbulk II AS v PT Humpuss Intermoda Transportasi TBK* [2011] EWHC 3143 (Comm), at [38] (Gloster J). See also *Derby & Co v Weldon (Nos 3 & 4)* [1990] Ch 65, at 76 (Lord Donaldson MR); *Camdex International Ltd v Bank of Zambia (No 2)* [1997] 1 All ER 728, at 733 (Sir Thomas Bingham MR).

[237] *Derby & Co Ltd v Weldon* [1990] Ch 48, at 57.

[238] *The Niedersachsen* [1983] 1 WLR 1412; *Elektromotive Group Ltd v Pan* [2012] EWHC 2742 (QB), at [33].

[239] *Third Chandris Shipping Corpn v Unimarine SA* [1979] QB 645; *Dadourian Group International Inc v Simms* [2009] EWCA Civ 169. See also *Negocios Del Mar SA v Doric Shipping Corpn SA, The Assios* [1979] 1 Lloyd's Rep 331; *Brinks-MAT Ltd v Elcombe* [1988] 3 All ER 188; *Tate Access Floors Inc v Boswell* [1990] 3 All ER 303.

[240] *Z Ltd v A–Z* [1982] QB 558, at 585. *VTB Capital Plc v Nutritek International Corp and ors* [2011] EWHC 3107 (Ch), at [227]-[230].

[241] 'Assets' includes a wide range of chattels. See *Allen v Jambo Holdings Ltd* [1980] 1 WLR 1252 (aeroplanes); *The Rena K* [1979] QB 377 (ships); *Rasu Maritima SA v Persuahaan Pertambangan Minyak Dan Gas Bumi Negara* [1978] QB 644 (machinery); *CBS United Kingdom Ltd v Lambert* [1983] Ch 37 (jewellery, *objets d'art*, other valuables, and choses in action); *Darashah v UFAC (UK) Ltd* (1982) *The Times*, 30 March, CA (goodwill of a business).

[242] *Derby & Co Ltd v Weldon (Nos 3 and 4)* [1990] Ch 65 (disposition of a freehold interest in a house).

[243] In *Dadourian Group International Inc v Simms (No 2)* [2006] 1 WLR 2499 at 2502–2508 the Court of Appeal laid down some guidance ('the Dadourian guidelines') on the factors the court should consider in deciding whether to grant a worldwide freezing order (WFO): see Meisel 'Worldwide Freezing Orders—The Dadourian Guidelines' (2007) 26 CJQ 176.

[244] *NML Capital Ltd v Argentina* [2011] UKSC 31, at [150]. See also *Madoff Securities International Ltd v Raven* [2011] EWHC 3102 (Comm).

[245] *Elektromotive Group Ltd v Pan* [2012] EWHC 2742 (QB), at [88].

(4) **Operation of a freezing order**

Where a freezing injunction is granted the defendant is entitled to draw upon his assets to fund his legitimate expenses,[246] including his reasonable legal expenses in defending the subsequent action, but is otherwise prohibited from removing from the jurisdiction, or from dealing with, disposing of or reducing the value of his assets up to the sum specified in the order.[247] The standard form of a freezing order applies to all the assets of a defendant, which can include assets of which he is, ostensibly, only a trustee or nominee[248] or which are held by a company which he owns or controls.[249] The order does not, however, give the claimant security for the claim, for instance through charging the assets.[250] The order does not apply to an unsecured loan facility, even though, by using such a facility, a defendant may increase his general indebtedness.[251] Nor does it apply to articles which have no commercial value.[252] However, 'the court will, on appropriate occasions, take drastic action and will not allow its orders to be evaded by manipulation of shadowy offshore trusts and companies formed in jurisdictions where secrecy is highly prized and official regulation is at a low level.'[253] This has been described as the 'flexibility principle'.[254] Failure to comply with a freezing order is a contempt of court and can lead to civil committal proceedings.[255]

Because of the potentially draconian effect of a freezing order on a defendant who has not yet been found liable in substantive proceedings, a freezing order 'should be clear and unequivocal, and should be strictly construed'.[256]

(5) **Undertaking in damages**

A freezing injunction is not permanent, but is only intended to protect a claimant until the trial of the main issue. There is normally a requirement that the claimant undertakes to compensate the defendant if he fails to establish his case at trial.[257]

---

[246] Cf *Fitzgerald v Williams* [1996] 2 All ER 171, where the Court of Appeal held that a defendant was not permitted to draw on frozen funds, to which the plaintiff asserted a proprietary claim, unless he had no other funds on which he could draw.

[247] In an exceptional case there may be no such limit: *London and Quadrant Housing Trust v Prestige Properties Ltd* [2013] EWCA Civ 130.

[248] *JSC BTA Bank v Solodchenko* [2010] EWCA Civ 1436, [2011] 1 WLR 888.

[249] *Group Seven Ltd v Allied Investment Corporation Ltd* [2013] EWHC 1509 (Ch), at [80]–[81].

[250] *Z Ltd v A-Z* [1982] QB 558, at 571 and 585 (per Lord Denning MR and Kerr LJ).

[251] *JSC BTA Bank v Ablyazov (Rev 1)* [2013] EWCA Civ 928, at [102].

[252] In *Camdex International Ltd v Bank of Zambia (No 2)*, [1997] 1 All ER 728. the Court of Appeal refused an order preventing the export of newly printed Zambian banknotes since they had no value until issued. It was inappropriate to use a freezing order merely to hold a defendant to ransom.

[253] *ICIC v Adham* [1998] BCC 134 (Robert Walker J).

[254] *JSC BTA Bank v Ablyazov*) [2013] EWCA Civ 928, at [36].

[255] See *Daltel Europe Ltd v Makki* [2006] EWCA Civ 94.

[256] *JSC BTA Bank v Ablyazov* [2013] EWCA Civ 928, at [37] citing *Haddonstone v Sharp* [1996] FSR 767, at 773 and 775 (per Rose and Stuart-Smith LJJ) and *Anglo Eastern Trust Ltd and another v Kermanshahchi* [2002] EWHC 1702 (Ch) (Neuberger J).

[257] *Third Chandris Shipping Corpn v Unimarine SA* [1979] QB 645; *The Financial Services Authority (FSA) v Sinaloa Gold plc* [2013] UKSC 11, at [15]–[18].

An undertaking to compensate affected third parties is also normally required, and in this case, there may be liability to 'innocent' third parties, even if the injunction is justified.[258] However, as was made clear in *Balkanbank v Taher*,[259] the undertaking is made to the court and not the defendant and the 'court has a discretion whether to order the plaintiff to pay damages where the defendants have sustained loss caused by the injunction'.[260] The court is not bound to order damages, and whether it does will depend on the circumstances of the case. Where the injunction is sought by a public authority exercising its statutory functions, there is no general rule that an undertaking in damages is required, unless the particular circumstances require it.[261]

(6) **Appointment of receiver**

In exceptional cases a receiver can be appointed to administer the assets. [262]

(7) **History**

The freezing injunction is a relatively recent creation of equity.[263] It was traditionally thought that *Lister & Co v Stubbs*[264] prevented the court from granting the claimant such an injunction, but in *Nippon Yusen Kaisha v Kaageorgis* and *Mareva Compania Naviera SA v International Bulkcarriers SA*[265] the Court of Appeal held that the court enjoyed the jurisdiction to grant just such an order under the predecessor to s 37(1) of the Supreme Court Act 1981.[266] Lord Denning MR described the development of the order as 'the greatest piece of judicial law reform in my time'.[267]

9 Search orders

(1) **Definition**

A search order prevents a defendant from destroying vital evidence before an issue comes to trial by requiring him to allow the plaintiff to enter his premises and search for, examine, remove, or copy articles specified in the order.[268] Previously, such injunctions were known as Anton Piller orders, and the new nomenclature was introduced by

---

[258] *The Financial Services Authority (FSA) v Sinaloa Gold plc* [2013] UKSC 11, at [18]–[19].

[259] [1994] 4 All ER 239.

[260] Per Clarke J. See also *Yukong Line v Rendsburg Investments Corp* [2001] 2 Lloyd's Rep 113, at [32] to [34].   [261] *The Financial Services Authority (FSA) v Sinaloa Gold plc* [2013] UKSC 11.

[262] *JSC BTA Bank v A* [2010] EWCA Civ 1141.

[263] However, in *The Siskina* [1979] AC 210 Lord Denning MR suggested that the Mareva injunction was a 'rediscovery' of the earlier procedure of 'foreign attachment'.   [264] (1890) LR 45 Ch D 1.

[265] [1980] 1 All ER 213, [1975] 2 Lloyd's Rep 509. A 'Mareva' injunction was first granted in the earlier case of *Nippon Yusen Kaisha v Karageorgis* [1975] 1 WLR 1093.

[266] Supreme Court of Judicature (Consolidation) Act 1925, s 45(1).

[267] *The Due Process of Law* (1980), p 134.

[268] For an approved specimen see *UL v BK* [2013] EWHC 1735 (Fam).

the Civil Procedure Rules. The rationale for the order was explained by Lord Denning MR in *Anton Piller KG v Manufacturing Processes Ltd*:

> such an order can be made by a judge ex parte, but it should only be made where it is essential that the plaintiff should have inspection so that justice can be done between the parties: and when, if the defendant were forewarned, there is a grave danger that vital evidence will be destroyed, that papers will be burnt or lost or hidden.[269]

The first such order was granted in *EMI Ltd v Kishorilal Pandit*,[270] and the first by the Court of Appeal in *Anton Piller KG v Manufacturing Processes Ltd*.[271] They were approved by the House of Lords in *Rank Film Distributors Ltd v Video Information Centre*.[272] Search orders have been particularly appropriate in cases where it is suspected that 'pirating' of music or films has taken place.[273]

(2) Preconditions to the grant of a search order

Search orders are granted ex parte, as the element of surprise is essential to prevent defendants destroying or hiding the evidence. As was said in *Rank Film Distributors Ltd v Video Information Centre*:[274]

> If the stable door cannot be bolted, the horse must be secured … If the horse is liable to be spirited away, notice of an intention to secure the horse will defeat the intention.[275]

Given the powerful effect of the order, as well as the fact that it will be granted without hearing the defendant, the court has laid down relatively strict criteria that the claimant must satisfy. In *Anton Piller KG v Manufacturing Processes Ltd*,[276] Ormrod LJ said that there are 'three essential pre-conditions' for the granting of an order. To these a fourth requirement suggested by Lord Denning MR can be added.

(a) Strong prima facie case

There must be 'an *extremely* strong prima facie case'. This represents a much higher standard than that required for other interlocutory injunctions following *American Cyanamid*.

(b) Serious potential damage

The damage, potential or actual, must be very serious for the applicant.

(c) Real possibility evidence will be destroyed

There must be clear evidence that the defendants have in their possession incriminating documents or things, and that there is a real possibility that they may destroy such material before any application inter partes can be made.

---

[269] [1976] Ch 55, at 61.   [270] [1975] 1 All ER 418.
[271] [1976] Ch 55.   [272] [1982] AC 380.
[273] Eg *Ex p Island Records Ltd* [1978] Ch 122, CA; *Rank Film Distributors Ltd v Video Information Centre* [1982] AC 380; *Columbia Picture Industries Ltd v Robinson* [1986] 3 All ER 338.
[274] [1982] AC 380.   [275] [1982] AC 380, at 418, per Templeman LJ.   [276] [1976] Ch 55, at 62.

(d) No real harm to the defendant

Lord Denning held that an order should only be granted when it 'would do no real harm to the defendant or his case'. In *Coca-Cola v Gilbey*,[277] Lightman J held that the risk of violence against a defendant if forced to disclose information will not generally justify the refusal to award an Anton Piller order. An order had been granted against the defendant, who had been involved in an operation to counterfeit Coca-Cola products, but he refused to disclose information concerning the operation because such disclosure would jeopardize his safety and that of his family. Lightman J held that such threats were 'a factor' to be considered when deciding whether to grant an order, but that in most cases it would be outweighed by the interests of justice:

> I cannot think that in any ordinary case where the plaintiff has a pressing need for the information in question, the existence of the risk of violence against the potential informant should outweigh the interest of the plaintiff in obtaining the information. In case of any unlawful threat or action directed at a party, a witness or their families, the rule of law requires that the law should in no wise be deflected from following its ordinary course and the court should proceed undeterred. Police protection is the appropriate remedy...[278]

(3) Protection for the defendant

Because of the 'draconian and essentially unfair nature of search orders from the point of view of the defendant'[279] there are a number of limitations and restrictions as to its execution intended to protect the defendant. Many of these were stated by Dillon LJ in *Booker McConnell plc v Plascow*[280] and Scott J in *Columbia Picture Industries v Robinson*, who recognized that:

> a decision whether or not an Anton Piller order should be granted requires a balance to be struck between the plaintiff's need that the remedies allowed by the civil law for the breach of his rights should be attainable and the requirement of justice that a defendant should not be deprived of his property without being heard.[281]

Many of these limitations are incorporated in the standard form order issued under a *Practice Direction* under the Civil Procedure Rules 2005.[282]

(a) Service and explanation by a solicitor

The order must be served by an independent supervising solicitor accompanying the plaintiff,[283] who must also explain what it means to the defendant in everyday language.[284] If the premises are likely to be occupied by an unaccompanied woman

---

[277] [1995] 4 All ER 711.   [278] [1995] 4 All ER 711, at 716.
[279] *Columbia Picture Industries Ltd v Robinson* [1986] 3 All ER 338, at 371. See also *Lock International plc v Beswick* [1989] 1 WLR 1268; *Bhimji v Chatwani* [1991] 1 WLR 989.   [280] [1985] RPC 425, CA.
[281] [1986] 3 All ER 338.
[282] PD10 *Practice Direction on Interim Injunctions* (1 October 2009) Para 7.1.
[283] *ITC Film Distributors Ltd v Video Exchange Ltd* [1982] Ch 431.
[284] *Bhimji v Chatwani* [1991] 1 WLR 989.

and the supervising solicitor is a man, one of the persons accompanying him must be a woman.

(b) Times of service

The order may normally only be served between 9.30 am and 5.30 pm on a weekday. This is to allow the respondent of the order to seek legal advice.

(c) Application to vary or discharge

The defendant may apply to the court at short notice for variation or discharge of the order, provided that the plaintiff and his solicitor, and the supervising solicitor have been allowed to enter the premises, although not commenced the search.

(d) Items to be removed

No item may be removed from the premises until a list of the items to be removed has been prepared, and a copy of the list has been supplied to the person served with the order, and he has been given a reasonable opportunity to check the list.

(e) Search in the presence of the defendant

The premises must not be searched, and items must not be removed from them, except in the presence of the defendant or a person appearing to be a responsible employee of the defendant.

(f) Undertaking in damages

The claimant must make an undertaking in damages to compensate the claimant for any loss he suffers as a result of the carrying out of the order if the court decides that he should be compensated.

(4) The privilege against self-incrimination

In *Rank Film Distributors Ltd v Video Information Centre*,[285] the House of Lords held that a claimant would not be granted a search order requiring the defendants to answer questions or disclose documents that would have the effect of incriminating him, as he is entitled to the privilege against self-incrimination.[286] In *IBM United Kingdom Ltd v Prima Data International Ltd*,[287] Sir Mervyn Davies QC refused to set aside sections of a search order made against a company director from whom IBM sought damages for conspiracy to extract goods without payment because the solicitor serving the order had adequately explained his right to claim privilege against self-incrimination. However, this privilege was removed as regards proceedings for

---

[285] [1982] AC 380.
[286] See also *Tate Access Floors Inc v Boswell* [1991] Ch 512; *IBM United Kingdom Ltd v Prima Data International Ltd* [1994] 4 All ER 748; *Cobra Golf Ltd v Rata* [1997] 2 All ER 150; *Den Norske Bank ASA v Antonatos* [1999] QB 271.   [287] [1994] 4 All ER 748.

the infringement of intellectual property rights and passing off by s 72 of the Senior Courts Act 1981.[288] In *Cobra Golf Ltd v Rata*,[289] Rimer J therefore held that a defendant had no right to assert an entitlement to the privilege against self-incrimination where proceedings for civil contempt had been commenced by a manufacturer of golf equipment alleging that he had infringed their trade marks.

---

[288] See *Istel (AT & T) Ltd v Tully* [1993] AC 45, HL.   [289] [1998] Ch 109.

PART II

Creating the Relationship

7

Substantive and formal requirements for the creation of express trusts

The preceding section has examined the history of equity, its contribution to English law and in particular the law relating to equitable remedies. This section will consider how the trust relationship is created. This chapter will consider the creation of express trusts, which are trusts brought into existence by the deliberate act of the owner of property. Implied trusts, which arise other than by the deliberate act of the owner, will be considered in Chapters 8 and 9, and the application of trusts to the family home will be considered in Chapter 10. The requirements of trusts and powers are also considered in Part IV of the book, and, where relevant, this is signposted in this chapter.

1 Creating a valid trust

A trust only arises where there is a separation of the legal and beneficial ownership of property; in other words, where a trustee holds property on trust for beneficiaries or recognized purposes.

(1) Two ways of creating an express trust

An express trust can be created in two ways (see Figure 7.1), which were identified by the Court of Appeal in *Milroy v Lord*.[1]

(a) Declaration of self as trustee

A trust will be created if the person who holds the legal title to property[2] effectively declares himself trustee of it in favour of specified beneficiaries. From the moment of the declaration he will hold the property on trust, and, although he retains the legal

---

[1] (1862) 4 De GF & J 264.
[2] If there is no trust already in existence, the person holding the legal title also holds the full beneficial title to the property, as the owner of the property. See Chapter 1.

(i) The absolute owner declares himself trustee

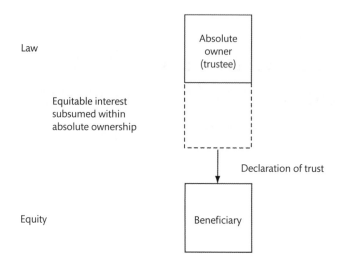

(ii) The absolute owner transfers the property to a trustee on trust

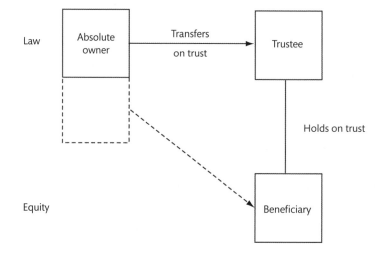

Figure 7.1 Creating a valid trust

title, the beneficiaries will enjoy the equitable interest in the property. If a trust is created by such a declaration, there is no need for any transfer of the property. Instead, the owner has simply changed his status vis-à-vis the property from that of absolute legal owner to that of trustee. The owner is known as the settlor, because he settles the property on trust.

(b) Transfer of the property on trust to trustees

If the legal owner of property, the settlor, wishes to subject it to a trust in favour of beneficiaries, but does not wish to serve as trustee himself, he can create a trust by transferring the property to someone else, requiring them to hold it as trustee for the intended beneficiaries. In such circumstances, the original owner ceases to have any interest in the property and the transferee of the property receives it as trustee subject to the trust obligations. After the transfer has occurred, the beneficiaries enjoy the equitable interest in the property.

(2) **Requirements of an express trust**

Whichever method is used to create the trust, a number of requirements must be satisfied.

(a) Intention

An express trust will only be created if the owner of property wishes it to be subjected to a trust obligation. Therefore, he must clearly intend to create the trust, whether by declaration or by transfer.

(b) Trust property

A trust obligation can only subsist in relation to specific property which is to be subject to the trust. Mere intention to create a trust will be of no effect if the settlor does not also make it clear what property is to be held on trust.

(c) Beneficiaries

It is a consequence of what is known as 'the beneficiary principle' that a trust can only exist in favour of individuals or legal persons. With some exceptions, the most notable of which is a trust for a charitable purpose, it is not possible to create a trust for abstract purposes with no ascertainable human beneficiaries.[3] Where the owner of property has indicated an intention to create a trust but has not specified who the beneficiaries are to be, no trust will come into existence and, if the property has been transferred to a third party as trustee, the equitable interest will revert back to the settlor by means of a resulting trust.[4] The 'beneficiary principle' is examined in detail in Chapter 14.

(d) Constitution

A trust will only come into existence if the intended separation between the legal and equitable title has in fact occurred. In the case of an express trust created by the owner of the property declaring himself to be a trustee, this will only be so if the declaration was effective. Alternatively, if the trust was intended to be created by transferring the property to the trustee, then the trust will only come into existence if the property was

---

[3] There are some limited exceptions, referred to as 'trusts of imperfect obligation'—see Chapter 14, Purpose Trusts.   [4] See further Chapter 8.

effectually transferred and the intention to impose a trust communicated. Provided that such a transfer and declaration are effective, the trust relationship comes into being and the trust is described as completely constituted. If there was no effective transfer, the trust relationship will not have come into being, and the trust is described as incompletely constituted. Constitution is thus concerned with the appropriate vesting of legal title in the trustees, and thus the separation of legal and equitable ownership.

(e) Formalities

Where the owner of property intends to create a trust of it during his lifetime, it may be necessary for him to comply with statutory provisions requiring the declaration to be made or evidenced by certain formalities. This is especially so if the intended trust property is land.[5] If these formalities are not followed, then the inter vivos declaration of trust may be void or unenforceable and the trust will not come into existence. Where the owner intends to make a trust of property on his death, he must comply with the statutory formalities required for a valid will. Formalities also apply where an existing equitable interest under a trust is transferred to new beneficiaries.

(f) Capacity

The settlor must also have the legal capacity to settle property on trust. This requires the settlor to be of sound mind in relation to the transaction involved, and where a transfer is involved, to have the legal standing to make it.

2 The requirement of certainty

(1) The three certainties

An express trust will not be validly created unless the 'three certainties'[6] are present. These classic requirements for a valid trust were identified by Lord Langdale MR in *Knight v Knight*,[7] where he said that a trust would only come into existence if there was certainty of words, certainty of subject matter, and certainty of objects.[8] If a trust is uncertain in any of these respects it will be invalid. In the case of a purported declaration of trust, the owner of the intended trust property will remain the outright owner thereof. If the property was transferred to a trustee, the equitable ownership will revert to the original owner by means of an automatic resulting trust.[9]

---

[5] Law of Property Act 1925, s 53.
[6] See *Re Kayford Ltd (In Liquidation)* [1975] 1 All ER 604, at 607; *Hunter v Moss* [1994] 3 All ER 215, at 219.   [7] (1840) 3 Beav 148, at 173.
[8] See *Wright v Atkyns* (1823) Turn & R 143, at 157, per Lord Eldon.
[9] See Chapter 18 for details of the allocation of funds on the failure of trusts. A failure to communicate any trust on a transfer will give the transferee title free from the trust.

(2) **Certainty of intention**

(a) **Meaning of the requirement**

The term 'certainty of words' was used by Lord Langdale MR in *Knight v Knight*,[10] but the modern meaning is probably better captured by the term 'certainty of intention'. The essence of the requirement is that an express trust will only arise if the owner of the property can be shown to have intended to subject it to a trust obligation. Where the trust is created by a document, the intention is deduced by examining the words used in the document purporting to create the obligation. As Megarry J said in *Re Kayford Ltd (In Liquidation)*:

> the question is whether in substance a sufficient intention to create a trust has been manifested.[11]

Hence, there is no special formula or technical phrasing necessary to create a trust. A trust can be created without ever using the word 'trust'. In *Re Kayford Ltd (In Liquidation)* itself, a mail-order company was in financial difficulties and used a separate bank account to deposit money received from customers whose goods had not yet been delivered. When the company became insolvent the question arose whether the money in that account was held on trust for the customers, in which case it would not form part of the general assets of the company. Megarry J held that a trust had been created, stating:

> As for the requisite certainty of words, it is well settled that a trust can be created without using the words 'trust' or confidence or the like...[12]

Similarly, the use of the word 'trust' will not of itself indicate the existence of an intention to create a trust, since the word may not have been used as a technical legal term.[13]

Since there is no requirement for a particular formula or phrase to be used to create a trust, an intention to create a trust must instead be deduced from the use of language that makes it clear that the recipient does not hold property for his own benefit, but holds it for the benefit of others. The words must demonstrate an intention to impose a mandatory obligation on the recipient of property as opposed to a purely moral obligation; an intention that the objects of the trust will benefit come what may. Finding an intention to create a trust is a question of fact that varies in every case on the construction of the particular language employed. However, some examples are useful to illustrate the approach of the courts. In *Re Snowden (Decd)*,[14] an elderly lady who could not decide how to leave her property among her nephews and nieces left it all to her brother, Bert, telling him that he would 'know what to do'. It was held that she had not intended to impose a mandatory obligation on him to hold the property on trust for her nephews and nieces, but merely expressed a moral obligation to distribute the property among her family. This can be contrasted with *Gold v Hill*,[15] where it was held that a man who orally directed the beneficiary of his life insurance policy to 'look after

---

[10] (1840) 3 Beav 148.   [11] [1975] 1 WLR 279, at 282.   [12] [1975] 1 All ER 604, at 607.
[13] See *Tito v Waddell (No 2)* [1977] Ch 106.   [14] [1979] 2 All ER 172.   [15] [1999] 1 FLR 54.

Carol [his former wife] and the kids' had intended to impose a mandatory obligation and created a trust. In *McPhail v Doulton*,[16] the House of Lords held that the mandatory character of the language used in a deed establishing a fund to provide for the benefit of the employees and ex-employees of a company, and their relatives and dependants, meant that the deed created a trust and not a mere power. The deed stated that the 'trustees shall apply the net income of the fund in making at their absolute discretion grants' to the specified class. The presence of the word 'shall' demonstrated that the recipients were under a mandatory duty to make grants, although they had a discretion in deciding to whom the grants would go. In *R v Clowes*,[17] it was held that a trust had arisen where an investment company had declared in its brochure that all monies received from clients would be held in a designated client account and only used to purchase specified government stock. In *Duggan v Governor of Full Sutton Prison*,[18] however, no trust was found to have been created where a prison governor held money in an account for a life prisoner in accordance with r 43(3) of the Prison Rules 1999. These rules provide that any cash which a prisoner had at a prison should be paid into an account under the control of the governor and the prisoner should be credited with the amount in the books of the prison. Hart J concluded that the language of the rules did not disclose an intention to create a trust, with a concomitant duty to 'invest' the money, but only to create the relationship of debtor and creditor. This must surely be correct, as it is unlikely that the draftsmen behind the rules intended a trust to arise in such circumstances. In *Shah v Shah*, Arden LJ demonstrated that the actions of the settlor provide an important context to decide the meaning of the language used as the court must consider 'the intentions of the maker as manifested by the words he has used in the context of all the relevant facts'.[19] Here, an incomplete transfer of shares was found to be held on a validly declared trust as the delivery of a signed letter alongside a shared stock transfer form bolstered language used in relation to the shares to demonstrate the required, mandatory duty.

Even if the language used in an agreement is inadequate in itself to create a trust, a trust may be held to have been created if this would fulfil the settlor's overriding intention. In *Don King Productions Inc v Warren (No 1)*,[20] Lightman J held that such an intention could be deduced as a 'matter of business common sense' from the commercial background and the commercial purpose of agreements for the assignment of promotion and management of a number of boxers.[21]

(b) Precatory words

In older authorities it was held that if a settlor or testator used certain key words or phrases, called 'precatory words', this would create a trust.[22] For example, if a testator

---

[16] [1971] AC 424.   [17] [1994] 2 All ER 316.   [18] [2003] 2 All ER 678.
[19] [2010] EWCA Civ 1408, at [13].   [20] [1998] 2 All ER 608; affd [2000] Ch 291, CA.
[21] [1998] 2 All ER 608; affd [2000] Ch 291, CA, at 625.
[22] Even if the terms of the gift seemed to be absolute: *Gully v Cregoe* (1857) 24 Beav 185; *Curnick v Tucker* (1874) LR 17 Eq 320. The Court of Chancery originally held that such words created a trust, because of historical reasons relating to the possibility of abuse by executors of wills.

had expressed his 'confidence', 'desire', 'wish', or 'hope' that a gift in his will be used in a particular way, this would be held to impose a trust on the recipient of the gift. The difficulty with this approach is that such words do not seem to impose any obligation on the recipient of the property, but merely express the wish of the transferor or testator as to how he would like to see the property used. They imply a purely moral obligation[23] and not the legally enforceable mandatory obligation which is the essential characteristic of a trust.

The lack of an intention to impose a legally binding obligation was recognized in a number of late nineteenth-century cases, and it was held that a trust could no longer be created merely through the use of 'precatory words'.[24] In *Re Adams and Kensington Vestry*,[25] for example, a testator left all his property to his wife 'in full confidence that she would do what was right as to the disposal thereof between his children'. The question was whether this language was effective to create a trust in favour of the children, or whether the wife took the property absolutely. The Court of Appeal held that the precatory words alone were insufficient to give rise to a trust. The position was summarized by Cotton LJ:

> I think that some of the older authorities went a deal too far in holding that some particular words appearing in a will were sufficient to create a trust. Undoubtedly confidence, if the rest of the context shows that a trust is intended, may make a trust, but what we have to look at is the whole of the will which we have to construe, and if the confidence is that she will do what is right as regards the disposal of the property, I cannot say that that is, on the true construction of the will, a trust imposed upon her.[26]

The consequence of these decisions is not that precatory words can never create a trust, but that such words are now just part of the evidence used to discover an intention to create a trust. A trust will be created if, on the proper construction of the whole instrument purporting to create a trust, including any precatory words, an intention can be found to subject the property to mandatory obligations.[27]

In the rather unusual case of *Re Steele's Will Trusts*,[28] it was held that precatory words were sufficient to create a trust. A testatrix left a diamond necklace to her son by will. Her will contained a clause intended to make the necklace a family heirloom that ended with the expression 'I request my said son to do all in his power by his will or otherwise to give effect to this my wish.' This form of words had been copied exactly from the will at issue in the earlier case of *Shelley v Shelley*,[29] where they had been held effective to create a trust. Wynn-Parry J concluded that although subsequent cases had held that mere precatory words were not sufficient to create a trust, in

---

[23] In *Mussoorie Bank Ltd v Raynor* (1882) 7 App Cas 321, at 331 the use of precatory words such as 'confidence' was described simply as an 'appeal to the conscience of the taker'. See also *Re Snowden (Decd)* [1979] Ch 528.

[24] See *Lambe v Eames* (1871) 6 Ch App 597; *Re Hutchinson and Tenant* (1878) 8 Ch D 540; *Mussoorie Bank Ltd v Raynor* (1882) 7 App Cas 321; *Re Diggles* (1888) LR 39 Ch D 253; *Re Hamilton* [1895] 2 Ch 370; *Re Johnson* [1939] 2 All ER 458.   [25] LR (1884) 27 Ch D 394.

[26] LR (1884) 27 Ch D 394, at 410.   [27] *Comiskey v Bowring-Hanbury* [1905] AC 84, HL.

[28] [1948] Ch 603.   [29] (1868) LR 6 Eq 540.

the circumstances a trust had been created. The very fact that the precedent of *Shelley v Shelley* had been followed verbatim afforded the strongest indication that the testatrix had intended to create a trust. Thus, the rationale for this decision was not the use of the precatory words per se, but the intention evidenced by following an established precedent for the creation of a trust of a family heirloom. It is unlikely that anyone would now be sufficiently foolish to attempt to create a trust in the same way.

(c) 'Sham' intention

Although an express intention will usually be effective to create a trust, provided that the appropriate formalities have been observed, the court may refuse to find that a trust was validly created if such an intention was a 'sham' and at the time it was made the owner had no real intention to subject his property to a trust. In *Midland Bank plc v Wyatt*,[30] Mr and Mrs Wyatt were the joint legal owners of their matrimonial home. In 1987 they executed a formally valid declaration of trust of the house in favour of Mrs Wyatt and their daughters. The trust deed was dated 17 June 1987 and signed by both husband and wife, although Mrs Wyatt had not been aware of its effect. The declaration of trust was not acted upon in any way but was placed in a safe. Subsequently, Mr Wyatt obtained loans to finance his business, secured by his interest in the house. The banks were unaware of the existence of the declaration. The declaration was only produced after the business had gone into receivership and the secured creditors sought a charging order against the house. D E M Young QC held that in these circumstances the purported declaration of trust in favour of the wife and children was a sham and had therefore been ineffective to divest the husband of the entire beneficial interest in the house:

> I do not believe that Mr Wyatt had any intention when he executed the trust deed of endowing his children with his interest in Honer House, which at the time was his only real asset. I consider the trust deed was executed by him, not to be acted upon but to be put in the safe for a rainy day…As such I consider the declaration of trust was not what it purported to be but a pretence or, as it is sometimes referred to, a 'sham'…Accordingly, I find that the declaration of trust sought to be relied upon by Mr Wyatt is void and unenforceable.[31]

Midland Bank plc v Wyatt concerned a situation where a settlor purported to declare himself a trustee. Where the settlor and the trustee are distinct, the trust will only be invalidated on the basis of a sham intention if the trustee shared the intention of the settlor.[32]

(d) Importance of evidence

Questions of intention can often turn on difficult, practical issues of evidence. In *Moore v Williamson*,[33] the question before the court was as to the ownership of a single share in a company. This share had originally been retained by Mr Moore, who had

---

[30] [1995] 1 FLR 696.   [31] [1995] 1 FLR 696, at 707.
[32] *Shalson v Russo (Tracing Claims)* [2005] Ch 281; *Re Esteem Settlement* [2004] WTLR 1.
[33] [2011] EWHC 672 (Ch).

transferred his remaining shares in a previous company to Mrs Williamson on the basis that she would hold them on his behalf and they would be equal owners of a new company. Mr Moore had, due to difficulties with registration of this new company formed from his and Mrs Williamson's share holding, transferred his single share to Jason, a director of the new company and Mrs Williamson's son. An entirely new company was duly formed by Jason and Mrs Williamson from the shareholding, without informing Mr Moore. There were two issued shares of this new company, one each of Jason and Mrs Williamson.

It was contended by Mr Moore that the share he had transferred to Jason was held in trust for him on the basis of either an oral or written declaration of trust by Jason, and that it therefore entitled him to a 50 per cent shareholding in the newly formed company. Picking through a tangled web of evidence through unreliable and conflicting testimony from key and supporting witnesses, David Cooke J found that no written trust declaration ever existed. He did, however, find for Mr Moore on the basis of the existence of an oral declaration of trust, based on express statements made by Jason to Mr Moore as to the ownership of the shares and evidenced by Mr Moore's continued involvement in the affairs of the new company. He rejected the contention that the purpose of founding the new company had been to cut Mr Moore out of the business and his continued involvement was simply as an employee, not a part-owner of the company.

(e) Failure of intention

If the words used in the instrument purporting to create a trust do not evince an intention to create a trust, then a trust cannot be created. If the words alleged to create a trust were associated with a transfer of the property inter vivos or by will, then in most cases the transfer or will gift remains effective to transfer the property and the recipient acquires the property free of any trust. If the words were alleged to constitute a declaration of the settlor himself as trustee, but show no such intention, then the settlor remains the outright owner. In some cases, where there is no disclosed intention to create a trust, the words used may confer on a third party a power of appointment[34] giving the donee of the power a discretion to distribute property to other named individuals or a class of potential objects.[35]

(3) Certainty of subject matter

A trust only exists if a separation of the legal and equitable ownership of property was brought about. Specific property must be identified which is intended to be subject to the trust obligation. An imprecise definition of the intended trust property will render the trust invalid for uncertainty of subject matter.

---

[34] See Chapter 2, Classification of Equitable Obligations, for a discussion of the difficulties that can accrue in determining whether a trust or power was intended from the wording used by the would-be settlor.

[35] See further Chapter 16 for a discussion of the distinction between trusts and powers.

(a) No specific property has been indicated

Since a trust cannot exist in abstract, but only in relation to specific assets, the failure to identify any specific property as the trust property will prevent the creation of a valid trust. In *Hemmens v Wilson Browne (a firm)*,[36] which primarily concerned the duty of care owed by a solicitor, it was held that an agreement allowing a person to call for a payment of £110,000 at any time could not create a trust of such a sum arising over their general assets because no specific property had been identified as the subject matter of the obligation. As Judge Moseley QC observed: 'there was no identifiable fund to which any trust could attach'.[37]

(b) A definition is too vague

A trust will fail for uncertainty if it is impossible to ascertain the property intended to be subject to it from the definition given. In essence, there must be no 'conceptual uncertainty' as to the subject matter of the trust. In *Palmer v Simmonds*,[38] for example, a testatrix attempted to create a trust of 'the bulk of my said residuary estate'. Kindersley V-C held that this did not create a trust because the term 'bulk' did not identify a definite, clear, and certain part of her estate. Similarly, in *Re Jones*,[39] it was held that a gift by a testator of the parts of his residuary estate which were not spent or disposed of by his wife did not create a trust.[40] In *Anthony v Donges*,[41] a husband made a gift to his wife by will of 'such minimal part of my estate of whatsoever kind and wheresoever situate save as aforesaid she may be entitled to under English law for maintenance purposes'. Lloyd J held that this provision was void for uncertainty on the grounds that it was impossible to determine what she was entitled to under English law for maintenance purposes.

In contrast, if the property is capable of being ascertained from the definition used a valid trust will be created. So, Herman can create a trust by his will of 'the residue of my estate' because the residue can be calculated. It is what is left of the estate after other bequests or testamentary gifts have been made. A more sophisticated operation of this principle is illustrated in *Re Golay's Will Trusts*.[42] Here, a testator provided in his will that a legatee was to receive a 'reasonable income' from his properties. Ungoed-Thomas J held that this was not uncertain because the term 'reasonable income' was sufficiently objective to be capable of quantification, noting that the court is regularly required to make objective assessments of what is reasonable.[43] In *T Choithram International SA v Pagarani*,[44] the Privy Council expressed no view as to whether a settlor's gift of 'all my wealth' was void for uncertainty, as the particular assets at issue in the case had been

---

[36] [1995] Ch 223.   [37] [1995] Ch 223, at 232.   [38] (1854) 2 Drew 221.

[39] [1898] 1 Ch 438.

[40] See also *Sprange v Barnard* (1789) 2 Bro CC 585; *In the Estate of Last* [1958] P 137. The authorities on mutual wills are developing in a way which suggests that (at least in some cases) a valid trust can exist where a beneficiary has a limited entitlement to draw down capital. See Chapter 13.

[41] [1998] 2 FLR 775.   [42] [1965] 2 All ER 660.

[43] See *Jackson v Hamilton* (1846) 3 Jo & Lat 702.   [44] [2001] 2 All ER 492, [2001] 1 WLR 1.

clearly identified by the settlor as being included in the gift, and they were therefore held on trust.

(c) **No means of identification has been provided**

A trust will fail for uncertainty if it is impossible to identify the property subject to the trust. In *Boyce v Boyce*,[45] a testator bequeathed his two houses to trustees, one to be held on trust for each of his two daughters. The terms of the trust required the trustees to convey to Maria whichever house she chose and then to convey the other house to Charlotte. However, as Maria had died during his lifetime the court held that no valid trust of either house was created in favour of Charlotte because it was impossible to ascertain which should comprise the trust property. Uncertainty could also arise where identifiable property is to be shared unequally between several beneficiaries, but the size of each share has not been quantified. Where there is a discretionary trust, and the trustees have the discretion to determine the extent of the beneficiaries' entitlement to the trust property, no such uncertainty will occur.[46]

(d) **The trust property has not been earmarked or segregated**

Where only part of a larger bulk of property is to be held on trust, the trust may fail if there has been insufficient earmarking or segregation of the trust property.[47] In *Re London Wine Co (Shippers) Ltd*,[48] a wine merchant held large stocks of wine in various warehouses. When a customer ordered a consignment, it was intended that the bottles ordered should become the property of the customer and that from that moment they would be held on trust for him by the company. However, there was no segregation of the bottles ordered from the general stocks until actual delivery to the customer. No beneficiary was able to identify which of the bottles were his or hers. In these circumstances, Oliver J held that the intended express trust of wine in favour of customers whose orders had not yet been delivered failed for lack of certainty of subject matter because the wine had not been appropriated from the general stock.[49] The same requirement was affirmed and applied by the Privy Council in *Re Goldcorp Exchange Ltd (In Receivership)*,[50] where a company dealing in gold and other precious metals had used investors' money to acquire bullion. The company had not appropriated or segregated any specific parcels of bullion to the individual purchasers, but rather held it in bulk. The Privy Council held that it was not held on trust for the investors. Thus, when the company became insolvent they ranked merely as general unsecured creditors. A comparable problem arose in *MacJordan Construction Ltd v Brookmount Erostin Ltd*,[51] where a builder's employer was entitled by contract to retain 3 per cent of the contract price as trustee for a builder, to ensure that the work done was satisfactory.

---

[45] (1849) 16 Sim 476.   [46] See Chapter 16, Essential validity of discretionary trusts.
[47] See Parkinson 'Reconceptualizing the Express Trust' [2002] 61 CLJ 657, at 667–676.
[48] (1975) 126 NLJ 977.
[49] Compare *Re Stapylton Fletcher Ltd (In Administration Receivership)* [1995] 1 All ER 192, where a legal tenancy in common was found because bottles of wine for a group of customers had been segregated from the bulk.   [50] [1995] 1 AC 74.
[51] [1992] BCLC 350.

The employer became insolvent, but had failed to earmark or put aside a separate retention fund of specific money due under the contract. The trust failed because it was impossible to identify any specific money as subject to the trust obligation.

A rather different view was taken in *Hunter v Moss*.[52] The Court of Appeal held that an oral declaration of trust by Mr Moss, who owned 950 shares in a private company, of 5 per cent of the issued share capital in favour of Mr Hunter, was not void for want of certainty of subject matter because the shares had not been segregated or appropriated. The issued share capital was 1,000 shares, so Moss held 50 of his shares on trust for Hunter. Since the shares had been sold, he was accountable for an equivalent percentage of the consideration received. The reason for this decision is not entirely clear. One interpretation is that the requirement of the appropriation of the trust property from a common stock only applies in the case of tangible property but has no application to intangible property, provided that there is an identifiable bulk from which the property allegedly subject to the trust can be drawn. This interpretation is inconsistent with the *MacJordan Construction* case. Another, more plausible, interpretation is that the declaration of trust was to be treated as of a fractional share of Mr Moss's holding, like a tenancy-in-common. While it could be objected that, even in this situation, the shares could have been segregated, there could be technical problems with segregating the shareholding into two separate holdings—it was likely, for instance, that Mr Moss's holding was represented by a single share certificate. An analogy could be drawn with trusts of land, where it is abundantly clear that the legal owner of land can declare a trust of a proportional share of the beneficial ownership without needing physically to divide the land in any way.

Hunter v Moss had been argued and decided before the decision had been given in *Re Goldcorp Exchange Ltd*. It has therefore been subjected to criticism[53] on the grounds that it is inconsistent with the ringing endorsement by the Privy Council of *Re London Wine Co (Shippers) Ltd*. However, in *Re Harvard Securities Ltd (In Liquidation)* Neuberger J held that he was required to follow the decision in *Hunter*, and that it could be distinguished from the earlier cases on the grounds that it concerned shares and not chattels.[54] It is submitted that this is not a strong ground for distinguishing the two cases, and that the better basis for making a distinction is that property is sufficiently identified if a trust is declared of a defined fractional share of a clearly identified whole. It should be noted that as a consequence of the Sale of Goods (Amendment) Act 1995 purchasers of unascertained goods held in bulk become tenants in common of the legal title if the goods are interchangeable. Although this does not generate a trust, it ensures that the purchaser enjoys a proprietary interest in the goods purchased, with the consequence that they will enjoy priority over other general creditors if the seller subsequently becomes insolvent before the goods are segregated from the bulk.

---

[52] *Hunter v Moss* [1994] 1 WLR 452; Hayton 'Uncertainty of Subject-Matter of Trusts' (1994) 110 LQR 335; Martin 'Validity of Trust of Unidentified Shares' [1996] Conv 223.

[53] See Goode 'Are Intangible Assets Fungible?' [2003] LMCLQ 379.

[54] [1997] 2 BCLC 369, 381–384.

(e) Future property

It is impossible for a settlor to create a presently existing trust of future property. 'Future property' means property which a person does not presently own, but which he hopes or expects will come into his ownership sometime in the future. Examples of future property include: the interest a person hopes to receive under the will or on the intestacy of a living person;[55] property a person may receive under the exercise of a special power of appointment;[56] future royalties;[57] a part, rather than a share, of future income;[58] and damages expected to be recovered in future litigation.[59]

In *Re Ellenborough*,[60] Miss Emily Towry Law, who was the sister of Lord Ellenborough, had executed a settlement in 1893 granting trustees any property to which she might become entitled on the deaths of her brother and sister. When her brother died in 1902 she decided not to transfer the property to the trustees. Buckley J held that no trust had been created by the execution of the settlement. It amounted rather to a mere promise to create a trust. The trustees could not compel her to transfer the property to the trustees because no consideration had been given for the promise and 'equity will not assist a volunteer'.[61] Similarly, in *Re Brooks' Settlement Trusts*[62] in 1929 a son assigned to trustees all the property which he might receive under the exercise of a power of appointment by his mother over property held on her marriage settlement. An appointment of £3,517 was made in his favour in 1939. Farwell J held that no trust had been created in 1929 because the property was a 'mere expectancy' and that since the settlement had been voluntary it could not be enforced.[63]

Future property should be distinguished from a residuary interest where a property right has already been conferred subject to the expiry of some prior right. A person with a vested or contingent right to property at some future date has an immediate proprietary interest in the property. Since it is not 'future property', he may subject it to an immediate trust.[64] For example, the person entitled to the remainder interest of property subject to a life interest may create a trust of his remainder interest.

A gift in an existing settlement to a class of persons on the expiry of a prior interest will be a vested or contingent interest rather than a mere expectancy: entitlement is based on an irrevocable trust rather than a mere hope or expectation of a future interest. This appears to have been misunderstood by Mark Herbert QC, sitting as a Deputy High Court Judge, in *Re Erskine 1948 Trust*.[65] Under this trust, the settlor expressly provided that in certain circumstances, the funds would devolve to the 'statutory next

---

[55] *Re Ellenborough* [1903] 1 Ch 697; *Re Lind* [1915] 2 Ch 345.
[56] *Re Brooks' Settlement Trusts* [1939] Ch 993. See Chapter 16.   [57] *Re Trytel* [1952] 2 TLR 32.
[58] *Williams v IRC* [1965] NZLR 395: the settlor assigned the first £500 of his income to a charitable purpose. The New Zealand Court of Appeal held that this was future property, because it was not certain there would be such income. If he had assigned a proportion of his annual income, this would have been valid.
[59] *Glegg v Bromley* [1912] 3 KB 474.   [60] [1903] 1 Ch 697.
[61] The concept of the volunteer in equity is discussed later in this chapter.   [62] [1939] Ch 993.
[63] See also *Norman v Federal Comr of Taxation* [1964] ALR 131; *Williams v IRC* [1965] NZLR 395.
[64] *Re Midleton's Will Trusts* [1969] 1 Ch 600; *Re Ralli's Will Trusts* [1964] Ch 288.
[65] [2012] 3 All ER 532.

of kin' of the principal beneficiary. As the judge accepted, the reference to the statutory next of kin was to be treated as if the words of the relevant Act had been incorporated into the settlement. Despite this, the judge thought—without citing any authority—that the next of kin had 'by definition'[66] only an expectancy. That aspect of his decision was erroneous, because their rights could not be destroyed by a new will. The reason why the next of kin (or a beneficiary under the will) of a living person have only an expectancy is because their expectations may be wholly defeated by the making of a will (or the changing of an existing will).

(f) The interrelationship between certainty of intention and of subject matter

Although the certainties of 'intention' and 'subject matter' refer to different aspects of the trust relationship, they are not to be considered independently of each other. Doubt over the certainty of the subject matter of a trust will exacerbate any doubt over the certainty of intention. This was recognized by the Privy Council in *Mussoorie Bank Ltd v Raynor*,[67] where the question at issue was whether the use of precatory words had been effective to create a trust:

> Now these rules are clear with respect to the doctrine of precatory trusts, that the words of gift used by the testator must be such that the court finds them to be imperative . . . If there is uncertainty as to the amount or nature of the property that is given over, two difficulties at once arise . . . the uncertainty in the subject of the gift has a reflex action upon the previous words and throws doubt upon the intention of the testator, and seems to show that he could not possibly have intended his words of confidence, hope, or whatever they may be . . . to be imperative words.[68]

(g) Effect of uncertainty of subject matter

Uncertainty as to the subject matter of a trust prevents the trust taking effect. If it has been claimed that a settlor has declared himself to be a trustee, the settlor will remain outright owner free of any trust. If the uncertainty relates to property which has already effectively been given to a third party (for instance where a gift of the settlor's entire estate has been made to a third party with a direction which applies only to an unascertained part), the effect of the trust failing will be to make the gift outright and free from a trust. Finally, if the uncertainty defines not only the property subject to a trust, but also the property contained in a transfer, the uncertainty will prevent the transfer taking effect.

(4) Certainty of objects

(a) General

With the exception of charitable trusts (and the small number of anomalous unenforceable trusts which are valid as exceptions to the beneficiary principle) a trust will only be valid if it exists for the benefit of identified legal persons who possess the locus

---

[66] At [55].   [67] (1882) 7 App Cas 321.   [68] (1882) 7 App Cas 321, at 331.

standi to enforce the trust obligations, and for whom the property is held. If an owner of property attempts to declare himself trustee without specifying any valid beneficiaries, he will retain the outright ownership of his property. If, instead, he attempts to create a trust by transferring the property to a trustee without specifying any valid beneficiaries, the equitable interest in the property transferred will revert back to him by means of a resulting trust.[69] The beneficiaries must be defined in such a way that it is possible for the trustees, or in the event of their default the court, to know who they are. The trustee will only be capable of performing his functions, by allocating and transferring the trust property to the beneficiaries, if they are capable of certain identification. Problems of uncertainty generally arise where the beneficiaries are defined by means of a 'class definition'. Such a definition must be sufficiently certain, and the criterion used to identify the class sufficiently objective, to enable determination of who is within, and who is outside, the class, thus ensuring that allocations of trust property are only made to genuine beneficiaries. There are two elements to sufficient certainty of objects.

(i) Conceptual certainty

Conceptual certainty refers to the semantic clarity of the description of beneficiaries. If there is any ambiguity in the words used to define a class of objects or if the definition is not objective, so that the court or the allocator cannot determine without a doubt whether a person is within the class or not, it will be conceptually uncertain. For example, 'tall men' is conceptually uncertain because there is no way of telling what is 'tall'. 'Men over 6 ft' would be conceptually certain, because it is possible to say clearly of every man whether he is over 6 ft and within the class, or 6 ft or under and outside it. Similarly, a class of 'old ladies', 'good friends' or 'regulars' at a local pub would be conceptually uncertain. In *Re Baden's Deed Trusts (No 2)*[70] Sachs LJ gave as examples of conceptually certain classes 'first cousins', 'members of the X trade Union', and 'those who have served in the Royal Navy'. Browne-Wilkinson J expressed the problem clearly with regard to the word 'friends' in *Re Barlow's Will Trusts*:

> ['Friends'] has a great range of meanings; indeed its exact meaning probably varies from person to person. Some would include only those with whom they had been on intimate terms over a long period; others would include acquaintances who they liked. Some would include people with whom their relationship was primarily one of business; others would not. Indeed, many people, if asked to draw up a complete list of their friends, would probably have some difficulty in deciding whether certain of the people they knew were really 'friends' as opposed to 'acquaintances' ...[71]

This requirement is therefore about the precision of language used to define the class of persons the settlor intends to benefit and it can be a difficult question, as it is concerned with linguistics and semantics. 'Nobel Prize winners' would be one example of a conceptually certain class, as it would be easy to determine whether someone was

---

[69] See Chapter 8.   [70] [1973] Ch 9, at 20.   [71] [1979] 1 WLR 278, at 298.

Obligation	Test of certainty	Authority	Requirements
Power	It must be possible to say whether any given individual is or is not a member of the class	*Re Gulbenkian* [1968] Ch 126	Conceptual certainty
Discretionary trusts	It must be possible to say whether any given individual is or is not a member of the class	*McPhail v Doulton* [1971] AC 424; *Re Baden (No 2)* [1972] Ch 607	Conceptual certainty
Fixed trusts	Complete list of all beneficiaries	*OT Computers Ltd v First National Tricity Finance Ltd* [2003] EWHC 1010 (Ch); [2007] WTLR 165	Conceptual and evidential certainty
Conditional gifts (conditions precedent)	Condition valid for those who can prove they satisfy the condition	*Re Barlow's Will Trust* [1979] 1 WLR 278	Individual proof

Figure 7.2 Tests for certainty of objects

or was not within that class. Similarly, 'David's descendants' would be conceptually certain.

(ii) *Evidential certainty*

This describes the extent to which the evidence in a particular case enables specific persons to be identified as members of a particular class of objects. For example, one could prove that one was a 'Nobel Prize winner' by providing the necessary documentary evidence that the prize had been awarded. In the case of 'David's descendants', although the test is conceptually certain—you are either one of David's children or grandchildren or you are not—until the advent of DNA fingerprinting there could have been evidential difficulties in individual cases of proving paternity. If the children have moved away from home and not kept in touch, there could also be difficulties in finding all of the descendants, although this is not strictly a question of certainty. The requirement of certainty of objects will be fully considered in Part IV, with reference to the different types of equitable obligation.[72] This section will only briefly review the relevant tests of certainty applying to trusts shown in Figure 7.2.

(b) **Fixed trusts**

In the case of a fixed trust,[73] where the beneficial interests of each beneficiary have been predetermined by the settlor, it must be possible to draw up a 'complete list' of

---

[72] Certainty is also required for powers of appointment, for example.   [73] See Chapter 15.

all the beneficiaries.[74] This is sometimes referred to as the 'class ascertainability' test. This means that the definition of the beneficiaries must be both conceptually certain and that there must also be evidential certainty of who is within the class. The reason for this is obvious: an obligation to divide the property in equal shares between the members of the class requires that the trustees should know how many there are in the class.

(c) Discretionary trusts

In the case of discretionary trusts,[75] the trustees enjoy the discretion to determine how the trust property should be allocated among the class of potential beneficiaries. Originally, the test for certainty of objects was the same as for fixed trusts, but in *McPhail v Doulton*,[76] the House of Lords held that the test for certainty of beneficiaries in discretionary trusts should be 'similar' to that used for the certainty of objects of powers,[77] namely, that it must be possible to say of any given individual that he is, or is not, within the class. This is known as the 'individual ascertainability' test. This requires that the class be specified with conceptual certainty. The disposition in question in *McPhail v Doulton* was 'to or for the benefit of any of the officers and employees or ex-officers or ex-employees of the company or to any relatives or dependants of any such persons'. The House of Lords held that the class had been specified with appropriate certainty, despite the potential problems raised by the words 'dependants' and 'relatives'. The case was remitted to the Chancery Division to apply the new test to the facts, and the application reached the Court of Appeal as *Re Baden's Deed Trusts (No 2)*.[78] They confirmed that the class was conceptually certain, and said that the requirement of certainty would be fulfilled if:

> as regards at least a substantial number of objects, it can be said with certainty that they fall within the trust, even though, as regards a substantial number of others it could not be proven whether they are in or out.

Thus, what was needed was not complete conceptual certainty, but enough certainty in the language for distribution to be made to identifiable persons.[79] The Court of Appeal also held that, if there was conceptual certainty, a discretionary trust would not be invalidated by the absence of evidential certainty. In order to distribute the funds, the trustees of a discretionary trust do not need to know the identity of every member of the class, nor the exact number of the beneficiaries.

A discretionary trust will also be invalid if it is administratively unworkable because of the sheer size of the class of potential beneficiaries.[80] This means that an otherwise valid trust can be invalidated if it would be too difficult, expensive, or time-consuming

---

[74] *IRC v Broadway Cottages Trust* [1955] Ch 20, CA. Note, what is required is that the total number of beneficiaries are known—they need not be individually named.   [75] See further Chapter 16.

[76] [1971] AC 424.   [77] *Re Gulbenkian's Settlement Trusts (No 1)* [1968] Ch 126. See Chapter 16.

[78] [1972] Ch 607.   [79] See further Chapter 16, The duties of trustees of discretionary trusts.

[80] *McPhail v Doulton* [1971] AC 424; *R v District Auditor, ex p West Yorkshire Metropolitan County Council* [1986] RVR 24.

for the trustees to make distributions within the class, even though the class is both conceptually and evidentially certain.

(d) Uncertainty of objects

If there are no certain objects, and property has left the hands of the settlor, the equitable title must revert to the settlor or the settlor's estate by means of a resulting trust.

3 Constitution of trusts

(1) The meaning of constitution

(a) Fully constituted trusts

We have already seen that there are two methods by which the owner of property, termed the settlor, can create a trust over it. He may either declare himself to be the trustee of the property, or alternatively transfer it to a third party who is intended to hold it on trust for the specified beneficiaries and not to enjoy the benefit himself. If such a declaration is made, or transfer occurs, the trust is brought into existence, and from that moment the trustee holds the legal title to the property subject to the trust obligations, and the beneficiaries enjoy the equitable ownership of the trust property, provided the three certainties are also present. Such a trust is described as 'fully constituted', meaning simply that the trust has in fact come into existence, because legal title to the property has been properly vested in the trustees and beneficial title in the proposed beneficiaries. Because a perfect trust has been created, the settlor cannot reclaim the property at a later date.

(b) Incompletely constituted trusts

In contrast, if for any reason the settlor fails effectively to declare himself trustee of the intended trust property, or if the property is never transferred by the settlor to the intended trustee, the trust does not come into being. The settlor remains the owner of the property and it is not held by him subject to the trust obligations. In consequence, the beneficiaries have no proprietary entitlement to the intended trust property. Legal title has not vested in the trustees, to be held for the benefit of the beneficiaries in equity. In such circumstances, the trust is described as 'incompletely constituted'. This terminology may be confusing, as in fact no trust exists.

(c) Beneficiaries' remedies

If a trust has been completely constituted, the beneficiaries have an equitable interest in the property, and may enforce the trust obligations. However, where a trust remains incompletely constituted, the reality is often that a settlor has previously promised that he will create a trust in favour of the proposed beneficiaries, but he has not fulfilled his promise by making an effective declaration or transfer. In such circumstances, the main concern of the proposed beneficiaries will be whether they have any means of requiring the settlor to constitute the trust in their favour. The basic position is that the beneficiaries cannot force the settlor to constitute the trust if they are volunteers, due to the rule that 'equity will not assist a volunteer'. Potential beneficiaries will be volunteers if they have not provided valuable consideration in return for the settlor's promise to settle the property on trust for them. It is worth noting that the majority of potential beneficiaries will be volunteers, as it is rare that a beneficiary pays for the benefit acquired under a trust. However, it will be seen that the general restriction against enforcing a promise to create a trust is subject to a number of limited exceptions. Alternatively, even if the beneficiaries are volunteers and not entitled to any equitable remedies, they may be able to seek common law remedies to compensate them for the loss they have suffered because the trust has not been constituted.

(2) **Constituting the trust by declaration**

(a) **Requirements of effective declaration**

In *Re Cozens*, Neville J indicated what would be required by the court to establish that a settlor had declared himself trustee of his property:

> in each case where a declaration of trust is relied on the Court must be satisfied that a present irrevocable declaration of trust has been made.[81]

This emphasizes that an expression of intent to create a trust in the future does not create an immediate fully constituted trust. In *Richards v Delbridge*, Jessel MR made clear that the settlor does not need to use particular words or technical expressions to create a trust by declaration:

> he need not use the words 'I declare myself a trustee', but he must do something which is equivalent to it, and use expressions which have that meaning.[82]

In *Paul v Constance*, Scarman LJ accepted as a statement of principle that 'there must be clear evidence from what is said or done of an intention to create a trust'.[83]

(b) **Formalities**

In general, an inter vivos declaration of trust will be valid and effective to create a fully constituted trust, even though it is made orally and without consideration.[84] No transfer of property is necessary; the settlor is simply changing the nature of his ownership of the property from owning it as himself to owning it as a trustee acting for named beneficiaries. The legal title does not move anywhere; the effective declaration of a trust separates the legal and equitable ownership of the property.

However, in the case of land, s 53(1)(b) of the Law of Property Act 1925 provides:

> a declaration of trust respecting any land or any interest therein must be manifested and proved by some writing signed by some person who is able to declare such trust or by his will.

---

[81] [1913] 2 Ch 478, at 486.   [82] (1874) LR 18 Eq 11, at 14.   [83] [1977] 1 WLR 527, CA.
[84] See *Jones v Lock* (1865) LR 1 Ch App 25, at 28, per Lord Cranworth LC: 'a parol declaration of trust of personality may be perfectly valid even when voluntary'.

A purported declaration of a trust of land which is not evidenced in writing will generally be ineffective, although this general rule is subject to exceptions, which are discussed later in the context of the formalities required for the creation of express trusts.

(c) Cases illustrating effective declaration

It is ultimately a question of fact whether in any particular case an effective declaration of trust has occurred. A number of general indications can be drawn from the authorities:

(i) Loose conversation

Jones v Lock[85] suggests that words spoken in what was merely 'loose conversation' will not amount to an effective declaration of trust because the necessary intention to create a trust is lacking. Jones was an ironmonger who had returned from a business trip to Birmingham. The nurse of his infant son complained that he had not brought anything back as a present for the baby. Jones then produced a cheque for £900, payable to himself, which was the result of his business negotiations and handed it to the baby saying: 'Look you here, I give this to baby; it is for himself, and I am going to put it away for him, and will give him a great deal more along with it.' A few days later he died. The question was whether in the circumstances the father had created a trust of the money represented by the cheque for the son. The cheque had not been effectively transferred to the son, as this would have required the father's endorsement (naming the son on the back of the cheque and signing it to confirm the transfer). Lord Cranworth LC held that there was equally no effective declaration of trust:

> the case turns on the very short question whether Jones intended to make a declaration that he held the property in trust for the child; and I cannot come to any other conclusion than that he did not. I think it would be of very dangerous example if loose conversation of this sort, in important transactions of this kind, should have the effect of declarations of trust.[86]

(ii) Words repeated over a period of time

Although isolated 'loose conversation' will not alone effect a valid declaration of trust, *Paul v Constance*[87] suggests that the repetition of similar words in conversation over a period of time may be sufficient to create a trust. Dennis Constance was separated from his wife and living with Doreen Paul. In 1974 he received £950 damages as compensation for an injury he had sustained at work. He deposited the money in a bank account and on a number of occasions told Paul that the money was 'as much yours as mine'. Constance died without leaving a will and his wife, from whom he had not been divorced, claimed that she was entitled to the money in the account on the grounds that it formed part of his estate, to which she was entitled by the rules of intestate succession. The Court of Appeal held that she was not entitled to the money because it was held upon a validly declared express trust in favour of Paul. Scarman LJ said that

---

[85] (1865) LR 1 Ch App 25.   [86] (1865) LR 1 Ch App 25, at 28–29.   [87] [1977] 1 WLR 527.

although 'it is not easy to pin-point a specific moment of declaration' the 'use of those words on numerous occasions' between Constance and Paul was sufficient to constitute an express declaration of trust. Nevertheless, Scarman LJ indicated that this was very much a borderline case.

Paul v Constance has since been followed in *Rowe v Prance*.[88] Mr Prance and Mrs Rowe had conducted a relationship over many years. Although Prance had promised to divorce his wife to live with Mrs Rowe, he had remained married. He purchased a yacht where he said he would live with Mrs Rowe, and in which they could sail the world. The yacht was registered in his sole name, allegedly because Mrs Rowe did not have an Ocean Master's certificate. Over a period of time Mr Prance regularly used the word 'our' in relation to the yacht. Nicholas Warren QC held that in these circumstances the yacht was held on trust by Mr Prance for himself and Mrs Rowe in equal shares.

(iii) Words of gift by the settlor to himself

In *Choithram (T) International SA v Pagarani*,[89] the Privy Council was forced to consider what appeared to be a novel situation that did not fall squarely within either of the methods of constitution identified in *Milroy v Lord*. The case concerned a wealthy philanthropist ('TCP') who wished to set up a charitable foundation to receive much of his wealth, consisting of company shares and deposit balances, when he died. In February 1992, knowing that he was dying, he signed a trust deed establishing the foundation. The deed stated that he was the settlor, and appointed seven trustees, of which he was one. After signing the deed he orally stated that he was giving all his wealth to the foundation. He died a month later, but had not executed any share transfers to the foundation, nor had he executed a formal declaration of trust. The judge at first instance, and the Court of Appeal of the British Virgin Islands, held that no trust had been created because of the absence of either an effective declaration or an effective transfer. The Privy Council allowed an appeal, advising that the settlor had constituted the trust. Lord Browne-Wilkinson explained that his words of gift to the foundation could only have been intended to establish a trust:

> Although the words used by TCP are normally appropriate to an outright gift—'I give to X'—in the present context there is no breach of the principle in *Milroy v Lord* if the words of TCP's gift (ie to the foundation) are given their only possible meaning in this context. The foundation has no legal existence apart from the trust declared by the foundation trust deed. Therefore the words 'I give to the foundation' can only mean 'I give to the trustees of the foundation trust deed to be held by them on the trusts of the foundation trust deed.' Although the words are apparently words of outright gift they are essentially words of gift on trust.[90]

In effect the settlor made a gift of the intended trust property to himself in his capacity as trustee, which had the effect of constituting the trust. The trust was enforceable even though the trust property had only been vested in one of the trustees. Since it is

---

[88] [1999] 2 FLR 787.   [89] [2001] 1 WLR 1.   [90] [2001] 1 WLR 1, at 11–12.

somewhat artificial to regard the settlor as having made a gift to himself, as there was no need for any transfer of the assets concerned, it might be better to treat the settlor as having declared himself a trustee of the assets which were already his.[91] Thus, words of gift by the settlor to himself on trust should be regarded in substance as a declaration of self as trustee.

(iv) Declaration by conduct

It seems an effective declaration of trust may also be inferred from conduct, even though no words approximating to such a declaration are actually used. In *Re Vandervell's Trust (No 2)*,[92] the Vandervell Trust Company held a share option on trust for Mr Vandervell. The option was exercised using £5,000 that the trust company held on separate trusts for Vandervell's children. Thereafter, the trustees wrote to the Inland Revenue saying that the shares would be held on trust for the children's settlement, and dividends arising from the shares were henceforth paid into the children's settlement. Given that this was all done with the full assent of Mr Vandervell, the Court of Appeal held that the evidence of the intention to declare a trust was clear and manifest and that the trustee company held the shares on trust for the children. Unless the trustees can be treated as acting as agents for Mr Vandervell in declaring the trust, the reasoning in this case is unconvincing, as passive assent by Mr Vandervell does not suggest a clear and present irrevocable declaration of trust, or, indeed, unequivocal conduct suggesting such a declaration.[93] This aspect of effective declaration of a trust should therefore be treated with caution.

(v) Overarching intention to create a trust

In *Don King Productions Inc v Warren (No 1)*,[94] Lightman J was faced with the task of interpreting two multi-million pound contracts between the leading boxing promoters in the UK and the USA. The judge remarked that 'the drafting of the first agreement is somewhat primitive for a transaction of this size and importance for the parties'.[95] By the agreements, Frank Warren, the UK boxing promoter, purported to assign his promotion, management, and associated contracts ('PMA contracts') to a partnership with Don King, the 'larger than life' American promoter. The contracts related to personal services, so no assignment could take place. However, Lightman J held that the benefit of the PMA contracts had been subjected to a trust in favour of the partnership since this had been the overriding intention of the parties:

> the clear intent of the parties manifested in the first and second agreements was that the promotion management and associated agreements should be held by the partnership or by the partners for the benefit of the partnership absolutely, and that this intent should be

---

[91] See Ricketts 'Completely Constituting an Inter Vivos Trust: Property Rules?' [2001] Conv. 515, where it is suggested that this was not a novel set of facts at all, and should have been considered as a transfer of property to trustees, given that title was being transferred to third parties.   [92] [1974] Ch 269.
[93] See also Battersby 'Formalities for the Disposition of Equitable Interests under a Trust' [1979] Conv 17.
[94] [1998] 2 All ER 608.   [95] [1998] 2 All ER 608, at 615.

given the fullest possible effect. The agreements have accordingly at all times been held by the partners as trustees for the partnership.[96]

(3) **Constituting the trust by transfer**

(a) **Requirements for effective transfer**

Where a settlor wishes to create a trust of which a third party is the trustee, the trust will only be constituted if the trust property is vested in the trustee by means of an effective transfer of his legal or beneficial title. In *Choithram (T) International SA v Pagarani*, the Privy Council held that where the settlor intends to establish a trust with a body of trustees it will be sufficient to constitute the trust if the property is transferred to at least one of the intended trustees, since that recipient will be bound by the trust and must give effect to it by transferring the trust property into the name of all the trustees.[97] The requirements for an effective transfer of the settlor's title vary, depending on the type of property that has to be transferred.

(i) *Land*

By s 52 of the Law of Property Act 1925 all conveyances of land, or of interests in land, are void unless made by deed. An attempted oral transfer of land, a transfer by mere writing, or even granting the trustees physical possession of the land will thus be insufficient to create a constituted trust. In *Richards v Delbridge*,[98] a grandfather attempted to create a trust of a leasehold interest for his grandson by assigning the lease to the boy's mother. Although the assignment was in writing, it was not made by deed. There was therefore no effective transfer of the lease and the trust remained incompletely constituted. With some exceptions for short leases, the transfer of the legal title to land must be perfected by the registration of the transferee as the 'registered proprietor' at the Land Registry.[99]

(ii) *Shares*

Shares are owned at law by the person who is registered as the owner thereof on the 'share register' of the company to which they relate. The legal ownership of shares can only be validly transferred by means of the registration of the transferee on the share register of the company issuing them. The possession of share certificates is merely evidence of the ownership of the shares but does not itself constitute ownership. Registration of a transferee as legal owner of the shares may occur either following the completion of an appropriate share transfer form,[100] or by means of an appropriate instruction if the shares are held electronically in the CREST system.[101] In either case, simple delivery of the share certificates by the settlor to an intended trustee will

---

[96] [1998] 2 All ER 608, at 635.

[97] [2001] 2 All ER 492, at 502. See also *Re Ralli's Will Trust* [1964] Ch 288, considered later in the chapter.

[98] (1874) LR 18 Eq 11.

[99] See Land Registration Act 2002; *Mascall v Mascall* (1984) 50 P & CR 119, CA.

[100] Companies Act 2006, ss 770–771; Stock Transfer Act 1963, s 1.

[101] Pinner 'CREST—The New Settlement System' (1996) 146 NLJ 964.

not create a completely constituted trust. This was established in the leading case, *Milroy v Lord*.[102] Thomas Medley attempted to create a trust of 50 shares in the Bank of Louisiana in favour of the plaintiffs by transferring them on trust to Samuel Lord. By the constitution of the bank, the shares were only transferable in the books of the company. Although Medley had executed a deed of assignment and delivered the share certificates to Lord, the view of the court was that title had not been effectively transferred and the trust remained incompletely constituted.

(iii) Copyrights

By s 1 of the Copyright, Designs and Patents Act 1988, a copyright must be transferred in writing.

(iv) Chattels

Title to chattels, ie tangible personal property, may be effectively transferred by means either of a deed or gift, or delivery of possession of the chattel to the intended transferee.

(v) Bills of exchange and cheques

A bill of exchange or cheque may only be transferred by endorsement, namely by the holder of the bill of exchange or cheque writing the name of the person to whom the debt is transferred and signing to confirm the transfer. Mere physical delivery to the intended trustee will not constitute the trust. This was evident in *Jones v Lock*,[103] where the mere fact that the father had handed his cheque to his infant son was insufficient to transfer title to him.

(vi) Equitable interests

If the intended trust property is an equitable interest enjoyed in property by the settlor, it can only be transferred to the trustee by writing, as required by s 53(1)(c) of the Law of Property Act 1925, which provides:

> a disposition of an equitable interest or trust subsisting at the time of the disposition, must be in writing signed by the person disposing of the same, or by his agent thereunto lawfully authorised in writing or by will.

(b) Transfers where registration by a third party is required

The legal title to some forms of property such as shares or land can only be transferred by registration of the transferee as the new legal owner. Prior to the decision of the Court of Appeal in *Pennington v Waine*,[104] it was thought that the mere completion of the relevant transfer documents by the transferor would be ineffective to transfer any interest to a volunteer transferee, since equity would not act to perfect an imperfect gift. The only exception, known as the rule in *Re Rose*, was that equity would treat a transfer as complete if the transferor had done everything in his power to transfer the

---

[102] (1862) 4 De GF & J 264.   [103] (1865) LR 1 Ch App 25.
[104] [2002] 1 WLR 2075; [2002] LMCLQ 296 (Tijo & Yeo); (2003) 17 TLI 35 (Ladds); (2003) 62 CLJ 263 (Doggett); [2003] Conv 364 (Garton); [2003] Con 192 (Halliwell).

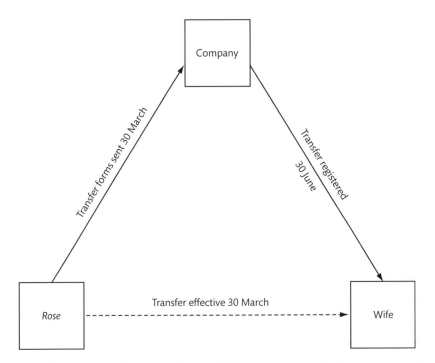

Figure 7.3 The settlor has done everything within his power to transfer the property: *Re Rose*

property to the transferee. However, in *Pennington v Waine* the Court of Appeal held that mere completion of the relevant transfer documents may be capable of giving rise to an equitable assignment of the property concerned, even where the transferor has not strictly done everything in his power to transfer the property.

(i) Transfer complete in equity when the transferor has done everything in his power to transfer the legal title to the transferee

It is well established that where the legal title to property can only be effectively transferred by registration of the transferee as the substitute owner on a register maintained by a third party, equity will treat the transfer as complete from the moment that the transferor has done 'everything within his power' to facilitate the transfer of the property.[105] This principle emerged in *Re Rose (Decd)*,[106] where Eric Rose had transferred 10,000 shares to his wife. The share transfer form was completed on 30 March 1943 and forwarded to the company. The transfer was registered in the books of the company on 30 June. To avoid estate duty the transfer would have had to have been completed prior to 10 April. The Court of Appeal held that the transfer had in fact been completed on 30 March, since at that time the transferor had done everything within his power to divest himself of his interest in the shares (see Figure 7.3). Estate duty was not therefore payable.

---

[105] See [1998] CLJ 46 (Lowrie and Todd). See also *Hunter v Moss* [1994] 3 All ER 215, 220; *Re Harvard Securities Ltd (In Liquidation)* [1997] 2 BCLC 369, 375.   [106] [1952] Ch 499.

The concept of the transferor having done 'everything within his power' to transfer legal title to his property does not merely mean that he had done all that he was practically able to do, or had been capable of doing, in the circumstances he faced. The rule in *Re Rose* operates where the only acts which remain to achieve the transfer of the legal title to the transferee are those of third parties. The transferor must have gone beyond the point of no return so that he is no longer able to prevent the transfer being completed. The principle was explained by Jenkins LJ:

> [Rose] had done all in his power to divest himself of and to transfer to the transferees the whole of his right, title and interest, legal and equitable, in the shares in question. He had, moreover, complied strictly with the procedure prescribed by the company's articles. Nevertheless, he had not transferred the full legal title, nor could he do so by the unaided operation of any instructions of his…[He] had thus done all he could, in appropriate form, to transfer the whole of his interest, but so far as the legal title was concerned, it was not in his power himself to effect the actual transfer of that, inasmuch as it could only be conferred on the transferees in its perfect form by registration of the transfers.[107]

The rule did not operate in *Re Fry*[108] because in that case the transferor had failed to do everything which was necessary to transfer title. The owner of shares in an English company, who was domiciled in America, had executed a share transfer form and sent it to England to be registered. Under wartime legislation in force, the company was prohibited from registering the transfer without the consent of the Treasury. Although the transferee had obtained, completed, and returned the appropriate forms seeking such consent, he had died before it was given. In these circumstances, Romer J held that he had not done everything within his power to transfer title to the shares, and that they therefore remained his at the date of his death:

> Now I should have thought it was difficult to say that the testator had done everything that was required to be done by him at the time of his death, for it was necessary for him to obtain permission from the Treasury for the assignment and he had not obtained it. Moreover the Treasury might in any case have required further information of the kind referred to in the questionnaire which was submitted to him, or answers supplemental to those which he had given in reply to it.[109]

In *Zeital v Kaye*,[110] a donor was held not to have met the strictures of the rule in *Re Rose*, when he handed the donee an incomplete but signed share transfer form, but not the share certificate.[111]

The rule in *Re Rose* was applied to a transfer of registered land in *Mascall v Mascall*.[112] William Mascall wanted to transfer his house to his son. He filled in all the relevant parts of a form of transfer supplied by the Land Registry to effect a transfer of the land and handed it to his son. The son completed those parts that the intended transferee was required to complete and sent the form to the Stamp Office, a necessary step prior to sending the form for registration. He then had a row with his father, who sought a

---

[107] [1952] Ch 499, at 515.   [108] [1946] Ch 312.   [109] [1946] Ch 312, at 317–318.
[110] [2010] EWCA Civ 159.   [111] [2010] EWCA Civ 159, at [43].   [112] (1984) 50 P & CR 119.

declaration that the transfer was void. The transfer form had not yet been sent to the Land Registry. The Court of Appeal held that the father had done everything in his power to transfer the title to his son, and that the transfer was therefore completed when he handed the transfer form to him, having completed all the parts that were required of the transferor. Although it had not yet been sent to the Land Registry, this was the responsibility of his son as transferee, and therefore the father had done everything within his power, or more precisely everything that was necessary by him, to transfer the title. All that remained were the acts of third parties, the son sending the form to the Land Registry and their registering him as the proprietor, which were out of the father's control. The principle was stated by Browne-Wilkinson LJ:

> A gift is complete as soon as the settlor or donor has done everything that the donor has to do, that is to say, as soon as the donee has within his control all those things necessary to enable him, the donee, to complete his title.[113]

Re Rose[114] and *Mascall v Mascall*[115] concerned absolute transfers of property by way of outright gift, but the rule would equally operate in favour of a transferee who was intended to acquire the legal title as a trustee. In such a case, the trust would be completely constituted from the very moment that the settlor had done everything within his power to transfer title. Technically, this is not an exception to the rule that 'equity will not assist a volunteer', because there is no need for the court to intervene and order the trust to be constituted on behalf of the beneficiaries. Nevertheless, in practical terms the rule in *Re Rose*[116] does indirectly operate to assist volunteers by widening the circumstances in which equity will regard a trust as having come into existence.

(ii) Transfer complete in equity when it would be unconscionable for the transferor to recall the gift to the transferee

It used to be considered that an attempted transfer of shares would only be regarded as complete if the strict requirements of the rule in *Re Rose* were satisfied. However, in *Pennington v Waine*[117] the Court of Appeal held that, in appropriate circumstances, the execution of a share transfer form might in itself be sufficient to give rise to an equitable assignment of the beneficial interest in the shares. The result would be that the transferor would hold the shares on trust for the transferee, even though the completed form has not been delivered to the transferee or the company's registrar. The facts are important to consider what these appropriate circumstances might be.

In September 1998, Ada Crampton executed a share transfer form in favour of her nephew, Harold Crampton, in respect of 400 shares in a family company. The share transfer form had been drawn up for her by a partner in the company's auditors. She returned the form to him and it was placed on the company's file. Ada also wanted Harold to become a director of the company, and the auditor wrote to him enclosing instructions to complete form 288A (a prescribed form of consent to act as a director), and also stating that Ada had instructed him to arrange the transfer to him of 400 shares in

---

[113] (1984) 50 P & CR 119, at 126.   [114] [1952] Ch 499.   [115] (1984) 50 P & CR 119.
[116] [1952] Ch 499.   [117] [2002] 1 WLR 2075.

the company, adding that this did not require any action on his part. The auditor took no further action to transfer the shares prior to Ada's death in November 1998. It was clear that Ada had not done everything in her power to effect transfer of the shares, because the transfer form had not been delivered to Harold or submitted to the company for registration. Nevertheless, the Court of Appeal held that the gift of the shares was effective in equity. Arden LJ, with whom Schiemann LJ agreed, held that the gift was complete because Ada had intended to make an immediate gift and it would have been unconscionable for her to recall the gift.[118] Clarke LJ instead held that the execution of the share transfer form could be taken as a complete assignment of her equitable interest in the shares, thus generating a trust under which she could have been compelled to procure the registration of the shares in Harold's name.[119]

In the view of the majority, the crucial element that renders a transfer complete in equity is that it would be unconscionable for the transferor to recall the gift. Arden LJ identified the circumstances which she considered had made it unconscionable for Ada to recall the gift:

> There can be no comprehensive list of factors which makes it unconscionable for the donor to change his or her mind: it must depend on the court's evaluation of all the relevant considerations. What then are the relevant facts here? Ada made the gift of her own free will: there is no finding that she was not competent to do this. She not only told Harold about the gift and signed a form of transfer which she delivered to Mr Pennington for him to secure registration; her agent also told Harold that he need take no action. In addition Harold agreed to become a director of the Company without limit of time, which he could not do without shares being transferred to him. If Ada had changed her mind on (say) 10 November 1998, in my judgment the court could properly have concluded that it was too late for her to do this as by that date Harold signed the form 288A.[120]

It is submitted that this case dangerously undermines the established principles that equity will not act to perfect an imperfect gift nor assist a volunteer. A finding that a donor intended to make an immediate gift does not mean that an immediate gift was made. The established equitable principles enable a transferor to change his or her mind whether to make a gift even after they have completed many of the steps necessary to effect a transfer. While it might have been clear on the particular facts in *Pennington v Waine* that Ada had not changed her mind about the intended transfer, in other cases the evidence will be more equivocal. The effectiveness of alleged transfers of property should not be determined by the vagaries of whether the court considers that it would be 'unconscionable' for the transferee to change his or her mind.[121]

Arden LJ held that if she had been wrong to hold that the delivery of the share transfers to the company or donee was not required, then the case could have been decided

---

[118] [2002] 1 WLR 2075, at [66].

[119] [2002] 1 WLR 2075, at [110]. It is submitted that this seems to directly contravene *Re Rose* itself, where no such trust was found, and is therefore dubious reasoning.   [120] [2002] 1 WLR 2075 at [64].

[121] See further Halliwell 'Perfecting Imperfect Gifts and Trusts: Have We Reached the End of the Chancellor's Foot?' [2003] Conv 192. Cf Garton 'The Role of the Trust Mechanism in the Rule in *Re Rose*' [2003] Conv 364, who favours the flexibility and conceptual clarity that an approach based on unconscionability might bring over the existing equitable principles.

the same way by finding that Ada and the company auditor had become agents for Harold for the purpose of submitting the share transfer to the company.[122] It is submitted that this analysis would have been preferable to the amelioration of the strict requirements of the rule in *Re Rose*, although it may be stretching the concept of agency somewhat to accommodate it.[123] Alternatively, it might have been argued that Harold had provided valuable consideration by agreeing to become a director of the company without limit of time in return for the gift of shares, thus entitling equity to act on his behalf. It still remains to be seen whether the new approach founded on unconscionability finds favour with higher courts.[124]

(iii) Reinterpreting unconscionability

The potentially unruly approach of unconscionability in *Pennington v Waine* was considered at first instance by Biggs J in *Curtis v Pullbrook*.[125] The case concerned the validity of a purported gift of shares to Mr Pullbrook's wife and daughter, which otherwise would be part of a settlement for the claimant beneficiaries against Mr Pullbrook for breach of trust. Biggs J found that, despite Mr Pullbrook having done 'his incompetent best'[126] to validly transfer legal title in the shares to his wife and daughter as managing director of the company, the power to issue and record share transfers was a power of the company board which had not been delegated to Mr Pullbrook. Mr Pullbrook had not satisfied the requirements of *Re Rose*, as he had not done all he could do to transfer the shares, as he had not deposited the share transfer forms with the company solicitors. In considering the question whether it would be unconscionable to resile from the gift, Biggs J treated the question as a matter of detrimental reliance.[127] Hence, where there is detrimental reliance by the donee that may bind the conscience of the donor to justify the imposition of a constructive trust. In the present case, there was no evidence of any reliance, detrimental or otherwise, by the wife or daughter on Mr Pullman's purported gift of the shares.

In explicitly linking the question of unconscionability to detrimental reliance by the donee, this potentially has the benefit of qualifying when it may be unconscionable for the donor to recall a gift or to and make its impact less unruly.[128] It does at least bring the rule in line with other areas where equity imposes a constructive trust on another.[129] However, it is still difficult to see what advantages even this reinterpreted approach to upholding an imperfect gift, if followed, adds to the certainty and

---

[122] [2002] 1 WLR 2075 at [67].

[123] See Halliwell 'Perfecting Imperfect Gifts and Trusts: Have We Reached the End of the Chancellor's Foot?' [2003] Conv 192.

[124] The issue did arise for discussion in *Zeital v Kaye* [2010] EWCA Civ 159, where Rimer LJ simply stated that the issue was of no help on the facts (at [40]) and otherwise appeared to treat the case as similar to the rule in *Re Rose*. 　　　　　　　　　　　　　　　　　　　　　　[125] [2011] EWHC 167 (Ch).

[126] [2011] EWHC 167 (Ch), at [42]. 　　　　[127] [2011] EWHC 167 (Ch), at [43].

[128] See further Luxton 'In search of perfection: the *Re Rose* rationale' [2012] Conv 70; who opines that this means that there is no longer a separate 'unconscionability test'; instead this is an example of the operation of proprietary estoppel. This remedy is considered in the context of the family home in Chapter 10.

[129] Constructive trusts are considered in Chapter 9.

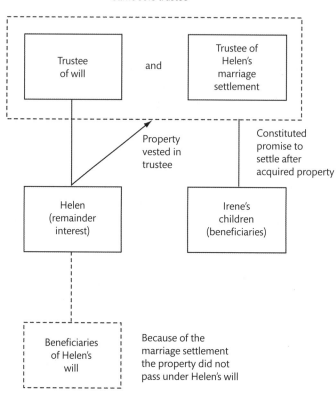

Figure 7.4 *Re Ralli's Will Trusts*

predictability of the rule in *Re Rose* and a decision of a higher court is still awaited to determine the fate of unconscionability.[130]

(4) **Constitution of a trust through coincidental receipt of the trust property by the trustee**

In most cases, a trust will only be fully constituted if the trust property is transferred to the trustee by the deliberate act of the settlor. However, in some very rare cases it seems that a trust will be fully constituted if the trustee received the legal title to the trust property as a matter of coincidence. In *Re Ralli's Will Trusts*,[131] a number of trusts were created by the members of a family (see Figure 7.4). The patriarch, Ambrose Ralli, died in 1899. Under his will his wife was to enjoy a life interest of his residuary estate which was to be held on trust, and on her death it would pass to his daughters, Helen and Irene, in equal shares. In 1924 Helen executed a marriage settlement, under which she promised to settle any after-acquired property for the benefit of the beneficiaries of

---

[130] It is worth noting that Biggs J in *Curtis v Pullbrook* did not feel there was any clear rationale or objective for equitable intervention perfect imperfect gifts of shares (at [47]), suggesting he was also dismissive of the rule in *Re Rose*.   [131] [1964] Ch 288.

the settlement. This would include the remainder interest in her father's estate to which she would become entitled on the death of her mother. The beneficiaries under the marriage settlement were her sister Irene's children. Helen died in 1956 and the testator's widow in 1961. The plaintiff, who had been appointed a trustee of Ambrose Ralli's will in 1946, was at that date the sole surviving trustee of the trusts established under the will. He was, coincidentally, also the sole surviving trustee of Helen's marriage settlement. On Ambrose's widow's death, the remainder interest in his residuary estate was vested in him as trustee under the will. The central question was whether he held Helen's half share as part of Helen's estate, in which case it would pass under her will, or whether he held it under the terms of her marriage settlement, in which case it would pass to Irene's children. Although there had been no intentional transfer of the property to the plaintiff in his capacity as trustee of the marriage settlement, Buckley J held that the fact that he had received it in his capacity as the trustee of the will was sufficient to constitute the trust, and the property was therefore held on the terms of the marriage settlement. He concluded that it did not matter how the trustee had come to receive the legal title to the trust property, it was sufficient that the title had vested in him:

> In my judgment the circumstance that the plaintiff holds the fund because he was appointed a trustee of the will is irrelevant. He is at law the owner of the fund, and the means by which he became so have no effect on the quality of his legal ownership. The question is: For whom, if anyone, does he hold the fund in equity?[132]

In the circumstances that transpired, it was a fortuitous coincidence that the plaintiff had enjoyed a double capacity as trustee of both the will and of the marriage settlement. It meant that Helen could not claim the property from him without breaking her promise to give it to him on trust. On a narrow reading of the case this was an essential part of the decision. On a wider reading, the case supports the view that it is not essential for a trustee to obtain the legal title to the trust property by way of a deliberate transfer from the settlor.

As with the principle in *Re Rose*[133] examined earlier, *Re Ralli's Will Trusts*[134] does not provide an example of equity assisting a volunteer. The trust is completely constituted, so there is no need for equity to assist the beneficiaries. Again, the practical effect of the principle is to broaden the circumstances in which equity will regard a trust as having been constituted, which indirectly assists the position of volunteers.

(5) **Relationship between constitution by transfer and constitution by declaration**

It has been seen that a fully constituted trust may be created either by an effective declaration of self as trustee, or by an effective transfer of the property to the trustee on trust. If there was an intention by the settlor to create a trust in favour of the beneficiaries by transferring the trust property to trustees, but an attempt to constitute the trust was ineffective because the property has not been transferred, the question arises

---

132 [1964] Ch 288, at 301.   133 [1952] Ch 499.   134 [1964] Ch 288.

whether equity should treat the settlor as holding the property on trust. This would have the advantage of ensuring that the beneficiaries were able to enforce their equitable entitlement to the trust property, which seems to have been the settlor's intention. However, in such circumstances equity will not construe an ineffective transfer as a declaration of trust by the settlor. This was made clear in *Milroy v Lord*[135] where, as was noted earlier, the settlor who intended to create a trust of shares had failed to transfer title to the intended trust, because he had merely handed the share certificates to him and he had not been registered as the owner thereof on the company share register. The Court of Appeal held that there had been no effective declaration of trust by the settlor. The principle was stated by Turner LJ:

> it is plain that it was not the purpose of this settlement, or the intention of the settlor, to constitute himself a trustee of the bank shares. The intention was that the trust should be vested in... Samuel Lord, and I think therefore that we should not be justified in holding that by the settlement, or by any parol declaration made by the settlor, he himself became a trustee of these shares for the purposes of the settlement. By doing so we should be converting the settlement or the parol declaration to a purpose wholly different from that which was intended to be created by it, and, as I have said, creating a perfect trust out of the imperfect transaction.[136]

In *Choithram (T) International SA v Pagarani*,[137] which was also discussed earlier, the Privy Council dealt with a situation which did not easily fit into the two categories identified in *Milroy v Lord*. The decision does not, however, undermine the traditional principle that a failed transfer will not be construed as a declaration of trust. Instead it is submitted that the highly unusual situation of a settlor's words of gift to himself should be construed in substance as a declaration of trust.

(6) **Enforcing a trust**

(a) **Enforcing fully constituted trusts**

Where a trust has been fully constituted, whether in consequence of a settlor's declaration or through an effective transfer of the intended trust property to trustees, the beneficiaries are immediately entitled to the equitable interest in the property held on trust for them. They can seek the aid of equity to compel the trustees to perform the trust obligations by virtue of their interest as beneficiaries, irrespective of whether they were volunteers or whether they had provided consideration to the settlor in return for the creation of the trust. Once the trust has been created, the settlor cannot change his mind.[138]

This can be seen from the following two cases. *Paul v Paul*[139] concerned a marriage settlement executed by parties who had since separated. Under the terms of the

---

[135] (1862) 4 De GF & J 264.   [136] (1862) 4 De GF & J 264, at 275.   [137] [2001] 1 WLR 1.
[138] See *Jefferys v Jefferys* (1841) Cr & Ph 138; *Bentley v Mackay* (1851) 15 Beav 12; *Kekewich v Manning* (1851) 1 De GM & G 176; *Milroy v Lord* (1862) 4 De GF & J 264; *Richardson v Richardson* (1867) LR 3 Eq 686; *Henry v Armstrong* (1881) 18 Ch D 668.   [139] (1882) 20 Ch D 742, CA.

settlement as husband and wife, they were entitled to enjoy the income derived from the trust property for life, with the remainder interest passing on their deaths to the children of the marriage. If there were no children and the wife predeceased her husband she enjoyed a general power to appoint over the trust property by will, subject to an express provision in default of appointment in favour of her next of kin. As there were no children, the husband and wife applied to have the capital of the trust paid over to themselves, arguing that the only other persons with any interest in it were the next of kin, who were volunteers. The Court of Appeal held that although the next of kin were volunteers, they enjoyed an immediate equitable interest in the capital because the trust was fully constituted and they were beneficiaries under it. As such, the trust could not be brought to an end without their consent. In *Re Bowden*,[140] Catherine Bowden agreed to settle any property to which she might become entitled under her father's will on trust. Her father died in 1869, and between 1871 and 1874 the property to which she was entitled under his will was transferred to the trustees. In 1935 she requested that the trustees transfer the trust funds to her absolutely. Bennett J held that she was not entitled to the transfer because the property had become impressed with the trust the moment that it had been received by them.

(b) Enforcing incompletely constituted trusts

As mentioned earlier, where a settlor has neither declared himself trustee of the trust property nor transferred it to trustees, the trust is said to be incompletely constituted. In reality, no trust exists. The trust property is not subject to any obligations, and the legal and equitable ownership are not separated. The settlor remains the owner of the property. The intended beneficiaries enjoy no entitlement to the putative trust property, nor can they enforce the trust obligations against the intended trustees, because there is no trust. In substance, the intended beneficiaries are merely the victims of the settlor's unfulfilled promise to create a trust in their favour. In such circumstances, the question arises as to whether there are any means by which the intended beneficiaries can compel the settlor to carry out his promise to subject the property to a trust in their favour, by in effect requiring specific performance thereof. The basic principle is that if the intended beneficiaries have provided valuable consideration in return for the settlor's promise to create a trust in their favour, then equity will compel the settlor to constitute the trust. However, if they are volunteers the rule that 'equity will not assist a volunteer' operates to prevent them compelling the settlor to constitute the trust.

(i) Beneficiaries of an incompletely constituted trust who have given valuable consideration

Where the potential beneficiaries have given valuable consideration, equity will come to their assistance and compel the settlor to constitute the trust.[141] Equity does not take the same view of consideration as the common law and will not enforce a promise made in return for merely nominal consideration. Instead, equity requires 'valuable consideration'.

---

[140] [1936] Ch 71.   [141] See *Donaldson v Donaldson* (1854) Kay 711; *Lee v Lee* (1876) 4 Ch D 175.

'Valuable consideration' is a technical term requiring either 'money or money's worth'[142] or marriage consideration.[143] As well as excluding nominal consideration, it also excludes a deed (a covenant) which is enforceable at common law by the covenantee even where no consideration at all has been provided. The ability of equity to compel the creation of trusts which are not completely constituted on behalf of those who have provided valuable consideration can be illustrated from the context of marriage settlements. In *Pullan v Koe*,[144] a wife covenanted to settle after-acquired property of a value greater than £100 on the trusts established under her marriage settlement. She subsequently received a gift of £285 from her mother, which she failed to transfer to the trustees and which was instead invested in bonds. On the death of her husband, the bonds were in the possession of his executors. Swinfen Eady J held that the trustees were entitled to enforce the trust on behalf of her children because they were within the scope of the marriage consideration and not mere volunteers. (It may be a surprising concept nowadays, but it is well accepted that a contract made in expectation of marriage can be enforced by the parties to the marriage and any of their children.) The bonds were held on the terms of the marriage settlement, even though they had not been transferred to the trustees.

(ii) Volunteer beneficiaries of an incompletely constituted trust

In contrast, where the beneficiaries of an incompletely constituted trust are volunteers who have provided no valuable consideration in return for the settlor's promise to create a trust, equity will not compel the constitution of the trust.[145] This is an application of a more general principle that equity will not act to complete an imperfect gift, which was explained by Page-Wood V-C in *Donaldson v Donaldson*:

> [Where there is an imperfect gift] which requires some other act to complete it on the part of the assignor or donor, the court will not interfere to require anything else to be done by him.[146]

This limitation prevented the enforcement of a trust in *Re Plumptre's Marriage Settlement*,[147] which, like *Pullan v Koe* (see earlier), also concerned a wife's covenant in her marriage settlement to transfer any after-acquired property to the trustees. She was subsequently given certain stocks by her husband, but they were never transferred to the trustees of the marriage settlement. On her death her next of kin sought to enforce the trust. It was held that they were unable to do so because they were outside of the scope of the marriage consideration and volunteers in equity. The stocks therefore remained free of the marriage settlement trusts and formed part of her estate. Similarly, in *Re Cook's Settlement Trusts*,[148] it was held that volunteer beneficiaries

---

[142] If value was given, it is irrelevant whether the consideration was adequate: *Bassett v Nosworthy* (1673) Cas temp Finch 102.

[143] Marriage consideration exists where gifts are made in contemplation of, or at the time of, marriage of the potential beneficiaries. Only the husband, wife, and direct issue (children) of the marriage are within the marriage consideration: *De Mestre v West* [1891] AC 264; *A-G v Jacobs-Smith* [1895] 2 QB 341, CA; *Rennell v IRC* [1962] Ch 329; *Re Cook's Settlement's Trusts* [1965] Ch 902.   [144] [1913] 1 Ch 9.

[145] See *Jefferys v Jefferys* (1841) Cr & Ph 138; *Dening v Ware* (1856) 22 Beav 184; *Re D'Angibau* (1880) LR 15 Ch D 228; *Harding v Harding* (1886) 17 QBD 442; *Re Earl of Lucan* (1890) 45 Ch D 470.

[146] (1854) Kay 711, at 718.   [147] [1910] 1 Ch 609.   [148] [1965] Ch 902.

were not entitled to enforce a settlor's promise to create a trust, even though other beneficiaries had given consideration. Sir Francis Cook executed a covenant that he would settle the proceeds of sale of any picture he had received from his father, and which he sold in his lifetime, on trust for members of his family. The beneficiaries provided no consideration for this covenant. During his lifetime he gave Rembrandt's 'Titus' to his wife, which she wished to sell. The trustees sought the opinion of the court as to the steps they should take if the picture was sold and the proceeds were not paid over to them. Buckley J held that since the potential beneficiaries were volunteers, equity would not enforce the trust if it was not completely constituted by the promised transfer of the proceeds of sale.[149]

(iii) Volunteer beneficiaries of an incompletely constituted trust who are able to obtain specific performance of a contract to create a trust

Where a settlor has entered a contract with a third party promising to settle specified property on trust for beneficiaries, the potential beneficiaries will generally be unable to obtain specific performance because they are volunteers. However, in exceptional circumstances, the potential beneficiaries might be able to stand in the position of the third party to whom the contractual promise was made and obtain specific performance to enforce the trust. In *Beswick v Beswick*,[150] Peter Beswick contracted to transfer his business to his nephew, John, in return for his promise to pay an annuity of £5 per week to his wife. The business was transferred, but after Peter died John refused to pay the annuity. The House of Lords held that Mrs Beswick, although a volunteer who was not privy to the contract, was entitled to an order of specific performance to compel the nephew to pay the annuity. She was not, however, entitled to this remedy in her own right, but rather, because she stood in the shoes of her husband as she was the administrator of his estate. It was therefore as if Peter Beswick himself were seeking the remedy. *Beswick v Beswick* did not in fact involve a trust, but if the nephew had agreed to settle property on Mrs Beswick, as administratrix, she would have been similarly able to obtain an order of specific performance, enforcing the trust. Her status as administratrix meant she was able to obtain indirectly what she was not entitled to obtain directly.

(7) Exceptions to the rule that 'equity will not assist a volunteer'

(a) Importance of the exceptions

In limited circumstances equity is prepared to assist a volunteer transferee of property where a transferor has failed effectively to transfer the legal title to him. These exceptions to the rule that 'equity will not assist a volunteer' operate whether the ineffective transfer was intended as an absolute gift or whether the property was intended to be held by the transferee on trust for third party beneficiaries. If the transferee was

---

[149] The abrogation of the doctrine of privity of contract by the Contracts (Rights of Third Parties) Act 1999 would enable the beneficiaries to obtain common law damages for breach of contract in such a situation, but does not enable them to obtain specific performance.   [150] [1968] AC 58.

intended to hold the property as trustee, the effect of equity compelling the perfection of the imperfect transfer is to constitute the trust.

(b) The rule in *Strong v Bird*

If a donor makes an imperfect gift during his lifetime, so that the donee does not receive the legal title to the property, the rule in *Strong v Bird*[151] operates to perfect the gift if the donee is appointed the donor's executor, or becomes his administrator on intestacy. The gift is perfected because the donee receives legal title to all the donor's property in his capacity as executor or administrator, including the property that was the intended subject matter of the gift. This has the effect of completing the imperfect transfer, by vesting the necessary legal title in the trustee.[152] *Strong v Bird*[153] concerned an incomplete release of a debt. Strong had borrowed £1,100 from his step-mother, who lived in his house and paid board to him. It was initially agreed that he would repay the sum to her by means of a deduction of £100 from the board she paid quarterly. After two quarters where the deduction was made, she told him that she did not want the money returned and reverted to paying full board. This was not effective as a release of the debt at common law, which required a deed, and Strong had not provided any consideration for the release. Four years later, the step-mother died. Strong was appointed sole executor in her will. The court held that his appointment operated to perfect the imperfect release of the debt, so that Strong was not liable to repay the loan to the estate. The principle was stated by Jessel MR:

> it appears to me that there being a continuing intention to give, and there being a legal act which transferred the ownership or released the obligation—for it is the same thing—the transaction is perfected, and he does not want the aid of a court of equity to carry it out, or to make it complete, because it is complete already, and there is no equity against him to take the property away from him.[154]

This principle was subsequently applied in *Re James*.[155] Sarah James had been the housekeeper of James for some nineteen years. Although she received no payment, he told her that his house and furniture were to be hers on his death. When he died his son John inherited the property and gave Sarah the title deeds of the house, where she continued to live with her husband. John later died intestate and Sarah was granted letters of administration. Farwell J held that this had the effect of perfecting the gift of the house, which was imperfect because there had been no conveyance to her. He held that:

> by her appointment as one of the administratrixes she got the legal estate vested in her...she needs no assistance from equity to complete her title.[156]

A number of conditions must be satisfied before the rule in *Strong v Bird* will operate to perfect an imperfect gift—these are considered in the following paragraphs.

---

[151] (1874) LR 18 Eq 315; Kodilinye 'A Fresh Look at the Rule in *Strong v Bird*' [1982] Conv 14.
[152] See *Re Ralli's Will Trusts* [1964] Ch 288.   [153] (1874) LR 18 Eq 315.
[154] (1874) LR 18 Eq 315, at 319.   [155] [1935] Ch 449.   [156] [1935] Ch 449, at 451.

(i) The donor must have intended to make an inter vivos gift

The rule will only apply if an immediate inter vivos gift of the property had been intended by the donor, which failed because the transfer was ineffective given the nature of the property. The rule has no application where the donor intended to make a gift which would only take effect on his death.

(ii) The donor's intention to make the gift must have continued until his death

The rule will only operate if the donor who had failed to make an effective gift of the property had a 'continuing intention' to make the gift at the time of his death. This was emphasized in *Strong v Bird*[157] and also in *Re James*,[158] where Farwell J concluded that he was 'completely satisfied that there was a continuing intention in the donor up to the time of his death to give the property to the defendant'.[159] In contrast, in *Re Gonin*[160] it was held that the donor had no continuing intention, and the rule could not operate. The plaintiff, Lucy Gonin, had returned home in 1944 to look after her parents. They promised that in return she should have their house when they died. Because Lucy had been born illegitimate, her mother mistakenly believed that she could not leave the property to her by will. In 1962 she drew a cheque for £33,000 in Lucy's favour, which she left in an envelope that was discovered after her death. Lucy claimed that in these circumstances the imperfect gift of the house was perfected when she was granted letters of administration over her mother's estate. Walton J held that the rule in *Strong v Bird* could not apply because her mother had not had a continuing intention to make a gift of the house at the time of her death:

> so far as the land is concerned no such continuing intention can be found…I think that the intention changed by the latest in 1962 when the deceased drew her cheque in favour of her daughter. I find it impossible to think that from then on what she really had in mind was anything other than that the plaintiff would inherit the cheque on the deceased's death—no immediate gift, and no gift of land.[161]

(iii) The donee must have been appointed an executor or granted letters of administration

The perfection of an imperfect gift by the rule in *Strong v Bird* is only effected by the vesting of the legal title to the intended subject matter in the donee in his capacity as the executor or administrator of the donor. It is irrelevant whether the donee is a sole executor, or one of several joint executors.[162] Some doubts were expressed in *Re Gonin*[163] as to whether the rule should apply to administrators, because 'it is often a matter of pure chance which of many persons equally entitled to a grant of letters of administration finally takes them out'.[164] However, Walton J was unwilling to determine the issue and noted that the rule was applied to an administrator in *Re James*,[165] which had been cited without dissent by Buckley J in *Re Ralli's Will Trusts*.[166]

---

[157] (1874) Lr 18 Eq 315.   [158] [1935] Ch 449.

[159] See also *Re Freeland* [1952] Ch 110; *Re Wale* [1956] 1 WLR 1346; *Choithram (T) International SA v Pagarani* [2001] 2 All ER 492.   [160] [1979] Ch 16; (1977) 93 LQR 488.

[161] [1979] Ch 16, at 35.   [162] *Re Stewart* [1908] 2 Ch 251.   [163] [1979] Ch 16.

[164] [1979] Ch 16, at 35.   [165] [1935] Ch 449.   [166] [1964] Ch 288, at 301.

(iv) The intended subject matter of the gift must have been capable of enduring the death of the donor

Most property, whether tangible or intangible, is capable of enduring past the death of its owner. However, a cheque which has not been endorsed by the payee constitutes nothing more than a revocable mandate of the customer on whose account it was drawn, to his bank, requesting them as his agents to make payment to the payee. On the death of the customer, this mandate is automatically terminated. It follows that a cheque which remains uncashed at the date of death of the drawer will be incapable of passing title to the money instructed to be transferred, even if the payee is appointed the executor or administrator of the estate. Thus, in *Re Gonin*[167] the daughter had no entitlement to the £33,000 cheque her mother had left for her. If, however, a cheque is endorsed by its payee, it becomes a negotiable instrument and is a species of property capable of enduring despite the death of the drawer.

Although the rule in *Strong v Bird*[168] is commonly cited as an example of an exception to the rule that equity will not assist a volunteer, it is questionable whether this is genuinely the case. Instead, like the principles identified in *Re Rose*[169] and *Re Ralli's Will Trusts*,[170] it may be viewed as an example of widened circumstances in which equity is willing to find that a transfer has in fact been completed.

(c) Donatio mortis causa (gift on account of death)

The donatio mortis causa (sometimes referred to as a 'deathbed' gift) provides a genuine exception to the principle that equity will not assist a volunteer. It operates where an owner wants to make a gift of property to the donee that is only intended to take effect if he dies. If, in such circumstances, the donor failed to make an effective transfer of the property to the donee during his lifetime, equity will act to compel his executors, or administrators, to perfect the donee's imperfect title. It does not matter that the donee is a volunteer. If the donee was intended to receive the property as a trustee, the operation of the donatio mortis causa will have the effect of constituting the trust.

In its simplest form, a donatio mortis causa is merely a gift which is conditional upon death. Where the intended subject matter of a gift is personal property, a straightforward gift (such as a birthday present) is normally made by handing the property to the recipient with the intention to make a gift. The intention will normally be unconditional. However, it is possible for the intention to be subject to some condition being satisfied. For instance, a doting father might lend a car to his daughter, telling the daughter that she can keep it if she passes her examinations. If the daughter does pass, then the gift is completed. Where the condition which has to be satisfied is the death of the donor, the gift could be described as a donatio mortis causa. In extended forms of the donatio mortis causa the gift may go beyond the simple characteristics of such a conditional gift, as will be seen from the cases described below.

---

[167] [1979] Ch 16.   [168] (1874) LR 18 Eq 315.   [169] [1952] Ch 499.   [170] [1964] Ch 288.

The essential conditions of a valid donatio mortis causa were stated by Lord Russell CJ in *Cain v Moon*:[171]

(i) 'The gift or donation must have been made in contemplation, though not necessarily in expectation of death'

The special treatment granted to the donee of a donatio mortis causa is only warranted because of the unique circumstances in which the gift was made. Only if the donee made the gift in contemplation of death can a valid donatio occur. This requires something more specific than a realization of the general truth that we are all going to die eventually. As Hale J said in the Australian case, *Smallacombe v Elder's Trustee & Executor Co Ltd*:

> the donor must have been contemplating a comparatively early death from some cause or other, whether it be an existing illness, a dangerous journey[172] or even extreme old age. While an immediate expectation of immediate death is not required, nevertheless something more is required than a mere recognition of the inevitability of death itself.[173]

Where a gift is made by a donor in contemplation of death from a specific cause, it is irrelevant if he in fact dies from different causes, and this does not prevent the validity of the donatio. In *Wilkes v Allington*[174] the donor was diagnosed as suffering from cancer in 1922. Although he continued to farm, he considered himself under a sentence of death. He therefore made several incomplete gifts to his nieces. In January 1928, after coming home in a bus from Worcester market, he caught a chill and died of pneumonia. Lord Tomlin held that there was a valid donatio, even though the precise cause of death was different to the contemplated cause.

It seems that a gift made in contemplation of suicide will not operate as a valid donatio mortis causa.[175] However, the Irish case *Mills v Shields*[176] held that a gift in contemplation of death by natural causes was a valid donatio even if the donor subsequently committed suicide.

(ii) 'There must have been delivery to the donee of the subject matter of the gift'

An imperfect inter vivos gift will only be perfected as a donatio mortis causa if the donor had delivered the property intended to be the subject matter of the gift to the donee before his death.[177] The requirement is delivery, not a transfer of title, so any formalities necessary validly to transfer title to the property in question are not necessary. In the case of chattels, delivery can usually be achieved by handing physical possession of the property to the donee.[178] However, by way of one extension of the simple concept of a conditional gift, it will also be sufficient if the donor hands the donee

---

[171] [1896] 2 QB 283. See also *Re Johnson* (1905) 92 LT 357, per Farwell J; *Re Craven's Estate (No 1)* [1937] Ch 423, per Farwell J; *Delgoffe v Fader* [1939] Ch 922, per Luxmore LJ; *Birch v Treasury Solicitor* [1951] Ch 298.

[172] See *Thompson v Mechan* [1958] OR 357: the ordinary risks of air travel are not sufficient for a valid donatio.   [173] [1963] WAR 3, at 4–5.

[174] [1931] 2 Ch 104.

[175] *Agnew v Belfast Banking Co* [1896] 2 IR 204, CA; *Re Dudman* [1925] Ch 553. This is because the act of suicide is an illegal act.   [176] [1948] IR 367.

[177] *Ward v Turner* (1752) 2 Ves Sen 431.   [178] *Miller v Miller* (1735) 3 P Wms 356.

'dominion' over the property by granting him the means to control it. Such dominion would have been given, for example, if the property had been kept in a locked box and the donor had handed the key to the donee.[179] In *Re Lillingston*,[180] the donor gave the donee the key to a trunk, which contained the key to a safe deposit at Harrods, which in turn contained the key to a safe deposit at the National Safe Deposit and Trustee Co. It was held that there was a valid donatio mortis causa of jewellery in the trunk and the contents of the two safe deposit boxes. In *Woodard v Woodard*,[181] the Court of Appeal held that there was a valid donatio of a car where the donor had given the donee a set of keys, since these constituted sufficient dominion.

When the intended subject matter of the gift is land or intangible property it is impossible for the donor to physically deliver it to the donee, or grant him dominion over it. Here, the prerequisite of a valid donatio is that the donor delivered the 'essential indicia or evidence of title'[182] to the donee, or gave him dominion over such indicia. For money held in a bank deposit account,[183] post office saving account,[184] or national saving certificates,[185] the relevant pass-book or certificates are the necessary indicia. In *Sen v Headley*,[186] the Court of Appeal held that in the case of unregistered land the deeds were the essential indicia of title, and that the passing of dominion over the deeds effected a valid donatio mortis causa of the unregistered land.

In respect of shares in a public company, *Staniland v Willott*[187] suggests that handing the donee an executed share transfer form is sufficient for a valid donatio of the shares, even though the formal transfer of such rights requires the appropriate form of assignment. It is unclear whether mere delivery of a share certificate will suffice, although Australian authority suggests that it will,[188] as does reasoning by analogy from *Sen v Headley*.

A second extension to the concept of the simple conditional gift is that where there is a valid donatio mortis causa of property such as land, or money in a deposit account, where the transfer of dominion is purely symbolic, equity will intervene to compel the personal representatives of the deceased's estate to do whatever is necessary to complete the formal transfer of the property.

(iii) 'The gift must be made under such circumstances as show that the thing is to revert to the donor in case he should recover'

There will be no valid donatio unless the donor only intended the gift to take effect in the event of his death. Otherwise, the gift is simply an ineffective inter vivos transfer.

---

[179] See *Re Wasserberg* [1915] 1 Ch 195; *Re Cole (A Bankrupt)* [1964] Ch 175; *Sen v Headley* [1991] Ch 425, CA.
[180] [1952] 2 All ER 184.   [181] [1991] Fam Law 470.
[182] *Birch v Treasury Solicitor* [1951] Ch 298, CA.
[183] *Re Dillon* (1890) 44 Ch D 76; *Birch v Treasury Solicitor* [1951] Ch 298.
[184] *Re Thompson's Estate* [1928] IR 606; *Re Weston* [1902] 1 Ch 680.
[185] *Darlow v Sparks* [1938] 2 All ER 235.   [186] [1991] Ch 425.   [187] (1852) 3 Mac & G 664.
[188] *Duffcy v Mollica* [1968] 3 NSWR 751. Compare the Irish case of *Mills v Shields (No 2)* [1950] IR 21, where Gavan Duffy P held that delivery of share certificates was not sufficient to constitute a valid donatio of the shares.

Thus, there will be no effective donatio mortis causa if the donor intended the donee to have the property at all events. As Wynn-Parry J said in *Re Lillingston*:

> The gift should be conditional, ie, on the terms that, if the donor should not die, he should be entitled to resume complete dominion of the property the subject matter of the gift.[189]

A donatio will not be invalid merely because the donor knows that he will not recover, and in such cases the intention to make a revocable gift is implied.[190] Where the donatio has been made in contemplation of death from an illness, the gift is automatically revoked by the donor's recovery.[191] The donor may also revoke the gift at any time during his lifetime, for example by retaking dominion over the property,[192] or giving the donee notice of revocation.[193] However, he cannot revoke the gift by will, since his death completes the gift.[194] In *Vallee v Birchwood*,[195] another unregistered land case, the High Court had to consider whether the continued enjoyment of a house by the donor for a further four months after he had transferred the title deeds and keys to the property to the donee was incompatible with the intention to make a valid donatio mortis causa. Deputy Judge Jonthan Gaunt held that enjoyment of the house did not defeat the gift, on the basis that:

> [a] gift by way of *donatio* does not become effective until the death of the donor, so the property remains both in law and equity the property of the donor. There seems to be no reason why acts of continued enjoyment of his own property should be regarded as incompatible with his intention to make an effective gift on his death…The delivery of the deeds would put it out of his power to transfer [the property] and the handing over of the key as well would give the donee access to the house and diminish to some extent the donor's control.[196]

A fourth requirement may be added to the three set out by Lord Russell:[197]

(iv) The property must be capable of forming the subject matter of a donatio mortis causa

Even if the preceding three conditions are satisfied, it has been held that some types of property are not capable of forming the subject matter of a valid donatio mortis causa. A cheque payable to the donor is capable of forming the subject matter of a donatio,[198] but a cheque written by the donor cannot,[199] because it is merely a revocable mandate to his bank which automatically terminates on death. Similarly, the donor's promissory note is incapable of forming the subject matter of a donatio.[200] A conflict of

---

[189] [1952] 2 All ER 184, at 187.
[190] *Wilkes v Allington* [1931] 2 Ch 104; see also *Sen v Headley* [1991] Ch 425, where the gift was made by the donor two days after he had been readmitted to hospital, when he knew he did not have long to live and when there could have been no practical possibility of his ever returning home.
[191] *Gardner v Parker* (1818) 3 Madd 184; *Staniland v Willott* (1852) 3 Mac & G 664; *Keys v Hore* (1879) 13 ILT 58.   [192] *Bunn v Markham* (1816) 7 Taunt 224; *Staniland v Willott* (1852) 3 Mac & G 664.
[193] *Bunn v Markham* (1816) 7 Taunt 224.   [194] *Jones v Selby* (1710) Prec Ch 300.
[195] [2013] EWHC 1449 (Ch).   [196] [2013] EWHC 1449 (Ch), at [27].
[197] *Cain v Moon* [1896] 2 QB 283.   [198] *Re Mead* (1880) LR 15 Ch D 651; *Re Mulroy* [1924] 1 IR 98.
[199] *Re Beaumont* [1902] 1 Ch 886.   [200] *Re Leaper* [1916] 1 Ch 579.

authorities renders it unclear whether shares are capable of forming the subject matter of a donatio. Some cases adopt the view that shares cannot be the subject of a valid donatio,[201] but in *Staniland v Willott*[202] it was held that there could be a valid donatio of shares in a public company. There seems to be no reason in logic or principle why shares should not be able to form the subject matter of a donatio mortis causa.[203]

Following dicta of Lord Eldon in *Duffield v Elwes*,[204] land was traditionally regarded as incapable of forming the subject matter of a valid donatio mortis causa because it was not thought possible to grant dominion to the donee. In *Sen v Headley*,[205] the Court of Appeal held that it was possible to part with dominion over the essential indicia of title of unregistered land, namely the title deeds, and that to refuse to permit a valid donatio of land would create an anomalous exception.[206] Mrs Sen had lived with Mr Hewitt for ten years and had remained very close to him after this. When he was dying he told her that his house, title to which was unregistered, was hers, and he gave her the keys to a steel box which contained the deeds. It was held that in these circumstances a valid donatio had been made in her favour, and she was therefore entitled to compel the administrator of his estate to transfer the legal title of the house into her name. Although the case concerned unregistered land, where title is constituted by the title deeds, there seems no reason why the same principle should not apply to registered land where a land certificate has been issued, particularly as the object of the court was to avoid anomalous exceptions. Although the land certificate to registered land is only evidence of title,[207] it is sometimes treated as the equivalent of the title deeds to unregistered land.[208] However, it is no longer the practice to issue a land certificate, and this will therefore have the effect of preventing a donatio mortis causa of registered land.[209]

(8) **Common law remedies which may be available to the beneficiary of an incompletely constituted trust**

(a) Significance of common law remedies

If a volunteer is unable to get help from equity to enforce the settlor's promise to create a trust, he may instead be entitled to sue the settlor at common law and recover compensatory damages for the failure to constitute the trust. Where damages at common law are available, the measure recoverable will be the quantum of loss suffered in consequence of the settlor's failure to constitute the trust, which will generally be the value

---

[201] *Ward v Turner* (1752) 2 Ves Sen 431 (South Sea annuities); *Moore v Moore* (1874) LR 18 Eq 474 (railway stock); *Re Weston* [1902] 1 Ch 680 (building society shares). [202] (1852) 3 Mac & G 664.

[203] See Samuels 'Donatio Mortis Causa of a Share Certificate' (1966) 30 Conv 189.

[204] (1823) 1 Sim & St 239. See also *Wilkes v Allington* [1931] 2 Ch 104.

[205] [1991] Ch 425; [1991] Conv 307 (Halliwell); (1991) 50 CLJ 404 (Thornely); All ER Rev 1991, p 207 (Clarke); (1991) 1 Carib LR 100 (Kodilinye); (1993) 109 LQR 19 (Baker).

[206] [1991] Ch 425, at 440, per Nourse LJ. [207] Land Registration Act 2002, Sch 10, para 4.

[208] See, for example. Land Registration Act 1925, s 66; *Thames Guaranty Ltd v Campbell* [1985] QB 210, at 233.

[209] See further Roberts 'Donatio mortis causa in a dematerialised world' [2012] Conv 113,

of the promised trust property. Historically, the possibility of obtaining common law damages arose because equity and the common law treated the concept of consideration differently. At common law, a promise to create a trust would be enforceable if it was contained in a covenant (ie a deed)[210] or was accompanied by even nominal consideration. In neither instance would equity treat the agreement as enforceable. Such a contract or covenant might have been entered between the settlor and the intended beneficiaries, or between the settlor and the intended trustees. The ability of volunteer beneficiaries to obtain a remedy at common law has recently been significantly widened by the Contracts (Rights of Third Parties) Act 1999, which has had the effect of abrogating the doctrine of privity of contract. This will prove especially significant where a settlor has covenanted or contracted to create a trust with the intended trustees but not the beneficiaries. The new regime applies to contracts entered into on or after 11 May 2000.[211]

It is important to realize that the beneficiaries' entitlement to claim damages at common law is not a means by which they can constitute the trust, thus circumventing the rule that equity will not assist a volunteer. Any damages recovered are compensation for the fact that no trust was ever created in their favour, and they will receive such damages absolutely and free from any trust. By contrast, where a beneficiary who has given consideration recognized by equity brings a suit, the remedy will normally be to compel the constitution of the trust which will, of course, also work to the advantage of the beneficiaries who have provided no consideration. Whether beneficiaries are in fact able to recover damages for the settlor's breach of covenant will depend on the circumstances of the case.

(b) Common law compensation on or after 11 May 2000

(i) Settlor covenanted or contracted with the beneficiary to create a trust

Where a settlor has entered into a covenant to create a trust with the intended beneficiary, or has entered into a contract with the beneficiary for nominal consideration, the beneficiary will be entitled to sue to recover damages at common law if he fails to fulfil his promise to constitute the trust. As the intended beneficiary is a party to the covenant or contract, there is no difficulty of privity. Such situations will be rare, as most settlors do not enter into contracts with beneficiaries to create trusts.

(ii) Settlor covenanted or contracted with the trustee to create a trust

The Contracts (Rights of Third Parties) Act 1999, s 1(1) provides that a third party is entitled to enforce a term of a contract if it expressly provides that he may, or if it purports to confer a benefit on him. Where a settlor enters into a covenant[212] or contract to create a trust with the intended trustee, the beneficiary will be entitled to sue to recover damages at common law if he fails to fulfil his promise, unless the contract made clear that it was not intended to be enforceable by him.[213] Although

---

[210] See Law of Property (Miscellaneous Provisions) Act 1989, s 1.
[211] Contracts (Rights of Third Parties Act) 1999, s 10(2).   [212] S 7(3).   [213] S 1(2).

s 1(5) provides that a third party is entitled to obtain any remedy that would have been available to him in an action for breach of contract if he had been a party to the contract, the better view appears to be that this does not mean that the beneficiary can obtain specific performance, as the rule that equity will not assist a volunteer has not been abrogated.[214]

(c) Common law compensation where the settlor covenanted to create a trust before 11 May 2000

The Contracts (Rights of Third Parties) Act 1999 does not apply to covenants granted prior to 11 May 2000. The rights of the beneficiaries to enforce such a covenant will continue to be determined by the traditional rules.

(i) Beneficiary was a party to the settlor's covenant to create a trust

If a beneficiary is a party to a settlor's covenant to create a trust in his favour, it is clear from *Cannon v Hartley*[215] that he can recover damages for breach of covenant against the settlor if the latter subsequently fails to constitute the trust. Bernard Hartley executed a covenant on his separation from his wife, to which his wife and daughter were parties. He agreed that he would settle any money or property worth more than £1,000 which he subsequently received on the death of his parents on trust for his daughter. When his parents died, he received a substantial amount of money but refused to transfer it to trustees. Romer J held that although the daughter was a volunteer, and therefore unable to enforce the incompletely constituted trust in equity, she was entitled to receive damages for breach of covenant:

> The plaintiff, although a volunteer, is not only a party to the deed of separation but is also a direct covenantee under the very covenant upon which she is suing. She does not require the assistance of the court to enforce the covenant for she has a legal right herself to enforce it. She is not asking for equitable relief but for damages at common law for breach of covenant.[216]

(ii) Common law compensation where the trustee was party to the settlor's covenant to create a trust

The proposed beneficiary's position is much less certain if the intended trustee of the settlement was a party to the settlor's covenant to create a trust, but he himself was not. The beneficiary cannot sue the settlor for breach in his own right, as he has no privity of contract to do so. Unless the intended trustees hold the benefit of the covenant on trust for him[217] he similarly cannot compel them to bring an action for breach against the settlor. The central question in these cases is whether the intended trustee is able to sue the settlor if he so wishes and, if so, as to the quantum of damages recoverable.

---

[214] Hanbury and Martin, *Modern Equity* (18th edn, 2009), p 762. See also Andrews 'Strangers to Justice No Longer: The Reversal of the Privity Rule under the Contracts (Rights of Third Parties) Act 1999' (2001) 60 CLJ 353.   [215] [1949] Ch 213.

[216] [1949] Ch 213, at 223.

[217] This is referred to as a 'trust of a promise' and is discussed later in this chapter.

It is well established that where a trustee who is party to the settlor's covenant seeks the court's direction whether he should sue, he will be directed not to take proceedings to enforce the covenant. In *Re Pryce*,[218] Eve J directed the trustees of a marriage settlement to take no proceedings to enforce a covenant to settle after-acquired property. In *Re Kay's Settlement Trusts*,[219] Simonds J followed the decision in *Re Pryce* and held that where a spinster had failed to perform her voluntary covenant to settle after-acquired property, the trustees should be directed not to take any proceedings to enforce the covenant by an action for damages for breach. These authorities were approved in *Re Cook's Settlement Trusts*,[220] where Buckley J held that volunteer beneficiaries could not compel the trustees to sue on the settlor's covenant to settle the proceeds of sale of certain paintings, even though other beneficiaries had given consideration. The rationale underlying these decisions is that to allow trustees to recover under the settlor's deed at common law would indirectly assist volunteers who are not entitled to the direct assistance of the court in equity.[221]

If an intended trustee were to decide to sue the settlor on their own initiative, rather than asking the court for a direction, it is debatable whether they would be entitled to recover substantial damages. One view, supported by the Canadian decision of *Re Cavendish Browne's Settlement Trusts*,[222] is that the trustee in such circumstances should be entitled to recover damages equivalent to the value of the property that was to be settled on trust, and hold those damages on trust for the beneficiaries.[223] The case concerned a covenant entered into with the intended trustees to settle land on beneficiaries who were volunteers, and the court held that the trustees were entitled to damages to the value of the land, to be held on trust for the intended beneficiaries.[224]

In the English cases, it has been argued that, as a matter of principle, a covenantee is only entitled to recover damages as compensation for his own personal loss[225] resulting from breach of the covenant to which he was a party. It follows that, as a trustee derives no personal gain from a trust, the personal loss suffered is minimal, so the intended trustee would be entitled to recover only nominal damages from the settlor. Furthermore, even if a trustee were held entitled to recover substantial damages, it has been suggested that he should hold them on a resulting trust for the settlor, rather than for the volunteer beneficiaries.[226] It is suggested that it would be a brave trustee who decided to sue on their own initiative, knowing that the English court would not direct such an action if asked. This perhaps explains why the questions over the action remain unanswered.

---

[218] [1917] 1 Ch 234.   [219] [1939] Ch 329.   [220] [1965] Ch 902.

[221] See *Re Pryce* [1917] 1 Ch 234, at 241, per Eve J.

[222] [1916] WN 341; (1979) 32 CLP 1 (Rickett).

[223] See (1960) 76 LQR 100 (Elliott); (1975) 91 LQR 236 (Barton); [1982] Conv 280 (Friend); [1988] Conv 18 (Goddard).

[224] However, *Re Cavendish Browne's Settlement Trusts* is distinguishable from *Re Pryce*, *Re Kay* and *Re Cook* as it involved a covenant to settle identified specific property rather than after-acquired property.

[225] *Woodar Investment Developments Ltd v Wimpey Construction UK Ltd* [1980] 1 WLR 277; *Panatown Ltd v Alfred McAlpine Construction Ltd* [2000] 4 All ER 97.

[226] Lee 'Public Policy of *Re Cook's Settlement Trusts*' (1969) 85 LQR 213.

(iii) *Common law compensation where the trustees hold the benefit of the settlor's covenant on trust for the beneficiary*

It is accepted that beneficiaries who are not party to the settlor's covenant to settle cannot compel trustees who are parties to take proceedings. However, if the trustees can be shown to hold the 'benefit of the covenant' on trust for the beneficiaries, they can sue in their own right as the beneficiaries of a completely constituted trust of the covenant, and the trustees can either join their action as co-plaintiffs or be joined as co-defendants. Such a trust of the benefit of the covenant is possible because a covenant is a 'chose in action', which is a form of intangible property. Given that it is property, it is capable of forming the subject matter of a trust. It can be held on a completely constituted trust, as no particular formalities are required to vest title to a chose in action in the trustees and beneficiaries. The possibility of a trust of the benefit of a covenant therefore provides a clever device to avoid the restrictive implications of the privity doctrine, which prevents an intended beneficiary suing in his own right. This type of situation is sometimes referred to as the trust of a promise.

The concept of a 'trust of the benefit of a covenant', which enables a beneficiary to enforce a settlor's covenant with the trustees, was accepted by Wigram V-C in the mid-nineteenth-century case, *Fletcher v Fletcher*:

> One question made in argument has been whether there can be a trust of a covenant the benefit of which shall belong to a third party; but I cannot think there is any difficulty in that…The proposition, therefore, that in no case can there be a trust of a covenant is clearly too large, and the real question is whether the relation of trustee and [beneficiary] is established in the present case.[227]

Ellis Fletcher had executed a voluntary covenant to settle £60,000 on trust for his illegitimate sons, John and Jacob, if they survived him. He retained the deed and did not make known its existence either to the trustees with whom it was made or to his sons. The deed was found among his papers after his death. Jacob, who had survived his father and attained the age of 21, sued the executors of his father's estate for £60,000. Wigram V-C held that although Jacob was not a party to the deed himself he was entitled to recover the £60,000 from the executors because the trustees held the benefit of the covenant on trust for him. The legitimacy of the concept of a 'trust of a promise' has been confirmed by the courts in a large number of cases;[228] including *Don King Productions v Warren*,[229] where Lightman J cited the dicta of Lord Shaw in *Lord Strathcona Steamship Co Ltd v Dominion Coal Co Ltd*:

> The scope of the trusts recognized in equity is unlimited. There can be a trust of a chattel, or of a right or obligation under an ordinary legal contract, just as much as a trust of land.[230]

---

[227] (1844) 4 Hare 67.

[228] See *Lloyd's v Harper* (1880) 16 Ch D 290, CA; *Vandepitte v Preferred Accident Assurance Corpn of New York* [1933] AC 70, PC; *Re Schebsman (Decd)* [1944] Ch 83, CA; *Re Cook's Settlement Trusts* [1965] Ch 902; *Swain v Law Society* [1983] 1 AC 598, HL.   [229] [1998] 2 All ER 608.

[230] [1926] AC 108, at 124.

However, while *Fletcher v Fletcher*[231] clearly establishes that the benefit of a covenant may form the subject matter of a trust, such trusts are not commonplace. There is great difficulty is establishing that such a trust has come into existence. There is a marked reluctance to find that such trusts have been created because they are capable of undermining the doctrine of privity of contract. *Fletcher v Fletcher* is open to criticism in that there was no evidence on the facts of an intention to create a trust of the benefit of the covenant. There was no evidence that Fletcher intended to create such a trust, and the trustees and beneficiaries were unaware of the existence of the covenant. How could the trustees be said to be holding the benefit of a covenant, the existence of which they were unaware of, on trust for beneficiaries for whom they did not know they were trustees? In more recent cases the courts have held that a trust of a covenant will only be created by clear express intention. In *Vandepitte v Preferred Accident Insurance Corpn of New York*,[232] the Privy Council held that to establish a trust of the benefit of an insurance contract 'the intention to constitute the trust must be affirmatively proved', and that such an intention could not necessarily be inferred from the words of the policy. There was therefore no intention that the policy holder had any intention to create a trust in favour of the plaintiff. Similarly, in *Re Schebsman*[233] Lord Greene MR held that it was 'not legitimate to import into the contract the idea of a trust when the parties have given no indication that such was their intention'.[234] These cases suggest that a trust of the benefit of a promise will not be implied merely from the fact that a promise has been made between two parties for the benefit of a third. Such a trust will only arise if there is clear evidence of an intention on the part of the parties to the promise to create such a trust.[235] It clearly cannot arise if the contract contains a term prohibiting such a declaration.[236]

One further anomalous restriction on the scope of the concept of a trust of the benefit of a covenant is that it has been held that a covenant to settle future property is incapable of forming the subject matter of a trust. In *Re Cook's Settlement Trusts*[237] Sir Francis Cook covenanted to settle the proceeds of sale of certain pictures sold during his lifetime. This covenant did not create a property right that would have been capable of being the subject matter of an immediate trust, so Buckley J held that no trust of the covenant could have been created:

> this covenant upon its true construction is...an executory contract to settle a particular fund or particular funds of money which at the date of the covenant did not exist and which might never come into existence. It is analogous to a covenant to settle an expectation or to settle after-acquired property. The case, in my judgment, involves the law of contract, not the law of trusts.[238]

---

[231] (1844) 4 Hare 67.   [232] [1933] AC 70.   [233] [1944] Ch 83.   [234] [1944] Ch 83, at 89.
[235] *Swain v Law Society* [1983] 1 AC 598.
[236] *Don King Productions v Warren* [1998] 2 All ER 608, at 632–633.   [237] [1965] Ch 902.
[238] [1965] Ch 902, at 914.

This limitation has been severely criticized,[239] since although the covenant concerns future property, which could not itself form the subject matter of a trust, it is no less a valid chose in action than a covenant to settle existing property. The promise itself is the subject matter of a trust of the benefit of a covenant, not the property to which the promise relates.

The mechanism of a trust of a promise may become of increasingly marginal utility given the requirement of a clearly demonstrated intention to create a trust, which is not something a settlor is often likely to do, and the impact of the enactment of the Contracts (Rights of Third Parties) Act 1999.

4 Formalities required for the creation of trusts

A valid trust may be created either by the self-declaration of the legal owner, or by the transfer of the legal title to trustees upon trust. The trust may be created either inter vivos or by will. In some circumstances, legislation requires the observance of specified formalities to create a valid or enforceable trust.

(1) Inter vivos declarations of trust

(a) Trusts of land

(i) Formalities required

Section 53(1)(b) of the Law of Property Act 1925[240] provides:

> a declaration of a trust respecting any land or any interest therein must be manifested and proved by some writing signed by some person who is able to declare such a trust or by his will.

Formalities are required for declarations of trusts of land to prevent the disputes and inconvenience which would result if purely oral declarations were allowed. In essence s 53(1)(b) imposes an evidential safeguard. It is important to note that a purported oral declaration of a trust of land is not void, but only unenforceable.[241] The requirement of writing applies whether the trust is created by the land owner declaring himself trustee or transferring the land to trustees. It is not necessary that the actual declaration of the trust be made in writing, nor need the writing which evidences the declaration be contemporaneous with the declaration of the trust.[242] However, the written evidence must contain all the material terms of the trust, namely the beneficiaries, the trust

---

[239] (1965) 24 CLJ 46 (Jones); (1969) 85 LQR 213 (Lee); (1979) 32 CLP 1 and (1981) 34 CLP 189 (Rickett); (1982) 98 LQR 17 (Feltham); [1982] Conv 280 (Friend); [1982] Conv 352 (Smith).

[240] Re-enacting the Statute of Frauds 1677, s 7.

[241] *Gardner v Rowe* (1828) 5 Russ 258; *Gissing v Gissing* [1969] 2 Ch 85, at 99; *Cowcher v Cowcher* [1972] 1 WLR 425, at 430–431; *Midland Bank plc v Dobson* [1986] 1 FLR 171, at 175.

[242] *Forster v Hale* (1798) 3 Ves 696; *Rochefoucauld v Boustead* [1897] 1 Ch 196.

property, and the nature of the trust.[243] Unlike the parallel provision s 53(1)(c), s 53(1)(b) will not be satisfied if the writing was signed by an agent. However, if the land is transferred subject to a trust, the transferee of the land may sign the written evidence of the declaration.[244]

(ii) The rule in Rochefoucauld v Boustead

Although s 53(1)(b) renders an orally declared trust of land unenforceable in the absence of substantiating writing, this requirement is not always strictly enforced.[245] The courts have held that where insistence upon writing would allow the statute to be used as 'an instrument of fraud' the trust will be enforced, irrespective of the lack of writing. A fraud arises if a person to whom land was conveyed, subject to an oral understanding that it was to be held on trust, seeks to deny the trust, and claims to be absolutely entitled to the land because the requisite formalities are lacking. In *Rochefoucauld v Boustead*[246] the Comtesse de la Rochefoucauld owned the Delmar Estates in Ceylon, subject to a mortgage of £25,000. The land was sold by the mortgagee to the defendant, who was intended to take as trustee for the Comtesse. He subsequently mortgaged the land for a further £70,000 without her consent. The Comtesse sought a declaration that the defendant had acquired the land subject to a trust in her favour. The defendant claimed that the alleged trust had not been proved by any writing signed by him, as required by the Statute of Frauds, s 7.[247] The Court of Appeal held that, despite the lack of formalities compliant with the statutory provision, evidence other than writing signed by the defendant would be admitted to prove the trust, since otherwise the defendant would be committing a fraud against the Comtesse. The principle was stated by Lindley LJ:

> the Statute of Frauds does not prevent the proof of a fraud; and it is a fraud on the part of a person to whom land is conveyed as a trustee, and who knows it was so conveyed, to deny the trust and claim the land himself. Consequently, notwithstanding the statute, it is competent for a person claiming land conveyed to another to prove by parol evidence that it was so conveyed upon trust for the claimant, and that the grantee, knowing the facts, is denying the trust and relying upon the form and conveyance and the statute, in order to keep the land himself.[248]

Although the principle applies where a third party seeks to deny that he received the legal title to land as a trustee, it is less likely that a fraud will be committed if the owner of land orally declares himself a trustee in favour of a volunteer beneficiary. In such a case there is no justification for finding that a fraud had been perpetrated against the purported beneficiary.

---

[243] *Smith v Matthews* (1861) 3 De GF & J 139; *Rochefoucauld v Boustead* [1897] 1 Ch 196.

[244] *Gardner v Rowe* (1828) 5 Russ 258; *Smith v Matthews* (1861) 3 De GF & J 139.

[245] See Youdan 'Formalities for Trusts of Land, and the Doctrine in *Rochefoucauld v Boustead*' [1984] CLJ 306; McFarlane 'Constructive Trusts Arising on a Receipt of Property *Sub Conditione*' (2004) 120 LQR 667. [246] [1897] 1 Ch 196.

[247] Predecessor of s 53(1)(b) of the Law of Property Act 1925. [248] [1897] 1 Ch 196, at 206.

The principle adopted in *Rochefoucauld v Boustead* has the merit of justice, but clearly runs contrary to the wording of the statute. Subsequent cases have tended to treat the principle as an example of where a constructive trust is imposed, so that the intended trustee cannot rely on the absence of writing to deny the trust because he is already a constructive trustee of the land for the intended beneficiary.[249] In *Bannister v Bannister*, for example, Scott LJ described the principle as:

> the equitable principle on which a constructive trust is raised against a person who insists on the absolute character of a conveyance to himself for the purpose of defeating a beneficial interest.[250]

This analysis of the rule in *Rochefoucauld v Boustead* has the attraction of not seeming to contradict the wording of s 53(1)(b) of the Law of Property Act 1925, as s 53(2) provides that formalities are not required for the creation of 'resulting, implied or constructive trusts'. Therefore, if a constructive trust of the land can be found, the court will not be seen to be enforcing a trust that the clear words of s 53(1)(b) render unenforceable. However, in *Rochefoucauld v Boustead*[251] itself, the Court of Appeal was of the view that an express trust was being enforced, despite the lack of statutory formalities. Lindley LJ stated that 'the trust which the plaintiff has established is clearly an express trust'. Given this, it seems more satisfactory to regard *Rochefoucauld v Boustead* as authority for the proposition that the court will enforce an express trust of land, despite an absence of writing, where to do otherwise would be to allow the statute to facilitate a fraud.

(b) Trusts of personal property

Section 53(1)(b) has no application to declarations of trusts of personal property. An absolute owner may orally declare himself the trustee of such property without the need for any further formalities.[252]

(c) Declaration of a sub-trust

Where property is already held on trust, the beneficiary enjoys an immediate proprietary interest in the trust property. Since equitable proprietary interests are themselves capable of forming the subject matter of a trust, the beneficiary is entitled to declare himself a trustee of his interest under the trust, creating a sub-trust. If the property held under the head trust is land, any declaration of a sub-trust will only be enforceable by the sub-beneficiary if it is evidenced in writing in compliance with s 53(1)(b), since the trust property consists of an 'interest in land'. If the property held under the head trust is personalty, formalities will only be required to create the sub-trust if s 53(1)(c) applies. This section stipulates that dispositions of subsisting equitable interests can only be made in writing. The central question is whether a declaration of a sub-trust is to be characterized as effecting a 'disposition' of the original beneficiary's equitable

---

[249] *Bannister v Bannister* [1948] 2 All ER 133; *Neale v Willis* (1968) 19 P & CR 836; *Re Densham (A Bankrupt)* [1975] 1 WLR 1519.   [250] [1948] 2 All ER 133.
[251] [1897] 1 Ch 196.
[252] See, for example, *Re Kayford Ltd* [1975] 1 WLR 279; *Paul v Constance* [1977] 1 WLR 527, CA.

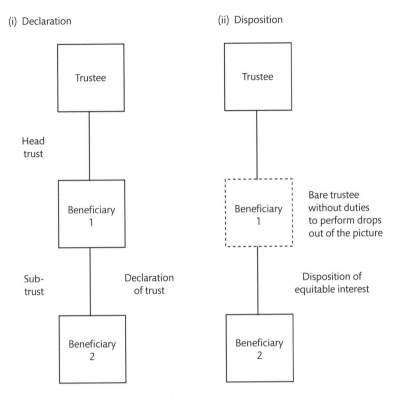

Figure 7.5 The declaration of a 'sub-trust'

interest under the head trust. If so, any purported declaration which is not effected in writing will be of no effect. In addressing this question, it seems that the courts have drawn a distinction between genuine declarations of a sub-trust, and transactions which, though in the form of a declaration of sub-trust, are in substance a disposition of the beneficiary's equitable interest. If the sub-trust declared is a bare trust,[253] so that the sub-trustee has no active duties to perform because the sub-beneficiary's entitlement to the trust property is identical to his own, he will be regarded as having effected a disposition of his interest. The sub-trust would merely amount to a duplication of the head-trustee's duties, so the sub-trustee is said to drop out of the picture and the head trustee holds the property on trust for the newly declared beneficiary (see Figure 7.5). This principle was recognized in *Grainge v Wilberforce*.[254] More significantly, it was accepted in *Grey v IRC*,[255] where Upjohn J used the language of a sub-trustee 'disappearing from the picture'[256] when a sub-trust is declared. Where a beneficiary who declares a sub-trust 'drops out of the picture' in this manner, the reality of the transaction is that he has effected a disposition of his equitable interest under the trust to the

---

[253] Bare trusts are discussed in Chapters 15 and 19.
[254] (1889) 5 TLR 436. See also: *Re Lashmar* [1891] 1 Ch 258, CA; Law Com No 260, *Trustees' Powers and Duties* (1999), para 5.4, fn 3. [255] [1958] Ch 375.
[256] [1958] Ch 375, at 382, per Upjohn J.

intended sub-beneficiary, and therefore the transaction will be ineffective unless the declaration is effected in writing.

In contrast, if an intended sub-trustee has active duties to perform under the sub-trust, he does not drop out of the picture and there is no disposition. Instead, a genuine sub-trust arises. This would be the case, for example, if a beneficiary created a life-interest of his interest under the trust in favour of a sub-beneficiary. Provided that the trust property is not land, in such circumstances there is no need for the declaration to be made in writing under s 53(1)(c). A purely oral declaration of the sub-trust will be sufficient.[257]

(2) **Declarations of trusts by will**

A valid declaration of trust can be made by will for any property, whether land or personalty.[258] The requirements of a valid will are set out in s 9 of the Wills Act 1837. A will is only valid if it is made in writing,[259] which is signed by the testator (or by some other person acting at his direction in his presence)[260] in the presence of two witnesses, who themselves attest and sign the will (or acknowledge their signature) in the presence of the testator.[261]

(3) **Dispositions of subsisting equitable interests**

(a) **The requirement of writing**

It has already been noted in the context of the difficulties associated with the declaration of sub-trusts discussed earlier that a different formality requirement applies to dispositions of existing equitable interests. Section 53(1)(c) of the Law of Property Act 1925 provides that:

> a disposition of an equitable interest or trust subsisting at the time of the disposition must be in writing signed by the person disposing of the same, or by his agent thereunto lawfully authorised in writing or by will.

This section applies whenever the beneficiary of a trust attempts to transfer his equitable interest in the trust property to someone else. In *Vandervell v IRC*, Lord Upjohn provided an explanation of why formalities are required to effect such dispositions of a beneficiary's interest under a trust:

> the object of the section, as was the object of the old Statute of Frauds, is to prevent hidden oral transactions in equitable interests in fraud of those truly entitled, and making it difficult, if not impossible, for the trustees to ascertain who are in truth his beneficiaries.[262]

It is questionable whether it is truly correct that the requirement of writing prevents hidden transactions, as there is no obligation on the part of the transferor or transferee to bring the transfer to the attention of the trustees.[263] Writing is required

---

[257] Green 'Grey, Oughtred and Vandervell—A Contextual Reappraisal' (1984) 47 MLR 385.
[258] S 53(1)(b) and (c).   [259] S 9(a).   [260] S 9(a).   [261] S 9(c) and (d).
[262] [1967] 2 AC 291, at 311.   [263] See Harris (1975) 38 MLR 557.

because, as in the case of other forms of intangible property such as copyrights, there is no other means of effecting a transfer, as the property cannot be physically possessed or delivered. Unlike s 53(1)(b), where the effect of a lack of written evidence is merely to render an oral declaration of a trust of land unenforceable, a failure to comply with s 53(1)(c) renders the purported disposition void.[264] As such, the transferee-beneficiary will have failed to divest himself of his equitable interest in the trust property.

The following aspects of the requirement deserve attention.

(i) 'Disposition'

Section 53(1)(c) only applies to dispositions of subsisting equitable interests. It therefore has no application to declarations of trust, otherwise s 53(1)(b) would be redundant in requiring a declaration of a trust of land to be evidenced in writing. It is clear that an assignment of a subsisting equitable interest must be made in writing, as was held in *Re Danish Bacon Co Ltd Staff Pension Fund Trusts*.[265] Nevertheless, the meaning of the term 'disposition' has been the subject of much debate, as beneficiaries have sought to avoid compliance with the requirement of writing for tax reasons. The tax in question in many of the cases before the courts was ad valorem stamp duty.[266] This tax, which was calculated as a proportion of the value of the subsisting equitable interest being transferred, was payable if and only if the equitable interest was transferred in writing. Stamp duty was levied not on the transaction, but on a written document of transfer. Accordingly, if the transfer could be effected orally, and was later evidenced in writing, no tax was payable. The fact that only a 'disposition' of a subsisting equitable interest was required to be in writing, and the fact that no statutory definition of 'disposition' was provided in the Law of Property Act 1925, led to many ingenious methods which sought to effect transfers of interest without them being classed as 'dispositions' required to be in writing and subject to tax.[267]

The scope of a 'disposition' was considered by the House of Lords in *Grey v IRC* (see Figure 7.6),[268] where it was held that it should be given its 'natural meaning'.[269] The appellants held 18,000 shares on a bare trust as nominees for Mr Hunter. On 18 February 1955, Hunter orally directed them to henceforth hold the shares under six trusts, of 3,000 shares each, in favour of his grandchildren. On 25 March, the trustees executed a declaration of trust to that effect. The central question was whether the oral direction of 18 February was effective to transfer the equitable interest in the shares to the grandchildren. The Revenue argued that without writing the oral direction was void and ineffective to transfer the equitable interest in the shares. The trustees responded that the transaction did not require a written instrument because there

[264] See *Grey v IRC* [1960] AC 1; *Oughtred v IRC* [1960] AC 206.   [265] [1971] 1 WLR 248.
[266] Finance Act 1910, s 74.
[267] Stamp duty was abolished by the Finance Act 2003 in respect of shares, though stamp duty land tax was introduced in respect of land. The incentive to arrange matters to be effected without writing is now greatly reduced.
[268] [1960] AC 1; (1960) CLJ 31 (Thornely); see also *Re Danish Bacon Co Ltd Staff Pension Fund Trusts* [1971] 1 WLR 248, at 254, per Megarry J; *Halley v The Law Society* [2003] WTLR 845.
[269] [1960] AC 1, at 13, 15, per Lord Simmonds.

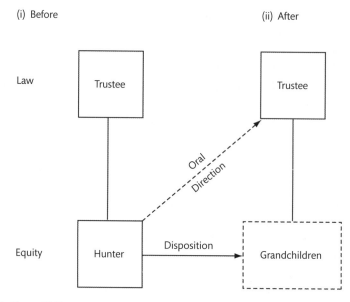

Figure 7.6 *Grey v IRC*

had been no 'disposition' within the meaning of s 53(1)(c). They alleged that the Law of Property Act 1925 was merely a consolidating act, and that the word 'disposition' should be given no wider meaning than that accorded to the words 'grants and assignments' in the Statute of Frauds.[270] The House of Lords rejected this argument and held that the word 'disposition' should be given its natural meaning, in which case the oral direction to the trustees had been a disposition and was void and ineffective to transfer the equitable interest in the shares to the children. Lord Radcliffe stated:

> if there is nothing more in this appeal than the short question whether the oral direction that Mr Hunter gave to his trustees on February 18th 1955 amounted in any ordinary sense to a 'disposition of an equitable interest or trust subsisting at the time of the disposition', I do not feel any doubt as to my answer. I think that it did. Whether we describe what happened in technical or in more general terms the full equitable interest in the 18,000 shares concerned, which at that time was his, was…diverted by his direction from his ownership into the beneficial ownership of [his grandchildren]…[271]

As the oral directions of 18 February were ineffective because of the absence of writing, the transfer of the equitable interest in the shares had only been effected by the deed executed on 25 March. This written declaration was instead the disposition and therefore liable to ad valorem stamp duty. It is worth considering whether the decision in this case might have been different if the spectre of illegitimate tax avoidance had not haunted the minds of their Lordships. This was not a case where it could be suggested that there was a hidden oral transaction which could give rise to a fraud.

---

[270] Statute of Frauds 1677, s 9.   [271] [1960] AC 1, at 15.

All parties concerned were aware from the oral direction of the proposed change of ownership.

Hunter may have dropped out of the picture, but the trustees and Hunter were aware of this.

A disclaimer of an equitable interest will not be regarded as a 'disposition' requiring writing,[272] whereas a surrender of an equitable interest is a disposition and will fall within the ambit of s 53(1)(c).[273]

(ii) Of an equitable interest or trust subsisting at the time of the disposition

Section 53(1)(c) only applies to beneficial interests which actually exist at the date of the disposition. In *Re Danish Bacon Co Ltd*,[274] an employee had nominated someone to receive pension benefits if he died in pensionable service. Megarry J suggested that in these circumstances s 53(1)(c) did not apply because the employee had been dealing with something that could never be his. He had no subsisting equitable interest in the benefits he was allocating.

(iii) In writing

Unlike s 53(1)(b), which only requires that a declaration of trust be evidenced in writing, s 53(1)(c) requires that a disposition actually be made in writing. This writing must obviously be contemporaneous with the intended disposition, although the disposition may be found in two or more separate documents, provided they are sufficiently connected.[275] The requirements of writing and signing may be satisfied by an electronic document.[276] This will be important where, for example, shares are held in trust and are traded electronically.

(iv) Signed by the person disposing of the same or his agent

Again, in contrast to s 53(1)(b), the written instrument effecting a disposition need not be personally signed by the beneficiary or other person disposing of the equitable interest. It will be effective if signed by his lawfully authorized agent (such as the trustees in *Grey v IRC*).

(v) By will

A disposition of a subsisting equitable interest may be effected by will. The requirements of a valid will are considered in Chapter 13.

(b) Exceptions to s 53(1)(c)

Although the requirement of writing under s 53(1)(c) appears comprehensive, in a number of situations the courts have concluded that writing was not required to effect

---

[272] *Re Paradise Motor Co Ltd* [1968] 1 WLR 1125.

[273] See *Newlon Housing Trust v Al-Sulaimen* [1999] 1 AC 313 in the context of Matrimonial Causes Act 1973, s 37.   [274] [1971] 1 WLR 248.

[275] *Re Danish Bacon Co Ltd Staff Pension Fund Trusts* [1971] 1 WLR 248, at 254–255.

[276] See Electronic Communications Act 2000, s 8; Pt 3 of the Advice from the Law Commission, *Electronic Commerce: Formal Requirements in Commercial Transactions* (2001).

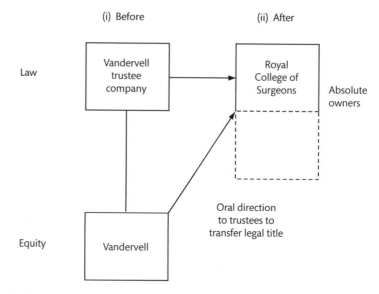

Figure 7.7 *Vandervell v IRC*

a transaction which was in substance a disposition of an equitable interest. These cases have largely arisen in the context of taxation, where, as we have seen, transferees have sought to avoid stamp duty by effecting transfers of their equitable interest without using a written instrument that will attract duty. In some cases, the courts have held that writing was not necessary to effect the transfer, but generally they have also found that tax remained payable.

The cases suggest that writing will not be required to effect a transfer of a subsisting beneficial interest in the following circumstances.

(i) The beneficiary of a bare trust directs the trustees to transfer the legal title

In *Vandervell v IRC*,[277] the House of Lords held that s 53(1)(c) did not have to be satisfied where a beneficiary with a subsisting equitable interest under a bare trust directed the trustees to transfer the legal title to a third party and the transaction was completed (see Figure 7.7). The facts are complicated but important. Mr Vandervell was the sole beneficiary of a bare trust of shares in his company, Vandervell Products Ltd, of which Vandervell Trustees Ltd was the trustee. He decided to endow a chair of pharmacology at the Royal College of Surgeons. At the time income tax (surtax) rates were very high and there was no tax relief for gifts to charity. Mr Vandervell wished to save tax on his gift. His scheme was to transfer shares in his company to the Royal College of Surgeons, and to fund the new professorship by declaring a sufficiently large dividend on the shares. He therefore directed the trustee company to execute a share transfer form for the shares and to pass it to him, leaving the name of

---

[277] [1967] 2 AC 291; (1966) 24 CLJ 19 (Jones); (1967) 31 Conv (NS) 175 (Spencer); (1967) 30 MLR 461 (Strauss); (1975) 38 MLR 557 (Harris). Nolan has argued that the decision can be explained on the basis of overreaching: '*Vandervell v IRC*; A Case of Overreaching' [2002] 61 CLJ 169.

the transferee blank. The trustees duly completed the transfer form and handed it to Mr Vandervell, who entered the name of the Royal College of Surgeons as transferee. The College was then registered as the owner of the shares on the company share register. In return for the transfer of the shares, the college granted the trustees an option to repurchase the shares for £5,000. Dividends of some £250,000 were subsequently declared on the shares to provide the endowment for the chair. The Revenue claimed that Mr Vandervell was liable to pay surtax on these dividends, arguing that the transaction amounted to a settlement of property in which the settlor had not absolutely divested himself of his interest in the property.[278] One ground of the Revenue's case was that Vandervell had failed to divest himself of his equitable interest in the shares because the disposition had not been effected in writing.

Addressing this argument, the House of Lords held that, in the circumstances, writing had not been necessary to effect a transfer of Vandervell's equitable interest in the shares to the college. As the beneficiary of a bare trust he was entitled to direct the trustee to transfer the legal title to the trust property, and there was no need for a separate disposition to transfer the equitable title. As Lord Wilberforce said: 'No separate transfer... of the equitable interest ever came to or needed to be made and there is no room for the operation of the subsection.'[279] The rationale was more fully explained by Lord Upjohn:

> I cannot agree...that prima facie a transfer of the legal estate carries with it the absolute beneficial interest in the property transferred; this plainly is not so, e.g., the transfer may be on a change of trustee; it is a matter of intention in each case. But if the intention of the beneficial owner in directing the trustee to transfer the legal estate to X is that X should be the beneficial owner I can see no reason for any further document or further words in the document assigning the legal estate also expressly transferring the beneficial interest; the greater includes the less. X may be wise to secure some evidence that the beneficial owner intended him to take the beneficial interest in case his beneficial title is challenged at a later date but it certainly cannot, in my opinion, be a statutory requirement that to effect its passing there must be some writing under section 53(1)(c).[280]

He also held that a transfer without writing in such circumstances would not offend against the policy underlying the formality requirement noted earlier, namely to prevent hidden oral transactions in equitable interests in fraud of those truly entitled and which might make it difficult or impossible for the trustees to ascertain their beneficiaries:

> when the beneficial owner owns the whole beneficial estate and is in a position to give directions to his bare trustee with regard to the legal as well as the equitable estate there can be no possible ground for invoking the section where the beneficial owner wants to deal with the legal estate as well as the equitable estate.[281]

This does make perfect sense, as in this situation, the trust itself is coming to an end, as both Vandervell and his trustees dropped out of the picture. Had it not been for

---

[278] Income Tax Act 1952, Pt XVIII.   [279] [1967] 2 AC 291, at 330.
[280] [1967] 2 AC 291, at 311.   [281] [1967] 2 AC 291, at 311.

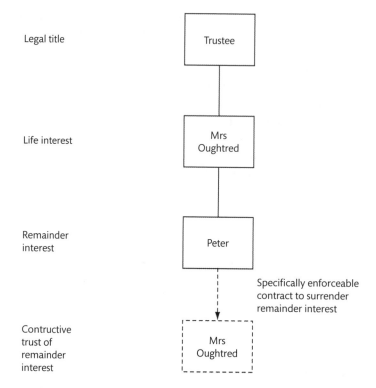

Figure 7.8 *Oughtred v IRC*

the option to repurchase the shares, Vandervell would have had no rights to recover any interest in the shares, as the Royal College of Surgeons were the outright owners in law and equity of the shares. This dealt with the issue of formalities under s 53(1)(c). Nevertheless, while Vandervell was able to avoid ad valorem stamp duty on the transfer of his equitable interest in the shares, the majority of the House of Lords went on to find Vandervell liable to surtax on the dividends declared. They held that the option to repurchase the shares granted by the College to the trustee company was, in the absence of an express declaration of trust, held on an automatic resulting trust for Vandervell himself.[282] Since he was the beneficiary of the option he had failed to fully divest himself of all interest in the shares, thus attracting liability to surtax.

(ii) A specifically enforceable contract for the transfer of the subsisting equitable interest

Where a beneficiary enters a specifically enforceable contract to transfer a subsisting equitable interest under a trust, that interest passes to the intended transferee immediately on the making of the contract by means of a constructive trust. Since the transferee obtains the equitable interest by means of the constructive trust arising from the contract, there is no need for further writing under s 53(1)(c). In *Oughtred v IRC*,[283] shares in a private company were held on trust for Mrs Oughtred for life with

---

[282] For a discussion of automatic resulting trusts, see Chapter 8.   [283] [1960] AC 206.

remainder to her son, Peter (see Figure 7.8). On 18 June, they entered an oral contract in which Peter agreed to release his interest in the shares subject to the settlement, so that his mother would be absolutely entitled to them, in return for which she would transfer 72,700 shares, of which she was already the absolute owner, to nominees for him. A deed of release was executed on 26 June. The central question before the House of Lords was whether ad valorem stamp duty was payable on this deed, which depended on whether the deed was a 'transfer on sale' within the provisions of the Stamp Act 1891.[284] The Oughtreds argued that the deed was not a 'transfer on sale' because the equitable remainder interest in the shares had passed to Mrs Oughtred by virtue of the contract to transfer, since, from the moment of the agreement, Peter held his interest on constructive trust. The majority of the House of Lords[285] held that irrespective of any constructive trust the deed of 26 June was a 'transfer on sale' for the purposes of the Stamp Act, and that stamp duty was therefore payable.[286] However, Upjohn J at first instance, and Lord Radcliffe in the House of Lords, took the view that the oral contract had given rise to a constructive trust which effected a transfer of the remainder interest in the shares to Mrs Oughtred without the need for further writing. Lord Radcliffe explained:

> The reasoning of the whole matter, as I see it, is as follows: On June 18 1956 the son owned an equitable reversionary interest in the settled shares: by his oral agreement of that date he created in his mother an equitable interest in his reversion, since the subject-matter of the agreement was property of which specific performance would normally be decreed by the court. He thus became a trustee for her of that interest sub modo: having regard to subsection (2) of section 53 Law of Property Act 1925, subsection (1) of that section did not operate to prevent that trusteeship arising by operation of law...[287]

There has been some question whether Lord Radcliffe's comments establish that a specifically enforceable contract to transfer a subsisting equitable interest passes the interest by way of a constructive trust without the need for further writing, because the other members of the House of Lords did not express an opinion. However, his approach seems to have been adopted as correct in subsequent cases. It was accepted by Megarry J in *Re Holt's Settlement*[288] and by the Court of Appeal in *Neville v Wilson*.[289] This case concerned a trust of 120 shares in a company (U Ltd), which were held by the directors of the company as nominees for a separate family company (J Ltd). In 1969 J Ltd had been struck off the register because it had become defunct. It was claimed that in 1969 an oral agreement had been reached between the shareholders of J Ltd that the assets of the company should be divided among the shareholders rateably. The

---

[284] Stamp Act 1891, s 54, Sch 1. Note that stamp duty was abolished by the Finance Act 2003.
[285] With the exception of Lord Denning.
[286] Per Lords Keith, Denning and Jenkins, Lords Radcliffe and Cohen dissenting.
[287] [1960] AC 206, at 227.
[288] [1969] 1 Ch 100. See *DHN Food Distributors Ltd v London Borough of Tower Hamlets* [1976] 3 All ER 462 (1977) 93 LQR 170 (Sugarman and Webb); *Chinn v Collins (Inspector of Taxes)* [1981] 1 All ER 189, HL.
[289] [1997] Ch 144; (1996) 55 CLJ 436 (Nolan); [1996] Conv 368 (Thompson); (1997) 113 LQR 213 (Milne). See also *Bishop Square Ltd v IRC* (1999) 78 P & CR 169, where the Court of Appeal applied *Oughtred v IRC* to a very similar fact situation.

central question was whether this oral agreement gave rise to a constructive trust of the 120 shares in favour of the shareholders of J Ltd or whether it was void for failure to comply with the requirements of s 53(1)(c). If no such constructive trust had arisen, the shares would pass to the Crown as bona vacantia. The Court of Appeal held that the oral agreement of the shareholders had produced a constructive trust of the shares, so that they were held by the directors of U Ltd on behalf of the shareholders of J Ltd. Nourse LJ explained:

> The simple view of the present case is that the effect of each individual agreement was to constitute the shareholder an implied or constructive trustee for the other shareholders, so that the requirement for writing contained in sub-s (1)(c) of s 53 was dispensed with by sub-s (2). That was the view taken by Upjohn J at first instance and by Lord Radcliffe in the House of Lords in *Oughtred v IRC*…So far as it is material to the present case, what sub-s (2) says is that subs-s (1)(c) does not affect the creation or operation of implied or constructive trusts. Just as in *Oughtred v IRC* the son's oral agreement created a constructive trust in favour of the mother, so here each shareholder's oral or implied agreement created an implied or constructive trust in favour of the other shareholders. Why then should sub-s (2) not apply? No convincing reason was suggested in argument and none has occurred to us since. Moreover, to deny its application in this case would be to restrict the effect of the general words when no restriction is called for, and to lay the ground for fine distinctions in the future. With all the respect which is due to those who have thought to the contrary, we hold that sub-s (2) applies to an agreement such as we have in this case.

Following *Neville v Wilson*, it seems clear that there is a general principle that where a subsisting equitable interest is the subject of an oral contract to transfer which gives rise to a constructive trust, there is no need for further writing in satisfaction of s 53(1)(c) because the constructive trust itself effects the disposition of the subsisting equitable interest to the transferee. However, in practice this possibility will be of relatively limited scope. It will only apply to oral contracts which are specifically enforceable. While contracts to transfer interests in land are specifically enforceable, giving rise to a constructive trust, there is no possibility of an oral contract to transfer a subsisting equitable interest under a trust of land avoiding formality provisions altogether, because the contract itself must be in writing.[290] In the case of personal property, contracts are not specifically enforceable unless the subject matter of the contract is unique because no market substitute is available. For example, a contract to transfer shares in a public company is not usually thought to give rise to a constructive trust.[291] In *Oughtred v IRC*,[292] the contract was specifically enforceable because the shares were in a private company and were not freely available in the market.

---

[290] Law of Property (Miscellaneous Provisions) Act 1989, s 2.

[291] See, however, *Chinn v Collins (Inspector of Taxes)* [1981] AC 533, which provides some authority that even in the case of shares in a public company a constructive trust will arise. Lord Wilberforce considered the effect of a contract to transfer the equitable interest in shares in a public company quoted on the London Stock Exchange which were held on trust by a nominee. He regarded the agreement as giving rise to a constructive trust so that dealings with the equitable interest did not require formalities. He seemed to regard it as irrelevant whether the contract would have been specifically enforceable. However, *Oughtred v IRC* was not cited.   [292] [1960] AC 206.

(iii) Extinction of a subsisting equitable interest under a resulting trust

It further seems that there is no need for writing in satisfaction of s 53(1)(c) if the act of a third party has the effect of extinguishing a subsisting equitable interest which has arisen under an automatic resulting trust. It has already been seen how, in *Vandervell v IRC*,[293] Mr Vandervell failed to divest himself absolutely of his interest in shares transferred to the Royal College of Surgeons because the option to repurchase was held on resulting trust for him by the Vandervell Trustee Company. The trustee company subsequently exercised this option using money they held on other trusts for Vandervell's children. They then informed the Revenue that they held the re-acquired shares on trust for the children, and all dividends deriving from those shares were paid to the children's settlement. In *Re Vandervell's Trusts (No 2)* (see Figure 7.9),[294] the Revenue claimed that Vandervell was liable to pay surtax on these dividends as well, on the grounds that he had still not divested himself absolutely of his interest in the shares. Their argument that there had been no effective declaration of trust in favour of the children was accepted by Megarry J, at first instance, but rejected by the Court of Appeal, which held that the conduct of the trustees was sufficient to amount to a declaration of trust in favour of the children. The Revenue further argued that Vandervell had never effectually disposed of his equitable interest under the resulting trust of the option, because he had never done so in writing as required by s 53(1)(c). The Court of Appeal also rejected this argument, holding that there had been no need of a written instrument to extinguish Vandervell's resulting trust interest. Lord Denning MR based his conclusion on the nature and function of the resulting trust:

> A resulting trust for the settlor is born and dies without any writing at all. It comes into existence whenever there is a gap in the beneficial ownership. It ceases to exist whenever that gap is filled by someone becoming beneficially entitled. As soon as the gap is filled by the creation or declaration of a valid trust, the resulting trust comes to an end. In this case, before the option was exercised, there was a gap in the beneficial ownership. So there was a resulting trust for Mr Vandervell. But as soon as the option was exercised and the shares registered in the trustee's name, there was created a valid trust of the shares in favour of the children's settlement...[295]

Lawton LJ took the view that the declaration of the trust of the shares in favour of the children's settlement had the effect of extinguishing Vandervell's interest under the resulting trust of the option. An extinction was not a 'disposition' and therefore writing was not required:

> The exercise of the option and the transfer of the shares to the trustee company necessarily put an end to the resulting trust of the option. There could not be a resulting trust of a chose in action which was no more. The only reason why there ever had been a resulting trust of the option was the rule that the beneficial interest in property must be held for some one if the legal owner is not entitled to it. The legal but not the beneficial interest in the option had vested in the trustee company. The beneficial interest had to be held for some one and as the trustee company had declared no trusts of the option, the only

---

[293] [1967] 2 AC 291.   [294] [1974] Ch 269; (1975) 38 MLR 557 (Harris).   [295] [1974] Ch 269, at 320.

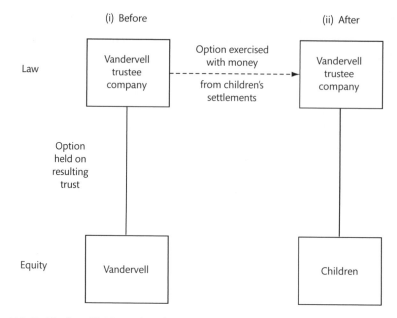

Figure 7.9 *Re Vandervell's Trusts (No 2)*

possible beneficiary was Mr Vandervell. Once the trustee company took a transfer of the shares the position was very different. The legal title to them was vested in the trustee company and by reason of the facts and circumstances to which I have already referred it held the beneficial interest for the trusts of the children's settlement. There was no gap between the legal and beneficial interests and in consequence no need for a resulting trust in favour of Mr Vandervell to fill it. Neither the extinction of the resulting trust of the option resulting from its exercise nor the creation of a beneficial interest in the shares by the declaration of trust amounted to a disposition of an equitable interest or trust within the meaning of sections 53(1)(c) and 205(1)(ii) of the Law of Property Act 1925.[296]

The precise impact of the decision in *Re Vandervell's Trusts (No 2)*[297] is open to question, as is the reasoning within it. It is doubtful whether, in reality, the acts of the trustee company were of themselves sufficient to divest Vandervell of his resulting trust of the option. As Megarry J had commented at first instance:

> That issue is, in essence, whether trustees who hold an option on trust for X will hold the shares obtained by exercising that option on trust for Y merely because they used Y's money in exercising the option. Authority apart, my answer would be an unhesitating no. The option belongs to X beneficially, and the money merely exercises rights which belong to X. Let the shares be worth £50,000 so then an option to purchase those shares for £5,000 is worth £45,000, and it will be at once seen what a monstrous result would be produced by allowing trustees to divert from their beneficiary X the benefits of what they hold for him merely because they used Y's money instead of X's.

---

[296] [1974] Ch 269, at 326.   [297] [1974] Ch 269.

More significantly, it is questionable whether the mere fact that the beneficial interest in the option arose under a resulting trust should provide a justification for the
inapplicability of s 53(1)(c). There is no conceptual imperative for treating a disposition of a subsisting equitable interest which has arisen by way of a resulting trust any
differently from a disposition of an interest arising under an express trust. The court's
reasoning that the resulting trust is somehow eliminated by the act of the trustee identifying new beneficiaries is spurious. While it is true that the original resulting trust
arose because Vandervell had failed to specify who was to be the beneficial owner of the
option, the trust is only a 'resulting trust' to the extent that it was not expressly created,
and this characterization should not colour its nature for the whole of its existence. The
prime duty of a trustee, whether of a bare or active trust, is to preserve the trust fund for
the beneficiary. The beneficiary's interest cannot be transferred to different beneficiaries by the mere act of the trustees without assignment by the beneficiary, otherwise the
trustee would be able to dispose of the beneficial interests under the trust without reference to the beneficiary. For example, if two friends (X and Y) contributed equally to the
purchase of shares valued at £100,000 acquired in the name of X alone, surely X should
not be able to eliminate Y's beneficial half-interest under a resulting trust merely by
declaring that henceforward he regards himself as holding the shares on trust for Z. To
conclude that interests subsisting behind resulting trusts can be disposed of without
writing would also provide an easy means of evasion of the ruling in *Grey v IRC*, which
concerned an equitable interest subsisting under an express bare trust. If a settlor were
to transfer property to a nominee, without specifying a beneficiary and thus giving rise
to a resulting trust in his favour, he could then transfer the equitable interest to new
beneficiaries by merely orally directing the trustees to declare new trusts.

If any general principle can be construed from *Re Vandervell's Trusts (No 2)* it would
therefore seem that it should be limited to a case where the extinction of the equitable
interest arising under a resulting trust is the act of a third party, and not of the person
who enjoys the interest. It was only because the declaration of trust was made by the
trustees that there was no need for writing. If Vandervell himself had sought to transfer his equitable interest under the resulting trust, writing would surely have been
required in satisfaction of s 53(1)(c).

(4) **Resulting and constructive trusts**

The formality requirements of s 53(1) only apply in respect of declarations of express
trusts and dispositions of existing equitable interests. As will be evident in the following chapters, they have no application to resulting or constructive trusts. This is the
effect of s 53(2), which provides:

> This section does not affect the creation or operation of resulting, implied or constructive
> trusts.

8

Resulting trusts

The previous chapter has examined the circumstances in which a trust relationship may be created by the deliberate intention and act of the settlor. Such trusts are known as 'express trusts'. However, in some situations property will be regarded as subject to a trust despite the absence of any express intention on the part of the settlor. In English law 'resulting trusts' are one of the two main categories of such informal trusts, the other being that of 'constructive trusts' (considered in the next chapter). In general, resulting trusts arise to give effect to the implied intention of the owner of property that someone else should not enjoy the benefit of it. The application of resulting trusts is also considered in the context of acquiring rights in the family home in Chapter 10.

1 Introduction to resulting trusts

(1) **What are resulting trusts?**

The circumstances in which property will become subject to a resulting trust were examined by the House of Lords in *Westdeutsche Landesbank Girozentrale v Islington London Borough Council*.[1] Lord Browne-Wilkinson identified two circumstances in which a resulting trust would arise:

> Under existing law a resulting trust arises in two sets of circumstances: (A) where A makes a voluntary payment to B or pays (wholly or in part) for the purchase of property which is vested either in B alone or in the joint names of A and B, there is a presumption that A did not intend to make a gift to B; the money or property is held on trust for A (if he is the sole provider of the money) or in the case of a joint purchaser by A and B in shares proportionate to their contributions. It is important to stress that this is only a *presumption,* which presumption is easily rebutted either by the counter presumption of advancement or by direct evidence of A's intention to make an outright transfer...(B) Where A transfers property to B *on express trusts*, but the trusts declared do not exhaust the whole beneficial interest.[2]

---

[1] [1996] AC 669. See Birks 'Trusts Raised to Avoid Unjust Enrichment: The *Westdeutsche* Case' [1996] RLR 3.

[2] [1996] AC 669, at 708. See Chambers, *Resulting Trusts* (1997); Swadling 'Explaining Resulting Trusts' (2008) LQR 72.

Resulting trusts of the second type will be examined in Chapter 18, where it will be seen that they operate to 'fill the gap' in the beneficial ownership of property where an express trust fails. This chapter will be concerned largely with resulting trusts of the first type, commonly termed 'presumed resulting trusts'.

(2) Distinguishing resulting and constructive trusts

In some cases, the House of Lords seem to have used 'resulting' and 'constructive' trusts as interchangeable terms,[3] suggesting that it is not necessary to distinguish between them. However, it is submitted that they are fundamentally different, operating on different principles, and that they need to be strictly differentiated.

Constructive trusts[4] are imposed by the court as a consequence of the conduct of the party who becomes a trustee. Resulting trusts are not imposed as a response to the conduct of the trustee, but to give effect to the implied intentions of the owner. Where a transfer of property has occurred and the legal title has been transferred, but the transferor has failed to show an intention to divest himself fully of all his interest in that property, the transferee will not be permitted to receive the property absolutely for his own benefit. Instead, he will hold it on trust for the transferor. The equitable interests are said to 'result back' to the transferor, thus ensuring that he retains his interest in the property.

Practical imperatives may also demand that a distinction be drawn between beneficial entitlements taking effect under resulting and constructive trusts. *Re Densham (A Bankrupt)*[5] concerned a dispute as to the ownership of a matrimonial home. While the husband was the sole legal owner of the house, his wife had contributed towards the purchase price and they had also agreed that the ownership should be jointly shared. Goff J held that, in consequence of the agreement, the wife was prima facie entitled to a beneficial half share in the ownership of the house by way of a constructive trust, and that through her direct financial contribution to the purchase price she was also entitled to a ninth share of the beneficial ownership by way of a resulting trust. However, because the husband was bankrupt, she was held unable to assert any entitlement by way of the constructive trust, because it was not a settlement made for 'valuable consideration' and therefore void against his trustee in bankruptcy.[6] Nevertheless, she was able to assert her entitlement by way of the resulting trust.

Re Densham therefore illustrates the need to distinguish between the operation of resulting and constructive trusts. This need was reiterated by the Court of Appeal in *Drake v Whipp*,[7] where the central issue was as to the proportion of the equitable interest that the plaintiff enjoyed in a barn owned by her erstwhile partner by virtue of her contributions to the purchase price and work done, where there was also a

---

[3] For example, *Gissing v Gissing* [1971] AC 886, at 905, per Lord Diplock; *Tinsley v Milligan* [1993] 3 All ER 65, at 86–87, per Lord Browne-Wilkinson. [4] See Chapter 9.
[5] [1975] 1 WLR 1519. [6] Bankruptcy Act 1914, s 42. [7] [1996] 1 FLR 826.

common intention that she was to enjoy a share of the ownership. Peter Gibson LJ
remarked:

> A potent source of confusion, to my mind, has been suggestions that it matters not
> whether the terminology used is that of the constructive trust, to which the intention,
> actual or imputed, of the parties is crucial, or that of the resulting trust which operates
> as a presumed intention of the contributing party in the absence of rebutting evidence of
> actual intention.[8]

Thus, while by means of a resulting trust the plaintiff would only be entitled to a share
of the beneficial interest directly equivalent to the proportion of her contribution to
the purchase price of the barn (which was 19.4 per cent), by way of a constructive trust
she was entitled to a third interest.[9]

Most cases involving resulting trusts have involved the family home. In this context, there has been some blurring of the distinction between resulting trusts and constructive trusts. In some cases, the courts have treated any financial contribution to
the family home as opening up to the court the option to confer on the contributor a
share of ownership which is not calculated arithmetically by reference to the financial
contribution, but which is a 'fair share' on the basis of all the parties' dealings with the
property. An illustration is provided by the decision of the Court of Appeal in *Oxley
v Hiscock*.[10] Ms Oxley had contributed 22 per cent of the cost of acquiring the family
home, but the Court of Appeal held that she was entitled to a 40 per cent share of the
value of the home even though there had never been any discussion about what share
she should have. It would be unwise to see such cases as this as establishing a general
principle applicable in all situations where a resulting trust arises; not least because
the use of the resulting trust has become subsumed into the wider concept of a constructive trust and it has fallen out of favour as a device used to create interests in the
family home.[11] What is happening in the family home context, it would seem, is the
development of a special jurisprudence applicable to cohabiting couples from which
the resulting trust is excluded. This jurisprudence is explored in Chapter 10.

(3) **Rationale of resulting trusts**

In *Westdeutsche Landesbank Girozentrale v Islington London Borough Council*[12] Lord
Browne-Wilkinson stated that resulting trusts arise to fulfil the implied intentions of
the parties:

> Both types of resulting trust are traditionally regarded as examples of trusts giving effect
> to the common intentions of the parties. A resulting trust is not imposed by law against
> the intentions of the trustee (as is a constructive trust) but gives effect to his presumed
> intention.[13]

---

[8] [1996] 1 FLR 826, at 827.   [9] See also *Midland Bank Plc v Cooke* [1995] 4 All ER 562.
[10] [2004] EWCA Civ 546.
[11] See *Stack v Dowden* [2007] 2 AC 437(HL) ; *Jones v Kernott* [2012] 1 AC 776 (SC).
[12] [1996] AC 669.   [13] [1996] AC 669, at 708.

However, this formulation is open to question. While it is certainly the case that a presumed resulting trust arises in consequence of the presumed intention of the transferor of the trust property (or contributor to its purchase, as the case may be) it is not necessarily the case that the trustee who received the legal title intended the property to be held on trust. In many cases, a resulting trust has been found in circumstances where the transferee of the legal title anticipated that a gift had been made divesting the transferor of his entire interest in the property. This can be seen from the fact that many cases involve a dispute as to whether a presumption of resulting trust has been rebutted. As Lord Browne-Wilkinson himself observed, a resulting trust of the first type arises because 'there is a presumption that A did not intend to make a gift to B'.[14] A resulting trust will arise in favour of A in such circumstances even though B anticipated that he was the beneficiary of an absolute gift, and in this sense B will be required to hold the property on resulting trust against his intentions. More significantly, a resulting trust may even arise where the transferee of property was unaware that the transfer had occurred.[15] Therefore, it should not be thought that a resulting trust will only arise on the basis of the mutual intention of the parties. Instead, a resulting trust should arise whenever a transferee (or contributor) cannot be shown to have possessed the intention to make a gift. As Lord Goff stated, a presumed resulting trust arises when there are:

> voluntary payments by A to B, or for the purchase of property in the name of B or in his and A's joint names, where there is no presumption of advancement or evidence of intention to make an out-and-out gift.[16]

A number of earlier cases provide a less confusing analysis of the rationale for the creation of resulting trusts. In *Re Sick and Funeral Society of St John's Sunday School, Golcar*[17] Megarry V-C stated that:

> A resulting trust is essentially a property concept: any property that a man does not effectually dispose of remains his own.

This clearly recognizes that a resulting trust arises because of the failure of the transferor to make an absolute gift of his property. As Lord Reid observed in *Vandervell v IRC*:

> where it appears to have been the intention of the donor that the donee should not take beneficially, there will be a resulting trust in favour of the donor.[18]

A more nuanced understanding of the operation of resulting trusts was provided by the Privy Council in *Air Jamaica Ltd v Charlton*, where Lord Millett stated:

> Like a constructive trust, a resulting trust arises by operation of law, although unlike a constructive trust it gives effect to intention. But it arises whether or not the transferor intended to retain a beneficial interest—he almost always does not—since it responds to the absence of any intention on his part to pass a beneficial interest to the recipient.[19]

---

[14] [1996] AC 669, at 708.
[15] As, for example, in *Re Vinogradoff* [1935] WN 68. See Chambers, *Resulting Trusts* (1997), p 37.
[16] [1996] AC 669, at 689.   [17] [1973] Ch 51.   [18] [1967] 2 AC 291, HL.
[19] [1999] 1 WLR 1399, at 1412.

2 Presumed resulting trusts

Presumed resulting trusts arise where the transferor of property did not intend to dispose of his entire ownership interest in the property transferred. Under English law there is a rebuttable presumption that a transferor of property does not intend to make a gift of it, and unless this presumption is rebutted the transferee will hold it on resulting trust for the donor. However, in some circumstances the nature of the relationship between the transferor and the transferee gives rise to an opposite presumption, namely that the transferor did intend to benefit the transferee, in which case unless the presumption of a gift is rebutted there will be no resulting trust. This counter-presumption is known as the 'presumption of advancement'.

(1) The basic presumption of resulting trust

English law adopts two basic presumptions about the intentions of property owners, both of which are rebuttable by evidence of a contrary intention.

(a) A presumption against gifts

First, it is presumed that, outside of certain relationships, an owner of property never intends to make a gift. If an owner voluntarily transfers the legal title of his property to a third party without receiving any consideration in return, he is presumed to have intended to retain the equitable interest for himself. The transferee will therefore hold the property on resulting trust for him. This presumption was invented by equity to defeat the misappropriation of property as a consequence of potentially fraudulent or improvident transactions.[20]

(b) A presumption in favour of the provider of purchase money

By extension of this first presumption, it is also presumed that a person who provides the money required to purchase property intends to obtain the equitable interest in the property acquired. Therefore, when the property is purchased in the name of someone who did not provide the purchase money, he will be presumed to hold the legal title on trust for the provider thereof. This presumption is long established and was recognized in *Dyer v Dyer*, where Eyre CB stated:

> the trust of a legal estate ... whether taken in the names of the purchasers and others jointly, or in the names of others without that of the purchaser; whether in one name or several; whether jointly or successive, results to the man who advances the purchase-money.[21]

Where a person has only contributed a part of the purchase price of property, a resulting trust will be presumed in his favour of an equivalent proportion of the equitable interest.[22] *Tinsley v Milligan*[23] (see Figure 8.2) provides an example.

---

[20] *Lynch v Burke* [1995] 2 IR 159, per O'Flaherty J.   [21] (1788) 2 Cox Eq Cas 92, at 93.
[22] *Midland Bank plc v Cooke* [1995] 4 All ER 562; *Drake v Whipp* [1996] 1 FLR 826.
[23] [1993] 3All ER 65.

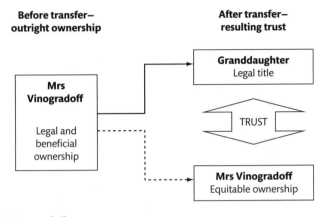

Figure 8.1 *Re Vinogradoff*

(2) **Voluntary transfers of property**

Where an owner makes a voluntary transfer of property, either into the sole name of the transferee or into the joint names of himself and the transferee, without receiving any consideration in return, a resulting trust will be presumed in his favour unless rebutted by evidence that he intended to make a gift. The presumption of a resulting trust clearly operates in the context of voluntary transfers of personal property, but it is less certain whether it operates in respect to voluntary transfers of land.

(a) **Operation of the presumption of resulting trust in the context of personal property**

The operation of the presumption of a resulting trust is well illustrated by *Re Vinogradoff* (see Figure 8.1).[24] Mrs Vindogradoff transferred £800 War Loan stock into the joint names of herself and her infant granddaughter. Farwell J held that the stock was held on resulting trust for her,[25] and that therefore on her death it belonged in equity to her estate. In *Thavorn v Bank of Credit and Commerce International SA*[26] a resulting trust was found to exist where a woman opened a bank account in favour of her infant nephew. In 1981 Mrs Thavorn opened an account with some £20,000 in her nephew's name. She had directed the bank that she alone was to operate the account. Lloyd J held that in these circumstances there was no evidence to rebut the presumption of a resulting trust:

> There was not the slightest evidence on which I could hold that, by opening the account in his name, she intended to transfer any beneficial interest to him during her lifetime.[27]

The bank was therefore liable to pay damages when they paid the money into his current account. A presumption of resulting trust will also arise where a person transfers money into a bank account in joint names. In *Aroso v Coutts*[28] it was held that

---

[24] [1935] WN 68. See also *Re Muller* [1953] NZLR 879.
[25] The granddaughter was held to be a trustee of the resulting trust despite her minority. See Law of Property Act 1925, s 20.   [26] [1985] 1 Lloyd's Rep 259. Compare also *Re Howes* (1905) 21 TLR 501.
[27] [1985] 1 Lloyd's Rep 259, at 263.   [28] [2002] 1 All ER (Comm) 241.

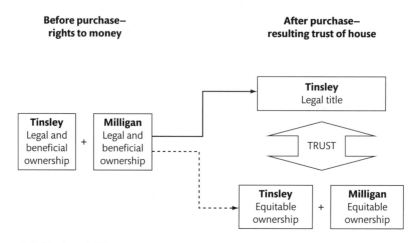

Figure 8.2 *Tinsley v Milligan*

the presumption of resulting trusts operated when Sr Aroso transferred money into a joint account opened in the names of himself and his nephew, although the presumption was held to have been rebutted by evidence that a gift had been intended. In *Re Northall (Deceased)*,[29] the presumption of resulting trust was used to identify money paid in by a testatrix into a joint account with one of her sons as part of her residuary estate. Richards J in giving judgment noted that 'there was no dispute as to the applicable rules'[30] in such cases, and as the testatrix had made all the payments into the account and no contrary intention was evident, ownership in the joint account resulted to her estate.

(b) Operation of the presumption of resulting trust in the context of land

While the presumption of resulting trust clearly operates in respect of voluntary transfers of personal property, a more difficult question is whether the presumption against gifts continues to apply in the context of voluntary transfers of land. Section 60(3) of the Law of Property Act 1925 provides:

> In a voluntary conveyance a resulting trust for the grantor shall not be implied merely by reason that the property is not expressed to be conveyed for the use or benefit of the grantee.

There has been much debate as to whether this provision was enacted to remove the presumption of resulting trust where land is conveyed voluntarily,[31] or whether it was merely intended to remove a conveyancing inconvenience. Prior to the enactment of s 60(3), it was necessary to declare in a voluntary conveyance that land was granted 'unto and to the use of' the grantee to ensure an effective transfer. It has therefore been

---

[29] [2010] EWHC 1448 (Ch).   [30] [2010] EWHC 1448 (Ch), at [8].
[31] Chambers, *Resulting Trusts* (1997), pp 18–19; Mee 'Resulting trusts and voluntary conveyances of land' [2012] Conv 307. Mee also suggests that there may have been no presumption of resulting trust before 1926 on a review of the case law.

argued that s 60(3) was intended to render such a declaration unnecessary, so that the mere absence of it will not alone lead to a resulting trust, while leaving the operation of the presumption intact.[32] The true effect of s 60(3) has not fallen for a convincing determination by the higher courts. In *Tinsley v Milligan*[33] Lord Browne-Wilkinson commented that it was 'arguable that the position has been altered by the 1925 property legislation',[34] and in *Hodgson v Marks*[35] the Court of Appeal held that a resulting trust arose in favour of an elderly lady who had transferred the legal title to her house to her lodger on the basis of an oral understanding that he would look after her affairs. However, in *Lohia v Lohia*,[36] Nicholas Strauss QC held that although both proposed interpretations of s 60(3) could reasonably be adopted by the court, on a 'plain reading' the presumption of resulting trust had been abolished in respect of a voluntary conveyance of land. Thus a presumption of resulting trust will only arise if there is some fact in addition to the lack of consideration, such as that the parties are strangers. In the light of this interpretation, he held that no resulting trust had arisen where a son had conveyed his share in the family home to his father. The mere fact that there was no evidence of any sensible reason why he had so conveyed his share in the house to his father, and that he had continued to share mortgage payments and rental income, was not sufficient to lead to the inference of a resulting trust. On appeal in *Lohia v Lohia*,[37] their Lordships agreed with the finding of a resulting trust on the facts, but were more cautious as to the survival of the presumption of resulting trust. Mummery LJ refused to pronounce on the matter 'without having heard very extensive argument'[38] and Sir Christopher Slade acknowledged that it was a 'knotty issue'[39] but similarly refused to give an opinion. Nevertheless, in the subsequent decision of the Court of Appeal in *Ali v Khan*,[40] Morritt VC followed the view of Nicholas Strauss QC that the presumption of resulting trust had been abolished on voluntary conveyances of land and could only be established by additional evidence. However, as Mee argues, it does not appear that Morrit VC was aware of the approach of the Court of Appeal in *Lohia*, which weakens the strength of the authority.[41]

Where does that leave the law? There are some indications in the cases that the approach that the presumption is gone and evidence must be demonstrated from which the existence of a trust can be inferred. It is submitted, however, that the alternative interpretation is preferable and the presumption should remain. As Nicholas Strauss QC himself indicated, it is doubtful whether the differences between

[32] See Cheshire and Burn, *Modern Law of Real Property* (15th edn, 1994), p 161.

[33] [1993] 3 All ER 65, HL.

[34] See also *Hodgson v Marks* [1971] Ch 892, where Russell LJ described the proposition that s 60(3) has put an end to the presumption, resulting trusts of land as 'debatable'.

[35] [1971] Ch 892. This decision has been quite contentious—see, for example, Swadling in Birks and Rose, *Resulting Trusts and Equitable Compensation* (2000, Oxford), p 61, where it is suggested that the decision should have been reached on an application of express trust principles.   [36] [2001] WTLR 101.

[37] [2001] EWCA Civ 1691.   [38] [2001] EWCA Civ 1691, at [24].

[39] [2001] EWCA Civ 1691, at [34].   [40] [2002] EWCA Civ 774.

[41] See Mee [2012] Conv 307, who suggests that the Court of Appeal appeared not to have appreciated the more cautious approach adopted by the judges on the appeal of *Lohia*.

land and personalty, and between methods of making apparent gifts, provide meaningful bases for distinction.[42] The presumptions of resulting trust and advancement
operate in practice primarily to allocate the burden of proof where property has been
transferred and there is a dispute as to the effect of the transfer. To eliminate the presumption of resulting trust in relation to land is, in effect, to introduce something akin
to the presumption of advancement where land has been voluntarily conveyed. The
transferor will therefore have to bring forward evidence to show that the beneficial
interest was not intended to be transferred. The facts of *Lohia v Lohia* demonstrate
that it may prove difficult to discharge such a burden. It is clearly desirable that any
transfer of land where no consideration is paid should make it explicit whether or not
a gift is intended.

(3) Purchase money resulting trusts

The presumption of a resulting trust in favour of a contributor to the purchase price of
property applies to both personal property and land.

(a) Purchase money resulting trust of personal property

The presumption of a resulting trust of personal property was raised in *Fowkes
v Pascoe*.[43] John Pascoe was the grandson of Sarah Baker. Over a period of some
five years, Sarah Baker purchased annuities totalling £7,000 in the joint names
of herself and John Pascoe. The Court of Appeal accepted that there was thus a
presumption of a resulting trust in favour of Sarah Baker, but held the evidence
rebutted this presumption and demonstrated that a gift had been intended. In *The
Venture*,[44] a resulting trust was held to have arisen in favour of a contributor to the
purchase price of a yacht. In *Abrahams v Trustee in Bankruptcy of Abrahams*,[45] it
was held that a presumption of resulting trust operated where a wife, who was separated from her husband, contributed to a syndicate purchasing National Lottery
tickets in the name of her husband. Since the presumption was not rebutted the
husband held his share of the winnings, some £242,000, on resulting trust for
his wife.

The important case of *Foskett v McKeown*[46] concerned the question whether a contributor to the premiums of a life insurance policy thereby gained a proportionate
share of the proceeds of the policy. Mr Murphy had taken out a life insurance policy
in 1986 that would provide a death benefit of £1 million. He paid the annual premiums for the first two years using his own money, but paid subsequent premiums
using misappropriated trust money. He committed suicide in 1991, at which point at
least 40 per cent of the premiums had been paid using trust money. The question was
whether the beneficiaries were entitled to a proportionate share of the proceeds of the

---

[42] Cf Mee [2012] Conv 307 who argues (at 325–326) that there is a justifiable difference between land and
personalty, and that the coherence of the law is better served by the removal of the presumption.
[43] (1875) 10 Ch App 343.   [44] [1908] P 218.   [45] [1999] BPIR 637.   [46] [2001] 1 AC 102.

policy. While there was no doubt that the trust money had been used to pay premiums, under the terms of the policy the death benefit would still have been payable even if they had not been made, due to the payment of the earlier premiums. In *Re Policy No 6402 of the Scottish Equitable Life Assurance Society*[47] Joyce J had held that resulting trust principles were applicable to a life policy. In the Court of Appeal[48] Scott V-C held that this case was distinguishable because the contributions giving rise to the resulting trust had been made from the outset of the policy, so that it did not apply in favour of contributors of later premiums which would have the effect of divesting those already entitled to the proceeds of the policy.[49] Morritt LJ dissented and, while he was unwilling to decide whether a resulting trust could arise from the payment of some premiums due on an insurance policy taken out in the name of another,[50] he held that contributions to the purchase of property by instalments could give rise to a resulting trust:

> in principle if property is acquired by a series of payments a resulting trust in respect of the due proportion may arise from the payment of one or more in the series; hire purchase or instalment payment transactions would be examples.[51]

The majority of the House of Lords approved the dissenting judgment of Morritt LJ, and held that the beneficiaries were entitled to a proportionate share of the proceeds of the policy. Lord Millett explained:

> It is true that the last two premiums were not needed to provide the death benefit in the sense that in the events which had happened the same amount would have been payable even if those premiums had not been paid…But the fact is that Mr Murphy, who could not foresee the future, did choose to pay the last two premiums, and to pay them with the purchaser's money; and they were applied by the insurer towards the payment of the internal premiums needed to fund the death benefit. It should not avail his donees that he need not have paid the premiums, and that if he had not then (in the events which happened) the insurers would have provided the same death benefit and funded it differently.[52]

Contribution to the premiums required under an insurance policy will therefore entitle the contributor to a proportionate share of the proceeds.

However, *Foskett v McKeown*[53] also illustrates the potential problems of determining the exact extent of an interest acquired by resulting trust where contributions have been made to a purchase by instalments. Lords Hoffman and Browne-Wilkinson held that the extent of the interest in the proceeds of the policy should be proportionate to the contributions the parties had made to the premiums. Lord Millett considered that, since the policy was unit-linked in nature, the appropriate division was in proportion to the number of units that were acquired by the respective premiums.

---

[47] [1902] 1 Ch 282.   [48] [1997] 3 All ER 392.   [49] [1997] 3 All ER 392, at 406.
[50] [1997] 3 All ER 392, at 424–425.   [51] [1997] 3 All ER 392, at 423.
[52] [2001] 1 AC 102, at 138.   [53] [2001] 1 AC 102.

(b) Purchase money resulting trust of land

In the context of the acquisition of land it is clear that a presumed resulting trust will arise in favour of a contributor to the purchase price.[54] The general principle was stated by Lord Reid in *Pettitt v Pettitt*:

> in the absence of evidence to the contrary effect, a contributor to the purchase-price will acquire a beneficial interest in the property.[55]

This was reiterated by Lord Pearson in *Gissing v Gissing*, where the issue was whether a wife was entitled to a share of the ownership of her matrimonial home, which had been purchased in the sole name of her husband:

> If [the wife] did make a contribution of a substantial amount towards the purchase of the house, there would be a resulting trust in her favour. That would be the presumption as to the intention of the parties at the time or times when she made and he accepted the contributions. The presumption is a rebuttable presumption: it can be rebutted by evidence showing some other intention...[56]

It is in relation to the ownership of the family home that presumed resulting trusts have most often been employed to allow a non-legal owner to acquire a beneficial interest, though, as indicated earlier, they now have a significantly limited role to play in that context due to the development of a particular form of constructive trust into which they have been subsumed. This is discussed in Chapter 10, but it appears that the role for the resulting trust in the family home is now limited to determining the ownership on the dissolution of the relationship in situations where parties living together buy property as an investment rather than a home, and so are not afforded the special treatment awarded to the purchase of a property as a family home.[57] What follows is an overview of the major areas of interest in the application of these trusts to the acquisition of interests in land outside the domestic, family home context.

(i) Nature of contributions

The major area of controversy has concerned the nature of 'contributions' sufficient to give rise to the presumption. While 'indirect' contributions may, in certain circumstances, constitute sufficient detriment to call for the imposition of a constructive trust [58] only 'direct' contributions to the purchase price will give rise to a presumption of resulting trust in favour of the contributor. Thus, paying for the cost of renovations or repairs to a property may give rise to the presumption,[59] while contributing to the household expenses[60] or working for a low wage[61] will not, but may lead to the

---

[54] See Stevens and Pearce, *Land Law* (5th edn, 2013), pp 303–319.

[55] [1970] AC 777, at 794. See Chapter 10.   [56] [1971] AC 886.

[57] See *Jones v Kernott* [2012] 1 AC 776, at [53]; *Geary v Rankine* [2012] EWCA Civ 555 (CA), at [18]; *Favor Easy Management Ltd v Wu* [2012] EWCA Civ 1464 (CA).

[58] Such constructive trusts are now referred to as 'constructive trusts of common intention' and are the device used to create interests in the family home, and are therefore discussed in Chapter 10.

[59] *Drake v Whipp* [1996] 1 FLR 826.   [60] *Burns v Burns* [1984] Ch 317.

[61] *Ivin v Blake* (1994) 67 P & CR 263 (no resulting trust where daughter worked in her mother's pub).

imposition of a constructive trust. Mortgage payments have caused considerable difficulties, and yet most properties are now purchased with the help of a mortgage loan. Quite apart from the practical difficulties of quantifying the beneficial share from mortgage repayments,[62] unless there is a repayment agreement made before the mortgage was entered into, payment of the mortgage instalments on a property will not give rise to the presumption of resulting trust, as they are technically not payments to the purchase price, but the reduction of an existing monetary debt.[63]

(ii) Size of beneficial share

The issue of quantification has been of major significance in this area of the law. The application of a strict resulting trust analysis would, as we have seen, fix the share of the beneficial interest in property in direct proportion to the money advanced towards the purchase price. In cases involving the family home, the courts have often conferred a larger share.[64] This reached its apex in the Court of Appeal decision in *Oxley v Hiscock*[65] where it suggested that the size of a beneficial share awarded by means of a resulting trust should represent a 'fair share' on the basis of all the parties' dealings with the property. The approach to fairness in *Oxley* has been explicitly adopted by the Supreme Court in *Jones v Kernott*,[66] in relation to imputing a common intention to decide on the size of the beneficial share in a common intention constructive trust where no objective common intention between them can be inferred. However, the same decision makes it clear that it does not apply to a resulting trust, as resulting trusts are no longer to be used in the acquisition or quantification of interests in the family home,[67] as we have seen.

(4) Rebutting the presumption of resulting trust

In *Pettitt v Pettitt* Lord Diplock observed that the presumptions of resulting trust and advancement are:

> no more than a consensus of judicial opinion disclosed by reported cases as to the most likely inference of fact to be drawn in the absence of any evidence to the contrary.[68]

It therefore follows that they can be rebutted by evidence that in a specific situation the 'most likely inference' was not, in fact, intended. The presumption of a resulting trust, whether arising from a voluntary transfer or a contribution to the purchase price of property, will be rebutted by evidence that the transferor or contributor had no intention to retain any beneficial interest in the property. The strength of the evidence required to rebut the presumption of a resulting trust will depend upon the strength of

---

[62] See *Marsh v Von Sternberg* [1986] 1 FLR 526.
[63] *Curley v Parkes* [2004] EWCA Civ 1515. See also *Barrett v Barrett* [2008] EWHC 1061 (Ch), at [24].
[64] *Midland* Bank v Cooke [1995] 4 All ER 562, where the wife had contributed only 6.74 per cent of the purchase cost of the family home through a direct contribution, but she was entitled to one-half share of the beneficial ownership of the property.   [65] [2004] EWCA Civ 546,
[66] [2012] 1 AC 776, at [51]–[52].   [67] [2012] 1 AC 776, at [57].   [68] [1970] AC 777, at 823.

the presumption, which will in turn depend upon the facts and circumstances which gave rise to it.[69]

(a) Circumstances rebutting the presumption of resulting trust

(i) Evidence a gift was intended

It was noted earlier that in *Fowkes v Pascoe*[70] a presumption of a resulting trust was raised when Sarah Baker purchased annuities in the joint names of herself and John Pascoe. However, this presumption was rebutted by evidence indicating that a gift had been intended. Two initial purchases of stock were made by Sarah, one of £250 in the joint names of herself and John Pascoe, and another of £250 in the joint names of herself and her companion. She also held large quantities of the same stock in her own name, besides other property. The court considered this 'absolutely conclusive' that a gift was intended. As James LJ said:

> Is it possible to reconcile with mental sanity the theory that she put £250 into the names of herself and her companion, and £250 into the names of herself and [John Pascoe], as trustees upon trust for herself? What…object is there conceivable in doing this?[71]

In *Re Young*[72] it was similarly held that the presumption of a resulting trust had been rebutted. Colonel and Mrs Young had a joint bank account, which contained money derived from Mrs Young's separate income. The account was used to pay for household expenses, and Colonel Young, with his wife's consent, withdrew money to purchase investments in his own name. Pearson J held that the evidence showed that the money in the account was intended to be joint, and that the investments purchased in his own name were his own property, and were not held on resulting trust for his wife.

In *Aroso v Coutts & Co*[73] Collins J held that the presumption of resulting trust was rebutted where a wealthy Portuguese gentleman had transferred money into a joint account in the names of himself and his nephew. The evidence, primarily the mandate establishing the account that clearly stated that the beneficial interest was to be held jointly and the evidence of the bank client relationship officer who had explained the effect of the account, established that he had intended the nephew to take the property beneficially.

It appears that a presumption of resulting trust may be rebutted even where money has been paid into a joint bank account with the intention that the transferee is not allowed to draw on the account until the death of the transferor. This approach was adopted in *Russell v Scott*,[74] where an aunt had opened a joint account in the names of herself and her nephew, but did not intend her nephew to benefit during her lifetime. The Australian High Court held that she had nevertheless conferred an immediate beneficial interest on him that would only fall into possession on her death through the operation of the right of survivorship. Because of her control over

---

[69] *Vajpeyi v Yijsaf* [2003] EWHC 2339, per Peter Prescott QC, at [71].
[70] (1875) LR 10 Ch App 343.   [71] (1875) LR 10 Ch App 343, at 349.
[72] (1885) 28 Ch D 705.   [73] [2002] 1 All ER (Comm) 241.   [74] (1936) 55 CLR 440.

the account, the interest that she conferred on him remained revocable by her during her lifetime. This decision was followed in England in *Young v Sealey*.[75] In contrast, in Ireland it was held in *Owens v Greene*[76] that the presumption of resulting trust could not be rebutted in such cases because the transferor's intention amounted to an intention to make a testamentary gift, and that evidence of this intention was not admissible, since otherwise the requirements for making a will would be avoided. However, as many commentators have observed,[77] rebutting the presumption of resulting trust in such circumstances is no more offensive to the policy of the Wills Act than the recognition of secret trusts. *Owens v Greene* has since been overruled by the Irish Supreme Court in *Lynch v Burke*.[78] In *Aroso v Coutts & Co*[79] Collins J indicated that he would have followed *Russell v Scott* and *Young v Sealey*, but the point did not arise for decision.

In *Drakeford v Cotton*[80] Morgan J applied the principles explained in previous paragraphs to hold that where a mother had transferred a building society account into the joint names of herself and her daughter, initially on trust for herself, but later changed her mind and indicated that she wished the daughter to become sole owner on the mother's death, this constituted a new declaration of trust which changed the beneficial interests, was not a testamentary disposition, and did not need to be in writing since it was not the disposition of an existing equitable interest.[81]

(ii) Evidence a loan was intended

The presumption of a resulting trust will also be rebutted where evidence shows that money was advanced by way of a loan. In *Re Sharpe (a bankrupt)*[82] Mr and Mrs Sharpe lived in a maisonette with their 82-year-old aunt, Mrs Johnson. The property had been purchased in the name of Mr Sharpe for £17,000. Mrs Johnson had contributed £12,000 towards the purchase price, while the remainder was raised by way of a mortgage. Mr and Mrs Sharpe were subsequently declared bankrupt and Mrs Johnson claimed to be entitled to a proprietary interest in the maisonette by means of a resulting trust presumed from her contribution to the purchase price. Browne-Wilkinson J held that the money had in fact been advanced by way of a loan, with the intention that it would be repaid. She was not therefore entitled to any share of the equitable interest of the property. A presumption of a resulting trust was also rebutted by evidence that a loan was intended in *Vajpeyi v Yijaf*.[83] In this case, the claimant provided the defendant, who was her lover, with £10,000 to enable him to purchase a house in his sole name. At the time of the purchase in 1980 the defendant was a young man of limited means. The claimant alleged that by virtue

---

[75] [1949] Ch 278.   [76] [1932] IR 225.

[77] See Delaney, *Equity and Trusts in the Republic of Ireland* (1995), p 133.

[78] [1995] 2 IR 159. See (1996) ILSI Gazette March, p 70 (Mee).

[79] [2002] 1 All ER (Comm) 241.   [80] [2012] 3 All ER 1138.

[81] If it was a disposition of an existing equitable interest, Law of Property Act 1925 s 53(1)(c) would have required the disposition to be in writing.

[82] [1980] 1 WLR 219. See also *Blue Sky One Ltd v Blue Airways LLC* [2009] EWHC 3314 (Comm) at [255]–[257].   [83] [2003] EWHC 2339.

of this payment she was entitled to a 33.89 per cent share of the equitable ownership of the property on the basis of a presumed resulting trust, whereas the defendant claimed that the money had been advanced by way of a loan, which he had repaid. Peter Prescott QC held that the following factors had rebutted the presumption of a resulting trust in favour of a loan: the fact that the defendant had been a young man of limited means who was anxious to get on the property ladder whereas the claimant was a lady who was already on the property ladder when the money was advanced; the fact that the claimant had tolerated the defendant collecting rents from the property and keeping them for himself for some twenty-one years; the fact that the claimant had failed to propound her claim to an interest for twenty-one years, and the fact that she had never said anything about her alleged interest in the house when it was mortgaged by the defendant to enable him to purchase her matrimonial home some years previously.

(b) Evidence required to rebut the presumption of resulting trust

Fowkes v Pascoe[84] makes clear that the quality of evidence required to rebut a presumption of a resulting trust will vary depending on the circumstances in question, because the presumption of resulting trust will be given varying weight depending upon the context. As Mellish LJ stated:

> the presumption must…be of very different weight in different cases. In some cases it would be very strong indeed. If, for instance, a man invested a sum of stock in the name of himself and his solicitor, the inference would be very strong indeed that it was intended solely for the purpose of a trust, and the court would require very strong evidence on the part of the solicitor to prove that it was intended as a gift; and certainly his own evidence would not be sufficient. On the other hand, a man may make an investment of stock in the name of himself and some person, although not a child or wife,[85] yet in such a position to him as to make it extremely probable that the investment was intended as a gift. In such a case, although the rule of law, if there was no evidence at all, would compel the Court to say that the presumption of trust must prevail, even if the court might not believe that the fact was in accordance with the presumption, yet, if there is evidence to rebut the presumption, then, in my opinion, the court must go into the actual facts.[86]

(c) Admissibility of evidence to rebut a presumption of resulting trust

Any acts or declarations by the parties forming part of the transaction to which the presumption of a resulting trust relates will be admissible in favour of, or against, the parties performing them. However, in *Shephard v Cartwright*[87] the House of Lords held, in the context of the rebuttal of a presumption of advancement, that subsequent acts and declarations are admissible only as evidence against the party who made them, and not in his favour.

---

[84] (1875) LR 10 Ch App 343.   [85] Where the presumption of advancement would apply.
[86] (1875) LR 10 Ch App 343, at 352–353.   [87] [1955] AC 431.

(5) **Presumed resulting trust arising in the context of an illegal purpose**

In *Tinsley v Milligan*[88] the House of Lords was faced with the question whether a plaintiff was entitled to rely on a presumption of resulting trust arising in the context of a transaction entered to facilitate an illegal purpose. A house had been purchased in the sole name of Tinsley, using money which both Tinsley and Milligan, a cohabiting lesbian couple, had raised from the sale of a previous property, augmented by a mortgage loan. The reason for this was to enable Milligan to appear to be a mere lodger in the property, rather than a co-owner, so that she could make false claims for various state social welfare benefits. After the breakdown of their relationship, Milligan claimed that Tinsley held the house on trust for them in equal shares. Tinsley claimed that the court should not enforce Milligan's claim because of the illegal purpose underlying the transaction, demanding a strict application of the maxim that 'he who comes to equity must come with clean hands'. This would obviously have the consequence that Tinsley was solely entitled to the house, despite the fact that she had been as much party to the illegality as Milligan. While this might have seemed a harsh result between the specific parties, especially given that the falsely claimed social security money had been repaid, the strict rule was intended to operate as a deterrent to those who might be tempted to involve themselves in illegal transactions.

The majority of the Court of Appeal rejected the application of such a strict principle in favour of the adoption of a 'public conscience test', which would vest the court with a discretion to balance the consequences of either granting or refusing relief to the person seeking to claim an interest.[89] The House of Lords in turn rejected this discretionary approach, favouring the application of a strict rule to determine when a plaintiff could assert an interest. However, it was divided as to the appropriate rule. Lord Goff and Lord Keith held that the equitable maxim requiring clean hands should be strictly applied. Lord Goff explained how this would operate:

> once it comes to the attention of a court of equity that the claimant has not come to the court with clean hands, the court will refuse to assist the claimant, even though the claimant can prima facie establish his claim without recourse to underlying fraudulent or illegal purpose.[90]

In contrast, the majority adopted an evidential approach, whereby a claimant is entitled to enforce an equitable interest provided that he or she did not have to rely on the fact of the illegal purpose in order to establish that interest. Lord Browne-Wilkinson stated the principle:

> In my judgement the time has come to decide clearly that the rule is the same whether a plaintiff founds himself on a legal or equitable title: he is entitled to recover if he is not forced to plead or rely on the illegality, even if it emerges that the title on which he relied was acquired in the course of carrying through an illegal transaction.[91]

---

[88] [1994] 1 AC 340.   [89] [1992] 2 All ER 391.   [90] [1993] 3 All ER 65, at 75.
[91] [1993] 3 All ER 65, at 91.

He explained how this principle applied where the alleged equitable interest had arisen through the operation of a presumption of a resulting trust:

> The presumption of resulting trust is…crucial in considering the authorities. On that presumption…hinges the answer to the crucial question: does a plaintiff claiming under a resulting trust have to rely on the underlying illegality? Where the presumption of resulting trust applies, the plaintiff does not have to rely on the illegality. If he proves that the property is vested in the defendant alone but that the plaintiff provided part of the purchase money, or voluntarily transferred the property to the defendant, the plaintiff establishes his claim under a resulting trust unless either the contrary presumption of advancement displaces the presumption of resulting trust or the defendant leads evidence to rebut the presumption of resulting trust. Therefore, in cases where the presumption of advancement does not apply, a plaintiff can establish his equitable interest in the property without relying in any way on the underlying illegal transaction.[92]

Applying this principle it was therefore held that Milligan was entitled to assert her entitlement to a half-share of the equitable ownership of the house, since all she needed to do to establish her interest was to prove that she had contributed to the purchase price. This would give rise to a presumption of resulting trust in her favour, and she did not need to rely on the illegal purpose underlying the transaction.

The evidential approach adopted in *Tinsley v Milligan* has been applied in subsequent cases. In *Silverwood v Silverwood*[93] an elderly lady had transferred money to her grandchildren to enable her to claim income support to contribute towards the costs of her residential care. The Court of Appeal held that the plaintiff, who was a beneficiary under her will, was entitled to maintain that the money was held on resulting trust by the recipients, as he did not need to rely on the illegality to establish the resulting trust. Peter Gibson LJ also stated that it would be absurd and unjust if he could not lead evidence of fraud in order to disprove a spurious defence by the recipients. In *Lowson v Coombes*[94] a man had purchased a flat together with his mistress, but it was conveyed into her sole name so that his wife would not be able to maintain any claim to it. The Court of Appeal held that he was entitled to assert a half-interest by way of a resulting trust, despite the illegal purpose of frustrating any potential claim under the Matrimonial Causes Act 1973, because he did not need to rely on the illegal purpose to establish his entitlement. In *Zabihi v Janzemini & Ors*[95] Blackburne J held that it was no defence to a claim for the return of jewellery entrusted by the claimant to the defendant that the jewellery might have been imported illegally:

> The illegal importation of the jewellery, assuming that to have happened, is irrelevant to the claim against Mr Janzemini in that it is not necessary to the establishment of Mr Zabihi's title to the jewellery and thus to his claim to recover it or its value that he should have to rely on its illegal importation.[96]

---

[92] [1993] 3 All ER 65, at 87.   [93] (1997) 74 P & CR 453.   [94] [1999] Ch 373.
[95] [2008] EWHC 2910.   [96] [2008] EWHC 2910, at [286].

However, it has also been subjected to criticism. In *Silverwood v Silverwood*[97] itself, Nourse LJ described the principle adopted in *Tinsley v Milligan* as a 'straitjacket' and indicated that he would have preferred a more flexible approach. In particular the approach adopted by the House of Lords arbitrarily differentiates between situations where a presumption of resulting trust and a presumption of advancement are operative. While Milligan was held able to assert her interest by way of a presumed resulting trust without the need to rely on the fact of her illegal conduct, a more difficult problem would have arisen if the countervailing presumption of advancement had applied between Tinsley and herself. In such circumstances she would only have been entitled to assert her interest if she could rebut the presumption, which would require evidence of the illegal purpose of the transaction. The Court of Appeal was forced to grapple with such a difficulty in *Tribe v Tribe*,[98] where a presumption of advancement did arise between the parties. As Nourse LJ observed in *Silverwood v Silverwood*:

> It is not at all easy to understand or to see any public or other policy or advantage behind a rule which regulates the claimant's right of recovery solely according to whether the other party to the transaction is his wife, child or fiancée on the one hand or his brother, grandchild or anyone else on the other.[99]

Lord Goff, in his dissenting judgment, also pointed to the arbitrary consequences that might follow from the application of the principle adopted by the majority in *Tinsley v Milligan*:

> But it is not to be forgotten that other cases in this category will not evoke the same sympathy on the part of the court. There may be cases in which the fraud is far more serious than that in the present case, and is uncovered not as a result of a confession but only after a lengthy police investigation and a prolonged criminal trial. Again there may be cases in which a group of terrorists, or armed robbers, secure a base for their criminal activities by buying a house in the name of a third party not directly implicated in those activities. In cases such as these there will almost certainly be no presumption of advancement. Is it really to be said that criminals such as these, or their personal representatives, are entitled to invoke the assistance of a court of equity in order to establish an equitable interest in property?[100]

In the light of such criticisms the law regarding illegality, alongside defences to illegality in contract and tort, has been reviewed by the Law Commission, who have recommended the abandonment of the 'reliance principle' adopted in *Tinsley v Milligan* in favour of granting the court a discretion to determine that a beneficiary ought not to be allowed to enforce the equitable interest.[101] The operation of this proposed discretion is discussed in more detail later in the context of the operation of the presumption of advancement, since this has provided the context for the more serious difficulties.

---

[97] (1997) 74 P & CR 453.   [98] [1996] Ch 107.   [99] (1997) 74 P & CR 453, at 458.
[100] [1993] 3 All ER 65, at 79.
[101] 'The Illegality Defence'. Law Com No 320, following 'Illegal Transactions: The Effect of Illegality on Contracts and Trusts' (1999), Law Com CP No 154.

3 The presumption of advancement

(1) Nature of the presumption

In some circumstances where a person voluntarily transfers property into the name of another, or contributes to its purchase, the law presumes that a gift was intended and that the transferor/contributor did not intend to retain any interest in the property concerned. This presumption, known as the 'presumption of advancement', displaces the presumption of resulting trust. The presumption of advancement arises as a consequence of a pre-existing relationship between the parties to the transfer or acquisition, where the transferor/contributor is regarded as morally obliged to provide for the person benefiting. As Lord Eldon stated in *Murless v Franklin*:

> The general rule that on a purchase by one man in the name of another, the nominee is a trustee for the purchaser, is subject to exception where the purchaser is under a species of natural obligation to provide for the nominee.[102]

The range of relationships where equity recognizes a presumption of advancement reflects a nineteenth-century understanding of family responsibility, and it is clear that, today, the strengths of the presumptions vary to reflect differing social circumstances. However, the state of the law in this area remains far from satisfactory.

The presumption of advancement may at some time be relegated to legal history. Section 199 of the Equality Act 2010[103] would abolish the presumption of advancement with prospective effect.[104] The reason for the abolition of the presumption is motivated not by the concern that the presumption is seen as antiquated and outmoded in the modern day, but by the suggestion that it was in breach of Article 5 of Protocol 7 of the European Convention on Human Rights and Fundamental Freedoms 1950 and therefore needed to be abolished should the UK choose to accede to that Protocol.

The need for the provision has been questioned,[105] and there has also been such a long delay in implementing this (and some other provisions of the Act) that it is an open question when, if ever, it will come into force. At the time of writing, this

---

[102] (1818) 1 Swan 13, at 17.

[103] This section is part of a package of provisions relating to family property, located in Part 15 of the Act.

[104] See s 199(2) relating to property transfers undertaken before the commencement of the section (s 199(2)(a)) or acts done in pursuance of an obligation arising under a pre-existing obligation under the presumption of advancement (s 199(2)(b)).

[105] See further Glister 'Section 199 of the Equality Act 2010: How Not To Abolish The Presumption of Advancement' (2010) 73 MLR 807; where is it is argued that the presumption does not breach Article 5 of Protocol 7 and, at any rate, the drafting of s 199 (particularly s 199(2)(a)) means that abolition will not have this effect and should only be enacted in part, if at all.

section is not yet in force and is still awaiting an order of the Lord Chancellor to commence it.[106]

(2) Relationships giving rise to the counter-presumption of advancement

(a) Father and child

Traditionally, there was a strong presumption of advancement between a father and his child.[107] In *Re Roberts (Decd)*[108] Evershed J held that the presumption of advancement applied where a father had made payments on a policy of assurance taken out on his son's life. He said that:

> It is well established that a father making payments on behalf of his son prima facie, and in the absence of contrary evidence, is to be taken to be making and intending an advance in favour of the son and for his benefit.[109]

In *B v B*[110] a Canadian court held that the presumption of advancement applied where a father had purchased a winning lottery ticket in the name of his 12-year-old daughter. She was therefore entitled to the winnings absolutely. The rationale for the presumption of advancement between a father and child is that a father, by the very nature of his position, is under a duty to provide for his child.[111] This may include the child's mother if she stands in loco parentis. There is no presumption of advancement in the case of other family relationships.[112]

The strength of this presumption of advancement between a father and child was questioned by the Court of Appeal in *McGrath v Wallis*,[113] where Nourse LJ stated:

> Ever since the decision in *Pettitt v Pettitt* it has been my understanding that, in its application to houses acquired for joint occupation, the equitable presumption of advancement has been reclassified as a judicial instrument of last resort, its subordinate status comparable to that of the contra proferentem rule in the construction of deeds and contracts... For myself, I have been unable to recollect any subsequent case of this kind in which the presumption has proved decisive...[114]

---

[106] The time of writing is August 2014. See s 216—this is true of all of Part 15 (ss 198–201). The Act received Royal Assent on 8 April 2010, but there is a detailed series of commencement orders relating to different parts and sections of the Act—many provisions came into force on 1 October 2010, but many provisions are not yet implemented.

[107] See *Shephard v Cartwright* [1955] AC 431. In *Oliveri v Oliveri* (1995) 38 NSWLR 665 Powell J suggested that a presumption of advancement could operate between a stepfather and stepchild.

[108] [1946] Ch 1.

[109] [1946] Ch 1, at 5. See also, in more recent times, *Antoni v Antoni* [2007] UKPC 10, which concerned the transfer of company shares between father and child.   [110] (1976) 65 DLR (3d) 460.

[111] *Bennet v Bennet* (1879) LR 10 Ch D 474, at 476, per Jessel MR. This has led some other jurisdictions to hold the presumption of advancement inapplicable to children of adult age, as they are not in need of support—see Glister 'The Presumption of Advancement to Adult Children' [2007] Conv 370; Low 'Apparent Gifts: Re-Examining The Equitable Presumption' (2008) 124 LQR 369.

[112] See, for example, sister (*Noack v Noack* [1959] VR 137; *Gorog v Kiss* (1977) 78 DLR (3d) 690); son-in-law (*Knight v Biss* [1954] NZLR 55); and nephew (*Dury v Dury* (1675) 75 SS 205; *Russell v Scott* (1936) 55 CLR 440).

[113] [1995] 2 FLR 114.   [114] [1995] 2 FLR 114, at 115.

(b) Persons standing in loco parentis

A presumption of advancement also arises between a child and a person standing in loco parentis.[115] The rationale for this extension of the presumption was stated by Jessel MR in *Bennet v Bennet*:

> as regards a child, a person not the father of the child may put himself in the position of loco parentis to the child, and so incur the obligation to make provision for the child…[116]

(c) Husband and wife

The presumption of advancement also arises between a husband in favour of his wife (but not vice versa). The principle was stated in *Re Eykyn's Trusts*, by Malins V-C:

> The law of this court is perfectly settled that when a husband transfers money or other property into the name of his wife only, then the presumption is, that it is intended as a gift or advancement to the wife absolutely at once, subject to such marital control as he may exercise. And if a husband invests in money, stocks, or otherwise, in the names of himself and his wife, then also it is an advancement for the benefit of the wife absolutely if she survives her husband…[117]

The operation of the presumption in this context reflects a nineteenth-century social understanding of a husband's obligation to provide for his wife.

Although these comments were cited in *Pettitt v Pettitt*,[118] the House of Lords acknowledged that the presumption between husband and wife had reduced in significance.[119] Lord Reid suggested that the only reasonable basis for the presumption had been the economic dependence of wives on their husbands, and that given the changes in social circumstances 'the strength of the presumption must have much diminished'.[120]

Lord Diplock considered that it was not appropriate that transactions between married couples should be governed by presumptions 'based upon inferences of fact which an earlier generation of judges drew as to the most likely intentions of earlier generations of spouses belonging to the propertied classes of a different social era'.[121] The presumption of advancement also applies between a man and his fiancée.[122] In recent cases, the operation of the presumption in this context has come under further attack,[123] and Arden LJ has suggested in *Gibson v Revenue and Customs Prosecution*

---

[115] *Hepworth v Hepworth* (1870) LR 11 Eq 10; *Re Orme* (1883) 50 LT 51; *Shephard v Cartwright* [1955] AC 431; *Re Paradise Motor Co Ltd* [1968] 1 WLR 1125, CA.

[116] (1879) LR 10 Ch D 474.   [117] (1877) 6 Ch D 115, at 118.

[118] [1970] AC 777, at 815, per Lord Upjohn.

[119] See *Silver v Silver* [1958] 1 All ER 523, at 525, per Evershed MR. The presumption of advancement between husband and wife also applies in Ireland and Australia: *Heavey v Heavey* [1971] 111 ILTR 1; *M v M* [1980] 114 ILTR 46; *Doohan v Nelson* [1973] 2 NSWLR 320; *Napier v Public Trustee (Western Australia)* (1980) 32 ALR 153.   [120] [1970] AC 777, at 792.

[121] [1970] AC 777, at 792.

[122] *Moate v Moate* [1948] 2 All ER 486; *Silver v Silver* [1958] 1 WLR 259; *Tinker v Tinker (No 1)* [1970] P 136; *Mossop v Mossop* [1989] Fam 77.

[123] *Stack v Dowden* [2007] 2 AC 432, at [16] per Lord Walker and at [101] per Lord Neuberger. See also Lord Walker and Lady Hale in *Jones v Kernott* [2011] UKSC 53, at [24].

Office that the presumption of advancement no longer has any application where legal title to property is co-owned:

> the function of the presumption of advancement is now performed by the presumption of equal beneficial ownership of property held in joint names laid down in *Stack v Dowden*.[124]

(3) Relationships where no presumption of advancement arises

(a) Mother and child

No presumption of advancement arises between a mother and her child,[125] and there-fore if a mother transfers property voluntarily to her child the counter presumption of resulting trust will apply.[126] In *Bennet v Bennet*[127] Jessel MR explained the absence of the presumption on the basis that 'there is no moral legal obligation…no obligation accord-ing to the rules of equity—on a mother to provide for her child'.[128] Again, such reason-ing reflects nineteenth-century concepts of the family, and in modern social conditions mothers almost invariably share the responsibility to provide for their children.[129] Despite the socially archaic rationale, more modern cases have confirmed that there continues to be no presumption of advancement between a mother and child.[130] The presumption of resulting trust was applied by the Court of Appeal in *Gross v French*,[131] and by Hoffmann J in *Sekhon v Alissa*.[132] In the latter case, a mother had provided £22,500 to help her daugh-ter purchase a house. In the absence of sufficient evidence to rebut the presumption of a resulting trust, the mother was held entitled to an interest in the property.

Despite the absence of a presumption of advancement between mother and child, the presumption of resulting trust arising in default is relatively weak and easily rebut-ted. As Jessel MR said in *Bennet v Bennet*:

> We arrive then at this conclusion, that in the case of a mother…it is easier to prove a gift than in the case of a stranger: in the case of a mother very little evidence beyond the rela-tionship is wanted, there being very little additional motive required to induce a mother to make a gift to her child.[133]

In *Nelson v Nelson*[134] the Australian High Court has held that a presumption of advancement should operate between a mother and child.[135] In England the decision in *Re Cameron (Decd)*[136] suggests a possible avenue by which it might be found that the

---

[124] [2008] EWCA Civ 645, at [27].

[125] See Dowling 'The Presumption of Advancement between Mother And Child' [1996] Conv 274.

[126] *Re De Visme* (1863) 2 De GJ & Sm 17; *Bennet v Bennet* (1878–79) LR 10 Ch D 474. See also: *Sayre v Hughes* (1867–68) LR 5 Eq 376; *Gore-Grimes v Grimes* [1937] IR 470.   [127] (1879) LR 10 Ch D 474.

[128] (1879) LR 10 Ch D 474, at 478.   [129] Compare *Dullow v Dullow* [1985] 3 NSWLR 531.

[130] See, however, *Close Invoice Company Ltd v Abowa* [2010] EWHC 1920 (QB), where Deputy Judge Mr Simon Picken QC felt that, as in Australian law, there the presumption of advancement should apply between mother and child.   [131] (1975) 238 Estates Gazette 39.

[132] [1989] 2 FLR 94.

[133] (1879) 10 Ch D 474, at 480. See, however, *Sekhon v Alissa* [1989] 2 FLR 94, where Hoffmann J held that the evidence was inconsistent with there being a gift.   [134] (1995) 132 ALR 133.

[135] In *Re Dreger Estate* (1994) 97 Man R (2d) 39 it was held that in modern conditions the presumption of advancement ought to be applicable between mother and child.   [136] [1999] 2 All ER 924.

presumption should operate between a mother and child. Lindsay J held that, in the light of the difference between Victorian and modern attitudes to the ownership and ability to dispose of property, it would be appropriate nowadays to take both parents to be in loco parentis for the purposes of the succession rule against double portions unless the contrary is proved.[137]

(b) Wife and husband

Similarly, no presumption of advancement operates between a wife and her husband, so that in orthodox theory if a wife voluntarily transfers property into the name of her husband, or contributes to the purchase of property in his name, a presumption of resulting trust arises. Thus, in *Re Curtis*,[138] in the absence of evidence that a gift was intended, a wife was presumed to enjoy the equitable interest in shares, which she had voluntarily transferred into the name of her husband, by way of a resulting trust.[139] The absence of the presumption seems to have been accepted in the more recent case of *Mossop v Mossop*,[140] and led to the presumption of a resulting trust in *Abrahams v Trustee in Bankruptcy of Abrahams*,[141] where a wife contributed to a syndicate purchasing National Lottery tickets in the name of her husband.

The absence of the presumption of advancement between a wife and her husband reflects nineteenth-century social circumstances. As was noted earlier, in *Pettitt v Pettitt*[142] the House of Lords held that the presumption of resulting trust between a wife and her husband was of much diminished strength and would be rebutted by very slight evidence that a gift was intended. Following *Stack v Dowden*[143] and *Jones v Kernott*,[144] no presumption of resulting trust arises where a property is acquired in the joint names of husband and wife as their family home since this now gives rise to a presumption of ownership in equal shares. Even outside this narrow context, the jurisprudence being developed by the courts in relation to the family home has regard to such a wide range of factors that there will rarely be any place for the application of classical presumptions of advancement in this context.

(c) Cohabiting couples/mistresses

There is no presumption of advancement between cohabiting couples (whether heterosexual or homosexual),[145] nor between a man and his mistress.[146] The presumption of resulting trust will therefore apply if property is voluntarily transferred in such cases, except where the jurisprudence relating to the acquisition of a family home produces a different result.

---

[137] [1999] 2 All ER 924, at 939.   [138] (1885) 52 LT 244.

[139] See also *Mercier v Mercier* [1903] 2 Ch 98; *Pearson v Pearson* (1965) *The Times*, 30 November; *Pettitt v Pettitt* [1970] AC 777; *Heseltine v Heseltine* [1971] 1 WLR 342; *Northern Bank Ltd v Henry* [1981] IR 1; *Allied Irish Banks Ltd v McWilliams* [1982] NI 156.

[140] [1988] 2 All ER 202, at 206, where Lawton LJ cited the relevant principles from Snell, *Principles of Equity* (28th edn, 1982), p 183.   [141] [1999] BPIR 637.

[142] [1970] AC 777.   [143] [2007] 2 AC 432.   [144] [2012] 1 AC 776.

[145] *Rider v Kidder* (1805) 10 Ves 360; *Soar v Foster* (1858) 4 K & J 152; *Allen v Snyder* [1977] 2 NSWLR 685; *Calverly v Green* (1984) 56 ALR 483.   [146] *Diwell v Farnes* [1959] 1 WLR 624.

(4) **Rebutting a presumption of advancement**

(a) **Evidence required to rebut a presumption of advancement**

A presumption of advancement will be rebutted by evidence that the transferor (or contributor) did not intend to make a gift but wished to retain an interest in the property transferred or acquired. In *Re Gooch*[147] Sir Daniel Gooch transferred shares into the name of his eldest son. The son paid the dividends from the shares to his father, who also retained the share certificates. Kay J held that the presumption of advancement was rebutted by evidence that the shares had been transferred to qualify the son to become a director of the company, and that no gift had been intended. In *Warren v Gurney*,[148] a father purchased a house in the name of his daughter prior to her wedding. He retained the title deeds until his death. The Court of Appeal held that the presumption of advancement was rebutted by evidence that at the time of the transaction the father had intended her husband to repay the money. The retention of the title deeds was considered a very significant fact, as 'one would have expected the father to have handed them over either to [his daughter] or her husband, if he had intended the gift'.[149] In *McGrath v Wallis*[150] a house was acquired for joint occupancy by a father and son in the sole name of the son. The purchase price was provided partly by the proceeds of sale of the father's previous house and partly by means of a mortgage. The Court of Appeal held that the presumption of advancement was rebutted by evidence that the father had intended to retain an interest in the ownership of the house, including an unsigned declaration of trust which would have shared the beneficial ownership in the proportions represented by the deposit and mortgage, respectively.

The mere fact that any rents and profits generated from the property concerned are returned to the purchaser or transferor will not conclusively rebut a presumption of advancement. In *Stamp Duties Comrs v Byrnes*[151] a father had purchased property in Australia in the name of his sons. They paid over to him the rents received from the properties, and he paid for rates and repairs. The Privy Council held that as it was not unusual for a father to transfer property to a son while continuing to receive any rents and profits during his lifetime, the presumption of advancement had not been rebutted:

> Having regard to the state of the family and the relations subsisting between Mr Byrnes and his two sons who were living at home, it seems very natural that the sons receiving advances should yet feel a delicacy in taking the fruits during their father's lifetime. They had all they wanted as things were, and if they were unduly favoured it might possibly have created some feeling of jealousy among the rest.[152]

Although the opening of a bank account by a husband in the joint names of himself and his wife will lead to the presumption of a joint tenancy of the money therein,[153]

---

[147] (1890) 62 LT 384.
[148] [1944] 2 All ER 472. See also *Webb v Webb* [1992] 1 All ER 17; refd [1994] 3 All ER 911.
[149] [1944] 2 All ER 472, at 473, per Morton LJ.   [150] [1995] 2 FLR 114.   [151] [1911] AC 386.
[152] [1911] AC 386, at 392.   [153] See *Re Bishop* [1965] Ch 450; *Re Figgis* [1969] 1 Ch 123.

the presumption of advancement operating between them may be rebutted. In the nineteenth-century case of *Marshal v Crutwell*[154] it was held that the presumption of advancement was rebutted where a husband had transferred his bank account into the joint names of himself and his wife. The court held that the transfer was merely for convenience, since the husband was in ill health and could not draw cheques himself. His wife was not therefore entitled to the balance in the account on his death. In *Anson v Anson*[155] the presumption of advancement was rebutted where a husband had entered a guarantee of an overdraft on a bank account in his wife's name. After their divorce he was called to pay £500 to the bank under the guarantee, and demanded repayment from his wife. Pearson J held that the intention was that the debt would remain her debt, and the guarantee to the bank was not intended to relieve her of her obligation but merely to solve her immediate banking emergency.

(b) Rebuttal of a presumption of advancement by evidence of an illegal purpose

(i) The general rule

It has been seen earlier that, as a general rule, a plaintiff will not be permitted to rely on evidence of his own illegal conduct to rebut a presumption of resulting trust.[156] He will similarly be prevented from relying on evidence of an illegal purpose to rebut a presumption of advancement. In *Gascoigne v Gascoigne*[157] a husband took a lease of land in his wife's name. The judge at first instance held that the presumption of advancement was rebutted by evidence that he had not intended to make a gift of the lease to his wife because it had been taken in her name only to defeat the claims of his creditors. However, the Court of Appeal held that he was not entitled to rebut the presumption by raising evidence of the illegal purpose underlying the transaction:

> what the learned judge has done is this: He has permitted the plaintiff to rebut the presumption which the law raises by setting up his own illegality and fraud, and to obtain relief in equity because he has succeeded in proving it. The plaintiff cannot do this...[158]

This restriction was followed by the Court of Appeal in *Tinker v Tinker (No 1)*,[159] where a husband had purchased a house in the name of his wife, on the advice of his solicitor, again with the intention of preventing the house being seized by creditors if his business failed. On the breakdown of the marriage it was held that he could not rebut the presumption of advancement. Lord Denning MR stated:

> he cannot say that the house is his own and, at one and the same time, say that it is his wife's. As against his wife, he wants to say that it belongs to him. As against his creditors, that it belongs to her. That simply will not do. Either it was conveyed to her for her own use

---

[154] (1875) LR 20 Eq 328.   [155] [1953] 1 QB 636.
[156] See *Tinsley v Milligan* [1993] 3 All ER 65, at 90. See J D Davies, 'Presumptions and Illegality' in Oakley, *Trends in Contemporary Trust Law* (1996).   [157] [1918] 1 KB 223.
[158] [1918] 1 KB 223, at 226.   [159] [1970] P 136.

absolutely; or it was conveyed to her as trustee for her husband. It must be one or the other. The presumption is that it was conveyed to her for her own use: and he does not rebut that presumption by saying that he only did it to defeat his creditors...[160]

In *Re Emery's Investments Trusts*[161] a husband was held unable to rebut a presumption of advancement when he had purchased American stock in the name of his American wife to avoid taxation under American Federal law, and in *Chettiar v Chettiar*[162] a father could not rebut a presumption of resulting trust where he had purchased a rubber estate in the name of his son to avoid a provision restricting the maximum area of land in a rubber plantation that an individual could own.

(ii) A modified approach

While the policy objective of this strict approach is to discourage persons from entering illegal transactions, in the more recent case of *Tribe v Tribe*[163] the Court of Appeal demonstrated a marked reluctance to disallow a father from rebutting the presumption of advancement arising when he had transferred property voluntarily to his son to achieve an illegal purpose. The father was the owner of a majority shareholding in a family company and the tenant of two properties occupied by the company as licensee. The landlord of these premises served notice of various alleged dilapidations on the father, requiring him to carry out substantial repairs. The father was advised by his solicitor that, if the claims were valid, he might be forced to sell the company shares to pay for the repairs. He therefore transferred them to his son as a means of safeguarding his assets. The transfer was stated to be made for a consideration of £78,030, but no money was ever paid. In the event, the father was never required to carry out the repairs and he sought to recover the shares from his son. The son refused to retransfer them to him, and the father alleged that he held them on bare trust for him. The son argued that the presumption of advancement applied in his favour and that the father could not rebut it by evidence of the illegal attempt to evade his creditors. While accepting that the decision of the House of Lords in *Tinsley v Milligan*[164] had the general effect that a presumption of advancement cannot be rebutted by evidence of an underlying illegal purpose, the Court of Appeal held that this general rule was subject to an exception if the 'illegal purpose has not been carried into effect'. As Nourse LJ explained:

> The judge found that the illegal purpose was to deceive the plaintiff's creditors by creating an appearance that he no longer owned any shares in the company. He also found that it was not carried into effect in any way. [Counsel for the defendant] attacked the latter finding on grounds which appeared to me to confuse the purpose with the transaction. Certainly the transaction was carried into effect by the execution and registration of the transfer. But *Wright's*[165] case shows that that is immaterial. It is the purpose which has to be carried into effect and that would only have happened if and when a creditor of the

---

[160] [1970] P 136, at 141.   [161] [1959] Ch 410.   [162] [1962] 1 All ER 494.
[163] [1995] 4 All ER 236; (1996) 112 LQR 386 (Rose); [1996] CLJ 23 (Virgo); (1997) 60 MLR 102 (Creighton). See also (1995) 111 LQR 135 (Enonchong); [1996] RLR 78 (Enonchong).   [164] [1993] 3 All ER 65.
[165] *Perpetual Executors and Trustees Association of Australia Ltd v Wright* (1917) 23 CLR 185.

plaintiff had been deceived by the transaction. The judge said there was no evidence of that and clearly he did not think it appropriate to infer it. Nor is it any objection to the plaintiff's right to recover the shares that he did not demand their return until after the danger had passed and it was no longer necessary to conceal the transfer from his creditors. All that matters is that no deception was practised on them. For these reasons the judge was right to hold that the exception applied.[166]

Millett LJ reached the same conclusion but stated the principle more broadly, holding that a person is entitled to recover property transferred for an illegal purpose if he withdrew from the transaction before it was carried out. He attempted to formulate a single unitary principle derived from the equitable doctrines regarding the rebuttal of presumptions of resulting trust and advancement and common law cases where it had been held that a party was entitled to withdraw from an illegal contract. While he made clear that effectual withdrawal from a transaction did not require 'genuine repentance' on the part of the wrongdoer, he held that he must have withdrawn voluntarily. There would therefore be no effective withdrawal if 'he is forced to [withdraw] because his plan has been discovered'.[167]

Despite the superficial attraction of simplicity, this proposed general approach is inadequate because it is unclear when a transaction has been carried into effect so as to prevent withdrawal. As Millett LJ noted, early common law cases indicated that a party to an illegal contract could withdraw only so long as it has not been completely performed, whereas later decisions held that any recovery under the contract was barred once partial performance had occurred.[168] He formulated his general proposition in the following terms:

> The transferor can lead evidence of the illegal purpose whenever it is necessary for him to do so provided that he has withdrawn from the transaction before the illegal purpose has been *wholly or partly* carried into effect.[169]

It is suggested that this is extremely confusing, as it does not clarify whether withdrawal is possible in cases where the transaction was partially carried into effect.

(iii) Explaining the modified approach

Tribe v Tribe should only be considered good authority to the extent that it decides that evidence of an illegal purpose may be admitted to rebut a presumption of advancement if the illegal purpose has not been carried into effect at all. Nonetheless, even when assessed in the light of this limited proposition, the decision remains unsatisfactory. The conclusion that the illegal purpose had not been carried into effect was artificial, as in reality the act which was intended to achieve the illegal purpose was the transfer of the legal title of the shares to the son, thus on the face of it divesting the father of any interest. It is arguable that the illegal object was carried into effect at the very moment that the legal title was effectually transferred to the son. Far from

---

[166] [1995] 4 All ER 236, at 248.   [167] [1995] 4 All ER 236, at 259.
[168] *Kearley v Thomson* (1890) 24 QBD 742.   [169] [1995] 4 All ER 236, at 259.

rebutting the presumption of advancement, the very act of transferring the shares to the son with the illegal aim of defeating the creditors actually reinforces the presumption of a gift to the son. As Millett LJ stated:

> The only way in which a man can protect his property from his creditors is by divesting himself of all beneficial interest in it. Evidence that he transferred the property in order to protect it from his creditors, therefore, does nothing by itself to rebut the presumption of advancement; it reinforces it. To rebut the presumption it is necessary to show that he intended to retain a beneficial interest and conceal it from his creditors.[170]

The reality is that, in both *Tribe v Tribe* and *Tinsley v Milligan*,[171] the respective courts were attempting to avoid the perceived unfairness that would result from the application of a strict rule against illegality intended to serve a general public policy of deterring wrongdoers. It would seem unfair if Milligan were to be prevented from asserting any entitlement to an equitable share of the house owned at law by Tinsley when they were both parties to the illegal purpose, and the consequence would be that Tinsley received a large windfall gain at Milligan's expense. The majority of the House of Lords was conveniently able to avoid such a result by exploiting the logic that Milligan merely needed to prove that she had contributed to the purchase price of the house to raise a presumption of resulting trust in her favour. While achieving justice between the parties, the decision represented a departure from the traditional position that a transferor could not recover property transferred in pursuit of an illegal purpose irrespective of whether the presumption of advancement or the presumption of resulting trust applied. *Tinsley v Milligan* therefore introduced an arbitrary distinction, whereby the general rule would apply where there was a presumption of advancement between the parties, but not where there was a presumption of resulting trust. As has been noted earlier, the circumstances in which a presumption of advancement arises are largely derived from out-dated conceptions of family responsibility. They are riddled with inconsistency, to such an extent that the courts have tended to treat them as of relatively little weight and easily rebutted. Given the inadequacy of the law determining the circumstances in which a presumption of advancement arises, any differentiation between the effects of illegality on such grounds is highly unsatisfactory. As Judge Weekes stated at first instance in *Tribe v Tribe*:

> Finally, it is not for me to criticise their Lordship's reasoning, but with the greatest respect I find it difficult to see why the outcome in cases such as the present one should depend to such a large extent on arbitrary factors, such as whether the claim is brought by a father against a son, or a mother against a son, or a grandfather against a grandson.[172]

It is also worth noting that, if the facts of *Tinsley v Milligan* were to be retried following the decisions of he highest courts in *Stack v Dowden*[173] and *Jones v Kernott*,[174] it is extremely unlikely that the presumption of a resulting trust could have been used to

---

[170] [1995] 4 All ER 236, at 259.   [171] [1994] 1 AC 340.
[172] Quoted by Nourse LJ [1995] 4 All ER 236, at 244. See also *Collier v Collier* [2003] WTLR 617, at 654–655, per Mance LJ.   [173] [2007] 2 AC 432.
[174] [2012] 1 AC 776.

facilitate Milligan's entitlement to an interest. It was suggested in these cases that the resulting trust analysis should be abandoned in cases relating to interests in the family home, otherwise than where the property was purchased as an investment.

(iv) The call for reform

The arbitrary operation of the rules on illegality established by *Tinsley v Milligan* can hardly be considered satisfactory.[175] One solution would be an approach which operates consistently, irrespective of the nature of the presumption applicable. Such consistency could have been obtained by retention of the traditional rule that an equitable interest cannot be asserted by a transferor of property if the purpose of the transfer was to give effect to an illegal purpose, irrespective of any presumption, be it advancement, resulting trust, or any other.[176] Instead, the estate would 'lie where it falls'. However, this approach was rejected by the majority in *Tinsley v Milligan* precisely because it would lead to unfairness in individual cases. It was also rejected by the High Court of Australia in *Nelson v Nelson*,[177] where Deane and Gummow JJ described it as a 'harsh and indiscriminate principle'. In that case, the approach of the House of Lords in *Tinsley v Milligan* was also rejected on the grounds that it generated different results which were 'entirely fortuitous being dependent upon the relationship between the parties', and therefore 'wholly unjustifiable on any policy ground'.[178] The High Court held that a person should only be prevented from asserting an equitable right if to allow him to do so would be inconsistent with the public policy applicable to the specific right claimed. Applying this test, the High Court held that public policy did not prevent a mother asserting an equitable interest in property she had transferred to her children. Mrs Nelson had provided the purchase money for a house which was transferred into the names of her two children to enable her to obtain a subsidized advance towards the purchase of another house under the Australian housing legislation. To obtain such an advance she had to declare that she did not own, or have an interest, in any other house. After she had received the advance the first house was sold, and one of the children claimed that he was entitled to half the proceeds of sale. It was held that Mrs Nelson could rebut the presumption of advancement operating in favour of the children because the policy of the particular legislation concerned would 'not be defeated if the court enforces her equitable right'. Thus, the court was willing to allow Mrs Nelson to assert her equitable entitlement even though the illegal purpose had been carried into effect, a result which would not have been possible through an application of the principles adopted in *Tribe v Tribe*. However, the majority further held that her right to assert her equitable interest should be conditional on repayment of her unlawful benefit to the state.

While there are undoubtedly problems with the current law, it should be noted that all members of the House of Lords in *Tinsley v Milligan* rejected a discretionary

---

[175] See also *Moore Stephens (a firm) (Respondents) v Stone Rolls Limited* [2009] UKHL 39, at [130], where Lord Phillips described *Tinsley v Milligan* as 'in some ways a difficult and controversial decision'.
[176] If the parties own the legal title jointly, there is a presumption of equal beneficial ownership—see *Jones v Kernott* [2012] 1 AC 776.   [177] (1995) 132 ALR 133.
[178] (1995) 132 ALR 133, at 166, per Dawson J.

approach to the effect of illegality on equitable property rights, preferring strict rules which would determine whether a right could be asserted. The law regarding illegality has been reviewed by the Law Commission.[179] Given its unsatisfactory nature, the Law Commission recommended in its earlier report the abandonment of the 'reliance principle' adopted in *Tinsley v Milligan* in favour of granting the court a discretion to declare a trust illegal or invalid.[180] This discretion would be structured so that a court would have to take into account a number of specified factors in reaching its decisions:

> those factors should be: (a) the seriousness of the illegality; (b) the knowledge and intention of the illegal trust beneficiary; (c) whether invalidity would tend to deter the illegality; (d) whether invalidity would further the purpose of the rule which renders the trust 'illegal'; and (e) whether invalidity would be a proportionate response to the claimant's participation in the illegality.[181]

The Law Commission's final report advocates a modified and much more restrictive version of the statutory discretion scheme it had previously advocated.[182] The proposed discretion is limited to cases where a trust was created, or subsequently continued, in order to conceal the true beneficial ownership of the trust property in connection with the commission of an offence.[183] The Law Commission's view is that an illegality should only have an effect on the beneficial entitlement under the trust when the court considers that there are exceptional circumstances.[184] The draft Bill sets out a list of relevant factors.[185]

(c) Admissibility of evidence to rebut a presumption of advancement

As in the case of the rebuttal of presumptions of a resulting trust, only evidence of the plaintiff's acts and declarations contemporaneous with the transaction are admissible in his favour to rebut the presumption of advancement. Evidence of subsequent acts and declarations are only admissible as evidence against him. This principle was stated and applied by the House of Lords in *Shephard v Cartwright*,[186] where Lord Simmonds approved a summary of the law in Snell's *Equity*:

> The acts and declarations of the parties before or at the time of the purchase, or so immediately after it as to constitute a part of the transaction, are admissible in evidence either for or against the party who did the acts or made the declaration... But subsequent declarations are admissible as evidence only against the party who made them, and not in his favour.[187]

---

[179] 'The Illegality Defence'. Law Com No 320; Davis 'The Illegality Defence: Turning Back The Clock' [2010] Conv 282.

[180] 'Illegal Transactions: The Effect of Illegality on Contracts and Trusts' (1999), Law Com CP No 154.

[181] Enonchong 'Illegal Transactions: The Future?' [2000] RLR 82, at para 8.63.

[182] 'The Illegality Defence'. Law Com 320.

[183] 'The Illegality Defence'. Law Com 320, at paras 2.24–2.35.

[184] 'The Illegality Defence'. Law Com. 320, at para 2.61.

[185] Part of the reasoning behind this is to accommodate the effect of *Stack v Dowden* on acquisitions of property.   [186] [1955] AC 431.

[187] [1955] AC 431, at 445; Snell, *Principles of Equity* (24th edn, 1990), p 153.

In 1929 Philip Shephard subscribed for shares in the name of his children. In 1934 the shares were sold to a company promoted by him, and the children signed the requisite documents at his request without knowing what they were doing. The proceeds of sale were paid into separate deposit accounts in the children's names. They later signed documents, unaware of their contents, authorizing him to withdraw money from the accounts, whereupon he withdrew money from them without their knowledge. In an action by the children against his executors the central issue was whether the presumption of advancement had been rebutted. The House of Lords held that evidence of the father's acts after the transaction of 1929 were not admissible to prove the rebuttal of the presumption of advancement as they did not form part of the original transaction.[188]

4 Reform of presumed resulting trusts

The presumptions of resulting trusts largely operate as a mechanism for allocating the burden of proof when there is a dispute as to intended effect of a transaction on the beneficial ownership of property. As the Australian High Court stated in *Russell v Scott*:

> The presumption of resulting trusts does no more than call for proof of an intention to confer beneficial ownership.[189]

Thus where the presumption of resulting trust applies, a transferee will have to discharge the burden of proof by demonstrating that a gift was intended, whereas if the presumption of advancement applies the transferor will bear the burden of proving that no gift was intended. The presumptions may serve the purpose of protecting vulnerable individuals where property has been transferred, or contributions made, in circumstances where there was very little evidence as to the intended nature of the transaction. It has already been noted that the role of the purchase money resulting trust appears to have been irreversibly altered in relation to the acquisition of interests in the family home, and discussion of this aspect, alongside potential legislative solutions to the issue, are considered in Chapter 10.

5 Resulting trusts operating to reverse unjust enrichment?

At the beginning of this chapter it was noted that there are two categories of resulting trusts recognized in English law, historically differentiated as 'presumed' and 'automatic' resulting trusts. However, a great deal of recent debate has been addressed to the question whether a third type should be recognized, namely, a

---

[188] Similarly, evidence of the children's acts in signing the documents at their father's request was not admissible against them, because they had been unaware of the contents.

[189] (1936) 55 CLR 440, per Dixon and Evatt JJ.

restitutionary resulting trust, which arises for the purpose of reversing unjust enrichment. Although English law did not historically recognize a right to restitution founded on a general principle against unjust enrichment, in *Likpin Gorman v Karpnale Ltd*[190] the House of Lords held that 'unjust enrichment' should be recognized as a valid autonomous cause of action. This recognition has been reiterated in many subsequent decisions[191] and is now beyond doubt. A claimant will be entitled to restitution whenever he can demonstrate that the defendant was unjustly enriched at his expense. Where a claimant can demonstrate an entitlement to receive restitution from the defendant, the question arises as to the nature of the remedy available to him to effect such restitution. The claimant will generally be entitled to a personal remedy, requiring the defendant to pay over to him an amount equivalent to the enrichment that had been received, but this remedy will be of little use if the defendant is insolvent. If, however, it can be shown that property constituting the enrichment received by the defendant was subjected to a trust, the plaintiff will be able to assert a proprietary claim to any assets remaining in the defendant's hands which are the traceable proceeds of the enrichment received. Such a trust will not arise expressly and there would be no grounds for finding a presumed resulting trust.

However, in a significant article, Professor Birks argued that a resulting trust should arise whenever a defendant receives an unjust enrichment conferred by mistake or under a contract the consideration for which wholly fails.[192] If such a resulting trust were to arise from the mere fact of enrichment in such cases the claimant would be entitled to a proprietary remedy. This thesis was considered in *Westdeutsche Landesbank Girozentrale v Islington London Borough Council*,[193] where it was comprehensively rejected by the House of Lords, which preferred the critical approach of William Swadling.[194] The case involved an interest rate swap agreement entered into between the plaintiff bank and the defendant local authority. Under the agreement the bank made a payment of £2.5m to the authority. However, as a consequence of the decision of the House of Lords in *Hazell v Hammersmith and Fulham London Borough Council*,[195] the contract between the parties was ultra vires the local authority and therefore void. The bank sought restitution of the balance of the payment it had made, less the repayments the authority had already made, together with interest. In the House of Lords the sole remaining question was as to the nature of the interest payable on the award of restitution. If the bank was only entitled to restitution at common law then the court had no jurisdiction to award compound interest. However, the

---

[190] [1991] 2 AC 548. See Birks 'English Recognition of Unjust Enrichment' [1991] LMCLQ 473.

[191] See *Woolwich Equitable Building Society v IRC* [1993] AC 70; *Westdeutsche Landesbank Girozentrale v Islington London Borough Council* [1996] AC 669; *Kleinwort Benson Ltd v Glasgow City Council* [1999] 1 AC 153, HL.

[192] Birks, 'Restitution and Resulting Trusts', in Goldstein (ed), *Equity: Contemporary Legal Development* (1992). See also Chambers, *Resulting Trusts* (1997), pp 93–219.

[193] [1996] AC 669; (1996) 112 LQR 521 (Cape); [1996] CLJ 432 (Jones); [1997] LMCLQ 441 (Stevens).

[194] (1996) 16 LS 133.   [195] [1992] 2 AC 1.

bank alleged that the payment had been received subject to a resulting trust, because the contract under which it was made was void, thus rooting their claim in equity and entitling the court to award compound interest. Lord Browne-Wilkinson explained that the circumstances of the payment could not have given rise to a resulting trust:

> Applying these conventional principles of resulting trust to the present case, the bank's claim must fail. There was no transfer of money to the local authority on express trusts: therefore a resulting trust of type (B) above could not arise. As to type (A) above, any presumption of resulting trust is rebutted, since it is demonstrated that the bank paid, and the local authority received, the upfront payment with the intention that the moneys so paid should become the absolute property of the local authority. It is true that the parties were under a misapprehension that the payment was made in pursuance of a valid contract. But that does not alter the actual intentions of the parties at the date the payment was made...[196]

He further elucidated three reasons for rejecting Professor Birks' thesis that the concept of the resulting trust should be extended to provide a plaintiff with a proprietary remedy whenever he had transferred value to a defendant under a mistake or subject to a condition which is not subsequently satisfied. First, he held that trust interests could not arise in relation to the restitutionary concept of 'value transferred' but only in relation to defined property. Second, he considered that a trust would only arise at the moment that a defendant received a payment if he was aware of the circumstances alleged to give rise to the trust. Since a recipient of a payment subsequently found void for mistake or failure of consideration will not have been aware of the circumstances rendering it void at the date of receipt, his conscience cannot have been affected so as to generate a trust. Thirdly, he noted that the thesis was flawed by the need to artificially exclude cases of partial failure to perform a contract, despite the fact that the wider concept logically led to a resulting trust in such cases.

Alongside these conceptual objections to the recognition of restitutionary resulting trusts, the House of Lords considered that the consequential expansion in proprietary entitlements would have unacceptable practical consequences for third parties.[197] For example, if money paid under a void contract was subject to a resulting trust, third parties who entered into transactions with the recipient of the payment might be affected by the trust interest of the payor, even though no one knew that the contract was void, so that they could not have been aware of the supposed trust. In the light of these considerations Lord Browne-Wilkinson concluded:

> If adopted, Professor Birks' wider concepts would give rise to all the practical consequences and injustice to which I have referred. I do not think it right to make an unprincipled alteration to the law of property (ie the law of trusts) so as to produce in the law of unjust enrichment the injustices to third parties...and the consequential commercial

---

[196] [1996] AC 669, at 708.
[197] See Burrows 'Swaps and Friction between Common Law and Equity' [1995] RLR 15 for a fuller consideration of the practical implications of the adoption of restitutionary resulting trusts.

uncertainty which any extension of proprietary interests in personal property is bound to produce.[198]

Although the House of Lords has rejected the adoption of a wider restitutionary resulting trust, this does not mean that a trust interest will never be raised for the purpose of reversing an unjust enrichment. Lord Browne-Wilkinson stated:

> Although the resulting trust is an unsuitable basis for developing proprietary restitutionary remedies, the remedial constructive trust, if introduced into English law, may provide a more satisfactory road forward.[199]

The nature of the remedial constructive trust is examined in Chapter 9.

---

[198] [1996] AC 669, at 709.   [199] [1996] AC 669, at 716.

9

Constructive trusts

This chapter considers the operation of constructive trusts, and the situations in which such trusts are found to arise under equitable principles to counter unconscionable conduct. Constructive trusts arise in various, defined circumstances wherever justice and good conscience require it, as English law has yet, despite increasing support in some quarters, to develop the concept of a 'remedial' constructive trust.

1 Introduction to constructive trusts

(1) Terminology

The major obstacle to any analysis of the English doctrine of constructive trusts is the wide number of circumstances described by the term 'constructive trust'. This has led Sir Peter Millett to comment that 'the use of the language of constructive trust has become such a fertile source of confusion that it would be better if it were abandoned'.[1] It has been used to describe a range of situations as diverse as the remedy available against a fiduciary who has made an unauthorized profit in breach of his duty, to the creation of a trust where parties make mutual wills. At its simplest, the term 'constructive trust' describes the circumstances in which property is subjected to a trust by operation of law. Unlike an expressly declared trust, a constructive trust does not come into being solely in consequence of the express intention of a settlor. Unlike a resulting trust, it is not the product of an implied or presumed intention.[2] In *Westdeutsche Landesbank Girozentrale v Islington London Borough Council*[3] Lord Browne-Wilkinson identified a constructive trust as a trust 'which the law imposed on [the trustee] by reason of his unconscionable conduct'.[4]

---

[1] McKendrick, *Commercial Aspects of Trusts and Fiduciary Obligations* (1992), p 3.

[2] But see, however, *Midland Bank plc v Cooke* [1995] 4 All ER 562, where the Court of Appeal failed to maintain a strict distinction between resulting and constructive trusts. The use of constructive trusts of common intention to provide a non-legal owner of a family home with a beneficial interest in equity does depend on an implied or imputed intention of the settlor and claimant, but does arise without the need for court intervention—this is explored further later in the chapter. The operation of trust in the family home is explored in detail in Chapter 10.

[3] [1996] AC 669; (1996) 112 LQR 521 (Cape); [1996] CLJ 432 (Jones); [1997] LMCLQ 441 (Stevens).

[4] [1996] AC 669, at 705. See also *Paragon Finance plc v D B Thakerar & Co* [1999] 1 All ER 400, 409, where Millett LJ stated that a 'constructive trust arises by operation of law whenever the circumstances are such

(2) **The English concept of the 'constructive trust'**

Although the terminology of 'constructive trust' is used throughout common law jurisdictions, it does not describe identical concepts. Different jurisdictions have developed widely differing views as to the nature of constructive trusts and the circumstances in which they come into existence. One of the most significant conceptual distinctions is between what are described as 'institutional' and 'remedial' constructive trusts.

(a) **The 'institutional' constructive trust**

An institutional constructive trust is a trust that is brought into being on the occurrence of specified events, without the need for the intervention of the court. The trust comes into being if the facts that are necessary to give rise to it are proved to have occurred. It exists from the time that the relevant events occurred.[5] The court does not impose the trust, but rather, recognizes that the beneficiary enjoys a pre-existing proprietary interest in the trust property. The court has no discretion to decide whether or not the property should be subject to a trust. Since an institutional constructive trust does not arise from the judgment of the court, it is capable of gaining priority over any interests acquired by third parties in the trust property during the period between the creation of the trust and its recognition by the court.

(b) **The 'remedial' constructive trust**

In contrast to the 'institutional' constructive trust, some other jurisdictions have come to regard constructive trusts as one of a range of remedies to facilitate restitution where a defendant has been unjustly enriched at the expense of a plaintiff. Having found that there has been an unjust enrichment, the court can, in its discretion, impose a constructive trust over assets representing any remaining enrichment in the hands of the defendant if appropriate, or alternatively award a monetary remedy. A remedial constructive trust is imposed by the court, which does not merely recognize a pre-existing proprietary right. The trust arises from the date of the court's judgment and it will not therefore gain automatic priority over the rights of third parties. These characteristics of a 'remedial' constructive trust were recognized in *Metall and Rohstoff AG v Donaldson Lufkin & Jenerette Inc*,[6] where Slade LJ stated:

> the court imposes a constructive trust *de novo* on assets which are not subject to any pre-existing trust as a means of granting equitable relief in a case where it considers it just that restitution should be made.[7]

---

that it would be unconscionable for the owner of property (usually but not necessarily the legal estate) to assert his beneficial interest in the property'.

[5] *Re Sharpe* [1980] 1 All ER 198, at 203, per Browne-Wilkinson J.   [6] [1990] 1 QB 391.
[7] [1990] 1 QB 391, at 478. See also *Re Polly Peck (No 2)* [1998] 3 All ER 812, at 831, where Nourse LJ defined a remedial constructive trust as 'an order of the court granting, by way of remedy, a proprietary right to someone who, beforehand, had no proprietary right'.

At present, despite some dicta in cases to the contrary,[8] English law only recognizes the 'institutional' constructive trust and has not been willing to adopt the remedial constructive trust.[9] Other jurisdictions, in particular Canada, have adopted an unjust enrichment analysis to explain the availability of constructive trusts, and the operation of the remedial constructive trust will be examined in detail at the end of this chapter.

(3) The search for a coherent theory

Given that the terminology of constructive trusts is utilized in so many different contexts, it is difficult to provide any coherent unifying theory that will adequately explain their incidence. English law has tended to take the view that constructive trusts arise in a range of relatively well circumscribed conditions in which the trustee's conduct is considered unconscionable. A previous edition of Snell's *Equity* concluded:

> For the present...constructive trusts fall for the most part in well-established categories, and it is only occasionally and in unusual circumstances that it would be necessary to take refuge in such a broad and fundamental principle [ie of unconscionability].[10]

In the case of the remedial constructive trust, the unifying fundamental principle is that of the reversal of unjust enrichment. Although superficially attractive as a touchstone, this merely shifts the goal posts, since it becomes necessary to define when an enrichment is 'unjust'. This would require the identification of common fact situations where enrichment is regarded as 'unjust', which may of themselves have no greater coherency than those regarded as giving rise to constructive trusts in English law. In this sense the restitutionary approach may simply reinvent the wheel under a different name.

Despite the difficulty of providing any single coherent theory for the enforcement of constructive trusts, the factor that appears to connect the circumstances in which the court will find that a constructive trust has arisen is an emphasis on the conduct of the party who is required to hold property subject to the constructive trust. Constructive trusts are imposed by equity in order to satisfy the demands of justice and good conscience,[11] and where it would be unjust to allow the trustee to assert an absolute entitlement to property. As Lord Denning MR observed in *Binions v Evans*,[12] quoting the words of an American judge:

> A constructive trust is the formula through which the conscience of equity finds expression. When property has been acquired in such circumstances that the holder of the legal title may not in good conscience retain the beneficial interest, equity converts him into a trustee.[13]

---

[8] See, particularly, *Thorner v Major* [2007] 2 AC 432; *Clarke v Meadus* [2010] EWHC 3117 (Ch).
[9] See *Metall und Rohstoff AG v Donaldson Lufkin & Jenrette Inc* [1990] 1 QB 391; *Westdeutsche Landesbank Girozentrale v Islington London Borough Council* [1996] AC 669; *Re Polly Peck (No 2)* [1998] 3 All ER 812.
[10] Snell, *Principles of Equity* (29th edn, 1990), p 197.
[11] *Carl-Zeiss-Stiftung v Herbert Smith & Co (No 2)* [1969] 2 Ch 276, at 301, per Edmund Davies LJ.
[12] [1972] Ch 359, at 386.
[13] *Beatty v Guggenheim Exploration Co* 225 NY 380 (1919), at 386 per Cardozo J.

The concept of 'justice and good conscience' is too broad to be of direct practical value.[14] Analysis of the precise conduct justifying the imposition of a constructive trust can only realistically be attempted in the context of the common circumstances where constructive trusts have been found to arise. This chapter will therefore follow the common approach of identifying and describing the circumstances in which English law will find that a constructive trust has been created.

(4) **The significance of constructive trusts**

(a) **Creation of proprietary interests**

Constructive trusts inherently create equitable proprietary interests in favour of identifiable beneficiaries. A trust cannot arise in abstract, but only in respect of defined property.[15] Constructive trusts therefore provide a means by which a legal owner will be required to hold property on trust for beneficiaries, despite the lack of any express or implied intention that he should do so, or where an intention to create a trust is ineffective because it is not expressed in compliance with the appropriate statutory formalities.[16] This ability of constructive trusts to generate proprietary interests has been especially significant in the context of the ownership of land. Alongside resulting trusts, constructive trusts provide a means by which a person can obtain a share of the beneficial ownership where no formal declaration of trust has been made in their favour.[17] Where constructive trusts do give rise to proprietary interests, they may have far-reaching effects, especially by detracting from the interests that third parties may have acquired after the trust had arisen, for example if land subject to a constructive trust has been mortgaged, and by gaining automatic priority over the rights of other creditors if the trustee is insolvent. The institutional nature of the constructive trust gives the court no flexibility to consider the potential effects of the constructive trust on such third parties or creditors.

(b) **Preservation of pre-existing equitable interests**

Constructive trusts also operate to preserve the interest of the beneficiaries of an existing trust, however created, if the legal title to the trust property is wrongly transferred by the trustee. A third party who purchases the legal title to the trust property from a trustee will take free from the pre-existing trust interests of the beneficiaries if he was a bona fide purchaser for value without notice. However, if the requirements of the doctrine of notice are not fulfilled, either because the transferee of the legal title was a volunteer who had not provided consideration, or because he had notice (whether

---

[14] See *Snell's Equity* (13th edn, 2000), p 221.

[15] *Westdeutsche Landesbank Girozentrale v Islington London Borough Council* [1996] AC 669, at 709, per Lord Browne-Wilkinson.

[16] *Rochefoucauld v Boustead* [1897] 1 Ch 196. See also, in this context, *Re Rose (Deceased)* ([1952] Ch 499), where it was held that a constructive trust arose once a transferor had done all he could do to transfer legal title to property—see further Chapter 7.

[17] This topic is explored fully in Chapter 10. See also Howard and Hill 'The Informal Creation of Interests in Land' (1995) 15 LS 356.

actual or constructive) of the existence of the trust, the transferee will hold the property as constructive trustee for the beneficiaries. By this means their pre-existing entitlements are preserved and the recipient will not be entitled to treat the property as if he were the absolute owner.

(c) Misappropriated property

Constructive trusts have increasingly come to prominence in commercial contexts where property has been misappropriated from its true owner. If the misappropriated property was not previously subject to a trust, it may be rendered subject to a constructive trust in the hands of the recipient if it was misappropriated by a person standing in a fiduciary relationship to the owner,[18] or if it was received in circumstances generating a fiduciary relationship between the recipient and the owner.[19] By means of such a constructive trust, the entitlement of the true owner is preserved in equity. In *Westdeutsche Landesbank Girozentrale v Islington London Borough Council*[20] Lord Browne-Wilkinson held that a thief would hold the money he had stolen on constructive trust for the victim.[21]

(d) Receipt of an unauthorized profit by a fiduciary

A constructive trust may also arise whenever a fiduciary receives an unauthorized profit in breach of the duty of loyalty that is owed to his principal, but only where the receipt involves a clear misuse of the beneficiary's assets (such as misappropriating the principal's property) or taking advantage of opportunities that were properly those of the principal.[22] Simple receipt of an unauthorized profit will not give rise to a constructive trust.[23] Instead, such parties may simply be liable to account for the profit. The distinction is important, as only where a constructive trust is imposed does the principal have an equitable proprietary interest in the unauthorized profits or their traceable proceeds. The intense debate over the availability of proprietary and personal remedies available against a fiduciary will be fully considered in Chapter 28.

---

[18] As, for example, in *Agip (Africa) v Jackson* [1991] Ch 547.

[19] *Chase Manhattan Bank NA v Israel-British Bank (London) Ltd* [1981] Ch 105.

[20] [1996] AC 669.

[21] [1996] AC 669, at 716. See *Twentieth Century Fox Film Corp v Harris* [2013] EWHC 159 (Ch), where it was held that while copyright materials (in this case, films and related media) could be the subject matter of a constructive trust, there was no proprietary right to the proceeds of infringement of copyright materials, as such a right was not akin to theft of property.

[22] See *Sinclair Investments (UK) Ltd v Versailles Trade Finance* [2012] Ch 453; affirming the approach in Lister & Co v Stubbs (1890) 35 Ch D 1 (CA).

[23] It was thought that English law would follow the Privy Council's decision in *AG for Hong Kong v Reid* [1994] 1 AC 324, which imposed a constructive trust on any unauthorized profit by a fiduciary, however obtained. This decision was not followed by the Court of Appeal in *Sinclair*. This has not meet with universal approval in later cases—see, for example, *FHR European Ventures LLP v Mankarious* [2013] EWCA Civ 1, where the Court of Appeal suggested the Supreme Court should revisit the decision. See also Lord Millett, writing extra-judicially in support of the approach in *Reid*—Millett 'Bribes and Secret Commissions Again' (2012) CLJ 583.

(e) Personal liability to account as a constructive trustee

Historically, English law utilized the concept of the constructive trust to impose a personal liability to account upon a fiduciary who had received an unauthorized profit, a stranger to a trust who had knowingly received and dissipated trust property, and a stranger who had knowingly assisted in the commission of a breach of trust. However, in *Paragon Finance plc v D B Thakerar & Co*[24] Millett LJ considered that the terminology of constructive trusts was inappropriate to describe such liability. He distinguished between two categories of constructive trusts. The first category were those situations in which a person had assumed the duties of a trustee even though he had not been expressly appointed as such. The second were circumstances in which the defendant was implicated in a fraud. In respect to this second category of cases he considered that the language of constructive trusts was inappropriate:

> The second class of case is different. It arises when the defendant is implicated in a fraud. Equity has always given relief against fraud by making any person sufficiently implicated in the fraud accountable in equity. In such a case he is traditionally though I think unfortunately described as a constructive trustee and said to be 'liable to account as a constructive trustee'. Such a person is not in fact a trustee at all, even though he may be liable to account as if he were. He never assumes the position of a trustee, and if he receives the trust property at all it is adversely to the plaintiff by an unlawful transaction which is impugned by the plaintiff. In such a case the expressions 'constructive trust' and 'constructive trustee' are misleading, for there is no trust and usually no possibility of a proprietary remedy; they are 'nothing more than a formula for equitable relief': *Selangor United Rubber Estates Ltd v Craddock (No 3).*[25]

While it is certainly correct that the personal liability of a person who has assisted in the commission of a breach of trust should not be characterized as the liability of a constructive trustee, as the assistor will usually never have held the trust property, it is less obvious that the terminology is inappropriate to describe the personal liability of a fiduciary who has received an unauthorized profit, or a stranger who has received and dissipated trust property. In both situations the liability arises because the fiduciary or stranger has failed to preserve the property that he held on trust. However, given the confusion of terminology, the personal liability of a fiduciary to account for unauthorized profits, or of a stranger to account for the value of trust property he has received, are better analysed as examples of claims to restitution in equity.[26]

Millett LJ's distinction was affirmed by the Supreme Court in *Williams v Central Bank of Nigeria*[27] which confined the second category (Class 2) constructive trusts to the two types of accessory liability, knowing receipt of trust property, and dishonest assistance in breach of trust. The personal remedies available against a fiduciary are

---

[24] [1999] 1 All ER 400.   [25] [1999] 1 All ER 400, at 409.
[26] As, for example, in *Re Montagu's Settlement Trusts* [1987] Ch 264.
[27] *Williams v Central Bank of Nigeria* [2014] UKSC 10.

considered in Chapter 28, and those against a stranger who has received trust property in Chapter 29.

2 Preventing benefit from crime

(1) The principle that no criminal may benefit from his crime

It is a basic principle of English Law that no criminal should be entitled to retain a material benefit derived from his crime.[28] As Fry LJ said in *Cleaver v Mutual Reserve Fund Life Association*:

> no system of jurisprudence can with reason include among the rights which it enforces rights directly resulting to the person asserting them from the crime of that person…This principle of public policy, like all such principles, must be applied to all cases to which it can be applied without reference to the particular character of the right asserted or the form of its assertion.[29]

The principle operates to prevent property coming into the hands of a criminal as a result of his crime, and instead deflects it to others who would be entitled in his place by forfeiting his entitlement. The potentially harsh operation of the rule was illustrated in *Re D W S (Decd)*,[30] where a person killed both his parents, neither of whom left a will. Following the forfeiture rule, the Court of Appeal decided that not only the killer, but also his son, was excluded from inheriting. The inheritance went instead to the couple's other relatives. The outcome of this case led the Law Commission to recommend that the rule be reformed[31] and these suggestions have subsequently been enacted in the Estates of Deceased Persons (Forfeiture Rule and Law of Succession) Act 2011.[32]

Where, however, a criminal has already received property into his hands in consequence of his crime, it will be subjected to a constructive trust in favour of those who would have been entitled to it in his place. Suppose, for example, a man kills his wife and subsequently inherits property that she bequeathed to him in her will. If it is later discovered that she was murdered, he will hold what remains of the property, or its traceable proceeds, on constructive trust. The imposition of this constructive trust has the effect of depriving him of the beneficial interest in the property, although he will continue to hold the legal title as trustee.

The principle that a criminal cannot benefit from his crime could have application in two main circumstances; first, where a person receives property by theft,

---

[28] See Oakley, *Constructive Trusts* (3rd edn, 1996), pp 46–53; Goff and Jones, *The Law of Restitution* (5th edn, 1998), pp 802–814; Youdan 'Acquisition of Property by Killing' (1973) 89 LQR 235; Earnshaw and Pace 'Let the Hand Receiving It Be Ever So Chaste' (1974) 37 MLR 481.   [29] [1892] 1 QB 147, at 156.
[30] [2001] Ch 568.
[31] *The Forfeiture Rule and the Law of Succession*, Law Com No 295 (2005), paras 1.14–1.15.
[32] This is discussed later in this chapter.

and second where a person acquires property (whether by succession or survivorship) from someone who has died in consequence of a crime committed by that person.

(2) **Property obtained by theft**

The principle has little practical application to the area of theft because a thief does not normally acquire legal title to the property that he steals.[33] Under s 28 of the Theft Act 1968 the court has power to order a person convicted of theft to return the property to its owner. The equitable rules of tracing may be helpful in following the property into the hands of a third party where the thief has disposed of it.[34] The process of tracing is considered in Chapter 30.

(3) **Property acquired by a crime causing death**

A person who unlawfully kills another will not be entitled to retain property received as a result of his victim's death, whether under the victim's will, on intestacy, or through the operation of survivorship in the context of jointly owned property. Similarly, an unlawful killer will not be able to recover under an insurance policy covering the consequences of the death of the unlawfully killed person. In each of these cases the courts intervene to prevent the criminal obtaining a benefit.

(a) **Must the criminal have used or threatened violence?**

The principle of forfeiture by imposition of a constructive trust will apply where a person has received property from a victim he has unlawfully killed. Unlawful killing obviously includes murder, but forfeiture will not operate against a killer found innocent on the grounds of insanity because such a verdict constitutes an acquittal.[35] It has been less clear whether forfeiture applies where a killer has committed manslaughter, which:

> [Is] a crime which varies infinitely in its seriousness. It may come very near to murder or amount to little more than inadvertence, although in the latter class of case the jury only rarely convicts.[36]

Rather than distinguish between cases of 'voluntary manslaughter' and 'involuntary manslaughter',[37] the law instead considered that the forfeiture rule would be

---

[33] A purchaser from a thief will only obtain good title in a few cases. See Bradgate, *Commercial Law* (3rd edn, 2000).   [34] See *Westdeutche Landesbank v Islington Borough Council* [1996] AC 669.

[35] Criminal Procedure (Insanity) Act 1964, s 1.

[36] *Gray v Barr* [1971] 2 QB 554, at 581 per Salmon LJ

[37] Voluntary manslaughter is where what would otherwise be murder is reduced to manslaughter by provocation or diminished responsibility, or because the death occurred in pursuance of a suicide pact. Involuntary manslaughter is where an unlawful killing is reduced to manslaughter because there was no intent to kill or to do grievous bodily harm: see *Re K* [1985] Ch 85, at 98.

applicable in manslaughter cases only where the killer used violence, or threats of violence, against his victim, even if the death was accidental.[38]

In *Gray v Barr*,[39] Mr Barr confronted Mr Gray believing that his wife, with whom Mr Gray had been having an affair, was present. He involuntarily shot Mr Gray after falling backwards while threatening him with a loaded shotgun. The Court of Appeal held that in these circumstances the principle of forfeiture should apply.

At first instance, Geoffrey Lane J had held that the forfeiture rule should apply if a person was 'guilty of deliberate, intentional and unlawful violence or threats of violence'. The Court of Appeal agreed.[40] This test was cited with approval and applied by Vinelott J in *Re K*,[41] where a wife had intended to threaten her husband with a loaded shotgun following domestic violence, but had accidentally shot and killed him when she removed the safety catch.

However, in *Dunbar v Plant*[42] the Court of Appeal rejected the view that forfeiture only operates where deliberate violence, or threats of violence, have been used and concluded that it applied where a woman had aided and abetted the suicide of her fiancé. The facts of the case were tragic. Miss Plant, who was facing a trial for theft from her employers, decided to commit suicide rather than face the prospect of jail. Mr Dunbar, her fiancé, said that he could not contemplate life without her, so they agreed that they would commit suicide together. An initial attempt to gas themselves in a car failed, as did an attempt to hang themselves with cable. On a further attempt to hang themselves with sheets, Dunbar was successful but Plant survived. Further suicide attempts, including cutting her throat and jumping out of a window, were also unsuccessful. The case concerned the question whether forfeiture should operate to prevent her obtaining the benefit of Dunbar's life insurance policy, of which she was the beneficiary. Counsel for Plant argued that the forfeiture rule should not apply at all because she had not used or threatened violence against Dunbar. This was rejected unanimously by the Court of Appeal, which held that the forfeiture rule prima facie applied. Mummery LJ explained:

> In my judgment…the presence of acts or threats of violence is not necessary for the application of the forfeiture rule. It is sufficient that a serious crime has been committed deliberately and intentionally. The references to acts or threats of violence in the cases are explicable by the facts of those cases. But in none of those cases were the courts legislating a principle couched in specific statutory language. The essence of the principle of public policy is that (a) no person shall take a benefit resulting from a crime committed by him or her resulting in the death of the victim and (b) the nature of the crime determines the application of the principle. On that view, the important point is that the crime that had

---

[38] There was some earlier evidence that forfeiture might be inapplicable to manslaughter in death through reckless driving cases, as drivers were held able to claim on insurance policies—see *Tinline v White Cross Insurance Association Ltd* [1921] 3 KB 327; *James v British General Insurance Co Ltd* [1927] 2 KB 311. However, in such cases of 'motor manslaughter' the forfeiture rule has applied if the driver's conduct had been wilful—see *Hardy v Motor Insurers' Bureau* [1964] 2 QB 745.

[39] [1971] 2 QB 554.   [40] [1971] 2 QB 554, at 581 per Salmon LJ.

[41] [1985] 2 WLR 262, at 276.   [42] [1998] Ch 412.

fatal consequences was committed with a guilty mind (deliberately and intentionally). The particular means used to commit the crime (whether violent or non-violent) are not a necessary ingredient of the rule.[43]

Given that violence was not required, it was held that the forfeiture rule operated where the offence of aiding and abetting suicide contrary to s 2(1) of the Suicide Act 1961 had been committed in the context of a suicide pact. Miss Plant had encouraged Dunbar to commit suicide, thus committing the offence and attracting the operation of the forfeiture rule. In *Dalton v Latham*,[44] Patten J held that *Dunbar v Plant*:

> must now be taken to be a binding statement of the law as to the application of the rule of public policy. It applies to all cases of unlawful killing, including manslaughter by reason of diminished responsibility or by reason of provocation. The only possible exception is where the defendant is found to be criminally insane, which leads to an acquittal...[45]

In *Dalton v Latham*, the claimant was acquitted of murder on the grounds of diminished responsibility but pleaded guilty to manslaughter. In *Land v Land*[46] the forfeiture rule was again applied, on this occasion to a man, assessed as probably having a developmental disorder, who had pleaded guilty to manslaughter after failing to call for medical assistance to aid his domineering mother, who was terminally ill and bedridden with breast cancer. According to HHJ Alastair Norris QC, sitting as a High Court judge:

> Following *Dunbar*...it is no longer possible to discriminate in the application of the rule, only to mitigate its effects where the ends of justice require. The rule will accordingly be applied even where the public interest does not require it (and even where its application may be contrary to the public interest), but in some circumstances its effects may be mitigated.[47]

As is evident from *Dunbar v Plant*, where Miss Plant had not been convicted of the offence of aiding and abetting, the forfeiture rule will apply even though the person causing death has not been convicted of a criminal offence. This may be because it has not been possible to bring him to trial, for example because of his own suicide.[48] In *Gray v Barr*,[49] the Court of Appeal held that the forfeiture rule should apply even though Mr Barr had been acquitted at trial of both murder and manslaughter. In the civil trial the lower evidential standard of the 'balance of probabilities' applied. For this reason, Lord Denning MR was able to conclude: 'there is no doubt, to my mind, that Mr Barr was guilty of manslaughter'.[50]

(b) Forfeiture of entitlement under the victim's will

Where the forfeiture rule operates, a criminal will not be permitted to derive any benefit under the will of his victim. In *Re Sigsworth*[51] a coroner's inquest found that Mary

---

[43] [1997] 4 All ER 289, at 300. Mummery LJ cited the Canadian case *Whitelaw v Wilson* [1934] OR 415, where it had been held that the forfeiture rule applied to the survivor of a suicide pact in which a husband and wife both drank poison.

[44] [2003] EWHC 796.   [45] [2003] EWHC 796, at [9].   [46] [2006] EWHC 2069.

[47] [2006] EWHC 2069, at [18].   [48] See *Re Sigsworth* [1935] Ch 89.   [49] [1971] 2 QB 554.

[50] [1971] 2 QB 554, at 568.

[51] [1935] Ch 89. See also *Re Callaway* [1956] Ch 559; *Re Peacock* [1957] Ch 310.

Sigsworth had died as a result of a fractured spine caused by her son, Thomas. He subsequently committed suicide before he could be brought to trial. She had left the whole of her property to him. On the assumption that he had murdered his mother,[52] Clauson J held that Thomas was not entitled to take any interest under the will. He stated the principle:

> the claim of the [son], to the estate of the mother under her will is bound to fail by reason of the well-settled principle that public policy precludes a sane murderer from taking a benefit under his victim's will.[53]

(c) Forfeiture of entitlement arising on the victim's intestacy

Similarly, the forfeiture rule operates to preclude the criminal receiving any property to which he would ordinarily have been entitled on the intestacy of the deceased. In *Re Crippen*,[54] Harvey Crippen was executed following his conviction for the murder of his wife, Cora. She had left no will. Before his execution he made a will leaving all his property to his mistress, Ethel Le Neve. The court held that Le Neve was not entitled to receive the property to which Crippen would have been entitled from his wife's estate under the rules of intestacy. The principle was again stated by Clauson J in *Re Sigsworth*:

> the principle of public policy which precludes a murderer from claiming a benefit conferred on him by his victims will preclude him from claiming a benefit conferred on him, in case of his victim's intestacy, by statute.[55]

(d) Forfeiture of entitlement by survivorship

Where property is held by co-owners as joint tenants, the principle of survivorship (the ius accrescendi) operates, so that the property vests automatically in the surviving joint tenant or tenants. This will apply whether the joint tenancy is of the legal or the equitable title to property. Therefore, if Harry and Joan are the joint tenants of a house in law and in equity, and Harry dies, the title will vest automatically in Joan. It will make no difference if he had left all his property by will to charity, as the operation of survivorship takes precedence over the disposition by will. However, if Joan unlawfully killed Harry and survivorship were allowed to operate, she would benefit from her crime. Therefore, the forfeiture rule is applied and the principle of survivorship will not operate between the joint tenants.[56] In *Re K*,[57] Vinelott J held that the principle of forfeiture applied so that a wife who was guilty of the manslaughter of her husband was not entitled to their jointly owned matrimonial home by the operation of survivorship between them. Instead, she held the house on trust for herself

---

[52] The verdict of the coroner's jury was not conclusive, and the judge stressed that if the administrator of the estate acted upon his judgement he would have to take the risk that the assumption of fact may conceivably turn out to be erroneous.

[53] [1935] Ch 89, at 92.   [54] [1911] P 108.   [55] [1935] Ch 89, at 92.

[56] It should be noted that the rule does not deprive the killer of his or her own presumptive share under the joint tenancy.   [57] [1985] Ch 85.

and her husband's next of kin in equal shares as tenants-in-common.[58] Similarly, in *Dunbar v Plant*[59] the forfeiture rule prima facie excluded the operation of survivorship in respect of a jointly owned house.

(4) The court's jurisdiction to grant relief from forfeiture

Although the forfeiture rule prima facie applies where a person has died in consequence of a crime, under the Forfeiture Act 1982 the court has the discretion to grant relief from the effects of the rule. Section 2(1) provides that where the forfeiture rule has precluded a person who has unlawfully killed another from acquiring any interest in property: 'the court may make an order…modifying the effect of that rule'. This jurisdiction applies to property in the form of beneficial interests under the deceased's will, intestacy, a donatio morits causa, or under a trust. The section has no application to persons convicted of murder.[60] Under s 2(2) the court may only exercise its jurisdiction to grant relief if satisfied that:

> having regard to the conduct of the offender and of the deceased and to such other circumstances as appear to the court to be material, the justice of the case requires the effect of the rule to be modified in that case.

The jurisdiction was exercised in *Re K*.[61] Vinelott J held that the discretion conferred by the Act requires the court to investigate the moral culpability of the killing, and he concluded that, because of the tragic circumstances of the case, and the fact that a loyal wife had suffered grave violence at the hands of her husband, it was appropriate for the court to grant relief so that she would not be deprived of the provision which her husband had made for her under his will or of the matrimonial home under the operation of survivorship. He also considered that it was relevant to take into account the relative financial position of persons claiming relief under the Act and those who would be entitled if the forfeiture rule was applied.

In *Dunbar v Plant*[62] the Court of Appeal also held that Miss Plant should be granted relief against forfeiture of the proceeds of Dunbar's life insurance policy, even though this was contested by his father. It was unanimously held that the approach of the first instance judge, who had sought to 'do justice between the parties', was an inappropriate approach to the exercise of the jurisdiction. The majority went on to conclude that, in the case of suicide pacts which were the result of irrational depression or desperation, total relief from forfeiture would be appropriate. Phillips LJ, with whom Hirst LJ agreed, concluded that there was nothing in the circumstances to require a different approach:

> The desperation that led Miss Plant to decide to kill herself, and which led to the suicide pact, was an irrational and tragic reaction to her predicament. I do not consider that the

---

[58] See also *Schobelt v Barber* (1966) 60 DLR (2d) 519; *Re Pechar* [1969] NZLR 574. Although the forfeiture rule operates simply where there are only two joint tenants, it is much more complicated where there are three or more and one joint tenant kills another. See *Rasmanis v Jurewitsch* [1970] 70 SRNSW 407.

[59] [1997] 4 All ER 289.

[60] S 5.   [61] [1985] Ch 85, Vinelott J; affd [1986] Ch 180, CA.   [62] [1997] 4 All ER 289.

nature of Miss Plant's conduct alters what I have indicated should be the normal approach when dealing with a suicide pact—that there should be full relief against forfeiture. The assets with which this case is concerned were in no way derived from Mr Dunbar's family. They are the fruits of insurance taken out by Mr Dunbar for the benefit of Miss Plant.[63]

In *Land v Land*[64] judge Alastair Norris QC mitigated the impact of forfeiture by making an order for the claimant under the Inheritance (Provision for Family and Dependants) Act 1975 as envisaged by s 3(1) of the Forfeiture Act 1982. *Mack v Lockwood*[65] provides an example where relief against forfeiture was refused. An 80-year-old man had killed his wife by stabbing her repeatedly some fifty-four times. While the defence of provocation was established in relation to the killing, the deputy judge Geraldine Andrews QC considered that it remained both a deliberate and brutal killing and that it would therefore not be unjust for the husband to be prevented from inheriting his wife's interest.

(5) Reform of the forfeiture rule

Where the forfeiture rule operates, *Re DWS (Decd)*[66] established that neither the perpetrator of the offence nor anyone claiming through him can benefit under the will or intestacy. In this case a son had murdered his parents, who had died intestate. Clearly the son was disqualified from inheriting their estates. The Court of Appeal held that his illegitimate son was also unable to inherit his grandparent's estate because the rules of intestacy state that 'no issue shall take whose parent is living at the date of the intestate'.[67] Their estates passed to more distant relatives. This harsh consequence led the Law Commission to recommend that the rule be reformed. The Commission suggested that the forfeiture rule be replaced by a 'deemed predecease' rule,[68] so that the property of the intestate would be distributed as if the killer had died immediately before the deceased. The rule would also extend to situations where the deceased had made a will and the potential beneficiary is excluded because he or she claims through the person who killed the deceased.[69] The Estates of Deceased Persons (Forfeiture Rule and Law of Succession) Act 2011, which came into force on 1 February 2012, implements these recommendations. Section 1 of the 2011 Act amends Part 4 of the Administration of Estates Act 1925 by inserting a new s 46A in relation to intestacy:

> (1) This section applies where a person—
>
>> (a) is entitled in accordance with section 46 to an interest in the residuary estate of an intestate but disclaims it, or
>>
>> (b) would have been so entitled had the person not been precluded by the forfeiture rule from acquiring it.

---

[63] [1997] 4 All ER 289, *at 313*.   [64] [2006] EWHC 2069.
[65] [2009] EWHC 1524.   [66] [2001] Ch 568.
[67] Administration of Estates Act 1925, s 47(1)(i).
[68] The Forfeiture Rule and the Law of Succession, Law Com No 295 (2005), paras 1.14-1.15.
[69] The Forfeiture Rule and the Law of Succession, Law Com No 295 (2005), para 1.16.

(2) The person is to be treated for the purposes of this Part as having died immediately before the intestate.

The court, by s 46A(3) of the Administration of Estates Act 1925, still retains the power to set aside the operation of the forfeiture rule. Section 2 of the 2011 Act inserts s 33A into the Wills Act 1837 to similar effect:

(1) This section applies where a will contains a devise or bequest to a person who—

    (a) disclaims it, or

    (b) has been precluded by the forfeiture rule from acquiring it.

(2) The person is, unless a contrary intention appears by the will, to be treated for the purposes of this Act as having died immediately before the testator.

Neither the Law Commission's proposals, nor the subsequent Act, have any application to the operation of the survivorship rule in joint tenancies since the deemed predecease rule would be confined to the construction of the intestacy legislation and of wills.[70]

3 Specifically enforceable contract to sell property

From the very moment that a vendor enters a specifically enforceable contract to sell property, he holds it on constructive trust for the purchaser. The reason for the imposition of the trust in these circumstances is that the contract of sale renders the vendor subject to an obligation to transfer the property to the purchaser that will be enforced in equity by means of the remedy of specific performance. By applying the maxim that 'equity treats as done that which ought to be done', the constructive trust ensures that the purchaser is entitled to the equitable interest immediately, even though he will not become the full absolute owner until the vendor transfers the legal title in fulfilment of the contract. The operation of such constructive trusts was explained in *Lysaght v Edwards*[71] by Jessel MR:

the moment you have a valid contract for sale the vendor becomes in equity a trustee for the purchaser of the estate sold, and the beneficial ownership passes to the purchaser...[72]

As has been seen in Chapter 5, such constructive trusts will most commonly arise in the context of contracts for the purchase of land, as the majority of contracts for the purchase of personal property are not specifically enforceable because the subject matter is not unique. However, if specific performance would be available, a constructive trust will arise. Such a constructive trust was found to have arisen in *Oughtred v IRC*,[73]

---

[70] The Forfeiture Rule and the Law of Succession, Law Com No 295 (2005), para 2.29.

[71] (1876) 2 Ch D 499; see also *Haywood v Cope* (1858) 25 Beav 140.

[72] Compare *Rayner v Preston* (1880–81) LR 18 Ch D 1, CA, where Brett LJ held that a trust did not arise; *KLDE Pty Ltd v Stamp Duties Comr (Queensland)* (1984) 155 CLR 288.

[73] [1960] AC 206. See also *Re Holt's Settlement* [1969] 1 Ch 100.

for example, which involved a contract for the sale of shares in a private company. This decision was reaffirmed by the Court of Appeal in *Neville v Wilson*.[74]

From the moment of contract, a genuine trust relationship is created, so that the vendor holds the title of the property on trust for the purchaser. His duties are not the same as those of an ordinary trustee,[75] for example he is entitled to retain profits arising from the property before completion of the contract.[76] However, he is under a duty to 'use reasonable care to preserve the property in a reasonable state of preservation'.[77]

4 Mutual wills

It is a fundamental principle that a man is entitled to make a will leaving his property to whomsoever he chooses. Any will he makes remains revocable until his death. However, if two persons enter into a contract to execute wills in a common form, and the survivor subsequently changes his will, the court will impose a constructive trust on the property in the hands of the executors of the survivor in favour of the beneficiaries of the mutual wills. The doctrine of mutual wills is considered in Chapter 15.

5 Acquisition of land expressly subject to the interests of a third party

One of the central objectives of land law is to determine whether a transferee of land is bound by third party interests in the land that were valid against the transferor. Where title to the land is registered, the equitable doctrine of notice has been replaced by a scheme of registration.[78] Lesser interests must be protected by means of an entry on the register of the title to which they relate. If an interest is unprotected, a transferee for valuable consideration of the legal title will acquire the land free from it,[79] unless it is an 'overriding interest',[80] in which case it will bind the transferee irrespective.

However, it has been held that if a transferee of the land expressly agrees that he will honour the rights of a third party, he will be bound by those rights under a constructive

---

[74] [1996] 3 All ER 171; (1996) 55 CLJ 436 (Nolan); [1996] Conv 368 (Thompson).

[75] *Shaw v Foster* (1872) LR 5 HL 321; *Earl of Egmont v Smith* (1877) 6 Ch D 469; *Royal Bristol Permanent Building Society v Bomash* (1887) LR 35 Ch D 390; *Cumberland Consolidated Holdings Ltd v Ireland* [1946] KB 264; *Engelwood Properties v Patel* [2005] 3 All ER 307.

[76] *Cuddon v Tite* (1858) 1 Giff 395.

[77] *Clarke v Ramuz* [1891] 2 QB 456, at 459–460, per Lord Coleridge CJ. See also *Royal Bristol Permanent Building Society v Bomash* (1887) LR 35 Ch D 390; *Phillips v Lamdin* [1949] 2 KB 33; *Lucie-Smith v Gorman* [1981] CLY 2866.   [78] Stevens and Pearce, *Land Law* (5th edn, 2013), Chapter 6.

[79] Land Registration Act 2002, s 29.

[80] Land Registration Act 2002, Sch 3. If the transfer triggers first registration of an unregistered title to land, the category of overriding interests is wider—see Sch 1.

trust even though it had not been properly protected on the register. This constructive trust prevents the purchaser taking advantage of his strict rights under the statute. Such a constructive trust was held to have arisen in *Lyus v Prowsa Developments*.[81] Mr and Mrs Lyus entered a contract to purchase a house that was to be built on a new estate. The developers subsequently went into liquidation and the bank that held a mortgage of the land sold it to another developer. This second developer agreed in the contract to take the land 'subject to, but with the benefit of the contract made with Mr and Mrs Lyus'. This developer subsequently sold the land to a third, who agreed to the same terms. The contract entered between the first developer and Mr and Mrs Lyus was an interest in land which should have been protected on the register as a minor interest. Even though it had not been protected appropriately, Dillon J held that the developers who had purchased the land were bound by it. They had expressly agreed to take subject to the interest and therefore a constructive trust was raised to 'counter unconscionable conduct or fraud'.[82] Dillon J stressed that the agreement was not a general agreement to take the land subject to possible encumbrances but a positive stipulation in favour of a particular identified interest.

The operation of such a constructive trust was further considered in *Ashburn Anstalt v Arnold*.[83] The Court of Appeal addressed, obiter, the question whether a purchaser could be bound by a constructive trust when he had expressly agreed to acquire land subject to a third party's contractual licence. The court accepted that a constructive trust could arise in such circumstances, but stated that 'the court will not impose a constructive trust unless it is satisfied that the conscience of the estate owner is affected'.[84] The mere fact that land was expressly said to be conveyed 'subject to' a contractual right would not suffice alone:

> We do not think it is desirable that constructive trusts of land should be imposed in reliance on inference from slender materials.[85]

It was suggested that other factors would be necessary to justify the imposition of a constructive trust, for example evidence that the purchaser paid a lower price for the land as a consequence of the express agreement to take subject to the interest. The essence of the constructive trust is the purchaser's voluntary acceptance of obligations in favour of the third party.[86] The appropriate test, following the Court of Appeal decision in *Lloyd v Dugdale*, is whether the purchaser has:

> undertaken a new obligation, not otherwise existing, to give effect to the relevant encumbrance or prior interest. If, but only if, he has undertaken such a new obligation will a constructive trust be imposed.[87]

---

[81] [1982] 1 WLR 1044. This case deals with registered title. There is no reason to suspect that, had the facts arisen in unregistered title, the decision would have been any different—see further Stevens and Pearce, *Land Law* (5th edn, 2013), pp 118–119.

[82] [1982] 1 WLR 1044, at 1052.

[83] [1989] Ch 1; [1988] Conv 201 (Thompson); (1988) 51 MLR 226 (Hill); (1988) 104 LQR 175 (Sparkes).

[84] [1989] Ch 1, at 25.   [85] [1989] Ch 1, at 25, at 26.

[86] There is a clear analogy with cases such as *Bannister v Bannister* [1948] 2 All ER 133 and *Binions v Evans* [1972] Ch 359. See also McFarlane 'Constructive Trusts Arising on a Receipt of Property *Sub Conditione*' (2004) 120 LQR 667.   [87] [2002] 2 P & CR 13, at [52] per Slade LJ.

In *Chaudhary v Yavuz*,[88] Lloyd LJ sought to further limit the application of an imposition of a constructive trust in such situations. First, his Lordship made clear that there must be a very specific reference to the interests over which a constructive trust is sought. It was not enough, on the facts of that case, that the transfer states that it is 'subject to' the rights of the licensee, even if coupled with an indemnity clause, because these are standard terms in a contract of sale, often intended simply to protect the seller. Second, Lloyd LJ felt that a party's failure to protect a registerable interest by registration might either preclude or limit the finding of a constructive trust in their favour, on the basis that, as he stated, he was unaware of any English precedent in which *Lyus v Prowsa* had been successfully argued to make binding on a purchaser of land an interest which could have been, but was not, protected by registration.[89] While the first point simply restates the concern that the constructive trust should not be imposed lightly, the second would seem to be an unjustifiable limitation on the operation of constructive trusts. It is difficult to see how the status of registration directly relates to whether the facts support a finding that the purchaser has undertaken a new obligation which binds his conscience as required by *Lloyd v Dugdale*.[90] In the later case of *Groveholt v Hughes*,[91] Richards J cited the dicta of Lloyd LJ in *Chaudhary* as a qualification on the operation of constructive trusts, which meant that *Lyus v Prowsa* 'must be regarded as being on the outer edge of circumstances in which a constructive trust will be found to exist'.[92] On the facts, Richards J did not need to consider whether to apply those qualifications as there was no possible finding of a constructive trust as the agreement in question contained no express provision as to the contested right to retransfer property. It is suggested that it is unlikely that Lloyd LJ's dicta in relation to the relevance of unprotected registerable rights will be followed in later cases. The question will remain whether the purchaser has entered into a new obligation with the vendor to protect the otherwise unprotected interest.

6 Common intention to share the ownership of land

One of the most significant areas of operation of the doctrine of constructive trusts in the past sixty years has been in the context of land ownership, and especially the ownership of the family home.[93] Constructive trusts provide a means by which a person may obtain a share of the ownership of land despite the lack of any express declaration of trust in his favour.

---

[88] [2011] EWHC Civ 1314.

[89] [2011] EWHC Civ 1314 at [61]. See, however, *Bahr v Nicolay (No.2)* (1988) 78 ALR 1, where the Australian High Court found a constructive trust to arise in similar circumstances to *Lyus v Prowsa*.

[90] McFarlane 'Eastenders, Neighbours and Upstairs Downstairs: *Chaudhary v Yavuz*' [2013] Conv 74 at 81–2.

[91] [2012] EWHC 3351   [92] [2012] EWHC 3351,at [17].

[93] See, generally, Stevens and Pearce, *Land Law* (5th edn, 2013) Ch 11, pp 322–356.

The House of Lords affirmed the use of constructive trusts as a means to acquire an interest for the non-legal owner of property in the landmark decision of *Gissing v Gissing*:

> A…constructive trust…is created by a transaction between the trustee and the [beneficiary] in connection with the acquisition by the trustee of a legal estate in land, whenever the trustee has so conducted himself that it would be inequitable to allow him to deny to the [beneficiary] a beneficial interest in the land acquired.[94]

Lord Diplock emphasized that a legal owner would only have acted so as to justify the imposition of a constructive trust:

> if by his words or conduct he has induced the [beneficiary] to act to his own detriment in the reasonable belief that by so acting he was acquiring a beneficial interest in the land.[95]

This very broad principle has been developed and refined in subsequent cases, notably *Lloyds Bank v Rosset*,[96] to create the distinctive, but inaccurately named, 'common intention constructive trust'. This branch of equity has emerged in response, in part, to the changing patterns of home ownership following the Second World War, and the fact that there is no concept of 'common law' marriage for unmarried cohabiting couples that gives a non-legal owner rights over the property on the cessation of the relationship. Many couples still operate under the mistaken belief that following a period of time together they will acquire some rights in any home they share. In the absence of marriage or, in the case of same-sex couples, registering as civil partners, which give statutory powers to redistribute property at the end of a relationship, cohabiting couples do not enjoy any rights without the intervention of equity.

The principle underlying the common intention constructive trust is that the constructive trust will be imposed where the owner of land (usually the husband or the male partner in a relationship) has promised his cohabitant that she will have a share of the beneficial ownership, and she has acted upon that promise, usually by making a financial contribution. In some circumstances, even where no express promise has been made, a promise can be implied from conduct. Constructive trusts of common intention are thus based on the express or implied intention of the parties. They are the counterpart, in the context of domestic property, of the trust imposed in cases like *Lyus v Prowsa Developments*,[97] discussed earlier.

The traditional rationale for the common intention constructive trust is that it is inequitable for the owner of land to resile from an expectation that he has created or encouraged. The courts are not inventing intention, but finding it from the express discussions of the parties, or inferring it from their actions. The actions that will suffice to establish a constructive trust, where there has been no express discussion about ownership, are very limited, and it may be that only a direct financial contribution towards the acquisition of the property will suffice. However, the cases demonstrate that once a constructive trust has been established, a much wider range of factors can

---

[94] [1971] AC 886, at 905.   [95] [1971] AC 886, at 905.   [96] [1971] AC 886.
[97] [1982] 1 WLR 1044.

be taken into account in quantifying the size of the beneficial share of the property to be awarded to the cohabitant. Household labour by one party may not, for example, support a claim to an interest, but may be used to quantify it.

The common intention constructive trust is an area of fertile litigation, both in relation to acquiring and quantifying a beneficial interest. The applicability of constructive trusts as a mechanism for allowing a cohabitant to gain an interest has attracted considerable criticism for various reasons, not least that as a method of property management it is ill-suited to protecting the financial needs of family members, which extend to children from a relationship, or that it stretches the concept of constructive trust too far. Indeed, recent decisions from the highest courts in *Stack v Dowden*[98] and *Jones v Kernott*[99] threaten to create an entirely new form of distributive mechanism in the family home, which better suits family needs but is difficult to justify as a constructive trust at all—this intriguing set of developments is explored in Chapter 10. The Law Commission has undertaken projects either to place the existing equitable rules on a statutory footing or to replace them with a statutory scheme, giving cohabitants similar rights to married couples and registered civil partners. To date, none of these proposals have been enacted and cohabitants must rely on equitable methods.[100]

There is a close relationship between common intention constructive trusts and purchase money resulting trusts (discussed in Chapter 8). The decisions in *Stack v Dowden*[101] and *Jones v Kernott*[102] have suggested that resulting trusts in this context have been entirely subsumed within the common intention constructive trust, except where property has been bought by the parties purely as an investment rather than as the family home. There are also strong parallels between the common intention constructive trust and the equitable doctrine of proprietary estoppel. The interaction between common intention constructive trusts, purchase money resulting trusts, and proprietary estoppel is also considered in detail in Chapter 10.

7 The 'remedial constructive trust'

(1) Defining the 'remedial constructive trust'

The English doctrine of constructive trusts has been subjected to much criticism. As has been seen in the context of trusts of co-owned land, English law adopts an 'institutional' form of constructive trust, whereby the court merely recognizes a pre-existing equitable interest. There is little scope for flexibility, other than by manipulation of the

---

[98] [2007] 2 AC 432.   [99] [2012] 2 AC 776.

[100] The Inheritance and Trustees' Powers Act 2014, which provides intestacy rights for cohabitants who have lived together for five years and are not also married or in a civil partnership, has now received Royal Assent. This is a limited step towards recognition of cohabitants' rights.   [101] [2007] 2 AC 432.

[102] [2012] 2 AC 776.

criteria that must be satisfied for the creation of a constructive trust, and the nature of the claim predetermines the remedial outcome.[103]

In other jurisdictions, an entirely different approach towards constructive trusts has emerged. An equitable proprietary right is regarded as one possible remedial response to effect restitution where a defendant has been unjustly enriched. Restitution may be effected either by a personal remedy requiring the enriched defendant to pay a monetary sum equivalent to the value of the enrichment he received to the plaintiff, or by the award of a proprietary remedy over any assets representing the enrichment which remain in the defendant's hands. The essence of the 'remedial' constructive trust[104] is that the court enjoys the discretion to determine whether or not a proprietary remedy should be awarded. If the court exercises its discretion to award a constructive trust, the resulting beneficial entitlement can be said to have been 'imposed' by the court, which does not merely recognize a pre-existing proprietary interest. The plaintiff's equitable proprietary interest does not therefore arise from the facts per se, which establish a cause of action in unjust enrichment, but from the exercise of its discretion to award such a remedy.

(2) Development of the remedial constructive trust

The Commonwealth approaches to resolving issues concerning the ownership of the family home suggest a movement away from the institutional approach to constructive trusts, towards a more remedial understanding. The courts of Canada seem to have taken the greatest steps towards the recognition and acceptance of a general remedial constructive trust, not merely within the context of familial or quasi-familial property, but also in commercial situations. The best description of how the remedial nature of the constructive trust came to be recognized in Canada is found in the judgment of Dickson CJC in *Hunter Engineering Co Inc v Syncrude Canada Ltd*:

> The constructive trust has existed for over two hundred years as an equitable remedy for certain forms of unjust enrichment. In its earliest form, the constructive trust was used to provide a remedy to claimants alleging that others had made profits at their expense. Where the claimant could show the existence of a fiduciary relationship between the claimant and the person taking advantage of the claimant, the courts were receptive... Equity would not countenance the abuse of the trust and confidence inherent in a fiduciary relationship and imposed trust obligations on those who profited from abusing their position of loyalty. The doctrine was gradually extended to apply to situations where other persons who were not in a fiduciary relationship with the claimant acted in concert with the fiduciary or knew of the fiduciary obligations. Until the decision of this court in *Pettkus v Becker*, the constructive trust was viewed largely in terms of the law of trusts, hence the need for the existence of a fiduciary relationship. In *Pettkus v Becker*

---

[103] The considerable debate over determining the size of the beneficial share does not alter the nature of the right—the court is only seeking to decide the extent of the pre-existing beneficial interest.

[104] See Birks (ed), *The Frontiers of Liability* (1994) Vol 2, pp 163–223; (1998) 114 LQR 399 (Sir Peter Millett).

the court moved to an approach more in line with restitutionary principles by explicitly recognising a constructive trust as one of the remedies for unjust enrichment. In finding unjust enrichment the court…invoked three criteria: namely (1) an enrichment (2) a corresponding deprivation, and (3) absence of any juristic reason for the enrichment. The court then found that in the circumstances of the case a constructive trust was the appropriate remedy to redress the unjust enrichment.[105]

Several key points of this restatement of principle require examination.

(a) A restitutionary cause of action

A remedial constructive trust can only be imposed against a person who has been unjustly enriched. 'Unjust enrichment' is therefore the cause of action for which the constructive trust is available as a remedy. In the absence of an unjust enrichment, a constructive trust will not be imposed. For this reason a constructive trust was not imposed in *Hunter Engineering Co v Syncrude Canada Ltd*.[106] Syncrude ordered some specialist gearboxes from Hunter Canada Ltd, a company which fraudulently misrepresented that it acted on behalf of an American company, Hunter US. Hunter Canada placed a contract for the gearboxes with a subcontractor, Alco Sales and Engineering. When Hunter US discovered the circumstances they immediately alerted Syncrude and began an action against Hunter Canada for 'passing off'. Fearing a delay in the production of the gearboxes, Syncrude set up a trust fund into which they paid all the moneys which would have been payable to Hunter Canada, and agreed to pay Alco the contract price of the subcontract from this fund. The balance, representing the profit which Hunter Canada would have made, was to be distributed according to the outcome of the litigation between Hunter Canada and Hunter US. In these circumstances, Hunter US claimed that the balance of the fund was held on constructive trust for them, because it represented the profit that Hunter Canada would have made through passing themselves off as their authorized representatives. The majority of the Supreme Court allowed an appeal against the judgment of the Court of Appeal which had imposed a constructive trust under the principle of *Pettkus v Becker*.[107] They held that there had been no enrichment of Hunter Canada that would call for restitution, and therefore that a constructive trust could not be justified. Any claim of Hunter US could only arise as a result of Hunter Canada's actions, and Hunter Canada would only be entitled to the surplus in the trust fund on the basis of their contract with Syncrude. Since that contract had been terminated because of the fraudulent misrepresentation, Hunter Canada was no longer entitled to any payment under the contract, and Hunter US could not be in a better position vis-à-vis Syncrude than Hunter Canada. In conclusion, rather than reversing an enrichment received by Syncrude, Dickson CJC considered that:

> if Hunter US's claim prevailed (i) Hunter US would be enriched (ii) with a corresponding deprivation of Syncrude (iii) and for no juristic reason that I am able to detect.[108]

---

[105] (1989) 57 DLR (4th) 321, at 348.   [106] (1989) 57 DLR (4th) 321.
[107] (1980) 117 DLR (3d) 257.   [108] (1989) 57 DLR (4th) 321, at 353.

(b) A range of remedial responses

Once liability has been established by demonstrating an unjust enrichment which calls for restitution, the court is entitled to select the appropriate remedy to effect restitution. It may conclude that a proprietary remedy is appropriate. Alternatively, a purely personal monetary award may be made. This flexibility was recognized by the Supreme Court in *Sorochan v Sorochan*, where Dickson CJC stated:

> The constructive trust constitutes one important judicial means of remedying unjust enrichment. Other remedies, such as monetary damages, may also be available to rectify situations of unjust enrichment. We must, therefore, ask when and under what circumstances it is appropriate for a court to impose a constructive trust…[109]

This remedial flexibility was similarly adopted in *Rawluk v Rawluk*.[110] McLachlin J explained:

> The significance of the remedial nature of the constructive trust is not that it cannot confer a property interest, but that the conferring of such an interest is discretionary and dependant on the inadequacy of other remedies for the unjust enrichment in question. The doctrine of constructive trust may be used to confer a proprietary remedy, but that does not automatically presuppose a possessory property right. Thus, even where the tests for constructive trust are met—unjust enrichment, corresponding deprivation, and no juridical justification for the enrichment—the property interest does not automatically arise. Rather, the court must consider whether other remedies to remedy the injustice exist which make the declaration of a constructive trust inappropriate.[111]

The most important decision concerning the nature and function of remedial constructive trusts is that of the Supreme Court in *LAC Minerals Ltd v International Corona Resources Ltd*.[112] This case concerned the application of the remedial constructive trust to a commercial situation rather than to the specialized circumstances of the family home. Corona owned the mining rights over land, and approached LAC with a view to negotiating a joint venture to exploit mineral deposits. In the course of these negotiations Corona revealed results from their exploratory drilling, from which it was clear that adjacent land was also likely to contain mineral deposits. Corona sought to purchase the neighbouring land but were defeated by a competing bid by LAC, which proceeded to exploit the deposits alone. The court held that in these circumstances LAC had been unjustly enriched by misuse of the confidential information they had received from Corona. The central question was as to the nature of the remedy that should be awarded to effect restitution and reverse their unjust enrichment. To give some idea of the size of the claims involved, the trial judge had valued the land at $700m. The Supreme Court emphasized that as the plaintiff's right to restitution had been established it possessed a remedial discretion:

> The court can award either a proprietary remedy, namely that LAC hand over the [land], or award a personal remedy, namely a monetary award. The constructive trust does not

---

[109] (1986) 29 DLR (4th) 1.   [110] (1990) 65 DLR (4th) 161.
[111] (1990) 65 DLR (4th) 161, at 185–186.   [112] (1989) 61 DLR (4th) 14.

lie at the heart of the law of restitution. It is but one remedy, and will only be imposed in appropriate circumstances.[113]

The majority of the court held that, in the circumstances, a constructive trust was appropriate, and that LAC should hold the land on trust for Corona.

(3) **Difficulties associated with the remedial constructive trust**

Although superficially attractive, in that it seems to provide a single coherent theory to explain the imposition of constructive trusts, as well as providing flexibility of remedies, the remedial constructive trust poses difficulties that cannot be ignored. The essential problem is one of uncertainty, which arises both at the level of the cause of action and at the level of the court's remedial discretion. For these reasons, the English courts have not yet followed the Canadian lead and adopted the 'remedial constructive trust'. Whilst some English judges have suggested that the remedial constructive trust might be introduced in the future, most cases have refused to countenance its adoption.

(a) **Uncertainty as to the cause of action**

The remedial constructive trust is seen as one means by which restitution may be effected. The cause of action which gives rise to it is not therefore breach of fiduciary duty or inequitable conduct, which are the triggers for a constructive trust in English law, but unjust enrichment.[114] The Canadian courts have been quick to develop and recognize a general principle of unjust enrichment, whereas in England there has been a historic reluctance to adopt what has been seen as a vague and amorphous concept. In *LAC Minerals Ltd v International Corona Resources Ltd*[115] the Supreme Court stressed that unjust enrichment was not simply a vague concept of fairness. La Forest J was keen to point out that:

> The determination that the enrichment is 'unjust' does not refer to abstract notions of morality and justice, but flows directly from the finding that there was a breach of a legally recognised duty for which the courts will grant relief. Restitution is a distinct body of law governed by its own developing system of rules.[116]

The remedial constructive trust is therefore dependent upon a highly developed and well-defined concept of unjust enrichment. Otherwise, it would evolve into the 'palm tree justice' that the courts have been so keen to avoid, and which was the prime reason for the rejection of Lord Denning's new model constructive trust. In *Korkontzilas v Soulos*[117] the majority of the Supreme Court of Canada held that a remedial constructive trust was available even where there had been no unjust enrichment, and that it could be imposed where good conscience requires. If uncertainty is to be avoided, the

---

[113] (1989) 61 DLR (4th) 14, at 48, per La Forest J.
[114] See Delaney and Ryan 'Unconscionability: A Unifying Theme in Equity' [2008] Conv 401.
[115] (1989) 61 DLR (4th) 14.   [116] (1989) 61 DLR (4th) 14, at 45.
[117] (1997) 146 DLR (4th) 214.

view of the dissenting minority that a constructive trust may only be imposed where there has been an unjust enrichment should be preferred.

(b) Uncertainty as to the remedy

Once unjust enrichment has been established, it is for the court to determine the appropriate remedy. It is therefore impossible for the parties to determine whether a constructive trust will be imposed from the fact than an unjust enrichment had been received, although precedents might provide some guidance as to the likely remedy. In *LAC Minerals v International Corona Resources Ltd* the court was aware of the problems of uncertainty attendant on the remedial constructive trust. La Forest J observed that:

> There is no unanimous agreement on the circumstances in which a constructive trust will be imposed.[118]

The approach advocated by Goff and Jones, who had argued that a restitutionary proprietary remedy should be awarded when it is 'just, in the particular circumstances of the case, to impose a constructive trust',[119] was rejected unless further guidance could be given as to what those circumstances might be.[120] However, some guidelines were suggested, and it was held that there was no need to demonstrate a special relationship between the parties as a prerequisite of a constructive trust, nor that there must have been a pre-existing property right. La Forest J suggested that 'a constructive trust should only be awarded if there is reason to grant the plaintiff the additional rights that flow from the recognition of a right of property'.[121] A number of factors were identified which may be relevant in determining whether to award a proprietary remedy:

> Amongst the most important of these will be that it is appropriate that the plaintiff receive the priority accorded to the holder of a right of property in a bankruptcy. More important in this case is the right of a property owner to have changes in value accrue to his account rather than to the account of the wrongdoer...The moral quality of the defendant's acts may also be another consideration in determining whether a proprietary remedy is appropriate. Allowing the defendant to retain a specific asset when it was obtained through conscious wrongdoing may so offend a court that it would deny to the defendant the right to retain the property.

Having considered these factors, La Forest J, with whom the majority concurred, concluded that a constructive trust should be imposed:

> [the constructive trust] is but one remedy, and will only be imposed in appropriate circumstances. Where it could be more appropriate than in the present case, however, it is difficult to see.[122]

However, the absolute certainty of the rightness of a proprietary remedy in this statement only serves to emphasize the difficulty of uncertainty, for whilst La Forest J and

---

[118] (1989) 61 DLR (4th) 14, at 49.   [119] Goff and Jones, *The Law of Restitution* (3rd edn, 1986), p 78.
[120] (1989) 61 DLR (4th) 14, at 51.   [121] (1989) 61 DLR (4th) 14.
[122] (1989) 61 DLR (4th) 14, at 48.

the majority considered that the facts provided the clearest possible case for a propri-etary remedy, Sopinka J and McIntyre J dissented and held that a personal monetary award of restitution was sufficient to reverse the unjust enrichment.[123] This uncertainty about the correct remedy was also evident in the more recent case of *Korkontzilas v Soulos*,[124] where the Supreme Court considered whether a constructive trust should be awarded against a gratuitous agent who had acted in breach of his fiduciary obliga-tions. The majority held that a constructive trust should be awarded, whereas the dis-senting minority held that it should not.

(c) The rise and fall of the 'new model' constructive trust

During the 1970s, Lord Denning MR advocated a novel approach whereby a construc-tive trust should be imposed simply to achieve perceived justice between cohabitants in the family home in acquiring an interest in land. He described this principle as a 'new model' constructive trust.[125] In *Hussey v Palmer* he expounded the nature and operation of such a trust:

> it is a trust imposed by law whenever justice and good conscience require it. It is a liberal process, founded on large principles of equity, to be applied in cases where the defendant cannot conscientiously keep the property for himself alone, but ought to allow another to have the property or a share in it. The trust may arise at the outset when the property is acquired, or later on, as the circumstances may require. It is an equitable remedy by which the court can enable an aggrieved party to obtain restitution.[126]

In essence, the 'new model' constructive trust was a trust imposed to achieve restitu-tion, in other words to prevent the legal owner of land being unjustly enriched by refus-ing to acknowledge that the beneficiary was entitled to an interest. The 'new model' constructive trust was derived from the American model of constructive trusts, as stated in the Restatement of Restitution:

> Where a person holding title to property is subject to an equitable duty to convey it to another on the ground that he would be unjustly enriched if he were permitted to retain it, a constructive trust arises.[127]

Lord Denning even claimed that in advocating the 'new model' constructive trust he was merely extending the concept that had been approved by the House of Lords in *Gissing v Gissing*.[128] In *Eves v Eves* he stated:

> Equity is not past the age of child bearing. One of her latest progeny is a constructive trust of a new model. Lord Diplock brought it into the world[129] and we have nourished it...[130]

---

[123] See also Tang 'Confidence and the Constructive Trust' (2003) 23 LS 135, who argues that a construc-tive trust should not have been imposed.   [124] (1997) 146 DLR (4th) 214.
[125] *Eves v Eves* [1975] 1 WLR 1338, at 1341. See also *Binions v Evans* [1972] Ch 359; *Cooke v Head (No 1)* [1972] 1 WLR 518; *Hussey v Palmer* [1972] 1 WLR 1286.
[126] *Hussey v Palmer* [1972] 3 All ER 744, at 747; (1973) 37 Conv (Hayton); (1973) 89 LQR 2; (1973) 32 CLJ 41 (Fairest); (1973) 36 MLR 426 (Ridley); (1973) 26 CLP 17 (Oakley); (1978) 8 Sydney LR 578 (Davies).
[127] Para 16.   [128] [1971] AC 886.   [129] In *Gissing v Gissing* [1971] AC 886.
[130] [1975] 1 WLR 1338, at 1342.

However, on careful reading, his citation of Lord Diplock's comments was extremely selective and, as will be seen later, the House of Lords did not suggest anything approximating to the 'new model' constructive trust. What Lord Denning was advocating was a form of remedial constructive trust, which arises as a remedy to correct a wrong, rather than an institutional constructive trust which arises on a particular set of legal principles.

The 'new model' constructive trust has been comprehensively rejected by the English courts. The main objection has been the absence of a coherent principle by which it can be decided whether the imposition of a constructive trust is warranted in any particular situation, which would lead to uncertainty and unpredictability in proprietary rights. After Lord Denning had retired, the Court of Appeal held in a number of cases that, whilst the actual decisions where he had advocated the 'new model' constructive trust could be justified on other grounds, Lord Denning's reasoning was inconsistent with earlier authorities. For example, in *Grant v Edwards*[131] Nourse LJ suggested that Lord Denning's decision in *Eves v Eves*[132] had been 'at variance with the principles stated in *Gissing v Gissing*'.[133]

The main objection raised against the new model constructive trust was the fear that such an approach to proprietary entitlements would create uncertainty, and that decisions would depend on the personal moral feelings of the individual judge. This danger was clearly expressed by Bagnall J in *Cowcher v Cowcher*,[134] where he considered the argument that injustice could result from the narrow criteria required for a constructive trust by the House of Lords in *Pettitt v Pettitt*[135] and *Gissing v Gissing*:[136]

> In any individual case the application of these propositions may produce a result which appears unfair. So be it; in my view, that is not an injustice. I am convinced that in determining rights, particularly property rights, the only justice that can be attained by mortals, who are fallible and are not omniscient, is justice according to law; the justice which flows from the application of sure and settled principles to proved or admitted facts. So in the field of equity the length of the Chancellor's foot has been measured or is capable of measurement. This does not mean that equity is past the age of child bearing: simply that its progeny must be legitimate—by precedent out of principle. It is well that this should be so; otherwise no lawyer could safely advise on his client's title and every quarrel would lead to a law suit.

This attitude was echoed in *Springette v Defoe*,[137] where Dillon LJ proclaimed:

> The court does not as yet sit, as under a palm tree, to exercise a general discretion to do what the man in the street, on a general overview of the case, might regard as fair.

The new model constructive trust was also initially rejected by some Commonwealth jurisdictions on similar grounds of uncertainty and lack of principle. In Australia,

---

[131] [1986] Ch 638, at 647.   [132] [1975] 1 WLR 1338.   [133] [1971] AC 886.
[134] [1972] 1 WLR 425, at 430.   [135] [1970] AC 777.   [136] [1971] AC 886.
[137] [1992] 2 FLR 388, at 393.

Allen v Snyder[138] doubted whether the new model constructive trust could be supported from *Gissing v Gissing*,[139] and the High Court rejected it in *Muschinski v Dodds*.[140] In New Zealand the 'new model' constructive trust was described in *Carly v Farrelly*[141] by Mahon J as:

> a supposed rule of equity which is not only vague in its outline but which must disqualify itself from acceptance as a valid principle of jurisprudence by its total uncertainty of application and result.

It is somewhat ironic that, as we have seen, these jurisdictions have subsequently adopted forms of constructive trust which are imposed as remedies to prevent 'unjust enrichment' similar to the new model constructive trust as Lord Denning described it Some would also argue that the broad and imprecise criteria adopted by a majority of the House of Lords in *Stack v Dowden*[142] and advanced in *Jones v Kernott*[143] for inferring an intention to create a common intention constructive trust have resulted in the introduction of a new model constructive trust in all but name; or something which has that effect.

(4) Prospects for the remedial constructive trust in England

While the remedial constructive trust developed in Canada has to some degree been adopted in other commonwealth jurisdictions, it has yet to find a place in English law.[144] As has been evident throughout this chapter, English law seems to have been particularly sensitive to the difficulties of uncertainty, especially in the field of proprietary rights. The ability of a legal system to incorporate a concept such as the remedial constructive trust may largely be determined by the prevailing legal culture and its ability to accept a degree of remedial discretion in the interests of individual justice at the expense of absolute certainty. However, the emergence of a coherent doctrine of unjust enrichment in England has opened the door to the possible acceptance of a remedial style of constructive trust in the future. In *Lipkin Gorman v Karpnale Ltd*[145] the House of Lords took the momentous step of acknowledging the existence of an autonomous cause of action in unjust enrichment, which has been consistently affirmed in subsequent decisions.[146] The precise scope of the principle against unjust enrichment has been the subject of intense academic scrutiny, and as restitutionary claims are more frequently considered judicially it is inevitable that it will attain

---

[138] [1977] 2 NSWLR 685.   [139] [1971] AC 886.

[140] (1985) 160 CLR 583, 62 ALR 429, at 452.

[141] [1975] 1 NZLR 356; (1978) 94 LQR 347 (Samuels). See also *Avondale Printers & Stationers Ltd v Haggie* [1979] 2 NZLR 124.

[142] [2007] 2 AC 432.   [143] [2012] 2 AC 776.

[144] The possible existence of the remedial constructive trust was left open by the Privy Council in *Re Goldcorp Exchange Ltd (In Receivership)* [1995] 1 AC 74.   [145] [1991] 2 AC 548.

[146] See *Woolwich Equitable Building Society v IRC* [1992] 3 All ER 737; *Westdeutsche Landesbank Girozentrale v Islington London Borough Council* [1996] AC 669; *Kleinwort Benson Ltd v Glasgow City Council* [1999] 1 AC 153.

greater clarity. Whilst some areas remain vague, for example the practical scope of the restitutionary defence of change of position, it seems clear that English law has developed an independent law of restitution, founded on the principle against unjust enrichment, which is the necessary prerequisite of the adoption of the remedial constructive trust. The adoption of a cause of action in unjust enrichment inevitably raises the question as to the nature of the remedies available to effect restitution. Whilst personal restitutionary remedies are available, it is less clear when restitution may be effected by the award of a proprietary remedy. Traditionally, such proprietary remedies have only been available where an enrichment has been received in breach of fiduciary duty, or if the defendant enjoyed a pre-existing proprietary right, or 'proprietary base'[147] in the property from which the enrichment was derived. It was noted in the preceding chapter how Professor Birks proposed an extension of the concept of the resulting trust as a vehicle to effect restitution, which would have led to a significant expansion in the circumstances in which a proprietary remedy was available against an enriched defendant. Although this thesis was rejected by the House of Lords in *Westdeutsche Landesbank Girozentrale v Islington London Borough Council*,[148] Lord Browne-Wilkinson took the opportunity to suggest that English law may yet decide to adopt the remedial constructive trust:

> Although the resulting trust is an unsuitable basis for developing proprietary restitutionary remedies, the remedial constructive trust, if introduced into English law, may provide a more satisfactory road forward. The court by way of remedy might impose a constructive trust on a defendant who knowingly retains property of which the plaintiff has been unjustly deprived. Since the remedy can be tailored to the circumstances of the particular case, innocent third parties would not be prejudiced and restitutionary defences, such as change of position, are capable of being given effect. However, whether English law should follow the United States and Canada by adopting the remedial constructive trust will have to be decided in some future case when the point is directly in issue.[149]

However, in subsequent cases the Court of Appeal has rejected any suggestion that English law should introduce the remedial constructive trust. In *Halifax Building Society v Thomas*[150] Peter Gibson LJ refused to impose a constructive trust where a defendant had obtained a profit by purchasing a house, which had subsequently risen in value, using a fraudulently obtained mortgage. He stated that English law had not followed other jurisdictions where the constructive trust has become a remedy for unjust enrichment, and indicated that, in the light of Parliamentary action that presupposed that a criminal might keep the benefit of his crime without statutory intervention, the courts should not indulge in such judicial creativity.[151]

Such objections were stated even more strongly in *Re Polly Peck (No 2)*.[152] The applicants, who were the owners of land in Cyprus, applied for leave, pursuant to s 11(3)(d)

---

[147] *Lonhro plc v Al-Fayed (No 2)* [1992] 1 WLR 1.

[148] [1996] AC 669; (1996) 112 LQR 521 (Cape); [1996] CLJ 432 (Jones); [1996] LMCLQ 441 (Stevens). See [1996] RLR 3 (Birks).   [149] [1996] AC 669, at 716.

[150] [1996] Ch 217.   [151] [1995] 4 All ER 673, at 682.   [152] [1998] 3 All ER 812.

of the Insolvency Act 1986, to commence proceedings by writ against the administrators of Polly Peck International. They claimed that they were entitled to a remedial constructive trust of the profits which Polly Peck had obtained by wrongful exploitation
of their land after it had been misappropriated by the Turkish Republic of Northern
Cyprus. As Polly Peck was in administration, the grant of such a proprietary remedy
would enable them to gain priority over other creditors. The Court of Appeal held
that there was no prospect that the court would grant the order requested. It would
impose a retrospective proprietary interest on the assets of the insolvent company,
excluding those assets from pari passu distribution amongst the general creditors,
thereby modifying the statutory scheme for the distribution of the company's assets
under the Insolvency Act. Nourse LJ held that the remedial constructive trust could
only be introduced into English law by an Act of Parliament.[153] Having noted that Lord
Browne-Wilkinson had accepted the possibility that the remedial constructive trust
may become part of English Law in *Westdeutsche Landesbank Girozentrale v Islington
London Borough Council*, he continued:

> such observations, being both obiter and tentative, can only be of limited assistance when
> the question has to be decided, as it does here. There being no earlier decision, we must
> turn to principle. In doing so, we must recognise that the remedial constructive trust
> gives the court a discretion to vary proprietary rights. You cannot grant a proprietary
> right to A, who has not had one beforehand, without taking some proprietary right away
> from B. No English court has ever had the power to do that, except with the authority of
> Parliament…It is not that you need an Act of Parliament to prohibit a variation of pro-
> prietary rights. You need one to permit it: see the Variation of Trusts Act 1958 and the
> Matrimonial Causes Act 1973.[154]

He further indicated that, in his opinion, the possibility of a remedial constructive
trust would not have been seriously arguable even if Polly Peck had been solvent and
there was no direct conflict with the provisions of the Insolvency Act.

In the light of these cases, some commentators have suggested that there is no prospect that the remedial constructive trust will be introduced in England.[155] However,
the prospect has not disappeared and has gained some ground more recently. Writing
extra-judicially, Etherton LJ has suggested that the recent House of Lords decision in
Stack v Dowden[156] has introduced a remedial constructive trust in the family home
by introducing a new method of acquiring a proprietary interest without the need
for detrimental reliance, a change 'driven by social policy rather than strict adherence to precedent'.[157] This view almost certainly goes too far since it is based on obiter

---

[153] This almost certainly underestimates the power of the House of Lords, and now the Supreme Court,
to develop the law. No such statutory authority was required in Canada.

[154] [1998] 3 All ER 812, at 831. Nourse LJ placed particular reliance on the judgment of Lord Simmond
LC in *Chapman v Chapman* [1954] AC 429.

[155] Birks 'The End of the Remedial Constructive Trust?' (1998) 12 *Trusts Law International* 202; Wright
'Professor Birks and the Demise of the Remedial Constructive Trust' [1999] RLR 128.

[156] [2007] 2 AC 432.

[157] Etherton 'Constructive Trusts and Proprietary Estoppel: The Search for Clarity and Principle' [2009]
Conv 104.

comments and is inconsistent with earlier decisions of the House of Lords, like *Gissing v Gissing*,[158] which have not been overruled. Lord Scott, using a technique reminiscent of Lord Denning, has also laid down a 'marker' which could enable courts in the future to adopt the remedial constructive trust. In *Thorner v Major*,[159] the House of Lords applied the doctrine of proprietary estoppel to compel a farmer to honour his promise to leave his farm to a cousin who had provided unpaid assistance for many years. Giving his opinion, Lord Scott, whilst concurring in that view, expressed his preference for using a 'remedial constructive trust'. He said:

> The possibility of a remedial constructive trust over property, created by the common intention or understanding of the parties regarding the property on the basis of which the claimant has acted to his detriment, has been recognised at least since *Gissing v Gissing*[160] (see particularly Lord Diplock, at p 905).[161]

This view is open to challenge on a number of counts. First, he has taken a view about proprietary estoppel that is not shared by his peers.[162] Second, he adopts a highly idiosyncratic view of Lord Diplock's comments, since the passage to which he refers has always been taken to relate to an institutional rather than a remedial constructive trust. Third, if Lord Scott is merely renaming the common intention constructive trust, then it is confusing and unnecessary. Finally, it is noteworthy that none of the other Law Lords passed comment on this view. It cannot be taken to be the view of the most senior court yet.

Lord Scott's comments in relation to the possible existence of a remedial constructive trust in English law have been endorsed by the summary judgment of Warren J in *Clarke v Meadus*.[163] This case concerned a claim, either through proprietary estoppel or a constructive trust, to a beneficial interest in property arising after such interests had already been declared in an earlier, express trust. In holding that an express declaration of trust did not preclude a claim through proprietary estoppel arising as a result of promises and representations made after the deeds of trust were executed, Warren J noted that the constructive trust argument in this case relied on 'a *remedial* constructive trust, a juridical beast which English case law has set its face against'.[164] Nevertheless, he felt Lord Scott's dicta in *Thorner* lent 'support to the view that such a remedy should be available in cases of this sort'[165] and that:

> ...Proprietary estoppel and remedial constructive trust are simply different routes to the same result which is to give Mrs Clarke an interest in the property going beyond the half share which she already has...the authorities, in particular *Stack v Dowden*,[166] do not in

---

[158] [1971] AC 886.   [159] [2009] UKHL 18.   [160] [1971] AC 886.

[161] [2009] UKHL 18, at [20].

[162] See the comments made by Lord Walker in *Thorner v Major* [2009] UKHL 18, at [67] on Lord Scott's observations about proprietary estoppel in *Yeoman's Row Management Ltd v Cobbe* [2008] UKHL 55.

[163] [2010] EWHC 3117 (Ch).

[164] [2010] EWHC 3117 (Ch) at [82] (the emphasis on the word 'remedial' is contained in the text of the judgment and has not been added).   [165] [2010] EWHC 3117 (Ch).

[166] [2007] 2 AC 432.

my view preclude a remedial constructive trust once Mrs Clarke has jumped the hurdle of establishing the availability of such a remedy as a matter of English law.[167]

In relation to the latter point, it is still suggested that establishing the availability of a remedial constructive trust in English law remains an almost insuperable hurdle for a claimant to overcome.[168] Certainly, comments made in a summary judgment or obiter in the higher courts will not alter years of binding precedent, but it suggests that the dicta of Lord Scott in *Thorner* and, to no lesser extent of Lady Hale in *Stack* and *Kernott*, have put up a marker that cannot simply be ignored. Cynics might also suggest that there is no material difference between a remedial constructive trust and an 'ambulatory' institutional constructive trust where the shares of the beneficial owners in the family home remain uncertain and in flux until a decision of the court implying or imputing those shares. These arguments are explored in the treatment of constructive trusts of the family home in the next chapter.

[167] [2010] EWHC 3117 (Ch), at [83].

[168] See, for instance, *Cook v Thomas* [2010] EWCA Civ 227 (an appeal on findings of fact concerning an estoppel claim), in which Lloyd LJ suggested that Lord Scott was 'on his own' (at [105]) in his view of (remedial) constructive trusts as a better way of interpreting claims than estoppel.

PART III

Application of Trusts

10

Interests in the family home

This chapter explores how it is possible for someone living in a family home to acquire an interest in it. This can be done formally and documented in writing, but even where this is not the case, it is possible for an interest in the family home to be acquired informally through the application of equitable principles and doctrines. These include implied trusts (resulting and constructive) and the equitable remedy of proprietary estoppel. This has been a highly contentious area of law, and has generated significant judicial and academic interest over a sustained period. However, as will be demonstrated, the principles applicable now appear to be relatively settled, if complex, and it may well be that the law in this area enters a period of relative quietude. In view of the fact that this is a complex area, the chapter considers the significance of the context of the family home, before we look at each equitable mechanism in turn.

1 Equity and the family home

Before the Second World War, most people in Britain rented the house in which they lived. Now most people live, or aspire to live, in houses that are owned by one of the people living there.[1] Since the average house is now worth over £165,441,[2] the family home represents the most substantial tangible asset in most households. Despite this, it is surprisingly common for very little thought to be given to the arrangements for its ownership, or for any arrangements to be informal and unrecorded. This can give rise to problems where one of the occupiers dies, or where there is a breakdown in family relationships.

The most common situation that will provide the focus of this chapter is where a couple cohabit in a property that has been acquired in the name of one of them only (historically the male partner). There are other situations at which we will be looking, such as where a person has contributed to the cost of acquiring a family home, or to the expenses of life in the family home, or where a person has been led to believe that for some other reason they are acquiring a stake in the home. In most of these cases, the problem would not have arisen if the parties had given sufficient thought to the

---

[1] See *Cohabitation: The Financial Consequences of Relationship Breakdown* Law Com No 207 (2007), Parts I and II. [2] Land Registry House Price Index, November 2013.

issue and had chosen to create an express trust, declaring how the beneficial interests in the property would be held.[3] Although the legal principles that are discussed in this chapter are in most cases capable of conferring rights on parties other than married or unmarried cohabiting couples, this kind of relationship is the most typical situation in which these issues arise. For convenience, the discussion therefore assumes that this is the relationship between the parties in dispute. There are, however, many reported cases in which different relationships are considered, especially in relation to propri-etary estoppel. For instance there are a number of cases where someone has been per-suaded to provide support for an older person by providing unpaid personal care, or by working on their farm without being fairly paid. They may be able to acquire rights using the same principles as those that apply between couples.

(1) **The social and legal context**

(a) **The emancipation of women**

Changes in the pattern of home ownership and the emancipation of women have made the acquisition of an interest in the family home a matter of increasing importance since the middle of the twentieth century. Before the Married Women's Property Act 1882, a wife did not have a separate legal existence to her husband, and in consequence property vested in the husband alone. During the first half of the twentieth century, the majority of matrimonial homes were purchased in the sole name of the husband, who generally worked to provide the family income while the wife brought up their children and took care of the domestic needs of the family. Divorce was less common than it is now and it was often unnecessary to determine whether the wife had any independent interest in the property. The increasing recognition of the equal place of women, their growing economic contribution to marriage through their participation in the labour market, and especially the growth in divorce, made it essential to determine when a wife enjoyed a share of the ownership of her matrimonial home.[4] This was particularly important in the context of divorce, since under early divorce laws the court possessed no jurisdiction to divide the matrimonial property between the parties. If the husband was the sole owner of the matrimonial home, it would remain his on divorce. Since the Matrimonial Causes Act 1973, divorce laws do now contain provisions for the alloca-tion of assets between married couples on the dissolution of marriage, and there is also special protection for marital relationships on the death of one of the parties.[5]

(b) **Non-marital heterosexual relationships**

From around the third quarter of the twentieth century there has been significant growth in the number of heterosexual people living together as a couple without marrying. By 2010, around 7.5 million people were living in cohabiting families,

---

[3] Land Registration Rules 2003, TR 1 and Declarations form.
[4] See Cretney, *Family Law in the Twentieth Century* (2003).
[5] A discussion of such legislation is outside the scope of this book—see further Welstead and Edwards, *Family Law* (4th edn, 2013), Chs 6, 7, and 8.

representing more than 15 per cent of all family relationships.[6] It is estimated that the number of cohabiting couples in England and Wales will increase from 2.3 million in 2008 to 3.8 million in 2033.[7] The divorce legislation has no application to 'common law marriage',[8] despite a sustained and mistaken belief of a large proportion of the population that such relationships are given special recognition.[9] There is currently no other legislation similar to the divorce legislation in such circumstances. Proposals to introduce legislation have been controversial, and any legislation would in any event be incapable of covering the whole range of possibilities. There has been, since 1995, limited protection for the maintenance of a cohabitant on the death of their partner under the Inheritance (Provision for Family and Dependants) Act 1975. On 29 October 2009, the Law Commission published a consultation paper on a review of the law of intestacy, entitled 'Intestacy and Family Provision Claims on Death', which proposed that certain cohabitants should have entitlements similar to those of married couples when one of the cohabitants dies intestate.[10] A draft Bill followed in the Commission's final report, which, in Part 8, contained a draft Inheritance (Cohabitants) Bill.[11] The Inheritance and Trustees' Power Act 2013, which implements the Commissions recommendations in Parts 2 to 7 of the report received Royal Assent on 14 May 2014, but the government announced that the recommendations in Part 8 would not be implemented during the current Parliament.[12] That may well be the death-knell (no pun intended) for cohabitants' rights on death. The proposals, when made, did not enjoy fulsome support, highlighting the difficulties of introducing even specific rights for non-married cohabitants:

> There is no overwhelming consensus in favour of reform, and that is perhaps to be expected. For some people, the granting of legal rights to the survivor of an unmarried couple is simply unacceptable, notwithstanding that many cohabitants already inherit when a partner dies intestate, through a claim for family provision. For many who take this view, the concern is that greater legal equivalence between marriages and civil partnerships on the one hand, and cohabiting relationships on the other, risks undermining the institution of marriage. We appreciate those concerns but do not share them.[13]

---

[6] Office for National Statistics, *Social Trends (Households and families)* (2011), pp 7–8.

[7] Office for National Statistics, *Marital Status population projections: 2008-based, Statistical Bulletin* (2010), p 4.

[8] Probert 'Why Couples Still Believe in Common-Law Marriage' (2007) 37 Family Law 403.

[9] The British Social Attitudes survey in 2006 found that 51 per cent of respondents believed that an unmarried couple who live together for some time 'definitely' or 'probably' have a 'common law marriage' which gives them the same legal rights as married couples: see Barlow, Burgoyne, Clery, and Smithson, 'Cohabitation and the Law: Myths, Money and the Media', in Park, Curtice, Thomson, Phillips, Johnson, and Clery (eds), *British Social Attitudes: The 24th Report* (2008), pp 40–42.

[10] Consultation Paper No 191. This also included proposals on reform of the eligibility requirements under the Inheritance (Provision for Family and Dependents) Act 1975.

[11] Law Com No 331, *Intestacy and Family Provisions Claims on Death* (December 2011).

[12] The reforms within this Bill to the existing intestacy regime will be covered in Chapter 13 of this book; the proposed general changes to trustees' powers of advancement and maintenance in Chapter 15.

[13] Law Com No 331, at para 8.36.

(c) **Same-sex relationships**

Until the Sexual Offences Act 1967 male homosexual activity was illegal (lesbian activity has never been illegal). Since that date there has been further harmonization of same-sex relationships with heterosexual relationships, and since 2004 same-sex couples have, under the Civil Partnerships Act 2004 been able to enter into a civil partnership, which is treated in the same way as a marriage between a heterosexual couple. A same-sex couple who have not entered into a civil partnership are treated in the same way as an unmarried cohabiting heterosexual couple. It is now possible for same-sex couples to marry on the same basis as heterosexual couples, following the coming into force of the Marriage (Same-Sex) Couples Act 2013.[14]

(d) **Express agreement**

Most disputes about ownership of the family home would have been resolved, as has been said, if the parties had formally recorded their understanding or agreement about ownership. This would not, of course, displace the jurisdiction of the courts to vary the arrangements on divorce or death, but it would avoid most of the difficulties that arise in other situations. The agreement would usually need to take the form of an express trust, since even where the legal ownership of the property is vested in the parties jointly, this does not automatically exclude the possibility of the beneficial interests being held in some other way or in unequal shares.

(e) **Equity fills the gap**

It has already been stated that in a surprisingly high proportion of cases the arrangements concerning rights to the family home are not formally recorded, either through inadvertence or through ignorance.[15] In the absence of any legislative provisions, the courts have had to deal with the problems to which this gives rise. Equity has filled the gap, and this is an area where the creativity of equity is ably demonstrated,[16] as equity has adapted existing principles and doctrines (with varying degrees of success) to meet a problem caused by changes in lifestyle and the family unit since the middle of the last century.

The first innovation in this area was the 'deserted wife's equity', invented by Lord Denning to prevent a husband from evicting a wife he has deserted from his home. This device was emphatically rejected by the House of Lords in National *Provincial Bank v Ainsworth*,[17] where it was insisted that conventional principles of property law needed to be applied.

---

[14] It is not currently possible for same-sex marriages to be conducted in the Church of England or Wales, but the Act does not make provision to allow any other religious organization to do so, should they so wish.

[15] See *Cohabitation: The Financial Consequences of Relationship Breakdown*, Law Com No 207 (2007); Barlow, Duncan, James, and Park, *Cohabitation, Marriage and the Law* (2005). See also Cooke 'Cohabitants, Common Intention and Contributions (Again)' [2005] Conv 555.

[16] See Chapter 1.   [17] [1965] AC 1175.

(f) Creation and quantification of interests

Traditionally, and what most of this chapter will deal with, the enquiry of the judiciary has concerned whether the a cohabitant who is not also on the legal title to property is entitled to an interest in the property and no express trust has been created to indicate beneficial co-ownership in equity. The question arises in a variety of situations, but more often than not when the relationship between the cohabiting parties has reached an end or where a third party, such as a mortgagee, seeks to realize their security on the default of the legal owner as mortgagor. The courts in the past have construed this question as a matter of traditional property law—a reason or method has had to be found that allows departure from the legal fact that, without intervention, the legal owner is also the full beneficial owner of the property. The court has therefore been concerned with the creation of interests in the family home. Today, however, much of the case law concerns a second, but related question of entitlement to the home—the size of the beneficial share of the home enjoyed by the cohabitants. This arises not only in the cases listed earlier, where the next stage having identified that the non-legal owner is entitled to an interest is to quantify the size of the beneficial entitlement, but also in the express co-ownership cases. Traditionally, where there is express co-ownership in equity; the beneficial entitlements have been determined either according to the terms of the express trust or, in their absence, on the principle equality is equity. Following the House of Lords decision in *Stack v Dowden*[18] and the subsequent Supreme Court decision in *Jones v Kernott*,[19] it appears that the general rule of equal distribution may now be challenged, where the beneficiaries can demonstrate that their circumstances have changed sufficiently by the time of any dispute to render earlier distributions of the beneficial entitlement invalid, allowing the court to exercise a structured, judicial discretion to set the entitlements by what is considered fair between the parties. The application of such principles to vary the terms of an existing express trust is doubtful, but not impossible. The intervention of the courts in the family home is no longer limited to providing entitlements to those who, without equity's assistance, would have no legal rights over the home, but extends to the entitlement under a trust.

(g) Context and the straining of principles

The courts have insisted that they have not developed new or special rules, and that they have simply applied existing rules to new situations. Proponents of this approach suggest that if a couple cohabiting outside of marriage choose to acquire property in which they live, they should be governed by the same rules as would apply to a couple acquiring a property as a business venture. To do more would be seen as an illegitimate intrusion by the courts into the domain of law reform that is the responsibility of Parliament, and the demotion of the status of marriage in regulating domestic relationships. The counter-position is that equity has allowed the creation of a special regime for property acquired or used as a family home, which recognizes that there is a social and legal problem that must be addressed. There is strong judicial support for

---

[18] [2007] 2 AC 432.   [19] [2011] UKSC 53.

this approach at the very highest level in the latest Supreme Court decision in *Jones v Kernott*[20] and subsequent decisions of the first instance and appellate courts.

So, where is English law now? This is a question to which we need to return towards the end of this chapter but it is worth noting that, for many, the reality appears to be that a new jurisprudence is being created to resolve problems relating to ownership of the family home. In the words of Etherton LJ:

> [The] line of cases on the common law constructive trust can be seen clearly in retrospect as a specific jurisprudential response to the problem of a presumption of resulting trust and the absence of legislation for resolving disputes over property ownership where a married or unmarried couple have purchased property for their joint occupation as a family home.[21]

At the very least, existing principles have been strained to their absolute limits to provide solutions in this difficult area. The issues with which the courts are dealing are complex, so it is not surprising that there have been some false starts, and that there has been uncertainty or inconsistency.

(h) A clash of legal cultures: property and family law

The area also lies at the intersection of two areas of legal discourse: property law and family law. The approach of the court has been founded on property law principles, concerned with identifying interests in property under rules designed to promote certainty, whereas family law is based more on entitlements arising from the status of the home as family property and of the members of the family unit (however diverse that might be). The status of the family home itself encapsulates this difference of approach, as it is more than simply another part of an individual's property portfolio; there is an emotional connection and investment in the home that is not captured in traditional property-based thinking.[22] In seeking to give some judicial protection to the practical realities of family property, a variety of equitable devices have been employed to answer the question relating to property entitlements in the home, including the equitable remedy of proprietary estoppel. Predictability has therefore proved difficult, meaning that giving good advice in this area has been challenging. Recent decisions, have, arguably, made the position clearer for cohabitants, but not necessarily for the law. As Dixon succinctly puts it:

> If we look for an explanation of the role and impact of [recent] cases within the jurisprudence of property law, we will not find it ... [perhaps] what we now have, is a reasonably structured judicial discretion to vary the property rights of cohabitants and other property sharers that is not based on property law at all. It is something else: call it family law, call it an exercise of the court's inherent equitable jurisdiction, but, maybe, do not call it property law.[23]

---

[20] [2011] UKSC 53 per Lord Walker and Lady Hale; Lord Collins at [60]; Lord Kerr at [68].
[21] [2011] EWCA Civ 1619, at [85].
[22] See, generally, Fox, *Conceptualising Home: Theories, Laws and Policies* (2007).
[23] [2012] Conv 1 (Editorial), 2–3.

(i) No easy legislative solution

The contentious nature of legislative intervention has already been outlined. Yet, Parliament's failure to legislate in this area has been widely criticized, including recently by Lady Hale in *Gow v Grant*:

> There is some reason to think that a family law remedy such as that proposed by the Law Commission would be less costly and more productive of settlements as well as achieving fairer results than the present law.[24]

The Law Commission had proposed a partial legislative solution,[25] but this was neither comprehensive nor uncontroversial and it was rejected by government,[26] There is little hope that this particular reform will ever now become law.

2 Equitable mechanisms and understanding entitlements

It is worth appreciating that there are essentially two stages to the creation of an interest in the family home for the non-legal owner. These are (1) the acquisition of an interest in the family home through one of the equitable mechanisms used in this area of law, and, as a distinct step, (2) the quantification of the interest granted, in terms of the size or nature of the interest granted. In the past, the courts did not always make it clear that they were following this two-stage process, but it provided a useful, analytical structure to understand what was happening in the decisions. The two stages of acquisition and quantification have now been officially recognized and adopted by the Court of Appeal in *Geary v Rankine*.[27]

Conflation of the two stages in addressing the entitlements of cohabitants can lead to problems, and, as will seen, sometimes the judiciary themselves provide exemplars of the danger of such conflation in their judgments. The courts have used, in rough chronological order, resulting trusts, constructive trusts, and the remedy of proprietary estoppel as the three main methods of equitable intervention to assist the non-legal cohabitant in gaining an interest in the family home. The first two mechanisms, as we have seen in previous chapters, are species of implied trust; the latter is a particular species of estoppel that allows the creation of new rights, rather than the traditional role of estoppel to protect existing rights. It is, of course, possible to create interests in the family home expressly, but, as noted, many cohabiting couples do not choose to do so for various reasons. Figure 10.1 provides a diagrammatic overview of the acquisition and quantification of interests in the home. It does not include the position where there is joint legal ownership between the cohabitants, as that is dealt with separately later (see Figure 10.4).

---

[24] [2012] UKSC 29, at [47].
[25] *Cohabitation: The Financial Consequences of Relationship Breakdown*, Law Com No 207 (2007).
[26] See Law Com 307, Cm 7182.   [27] [2012] EWCA Civ 55 (CA) per Lewison LJ, at [19] and [20].

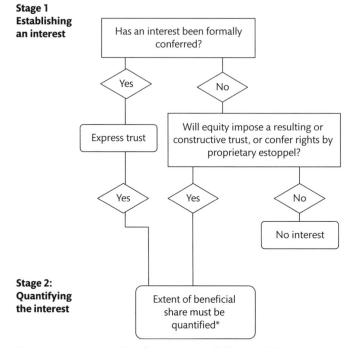

Figure 10.1 Acquiring an interest in the family home

Most of the important decisions in the last few years have concerned themselves with the quantification stage of the creation of interests in the family home. This is not to say that the acquisition of interests is a matter of settled law and principle, but the extent of beneficial (or, in the case of estoppel, other) entitlement has exercised judicial reasoning more often of late. Most significantly, the latest two highest decisions, *Stack* v *Dowden*[28] in the House of Lords and *Jones v Kernott*[29] in the Supreme Court, are both cases in which there was no question of acquisition of interests as both parties were express co-owners of the legal title; the decisions strictly concerned the question of quantification. It is easy to forget this when reading the decisions, as both are replete with dicta relating to the acquisition of interests, but it is important to remember that such dicta do not have the force of law, though they have often been treated in practice as if they did.

Quantification also means different things depending on the equitable device used, as we shall see. With trusts, quantification is about the size of the beneficial share the cohabitant enjoys under the trust; with proprietary estoppel the quantification stage is where the court gives form to the right granted to the parties, as the acquisition stage gives the cohabitant an 'estoppel equity', which awaits a court order to give it shape and substance.

---

[28] [2007] 2 AC 432.   [29] [2011] UKSC 53.

In considering the creation of interests—the entitlement of the non-legal cohabitant to claim some right in the family home—it is instructive to first consider trusts.

3 Express trusts

The most straightforward way for a cohabitant to acquire an interest in the family home is by means of a formally created express trust. An express trust arises where the parties have agreed on their shares in the property, and have recorded this agreement. This trust might be created at the time the family home is acquired, or subsequently. Given the trust relates to land, it must be declared or evidenced in writing[30] and it must also comply with the general rules that apply to the creation of any express trust.[31]

(1) **When an express trust can be created**

The most common form of express trust will be where there are joint legal owners, and an express declaration is made at the time of the purchase stating what their interests are. It is equally possible for a sole legal owner to create an express trust in favour of himself or herself and their partner or spouse, again declaring their interests. Although less common, there is nothing to prevent an express trust being declared after the purchase has been completed. The creation of an express trust relating to the family home is now encouraged in relation to registered land. For current transactions in registered land, the registration form (TR1) provides a box for the transferees to declare the trusts on which they wish to hold the property.[32] If this express declaration were made in every situation, the scope for dispute would be much diminished, a point made forcibly by Lady Hale in *Stack v Dowden* in relation to the role played by legal advisors.[33] In a belated response, on 14 January 2013 the Law Society and Law Registry issued a Practice Note,[34] which explains the introduction of a new Form (JO) for registered title. This form may be completed at the time of purchase and allows joint purchasers the ability to record, in effect by way of declaration of trust, their shares in the property.

A declaration of trusts remains optional through either the TI or JO forms, so that a legal adviser cannot insist that trusts are declared,[35] but hopefully the impact of the latest practice direction and the ease with which trusts can now be declared will lead to the creation of more express trusts. Prevention is much better than cure.

---

[30] Law of Property Act 1925, s 53(1)(b).

[31] The property must be vested in the trustee, there must be a clear intention to create a trust, and the terms of the trust must be clear. See Chapter 7.

[32] Land Registry Form, TR1 (updated October 2009).   [33] [2007] 2 AC 432, at [48].

[34] See www.lawsociety.org.uk.ezproxy.liv.ac.uk/news/stories/new-practice-note-on-joint-ownership/.

[35] See further Moran 'Anything to Declare? Express Declarations of Trust on Land Registry Form TR1: The Doubts Raised in *Stack v Dowden*' [2007] 71 Conv 364.

(2) **Functions of an express trust**

An express trust usually serves two functions: it both establishes the existence of an equitable interest (fulfilling the acquisitive stage of creation of the beneficial interests), and simultaneously quantifies that interest. A beneficial interest in the family home is an interest in land, and is therefore a proprietary interest. The nature of the beneficial shares in land will depend on the method of co-ownership declared under an express trust. There are two possibilities in equity, either that the beneficiaries hold under a joint tenancy or a tenancy in common.[36] Where the trust properly creates an equitable joint tenancy, there is no division of ownership as both joint tenants are seen as together owning the whole of the property. On the dissolution of any relationship between the parties during their lifetime, the presumption of equal shares applies in relation to the parties' respective entitlements in the home. It is only where there is a validly created tenancy in common that the beneficial co-owners can have a declared and separate share in the property.

(3) **Express trust declaring beneficial interests**

Where the claimant is a party to the expressly declared trust, the terms of the trust will normally be conclusive of the interest which that party has unless it is set aside or rectified on the basis of fraud, mistake, or undue influence, or varied by subsequent agreement.[37] The effect of an express declaration was explained by Slade LJ in *Goodman v Gallant*:

> If, however, the relevant conveyance contains an express declaration of trust which com-prehensively declares the beneficial interests in the property or its proceeds of sale, there is no room for the application of the doctrine of resulting implied or constructive trusts unless and until the conveyance is set aside or rectified; until that event the declaration contained in the document speaks for itself.[38]

It appeared to have been suggested in *Stack v Dowden*[39] that it would be possible for the parties to vary their original shares as declared in the trust instrument, without the need for a supplemental deed of variation. Compelling evidence would be needed to show such an intention, involving:

> [D]iscussions, statements or actions, subsequent to the acquisition, from which an agree-ment or common understanding as to such a change could properly be inferred.[40]

There is reason to doubt that this was ever the intention of the House of Lords in *Stack*, as Lady Hale supported the express trust as a solution to the problems of quantifying

---

[36] For a succinct account of the rules relating to the different forms of co-ownership, including how they may validly be created, see Stevens and Pearce, *Land Law* (5th edn, 2013), Chapter 12 pp 386–371.

[37] This variation would normally have to comply with s 53(1)(b) of the Law of Property Act 1925.

[38] [1986] Fam 106, at 110–111. See also *Clarke v Harlowe* [2005] EWHC 3062.

[39] [2007] 2 AC 432.

[40] [2007] 2 AC 432, at 475 [138] per Lord Neuberger, who was in dissent, but is unlikely to be doubted on this issue. See also *Bedson v Bedson* [1965] 3 All ER 307, at 316 per Davies LJ: 'whatever the documents say on their face, the court may reach the conclusion that, in reality, by express or impled agreement the true position was something different from that appearing on the face of the documents.'

interests in the family home, on the basis that where interests are clearly defined 'no one thinks that such a declaration can be overturned, except in cases of fraud or mistake'.[41] Nevertheless, the suggestion that the parties intentions might change over time, led to questions being asked in later decisions, such as *Clarke v Meadus*,[42] as to the extent to which subsequent conduct may permit inferred or imputed intentions to alter the provisions of an earlier express declaration of trust in relation to the beneficial shares. The point was repeated in *Jones v Kernott*[43] by the Supreme Court, who agreed that the parties' intentions might change over the passage of time. Mummery LJ has now clarified the position in *Pankhania v Chandegra*:

> [R]eliance on *Stack v. Dowden* and *Jones v. Kernott* for inferring or imputing a different trust in this and other similar cases which have recently been before this court is misplaced where there is an express declaration of trust of the beneficial title and no valid legal grounds for going behind it.[44]

It may, however, be possible for the courts to show such valid legal grounds to vary the terms of an express trust in exceptional cases where the remedy of proprietary estoppel would be available. In *Clarke v Meadus*,[45] the parties were mother and daughter, and the daughter claimed entitlement to the whole beneficial interest in the home of which she was already a half owner under an express trust on the basis of detrimental reliance on assurances made by her mother to that effect. In holding that Master Bragg at first instance had been wrong to strike out the estoppel claim, Warren J opined:

> [E]xpress trusts…are capable of being overridden by a proprietary estoppel…as a result of promises and representations…It cannot, in my judgment, sensibly be argued that once beneficial interests have been declared in a formal document, those interests become immutable and incapable of being affected by a proprietary estoppel.[46]

It remains to be seen whether this decision will be followed in later cases,[47] but since proprietary estoppel permits the creation of new rights, it is suggested that on this point Warren J is correct and this is just an exceptional method of varying the terms of the original express trust. The requirements to establish a valid claim to an interest through proprietary estoppel are discussed later in this chapter.

(4) **Express trust not declaring beneficial interests**

It is possible for the parties buying a home to declare that they are joint legal owners and that they hold the property on trust, without defining the nature or extent of

---

[41] *Stack v Dowden* [2007] 2 AC 432 (HL), at [49].

[42] [2010] EWHC 3117 (Ch). The case was discussed in Chapter 9 in relation to Warren J's support for a remedial constructive trust.　　　　　　　　　　　　　　　　　　　　　　　　　[43] [2011] UKSC 53.

[44] [2012] EWCA Civ 1438. at [28]. The leading speech in that case was delivered by Patten LJ, with whom Mummery LJ agreed.　　　　　　　　　　　　　　　　　　　　　　　[45] [2010] EWHC 3117 (Ch).

[46] [2010] EWHC 3117 (Ch).

[47] See Pawlowski 'Informal variation of express trusts' [2011] Conv 245. Estoppel was not argued on the facts of *Pankhania v Chandegra* [2012] EWCA Civ 1438, nor was *Meadus* cited in argument or the opinion of the court.

their beneficial interests. These situations might occur less often if the latest practice direction on purchases of registered land is properly applied, but there will be situations where it arises. In that case, quite obviously, the declaration of trust is not conclusive about the quantification of the beneficial interests of the parties, since this is a matter on which it is silent. It is worth noting in this context that stating whether or not the survivor of the relationship can give a good receipt for capital monies on the old Land Registry form[48] where the house is registered in joint names is not evidence of an express declaration of a beneficial joint tenancy.[49] In such cases, following clarification in *Jones v Kernott*,[50] the presumption of equal shares is the starting point to determine the respective entitlements of the parties, though this presumption may be displaced. This is discussed under the discussion of constructive trusts later in the chapter.

4 Resulting trusts

The purchase money resulting trust, as this type of implied trust is known, has already been discussed in detail in Chapter 8. It is worth remembering before considering the rules relating to the operation of resulting trusts that it would appear that the utility of resulting trusts themselves in the family home has been severely restricted by key decisions of the House of Lords and the Supreme Court. This position, to which the courts had in any event been moving, albeit slowly, leaves the application of resulting trusts to affect property bought during a familial relationship to those cases where that property is bought as an investment rather than as the family home. However, despite the judicial pronouncements of the death of the resulting trust, it is important to understand the contribution it has made to securing interests in the family home.

(1) Basis: a reminder

(a) Operation

A resulting trust is an implied trust that confers a share of beneficial ownership on a person who has contributed to the acquisition of the property, but is not named as a legal owner and there has been no declaration of an express trust.[51] The resulting trust thus seeks to 'fill the gap' in the beneficial ownership. The trust arises at the date on which a property is acquired, and in principle is based exclusively upon contributions made at that date rather than subsequently.

---

[48] This form was used for conveyances prior to 1 April 2008.

[49] It does not determine that the parties will have identical rights when one of the couple dies: the entire property passes to the survivor—see *Stack v Dowden* [2007] 2 AC 432 (HL), at 452 [51] per Baroness Hale, approving the earlier decisions of the Court of Appeal on this point—*Harwood v Harwood* [1991] 2 FLR 274; *Huntingford v Hobbes* [1993] 1 FLR 736.   [50] [2011] UKSC 53.

[51] The other broad possibility is to remedy a failure of the settlor to fully divest himself of his equitable interest in property on the creation of an express trust, which is less applicable here.

(b) Resulting trust is based on a presumption

The resulting trust is based on a presumption that the purchaser would not have financed the transaction without wishing to retain a share of the beneficial ownership. The general principle was stated by Lord Reid in *Pettitt v Pettitt*:

> in the absence of evidence to the contrary effect, a contributor to the purchase-price will acquire a beneficial interest in the property.[52]

The presumption can apply where a family home is bought in the name of one of the couple only, or where it is bought in their joint names and there is no express declaration of the beneficial interests.

(2) **Creation of interests: acquisition**

(a) **Contribution to the purchase price**

The acquisition of the interest under a presumed resulting trust is based on a contribution to the purchase price of land (see Figure 10.2).[53] The major area of controversy has concerned the nature of the 'contributions' sufficient to give rise to the presumption. While 'indirect' contributions may constitute sufficient detriment to support claims based on constructive trust or proprietary estoppel, only 'direct' contributions to the purchase price have been held to give rise to a presumption of resulting trust in favour of the contributor.

(b) **Contribution to mortgage repayments**

In the majority of cases land is not purchased outright but with the help of a mortgage. In such circumstances it might be thought that a person who contributes to the mortgage repayments should be treated as having contributed to the purchase price, thus raising a presumption of resulting trust in his or her favour in proportion to his contributions. However, the principle traditionally taken as a starting point is that the amount paid through mortgage is treated in the same way as a cash contribution by the person taking out the mortgage, since that person has a legal liability to repay it.[54] That principle can be modified if there is an agreement at the time the mortgage is taken out that the sum raised by mortgage will be treated as a joint contribution to the purchase price. In this case the payment of mortgage instalments will be taken to give rise to a resulting trust. This was explained in *Cowcher v Cowcher*, where Bagnall J considered the consequences of a conveyance of a house to A for £24,000, where A had provided £8,000 of his own money and the remainder was provided by a mortgage taken out in the name of B:

> suppose that at the time A says that as between himself and B he, A, will be responsible for half the mortgage repayments... Though as between A and B and the vendor A has

---

[52] [1970] AC 777, at 794. See also *Gissing v Gissing* [1971] AC 886.

[53] *Tinsley v Milligan* [1994] 1 AC 340, where a lesbian couple purchased a house in the sole name of Tinsley, but a direct contribution of half the deposit gave rise to a presumption of a resulting trust in favour of Milligan of one-half share in the house.

[54] This view still has judicial support—see *Barrett v Barrett* [2008] EWHC 1061 (Ch), at [6]–[7] and [24] per David Richards J.

provided £8,000 and B £16,000, as between A and B themselves A had provided £8,000 and made himself liable for the repayment of half the £16,000 mortgage namely a further £8,000, a total of £16,000; the resulting trust will therefore be as to two-thirds for A and one-third for B.[55]

Applying this principle, Bagnall J held that a resulting trust was presumed in favour of a wife who had made some of the repayments on a mortgage taken out by her husband. Similarly in *Tinsley v Milligan*[56] the House of Lords held that there was evidence to support finding a resulting trust where the parties had agreed that the mortgage repayments would be made from an account containing the proceeds of their joint business operation, even though this was in the sole name of Tinsley.

(c) Mortgage contributions not referable to agreement prior to purchase

In the absence of any agreement prior to purchase that the mortgage is to be treated as finance provided by both parties, the payment of mortgage instalments subsequent to the initial acquisition of the property will not give rise to any interest by way of a resulting trust, since they are not regarded as being contributions to the purchase price of the property. This was so held by the Court of Appeal in *Curley v Parkes*.[57] In this case Mr Curley and Miss Parkes were living together. A house was purchased in 2001 in the sole name of Parkes. The purchase was funded exclusively by the proceeds of sale of her previous solely owned house, cash she provided and a mortgage of £138,000 which was taken out in her sole name. Curley subsequently paid some £9,000 into Park's bank account, from which the mortgage instalments were paid, as a way of assisting her with the huge commitments she was taking on. Curley claimed that these payments entitled him to an 8.5 per cent share of the equitable ownership of the house by way of a resulting trust. The Court of Appeal rejected his claim to an interest on this basis, holding that the payments could not be regarded as a contribution to the purchase price. Peter Gibson LJ explained the relevant principles:

> The relevant principle is that the resulting trust of a property purchased in the name of another, in the absence of contrary intention, arises once and for all at the date on which the property is acquired. Because of the liability assumed by the mortgagor in a case where monies are borrowed by the mortgagor to be used on the purchase, the mortgagor is treated as having provided the proportion of the purchase price attributable to the monies so borrowed. Subsequent payment of the mortgage instalments are not part of the purchase price already paid to the vendor, but are sums paid for discharging the mortgagor's obligations under the mortgage.[58]

Since it will frequently be the case that there is no direct evidence of an agreement to treat mortgage payments as a joint contribution to the cost of acquiring the family home, it may be possible for the payments themselves to be treated as evidence from which such an agreement can be inferred. This may be the correct interpretation of

---

[55] [1972] 1 WLR 425.   [56] [1994] 1 AC 340.   [57] [2004] EWCA Civ 1515.
[58] [2004] EWCA Civ 1515, at [14].

McQuillan v Maguire,[59] where a wife was held to be entitled to a 50 per cent share of a matrimonial home bought in the husband's name because she had subsequently contributed indirectly to the discharge of the mortgage. Lord Neuberger, in his dissenting speech in *Stack v Dowden* suggested that it might be possible to classify mortgage repayments as direct contributions, particularly where property is bought almost exclusively by means of a mortgage as:

> repayments of mortgage capital may be seen as retrospective contributions towards the cost of acquisition, or as payments which increase the value of the equity of redemption.[60]

These comments have yet to be followed in any later decisions, and while superficially attractive, it is suggested that the orthodox rule is to be preferred not least for reasons of certainty.

(d) Impact of excluding mortgage contributions

The importance of resulting trusts in determining the ownership of the family home was very much diminished by the decision to exclude payments subsequent to the date of purchase, except where these can be referred back to an agreement at the date of purchase. On the other hand, it avoided the need for difficult calculations to determine the proportion of the ownership of property acquired by way of subsequent contributions to mortgage payments, a difficulty which was acknowledged by the House of Lords in *Gissing v Gissing*, and for which no easy solution had been found.[61] However, even though such contributions may be insufficient to gain an interest by way of a resulting trust, they may be relevant for the purposes of a constructive trust, discussed later.

(e) Contribution by qualification for a discount in the purchase price

If a house is purchased at a discounted price, the amount of the discount is regarded as a contribution to the purchase price. Therefore, the person who qualified for the discount will be presumed to be the beneficiary of a resulting trust to that extent in the property. In *Marsh v Von Sternberg*[62] Bush J held that a discount gained on the market value of a long lease because one of the parties was a sitting tenant was to be treated as a contribution to the purchase price in assessing their respective interests under a resulting trust. In *Springette v Defoe*[63] a discount of 41 per cent of the market value of a council flat obtained because the plaintiff had been a tenant for more than eleven years was counted as a contribution to the purchase price by the Court of Appeal.

---

[59] [1996] 1 ILRM 394.   [60] [2007] 2 AC 431, at [117].

[61] [1971] AC 886, at 987, per Lord Reid: 'where [the contributor] does not make direct payments towards the purchase it is less easy to evaluate her share. If her payments are direct she gets a share proportionate to what she has paid. Otherwise there must be a more rough and ready evaluation. I agree that this does not mean that she would as a rule get a half-share... There will of course be cases where a half-share is a reasonable estimation, but there will be many others where a fair estimate might be a tenth or a quarter or something even more than a half.'   [62] [1986] 1 FLR 526.

[63] [1992] 2 FLR 388.

(f) Contributions to the cost of repairs or renovation

Where, contemporaneously with the purchase, the property is repaired or renovated, and its value is thereby increased, a person who contributes towards the cost of such repairs or renovations will be entitled to an interest in the land by way of a resulting trust proportionate to the extent to which the increase was attributable to their contribution.[64] Improvements made much later than the date of purchase may give rise to a constructive trust.

(g) Contributions to general household expenses

In contrast to indirect contributions to the purchase price of land, it seems that contributions made to general household expenses will not give rise to a presumption of resulting trust in favour of the contributor because they are not sufficiently referable to the purchase price. In *Burns v Burns*[65] Mr and Mrs Burns began living together as man and wife in 1961. In 1963 a house was purchased in the sole name of Mr Burns, who financed the purchase by way of a mortgage. Mrs Burns began to work in 1975. She used part of her earnings to pay the rates and telephone bills and to buy various domestic chattels for the house. When they split up in 1980, she claimed to be entitled to an equitable interest in the house by reason of her contributions. The Court of Appeal held that she was not entitled to an interest by way of resulting trust because she had 'made no direct contribution to the purchase price'.[66] It should be noted that although such contributions to family expenses will not give rise to a presumption of resulting trust, they may, if substantial, constitute sufficient detriment to lead to the imposition of a constructive trust.

(h) Contributions to removal expenses

In *Curley v Parkes*[67] the Court of Appeal held that neither the payment of solicitor's fees and expenses, nor the payment of removal costs, were capable of giving rise to a resulting trust. Although such costs might be substantial, they do not form any part of the purchase price of the property itself, and hence do not give rise to a presumption of resulting trust. They may, however, be relevant for the purposes of a constructive trust.

(i) Contributions otherwise explained as loans

Even where there is a direct contribution towards the cost of acquiring a property which would normally lead to a resulting trust, the presumption of a resulting trust will be rebutted where evidence shows that money was advanced by way of a loan. In *Re Sharpe (a bankrupt)*[68] Mr and Mrs Sharpe lived in a maisonette with their 82-year-old aunt, Mrs Johnson. The property had been purchased in the name of Mr Sharpe for £17,000. Mrs Johnson had contributed £12,000 towards the purchase price, while the remainder was raised by way of a mortgage. Mr and Mrs Sharpe were subsequently declared bankrupt and Mrs Johnson claimed to be entitled to a proprietary interest in the maisonette by means of a resulting trust presumed from her contribution to the purchase price.

---

[64] *Drake v Whipp* [1996] 1 FLR 826.   [65] [1984] Ch 317.
[66] [1984] Ch 317, at 326, per Fox LJ.   [67] [2004] EWCA Civ 1515.   [68] [1980] 1 WLR 219.

Browne-Wilkinson J held that the money had in fact been advanced by way of a loan, with the intention that it would be repaid. She was not therefore entitled to any share of the equitable interest of the property. A presumption of a resulting trust was also rebutted by evidence that a loan was intended in *Vajpeyi v Yijaf*.[69] In this case the claimant provided the defendant, who was her lover, with £10,000 to enable him to purchase a house in his sole name. At the time of the purchase in 1980 the defendant was a young man of limited means. The claimant alleged that by virtue of this payment she was entitled to a 33.89 per cent share of the equitable ownership of the property on the basis of a presumed resulting trust, whereas the defendant claimed that the money had been advanced by way of a loan, which he had repaid. Peter Prescott QC held that the following factors had rebutted the presumption of a resulting trust in favour of a loan: the defendant had been a young man of limited means who was anxious to get on the property ladder, whereas the claimant was a woman who was already on the property ladder when the money was advanced; the claimant had tolerated the defendant collecting rents from the property and keeping them for himself for some twenty-one years; the claimant had failed to propound her claim to an interest for twenty-one years; and she had never said anything about her alleged interest in the house when it was mortgaged by the defendant to enable him to purchase her matrimonial home some years previously.

(j) Contributions otherwise explained as gifts

The normal presumption that a contribution to the purchase price of property creates a resulting trust will also be rebutted where there is evidence that the payment was made by way of gift. The presumption of resulting trust can also be rebutted by the presumption of advancement, which holds that in certain relationships a contribution towards the acquisition of property was intended to be an outright gift. Of relevance here has traditionally been such a presumption (the presumption of advancement) in where a husband makes a transfer to, or contributes towards the cost of purchase in the name of, his wife. There is no presumption from wife to husband or between mother and child. It has already been seen that the presumption of advancement is extremely weak,[70] and the development of acquisition of interest in the family home led Lord Diplock to refer the presumption as a judicial instrument of last resort in *Pettitt v Pettitt*.[71] Indeed, even stronger doubt has come in later cases,[72] and Arden LJ confirmed in *Gibson v Revenue and Customs Prosecution Office*,[73] that the presumption of advancement, like the presumption of resulting trust, is displaced by the presumption that that beneficial ownership follows legal ownership, discussed later in this chapter.[74] In consequence, there is no compelling reason to think that the presumption has any further utility even in cases of single legal ownership. The presumption is now only likely to be employed on behalf

---

[69] [2003] EWHC 2339.

[70] The high point in recent memory was Lord Denning's use of the presumption in *Tinker v Tinker* [1970] 2 WLR 331. to frustrate a husband who had conveyed property into his wife's name to shield the family assets from his creditors, and later wished to claim the property back.   [71] [1970] AC 777.

[72] *Stack v Dowden* [2007] 2 AC 432 at [16] per Lord Walker; [101] per Lord Neuberger.

[73] [2008] EWCA Civ 645.

[74] [2008] EWCA Civ 645, at [27]. Confirmed in *Jones v Kernott* [2012] 1 AC 776.

of a claimant in the most desperate or extreme of circumstances, and even then, some supporting evidence is likely to be needed if the claim is to succeed. It is also, as we saw in Chapter 8, an order of the Lord Chancellor away from becoming a footnote in legal history, thanks to s 199 of the Equality Act 2010.

(3) Quantifying the interest

The normal method of quantifying an interest arising out of a resulting trust is an arithmetical calculation, so that the share of the beneficial ownership attained is proportionate to the share of the purchase price contributed (see Figure 10.2). This was one of the weaknesses of the resulting trust approach when compared to the common intention constructive trust, which has always allowed a wider range of factors to be considered in determining a share of the beneficial interest. This did not go unnoticed in the case law, and there were some instances where different approaches to quantification have been adopted.

(a) Utilizing the constructive trust analysis

In *Midland Bank v Cooke*,[75] the Court of Appeal found that the circumstances that established a resulting trust also sufficed to establish a constructive trust; a possibility opened up by Lord Bridge's suggestion that a direct contribution was necessary to demonstrate a common intention constructive trust through conduct.[76] Moving quantification to a constructive trust allowed for a more holistic approach to considering the factors applicable to determining the size of the beneficial share:

> [T]o determine (in the absence of express evidence of intention) what proportions the parties must be assumed to have intended for their beneficial ownership, the duty of the judge is to undertake a survey of the whole course of dealing between the parties relevant to their ownership and occupation of the property and their sharing its burdens and advantages. That scrutiny will not confine itself to a limited range of acts of direct contribution of the sort that are needed to found a beneficial interest in the first place. It will take into consideration all conduct which throws light on the question what shares were intended.[77]

On the facts of that case, Mrs Cooke was entitled to a 50 per cent share of the property, though her direct contribution to the purchase price would have entitled her only to a 6.74 per cent share. Subsequent decisions confirmed that the only way for a cohabitant to enjoy an interest greater than the exact mathematical equivalent of the contribution was to demonstrate that the land was held on constructive trust,[78] and the approach, which may be termed 'the assumed intention approach' gathered favour.[79] It has already been seen in Chapter 8 that this approach reached its apex in the Court of

---

[75] [1995] 4 All ER 562; (1995) 27 HLR 733; (1997) 60 MLR 420 (O'Hagan); [1997] Conv 66 (Dixon). See also *McHardy and Sons (A firm) v Warren* [1994] 2 FLR 338.

[76] *Lloyds Bank v Rosset* [1991] 1 AC 107 at 133. This is discussed under the treatment of common intention constructive trusts later in the chapter.   [77] (1995) 27 HLR 733, at 745.

[78] See *Drake v Whipp* [1996] 1 FLR 826.   [79] See, for example, *Le Foe v Le Foe* [2001] 2 FLR 970.

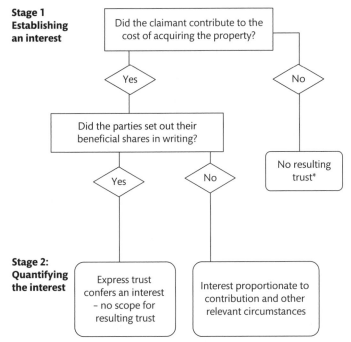

Stage 1
Establishing
an interest

Did the claimant contribute to the
cost of acquiring the property?

Yes   No

Did the parties set out their
beneficial shares in writing?

Yes   No

No resulting
trust*

Stage 2:
Quantifying
the interest

Express trust
confers an interest
– no scope for
resulting trust

Interest proportionate to
contribution and other
relevant circumstances

*The claimant may have a remedy in constructive trust or proprietary estoppel.

Figure 10.2 Resulting trusts of the family home

Appeal decision in *Oxley v Hiscock*.[80] Chadwick LJ adopted a new broad principle that
the beneficial interests of the parties should be determined by the court on the basis of
what seemed 'fair' in the light of all the circumstances:

> It must now be accepted (at least in this Court and below) the answer is that each is entitled
> to that share which the court considered fair having regard to the whole course of dealing
> between them in relation to the property. And, in that context, the 'whole course of deal-
> ing between them in relation to the property' includes the arrangements which they make
> from time to time in order to meet the outgoings (for example, mortgage contributions,
> council tax and utilities, repairs, insurance and housekeeping) which have to be met if
> they are to live in the property as their home.[81]

On the facts, Ms Oxley, who had contributed 22 per cent of the purchase price, was
awarded a 40 per cent share to reflect the fact that Mr Hiscock had contributed nearly
twice as much to the purchase price of the home and that the parties' conduct was:

> consistent with an intention to share the burden of the property (by which she must,
> I think, have meant the outgoings referable to ownership and cohabitation), it would be
> fair to treat them as having made approximately equal contributions to the balance of the
> purchase price (£30,000).[82]

---

[80] [2005] Fam 211.   [81] [2005] Fam 211, at [69].   [82] [2005] Fam 211, at [74].

This form of what may be termed 'judicial discretion' was applied in subsequent cases, *Cox v Jones*[83] and *Pinfield v Eagles*.[84] It was rejected in relation to the *inference* of a common intention between the parties when quantifying an interest.[85] It has, however, been explicitly adopted by the Supreme Court in *Jones v Kernott*,[86] in relation to *imputing* a common intention to decide on the size of the beneficial share in a common intention constructive trust where no objective common intention between them can be inferred. The difference between inferring and imputing intention may seem semantic at first glance, but as we shall see in the discussion of constructive trusts, there is a difference of approach and principle underlying it. Importantly, neither of these approaches, be it 'judicial discretion' or 'assumed intention', are strictly relevant to the resulting trust.

(b) Constructive trusts subsume purchase money resulting trusts

It was in these cases (which are considered in more detail in relation to the common intention constructive trust) that a 'muddying' of the boundary lines between a resulting trust and a constructive trust of common intention was most evident, and the sublimation of the identity of the resulting trust into the constructive trust really began. Consider this. Aida made a small direct contribution to the purchase price of a family home in Philbert's name alone, but, after many happy years, the relationship has broken down irretrievably. Aida wants the home to be sold. If Aida argued that her small direct contribution raised a presumption of resulting trust, she ran the danger that, without more, her interest in the home would be in direct proportion to the money she advanced on traditional resulting trusts principles. If, however, Aida argued that the payment demonstrated an objectively inferred common intention to share the property, in which her small contribution merely supplied the missing element of detriment which is traditionally needed,[87] then her interest would be quantified in a much more generous way. It is not difficult to see why Aida might have preferred to argue the constructive trust route over the resulting trust one.[88]

(4) The scope of resulting trusts after *Jones v Kernott*

(a) The challenge to resulting trusts

In *Stack v Dowden*,[89] the majority of the House of Lords dismissed resulting trusts as no longer an appropriate tool to discover common intention.[90] Lord Walker was emphatic:

---

[83] [2004] EWHC 1486; Probert 'Land, Law and Ex-Lovers' [2005] Conv 168.

[84] [2005] EWHC 447.

[85] See *Stack v Dowden* [2007] 2 AC 432, at [127] per Lord Neuberger, affirming the view expressed by Lady Hale at [61]; *Jones v Kernott* [2012] 1 AC 776, at [51] per Lady Hale and Lord Walker.

[86] [2012] 1 AC 776, at [51]–[52].

[87] Detriment is traditionally needed alongside a common intention to meet the acquisition stage of the creation of an interest by means of a constructive trust of common intention.

[88] See, however, *McHardy v Warren* [1994] 2 FLR 338, which resisted the co-mingling of resulting and constructive trusts and argued that they should both be treated, quite correctly, as entirely separate equitable devices.   [89] [2007] 2 AC 432.

[90] [2007] 2 AC 432, at [60] per Baroness Hale, citing with approval Lord Walker's discussion at [19]–[31]. See also *Fowler v Barron* [2008] EWCA Civ 377 (CA), where Arden LJ agreed, at least in relation to cases of joint legal ownership. Lord Walker's comments go further.

In a case about beneficial ownership of a matrimonial or quasi-matrimonial home (whether registered in the names of one or two legal owners) the resulting trust should not in my opinion operate as a legal presumption, although it may (in an updated form which takes account of all significant contributions, direct or indirect, in cash or kind) happen to be reflected in the parties' common intention.[91]

Lord Neuberger was alone in *Stack v Dowden* in considering that there was a continuing role for resulting trusts in relation to the family home. He agreed with the conclusion of the majority in *Stack*, but dissented on the reasoning; he felt that the resulting trust approach was to be favoured as part of the process of determining the rights of parties acquiring a family home. In his view, which provided a masterly reconciliation of the legal principles, one should start by identifying the parties' shares at the time of acquisition. This would be done by applying a presumption of sole or joint ownership (depending on how legal title was acquired), and then modifying this by an application of classic resulting trust principles to give the parties (in the absence of express agreement) beneficial interests proportionate to their contributions. This starting point could then be subject to further modification using constructive trust principles if there was evidence of a contrary intention, inferred not imputed, as imputation would be 'not only be wrong in principle but it would also involve a judge in an exercise which was difficult, subjective and uncertain'. This analysis has not been supported in later cases.

The abandonment of resulting trust principles drew some criticism, not least because it was, in Swadling's words, 'made with the benefit of almost no reasoning.'[92] The same comment cannot be made of the latest Supreme Court decision in *Jones v Kernott*,[93] where at least some analysis of the legal position was undertaken.[94]

(b) Common intention to be found by constructive trust alone

In *Jones v Kernott*, Lord Walker and Lady Hale make it quite explicit that there is no place for resulting trusts to determine beneficial interests:

in the case of the purchase of a house or flat in joint names for joint occupation by a married or unmarried couple, where both are responsible for any mortgage.[95]

---

[91] [2007] 2 AC 432, at [31].

[92] Swadling 'The Common Intention Constructive Trust in the House Of Lords: An Opportunity Missed' [2007] LQR 511, at 518.

[93] [2012] 1 AC 776 per Lord Walker and Lady Hale, at [15] and [51].

[94] [2012] 1 AC 776 per Lord Walker and Lady Hale, at [23]–[24]; suggesting that the constructive trust was the better approach.

[95] [2012] 1 AC 776 at [25]. Resulting trusts can still apply in business contexts, even where the business partners are domestic partners ([2012] 1 AC 776, at [31]), and the way in which Lord Walker and Lady Hale express their proposition raises the intriguing possibility that the presumption of a resulting trust might apply where no mortgage is required for a purchase (see also the summary at [51](1) where joint responsibility for a mortgage is again referred to by Lord Walker and Lady Hale as a prerequisite for the application of the principles). It is suggested this is a theoretical possibility only, given that case law subsequent to *Kernott* dealing with resulting trusts has missed this subtlety of language—see, for example, *Geary v Rankine* [2012] EWCA Civ 555.

Later in the same speech, they repeat the point for clarity:

> The assumptions as to human motivation, which led the courts to impute particular inten-
> tions by way of the resulting trust, are not appropriate to the ascertainment of beneficial
> interests in a family home.'[96]

There is even no solace for the resulting trust in situations where the property has been
purchased in joint names, but the size of the shares is not determined between the parties. In the past, unequal contributions to the purchase of property provided evidence
of an intention to create undivided shares proportionate to the contributions.[97] This is
no longer the case as Lord Walker and Lady Hale make clear that where a property is
acquired by a cohabiting couple in joint names, but there is no express declaration of
their beneficial interests, there is a presumption that the beneficial ownership is similarly held jointly in equal shares. This presumption of joint ownership is incompatible
with a presumption of a resulting trust based on unequal contributions. The presumption of joint ownership can, in turn, be rebutted by a party asserting a different share,
but clear evidence will be needed to support such a claim.[98]

(c) Judicial resistance?

Nevertheless, the judiciary has shown itself unwilling to give up on the resulting trust
as a concept. In *Ullah v Ullah*,[99] in a case involving an alleged agreement that property
assigned to Mr Ullah's sons to avoid bankruptcy claims would be held beneficially for
him, John Martin QC suggested that, if Mr Ullah could not establish a common intention constructive trust then he might instead use find a resulting trust. This would, of
course, need a direct contribution to the purchase price, and there was no such contribution on the facts.

(d) A continuing role for resulting trusts?

A common feature of both *Stack* and *Kernott* is that they were not concerned with the
law relating to the acquisition of an interest, simply in quantifying it. Property had
been purchased in joint names in both cases, so there was no dispute as to the fact
of joint ownership in equity, only to the size of the respective beneficial interests. It
might therefore be argued that the statements made in relation to acquisition of rights
by means of a presumed resulting trust were obiter dicta. Also, in neither case was
the earlier decision of *Gissing v Gissing*[100] overruled, suggesting that resulting trusts
might, technically, have a role to play in the family home. Moreover, since the circumstances which give rise to a presumed resulting trust could also support the conclusion
that there is a common intention to share the premises giving rise to a constructive
trust, on the basis that a direct contribution to the purchase price could infer a common intention to share the premises,[101] it is submitted that the resulting trust still has a

---

[96] [2012] EWCA Civ 555, at [53].
[97] See, for example, *Gissing v Gissing* [1971] AC 886.   [98] [2012] 1 AC 773 at [15], [23], and [51].
[99] [2013] EWHC 2296 (Ch).   [100] [1971] AC 886.
[101] This was part of the inference made by Holman LJ in the post-*Kernott* decision in *CPS v Piper* [2011]
EWHC 3570 (Admin) in finding a common intention constructive trust on the basis of the wife's financial
contributions. Holman LJ did not, however, recognize that he was in any way using resulting trust principles.

life, albeit disguised by the language of constructive trust. On this basis, Bailey-Harris has argued:

> In essence, the judgment clarifies the method by which the extent of each party's benefi-
> cial interest is quantified, once the existence of those interests has been established…In
> effect and for practical purposes, the constructive trust 'overrides' the resulting trust.[102]

This is essentially to support the idea that the constructive trust of common intention has subsumed the resulting trust within it. Practically, therefore, a claimant such as Aida in our example would not notice or even know that the mechanism she was rely-ing on to get a share of the home was a resulting trust. Also, subsequent decisions, both at first instance and in the Court of Appeal, have embraced the view that resulting trusts no longer have a role to play in determining the interests of cohabitants who live together as a family, and instead look simply to constructive trusts as clearly guided by *Kernott*.[103]

(e) Property purchased as an investment

Where property is bought as a family home the constructive trust analysis prevails. However, where property is bought in a domestic relationship as an investment, the correct approach would appear to be to apply the presumption of resulting trust. In *Laskar v Laskar*[104] property was bought by a mother and her daughter primarily as an investment, not as a home in which to live together. According to Lord Neuberger (sitting as a Lord Justice of Appeal in the Court of Appeal), the correct approach to determine the beneficial ownership of the investment asset on the breakdown of the relationship is to apply the presumption of resulting trust:

> It would not be right to apply the reasoning in *Stack v Dowden* to such a case as this, where
> the parties primarily purchased the property as an investment for rental income and capi-
> tal appreciation, even where the relationship is a familial one.[105]

None of the judges in *Jones v Kernott* cast doubt on this. Lady Hale and Lord Walker were content to say that while resulting trusts were not appropriate to the family home '[w]hether they remain appropriate in other contexts is not the issue in this case.'[106]

Further support for the existence of the resulting trust in the investment context was provided by the Court of Appeal in *Geary v Rankine*.[107] Mrs Geary claimed an inter-est in the guest house which had been purchased by Mr Rankine in his sole name and with his own funds as a business venture. The couple had been cohabiting elsewhere, but had taken up residence in the guest house following the departure of an unsuc-cessful manager, and Mrs Geary had helped run the business. Her claim failed. In reaching judgment, Lewison LJ opined that the burden of establishing a constructive trust was 'all the more difficult to discharge where, as here, the property was bought

---

[102] 'Property' [2004] Fam Law 569.

[103] See, for example, *Aspden v Elvy* [2012] EWHC 1387; *Geary v Rankine* [2012] EWCA Civ 555; *Thompson v Hurst* [2012] EWCA Civ 1752.   [104] [2008] EWCA Civ 347.

[105] [2008] EWCA Civ 347, at [17].   [106] [2012] 1 AC 776, at [53].   [107] [2012] EWCA Civ 555.

as an investment rather than as a home' and that the presumption of a resulting trust 'may arise where the partners are business partners as well as domestic partners'.[108]

Favor Easy Management Ltd v Wu[109] also proceeded on the basis that a resulting trust was applicable to property purchased as an investment between cohabitants and that the constructive trust was properly applied where the property was purchased as their home. It was difficult on the facts to decide which approach to adopt, not least because of serious evidential difficulties due to the vehement disagreement between the cohabitants as to the circumstances of the purchase of the property. More significantly, as highlighted by Yip & Lee, the case concerned 'a culturally Chinese type of sexual relationship...the relationship is personal, not familial' which also made applying the appropriate device, constructive or resulting trust, difficult.[110] The argument that follows is that that the dual distinction means that '[t]he courts will have to engage in a difficult exercise of forcing the case into one of two categories of hard cases'.[111] Such situations may be rare, however.

(f) The fate of resulting trusts in the family home

So, where does that leave the resulting trust in relation to the family home? Overtly, the answer is very clear. Barring some intervention by the Supreme Court, the resulting trust is, in practice at least, now of historical interest only in the acquisition of interests. It is only where there is a commercial context to the purchase of the home, as where the property is bought for investment purposes, that the resulting trust still has a spark of life. This is because the property does not attract any special considerations, which have grown up around the family home, and is seen as the general purchase of any other piece of land.

Covertly, it might be argued that the resulting trust lives on in the family home, as one of the factors in identifying a common intention based on conduct, clothed in the language of the constructive trust, though, as we have seen, increasingly this argument might be technically meritorious but is increasingly bereft of practical impact. It simply forms part of the analysis of constructive trusts and ceases to have any independent existence.

There remains good reason to suggest that a resulting trust, free of the shackles of constructive trust language, should continue to exist, not least Lord Neuberger's intelligent, compelling and overlooked dissenting reasoning in *Stack* which permits both the arithmetical calculation and the ability to look to other factors to rebut the arithmetical formula when it is necessary to take a wider range of circumstances into account. Commentators, in the post-*Kernott* world, have not mourned the loss of the resulting trust, which is a perhaps a reflection that the tide has come in and swallowed property concepts such as the resulting trust in the creation of a special kind of discretion applicable only to interests in the family home which is more about discretion and flexibility than it is about hard and immutable rules of property law. This is a point to which we will return towards the end of this chapter, once the development and operation of the other equitable mechanisms has been considered.

5 Common intention constructive trusts

Constructive trusts were considered in Chapter 9. The form of constructive trust that has been employed in the context of the family home, and indeed that has been developed almost exclusively in the context of the family home, is the common intention constructive trust. The trust is so called because Lord Diplock in *Pettitt v Pettitt*[112] said that the approach to be adopted in cases involving the family home should be based upon seeking the common intention of the parties. This form of constructive trust has been seen as more apt for resolving disputes relating to ownership of the family home than resulting trusts. It has the advantage of greater flexibility and the ability to resolve issues about ownership both at the time of acquisition of the family home and later.

(1) The development of the constructive trust in the family home in sole legal owner cases

(a) The traditional use of constructive trusts

Although the House of Lords held in *Gissing v Gissing*[113] that a constructive trust should be imposed whenever it is 'inequitable' for a legal owner to deny the beneficiary an equitable interest in land, the circumstances in which this test would be met were closely defined. Lord Diplock emphasized that a legal owner would only have acted so as to justify the imposition of a constructive trust:

> if by his words or conduct he has induced the [beneficiary] to act to his own detriment in the reasonable belief that by so acting he was acquiring a beneficial interest in the land.[114]

This formulation captures the essential elements of the constructive trust, namely that the court is acting to fulfil the reasonable expectations of the beneficiary, who is entitled to have his expectation fulfilled because he has acted to his detriment in the belief that they would be fulfilled. The legal owner cannot be allowed to enjoy the benefit conferred by the beneficiary's detrimental reliance without also allowing him to enjoy the expected interest.

(b) The criteria developed

The criteria for a common intention constructive trust first set out in *Gissing v Gissing* have been subject to considerable discussion and development. The principles expounded in *Gissing v Gissing* were extremely traditional and represented a strict

---

[112] [1970] AC 777.   [113] [1971] AC 886.   [114] [1971] AC 886, at 905.

property-based approach which was more concerned with the nature of the parties' contributions to the property rather than to the nature of their relationship. Under this approach, contributions to family life which could not be related to ownership of a house, such as child-rearing or the performance of the usual domestic tasks that partners ordinarily have to do around the home, would not be sufficient to gain an interest in the property. Some judges preferred a less rigorous and limiting approach to the determination of constructive trust interests, and Lord Denning in particular was responsible for attempting to introduce a radically different approach by giving the court a wide discretion to determine on the facts of any given case whether a person should be entitled to an interest by way of a constructive trust. On his approach the chief criterion was that of 'justice' and not the type of contribution that had been made. The death of Lord Denning's new model constructive trust has already been explored in the previous chapter.

(c) The classic reformulation: *Lloyds Bank v Rosset*

For many years the classic statement of the criteria, following the death of the 'new model constructive trust' was contained in the speech of Lord Bridge in *Lloyds Bank plc v Rosset*.[115] Lord Bridge, with the agreement of the rest of the House of Lords, rationalized the case law up until that point. He stated that to displace the presumption that beneficial ownership follows legal title (so that a sole legal owner would be enjoy the whole of the beneficial interest in the property), the parties had to demonstrate a common intention for a constructive trust to give effect to these intentions. The House of Lords drew a sharp distinction between two different methods through which this common intention could be demonstrated.

(i) Express common intention: agreement

The first category of circumstances in which a constructive trust could arise is where there was an express common intention between the parties that they were to share the ownership of the land. The establishment of such an express intention is a matter of evidence of what the parties said to each other at the time that the property was purchased and thereafter:

> The first and fundamental question which must always be resolved is whether...there has at any time prior to the acquisition, or exceptionally at any later date, been any agreement, arrangement or understanding reached between them that the property is to be shared beneficially. The finding of an agreement or arrangement to share in this sense can only, I think, be based on evidence of express discussions between the partners, however imperfectly remembered and however imprecise their terms may have been.[116]

(ii) Common intention inferred from conduct

Although Lord Bridge stated the circumstances in which a common intention would have to be inferred, he also made it clear that this would be difficult without a direct contribution to the purchase price:

---

[115] [1991] 1 AC 107.   [116] [1991] 1 AC 107, at 132.

In sharp contrast [to the case where there is an express common intention] is the very different one where there is no evidence to support a finding of an agreement or arrangement to share, however reasonable it might have been for the parties to reach such an arrangement if they had applied their minds to the question, and where the court must rely entirely on the conduct of the parties both as the basis from which to infer a common intention to share the property beneficially and as the conduct relied on to give rise to a constructive trust. In this situation direct contributions to the purchase price by the partner who is not the legal owner, whether initially or by payment of the mortgage instalments, will readily justify the inference necessary to the creation of a constructive trust. But, as I read the authorities, it is at least extremely doubtful whether anything less will do.[117]

(iii) Detrimental reliance

Once a common intention was demonstrated, the claimant would then need to show 'that he or she has acted to his or her detriment or significantly altered his or her position in reliance on the agreement in order to give rise to a constructive trust or a proprietary estoppel'.[118] In situations where a common intention was inferred from a direct contribution to the purchase prices, detriment was not a major issue, as in paying the money the contributor would clearly have acted to his detriment sufficiently to justify a constructive trust.

(iv) Quantification

Once this had been done, the court would then quantify the interest by reference to the express or inferred common intention, which, as we have seen under the treatment of resulting trusts, allowed for a greater share of the property than the value of any financial contributions made to the purchase or upkeep of the property.

(v) Impact of dual approach

This dual approach of express or inferred common intention supported by detrimental reliance, as we shall see, dominated analysis of the rights of cohabitants in the absence of an express declaration of trust and the development of the law for some sixteen years. No distinction was drawn between those situations where a property had been purchased in the sole name of one of the parties, or in joint names.

(2) Purchase in joint names and a new start for common intention constructive trusts

(a) Presumption of joint equitable ownership

However, following *Stack v Dowden*[119] and *Jones v Kernott*,[120] a new approach was proposed for situations where the family home had been purchased in joint names but no express trust had been declared as to the respective shares of beneficial ownership. At its simplest, *Stack v Dowden* establishes that 'a "common intention" trust, for the

---

[117] [1991] 1 AC 107, at 132–133.   [118] [1991] 1 AC 107, at 132–133.
[119] [2007] 2 AC 432.   [120] [2011] UKSC 53.

cohabitants' home to belong to them jointly in equity as well as on the proprietorship register, is the default option in joint names cases.'[121] This modern presumption (or assumption[122]) is likely in most cases to provide an accurate means of ascertaining the parties' intention at the time of acquisition, as many lay people will think that if they purchase a house jointly, they own it jointly. The initial presumption of joint ownership can, however, be displaced by evidence of a different common intention as to ownership.

(b) Rebutting the presumption: finding another common intention

Whilst the initial presumption is very strong, and not to be displaced lightly, there is no limit on the kind of evidence that can be adduced to show that the parties did have a different intention, though there are some guidelines or factors to help shape the enquiry, as set out by Lady Hale in *Stack*. Where it is argued that the presumption should be displaced, 'the task...is to ascertain the parties' common intentions as to what their shares in the property would be, in the light of their whole course of conduct in relation to it.[123]

The requirement of evidence of an express agreement or understanding, or of a direct financial contribution, as set out in *Lloyds Bank v Rosset*[124] seems to have been abandoned here. A separation of the parties' financial affairs may be a pointer, but is neither necessary nor sufficient.

(c) An ambulatory constructive trust

It is clear that, in inferring or imputing the parties intentions, the enquiry is not limited to their intentions at the date of the purchase of the property, but at any subsequent date, therefore creating 'an "ambulatory trust" in which the beneficial interests vary, depending upon the circumstances at the relevant time'.[125]

(d) Quantifying the common intention: inferring and imputing

Once any initial presumption of equality has been displaced, the courts will look at the whole of the circumstances to decide what the parties intended. Where there is evidence of the parties' intentions, 'deduced objectively from their words and their actions', it is not the role of the court to substitute a decision which it considers to be fair.[126] The court is therefore inferring an agreement. However, imputation is permitted 'where it is clear that the beneficial interests are to be shared, but it is impossible to divine a common intention as to the proportions in which they are to be shared'.[127] In these situations, the court may have no alternative but to ask what the parties' intentions as reasonable and just people would have been had they thought about it at the time.[128]

---

[121] *Jones v Kernott*, at [15], per Lord Walker and Lady Hale.   [122] *Jones v Kernott*, at [17].
[123] Lord Walker and Lady Hale, at [13].   [124] [1991] 1 AC 107.
[125] [1991] 1 AC 107, at [14] and [47].   [126] [1991] 1 AC 107, at [46].
[127] [2011] UKSC 53, at [31].   [128] [2011] UKSC 53, at [47].

(e) Basis of quantification

Where the court is obliged to impute an intention, it cannot do so by reference to the parties' actual intentions. So how, instead, should the shares be determined? In *Stack v Dowden,* Lady Hale had expressed agreement with the approach adopted in *Oxley v Hiscock*.[129] There, Chadwick LJ had said that where the evidence did not permit the court to identify the parties' actual intentions, they were entitled to that share which the court considers fair having regard to the whole course of dealing between them in relation to the property.' The Supreme Court in *Jones v Kernott*[130] adopted the same approach. This resolves some of the uncertainty that was left by *Stack v Dowden* since in that case, despite Baroness Hale's approval of Chadwick LJ's approach, some of her remarks suggested that she did not agree that this meant that the search was for 'fair shares'.

(f) Detriment?

There is no mention of reliance or detriment as a requirement in either *Stack v Dowden*[131] or *Jones v Kernott*.[132] This may suggest that proof of detrimental reliance is no longer necessary, although it will be present in the overwhelming majority of cases, and indeed could easily have been found in both *Stack* and *Kernott*.

(g) A special form of constructive trust for family homes

This approach strongly suggests that there is a special regime that applies to property acquired or used as a family home, as was suggested in the introduction to this chapter. What does this new analysis mean for those cases where there is no joint ownership of the legal title?

(3) Application of the new approach to sole legal ownership cases

(a) Questions left unanswered

In the wake of *Stack*, and before *Kernott* was decided, questions were being asked in the courts as to whether the traditional constructive trust analysis in sole name cases could survive. This concern was ably demonstrated when the Privy Council (constituted by many of the members who had decided *Stack*) addressed the issue in *Abbott v Abbott*.[133] Here the husband's mother transferred the plot of land on which the matrimonial home was later built to the husband, who held title as sole legal owner. The construction costs were paid by the husband and wife taking out a bridging loan and then a mortgage, and the husband's mother also contributed. Following acquisition, the wife made herself jointly and severally liable for the repayment of principal and interest on the mortgage. The couple had a joint bank account and all payments were made from it. The wife did not work for a period of nearly nine years. The parties ultimately divorced, and the question before the court was to consider the extent of the

---

[129] [2005] Fam 211.   [130] [2011] UKSC 53.

[131] Except in Lord Neuberger's dissenting opinion at [124].   [132] [2011] UKSC 53.

[133] [2008] Fam Law 215 (PC).

wife's beneficial interest. In deciding that the parties shared the beneficial ownership equally, the Privy Council disapproved *Rosset* and said that the parties' whole course of conduct in relation to the property had to be taken into account in determining their shared intentions as to its ownership, as with *Stack v Dowden*. Equal division was the correct inference (without more) from the fact that gift by the husband's mother was intended for both of them, and that was backed up by the conduct of the couple throughout their marriage, as they arranged their finances jointly and undertook joint liability on the mortgage.

(b) **The technical, legal context**

Stack v Dowden and *Jones v Kernott* were both cases of joint acquisition, not situations where a property has been acquired in the sole name of one party, or was already owned by one party before the relationship began. The parties in both cases were joint legal owners of the property, and the fact that they had some entitlement to a beneficial interest in the family home was not contested. Instead, the issue was one of quantification as to the extent of their entitlements. Hence, it would be expected that anything related to quantification would have some impact on the approach in sole legal owner cases. Indeed, in some cases, whilst it will be clear that the parties intended to share beneficial ownership, it will not be possible to objectively ascertain the parties' actual intentions as to their respective shares, so an imputation might be needed. Beyond this, any comments made in relation to acquisition principles are strictly obiter. *Abbott* was of persuasive authority only, as a Privy Council decision. Moreover, at no time in either judgment, as with resulting trusts, were any of the key decisions like *Rosset* or *Gissing* overruled, so following a strict view of precedent, those cases should continue to provide the answer to whether a cohabitant is entitled to a beneficial interest in the family home in the absence of an express trust and they are not joint legal owners.

(c) **The practical realities**

Whatever the legal technicalities, it would be illogical for some of the principles set out in the two cases not to apply to sole legal owner case. The approach that the parties' intentions can change after the initial purchase of the family home, for example, marks a major departure from previous constructive trust analysis, which appears to have assumed a consistent and continuing common intention. The starting point is inevitably different, as there is no joint ownership at law. Indeed, if there is a presumption, it is that equity follows the law, so that the legal owner is entitled to the whole of the beneficial interest. Is the approach in *Lloyds Bank v Rosset*[134] still relevant to determine the question? Is it only once an intention to share ownership has been found that it is possible to apply the wider principles about inferring or imputing intention set out in *Stack v Dowden* and *Jones v Kernott*? Or does the court simply infer or even impute a common intention in these circumstances, on the basis that the home is shared?

---

[134] [1991] 1 AC 107.

(d) A continuing role for *Rosset*

Baroness Hale indicated in *Stack v Dowden,* in cases of sole ownership 'the claimant had first to surmount the hurdle of showing that she had any beneficial interest at all, before showing exactly what that interest was'.[135] Neither Lord Walker nor Lady Hale sought to overturn *Lloyds Bank v Rosset,* and instead recognized that such cases have a different 'starting point...because the claimant...has the burden of establishing some sort of implied trust'.[136] Further, in their concluding comments they noted that there is no presumption of joint ownership in sole legal owner cases, and the principles applicable to determining the size of the beneficial interest for joint legal owners only apply where 'the evidence shows a common intention to share beneficial ownership but does not show what shares were intended'.[137]

Read together, these statements suggest that the impact of the Supreme Court decision to sole legal owner cases is simply to clarify the principles applicable to the quantification of property interests post-*Stack v Dowden* once the claimant has established an interest to the home. It does not appear to alter those principles upon which the property entitlement is acquired. The two-stage approach set out in *Lloyds Bank v Rosset* still applies. Crossing the hurdle of establishing some beneficial interest therefore still requires either proof of an express agreement or understanding, or proof of a direct financial contribution.

(e) *Rosset* or *Kernott*? The debate continues

Cases of the lower and higher courts have demonstrated that there is still some disquiet in the courts about how to apply *Rosset* principles in the wake of the change of approach to family homes in both *Stack* and *Kernott.* Despite what appears to have been clear evidence that the *Rosset* test survived the evolution of principles for the cohabitant to acquire an interest in the sole legal owner cases, it is apparent that there is some support to allow for an inferred common intention as to the acquisition of an interest, not just the quantification.

(i) Inconsistency in applying the two stage approach

In *Aspden v Elvy,*[138] although the judge adopted a two-stage approach, it is less clear that he applied different criteria at each stage. The facts were both complex and unusual, but the essence of the case was that Mr Aspden made a substantial contribution in money and personal work to the conversion into a dwelling of a barn owned by Ms Elvy.[139] Judge Behrens considered 'that the proper inference from the whole course of dealing is that there was a common intention that Mr Aspden should have some interest in Outlaithe Barn as a result of the very substantial contributions made to

---

[135] [2007] 2 AC 432, at [61].   [136] [2011] UKSC 53, at [17].   [137] [2011] UKSC 53, at [52].
[138] [2012] EWHC 1387.
[139] The barn had previously been owned by Mr Aspden but the judge, resolving a conflict in the evidence, considered that the transfer to Ms Elvy was intended to be an outright transfer of his legal and beneficial interest in it.

the conversion works.'[140] It is to be noted that this was not a contribution to the initial acquisition, but a subsequent contribution, albeit significant.

(ii) The Rosset orthodoxy confirmed

A number of cases have confirmed the *Rosset* approach to acquisition, and that quantification issues are now being addressed on the basis of what is fair in the light of the whole course of dealing between the parties. In *Re Ali*,[141] which concerned property disputes arising out of a money laundering case, Dobbs J followed the reasoning in *Kernott* that 'there were two questions to be asked—namely whether it was intended that the other party have any beneficial interest in the property at all and, if he does, the second issue is what that interest is.'[142] Dobbs J held that 'in order to show a beneficial interest in a property, a claimant must demonstrate either a financial contribution to its purchase (demonstrating an interest under a resulting trust)', or 'evidence of an actual agreement, arrangement or understanding'[143] with reliance to the claimant's detriment.[144] There was no question that the creation of the beneficial interest could be inferred simply by looking at the whole course of dealings between the parties.[145]

In *Thompson v Hurst*[146] the Court of Appeal applied the same principles where property had been purchased in a sole name, on the basis that as one party was unemployed, the couple were advised that it might impact on securing mortgage finance if he appeared on the legal title. Etherton LJ said that the claimant in a sole name case must establish that it was intended that he or she have an interest in the property, which 'can only be achieved by evidence of the parties' actual intentions, express or inferred, objectively ascertained.'[147] It is not, at this stage, permissible for the court to impute to the parties an intention that they did not have nor to impose a solution upon them which it considers fair. It is only where 'such evidence does show a common intention to share beneficial ownership, but does not show what shares were intended, then each of them is to have that share which the court considers fair, having regard to the whole of dealing in relation to the property.'[148]

(iii) Concerns with inferred common intention

The orthodox *Rosset* analysis is that, while it is possible to infer a common intention from the conduct of the parties in the absence of an express agreement, the House of Lords suggested this could only happen where there was a direct contribution to the purchase price, or an equivalent payment. A major criticism of the law is that this approach undervalues non-financial contributions to cohabitation. In *Stack v Dowden*,[149] Lord Walker opined that the law should take a wide view of what is capable of counting as a contribution towards the acquisition of a residence, while remaining skeptical about the value of alleged improvements that are really insignificant, or

---

[140] [2012] EWHC 1387, at [125].　　　[141] [2012] EWHC 2302 (Admin)
[142] [2012] EWHC 2302 (Admin), at [104].　　　[143] [2012] EWHC 2302 (Admin).
[144] [2012] EWHC 2302 (Admin), at [108].　　　[145] [2012] EWHC 2302 (Admin), at [148] and [154].
[146] [2012] EWCA Civ 1752.　　　[147] [2012] EWCA Civ 1752, at [22].
[148] [2012] EWCA Civ 1752.　　　[149] [2007] 2 AC 432.

elaborate arguments (suggestive of creative accounting) as to how the family finances were arranged.[150] He added:

> Whether or not Lord Bridge's observation was justified in 1990, in my opinion the law has moved on, and your Lordships should move it a little more in the same direction, while bearing in mind that the Law Commission may soon come forward with proposals which, if enacted by Parliament, may recast the law in this area.[151]

Perhaps, unsurprisingly, it is this element of the *Rosset* test that some courts have found difficult to apply in the light of *Kernott*, and it has led to a search for a wider frame of inference of common intention.

(iv) A role for wider inference?

In *CPS v Piper*,[152] which was decided only a month after *Kernott*, the parties' home was vested in Mr Piper as sole legal owner, although Mrs Piper had contributed to its acquisition. The question was whether Mrs Piper had a beneficial interest so as to limit the effect of a confiscation order against her husband. Holman LJ first asked whether there was any common intention that Mrs Piper should have any beneficial interest at all. This could be inferred from their conduct, in particular from the wife's financial contribution. Then, Holman LJ addressed the question of quantifying Mrs Piper's share, which followed the principles enunciated in *Kernott*, that if a common intention as to the size of the share could be deduced 'by direct evidence or by "inference" then that should be given effect by the court.'[153]

The issue here relates to the inference of the common intention to create the interest. Rather than treat the direct contribution as the only evidence capable of demonstrating an inferred common intention, Holman LJ had considered it only as part of the evidence from which he could infer an express common intention. Although their respective interests in the property had rarely been discussed, everything about their interaction, together with contemporaneous documentation from 1996 and 1997, led to the conclusion that the wife had an interest which amounted to co-ownership even though neither party had consciously formed such an intention.[154] This was very much wider than was permitted in *Rosset*. There was also no major discussion of detriment, but, of course, it would have been present because of the direct contribution to the purchase price. Dixon argues that this approach, that a common intention can be deduced objectively from the parties conduct, means that 'we can still argue, but it is difficult to see a return to the *Rosset* approach now that the genie is out of the bottle.'[155]

The Court of Appeal in *Geary v Rankine*,[156] a case involving a supposed change of common intention after purchase in the sole name of the owner of a guesthouse,

---

[150] [2007] 2 AC 432, at [34].   [151] 285 [2007] 2 AC 432, at [26].   [152] [2011] EWHC 3570 (Admin).
[153] [2011] EWHL 3570 (Admin), at [12].   [154] [2011] EWHL 3570 (Admin), at [77]–[79].
[155] Dixon [2012] Conv 1 (Editorial) 1; at 2.   [156] [2012] EWCA Civ 555.

Lewison LJ set out the principles which applied to sole ownership cases following *Stack v Dowden* and *Jones v Kernott*:

> Whether the beneficial interests are to be shared at all is still a question of a party's actual shared intentions. An imputed intention only arises where the court is satisfied that the parties' actual common intention, express or inferred, was that the beneficial interest would be shared, but cannot make a finding about the proportions in which they were to be shared. [157]

So far, so orthodox. However, on the facts there had been no payment towards the purchase of the guesthouse and Mrs Geary was unsuccessful in showing a common intention to share the property. The enquiry did not stop there. Instead, Lewison LJ considered whether any of her conduct since purchase was sufficient for him to infer a change of common intention as to the beneficial ownership, as 'the common intention is to be deduced objectively from [the claimant's] conduct'.[158] Hence, as Lees convincingly argues:

> The effect of *Stack* and *Kernott* then, at least insofar as sole name cases are concerned, is that the second branch of common intention constructive trusts in *Rosset*, that of inference, is expanded... The quest (with respect to acquisition) remains the same. It is simply that a broader range of tools (factors) are utilised. *Rosset* did not require overruling on either the question of acquisition or the factors to be taken into account in inferring that common intention.[159]

However, again, the claim was unsuccessful, so it is difficult to know how detrimental reliance would be supplied if evidence had been found.

(v) Conclusions

So, where does that leave the law? It appears now to be relatively clear that in the absence of a declaration of trust there is a two stage process in all cases involving disputed claims about the beneficial ownership of the family home. The first stage is to ascertain whether the claimant has any kind of beneficial interest. That can be presumed where the purchase is in joint names, but needs to be established by evidence in other cases. That evidence may be of an express agreement, understanding or arrangement, or inferred from the conduct of the parties. Once the first stage has been satisfied, the cases all now point to the respective shares being settled by reference to any express agreement or to what the court considers fair in the light of all the parties' dealings in relation to the property and, almost certainly, looking at factors considered by the courts, to their lives more generally. The approach in *Rosset* has not been swept away, but modified.

It is the extent of this modification to the operation that is still unclear. Those who are proponents of the more rights based approach evident in *Kernott* will favour an

---

[157] [2012] EWCA Civ 555, at [19].

[158] [2012] EWCA Civ 555, at [20]. See also *Ullah v Ullah* [2013] EWHC 2296 (Ch) where a similar approach was adopted.

[159] Lees '*Geary v Rankine*: Money isn't Everything' [2012] Conv 412, at 417.

inference (though not imputation) of a common intention from any conduct, without the need for a direct payment. If it was permissible to infer a common intention as to ownership based on both parties' entire relationship with the other, this would represent a significant move towards entitlement to a property right in the family, rather than a need to establish one, and a move to a family based entitlement's analysis, rather than a property one. With respect to these arguments, they are not supported legally, as the issue of detrimental reliance, and how it could be proved in such cases, has yet to be addressed. There is no indication that detrimental reliance is no longer a consideration, though it has not been addressed directly in most of the cases since *Kernott*.[160] Hence, there still, for the moment, remains a distinction between sole and joint legal owner cases in the approach applicable. Practice, may, however, have already moved on and it is doubted that the lack of detrimental reliance will stop the courts successfully finding an inferred common intention to acquire an interest, but, as has been said, we are not quite there yet.

(4) The 'conventional' constructive trust: sole legal owner

Having recognized that the *Rosset*-style constructive trust still has a life of its own, it is necessary to consider in a little more detail what is needed for the finding of an express and inferred common intention, and to consider the quantification principles more clearly (see Figure 10.3).

(a) Acquisition: The need for a common intention

(i) Establishing a common intention

Establishing the presence of a common intention is often the greatest hurdle to establishing a constructive trust.[161] In *Lloyds Bank plc v Rosset*[162] Lord Bridge recognized that one barrier to the establishment of a common intention is that 'spouses living in amity will not normally think it necessary to formulate or define their respective interests in the property in any precise way'.[163] Although the expectation of the parties to a happy marriage is generally that they will share the practical benefits of occupying the matrimonial home, whoever owns it, he maintained that this is not identical to a common intention to sharing the ownership of the property. A true common intention to share ownership sufficient to found a constructive trust may be established either from the expressed sentiments of the parties or by inference from their conduct.

(b) The framework to establish a common intention

In *Lloyds Bank plc v Rosset*,[164] the House of Lords provided a framework for determining when such trusts will arise, as we have seen. The facts of the case concerned a

---

[160] An exception is *Aspden v Elvy* [2012] EWHC 1387, at [129] where Judge Behrens said 'The valuation of the equity requires me to do justice having regard to the proportionality between the expectation and the detriment.'   [161] [2012] EWHC 1387, at 647.
[162] [1991] 1 AC 107.   [163] [1991] 1 AC 107, at 127–128.   [164] [1991] 1 AC 107.

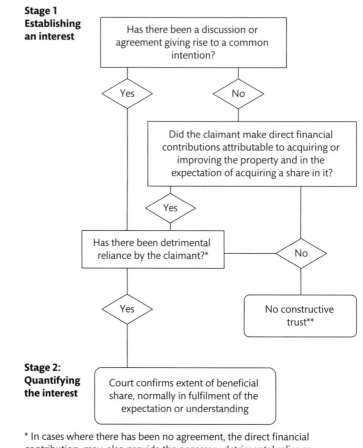

Stage 1 Establishing an interest

Has there been a discussion or agreement giving rise to a common intention?

Yes   No

Did the claimant make direct financial contributions attributable to acquiring or improving the property and in the expectation of acquiring a share in it?

Yes

Has there been detrimental reliance by the claimant?*   No

Yes   No constructive trust**

Stage 2: Quantifying the interest

Court confirms extent of beneficial share, normally in fulfilment of the expectation or understanding

* In cases where there has been no agreement, the direct financial contribution may also provide the necessary detrimental reliance.
**The claimant may have a remedy in proprietary estoppel.

Figure 10.3 Constructive trusts of the family home: sole legal owner cases

married couple, and the central issue was whether the wife had acquired an interest in her matrimonial home by way of a constructive trust that was capable of gaining priority over a legal mortgage of the house that the husband had granted to a bank. Mr and Mrs Rosset were married in 1972. In 1982 Mr Rosset became entitled to a substantial sum of money under a trust fund established by his grandmother in Switzerland. They found a house that required complete renovation. It was purchased for £57,500 in the sole name of Mr Rosset because the Swiss trustee had refused to advance the money for a purchase in joint names. The cost of the renovation work was also provided by Mr Rosset alone, so that his wife made no direct financial contribution to the purchase. Mrs Rosset had, however, helped with the renovation work. She had decorated some bedrooms and prepared others for decoration. She had also supervised the work of builders who were carrying out the renovation work. In the light of this she claimed to be entitled to a share of the ownership by way of a constructive trust.[165] The judge at first instance held that, although there was no express agreement that Mrs Rosset was intended to enjoy a share of the beneficial ownership, he could infer a common intention to share from the fact that she had assisted with the renovations, as this had been work 'upon which she could not reasonably have been expected to embark unless she was to have an interest in the house'. However, the House of Lords held that no such intention could be inferred from the work she had done, and that, in the absence of an express common intention, no constructive trust had arisen in her favour and Mr Rosset remained the absolute owner of the house. In consequence, Mrs Rosset had no proprietary interest that could take priority over the rights of the mortgagee bank.

(c) Finding an express common intention

The first category of circumstance in which a constructive trust may arise is where there was an express common intention between the parties that they were to share the ownership of the land. The establishment of such an express intention is a matter of evidence of what the parties said to each other at the time that the property was purchased and thereafter.[166]

(i) The agreement must be operative

The agreement must, of course, be operative at the relevant date. In *Clarke v Corless*[167] three landowners had made an express agreement to acquire a strip of land that provided an access to their properties. Two of them later acquired parts each in their own right, and the third objected to one of these purchases. Proudman J held that there was no constructive trust because at the time of the purchase the agreement had been abandoned, and also had not been relied upon by the claimants.

(ii) Express agreement to share ownership amounts to a declaration of trust

Where a genuine express agreement to share the ownership of land is found, in substance the legal owner has expressly declared, or agreed to declare, a trust in favour of the claimant. However, such a declaration would be merely oral and therefore ineffective to create an enforceable trust due to the absence of compliance with the formality requirements of s 53(1)(b) of the Law of Property Act 1925.[168] Although there is no enforceable express declaration of trust, a constructive trust will be imposed if the claimant acted to her detriment on the basis of the express agreement, as it would be inequitable to allow the legal owner to deny a trust which would give effect to his intentions.

---

[165] The issue did not arise on a divorce of the parties, where it would have been open to the court to adjust their interests in the property. Instead, Mr Rosset had mortgaged the property without his wife's consent, and she was seeking to establish an overriding interest that would bind the bank and therefore prevent them from enforcing the sale of the house. To establish the overriding interest, Mrs Rosset would have to show that she had an interest in the property, which she claimed to have by way of a constructive trust. See Stevens and Pearce, *Land Law* (5th edn, 2013), Chapter 11.   [166] [1991] 1 AC 107, at 132.

[167] [2009] EWHC 1636 (Ch).   [168] Law of Property Act 1925.

(iii) Examples of 'common intention'

Lord Bridge considered that the earlier cases of *Eves v Eves*[169] and *Grant v Edwards*[170] were 'outstanding examples'[171] of constructive trusts created through an express common intention. In *Eves v Eves*[172] an unmarried couple, Janet and Stuart Eves,[173] moved to a new house. It was purchased solely in the name of Stuart, who told Janet that it was to be their house, and a home for themselves and their children. He also told her that the purchase could not be completed in their joint names because she was under 21, but that if she had been of age it would have been purchased in their joint names. In *Grant v Edwards*[174] a man purchased a house in his name alone to provide a home for himself and his lover. He told her that he had not purchased it in their joint names because that would prejudice her divorce proceedings.

However, in both of these cases the supposed 'common intention' was in reality merely an appearance of common intention. Neither of the male parties genuinely wished their partners to enjoy a share of the ownership of their respective houses. Better examples of a true common intention can be found in the subsequent cases of *Yaxley v Gotts* and *Banner Homes plc v Luff Developments Ltd*. In *Yaxley v Gotts*,[175] a case that was in fact decided on the grounds of proprietary estoppel, the Court of Appeal held that a constructive trust could have been established where a builder had carried out work to convert and refurbish a house into flats on the basis of an oral understanding that he would acquire the ground floor flat. In *Banner Homes plc v Luff Developments Ltd*[176] the Court of Appeal held that a constructive trust arose where two development companies reached an understanding that they would acquire a site as a joint venture, but one went ahead and developed the site alone. These cases also demonstrate that the principles of constructive trusts are not confined to domestic situations, but are of general application. A more recent example of what constitutes an agreement can be found in *HSBC Bank plc v Dyche*.[177] Here, when Mr Collelldevall had been made bankrupt, he had (with the consent of his trustee in bankruptcy) transferred his jointly owned family home to his daughter and son-in-law (Mr and Mrs Dyche) for much less than its open market value. The Collelldevalls remained in the house, and alleged that an agreement had been reached that the property would be held by the Dyches for them and that it would be transferred back when a loan taken out to finance the transfer had been repaid. Judge Purle QC (sitting as a High Court judge) found an agreement on the evidence which gave rise to a common intention constructive trust. The claimant had agreed to transfer the property upon faith of a clear agreement or understanding that it would thereafter be held for him and his wife (who had since died). That agreement had been acted upon by his transferring the property, at a price that bore no relationship to its true value, to his daughter and

---

[169] [1975] 1 WLR 1338.   [170] [1986] Ch 638.

[171] [1991] 1 AC 107, at 133. See also *Hammond v Mitchell* [1992] 2 All ER 109.

[172] [1975] 1 WLR 1338.

[173] Although they shared the same name, they were unmarried. She had changed her name to his by deed poll.   [174] [1986] Ch 638.

[175] [2000] Ch 162.   [176] [2000] 2 All ER 117.   [177] [2009] EWHC 2954 (Ch).

son-in-law and by making repayments to his son corresponding broadly to the sums falling due under the mortgage. The requisite common intention was to be inferred also from the simple fact that the claimant had continued to have sole beneficial use of the property as his home.

(iv) Agreement on shares is not essential

In *Drake v Whipp*,[178] the Court of Appeal stressed that the principles identified in *Lloyds Bank plc v Rosset* did not require the parties to have reached a common intention 'as to the respective shares to be taken by the beneficial owners'.[179] Peter Gibson LJ stated:

> All that is required for the creation of a constructive trust is that there should be a common intention that the party who is not the legal owner should have a beneficial interest and that that party should act to his or her detriment in reliance thereon.[180]

(v) Agreement is not imputed

As we have seen earlier, while the evidence needed to support a finding of a 'common intention' falls short of that needed to support the finding that there was a legally binding contract,[181] the courts have been clear that they are finding an express agreement that the parties had, not imputing an agreement to them. In *Gissing v Gissing*, Lord Morris stated categorically:

> The courts cannot devise agreements which the parties never made. The court cannot ascribe intentions which the parties in fact never had.[182]

This proposition is illustrated by *James v Thomas*.[183] A couple separated after fifteen years together. Ms James worked unpaid for Mr Thomas, in a business run from home. The profits went into Thomas's bank account and all payments were made from this account. Later, they entered into a partnership, which was dissolved, and then became joint account holders of the bank account. To demonstrate a common intention, Ms James relied on improvements made to the property and the fact that Mr Thomas had said she would be well provided for in the event of his death. The Court of Appeal held that Ms James had no interest under an express common intention constructive trust. In relation to the improvements, they held that the improvements made to the property, using money from the joint account, were not referable to the acquisition of an interest in the property, but were instead about the quality of life of the parties inhabiting the property, and the assurance about provision after death was made on the 'common assumption' that the parties would be living together on the occurrence of that (unfortunate) event.[184] Moreover, clear evidence of Mr Thomas's evasiveness when Ms James asked about transferring title to the property into joint names was

---

178 [1996] 1 FLR 826.   179 [1996] 1 FLR 826, at 830, per Peter Gibson LJ.
180 [1971] AC 886, at 898.   181 *Clarke v Corless* [2009] EWHC 1636 (Ch), at [22].
182 [1996] 1 FLR 826, at 830.   183 [2007] EWCA Civ 1212.
184 Compare this approach to that adopted in *Grant v Edwards* [1986] Ch 638.

adduced as evidence that he did not intend to share the beneficial interest. In the words
of Chadwick LJ:

> Although it is possible to envisage circumstances in which the fact that one party began to
> make contributions to capital repayments due under a mortgage might evidence an agree-
> ment that the party was to have a share in the property, the circumstances of this case are
> not of that nature…That is not to undervalue her contribution; which, as Mr Thomas
> recognised, was substantial. But it is to recognise that what she was doing gives rise to no
> inference that the parties had agreed (or had reached a common understanding) that she
> was to have a share in the property: what she was doing was wholly explicable on other
> grounds.[185]

This approach has drawn criticism from Greer, noting the distinction between this
and cases such as *Eves v Eves*:

> In all of these cases, including *James [v Thomas]*, the clear intention of the male partner
> was to avoid joint ownership of the property, yet in all but this case the claimant suc-
> ceeded. Ms James would have been more successful if Mr Thomas had simply lied to avoid
> putting the property in joint names, rather than evaded the issue, which seems to make
> nonsense of the law.[186]

In Geary v Rankine,[187] Lewison LJ was also clear that the role of the courts was not to
impute an agreement:

> Whether the beneficial interests are to be shared at all is still a question of a party's actual
> shared intentions. An imputed intention only arises where the court is satisfied that the
> parties' actual common intention, express or inferred, was that the beneficial interest
> would be shared, but cannot make a finding about the proportions in which they were to
> be shared.[188]

(vi) Is the evidence for an agreement adequate?

Although the courts have repeatedly indicated that they are not imputing an agreement or common intention to the parties, it is worth noting that one of the major
criticisms of the common intention constructive trust is that, whether intentionally
or otherwise, the court is devising an agreement from scraps of conversation between
the parties and construing their words out of context.[189] Indeed, there is much force in
the contention that if the parties had expressly agreed to share the beneficial interest,
then they would probably also have decided to declare that in a trust or by deciding
to share the legal title. At best, the courts are inferring a common intention from
what the parties have said. The difference between inference and imputation is that
with the former, the court is trying to decide what the parties actually decided, even
if they may not have put their understanding clearly into words. With imputation,

---

[185] [2007] EWCA Civ 1212, at [27].   [186] Greer 'Back to the Bad Old Days' (2008) 158 NLJ 174.
[187] [2012] EWCA Civ 555.   [188] [2012] EWCA Civ 555, at [19].
[189] See, for example, Clarke 'The Family Home: Intention and Agreement' [1992] Fam Law 72.

the court decides what they should be taken to have decided, having regard to all the circumstances.

(vii) Assurance rather than common intention?

Even more compelling, particularly when considering that an excuse to exclude a partner from the legal title was construed as an express common intention to grant an interest in *Grant v Edwards*,[190] is the suggestion that what the court is really looking for is a representation or assurance from the legal owner, or a reasonable expectation on the part of the claimant, even if the other party never meant what they said. That certainly appears to have been the case in *Eves v Eves*[191] and *Grant v Edwards*.[192] More recently, in the Northern Irish case of *Bank of Scotland v Brogan*[193] Deeny J found an express intention or understanding to share ownership of a farmhouse between a husband and wife. His remarks about 'that what was hers was his and his hers' had been repeated a number of times and were accompanied by a range of other circumstances, not least, as Deeny J said 'in the context of [the husband] obtaining cash from her before going out for an evening.'[194] This is really at the crux of the express common intention demonstrated through an agreement, and explains the overlap with proprietary estoppel, where a detrimental reliance on a representation or assurance is part of the test (this is discussed further later in the chapter).

(d) Inferring a common intention from the parties' conduct: the orthodox view

We have already seen that this is where there is considerable disquiet after *Stack v Dowden* and *Jones and Kernott* as to from what conduct a common intention to share the property can be inferred. The traditional approach, as we have seen, is that only financial value in the form of some sort direct or indirect contribution to the purchase prices, which matters, not least on the basis that this will provide the necessary detrimental reliance. Other cases have wished to go wider than financial contributions, though it is not clear how the detriment requirement could be met. Lord Bridge in *Lloyds Bank v Rosset* was clear that more than a change of position was needed, and he was reviewing a large corpus of case law in doing so.

(i) Direct contribution to the purchase price

In *Lloyds Bank plc v Rosset*, the House of Lords significantly concluded that a common intention should only be inferred where a claimant had made direct contributions to the purchase price of the property concerned. A common intention will be inferred in circumstances where a presumption of resulting trust might have arisen. A common intention will be inferred where a person has made a financial contribution to the purchase of the property, has enabled the property to be purchased at a discounted

---

[190] [1986] Ch 638.   [191] [1975] 1 WLR 1338.   [192] [1986] Ch 638.   [193] [2012] NICh 21.
[194] At [31].

price,[195] or had increased the value of the property by undertaking or contributing to the cost of significant improvements.[196]

(ii) Contributions after the date of purchase

A difference between resulting trusts and the common intention constructive trust is that a common intention could be inferred from a contribution referable to the acquisition or improvement of the family home made after the date of its purchase. For instance, a wife who pays for the construction of a house on land, which has been inherited by her husband should, in principle, be able to make a claim on the basis of an intention inferred from conduct. However, relatively insignificant improvements will not be sufficient to give rise to an inference of a common intention. In *Lloyds Bank plc v Rosset* itself, the House of Lords held that Mrs Rosset's assistance with the decoration of the house 'could not possibly justify' the inference of a common intention that she was to gain a share of the ownership thereof:

> Mrs Rosset was extremely anxious that the new matrimonial home should be ready for occupation before Christmas if possible. In these circumstances it would seem the most natural thing in the world for any wife, in the absence of her husband abroad, to spend all the time she could spare and to employ any skills she might have, such as the ability to decorate a room, in doing all she could to accelerate progress of the work quite irrespective of any expectation she might have of enjoying a beneficial interest in the property.[197]

The monetary value of her work, in the light of a total purchase price exceeding £70,000, was also said to have been 'so trifling as to be almost de minimis'.[198] Cases subsequent to *Lloyds Bank plc v Rosset* have also held that the words of Lord Bridge requiring a 'direct financial contribution to the purchase price' should not be interpreted so strictly as to exclude the possibility of an inference of a common intention where a person has contributed to the payment of household expenses and this has enabled the legal owner to pay the mortgage. In *Le Foe v Le Foe*[199] Nicholas Mostyn QC held that the financial contributions of a couple to the acquisition of their home should be viewed as a whole, so that a wife's contributions towards the household expenses could be regarded as an indirect contribution to the purchase price of the property:

> Although I am sure that H earned more than W ... I have no doubt that the family economy depended for its function on W's earnings. It was an arbitrary allocation of responsibility that he paid the mortgage, service charge and outgoings, whereas W paid for day-to-day

---

[195] As was the case in *Oxley v Hiscock* [2005] Fam 111.

[196] Note that s 65 of the Civil Partnerships Act 2004 expressly provides that a civil partner who contributes in money or money's worth to the improvement of property will be entitled to a share, or an increased share, of the beneficial ownership of the property, either on the basis of what may have been agreed between the parties, or in default of such agreement on the basis of what may seem just to the court in all the circumstances.   [197] [1991] 1 AC 107, at 131.

[198] See also *W v G* (1996) 20 Fam LR 49; (1997) 113 LQR 227 (Bailey-Harris)—where the NSW Supreme Court held that a contribution of $500 towards the deposit of a house was de minimis and therefore incapable of establishing an interest by way of a constructive trust. Contrast, however, *Midland Bank plc v Cooke* [1995] 4 All ER 562, where a small contribution to the purchase price of property derived from a joint gift was sufficient to establish a common intention.   [199] [2001] 2 FLR 970.

domestic expenditure. I have clearly concluded that W contributed indirectly to the mortgage repayments, the principal of which furnished part of the consideration of the initial purchased price.[200]

Thus contributions to the purchase price that are, strictly speaking, indirect, may still be capable of leading to the inference of a common intention if they enabled the other party to make a direct contribution. In *Aspden v Elvy* a substantial contribution to the renovation of a property in the expectation of being able to live there and to have a share in it was held by Judge Behrens to be enough to justify implying a common intention,[201] though, as suggested earlier, the case is not an entirely convincing application of the *Rosset* approach as it seems to conflate the acquisition stage with quantification stage.

(iii) Contributions towards mortgage payments

Despite some cases suggesting that direct or indirect contributions towards mortgage payment can be relevant in inferring a common intention, the decision of the Court of Appeal in *Curley v Parkes*[202] has called into question whether contributions to the payment of a mortgage, whether direct or indirect, made subsequent to the acquisition of the property can be regarded as a contribution to the purchase price at all. The case itself concerned a claim to an interest by way of a resulting trust. The Court of Appeal held that contributions made toward the payment of mortgage instalments subsequent to the acquisition of a property are simply sums paid to discharging the mortgagor's obligations under the mortgage, and as such are not a contribution to the purchase price. It is unclear whether the same principle will apply in the context of constructive trusts. There is no theoretical reason why contributions subsequent to the purchase should be ignored, even if not envisaged at the time of purchase, since the theory which underpins a constructive trust is different from that which underpins a resulting trust. A resulting trust adopts the principle that a person is entitled to keep what they have paid for, unless there is some other explanation for their payment. A constructive trust is based on the undertaking by a legal owner, evidenced by the common intention, to confer an interest on the other party. In some cases since *Curley v Parkes* the possibility of a common intention being inferred from contributions to mortgage payments has been entertained without question.[203] However, in *Driver v Yorke*[204] it was held that occasional contributions to the mortgage instalments made by the two sons of the purchaser of a flat would not give rise to an inference of a common intention because the payments did not have sufficient connection with the purchase to be treated as a contribution to the purchase price. If the dicta in *Curley v Parkes* are strictly applied, a claimant who moved in with an owner of a mortgaged property and then contributed to the mortgage instalments—even paying them all—would not be able to establish an inferred common intention to share the ownership from the

---

[200] [2001] 2 FLR 970, at 973.   [201] [2012] EWHC 1387, at [123] to [124].
[202] [2004] EWCA Civ 1515.
[203] *Lightfoot v Lightfoot-Browne* [2005] EWCA Civ 201.   [204] [2003] 2 P & CR 210.

payments alone, and so would only be able to maintain a constructive trust if the payments were made on the basis of an express common intention to share the ownership. Since this is one of the most common scenarios in which cohabitation may occur without the parties giving any express consideration to their respective property rights, such an application would severely reduce the ability of home sharers to establish an interest by way of a constructive trust. The Privy Council in *Abbott v Abbott*[205] were firmly of the belief that assumption of the mortgage responsibilities by the cohabitant was sufficient detriment, though this case itself took the view that the *Rosset* test itself need not be applied, so is perhaps of quite limited persuasive authority.

(iv) Financial contribution alone may not establish common intention

The mere fact that a financial contribution has been made towards the purchase price of property does not in itself guarantee that a common intention will be inferred. No constructive trust will arise if the contribution is made in circumstances that demonstrate that there was no intention on the part of the contributor to obtain an interest in the property. A common intention will not therefore be inferred if the parties have merely done what spouses or partners would ordinarily do. As Lord Diplock observed in *Pettitt v Pettitt*:[206]

> It is common enough nowadays for husbands and wives to decorate and to make improvements in the family home themselves, with no other intention than to indulge in what is now a popular hobby, and to make the home pleasanter for their common use and enjoyment. If the husband likes to occupy his leisure by laying a new lawn in the garden or building a fitted wardrobe in the bedroom while the wife does the shopping, cooks the family dinner or bathes the children, I, for my part, find it quite impossible to impute to them as reasonable husband and wife any common intention that these domestic activities or any of them are to have any effect upon existing proprietary rights in the family home on which they are undertaken.[207]

In *Lloyds Bank plc v Rosset*[208] the decisions of the Court of Appeal in *Eves v Eves* and *Grant v Edwards* were reviewed. In *Eves v Eves*[209] Lord Denning had considered that Janet had done 'a great deal of work to the house and garden...much more than many wives would do',[210] including stripping the hall of wallpaper, painting the woodwork in the lounge and kitchen, painting the kitchen cabinets, painting the brickwork, breaking up concrete in the front garden, and demolishing a shed. In *Grant v Edwards*[211] Linda Grant had made a substantial contribution to housekeeping expenses. However, Lord Bridge concluded that the conduct of neither of the respective claimants had been sufficient to infer a common intention. The constructive trusts in each case were

---

[205] [2008] Fam Law 215 (PC).   [206] [1970] AC 777, at 826.
[207] See also *Burns v Burns* [1984] Ch 317, at 344, where May LJ said: 'The court is only entitled to look at the financial contributions or their real and substantial equivalent to the acquisition of the house; that the husband may spend this weekend redecorating or laying a patio is neither here nor there, nor is the fact that the woman has spent so much of her time looking after the house, doing the cooking and bringing up the family.'   [208] [1991] 1 AC 107.
[209] [1975] 1 WLR 1338.   [210] 1975] 1 WLR 1338, at 1340.   [211] [1986] Ch 638.

only justifiable on the basis of an express common intention. In *Driver v Yorke*[212] it was held that a person who had acted as a guarantor of the mortgage on behalf of the purchaser of a flat had not made any contribution to the purchase price because he had not shown any intention of being liable for the mortgage instalments. Similarly, a contribution to the purchase of property by way of a loan or a gift cannot give rise to an inference of a constructive trust.[213] Nor will a common intention be inferred where a person has made a contribution to the purchase price without the knowledge of the legal owner. In *Lightfoot v Lightfoot-Browne* a claimant who had made a payment of £41,000 towards the mortgage of a property without the knowledge of the sole legal owner was therefore held unable to establish a common intention by inference from the payment.[214]

(v) Payments not referable to acquisition of home

In the orthodox view, payments that do not contribute to the purchase price of property, for example the payment of removal costs or solicitors' fees,[215] will clearly be insufficient to generate an inferred common intention, as they are not regarded as a contribution to the purchase price. Nor will a constructive trust be inferred from conduct that, though costly in time and effort, does not contribute financially at all. Thus a constructive trust will not be inferred in favour of a person who undertakes domestic responsibilities, bears children, provides child-care or looks after sick or elderly relatives. However, such non-financial contributions are not entirely irrelevant, as they can be taken into account in determining the extent of the beneficial interest that will arise under a constructive trust established on the basis of a common intention inferred from a direct financial contribution. Thus, such non-financial conduct will only be irrelevant in a case where a person has acted in the absence of an express common intention and they have not made any financial contribution of any kind, no matter how small, to the purchase price of the property.

(e) Inferring a common intention from the parties' conduct: the wider view

(i) More factors from which to infer intention

The concept is easily stated. It is that, in the absence of an express common intention between the parties, it should be possible to infer a common intention as to acquire an interest in the home in sole legal owner cases, based on both parties' entire relationship with the other, just as it already is possible to infer from the same conduct what their respective shares should be, if they had acquired an interest. This is supported, as we have seen, by the Court of Appeal in *Geary v Rankine*,[216] and by various dicta.[217]

---

[212] [2003] 2 P & CR 210.   [213] See *Re Sharpe (A Bankrupt)* [1980] 1 WLR 219.
[214] [2005] EWCA Civ 201. Note that in the light of *Curley v Parkes* [2004] EWCA Civ 1515 such a contribution to the discharge of the mortgage might not have been considered a contribution to the purchase price in any event.
[215] *Curley v Parkes* [2004] EWCA Civ 515.   [216] [2012] EWCA Civ 555.
[217] In *Stack v Dowden* [2007] 2 AC 432, Lady Hale suggested that Lord Bridge's statements concerning direct purchase money were strictly obiter, but she did not expressly overrule them (at [34]).

(ii) The impact of wider factors

Even if we assume this to be the correct position, despite this apparent lowering of the hurdle, constructive trusts of common intention based on conduct alone will be found only in exceptional circumstances and the court will be slow to infer from conduct alone that the parties intended to vary beneficial interests established at the time of acquisition. In *Morris v Morris*,[218] the Court of Appeal held that in cases such as this the courts should be slow to interpret conduct of spouses or cohabitants as meaning that a beneficial interest of some sort should be acquired. The respondent and his mother were joint owners of a farmhouse that was part of the family farm. The claimant married and moved in with the respondent and contributed without remuneration to the family farming business. She also provided the money to purchase an enclosure and started her own riding school funded partly by a free loan made by the respondent and his mother. The conduct was not exceptional, as required in post-acquisition cases, partly because she had received benefits towards her own business.[219]

(f) Reliance or detriment

We have already seen that the mere fact of a 'common intention' will not alone give rise to a constructive trust. The criteria as set out by Lord Bridge in *Lloyds Bank v Rosset*,[220] following a similar requirement described in *Gissing v Gissing*,[221] is that a constructive trust will only arise in favour of a person who acted to his detriment, or substantially changed his position in reliance on the common intention.

(i) Rationale underpinning the need for detrimental reliance

The constructive trust arises because it would be inequitable to allow the legal owner to refuse to give effect to the intention when the claimant has acted in a personally detrimental manner. It is absolutely essential to grasp that the standard of conduct sufficient to establish detrimental reliance is different from the standard of conduct required to justify an inference of a common intention. While only a direct contribution to the purchase price will justify the inference of a common intention, in orthodox thinking, a much wider range of conduct will constitute sufficient detriment to lead to the imposition of a constructive trust if there was an express common intention.

(ii) Detriment where there is an express common intention

Lord Bridge in *Rosset* summarized what was required in the way of detriment to establish a constructive trust founded upon an express common intention to share the ownership of the property:

> it will only be necessary for the partner asserting a claim to a beneficial interest against the partner entitled to the legal estate to show that he or she has acted to his or her detriment or significantly altered his or her position in reliance on the agreement in order to give rise to a trust…[222]

---

[218] [2008] EWCA Civ 257.   [219] [2008] EWCA Civ 257.   [220] [1991] 1 AC 107.
[221] [1971] AC 886.   [222] [1971] AC 886, at 132.

This clearly adopts a much lower standard than the restrictive threshold of conduct from which it is possible to infer a common intention. The cases clearly support the proposition that conduct other than a direct contribution to the purchase price of the property will suffice to establish a constructive trust if there was an express common intention that the ownership of the land be shared. In *Lloyds Bank plc v Rosset*[223] itself the House of Lords held that there was no express common intention between the husband and wife as to the ownership of the house and therefore the question whether Mrs Rosset's activities would have been sufficient detriment or change of position was not addressed. The leading authority therefore remains *Grant v Edwards*,[224] where it was held that there was an express common intention that Linda Grant was to enjoy a share of the ownership of the house she cohabited with George Edwards. While Edwards paid the mortgage instalments, Grant made a substantial contribution from her own wages to the housekeeping and bringing up the children. The Court of Appeal held that her conduct amounted to sufficient detriment to justify a constructive trust.

(iii) Must the conduct be referable to the expected interest?

A difference of opinion appears in the judgments in *Grant v Edwards* as to whether the conduct alleged to represent reliance or detriment needed to be directly linked to the interest claimed. Nourse LJ addressed the question as to the nature of conduct required and concluded:

> In my judgment it must be conduct on which the woman could not reasonably have been expected to embark unless she was to have an interest in the house.[225]

He held that Grant's contribution to the housekeeping amounted to an indirect contribution to the mortgage instalments, as it enabled Edwards to pay them from his own wages. This was conduct that could not have been reasonably expected unless she was to have an interest in the house. Sir Nicholas Browne-Wilkinson V-C took a more liberal view:

> Once it has been shown that there was a common intention that the claimant should have an interest in the house, any act done by her to her detriment relating to the joint lives of the parties is, in my judgment, sufficient detriment to qualify. The acts do not have to be referable to the house.[226]

He emphasized the practical difficulties attendant on a test that required the court to find that the claimant's conduct could only be explained on the basis that a beneficial interest in the property would be thereby acquired:

> In many cases of the present sort, it is impossible to say whether or not the claimant would have done the acts relied on as a detriment even if she thought she had no interest in the house. Setting up house together, having a baby, making payments to general housekeeping expenses (not strictly necessary to enable the mortgage to be paid) may all be referable

---

[223] [1991] 1 AC 107.   [224] [1986] Ch 638.   [225] [1986] Ch 638 at 648.
[226] [1986] Ch 638, at 657. Compare the similar debate on part performance in *Steadman v Steadman* [1976] AC 536.

to the mutual love and affection of the parties and not specifically referable to the claimant's belief that she has an interest in the house.[227]

Given that Lord Bridge indicated in *Lloyds Bank plc v Rosset*[228] that 'a significant change of position by the claimant' was sufficient detriment to support a constructive trust in fulfilment of an express common intention, it seems that the more liberal approach of Browne-Wilkinson V-C is to be preferred. This also follows from the growing recognition that the detriment required in the case of a constructive trust based on an express common intention is analogous to that required to sustain a claim to a remedy under the principles of proprietary estoppels.[229] This is considered further later in the chapter.

(iv) Detriment where a common intention is inferred

Where there was no express common intention but the criteria are satisfied to entitle the court to infer a common intention, the element of detriment presents much less difficulty in the orthodox view. Given that the court can only infer a common intention from conduct constituting a direct contribution to the purchase price of the property,[230] the contributor will clearly have acted to his detriment sufficiently to justify a constructive trust. Indeed, it is this essential fact which demonstrates how resulting trusts can be clothed in the language and trappings of common intention, as the necessary payment to the purchase price which gives rise to the presumption of resulting trust provides both the intention and necessary detriment to be awarded a constructive trust. The nature of the detriment will, however, be crucial to the determination of the extent of the beneficial interest thereby acquired and it is here that the attractiveness of arguing an inferred common intention rather than resulting trust manifests itself. If a wider range of situations in which a common intention to acquire an interest can be inferred takes hold, there will be the need to demonstrate detrimental reliance separately. It will be interesting to see how, if at all, this differs from change of position in the express agreement cases.

(g) Quantifying the beneficial interest under a common intention constructive trust

(i) When is it necessary for the court to quantify the beneficial interests?

Where the evidence establishes that the parties had reached an express agreement as to the ownership of the property, the constructive trust will operate to fulfil that agreement. In many cases the parties will have expressly agreed to share the property equally, and the claimant will be entitled to one half-share of the equitable interest. However, where there is no express common intention as to the respective shares of the parties in the property, either because they had an express common intention to share

---

[227] [1986] Ch 638, at 657.   [228] [1991] 1 AC 107.
[229] *Lloyds Bank plc v Rosset* [1991] 1 AC 107, at 132. See also *Grant v Edwards* [1986] Ch 638, at 656, where Browne-Wilkinson V-C thought that 'useful guidance may in future be obtained from the principles underlying the law of proprietary estoppel which in my judgment are closely akin to those laid down in *Gissing v Gissing*'.   [230] *Lloyds Bank plc v Rosset* [1991] 1 AC 107, at 133.

the ownership of the property but had not discussed the specific proportions in which the ownership was to be shared,[231] or because the common intention to share has had to be inferred from a contribution to the purchase price, the extent of the equitable interest arising under the constructive trust will have to be determined by the court.

(ii) How should the court quantify the beneficial interests?

The starting point for analysis is the basic principle that constructive trusts arise to fulfil the intentions of the parties, so as Browne-Wilkinson V-C stated in *Grant v Edwards*,[232] 'prima facie the interest of the claimant will be that which the parties intended'.

(iii) Approach has never been based on relative size of contributions

The approach to the quantification of an interest in a constructive trust can be distinguished from the resulting trust. In the case of a presumed resulting trust, the extent of the claimant's beneficial entitlement will be determined solely by the amount of contribution made to the purchase price of the property, whereas in the case of a constructive trust the claimant may gain a share of the equitable interest far in excess of the proportion they have contributed to the purchase price, or of the value of their action which constitutes the necessary detriment.

(iv) Principles to be adopted: the original debate

We have already explored under resulting trusts the alternative methods of quantification suggested in *Midland Bank plc v Cooke*[233] and *Oxley v Hiscock*,[234] to permit the court to take into account all the aspects of the parties' relationship. In *Cooke* the basis was assumed or imputed agreement, in *Oxley*, what the court adjudged to be a fair share in all the circumstances of the case. In *Oxley*, Chadwick LJ stated the principle by which he thought that the court should determine the appropriate beneficial interests of the parties where there is no evidence of what their intentions were:

> It must now be accepted (at least in this Court and below) the answer is that each is entitled to that share which the court considers fair having regard to the whole course of dealing between them in relation to the property. And, in that context, the 'whole course of dealing between them in relation to the property' includes the arrangements which they make from time to time in order to meet the outgoings (for example, mortgage contributions, council tax and utilities, repairs, insurance and housekeeping) which have to be met if they are to live in the property as their home.[235]

There is a divergence between the 'assumed intention' approach adopted by the Court of Appeal in *Midland Bank v Cooke* and the seeming 'judicial discretion' approach adopted in *Oxley v Hiscock*. These decisions have both been subject to academic and judicial criticism, not least that the determination of the beneficial interest arising

---

[231] As in *Cox v Jones* [2004] EWHC 1486 and *Pinfield v Eagles* [2005] EWHC 477.
[232] [1986] Ch 638, at 657.
[233] [1986] Ch 638; O'Hagan 'Quantifying Interests under Resulting Trusts' (1997) 60 MLR 420.
[234] [2005] Fam 211.   [235] [2004] EWCA Civ 546, at [69].

under a constructive trust will ultimately turn on subjective value judgements rather than legal principles. The approach adopted in *Oxley v Hiscock* owes more to the principles of proprietary estoppel than to the principles of constructive trusts, and indeed Chadwick LJ relied primarily on estoppel authorities to conclude that the court should determine what was 'fair' between the parties.[236]

(v) The debate settled: quantification after Stack and Kernott

We have already noted the confusion over which approach to apply to quantification. However, it is clear following *Jones v Kernott*,[237] that the court will strive to infer the size of the shares each party intended to have by objectively considering their words and actions, but will impute fair shares 'where it is clear that the beneficial interests are to be shared, but it is impossible to divine a common intention as to the proportions in which they are to be shared'.[238]

(vi) The current approach stated

In quantifying the parties' interests there is a significant distinction in approach between joint name and sole name cases. In sole names cases, once the claimant has overcome the first hurdle by establishing that he or she has an interest in the property the question is 'what is the extent of the party's beneficial interest?'; there is no presumption of equal distribution.

Within sole name cases, the approach differs slightly, at least in theory, dependent on whether the interest was acquired through an express common intention or an inferred common intention. In the express common intention cases, the court is meant to objectively infer the size of the share from all the circumstances of how the parties lived together, in other words by construing the agreement in the light of all the evidence. It is not, at this stage, permissible for the court to impute to the parties an intention that they did not have nor to impose a solution upon them which the court considers fair. It is only where 'such evidence does show a common intention to share beneficial ownership, but does not show what shares were intended, then each of them is to have that share which the court considers fair, having regard to the whole of dealing in relation to the property.'[239] Where the common intention is inferred, the court will need to impute rather than imply an intention more often than not, as, at least in the orthodox view of inferred intention, there will no objective agreement demonstrated from financial contributions. The distinction may well be illusory in practice, though it is clear the courts will strive to infer rather than impute intentions, where possible.

(vii) Factors to be considered

In *Stack v Dowden*,[240] Baroness Hale said that in determining the size of a beneficial share in the property, the court should have recourse to the following indicative list of factors:

---

[236] In particular he relied on *Yaxley v Gotts* [2000] Ch.162. See [2004] EWCA Civ 546, at [70].
[237] [2011] UKSC 53.   [238] [2011] UKSC 53, at [31].
[239] [2011] UKSC 53.   [240] [2007] 2 AC 432.

any advice or discussions at the time of transfer which cast light on their intentions then; the reasons why the home was acquired in their joint names; the reasons why (if it be the case) the survivor was authorised to give a receipt for the capital moneys; the purpose for which the home was acquired; the nature of the parties' relationship; whether they had children for whom they both had responsibility to provide a home; how the purchase was financed, both initially and subsequently; how the parties arranged their finances, whether separately or together or a bit of both; how they discharged their outgoings on the property and their other household expenses.[241]

These were not intended to be exhaustive, just useful guidelines.

(viii) *Applying the criteria: determining the beneficial share in sole owner cases*

In the absence of many cases dealing with quantification, it is worth considering what happened in the key decisions, before considering the somewhat less satisfactory decision in *Aspden v Elvy*.[242]

(ix) Stack v Dowden

On the facts of *Stack v Dowden* itself, a couple had lived together for twenty-five years, and had four children. The original family house had been purchased by Ms Dowden alone, using £8,000 savings and a mortgage of £22,000. Ms Dowden paid all the mortgage repayments and Mr Stack helped with improvements. On sale, title to the new house was registered in both names. The purchase was funded 65 per cent from Ms Dowden (proceeds of sale and savings) and the remainder from an endowment mortgage loan. Mr Stack paid the interest on the loan. Capital was repaid by lump sums, of which Mr Stack contributed £27,000, and Ms Dowden the remaining £38,000. The parties kept their financial affairs entirely separate throughout their relationship together. On the breakdown of the relationship, Mr Stack sought an order for sale and equal division of any proceeds of sale. Following the decision in *Oxley v Hiscock*, the Court of Appeal had divided the proceeds of sale 65 per cent to Ms Dowden, 35 per cent to Mr Stack as representing a fair share of the course of dealings between the parties, with which the House of Lords agreed.

Baroness Hale concluded that this was an unusual case and that Ms Dowden had successfully rebutted the strong presumption of joint beneficial ownership. The couple kept their affairs 'rigidly separate'[243] and Ms Dowden had contributed much more to the financial acquisition of the property than Mr Stack had done:[244]

> This is not a case in which it can be said that the parties pooled their separate resources, even notionally, for the common good … they undertook separate responsibility for that part of the expenditure which each had agreed to pay.[245]

Mr Stack had not agreed to pay for 'consumables and child minding' so it was not 'possible to deduce some sort of commitment that each would do what they could'.[246]

---

[241] [2007] 2 AC 432, at [69] and [70].   [242] [2012] EWHC 1387.
[243] [2007] 2 AC 432, at [92].   [244] [2007] 2 AC 432, at [89].
[245] [2007] 2 AC 432, at [90]–[91].   [246] [2007] 2 AC 432, at [91].

(x) Cases following Stack

In *Fowler v Barron*,[247] Mr Barron was the 'breadwinner' and paid all property-related expenses, whereas Ms Fowler paid for the 'extras', such as school trips for the children, holidays, and clothing. Arden LJ affirmed that the emphasis of the courts' approach is on finding the parties' shared intentions. On the instant facts, the lack of financial contributions was only one factor, and not necessarily a 'critical factor'[248] in determining the beneficial share, and it was decided that the property should be shared equally. Other factors to which Arden LJ had recourse included that the property was the only real asset of the parties, and the mortgage liability was joint even though it was discharged by one of them.

(xi) Jones v Kernott

In *Jones v Kernott*,[249] Ms Jones and Mr Kernott started living together in 1983, initially living together in a mobile home which Ms Jones had bought in her own name two years earlier. In 1985 the mobile home was sold, and the proceeds of sale were used as a deposit for a house in Thundersley, Essex, which was bought in their joint names. Whilst Ms Jones paid the mortgage (which was in joint names) Mr Kernott met most of the cost of an extension which significantly increased the value of the house. He also made a significant contribution towards the family's household expenses. The couple (who by now had two children) separated in 1993. Mr Kernott made no further contribution towards the house or household expenses (nor very much towards the support of the children). An attempt was made to sell the Thundersley house, and when this proved unsuccessful, the parties cashed in an insurance policy, and Mr Kernott used his share of the proceeds as the down payment of another home of his own in Benfleet. There was no discussion about how the parties' affairs should be resolved until Mr Kernott in 2008 claimed a half share of the Thundersley property.

There had been some difficulty in the lower courts in applying the principles set out in *Stack v Dowden*. The trial judge, and on appeal, the High Court judge, had concluded that Mr Kernott should have only a 10 per cent share of the Thundersley house. Although it might initially have been the parties' intention to share it equally, Mr Kernott had effectively turned his back on it for over fourteen years, during which the majority of the increase in value had occurred, and he had benefited from being able to buy another property of his own. In those circumstances the parties could not have intended the original shares to remain the same. The High Court judge agreed with the trial judge that 'in the absence of any indication by words or conduct as to how they should be altered, the appropriate criterion was what he considered to be fair and just.'[250] The Court of Appeal disagreed, the majority holding that there was nothing to indicate that the parties had substituted an agreement to share otherwise than equally, and such an intention could not be imputed.

---

[247] [2008] EWCA Civ 377.   [248] [2008] EWCA Civ 377, at [41].   [249] [2011] UKSC 53.
[250] Nicholas Strauss QC sitting as a Deputy Judge [2009] EWHC 1713, at [49].

Lord Walker and Lady Hale concluded that it was a reasonable inference from the aborted decision to sell the Thundersley house that the parties had intended their shares to crystallize at that date. 'Insofar as the judge did not in so many words infer that this was their intention, it is clearly the intention which reasonable people would have had had they thought about it at the time.'[251] In short, in cases where no inference is possible, an imputation of intention is permissible. This was the view of the majority of the court. The outcome if the parties' shares had been crystallized in 1993 was so close to the outcome reached by the judge that it would be inappropriate to change it.

(xii) Relevance of money paid

If the court is inferring an intention, there may be a continued role for monetary payments in making a decision, as was the case in *Aspden v Elvy*.[252] Lee argues that since 'judges are asked to produce their quantifications from the ether, it is understandable that they may wish to anchor their analysis in the financial contributions, which "are relevant but there are many other factors which may enable the court to decide what shares were either intended".'[253] The problem is in predicting the outcome of this wider consideration. Except in exceptional cases, it is suggested, it will normally be more than the value of any money advanced by the sole legal owner towards the purchase price, as this is part of a holistic analysis and is consistent with the approach since *Rosset*.

(5) The constructive trust of common intention: joint names

Very little needs to be said here, as the principles are tolerably clear and have already been explained in some detail earlier in the chapter. The purchase in joint names analysis does not really fall within the 'acquisition' and 'quantification' distinction very easily, as there is no acquisition as such, only a change of intention to rebut the presumption of joint ownership that follows the joint legal title in the absence of an express trust.

The view of the Supreme Court in *Jones v Kernott*[254] strongly suggests that there is a special regime that applies to property acquired or used as a family home. In the absence of legislation governing the property rights of cohabitants the courts have been obliged to develop their own rules, and they have done so through the development of the common intention constructive trust. The rules relating to these trusts may not be transferrable to situations outside that of disputes relating to ownership of the family home.

A number of propositions can be put forward with a degree of assurance:[255]

(1) Where a family home is acquired in joint names, there is a presumption, in the absence of any express declaration of trust, that the beneficial interests are also held in joint tenancy.

---

[251] [2011] UKSC 53, at [48].   [252] [2012] EWHC 1387.   [253] Lee [2012] 5 Conv 421, at 427.
[254] [2011] UKSC 53.   [255] Lord Walker and Lady Hale; Lord Collins, at [60]; Lord Kerr, at [68].

(2) This presumption is not normally displaced by unequal contributions to the purchase price.

(3) It should generally be rare for the presumption of a joint tenancy to be displaced, and very unusual facts will be needed to establish this.

(4) Where it is argued that the presumption should be displaced, 'the task...is to ascertain the parties' common intentions as to what their shares in the property would be, in the light of their whole course of conduct in relation to it'.[256]

(5) Where there is evidence of the parties' intentions, 'deduced objectively from their words and their actions', it is not the role of the court to substitute a decision which it considers to be fair.[257]

(6) If the court cannot deduce exactly what shares were intended, it may have no alternative but to ask what the parties' intentions as reasonable and just people would have been had they thought about it at the time.[258]

(7) The parties' intentions may change from time to time, creating an 'ambulatory trust' in which the beneficial interests vary, depending upon the circumstances at the relevant time.[259]

We have already seen, under traditional constructive trusts, the factors that may demonstrate a change of intention in the key cases, and how the courts quantify the beneficial share, and the principles applicable where they infer or impute it.

(6) Presumed constructive trust of common intention: a common approach?

Only one question remains unaddressed—should inference and imputation not be a common approach across all types of constructive trust in the family home, not just in the joint purchase cases? Or, to put it another way, is there still any need for the two-stage approach in *Rosset* and can we not move instead to an objective inference? The debate, which would range across a variety of property law and family law views, is too large to capture in anything but the vaguest outline here, but some commentators have a very strongly held view that the current property-based approach to identifying the interests of cohabitants in the family home has a discriminatory effect, since it is said to be more common for the sole legal owner to be the male partner in a heterosexual relationship than the female partner. To redress this discrimination they would support a presumption in favour of shared ownership in all cases involving the home in which a cohabiting couple live. Mark Tattershall, for example, said:

> If an intention can be imputed in a joint names case, is there any reason in logic or in principle why it cannot be imputed in a sole name case?[260]

---

[256] Lord Walker and Lady Hale, at [13]. [257] Lord Walker and Lady Hale, at [46].
[258] Lord Walker and Lady Hale, at [47]. [259] Lord Walker and Lady Hale, at [14] and [47].
[260] '*Stack v Dowden*: Imputing an Intention' [2008] Fam Law 249, at 250.

But what imputed intention should this be? One argument is that since relationships are, by definition, about sharing lives, both parties are likely also to have intended to share their property, whoever happens to be the legal owner. The converse argument is that the choice of sole legal ownership is indicative of an intention to keep the assets separate. It is the latter view that Lady Hale espoused in *Stack* and that has been adopted by Lady Hale, Lord Walker and the rest of the Supreme Court in *Kernott*. There is clear support for the extension of this approach, but, as said earlier, we are not there yet.

Figure 10.4 attempts to show what a unified approach would look like in terms of the traditional, two-stage analysis. It will be seen that again the question of detrimental reliance looms large over the debate. The relevance of detriment, it is suggested, is what delineates rights as against entitlements. If someone without an express beneficial or legal interest seeks to have an interest in what is otherwise someone else's sole property, in terms of property law at least, then they need to show something more than an intention, actual or inferred, to do so. If someone is to be entitled to property simply by the fact that they share the property as the family home, then detriment is not relevant, except in helping to work out objectively what the parties agreed between themselves as to ownership or to guide the courts in imputing a fair solution on dissolution of the relationship. The latter would be a very significant change in the law indeed, alongside what has already been a significant straining, even in a 'strictly *Rossetian*' terms, of the constructive trust context. The right we now have, and whether we can still describe it as a constructive trust, is now worth considering.

(7) **Criticism of the 'common intention' constructive trust**

(a) **Is finding a common intention an artificial exercise?**

Although the common intention approach to constructive trusts was firmly entrenched by *Lloyds Bank plc v Rosset*,[261] it has been subjected to extensive criticism.[262] The major objection is that the whole process of finding, and then enforcing, the 'common intention' of the parties, is highly artificial. Thus, whereas Lord Bridge described *Eves v Eves*[263] and *Grant v Edwards*[264] as 'outstanding' examples of express common intention, the facts would suggest that there was no real agreement between the parties to share the ownership of the property concerned. In both cases the men concerned had no real intention that their partners should enjoy an interest in the property. Stuart Eves refused to put Janet on the title of the house, using the excuse that she was under 21. Grant would not put Edwards on the title because he said that it would prejudice her forthcoming matrimonial proceedings. Both of these excuses covered the real intention of the men that their partners were not to receive any proprietary interest in the house. They were to remain the owners and to enjoy the power and control that are

---

[261] [1991] 1 AC 107.
[262] Gardner 'Rethinking Family Property' (1993) 109 LQR 263; Riniker 'The Fiction of Common Intention and Detriment' [1998] Conv 202.   [263] [1975] 1 WLR 1338.
[264] [1986] Ch 638.

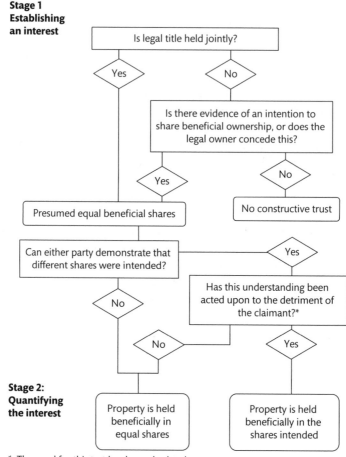

Stage 1
Establishing
an interest

Is legal title held jointly?

Yes / No

Is there evidence of an intention to share beneficial ownership, or does the legal owner concede this?

Yes / No

Presumed equal beneficial shares

No constructive trust

Can either party demonstrate that different shares were intended?

Yes

Has this understanding been acted upon to the detriment of the claimant?*

No

No / Yes

Stage 2:
Quantifying
the interest

Property is held beneficially in equal shares

Property is held beneficially in the shares intended

* The need for this test has been doubted.

Figure 10.4 Constructive trusts of the family home: presumed common intention

necessarily commensurate with such ownership. If the relationship broke down, they wanted to be able to remove their erstwhile partner and not to be encumbered by their presence in the house. To describe the parties in these cases as enjoying a 'common intention' to share the ownership is nothing short of a fiction. The inference of common intention is similarly fraught with the danger that the court is merely inventing a justification for imposing a constructive trust.

Where there is no express common intention the process of inferring or imputing an intention is even less authentic. The court is at best engaged in a process of creative assessment of the parties' desires and it is simply false to suggest that the court is in any way responding to what they would have wanted, or thought they would have wanted. This is even less so where the court identifies what is fair having regard to the circumstances. In many of the cases the dispute has only reached court because one of the parties is behaving unfairly, and may have been doing so throughout the relationship.

(b) Are we still really talking about a recognizable concept of constructive trust?

It is increasingly difficult to resist the conclusion that developments in relation to the common intention constructive trust have moved beyond even equity's wide conception of a constructive trust as a concept. That is, of course, not the only arena in which common intention constructive trusts operate: we have seen the operation of constructive trusts in Chapter 9, and will see them applied to allow trust property to be identified in the hands of people who receive or assist in a trustee's breach of trust in Chapter 29. In none of these areas does the constructive trust work as flexibly as the constructive trust of common intention.

(c) Away from property law?

The rights in favour of cohabitants generated by the common intention constructive trust appear in many cases to have more affinity to the rights of spouses when a financial adjustment order is made on divorce than to conventional property rights. A cynic might even see recent developments as a revival of Lord Denning's once discredited new model constructive trust. Perhaps, rather than considering questions such as 'do we need detrimental reliance?' the time has come to stop trying to subject the trust of the family home to any form of property-law analysis:

> To put it another way, one reason why *Stack* and *Kernott* raise so many property law questions, and fail to answer them, could be that the cases are not really about property law at all. Not any more. If we look for an explanation of the role and impact of these cases within the jurisprudence of property law, we will not find it.[265]

6 Proprietary estoppel

Attention now turns to the final equitable device used to give a cohabitant rights in the family home, proprietary estoppel.[266]

(1) The nature of proprietary estoppel

(a) What is it?

Proprietary estoppel is an entirely different equitable device from either the constructive or resulting trust, because it does not operate by recognizing the existence of a beneficial interest already created by the parties themselves. Instead, it provides an equitable remedy, even though the remedy may allow a party to acquire an interest in the property. It provides a means by which a person may become entitled to a proprietary right despite the absence of appropriate formalities.[267]

---

[265] Dixon [2012] Conv 1 (Editorial) 2; at 3.
[266] Stevens and Pearce, *Land Law* (5th edn, 2013), Chapter 20.   [267] (1984) 100 LQR 376, at 381.

(b) Overlap with constructive trusts

There is a substantial overlap between constructive trusts and proprietary estoppel. This means that the same facts might give rise either to the recognition of a constructive trust, or to the award of an estoppel remedy. The overlap has in the past led the judiciary to enquire whether there is any substantive difference between the two.[268] Nevertheless, it is not unusual for a claimant to have two alternative bases of claim on the same facts.[269]

(c) Distinguishing constructive trusts and proprietary estoppel

Even if there may be circumstances in which both mechanisms operate, Lord Hope in *Stack v Dowden* correctly identified that the two doctrines are different in both approach and outcome:

> Proprietary estoppel typically consists of asserting an equitable claim against the conscience of the 'true' owner. The claim is a 'mere equity'. It is to be satisfied by the minimum award necessary to do justice…which may sometimes lead to no more than a monetary award. A 'common intention' constructive trust, by contrast, is identifying the true beneficial owner or owners, and the size of their beneficial interests.[270]

In some cases, as we shall see, the court has felt that it is appropriate to award the claimant the full fee simple ownership of the land concerned. In other cases a lesser interest, such as a right to occupy, has been granted. The court has also awarded merely monetary compensation. Since *Jones v Kernott*, this is less a point of distinction between the two doctrines, at least in cases where the court must assess what share is just, although the only available remedy with a constructive trust is a finding of a share of beneficial ownership. Thirdly, whereas a constructive trust arises at the moment when the common intention is acted upon, which means that it may bind third parties acquiring interests in the land after that time but before the court has recognized the entitlement, any interest by way of proprietary estoppel may only arise after it has been awarded by the court.

(2) Acquiring an interest: establishing the equity

(a) The essence of proprietary estoppel

The essence of proprietary estoppel is that if the legal owner of property has so conducted himself (whether by encouragement or representations) that the claimant believes that he has, or will obtain, some rights in respect of the land, and he has acted to his detriment on the basis of his induced belief, it would be unconscionable for the legal owner to assert his strict legal entitlement to the property, and equity will therefore intervene to prevent this.[271] The remedy granted in satisfaction of the

---

[268] See, for example the obiter statements of Chadwick LJ in *Oxley v Hiscock* [2005] Fam 211, at [66]: 'it may be more satisfactory to accept that there is no difference, in cases of this nature, between constructive trust and proprietary estoppel.'

[269] For instance, a person injured by a defective product may have both a claim for breach of contract and a claim for negligence.

[270] [2007] 2 AC 432, at 448 [37].

[271] See Snell, *Principles of Equity* (29th edn, 1990), pp 573–574.

estoppel equity is therefore awarded because the claimant has experienced a 'frustrated expectation'.[272]

(b) When will conduct be 'unconscionable'?

Although the principle of proprietary estoppel has a long historical pedigree, dating from before the nineteenth century,[273] it was only towards the end of the twentieth century that the full scope of the doctrine was recognized and that the courts formulated the key requirements in a general way. The most important question is to identify the circumstances in which a legal owner's conduct can be regarded as 'unconscionable', thus calling for the court to provide the claimant with a remedy and preventing him from asserting his legal rights.

(i) Strict criteria: the 'five probanda'

In the late nineteenth century, the courts held that there were strict and rigid criteria that must be met before an estoppel equity was raised. Despite earlier and broader statements of principle in *Ramsden v Dyson*,[274] in *Willmott v Barber* Fry J stipulated five essential elements which had to be established before the court would restrain a defendant from asserting his legal rights over property:

> A man is not to be deprived of his legal rights unless he has acted in such a way as would make it fraudulent for him to set up those rights. What, then are the elements or requisites necessary to constitute fraud of that description? In the first place the plaintiff must have made some mistake as to his legal rights. Second, the plaintiff must have expended some money or must have done some act (not necessarily upon the defendant's land) on the faith of his mistaken belief. Thirdly, the defendant, the possessor of the legal right, must know of the existence of his own right which is inconsistent with the right claimed by the plaintiff. If he does not know of it he is in the same position as the plaintiff, and the doctrine of acquiescence is founded upon conduct with a knowledge of your legal rights. Fourthly, the defendant, the possessor of the legal right, must know of the plaintiff's mistaken belief of his rights. If he does not, there is nothing which calls upon him to assert his own rights. Lastly, the defendant, the possessor of the legal right, must have encouraged the plaintiff in his expenditure of money or in the other acts which he has done, either directly or by abstaining from asserting his legal right. Where all these elements exist, there is fraud of such a nature as will entitle the court to restrain the possessor of the legal title from exercising it, but, in my judgment, nothing short of this will do.[275]

These five 'probanda' came to be regarded as essential requirements of estoppel, and claims failed where it was not possible to establish all five.[276] In *Crabb v Arun District Council*[277] Scarman LJ considered that the five requirements were 'a valuable guide as to

---

[272] Gray, *Elements of Land Law* (2nd edn, 1993), p 356.

[273] See *Bridges v Kilburne* (1792) (referred to in *Jackson v Cator* (1800) 5 Ves 688); *Dillwyn v Llewelyn* (1862) 4 De G F & J 517; *Ramsden v Dyson* (1866) LR 1 HL 129.

[274] (1866) LR 1 HL 129, at 152 (Lord Cranworth LC) and at 170 (Lord Kingsdown).

[275] (1880) 15 Ch D 96, at 105–106.

[276] See *Kammins Ballroom Co Ltd v Zenith Instruments (Torquay) Ltd* [1971] AC 850, at 884; *E and L Berg Homes Ltd v Grey* (1979) 253 *Estates Gazette* 473.   [277] [1976] Ch 179.

the matters of fact which have to be established in order that a plaintiff may establish this particular equity' and they became entrenched within the law.

(ii) A broader understanding of what is unconscionable

The restrictive approach of *Willmott v Barber*[278] has largely given way to a much broader understanding of proprietary estoppel.[279] In *Taylor Fashions Ltd v Liverpool Victoria Trustees Co Ltd*[280] Oliver J restated the requirements of proprietary estoppel:

> the recent cases indicate,[281] in my judgment, that the application of the *Ramsden v Dyson* principle—whether you call it proprietary estoppel, estoppel by acquiescence or estoppel by encouragement is really immaterial—requires a very much broader approach which is directed rather at ascertaining whether, in particular individual circumstances, it would be unconscionable for a party to be permitted to deny that which, knowingly or unknowingly, he has allowed or encouraged another to assume to his detriment than to inquiring whether the circumstances can be fitted within the confines of some preconceived formula serving as a universal yardstick for every form of unconscionable behaviour.[282]

Therefore, rather than determining whether an equity had been established by application of a rigid list of requirements which must be satisfied, he held that the appropriate inquiry was simply whether the defendant's conduct had been, in all the circumstances of the case, 'unconscionable'.[283]

In *Gillett v Holt*, Robert Walker LJ similarly emphasized that the prevention of 'unconscionability' is the essence of proprietary estoppel:

> Moreover, the fundamental principle that equity is concerned to prevent unconscionable conduct permeates all the elements of the doctrine. In the end the court must look at the matter in the round.[284]

(c) Application of the modern requirements

Although the approach taken in *Taylor Fashions*[285] explains the doctrine of proprietary estoppel on the general principle of 'unconscionability', to establish an equity the courts have held that the three key elements of 'assurance', 'reliance', and 'detriment or change of position' must be present.[286] Although these elements can be separated

---

[278] (1880) 15 Ch D 96.

[279] However, in the recent case of *Taylor v Dickens* [1998] 1 FLR 806, Judge Weeks QC rejected the notion of a broad doctrine of estoppel founded on the principle of 'unconscionability' and said that the existence of such a doctrine would mean that 'you might as well forget the law of contract and issue every judge with a portable palm tree'. His comments appear to be inconsistent with the majority of modern cases and have been severely criticized: [1998] Conv 213 (Thompson).

[280] [1982] QB 133; *McMahon v Kerry County Council* (1981) ILRM 419; (1985) 79 ILSI Gaz 179 (Pearce).

[281] See *Inwards v Baker* [1965] 2 QB 29; *ER Ives Investment Ltd v High* [1967] 2 QB 379; *Crabb v Arun District Council* [1976] Ch 179; *Moorgate Mercantile Credit Co Ltd v Twitchings* [1976] QB 225, CA; *Shaw v Applegate* [1977] 1 WLR 970, CA.

[282] See also *Amalgamated Investment and Property Co Ltd (in liquidation) v Texas Commerce International Bank Ltd* [1982] QB 84.   [283] [1982] QB 84, at 155.

[284] [2000] 2 All ER 289, at 301.   [285] [1982] QB 133n.

[286] See *A-G of Hong Kong v Humphreys Estate (Queen's Gardens) Ltd* [1987] AC 114, PC; *Gillies v Keogh* [1989] 2 NZLR 327, at 346, per Richardson J. There is also the requirement, rarely emphasized in the case

for analytical purposes, in *Gillett v Holt*[287] Robert Walker LJ suggested that in practice they are often interrelated because 'the quality of the relevant assurances may influence the issue of reliance' and that 'reliance and detriment are often intertwined'.[288]

(i) 'Assurance'

No estoppel 'equity' will arise unless the claimant can establish that the legal owner of land made a representation, or created or encouraged an expectation that he was presently entitled, or would become entitled,[289] to an interest in the land. An assurance may be given 'actively' through the acts of the legal owner, or 'passively' through his silence and failure to disabuse the claimant of his belief that he is entitled to an interest in the land.[290] To be valid, the assurance must be:

> unambiguous and must appear to have been intended to be taken seriously. Taken in its context, it must have been a promise which one might reasonably expect to be relied upon by the person to whom it was made.[291]

In some cases the assurance may take the form of an actual agreement between the parties. In others there may be a promise that falls short of an agreement, and in others again there may be no more than an understanding or even a course of dealing that shows that a particular state of affairs was assumed or accepted.

(ii) Active assurance

In *Pascoe v Turner*[292] the plaintiff made an active assurance to the defendant, a woman with whom he was living. The defendant had moved in with the plaintiff in 1964. In 1973 he left the house when he started an affair with another woman, but the evidence showed that he had visited the defendant and had declared to her that she had nothing to worry about, as the house was hers and everything in it. The Court of Appeal held that the evidence established an assurance sufficient to found an estoppel equity, and since she had acted to her detriment in reliance upon it she was entitled to a remedy by way of proprietary estoppel. In *Inwards v Baker*[293] Mr Baker's son, Jack, was intending to build a bungalow. He was persuaded by his father to build the bungalow on his land, which he subsequently did. The Court of Appeal held that this amounted to a sufficient inducement or encouragement to give rise to an estoppel. In *Griffiths v Williams*[294] the Court of Appeal held that an estoppel equity was established where a mother had assured her daughter that she would be entitled to live in her house for the whole of her life. An active assurance will certainly have been given if the legal owner of property promised that the claimant was, or would become, entitled to some interest in it.[295]

---

law, that, as with other equitable remedies, there must be no bar to the equity, so that the court is free to intervene. In other words, the acts of the claimant must be free of the taint of unconscionability if they are to be provided with relief through estoppel.   [287] [2000] 2 All ER 289, at 301.

[288] See also *Jennings v Rice* (2003) 1 P & CR 8 and *Henry v Henry* [2010] 1 All ER 998 at [55].

[289] *Re Basham (Decd)* [1987] 1 All ER 405.

[290] *Warnes v Headley* (31 January 1984, unreported), CA.

[291] [2009] UKHL 18, at [56] per Lord Walker, approving the words of Hoffmann LJ in *Walton v Walton* (unreported).   [292] [1979] 1 WLR 431.

[293] [1965] 2 QB 29.   [294] (1977) 248 *Estates Gazette* 947.   [295] *Wayling v Jones* (1993) 69 P & CR 170.

(iii) Can an agreement be enforceable if it is void as a contract?

In *Yaxley v Gotts*[296] a builder had entered into an oral agreement with the owner to refurbish and convert a house into flats in return for his acquiring the ground floor flats. The Court of Appeal held that, although this agreement was unenforceable as a contract for lack of formalities,[297] it could give rise to a claim by way of proprietary estoppel. Lord Scott suggested in *Yeoman's Row v Cobbe*,[298] that 'proprietary estoppel cannot be prayed in aid in order to render enforceable an agreement that statute has declared to be void',[299] such as a contract to grant an interest in land which has not been made in writing. At face value, this would have robbed proprietary estoppel of any real utility in the family home (and beyond),[300] but the case was never likely to be decisive in domestic cases. *Yeoman's Row v Cobbe* was a commercial case where a property developer was led to believe that he would be able to contract to buy land for redevelopment if he succeeded in gaining planning permission. He spent considerable time and money in securing planning permission, only to find that the landowner then wished to increase the price that had been discussed and agreed. Lord Scott's principal reason for rejecting proprietary estoppel as a basis for a remedy[301] was that, even if the developer's expectation was fulfilled, all that he would receive would have been a contract to purchase the development property, some of the important terms of which remained to be agreed. This could not found a claim in proprietary estoppel, for which, in his view, there had to be a claim to a 'certain interest in land' which the party estopped was prevented from denying. A contract to purchase a property was not a certain interest in land. In addition, the claimant knew that he was taking a risk. Lord Scott's observation about proprietary estoppel not being available to enforce a contract that is required to be made in writing was therefore not necessary for a decision in the case. Lord Walker suggests in his judgment that a distinction should be drawn between commercial cases involving individuals who are aware of their rights and who may well have taken legal advice, and domestic cases where the claimant is much less likely to be legally advised and where expectations and understandings might be much less clearly formulated.[302]

Thorner v Major[303] is a later House of Lords' decision. For nearly thirty years David Thorner worked without pay on the farm of his father's cousin, Peter. Although no express promise had been made, the clear understanding between David and Peter was that David would inherit the farm on Peter's death. In the event, Peter died without making a will. The House of Lords held that David's reasonable belief that he would inherit the farm should be fulfilled since he had acted on that belief by

---

[296] [2000] 1 All ER 711.   [297] Law of Property (Miscellaneous Provisions) Act 1989, s 2.
[298] [2008] UKHL 55.   [299] [2008] UKHL 55, at [29].
[300] Etherton 'Constructive Trusts and Proprietary Estoppels: The Search for Clarity and Principle' [2009] Conv 104, at 120.
[301] The claimant did not go without a remedy. It was held that he was entitled to reasonable remuneration for the time and effort which he had spent on a *quantum meruit* basis.
[302] [2008] UKHL 55, at [68], [81], and [87].   [303] [2009] UKHL 18.

foregoing other opportunities. The view of the majority was that this was in most respects a straightforward instance of proprietary estoppel, although Lord Scott, while agreeing that the requirements of proprietary estoppel had been met would have found it 'easier and more comfortable to regard David's equity as established via a remedial constructive trust'.[304] Lord Walker and Lord Neuberger both indicated that the assurance or understanding on which a claimant relied did not need to be expressed with precise and exact definition.[305] Lord Neuberger was forthright in his view that Lord Scott's observations about the difficulty of using proprietary estoppel to render enforceable a contract that was void because it was not in writing had no relevance in a case with no contractual connection.[306] Some emphasis is placed in *Thorner v Major* on the commercial nature of the transaction in *Yeoman's Row v Cobbe*, the sophistication of the parties, and their awareness of the risks in undertaking work on the basis of a promise they both knew could not be enforced as a contract. Lord Walker, in a postscript, expressed his difficulty with Lord Scott's alignment in *Yeoman's Row* of proprietary estoppel with the requirements of promissory estoppel (including the requirement of a 'clear and unambiguous' representation). In *Thompson v Foy*,[307] Lewison J followed the guidance of Lords Walker and Scott in *Thorner v Major*. In this case, the relevant assurance related to the building of an extension to the family home by Mrs Foy. Lewison J, held that, despite there being no evidence of specific conversations between Mrs Thompson and Mrs Foy, it was 'clear enough'[308] that there was a 'mutual understanding'[309] that the extension would belong to Mrs Foy. The more flexible approach has been cited recently with approval in a number of first instance decisions. In *Clarke v Corless*, Proudman J held that:

> there must be a clear agreement on the basic details of the arrangement without difference of principle[310]

Similarly, in *Gill v Woodall*, Deputy Judge James Allen QC stated:

> The relevant assurance must be clear enough but what amounts to sufficient clarity in a case of this kind is hugely dependent upon context. A representation can be sufficient to found proprietary estoppel even if it is not made expressly. It may be made in oblique and allusive terms providing it was reasonable for the person to whom it was made, given his knowledge of the maker and background circumstances, to have understood the maker not merely that his present intention was to leave the property to the other but that he would definitely do so.[311]

It seems that the impact of *Cobbe* on the family home has been mitigated.[312]

---

[304] [2009] UKHL 18, at [14].   [305] See, for example, [2009] UKHL 18, at [98].

[306] [2009] UKHL 18, at [96]–[98] per Lord Neuberger.

[307] [2009] EWHC 1076 (Ch).   [308] [2009] EWHC 1076 (Ch), at [90].

[309] [2009] EWHC 1076 (Ch), at [92].   [310] [2009] EWHC 1636, at [23].

[311] [2009] EWHC 834, at [51].

[312] See also *Whittaker v Kinnear* [2011] EWHC 1479 (QB), at [30] per Bean J.

(iv) Passive assurance

It seems that if a legal owner merely stands by while the claimant acts to his detriment, in the belief that he is entitled to an interest in the land, this will constitute a sufficient assurance to give rise to an estoppel equity.[313] Although it is not strictly essential[314] that the owner knew of the claimant's action and mistaken belief, and of his own rights to intervene,[315] these are relevant issues and it will be easier to establish an equity where they are present. In *St Pancras and Humanist Housing Association Ltd v Leonard*,[316] Mr Leonard (described by the judge as a seasoned squatter) had, for over twelve years, been in exclusive possession of a garage close to a group of houses that had been acquired from Camden Council by a cooperative of which he was a member. He attended a meeting of the cooperative in which the decision was taken to seek a lease of land, including the garage from the Council, for the benefit of all the members. He raised no objection. The trial judge, upheld by the Court of Appeal, held that Mr Leonard was later estopped from asserting his claim to exclusive rights to the garage, even though he was not aware at the time of the meeting that his adverse possession gave him a right to claim title. He did believe at the time that he had the right to prevent other cooperative members from using the garage, and his failure to assert this was enough to make his silence at the meeting an acceptance that the garage would become a communal asset.

(v) Assurance relating to specific assets

Whether the assurance is active or passive it will only generate an equity if it is given with respect to particular assets. In a sense, this limitation operates as an equivalent of the rule that a trust can only be validly created if there was 'certainty of subject matter'. In *Layton v Martin*[317] a man had given a woman who had moved in with him a general assurance that he would provide her with 'financial security'. It was held that this assurance was too amorphous and insufficiently connected with specific property to give rise to an estoppel equity.

In *Re Basham (Decd)*[318] it was held that a plaintiff was able to claim a right by way of proprietary estoppel to the residuary estate of the defendant who had made an assurance to that effect, on the basis that it could extend to the 'the whole of A's estate',[319] rendering it clearly identifiable.

Appropriate identification of assets was an important issue before their Lordships in *Thorner v Major*.[320] Peter Thorner had led his nephew David to believe that he would inherit his farm on his death. Over the thirty-year period in which the claimant had worked without payment on the farm there had been a number of disposals and acquisitions of parcels of land. It was argued before their Lordships that the property

---

[313] *Ramsden v Dyson* (1866) LR 1 HL 129.

[314] *Shaw v Applegate* [1978] 1 All ER 123, CA; *Taylor Fashions Ltd v Liverpool Victoria Trustees Co Ltd* [1982] QB 133; *Thorner v Major* [2009] UKHL 18.

[315] Compare *Armstrong v Sheppard & Short Ltd* [1959] 2 QB 384, CA.

[316] [2008] EWCA Civ 1442.   [317] [1986] 2 FLR 227.   [318] [1986] 1 WLR 1498.

[319] [1986] 1 WLR 1498, at 1510.   [320] [2009] UKHL 18.

had not been established with sufficient certainty. Their Lordships, while noting the requirement of certainty, felt that the fluidity of the farm holding did not stop it being identified as the proprietary subject of the assurance. Lord Neuberger opined that:

> It would represent a regrettable and substantial emasculation of the beneficial principle of proprietary estoppel if it were to be artificially fettered so as to require the precise extent of the subject of the alleged estoppel to be strictly defined in every case…focusing on technicalities can lead to a degree of strictness—inconsistent with the fundamental aims of equity.[321]

His Lordship was responding, in part, to the contention in the earlier speech of Lord Scott in *Yeoman's Row v Cobbe*[322] which suggested that a contractual level of certainty as to assets identified was required in estoppel claims.

(vi) Assurance relating to a grant of future rights

An estoppel equity can arise when an assurance is made concerning the future grant of rights in specific property. This will most commonly occur where an owner had made assurances that he will leave property to the claimant in his will. For example, an estoppel equity was established in *Wayling v Jones*,[323] where the owner of a hotel had promised his partner that he would leave it to him by will on his death. *Thorner v Major*[324] is another example.

However, in *Taylor v Dickens*[325] it was held that there was no claim by way of proprietary estoppel where an elderly lady had said that she would leave her estate to her gardener, but changed her mind without telling him after he had stopped charging her for his help. Judge Weeks QC held that, in light of the inherent revocability of testamentary dispositions, such an assurance would only give rise to an estoppel equity if it created or encouraged the claimant to believe that the owner would not exercise her right to change her will. This decision was subjected to severe academic criticism,[326] which was accepted by the Court of Appeal in *Gillett v Holt*.[327] In this case Gillett had worked for Holt, who was a gentleman farmer, for nearly forty years. On seven separate occasions Holt had assured him that he would leave his entire estate to him, and that he and his family could therefore be sure of a secure future. Robert Walker LJ explained that these assurances were sufficient to give rise to an estoppel equity, even though they did not include an explicit assurance that the owner would not alter his will:

> But the inherent revocability of testamentary dispositions (even if well understood by the parties, as Mr Gillett candidly accepted that it was by him) is irrelevant to a promise or

---

[321] [2009] UKHL 18, at [98].   [322] [2008] UKHL 55.

[323] (1993) 69 P & CR 170. See also *Gillett v Holt* [1998] 3 All ER 917, where it was held that an assurance that the defendant would leave his estate to the plaintiff was capable of founding an entitlement by way of proprietary estoppel. However, in the event Carnwath J held that a claim failed because the defendant had only expressed a mere intention to leave his estate by will to the plaintiff and not an irrevocable promise that he would inherit regardless of any changes in circumstances.   [324] [2009] UKHL 18.

[325] [1998] 3 FCR 455.

[326] Thompson 'Emasculating Estoppel' [1998] Conv 220; Swadling 'Case Note on *Taylor v Dickens*' [1998] RLR 455.   [327] [2000] 2 All ER 289.

assurance that 'all this will be yours'…Even when the promise of assurance is in terms linked to the making of a will…the circumstances may make clear that the assurance is more than a mere statement of present (revocable) intention, and is tantamount to a promise.[328]

The Court of Appeal addressed the same issue in *Bradbury v Taylor*.[329] Bill Taylor had encouraged his nephew, Roger, and his partner and children to move into his house on the basis of oral promises that he would leave the house to them after his death. The house was sufficiently large for them to live together. Some years later relations soured and Roger eventually discovered that Bill had changed his will and was not intending to leave the property to his family as promised. Bill applied for a declaration that Roger and family had no beneficial interest and for an injunction to allow him access to the whole property. He made a witness statement, but died the day before trial. At first instance, the trial judge found Bill's earlier wills and a draft letter confirmed that Roger and family had moved to the property on the basis of Bill's promises to leave the house to them subject to certain conditions, including that they had to continue living there for seven years after Bill's death. The Court of Appeal did not set aside this finding of fact.[330]

(vii) Assurance not required to have been intended to be acted upon

It is not necessary for the party making the assurance to intend that the assurance be acted upon. This was confirmed by Lord Scott in *Thorner v Major*:

> If it is reasonable for a representee to whom representations have been made to take the representations at their face value and rely on them, it would not in general be open to the representor to say that he or she had not intended the representee to rely on them.[331]

(viii) Resolving ambiguity in an assurance

It has been noted that an assurance must be sufficiently clear and relate to specific assets. Nevertheless, as the House of Lords indicated in *Thorner v Major*,[332] the requirement of clarity must not be used to defeat otherwise meritorious claims. Lord Neuberger, exploring this issue in detail,[333] opined that any assurance needs to be adjudged according to three separate (though related) criteria: (1) in context; [334] (2) without rigidity;[335] and (3) that any ambiguity, such as where the assurance has more than one possible meaning, should be taken into account in quantifying the estoppel interest, rather than to negative the assurance.

---

[328] [2000] 2 All ER 289, at 304. Pawlowski and Brown argue that an estoppel equity would also arise where a testator promises to create a secret trust and then subsequently changes his will so that the property is not left to the secret trustee: 'Constituting a Secret Trust by Estoppel' [2004] Conv 388.

[329] [2012] EWCA Civ 1208.

[330] For a trenchant criticism of the validity of the oral assurance in this case, see Mee 'Proprietary estoppel and influence: enough is enough?' [2013] Conv 280.   [331] [2009] UKHL 18, at [17].

[332] [2009] UKHL 18.   [333] [2009] UKHL 18, at [84]–[86].

[334] See *Cook v Thomas* [2010] EWCA Civ 227, at [99].

[335] [2010] EWCA Civ 227, at [85]: 'The court should not search for ambiguity or uncertainty, but should assess the question of clarity and certainty practically and sensibly, as well as contextually.'

Whether a subsequent written agreement, fulfilling most of the parties understanding, but missing out some important element, will override the effect of an earlier assurance which included the missing element has not yet come before the courts for a decision.[336] It is suggested that the answer would depend upon the particular intentions of the parties in making the agreement.

(ix) Assurances and false representations

As befits a doctrine based on the equitable concept of unconscionability, it is clear that it is not possible to rely on an assurance which has been obtained by dishonest conduct and through false representations. In *Murphy v Rayner*,[337] Mrs Murphy had been Mr Raynor's carer for many years and had all her expenses paid by him. Mr Rayner had given gifts and provided food and other necessities to Mrs Murphy. He frequently told her that he intended to give her his property and a percentage of his investments after death. Mrs Murphy had falsely represented that an adult family relative was her daughter, and Mr Raynor had made payments for her education in India and assisted in the purchase of property for her. Mr Rayner's family became suspicious, and following an investigation which revealed that there was no daughter, Mrs Murphy was dismissed. Mrs Murphy claimed that she was entitled to live in the property during Mr Rayner's lifetime and to have it transferred to her on his death by means of estoppel, as well as to a share of the investments. Jeremy Cousins QC held that in light of her dishonest conduct, Mrs Murphy could not rely on the assurances that had been induced on the basis of false representations of fact.[338]

In a similar vein, it will be more difficult for an interest to be acquired through proprietary estoppel where the claimant is a trustee under a family trust and the right alleged is being acquired in breach of duty against beneficiaries who are said to have acquiesced.[339]

(x) Assurances and common intention

There is significant overlap between the requirements necessary to demonstrate an express common intention to acquire an interest by means of a constructive trust and a representation or assurance to found a claim through proprietary estoppel. Neither requires a contractual style of agreement in the family homes context and both require that the understanding or assurance relates to a right in particular property. An important distinction is that in proprietary estoppel the courts are focusing on finding an assurance or representation by the representor; in the constructive trusts context the courts are supposedly seeking the common intention of the parties. That distinction may be narrower than appears at first blush since analysis of the case law on common intention suggests that the courts are in fact concerned only with a

---

[336] See *Whittaker v Kinnear* [2011] EWHC 1479 (QB), at [33].   [337] [2011] EWHC 1 (Ch).
[338] The same would not appear to true with innocent misrepresentations of fact, which are to be treated as one of the factors in considering all aspects of whether a valid estoppel claim has been made out—see *Qayyum v Hameed* [2009] EWCA Civ 352.
[339] See *Sinclair v Sinclair* [2009] EWHC 926 (Ch), at [71].

representation from the legal owner which the claimant relies upon. It would be rare for circumstances which give rise to the finding of an express common intention to not also give rise to an assurance in proprietary estoppel.[340]

(d) 'Reliance'

(i) Requirement of reliance

An essential element of proprietary estoppel is that the claimant must have acted in reliance upon the assurance in relation to which the claim is being made.[341] It is not unconscionable to make an assurance if it is not acted upon.

(ii) 'Reliance' as a causal connection

Reliance connects the assurance with the detriment. It demonstrates that the assurance caused the claimant to act to his detriment. As Balcombe LJ stated in *Wayling v Jones*:

> There must be a sufficient link between the promises relied upon and the conduct which constitutes the detriment.[342]

(iii) Burden of proving reliance

In order to establish an estoppel equity a claimant must demonstrate[343] not merely that an assurance was made by the legal owner of land, but also that he relied upon the assurance made. In *A-G of Hong Kong v Humphreys Estate (Queen's Gardens) Ltd*[344] the Privy Council stated that it was necessary for the claimants to 'show' that they had relied on an expectation that had been encouraged by the landowner. In *Lim Teng Huan v Ang Swee Chuan*[345] the Privy Council held that the requisite reliance could be established by an 'inevitable'[346] inference drawn from the facts. In *Wayling v Jones* Balcombe LJ held:

> Once it has been established that promises were made, and that there has been conduct by the plaintiff of such a nature that inducement may be inferred then the burden of proof shifts to the defendant to establish that he did not rely on the promises.[347]

(iv) Establishing reliance

A claimant will thus fail to establish an estoppel equity if it can be shown that he acted as he did for reasons other than the assurance. In *Coombes v Smith*[348] Mrs Coombes had an unhappy marriage and fell in love with Mr Smith. He bought a house where it was

---

[340] Dixon 'Invalid Contracts, Estoppel and Constructive Trusts' [2005] Conv 247.

[341] See further Robertson 'The Reliance Basis of Proprietary Estoppel Remedies' [2008] Conv 295.

[342] (1993) 69 P & CR 170, at 173. See also *Eves v Eves* [1975] 1 WLR 1338, at 1345, per Brightman J; *Grant v Edwards* [1986] Ch 638, at 648–649, 655–657, 656, per Nourse LJ and per Browne-Wilkinson V-C; *Gillett v Holt* [2000] 2 All ER 289, 306.

[343] See *Greasley v Cooke* [1980] 1 WLR 1306, where Lord Denning MR considered that there is a presumption of reliance once a representation has been established.   [344] [1987] AC 114.

[345] [1992] 1 WLR 113.   [346] [1992] 1 WLR 113, at 118.   [347] (1993) 69 P & CR 170, at 173.

[348] [1986] 1 WLR 808.

intended they should live together. She became pregnant by him, and moved into the house. Mr Smith never moved in with her, but visited regularly. The house was sold and another purchased, which Mrs Coombes decorated. After their relationship had broken down, Mrs Coombes claimed an interest in the house by way of proprietary estoppel. Jonathon Parker QC held that even if an assurance had been made, Mrs Coombes had not acted in reliance on it. As to her becoming pregnant, he considered:

> it would be wholly unreal, to put it mildly, to find on the evidence adduced before me that the plaintiff allowed herself to become pregnant by the defendant in reliance on some mistaken belief as to her legal rights. She allowed herself to become pregnant because she wished to live with the defendant and bear his child.[349]

Likewise, leaving her husband was not because of any assurance that Mr Smith had made but because 'she preferred to have a relationship with…the defendant rather than continuing to live with her husband…There is no evidence that she left her husband in reliance on the defendant's assurance that he would provide for her if and when their relationship came to an end.' Even the decorating she carried out failed to demonstrate reliance, since it was done 'by the plaintiff as occupier of the property, as the defendant's mistress, and as [the child's] mother, in the context of a continuing relationship with the defendant…'[350]

However, it may be that *Coombes v Smith* adopts an unduly restrictive approach to the concept of reliance and an over-optimistic confidence in the ability of the court to determine the true rationale for the claimant's actions. Motives are invariably mixed rather than pure, and it would not be unreasonable to suggest that Mrs Coombes' actions were at least partially influenced by the assurances she had received from her lover. Only with the promise of security was she prepared to continue her relationship and have a child. Subsequent cases have tended to take a more generous attitude towards questions of reliance. In *Matharu v Matharu*[351] a wife returned to live with her husband on the mistaken basis that the matrimonial home was as much hers as his. She later discovered that it was in fact owned by his father. She subsequently acted to her detriment by installing a new kitchen. The Court of Appeal held that this indicated that she had acted in reliance upon an assurance by her father-in-law, through his conduct, that he would abstain from asserting his legal rights to the house, even though the expenditure had been incurred after she was aware of her mistaken assumption as to the ownership of the property.

Similarly, in *Wayling v Jones*[352] the plaintiff and deceased defendant had cohabited in a homosexual relationship. The defendant ran a hotel business in which he was helped by the plaintiff, who acted as his companion and chauffeur in return for pocket money and the promise that the defendant would leave the business to him on his

---

[349] [1986] 1 WLR 808, at 820.

[350] Compare the House of Lords' views of the wife's activities in *Lloyds Bank plc v Rosset* [1991] 1 AC 107. For similar reasoning, see also *Stilwell v Simpson* (1983) 133 NLJ 894; *Layton v Martin* [1986] 2 FLR 227.

[351] (1994) 68 P & CR 93.

[352] (1994) 68 P & CR 93; Cooke 'Reliance and Estoppel' (1995) 111 LQR 389; Davis 'Estoppel—Reliance and Remedy' [1995] Conv 409.

death. When the defendant died he had left the plaintiff only a motor car valued at £375. The Court of Appeal held that sufficient reliance was demonstrated and could be established by inference from the plaintiff's conduct. Balcombe LJ stated the principle:

> The promises relied upon do not have to be the sole inducement for the conduct: it is sufficient if they are an inducement.[353]

Nevertheless, in *James v Thomas*,[354] the reasoning is as restrictive as in *Coombes*. Peter Thomas had acquired a cottage, previously owned by his parents, by buying out the shares of his brother and sister in 1986. In 1989, he developed a relationship with Sharon James, and she moved to live with him. Sharon worked without pay in Peter's business. She also helped with the manual work involved in carrying out improvements. Peter told Sharon that these actions 'will benefit us both' and he told her he would ensure that she was provided for if he died. The relationship broke down in 2005 and Sharon claimed an interest in the cottage. It was argued that the defendant had created an expectation that the claimant would acquire a proprietary interest in property, on which the claimant had acted to her detriment. Sir John Chadwick, in the Court of Appeal, held that the trial judge was correct to form the conclusion that Peter had not given any assurance that Sharon would acquire an interest in the cottage. He added:

> for completeness, I should add that the factors which lead to the conclusion that the assurances were not intended or understood as a promise of some property interest lead, also, to the conclusion that it would be unreal to think that Miss James did what she did in reliance on such a promise. The true position, as it seems to me, is that she worked in the business, and contributed her labour to the improvements to the property, because she and Mr Thomas were making their life together as man and wife. The Cottage was their home: the business was their livelihood. It is a mistake to think that the motives which lead parties in such a relationship to act as they do are necessarily attributable to pecuniary self-interest.[355]

Whether there has been reliance will therefore be very much a question of fact in every case, and it is relatively easy to find apparent inconsistencies in the approach of individual members of the judiciary.

(v) Reasonableness of reliance

The reliance on the assurance must be reasonable and not be so far divorced from the assurance or expectation given as to render it irrelevant. Nevertheless, whether a reliance is reasonable must be considered on a holistic appraisal of all the facts, not just those known at the time of the reliance:

> Past events provide context and background for the interpretation of subsequent events and subsequent events throw retrospective light upon the meaning of past events. The owl of Minerva spreads its wings only with the falling of dusk. The finding was that [the

---

[353] (1995) 69 P & CR 170, at 173.   [354] [2007] EWCA Civ 1212.
[355] [2007] EWCA Civ 1212, at [36].

appellant] reasonably relied upon the assurance from 1990, even if it required later events to confirm that it was reasonable for him to have done so.[356]

(e) 'Detriment or change of position'

(i) Assurance and reliance insufficient without detriment or change of position

An estoppel equity calling for a remedy will only be established if a claimant can show that he acted to his detriment in reliance upon the assurance that was made. This final element of detriment renders it 'unconscionable' for the legal owner to assert his strict rights.[357] If the owner had created an expectation on the part of the claimant, but the claimant had done nothing in response, there would be no reason why he should not be entitled to assert his rights. Rights over land are not created by mere representations, which do not amount to either a contract or a declaration of trust.[358]

(ii) Detriment and change of position

The courts have tended to express the requirement of detriment in terms of 'change of position'[359] and to highlight that 'the categories of detriment [are] not closed'.[360] In *Gillett v Holt* Robert Walker LJ summarized what detriment requires:

> The overwhelming weight of authority shows that detriment is required. But the authorities also show that it is not a narrow or technical concept. The detriment need not consist of the expenditure of money or other quantifiable financial detriment as long as it is something substantial. The requirement must be approached as part of a broad inquiry as to whether repudiation of an assurance is or is not unconscionable in all the circumstances.[361]

This detriment must therefore be considered together with the question of unconscionability, such that a change of position will only be sufficiently substantial if it means it would be unjust or inequitable to withdraw the assurance or expectation. This has been criticized by Wells, on the basis that it is destroying existing categories and principles of detriment and thereby creating uncertainty.[362] Nevertheless, Robert Walker LJ's words have been affirmed directly in *Campbell v Grifffin*[363] and *Parker v Parker*[364] and tacitly by the House of Lords in their most recent decision in *Thorner v Major*.[365] In *Suggitt v Suggitt*, Arden LJ also affirmed the need for detrimental reliance in unequivocal terms:

> The overwhelming weight of authority shows that detriment is required. But the authorities also show that it is not a narrow or technical concept. The detriment need not consist

---

[356] *Thorner v Major* [2009] UKHL 18, at [8] per Lord Hoffmann.

[357] See *Grundt v Great Boulder Pty Gold Mine Ltd* (1937) 59 CLR 641.

[358] It will be remembered that in the case of a declaration of a trust of land there is a need for evidence in writing under s 53(1)(b) of the Law of Property Act 1925. A contract for the creation of an interest in land must be made in writing in accordance with s 1 of the Law of Property (Miscellaneous Provisions) Act 1989.

[359] See *ER Ives Investment Ltd v High* [1967] 2 QB 379, CA; *Bhimji v Salih* (4 February 1981, unreported), CA; *In Re Basham (Decd)* [1986] 1 WLR 1498, at 1504; *Lloyds Bank v Rosset* [1991] AC 107, at 132.

[360] *Watts v Storey* (1983) 134 NLJ 631.   [361] [2000] 2 All ER 289, at 308.

[362] 'The Element of Detriment in Proprietary Estoppel' [2001] Conv 13.   [363] [2001] WTLR 981.

[364] [2003] EWHC 1846.   [365] [2009] UKHL 18.

of the expenditure of money or other quantifiable financial detriment, so long as it is something substantial. The requirement must be approached as part of a broad inquiry as to whether repudiation of an assurance is or is not unconscionable in all the circumstances... The issue of detriment must be judged at the moment when the person who has given the assurance seeks to go back on it. Whether the detriment is sufficiently substantial is to be tested by whether it would be unjust or inequitable to allow the assurance to be disregarded—that is, again, the essential test of unconscionability. The detriment alleged must be pleaded and proved.[366]

The cases have found that a wide range of conduct is sufficient 'detriment' to give rise to an equity. It is also worth noting that the requirement of change of position is similar to the level of detriment required to give effect to an express common intention to found an interest by means of a constructive trust,[367] but, as will be seen, the range of factors which may be taken into account in demonstrating change of position are wider, as they do not have to relate directly to the purchase of the family home.

(iii) Improvement of the legal owner's land

Sufficient detriment will be demonstrated if the claimant had expended money improving the land in respect of which an assurance was given.[368] For example, in *Inwards v Baker*[369] it was held that a son had acted to his detriment by building a bungalow on his father's land in reliance on an assurance he had received. In *Pascoe v Turner*[370] an equity was raised where the claimant had spent money on redecoration, improvements, and repairs to a house that was owned by her former lover, while he passively assured by his acquiescence that she had an interest in the house. In *Matharu v Matharu*[371] it was held that a wife had acted to her detriment when she installed a new kitchen in a house owned by her father-in-law in reliance upon an assurance that it belonged to her husband and that she would have an interest in it. In *Gillett v Holt*[372] one of the ways in which the claimant had acted to his detriment was by incurring substantial expenditure improving the farmhouse he occupied. In *Thompson v Foy*,[373] the claimant had acted to her detriment by building and paying for an extension to the family home. Incurring liability to repay a mortgage has been held as sufficient detriment where a claimant was promised a half share in the property in *Qayyum v Hameed*.[374]

(iv) Improvement of the claimant's own land

A claimant will also be held to have acted to his detriment if he improved his own land in reliance upon an assurance that he is to enjoy a right over the land of the legal

---

[366] [2012] EWCA Civ, at [34]. Ironically, the apparent lack of detriment on the facts in what was a successful estoppel claim has drawn considerable criticism—see Mee 'Proprietary estoppel and influence: enough is enough?' [2013] Conv 280.

[367] [1970] AC 777.   [368] See *Voyce v Voyce* (1991) 62 P & CR 290, CA.   [369] [1965] 2 QB 29.

[370] [1979] 1 WLR 431.   [371] (1994) 68 P & CR 93.   [372] [2000] 2 All ER 289, at 309–310.

[373] [2009] EWHC 1076 (Ch).   [374] [2009] EWCA Civ 352.

owner. In *Rochdale Canal Co v King*[375] a mill owner built a mill on his own land after having applied to the canal company to take water from the canal to operate his steam engines. The company did not refuse the application and pipes were laid in the presence of their engineers. The court held that, due to their acquiescence, they were not entitled to an injunction restraining the mill owner from drawing water from the canal.[376]

(v) Acquisition of new land by the claimant

In *Salvation Army Trustees Co Ltd v West Yorkshire Metropolitan County Council*[377] the council informed the Salvation Army that the site of their hall would be required for a proposed road-widening scheme. Although there was no contract for the sale of the hall to the council, the Salvation Army acquired a new site and built a new hall. The council subsequently informed them that the proposed scheme would not be adopted for some years and that they would not therefore be acquiring the old site. Woolf J held that the Salvation Army was entitled to a claim on the basis of proprietary estoppel. He held that the principle of proprietary estoppel was:

> capable of extending to the disposal of an interest in land where that disposal is closely linked by an arrangement that also involves the acquiring of an interest in land.[378]

(vi) Working without adequate remuneration

In *Wayling v Jones*[379] it was held that an estoppel equity was established where the claimant had helped his homosexual partner to run a cafe and hotel in reliance upon the assurance that it would be left to him by will. The fact that he received 'little more than pocket money' as remuneration for his work was sufficient to constitute the necessary element of detriment. Similarly, in *Thorner v Major*[380] the House of Lords held that the claimant had acted to his detriment by doing substantial farm work for thirty years without pay, for most of that time in reliance on an assurance that he would inherit the farm. Along similar lines, giving up a job and moving to a new area has been held to be a sufficient change of position.[381]

(vii) Personal disadvantage

A claim may arise by way of proprietary estoppel even if the claimant did not act to his detriment financially by incurring the expenditure of money. In a number of cases purely personal disadvantage, such as being 'deprived of the opportunity of a better life elsewhere',[382] has been held sufficient to give rise to an equity. A classic example is

---

[375] (1853) 16 Beav 630.　　[376] See also *Cotching v Bassett* (1862) 32 Beav 101.
[377] (1980) 41 P & CR 179.　　[378] (1980) 41 P & CR 179, at 192.
[379] (1993) 69 P & CR 170. See also *Gillett v Holt* [1998] 3 All ER 917, where Carnwath J accepted that a 'lower salary than would otherwise have been appropriate would have been sufficient detriment to establish a claim by way of proprietary estoppel'. However, there was no evidence to prove that the plaintiff had received a lower salary and the claim therefore failed.　　[380] [2009] UKHL 18.
[381] See *Jones v Jones* [1977] 1 WLR 438.　　[382] *Henry v Henry* [2010] UKPC 3, at [61].

Greasley v Cooke.[383] Doris Cooke moved into the house of Arthur Greasley as a maid-servant in 1938. She lived with one of his sons, Kenneth, from 1946. Throughout that time she looked after the son and his mentally disabled sister, Clarice. When Kenneth died in 1975 the members of the family who had inherited the house asked her to leave. The trial judge found that she 'reasonably believed and was encouraged by members of the family to believe that she could regard the property as her home for the rest of her life', but held that she had not acted to her detriment. The Court of Appeal allowed her appeal. Lord Denning MR stated that it was not necessary that the change of position take the form of expenditure of money. He held that:

> It is sufficient if the party, to whom the assurance is given, acts on the faith of it in such circumstances that it would be unjust and inequitable for the party making the assurance to go back on it.[384]

The importance of cumulative detriment was emphasized in *In Re Basham (decd)*,[385] in which acts such as refraining from taking a job outside the area, paying legal expenses for boundary disputes, and spending time and money on the upkeep of the property, while individually not particularly significant, collectively demonstrated acts beyond 'normal love and affection' that supported a finding of detrimental reliance as the claimants had 'subordinated their own interests to the wishes of the deceased'.[386] Similar evidence of personal detriment was approved to support financial detriment by the Court of Appeal in *Gillett v Holt*,[387] including the claimant and his wife performing tasks beyond the normal scope of an employee's duties and subordinating their wishes to those of *Holt*, such as the decision as to the school their son would attend.

The most important comments regarding the relevance of non-monetary detriment were made by Browne-Wilkinson V-C in *Grant v Edwards*.[388] The case concerned a common intention constructive trust[389] but he considered that 'useful guidance may be obtained from the principles underlying the law of proprietary estoppel'. On the question of detriment he stated:

> In many cases of the present sort, it is impossible to say whether or not the claimant would have done the acts relied on as a detriment even if she thought she had no interest in the house. Setting up house together, having a baby, making payments to general housekeeping expenses (not strictly necessary to enable the mortgage to be paid) may all be referable to the mutual love and affection of the parties and not specifically referable to the claimant's belief that she has an interest in the house. As at present advised, once it has been shown that there was a common intention that the claimant should have an interest in the house, any act done by her to her detriment relating to the joint lives of the parties is, in my judgment, sufficient detriment to qualify.[390]

---

[383] [1980] 1 WLR 1306.
[384] [1980] 1 WLR 1306, at 1311.   [385] [1986] 1 WLR 1498.   [386] [1970] AC 777.
[387] [2000] 2 All ER 289, at 309–310.
[388] [1986] Ch 638; Hayton 'Equity and the Quasi-Matrimonial Home'[1986] CLJ 394; Warburton 'Interested or Not?' [1986] Conv 291.   [389] See Chapter 8.
[390] [1986] Ch 638, at 657.

Applying the test of 'any act done by her relating to the joint lives of the parties' to proprietary estoppel claims,[391] a whole range of non-monetary detriment would be sufficient to raise an equity.

However, as has been noted earlier, some cases have taken a much narrower attitude towards non-monetary detriment. In particular, in *Coombes v Smith*[392] Jonathon Parker QC held that a woman who had left her husband to live with her lover, became pregnant by him, gave birth to their child, and looked after the shared property and their daughter had not 'acted to her detriment' in reliance on an assurance that she was entitled to an interest in the house. As has been discussed earlier, this may be because these acts could not be seen as performed 'in reliance' on an assurance, rather than because they were not detrimental per se.[393]

(viii) Weighing detriment against any benefits derived

Whether there has, in fact, been a detriment depends upon a balance in which the courts weigh any benefits gained in acting on an assurance against the claimed detriment. If the balance is a detriment overall, then a claim may succeed. In *Watts v Storey*[394] the claimant was persuaded by his grandmother to give up a tenancy of a house in Leeds and move into her home, Apple House, in Nottinghamshire, following her move to the Isle of Wight. He gave up his prospects of finding employment in Leeds. Although the Court of Appeal found that there was an assurance that Apple House would be left to him by will, it held that there was insufficient detriment to found a claim by way of proprietary estoppel:

> when the benefits derived by him from his rent-free occupation…are set against any detriments suffered by him as a result of making the move from his protected flat in Leeds, he has not on balance suffered any detriment in financial or material terms.

In *Powell v Benney*,[395]—at first instance the judge had awarded £20,000 to a couple who had acted to their detriment in reliance on a promise of an elderly gentleman to leave two properties to them in his will. The couple appealed on the basis that they should have been entitled to the freehold of the properties. In dismissing the appeal, Sir Peter Gibson factored in the use of the premises during lifetime and found that '[i]t would offend common sense to leave out of account a benefit received in connection with a detriment when considering the detriment for the purpose of proprietary estoppel.'

In *Henry v Henry*,[396] the claimant had been living and cultivating land in St Lucia for over thirty years. It was his case that Mrs Henry had promised to leave him the

---

[391] Although Browne-Wilkinson J did not rest his judgment on the analogy between common intention constructive trusts and proprietary estoppel because the point had not been fully argued.

[392] [1986] 1 WLR 808.

[393] In the Australian case *W v G* [1996] 20 Fam LR 49, the NSW Supreme Court held that a lesbian partner had acted to her detriment where she had agreed to have a child by way of artificial insemination on the basis of an assurance that her partner would assist in the upbringing of the child. The court did not, however, find that having a child per se was a detriment: see Bailey-Harris 'Equity Still Childbearing in Australia?' (1997) 113 LQR 227.   [394] (1983) 134 NLJ 631.

[395] (2008) 1 P & CR DG 12.   [396] [2010] UKPC 3 (PC).

land on her death and that he had acted to his detriment by working on the land, and taking care of Mrs Henry until she died. The claim had been dismissed at first instance, on the basis that rather than suffer a detriment, he had positively benefited from living there and reaping its produce. Sir Jonathan Parker upheld the claim by estoppel. It was clear from the evidence that, by remaining on the land, Mr Henry had deprived himself of the opportunity of a better life elsewhere. That detriment had not been outweighed by the advantages he enjoyed as a result of remaining on the land.[397]

(3) Quantification: satisfying the equity

(a) A range of remedial responses

(i) Court must identify the appropriate remedy

Once a claimant has established an estoppel equity by demonstrating the elements of assurance, reliance, and detriment, the question arises as to his remedial entitlement. The mere fact that he has established an equity does not entitle him to any particular remedy, or even to a remedy at all. It is for the court to determine, in its discretion, whether the estoppel equity requires the award of a remedy, and if so the type of remedy that would be appropriate to achieve justice between the parties. This process of determining the appropriate remedial response is described as 'satisfying the equity'. This terminology is long established, as in *Plimmer v Wellington Corpn* the Privy Council stated that:

> the court must look at the circumstances in each case to decide in what way the equity can be satisfied.[398]

Where an estoppel equity has been established, the courts have awarded a wide range of remedies in satisfaction. The process and criteria by which the court determines the appropriate remedy will be examined later, but this emphasizes that the creation of any right is by court order. The right granted may be lesser or greater than the parties expected or might have wished.

(ii) Transfer of the legal ownership of land

The most powerful remedy by which the court may satisfy an estoppel equity is to order the legal owner to transfer his land to the claimant. In *Dillwyn v Llewelyn*[399] and *Pascoe v Turner*[400] the legal owner was ordered to convey the fee simple in his house to the claimant.[401] In *Gillett v Holt*[402] the court ordered Holt to transfer the freehold of the farm they occupied to the claimant in part satisfaction of his estoppel interest. The

---

[397] [2010] UKPC 3 (PC), at [61].   [398] (1883–84) LR 9 App Cas 699, at 714.
[399] (1862) 4 De GF & J 517.   [400] [1979] 1 WLR 431.
[401] See also *Thomas v Thomas* [1956] NZLR 785; *Cameron v Murdoch* [1983] WAR 321; *Riches v Hogben* [1986] 1 Qd R 315; *Re Basham (Decd)* [1987] 1 All ER 405; *Voyce v Voyce* (1991) 62 P & CR 290, CA; *Durant v Heritage and Hamilton* [1994] NPC 117; *Walton v Walton* (20 July 1994, unreported), Ch Div.
[402] [2001] Ch 210.

court may also be able to award a conditional or determinable fee simple, specifying the conditions on which the right will come to an end. In *Williams v Staite*[403] Goff LJ stated that:

> the court might hold in any proper case, that the equity is in its nature for a limited period only or determinable upon a condition certain. In such a case the courts must then see whether, in the events which have happened, it has determined or it has expired or been determined by the happening of that condition.[404]

More recently, Lewison J in *Thompson v Foy*,[405] emphasized that the satisfaction of an equity was a remedy for the courts,[406] and therefore granted ownership of an extension built by Mrs Foy, rather than a licence to occupy it, which, it was argued by Mrs Foy's mother, was the minimum equity to do justice between the parties. This was in line with what his Lordship considered the underlying expectation between the parties.

(iii) Transfer of an undivided share in the land

Where land is held on trust the court may order one joint tenant to transfer his undivided share in the land to another in satisfaction of an estoppel equity. In *Lim Teng Huan v Ang Swee Chuan*[407] the plaintiff and the defendant were the equitable joint tenants of land in Brunei. The defendant built a house on the land believing (wrongly) that a contract had been entered between himself and the plaintiff. The Privy Council held that the plaintiff was therefore estopped from claiming his title to the land, and that the land should belong outright to the defendant, subject to him paying compensation for the value of the land.

(iv) Grant of a lease

In some cases the court has awarded a leasehold estate in satisfaction of proprietary estoppel, as for example in *Siew Soon Wah v Yong Tong Hong*.[408] In *Grant v Williams*[409] a daughter who had lived for most of her life in her mother's house and had cared for her and incurred expenditure improving the property on the basis of a representation that she would be entitled to live in it for the rest of her life was granted a long lease at a nominal rent, determinable on death, in satisfaction of her estoppel equity. In *Yaxley v Gotts*[410] the Court of Appeal upheld the grant of a long lease in satisfaction of an estoppel equity where a builder had refurbished and converted a house into flats in reliance upon an assurance from the owner that he would thereby acquire the ground floor flats.

(v) Right of occupancy

In the majority of cases the courts have stopped short of awarding a claimant full ownership of the property and have granted some form of a right of occupancy. For example, in *Greasley v Cooke*,[411] the Court of Appeal held that the claimant should be

---

[403] [1979] Ch 291.   [404] [1979] Ch 291, at 300.

[405] [2009] EWHC 1076 (Ch).   [406] *Thompson v Foy* [2009] EWHC 1076 (Ch), at [96].

[407] [1992] 1 WLR 113.   [408] [1973] AC 836.   [409] (1977) 248 *Estates Gazette* 947.

[410] [2000] 1 All ER 711.   [411] [1980] 1 WLR 1306.

entitled to remain in the house rent free for as long as she wished. Similarly, in *Inwards v Baker*[412] the son, who had built his bungalow on his father's land, was held entitled to remain there as long as he wanted. In *Matharu v Matharu*[413] the Court of Appeal held that a claimant was entitled to 'a 'a licence . . . to remain in this house for her life or such shorter period as she may decide'[414] Such rights of occupation virtually amount to the grant of a 'life interest'. Prior to the introduction of trusts of land under the Trusts of Land and Appointment of Trustees Act 1996, such a right would have tended to create a strict settlement under the provisions of the Settled Land Act 1925.[415] The grant of a lease in *Griffiths v Williams*[416] was a means of avoiding the unsatisfactory consequences of a strict settlement. With the introduction of the trust of land, the courts may become more willing to utilize the equitable life interest as a means of satisfaction of an estoppel equity. Unlike the Irish courts, the English courts have not recognized rights of residence not conferring exclusive possession as proprietary interests in land.

(vi) Financial compensation

In some other cases, the courts have awarded a claimant only financial reimbursement in satisfaction of his estoppel equity. In *Dodsworth v Dodsworth*[417] the legal owner of a bungalow allowed the claimants, her brother and his wife, to live in it on their return from Australia. They spent £700 on improvements in the expectation that they would be able to remain in the bungalow as long as they wished. After a breakdown in the relationship between the parties, the Court of Appeal held that the claimants were not entitled to occupy rent-free for life, but were entitled to be repaid their outlay on improvements. The court may award the claimant a lien or a charge over the property to the value of the improvements made.[418] In *Wayling v Jones*[419] the Court of Appeal held that the claimant should be entitled to recover the proceeds of sale of the hotel that his partner had promised to leave him by will. In *Jennings v Rice*[420] the Court of Appeal held that a gardener who had acted to his detriment by looking after an elderly lady in reliance upon her assurance that she would 'see to it' that he would be alright in her will should receive £200,000 from her estate.

(vii) Grant of easement

Where appropriate, the courts have held that a claimant is entitled to the grant of an easement over the land of the person estopped, as, for example, in *ER Ives Investment Ltd v High*[421] and *Crabb v Arun District Council.*[422] The loss of an easement is also possible, as in *Lester v Woodgate.*[423]

---

[412] [1965] 2 QB 29.   [413] (1994) 68 P & CR 93.   [414] (1994) 68 P & CR 93, at 103.
[415] See *Dodsworth v Dodsworth* (1973) 228 *Estates Gazette* 1115; *Ungurian v Lesnoff* [1990] Ch 206; *Costello v Costello* (1994) 70 P & CR 297.   [416] (1977) 248 *Estates Gazette* 947.
[417] (1973) 228 *Estates Gazette* 1115.
[418] *Unity Joint Stock Mutual Banking Association v King* (1858) 25 Beav 72; *Taylor v Taylor* [1956] NZLR 99.
[419] (1995) 69 P & CR 170.   [420] 2002 WL 45443, [2002] NPC 28.
[421] [1967] 2 QB 379, CA.   [422] [1976] Ch 179, CA.
[423] [2010] EWCA Civ 199 (acquiescence in blocking of right of way).

(viii) Composite remedy

On occasion, the court has awarded a composite remedy. For example, in *Re Sharpe (a bankrupt)*[424] Dorothy Johnson moved into a house, with her nephew Thomas Sharpe, which had been purchased in his name. She provided £12,000 of the purchase price of £17,000 by way of a loan to him. Browne-Wilkinson J held that since the payment was made by way of loan, there was no possibility of a resulting trust, but that she was entitled to an interest under the principles of proprietary estoppel. He held that she should have the right to live in the house until her loan was repaid.[425] As has been seen, in *Gillett v Holt*[426] the Court of Appeal awarded the claimant the freehold of the farm he occupied. In addition he was also awarded a sum of £100,000 to compensate him for his exclusion from the rest of the farming business carried on by Holt.

(ix) Imposition of a constructive trust

Although the courts have not yet awarded an interest by way of a constructive trust in satisfaction of an estoppel equity, there appears to be no reason in principle why this would not be possible. The effect would be similar to an order to transfer the legal ownership of land, in that the claimant would receive an ownership interest in the property, only in the form of a share of the beneficial ownership behind a trust of land. There are indications in dicta that a constructive trust may be awarded as a remedy. Originally, these came from Lord Denning MR in *Hussey v Palmer*,[427] in which his Lordship suggested his now discredited new model constructive trust. However, in *Re Basham (Decd)*[428] Edward Nugee QC also took the view that a constructive trust was an appropriate remedy for cases of proprietary estoppel:

> The plaintiff relies on proprietary estoppel, the principle of which, in its broadest form, may be stated as follows: where one person, A, has acted to his detriment on the faith of a belief, which was known to and encouraged by another person, B, that he either has or is going to be given a right in or over B's property, B cannot insist on his strict legal rights if to do so would be inconsistent with A's belief. But in my judgment at all events where the belief is that A is going to be given a right in the future, it is properly to be regarded as giving rise to a species of constructive trust...[429]

In *Matharu v Matharu*[430] the first instance judge held that the claimant was entitled to a share of the beneficial ownership of her matrimonial home by way of proprietary estoppel. This could only take effect by means of a trust.

If the court does possess the jurisdiction to award an equitable interest by way of a constructive trust in satisfaction of an estoppel equity, such a constructive trust would be radically different to the 'institutional' common intention constructive trust generated under the principles set out in *Lloyds Bank plc v Rosset*.[431] A constructive trust imposed by the court by way of proprietary estoppel would be akin to the remedial

---

[424] [1980] 1 WLR 219.

[425] See also *Dodsworth v Dodsworth* (1973) 228 *Estates Gazette* 1115, CA; *Stratulatos v Stratulatos* [1988] 2 NZLR 424.   [426] [2001] Ch 210.

[427] [1972] 3 All ER 744.   [428] [1986] 1 WLR 1498.   [429] [1986] 1 WLR 1498, at 1503–1504.

[430] (1994) 68 P & CR 93.   [431] [1991] 1 AC 107.

constructive trust adopted in other jurisdictions, since the claimant's equitable interest would only arise at the date of judgment, and not at the date of the assurance,
reliance, and detriment.[432] We have already seen that in some recent cases the courts
have considered that estoppel and trusts are interchangeable methods of quantifying
an interest. Indeed, in the House of Lords' decision in *Thorner v Major*,[433] Lord Scott
talked in terms of the overlap between constructive trusts and estoppel, and suggested
that a set of facts which he agreed gave rise to a proprietary estoppel could also give
rise to a 'remedial constructive trust'.[434] Any suggestion that the principles of constructive trusts and proprietary estoppel have melded to create a remedial trust should
be treated with extreme caution, as this does not yet reflect the orthodox view.[434a]
Lord Scott's preference for circumscribing resulting trusts and proprietary estoppel
in favour of a remedial constructive trust doctrine has yet to receive majority support.

(x) No remedy because the claimant has already received 'full satisfaction'

In some cases it appears that the courts may find that a claimant does not require the award
of any remedy at all in order to satisfy an estoppel equity because he has already received
advantages which have fully satisfied his claim. In *Sledmore v Dalby*[435] Mr Dalby had lived
in a house owned by his parents-in-law since 1965. Initially, he and his wife paid rent,
but in 1976 they ceased to do so because his wife became seriously ill. He subsequently
substantially improved the property, having been encouraged to do so by Mr and Mrs
Sledmore. Following the death of his wife, he continued to live in the house, which was
then owned by Mrs Sledmore alone, rent free. In 1990 she gave him notice to quit. At first
instance Mr Dalby was held entitled to a non-assignable licence to occupy the house for
life on the grounds of proprietary estoppel, but the Court of Appeal held that, although he
was entitled to an estoppel equity, it had been fully met. Although he had spent money on
the property, he had enjoyed the benefits of that expenditure through more than fifteen
years' rent-free occupation. Roch LJ also took account of the parties' respective situations,
weighing the fact that Mrs Sledmore was a widow dependent upon benefit, who urgently
wanted to sell the house, against the fact that Mr Dalby was employed and currently making minimal use of the house because he enjoyed accommodation elsewhere.

(b) Determining the appropriate remedy

(i) Is the court's discretion narrow or broad?

As is clear from the preceding section, the courts have awarded a wide range of remedies in satisfaction of estoppel equities. The central question is therefore whether there
is any coherent principle underlying the process by which the remedy is selected in
each case.[436] Two main opposing views have been advocated to explain the function of

---

[432] If an equitable proprietary interest was created as an automatic consequence of the assurance, reliance and detriment, the constructive trust would similarly arise automatically and would be recognized,
rather than created, by the court.   [433] [2009] UKHL 18.
   [434] [2009] UKHL 18, at [18].   [434a] See *Cook v Thomas* [2010] EWCA Civ 229, at [105].
   [435] (1996) 72 P & CR 196; Pawlowski 'Proprietary Estoppel—Satisfying the Equity' (1997) 113 LQR 232.
   [436] See especially Gardner 'The Remedial Discretion in Proprietary Estoppel' (1999) 115 LQR 438; Bright
and McFarlane 'Proprietary Estoppel and Property Rights' [2005] 64 CLJ 449.

the court in the determination of the appropriate remedy. The narrow approach considers that the court is simply required to carry into effect the parties' own 'reasonable expectations'. Under this view, the court is left with a highly circumscribed discretion as to the remedy that is appropriate. The flexible approach argues that the court has a wide discretion to decide the appropriate remedy in the circumstances. In *Jennings v Rice*[437] the Court of Appeal considered the merits of these alternatives and concluded that a composite approach should be adopted which would ensure that there was proportionality between the remedy awarded and the detriment experienced.

(ii) Fulfilment of the claimant's 'reasonable expectation'

A number of academics have argued that when the court satisfies an estoppel equity, it invariably selects the remedy which as far as possible fulfils the reasonable expectations of the claimant.[438] It is alleged that this analysis is capable of rationally explaining the apparent conflict in outcome between *Dillwyn v Llewelyn*[439] and *Pascoe v Turner*,[440] where the court ordered the transfer of the fee simple to the claimant, and *Inwards v Baker*[441] and *Williams v Staite*,[442] where only a lesser right of occupancy was awarded. The crucial distinguishing feature is said to be the nature of the claimant's expectation raised by the assurance of the legal owner. In *Pascoe v Turner*[443] the assurance given to Mrs Turner was that 'the house is yours and everything in it'. Therefore, her reasonable expectation was that she owned the house and, having acted to her detriment in reliance on that assurance, the court acted to fulfil her expectation. In contrast, in *Inwards v Baker*[444] the father's representation to his son was simply 'Why not put the bungalow on my land and make the bungalow a little bigger?' Although this amounted to a clear indication that the son would be entitled to remain on the land, it cannot be taken as an assurance that the son would own the land. The award of a right to occupy for as long as he wished therefore fulfilled the reasonable expectation raised by the assurance he received. Similarly, in *Williams v Staite*[445] the representation was merely that 'you can live here as long as you like', and on the basis of such a representation there could be no reasonable expectation of ownership.

(iii) How can financial remedies be explained?

Slightly more difficult to analyse on this 'expectation model' are cases where the claimant was awarded merely monetary compensation for detriment suffered, as for example in *Dodsworth v Dodsworth*.[446] However, in these cases financial compensation seems to operate as a default remedy when the circumstances prevent the fulfilment of the

---

[437] 2002 WL 45443, [2002] NPC 28.

[438] See (1984) 100 LQR 376 (Moriarty); (1997) 17 LS 258 (Cooke). However, in *Sledmore v Dalby* (1996) 72 P & CR 196, Hoffmann LJ adopted the view that there must be 'proportionality' between the detriment experienced and the remedy awarded, so that the claimant's expectations will not be fulfilled if to do so would be disproportionate to the amount of detriment he had experienced: see (1997) 113 LQR 232 (Pawlowski). See also [1998] Conv 213, where Mark Thompson suggests that there is no need for an expectation to be satisfied in full where an estoppel equity is raised.   [439] (1862) 4 De GF & J 517.

[440] [1979] 1 WLR 431, CA.   [441] [1965] 2 QB 29, CA.   [442] [1979] Ch 291, CA.

[443] [1979] 1 WLR 431, CA.   [444] [1965] 2 QB 29, CA.   [445] [1979] Ch 291, CA.

[446] (1973) 228 *Estates Gazette* 1115: see also *Taylor v Taylor* [1956] NZLR 99; *Re Sharpe* [1980] 1 WLR 219.

claimant's legitimate expectation. In *Dodsworth*[447] the plaintiff's brother and sister-in-law moved into her bungalow with her on their return from Australia, and spent £700 on improvements in reliance on the assurance by the plaintiff that they would be able to remain in the bungalow as their home for as long as they wished. Obviously, this representation is comparable to that made in *Williams v Staite*[448] and a similar remedy of a right of occupancy would be expected. However, the court awarded the defendants only monetary compensation for their improvements. The explanation may well be that it was impossible to fulfil the claimants' reasonable expectation, namely the right to reside in the bungalow with the plaintiff, because the relationship between them had broken down.[449] As Russell LJ observed, the consequence of awarding the defendants a right of occupancy would be that the plaintiff:

> would have to continue sharing her home for the rest of her life with the defendants with whom she was, or thought she was, at loggerheads.

The award of monetary compensation is therefore a default remedy given where a reasonable expectation of shared occupation is no longer a realistic possibility. This analysis is also capable of explaining the award of monetary compensation in *Hussey v Palmer*;[450] *Re Sharpe*;[451] and *Burrows and Burrows v Sharp*.[452] Moriarty summarizes the argument as follows:

> The remedies granted [for proprietary estoppel] are not the product of an unpredictable discretion; but are selected in accordance with well-established principles of English property law. Normally, therefore, a remedy will be chosen which gives the party precisely what he has been led to expect, but occasionally, where joint rights to land have been represented, he may get money instead.[453]

(iv) Criticism of expectation analysis

Although the 'fulfilment of the reasonable expectation' analysis has the attractive merit of certainty, a number of criticisms may be made. First, it ignores a large number of judicial statements that emphasize the court's flexibility in determining the appropriate remedy.[454] Second, it assumes that it is possible to correctly identify the reasonable expectations of the claimant, whereas the reality is often that the assurance, and therefore the derived expectation, are ambiguous. The informal circumstances and terms in which the assurance is given cannot always be taken as sufficiently certain to determine the remedy. To some extent, the court is engaged in the business of

---

[447] (1973) 228 *Estates Gazette* 1115.   [448] [1979] Ch 291, CA.

[449] See *Thompson v Park* [1944] KB 408.

[450] [1972] 1 WLR 1286, CA. Although the plaintiff was only claiming monetary compensation, there had been a breakdown of the sharing relationship between the mother-in-law and son-in-law.

[451] [1980] 1 WLR 219. Although the sharing relationship between aunt and nephew had not broken down, it was the nephew's trustee in bankruptcy who was seeking to evict the aunt.

[452] [1991] Fam Law 67; [1992] Conv 54.   [453] (1984) 100 LQR 376, at 412.

[454] See *Plimmer v Wellington Corpn* (1883–84) LR 9 App Cas 699; *Crabb v Arun District Council* [1976] Ch 179, CA; *Griffiths v Williams* (1977) 248 *Estates Gazette* 947; *Denny v Jensen* [1977] 1 NZLR 635; *Greasley v Cooke* [1980] 1 WLR 1306, CA; *Morris v Morris* [1982] 1 NSWLR 61.

rationalizing the claimant's expectation, and an element of discretion is simply built into that process. For example, is it strictly accurate to conclude from the language used by the father in *Inwards v Baker*[455] that the son's expectation was only of a right to remain on the land rather than to own it? The extent of his detriment, building a house, could surely indicate that something more substantial than a right of occupancy was expected. As Lord Westbury LC said in *Dillwyn v Llewelyn*:

> No one builds a house for his own life only, and it is absurd to suppose that it was intended by either party that the house at the death of the son, should become the property of the father.[456]

The heart of the problem is that, in the informal (and often family) context, the parties rarely formulate precisely the extent of the entitlement being represented, and it is only after the events that the court is called to analyse what has taken place. Determining the claimant's expectation is not therefore an exact science. Moriarty's claim that 'we can get quite some way towards explaining the court's intuitive choice of remedy by merely paying closer attention to the precise content of the representation'[457] is an overstatement.

(v) Composite approach

In the light of such criticisms the Court of Appeal held in *Jennings v Rice*[458] that a pure 'fulfilment of expectations' approach was not the appropriate means of determining the remedy to satisfy an estoppel equity. The case concerned a gardener who had taken care of an elderly lady without remuneration, relying upon her assurance that she would 'see to it' that he was alright, and her statements to him that her house would 'all be yours one day'. At first instance Judge Weeks held that he was entitled to a claim by way of proprietary estoppel, but that he should receive a sum of £200,000 rather than the freehold of the house and its furniture, which was worth considerably more. On appeal it was argued that he should have been entitled to the house and furniture on the grounds that an estoppel equity should be satisfied by making good the expectation of the claimant. The Court of Appeal held that while the nature of the expectation was a relevant consideration, it did not alone determine the appropriate remedy. The court was rather required to do justice by ensuring that there was proportionality between the remedy and the detriment. The importance of proportionality was emphasized in *Malik v Kalyan*,[459] *Henry v Henry*,[460] and *Gow v Grant*.[461]

(vi) Broad discretion approach

In contrast to the 'expectation' analysis, other academics have argued[462] that the court possesses a broad discretion to select whichever remedy it feels is appropriate in the circumstances of each case. The 'equity' of the claimant arises as a result of the assurance,

---

[455] [1965] 2 QB 29.   [456] (1862) 4 De GF & J 517, at 522.   [457] (1984) 100 LQR 376, at 383.

[458] 2002 WL 45443, [2002] NPC 28.   [459] [2010] EWCA Civ 113.

[460] [2010] UKPC 3, at [65].   [461] [2012] UKSC 29 (Scotland).

[462] See Thompson 'Estoppel and Clean Hands' [1986] Conv 406; Dewar 'Licences and Land Law: An Alternative View' (1986) 49 MLR 741.

reliance, and detriment, and that equity remains 'inchoate' until the court determines a remedy to satisfy it. In this sense, the court is acting in a similar way to the courts of other jurisdictions where the remedial constructive trust is recognized.[463] The cause of action is proprietary estoppel, and, if established, the court selects the appropriate remedy.

Dicta in a significant number of cases support the suggestion that the court possesses a wide discretion to determine the appropriate remedy. In *Plimmer v Wellington Corpn*[464] Sir Arthur Hobhouse stated that 'the court must look at the circumstances in each case to decide in what way the equity can be satisfied'. In *Crabb v Arun District Council*[465] Lord Denning MR emphasized that in answering the question how an established equity should be satisfied, 'equity is displayed at its most flexible'. He also restated the principle in *Greasley v Cooke*:

> The equity having thus been raised...it is for the courts of equity to decide in what way that equity should be satisfied.[466]

Such flexibility was also emphasized in *Griffiths v Williams*,[467] where Goff LJ answered the question 'What is the relief appropriate to satisfy the equity?' in this way:

> the next question is one upon which the court has to exercise a discretion. If it finds that there is an equity, then it must determine the nature of it, and then, guided by that nature and exercising discretion in all the circumstances, it has to determine what is the fair order to make between the parties for the protection of the claimant.[468]

The wide discretion of the court was also stressed in New Zealand in *Stratulatos v Stratulatos*,[469] where McGehan J said that 'the range of available remedies should not be cluttered by arbitrary rules'.

(vii) Criticism of discretionary approach

As with any area in which the court possesses a wide remedial discretion, the key criticism has been that of uncertainty.[470] If the remedy is entirely within the choice of the courts, without any defined criteria as to how that choice will be made, it will not be possible to advise accurately on the likely remedy, which could range from a transfer of the fee simple to mere monetary compensation. The courts seem to be aware of the danger of uncertainty, as was indicated by Browne-Wilkinson J in *Re Sharpe*.[471] Having held that the claimant was entitled to occupy the property until the loan was repaid, he noted:

---

[463] See Chapter 9.   [464] (1883–84) LR 9 App Cas 699, at 714.   [465] [1976] Ch 179, at 189.
[466] [1980] 1 WLR 1306, at 1312.   [467] (1977) 248 *Estates Gazette* 947.
[468] See also *Williams v Staite* [1979] Ch 291, at 298, where Goff LJ said: 'In the normal type of case...whether there is an equity and its extent will depend...simply upon the initial conduct said to give rise to the equity, although the court may have to decide how, having regard to supervening circumstances, the equity can best be satisfied.'   [469] [1988] 2 NZLR 424.
[470] See *Cowcher v Cowcher* [1972] 1 WLR 425, at 430, where Bagnall J said: '[justice] flows from the application of sure and settled principle for proved or admitted facts'; *Taylor v Dickens* [1998] 1 FLR 806; [1998] Conv 210 (Thompson).   [471] [1980] 1 WLR 219.

I reach this conclusion with some hesitation since I find the present state of the law very confused and difficult to fit in with established equitable principles. I express the hope that in the near future the whole question can receive full consideration in the Court of Appeal, so that, in order to do justice to the many thousands of people who never come into court at all but who wish to know with certainty what their proprietary rights are, the extent to which these irrevocable licences bind third parties may be defined with certainty. Doing justice to the litigant who actually appears in the court by the invention of new principles of law ought not to involve injustice to the other persons who are not litigants before the court but whose rights are fundamentally affected by the new principles.[472]

Such fears of uncertainty also led the Court of Appeal to reject a purely discretionary approach in *Jennings v Rice*.[473] While it was accepted that equity acts flexibly to do justice by preventing unconscionability, Robert Walker LJ rejected any notion of an unfettered discretion:

> It cannot be doubted that in this as in every other area of the law, the court must take a principled approach, and cannot exercise a completely unfettered discretion according to the individual judge's notion of what is fair in any particular case.

(viii) *Proportionality between the remedy and the detriment*

It has now been recognized that it is a false dichotomy to set the two views explained above against each other as if only one were correct.[474] In *Jennings v Rice*[475] the Court of Appeal has confirmed that elements of both are discernible in the decided cases, so that although the courts articulate a flexibility to determine the appropriate remedy to satisfy an estoppel equity, they do so in a circumspect way that takes account of the claimant's expectations. Robert Walker LJ stated the underlying principle as follows:

> once the elements of proprietary estoppel are established an equity arises. The value of that equity will depend upon all the circumstances including the expectation and the detriment. The task of the court is to do justice. The most essential requirement is that there must be proportionality between the expectation and the detriment.[476]

In applying this underlying principle he drew a distinction between a situation where the assurance and reliance related to specific property and had a consensual character falling not far short of an enforceable contract,[477] and a situation where the claimant's expectation was more uncertain and did not focus on any specific property. In cases falling within the first category, he considered that the court should act to fulfil the expectation of the claimant, on the grounds that the 'consensual element of what has happened suggests that the claimant and the benefactor probably regarded the expected benefit and the accepted detriment as being (in a general, imprecise way) equivalent, or at any rate not obviously disproportionate'.[478] He suggested that the situation where an elderly benefactor reaches a clear understanding with the claimant that, if the claimant

---

[472] [1980] 1 WLR 219, at 226.   [473] [2003] 1 P & CR 8.

[474] See Bright and McFarlane 'Proprietary Estoppel and Property Rights' [2005] 64 CLJ 449.

[475] [2003] 1 P & CR 8.   [476] [2003] 1 P & CR 8, at [36].

[477] As, for example, in *Yaxley v Gotts* [2000] Ch 162.   [478] [2003] 1 P & CR 8, at [45].

resides with and cares for the benefactor, the claimant will inherit the benefactor's house, was a typical case where the expectations should be fulfilled. However, in cases falling within the second category, where the expectations are uncertain and do not relate to specific property, he considered that the claimant's expectations should be regarded as 'no more than a starting point' for the determination of the remedy:

> But if the claimant's expectations are uncertain, or extravagant, or out of all proportion to the detriment which the claimant has suffered, the court can and should recognise that the claimant's equity should be satisfied in another (and generally more limited) way.[479]

In such cases the court must exercise 'a wide judicial discretion'[480] to determine the appropriate remedy. While the claimant's expectations remain relevant, the court must also consider the detriment suffered and exercise its discretion so as to ensure that a disproportionate remedy is not awarded. While unwilling to provide a comprehensive enumeration of the factors relevant to the exercise of the court's discretion, Robert Walker LJ did indicate a number of factors which should be taken into account: the misconduct of the claimant; particularly oppressive conduct on the part of the defendant; the court's recognition that it cannot compel people who have fallen out to live peaceably together; alterations in the benefactor's assets and circumstances; the likely effects of taxation; and (to a limited degree) the other claims (legal or moral) on the benefactor or his or her estate.[481]

Having established the appropriate principles, the Court of Appeal concluded that the first instance judge had exercised his discretion correctly in awarding the claimant £200,000 rather than ownership of the benefactor's house and its furniture. He had been unaware of the extent of her wealth, the actual value of her estate was out of all proportion to what he might reasonably have charged for the services he had provided free, and the nature of the house was such that it was unsuitable for him to reside in on his own.

(ix) Confirmation of the intermediate approach

Other cases also illustrate that the court neither possesses an unbridled discretion, nor determines remedies on a purely mechanistic formula. In *Burrows and Burrows v Sharp*[482] an equity was established when the plaintiff and her family moved in with her grandmother. The relationship broke down and it fell to the court to determine how the equity should be satisfied. The judge at first instance had held that the plaintiff was entitled to continue to reside in the house. The Court of Appeal held that this was unworkable, and instead ordered that the grandmother make financial compensation for the expenditure the plaintiff had incurred. In discussing the appropriate remedy, Dillon LJ emphasized that the court 'had a discretion as to how the equity should be satisfied',[483] and that the appropriate remedy 'had to be decided in the light of the circumstances at the date of the hearing, taking into account, if appropriate, the conduct of the parties up to that date'. As a prime principle he held that it was often appropriate to satisfy the equity by granting the claimant the interest he was intended to have.

---

[479] [2003] 1 P & CR 8, at [50].   [480] [2003] 1 P & CR 8, at [51].   [481] [2003] 1 P & CR 8, at [51].
[482] [1991] Fam Law 67.   [483] Citing *Griffiths v Williams* (1977) 248 *Estates Gazette* 947, CA.

This emphasizes that the claimant's 'reasonable expectation' is the key factor which circumscribes the court's discretion. However, he admitted that in some cases it was not practicable for the court to order that the intention be fulfilled and that in such cases the court must do the best it could. This might mean that 'the way in which an equity should be satisfied might take a wholly different form from what had been intended when the parties were on good terms'. Along with the nature of the claimant's expectations, other factors which should be taken into account in determining the remedy include: the extent of reliance; the relative wealth of the parties; the existence of children; and inequitable conduct by either party.[484]

A similar approach was taken by the Court of Appeal in *Gillett v Holt*.[485] Having concluded that an estoppel equity was established, Robert Walker LJ stated that the 'court must decide what is the most appropriate form for the relief to take'.[486] While this might suggest a broad discretion, he proceeded to undertake a two-stage process to determine appropriate relief. First he identified the extent of the owner's property in respect of which the equity was established. This, it appears, was determined by the expectations that had been generated by the assurances given, namely, Holt's farming business. However, having established the maximum extent of the equity he held that the court should determine the 'minimum required to satisfy it and do justice between the parties'.[487] Thus the court does not possess an unbridled discretion, but is required to exercise its discretion to determine an appropriate remedy within the limits of the expectations that have been created by the assurances. In exercising its discretion to determine the minimum required he held that the court should look at all the circumstances, including the need to achieve a 'clean break' between the parties and to avoid or minimize future friction. Another good example is *Parker v Parker*,[488] where the court had to consider the right of Lord Macclesfield to live in Shirburn Castle. There had been a representation by the company owning the castle that it would negotiate and agree terms for Lord Macclesfield's occupation of the castle, in reliance on which Lord Macclesfield gave up the tenancy of a farm. By the time of the action, relationships between the parties had broken down to such an extent that the court felt ordering them to live together would have been inadvisable. Instead, they held that Lord Macclesfield was entitled to occupation until given at least two years' notice to quit, to allow his Lordship the time necessary, from the evidence, to catalogue and remove his chattels and find alternative accommodation.

There can still be difficulties in this approach. In *Suggitt v Suggitt*,[489] Arden LJ supported as not disproportionate the findings of a trial judge to award property a farm and farmhouse worth some £3.3m on the basis of questionable detrimental reliance of some work done on the farm, 'for lower wages than he might have expected had he been an agricultural worker'.[490] In Arden LJ's view this was compliant with the minimum equity to do justice between the parties:

---

[484] Thompson 'Estoppel and Clean Hands' [1986] Conv 406.   [485] [2000] 2 All ER 289.
[486] [2000] 2 All ER 289, at 311.   [487] [2000] 2 All ER 289, at 312.   [488] [2003] EWHC 1846.
[489] [2012] EWCA Civ 1140.   [490] [2012] EWCA Civ 1140, at [22].

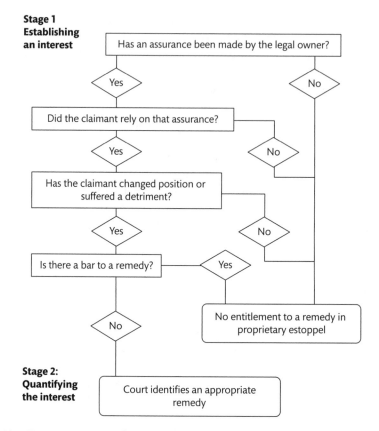

Figure 10.5 Proprietary estoppel

Since the promise was that [the claimant] should have the farmland unconditionally, I do not consider that to grant him the farmland…could be said to be out of all proportion.[491]

(4) **Bars to a remedy**

It follows from the fact that proprietary estoppel is an equitable remedy, based on the conscience of the parties, that there must be no bar in any given case to the claimant seeking to rely on an estoppel to found an interest (see Figure 10.5).

Hence, the claimant must 'come with clean hands', so that if the original representation was procured through any falsehood on the part of the claimant, no claim to an interest by estoppel will be supported by the courts. Similarly, unreasonable delay in bringing an action under estoppel may bar a claim to a remedy.[492]

---

[491] [2012] EWCA Civ 1140, at [45].
[492] See, eg, *Voyce v Voyce* (1991) 62 P & CR 290, where, on the facts, there was no unreasonable delay.

11

Charities

Charity has a legal meaning, well beyond the everyday concept of helping the underprivileged in society. Trusts set up for recognized charitable purposes and other legally recognized forms of charities receive financial benefits from the state in the form of tax exemptions, and also legal advantages over trusts set up for private beneficiaries. The restrictions of charity law mean that many activities that the public may consider 'charitable' are not so in law, but are instead carried out by non-charitable voluntary organizations. Charities do not have named beneficiaries, so the law is enforced by the Attorney-General and the Charity Commission on behalf of the public. Charities must demonstrate that they carry out their activities for the benefit of the public at large. This chapter considers the nature and benefits of an organization gaining charitable status, as well as an in-depth look at the legal requirements to be granted charitable status.

Schemes for dealing with surplus property for charities are detailed in Chapter 18, and specific restrictions on charity trustees in the discharge of their duties, particularly in relation to investment, and the regulation of charitable activity by the Charity Commission, are considered in the relevant chapters of Part VII of this book.

1 Introduction

The majority of trusts and equitable mechanisms examined so far are used by owners to allocate their property to individuals, whether by mechanisms which allocate fixed shares, or those which grant others the discretion how the property should be allocated. Owners do not always wish to dispose of their property to individuals, but may also wish to give to purposes that they consider worthy, whether to their church, their school parent-teachers' association, the local animal refuge, an appeal following a major disaster, or to a political party which they support. In Chapter 7 it has already been seen that, except for some anomalous exceptions, gifts for purposes will fail by virtue of the 'beneficiary principle'. The most significant exception to this is the area of charitable trusts, where the law upholds and encourages giving to purposes that are regarded in law as charitable. Some, but not all, of the purposes outlined above would be considered to be charitable.

(1) **The social context of charitable giving**

The significance of charity to society is self-evident, but the extent and value of charitable activity is worth noting. There is a point at which many people have real, if unknowing, contact with the law of trusts, whether they are putting a small donation into collection boxes or envelopes, putting something into a collection at church, signing a Gift Aid declaration on admission to zoological gardens or National Trust properties, contributing regularly through payroll giving schemes, or responding to major disaster appeals. A high proportion of total charity funds are held by a small number of very large charities, such as the Wellcome Trust (the UK's largest charity), which has investments of £13bn and spends £600m each year on scientific research. At the other end of the scale there are a large number of charities with very small funds, or even no investments at all. By the end of March 2008, there were over 190,000 registered charities,[1] with an annual income of over £48bn. In the year 2012–2013 the Charity Commission registered 4,714 new charities, and a slightly smaller number were removed from the register.[2] The largest single category of new registrations related to education and training.

(2) **Mechanisms for charitable giving**

Owners of property may decide to apply it for the furtherance of charitable purposes in a variety of ways.

(a) **Outright gifts to charitable organizations**

An owner may make a gift to an organization which enjoys charitable status, whether an unincorporated association, or a charitable corporation. Charitable corporations may be established by Royal Charter (as is the case with many of the older universities); as a company limited by guarantee; by virtue of specific legislation (as is the case with Further Education Corporations); or, following the Charities Act 2006 (consolidated in the Charities Act 2011 Part 11), as a charitable incorporated organization registered as such by the Charity Commission.[3] The organization will receive the property, and apply it to its charitable purposes. A gift to Cancer Research UK, Oxfam GB (both companies limited by guarantee), or to a particular educational establishment would be such a gift.

(b) **Trusts in favour of defined charitable objects**

Alternatively, an owner may transfer property to trustees to be used for specified charitable purposes. In such a case the trustees will be subject to a duty to apply the funds

---

[1] Charity Commission Annual Report 2008–2009.
[2] Charity Commission Annual Report 2012–2013.
[3] The operation, regulation, and potential benefits of the CIO are beyond the scope of this text, but in essence the structure seeks to provide the advantages of a corporate structure (including limited liability) without the burden of regulation under company law.

to those purposes only. A gift by will to trustees to be applied for the education of the testator's poor relations would be an example.

(c) Discretionary trusts in favour of charitable objects

An owner may alternatively transfer the property to trustees granting them the discretion as to the charitable purposes to which the fund may be applied. This may be a wide discretion, for example a gift of '£100,000 to trustees to be applied to such charities as they see fit', or the owner may place limits on the width of the discretion, for example 'for such educational charities as they see fit'.

(d) All charitable institutions are treated similarly

Whether a charity exists as an incorporated or unincorporated body, or as a trust, it is governed by essentially similar rules.[4]

(3) **The unity of charity**

Although there are numerous charitable organizations, and distinct charitable purposes covering wide ranges of human activity, in some senses the law regards all property dedicated to charity as comprising a single fund, a 'common pot'. This is evident in the way that a gift 'to charity' will be upheld, despite the absence of any indication of the giver's intention as to how it should be used. In such circumstances, the Crown disposes of the property to charitable purposes by sign manual. Similarly, if a charity fails, or a charitable purpose comes to an end, any property dedicated to that charity or purpose will be applied to other similar charitable purposes under the principle of cy-près.[5] The property, once dedicated to charity, is seen as placed into the 'common pot', and cannot be removed from it, but will be applied to other purposes. Hence, it is not possible for an organization that has become a charity to voluntarily cease operating as a charity, taking with it its assets, as the property is held for charitable purposes.

(4) **Regulation and control of charities**

Given both the quantity of money concerned and the dangers of abuse and misuse,[6] the area of charities is regulated by the government. The Attorney-General enforces charitable trusts in the name of the Crown, but they are regulated and overseen by the Charity Commission,[7] which plays the predominant role in the supervision and regulation of charities. This regulation and supervision will be examined in Chapter 28. The law concerning the regulation of charities was consolidated and amended by the

---

[4] This chapter is concerned with charitable trusts, though many of the rules also apply to charitable corporations. Charitable companies are also subject to the rules of company law, which means that they are subject to two regulatory regimes. [5] Discussed in Chapter 18.

[6] See, for example, the case of the Hospital Fund, where some £2.7m of the charity's funds were stolen by the chief fundraiser, reported by the Charity Commissioners in their Report for 1992, paras 91–96.

[7] Prior to the Charities Act 2006 that constituted the Charity Commission as an incorporated body, the functions of the Commission were vested in the Charity Commissioners.

Charities Act 1993, further amended by the Charities Act 2006, and in turn consolidated in the Charities Act 2011. Regulation also provides an important public validation of charitable organizations, and a safeguard for those contributing to worthy causes. Thus, it is said that 'trust is the voluntary sector exchange rate',[8] so that an effective charity 'is accountable to the public and other stakeholders in a way that is transparent and understandable'.[9]

Most charities are required to be registered,[10] and the Charity Commission also undertakes the process of registration and the maintenance of the register.

(5) Charities and the Third Sector

Charities form a very significant part of a wider Third Sector,[11] which includes 'not for profit', voluntary and community sector, social enterprise, and mutual societies or organizations, cooperatives, and non-governmental organizations all working independently of direct governmental direction. Charities, as part of the Third Sector, are an essential component of social provision,[12] as they encourage and create 'new services … [plug] gaps in delivery … and often focus on meeting the needs of the disadvantaged and socially excluded'.[13] The current welfare system in Britain, which includes the National Health Service and free school education for all, developed as a state system following the example of charitable organizations working in these fields in the nineteenth century.[14]

The success of charitable organizations in carrying out their purposes has led to a view that charities (and other voluntary organizations) should be utilized in providing front-line public services, such as social housing, rather than the traditional view of charities as providing additional or complementary services to those for which the state has responsibility. This initiative, originally referred to as 'the Third Way' and now as the 'Big Society',[15] seeks to make charities enablers and providers of public services organization. In an important registration decision[16] the Charity Commission decided that charities should be free to undertake public services of whatever nature, provided the normal characteristics of a charity are present and that the charity remains independent.

---

[8] NCVO, 'Blurred vision' in *Research Quarterly Issue* 1, January 1998.

[9] Charity Commission, CC10, *The Hallmarks of an Effective Charity* (July 2008), p 11.

[10] Each registered charity is given a unique registration number. The register is open to public inspection, and is now computerized.

[11] The other two sectors are referred to as the private sector and public sector.

[12] See HM Treasury, *Exploring the Third Sector In Public Service Delivery and Reform: A Discussion Document* (2005), Chapter 1.

[13] FCO, 'Implementing the Cross Cutting Review on "The Role of the Voluntary and Community Sector in Service Delivery"' (2004).

[14] See Jones, *History of the Law of Charity* (1969); Weiner (1978) 12 *Journal of Social History* 314.

[15] Cabinet Office, *Building The Big Society* (May 2010); Holt 'The Big Idea' (2011) Solicitor's Journal, Charity & Appeals Supplement, February.

[16] Charity Commission, Decisions of the Charity Commission for England and Wales, Applications for Registration (i) Trafford Community Leisure Trust; and (ii) Wigan Leisure and Culture Trust, April 2004.

However, the desirability of this sort of initiative has been questioned, both in terms of the charity sector's capacity to do what is asked of it[17] against a backdrop of huge public service cuts and at a more theoretical level.[18]

(6) **Negative perceptions of charity**

While the social importance of charities is self-evident and recognized by equity in allowing trusts for a charitable purpose, the concept of 'charity' is not without difficulty in modern times. Few, if any, beneficiaries of charitable endeavours would like to be referred to as 'objects of charity', as there are evident negative connotations in that status. Similarly, research undertaken for the Charity Commission suggests that a significant proportion of the public are not inclined to donate funds, property, or time to charities.[19] The reasons provided include negative attitudes towards the helping of others; fears that charities might be used to facilitate money-laundering, the concern that charitable organizations are using intrusive fundraising methods;[20] the use of for-profit enterprises in the collection of donations; distrust of the ways in which some charitable organizations carry out their functions; and a view that charities should not be using public money to pay for a service that the public purse was already financing, as there was a duty on the government to provide the service directly through public sector organizations. There is also a widely held view that there are too many charities.[21]

Nevertheless, while donations to charity are no longer exclusively motivated by altruism,[22] and the nature of the sector has undoubtedly altered significantly since the Victorian era of philanthropy, the continued importance of charities cannot be denied. The Charities Act 2006, now consolidated in the 2011 Act, which brought some significant changes to the regulation of charities and to the promotion of the work that they do, seeks to address some of the more negative aspects of the charity 'brand'.[23]

---

[17] See Morris 'Charities and the Big Society: A Doomed Coalition?" [2012] Legal Studies 132; and in a narrower context of social housing, Barr, 'The Big Society and Social Housing: Never the Twain Shall Meet?' in Hopkins (ed), *Modern Studies in Property Law: Volume 7*, (2013), Chapter 3.

[18] See Glover-Thomas and Barr 'Enabling or Disabling? Increasing Involvement of Charities in Social Housing' [2009] Conv 209.

[19] Charity Commission, *Charity Commission Study into Public Trust and Confidence in Charities* (2008).

[20] A finding reiterated in subsequent surveys. See Ipsos Mori, *Public Trust and Confidence in Charities* (2012), p 34.

[21] MORI/Charity Commission, *The Work of the Charity Commission. A Survey of Public Attitudes and Knowledge* (1999); (58 per cent of those surveyed thought that there were too many charities); see also [2001–2002] Ch Com Rep, at 21. Buzzacott and Third Sector, *Major Issues Facing Charities in 2000* (75 per cent of businesses responding felt that charities with similar purposes should merge). Warburton and Barr 'Charity Mergers—Property Problems' [2002] Conv 531.

[22] See Warburton, 'Trusts: Still Going Strong 400 Years after the Statute of Charitable Uses' in Hayton (ed), *Extending The Boundaries of Trusts and Similarly Ring-Fenced Funds* (2002).

[23] The Act is concerned with the modernization of both the regulatory framework for charities and, to a lesser extent, the rationalization of the legal principles underpinning charity law. The Act has a chequered history, explored further later, but in essence it arose following a process of review undertaken by the Charity Commissioners and, more significantly, a report of the Cabinet Office Strategy Unit, *Private Action, Public Benefit, A Review of Charities and the Wider Not-For-Profit Sector* (2002). Challenges to the charity brand are considered alongside regulation of charities in Chapter 26.

(7) **Charities, the Charity Commission and the law**

It has been noted that the Charity Commission, as well as acting as regulator of the charity sector, also maintains the register of charities. This means that it is the Charity Commission that decides whether an organization can be registered as charitable. It is important to recognize, however, that the Charity Commission does not make the law. In deciding whether an organization can be registered as a charity, the Commission is bound by the case law and must apply the law as set down by the courts, and its decisions are open to appeal to the First Tier Tribunal (Charity) and from there to the Upper Tribunal and to the Court of Appeal. It is vital to appreciate that although the Charity Commission does interpret and apply the law on an everyday basis, it is not empowered to change the law, and its application of the law may be tested in the legal system. However, the Charity Commission does not simply 'rubber-stamp' every application that comes its way; there is a great deal of interpretation required to match the legal principles to the facts, not least because there are gaps and ambiguities in the legal framework. Indeed, the Charity Commissioners have developed the law by analogy to existing charitable purposes, a role explored in detail later in the chapter. Moreover, many decisions as to registration will not be appealed, so that the decision of the Charity Commission in effect decides the issue of charitable status for many applicants. Reasons for not appealing a decision may include the cost in time and money of mounting such an action, so that important issues of charitable status may not always reach the legal system. For example, the Charity Commission extended the range of religions that it would accept as charitable long before the issue was addressed by the law courts.

Similarly, when the Charity Commission publishes guidance on legal matters, such as the requirements of registration for a charity and public benefit, such guidance does not have the force of law, and cannot change or depart from existing case law or statutory enactments on the relevant issues.[24]

2 **Privileges enjoyed by charitable trusts**

Charities and charitable trusts are granted various privileges that are not enjoyed by other private trusts. In *Dingle v Turner*,[25] Lord Cross observed that the privileges enjoyed by charitable trusts were of 'two quite different sorts', namely privileges as to their essential validity, and financial privileges through exemption from some forms of taxation. Underlying this privileged status of charitable trusts is public policy, which seeks to encourage benevolent giving to purposes that are in the public interest.

---

[24] See *Catholic Care v Charity Commission* [2010] EWHC 520 (Ch), at [68].   [25] [1972] AC 601.

(1) Privileges as to essential validity

Charitable trusts enjoy exemption from various requirements that would render a non-charitable trust invalid.

(a) Purpose trusts

It is a trite proposition that private non-charitable trusts must be for the benefit of persons and not purposes.[26] Charitable trusts are thus the major exception to this 'beneficiary principle'. However, since a mechanism for the enforcement of charitable trusts is provided by the state, the chief objection to purpose trusts (that there is nobody in whose favour the court can decree performance of the trust)[27] does not apply. Charitable trusts are enforced by the Charity Commission or by the Attorney-General in the name of the Crown.

(b) Certainty of objects

While non-charitable trusts must have objects that are certain, gifts made exclusively for charitable purposes are valid even though the exact purposes have not been identified with certainty. Thus, a gift to trustees 'for charity' will be valid. This follows from the fact that the law regards 'charity' as if it were a single common pot, and since the gift was certainly intended for that common pot, it will be upheld. If the exact charitable purposes to which the owner of the property intends to give are uncertain, the Charity Commission[28] and the court have jurisdiction to draw up a scheme to apply the funds.

(c) Perpetuity

Charitable trusts are valid even though they may last for an indefinite period of time. They are exempt from the rule against inalienability, by which trusts requiring capital to be retained for a period longer than the perpetuity period of a life in being plus twenty-one years are invalid. However, the rule against remoteness of vesting applies to gifts to charities as to other gifts. This rule requires that all property given to the trust must vest during the perpetuity period of 125 years laid down by the Perpetuities and Accumulations Act 2009. Under the previous law there was an exception where there is a gift over from one charity to another charity. The gift to the second charity will be valid even though it takes place outside of the perpetuity period. The exception was used in *Re Tyler*[29] to give effect indirectly to a non-charitable purpose. Sir James Tyler left £42,000 of stock to the London Missionary Society, with the condition that they were to maintain his family vault. If the condition was broken, there was a gift over in favour of the Blue Coat School. The gift over did not render the gift void for perpetuity, even though it could conceivably have vested outside of the perpetuity

---

[26] There are a small number of anomalous exceptions.
[27] *Morice v Bishop of Durham* (1804) 9 Ves 399.   [28] Charities Act 2011, Part 6.
[29] [1891] 3 Ch 252, CA.

period. Although the London Missionary Society could not be compelled to maintain the vault, they would have had a strong financial incentive to do so.

(2) Financial privileges

Charities and charitable trusts enjoy tremendous financial advantages over private trusts. It is difficult to be certain of the precise value of these privileges, but the Inland Revenue estimated that in the year 2007–2008, the value of tax relief for charities was around £2.19bn.[30] This is likely to be a conservative estimate, and does not include the value of tax advantages (excluding Gift Aid) that are provided to donors to promote donation to charity, either corporate or as private individuals.[31] Charities are exempt from tax on income and capital gains from most sources, and may be exempt from tax on certain trading activities, such as running a charity shop.[32] Gifts to charities are exempt from inheritance tax.[33] Charities also benefit from Gift Aid donations, whereby the charity can reclaim the basic rate of tax on the gift.[34] There is an 80 per cent exemption from non-domestic rates on properties they occupy.[35] Charities are not exempt from VAT. These financial privileges amount to a massive state subsidy of charitable trusts. Some charities may even enjoy exceptional financial privileges. For example, in *Scott v National Trust*[36] Robert Walker J observed that the trust, which was established by statute, is a charity 'whose special place in the affairs of the nation has been recognized by tax exemptions and reliefs (especially in connection with capital taxation) going well beyond those accorded to charities generally'.[37]

(3) Assessment of the privileges enjoyed by charities

It is clear that charitable trusts enjoy tremendous advantages over non-charitable trusts through their enjoyment of these privileges. The justification for such advantageous treatment is that charitable purposes are of sufficient importance to the community at large that they deserve both to be upheld and encouraged. It is for this reason that the definition of charity focuses on the notion of 'public benefit', for only

---

[30] HMRC, *Annual Report Tables & Statistics 2007–2008*, Table 10.2.

[31] These include, for private individuals, employer payroll deduction schemes, whereby employees can obtain tax relief for donations to charity deducted from their wages (see Income Tax (Earning and Pensions) Act 2003, ss 713–715). Corporate donations may be deductible from taxable profits for the purposes of corporation tax, for example, through Gift Aid (Income and Corporations Tax Act 1988, s 339).

[32] See HMRC guidance note at www.hmrc.gov.uk/charities/guidance-notes/annex1/annex_i.htm.

[33] Inheritance Tax Act 1984, ss 23 and 76.

[34] See Income Tax Act 2007, ss 413–430 and 520–522 (individuals); Corporation Tax Act 2010 ss 191–202 (corporations). The gift aid rules were exploited to generate large gains for both a charity and the donors in the Cup Trust case *Mountstar (Plc) Ltd v Charity Commission for England and Wales*, First-tier Tribunal (General Regulatory Chamber), 17 October 2013. See Keylock, 'A Question of Confidence' (2014) 153 TEL & TJ 8–11.

[35] Local Government Finance Act 1988, s 43(5); under s 47 the rating authority has discretion to relieve up to the whole amount payable.   [36] [1998] 2 All ER 705.

[37] [1998] 2 All ER 705, at 710.

those purposes that can be said to be of benefit to the public as a whole can be considered worthy of such special treatment. However, it is questionable whether all charities and charitable trusts need be treated alike. At the moment, every charitable trust enjoys not only the privileges as to essential validity, but also the financial privileges. There is no necessary reason why every charitable trust should automatically enjoy the financial privileges, a conclusion that Lord Cross described in *Dingle v Turner*[38] as 'unfortunate'. Obviously, all must receive the privileges as to validity; otherwise, most would fail under the beneficiary principle. The proposal that only some charities should enjoy financial privileges was made by the Radcliffe Commission in 1956[39] and, as many charities begin to act more like companies, operating in a commercial manner, running what are often multimillion pound trading operations, it is perhaps time that the question of universal financial privilege was re-examined. The financial privileges available to public schools such as Eton and Harrow are a particularly contentious issue, and were the subject of extensive debate in the progress of the Charities Act 2006 through Parliament.

It is also an open question whether the availability of financial privilege is a factor to be taken into account when the court is considering if a trust is charitable. In *Dingle v Turner*[40] Lord Cross took the view that, in considering whether a trust was for the benefit of the 'public', regard should be had to the availability of fiscal privileges. However, the other four members of the House expressed doubts as to its relevance. The issue is not resolved by the Charities Act 2011.

3 Defining charitable trusts

(1) When is a trust charitable?

For a trust to be charitable in law, it must be of a charitable character. In other words, it must be for a purpose that is considered in law to be prima facie charitable. The purposes considered to be charitable are all purposes that in a general sense can be considered to be beneficial. In addition to this requirement, the particular application contained in the trust must be for the public benefit. The rationale is that even if a purpose can be considered in a general sense to be beneficial, it should only secure the privileges of charitable status if benefits are conferred upon the public, rather than being confined to a small group of private individuals. Finally, if it is possible for funds to be applied in ways that are not considered to be charitable, this will prevent the whole trust from being considered to be charitable, even if parts, taken alone, could have been held charitable. This is often referred to as the requirement that the organization's activities must be 'exclusively charitable'.

---

[38] [1972] AC 601, HL.
[39] *Royal Commission on Taxation of Profits and Income* (1955) Cmd 9474, ch 7.
[40] [1972] AC 601, HL.

(2) **Statutory definition of 'charity'**

The Charities Act 2006, introduced the first statutory definition of charity (apart from the descriptive list contained in the Statute of Charitable Uses 1601). Until then the meaning of 'charity' as a legal concept was determined by reference to judicial precedents.

The statutory definition of charity is now contained in ss 1 to 5 of the Charities Act 2011.

Section 1 of the Charities Act 2011 states that, '"charity" means an institution which…is established for charitable purposes only…'. Section 2 in turn says that a charitable purpose is one which is described in s 3 and is for the public benefit. Section 3 then sets out a list of charitable purposes. The definition essentially consolidates the previous law by reclassifying existing recognized purposes with almost no change. It preserves the flexibility that was a fundamental feature of the previous categorization of charitable purposes. The main drawback with the list is that, because it incorporates a reference to the old law, it is necessary to have regard to most of the case law prior to its enactment.

(a) **Relevance of previous law**

The Charities Act 2011, s 3 provides a list of purposes which are prima facie considered to be charitable, but then states that any purposes which do not fall within the specific categories in the list shall be recognized as charitable if they are 'recognised as "charitable purposes" under the old law', meaning 'the law relating to charities in England and Wales as in force immediately before 1 April 2008', the date on which the Charities Act 2006 came into force.[41] The statutory definition therefore adds to rather than replaces existing law.

(b) **List is not closed**

The Charities Act retains the dynamism of the previous concept of charitable purposes. The old law recognized the possibility of development by analogy or because of changes in society and public attitudes. For example, in *Scottish Burial Reform and Cremation Society v Glasgow City Corpn*[42] a trust to promote cremation as a method of disposal of the dead was held charitable by the House of Lords, as it was analogous to earlier cases in which it had been held that trusts for the maintenance of graveyards were charitable. Development was possible even where previous case law suggested that a purpose would not, in the past, have been considered to be charitable. For instance in *Funnell v Stewart*[43] Hazel Williamson QC held that faith healing had 'become a recognised activity of public benefit' so as to be charitable, even though an earlier decision had held that a trust to promote faith healing was non-charitable.[44] Preservation of this ability to develop charitable purposes is essential, as, in the words

---

[41] Charities Act 2006, s 2(2)(m) and s 2(4).   [42] [1968] AC 138.
[43] [1996] 1 WLR 288.   [44] *Re Hummeltenberg* [1923] 1 Ch 237.

of Viscount Simonds in *IRC v Baddeley*, 'there is no limit to the number and diversity of the ways in which man will seek to benefit his fellow man'.[45]

The concept of development by analogy (and by analogy upon analogy) is recognized by s 3(1)(m) of the Charities Act 2011. The extraordinary effect of the statutory definition is therefore that it retains all the elements of the previous law. The only change effected by the statutory definition is that the list of purposes which it contains can be changed only by legislation: under the previous law it was possible for a purpose which was once considered to be charitable to cease to be charitable because of changing social conditions. As Lord Wilberforce observed in *Scottish Burial Reform and Cremation Society v Glasgow City Corpn*,[46] 'the law of charity is a moving subject' which evolves over time. This was also recognized by Lord Simmonds in *National Anti-Vivisection Society v IRC*,[47] where a society which promoted the suppression of vivisection was held not to be charitable, as the court found that the advantages of reduced cruelty to animals were outweighed by the detriments to medical research that would be caused if the purpose was accomplished. He said that:

> A purpose regarded in one age as charitable may in another be regarded differently ... I conceive that an anti-vivisection society might at different times be differently regarded.

This flexibility to take into account changes in society and in public attitudes by restricting the range of charitable purposes can now only be exercised by legislative change or through the application of the public benefit requirement.

(3) The categories of charitable purpose

Prior to the Charities Act 2006, there were three sources from which the categories of charitable trust were drawn: a long-repealed ancient Act of Parliament which contained a descriptive list; the decisions of the courts, which were categorized into four groups by a leading nineteenth-century judgment; and the determinations of the Charity Commissioners. These original sources can still be discerned in the list provided by the new law.

(a) The Charitable Uses Act 1601

The Charitable Uses Act 1601[48] did not set out to define charity, but rather, to correct abuses in the administration of charitable trusts. However, the preamble to the Act contained a list of the objects that the law regarded as charitable in 1601, which became a guide to which the courts referred to determine whether purposes were charitable. Although the preamble was repealed in 1960,[49] it has continued to provide guidance in defining charity until the changes made by the Charities Act 2006 as consolidated in the 2011 Act.

---

[45] [1955] AC 572.   [46] [1968] AC 138.   [47] [1948] AC 31, HL.   [48] 43 Eliz, c 4.
[49] Charities Act 1960, s 38(1).

(b) *Income Tax Special Purposes Comrs v Pemsel*

In *Income Tax Special Purposes Comrs v Pemsel*,[50] Lord Macnaghten provided an organizing classification of charitable purposes. He identified four 'heads' of charity:

> Charity in its legal sense comprises four principal divisions; trusts for the relief of poverty; trusts for the advancement of education; trusts for the advancement of religion; and trusts for other purposes beneficial to the community, not falling under any of the preceding heads.

This classification was not an exhaustive definition of the law of charity, but a convenient grouping of the cases into areas of benefit that the law regards as charitable, with the exception of the fourth division which is obviously a 'catch-all' category. The categories themselves did not provide the answers as to whether a particular purpose was indeed charitable. In *Scottish Burial Reform and Cremation v Glasgow City Corpn* Lord Wilberforce gave three cautions about its use:

> first that, since it is a classification of convenience, there may well be purposes which do not fit neatly into one or other of the headings; secondly, that the words used must not be given the force of a statute to be construed; and thirdly, that the law of charity is a moving subject which may well have evolved even since 1891.[51]

The Macnaghten classification may still be relevant in relation to the operation of the public benefit requirement.

(c) The role of the Charity Commission in defining 'charity'

The Charity Commission plays an increasingly important role in shaping the development of the definition of charitable purposes. The Commission has the legal obligation to keep a register of institutions that are charitable.[52] The Commission has the power to recognize a new purpose as charitable in circumstances where it believes that the courts of law would do so, and it therefore has in practice (even if not in law) similar powers as a court to take into account changing social and economic circumstances in determining whether an organization is charitable or not. The Commission has recognized a number of new charitable purposes (such as the promotion of urban and rural regeneration in areas of social and economic deprivation and the conservation of the environment) that have now been included in the list contained in the Charities Act 2006. The Commission has also decided that some previously charitable purposes should lose their charitable status. For example, civilian rifle and pistol clubs had historically enjoyed charitable status on the grounds that they promoted the defence of the realm by encouraging skill in shooting. However, in 1993 the Commission decided that gun clubs could no longer be regarded as a reserve for the armed forces.

---

[50] [1891] AC 531. See Mummery '*The Commissioners for Special Purposes of Income Tax v Pemsel*' (2013) 16 CLPR 1.   [51] [1968] AC 138, at 223.

[52] Charities Act 1993, s 3. Under s 4(1) of the Act, the register is deemed conclusive of the charitable nature of an organization. Certain charities are not required to be registered. These include exempt charities (see s 3A(2)(a) and Sch 2) who are organizations that are subject to another form of regulatory or supervisory control, eg universities, national galleries, and museums. Small charities, defined by having a total income of less than £5,000 a year, are also not required to register (s 3A(2)(d)) but may choose to do so. See further Lloyd, *Charities—The New Law 2006: A Practical Guide To The Charities Acts* (2007), Ch 3.

The role of the Commission in determining whether a purpose is charitable confers on it the ability to develop the law, subject to the possibility of its decisions being challenged through the tribunal system and ultimately the courts. For instance, using reasoning by analogy, the Commissioners decided in 2003–2004 that the promotion of restorative justice was charitable. The Commissioners concluded that 'the promotion of restorative justice was analogous to the charitable purposes of the preservation of public order and the prevention of breaches of the peace, the protection of life and property and the promotion of the sound administration of the law, and as such was for the public benefit'.[53] The Commission has been prepared to make decisions in some potentially contentious areas. For instance, it registered religious charities that do not involve belief in a deity, before there was judicial (and now legislative[54]) recognition that this was possible, and even though belief in a deity had been stated as a requirement in the previous case law. While it can be argued that the authority given to the Charity Commission does not enable it to change the law since any guidance issued or decisions made on registration only have effect unless and until they are tested in the courts, it is nevertheless the case that many registration decisions will not be appealed immediately or at all.[55] In consequence, there is little choice for organizations seeking registration other than to follow existing Commission decisions in contentious areas.

(4) **The new list of charitable purposes**

The list is essentially an extended formulation of the classification provided by Lord Macnaghten, even to the extent of including the first three substantive categories, and after an additional group of substantive categories, a 'catch-all' category. This catch-all category includes any other purposes currently considered to be charitable, but which are not included in the previous paragraphs, as well as any other purposes which could on the basis of analogy (and by analogy from analogy) be considered to be charitable. The new list, like Lord Macnaghten's, is no more than a classification. However, being statutory, it is an authoritative classification. Like Lord Macnaghten's list, it does not follow automatically that a trust is charitable because it falls within the list. The test of public benefit still has to be satisfied.

The list of charitable purposes is set out in s 3 of the Charities Act 2011 as follows:

"(a) the prevention or relief of poverty;

(b) the advancement of education;

(c) the advancement of religion;

(d) the advancement of health or the saving of lives;

(e) the advancement of citizenship or community development;

---

[53] *Annual Report of the Charity Commissioners for England and Wales 2003–2004*, p 11.

[54] Charities Act 2011, s 3(2).

[55] Before the introduction of the Tribunal service, any appeal on a registration decision had to be taken to the High Court, with the attendant expense. It should come as no surprise that appeals were few and far between, particularly as organizations seeking charitable status were unlikely to have the will or resources to mount such an appeal.

(f) the advancement of the arts, culture, heritage or science;

(g) the advancement of amateur sport;

(h) the advancement of human rights, conflict resolution or reconciliation or the pro-
     motion of religious or racial harmony or equality and diversity;

(i) the advancement of environmental protection or improvement;

(j) the relief of those in need because of youth, age, ill-health, disability, financial
     hardship or other disadvantage;

(k) the advancement of animal welfare;

(l) the promotion of the efficiency of the armed forces of the Crown or of the effi-
     ciency of the police, fire and rescue services or ambulance services;

(m) any other purposes [recognized under the old law, or development by analogy
     from it, or recognized as recreational trusts under s 5 of the Act].

The list relies heavily upon existing case law. The Act states that where the list contains
a term which 'has a particular meaning under the law relating to charities in England
and Wales, the term is to be taken as having the same meaning where it appears in that
provision'.[56] Even where this is not the case, previous case law is a guide to the scope
and effect of some of the categories. In one of the first reported cases involving the Act,
a case involving an animal welfare charity, Lewison J observed that 'I do not regard
this as amounting to any change in the substance of the law.'[57] If this view is taken by
other judges, then the list of charitable purposes in the Act may have had no more
impact than to have provided a useful categorization.

   In considering the categories, for convenience, each will be taken separately.

4 Charitable purposes

(1) Trusts for the prevention or relief of poverty

The first general head of charitable purposes identified by Lord Macnaghten and
repeated in the list in the Charities Act 2011 was that of the 'relief of poverty', a
description now extended to include the prevention of. In a social era when there was
no welfare state and little other state provision for those at the bottom of society, it was
obviously 'beneficial' for private individuals to provide for them. Thus, the law has
always regarded the relief of poverty as a charitable purpose to be encouraged.

   The preamble to the Statute of Charitable Uses 1601 referred to the relief of poverty
in a wider context, including the 'relief of aged, impotent [ie infirm or disabled] and
poor people'. As a result, trusts dealing with the relief of problems arising from age or
infirmity were recognized as charitable. Trusts for these purposes are now covered by
separate categories in the statutory list.

---

[56] Charities Act 2011, s 2(3).
[57] *Hanchett-Stamford v Attorney-General* [2009] Ch 173, at [14] and [23].

(a) The meaning of 'poor'

Poverty is not defined or explained in the Charities Act 2011. Case law prior to 2006 indicated that it is a relative concept, and that what a society regards as 'poor' will vary with changes in social circumstance and what is regarded as a 'normal' level of income and ownership of consumer products. 'Charity law treats poverty as a relative, rather than an absolute, concept.

A good starting point in understanding the charity law meaning of poverty is *Re Coulthurst*,[58] where Sir Raymond Evershed MR made clear that in this context 'poverty' is not synonymous with destitution:

> It is quite clearly established that poverty does not mean destitution; it is a word of wide and somewhat indefinite import; it may not unfairly be paraphrased for present purposes as meaning persons who have to 'go short' in the ordinary sense of that term, due regard being had to their status in life.

This means that poverty is not to be understood as something experienced only by those at the very bottom of society, and the concept of 'going short'[59] will mean different things to people at different social levels. Those who are middle-class yet have fallen on hard times may well fall within this understanding of poverty, since they 'go short' compared to their social peers, although there may be others with similar financial circumstances who are not regarded as poor, because in the light of their social and economic background they do not 'go short'. Thus, gifts in favour of 'distressed gentlefolk'[60] or persons of 'moderate means'[61] have been held to fall within this understanding of 'poor'. In *Re De Carteret*[62] the Bishop of Jamaica left property on trust to pay an annuity of £40 per annum to widows and spinsters in England whose income was between £80 and £120. Although this excluded widows with an income lower than £80, who seem to be poorer in an absolute sense, the gift was upheld as a valid charitable gift for the relief of poverty. Maugham J expressed some hesitation at this conclusion, and emphasized that the gift expressed the Bishop's preference that the annuities be paid to widows who had children dependent upon them. In contrast, in *Re Gwyon*[63] a gift for the provision of clothing for children was held not charitable since the terms of the gift did not exclude children who were from affluent backgrounds. In *Re Segelman (Decd)*,[64] Chadwick J held that the beneficiaries of a trust had been selected on the basis of potential 'poverty' where they were presently 'comfortably off—in the sense that they are able to meet their day-to-day expenses out of income—but not affluent', but where they might need financial help in the future:

> Like many others in similar circumstances, they need a helping hand from time to time in order to overcome an unforeseen crisis: the failure of a business venture, urgent repairs to a dwelling house or expenses brought on by reason of failing health.[65]

---

[58] [1951] Ch 661, CA.

[59] This term was approved by Lightman J in *IRC v Oldham Training and Enterprise Council* [1996] STC 1218, at 1233.   [60] *Re Young* [1951] Ch 344.

[61] *Re Clarke* [1923] 2 Ch 407.   [62] [1933] Ch 103.   [63] [1930] 1 Ch 255.

[64] [1995] 3 All ER 676.   [65] [1995] 3 All ER 676, at 690.

He further considered that minors who became students would be likely to experience 'relative poverty' when their income from grants or parental resources fails to cover their expenditure on 'their actual or perceived needs'.[66] One of the issues in *Cawdron v Merchant Taylors' School*[67] was whether a trust was for the relief of poverty. Funds were available to pay for the education of sons of Old Merchant Taylors (a public school which charges substantial fees) who had been killed or injured in the First World War and to provide assistance to the dependent relatives of such killed or injured Merchant Taylors. Blackburne J held that (even though those eligible were likely to have relatively privileged backgrounds), the references to assistance and dependency showed that relief could only be given to those who were in financial need, or in other words those who would otherwise 'go short'.[68]

In *Re Sanders' Will Trusts*[69] money was given to provide dwellings for 'the working classes and their families'. Harman J held this was not charitable, since the term 'the working classes' did not indicate poor persons. In *Re Niyazi's Will Trusts*[70] Megarry V-C held charitable a gift of £15,000 for the construction of a 'working men's hostel' in Cyprus. He distinguished *Re Sanders' Will Trusts* on the basis that 'hostel' meant modest, temporary accommodation for those with a relatively low income, whereas 'dwellings' were ordinary houses which may be inhabited by the well-to-do as much as the relatively poor. In *IRC v Oldham Training and Enterprise Council*, Lightman J held that a trust to help the unemployed would be a charitable trust for the relief of poverty:

> So far as the object...is to set up in trade or business the unemployed and enable them to stand on their own feet, that is charitable as a trust for the improvement of the conditions in life of those 'going short' in respect of employment and providing a fresh start in life for those in need of it.[71]

Two simple propositions can be drawn from the cases. First, that the legal concept of poverty is a relative one, and 'that poverty is to be judged in relation to whether a person is suffering hardship having regard to their social and economic position and other circumstances. Second, that to be a valid gift for the relief of poverty, the gift must be exclusively for the benefit of those who are experiencing hardship. If those who are not considered poor in this sense fall within the scope of the gift, then it will not be charitable.

In its guidance, the Charity Commission recognizes the contextual meaning of poverty. It gives some examples of what may constitute the relief of poverty: for instance where an elderly person who owns their own house has insufficient income to meet the costs of a heating bill during the winter; similarly a person who suffers financial hardship as a result of a redundancy, illness, accident or death in the family.[72]

---

[66] [1995] 3 All ER 676, at 690. Under the current student loan system and tuition fees system operating in the UK, which forces an undertaking of debt to pursue higher education study, students might find this a comforting concept.   [67] [2009] EWHC 1722 (Ch).

[68] [2009] EWHC 1722 (Ch), at para [33].   [69] [1954] Ch 265.

[70] [1978] 1 WLR 910.   [71] [1996] STC 1218, at 1233.

[72] CC4, *Charities for the Relief of the Poor* (2008) section C1, p 8. This guidance is under review.

The guidance recognizes that poverty is not confined to the destitute and that 'people may qualify for assistance from a poverty charity whether or not they are eligible for state benefits'.[73] In previous guidance, the Commission had warned that charity resources should not be used simply to replace state benefits, as this would not make the recipients any better off.[74] This is not repeated in the current guidance, but would seem to be a sensible interpretation of the law.

(b) The meaning of 'relief' or 'prevention'

Under the first category, a gift is not charitable merely because it is for the benefit of the poor. It must also relieve a need that they have as a result of their condition of poverty or must operate to prevent poverty. The concept of relief has been well explored in the courts, but the concept of prevention has been added by the Charities Act and has therefore not yet been tested. The requirement of relief is best explained in a wider context than that of the relief of poverty. In *Joseph Rowntree Memorial Trust Housing Association Ltd v A-G*[75] the housing association wished to build small dwellings for elderly people, who would be able to purchase them on long leases. The elderly would pay 70 per cent of the purchase price of the premises, with the remainder being paid by the housing association. To be charitable Peter Gibson J emphasized that:

> there must be a need which is to be relieved by the...gift, such need being attributable to the aged...condition of the person to be benefited.

Therefore, as counsel for the Attorney-General had argued, a gift for the 'aged millionaires of Mayfair' would not be charitable as it would not relieve a need that such millionaires experienced as aged people. The fact that the housing association was providing a specialist type of accommodation for the elderly meant that a need was being relieved and the purpose was charitable.[76]

The distinction between the relief and prevention of poverty has been considered by the Charity Commission in their current guidance, as follows:

> the prevention of poverty includes preventing those who are poor from becoming poorer, and preventing people who are not poor from becoming poor.[77]

Therefore, in the Commission's view, the relief and prevention of poverty are generally interchangeable terms, but, where a charity is set up purely for the prevention of poverty, it will 'tend to take a very specific approach to poverty, which usually involves tackling its root causes'.[78]

Examples of purposes for the prevention of poverty are thus providing money management training or services to someone at actual risk of being in poverty or at risk of

---

[73] CC4, *Charities for the Relief of the Poor* (2008) section C1, p 8.

[74] CC4, *Charities for the Relief of the Poor* (2001), para 1. See, generally, Dunn 'As "Cold as Charity"?: Poverty, Equity and the Charitable Trust' (2000) LS 222.   [75] [1983] Ch 159.

[76] See also the Garfield Poverty Trust, which provided interest-free loans to assist poor members of the Exclusive Brethren to purchase housing; Report of the Charity Commissioners for England and Wales 1990, para 13, App A.   [77] CC4, *Charities for the Relief of the Poor* (2008) section C1, p 8.

[78] CC4, *Charities for the Relief of the Poor* (2008) section C1, p 8.

becoming impoverished due to natural disaster or famine.[79] There would seem to be considerable sense in this approach, and it is unlikely that the courts would take issue with this guidance.

(2) Trusts for the advancement of education

(a) A broad concept of 'education'

Under the second head of the classification of charity, gifts for the advancement of education will be charitable. The preamble to the 1601 Act included the 'maintenance of schools of learning, free schools and scholars in the universities' and 'the education and preferment of orphans'. The law takes a wide view of what may be regarded as for the advancement of education, and education is not confined to teaching in schools and colleges. In *IRC v McMullen* Lord Hailsham spoke of the education of the young as:

> a balanced and systematic process of instruction, training and practice containing…both spiritual, moral, mental and physical elements.[80]

Education thus covers skills and understanding, as well as knowledge. This wide concept of education has been reflected in the cases that have held that not only gifts to advance academic study but also for research, culture, and sport may be charitable. The Charities Act 2011 contains separate heads that cover some of these areas.

(b) Teaching

The advancement of school and tertiary level teaching and of institutions that provide such teaching is clearly charitable. Charitable gifts have included: the founding of a professorial chair (*A-G v Margaret and Regius Professors in Cambridge*[81]); the endowments of schools and colleges (*A-G v Lady Downing*;[82] *Abbey Malvern Wells Ltd v Ministry of Local Government and Planning*;[83] and the payment of teachers and administrative staff of an institution (*Case of Christ's College Cambridge*).[84] In *Customs and Excise Comrs v Bell Concord Educational Trust Ltd*[85] it was held that trusts endowing fee-paying schools are charitable, provided that the school is non-profit making, or uses its profits for school purposes only. Purposes ancillary to teaching institutions may also be charitable, as for example in *A-G v Ross*,[86] where the students' union at a polytechnic was held charitable as it furthered the educational function of the institution.

---

[79] CC4, *Charities for the Relief of the Poor* (2008) section C1, p 8. Annex A, at p 20. Usefully, this Annex contains examples of charitable purposes that would be for the relief or prevention of poverty. Two Pennies (Worcester Cash Community Advice Support and Help) and Christians Against Poverty are examples of such charities.   [80] [1981] AC 1, HL.

[81] (1682) 1 Vern 55.   [82] (1766) Amb 550.   [83] [1951] Ch 728.

[84] (1757) 1 Wm Bl 90.   [85] [1990] 1 QB 1040, CA.   [86] [1986] 1 WLR 252.

(c) Industrial training and professional bodies

The advancement of industrial and technical training has also been held charitable (*Re Koettgen's Will Trusts*[87] and *Construction Industry Training Board v A-G*).[88] In *IRC v White*[89] an association with the purpose of encouraging craftsmanship and maintaining the standards of the modern and ancient crafts was held to be charitable. The Royal College of Surgeons, which exists to promote the study and practice of the art of surgery, has been held charitable,[90] as has the Royal College of Nursing, whose objects are the better education and training of nurses and to promote nursing as a profession.[91] In contrast, the General Nursing Council, which was established by statute to regulate the nursing profession, has been held not charitable[92] since its objects included the enhancement of the status of nurses, which is analogous to the objectives of trade unions to advance the interests of their members.

(d) Research

The advancement of education extends beyond mere teaching to include research activity.[93] But not all research will be charitable. The courts have sought to distinguish research which is of truly educational value and worthy of charitable status, from that which is not. Research that is of no educational value, or of purely esoteric value to the researcher, will not be charitable. The three criteria laid down by Slade J in *Re Besterman's Will Trusts*[94] summarize the present state of the law. For a trust for research to be charitable:

(1) the subject matter of the research must be a useful subject of study;

(2) the knowledge acquired by the research must be disseminated to others; and

(3) the trust must be for the benefit of the public, or a sufficiently important section of the public.

The case concerned a trust for research into the works of Voltaire and Rousseau, and since the three criteria were met it was held to be charitable. In the earlier case of *Re Shaw*,[95] Harman J had held that a gift by George Bernard Shaw in his will for research into a 40-letter alphabet, and translation of one of his plays into it, was not charitable. However, Harman J seems to have taken a very narrow view of education, stating that:

> if the object [of the research] be merely the increase of knowledge, that is not in itself a charitable object unless it be combined with teaching or education.[96]

---

[87] [1954] Ch 252.   [88] [1973] Ch 173, CA.   [89] [1980] TR 155.
[90] *Royal College of Surgeons of England v National Provincial Bank Ltd* [1952] AC 631, HL.
[91] *Royal College of Nursing v St Marylebone Corpn* [1959] 1 WLR 1077, CA.
[92] *General Nursing Council for England and Wales v St Marylebone Borough Council* [1959] AC 540, HL.
[93] The case law on this purpose now overlaps to some degree with the distinct purpose of the advancement of arts, culture, heritage, or science under the Charities Act 2011 s 3(1)(f).
[94] (1980) *The Times*, 21 January.   [95] [1957] 1 WLR 729.
[96] [1957] 1 WLR 729, at 737.

It is questionable whether the same result would have been reached under the principle applied in the later case of *Re Hopkins' Will Trusts*,[97] which concerned a gift to the Francis Bacon Society to be used to find manuscripts proving that the plays of Shakespeare were written by Francis Bacon. Holding the purpose charitable, Wilberforce J stated that the research 'must either be of educational value to the researcher or must be so directed as to lead to something which will pass into the store of educational material, so as to improve the sum of communicable knowledge in an area which education may cover'. This test has now evolved into the three criteria set out by Slade J in *Re Besterman's Will Trusts*.[98]

Propaganda—the promotion of a single view-point or a set of singular views—masquerading as research will not be charitable. The educational value of research comes from the presentation of a balanced argument, reaching conclusions through analysis of evidence and considering competing arguments. This does not mean that research cannot be value-driven, provided that it does not amount to campaigning for a particular view. Thus, in *Re Hopkinson*,[99] a proposed trust for educating adults in the views of a single political party was not held charitable.[100] The issue often overlaps with the promotion of political purposes or campaigning, which is discussed further later in the chapter.

In summary, it is essential that the subject of proposed research must be of some usefulness. This requires a value judgement on the part of the court or the Charity Commission. The results of the research must also enter the public domain, usually by publication, and if the information is kept purely for the benefit of the researcher alone it will not be charitable, as there is no advancement of education in non-disseminated work. Similarly, research carried out by companies and intended for their exclusive commercial use will not be charitable, as it is not publicly available. Nor will it be charitable for a university to conduct research on behalf of a corporation if the results of the research cannot enter the public domain. It is worth noting that the requirement of research being in the public domain in this context means that the research must be available to the public, not in the technical sense understood in copyright law of it being free of author's copyright.

(e) Advancement

It is clear from the preceeding discussion that, however broad a view is taken of what is understood as 'education', it will only be a charitable if the proposed charitable activities actually *advance* education. In the words of guidance issued by the Charity Commission this means 'to promote, sustain and increase' individual and collective knowledge and understanding of specific areas of study, skills and expertise.[101] The Commission also provides a list of example purposes that they would consider to be

---

[97] [1965] Ch 669.   [98] (1980) *The Times*, 21 January.   [99] [1949] 1 All ER 346.

[100] It is also possible to view the decision in *Re Shaw* [1957] 1 WLR 729 in this light, as the proposed bequest was for the promotion of George Bernard Shaw's alphabet, not really to research the benefits of the Shaw alphabet as compared to the existing Roman system.

[101] Charity Commission, *Advancement of Education for the Public Benefit* (December 2008), p 8.

charitable,[102] which draw upon the legal decisions reached in the previously discussed cases.

(3) **The advancement of religion**

Trusts for the advancement of religion fall into the third of Lord Macnaghten's categories that have been retained by the Charities Act 2011. The law assumes that any religious activity, provided it is carried on in the public domain,[103] is charitable. There is no need at this first stage of the test as to whether a purpose is charitable for the particular religion in issue to prove its value, or for the court to weigh the validity of its beliefs. This was emphasized by Lord Reid, who stated in *Gilmour v Coats*, that:

> A religion can be regarded as beneficial without it being necessary to assume that all its beliefs are true, and a religious service can be regarded as beneficial to all those who attend it without it being necessary to determine the spiritual efficacy of that service or to accept any particular belief about it.[104]

Thus, in *Funnell v Stewart*[105] a gift to further the work of a small group of faith healers was not denied charitable status merely because there was no evidence that anyone had ever been healed, as was argued by the testatrix's next of kin, who alleged that the bequest was invalid. Hazel Williamson QC upheld the argument of the Attorney-General that there was no need to prove public benefit, as it was presumed. Even a religious sect which holds beliefs which contain 'elements of detriment' can be charitable in law. The Charity Commission reported in January 2014 that, despite considerable controversy, and evidence which 'suggests that "there were elements of detriment and harm" associated with the doctrines and practices of the Plymouth Brethren Christian Church, especially its disciplinary practices, which include socially isolating members who have not complied with strict codes of behaviour', it had agreed to register the Preston Down Trust, which supported a Plymouth Brethren meeting hall.[106]

(a) **The meaning of 'religion'**

Although the position has now been changed, the courts originally defined religion so as to require belief in a divine being. Indeed, in *Bowman v Secular Society*[107] Lord Parker suggested that only monotheistic faiths would count as religions for the purposes of charity. It therefore follows that groups that merely promoted a moral lifestyle without a spiritual dimension would not be charitable for the advancement of religion. That seemed somewhat ironic given that the assumed benefit of religion is that citizens will adopt a more moral lifestyle as a result of their beliefs and not the essential validity

---

[102] Charity Commission, *Advancement of Education for the Public Benefit* (December 2008), Annex A, pp 23–24.　　　　　　　　　　　　　　　　　　　[103] See *Gilmour v Coats* [1949] AC 426.
[104] [1949] AC 426, at 862. See also: *Re Watson* [1973] 1 WLR 1472; *Funnell v Stewart* [1996] 1 WLR 288.
[105] [1996] 1 WLR 288.
[106] Charity Commission, news release, 9 January 2014. This case is further discussed in relation to public benefit, later in the chapter.　　　　　　　　　　　　　　　[107] [1917] AC 406, HL.

of the spiritual truths they profess. In *Re South Place Ethical Society*[108] Dillon J expressed the view that religion is 'concerned with man's relations with God' and therefore a society that had the purpose of promoting the 'study and dissemination of ethical principles' did not advance religion.[109]

The view that religion requires belief in a divine being would exclude the possibility of recognizing Buddhism as a religion.[110] Equally, if religion requires belief in a single god, then neither could Hinduism be recognized as a religion. This would be an odd conclusion in an open and liberal society in which differences are respected and cherished. It is therefore no surprise that the Charities Act 2011 states that:

'religion' includes—

    (i)   a religion which involves belief in more than one god, and

    (ii) a religion which does not involve belief in a god;[111]

This confirms the practice which the Charity Commission had already adopted of registering Hindu and Buddhist trusts,[112] although in many but by no means all cases the organizations included additional objects such as the advancement of education or the relief of poverty, and could therefore have been considered charities on that basis. It is worth noting that even in *Re South Place Ethical Society*,[113] although Dillon J considered that ethics did not constitute a religion, he considered that the South Place Ethical Society was a charity because the promotion of ethical values and philosophies are charitable as for the advancement of education.

The Charity Commission practice, if tested in the courts, would almost certainly have been approved even before the legislative change. For instance in *Varsani v Jesani*[114] the Court of Appeal had to adjudicate on how to deal with the property of a Hindu sect established to follow the teachings of Shree Swaminarayan Bhagwan, who was believed by adherents to have been the incarnation or manifestation of the Supreme Being. The sect had become irretrievably divided. The Court of Appeal had so little doubt that the sect, and both of the divisions which had emerged from it, were charitable that the question of whether Hinduism could be recognized as charitable did not even feature in debate.

In 1999 the Charity Commission rejected the application of the Church of Scientology for registration as a charity.[115] It held that a body would only be charitable for the advancement of religion if it engaged in the worship of a divine being.[116]

---

[108] [1980] 1 WLR 1565.

[109] Although it could be, and was, in this particular case, held to be charitable under Lord Macnaghten's fourth category of other purposes beneficial to the public.

[110] See the doubts expressed by Dillon J in *Re South Place Ethical Society* [1980] 1 WLR 1565.

[111] S 2(3)(a).

[112] See, for instance, *Gaudiya Mission v Brahmachary* [1997] EWCA Civ 2239; *Varsani v Jesani* [1998] EWCA Civ 630; *Muman v Nagasena* [1999] EWCA Civ 1742. A search of the register of charities discloses many more examples.   [113] [1980] 1 WLR 1565.

[114] [1999] 1 Ch 219.

[115] For interesting commentaries of the Charity Commission's decision from the perspective of human rights, see Quint and Spring 'Religion, *Charity Law* and Human Rights' (1999) *Charity Law and Practice Review* 153; Harding 'Trusts for Religious Purposes and the Question of Public Benefit' (2008) MLR 159.

[116] Decision of the Charity Commissioners for England and Wales made on 17 November 1999. See also *R v Registrar General, ex p Segerdal* [1970] 2 QB 697.

While it was accepted that the Church of Scientology believed in the existence of a divine being, its activities did not exhibit the defining characteristics of worship, namely, the 'reverence or veneration for that supreme being'. The activities of Scientology consisted of 'auditing', which was found to be very much akin to counselling, and 'training', which involved the detailed study of the works of L Ron Hubbard.[117]

In *R (on the application of Hodkin) v Registrar General of Births, Deaths and Marriages*[118] the Supreme Court held unanimously that a Church of Scientology chapel was 'a place of meeting for religious worship'. The decision arose in a different context from charity law, but will nevertheless be influential. The court considered that there has never been a universal legal definition of religion in English law, given the variety of world religions, changes in society, and the different legal contexts in which the issues arise. Belief in deity or a supreme being was not an essential requirement. Lord Toulson said that religion could be described in summary as:

> a spiritual or non-secular belief system, held by a group of adherents, which claims to explain mankind's place in the universe and relationship with the infinite, and to teach its adherents how they are to live their lives in conformity with the spiritual understanding associated with the belief system.[119]

He added that in his view 'spiritual or non-secular'

> means a belief system which goes beyond that which can be perceived by the senses or ascertained by the application of science…Such a belief system may or may not involve belief in a supreme being, but it does involve a belief that there is more to be understood about mankind's nature and relationship to the universe than can be gained from the senses or from science.

With this approach to religion, Scientology was clearly a religion for the purpose under consideration.[120] It does not follow that it will now similarly be recognized in charity law, because the test for charity requires a consideration of public benefit. However, the view of the Supreme Court is likely to have an impact on the approach of any court or of the Charity Commission should the question arise again. It is also relevant that Charity Commission guidance recognizes that worship is not an essential element in the recognition of a religion. It states that a religion which does not involve worship could be recognized where it instills a sense of 'connectedness' with the spiritual belief system or the force or power extending beyond the self, particularly where this 'might motivate or be expressed through the quality of life led by adherents, especially activity which involves helping others and inspiring others to do likewise'.[121] The Commission cite Jainism as an example, where there is no worship of a supreme

---

[117] See also O'Brien 'Rastafarianism as Religion' (2001) 252 NLJ 509.   [118] [2013] UKSC 77.

[119] [2013] UKSC 77 at [57].

[120] [2013] UKSC 77, at [60]. In Australia Scientology has been held to be a religion and entitled to charitable status and tax exemptions: *Church of the New Faith v Comr of Pay-Roll Tax* (1983) 49 ALR 65.

[121] Charity Commission, *The Advancement of Religion for the Public Benefit* (December 2008), Annex A, p 23.

being, but the teaching of a supreme being or entity serves to inspire followers to lead better lives.[122] This appears to be a correct view since public worship is just one way of demonstrating public engagement and benefit which lies at the foundation of the recognition of religion in charity law.

(b) Equal treatment of different religions

Given that the benefit the court assumes to derive from a trust for the advancement of religion is the benefit of an improved life through religious belief, it follows that the precise nature of the religious belief is not important, and the law does not discriminate between different faiths and traditions. This was expressed by Cross J in *Neville Estates Ltd v Madden*:

> as between different religions the law stands neutral, but it assumes that any religion is at least as likely to be better than none.

The promotion of the Christian religion in all its denominational forms is clearly charitable, and despite little authority it seems that the mainstream non-Christian religions will be treated similarly.[123] In contrast to their willingness to attempt to assess the value of research or supposed art, the courts have not in the past weighed the merits of religious belief. Thus, in *Re Watson*[124] a trust to promote the works of H G Hobbs, the leader of a small group of non-denominational Christians comprising only members of his family, was held charitable despite the unanimous conclusion of expert evidence that they were of no value.

If past authority is followed, it seems that sects and cults will be charitable provided that they are not destructive to the whole concept of religion or contrary to the foundations of society, no matter how obscure or foolish their beliefs. In *Thornton v Howe*[125] a trust to promote the publication of the works of Johanna Southcote, who claimed that she was the mother of the second messiah, was held charitable. The Unification Church (commonly known as the 'Moonies') has been registered as a charity.

(c) Purposes ancillary to religion

Purposes ancillary to the advancement of religion will also be charitable. The construction or maintenance[126] of religious buildings, and even the provision of bells,[127] have been held charitable. Provision for the benefit of religious ministers, retired missionaries,[128] and the church choir[129] have also been held charitable.

---

[122] Charity Commission, *The Advancement of Religion for the Public Benefit* (December 2008), Annex A, p 23.

[123] See the discussion earlier in relation to Buddhism and Hinduism. See *Straus v Goldsmid* (1837) 8 Sim 614; *Re Michel's Trust* (1860) 28 Beav 39; and *Neville Estates Ltd v Madden* [1962] Ch 832 for the promotion of Judaism. The Charity Commission has also registered organizations or trusts for the promotion of Islam.

[124] [1973] 1 WLR 1472.   [125] (1862) 31 Beav 125.

[126] *Re Hooper* [1932] 1 Ch 38—trust to upkeep a tablet and a window in a church.

[127] *Re Pardoe* [1906] 2 Ch 184.   [128] *Re Mylne* [1941] Ch 204.

[129] *Re Royce* [1940] Ch 514.

(d) Gifts to religious leaders

Gifts made to religious leaders in their capacity as such will be considered charitable gifts for the advancement of religion, provided that the gifts are exclusively for the spiritual work of the leader. In *Re Flinn*[130] a gift to the Archbishop of Westminster for 'such purposes as he shall in his absolute discretion think fit' was held charitable, as was a gift to the Bishop of the Windward Islands 'to be used by him as he thinks fit in his diocese'.[131] In *Farley v Westminster Bank*[132] a gift to a vicar for his 'work in the parish' was held charitable, but in *Re Simson*[133] a gift to a vicar for his 'parish work' was held not to be charitable, since as a matter of construction it was held that his 'parish work' may include work which was not exclusively charitable. This distinction is tenuous, if not spurious.

(e) Advancement, not merely belief

A purpose will not be charitable simply because it involves belief in a religion. It must be for the *advancement* of religion. In other words, the activities involved must in some way promote, maintain, or practise the religion or encourage or increase belief in the faith concerned.[134] In *United Grand Lodge of Ancient Free and Accepted Masons of England v Holborn Borough Council*,[135] freemasonry was held not to be charitable because it did not advance religion as such, but merely encouraged its members to lead a good moral life. Current examples of purposes that advance religion can be found in Annex B to the Charity Commission guidance, *The Advancement of Education for the Public Benefit*.[136]

(4) Advancement of health or the saving of lives

(a) Medical and healthcare charities

This is the first of the new categories of charitable purpose added by the Charities Act 2006. It does not represent an entirely new category, but simply a subdivision of what in Lord Macnaghten's classification would have been considered 'other purposes beneficial to the community'. The preamble to the Statute of Charitable Uses referred to the relief of the 'aged, impotent and poor'. The word 'impotent' in this context does not have its modern meaning relating to sexual function, but was used in a more general but now archaic sense to refer to incapacity, infirmity, or illness. In *Joseph Rowntree Memorial Trust Housing Association Ltd v A-G*,[137] it was held that the words of the preamble were to be read disjunctively. It has therefore been recognized for four centuries that the provision of medical care is a charitable purpose.[138] In *Re Smith's Will Trusts*[139]

---

[130] [1948] Ch 241.   [131] *Re Rumball* [1956] Ch 105.   [132] [1939] AC 430, HL.
[133] [1946] Ch 299.
[134] Charity Commission, *The Advancement of Religion for the Public Benefit* (December 2008), p 8.
[135] [1957] 1 WLR 1080.   [136] (2008, as amended December 2011), at pp 24–26.
[137] [1983] Ch 159.
[138] See more recently the Charity Commission publication CC6—*Charities for the Relief of Sickness* (2000).   [139] [1962] 2 All ER 563.

the Court of Appeal held that a gift to be applied to the benefit of such hospitals as the trustees in their absolute discretion thought fit was charitable. The court considered that the testator, who had made his will before the creation of the National Health Service, had meant hospitals dependent on voluntary contributions and not nursing homes run for private profit, which would not be charitable.[140] The provision of health-care is not confined to conventional treatment. In *Funnell v Stewart*[141] the court held that a trust to further the work of a group offering faith healing was charitable. The view of the Charity Commission is that the promotion of alternative and complemen-tary therapies can be charitable, but evidence is required of its efficacy:

> Assessing the efficacy of different therapies will depend upon what benefits are claimed for it (ie whether it is diagnostic, curative, therapeutic and/or palliative) and whether it is offered as a complement to conventional medicine or as an alternative. Each case is con-sidered on its merits, but the Report on complementary and alternative medicine provides a useful guide.[142]

It also seems clear that this category of charitable purpose extends beyond formal healthcare to include services to ease the suffering of the sick, disabled, or infirm.[143] A hospice providing palliative care for the terminally ill would therefore fall within this category.

(b) Imposition of fees or charges for treatment

Hospitals which charge fees for the treatment they provide can be charitable, even if as a result their services are only available to those who are capable of paying or have insurance.[144] In *Re Resch's Will Trusts*[145] a gift of $8m was made to the St Vincent's Private Hospital. The Privy Council held that this was a valid charitable gift, and that there was sufficient benefit to the community resulting from 'the beds and medical staff of the general hospital, the availability of a particular type of nursing and treatment which supplements that provided by the general hospital and the benefit to the standard of medical care in the general hospital which arises from the juxtaposition of the two institutions'.[146] It was emphasized that if the hospital was carried on as a commercial venture, with a view to making profits for individuals, then it would not be charitable.[147] This means that the majority of privately owned and run nursing homes and old people's homes will not be charitable. This is sen-sible, since profit-making ventures do not warrant the tax privileges granted to charities.

---

[140] [1962] 2 All ER 563., at 564, per Lord Denning MR.   [141] [1996] 1 WLR 288.

[142] Charity Commission Guidance on the advancement of health or the saving of lives. *The Report referred to is the* 6th Report of the House of Lords Report Select Committee on Science and Technology (Session 1999–2000).

[143] Charity Commission Guidance on the advancement of health or the saving of lives, at para 26. There is thus likely to be some overlap between this category and the relief of those in need in s 2(2)(j) of the Charities Act 2006.

[144] See also the discussion later in the chapter on the impact of fees upon public benefit.

[145] [1969] 1 AC 514.   [146] [1969] 1 AC 514, at 540, per Lord Wilberforce.

[147] [1969] 1 AC 514.

(c) Saving lives (and property)

Trusts for the protection of human life and property have been held to be charitable as falling within the 'spirit and intendment' of the preamble. For example, in *Re Wokingham Fire Brigade Trusts*[148] the provision of a voluntary fire brigade was held charitable. The Royal National Lifeboat Institution is also charitable.[149] Clearly, such services must not exist to make profits for individuals, which would rule out commercial organizations offering emergency services such as most (or all) motoring assistance agencies. The Charity Commission considers that a trust for the provision of emergency services or services assisting the emergency services, or for the provision of life-saving or self-defence classes, could be considered charitable purposes under this head.[150]

(d) Analogous and ancillary purposes

The Charities Act 2011 makes it clear that the advancement of health is to be given an expansive meaning. It states that it 'includes the prevention or relief of sickness, disease or human suffering'.[151] As with trusts for the advancement of education and religion, purposes ancillary to the provision of medical care are charitable, so in *Re Bernstein's Will Trusts*[152] a surgeon's gift of part of his residuary estate to provide extra comforts at Christmas for the nurses of a specified hospital was held charitable. In *London Hospital Medical College v IRC*[153] a students' union at a medical school was held charitable as being a practical necessity to the efficient functioning of the school. The Charity Commission has also decided that the General Medical Council should be registered as a charity on the grounds that it was established for the charitable propose of 'the protection, promotion and maintenance of the health and safety if the community' by ensuring proper standards in the practice of medicine.[154]

(5) Advancement of citizenship or community development

The Charity Commission considers that this head of charity covers a broad range of purposes 'directed towards support for social and community infrastructure which is focused on the community rather than the individual'.[155]

(a) Rural or urban regeneration

Section 3(2)(c) of the Charities Act 2011 states that this head of charitable purpose 'includes rural or urban regeneration'. This is a category of charity recognized by the Charity Commission[156] before the passing of the 2006 Act and is an area of activity on which the Commission has issued guidance.[157] In order to attain charitable status,

---

[148] [1951] Ch 373.   [149] *Re David* (1889) 43 Ch D 27.

[150] Charity Commission, *Commentary on the Descriptions of Charitable Purposes in the Charities Act 2006* (August 2009), para 28.   [151] S 3(2)(b).   [152] (1971) 115 Sol Jo 808.

[153] [1976] 1 WLR 613.   [154] Decision of the Charity Commissioners, 2 April 2001.

[155] Charity Commission, *Commentary on the Descriptions of Charitable Purposes in the Charities Act 2006* (August 2009), para 29.   [156] See *Charity Commission Annual Report 2003–2004*, p 8.

[157] RR2—*Promotion of Urban and Rural Regeneration* (1999)

an organization must seek to maintain or improve 'the physical, social and economic infrastructure' and assist people 'who are at a disadvantage because of their social and economic circumstances'. Such purposes might include: providing financial assistance to people who are poor; providing or improving housing standards; helping people find employment; providing education, training, and retraining; providing assistance to businesses, including land and buildings on favourable terms; providing and maintaining roads and transport; providing, maintaining, and improving recreational facilities; preserving historic buildings in the area; providing public amenities.[158]

(b) Promotion of community capacity building

The Charity Commission has decided that the promotion of community capacity building in relation to communities that are socially or economically disadvantaged should be recognized as charitable.[159] Community capacity building means 'developing the capacity and skills of the members of a community in such as way that they are better able to identify, and help meet, their needs and to participate more fully in society'.[160] This might involve: equipping people with skills and competencies; realizing existing skills and developing potential; promoting people's increased self-confidence; promoting people's ability to take responsibility for identifying and meeting their own, and other people's, needs; encouraging people to become involved in their community and wider society in a fuller way.[161]

(c) Civic responsibility and good citizenship[162]

Organizations such as the Guides and Scouts would be considered charitable under this category. Another example, reported by the Charity Commission in their Annual Report for 2004–2005 is 'Funky Dragon', the Welsh youth parliament.

(d) Promoting ethical standards in business and corporate responsibility

Despite the extensiveness of the list of charitable purposes set out in the Charities Act 2006, there are many examples of charitable activity that are hard to classify. For instance, even though there was no direct judicial authority, the Charity Commission has decided to recognize as charitable organizations which promote the incorporation of ethics into business practice, and which advise and protect vulnerable employees faced with ethical dilemmas in the course of their work. In the light of this, the Commission considered that the objects of the Centre of Corporate Accountability, which sought to promote safety by encouraging corporate accountability for breaches of health and safety laws, were capable of being charitable, although the organization itself was held not to be charitable because its objects were also political.[163]

---

[158] RR2—*Promotion of Urban and Rural Regeneration* (1999), para 7.
[159] RR5—*The Promotion of Community Capacity Building* (Nov 2000).
[160] RR5—*The Promotion of Community Capacity Building* (Nov 2000), para 7.
[161] RR5—*The Promotion of Community Capacity Building* (Nov 2000), para 13.
[162] The promotion of civic responsibility is specifically included within this head by the Charities Act 2011, s 3(2)(c)(ii).
[163] Decision of the Charity Commission for England and Wales, Application for Registration of the Centre for Corporate Accountability, 24 August 2001.

(e) Volunteering and the voluntary sector

Volunteering consists of engaging in action which is not compulsory, for which financial reward is not the primary motivation, and which benefits others or society.[164] According to the Home Office Citizenship Survey in 2003, more than 50 per cent of the adult population volunteers.[165] Volunteering makes a very substantial contribution to many areas of life, including culture and the arts, sport and recreation, conservation and regeneration, health and care, and politics. Some volunteering is done on an individual basis, but much operates through what is called the voluntary sector. The voluntary sector comprises organizations which are 'formally constituted, independent of government, self-governing, not profit distributing, primarily non-business and that benefit from voluntarism'.[166] These organizations are established for purposes that add value to the community. Some, but not all voluntary sector organizations are charitable. For instance, housing associations providing social housing for disadvantaged groups and community care associations providing care in the community for individuals with disabilities or mental health problems may be either charitable or non-charitable, depending upon their objects. Section 3(2)(c)(ii) of the Charities Act 2011 includes the promotion of volunteering and the voluntary sector in this head of charity.

(f) Promoting the efficiency of charities

Promoting the effectiveness or efficiency of charities is included in the list of charitable purposes under this head by s 3(2)(c)(ii)of the Charities Act 2011. While this is a slightly unusual categorization, there could be little doubt that trusts seeking to enhance the effectiveness of charities would be recognized as beneficial to the public, since they could only be encouraging the better performance of functions which have already been held, themselves, to be charitable.

(6) Advancement of the arts, culture, heritage, or science

(a) Art, culture, and education

Trusts which promote an appreciation of the arts and other cultural activities have long been held to be charitable. Prior to the re-categorization of charities by the Charities Act 2006, this was because such purposes were considered to be extensions of Lord Macnaghten's category of trusts for the advancement of education. A trust to promote the works of William Shakespeare has been held charitable,[167] as has a trust to hold exhibitions of Egyptian archaeological finds.[168] In *Royal Choral Society v IRC*[169] the

---

[164] See the definition contained in the United Nations Volunteers Report, prepared for the UN General Assembly Special Session on Social Development, Geneva, June 2004 and cited in the Russell Commission Report 2005, p 13. The Russell Commission was established in May 2004 by the then Home Secretary, David Blunkett, and the Chancellor of the Exchequer, Gordon Brown, to develop a new national framework for youth action and engagement. A new charity, 'V' (registered charity no: 1113255) was set up as a result in May 2006.   [165] Russell Commission Report 2005, p 19.

[166] RR13—*The Promotion of the Voluntary Sector for the Benefit of the Public* (September 2004), para 3.

[167] *Re Shakespeare Memorial Trust* [1923] 2 Ch 398.

[168] *Re British School of Egyptian Archaeology* [1954] 1 WLR 546.   [169] [1943] 2 All ER 101.

society, whose purposes were 'to form and maintain a choir in order to promote the practice and performance of choral works', was held charitable by the Court of Appeal. Lord Greene MR rejected the narrow view of education as teaching that had been proposed by counsel for the Inland Revenue, and stated that 'the education of artistic taste is one of the most important things in the development of a civilised human being'. This approach was followed in *Re Delius (Decd)*,[170] where Roxburgh J held charitable a trust to promote the music of the composer Frederick Delius. In *IRC v White*[171] the Clerkenwell Green Association of Craftsmen, which existed to further crafts and craftsmanship, was held charitable. Charitable purposes within this head can include societies supporting the arts, local or national history or archaeology, the establishment or support of museums, the preservation of ancient sites or buildings, or an individual monument.[172] Purposes that are too vague and uncertain will not be held charitable. So in *Associated Artists Ltd v IRC*[173] the promotion of 'artistic dramatic works' was not considered charitable.

(b) Monuments

A trust to erect a public statue of Earl Mountbatten of Burma was considered charitable by the Charity Commissioners.[174] The chief consideration was that the person to be commemorated could be said to be a figure of historical importance. The benefit of such a statue was that it would foster patriotism and good citizenship, and act as an incentive to heroic and noble deeds. Memorials to private individuals of no such historical importance will not be charitable.[175] The Charity Commission accepted in 2003 that an appeal to provide a new statue in Banbury to celebrate the nursery rhyme 'Ride a cock horse to Banbury Cross, to see a fine lady upon a white horse' was charitable on the grounds of a trust for the enhancement of a locality and raising artistic taste, even though it was not accepted that the associated activities proposed in the application for registration were of educational value.[176] It is suggested that this decision might now be explained as an example of the preservation of heritage,[177] as an activity 'concerned with preserving or maintaining a particular tradition where the benefit to the public in preserving it can be shown'.[178]

(c) A requirement of merit

Despite the desire to uphold gifts that genuinely advance artistic and cultural appreciation, the Charity Commission and the courts are astute to ensure that gifts that

---

[170] [1957] Ch 299.   [171] [1980] TR 155.

[172] See Charity Commission, *Commentary on the Descriptions of Charitable Purposes in the Charities Act 2006* (August 2009), para 35.   [173] [1956] 1 WLR 752.

[174] Report of the Charity Commissioners for England and Wales 1981, paras 68–70.

[175] See *Re Endacott* [1960] Ch 232, CA.

[176] *Re The Fine Lady Upon A White Horse Appeal* [2006] WTLR 59.

[177] See Charity Commission RR9, *Preservation and Conservation* (February 2001).

[178] Charity Commission, *Commentary on the Descriptions of Charitable Purposes in the Charities Act 2006* (August 2009), para 33.

promote purposes of no artistic merit are not held charitable. The very nature of art makes it difficult for the courts to exercise objective judgments as to what is artistically valuable, and what is not. One man's masterpiece is another man's rubbish. In *Re Delius*[179] it was suggested that the subjective nature of such a judgment would mean that the court would have no option but to hold charitable a trust to promote the work of even an inadequate composer. On the facts, the issue did not arise because the high standard of Delius's work was not challenged. However, it is now clear that the court will take expert advice as to the value of work of supposed artistic merit, and if the expert advice is unanimous that it is of no value, then the courts will not find that there is a charity for the advancement of education.[180] In *Re Pinion (Decd)*[181] Harry Pinion had been a prolific collector of paintings, furniture, china, glass, and other objets d'art. On his death he left his residuary estate to trustees to open his studio as a museum housing the collection. Expert witnesses considered the merits of the collection, and were unanimous in their conclusion that it was of no value. Indeed, one expert expressed his surprise that such a voracious collector had not even managed to pick up a single meritorious piece by accident. In the light of this evidence the Court of Appeal held that the trust was not charitable. Harman LJ concluded 'I can conceive of no useful object to be served in foisting upon the public this mass of junk.'

(d) Can the vernacular and the popular have merit?

There is an increasing interest in the study of the vernacular, and of the need to preserve historical evidence of the way of life of ordinary people in the past. The National Trust, for instance, has preserved an ordinary terraced house in the North of England, using it to reflect a comparatively recently bygone way of life.[182] Industrial and folk museums have developed substantially over recent decades. No doubt all of these could be considered charitable, even though they reflect 'ordinary' rather than 'high' culture. What the courts have yet to address specifically, however, is whether the promotion and assistance of popular culture and music can be charitable. Why should promoting opera, choral music, and the works of Delius be considered charitable if promoting the musical compositions of the Beatles or Lady GaGa is not? Are the only values that the law should uphold as charitable those which are held by the elite and not those held by the masses? The courts have not yet made this clear, nor can anything be inferred from Charity Commission guidance on the issue, which simply refers to 'the arts of drama, ballet, music, singing, literature, sculpture, painting, cinema, mime, etc.'.[183]

---

[179] [1957] Ch 299.

[180] This is reflected in the Charity Commission's review of the register, which sets out the selection requirements of such experts—Charity Commission, RR10 *Museums and Art Galleries* (August 2002), paras A12–A17. [181] [1965] Ch 85.

[182] 20 Forthlin Road, Liverpool (Paul McCartney's former council house home) has been opened to the public by the National Trust.

[183] See Charity Commission, *Commentary on the Descriptions of Charitable Purposes in the Charities Act 2006* (August 2009), para 35.

(7) Advancement of amateur sport

(a) Promotion of sport per se

It was originally considered that trusts encouraging the playing of sport would not in themselves be considered charitable. The leading case was *Re Nottage*,[184] in which it was held that establishing a prize for ocean yacht racing was not charitable. There had to be some factor other than the playing of sport that justified a conclusion that the purpose was charitable. For instance, in an era when archers formed an essential part of the armed forces, a trust to promote archery practice would have been considered charitable since it helped to promote the defence of the realm by providing a cadre of skilled archers.

(b) Sport and the advancement of education

A line of authority supported the view that the promotion of sport in schools and universities would be regarded as for the advancement of education, since, as Lord Hailsham indicated in *IRC v McMullen*,[185] education includes 'spiritual, moral, mental and physical elements'. In *Re Mariette*[186] a gift to provide fives and squash courts at a specific school was held charitable. In *IRC v McMullen*[187] the Football Association had established a trust for the promotion of football and other games or sports in schools and universities. This was held charitable for the advancement of education by the House of Lords, even though the gift was not for the benefit of any specific institution. The promotion of intellectually stimulating games was also held to be charitable, and in *Re Dupree's Deed Trusts*[188] the gift of a prize for chess to boys and young men resident in Portsmouth was held charitable. In contrast, in 1989 the Charity Commissioners refused charitable status to the Birchfield Harriers, a leading athletic club, on the basis that there was an insufficient element of education in their activities.[189]

(c) Sport, health, and community interest

In November 2002 the Charity Commissioners decided that Community Amateur Sports Clubs (CASCs) should be recognized as charitable:

> As part of our *Review of the Register* project, we have looked at the relationship between sport and charity in the light of modern social conditions. We have taken account of the enormous public interest in sport as a means of promoting health and the vital role that sport plays in improving the health of the nation. We have concluded that, within the law as it stands, we can properly recognise as charitable bodies that set out to encourage community participation in healthy sports.[190]

---

[184] [1895] 2 Ch 649, CA. It may be wondered whether the nature of the sport was relevant. Ocean yacht racing has sometimes been described as being as pleasurable as standing under a cold shower tearing up £50 notes. However, cases subsequent to *Re Nottage* have held that even sports of the common man, such as athletics and football, are not charitable.   [185] [1981] AC 1, HL.
[186] [1915] 2 Ch 284.   [187] [1981] AC 1.   [188] [1945] Ch 16.
[189] Report of the Charity Commissioners for England and Wales 1989, para 52.
[190] RR11—*Charitable Status and Sport* (April 2003), para 5.

By the date of the Charity Commission's *Annual Report for 2003–2004*, 120 CASCs had been registered.[191] It was this development that formed the basis for the head of promotion of amateur sport contained in the Charities Acts 2006 and 2011.

(d) Healthy recreation

The Charity Commission view was that 'it is the close and obvious connection between physical exercise and physical health that makes the provision of facilities for healthy recreation charitable'.[192] The test that the Charity Commission applied was that:

> Sports that are capable of providing 'healthy recreation' are those sports which, if practised with reasonable frequency, will tend to make the participant healthier, that is, fitter and less susceptible to disease. Fitness includes elements of stamina, strength and suppleness (there may be others), but it will be enough if a sport contributes to just one of these elements.[193]

(e) Statutory extension of the promotion of sport

The Charities Act 2011 extends the category of sporting activity that can be held to be charitable. By s 3(1)(g) the promotion of amateur sport is a charitable purpose. Only sports that involve 'physical or mental skill and exertion' are charitable under this head.[194] This reflects the similar restriction that the Charity Commission applied to the recognition of Community Amateur Sports Clubs. It is unlikely that promoting the playing of darts or snooker would be considered to be charitable under this head. More difficulty might be experienced with a game such as croquet, where the extent of exertion required is modest. A bridge club has been held charitable: even though this card game involves minimal physical skill, it presents considerable mental challenge.[195]

(f) Not all amateur sports clubs are charitable

It does not follow that because it is possible for an amateur sports club to be charitable that all clubs will satisfy the requirements to be charitable. This might be because benefits are confined to a small, private, group of members, as may be the case with some golf clubs. It might be because the sport does not satisfy the test of promoting health or involving physical exertion and skill. It might be because the sport is insufficiently inclusive. For instance, ocean yacht racing has been described as a sport for those who enjoy tearing up £50 notes while standing under a cold shower. It is an expensive sport that is generally confined to people with significant means,. Without evidence that people from all levels of society, perhaps through sponsorship, have the potential to participate, it is likely that a trust to provide an annual prize for ocean yacht racing would still not be considered to be charitable.[196] Polo and motor racing may also be

---

[191] *Charity Commission Annual Report for 2003–2004*, p 5.
[192] RR11—*Charitable Status and Sport* (April 2003), para 8.
[193] RR11—*Charitable Status and Sport* (April 2003), paras 8 and 9.
[194] Charities Act 2011, s 3(2)(d)).
[195] See Charity Commission Registration decision for Hitchin Bridge Club.
[196] See *Re Nottage* (discussed earlier).

considered to be 'elite' sports which fail to satisfy the test of public benefit, unless a trust to promote these sports includes measures which enable participation by people who, without the support offered by the trust, could not afford to acquire the expensive equipment needed.[197] The Charity Commissioners refused charitable status to the Birchfield Harriers, a leading athletics club, since they existed to promote competitive sport, rather than to provide sporting facilities to the public.[198] Certain amateur sports clubs can register with HM Customs & Revenue as a Community Amateur Sports Club (CASC) in order to gain tax-exempt status, but it is not possible following the Charities Act 2011 for a club to be both registered in this way and to be a registered charity, even if the club was established for charitable purposes.[199]

(8) **Advancement of human rights, conflict resolution, and equality**

(a) **A broad category**

This new head of charity contained in the Charities Act 2011 has the longest description. It comprises 'the advancement of human rights, conflict resolution or reconciliation or the promotion of religious or racial harmony or equality and diversity'. This is a category of charitable purpose that, perhaps more than any other, reflects changes in society and social attitudes. The category is clearly of considerable scope.

(b) **Advancement of human rights**

The advancement of human rights is now seen as being charitable by analogy with other charitable purposes,[200] a position confirmed by the Charities Act 2011. The Charity Commission has provided detailed guidance on the recognition of human rights charities, and revised this guidance following the recommendation of the Prime Minister's Strategy Unit in *Private Action, Public Benefit*[201] that the Commission should take a more positive approach to campaigning by charities. The problem is that the promotion of human rights may often require advocating a change in the law, and advocating such a change has been held to be a political purpose that cannot therefore be charitable.[202] By adopting a less cautionary view of what is permissible in relation to political campaigning, the Charity Commission has enabled human rights charities to be registered, even if seeking to influence government policy or to change the law may be activities that the charity will undertake. The Commission has provided what it considers a model set of objects for a human rights charity.[203] This sets out a range of

---

[197] RR11—*Charitable Status and Sport* (April 2003), para 26.
[198] *Report of the Charity Commissioners for England and Wales 1989*, para 54.
[199] Charities Act 2011, s 6.
[200] RR12—*The Promotion of Human Rights* (January 2005), para 8: 'Given that respect for human rights is widely regarded as a moral imperative, the well-established charitable purpose of promoting the moral or spiritual welfare and improvement of the community provides a sufficient (but not the only) analogy for treating the promotion of human rights generally as charitable.'   [201] September 2002.
[202] Charities and political purposes are considered further below, at pp 621–627.
[203] Charity Commission RR12—*The Promotion of Human Rights* (January 2005), para 37. This is supplemented by *Commentary on the Descriptions of Purposes under the Charities Act 2006* (August 2009), paras 39–42.

ways in which human rights can be promoted without engaging in political activity, and then adds that

> In furtherance of that object but not otherwise, the trustees shall have power to engage in political activity provided that the trustees are satisfied that the proposed activities will further the purposes of the charity to an extent justified by the resources committed and the activity is not the dominant means by which the charity carries out its objects.

(c) Advancement of conflict resolution or reconciliation

This description would include a trust seeking to resolve national or international conflicts, and also a trust promoting restorative justice 'where all the parties with a stake in a particular conflict or offence come together to resolve collectively how to deal with its aftermath and its implications for the future'.[204]

(d) The promotion of religious or racial harmony or equality and diversity

The Charity Commission has indicated that this head will include a broad range of charitable activities, including enabling people to understand the religious beliefs of others, promoting equality and diversity by eliminating discrimination on the grounds of age, sex, or sexual orientation, as well as the promotion of good relations between different groups.[205]

The promotion of equality between men and women was held charitable in *Halpin v Steear*.[206] The promotion of good community relations has more recently come to be recognized as a charitable purpose, demonstrating that the law of charity is able to develop to meet the social needs of the day, and to reflect the current moral agenda.[207] In *Re Strakosch (Decd)*[208] a gift to be used to appease racial feeling between the Dutch- and English-speaking sections of the South African community was held not to be charitable on the basis that it was a political purpose, too vague, and might include very wide objects, some of which would not be charitable. It had at one time been thought that this decision rendered the promotion of racial harmony a non-charitable object. However, even before the statutory provision, the Charity Commissioners took the view that the promotion of racial harmony and endeavouring to eliminate race discrimination is analogous to other purposes that the courts have held charitable and are therefore charitable purposes.[209] The promotion of religious harmony was accepted as charitable by the Charity Commission in 2002 when it registered The Friends of Three Faiths Forum, an organization intended to promote religious harmony by enabling people of one faith to understand the religious beliefs of others. The three faiths concerned were Christianity, Judaism, and Islam. The Commissioners

---

[204] Charity Commission, *Commentary on the Descriptions of Charitable Purposes in the Charities Act 2006* (August 2009), para 40. The promotion of restorative justice was recognized as a charitable purpose by the Charity Commission in 2003: *Charity Commission Annual Report 2003–2004*, p 11.

[205] Charity Commission, *Commentary on the Descriptions of Charitable Purposes in the Charities Act 2006* (August 2009), para 42.   [206] (27 February 1976, unreported).

[207] RR1—*The Review of the Register of Charities* (2001), para B1.   [208] [1949] Ch 529, CA.

[209] Report of the Charity Commissioners for England and Wales 1983, paras 18–20.

considered that the purposes were charitable by virtue of the analogy 'to the existing purposes of promoting equality of women with men, promoting racial harmony and promoting the moral or spiritual welfare or improvement of the community'.[210]

(9) **Advancement of environmental protection or improvement**

The preservation of national heritage and conservation of the environment are charitable purposes under the 2011 Act. The National Trust is charitable,[211] since its objects of 'promoting the permanent preservation for the benefit of the nation of lands and tenements (including buildings) of beauty or historic interest and as regards lands for the preservation since of their natural aspect features and animal and plant life'[212] are for the public benefit. Where the organization is set up to maintain a particular building, site, or habitat, the element of public benefit will normally only be satisfied if the public have access. However, if there are valid reasons for limiting or excluding such access the public benefit element may be satisfied if the organization puts in place alternative means of informing the public about its activities.[213]

In their 1973 *Annual Report* the Charity Commissioners reported that they had registered as charitable the Advisory Committee on Oil Pollution of the Sea, which sought to preserve the sea in general, and especially the seas around the United Kingdom from pollution.[214] In 2001, the Charity Commission recognized the conservation of the environment as a charitable purpose in its own right, including organizations that conserve the environment by promoting biodiversity.[215] In April 2002 the Charity Commission therefore decided that Recycling in Ottery, a company which sought to 'protect and safeguard the environment particularly through the promotion of re-use and recycling and the provision of recycling facilities', and which ran a scrap yard where members of the public could bring items for recycling, was charitable.[216] However, environmental campaign groups that have primarily political purposes will not enjoy charitable status.

(10) **Relief of need**

It has already been seen that the Statute of Charitable Uses recognized that charitable purposes included the relief of poverty, infirmity, and illness. These are merely examples of need, and other (mainly now archaic) examples are contained in the preamble to the 1601 Statute. The Charities Act 2011 states that it is a charitable purpose to provide relief for those in need 'by reason of youth, age, ill-health, disability, financial hardship

---

[210] *Charity Commission Annual Report 2002–2003*, p 22.
[211] *Re Verrall* [1916] 1 Ch 100.   [212] National Trust Act 1907, s 4(1).
[213] RR9—*Preservation and Conservation* (Feb 2001), paras A18–A20.
[214] Report of the Charity Commissioners for England and Wales 1973, para 40.
[215] RR1—*The Review of the Register of Charities* (2001), para B9.
[216] Decision of the Charity Commissions for England and Wales, *Application for Registration of Recycling in Ottery*, April 2002.

or other disadvantage'.[217] This 'includes relief given by the provision of accommodation or care to the persons mentioned in that paragraph'.[218]

(a) Examples of the relief of need

There is clearly considerable overlap between this head of charity and the head relating to the relief of poverty and the advancement of health, and many trusts that are charitable under those heads would also be charitable within this category. The provision of social housing is expressly included in the category. In *Joseph Rowntree Memorial Trust Housing Association Ltd v A-G*,[219] the Housing Association, which wished to build small dwellings for sale to the elderly, was considered charitable even though those who would benefit by purchasing the dwellings would not fall within the definition of 'poor'. Other forms of assistance to disadvantaged groups would also be charitable. For example, the relief of unemployment was not historically a charitable object in itself, though organizations that have helped unemployed people have been considered charitable under the categories of advancing education or relieving poverty. As part of its review of the Register, the Charity Commission decided in 1999 that an organization for the relief of unemployment would be charitable per se if it can be demonstrated that it is tackling unemployment, either generally or for a significant section of the community. Acceptable activities include the provision of: advice and training to unemployed individuals; practical support for unemployed people by way of accommodation, child care facilities, or assistance with travel; land, and buildings at below market or subsidized rents to businesses starting up; capital grants or equipment to new businesses; and payments to an existing commercial business to take on additional staff.[220]

It is not necessary that the needs relieved relate only to the United Kingdom. The Charity Commission has held the promotion of trading fairly is a charitable purpose. Thus in 1995 it registered as a charity an organization which would award a 'fair trade mark' on the packaging of goods sold in supermarkets, which would have the effect of relieving the conditions of life of third-world workers.[221]

(b) Provision of recreational facilities

Until the position was changed by the Recreational Charities Act 1958, the provision of recreational facilities was not, in itself, charitable, even if those facilities are provided to the public at large. This position was established by three decisions of the House of Lords in the mid-twentieth century. In *Williams' Trustees v IRC*[222] a trust was established to promote Welsh interests in London, including the provision of a meeting place to promote the 'moral, social, spiritual and educational welfare of Welsh people'. The House of Lords held that this was not charitable because of the 'social' purposes, although many of the other purposes of the society would be charitable. In *IRC v City of Glasgow Police Athletic Association*,[223] an association which existed 'to encourage

---

[217] Charities Act 2011, s 3(1)(j).   [218] S 3(2)(e).   [219] [1983] Ch 159.
[220] RR3—*Charities for the Relief of Unemployment* (1999).
[221] RR1—*The Review of the Register of Charities* (2001), para B17.
[222] [1947] AC 447, HL.   [223] [1953] AC 380.

and promote all forms of athletic sports and general pastimes' among members of the force claimed charitable status and tax exemption on the grounds that it promoted the efficiency of the police force, which would be a charitable object. The House of Lords held that the provision of recreation for the members was not purely incidental to the charitable purpose of promoting the efficiency of the force, and therefore the association was not entitled to charitable status. In *IRC v Baddeley*[224] a gift of land was made to a Methodist Mission, including an area laid out as a playing field complete with a pavilion and groundsman's bungalow. The purposes of the gift included 'the provision of facilities for religious services and instruction and for the social and physical training and recreation' of persons resident in West Ham and Leyton. The House of Lords held that this was not a gift made exclusively for charitable purposes, following *Williams' Trustees v IRC*.[225]

A number of cases have held that gifts for the provision of public recreation grounds can be charitable, for example in *Re Hadden*,[226] where a gift was made for the provision of playing fields, parks, and gymnasiums in Vancouver, and in *Re Morgan*,[227] where a gift for the provision of a public recreation ground for a particular parish was held charitable. In *Brisbane City Council v A-G for Queensland*[228] a trust to provide an area for 'a park and recreation purposes' was also held charitable. Viscount Simmonds in *IRC v Baddeley* was careful to stress that the provision of recreation grounds would still be charitable.[229]

The decision in *IRC v Baddeley* gave rise to concern that Women's Institutes and similar organizations, previously considered to be charitable, would no longer qualify for that status. To eliminate any uncertainty, the Recreational Charities Act 1958 (now consolidated in the Charities Act 2011, s 5) was enacted. This Act was not intended to enlarge the definition of charity, but instead to give statutory confirmation of purposes already recognized as charitable. The statute covers the provision of 'facilities for recreation or other leisure-time occupation' and specific mention is made of facilities at 'village halls, community centres and women's institutes'. The key provision of the Act is that the facilities must be provided in the 'interests of social welfare'. This requirement cannot be met unless the facilities provided have the object of 'improving the conditions of life for the persons for whom the facilities are primarily intended' and those persons must fall within either of the two groups specified:

(1) persons needing such facilities because of their youth, age, infirmity or disability, poverty or social and economic circumstances;

(2) the public at large or the male[230] or female members of the public.

---

[224] [1955] AC 572.   [225] [1947] AC 447.   [226] [1932] 1 Ch 133.

[227] [1955] 1 WLR 738.   [228] [1979] AC 411, PC.

[229] [1955] AC 572, at 559: 'I think it right to say that, in my opinion, a gift of land for the use as a recreation ground by the community at large or by the inhabitants of a particular geographical area may well be supported as a valid charity.'

[230] Male members of the public were included by the Charities Act 2006, s 5(2) (now the Charities Act 2011, s 5(3)). Prior to this, benefits could be confined to female members of the public, but not to male members of the public. While the difference in treatment would now be considered indefensible under

Thus, private clubs, such as golf clubs, which provide facilities only for their members and which therefore lack altruism,[231] will not attract charitable status and the consequent tax privileges. A club confined to a single sport may also be less likely to be considered charitable.[232] Only facilities provided for the public in general, for female members of the public (an early example of positive discrimination), and now male members of the public, or to groups in some way disadvantaged will attract charitable status. For example, in their 1984 Report the Charity Commissioners considered as charitable a company with the object of providing an ice-rink in Oxford that would be available to members of the public at large.[233] Although the Act does not specifically mention ethnic or minority groups, the Charity Commission has considered that it would be charitable to set up a community association or other recreational organization primarily for the use of some identifiable racial minority group.[234] The statute does not exactly define 'social welfare',[235] stating instead the essential elements that must be present. At first instance in *IRC v McMullen*[236] Walton J took the view that 'social welfare' indicates that there must be some kind of deprivation and that as a class, pupils at schools and universities cannot be described as 'deprived'.[237] In the Court of Appeal[238] Bridge LJ rejected that view, stating 'the village hall may improve the conditions of life for the squire and his family as well as for the cottagers'. This was the view of the Charity Commissioners,[239] and was approved by the House of Lords in *Guild v IRC*.[240] Lord Keith expressly stated that Walton J's approach had been incorrect, and that 'persons in all walks of life and all sorts of social circumstances may have their conditions of life improved by the provision of recreational facilities of a suitable character'.[241] A gift for use in connection with a sports centre in North Berwick was therefore held charitable. The fact that patrons must pay reasonable charges for the use of the facilities did not deprive the activity of its charitable status.

(11) **Advancement of animal welfare**

Gifts to specific animals may be upheld as valid unenforceable purpose trusts since they are recognized as anomalous exceptions to the beneficiary principle.[242] In contrast, trusts that promote the welfare of animals in general are charitable. This was recognized before the 2006 Act, which according to Lewison J in *Hanchett-Stamford*

---

the Human Rights Act, at the time of the original enactment of the Recreational Charities Act 1958, it was intended to protect the charitable status of women's institutes.

[231] A characteristic considered necessary by the Charity Commission: See RR4—*The Recreational Charities Act 1958* (2000), paras A13–A14 and A34–A35.

[232] RR4—*The Recreational Charities Act 1958* (2000), paras A24–A25.

[233] *Report of the Charity Commissioners for England and Wales for 1984*, para 19.

[234] RR1A—*Recognising New Charitable Purposes* (October 2001), para B14.

[235] See *Valuation Comr for Northern Ireland v Lurgan Borough Council* [1968] NI 104, at 126–127, per Lord MacDermott LCJ.   [236] [1978] 1 WLR 664.

[237] 1978] 1 WLR 664, at 675.   [238] [1979] 1 WLR 130.

[239] *Report of the Charity Commissioners for England and Wales 1989*, para 55.

[240] [1992] 2 AC 310, [1992] 2 All ER 10.   [241] [1992] 2 All ER 10, at 17.   [242] See Chapter 14.

v Attorney-General,[243] has not effected 'any change in the substance of the law'.[244] In *Re Wedgwood*[245] Frances Wedgwood left property to her brother on secret trust for the protection and benefit of animals. She had discussed with him the possible use of the money to forward the movement for humane slaughtering of animals, which the Court of Appeal held to be a valid charitable object. The necessary element of public benefit was not found in any benefits to the animals themselves, but in the beneficial effects that the relief of cruelty to animals was expected to have on public morality. This was emphasized by all the members of the Court of Appeal. For example, Swinfen Eady LJ explained that:

> a gift for the benefit and protection of animals tends to promote and encourage kindness towards them, to discourage cruelty and to ameliorate the condition of the brute creation, and thus to stimulate humane and generous sentiments in man towards the lower animals, and by these means promote feelings of humanity and morality generally, repress brutality, and thus elevate the human race.[246]

This reasoning was accepted without question by Nourse J in *Re Green's Will Trusts*.[247] It is artificial to justify animal welfare charities on the unproven and far from self-evident basis that they 'elevate the human race'. It would be rather better to accept them as charitable simply because they benefit the animals themselves, the approach taken in Ireland.[248]

In *Re Moss*[249] the welfare of cats and kittens was held charitable, as was a home for lost dogs.[250] In *Tatham v Drummond*[251] the RSPCA was held charitable, and more recently in *Re Green's Will Trusts*[252] a trust for the rescue, maintenance, and benefit of cruelly treated animals was held charitable. Gifts for animal sanctuaries have been held charitable, as in *Re Murawski's Will Trusts*,[253] where a gift was made to the Bleakholt Animal Sanctuary, whose constitution adopted the objects of 'the provision of care and shelter for stray, neglected and unwanted animals of all kinds and the protection of animals from ill-usage, cruelty and suffering'. However, it seems that the sanctuary must either relieve cruelty or provide access to the public to view the animals if it is to be regarded as for the benefit of the public. Thus, in *Re Grove-Grady*[254] the Court of Appeal considered that a gift to found the 'Beaumont Animal Benevolent Society' was not charitable. Its purposes were to provide a refuge where animal life of all types might be completely undisturbed by man. The court held that the public derived no benefit from such a refuge, since the purpose was not the reduction of pain or cruelty to the animals and the public could be excluded from entering the area or even looking into it. Russell LJ considered that there was no public benefit when:

> all that the public need know about the matter would be that one or more areas existed in which all animals (whether good or bad from man's point of view) were allowed to live free

[243] [2009] Ch 173.   [244] [2009] Ch 173, at [22].
[245] [1915] 1 Ch 113.   [246] [1915] 1 Ch 113, at 122.   [247] [1985] 3 All ER 455, at 458.
[248] *Armstrong v Reeves* (1890) 25 LR Ir 325.   [249] [1949] 1 All ER 495.
[250] *Re Douglas* (1887) 35 Ch D 472.   [251] (1864) 4 De GJ & Sm 484.
[252] [1985] 3 All ER 455.   [253] [1971] 1 WLR 707.   [254] [1929] 1 Ch 557.

from any risk of being molested or killed by man; though liable to be molested and killed by other denizens of the area.[255]

It is questionable whether this attitude would still prevail, given greater awareness and concern about environmental and conservation issues (a specific category of charity following the Charities Act 2006) and of the desirability of maintaining genetic diversity.

An organization promoting the welfare of animals will not be a charity if its principal purpose is to campaign for a change in the law. In *Hanchett-Stamford v Attorney-General*,[256] Lewison J held that the Performing and Captive Animals Defence League was not charitable because the achievement of its purposes required a change in the law.

(12) **Promotion of the efficiency of the defence and rescue services**

Gifts that promote the efficiency of the armed forces have long been held charitable under the fourth head. This was held to follow from the 'spirit and intendment' of the preamble, which mentioned the 'setting out of soldiers'. By analogy, it has been held that gifts which promote the efficiency of the police force will also be charitable.[257] The statutory list includes the armed forces, and the police, fire and ambulance services.[258]

Some of the older cases need to be followed only with caution. In *Re Good*[259] a gift of plate for an officers' mess was held charitable, and in *Re Gray*[260] a gift for the promotion of shooting, fishing, cricket, football, and polo for a regiment was held charitable, as it promoted the physical efficiency of the army.[261] 'The more recent cases suggest that the prime object of the purposes must be to promote efficiency if a gift is to be charitable. In *IRC v City of Glasgow Police Athletic Association*[262] a gift to promote sport and athletic pastimes in the police force was held not charitable because, although similar to the facts of *Re Gray*,[263] the promotion of efficiency was only incidental to the promotion of sport.[264] The Charity Commission's guidance suggests that charitable activities would include providing equipment or services, or encouraging recruitment to the services.[265] The provision of RAF playgroups and ex-servicemen's associations have been recognized as charitable.[266]

(13) **Other purposes beneficial to the community**

Notwithstanding the length of the list contained in the Charities Act 2011, there are many instances of charity which do not fall under any of these categories, but which

---

[255] [1929] 1 Ch 557, at 586.   [256] [2009] Ch 173.

[257] *IRC v City of Glasgow Police Athletic Association* [1953] AC 380.

[258] Fire and rescue services are as defined in Part 2 of the Fire and Rescue Services Act 2004.

[259] [1905] 2 Ch 60.   [260] [1925] Ch 362.   [261] [1925] Ch 362, at 365, per Romer J.

[262] [1953] AC 380.   [263] [1925] Ch 362.

[264] Essentially, the gift was not exclusively charitable. This requirement is considered later in this chapter.

[265] Charity Commission, *Commentary on the Descriptions of Charitable Purposes in the Charities Act 2006* (August 2009), para 50.

[266] Charity Commission for England and Wales, *Annual Report 1997*, para 90.

will remain charitable because of the preservation of the current law by s 3(1)(m). For instance, a number of cases hold that the promotion of trade and industry can be charitable. In *Construction Industry Training Board v A-G*[267] the Board, which was to make provision for the training of those employed in the construction industry, was held charitable. In *IRC v Yorkshire Agricultural Society*[268] the society, which existed for the general promotion of agriculture, was held charitable, as was the provision of a 'showground'[269] that would encourage agriculture. In their annual report for 1973[270] the Charity Commissioners considered that the Council of Industrial Design, which seeks to improve the design of industrial products, was charitable, since it was clearly of benefit to the public at large. However, the promotion of the interests of individuals rather than industry in general will not be charitable. In *Hadaway v Hadaway*[271] a trust to 'assist planters and agriculturists' by the provision of loans at favourable rates of interest was held non-charitable by the Privy Council because it was directed at conferring private benefits. Similarly, in *IRC v Oldham Training and Enterprise Council*[272] Lightman J held that a trust to promote 'trade commerce and enterprise' in the Oldham area by providing 'support services and advice to and for new businesses' was not exclusively charitable because of the private benefits. The purposes would enable the TEC to 'promote the interests of individuals engaged in trade commerce or enterprise and provide benefits and services to them'.[273]

Other charitable purposes which cannot easily be located in any other category include establishing and running a Cyber Café in a socially deprived area,[274] and operating an internet content rating service.[275]

5 Recognizing new charitable purposes

Since the list of charitable purposes is not closed, a question arises as to how new charitable purposes will be recognized. The Charities Act 2011, s 3(1)(m) allows the recognition not only of those charitable purposes 'which are listed in the Act and those recognized under the old law before the Charities Act 2006, but also any purposes 'analogous to or within the spirit of' those purposes or any new recognized purposes.

(1) The 'spirit and intendment' of the Statute of 1601

The Charities Act appears to exclude a method of reasoning which has been extensively used in the past. Traditionally, the 'spirit and intendment' of the preamble to the

---

[267] [1971] 1 WLR 1303. See also *Crystal Palace Trustees v Minister of Town and Country Planning* [1951] Ch 132, where a trust with the purpose of the promotion of industry commerce and art was held charitable.
[268] [1928] 1 KB 611.   [269] *Brisbane City Council v A-G for Queensland* [1979] AC 411.
[270] *Report of the Charity Commissioners for England and Wales 1973*, paras 69–70.
[271] [1955] 1 WLR 16.   [272] [1996] STC 1218.   [273] [1996] STC 1218, at 1235.
[274] Charity Commissioners, *Decision on Community Server*, September 2003.
[275] Charity Commissioners, *Decision on the Internet Rating Association*, September 2002.

Statute of 1601 has acted as the benchmark to determine which purposes benefit the public in ways which are charitable. In *Williams' Trustees v IRC*,[276] where the House of Lords held that a trust for promoting Welsh interests in London was not charitable, Lord Simmonds said that:

> it is still the general law that a trust is not charitable and entitled to the privileges which charity confers, unless it is within the spirit and intendment of the preamble to the Statute of Elizabeth.

The continued significance of the preamble was reiterated by the Privy Council in *A-G of the Cayman Islands v Wahr-Hansen*,[277] where Lord Browne-Wilkinson took it for granted that it was necessary to decide whether a purpose specified by a donor fell within the spirit and intendment of the preamble. However, the preamble cannot possibly anticipate the needs of society in the twenty-first century, and is an inadequate vehicle for determining charitable status. As Lord Upjohn commented in *Scottish Burial Reform and Cremation Society Ltd v Glasgow City Corpn*,[278] 'the authorities show that the spirit and intendment of the preamble to the Statute of Elizabeth have been stretched almost to breaking point'.

(2) **Development by analogy**

The practice of development by analogy, incorporated in the Charities Act, has become the predominant means of ascertaining whether a new purpose can be considered charitable. Lord Wilberforce in the *Scottish Burial Reform* case examined how the principle of the spirit and intendment had been applied in practice:

> the courts appear to have proceeded first by seeking some analogy between an object mentioned in the preamble and the object with regard to which they had to reach a decision. And then they appear to have gone further and to have been satisfied if they could find an analogy between an object already held to be charitable.[279]

The Goodman Committee in 1976 recommended that the preamble should be replaced by a modern list of purposes deemed charitable to serve as a new benchmark for further development.[280] It took thirty years for the Committee's recommendations to be implemented.

(3) **Purposes without an analogy**

A new situation will occasionally arise in which, although there appears to be a public benefit, there is no obvious analogy. The problem may then arise as to whether this can be considered charitable. In *Williams' Trustees v IRC*, Lord Simmonds said, 'it is not enough to say that the trust in question is for public purposes beneficial to the

---

[276] [1947] AC 447.   [277] [2001] 1 AC 75, [2000] 3 All ER 642.
[278] [1968] AC 138, at 153.   [279] [1968] AC 138, at 147.
[280] Report of the Goodman Committee: *Charity Law and Voluntary Organisations* (1976), para 32.

community or for the public welfare; you must show it to be a charitable trust'.[281] How is this to be done in the absence of any analogy? An approach which has been suggested is that trusts which are for purposes manifestly for the public benefit should be prima facie charitable, unless there are any reasons why they should not be. In *Incorporated Council of Law Reporting for England and Wales v A-G*[282] Russell LJ recognized the inadequacies of the 'spirit and intendment' principle and proposed instead that purposes which 'cannot be thought otherwise than beneficial to the community and of general public utility' should be charitable in law 'unless there are any grounds for holding it to be outside of the equity of the Statute [of 1601]'. This proposal was embraced by Sachs and Buckley LJJ. Applying this principle, it was held that the Incorporated Council of Law Reporting was registrable as a charity since its object of the production of law reports was clearly of general public utility and there were no grounds on which it should not be held charitable.

This approach has much to commend it, as the Privy Council indicated in *A-G of the Cayman Islands v Wahr-Hansen*.[283] It provides the capability to embrace new charitable purposes justified by changing social conditions. However, in *Barralet v A-G* Dillon J expressed doubt whether it is consistent with the decision of the House of Lords in *Williams' Trustees v IRC*[284] and concluded:

> it seems to me that the approach to be adopted in considering whether something is within the fourth category is the approach of analogy from what is stated in the preamble to the Statute of Elizabeth or from what has already been held to be charitable within the fourth category.[285]

The Court of Appeal in *Helena Partnerships v HMRC*[286] also thought that reasoning by analogy or by reference to the spirit of the preamble was essential, and that the decision in the *Incorporated Council of Law Reporting* case did not depart from that view, given the reference by Russell LJ to the 'equity of the Statute'. The language of s 3(1)(m) of the Charities Act 2011 does not help since it is capable of being interpreted to include both reasoning by analogy and 'any other purposes recognised as charitable purposes . . . under the old law' by whatever means of reasoning.

6 Charitable purposes overseas

A trust is not denied charitable status merely because any benefit from its execution will be experienced abroad rather than within the jurisdiction. Examples of charities with an international dimension include: a gift to the German government for the benefit of soldiers disabled in the Great War;[287] a trust for aid to churches, hospitals, and schools and for the assistance of the poor and aged in Cephalonia;[288] a trust for

---

[281] [1947] AC 447.   [282] [1972] Ch 73, CA.
[283] [2001] 1 AC 75, [2000] 3 All ER 642.   [284] [1947] AC 447.
[285] [1980] 3 All ER 918.   [286] [2012] EWCA Civ 569 at [61]–[63].
[287] *Re Robinson* [1931] 2 Ch 122.   [288] *Re Vagliano* [1905] WN 179.

planting a grove of olive trees in Israel;[289] and a trust for a working men's hostel in Cyprus.[290]

The approach to benefits outside the United Kingdom has evolved. In their *Annual Report* for 1963 the Charity Commissioners had no doubt that the advancement of religion, the advancement of education, and the relief of poverty are charitable in any part of the world.[291] For charities within Lord Macnaghten's fourth head of 'other purposes beneficial to the community', however, they said that there must be some benefit to the community of the United Kingdom, and not merely to the foreign country, reflecting a dictum of Lord Evershed MR in *Camille and Henry Dreyfus Foundation Inc v IRC*.[292] The Commissioners suggested that this might be more easily found in benefits to a Commonwealth country.[293] In their report for 1990, the Commissioners noted the trend toward a European and international dimension in new charities illustrated by the registration of the Gdansk Hospice Fund, the Nairobi Hospice Trust, and the USSR Support Charity.[294]

In their *Annual Report* of 1992 the Charity Commissioners went further and rejected the complex concepts of tangible and intangible benefit to the community of the United Kingdom. In future, the Commissioners indicated that a charity of any type operating abroad will be presumed charitable in the same way as if its operations were confined to the United Kingdom.[295] This presumption will be rebutted if it would be contrary to public policy to recognize the charity.[296] There is nothing in the Charities Act 2011 that challenges this practice.

7 Trusts with political objects

The fundamental principle behind the definition of charity is that purposes that are charitable must be for the public benefit. However, even if a purpose falls within one of the previously discussed categories, and is therefore considered as beneficial, it will not be charitable if it is for political purposes. Lord Parker in *Bowman v Secular Society*[297] stated that equity had always refused to recognize as charitable 'purely political objects'. This restriction was applied by Slade J in *McGovern v A-G*.[298] Amnesty International wanted to set up a trust with four main objects:

(1) the relief of needy relatives and dependants of prisoners of conscience;

---

[289] *Re Jacobs* (1970) 114 Sol Jo 515.   [290] *Re Niyazi's Will Trusts* [1978] 1 WLR 910.

[291] *Report of the Charity Commissioners for England and Wales 1963*, para 72.

[292] [1954] Ch 672, at 684.

[293] *Report of the Charity Commissioners for England and Wales 1963*, para 72.

[294] *Report of the Charity Commissioners for England and Wales 1990*, paras 32 and 33.

[295] The Commissioners adopted an approach which had already been adopted in some Commonwealth jurisdictions. See *Re Lowin* [1967] 2 NSWR 140, CA; *Re Stone* (1970) 91 WNNSW 704 (SC); *Lander v Whitbread* [1982] 2 NSWLR 530: *Re Levy Estate* (1989) 58 DLR (4th) 375.

[296] *Report of the Charity Commissioners for England and Wales 1992*, para 76.   [297] [1917] AC 406.

[298] [1982] Ch 321. See Dunn '*McGovern v Attorney-General*' (2013) 16 CLPR 105.

(2) attempting to secure the release of prisoners of conscience;

(3) procuring the abolition of torture or inhuman or degrading treatment or punishment;

(4) undertaking, and disseminating the results of research into the observance of human rights.

The Charity Commissioners had refused to register the trust as a charity, and their decision was affirmed by Slade J, who held that the main purpose was political.

(1) **Meaning of 'political objects'**

In the course of his judgment Slade J identified the circumstances in which a court would regard a trust as political. The tests he proposed were later approved (although in a different context) by the Court of Appeal in *R v Radio Authority, ex p Bull*.[299] According to Slade J, a trust will be regarded as political if it has as a direct or principal purpose supporting a political party, changing the law, or changing government policy.

(a) **To further the interests of a political party**

In *Re Ogden*[300] a trust to promote 'Liberal principles' in politics was held not to be charitable.[301] The Charity Commissioners refused to register 'Youth Training' as a charity, since its purpose was to assist the Workers' Revolutionary Party.[302]

(b) **To procure changes in the laws of this country**[303]

A ground for the decision of the House of Lords in *National Anti-Vivisection Society v IRC*[304] was that the society's object of the abolition of vivisection would necessitate a change in the law of the land. This, it was held, would not be charitable. Summarizing the law and the rationale for this principle, Slade J said:

> the court will not regard as charitable a trust of which the main object is to procure an alteration of the law of the United Kingdom for one of two or both of two reasons; first, the court will ordinarily have no sufficient means of judging as a matter of evidence whether the proposed change will or will not be for the public benefit.[305] Secondly, even if the evidence suffices to enable it to form a prima facie opinion that a change in the law is desirable, it must still decide the case on the principle that the law is right as it stands since to do otherwise would usurp the functions of the legislature.

---

[299] [1998] QB 294; Stevens and Feldman 'Broadcasting Advertisements by Bodies with Political Objects, Judicial Review, and the Influence of Charities Law' [1997] PL 615. [300] [1933] Ch 678.

[301] See also *Bonar Law Memorial Trust v IRC* (1933) 49 TLR 220.

[302] Charity Commissioners for England and Wales, *Annual Report 1982*, paras 451–651.

[303] *IRC v Temperance Council of Christian Churches of England and Wales* (1926) 10 TC 748; *National Anti-Vivisection Society v IRC* [1948] AC 31. [304] [1948] AC 31.

[305] See *Bowman v Secular Society* [1917] AC 406, at 443, per Lord Parker of Waddington: 'a trust for the attainment of political objects has always been held invalid, not because it is illegal... but because the court has no means of judging whether a proposed change in the law will or will not be for the public benefit'. See also [1973] Anglo-American Law Review 47 (Sheridan).

The promotion of the present status quo by maintaining the existing law or policy is equally a political purpose,[306] unless the effect of the law or policy concerned is to promote a charitable purpose.[307]

(c) To procure changes in the law of a foreign country

Although there is no obligation on the court to assume that foreign law is right as it stands, Slade J considered that it was still impossible to judge whether a change in foreign law would be beneficial to the community, and therefore such purposes are not charitable. In *R v Radio Authority, ex p Bull*[308] it was held that even the attempt to persuade countries to implement human rights in accordance with their obligations through international treaties was political.

(d) To procure a reversal of government policy or of particular decisions of governmental authorities in this country

The courts are also unwilling to encroach on the functions of the executive. Therefore, and also because it is impossible to determine whether any changes would result in a public benefit, Slade J held that such purposes would not be charitable.

(e) To procure a reversal of government policy or of particular decisions of governmental authorities in a foreign country

Similarly, the court has no satisfactory means of judging whether there is any public benefit from such a reversal.

(2) Application of the restriction

Whatever the category of charitable purpose, if a trust or organization has political purposes, it cannot be recognized as charitable. In *Re Hopkinson*[309] a gift was made for the advancement of adult education on the lines of a Labour Party memorandum. Vaisey J held that the purpose was 'political propaganda masquerading as education' and therefore not charitable.[310] In *Re Bushnell*[311] a trust for the promotion of socialized medicine through the publishing and distribution of books was held to be political, rather than for the provision of medical care. In contrast, in *Re Koeppler Will Trusts*[312] a gift to 'Wilton Park', an institution which was not party political and sought to promote greater cooperation in Europe, was held charitable. The Court of Appeal emphasized that the discussions it organized were neither party political nor propagandist. The Charity Commission has decided that the Centre for Corporate Accountability was not exclusively charitable because, although it was established for the charitable

---

[306] *Re Hopkinson* [1949] 1 All ER 346; *Re Koeppler Will Trusts* [1984] Ch 243.

[307] *Re Vallance* (1876) 2 *Seton's Judgments* (7th edn) 1304; *Re Herrick* (1918) 52 ILT 213.

[308] [1998] QB 294; Stevens and Feldman 'Broadcasting Advertisements by Bodies with Political Objects, Judicial Review, and the Influence of Charities Law' [1997] PL 615.   [309] [1949] 1 All ER 346.

[310] However, in *Re Trust of Arthur McDougall Fund* [1956] 3 All ER 867 it was held that a trust for the education of the public in forms of government and in political matters generally was charitable.

[311] [1975] 1 WLR 1596.   [312] [1986] Ch 423.

purpose of promoting public safety, it sought to do so by advocating changes to the law of corporate killing and influencing the prosecutions and investigations policy of the Crown Prosecution Service and the Health and Safety Executive.[313] Charities have been held not to be entitled to engage in public campaigning on political issues unrelated to their charitable objects. In *Baldry v Feintuck*[314] a student union was held to have applied money to a non-charitable object when it supported a campaign against the government policy of ending free milk in schools. Similarly, in *Webb v O'Doherty*[315] support by a student union of a campaign against the Gulf War was held non-charitable. In *R v Radio Authority, ex p Bull*,[316] Lord Woolf pointed out that an activity that was not in itself political could be considered to become political if it had the objective of promoting a political purpose. 'It takes its nature from the principal objective.'[317]

In *Hanchett-Stamford v Attorney-General*[318] a society was established to prevent cruelty to animals by prohibiting their use for performances on stage or in films. The association had been denied the benefits of charitable status in the past, on the basis that it was campaigning for a change in the law. Lewison J held that the:

> Charities Act 2006 has not changed the fundamental principle that if one of the objects or purposes of an organisation is to change the law, it cannot be charitable.[319]

(3) **Ancillary political activities**

Slade J's decision in *McGovern v A-G*[320] initially gave many charities cause for concern. Amnesty International had taken professional advice in drawing up their trust deed. The whole intention was 'that there should be hived off into a trust those purposes which they had been advised would be charitable'.[321] The decision of Slade J was therefore something of a surprise. It affected not just Amnesty International, but also other charities, like Oxfam or Shelter, which, in addition to fulfilling their main purpose of providing relief or care services, would also seek to influence government opinion in favour of the causes which they espoused. Slade J had recognized that a limited degree of political activity was permissible, provided that it was not a main purpose of the trust. He said:

> Trust purposes of an otherwise charitable nature do not lose it merely because the trustees, by way of furtherance of such purposes, have incidental powers to carry on activities which are not themselves charitable rust pIf all the main objects of the trust are exclusively charitable, the mere fact that the trustees may have incidental powers to employ political means for their furtherance will not deprive them of their charitable status.[322]

---

[313] Decision of the Charity Commissioners for England and Wales, *Application for Registration of the Centre for Corporate Accountability* (24 August 2001).   [314] [1972] 2 All ER 81.
[315] (1991) *The Times*, 11 February.   [316] [1997] 2 All ER 561.
[317] [1997] 2 All ER 561, at 572.   [318] [2009] Ch 173.
[319] [2009] Ch 173, at 181.   [320] [1982] Ch 321.
[321] [1981] 3 All ER 493, at 500, per Slade J. Amnesty did ultimately come up with a scheme for a trust which satisfied the Charity Commissioners: see [1997] 2 All ER, at 581 and 584.
[322] [1981] 3 All ER 493, at 509 and 511.

In *R v Radio Authority, ex p Bull*, Brooke LJ commented on the impact of this exception:

> Many charitable trusts today—national charities concerned with children, or the physic-
> ally or mentally disabled, or with housing the homeless, for example—are prominent in
> their espousal of political means to attain their ends.[323]

(4) Legitimate political activity by charities

It is obviously correct that purposes of a truly political nature should not receive the state subsidy in effect granted to charities through tax privileges. However, it is also the case that many well-established charities engage in political activity of some type, whether campaigning, lobbying Parliament, or advocating changes in the law. For example, the housing charity Shelter may challenge government housing policy, and relief agencies may demand a different attitude by government towards the Third World. A fine balance must be drawn between legitimate political activity by charities, and political activism that is incompatible with the retention of charitable status—any political activity must be purely ancillary to their main charitable objects. This was the theme of the advice given to charity trustees by the Charity Commissioners in guidelines published in their 1981 Report.[324]

In 1999 the Charity Commissioners provided updated comprehensive guidance to charity trustees in their publication *Political Activities and Campaigning by Charities*.[325] Their advice was further updated following the Prime Minister's Strategy Unit report, *Private Action, Public Benefit*—a review of charities and the wider not-for-profit sec-tor.[326] This recommended that the Charity Commission's guidance on political cam-paigning should place a greater emphasis on the campaigning activities that charities can undertake because:

- their strong links into local communities means that charities are well placed to monitor, evaluate, and comment upon policies as they are implemented;
- the high levels of public trust and confidence they command means that charities are well placed to offer alternative ways of engaging with the public policy debate and the processes of democracy; and
- the diversity of causes they represent, [enables] charities to give voice to a far wider range of political perspectives, including those of minority groups or inter-ests, than might otherwise be heard by government.[327]

The Charity Commission's guidance was revised in September 2004 following these recommendations, and again in March 2008 following the enactment of the Charities Act 2006. This most recent guidance is far less cautionary in tone, and less directive.

---

[323] [1997] 2 All ER 561, at 580.
[324] *Report of the Charity Commissioners of England and Wales for 1981*, paras 53–56.
[325] CC9—*Political Activities and Campaigning by Charities* (September 1999).
[326] September 2002.
[327] CC9—*Political Activities and Campaigning by Charities* (September 2004), para 5.

Instead of telling charity trustees what they are or are not permitted to do, the guidance is more general, leaving the ultimate decision on appropriateness of any given activity to the organization itself.

The Commission acknowledges that, while an organization can never be a charity if it is established solely for political purposes, so long as a charity is 'engaging in campaigning or political activity solely in order to further or support its charitable purposes, and there is a reasonable likelihood of it being effective, it may carry out campaigning and political activity'.[328] Charity trustees must consider that the methods used are lawful and an effective use of charity resources,[329] and be satisfied that the activities are permitted under the governing document of the charity.[330] A charity may seek to influence government.[331] It may provide and publish comments on possible or proposed changes in the law or government policy,[332] and advocate a change in the law or public policy, provided that these activities do not become the dominant means by which it carries out its purposes.[333] The evaluation of risk is a key feature of the guidance,[334] as when considering campaigning and political activity charity trustees must carefully weigh up the possible benefits against the costs and risks in deciding whether the campaign is likely to be an effective way of furthering or supporting the charity's purposes.[335] Similarly, the decision whether to use emotive or controversial material is a value judgement for the trustees, taking into account whether it is justifiable in the context of the campaign and has a legitimate evidence base to support the claims made.[336]

Additionally, although charities may not support a political party, they may support specific policies advocated by political parties if the policy would help them achieve their charitable purpose.[337] Moreover, it appears that a charity may focus most or all of its resources on political activity for a period, if this is the best way to support the charity's purposes and does not become the reason for the charity's existence.[338]

The interpretation given by the Charity Commission of what political activities are permitted go significantly beyond the limits set out by Slade J in *McGovern v A-G*,[339] even as subsequently glossed in *Re Koeppler's Will Trusts*.[340] They seek to add clarity to what is permissible activity by charity trustees. It remains to be seen, however, whether this very considerable extension is recognized by the courts if and when they are faced with such activities.

---

[328] CC9—*Speaking Out: Guidance on Political Activities and Campaigning by Charities* (March 2008), para D1.   [329] CC9—*Speaking Out* (2008), para G2.
[330] CC9— *Speaking Out* (2008), paras D1 and D4.
[331] CC9—*Speaking Out* (2008), para D9.   [332] CC9— *Speaking Out* (2008), para D7.
[333] CC9— *Speaking Out* (2008), paras D3 and D7.
[334] See further Atkinson 'Charities and Political Campaigning, The Impact of Risk-based Regulation' (2008) *Liverpool Law Review* 143.   [335] CC9—*Speaking Out* (2008), para F1.
[336] CC9—*Speaking Out* (2008), para G4.
[337] CC9—*Speaking Out* (2008), para D5.   [338] CC9—*Speaking Out* (2008), para D8.
[339] [1982] Ch 321.   [340] [1986] Ch 423.

(5) **Critique of the political purposes test**

A larger question than the limits on political campaigning is whether the judicial aversion to political trusts is well founded. Slade J in *McGovern v A-G*[341] spoke of the difficulty of judges in identifying whether a change in the law is for the public benefit and of the danger of usurping the functions of the legislature. The objection that Slade J gives to party political purposes is that:

> Since their nature would ex hypothesi be very controversial, the court could be faced with even greater difficulties in determining whether the objects of the trust would be for the public benefit; correspondingly, it would be at even greater risk of encroaching on the functions of the legislature and prejudicing its reputation for political impartiality, if it were to promote such objects by enforcing the trust.[342]

Slade J gave almost identical reasons for objecting to trusts that sought to achieve their objective through influencing opinion. There would again be no way of telling whether a reversal of government policy was for the public benefit 'and in any event [the court] could not properly encroach on the functions of the executive, acting intra vires, by holding that it should be acting in some other manner'.[343]

The objections that Slade J sets out are almost certainly overstated. His aversion to comment on whether the changes in the law are for the public benefit does not seem to have prevented the judges shaping the law through the development of new rules and principles,[344] nor has it prevented them, on occasions, from making suggestions for law reform in their judgments. Judges have also taken a leading role in law reform through chairmanship of the Law Commission. Lord Woolf in *R v Radio Authority ex p Bull*[345] acknowledged that a campaign to seek a change in the law would be political even though it could also be commendable. Fine distinctions have also been made. Slade J had no difficulty in reconciling *Jackson v Phillips*[346] with his view of political purposes. There the Massachusetts Supreme Court had upheld as charitable a trust to campaign against slavery before slavery was prohibited in the United States. Slade J took the view that 'the pressure was to be directed by the trustees against individual persons, rather than governments with a view to obtaining the "voluntary manumission" of the slaves belonging to such individuals'.[347]

Much of the objection to the court 'taking sides' would be overcome if the court adopted the policy of accepting purposes as being for the public benefit if they are not immoral, illegal, or subversive and are adopted by a significant proportion of the public. It would then be possible for opposing views both to be capable of being considered charitable. It may also be that a distinction needs to be made between propagandist trusts and those which seek to influence public and governmental opinion, and perhaps even influence changes in laws, not through any pre-ordained view of what is right and wrong (which is the position taken in many 'political' activities), but only

---

[341] [1982] Ch 321.   [342] [1981] 3 All ER 493, at 507.   [343] [1981] 3 All ER 493, at 508.
[344] See the discussion in Chapter 2.   [345] [1997] 2 All ER 561, at 571.
[346] 96 Mass 539 (1867).   [347] [1981] 3 All ER 493, at 514.

after careful and considered debate. After all, why should a trust to promote the work of the Law Commission not be held charitable, even though the whole purpose of the Commission is to change the law?

Strong support for the view that such a distinction should be made can be found in *Re Koeppler's Will Trusts*.[348] The testator had left a substantial gift to support the work of 'Wilton Park', in making 'a British contribution to the formation of an informed international public opinion and to the promotion of greater co-operation in Europe and the West in general'. The organization worked by bringing together in conferences a broad range of politicians, academics, civil servants, industrialists, and journalists to exchange views on political, economic, and social views of common interest. Peter Gibson J, at first instance, having considered the *McGovern* case, held that:

> trusts aimed at securing better international relations, including co-operation in a par-
> ticular part of the world, can properly be called political causes...Whether there should
> be better relations and co-operation and, if so, how it should be achieved and with whom
> are matters for government decision, not for the court.[349]

This view was overruled by the Court of Appeal. The judgment of the court was given by Slade LJ (who had now been promoted to the Court of Appeal). He distinguished the case from his previous decision in *McGovern*:

> In the present case the activities of Wilton Park are not of a party political nature. Nor,
> as far as the evidence shows, are they designed to procure changes in the laws or gov-
> ernmental policy of this or any other country: even when they touch on political mat-
> ters, they constitute, so far as I can see, no more than genuine attempts in an objective
> manner to ascertain and disseminate the truth. In these circumstances I think that no
> objections to the trust arise on a political score...the court is entitled to presume that
> the trustees will only act in a lawful and proper manner appropriate to the trustees of
> a charity and not, for example, by the propagation of tendentious political opinions.[350]

For Slade LJ to say in this case that there was no intention to change laws or governmental policy seems rather disingenuous. A large part of the reason for bringing together distinguished conference participants capable of influencing opinion in
Europe and the West must surely have been to act as a driver for cooperation between
states and governments. If that is not 'political' at an international level, it is hard
to see what could be. The major significance of this judgment must therefore be the
recognition that a distinction can be drawn between 'the propagation of tendentious
political opinions' which the court will not consider to be charitable, and 'genuine
attempts objectively to ascertain and disseminate the truth', even in a political context, which can be charitable. Applying this test, a trust to promote the work of the Law
Commission could be charitable, even if a trust to reform the rule against perpetuities
would not.

---

[348] [1986] Ch 423.   [349] [1984] 2 All ER 111, at 124.   [350] [1985] 2 All ER 869, at 878.

8 The requirement of public benefit

(1) General principles

The principle of public benefit suffuses the whole of charity law.[351] It is not enough for
a trust to be charitable that it falls within one of the categories in s 3 of the Charities
Act 2011, even though, as has already been seen, it will only do so if the purpose can in
a general sense be seen as beneficial. More is required. The way in which that purpose
is to be fulfilled must be one which confers public benefit. That in turn requires public
benefit in two respects: the specific form of the general purpose must be beneficial
in nature, and the way in which it is proposed to implement that purpose must confer benefits on a sufficiently numerous and broad group of beneficiaries to constitute
public rather than private benefit. Finally, once a gift, trust, or organization has been
recognized as charitable, it must continue to operate in a way which is charitable.
That requires ongoing benefits to be conferred on the public. Thus, a trust to preserve
a significant building is in principle beneficial; however this will be the case only if
the specific building involved (like Sir Edward Heath's former home Arundells[352]) is
indeed of architectural, historic, or cultural significance and thus preserving it is of
public benefit; in addition, there must be some way in which the virtues of the preserved building are delivered to the public, for instance through opening the building to the general public; there must also be ongoing public benefit such as through
maintaining access. This multi-faceted requirement of public benefit has been the case
for many years (even if not always clearly articulated), but that requirement has been
given statutory force by the Charities Act 2011, ss 2(1)(b) and 4. There is no new statutory definition, so public benefit is defined as having the same meaning as under the
previous law.[353]

(a) When does the public benefit test apply?

The public benefit test applies to new organizations or trusts seeking to be registered
as a charity. It also applies to existing charities, which must continue to satisfy the
public benefit test and must demonstrate that they do so. Charities are now required
to report on public benefit as part of the Trustees' *Annual Report*. This information
must be set in the context of the charity's aims, and must demonstrate how in practice
each purpose of the charity has been carried out for the public benefit. The focus, of
course, is upon a charity's continuing operations rather than in reiterating the information which is necessary to establish whether a charity meets the criteria for registration. Following some initial assessments of the way in which charities were fulfilling

---

[351] See Warburton 'Charities and Public Benefit—From Confusion to Light? (2008) *Charity Law and Practice Review* 1; Hackney 'Charities and Public Benefit' (2008) 124 LQR 347.

[352] Registered Charity 1112773—THE SIR EDWARD HEATH CHARITABLE FOUNDATION.

[353] Charities Act 2011, s 4(3).

the public benefit requirement,[354] the Charity Commission published some emerging findings in 2009.[355]

(b) Charity Commission guidance

To assist trustees, the Charity Commission, as it was required to do under s 4 of the Charities Act 2006 (now s 17 of the Charities Act 2011), published guidance. The content of this guidance was challenged by the Independent Schools Council. The dispute went to the Upper Tribunal which, in a landmark decision, concluded that material aspects of the guidance were incorrect in law or obscure[356] and that parts of the guidance should be withdrawn.[357] The significance of the guidance is that 'the charity trustees of a charity must have regard to any such guidance when exercising any powers or duties to which the guidance is relevant'.[358] Trustees are also obliged to report as to whether they have complied with the duty to have due regard to the guidance.[359]

New general guidance was issued in September 2013. It comprises three sections or guides explaining public benefit in three different contexts: the requirement as it applies to the recognition of charities (*Public benefit: the public benefit requirement* (PB1)): the requirement as it applies to the operation of a charity (*Public benefit: running a charity* (PB2)); and a guide to reporting on a charity's work (*Public benefit: reporting* (PB3)). This guidance has clear and close regard to the decision of the Upper Tribunal in the *Independent Schools* case. The Charity Commission has produced guides on a number of specific charitable purposes, but some of these, issued before the *Independent Schools* case, no longer form part of its statutory guidance to which trustees must have regard. They comprise the three guides covering the substantive Macnaghten categories of charitable purpose: *The Prevention or Relief of Poverty for the Public Benefit*,[360] *The Advancement of Education for the Public Benefit*,[361] and *The Advancement of Religion for the Public Benefit*.[362]

(c) Consequences of failing the public benefit test

Where a proposed charity does not meet the public benefit test, it will not be a charity and will not therefore enjoy the benefits and advantages of that status. It may be possible for the objectives or purposes of the trust or organization to be amended to satisfy the test.

Where an existing charity fails to satisfy the public benefit test, the trust or organization will have essentially one of three choices. It could challenge the Charity Commission's interpretation of the requirements of public benefit. It may amend its purposes and modify its activities in order to comply with the Charity Commission

[354] Charity Commission, *Public Benefit Assessment Report—Methodology* (July 2009).
[355] Charity Commission, *Public Benefit Assessments: Emerging Findings for Charity Trustees from the Charity Commission's Public Benefit Assessment Work: 2008–09* (July 2009).
[356] *The Independent Schools Council v The Charity Commission* [2011] UKUT 421 (TCC) (13 October 2011).   [357] *Independent Schools Council v HMRC* [2011] UKUT B27 (TCC) (2 December 2011).
[358] Charities Act 2006, s 4(6). Now the Charities Act 2011 s 17(5).
[359] Charities (Accounts and Reports) Regulations 2008, SI 2008/629.
[360] December 2008.   [361] December 2008.   [362] December 2008.

guidance, and may be required to do this by the Charity Commission. Finally, if it is not possible to make such changes, it could cease to be a registered charity. The impact of the last course of action could be catastrophic for the entity concerned. Once assets have irrevocably been devoted to charitable purposes, they cannot be used for any non-charitable purposes, but must, in the event of an organization ceasing to be charitable, be applied to other charitable purposes.[363] Thus, if a public school lost its charitable status, and wished to operate as a private sector school, it would not be able to transfer its assets to the new non-charitable entity. The new entity would either have to purchase the assets or acquire new premises and facilities. That would inevitably have a dramatic and negative impact upon the level of fees that the new entity would need to charge, or upon the quality of the provision which it could offer.

(2) **What is 'public benefit'?**

What constitutes public benefit is very much dependent upon the context, and it is not easy to describe criteria which are of general application. It is stating the obvious to observe that public benefit has two dimensions: whether the proposed charity provides benefits; and whether those benefits are conferred upon the public. It used to be thought that there was a presumption of public benefit in relation to purposes which fell within the first three of the Macnaghten categories, namely the advancement of education, the relief of poverty, and the advancement of religion.[364] However, according to the *Independent Schools* case,[365] establishing whether there is a benefit is a question of fact in every case. That will be a decision which must be based upon the evidence presented to the Charity Commission, tribunal, or court, although there may be some cases (for instance, mainstream education available to all free of charge) where the answer as to whether there is a benefit is self-evident and is a matter on which a judge can take judicial notice.

(a) **Purpose must be beneficial in nature**

It does not follow that because a proposed purpose falls within one of the recognized categories of charitable purpose the specific way in which that purpose will be implemented (or is being implemented) is charitable.[366] It could be argued that a trust to provide training to the Taliban in making explosive devices is 'educational', but it is hardly a charitable purpose to train terrorists. There would be no public benefit from the particular form of education proposed.[367]

---

[363] Charity Commission, *Public Benefit—The Charity Commission's Approach* (January 2005), para 22.

[364] See Charity Commission, *Public benefit: analysis of the law relating to public benefit* (September 2013), para 12.

[365] *The Independent Schools Council v The Charity Commission* [2011] UKUT 421 (TCC) (13 October 2011), at [70].

[366] For the use of the term 'beneficial in nature' see *Attorney-General v Charity Commission (The Poverty Reference)* [2012] WTLR. 977, at [32].

[367] See *R (Independent Schools Council) v Charity Commission* [2012] Ch 214 and *Attorney General v Charity Commission (The Poverty Reference)* [2012] WTLR 977, at [66]–[67] where the examples of

(i) Form of benefit may be practical or intangible

The public benefit may consist of practical assistance, as in most cases involving the relief of need, for instance through the provision of housing to the homeless, financial assistance to the poor, or advocacy for those who lack the mental capacity to represent themselves. The benefit may also be of an intangible or moral nature. For instance, the promotion of fine music or the preservation of the cultural heritage may have no direct practical benefits, but they may help to improve the human condition in a moral or intellectual sense. It used to be considered that the provision of overseas aid was justified on moral, rather than practical grounds, although a different view is now taken. The personal views of the founder are not relevant either in interpreting the disposition[368] or in determining that the purpose is beneficial.[369]

(ii) Benefit may be direct or indirect

It is possible for indirect benefits to be taken into account in deciding whether there is public benefit. A trust to train teachers in the use of sign language provides services directly to the individuals who are trained, but the greater benefits are to the pupils who will benefit from having teachers who have the skills that they need for their education. A hospice providing care for the terminally ill confers benefits not only on the patients who may receive care more closely aligned to their needs than would otherwise be the case; it also relieves the burden which the National Health Service would need to carry, and it provides assistance to the family of the patient who might find it difficult to cope in providing the level of intensive support which a patient needs. All of these factors can be weighed in the balance in deciding whether there is a benefit to the public.[370] However, there are some cases where indirect benefits will be insufficient to carry the day because they are outweighed by direct non-charitable benefits to individuals.[371] Thus in a case involving a housing association established 'for the benefit of the community', the Court of Appeal held that the general public interest in the provision of good quality housing was insufficient to make the purposes of a housing association charitable; it would be necessary for the objects of the association to confine provision to those who had some special need, for instance by reason of disability or other disadvantage.[372]

(iii) Benefit must be recognized as charitable

It is so obvious that it hardly needs saying that for a benefit to be recognized by law, it must be of a kind which promotes a purpose which has been recognized by law as

non-charitable purposes are a school for pickpockets and a library of pornography. The examples are drawn from observations in *Re Macduff* [1896] 2 Ch 451, at 474 (Rigby LJ) and in *Re Pinion* [1965] Ch 85, at 106 (Harman LJ).

[368] *Helena Partnerships Ltd v HMRC* Upper Tribunal (Tax and Chancery) [2011] STC 1307 [16–22]; affd [2012] EWCA (Civ) 569, [2012] PTSR 1409.   [369] *Re Hummeltenberg* [1923] 1 Ch 237.
[370] *R (Independent Schools Council) v Charity Commission* [2011] UKUT 421 (TCC), at [37]; *Helena Partnerships Ltd v HMRC* [2012] EWCA Civ 569, at [78].
[371] *Helena Partnerships Ltd v HMRC* [2012] EWCA Civ 569, at [108].
[372] *Helena Partnerships Ltd v HMRC* [2012] EWCA Civ 569. See also *Inland Revenue Commissioners v Oldham Training and Enterprise Council* [1996] STC 1218 where a similar conclusion was reached.

charitable. Acting illegally cannot be considered to be beneficial. A proposed trust to provide cannabis to chronic sufferers of arthritis would not be charitable, even if it could be proved that the drug would improve the condition of life of those receiving the treatment. In a less extreme situation, a trust to build a private (for profit) hospital would not be charitable because even if it could be considered as for the advancement of health, doing so for profit is not considered to be charitable.

(iv) Benefit must relate to the aims of the charity

Although benefits can be indirect, they must be sufficiently related to the primary activities or purposes of the organization or trust. For example, worthless education would not be redeemed because the educational institution was based in an historical building worthy of protection. In *IRC v Oldham Training and Enterprise Council*[373] an organization established to provide 'support services and advice to and for new businesses' in the Oldham area was principally directed as raising the profitability of local businesses. However, this would indirectly improve employment prospects in the area. Lightman J held that these indirect 'benefits to the community conferred by such activities are too remote'.[374] This may just be another way of saying that the private benefits outweigh the public benefit.[375]

(b) Assessing benefit

Different views can be taken about what constitutes a benefit. Some purposes or activities may be beneficial in the eyes of some but detrimental in the eyes of others. For example, some members of the community may think that public health would be promoted by campaigning to promote vegetarianism, but others may think that advocating the eating of red meat would be in the public interest for similar reasons. How can the Charity Commission or the court determine whether there is a public benefit without simply making a value judgement? Different approaches are possible.

(i) Assessment of benefit can be controversial

The assessment of benefit is not free from controversy. A particularly contentious issue which took up much time in debate over the Charities Act 2006 in both Lords and Commons concerns the charitable status of public schools. The government essentially passed this thorny issue to the Charity Commission for resolution. The Charity Commission, which anticipated the possibility of challenge,[376] published its initial views, following considerable consultation, in December 2008 in three separate reports, *Public Benefit and Fee-Charging*, an *Analysis of the Law underpinning Public Benefit and Fee Charging*, and *The Advancement of Education for the Public Benefit*. It published its first Public Benefit Assessments of some independent schools in 2009.

---

[373] [1996] STC 1218.   [374] [1996] STC 1218, at 1235.

[375] This was how Lloyd LJ interpreted the decision in *Helena Partnerships Ltd v HMRC* [2012] EWCA Civ 569.

[376] *Public Benefit—The Charity Commission's Position on How Public Benefit Is Treated in the Charities Act* (July 2005).

The Commission was accused by a leading independent school headmaster of making 'politically motivated' judgements and adopting 'a blinkered approach', and aspects of the Charity Commission guidance were found to be unlawful in a successful challenge by the Independent Schools Council. The Commission had not (in Spring 2014) published revised guidance on public benefit and education.

(ii) The view of the public

What benefits the public could be judged by public opinion—an 'ask the audience' approach. This is not the approach used in the United Kingdom. Public opinion is not easy to measure, and it can change frequently. In the Canadian case of *Everywoman's Health Centre Society (1988) v Minister of National Revenue*[377] the court said that:

> to define charity through public consensus would be a most imprudent thing to do. Charity and public opinion do not always go hand in hand . . . Courts are not well equipped to assess public consensus, which is a fragile and volatile concept. The determination of the charitable character of an activity should not become a battle between pollsters.

While public opinion may not be the primary test for identifying whether there is a benefit, there are instances where public views are relevant. Lord Wright in *National Anti-Vivisection Society v IRC*[378] said that whether there was a benefit could be judged on the basis of 'approval by the common understanding of enlightened opinion for the time being' that there is benefit to the public, and in *Funnell v Stewart*[379] it was held that a trust to advance the practice of faith healing was charitable on the grounds that it had become 'a recognised activity of public benefit'. This suggests that the attitude of the public cannot be disregarded in determining whether an activity should be characterized as for the public benefit, but the way in which wider opinion is referred to leaves a subjective value judgement to be made by the court.

(iii) A subjective assessment of benefit

Another possibility is for the court to adopt a subjective test, and uphold the gift if the donor thought the activity confers public benefit. This approach seems to have been applied by Chitty J in *Re Foveaux*,[380] where a gift to the International Society for the Total Suppression of Vivisection was held charitable. He acknowledged that vivisection was a practice over which opinion was divided, and said that it was not for the court to 'enter into or pronounce any opinion on the merits of the controversy which subsists between the supporters and opponents of the practice of vivisection'. Instead, when 'humane men and women of a high order of intelligence and education are found in the ranks on either side the law stands neutral'. This reluctance to judge the merits of questions of morals where men's minds reasonably differ was also reflected in the Irish case of *Re Cranston*,[381] which concerned a gift to a vegetarian society. Fitzgibbon LJ took the view that it would be charitable provided the purpose was one which the founder of the society believed to be to public advantage, and that his belief 'be at least

---

[377] [1992] 2 FC 52, at 68–69.   [378] [1948] AC 31, at 49   [379] [1996] 1 WLR 288.
[380] [1895] 2 Ch 501.   [381] [1898] 1 IR 431.

rational and not contrary either to the general law of the land or to the principles of morality'. The key factor is the subjective belief of the donor, within certain objective limits, that the purpose is beneficial. In neither of these two cases was the court willing to weigh the alleged benefits of the purpose against its alleged drawbacks.

(iv) An objective assessment of benefit

In *National Anti-Vivisection Society v IRC*[382] the House of Lords overruled the decision in *Re Foveaux*[383] and held that a gift to the society, whose object was the suppression of vivisection, was not charitable. They adopted an objective approach to the question of public benefit. Lord Simmonds stated:

> Where on the evidence before it the court concludes that, however well-intentioned the donor, the achievement of his object will be greatly to the public disadvantage, there can be no justification for saying that it is a charitable object.[384]

The House was faced by the decision of fact of the Special Commissioners for Income Tax that any benefit 'was far outweighed by the detriment to medical science and research and consequently to the public health which would result if the society succeeded in achieving its objects'.[385]

The *National Anti-Vivisection Society* decision suggests that the underpinning requirement for all kinds of public benefit is that the benefit must be capable of proof. The classic formulation of this requirement can be found in the judgment of Slade J in *McGovern v AG*:

> The question whether a purpose will or may operate for the public benefit is to be answered by the court forming an opinion on the evidence before it ... No doubt in some cases a purpose may be so manifestly beneficial to the public that it would be absurd to call evidence on this point.[386] In many other instances, however, the element of public benefit may be much more debatable. Indeed, in some cases the courts will regard this element [as] being incapable of proof one way or the other and thus will inevitably decline to recognise the trust as being of a charitable nature.[387]

(v) Balance of benefit and detriment

Nearly all activities have both positive and negative impacts. For an activity to be charitable, it is not necessary for there to be unqualified benefits. It is sufficient if, on balance, the benefits sufficiently outweigh the disadvantages. For instance, promoting the playing of amateur sport in schools can be charitable, even though there is an inevitable risk of injury. If the risk of injury is managed, it is outweighed by the positive benefits of healthy exercise.[388] The balancing process is well illustrated in *National Anti-Vivisection Society v IRC*,[389] where the evidence before the House of Lords was

---

[382] [1948] AC 31.
[383] [1895] 2 Ch 501.   [384] [1948] AC 31, at 65–66.   [385] [1948] AC 31, at 65–66.
[386] See an identical observation by Vaisey J in *Re Shaw's Will Trusts* [1952] Ch 163, at 169.
[387] [1981] 3 All ER 493, at 504.
[388] Charity Commission online guidance, *Charities and Public Benefit* (January 2008), para E4.
[389] [1948] AC 31.

that the benefits achievable through medical research from experimentation on animals far outweighed the moral benefits in preventing vivisection of animals. It has
been said judicially that there will be a predisposition to discount alleged disadvantages arising from what would otherwise be a beneficial purpose unless those disadvantages have been clearly demonstrated.[390]

(vi) Can benefit always be measured objectively?

The objective approach adopted in the *National Anti-Vivisection* case assumes that
the court is competent to make judgements of what is in the public interest. This is
questionable as a universal proposition, since there are many instances where the issue
of whether there is a benefit to the public is a matter of opinion. This is especially
the case if fine moral issues over which there is a real divergence of opinion in society are involved, and at best the court can only give its own value judgement on the
issue. There are also some very interesting examples of activities held to be charitable despite no evidence having been provided to demonstrate public benefit. These
include religious organizations engaged in public worship and societies promoting
the humane treatment of animals. In both of these instances the courts have been
prepared to assume public benefit without any form of proof of benefit being offered.
In both cases, quantification or measurement of the benefits (if they exist) would be
difficult or impossible.

(vii) Is a hybrid approach preferable?

The subjective approach, with objective limitations, suggested in *Re Cranston*[391] provides a more attractive alternative than a purportedly purely objective approach.
There is no need for the court—or the Charity Commission—to make its own value
judgements about relative merits. Is it not possible that both a trust for the prevention
of animal experimentation and a trust for the promotion of medical research could be
considered charitable, although their objects are to some extent in conflict? Similarly,
could not a trust for the promotion of the health benefits of vegetarianism be charitable alongside a trust for the promotion of the health benefits of eating meat? All that
is really needed is a test that will eliminate those purposes that are in no sense in the
public interest or are of benefit only to small and obscure groups and sects. A test
which upholds purposes that a substantial body of public opinion regards as beneficial
would be adequate for this purpose, and more honest than a spurious claim to make
all judgements objectively.

(c) Assessing benefit in the light of modern conditions

There is not the slightest doubt that the concept of what constitutes a public benefit
has changed over the years, and that this is reflected in the decisions of the courts
and of the Charity Commission. For instance, it is now recognized that charities that

---

[390] *R (Independent Schools Council) v Charity Commission* [2012] Ch 214, at [106].
[391] [1898] 1 IR 431.

operate overseas can be justified on the basis of the benefits that they confer on their overseas beneficiaries, without needing to show a benefit to the public in the United Kingdom.[392] Views relating to the conservation of the built and natural heritage have changed. There is now, for instance, a belief that the protection of biodiversity could in itself be of value without needing to establish immediate practical benefits.[393]

Changes in social conditions and emerging scientific findings can change the view of what will be considered to be a public benefit. The Charity Commission gave an example in its 2008 analysis of the law:

> for a long time in the earlier part of the 20th century, the supply of cigarettes to sick people in hospital was regarded as charitable. During the First World War, major charities, in carrying out such a charitable aim, would provide cigarettes as 'useful sedatives for sick or wounded men'... Today, we would not regard the provision of cigarettes to hospital patients as being charitable for the public benefit. Any apparent benefits from the cigarettes acting as a sedative would be more than outweighed by the very real and considerable detriment caused to the patients and others by cigarette smoke.[394]

(d) Benefit to the public

It might seem fairly obvious as to whether there is a benefit to the public, but in many cases it is hard to determine whether benefits are genuinely public. For instance, the provision of a park in Lampeter is unlikely to be of much value to the residents of Birmingham, Liverpool, or Worcester. Does it therefore confer benefits on the public? If a trust provides advice and guidance to people suffering from a rare disease, can that be considered to be providing benefits on the public? The answer in both cases is likely to be that the activities concerned are for the public benefit, but they are clearly not for the benefit of the whole of the public, if by that we mean the whole population of England and Wales, or of the United Kingdom. Benefits can be public, therefore, even if they are available only to part of the public. But, if benefits are available only to part of the public, how can we determine whether those benefits are to the public or merely to a group of private individuals? The cases on public benefit have, in the past, distinguished between different heads of charity. They raise complex issues and are not always easy to reconcile. Nevertheless, there are some recurrent themes and common principles. These include what is known as the 'personal nexus' rule, and the need for a class of beneficiaries which is sufficiently large.

(e) A sufficiently large group

For a class or group to constitute a section of the public it must not be 'numerically negligible'.[395] In Re Duffy[396] Roth J held that a trust to provide amenity benefits for the residents and staff of a single residential care home, even if a beneficial purpose, could

---

[392] *Report of the Charity Commissioners for England and Wales 1992*, para 76.
[393] RR1—*The Review of the Register of Charities* (2001), para B9.
[394] *Charities and Public Benefit* (January 2008), para D6.
[395] *Oppenheim v Tobacco Securities Trust Co Ltd.* [1951] AC 297.   [396] [2013] EWHC 2395 (Ch).

not be charitable because a gift for the benefit of no more than thirty-three residents at a particular care home could not be regarded as a gift to a sufficient section or class of the community as to meet the public benefit requirement. This rule is not applied to trusts for the relief of poverty.

(f) The 'personal nexus' rule

It is rather more difficult than it might seem to distinguish between public and private benefits. There is, of course, no difficulty at the extremes. Funding research into a cure for cancer on terms that the research is to be made publicly available is obviously for the public benefit. Conversely, a trust for a named individual will be considered to confer only private benefits, even if the gift will transform the life of a person who is in poor health, badly housed, badly educated, and impecunious. A trust to educate the members of a single family will also be considered to confer only private benefits, even if the family is very large. One test to distinguish public from private benefits is the 'personal nexus' test, but it will be seen that this test has drawbacks.

(i) Meaning of the 'personal nexus' rule

This test has its foundation in the decision of the House of Lords in *Oppenheim v Tobacco Securities Trust Co Ltd*.[397] John Phillips was a large shareholder in British American Tobacco (BAT), and on his death he left property on trust to use the income for the education of the children of the employees or ex-employees of BAT. The House of Lords took the view that this group was not a section of the public but a private class, and that the trust was therefore non-charitable. The principle was stated by Lord Simmonds, who identified two characteristics that would render a class of beneficiaries a 'section of the public'. First (as has just been considered), such a class would have to be 'not numerically negligible'. Second, the identity of the members of the class could not be defined by means of a personal nexus. He explained that:

> the quality which distinguishes [the potential beneficiaries] from other members of the community, so that they form by themselves a section of it, must be a quality which does not depend on their relationship to a particular individual.[398]

Thus, although the employees and ex-employees formed a class of some 110,000 persons, they were not a section of the public because they were identified by their personal contractual relationship with BAT. As Lord Simmonds said:

> A group of persons may be numerous but, if the nexus between them is their personal relationship to a single propositus or to several propositi, they are neither the community nor a section of the community for charitable purposes.[399]

(ii) Impact of the personal nexus rule

Lord Simmonds did not qualify the 'personal nexus' rule so that it appears to offer provides a conclusive test of whether a class should be regarded as a section of the public.

---

[397] [1951] AC 297.   [398] [1951] AC 297, at 306.   [399] [1951] AC 297.

Thus if the identifying feature of the class is the members' nexus or relationship to a particular individual or group of individuals, they cannot constitute a section of the public. So the employees of a company would not constitute a section of the public, nor would the relatives of an individual[400] or the members of a trade union.[401] A strict application of the test might mean that the patients of a particular general medical practice, the clients of a firm of solicitors, and the members of a university and other similar classes would all be considered to be private groups. The rule can apply even if the class of beneficiaries is identified in a way which does not require specific reference to a single 'propositus'. In *IRC v Educational Grants Association Ltd*.[402] Metal Box Ltd established and funded the EGA, which had the object of advancing education by providing grants for individuals to attend university or private schools. Between 76 per cent and 85 per cent of the grants made by the EGA were made to children of employees of Metal Box, although Metal Box was not mentioned in the memorandum of association of the EGA. The Court of Appeal held that in practice there was a personal nexus, and that the EGA was not exclusively charitable. In *Re Koettgen's Will Trusts*[403] an educational trust was open to the public at large, subject to a direction that the trustees were to give preference to the families of employees, up to a maximum of 75 per cent of the income. This was held to be valid, although Pennycuick J in *IRC v Educational Grants Association* expressed considerable difficulty with it. In *Caffoor v Income Tax Comr for Columbo*[404] it was held that a preference for the grantor's family made an educational trust non-charitable. This seems to be the better view, although it must be a question of degree in each case whether the extent of a preference is sufficient to deprive an otherwise charitable trust of its charitable status.

(iii) Criticism of the personal nexus test

The rationale behind the personal nexus test is understandable, namely that purely private groups should not receive the tax privileges enjoyed by charities. If BAT had attempted to set up a similar trust in favour of its own employees, charitable status should not have been granted, as the company would have been seeking to provide its employees with a tax-free benefit. This was, in effect, what had been done in the *Metal Box* case. However, the facts of *Oppenheim* were essentially different. The trust was established by a man whose only interest in the company was that he owned a substantial shareholding,[405] and in no sense was there an attempt by the company to give their employees a tax-free perk. In such circumstances, where the gift was made by an outside donor to a substantial class, there is less justification for refusing charitable status.

The philosophy of providing rigid tests for public benefit is also questionable, since it is impossible to devise a rule that will cover all circumstances and not lead

---

[400] See *Re Compton* [1945] Ch 123, where the Court of Appeal held that a trust for the education of the descendants of three named persons was not charitable.

[401] *Re Mead's Trust Deed* [1961] 1 WLR 1244.   [402] [1967] Ch 993.

[403] [1954] Ch 252.   [404] [1961] AC 584.

[405] See [1951] AC 297, at 299, where it is recorded that 'no evidence was given of any connection of the grantors with the company except that John Phillips was a large stockholder'.

to anomalous results. For this reason, Lord MacDermott dissented from the decision of the other members of the House of Lords in *Oppenheim*, and rejected the personal nexus test. He pointed out that historically there had been no single conclusive test as to what constituted a sufficient section of the public, but that instead:

> The usual way of approaching the issue…was…to regard the facts of each case and to treat the matter very much as one of degree.[406]

He pointed out that far from proving conclusive, the 'personal nexus' test would produce unacceptable anomalies: would a trust for miners in the service of the National Coal Board (at the time the only employer of coal miners, and therefore a group which would include all miners throughout the UK) be for private purposes but a trust for miners at a particular pit or of a particular district (merely a subset of the previous group) constitute a section of the public?[407] The force of Lord MacDermott's criticisms was felt by all members of the House of Lords in *Dingle v Turner*,[408] which is discussed below.

(iv) Continued relevance of the personal nexus test

Despite these criticisms, the personal nexus test has continued to be applied and is contained (without qualification) in the Charity Commission guidance on public benefit.[409] However, in the Commission's legal analysis of public benefit, in 2005 and 2008[410] the Commission indicated that the rule should be applied with caution and flexibility, and in its 2013 analysis it suggests, citing *Dingle v Turner*,[411] that the rule has been 'assumed' by the House of Lords to apply to trusts in Lord Macnaghten's fourth category only. That, as will shortly be seen, is a very weak foundation for the proposition.

(v) The scope of the 'personal nexus' rule

The personal nexus test has not been applied to all categories of charity. *Oppenheim v Tobacco Securities Trust Co Ltd* and *IRC v Educational Grants Association* (the *Metal Box* case) both concerned trusts for the advancement of education, and the test clearly applies to that head. It was also applied to charities within Lord Macnaghten's fourth head of 'other purposes beneficial to the community'.[412] It was not applied to trusts for the advancement of religion, provided that the religiously affected people lived their lives among the community at large (an illustration of the acceptance of indirect benefits). Most significantly, it did not apply to charities that fell under the head of relief of poverty. Thus, as Chadwick J observed in *Re Segelman (Decd)*:

---

[406] [1951] AC 297, at 314.   [407] [1951] AC 297, at 318.   [408] [1972] AC 601.

[409] Charity Commission, *Public Benefit; The Public Benefit Requirement (PB1)* (2013) Part 5: Benefiting the public or a sufficient section of the public.

[410] Charity Commission, *Public Benefit—The Legal Principles* (January 2005), para 23; *Analysis of the Law Relating to Public Benefit* (September 2013), para 71. See also the Law Commission document, *Analysis of the Law Underpinning Charities and Public Benefit* (2008) v 1.1.1, para 3.45.

[411] *Dingle v Turner* [1972] AC 601, at 625D.

[412] See *Re Drummond* [1914] 2 Ch 90, where a gift to provide the holiday expenses of the workpeople of a spinning company was held not charitable, since it was not for general public purposes.

a gift for the relief of poverty is no less charitable because those whose poverty is to be relieved are confined to a particular class limited by ties of blood or employment.[413]

This exception enjoyed an insurmountable historical pedigree. The special treatment of trusts for the relief of poverty does not seem to apply to trusts relieving needs of other types. Thus in *Re Mead's Trust Deed*[414] a trust to provide a home for aged members of a trade union and to provide a sanatorium for members suffering from tuberculosis was held not to be charitable because the members of a trade union are not a section of the public. In *Attorney General v Charity Commission (The Charity Commission Poverty Reference)*[415] the Upper Tribunal accepted that different tests for public benefit could apply to different types of charity.

(vi) Poor relations

In *Re Compton*,[416] where the personal nexus test was first suggested, Lord Greene MR referred to a series of cases where gifts to the 'poor relations' of an individual had been held charitable.[417] He concluded that although these cases would fail under the personal nexus test, they were to be regarded as 'anomalous'[418] exceptions to the principle. In *Oppenheim*, Lord Simmonds was similarly unwilling to 'harmonise' and overturn the 'poor relations' cases.[419] It might be thought that members of a family are just the type of class that is private rather than public, and therefore not deserving of charitable status. The exception can only be justified on public policy grounds that the relief of poverty is such an important object to society that any gift that seeks to relieve it will be encouraged and upheld[420] or that the relief of poverty, even for a very small number of individuals, provides significant indirect benefit to the public as a whole.[421] Thus, in *Re Scarisbrick's Will Trusts*[422] Bertha Scarisbrick left her residuary estate to trustees upon trust for her relations 'in needy circumstances'. The Court of Appeal held that this was a valid charitable trust. In *Dingle v Turner*,[423] this exception was confirmed by the House of Lords. Frank Dingle left his residuary estate to trustees, the income to be used to pay pensions to the 'poor employees' of E Dingle & Co, a company that he jointly owned. The House of Lords held unanimously that the personal nexus rule had no application to trusts for the relief of poverty.[424] The exemption was re-affirmed in *Re Segelman*,[425] where a testator left property in his will to be used for a period of

---

[413] [1996] Ch 171, [1995] 3 All ER 676, at 687.   [414] [1961] 1 WLR 1244.

[415] [2012] WTLR 977, at [34].   [416] [1945] Ch 123.

[417] *Isaac v DeFriez* (1754) Amb 595; *A-G v Price* (1810) 17 Ves 371; *Bernal v Bernal* (1838) 3 My & Cr 559; *Browne v Whalley* [1866] WN 386; *Gillam v Taylor* (1873) LR 16 Eq 581; *A-G v Duke of Northumberland* (1877) 7 Ch D 745.   [418] [1945] Ch 123, at 139.

[419] [1951] AC 297, at 308.

[420] See *Re Scarisbrick* [1951] Ch 622, at 639, per Evershed MR: 'The "poor relations" cases may be justified on the basis that the relief of poverty is of so altruistic a character that the public element may necessarily be inferred thereby, or they may be accepted as a hallowed, if illogical, exception.'

[421] See *Gibson v South American Stores (Gath & Chaves) Ltd* [1949] Ch 572, at 576.

[422] [1951] Ch 622.   [423] [1972] AC 601.

[424] [1972] AC 601, at 623, per Lord Cross: 'it must be accepted that whatever else it may hold sway the *Compton* rule has no application in the field of trusts for the relief of poverty'.

[425] [1996] Ch 171, [1995] 3 All ER 676; Bennett Histed 'Rectification of Wills and Charitable Trusts for Poor Relations: Broadening the Boundaries' [1996] Conv 379.

twenty-one years for the benefit of the poor and needy members of his family. A schedule was drawn up in which he named six members of his extended family and the
issue of five of them as comprising the class of beneficiaries. Chadwick J held that this
created a valid charitable gift, falling within the scope of the exception, because it was
'a gift to particular poor persons, the relief of poverty among them being the motive
for the gift'.[426]

The argument that there are substantial benefits to the public which outweigh the
personal benefit to a small and narrowly defined group of individuals of being kept
in a lifestyle determined by reference to their former conditions of life rather than by
reference to any objective assessment of poverty must be tenuous. Similarly, nor does
a trust for financial provision for the members of one's own family have the characteristic of altruism that is normally the hallmark of charitable activity. It might
therefore be thought that the anomalous treatment of poverty could not survive the
abolition of the presumption of public benefit in the Charities Acts 2006 and 2011.
Nevertheless, in *Attorney General v Charity Commission (The Charity Commission
Poverty Reference)*[427] the Upper Tribunal came to the firm and clearly expressed view
that there was no requirement for a trust for the relief of poverty to satisfy the public benefit requirement by benefiting a sufficiently large and appropriately described
part of the community or public; it was sufficient if the trust met the test of being
charitable in nature.[428] The Tribunal did not consider it necessary to decide whether
poverty charities were anomalous or whether, as a question of fact, the indirect public
benefit of relieving poverty, even for small groups, was sufficient. The Upper Tribunal
decision is consistent with *Cawdron v Merchant Taylors' School*,[429] decided after the
2006 Act, where Blackburne J saw no objection to holding charitable a gift to provide
assistance (including scholarships) for the sons and other dependant relatives of Old
Merchant Taylors killed or disabled in the First World War—a class defined by reference to a single propositus.

(vii) Prevention of poverty

The Upper Tribunal in the *Charity Commission Poverty Reference* case considered
that logic and coherence would normally require the same principles to be applied to
trusts for the prevention of poverty as to those for the relief of poverty. The two objects
would often be combined, and it would likely be illogical to apply different public
benefit rules to a charity established purely for the prevention of poverty. However,
there might be some (undefined) circumstances in which a different rule might be
logical and appropriate.[430]

(g) Distinguishing between public and private benefit: a flexible approach

In contrast to the strict approach to questions of public benefit in the personal nexus
test outlined earlier, others have advocated a more flexible response, arguing that strict

---

[426] [1995] 3 All ER 676, at 688.
[427] [2012] WTLR 977.   [428] [2012] WTLR 977, at [64].   [429] [2009] EWHC 1722 (Ch).
[430] *Attorney General v Charity Commission (The Poverty Reference)* [2012] WTLR 977, at [69]–[82].

tests are unworkable in practice and lead to anomalous results. They consider that each situation should be considered on its own facts, with a variety of circumstances being taken into account before an impressionistic judgement is made whether a class constitutes a section of the public or not.

As was noted earlier, in *Oppenheim v Tobacco Securities Trust Co Ltd* Lord MacDermott dissented from the decision of the majority and held that the personal nexus rule should not alone govern the question of public benefit. He considered that to separate the attributes dividing human beings into classes of those purely personal and those purely impersonal was a task 'no less baffling and elusive than the problem to which it is directed, namely, the determination of what is and what is not a section of the public'.[431] He also pointed out the anomalous results that would follow from such a rigid approach, so that a trust framed to provide for the education of children of those employed in the tobacco industry in a named town would be charitable, even though the class of potential beneficiaries may have been appreciably smaller than that under the trust in question. It would also call into question long-standing charities, for example gifts for the education of the daughters of missionaries or children sent to a particular school. He advocated a flexible approach whereby the court would 'regard the facts of each case and ... treat the matter very much as one of degree', with a process of 'reaching a conclusion on a general survey of the circumstances and considerations regarded as relevant rather than of making a single, conclusive test'.[432] On such an approach he would have held the trust charitable, taking into account the numerical size of the class and the fact that it was not limited to present employees but also ex-employees. The intention of the donor was to 'advance the interest of the class described as a class rather than as a collection or succession of particular individuals'.[433]

In *Dingle v Turner*[434] Lord Cross, who delivered the leading judgment, expressed his dissatisfaction with the strict approach taken in *Oppenheim*. He accepted the force of the criticisms of Lord MacDermott, and acknowledged that he himself would 'prefer to approach the problem on much broader lines'.[435] He considered that the distinction between personal and impersonal relationships was unsatisfactory, and concluded that 'at the end of the day one is left where one started with the bare contrast between "public" and "private"'.[436] Like Lord MacDermott, he accepted that the question whether a trust was for the benefit of the public was a question of degree[437] and that a variety of factors would be taken into account. He suggested that a number of factors were significant:

(i) The size of the class

Obviously, the larger the class of potential beneficiaries the more likely it is that they will constitute a section of the public. Thus, the employees of a fairly small firm are less

---

[431] [1951] AC 297, at 317.   [432] [1951] AC 297, at 314.
[433] [1951] AC 297, at 315.   [434] [1972] AC 601.   [435] [1972] AC 601, at 623.
[436] [1972] AC 601, at 623.   [437] [1972] AC 601 at 624.

likely to be a section of the public than the employees of large companies like ICI and GEC, which employ many thousands of men and women who are largely unknown to each other.[438]

(ii) The purpose of the trust

The objects of the trust will exert a major influence on whether it should be regarded as charitable. Lord Cross explained that there was an intrinsic relationship between the size of the class and the objects of the trust:

> It may well be that, on the one hand, a trust to promote some purpose, prima facie char-
> itable, will constitute a charity even though the class of potential beneficiaries might
> fairly be called a private class and that, on the other hand, a trust to promote another
> purpose, also prima facie charitable, will not constitute a charity even though the class
> of potential beneficiaries might seem to some people fairly describable as a section of
> the public.[439]

Unfortunately, he did not give any illustration of how this principle might apply in practice.

(iii) The fiscal privileges enjoyed as a consequence of charitable status

Lord Cross further indicated that the question of charitable status cannot be determined in isolation from the benefits that such status will bring, so that regard to the
fiscal privileges attendant upon charitable status cannot be avoided. He was of the
view that the decisions in *Re Compton* and *Oppenheim* were influenced by the 'consideration that if such trusts as were there in question were held valid they would
enjoy an undeserved fiscal immunity'.[440] However, Lord MacDermott expressed doubt
whether fiscal privilege was a factor to be taken into account in determining whether
a class constitutes a section of the public, and Viscount Dilhorne and Lord Hodson
concurred with his reservation.

(h) The unsatisfactory state of the current law on public benefit

While the judgment of Lord Cross in *Dingle v Turner*[441] highlights the deficiencies of
the *Oppenheim* test, it sadly fails to eliminate the difficulties the test causes.[442] Its status is in doubt. Although all the members of the House of Lords expressly concurred
with the opinion of Lord Cross, their comments vis-à-vis the *Oppenheim* test were
purely obiter because the trust in question fell within the 'poverty' exception to the
personal nexus rule. It is unfortunate that the law is in such a state of uncertainty, and
an early resolution of the issue, although unlikely, would be desirable. Given the arbitrary character of the strict 'personal nexus' approach advocated by Lord Simmonds,
the 'impressionistic' approach advocated by Lord MacDermott and Lord Cross, which
takes into account a wide range of factors, is preferable. There is no reason why fiscal
privilege should not be considered as a factor, since the very reason why the law insists

---

[438] [1972] AC 601, at 624.   [439] [1972] AC 601, at 624.   [440] [1972] AC 601, at 625.
[441] [1972] AC 601.   [442] Jones 'Charitable Trusts. What is Public Benefit?' (1974) 33 CLJ 63.

that a charity must benefit the public or a section of the public is that private groups should not be entitled to massive state subsidy at the expense of the taxpayer.

(i) Impact of conditions or restrictions on benefit

(i) Assumption that benefits will be available to all in need

Even where a group or class may prima facie constitute a section of the public, there may be conditions, restrictions or aspects of the disposition or association which deprive it of charitable status. The starting point for this is that, once it has been determined that a purpose is in its nature charitable, there is an assumption that the benefits should be available to all those in need, and that it would be illogical to restrict the benefits in an arbitrary way.

(ii) Some restrictions may be justified

It is not inconsistent with charitable status for limits to be provided on access to benefits, provided that these limits are not irrational or unreasonable, and they can be justified by reason of the nature of the charity. It is inevitable that many charitable purposes are not available to every single member of the public. Trusts for the benefit of the blind or the disabled are not available to every member of the community because not every member of the community is blind or disabled. Trusts to provide for sea defences are not of direct benefit to members of the public living inland.[443]

There can also legitimately be limits that are not dictated simply by the nature of the benefit conferred. The provision of almshouses or sheltered accommodation could reasonably be confined to residents of a geographical area, since this is a rational way of allocating a limited provision. Participation in an orchestra might be confined to those who reach a satisfactory musical standard, since otherwise the quality of the musical experience might be affected. Membership of a debating society, while open to the public as a whole, might be limited at any one time to the number of seats in the debating chamber.

(iii) Equality Act 2010

The Equality Act 2010 prohibits discrimination by reference to a protected characteristic, namely age, disability, gender reassignment, marriage and civil partnership, pregnancy and maternity, race, religion or belief, sex, or sexual orientation. There is an exception for charities which by their constitution are permitted to provide benefits only to a group sharing a protected characteristic, and either the object of the trust is to tackle a disadvantage relating to that characteristic, or there is some other legitimate aim which the charity is addressing in a proportionate way. The Charity Commission may approve a change in the governing instrument of a charity to permit discrimination by reference to a protected characteristic, but it refused to do so for the Catholic Care charity, which offered an adoption service for 'hard to place' children, but was willing to do so only for heterosexual couples. For mainly religious reasons, the charity was not prepared to place

---

[443] See *IRC v Baddeley* [1955] AC 572.

children for adoption with homosexual couples. The charity failed in its appeals from the Charity Commission since it did not succeed in showing that there were sufficiently weighty reasons to justify the discrimination it proposed to engage in.[444]

(iv) Arbitrary restrictions are not permitted

Even apart from the Equality Act 2010 restrictions that operate arbitrarily are not permitted. The Charity Commission has suggested in past guidance that a restriction would be inappropriate if it was unrelated to an organization's purpose, for example 'by hair colour or support for a particular football team'.[445] The bar on arbitrary restrictions is illustrated by *IRC v Baddeley*.[446] In this case a gift to a Methodist Mission in London for the promotion of the 'religious, social and physical training' of persons resident in West Ham and Leyton 'who were or were likely to become members of the Methodist Church' was held non-charitable because of the inclusion of social and recreational purposes. However, the House of Lords also held that the class of potential beneficiaries did not constitute a section of the public, so that there was insufficient 'public benefit'. There is no doubt that the residents of a particular area will be regarded as constituting a section of the public, but Viscount Simmonds drew a distinction between 'a form of relief extended to the whole community yet by its very nature advantageous only to the few and a form of relief accorded to a selected few out of a larger number equally willing and able to take advantage of it'.[447] He said that it would be charitable to provide a bridge, available to the public at large, but only used by a very small number. However, it would be different for 'a bridge to be crossed only by impecunious Methodists'. He held that the proposed gift fell within the second category because it was not available to all the residents of West Ham and Leyton but only those who were, or were likely to become, members of the Methodist Church. The principle has sometimes been described as a prohibition on having 'a class within a class'. Its scope is uncertain.

(v) A 'class within a class' is not permitted?

The description of the principle as preventing the creation of a 'class within a class' goes too far, since there are many cases where a charitable trust operates despite a double limitation on eligibility. For instance, a trust for poor widows in Rotherhithe was charitable despite there being three limitations on eligibility.[448] The real objection, it is submitted, is the introduction of an arbitrary limitation on eligibility. There is no objection to funding a church for the use of Methodists, or a synagogue for the use of Jews. But to limit the use of a bridge to Methodists (even poor Methodists) is an arbitrary and capricious restriction in the use of a facility that should be made available to all.

---

[444] *Catholic Care (Diocese of Leeds) v Charity Commission* [2012] UKUT 395 (TCC); *Catholic Care (Diocese of Leeds) v Charity Commission* [2010] EWHC 520 (Ch).

[445] *Public Benefit—The Legal Principles* (January 2005), para 23. See also RR8—*The Public Character of Charity* (February 2001), para 11.   [446] [1955] AC 572.

[447] [1955] AC 572, at 592. Lord Reid dissented on this point and Lords Tucker and Porter expressed no opinion: [1955] AC 572, at 612, 614, and 593.   [448] *Re Faraker* [1912] 2 Ch 488.

(vi) Excluding the less well-off

There are many cases that demonstrate that it is not inimical to charitable status for charges to be made by a charity for the services which it provides. It has already been seen earlier that this has been held to be the case for a housing charity, a health-care charity, for a sports centre, and for educational charities. Nevertheless, there is continuing disquiet in some circles about charities such as public schools or private hospitals that impose charges for their services, with the result that benefits are only available to those who can afford to pay for these services. The fact that these organizations make no private profit, or that any profit that they do make is ploughed back into the further enhancement of their provision, does not silence their critics. In *Re Resch's Will Trusts*[449] it was made clear that the assessment of public benefit in the case of a fee-charging organization need not be confined to an assessment of the benefits to the direct recipients of the services. Indirect benefits to the public can also be taken into account. However, if an organization excludes the less well-off from both direct and indirect benefits, this is likely to affect its charitable status. In *R (Independent Schools Council) v Charity Commission*,[450] the Upper Tribunal considered a challenge by independent schools to the Law Commissions somewhat prescriptive guidance on public benefit. The Upper Tribunal, chaired by Warren J, after a careful review of the case law, considered that the activities of independent schools were of a character that they would be charitable if provided by a free school open to all. The essential question was, therefore, whether the fact that the schools charged fees affected their charitable status. This was a question as to whether the application of the charitable purposes conferred sufficient public benefit.[451] The tribunal considered the hypothetical case of a school which had the sole object of advancing the education of children whose families can afford to pay fees representing the cost of the provision of their education. The tribunal's view was that such a school would not have purposes which provide that element of public benefit necessary to qualify as a charity.[452] The reason for this is that 'a trust which excludes the poor from benefit cannot be a charity'.[453] Few schools were likely to have constitutions which excluded the poor, so defined, but they were also required to operate in a way which did not exclude the poor.[454] It was not, however, an objection that a trust charges fees which equate to the full cost of the provision of its services; the problem arose only where the level of fees was such that only the richer members of the public could afford to pay them.[455] The test in such a case would be whether the fees were affordable to the 'not very well off.'

Provided that a school was not established with a restriction on benefits excluding the poor, and the poor were not de facto excluded, there were a number of ways in which public benefit could be demonstrated by a school with fees higher than those which people of modest means could afford:[456]

---

449 [1969] 1 AC 514.   450 *R (Independent Schools Council) v Charity Commission* [2012] Ch 214.
451 At [112].   452 At [177].   453 At [178].   454 At [215].   455 At [179].
456 At [196]–[205].

(1) through the provision of scholarships and bursaries enabling children from poorer families to attend, whether funded from the school's own resources, or from associated or independent trusts or other grant making bodies;[457]

(2) through arrangements under which students from local state schools can attend classes in subjects not otherwise readily available to them;

(3) by sharing of teachers or teaching facilities with local state schools;

(4) by making available (whether on the internet or otherwise) teaching materials used in the school;

(5) by making available to students of local state schools other facilities such as playing fields, sports halls, swimming pools, or sports grounds.

Taking children out of the state sector who would otherwise have to be educated at public expense might be a minor benefit, but was not in itself sufficient public benefit.[458] Overall, in order to demonstrate public benefit, fee-charging schools needed to demonstrate that they were doing enough for those who cannot afford fees. This required at least that the school admitted a non-token number of children from less well off families,[459] but also that it engaged in such other activities in the interests of the community as a whole (such as those just described) as were appropriate to its own individual circumstances:[460]

> It is for the charity trustees of the school concerned to address and assess how their obligations might best be fulfilled in the context of their own particular circumstances...It is not for the Charity Commission or the Tribunal or the court to impose on trustees of a school their own idea of what is, and what is not, reasonable.[461]

The nature and extent of the benefits which needed to be provided to the wider community would be greater where a school provided facilities and services at the luxury end of the spectrum than in the case of a school with more modest provision.[462]

(j) Non-charitable benefits must be incidental

(i) The 'exclusively charitable' rule

It has already been seen that a trust that combines both charitable and non-charitable objects will not be considered to be charitable. The same principle applies to the way in which the charity operates and the benefits which it confers. By definition, a charity exists for the public benefit. A trust which confers only private benefits cannot be a charitable trust, nor can a trust which provides a mixture of both public and private benefits, unless the private benefits can be seen as being no more than ancillary or subordinate to the public benefits. There can therefore be issues relating to the relative balance of benefits, particularly in the case of membership organizations or trusts that confer benefits on a narrow range of beneficiaries. The essential test with a membership organization is whether the organization has an altruistic purpose with

---

[457] At [184].　　[458] At [205]–[207].　　[459] At [215].　　[460] At [215]–[216].
[461] At [217] and [220].　　[462] At [219].

a membership structure adopted as an effective way of delivering charitable benefits or for administrative convenience, or whether the purpose is primarily self-help.[463]

(ii) Incidental private or non-charitable benefits

Although as a general rule a trust will only be charitable if its objects are exclusively charitable, the courts have held that there is an element of leeway such that a trust is not invalidated merely because it contains some non-charitable objects that are sub-sidiary or ancillary to the main charitable purposes. Thus, in *IRC v City of Glasgow Police Athletic Association*[464] Lord Cohen posed the question whether 'the main pur-pose of the body…is charitable and the only elements in its constitution and oper-ation which are non-charitable are merely incidental to that purpose'.[465] The House of Lords held that, in the circumstances, the promotion of sport was not purely ancillary to the purpose of promoting the efficiency of the police force. The decision would have been different if the non-charitable benefits had been only incidental. It is, for instance, possible for universities as charitable bodies to pay their teaching and sup-port staff, even though this confers private benefits, provided that the payments made represent a fair payment for services rendered. In *Re Coxen*[466] a charitable trust was upheld despite the presence of some non-charitable elements. A previous Lord Mayor of London left some £200,000 to the Court of Aldermen on trust to apply the income to the following purposes:

(1) a sum not exceeding £100 for a dinner for the Court of Aldermen meeting on trust business;

(2) to pay one guinea to each alderman attending a committee in connection with the trust; and

(3) the balance for the benefit of orthopaedic hospitals.

If the first two purposes had not been charitable, Jenkins J would have regarded them as purely ancillary to the main charitable gift. In the event, he held that they were charitable as promoting the better administration of the charity. In *London Hospital Medical College v IRC*[467] a students' union[468] that provided social, cultural, and ath-letic activities for the students of a London teaching hospital was held charitable. Brightman J considered that the prime object of the union was the furtherance of the purposes of the medical college and not the private and personal benefit of the students, which was ancillary.[469] Similarly, in *Re South Place Ethical Society*[470] Dillon J regarded the organization of social activities by the society as purely ancillary to the society's main object of the promotion of ethical principles.[471]

---

[463] Charity Commission, *Public benefit: analysis of the law relating to public benefit* (2013) para 72; see also *Charities and Public Benefit* (January 2008), para F12.   [464] [1953] AC 380.

[465] [1953] AC 380, at 405.   [466] [1948] Ch 747.   [467] [1976] 1 WLR 613.

[468] See also *A-G v Ross* [1986] 1 WLR 252, where the students' union of North London Polytechnic was held charitable despite some non-charitable activities which were regarded as ancillary.

[469] [1976] 1 WLR 613, at 623.   [470] [1980] 1 WLR 1565.   [471] [1980] 1 WLR 1565, at 1569.

In *Funnell v Stewart*[472] the testatrix had left a substantial sum of money to a faith-healing group which held private religious services but which saw its raison d'être as 'the healing work it did for members of the community'.[473] Hazel Williamson QC held that despite the non-charitable nature of the private services, the trust as a whole was charitable because the private services were 'clearly ancillary or subsidiary to the public faith healing part of the group's work, which was its predominant function'.[474] A similar distinction between primary and ancillary purposes was made in *Longridge on the Thames v Revenue and Customs Commissioners*[475] (a tax tribunal decision) where it was held that making charges below commercial cost was ancillary to the primary educational purposes of a youth training centre in water-based activities.

(iii) Severance of non-charitable elements

In some cases it will be possible to sever the non-charitable or private elements in a trust. Where a gift is made in favour of some charitable and other non-charitable purposes, the court may sever the good from the bad. In *Salusbury v Denton*[476] a gift to the testator's widow was to be applied partly toward charitable objects and the rest to his relatives. The widow died without making any appointments, and the court held that there could be a division of the fund between the charitable and non-charitable objects. Page-Wood V-C applied the maxim 'equality is equity' and divided the fund into two equal shares. However, where severance is possible equal division may not always be the most appropriate solution. In *Re Coxen*[477] Jenkins J held that if he had not been able to find that the object of providing a dinner for the aldermen was charitable, he would have been prepared to divide the fund unequally so as to sever the charitable from the non-charitable objects.

(3) Public benefit in particular circumstances

(a) Public benefit can be self-evident

The Upper Tribunal has rejected the view that prior to the Charities Act 2006 there were any presumptions about public benefit in relation to education[478] or to poverty.[479] It has taken the view that a decision is taken in each case on the basis of the evidence, although there are some cases (such as in relation to the provision of mainstream education open to all without the payment of a fee) where it is so obvious that there is a public benefit that evidence may not be required. As Vaisey J said in *Re Shaw's Will Trusts*

> ...there are many cases on this question of whether a bequest is 'charitable' or 'non-charitable' where the purpose is so obviously beneficial to the community that to ask for evidence would really be quite absurd.[480]

---

[472] [1996] 1 WLR 288.   [473] [1996] 1 WLR 288, at 296.   [474] [1996] 1 WLR 288, at 296.
[475] [2013] UKFTT 158 (TC).   [476] (1857) 3 K & J 529.
[477] [1948] Ch 747.   [478] *R (Independent Schools Council) v Charity Commission* [2012] Ch 214.
[479] *Attorney General v Charity Commission (The Poverty Reference)* [2012] WTLR 977.
[480] [1952] Ch 163, at 169.

(b) Public benefit in relieving poverty

Trusts for the relief of poverty are treated more favourably in applying the public benefit requirement than other trusts. It has been seen that this is either because they are
anomalous, or because there is such a substantial indirect public benefit in relieving
poverty that there is no need to demonstrate direct benefit to a class which is not
numerically insignificant and which constitutes a section of the community. If the
latter is the case, this proposition appears to have been established without any need
for formal proof.

(c) The public benefit of religion

There is undoubtedly a requirement for trusts for the advancement of religion to
demonstrate public benefit in order to be charitable,[481] but the case law does not
always distinguish between the need for a purpose to be beneficial in nature and
for it to be beneficial in operation. In *Neville Estates v Madden*[482] Cross J famously
said that 'as between different religions the law stands neutral, but it assumes that
any religion is at least likely to be better than none' and in *Re Watson*[483] a trust
to promote Christian spiritual works which experts unanimously considered to be
worthless was held to be charitable. From this it might be thought that the public benefit requirement applies only to the operation of the charity. However, the
Charity Commission has refused to register some alleged religions on the basis that
they 'must tend directly or indirectly to the moral or spiritual improvement of the
public' and have 'an identifiable positive, beneficial, moral or ethical framework',
conditions which were not met in the case of Gnosticism and Druidry.[484] Whilst
these requirements may be sensible, they are not directly supported by the later
Supreme Court decision in *R (on the application of Hodkin) v Registrar General of
Births, Deaths and Marriages*,[485] and it has been argued that they are not justified
in law.[486] There is a difficulty for the law in recognizing new religions or religious
sects because it can involve examining matters of spiritual belief which according
to the Court of Appeal in *Shergill v Khaira*[487] are non-justiciable because they are
not matters of law at all, but subjective inward matters incapable of proof by direct
evidence or by inference. According to the court it is therefore inappropriate for a
court to pronounce on matters of religious doctrine and practice, although there
may be rare occasions on which they have to foray into such matters to resolve issues
of property rights.

The question of public benefit in the operation of a religion is, however, one which
requires legal resolution on the basis of forensic proof. Contemplative religious orders
that are cloistered and have no contact with the community at large have been held not

---

[481] *Gilmour v Coats* [1949] AC 426 and *Neville Estates Ltd. v Madden* [1962] Ch 832.

[482] [1962] Ch 832, at 853.   [483] [1973] 1 WLR 1472.

[484] See Luxton and Evans 'Cogent and cohesive? Two recent Charity Commission decisions on the
advancement of religion' [2011] 75 Conv 144.   [485] [2013] UKSC 77.

[486] See Luxton and Evans 'Cogent and cohesive? Two recent Charity Commission decisions on the
advancement of religion' [2011] 75 Conv 144.   [487] [2012] EWCA Civ 983, at [69]–[70].

to be charitable. In *Gilmour v Coats*[488] a gift of £500 was made to a priory of Carmelite nuns, who were cloistered and devoted their lives to prayer. The House of Lords held that they were not a charity because there was not the necessary element of benefit to the public. There was no interaction between the nuns and the community and Lord Simmonds rejected as 'too vague and intangible' any claimed edification of the public through the example of their spiritual lives and sacrifice. He also rejected the alleged benefit to the community of their intercessory prayer according to Roman Catholic doctrine, as evidenced by an affidavit of the Archbishop of Westminster. This alleged benefit was dismissed as 'manifestly not susceptible of proof', and he stated that the court does not accept as fact whatever a particular religion believes. In *Leahy v A-G of New South Wales*[489] a gift to religious orders which could have included contemplative orders would have been held invalid by the Privy Council as not being exclusively for charitable purposes if it had not been saved by the New South Wales Conveyancing Act 1919–54.

By contrast, the courts have consistently taken the view that public religious worship will provide sufficient public benefit. This may well be capable of forensic proof, but it is not self-evident to many atheists and agnostics, nor is it a matter on which the courts have ever expected evidence to be presented. In *Neville Estates Ltd v Madden* this attitude was reflected by Cross J, who said:

> the court is…entitled to assume that some benefit accrues to the public from the attendance at places of worship of persons who live in this world and mix with their fellow citizens.[490]

This was echoed by Sir Nicholas Browne-Wilkinson V-C in *Re Hetherington (Decd)*:

> The celebration of a religious rite in public does confer a sufficient public benefit because of the edifying and improving effect of such a celebration on the members of the public who attend.[491]

He therefore held that the saying of masses for the dead was prima facie charitable since the invariable practice is that they are said in public, 'which provides a sufficient element of public benefit'. No evidence was presented as to the nature of the benefit either to the dead or to the living.

The Charities Acts 2006 and 2011 will not have changed this position.

(d) The public benefit of animal welfare

A similar issue about public benefit arises in relation to animal welfare charities, where judicial notice was taken *Re Wedgwood*[492] of the elevating effect on the human race of providing animal welfare. However, some animal welfare organizations show scant regard for the welfare of humans, and if evidence acceptable to a court of law is required to demonstrate the public benefit of a ban on experimentation on animals,[493] why should there be no need of such proof of the benefits of the provision of animal welfare?

---

[488] [1949] AC 426.   [489] [1959] AC 457.   [490] [1962] Ch 832.   [491] [1990] Ch 1.
[492] [1915] 1 Ch 113.   [493] *National Anti-vivisection Society v IRC* [1948] AC 31.

9 Interpreting charitable gifts

(1) Purposes must be exclusively charitable

For a trust to be upheld as a valid charitable trust it must be for exclusively charitable purposes. None of the trust property must be applicable to non-charitable objects. Similarly, a corporation or unincorporated association will only be a charity if its purposes are exclusively charitable. If there is a combination of purposes, some charitable and others not, then it will not be charitable and will not enjoy the privileges outlined earlier. Thus, in *IRC v Oldham Training and Enterprise Council*[494] Lightman J held that an organization to support business development was not a charitable body because its objects included some non-charitable elements, including the promotion of the interests of individuals rather than of the community in general. Similarly, in *McGovern v A-G*[495] the trust established by Amnesty International included some charitable objects, but also some non-charitable political purposes, and was not held charitable. In *Williams' Trustees v IRC*[496] the objects included many that were charitable, but also the promotion of social activities that are not. In *IRC v Baddeley*[497] the promotion of Methodism was a charitable purpose but the promotion of sport and recreation were not.

(2) Ordinary rules of construction

The starting point for construing a charity's governing documents is that ordinary principles of construction apply. According to Lord Hoffman in *Attorney General of Belize v Belize Telecom Ltd*: [498]

> It is the meaning which the instrument would convey to a reasonable person having all the background knowledge which would reasonably be available to the audience to whom the instrument is addressed.

(3) Benignant construction in cases of ambiguity

There are some circumstances where the court may take a generous approach and give a disposition a 'benignant construction'.[499] This means that, where there is an ambiguity such that a gift is capable of two constructions, one of which would make it void and the other effectual, the court will uphold it. This approach was confirmed by the House of Lords in *Guild v IRC*.[500] The precise scope of the principle permitting a benignant

---

[494] [1996] STC 1218.   [495] [1982] Ch 321.   [496] [1947] AC 447.   [497] [1955] AC 572.

[498] [2009] UKPC 10 at 16. Although this was a case involving the interpretation of a written contract, the principles are considered to be of general application. See also *Investors Compensation Scheme Ltd v West Bromwich Building Society* [1998] 1 WLR 896 for a statement of canons of interpretation.

[499] *IRC v McMullen* [1981] AC 1, at 14, per Lord Hailsham LC; *Weir v Crum-Brown* [1908] AC 162, at 167, per Lord Loreburn LC.   [500] [1992] 2 AC 310, at 322.

construction was considered by Hazel Williamson QC in *Funnell v Stewart*.[501] She indicated that it would not save a 'dual purpose gift' where one identifiable object was clearly present but plainly not charitable, as the court could not simply ignore the non-charitable element of the trust. However, it would enable the court to save a gift which had a single purpose which was capable of being carried into effect in two different ways, one of which would be charitable and the other of which would not.[502]

(4) **Statutory amendment**

Where a charitable instrument limits benefits to persons defined by colour, then under the Equality Act 2010, s 193 (4)[503] the instrument will operate as if there had been no reference to skin colour. This provision was applied in *Re Harding*.[504] A dying nun made a will leaving her property to be held 'in trust for the black community of Hackney, Haringey, Islington and Tower Hamlets'. Lewison J held that the gift was charitable in character as a gift for the benefit of a local area, and that, applying the statutory provision, the restriction to the black community should be removed. Since there was no specific scheme for the use of the funds, this could be resolved by the approval of a scheme by the Charity Commission.[505]

(5) **Conjunctions**

Where a trust lists a variety of purposes, the conjunctions used may determine whether the gift is to be construed as exclusively for charitable purposes. The word 'or' is usually given a disjunctive construction, so that 'charitable or benevolent' purposes are not exclusively charitable. In contrast, the word 'and' is usually given a conjunctive construction so that 'charitable and benevolent' purposes would be exclusively charitable. Although providing a strong prima facie indication, these are not binding rules of construction and each case must be examined in the light of the surrounding circumstances.

(a) 'And'

In *Re Sutton*[506] a gift to 'charitable and deserving' objects was held exclusively charitable. The word 'and' was given a conjunctive interpretation so that only deserving objects which were also charitable were contemplated. In *Re Best*[507] a gift to 'charitable and benevolent' institutions was similarly held exclusively charitable. The conjunctive construction is only a prima facie guide that may be displaced. In *A-G of the Bahamas v Royal Trust Co*,[508] a gift for purposes connected with the 'education and welfare' of Bahamian children was, in the light of all the circumstances, construed disjunctively and the gift therefore failed since it permitted the application of funds for

---

[501] [1996] 1 WLR 288, at 296–297.   [502] See also *Re Hetherington* [1990] Ch 1.
[503] Replacing Race Relations Act 1976, s 34.   [504] [2008] Ch 235.
[505] [2008] Ch 235, at [27].   [506] (1885) 28 Ch D 464.
[507] [1904] 2 Ch 354.   [508] [1986] 1 WLR 1001.

educational purposes alternatively for welfare purposes, which need not necessarily be educational.[509]

(b) 'Or'

In *Blair v Duncan*[510] a testatrix gave her trustee discretion to apply part of her residuary estate to 'charitable or public purposes'. The House of Lords held that this was to be read disjunctively, so that the gift included 'public purposes', which may fall outside the scope of charity. The gift therefore failed. A similar result was reached in *Houston v Burns*,[511] where a gift was made for 'public, benevolent or charitable purposes'. In *Chichester Diocesan Fund and Board of Finance v Simpson*[512] a gift in favour of 'charitable or benevolent objects'[513] was reluctantly held not to be exclusively charitable. The House of Lords could not find a more favourable interpretation than that the purposes were to be considered disjunctively.[514] Subsequently, in *A-G of the Cayman Islands v Wahr-Hansen*[515] the Privy Council advised that a trust established for the benefit of 'any one or more religious, charitable or educational institution or instructions or any organizations or institutions operating for the public good' was not exclusively charitable.

In some circumstances, on the construction of a gift as a whole, the word 'or' may not be read in this disjunctive way. In *Re Bennett*[516] a gift to educational purposes and 'other objects of charity, or any other public objects in the parish of Farringdon' was held to be exclusively charitable. Taken as a whole, and especially noting the word 'other', Eve J held that it was not to be construed disjunctively but to mean other public purposes that are also charitable.

(6) Charitable Trusts (Validation) Act 1954

This Act mitigates the impact of *Chichester Diocesan Fund v Simpson*[517] by treating similar cases as if the trust had been exclusively charitable. It retrospectively validates trusts coming into effect prior to 16 December 1952. The Act has no application to trusts coming into effect after 15 December 1952. Equally, the Act does not apply where the primary purpose of a trust is to provide non-charitable benefits. In *Re St Andrew's (Cheam) Lawn Tennis Club Trust*[518] land was held on trust for a range of purposes including both providing premises for a tennis club associated with the local church, and also for the benefit of the church. Arnold J held that the trust could not be treated as wholly charitable by the 1954 Act since it would have deprived the club of the benefit it was intended to receive. He approved the test set out by Hart J in *Ulrich v Treasury Solicitor*,[519] that the Act did not apply where it 'would flout either

---

[509] See also *Re Eades* [1920] 2 Ch 353, 'religious, charitable and philanthropic objects' held not exclusively charitable.   [510] [1902] AC 37.

[511] [1918] AC 337.

[512] [1944] AC 341, HL.   [513] See also *Oxford Group v IRC* [1949] 2 All ER 537, CA.

[514] See also *Re Macduff* [1896] 2 Ch 451, where a gift to charitable or philanthropic purposes was held not exclusively charitable.   [515] [2001] 1 AC 75.   [516] [1920] 1 Ch 305.

[517] [1944] AC 341, HL.   [518] [2012] EWHC 1040 (Ch).   [519] [2005] EWHC 67 (Ch).

the intention of the settlor or the legitimate expectations of those interested under the non-charitable objects' for the trust to be confined to those purposes which were charitable.

Apart from the 1954 Act, there is no legislation in England allowing a gift which is partly charitable and partly non-charitable to be upheld in so far as it is charitable.[520]

(7) **Trusts for the benefit of a locality**

For reasons which have now become obscure, the courts have adopted a benevolent construction towards gifts made in general terms for the benefit of a named locality or its inhabitants. Such gifts are construed to be impliedly limited to charitable purposes in the specified community. Thus a gift to a particular parish,[521] or for the good of a particular country,[522] such as a gift for 'the benefit and advantage of Great Britain',[523] will be upheld as a valid charitable trust. However, in *A-G of the Cayman Islands v Wahr-Hansen*[524] the Privy Council advised that this generous rule of construction should not be extended to encompass all cases where there are general statements of benevolent or philanthropic objects.

---

[520] There is legislation to this effect in the Republic of Ireland: Charities Act 1960, s 49. See also *Leahy v A-G for New South Wales* [1959] AC 457, where similar Australian legislation was applied.

[521] *West v Knight* (1669) 1 Cas in Ch 134.

[522] *A-G v Earl of Lonsdale* (1827) 1 Sim 105; *Re Smith* [1932] 1 Ch 153.

[523] *Nightingale v Goulburn* (1847) 5 Hare 484.   [524] [2001] 1 AC 75.

12

Clubs and societies

Most people would not give the issues about how clubs and societies can hold and manage property much thought. However, since some forms of club do not have a legal personality as such, there is a real issue about how they can deal with property, whether this concerns everyday management, the receipt of gifts, or who is entitled to the club's property if the club is dissolved. Trusts play a role in providing an explanation.

1 Types of clubs and societies

English law does not accord automatically an independent status to clubs, societies, or other unincorporated associations. The question that arises from this is how a society with no legal status as such can hold or manage property. Equity, as is so often the case in relation to the management of property, has sought to supply the answer. It is desirable first, however, to distinguish four different kinds of club or society.

(1) Proprietary clubs

A proprietary club is privately owned by an individual or company. The owner permits members to use the facilities in return for membership and other fees. A hotel with leisure facilities that permits members of the public to use the swimming pool and exercise rooms in return for an annual fee, describing those subscribing in terms such as members of the 'Park Hotel Health Club' would be a club of this kind. Since all the club assets belong to the owner, there are no special considerations for the involvement of equity.

(2) Incorporated clubs and societies

A variant of the proprietary club is where the proprietor that owns the club assets is a company and its shareholders are also the members of the club. In such a case, each member of the club may be required to acquire a share in the company owning the club assets at the time of being admitted as a member. On leaving membership, the member may then be required to surrender the share. In this way, only members of the club are shareholders and through their shareholdings, they own and control the club assets, although it is the company that will be treated as owner for such legal purposes as bringing and defending legal actions. On the dissolution of the club, any club assets will be distributed in accordance with company law.

(3) **Members' club**

Another type of club is a members' club. The club assets are neither owned by a company nor an individual, whether associated with the membership or not. It is in this situation that the issue arises of who owns and controls the club assets. Clubs and societies belonging to this category are generally described as unincorporated associations. They are a group of individuals, bound together in some way by club rules, but without having acquired separate legal personality for the group by incorporation or in some other way such as registration as a friendly society.

(4) **Societies that are not unincorporated associations**

After we have considered the theory upon which unincorporated associations legally own and manage property, we shall see that there is, in fact, a further type of association or society which cannot fit within the ordinary principles created by equity, and a further set of extraordinary principles have had to be developed to cover this situation.

2 The 'problem' of asset holding and management

The absence of an independent legal personality for an unincorporated association creates only a theoretical problem of asset holding and management.[1] Most clubs and societies get along perfectly well, raising funds by subscriptions from members and by fundraising events such as cake sales, car boot sales, and other activities. They will find little difficulty in opening a bank or building society account. A problem arises only when someone leaves a legacy by will to an unincorporated association, and the next of kin or residuary beneficiary challenges the validity of the legacy; or when the association is being wound up and there is a dispute between the members; or in some similar situation.

The courts have been prevented by precedent and English legal tradition from saying that an unincorporated association, as such, is capable of owning property. Yet were the courts to say that the association is incapable of enjoying or managing property, they would be flying in the face of reality. The courts have therefore had to invent or construct[2] a solution to the 'problem' in order to justify the fact that in practice unincorporated associations can enjoy and manage, and receive by subscription or gift (sometimes substantial) funds and assets.

---

[1] See Warburton, *Unincorporated Associations: Law and Practice* (2nd edn, 1992), Ch 5.
[2] See Hackney, *Understanding Equity and Trusts* (1987), pp 75–82.

(1) **The purpose trust theory**

It will be seen in Chapter 14 that, except in the case of charities, English law does not permit the creation of a trust that has no beneficiaries, with the exception of a few narrowly defined categories. One such exception used to apply to gifts to unincorporated associations[3] which were considered valid as gifts for the purposes of the association provided that the association was free to dispose of its assets at any time.[4] If the terms of the gift, or the rules of the association to which it was made, did not permit the association to be wound up and its assets disposed of within a period of lives in being, plus up to a further twenty-one years, then the disposition would be invalid for infringing the rule against perpetual trusts, otherwise known as the rule against inalienability.[5]

Judicial doubt has been expressed as to whether, even if the gift to an unincorporated association were limited to the perpetuity period, it could take effect as a gift for the purposes of the society. In *Leahy v A-G of New South Wales*,[6] Viscount Simonds expressed the firm opinion that a gift upon trust for the purposes of an unincorporated association would be invalid for want of beneficiaries. Viscount Simonds believed that the cases upholding gifts to unincorporated associations could be upheld on a different principle, namely, that they were beneficial gifts to the members of the society. This analysis is considered later.

It has been suggested by Goff J in *Re Denley's Trust Deed*[7] that a gift for non-charitable purposes would not fall foul of the beneficiary principle if the purposes were directly or indirectly for the benefit of an individual or individuals. This may mean that, subject to the gift being confined to the perpetuity period, a gift for the purposes of an unincorporated association that benefits the members of that association can be valid notwithstanding Viscount Simonds' observations.

(2) **Gift to members**

The theory that Lord Simonds believed explained the unincorporated association cases was that the law treated a gift to an association as valid if the gift could be treated as to the present members rather than upon trust for the purposes of the society. The case before the Privy Council in *Leahy v A-G of New South Wales*[8] concerned a gift by will of a homestead and land upon trust to whatever order of Roman Catholic nuns or Christian Brothers his executors might select. The gift could not be treated as wholly charitable, because his executors were at liberty to select a purely contemplative order of nuns.[9] Could the gift be treated as a valid private trust in favour of a contemplative order of nuns if the executors wished to choose such a group? The Privy Council advised that it could not. The gift could not be valid as a gift for the purposes of such a

---

[3] See *Re Endacott* [1960] Ch 232.

[4] *Re Drummond* [1914] 2 Ch 90; *Re Clarke* [1901] 2 Ch 110; *Re Taylor* [1940] Ch 481; *Re Price* [1943] Ch 422.   [5] *Carne v Long* (1860) 2 De GF & J 75; *Re Macaulay' Estate* [1943] Ch 435.

[6] [1959] AC 457.   [7] [1969] 1 Ch 373.   [8] [1959] AC 457.

[9] The necessary element of demonstrable public benefit for the advancement of religion was lacking: see Chapter 11.

group. It could therefore be upheld only if it were a gift to the members of the chosen order. In the opinion of the Privy Council, a gift to an unincorporated association was to be treated prima facie as a gift to the individual members of that association at the time of the gift so that they could together dispose of it as they thought fit. On that footing, a gift to an unincorporated association would be valid.

But that interpretation of the gift was not possible in this case, and the gift was invalid in so far as a contemplative order of nuns could be selected. The testator had not made a gift to the members of a selected order, but upon trust for the order itself; the order could be numerically very large and spread over the whole world, and although the homestead had twenty rooms and there were 730 acres of land, it was unrealistic to expect this to be shared beneficially by the members of a religious order. The Privy Council believed that:

> ...however little the testator understood the effect in law of a gift to an unincorporated
> body of persons by their society name, his intention was to create a trust not merely for
> the benefit of the existing members of the selected order but for its benefit as a continuing
> society and for the furtherance of its work.[10]

To give effect to this, the gift would have to include future as well as present members of the order. It would then fail for perpetuity. The statement by Viscount Simonds exposes one of the difficulties with the theory that he adopted. The court was obliged to frustrate the intentions of the testator because of the lack of an adequate theory to explain how a contemplative order of nuns could receive, hold, and manage assets. Yet there are contemplative orders with substantial property interests. The theory is clearly inadequate to explain this.

There are other problems. If a gift to a club or society is treated as a gift to the individual members beneficially, it enables them to deal with it collectively however they wish. But if they are tenants-in-common of the gift, each member could claim payment directly of his share, and if joint tenants, each member could do the same after an act of severance converting his interest into that of a tenant-in-common. Again, the theory does not explain how club or society assets should be dealt with when new members join or existing members resign.[11] An existing member with a share as tenant-in-common or joint tenant of property derived from gifts to which the *Leahy* analysis applies would continue to be entitled to it even after leaving membership of the club, unless there was an assignment of the share to the continuing members, which would require writing.[12]

---

[10] [1959] AC 457, at 486.

[11] In *Hanchett-Stamford v Attorney-General* [2009] Ch 173, Lewison J rejected any suggestion that members of unincorporated associations held under any specialized form of co-ownership: 'Megarry & Wade, *The Law of Real Property* (6th edn, 2000), para 9–095 accuses the courts of having developed "a new form of property holding by unincorporated associations" in order to escape from technical difficulties of the classic models of joint tenancies and tenancies in common. I do not think that the courts have purported to do so...the "ownership" of assets by an unincorporated association must, somehow, fit into accepted structures of property ownership' (at 183 [31]).

[12] The assignment of any existing equitable interest requires a written disposition: Law of Property Act 1925, s 53(1)(c). See Chapter 7.

(3) **Mutual contract theory**

In *Neville Estates Ltd v Madden*,[13] Cross J put forward a refined version of the *Leahy* theory that goes some way to meet the objections. He said that a gift could be construed as:

> ...a gift to the existing members not as joint tenants, but subject to their respective con-
> tractual rights and liabilities towards one another as members of the association. In such
> a case a member cannot sever his share. It will accrue to the other members on his death
> or resignation, even though such members include persons who became members after
> the gift took effect. If this is the effect of the gift, it will not now be open to objection on
> the ground of perpetuity or uncertainty unless there is something in its terms or circum-
> stances or in the rules of the association which precludes the members at any given time
> from dividing the subject of the gift between them on the footing that they are solely
> entitled to it in equity.[14]

Cross J did not need to apply the analysis to the case before him, since he was concerned with a charitable association in relation to which it is clear that property may validly be held upon trust for the purposes of the association. The analysis was, however, adopted by Brightman J in *Re Recher's Will Trusts*,[15] the case with which this theory is most frequently associated. In that case, Brightman J held that a gift by will to the London and Provincial Anti-Vivisection Society would have been valid on this interpretation if the society had still been in existence at the date of the testatrix's death. Other cases subsequently have adopted the same analysis and it is now generally accepted as the proper way in which to explain how unincorporated associations receive gifts, hold their assets, and distribute them on the winding-up of the association. As Walton J said in *Re Bucks Constabulary Fund (No 2)*:[16]

> I can see no reason for thinking that this analysis is any different whether the purpose
> for which the members of the association associate are a social club, a sporting club, to
> establish a widows' and orphans' fund, to obtain a separate Parliament for Cornwall, or
> to further the advance of alchemy. It matters not. All the assets of the association are held
> in trust for its members (of course subject to the contractual claims of anybody having a
> valid contract with the association) save and except to the extent to which valid trusts have
> otherwise been declared of its property.

The theory allows the club or society to own assets by deeming them to be vested bene-ficially in the members, although legal title will normally be held by some trustee, such as the treasurer, who will hold the assets upon trust to deal with them in accordance with the instructions of the committee of management[17] and ultimately the members; but it prevents members from withdrawing their share of the assets from the society by

---

[13] [1962] Ch 832.   [14] [1962] Ch 832, at 849.   [15] [1972] Ch 526.

[16] [1979] 1 All ER 623.

[17] It is desirable that a gift by will to an unincorporated association should provide that the receipt of the treasurer or other officer is a sufficient discharge, for if this is not provided for by the rules of the society, the administrators of the estate should technically obtain the discharge by way of receipt from every member.

treating the rules of the society as paramount, which members have mutually agreed by contract to observe.[18]

In *Hanchett-Stamford v Attorney-General*,[19] Leahy J affirmed this analysis in dealing with the proprietary entitlements of the sole survivor of an unincorporated association established for the purpose of securing a ban on the use of performing animals in film. In holding that all property vested in the sole surviving member under the rules of survivorship of a joint tenancy, he held:

> It is true that this is not a joint tenancy according to the classical model; but since any collective ownership of property must be a species of joint tenancy or tenancy in common, this kind of collective ownership must, in my judgment, be a subspecies of joint tenancy, albeit taking effect subject to any contractual restrictions applicable as between members. In some cases... those contractual restrictions may be such as to exclude any possibility of a future claim. In others they may not. The cases are united in saying that on a dissolution the members of a dissolved association have a beneficial interest in its assets... I cannot see why the legal principle should be any different if the reason for the dissolution is the permanent cessation of the association's activities or the fall in its membership to below two. The same principle ought also to hold if the contractual restrictions are abrogated or varied by agreement of the members.[20]

(4) Limits to the mutual contract theory

(a) Restriction on dissolving the society

The mutual contract theory explained in *Neville Estates Ltd v Madden* and *Re Recher's Will Trusts* can only apply, as Cross J explained, where there is nothing in the terms of the gift or in the rules of the society that will prevent the distribution of the association's assets. If there is, then even under this analysis, any gift will fail under the rule against perpetual trusts. In *Carne v Long*[21] a testator had made a gift of his house to the trustees of the Penzance Public Library, a subscription library. The rules of the library provided that it could not be broken up as long as ten members remained. The House of Lords held that, under the rules, the library was intended to be a perpetual institution, so that the gift could not be upheld.

(b) Members do not have control of the assets

In the leading case of *Re Grant's Will Trusts*[22] a testator left property 'to the Labour Party Property Committee for the benefit of the Chertsey Headquarters of the Chertsey and Walton Constituency Labour Party'. Under the rules of the Constituency Labour Party, its constitution could not be altered without the consent of the National Labour Party, to which it was subordinate. Vinelott J held that the element of control by an outside body meant that the gift infringed the rule against perpetual trusts, since the

---

[18] As in *Clarke v Earl of Dunraven and Mount-Earl* [1897] AC 59.   [19] [2009] Ch 173.
[20] [2009] Ch 173, at 188.   [21] (1860) 2 De GF & J 75.   [22] [1980] 1 WLR 360.

Constituency Party was not at liberty to dissolve itself.[23] This reasoning was distinguished by Lawrence Collins J in *Re Horley Town Football Club*,[24] who held that the ability of a body, not itself the member of the unincorporated association, to vote at meetings of the Club was not sufficient to defeat the application of the contract-holding theory. The case concerned identifying the nature of the members of Horley Town Football Club's entitlement to property settled on trust for the purpose of securing a permanent football ground for the team. On the facts of the case, the relevant rules of the association had been altered in 2000, so that independently constituted clubs enjoying associate membership were to be entitled to attend the AGM and to cast one vote, and it was argued that this prevented the entitlement of any members after the rule change to the property, as the mutual contract-holding theory could not apply. The distinction Lawrence Collins J reached was a technical one. He contrasted the situation in the instant case with the seriousness of the voting rights in *Re Grants Will Trusts*, and therefore held that the members could hold the property on mutual contracts on a per capita basis:

> I do not consider that it matters that the Rules were changed in 2000 to confer a right to vote on a body which is not itself a member, namely the club of which Associate Members are members. This is far from the case of *Re Grant's Will Trusts*, where Vinelott J held that the influence of a body (not itself a member) on the rules and the destination of Club property was fatal to the argument that a gift should be analysed as one within [mutual contract theory]…[25]

(c) Assets held for mixed purposes

In *Re St Andrew's (Cheam) Lawn Tennis Club Trust*[26] land had been acquired by trustees on trusts which included the provision of land for a tennis or sports ground, and also charitable purposes. Arnold J held that the land could not be treated as belonging to the members of the club because the trust was for mixed purposes, nor could it be treated as a purely charitable trust because this would defeat the primary purpose of providing a tennis ground. The trust deed was an attempt to achieve the legally impossible: a perpetual trust for a non-charitable purpose, namely to enable the members of the club to play tennis. The trust failed, and the property had to go on a resulting trust.

(d) Lack of identifiable membership

The theory can only apply where there is an identifiable membership, who are capable (in theory) of being beneficial owners subject to the rules of membership. This

---

[23] Compare *News Group Newspapers Ltd v Society of Graphical and Allied Trades* [1986] ICR 716, CA, where, although the local branch of a trade union was subordinate to the national union, it was in theory possible for the local branch to secede from the union and dissolve itself. It may be that even where there is no provision under the rules of an association for amendment and dissolution, this would be permitted by the unanimous agreement of the members: see *Universe Tankships Inc of Monrovia v International Transport Workers Federation* [1983] 1 AC 366, HL.   [24] [2006] EWHC 2386 (Ch).

[25] [2006] EWHC 2386 (Ch), at [117]. See further, in support, Luxton 'Gifts to Clubs: Contract-Holding Is Trumps' [2007] Conv 274.   [26] [2012] EWHC 1040 (Ch).

presented a problem in *Conservative and Unionist Central Office v Burrell*.[27] The party was considered by the Court of Appeal to be a combination of a number of elements that could not be considered an unincorporated association because of the lack of a body of mutual rights and duties binding those elements together.

(e) Conditions attached to gifts to unincorporated associations

There may be something in the terms of a gift rather than in the rules of an association that makes the mutual contract theory inapplicable. The theory cannot apply if the terms of the gift exclude the possibility of the members of the association taking beneficially. This was considered by Oliver J in *Re Lipinski's Will Trusts*.[28] Harry Lipinski had left his residuary estate to an unincorporated association, the Hull Judeans (Maccabi) Association, 'in memory of my late wife to be used solely in the work of constructing new buildings for the association and/or improvements to the said buildings'. The next-of-kin disputed the validity of this gift. Their counsel argued that the terms of the gift meant that the members of the association could not take beneficially, since the money had to be used for a particular purpose and because there was an intention to create a permanent endowment. Oliver J rejected the argument that the words of the gift showed an intention to create a permanent endowment: the whole of the money could be spent immediately. Nor did he think that the direction of Harry Lipinski as to how the money should be spent was binding on the association. The association was free within its rules to alter its constitution and to divide the whole of its assets between the members.[29] Oliver J therefore believed that there was nothing to prevent the application of the mutual contract theory. As an alternative, he considered that, even if the association was bound to apply the money for a particular purpose, on the authority of *Re Denley's Trust Deed* 'a trust which, though expressed as a purpose, was directly or indirectly for the benefit of an individual or individuals was valid provided that those individuals were ascertainable at any one time and the trust was not otherwise void for uncertainty'.[30]

The latter analysis might ensure that Harry Lipinski's bounty was used as he intended, although even in this case some of Oliver J's remarks suggest that the members of the association would be free as both trustees and beneficiaries of the gift to treat it as an absolute one.[31] In order to sustain the validity of Harry Lipinski's gift, Oliver J is thus permitting the association to disregard his directions. One wonders if Harry Lipinski would have turned in his grave at the suggestion that the members of the association would be free to divide the legacy among themselves, rather than

---

[27] [1982] 1 WLR 522.   [28] [1976] Ch 235.

[29] He drew an analogy with *Re Bowes* [1896] 1 Ch 507, where it was held that a gift by will to be used for planting trees on the Wemmergill Estate could be used in any way which the landowner chose.

[30] This analysis of the gift appears to represent a return to the purpose trust theory that was rejected in *Leahy v A-G for New South Wales*. Some doubt about the decision in *Re Denley* was expressed by Lawrence Collins J in *Re Horley Town Football Club* [2006] EWHC 2386 (Ch), at [99] and [131] because 'there are difficulties with regard to termination of such a trust which make it an unsafe basis for decision'.

[31] By analogy with *Re Turkington* [1937] 4 All ER 501. This appears to be an application of the rule in *Saunders v Vautier* (1841) 10 LJ Ch 354.

building as he requested. If he intended an absolute gift to the members, why did he seek to impose a direction as to how it was to be used?

There might be situations in which the addition of a direction in a gift to an unincorporated association could not be overcome in one of the ways suggested by Oliver J in *Re Lipinski's Will Trusts*.[32] If a gift to an unincorporated association imposes in clear terms a trust to use that gift in a way which is neither directly nor indirectly for the benefit of the members, it would be rather more difficult to treat the gift as an absolute one to the members of the association subject to its rules, since the members would not also be beneficiaries. This is one way in which *Re St Andrew's (Cheam) Lawn Tennis Club Trust*[33] could be viewed. Even in this case, however, if the purposes of the trust were within the purposes of the society (which was not so in the *St Andrew's* case), it might be possible to take the view that the direction to hold upon trust was otiose and could therefore be disregarded. There is persuasive authority that in the case of benevolent associations established for altruistic purposes the mutual contract analysis is the one which prima facie applies to the assets of the association.[34]

(f) Charitable unincorporated associations

It is possible for a charity to be established via the mechanism of an unincorporated association. In this case, the assets of the association are dedicated to charitable purposes and are not available to the members individually.

(5) Associations without mutual contract status

Mention has already been made of *Conservative and Unionist Central Office v Burrell*,[35] a case that involved the tax status of the Conservative Party. If it was an unincorporated association, then the treasurer would have been liable to pay corporation tax on behalf of the association. The Court of Appeal held that the Conservative Party was not an unincorporated association because, although it was an association of individuals, it lacked a set of rules regulating its affairs and binding its members together by means of mutually enforceable rights and obligations.[36] Since the existence of such a body of rules is essential to the mutual contract analysis of property-holding by clubs and societies, the court felt obliged to offer a solution as to how the Conservative Party was legally entitled to manage its finances. In the High Court,[37] Vinelott J put forward the suggestion that a person making a donation to the party entered into a contract with the treasurer under which the latter would be in breach of contract if he failed to apply the sums received for the purposes of the party, and that the treasurer might

---

[32] [1976] Ch 235.   [33] [2012] EWHC 1040 (Ch).

[34] *Re Bucks Constabulary Widows' and Orphans' Fund Friendly Society (No 2)* [1979] 1 All ER 623, where Walton J believed that nothing turned upon the status of the benevolent fund as a Friendly Society in deciding how its property was held for the purpose of distribution on its dissolution.

[35] [1982] 1 WLR 522, CA.

[36] The Court of Appeal also suggested that an unincorporated association required a defined date upon which it had come into existence, and that members should be free to join or to leave at will. The necessity for these requirements may be doubted.   [37] [1980] 3 All ER 42.

also be under some special equitable obligation akin to that of an executor. Without commenting on these possibilities, Brightman LJ in the Court of Appeal put forward another possibility. He suggested that the contributor would confer an irrevocable mandate on the party treasurer[38] to add the donation or subscription to the general funds of the party. The contributor would have the right to prevent a misapplication of the general funds, or to have a misapplication remedied, until on ordinary accounting principles no part of the contributor's donation is represented in the general funds.[39]

Brightman LJ acknowledged that the mandate theory could not easily support donations by will, since mandate and agency relationships can subsist only during the lifetime of the principal.[40] It would, however, be possible for a testator to authorize his personal representatives to enter into a mandate on his behalf.

The potential of the mandate theory to explain and justify gifts where there is no obvious beneficiary has yet to be fully explored or exploited. For instance, there is no reason why mandate or agency theory could not equally apply to gifts to unincorporated associations with clear rules as it does to less formally constituted groups. The mandate theory could also make a gift for purposes effective even without any ascertainable human beneficiaries.[41] The willingness of the court to put the theory forward in the *Conservative Central Office* case, even though any such theory is unlikely to have been in the mind of many Conservative Party members, is an indication of how the courts will stretch legal theory to solve a problem which legal theory has itself created.

3 Dissolution of unincorporated associations

An incorporated body is wound up in accordance with the principles which apply to that type of body. For instance a limited company can be wound up in accordance with the Companies Act 2006, and a charitable incorporated organization established under the Charities Act 2011 can be wound up or dissolved in accordance with the procedures set out in that Act.

Unincorporated associations as groups of individuals bound together by mutual agreement can be wound up in accordance with the rules which form the contractual bond making the individuals into an association, and if the rules make no provision for dissolution, by unanimous agreement of all members.[42] Hogan J held in In *Dunne v Mahon* [43] held that, even in the absence of specific provision in the rules of a club permitting dissolution, it was to be implied that the club could dissolve on the basis of a

---

[38] The effect of the mandate would be to make the treasurer the contributor's agent in relation to the funds transferred.

[39] There are parallels between this analysis and *Quistclose* trusts, discussed in Chapter 18.

[40] See *Re Wilson* [1908] 1 Ch 839. There might also be difficulty where a new treasurer took office, since the relationship between principal and agent is essentially a personal one.   [41] See Chapter 14.

[42] *Re William Denby & Sons Ltd. Sick and Benevolent Fund* [1971] 1 WLR 973, at 978–979.

[43] [2012] IEHC 412.

majority decision. He considered that it was reasonable to imply a term that a changes to the rules of a society could be agreed by a majority, except so far as this affected the vested rights of existing members.[44] The association also ceases to exist if all its members die or leave, or if the number of members is reduced to one.[45] An unincorporated association is not dissolved spontaneously merely by inactivity. In *Trustees of the Graphic Reproduction Federation v Wellcom London Ltd*[46] it was held that a printing trade association which had engaged in no significant activity for twenty-seven years was still in being, 'But inactivity may be so prolonged or so circumstanced that the only reasonable inference is that the club has become dissolved.'[47] This is likely to be the case where a club has become incapable of carrying out any of its objects. It is possible, although likely to be rare, that a court can infer a mutual agreement between the members to regard a club as having ceased to exist.[48]

In addition to winding up by the members in accordance with the rules, the court has an inherent equitable jurisdiction to wind up an unincorporated association.[49] This jurisdiction was exercised in *Re Enniskillen Trust*[50] to wind up an insolvent charitable unincorporated association. The jurisdiction can be exercised even when it is still open to the members to wind up by mutual agreement, but in fairness this should be on terms which are no less favourable to the members than if they had wound up voluntarily, and the court should not disturb the existing property rights of members.[51]

4 Surplus funds on the dissolution of unincorporated associations

(1) Property holding by unincorporated associations

Problems can arise as to what should happen to the assets of an unincorporated association that is dissolved. As we have seen, the usual modern solution is that the officers of the association hold the assets for the members on the basis of their contract inter se, which is formed by the rules of the association.[52] The members' rights over the assets are therefore governed primarily by contract and not by trust. The question of how any assets should be distributed when an association is dissolved is therefore governed by the rules of the association. Some early cases decided that any surplus funds would be

---

[44] This restriction invalidated a purported rule change requiring any surplus funds on disbanding the club to be donated to charity.   [45] *Hanchett-Stamford v Attorney-General* [2009] Ch 173.

[46] [2014] EWHC 134 (Ch).

[47] *Re GKN Bolts and Nuts Sports and Social Club* [1982] 2 All ER 855, at 779 (Sir Robert Megarry VC).

[48] *Re GKN Bolts and Nuts Sports and Social Club* [1982] 2 All ER 855, at 782 (Sir Robert Megarry VC).

[49] *Re William Denby & Sons Ltd. Sick and Benevolent Fund* [1971] 1 WLR 973; *Butts Park Ventures (Coventry) Ltd v Bryant Homes Central Ltd* [2003] EWHC 2487 (Ch), at [18]. There is a power to appoint a liquidator.   [50] [2013] NI Ch 10.

[51] *Trustees of the Graphic Reproduction Federation v Wellcom London Ltd* [2014] EWHC 134 (Ch).

[52] *Leahy v A-G for New South Wales* [1959] AC 457, PC; *Neville Estates Ltd v Madden* [1962] Ch 832; *Re Recher's Will Trusts* [1972] Ch 526; *Re Lipinski's Will Trusts* [1976] Ch 235; *Re Grant's Will Trusts* [1980] 1 WLR 360.

held on a resulting trust for those who had contributed.[53] However, cases adopting a resulting trust approach pre-date the more recent authorities adopting the contractual analysis of property holding by unincorporated associations.

(2) *Re West Sussex Constabulary's Trusts*: partial rejection of the resulting trust approach

Re West Sussex Constabulary's Widows, Children and Benevolent (1930) Fund Trusts[54] is one of the early cases. A fund to provide benefits to the widows of members of the West Sussex police force was wound up when the force was amalgamated with others, leaving a surplus of £35,000. The club's revenue was derived from: (a) members' subscriptions; (b) legacies and donations from outsiders; and (c) proceeds of entertainments and collecting-boxes. The question arose as to how the surplus should be distributed. Goff J dealt separately with each type of revenue (see Figure 12.1).

(i) Members' subscriptions

Goff J held that the members were not entitled to take any share of the surplus on the basis of resulting trusts because they had made their contributions on the basis of contract and not trust.[55] They had received all that they had bargained for from their membership of the club. Therefore this property went bona vacantia to the Crown.

(ii) Outside legacies and donations

Since these were not given on the basis of contract, Goff J held there should be a resulting trust in favour of those who had contributed, in so far as the surplus was attributable to their contributions.[56] He considered that this aspect of the case was indistinguishable from *Re Abbott Fund Trusts.*[57]

(iii) Proceeds of entertainments and collecting-boxes

Because the donors of these funds could not be identified, Goff J held that there could be no resulting trust of the surplus attributable to revenue from these sources, and they thus passed bona vacantia to the Crown.[58]

The result of this decision is that the majority of the surplus passed bona vacantia to the Crown, with the members seeming to receive nothing for their contributions. The reason for this may be that, although the contractual analysis was argued so as to defeat any claim by the members to a resulting trust, there was no argument that the members had any contractual rights to the surplus. Goff J observed in his judgment:

> The surviving members...may well have a right in contract on the ground of frustration or total failure of consideration, and that right may embrace contributions made by past

---

[53] *Re Printers and Transferrers Amalgamated Trades Protection Society* [1899] 2 Ch 184; *Re Lead Co's Workmen's Fund Society* [1904] 2 Ch 196; *Tierney v Tough* [1914] 1 IR 142; *Re Hobourn Aero Components Air Raid Distress Fund* [1946] Ch 86.   [54] [1971] Ch 1.
[55] Following *Cunnack v Edwards* [1896] 2 Ch 679; *Re Gillingham Bus Disaster Fund* [1958] Ch 300.
[56] [1971] Ch 1, at 14–16.   [57] [1900] 2 Ch 326.   [58] [1971] Ch 1, at 11–14.

(i) *Re West Sussex*

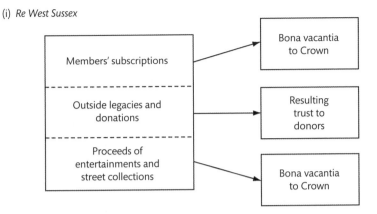

(ii) *Re Bucks Constabulary*

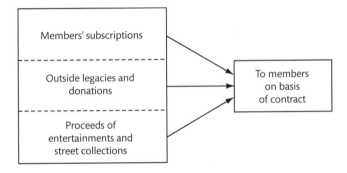

Figure 12.1 Distribution of assets on the dissolution of an unincorporated association

members, though I do not see how it could apply to moneys raised from outside sources. I have not, however, heard any argument based on contract...[59]

If Goff J was right in his analysis that most of the association's funds had no owner on the association's dissolution, it would have followed as a matter of logic that there was no owner immediately before the association's dissolution. If that was indeed the case, it is hard to see how any of the association's purposes could have been achieved.

(3) *Re Bucks Constabulary Fund (No 2)*: distribution of surplus funds to the members of the association

A later case with similar facts but a different conclusion is *Re Bucks Constabulary Fund (No 2)*,[60] where it was held that the members of an unincorporated association enjoyed contractual rights to surplus assets (see Figure 12.1). The case concerned a society

---

[59] [1971] Ch 1, at 10: this did not prevent the property being paid over as bona vacantia, as the Crown had offered a full indemnity to the trustees. [60] [1979] 1 WLR 936.

registered under the Friendly Societies Act 1896, which was wound up because of the amalgamation of the Buckinghamshire Constabulary, leaving a surplus. Given that an unincorporated association derives its existence from an 'implied contract between all the members inter se governed by the rules of the society',[61] Walton J held that this contract should govern the distribution of the surplus:

> as on dissolution there were members of the society...in existence, its assets are held on trust for such members to the total exclusion of any claim on behalf of the Crown.

This is entirely consistent with the reasoning that unincorporated associations hold their property on the basis of the contract between the members,[62] and that they must be able to alter the rules of the association so as to put the assets into their own pockets.[63] Since this shows that 'the money was theirs all the time',[64] they should be entitled to what is theirs on the winding-up of the association. This reasoning excludes any possibility of a resulting trust, either of the members' own contributions, or of the donations of outsiders,[65] and provides the members with a basis for entitlement to the surplus which was not found in *Re West Sussex Constabulary's Widows, Children and Benevolent (1930) Fund Trusts*.[66] Therefore, none of the assets of the association, whatever their source, should pass under a resulting trust or as bona vacantia. The only circumstance in which Walton J anticipated the surplus would pass bona vacantia to the Crown was when the society had spontaneously dissolved by being reduced to a single member,[67] although we shall see that this situation has arisen and a different solution was applied.

(a) Who are the members?

The members of an unincorporated association for the purpose of any distribution of assets are those who are (or were) members at the time of the dissolution. The identity of the members at that date will be governed by the rules of the association, as indeed will the extent of their shares (discussed later). Thus honorary or associate members may participate differently, or not at all, compared with full members.[68]

---

[61] [1979] 1 WLR 936, at 943.

[62] *Re Sick and Funeral Society of St John's Sunday School, Golcar* [1973] Ch 51, at 60, per Megarry J: 'membership of a club or association is primarily a matter of contract. The members make their payments, and in return they become entitled to the benefits of membership in accordance with the rules. The sums they pay cease to be their individual property, and so cease to be subject to any concept of resulting trust. Instead, they become the property, through the trustees of the club or association, of all the members for the time being, including themselves.'

[63] See *Re Lipinski* [1976] Ch 235; *Re Grant's Will Trusts* [1980] 1 WLR 360.

[64] *Re Bucks Constabulary Widows' and Orphans' Fund Friendly Society (No 2)* [1979] 1 WLR 936, at 951; *Dunne v Mahon* [2012] IEHC 412.

[65] Since these too are held by the association on the basis of the contract for the members absolutely. See *Re Lipinski's Will Trusts* [1976] Ch 235, where Mr Lipinski's gift to the association was held to be a gift to the members subject to their contract inter se, which they could decide to distribute among themselves.

[66] [1971] Ch 1.   [67] [1979] 1 WLR 936, at 943.

[68] See *Re Horley Town Football Club* [2006] EWHC 2386 (Ch), in which Lawrence Collins J, in considering the entitlement of members to land settled on trust to provide a permanent ground for Horley FC, applied the contractual theory to find that property was settled on a bare trust for the full-time members on a per capita basis, to the exclusion of associate and temporary members.

A person who was a member of the association, even for many years, but who had ceased to be a member at the date of dissolution, will not be entitled to a share. In the case of corporate members, corporations which themselves have dissolved before the dissolution of the association will not be entitled to a share of the assets: 'Entitlement goes with membership. If membership goes, entitlement to any funds goes.'[69]

(b) The members' contractual rights

The exact entitlement of each surviving member on a distribution of the surplus assets of an association depends on its rules. In the absence of express rules providing for dissolution, the surviving members at the date of dissolution will have prima facie entitlement to the surplus in equal shares, and not proportionately to their contributions.[70] This was the conclusion reached by Walton J in *Re Bucks Constabulary Fund (No 2).*[71] However, the rules of the society may expressly or impliedly indicate that something other than equal division was intended. In *Re Sick and Funeral Society of St John's Sunday School, Golcar*[72] a society existed to provide members with sickness allowances and death benefits. Members aged five to twelve paid half-contributions and were only entitled to half-benefits. Megarry J held that since this inequality was written into the rules, dividing the members into different classes, it should be applied to the surplus funds on dissolution. Those paying half-contributions were only entitled to half-shares in the surplus.[73]

(c) Last surviving member of an association

The question of what happens when an unincorporated association comes to an end because all but one of its members have died or resigned arose in *Hanchett-Stamford v A-G.*[74] The Performing and Captive Animals Defence League had been established in 1914 to seek to prevent animals being used in performances. Lewison J held that the League was not charitable because it was campaigning to change the law. The question was what should happen to its assets, which consisted mainly of a house, Sid Abbey (worth around £675,000), purchased to provide offices and investments (worth approximately £1.77m), with Mr Hanchett-Stamford and a Mr Hervey registered as trustees for the League. Although at one time there had been 250 members, when Mr Hervey and then Mr Hanchett-Stamford died the only traceable member was Mrs Hanchett-Stamford. Who was entitled to the assets? If Mrs Hanchett-Stamford was entitled to the funds, she intended to follow her late husband's wishes and to apply the funds to another animal charity, the Born Free Foundation. Lewison J accepted that Walton J's analysis of the way in which an unincorporated society held its assets

---

[69] *Trustees of the Graphic Reproduction Federation v Wellcom London Ltd* [2014] EWHC 134 (Ch), at [30].

[70] See *Brown v Dale* (1878) 9 Ch D 78; *Re Printers and Transferrers Amalgamated Trades Protection Society* [1899] 2 Ch 184; *Re Lead Co's Workmen's Fund Society* [1904] 2 Ch 196; *Tierney v Tough* [1914] 1 IR 142; *Feeny and Shannon v MacManus* [1937] IR 23; *Re Blue Albion Cattle Society* [1966] CLY 1274; *Re St Andrew's Allotments Association's Trusts* [1969] 1 WLR 229.   [71] [1979] 1 WLR 936, at 951–955.

[72] [1973] Ch 51.

[73] See also *Re St Andrew's Allotments Association's Trusts* [1969] 1 WLR 229 and *Re Horley Town Football Club* [2006] EWHC 2386 (Ch).   [74] [2008] EWHC 330 (Ch).

was correct and that where no express restriction had been placed on the funds, 'the members for the time being of an unincorporated association are beneficially entitled to "its" assets, subject to the contractual arrangements between them'.[75] Lewison J saw no basis for restricting this principle to cases only where there were two members or more. It would breach human rights law to deprive the surviving member of the assets on the death of the last-but-one member. The League was still active up to the death of Mr Hanchett-Stamford. In the view of Lewison J:

> I consider that the League ceased to exist upon his death in January 2006, when its membership fell below two. Since Mrs Hanchett-Stamford is the sole surviving member of the League, she is, in my judgment, entitled to its assets. She is therefore entitled to be registered as proprietor of Sid Abbey and as shareholder of the shares now held in the League's name. Her entitlement is free from any restrictions imposed by the rules of the League, which must have ceased to bind on the death of her husband. It follows that she is free, if she so chooses, to give all the former assets of the League to the Born Free Foundation.[76]

(d) Special cases

The solution of dividing the assets of a dissolved unincorporated association between its members at the time of dissolution can apply only where the members could claim a beneficial entitlement immediately before that date. It could not apply, therefore, in a case like *Re St Andrew's (Cheam) Lawn Tennis Club Trust* [77] where the land on which the club played tennis was held on trusts for purposes which excluded any claim by the members to have full ownership. Where a charitable unincorporated association is dissolved, the assets of the association are not available for distribution between the members because of the principle that assets dedicated to charitable purposes are dedicated to charity in perpetuity. The assets will instead be applied to another charity in accordance with the rules of the association or a scheme approved by the Charity Commission or the court.[78]

(e) Mutual contract theory doubted?

In *Davis v Richards and Wallington Industries Ltd*,[79] Scott J had to decide what happened to surplus funds in a pension scheme to which employees had made contributions in return for defined retirement and other benefits, and the employer made additional payments. On the termination of the scheme there was a surplus of £3m after allowing for the payment of all contractually due payments. Although this situation was similar to that involving the police benevolent funds, and counsel had argued that a pension fund should be treated as similar to an unincorporated association (but without it seems arguing for the mutual contract theory), Scott J applied a resulting trust analysis which ignored *Re Bucks Constabulary Fund (No 2)*,[80] even though

---

[75] [2008] EWHC 330 (Ch), at [31].
[76] [2008] EWHC 330 (Ch), at [50]. See Griffiths 'Hanchett-Stamford v Attorney General: Another Twist in the Tale—Unincorporated Associations and the Distribution of Surplus Funds' [2009] 73 Conv 428; Panesar 'Surplus Funds and Unincorporated Associations' (2008) *Trusts and Trustees* 698.
[77] [2012] EWHC 1040 (Ch).   [78] See Chapter 18.   [79] [1991] 2 All ER 563.
[80] [1979] 1 WLR 936.

the case had been cited in argument, and instead referred with approval to *Re West Sussex Constabulary's Widows, Children and Benevolent (1930) Fund Trusts*.[81] Scott J held that because, in his view, the surplus had been generated primarily by employer contributions (since the employer was only required to contribute to top-up the fund if the employee contributions were insufficient), the employer had the first claim. Even if the employees could show that their contributions had created or contributed to the surplus, they should still have no claim to it both because no workable method could be identified for distributing funds between members with greatly differing contractual rights, and because benefits payable to pension scheme members are limited by Inland Revenue rules. This part of the surplus would therefore go to the Crown as bona vacantia. Scott J's reasoning was rejected by the Privy Council in *Air Jamaica Ltd v Charlton*,[82] but the Privy Council still adopted a resulting trust analysis and held that the surplus on a winding up of a pension scheme, in so far as it was attributable to contributions made by members, should be returned to them pro rata and in proportion to the amounts they had contributed to the scheme. Payments should include the estates of deceased as well as surviving members, and should take no account of any benefits received. This scheme of payment was clearly very different from the payments which would be made under the mutual contract theory.

There are considerations which apply to pension funds which may not apply to some clubs and societies, but pension fund schemes do not differ markedly from some benevolent societies such as the one in *Re Sick and Funeral Society of St John's Sunday School, Golcar*.[83] The very different treatment of such associations from pension schemes highlights the artificiality of the reasoning which the courts are obliged to employ to resolve issues about property ownership.

5 Critique

Most people joining a club do so because they wish to engage in the activities which the club supports. Unless they have studied this branch of the law they would probably be surprised to discover that by joining the club they have acquired a share of the club's assets. Members who supported the club in its early years, but who have left because they have moved from the area or for any other reason would probably be equally surprised to discover that their successors could close the club and share all the assets. The windfall gains are potentially very large. The sale of the RAC rescue service division in 1998 produced in the order of £30,000 for each of the Club's members; the assets held by the Performing and Captive Animals Defence League when it ceased to exist were worth more than £2m.

These windfall gains are all the more surprising where an association has benevolent purposes. If the association is charitable, then the association's assets would have

---

[81] [1971] Ch 1.   [82] [1999] 1 WLR 1399.   [83] [1973] Ch 51.

to be applied to other similar purposes rather than be shared by the members. It may be asked why a slight difference in purposes can lead to such a difference in result. Returning the funds to the original donors or contributors is in many cases impractical or impossible, so in most instances the only real alternative is that the assets will become bona vacantia. Dividing the assets between the current members may be the least worst solution; an economist might also say that it is also efficient, because it provides an incentive to members to use assets in the most productive way. If a sports club holds land suitable for housing development, selling it for that purpose might be better in terms of economic efficiency than retaining the land undeveloped.

13

Testate and intestate succession

It is a simple truth that a man cannot take his property with him when he dies. 'We brought nothing into the world, and we can take nothing out of it.'[1] We may, however, want to decide to whom our property should pass on our death.

When a person dies, some of their property rights die with them. For instance a person's retirement pension payments normally end on their death, and if they had the right under a trust to live in a house during their lifetime, the use of the house will pass on their death to the next person entitled. Similarly the property rights of a joint tenant ends on their death. However, most of a person's property endures beyond their death, and although we cannot enjoy our worldly goods from our graves, as owners of property we can influence (even if not fully control) who will be entitled to our property after our death. This chapter is concerned with the arrangements which people can make to choose who will benefit from their property after their death. It has been said that only two things are certain in life: death and taxes. The two are linked in another way, because death is an occasion on which the state levies taxes, primarily through inheritance tax. The tax treatment of inheritance arrangements is important and has considerable influence on the way in which people arrange their affairs, but it is a specialist subject not covered in this book.

1 Methods of making provision after death

There are several ways in which a person can choose who will benefit from their property after their death.

(1) Lifetime gift

The owner of property can make a gift of property during his lifetime. The effect of this is to pass ownership immediately to the beneficiary. If the gift is complete, the donor cannot change his mind and ask for the property back, even if his circumstances change. So if Andy transfers his farm to his son Barry, but then the two of them fall

---

[1] St Paul, First Letter to Timothy, Ch 6, v 7.

out, or if Andy needs expensive drug therapy which is not available on the NHS, Barry cannot be compelled to return the farm or to sell it to support his father.

(2) **Donatio mortis causa**

It is possible to make a gift which is made in expectation of death and which is conditional upon the donor dying. Such gifts are instances where equity will complete an imperfect gift and are discussed in Chapter 7.

(3) **Lifetime trust**

The owner of property can also create a lifetime trust and transfer funds to it. In this case, like a gift, provided the trust is complete, there is nothing the settlor can do to change the terms of the trust or to revoke it, unless the power to do so has been expressly reserved as a term of the trust.[2] Life insurance policies are sometimes 'written in trust' so that the policyholder declares who is to benefit from the payment when the policy matures.

(4) **Joint tenancy**

Where property is vested jointly in the deceased and another person or persons, and one of the joint tenants dies, the rights to that property pass automatically to the survivors. It is possible for most forms of property to be enjoyed through a joint tenancy. In the case of land a trust is required; in the case of most other property (including bank accounts) it is possible for a joint tenancy to be created directly. However, a joint tenancy will not always operate to confer a beneficial interest on the survivor. In *Re Vinogradoff*[3] an aunt had transferred government stock into the names of herself and her young granddaughter. It would not be unreasonable to assume that the purpose was to permit her granddaughter to acquire the property by survivorship on her death, but because there was no evidence of an intention to make a gift, it was held that there was a resulting trust in favour of the grandmother. In *Young v Sealey*[4] and in *Aroso v Coutt*[5] the method succeeded in similar circumstances because there was sufficient evidence of an intention to make a gift. Romer J in *Young v Sealey* rejected the argument that this method of giving was invalid because it attempted to circumvent the rules relating to making wills.

(5) **Nominations and expressions of wishes**

Some pension fund schemes provide for the payment of a death benefit when a member of the scheme dies. Some of these schemes allow the member to nominate the person who is to receive the payment on the member's death. This enables the payment to

---

[2] *Paul v Paul* (1882) 20 Ch D 742, CA.   [3] [1935] WN 68.   [4] [1949] Ch 278.
[5] [2002] 1 All E.R. (Comm) 241.

be made without the need for probate. A similar method, which may have tax advantages, is where the trustees of the scheme have discretion as to whom to make the payment, but where they will take into account a non-binding expression of wishes by the member.

(6) **Will and testament**

The most obvious way in which a person can control their property beyond the grave is through making a will. A person making a will is known as either a testator or testatrix (if male or female, respectively) and is said to die testate. When a testator dies, the will must be proved (ie checked and registered) by the Probate Registry (part of the Family Division of the High Court). It is then available for public inspection. For this reason it was possible for reporters to discover the exact details of the will of Diana, Princess of Wales. There is no requirement in England and Wales for a will to be registered prior to a testator's death.

(7) **Intestacy**

Where a person does not make a will, then any property to which they are entitled on their death passes to their next of kin under statutory intestacy wills. A person who dies without a will is said to die intestate.

(8) **Partial intestacy**

If a person has made a will, but this does not deal with the whole of that person's property, the person is said to die partially testate. The rules which then apply are a combination of the rules relating to wills and the intestacy rules.

(9) **Provision for family and dependants**

In some jurisdictions (for instance in France and in the Republic of Ireland) a person is not free to dispose of all his or her property on death. Instead, close family members (in France children, and in Ireland a surviving spouse) are automatically entitled to a share of the estate (this is called the legal right share in Ireland). A testator is free to dispose of the balance of the estate. The rule in England and Wales is different. A testator is free to cut his family out of his estate entirely. However, under the Inheritance (Provision for Family and Dependants) Act 1975, as amended by the Inheritance and Trustees' Powers Act 2014,[6] a surviving spouse or civil partner, or a child, or a person who was dependent upon the deceased, may apply to court to have an order made requiring reasonable provision to be made for them out of the estate. The Act also allows an application where a cohabitant has been living with the deceased 'as husband and wife' for at

---

[6] S 6, implementing the substantive changes in Sch 2 of the 2014 Act.

least two years at his death. So, in *Baker v Baker*,[7] a man who was dying from liver cancer made a will shortly before his death. He left everything to the woman with whom he was living. His daughter successfully challenged the will on the basis that her father did not have mental capacity at the time. The court, however, ordered that his domestic partner should have a life interest in his house. In view of her limited means, reasonable provision for her required the provision of a home for her lifetime.

2 Probate

None of the property to which a deceased is entitled passes automatically to those entitled on the death by virtue of a will or intestacy. Instead, the assets of the deceased vest in personal representatives whose function it is to ascertain if there is a will; to dispose of the deceased's remains (for instance by organizing a funeral and burial or cremation); to collect together all the assets; to pay all the debts including any taxes due including inheritance tax; and then, only if there are sums remaining, to distribute them amongst those entitled. The personal representatives are either executors (if they are named in the deceased's will) or administrators, but there is no difference in their function. The personal representatives derive their authority from a grant of representation made by the Probate Registry. The grant of representation may also be called a grant of probate (where executors prove that there is a valid will); or a grant of letters of administration with will attached (where a will is proved by representatives who are not named in the will); or letters of administration (where there is no will).

3 Intestacy

The modern rules of intestate inheritance were first introduced by the Administration of Estates Act 1925, s 46 and have been modified a number of times, but an overhaul was proposed by the Law Commission and a Bill to effect these changes was introduced to the House of Lords in 2013 (the Inheritance and Trustees' Powers Bill). The Bill has now become law, following the enactment of the Inheritance and Trustees' Powers Act 2014.

(1) The intestacy rules

(a) Principles of inheritance

Under the rules for the distribution of a person's estate where there is no will, any surviving spouse or civil partner has the first claim. The extent of that claim depends

---

[7] [2008] EWHC 937 (Ch).

upon whether the deceased is survived by issue (ie children, grandchildren and any other direct lineal descendants). Only if there is neither spouse (or civil partner) nor issue do other relatives inherit. The relatives who can then inherit are set out in an ordered list. Although these rules seem complicated, the principle is simple—closer relatives are preferred to more distant relatives. If there are no surviving relatives in any of the categories enumerated, then the estate goes to the Crown in default of heirs or successors. Only blood relatives inherit (although adopted children are treated as if they were natural children of their adoptive parents). No distinction is made between children born in wedlock and children whose parents are not married.

(b) Spouse inherits personal chattels

The surviving spouse or civil partner always inherits all the personal chattels which belonged to the deceased. These are defined in the Bill and include all the deceased's 'tangible movable property' with three exceptions. First, personal chattels do not include money and securities for money. Secondly, they do not include property of the deceased used solely or mainly for business purposes. Thirdly, they do not include property held solely as an investment. Gold bars kept as an investment would fall into this exception, but expensive jewelry, if used occasionally, would not, even if it was normally stored in a bank vault for safety.

(c) Spouse survives with no issue

If the deceased has a surviving spouse or civil partner, but leaves no surviving issue, then the whole of the estate goes to the surviving spouse or civil partner. A partner who has not married or entered into a civil partnership with the deceased has no claim under the intestacy rules.

(d) Issue and no spouse

If there are surviving issue, but no surviving spouse or civil partner, then the issue take the whole estate.

(e) Division between spouse and issue

Where a deceased is survived by both a surviving spouse or civil partner and by issue, then the estate is shared between them. The surviving husband, wife or civil partner takes all the personal chattels and the remaining assets, up to a value of £250,000 (although this is a figure which will be reviewed in line with inflation measured by the Consumer Prices Index). The remainder of the estate is divided equally with half of the remainder going to the spouse or civil partner and the other half going to the descendants in equal shares by line of descent (*per stirpes*).

(f) How the issue share

Where issue are entitled to a share of the estate, they take by line of descent. What this means is that if the deceased had three children, but one has died, the two surviving children will take one third each. The remaining third will be taken by the deceased child's children or grandchildren. They will take shares determined in the same way.

(g) Order of inheritance

The order in which remoter relatives inherit is: parents; full blood brothers and sisters (ie brothers and sisters who share both parents); half-blood brothers and sisters (ie brothers and sisters who share just one parent); grandparents; uncles and aunts by full blood (ie full blood brothers or sisters of a parent of the deceased); half-aunts and half-uncles (ie a half brother or half sister of a parent of the deceased). Relatives only inherit if they are still living when the deceased died (even if they have died subsequently before receiving their share). Where brothers and sisters or aunts and uncles have died before the deceased, then any share which they would have received if they survived would be taken instead by their living descendants, taking by line of descent.

(2) Partial intestacy

The rules set out above apply to a partial intestacy. It used to be the case that in some circumstances a doctrine called hotchpot applied, and allowance had to be made for any gift received by will against any sums which would be payable on intestacy. That rule was abolished in relation to partial intestacy by the Law Reform (Succession) Act 1995.

(3) Problems raised by including only blood relations

The restriction of next of kin on intestacy to blood relations is, in many ways, understandable, and has the advantage of certainty. However, it can in some circumstances cause problems. For instance if a couple, who both have children from a previous relationship, marry or remarry, on the death of the first to die intestate the surviving spouse will inherit a substantial part of the estate, or the whole of a smaller estate. When the surviving spouse then dies, only the blood relations of that person will inherit on intestacy. The children from the first marriage of the first deceased will receive nothing under the intestacy rules. This underlines the importance of making wills, but even then there can be problems, because even if the wills made by a remarrying couple make provision for each other's children, the rules relating to wills permit the survivor to make a new will excluding the children of their spouse. For this reason, some remarrying couples may choose to make mutual wills which contain an agreement not to revoke the provision in favour of each other's children.[8] Mutual wills are considered later in this chapter.

4 Wills

A will is an expression of a person's wishes intended to take effect on their death. Whilst we normally associate wills with the disposition of property, they may also

---

[8] See, as an example, *Fry v Densham-Smith* [2010] EWCA Civ 1410.

deal with matters such as the wishes of the deceased concerning their funeral, or the custody and care of their children or pets. Most of the requirements relating to wills are set out in the Wills Act 1837 as amended. As an exception to the normal requirements, it is possible for a soldier in actual military service, members of the naval or marine forces in actual military service, and any mariner or seaman at sea to make a will without complying with the normal rules. Indeed, a privileged will can be made, with the necessary intention and capacity, by an oral statement.[9]

(1) Capacity to make wills

(a) Age

Under the Wills Act 1837, s 7 a person must be an adult (have attained the age of 18) in order to make a normal will (this requirement does not apply to privileged wills[10]).

(b) General test for capacity

The testator must also have testamentary capacity. Where a person does not have testamentary capacity any will they make has no effect,[11] but the loss of mental capacity after a will has been made does not affect it. The test for testamentary capacity was set out in *Banks v Goodfellow*.[12] Lord Cockburn CJ said:

> It is essential to the exercise of such a power that a testator shall understand the nature of the act and its effects; shall understand the extent of the property of which he is disposing; shall be able to comprehend and appreciate the claims to which he ought to give effect; and with a view to the latter object, that no disorder of the mind shall poison his affections, pervert his sense of right, or prevent the exercise of his natural faculties—that no insane delusion shall influence his will in disposing of his property and bring about a disposal of it which, if the mind had been sound, would not have been made.

The requirement can be summarized by saying that the testator must be 'of sound mind, memory and understanding.'[13] There are four elements:

(1) the testator must know that he is making a document that will deal with his property on his death;

(2) the testator must have a general awareness of the extent of his property;

(3) the testator must understand and recall those who have a moral claim to his estate, even if he does not intend to make provision for them in the will;

(4) the testator must not be suffering from any illness which may impair his judgement in regard to disposing of his property.

---

[9] Wills Act 1837, s 11 as explained and extended by Wills (Soldiers and Sailors) Act 1918.

[10] Wills (Soldiers and Sailors) Act 1918, s 1. The provision was enacted to allay any doubts about the validity of informal wills made by young soldiers in the Great War.   [11] *Bunter v Coke* 91 ER 210.

[12] (1869–70) LR 5 QB 549.

[13] See *Mortimer on Probate, Law and Practice* (1st edn, 1911), p 42 (quoted regularly in the courts, for instance in *Perrins v Holland* [2010] EWCA Civ 840 at [13]).

There is no fixed standard of testamentary capacity. Where the testator's affairs are simple, a lower standard will apply than where his affairs are complex and more complex provision is made (or is required) in the will.[14] It is also possible for a person to execute a will during a lucid interval, even if they periodically lack capacity.[15]

(c) Presumption of capacity

Testamentary capacity does not have affirmatively to be proved unless there is something in the circumstances to question it.[16] So if the testator had general mental capacity at the time the will was made, and the will is rational, capacity will be presumed. This common law position is confirmed by the Mental Capacity Act 2005, s 1 which states that a person is assumed to have capacity unless it is established that he lacks capacity.

(d) Will can be perverse

A testator is not required to make a rational will: 'The law does not say that a man is incapacitated from making a will if he proposes to make a disposition of his property moved by capricious, frivolous, mean, or even bad motives'.[17] However, the fact that the will appears irrational is likely to mean that proof of capacity will be required.

(e) The 'golden rule'

In circumstances where the testator's mental capacity is in doubt, perhaps because of the onset of dementia, or because an elderly person has suffered a serious illness, it is wise to follow a 'golden if tactless rule'[18] that the will 'ought to be witnessed or approved by a medical practitioner who satisfied himself of the capacity and understanding of the testator, and records an preserves his examination and finding.'[19] Whilst this is not the only way of ensuring that the testator's capacity can be proved, it will provide strong supporting (but not conclusive) evidence.[20]

(f) Undue influence or fraud

A will which has been procured through fraud or undue influence will be set aside.[21] *Schrader v Schrader*[22] sets out the principles which apply when deciding whether undue influence has been applied to a person making a will.

(2) Execution of wills

(a) Statement of rules

The rules for the execution of a will are found in the Wills Act 1837, s 9 as substituted by the Administration of Justice Act 1982, s 17:

---

[14] *In the Estate of Park* [1954] P 112.   [15] *In the Estate of Walker* (1912) 28 TLR 466.
[16] *Symes v Green* 164 ER 785.   [17] *Boughton v Knight* (1872–1875) LR 3 P & D 64.
[18] *Kenward v Adams, The Times*, 29 November 1975.
[19] *Re Simpson (Decd)* (1977) 121 SJ 224 (Templeman J).
[20] *Perrins v Holland* [2009] EWHC 2558 (Ch), at [10]; *Re Watson (Probate)* [2008] EWHC 2582 (Ch).
[21] See Chapter 4.   [22] [2013] EWHC 466 (Ch).

No will shall be valid unless—

(a) it is in writing, and signed by the testator, or by some other person in his presence and by his direction; and

(b) it appears that the testator intended by his signature to give effect to the will; and

(c) the signature is made or acknowledged by the testator in the presence of two or more witnesses present at the same time; and

(d) each witness either—

    (i) attests and signs the will; or

    (ii) acknowledges his signature, in the presence of the testator (but not necessarily in the presence of any other witness),but no form of attestation shall be necessary.

(b) 'In writing'

With the exception of privileged wills, all wills must be in writing. There is no general requirement that it should be dated, but it is good practice to date a will because where a testator has made more than one will it helps to identify which is the most recent.

(c) 'Signed by the testator'

The testator may sign personally. Any mark intended as a signature will suffice. It is also possible for the will to be signed on the testator's behalf. Where someone signs on the testator's behalf, it is essential that there is something which constitutes a 'direction' to do so. In *Barrett v Bem*[23] the hand of the testator, who was seriously ill in hospital, was shaking too much for him to sign a will which had been prepared for him by his niece Hanora. Although what happened then was not easy to know, the judge concluded that Hanora's mother Anne, the only beneficiary in the will, and the sister of the testator, took the pen and completed the signature. The Court of Appeal held that the absence of any instruction to do this meant that Anne did not sign on his behalf 'and by his direction'. 'The testator must make some positive communication of his desire that someone else should sign the will on his behalf.'[24]

(d) 'Intended...to give effect to the will'

The testator must know that what is being signed is a document containing instructions for the disposition of the testator's property on death, and must also be aware of the instructions contained in the will.[25] Normally, this can be assumed, but if the testator is illiterate or blind, evidence may be required to prove that the testator was aware of the contents. This could have been done through the will being read to him. It is wise to include a statement to this effect as part of the attestation (the description alongside the signatures). Evidence that the testator was aware of the contents of the will and intended to approve them would also be necessary where the will was

---

[23] [2012] EWCA Civ 524.   [24] [2012] EWCA Civ 524, at [24] and [36].
[25] *Cleare v Cleare* (1865–1869) LR 1 P&D 655.

prepared by someone who benefits from it or there are other factors which 'excite the suspicion of the court'.[26]

It used to be a requirement that the signature appear 'at the foot or end of the will', but that requirement no longer applies, it being sufficient, wherever the signature appears, that it is intended to give effect to the will.

(e) An interesting problem

In *Marley v Rawlings*[27] a husband and wife had made almost identical wills, differing only in the references to each other. By mistake each signed the other's will and this only came to light after their deaths. The Court of Appeal held that their signatures did not give effect to the relative wills because 'Mr Rawlings did not authenticate the document as his will and he did not intend it to operate as his will.'[28] In a victory for common sense the Supreme Court held that the documents were valid wills because they had been signed with the intention that they should be the parties' wills. The contents of the will concerned could be rectified since the solicitor involved had candidly admitted that he had made a 'silly mistake' in giving the husband and wife the wrong wills to sign. This constituted a clerical error which the court was permitted to correct.

(f) Witnesses

There must be two witnesses who are both present physically and mentally[29] when the testator signs or acknowledges his signature. The witnesses do not have to be present together when they, in turn, sign the will, but they must each sign in the presence of the testator. The witnesses must have been in a position to see the testator sign or to have seen his signature if he is acknowledging it, but they do not need to have taken advantage of that opportunity or even to know that the signature was on a will.[30] Because of the requirement of being able to see the signature, a blind person cannot act as a witness.[31]

It is possible for the testator to acknowledge to the witnesses a signature which he has already made. Similarly, it is possible for the witnesses to acknowledge to the testator a signature which has been made in his absence, but the order of events is still important because the witnesses' function is to verify that the signature of the testator is indeed his or one which he acknowledges as his. An acknowledgment can be in either words or conduct, for instance in *Weatherhill v Pearce*[32] Mrs Weatherhill handed the two witnesses a will which she had already signed and asked them to witness it. The judge said:

> It is plain that a signature which has already been written can be acknowledged in many ways and no set form is required. It is sufficient to proffer a document which all concerned know is a will for the witnesses to sign, and no express declaration is necessary.

---

[26] *Sherrington v Sherrington* [2005] EWCA Civ 326, at [69].

[27] [2012] EWCA Civ 61, [2013] Ch 271; on appeal [2014] UKSC 2.

[28] [2012] EWCA Civ 61, at [105] (Thomas LJ).   [29] *Hudson v Parker* (1844)163 ER 948.

[30] *Smith & Smith v Smith* (1869) LR 1 P&D 143; *Cooke v Henry* [1932] IR 574; *Kavanagh v Feegan* [1932] IR 566.   [31] *Re Gibson* [1949] P 434.

[32] [1995] 1 WLR 592.

(g) Who can be a witness?

There is no age requirement for a person to act as a witness, but since the witnesses 'attest' the will, that is they validate and bear witness to the testator's signature,[33] they must have the capacity and understanding to know that this is what they are doing.

A beneficiary is not, as such, prevented from acting as a witness, but the consequence of a person being a witness is that they and any spouse or civil partner is disqualified from receiving a benefit under the will.[34] The effect of this in the past was that a person signing, not as witness, but only to confirm that they were content with the provisions of the will, would not be disqualified from taking a gift, but it was presumed that any person signing at the end of a will was doing so as a witness.[35] For this exception to operate, there needed to be at least two other witnesses who were not also beneficiaries. The Wills Act 1968 extends the exception so that provided that there are at least two witnesses who are not also beneficiaries, the attestation of a will by a person who is also a beneficiary can be disregarded.

(h) Attestation

There is no statutory requirement for a will to contain an attestation clause—that is to contain a statement alongside the signatures of the testator and witnesses explaining how and why they were signing the will. However, a description to this effect can help in providing evidence that the requirements of the Wills Act have been met, and so it is common and good practice to use an attestation clause such as:

> Signed by the said testator [name] in the presence of us both present at the same time who at her request in her presence and in the presence of each other have subscribed our names as witnesses.[36]

In the absence of any evidence to the contrary (which may come from the will itself, or from extrinsic evidence), there is a strong presumption that a will that contains an attestation clause has been properly executed.[37] Without an attestation clause, affidavit evidence of compliance with the Wills Act 1837 requirements may be needed before a will is accepted by the Probate Registry.

(3) Incorporation

It is possible for a will to include supplementary documents where these are appropriately referred to in the main will. These supplementary documents do not themselves have to be signed and witnessed if they are 'incorporated by reference'. Where a document is effectively incorporated into the will, it 'becomes part of the will'.[38] As such,

[33] *Sherrington v Sherrington* [2005] EWCA Civ 326, at [38].   [34] Wills Act 1837, s 15.
[35] *In the Estate of Bravda* [1968] 1 WLR 479.
[36] This was substantially the form of the clause used in *Weatherhill v Pearce* [1995] 1 WLR 592.
[37] *Sherrington v Sherrington* [2005] EWCA Civ 326 at [63]
[38] *Re Smart's Goods* [1902] P 238, at 240.

the incorporated document must also be admitted to probate, and thereby becomes a public document in the same way as the will itself.

A document will only be incorporated by reference into a will if the conditions stated by Gorell-Barnes P in *Re Smart's Goods*[39] are met.

(i) Incorporated document was in existence at the date of the will

Only a document that was in existence at the date the will was executed can be incorporated by reference, thus becoming part of the will.[40] A document may be incorporated if it was written after the will was executed provided that a subsequent properly executed codicil is added confirming that it is to be incorporated.

(ii) Incorporated document is referred to in the will

To be incorporated into a will a document must not only exist at the date of the will, but it must also be referred to in the will as existing at that date. In *Re Smart's Goods*[41] the testatrix, Caroline Smart, executed a will in 1895 leaving her property to the friends she might designate in a book or memorandum. At the time that the will was executed no such book or memorandum existed. A book was written between 1898 and 1899, and in 1900 a codicil was added to the will. However, although this book was in existence at the date of the execution of the codicil it was held that it was not incorporated into the will because the codicil made no reference to it as existing at the date that it was executed. The will continued to refer to the book as a future document.[42]

(iii) Incorporated document must be clearly identified in the will

A document will only be incorporated by reference if it is clearly identified in the will.[43]

(4) **Alterations**

Alterations made to a will before it has been executed will be validated by the execution of the will. Since it may not always be evident when alterations have been made, it is good practice to make a note of the alterations, confirming that they were made prior to execution, alongside the attestation clause. Without this, extrinsic evidence may be needed to confirm when the alterations were made. There are three ways in which alterations can be made to a will after it has been executed.

(a) **New will or codicil**

The provisions of an existing will can be amended or modified by a new will. The second will must comply with the same rules as to formal validity as apply to an original

---

[39] [1902] P 238.   [40] *Singleton v Tomlinson* (1878) 3 App Cas 404, HL.   [41] [1902] P 238.
[42] See also *University College of North Wales v Taylor* [1908] P 140; *Re Bateman's Will Trusts* [1970] 3 All ER 817.
[43] See *Croker v Marquis of Hertford* (1844) 8 Jur 863; *Re Balmes' Goods* [1897] P 261; *Re Saxton's Estate* [1939] 2 All ER 418; *Re Mardon's Estate* [1944] P 109.

will under the Wills Act 1837. Where the second will acts simply as a supplement to a previous will, it is called a codicil.

(b) Alterations on the will itself

It is possible for textual amendments to be made to the original will, but under the Wills Act 1837, s 21 these all need to comply with the same formalities as for an original will.

(c) Obliteration of words in the will

A limited form of alteration can be made in accordance with the Wills Act 1837, s 21 where words in a will are obliterated to such an extent that 'the words or effect of the will before such alteration shall not be apparent'. Scientific methods now make it much easier to decipher obliterated text than when the Wills Act 1837 was enacted, but according to Sir Francis Jeune P in *Ffinch v Combe*:[44]

> The result of the authorities, therefore, appears to be that the words beneath obliterations, erasures, or alterations on a testamentary document are 'apparent' within the meaning of the Wills Act, if experts, using magnifying-glasses, when necessary, can decipher them and satisfy the court that they have done so; but that it is not allowable to resort to any physical interference with the document, so as to render clearer what may have been written upon it.

Applying these principles, in *Re Itter (No 2)*[45] it was held that words had been obliterated where a testatrix had tried to increase the sums of various gifts by sticking slips of paper containing new amounts over the original amounts. The gifts were only saved from failing altogether because the judge held that a deletion was only effective if it was made with the intention to revoke that particular gift. In the circumstances, it could be inferred that the testatrix intended to revoke the part of the bequest covered by the slips only if new bequests were effectually substituted. The substitution was not effective because it had not been signed and witnessed as required for an alteration.

(5) Interpretation

(a) Will 'speaks from death'

The Wills Act 1837, s 24 provides that a will 'shall be construed, with reference to the real estate and personal estate comprised in it, to speak and take effect as if it had been executed immediately before the death of the testator, unless a contrary intention shall appear by the will.' This means that the will can apply to property acquired by the testator between the date of the will and his death, and not just property owned by the testator when he made the will.

---

[44] [1894] P 191, at 199. See also *Re Adams (Deceased)* [1990] Ch 601.   [45] [1950] P 130.

(b) Principles of interpretation

The Supreme Court held in *Marley v Rawlings*[46] that wills should be interpreted using the same canons of construction as other documents: 'Whether the document in question is a commercial contract or a will, the aim is to identify the intention of the party or parties to the document by interpreting the words used in their documentary, factual and commercial context.' This means that:

> the court is concerned to find the intention of the party or parties, and it does this by identifying the meaning of the relevant words, (a) in the light of (i) the natural and ordinary meaning of those words, (ii) the overall purpose of the document, (iii) any other provisions of the document, (iv) the facts known or assumed by the parties at the time that the document was executed, and (v) common sense, but (b) ignoring subjective evidence of any party's intentions.[47]

(c) Evidence of intention

The Administration of Justice Act 1982, s 21 contains some general rules relating to the evidence which can be admitted to aid in the interpretation of wills. These go further than the general rules of interpretation by allowing evidence of the testator's intention to be admitted to assist in the interpretation of a will where any part of a will is meaningless, the language used in the will is ambiguous, or there is evidence (other than evidence of the testator's intention) which 'shows that the language used in any part of it is ambiguous in the light of surrounding circumstances.'

(d) Lapse

The ordinary rule is that if a beneficiary named in a will does not survive the testator, the gift lapses, that is, it does not take effect.[48] This rule about lapse will not apply where a contrary intention appears, nor does it apply where a testator makes a gift to one of his own children or other issue who have predeceased him, but have left issue of their own who have survived the testator.[49] Suppose Bill makes a will in 2001 leaving '£100,000 to each of my children', but one of his children, Pat, dies shortly after giving birth to her son Robbie in 2005. If Bill dies in 2014 Pat's £100,000 will go to Robbie (who will share it with any other of Pat's children). Had the gift been made to Bill's housekeeper, who died before him, the gift would lapse.

(e) Rectification

Under the Administration of Justice Act 1982, s 20 the courts may rectify a will if it is satisfied that the will is so expressed that it fails to carry out the testator's intentions in consequence of a clerical error or of a failure to understand his instructions. This jurisdiction was invoked by the Supreme Court in *Marley v Rawlings*,[50] described earlier. The Supreme Court took the view that the expression 'clerical error' should be given

---

[46] [2014] UKSC 2, at [20]. [47] [2014] UKSC 2, at [19].
[48] *Elliott v Davenport* (1705) 1 P Wms 83; *Mabank v Brooks* (1780) 1 Bro CC 84.
[49] Wills Act 1837, s 33. [50] [2014] UKSC 2.

a broad interpretation to cover mistakes such as that involved in *Marley v Rawlings* as well as the correction of typographical errors.

(6) Revocation

(a) Revocability of wills

It is a cardinal rule relating to wills that they can be changed or revoked by the testator at any time up to his death. As was said in *Vynior's case*:

> If a man makes his testament and last will irrevocably, yet he may revoke it; for his acts or his words cannot alter the judgement of the law, to make that irrevocable which, of its own nature, is revocable.[51]

Even if a will states that the testator cannot amend or revoke it, this will not prevent subsequent changes or revocation. Similarly, even if a testator enters into what would otherwise be a legally binding contract not to change his will, he cannot be prevented from doing so. However, this rule can be circumvented in a number of ways. First, a contract not to change a will could give rise to liability in damages. Secondly, the rules relating to mutual wills (to be considered shortly) may impose a trust on some or all of the testator's assets.[52] Thirdly, as was seen in Chapter 10, the doctrine of proprietary estoppel may bind a testator's estate where a promise has been made in relation to his assets, and it would be inequitable for the promise not to be honoured. In some instances, more than one ground of claim may be possible.[53]

(b) How wills can be revoked

There are four ways in which a will can be revoked.

(i) Marriage

Where a testator who has made a will marries or enters into a civil partnership, the effect is to revoke any earlier will except for one which has been made in contemplation of the particular marriage or civil partnership concerned.[54] It must appear from the will itself that the testator was expecting to be married to a particular person, and that is the marriage which took place.

(ii) Divorce

The dissolution or annulment of a marriage does not revoke the whole of a will, but it does have the effect of revoking any gift in a will by treating the gift as if the spouse or concerned had predeceased the testator, unless a contrary intention appears in the will.[55]

---

[51] (1610) 8 Co Rep 80a.
[52] *Shovelar v Lane* [2011] EWCA Civ 802 makes it clear at [44] that a claim based on mutual wills is a trusts, not a probate, issue.
[53] *Fox v Jewell* [2013] EWCA Civ 1152 (claim made on the basis of both mutual will and proprietary estoppel). [54] Wills Act 1837, s 18.
[55] Wills Act 1837, s 18A.

(iii) New will or document in the form of a will

Under the Wills Act 1837, s 20 an existing will is revoked by a new will or codicil made in proper form. If the new will contains a clause expressly revoking all previous wills, then that will have effect, otherwise any existing will is revoked to the extent that it is inconsistent with the later will or codicil. The same section permits a declaration revoking a will to be made in the same form (ie complying with the requirements of the Wills Act 1837, s 9) without the need to substitute any new will.

(iv) Destruction

A will can also be revoked in accordance with the Wills Act 1837, s 20 by 'the burning, tearing, or otherwise destroying the same by the testator, or by some person in his presence and by his direction, with the intention of revoking the same.'

It will be seen that two elements are required: the destruction and an intention to revoke. In *Cheese v Lovejoy*[56] the testator had written 'This is revoked' across his will and thrown it into a pile of scrap papers. It was retrieved by a housemaid and kept for several years until his death. It was held that the will had not been revoked. James LJ adopted the argument of counsel: 'All the destroying in the world without intention will not revoke a will, nor all the intention in the world without destroying: there must be the two.'

(b) Revival of a revoked will

A revoked will can only be revived by being re-executed as if it were a new will, or by a new will or codicil declaring that it is revived.[57]

(7) Liability of draftsman for negligence

Where a legal professional offers support in the preparation of a will, that person can be liable to a disappointed beneficiary in negligence if through a lack of care the will is invalid or for some other reason an intended gift cannot take effect. This is a duty which applies as much to a will writing business[58] as it does to solicitors.[59] Liability has been imposed for failing to ensure that a will was properly executed;[60] failing to ensure that a beneficiary's husband was not a witness;[61] and failing to advise a client that a joint tenancy should be severed in order to dispose of a share in jointly held property.[62] It might well have been the case that the solicitor in *Marley v Rawlings*[63] could have been held liable to the disappointed beneficiary for his admitted mistake in giving the husband and wife the wrong wills to sign, had the will not been rectified.

---

[56] (1877) 2 PD 251.   [57] Wills Act 1837, s 22.
[58] *Esterhuizen v Allied Dunbar Assurance Plc* [1998] 2 FLR 668.
[59] *Ross v Caunters* [1980] Ch 297; *White v Jones* [1995] 2 AC 207.
[60] *Esterhuizen v Allied Dunbar Assurance Plc* [1998] 2 FLR 668.
[61] *Ross v Caunters* [1980] Ch 297.   [62] *Carr-Glynn v Frearsons (A Firm)* [1999] Ch 326.
[63] [2014] UKSC 2.

5 Mutual wills

(1) **The practical problem**

The potential revocability of a will presents a significant obstacle if an owner wishes to leave property to one person absolutely, subject to a requirement that the recipient bequeaths it to an agreed third person. For example, if a husband and wife have one child the husband may want his wife to enjoy all his property if he predeceases her, but also to ensure that it is ultimately left to their daughter. If he simply executes a will leaving his property to his wife, it will become her absolute property on his death and she will be free to execute her own will leaving the property to whomsoever she chooses, perhaps to the children of a second marriage or to some charitable object. To try to avoid such difficulties they may decide to execute wills with identical terms, leaving their property to each other in the event that they predecease, but to their daughter if they survive. However, even where identical wills have been executed, the survivor will remain free to revoke the former will and leave the property to others.

These practical difficulties are well illustrated by the facts of *Re Cleaver*.[64] Arthur and Flora Cleaver had married in 1967, when he was 78 and she was 74. He had three children by a previous marriage and she had none. They executed identical wills, leaving the bulk of their estates[65] to the survivor absolutely, and in default of their survival to the three children.[66] Arthur died in 1975. The will was proved and Florence became entitled to his estate absolutely. She subsequently executed a new will leaving her entire estate, which included the property she had inherited from Arthur, to only one of the children. While Arthur had clearly intended that the property bequeathed to his wife should ultimately be left by her to the children equally,[67] it was impossible to prevent his widow revoking her will and executing a replacement with different terms. If the terms of the new will were allowed to operate, Arthur's intentions would have been defeated by his wife's subsequent change of mind.

While these difficulties can be avoided by bequeathing property directly to the intended ultimate beneficiaries, or through the use of a life interest that will ensure that the survivor is only entitled to utilize the income derived from the property but not the capital, in reality these are often impracticable solutions. Where the testators do not possess great wealth, the survivor may need to make use of the property bequeathed to them, for example to provide retirement income or to pay for nursing care if needed, and solutions which do not enable them to do so are inadequate to fulfil their intentions.[68] What is required is a mechanism which enables the survivor

---

[64] [1981] 2 All ER 1018.   [65] The remainder after certain specific legacies.

[66] Two of the children were to receive one-third shares absolutely, with the daughter receiving only a life interest in the remaining third.

[67] [1981] 2 All ER 1018, at 1029. Nourse J described him as 'a very determined man' and that 'everything suggests that he would, so far as he could, have wanted to ensure that anything which was left at [his wife's] death should go back to his side of the family'.

[68] See Stevens 'Avoiding Disinheritance' (1996) NLJ 961.

to enjoy the property inherited from the first to die, if necessary, but which prevents the survivor from making an effective bequest of any of that property remaining at the date of their death to anyone other than the agreed beneficiary. Equity provides such a mechanism through the doctrine of 'mutual wills'.

(2) **The doctrine of mutual wills**

The essence of the doctrine of mutual wills was stated by Morritt J in *Re Dale (Decd)*:

> The doctrine of mutual wills is to the effect that where two individuals have agreed as to the disposal of their property and have executed mutual wills in pursuance of the agreement, on the death of the first (T1) the property of the survivor (T2), the subject matter of the agreement is held on an implied trust for the beneficiary named in the wills. The survivor may thereafter alter his will, because a will is inherently revocable, but if he does his personal representatives will take the property subject to the trust.[69]

Where mutual wills have been executed, equity does not prevent the survivor from changing his will.[70] Instead, the executors of the new will hold any property that was intended to be left to the beneficiary of the mutual wills on constructive trust. By means of this trust the property will be held for the beneficiary named in the original mutual wills, and will not pass to those named in the new will. As the Privy Council stated in *Gray v Perpetual Trustee Co Ltd*:

> If two persons simultaneously make wills to the same effect, and in that sense mutually, a second will be made by one of them after succeeding to the other's estate under the originally made will is precluded from being treated as effective to interfere in equity with the existing disposition.[71]

Returning to the example of *Re Cleaver*,[72] it was held that the wills executed by Arthur and his wife had been 'mutual wills', so that the equitable doctrine applied and a constructive trust had come into existence. The widow's executors therefore held the property she had received under her husband's will on constructive trust for the three children in equal shares.

(3) **Rationale for the imposition of a constructive trust**

A constructive trust will be imposed if the testators executed mutual wills on the basis of an agreement not to revoke. The rationale for imposing a constructive trust in such circumstances is that equity will not permit the survivor to commit a fraud by going back on his agreement. Since the property he received on the death of the first testator had only been bequeathed to him on the basis of the agreement not to revoke his own will, it would be a fraud for him to take the benefit while failing to observe the agreement, and equity intervenes to prevent this fraud.[73] This rationale is evident from the

[69] [1993] 4 All ER 129, at 132.   [70] See *Re Hey's Estate* [1914] P 192.
[71] [1928] AC 391, at 399.   [72] [1981] 2 All ER 1018.
[73] See *Re Dale (Decd)* [1993] 4 All ER 129, at 142, per Morritt J.

judgment of Lord Cottenham LC in the early case of *Dufour v Pereira*, where there was an express reference to fraud as the basis for equity's intervention.[74]

In *Re Dale (Decd)*, Morritt J reiterated the fraud justification for the imposition of a constructive trust:

> There is a contract between the testators which on the death of T1 is carried into effect by him, that T1 dies with the promise of T2 that the agreement will stand and that it would be a fraud on T1 to allow T2 to disregard the contract which became irrevocable on the death of T1.[75]

The reasoning in *Re Dale (Decd)* was cited with approval by the Court of Appeal in *Olins v Walters*.[76]

Given that the mutual wills operate to prevent the survivor acting fraudulently, the question has arisen whether the doctrine of mutual wills operates if the surviving testator gains no personal benefit under the will of the first testator who predeceases him. In the majority of cases this question will not arise because the mutual wills provide that the survivor is to inherit the estate of the predeceasing party absolutely, or receive a life interest in it. However, the problem did arise in *Re Dale (Decd)*.[77] Norman and Monica Dale executed mutual wills in September 1988. They had two children, a son Alan and a daughter Joan. Under the terms of the mutual wills all their property, real and personal, was to be divided equally between their children. They left nothing to each other. Norman died in November 1988 and his estate was worth about £18,500. Monica died in 1990, having made a new will earlier that year leaving £300 to Joan and everything else to Alan. Her estate was valued at £19,000. Joan claimed that the doctrine of mutual wills applied so that Alan, as executor, held Monica's estate on constructive trust in accordance with the terms of the mutual wills. Alan argued that the doctrine could not operate because Monica had derived no personal benefit under Norman's will. After reviewing the authorities, Morritt J concluded that the doctrine of mutual wills could operate even where the surviving testator received no benefit under the first testator's will:

> As all the cases show the doctrine applies when T2 benefits under the will of T1. But I am unable to see why it should be any the less a fraud on T1 if the agreement was that each testator should leave his or her property to particular beneficiaries, for example their children, rather than to each other. It should be assumed that they had good reason for doing so and in any event that is what the parties bargained for. In each case there is the binding contract. In each case it has been performed by T1 on the faith of the promise of T2 and in each case T2 would have deceived T1 to the detriment of T1 if he, T2, were permitted to go back on his agreement. I see no reason why the doctrine should be confined to cases where T2 benefits when the aim of the principle is to prevent T1 from being defrauded.[78]

---

[74] (1769) 2 Hargreave's Juridical Arguments 304. The key passage was cited by Morritt J in *Re Dale (Decd)* [1993] 4 All ER 129, at 135–136.

[75] [1993] 4 All ER 129, at 136; Brierley 'Mutual Wills—Blackpool Illuminations' (1995) 58 MLR 95.

[76] [2009] Ch 212, at 221 [37].

[77] [1993] 4 All ER 129; O'Hagan 'Mutual Wills' [1994] NLJ 1272.

[78] [1993] 4 All ER 129, at 142. In the Canadian case *Lynch Estate v Lynch Estate* (1993) 8 Alta LR (3d) 291, it was held that a 'disposition agreement' was generally only enforceable against someone who had taken a benefit under it.

(4) **Establishing mutual wills**

(a) Necessity of a contract

The doctrine of mutual wills will only operate if the testators had agreed that their wills would not be revoked. In the absence of such an agreement there will be no fraud if the surviving testator revokes his will. As Lord Loughborough LC indicated in *Walpole v Lord Orford*,[79] the principal difficulty in establishing that wills were intended to be mutual is determining whether the testators had entered a legally binding obligation not to revoke their wills rather than a mere 'honourable engagement'. In *Re Cleaver* Nourse J stated:

> I would emphasise that the agreement or understanding must be such as to impose on the donee a legally binding obligation to deal with the property in the particular way.[80]

More recent cases have held that this agreement between the parties must take the form of a valid contract. In *Re Dale (Decd)*[81] Morritt J held that 'there is no doubt that for the doctrine to apply there must be a contract at law'. The requirement of a contract was reiterated in *Goodchild v Goodchild*,[82] where it had been argued that a contract should not be required because it was not an essential element of the establishment of a constructive trust. The Court of Appeal rejected the purported analogy between the operation of mutual wills and secret trusts and concluded that a contract was required. Morritt LJ stated:

> As Leggatt LJ has pointed out, a consistent line of authority requires that for the doctrine of mutual wills to apply there must be a contract between the two testators. In delivering the advice of the Privy Council in *Gray v Perpetual Trustee Co Ltd*[83] such requirement was made abundantly clear by Viscount Haldane. Counsel…suggests that this test is too high. He does so by reference to the requirements for a secret trust or for the imposition of a constructive trust. I do not accept that there is any justification to be found in those areas of equity such as would justify departing from the clear statement of Viscount Haldane.[84]

While critics have suggested that Morritt LJ misrepresented the earlier cases cited in support of his conclusion that a contract is required,[85] and argued that the doctrine of mutual wills should operate whenever testators have reached an agreement or understanding not to revoke their wills,[86] subsequent decisions make clear that a contract (or in one case 'what amounts to a contract'[87]) will be required.[88] The courts have enjoyed ample opportunity to adopt a lower threshold but have pointedly, and

---

[79] (1797) 3 Ves JR 402, at 419. Cited by Nourse J in *Re Cleaver* [1981] 2 All ER 1018, at 1024.
[80] [1981] 2 All ER 1018, at 1024.   [81] [1993] 4 All ER 129, at 133.
[82] [1997] 3 All ER 63; Grattan 'Mutual Wills and Remarriage' [1997] Conv 153.
[83] [1928] AC 391, at 400.   [84] [1997] 3 All ER 63, at 75.
[85] *Dufour v Pereira* (1769) 1 Dick 419; *Walpole v Lord Orford* (1797) 3 Ves JR 402; *Gray v Perpetual Trustee Co Ltd* [1928] AC 391; *Birmingham v Renfrew* (1937) CLR 666; *Re Cleaver* [1981] 2 All ER 1018.
[86] Harper 'A Retreat from Equitable Mutuality?' [1997] Conv 182; Grattan 'Mutual Wills and Remarriage' [1997] Conv 153.   [87] *Charles v Fraser* [2010] EWHC 2154 (Ch), at [59].
[88] See also *Birch v Curtis* [2002] FLR 1158. In New Zealand it was held that the doctrine of mutual wills may be founded either on the basis of contract or restitution: *Re Newey* [1994] 2 NZLR 590.

repeatedly, chosen not to do so. For example, in *Olins v Waters*,[89] Mummery LJ reiterated that it 'is a legally *necessary* condition of mutual wills that there is clear and satisfactory evidence of a contract between two testators'.[90] This decision must in principle be correct. The effect of a finding that there are mutual wills is to impose a binding legal obligation in respect of the property affected. To give rise to this, even if a contract is not required, there must be an agreement intended to have legal effect. The difference between such an agreement and a contract is no more than semantic.

(b) Necessity of consideration

In order to establish that the testators had entered into a binding contract not to revoke their wills, it is necessary to show that consideration was provided. In *Re Dale (Decd)*[91] the defendants argued that consideration was only given for the promise not to revoke if the first testator to die had provided a benefit to the survivor other than his promise not to revoke his own will. Morritt J rejected this submission and held that a testator has acted sufficiently to his detriment to constitute consideration where he has performed his promise by executing the mutual will, and not subsequently taken advantage of his legal right to revoke it.

(c) Absence of any contract

In the absence of a contract the testators' wills will not be mutual, and a constructive trust cannot arise.[92] In *Re Oldham*,[93] Mr and Mrs Weldon executed similar wills in 1907. In 1914 the husband died. As a result his estate passed to his wife absolutely. In 1921 she married Mr Oldham, who was some thirty-five years her junior, and altered her will to grant him a life interest in a large portion of her estate. She died in 1922, leaving some £108,000, all but £10,000 of which had come from her first husband's estate. Astbury J held that there was no evidence of an agreement that the 'mutual' wills should be irrevocable, and therefore there was no trust raised in favour of the beneficiaries named in them.

In *Healey v Brown*,[94] a question arose about the effect of s 2 of the Law of Property (Miscellaneous Provisions) Act 1989 (which requires contracts relating to interests in land to be made in writing). Thomas and Mary Theresa Brown, in accordance with an oral agreement, had made identical mutual wills under which, on the death of the survivor, the flat which they jointly owned was to go to Mary's niece, Jacqueline. David Donaldson QC, sitting as a Deputy High Court judge, held that Jacqueline's claim based on the mutual wills was precluded by the fact that there was no written contract signed by both Thomas and Mary. In his view if there was no enforceable

---

[89] [2009] Ch 212, at 221 [36].

[90] Oddly, in *Fry v Densham-Smith* [2010] EWCA Civ 1410 Mummery LJ did not refer expressly to the need for a contract, but referred to the need for an 'express agreement' 'to become irrevocable on the death of the first to die' (at [4]) and later to a 'bilateral agreement' (at [35]). It is hard to see how a bilateral agreement which is intended to be irrevocable is anything other than a contract.

[91] [1994] Ch 31.   [92] *Birch v Curtis* [2002] FLR 1158.   [93] [1925] Ch 75.

[94] [2002] EWHC 1405 (Ch).

contract, the mutual wills doctrine could not apply. He was, however, prepared to hold that the half-share in the flat which Thomas had acquired from Mary on her death was subject to a constructive trust—akin to either a secret trust or a common intention constructive trust. With respect, this decision is mistaken for two reasons. First, s 2 of the 1989 Act applies only to contracts 'for the sale or other disposition of an interest in land'. A mutual wills contract does not dispose of an interest in land, but has a freezing effect on the terms of the agreed wills.[95] Secondly, s 2 of the 1989 Act preserves the effect of implied, constructive, or resulting trusts. Since mutual wills agreements are enforced as constructive trusts of the property subject to the agreement, they should not be rendered unenforceable merely by the absence of a single document signed by both parties. This is an issue which would merit reconsideration by a higher court.

(d) Breach of contract by revocation

As mutual wills are executed on the basis of a contract not to revoke, a testator who unilaterally revokes his will before either has died will have acted in breach of his contractual obligations. As such, he will be prima facie liable to pay damages to his fellow testator, and if he has died his estate will be liable to the survivor.[96] There will be no liability for breach if the revocation occurred by operation of law, for example where the testator married or divorced, but the relevant property may still be subject to a constructive trust.

(e) The standard of proof

In *Re Cleaver*[97] Nourse J held that the agreement not to revoke the mutual wills can only be established by 'clear and satisfactory evidence' and that the burden of proof is the ordinary civil standard of the balance of probabilities.

(f) Mere fact of identical wills

In *Dufour v Pereira*[98] Lord Cottenham LC had suggested that, where identical wills had been executed, it was possible to infer that the parties had agreed that they should not be revoked because 'the instrument itself is the evidence of the agreement'. However, it is clear from more recent cases a contract cannot be implied from the testators having simultaneously executed identical wills. In *Gray v Perpetual Trustee Co Ltd*[99] the Privy Council concluded that:

> the mere simultaneity of the wills and the similarity of their terms do not appear, taken by themselves, to have been looked on as more than some evidence of an agreement not to revoke. The agreement...was a fact which had in itself to be established by evidence, and in such cases the whole of the evidence must be looked at.[100]

---

[95] Compare *Yeates v Line* [2012] EWHC 3085 (Ch).
[96] *Robinson v Ommanney* (1883) 23 Ch D 285.   [97] [1981] 2 All ER 1018, at 1024.
[98] (1769) 1 Dick 419; see also *Walpole v Lord Orford* (1797) 3 Ves JR 402.
[99] [1928] AC 391, at 400.   [100] [1928] AC 391, at 400.

This statement of principle was approved by Nourse J in *Re Cleaver*.[101] For this reason, no constructive trust was established in *Re Oldham*,[102] the facts of which were noted earlier. The only evidence of an agreement came from the fact that identical wills had been executed and Astbury J held that this was insufficient. He regretted his conclusion, because he was sure that the testator would have made a different will if he had foreseen that after his death his wife 'would marry a young man and leave the whole of her first husband's property to that young man and her own relatives'.[103] He added that a mutual will agreement was not the only possible interpretation of what happened:

> Each may have thought it quite safe to trust the other, and to believe that, having regard to their ages, nothing was likely to occur in the future substantially to diminish the property taken by the survivor, who could be trusted to give effect to the other's obvious wishes. But that is a very different thing from saying that they bound themselves by a trust that should be operative in all circumstances and in all cases.[104]

Although the mere fact of the execution of mutual wills is not alone sufficient to prove the necessary contract, it may provide a strong indication that a contract had been concluded between the testators.[105] This was recognized even in *Re Oldham*.[106]

(g) Additional evidence of agreement

Since a contract will not be inferred from the mere execution of identical wills, additional evidence will have to be provided to demonstrate that the testators had concluded a contract not to revoke. A constructive trust will be established if the mutual wills themselves contain a statement that they have been executed on the basis of an agreement, as was the case in *Re Hagger*.[107] Written evidence outside of the wills, for example a memorandum stating the testators' intentions, will also support the establishment of a mutual wills constructive trust. In *Olins v Walters*,[108] a statement in the wills that they were intended to be mutual wills was supported by an attendance note from the testators' solicitor (who was also their grandson and a beneficiary), and by his oral evidence.

It is possible for a mutual wills agreement to be established by oral evidence, but this will be no easy task. Factors which may help to establish the agreement are similarities in the wills, particularly where they are unusually detailed, and evidence of family conversations[109] or statements to friends.[110] There will be particular difficulty about establishing the essential agreement not to revoke,[111] but the conduct of the survivor

---

[101] [1981] 2 All ER 1018, at 1022. [102] [1925] Ch 25. [103] [1925] Ch 25. at 87.

[104] [1925] Ch 25, at 88–89.

[105] [1925] Ch 25, at 88–89, at 87, where Astbury J said: 'Of course it is a strong thing that these two parties came together, agreed to make their wills in identical terms and in fact so made them. But that does not go nearly far enough.' The approach of Astbury J was approved by the Privy Council in *Gray v Perpetual Trustee Co Ltd* [1928] AC 391, at 400. [106] [1925] Ch 75.

[107] [1930] 2 Ch 190. [108] [2009] Ch 212. [109] *Re Cleaver* [1981] 2 All ER 1018.

[110] *Charles v Fraser* [2010] EWHC 2154 (Ch)

[111] *Charles v Fraser* [2010] EWHC 2154 (Ch), at [70].

may help to establish this.[112] In *Re Cleaver*,[113] Nourse J held that his conclusion was helped by the attitude of Mrs Cleaver after her husband's death, which seemed to suggest that she was aware that she was under an obligation to dispose of her estate in accordance with the terms of their mutual wills, and not merely an honourable engagement.[114] It was only later that she adopted the attitude that she did not have to worry about promises made to her husband because he was dead and could do nothing about it.[115] Contradictory evidence, particularly from the attending solicitor, will carry some weight. In *Goodchild v Goodchild*[116] family members and friends gave evidence that the wills were intended to be mutually binding.[117] However, this body of anecdotal evidence was weighed against the evidence of the family solicitor who had drawn up the wills in question. He claimed that it was not his normal practice to draw up mutually binding wills, but rather to grant a life interest to the survivor. He claimed to have discussed the matter with them and that they clearly intended the survivor to be free to deal with the property during his or her lifetime.

Faced with this conflict of evidence, Carnwath J placed greater weight on the evidence of the solicitor. He concluded that in the circumstances no agreement had been proved.

The Court of Appeal upheld his conclusion that there was insufficient evidence to establish anything beyond a mere moral obligation.

It should be noted that the overriding difference between the evidence presented in the cases of *Re Cleaver* and *Goodchild v Goodchild* was as to the evidence of the respective solicitors. In *Re Cleaver* the solicitor's evidence was relatively weak.[118] In contrast, in *Goodchild* the solicitor was adamant that no agreement had been intended, and that he had expressly outlined to the testators the various options as to how they could ensure that the estate passed to the son, and that they had decided to opt for the identical, but not mutual, wills, which he had explained would mean that the survivor was still free to dispose of the property freely as they chose.

(h) Certainty of subject and objects

In *Re Cleaver*,[119] Nourse J also emphasized that there must be certainty of subject matter and of objects for a constructive trust to arise on the basis of mutual wills. He considered that these requirements 'are as essential to this species of trust as they are to any other'. It is not necessary, however, that the mutual wills agreement should deal with every eventuality. In *Olins v Walters*[120] counsel argued that there was no binding mutual wills agreement because there were some unanswered questions, such as the extent to which the survivor could use any property they inherited for their own purposes. This argument about insufficiency of terms was roundly rejected by Mummery LJ, who said:

---

[112] *Charles v Fraser* [2010] EWHC 2154 (Ch), at [69].   [113] *Re Cleaver* [1981] 2 All ER 1018.
[114] *Re Cleaver* [1981] 2 All ER 1018, at 1027.   [115] *Re Cleaver* [1981] 2 All ER 1018, at 1027–1028.
[116] [1997] 3 All ER 63.   [117] [1997] 3 All ER 63, at 679.
[118] As it was in *Charles v Fraser* [2010] EWHC 2154 (Ch), another case in which a mutual wills agreement was established on the basis of oral evidence.   [119] [1981] 2 All ER 1018.
[120] [2009] Ch 212.

Possible, and as yet unexplored, legal consequences of the application of the equitable principles do not negative the existence of the foundation contract or prevent a constructive trust from arising by operation of law on the death of the Deceased.[121]

(5) The operation of mutual wills

While English law clearly accepts the doctrine of mutual wills, there are many theoretical and practical difficulties concerning the nature of the trust interest established thereby. In *Goodchild v Goodchild*[122] Morritt LJ emphasized that 'the doctrine of mutual wills is anomalous',[123] and for this reason uncertainties and inconsistencies are tolerated which would render a more conventional trust void.

(a) Date of creation of the constructive trust

When it is established that wills were intended to be mutual, it has been seen that a constructive trust will arise to prevent the survivor disposing of his property in contravention of his contractual agreement not to vary his will. While it is clear that equity imposes a constructive trust, it is less clear when the trust arises.[124] A number of alternatives present themselves.

(b) Date the mutual wills are executed

As a matter of logic, this cannot be the date at which the constructive trust arises. The parties remain free to revoke their wills by agreement at any time before the death of the first testator.[125] It may even be that a revocation without agreement will prevent a constructive trust arising. Sir Gorell Barnes P held in *Stone v Hoskins*[126] that the survivor has no claim to a constructive trust where the testator who has died revoked his mutual will and executed another in a different form.

(c) Date of the death of the survivor

The date of death of the surviving testator cannot be the relevant date for the establishment of the constructive trust, as it has been held that the interest of a beneficiary of a mutual will who survives the first testator but predeceases the second does not lapse. In *Re Hagger*[127] John and Emma Hagger executed mutual wills leaving one-sixth interests in their estates to Edward Adams, Eleanor Palmer, and Alice Young. All three survived Emma's death in 1904, but predeceased John, who died in 1928. Clauson J held that their respective interests had not lapsed because the trust took effect from the date of the wife's death.

---

[121] [2009] Ch 212, at 221, [41].   [122] [1997] 3 All ER 63.   [123] [1997] 3 All ER 63, at 76.

[124] See (1951) 14 MLR 137 (Mitchell).

[125] However, if the testator revokes his will before death, he will have committed a breach of contract and his estate will be liable to the survivor in damages: see *Robinson v Ommanney* (1883) LR 23 Ch D 285.

[126] [1905] P 194.   [127] [1930] 2 Ch 190.

(d) Date of the first testator's death

It therefore seems that a constructive trust imposed on the basis of the doctrine of mutual wills arises on the date of the death of the first of the testators who executed them. In *Thomas and Agnes Carvel Foundation v Carvel*,[128] Thomas and Agnes Carvel made mutual, identical wills, each leaving their estate on trust to the other for life, with the remainder on trust for the claimant, an American corporation. By a reciprocal will agreement they agreed not to alter the provisions of their wills without the consent of the other, and that the survivor would not make any alterations. Following the death of Thomas in America, Agnes made two further wills, the last of which revoked all previous wills. When Agnes died in England the claimant instituted proceedings in the United States of America to enforce the reciprocal will agreement. By the time the case reached the English High Court, the main issue before the court was the potential removal of Agnes's personal representative for failing to administer the estate as required by the mutual will. Lewison J had to determine whether the claimant foundation had any interest under the will, to determine whether the personal representative was acting improperly. He concluded that the mutual will arose on the time of the first testator's death, therefore binding Agnes from that point. In his view:

> The essential point, to my mind, is that the trust does not arise under the will of the surviving testator. Nor does it arise under any previous will of the surviving testator. It arises out of the agreement between the two testators not to revoke their wills, and the trust arises when the first of the two dies without having revoked his will. In so far as there is an 'operative will', it seems to me that it is the will of the first testator (and his death with that will unrevoked) which brings the trust into effect.[129]

(6) The beneficial interest under the constructive trust

(a) What property is subject to the trust?

Although it seems that a constructive trust arises on the death of the first testator, it is more difficult to identify the precise nature and extent of the beneficial interest subsisting under the trust. There are two questions here, the first being what property is subject to the trust, the second, how the trust affects that property. On the first question the only logical answer is that it depends on the agreement of the testators,[130] although some cases seem to make assumptions. In *Re Hagger*[131] Clauson J held that a mutual will trust applied only to the property received by the survivor after the death of the first testator. However, in *Goodchild v Goodchild*[132] the Court of Appeal treated a trust affecting all the testator's property as the normal mutual wills arrangement. There is no reason in principle why, if it is based on the agreement of the parties, the trust should not encompass property acquired by the survivor after the death of

---

[128] [2008] Ch 395.   [129] [2008] Ch 395, at 404 [27].   [130] *Re Cleaver* [1981] 2 All ER 1018.
[131] [1930] 2 Ch 190.   [132] [1997] 3 All ER 63.

the first testator, for example through receipt of a windfall profit such as gambling winnings.[133]

(b) How does the trust affect the property?

This second question is more difficult. It would defeat the intentions of most testators if the effect of mutual wills is to make the survivor an immediate bare trustee for the ultimate beneficiaries and with no personal interest in the property. If this was what was intended, the will of the first to die could have made the gifts to the ultimate beneficiaries directly, and the ultimate beneficiaries would be able to call for the property to be transferred to them immediately. An alternative is that the survivor has only a life interest in the property affected. This was the view of Clauson J in *Re Hagger.*[134] That interpretation is more plausible in the case of a trust affecting only the interest of the first to die, but less plausible where it affects the whole of the property of the survivor, whether inherited from the first to die or not. Having a life interest only gives no right to the capital. What if the survivor faces expensive medical bills which are not covered by the NHS, or needs constant care and attention in a nursing home? Could capital be used for this purpose?

The practical reality is that, in most cases, the underlying intention of the mutual wills is to allow the survivor to use the property inherited, including the capital, for his or her own support and maintenance during their lifetime, but that the residue remaining at their death will be bequeathed to the agreed beneficiaries, rather than to others. As Nourse J observed in *Re Cleaver,*[135] Mr Cleaver wanted Mrs Cleaver to enjoy 'the security after his death which a free power of disposal over his estate would give her' and at the same time 'to ensure that anything which was left at her death should go back to his side of the family'.

(c) What are the rights of the beneficiaries?

If the survivor has the use of capital, and only the residue goes to the ultimate beneficiaries, then this suggests that the property rights of the beneficiaries of the mutual wills cannot crystallize until the date of the death of the survivor. If the trust were to fix unconditionally on the death of the first testator, ludicrous and unintended results could follow. Although the issue was not considered in *Re Dale (Decd),*[136] the facts of that case can be used as an illustration. If the beneficiaries' interests had crystallized as absolute rights at the date of their father's death, their mother would have held all her property, which was the subject matter of the trust, on trust for the children in equal shares, and she would in effect have no longer owned anything at all. Alternatively, if they crysallized then, but the mother retained a life interest, she would have no right to use any capital for her own needs.

An alternative model is therefore required to explain the nature of the entitlement of the beneficiaries of a constructive trust arising under mutual wills. The cases which

---

[133] The issue was raised in *Olins v Walters* [2009] Ch 212, but had not been pleaded on the facts, so neither the trial judge nor the Court of Appeal expressed any binding view on the matter.

[134] [1930] 2 Ch 190.   [135] [1981] 2 All ER 1018, at 1029.   [136] [1994] Ch 31.

have explored this problem have suggested that the property in the hands of the survivor affected by the mutual wills is rendered subject to a floating trust which arises at the date of death of the first testator, but which does not crystallize in favour of the beneficiaries until the death of the survivor. The possibility of such a 'floating trust' was raised by Dixon J in the Australian case *Birmingham v Renfrew*:

> The purpose of an arrangement for corresponding wills must often be, as in this case, to enable the survivor during his life to deal as absolute owner with the property passing under the will of the party first dying. That is to say, the object of the transaction is to put the survivor in a position to enjoy for his own benefit the full ownership so that, for instance, he may convert it and expend the proceeds if he chooses. But when he dies he is to bequeath what is left in the manner agreed upon. It is only by the special doctrines of equity that such a floating obligation, suspended, so to speak, during the lifetime of the survivor can descend upon the assets at his death and crystallise into a trust.[137]

The concept of such a 'floating', uncrystallized, trust was raised in England in *Ottaway v Norman*[138] in the context of a fully secret trust.[139] Harry Ottaway left his bungalow by will to Eva Hodges, a woman he had been living with, having communicated his intention that on death she should leave it to his son, William. Although argued and decided on the basis that a fully secret trust had been created, this does not easily accord with the facts. It was not the intention of Harry that Eva should hold the bungalow on trust for William from the moment of his death. Nor were there mutual wills. Despite an expectation that Eva would leave the bungalow by will to William, she made no simultaneous will alongside Harry. Having held that a secret trust had arisen, Brightman J considered the nature of the beneficiary's rights during the lifetime of Eva, the trustee:

> I am content to assume for present purposes but without so deciding that if property is given to the primary donee on the understanding that the primary donee will dispose by his will of such assets, if any, as he may have at his command at his death in favour of the secondary donee, a valid trust is created in favour of the secondary donee which is in suspense during the lifetime of the primary donee, but attaches to the estate of the primary donee at the moment of the latter's death.[140]

It therefore seems best to regard mutual wills as creating some type of floating trust, which allows the survivor to dispose of the property subject to it if necessary but crystallizing over whatever remains at his death[141] or on any asset subject to an unauthorized voluntary disposition prior to death.[142] This approach was also assumed by Astbury J in *Re Oldham*.[143] Most significantly, in *Goodchild v Goodchild*[144] Leggatt LJ assumed that mutual wills operated to create a floating trust. In the course of his comments concerning the need for a contractual agreement between the testators, he stated:

---

[137] (1937) CLR 666.   [138] [1972] Ch 698.   [139] See Chapter 8.
[140] [1972] Ch 698, at 713.
[141] As has been seen in Chapter 7, a number of cases hold that such a trust, if created expressly, would fail for lack of certainty.   [142] *Healey v Brown* [2002] EWHC 1405 (Ch), at [13].
[143] [1925] Ch 25, at 88.   [144] [1997] 3 All ER 63.

The fact that each expected that the other would leave them to him is not sufficient to impress the arrangement with a floating trust.[145]

(d) Use of the property subject to the 'floating' trust by the survivor

Where the doctrine of mutual wills operates so that property in the hands of the surviving testator is subject to a floating constructive trust, the question arises as to duties of the survivor as trustee. The doctrine of mutual wills clearly operates to prevent the survivor disposing of the trust property by will in a manner inconsistent with the mutual wills, but the more significant issue is whether he is prevented from disposing of it during his lifetime. In *Re Oldham*[146] Astbury J was of the opinion that the survivor could dispose of the property inter vivos. However, it is clear that there must be limits to the power of the survivor to dispose of the property subject to the trust, otherwise the entire purpose of the arrangement could easily be defeated. This difficulty was recognized by Dixon J in *Birmingham v Renfrew*:

> No doubt gifts and settlements, inter vivos, if calculated to defeat the intention of the compact, could not be made by the survivor and his right of disposition, inter vivos, is, therefore, not unqualified. But, substantially, the purpose of the arrangement will often be to allow full enjoyment for the survivor's own benefit and advantage upon condition that at his death the residue shall pass as arranged.[147]

Adopting this analysis, the position would be very similar to a floating charge over the assets of a company.[148] So long as the survivor continued to behave in an ordinary way that was in accordance with his means and circumstances, he would continue to have freedom of disposition over the assets subject to the inchoate trust. The trust would, however, crystallize and settle on the assets upon his death, and even during his lifetime he could be called upon to account for any extraordinary transaction inappropriate to his circumstances. If a purported extraordinary transaction was identified in time, a beneficiary affected by it could presumably take steps to restrain it. If the transaction has already taken place, the recipient could be held subject to a constructive trust. For instance, in *Healey v Brown*[149] Thomas Brown put into joint names with his son a flat which Thomas had agreed with his wife to leave to her niece (the claimant) on his death. The deputy High Court judge took the view that, if a mutual wills agreement had been established, Thomas's son would have held the flat on constructive trust for the niece. The judge, David Donaldson QC, observed:

> Had Mr Brown sold the flat and used the proceeds to fund a place in a nursing home, there would have been no basis for complaint. But to give away the flat to his son—with immediate effect as to a 50% undivided share, and with effect on death as to the remainder by operation of the doctrine of survivorship—could scarcely run more directly and fully counter to the intention of the mutual will compact that the flat should pass to his deceased's wife niece on his own death. Subject therefore to the impact of the 1989 Act

---

[145] [1997] 3 All ER 63, at 71.   [146] [1925] Ch 25, at 88.   [147] (1937) CLR 666.
[148] *Re Panama, New Zealand and Australian Royal Mail Co* (1870) 5 Ch App 318.
[149] [2002] EWHC 1405 (Ch).

[the need for a contract disposing of land to be in writing] I have no doubt that the mutual wills doctrine would apply in the present case so as to impose in favour of the Claimant a constructive trust attaching to the flat.[150]

6 Secret trusts

(1) Introduction to secret trusts

Exactly how secret trusts should be categorized is a matter on which there are different views. The most widely held theory is that they are forms of lifetime trusts set up outside a will, but depending upon the will for their operation. Some of the cases suggest that they are a mechanism for making provision via a will for illegitimate children or mistresses which avoids the publicity of describing the gift in the will,[151] but there are more secure and effective means of concealing the identity of a beneficiary by making lifetime gifts or creating lifetime trusts. More often than not secret trusts are used to provide for a beneficiary who has been forgotten, and in some cases because the testator was unsure as to who should be the ultimate beneficiary when he made his will. What is secret about a secret trust is not that no one knows about it—there would be problems relating to enforcement if that were the case—but that the existence or the terms of the trust are not disclosed in the will.

(2) Types of secret trust

English law recognizes two categories of secret trust, namely 'fully secret trusts' and 'half-secret trusts'. The central difference between these categories is the extent to which the testator's will discloses that the person named as the recipient of a bequest is intended to take the property as a trustee rather than for himself. While the difference might appear slight, for a long period of time it was held that only fully secret trusts should be recognized as valid, and even though half-secret trusts are now accepted, the rules governing their creation are somewhat more restrictive.

(a) Fully secret trusts

A fully secret trust is created when a testator leaves property to a specified person in his will who has agreed that he will hold the property left to him on trust for a third party. In a fully secret trust, neither the fact of the trust nor the identity of the beneficiary under the trust are revealed in the will. For example, imagine that George wants to leave something to his first wife, Henrietta, without his second wife discovering her existence. He therefore leaves £50,000 in his will to his close friend, Ian, who has agreed that he will ensure that Henrietta receives the money. On the face of George's

---

[150] [2002] EWHC 1405 (Ch), at [14]–[15].
[151] Eg, *Re Boyes* (1884) LR 26 Ch D 531; *Blackwell v Blackwell* [1929] AC 318.

will, it appears that Ian is the absolute beneficiary of the bequest, whereas in fact, behind the scenes, Henrietta is intended to benefit. This arrangement would give rise to a fully secret trust. On the death of George, Ian will receive the money under the terms of the will, but he will be required to hold it as trustee for Henrietta. Ian is therefore the trustee of the secret trust, and Henrietta the beneficiary.

(b) Half-secret trusts

The performance of a fully secret trust is to some extent dependent on the integrity of the beneficiary who has agreed to act as the secret trustee. There is always a danger that the secret trustee will ignore the trust and take the property as his own. This danger can be avoided by confirming the instructions in writing, asking the trustee to sign this, and giving a copy to the intended beneficiary. Alternatively, if the testator indicates in his will that the recipient of the bequest is intended to take the property as a trustee it is impossible for the trustee recipient to deny the existence of a trust. The identity of the beneficiary can be disclosed separately. Amending the example used above, if George were to leave £50,000 to Ian in his will 'on trust', without disclosing that Henrietta was the ultimate beneficiary, a half-secret trust would have been created. The trust is described as 'half-secret' because the fact that the property is subject to a trust obligation appears on the face of the will, but the identity of the true beneficiary remains secret.

(c) Secret trusts arising on intestacy

Although secret trusts generally arise in the context of a testamentary disposition, a secret trust may arise in a case of intestacy,[152] provided that the person entitled to the deceased's estate on his intestacy had agreed that he would receive the specified property as a trustee and not for himself absolutely. As Romer J stated in *Re Gardner (No 2)*:

> The principle has been applied...where the owner of property refrains from making a will and so allows the property to pass to the donee as on an intestacy.[153]

Therefore, if, under the rules of intestacy, Ian was entitled to receive a share of George's estate, George could ask him to hold that share for the benefit of Henrietta. Provided that Ian agreed, and George died without making a will, Ian would hold whatever he received from the administration of George's estate on trust for Henrietta.

(d) Secret trust arising on transfer by survivorship in joint tenancy

A secret trust can probably also arise where a person acquires an enlarged interest in property through survivorship to a joint tenancy. In *Healey v Brown*[154] David Donaldson QC (sitting as a Deputy High Court Judge) held that a constructive trust applied to the half interest in a flat to which Mr Brown had succeeded as a joint tenant on the death of his wife, after he had promised to leave the flat to a named beneficiary on his own death. David Donaldson observed that 'the present case differs from the

---

[152] *Stickland v Aldridge* (1804) 9 Ves 516.   [153] [1923] 2 Ch 230, at 233.
[154] [2002] EWHC Ch 1405.

ordinary case of secret trusts, since the property passed outside the will and by operation of law rather than pursuant to a bequest. But to my mind that is a matter of form
without substantive significance.'[155]

(3) **Requirements for the creation of secret trusts**

The essential requirements of 'intention, communication and acceptance' must be satisfied to create a valid fully secret, or half-secret, trust. It has been questioned whether
the creation of a secret trust requires a contract between the testator and the intended
trustee, whereby the trustee agrees to hold the property bequeathed to him on trust
for the indicated beneficiary. In *Re Goodchild (Decd)*[156] Morritt LJ suggested that the
'principles applicable to cases of a fully secret trust do, in substance, require the proof
of a contract,' although he accepted that they do not 'require exactly the same degree
of agreement as does a contract at law'.[157] While many of the authorities elucidating
the meaning of these requirements are applicable to both categories of secret trust, it
should be noted in advance that there are significant differences regarding the application of the requirement of communication to half-secret trusts.

(4) **Fully secret trusts**

The leading authority stating the requirements of a fully secret trust is *Ottaway v
Norman*.[158] Harry Ottaway cohabited with Miss Hodges in his house, 'Ashcroft'. On his
death, 'Ashcroft' was left to Miss Hodges in his will, and she left it in her will to Mr and
Mrs Norman. Harry's son, William, claimed that the house had been left to Miss Hodges
on the understanding that she would leave it to him on her death. He claimed that a
secret trust had been created in his favour, so that Miss Hodges held the house on trust
for him and that it had not therefore formed part of her estate. Although the case is open
to criticism on the grounds that it did not really involve a secret trust, as Miss Hodges
was not subjected to an immediate obligation to hold the house on trust for William on
the death of Harry, it was argued and decided on the basis that the existence of a secret
trust was in issue. Having examined the facts, Brightman J concluded that a fully secret
trust had been created. In the course of his judgment he referred to the secret trustee as
the 'primary donee' (who would take the property under the will) and the secret beneficiary as the 'secondary donee'.[159] He held that subjection of property to a fully secret trust
required the three elements of intention, communication, and acceptance.

(a) **Intention**

Brightman J stated that a secret trust would not be created unless it was 'the intention
of the testator to subject the primary donee to an obligation in favour of the secondary

---

[155] [2002] EWHC Ch 1405, at [29]. While this remark referred to secret trusts, most of the judgment
concerns mutual wills—see earlier.   [156] [1997] 3 All ER 63.
    [157] [1997] 3 All ER 63, at 75.   [158] [1972] Ch 698; (1972) 36 Conv 129.
    [159] [1972] Ch 698, (1972) 36 Conv 129, at 711.

donee'.[160] This requirement is no different from the requirement that conventional express trusts must demonstrate sufficient 'certainty of intention' to create a trust.[161] It must be shown that the testator intended to subject the secret trustee to a mandatory obligation to hold the property for the benefit of the secret beneficiary. An intention to impose a purely moral obligation is insufficient, as can be seen in *Re Snowden (Decd)*,[162] where an elderly testatrix left her entire residuary estate to her older brother because she was uncertain as to how she should leave her property among her relatives, and she said that her brother would 'know what to do'. She died without changing her will, and six days later her brother also died, leaving all his property to his only son. The question was whether the brother had taken Mrs Snowden's residuary estate on secret trust for her nephews and nieces equally. Megarry V-C concluded that she had not possessed the necessary intention to impose a trust on her brother, but that she had merely intended to impose on him a 'moral obligation' to do what he thought best. As a result no secret trust was established, and the brother's son was entitled to the entire residue absolutely.

(b) Communication

The mere fact that a testator intends to create a secret trust is insufficient on its own to subject the recipient of the trust property under his will to an enforceable secret trust. As Brightman J stated in *Ottaway v Norman*, creation of a valid secret trust requires 'communication of that intention to the primary donee'.[163] The conscience of a beneficiary under the will is only affected, so as to justify the imposition of a trust, if the testator made him aware that he was to receive the property bequeathed as a trustee.

Communication will only be effective to create a fully secret trust if it satisfies the following criteria.

(i) Communication of both the fact of the trust and the terms of the trust

A fully secret trust will only arise if the testator makes the intended trustee aware of both the fact that he is to hold the property bequeathed to him on trust, and the identity (or the means of discovering the identity) of the intended trust beneficiary. Where either of these elements is missing, the property will not be held on trust. For example, in *Re Boyes*[164] George Boyes left his entire estate by will to his solicitor, Frederick Carritt. Prior to his death Boyes had informed Carritt that he was to hold the property on trust, the terms of which he said he would communicate to him by letter. No communication of the terms of the trust was made during the testator's lifetime, but after his death papers were discovered directing Carritt to hold the property for his mistress and illegitimate child. Kay J held that in these circumstances a secret trust had not been established in favour of the mistress and child. However, as the solicitor had admitted that he had agreed to receive the property left to him as a trustee, he was not

---

[160] [1972] Ch 698, (1972) 36 Conv 129.   [161] See Chapter 7.

[162] [1979] 2 All ER 172. Similar cases are *Taylor v HMRC* [2008] STC (SCD) 1159 and *Davies v HMRC* [2009] UKFTT 138 (TC).   [163] *Ottaway v Norman* [1972] Ch 698, at 711.

[164] (1884) LR 26 Ch D 531.

entitled to take it absolutely for himself, and therefore he held it on a resulting trust for Boyes' next of kin.

While a complete failure to communicate the terms of the trust before the testator's death prevents the creation of a valid secret trust, communication of the terms of the trust by means of a sealed envelope, given to the trustee during the testator's lifetime with the stipulation that it was not to be opened until after his death, will be sufficient to create a secret trust. This was accepted by the Court of Appeal in *Re Keen*,[165] where Lord Wright MR considered such communication analogous with that of a ship sailing under sealed orders, which he considered is 'sailing under orders though the exact terms are not ascertained by the captain till later'.

(ii) Communication of the extent of the trust

A secret trust will only affect property bequeathed to the intended trustees to the extent that effective communication had been made. In *Re Cooper*[166] a testator left £5,000 by will to two trustees. He had previously communicated the terms of the trust to them both. He subsequently added a codicil to his will, increasing the amount of the gift to £10,000, but without communicating this alteration to the trustees. The Court of Appeal held that only £5,000 of the money bequeathed to the trustees was subject to the secret trust.[167]

(iii) Communication must be made before the death of the testator

A valid fully secret trust will be created provided that effective communication was made to the trustee at any time prior to the death of the testator. It has already been seen how failure to communicate the terms of the intended trust before the testator's death prevented the finding of a secret trust in *Re Boyes*.[168] In *Wallgrave v Tebbs*[169] William Coles left property by will to the defendants. From a letter he had written it appeared that he had intended that it should be applied by them for the charitable purpose of endowing a church. However, as this intention had not been communicated to them during his lifetime, Page-Wood V-C held that no trust had been created, and that the defendants were entitled to take the property bequeathed to them absolutely.

(iv) Communication to joint trustees

Particular difficulties of communication emerge if a testator intends to subject property to a secret trust bequeathed to two or more persons jointly in his will. The question arises whether the joint beneficiaries under the will are bound by the secret trust if communication had been made to only some of them. In answering this dilemma the law distinguishes between bequests made to the intended trustees as joint tenants, and bequests made to them as tenants-in-common. The principles were stated

---

[165] [1937] Ch 236. See also *Re Boyes* (1884) LR 26 Ch D 531, at 536; *Re Bateman's Will Trusts* [1970] 1 WLR 1463.   [166] [1939] Ch 811.
[167] As it was a half-secret trust, the remaining £5,000 was held on resulting trust for the testator's residuary legatees. If it had been an attempted fully secret trust, the intended trustees would have been entitled to the remaining £5,000 absolutely.   [168] (1884) LR 26 Ch D 531.
[169] (1855) 2 K & J 313.

by Farwell J in *Re Stead*.[170] Where the intended trust property is bequeathed to two or more persons as tenants-in-common, a secret trust will only bind the respective shares of those tenants-in-common to whom the testator had communicated the terms of the trust. Those to whom the trust had not been communicated are entitled to receive their respective shares of the bequeathed property absolutely.[171] In *Re Stead*, Mrs Stead had left property to Mrs Witham and Mrs Andrews as tenants-in-common. She informed Mrs Witham that £2,000 was to be held on trust for John Collett, but made no communication to Mrs Andrews. It was held that Mrs Andrews took her share of the property free from any trust. Where the intended trust property is bequeathed to joint tenants, a further distinction is made on the grounds of the timing of any communication of the trust. Farwell J held that if a testator made effective communication to any one of the joint tenants before executing the will, they would all be bound by the secret trust.[172] However, he held that where communication occurred after the will had been executed, only those to whom communication had been made would be bound by the trust, and that therefore those tenants-in-common to whom no communication had been made would be entitled to take their respective shares of the bequeathed property absolutely.[173] Although clearly representing the present law, it has been persuasively argued that the rules expounded in *Re Stead*[174] are incorrect because Farwell J developed his reasoning from a misunderstanding of earlier cases cited as authority.[175] It is suggested that, rather than distinguishing between joint tenants and tenants-in-common (and in the latter case also between communication before and after the execution of the will), the question in each case should be whether the testator was induced to make the joint bequest only because of the promise of some of those entitled that the property would be held on trust.[176] Clearly, it will be more difficult to show that the gift was so induced if it was made to tenants-in-common, or if the promise was only made after the will had been executed.

(c) Acceptance

A secret trust is not imposed on property left to an intended secret trustee merely because the testator effectively communicated his intention that it should be held on trust. The property will only be subject to a secret trust if the intended trustee accepted that he would hold it on trust. As Brightman J said in *Ottaway v Norman*,[177] the third essential element for the creation of a fully secret trust is 'the acceptance of that obligation by the primary donee either expressly or by acquiescence'. Such acceptance does not need to be active. It has been held that if the terms of the trust have been communicated to the intended trustee, his silence will be taken to be an acceptance

---

[170] [1900] 1 Ch 237.

[171] See *Tee v Ferris* (1856) 2 K & J 357; *Rowbotham v Dunnett* (1878) LR 8 Ch D 430; *Re Young (Decd)* [1951] Ch 344. Compare also *Geddis v Semple* [1903] 1 IR 73.

[172] *Russell v Jackson* (1852) 10 Hare 204; *Jones v Badley* (1868) 3 Ch App 362.

[173] *Burney v Macdonald* (1845) 15 Sim 6; *Moss v Cooper* (1861) 1 John & H 352.

[174] [1900] 1 Ch 237.   [175] Perrins 'Can You Keep Half a Secret?" (1972) 88 LQR 225.

[176] Applying the principle of *Huguenin v Baseley* (1807) 14 Ves 273 that 'No man may profit by the fraud of another.'   [177] [1972] Ch 698, at 711.

of the trust. In *Moss v Cooper*[178] John Hill left property in his will to James Gawthorn, William Sedman, and James Owen. He communicated his intention to all three that the property should be used for the benefit of certain charities. The trust was accepted by Gawthron and Sedman. However, Owen remained silent. Page-Wood V-C held that, having learned of the testator's intention, such silence amounted to an acceptance of the trust. He justified this conclusion on the grounds that 'the legatees, as soon as they learned the intention of the testator, would be bound to elect whether they would undertake the trust or not'.

(5) **Half-secret trusts**

The creation of a valid half-secret trust is dependent upon satisfaction of the same three elements of intention, communication, and acceptance. However, there are significant differences concerning the application of the requirement of communication. The leading case stipulating the requirements for half-secret trusts is *Blackwell v Blackwell*,[179] where Lord Sumner stated that the essential criteria were 'intention, communication and acquiescence'.[180] As the criteria of intention and acceptance are identical to those required for a valid fully secret trust, which have been discussed earlier, only the element of communication will be examined.

(a) **Communication must be made before the execution of the will**

It has already been seen that property bequeathed to an intended trustee will be subject to a fully secret trust if the testator made effective communication of the trust at any time before his death. In contrast, in the case of half-secret trusts it has been held that the testator must make communication to the intended trustee before his will is executed. Communication subsequent to the execution of the will, even though prior to the testator's death, will not subject the bequeathed property to an enforceable half-secret trust. This follows from the judgment of Lord Sumner in *Blackwell v Blackwell*,[181] who stated:

> A testator cannot reserve to himself a power of making future unwitnessed dispositions by merely naming a trustee and leaving the purposes of the trust to be supplied afterwards...

His comments in this respect were strictly obiter, because the trust in question had been communicated to the intended trustee before the testator's will was executed. However, the limitation was accepted by the Court of Appeal in *Re Keen*,[182] and followed in *Re Bateman's Will Trusts*.[183] It is hard to see the logic for this differentiation between fully and half-secret trusts.[184] In *Gold v Hill*,[185] a man who had separated from his wife nominated a solicitor as the beneficiary of a life insurance policy, having communicated to him that the proceeds were to be held on trust for his partner and her children. This nomination and communication had taken place after the execution of

---

[178] (1861) 1 John & H 352.   [179] [1929] AC 318, HL.   [180] [1929] AC 318, HL, at 334.
[181] [1929] AC 318, HL, at 339.   [182] [1937] Ch 236.   [183] [1970] 1 WLR 1463.
[184] Holdsworth 'Secret Trusts' (1937) 53 LQR 501.   [185] [1999] 1 FLR 54.

his will, which had left his estate to his wife. Carnwath J held that the situation was analogous to that of a half-secret trust, but held that any doubts as to the effectiveness of communication after the execution of a will were derived from the particular rules applying to wills and should not create difficulties for nominations. Even in the case of wills it is hard to see a convincing justification. It may be that the insistence on communication before the execution of the will arises by analogy between the doctrine of half-secret trusts and the principle of incorporation by reference. As was explained earlier, a document can only be incorporated into a will if it was in existence when the will was executed. It is submitted that this analogy is false, and that there is no reason for maintaining a distinction between the rules of communication applicable to fully and half-secret trusts. A document incorporated by reference becomes part of the will itself, whereas according to the prevailing theory a secret trust, whether fully or half-secret, arises wholly outside of the terms of the will.[186] It may yet be open to the House of Lords to find that a half-secret trust can be validly created by communication at any time before the death of the testator, and other jurisdictions have rejected the distinction and held that the same rule applies to both fully and half-secret trusts.[187] In the Irish case *Riordan v Banon*,[188] Chatterton V-C seems to have suggested that a valid half-secret trust can be created by communication after the date of the will but before the testator's death, and this has been supported by later cases.[189]

(b) Communication must be consistent with the will

Even if a testator communicates the trust to the intended trustee of a half-secret trust before executing his will, evidence of such communication will not be admitted to establish the trust if it is inconsistent with the face of the will. Therefore, evidence of a communication inconsistent with the manner in which the will stated that communication would be made will not be admissible to prove the existence of a half-secret trust. The application of this rule had the effect of preventing the creation of a half-secret trust in *Re Keen*.[190] While the terms of the trust had in fact been communicated to the trustee before the execution of the will, by means of a sealed envelope, the Court of Appeal held that evidence of the communication was inadmissible because clause 56 of the will anticipated that communication would only be made after the will had been executed. Therefore, evidence of the prior communication was inconsistent with the face of the will. In *Re Spence*[191] a testator had communicated the trust to some of the four trustees to whom he had jointly bequeathed the intended property. While such communication would have been sufficient to establish a fully secret trust, it was held that evidence of the communication was inadmissible to establish a half-secret trust. It was inconsistent with the terms of the will, which stated that communication had been made to them all.

---

[186] See discussion later in the chapter.
[187] See Scott, *Law of Trusts* (4th edn, 1988), para 55.8.   [188] (1876) 10 IrR Eq 469.
[189] See *Re King's Estate* (1888) 21 LR Ir 273; *Re Browne* [1944] IrR 90; *Re Prendeville* (5 December 1990, unreported) (Irish High Court). See [1992] Conv 202 (Mee).   [190] [1937] Ch 236.
[191] [1949] WN 237.

The validity of this restriction should also be questioned. It is inconsistent with the approach applied to fully secret trusts, where parol evidence of communication is admissible to prove the secret trust, despite the fact that it is always inconsistent with the face of the will, which suggests that an absolute gift has been made. The inconsistency should only be material where it casts significant doubt upon whether the testator had intended the communication to be an effective expression of his wishes.

(6) **The burden of proof required to establish a secret trust**

The level of proof necessary to establish a secret trust has been a matter of some debate. Traditionally, secret trusts were thought to be imposed by the court to prevent the secret trustee committing a fraud by denying the existence of the trust. In *McCormick v Grogan*[192] Lord Westbury therefore held that an extremely high burden of proof must be discharged before the court would impose a secret trust:

> Now, being a jurisdiction founded on personal fraud, it is incumbent on the court to see that a fraud, a malus animus, is proved by the clearest and most indisputable evidence...You are obliged, therefore, to show most clearly and distinctly that the person you wish to convert into a trustee acted mala animo. You must show distinctly that the testator or the intestate was beguiled and deceived by his conduct...

As will be seen later, this view of secret trusts imposed to prevent personal fraud has been rejected by more modern cases in favour of the theory that they are inter vivos trusts arising wholly outside of the testator's will. It is therefore illogical to require the same special standard of proof as that which applies to an allegation of fraud. In *Ottaway v Norman*,[193] Brightman J suggested that what was required was a standard of proof 'analogous to that required before the court would rectify a written instrument'. This is higher than the usual civil law standard of proof on the balance of probabilities. However, in *Re Snowden*[194] Megarry V-C considered that even this was inappropriate, since it demanded a higher threshold than the ordinary civil standard of proof, and it was founded upon a false analogy between rectification of documents and the operation of secret trusts. He concluded that the standard of proof required to establish a secret trust was simply the 'ordinary standard of evidence required to establish a trust'.[195] The higher standard appropriate for fraud would only need to be satisfied in circumstances where the secret trust could only be established by holding the legatee guilty of fraud.

(7) **Failure of secret trusts**

Where a testator has left property in his will intending that it should be subject to a secret trust, but has failed to satisfy the requisite criteria, the ultimate location of the

---

[192] (1869) LR 4 HL 82.   [193] [1972] Ch 698, at 699.   [194] [1979] 2 All ER 172.
[195] [1979] 2 All ER 172, at 178.

ownership of the intended trust property will depend upon whether the trust was fully or half-secret.

(a) Failure of a fully secret trust

If a testator fails to establish a valid fully secret trust, the intended secret trustee will be entitled to take the property for himself absolutely. This is nothing other than his entitlement under the will because the fact of the trust does not appear from the face of the will.[196] The intended trustee will only be required to hold the property on resulting trust for the testator's residuary legatees or next of kin[197] if he admits that he was intended to receive the property as a trustee.

(b) Failure of a half-secret trust

Unlike a fully secret trust, a half-secret trust is evident from the face of the will. If the trust fails for any reason the trustee will therefore be prevented from retaining the property bequeathed to him by the will. Instead, he will hold it on resulting trust, either for the residuary legatees under the will or, if the bequest is of the residuary estate, for the testator's next of kin.[198]

(8) Death or disclaimer of the secret trustee

A secret trust does not come into existence until the death of the testator who has bequeathed the trust property in his will to the intended secret trustee. Inevitably there is therefore a period of time, which in some cases may be substantial, between the communication and acceptance of the trust and the death of the testator. This time interval will give rise to practical difficulties if the intended secret trustee predeceases the testator, or disclaims the trust on the death of the testator. In either event, the question will arise whether the intended trust property is subject to a valid trust on the death of the testator. The answer will be determined primarily by the nature of the secret trust concerned.

(a) Secret trustee predeceases the testator

(i) Fully secret trust

Under the law of succession, a bequest lapses and fails if the beneficiary predeceases the testator. As a matter of logic, the predeceased of a trustee of a fully secret trust should therefore cause the trust to fail. This was accepted in *Re Maddock*,[199] where Cozens-Hardy LJ stated that a fully secret trust will fail if the trustee dies during the lifetime of the testator. This is consistent with the modern explanation of the operation of secret trusts discussed later, namely, that a secret trust is an expressly declared inter vivos trust which remains unconstituted until the testator's will operates to transfer

---

[196] Eg *Wallgrave v Tebbs* (1855) 2 K & J 313; *Jones v Badley* (1868) 3 Ch App 362; *McCormick v Grogan* (1869) LR 4 HL 82; *Re Pitt Rivers* [1902] 1 Ch 403.   [197] *Re Boyes* (1884) LR 26 Ch D 531.
[198] See *Re Cooper* [1939] Ch 811, CA.   [199] [1902] 2 Ch 220, at 231.

the legal title to the trust property to the trustee. Since the predecease of the trustee causes the gift to lapse, the testator's will fails to effect a constitution of the trust.

(ii) Half-secret trusts

In the case of a fully secret trust, the existence of the intention to subject the property bequeathed to a trust is entirely absent from the face of the will. In contrast, where the trust is half-secret, the fact that the property bequeathed was intended to be subject to a trust is apparent from the will itself. It is therefore clear that the legatee was never intended to enjoy the property left to him absolutely. If the intended trustee of a half-secret trust predeceases the testator, equity will not allow the trust to fail for want of a trustee. The testator's personal representative will act as trustee in his place.[200] Provided that it is still possible to identify the terms of the half-secret trust, it will not fail.

(b) Secret trustee dies after the testator

If the trustee of a secret trust, whether half- or fully secret, dies after the testator, the trust will not fail. In both cases the testator's will operates according to its terms to transfer the legal title of the property bequeathed to the secret trustee at the moment of the testator's death, thus constituting the trust. As the trust is fully constituted from the death of the testator, it will not fail for want of a trustee. However, if the death of the secret trustee renders it impossible to identify the beneficiary of the trust, the property will pass by resulting trust to the testator's residuary legatees or next of kin.

(c) Secret trustee disclaims the trust

(i) Revocation of acceptance before the death of the testator

It has been seen that a secret trust will only be established if the intended trustee accepts that he will hold the property bequeathed to him on trust. His acceptance, however, is not irrevocable. A secret trustee is entitled to revoke a previous acceptance of the trust at any time before the death of the testator. If the trust was fully secret, a trustee who has revoked the trust will be entitled to take the property bequeathed to him in the will absolutely for his own benefit. In contrast, if the trust was half-secret, the intended trust property will be held on resulting trust for the testator's residuary legatees or next of kin. To be effective, the trustee must communicate his change of mind to the testator. He will otherwise be estopped from asserting his revocation of the agreement to hold upon trust.

(ii) Disclaimer after the death of the testator

While a secret trustee may revoke his acceptance of the secret trust at any time before the death of the testator, in principle disclaimer after the will has taken effect should not invalidate the trust. Despite dicta to the contrary by Cozens-Hardy LJ in *Re Maddock*,[201] dicta of Lord Buckmaster and Lord Warrington in *Blackwell v Blackwell*[202]

---

[200] See *Mallott v Wilson* [1903] 2 Ch 494.   [201] [1902] 2 Ch 220.
[202] [1929] AC 318, at 328, 341.

suggest that a secret trust will not fail if the trustee disclaims the trust subsequent to the testator's death. This is logical because the trust is constituted by the operation of the testator's will, thus crystallizing the secret beneficiary's equitable entitlement to the trust property. Since the trust has come into existence, it should not be allowed to fail for want of a trustee.

(9) Can a secret trustee benefit from a secret trust?

In some cases, the trustee of a secret trust will enjoy no personal entitlement to the trust property and will hold it entirely for others. However in others the testator may also wish to grant the trustee some entitlement to the trust property, either as a joint beneficiary of the secret trust, or by way of a right to retain any surplus funds remaining after the beneficiaries have been allocated their interests. In *Irvine v Sullivan*[203] it was held that the trustee of a fully secret trust was entitled to retain the surplus of the trust property remaining after the trusts had been carried out. In contrast, in *Re Rees' Will Trusts*[204] the Court of Appeal held that the trustee of a half-secret trust was not entitled to assert any entitlement to such a surplus because this would be inconsistent with the terms of the will, which suggested that all the property bequeathed to him was subject to the trust. This decision was doubted by Pennycuick J in *Re Tyler's Fund Trusts*[205] and there is no logical justification for maintaining this differentiation between fully secret and half-secret trusts.[206] It may be significant that in *Re Rees' Will Trusts* the trustee was the testator's solicitor and a beneficial gift was therefore inherently less likely.[207]

(10) Justifying the enforcement of secret trusts

While it is easy to appreciate the practical advantages that have contributed to the evolution of secret trusts as mechanisms for allocating property on death, it is less easy to provide an adequate explanation of the legal principles justifying their enforcement. They appear to operate in contradiction of the clear policy of the Wills Act since such enforcement appears to permit a testamentary disposition (ie a disposition intended to take effect only on death) without satisfaction of the requisite formalities. Equity's effort to provide an adequate explanation for the enforcement of secret trusts is an ex post facto rationalization of a mechanism that had already developed. It has already been noted that historically, equity enforced secret trusts on the grounds that to fail to do so would allow the Wills Act to be used as an instrument of fraud. This historic explanation has been eclipsed by a more fashionable alternative. Cases after the decision of the House of Lords in *Blackwell v Blackwell*[208] have held that they are enforced as valid inter vivos trusts arising outside (dehors) the will. The advantage of this explanation is that it does not predicate a conflict between the enforcement of secret

---

[203] (1869) LR 8 Eq 673.   [204] [1950] Ch 204.   [205] [1967] 1 WLR 1269.
[206] See Oakley, *Constructive Trusts* (3rd edn, 1997), p 259.
[207] See [1950] Ch 204, at 211, per Lord Evershed MR.   [208] [1929] AC 318.

trusts and the requirements of the Wills Act 1837, s 9. However, even this theory is not wholly satisfactory.

(a) Secret trusts enforced to prevent fraud

In the nineteenth century equity accepted that secret trusts were enforced in order to prevent fraud. The secret trustee had induced the testator to leave property to him on the understanding that he would apply it for the benefit of the secret beneficiary. If the secret trustee were permitted to deny the trust, because of a lack of testamentary formalities, and to assert a personal entitlement to the property bequeathed to him in the testator's will, he would be using the Wills Act as an instrument of fraud. To prevent such a fraud, equity would allow the admission of parol evidence on behalf of the beneficiary to prove that the bequest had been subject to a trust. This rationale was accepted by the House of Lords in *McCormick v Grogan*,[209] where Lord Hatherley LC described the enforcement of secret trusts as:

> a doctrine which involves a wide departure from the policy of…the [Wills Act] and it is only in clear cases of fraud that this doctrine has been applied—cases in which the court has been persuaded that there has been a fraudulent inducement held out on the part of the apparent beneficiary in order to lead the testator to confide to him the duty which he so understood to perform.[210]

Lord Westbury also emphasized that the enforcement of secret trusts was 'founded altogether on personal fraud'.[211] However, despite the early acceptance of the fraud explanation by the House of Lords, it came to be thought that the fraud theory was inadequate as a justification for the enforcement of secret trusts.[212] A number of defects were identified. First, the fraud theory accepts that the enforcement of secret trusts is in direct conflict with the provisions and policy of the Wills Act. Although such conflict has been tolerated in other areas, for example where the principle of *Rochefoucauld v Boustead*[213] operates to enforce an oral declaration of a trust of land despite the lack of writing, the courts today are reluctant to adopt an analysis so directly opposed to the terms of legislation. Second, a major defect of the fraud theory was that it did not provide an adequate justification for the enforcement of half-secret trusts. In the case of a half-secret trust, the fact of the trust is evident from the face of the will, so that there is no possibility of fraud. The secret trustee cannot take the property absolutely for himself. Fraud would easily be avoided by the secret trustee holding any property received under the will on resulting trust for the residuary legatees or the testator's next of kin. Third, it is questionable whether the fraud theory is also capable of explaining why a fully secret trust should be enforced in favour of the secret beneficiary. While it might justify the refusal to allow the secret trustee to take the property bequeathed to him by the testator absolutely, it is less easy to see why the possibility of fraud justifies enforcement of the trust in favour of the secret beneficiary. Any fraud could equally

---

[209] (1869) LR 4 HL 82.   [210] (1869) LR 4 HL 82, at 89.   [211] (1869) LR 4 HL 82, at 99.
[212] See Hodge 'Secret Trusts: the Fraud Theory Revisited' [1980] Conv 341.
[213] [1897] 1 Ch 196, CA.

be prevented if the trustee was required to hold the property on resulting trust for the residuary legatees under the will or the testator's next of kin. This would prevent the trustee benefiting by his fraud, but would not contradict the provisions of the Wills Act. Fourth, as has been noted earlier, adoption of the fraud theory had the effect that an unduly high burden of proof needed to be discharged if a beneficiary was to establish that property was held on secret trust. In consequence of these inadequacies, the fraud analysis has been rejected in more modern cases.

However, the fraud theory continues to enjoy the support of some academics. Critchley has argued that the modern theory that secret trusts arise outside of the will is implausible, and argues that secret trusts are upheld to prevent fraud where this is demanded by legal policy.[214] Such enforcement will only be justified where there is a combination of personal wrongdoing on the part of the trustee, and harm would be caused to beneficiary and/or testator if the trust were not enforced. The requisite element of personal wrongdoing would only be satisfied if 'the trustee was fully aware that the property was only to be transferred to him on trust, but that he took no steps to deny this understanding until the transfer was completed beyond the recall of the testator'.[215] However, this argument does not address all of the problems identified earlier. Critchley concludes that while the fraud maxim might justify the enforcement of a fully secret trustee where the trustee actively seeks to deny the trust, it is 'less overwhelmingly supportive' of justifying the enforcement of other fully and half-secret trusts. She therefore suggests that these other secret trusts must be allowed to tag along in the wake of those which can be justified on the basis of fraud, since otherwise further problems, such as the increase of opportunities for fraud, or of litigation over the construction of the will, seem likely, if not bound, to emerge.[216] It is submitted that this concedes that the fraud theory, even articulated in a more sophisticated form, is incapable of adequately justifying the enforcement of secret trusts.

(b) Secret trusts arise outside of the testator's will

The modern justification of the enforcement of secret trusts was neatly summarized by Megarry V-C in *Re Snowden*:[217]

> the whole basis of secret trusts, as I understand it, is that they operate outside the will, changing nothing that is written in it, and allowing it to operate according to its tenor, but then fastening a trust on to the property in the hands of the recipient.

This explanation evolved from the decision of the House of Lords in *Cullen v A-G for Ireland*, where Lord Westbury said:

---

[214] 'Instruments of Fraud, Testamentary Dispositions, and the Doctrine of Secret Trusts' (1999) 115 LQR 631.

[215] 'Instruments of Fraud, Testamentary Dispositions, and the Doctrine of Secret Trusts' (1999) 115 LQR, at 647.

[216] 'Instruments of Fraud, Testamentary Dispositions, and the Doctrine of Secret Trusts' (1999) 115 LQR, at 653.   [217] [1979] 2 All ER 172, at 177.

> I think it very material to point out that where there is a secret trust...the title of the party claiming under the secret trust...is a title dehors the will, and which cannot be correctly termed testamentary.[218]

It was utilized and developed by the House of Lords in *Blackwell v Blackwell*[219] to justify the enforceability of half-secret trusts. Its overwhelming advantage is that it does not presuppose a contradiction between the enforcement of secret trusts and the Wills Act.[220]

The essence of this modern justification for the enforcement of secret trusts is that they come into existence entirely outside of the operation of the will to which they relate, so that the equitable interest enjoyed by the secret beneficiary is not a species of testamentary disposition. The modern theory postulates two distinguishable stages in the creation of a valid secret trust. First, the testator communicates to the secret trustee his intention to subject the property bequeathed to a trust, at which point the secret trustee accepts the trust obligation. However, at this point the secret trust has not yet come into existence. The intended subject matter of the trust remains the absolute property of the testator, and the legal title to it has not been transferred to the trustee. In effect the testator and trustee have agreed that the property will be subject to a trust when it comes into the hands of the trustee but at present the trust remains incompletely constituted. Second, when the testator dies his will operates according to its terms to transfer the legal title to the secret trustee. His receipt of the property in this way has the effect of constituting the incompletely constituted trust.[221] He henceforth holds the property on trust for the secret beneficiary (see Figure 13.1). The secret trust does not therefore arise completely independently of the testator's will. As Kincaid has commented:

> A secret trust relies on the death of the settlor to constitute the trust and the terms of the will or the rules of intestate succession to vest the property in the hands of the secret trustee or legatee. The trust can be revoked until the death of the settlor and therefore it does not stand alone until it is properly constituted either *inter vivos* or on the death of the settlor.[222]

This explanation appears to involve no element of conflict between the enforcement of a secret trust and the provisions of the Wills Act. The testator's will operates according to its terms, transferring ownership of the bequeathed property to the legatee. The trust is enforced not under the will, but because the legatee has previously agreed that he will observe the terms of the trust which were communicated to him by the testator. In a sense the secret trust is constituted by a mechanism similar to the rule in *Strong v Bird*[223] examined in Chapter 7.

The practical operation of the modern theory for the enforcement of secret trusts is clearly seen in *Re Young (Decd)*.[224] Roger Young left his entire estate to his wife, Eveleen. Prior to his death he informed her of his intention that his chauffeur, Thomas

---

[218] [1866] LR 1 HL 190, at 196.   [219] [1929] AC 318.   [220] [1929] AC 318, at 340.

[221] Critchley, however, argues that this analysis is 'implausible': (1999) 115 LQR 631, at 634.

[222] 'The Tangled Web: The Relationship between a Secret Trust and the Will' [2000] Conv 420, at 442.

[223] (1874) LR 18 Eq 315.   [224] [1951] Ch 344.

(i) The trust is declared inter vivos but remains unconstitued

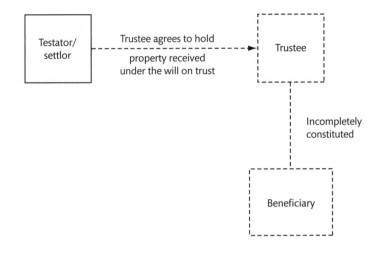

(ii) The trust is constituted by the operation of the settlor's will

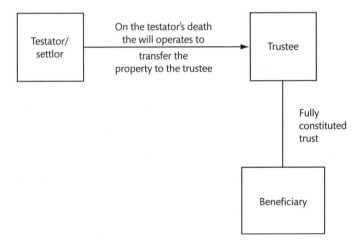

Figure 13.1 The operation of secret trusts

Cobb, should receive a legacy of £2,000. This prima facie established a fully secret trust in Cobb's favour. However, Cobb was coincidentally one of the witnesses to Roger's will. By the Wills Act 1837, s 15 a legacy to a person attesting a will is forfeit. The central question was, therefore, whether Cobb's entitlement to the £2,000 subject to the secret trust should be characterized as a legacy under the will, in which case it would be void. Danckwerts J held that the chauffeur was entitled to receive the money because his entitlement was by way of a secret trust which had arisen wholly outside of the will:

The whole theory of the formulation of a secret trust is that the Wills Act has nothing to do with the matter because the forms required by the Wills Act are entirely disregarded, since the persons do not take by virtue of the gift in the will, but by virtue of the secret trusts imposed upon the beneficiary, who does in fact take under the will.[225]

(11) Date of accrual of the beneficial interest under a secret trust

A further practical problem that has arisen relates to the time at which the beneficiary of a secret trust acquires the property subject to the trust. In principle, because a secret trust is only fully constituted when the testator's will operates to transfer the bequeathed property to the trustee, a secret beneficiary should not be entitled to any interest in the putative trust property until the death of the testator. Prior to his death, the testator retains the right to change his will, enabling him to subvert the trust by bequeathing the property to someone other than the secret trustee, thus ensuring that the trust is never constituted.[226] The logic of this argument was not, however, followed in *Re Gardner (No 2)*.[227] A testatrix made a will leaving all her property to her husband for life, with the remainder subject to a secret trust in favour of her two nieces and nephew. At the date of the testatrix's death she had been predeceased by one of her nieces. The court was required to decide whether the personal representative of the niece was entitled to a third share of the remainder interest by way of the secret trust. Romer J held that, as a secret beneficiary, the niece had been entitled to her share of the trust property from the moment that the husband had accepted the terms of the trust. Her third share was therefore held on trust for her personal representative, notwithstanding that she had predeceased the testator. This case is open to the criticism that the niece cannot have gained an interest in the testatrix's estate until her death, since a secret trust remains unconstituted until the will operates to transfer the trust property to the trustee.[228] Prior to the testator's death, the trust does not exist. It is therefore submitted that the decision in *Re Gardner (No 2)* is incorrect and that a secret beneficiary enjoys no entitlement to the putative trust property until the trust is fully constituted through the operation of the testator's will.

(12) Problems associated with the modern theory

The currently fashionable theory for explaining secret trusts is less elegant than it may seem and has attracted academic criticism. There appears to be no reason why the testator should not change his mind about the creation of the trust prior to his death, either by informing the trustee that he no longer wishes to create a trust, or by an amendment to his will. The secret trust therefore shares one of the characteristics

---

[225] [1951] Ch 344, at 350.

[226] Pawlowski and Brown argue, however, that an estoppel equity may arise from the moment that the testator departs from his promise to benefit the secret beneficiary and changes his will: 'Constituting a Secret Trust by Estoppel' [2004] Conv 388.   [227] [1923] 2 Ch 230.

[228] See Pawlowski and Brown, 'Constituting a Secret Trust by Estoppel' [2004] Conv 388.

of a testamentary gift, namely, that it is revocable at any time prior to the testator's death. Furthermore, secret trusts are clearly intended to become operative only on the testator's death, so that they do not in any way inhibit the testator's power to deal as he wishes with his property during his lifetime. This is also a characteristic of a testamentary gift. Finally, in *Re Maddock*[229] a gift by way of a secret trust was treated as if it had been made by will in a case where the estate was insufficient to meet all the specific gifts made by the testator. The case for treating gifts under a half-secret trust in this way would be even stronger.

Critchley has therefore argued that the *dehors* (outside) the will theory cannot justify the enforcement of secret trusts.[230] She submits that secret trusts are testamentary dispositions because they possess the characteristics of being ambulatory and revocable, in that they do not take effect until the death of the testator, and the testator can change his mind:

> the *dehors* theory seems to be fatally flawed. In essence the mistake is to confuse 'outside the will' with 'outside the Wills Act'. The *dehors* theory needs—and fails—to demonstrate the trust of the latter and too often ends up resting merely upon the former, which is wholly inadequate as a justificatory argument.[231]

It would be possible to treat secret trusts as well-established anomalies which do not fit easily with any justification. It is also possible to argue that as unjustifiable anomalies, they should no longer be recognized.[232] Aside from these extremes, whilst the fashionable modern theory explaining their operation is imperfect, it has the merit of pragmatism and it is certainly the explanation that commands the support of the authorities.

(13) **The juridical nature of secret trusts**

The accepted modern justification for enforcement of secret trusts is that they arise inter vivos outside of the will. However, the acceptance of this theory does not of itself answer the question whether secret trusts should be characterized as express or constructive trusts. This is not an entirely esoteric academic question. If secret trusts are characterized as express in nature, practical difficulties arise where the intended trust property is land or an interest in land, as s 53(1)(b) of the Law of Property Act 1925 renders an oral declaration of a trust of land unenforceable without substantiating evidence in writing. In contrast, if they are characterized as constructive in nature,

---

[229] [1902] 2 Ch 220.

[230] 'Instruments of Fraud, Testamentary Dispositions, and the Doctrine of Secret Trusts' (1999) 115 LQR 631.

[231] 'Instruments of Fraud, Testamentary Dispositions, and the Doctrine of Secret Trusts' (1999) 115 LQR 631, at 641.

[232] Emma Challinor has argued that no logical rationale for the enforcement of secret trusts may be discerned, and that they are covert devices by which the courts avoid the statutory formalities of the Wills Act 1837, thus subverting the policy of the Wills Act: 'Debunking the Myth of Secret Trusts?' [2005] Conv 493. She therefore proposes abolition or fundamental revision of the law relating to secret trusts.

a secret trust of land will be enforceable without the need for further formalities as s 53(2) exempts all constructive trusts from the need of writing.

(a) Secret trusts characterized as express trusts

The modern theory that secret trusts arise inter vivos outside of the testator's will would logically suggests that they are express in nature. The acceptance of the trust by the secret trustee amounts to an express *inter vivos* declaration of trust. This view has been favoured in the past by most academic writers.[233] However, such a characterization could produce the unsatisfactory implication of rendering an oral agreement to hold land subject to a secret trust unenforceable through the absence of writing, as required by s 53(1)(b) of the Law of Property Act 1925.[234] Thus, in *Re Baillie*[235] North J held a secret trust of land unenforceable because the Statute of Frauds applied and the trust had not been indicated in writing. In other cases, for example *Ottaway v Norman*,[236] orally declared secret trusts of land have been enforced without question. Of itself the enforcement of the trusts in such cases fails to prove the point, since a trust will not fail for lack of formalities unless the absence of writing is specifically pleaded as a ground of invalidity.[237] However, even if secret trusts are characterized as express trusts, it is submitted that an orally declared secret trust of land should not fail merely because of the lack of writing. The court should invoke the well-established doctrine of *Rochefoucauld v Boustead*,[238] namely, that equity will not allow the statute requiring trusts of land to be evidenced in writing to be used as an instrument of fraud, to prevent the secret trustee denying the trust because of the absence of writing. This would not mark a reversion to the fraud explanation of the enforcement of secret trusts in conflict with the terms of the Wills Act, as the rule in *Rochefoucauld v Boustead* would only be employed to prevent the use of s 53(1)(b) of the Law of Property Act as an instrument of fraud.

(b) Secret trusts characterized as constructive trusts

Despite traditional academic consensus that secret trusts are express in nature, in *Re Cleaver*[239] Nourse J characterized them as constructive trusts. As the case concerned the doctrine of mutual wills, his expression of opinion is strictly obiter. A number of commentators have adopted the view that secret trusts are gratuitous promises enforced as constructive trusts on the grounds of fraud or unconscionability.[240]

---

[233] See Snell, *Principles of Equity* (30th edn, 2000), pp 132–136; Pettit, *Equity and the Law of Trusts* (12th edn, 2009); Oakley, *Constructive Trusts* (3rd edn, 1997), p 263; (1991) 5 Tru LI 69 (Caughlon). See also Sheridan 'English and Irish Secret Trusts' (1951) 67 LQR 314—where half-secret trusts are held to be express, but fully secret trusts to be constructive.

[234] See Chapter 7.   [235] (1886) 2 TLR 660.   [236] [1972] Ch 698.

[237] *North v Loomes* [1919] 1 Ch 378.   [238] [1897] 1 Ch 196, CA.   [239] [1981] 1 WLR 939.

[240] McFarlane 'Constructive Trusts Arising on a Receipt of Property Sub Conditione' (2004) 120 LQR 667.

PART IV

Allocation of Benefit

14

Introduction to allocation

1 General

The nature of the allocation of a trust fund will be dependent upon the type of equitable obligation which has been created, whether a power of appointment, fixed trust, or discretionary trust. The original owner may have specified how the fund should be allocated himself or, alternatively, he may have given to someone else the task of deciding how the allocation should be made by granting a discretion. Each of these mechanisms will be examined in detail in the following chapters. This chapter will sketch some of the recurrent themes that run through the area.

2 Certainty of objects

(1) Nature of the problem

Whenever an equitable mechanism is used to allocate the ownership of a fund, it must be possible for the allocation to be carried out in practice. If it cannot, then the mechanism will fail and the property returns from the fund to the original owner, or his successor in title, by means of a resulting trust.[1] It must also be possible for the court to be able to supervise allocations from the fund to ensure that the owner's wishes are followed and that the fund is not allocated to persons who were never intended to benefit from it. The problem arises particularly where the original owner has defined the potential objects as a class, using a generic description rather than naming them as individuals. For example, if George was to leave £10,000 to his wife, Mildred, to be divided equally among his 'good friends', it would be impossible for his directions to be carried out. How would Mildred know what was meant by a 'good friend'? The concept is not capable of objective definition. To allocate the fund according to his instructions she would have to ascertain the identity of all George's 'good friends' before she could know how much to allocate to each 'good friend'. No doubt there would be many obvious candidates, but that would not be sufficient to make the gift workable. There is bound to be a grey area where it is unclear whether someone is a

---

[1] See Chapter 6.

'good friend' or not. The rights of any specific 'good friend' cannot be determined until the entire class is known.

If George had given Mildred a discretion to allocate the fund among 'whichever of my good friends she chooses', the problem remains, although in a less extreme form. Clearly, the terms of the gift only permit allocation to 'good friends', and to prevent fraud the court must ensure that it is so allocated. If Mildred were to make an allocation of £1,000 to Brian, who was a childhood friend of George but has not seen him for twenty years, how could the court decide whether she had acted within the terms of the discretion? Is Brian a 'good friend' or not?

The very fact that this question is unanswerable is the problem addressed by the requirement that the objects of an equitable obligation to allocate the fund must be certain. This means that the class of people who are potential recipients from the fund are capable of being identified sufficiently clearly for the allocator to carry out his duty and the court effectively to scrutinize any allocations made. Such a term as 'good friends' would not be regarded as sufficiently certain, because it has no clear objective meaning.[2] The precise requirement of certainty of objects differs with the variety of equitable obligation in issue.[3] The test for powers of appointment and discretionary trusts is different from that for fixed trusts. Although the details differ, the principle is the same, namely, that the objects (or potential objects) of allocation must be certain.

(2) Types of certainty

In *Re Baden's Deed Trusts (No 2)*,[4] the Court of Appeal drew a distinction between 'conceptual' certainty and 'evidential' certainty. Understanding this distinction is an essential prerequisite to understanding the requirements of certainty applicable to different equitable obligations.

(a) Conceptual certainty

This concept, discussed in relation to express trusts in Chapter 7, concerns the precision of language used to define the class of persons the settlor intends to benefit. It can be a difficult question, as it is concerned with linguistics and semantics. 'Nobel Prize winners' would be one example of a conceptually certain class, as it would be easy to determine whether someone was or was not within that class. By contrast, 'persons leading a useful life' would be conceptually uncertain. No equitable mechanism, whether a power, trust or discretionary trust, is valid if the class of objects is not conceptually certain.[5]

(b) Evidential certainty

Evidential certainty is concerned with proving whether a person falls within the specified class of objects of an equitable obligation. The class may be conceptually

---

[2] See *Re Baden's Deed Trusts (No 2)* [1973] Ch 9.   [3] See *McPhail v Doulton* [1971] AC 424, HL.
[4] [1973] Ch 9.
[5] *Re Baden's Deed Trusts (No 2)* [1973] Ch 9. See also Emery 'The Most Hallowed Principle: Certainty of Beneficiaries of Trusts and Powers of Appointment' (1982) 98 LQR 551.

certain, as for example 'relatives', but unless some scientific process such as genetic fingerprinting can be used, it may be difficult or impossible for some persons to prove whether they are relatives or not. Thus, it may be conceptually certain that any given individual 'is or is not' a relative, but it is impossible to prove to which category a specific person belongs. Fixed trusts require every beneficiary to be identified in fact, and are invalid if evidential certainty is lacking.[6] Powers and discretionary trusts do not require evidential certainty.[7]

3 Beneficial entitlement and ownership

A second recurrent theme is the question of the nature of the rights enjoyed by the potential objects of allocation in the fund. This has been explored in Chapter 2, but to recap this will again depend on the exact nature of the equitable mechanism that has been created, and will range from a subsisting property interest in a share of the fund, to no property right at all in the fund. For example, Oliver has four children, Peter, Quentin, Robert, and Stuart. He leaves £100,000 to their godparents, Tristan and Una, to be allocated between them. The exact rights that the children have in the fund will depend on the type of equitable obligation that has been created.

(1) Fixed trust

At one end of the scale is the fixed trust,[8] where Oliver stipulates that Tristan and Una are to hold the fund on trust for the children in equal shares. From the very moment that the trust is created, when the property comes into the hands of the trustees, the children have an immediate proprietary interest in the fund. They are each the owners in equity of a quarter of the trust property. They are liable for tax on their interest,[9] and it will be protected as against third parties who are not bona fide purchasers for value of a legal estate without notice. The important decision of *Saunders v Vautier*[10] states that, as a consequence of having an immediate proprietary interest in the fund, the beneficiaries of a fixed trust can together demand that the legal title is transferred to them by the trustee. This means that if the four children were all of age and mentally competent they could demand that Tristan and Una convey the legal title to them.

(2) Power of appointment

At the other end of the scale is the power of appointment. If Oliver provides that Tristan and Una are to hold the property and that they have the power to appoint

---

[6] *IRC v Broadway Cottages Trust* [1954] 3 WLR 438; affd [1955] Ch 20, sub nom *Broadway Cottages Trust v IRC* [1954] TR 295, C; *O T Computer Ltd v First National Tricity Finance Ltd* [2003] EWHC 1010.
[7] *Re Gulbenkian's Settlement Trusts* [1970] AC 508; *McPhail v Doulton* [1971] AC 424; *Re Baden's Deed Trusts (No 2)* [1973] Ch 9.   [8] See Figure 2.1, which shows the scale of equitable obligations.
[9] See Chapter 3.   [10] (1841) 4 Beav 115.

it in favour of such of his children as they may choose, then the children have no immediate proprietary interest in the fund at all.[11] None of them has any interest in the fund unless and until Tristan and Una exercise their power and make an appointment in favour of all or some of them.[12] If they make an appointment of £50,000 in favour of Robert, then Robert will have a proprietary right in the proportion of the fund that has been allocated to him, but he and the others continue to have no interest in the £50,000 comprising the other half of the fund. If there are no appointments the fund will pass by resulting trust[13] to the residuary legatees under Oliver's will.[14]

(3) **Discretionary trust**

Between these two extremes lies the discretionary trust, where the exact nature of the potential beneficiaries' right is unclear. The beneficiaries do not have immediate proprietary rights to specific shares of the fund, but they are not without any proprietary right in the fund as a whole. Oliver may have left the fund to Tristan and Una on trust to 'distribute among my children as they in their discretion think fit'. As a class, the children have proprietary rights to the fund, but as individuals they could not identify any particular share of the fund as their own, unless and until it was allocated to them by the trustee.

They can, if they all come together, call for the transfer of the legal title under the rule in *Saunders v Vautier*,[15] as was done in *Re Smith*.[16] In practice, this would be almost impossible if the class were a large group, for example in the case of a discretionary trust for the benefit of 'all the employees and ex-employees' of a company. The position taken in *Gartside v IRC*[17] and *Sainsbury v IRC*[18] was that the potential beneficiary of a discretionary trust has no actual proprietary interest in the fund. Instead, he or she merely has a right to be considered as a beneficiary by the trustees. Once a selection has been made, the beneficiary has entitlement to the share allocated to him or her. This means that under a discretionary trust the beneficial interest in the property is held 'in the air' without a specific group who have proprietary rights in the fund, until allocations are made by the trustee.

4 Purpose trusts

Since a trust creates a proprietary interest in favour of the beneficiaries, it is a cardinal principle that it must have beneficiaries who are capable of owning property and enforcing the trust. For this reason, the law insists that trusts must be for the benefit of

---

[11] *Vestey v IRC* [1980] AC 1148, HL.   [12] *Re Brookes' Settlement Trusts* [1939] Ch 993, at 997.
[13] See Chapter 8.
[14] Unless the rule in *Burrough v Philcox* (1840) 5 My & Cr 72 applies. See Chapter 16.
[15] (1841) 4 Beav 115.   [16] [1928] Ch 915.   [17] [1968] AC 553.   [18] [1970] Ch 712.

legal persons[19] and not merely for the object of carrying out purposes. This limitation is not, however, absolute.[20] By far the most significant exception to this rule is the area of charity, already covered in Chapter 11, where purpose trusts are upheld as valid and a mechanism to supervise and enforce them is provided by the state for reasons of public policy.[21] There are also several minor exceptions that are considered later in the chapter.

(1) **The beneficiary principle**

The rule against purpose trusts is long established. In *Morice v Bishop of Durham* Sir William Grant MR stated that:

> Every…trust must have a definite object. There must be somebody, in whose favour the court can decree specific performance.[22]

Similarly, in *Bowman v Secular Society*[23] Lord Parker of Waddington said that 'for a trust to be valid it must be for the benefit of individuals'.[24]

(a) **Rationale for the beneficiary principle**

There are three main problems with the validity of purpose trusts that have led to the adoption of the beneficiary principle.

(i) *Without beneficiaries there is no owner*

In its simplest form, a trust makes the beneficiaries into equitable owners. However, as has been seen, the principle that a trust fund 'belongs' to the beneficiaries is not absolute. There are many cases where property may—at least for a time—have no owner in equity. For instance, a trust in favour of Sandra's grandchildren will have no ascertained beneficiaries before at least one grandchild has been born. Similarly, a trust to invest and accumulate a fund for the first woman to land on the moon has no owner in equity until the condition has been satisfied.[25] A discretionary trust in favour of a large class defined in a conceptually certain way, but too large to list, has no identifiable owner. Yet again, it has been held that there is no beneficial owner of the estate of a deceased person until the completion of the administration of the estate. In *Stamp Duties Comr (Queensland) v Livingston*[26] a husband had died, leaving all his property by will to his wife, who had died shortly thereafter, and before the administration of her husband's estate had been completed. The Privy Council held that the wife's estate was not liable to pay death duties on the property she was expected to receive on the completion of the administration of her husband's estate because, until the administration

---

[19] See Naffine 'Who are Law's Persons? From Cheshire Cats to Responsible Subjects' (2003) 66 MLR 346.

[20] See Matthews 'The New Trust: Obligations without Rights?' in Oakley, *Trends in Contemporary Trust Law* (1996).   [21] See Chapter 26 concerning the enforcement of obligations against charities.

[22] (1804) 9 Ves Jr 399, at 405.   [23] [1917] AC 406, at 441.

[24] See also *Leahy v A-G for New South Wales* [1959] AC 457, per Viscount Simmonds: 'a trust may be created for the benefit of persons as cestui que trust but not as a purpose or object unless the purpose or object be charitable'.

[25] The rule against perpetuities requires a perpetuity period to be specified.   [26] [1965] AC 694.

was complete, she had no equitable title to the property. The personal representatives were the legal owners and there was no separate equitable owner; the personal representatives merely owed enforceable duties to the 'beneficiaries' of the will or intestacy to see that the administration of the estate was conducted properly. Since the personal representatives had no beneficial interest in the property—they could not keep it for their own use—it follows that, during administration of a deceased's estate, there is no equitable beneficial owner. The concept of property being subject to enforceable obligations but having no immediate beneficial owner is thus well established. This should not be an objection to purpose trusts.

(ii) The trust cannot be enforced by the court

Where a trust is created to carry out a purpose there is no person with locus standi to apply to the court to ensure that the terms of the trust are being carried out and that the trustees do not act in breach of trust, for example by misappropriating the trust property for themselves. The supervision of trusts relies first and foremost on the beneficiaries, as the persons most interested in the proper administration of the trust, bringing abuses to the attention of the court.[27]

(iii) The trust will violate the rule against perpetuity

The law has always been reluctant to allow property to become subject to restrictions that would unduly prevent its free marketability. Where property is subject to a trust, it is not freely available and the terms of the trust may prevent its most efficient use. For this reason the law provides that property may not be subject to a trust for an excessive period of time. This rule is known as the rule against inalienability. A private trust (as opposed to a charitable trust) must not exceed the perpetuity period, which has been defined to consist of the duration of a human life in being at the date that the trust was established plus an additional period of twenty-one years. If a trust were created for the carrying out of a purpose, there is no guarantee that the purpose would ever be completed so as to bring the trust to an end. The property would therefore be perpetually held on trust. If property is subject to a trust for persons, the perpetuity period is less likely to be violated, as the beneficiary will be a life in being and the trust will not endure beyond his death, although problems may occur if successive interests are created behind a trust. If a trust offends against the perpetuity period it is void ab initio.[28]

(b) Application of the beneficiary principle

The beneficiary principle was applied so as to invalidate the trust in *Re Astor's Settlement Trusts*.[29] A settlement was made by Viscount Astor of all the issued shares of the *Observer* newspaper. The terms of the trust were that the income was to be

---

[27] See Chapter 26. See also *Re Astor's Settlement Trusts* [1952] Ch 534, at 549; *Re Shaw* [1957] 1 WLR 729, at 744–746.

[28] The more relaxed rules to be found in either the Perpetuities and Accumulations Act 1964 (for trusts arising before 6 April 2010) or the Perpetuities and Accumulations Act 2009 (for trusts arising on or after 6 April 2010) only apply to the rule against remoteness of vesting and accumulation, not to the rule against perpetual trusts.   [29] [1952] Ch 534.

applied for the 'maintenance ncome of good understanding between nations' and 'the preservation of the independence and integrity of the newspapers', purposes which were considered not to be charitable. Roxburgh J held that the trust was invalid on two grounds, first that it offended against the beneficiary principle, and second that the purposes were uncertain. He examined the principle laid down by Lord Parker in *Bowman v Secular Society*[30] and concluded that it was not susceptible to attack from a base of principle,[31] and that it was well established in authority.[32] He referred to *Re Wood*,[33] where Harman J had asserted the orthodox position that 'a gift on trust must have a cestui que trust'.[34] Since the purposes did not fall within any of the exceptions to the beneficiary principle, the trust was void.

In *Re Shaw*[35] George Bernard Shaw left his residuary estate to trustees to apply the income to purposes including research into a proposed 40-letter alphabet, and the transliteration of one of his plays into such an alphabet. These were held not to be charitable purposes, and they failed as purpose trusts. Harman J indicated some dissatisfaction with the 'beneficiary principle',[36] but felt himself bound by the higher authority of the House of Lords and Court of Appeal.[37] In *Re Endacott*[38] Harman LJ in the Court of Appeal applied the beneficiary principle to a gift by Albert Endacott to the North Tawton Devon Parish Council 'for the purposes of providing some useful memorial to myself'. He did not indicate any of the doubts he had mentioned in *Re Shaw*[39] but instead applauded the 'orthodox sentiments expressed by Roxburgh J in the *Astor* case'.[40] The Court of Appeal held that the gift was a non-charitable purpose trust that did not fall within any of the exceptions to the beneficiary principle.

(2) Exceptions to the beneficiary principle

Whilst the cases cited earlier confirm the existence of the 'beneficiary principle' rendering non-charitable purpose trusts void, English law recognizes a number of exceptions where pure non-charitable purpose trusts will be upheld despite the lack of beneficiaries. There is no logical rationale for these exceptions, and in this sense they are said to be anomalous. In *Re Astor's Settlement Trusts*, Roxburgh J reviewed the exceptions and commented that they were 'anomalous and exceptional J reviconcessions to human weakness or sentiment'.[41] In Re *Endacott*[42] Harman LJ confirmed their anomalous nature, and indicated that the number of exceptions should not be increased. They are decisions:

> which are not really to be satisfactorily classified, but are perhaps merely occasions where Homer has nodded, at any rate these cases stand by themselves and ought not to be increased in number, nor indeed followed, except where the one is exactly like the other.[43]

---

[30] [1917] AC 406.   [31] [1917] AC 406, at 541.   [32] [1917] AC 406, at 546.   [33] [1949] Ch 498.
[34] [1949] Ch 498, at 501.   [35] [1957] 1 WLR 729.   [36] [1957] 1 WLR 729, at 745.
[37] *Bowman v Secular Society* [1917] AC 406; *Re Diplock* [1941] Ch 253, at 259; *IRC v Broadway Cottages Trust* [1955] Ch 20, CA.   [38] [1960] Ch 232.
[39] [1957] 1 WLR 729.   [40] *Re Endacott* [1960] Ch 232, at 250.
[41] [1952] Ch 534, at 547.   [42] [1960] Ch 232, CA.   [43] [1960] Ch 232, CA, at 250–251.

Even where a trust falls within the ambit of one of the anomalous exceptions, it will be void if it offends the rule against perpetual trusts because it might exceed the perpetuity period. Opinion differs as to the exact juridical status of the exceptions but they are best regarded as valid unenforceable trusts ('trusts of imperfect obligation').[44] As such, they are not void, but the trustees cannot be required to carry out the trust, though the court will prevent them from misapplying the trust property.

(a) Care of particular animals

A trust for the welfare of animals in general, or of a particular class of animals, will be charitable. A trust for the maintenance of a specific animal is not charitable but may be upheld as an anomalous exception to the beneficiary principle, provided that it does not offend against the perpetuity period. In *Pettingall v Pettingall*[45] a gift by a testator of £50 per annum for the upkeep of his favourite black mare was upheld. In *Mitford v Reynolds*[46] a gift for the upkeep of the testator's horses was upheld. In *Re Dean*[47] William Dean left his eight horses and his hounds to his trustees, and charged his freehold estates with an annuity of £750 per year for fifty years, if they should live that long, to be paid to the trustees for their upkeep. North J held that this was a valid non-charitable trust. However, he seemed to reject the 'beneficiary principle' entirely, stating that he did not assent to the view that a trust is not valid if there is no cestui que trust to enforce it.[48] Although *Re Dean* has been taken as authority for the upholding of trusts for the maintenance of particular animals, the reasoning is incompatible with the beneficiary principle.

Another difficulty with *Re Dean*[49] is that it seems to offend against the perpetuity period. A non-charitable trust must not last beyond the period of lives in being plus twenty-one years. In *Re Dean* the gift to the horses and hounds was for a maximum of fifty years, which exceeds the perpetuity period. One possible solution would be to measure the perpetuity period by reference to an animal life, but this was rejected by Meredith J in *Re Kelly*,[50] who said 'there can be no doubt that "lives" means lives of human beings, not of animals or trees in California'. In some cases the courts have taken judicial notice that an animal's lifespan is less than twenty-one years,[51] or that the particular animal has less than twenty-one years to live. Again, this approach was questioned in *Re Kelly*.[52] It would still leave problems with animals that clearly have a life expectancy beyond twenty-one years.

The most common circumstance in which a trust will be established for a particular animal is where a testator leaves property for the benefit of his favourite

---

[44] See (1953) 17 Conv (NS) 46 (Sheridan); (1953) 6 CLP 151 (Marshall); (1970) 34 Conv (NS) 77 (Lovell); (1973) 37 Conv (NS) 420 (McKay); (1971) 87 LQR 31 (Harris); (1970) 40 MLR 397 (Gravells); (1977) 41 Conv (NS) 179 (Widdows).   [45] (1842) 11 LJ Ch 176, at 177.

[46] (1848) 16 Sim 105.   [47] (1889) 41 Ch D 552.   [48] (1889) 41 Ch D 552, at 556–557.

[49] (1889) 41 Ch D 552.   [50] [1932] IR 255, at 260–261.

[51] See *Re Haines* (1952) *The Times*, 7 November, where Danckwerts J took judicial notice that a cat would not live for more than twenty-one years and upheld the gift.

[52] Meredith J: 'It was suggested that the last of the dogs could in fact not outlive the testator by more than twenty-one years. I know nothing of that. The court does not enter into the question of a dog's expectation of life. In point of fact neighbours' dogs and cats are unpleasantly long lived…'

pet.[53] It should not be forgotten in such circumstances that the animal also constitutes property and ownership of it will also devolve on the testator's death. The new owner will have the prime responsibility to care for the animal and failure of the trust does not necessarily mean that there is no one to care for the animal.

It must not be forgotten, either, that a gift to an individual with a statement that it is to be used for a particular purpose will often be treated as an absolute gift. The expression of the purpose is considered to be no more than the motive for the gift, imposing a moral obligation rather than a legally binding trust obligation.

(b) Maintenance of specific graves and monuments

Trusts to provide for the maintenance of specific graves and monuments have been upheld as valid and unenforceable despite the lack of a beneficiary who can enforce them.[54] In *Mitford v Reynolds*[55] a gift for the erection of a monument was upheld as valid. In *Pirbright v Salwey*[56] a gift of £800 for the upkeep of the burial enclosure of a child in a churchyard for 'as long as the law permitted' was upheld for at least twenty-one years from the testator's death. In *Re Hooper*[57] a testator left £1,000 to his executors to use the income for the upkeep of various family graves and monuments for 'so long as they legally can do so'. Following *Pirbright v Salwey*[58] Maugham J held that the trust was valid for twenty-one years from the testator's death. If the purpose exceeds the perpetuity period, the trust will be void. In *Mussett v Bingle*[59] a testator gave £300 for the erection of a monument and £200 to provide income for its upkeep. This second gift was held void for perpetuity.[60]

This exception did not apply in *Re Endacott* because no specific memorial was identified: 'some useful memorial' was too vague. Even though suitable projects like a bus shelter, a park bench, or public conveniences might come to mind, there was insufficient guidance to enable the trustees to direct the property to a specific project.

(c) Saying masses for the dead

According to Catholic theology, on death the soul does not go direct to heaven but to purgatory, a place of punishment where unforgiven sins must be paid for before the soul can go to heaven. The saying of masses for the dead soul may reduce the length of time that must be spent in purgatory. Thus, testators may seek to leave money to provide for the saying of masses for the benefit of their own souls, or those of their relatives. The saying of masses for the dead was held to be a charitable activity for the advancement of religion in *Re Hetherington (Decd)*,[61] provided they are celebrated in

---

[53] See Brown 'What Are We To Do with Testamentary Trusts of Imperfect Obligation?' [2007] Conv 148, where a survey of probate practitioners demonstrated that such trusts are still common, along with testamentary trusts for the maintenance of specific graves or monuments.

[54] See *Trimmer v Danby* (1856) 25 LJ Ch 424 (testator gave £1,000 to his executors to erect a monument to himself in St Paul's Cathedral).   [55] (1848) 16 Sim 105.

[56] [1896] WN 86.   [57] [1932] 1 Ch 38.   [58] [1896] WN 86.   [59] [1876] WN 170.

[60] By s 1 of the Parish Councils and Burial Authorities (Miscellaneous Provisions) Act 1970 a burial authority may agree, for the payment of a sum, to maintain a grave or monument for a period not exceeding 99 years.   [61] [1990] Ch 1.

public. Thus, a trust for the saying of masses may be valid as a charity. However, it is possible that a gift for the saying of masses in private will be a valid, unenforceable purpose trust even though it is not charitable. Such an approach is suggested by the decision of the House of Lords in *Bourne v Keane*.[62] Again, the duration of the gift must not exceed the perpetuity period.

The exception may also extend to the provision of other non-charitable rites. In *Re Khoo Cheng Teow*,[63] a gift for the performance of ceremonies called Sin Chew to perpetuate the testator's memory during the perpetuity period was upheld by the Supreme Court of the Straits settlement.

(3) Policy limitations on purpose trusts

Even if a purpose trust falls within the anomalous exceptions, it appears that it will be invalid if it is for capricious or useless purposes. In *Brown v Burdett*[64] a trust to block up all the rooms of a house for twenty years was held void. The Scottish courts have been astute to hold that trusts for useless purposes are invalid on grounds of public policy. In *M'Caig v University of Glasgow*[65] a trust to erect statues of the testator and 'artistic towers' on his estates was set aside. In *M'Caig's Trustees v Kirk-Session of United Free Church of Lismore*[66] a trust to erect bronze statues of the testatrix's parents and their children was void on grounds of public policy, since it involved 'a sheer waste of money'.[67]

(4) Trusts for purposes that will benefit an identifiable class of persons

Whilst a non-charitable purpose trust will generally be void unless it falls within the limited categories of the anomalous exceptions, a trust will not be void merely because it is expressed to be for the carrying out of a purpose if it will in fact benefit identifiable individuals who possess sufficient locus standi to enforce it. The central question is whether the carrying out of the specified purpose directly or indirectly benefits an ascertainable and certain group of individuals.

(a) The rule in *Re Denley's Trust Deed*

In *Re Denley's Trust Deed*[68] the court upheld a gift that appeared to establish a purpose trust. Charles Denley had transferred land to trustees to be maintained and used as a sports field for the employees of a company. Goff J took the view that, although the

---

[62] [1919] AC 815; see also *Re Hetherington (Decd)* [1989] 2 All ER 129, at 132.
[63] [1932] Straits Settlements LR 226.   [64] (1882) 21 Ch D 667.   [65] 1907 SC 231.
[66] 1915 SC 426.
[67] Per Lord Salvesen. Other cases include *Aitken's Trustees v Aitken* 1927 SC 374 (erection of a massive bronze equestrian statue); *Lindsay's Executor v Forsyth* 1940 SC 568 (£1,000 on trust to provide weekly supply of flowers to own and mother's graves).
[68] [1969] 1 Ch 373. For comment on *Re Denley's Trust Deed* see Jaconelli 'Independent Schools, Purpose Trusts and Human Rights' [1996] Conv 24; Matthews, 'The New Trust: Obligations without Rights' in Oakley, *Trends in Contemporary Trust Law* (1996), pp 13–15.

trust was expressed to be for a purpose, it was in fact for the benefit of individuals (the employees of the company) because they would benefit, directly or indirectly, from the carrying out of the purpose. As such, it was outside the mischief of the beneficiary principle.[69] Since the employees were an ascertainable and certain class, they had locus standi to apply to the court to enforce the trust. He emphasized that the employees gained a direct benefit from the carrying out of the purposes, and warned that if the benefit was not so direct or intangible the beneficiary principle would invalidate the trust.[70] The trust was therefore upheld because the court could act to enforce it at the suit of the beneficiaries, either negatively by restraining any improper disposition or use of the land, or positively by ordering the trustees to allow the employees to use the land for recreation.[71]

Although the decision prevents the trust falling foul of the beneficiary principle by finding that the employees can enforce the trust, it does not answer the problem of the beneficial ownership of the land. Do the trustees hold the land on trust for the employees? If so, the employees could together demand the transfer of the land to them under the principle of *Saunders v Vautier*,[72] for example if they wanted to sell it to a supermarket for a lucrative development. If that were the case, it would defeat the settlor's intention in establishing the trust. The only other logical conclusion from the decision is that the beneficial interest is suspended for the duration of the trust, which must be limited to the perpetuity period.

(b) Application of the principle to an unincorporated association

Re Denley's Trust Deed was applied in slightly different circumstances by Oliver J in *Re Lipinski's Will Trusts*.[73] Harry Lipinski left his residuary estate to the Hull Judeans (Maccabi) Association in memory of his wife, to be used solely in constructing new buildings for the association. As the gift was made to an unincorporated association the only way it could be upheld was if it was a gift to the individual members of the association.[74] However, it would be difficult to construe a gift for a purpose as a gift to the individual members. Oliver J adopted *Re Denley's Trust Deed* with approval, and concluded that although this gift was expressed as a gift for a purpose (the new buildings) it was directly for the benefit of the members of the Association and could be construed as a gift to them as individuals. He summarized the principle of the case:

> A trust which, though expressed as a purpose, was directly or indirectly for the benefit of an individual or individuals was valid provided those individuals were ascertainable at any one time and the trust was not otherwise void for uncertainty.[75]

In conclusion, this means that although a gift may be expressed as a gift to a purpose, the court can find that it is really a gift for the benefit of individuals if there is a certain and ascertainable class who will benefit sufficiently directly from its performance. Provided it is not void for perpetuity, it will be upheld.

---

[69] [1969] 1 Ch 373, at 383–384.   [70] [1969] 1 Ch 373, at 383.   [71] [1969] 1 Ch 373, at 388.
[72] (1841) 4 Beav 115.   [73] [1976] Ch 235.   [74] See Chapter 22.   [75] [1976] Ch 235, at 248.

(c) Inapplicability of the *Denley* principle to an administratively unworkable class

The principle in *Re Denley's Trust Deed* will not apply if the class of beneficiaries is administratively unworkable through being too wide to form anything like a class. In *R v District Auditor, ex p West Yorkshire Metropolitan County Council*[76] a trust was established to assist economic development, youth, and community projects and encourage ethnic and minority groups for 'the benefit of all or any or some of the inhabitants of West Yorkshire'. It was held invalid as a private purpose trust, and it could not be upheld on the basis of the *Denley* principle. This is because there were no 'ascertained or ascertainable beneficiaries', as the court had also held that with some 2.5 million potential beneficiaries, the trust was administratively unworkable.[77]

(5) Criticism of the beneficiary principle

The central reason for the beneficiary principle is that if a trust does not have beneficiaries then the court will not be able to enforce and supervise it. As Roxburgh J said in *Re Astor's Settlement Trusts*:

> a court of equity does not recognise as valid a trust which it cannot both enforce and control.[78]

Where there is no beneficiary, there is no one in whose favour the court can order performance. There is also no one who is interested in the performance of the trust to apply to the court if the obligation is not being appropriately performed. The court relies on the self-interest of beneficiaries to police trusts and bring any wrongdoing on the part of the trustees to their attention.

However, the force of these objections may have been overstated.[79] Where a trust is made for a purpose, there is always someone who will be entitled to the property in default if the purpose is not carried out,[80] whether the residuary legatee under a will or the owner of the property himself under a resulting trust. Such a person would have sufficient interest to apply to the court if the property were being misapplied by the trustee. This would provide a potential mechanism for control and enforcement.[81] Roxburgh J noted in *Re Astor's Settlement Trusts* that in many of the cases of exceptions to the beneficiary principle there was a residuary legatee who would be able to ensure that the purpose was carried out.[82] Such a mechanism for enforcement seems

---

[76] [1986] RVR 24.

[77] See Harpum 'Administrative Unworkability and Purpose Trusts' (1986) 45 CLJ 391.

[78] [1952] Ch 534, at 549.

[79] See Hayton 'Developing the Obligation Characteristic of the Trust' (2001) 117 LQR 96.

[80] Although that person will not always be immediately ascertainable, as where the residuary beneficiary is whoever happens to be the Vice-Chancellor of the University of Buckingham twenty-one years from the death of the testator.

[81] See Brown 'What are We to Do with Testamentary Trusts of Imperfect Obligation?' [2007] Conv 148, at 159–160.

[82] *Pettingall v Pettingall* (1842) 11 LJ Ch 176; *Mitford v Reynolds* (1848) 16 Sim 105; *Re Dean* (1889) 41 Ch D 552; *Re Hooper* [1932] 1 Ch 38; *Pirbright v Salwey* [1896] WN 86. See also *Re Astor's Settlement Trusts* [1952] Ch 534, at 542–545.

to have been applied in *Re Thompson*.[83] The testator bequeathed £1,000 to his friend, George Lloyd, to be applied for the promotion of fox hunting.[84] The residuary legatee under the will was Trinity Hall, University of Cambridge. Clauson J ordered that the executors pay the money to Lloyd, on his giving an undertaking that he would so apply the money. Trinity Hall would be at liberty to apply to the court if the property was misapplied. Although this seems to offer a way of avoiding the beneficiary principle, the case is of limited value. The case was uncontested, and both parties wanted to see the gift upheld. The court only granted the order that they together requested. The result would have been different if the residuary legatee had not wanted to see the purpose performed, but had wanted to see the gift fail so that they would receive the £1,000 as part of the residue.

The problem with this mechanism for enforcement is that in most cases the residuary legatees, who would be able to apply to the court to prevent misapplication of the funds, are the very people who will benefit if the purpose is not carried out and therefore have no incentive to ensure that the testator's wishes are followed. In fact, in most cases they are actively challenging the validity of the purpose trust because they will be entitled to the property in default. Under a trust, the beneficiaries stand to gain if the trust is properly administered, but the residuary legatee under a purpose trust will not gain from the performance of the purpose. The motivation of self-interest is the key to the proper supervision of trusts, and in the case of purpose trusts that self-interest is not present. This mechanism for enforcement would only be able to ensure that the property was not misapplied, but would not be able to ensure that the trustee carried out his duty to perform the trust.

In the light of these difficulties, other jurisdictions have introduced statutory schemes that facilitate the enforcement of non-charitable purposes trusts.[85] The essence of many such schemes is the introduction of a third party 'enforcer' who is empowered to act to ensure that the trustees carry out their duties. For example, under the Cayman Islands Special Trusts (Alternative Regime) Law 1997[86] the 'enforcer' of a trust, who may not himself enjoy any interest in the trust property, is granted 'the same personal and proprietary remedies against the trustee and against third parties as a beneficiary of an ordinary trust'.[87] The enforcer therefore performs a similar function to that of the Crown in relation to the oversight and enforcement of charitable trusts. Whilst such regimes have been adopted in many offshore jurisdictions,[88] no equivalent has yet been adopted in England.[89]

---

[83] [1934] Ch 342.

[84] Such a gift could no longer be upheld, as fox hunting with hounds is now illegal, following the Hunting Act 2004.

[85] For example, Jersey, Bermuda, Isle of Man, Cayman Islands, British Virgin Islands.

[86] See Duckworth, *STAR Trusts* (1998).   [87] S 7(1).

[88] Note also that the Ontario Perpetuities Act 1966 enacts that trusts for non-charitable purposes should be construed as powers, thus overcoming the beneficiary principle, and that the US Uniform Trust Code permits purpose trusts for twenty-one years.

[89] See Pawlowski and Summers 'Private Purpose Trusts—A Reform Proposal' [2007] Conv 440, advocating proposals for statutory reform of private purpose trusts along similar lines to those found in the offshore jurisdictions listed.

(6) **The beneficiary principle and certainty of objects**

There is a very close relationship between the beneficiary principle and the require-ment that the objects of a trust must be certain. In both cases, the requirement follows from the fact that the court must be able to supervise and enforce the operation of the trust. It is possible to re-analyse the cases that have offended against the beneficiary principle as cases of uncertainty. Where the purpose is so uncertain that the court could not properly supervise or enforce its execution, then it will not be valid. If the purpose is sufficiently certain and its performance is capable of judicial scrutiny, then it should be valid and upheld.

In *Re Thompson*[90] Clauson J emphasized that the purpose was 'defined with suffi-cient clearness and is of a nature to which effect can be given'.[91] Similarly, the anoma-lous exceptions that have been recognized are all sufficiently certain to enable a court to determine whether the property is being applied to the purpose specified. The court can objectively assess whether specified graves are being maintained, animals cared for, or masses said. In contrast, *Re Astor's Settlement Trusts*,[92] *Re Shaw*[93] and *Re Endacott*[94] are all explicable on the basis of uncertainty. It would have been impossible for the court to scrutinize whether the trust property was being applied to the 'mainte-nance rust pof good understanding f goodbetween nations', or 'the preservation of the independence and the integrity of newspapers', because these concepts are themselves uncertain.[95] Similarly, a trust to provide 'some useful memorial to myself' is unen-forceable because it is uncertain.[96] How would the court be able to decide whether the terms of the trust had been carried out?

Although this analysis on the basis of certainty is attractive, and would eliminate the beneficiary principle as an independent requirement, it is not supported by pre-sent authority. Uncertainty was a secondary ground for the decision in *Re Astor's Settlement Trusts*[97] and the objection that there were no beneficiaries was treated separately. In *Re Endacott* Lord Evershed MR made absolutely clear that there was a separate 'beneficiary principle':

> No principle perhaps has greater sanction or authority behind it than the general proposi-tion that a trust by English law, not being a charitable trust, in order to be effective must have ascertained or ascertainable beneficiaries.[98]

5 Charitable and benevolent giving

Although purpose trusts are not as a general rule valid, it is often the case that owners wish to allocate their property to purposes rather than to specific individuals. This is

---

90 [1934] Ch 342.   91 [1934] Ch 342, at 344.   92 [1952] Ch 534.
93 [1957] 1 WLR 729.   94 [1960] Ch 232.   95 See [1952] Ch 534, at 548.
96 [1960] Ch 232, at 247, per Lord Evershed MR: 'though this trust is specific, in the sense that it indicates a purpose capable of expression, yet it is of far too wide and uncertain a nature…'
97 [1952] Ch 534.   98 [1960] Ch 232, at 246.

particularly so when owners want to support causes that they consider to be worthy. The law provides that certain purposes are charitable and gifts and trusts for these purposes are valid, even though there are no beneficiaries as such. The purposes considered charitable are those that have come to be recognized as for the 'public good', and which are now listed in s 3 of the Charities Act 2011.

Charitable trusts are not only valid but also enjoy extensive financial support through government grants and tax exemptions, as explored in Chapter 11. The state provides a mechanism by which they can be enforced and supervised, thus preventing their invalidity under the beneficiary principle. They are enforced by the Attorney General or Charity Commission in the name of the Crown. The general administration of charities is supervised by the Charity Commission. All this state support of purpose trusts is provided in the interests of encouraging giving to worthy causes.

6 The duty to act even-handedly

(1) A general duty

Where a trust has been created for the benefit of multiple beneficiaries, the trustees who have the task of allocating the property have a duty to act even-handedly between them, so that they are all treated impartially and no favouritism is shown to one beneficiary or category of beneficiaries. In *Lloyds Bank plc v Duker*[99] John Mowbray QC stated that there was a general principle that:

> trustees are bound to hold an even hand among their beneficiaries and not to favour one as against another.[100]

This clearly means that a trustee must not be partisan to the interests of one beneficiary at the expense of others.[101] The Law Reform Committee in its 23rd Report[102] recommended that trustees be under a statutory duty to hold a fair balance between beneficiaries.[103]

The need to maintain even-handedness between beneficiaries is particularly acute in two contexts: first, in the context of discretionary trusts where the trustee is entitled to decide how the trust property should be allocated among the class of beneficiaries; and, secondly, where a trust creates successive interests so that a life tenant is to enjoy the income generated by the trust property for his lifetime, but the person entitled to the remainder interest will receive the capital of the fund on his death.

---

[99] [1987] 1 WLR 1324.
[100] [1987] 1 WLR 1324, at 1330–1331, citing *Snell's Principles of Equity* (28th edn, 1982), p 225.
[101] See *Simpson v Bathurst* (1869) 5 Ch App 193, at 202.   [102] Cmnd 8733.
[103] Cmnd 8733, at para 3.36.

(2) **The duty to act even-handedly in the context of a discretionary trust**

The trustees' duty to act even-handedly in the context of a discretionary trust was examined by the Court of Appeal in *Edge v Pensions Ombudsman*.[104] The case concerned a decision by the trustees of a pension scheme to increase the benefits payable to members in service on a particular date. Pensioners who had been in service prior to this date complained to the ombudsman that the changes in the rules introduced were unjust. At first instance, Scott V-C concluded that the trustees were under a duty to act impartially between the different beneficiaries, and that they had acted with 'undue partiality' towards those preferred by the rule change. He rejected any notion of a general duty to act impartially in the context of a discretionary trust as the very essence of the trust is that the trustees select some to benefit from the wider class of potential beneficiaries. Instead, he held that the trustees were under a duty not to take into account irrelevant, irrational, or improper factors. Chadwick LJ, delivering the opinion of the Court of Appeal, cited Scott V-C's words with approval and agreed that the trustees had properly exercised their discretion and had in fact considered the position of those pensioners who would not benefit. The Pensions Ombudsman and the court had no right to interfere in the proper exercise of a discretionary trust. He concluded:

> Properly understood, the so-called duty to act impartially . . . is no more than the ordinary duty which the law imposes on a person who is entrusted with the exercise of a discretionary power: that he exercises the power for the purpose for which it is given, giving proper consideration to the matters which are relevant and excluding from consideration matters which are irrelevant. If pension fund trustees do that, they cannot be criticised if they reach a decision which appears to prefer the claims of one interest—whether that of employers, current employees or pensioners—over others. The preference will be the result of a proper exercise of the discretionary power.[105]

(3) **The duty to act even-handedly in the context of successive interests**

Where property is subject to a life interest behind a trust it is important to ensure that both the life tenant and those entitled to the remainder receive a fair share of the fruits of the trust fund, and that the fund is not invested and allocated in such a way that income is generated at the expense of the preservation of the capital, or that the capital is preserved but no income is generated. Equity has tackled this problem by means of rules designed to ensure that the trust fund is invested in such investments as by their very nature will operate fairly in producing income whilst preserving capital. These rules have become known as rules of apportionment and have been subject to considerable reform through the enactment of the Trusts (Capital and Income) Act 2013. It is still important to appreciate the existing equitable rules, as they apply to trusts already in existence before the passing of the 2013 Act, and may survive the legislative reforms

---

[104] [2000] Ch 602.   [105] [2000] Ch 602, at 627.

by express incorporation of the rules into the trust instrument in trusts arising after the 2013 Act.

(a) The duty to convert investments

(i) The rule in Howe v Earl of Dartmouth

As will be seen in Chapter 21, the trustees may be under a duty to convert unauthorized investments. This duty may be expressly imposed in the trust instrument or, in the case of a residuary bequest in a will in a trust arising before 1 October 2013,[106] implied[107] under the rule in *Howe v Earl of Dartmouth*.[108] This rule, where it still has application, has the effect that the trustee must sell unauthorized investments that by their very nature operate unfairly between the life tenant and the remainderman and then reinvest the realized funds in authorized investments. For example, if the trust fund consists of wasting assets, for example copyrights,[109] the consequence of retaining them would be that they would generate a large income for the life tenant, but would be of rapidly depreciating capital value, leaving perhaps little or nothing for the remainderman. The introduction of a general power of trustees to invest as if absolutely entitled to the assets of the trust in the Trustee Act 2000 has vastly extended the range of authorized investments, so that the circumstances in which the rule in *Howe v Earl of Dartmouth* would apply have been significantly restricted.[110]

(ii) Reform of the rule in Howe v Earl of Dartmouth

In May 2009, the Law Commission issued a report recommending that the rule in *Howe v Earl of Dartmouth* requiring the trustees to convert unauthorized investments (as well as some other equitable rules) be abolished in all new trusts.[111] This has since been enacted in the Trusts (Capital and Income) Act 2013, which came into force on 1 October 2013. The rule no longer applies to trusts created after commencement[112] unless expressly included in the trust instrument.[113] The obligation to sell such investments has thus been removed in new trusts, but the Act clarifies that the trustees still retain a power to sell the investments.[114]

(b) Apportionment between income and capital

(i) The general equitable rules

Where the trustees are subject to a duty to convert the trust property, it is inevitable that there will be some delay between the time that the trustee receives the property as comprising part of the fund and when he is able to convert it. When the property has

---

[106] The commencement date of The Trusts (Capital and Income) Act 2013.

[107] Unless it is excluded by contrary intention of the testator: *Hinves v Hinves* (1844) 3 Hare 609; *Re Pitcairn* [1896] 2 Ch 199.   [108] (1802) 7 Ves JR 137.

[109] *Re Sullivan* [1930] 1 Ch 84.

[110] *Capital and Income in Trusts: Classification and Apportionment*, Law Com CP No 175 (2004), para 3.8.

[111] *Capital and Income in Trusts: Classification and Apportionment*, Law Com No 315 (2009) para 6.65.

[112] Trusts (Capital and Income) Act 2013; s 1(2).

[113] Trusts (Capital and Income) Act 2013; s 1(4).

[114] Trusts (Capital and Income) Act 2013; s 1(3).

been converted and its value realized, the question arises as to how it should then be allocated between the life tenant and the remainderman. It would not be fair for the whole of the proceeds of the converted assets to be applied entirely to capital, since if it was a non-income-generating asset the life tenant would have been entitled to receive some income from it during the period of time that it had not yet been converted. The equitable rules of apportionment determine how an allocation is to be made of the realized value of the converted asset between income and capital. Obviously, any express intentions of the testator or settlor have always taken priority over the implied rules of apportionment. That is no longer necessary in trusts created after 1 October 2013, so-called 'new trusts', as the equitable rules will only apply where they are expressly incorporated into the trust instrument. The exact application of the equitable rules would depend upon the type of property that was converted.

The basic position at equity was that when unauthorized investments were converted, the life tenant was entitled to receive the income that he would have received if they had been authorized investments all along. This has been held to an income of 4 per cent per annum on the value of the converted asset from the date of the death of the testator to the date of the conversion.[115] The remainder of the value realized by the conversion was to be reinvested as capital of the fund. For example, if the asset was of a wasting nature that created a large income, it is possible that the actual income generated between the death of the testator and the conversion would be greater than 4 per cent of the value of the asset. In such a case, the life tenant would only be entitled to receive the equivalent of 4 per cent and the remainder would be applied to capital. However, if the asset did not generate income equivalent to 4 per cent, the life tenant would be entitled to receive such an amount from the realized value, and the remainder would then be applied to capital.

One crucial question was the date at which the value of the converted asset is to be calculated, so as to enable apportionment to take place. This would depend on whether the trust instrument granted the trustees an express power to postpone conversion. Where there was no power to postpone conversion, the trustees were expected to convert the assets within the 'executor's year'. If the assets were converted within the year, the relevant value is the actual amount realized on conversion.[116] However, if they were not sold within the year, the relevant value was the value one year from the date of death.[117] The life tenant was then entitled to the equivalent of 4 per cent per annum interest on that value and the remainder would be applied to capital. Where the trustees had the power to postpone the conversion, the relevant date for valuing the asset was the date of the testator's death.[118]

The operation of these rules is neatly illustrated by the facts of *Brown v Gellatly*.[119] An estate consisted of several unauthorized assets to which a duty to convert applied, including some ships. With respect to the ships, there was a power to postpone the

---

[115] *Re Fawcett* [1940] Ch 402.   [116] [1940] Ch 402.   [117] *Dimes v Scott* (1828) 4 Russ 195.
[118] *Brown v Gellatly* (1867) 2 Ch App 751; *Re Owen* [1912] 1 Ch 519; *Re Parry* [1947] Ch 23; *Re Berry* [1962] Ch 97.   [119] (1867) 2 Ch App 751.

conversion. Therefore, the relevant date for valuation of the ships was the date of death, but the relevant date for the other unauthorized investments was a year from the testator's death.

(ii) Rules applicable to a reversionary interest

Where the assets of the trust include a reversionary interest and there is a duty to convert by selling and reinvesting in authorized investments, a different rule of apportionment used to apply in all trusts. In *Re Earl of Chesterfield's Trusts*[120] it was held that the sum to be allocated to capital was the sum which, if it had been invested at 4 per cent per annum compound interest, taking account of income tax, would have produced the sum which was actually realized by the sale of the interest. The remainder of the realized value is then to be paid to the life tenant as income. This rule may be displaced, and if the will demonstrates the testator's intention that the life tenant was to receive the actual income generated, he will receive nothing by way of income.[121]

(iii) Reform of apportionment

The equitable rules governing apportionment had been criticized on the grounds that they were rigid, technical, and outdated.[122] They required very complex calculations affecting small amounts of money. The rate of interest used to calculate the respective allocations to income or capital may also be criticized. A figure of 4 per cent may be appropriate in times of low inflation and low interest rates, but is wholly inappropriate when there is high inflation. In other areas a more flexible approach has been developed, for example the interest payable by a trustee for breach of trust is the same as that paid on the court's short-term investment account. In the light of these criticisms the Law Commission issued a report, proposing the abolition of all existing equitable rules of apportionment in all new trusts, subject to any contrary provision in the trust instrument.[123] This has since been enacted[124] and the sale and reinvestment of trust property now forms part of a trustee's general investment duties under the Trustee Act 2000. The creation of a general discretion or power simply to replace the equitable rules was originally considered and rejected for tax considerations.[125] The Commission also felt unable to provide a series of limited discretions to cover the circumstances existing under the existing equitable rules of allocation,

[120] (1883) LR 24 Ch D 643.

[121] *Mackie v Mackie* (1845) 5 Hare 70; *Rowlls v Bebb* [1900] 2 Ch 107, CA.

[122] *Capital and Income in Trusts: Classification and Apportionment*, Law Com No 315(2009), para A.6: 'Professionally drafted trust instruments generally exclude them. In most trusts where they have not been excluded they are either ignored or cause considerable inconvenience by requiring complex calculations in relation to very small sums of money.'

[123] *Capital and Income in Trusts: Classification and Apportionment*, Law Com No 315 (2009), paras 6.54–6.65 and cl 1(2)(a)–(2b) (*Howe v Early of Dartmouth* rules) and cl 1(3) (*Re Earl of Chesterfield's Trusts* rule).

[124] Trusts (Capital and Income) Act 2013, s 1(1) (removing general equitable rules), s 1(2)(b) (removing the rule in *Re Earl of Chesterfield's Trusts*).

[125] *Capital and Income in Trusts: Classification and Apportionment*, Law Com No 315 (2009), para. 6.61. The potential tax problems included the re-categorization of trusts with the statutory power as non-interest in possession trusts for the purposes of Income Tax and Inheritance Tax. See further para 5.79.

as, while desirable, they would be too cumbersome and likely to be excluded in trust instruments.[126]

(c) Corporate receipts received as a 'windfall' by the trust

Problems of allocation between the life tenant and remainderman may arise if the trust receives a 'windfall' because of the assets held. This is particularly the case when the trust holds shares in a company which either makes cash payments to shareholders as a 'capital profits dividend', capitalizes its profits and issues bonus or scrip dividend shares to the existing shareholders, or demerges and gives shares in the new company to the original shareholders.[127] The question arises whether these payments or shares should be allocated to capital or income. In the event of liquidation, all payments to the trustees who hold shares are regarded as capital.[128]

(i) Cash payments

If a company decided to distribute some form of cash bonuses to shareholders, any payments received by trustees who hold shares as part of trust assets are to be regarded as income and therefore allocated to the life tenant. In *Re Bates*[129] a company distributed cash bonuses to shareholders after selling some vessels at prices exceeding their value in the company balance sheets. Eve J held that the life tenant of a trust holding shares in the company was entitled to receive the entire payment as income.[130]

(ii) Bonus shares

If the company decides to capitalize its profits and issue bonus shares to the present shareholders and they are received by the trustees, then they are to hold them as part of the capital of the trust. This was so held by the House of Lords in *Bouch v Sproule*,[131] where it was emphasized that the decision whether to distribute cash or to capitalize was for the company alone. The result would no doubt be different if the trustees were entitled to elect to take a dividend either in cash or in the form of additional shares.[132]

(iii) Demergers

The allocation between capital and income where a company demerges is complex, and a distinction may be drawn between a direct and an indirect demerger. A direct demerger occurs where the original company allocates the shares in the new company to its shareholders. In such cases the Inland Revenue views the shares distributed as income. An indirect demerger occurs where the new company allocates its own shares to the shareholders of the original company. In *Sinclair v Lee*[133] it was held that new shares were to be treated as capital assets.

---

[126] *Capital and Income in Trusts: Classification and Apportionment*, Law Com No 315 (2009), para 6.63.
[127] See *Sinclair v Lee* [1993] Ch 497.
[128] *Re Armitage* [1893] 3 Ch 337; *IRC v Burrell* [1924] 2 KB 52.   [129] [1928] Ch 682.
[130] See also *Re Whitehead's Will Trusts* [1959] Ch 579.   [131] (1887) 12 App Cas 385.
[132] For the treatment of scrip dividend shares, see *Pierce v Wood* [2009] EWHC 3225 (Ch).
[133] [1993] Ch 497.

(iv) Reform of the allocation of corporate receipts

The Law Commission also sought to address this issue. It considered that the law regarding the classification of corporate receipts as capital or income did not rest on principle, and failed to deliver either certainty or fairness. The Law Commission would have liked to propose an abolition of the existing rules and the introduction of a more appropriate regime allowing more flexible treatment of trust receipts, but it felt it was constrained from doing so by the tax implications of these changes.[134] It therefore proposed only that the distinction between direct and indirect demergers should be abolished, a measure which would be tax neutral. This has been adopted, so that income from either set of demerger is now classed as capital under s 2(1) of the Trusts (Capital and Income) Act 2013 in all trusts, whether created before or after the commencement of the Act.[135] Like the other reforms under this Act, the original equitable rules may be expressly incorporated within the trust instrument.[136] The Act also provides the trustees with the power to make a compensatory payment out of the capital where a beneficiary has been prejudicially affected by the classification of the income as a capital sum.[137]

---

[134] *Capital and Income in Trusts: Classification and Apportionment*, Law Com No 315 (2009), para 5.83.
[135] Trusts (Capital and Income) Act 2013, s 2(5).
[136] Trusts (Capital and Income) Act 2013, s 2(2).
[137] Trusts (Capital and Income) Act 2013, s 3.

15

Defined interests and powers of advancement and maintenance

This chapter considers the mechanisms for the distribution of a trust fund where the trustees have no discretion as to how the fund is to be allocated. The interests of the objects of the fund, that is who is to benefit and in what proportions, have already been fixed, or defined, by the creator of the trust. The role of the trustees is merely to carry out those instructions, and carry into effect the owner's intentions. This chapter also deals with the related question of when a settlor creates interests under a fixed trust which are contingent upon the happening of a future event. In such circumstances the question arises what to do with the income generated by the trust until the interest vests in the beneficiaries. There may be good reason to allow the contingent beneficiaries to receive the income or a share of the capital, as for example where the beneficiaries may need income to meet living expenses. This is permitted in certain circumstances by the use of inherent, statutory, or express powers of maintenance (income) and advancement (capital).

1 Introduction to defined interests

(1) **Meaning of defined interests**

The type of equitable obligation where the interests in the fund are already defined is the fixed trust. The settlor of the trust himself defines the beneficial interests which the beneficiaries under the trust are to enjoy in the trust instrument. The trustee must carry out those terms and distribute the fund as has been specified.

(a) **Example of fixed trusts**

If David leaves 10,000 shares in a public company to Elizabeth on trust for his three children, Frieda, Graham, and Henrietta, in equal shares, Elizabeth has no discretion as to how the fund is to be allocated as the beneficial interests of the three children have already been defined by David. They will each have an immediate beneficial entitlement to a third of the fund (see Figure 15.1). It is Elizabeth's duty to allocate them their respective shares. If David provides that the children should take in unequal proportions, for example that Frieda should be entitled to 5,000 shares and the others 2,500 each, Elizabeth would have to allocate in those defined shares.

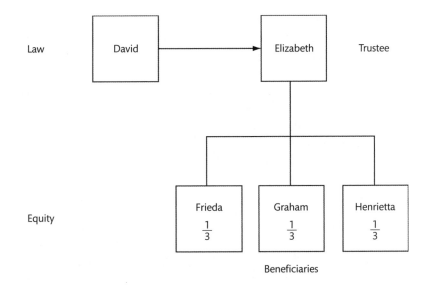

Figure 15.1 An example of fixed trusts

(b) Fixed trusts in favour of a class of beneficiaries

The interests granted under a fixed trust may also be specified by means of a class definition rather than by listing each individual who is intended to benefit. Instead of naming Frieda, Graham, and Henrietta as beneficiaries, David could have left the shares to Elizabeth 'on trust for such of my children who survive me', or alternatively 'to all the present employees at the date of my death' of a particular company. The presumption would be that the members of the class would take the property in equal shares. If such a class definition is used, the trust will only be valid if the objects of the trust are sufficiently certain to enable the trustee, or if necessary the court, to carry out the trust. The trust must, in addition, be administratively workable.

2 Defined interests under trusts

(1) Bare trusts

A bare trust arises where there is a trustee who holds the trust property on trust for the benefit of a single beneficiary. In a bare trust the trustee has no active duties to perform but merely holds the property on trust for the benefit of the person entitled. The trustee acts exclusively at the direction of the beneficiary, who is able to demand the legal title to be conveyed to him at any time under the principle of *Saunders v Vautier*.[1] The trustee is, in effect, the nominee of the beneficiary and acts at his discretion. For example, in *Vandervell v IRC*[2] the National Provincial Bank held stock in Vandervell

---

[1] (1841) 4 Beav 115.   [2] [1967] 2 AC 291, HL.

Products Ltd for Mr Vandervell. This was a bare trust, and the bank was acting as his nominee. It was obliged to follow his directions, and thus when he asked them to complete a share transfer form to enable him to transfer the shares to the Royal College of Surgeons they acted at his request. The allocation of the fund is not necessarily the prime purpose of a bare trust. It is a very simple mechanism for hiding the true owner of property from the world. The trustee appears to be the legal owner and the beneficiary can remain hidden from the management of the property. In practice, the trustee acts at the beneficiary's direction, who therefore himself keeps control of the management of the property.

(2) **Fixed trusts**

Unlike a bare trust, the prime purpose of a fixed trust is to allocate the trust fund, or limited interests in the fund, to others. The flexibility of the trust, and the equitable interests in property which subsist behind it, facilitate such allocation. Interests in the fund can be allocated concurrently between two or more beneficiaries, or consecutively, so that different beneficiaries will enjoy the property at different times.

(a) **Concurrent interests**

The fixed trust can be used to allocate concurrent interests in the same assets. Often the property comprised in a fund is physically indivisible, and the only way that more than one person can enjoy shares in it is through the allocation of the beneficial interest. For example, it is not possible for people to enjoy shared ownership of land other than behind a trust. If Robert wanted to leave his house to his sons, Steven and Timothy, in equal shares, it is unlikely to be possible for the house to be physically divided between them. Instead, he can leave it to them on trust as tenants-in-common in equity of equal shares. From the moment that the trust comes into being, they enjoy equal shares of the equitable interest in the house under a trust of land.[3] The fixed trust can also be used to delay allocation of concurrent interests in the trust fund until the future. Rashid, who is dying, has two small children, Khalid and Fatima, and wants to make provision for them. He leaves his property to his brother, Karim, on trust for them until they reach the age of 21. Here Karim would hold the legal title and enjoy the powers of management over the property described in the previous section, but he would be under a duty to allocate the fund to the children equally when they reach the stated age. Whatever the terms of the trust for the timing of the allocation, the trustee must follow them. Karim cannot allocate the fund to his own children when they reach 21, and to do so would be a breach of trust that the court would intervene to prevent or remedy.

---

[3] Trusts of Land and Appointment of Trustees Act 1996, s 1.

(b) **Consecutive interests**

Fixed trusts also enable interests in the property to be divided by time, so that one person may enjoy the use of the property for the present, but another has an interest for the future. Alexander dies and leaves his property to trustees on trust for his wife, Becky, for life, and then to his children, Charles and Delia, in equal shares. His wife enjoys an immediate life interest in the property, which will entitle her to the income from it. His children do not have any immediate entitlement to the capital of the fund so they cannot demand that the trustees transfer the legal title to them now, but they enjoy a remainder interest in the fund and will be entitled to the capital in equal shares on the death of their mother. This is a proprietary right that they can sell or assign to others, and if they die it will pass to their own heirs. The task of the trustees is to obey the terms of the trust by investing the fund and by paying the income to Becky, and when she dies by allocating it equally between the children. If they fail to do so they have committed a breach of trust.

3 **Beneficial entitlement to defined interests**

The beneficiaries under a fixed trust may be either immediately ascertainable or ascertainable only in the future. In the example just given, Alexander identified all of the beneficiaries of his trust by name. They are immediately ascertainable. However, if Sandra creates a trust for her grandchildren equally, the beneficiaries are not yet ascertainable since, even if Sandra already has some grandchildren, she might have more who have not yet been born.

Beneficiaries under a fixed trust may also have vested or contingent interests. They have vested interests where they are immediately ascertainable, and do not have to satisfy any conditions in order to benefit. An interest can be vested even if enjoyment is postponed to a future date. For instance, in Alexander's trust, Charles and Delia have vested interests even though they will only get the capital of the fund when Becky dies. If they die before Becky, they may not be able to enjoy their capital share personally, but it will form part of their estate to be dealt with by will or intestacy. A contingent interest, by contrast, is one where, even though a beneficiary is immediately ascertainable, some further condition has to be satisfied. For instance, if Alexander specified that Charles and Delia had to be living when Becky died in order to take a share of capital, their rights to the capital would be contingent during Becky's life, and would vest only on her death (if they survived her). This is because surviving Becky has been made a condition of taking the gift.

Immediately ascertainable beneficiaries with a vested interest under a fixed trust have immediate proprietary interests in the assets of the fund. If they are of full age, mentally competent and entitled to an immediate interest in the property, they can require the trustee to transfer the legal title to them under the principle of *Saunders v*

Vautier.[4] If the beneficiaries are not immediately entitled but have a vested or contingent future interest, they will have to wait until they have an immediate entitlement before they can exercise this right. Thus, a remainder interest behind a life interest in the trust fund does not entitle the beneficiary to call for the legal title. However, when the life tenant dies he becomes the sole beneficiary and can demand the conveyance of the legal title.

As the holder of a proprietary interest in the fund, a beneficiary with an immediate vested interest is liable to taxation on his interest.[5] If he dies it will form part of his estate and be subject to inheritance tax. If the property comprising the fund is wrongfully transferred to others by the trustee, not only will all the beneficiaries have personal remedies against the trustee for breach of trust, but their proprietary rights over the fund will be preserved into the hands of all except a bona fide purchaser for value of the fund.[6]

4 Certainty of objects

It has already been noted in Chapter 7 that a valid trust requires certainty of intention, certainty of subject matter, and certainty of objects.[7] It is also a cardinal principle that the court must be able to carry out the trust if the trustee is unable and unwilling to do so. This reflects the mandatory nature of the trust obligation. If the objects of the trust are not sufficiently certain, it is impossible for the trustee to carry out his duty of allocation, nor can the court carry out the trust in the event of his default if necessary.

Under a fixed trust the beneficial interests of each and every beneficiary are predefined by the settlor. If these are named then there is no uncertainty. The problem arises where the beneficiaries are defined by means of a 'class definition'. Imagine that Wendy leaves £20,000 to Lucy on trust for 'my children in equal shares'. To be able to carry out the trust it must be possible to identify each and every person who falls within the class of 'Wendy's children', because the share of each child in the fund cannot be determined until the full extent of the class is identified. If Lucy were to distribute the fund in equal shares to the first three people who showed themselves to be children of Wendy, she would be in breach of trust if it subsequently came to light that there was a fourth child who should also have received a share. If it fell to the court to carry out the trust and allocate the fund they would also have to be able to identify each and every child.

The problem of uncertainty is generally slight in the context of fixed trusts because they are usually only appropriate for small, well-defined, classes. For larger classes, for example 'all the employees and ex-employees' of a company, a discretionary trust would tend to be used. However, if a fixed trust was intended in such circumstances it

---

[4] (1841) 4 Beav 115.   [5] See Chapter 2.   [6] See Chapter 3.
[7] Referred to as the 'three certainties'—*Knight v Knight* (1840) 3 Beav 148.

would not be possible to carry out the trust and allocate the fund unless each and every employee and ex-employee were identified.

(1) The 'complete list' test

In order to carry out the terms of the trust and allocate the fund in accordance with the settlor's intentions, the trustee must be able to ascertain each and every person who is entitled to a defined interest in the fund. If he cannot do so then he cannot carry out the terms of the trust. Wynn-Parry J stated in *IRC v Broadway Cottages Trust*[8] that the class must be 'capable of ascertainment'.[9] He took this to mean that the trustee must be able to draw up a 'complete list'[10] of all the beneficiaries of the trust, and that the trust will fail if such a list cannot be drawn up.[11]

The 'complete list' test is almost universally accepted as the requisite test of certainty of objects for fixed trusts.

However, it has been argued that the 'complete list' test is a 'heresy' that has grown from a misunderstanding of judicial statements,[12] and that the test for fixed trusts should be the same as that for discretionary trusts.[13] This argument runs against principle, logic, and authority, and fails to take sufficient account of the differences between the duty of trustees of a fixed trust to allocate the fund and that of trustees under a discretionary trust.[14] The 'complete list' test is supported both in principle and in logic. The very nature of the fixed trust where the beneficiaries are defined as a class requires that a 'complete list' be drawn up before the trustee can allocate the fund. If such a list cannot be drawn up, it is absolutely impossible for the trustee to carry out his duty to allocate the fund, or for the court to act on his default. Lord Upjohn expressed the problem clearly in *Re Gulbenkian's Settlement*:

> Suppose the donor directs that a fund be divided equally between 'my old friends', then unless there is some admissible evidence that the donor has given some special 'dictionary' meaning to that phrase which enables the trustees to identify the class with sufficient certainty, it is plainly bad as being too uncertain. Suppose that there appeared before the trustees (or the court) two or three individuals who plainly satisfied the test of being among 'my old friends', the trustees could not consistently with the donor's intentions accept them as claiming the whole or any defined part of the fund. They cannot claim the whole fund for they can show no title to it unless they prove they are the only members of the class, which they cannot do, and so, too, by parity of reasoning they cannot claim any

---

[8] [1954] 1 All ER 878.   [9] [1954] 1 WLR 659, at 664.   [10] [1954] 1 All ER 878, at 881.
[11] See Hopkins 'Continuing Uncertainty as to Certainty of Objects of Trust Powers' (1971) 29 CLJ 68, at 81.   [12] Matthews 'A Heresy and a Half in Certainty of Objects' [1984] Conv 22.
[13] Requiring only 'conceptual certainty' and not a 'complete list' to be in fact drawn up. See also Matthews 'The Comparative Importance of the Rule in *Saunders v Vautier*' (2006) LQR 268, at 276: 'there is no sensible basis for applying a different test of certainty for different kinds of equitable owners. The size or stability of the equitable interest concerned is not a sufficient reason. All interests having a *Saunders v Vautier* value (however big or small) should be judged by the same criteria of certainty.'
[14] Martin 'Certainty of Objects—What Is Heresy?' [1984] Conv 304; Hayton 'Certainty of Objects—What Is Heresy?' [1984] Conv 307.

defined part of the fund and there is no authority in the trustees or the court to make any distribution among a smaller class than that pointed to by the donor.[15]

Re Gulbenkian's Settlement involved a power, not a trust, so the observations do not form part of the ratio decidendi. Other cases supporting the 'complete list' test[16] pre-dated the decision of the House of Lords in *McPhail v Doulton*,[17] which rejected this test for discretionary trusts. The cases themselves also involved discretionary trusts. This meant that there was a lack of direct authority. It now seems that the matter is settled, as the 'complete list' test was applied to a fixed trust in *OT Computers Ltd v First National Tricity Finance Ltd*.[18] Pumphrey J, in considering that a proposed fixed trust of a supplier's deposit account was uncertain, stated that a complete list of beneficiaries was necessary so that the property could vest immediately under the trust:

> At this point, it is important to remember that the trust which is proposed is a fixed trust. Accordingly, it must be possible to identify each member of the class of beneficiaries. It is not sufficient to be able to say whether or not any identified person is or is not a member of the class entitled to be considered: the purpose of the trust in the present case is to vest an immediate interest in the suppliers in question.[19]

Significantly, Pumphrey J cited *McPhail v Doulton*[20] as authority for this statement of the law, demonstrating that the 'complete list' test has survived that decision. In the absence of a contrary decision of a higher court, the law now accords with principle and logic.

(2) **Application of the 'complete list' test**

Application of the 'complete list' test means that a fixed trust will be void unless the objects are defined with conceptual certainty *and* can be identified with evidential certainty.[21] Provided that these two elements of certainty are present, it is not necessary that the beneficiaries be immediately ascertainable.

(a) 'Conceptual certainty'

If a 'complete list' of beneficiaries must be drawn up, it is essential that any class is defined in conceptually certain terms. This means that there must be a clear objective definition that will enable the trustee or court to determine whether any given individual falls within the class or is outside it. Without such 'conceptual certainty' it is impossible for a 'complete list' to be drawn up. This was emphasized in the example provided by Lord Upjohn in *Re Gulbenkian's Settlements* noted earlier. A trust to divide a fund equally between 'my old friends' is void for uncertainty, because the class

---

[15] [1970] AC 508, at 524.
[16] *IRC v Broadway Cottage Trust* [1954] 1 All ER 878 affirmed by the Court of Appeal [1955] Ch 20 and followed by Upjohn J in *Re Sayer* [1957] Ch 423, at 430.   [17] [1971] AC 424.
[18] [2003] EWHC 1010 (Ch); [2007] WTLR 165.   [19] [2003] EWHC 1010 (Ch), at [21].
[20] Referred to as *Re Baden* [1971] AC 424.
[21] Emery 'The Most Hallowed Principle: Certainty of Beneficiaries of Trusts and Powers of Appointment' [1982] 98 LQR 551.

is 'conceptually uncertain'. It is impossible to define what is mean by an 'old friend', and it is impossible for the trustee or the court to say of any individual whether he is, or is not, an 'old friend' because they have no criteria on which to make such a judgement.

In *OT Computers Ltd v First National Tricity Finance Ltd*,[22] a proposed trust in favour of 'urgent suppliers' failed as it did not create a conceptually certain class. The case concerned the collapse of the Tiny Computer retailer, owned by the claimant, OT Computers Ltd. To protect its customers and suppliers from creditors in difficult trading conditions, the claimant had instructed the defendant bank to set up two separate bank accounts, one for customers and one for monies owed to its suppliers. The company also created two schedules, which listed the names of its customers and a selection of its suppliers, respectively. When the claimant company went into receivership, the defendant sought to reclaim a loan due to it from the money in the two deposit accounts. The claimant argued that trusts had been validly declared of the monies in the bank accounts. Pumphrey J upheld a fixed trust of the customer account, as all the beneficiaries could be clearly identified due to the payments made by them to the claimant company. However, in relation to the supplier account, the schedule did not list all suppliers, but referred instead to 'urgent suppliers'. Pumphrey J held that the term 'urgent suppliers' was an insufficiently conceptually certain description of a class, so that the trustees could not draw up a complete list. The term 'urgent' was simply too vague. The money in the suppliers account remained part of the company assets.

(b) 'Evidential certainty'

A 'complete list' of beneficiaries can only be drawn up if it is possible to identify each and every member of the class in fact. This means that there must be absolute 'evidential certainty'. If the trust is created in favour of all the 'employees and ex-employees' of a company, it must be possible to identify each and every employee and ex-employee. In *Re Sayer*[23] a trust in favour of the employees and ex-employees of Sayers (Confectioners) Ltd was held void for uncertainty[24] because it was impossible to draw up a complete list of the persons employed by the company since its incorporation. The company had found it impossible to keep accurate records of its ex-employees.[25] Lord Upjohn also gave an example of a fixed trust void for evidential uncertainty in *Re Gulbenkian's Settlements*:

> If a donor...directs trustees to make some specified provision for 'John Smith', then to give legal effect to that provision it must be possible to identify 'John Smith'. If the donor knows three John Smiths then by the most elementary principles of law neither the trustees nor the court in their place can give effect to that provision; neither the trustees nor

---

[22] [2003] EWHC 1010 (Ch); [2007] WTLR 165.   [23] [1957] Ch 423.

[24] *Re Sayer* involved what today would be regarded as a discretionary trust and the test adopted in the House of Lords in *McPhail v Doulton* [1971] AC 424, HL would now be applied. As interpreted in *Re Baden (No 2)* [1973] Ch 9 the trust would be upheld, as for a discretionary trust the class of beneficiaries must be 'conceptually' certain but need not be 'evidentially' certain..

[25] [1957] Ch 423, at 430: because of its large number of shops (seventy), and the nature of its workforce, which consisted of a large number of female shop assistants who tended to change employment frequently.

the court can guess at it. It must fail for uncertainty unless of course admissible evidence is available to point to a particular John Smith as the object of the donor's bounty.[26]

The relevant date for the drawing up of the complete list is the date of execution of the trust, not the date of its creation.[27]

(c) 'Ascertainability'

A class may enjoy 'evidential certainty', so that it is possible to draw up a 'complete list' of the beneficiaries, even though it may be impossible to ascertain where some of those who appear on the list are, or whether they are still alive. If Francis leaves all her property to Eric on trust to be divided equally among her cousins, this will create a valid fixed trust. The class is conceptually certain, and it is known that Francis had seven cousins. One of the seven, Graham, left for South America in 1987 and has not been seen or heard from since. Would the fact that it is not known whether he is alive or cannot be found, invalidate the trust? Although this looks similar to the problem of 'evidential uncertainty', it is a quite different problem, one of 'ascertainability'.[28] The distinction was drawn by Lord Upjohn in *Re Gulbenkian's Settlements*, where he said:

> If the class is sufficiently defined by the donor the fact that it may be difficult to ascertain the whereabouts or continued existence of some of its members at the relevant time matters not.[29]

Lord Wilberforce echoed this distinction in *McPhail v Doulton*:

> as to the question of certainty, I desire to emphasise the distinction clearly made and explained by Lord Upjohn, between linguistic or semantic uncertainty...and the difficulty of ascertaining the existence or whereabouts of members of the class...[30]

Problems of the 'ascertainability' of beneficiaries will not render the trust void for uncertainty. This is consistent with principle. If a complete list can be drawn up, then the minimum share to which each beneficiary is entitled is known and the fund can be allocated on that basis. In our example, because it is known that Francis had seven cousins, each cousin is certainly entitled to a seventh share in the fund, and Eric can allocate it on that basis. As to the seventh share to which Graham may be entitled, Eric can 'apply to the court for directions or pay a share into court'.[31] In the case of unascertainable beneficiaries who are thought to be dead, the court can make a 'Benjamin order'. This entitles the trustees to allocate the fund on the presumption that the beneficiary had predeceased the testator. In *Re Benjamin*[32] David Benjamin left his residuary estate to his children in equal shares. He had twelve children surviving him, but

---

[26] [1970] AC 508, at 523.

[27] See, for example, *Swain v Law Society* [1981] 3 All ER 797. Thus a trust may be created now for the benefit of persons as yet unborn or unascertained, but it must be possible to draw up a complete closed list on the due date of execution.

[28] See Emery 'The Most Hallowed Principle: Certainty of Beneficiaries of Trusts and Powers of Appointment' [1982] 98 LQR 551, at 556.   [29] [1970] AC 508, at 524.

[30] [1971] AC 424, at 457.

[31] *Re Gulbenkian's Settlement Trusts* [1970] AC 508, at 524, per Lord Upjohn.   [32] [1902] 1 Ch 723.

one had disappeared while on holiday in France a year before the testator's death. Joyce J held that, in the absence of any evidence to the contrary, he must be presumed to be dead and his share was to be allocated accordingly. If it subsequently turns out that the unascertained beneficiary is alive, he may trace his share of the fund into the hands of those who received it,[33] and the trustees are not liable for breach of trust. The court order protects them.

(3) **Resolving uncertainty**

There are some ways in which a gift that would otherwise fail on grounds of uncertainty might be found to be valid. What might appear to be a gift to an ill-defined group such as 'my old friends' might perhaps be treated as a series of separate gifts that can be considered as if they stood alone. For instance, in *Re Barlow's Will Trusts*,[34] Helen Alice Dorothy Barlow died leaving a valuable collection of paintings. She gave instructions in her will that 'any members of my family and any friends of mine' could buy any of the paintings at the prices contained in a catalogue of valuations made some five years before her death. These prices were significantly below the value of the paintings after her death. Browne-Wilkinson J held that the instruction was not invalid for uncertainty. This was not a gift to a class. It was properly to be regarded as a series of individual gifts to persons answering the description of friend or family member. The test which applies to class gifts 'has no application to a case where there is a condition or description attached to one or more individual gifts; in such cases, uncertainty as to some other persons who may have been intended to take does not in any way affect the quantum of the gift to persons who undoubtedly possess the qualification'.[35] Accordingly, 'anyone who can prove that by any reasonable test he or she must have been a friend' of Helen Barlow would be entitled to purchase a picture. Anyone who did not satisfy this stringent test would not be entitled to take advantage of the option created by the will. Similarly, anyone who could prove a blood relationship to Helen Barlow would qualify as a family member. The fact that there might be considerable areas of uncertainty did not defeat the provision for those who clearly satisfied it.

Another way in which problems of uncertainty can be resolved is where the gift itself provides a mechanism for resolving that uncertainty. Thus, a gift to 'intelligent people' would normally fail for lack of certainty because there is no clear definition of intelligence. However, a gift to people who, in the opinion of the President of Mensa, are intelligent, would probably be held to be valid. For instance, in *Re Tuck's Settlement Trusts*,[36] Sir Adolf Tuck, a Jew, was made a baronet in 1910. He wanted to make sure that future descendants inheriting the title of baronet remained in the Jewish faith. To this end, he specified that future baronets would inherit the funds he left by will only if they married a wife of Jewish blood who at the time of her marriage 'continues to worship according to the Jewish faith'. He added that in case of dispute 'the decision

---

[33] Subject to the Limitation Act 1980, ss 18, 21(3), and 22.   [34] [1979] 1 WLR 278.
[35] [1979] 1 WLR 278, at 281–282.   [36] [1978] Ch 49, [1978] 1 All ER 1047.

of the Chief Rabbi in London shall be conclusive'. Eveleigh LJ in the Court of Appeal had some doubt as to whether the condition as to the Jewish faith would in itself have been sufficiently clear. However, the reference to the Chief Rabbi operated to make it clear: 'Different people may have different views or be doubtful as to what is "Jewish faith" but the Chief Rabbi knows and can say what meaning he attaches to the words.'[37]

There has been some debate about the reasoning lying behind this decision. Eveleigh J suggested that the Chief Rabbi would have a clear understanding of what was meant by the Jewish faith and could provide it if asked. But it is more than likely that, even for the Chief Rabbi, there could be areas of conceptual doubt. In that case, does reference to him for a decision resolve any uncertainty? It may be that providing for a decision to be made by a third party means that an inherently uncertain concept (for instance, who is intelligent?) is replaced by the certain test (eg those persons stated by the President of Mensa to be intelligent). In that case, what can be done if a decision is taken by the third party arbitrarily—for instance, if the President of Mensa states that someone is intelligent when they are clearly not? The courts are reluctant to see their jurisdiction ousted. If they retain a supervisory jurisdiction, then they need to be able to control the arbitrary exercise of the decision-making authority conferred on the third party. Yet they can only decide if the decisions he or she makes have been properly made if the test itself is sufficiently certain to be applied by the court. That takes us back to where we began.[38]

The answer to this problem is contained in the common-sense judgment of Lord Denning. Even if there is conceptual uncertainty, it can be cured by a provision stating that any uncertainty may be resolved by the decision of a competent third party:

> So long as he does not misconduct himself or come to a decision which is wholly unreasonable, I think his decision should stand...As this very case shows, the courts may get bogged down in distinctions between conceptual uncertainty and evidential uncertainty...The testator may want to cut out all that cackle, and let someone decide it who will really understand what the testator is talking about, and thus save an expensive journey to the lawyers and the courts. For my part, I would not blame him. I would give effect to his intentions.[39]

5 Policy limits

Although a prime purpose of the law of equity is to enable owners to deal with their property as they wish, there are certain policy-motivated limits which constrain their freedom. The rule against perpetuities prevents owners tying their property up outside of the market for too long a period of time. Conditional and determinable

---

[37] [1978] 1 All ER 1047, at 1057.
[38] It may be possible to classify this decision as one of evidential uncertainty, rather than conceptual uncertainty, but doing so does not resolve the issues raised earlier, as the same concerns about arbitrary decision-making by the nominated third party remain.   [39] [1978] 1 All ER 1047, at 1053–1054.

interests, where the conditions are designed to influence the beneficiaries' behaviour in a way that is contrary to public policy, are also restricted. These limitations are equally applicable to varieties of equitable obligations other than the fixed trust. Legislation also provides that trusts may be set aside if they are established with the object of defrauding the creditors of the settlor.

(1) **The rule against perpetuities**

The rule against perpetuities was examined by the Law Commission, which recommended significant legislative reform.[40] The new scheme, which was finally enacted[41] on 12 November 2009 as the Perpetuities and Accumulations Act 2009, only has prospective effect,[42] so that trusts executed before the new legislation came into force on 6 April 2010 will continue to be administered under the old scheme.[43] The existence of separate schemes complicates the law, but was part of the price paid for simplification.[44]

(a) **The perpetuity rules**
(i) Remoteness of vesting

The law require that gifts of property vest within a certain period of time, the perpetuity period. This prevents property being tied up, and hence kept outside the economy, for long periods.[45] At common law, if the property might vest outside of the perpetuity period, the gift would be void. The relevant perpetuity period was a life in being plus twenty-one years. This meant that the gift must not vest outside of a period of twenty-one years after the lifetime of a human person living at the date of the creation of the interest.[46]

The common law rule preventing remoteness of vesting was reformed by the Perpetuities and Accumulations Act 1964.[47] Under s 1, a settlor could specify the relevant perpetuity period in the trust instrument instead of a perpetuity period of a life in being plus twenty-one years, up to a period of eighty years. This was obviously simpler than the requirement of a life in being and was a more attractive option than the 'royal lives' clauses previously regularly used in trust instruments.[48] Where no

[40] Law Com No 251, *The Rules Against Perpetuities and Excessive Accumulations* (1998).

[41] The Law Commission's recommendations were accepted by the government in 2001, but no time was found to implement them. In 2008, the Bill was proposed as the first in the trial of the new House of Lords' procedure for Law Commission Bills (HL Paper 63, *1st Report of Session 2007–08: Law Commission Bills.*), which, in essence, is a streamlined procedure for enacting uncontroversial Law Commission Bills that allows them to be taken in Committee, off the floor of the House.

[42] Perpetuities and Accumulations Act 2009, s 15 and Perpetuities and Accumulations Act 2009 (Commencement) Order 2010, SI 2010/37.

[43] There are limited opt-in opportunities for existing trusts, so that they may be administered under the statutory scheme—see Perpetuities and Accumulations Act 2009, s 12.

[44] For a critique, see T P Gallanis 'The Rule Against Perpetuities and the Law Commission's Flawed Philosophy' [2000] 59 CLJ 284.   [45] See Maudsley, *The Modern Law of Perpetuities* (1979).

[46] Gray on *Perpetuities*, §201.

[47] This Act has not been repealed, as it applies to trusts arising before the commencement of the Perpetuities and Accumulations Act 2009, although, by s 16 of the 2009 Act, the 1964 Act has no application to trusts falling under the new statutory perpetuity regime.

[48] These clauses defined the perpetuity period by reference to the lives of the living descendants of a member of the royal family such as Queen Victoria.

perpetuity period was specified under s 1, and the trust would have been invalid under the common law rule because it might have vested outside of the perpetuity period,[49] s 3 provided a 'wait and see' procedure. The trust would only be void if it does not in fact vest within the perpetuity period.[50] Section 3 provided its own list of statutory lives by which the perpetuity period is to be measured.

(ii) Excessive accumulations

At common law, the rules of perpetuity applied equally to accumulations of income, so that income could not be accumulated on capital for longer than the perpetuity period.[51] However, with the passing of the Accumulations Act 1800, a complicated statutory rule was introduced which created a new rule against 'excessive accumulations' of income.[52] This statutory code, though repealed, forms the basis of the provision of six permitted periods of accumulation of income under what is now s 164 of the Law of Property Act 1925. These are:

(i)   the life of the grantor or settlor; or

(ii) a term of twenty-one years from the death of the grantor, settlor or testator; or

(iii) the duration of the minority (or respective minorities) of any person living or en ventre sa mère at the death of the grantor, settlor testator, or

(iv) the duration of the minority (or respective minorities) of any person who under the limitation of the trust or will if of full age would be entitled to the income directed to be accumulated; or

(v)   twenty-one years from the making of the disposition;[53] or

(vi) the minority (or respective minorities) of any person in being at the date of the disposition.

(iii) Rule against inalienability

In addition to the other two rules, the law does not allow property to be tied up, and hence become inalienable,[54] forever. A trust must not have a duration longer than the perpetuity period of a life in being plus twenty-one years. This has already been examined in the previous chapter in the context of non-charitable purpose trusts. Charitable trusts are exempt from this requirement and may be perpetual. The Perpetuities and Accumulations Act 1964 did not affect the rule against inalienability (or 'the rule against perpetual trusts', as it is sometimes known), nor did the Law

---

[49] It will be invalid, even though it may be highly likely in fact to vest within the perpetuity period.

[50] In other words, it is not sufficient to invalidate the gift that it might not vest within the perpetuity period; it must actually fail to vest.

[51] The distinction between income and capital was considered previously in Chapter 14.

[52] The Act was a direct, Parliamentary response to the decision in *Thellusson v Woodford* (1799) 4 Ves 227; 11 Ves 112. See further Polden 'Panic or Prudence? The Thellusson Act 1800 and Trusts for Accumulation' (1994) 45 NILQ 13.   [53] These last two periods were inserted by the 1964 Act.

[54] This means that the property cannot be transferred or sold (alienated) and enter the general property market.

Commission consider the rule as part of its reform, on the basis that its only real application was to non-charitable purpose trusts and unincorporated associations. These rules are unaffected by the new statutory scheme,[55] so the same period of life in being plus twenty-one years applies.

(b) Perpetuity rules on or after 6 April 2010

The Law Commission recommended that the rule against perpetuities be retained so as to ensure that there is 'some restriction on the freedom of one generation to control the devolution of property at the expense of the generations that follow'. The major components of the reform of the rule are:

(1) Under s 1 of the Perpetuities and Accumulations Act 2009, the perpetuity rule, with limited exceptions, only applies to private trusts and operates to exclude all previous common law rules.[56]

(2) Where the rule applies, under s 5 of the 2009 Act a single perpetuity period of 125 years is adopted, and applies whether or not adopted in the express wording of the trust instrument.

(3) In respect of the rule against remoteness of vesting, under s 7 of the 2009 Act the 'wait and see' principle will continue to operate.

(4) In respect of excessive accumulations, s 13 abolishes the statutory permitted periods for accumulation, and income can now be accumulated for the perpetuity period.

(5) There are restrictions on accumulation for charitable trusts under s14, justifiable on the basis that there is a public interest in making sure that charities should use income to further their charitable purposes, not simply to add to the capital value of the charity. Charitable trusts may only accumulate income for twenty-one years from the date the trustees had the power to or were directed to accumulate income or for the life of the settlor or settlors. The restriction on accumulations does not apply if the court or the Charity Commission provide for a different period of accumulation.

There is a possibility in limited circumstances for a private trust created before 6 April 2010 to be partially brought within the scheme. Section 12 of the 2009 Act gives trustees of an existing trust a fiduciary power[57] to adopt by deed a perpetuity period of 100 years (and no other period) *if* the trust contains an express perpetuity period of lives in being plus twenty-one years *and* they believe that it is difficult or impracticable to ascertain the existence or whereabouts of the measuring lives.

---

[55] Perpetuities and Accumulations Act 2009, s 18.

[56] The perpetuity period will cease to apply to commercial dealings or interests in property such as options to purchase, and occupational pension schemes are also exempt from the rule.

[57] Hence, the trustees are under a duty to consider whether to opt in to the new statutory regime. The duties of donees of fiduciary powers are discussed further in Chapter 16.

(c) Complexity

Unfortunately, while the 2009 Act is a welcome simplification and modernization of the law, the fact that many existing trusts fall outside the scheme means that students and practitioners alike will have to struggle with three different sets of perpetuity rules and periods (two different schemes for remoteness of vesting and accumulations, plus a different time period for the inability rules) for some time into the future.

(2) Conditional and determinable interests

Owners may choose not to make absolute gifts to others, but instead to make gifts that are subject to conditions subsequent or determinable on the happening of a particular event. For example, Terrance may leave his cottage to trustees on trust for his mistress, Joyce, on the condition that she does not marry. This is a very powerful method of controlling a donee's behaviour, since he has a strong financial incentive not to breach the condition and forfeit the interest. However, if the condition is illegal, or one that would constrain the donee's behaviour in a way contrary to public policy, it will be void.

(a) Conditions void for uncertainty

If the condition or determining event is uncertain, then it will be void. Lord Cranworth stated the principle in *Clavering v Ellison*[58] that the court must be able to 'see from the beginning, precisely and distinctly, upon the happening of what event it was that [the gift] was to determine'.[59] Conditions which have been held void for uncertainty include: a requirement that the donee 'conform to' the Church of England;[60] not marry a person 'not of Jewish parentage';[61] not have a 'social or other relationship with a named person',[62] 'continue to reside in Canada'[63] or 'take up permanent residence in England'.[64]

(b) Conditions void as contrary to public policy

Certain types of condition have also been held to be void because they offend against public policy.

(i) Conditions restricting alienation

If a condition attached to a gift is tantamount to a complete restriction on alienation or transfer of the property, it will be void as contrary to public policy.[65] In *Re Brown*[66]

---

[58] (1859) 7 HL Cas 707.   [59] (1859) 7 HL Cas 707, at 725.   [60] *Re Tegg* [1936] 2 All ER 878.
[61] *Clayton v Ramsden* [1943] AC 320, HL.   [62] *Re Jones* [1953] Ch 125.
[63] *Sifton v Sifton* [1938] AC 656.   [64] *Re Gape* [1952] Ch 743.
[65] *Muschamp v Bluet* (1617) J Bridge 132; *Hood v Oglander* (1865) 34 Beav 513; *Re Rosher* (1884) 26 Ch D 801; *Corbett v Corbett* (1888) 14 PD 7; *Re Dugdale* (1888) LR 38 Ch D 176; *Re Cockerill* [1929] 2 Ch 131.
[66] [1954] Ch 39.

a father bequeathed his freehold properties to his four sons in equal shares, with a condition that they were not to alienate their shares other than to each other. Harman J held that this amounted to a general prohibition on alienation because they were a small and diminishing class, and the condition was void.[67]

(ii) Conditions restraining marriage

Marriage has always been the fundamental building block of society, and conditions which seek to undermine marriage are void as contrary to public policy.[68] Conditions that completely restrain the donee's freedom to marry are void.[69] However, conditions that restrain the donee's freedom to *remarry* have in the past been upheld.[70]

Conditions that restrain marriage to particular individuals[71] or classes are also valid. In *Jenner v Turner*[72] a testatrix left property to her brother on condition that he did not marry a 'domestic servant'. This was held to be a valid condition by Bacon V-C. In *Duggan v Kelly*[73] a condition not to marry a 'Papist' was upheld, as was a condition not to marry a 'Scotchman' in *Perrin v Lyon*.[74] Conditions that encourage separation or divorce of husband and wife are void.[75] Thus, in *Re Johnson's Will Trusts*[76] a donor established a trust in favour of his daughter which would pay her £50 per year as long as she continued to be married to her husband, but would pay her the full income from the fund if she were divorced or separated. Buckley J held that the condition was void as it amounted to an incentive to the break-up of the marriage.[77]

(iii) Conditions restraining religion[78]

Conditions that restrict the choice of religion of a beneficiary have never been regarded as void because they offend against public policy.[79] In *Blathwayt v Baron Cawley*[80] a condition that a beneficiary forfeit his interest if he 'be or become a Roman Catholic'

---

[67] Contrast *Re Macleay* (1875) LR 20 Eq 186, where a restriction to alienation within 'the family' was upheld. Harman J considered that this was a large and indeterminable group of people that may increase.

[68] See *Long v Dennis* (1767) 4 Burr 2052, at 2059, per Lord Mansfield: 'conditions in restraint of marriage are odious…'.

[69] *Low v Peers* (1770) Wilm 364, at 372: an absolute restraint on marriage 'tends to evil and the promoting of licentiousness; it tends to depopulation, the greatest of all political sins…'.

[70] *Jordan v Holkham* (1753) Amb 209: provision of testator's will that his wife would forfeit her interest if she remarried was upheld. Contrast the Irish case of *Duddy v Gresham* (1878) 2 LR Ir 442, where a condition in the testator's will that his wife not remarry but enter a convent of her choice was held void.

[71] *Re Bathe* [1925] Ch 377; *Re Hanlon* [1933] Ch 254: a gift by testator to her daughter subject to the condition that she does not 'intermarry with AB' upheld by Eve J.   [72] (1880) 16 Ch D 188.

[73] (1848) 10 I Eq R 473.   [74] (1807) 9 East 170.

[75] *Wren v Bradley* (1848) 2 De G & Sm 49; *Re Moore* (1888) 39 Ch D 116; *Re Caborne* [1943] Ch 224; *Re Johnson's Will Trusts* [1967] Ch 387; *Re Hepplewhite Will Trust* [1977] CLY 2710.

[76] [1967] Ch 387.   [77] [1967] Ch 387, at 396.

[78] See later in the chapter about the impact of the Equality Act 2010.

[79] The boundary between race and religion is uncertain. In *Mandla v Dowell Lee* [1983] 2 AC 548 Sikhs were held to be a racial group, and in *King-Ansell v Police* [1979] 2 NZLR 531 Jews were also held to be a racial group. However, the distinction is of no practical importance for the law of trusts since conditions on grounds of neither religion nor of race are invalid.   [80] [1976] AC 397, HL.

was upheld by the House of Lords. It was neither uncertain nor contrary to public policy. Lord Wilberforce explained that:

> to introduce for the first time a rule of law which would go far beyond the mere avoidance of discrimination on religious grounds...would bring about a substantial reduction of another freedom, firmly rooted in our law, namely that of testamentary disposition. Discrimination is not the same thing as choice: it operates over a larger and less personal area, and neither by express provision nor by implication has private selection yet become a matter of public policy.[81]

However, if the condition restrictive of religion is uncertain it will not be binding. In *Clayton v Ramsden*[82] a provision forfeiting the beneficiary's interest on marriage to a person 'not of Jewish parentage' was held void for uncertainty.[83]

(iv) Conditions affecting parental duties

Conditions which seek to separate parent from child are void as contrary to public policy.[84] In *Re Sandbrook*[85] the condition that a gift of the income of a fund was to be forfeited if children lived with their father was held void. Such a condition is void even if the parents are divorced.[86] Some cases have suggested that conditions that interfere with the exercise of parental duties are void. In *Re Borwick*[87] a condition that a minor forfeit an interest if she 'become a Roman Catholic or not be openly or avowedly Protestant' was held void as it operated to interfere with the exercise of a parent's duty in the religious instruction of his children.[88] In *Blathwayt v Baron Cawley*[89] the House of Lords limited the range of this principle, holding that:

> To say that any condition which in any way might affect or influence the way in which a child is to be brought up, or in which parental duties are exercised, is void seems to me to state far too wide a rule.[90]

(v) Conditions discriminatory on grounds of religion, race, sex and other protected characteristics under the Equality Act 2010

Whilst it is probably the case that the Equality Act 2010, which generally prohibits discrimination on the grounds of religion, race, sex and other protected characteristics,[91] does not apply to private trusts, it is also unlikely that a court would enforce a discriminatory trust. This may mean that discriminatory clauses in private trusts are valid but unenforceable.

---

[81] [1976] AC 397, HL, at 426.   [82] [1943] AC 320, HL.

[83] See also *Re Tegg* [1936] 2 All ER 878, where a condition 'to conform' to the Church of England was held void for uncertainty.   [84] See *Re Morgan* (1910) 26 TLR 398; *Re Boulter* [1922] 1 Ch 75.

[85] [1912] 2 Ch 471.

[86] *Re Piper* [1946] 2 All ER 503, which concerned a gift by will to children provided they do not live with their father before attaining the age of 30. Mother had divorced father before the date of the will.

[87] [1933] Ch 657.   [88] The condition was also held void on the grounds of uncertainty.

[89] [1976] AC 397.   [90] [1976] AC 397, at 426, per Lord Wilberforce.

[91] Equality Act 2010, s 4 lists the protected characteristics.

(vi) *Impact of the Human Rights Act*

Many of the decisions in this area date from the nineteenth century, and some may be open to reconsideration in the light of changing social mores and more specifically as a consequence of the incorporation of the European Convention on Human Rights and Fundamental Freedoms 1950 into British law by the Human Rights Act 1998. Whilst the Act, and therefore the Convention, are not directly applicable to private trusts, the fundamental rights and freedoms set out in the Convention may have an impact upon judicial views of public policy. Conditions which aim to restrain marriage to particular individuals, or encourage divorce, could be characterized as an interference with the right to respect for private and family life under Article 8 ECHR, or the right to marry under Article 9, and would reinforce the current approach of the courts to such clauses.

(c) **Effect of an invalid condition**

The exact consequences of a condition being found to be void will depend on whether the gift was made subject to a condition subsequent or was a determinable interest.

(i) *Determinable interests*

If the gift is characterized as 'determinable' and the determining event is unlawful for reasons of public policy, the gift will fail and the property reverts to the original owner. Thus, in *Re Moore*[92] a trust to pay a weekly sum to a woman 'whilst. whilst whilst. whil sta weekly sum to a woman 'whilst. he detle interest and the gift was void.

(ii) *Conditional interests*

If the gift is subject to a condition subsequent and the condition is unlawful, the gift is not void and the condition is merely struck out. The gift will thus become absolute.[93] In *Re Beard*[94] a testator made a gift of his estates to his nephew, Herbert, 'provided that he does not enter into the naval or military services of the country'. As the condition was held contrary to public policy,[95] it was struck out and the nephew took an absolute interest in the estates.

(d) **Distinguishing conditional and determinable gifts**

Given the different consequences for determinable and conditional gifts, if the condition or determining event is unlawful, it is necessary to distinguish between them. The distinction is notoriously difficult to pin-point and has been described as 'little short of disgraceful to our jurisprudence'.[96] The essence of the distinction is that a determinable gift is defined as lasting only for the duration of a certain state of affairs, whilst a conditional gift is one which may be cut short if a given event occurs. For instance,

---

[92] (1888) 39 Ch D 116.   [93] See *Re Croxon* [1904] 1 Ch 252; *Re Turton* [1926] Ch 96.
[94] [1908] 1 Ch 383.
[95] [1908] 1 Ch 383, at 387, per Swinfen Eady J: 'there can be few, if any, provisions more against public good and the welfare of the State than one tending to deter persons from entering the naval or military service of the country'.   [96] Porter MR in *Re King's Trusts* (1892) 29 LR Ir 401, at 410.

a gift to Myfanwy 'whilst she remains a widow' would be a determinable gift; on the other hand a gift to Myfanwy 'provided that she does not remarry' would be a gift subject to a condition subsequent.

Put another way, in a determinable gift the gift is never contemplated as being absolute, but only as lasting until the determining event occurs.[97] Thus, a gift to George 'until he becomes a brain surgeon' will be a determinable gift. If the determining event occurs, the gift will automatically revert to the original donor. In a conditional gift, the gift is contemplated as being absolute from the very beginning, but the occurrence of the condition brings it to an end. A gift to George 'unless he becomes a brain surgeon' would be a conditional gift. In cases concerning conditional gifts of land, it has been held that a gift does not end automatically when the condition occurs, but that the donor or his successor in title must 're-enter' by taking steps to terminate the interest.[98] This dogma has no application to a conditional gift by way of trust, where the condition represents a direction to trustees that they will carry out without any further intervention by the original donor.

6 Introduction to powers of advancement and maintenance

A testator with young children may leave his estate to them subject to a stipulation that they will only become entitled to the property on attaining the age of 21. Although the trustees will hold the fund on trust for them from the time of his death, they will not be entitled to the capital until they attain the specified age and the trustees will be under no duty to transfer it to them. However, whilst the settlor may have created such a contingent interest with the object of preventing his children receiving their inheritance before they are sufficiently mature to manage it for themselves, such an arrangement may cause practical difficulties. In our example, the children may have no actual income on which to live in the interim period before they are entitled to their share of the fund.

To overcome such difficulties, the law grants trustees powers that enable them to apply the fund on behalf of beneficiaries even where they have not yet satisfied the specified contingency. The power of maintenance allows the trustees to apply the income generated by the fund on behalf of the beneficiary, and the power of advancement, as amended by the Inheritance and Trustees' Powers Act 2014, allows the trustees to transfer or apply part or all[99] of the capital money, or other property forming part of the capital of the trust, for the benefit of a beneficiary. Although both such powers can be granted expressly in a trust deed, the Trustee Act 1925 grants trustees powers

---

[97] If the determining event becomes impossible in fact, the gift automatically becomes absolute: *Re Leach* [1912] 2 Ch 422.   [98] See Challis's *Real Property* (3rd edn, 1911), pp 219, 261.
[99] There is a distinction between trusts arising before and after the commencement of the 2014 Act— this will be discussed later in this chapter.

of maintenance[100] and advancement[101] which, following reform, will usually be sufficient. The court also possesses an inherent jurisdiction to provide advancement and maintenance. Reform to the powers of maintenance and advancement followed from two consultation exercises undertaken by the Law Commission.[102] Originally, changes had only been suggested to the statutory trusts that arose on intestacy, but consultation suggested a change to power of trustees of all trusts, including those made by will or during lifetime. This is what was recommended by the Commission in its final report and Bill, which has now been enacted.[103] Most of these reforms have prospective effect only, but existing trusts may be brought within the scheme under certain circumstances,[104] for example, where a new trust interest is created by a trustee exercising a power of appointment amongst a class of beneficiaries.[105]

7 The trustees' power of maintenance

(1) Express powers of maintenance

A settlor may include express powers of advancement in the trust instrument. However, given the width of the statutory powers it is not usually necessary to do so.[106]

(2) Trustee Act 1925, s 31

Section 31 of the Trustee Act 1925[107] draws a distinction between the position of a minor who is contingently interested under a trust, and the position of an adult who is similarly contingently interested.[108]

(a) The position of a contingently interested minor—s 31(1)(i)

Section 31(1)(i) grants the trustees of every trust where property is held for any person, whether their interest is vested or contingent, the power to apply the whole

---

[100] Trustee Act 1925, s 31; as amended by Inheritance and Trustee's Powers Act 2014, s 8.

[101] Trustee Act 1925, s 32; as amended by the Inheritance and Trustees' Powers Act 2014, s 9.

[102] Law Com Consultation Paper No 191, *Intestacy and Family Provision Claims on Death*, (2009) and Consultation Paper No 191 (Supplemental), *Intestacy and Family Provisions Claims on Death: Sections 31 and 32 of the Trustee Act 1925*, (May 2011).

[103] Law Com No. 331 *Intestacy and Family Provision Claims on Death* (2011).

[104] Inheritance and Trustees' Powers Act 2014, s 10(5). At the time of writing, the Act has not received a commencement order. The forgoing treatment assumes the provisions of the Act are in force.

[105] Such powers, which have been considered in earlier chapters, are addressed in detail in the next chapter, alongside discretionary trusts.

[106] Where express maintenance provisions are inserted, the major issue is normally whether they create fiduciary powers or impose trust obligations—see, for example, *Wilson v Turner* (1883) 22 Ch D. 521.

[107] Trustee Act 1925, s 31 replaces the Conveyancing Act 1881, s 43 (which still applies to instruments coming into force before 1926), which itself replaced a provision in Lord Cranworth's Act of 1860.

[108] By s 31(4) the same principles are applied to income generated by an annuity vested in a minor, with the exception that s 31(2)(ii) has no application and the accumulated income is the absolute property of the infant.

or the part of the income generated by the fund to his parent or guardian for his 'maintenance education or benefit'.[109] This power is to be exercised solely at their discretion, though the exercise was required to be 'reasonable' as well as for the benefit of the minor[110] Following the Inheritance and Trustees' Powers Act 2014, for all trusts created after the commencement of that Act, the requirement of reasonableness is removed, as the words 'as they trustees think fit' replace the original statutory wording.[111]

(b) The position of a contingently interested adult—s 31(1)(ii)

Section 31(1)(ii) directs that if the beneficiary has reached the age of majority,[112] the trustees are to pay the income generated by the fund to him, until his interest either vests or fails. Payment of such income is not a matter for the trustees' discretion, although it may be excluded if there is a counter-intention indicated by the testator in the trust document.[113]

It has been held that the power to pay over the income to an adult beneficiary who is contingently interested in the fund is excluded if there is a direction in the trust instrument to accumulate the income.[114] Thus, in *Re Turner's Will Trusts*[115] the Court of Appeal held that a beneficiary who was 24 years old was not entitled to the income from a fund in which he would obtain a vested interest on attaining the age of 28 yeard old because the settlor had directed that the income be accumulated.[116] Similarly, in *Re Erskine's Settlement Trusts*[117] a direction to accumulate the income from a fund was held to exclude the power under s 31, even though the direction was itself void under s 164 of the Law of Property Act 1925. Even in the absence of a direction to accumulate, the obligation to pay over the income under s 31(1)(ii) may be excluded. In *Re McGeorge*[118] a gift of agricultural land by a testator to his daughter, which was not to take effect until the death of his wife, was held to express a contrary intention because 'by deferring the enjoyment of the devise until after the widow's death the testator has expressed the intention that the daughter shall not have the immediate income'.[119]

---

[109] S 31(1)(i). See *Fuller v Evans* [2000] 1 All ER 636 (it does not matter if there is also an incidental benefit to the parent or guardian, as here where the father was under a requirement to pay tuition fees as part of a divorce settlement).   [110] See *Wilson v Turner* (1883) 22 Ch D 521.

[111] Inheritance and Trustees' Powers Act 2014, s 8(a).   [112] That is, 18 years of age.

[113] As the Trustee Act 1925 makes clear by s 69(2): 'All the powers conferred by this Act on trustees are in addition to the powers conferred by the instrument, if any, creating the trust, but those powers unless otherwise stated, apply, if and so far only as a contrary intention is not expressed in the instrument, if any, creating the trust, and have effect subject to the terms of that instrument.'

[114] See *Re Watt's Will Trusts* [1936] 2 All ER 1555; *Re Turner's Will Trusts* [1937] Ch 15; *Re Ransome* [1957] Ch 348; *Re Erskine's Settlement Trusts* [1971] 1 WLR 162.   [115] [1937] Ch 15.

[116] Although he had granted the trustees an express power to apply the income for the 'maintenance, benefit and education' of the beneficiaries, and it was the surplus income which was to be accumulated.

[117] [1971] 1 WLR 162.   [118] [1963] Ch 544.

[119] [1963] Ch 544, at 552–553, per Cross J. He also held that s 31 did not apply because the daughter's interest was not contingent, but rather, subject to being divested.

(c) Gifts carrying intermediate income

By s 31(3) the powers of maintenance granted to trustees under s 31(1) are only available if the contingent interest 'carries the intermediate income'. This means that the beneficiary must be entitled to the income earned by the share of the fund to which he is contingently entitled between the date of the gift and the date when his share is paid over to him.[120] Whether a gift carries the intermediate income depends on a series of technical rules, derived from both statute and cases.

(i) Vested gifts

A gift that is vested carries the intermediate income unless there is a contrary intention, for example if the income is directed to be applied to someone else.[121]

(ii) Contingent gifts of residuary personalty

A contingent gift of residuary personal property[122] made by will always carries the intermediate income from the date of the testator's death.[123] This was explained in *Re Adams*,[124] where North J stated that since the income was 'undisposed of' it would itself become part of the residue. However, if the gift is deferred to 'a future date which must come sooner or later',[125] it does not carry the intermediate income.[126]

(iii) Specific devises or bequests

Section 175 of the Law of Property Act 1925 provides that contingent or future specific devices or bequests of property, whether personal or real, carry the intermediate income from the date of the death of the testator unless that income has been otherwise expressly disposed of.[127] The section has been held not to apply to pecuniary legacies.[128]

(iv) Contingent pecuniary legacies

Since pecuniary legacies are not included within the scope of s 175, as a general principle a contingent pecuniary legacy will not carry the intermediate income.[129] There are three exceptions to this principle. First, gifts by fathers to their children. If a pecuniary legacy is left by a father to his child, the gift carries the intermediate income if there is no other fund provided for the child's maintenance,[130] and the contingency is the child attaining the age of majority.[131] The rationale behind this exception is clearly

---

[120] (1953) 17 Conv 273 (Ker); PVB 'Carrying the Intermediate Income' (1963) 79 LQR 184.

[121] A direction to accumulate merely indicates an exclusion of the power of maintenance, and not that the gift does not carry the intermediate income.

[122] This includes leasehold property, which ranks as personal property: *Guthrie v Walrond* (1883) 22 Ch D 573; *Re Woodin* [1895] 2 Ch 309.

[123] *Countess of Bective v Hodgson* (1864) 10 HL Cas 656; *Re Taylor* [1901] 2 Ch 134.

[124] [1893] 1 Ch 329.   [125] *Re McGeorge* [1963] Ch 544, at 551, per Cross J.

[126] *Re Gillett's Will Trust* [1950] Ch 102; *Re Geering* [1964] Ch 136; *Re McGeorge* [1963] Ch 544; *Re Nash* [1965] 1 All ER 51. Compare also *Re Lindo* (1888) 59 LT 462.

[127] *Re Reade-Revell* [1930] 1 Ch 52; *Re Stapleton* [1946] 1 All ER 323.

[128] *Re Raine* [1929] 1 Ch 716.   [129] *Re George* (1877) 5 Ch D 837, CA.

[130] *Re Moody* [1895] 1 Ch 101; *Re George* (1877) 5 Ch D 837; *Re West* [1913] 2 Ch 345.

[131] *Re Abrahams* [1911] 1 Ch 108.

similar to that which reveals itself in the presumption of advancement which rebuts an inference of a resulting trust when a gift is made by a father to his child,[132] namely, the obligation of the father to provide. The exception will also apply when a gift of a contingent pecuniary legacy is made by a person standing in loco parentis to the minor.[133] Second, gifts made with the intention of providing maintenance. If the will expressly or impliedly indicates that the income be used for the maintenance of the minor, the gift will carry the intermediate income. In *Re Churchill*[134] a gift of a pecuniary legacy to a grandnephew was held to carry the intermediate income where the will directed the trustees at their discretion to pay any part of it 'towards the advancement in life or otherwise for the benefit' of the legatee.[135] It is not necessary that the legacy be contingent upon the attainment of majority.[136] Third, 'set aside' gifts. Where a pecuniary legacy is set aside by the testator[137] as a segregated fund for his benefit, to be available on the happening of the contingency, the gift will carry the intermediate income.[138]

(d) Undistributed income

Since s 31(1)(i) grants the trustee a discretion to pay maintenance out of the intermediate income to the parent or guardian of a minor who has a contingent interest, the question arises as to what should happen to any surplus income the trustees decide not to apply for the beneficiary's maintenance. Such eventuality is covered by the provisions of s 31(2).

(i) Accumulation of surplus income

Under s 31(2) the trustees are directed to accumulate and invest any income from the fund which has not been applied to a beneficiary's maintenance. Such accumulated income is then available to be distributed for the beneficiary's maintenance, and may be applied as if it were income arising in the current year.

(ii) Beneficiary's entitlement to accumulated surplus income

Section 31(2)(i)(b) provides that if the beneficiary is entitled to a vested interest in the capital of the fund on attaining his majority (or on marriage under that age), he will be entitled to the accumulated surplus income. If, however, his interest is not vested, or liable to be determined, he will not be entitled to the accumulated income.[139] One anomalous result of the wording of s 31(2)(i)(b) is that a distinction is drawn between determinable gifts of realty and personalty. The section states that the beneficiary must be entitled to the property from which the income arose 'in fee simple, absolute or determinable, or absolutely enefic' In *Re Sharp's Settlement Trusts*[140] it was held that the words 'in fee simple, absolute or determinable' apply only to realty, and the

---

[132] This was discussed in Chapter 8.   [133] *Re Eyre* [1917] 1 Ch 351.   [134] [1909] 2 Ch 431.
[135] See also *Re Selby-Walker* [1949] 2 All ER 178.   [136] *Re Jones* [1932] 1 Ch 642.
[137] *Re Judkin's Trusts* (1884) 25 Ch D 743.
[138] *Re Medlock* (1886) 54 LT 828; *Re Clements* [1894] 1 Ch 665; *Re Woodin* [1895] 2 Ch 309, CA. Compare also *Re Judkin's Trusts* (1884) 25 Ch D 743.   [139] *Re Sharp's Settlement Trusts* [1973] Ch 331.
[140] [1973] Ch 331; (1972) 36 Conv 436 (Hayton).

word 'absolute' applies exclusively to 'personalty'. This means that a beneficiary has no entitlement on reaching majority to the accumulated income on a fund of personal property in which he has only a determinable interest. On the facts, a beneficiary who had attained the age of 21 was not entitled to the accumulated income from the fund because his contingent interest was liable to be defeated by the exercise of a power of appointment.[141]

(iii) Death of a minor before attaining a vested interest

Where a beneficiary dies before attaining majority (or earlier marriage) and income has been accumulated on his behalf, s 31(2)(ii) provides that the accumulated income should be added to the capital of the fund, and not pass as part of the minor's estate.[142] This provision will not apply if a contrary intention is shown from the trust instrument.[143] Thus in *Re Delamere's Settlement Trusts*[144] the trustees of a settlement appointed the income from a trust fund to six infant beneficiaries 'in equal shares absolutely'. The Court of Appeal held that this excluded the operation of s 31(2)(ii) and that the infant beneficiaries had indefeasible interests in the accumulated income.

(3) The court's inherent jurisdiction

The court has an inherent jurisdiction to allow trust income to be used for a minor's maintenance,[145] and in exceptional circumstances the court may even allow capital to be so used.[146] The courts have generally refused to allow trust income to be used for a child's maintenance where the father has sufficient means to provide for the child.[147] The width of the general statutory power of maintenance has rendered the court's inherent jurisdiction insignificant.

8 The trustees' power of advancement

(1) Meaning of advancement

A power of maintenance enables the trustees to apply the income generated by a trust fund for the maintenance of the beneficiaries, even where they are not as yet entitled to the capital of the fund. A power of advancement enables the trustees to advance part of the capital, whether as monetary funds or by transfer of property to beneficiaries who are contingently interested in the trust fund. As Lord Radcliffe observed

---

[141] See also *Phipps v Ackers* (1842) 9 Cl & Fin 583; *Re Heath* [1936] Ch 259; *Re Kilpatrick's Policies* [1966] Ch 730; *Brotherton v IRC* [1978] 1 WLR 610.   [142] *Re Joel's Will Trusts* [1967] Ch 14.
[143] Trustee Act 1925, s 69(2).   [144] [1984] 1 WLR 813; [1985] Conv 153 (Griffith).
[145] *Wellesley v Wellesley* (1828) 2 Bli 124, at 133–134, per Lord Redesdale.
[146] *Ex p Green* (1820) 1 Jac & W 253; *Ex p Chambers* (1829) 1 Russ & M 577; *Robinson v Killey* (1862) 30 Beav 520.   [147] *Douglas v Andrews* (1849) 12 Beav 310, at 311.

in *Pilkington v IRC*, the purpose of a power of advancement is that the trustees can in a proper case:

> anticipate the vesting in possession of an intended beneficiary's contingent or reversionary interest by...paying or applying it immediately for his benefit. By so doing they released it from the trusts of the settlement and accelerate the enjoyment of his interest...[148]

(2) Express powers of advancement

A settlor may grant the trustees express powers of advancement in the trust instrument. However, since the enactment of a statutory power,[149] which grants the trustees of a power of advancement modeled on the standard form of such express powers, express powers have only been necessary if a settlor wishes the trustees to have wider powers than those granted by the statute. In the past, this was in fact often to give the trustees power to advance more than half a beneficiary's presumptive share,[150] but this limitation has been removed in all trusts created after the commencement of the Inheritance and Trustees' Powers Act 2014.[151] It is questionable, therefore, how often express powers will be used in the future.

(3) Trustee Act 1925, s 32

(a) Scope of the statutory power of advancement

Section 32(1) grants trustees the power, in their absolute discretion, to apply the capital of a trust fund or transfer or apply any other trust property making up the capital on behalf of any beneficiary who has an absolute or contingent interest in the fund. Originally, it was only possible to advance capital monies, but the Law Commission recommended an expansion of the wording to avoid the practice where a trustee, wishing to transfer a property asset to the beneficiary under this power, instead had to advance cash to the beneficiary for them to purchase the asset.[152] This alteration of the wording has both prospective and retrospective effect, so that it applies to all trusts, whether created before or after the commencement of the Inheritance and Trustee's Powers Act 2014.[153]

It makes no difference that the beneficiary's contingent interest may at some later date be defeated, for example by the exercise of a power of appointment, or that his precise share of the fund may diminish because of an increase in the number of a class to

---

[148] [1964] AC 612, at 633.

[149] Trustee Act 1925, s 32, as amended by the Inheritance and Trustees' Powers Act 2014, s 9.

[150] See Trustee Act 1925, s 32(1)(a), as originally enacted. The Law Commission found in its second consultation exercise on reform of powers of maintenance that professionally drafted trusts expressly widened this power as a matter of course (see *Analysis of Responses*, paras 5.32–5.50; 8.20–8.28); strengthening the proposal for reform.

[151] S 10(3), giving effect to s 9(3)(b), which amends the wording of the Trustee Act 1925, s 32(1)(a) to that effect.   [152] See *Re Collard's Will Trusts* [1961] Ch 293.

[153] S 10(2), giving effect to all parts of s 9 (except s 9(3)(b)), which amends all relevant subsections of s 32 to include the application or transfer of property.

which he belongs.[154] The section introduces some practical limitations on the trustee's power of advancement:

(i) Proportion of share which may be advanced

Section 32(1)(a), as we have seen, originally provided that the trustees must not advance to a beneficiary more than a half of his presumptive or vested interest under the fund.[155] This has since been altered in any trust arising after the commencement of the Inheritance and Trustees' Powers Act 2014 to allow the power to be extended to the whole of the beneficiary's share in the trust fund.[156]

(ii) Accounting for advancements in the final distribution of the trust fund

Where a beneficiary is contingently entitled to a share of the trust fund, s 32(1)(b) provides that any property advanced be taken into account in calculating the size of any share to which he becomes absolutely entitled.[157] This obviously prevents unfairness between the beneficiaries.

(iii) Protection of those with a prior interest in the trust fund

Where an advancement would be to the prejudice of those who have a prior life or other interest in the fund, s 32(1)(c) requires that they give consent in writing to any advancement.[158] This protects, for example, a life tenant, who is entitled to the income of the fund during his lifetime. Clearly, if an advancement of capital is made to a contingently entitled remainderman, the life tenant will suffer as the income generated by the fund will decrease with the reduction in the capital.

(b) Type of fund where capital may be advanced

Section 32(2) provides that the power of advancement does not apply to funds consisting of capital money under the Settled Land Act 1925.

(c) The requirement of benefit

The most important restriction of the trustees' power of advancement is the requirement that the application of capital must be for the 'advancement or benefit' of the

---

[154] For example, a trust may grant contingent interests to the children of the settlor, and the class may subsequently increase with the birth of further children.

[155] See *Re Marquess of Abergavenny's Estate Act Trusts* [1981] 1 WLR 843; [1982] Conv 158 (Price). There will therefore no longer be any need to approve a variation of trusts which will allow the advancement of more than a half of the trust fund if this would be of 'benefit' to the beneficiary, as happened in *CD (A Child) v O* [2004] 3 All ER 780. This will be covered in Chapter 17.

[156] S 9(3)((b), which removes the phrase 'one-half of' from the Trustee Act 1925, s 32(1)(a) so that it reads that the advancement 'must not, altogether, represent more than the presumptive or vested share or interest of that person in the trust property'.

[157] See *Re Fox* [1904] 1 Ch 480. The Inheritance and Trustees' Powers Act 2014 adds, by s 10(6), s 32(1A) into the Trustee Act 1925 which sets out a requirement to add together all cash and non-cash advancements to find the total amount advanced for this purpose.

[158] The court cannot dispense with the need for consent: *Re Forster's Settlement* [1942] Ch 199. A member of a discretionary class does not need to give consent: *Re Harris's Settlement* (1940) 162 LT 358; *Re Beckett's Settlement* [1940] Ch 279.

beneficiary. The meaning of this phrase was considered by Lord Radcliffe in *Pilkington v IRC*, where he held that the phrase 'advancement and benefit':

> means any use of the money which will improve the material situation of the beneficiary.[159]

The case concerned a proposed advancement of part of the contingent share of an infant beneficiary, Penelope Pilkington. She was entitled to a share of a fund established by her great uncle, provided she reached the age of 21, but the trustees wanted to advance £7,600, to be settled on different trusts in her favour, to avoid death duties. The House of Lords held that this was a proper exercise of the statutory power of advancement, and that there was a benefit to the infant in the avoidance of taxation. Lord Radcliffe observed:

> if the advantage of preserving the funds of a beneficiary from the incidence of death duty is not an advantage personal to that beneficiary, I do not see what is.[160]

It did not matter that the advanced money was to be resettled on different trusts for the infant.[161]

A wide range of purposes have been held to be sufficiently beneficial to permit an advancement. In the nineteenth century, typical examples included the provision of an apprenticeship, the purchase of a commission in the army, or an interest in a business.[162] Benefits have included the discharge of the beneficiary's debts,[163] an advancement to a wife who helped her husband set up in business,[164] an advancement to a girl on her marriage,[165] and an advancement to provide for the beneficiary's maintenance and education.[166] In *Re Halstead's Will Trusts*[167] the court approved an advancement to a man so that he could make provision for his wife and child in the future by settling a sum upon himself for life; and after his death for his wife for life, remainder to his children. Farwell J held that this was within the 'very wide terms in which the word "benefit" has been construed in the past'. The purchases of house and furniture have also been held to be for the benefit of a beneficiary.[168]

In *Re Clore's Settlement Trusts*[169] an advancement to enable a contingently entitled beneficiary to make a donation to charity which they felt morally obliged to make was held to be a benefit. However, in *X v A*,[170] it was held that an advancement of the whole of the trust fund to enable a charitable donation was not of benefit. Hart J reasoned that the extent of the gift meant that the contingently entitled beneficiary would not have their material situation improved by the advancement as required under *Pilkington v IRC*, as the beneficiary would not have been able to meet the moral obligation from their own resources.

---

[159] [1964] AC 612, at 635.   [160] [1964] AC 612, at 640.
[161] *Roper-Curzon v Roper-Curzon* (1871) LR 11 Eq 452; *Re Halstead's Will Trusts* [1937] 2 All ER 57; *Re Ropner's Settlement Trusts* [1956] 1 WLR 902.   [162] *Pilkington v IRC* [1964] AC 612, at 634.
[163] *Lowther v Bentinck* (1874) LR 19 Eq 166.   [164] *Re Kershaw's Trusts* (1868) LR 6 Eq 322.
[165] *Lloyd v Cocker* (1860) 27 Beav 645.
[166] *Re Breed's Will* (1875) 1 Ch D 226; *Re Garrett* [1934] Ch 477.   [167] [1937] 2 All ER 57.
[168] *Re Pauling's Settlement Trust* [1964] Ch 303, CA.   [169] [1966] 1 WLR 955.
[170] [2006] 1 WLR 741.

(d) Fiduciary nature of the power of advancement

A power of advancement is a fiduciary power, and must therefore be exercised by the trustee in a fiduciary manner. In *Re Pauling's Settlement Trusts*,[171] in the context of an express power, the Court of Appeal held that this means that before exercising the power the trustees must 'weigh on the one side the benefit of the proposed advancee, and on the other hand the rights of those who are or may hereafter become interested under the trusts of the settlement'.[172] The trustees are also subject to a duty to ensure that money advanced is applied by the beneficiaries for the purposes for which it was advanced.[173]

(4) The court's inherent jurisdiction

The court possesses an inherent jurisdiction to apply capital[174] for the maintenance or advancement of an infant. For example, in *Clay v Pennington*[175] the court advanced a sum of £125 to cover the cost of an infant's passage to India.[176]

---

[171] [1964] Ch 303.   [172] 1964] Ch 303, at 333, per Willmer LJ.   [173] 1964] Ch 303, at 334.
[174] *Barlow v Grant* (1684) 1 Vern 255.   [175] (1837) 8 Sim 359.
[176] See also *Re Mary England's Estate* (1830) 1 Russ & M 499.

16

Powers of appointment and discretionary trusts

This chapter considers the key features of a discretionary trust, and the similar looking powers of appointment, which are both equitable mechanisms that facilitate the management and allocation of property. They both enable a person who is not the owner of property to identify who will benefit from it. Powers may be held by trustees or independently, discretionary trusts only by trustees. The key feature of both powers of appointment and discretionary trusts is that they are discretionary in character. Trusts, while very similar in nature to powers, differ in that, unlike a power of appointment, a trustee must make a distribution to the identified class, and the court will step in to compel the exercise of a discretionary trust. This chapter explores in detail the nature, creation, use and rights, and obligations imposed by both powers and discretionary trusts. It is sensible to consider powers first, as many of the concepts of discretionary trusts build on powers.

1 Powers of appointment and redistribution

(1) The nature of powers of appointment

Powers of appointment confer on a person who does not own property the authority to choose who shall become the owner. The key feature of a power of appointment is that it is discretionary in character. The donee of a power is under no enforceable obligation to make any appointments of the fund at all. Even if the donee were never to make any appointments at all, he would not be in breach of a duty owed either to the donor or to the potential objects of the power. The court will not step in to compel the exercise of the power, but it will exercise a supervisory jurisdiction to ensure that, if the donee does decide to exercise the power, he does so properly. Powers of appointment are commonly used as a mechanism to determine the allocation of the surplus remaining in a trust fund after the beneficiaries have received their defined interests. Many older cases concern family trusts where the property of a testator was left on trust for a spouse for life, with a power of appointment granted over the remainder interest (see Figure 16.1).[1] This allows the donee of the power to decide how the capital

---

[1] *Re Weekes' Settlement* [1897] 1 Ch 289.

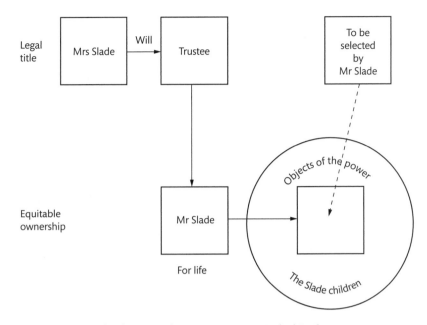

Figure 16.1 An example of powers of appointment: *Re Weekes' Settlement*

of the fund should be allocated on the death of the life tenant. The discretionary nature of the power means that the testator does not have to predetermine how the remainder interest should be distributed, and allows the donee of the power to take account of changing circumstances between the death of the testator and the death of the life tenant. Later cases have tended to concern pension funds, where the donee is given a power of appointment over any surplus that remains after the contributors have received their contractual entitlements.[2] Although the position has now changed, with many pension funds operating in deficit, in the 1990s some pension funds had assets exceeding their liabilities. The power to allocate the surplus by exercise of a power of appointment, whether to the pensioners or the company, was therefore an extremely valuable right.

(a) Classification of powers of appointment

Though all powers of appointment share their discretionary character, several sub-categories of power can be identified, which are differentiated by the nature of the class of potential objects and by the exact duties of the donee.

(i) Classification by the nature of the class of objects

There are three types of power of appointment: general, special, and hybrid powers. They are differentiated by the range of potential objects in whose favour the power may be exercised:

---

[2] *Hillsdown Holdings plc v Pensions Ombudsman* [1997] 1 All ER 862; *Edge v Pensions Ombudsman* [1998] 2 All ER 547; *Pitt v Holt* [2012] Ch 132.

General powers

Under a general power of appointment the donee enjoys the right to allocate the property by appointment to anyone he wishes. The donee may even appoint the property to himself. This extremely wide power is tantamount to absolute ownership by the donee.

Special powers

Where the donor of a power has specified that it should only be exercised in favour of a class of people, it is said to be a special power. The donee has absolute discretion whether to make any appointments of the property but any appointments made must be to persons within the specified class. In *Re Weekes' Settlement*,[3] Mrs Slade granted a life interest of her estate to her husband and gave him a power of appointment over the reversionary interest in favour of their children (see Figure 16.1). This created a special power in favour of the class of their eight surviving children. Mr Slade had discretion whether to make appointments at all, but he could only make appointments to those who fell within the class of potential objects (see Figure 16.1).

Hybrid powers

A hybrid,[4] or intermediate,[5] power is the inverse of a special power. The donee is entitled to make appointments in favour of anyone except the members of a specified class. In *Re Byron's Settlement*[6] a power of appointment was given by the testatrix to her daughter in favour of anyone except 'her present husband or any friend or relative of his'. In *Re Lawrence's Will Trusts*[7] Mr Lawrence granted his wife a power of appointment over his residuary estate in favour of anyone except her relatives.[8]

(ii) Classification by donee's duties

Powers may also be divided into those where the donee owes no duty of a fiduciary nature to the potential objects of the power, and those where some fiduciary duties are owed. Although in both cases the power remains essentially discretionary, there is a slight difference in the duties owed. This difference normally arises because the donee is also a trustee.

Bare or mere powers

If the donee of the power does not hold the power in a fiduciary capacity, then he owes no duties to the objects concerning its exercise. He is under no duty to exercise it, and need not even consider whether he should exercise the power. He can completely

---

[3] [1897] 1 Ch 289. See also *Re Gestetner Settlement* [1953] Ch 672 (wide class including named persons, named charitable bodies, and employees and ex-employees of the settlor's company); *Re Sayer* [1957] Ch 423 (class in favour of employees, ex-employees, and widows and infant children of Sayers Confectionary Ltd).

[4] See *Re Lawrence's Will Trusts* [1972] Ch 418, at 423.

[5] See *Re Manisty's Settlement* [1974] Ch 17, where Templeman J described a power to appoint anyone in the world except the settlor, his wife and other excepted persons as an 'intermediate power'.

[6] [1891] 3 Ch 474.   [7] [1972] Ch 418.

[8] See also *Re Park* [1932] 1 Ch 580; *Re Abrahams' Will Trusts* [1969] 1 Ch 463; *Re Manisty's Settlement* [1974] Ch 17.

forget that he has it, and never apply his mind to the question whether he should exercise it. This type of power is known as a bare or mere power.

Fiduciary powers

If the donee holds the power of appointment in a fiduciary capacity, most commonly because it is a power which arises under a trust of which he is the trustee, then he owes limited fiduciary duties to the potential objects of the powers.[9] He must periodically consider whether to exercise the power, although it remains entirely discretionary and he is under no enforceable obligation to make appointments.[10] If he does decide to exercise the power, he must first survey the range of potential objects before making particular appointments. The fact that the donee has fiduciary obligations does not mean that he is a trustee. Although there is a wide spectrum of fiduciary duties, some of which are analogous to or akin to the duties of a trustee,[11] there can be 'considerable differences between the office or the capacity of a trustee and the position of a donee of a fiduciary power'.[12]

(b) Duties of the donee of a power

The donee of a bare power is under no duty to exercise the power because it is entirely discretionary. If he makes no appointments at all he is not in breach of any duty. In *Re Weekes' Settlement*,[13] Mr Slade failed to make any appointments in favour of his children and had not committed any breach thereby. The donee does not even have to consider whether or not to exercise the power. By way of exception, if the power is held by someone who is also a trustee, then he holds the power in a fiduciary capacity, and he must from time to time consider whether or not to exercise the power in favour of the objects.[14] If the donee of a mere power does choose to exercise the power, he must not act outside of the terms of the power and appoint in favour of non-objects. Such an appointment to non-objects is known as 'excessive exercise' because it exceeds the scope of the power. He must exercise the power honestly and not fraudulently.

(c) Rights of the objects of powers

In Chapter 14 it was seen that the beneficiaries of a fixed trust have an immediate proprietary interest in the share of the fund which is earmarked for them and, if of age and legally competent, they can demand that the trustees transfer the property to them.[15] The potential objects of a power of appointment have no immediate proprietary interest in the property over which the donee has power.[16] An object only gains

---

[9] See *Re Hay's Settlement Trusts* [1982] 1 WLR 202.

[10] See *Re Allen-Meyrick's Will Trusts* [1966] 1 WLR 499, where the court refused to intervene to compel trustees to exercise a power that they held over a fund in favour of the settlor's husband.

[11] See *Gomez and others v Gomez-Monche Vives and others* [2008] EWCA Civ 1065, [2009] Ch 245 (CA), at [94].

[12] *Gomez and others v Gomez-Monche Vives and others* [2008] EWCA Civ 1065, [2009] Ch 245 (CA), at [94].   [13] [1897] 1 Ch 289.

[14] See *Re Abrahams' Will Trusts* [1969] 1 Ch 463, at 474 per Cross J; *Re Hay's Settlement Trusts* [1982] 1 WLR 202. Fiduciary powers are discussed later in this chapter.

[15] *Saunders v Vautier* (1841) 4 Beav 115.   [16] *Vestey v IRC* [1980] AC 1148, HL.

a proprietary interest in any property which is allocated to him by the donee. In *Re Brooks' Settlement Trusts* Farwell J said of the position of a son who was a potential object of a special power under his mother's marriage settlement:

> It is…impossible to say that until an appointment has been made in favour of this son that the son had any interest under his mother's settlement other than an interest as one of the people entitled in default of appointment.[17]

(2) The validity of powers of appointment

(a) Certainty of objects

(i) Comparison with fixed trusts

In the case of a fixed trust[18] it must be possible to draw up a 'complete list' of each and every beneficiary.[19] If this is not possible, the trust is void for uncertainty because neither the trustee nor the court could carry out the trust. If the beneficiaries are defined as a class, then a complete list can only be drawn up if the class is both conceptually and evidentially certain. In the case of powers, the test of certainty is less stringent. There is no need for the donee to be able to draw up a complete list of every potential object to exercise the power properly. In the case of a general power, such a requirement would entail the production of a list of the entire population of the world! Equally, the court will not step in to exercise the power if the donee defaults because it is purely discretionary. However, the court must be able to supervise any exercise of the power. In the case of a special power, this means that the court must be able to determine whether any person selected by the donee was within the class, and therefore entitled to enjoy the benefit of the exercise. As Lord Upjohn observed in *Re Gulbenkian's Settlement*:

> those entitled to the fund in default [of appointment] must clearly be entitled to restrain the trustees from exercising it save amongst those within the power. So the trustees, or the court, must be able to say with certainty who is within and who without the power.[20]

If an appointment is made to a person who is outside the class of objects, then the exercise is excessive and void. The test for certainty of objects for powers of appointment has developed to meet this necessity.

(ii) The 'is or is not' test

The test of certainty for powers of appointment was laid down by the House of Lords in *Re Gulbenkian's Settlement (No 1)*.[21] A special power of appointment was granted in favour of a class consisting of Nubar Gulbenkian, his wife and children, and 'any person or persons in whose house or apartments or in whose company or under whose

---

[17] [1939] Ch 993, at 997.   [18] See Chapter 15.
[19] See *IRC v Broadway Cottages Trust* [1954] 1 All ER 878, discussed in Chapter 15.
[20] [1970] AC 508, at 525.
[21] [1970] AC 508.

care or control or by whom or with whom he may from time to time be employed or residing'. This was upheld as sufficiently certain. Lord Upjohn stated the relevant test of certainty:[22]

> a mere or bare power of appointment among a class is valid if you can with certainty say whether any given individual is or is not a member of the class: you do not have to be able to ascertain every member of the class.[23]

This test had been propounded by Harman J in *Re Gestetner Settlement*[24] and approved by the Court of Appeal in *IRC v Broadway Cottages Trust*.[25] Lord Upjohn rejected[26] a broader test of certainty put forward by Lord Denning MR in the Court of Appeal that a power of appointment would be valid if it could be said with certainty of any one person that he was clearly within the class, even if it may be difficult to say in other cases whether a person is within the class or not.[27] In *Re Gresham*[28] Harman J had held that a power with similar terms to that in *Re Gulbenkian* was void for uncertainty, but the Court of Appeal and House of Lords overruled the decision. Mere difficulty in determining whether an individual is within or without the class is not sufficient to invalidate the power, and the court can rule on borderline cases.[29] It is only insuperable difficulty that will render the power void for uncertainty.

The *Gulbenkian* test is consistent with established principle and logic. It requires that the court must be able to determine with absolute certainty whether any given individual is or is not a member of the class of potential objects. This is essential if the court is to determine whether the power has been exercised properly. If Toby grants Stephanie a power of appointment over his residuary estate in favour of 'old men', it would be impossible for the court to determine if an appointment in favour of Robert, who is 64, was excessive. It is not possible to say of every individual whether they are 'old' or not, because 'old' has no clear objective meaning. A power in favour of 'men aged over 65' is clearly valid because it is possible to say of every man whether he is over 65 or not.

(iii) Application of the 'is or is not' test

The test for certainty of objects[30] for powers laid down in *Re Gulbenkian*[31] was adopted for discretionary trusts by the House of Lords in *McPhail v Doulton*.[32] It

---

[22] Lord Hodson and Lord Guest agreed with Lord Upjohn; Lord Reid delivered a similar opinion; Lord Donovan agreed with Lord Upjohn but reserved his opinion on whether the test proposed by the Court of Appeal that the power should be valid if it could be said of any one person that he was within the class, although he was 'inclined to share' Lord Upjohn's view.   [23] [1970] AC 508, at 521.

[24] [1953] Ch 672; followed by Roxburgh J in *Re Coates (Decd)* [1955] Ch 495 and Upjohn J in *Re Sayer* [1957] Ch 423.

[25] [1955] Ch 20. See also *Re Hain's Settlement* [1961] 1 WLR 440, at 445, per Lord Evershed MR.

[26] [1970] AC 508, at 134.   [27] [1968] Ch 126, at 134.   [28] [1956] 1 WLR 573.

[29] [1970] AC 508, at 523.

[30] See Hopkins 'Continuing Uncertainty as to the Certainty of Trust Powers' [1971] CLJ 68; Emery 'The Most Hallowed Principle: Certainty of Beneficiaries of Trusts and Powers of Appointment' (1982) 98 LQR 551.   [31] [1970] AC 508.

[32] [1971] AC 424 (also referred to as *Re Baden's Deed Trusts (No 1)*).

was subsequently examined and applied by the Court of Appeal in *Re Baden's Deed Trusts (No 2)*.[33] It follows that, although these cases concerned discretionary trusts, they are the main authorities considering the implications of the *Re Gulbenkian* test for powers of appointment. They indicate that while the 'is or is not' test requires conceptual certainty, a special power will not be invalid for reasons of evidential uncertainty.

'Conceptual certainty'

The class of a special power must be defined with conceptual certainty.[34] This means that the class must be defined by objective criteria by which the court can judge whether any given individual is within the class. Thus, a power of appointment in favour of 'my good friends' or 'my business associates' would be void for uncertainty. In contrast, a power of appointment in favour of 'the fellows of Oriel College, Oxford University' or 'members of the National Union of Students' would create an objectively certain class.

'Evidential certainty'

In *Re Baden's Deed Trusts (No 2)*[35] the majority of the Court of Appeal held that a discretionary trust which was conceptually certain was not defeated by evidential uncertainty. In other words, provided the class criteria are clear-cut it does not matter that it is not possible to prove of every individual whether they meet the criteria or not.[36] For example, a class defined as 'Medwin's children' is conceptually certain, even though before DNA profiling it might have been difficult to prove paternity for every child. Since the test is the same for powers of appointment, it is not necessary that the class of a special power be evidentially certain. The lack of a requirement of strict evidential certainty follows from the fact that the donee of the power does not have to consider every single potential object in exercising his discretion to appoint the property. His complete discretion means that his only duty is to ensure that any appointments are made to persons within the class of objects and not to exercise the power excessively.[37]

(iv) Criticism of the 'is or is not' test

Following *Re Gulbenkian*,[38] *McPhail v Doulton*,[39] and *Re Baden (No 2)*,[40] the same requirement of conceptual certainty applies to fixed trusts, discretionary trusts, and powers of appointment. Equitable obligations of any of these types will be void if there is no conceptual certainty. This could lead to some unsatisfactory results, and it remains questionable whether the same strict test should apply to powers of appointment, which are discretionary, and trusts, which are in essence mandatory equitable

---

[33] [1973] Ch 9.   [34] See Chapter 14.   [35] [1973] Ch 9.   [36] See Chapters 14 and 17.
[37] With the exception of a fiduciary power, where the trustee who holds the power of appointment is under a duty to have an appreciation of the width of the field of potential objects when he exercises it. See *Re Hay's Settlement Trusts* [1982] 1 WLR 202.   [38] [1970] AC 508.
[39] [1971] AC 424.   [40] [1973] Ch 9.

obligations. There is much to commend a modified version of the broader proposition of Lord Denning MR in the Court of Appeal, who proposed that:

> if the [donees] can say of a particular person: 'He is clearly within the category', the gift is good, even though it may be difficult in other cases to say whether a person is or is not within the category.[41]

In *Re Gibbards Will Trusts*[42] a testator gave his trustees a power of appointment over his residuary estate in favour of 'any of my old friends'. Plowman J concluded that 'there is not a sufficient degree of uncertainty about the expression'[43] to hold the power void for uncertainty. Similarly, in *Re Coates (Decd)*[44] a power to appoint a specified sum to 'friends' was upheld as valid. Roxburgh J held that the word 'friend' was not too vague, although he recognized that 'friendship' was a phrase 'particularly blurred in outline'.[45] It is unclear whether these cases could be decided similarly today. Definitions such as 'old friends' would probably not be sufficiently conceptually certain[46] under the test propounded in *Re Baden (No 2)*.[47] A fixed trust for 'my old friends' would certainly not be valid as it would not be possible to identify the full extent of the class. *Re Gibbard*[48] was decided on the basis of the test rejected by the House of Lords in *Re Gulbenkian* that it must be possible to say of at least some persons that they are certainly within the class, even if it were not possible to say of others whether they are or not.

(v) An alternative to the 'is or is not' test for powers?

Ultimately, it is a question of policy whether a purely discretionary power should fail for lack of complete conceptual certainty. If a donor grants a power to appoint his property in favour of his 'old friends', there are clearly some people who are without question within the class. Should the power fail and the donor's intention be defeated merely because there are others about whom it cannot be definitely stated whether they are 'old friends' or not? It would be more in keeping with the donor's intentions that appointments can be made in the donee's discretion to those who are definitely objects. An analogy can be drawn from the requirement of certainty applicable to a gift subject to a condition precedent. In *Re Barlow's Will Trusts*[49] Browne-Wilkinson J held that, if such gifts are made to a class, then they are valid if 'it is possible to say of one or more persons that he or they undoubtedly qualify even though it may be difficult to say of others whether or not they qualify'.[50] The case concerned a testatrix who directed her executor to sell valuable paintings at a considerable undervalue to her family and 'friends'. These gifts were valid because it was possible to say of some people that 'on any reasonable basis' they were friends, and would therefore be entitled

---

[41] *Re Gulbenkian's Settlement* [1968] Ch 126, at 134.   [42] [1966] 1 All ER 273.
[43] [1966] 1 All ER 273., at 281.   [44] [1955] Ch 495.   [45] [1955] Ch 495, at 499.
[46] See *Re Barlow's Will Trusts* [1979] 1 WLR 278, at 298, per Brown-Wilkinson J: '["Friends"] has a great range of meanings; indeed, its exact meaning probably varies slightly from person to person...'.
[47] [1973] Ch 9.   [48] [1966] 1 All ER 273.   [49] [1979] 1 WLR 278.
[50] [1979] 1 WLR 278., at 281, following *Re Allen* [1953] Ch 810.

to purchase. Provided a potential purchaser satisfied the condition of proving that he was definitely a friend, it did not matter that it was impossible to say whether others were friends or not.

If this approach was applied to powers of appointment it might provide a better balance between upholding the donor's intentions and ensuring that the court can supervise the execution of the power. The court will not intervene if the power is not exercised, so there is no possibility of the court exercising the power itself.[51] The court could prevent excessive exercise by upholding only appointments to those shown definitely to be within the class on any reasonable basis. In cases of doubt, the donee of the power could apply to the court for determination whether a person falls indisputably within the class. Such an approach would be entirely inappropriate for fixed or discretionary trusts, where the court may have to carry out the terms of the trust. For powers of appointment it would provide a less stringent test than that declared by the House of Lords in *Re Gulbenkian*,[52] and would be similar to the rejected test applied by the Court of Appeal in that case. One disadvantage is that it would again create a distinction between the test of certainty applying to discretionary trusts and powers, which would make the question of whether a particular instrument creates a trust or a power far more significant, since that may determine its validity. That danger could be prevented by the court taking a strict view and not succumbing to the temptation of construing an invalid trust as a valid power.[53]

(b) Capriciousness

Even if a special power of appointment is sufficiently certain, it will be invalid if it is capricious in nature. The principle of capriciousness was considered applicable to special powers in *Re Manisty's Settlement*,[54] where Templeman J suggested that a special power in favour of the 'residents of Greater London' would be capricious 'because the terms of the power negated any sensible intention on the part of the settlor'.[55] Capriciousness does not invalidate a power merely because of its width of the power, as a general power is valid even though the donee has the discretion to make appointments to anyone in the whole world. Instead, it invalidates a special power because there is no rational reason why the donor selected the specified class, and consequently the donee has no rational basis on which he can exercise his discretion.[56] 'Residents of Greater London' would be capricious because the class was 'an accidental agglomeration of persons who have no discernible link with the settlor or with any institution'.[57] If there were a link between the donor of the power and the class of potential objects, the power would not be open to the charge of capriciousness. In *Re Hay's Settlement*

---

[51] Unlike a discretionary trust. See *McPhail v Doulton* [1971] AC 424.   [52] [1970] AC 508.
[53] As was taken in *McPhail v Doulton* [1971] AC 424.   [54] [1974] Ch 17.
[55] [1974] Ch 17, at 27.
[56] [1974] Ch 17. 'A capricious power negatives a sensible consideration by the trustees of the exercise of the power.'   [57] [1974] Ch 17.

Trusts[58] Megarry V-C suggested that a power in favour of 'the residents of Greater London' would not be capricious if the donor were a former chairman of the Greater London Council. In *R v District Auditor ex p West Yorkshire Metropolitan County Council*[59] it was held that a discretionary trust created by the council for the benefit of the residents of West Yorkshire was not capricious.[60]

Where a power is found to be capricious it will be rendered void. Capriciousness will only invalidate a special power, and the principle has no application to a general power, or a hybrid power.[61] As both *Re Manisty's Settlement* and *Re Hay's Settlement Trusts* concerned fiduciary powers, where the donee of the power has additional fiduciary duties, the principle may not apply to bare powers where the donee has no obligations of a fiduciary nature.

(3) Exercise of powers of appointment

(a) Formalities

As a general rule, no special formalities are required for the valid exercise of a power of appointment. However, the donee of the power must intend to allocate the fund or part of the fund to an object of the power. Where the power is granted in relation to land an appointment must be evidenced in writing signed by the donee, in accordance with s 51(1)(b) of the Law of Property Act 1925. In some circumstances additional formalities may be required.

(i) Formalities required by the terms of the power

The terms of the power may require it to be exercised in a particular form, for example by deed. If so, the power can only be exercised in that form. Where it is stipulated that a power must be exercised by deed, a purported exercise by will be ineffective.[62] Similarly, a power which can only be exercised by will cannot be exercised inter vivos.[63]

(ii) Limitations on additional formalities

Although the terms of the power may specify additional formalities, legislation has limited the range of stipulations which must be observed to effect a valid exercise. Under s 159(1) of the Law of Property Act 1925, where a power is exercised inter vivos the exercise will be valid if the donee executed by a valid deed,[64] even though the terms of the power required some 'additional or other form of execution or attestation or solemnity'. This does not exclude the necessity for the donee to comply with any terms of the power requiring him to gain the consent of another individual, or performing

---

[58] [1982] 1 WLR 202.   [59] [1986] RVR 24.

[60] It was, however, found to be 'administratively unworkable', demonstrating that 'capriciousness' and 'administrative unworkability' are distinct concepts

[61] See *Re Manisty's Settlement* [1974] Ch 17, at 27; *Re Hay's Settlement Trusts* [1982] 1 WLR 202, at 212.

[62] *Re Phillips* (1889) LR 41 Ch D 417.

[63] *Re Evered* [1910] 2 Ch 147, at 156, per Cozens-Hardy MR.

[64] Executed in the presence of and attested by two or more witnesses (Law of Property (Miscellaneous Provisions) Act 1989, s 1).

an act not relating to the mode of executing the deed.[65] In the case of a will, s 10 of the Wills Act 1837 provides that the exercise of a power by a valid will is effective notwithstanding the absence of any additional formalities required by the terms of the power.[66]

(b) Defective exercise

In general, a defective exercise of a power is void, and the purported appointment of the fund does not take place. However, equity may validate a defective exercise if the donee 'in discharge of moral or natural obligations shows an intention to execute [a] power'.[67] This will only apply in favour of purchasers for value, creditors, charities, and persons to whom the donee is under a natural or moral obligation to provide. Some key elements must be proved if the defective exercise is to be upheld:

> the intention to pass the property...the persons to be benefited...the amount of the benefit...good consideration.[68]

(c) Contracts to exercise

A contract to exercise a power of appointment will operate in equity as a valid exercise of the power, provided that the contract is specifically enforceable. This is an application of the maxim that 'equity treats as done that which ought to be done'. Since a contract to exercise a testamentary power is not specifically enforceable,[69] it does not operate as an effective exercise of the power, and the only remedy available to the disappointed object is an action for damages for breach of contract against the estate.

(d) Excessive exercise

The exercise of the power will be excessive if the donee makes an appointment to a person outside of the potential objects of the power. In the case of a special power, appointments can only be made to members of the specified class, while in the case of a hybrid power, appointments must not be made to members of the excluded class. Any such excessive appointments are void and of no effect.

If an appointment is made which is partly good and partly bad, the court will sever the good from the bad if possible. In *Re Kerr's Will Trusts*[70] Maria Young had a special power of appointment over a fund in favour of the children of her marriage. By will, she appointed the fund to two of her children, Charlotte and Catherine. Catherine was a child of the marriage and within the power, but Charlotte was an illegitimate child of Maria before she married. The exercise was thus excessive, but the court applied severance and Catherine took the share of the fund appointed to her. The remainder of the fund was divided equally among those entitled in default of appointment.

---

[65] Law of Property Act 1925, s 159(2).   [66] See also Wills Act 1963, s 2.
[67] *Farwell on Powers* (3rd edn, 1916), p 378; *Chapman v Gibson* (1791) 3 Bro CC 229.
[68] *Farwell on Powers* (3rd edn, 1916), p 379.
[69] *Re Bradshaw* [1902] 1 Ch 436; *Re Cooke* [1922] 1 Ch 292.   [70] (1877) 4 Ch D 600.

In *Re Holland*[71] an appointment was made with attached conditions which rendered the exercise excessive. The conditions were severed from the appointment and it was upheld as a valid exercise.[72] If it is impossible to sever the condition from the appointment, the exercise will be excessive and void.[73]

(e) Effect of valid exercise

The effect of a valid exercise of the power is to allocate the share of the fund appointed to the person in whose favour the donee has exercised the power. The appointee will then be entitled to an immediate proprietary interest in the share of the fund which has been allocated.[74] In *Churchill v Churchill*,[75] Lord Romilly MR held that the effect of an appointment by Sir Orford Gordon under a special power of a fund to his three daughters in equal shares was to vest in them absolute interests in the appointed fund.

(4) Duties of the donee of a mere power of appointment

(a) No duty to exercise the power

The donee of a mere power of appointment is under no duty to exercise the power and make appointments in favour of the potential objects. He has complete discretion and the court will not compel him to exercise the power, nor even to consider periodically whether he should exercise the power. If he fails to make any appointments at all he is not in breach of any duty owed either to the donor of the power or to the potential objects, and they in turn have no cause for complaint against him.

(b) No duty to consider the width of the field

If the donee of the mere power does decide to exercise it, he has no duty to survey and consider the range of potential objects of the power before exercising his discretion in favour of any one object. He may appoint to whomsoever he wishes, provided they are within the class, without having to take account of others who could benefit if he were to exercise his discretion in their favour. If he is within the scope of the power, the donee may appoint the fund entirely to himself without even considering the other potential objects. Thus, in *Re Penrose*[76] an exercise of a special power of appointment by the donee in favour of himself, where he was an object, was upheld.

(c) Duty not to delegate the exercise of the power

The donee must not delegate the power of appointment to others except in so far as this is authorized by the terms of the grant: *delegatus non potest delegare* (a delegate has no power to delegate).

---

[71] [1914] 2 Ch 595.
[72] See also *Churchill v Churchill* (1866–67) LR 5 Eq 44; *Price v William-Wynn* [2006] EWHC 788 (Ch) (a clause inserted into deeds of appointment and revocation, which was held to exceed the powers given to trustees under a settlement, was therefore severed from each of the affected deeds so that they could validly be read without the offending clause). [73] *Re Cohen* [1911] 1 Ch 37.
[74] See *Vestey v IRC* [1980] AC 1148, HL. [75] (1866–67) LR 5 Eq 44. [76] [1933] Ch 793.

(d) Duty not to exercise the power excessively

The donee of the power is under a duty to make appointments only to those who are objects of the power. As has been seen, any appointments which are excessive will be void.

(e) Duty not to exercise the power fraudulently

Even if the donee exercises the power and makes appointments which appear to be within the scope of the power, they will be void if the exercise amounts to a 'fraud on the power'. The power must be exercised honestly, and the court will look to the motives and intentions of the donor of the power to ensure that they are not improper. As Lord Parker of Waddington observed in *Vatcher v Paull*:

> The term fraud in connection with frauds on a power does not necessarily denote any conduct on the part of the appointor amounting to fraud in the common law meaning of the term or any conduct which could be properly termed dishonest or immoral. It merely means that the power has been exercised for a purpose or with an intention, beyond the scope of or not justified by the instrument creating the fraud...[77]

Thus, in *Hillsdown Holdings plc v Pensions Ombudsman*[78] an exercise of a power was held to constitute a 'fraud', despite the fact that the donee and all parties had acted honestly and with good intentions. In *Edge v Pensions Ombudsman*[79] Scott V-C held that pension trustees were required to 'exercise their discretionary power honestly and for the purpose for which the power was given and not so as to accomplish any ulterior purpose'.

 Where the exercise of a power is held invalid on the grounds of fraud, the court acts to protect the interests of those who would be entitled to the fund if no appointments are made. They are the victims of the fraud if appointments are made with improper motives, since they are thereby divested of an interest in the fund to which they would otherwise have become entitled.[80] The effect of fraud is to render the exercise of the power void, not merely voidable.[81]

 In *Vatcher v Paull*[82] Lord Parker indicated three circumstances in which the exercise of a power would amount to a fraud. The essence of each is that the benefit is not exclusively conferred upon objects of the power.[83] Clearly, these limitations apply only to special powers and not to general powers, since in the case of a general power there are no persons outside of the scope of the power and the donee may even appoint in his own favour.

 The obligation not to exercise a power for an improper purpose applies to administrative as well as to dispositive powers. In *Dalriada Trustees v Faulds*[84] Bean J held that even if a power of investment allowed for money to be advanced on unsecured personal loans, it did not permit six HMRC[85] registered pension funds to make reciprocal loans

---

[77] [1915] AC 372, at 378.   [78] [1997] 1 All ER 862.   [79] [1998] 2 All ER 547, at 569.
[80] *Re Brooks' Settlement Trusts* [1939] Ch 993.   [81] *Cloutte v Storey* [1911] 1 Ch 18, CA.
[82] [1915] AC 372, at 378.   [83] See *Re Merton* [1953] 1 WLR 1096.
[84] [2012] 2 All ER 734. See also Chapter 21.   [85] Her Majesty's Revenue and Customs.

to the members of the other schemes in order to circumvent the fiscal rules of HMRC barring members of pension schemes from obtaining access to their pension capital prior to retirement. The loans were beyond the scope of the pension fund trustees' powers, and 'the fact that everyone involved with the transactions wished to validate [the] loans does not prevent the loans from being a fraud on the trustees' powers.'[86]

(i) Where the exercise is due to some bargain between the appointor and the appointee

If an appointment is made on the basis of a prior agreement between the donee/ appointor and the appointee as to how the appointed share of the fund should be used, the appointment is void. The purpose of the bargain may be for the donee to gain some benefit for himself, or for a non-object of the power. The objection to such a bargain is 'that the power is used not with the single purpose of benefiting its proper objects'.[87] In *Hillsdown Holdings plc v Pensions Ombudsman*,[88] Hillsdown plc participated in a pension scheme (the FMC scheme) which had accumulated an actuarial surplus of some £20m. The scheme contained no power allowing the trustees to repay any surplus to employers participating in the scheme, and the scheme could not be amended to confer such a power. After an agreement had been negotiated between Hillsdown and the FMC trustees to augment the benefits of FMC pensioners and to transfer to the company £11m of the surplus, the trustees exercised a power under the scheme to transfer the entire fund to another scheme (the HF scheme), the rules of which were changed to allow the surplus to be paid to Hillsdown. Knox J held that the FMC trustees' exercise of the power, transferring the assets to HF was a fraud on the power as it amounted to 'an improper use of the power for a collateral purpose'[89] of paying the surplus to Hillsdown.

There is no objection to an appointment made on the basis of a bargain with those who are entitled in default of any appointment being made.[90] Where an appointment is a fraud because it was made on the basis of such a bargain, the court may sever the good from the bad provided that it:

> can clearly distinguish between the quantum of the benefit bona fide intended to be conferred on the appointee and the quantum of benefit intended to be derived by the appointor or to be conferred on a stranger.[91]

(ii) The appointor's purpose and intention is to secure a benefit for himself

Even where there was no explicit bargain between the donee/appointor and appointee, the exercise will constitute a fraud if the purpose of the appointment was to enable the appointor to receive a benefit. Thus, if an appointor makes an appointment in favour of a child they know to be dying, with the intention that they will gain the benefit of that sum on the death of the child, the appointment is a fraud on the power. In *Lord Hinchinbroke v Seymour*[92] a father appointed £10,000 in favour of his daughter

---

[86] At [72].   [87] *Vatcher v Paull* [1915] AC 372, at 379.   [88] [1997] 1 All ER 862.
[89] [1997] 1 All ER 862, at 883.   [90] [1915] AC 372, at 379.   [91] [1915] AC 372, at 378.
[92] (1784) 1 Bro CC 395.

who was 14 and dying of consumption. The intention of the appointment was that the father would take the money as administrator of the child. It was 'as plain a case of gross fraud on a power as can well be imagined', and 'it was quite obvious what the motive was. It could not have been for the benefit of the child, because she was already provided for.'[93] An appointment made to a child who is healthy is not a fraud, even though the appointor stands to gain if the child subsequently dies.[94]

(iii) The appointor's purpose is to benefit for some other person not an object of the power

An appointment in favour of an object of the power will be fraudulent if the real intention of the donee/appointor was to benefit a non-object. In *Re Dick*,[95] Mrs Sherman was the donee of a special power of appointment over property left on trust by her father in favour of her brothers or sisters and their issue. She exercised the power by will in favour of her sister, Miss Dick, but contemporaneously with the will executed a formal memorandum desiring her sister provide an annuity of £800 per annum for her gardener Mr Claydon, who was not an object. The memorandum expressly stated that it did not impose a 'trust or legal obligation' on Miss Dick, so that there was no bargain between the appointor and appointee. Nevertheless, the Court of Appeal held that this amounted to an excessive exercise of the power. Evershed MR stated that the central question was:

> whether the right inference is that what Mrs Sherman intended to do, her real deliberate purpose which she wanted and set out by all means that were possible to achieve, was to benefit the Claydons via her relations...or whether her purpose was really to benefit her relations subject only to this, that she had indicated to them that she hoped...they would so something for the Claydons on the lines she had suggested.[96]

The court held that in all the circumstances the real intention was to benefit the non-object. This case suggests that the court will weigh the appointor's motives and intentions from all the available evidence, a principle that was established by Cohen LJ in *Re Crawshay (Decd) (No 2)*.[97] This is notoriously difficult, as evidenced by the large number of indications and counter-indications considered by the Court of Appeal in *Re Dick*.

(5) Failure to exercise the power

Since a power of appointment is purely discretionary in nature, a donee is under no obligation to exercise it, and the objects have no rights to the fund unless it is appointed to them. If the power is not exercised, the fund passes to those entitled in default. Usually this will occur where a donee has been granted a power but has died without making any valid appointments, either inter vivos or by will (see Figure 16.2).

---

[93] *Henty v Wrey* (1882) LR 21 Ch D 332, at 342, per Jessel MR.   [94] (1882) LR 21 Ch D 332.
[95] [1953] Ch 343.   [96] [1953] Ch 343, at 363.   [97] [1948] Ch 123.

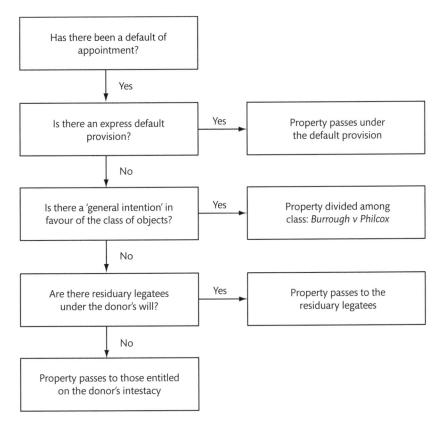

Figure 16.2 Effect of default of appointment

(a) Express gift over in default of appointment

The power of appointment may itself contain an express stipulation of who is to receive the fund if no appointments are made. Such an express provision will determine how the fund should be distributed.

(b) No express gift over in default

If the power does not contain an express gift over in default, the fund will fall to be distributed according to the general principles governing the distribution of surplus funds.[98] If the fund was created by will, the property passes to those entitled to the residuary estate under the will. If the fund was created by an inter vivos settlement, it will result back to the settlor, or his heirs, by a resulting trust. There may, however, be an implied trust producing a different result.

(c) An implied trust in default

In some circumstances, even though no appointment has been made, the court may hold that the fund should be divided among the objects rather than passing to the

---

[98] See Chapter 18.

residuary legatees or by resulting trust. This will only be possible if the court can find that there was a 'general intention' by the donee of the power to benefit a class. The leading case is *Burrough v Philcox*.[99] John Walton granted his surviving daughter, Ann, a power of appointment over his property in favour of his nephews and nieces. The power contained no express gift over in default and Ann died without making any appointments. Under the rules of succession, the testator's next of kin would be entitled to the fund. However, Lord Cottenham LC held that the effect of the arrangement was to create a trust in favour of the nephews and nieces subject to Ann's power of selection, so that when Ann died without having made any appointments, they each took an equal share in the fund. The principle was stated by Lord Cottenham:

> where there appears a general intention in favour of a class, and a particular intention in favour of individuals of a class to be selected by another person, and the particular intention fails, from that selection not being made, the court will carry into effect the general intention in favour of the class.[100]

The key element is the finding of a general intention in favour of the class. In effect, the court is concluding from the circumstances of the creation of the power that if it has not been exercised the donor would have wanted the fund to go to the objects. In this sense the operation of the implied trust in default is somewhat similar to an application cy-près, where a charitable gift has failed initially on the grounds that the donor had an overriding charitable intention.[101]

(i) Demonstrating a general intention

An implied trust in default will only arise if it can be shown that the donor of the power possessed a general intention to benefit the objects thereof. If the power contained an express gift in default, then the court cannot conclude that there was a general intention in favour of the class of objects because the donee had already expressed his intention vis-à-vis the fund in default of any appointments.[102] It is not inevitable that the absence of an express gift over in default will lead to the finding of a general intention in favour of the objects. In *Re Weekes' Settlement*[103] Mrs Slade granted her husband a power of appointment over a fund established under her marriage settlement. Mr Slade died without making any appointments, and the children of the marriage claimed to be equally entitled to the fund. Romer J held that there was no general intention in favour of the class, and the fund therefore passed to the eldest son, who was Mrs Slade's heir at law. He stated:

> The authorities do not show... that there is a hard and fast rule that a gift to A for life with a power to appoint among a class and nothing more must, if there is no gift over in the will, be held a gift by implication to the class in default of the power being exercised... you must find in the will an indication that the testatrix did intend the class or some of the class to take—intended in fact that the power should be regarded in the nature of a trust.[104]

---

[99] (1840) 5 My & Cr 72.   [100] (1840) 5 My & Cr 72 at 92.
[101] See Chapter 18, Surplus funds on the failure of a charity.   [102] *Re Mills* [1930] 1 Ch 654.
[103] [1897] 1 Ch 289.   [104] [1897] 1 Ch 289 at 292.

No general intention in favour of the class was found in *Re Combe*[105] or *Re Perowne (Decd)*.[106] Such a general intention is only likely to be found where the power is in favour of a small and well-defined class, especially a close family group.

(ii) Juridical nature of the implied trust in default

There remains confusion as to the basis under which the fund subject to a power is distributed to the objects under the rule in *Burrough v Philcox*. One analysis is that the power is in fact a discretionary trust under which the donee is under an obligation to make an appointment. Thus, in *Burrough v Philcox* Lord Cottenham LC cited the dictum of Lord Eldon in *Brown v Higgs*[107] that the power is given so as to:

> make it the duty of the donee to exercise it; and, in such case, the court will not permit the objects of the power to suffer by the negligence or conduct of the donee, but fastens upon the property a trust for their benefit.[108]

Similarly, in *Re Weekes' Settlement*[109] Romer J considered that if there had been a general intention in favour of the class this would have rendered the power in the nature of a trust.

A second analysis is that the general intention in favour of the class creates a fixed trust in favour of the whole class, so that from the very beginning the objects/beneficiaries enjoy equal shares in the fund, but that the donor of the power is entitled to divest them of their interests by the exercise of the power.

A third analysis is that the trust in favour of the whole class applies only in default of appointment, just as would be the case if the trust had contained an express gift over in default of appointment. In this situation the beneficiaries of the trust in default of appointment do not have vested, but only contingent, interests which depend for their vesting and fulfilment on the power not being exercised.

The confusion has arisen because the rule only comes into play after there has been a failure on the part of the donee to exercise the power. If appointments had been made, no difficulties would arise. It is better to regard the court as acting *ex post facto*, and implying a trust in favour of the objects of power in the event of no appointment being made, rather than to construe a trust in their favour from the beginning. This was the approach taken by Buckley J in *Re Wills' Trust Deeds*.[110] He considered that a trust in favour of the objects only arose in the event of default:

> A perusal of these cases…leads to the conclusion that they really turn on the question whether on the particular facts of each case it was proper to infer that there was a trust in default of appointment for the objects of the power. The court did not, and I think, could not compel the donee personally to exercise the power but carried what it conceived to be the settlor's intention into effect by executing an implied trust in default of appointment.[111]

---

[105] [1925] Ch 210.   [106] [1951] Ch 785.   [107] (1803) 8 Ves 561.
[108] (1840) 5 My & Cr 72, at 92.   [109] [1897] 1 Ch 289.   [110] [1964] Ch 219.
[111] [1964] Ch 219, at 230.

It therefore seems that the best analysis is that a power is given to the donee, which he is under no duty to exercise, but that in the event of there being no exercise the court implies a trust in favour of the class on the basis of a general intention in their favour on the part of the donor. The objects thus have no beneficial entitlement to the fund until the trust is implied and the donee of the power has no enforceable duties and is not in breach by failing to make appointments.

(6) **Fiduciary powers**

(a) Definition

If a power of appointment is held by the donee in a fiduciary capacity, the power is a 'fiduciary power'. This will normally occur because the donee is also a trustee of the property subject to the power. In *Re Hay's Settlement Trusts*[112] David Greig and Colin Oliver were the trustees of a settlement made by Lady Hay. As part of the settlement they enjoyed a general power of appointment over the property subject to the trust. As they were trustees, they held their power in a fiduciary capacity.[113] In *Mettoy Pension Trustees Ltd v Evans*[114] Warner J described such an obligation as a 'fiduciary power in the full sense',[115] which he defined as:

> comprising any power conferred on the trustees of the property or any other person as a trustee of the power itself.

The case concerned the pension fund of a company, Mettoy plc, which had gone into liquidation. After the fund had met the fixed entitlements of pensioners, there was a surplus of some £9m remaining in the fund. Rule 13(5) of the fund's rules granted a power of appointment over any surplus, which could be exercised to increase the entitlements of the pensioners. This power was held by the company and not by the separate trustee of the fund. If the power was not exercised, an undistributed surplus would pass to the company itself (see Figure 16.3). In these circumstances Warner J concluded that the power was a fiduciary power, even though the trustee was not the donee.[116] He relied on two main factors to reach this conclusion. First, he considered that if the power were a mere power and not a fiduciary power, any supposed discretion by the company to appoint increased entitlements to the pensioners would be 'illusory', since the company would in effect only be making ex gratia gifts from property which they owned absolutely.[117] Second, the objects of the power were not volunteers, as the fund surplus had arisen partially from their own pension contributions and not from successful investment or over-contribution by the company alone.[118]

---

[112] [1982] 1 WLR 202.   [113] See also *Breadner v Granville-Grossman* [2001] Ch 523.

[114] [1990] 1 WLR 1587. See Gardner 'Fiduciary Powers in Toytown' (1991) 107 LQR 214. The reasoning as it relates to the setting aside of decisions by trustees (the rule in *Re Hastings Bass*) was restricted by *Pitt v Holt* [2011] EWCA Civ 197, but the case remains relevant on the points cited.

[115] Using the language of Chitty J in *Re Somes* [1896] 1 Ch 250.

[116] This finding of a fiduciary duty has been subject to criticism—see Barkley 'The content of the trust: what must a trustee be obliged to do with the property?' (2013) Trusts & Trustees 452.

[117] Barkley 'The content of the trust', at 547.   [118] [1993] OPLR 171.

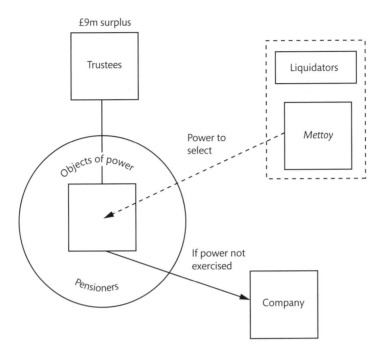

Figure 16.3 Fiduciary powers: *Mettoy Pension Trustees v Evans*

(b) Duties of the donee of fiduciary powers

The key difference between a 'fiduciary power' and a 'mere power' is that the donee of a fiduciary power owes limited duties to the objects. In *Re Hay's Settlement Trusts*[119] Sir Robert Megarry V-C held that there were three additional duties owed by the donee to the objects of a fiduciary power. These duties point to the fact that the donee of a fiduciary power must have a greater sensitivity to the nature of the discretion that he holds.

(i) Duty periodically to consider whether or not he should exercise the power

Unlike a mere power, which the donee need never consider whether or not to exercise, Megarry V-C held that the donee of a fiduciary power cannot 'simply fold his hands and ignore it, for normally he must from time to time consider whether or not to exercise the power'.[120] This duty is enforceable by the court, which may direct the donee to consider whether he should exercise the power.[121]

(ii) Duty to consider the range of objects of the power

The fiduciary nature of the position of the donee also affects the manner in which a donee makes appointments. Following the decision of the House of Lords in *McPhail v Doulton*,[122] which concerned the duties of trustees of a discretionary trust, Megarry

---

[119] [1982] 1 WLR 202. [120] [1982] 1 WLR 202, at 209. [121] [1982] 1 WLR 202.
[122] [1971] AC 424.

V-C held that the donee of a fiduciary power must 'make such a survey of the range of objects' as will enable him to carry out his fiduciary duty.[123] This does not mean that he has to identify every single member of the class of objects before making any allocations of the fund, but that he must find out 'the permissible area of selection'. He cannot make an appointment to the first object who comes to mind.

(iii) Duty to consider the appropriateness of individual appointments

Having considered the range of potential objects, the donee of a fiduciary power must 'then consider responsibly, in individual cases, whether a contemplated beneficiary was within the power and whether, in relation to other possible claimants, a particular grant was appropriate'.[124]

(iv) Duty to make trust documents available to the objects

In *Schmidt v Rosewood Trust Ltd*[125] the Privy Council held that the objects of a fiduciary power of appointment may be entitled to seek disclosure of trust documents of the trust to which the power relates, so as to ensure the proper administration of the trust. However, this right is not absolute as disclosure is ordered under the inherent jurisdiction of the court, and the entitlement to disclosure may be limited or safeguarded so as to protect personal or commercial confidentiality, or to balance the competing interests of different beneficiaries, trustees, or third parties. At all events, the object of a power of appointment will not be granted access to trust documents which would reveal the trustees' reasons for exercising, or not exercising, the power.[126]

(v) Different duties in different contexts

There is a degree of circularity in identifying whether a power is fiduciary and what duties are imposed on the donee. The power is fiduciary because the donee is subject to duties; but it follows that if the power is fiduciary, the donee is subject to duties. Sir Robert Megarry's analysis in *Re Hay's Settlement Trusts*[127] of the duties of a donee of a fiduciary power tends to assume that all fiduciary powers involve the same duties. The decision of the Court of Appeal in *Gomez and others v Gomez-Monche Vives*[128] accepts that there is a wide range of fiduciary duties, some analogous to those of a trustee, and some less so. This means that a more sophisticated analysis of fiduciary powers is required: a power will be fiduciary if the donee is subject to duties, but the nature of those duties will depend upon an analysis of the instrument creating the power and any other relevant circumstances.

---

[123] Per Lord Wilberforce, quoted by Sir Robert Megarry V-C in *Re Hay's Settlement Trusts* [1982] 1 WLR 202, at 209.

[124] *McPhail v Doulton* [1971] AC 424, at 457, quoted by Sir Robert Megarry in *Re Hay's Settlement Trusts* [1982] 1 WLR 202, at 209.

[125] [2003] 2 AC 709; followed by Briggs J in *Breakspear v Auckland* [2009] Ch 32

[126] See Chapter 25 for a fuller discussion of the right to disclosure of trust documents.

[127] [1982] 1 WLR 202.   [128] [2008] EWCA Civ 1065; [2009] Ch 245 (CA).

(c) Supervision by the court of fiduciary powers

Since the donee of a fiduciary power owes duties to the objects, the court will ensure that these duties are properly performed.

(i) Appointments made without due consideration

If appointments are made by the donee without proper consideration of the range of objects and the appropriateness of the particular appointments being made, then such appointments will be void as an invalid exercise of the power. In *Turner v Turner*[129] the trustees of a settlement made appointments by deed under a power of appointment they held in their capacity as trustees. They had executed the deeds at the request of the solicitors acting for the settlor without reading or understanding what they were signing, and without making a decision to appoint. Mervyn Davies J held that these appointments should be set aside because they had been made 'in breach of their duty, in that it was their duty to "consider" before appointing, and this they did not do'.[130]

(ii) Failure to exercise the power

Where the donee of a fiduciary power has failed to make any appointments, the question arises whether the court can intervene to compel them to carry out their duties. In *Re Hay's Settlement Trusts*[131] Sir Robert Megarry V-C indicated that the courts would compel the donee of a fiduciary power to consider exercising it.[132] However, the courts have been reluctant to suggest that they would compel the donee to *exercise* the power, as this is inconsistent with its discretionary character. In *McPhail v Doulton*[133] Lord Wilberforce cited the judgment of Lord Upjohn in *Re Gulbenkian's Settlement*[134] and stated:

> although the trustees may … be under a fiduciary duty to consider whether or in what way they should exercise their power the court will not normally compel its exercise.[135]

However, in the *Mettoy*[136] case Warner J considered that in some circumstances the court might be willing to step in and compel the exercise of a fiduciary power. On the facts of *Mettoy*, the company donee was incapable of exercising the power itself, and it was held by the liquidators. They would be unable to exercise it because of a conflict between their duty to give proper consideration to exercising it in favour of the pensioners and their duty to the company's creditors, which would require them to exercise the power to enable the company to take the surplus in default. Warner J held that, since there was no one remaining who could exercise the power, the court should step in. He held that in such circumstances the court could exercise the fiduciary power in the same way that it was entitled to intervene if the trustees of a discretionary trust were failing to carry out their duties.

It is suggested caution is needed. The traditional distinction between trusts, which the court will enforce, and powers, which it will not, would be all but abolished if

---

[129] [1983] 2 All ER 745.   [130] [1983] 2 All ER 745, at 752.   [131] [1982] 1 WLR 202.
[132] [1982] 1 WLR 202, at 209.   [133] [1971] AC 424.   [134] [1970] AC 508.
[135] [1971] AC 424, at 456–457.   [136] [1990] 1 WLR 1587.

the courts are willing to enforce fiduciary powers in exactly the same way that they will enforce discretionary trusts. The limitation seems to be the recognition that this procedure is only available in the limited exceptional circumstances where the power cannot be exercised because there is no donee able to make any appointments.

A different problem arises where the donee of a fiduciary power has failed to make any appointments because he has not fulfilled his duty to consider whether or not to exercise the power. In *Breadner v Granville-Grossman*[137] the two trustees of a discretionary trust were granted a power of appointment in 1976. Under the terms of the trust this power had to be exercised before a specified date, namely, 2 August 1989. At a late stage one of the trustees prepared a deed appointing the entire beneficial interest to one beneficiary, which he only explained to his co-trustee on the day that the deed was executed, which was 2 August 1989, in other words after the last day for exercising the 1976 power. The beneficiary claimed that the appointment was still effective in equity, on the grounds that the trustees had failed to comply with their duty to consider exercising it. Park J held that, while the trustees had failed to perform their duty to consider exercising the power, the court could not intervene because the power had ceased to be exercisable, even though they would have made the appointment if they had performed their duty.

(d) Validity of fiduciary powers

(i) Certainty

The test for certainty of objects of a fiduciary power is the same as that for a mere power, namely, the 'is or is not' test.

(ii) Capriciousness

It is clear from *Re Manisty's Settlement*[138] and *Re Hay's Settlement Trusts*[139] that a fiduciary power will be void if it is capricious in nature.

(iii) Administrative unworkability

In *McPhail v Doulton*[140] Lord Wilberforce suggested that a discretionary trust which is not void for uncertainty may yet be void for 'administrative unworkability'[141] if the class is 'too wide to form anything like a class'.[142] In *Re Hay's Settlement Trusts*[143] Sir Robert Megarry V-C considered that the principle of 'administrative unworkability' was directed only towards discretionary trusts and had no application to fiduciary powers.

(7) Release of powers

The donor of a power of appointment, whether a bare power or a fiduciary power, may wish to release it. As a consequence of release he will cease to be able to make any

---

[137] [2000] 4 All ER 705.   [138] [1974] Ch 17.   [139] [1982] 1 WLR 202.
[140] [1971] AC 424.
[141] [1971] AC 424, at 444. See Gardner 'Fiduciary Powers in Toytown' (1991) 107 LQR 214
[142] [1971] AC 424, at 457.   [143] [1982] 1 WLR 202.

appointments of the fund. This has the same effect on the ownership of the property subject to the power as if the power had not been exercised. Therefore, on release those entitled in default will automatically become entitled to the property previously held subject to the power. Sometimes a power may be released to remove persons from the class of potential recipients of the property if the possibility of their receiving a benefit would result in tax disadvantages. For example, it may be advantageous to exclude the settlor from the class of objects of a power to avoid inheritance tax under the 'reservation of benefit' rules.[144] Similarly, a settlement may be liable to income tax if the settlor or his wife may benefit from the exercise of a power of appointment in their favour. In *Muir v IRC*[145] the Court of Appeal held that the trustees had released their power to pay income from the trust towards the payment of premiums of insurance policies held by persons including the settlor, and that therefore the settlor had no interest in the income from the settlement and was not liable to surtax. In *Re Wills' Trust Deeds*[146] property was held on trust for such of the issue of the testator or charitable institutions as the trustees should appoint. The trustees sought to release the power in favour of the testator's issue so that the trust would be for exclusively charitable objects.

(a) The consequences of release

If property is gifted to persons subject to a power of appointment which may divest them of their interest, on the release of the power their interests will become indefeasible. This was seen in *Re Mills*,[147] which concerned the will of Algernon Mills. His residuary estate was to be held for the benefit of such of his father's children and remoter issue that his brother should appoint or, in default of any such appointment, for his brother absolutely. The brother made a number of appointments and then released the power by deed. The Court of Appeal held that this was a valid release, and the consequence was that the brother became absolutely entitled to the property under the default provision.

(b) Authority to release

Not every power is capable of being released by the donee. The leading authority concerning the circumstances in which a power may be released is the judgment of Buckley J in *Re Wills' Trust Deeds*.[148] Generally, a donee will only be able to release a power which he is under no obligation to exercise or to consider exercising.

(i) Mere powers

In the case of a bare or mere power, which is not held in any fiduciary capacity and where there is no express or implied trust in favour of the objects in default of appointment, the donee may release the power. As Buckley J said:

> Where a power is conferred on someone who is not a trustee of the property to which the power relates or, if he is such a trustee, is not conferred on him in that capacity, then in

---

[144] See Chapter 3.   [145] [1966] 1 WLR 1269.   [146] [1964] Ch 219.
[147] [1930] 1 Ch 654, CA.   [148] [1964] Ch 219.

the absence of a trust in favour of the objects of the power in default of appointment, the donee is, at any rate prima facie, not under any duty recognisable by the court to exercise a power such as to disenable him from releasing the power.[149]

Mere powers fall within the ambit of s 155 of the Law of Property Act 1925, which provides:

> A person to whom any power, whether coupled with an interest or not, is given, may by deed release, or contract not to exercise, the power.[150]

(ii) Mere powers with a trust in favour of the objects in default of appointment

Where there is a trust in default of appointment under the power, according to Buckley J, the donee is not entitled to release the power so as to defeat the trust. This will be so whether the trust in default is express or implied under the rule in *Burrough v Philcox*.[151] This was explained by Buckley J:

> if a power is granted to appoint among a class of objects and in default of appointment there is a trust, express or implied, in favour of the members of that class, the donee of the power cannot by failure to appoint or by purporting to bind himself not to appoint or, which comes to the same thing, by purporting to release his power, defeat the interests of the members of the class of objects. This proposition really needs only to be stated to be accepted. The problem in such cases, where there is no express trust in default of appointment, is whether such a trust should be inferred...[A] power of the kind just mentioned cannot be released, for the donee is under a duty to exercise it, notwithstanding that the court may not be able to compel him personally to perform that duty, and can remedy his default only be executing the trust in default of appointment.[152]

Buckley J's view that a power cannot be released in this situation is based on the assumption that the trust in favour of the members of the class arises from an obligation to exercise the power. As has already been explained, this may not be the best interpretation of *Burrough v Philcox*. Despite his view to the contrary, the logic of his statement that the power cannot be released also cannot apply to an express trust by way of gift over in default in favour of the class of objects. Such release will accelerate the gift in favour of the class. In *Re Radcliffe*[153] a father held a power of appointment in favour of the class of objects of his children, with an express trust in favour of them equally in default of appointment. One of the three children had died in infancy, and the father was entitled as his administrator. The father released the power of appointment by deed and demanded that the trustees pay a third of the trust property to him. The Court of Appeal, following the earlier case of *Smith v Houblon*,[154] held that there had been a valid release and that, subject to the father surrendering his life-interest over the trust, he was entitled to the third to be transferred to him.

---

[149] [1964] Ch 219, at 237.
[150] Law of Property Act 1925, s 160 provides that s 155 applies to 'powers created or arising either before or after the commencement' of the Act.   [151] (1840) 5 My & Cr 72.
[152] [1964] Ch 219, at 236.   [153] [1892] 1 Ch 27.   [154] (1859) 26 Beav 482.

(iii) Fiduciary powers

Fiduciary powers with no authorization to release

Where a power is held in a fiduciary capacity, whether by a trustee or other fiduciary, the donee may not release it unless release is authorized by the instrument creating the power. When the predecessor to s 155 of the Law of Property Act 1925 was enacted in 1881,[155] the courts held that it did not apply to trusts held in a fiduciary capacity.[156] This was followed by the Court of Appeal in *Re Mills*[157] and in *Re Wills' Trust Deeds*, where Buckley J said:

> [W]here a power is conferred on trustees virtute officii in relation to their trust property, they cannot release it or bind themselves not to exercise it…[T]he same is true if the power is conferred on persons who are in fact trustees of the settlement but is conferred on them by name and not by reference to their office, if on the true view of the facts they were selected as donees of the power because they were the trustees.[158]

This principle was applied by Millett J in *Re Courage Group's Pension Schemes*,[159] where he held that a committee of management of a pension scheme could not release their powers or discretion so as to deprive their successors of the right to exercise them as they were vested in the committee in a fiduciary capacity. This restriction will also apply where the power is held in a fiduciary capacity, even though the donees are not trustees, as in *Mettoy Pension Trustees v Evans*,[160] the company, although not a trustee of the fund, held a power of appointment in a fiduciary capacity and could not release it.

Fiduciary powers with authorization to release

The donee of a fiduciary power will be entitled to release it if the instrument creating the power gives him the authority to do so. The principle was stated by Harman LJ in *Muir v IRC*,[161] where he commented on the judgment of Buckley J in *Re Wills' Trusts Deeds*:[162]

> I would agree that, if a power is conferred on trustees virtute officii, that is to say, if it be a [fiduciary] power which the trustees have the duty to exercise, they cannot release it in the absence of words in the trust deed authorising them to do so…[163]

On the facts he found that the trust instrument did authorize a release.[164]

(iv) Discretionary trusts

Due to the evolutionary development of concepts and terminology, some early cases referring to 'trust powers' would today be recognized as 'discretionary trusts'. Clearly, these cannot be released because the obligation is in the nature of a trust, and the court will compel its exercise.

---

[155] Conveyancing Act 1881, s 52.
[156] See *Weller v Kerr* (1866) LR 1 Sc & Div 11; *Re Eyre* (1883) 49 LT 259; *Saul v Pattinson* (1886) 55 LJ Ch 831.   [157] [1930] 1 Ch 654.
[158] [1964] Ch 219.   [159] [1987] 1 WLR 495.   [160] [1991] 2 All ER 513.
[161] [1990] 1 WLR 1587.   [162] [1964] Ch 219.   [163] [1966] 1 WLR 1269, at 1283.
[164] See also *Blausten v IRC* [1972] Ch 256, CA.

(c) Means of release

It seems clear that a purely oral release will be ineffective to release a power.[165] However, if a donee of a power of appointment possesses the jurisdiction to release the power, he may do so by deed, as provided in s 155 of the Law of Property Act 1925. Alternatively, a power may be released by the donee entering into a contract not to exercise the power, as also provided in s 155. It seems that a power will also be released where there has been any dealing with the property subject to it which is inconsistent with the exercise of the power. In *Foakes v Jackson*[166] a power was held jointly by a husband and wife, and the survivor had a separate power. A deed was executed in 1886 by the husband, wife, and those beneficially entitled to the property assigning it to one of the objects. In 1899, after the wife's death, the husband purported to appoint the property to a different object. Farwell J held that the earlier deed which, with the intention of the donees and the parties entitled in default, had the effect of passing the property absolutely to the object operated as a release of the power. Similarly, in *Re Courtauld's Settlement*[167] Plowman J held that where there had been an application to vary a settlement so that a power was extinguished, there was no need to execute a separate deed of release. Trustees may surrender their trusts and powers by paying the trust property into court, as provided in s 63 of the Trustee Act 1925.

(d) Release and fraud on a power

The equitable doctrine that will invalidate the fraudulent exercise of a power has no application to the release of a power of appointment, and therefore a donee may release a power even though he thereby derives a personal benefit. In *Re Somes*[168] a father held a power of appointment over property held on his marriage settlement. In default, his daughter was absolutely entitled. He was suffering financial difficulties and therefore released the power and he and his daughter then mortgaged their interests in the fund for £10,000, which was paid to the father. Chitty J held that this was a perfectly valid release:

> it appears to me that there is a fallacy in applying to a release of a power of this kind the doctrines applicable to the fraudulent exercise of such a power. There is no duty imposed on the donee of a limited power to make an appointment; there is no fiduciary relationship between him and the objects of the power beyond this, that if he does exercise the power of appointment, he must exercise it honestly for the benefit of an object or the objects of the power, and not corruptly for his own personal benefit; but I cannot see any ground for applying that doctrine to the case of a release of a power; the donee of the power may, or he may not, be acting in his own interest, but he is at liberty, in my opinion, to say that he will never make any appointment under the power, and to execute a release of it.[169]

Obviously, this will only apply if the power is of a type which may be released, and the court finds that the power is not subject to fiduciary duties excluding such a release.

[165] See *Re Christie-Miller's Settlement Trusts* [1961] 1 All ER 855n; *Re Courtauld's Settlement* [1965] 2 All ER 544n. [166] [1900] 1 Ch 807.
[167] [1965] 2 All ER 544n.   [168] [1896] 1 Ch 250.   [169] [1896] 1 Ch 250, at 255.

2 **Discretionary trusts**

(1) **Introduction**

(a) The nature of discretionary trusts

(i) The definition of discretionary trusts

Discretionary trusts were usefully defined by Warner J in *Mettoy Pension Trustees Ltd v Evans* as:

> cases where someone, usually but not necessarily the trustee,[170] is under a duty to select from among a class of beneficiaries those who are to receive, and the proportions in which they are to receive, income or capital of the trust property.[171]

They are mechanisms by which an owner of property can grant to others the power to allocate a fund among a defined group of individuals. As in a power of appointment, the allocator has complete discretion how the fund should be allocated, either or both in terms of the persons who should receive shares of the fund, and the size of the shares they should receive. However, unlike powers of appointment, the allocator is under a mandatory duty to make allocations in accordance with the terms of the trust. The court will intervene to ensure that this duty is discharged.

(ii) The flexibility of discretionary trusts

The discretionary trust is therefore an extremely flexible mechanism for the distribution of property. It combines all the advantages of the power of appointment in permitting the owner of property not merely to delegate the task of transferring his property to others, but also of delegating the responsibility for deciding how that property should be distributed. Yet it avoids the potential pitfalls of the mere power because the trustees are under a duty to distribute according to the terms of the trust, which is enforceable by the court. This inherent flexibility, coupled with the security of enforcement by the court, has made the discretionary trust ideal as a means of allocating large funds among large potential classes of beneficiaries. For example, in the leading case of *McPhail v Doulton*,[172] Bertram Baden established a trust in 1941 to provide benefits for the staff of Matthew Hall & Co Ltd and their relatives and dependants (see Figure 16.4). Clause 9(a) of the deed stated that:

> The trustees shall apply the net income of the fund in making at their absolute discretion grants to or for the benefit of any of the officers and employees or ex-officers and ex-employees of the company or to any relative or dependants of any such person in such amounts... as they think fit.

In 1941 the company employed some 1,300 people. By 1962 the fund contained assets valued at £163,000, which had risen to £463,000 in 1972. Clearly, it was never the

---

[170] This exception is probably intended to recognize the possibility of there being separate management and custodian trustees.   [171] [1990] 1 WLR 1587.

[172] [1971] AC 424.

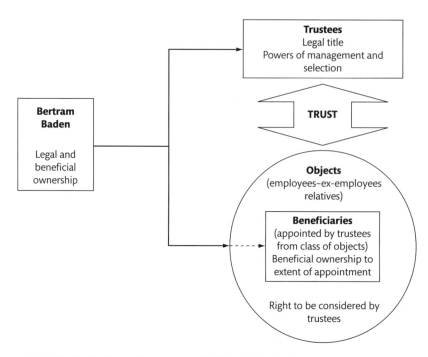

Figure 16.4 The *Baden* discretionary trust (*McPhail v Doulton*)

intention of Mr Baden that each and every member of the specified class should receive payments from the fund, but that those appointed trustees should have the discretion to select some to benefit. Equally, it was not his intention that the trustees be able to sit idly by and fail to make any allocations at all. The language of the deed clearly indicated an obligation, or duty, to distribute the income of the fund. The House of Lords held that a discretionary trust had been created. Although the trustees had complete discretion which particular members of the class specified were to receive shares of the income produced by the fund, they had no freedom to refuse to carry out the trust.

(b) The development of the discretionary trust

Although the terminology of the 'discretionary trust' is a more recent development, the underlying concept of an equitable obligation which is discretionary in part while remaining predominantly mandatory is well established and has a strong historical pedigree.[173] In *Brown v Higgs*[174] Lord Eldon, the Lord Chancellor, held that equitable obligations could not simply be categorized as trusts or powers:

> But there are not only a mere trust and a mere power, but there is also known to this court a power which the party to whom it is given is entrusted and required to execute; and with regard to that species of power the court consider it as partaking so much of the nature

and qualities of a trust that, if the person who has that duty imposed upon him does not discharge it, the court will, to a certain extent, discharge the duty in his room and place.[175]

In essence, he was describing what today would be termed a discretionary trust. The older cases often use the phrase 'trust power'. This term has been the source of some confusion, since it is used interchangeably in the cases to describe both a trust implied in default of the exercise of a power of appointment under the principle of *Burrough v Philcox*,[176] and an obligation which would today be characterized as a discretionary trust.

> In *Crockett v Crockett*,[177] Lord Cottenham found that a possible construction of a will where a husband left all his property 'at the disposal of his wife, for herself and children', was that she was 'as between herself and her children found a trustee, with a large discretion as to the application of the fund'.[178] This analysis was followed by Sir John Romilly MR in *Hart v Tribe*.[179] Even in the leading case of *McPhail v Doulton*[180] the House of Lords spoke of the obligation created by Baden's deed as a 'trust power',[181] although when the case returned to the Court of Appeal as *Re Baden's Deed Trusts (No 2)*[182] the term 'discretionary trust' was used. It is important to be alive to the different terminology used.[183]

(c) Types of discretionary trusts

There are two types of discretionary trust: 'exhaustive' and 'non-exhaustive'.

(i) Exhaustive discretionary trusts

In an exhaustive discretionary trust the trustees are subject to a duty to distribute the whole of the trust fund, or its income, to the potential beneficiaries. They have no power to decide not to distribute part of the fund. An example of an exhaustive discretionary trust is found in *Re Locker's Settlement Trusts*,[184] where a discretionary trust was established in favour of a class of individuals, charities, and other institutions. The trustees were regarded as being in breach of trust when they failed to distribute the trust income within a reasonable period of time.[185] An exhaustive discretionary trust will arise, as in *Re Gourju's Will Trusts*,[186] whenever the trustees are not given an express power to retain all or part of the income from the fund.

(ii) Non-exhaustive discretionary trusts

In a non-exhaustive discretionary trust the trustees are not obliged to distribute the whole of the trust fund income among the class of beneficiaries but may, in their

---

[175] (1800) 5 Ves 495 at 570.
[176] (1840) 5 My & Cr 72.   [177] (1848) 2 Ph 553.   [178] (1848) 2 Ph 553, at 561.
[179] (1854) 18 Beav 215.   [180] [1971] AC 424.
[181] Lord Wilberforce did on one occasion refer to 'discretionary trusts': see [1971] AC 424, at 452.
[182] [1973] Ch 9.
[183] See also *Mettoy Pensions v Evans* [1991] [1990[1 WLR 1587, for a useful discussion of the various terminologies used in the cases, and the potential for confusion between trusts and powers.
[184] [1977] 1 WLR 1323.   [185] [1977] 1 WLR 1323, at 1325.   [186] [1943] Ch 24.

discretion, decide to accumulate it. This is only possible if the trustees are expressly given the power to retain and accumulate the income, or part of the income, from the trust fund by the terms of the trust. *McPhail v Doulton*[187] is an example of a non-exhaustive discretionary trust. The trust deed did not require the trustees to distribute all the income generated by the fund to the employees, ex-employees, relatives, and dependants, but granted them the power to retain and accumulate it.[188] In many ways a non-exhaustive discretionary trust is extremely similar in practice to a fiduciary power. In neither case is the allocator of the fund obliged to distribute the fund or its income to the class of potential objects or beneficiaries. This leads to the question whether there is any real distinction between them.[189] Analytically, a distinction can be drawn on the basis of the nature of the duties owed by the allocator in each case. Under a non-exhaustive discretionary trust, the prime duty of the trustee is to distribute the fund income among the class of beneficiaries, although there is a power to retain and accumulate.[190] Whether the trustee has exercised that power properly is open to the supervision of the court under an objective test, that he must have acted in the best interests of the class of beneficiaries. In the case of a power of appointment, the donee of the power has no prime duty, as it is purely within his discretion whether he allocates the property subject to the power. He owes no objective duties that the court can supervise, but purely a subjective duty to act as he thinks best. Provided he acts genuinely, the court cannot question his decision. This is a fine distinction, but it demonstrates that the non-exhaustive discretionary trust remains in essence a trust, although it is extremely close on the scale of equitable obligations to the fiduciary power.[191] A further distinction is that, under a discretionary trust, the legal title to the trust fund will normally be vested in the trustees, who will thus also be required to invest and manage the trust property. In contrast, a fiduciary power may be held by a person with no rights of ownership to the fund. Thus, in *Mettoy Pension Trustees Ltd v Evans*[192] a power of appointment over a pension fund surplus was held in a fiduciary capacity by a company which was not simultaneously the trustee thereof. However, in the majority of cases a fiduciary power will be held by a trustee, since the donee's status as a trustee invests the power with fiduciary characteristics.

(2) **Essential validity of discretionary trusts**

A discretionary trust will only be validly created if it satisfies the requirements for the validity of trusts in general. It must have certainty of subject matter and objects, and

---

[187] [1971] AC 424.

[188] Clause 9(b) of the deed creating the Matthew Hall Staff trust fund stated: 'The trustees shall not be bound to exhaust the income of any year or other period in making grants…' and granted them a power to invest the undistributed surplus under clause 6(a).

[189] See [1970] ASCL 187 (Davies); Grbich '*Baden*: Awakening the Conceptually Moribund Trust' (1974) 37 MLR 643; (1976) 54 CBR 229 (Cullity).

[190] Compare eg a trust for sale of land, where the trustees are under a duty to sell but have a power to postpone sale. See Chapter 1.   [191] See Chapter 2.

[192] [1990] 1 WLR 1587.

it must comply with the beneficiary principle. The trust must not exist for a period exceeding the duration of the perpetuity period.[193] Some aspects of these general requirements warrant detailed attention in the context of discretionary trusts, and there are also some additional requirements which are specific to such trusts, especially that they must not be 'administratively unworkable'.

(a) Certainty of objects

(i) The test for certainty prior to McPhail v Doulton

When the trust fund is subject to a fixed trust, the trustees hold the fund on trust for the beneficiaries in the shares and proportions determined by the settlor who created the fund. They have no discretion as to how the fund should be allocated. Where the beneficiaries are defined as a class, a fixed trust will be void for uncertainty unless it is possible to draw up a 'complete list' of each and every person who is a member of the specified class. This is because the trustee (or the court in the event of his default) must know the full extent of the class before he is able to determine the individual shares of each beneficiary and carry out the trust. Prior to the leading case of *McPhail v Doulton*,[194] this test was also applied to discretionary trusts. Thus, in *IRC v Broadway Cottages Trust*[195] the Court of Appeal held that a discretionary trust in favour of a class of beneficiaries that could not be completely ascertained at any one moment was void for uncertainty. There were two essential rationales for the application of the 'complete list' test to discretionary trusts:

The court must be able to exercise the trust

In *Morice v Bishop of Durham*,[196] Lord Eldon stated that a trust is only valid if the court is able to execute it in the event of a failure by the trustee to carry out their obligation so to do, whether through death, neglect, or refusal. The 'complete list test' was applied to discretionary trusts because it was thought that the only method the court could employ to carry out the trust in the event of the trustee's default was to order equal division of the fund between all the potential beneficiaries. Obviously, such equal division would require a complete list of the beneficiaries. However, some early cases had adopted a more flexible approach, holding that the court could exercise its discretion in the event of the trustee's failure. In *Moseley v Moseley*[197] an estate was held on trust by two trustees for such of the testator's relatives as they should think fit. When the trustees failed to exercise their discretion to allocate the property, the court ordered that it be conveyed into court, rather than divided equally among the class of potential beneficiaries.[198] In *Warburton v Warburton*[199] trustees held a fund on discretionary trust for the testator's children. The House of Lords ordered that the eldest child be given a double share. In *Hart v Tribe*[200] a testator's wife held £4,000 on discretionary trust for herself and his children. She refused to award any of the income from the fund for

---

[193] *Re Coleman* [1936] Ch 528.   [194] [1971] AC 424.   [195] [1955] Ch 20.
[196] (1805) 10 Ves 522, at 539–540.   [197] (1673) Cas temp Finch 53.
[198] See also *Clarke v Turner* (1694) Freem Ch 198.   [199] (1702) 4 Bro Parl Cas 1.
[200] (1854) 19 Beav 149.

the education and maintenance of his son by another marriage. Sir John Romilly MR directed that the boy receive £30 a year from the fund. Although explicable as a case where the trustees' discretion had not been exercised bona fides, this decision does seem to amount to an exercise of the discretion by the court. In earlier proceedings[201] the Master of the Rolls had indicated that, although the normal means by which the court can execute the trust is equal division between the beneficiaries, this is only one method, and that the court can compel the trustees to exercise their discretion.[202] However, the orthodox position was reiterated in *Gray v Gray*,[203] where Thomas Smith MR held that the only way the court could exercise a discretionary trust where the trustee had failed to do so was by ordering equal division between all the members of the class, and a similar view was taken by Sir Richard Arden in *Kemp v Kemp*.[204] The cases which adopted a more flexible approach were condemned as anomalous by the Court of Appeal in *IRC v Broadway Cottages Trust*.[205] Jenkins LJ asserted the principle that 'a trust for such members of a given class of objects as the trustees shall select is void for uncertainty, unless the whole range of objects eligible for selection is ascertained or capable of ascertainment'.[206] The court rejected the view that it could execute the trust in any way other than by the equal division of the fund among all the potential beneficiaries:

> it might be assumed that the trustees for some reason or other might fail or refuse to make any distribution, and see whether the court could execute the trust in that event. Consideration of the case on that assumption shows that the most the court could do would be to remove the inert or recalcitrant trustees and appoint others in their place. That, however, would not be execution of the trust by the court, but a mere substitution for one set of trustees invested with an uncontrollable discretion of another set of trustees similarly invested, who might be equally inert or recalcitrant.[207]

The trustee must be able to exercise his discretion

In the case of a discretionary trust the trustee is subject to an obligation to exercise his discretion to distribute the fund among the class of potential beneficiaries.[208] An underlying assumption of the cases prior to *McPhail v Doulton*[209] was that the trustee would not be able properly to exercise his discretion without drawing up a complete list of the class before making decisions as to how he should allocate the fund. Unlike the donee of a mere power of appointment, who owes no fiduciary duty to the objects, the trustee of a discretionary trust owes the class of beneficiaries fiduciary duties and for this reason would be expected to consider them individually before exercising his discretion. This would require a complete list.

---

[201] *Hart v Tribe* (1854) 18 Beav 215.
[202] See also *Richardson v Chapman* (1760) 7 Bro Parl Cas 318.   [203] (1862) 13 I Ch R 404.
[204] (1801) 5 Ves Jr 849.   [205] [1955] Ch 20.   [206] [1955] Ch 20, at 36.
[207] [1955] Ch 20, at 31.
[208] Although in the case of a non-exhaustive discretionary trust he has the power to accumulate rather than distribute.   [209] [1971] AC 424.

(ii) Criticism of the 'complete list' test

The 'complete list' test applied to discretionary trusts in *IRC v Broadway Cottages Trust*[210] was open to two major criticisms. First, it failed to take account of the developing social function of discretionary trusts. While it might have been appropriate for 'family'-style discretionary trusts, where there was a small class of potential beneficiaries, so that in the event of default by the trustee equal division would be a sensible and fair solution, it was entirely inappropriate for discretionary trusts designed to allocate benefits from a fund among a large class of potential beneficiaries. The 'complete list' test was simply unworkable for trusts such as that established in *McPhail v Doulton*,[211] since it would never be possible to draw up a list of every single individual who fell within the class of employees, ex-employees, and relatives and dependants. The continued application of the 'complete list test' would stagnate the developing social function of the discretionary trust as a means of allocating property. Secondly, it placed too much emphasis on the distinction between trusts and powers of appointment. An inevitable consequence of the adoption of the complete list test for discretionary trusts was that it became essential to tell if a particular obligation was a trust or a power. If it were characterized as a power, then it would probably be valid, as the test of certainty in *Re Gulbenkian's Settlement Trusts*[212] would apply. If it were characterized as a trust, then the much more demanding complete list test would render it void. This placed an undue significance to the question of characterization, especially since the obligations are in essence very similar to each other. This problem is well illustrated by the history of the litigation in *McPhail v Doulton*.[213] Goff J, at first instance, and the majority of the Court of Appeal, held that a valid power had been created. This was despite the fact that the language creating the obligation was clearly of a mandatory character, and therefore the House of Lords unanimously held that it was a discretionary trust. The factor that had influenced the decisions of the lower courts was the problem that, as a result of the *Broadway Cottages*[214] test, to characterize the obligation as a trust would be to render it completely void for uncertainty, as indeed the minority of Lord Hodson and Lord Guest held. It was clearly unsatisfactory that the question of the validity of an obligation should depend upon the fine distinction between powers and discretionary trusts. As Lord Wilberforce observed:

> It is striking how narrow and in a sense artificial is the distinction, in cases such as the present, between trusts or as the particular type of trust is called, trust powers, and powers...It is only necessary to read the learned judgment in the Court of Appeal to see that what to one mind may appear as a power of distribution coupled with a trust to dispose of the undistributed surplus, by accumulation or otherwise, may to another appear as a trust for distribution coupled with a power to withhold a portion and accumulate or otherwise dispose of it. A layman and, I suspect, also a logician would find it hard to understand what the difference is.[215]

Given this artificiality, the majority of the House of Lords radically altered the test of certainty applicable to discretionary trusts.

---

[210] [1955] Ch 20, CA.   [211] [1971] AC 424.   [212] [1970] AC 508.   [213] [1971] AC 424.
[214] [1955] Ch 20.   [215] *McPhail v Doulton* [1971] AC 424, at 448.

(iii) McPhail v Doulton

The effect of the decision of the majority of the House of Lords in *McPhail v Doulton*[216] was briefly summarized by Lord Wilberforce:

> the rule recently fastened upon the courts by *IRC v Broadway Cottages Trust* ought to be discarded and the test for the validity of [discretionary trusts][217] ought to be similar to that accepted by this House in *Re Gulbenkian's Settlement* for powers, namely, that the trust is valid if it can be said with certainty that any given individual is or is not a member of the class.[218]

Thus, it is no longer necessary that it be possible to draw up a 'complete list' of potential beneficiaries. To reach this conclusion Lord Wilberforce, with whom Lord Reid and Viscount Dilhorne concurred, had to overcome the perceived obstacles which had led to the adoption of the 'complete list test'.

Equal division was inappropriate if the trustee defaulted in his duty

The rationale for the adoption of the 'complete list' test was that the court could only intervene to enforce the trust by 'equal division' of the fund between the class of potential beneficiaries. While conceding the applicability of equal division to 'family trusts', Lord Wilberforce demonstrated how it was wholly inappropriate to large-scale discretionary trusts of the type in issue:

> As a matter of reason to hold that a principle of equal division applies to trusts such as the present is certainly paradoxical. Equal division is surely the last thing the settlor ever intended: equal division among all may, probably would, produce a result beneficial to none…[219]

This represents a recognition that the social function of discretionary trusts had evolved to enable property owners to 'confer benefits on deserving cases among large constituencies—in the same sort of way as charitable trusts'.[220] Clearly, there was never any intention by Bertram Baden that every single employee, ex-employee, relative, and dependant should benefit from the fund he had established in their favour, but that the nominated trustees should choose some from that class to receive substantial benefits. The settlor's purpose in creating the fund would be completely defeated if, in the event of the trustees' default, each and every member of the class were to receive an insignificant payment which was far outweighed by the administrative costs of determining the full extent of the class.

The court could enforce the trust other than by ordering equal division

Although 'equal division' might be inappropriate, cases such as *Gray v Gray*[221] and *Kemp v Kemp*[222] suggested that the courts had no alternative. In *McPhail v Doulton*[223]

---

[216] [1971] AC 424.   [217] Lord Wilberforce actually used the term 'trust powers'.

[218] [1971] AC 424, at 456.   [219] [1971] AC 424, at 451.

[220] Gardner, *An Introduction to the Law of Trusts* (2nd edn 2003), pp 199–200.

[221] (1862) 13 I Ch R 404.   [222] (1795) 5 Ves 849.   [223] [1971] AC 424, at 457.

Lord Wilberforce noted the early cases where the courts had taken a more flexible approach,[224] and concluded that:

> the court, if called upon to execute the [discretionary trust],[225] will do so in the manner best calculated to give effect to the settlor's or testator's intentions ...

He suggested three alternative means by which the court is able to ensure that the trust is enforced:

> It may do so by appointing new trustees, or by authorising or directing representative persons to the classes of beneficiaries to prepare a scheme of distribution, or even, should the proper basis for distribution appear by itself directing the trustees so to distribute.

The trustee does not need a 'complete list' of the potential beneficiaries to exercise his discretion

The suggestion that the trustee must have a complete list of all the potential beneficiaries of the discretionary trust before he can exercise his discretion in favour of any particular beneficiary was also rejected by Lord Wilberforce:

> a trustee with a duty to distribute, particularly among a potentially very large class, would surely never require the preparation of a complete list of names, which anyhow would tell him little that he needs to know.[226]

Instead, the trustee has a duty of 'inquiry or ascertainment' so 'in each case the trustees ought to make such a survey of the range of objects or possible beneficiaries as will enable them to carry out their fiduciary duty'.[227]

(iv) Application of McPhail v Doulton

The House of Lords in *McPhail v Doulton*[228] settled the theoretical question: namely, which test for certainty of objects should govern discretionary trusts? The case was remitted to the Chancery Division for consideration as to whether the terms of the Baden trust met the new requirements, and the case reached the Court of Appeal under the name *Re Baden's Deed Trust (No 2)*.[229] The central question was whether the application of the 'is or is not' test adopted by the House of Lords from *Re Gulbenkian's Settlement Trusts*[230] requires positive proof of the negative limb, so that it can be categorically stated that any individual in the world 'is not' a member of the given class. Counsel[231] for Baden's personal representatives, who claimed the trust was void for uncertainty, argued that as 'relative' in its widest sense means 'descended from a common ancestor' it is impossible to prove that any given individual is not a 'relative'. Therefore, the trust should fail, since it is impossible to say with certainty of any given individual that 'he is not' a member of the class.

---

[224] [1971] AC 424, at 451. See also *Moseley v Moseley* (1673) Cas temp Finch 53; *Clarke v Turner* (1694) Freem Ch 198; *Warburton v Warburton* (1702) 4 Bro Parl Cas 1; *Richardson v Chapman* (1760) 7 Bro Parl Cas 318, HL.   [225] Lord Wilberforce used the term 'trust powers'.
[226] [1971] AC 424, at 449.   [227] [1971] AC 424, at 457.   [228] [1971] AC 424.
[229] [1973] Ch 9.   [230] [1970] AC 508.   [231] John Vinelott QC and Rupert Evans.

The majority of the Court of Appeal took the view that this was not the intended effect of the *Gulbenkian* test, and that it is not necessary to be able to prove that any given individual is not within the class. Sachs and Megaw LLJ distinguished 'conceptual' and 'evidential' certainty, and said that the test is satisfied provided the class is conceptually certain. As Sachs LJ observed:

> 'the court is never defeated by evidential uncertainty', and it is in my judgment clear that it is conceptual certainty to which reference was made when the 'is or is not a member of the class' test was enunciated ... The suggestion that such trusts could be invalid because it might be impossible to prove of a given individual that he was not in the relevant class is wholly fallacious ...[232]

Both Sachs and Megaw LLJ took the view that since the words 'relatives' and 'dependants' were conceptually certain in their widest possible meanings, the trust was valid and not void for uncertainty. However, they took slightly differing approaches to the problem of 'evidential certainty' (see Figure 16.5).[233] Sachs LJ took the view that if a class was 'conceptually certain' then there was in essence no evidential difficulty because of the operation of a presumption that anyone not positively proved to be within the class is outside of it. The burden falls on potential claimants to prove they fall within the class. Megaw LJ did not employ such a simple evidential presumption, but considered that there were three groups of persons: ie those positively proved within the class; those positively proved to be outside the class; and those about whom, if they were to be considered, it would have to be said they are not proven to be inside or outside the class. He concluded that the trust would be valid provided 'as regards a substantial number of objects, it can be said with certainty that they fall within the test'.[234] Stamp LJ took a differing view to that of the other members of the Court of Appeal. He accepted the argument that it must be possible to say of any individual that 'he is not a member of the class' and on that basis alone would have found the trust void for uncertainty.[235] However, he followed *Harding v Glyn*,[236] a previous authority where 'relations' had been treated by the court as meaning next of kin. He applied this to the Baden trust and concluded that 'relations' meant 'next of kin', which was sufficiently certain.[237]

To summarize, the effect of the decision of the Court of Appeal in *Re Baden's Deed Trusts (No 2)*[238] is that the application of the 'is or is not' test merely requires that the class of potential beneficiaries is conceptually certain. If the class is not conceptually certain, then the trust will be void, but it will not be rendered void merely by evidential uncertainty.[239]

(b) Administrative unworkability

(i) Definition

Even though a discretionary trust has sufficiently certain objects, it may still be void if it is 'administratively unworkable'. This concept was first proposed

---

[232] [1973] Ch 9, at 20.
[233] Criticized Hopkins 'Continuing Uncertainty as to Certainty of Objects of Trust Powers' [1973] CLJ 36; (1972) 36 Conv (NS) 351, 352.   [234] [1973] Ch 9, at 24.
[235] [1973] Ch 9, at 28.   [236] (1739) 1 Atk 469.   [237] [1973] Ch 9, at 28–29.   [238] [1973] Ch 9.
[239] See Emery 'The Most Hallowed Principle: Certainty of Beneficiaries of Trusts and Powers of Appointment' (1982) 98 LQR 551.

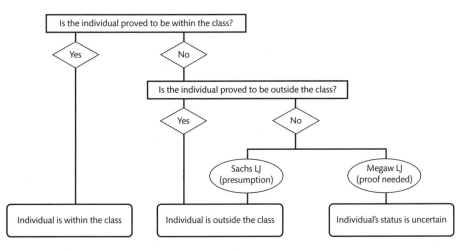

Figure 16.5 Dealing with evidential certainty

by Lord Wilberforce in *McPhail v Doulton*, where he suggested there may be classes where:

> the meaning of the words used is clear but the definition of the beneficiaries is so wide as to not form 'anything like a class' so that the trust is administratively unworkable wide [240]

He hesitated to give any example, but suggested that a discretionary trust in favour of 'all the residents of Greater London' would fall within the category of administratively unworkable trusts. The principle has been criticized because it is not clear precisely what evil it is seeking to prevent.[241] However, the cases suggest that the sheer size of the class is the most relevant factor. If a class is too vast in number, it is impossible for the trustees to carry out their duty to survey the range of the beneficiaries of the trust in any real sense, and in the event of their default the court would likewise be unable to carry out the distribution of the fund.

(ii) Application

In *Re Hay's Settlement Trusts*[242] Sir Robert Megarry V-C considered obiter that a discretionary trust with a class similar to that of an intermediate power, namely for all the people in the world except for an excluded class, would be administratively unworkable. In *R v District Auditor ex p West Yorkshire Metropolitan County Council*[243] the Council attempted to create a discretionary trust over a fund of £400,000 in favour of the 'inhabitants of the County of West Yorkshire'. The Council's purpose was to defeat government legislation which prevented them incurring expenditure prior to their being abolished. The Divisional Court held that, although the class was conceptually

---

[240] [1971] AC 424, at 457.
[241] See Harris 'Trust, Power and Duty' (1971) 87 LQR 31; McKay '*Re Baden* and the Third Class of Uncertainty' (1974) 38 Conv 269.
[242] [1982] 1 WLR 202.
[243] [1986] RVR 24; Harpum 'Administrative Unworkability and Purpose Trusts' [1986] CLJ 391.

certain the range of objects, comprising some 2.5 million potential beneficiaries, was so wide as to be 'incapable of forming anything like a class'. It was thus administratively unworkable and void. Drawing from Lord Wilberforce's example of 'all the residents of Greater London', and the facts of this case, it can be surmised that 'administrative unworkability' will only render discretionary trusts void which have a class ranging in the magnitude of millions. Where the line is to be drawn between trusts falling foul of the principle and those which are valid is impossible to predict. It is easier to understand the concept of administrative unworkability in the context of a fixed trust. There, in the case of a small gift to a large class, the costs of ascertainment and distribution could easily take up the whole, or a disproportionately large part, of the fund. With a discretionary trust it must be rare that a fund would be so small that no rational scheme could be devised. However, it is possible that with a small gift to a large class it might prove impossible to devise any scheme that could have sufficient regard to the interests of the class as a whole, to which the trustees owe fiduciary duties. That would surely then be a case of administrative unworkability. Unworkability could be avoided if, despite the smallness of the gift, the settlor gave some instruction as to the principles upon which the trustees should exercise their discretion.

(c) Capriciousness

A discretionary trust will also be void if it is capricious (see Figure 16.6). This principle was suggested in *Re Manisty's Settlement*[244] in the context of fiduciary powers, when Templeman J indicated that a power in favour of the 'residents of Greater London' might be capricious. The concept was developed in *Re Hay's Settlement Trusts*,[245] where Sir Robert Megarry V-C suggested that a power in favour of the 'residents of Greater London' would not be void for capriciousness if the donor of the power were, for example, a former mayor of the Greater London Council. It seems that a gift to members of a class will be capricious if there is absolutely no rational reason for making the gift to that class, and that the person charged with allocating the fund has no rational basis on which to make allocations. It is clear that capriciousness is a principle which applies to discretionary trusts and that it is a concept distinct from administrative unworkability. The discretionary trust in *R v District Auditor ex p West Yorkshire Metropolitan County Council*[246] was not regarded as capricious because the Council had every reason to create a fund in favour of its residents.

(3) Rights of beneficiaries of discretionary trusts

(a) A proprietary interest in the fund

In the case of a power of appointment, it is clear that the objects of the power have no proprietary interest in the fund unless an appointment is made in their favour. In the case of a fixed trust the beneficiaries have equitable title to the property held on trust for them, and may compel the trustees to transfer the legal title to them under

---

[244] [1974] Ch 17.   [245] [1982] 1 WLR 202.   [246] [1986] RVR 24.

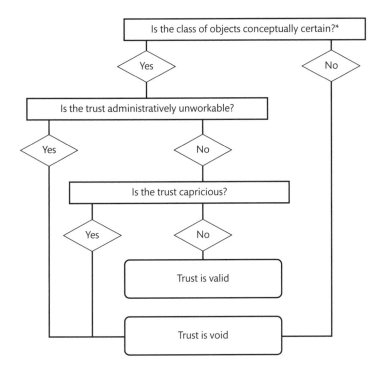

*Evidential uncertainty does not affect the validity of the trust.

Figure 16.6 The validity of discretionary trusts

the rule in *Saunders v Vautier*.[247] The position of the beneficiaries of a discretionary trust is not so clear cut, and has led some commentators to suggest that they have a 'quasi-proprietary' right.[248] The rights of the class as a whole are essentially different from the rights of any individual members of the class.

(i) A proprietary right for the class as a whole

By analogy with fixed trusts, since a discretionary trust is a mandatory equitable obligation and the trustees must distribute the fund among the beneficiaries, it would seem logical that the equitable title to the property is vested in the class of potential beneficiaries as a whole. This approach was taken in *Re Smith*,[249] where property was held by trustees on discretionary trust for Mrs Aspinall and her three children. Romer J, following the Court of Appeal decision in *Re Nelson*,[250] held that the class as a whole could have come to the trustees and demanded the transfer of the legal title. He suggested that the principle for the class of such a discretionary trust was to 'treat all the people put together just as though they formed one person, for whose benefit the trustees were directed to apply the whole of a particular fund'.[251] However, despite its

---

[247] (1841) Cr & Ph 240.   [248] [1982] Conv 118.
[249] [1928] Ch 915.   [250] [1928] Ch 920.   [251] [1928] Ch 920.

credentials in logic, this proprietary interest approach was rejected by the House of Lords in *Gartside v IRC*.[252] The case concerned a non-exhaustive discretionary trust in favour of John Gartside and his wife and children. The central question was whether estate duty was payable on the trust fund, which had not yet been distributed at the date of John's death. The relevant legislation[253] would render the fund liable to estate duty if he was regarded as having an 'interest' in the fund. In these circumstances, the House of Lords held that the deceased beneficiary had no 'interest' in the fund and that estate duty was not payable. To reach this conclusion it rejected any possibility of a 'group interest' in the fund. Lord Reid said that 'two or more persons cannot have a single right unless they hold it jointly or in common. But clearly objects of a discretionary trust do not have that: they each have individual rights: they are in competition with each other and what the trustees give to one is his alone.'[254] Lord Wilberforce echoed this thinking, stating that although it was correct that a beneficiary had more than a mere hope[255] of a right:

> that does not mean that he has an interest which is capable of being taxed by reference to its extent in the trust's income: it may be a right, with some degree of concreteness or solidity, one which attracts the protection of a court of equity, yet it may still lack the necessary quality of definable extent which must exist before it can be taxed.[256]

The case is therefore best understood as a reaction against the prospect of the taxation of the entire balance of the fund which has not yet been allocated every time that a member of the class who is a potential beneficiary dies. This would have been the consequence of holding that the members of the class had a group 'interest' in the trust property.

While the analysis adopted in *Gartside v IRC*[257] was applied to exhaustive discretionary trusts in *Re Weir's Settlement*[258] and *Sainsbury v IRC*,[259] it is arguable that the root problem lay with the drafting of the relevant taxing provisions, which would lead to a ludicrous result, rather than with the suggestion that the class of beneficiaries of a discretionary trust hold the equitable title to the property. As Lord Reid observed in *Gartside*, 'it may be that in 1894 discretionary trusts were not so common that the draughtsman of the legislation must have had them in mind'.[260] The tax has now been abolished. It is submitted that, despite the authority of the House of Lords, the equitable interest of property subject to a discretionary trust does not remain inchoate, or 'in the air', but vests in the class of potential beneficiaries as a whole. There is support for this view in the approach which is taken in relation to the variation of trusts with the consent of the beneficiaries.[261] In the case of an exhaustive discretionary trust, the

---

[252] [1968] AC 553.   [253] Finance Act 1940, s 43(1).   [254] [1968] AC 553, at 605–606.
[255] Lord Wilberforce used the Latin word 'spes' in his speech.   [256] [1968] AC 553, at 618.
[257] [1968] AC 553.
[258] [1969] 1 Ch 657, at 682. Cross J stated: 'I do not think that Lord Reid was intending to suggest that the distinction [between exhaustive and non-exhaustive discretionary trusts] was relevant to his discussion of the "group theory". Even if the trust is exhaustive and there is no power to withhold income, the objects have individual competing interests, not concurrent interests in the income.'   [259] [1970] Ch 712.
[260] [1968] AC 553, at 606.   [261] See Chapter 17.

class would theoretically be able to demand the transfer of the legal title by the trustees. In reality, this will often be impossible, as the class may be incapable of complete ascertainment.

(ii) A proprietary right for individual beneficiaries

Although the class of beneficiaries of a discretionary trust may be regarded as having a collective proprietary entitlement to the fund, it is clear that members of the class cannot claim an individual proprietary entitlement to the fund or any part of the fund unless the trustees exercise their discretion to appoint property in their favour. As Lord Reid observed in *Gartside v IRC*:

> you cannot tell what any one of the beneficiaries will receive until the trustees have exercised their discretion.[262]

(b) The right to be considered as a potential beneficiary

The most concrete right that the members of a class of beneficiaries of a discretionary trust possess is the right to be considered as potential recipients from the fund by the trustees.[263] They also have the right to have the trustees exercise their discretion 'bona fides',[264] 'fairly', 'reasonably', or 'properly'.[265]

(4) The duties of trustees of discretionary trusts

The prime obligation of the trustee of a discretionary trust is to carry out the terms of the trust and allocate the fund among the class of potential beneficiaries. In the case of an exhaustive discretionary trust, the trustees must allocate the whole of the fund or its income, whereas in the case of a non-exhaustive discretionary trust they have the power to retain and accumulate all or part of the fund or income. The central issues concern the question how the trustees should go about their obligation to allocate in practice.

(a) The duty to conduct a survey of the range of the objects

The trustees of a discretionary trust are subject to a duty to consider the members of the class as potential recipients of benefit from the trust fund. In the case of a trust with a fairly small class of beneficiaries it may be practicable for the trustees to consider the circumstance of each and every member of the class before deciding on any allocations of benefit. However, in the case of discretionary trusts with a large class it is impossible for the trustees to consider the circumstances of each and every member of the class of potential beneficiaries. For example, the trustees of the Baden trust could not have considered the position of each employee, ex-employee, or their relatives and dependants, particularly since many within the class would remain unknown to the trustees at the moment they exercised their discretion.

---

[262] *Gartside v IRC* [1968] AC 553.
[263] *Gartside v IRC* [1968] AC 553, at 606, per Lord Wilberforce.
[264] [1968] AC 553, at 606, per Lord Reid.   [265] [1968] AC 553, at 618, per Lord Wilberforce.

The requirement that the trustees 'consider' allocations in favour of members of the class of beneficiaries has thus been developed in a way which reflects what can reasonably be expected of them in practice. The exact degree of consideration required of the trustees will depend on the type of the discretionary trust concerned, and in particular the size of the class of potential beneficiaries. The larger the class, the less onerous the duty to consider becomes. In *McPhail v Doulton*[266] Lord Wilberforce stated that trustees must 'make such a survey of the range of objects or possible beneficiaries as will enable them to carry out their fiduciary duty'. In the course of his judgment he sought to elucidate what that duty required:

> Any trustee would surely make it his duty to know what is the permissible area of selection and then consider responsibly, in individual cases, whether a contemplated beneficiary was within the power, and whether, in relation to other possible claimants, a particular grant was appropriate.[267]

In the case of a discretionary trust with a large class of beneficiaries, the factors that will be taken into account in determining the extent of the trustees' duty to survey the range of objects include the size of the class and the size of the fund available for distribution. As Lord Wilberforce observed:

> a trustee with a duty to distribute, particularly among a potentially very large class, would surely never require the preparation of a complete list of names, which anyhow would tell him little that he needs to know. He would examine the field by class and category; might indeed make diligent and careful enquiries, depending on how much money he had to give away and the means at his disposal, as to the composition and needs of particular categories and of individuals within them; decide upon certain priorities or proportions, and then select individuals according to their needs or qualifications.[268]

The test is therefore extremely flexible, and appropriate to the modern usage of discretionary trusts as a mechanism to distribute relatively small funds among selected members of a potentially vast class. As Sachs LJ observed in *Re Baden's Deed Trusts (No 2)*:

> The word 'range'...has an inbuilt and obvious element of elasticity, and thus provides for an almost infinitely variable range of vision suitable to the particular trust to be considered. In modern [discretionary] trusts as an it may be sufficient to know whether the range of potential postulants runs into respectively dozens, hundreds, thousands, tens of thousands or even hundreds of thousands...Assessing in a businesslike way 'the size of the problem' is what the trustees are called on to do.[269]

In practical terms, what this means is that the trustee must not make an allocation from the fund to an individual beneficiary without first assessing the appropriateness

---

[266] [1971] AC 424, at 457.   [267] [1971] AC 424, at 449.   [268] [1971] AC 424, at 449.
[269] [1973] Ch 9, at 20. See also *Re Hay's Settlement Trusts* [1982] 1 WLR 202, at 210, where Sir Robert Megarry V-C considered that the analogous duties of the trustee of a fiduciary power are to: 'consider the range of the objects of the power; and...consider the appropriateness of individual appointments'.

of that allocation in the light of the claims of other possible beneficiaries. It would be inappropriate for the trustees of a fund of £1m held on an exhaustive discretionary trust for a class of ten beneficiaries to allocate only to three or four individuals without first considering the claims of all the members of the class. In the case of a fund of £1m to be divided among a class of a hundred thousand, the trustees would not need to consider the case for each member of the class, provided they bear in mind the number of potential claimants from the class and the purposes of the fund when deciding whether to make any individual allocations.

(b) The duty not to make allocations outside of the class of potential objects

The trustees must not allocate the trust fund to persons who do not fall within the class of beneficiaries. Any such allocations will be held void by the court because they fall outside of the terms of the trust, and the trustees will be in breach of trust. If such an allocation is made the beneficiaries may enforce remedies against the trustees[270] and the wrongful recipient of the trust property.[271]

---

[270] See Chapter 27.   [271] See Chapter 29.

17

Variation of beneficial interests

The original terms of a trust may no longer serve the purposes of the beneficiaries of a trust or operate as intended by the settlor. It is possible in some cases to amend the trusts by varying the beneficial interests. Variation of existing beneficial interests normally requires the consent of all the current and prospective beneficiaries. The general principles and the exceptions are explored in this chapter.[1]

1 Introduction

(1) **Allocation of beneficial interests under trusts**

In the case of discretionary trusts the allocation of benefit in the trust fund is within the discretion of the trustee. The original owner of the property who created the trust has not specified precisely how the fund is to be allocated among the class of beneficiaries. In the case of a fixed trust the interests of the beneficiaries have been specified by the settlor, and the trustee's obligation is merely to carry out the trust according to its terms. However, it may well be that it is in the interests of the beneficiaries that the trust be carried out in a way which is different to that specified by the settlor. For example, circumstances may have changed since the trust was created so that what was once a tax-advantageous settlement now has disastrous tax consequences.[2] This chapter examines how the allocation of benefit under a trust can be altered from what was originally specified by the settlor.

(2) **The primacy of the settlor's intention?**

It is a basic principle that a trust must be carried out according to its terms, and that any deviation from them constitutes a breach of trust. In *Re New*, Romer LJ stated that:

---

[1] See Harris, *Variation of Trusts* (1975).
[2] As Lord Denning MR observed in *Re Weston's Settlements* [1969] 1 Ch 223, at 245: 'Nearly every variation that has come before the court has tax avoidance as its principal object.'

As a rule, the court has no jurisdiction to give, and will not give, its sanction to the perform-ance by the trustees of acts with reference to the trust estate which are not, on the face of the instrument creating the trust, authorised by its terms.[3]

This 'primacy to the settlor's intention' was also expressed by Farwell J in *Re Walker*,[4] where he declined 'to accept any suggestion that the court has an inherent jurisdiction to alter a man's will because it thinks it beneficial'. However, this commitment to the primacy of the settlor's intention has to be balanced against giving effect to the present wishes and interests of the beneficiaries, and it has never been a principle which has been rigidly applied. Instead, the wishes of the beneficiaries are given primacy over the intentions of the settlor. In *Goulding v James*,[5] the Court of Appeal held that the beneficiaries were entitled to vary a trust in a way that entirely undermined the inten-tions of the settlor.

(3) **The primacy of the beneficiaries' wishes**

It has long been recognized that the beneficiaries of a trust can consent to the execution of the trust in a manner other than that specified by the settlor. A trustee will not be liable for breach of trust if he acts at the request, or with the consent, of the beneficiaries.[6] If the trustees so act and in effect vary the trust by performing it inconsistently with the settlor's intentions, the court will not intervene. At its most dramatic, this enables the beneficiaries to bring the trust to an end. Under the principle of *Saunders v Vautier*[7] the beneficiaries, provided they are absolutely entitled, sui juris and of age, may call for the legal title to the trust property.[8] In *Re Smith*[9] the beneficiaries of a discretionary trust were held able to compel the trustees to transfer the legal title to them. In *Saunders v Vautier*,[10] Daniel Vautier was the sole beneficiary of a trust of East India stock established by Richard Wright. The settlor directed in the terms of the trust that dividends from the stock be accumulated by the trustees until Daniel attained the age of 25. The court held that as he was solely entitled to the fund, and the accumulation was for his benefit alone, he was entitled to the fund at the age of 21. In effect, primacy was given to the beneficiary's wishes, rather than the settlor's expressed intentions. In *Goulding v James*, Mummery LJ identified the principle embodied in the rule in *Saunders v Vautier*:

> The principle recognizes the rights of beneficiaries, who are sui juris and together entitled to the trust property, to exercise their proprietary rights to overbear and defeat the inten-tion of a testator or settlor to subject property to the continuing trusts, powers and limita-tions of a will or trust instrument.[11]

---

[3] [1901] 2 Ch 534, at 544.   [4] [1901] 1 Ch 879, at 885.

[5] [1997] 2 All ER 239, at 247; Luxton 'Variation of Trusts: Settlors' Intentions and the Consent Principle in *Saunders v Vautier*' (1997) 60 MLR 719.

[6] *Re Pauling's Settlement Trusts* [1964] Ch 303, CA. See Chapter 29.   [7] (1841) Cr & Ph 240.

[8] See *Re Chardon* [1928] Ch 464; *Re Smith* [1928] Ch 915; *Re Nelson* [1928] Ch 920; *Re Beckett's Settlement* [1940] Ch 279; *Re AEG Unit Trusts (Managers) Ltd's Deed* [1957] Ch 415.

[9] [1928] Ch 915.   [10] (1841) Cr & Ph 240.   [11] [1997] 2 All ER 239, at 247.

(4) Limits to consensual variation

The primacy of the beneficiaries' wishes established by *Saunders v Vautier*[12] enables them to vary the beneficial entitlements under a trust. However, their right to do so is subject to severe practical restrictions and is often inadequate to authorize a variation of the beneficial interest. A consensual variation of trust can only take place where there is the unanimous consent of all the actual and potential beneficiaries of the trust, since if any beneficiary fails to give consent the trustees will remain open to liability for breach of trust to any who have not consented. Therefore, consensual variation will not be possible if some of the beneficiaries are minors and unable to give consent, or alternatively unidentifiable or not yet in existence, for example if the class of beneficiaries includes children as yet unborn or the future spouses of present beneficiaries. This will often be the case if the trust creates successive interests, as in *Goulding v James*[13] itself, where the potential beneficiaries of the remainder interest behind a life interest were the (as yet) unborn great-grandchildren of the testator. To overcome these limitations the law has developed various means by which the court can approve a variation of trust when the beneficiaries are not able to do so themselves.

2 Variation under the inherent jurisdiction of the court

In *Chapman v Chapman*,[14] the House of Lords recognized that in four situations the court possesses an inherent jurisdiction to authorize a variation of the terms of a trust.[15] However, even in these situations the court has no real jurisdiction to alter the beneficial interests under the trust.

(1) Conversion jurisdiction

The court has the power to authorize the conversion of property in which an infant has an equitable interest from personalty or realty.[16] Lord Morton emphasized that even this limited jurisdiction was exceptional in nature,[17] and its exercise would in no way affect the infant's beneficial entitlement.[18] The very wide powers of investment now given to trustees mean that this jurisdiction will very rarely be required.

(2) Emergency jurisdiction

The court has jurisdiction to authorize transactions involving the trust property which are not authorized by the trust if a 'peculiar set of circumstances arises'[19] for which no

---

12 (1841) Cr & Ph 240.   13 [1997] 2 All ER 239, at 247.   14 [1954] AC 429.
15 [1954] AC 429, at 445, per Lord Simmonds LC.
16 See *Earl of Winchelsea v Norcloffe* (1686) 1 Vern 435; *Pierson v Shore* (1739) 1 Atk 480; *Bridges v Bridges* (1752) 12 App Cas 693n; *Inwood v Twyne* (1762) Amb 417; *Lord Ashburton v Lady Ashburton* (1801) 6 Ves 6.
17 *Re Jackson* (1882) 21 Ch D 786; *Glover v Barlow* (1831) 21 Ch D 788n.
18 [1954] AC 429, at 451.   19 *Re New* [1901] 2 Ch 534, at 534, per Romer LJ.

provision was made in the trust instrument. In *Re New*,[20] the trust fund consisted of ordinary shares in a private limited company. A company reorganization was proposed in which ordinary shares would be transferred for preference shares and debentures. As the trust instrument did not give the power to invest in such securities, the Court of Appeal authorized the investment acting under their inherent jurisdiction. Romer LJ emphasized that the variation must be for the 'benefit' of the beneficiaries. As in the case of the 'conversion jurisdiction', this 'emergency jurisdiction' does not give the court power to vary the interests of the beneficiaries. The wider powers of investment now enjoyed by trustees will similarly make the exercise of this jurisdiction exceedingly rare.

(3) Maintenance jurisdiction

Where the settlor directed that income from the trust fund should be accumulated for the beneficiaries, the court has the jurisdiction to authorize the advancement of the income to provide for their maintenance. Usually, although not necessarily, this will be in the case of infant beneficiaries.[21] The maintenance jurisdiction does not give the court the power to alter the beneficial interests of the beneficiaries.[22] The statutory powers of advancement and maintenance, as amended by the Inheritance and Trustees' Powers Act 2014, (already considered in Chapter 15) make this power less significant than it was in the nineteenth century and before.

(4) Compromise jurisdiction

The court also has inherent jurisdiction to approve on behalf of those who cannot consent for themselves[23] a compromise agreement between the beneficiaries where there has been a 'genuine dispute' about the extent of the rights of the beneficiaries. Prior to the decision of the House of Lords in *Chapman v Chapman*,[24] this 'compromise jurisdiction' had been given a wide meaning so that it could be used to authorize variations in the beneficial interest of the beneficiaries. For example, in *Re Downshire Settled Estates*[25] the Court of Appeal authorized a scheme restructuring the beneficial interests of a settlement for tax reasons. Evershed MR took the view that 'the word "compromise" should not be narrowly construed so as to be confined to "compromises" of disputed rights'.[26] In his dissenting opinion Denning LJ advocated a very general jurisdiction to vary:

> The jurisdiction is not confined to cases where there is a dispute about the extent of the beneficial interests, nor to cases of emergency or necessity, but extends wherever there is

---

[20] [1901] 2 Ch 534. See also *Re Tollemache* [1903] 1 Ch 955, CA.

[21] See *Revel v Watkinson* (1748) 1 Ves Sen 93; *Cavendish v Mercer* (1776) 5 Ves 195n; *Greenwell v Greenwell* (1800) 5 Ves 194; *Errat v Barlow* (1807) 14 Ves 202; *Haley v Bannister* (1820) 4 Madd 275; *Havelock v Havelock* (1881) 17 Ch D 807; *Re Collins* (1886) 32 Ch D 229.

[22] *Chapman v Chapman* [1954] AC 429, at 456, per Lord Morton.

[23] [1954] AC 429, at 457 per Lord Morton, the jurisdiction had been exercised on behalf of 'infants interested under a will or settlement and on behalf of possible after-born beneficiaries'.

[24] [1954] AC 429.   [25] [1953] Ch 218.   [26] [1953] Ch 218, at 239.

a bargain about the beneficial interests which is for the benefit of the infants or unborn persons.[27]

However, in *Chapman v Chapman*[28] the House of Lords asserted that the court only has the inherent jurisdiction to approve a compromise altering beneficial interests if there is a 'genuine dispute' as to the beneficial entitlements of the beneficiaries. In essence, this means that the court does not possess any jurisdiction to 'vary' the beneficial entitlement of beneficiaries, but merely a jurisdiction to clarify them when there is a dispute about their extent. In the words of Lord Morton:

> ...the court's jurisdiction to sanction a compromise in the true sense, when the beneficial interests are in dispute, is not a jurisdiction to alter these interests, for they are still unascertained. If, however, there is no doubt as to the beneficial interests, the court is, to my mind, exceeding its jurisdiction if it sanctions a scheme for their alteration...[29]

The decision in *Chapman v Chapman*[30] thus deprived the courts of any real jurisdiction to authorize variations in the beneficial interests under trusts. For example, in *Re Powell-Cotton's Resettlement*[31] an alleged dispute over an investment clause in the trust instrument was held not to be a 'genuine dispute' and the Court of Appeal refused to authorize a compromise agreement.[32] The restriction of the court's inherent jurisdiction led to the enactment of the Variation of Trusts Act 1958, which gives the court a 'very wide and, indeed, revolutionary discretion'[33] to approve variations of trusts, including the variation of beneficial interests.

3 Statutory powers of variation other than the Variation of Trusts Act 1958

(1) Trustee Act 1925, s 57[34]

By this section the inherent 'emergency jurisdiction' is extended to cases where a transaction is merely 'expedient' in the opinion of the court. The section is expressly limited to matters of 'the management and administration' of the trust property, and does not enable the variation of beneficial interests under the trust.[35] This distinction is not always easy to maintain in practice. In *Sutton v England*,[36] a scheme to create a sub-trust to benefit US beneficiaries of a family trust shared with UK resident beneficiaries was held by the Court of Appeal to fall within the emergency jurisdiction.

---

[27] [1953] Ch 218, at 274.   [28] [1954] AC 429.
[29] [1954] AC 429, at 461.   [30] [1954] AC 429.   [31] [1956] 1 WLR 23.
[32] See also *Allen v Distillers Co (Biochemicals) Ltd* [1974] QB 384; *Mason v Farbrother* [1983] 2 All ER 1078.   [33] *Re Steed's Will Trusts* [1960] Ch 407, at 420–421, per Evershed MR.
[34] See *Re Beale's Settlement Trusts* [1932] 2 Ch 15; *Re Thomas* [1930] 1 Ch 194; *Re Harvey* [1941] 3 All ER 284; *Re Power* [1947] Ch 572; *Re Cockerell's Settlement Trusts* [1956] Ch 372; *Re Shipwrecked Fishermen and Mariners' Royal Benevolent Society* [1959] Ch 220.
[35] *Re Downshire Settled Estate* [1953] Ch 218.   [36] [2011] 2 P & CR DG15.

This has been refused at first instance, on the basis that, while expedient, conferring the necessary power to partition the trust property to create the sub-trust required an alteration of the beneficial interests of the trust, and was therefore outside the powers conferred under s 57(1). Mummery LJ, while supporting a cautious approach to the intervention of the court in these matters, held that the impact on beneficial interests was incidental only as a result of due management and administration of the trust as it did not alter the nature of the beneficial entitlements and was therefore permissible.[37]

(2) Settled Land Act 1925, s 64(1)

This section enables the court to authorize 'any transaction affecting or concerning the settled land' by the tenant for life, provided that the transaction is, in the opinion of the court, for 'the benefit of the settled land'. Although limited to settled land, this provision allows the court to authorize alterations in beneficial interests, as for example in *Re Downshire Settled Estates*.[38] It has not been possible to create new settlements governed by the Settled Land Act 1925,[39] so this provision is of limited and decreasing importance.

(3) Trustee Act 1925, s 53

This section extends the court's inherent 'maintenance jurisdiction' in favour of infants and gives the court power to order the application of the capital or income from the trust for the 'maintenance, education or benefit of the infant'.[40]

(4) Matrimonial Causes Act 1973

This Act grants the court wide powers to make orders concerning the parties to matrimonial proceedings. By s 24 this includes the powers to order the making of a settlement for the benefit of the 'other party to the marriage and of the children of the family',[41] and to vary the beneficial interests under 'any ante-nuptial or post-nuptial settlement'.[42] This power was exercised by the court in *E v E (Financial Provision)*,[43] where the court ordered that £200,000 should be paid to a wife, on her divorce, from a post-nuptial settlement of the matrimonial home on discretionary trusts in favour of the husband, wife, and children, thus varying the beneficial interests. It was also exercised in *Brooks*

---

[37] [2011] 2 P & CR DG15, at [34]–[43]. Mummery LJ also made reference to *Re Downshire*, where Lord Evershed said that a scheme which had an incidental effect on the beneficial interests was permissible— see [6].   [38] [1953] Ch 218. See also *Hambro v Duke of Marlborough* [1994] Ch 158.

[39] The creation of new Settled Land Act settlements is prohibited under the Trusts of Land And Appointment of Trustees Act 1996, s 2(1).

[40] See *Re Meux* [1958] Ch 154; *Re Gower's Settlement* [1934] Ch 365; *Re Bristol's Settled Estates* [1964] 3 All ER 939; *Re Lansdowne's Will Trusts* [1967] Ch 603; *Re Heyworth's Contingent Reversionary Interest* [1956] Ch 364.   [41] S 24(1)(a)–(b).

[42] S 24(1)(c)–(d): *C v C (Ancillary relief: Nuptial Settlement* [2005] 2 WLR 241; Bennett 'Variation of Ante and Post Nuptial Settlements' (2007) Fam Law 916.   [43] [1990] 2 FLR 233.

v Brooks,[44] where the House of Lords held that a husband's pension scheme constituted a 'post-nuptial' settlement, thus bringing it within the scope of s 24(1)(c) and allowing the court to vary it so that his ex-wife was entitled to receive a pension from its surplus. However, Lord Nicholls was at pains to stress that this approach did not provide a solution to the problem of splitting pension rights on divorce:

> This decision should not be seen as a solution to the overall pensions problem. Not every pensions scheme constitutes a marriage settlement. And even when a scheme does fall within the court's jurisdiction to vary a marriage settlement, it would not be right for the court to vary one scheme member's rights to the prejudice of other scheme members…A feature of the instant case is that there is only one scheme member and, moreover, the wife has earnings of her own from the same employer which will sustain provision of an immediate pension for her. If the court is to be able to split pension rights on divorce in the more usual case of a multi-member scheme where the wife has no earnings of her own from the same employer, or to direct the taking out of life insurance, legislation will still be needed.[45]

(5) **Mental Capacity Act 2005, s 18(1)(h)**

This section, which came into force in October 2007,[46] gives the court power to make a settlement on behalf of a person who lacks capacity, and to vary it if any material fact was not disclosed when the settlement was made, or if there has been any substantial change in circumstances.

4 The Variation of Trusts Act 1958

(1) **Introduction**

The Variation of Trusts Act was passed in the aftermath of the decision of the House of Lords in *Chapman v Chapman*,[47] which severely restricted the 'compromise jurisdiction' that the courts had construed to give themselves a wide jurisdiction to vary trusts. The matter was referred to the Law Reform Commission, which concluded that:

> the only satisfactory solution to the problem is to give the court the unlimited jurisdiction to sanction such changes which it in fact exercised in the years preceding the decision in *Chapman v Chapman*.

The subsequently enacted Variation of Trusts Act gives the court a 'very wide discretion'[48] to authorize the variation of trusts, including the adjustment of the beneficial interests thereunder.[49]

---

[44] [1996] AC 375; Thomas 'Divorce and Pension Funds' [1997] Conv 52.
[45] [1996] AC 375, at 396. See Family Law Act 1996.
[46] This section replaced a similar provision under the Mental Health Act 1983.
[47] [1954] AC 429.
[48] *Re Steed's Will Trusts* [1960] Ch 407, at 420–421, per Evershed MR.
[49] The problem of whether an English court might vary a trust governed by a foreign law is examined by Harris in the light of *Charalambous v Charalambous* [2004] EWCA Civ 103; (2005) 121 LQR 16.

(2) **Scheme of the Variation of Trusts Act**

The Variation of Trusts Act operates alongside the principle of consensual variation, by which the beneficiaries can consent to the trust being performed in a manner different to that stipulated by the settlor in the trust instrument. The court is given the power to approve 'any arrangement[50] varying or revoking all or any of the trusts, or enlarging the powers of the trustees of managing or administering any of the property subject to the trusts',[51] on behalf of the categories of persons specified in s 1 who are not able to consent on their own behalf.[52] In this sense, the court acts as a 'statutory attorney'[53] for those who cannot consent for themselves, and it enjoys no power to consent on behalf of persons who are able to consent for themselves.[54] As a safeguard to ensure that the interests of those on whose behalf the court can approve a variation are not prejudiced, the arrangement approved must be for their 'benefit'. Thus the Act achieves flexibility, by allowing trusts to be varied to take account of changing circumstances, while preserving the right of parties who can consent on their own behalf to make their own decisions, and protecting the interests of those who cannot. The operation of the jurisdiction was most recently considered by the Court of Appeal in *Goulding v James*,[55] where Mummery LJ explained the role of the court and the relationship between the statutory jurisdiction and the rule in *Saunders v Vautier*:

> First, what varies the trust is not the court, but the agreement or consensus of the beneficiaries. Secondly, there is no real difference in principle in the rearrangement of the trusts between the case where the court is exercising its jurisdiction on behalf of the specified class under the 1958 Act and the case where the resettlement is made by virtue of the doctrine in *Saunders v Vautier* and by all the adult beneficiaries joining together. Thirdly, the court is merely contributing on behalf of infants and unborn and unascertained persons the binding assents to the arrangement which they, unlike an adult beneficiary, cannot give. The 1958 Act has thus been viewed by the courts as a statutory extension of the consent principle embodied in the rule in *Saunders v Vautier*.[56]

While the Variation of Trusts Act enables the courts to approve a proposed variation of the allocation of benefit behind a trust, it has been held that the courts do not possess the jurisdiction to approve a 'resettlement' of the trusts, so that the trust is completely reshaped. There is a line to be drawn somewhere between what amounts to a genuine variation and what is a resettlement.

---

[50] In *Re Steed's Will Trusts* [1960] Ch 407 Evershed MR held that the word 'arrangement' should be given the 'widest possible sense … to cover any proposal … put forward'. See also *Ridgwell v Ridgewll* [2007] EWHC 2666 (Ch), where Behrens J confirmed this wide interpretation in considering whether the addition of a life interest was an arrangement within s 1.   [51] S 1(1).

[52] See *Re Holt's Settlement Trusts* [1969] 1 Ch 100.

[53] *Goulding v James* [1997] 2 All ER 239, at 249 per Mummery LJ.

[54] S 1(1) specifically states that the court's power to approve is given irrespective of 'whether or not there is any other person beneficially interested who is capable of assenting thereto'. See also *IRC v Holmden* [1968] AC 685, at 701, per Lord Reid.   [55] [1997] 2 All ER 239, at 247.

[56] [1997] 2 All ER 239, at 247.

(a) A 'resettlement' rather than a 'variation'

On one side of the line falls *Re T's Settlement Trusts*.[57] A trust provided that an infant would become entitled to a quarter of the trust income on attaining her majority. The child was irresponsible and immature, and the court's consent was sought to a variation which would transfer her share of the trust fund to new trustees to be held on protective trusts for her life, with remainder to her issue. Wilberforce J held that he did not have jurisdiction to approve this arrangement:

> It is obviously not possible to define exactly the point at which the jurisdiction of the court under the Variation of Trusts Act stops or should not be exercised. Moreover, I have no desire to cut down the very useful jurisdiction which this act has conferred upon the court. But I am satisfied that the proposal as originally made to me falls outside it. Though presented as a 'variation' it is in truth a complete new resettlement. The former trust funds were to be got in from the former trustees and held upon wholly new trusts such as might be made by an absolute owner of the funds. I do not think that the court can approve this.[58]

(b) A genuine variation

Re Holt's Settlement[59] falls on the other side of the line. A trust had been created for Mrs Wilson for life, with remainder to her children who attained the age of 21. A variation was proposed under which Mrs Wilson would surrender her life interest in a half of the income in favour of the children, but also to postpone the children's entitlement to capital until each child attained the age of 30.[60] Megarry J felt that this amounted to a genuine variation and not a resettlement:

> It is not, of course, for the court to draw the line in any particular place between what is a variation and what, on the other hand, is a completely new settlement. A line may, perhaps, one day emerge from a sufficiently ample series of reported decisions; but for the present all that is necessary for me to say is whether the particular case before me is on the right side or the wrong side of any reasonable line that could be drawn. In this case I am satisfied that the arrangement proposed falls on the side of the line which bears the device 'Variation'.[61]

In the later case of *Re Ball's Settlement Trusts* Megarry J laid down a general test to distinguish between 'variations' and 'resettlements', namely, the 'substratum test':

> If an arrangement changes the whole substratum of the trust, then it may well be that it cannot be regarded merely as varying the trust. But if an arrangement, while leaving the substratum, effectuates the purpose of the trust by other means, it may still be possible to regard that arrangement as merely varying the original trusts, even though the means employed are wholly different and even though the form is completely changed.[62]

---

[57] [1964] Ch 158.   [58] [1964] Ch 158, at 162.   [59] [1969] 1 Ch 100.
[60] See also *Goulding v James* [1997] 2 All ER 239, where the Court of Appeal approved a variation in which the life tenant and remainderman agreed that 90 per cent of the trust capital should be divided between themselves, thus defeating the life interest under the trust.   [61] [1969] 1 Ch 100, at 118.
[62] [1968] 1 WLR 899, at 905.

In *Wyndham v Egremont*,[63] Blackburne J did not find this statement particularly help-ful, since it left unanswered what was meant by the 'substratum'. He had been asked to approve a variation of a trust made concerning the ancestral estates around Petworth House in West Sussex. The variation was intended to defer a very considerable tax liability and to ensure that the ancestral estates continued to devolve down the senior male line with the baronies of Egremont and Leconfield. Blackburne J concluded that this was not a resettlement and that he could and should approve it. He referred to a statement of Lord Wilberforce, in a different context (whether a new settlement had been created giving rise to a capital gains tax liability):

> I think that the question whether a particular set of facts amounts to a settlement should be approached by asking what a person, with knowledge of the legal context of the word under established doctrine and applying this knowledge in a practical and common-sense manner to the facts under examination, would conclude.[64]

Applying this test (which can scarcely be considered to be any clearer than the substra-tum test), Blackburne J concluded that he was being asked to approve only a variation:

> The trustees remain the same, the subsisting trusts remain largely unaltered and the administrative provisions affecting them are wholly unchanged. The only significant changes are (1) to the trusts in the remainder, although the ultimate trust in favour of George and his personal representatives remains the same, and (2) the introduction of the new and extended perpetuity period.[65]

The restriction that the court cannot approve a resettlement is a remaining vestige of the 'primacy of the settlor's intention'.

(3) Persons on whose behalf the court may approve an arrangement

The court may approve a variation of trust on behalf of four groups of persons identi-fied in s 1 of the Variation of Trusts Act 1958.

(a) Persons incapable of consenting for reasons of infancy or incapacity

By s 1(1)(a) the court can consent on behalf of:

> any person having, directly or indirectly, an interest, whether vested or contingent under the trusts who by reason of infancy or other incapacity is incapable of assenting.

(b) Unascertained persons

By s 1(1)(b) the court may consent on behalf of:

> any person (whether ascertained or not) who may become entitled, directly or indirectly, to an interest under the trusts as being at a future date or on the happening

---

[63] [2009] EWHC 2076 (Ch).
[64] *Roome v Edwards* [1982] AC 279, at 292–293.   [65] [2009] EWHC 2076 (Ch), at [24].

of a future event a person of any specified description or a member of any specified class of persons, so however that this paragraph shall not include any person who would be of that description, or a member of that class, as the case may be, if the said date had fallen, or the said event had happened at the date of the application to the court.

This complicated section is designed to cover the case of beneficiaries who are unascertainable, in the sense that it is not known who they are because the circumstances that would bring them within the class have not yet occurred. Since they are unascertainable, they cannot give consent to variations which affect their position, and the court can consent on their behalf. In *Re Clitheroe's Settlement Trust*,[66] for example, a variation of a discretionary trust was approved by the court. The trust was established by Lord Clitheroe in favour of 'the descendants of Sir Ralph Cockayne Assheton [his father] or the spouse of any of them'. Consent was given to a tax advantageous variation by the court under s 1(1)(b) on behalf of any future wife that Lord Clitheroe might have, who would thereby become a beneficiary of the trust. Two features of this section are worthy of special attention.

(i) The court has no jurisdiction on behalf of persons who have an existing contingent interest in the trust

The court only has jurisdiction under s 1(1)(b) to grant approval on behalf of persons who 'might become entitled) to gto an interest' under the trust in the future. In *Knocker v Youle*[67] it was held that this means that the court cannot consent for persons who have a current interest in the trust, no matter how remote, even though it is impracticable to seek their consent. The case concerned a trust created in 1937 in favour of the settlor's daughter, with default clauses that could cause the property to be held on trust for her cousins. As Warner J noted, these were very numerous[68] and some lived in Australia, so that it was not practical to get their approval to a proposed variation. However, he held that he did not have the jurisdiction to grant approval on their behalf because 'a person who has an actual interest directly conferred upon him or her by a settlement, albeit a remote interest, cannot properly be described as one who "may become" entitled to an interest',[69] and is therefore not within the scope of s 1(1)(b).

(ii) Section 1(1)(b) implies a 'double contingency' test

The second part of the definition in s 1(1)(b) adds a 'proviso'[70] that the court cannot consent on behalf of persons who would have interests in the trust if the event that would render them a beneficiary had in fact occurred at the date of the application. This means that the court only has jurisdiction to approve variation on behalf of persons who become entitled in the event of a 'double contingency'. This perceived

---

[66] [1959] 1 WLR 1159.
[67] [1986] 1 WLR 934; Riddall 'Does It or Doesn't It?—Contingent Interests and the Variation of Trusts Act 1958' [1987] Conv 144.   [68] There were seventeen.
[69] [1986] 1 WLR 934, at 937.   [70] [1986] 1 WLR 934, at 937, per Warner J.

'proviso' was applied in *Re Suffert*.[71] A trust was established for Elaine Suffert for life, with the remainder to such of her issue as she should appoint, and in the event of default to those who would be entitled if she died intestate. She was a spinster, without issue, and had three adult cousins. She sought to vary the trust, one cousin consented, and the approval of the court was sought on behalf of all unascertained persons who might become entitled under the trusts. Buckley J held that he could not grant approval on behalf of the two adult cousins because they fell within the proviso to s 1(1)(b), since if the event under which they would become entitled, namely the death of Elaine Suffert, had occurred at the date of the application, they would have been beneficiaries of the trust. Similarly, in *Re Moncrieff's Settlement Trusts*[72] a trust was established in favour of Anne Moncrieff, then for such of her issue as she appointed, and in default of appointment, to those entitled on intestacy. The court's approval to a variation was sought on behalf of her adopted son and her next of kin. Buckley J held that there was no jurisdiction to grant approval on behalf of the adopted son, as he fell within the limitation to s 1(1)(b), and would have been entitled at the date of the application if his mother had died. However, the court could consent on behalf of the other next of kin since they would only be entitled on the occurrence of a 'double-contingency', meaning both the death of the mother and the predecease of the adopted son. If the mother alone had died at the date of the application, they would still not have been entitled. *Re Suffert*[73] and *Re Moncrieff's Settlement Trusts*[74] were cited and followed by Warner J in *Knocker v Youle*.[75]

(c) Persons unborn

By s 1(1)(c) the court can consent on behalf of 'any person unborn'. If it is clearly the case that a person is past the age of childbearing and the chance of further beneficiaries arising is an impossible contingency, it is inappropriate to apply to the court to approve a variation under the Variation of Trusts Act. Thus, in *Re Pettifor's Will Trusts*[76] Pennycuick J refused to approve a variation on behalf of the unborn children of a woman of 78.

(d) Persons contingently interested under protective trusts

By s 1(1)(d) the court can consent on behalf of:

> any person in respect of any discretionary interest of his under protective trusts where the interest of the principal beneficiary has not failed or determined.

The important feature of this paragraph is that the court's jurisdiction is not limited to variations which are 'for the benefit' of the person on whose behalf approval is given. If a person falls within the scope of either paras (a)–(c), where the requirement of benefit applies, or para (d), where there is no need to prove benefit, the court may act under paragraph (d).[77]

---

[71] [1961] Ch 1.   [72] [1962] 1 WLR 1344.   [73] [1961] Ch 1.
[74] [1962] 1 WLR 1344.   [75] [1986] 1 WLR 934.   [76] [1966] Ch 257.
[77] *Re Turner's Will Trusts* [1968] 1 All ER 321.

(4) **The requirement of benefit**

Under s 1 the court may only grant approval to a scheme of variation on behalf of a person within the categories set out in s 1(1)(a)–(c) if: 'the carrying out thereof would be for the benefit of that person'.

(a) **Recognized benefits**

The courts have recognized that a variety of different types of benefit will be sufficient to allow them to authorize variations:

(i) *Financial benefit*

There is no doubt that the court will grant approval on behalf of persons who would benefit financially from a proposed variation. In *CD (A Child) v O*,[78] for example, Lloyd J approved a variation which would insert a power of advancement into a trust allowing the advancement of the whole capital of the fund to an infant beneficiary to be applied to pay school fees. However, the financial benefit sought in most cases has been a reduction in tax liability. As Lord Denning MR observed in *Re Weston's Settlement*, 'nearly every variation that has come before the court has tax-avoidance for its principal object'.[79] In *Re Weston's Settlement*[80] Stamp J did seem to suggest that the court would not sanction 'illegitimate tax avoidance'. He described the proposed variation in a family trust as 'a cheap exercise in tax avoidance which I ought not to sanction, as distinct from a legitimate avoidance of liability to taxation'.[81] However, the Court of Appeal in *Chapman v Chapman*[82] had not objected to a variation which had as its prime object the reduction of tax liability. In principle all attempts to avoid tax, provided they are lawful, should be legitimate and a 'benefit'. This approach was approved and followed in *Ridgwell v Ridgwell*,[83] which concerned variations that sought to defer the date at which any current and future children of the life tenant under a trust fund would obtain a vested interest in the fund. Behrens J, in approving the arrangement, held that the changes would confer a benefit on the current and unborn children, due to the savings in Capital Gains Tax and inheritance tax arising from the variations.[84]

(ii) *Non-financial benefits*

The courts have also approved variations where the benefit derived is of a social or moral nature. In *Re T's Settlement Trusts*[85] Wilberforce J held that the advantage of postponing the age at which a minor who was irresponsible and immature would

---

[78] [2004] 3 All ER 780. Following the commencement of the Inheritance and Trustees' Powers Act 2014, a power of advancement will now extend by default to the whole of the capital fund—this was discussed in Chapter 15. It is only in relation to trusts in existence before the commencement of that Act that are subject to the original statutory power in the Trustee Act 1925 s 32(1)(a) where such a scheme would still be needed.

[79] [1969] 1 Ch 223, at 245.   [80] [1969] 1 Ch 223.   [81] [1969] 1 Ch 223, at 234.

[82] [1953] Ch 218.   [83] [2007] EWHC 2666.

[84] [2007] EWHC 2666, at [36]. There was also a possibility of cheaper life insurance being obtained through the variation.   [85] [1964] Ch 158.

become entitled to an interest under the trust was 'the kind of benefit which seems to be within the spirit of the Act'.[86] In *Re Holt's Settlement*[87] Megarry J granted approval to a variation which deferred the interests of the infant beneficiaries until they attained the age of 30. He considered that 'the word "benefit" is plainly not confined to financial benefit, but may extend to moral or social benefit',[88] and that it would therefore be a benefit to the children not to receive an income from the trust which would make them independent of the need to work before they had become reasonably advanced in their careers and settled in life. In *Re Remnant's Settlement Trusts*[89] a family trust contained a forfeiture clause which would forfeit the interests of members of the family who became, or married, Roman Catholics. A variation removing this clause was approved by the court, which found a benefit to the children in that they would no longer be deterred from marrying a Roman Catholic if they so chose, and that the clause could be a source of future family dissension.[90] Facilitating the administration of the trust will also amount to a benefit, so in *Re Seale's Marriage Settlement*[91] Buckley J approved on behalf of an infant the transfer of a trust to a Canadian trustee where the family had moved permanently to Canada.

(b) Conflicting benefits

The court may be faced with a situation where the proposed variation is beneficial in some ways but disadvantageous in others. For example, there may be great social or moral benefits, but financial disadvantages. In such circumstances the court will weigh the benefits to determine whether the variation is 'for the benefit' of the persons on whose behalf the court is asked to consent. In *Re Weston's Settlement*[92] the court's approval was sought on behalf of the infant beneficiaries of a marriage settlement to a variation which would transfer the trust to Jersey. Although this would produce a financial benefit of some £800,000, the Court of Appeal held that this was outweighed by the social benefits of the children remaining in England. Lord Denning MR explained how he had weighed the different benefits:

> The court should not consider merely the financial benefit to the infants or unborn children, but also their educational and social benefit. There are many things in life more worthwhile than money. One of these things is to be brought up in this our England, which is still 'the envy of less happier lands'. I do not believe it is for the benefit of children to be uprooted from England and transported to another country simply to avoid tax.[93]

This weighing of 'benefit' obviously involves a value judgement on the part of the court of the relative merits of the benefits and disadvantages associated with a

---

[86] [1964] Ch 158, at 162. Wilberforce J held on the facts he did not have the jurisdiction to approve the proposed variation.   [87] [1969] 1 Ch 100.
[88] [1969] 1 Ch 100, at 121.   [89] [1970] Ch 560.
[90] There was also a financial benefit to the children in having their interests under the trust advanced.
[91] [1961] Ch 574.   [92] [1969] 1 Ch 223.   [93] [1969] 1 Ch 223, at 245.

proposed variation. In *Ridgwell v Ridgwell*,[94] for example, Behrens J considered that the long-term tax benefits of a proposed variation outweighed any disadvantage of a postponement of the current and unborn children's entitlement to interests in remainder under a settlement.[95]

(5) A discretion to vary

The Variation of Trusts Act provides that the court 'may if it thinks fit' approve a proposed variation. This clearly gives the court a discretion, and the court is not obliged to approve a variation, even if the requisite element of benefit can be shown. In some recognized circumstances the court will not exercise its discretion to approve a variation.

(a) Fraud on a power

The court will not approve a variation which amounts to a fraud on a power.[96] Megarry J stated the principle in *Re Wallace's Settlements*:

> If it is clear that a fraud on the power is involved, then plainly the court ought to withhold its approval. The power of the court under the Act is a discretionary power exercisable if the court 'thinks fit'; and I cannot conceive that it would be fitting for an arrangement to be approved if that arrangement had been made possible by a manifest fraud on a power, or was in some way connected with such a fraud.[97]

Difficulty arises where a life tenant holds a life interest over a fund and special power of appointment over the remainder interest. To avoid inheritance tax the life tenant has exercised the power in favour of the objects, and then sought the court's approval to bring the life interest to an end, and divide the fund between himself and the objects of the power. The danger is that the life tenant himself benefits by receiving a share of the capital of the fund, and this may be the prime motivation for exercising the power. In determining whether there has been a fraud on the power an important factor has been the extent to which the life tenant benefits by a division of the fund. If the life tenant receives a share of the fund which is greater than the actuarial value of his life interest[98] then this suggests a fraud on a power. In *Re Brook's Settlement*[99] Stamp J took a very strict approach and held that if the purpose of the exercise of a power of appointment was that the life tenant should gain a share of the fund, then there was a fraud on the power even though the life tenant may gain a share of the fund lower than the market value of his life interest.[100] However, a more flexible approach was adopted by Megarry J in *Re Wallace's Settlements*,[101] where he approved a variation when there had been an exercise of a power of appointment, even though the life tenant received a share of the fund slightly greater than the actuarial value of her life interest. On the

---

[94] [2007] EWHC 2666.   [95] [2007] EWHC 2666, at [36].   [96] See Chapter 15.
[97] [1968] 1 WLR 711, at 717–718.
[98] The actuarial value of the life interest is the sum that would be necessary to purchase an annuity producing the same annual income.   [99] [1968] 1 WLR 1661.
[100] [1968] 1 WLR 1661, at 1669.   [101] [1968] 1 WLR 711.

facts, he held that the exercise of the power had been long intended and was for the benefit of the beneficiaries, and therefore there was no fraud.

(b) Undermining protective trusts

It seems that the courts will not approve a proposed variation that would have the effect of reducing the protection enjoyed by the beneficiary of a protective trust. In *Re Steed's Will Trusts*[102] the Court of Appeal refused to approve a variation which would effectively remove the protective element from a protective trust of property left by a testator to his housekeeper. The court took the view that the protective element was part of the 'testator's scheme' and it had been his desire and intention that she enjoy that protection.[103]

(c) Manifest benefit

It is not enough that those on whose behalf the court is asked to grant approval to a proposed variation gain a benefit from the variation. The extent of their benefit must reflect that they are bargaining from a position of strength. This requirement prevents their position being exploited. In *Re Van Gruisen's Will Trusts*,[104] Ungoed Thomas J held that it would not be sufficient for the infants and unborn children on whose behalf he was asked to consent merely to receive the actuarial value of their remainder interest in the trust fund. Instead, the court must make 'a practical and business-like consideration of the arrangement including the total amounts of the advantages which the various parties obtain and their bargaining strength'. On the facts, he held that the share of the infants and unborn did adequately exceed their actuarial value.

(d) Relevance of the settlor's intentions

Where the court is requested to grant approval of a variation for persons unable to consent on their own behalf, it is not entitled to refuse a variation which would be for their benefit merely because the variation would contravene the intentions of the original settlor. In such circumstances the intentions and wishes of the original settlor are of 'little, if any, relevance or weight'[105] to the question whether approval should be given. In *Goulding v James*,[106] the testatrix left her residuary estate on trust for her daughter for life, with remainder to her grandson on his attaining the age of 40. It was further provided that if he failed to attain the age of 40 the residuary estate should pass to such of his children (ie her great-grandchildren) as were living at the date of his death. She had established this trust with the express object of preventing her daughter touching the capital of her estate, because she did not trust her son-in-law. She had postponed her grandson's interest until he was 40 because he was presently living with an artistic community in Nantucket and she considered him a 'free spirit' who had not yet

---

[102] [1960] Ch 407.

[103] [1960] Ch 407, at 421–422: the purpose of the protection was to prevent the housekeeper being 'sponged upon' by her brothers.   [104] [1964] 1 All ER 843n.

[105] *Goulding v James* [1997] 2 All ER 239, at 251–252, per Mummery LJ.

[106] [1997] 2 All ER 239.

settled down. The daughter and grandson sought to vary the trusts under the will so that they would receive a 45 per cent share each of the residuary estate absolutely, with the remaining 10 per cent on trusts for any great-grandchildren. As they were adults, the daughter and grandson were perfectly entitled to agree to such variation, but they sought the approval of the court on behalf of the as yet unborn great-grandchildren. Although the variation was for their benefit, because actuarial valuation showed that the current value of the contingent interest of the great-grandchildren was only 1.85 per cent of the residuary estate, Laddie J held that the court should refuse to exercise its discretion to grant approval because the object of the arrangement was the complete opposite of what the testatrix had intended.[107] However, the Court of Appeal held that approval should have been forthcoming. Mummery LJ held that the testatrix's intentions were all but irrelevant in deciding whether the discretion should be exercised:

> In my judgment the legal position is as follows. (1) The court has a discretion whether or not to approve a proposed arrangement. (2) That discretion is fettered by only one express restriction. The proviso to s 1 prohibits the court from approving an arrangement which is not for the benefit of the classes referred to in (a) (b) or (c). The approval of this arrangement is not prevented by that proviso, since it is plainly the case that it is greatly for the benefit of the class specified in s 1(1)(c).[108]

Ralph Gibson LJ similarly explained that the settlor's original intention was irrelevant:

> Where there is an application under the Variation of Trusts Act 1958 for approval of an arrangement agreed by the beneficiaries, capable of giving assent, it is not clear to me why evidence of the intention of the testator can be of any relevance whatever if it does no more than explain why the testator gave the interests set out in the will and the nature and degree of feeling with which such provisions were selected. The fact that a testator would not have approved or would have disapproved very strongly does not alter the fact that the beneficiaries are entitled in law to do it and, if it be proved, that the arrangement is for the benefit of the unborn. If, of course, it can be shown that the arrangement put forward constitutes, for example, a dishonest or inequitable or otherwise improper act on the part of one or more of the beneficiaries, then such evidence would clearly be relevant to the question whether the court would 'think fit' to approve it on behalf of a minor or unborn persons. In this case, the evidence of intention of this testatrix seems to me to have been of no relevance.[109]

The decision in *Goulding v James*[110] is at odds with the decision in *Re Steed's Will Trusts*,[111] where the court refused to vary a protective trust because, among other reasons, this was part of the testator's scheme. While the decision in *Goulding v James* may be better founded in logic, the power of the court to approve a variation is discretionary, and it is hard to see why the testator's motives should be wholly disregarded. On the other hand, treating the court as the 'statutory attorney' for those on whose behalf it consents, its task is not to adjudicate on the merits of the scheme as a whole, but only

---

[107] [1996] 4 All ER 854.   [108] [1997] 2 All ER 239, at 249.   [109] [1997] 2 All ER 239, at 252.
[110] [1997] 2 All ER 239, at 252, per Mummery LJ. See Luxton 'Variation of Trusts: Settlors' Intentions and the Consent Principle in *Saunders v Vautier*' (1997) 60 MLR 719.   [111] [1960] Ch 407.

on its impact on those for whom the court acts as a surrogate. From this point of view, why should those beneficiaries lose the benefits in kind they would receive from a variation unless those benefits are more than compensated by the non-pecuniary benefits of knowing that the testator's wishes have been respected?

(e) Widening powers of investment

The Variation of Trusts Act is not limited to the variation of beneficial interest, but may also be used to vary the powers of the trustees under the trust deed. In the past the courts held that they would not grant approval to a variation of the trustee's powers of investment which were wider than those contained in the Trustee Investment Act 1961.[112] However, the courts came to recognize that the Act was outdated and approved variations granting wider investment powers.[113] The Trustee Investment Act 1961 has now been replaced by the Trustee Act 2000, which grants trustees the power to make any kind of investment. This new legislative framework is likely to free the courts from any residual unwillingness to grant variations in the trustees' power of investment. The trustees' power of investment is discussed in Chapter 21.

(6) Effect of an order to vary

The question has arisen as to how precisely a variation of the beneficial interests under a trust take place. Does it occur by the order of the court, or as a result of the arrangement that is consented to by those who are able, and by the court on those who cannot consent for themselves? The difficulty is not merely theoretical because of the implications of s 53(1)(c) of the Law of Property Act, which requires that a disposition of a subsisting equitable interest 'must be in writing signed by the person disposing of the same'.[114] If the variation is considered a 'disposition',[115] and takes effect as a consequence of the arrangement and not the court order, is it necessary that all those who can consent for themselves do so in writing? Although there is some authority to the contrary,[116] the House of Lords has held that the variation takes effect through the arrangement and not by the order of the court. The principle was stated by Lord Reid in *IRC v Holmden*:

> Under the Variation of Trusts Act the court does not itself amend or vary the trusts of the original settlement. The beneficiaries are not bound by variations because the court has made the variation. Each beneficiary is bound because he has consented to the variation. If he was not of full age when the arrangement was made he is bound because the court was authorised to act on his behalf and did so by making an order. If he was of full age and did not in fact consent he is not affected by the order of the court and he is not bound. So the arrangement must be regarded as an arrangement made by the beneficiaries themselves.

---

[112] See *Re Kolb's Will Trusts* [1962] Ch 531.
[113] See *Mason v Farbrother* [1983] 2 All ER 1078; *Trustees of the British Museum v A-G* [1984] 1 WLR 418; *Steel v Wellcome Custodian Trustees Ltd* [1988] 1 WLR 167.   [114] See Chapter 7.
[115] *Grey v IRC* [1960] AC 1, HL.
[116] *Re Viscount Hambleden's Will Trusts* [1960] 1 All ER 353n, per Wynn-Parry J.

The court merely acted on behalf of or as representing those beneficiaries who were not in a position to give their own consent and approval.[117]

Whether the consenting beneficiaries must comply with s 53(1)(c) was considered by Megarry J in *Re Holt's Settlement*,[118] where he adopted two possible solutions to avoid the difficulty. First, he accepted that the express granting of the power to vary trusts to the courts by Parliament in the Variation of Trusts Act has 'provided by necessary implication an exception from s 53(1)(c)'.[119] Second, if the arrangement is an agreement made for valuable consideration, then because it is specifically enforceable the 'beneficial interests pass to the respective purchasers on the making of the agreement', by means of a constructive trust.[120] By virtue of s 53(2), writing is therefore not required.

---

[117] [1968] AC 685, at 701; *Re Joseph's Will Trusts* [1959] 1 WLR 1019.

[118] [1969] 1 Ch 100. It is worth noting that *Re Holt's Settlement Trusts* was decided prior to the House of Lords' decision in *Re Holmden's Settlement Trusts* and that Megarry J proceeded on the basis that it was the court order which varied the trusts.

[119] [1969] 1 Ch 100, at 115: Megarry J accepted that this was not the most natural construction and that he was 'straining a little at the wording in the interests of legislative efficiency'.

[120] [1969] 1 Ch 100, at 116, following *Oughtred v IRC* [1960] AC 206, HL.

18

Winding up of funds

When property is held as a fund for the benefit of other persons or purposes, it is inevitable in most instances that at some time the fund will come to an end. This may be a result of its exhaustion, as the property is properly applied. Alternatively, the purposes for which the fund was established may have failed or come to an end, leaving a surplus as yet undistributed. This chapter will consider the circumstances in which a fund comes to an end, and especially how the surplus of funds which have failed are applied.

1 Exhaustion and failure

Trusts can end both when the assets that are held on trust have been fully used, and also when, although assets remain, the purposes for which those assets were held on trust have become fulfilled or impossible. In the latter case, there will be a question as to who is entitled to the remaining assets.

(1) Initial failure

An attempt to create a trust in favour of, or to make a gift to, a person who does not exist, cannot operate as an effective disposition, and beneficial ownership will therefore remain in the donor. In *Omojole v HSBC Bank Plc*[1] a Nigerian company paid £3m into the account of a company with which it was associated without being aware that the company had been struck off for failing to file its returns. It was held that the money was held on resulting trust for the company which made the payment.

(2) Exhaustion of a fund

Clearly, a fund will come to an end if all the property within it has been appropriately applied. The most obvious example is a bare trust where the property has been transferred to the beneficiary, thus bringing the trust relationship to an end. Similarly, the trustees of a discretionary trust, either exhaustive or non-exhaustive in character, may have distributed the whole of the fund among the class of potential beneficiaries.

[1] [2012] EWHC 3102 (QB).

A charity may have spent all the money it possesses in pursuit of its purposes, and an unincorporated association may have exhausted its funds. In all such cases the fund has come to an end by process of exhaustion, and there is no longer any property left. There is no question of what should happen to an undistributed surplus, and the exhaustion of the fund brings the trust to an end.

(3) Subsequent failure of the fund

Alternatively, the fund may have to be wound up because of the failure of the purposes of the fund or the organization holding the fund. For example, a fund may have been established by the transfer of property to trustees on a trust which is subsequently found to be void for uncertainty, or a charitable organization holding funds may have closed.[2] In such circumstances, what happens to the surplus will depend on the nature of the fund and how it was held. In the event that there is no other person who is entitled to the surplus of a fund which has failed, it will pass to the Crown as bona vacantia.

(a) Failure of private trusts

Where a private trust fails, any surplus of the fund[3] will generally revert back to the original settlor of the property under a resulting trust.

(b) Dissolution of unincorporated associations

What happens when a non-charitable unincorporated association is dissolved was considered in Chapter 12. Normally any property held by the association will be divided among the remaining members of the association in accordance with its rules.

(c) Failure of charities

When a charitable purpose or particular charitable institution or organization comes to an end, any surplus held by the charity will be applied cy-près for an alternative charitable purpose.

2 Surplus funds on the failure of private trusts

(1) Operation of resulting trusts

When a trust is created, the property subject to it is held by trustees for the beneficiaries, who become the equitable owners. If for some reason the equitable ownership is not effectively transferred to the new beneficiaries, it will revert, or 'result back', to the previous equitable owner, normally the person who created the trust. The trustees will therefore hold the property on trust for the previous equitable owner to whom it

---

[2] *Re Slevin* [1891] 2 Ch 236, CA; *Re Rymer* [1895] 1 Ch 19, CA.
[3] Or the whole fund in the case of a trust fund void ab initio.

has resulted. The essence of a resulting trust was captured by Megarry J in *Re Sick and Funeral Society of St John's Sunday School, Golcar*:

> A resulting trust is essentially a property concept: any property a man does not effectually dispose of remains his own.[4]

The term 'resulting trust' is used to describe a number of different situations where property will revert back to its original owner, and it is important to distinguish the different senses in which the term is used. Resulting trusts were classified by Megarry J in *Re Vandervell's Trusts (No 2)*[5] into 'presumed' and 'automatic' resulting trusts.[6]

(a) Presumed resulting trusts

Presumed resulting trusts are those which arise as the result of the presumption that a property 'results to the man who advances the purchase money'.[7] For example, in *Tinsley v Milligan*[8] a house was purchased in the sole name of Tinsley, but part of the purchase price was provided by her lesbian lover, Milligan. It was held that there was a resulting trust and that Tinsley held the house on trust for herself and Milligan as joint tenants. The presumptions that give rise to such resulting trusts are not conclusive, and may be rebutted by evidence that the contributor intended to make a gift and not to retain any interest in the property purchased. In some cases, because of the nature of the relationship between the parties, the law presumes that a gift is intended, and a resulting trust does not arise unless the presumption is rebutted by evidence that a gift was not intended.[9]

(b) Automatic resulting trusts

Megarry J suggested that 'automatic' resulting trusts arise by operation of law, and not on the basis of any presumed intention on the part of the original owner of the property. As he observed:

> What a man fails effectually to dispose of remains automatically vested in him, and no question of a mere presumption can arise.[10]

Where a trust fails, unless expressly or impliedly excluded,[11] an automatic resulting trust determines how any remaining surplus should be applied. This can apply as much where a trust fails from the outset (as *Omojole v HSBC Bank Plc*[12] shows) as where a trust fails subsequently and a surplus remains.

In *Westdeutsche Landesbank Girozentrale v Islington London Borough Council*,[13] this twofold categorization of resulting trusts was broadly adopted.

---

[4] [1973] Ch 51, at 59.   [5] [1974] Ch 269.   [6] [1974] Ch 269 at 289 and 294–296.
[7] *Dyer v Dyer* (1788) 2 Cox Eq Cas 92, per Eyre CB.   [8] [1993] 3 All ER 65.
[9] The presumption of 'advancement'. See further Chapter 9.   [10] [1974] Ch 269, at 289.
[11] See *Davis v Richards and Wallington Industries Ltd* [1991] 2 All ER 563.
[12] [2012] EWHC 3102 (QB).
[13] [1996] AC 669. See Birks 'Trusts Raised to Avoid Unjust Enrichment: The *Westdeutsche* Case' [1996] RLR 3; Cape 'Compound Interest and Restitution' (1996) 112 LQR 521; Jones 'Ultra Vires Swaps: The Common Law and Equitable Fall-Out' [1996] CLJ 432; Stevens 'Simple Interest Only? Autonomous Unjust Enrichment and the Relationship between Equity and Common Law' [1997] LMCLQ 441.

However, Lord Browne-Wilkinson put forward an argument that all resulting trusts are based on intention. Describing an 'automatic resulting trust,' he said:

> Under existing law a resulting trust arises in two sets of circumstances…(B) Where A transfers property to B on express trusts, but the trusts declared do not exhaust the whole beneficial interest…Both types of resulting trust are traditionally regarded as examples of trusts giving effect to the common intentions of the parties. A resulting trust is not imposed by law against the intentions of the trustee (as is a constructive trust) but gives effect to his presumed intention. Megarry J in *Re Vandervell's Trusts (No 2)* suggests that a resulting trust of type (B) does not depend on intention but operates automatically. I am not convinced that this is right. If the settlor has expressly, or by necessary implication, abandoned any beneficial interest in the trust property, there is in my view no resulting trust: the undisposed of equitable interest vests in the Crown as bona vacantia.[14]

While these comments rightly observe that a resulting trust is not an inevitable result whenever an express trust fails, it is unlikely that Megarry J ever intended the term automatic resulting trust to carry this connotation. Such a resulting trust operates in effect as a form of trust implied in default. While it could be said that a failure to dispose of the entire equitable interest arises by interpreting the settlor's intentions, this is a rather forced interpretation of a case like Mr Vandervell's. The consequence of finding that he had not entirely parted with the beneficial interest in the shares was that he faced a huge tax bill. Had he been asked whether this was what he intended, he would certainly have denied it. It is more realistic to accept that resulting trusts arising in the event of the failure of an express trust do tend to arise automatically in practice, if not in theory. Cases where it can be shown that a settlor has expressly, or by necessary implication, abandoned any beneficial interest in the trust property will be quite exceptional,[15] except in cases, for instance, where small donations have been made anonymously in a collection box. Despite Lord Browne-Wilkinson's attempt to label resulting trusts as Types A and B it is therefore sensible to retain the more traditional classification into presumed and automatic.[16] Presumed resulting trusts were considered in Chapter 8. This chapter looks only at automatic resulting trusts, which have significantly different characteristics.

(2) When an automatic resulting trust will be implied

(a) Failure to declare the beneficial interests arising behind an express trust

If property is transferred to trustees upon trust but the settlor makes no effective declaration of the beneficial interests, so that the trustees do not know who they are to hold the property for, they will hold the property transferred on a resulting trust for the settlor, or if he is dead, for his successors in title.[17] The principle was stated by Lord

---

[14] [1996] AC 669, per Lord Goff, at 708.

[15] See *Simpson v Gowers* (1981) 32 OR (2d) 385; *Dennis v North Western Nat Bank* 81 NW 2d 254 (1957) (cases involving chattels).   [16] See Swadling 'Explaining Resulting Trusts' (2008) 124 LQR 72.

[17] See *Johnson v Ball* (1851) 5 De G & Sm 85; *Re Keen* [1937] 1 All ER 452 and *Re Boyes* (1884) 26 Ch D 531, where there were ineffective attempts to create secret trusts.

Wilberforce in *Vandervell v IRC*, where an option to repurchase shares was held by a trust company but no indication had been given as to the beneficiaries thereof:

> the option was vested in the trustee company as a trustee on trusts, not defined at the time, possibly to be defined later. But the equitable, or beneficial interest, cannot remain in the air: the consequence in law must be that it remains in the settlor...[18]

The option was therefore held by the trustee company on resulting trust for Mr Vandervell, who had been the original owner of the shares.

The operation of a resulting trust in such circumstances was examined by the Privy Council in *Air Jamaica Ltd v Charlton*.[19] Lord Millett explained that a resulting trust does not arise because the trustee wanted to retain a beneficial interest in the property:

> Like a constructive trust, a resulting trust arises by operation of law, though unlike a constructive trust it gives effect to intention. But it does arise whether or not the transferor intended to retain a beneficial interest—he almost always does not—since it responds to the absence of any intention on his part to pass a beneficial interest to the recipient. It may arise even where the transferor positively wished to part with the beneficial interest, as in Vandervell v IRC... The House of Lords affirmed the principle that a resulting trust is not defeated by evidence that the transferor intended to part with the beneficial interest if he has not in fact succeeded in doing so.[20]

(b) Failure of an express trust

If a valid trust is created but subsequently fails for some reason, any trust property that remains in the hands of the trustees will be held on resulting trust for the settlor. For example, in *Re Ames' Settlement*[21] Louis Ames created a marriage settlement of £10,000 on the marriage of his son in 1908. The marriage was declared 'absolutely null and void' in 1927 by the Supreme Court of Kenya, on the grounds of the husband's incapacity to consummate the marriage.[22] Vaisey J concluded that, since the marriage had been void ab initio, there was a total failure of the consideration for the marriage settlement and the property should result back to the father's estate. A resulting trust would also arise if a settlement was created in contemplation of a marriage which never took place.[23] In *Re Cochrane*[24] a marriage settlement was created in favour of a wife 'so long as she shall continue to reside with' her husband. They separated and the income was paid to the husband, who then predeceased her. It was held that the income should be held on resulting trust for the settlors in proportion to the contributions they had made to the fund.

Where a trust is void because it fails to comply with all the requirements necessary for the creation of a valid trust, the trust property will again be held on a resulting trust for the settlor or his estate. In *Chichester Diocesan Fund and Board of Finance Inc v Simpson*[25] Caleb Diplock created a discretionary trust in favour of charity. However,

---

[18] [1967] 2 AC 291, at 329.   [19] [1999] 1 WLR 1399.   [20] [1999] 1 WLR 1399, at 1412.
[21] [1946] Ch 217.   [22] See *Re d'Altroy's Will Trusts* [1968] 1 WLR 120; *Re Rodwell* [1970] Ch 726.
[23] *Essery v Cowlard* (1884) 26 Ch D 191; *Bond v Walford* (1886) 32 Ch D 238.
[24] [1955] Ch 309.   [25] [1944] AC 341.

because the trust included some non-charitable objects it was invalid and the property resulted back to his estate. In *Re Astor's Settlement Trusts*[26] a trust created in 1945 for the promotion of 'good understanding between the nations' and the 'preservation of the independence and integrity of newspapers' was held void because it contravened the beneficiary principle. The property was therefore held on resulting trust.

Where property has been held on trust for a charity that has failed, it may similarly result to the settlors or donors if there was no intention to make an outright charitable gift. For example, in *Re Ulverston and District New Hospital Building Trusts*[27] a fund had been created for the purpose of building a new hospital. The fund consisted of contributions from named donors, anonymous donors, street collections, and the proceeds of entertainments. The purpose became impossible, and it was held that the fund should be held on resulting trust for its donors because the donations had been made for only this purpose. It the donors' intentions had been more generally to support medical care, the gift property could have been applied to other charitable purposes under the cy-près doctrine, considered later in this chapter.

Deciding who the settlor is, or who the donors are, can be complicated. In *Re St Andrew's (Cheam) Lawn Tennis Club Trust*,[28] Arnold J, having held that a trust of land for use as a tennis club failed because it was for mixed charitable and non-charitable purposes, held that the land was held on resulting trust for the previous owner (Mr Tweddle), despite significant contributions by other parties, because 'Mr Tweddle appears to have been the largest single donor, and the donations made by the smaller donors were predicated upon Mr Tweddle's donation'.

(c) Trust fund has not been exhausted

Where a trust has been established for a specific purpose, any surplus funds that have not been exhausted on the completion of the purpose should in most cases be returned to the original contributors by way of a resulting trust in proportion to their contributions. The principle was stated by Harman J in *Re Gillingham Bus Disaster Fund*:

> The general principle must be that where money is held upon trust and the trusts declared do not exhaust the fund it will revert to the donor under what is called a resulting trust.[29]

In *Re Abbott Fund Trusts*[30] a fund was collected and established in 1890 for the support of two deaf and dumb ladies. On their death in 1899 a surplus remained in the fund. The court held that the surplus should be held for the benefit of those who had subscribed to the fund. Central to the decision was the finding by Stirling J that the fund was never 'intended to become the absolute property of the ladies'.[31] However, in subsequent cases the courts have construed gifts for beneficiaries with a description of purposes as if they were outright gifts, thereby excluding any possibility of a resulting trust to the contributors. In *Re Andrew's Trust*[32] the friends of a deceased clergyman subscribed to a fund for the education of his children. After all the children had

---

[26] [1952] Ch 534.   [27] [1956] Ch 622.   [28] [2012] EWHC 1040
[29] [1958] Ch 300, at 310.   [30] [1900] 2 Ch 326.   [31] [1900] 2 Ch 326, at 330.
[32] [1905] 2 Ch 48.

completed their education, there was a surplus of some £460 remaining in the fund. Kekewich J held that there should not be a resulting trust to the subscribers because the gift was to be construed as an absolute gift to the children, with the purpose being merely a motive for the gift. He took the view that the court always[33] construed such gifts in this way.[34] *Re Andrew's Trust*[35] was followed in *Re Osoba (Decd)*,[36] which concerned a trust established by a testator 'for the training of my daughter Abiola up to university grade and for the maintenance of my aged mother'. His mother had died and the daughter had completed her university education, leaving a surplus in the fund. The Court of Appeal held that the gift was an absolute gift and the reference to the purpose 'merely a statement of the testator's motive in making the gift'.[37] It is difficult to reconcile[38] *Re Abbott Fund Trusts*[39] with *Re Andrew's Trust*.[40] Ultimately, as was recognized by the Court of Appeal in *Re Osoba*,[41] each turns on its own facts, and it is of perhaps crucial importance that in *Re Abbott Fund Trusts*[42] the beneficiaries of the fund were deceased, and could derive no further benefit from it.[43]

The question is whether, on the facts, the settlor parted with all claim to the property. In this context it may be relevant that with only a few exceptions, the law does not recognize purpose trusts, and this may therefore predispose the courts towards interpreting trusts for the benefit of ascertainable beneficiaries as outright gifts. This is an approach which has also been taken in regard to gifts to unincorporated associations.[44]

(d) Pension fund surplus

Particular problems have arisen concerning the applicability of a resulting trust analysis to a surplus under a pension scheme trust.[45] There is only one kind of pension scheme where this can arise: where the scheme is paid from a fund into which the member and/or his employer have made contributions, and the pension is defined independently of the value of the investments. This type of pension is described as a funded defined benefit scheme. Most funded pension schemes pay a pension based on the value of the investments which are attributed to an individual member. By definition these cannot be in surplus. With a defined benefit scheme it is possible for there to be either a shortfall or a surplus. Falling investment returns and increased longevity

---

[33] See *Re Sanderson's Will Trust* (1857) 3 K & J 497; *Barlow v Grant* (1684) 1 Vern 255; *Webb v Kelly* (1839) 9 Sim 469; *Lewes v Lewes* (1848) 16 Sim 266; *Presant and Presant v Goodwin* (1860) 1 Sw & Tr 544.

[34] [1905] 2 Ch 48 at 52–53: 'If a gross sum be given, or if the whole income of the property be given, and a special purpose be assigned for that gift, this court always regards the gift as absolute, and holds the purpose merely as the motive of the gift, and therefore holds that the gift takes effect as to the whole sum or the whole income, as the case may be.'   [35] [1905] 2 Ch 48.

[36] [1979] 1 WLR 247; [1978] CLJ 219 (Rickett). See also *Re Lipinski's Will Trusts* [1976] Ch 235.

[37] [1979] 1 WLR 247 at 257, per Buckley LJ.

[38] See the judgment of Megarry V-C at first instance in *Re Osoba* [1978] 1 WLR 791.

[39] [1900] 2 Ch 326.   [40] [1905] 2 Ch 48.   [41] [1979] 1 WLR 247, at 251.

[42] [1900] 2 Ch 326.

[43] This was pointed out by Kekewich J in *Re Andrew's Trust* [1905] 2 Ch 48, at 52.

[44] *Re Lipinski's Will Trusts* [1976] Ch 235 discussed in relation to clubs and societies in Chapter 12.

[45] See Pollard 'Pensions Law and Surpluses: A Fair Balance between Employer and Members?' (2003) TLI 2.

have meant that few defined benefit pension schemes now have a surplus, but pension scheme surpluses were common in the 1990s and may still arise where a well-funded scheme is wound up. A variety of solutions have been adopted which demonstrate the unclear relationship between trust and contract.[46] Because the solution is so intimately connected with the way in which pension fund trusts are viewed, these solutions are considered in Chapter 22, which looks at these schemes more generally.

(e) Failure of a loan made for a specific purpose

One specialized application of the surplus-funds resulting trust can occur where money has been lent for a specific purpose that has failed. On the failure of the purpose the borrower may hold the money lent on a resulting trust for the lender. Such a result-ing trust is extremely significant if the borrower becomes insolvent, since the lender will be entitled to assert an equitable proprietary claim to the money lent and it will not form part of the assets of the creditor. The lender will not therefore merely rank among the general creditors of the borrower, which would have been his position in the absence of a trust because he would only have been entitled to a contractual claim for the repayment of the debt. It is not surprising that the principle originally evolved in cases where lenders were willing to make last-ditch loans to companies in extreme financial peril, since the added security of the resulting trust encourages them to make what would otherwise be extremely risky investments.

The implication of such a resulting trust was first recognized by the House of Lords in *Barclays Bank Ltd v Quistclose Investments Ltd*,[47] the case which has given its name to this type of trust. A company, Rolls Razor Ltd, was in severe financial difficulties. The company obtained a loan from Quistclose on the agreed condition that it would only be used to pay the dividend to shareholders, and for that purpose the money was to be kept in a separate bank account. Before the dividend could be paid, Rolls Razor went into voluntary liquidation. The House of Lords held that, because of the exclusive purpose for which the loan was made, the money was received by Rolls Razor in the fiduciary character of a trust to pay the dividend. Since that purpose had failed, there was a resulting trust in favour of the lenders. The principle was explained by Lord Wilberforce:

> There is surely no difficulty in recognising the co-existence in one transaction of legal and equitable rights and remedies: when the money is advanced, the lender acquires an equita-ble right to see that it is applied for the primary designated purpose: when the purpose has been carried out...the lender has his remedy against the borrower in debt: if the primary purpose cannot be carried out, the question arises if a secondary purpose (ie repayment to the lender) has been agreed, expressly or by implication: if it has, the remedies of equity may be invoked to give effect to it...[48]

---

[46] As Megarry J observed in *Re Sick and Funeral Society of St John's Sunday School, Golcar* [1973] Ch 51, many of the difficulties arise because of the confusion of property with contract.

[47] [1970] AC 567. See also Mitchell 'Subrogation, Tracing and the *Quistclose* Principle' [1995] LMCLQ 451; Matthews, 'The New Trust: Obligations without Rights' in Oakley, *Trends in Contemporary Trust Law* (1996), p 16.   [48] [1970] AC 567, at 581.

This principle has been developed and applied in subsequent cases,[49] and the House of Lords again considered whether such a trust was operative in *Twinsectra Ltd v Yardley*.[50] In this case, a finance company agreed to lend £1m to the prospective purchaser of residential land. The money was paid into the client account of the purchaser's solicitor, subject to an express undertaking that the money be utilized 'solely for the acquisition of property on behalf of our client and for no other purpose'. Contrary to the terms of this undertaking, £358,000 of the money was used for other purposes. One question was whether the arrangement had given rise to a trust of the money, a crucial prerequisite to the claim of dishonest assistance in a breach of trust that was being maintained by the finance company. The House of Lords held that the money was subject to a trust because it had been paid subject to an undertaking that it would only be used for a specific purpose.

While these cases establish that a trust will arise where money is lent for a specific purpose that fails, the exact nature of such a trust has been a matter of academic controversy. In particular it has been difficult to determine when the trust comes into existence, to identify the beneficiary, and to reconcile the existence of the trust with the beneficiary principle, since as it was described in the *Quistclose* case it appears to require the existence of a primary trust under the terms of which money is held for the carrying out of a purpose. These theoretical problems were not explored by the House of Lords in *Quistclose* itself. There are several possibilities, none of which is free from difficulty.

(i) Primary trust for intended recipients

First, a loan for a specific purpose may be regarded as creating a primary trust in favour of the persons intended to receive payment, for example specific creditors or shareholders, which gives rise to a resulting trust when the purpose fails. This approach seems to have been adopted by Megarry V-C in *Re Northern Developments (Holdings) Ltd*.[51] However, this analysis can be criticized[52] on the grounds that such loans are made to benefit the borrower, and not for the benefit of the creditors or shareholders as such, and that it cannot explain cases where the loan was made for an abstract purpose.[53]

(ii) Primary trust for a purpose

Second, the loan might create a primary trust to use the money for a purpose, with a resulting trust arising only when the purpose, and hence the primary trust, fails.

---

[49] *Carreras Rothmans Ltd v Freeman Mathews Treasure Ltd* [1985] Ch 207, at 222, per Peter Gibson J, who explained the trust as arising from the principle 'that equity fastens on the conscience of the person who receives from another property transferred for a specific purpose only and not therefore for the recipient's own purposes, so that such person will not be permitted to treat the property as his own or use it for other than the stated purpose'. See also *Re EVTR* [1987] BCLC 646.

[50] [2002] 2 AC 164; [2002] 2 All ER 377. See [2002] RLR 111 (Ricketts); [2002] Con 387 (Thompson); (2002) 16 TLI 165 (Penner); (2002) 16 TLI 223 (Glister); (2003) 119 LQR 8 (Yeo and Tijo); (2004) 63 CLJ 632 (Glister).   [51] (6 October 1978, unreported).

[52] *Twinsectra Ltd v Yardley* [2002] 2 All ER 377, at [85]–[89].

[53] For example, as in *Re EVTR* [1987] BCLC 646.

Under this approach, which was advocated by the Court of Appeal in *Twinsectra Ltd v Yardley*,[54] the equitable interest in the money might be regarded as being 'in suspense' until the stated purpose is carried out, so that neither the lender nor the borrower is, strictly speaking, the beneficiary. However, it has the difficulty of appearing to offend the beneficiary principle, and was subjected to criticism in the House of Lords on the grounds that it is unorthodox, fails to have regard to the role which resulting trusts play in equity, and fails to explain why the money is not simply held on resulting trust for the lender from the outset.[55]

(iii) No primary trust

Third, Chambers has argued that the loan does not create a primary trust at all. Rather, the borrower receives the entire beneficial ownership in the money lent, subject only to a contractual right in the lender to prevent the money being used otherwise than for the stated purpose, and a resulting trust springs into being only if the purpose fails.[56] This view has been criticized because it cannot explain cases of non-contractual payments, and it is inconsistent with the judgments in *Quistclose* that describe the borrower as under a fiduciary duty.[57]

(iv) Resulting trust throughout

Finally, the money lent for a specific purpose may be regarded as being held on resulting trust by the borrower for the lender from the very beginning, the resulting trust arising from the fact that the lender did not intend the borrower to enjoy the beneficial ownership in the money lent. This analysis has been advocated extra-judicially by Lord Millett,[58] and was therefore, unsurprisingly, adopted by him in *Twinsectra Ltd v Yardley*.[59] He explained what he considered to be the nature of the *Quistclose* trust:

> As Sherlock Holmes reminded Dr Watson, when you have eliminated the impossible, whatever remains, however improbable, must be the truth. I would reject all the alternative analyses, which I find unconvincing and hold the Quistclose trust to be an entirely orthodox example of the kind of default trust known as a resulting trust. The lender pays the money to the borrower by way of loan, but he does not part with the entire beneficial interest in the money, and in so far as he does not it is held on a resulting trust for the lender from the outset.... When the purpose fails, the money is returnable to the lender, not under some new trust in his favour which only comes into being on the failure of the purpose, but because the resulting trust in his favour is no longer subject to any power on the part of the borrower to make use of the money.[60]

---

[54] [1999] Lloyd's Rep Bank 438.

[55] *Twinsectra Ltd v Yardley* [2002] 2 All ER 377, at [90], per Lord Millett.

[56] Chambers, *Resulting Trusts* (1997), pp 68–89.

[57] Ho and Smart 'Reinterpreting the *Quistclose* Trust: A Critique of Chambers' Analysis' (2001) 21 OJLS 267. See also *Twinsectra Ltd v Yardley* [2002] 2 All ER 377, [95], per Lord Millett.

[58] Sir Peter Millett 'The *Quistclose* Trust: Who Can Enforce It?' (1985) 101 LQR 269.

[59] [2002] 2 All ER 377.   [60] [2002] 2 All ER 377, at 403.

While this analysis has the merit of simplicity, and of avoiding any problem of any conflict with the beneficiary principle, it is submitted that it is somewhat artificial to regard a resulting trust as subsisting from the very moment that the loan is made, prior to the failure of the purpose, unless the resulting trust is essentially an express trust based on the intentions of the parties. It is also unclear whether Lord Millett's analysis was supported by the majority of the House of Lords. Lord Hoffmann agreed that there was a trust, but did not specifically refer to the *Quistclose case*, and he appears to have regarded the arrangement as more akin to an express trust created by the under- taking. Lord Slynn agreed with Lord Hoffmann. Lord Hutton agreed with both Lords Hoffmann and Lord Millett that the money was subject to a trust, but did not comment further on their reasoning. Lord Steyn simply agreed with both Lords Hoffmann and Hutton. The basis of the decision is therefore open to debate, but it has been described as the characterization which 'probably holds sway'.[61]

(v) Mandate?

Another similar option is to view the arrangement in contractual terms. On this analy- sis, the bargain between the parties gives the borrower a mandate to use the loan for a particular purpose only, but unless and until the loan is used in this way, the money lent remains the property of the lender. Hildyard J in *Challinor v Juliet Bellis & Co (A Firm)*[62] described such a contractual arrangement as an escrow agreement, but thought that it might differ in some respects from a *Quistclose* trust since the latter does not depend upon the existence of a contract (although the two would usually coexist). The rationale is almost identical to Lord Millett's, but expressed in the language of contract rather than of trust. This analysis is supported by comments of Norris J approved on appeal by the Court of Appeal in *Bieber v Teathers Ltd*[63] and is the solution which was adopted in another context by the Court of Appeal in *Conservative Central Office v Burrell*.[64] It is also mirrored by the rules applying to the lien which a solicitor has for unpaid fees. The normal rule is that the firm will have a professional lien allowing it to retain any deed, paper, chattel, or money belonging to the client until the fees have been paid. The lien does not apply to any funds held by the solicitor subject to a trust for a particular purpose,[65] nor to funds subject to a court order which does not impose a trust, but which does restrict their use.[66]

(vi) Sui generis situation?

If there is no better justification, it might be better to acknowledge the essen- tially anomalous and sui generis nature of the *Quistclose* trust, rather than to

---

[61] *Challinor v Juliet Bellis & Co* [2013] EWHC 347 (Ch), at [543]

[62] [2011] EWHC 3249 (Ch). (Application for reverse summary judgment. The main judgment is referred to later.) [63] [2012] EWCA Civ 1466, at [14].

[64] [1982] 1 WLR 522. The context was that of an unincorporated organization which was not an unincor- porated association. See Chapter 12. [65] *Stumore v Campbell & Co* [1892] 1 QB 314.

[66] *Withers LLP v Langbar* [2012] 2 All ER 616.

search for the 'truth' as to its nature by fitting it within 'orthodox' categories. As Potter LJ suggested in the Court of Appeal, the *Quisclose*-type trust 'is in truth a "quasi-trust" '.[67]

(f) Criteria needed for *Quistclose* trusts

The essence of a *Quistclose* trust is that the terms of the arrangement are such that ownership of the money concerned does not pass to the recipient, but that the recipient is authorized to use it only in a defined way. *Bieber v Teathers Ltd*[68] contains a recent distillation of the criteria drawn from the *Quistclose* and *Twinsectra* cases, that has been adopted in other cases both in the United Kingdom[69] and Ireland.[70]

(i) Money advanced for a specific purpose

A *Quistclose* resulting trust will only arise if the loan or other payment[71] (such as money to be invested by the recipient[72]) was made exclusively[73] for an agreed specific purpose. In *Quistclose*, the purpose was the payment of a share dividend. In *Carreras Rothmans Ltd v Freeman Mathews Treasure Ltd (in liquidation)*[74] a resulting trust was held to arise where a loan had been made by Rothmans to their advertising agency, who were in financial difficulty, for the purpose of paying third parties with whom Rothmans' adverts had been placed. In *Re EVTR*[75] a resulting trust was found where a loan had been made to a company in financial difficulties for the purchase of new machinery.

(ii) Objective mutual intention to retain title

It is not enough that it is intended the money should be used in a particular way. The money must be advanced and on such terms or in such circumstances that it was made objectively clear 'that the funds transferred should not be part of the general assets of the recipient but should be used *exclusively* to effect particular identified payments'[76]. The recipient must be party to this agreement or understanding.[77] If the funds are at the free disposal of the recipient, there cannot be a *Quistclose* trust.[78]

---

   [67] [1999] Lloyd's Rep Bank 438, at [76].
   [68] [2012] EWCA Civ 1466, at [14] and [15]. The criteria are drawn from the first instance judgment of Norris J.
   [69] *Challinor v Juliet Bellis & Co* [2013] EWHC 347 (Ch); *Eleftheriou v Costi* [2013] EWHC 2168 (Ch); *Brown v Innovatorone Plc* [2012] EWHC 1321 (Comm).
   [70] *Harlequin Property (SVG) Ltd v O'Halloran* [2013] IEHC 362.
   [71] In *Patel v Mirza* [2013] EWHC 1892 (Ch), at [40]. David Donaldson QC would have been prepared to apply the principle to money advanced to make a bet on the IG Index were the transaction not affected by illegality because of insider dealing. *G v A* [2009] EWHC 11 (Fam) a *Quistclose* trust was applied to moneys payable for a particular purpose by way of financial provision on divorce.
   [72] *Wise v Jimenez* [2014] WTLR 163 and *Brown v Innovatorone Plc* [2012] EWHC 1321 (Comm) (trust established); *Bieber v Teathers Ltd* [2012] EWCA Civ 1466 (trust not established).
   [73] See *Gabriel v Little* [2013] EWCA Civ 1513, at [20] and [41]; *Soutzos v Asombang* [2010] EWHC 842 (Ch), at [144].   [74] [1985] Ch 207.
   [75] [1987] BCLC 646.   [76] *Bieber v Teathers Ltd* [2012] EWCA Civ 1466, at [14] and [15].
   [77] *Challinor v Juliet Bellis & Co* [2013] EWHC 347 (Ch), at [552].
   [78] *Re Goldcorp Exchange* [1995] 1 AC 74.

(iii) High level of certainty

It is also necessary that the particular purpose must be specified in terms which enable a court to say whether a given application of the money does or does not fall within its terms.[79] This is important to enable it to be identified whether the recipient has acted within the mandate or power and at what point the trust ceases. However, in *Twinsectra Ltd v Yardley* the purpose was expressed in relatively vague terms, namely, that the money was only to be used for the 'acquisition of property',[80] without specifying the particular property to be acquired. Carnwath J at first instance thought this too uncertain. In the House of Lords, Lord Millett held that the undertaking was stated with sufficient certainty:

> Provided that the power is stated with sufficient clarity for the court to be able to determine whether it is still capable of being carried out or whether the money has been misapplied, it is sufficiently certain to be enforced. If it is uncertain, however, then the borrower has no authority to make any use of the trust money at all and must return it to the lender under the resulting trust.[81]

(iv) Existence of trust must be compatible with terms of business

No *Quistclose* trust can arise if it is excluded by the terms of business between the parties. For instance, in *Bieber v Teathers Ltd*[82] the agreement between the parties was that the funds allegedly subject to a *Quistclose* trust were to be held as partnership assets. That was incompatible with their being a resulting trust.

> Once the partnership was in existence and their subscriptions had been paid into the partnership account...each investor's beneficial ownership of his or her individual subscription ceased and was replaced with a right to participate in the profits of the partnership and in its net assets on dissolution.

(v) Money kept in a separate bank account?

In both *Quistclose* and *Carreras Rothmans* the money lent was kept in a separate bank account. However, while this is obviously extremely clear evidence that the money is intended for the specified purpose only,[83] it is not essential. In *Re EVTR,*[84] *Twinsectra Ltd v Yardley*[85] and *Re Lehman Bros International (Europe)*[86] a trust was found even though the money was held in a general account rather than a separate account. Without a requirement for the money concerned to be segregated from the recipient's general funds, it is likely to be harder to establish the obligation to return them if they are not used for the specified purpose.[87] An unperformed obligation to segregate funds

---

[79] *Twinsectra Ltd v Yardley* [2002] 2 All ER 377, at [16]; *Bieber v Teathers Ltd* [2012] EWCA Civ 1466, at [14].   [80] [2002] 2 All ER 377.
[81] [2002] 2 All ER 377, at [101].   [82] [2012] EWCA Civ 1466, at [59].
[83] See *Challinor v Juliet Bellis & Co* [2013] EWHC 347 (Ch), at [559]–[572] where payment into a solicitor's client account was held to be a very strong indication that it was held on trust.
[84] [1987] BCLC 646.   [85] [2002] 2 All ER 377.   [86] [2012] 3 All ER 1.
[87] *Eleftheriou v Costi* [2013] EWHC 2168 (Ch), at [71].

may provide evidence of a trust obligation. In the *Lehman* case the firm had ignored the statutory rules for protecting client funds on a 'truly spectacular scale',[88] involving several billion pounds, and over a very considerable period. These rules required client funds to be segregated, and then to be subject to a statutory trust. No segregation took place, but a trust was still imposed on the funds. In some cases the lack of segregation may make it impossible to trace the funds subject to the trust.[89]

(vi) The purpose has failed?

In cases prior to *Twinsectra Ltd v Yardley* it was held that the resulting trust in favour of the lender only arises where the purpose, and thereby the primary trust, fails. In *Quistclose* and *Carreras Rothmans* this was when the borrower went into liquidation. The meaning of 'failure' was further considered by the Court of Appeal in *Re EVTR*.[90] If the explanation of the *Quistclose* trust adopted by Lord Millett in *Twinsectra Ltd v Yardley* is accepted, then it might be better to say that the trust subsists for as long as the purpose has not been carried out rather than arising only on failure of the purpose, since the resulting trust will simply remain in effect until the money is properly applied. If only part of the money is properly applied, a resulting trust will apply to the remaining balance.[91]

(g) Void transactions

In *Westdeutsche Landesbank Girozentrale v Islington London Borough Council*[92] the House of Lords considered whether a resulting trust would arise 'automatically' in situations other than where an express trust had failed. The case concerned an interest rate swap agreement that had been entered between a bank and a local authority, but which was ultra vires the local authority. The bank claimed that as the transaction was void the local authority was not merely subject to a personal common law obligation to make restitution but held the money received under the void contract on resulting trust. In such circumstances, the transfer of money by the bank had never been intended to be subject to an express trust, and therefore the House of Lords held that there were no grounds for finding that it was subject to a resulting trust merely because the contract was void. The argument for a generalized resulting trust to effect restitution was rejected. This has been examined in detail in Chapter 8.

(h) Analogous trusts

In *Challinor v Juliet Bellis & Co*[93] Hildyard J felt that the normal criteria applying to *Quistclose* trusts could be extended to allow the imposition of a trust in analogous circumstances. The essential question was as to whether there was an objective intention that negated the money belonging immediately to the recipient or a third party for whom the recipient was acting, 'such that the account holder is bound to

---

[88] [2012] 3 All ER 1, at [48].
[89] [2012] 3 All ER 1, at [2]. See Chapter 30.   [90] [1987] BCLC 646.
[91] *Latimer v Commissioner of Inland Revenue* [2004] 2 AC 164.   [92] [1996] AC 669.
[93] [2013] EWHC 347 (Ch), at [554].

hold such monies for the payer pending receipt or satisfaction of a clear direction or pre-stipulated event providing for or triggering transfer of ownership.'

(3) **Street collections and resulting trusts**

As Lord Browne-Wilkinson indicated in *Westdeutsche Landesbank Girozentrale v Islington London Borough Council*,[94] the mere fact than an express trust has failed does not inevitably mean that an automatic resulting trust will arise in favour of the settlor/contributor. For instance, where property is contributed to a fund in return for the provision of contractual benefits, this may impliedly exclude the possibility of a resulting trust in favour of the contributor. Where no contractual relationship is in issue, the presumption of an automatic resulting trust will be rebutted by evidence that the settlor had entirely abandoned his property. Thus, if he no longer intended to retain any interest in it from the moment that it was transferred by him, even by way of reverter in the event of failure of the express trust, any surplus will vest in the Crown as bona vacantia. In the absence of the settlor's express intention against a surplus-funds resulting trust, the most likely circumstance in which such a counter-intention will be implied is where an owner has made a donation which was so small as to indicate that he would not wish it to be returned in any event. Such cases might include trust surpluses consisting of anonymous small donations from street collections. In *Re Gillingham Bus Disaster Fund*[95] a fund had been established in the aftermath of an accident, in which twenty-four Royal Marine Cadets had been killed, to defray the funeral expenses of the dead and care for the disabled. Some £9,000 was raised, largely by anonymous contributors to street collections. After providing for the funerals and care, there was a large surplus of the fund remaining, and the question before the court was whether that surplus should be returned to the donors on the basis of a resulting trust, be applied cy-près to other charitable purposes, or pass as bona vacantia to the Crown. Harman J held that as the objects of the fund were not exclusively charitable there could be no application cy-près, and the surplus should be held on resulting trust for the contributors. He recognized the tremendous practical difficulty of this solution that many of those who had contributed were unknown, but concluded that this did not make a resulting trust unworkable because the trustees could pay the money into court.[96] However, this appears to be an inappropriate solution. The individual donors surely intended to part with their money when they contributed it to the fund. As such, they should have ceased to enjoy any interest in it, even the possibility of reverter by way of a resulting trust. This more realistic approach was adopted by Goff J in *Re West Sussex Constabulary's Widows, Children and Benevolent (1930) Fund Trusts*[97] in the context of an unincorporated association. He declined to follow the judgment of Harman J in *Re Gillingham Bus Disaster Fund*,[98] but followed the earlier cases of

---

[94] [1996] AC 669.   [95] [1958] Ch 300.
[96] [1958] Ch 300, at 314. In 1993 it was announced that the money was to be paid out and used for a memorial to the victims. See Hanbury and Martin, *Modern Equity* (18th edn, 2009), p 247.
[97] [1971] Ch 1.   [98] [1959] Ch 62.

Re Welsh Hospital (Netley) Fund[99] and *Re Hillier*,[100] which held that persons contributing to a fund through street collections parted with their money 'out-and-out'[101] and retained no interest in it. As PO Lawrence J had observed in *Re Welsh Hospital*:

> It is inconceivable that any person placing a coin in a collecting-box presented to him in the street should have intended that any part of the money so contributed should be returned to him. To draw such an inference would be absurd.[102]

In the light of this analysis it should perhaps be questioned whether a resulting trust should have arisen in favour of the donors in *Re Abbott Fund Trusts*.[103]

While the resulting trust analysis in such cases appears inappropriate, the alternative, whereby the surplus passes as bona vacantia to the Crown, is equally unattractive as an option. The contributors to the *Gillingham Bus Disaster Fund* surely would not have wanted the surplus to pass to the Crown, thus making an involuntary contribution to government income. The central problem with such cases is that they concerned non-charitable purpose trusts, and that there is no equivalent principle to that of cy-près by which any surplus can be applied to similar purposes.[104] If the donors to such purpose trusts are taken to have given their property out-and-out, it is right that a resulting trust should not be implied, but equity should provide a mechanism permitting the application of any such surplus by the trustees in a manner consistent with the original objectives of the trust.

3 Surplus funds on the failure of a charity

(1) Different types of failure

(a) Winding up of a charity

What happens if a charity is wound up, but still has assets? One possibility is that the assets should be returned to those who donated them on the basis of a resulting trust, in much the same way as a surplus on the failure of a private trust will return to the original contributors. However, charitable trusts are treated differently from private trusts because they have a public character. Although a whole range of different purposes may fall within the definition of 'charity', it is regarded as a unified area, so that property applied to any particular charitable purpose forms part of the 'common pot' of charity. The law thus regards property given for any specific charitable purpose as given not merely to that particular purpose but dedicated to charity

---

[99] [1921] 1 Ch 655.
[100] [1954] 1 WLR 9; on appeal [1954] 1 WLR 700, CA.
[101] *Re Hillier* [1954] 1 WLR 9 at 21–22, per Upjohn J; [1954] 1 WLR 700, at 714, per Denning LJ.
[102] [1921] 1 Ch 655, at 660.   [103] [1900] 2 Ch 326.
[104] If *Re Gillingham Bus Disaster Fund* had concerned a charitable trust the surplus remaining after the purposes had been satisfied would have been applied cy-près: *Re Wokingham Fire Brigade Trusts* [1951] Ch 373; *Re Ulverston and District New Hospital Building Trusts* [1956] Ch 622.

in the general sense. If the particular purpose for which the property was given fails, it will be applied, under a scheme drawn up by the Charity Commission,[105] to other similar charitable purposes and will not return to the donor under a resulting trust. This application to alternative charitable purposes is called 'cy-près'.[106] The principle was stated by Roxburgh J in *Re Lucas*:

> once a fund has been devoted to charitable purposes, it cannot be diverted from charity by any supervening impracticality but must be applied cy-près.[107]

(b) Subsequent failure

The situations just described involve 'subsequent' failure—funds have already been devoted to a charitable purpose when that purpose fails, for instance because the organization concerned is wound up. Subsequent failure can also arise where a charitable gift is made to an organization in existence at the date of a testator's death, but which is wound up before the personal representatives are able to transfer the gift.[108]

(c) Initial failure

There can also be problems with 'initial' failure, where a charitable purpose is from the outset incapable of achievement. This could apply where a testator makes a gift by will to a charity that has already ceased to exist, or a gift is too small to achieve the desired result. The principles determining whether the property will be applied cy-près operate differently, depending upon whether the failure was 'initial' or 'subsequent'.

(d) General charitable intent

The main difference between the treatment of initial failure and of subsequent failure is that since, in the latter, funds have already been devoted to charity, they remain devoted to charity unless the terms of the gift make it clear that the gift was limited in some way, for instance to a very specific purpose which can no longer be fulfilled. In the case of initial failure, for a gift to become effective at all, the gift has to be interpreted as impliedly extending to similar purposes, an implication which is based on finding a general charitable intent.

(e) Problems of interpretation

It is not uncommon for a testator to misdescribe a charity. This can happen for a variety of reasons. The charity may have a formal name, but is known by some less formal description. Equally, a testator may simply have guessed at the name, and guessed wrongly. If it is impossible to tell what charity a testator meant to support, the gift may still be capable of surviving where there is a general charitable intent, but it is

---

[105] Formerly, the scheme was drawn up by the court. This 'judicial' cy-près is to be contrasted with 'prerogative' cy-près, which is exercised by the Crown, where a gift is made to charity but not upon trust.

[106] See Sheridan and Delaney, *The Cy-près Doctrine* (1959); Sheridan and Keeton, *The Modern Law of Charities* (4th edn, 1992); *Nathan Committee Report* (Cmnd 8710), Ch 9; Garton 'Justifying the Cy-Près Doctrine' (2007) 21 *Trust Law International* 134.   [107] [1948] Ch 175, at 181.

[108] See eg *Phillips v The Royal Society for the Protection of Birds* [2012] EWHC 618 (Ch).

sometimes possible to escape this problem by using extrinsic evidence to make good any uncertainty in the will.[109]

(f) Failure of charitable appeals

Special statutory rules[110] apply where there is an appeal for funds for a specific charitable purpose but that purpose fails. Where a donor to the appeal cannot be identified or found after advertisement and inquiries, the funds may be applied cy-près as if the funds had been given for charitable purposes generally. Donors via collecting boxes or similar fundraising methods are conclusively treated as unidentifiable without the need for advertisement, and an appeal can contain a statement that donors must make a positive election if they are unwilling to have their donation applied to alternative purposes. These principles do not apply where an appeal is for non-charitable purposes, as was the case in *Re Gillingham Bus Disaster Fund*,[111] discussed earlier.

(2) Circumstances justifying cy-près application

(a) Impossibility or impracticality

Prior to legislative change, property would only be applied cy-près if a charitable purpose had become impossible or impracticable. For example, in *A-G v London Corpn*[112] a trust for 'the propagation of the Christian religion among the infidels of Virginia' was found to have become impossible, as Lord Thurlow LC held that there were no infidels left in Virginia. Similarly, in *Ironmongers' Co v A-G*[113] a trust for the redemption of British slaves in Turkey was impossible because there were no such British slaves remaining to be redeemed. In *Re Robinson*[114] a trust had been established to endow an Evangelical church in Bournemouth, subject to a condition that the preacher always wear a black gown. Since this was alienating the congregation, PO Lawrence J held that this rendered the purpose impracticable[115] and sanctioned a scheme dispensing with the condition.[116]

In order to extend the scope of this narrow jurisdiction, the courts did not insist strictly upon impossibility or impracticality.[117] In *Re Dominion Students Hall Trust*[118] a charity maintained a hostel for male students from the British Empire, but only those of European origin. The charity sought to remove the restriction. Evershed J held that 'the word 'impossible' should be given a wide significance'[119] and that in the circumstances the 'colour bar' did render the charity impossible since it would undermine its main objects. He therefore approved a scheme removing the bar. In *Re Lysaght (Decd)*[120] a bar on awarding medical studentships to Jews or Roman Catholics was removed because

---

[109] See *Marren v Masonic Havens Ltd* [2011] IEHC 525 (applying the slightly different rules as to interpretation of wills in the Republic of Ireland).   [110] Charities Act 2011, ss 63-66.

[111] [1958] Ch 300.   [112] (1790) 3 Bro CC 171.   [113] (1844) 10 Cl & Fin 908.

[114] [1921] 2 Ch 332. See also *Re Campden Charities* (1881) 18 Ch D 310, CA.

[115] See also *Re Weir Hospital* [1910] 2 Ch 124.

[116] In essence, he held that the paramount intention was to endow a church, and not to enforce the wearing of a black robe, and that the paramount intention would be rendered impossible by the condition. See *Re Lysaght* [1966] Ch 191, at 208.   [117] See *Re Weir Hospital* [1910] 2 Ch 124.

[118] [1947] Ch 183.   [119] [1947] Ch 183, at 186.   [120] [1966] Ch 191.

the trustee named in the will, the Royal College of Surgeons (RCS), refused to accept the gift with the restrictions, making the trust 'impossible'.[121] In *Re JW Laing Trust*[122] a trust of shares in favour of a variety of evangelical Christian purposes required all the funds to be disbursed within ten years of the settlor's death. On his death in 1978 the trust was worth some £24m. The court held that although the cy-près jurisdiction was not available, the court had an inherent jurisdiction to delete the time requirement, and should do so because the types of organizations that the trust had been supporting were unsuited to receiving large sums of capital.

(b) Charities Act 2011, s 62

Given the restrictive scope of the cy-près jurisdiction, the Nathan Committee recommended that the requirements for impracticality be relaxed.[123] A wider jurisdiction was thus introduced in s 13 of the Charities Act 1960, which has been re-enacted as s 62 of the Charities Act 2011. This section substantially broadens the occasions on which property can be applied cy-près to include situations where the original purposes have not just failed in whole or in part, but also where the funds could more effectively be used in other ways. Regard is to be had to a number of factors including changes in local boundaries, the suitability of restrictions in the gift, and especially, 'the spirit of the gift', and changed social and economic circumstances. It was held in *White v Williams* that 'the spirit of the gift, for the purposes of [this provision] is to be ascertained more broadly than by a slavish application of the language of the relevant trust deed'.[124] In that case it was held that, although individual church buildings had been acquired by a single church organization and were vested in a single group of trustees, the spirit in which those buildings had been acquired was to provide facilities for worship by local congregations. The consequence of a schism was that the existing arrangements inhibited that purpose being implemented.

A number of cases has shown how the statutory amendments have widened the cy-près jurisdiction. In *Re Lepton's Charity*[125] a trust established in 1716 provided for the payment of £3 per annum from the income generated by a piece of land to the minister of a dissenting church, with the remainder distributed among the poor. In 1716 the income was £5 but at the date of the case it was some £800. Pennycuick V-C held that, although the purpose of the trust had not failed, the circumstances fell within the new statutory jurisdiction and directed that £100 per annum be paid to the minister. In *Varsani v Jesani*[126] the Court of Appeal used the statutory rules in order to deal with the assets of a religious charity that had suffered an irretrievable schism. Chadwick LJ said that under the law as it stood before the statutory changes, the court could not direct a scheme:

> This is because it would still be possible to carry out the original purposes of the charity through the use of its property by the group who...had been found to be the adherents to

---

[121] See also *Re Woodhams* [1981] 1 WLR 493.   [122] [1984] Ch 143.
[123] *Report of the Committee on the Law and Practice relating to Charitable Trusts* (1952) (Cmd 8710), para 365.   [124] *White v Williams* [2010] EWHC 940 (Ch), at [20].
[125] [1972] Ch 276.   [126] [1999] Ch 219.

the true faith; and any application of any part of the property for use by the other group would be open to attack as a breach of trust.[127]

Because the original purposes 'are no longer a suitable and effective method of using the property'[128] the court ordered a scheme for the division of the funds between the two groups.

Conversely, it is possible that reference to the spirit of a gift may exclude cy-près application. When Sir Edward Heath, the former British Prime Minister, died, he left his home, Arundells, and his personal papers on charitable trusts. The trustees made a loss in opening Arundells to the public, and sought a scheme to allow its sale. The Charity Commission decided that the spirit of the gift 'was not simply the memorialisation of Sir Edward Heath. Arundells was a house of genuine historical and architectural merit, containing works of art and decorative features of worth, both intrinsically and culturally. Arundells was an essential and integral part of the trust's purposes, and since ways of making its opening to the public more viable had not been explored, it was inappropriate to approve a scheme to allow its sale.[129]

(c) Administrative schemes

Sometimes there is no need for a cy-près scheme because no change in purposes is required. In *Oldham Borough Council v A-G*[130] a council owned a piece of land 'upon trust to preserve and manage the same at all times hereafter as playing fields...for the benefit and enjoyment' of local inhabitants. The council wished to sell the land to developers and use the proceeds to purchase a different piece of land with better facilities. The Court of Appeal held that the planned sale and reinvestment for exactly the same purposes did not involve an alternation of the 'original purposes' of the charitable gift. The court could authorize the sale under its statutory or common law power relating to charities.

The same inherent powers were used in *Re JW Laing Trust*,[131] referred to earlier, where a stipulation that all the property of the trust be distributed within ten years of the settlor's death was removed. Similarly in *Varsani v Jesani*[132] the court held that, even if both groups remained true to the faith as prescribed in the original gift, the court had power under the inherent jurisdiction to authorize an administrative scheme 'for no alteration of the purpose of the Charity would arise'.

(3) Subsequent failure of charitable gifts

Where a testator leaves property to a charity in his will which fails after his death but before the administration of the estate is complete, it will be applied cy-près to other charitable purposes rather than resulting back to the residuary legatees, even though it was never in fact received by the charity. This is because the property was fully

---

[127] [1999] Ch 219, at 237.   [128] [1999] Ch 219, at 238.
[129] *Re Sir Edward Heath Charitable Trust* [2012] WTLR 1469.   [130] [1993] 2 All ER 432.
[131] [1984] Ch 143.   [132] [1998] 3 All ER 273, at 285, per Morritt LJ.

dedicated to charity from the very moment that the testator died. There is no requirement of a general charitable intent because, unless the gift was restricted, it is presumed that there was an outright and perpetual dedication to charitable purposes.[133]
A number of cases illustrate the operation of cy-près in the context of subsequent failure. In *Re Slevin*[134] a testator left a gift of £200 to St Dominic's Orphanage, Newcastle.
The orphanage closed after his death but before the legacy had been paid over. The
Court of Appeal held that the property should be applied cy-près, as it had become
the property of the charity from the date of the testator's death. The same result was
reached in *Phillips v The Royal Society for the Protection of Birds*[135] where a bird sanctuary, established as a company, had ceased operations before the death of the testatrix,
but was only dissolved a few days after her death.[136]

Property will also be applied cy-près without the need to show a general charitable
intention if it was given to accomplish a charitable purpose but the purpose has been
completed without the exhaustion of the property given. In *Re King*[137] property worth
£1,500 was bequeathed to install a window in a church, the cost of which could not
possibly exhaust that sum. Romer J held that the surplus should be applied cy-près.[138]
Similarly, in *Re Wokingham Fire Brigade Trusts*[139] a surplus derived from a public
appeal was held applicable cy-près without the need to demonstrate any general charitable intention on the part of the donors.[140]

(4) Initial failure of charitable gifts

A charitable gift will fail initially if the charity has ceased to exist before it receives any
interest in the property donated. This will happen when a testator bequeaths property
to a charity that ceases to exist before the date of his death. For example, in *Re Spence*[141]
a testatrix left part of her estate to 'The Old Folk's Home at Hillworth Lodge Keighley'
in a will that was executed in 1968. She died in 1972, but the Old People's Home had
closed down in 1971. In cases of initial failure the testator could have changed his will
to take account of the failure of the charity but has not done so, perhaps because of his
health, or through lack of knowledge that the charity has ceased to exist. The question
thus arises whether the property should be applied cy-près to other charitable purposes,
or whether it should pass by resulting trust to his residuary legatees. Since the testator
cannot be consulted, the law seeks to 'second-guess' what he would have wanted to

---

[133] See *Re North Devon and West Somerset Relief Fund Trusts* [1953] 2 All ER 1032; *Re Cooper's Conveyance Trusts* [1956] 1 WLR 1096.   [134] [1891] 2 Ch 236.

[135] [2012] EWHC 618 (Ch).

[136] See also *Re Wright* [1954] Ch 347; *Re Moon's Will Trust* (1948) 64 TLR 123; *Re Tacon* [1958] Ch 447.

[137] [1923] 1 Ch 243.

[138] See, however, *Re Stanford* [1924] 1 Ch 73, where Eve J held that a similar surplus should pass by way of a resulting trust to the residuary legatees.

[139] [1951] Ch 373. See also *Re Ulverston and District New Hospital Building Trusts* [1956] Ch 622.

[140] In *Re Welsh Hospital (Netley) Fund* [1921] 1 Ch 655 and *Re North Devon and Somerset Relief Fund Trusts* [1953] 1 WLR 1260 similar surpluses were held applicable cy-près because of the general charitable intention of the donors. However, it is doubtful that such an intention should be necessary, as the donors contributing to a public appeal surely dedicate their donation to charity at the moment it is made.

[141] [1979] Ch 483.

happen to the property. If it can be shown that he had a 'general charitable intention' when he made the gift in his will, the property will be applied cy-près. Such an intention indicates that the testator would have preferred the property to be applied to another charity rather than result back under his will. If there is no general charitable intention, then it is presumed that the testator intended to benefit only the specific charity that has failed, and that in the event of the failure he would have preferred his property to result back to the residuary legatees rather than pass to a replacement charity.

In *Kings v Bultitude*[142] the testatrix made a gift to a schismatic independent catholic church group[143] of which she was such an important member that it ceased to meet following her death. Proudman J held that this was a case of initial failure because on an interpretation of the will it was only intended to take effect if the group continued in existence after the death of the testatrix. The gift was not saved by a paramount or general charitable intent.[144]

(a) Has the charity actually failed?

An application cy-près will only be necessary if the charity to which a gift was made has actually failed. In some cases where it appears that a charity has failed the court has found a way of saving the gift by holding that the charity has in some way continued. If this is the case there is no need to apply the property cy-près and it will be applied to the charitable purposes in their continuing form.

(i) Amalgamation with other charities

The Charities Act 2011, s 311 contains provision for gifts to charities which have merged to be treated as gifts to the new organization. This applies both to direct gifts and to gifts on trust.[145] Even before this provision, the courts took a similar view, on the basis that a merged charity has not ceased to exist, but continues in a different form. In *Re Faraker*[146] a testatrix left £200 to Hannah Bayly's Charity. Hannah Bayly's Charity had been founded in 1756 for the benefit of the poor widows of Rotherhithe, but had ceased to exist as a separate entity in 1905, when it was amalgamated with other charities for the benefit of the poor of Rotherhithe. The Court of Appeal held that there had been no failure because Hannah Bayly's Charity had not ceased to exist but continued in the form of the amalgamated charity, which encompassed its objects. The principle was applied in *Re Lucas*,[147] where a testatrix, who died in 1942, left £550 to 'the Crippled Children's Home, Lindley Moor, Huddersfield'. The 'Huddersfield Home

---

[142] *Kings v Bultitude* [2010] EWHC 1795 (Ch).

[143] It was a church which refused to recognize the modernization of the Roman Catholic Church.

[144] See Picton 'Kings v Bultitude – a gift lost to charity' [2011] Conv 69. It is worth noting that two bank accounts, held by the testatrix in the name of the Church and separate from her personal bank accounts, were validly applied to charity cy-près. There was nothing to rebut the presumption that the testatrix held the accounts for charitable purposes, not beneficially, and they were held unconditionally for the church at a time when it was still functioning.

[145] *Berry v IBS-STL Ltd* [2012] EWHC 666 (Ch).

[146] [1912] 2 Ch 488. Expenditure is not confined to the purposes of the original charity.

[147] [1948] Ch 175; revsd [1948] Ch 24, CA.

for Crippled Children' had been founded in 1916, but was closed in 1941. However, its assets were applied to a new charity, 'The Huddersfield Charity for Crippled Children', under a scheme made by the Charity Commissioners. The Court of Appeal applied *Re Faraker*[148] and held that, rather than there being an initial failure, the legacy should pass to the new charity.[149] A more modern example might be the recent merger between the Imperial Cancer Research Fund and the Cancer Research Campaign to form Cancer Research UK.

The principle of *Re Faraker*[150] was not applied in *Re Roberts*.[151] Jane Roberts, who died in 1961, left a share of her residuary estate to the 'Sheffield Boys' Working Home'. The home had closed in 1945, at which point the trustees had transferred the majority of the assets to the 'Sheffield Town Trust', retaining only nominal funds themselves. Wilberforce J held that the property could not be applied to the Sheffield Town Trust on the basis of the principle of *Re Faraker*,[152] as the original charity was still in existence, although lacking the machinery to administer the legacy. It was therefore to be applied to the trustees of the home, and then applied cy-près.

Any funds received by the trustees of the amalgamated charity can be used for the general purposes of the charity. They are not limited to the specific purposes contemplated by the testator. It might therefore have surprised the testatrix in *Re Faraker* that not a penny of the funds she left need be spent on widows.

(ii) Unincorporated associations

Where a bequest is left to a charitable unincorporated association that ceased to exist before the death of the testator, the courts have held that the gift does not fail, because it should be construed as a gift to the continuing purposes of the association and not to the specific association as an entity. The rationale for this principle was considered by Buckley J in *Re Vernon's Will Trusts*:

> Every gift to an unincorporated charity by name without more must take effect as a gift for a charitable purpose. No individual or aggregate of individuals could claim to take such a bequest beneficially.[153] If the gift is to take effect at all, it must be as a bequest for a purpose, viz, that charitable purpose which the named charity exists to serve. A bequest which is in terms made for a charitable purpose will not fail for lack of a trust purpose.[154]

Since an unincorporated charity has no independent legal personality,[155] the gift is construed as a gift to the purposes of the association, and those purposes continue even though the particular association has ceased to exist.[156] The gift will only fail if

---

[148] [1912] 2 Ch 488.

[149] See also *Re Lucas* [1948] Ch 175; revsd [1948] Ch 242, CA; *Re Bagshaw* [1954] 1 All ER 227; *Re Slatter's Will Trusts* [1964] Ch 512; *Re Stemson's Will Trusts* [1970] Ch 16.   [150] [1912] 2 Ch 488.

[151] [1963] 1 WLR 406.   [152] [1912] 2 Ch 488.

[153] Although the usual interpretation of gifts to unincorporated associations is that the members take beneficially (see Chapter 22), this interpretation is excluded in the case of charities, since it is inconsistent with charitable status for the members of the charity to take a beneficial interest.

[154] [1972] Ch 300. See also *Re Morrison* (1967) 111 Sol Jo 758.   [155] See Chapter 22.

[156] This construction was approved by the Court of Appeal in *Re Koeppler Will Trusts* [1986] Ch 423 at 434, per Slade LJ.

the testator's intention to make the gift was dependent upon the named association to apply the gift.[157] The provisions in the Charities Act 2011, s 311 concerning mergers can apply to a merged unincorporated charity so that the gift takes effect in favour of the new entity.

(iii) Incorporated charities

In contrast, where a bequest is left to a charitable corporation it will be construed as a gift to that particular body, which has legal personality, and therefore if the corporation has ceased to exist the gift fails and the property will only be applied cy-près if a general charitable intention can be shown.[158] These principles were applied in *Re Finger's Will Trusts*.[159] Georgia Finger left a share of her residuary estate to a number of charitable organizations, including The National Radium Commission (NRC), an unincorporated charity, and The National Council for Maternity and Child Welfare (NCMCW), a corporate body. Both had ceased to exist before the death of the testator. Goff J held that since the gift to the NRC was a gift to an unincorporated charity, the gift should be construed as a gift to the purposes of the Commission, which had not failed. The gift to the NCMCW had failed, but the property was applied cy-près because there was a general charitable intention.

It is noteworthy that Australian courts have rejected any difference of construction of gifts made to charitable corporate and unincorporated bodies, and have held that there is a presumption that the gift is made for the purposes of the body in either case.[160] This removes the artificiality of the distinction.

(iv) Charitable company becomes insolvent

There is no cause for an application cy-près where a testator leaves property to a charitable company that has become insolvent and entered into liquidation before the date of his death, provided that it has not been dissolved. In *Re ARMS (Multiple Sclerosis Research) Ltd*[161] testators had left property to a charity that sought to promote research into a cure for multiple sclerosis which had gone into liquidation before their deaths, with debts of just under £1.5m. Neuberger J held that although the testators would not have wanted their gifts to take effect if they had known that the company was in liquidation at the date of their deaths, their gifts took effect because the company was still in existence, even if insolvent. Their bequests were therefore available to pay creditors, and were not able to be applied cy-près to other similar charitable purposes.

(b) Application cy-près where the charity has failed

Even where an initial charitable bequest fails, it is possible that the testator's will provides for what is to happen, for instance by a gift over to another charity.[162] Where even

---

[157] Eg *Re Spence* [1979] Ch 483.

[158] *Re Ovey* (1885) 29 Ch D 560; *Liverpool and District Hospital for Diseases of the Heart v A-G* [1981] Ch 193.   [159] [1972] Ch 286; (1972) 36 Conv 198 (Cotterell); (1974) 38 Conv 187 (Martin).

[160] *Sir Moses Montefiore Jewish Home v Howell & Co (No 7) Pty Ltd* [1984] 2 NSWLR 406.

[161] [1997] 1 WLR 877.

[162] As in *Games v Attorney-General* (2012) 14 ITELR 792 (Isle of Man).

this does not assist, a gift which suffers initial failure will only be applied cy-près if it can be shown that the testator had a 'general charitable intention'. 'General charitable intention' has a technical meaning, which encapsulates the idea that the testator was not so committed to the particular charity nominated in his will that, in the event of its failure, he would have preferred his gift to result back to the residuary legatees under his will rather than to be applied to similar charitable purposes. The principle was outlined by Sir Robert Megarry V-C in *Re Spence*:

> the essence of the distinction is in the difference between particularity and generality. If a particular institution or purpose is specified, then it is that institution or purpose, and no other, that is to be the object of the benefaction. It is difficult to envisage a testator as being suffused with a general glow of broad charity when he is labouring, and labouring successfully, to identify some particular specified institution or purpose as the object of his bounty. The specific displaces the general. It is otherwise where the testator has been unable to specify any particular charitable institution or practicable purpose, and so, although his intention of charity can be seen, he has failed to provide any way of giving effect to it. There, the absence of the specific leaves the general undisturbed succes[163]

This makes clear that whether a gift is made with general charitable intention or not is a matter of degree, and there is no single factor which will determine whether a gift falls on the 'particular' or 'general' side of the line. This will be determined in the light of all the circumstances of the gift. In assessing whether a gift was made with 'general charitable intention' the courts have taken account of the following factors.

(i) Gifts to specific institutions or bodies

Where a gift is made to a specific charitable institution or body, this is likely to indicate the absence of any general charitable intention. In *Re Rymer*[164] Horatio Rymer bequeathed a legacy of £5,000 to 'St Thomas' Seminary' in Westminster. The seminary had closed before his death, and the students had transferred to a seminary near Birmingham. The Court of Appeal held that there was no general charitable intention because the gift was a gift to a specific seminary.[165] In *Re Spence*[166] Beatrice Spence left half her residuary estate to the 'Old Folk's Home at Hillworth Lodge Keighley'. She died in 1972, and the home had closed in 1971. Megarry V-C held that this was a gift to a specific institution alone, and that there was no general charitable intention.

(ii) Gifts with an underlying general charitable intention

Even when a gift is made to a specific institution, if the court can see a 'clear general intention underlying the particular mode' of carrying the charitable purpose out[167] they will find a general charitable intention and apply the property cy-près. Thus, in *Biscoe v Jackson*[168] a gift was made by will for the establishment of a soup kitchen and cottage hospital in Shoreditch. This had become impossible, but Kay J held that the

---

[163] [1979] Ch 483, at 493.   [164] [1895] 1 Ch 19.
[165] See *Fisk v A-G* (1867) LR 4 Eq 521; *Clark v Taylor* (1853) 1 Drew 642.   [166] [1979] Ch 483.
[167] *Re Spence* [1979] Ch 483 at 495, per Megarry V-C.
[168] (1887) 35 Ch D 460. See also *A-G v Boultbee* (1794) 2 Ves 380; *Cherry v Mott* (1836) 1 My & Cr 123.

testator had a general charitable intention in that the underlying purpose of the gift was to benefit the poor of Shoreditch through the establishment of the soup kitchen and hospital. In *Re Woodhams (Decd)*[169] the court held that a testator who had left money for the musical education of boys from specific children's homes was held to have a paramount intention to benefit musical education. In *Re Spence*[170] Megarry V-C was unable to find any such underlying general intention because the purpose was to benefit the specific patients of the specific home, and not the aged in general.

(iii) 'Charity by association'[171]

Even though a gift is made to a specific institution, the court may find a general charitable intention if the gift is one of a number of charitable bequests, and it is clear that the testator intended all of the property so bequeathed to go to 'charity'. In *Re Knox*[172] Dorothy Knox left her residuary estate to three hospitals and to Dr Barnardo's Homes in equal shares. One hospital, the 'Newcastle-upon-Tyne Nursing Home', did not exist, and Luxmore J held that the quarter-share of the residuary estate should be applied cy-près. He found a general charitable intention in the context of the will, drawing from the fact that the residuary estate was divided among four beneficiaries, three of whom were undoubtedly charitable.[173] Similarly, in *Re Satterthwaite's Will Trusts*[174] a testatrix who hated all human beings left her residuary estate to be divided among nine specifically named animal charities, including the 'Animal Welfare Service'. There was no such charity. Russell LJ held that a general charitable intention could be discerned from the fact that the other eight-ninths of her estate was left to animal charities.[175] The principle of charity by association only applies where a charitable gift fails for lack of certainty or non-existence and has no application where one gift among a number of charitable gifts fails because it is non-charitable.

(iv) Specific charities that had never existed

It has been held that it is easier to find a general charitable intention where a gift is made to a specific charity that has never existed than to a charity that has ceased to exist.[176] In *Re Harwood*[177] a testatrix left bequests to a long list of charitable societies, including

---

[169] [1981] 1 All ER 202.   [170] [1979] Ch 483.

[171] The categorization of these cases by Megarry V-C in *Re Spence* [1979] Ch 483, at 494.

[172] [1937] Ch 109.

[173] Although the case could equally be explained on the principle of *Re Harwood* [1936] Ch 285, but it was not cited, and the judge reached his conclusion by looking to the other charitable gifts in the context of the will.   [174] [1966] 1 WLR 277.

[175] However, as Megarry V-C noted in *Re Spence*, *Re Satterthwaite's Will Trusts* is not such strong authority as *Re Knox* because Harman LJ had 'the gravest doubts' whether there was general charitable intention, and Diplock LJ agreed with both other judgments.

[176] *Loscombe v Wintringham* (1850) 13 Beav 87; *Re Clergy Society* (1856) 2 K & J 615; *Re Maguire* (1870) LR 9 Eq 632; *Re Rymer* [1895] 1 Ch 19; *Re Davis* [1902] 1 Ch 876; *Re Harwood* [1936] Ch 285: This construction was rejected by the Court of Appeal of New South Wales in *A-G for New South Wales v Public Trustee* (1987) 8 NSWLR 550, where the court held that there is no rule or principle that it is more difficult to conclude that a testator had a general charitable intention where there is a gift to a named charity which existed at the date of the will but which has ceased to exist before death than in the case where the named charity never existed at all.   [177] [1936] Ch 285.

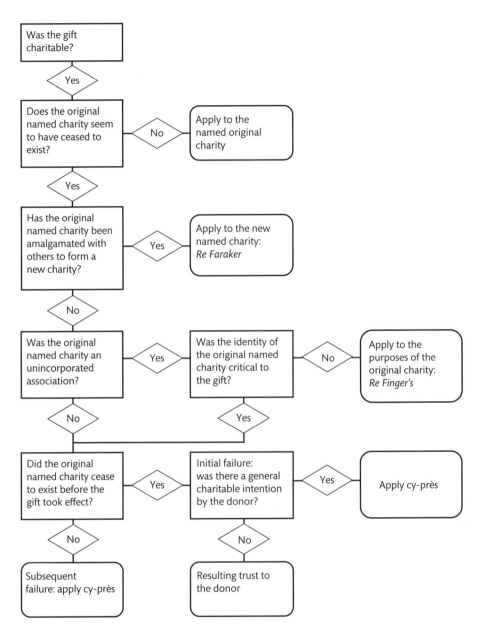

Figure 18.1 The operation of cy-près

those devoted to peace. Among these were a gift to the 'Wisbech Peace Society', which had ceased to exist before the testator's death, and the 'Peace Society of Belfast', which the evidence suggested had never existed. Farwell J held that the gift to the Wisbech society failed, and that as it was a gift to a specific institution the testatrix had no general charitable intention. In contrast, he held that because the Belfast society had never existed, she had demonstrated a general charitable intention for the purposes of peace in Belfast, and the gift was applied cy-près. The rationale behind this analysis is probably that, as the testatrix did not check whether a particular charity existed, she must have assumed that it did, and that her intention was therefore to benefit the purposes that the invented name suggested were being pursued.[178]

(5) Cy-près schemes

Where charity assets are applicable cy-près, the court or the Charity Commission may make or approve a cy-près scheme (see Figure 18.1). The Charities Act 2011, s 67 codifies and widens the common law principles. There are key criteria to be followed in deciding how funds should be applied. In making a scheme the court or the Charity Commission is required to have regard to:

(a) the spirit of the original gift;

(b) the desirability of securing that the property is applied for charitable purposes which are close to the original purposes; and

(c) the need for the relevant charity to have purposes which are suitable and effective in the light of current social and economic circumstances.

These criteria are closely intertwined with the criteria for deciding whether a cy-près application is justified. In *White v William*[179] the statutory provisions were used to make a scheme separating individual churches to enable them to be used by congregations which had split owing to a schism in their mother organization.[180]That was the only way of giving effect to the spirit in which the buildings had been acquired, namely, to provide facilities for worship available to the local congregations.

---

[178] Two difficulties arise with regard to the decision in *Re Harwood*. First, it was doubted in *Re Koeppler Will Trusts* [1984] 2 All ER 111 whether the purposes of a peace society are charitable because of their political nature. Second, in holding that there was no general charitable intention with regard to the gift to the Wisbech society the judge did not consider whether in the context of the will, and the large number of charitable bequests, there was a general charitable intention through the principle of 'charity by association'.

[179] [2010] EWHC 940 (Ch), at [20].

[180] The judge followed a similar course of action which had been taken in *Varsani v Jesani* [1999] Ch 219.

PART V

Asset Management

19

Holding trusts and nominee holdings

In Chapter 7 it was outlined how the trust can be used to enable property to be purchased by a nominee on behalf of a principal. Legal title to the property is held by the nominee or nominees as trustees, but the principal is the beneficial owner. This chapter will consider holding trusts in detail, namely the nature of such holdings, nominees' rights, and the execution and performance of holding trusts.

1 The nature of nominee holdings

The way in which a nominee arrangement will work in practice is that on any documents relating to legal ownership, it is the nominee's name that will appear. If the property concerned is land, the deed under which the land is acquired will state that it is transferred to the nominees. It is the nominees who will then be registered as owners with the Land Registry. If the property concerned consists of stocks or shares, again the document of transfer will be made out to the nominees, and it is their names that will be recorded in the register of shareholders kept by or on behalf of the company. If the property concerned is money deposited with a bank, the names appearing on the bank account will be that of the nominees. A nominee trust is a form of bare trust,[1] namely, a trust 'where property is vested in one person on trust for another where there are no active duties arising from the status of trustee'. [2]

In consequence of the nominees having legal title, any proceeds from the property, such as rent from land, dividends on shares, or interest on bank deposits, will be payable to the nominees. Only they can give a valid receipt for the income. Similarly, any dealings with the title to the property must be authorized by the nominees. They must:

(a) authorize any withdrawal of funds from a bank account;

(b) execute any transfer of land they hold as nominees; and

(c) execute any transfer of shares.

---

[1] See the definition in the Finance Act 2003, Sch 16.
[2] *Clutterbuck v Al Amoudi* [2014] EWHC 383 (Ch), at [458] (Asplin J).

If the property is disposed of by way of sale, the proceeds of the sale must be paid by the purchaser to the nominees, or in accordance with their instructions.

This does not mean, however, that the nominees are free to deal with the proceeds of the assets in any way they choose. The nominees hold the property on behalf of the principal, and must therefore deal with it for the principal's benefit. They must account to the principal both for the original property and for any income or capital derived from it.

Nominees therefore, like Janus, face two ways. As between themselves and the principal, it would not be misleading to describe the principal as the owner. It is he who will benefit from any gain (or bear any loss) in the value of the property. It is he who is entitled to the capital value of the assets, and to any income or revenue they produce. He may also transfer or otherwise deal with his equitable interest. This is, however, only one face of the nominees. As between the nominees and the outside world, it is the nominees who are, to most intents and purposes, the owners.

2 Rights and obligations of nominees

(1) Simple holding trusts

This twin aspect to a nominee holding is typical of the trust, and reflects the distinction that the trust permits to be made between powers of management and beneficial entitlement. The extent of the powers of management of the nominees will depend upon what was agreed at the time the relationship was established. In the usual case, the obligation of the nominees will be to act upon the instructions of the principal: the nominees therefore have no independent right to deal with the property, for instance by sale and reinvestment, and 'failure to deal with the property in the way instructed amounts to a breach of trust.'[3] An arrangement of this kind, in which the nominees or trustees must simply 'obey orders', may be described as a holding trust. It has two characteristics: the trustees have no discretion as to who will receive the benefit of the trust funds; and they have no authority to deal with the assets except upon instructions from the principal. In many cases the holding trust will be little more than a 'front' for the real beneficial owner.[4] In *Hardoon v Belilios*,[5] for instance, shares were acquired by a firm of stockbrokers in the name of one of their employees. Similarly, in *Arrow Nominees Inc v Blackledge*[6] the 'owner' of shares in a company held his shares via a trust of which Arrow Nominees Inc was the nominee. The same result can arise even if the parties are unaware that their arrangement has created a

---

[3] *Clutterbuck v Al Amoudi* [2014] EWHC 383 (Ch) at [458] (Asplin J). However, trustees cannot be required to act in a way which would be unlawful, for instance in breach of the terms of a lease which they hold on bare trust: *Clarence House Ltd v National Westminster Bank plc* [2009] EWCA Civ 1311 at [45].

[4] See *Young v Young* [2013] EWHC 3637 (Fam) at [24].

[5] [1901] AC 118.   See also *Sainsbury Plc v O'Connor (Inspector of Taxes)* [1991] 1 WLR 963 at 969.

[6] [2000] 1 BCLC 709.

trust. In *Pennington v Waine (No 1)*[7] the Court of Appeal held that a completed share transfer form, although never submitted to the company for registration, was nevertheless effective as an equitable assignment under which the transferor became a bare trustee for the transferee. Another illustration is provided by *Don King Productions Inc v Warren (No 1)*[8] where the leading boxing promoters in the USA and in the UK entered into a partnership agreement. Lightman J held that the effect of this was to make Frank Warren a trustee of promotion, management, and associated contracts (including a contract with Prince Naseem Hamed) for the benefit of the partnership.[9] There are a number of ways in which trusts of this kind can be described. A trust where the trustees hold upon trust for a single beneficiary absolutely (ie without conditions or qualifications), is generally described as a bare trust. Where there is more than one beneficiary, but the beneficial entitlements are set out in the trust documents, leaving no discretion as to the division of the property to the trustees, the trust is usually described as a fixed trust. It may also be described as an executed trust in that no further act is required to identify the rights of the beneficiaries. That there is more than one beneficiary does not necessarily affect the rights and obligations of the trustees, although it is more likely in such cases that the trustees will be given independent powers of management over the trust assets, and they must, of course, have regard to the interests of all the beneficiaries. Except where otherwise specified in the documents setting up the trusts, the beneficiaries can give binding instructions to the trustees.

The utility of the holding trust to conceal the identity of the 'true owner' has been greatly reduced under the Companies Act 2006. UK companies now have a right to ask any registered shareholder to disclose the beneficial ownership of shares.[10] Nevertheless, the nominee holding trust has become widely used as a means of purchasing shares. Under stock exchange rules, a person selling shares must supply the certificate for the shares sold very promptly after the sale has been made. In order to enable a shareholder to sell rapidly by telephone, many stockbroking firms will now arrange to register shares in the name of a nominee company controlled by the firm. The shares can then be sold by means of a written or oral instruction that simultaneously authorizes the nominee to release the share certificate. In some cases the nominee may consolidate the shareholdings of a number of principals under a single share certificate. Although this complicates the issue of identifying the legal title to which the principal's interest relates,[11] it does not affect the legal analysis. The position is not

---

[7] [2002] EWCA Civ 227, [2002] 1 WLR 2075.   [8] [1998] 2 All ER 608.

[9] The contract of partnership had purported to assign the contracts to the partnership, but the personal nature of the contracts prevented this. The judge held that because the contract of partnership manifested the clear intention that the promotion and management agreements should be held by the partnership absolutely, the agreement should be interpreted as creating a trust: [1998] 2 All ER 608, at 635.

[10] Companies Act 2006, ss 793 (notice by company requiring information about interests in its shares) and 820 (meaning of interest in shares). This would include beneficiaries behind holding trusts (see, in particular, s 820(4)(b)). It is suggested that the purpose of concealment may still be used to hide assets in the event of a hostile takeover—see Moffat, *Trusts Law* (5th edn, 2009), p 6.

[11] See Chapter 30, where the rights of a beneficiary to trace into assets acquired with his funds are discussed.

markedly different where ownership of shares is recorded through the new electronic CREST system, rather than in the traditional form of share certificates. Instead of the ownership of the nominee being evidenced by a share certificate, the shareholding is logged on the electronic register kept by the stock exchange. The position of the principal is not affected.

The appointment of nominees by trustees is expressly sanctioned by the Trustee Act 2000.[12] Prior to the enactment of this provision it was not clear whether trustees had the power to appoint a nominee except where there was an express provision in the trust permitting this. With the increasing use of nominees in share dealings, this change was a sensible modernization. The Trustee Act 2000 also permits the appointment of custodians by trustees.[13] Their function is to undertake safe (physical) custody of trust assets or any documents or records concerning trust assets. This could include, for instance, taking custody of valuable works of art belonging to the trust, bearer securities[14] (which must be deposited with a custodian),[15] or important documents such as share certificates or title documents relating to land. Custodians in this sense should not be confused with custodian trustees, described next. The Act authorizes the payment of nominees and custodians by trustees.[16] As with all cases of delegation (of which these are examples), the trustees must keep the arrangement under review.[17]

(2) Custodian trusts

A special form of holding trust displaying greater complexity than a nominee arrangement is a custodian trust. Whereas with a nominee arrangement the nominee normally holds a single asset or a single class of assets, the function of custodian trustees is to hold all the assets of the trust. The effect is to separate the legal ownership and custody of the trust assets from the function of managing those assets. The *custodian trustees* hold the assets to the order of other *management trustees* who have the powers of management (see Figure 19.1). The custodian trustees hold the legal title to the trust assets, but the management trustees make all the decisions relating to the administration of the trusts. This structure is used for the administration of unit trusts and many pension schemes.[18]

One advantage of a custodian trust is that the management trustees can be changed without the need to transfer all the trust property from the old trustees to the new.[19] Only the Public Trustee, the Official Custodian for Charities, and trust corporations[20]

---

[12] Trustee Act 2000, s 16(1).   [13] Trustee Act 2000, s 17(1).

[14] Ie securities such as investments in a company that are repayable to the person presenting the security document, unlike most investments, which are repayable to the person in whose name the investment is made.   [15] Trustee Act 2000, s 18(1).

[16] Trustee Act 2000, s 20.   [17] Trustee Act 2000, ss 21 and 22.

[18] See, for instance, *British Airways Pension Trustees Ltd v British Airways Plc* [2001] EWHC Ch 13, where Lloyd J was asked in litigation between the custodian trustees and the management trustees to resolve doubts and disagreements concerning the construction of the Airways Pension Scheme.

[19] See Maurice 'The Office of Custodian Trustee' (1960) 24 Conv (NS) 196; Pearce 'Directing the Trustee' (1972) 36 Conv (NS) 260, at 260–261.

[20] Trust corporations are companies specially authorized by statute to undertake trust business.

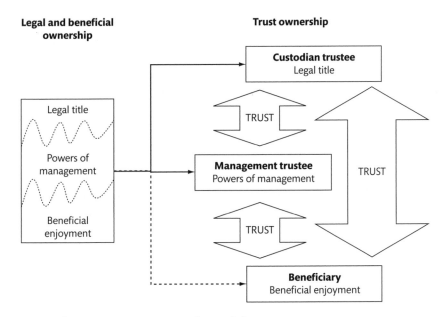

Figure 19.1 Separating management and custody by a trust

are authorized by statute to act as custodian trustees,[21] but there is no reason why a custodian trust should not be established where this is expressly permitted by the terms of the documents establishing a trust.[22] A sports club, for instance, may have taken the lease of a sports field and clubhouse in the names of up to four trustees. The trustees can hold that land upon trust to deal with in accordance with the directions of the club committee. There is no need to change the trustees every time the composition of the committee changes.

Trustees appointed as custodian trustees under the statutory scheme[23] are obliged to follow the instructions of the management trustees, except where to do so would amount to concurring in a breach of trust.[24] Bare trustees may not even have this freedom, for the terms of their appointment might require them to act upon any instruction of the principal.[25] Trustees appointed as custodian trustees without using the statutory scheme will not enjoy the statutory protection afforded to statutory

---

[21] Public Trustee Rules 1912, r 30, as substituted by the Public Trustee (Custodian Trustee) Rules 1975 (SI 1975/1189) and amended by the Public Trustee (Custodian Trustee) Rules 1976, 1981, 1984, and 1985 (SI 1976/836; SI 1981/358; SI 1984/109; SI 1985/132).

[22] See *Cadogan v Earl of Essex* (1854) 2 Drew 227 (trustees subject to directions as to investments). Before the enactment of the Companies Acts permitting companies to be incorporated through a registration procedure, a commonly adopted structure for joint stock companies was one in which, under a deed of settlement, the company's assets were held by trustees on trust for the investors in the company, with the firm being managed by a separate committee of directors.

[23] Established by the Public Trustee Act 1906.   [24] See *Brook v Brook Bond* [1963] Ch 357.

[25] See *IRC v Silverts Ltd* [1951] Ch 521, where the Court of Appeal distinguished custodian trusts from bare trusts on this ground.

custodian trustees, and they must use their own judgement in deciding whether to follow instructions given to them.[26] Where, however, the terms of the trust are so tightly drawn as to leave no scope for the exercise by them of their own judgement, it will not be a breach of trust for the trustees to follow binding instructions, even if the transaction would otherwise have been imprudent and so a breach of trust.[27]

(3) **Dealings with the trust assets**

Even in trusts where the trustees have no powers over the allocation of beneficial entitlement it is very common for the trustees to be empowered to manage the investment of the trust fund (as is the case with trusts of land created by the Trusts of Land and Appointment of Trustees Act 1996). Such powers of management are not a normal characteristic of a nominee trust. The absence of authorization to manage the investment of the trust fund will not, however, always prevent the nominees from disposing of the property. Since they have legal title, and appear to the outside world to be the owners, a stranger dealing with them is entitled to treat them as the owners they appear. A transfer from them, by way of cheque on a bank account, or by way of a transfer of land or shares in the proper form, will be effective to give legal title to the transferee. Whether the transferee will acquire that legal title subject to the rights of the principal depends mainly upon whether the transferee was aware of any impropriety at the time of the disposition. If he was not, and the transaction is one in which the stranger gives consideration, then he will normally acquire the property free from any claim of the principal. The extent to which a nominee or other trustee can dispose of the trust property to strangers is considered in Chapters 3 and 20.

Where an unauthorized disposition has been effective to transfer the trust property to a stranger, the principal will not be left without a remedy. An unauthorized transaction on the part of nominees will be a breach of trust and will expose them to personal liability to the principal for any loss that this has occasioned. The principal may also be able to recover, in lieu of the trust property any assets for which it was exchanged. These rights are considered in Part VII.

3 Execution and performance

The relationship of principal and nominee will continue for so long as the nominees hold the trust assets for the benefit of the principal. By way of agreement between the principal and the nominees (either at the time when the relationship was established, or subsequently) or, in the absence of agreement, under the rule in *Saunders v Vautier*[28] the

---

[26] *Beauclerk v Ashburnham* (1845) 8 Beav 322; *Re Hart's Will Trusts* [1943] 2 All ER 557 (trustees required to be satisfied that a directed investment was purchased at a fair price).

[27] *Re Hurst* (1890) 63 LT 665. See generally Pearce 'Directing the Trustees' (1972) 36 Conv (NS) 260.

[28] (1841) 4 Beav 115.

principal can call for the nominees to transfer the trust property to him. When they do so, the principal will acquire full legal and beneficial ownership, and the trust will be said to be executed (in other words, fully carried out).[29]

Similarly, by virtue of the original arrangement establishing the trust, or by subsequent agreement, the principal may call upon the nominees to transfer the trust property to a third party, or to deal with it in some other way. Where this is done with the intention of passing full legal and beneficial ownership to the third party, then the trust will equally come to an end. For instance, in *Vandervell v IRC*,[30] the National Provincial Bank Ltd held 100,000 'A' ordinary shares in Vandervell Products Ltd as bare trustees or nominees for the benefit of Guy Vandervell. Mr Vandervell wished to pay for the establishment of a chair in pharmacology at the Royal College of Surgeons. In a scheme devised to minimize his liability to pay tax, Mr Vandervell asked the bank, as his nominees, to transfer the shares to the college. Mr Vandervell then used his controlling interest in the company, through other share-holdings, to pay a dividend on the 'A' ordinary shares large enough to endow the chair in pharmacology. The Inland Revenue argued that Mr Vandervell had retained an equitable interest in the shares after the transfer, so that under the Income Tax Act 1952 he was liable to income tax and surtax (higher-rate income tax) on the dividends. The House of Lords held that the transfer of the shares to the Royal College of Surgeons was effective to give them both the legal title to the shares held by the bank, and Mr Vandervell's equitable beneficial interest. Whether the equitable beneficial interest passed on the transfer depended upon the intention of Mr Vandervell as the person entitled to the beneficial interest. There was no need for some separate transfer of Mr Vandervell's equitable rights. Mr Vandervell had not, therefore, retained an equitable interest in the shares.[31]

4 Dealing with the equitable interest

It is possible for the principal or beneficiary under a bare trust to deal with his equitable interest without terminating the trust. The same is true of a beneficiary under a fixed trust. Equity treats the beneficiary under a bare or fixed trust as having a beneficial proprietary interest, and not merely personal rights enforceable against the trustee.[32] That

---

[29] Note that a trust can also be described as executed rather than executory because the precise rights of the beneficiaries have already been identified, even though legal ownership has not yet been transferred to the beneficiaries.   [30] [1967] 1 All ER 1, HL.

[31] This was not enough, however, to enable Mr Vandervell to avoid the taxes. Because the Royal College of Surgeons had given the trustees of a Vandervell family trust an option to repurchase the shares, and there had been no declaration of who was to be the beneficiary of this option, the House of Lords considered that the trustees held the option on Mr Vandervell's behalf until he named some other beneficiary. Because Mr Vandervell therefore retained a power to control who would benefit from the shares once the option was exercised, he had sufficient power of disposition of beneficial entitlement to the shares to subject him to liability to tax.

[32] *Baker v Archer-Shee* [1927] AC 844. For an analysis of the debate as to whether equitable rights are properly characterized as in rem or in personam, see Waters 'The Nature of the Trust Beneficiary's Interest' (1967) 45 Can B R 219.

proprietary interest may be sold or given away, used as security for a loan, or itself held upon trust. The alienability of an equitable interest has many times been emphasized. According to Romer RJ in *Timpson's Executors v Yerbury (Inspector of Taxes)*,[33] an equitable interest in property in the hands of a trustee can be disposed of by the person entitled to it in favour of a third party in any one of four different ways:

The person entitled to it:

(1) can assign it to the third party directly;

(2) can direct the trustees to hold the property in trust for the third party;

(3) can contract for valuable consideration to assign the equitable interest to him; or

(4) can declare himself to be a trustee for him of such interest.

(1) Direct assignment

The Law of Property Act 1925, s 136 permits the assignment of choses in action. There is some authority that the section applies to equitable rights, including interests under a trust,[34] although the matter is not entirely free from doubt.[35] For the section to operate, the assignment must be an absolute assignment of the whole interest and not an assignment of part only of the interest or a charge extending only to part of the interest.[36] It must also be made in writing and signed by the assignor, and express notice in writing must be given to the trustee.[37]

Where an assignment fails to comply with the statutory provisions, it may nevertheless be effective as an assignment in equity. An equitable assignment does not need to be in any particular form, or to use any particular set of words or language.[38] It is enough if a clear intention is manifested, by words or conduct, to transfer the benefit of a clearly identified right from the assignor to the assignee.[39] The equitable assignment need not be communicated to the trustee,[40] although if the trustee has notice of the assignment it completes the transaction as to third parties, establishes priority on

---

[33] [1936] 1 KB 645, at 664. The statement was approved in *Sheffield v Sheffield* [2013] EWHC 3927 (Ch), at [80].

[34] *King v Victoria Insurance Co Ltd* [1896] AC 250, at 254; *Torkington v Magee* [1902] 2 KB 427, at 430–431, per Channell J (reversed on facts [1903] 1 KB 644); *Re Pain, Gustavson v Haviland* [1919] 1 Ch 38, at 44–45, per Younger J.   [35] *Snell's Principles of Equity* (30th edn, 2000), pp 84–86.

[36] *Durham Bros v Robertson* [1898] 1 QB 765, CA. A charge operating by way of a mortgage by assignment of the entire interest, with a proviso for reassignment on the discharge of the loan, is, however, within this section: *Tancred v Delagoa Bay and East Africa Rly Co* (1889) 23 QBD 239.

[37] *Campania Colombiana de Seguros v Pacific Steam Navigation Co* [1965] 1 QB 101; [1964] 1 All ER 216 (notice too late if served after commencement of action against debtor).

[38] *William Brandt's Sons & Co v Dunlop Rubber Co* [1905] AC 454, at 462, per Lord MacNaghten.

[39] *Voyle v Hughes* (1854) 2 Sm & G 18. See also *Pennington v Waine* [2002] 1 WLR 2075, where it was held that a share transfer form was capable of operating as an equitable assignment because it demonstrated an immediate and unconditional intention to transfer ownership.

[40] *Kekewich v Manning* (1851) 1 De GM & G 176; *Voyle v Hughes* (1854) 2 Sm & G 18.

the part of the assignee, and protects the assignee against any fraudulent receipt by the assignor.[41]

(2) **Directions to the trustees to hold on trust**

The alienation may take the form of instructions to the trustee to hold the property upon trust for some other person, as in *Tierney v Wood*.[42] Wood, the principal under a bare trust of property held by his nominee, Tierney, gave directions to his nominee by letter to hold the property upon trust for Wood's wife and daughters.[43] Where the directions impose upon the trustee an obligation more onerous than that required by the original terms of the trust, then it may be necessary for the trustee to agree to perform these obligations,[44] but the alienation is valid even if no consideration has been given, provided that the beneficiary has demonstrated an unconditional intention to make an outright transfer.[45] The alienation may also be of part only of the equitable interest in the property,[46] or be in some other way less than an outright transfer.[47]

(3) **Contract to assign**

Under the principle that 'equity treats as done that which ought to be done', a contract to transfer property, if specifically enforceable, will normally be effective to pass title in equity to the beneficiary of the contract.[48] Once any conditions which relate to the transfer have been satisfied, such as the identification of the property concerned, equity treats the transfer as if it had already been made.[49] In *Collyer v Isaacs*, for instance, Jessel MR said:

> A man can contract to assign property which is to come into existence in the future, and when it has come into existence, equity, treating as done that which ought to be done, fastens upon that property, and the contract to assign thus becomes a complete assignment.[50]

Where the contract is for the immediate transfer of existing and identifiable property, equity does not therefore distinguish between an equitable assignment and a contract to assign.[51]

The equitable maxim treating a contract to assign as an actual assignment applies only to contracts for value. It cannot be relied upon by volunteers who have

---

[41] *Kekewich v Manning* (1851) 1 De GM & G 176.　　[42] (1854) 19 Beav 330.

[43] Similar cases to the same effect are *Rycroft v Christy* (1840) 3 Beav 238; *Bentley v Mackay* (1851) 15 Beav 12; and *Paterson v Murphy* (1853) 11 Hare 88.　　[44] *Rycroft v Christy* (1840) 3 Beav 238.

[45] *Bentley v Mackay* (1851) 15 Beav 12; *Re Chrimes* [1917] 1 Ch 30.

[46] *Rycroft v Christy* (1840) 3 Beav 238.

[47] *Tierney v Wood* (1854) 19 Beav 330 (life interest followed by entailed interest in land created out of an interest in fee).

[48] *Wright v Wright* (1750) 1 Ves Sen 409, 412, (Lord Hardwicke); *Legard v Hodges* (1792) 1 Ves 477, (Lord Thurlow LC).

[49] *Tailby v Official Receiver* (1888) 13 App Cas 523; *Stephens v Green* [1895] 2 Ch 148, CA.

[50] (1881) 19 Ch D 342, at 351.　　[51] *Heap v Tonge* (1851) 9 Hare 90, at 104.

not themselves provided any consideration,[52] possibly even if there may have been someone else who has provided consideration but who does not seek to support the assignment.[53]

(4) **Declaration of subsidiary trust**

Although there may originally have been some doubt as to whether a trust could be created to fasten upon a beneficial interest under an existing trust,[54] it very soon became established that there was no objection to the imposition of such a trust.[55]

As with any trust, however, the trust will come into effect only if there is a clear intention to create an irrevocable trust, and an ineffective attempt to transfer the property will not be construed as a declaration of trust.[56] As Turner LJ observed in *Milroy v Lord*:[57]

> If it [a gift] is intended to take effect by transfer, the Court will not hold the intended transfer to operate as a declaration of trust, for then every imperfect instrument would be made effectual by being converted into a perfect trust.[58]

Where a sub-trust has been created, then the trustees of the head trust will be acting properly if they deal with the sub-trustees, but if the trust is a bare trust, they can also deal directly with the ultimate beneficiary.[59]

---

[52] *Re Anstis* (1886) 31 Ch D 596; *Re D'Angibau* (1879) 15 Ch D 228, at 242; *Re Plumptre's Marriage Settlement* [1910] 1 Ch 609, at 616.

[53] *Re Cook's Settlement Trusts* [1965] Ch 902. This case involved a promise to create a trust of the proceeds of sale of certain paintings should they ever be sold, rather than a contract to transfer an existing equitable interest. The judge held that such a promise did not create an existing proprietary interest capable of being held upon trust. The position concerning the assignment of an existing beneficial interest under a trust is therefore distinguishable.

[54] See the discussion in Simpson, *An Introduction to the History of the Land Law* (1961), pp 189–192.

[55] *Kekewich v Manning* (1851) 1 De GM & G 176. See also *Pulvertoft v Pulvertoft* (1811) 18 Ves 84, at 99, per Lord Eldon LC; *Meek v Kettlewell* (1842) 1 Hare 464, at 470–471, per Wigram VC.

[56] *Edwards v Jones* (1835) 1 My & Cr 226; *Antrobus v Smith* (1805) 12 Ves 39; *Searle v Law* (1846) 15 Sim 95; *Jones v Lock* (1865) 1 Ch App 25.   [57] (1862) 4 De GF & J 264, at 274.

[58] See further the discussion concerning the constitution of trusts in Chapter 7.

[59] *Sheffield v Sheffield* [2013] EWHC 3927 (Ch), at [82]–[86].

20

Management powers

This chapter considers the powers, express and implied, which are given to trustees to manage trust property. It also considers why management of trust property might be necessary, and details those trust holdings where management powers may not be necessary. In some textbooks, no distinction is made between the dispositive powers of trustees to allocate equitable interests (for instance through a power of appointment and through powers of advancement and maintenance) from their management powers. The operation and effect of dispositive and management powers, however, is quite different, and it is for that reason that they are considered separately in this book. Distributive powers have already been considered in Chapters 15 and 16.

1 Trusts with no management powers

With some kinds of property, such as a valuable painting which it is intended should be kept as a family heirloom, trustees might be directed to hold the property upon trust in its original form without any powers of disposition over the property. The purpose of the trust is to prevent the property—in this case, the painting—from being sold. The beneficial interests have been specified in advance by the settlor, who has left the painting on trust for his eldest child for life, and on her death for her eldest child. Since limited interests cannot be granted directly, the trust is necessary to give effect to the gift, but the trustees have no other real function. The trust can be used in a similar fashion to enable shares to be kept unsold for the benefit of future generations of a family, although in this case the trustees will receive dividend payments from the shareholding which they must pass on to the beneficiaries.

A common form of trust in which the trustee has no powers of disposition or management is a trust of a life insurance policy. When a person takes out a contract of life insurance, under which the insurance company undertakes to pay a sum of money on the death of the person insured, that sum is payable to the personal representatives of the person taking out the insurance contract, and forms part of that person's estate. Since most people taking out this form of life insurance intend their family to benefit from the proceeds of the policy, they may declare that they hold it in trust for their family.[1] The effect of this is that, on their death,[2] the insurance company may make the payment directly to the family members who have been named as beneficiaries,[3] rather than to the personal representatives. This can speed up payment. In addition, the proceeds of the policy do not form part of the estate of the deceased for inheritance tax purposes, and are not available to meet any debts which the insured may have owed. This is one of the reasons why, in *Foskett v McKeown*,[4] disappointed investors under a land investment scheme sought to trace their misused funds into an insurance policy taken out by the swindler in trust for his family. The proceeds from the policy would not otherwise have been available to meet their claim.

The disadvantages to the insured of creating a trust are that the insured will no longer be able to vary the terms of the policy without obtaining the consent of the beneficiary.[5] The insured must also act in the responsible way required of a trustee, considering the interests of the beneficiaries, for instance in considering whether to surrender the policy.[6]

2 The need for management

Unlike paintings and fully paid up insurance policies, some property cannot be left unmanaged: it requires active management. For instance, if land is held on trust, then, unless it is occupied by the beneficiary, the trustee will need to arrange for it to be let in order to produce an income. The trustee will also need to ensure that the rent is paid promptly and that proper steps have been taken to ensure that the property is properly maintained. Indeed, even a painting may need special measures to be taken to ensure that it is properly conserved, and it would be prudent to insure it. The necessary powers of management might be given to, or retained by, the beneficiaries, as is the case with nominee trusts, which were considered in the last chapter. The powers of management, though, may be conferred upon the trustees holding the title to the property, or in the special case of custodian trusts (also considered in the last chapter) by a separate group of trustees.

---

[1] A trust arises wherever a policy of life assurance on the life assured is expressed to be made for the benefit of the spouse or children of the insured: Married Women's Property Act 1882, s 11. In other cases, there must be an express intention to create a trust: compare *Re Webb, Barclays Bank Ltd v Webb* [1941] Ch 225 (trust created) and *Re Engelblach's Estate* [1924] 2 Ch 348 (no trust created).

[2] Or, in the case of an endowment policy, the date of maturity, if earlier: see *Re Ioakimidis' Policy Trusts* [1925] Ch 403.

[3] The spouse or children may be identified by name, in which case the proceeds of the policy are payable to their estate even if they predecease the insured: *Cousins v Sun Life Assurance Society* [1933] Ch 126. If the policy is expressed to be for the insured's spouse or children (or both) without naming them, it is construed as being for the benefit of those in that category who survive the insured: *Re Browne's Policy* [1903] 1 Ch 188.

[4] [1998] Ch 265.

[5] *Re Schebsman* [1944] Ch 83, CA. The contrary view expressed in *Hill v Gomme* (1839) 5 My & Cr 250 is wrong. If the matter remains in simple contract, then the insured will remain at liberty to vary the policy: *Green v Russell* [1959] 2 QB 226.

[6] *Re Equitable Life Assurance Society of US Policy and Mitchell* (1911) 27 TLR 213.

A trust might be created expressly for the purpose of conferring responsibility for active management on the trustees, as in the case of property being left on trust for a young child, or an adult who suffers from mental impairment. In other cases, for instance where there is complex beneficial entitlement, the need for powers of management might arise incidentally.

3 The extent of the powers

The powers of management[7] conferred upon a trustee are not the same in every case. Quite obviously, the powers of express trustees are likely to differ significantly from those of constructive trustees upon whom a trust has been imposed because of their improper conduct. In the latter case, the question of the trustees' powers rarely arises. They are wrongdoers who are, by definition, acting in breach of duty. How far they are authorized to act is therefore unlikely to be in issue.

Even in the case of express trustees, however, the powers of management of the trustees will differ markedly from one situation to another. The answer to the question about the extent of the management powers of the trustees depends primarily upon the terms of the individual trust instrument. Failing this, powers may be implied by statute or common law. Finally, the court has statutory and inherent powers to authorize management transactions. It is worth noting that since the Trustee Act 2000, which came into force from 1 February 2001, very broad general powers are now conferred on trustees, so that express provision in the trust instrument may be less important than in the past.

(1) **Express powers**

The trust instrument may set out in considerable detail the authority of the trustees. This is particularly likely to be the case with large, professionally drawn trust deeds such as those governing pension funds or unit trusts, or even large family trusts, especially where the assets pose distinctive issues of management.[8] For example, if the property which is held upon trust is a controlling interest in a private company which it is intended should be run by the trustees, or if it consists of an author's moral rights in literary works, it would be prudent and usual for the documents establishing the trust to define in detail the powers of the trustees.

Powers of management may or may not include a power to dispose of the property and to reinvest the proceeds. In the case of a trust for sale (described later in the

---

[7] It is important to distinguish powers of management which do not affect the beneficial interests in a fund from dispositive powers which allow trustees to dispose of interests in a fund, for instance through powers of appointment considered in Chapters 3 and 16, or through powers of maintenance and advancement considered in Chapter 15.

[8] For example, in *Re Duke of Norfolk's Settlement Trusts* [1982] Ch 610, CA, the trustees had powers of management which enabled them to carry out a substantial redevelopment of the Strand Estate which formed part of the settlement trusts.

chapter), the trustees are placed under an express obligation to sell the property and either to distribute or to reinvest the proceeds. Where the trust concerns land, the trustees will, in the absence of any express contrary intention, have both an automatic statutory power to sell the land and to postpone a sale.[9] This does not apply to trusts for sale of other kinds of property, although there can, of course, be an express power to postpone a sale.

(2) Implied powers

There are some cases where powers or duties can be implied from the context of a trust. Where a trust comprising money or quoted stocks and shares contains an express power of investment, but fails to provide express authority for sale for the purpose of reinvestment, it is reasonable to infer this power. The implication might, in some cases, go beyond the implication of a power and impose a duty on trustees.

Until it was abolished by the Trusts (Capital and Income) Act 2013,[10] the duty to convert under the rule in *Howe v Dartmouth*[11] was the best example of this. This rule required trustees to sell unauthorized trust assets in order to apply the proceeds into authorized investments. The Act also abolished the second rule in *Howe v Dartmouth* which imposed a duty to sell assets which did not fairly balance income with capital appreciation[12] between beneficiaries entitled in succession. These specific duties, which made sense when they developed, are now superseded by the general duty of trustees to keep investments under review.[13]

Other implied powers, such as the power of charity trustees to sell charity land with the consent of the court, will similarly not apply if this is inconsistent with the purpose of the trust. Thus, if a charitable trust is established to retain for the public benefit a particular house once owned by a particular historical figure or a particular building for its architectural merit, then a sale could not take place without altering the terms of the trust 'because after a sale the proceeds or any property acquired with the proceeds could not possibly be applied for the original charitable purpose'.[14]

(3) Specific statutory powers

Where a trust deed does not set out express powers of management or does not do so comprehensively, and no powers can be implied as a question of fact, the omission may

---

[9] Trusts of Land and Appointment of Trustees Act 1996, ss 4, 6, and 8.

[10] Implementing the recommendation of the Law Commission in *Capital and Income in Trusts: Classification and Apportionment*, Law Com No 319 (2009), para 6.65. The reform had also been proposed by the Law Reform Committee many years previously: 23rd Report (1982) Cmnd 8733.

[11] (1802) 7 Ves 137.

[12] Such as copyrights which have little prospect of keeping their capital value (*Re Sullivan* [1930] 1 Ch 84) or reversionary interests which produce no income (*Re Pitcairn* [1896] 2 Ch 199).

[13] Trustee Act 2000, s 4.

[14] *Oldham Borough Council v A-G* [1993] 2 All ER 432, at 439, per Dillon LJ. A similar decision was made in *Re Sir Edward Heath Charitable Trust* [2012] WTLR 1469.

be supplied by statute in one of two ways. First, there are some specific situations in which statutory powers of management are implied. The most notable of these are in trusts of land. Second, there are some general powers which are implied into all trusts by the Trustee Act 1925 and the Trustee Act 2000.

(a) Trusts of land

Since the Trusts of Land and Appointment of Trustees Act 1996, a single form of trust, the 'trust of land', applies to all trusts of land. The Act replaced the two previous types of trust of land (although preserving strict settlement trusts already in existence). The detailed technical rules governing trusts of land will be found in textbooks on land law, and need not detain us here. A few important features of the trusts are, however, worth pointing out.

(b) Powers of trustees of land

The trustees of a trust of land will often be the beneficiaries (in most cases of co-ownership), but can be specially appointed trustees (as is likely to be the case with land held on behalf of clubs and societies). Before the creation of the new trust of land under the Trusts of Land and Appointment of Trustees Act 1996, trustees of land had only the limited powers set out by the Settled Land Act 1925.

The powers conferred on trustees by the Trusts of Land and Appointment of Trustees Act 1996 are very much wider since, except where the powers are expressly excluded or curtailed, the trustees have all the powers of an absolute owner including the power to sell,[15] and a power to retain the property by postponing the sale for an indefinite period.[16] The power to retain applies even to an express trust to sell land, and is not capable of being excluded. There are some special provisions which do not apply to most trusts, and which reflect the reality that many trusts of land result from the beneficiaries combining to make a purchase of land for their own use. In exercising their powers, the trustees are required to consult the beneficiaries of full age and entitled in possession, and to give effect to the wishes of the majority by value, so far as this is consistent with the general interest of the trust.[17]

Beneficiaries with an interest in possession have a prima facie right to occupy the land.[18] Their rights of occupation are subject to the power of the trustees to exclude or restrict them.[19] The courts have jurisdiction to intervene in cases of dispute,[20] jurisdiction which may be needed more frequently than might be suggested by the rules about consultation, since trustees are required to act unanimously, and in cases of dispute a beneficiary who is also a trustee may be reluctant to concur with the majority.

---

[15] Trusts of Land and Appointment of Trustees Act 1996, s 6.
[16] Trusts of Land and Appointment of Trustees Act 1996, s 4.
[17] Trusts of Land and Appointment of Trustees Act 1996, s 11.
[18] Trusts of Land and Appointment of Trustees Act 1996, s 12.
[19] Trusts of Land and Appointment of Trustees Act 1996, s 13.
[20] Trusts of Land and Appointment of Trustees Act 1996, s 14.

(4) General statutory powers

The Trustee Act 1925 contains a small number of powers of management which are incorporated into all trusts. Additional management powers are conferred on trustees by the Trustee Act 2000. The Trustee Act 2000 also replaces the investment provisions of the 1925 Act with a new investment regime. The investment powers are of sufficient importance to merit a separate chapter.[21] Powers given to trustees to delegate trustee management functions are also considered in a separate chapter.[22] The 1925 Act also contains a number of general powers relating to the distribution of trust funds. Since these are distributive rather than management powers, they were considered in Part IV.[23]

(a) Sale

The Trustee Act 1925 contains various provisions governing sale which authorize trustees, for instance, to sell either by auction or by private contract.[24] While these provisions extend and expand upon any trust or power which a trustee may have to sell, they do not confer any authority upon the trustees to sell where it has not arisen in some other way. Similarly, the Trustee Act 2000, which extends the investment powers of trustees, does not include any provision authorising sale except for the purpose of varying an investment.[25] There is therefore no general statutory power of sale except in the case of trusts of land.

(b) Receipts

By s 14 of the Trustee Act 1925, a trustee may give a receipt in writing 'for any money, securities, or other personal property or effects payable, transferable, or deliverable to him under any trust or power' which is a sufficient discharge to the person making the transfer and which exonerates the transferee from having to enquire into the application of the property by the trustee. This power cannot be excluded by a contrary provision in the trust instrument, if any.[26] If there is more than one trustee, they must all, it seems, concur in the receipt because of the principle that trustees must act unanimously,[27] except where the trust instrument authorizes them to act by a majority[28] or, possibly, authorizes them to act individually. Charity and pension trustees are authorized by statute to act by a majority. Where capital money arises on a sale of land held upon trust, a minimum of two trustees are required to give a valid receipt, except where the trustee is a trust corporation.[29]

---

[21] See Chapter 21.   [22] See Chapter 23.   [23] Chapter 15.   [24] S 12.

[25] What constitutes investment and reinvestment is discussed in Chapter 21.   [26] S 14(3).

[27] *Attenborough v Solomon* [1913] AC 76.

[28] *Re Butlin's Settlement Trust* [1976] Ch 251; [1976] 2 All ER 483. Charitable trustees may act by a majority even if there is no express stipulation on the trust instrument: *Re Whiteley* [1910] 1 Ch 600, at 608.

[29] Trustee Act 1925, s 14(2), as amended by the Law of Property (Amendment) Act 1926 and the Trusts of Land and Appointment of Trustees Act 1996, Sch 3. See Settled Land Act 1925, s 94(1) and Law of Property Act 1925, s 27(2), as amended and re-enacted by the Law of Property (Amendment) Act 1926.

(c) Insurance

Trustees had no duty at common law to insure the trust property,[30] nor had they any power to do so. Section 19 of the Trustee Act 1925 conferred a limited power for trustees to take out insurance, and those powers were extended in 1996[31] and again by the Trustee Act 2000, which substituted a new s 19 for the original in the Trustee Act 1925. The new provision authorizes trustees to insure any trust property against the risks of loss or damage due to any event, and to pay the premiums out of the income or capital of the trust funds.[32] In the case of trusts where the beneficiaries are all of full age and capacity and together are absolutely entitled to the trust property, this power to insure is subject to any direction given by those beneficiaries.[33] If any payments are made out under the insurance policy, these payments will be treated as capital belonging to the trust, or may be used to reinstate the property lost or damaged.[34] The statutory duty to take reasonable care applies to the exercise of both the statutory and any express power to insure.[35]

(d) Compromises

A variety of powers relating to the management of property, including some enabling trustees to enter into a compromise or arrangement concerning a dispute, are contained in the Trustee Act 1925, s 15. In *Re Earl of Strafford (Decd)*[36] the sixth Earl of Strafford had left his mansion house, Wrotham Park, and his London home, together with most of his personal property, on a complex trust providing for a series of life interests. The trusts had subsequently been varied by transferring the property to Wrotham Park Settled Estates, an incorporated company.[37] There was some confusion as to whether a number of articles, amounting in value to over £170,000, belonged to the Earl of Strafford, and had been settled by him on trust, or whether they belonged to his wife, the Countess. The initial steps in litigation were taken in order to resolve the issue before the beneficiaries under the Countess's will proposed a compromise. The Court of Appeal held that the trustees were permitted by s 15 to agree to this proposed compromise even if other of their beneficiaries objected, and even though it involved a surrender of beneficial interests by those proposing the compromise. Buckley LJ said:

> The language of s 15 is, it appears to me, very wide. It would, I think, be undesirable to seek to restrict its operation in any way unless legal principles require this, for it seems to me to be advantageous that trustees should enjoy wide and flexible powers of compromising and settling disputes, always bearing in mind that such a power, however wide, must be exercised with due regard for the interests of those whose interests it is the duty of the trustees to protect. I see nothing in the language of the section to restrict the scope of the power.[38]

---

[30] *Re McEacharn* (1911) 103 LT 900.
[31] By the Trusts of Land and Appointment of Trustees Act 1996.
[32] Trustee Act 1925, s 19(1), as substituted by Trustee Act 2000, s 34.
[33] Trustee Act 1925, s 19(2).   [34] Trustee Act 1925, s 20.
[35] Trustee Act 2000, s 1 and Sch 1, para 5.   [36] [1979] 1 All ER 513.
[37] Subsequently involved in a leading case concerning the award of damages in lieu of an injunction for breach of a restrictive covenant: *Wrotham Park Estate Co v Parkside Homes Ltd* [1974] 2 All ER 321.
[38] [1979] 1 All ER 513, at 520.

The Court of Appeal held that the compromise could be approved provided that, when considered as a whole, it was for the benefit of all the beneficiaries in accordance with their several interests in the trust property. It is not a requirement of approving a compromise that a claim adverse to the trust would otherwise be certain to succeed.[39] There must, nevertheless, be a genuine dispute.[40] The trustees are also required to comply with the statutory duty to take reasonable care imposed by the Trustee Act 2000, s 1.

(e) Reversionary interests

Trustees are given wide powers under s 22 of the Trustee Act 1925 to enter into arrangements, agreements and other transactions concerning property to which the trust is entitled but which is not yet vested in the trustees. This would include, for instance, property which was payable to the trustees upon the winding up of a testator's estate. Once again, trustees must comply with the statutory duty to take reasonable care imposed by the Trustee Act 2000, s 1.

(5) Exceptional authority given by court

The express powers of trustees, as supplemented by the general and special statutory powers, may not cover every transaction which the trustees consider desirable. There is always the possibility of a situation arising which had not been anticipated: a valuable collection of modern art might, for instance, have started to deteriorate owing to the decomposition of some of the materials. Urgent restoration might be required in order to preserve the collection, yet no source of funds may be available to the trustees. In cases such as these, the trustees could enter into some otherwise unauthorized transaction (such as selling one piece of art to pay for repairs to the others), with the consent of all the beneficiaries. If some of the beneficiaries are unascertainable or unable to consent, or perhaps, where they decline consent, the trustees might need to apply to court for approval for an exceptional transaction.

(a) Statutory jurisdiction

The Trustee Act 1925, s 57 gives the court the jurisdiction to confer additional powers on trustees, either generally or in any particular instance. This jurisdiction may be exercised where the trustees or a beneficiary apply for authority for a transaction which is not otherwise authorized by the trust, and which 'is in the opinion of the court expedient'.[41] This statutory power does not authorize any alteration to the equitable entitlements of the beneficiaries,[42] and it does not require the consent or approval

---

[39] *Re Ridsdel* [1947] Ch 597.

[40] *Re Earl of Strafford* [1980] Ch 28; *Chapman v Chapman* [1954] AC 429, CA.

[41] A wider jurisdiction for the court to authorize specific transactions for the benefit of settled land or of the persons interested under the settlement is contained in the Settled Land Act 1925, s 64(1). This jurisdiction, which authorizes alterations in beneficial interests, applies only to settled land or land held upon trust for sale.

[42] *NBPF Pension Trustees Ltd v Warnock-Smith* [2008] EWHC 455 (Ch); *Re Downshire Settled Estates* [1953] Ch 218, CA.

of the beneficiaries. The court would not, however, consider that conferring additional powers upon the trustees was expedient unless it could be considered to be in the interest of the trust estate as a whole.[43] The object of the section is 'to secure that the trust property should be managed as advantageously as possible in the interests of the beneficiaries'.[44] A power conferred on trustees under the section is treated as if it were an overriding power contained in the original trust instrument.[45] The section has been used to extend the investment powers of trustees;[46] to amalgamate two funds held on identical trusts;[47] to authorize a sale of a reversionary interest[48] or other trust property where there was no other power of sale[49] or a necessary consent could not be obtained;[50] and to authorize the partition of land[51] and of other trust property.[52] In some cases which come close to trespassing upon the principle that beneficial interests may not be affected, sanction has been given for the release of capital to pay the debts of an income beneficiary, subject to the replacement of the capital on the income beneficiary's death by means of a policy of life assurance.[53]

(b) Inherent jurisdiction

The jurisdiction conferred upon the court by s 57 of the Trustee Act 1925 complements the inherent jurisdiction which the court has always enjoyed to ensure the good administration of trusts. Like the statutory jurisdiction this probably does not allow a variation of beneficial interests.[54] Lord Morton in the House of Lords in *Chapman v Chapman*[55] suggested that there were four situations in which the court could exercise an inherent jurisdiction. These were: where it authorized the conversion of freehold property to which an infant was beneficially entitled into personal property (which affected the devolution of the property on death until 1926 but is no longer of any significance); where it approves a compromise on behalf of an infant or an unborn beneficiary;[56] where it authorizes the use of accumulated income for the maintenance of an infant (although this may be doubted if it involves a modification of beneficial entitlement); and where 'the court has allowed the trustees of settled property to enter into some business transaction which was not authorised by the settlement'. Only this last category of the court's inherent jurisdiction is of consequence in this context.

---

[43] *Re Craven's Estate* [1937] Ch 423.

[44] *Re Downshire Settled Estates* [1953] Ch 218, at 248, per Evershed MR.

[45] *Re Mair* [1935] Ch 562.

[46] *Re Shipwrecked Fishermen and Mariners Royal Benevolent Society Charity* [1959] Ch 220; *Mason v Farbrother* [1983] 2 All ER 1078; *Anker-Petersen v Anker-Petersen* [1991] 16 LS Gaz R 32.

[47] *Re Harvey* [1941] 3 All ER 284; *Re Shipwrecked Fishermen and Mariners' Royal Benevolent Society Charity* [1959] Ch 220, not following the inconsistent decision in *Re Royal Society's Charitable Trusts* [1956] Ch 87.   [48] *Re Cockerell's Settlement Trusts* [1956] Ch 372.

[49] *Re Hope's Will Trust* [1929] 2 Ch 136.   [50] *Re Beale's Settlement Trusts* [1932] 2 Ch 15.

[51] *Re Thomas* [1930] 1 Ch 194. This would now be possible under the Trusts of Land and Appointment of Trustees Act 1996.   [52] *Sutton v England* [2011] EWCA Civ 637

[53] *Re Salting* [1932] 2 Ch 57; *Re Mair* [1935] Ch 562.

[54] *Re Philip Alexander Securities and Futures Ltd* (Unreported) Chancery Division (Companies Court), 25 July 2013.   [55] [1954] AC 429.

[56] Unlike s 15 of the Trustee Act 1925, the inherent jurisdiction permits the approval of a compromise between two beneficiaries which does not directly affect the trustees.

Lord Simonds LC in *Chapman v Chapman* limited the court's inherent jurisdiction to extend the authority of trustees to cases of salvage or emergency. In one series of cases, the court had approved the sale or mortgage of an infant's property to release funds for the preservation of what was retained where such action was absolutely necessary, for instance where buildings were in imminent danger of collapse or ruin.[57] Other cases extended this principle to situations where, although there was no absolute necessity, an emergency had arisen which the creator of the trust had not foreseen or anticipated, and where the best interests of the trust required the granting of exceptional authority. Romer LJ said in *Re New*:

> In the management of a trust estate...it not infrequently happens that some peculiar state of circumstances arises for which provision is not expressly made by the trust instrument, and which renders it most desirable, and it may be even essential, for the benefit of the estate and in the interest of all the cestuis que trust, that certain acts should be done by the trustees which in ordinary circumstances they would have no power to do. In a case of this kind, which may reasonably be supposed to be one not foreseen or anticipated by the author of the trust, where the trustees are embarrassed by the emergency that has arisen and the duty cast upon them to do what is best for the estate, and the consent of all the beneficiaries cannot be obtained by reason of some of them not being sui juris or in existence, then it may be right for the court, and the court in a proper case would have jurisdiction, to sanction on behalf of all concerned such acts on behalf of their trustees as we have above referred to.[58]

In that case the court authorized the trustees to agree to the reconstruction of the capital of a commercial company in which they had an interest. In *Re Tollemache*[59] the Court of Appeal said that *Re New* 'constitutes the high watermark of the exercise by the court of its extraordinary jurisdiction in relation to trusts', and refused to extend the powers of investment of the trustees to authorize the acquisition of a mortgage which would have enhanced the income of the trust. The fact that a proposed transaction would benefit one or even all of the beneficiaries is insufficient.[60] The jurisdiction which the court exercises in cases falling under the head of salvage or emergency is a jurisdiction to consent on behalf of beneficiaries who are not themselves sui juris by reason of infancy or mental incapacity. Unlike the statutory jurisdiction under s 57 of the Trustee Act 1925, which does not require the consent of adult beneficiaries, the court is probably unable, under its inherent jurisdiction, to override or to supply consent on behalf of those who are themselves legally competent to provide it.

(c) A broader jurisdiction?

There is some authority for suggesting that the inherent powers of the court could extend beyond cases of salvage and emergency. A lengthy series of cases, reviewed in *Re Duke of Norfolk's Settlement Trusts*,[61] establishes beyond doubt that the court has an inherent jurisdiction to authorize the payment of remuneration to trustees, and

---

[57] *Re Jackson* (1882) 21 Ch D 786; *Conway v Fenton* (1888) 40 Ch D 512; *Re Montagu* [1897] 2 Ch 8.
[58] [1901] 2 Ch 534, at 544.   [59] [1903] 1 Ch 955.   [60] *Re Montagu* [1897] 2 Ch 8.
[61] [1981] 3 All ER 220.

even, according to the latter case, increase the level of the remuneration. Fox LJ did not consider this to be inconsistent with the principles expressed in *Chapman v Chapman*, which was concerned with the power of the court to authorize variations in beneficial interests as such. He said:

> I appreciate that the ambit of the court's inherent jurisdiction in any sphere may, for his-torical reasons, be irrational and that logical extensions are not necessarily permissible. But I think that it is the basis of the jurisdiction that one has to consider. The basis, in my view, in relation to a trustee's remuneration is the good administration of trusts ... [I]t is of great importance to the beneficiaries that the trust should be well administered. If there-fore the court concludes, having regard to the nature of the trust, to the experience and skill of a particular trustee and to the amounts which he seeks to charge when compared with what other trustees might require to be paid for their services and to all the other circumstances of the case, that it would be in the interests of the beneficiaries to increase the remuneration, then the court may properly do so.[62]

The importance of the case in its immediate context is much reduced because the Trustee Act 2000 now allows trustees to be paid reasonable remuneration for services they provide if they are trust corporations or act in a professional capacity.[63] However, the principle of the case remains valid. The influence of the importance of the good administration of a trust is equally capable of application to administrative arrange-ments other than remuneration. Nor is authorization of payment for trustees the only instance in which the court enjoys jurisdiction to amend the operating arrangements for trusts. In *Re Ashton's Charity*,[64] followed in *Oldham Borough Council v A-G*,[65] Romilly MR held that, even where there is no applicable statutory authority, the Court of Chancery has a general jurisdiction to authorize the alienation of charity prop-erty where the court clearly sees that the transaction is for the charity's benefit and advantage. So, in the *Oldham* case, the Court of Appeal was prepared to authorize the sale for building development of a playing field held upon charitable trusts where the proceeds were to be used to acquire a new site with better facilities. This jurisdiction might relate only to the court's powers regarding the supervision of the administra-tion of charities, and it almost certainly does not extend to authorizing a sale which would have the consequence of changing the nature of a trust, as for instance where there is a trust to retain for the public benefit a tract of land of outstanding natural beauty. Nevertheless, when taken in association with the cases on salvage and emer-gency, the two examples just cited may evidence a wider equitable jurisdiction for the court to sanction transactions or arrangements which have been approved by all ben-eficiaries capable of concurring, and which are for the benefit of the trust viewed as a whole, and more particularly for those beneficiaries for whom the court is acting as a surrogate, provided that they do not amount to a rewriting of the beneficial interests.[66]

---

[62] [1981] 3 All ER 220., at 230.   [63] Ss 28 to 30.   [64] (1856) 22 Beav 288.

[65] [1993] 2 All ER 432. See also *Re Parke's Charity* (1842) 12 Sim 329; *Re North Shields Old Meeting House* (1859) 7 WR 541.

[66] Compare the dissenting judgment of Lord Denning in *Re Chapman's Settlement Trusts* [1953] Ch 218.

(6) **Correcting minor administrative errors**

The inherent jurisdiction of the courts over trusts enables the court to correct obvious minor administrative errors. In *HR Trustees Ltd v Wembley Plc (In Liquidation)*[67] only four out of five of a pension scheme's trustees had signed an amendment to its rules, despite all five having agreed to the amendment. It was held that the court could cure the defect by the application of the maxim that equity looked on matters as done which ought to be done, and therefore correct what had been an obvious administrative error. Without this correction the amendment would have been invalid.

---

[67] [2011] EWHC 2974 (Ch).

21

Investment and reinvestment

This chapter considers the powers and duties of trustees in relation to the investment of trust funds, including the range of permitted investments, and the objectives which trustees are expected to follow. Collective investment schemes and collective asset holding structures, including an outline of pension trusts, are considered in Chapter 22.

1 Introduction

Of their non-distributive functions, the powers and duties of trustees in relation to investment are undoubtedly the most important.[1] Except in the very simplest of trusts, it is the duty of the trustee to preserve the trust assets over a period for the benefit of a number of beneficiaries. In many cases, the property which is transferred to the trustee is transferred as a fund, rather than as a set of assets which are to be retained in their original form. The trustee is expected to preserve the value of that fund through proper investment. In some cases, such as with unit trusts, and to some extent with pension funds, investment is the primary purpose of the trust.

It is in the context of investment that the concept of the fund is at its most apparent. The beneficiaries are entitled to share in the wealth which the trust assets represent. The component parts of that wealth are very much less important to the beneficiaries than its aggregate value. Of course, there are exceptions. The member of the landed aristocracy who leaves the family mansion upon trust for future generations of the family will no doubt hope that the home will be preserved intact.[2] The married couple joining together in the purchase of a matrimonial home will no doubt intend to keep it as their dwelling. Even here, the land which constitutes the trust asset will be treated as a fund which can be sold and reinvested: so the new squire can sell some land on the fringe of the estate for building development and invest the proceeds in stocks and shares, or the married couple can 'up sticks' and sell to move to another area where they will buy another house, without in either case dissolving the original trust. The

---

[1] Note that trustees who are conducting investment business must be authorized under s 19 of the Financial Services and Markets Act 2000, or exempted. Breach of this requirement may be a criminal offence, and subject to up to two years imprisonment.

[2] See *Wyndham v Egremont* [2009] EWHC 2076, where the court approved a variation of trust to enable the Petworth estates to follow the titles to Leconfield and Egremont.

case of land is, perhaps, somewhat special, since the legislature has ensured that trustees of land will always have a power of sale and reinvestment, and as we have already seen in the previous chapter, there is no general power of sale in relation to property other than land which is vested in trustees.

It has already been described how the concept of the fund enables some assets to be disposed of, so that the purchaser acquires the assets free from the trust obligations, the trust obligations instead resting upon the price paid by the purchaser, or with whatever is purchased with the proceeds of the disposal. The issues which have to be addressed in the context of investment are first, when trustees are permitted to dispose of existing trust assets in order to substitute new assets; second, what assets may be substituted for the original ones; and third, the principles upon which those investments must be chosen. Overarching these issues is a fundamental question—what is the purpose of investment? It is with that question that we need to begin.

2 The purpose of investment

(1) Even-handedness between beneficiaries

As little as a century ago, one of the more common forms of trust was the family settlement, in which a man of property would settle funds for the benefit of his spouse and children for their lives, with entitlement to the capital then passing to the next generation. The duty of the trustees in such a case was to ensure that the capital was preserved for the benefit of the capital beneficiaries, while an income was produced for the settlor's wife and children. The trustees were obliged to keep a fair balance between the two, except where they had been given other instructions by the settlor. This rule of even-handedness between beneficiaries was at the root of the rule in *Howe v Dartmouth*, although, as we have seen in Chapter 14, this rule has been abolished in trusts created after 1 October 2013 by the Trusts (Capital and Income) Act 2013.

(2) The purpose of the trust

Not all trusts provide for successive interests, therefore requiring both income generation and preservation of capital. It is possible that a trust will provide for the accumulation of income for a limited period, with a view to conferring a lump sum benefit on a beneficiary at a future date. In such a case, it is of greater importance that the trust fund should produce capital appreciation than that it should provide a large income. For instance, in the case of an endowment fund for a major museum and art gallery, 'the desirability of having an increase of capital value which will make possible the purchase of desirable acquisitions for the museum despite soaring prices does something to justify the greater risks whereby capital appreciation may be obtained'.[3] On

---

[3] *Trustees of the British Museum v A-G* [1984] 1 All ER 337, at 343, per Megarry V-C.

the other hand, the investment of a pension fund will require a combination of investments which will provide some measure of protection against the ravages of inflation[4]
and of investments which will enable the payment of benefits to pensioners as and
when they fall due for payment, bearing in mind always the need to make a judgement
which takes account of the risks of the investments in question[5] and which has proper
regard to the need for security.[6] It may even be that, in considering investment policy,
the trustees will need to have regard to the circumstances of individual beneficiaries.
Trustees of land, for instance, may invest or apply trust funds in the purchase of property for occupation by a beneficiary,[7] a decision which can be made only after considering the circumstances of the beneficiaries. Also, in *Nestlé v National Westminster
Bank plc*,[8] Staughton LJ thought that it would be appropriate for trustees to take into
account the circumstances of the beneficiaries, as, for example, 'if the life tenant is living in penury and the remainderman already has ample wealth'.[9]

Expressed in general terms, it can be said that the purpose of investment is to enable
the fulfilment of the objectives of the trust. In one of the leading investment cases, Sir
Robert Megarry said:

> The starting point is the duty of trustees to exercise their powers in the best interests of
> the present and future beneficiaries of the trust, holding the scales impartially between
> different classes of beneficiaries. This duty of the trustees towards their beneficiaries is
> paramount... When the purpose of the trust is to provide financial benefits for the benefi-
> ciaries, as is usually the case, the best interests of the beneficiaries are normally their best
> financial interests. In the case of a power of investment, as in the present case, the power
> must be exercised so as to yield the best return for the beneficiaries, judged in relation to
> the risks of the investments in question; and the prospects of the yield of income and capi-
> tal appreciation both have to be considered in judging the return from the investment.[10]

This statement does not apply only to the exercise by trustees of their powers. The influence of the policy which underlies it can be seen also in the historical approach to trustees' general powers of permitted investment, and in the approach which the courts
have in the past adopted in considering extensions to trustees' powers of investment.

3 Powers of disposal

(1) Assets available for investment

Except where trustees are under an obligation to make an immediate distribution, the
trustees will have assets to invest where the funds they receive are in cash or currency.
It would rarely be appropriate for the trustees to retain large quantities of banknotes,

---

[4] *Mason v Farbrother* [1983] 2 All ER 1078, at 1086–1087.
[5] See *Cowan v Scargill* [1985] Ch 270.
[6] See Grosh 'Trustee Investment: English Law and the American Prudent Man Rule' (1974) 23 ICLQ 748.
[7] Trusts of Land and Appointment of Trustees Act 1996, s 6.   [8] [1993] 1 WLR 1260.
[9] [1993] 1 WLR 1260, at 1279.   [10] *Cowan v Scargill* [1985] Ch 270, at 286, per Megarry V-C.

uncleared cheques, or similar assets. Where the assets which the trustees receive are already in some form of investment, such as shares in a public company, a landholding, or some other enduring form, then it is less clear whether there is a power or even an obligation to realize those assets for the purpose of reinvestment. It has already been noted in the last chapter that there is no general power of sale. The power of sale for the purpose of reinvestment now needs to be examined more closely.

(2) **Trust for sale**

In some trusts, the trustees are placed under an obligation to sell the property in the form in which it is originally received, and either to distribute or to reinvest the proceeds of sale. Such a trust is called a trust for sale. A trust for sale may be imposed expressly by the settlor. Before the Trusts of Land and Appointment of Trustees Act 1996, it was also the statutory form of a trust of land, although that is no longer the case.

A trust for sale may, finally, have arisen under the rule in *Howe v Earl of Dartmouth*, explained in Chapter 13, where hazardous or wasting assets, or assets generating no income, and which formed part of a testator's residuary estate, were received by a trustee who is to hold the assets for beneficiaries entitled to successive interests. The Law Commission recommended the abolition of the rule in *Howe v Earl of Dartmouth* and of the implied trust for sale of unauthorized, hazardous, or wasting assets generated thereby,[11] which has now been enacted for any trust arising after 1 October 2013 when the Trusts (Capital and Income) Act 2013 came into force.[12] Express and statutory trusts for sale would be unaffected by this reform.

(3) **Other powers of sale and reinvestment**

A well-drafted trust will have anticipated the desirability of selling trust assets for the purpose of reinvestment, and will have made express provision. Trusts of land governed by the Settled Land Act 1925 confer upon the tenant for life, as trustee of the land, a power of sale,[13] with the proceeds of sale being treated as capital money which, if not otherwise required, is available for reinvestment.[14] Similarly, there is a power of sale[15] and a power indefinitely to postpone sale[16] in the case of trusts of land governed by the Trusts of Land and Appointment of Trustees Act 1996. This includes all trusts of land which are created on or after 1 January 1997, and all trusts of land arising before that date and which are not governed by the Settled Land Act 1925.

Strangely, the Trustee Act 2000, which introduced a new regime for investment of trust funds failed to make clear whether trustees had a power of sale for the purposes

---

[11] *Capital and Income in Trusts: Classification and Apportionment*, Law Com No 319 (2009), para 6.65.
[12] S 1(2)(a). The trustees retain the power to sell such investments, but are under no duty to do so—s 1(3).
[13] Settled Land Act 1925, s 38.   [14] Settled Land Act 1925, s 73.
[15] Trusts of Land and Appointment of Trustees Act 1996, s 6.
[16] Trusts of Land and Appointment of Trustees Act 1996, s 4.

of investment. The Act stated in s 3 that 'a trustee may make any kind of investment that he could make if he were absolutely entitled to the assets of the trust', but nowhere does it indicate when a trustee may or must make investments. The Trustee Investments Act 1961, which the Trustee Act 2000 largely replaces, did contain the more explicit statement that 'a trustee may invest any property in his hands, whether at the time in a state of investment or not that and may from time to time vary such investments'.[17] This omission is made all the more strange by the fact that s 8 of the Trustee Act 2000 confers a power on the trustees of personalty to purchase a legal estate in land as an investment.[18] In the absence of such a general provision, it will be a matter for the proper construction of the trust instrument as to whether the trustees are permitted or expected to invest the trust property. Such a conclusion could readily be reached if the trust assets are to be retained for any length of time, and the conferment of a statutory power of investment could be interpreted as implying a power to sell for the purpose of making an investment.[19] The indications are that the courts are likely to take a broad and common sense view of when property is available for investment. In *Gregson v HAE Trustees Ltd*[20] Henry Cohen, the founder of the Courts furniture group, set up a family trust in 1960 using company shares, with the intention that a wider family group should benefit from the success of the company. The trustees did not sell the shares and in 2004, when the Courts group collapsed, the shares became worthless. It was held that the shares constituted investments, even though it was not envisaged that they would necessarily be sold. Henry Cohen had not prohibited their sale, and indeed had given the trustees a power to sell them. The trustees should therefore have considered whether to diversify the trust's investments. The judge stated:

> It seems to me that on its natural reading 'the investments of the trust' comprise any asset of the trust which happens to be invested, whether it was in that state when originally settled or it came into that state of investment later.[21]

However, as has already been explained, there could be circumstances in which the power of sale is excluded because the trust requires the retention of the assets in a particular form.[22] Although there are authorities that suggested that there must be a clear exclusion of the statutory investment powers in express terms,[23] these were cases that sought to limit and not to exclude the trustee's powers of investment. It is submitted that the

---

[17] S 1(1).

[18] In fact, the section allows the purchase of land for purposes other than investment such as for occupation by a beneficiary (s 8(1)(c)) or for any other reason (s 8(a)).

[19] See Trustee Act 1925, s 16(1), which could be interpreted as conferring a power of sale in these circumstances. Compare *Hume v Lopes* [1892] AC 112; *Re Pratt's Will Trust* [1943] Ch 326.

[20] [2008] EWHC 1006 (Ch).

[21] [2008] EWHC 1006 (Ch), at [81] (Robert Miles QC sitting as a deputy High Court judge). The claim for breach of trust failed because the corporate trustees had no assets and the judge held that it was not possible for a beneficiary to make a direct ('dog leg') claim against the directors.

[22] See the now repealed s 1(3) of the Trustee Investments Act 1961, which stated that the previous statutory provisions are 'exercisable only in so far as a contrary intention is not expressed…'.

[23] *Re Rider's Will Trusts* [1958] 1 WLR 974; *Re Burke* [1908] 2 Ch 248; *Re Hill* [1914] WN 132.

implied statutory power to sell for the purpose of investment does not apply to property that it is the trustee's duty to retain.[24]

4 Authorized investments

(1) **Principles**

Except in those rare situations where a person is both trustee and beneficiary (as for instance in the case of co-ownership trusts of land), a trustee is investing property on behalf of others. This requires an approach to risk which may not be the same as that which might be adopted by a person making investments on his or her own behalf. Whilst an individual may consider it appropriate when making decisions on their own behalf to incur a high degree of risk, this is much less appropriate when dealing with the assets of others. To take an extreme example, a person can choose to gamble with their own money by buying lottery tickets, but this would not be a suitable application of trust funds. A 'turf investment' at the racecourse would not be a trustee investment.

There are two different methods which can be used to limit the investment decisions of trustees to investments which are suitable for trust funds. One is to provide a list of investments which are considered to be sufficiently secure and robust to be used for the investment of trust funds, limiting trustees to making a choice from this menu. The other is to impose a general duty on trustees only to select investments which meet the criteria of suitability. The first approach was at one time the approach adopted in Britain, but the Trustee Act 2000 implemented a sea change by sweeping away most of the previous restrictions on investment by trustees and adopting the second approach.

(2) **History**

The turbulence caused by the bursting of the South Sea Bubble in 1720 was the cause for a serious curtailment by the Court of Chancery of the investments which trustees were permitted to make. From the end of the eighteenth century onwards, it became the rule that a trustee would be liable to bear the deficiency if any loss resulted from making an investment in a way which was not authorized by the settlor or the beneficiaries, and which had gone beyond the range of investments contemplated by the courts or the legislature. Prior to the Trustee Act 2000, the investments authorized by the general law were conservative, placing considerable emphasis on the security of trust funds.

The policy adopted by legislation up to and including the Trustee Investments Act 1961 was to protect beneficiaries by limiting trustees to 'safe' forms of investment.

---

[24] Compare Settled Land Act 1925, s 67, under which heirlooms (defined as personal chattels settled so as to devolve with settled land) may be sold only pursuant to an order of the court, even where the purpose of sale is to invest the proceeds. In *Re Hope* [1899] 2 Ch 679 the court refused permission under this section to sell the 'Hope' diamond.

The Trustee Investments Act 1961 adopted a very much more constrained regulation of trustee investments than in some other jurisdictions, notably in North America, where the principal requirement is that in making investments, trustees should act as a prudent man would do when investing on behalf of others.[25] It also lagged substantially behind the practice of well-advised settlors inserting their own express investment powers. This, of course, limited the return that trustees could achieve through investment for the beneficiaries; as safety and high-income yield rarely go hand in hand.

Precisely to avoid the limitations on the powers of investment by trustees, settlors often included an express power of investment in a settlement. The trustees could also obtain the consent of the beneficiaries to investments which would not otherwise be authorized, although this course of action was only available if all the beneficiaries were capable of giving consent. Finally, the trustees could enlarge their investment powers by means of an application to court, either under the Variation of Trusts Act 1958, where the beneficiaries who are capable of consenting concur, or where this is not practicable, under s 57 of the Trustee Act 1925.

(3) **The new approach**

The new approach to investment has been embraced by the Trustee Act 2000. The approach was described in a Treasury consultation paper.[26] Rather than limit the kinds of investment which trustees can make, it is seen as more sensible to give the trustees more extensive powers of investment in relation to the selection of individual investments. The interests of the beneficiaries are then protected by requiring the trustees to take such expert advice as the nature of the trust requires and by charging them with responsibility to ensure that the portfolio of investments is properly balanced.

This new approach was first adopted by the Pensions Act 1995. This permits pension fund trustees to make any kind of investment as if they were absolutely entitled to the assets.[27] However, the trustees are required to maintain a statement of investment policy,[28] including information about the policy on risk, expected returns, and realization. The trustees are expected to secure and consider professional advice, to consider the need to maintain a balanced portfolio, and to consider the merits of each individual investment proposed.[29] The same approach has now been adopted by the Trustee Act 2000 as the general principle for most trusts.[30] Trustees are given the same

---

[25] See Grosh 'Trustee Investment: English Law and the American Prudent Man Rule' (1974) 23 ICLQ 748.   [26] Investment Powers of Trustees (May 1996).

[27] Pensions Act 1995, s 34.   [28] Pensions Act 1995, s 35.

[29] Pensions Act 1995, s 36. See also Occupational Pensions Schemes (Investment) Regulations, SI 2005/3378, which set out detailed regulations governing the exercise of the investment powers. There is special provision allowing the trustees to delegate some of these responsibilities: s 34.

[30] The general investment powers do not apply to occupational pension schemes, authorized unit trusts, or certain schemes under the Charities Act 1993: see Trustee Act 2000, ss 36–38. There are special statutory rules applying to these forms of collective investment.

power to invest trust funds, with some narrow exceptions, as if they owned the assets outright. They are, however, subject to an obligation to act in the best interests of the beneficiaries, to consider the need for diversification of investment, to consider the suitability of individual investments, and to take advice where appropriate.

The power of investment conferred by the Trustee Act 2000, described as the 'general power of investment', extends the powers of investment which may have been conferred upon trustees by other statutory provisions or by the trust instrument, but it can be excluded or restricted by the trust instrument or by legislation.[31] The general power of investment applies to existing trusts, not just those created after the passing of the 2000 Act.[32]

(4) Express powers of investment

(a) Interpretation

The need for express powers of investment is significantly reduced by the general power of investment conferred by Trustee Act 2000. Nevertheless, it is still common practice for professionally drafted trusts to contain express investment powers. The approach to the interpretation of such powers is demonstrated *by Re Harari's Settlement Trusts*.[33] Sir Victor Harari had transferred assets to trustees which fell outside the categories authorized by the general rules for trustees. Under an express provision in the trust deed, it was declared that:

> The trustees shall hold the said investments so transferred to them as aforesaid upon trust that they may either allow the same to remain in their present state of investment so long as the trustees may see fit or may at any time or times realise the said investments and invest the money produced thereby in or upon such investments as to them may seem fit with power to vary or transpose any investments for or into others.

It was argued before the judge that the investments which the trustees could select under this clause were limited to those generally authorized by law (which, of course, at the time were much narrower than they are now), since the clause did not clearly and unambiguously extend the range of investments beyond those permitted by statute. Jenkins J held, however, that the trustees were given a wider power of investment. In his view, he was free to construe the settlement according to what he considered to be the natural and proper meaning of the words used in their context, and he saw no justification for implying any restriction on the wide construction which the words themselves were sufficient to bear.[34]

(b) Limits to investment powers

Although it is clear from *Re Harari's Settlement Trusts*[35] that investment clauses will not be given a restrictive interpretation, there are still pitfalls for the draftsman. If the draftsman seeks to impose a limit on the range of permissible investments, that

---

[31] Trustee Act 2000, s 6.   [32] Trustee Act 2000, s 7.   [33] [1949] 1 All ER 430.
[34] See, to similar effect, *Re Peczenik's Settlement* [1964] 2 All ER 339.   [35] [1949] 1 All ER 430.

limit should be clearly and unambiguously expressed. Difficulties have occurred in the past with clauses limiting investments to stocks in 'any British colony or dependency' because of changes in the status of Commonwealth and former Commonwealth countries.[36] A clause authorizing investment in 'blue chip' securities has also been held to be ineffective on grounds of uncertainty.[37]

(c) Meaning of 'investment'

A number of cases, discussed in relation to the Trustee Act 2000 in the following paragraphs, have considered what is meant by the word 'investment'. The cases suggest that an application of funds will not be considered to be an investment unless the assets produce an income. It may be that in the light of changing investment practice, a different view would be taken today and that assets expected to produce a capital gain could be considered to be investments even if they were producing no income.[38] Nevertheless, good drafting will make clear that applications in non-income generating assets are permitted. The Universities' Superannuation Scheme Rules (the pension scheme for academic staff within the old universities), for instance, state that the trustee may apply its assets for the purchase of 'investments or property whether producing income or not':[39]

> All trust moneys in the fund shall either be placed on current or deposit account with a bank, or invested in the name or under the legal control of the trustee company in the purchase, or at interest upon the security, of such investments or property, whether involving liability or not, and *whether producing income or not*, or upon such personal credit, with or without security, as the trustee company shall think fit, to the intent that the trustee company shall have the same full and unrestricted powers of investing and transposing investments as if it was absolutely entitled to the fund beneficially. [emphasis added]

(d) Loans

In *Khoo Tek Keong v Ch'ng Joo Tuan Neoh*[40] the Privy Council held that trustees were not authorized to make an unsecured personal loan under a clause which permitted them 'to invest all moneys liable to be invested in such investments as they in their absolute discretion think fit'. Where security is given for the loan, it may be classed as

---

[36] *Re Maryon-Wilson's Estate* [1912] 1 Ch 55, CA; *Re Brassey's Settlement* [1955] 1 WLR 192; *Re Rider's Will Trusts* [1958] 1 WLR 974.   [37] *Re Kolb's Will Trusts* [1962] Ch 531.

[38] See *Cook v Medway Housing Society* [1997] STC 90, at 98 for support for this view. See however, *Dominica Social Security Board v Nature Island Investment Co* ([2008] UK PC 19, at [21]), referred to in *Dalriada Trustees v Faulds* [2012] 2 All ER 734, where Bean J, although accepting that the statement might be too limited in that it did not include assets acquired with a view to capital gain, held that an unsecured personal loan would not constitute an investment.

[39] Universities' Superannuation Scheme New Rules (1 October 2011), r 64.1. See also r 64.2.8, which expressly states that trust monies may 'be applied in any form of investment which may come to be developed, recognised and adopted as a new form of investment in reputable financial circles'.

[40] [1934] AC 529.

an investment under such a clause and, again, a suitably drafted clause can authorize the application of trust funds in unsecured personal loans.[41]

(5) **General power of investment under Trustee Act 2000**

(a) Meaning of 'investment'

The general power of investment conferred by the Trustee Act 2000 states that 'a trustee may make any kind of investment that he could make if he were absolutely entitled to the assets of the trust'.[42] The Act does not define what is meant by an investment, and this is therefore something to be resolved by reference to general principles of interpretation. The explanatory note to the Act states that an investment is something which is expected to produce an income or capital return. The case law on the use of the word in express investment clauses shows a narrower interpretation being adopted. In *Re Wragg*,[43] P.O. Lawrence J held that a clause authorizing investment in 'stocks funds shares and securities or other investments' was wide enough to include the purchase of land that was to be rented out to produce an income. He stated that 'to invest' includes as one of its meanings:

> to apply money in the purchase of some property from which interest or profit is expected and which property is purchased in order to be held for the sake of the income which it will yield.

In *Re Power*,[44] the court considered that the purchase of a house for occupation by a beneficiary was not permitted under a clause providing that 'All moneys requiring to be invested under this my will may be invested by the trustee in any manner in which he may in his absolute discretion think fit in all respects as if he were the sole beneficial owner of such moneys including the purchase of freehold property in England or Wales.' The reason for this was that land being occupied by a beneficiary would not be generating income, and it could not therefore appropriately be described as an investment.[45] Strict application of this interpretation of the meaning of 'investment' would preclude trustees from purchasing, in the absence of the conferral of an express power in the trust instrument, assets for investment which only have potential to appreciate in capital value but do not produce any income. This would include the purchase of precious metals, works of art, fine wine, or antiques. Premium bonds would also not be considered an investment.

The reason the Trustee Act 2000 is silent on a definition of 'investment' can be found in the Law Commission report on the powers and duties of trustees that preceded the Act. The Commission expressed the view that avoiding any definition of investment would permit the concept to evolve in ways which might be constrained were a definition to be given.[46] The explanatory notes accompanying the Act state that the power of

---

[41] *Re Laing's Settlement* [1899] 1 Ch 593. The Universities' Superannuation Scheme New Rules (1 October 2011) state that the trustee may apply funds 'upon such personal credit, with or without security, as the trustee company shall think fit' (r 64.1).   [42] Trustee Act 2000, s 3(1).   [43] [1919] 2 Ch 58.

[44] [1947] Ch 572.   [45] See also *Re Peczenik's Settlement Trusts* [1964] 1 WLR 720.

[46] *Trustees Powers and Duties*, Law Com Report No 260 (1999), p 22.

investment conferred by the Act permits trustees to invest so as to produce an income or capital return, but these do not form part of the Act and cannot be regarded as having overruled the definition of 'investment' in *Re Power*.[47] It would, however, be inconvenient if the word 'investment' in the Trustee Act 2000 were to be interpreted in the same restrictive way. Changing patterns of investment now mean that it is not uncommon for applications of funds to carry no rights to income. For instance, some companies adopt a policy of making no declaration of a dividend in order to rein-vest profits with the intention of increasing the value of their shares. Similarly, it is possible to purchase units in authorized unit trusts where all income is reinvested rather than being paid out to investors, again with the intention of producing capital growth. It is also possible to purchase capital bonds that are redeemable after a fixed period at a value higher than the purchase price, compensating for the lack of inter-est by this capital growth. All of these applications of funds generate potential capital growth and can have a place in a properly constructed investment portfolio. It would be unfortunate if trustees were not able to take advantage of them. As has already been indicated, it is possible that were the issue to be addressed today, a court would adopt the view set out in the explanatory memorandum and hold that the expression 'invest-ment' included any application of funds which produced either potential income or potential capital returns.[48]

(b) Traditional investments

There are certain types of investment which undoubtedly fall within the expression 'investment' as used in the Trustee Act 2000. These would include deposits in a bank or building society, the purchase of government stock, and the purchase of shares in publicly quoted companies. All of these forms of investment were permitted by the Trustee Investments Act 1961, which contained the list of authorized trustee invest-ments prior to the enlargement of investment powers given to trustees by the 2000 Act. The 1961 Act was the first Act to allow trustees to invest in company shares. This was a significant step, as a short analysis of different types of investment will indicate.

Where money is invested by deposit with a bank, the bank pays annual or other periodic interest, but undertakes only to return the sum originally deposited when the account is closed. Government stock is not repayable on demand, but is usually repayable at a fixed future date. Again, interest is payable periodically, but when the date for repayment of the stock falls due, it is repaid only at face value. Pending the date of repayment, the price at which the stock is traded will fluctuate in accordance with prevailing market interest rates and the period before redemption. A stock which offers a high fixed rate of interest on its nominal value, compared with market rates, will tend to trade at a premium (ie at a higher price than its nominal value), reflect-ing the advantage of the holder receiving the high income. Conversely, a stock which

---

[47] [1947] Ch 572.
[48] This view was taken in a different context in *Cook v Medway Housing Society* [1997] STC 90, at 98. See also Hicks 'The Trustee Act 2000 and the Modern Meaning Of Investment' (2001) 15 TLI 203, for the view that the 'portfolio' theory of investment permits more flexibility.

offers a low rate of nominal interest will tend to trade at a discount against its nominal value, reflecting the low yield of interest.

Shares (also referred to as 'equities') in public companies offer the advantage, compared with fixed interest securities and deposits, of offering the potential for both income and capital growth. The policy of most companies is to pay an annual dividend out of the profits which the company makes, while also retaining assets and profits which will enable the underlying capital value of the company to grow. As the net worth of the company increases, so its stock market value will tend to increase. The shareholder will thus receive an income and hope to participate in capital gains. The stock market can be volatile, particularly in the short term, so that, as investment advisers are required to warn, 'the value of your investment can fall as well as rise'. The share-market crash of October 2008 shows how dramatic the falls can be, with £93 billion wiped off the value of the FTSE 100 top companies in a day. Nevertheless, over the longer term, investments in shares have consistently outperformed bank and building society deposits and purchases of fixed interest securities. The ability of trustees, even in the absence of express extended powers of investment, to invest in shares, has been of considerable importance in enabling astute trustees to produce a reasonable income while providing a good measure of protection against inflation through capital appreciation.

(c) Financial instruments

The relatively recent past has seen an increase in the variety of financial instruments available. Some of these were created expressly for the purpose of providing investment vehicles, whilst others originated as mechanisms to help in managing the risks of exchange rate or share price fluctuations. Some appear to have evolved for purely speculative purposes. It is not clear whether all of these financial instruments would be considered to be investments permitted by the Trustee Act 2000. Some should fall within the meaning of the term, provided that it is not given too narrow an interpretation. Capital bonds, under which a company undertakes to repay a given sum at a fixed date in the future, but without any payment of interest in the meantime, have already been referred to. Since these bonds are sold at a price below their redemption value, the capital gain makes up for the loss of interest. There should be no reason why these capital bonds should not be considered valid trustee investments.

There are other financial instruments which are less readily considered to be investments within the ordinary meaning of the term. This includes, for instance, the so-called 'derivatives'. One form of derivative is the 'future' under which a person commits to the sale or purchase of shares or currency at a given date in the future at a fixed price. The other principal form is the 'option' under which the holder has the right, but not an obligation, to buy (purchase) or sell (put) at a fixed price on a future date. These instruments allow a jeweller, for instance, to reduce the risks of the price of gold going up or down by entering into an advance purchase contract or option. They would allow an exporter who knows that he will receive payment in a foreign currency in a year's time to reduce the risk of currency fluctuation by entering into a contract which effectively fixes the exchange rate. However, they also allow speculators to gamble on whether prices will go up or down.[49] There may be a place for this kind of speculation in some trusts, such as pension trusts, and banks were offering dealings in derivatives to private clients with substantial funds to invest. However, since they are extremely risky compared to most other forms of investment, they could well be considered to be outside the scope of authorized investment. Even if they were held to be 'investments' as that term is used in the Trustee Act 2000, a trustee would have to show that a properly informed decision had been made to apply trust funds in this fashion, and that the inherent risks were being managed, for instance by applying only a small part of the fund in this way.

(d) Purchase of land

The general power of investment does not in itself authorize trustees to invest in the purchase of land.[50] Section 8 of the Trustee Act 2000, however, contains authority for trustees (with some exceptions[51]) to purchase land. This extends to all trustees the power to apply trust funds to the purchase of land which was first conferred by statute on trustees of land by the Trusts of Land and Appointment of Trustees Act 1996.[52] There is now no distinction between trustees of land and trustees of personal property in this regard. Trustees may purchase land as an investment, for occupation by a beneficiary, or for any other reason. The purchase may be of a legal freehold or leasehold estate in the United Kingdom.[53] Trustees have no statutory authority to purchase land overseas, but the power to acquire such land could be conferred expressly by the trust instrument. Trustees who acquire land under the statutory power conferred by the Trustee Act 2000, s 8 have all the powers of an absolute owner in relation to the land for the purpose of exercising their functions as trustees.[54]

(e) Loans

Trustees have been permitted to invest in loans secured by way of a mortgage over the borrower's land for over one hundred years.[55] The Trustee Act 2000 continues to allow trustees to invest by way of loans secured on land,[56] but there is nothing in the Act which expressly confers any power to make unsecured loans. *Khoo Tek Keong v Ch'ng*

---

[49] It is also possible to gamble on prices going up or down through 'spread betting' where a gambler stakes money against the future price of a given share. If the share falls within the agreed band or spread of prices at the set date, the betting company pays out on the bet. It is unlikely that any convincing argument could be made that spread betting constitutes an investment within the meaning of the Trustee Act 2000.

[50] Trustee Act 2000, s 3(3).

[51] The power does not apply to trustees of settled land, who have the power to apply trust funds to the purchase of land under the Settled Land Act 1925, ss 73 and 75. Similarly, the power does not apply to occupational pension funds, authorized unit trusts, and certain charity investment funds: Trustee Act 2000, ss 36–38.

[52] S 6.

[53] Or the equivalent of a legal estate in the case of land in Scotland; Trustee Act 2000, s 8(2).

[54] This means, for instance, that trustees are able to grant leases, borrow against the security of the land, carry out building works, and so on.

[55] See Trustee Act 1925, s 8; Trustee Investments Act 2000, Sch 1, Pt II, para 13. Similar provisions appeared in the legislation which these Acts replaced.

[56] Although Trustee Act 1925, s 8 has been repealed, Trustee Act 2000, s 3(3) acknowledges that trustees may make loans secured on land.

Joo Tuan Neoh[57] suggests that unsecured loans would not be considered as investments without some express authority.

(f) Modification of the general power of investment

The general power of investment conferred on trustees by the Trustee Act 2000 is in addition to any express powers which might be conferred upon trustees,[58] but may also be restricted or excluded by an express provision.[59] It goes almost without saying that the general power of investment can be modified by legislation, although, out of an abundance of caution, the Act makes this clear.[60]

As was indicated earlier, the Act applies to trusts created before the commencement of the Act as well as to those created subsequently.[61] Where a trust instrument contains a phrase such as 'the trustees may invest in any investment authorized by law for the investment of trust property', this will be treated as conferring on trustees the general power of investment, whether the trust was made before or after the 2000 Act.[62] Express provisions contained in trust instruments made before 3 August 1961 (the day on which the Trustee Investments Act 1961 came into operation) are not to be treated as restricting or excluding the general power of investment.[63]

5 Widening of powers of investment

The substantial increase in the investment powers given to trustees by the Trustee Act 2000 should mean that it will be rare that they will consider their powers to be too narrow. However, there may be some instances in which they seek wider investment powers, for instance permitting the purchase of property overseas, or clarifying whether they are permitted to invest in assets which produce no income. There are a number of ways in which this may be possible.

(1) Power of variation in trust deed

Some trust deeds contain provisions under which alterations or amendments to the deed can be made. For instance, the Universities' Superannuation Scheme Rules provide that the rules can be altered by deed, with certain restrictions concerning maintaining the purpose of the scheme to provide pensions and other benefits for eligible employees, and subject to certain consents.[64]

---

[57] [1934] AC 529. The case is referred to above in relation to express powers of investment.
[58] Trustee Act 2000, s 6(1)(a).   [59] Trustee Act 2000, s 6(1)(b).
[60] Trustee Act 2000, s 6(1)(b).   [61] Trustee Act 2000, s 7(1).
[62] See Trustee Act 2000, s 7(3). A trust instrument made after the 2000 Act, which stated that trustees could invest in the manner authorized by the Trustee Investments Act 1961 would, however, be treated as limiting the investment powers of trustees to those permitted under the old rules set out in that Act.
[63] Trustee Act 2000, s 7(2).
[64] USS New Rules (1 October 2011), s 76. See also *British Coal Corpn v British Coal Staff Superannuation Scheme Trustees Ltd* [1995] 1 All ER 912.

(2) **Consent of beneficiaries**

Where all the beneficiaries of a trust are ascertainable, and, being competent to do so, give their consent, then new powers of investment proposed by the trustees may be adopted.

(3) **Variation of Trusts Act 1958**

Where it is not possible to obtain consent from all the beneficiaries of a trust, or some of the beneficiaries of the trust are not competent to give consent, and in certain other cases, the Variation of Trusts Act 1958 will apply. This enables the court to approve a variation of trust, including a variation of investment powers, on behalf of the unascertainable or incompetent beneficiaries.[65] The Act does not permit the court to consent to a variation on behalf of ascertainable and competent beneficiaries who have not been consulted (even where to do so would be inconvenient) or to override a refusal of consent by such a beneficiary.

(4) **Trustee Act 1925, s 57**

This section authorizes the court to approve a transaction, either exceptionally or generally,[66] and has been held to be wide enough in scope to authorize extended investment powers.[67] It has an advantage over the Variation of Trusts Act 1958 in that it does not require the beneficiaries to be consulted or to agree to the enlargement of the investment powers, although the court will not approve the variation unless it can be seen as being in the general interests of all the beneficiaries. In *Anker-Petersen v Anker-Petersen*[68] it was suggested that applications for extending powers of investment were more appropriately brought under s 57 than under the Variation of Trusts Act 1958. This was because it was more realistic for the court to consider the matter on behalf of the beneficiaries as a group rather than individually, as the 1958 Act required.

(5) **Principles on which court grants approval**

In a case decided shortly after the passing of the Trustee Investments Act 1961, *Re Kolb's Will Trusts*,[69] it was said that the investment powers in that Act should 'be taken to be prima facie sufficient and ought only to be extended if, on the particular facts, a special case for extending them can be made out'.[70] Subsequent cases departed from that view, and showed a greater willingness to entertain requests for enlarging powers of investment. Thus, in *Mason v Farbrother*,[71] Blackett Ord V-C approved a considerable widening of the powers of investment of the trustees of the Co-Operative Wholesale

---

[65] See Chapter 17.
[66] The Act applies to private trusts. The court has similar powers in respect of charitable trusts under the Charities Act 2011, s 105.   [67] *Mason v Farbrother* [1983] 2 All ER 1078.
[68] [1991] 16 LS Gaz R 32.   [69] [1962] Ch 531.   [70] [1962] Ch 531, at 540.
[71] [1983] 2 All ER 1078.

Society pension fund, and in *Trustees of the British Museum v A-G*[72] Megarry V-C approved the enlargement of the investment powers of the trustees of a museum of international importance. The first case was dealt with under the provisions of the Trustee Act 1925, s 57, and the latter under the Variation of Trusts Act 1958, but there does not seem to have been a difference in approach. Relevant factors included the quality of the advice available to the trustees, and the measures which were to be taken to balance risk and safety. The division of the trust fund into separate parts with different risk profiles was considered to be an important factor in granting approval. In *Steel v Wellcome Custodian Trustees*,[73] Hoffmann J approved almost unfettered investment powers, with no obligation to divide the fund into divisions for the trustees of an extremely large charitable foundation. He had regard to the size of the fund, the eminence and experience of the trustees, and the provisions in the proposed scheme for obtaining advice.

The width of the powers given by the 2000 Act might mean that there would be the same kind of reluctance to entertain an application as happened in *Re Kolb's Will Trusts*. Since the current legislative regime does not require any division of the trust fund, it is unlikely that a court would insist on it if granting enlarged powers, but the factors identified by Hoffmann J would still surely be relevant in deciding whether an extension of powers was appropriate. There are still circumstances, however, in which the courts will exercise their discretion, even after the passing of the Trustee Act 2000. Morgan J, in *Alexander v Alexander*,[74] ordered a sale of land under s 57(1) of the Trustee Act 1925 where no such power existed in the trust instrument. The trustees wanted to sell a cottage which had fallen into such a bad state of repair that it was uninhabitable, but the terms of the trust instrument expressly prohibited sale of the cottage, meaning no such power could be implied.[75] Morgan J held that normally where a transaction '. . . is expedient within the subsection, the court would exercise its discretion to confer power upon the trustees to effect the transaction'.[76] Though the settlor had expressed his wishes through a prohibition on sale in the trust instrument, he had provided the cottage for occupation by the beneficiaries of the trust, and since the beneficiaries also agreed on the trustee's course of action, there was no reason for the court not to exercise its discretion in the best interests of the beneficiaries.

6 Portfolio investment theory

(1) The responsibilities of trustees

The duties of trustees in relation to investment are now considered in detail. Foremost in those duties is a requirement to have regard to the fact that they are

---

[72] [1984] 1 All ER 337.   [73] [1988] 1 WLR 167.   [74] [2011] EWHC 2721 (Ch).
[75] Either under Trusts of Land and Appointment of Trusteees Act 1996, s 6 or the Trustee Act 2000, s 8.
[76] [2011] EWHC 2721, at [33].

dealing with money belonging to others, and therefore have a duty to safeguard it. They must also consider the appropriate balance between capital and income, and the need to protect the trust assets against erosion through inflation. If the trustees are holding only a small fund which they are expected to distribute in the near future, then the principal consideration will be safeguarding the assets in the short term whilst keeping the ability to draw on the fund for the purposes of distribution. Investing the money by way of deposit in a bank might be the simplest and most appropriate way of doing this. However, if the funds are larger and are to be retained for a longer period, then other considerations affecting the choice of investments come into play.

(2) **Risk management**

The advantage of depositing money with a bank is that the bank undertakes to return the same amount as was deposited with it, together with interest. The depositor runs only a very small risk that if the bank becomes insolvent, it may not be able to meet its obligations in full. That risk is made smaller still by government deposit protection schemes and the general unwillingness of governments to see deposit-taking institutions fail. The disadvantage is that the effect of inflation reduces the purchasing power of the cash sum which the bank returns to the depositor. How then is it possible for an investor to safeguard against inflation? A traditional means of doing this is to purchase company shares, which over the long term can be expected to increase in value in money terms, as well as providing an income through the dividends which the company pays. However, the risks associated with company shares are greater. The company may not flourish: it may be badly managed, or it may be operating in a sector which is generally in decline. In consequence, the risks that a single shareholding will fall in value are much greater than is the case with a bank deposit. The greater potential return from company shares is balanced by a greater element of risk. Trustees are permitted to take risks with trust funds. No investment is entirely risk free. However, it is the function of the trustees to manage the risks so that the balance of risk and profit is appropriate for the nature of the trust.

(3) **Investment portfolios**

One of the principles of investment policy is that you should not 'put all your eggs in one basket'. By investing in several companies, not just one, there is less chance that all will fail (although equally less chance that all will thrive). The risks are further reduced if the investments are made in different market sectors—for instance, buying shares in companies operating in different fields such as banking, oil distribution, business services, or supplying utilities. Portfolio investment theory is that where an investment fund is large enough, different parts of the fund should be invested in different ways to provide a balance of growth or income potential, and of security and risk. Instead of evaluating the profile or risk of individual investments, what matters is the balance across the portfolio as a whole—higher risks in some parts of the fund may be balanced by lower risks, or compensating considerations, in other parts of the fund. The exact balance will vary according to individual requirements. A pension fund investing for existing pensioners needs to tilt more towards income and security than, say, a trust fund, which is designed to accumulate to pay out a sum to a beneficiary in 20 years' time. The portfolio theory of investment was examined and discussed in *Nestlé v National Westminster Bank plc*.[77]

(4) Trustee Investments Act 1961

The Trustee Investments Act 1961 espoused the portfolio investment theory, but did so in a rigid way. Investments authorized for trustees were divided into three categories, and trustees who wished to invest in the riskier categories were obliged to take advice, and for certain investments (called wider-range investments) to create a separate part of the trust fund. The enlargement of the categories of permitted investment was welcome, but the way in which the Act required trustees to allocate investments was mechanical, cumbersome, and arbitrarily inflexible.[78] Certain aspects of the operation of the Act were rightly described as 'curious'.[79]

(5) Trustee Act 2000

The rigidity and capriciousness of the investment rules in the 1961 Act have been swept away by the 2000 Act. This permits trustees to invest in the way most appropriate for the circumstances of their trust, with none of the arbitrary limitations of the 1961 Act. In reviewing whether trustees have acted properly, the courts are likely to take account of the current theory of portfolio investment.[80]

(6) Total overall return

The return on an investment consists of either or both capital growth and income return. The total return which an investment makes is the combination of both of these elements. If £1,000 is invested in company shares and at the end of the first year of investment the shares have increased in value to £1,100, and the company has paid a dividend of £50, the total overall return on the investment is £150—the sum total of the capital growth and the income. If a person were investing for their own benefit, they

---

[77] [1993] 1 WLR 1260; Martin 'Investment Duties: A Victory for Complacency' (1992) 142 NLJ 1279; Kenny 'Are a Bank Trustee's Fees Performance Related?' [1993] Conv 63; Watt and Stauch 'Is There Liability for Imprudent Trustee Investment?' [1998] Conv 352.

[78] The Act initially required a division of the trust fund into two equal parts to enable the wider powers of investment to take effect (Trustee Investments Act 1961, s 2(1)), and this was later varied by the Trustee Investments (Division of Trust Fund) Order 1996, SI 1996/845 to permit three-quarters of the fund to be applied in the wider range of investments. Trustees could not choose some other division, such as two-thirds.

[79] *Nestlé v National Westminster Bank Ltd* [1993] 1 WLR 1260, at 1278, per Staughton LJ. See also Legair 'Modern Portfolio Theory: A Primer' (2000) 14 TLI 75.

[80] See further Hicks 'The Trustee Act 2000 and the Modern Meaning of Investment' (2001) 15 TLI 203.

might aim to get the best possible overall total return, regardless of the split between capital growth and income. If they need money, they can always cash in part of the investment if the income it produces is insufficient. Conversely, they could reinvest the income if they wanted to see their overall wealth increase. The same strategy could be adopted by a trust which has no beneficiaries currently entitled to the income, such as a charitable trust.[81] The trust invests for the best total overall return, and draws down a defined percentage of the fund each year. However, if the trust is one in which a beneficiary is entitled to the income, the strategy could operate unfairly since under current law the income is defined as the return the trust obtains through dividends and interest on its investments. Where there is an income beneficiary, the strategy would therefore only be appropriate where it is expressly envisaged by the trust instrument and a different means of identifying regular periodic sums which should be paid to the 'income' beneficiaries. This might be a fixed sum, possibly index-linked, or a fixed percentage of the value of the fund each year.

7 Duties of trustees in relation to investment

(1) The general duty of care

There is a substantial body of case law considering the duties of trustees in relation to investment, much of which remains relevant, although the Trustee Act 2000 imposes some statutory duties. The first of these statutory duties is the statutory duty of care. Trustees are required to exercise such care and skill in relation to investments as is reasonable in the circumstances.[82] As is explained elsewhere, a higher standard of care is expected from trustees acting in a professional capacity and where the trustee claims to have special knowledge or experience.[83] This is no more than a statutory restatement of the principles which had been established by the cases, with a clarification of the position of professional trustees. In *Speight v Gaunt*[84] Lord Blackburn stated that the general duty of trustees was to act honestly and fairly and to take 'all those precautions which an ordinary prudent man of business would take in managing similar affairs of his own'. In *Re Whiteley*[85] Lindley LJ refined this dictum as it applies to investment. He said:

> The duty of the trustee is not to take such care only as a prudent man would take if he had only himself to consider, the duty is rather to take such care as an ordinary prudent man would take if he were minded to make an investment for the benefit of other people for whom he felt morally bound to provide.[86]

---

[81] New statutory powers are conferred on charity trustees to effect total return investments—these are considered later under special considerations for charity investments.

[82] Trustee Act 2000, s 1(1).   [83] Trustee Act 2000, s 1(1). See the discussion in Chapter 26.

[84] (1883) 9 App Cas 1.

[85] (1886) 33 Ch D 347; affd sub nom *Learoyd v Whiteley* (1887) 12 App Cas 727.

[86] (1886) 33 Ch D 347, at 355.

Lord Watson on appeal to the House of Lords explained:

> Business men of ordinary prudence may, and frequently do, select investments which are more or less of a speculative character; but it is the duty of a trustee to confine himself to the class of investments which are permitted by the trust, and likewise to avoid all investments of that class which are attended by hazard.[87]

In addition to the specific duties relating to investment, trustees remain subject to their general fiduciary duties in making investment decisions.[88] This means that they should not act in a way which gives rise to a conflict of interest. Thus, in a Canadian case, it was held that the trustees were in breach of trust where they made a loan to a company owned by one of the trustees. Even though this application of the trust funds did not fall outside the investment powers of the trustees, the conflict of interest made the loan an improper investment.[89]

We have already seen that the rule in *Howe v Earl of Dartmouth*, if it has not been superseded by the Trustee Act 2000, may require immediate disinvestment by trustees of hazardous investments received under a residuary testamentary gift which is to be held for beneficiaries with successive interests in trusts arising before the commencement of the Trusts (Capital and Income) Act 2013.[90] However, in accordance with portfolio investment theory, as has already been explained, trustees may be entitled to retain or to make an investment which involves a measure of risk (as most investments inevitably do), provided that the risk involved in that investment is balanced by other elements in the portfolio. That is the tenor of most recent judgments on the investment powers of trustees. In *Nestlé v National Westminster Bank plc*,[91] Hoffmann J said that 'an investment which in isolation is too risky and therefore in breach of trust may be justified when held in conjunction with other investments'.

(2) The standard investment criteria

The Trustee Act 2000, s 4 requires all trustees exercising a power of investment, including trustees exercising express investment powers, to have regard to what are described as the 'standard investment criteria'.[92] There are two such criteria. First, the trustees must have regard to the suitability of the investment concerned, and second to the need for diversification. The trustees must have regard to these standard investment criteria both in making investments,[93] and also in periodically reviewing the investments.[94] The

---

[87] (1887) 12 App Cas 727, at 733.

[88] There is widespread concern about how fiduciary duties are interpreted in the context of investment—see Kay, *Final Report on UK Equity Markets and Long Term Decision Making* (November 2012), which was commissioned by the Department for Business and Skills. The Law Commission, as a result, opened a consultation on the fiduciary duties of investment intermediaries. The final report was published on 1 July 2014 (Law Com No 350 'Fiduciary Duties of Investment Intermediaries'), which calls for better guidance on fiduciary duties over legislative reform.

[89] *Re David Feldman Charitable Foundation* (1987) 58 OR (2d) 626.

[90] Section 1(2)(a) and (b) disapply the rules of apportionment for 'new trusts' arising on or after 5 October 2013. [91] [1993] 1 WLR 1260.

[92] These criteria are not new. They first appeared in the Trustee Investments Act 1961, s 6(1).

[93] Trustee Act 2000, s 4(3).   [94] Trustee Act 2000, s 4(1).

responsibilities of trustees in relation to investments are ongoing—they cannot invest funds and then forget them. They must keep the investment portfolio under periodic review. It is also clear that the duty to review extends to investments settled on the trustee at the creation of the trust, as well as investments made by trustees in pursuance of their powers of investment.[95]

When looking at the suitability of investments, the Trustee Act 2000 envisages a two-stage process. The trustees must consider the suitability for the trust of a particular kind of investment. For instance, should the trust invest in purchasing shares in a unit trust? The trustees must then consider the suitability of the particular investment proposed. For instance, having decided that investing in a unit trust would be suitable, which fund manager and which of that manager's investment funds should be selected?

(3) **The need for advice**

A further requirement of the Trustee Act 2000 is that trustees must normally take proper advice on investment decisions.[96] The Trustee Investments Act 1961 required trustees always to take advice before making all but a very limited range of investments. This requirement has been changed by the 2000 Act. Trustees can dispense with seeking advice if they reasonably conclude that in all the circumstances it is unnecessary or inappropriate to do so.[97] For instance, the trustees may consider the sums involved to be too small, or they may already have sufficient expertise available to them through fellow trustees or employees of the trust. However, for trustees to dispense with advice requires a conscious decision on the part of the trustees. It would be a breach of trust for trustees to fail to seek advice through oversight, even in a situation where advice was unnecessary, although it is hardly likely in such an instance that any action for breach of trust would be pursued.

'Proper advice' is defined by the Act as 'the advice of a person who is reasonably believed by the trustee to be qualified to give it by his ability in and practical experience of financial and other matters relating to the proposed investment'.[98] The trustees are not obliged to follow the advice which they are given. Their obligation is only to obtain and consider it. They would not be discharging their function if they followed the advice without applying their own minds to it,[99] but equally it would be unwise to disregard the advice without good reason.[100]

---

[95] See further *Gregson v HAE Trustees Ltd* [2008] EWHC 1006 (Ch), at [83], per Deputy Judge Robert Miles QC.

[96] Trustee Act 2000, s 5(1) (new investments) and s 5(2) (review of existing investments).

[97] Trustee Act 2000, s 5(3).

[98] Trustee Act 2000, s 5(4). A person acting as an investment adviser must be authorized under s 19 Financial Services and Markets Act 2000.

[99] See *Jones v AMP Perpetual Trustee Co NZ Ltd* [1994] 1 NZLR 690.

[100] See *Cowan v Scargill* [1985] Ch 270, at 289 (discussed later).

(4) Financial considerations

The object of investment is to produce a financial return from trust assets. The trustees are expected to adopt an investment strategy which has regard to the nature and purpose of the trust. This will affect whether the trustees should be maximizing income, maximizing capital growth, or balancing the two, and what balance there should be between risk and return. Where there are both income and capital beneficiaries, the trustees must seek a balance between high income and capital growth. It has been said that in all but the smallest fund, this will require a high proportion of the trust assets to be invested in company shares.[101] Where an income beneficiary would not be liable to tax on certain kinds of investment, however, this also should be considered by the trustees and would legitimately influence their investment decisions.[102] Because trustees must consider how to achieve a fair and proper balance between all the different classes of beneficiary, they will not be in breach of trust simply because their investment policy has resulted in greater erosion of the real capital value of the trust fund than would have been the case with a different investment strategy. Trustees are not under an absolute obligation to ensure that the capital value of the fund is maintained.[103] For instance, in *Nestlé v National Westminster Bank plc*[104] the heiress to the chocolate family fortune complained that, had the trustees invested differently, she could have received an inheritance four times greater than was the case. The Court of Appeal held that, although there had been errors of judgement on the part of the trustees, including a misunderstanding of the width of their powers of investment, and a failure to review the investments sufficiently often, there had not been any breach of trust resulting in liability to the heiress. It was also said that even if trustees had acted for the wrong reasons, they would still not be liable if their decision could be justified objectively by other, valid, reasons.[105] The case illustrates the difficulty which the beneficiary faces in seeking to prove a breach of trust in relation to investment by trustees.[106]

(5) Ethical considerations

The extent to which trustees may have regard to ethical considerations[107] was explored by Megarry V-C in *Cowan v Scargill*.[108] The National Coal Board pension fund was controlled by both management-appointed and union-appointed trustees. The union-appointed trustees objected to a proposed annual investment plan unless

---

[101] *Nestlé v National Westminster Bank plc* [1993] 1 WLR 1260.
[102] *Nestlé v National Westminster Bank plc* [1993] 1 WLR 1260.
[103] See *Jones v AMP Perpetual Trustee Co NZ Ltd* [1994] 1 NZLR 690.   [104] [1993] 1 WLR 1260.
[105] See also *Cowan v Scargill* [1985] Ch 270.
[106] See also *Jones v AMP Perpetual Trustee Co NZ Ltd* [1994] 1 NZLR 690, where trustees were held not liable for retaining shares in a falling market.
[107] See Lord Nicholls 'Trustees and Their Broader Community; Where Duty, Morality and Ethics Converge' (1995) 9 TLI 71; Luxton 'Ethical Investments in Hard Times' (1992) 55 MLR 587; Thornton 'Ethical Investments: A Case of Disjointed Thinking' (2008) CLJ 396.   [108] [1985] Ch 270.

it adopted the policy of withdrawing from overseas investment and from investment in industries in competition with coal. This led to a direct clash between the union-appointed trustees, led by Arthur Scargill—the National Union of Mineworkers General Secretary and a veteran of industrial disputes—and the other trustees, leading to the hearing in court. Eschewing the use of a barrister, Arthur Scargill chose to represent himself in court. Sir Robert Megarry held that the action of the union trustees was unreasonable. The duty of trustees was to optimize the benefits which the beneficiaries would receive. In the vast majority of cases, financial considerations would prevail. There could be rare cases where this was not so.

> Plainly the present case is not one of this rare type of case. Subject to such matters, under a trust for the provision of financial benefits, the paramount duty of the trustees is to provide the greatest financial benefits for the present and future beneficiaries.[109]

Trustees were not to be deflected from this duty to the beneficiaries merely because the policy of seeking the best financial returns conflicted with their personal opinions:

> Trustees may have strongly held social or political views. They may be firmly opposed to any investment in South Africa[110] or other countries, or they may object to any form of investment in companies concerned with alcohol, tobacco, armaments or other controversial products. In the conduct of their own affairs, of course, they are free to abstain from making any such investments. Yet under a trust, if investments of this type would be more beneficial to the beneficiaries than other investments, the trustees must not refrain from making the investments by reason of the views that they hold.[111]

It was not enough that they were honest and sincere in their cause. The general standard of conduct required of trustees demanded more:

> Honesty and sincerity are not the same as prudence and reasonableness. Some of the most sincere people are the most unreasonable; and Mr Scargill told me that he had met quite a few of them. Accordingly, although a trustee who takes advice on investments is not bound to accept and act on that advice, he is not entitled to reject it merely because he sincerely disagrees with it, unless in addition to being sincere he is acting as an ordinary prudent man would act.[112]

One of the cases which Megarry V-C thought might be exceptional and where ethical or moral considerations could legitimately sway the decision of the trustees was where all the beneficiaries were adults who shared the same moral values who 'might well consider that it was far better to receive less than to receive more money from what they consider to be evil and tainted sources'.[113]

Such a situation arose in *Harries v Church Comrs for England*,[114] which concerned the investment policy of the body controlling the investment funds of the Church of England. The revenue from these funds, together with contributions from parishes,

---

[109] [1985] Ch 270, at 288. [110] This remark was made before the end of apartheid.
[111] [1985] Ch 270, at 287. [112] [1985] Ch 270, at 289. [113] [1985] Ch 270, at 288.
[114] [1993] 2 All ER 300. See Nobles 'Charities and Ethical Investment' [1992] Conv 115.

was used to maintain churches and to meet the stipends of the clergy. The Church Commissioners operated an ethical investment policy, under which they chose not to invest in businesses which might be offensive to the Church, including armaments, gambling, tobacco, newspapers, and South Africa.[115] Sir Donald Nicholls V-C considered that these exclusions were appropriate and justified for a religious charity whose members were likely to support such a policy, but he rejected a call by the Bishop of Oxford for a much wider group of exclusions. Even though ethical considerations were legitimate for the Church Commissioners, provided that they left an adequate width of investment, where charity trustees held assets for investments, their principal duty was to seek the maximum return consistent with commercial prudence. If they did not do this, they would not be discharging their duty of furthering the purposes of the trust. If the Church Commissioners used their funds otherwise than for investment, how in the long term could they ensure that the clergy were paid and the Church's buildings maintained?

The danger of blind adherence to a political policy without considering the interests of the beneficiaries is illustrated by *Martin v Edinburgh District Council*,[116] where Lord Murray held that trustees were in breach of trust for pursuing a policy of disinvestment in South Africa prior to the end of apartheid 'without considering expressly whether it was in the best interests of the beneficiaries and without obtaining professional advice'. Trustees would only be entitled to adopt a blind policy of this nature where it was expressly permitted or required by the instrument establishing the trust. The decision to exclude a sector of possible investments in a way which 'runs contrary to the best financial indicators available at the time'[117] on political or ethical grounds is what constitutes the breach of trust. It is not relevant that the ethical investments may actually turn out to produce a reasonable return; the decision to invest in them should only have been made if other non-ethical investments were considered and rejected on the basis that they would not yield a greater return. Nevertheless, as Thornton suggests, there may be a disconnection between this legal orthodoxy and the ability of the beneficiaries to prove that pursuing an ethical investment policy necessarily resulted in loss to the trust.[118] There is also an arguable case that ethically based investments have a lower risk profile than other investments, or that in some instances (such as with investments in 'green' technology) that they have greater growth potential, which could justify a decision by trustees.[119]

---

[115] A very similar list of exclusions to those given by Megarry V-C in the passage cited earlier.

[116] 1988 SLT 329.

[117] Thornton 'Ethical investments: a case of disjointed thinking' (2008) CLJ 396.

[118] Thornton 'Ethical investments: a case of disjointed thinking' (2008) CLJ 396, pp 415–417.

[119] See McCormack 'Sexy But Not Sleazy: Trustee Investments and Ethical Considerations' (1998) 19 *Company Lawyer* 39, who argues that pursuing an ethical investment policy may not be a poor decision for trustees. This is in relation to ethically managed unit trusts and their relative performance on the stock market (FTSE).

(6) **Periodic review of investments**

The duty of trustees in relation to investment is a continuing one. They do not discharge their duty merely by giving proper consideration to the appropriateness of an investment at the time it is made or the asset acquired. They must also consider periodically whether the balance of investment is correct, and whether individual investments are retained. This responsibility is specifically imposed by the Trustee Act 2000, s 4(2), but would in any event apply on general trust principles. In *Bartlett v Barclays Bank Trust Co Ltd (No 2)*[120] trustees held a controlling shareholding in a property investment company. It was held that they were in breach of trust in failing to review the activities of the company and in permitting the directors to engage in a speculative and inadvisable development scheme. In *Jeffrey v Gretton*,[121] trustees where held to be in breach of the duty to review investments under s 4(2), on the basis that they should have considered selling a Grade II dilapidated property once the life tenant had given up his interest by deed of variation. Instead, the trustees had permitted the life tenant to remain in the property until his death and had, without professional advice, sought to refurbish the property. Mr Justice Blohm QC held that the trustees had failed in their duty to review the investments, as they should not have decided to defer sale as the life tenant had given up his entitlement under the deed of variation and should have considered professional advice on the financial merits of the plan to retain and refurbish the property.[122]

Provided that the trustees have given proper consideration to whether an investment should be retained, they will not be liable because it can be seen, with the benefit of hindsight, that they made a mistake. In *Re Chapman*[123] the trustees had properly invested in mortgages of agricultural land. The value of the land fell, placing the security of the mortgages at risk. The trustees nevertheless decided to retain them, hoping that the market would improve. Instead, land values fell still further. The Court of Appeal refused to find the trustees liable.

> There is no rule of law which compels the court to hold that an honest trustee is liable to make good loss sustained by retaining an authorized security in a falling market, if he did so honestly and prudently, in the belief that it was the best course to take in the interests of all parties. Trustees acting honesty, with ordinary prudence and within the limits of their trust, are not liable for mere errors of judgment.[124]

It is believed that this will continue to be the case, notwithstanding the omission by the Trustee Act 2000 of s 4 of the Trustee Act 1925, under which trustees were not to be held liable for breach of trust by reason only of continuing to hold an investment which has ceased to be authorized either by the trust instrument or by the general law.

---

[120] [1980] 1 All ER 139.   [121] [2011] WTLR 809.

[122] [2011] WTLR 809, at [69]–[72]. On the facts, though in breach of the duty, no loss had occurred on the market value of the property, which had not increased or decreased over the period in which the ex-life tenant had lived at the property.   [123] [1896] 2 Ch 763.

[124] See also *Jones v AMP Perpetual Trustee Co NZ Ltd* [1994] 1 NZLR 690.

(7) **Special rules for particular investments**

(a) Mortgages of land

In the nineteenth century, before building societies played the major role which they did in the first half of the twentieth century in financing the purchase of residential property, private mortgages were very common and a frequent type of investment for trustees. Modern conditions of inflation, and the ready availability of commercial funds from the building societies and banks make this form of investment much less popular for trustees, although it still occurs to a limited extent, and is envisaged by the Trustee Act 2000, s 3(3). Special rules used to be provided by the Trustee Act 1925, s 8 for trustees lending on mortgage. These rules protected trustees against liability for advancing too high a proportion of the value of the property if they lent no more than two-thirds of a valuation made by an independent surveyor or valuer. These rules have now been removed by the Trustee Act 2000 so that the question of whether a mortgage transaction was prudent and appropriate must be decided without recourse to any such guidelines.[125] It is not considered advisable for trustees to lend on the security of anything other than a first legal mortgage,[126] although it is possible that a loan on a properly registered second mortgage would not, in itself, be a breach of trust. The trust instrument may, of course, permit a loan on a second mortgage, or even an unsecured loan.

(b) Controlling interest in a company

Trustees who have a shareholding which gives them a controlling interest in a company are expected to take more than a passive interest in the affairs of the company. They should either ensure that one of the trustees is a member of the board (if not an executive director) or, at the very least, they should keep a watching brief lest the company seeks to act in an improvident way.[127]

(8) **Special considerations for charity investment**

(a) Charities Act 1993

The Charities Act 2011, s 96 authorizes the court or the Charity Commission to approve schemes for the establishment of common investment funds where trustees wish to pool the investments of two or more charitable trusts.[128] There should normally be some connection between the participating charities. Section 100 of the Act contains provisions for the establishment of common deposit schemes for charities.[129]

---

[125] See *Re Solomon* [1912] 1 Ch 261; *Re Dive* [1909] 1 Ch 328; *Shaw v Cates* [1909] 1 Ch 389.

[126] See *Chapman v Browne* [1902] 1 Ch 785, CA.

[127] *Re Lucking's Will Trusts* [1967] 3 All ER 726.

[128] For a common investment scheme approved under previous legislation see *Re University of London Charitable Trusts* [1964] Ch 282. Sections 97 to 103 set out the bodies that may participate in and the provisions and powers applicable to such schemes.

[129] Ss 101 to 103 set out the bodies that may participate and the provisions applicable to such schemes.

(b) Total return investments

We have already seen that charities may wish to make use of total return investments; to invest so as to obtain the best overall return to the charity and then decide how to allocate the overall return, both capital growth and income, This previously required a Charity Commission scheme to authorize such investments. From 1 January 2014, charities with a permanent endowment may now adopt a total returns policy under the Charities Act 2011, s 104A.[130] This follows the passing of the Charities (Total Returns) Regulations 2013, with which charities have to comply before passing and managing a 'total returns' portfolio. The regulation of charities is considered in Chapter 26.

(c) Social investments

Charities, in seeking to achieve their charitable purposes, normally either expend funds in the furtherance of those purposes (eg funding research into infectious diseases) or invest in the traditional sense to generate funds to supplement donations and other income to fund future expenditure on charitable purposes (eg through purchasing shares in a listed company). The Law Commission launched a consultation paper on 'social investment' by charities.[131] A social investment is one which seeks to achieve both a charitable purpose and an (often limited) financial benefit in one, composite transaction. A good example is a homelessness charity purchasing empty properties to be renovated and let at a low rent, thereby helping the homeless but also achieving a small financial return through rent and the increase in value of the purchased properties. Social investments are not new financial instruments in the sector, but there may be legal barriers to charity trustees making use of them either because of restrictions within charity law (such as the requirement not to provide anything other than incidental private benefits) or concerns within the general scope of trustee investment powers.

Concerns over the width of the statutory investment powers under the Trustee Act 2000, and the dubious position of ethical investments, have led the Law Commission to provisionally propose a new statutory power conferring on charity trustees the power to make social investments.[132] They also provisionally propose that the standard investment criteria under the Trustee Act 2000 should not apply to social investments by charities,[133] as they do not sit comfortably with social investments and may 'constitute a trap for the unwary' charity trustee.[134] The results of the consultation process are awaited with interest.[135]

---

[130] Inserted by the Trusts (Capital and Income) Act 2013, s 4.
[131] *Social Investment by Charities*, Law Com Consultation Paper No 216 (2014). The short consultation period opened on 24 April 2014 and closed on 18 June 2014.   [132] CP 216, para 4.12.
[133] CP 216, para 4.27.   [134] CP 216, para. 3.76.
[135] These results will not be available before this edition of the book goes to print, but will be considered in the online updates.

8 Delegation of investment decisions

(1) Authority to delegate investment management

Investment decisions and their execution are so complex that in many cases it will not be appropriate for trustees to manage the investment of trust funds themselves. This is more likely to be the case where large funds are under investment, or where the trustees do not themselves have investment experience. In such cases, the management of the investments might be delegated by the trustees. For instance, as the case of *Cowan v Scargill*[136] illustrated, the National Coal Board pension fund, one of the largest such funds, was not invested directly by the trustees. Instead, it was managed by professional financial advisers on behalf of the trustees, subject to the approval of an annual investment plan giving direction, which was prepared by the advisers for consideration by the board of trustees.

Prior to the Trustee Act 2000 it was not clear whether the delegation of investment management was permitted by general law, so that it was considered wise for a trust instrument expressly to authorize the delegation by trustees of investment management to professional portfolio managers.[137] The Pensions Act 1995 contains provisions enabling trustees to delegate certain of their functions concerning investment subject to a number of safeguards.[138] The Trustee Act 2000 has now extended to all trustees the explicit authority to delegate investment management.[139] This implements a proposal made by the Law Commission.[140] The change has been achieved by authorizing trustees to delegate any function relating to the trust, with certain exceptions.[141] Investment management is one of the functions which can be delegated.[142]

(2) Conditions

Where trustees do choose to delegate investment management, or *asset management,* to use the wider phrase used in the Trustee Act 2000, certain conditions must be satisfied. These conditions probably apply even in cases where this is done under an express power in the trust instrument rather than under the statutory power to delegate. First, the delegation to the agent must be in writing, or must be evidenced in writing.[143] Second, the trustees must produce a policy statement in writing, or evidenced in writing, which gives guidance as to how the asset management functions should be exercised.[144] This policy statement should, for instance, indicate what level of risk the

---

[136] [1985] Ch 270.   [137] See Hayton 'Investment Management Problems' (1990) 106 LQR 88.
[138] Pensions Act 1995, s 34.
[139] The powers granted in the Trustee Act 2000 do not, therefore, apply to pension trusts.
[140] *Trustees Powers and Duties,* Law Com Report No 260 (1999). This proposal adopts a recommendation of the Trust Law Revision Committee.   [141] Trustee Act 2000, s 11.
[142] Investment functions are included in the list of functions which can be delegated by trustees of a charitable trust, and are not excluded from the general authority given to other trustees.
[143] Trustee Act 2000, s 15(1).   [144] Trustee Act 2000, s 15(2)(a).

trustees consider acceptable, what balance is being sought between income and capital growth, and whether there are any types of investment that should be avoided. Third, the contract with the agent must require the agent to comply with the current policy statement given by the trustees.[145] Finally, the trustees must exercise reasonable care in the selection of the agent, since the selection of agents is one of the functions to which the statutory duty of care applies.[146]

In addition, the Act specifically imposes on the agent the obligation to have regard to the standard investment criteria, described earlier.[147] However, the agent is dispensed from the need to obtain advice if the agent is the sort of person from whom it would have been proper to seek advice.[148] Thus, where, as will often be the case, the trustees delegate investment management to a professional fund manager (such as an investment bank), the agent does not have to seek advice from other professionals. Professional fund managers will sometimes insist on a limitation of liability, or permission to act where there may be a potential conflict of interest, and the trustees are authorized by the Act to agree to such terms if it is reasonably necessary to do so.[149] The appointment of an agent will be valid notwithstanding any failure by the trustees to comply with the limits relating to the appointment,[150] but the trustees will thereby expose themselves to potential liability for breach of trust.

(3) **Supervision and review**

Just as the functions of trustees are not completed once they have made the initial investments of the trust fund, so their functions are not completed where they have appointed an agent. The trustees must keep the arrangement under review,[151] they must intervene if necessary by giving directions or terminating the agency,[152] and they must review and revise the investment policy statement.[153]

(4) **Related functions**

In addition to the delegation of investment management, trustees may also appoint nominees to act on their behalf, custodians to hold documents relating to trust assets or the trust assets themselves, and custodian trustees in whom the trust assets are vested. These arrangements were described in Chapter 19.

---

[145] Trustee Act 2000, s 15(2)(b).   [146] Trustee Act 2000, s 1 and Sch 1, para 3.
[147] Trustee Act 2000, s 13(1).   [148] Trustee Act 2000, s 13(2).
[149] Trustee Act 2000, s 14(2) and (3).   [150] Trustee Act 2000, s 24.   [151] Trustee Act 2000, s 22(1).
[152] Trustee Act 2000, s 22(1) and (4).   [153] Trustee Act 2000, s 22(2).

22

Collective assets and investments

This chapter considers collective investment vehicles. These are facilitated by the conceptual creation of equity, the fund, which enables a beneficiary's wealth to be considered to have an identity that is distinct from the assets in which that wealth may at any particular time be invested. The chapter considers a number of these collective asset schemes.

1 Introduction

The equitable conception of the fund can be used to enable a number of individuals to pool their assets, the advantage being that the combined assets of the investors can be used more effectively than the separate assets of the individuals. The group can take advantage of economies of scale, thereby reducing dealing and other management costs. It may also, because of the size of the combined fund, benefit from a wider spread of investments, thereby reducing risk through diversification and also enabling parts of the fund to be invested in higher risk sectors as part of a balanced portfolio.

The issues that arise from the establishment of groups for collective investment are similar to those that are raised by other forms of association. Not every association, whether for investment or other purposes, requires the assistance of equity. There are some forms of association that can enjoy the benefits of collective investment in other ways. These are considered briefly later in the chapter. Most rely upon the association acquiring some form of independent legal status. The great advantage of equity's fund and trust concepts is that the members of the group can enjoy the benefits of scale which have been described above and yet retain the security of direct beneficial ownership of the investments.

Most collective investment vehicles are now subject to regulation under the Financial Services and Markets Act 2000. The provisions of this Act are intended to safeguard the public, and a detailed consideration of the rules set out by the Act falls outside the scope of this book.

2 Bank deposits

The simplest way of individuals pooling resources is to use the services of a bank, which takes deposits on which it pays interest. The interest is generated by the bank in turn lending the money invested with it at a higher rate of interest that enables it to pay the investors and to cover its own operating costs and profits. Although banks may sometimes act as trustees, they do not normally do so in taking deposits (even if the bank is called a trustee savings bank). Instead the bank enters into a contract with the customer under which ownership of the money deposited is transferred to the bank and the depositor retains no proprietary interest in it. However, in return the bank contractually undertakes to repay an equivalent sum with interest. The law of trusts has no part to play in such a transaction, unless there is some special term in the contract.

3 Incorporation of a company

(1) **Incorporation**

One way in which a group of like-minded individuals can group together to acquire an asset or to make investments is to establish a company that is incorporated under the Companies Act 2006. The company then has an independent legal status, but is owned by the subscribing shareholders who can control the company by using the votes that most shareholdings confer. They will participate in the annual profits which the company makes through a distribution of dividends, and can benefit in any capital appreciation of the company's assets either through special distributions, or through a winding-up, dissolution, and distribution of the company's assets, or, more commonly, through the sale of their shareholding to a willing purchaser. Equity plays no special role in such arrangements although, before the introduction of the modern company through legislation, lawyers used the trust concept as the basis for the creation of the joint stock company,[1] the predecessor of the modern limited liability company.

(2) **Functions of companies**

Most companies are established for trading purposes, but they can be set up to make investments (and are then called investment trusts) or to acquire an asset as part of a joint venture (the company is then often called a special purpose vehicle).

(3) **Duties of directors**

Although the directors of a company are no longer considered to be trustees for the shareholders,[2] they are treated as being in a fiduciary position, and in this respect are

---

[1] The Joint Stock Companies Act 1856 allowed joint stock companies to be established with limited liability.

[2] See *Salomon v A Salomon & Co Ltd* [1897] AC 22. Compare the earlier case of *Smith v Anderson* (1880) 15 Ch D 247, in which the directors of a joint stock company were considered to be in the position of trustees for the members of the company.

subject to some of the obligations and liabilities that apply to trustees. Directors are now also under a series of statutory duties of care, introduced by the Companies Act 2006,[3] such as a duty to exercise 'reasonable care, skill and diligence'[4] in exercising any of their functions as directors. The existing case law on the fiduciary duties of directors remains relevant, as regard is to be had under s 171(4) to 'equitable principles in interpreting and applying the general duties'.[5]

4 Investment trusts

Despite the misleading nomenclature, these are not trusts at all, but companies quoted on the stock exchange whose purpose is not to trade directly, but instead to purchase shares in manufacturing or service companies. The word 'investment' is descriptive of the purpose of the corporation; the word 'trust' reflects the way in which joint stock companies were originally established, prior to modern company legislation permitting the statutory incorporation of companies. If the investments made by the company prosper, shareholders will receive dividends and see the value of their shareholding increase. Some investment trusts act as venture capital funds: providing capital for new or developing business ventures, and taking a stake in the companies in which they invest through shareholdings in them.

5 Open-ended investment companies

Investment trusts are closed-ended in that the company issues a fixed number of shares. If an investor who originally subscribed for those shares decides to realise his investment, he does so by selling his shareholding to a new investor. The company does not normally buy back the shareholding. Unless the company seeks exceptional power to buy back shares, or new shares are issued to raise additional capital, the number of shares issued remains unchanged.

Open-ended investment companies (or OEICs) operate differently.[6] The only purpose of an OEIC is to provide a vehicle for collective investment. The company issues shares to prospective investors, and uses the funds so raised to make investments through the purchase of shares and other securities. These assets are held by a depositary (effectively a custodian trustee) on behalf of the OEIC. New shares can be issued, or existing shares cancelled, to allow new investors to join, or existing investors to leave. The price at which the shares are bought or sold reflects the average asset value of the underlying investments.

---

[3] Pt 10, Ch 2, ss 170–181.   [4] Companies Act 2006, s 174.
[5] Duties of company directors are considered further in Chapter 28.
[6] See the Open-Ended Investment Companies Regulations 2001, 2005, 2008, 2009, and 2011.

6 Unincorporated associations

Although unincorporated associations have no independent legal status,[7] they are capable of owning property which is held by trustees on trust for the members as tenants-in-common subject to the rules. That form of ownership has been used in Ireland to permit the creation of common contractual funds which are held by custodian trustees on behalf of the investors as tenants-in-common, and managed by a management company appointed in accordance with the deed under which the common contractual fund has been established.

7 Mutual societies

The lack of any independent legal status for unincorporated associations has not prevented them being used for a wide variety of purposes, including benevolent functions (such as saving towards the cost of a modest funeral), but it did present difficulties for associations which wished to engage in commercial or quasi-commercial activities. To overcome these difficulties, legislation was enacted which enabled mutual associations, through a simple process of registration, to obtain limited independent legal personality, although they continued to be owned and governed by their members in accordance with their rules.[8] The legislation provided for a variety of different forms of association, for instance friendly societies set up to provide mutual insurance benefits;[9] and cooperative societies established to provide not-for-profit trading activities.[10] An example of the latter is the International Exhibition Co-operative Wine Society, which was set up in 1874 to supply good wines at fair prices to its members. Additional legislation covers specialist types of association, for instance credit unions,[11] building societies,[12] and housing associations.[13] Registration of an association as an industrial and provident society or as a friendly society was a convenient alternative to incorporation under the Companies Acts for mutual groups, many of which remain in operation today.

---

[7] See Chapter 12.

[8] See, for example, Friendly Societies Act 1896, s 49(1), which states: 'All property belonging to a registered society, whether acquired before or after the society is registered, shall vest in the trustees for the time being of the society, for the use and benefit of the society and the members thereof, and of all persons claiming through the members according to the rules of the society.'

[9] Friendly Societies Act 1829; Friendly Societies Act 1896. The current legislation is the Friendly Societies Act 1974 and the Friendly Societies Act 1992.

[10] Industrial and Provident Societies Act 1852; Industrial and Provident Societies Act 1862. See now the Industrial and Provident Societies Acts 1965 (as amended by the Industrial and Provident Societies Act 2002) and 1978.

[11] Now governed by the Credit Unions Act 1979 and the Co-operative and Community Benefit Societies and Credit Unions Act 2010

[12] Building Societies Act 1986, as amended by the Building Societies Act 1997.

[13] Housing Acts 1985, 1988, and 2004.

A difference between organizations incorporated under the Companies Acts and mutual organizations is that the subscribers to companies have shareholdings which they can sell, whilst with mutuals, the assets belong to the members for the time being, and those members lose any claim to the assets when they leave the mutual. Nevertheless, the property rights of members of a mutual organizations can be substantial, as we saw in Chapter 12.

The relevance of mutual societies in the present context—that of collective investment—is that many mutual societies have operated as vehicles for collective investment, albeit generally with some other social purpose. This is particularly evident with credit unions and building societies, both of which provided convenient vehicles for saving by small investors.

8 Building societies

Although they now operate in a very similar way to banks,[14] building societies were originally mutual organizations established for the purpose of enabling their members to build or acquire houses for residential use. The members would pool their savings. The fund thereby created would be used to make loans on mortgage to members for house purchase. Some building societies were set up for a limited period and were dissolved once the original membership had all acquired homes. Others were established on a permanent basis, and this was reflected in the name of the society, such as the Leeds Permanent Building Society.

Some early building societies took advantage of friendly society legislation, although they now have their own legislation.[15] Thus, they were able to obtain legal personality for the purpose of holding and managing property, for entering into contractual arrangements, and for bringing and defending legal actions. Nevertheless, as mutual organizations, they were—and in theory remain—controlled by their members (ie qualifying depositors and borrowers) without separate shareholders. The consequence of the controlling interest of the membership can be seen in what happens when it is proposed that a building society should merge with another, or be taken over by a public limited company. The members have to give their approval through a ballot to the proposed merger or takeover. Any payment made to the society will be distributed between the society's borrowers and depositors.

9 Endowment policies

The purchase of an endowment policy represents an indirect way of investing in the stock market and other assets. In return for either a single lump sum premium, or

---

[14] Northern Rock is a former building society that incorporated as a bank with public limited company status.
[15] Building Societies Act 1986 (as amended, including by the Building Societies Act 1997).

periodical premium payments, an insurance company offers a combination of life insurance and investment. In return for the life insurance element, the insurance company guarantees a lump sum payment if the policy-holder dies during a specified period. If the policy-holder does not die during that period, then the insurance company instead makes a lump sum payment to the policy-holder at the end of the term. This could either be a predetermined fixed sum (normally the same as that guaranteed on death), or a variable sum ('with profits') depending on the success of the investments made by the insurance company. With this latter form, each year the insurance company distributes a proportion of its profits between qualifying policy-holders. The policy-holders are not entitled to withdraw their allocated share of profits until their policy matures at the end of the specified period or earlier death. The allocated profits are therefore retained by the insurance company for this period and are available for it to lend at interest, to use for the purchase of property, or to invest on the stock market. These investments, in turn, will help to increase the insurance company's profits, which are again available for distribution between eligible policy-holders.

For many years, endowment policies were a popular way of repaying mortgages on residential property, but have now lost in popularity to unit trust arrangements.

10 Unit trusts

A unit trust is a complex form of equitable co-ownership.[16] An initial fund is established through subscriptions from investors. The fund thus established is used for the purchase of investments by the fund manager, the investments being held by a custodian trustee. The fund is valued, and on the basis of this valuation, notionally divided into units of equal value. Each investor is allocated a number of units proportionate to the amount that that investor originally subscribed. Although it is possible for a unit trust to contain no power of reinvestment,[17] most unit trusts permit the fund manager to alter the portfolio of investments, although often within special limits. The number of units can be increased or reduced to allow new investors to subscribe, or to allow existing investors to withdraw.

The rights of investors in a unit trust are a mix of contract and trust. The investment itself is made pursuant to a contract that defines the basis upon which units are bought and sold. The assets themselves are held on trust with the ultimate beneficiaries being the contributors as a whole,[18] although it is common for the contract to state that the investor acquires no proprietary right in the underlying assets in which investments are made. The effect of the contractual term is that no individual participant in a unit trust can call for the vesting in him or her of the property held in the scheme', thereby excluding the operation of the rule in *Saunders v Vautier*.[19]

---

[16] See *Costa & Duppe Properties Ltd v Duppe* [1986] VR 90.
[17] See *Re Municipal and General Securities Co Ltd's Trust* [1950] Ch 212.
[18] See *Re AEG Unit Trust Managers Ltd's Deed* [1957] Ch 415.   [19] (1841) 4 Beav 115.

11 Investment clubs

With this form of arrangement, a number of investors group into a syndicate. Each member of the syndicate subscribes an agreed amount each month or other agreed period. The members of the syndicate meet periodically and agree which investment will be acquired from the accumulated subscribed funds. The investment is purchased in the name of one or more of the syndicate who holds it upon trust for the others. The club rules provide what is to happen if the members of the syndicate fail to reach agreement, if they wish to wind the club up, or if one of them wishes to resign. An investment club is one type of unincorporated association. As described in Chapter 5, a syndicate purchasing tickets in the National Lottery works in a similar way. The organizer collects subscriptions from the members, and uses them to purchase tickets on behalf of the members. Any winnings will be held in trust for division between the members.

12 Pension funds and provision for retirement

(1) Methods of providing for retirement

In addition to the retirement pensions that are offered by the state and funded out of taxation,[20] individuals may make their own arrangements. They may do this either individually or through an occupational pension scheme, or through a combination of both. A very simple way of making individual provision is to save until retirement, and either to draw income and capital from the accumulated fund after retirement, or to use it to purchase an annuity. This is an arrangement with an insurance company under which the insurance company, in return for a lump sum, agrees to make annual[21] or other periodic payments at an agreed rate, either fixed or with provision for annual increases to allow for inflation, for the remainder of the annuitant's life. The arrangement is purely contractual. On the basis of actuarial information and advice, and a knowledge of current investment market conditions and returns, the insurance company can make a fairly accurate calculation of the cost of making the payments. In some cases, of course, the annuitant will live longer than expected, which will cost the insurance company more than the sum it received. If the insurance company has made its calculations correctly, however, these costs will be balanced by other cases in which the annuitant dies prematurely. The effect of an annuity is therefore to pass the risks of mortality on the erosion of the capital to the insurance company. Pensions provision is subject to a complex pattern of regulation which is beyond the scope of this book.[22]

---

[20] Including National Insurance contributions.   [21] Hence the term 'annuity'.
[22] Primarily contained in the Pension Schemes Act 1993 and the Pensions Acts 1995, 2004, 2007, 2008, and 2011. The 2004 Act has 325 sections and 13 schedules.

(2) **Types of pension scheme**

(a) **Personal pensions**

Instead of saving independently to raise the capital to purchase an annuity, most people planning to provide an income for retirement will do so through an arrangement with a financial services provider. One reason for doing this is that tax relief is available for qualifying pension savings plans. The investor gains the benefit of this tax relief, but cannot draw on the fund until retirement, and apart from a portion of the fund that can be drawn down tax-free, will pay tax on any benefits received.

(b) **Occupational pensions**

Occupational pensions were first introduced in the late nineteenth century, but became very much more important over the course of the twentieth century. A variety of forms were used for the introduction of such schemes. Some were, and in the public sector remain, unfunded. The pensions are then payable out of the annual revenue of the enterprise. The overwhelming majority of private occupational pension schemes, however, are funded.

(c) **Funded schemes**

Under a funded occupational pension scheme the employee and the employer generally both make contributions to an investment fund. That fund is then used to finance the payment of the pensions when they fall due. Although other means of providing for pensions are possible, the overwhelming majority of private sector pension funds are held by trustees under irrevocable trusts. One substantial reason for this was that the tax privileges accorded to 'approved schemes' used to be available only to pension schemes established in this way.[23] Funded schemes themselves divide into two main groups: money purchase schemes (otherwise known as defined contribution schemes) and defined benefit schemes.[24] There can in addition be special arrangements such as an 'executive pension plan' for a single employee.[25]

(i) *Money purchase schemes*

With a money purchase or defined contribution scheme, the pension fund of each member reflects the value of the investments purchased through the contributions relating to that individual.

(ii) *Defined benefit schemes*

Defined benefit schemes pay pensions based on a formula independent of the value of the investments held by the fund. This is usually a percentage of average earnings over

---

[23] Income and Corporation Taxes Act 1988, s 592, re-enacting a provision first found in Finance Act 1921, repealed by Finance Act 2004.

[24] Goode Report, paras 2.2.11–2.2.23. Some hybrid schemes have features of both defined-benefit and money-purchase. More detailed definitions are provided in Finance Act 2004, s 152.

[25] As in *Brooks v Brooks* [1996] AC 375. In this case, the House of Lords considered that special features of this bespoke pension plan meant that it constituted a marriage settlement that could be varied on divorce.

the period of pensionable service or (now more rarely) a percentage of final salary at the time of retirement. Most such schemes are 'balance of cost' schemes into which the employee pays a fixed contribution, with the employer being liable to supplement those contributions to the extent needed to make the scheme fully paid up. In the late twentieth century many of the schemes had an actuarial surplus (in other words the value of the investments exceeded the anticipated cost of pensions), but the combined effect of increased taxation, reduced investment returns, and increased life expectancy have meant that most schemes are now in deficit, and require substantially increased contributions over coming years if they are to continue to meet their liabilities.

(3) **Trusts and pension schemes**

(a) **The use of trusts in pension schemes**

The use of the trust as a means of providing for pensions enables the fund assets to be kept separate from the assets and liabilities of the employer. This offers some security in the event of the insolvency of the employer. The trust also means that where benefits are payable to someone other than the employee who is a member of the scheme, such as the employee's surviving spouse, the beneficiary has an enforceable claim which will not be barred by an absence of privity of contract. As explained earlier, it was previously a requirement for a scheme to qualify for tax benefits. Where the scheme is a defined benefit scheme, it might be wondered whether the trust vehicle is necessary at all. The benefits that the members will receive are defined by the rules of the scheme: the contributions that they make, and the benefits they will receive, are fixed. A simple contract could achieve the same. Similarly, the protection against the insolvency of the employer could equally be safeguarded by obtaining a guarantee from some third party, such as an insurance company or, indeed, by the contract for the provision of the pension being made directly by a third party such as an insurance company. It is now recognized that pension schemes, including occupational pension schemes, can operate without the use of a trust.

(b) **Characteristics of pension scheme trusts**

The trusts used in pension schemes have some distinctive characteristics. Pension schemes are not established by way of the generosity of a settlor, but as the result of contractual contributions which both the employer and the employee are contractually obliged to make. The beneficiaries therefore help to finance their own benefits:

> Even in a non-contributory scheme, the employer's payments are not bounty. They are part of the consideration for the services of the employee.[26]

The trustees are frequently interested in a pension fund as employers or employees,[27] rather than being wholly independent. Indeed, the Pensions Act 2004 requires that

---

[26] *McDonald v Horn* [1995] 1 All ER 961, at 973, per Hoffmann LJ.
[27] There is no reason why the trustees should not also be beneficiaries of the scheme: *Edge v Pensions Ombudsman* [1998] 2 All ER 547.

at least one-third of the total number of trustees must be trustees appointed by the members of the scheme (member-nominated trustees). The membership is not fixed, but open-ended. There is generally a wide power to alter the terms of the trust[28] and it is not uncommon for the pension fund to be established by an interim trust deed that is then replaced by a subsequent definitive trust instrument. It has been held that such a definitive trust deed operates retrospectively from the date of the establishment of the scheme,[29] but this has been described as 'controversial', and not applicable to alter vested rights.[30]

The special features of pension schemes could be expected to produce differences in the way in which trust law applies, and this is evident in the extensive special statutory rules and in some of the emerging case law,[31] although there are judges who have said that the administration of pension trusts should not be treated differently from the administration of other trusts. Speaking of investment, for instance, Sir Robert Megarry said:

> I can see no reason for holding that different principles apply to pension fund trusts from those which apply to other trusts. Of course, there are many provisions in pension schemes which are not to be found in private trusts, and to these the general law of trusts will be subordinated. But subject to that, I think that the trusts of pension funds are subject to the same rules as other trusts.[32]

Similarly, in *Re Trusts of Scientific Pension Plan* Ratee J, faced with a question as to the interpretation of a clause in a pension scheme, said:

> I accept that, as was said in *Mettoy Pension Trustees Ltd v Evans*,[33] 'the court's approach to the construction of documents relating to a pension scheme should be practical and purposive, rather than detached and literal', though I also accept that the ordinary principles of trust law apply to the terms of such a scheme once so construed.

The note, sounded in this statement, that a slightly different approach might be required from the ordinary for pension scheme deeds, was echoed in *Stevens v Bell*,[34] where Arden LJ, giving the sole opinion of the Court of Appeal on a complex issue of interpretation of the Airways Pension Scheme, said:

> A pension scheme should be construed so as to give a reasonable and practical effect to the scheme. The administration of a pension fund is a complex matter and it seems to me that it would be crying for the moon to expect the draftsman to have legislated exhaustively for every eventuality.[35]

---

[28] Pensions Act 1995, s 67 limits the extent to which such powers can be exercised, as amended by the Pensions Act 2004, s 262, which added s 67A-I detailing the exercise of these powers. Ss 68 and 69 (as amended) provide for pension schemes to be modified to implement the requirements of the Pensions Acts.

[29] *Re Imperial Foods Ltd Pension Scheme* [1986] 2 All ER 802 Walton J, Pen Schemes 23: Feb 2000.

[30] *Trustee Corpn Ltd v Nadir* [2001] BPIR 541 (Lawrence Collins J).

[31] See eg *Mihlenstedt v Barclays Bank plc* [1989] IRLR 522 and *Mettoy Pension Trustees Ltd v Evans* [1991] 2 All ER 513.

[32] *Cowan v Scargill* [1985] Ch 270, at 290. As we will see later in the chapter, such is the nature of the regulatory scheme under the Pensions Act 1995 relating to investment, it would be difficult to assert that pension trust investment is now subject to the same basic principles as other trusts.

[33] [1991] 2 All ER 513, at 537.   [34] [2002] EWCA 672.   [35] [2002] EWCA 672, at para 28.

The Goode Committee,[36] established to review the framework for occupational pension schemes in the wake of the Maxwell affair,[37] favoured the retention of trust law as the basis for providing and regulating such pensions.[38] The committee observed that 'trust law is indeed of considerable antiquity, but it has shown a remarkable ability to adapt itself to modern commercial requirements'.[39] The value of trust law lay in segregating assets for the protection of the beneficiaries; in providing a mechanism for the collective representation and protection of members of a group of people linked by a common interest; and in the embodiment of highly developed concepts of fiduciary responsibility. The committee therefore concluded:

> We therefore endorse the view expressed in the great weight of evidence submitted to us that trust law in itself is broadly satisfactory and should continue to provide the foundation for interests, rights and duties arising in relation to pension schemes. But, some of the principles of trust law require modification in their application to pensions.[40]

(c) Special duty of pension fund trustees

Most occupational pension schemes confer a wide measure of discretion upon the trustees. In accordance with ordinary principles of trust law, any powers that are held by a trustee will prima facie be held by them in a fiduciary capacity.[41] The trustees must therefore consider the best interests of the beneficiaries and exercise the power impartially and in accordance with its purpose.[42] The power will not be validly exercised if it has been exercised for an improper purpose, or as a result of illegitimate threats.[43] In *Re Courage Group's Pension Schemes* the Courage brewing group of companies had been taken over by Hanson Trust plc as part of the purchase of the Imperial Group. Hanson sought to be substituted as principal employer under the Courage Group scheme so that it could retain a surplus of approximately £70m on a sale of the Courage Group to Elders IXL Ltd, the brewers of Castlemaine XXXX. This surplus could then be used to fund pensions for other Hanson employees. Hanson sought to do this under a power in the pension trust deed that permitted variations that did not affect the main purpose of the fund. Millett J held that the power in the trust deed could be exercised only with the consent of the trustees,[44] and also that it would be improper for the trustees to give consent, since the exercise of the power in the present circumstances would

---

[36] *Report of the Pension Law Review Committee*, Chairman Professor Roy Goode (1993 Cm 2342) (the Goode Report).

[37] Robert Maxwell, who drowned in unexplained circumstances, had embezzled from his company pension schemes on a massive scale.   [38] Goode Report, para 4.1.14.

[39] Goode Report, para 4.1.9.

[40] Goode Report, para 4.1.14. The Pensions Acts from 1995 onwards have responded to this.

[41] *Re Hay's Settlement Trusts* [1981] 3 All ER 786.

[42] See Chapter 27 for a consideration on the exercise of powers by trustees.

[43] *Hillsdown Holdings plc v Pensions Ombudsman* [1997] 1 All ER 862.

[44] See also *Stannard v Fisons Pension Trust Ltd* [1992] IRLR 27, where the Court of Appeal held that transfer payments made in respect of a group of employees transferring to another scheme could not be determined solely by the scheme actuary, but had to be approved as fair by the trustees. See also *Re Imperial Food Ltd's Pension Scheme* [1986] 1 WLR 717.

be for a purpose inconsistent for that for which it was conferred.[45] The trustees were under an obligation to protect the interests of the employed members, pensioners, and deferred pensioners.[46] They would not be doing so if they permitted a variation in the trusts by the unilateral decision of a takeover raider. The employees, while having no legal right to any pension fund surpluses, were entitled to have them dealt with by consultation and negotiation.

(d) Duty to act in good faith

An attempt by Hanson Trust plc to capture a pension fund surplus again arose in *Imperial Group Pension Trust Ltd v Imperial Tobacco Ltd*.[47] The Imperial Group was taken over by Hanson plc. The Imperial Group pension scheme was very substantially in surplus. Hanson offered members the chance to transfer to a new pension scheme with enhanced guarantees against inflation, but under which the surplus could be transferred to Hanson instead of being used to augment pensions. Hanson did not appear to be prepared to consent to an amendment to the Imperial Group scheme to provide similar guarantees. Browne-Wilkinson V-C considered that it was a reasonable inference, although not a proven one, that Hanson was withholding its consent to the augmentation amendment under the Imperial scheme in order to seek control of the pension fund surplus by persuading members to transfer to the other scheme. In his view, if that were the case, Hanson would be withholding consent for a collateral purpose and would be acting unlawfully. Although in his view the power of the company to consent to variations in the scheme was not a fiduciary power, nor was it subject to an implied test of reasonableness, nevertheless pension schemes fell to be judged against the background of an employment relationship. As a matter of trust law:

> the pension trust deed and rules themselves are to be taken as being impliedly subject to the limitation that the rights and powers of the company can only be exercised in accordance with the implied obligation of good faith ... the company's right to give or withhold its consent to an amendment ... is subject to the implied obligation that the right shall not be exercised so as to destroy or seriously damage the relationship of confidence and trust between the company and its employees and former employees.[48]

There is a similar contractual obligation upon a company to act in good faith in regard to pension matters affecting employees and former employees.[49]

(e) Certain powers fiduciary

Browne-Wilkinson V-C held in the *Imperial Group* case that the power that the employer held was not fiduciary or subject to a test of reasonableness because such

---

[45] See also *Lock v Westpac Banking Corpn* (1991) 25 NSWLR 593.

[46] Deferred pensioners are members of a pension scheme who leave before retiring age, but are entitled under the rules of the scheme to receive a pension upon reaching normal retirement age. It is a requirement of legislation that retirement schemes should contain such a provision.   [47] [1991] 1 WLR 589.

[48] [1991] 1 WLR 589, at 598.

[49] *Mihlenstedt v Barclays Bank plc* [1989] IRLR 522; *National Grid plc v Mayes* [2001] 2 All ER 417, HL.

a limitation was not necessary to give business efficacy to the scheme. The question of implied limitations on powers held by employers must, however, be looked at in relation to each power individually. In *Mettoy Pension Trustees Ltd v Evans*[50] a provision in a pension trust provided that any surplus on dissolution 'may at the absolute discretion of the employer be applied to secure further benefits a pro and any further balance thereafter remaining' shall be paid to the employer. The company went into compulsory winding-up on insolvency. Warner J held that the power just set out was a fiduciary power. If the power was a beneficial one that the company was free to exercise or not as it chose, then it was meaningless. If there had been no power, and the company had been the beneficial owner under the rules of any surplus, then it would still have been able to augment the benefits of members if it chose. The company had therefore to be under some obligation in relation to the power if the rule was to have any consequence. Secondly, the members of the pension scheme were contributors, not volunteers. The power to augment pensions out of any surplus was something which they had contracted for; it was also unrealistic to suggest that their contributions had not played at least some role in the generation of the surplus.

Having concluded that the power was fiduciary, Warner J held that it would not vest in a receiver under a debenture issued by the company, since it did not form part of the company's beneficial assets. Neither could it be exercised or released by the liquidator, whose duties were to have regard primarily to the interests of the creditors and contributories of the company, which would create a conflict of interest between those persons and the beneficiaries under the pension scheme to whom the person exercising the power was also to have regard. Nor could the power be exercised by the directors of the company, since they lost all their powers on the appointment of the liquidator. Warner J was therefore led to the conclusion that in the absence of any other person to exercise the fiduciary power, it was for the court to do so.[51]

It has been suggested by one commentator that the cases concerning the exercise by trustees and employers of powers relating to the application of a pension fund surplus are swayed not just by ordinary principles of trust law, but also by the deeper-lying consideration that such surpluses should not be left at the mercy of company creditors and takeover predators.[52]

(f) Information

Members of pension schemes, like the beneficiaries under any trust, have the right to be given information about the administration of the trust.[53] Statutory regulations give flesh to that obligation so far as accounts and other financial information is concerned. David Hayton has argued that the common law should be developed, in recognition of

---

[50] [1991] 2 All ER 513. Parts of the decision were disapproved of in *Futter v Revenue and Customs* [2013] UKSC 26, but this does not affect the point discussed here.

[51] This was one of the options identified for the exercise of discretionary trusts by Lord Wilberforce in *McPhail v Doulton* [1970] 2 All ER 228, at 247. See Chapter 17.

[52] Gardner 'Fiduciary Powers in Toytown' (1991) 107 LQR 214.

[53] *Re Londonderry's Settlement* [1965] Ch 918, CA.

the differences between pension trusts and conventional private trusts, so as to impose a duty on pension trustees to give beneficiaries reasons for their decisions.[54]

(4) Pension fund surpluses

The notion that a pension fund might have a surplus may now seem unlikely, but it was not many years ago that the booming value of investments meant that many funds did indeed have actuarial surpluses. Where a pension scheme is wound up, the surplus is real in the sense that funds can remain even after fully making provision for meeting all pension liabilities by transferring responsibility for their payment to another financial organization. Where the fund is continuing, the surplus is more intangible since it represents simply an actuarial assessment that assets exceed liabilities. While the fund continues, there is always the possibility that some of the assumptions made by the actuary were mistaken. The salaries of scheme members might rise faster than the actuary has allowed, or the return on the fund's investments may be poorer than projected. Even a small difference in the assumptions in these matters can turn an apparently large actuarial surplus into a significant actual deficit. The calculation of surplus is therefore an imprecise matter.[55] But if it is confirmed that there is a surplus, who is entitled to it?

(a) Policy considerations
(i) Deferred remuneration?

A number of conflicting policy considerations enter into play. On the one hand, it has been said that occupational pensions reflect deferred remuneration: an employee is likely to accept lower wages where he will receive a pension on retirement than where he does not. An occupational pension is therefore an earned reward for employment.[56] The European Court of Justice has held that occupational pensions are to be regarded as deferred pay within the equal pay provisions of EU law.[57] The logic of this position is that the fund belongs to the employees, and not to the employer.

(ii) Relationship entirely contractual

Against this, it is said that pension scheme members have a contractual relationship with the pension scheme trustees in which the bargain is that the members make contributions and the scheme pays defined benefits in return. This bargain represents the whole of the relationship between the two, leaving no scope for a resulting trust.[58] This logic was applied in *Re West Sussex Constabulary's Widows, Children and Benevolent*

---

[54] 'Pension Trusts and Traditional Trust: Drastically Different Species of Trusts' [2005] Conv 229.

[55] See *Alitalia-Linee Aeree Italiane SPA v Rotunno* [2008] EWHC 185 (Ch).

[56] See *Parry v Cleaver* [1970] AC 1, at 16, per Lord Reid; *McDonald v Horn* [1995] 1 All ER 961, at 973; *The Halcyon Skies* [1977] QB 14.

[57] *Barber v Guardian Royal Exchange Insurance Group* [1991] 1 QB 344, ECJ.

[58] This principle was explained by A L Smith LJ in *Cunnack v Edwards* [1896] 2 Ch 679, at 683, a case which concerned the surplus funds of a society established to provide annuities for the widows of deceased members.

(1930) Fund Trusts[59] to a fund established to provide payments for the widows and dependants of policemen. When the fund was wound up, leaving a surplus, Goff J held that the members who had contributed to the fund could not recover back the share of the surplus attributable to their contributions because they had received all the benefit that they had contracted to receive. He similarly held that any fund surplus attributable to the proceeds of entertainments, raffles, sweepstakes, and other such fund-raising activities, should not be subject to a resulting trust because the participants had acted on the basis of a contractual bargain for services received:

> the relationship is one of contract and not of trust; the purchaser of a ticket may have the motive of aiding the cause or he may not; he may purchase a ticket merely because he wishes to attend the particular entertainment or to try for the prize, but whichever it be, he pays his money as the price of what is offered and what he receives.[60]

In later cases it has been held that a resulting trust analysis might be adopted in respect of a pension fund surplus, despite the contractual nature of the contributions made. In *Davis v Richards and Wallington Industries Ltd*[61] Scott J held that:

> the fact that a payment to a fund has been made under contract and that the payer has obtained all that he or she bargained for under the contract is not necessarily a decisive argument against a resulting trust.[62]

This approach was adopted by the Privy Council in *Air Jamaica Ltd v Charlton*,[63] which also concerned a pension fund surplus attributable to the contributions of the employers and employees of a company. Lord Millett explained that employees should not be excluded from obtaining an interest in a pension fund surplus merely because they had received what they had contracted to receive:

> Their Lordships would observe that, even in the ordinary case of an actuarial surplus, it is not obvious that, when employees are promised certain benefits under a scheme to which they have contributed more than was necessary to fund them, they should not expect to obtain a return of their excess contributions.[64]

A further weakness with the argument that the contract expresses the whole relationship is that if this is true of the employees there is no obvious reason why the same logic should not be applied to the employer leaving the fund with no owner. The surplus would therefore pass in its entirety to the Crown as bona vacantia.

(iii) Employer alone created the surplus

In a balance of cost scheme, it is arguable that since the employer tops up the fund to the extent to which it is in deficit, any surplus represents an overpayment by the employer, so that it should be returned to the employer. A different way of putting the

---

[59] [1971] Ch 1.   [60] [1971] Ch 1, at 11.
[61] [1991] 2 All ER 563; [1991] Conv 366 (Martin); Gardner 'New Angles on Unincorporated Associations' [1992] Conv 41.   [62] [1991] 2 All ER 563, at 593.   [63] [1999] 1 WLR 1399.
[64] [1999] 1 WLR 1399, at 1412.

same argument is that a surplus represents a mistaken overpayment by the employer that should be refunded. An alternative but similar argument in a balance of cost scheme is that since the employer bears the risk of having to increase contributions if the fund falls into deficit, then it is just that the employer should, by compensation, reap the benefit of any accrued surplus.

This argument has been adopted in some cases.[65] For instance in *Re Courage Group's Pension Schemes*[66] Millett J said:

> ...any surplus arises from past overfunding, not by the employer and the employees pro rata to their respective contributions, but by the employer alone to the full extent of its past contributions and only subject thereto by the employees.

However, in *Scully v Coley*[67] where the Privy Council had to decide how funds remaining on the winding up of a balance of cost scheme should be distributed, the argument was not even alluded to. The Privy Council held that the terms of the scheme required the funds to be distributed between the employee members at the time of the winding up and 'there is no surplus where the trustees have to use up the balance of the funds in the payment of benefits.' In addition, no direct claim appears to have been made by the employer.

(iv) Surplus reflects underpayments in the past

It could be argued that if a surplus arises, it is because the trustees have been too cautious in their decisions about such matters as augmenting pension payments to reflect inflation. To redress low past pension increases in circumstances where higher increases were affordable, the surplus should be used to augment benefits for pensioners.[68]

(v) Surplus reflects joint efforts

Finally, a more neutral policy argument is that the scheme has been created (in most cases) by contributions from both employees and employer, so the surplus has been contributed to by both. This was the view taken by the Privy Council in *Air Jamaica Ltd v Charlton*.[69]

(vi) Joint tenancy

The preceding arguments are based primarily on a resulting trust analysis of ownership of surplus funds. However a resulting trust analysis is not the only possible way of analysing entitlement to a pension fund surplus. It would be equally and perhaps more appropriate to apply the same analysis as that used to explain the ownership of the funds of unincorporated associations: namely that the members are beneficially

---

[65] See *Davis v Richards & Wallington Industries Ltd* [1990] 1 WLR 1511 and the cases cited in the next note.

[66] [1987] 1 WLR 495, at 515. See also *Wrightson Ltd v Fletcher Challenge Nominees Ltd* [2001] PLR 207 where Lord Millett made a very similar point.   [67] [2009] UKPC 29, at [45].

[68] This was the logic which underpinned the Pension Funds Second Amendment Act 2001 (South Africa).

[69] [1999] 1 WLR 1399.

entitled as tenants-in-common, subject to the rules by which the members are linked. This analysis is based, not on the origin of the funds, but on who is intended to benefit from them on receipt. Except where the terms of the scheme provide otherwise, it is not expected by contributors that they are doing anything other than making outright payments into the trust. Since the trustees cannot be beneficially entitled, only the members can be beneficial owners. In appropriate cases (and depending on the terms of the scheme), the employers might also have a share of the beneficial ownership. In the event of a winding up of the scheme it would be necessary to quantify the shares of the members. Scott J in *Davis v Richards and Wallington Industries Ltd*,[70] thought that it would be impossible to devise a scheme dividing any surplus equitably between the members in the event of a resulting trust distribution, but these concerns would not apply to a distribution which required no detailed analysis of the sums contributed by each member. Insurance companies routinely divide profits between 'with profits' investors who have contributed to an investment fund, and a distribution of the kind which Scott J thought was impractical was ordered in *Scully v Coley*.[71] However, while a pensions trust is still in operation there would be 'a range of conceptual and practical difficulties' which might well be insuperable in seeking to identify any specific part of a surplus to which any individual could claim entitlement.[72]

(vii) Do these arguments matter?

There is an argument that the way in which a pension fund surplus arises is irrelevant if one is considering how the rules of a scheme should be interpreted, and this is the primary task of the court.[73]

(b) Entitlement to pension fund surplus on winding up

When an employer ceases business, any associated pension scheme is likely to be closed to new members unless it either formed part of an industry-wide or group-wide scheme, or the whole scheme is transferred to another continuing scheme. The scheme could continue in existence until all pension entitlements are discharged in full. Alternatively the trustees could use the assets of the fund to purchase cover from an insurance company for the pensions which have or may become payable. In the latter two cases, if the scheme is solvent, a surplus will arise for distribution. There may be express provision for this in the scheme. For instance the scheme may well provide that any surplus is to be paid to the employer, once augmentation of benefits has been made to all members.[74] In *Scully v Coley*[75] the scheme provided that the whole of any surplus was to be applied, subject to the approval of the employer (a provision which

---

[70] [1991] 2 All ER 563. See also Chapter 20.   [71] [2009] UKPC 29.

[72] *Entrust Pension Ltd v Prospect Hospice Ltd* [2012] EWHC 1666 (Ch) (claim made on basis of interpretation of scheme rules).

[73] See *National Grid Co plc v Mayes* [2001] UKHL 20; *Stevens v Bell* [2002] EWCA Civ 672; *IMG Pension Plan HR Trustees Ltd v German* [2009] EWHC 2785 (Ch) at [110]. See also *The PNPF Trust Company Ltd v Taylor* [2010] EWHC 1573 (Ch) at [129].

[74] A clause similar to this was contained in the trust deed in *Bridge Trustees Ltd v Noel Penny (Turbines) Ltd* [2008] EWHC 2054.   [75] [2009] UKPC 29.

the court appears to have disregarded) in augmenting pension benefits. If there is no express provision, how should the surplus be applied? If no owner can be found, the surplus will pass as bona vacantia to the Crown. The courts are generally reluctant to choose this as a solution.[76] The question then remains as to how the balance should be divided between the only two other groups of potential claimant, the employers and the scheme members. In *Davis v Richards and Wallington Industries Ltd*,[77] Scott J chose to adopt a resulting trust analysis. The pension fund had been created by contributions from both employers and employees. In the absence of some term in the trust deed or rules excluding a resulting trust,[78] Scott J held that any surplus should revert to them as contributors.[79] However, he held that the employees should receive nothing because they had received the contractual benefits which were all they could expect to receive; their contributions could be seen as exhausted because their contributions alone would probably have been insufficient to provide those benefits; quantifying their shares would be impracticably difficult; and to give them any benefits would exceed the allowable limits under tax laws. The surplus had therefore been generated by contributions from the employer who, with hindsight, had contributed more than was necessary under the balance of cost provisions in the scheme. The whole of the surplus was therefore held upon trust for the employers. Much of Scott J's reasoning was rejected by the Privy Council in *Air Jamaica Ltd v Charlton*,[80] which also concerned a pension fund surplus attributable to the contributions of the employers and employees of a company. It was held that the fund should be divided between both. Lord Millett explained that employees should not be excluded from obtaining an interest in a pension fund surplus merely because they had received what they had contracted to receive:

> Their Lordships would observe that, even in the ordinary case of an actuarial surplus, it is not obvious that, when employees are promised certain benefits under a scheme to which they have contributed more than was necessary to fund them, they should not expect to obtain a return of their excess contributions.[81]

The Privy Council doubted that Scott J had been correct to exclude a resulting trust in favour of the employees. Rather than being required to value the benefits that each member had received in order to ascertain his share, the Privy Council held that the members' share of the surplus should be 'divided pro rata among the members and the estates of deceased members in proportion to the contributions made by each member without regard to the benefits each has received and irrespective of the dates on which the contributions were made'.[82] The company was also held entitled to a resulting trust

---

[76] *Jones v Williams* (15 March 1988, unreported) (Knox J), cited by Scott J in *Davis v Richard and Wallington Industries Ltd* [1991] 2 All ER 563; *Air Jamaica Ltd v Charlton* [1999] 1 WLR 1399.

[77] [1991] 2 All ER 563. See also Chapter 20.

[78] As in the decision of Foster J in *Re ABC Television Pension Scheme* [1989] PLR 21, to which he referred.

[79] Compare *Re Gillingham Bus Disaster Fund* [1958] Ch 300 and *Re West Sussex Constabulary's Widows, Children and Benevolent (1930) Fund Trusts* [1971] Ch 1, discussed earlier.

[80] [1999] 1 WLR 1399.

[81] [1999] 1 WLR 1399, at 1412.   [82] [1999] 1 WLR 1399, at 1413.

of the proportion of the surplus attributable to its contributions, despite the presence of a clause in the trust deed stating that 'no moneys which at any time have been contributed by the company under the terms hereof shall in any circumstances be repayable to the company'. The Privy Council considered that this clause only operated to prevent repayments to the company under the terms of the scheme, and did not exclude the possibility of a resulting trust if the scheme came to an end:

> Consequently their Lordships think that clauses of this kind in a pension scheme should generally be construed as forbidding the repayment of contributions under the terms of the scheme, and not as a pre-emptive but misguided attempt to rebut a resulting trust which would arise dehors the scheme. The purpose of such clauses is to preclude any amendment that would allow repayment to the company.[83]

(c) Entitlement to a surplus while the scheme continues

The Inland Revenue requires that a surplus should be eliminated within a set period[84] but it imposes no requirement as to how the surplus should be reduced. That is a matter for the rules of the trust or for any approved amendment. The rules may permit augmentation of pension benefits, a suspension or reduction of the contributions payable by the employer and sometimes also of the employee, or a cash payment to the employer. In most instances, more than one of these options will be available. In every case concerning the application of a surplus, the answer will depend upon the proper interpretation of the scheme rules.[85] For instance, in *British Coal Corpn v British Coal Staff Superannuation Scheme Trustees Ltd*[86] a question arose relating to a substantial actuarial surplus that had been built up within the coal industry pension scheme. Under the rules of the scheme, a surplus was to be applied, first, to provide full indexation for any pensions payable;[87] second, to reduce the contributions of the employer until the employer was reimbursed for any payments which had been made in respect of actuarial deficiencies in the fund; third, to meet any increase in pensions to reflect the cost of living in the next calendar year; and, finally, after retaining whatever reserve was considered desirable, to apply any remaining balance in equal parts for the benefit of members (by reducing contributions or increasing benefits) and for the benefit of the employer. The scheme contained a provision that permitted alterations to the rules, although a proviso prohibited any alteration 'making any of the moneys of the Scheme payable to any of the Employers'. As part of its plans to reduce its workforce, the Coal Corporation had entered into an agreement with the pension fund trustees to increase the benefits of employees made redundant by offering enhanced pensions. The Corporation agreed to fund these additional benefits by paying the additional costs to the pension fund trustees in instalments over a ten-year

---

[83] [1999] 1 WLR 1399, at 1412.

[84] The period allowed for the elimination of the surplus depends upon the means used to reduce it. For an account of the rules and recommendations for change, see the Goode Report, paras 4.3.20–4.3.37.

[85] Subject to limits imposed by the Pensions Act 1995, s 37 (as amended by the Pensions Act 2004). These are mentioned later in the chapter.   [86] [1995] 1 All ER 912.

[87] In other words, to increase pensions fully in line with any increase in the cost of living.

period. Before all the payments had been made, a revaluation of the fund showed that there was a surplus. The Corporation claimed to be able to set off the outstanding balance of the additional payments it had agreed to make against the part of the actuarial surplus that was to be applied to the employer. Vinelott J held that this was prohibited by the rules of the scheme. The Corporation had agreed to pay the trustees a lump sum. That could not be repaid to the Corporation under the rules. It made no difference that the sum was payable in instalments, since relieving the Corporation from liability in respect of an instalment would have the same effect as a repayment of an instalment already made.

An almost identical issue arose in *National Grid Co plc v Mayes*,[88] where the House of Lords was asked to rule whether the National Grid and International Power could use part of a pension fund surplus to meet the cost of supporting enhanced early retirement pensions which the companies had already agreed to pay by instalments, although they had not completed making those instalments. The House of Lords held that Vinelott J had come to the wrong conclusion in the *British Coal* case. The purpose of the prohibition on payments to the employers was to meet Inland Revenue restrictions that forbade the repayment of money contributed to the pension scheme, since those contributions had benefited from taxation privileges. That fiscal consideration did not apply to payments that, although agreed to be made, had not at that stage been paid. Moreover, it was not in dispute that the employer could take advantage of a surplus to reduce future contributions, if this was permitted by the rules of the scheme. There was no practical difference between reducing the standard rate of future contributions and cancelling instalment payments that had previously been agreed. Both actions had the same effect of reducing the total value of the fund. In the *National Grid* case, the House of Lords considered that, if it was necessary, the rules of the pension scheme could be amended to permit the payment of the surplus to the employers, since the rules conferred a power to make amendments, and did not forbid the use of the power to allocate the surplus in these circumstances.

(d) Who owns a pension fund?

Knott J in *London Regional Transport Pension Fund Trustee Co Ltd v Hatt*[89] has said that it is 'quite impossible, as well as simplistic, to try to identify the owner or owners of a surplus'. Pension funds are created to provide benefits not only for employees, but also for their dependants, some of whom may not be born. The true position with pension schemes may therefore be that the search for an 'owner' of the fund, in the sense that is possible with fixed trusts, is illusory. Just as with discretionary trusts,[90] or with the administration of estates,[91] it may be that the real claim of both employers and members of a pension scheme is not to ownership, but to the due administration of the scheme and trust.

---

[88] [2001] WLR 864.
[89] [1993] PLR 227.   [90] See *McPhail v Doulton* [1971] AC 424, HL.
[91] *Stamp Duties Comr (Queensland) v Livingston* [1965] AC 694, PC.

(5) **Enforcement of rights by members**

Employees, former employees, and pensioners are all beneficiaries under the trust deed in a pension scheme and therefore have the rights of any beneficiary to bring actions for breach of trust or in relation to the administration of the trust. The costs of the litigation can be substantial, with little direct benefit to an individual plaintiff. Plaintiffs might be assisted in bringing an action by a trade union, and there is also the possibility of the court ordering that the costs of a hearing should be borne out of the pension fund assets, whatever the outcome at trial.[92] Members of a pension scheme may also take complaints to the Pensions Ombudsman, who has statutory powers to deal with complaints concerning occupational and personal pension schemes.

---

[92] See *McDonald v Horn* [1995] 1 All ER 961.

PART VI

Administration of Trusts

23

Delegation by trustees

In consequence of his position, a trustee enjoys powers of control and management over the trust fund. In some situations, for example where property is subject to a discretionary trust, the trustee even enjoys the discretion to choose how the trust fund should be allocated amongst the beneficiaries. The precise duties and powers that a trustee will have depend upon the express terms of the trust deed creating the trust, or those that are implied by statute. In some circumstances it will be clear that the trustee is not the appropriate person to perform all the functions required of him as trustee, perhaps because he lacks the necessary expertise. He could obviously take advice and then carry out the function, but he may also wish to delegate the function to someone who can perform it properly for him. This chapter considers the authority, rights, and responsibilities involved in trustees delegating some or all of their trustee functions to third parties.

1 Introduction

Traditionally, equity has been reluctant to permit delegation by trustees of their powers in the absence of an express power provided in the trust instrument, but statutory powers of delegation have increasingly been available to trustees. The position for most trusts is now governed by the Trustee Act 2000, which has substantially changed the approach to delegation.

It should be noted that there are two forms of delegation. The trustees, acting together, may decide to delegate collectively a function to an agent. Alternatively, a single trustee may seek, for instance during a temporary period of absence, to assign his individual functions to a person to exercise on his behalf. This chapter looks first at collective delegation before considering individual delegation, although some elements of the discussion apply to both forms of delegation.

2 Delegation at common law

(1) **The general principle: no delegation of trustees' duties**

Traditionally, equity took the view that a trustee had no power to delegate his powers to an agent, either individually or collectively. As the Latin maxim expresses it: *delegatus non potest delegare*. This was emphasized by Lord Langdale MR in *Turner v Corney*,[1] which involved a trust where there was an express power of delegation. He stated that:

> trustees who take on themselves the management of property for the benefit of others have no right to shift their duty on other persons; and if they employ an agent, they remain subject to responsibility toward their cestui que trust, for whom they have undertaken the duty.

The rationale for this restriction was that the settlor had placed his confidence in the trustees he had chosen to perform the trust obligations.[2] As Lord Westbury stated in *Robson v Flight*:

> such trusts and powers are supposed to have been committed by the [settlor] to the trustees he appoints by reason of his personal confidence in their discretion, and it would be wrong to permit them to be exercised by [another].[3]

However, in consequence of the evolution of the law, this general principle must now be replaced by the more moderate position stated by Lord Radcliffe in *Pilkington v IRC*:[4] 'the law is not that trustees cannot delegate: it is that trustees cannot delegate unless they have authority to do so'. Thus, the central question is as to the circumstances in which trustees enjoy the authority to delegate their responsibilities.

(2) **A limited entitlement to delegate**

(a) **Delegation in the ordinary course of business**

During the eighteenth century the courts came to accept that, in some circumstances, delegation to an agent was required for reasons of commercial practicality. In *Learoyd v Whiteley*,[5] Lord Watson therefore stated a general principle permitting trustees to delegate their functions:

> whilst trustees cannot delegate the execution of the trust, they may...avail themselves of the services of others wherever such employment is according to the usual course of business.[6]

---

[1] (1841) 5 Beav 515. See also *Robson v Flight* (1865) 4 De GJ & SM 608, at 613, per Lord Westbury LC; *Speight v Gaunt* (1883) 22 Ch D 727, at 756, per Lindley LJ.

[2] *Speight v Gaunt* (1883) 9 App Cas 1, at 29, per Lord Fitzgerald.

[3] (1865) 4 De GJ & SM 608, at 613.

[4] [1964] AC 612, HL. See also Jones 'Delegation by Trustees: A Reappraisal' [1959] MLR 381.

[5] (1887) 12 App Cas 727.   [6] (1887) 12 App Cas 727, 734.

(b) Scope of the right to delegate

The common law power of trustees to delegate within the ordinary course of business did not, however, entitle trustees to delegate all of their functions or duties. The right to delegate extended only in respect of their ministerial acts, in other words those that did not require an exercise of discretion on their part. Trustees were not permitted to delegate their discretions,[7] such as the selection of trust investments,[8] or the decision whether or not to sell[9] or lease[10] trust property. Thus, whilst trustees were able to delegate the implementation of their decisions and the routine administration of the trust, they were required to continue to take all the basic decisions themselves.

(3) Trustees' liability for the acts of their agent

The mere fact that trustees were entitled to appoint an agent, whether because such an appointment was within the ordinary course of business or for reasons of necessity, did not mean that they were free from personal liability for any loss caused by the acts of the agent. Trustees would be personally liable for breach of trust if the agent they appointed was not appropriate, or if they failed to exercise adequate supervision, on the grounds that they had acted other than as reasonably prudent men of business.

(a) Agent employed outside of the scope of his business

A trustee who had legitimately delegated to an agent was liable to the trust if he employed an agent to carry out functions that were outside of the scope of his ordinary business.[11] As Kay J said in *Fry v Tapson*:[12]

> *Speight v Gaunt* did not lay down any new rule, but only illustrated a very old one, viz., that trustees acting according to the ordinary course of business, and employing agents as a prudent man of business would do on his own behalf are not liable for the default of an agent so employed. But an obvious limitation to that rule is that the agent must not be employed out of the ordinary scope of his business. If the trustee employs an agent to do that which is not the ordinary business of such an agent, and he performs that unusual task improperly, and loss is thereby occasioned, the trustee would not be exonerated.[13]

The trustees, who were considering investing trust funds on a mortgage, had delegated the task of selecting a valuer for the land concerned to their solicitors. The solicitors recommended a London surveyor, who did not have local knowledge of the area where the land was situated,[14] and who also had a pecuniary interest in the grant of the mortgage, as he would receive a commission of £75 if the mortgage was granted. He overvalued the property and the trustees lent £5,000, which was lost when the mortgagor

---

[7] *Speight v Gaunt* (1883) 9 App Cas 1. This limitation was restated in *Scott v National Trust* [1998] 2 All ER 705, at 717, per Robert Walker J.   [8] *Rowland v Witherden* (1851) 3 Mac & G 568.
[9] *Clarke v Royal Panopticon* (1857) 4 Drew 26; *Green v Whitehead* [1930] 1 Ch 38.
[10] *Robson v Flight* (1865) 4 De GJ & SM 608.
[11] See *Re Earl of Litchfield* (1737) 1 Atk 87; *Ghost v Waller* (1846) 9 Beav 497; *Rowland v Witherden* (1851) 3 Mac & G 568; *Re Gasquoine* [1894] 1 Ch 470.   [12] (1884) 28 Ch D 268.
[13] (1884) 28 Ch D 268, at 280.   [14] See also *Budge v Gummow* (1872) 7 Ch App 719.

became bankrupt. The trustees were held liable to replace this loss to the trust fund because it was out of the ordinary course of business of solicitors to appoint a valuer.

(b) Trustees' duty to supervise agents

Trustees who appointed an agent were under a duty properly to supervise his activities. The standard of care required was that of the ordinary prudence which a man uses in his own business affairs.[15] In *Rowland v Witherden*,[16] for example, trustees had committed the management of a trust fund completely to a solicitor, who had misapplied it. The Lord Chancellor held that the trustees were liable for their failure properly to supervise the solicitor's activities:

> The short result of the case is, that the trustees, instead of themselves seeing to the investment of the trust fund, delegated that duty to their solicitor, who misapplied the money…The trustees were bound to satisfy themselves in some way other than by the mere assurances of their solicitor, and by payments made by him as for interest, that the money was really advanced on mortgage. But they did not even require a sight of the mortgage deed, but simply paid the money to their solicitor and implicitly relied on his integrity…[17]

Similarly, in *Fry v Tapson*[18] Kay J held that the trustees would be liable for their acceptance of the valuation 'without attempting to check it'.[19]

3 Trustee Act 1925: a statutory right to delegate

Prior to the Trustee Act 1925 trustees were only entitled to appoint an agent when this was reasonably necessary or was within the ordinary course of business. The Trustee Act 1925[20] considerably extended the powers of trustees to delegate functions to agents by dispensing with the requirement that the delegation be reasonably necessary or in the ordinary course of business. However, the powers were still relatively restrictive—for instance only ministerial functions could normally be delegated—and the provisions of the Act relating to the liability of trustees where they had delegated a function were obscure to the point of unintelligibility. The leading case on the liability of trustees who had delegated functions to an agent was *Re Vickery*,[21] but even though this was reported in 1931, questions remained about the interpretation both of the statutory provisions and of this case some seventy years later. Few doubted that the position under the Act was unsatisfactory, not least the students who were required to grapple in examinations with the problems created by the statutory provisions or practitioners giving advice on them.[22]

---

[15] *Munch v Cockerell* (1840) 5 My & Cr 178; *Mendes v Guedalla* (1862) 2 John & H 259; *Speight v Gaunt* (1883) 22 Ch D 727.   [16] (1851) 3 Mac & G 568.   [17] (1851) 3 Mac & G 568, at 574.
[18] (1884) 28 Ch D 268.   [19] (1884) 28 Ch D 268, at 282.   [20] S 23 (now repealed).
[21] [1931]1 Ch 572.
[22] For a lively discussion and summary of the issues, see *Trustees' Powers and Duties* (1997) Law Com Consultation Paper No 146, Part IV.

In 1982 the Law Reform Committee considered whether the scope for delegation should be widened to encompass the trustees' discretions as well as ministerial functions, but concluded that the distinction between the delegation of administrative and managerial functions and of their discretions should be maintained.[23] However, in its Consultation Paper, *Trustees' Powers and Duties*, the Law Commission suggested that the climate of opinion had changed and that trustees should be entitled to delegate the task of managing the trust property to a fund manager, who would be entitled to make investment decisions within the context of an investment policy determined by the trustees:

> We consider that there is no longer any continued justification for the existing restrictions on trustees' powers of collective delegation. The principal objection to the present law is that trustees' powers of investment and certain of their powers of management (such as the power to sell, lease or mortgage trust property) are regarded in all respects as fiduciary. As such they must be exercised by the trustees alone and are non-delegable. This position was the product of a time when the decisions which trustees had to take were both comparatively straightforward and infrequent. However, it is increasingly unrealistic, given that many of these tasks (particularly in relation to investment) now arise regularly and often require speedy professional advice and execution. We consider that the 'exigencies of business' now justify the delegation of these discretions because adherence to the present restrictions is likely to frustrate the trustees' paramount duty to act in the best interests of the trust.[24]

Judicial notice was also taken of the difficulty caused by the inability of the trustees to delegate their discretions. In *Scott v National Trust* Robert Walker J stated:

> trustees may not (except in so far as they are authorised to do so) delegate the exercise of their discretions, even to experts. This sometimes creates real difficulties, especially when lay trustees have to digest and assess expert advice on a highly technical matter (to take merely one instance, the disposal of actuarial surplus in a superannuation fund).[25]

4 The current statutory framework

The Trustee Act 2000 now provides the framework for delegation by trustees. It distinguishes between two principal situations: delegation by charity trustees, and delegation by other trustees. The position the Act takes is much more radical in the latter case than it is in the former. There is also special provision for pension scheme trustees and some other special situations. Although not so described in the Act, the power of delegation conferred on most trustees can conveniently be called the general power of delegation.

---

[23] Law Reform Committee, *23rd Report* (Cmnd 8733), para 4.3.   [24] Para 5.16.
[25] [1998] 2 All ER 705, at 717.

(1) **General power of delegation**

The approach adopted by the Trustee Act 2000 to most trustees is radically new. Instead of specifying when trustees may appoint agents, the Act confers a general power to delegate any function other than certain non-delegable functions.[26] This is a complete reversal of the previous position.

The functions that *cannot* be delegated by trustees to an agent are:

(a) decisions concerning the distribution of the trust assets;[27]

(b) decisions as to whether costs or fees should be debited to capital or to income;[28]

(c) the appointment of new trustees;[29]

(d) any power to delegate trustee functions or to appoint a nominee or custodian.[30]

In addition, trustees of land who are obliged to consult the beneficiaries before exercising any of their powers may not delegate the obligation to carry out this consultation.[31] Should they delegate any function that involves a duty to consult, it must be on terms that enable the trustees to conduct that consultation and to give effect to the wishes of the beneficiaries.[32]

The connecting link between the matters that the trustees cannot delegate is that they are functions that lie at the heart of trusteeship and have a clear fiduciary content.[33] The functions that can be delegated include all ministerial acts (ie the implementation of decisions already taken), including the implementation of decisions relating to the distribution of trust funds. However, unlike the previous position, it is also possible for the trustees to delegate functions that may require the exercise of discretions or decisions. For instance, if Andrew and Brenda are appointed as trustees of a valuable collection of antiquarian books, some of which need rebinding, they could delegate to a librarian acquaintance the task of finding a craftsman with the appropriate skills. Similarly, they can delegate their investment functions, including the choice of which investments to make, although there are special rules applying to the delegation of asset management that were considered in Chapter 21.[34]

(2) **Delegation by charity trustees**

The Act maintains for charity trustees the position under the pre-existing law that the trustees can delegate only in prescribed situations.[35] The reason for limiting the

---

[26] Trustee Act 2000, s 11(1) and (2).   [27] Trustee Act 2000, s 11(2)(a).

[28] Trustee Act 2000, s 11(2)(b).   [29] Trustee Act 2000, s 11(2)(c).

[30] Trustee Act 2000, s 11(2)(d).   [31] Trustee Act 2000, s 13(3), (4), and (5).

[32] Trustee Act 2000, s 13(4).

[33] See further Chapter 28 for a discussion of the fiduciary duties imposed on trustees.

[34] In essence, this requires that the trustees make the delegation in writing or evidenced in writing, and prepare a policy statement giving guidance as to how the agent must exercise their investment functions in the best interests of the trust. Liability arises if the trustees fail to keep the appointment of the agent under review, and/or fail to intervene if a problem arises, under the general duty of care in s 1 and Sch 1 of the Trustee Act 2000.   [35] Trustee Act 2000, s 11(3).

powers of charity trustees to delegate is that there are some functions that are so central to the trust that it would not be appropriate for anyone other than the trustees to exercise them. For instance, the decision as to how to distribute funds by a charity established to make grants is something that should be under the immediate control of the trustees. The Explanatory Memorandum to the Act suggests that to have conferred a general authority on charity trustees to delegate, but to prohibit the delegation by charity trustees of distributive functions, or even of 'charitable functions', could unduly have narrowed the powers of charity trustees to appoint agents.

The delegable functions[36] of charity trustees are:

(a) carrying out a decision already made by the charity trustees;[37]

(b) investing the trust assets, or carrying out any function relating to investment;[38]

(c) carrying out any function relating to fund raising other than the raising of funds 'by means of profits of a trade which is an integral part of carrying out the trust's charitable purpose', the trade being something which is carried out as a primary purpose of the trust or is mainly carried out by the beneficiaries of the trust.[39]

This short list of delegable functions can be extended by delegated legislation made by the Secretary of State.[40]

The policy adopted by the Act is to allow the delegation of ministerial acts (executing decisions already taken). So far as discretions are concerned, the Act distinguishes between the functions of charity trustees relating to the generation of income to finance the charitable purposes (which can be delegated) and those relating to carrying out of the charitable purposes (which cannot be delegated). The proviso in s 13(3)(c) relating to trades which are conducted mainly by beneficiaries or which are a primary purpose of the trust is designed to prevent, say, the trustees of a school operating under a charitable trust from delegating their discretions relating to the running of the school. The trustees of a charitable housing association operating by way of trust would be in a similar position.

(3) Delegation by pension fund trustees and other special cases

The general power of delegation described earlier is restricted in its application to pension scheme trustees. Pension scheme trustees are not permitted to delegate investment functions under the general power,[41] or to appoint nominees or custodians,[42] although in other respects pension fund trustees may employ the general power of delegation. Another restriction on pension scheme trustees is that, in order to avoid

[36] Current guidance from the Charity Commission of the delegable functions by charity trustees can be found in OG86 B3, 'Power to Employ Agents and Delegate Functions to them' (Charity Commission, 2012).
[37] Trustee Act 2000, s 11(3)(a).   [38] Trustee Act 2000, s 11(3)(b).
[39] Trustee Act 2000, s 11(3)(c) and (4).   [40] Trustee Act 2000, s 11(3)(d) and (5).
[41] Trustee Act 2000, s 36(5).   [42] Trustee Act 2000, s 36(8).

potential conflicts of interest, they may not appoint as an agent an employer or a person who is connected with or an associate of an employer.[43]

The reason for excluding the power to delegate investment functions is that there are special provisions dealing with this in the Pensions Act 1995, which contains special safeguards to protect the rights of occupational pension scheme members. Section 34(2)(a) of the Pensions Act 1995 provides that the trustees of a pension trust scheme may delegate any decision about investments to a fund manager, who must be authorized to conduct investment business under the Financial Services and Markets Act 2000. Where such delegation occurs the trustees are required to prepare, maintain, and from time to time revise a written statement of the principles governing decisions about investments for the purpose of the scheme outlining their policy about the following matters: the kinds of investments to be held; the balance between different kinds of investments; risk; the expected return on investments; and the realization of investments.[44] Thus, the trustees are required to set the general policy that investment decisions should follow, but they can delegate the selection of specific investments to meet such a strategy to the fund manager. The trustees may also delegate decisions about investments to two or more of their number,[45] or to a fund manager operating outside the United Kingdom in respect of overseas investment business.[46]

The general power of delegation does not apply to trustees of authorized unit trusts[47] or to trustees of a common investment scheme or of a common deposit scheme made under the Charities Act 2011.[48]

(4) **Who may be appointed agent**

The trustees have a wide discretion as to whom they may appoint as an agent. They may even appoint one or more of the trustees as agent[49] (for instance four trustees might wish to delegate to one of their number the task of negotiating the terms of a lease for premises to be occupied by the trust), or a person who has already been appointed as a nominee or custodian.[50] The trustees may not authorize two different people to undertake the same function[51] unless they are appointed to exercise the function jointly. That is a matter of common sense. The trustees are also prohibited from appointing a beneficiary as an agent,[52] even if the beneficiary is also a trustee. This particular restriction does not apply to trusts of land, where under the Trusts of Land and Appointment of Trustees Act 1996, s 9 it is possible for trustees of land to delegate to a beneficiary of full age 'any of their functions as trustees which relate to the land'. This provision would enable trustees of land to delegate the functions relating to the management of the land to the beneficiary who is tenant for life for the time

---

[43] Trustee Act 2000, ss 36(6)–(7).   [44] Pensions Act 1995, s 35(1)–(3).
[45] Pensions Act 1995, s 34(5)(a).   [46] Pensions Act 1995, s 34(5)(b).
[47] Trustee Act 2000, s 37.   [48] Trustee Act 2000, s 38.   [49] Trustee Act 2000, s 12(1).
[50] Trustee Act 2000s 12(4).   [51] Trustee Act 2000, s 12(2).   [52] Trustee Act 2000, s 12(3).

being. It would not permit them to delegate to the beneficiary any function relating to the application of the proceeds from any dealings with the land.

(5) **Terms of agency**

The appointment of an agent by trustees does not have to be in writing, or evidenced in writing, except in the case of the delegation of asset management functions.[53] The terms of the appointment, including the remuneration of the agent, are at the discretion of the trustees[54] (although the amount of the remuneration must be reasonable),[55] with a number of significant caveats. The special restrictions applicable to the delegation of asset management functions are explained in Chapter 21. Another limitation on the power of trustees to set their own terms is that where a function being delegated is subject to any specific duties or restrictions attached to that function, then those duties or restrictions apply to the agent as they would have done to the trustee,[56] although if that restriction relates to obtaining advice, there is no need for the agent to seek advice if he is the kind of person who could have given it to the trustees.[57] For instance, a trust might authorize the trustees to take out insurance on buildings belonging to the trust only after consulting a qualified surveyor or valuer. If the trustees delegate this function to a chartered surveyor, there is no need for that agent to consult another valuer.

There are certain terms relating to the appointment of agents which can be agreed by trustees only if 'it is reasonably necessary for them to do so'.[58] These are terms:

(a) allowing the agent to appoint a substitute;[59]

(b) exemption clauses limiting the liability of the agent;[60]

(c) terms permitting the agent to act in circumstances giving rise to a conflict of interest.[61]

No definition is given in the Act of what is meant by the words 'reasonably necessary'.[62] Trustees will therefore need to act cautiously and to be prepared to demonstrate the basis on which they considered the inclusion of one of these terms to be reasonably necessary. This might be that it was usual business practice for specialists operating in a particular field to require such a provision. The Explanatory Memorandum to the Act provides an example:

> The appointment of a fund manager will often be essential to the efficient and effective management of the assets of the trust. Section 14(3)(a) flows from this. As the standard terms of business of fund managers generally require limits on liability and the ability to

---

[53] Trustee Act 2000, s 15, as discussed in Chapter 21.   [54] Trustee Act 2000, s 14.
[55] Trustee Act 2000, s 32(2).   [56] Trustee Act 2000, s 13.   [57] Trustee Act 2000, s 13(2).
[58] Trustee Act 2000, s 14(2).   [59] Trustee Act 2000, s 14(3)(a).
[60] Trustee Act 2000, s 14(3)(b).   [61] Trustee Act 2000 s 14(3)(c).
[62] See Hanbury and Martin, *Modern Equity* (18th edn, 2009), p 608, where it is suggested that these amendments were introduced to permit delegation to fund managers on their standard terms of business.

act despite a conflict of interest, the ability to appoint a manager would amount to little in practice if trustees were unable to accept such terms.

(6) Liability of agent

It has already been noted that powers and functions delegated to agents are subject to the same conditions and restrictions as applied to that power or function in the hands of the trustees. The Act does not apply any special statutory duty upon agents, so their position is governed by the contractual principles of agency. In most situations these will impose a duty upon the agent to exercise due care and diligence in the exercise of the functions assigned to him. Because these duties arise in contract, the agent's principal liability is to the trustees who appointed him. An unresolved issue is whether there might be some circumstances in which the agent might be directly liable to the beneficiaries, whether under the Contracts (Rights of Third Parties) Act 1999 or under common law or equitable principles arising from interference with the rights of third parties.[63] An analogous situation is where a solicitor negligently draws up a will for a testator, with the result that a beneficiary fails to obtain the benefit intended by the testator. It is now well established that the solicitor owes a duty of care in tort to the beneficiary, which is directly enforceable, in addition to the contractual duty owed to the testator.[64] However, a difference in this situation is that the testator (or his estate), although having a cause of action, has suffered no loss, and it is only if the beneficiary can sue that the wrongdoing solicitor can be held to account. In the case of a trust, any action brought by the trustees against an agent will enlarge the trust assets and so normally benefit the beneficiaries, reducing or even eliminating one of the justifications for conceding a direct cause of action. In addition, if the beneficiaries have a direct cause of action against an agent, it could give rise to potential double jeopardy, a matter that was of concern to the Court of Appeal in *Carr-Glyn v Frearsons*[65] when dealing with an action by a beneficiary under a will. The court in that case was able to resolve the issue by holding that any action by the testatrix's estate could only be complementary to that by the beneficiary: each could sue for their own loss only.

(7) Liability of trustees

(a) Liability in deciding whether or not to delegate

The Trustee Act 2000 adopts the same approach to the liability of trustees as at common law. Essentially trustees are obliged to exercise care in both the appointment and in the supervision of agents. This is achieved by the imposition of the statutory duty of care. The Act says nothing, however, about the duty of trustees in deciding whether or not to delegate. Trustees are therefore under no *statutory* duty to exercise due care in

---

[63] For a discussion of the liability of third parties who cause loss to a trust, see Chapter 29.

[64] See *Ross v Caunters* [1980] Ch 297; *White v Jones* [1995] 2 AC 207; *Carr-Glyn v Frearsons* [1999] Ch 326.

[65] [1999] Ch 326. See also *Worby v Rosser* [2000] PNLR 140.

deciding whether or not to delegate any of their functions, except in relation to decisions by trustees of land to delegate to a beneficiary.[66] They do not, for instance, need to demonstrate that it was reasonably necessary to delegate, nor that delegation was in the best interests of the beneficiaries. The fact that trustees can delegate even where there is no need to do so has been criticized, on the basis that it is unfair that the trustee should be able to delegate tasks to agents at the expense of the trust which he could easily and reasonably undertake himself. For this reason the Law Reform Committee recommended in their 23rd Report in 1982 that trustees should only be able to charge the trust for the expenses of delegation which were reasonably incurred.[67] There could also be the converse problem, where trustees unreasonably decide to undertake a specialist activity without appointing an agent. It remains to be seen whether the courts will impose a duty of care in such situations on the basis that the trustees are in breach of their general duty to act in the best interests of the beneficiaries.

(b) Duty of care in selection and appointment

Having made a decision to appoint an agent, the trustees are subject to the statutory duty to take reasonable care in selecting the agent, in determining the terms on which the agent is to act, and in preparing the investment policy statement where investment functions are delegated.[68] So, for instance, the trustees would be liable for appointing an agent to sell trust property who did not have the relevant expertise, if this is something that the trustees could reasonably have been expected to discover. Suppose that Stephanie is the trustee of a shop, which had been let to Rufus before Stephanie was appointed as a trustee. She needs to negotiate an increase in the rent under a rent review clause in the lease. Having no experience herself, she appoints a local estate agent to act on the trust's behalf. She fails to ask if he has any experience of dealing with commercial property, and his lack of experience causes a loss because the rent obtained on review is far below the level it should be. Stephanie will be liable for breach of trust.[69]

(c) Duty of care in supervision

The trustees are also under a statutory duty to keep an eye on the activities of the agent by keeping the arrangements for the delegation under review, monitoring the actions of the agent, considering whether to intervene, and taking appropriate action where necessary.[70] Imagine, for instance, that Veronica has employed an antiquarian book specialist to catalogue and value a collection of rare books that she holds on trust. Veronica allows the specialist free access to the collection for this purpose. When a scholar asks to see a book, it is discovered that this book and several others are missing. Veronica takes no action, and it later transpires that the specialist had yielded to

---

[66] Trusts of Land and Appointment of Trustees Act 1996, s 9A (added by Trustee Act 2000, Sch 2).
[67] Law Reform Committee, 23rd report (Cmnd 8733), para 4.6. See Trustee Act 2000, ss 14 and 32, concerning the reasonable remuneration of agents.　　　[68] Trustee Act 2000, s 1 and Sch 1, para 3.
[69] The agent will be liable for breach of his contractual duty of care.
[70] Trustee Act 2000, ss 21 and 22.

temptation by stealing a number of the books, something which would not have happened if his access had been supervised. Veronica could be liable for breach of trust for failure to review the arrangements if it is considered that in the circumstances she failed to exercise reasonable care. The position in this respect is just as it was at common law. For instance, in *Re Lucking's Will Trusts*,[71] Mr Lucking was the sole trustee of a trust fund which consisted of a majority shareholding in a private company. He appointed a Lieutenant-Colonel Dewar to manage the company, who sent a blank cheque which Lucking signed. Dewar subsequently misappropriated some £16,000. Cross J held that Lucking was liable for his own breach of trust in failing to supervise the activities of Dewar after he became aware of reasons to doubt his honesty.[72] The standard of care applied was that of *Speight v Gaunt*,[73] namely that the trustee is 'bound to conduct the business of the trust in such a way as an ordinary prudent man of business would conduct a business of his own'.[74] The duty so expressed is effectively the same duty as the statutory duty of care.

(d) Liability for failure to observe restrictions

Where trustees have failed to comply with one of the restrictions on the appointment of agents, for instance where they have agreed to a clause limiting the liability of the agent where it was not reasonably necessary to do so, the trustees will be in breach of trust. There may also be limitations on the appointment of agents contained in the trust instrument that they are required to observe at pain of committing a breach of trust. The fact that the trustees have exceeded their powers in authorizing a person to act as their agent does not, however, invalidate the appointment.[75]

(e) Vicarious liability

Where the trustees have exercised due care in the appointment and supervision of an agent, however, they are not liable merely because the agent does something which causes a loss to the trust. Section 23 of the Trustee Act 2000 exempts trustees who are not personally in breach of the statutory duty of care from what may be called vicarious liability.[76] For instance, in the example given earlier of the theft by a specialist of books from a valuable collection of which Veronica was the trustee, Veronica is not automatically liable because her agent was dishonest and stole the books. To hold her liable it has to be shown that she did not exercise reasonable care in selecting the specialist (perhaps she should have taken up references from other clients) or that she did not take appropriate action in supervising him.

---

[71] [1968] 1 WLR 866. *Bartlett v Barclays Bank Trust Co Ltd (Nos 1 & 2)* [1980] Ch 515 provides another example.

[72] Cross J considered that the statutory protection for trustees then in force gave no indemnity to trustees who were themselves at fault.   [73] (1833) 22 Ch D 727.   [74] (1833) 22 Ch D 727, at 874.

[75] Trustee Act 2000, s 24.

[76] The Law Commission in *Trustees' Powers and Duties* (1997) Law Com Consultation Paper No 146, paras 4.29–4.31 suggests that this description is not particularly helpful or accurate since there is no case in which a trustee has been held vicariously liable. However, the expression accurately conveys the concept of liability for the fault of others, even where there is no personal fault.

Section 23 may not be happily worded. It states that 'a trustee is not liable for any act or default of the agent' unless the trustee has failed to comply with the statutory duty 'when entering into the arrangements under which the person acts as agent' or 'when carrying out his duties' of keeping the appointment under review. On a literal interpretation, a trustee who fails to conduct a review at all, rather than carrying out a review badly, would not be liable. This interpretation, however, would undoubtedly be contrary to the policy of the Act, and it is likely that the courts will give the section a purposive interpretation to make trustees liable for unreasonable omissions as well as careless commissions.

(8) Liability of pension fund trustees

Trustees of a pension fund are not liable under the statutory duty of care imposed by the Trustee Act 2000 when delegating their investment functions, as they are not subject to the general powers of investment.[77] Instead, if the trustees of a pension fund exercise their right to delegate investment decisions to a fund manager their liability for the acts of their agent are specified by Pensions Act 1995, s 34(4):

> The trustees are not responsible for the act or default of any fund manager in the exercise of any discretion delegated to him he truif they have taken all such steps as are reasonable to satisfy themselves or the person who made the delegation on their behalf has taken all such steps as are reasonable to satisfy himself—
>
> (a) that the fund manager has the appropriate knowledge and experience for managing the investments in the scheme, and
>
> (b) that he is carrying out his work competently and complying with section 36.[78]

These obligations are very similar to the statutory duty of care imposed on other trustees who have appointed an agent, although the language used is not identical. If the delegation is made to a fund manager who is not authorized to conduct investments under the Financial Services and Markets Act 2000, such a delegation is still effective to vest the powers in the manager, but the trustees will normally be liable for the defaults and acts of such a person.[79]

(9) Liability of trustees of land for the acts of their agents

Where trustees of land have delegated their functions to a beneficiary under the special power to do so in the Trusts of Land and Appointment of Trustees Act 1996[80] they are subject to the statutory duty of care in respect of the decision to delegate and in the supervision of the arrangement.[81]

---

[77] Trustee Act 2000, s 36.
[78] See s 36 of the Pensions Act 1995, which requires the trustees to consider the need for diversification and to the suitability of investments.   [79] Pensions Act 1995, s 34(5).
[80] Trusts of Land and Appointment of Trustees Act 1996, s 9.
[81] Trusts of Land and Appointment of Trustees Act 1996, s 9A (inserted by Trustee Act 2000).

5 Individual delegation

In addition to the trustees acting together to appoint an agent, it is also possible for an individual trustee to delegate by appointing a substitute to exercise all or any of his powers. This was not something that was possible at common law, because of the principle *delegatus non potest delegare*. There is now statutory authority contained in Trustee Act 1925, s 25. As originally enacted, this section permitted delegation only during the absence of a trustee overseas. The section was substantially enlarged by the Powers of Attorney Act 1971 to confer a general authority to delegate trustee functions (including discretions), but only for a period not exceeding twelve months. The current provisions date from the Trustee Delegation Act 1999, which made further minor amendments. Section 25(l) of the Trustee Act 1925 (as amended) provides that:

> Notwithstanding any rule of law or equity to the contrary, a trustee may, by power of attorney,[82] delegate the execution or exercise of all or any of the trusts, powers and discretions vested in him as trustee either alone or jointly with any other person or persons.

The delegation may not exceed twelve months,[83] must be by made by deed,[84] and notice must be given to the other trustees and to the person entitled to appoint new trustees.[85] The purpose of this last requirement is to enable the trustees to consider whether the trustee making the delegation should be replaced. Where a trustee delegates his functions under s 25(1), he remains strictly liable for any losses caused by the agent, as s 25(7) provides that the donor of the power of attorney 'shall be liable for the acts or defaults of the donee in the same manner as if they were the acts or defaults of the donor'. Appointment of an agent under this section is thus a far less satisfactory course of action for a trustee than appointment of an agent under the powers of collective delegation provided by the Trustee Act 2000.

A delegation by means of a power of attorney will, like all such appointments of an agent, lapse should the principal cease to have full mental capacity, but the Trustee Delegation Act 1999[86] permits the power to be executed as a lasting power, which remains valid despite the incapacity of the principal.

---

[82] Discussed in Chapter 3.   [83] Trustee Act 1925, s 25(2)(a) (as amended).
[84] This is a requirement of all powers of attorney.   [85] Trustee Act 1925, s 25(4) (as amended).
[86] Trustee Delegation Act 1999, ss 6 and 9. The Act repeals Enduring Powers of Attorney Act 1985, s 3(3), which previously permitted the delegation of trustee functions by enduring power of attorney. See now Mental Capacity Act 2005, Sch 4.

24

Appointment, removal, and retirement of trustees

Previous chapters have considered the powers of trustees. This chapter turns to consider the rules and restrictions applicable to the appointment, removal, and retirement of trustees. Together these rules demonstrate the importance attached to the office of trustee, and the ongoing nature of the rights and obligations they owe to the beneficiaries of a trust. The rules seek to ensure that proper persons are appointed as trustees, and that such persons may be removed or replaced if they are not carrying out their obligations. The way in which the duties imposed upon trustees and those dealing with trust property are enforced will be considered in the following chapters of this book.

1 The appointment of the original trustees of a trust fund

(1) Appointment by the settlor

(a) Express trusts

When a trust of property is created, generally the settlor will appoint the initial trustees of the settlement. If he creates the trust inter vivos by declaring that he holds the property on trust for the beneficiaries, he will be the trustee. If he transfers the property to a third party subject to a trust, that person will become the trustee. Usually, the deed creating the trust will appoint the trustees. If the trust is testamentary, so that it is only created after his death, the testator will usually nominate the trustees in his will.

(b) Implied trusts

A trust may also come into being without the express intention of the original legal owner of the property. In some instances the recipient of the legal title of property will be deemed to hold it on trust for someone else. As has been seen, trusts which arise by implication from the circumstances or conduct of the parties are known as 'resulting' and 'constructive' trusts. The person who is deemed to hold property on either a constructive or resulting trust becomes a trustee, even though he may not be aware of the fact of the trust, provided he was aware of the circumstances affecting his conscience which gave rise to the trust.[1]

(c) Capacity to act as a trustee

Any legal person with legal capacity, whether an individual or corporation,[2] may act as a trustee. However, the Law of Property Act 1925, s 20 provides that: 'The appointment of an infant to be a trustee in relation to any settlement or trust shall be voidable'. This restriction only applies in respect of express trusts, and if a minor receives property in circumstances that would create a resulting or constructive trust he will become a trustee of the property.[3] However, this will only be possible in the case of personal property, as s 1(6) of the Law of Property Act 1925 provides that an infant cannot hold a legal estate in land. If a minor is appointed trustee of an express trust there are mechanisms which will enable the minor to be removed from his position and replaced.[4] Special rules are applicable to the appointment of trustees in a charitable purpose trust. Certain persons are disqualified from acting as trustees, to try and prevent fraud and maladministration of such trusts.[5] Therefore, persons convicted of an 'offence involving dishonesty or deception',[6] 'adjudged bankrupt',[7] or that have previously been removed from the office of trustee for mismanagement may not be appointed.[8]

(d) A trust will not fail for want of a trustee[9]

If a trust has been validly created by the transfer of the trust property to the trustees, or by the death of the testator who has specified trusts in his will, the trust will not fail if the nominated trustees disclaim the trust,[10] are incapable of acting as

---

[1] *Westdeutsche Landesbank Girozentrale v Islington London Borough Council* [1996] AC 669, at 705, per Lord Browne-Wilkinson. Although this judgment causes problems by suggesting that a person does not become a trustee of property until he is aware that he is intended to hold the property for the benefit of others, or of the factors which affect his conscience, it is probably better to regard Lord Browne-Wilkinson's comments as intimating that the trustee is not subject to the full fiduciary duties of trusteeship until he is aware of the existence of the trust. The trust exists irrespective of his knowledge in the sense that the property belongs in equity to the beneficiaries. However, the mere fact that there is a 'trust' in this sense does not mean that the trustee will be subject to personal liability for breach of trust if he acts in a manner inconsistent with the existence of the trust.

[2] See *A-G v St John's Hospital Bedford* (1865) 2 De GJ & Sm 621; *Re Thompson's Settlement Trust* [1905] 1 Ch 229; *Bankes v Salisbury Diocesan Council of Education Inc* [1960] Ch 631.

[3] See *Re Vinogradoff* [1935] WN 68.   [4] See, for example, Trustee Act 1925, s 36(1).

[5] This is enforced under s 183 of the Charities Act 2011, which makes it a criminal offence for a disqualified person to act as a trustee. S 184 provides that the Charity Commission may order such persons to repay any remuneration or expenses or benefit in kind received while acting as a charity trustee while disqualified.   [6] Charities Act 2011, s 178(1) Case A.

[7] Charities Act 2011, s 178(1) Case B.

[8] Charities Act 2011, s 178(1) Case C. There are three other classes of disqualified persons under s 178. It is worth noting that the Charity Commission may waive the disqualification of any person under s 181, except in certain matters relating to company directors detailed in s 181(5).

[9] *Robson v Flight* (1865) 4 De GJ & Sm 608.

[10] A person appointed trustee can disclaim the trust at any time before he has accepted it. He may disclaim by deed, although that is not necessary and a disclaimer can be inferred from his conduct: *Stacey v Elph* (1833) 1 My & K 195; *White v Barton* (1854) 18 Beav 192; *Holder v Holder* [1968] Ch 353. Once the trust

trustees,[11] or have predeceased the testator. Equity will not permit a trust to fail for want of a trustee and will seek to carry the settlor's intentions into effect as far as is possible. This principle operates in different ways, depending on whether the trust was created by an inter vivos or testamentary transfer.

(i) Inter vivos transfer of property to trustees upon trust

If the settlor effectively transferred the trust property to trustees by means of an inter vivos conveyance and the trustees disclaim, the trust property will revest in the settlor subject to the trusts. For example, in *Mallott v Wilson*[12] the settlor transferred land in 1866 to a trustee on trust. When the trustee executed a deed of disclaimer in 1867, it was held that the trust did not fail but that the property was automatically revested in the settlor by operation of law, and that he held the land subject to the trusts that had been validly created.[13] If the settlor has died since the trust was created, the property will revest in his personal representatives, who will again hold it subject to the trusts.

(ii) Testamentary transfers of property upon trust

If the trust was intended to be created by the testamentary transfer of the trust property to trustees and they predecease the testator, the deceased's personal representatives will hold the property on the terms of the trust that he had intended to create. For example, in *Re Willis*[14] a testatrix had left property on discretionary trusts for various charities. The trustee, who was to select how the property was to be allocated between the charities, had predeceased her. However, the court held that the trust did not fail but that the fund would vest in her executors and the court would select how the fund should be allocated.[15] Similarly, if the trustee survives the testator but then disclaims the trust, the property will also revest in the settlor's personal representatives, again subject to the trusts.

In either case the trust will not fail and the court has the power to appoint new trustees.[16] However, this principle is subject to the qualification that the trust will fail if the identity of the disclaiming trustee was essential to the trust. In *Re Lysaght (Decd)*[17] a testator left the residue of her estate to the Royal College of Surgeons to provide scholarships which were not to be awarded to Jews or Roman Catholics. In these circumstances the RCS, as trustee, refused to accept the trust. Buckley J held that the trust therefore failed, stating that:

> If it is of the essence of a trust that the trustees selected by the settlor and no one else shall act as the trustees of it and those trustees cannot or will not undertake the office, the trust must fail.

---

has been accepted, the trustee cannot disclaim: *Re Sharman's Will Trusts* [1942] Ch 311. A trustee cannot disclaim part of a trust, and therefore acceptance of part will amount to an acceptance of the whole: *Re Lord and Fullerton's Contract* [1896] 1 Ch 228; *Re Lister* [1926] Ch 149, CA.

[11] See *Re Armitage* [1972] Ch 438.   [12] [1903] 2 Ch 494.

[13] See also *Jones v Jones* [1874] WN 190.   [14] [1921] 1 Ch 44.

[15] See also *Moggridge v Thackwell* (1803) 7 Ves 36.

[16] *A-G v Stephens* (1834) 3 My & K 347; *Jones v Jones* (1874) 31 LT 535; *Mallott v Wilson* [1903] 2 Ch 494.

[17] [1966] Ch 191: see also *Reeve v A-G* (1843) 3 Hare 191; *Re Lawton* [1936] 3 All ER 378.

In the circumstances, because the gift was charitable and had failed, it was applied cy-près.[18]

(e) Limitation on the number of trustees

Where the trust fund consists of personal property there is no limit on the number of trustees that the settlor may appoint when the trust is created. However, in the case of a trust of land, the property legislation of 1925 restricts the number of persons who may hold the legal title. This restriction was introduced with the objective of increasing conveyancing efficiency. The Trustee Act 1925, s 34(2)[19] provides that for settlements created after 1925:

(a) the number of trustees thereof shall not in any case exceed four, and where more than four persons are named as such trustees, the four first named (who are able and willing to act) shall alone be the trustees, and the other persons named shall not be trustees unless appointed on the occurrence of a vacancy.

(b) the number of trustees shall not be increased beyond four.[20]

It is to be noted that those who are named after the first four persons named as trustees do not automatically become trustees if a vacancy arises, and they will only become a trustee if they are properly appointed by whoever has the authority to appoint replacement trustees. In the context of land it is also worth noting that although it is possible to have a sole trustee, overreaching of equitable trust interests cannot take place unless there is a payment to two trustees of land.[21] This is the case even where there are two trustees, but one has appointed the other as his attorney so that the attorney is acting in two capacities—on his own behalf and on behalf of the trustee for whom he is attorney.[22]

2 Retirement of trustees

(1) Voluntary retirement of trustees

Once a trustee has been appointed and has taken up his office, he may subsequently wish to retire from the trust. It is possible for the trust to contain an express power permitting retirement, but s 39 of the Trustee Act 1925 provides a general power which is usually adequate:

---

[18] See Chapter 18.   [19] See also Law of Property Act 1925, s 34(2) and (3).

[20] There are a number of very limited exceptions to the principle in s 34(3), primarily being land held on trust for 'charitable, ecclesiastical, or public purposes'.

[21] See Law of Property Act 1925, ss 2 and 27. Overreaching is the process by which interests in the land are transferred to the proceeds of sale, so that, for example, a beneficial interest in land does not bind a purchaser, but is instead expressed as a proportion of the price paid to the vendor. See further Stevens and Pearce, *Land Law* (2013), 3.15–3.33.

[22] Trustee Delegation Act 1999, s 7. The same applies where the attorney acts for two or more trustees and is not acting with another trustee.

Where a trustee is desirous of being discharged from the trust, and after his discharge there will be either a trust corporation or at least two individuals to act as trustees to perform the trust, then, if such trustee as aforesaid by deed declares that he is desirous of being discharged from the trust, and if his co-trustees and such other person, if any, as is empowered to appoint trustees, by deed consent to the discharge of the trustee, and to the vesting in the co-trustees alone of the trust property, the trustee desirous of being discharged shall be deemed to have retired from the trust, and shall, by the deed, be discharged therefrom under this Act, without any new trustee being appointed in his place.

This provision permits the retirement of a trustee without a replacement being appointed, but this will only be possible if at least two trustees, or a trust corporation remain. Where these conditions are not satisfied, a trustee may retire and be replaced under the power contained in s 36 of the Trustee Act 1925, which is considered later in the chapter. Retirement will not protect a trustee from liability for breaches of trust that he committed whilst he was a trustee, and he will be liable for breaches of trust committed after his retirement if he retired to facilitate those breaches.[23]

(2) **Compulsory retirement of trustees at the direction of the beneficiaries**

Historically, trustees could not be forced to retire by the beneficiaries of a trust, no matter how much the beneficiaries may have wished to have them replaced, and they could only be forcibly removed on grounds of incapacity or maladministration. However, where the beneficiaries are of age and legally competent it has been seen that they can demand that the trust be brought to an end under the rule in *Saunders v Vautier*.[24] If they wish they could therefore effectively remove the trustees and replace them by settling the property on new trusts. This process may be both costly (including potential liability to additional tax) and inefficient, as it requires a transfer of the legal title to the trust property from the original trustees to the beneficiaries, and then from the beneficiaries to the new trustees. Consequently, the Trusts of Land and Appointment of Trustees Act 1996 introduced a new statutory power enabling the beneficiaries of a trust to require a trustee to retire in circumstances where they could have taken advantage of the rule in *Saunders v Vautier* to achieve the same result. By s 19(2)(a) of the Act, the beneficiaries of a trust may give a written direction to a trustee or trustees to retire from the trust. This right is only exercisable if there is no person nominated for the purpose of appointing new trustees by the trust instrument,[25] and if the beneficiaries of the trust are of full age and capacity and, taken together, are absolutely entitled to the property subject to the trust.[26] This means that the right to direct retirement will not be available where there are infant beneficiaries of the trust, which will often be the case in respect of a discretionary trust. Where a trustee has been directed to retire by the beneficiaries, s 19(3) provides that he will be required

---

[23] See Chapter 27.   [24] (1841) 4 Beav 115.   [25] S 19(1)(a).
[26] Trusts of Land and Appointment of Trustees Act 1996, s 19(1)(b).

to make a deed declaring his retirement and shall be deemed to have retired and be discharged from the trust. However, he will only be required to retire if three conditions are satisfied:

(1)   reasonable arrangements have been made for the protection of any rights he has in connection with the trust;[27]

(2)   after he has retired there will be either a trust corporation or at least two persons to act as trustees to perform the trust;[28] and

(3)   either another person is to be appointed a new trustee on his retirement, or the continuing trustees consent by deed to his retirement.[29]

The power to compulsorily retire trustees under s 19 thus enables the beneficiaries to defeat the intentions of the settlor, who may have intended that a specific individual act as trustee. This ability to undermine the settlor's express intentions is the inevitable consequence of the rule in *Saunders v Vautier*. A settlor can, however, expressly exclude the right to compulsorily retire trustees under s 19,[30] and in reality a standard exclusion may be utilized in express trusts so that the statutory provision will only be applicable in respect of resulting and constructive trusts, especially of the family home.[31] Where trusts have come into existence before the commencement of the Act, the power to direct retirement can be excluded by the execution of a deed to that effect by the settlor, or surviving settlors, who created the trust.[32] If such a deed is executed, it is irrevocable in effect.[33]

3 The appointment of replacement or additional trustees

(1) The need for new appointments

It is inevitable that in the lifetime of many trusts circumstances may arise where it is necessary to appoint new trustees.

(a) Appointment of additional trustees

It may be necessary or beneficial for the number of original trustees appointed by the settlor to be increased by the appointment of additional trustees. This may be because of the workload that the trustees are experiencing, or for simple reasons of convenience. In the case of land, if the settlor has created a trust for sale with a single trustee it

---

[27] S 19(3)(b). This would include, for example, unpaid fees and expenses.
[28] S 19(3)(c). This is consistent with s 39 of the Trustee Act 1925.
[29] S 19(3)(d). In the event that the co-trustees refuse to consent to the retirement directed by the beneficiaries, the only means of removal of the trustee will be by order of the court exercising its jurisdiction under s 41 of the Trustee Act 1925.   [30] S 21(5).
[31] Although, even here, the provision cannot be exercised if one of the beneficiaries (who may also be the trustee) does not agree.   [32] Trusts of Land and Appointment of Trustees Act 1996, s 21(6).
[33] S 21(7).

may be necessary to appoint at least one additional trustee (or a trust corporation) so that, if the land is sold, the purchaser can gain the benefit of overreaching.[34]

(b) Appointment of replacement trustees

It may be necessary to appoint new trustees as replacements for those who are no longer able to act as such, for example because of death or mental incapacity, or who have retired from the trust.

(c) Removal of trustees

In some circumstances it may be necessary to remove a trustee from the trust against his will, for example if he proves to be incompetent or is frustrating the efficient exercise of the trust.

(2) Power to appoint new trustees

Having recognized that there may be a need in some circumstances to appoint new trustees, the central question is how such appointments can be made: who has the power to select and appoint new trustees, and in what circumstances can such powers be exercised?

(a) Express powers

In keeping with the fundamental philosophy that, as far as possible the settlor's intentions will be carried out, the trust deed may contain an express power authorizing the appointment of new trustees. Such a power will be strictly construed.[35] There is some question whether the donee of such a power can appoint himself as trustee of the settlement. In *Re Skeats' Settlement*[36] a trust contained an express power granting certain persons the power to appoint 'any other person' to be trustee. They exercised the power to appoint themselves. Kay J held that this was invalid since the power was fiduciary in character and it would thus be 'extremely improper for a person who has a power to appoint or select new trustees to appoint or select himself imsel'.[37] This principle was followed by Kekewich J in *Re Newen*,[38] but was doubted by Buckley J in *Montefiore v Guedalla*,[39] where he stated that:

> On the cases, I am clearly of opinion that it has not been laid down that the appointors are outside the class who can be appointed, although it has been said, and it is a very salutary rule, than an appointor ought not, save in exceptional circumstances, to appoint himself.[40]

However, in *Re Sampson*[41] Kekewich J considered that the decision in *Montefiore v Guedalla*[42] might require future reconsideration.[43]

---

[34] The Trustee Delegation Act 1999, s 7 makes it clear that the 'two trustee' rule is not satisfied if all of the trustees are represented by a single person acting under a power of attorney, or where the same single person is both a trustee and acts under a power of attorney for the other trustees.
[35] *Stones v Rowton* (1853) 17 Beav 308; *Re Norris* (1884) 27 Ch D 333.   [36] (1889) 42 Ch D 522.
[37] (1889) 42 Ch D 522, at 527.   [38] [1894] 2 Ch 297.   [39] [1903] 2 Ch 723.
[40] [1903] 2 Ch 723, at 725.   [41] [1906] 1 Ch 435.   [42] [1903] 2 Ch 723.
[43] *Re Sampson* concerned a statutory rather than an express power to appoint new trustees.

Today, express powers are of little significance because of the statutory powers that are available to provide for the appointment of new trustees. These statutory powers were themselves modeled on the express powers which had previously been included in trust deeds. If there is an express power providing for the removal of trustees from the trust, s 36(2) of the Trustee Act 1925 applies, which provides:

> Where a trustee has been removed under a power contained in the instrument creating the trust, a new trustee or trustees may be appointed in the place of the trustee who is removed, as if he were dead, or, in the case of a corporation, as if the corporation desired to be discharged from the trust, and the provisions of this section shall apply accordingly, but subject to the restriction imposed by this act on the number of trustees.

(b) Statutory powers

There are three important statutory provisions granting the power of appointment of new trustees.

(i) Trustee Act 1925, s 36

This section provides for the appointment of new trustees in a wide range of circumstances by persons either nominated in the trust deed by the settlor, or, in the absence of any such nomination, by the persons provided for by the section. The intervention of the court is not required for appointments made under the power contained in s 36.

(ii) Trustee Act 1925, s 41

This section grants the court a wide power to appoint new trustees either in addition to or in substitution for present trustees. The power is discretionary and may be exercised whenever the court considers it is expedient.

(iii) Trusts of Land and Appointment of Trustees Act 1996, ss 19 and 20

It has already been noted how the Trusts of Land and Appointment of Trustees Act 1996 has introduced a new statutory right enabling the beneficiaries of a trust to direct the compulsory retirement of a trustee. Section 19(2)(b) also grants the beneficiaries the right to direct the appointment of new trustees, and s 20 provides for the appointment of a replacement trustee where a trustee is mentally incapable of acting and there is no person willing and able to appoint a replacement under s 36(1) of the Trustee Act 1925.

4 Trustee Act 1925, s 36

(1) Appointing substitute trustees

(a) The power to appoint substitute trustees

The Trustee Act 1925, s 36(1) provides:

> Where a trustee, either original or substituted, and whether appointed by a court or otherwise, is dead, or remains out of the United Kingdom for more than twelve months, or

desires to be discharged from all or any of the trusts or powers reposed in or conferred on him, or refuses or is unfit to act therein, or is incapable of acting therein, or is an infant, then subject to the restrictions imposed by this Act on the number of trustees—

(a) the person or persons nominated for the purpose of appointing new trustees by the instrument, if any, creating the trust; or

(b) if there is no such person, or no such person able and willing to act, then the surviving or continuing trustees or trustee for the time being, or the personal representatives of the last surviving or continuing trustee;

may, by writing, appoint one or more other person (whether or not being the persons exercising the power) to be a trustee or trustees in the place of the trustee so deceased, remaining out of the United Kingdom, desiring to be discharged from the trust, and the provisions of this section shall apply accordingly, but subject to the restrictions imposed by this Act on the number of trustees.

(b) Circumstances in which the power may be exercised

Section 36 provides that the power to appoint new trustees may be exercised in seven well-defined circumstances, which cover many of the most likely situations in which new trustees would need to be appointed. It is to be noted that s 36 applies only to trustees and not to personal representatives.[44] An improper appointment not made in compliance with the statutory powers is invalid, so that no substitution takes place and the original trustees remain in office (or their personal representatives).[45]

(i) The trustee is dead

By s 36(8) the power of appointment under s 36(1) is also exercisable where a person who is nominated trustee in a will predeceases the testator. There is some authority[46] that the sections will also be operative in the unlikely event that the settlor attempts an inter vivos transfer to a trustee who is already dead. However, this will only be the case if the dead trustee was one of a number of others who were alive, since an attempt by the settlor to transfer property inter vivos to trustees who are all dead will not create a trust in the first place.

(ii) The trustee remains out of the United Kingdom for more than twelve months

The rationale for this provision was that the limited and slow means of communication and travel would prevent a trustee who was absent from the country from being able to properly carry out the trust business. It is possible under s 25 of the Trustee Act 1925 for a trustee to delegate his managerial functions and discretions by a power of attorney for up to twelve months, for instance, during absence abroad.[47] Today, with such instant means of communication as email, telephone, and fax, and with the availability of rapid air transport, it is questionable whether the absence of a trustee abroad

---

[44] See *Re Cockburn's Will Trust* [1957] Ch 438; *Re King's Will Trusts* [1964] Ch 542. However, the court has power to appoint a substituted person representative under the Administration of Justice Act 1985, s 50.

[45] See *Jasmine Trustees Ltd v Wells & Hind (A Firm)* [2008] Ch 194, at 216 [52], per Mann J.

[46] See *Re Hadley* (1851) 5 De G & Sm 67.   [47] Discussed in Chapter 23.

inevitably prevents him from conducting the business of the trust. The absence from the UK must be for a continuous period of twelve months. In *Re Walker*[48] Mr Walker was co-trustee of a settlement with Mrs Walker. He was out of the UK for more than a year from spring 1899, with the exception of one week in London in November 1899. In these circumstances Farwell J held that Mrs Walker could not exercise the power of appointment under what is now s 36(1).[49] The power enables a trustee to be removed against his will, as was held by Danckwerts J in *Re Stoneham's Settlement Trusts*.[50]

(iii) The trustee desires to be discharged from all or any of the trusts or powers reposed in or conferred on him

This provision means that a trustee can be discharged from only part of his trust responsibility, which prior to the Act was only possible through the court.[51]

(iv) The trustee refuses to act

This clearly covers the case where a trustee disclaims the trust.

(v) The trustee is unfit or incapable

This refers to any personal incapacity that would prevent the trustee acting as such. It clearly includes mental incapacity, so in *Re East*[52] the court held that there was a valid exercise of a power to appoint new trustees where one of three co-trustees became of unsound mind.[53] Similarly, in *Re Lemann's Trust*[54] age and infirmity were considered sufficient 'incapacity'. A trustee will also be considered unfit to act if he is bankrupt, as was held in *Re Wheeler and De Rochow*.[55] It seems that a trustee is not unfit to act merely through absence abroad.[56] However, in *Mesnard v Welford*[57] a trustee who had been absent in New York for twenty years was held to be incapable of acting for the purposes of an express power of appointment.[58] The cases holding that a trustee resident overseas may be incapable of acting all date from the nineteenth century, and improvements in communications and in the speed of international travel cast their current reliability into doubt.[59] In the case of the dissolution of a corporate trustee, s 36(3) provides:

> Where a corporation being a trustee is or has been dissolved olved then, for the purposes of this section ectio the corporation shall be deemed to be and to have been from the date of

---

[48] [1901] 1 Ch 259.   [49] Previously, Trustee Act 1893, s 10.   [50] [1953] Ch 59.

[51] See *Savile v Couper* (1887) 36 Ch D 520; *Re Moss's Trusts* (1888) 37 Ch D 513.

[52] (1873) 8 Ch App 735.

[53] It is possible for a trustee to execute a lasting power of attorney before becoming of unsound mind that has the effect of delegating to an agent his functions as a trustee of land and which operates in the event of his incapacity: Trustee Delegation Act 1999, s 1. See generally Mental Capacity Act 2005, ss 9–14 for the distinction between enduring powers of attorney (which have been repealed) and lasting powers of attorney (which must be registered to be effective).   [54] (1883) 22 Ch D 633.

[55] [1896] 1 Ch 315. See also *Re Roche* (1842) 1 Con & Law 306; *Re Hopkins* (1881) 19 Ch D 61.

[56] See *Withington v Withington* (1848) 16 Sim 104; *O'Reilly v Alderson* (1849) 8 Hare 101; *Re Harrison's Trusts* (1852) 22 LJ Ch 69; *Re Bignold's Settlement Trusts* (1872) 7 Ch App 223.

[57] (1853) 1 Sm & G 426.

[58] See also *Re Lemann's Trusts* (1883) 22 Ch D 633, where Chitty J gave the residence of a trustee abroad as one instance of incapacity.

[59] See the remarks by Millett J in *Richard v Mackay* (1997) 11 *Trust Law International* 22.

the dissolution incapable of acting in the trusts or powers reposed in or conferred on the corporation.

(vi) The trustee is an infant

Such an eventuality is only likely to arise in respect of a constructive or resulting trust of personal property, since in other cases the appointment of an infant as trustee is void.[60]

(vii) The trustee has been removed under an express power

If the trust instrument includes an express provision for the removal of trustees, any trustee who is so removed may be replaced under the powers of appointment of s 36 as if he were a trustee who had died.[61]

(c) Persons who may exercise the power to appoint new trustees

In addition to defining the circumstances in which new trustees may be appointed, s 36 of the Trustee Act also specifies who is to make any such appointments. The section adopts an order of priority as to who can exercise the power. It emphasizes the settlor's intentions by giving priority to any person nominated for the purpose in the trust instrument, but provides alternative mechanisms for appointment if there is no such person nominated.

(i) The person or persons nominated by the trust instrument

By s 36(1)(a), if the settlor has nominated a person or persons in the instrument creating the trust to exercise the power of appointment of new trustees, then it is they who can exercise the power to appoint under s 36(1). Such persons only fall within s 36(1) if they have a general power to make appointments[62] and not a power which is only granted in specific circumstances. In *Re Sichel's Settlements*[63] the nominated persons were given the power to appoint new trustees in the event of the present trustees becoming 'incapable to act'. Neville J held, following the decision of Kekewick J in *Re Wheeler and De Rochow*,[64] that they were not the appropriate persons to appoint a new trustee where one of the existing trustees was 'unfit' to act. Where several persons are jointly nominated, in the absence of a contrary intention[65] the survivor or survivors cannot exercise the power.[66] In that event, the power to appoint will be exercisable by those indicted in s 36(1). The same result will follow if the nominated persons are incapable of acting, for example because of disagreement.[67]

---

[60] Law of Property Act 1925, s 20.   [61] S 36(2).
[62] *Re Walker and Hughes' Contract* (1883) 24 Ch D 698.   [63] [1916] 1 Ch 358.
[64] [1896] 1 Ch 315. However, he did express his disagreement with the decision.
[65] *Re Harding* [1923] 1 Ch 182.
[66] This is subject to the exceptions that the survivors can exercise the power if the property is vested in them (*Re Bacon* [1907] 1 Ch 475), they hold the power as trustees (Trustee Act 1925, s 18(1)), or the power was granted to a class of which two or more members survive (*Jefferys v Marshall* (1870) 19 WR 94).
[67] *Re Sheppard's Settlement Trust* [1888] WN 234. Alternatively, because they cannot be found: *Cradock v Witham* [1895] WN 75.

(ii) The surviving or continuing trustee or trustees

If there are no persons nominated in the trust instrument, or if such persons are unable or unwilling to act, s 36(1)(b) provides that it is the 'surviving or continuing trustee or trustees for the time being' who may appoint new trustees. It has been held that the last surviving or continuing trustee includes a sole trustee.[68] The central difficulty concerns the questions as to who are the 'continuing trustees' where it is intended to remove a trustee who is alive and capable, since it is a basic principle that trustees must act with unanimity. It would prove impossible to remove a trustee against his will if he was to be regarded as a 'continuing trustee' and therefore had to be party to the decision to remove and replace him. The position is complicated by s 36(8), which provides that the continuing trustees include 'a refusing or retiring trustee, if willing to act in the execution of the provisions of this section'. This has the effect that a retiring sole trustee or retiring group of trustees are able to appoint their successors, although s 37(1)(c) means that two retiring trustees cannot be replaced by one, not being a trust corporation.[69] Whether a trustee should be regarded as 'refusing or retiring' was considered by Danckwerts J in *Re Stoneham's Settlement Trusts*.[70] He took the general view that a trustee who is being removed from the trust is not retiring and therefore does not fall within the scope of s 36(8):

> It seems to me, in the absence of any authority which binds me to decide otherwise, that a person who is compulsorily removed from a trust is not a person who retires and is not a retiring trustee.

Similarly, following *Re Coates to Parsons*,[71] he held that a trustee who has been abroad for more than twelve months was not a 'refusing or retiring trustee' within the meaning of s 38, and that therefore he was not a 'continuing trustee' and his concurrence was not needed for the appointment of a new trustee.

(iii) The personal representatives of the last surviving or continuing trustee

As a last resort, if there are no nominated persons who can make new appointments and there are no 'surviving or continuing' trustees, the statute pragmatically provides in s 36(1)(a) that the 'personal representatives of the last surviving or continuing trustee' have the power to appoint new trustees.

---

[68] *Re Shafto's Trusts* (1885) 29 Ch D 247. *Adam and Company International Trustees Ltd v Theodore Goddard (a firm)* [2000] WTLR 349; Barlow 'The Appointment of Trustees: A Disappointing Decision' [2003] Conv 15. See also *Jasmine Trustees Ltd v Wells & Hind (A Firm)* [2008] Ch 194, where it was held by Mann J that, in a trust subject to the older version of the wording of s 37(1)(c) existing before 1 January 1997, a company was not to be classed as a trustee, as it was not an 'individual' as required under the old wording of s 37(1)(c). The statutory provision now talks of 'persons' (following amendment by the Trust of Land and Appointment of Trustees Act 1996, Sch 3) and a company is a legal person.

[69] *Adam and Company International Trustees Ltd v Theodore Goddard (a firm)* [2000] WTLR 349; Barlow 'The Appointment of Trustees: A Disappointing Decision' [2003] Conv 15.   [70] [1953] Ch 59.

[71] (1886) 34 Ch D 370.

(d) No one is able to appoint a substitute trustee

In some extreme circumstances, even where there is a jurisdiction to appoint a substitute trustee under s 36 there will be no one who is capable of exercising it. Such a problem is especially likely where property is held by a sole trustee who has become mentally incapable. Since a sole incapable trustee is a surviving trustee, he alone is entitled to exercise the power to appoint a substitute for himself, and yet is incapable of so doing. In such circumstances where the power to appoint under s 36 is moribund, the court may exercise its jurisdiction to appoint new trustees under s 41. The Trusts of Land and Appointment of Trustees Act 1996 has conferred upon the beneficiaries of the trust the right to direct the appointment of a substitute. This jurisdiction is examined later in this chapter.

(2) Appointing additional trustees

(a) The power to appoint additional trustees

The Trustee Act 1925, s 36(6)[72] also provides for the appointment of additional trustees:

> Where, in the case of any trust, there are not more than three trustees—
>
>   (a) the person or persons nominated for the purpose of appointing new trustees by the instrument, if any, creating the trust; or
>
>   (b) if there is no such person, or no such person able and willing to act, then the trustee or trustees for the time being;
>
> may, by writing appoint another person or other persons to be an additional trustee or additional trustees, but it shall not be obligatory to appoint any additional trustees, unless the instrument, if any creating the trust, or any statutory enactment provides to the contrary, nor shall the number of trustees be increased beyond four by virtue of any such appointment.

(b) Circumstances in which the power may be exercised

Section 36(6) gives the trustee of a trust the option to increase the number of trustees to a maximum of four through the appointment of additional trustees. This power is subject to any express terms in the trust or by statute requiring the number of trustees to be increased.

(c) Persons who may appoint additional trustees

The mechanisms by which such appointments may be made are almost identical to those adopted under s 36(1).

(i) The person or persons nominated by the trust instrument

Priority is given to the settlor's express intention in the form of persons nominated for the purpose of appointing trustees in the trust instrument. Providing they are willing and able to act, they alone can exercise the power.

---

[72] As amended by Trusts of Land and Appointment of Trustees Act 1996, Sch 3, para 3(11).

(ii) The trustee or trustees for the time being

In the absence of any nominated persons the other trustees, whether a sole trustee or co-trustees, may appoint additional trustees. Obviously, if there are no trustees remaining because of death, the provisions of s 36(1) will operate. A limited power is available to the donee of an unregistered enduring power of attorney[73] or a registered lasting[74] power of attorney to exercise the functions of the trustees to appoint a new trustee if to do so is necessary to ensure that there are two trustees to receive capital money arising from a disposition of land.[75]

(3) Making appointments under s 36

(a) Persons who may be appointed

In the case of substitute appointments, under s 36(1) the persons who may exercise the power can appoint whoever they desire as trustees and it is specifically provided that they may appoint themselves if they wish. However, due to a slight difference in drafting, persons who are nominated to appoint additional trustees are not specifically permitted to appoint themselves under s 36(6), and in *Re Power's Settlement*[76] it has been held that they cannot appoint themselves. Where there are already two trustees, it is not possible for them to retire and to be replaced by a single trustee, unless that trustee is a trust corporation recognized under English law.[77]

(b) Relevance of the beneficiaries' wishes

The person (or persons) entitled to appoint new trustees are under no obligation to consult the beneficiaries of the trust and ascertain their wishes as to who should be appointed. In *Re Brockbank*[78] Vaisey J held that the person entitled to appoint under s 36 could not be compelled to do what the beneficiaries wanted, as the right to appoint belonged solely to those whom it was given by the statute and the court was unwilling to interfere with its exercise.[79] The only means by which the beneficiaries could compel the appointment of the persons they wanted to be trustees would be to put an end to the trust[80] under the rule in *Saunders v Vautier* or to make a direction under the Trusts of Land and Appointment of Trustees Act 1996.[81] The power to make a direction under the 1996 Act does not apply if the person entitled to appoint new trustees was nominated by the trust instrument.

---

[73] It is no longer possible to create enduring powers of attorney, although existing unregistered powers may still be used, if registered—Mental Capacity Act 2005, Sch 4, Pt 1 para 1.

[74] Added by the Mental Capacity Act 2005.

[75] Trustee Act 1925, s 36(6A)–(6D), as inserted by the Trustee Delegation Act 1999.

[76] [1951] Ch 1074, CA.

[77] See *Adam and Co International Trustees Ltd v Theodore Goddard* (2000) ITELR 634.

[78] [1948] Ch 206.   [79] See also *Re Gadd* (1883) 23 Ch D 134; *Re Higginbottom* [1892] 3 Ch 132.

[80] [1948] Ch 206, at 210.

[81] S 19. This jurisdiction is discussed later in this chapter.

(c) Formalities of appointment

The appointment of new trustees, whether substitute trustees under s 36(1) or additional trustees under s 36(6), must be made in writing. However, an appointment made by deed will have the effect of vesting the trust property in the new trustees under s 40 of the Trustee Act 1925, subject to registration of the trustees as legal owners in the case of land and shares.

(d) Effect of appointment

Section 36(7) provides that:

> Every new trustee appointed under this section as well before as after all the trust property becomes by law, or by assurance, or otherwise vested in him, shall have the same powers, authorities and discretions, and may in all respects act as if he had been originally appointed a trustee by the instrument, if any, creating the trust.

This provision applies equally to the appointment of additional or substitute trustees.

5 Trustee Act 1925, s 41

(1) The power of the court to appoint new trustees

Section 41(1) of the Trustee Act 1925 provides:

> The court may, whenever it is expedient to appoint a new trustee or new trustees, and if it is found inexpedient difficult or impracticable so to do without the assistance of the court, make an order appointing a new trustee or new trustees either in substitution for or in addition to any existing trustee or trustees, or although there is no existing trustee.

(2) Scope of the power under s 41

This provision gives the court a very wide discretion to appoint trustees, either in substitution for, or in addition to, existing trustees. However, a number of features should be noted.

(a) Relation to other powers of appointment of trustees

Appointments will generally only be made under the jurisdiction of s 41 where they cannot be made through the exercise of an express power within the trust instrument, nor under the statutory power granted by s 36 of the Trustee Act 1925.[82]

---

[82] *Re Soulby's Trusts* (1873) 21 WR 256; *Re Gibbon's Trusts* (1882) 45 LT 756; *Re Sutton* [1885] WN 122.

(b) 'Whenever it is expedient to appoint…if it is found inexpedient, difficult or impractical so to do without the assistance of the court'

This double-limbed test sets down the circumstances in which the court may exercise the power of appointment. It must be both expedient for a substitute or additional trustee to be appointed and in some sense, because of the circumstances, the assistance of the court must be necessary. Section 41(1) itself specifies some such circumstances where the jurisdiction may need to be exercised:

> In particular…the court may make an order appointing a new trustee in substitution for a trustee who lacks capacity[83] to exercise his functions as a trustee or is a bankrupt, or is a corporation which is in liquidation or has been dissolved.

A number of illustrations can be given of other circumstances in which the power has been exercised. In *Re Smirthwaite's Trust*[84] the court exercised its statutory power[85] to appoint new trustees when all of the trustees named in the settlor's will had predeceased him. In *Re May's Will Trust*[86] one of three trustees of a will was in Belgium during the time of the German invasion and had not escaped. It was held that there was no evidence that she was 'incapable of acting' within the meaning of s 36(1) so that she could not be replaced by the continuing trustees, but the court appointed a new trustee under s 41. The court may also act where an express power or the power under s 36 is incapable of being exercised, for example if the donee of an express power is an infant.[87] In *Re Rendell's Trusts*[88] the court exercised its power to appoint a trustee where one of the surviving trustees was opposed to the appointment.

(c) Removal of trustees against their will

It is clear that s 41 permits the court to remove trustees from the trust against their will. In *Re Henderson* Bennet J stated:

> I do not think that it is open to doubt that on the language of the sub-section the court has jurisdiction to displace a trustee against his will and to appoint a new trustee in substitution for him. Take the case of a trustee who is a convicted felon or a bankrupt whom the beneficiaries desire to have replaced by a new trustee. On the language of the sub-section, in my judgement, the court has a discretion, which it can exercise, if it regards it as expedient so to do, by appointing a new trustee in place of the trustee who has been convicted of felony, or who is a bankrupt…I do not doubt that the section gives the court jurisdiction in a proper case to appoint new trustees in place of and against the will of an existing trustee. Before exercising that jurisdiction the court must be satisfied that it is expedient to make such an appointment.[89]

He held that a trustee who had refused to retire in place of the Public Trustee should be removed against her will because she had previously agreed to retire but had changed

---

[83] The words were substituted for the original wording of the statute by the Mental Capacity Act 2005.
[84] (1871) LR 11 Eq 251.   [85] Under the Trustee Act 1850.   [86] [1941] Ch 109.
[87] *Re Parson's* [1940] Ch 973.   [88] (1915) 139 LT Jo 249.   [89] [1940] Ch 764, at 767.

her mind for no reason of substance. This was followed by Roxburgh J in *Re Solicitor, A*[90] where a bankrupt solicitor was replaced by the court acting under s 41.

One limitation to the principle that the court can remove a trustee against his will under s 41 is that there must be no dispute as to the facts. This was emphasized by Cotton LJ in *Re Combs*[91] and accepted by Bennet J in *Re Henderson*.[92]

(3) **Exercise of the court's discretion**

The court's power to appoint under s 41 is discretionary, and it must be satisfied that any appointments are 'expedient'. The question whether an appointment was 'expedient' was raised in *Re Weston's Settlement*,[93] where there was an attempt to move a trust from England to Jersey for tax reasons, and to replace the English trustees with trustees in Jersey. Applications were made under the Variation of Trusts Act 1958 in favour of the infant beneficiaries of the trust and under s 41 for the appointment of new trustees. The court refused to exercise its discretion under either of these provisions. As to s 41, Lord Denning MR said:

> with the appointment of new trustees the Trustee Act 1925 gives no guide. It simply says that the court may appoint new trustees 'whenever it is expedient'. There being no guidance in the statute, it remains for the court to do the best it can.[94]

Several reasons for the refusal of the court to appoint appear from the judgment. First, the proposed move of the trust to Jersey was solely for reasons of tax avoidance. Second, there was a relatively slight connection between the beneficiaries and Jersey. They had lived there for only a short time, and there was a high probability that they would move after the trust had been transferred. As Harman LJ said, they 'cannot be said to have proved that they truly intend to make Jersey their home'.[95] Finally, the court referred to the inadequacy of the law in Jersey for dealing with trusts. In these circumstances the court refused to appoint trustees, and instead held that 'these are English settlements and they should hould remain so unless some good reason connected with the trusts themselves can be put forward'.[96]

In contrast, it should be noted that in *Re Windeatt's Will Trusts*[97] the court was willing to approve a scheme for the variation of a trust, including the appointment of new trustees in Jersey, where the family had lived there for some nineteen years. In such circumstances it seems likely that the court would have equally found it 'expedient' to appoint new trustees under s 41 if that had been necessary. Given the significant improvement in communications, and the increased recognition of trusts overseas, it is quite possible that the courts would now be more willing to entertain the appointment of trustees overseas than they have in the past where there is some real overseas

---

[90] [1952] Ch 328.   [91] (1884) 51 LT 45.
[92] [1940] Ch 764. See also *Popoff v Actus Management Ltd* [1985] 5 WWR 660.
[93] [1969] 1 Ch 223.   [94] [1969] 1 Ch 223, at 245.   [95] [1969] 1 Ch 223, at 248.
[96] [1969] 1 Ch 223, at 284.   [97] [1969] 1 WLR 692.

connection or other justification.[98] In *Richard v The Hon A.B. Mackay*,[99] Millett J suggested that where trustees were exercising their own discretion to appoint an overseas trustee and seek merely approval from the court, the court should only need to be satisfied that the decision was 'not so inappropriate that no reasonable trustee could entertain it'. He recognized that social conditions had moved on and that international families with international interests 'are as likely to make their home in one country as in another and as likely to choose one jurisdiction as another for the investment of their capital'. The court should not act in a way that frustrated this.

(4) Persons the court will appoint trustees

(a) General principles guiding the court's selection

In *Re Tempest*,[100] which concerned the appointment of new trustees under a predecessor to s 41,[101] the Court of Appeal laid down three criteria that the court will apply in exercising its discretion to appoint new trustees. These were set out by Turner LJ.

(i) Regard to the wishes of the settlor

> First, the court will have regard to the wishes of the persons by whom the trust has been created, if expressed in the instrument creating the trust, or clearly to be collected from it.[102]

(ii) Regard to the interests of the beneficiaries

> Another rule which may, I think, safely be laid down is this—that the court will not appoint a person to be a trustee with a view to the interest of some of the persons interested under the trust, in opposition either to the wishes of the testator or to the interests of the other cestuis que trust. I think so for this reason that it is of the essence of the duty of every trustee to hold an even hand between the parties interested under a trust.[103]

(iii) Regard to the effective execution of the trust

> A third rule which, I think, may safely be laid down is this—that the court in appointing a trustee will have regard to the question, whether his appointment will promote or impede the execution of the trust, for the very purpose of the appointment is that the trust may be better carried into execution.[104]

(iv) Applying the principles

The Court of Appeal held that the proposed trustee, Mr Petre, should not be appointed. Although there could be no objection to him 'in point of character, position or ability',

---

[98] See *Re Beatty's WT (No 2)* (1997) 11 *Trust Law International* 77; *Richard v Mackay* (1997) 11 *Trust Law International* 22 (decided 1987).   [99] (1997) 11 *Trust Law International* 22.
[100] (1866) 1 Ch App 485.   [101] Trustee Act 1850.   [102] (1866) 1 Ch App 485, at 487.
[103] (1866) 1 Ch App 485, at 487.   [104] (1866) 1 Ch App 485, at 488.

he fell foul of the rules proposed. First, he was the nominee of the beneficiary of the trust, Charles Tempest, and the testator's intentions had been to exclude him 'from all connection with his estate'. Second, the court considered that he had been:

> proposed as a trustee…with a view to his acting in the trust in the interests of some only of the objects of it…and not with a view to his acting as an independent trustee for the benefit of all the objects of the trusts.

More recently in *Alkin v Raymond*,[105] the High Court refused to appoint the testator's daughter to the trust to replace existing trustees on the basis that it was against the wishes of her father as testator and that it would not be effective for the administration of the estate, as it would be difficult for her to hold a reasonably objective balance between the competing claims to the estate.

(b) Persons the court will not normally appoint trustees

There are some persons who, irrespective of their abilities, the court will not normally appoint as trustees because of their relationship to the trust and the likelihood of a conflict of interest. The court will not appoint, except in exceptional circumstances,[106] a beneficiary or a beneficiary's spouse as trustee,[107] nor the solicitor to the life tenant or the solicitor to an existing trustee.[108] Nor, according to a number of cases, will the court appoint a person living abroad unless the trust's property or the beneficiaries are also abroad,[109] although it may be that this attitude is changing.[110]

6 Trusts of Land and Appointment of Trustees Act 1996

(1) Appointment of trustees at the direction of the beneficiaries

It has been seen that ss 36 and 41 of the Trustee Act 1925 provide mechanisms for the appointment of new trustees, whether additional or replacement, in specified circumstances. However, in neither case do the beneficiaries of the trust have the right to require the appointment of a specific person as a trustee, as the right to appoint is vested in either other persons (the surviving or continuing trustees, or the personal

---

[105] [2010] WTLR 117.

[106] For example, where no independent person can he found to take up the office: *ex p Clutton* (1853) 17 Jur 988; *Re Clissold's Settlement* (1864) 10 LT 642; *Re Burgess' Trusts* [1877] WN 87; *Re Parrott* (1881) 30 WR 97; *Re Lightbody's Trusts* (1884) 33 WR 452.

[107] *Ex p Clutton* (1853) 17 Jur 988; *ex p Conybeare's Settlement* (1853) 1 WR 458; *Re Orde* (1883) 24 Ch D 271; *Re Kemp's Settled Estate* (1883) 24 Ch D 485, CA; *Re Coode* (1913) 108 LT 94.

[108] *Re Kemp's Settled Estates* (1883) 24 Ch D 485 27; *Re Norris* (1884) 27 Ch D 333; *Re Earl of Stamford* [1896] 1 Ch 288; *Re Spencer's Settled Estates* [1903] 1 Ch 75.

[109] *Re Guibert's Trust Estate* (1852) 16 Jur 852; *Re Hill's Trusts* [1874] WN 228; *Re Drewe's Settlement Trusts* [1876] WN 168; *Re Freeman's Settlement Trusts* (1887) 37 Ch D 148; *Re Liddiard* (1880) 14 Ch D 310; *Re Whitehead's Will Trusts* [1971] 1 WLR 833.

[110] See *Re Beatty's WT (No 2)* (1997) 11 *Trust Law International* 77; *Richard v Mackay* (1997) 11 *Trust Law International* 22.

representatives of the last surviving trustee) or the court. However, the Trusts of Land and Appointment of Trustees Act 1996, s 19 has granted the beneficiaries of a trust the right to direct the appointment of new trustees. Section 19(2)(b) provides that the beneficiaries can give:

> a written direction to the trustees or trustee for the time being (or, if there are none, to the personal representative of the last person who was a trustee) to appoint by writing to be a trustee or trustees the person or persons specified in the direction.

As in the case of the power to direct the retirement of trustees, this right to direct appointment can only be exercised if the beneficiaries would otherwise be entitled to take advantage of the rule in *Saunders v Vautier*[111] because they are of age, legally competent, and collectively entitled to the trust property.[112] The right to direct appointments is also excluded if the trust instrument expressly nominates a person for the purpose of appointing new trustees,[113] or if the right has been expressly excluded.[114] The beneficiaries' right to direct the appointment of new trustees cannot be exercised so as to appoint more than the maximum number of trustees permitted under the Trustee Act 1925.[115]

Problems remain concerning the practical implementation of the beneficiaries' right to direct the appointment of new trustees. Whereas s 19(3) makes clear that a trustee who is directed to retire must do so, there is no equivalent provision requiring the trustees (or the personal representative of the last surviving trustee) to carry into effect a direction to appoint. If the trustees are required to make the directed appointment, it is unclear whether they would be liable if the person nominated by the beneficiaries was unsuitable and the trust suffered a loss in consequence of the appointment. Presumably, the appointing trustees would be exempt from any liability for breach of trust in such circumstances because the appointment would have been made at the unanimous instigation of the beneficiaries.

(2) Appointment of a substitute for a mentally incapable trustee

It has already been noted that, where a trustee has become mentally incapable, the right to appoint a substitute trustee may have become moribund. This may be because the persons enjoying the right to appoint, whether under an express power or under s 36 of the Trustee Act 1925, are unwilling to do so, or because there is no one entitled to appoint a substitute: for example, where there is a sole trustee who has become incapable and the trust instrument does not include an express power of appointment. In order to facilitate the appointment of a substitute without the need for the court to intervene, s 20(2) of the Trusts of Land and Appointment of Trustees Act 1996 (as amended by the Mental Capacity Act 2005) provides that the beneficiaries of the trust may give 'a written direction to appoint by writing the person or persons specified in the direction to be a trustee or trustees in place of the incapable trustee'.

---

[111] (1841) 4 Beav 115.   [112] S 19(1)(b).   [113] S 19(1)(a).   [114] S 21(5)–(8).
[115] Trusts of Land and Appointment of Trustees Act 1996, s 19(5).

The right to give such a direction only arises where a trustee lacks capacity to exercise his functions as trustee,[116] and there is no person who is both entitled and willing and able to appoint a trustee in place of him under s 36(1) of the Trustee Act 1925.[117] The right to direct an appointment in such circumstances is only conferred upon the beneficiaries if they would otherwise be entitled to take advantage of the rule in *Saunders v Vautier*: they are of age, legally competent, and collectively entitled to the trust property.[118] The direction to appoint must be made to either a receiver of the incapable trustee,[119] or a person acting for him under an enduring or lasting power of attorney,[120] or a person with authority to act under the Court of Protection.[121] The beneficiaries' right to direct an appointment under s 20 may be expressly excluded in the trust instrument,[122] or, in the case of a trust created before the commencement of the Act, may be excluded by the execution of a deed to that effect by all the surviving settlors.[123]

7 Appointment of special trustees

A number of statutory provisions provide for the appointment of special trustees.

(1) Judicial Trustees Act 1896

(a) Nature of a judicial trustee

A judicial trustee is a trustee appointed by the court under s 1 of the Judicial Trustees Act 1896. The person appointed a judicial trustee is an officer of the court, and is therefore subject to its control and supervision. The purpose of appointing a judicial trustee is to ensure the proper execution of the trust, but without incurring the full expense of having the trust administered by the court. This was explained by Jenkins J in *Re Ridsdel*:[124]

> The object of the Judicial Trustees Act 1896…was to provide a middle course in cases where the administration of the estate by the ordinary trustees had broken down, and it was not desired to put the estate to the expense of a full administration of the estate…a solution was found in the appointment of a judicial trustee, who acts in close concert with the court and under conditions enabling the court to supervise his transactions.[125]

Although the judicial trustee may be given special directions by the court, and he may apply for the court's directions in his decisions, the purpose is not to 'reduce the

---

[116] S 20(1)(a). Capacity is defined under the Mental Capacity Act 2005, ss 1 and 2.
[117] S 20(1)(b).   [118] S 20(1)(c).   [119] S 20(2)(a).   [120] S 20(2)(b).
[121] S 20(2)(c) (as amended by the Mental Capacity Act 2005). For details of the Court of Protection, see Mental Capacity Act 2005.   [122] S 21(5).   [123] S 21(6).   [124] [1947] Ch 597.
[125] [1947] Ch 597, at 605.

administration of an estate by a judicial trustee to very much the same position as where an estate is being administered by the court and every step has to be taken in pursuance of the court's directions'.[126]

The appointment of a judicial trustee was particularly important prior to the enactment of s 50 of the Administration of Justice Act 1985, since it was the only way that a personal representative could be replaced. Although a judicial trustee is largely in the same position as any other trustee, for example he has the power to compromise claims,[127] he cannot appoint his successor under the provisions of s 36 of the Trustee Act 1925.

(b) Appointment of a judicial trustee

(i) The power to appoint

The Judicial Trustees Act 1896, s 1(1) provides that:

> Where application is made to the court by or on behalf of the person creating or intending to create a trust, or by or on behalf of a trustee or beneficiary, the court may, in its discretion, appoint a person (in this Act called a judicial trustee) to be a trustee, either jointly with any other person or as sole trustee, and if sufficient cause is shown, in place of any existing trustees.

The power to appoint a judicial trustee is therefore purely discretionary. It is also clear that a trustee may be removed against his will and replaced by a judicial trustee. In *Thomas and Agnes Carvel Foundation v Carvel*,[128] Lewison J held that the survivor of two persons who had made mutual wills and his personal representative was a trustee for the purposes of this section:

> As Clauson J made clear in *In re Hagger*[129] the survivor of two persons who make mutual wills is treated as a trustee, and as Lord Camden in *Dufour v Pereira*[130] said the trust binds those who claim under him. Accordingly, in my judgment the survivor and his executor are trustees in the usual sense of that word. A person entitled to enforce the trust thus imposed by law is, in my judgment, a beneficiary. In my judgment, therefore, although a person claiming under the English doctrine of mutual wills is not entitled to make an application under section 50 of the 1985 Act, he is entitled to apply under section 1 of the 1896 Act.[131]

(ii) Persons who may be appointed

Section 1(3) provides that:

> Any fit and proper person nominated for the purpose in the application may be appointed a judicial trustee, and, in the absence of such nomination, an official of the court may be appointed, and in any case a judicial trustee shall be subject to the control and supervision of the court as an officer thereof.

---

[126] *Re Ridsdel* [1947] Ch 597.   [127] *Re Ridsdel* [1947] Ch 597.   [128] [2008] Ch 395.
[129] [1930] 2 Ch 190, at 195.   [130] (1769) 21 ER 332.   [131] (1769) 21 ER 332, at 404 [29].

(iii) Remuneration of judicial trustees

Section 1(5) provides that the court may direct that the judicial trustee be remunerated for his services from the trust property.

(2) **Public Trustee Act 1906**

(a) Nature of the public trustee

The Public Trustee is a corporation sole which may act as an ordinary trustee, custodian trustee,[132] or judicial trustee.[133] He was established by the Public Trustee Act 1906, and one main function is to administer small estates. Once appointed, he has the same powers and duties, rights and liabilities as an ordinary trustee.

(b) Appointment of the public trustee

(i) Appointment as an ordinary trustee

Section 5(1) provides that the Public Trustee may be appointed trustee of any will or settlement:

> either as an original or as a new trustee, or as an additional trustee, in the same cases, and in the same manner, and by the same persons or court, as if he were a private trustee, with this addition, that, though the trustees originally appointed were two or more, the public trustee may be appointed sole trustee.

This is subject to the limitations that he may decline to accept any trust, although not on the grounds of the small value of the trust fund,[134] that he may not act as the trustee of any trust under a deed of arrangement for the benefit of creditors or as administrator of an insolvent estate,[135] and that he shall not accept any trust exclusively for religious or charitable purposes.[136] The court may order the appointment of the Public Trustee even if the trust instrument prohibits his appointment.[137]

(ii) Appointment as a custodian trustee

Section 4(1) provides that:

> Subject to rules under this Act the public trustee may, if he consents to act as such, and whether or not the number of trustees has been reduced below the original number, be appointed to be custodian trustee of any trust—
>
> (a) by order of the court made on the application of any person on whose application the court may order the appointment of a new trustee; or
>
> (b) by the testator, settlor or other creator of any trust; or
>
> (c) by the person having power to appoint new trustees.

---

[132] A custodian trustee holds the property of the trust fund and the documents relating to such property, but leaves the administration of the trust to the managing trustee. See Public Trustee Act 1906, s 4(2). See Chapter 21.   [133] Public Trustee Act 1906, s 2(1).

[134] S 2(3).   [135] S 2(4).   [136] S 2(5).   [137] S 5(3).

Circumstances	Relevant power	Exercised by?
Initial appointment	Own choice	Settlor/testator; Court (if original trustee disclaims the trust, or if the trust would otherwise fail for want of a trustee)
Appointment of additional trustee	Express power	Person nominated
	Trustee Act 1925, s 36(6)	Trustees for the time being
	TOLATA* 1996, s 19	Beneficiaries
Replacement of existing trustee	Express power	Person nominated
	Trustee Act 1925, s 36 (in specified circumstances)	'Surviving or continuing trustees' or personal representatives of last such
	TOLATA 1996, s 19	Beneficiaries
	TOLATA 1996, s 20 (Mentally incapable trustee)	Beneficiaries
	Trustee Act 1925, s 41	Court
Retirement without replacement	Trustee Act 1925, s 39	Retiring trustee with consent of others
	TOLATA 1996, s 19	Beneficiaries with consent of remaining trustees
Removal of trustee	Trustee Act 1925, s 36	'Surviving or continuing trustees' or personal representatives of last such
	TOLATA 1996, s 19	Beneficiaries (with consent of remaining trustees if not being replaced)
	Trustee Act 1925, s 41	Court
	Inherent jurisdiction	Court

* Trusts of Land and Appointment of Trustees Act 1996

Figure 24.1 Summary of powers to appoint and remove trustees

(iii) Intestate estates

The Public Trustee holds the estate of a person who dies intestate, pending the appointment of an administrator.[138]

8 The court's inherent jurisdiction to remove trustees

In addition to the statutory power to remove trustees under s 41 of the Trustee Act 1925, the court possesses an inherent jurisdiction to remove trustees in an action

---

[138] Law of Property (Miscellaneous Provisions) Act 1994, s 14.

begun by writ for the administration or execution of a trust.[139] Although there is little authority as to the exercise of this jurisdiction, the overriding consideration seems to be the welfare of the beneficiaries and the trust estate. Some guidance was provided by the Privy Council in *Letterstedt v Broers*,[140] where Lord Blackburn said:

> The reason why there is so little to be found in the books on this subject is probably that suggested by Mr Davey in his argument. As soon as all questions of character are as far settled as the nature of the case admits, if it appears clear that the continuance of the trustee would be detrimental to the execution of the trusts, even if for no other reason than that human infirmity would prevent those beneficially interested, or those who act for them, from working in harmony with the trustee, and if there is no reason to the contrary from the intentions of the framer of the trust to give this trustee a benefit or otherwise, the trustee is always advised by his own counsel to resign, and does so. If, without any reasonable ground, he refused to do so, it seems to their Lordships that the court might think it proper to remove him...[141]

The court may act under its inherent jurisdiction even where the facts are in dispute.[142] The inherent jurisdiction was used to remove three trustees against their will in *Clarke v Heathfield (No 2)*.[143] The case concerned a trust fund of money belonging to the National Union of Mineworkers. The three trustees transferred the funds abroad to prevent them being sequestrated as a result of the illegal industrial action by the union. Members of the NUM sought to have the trustees removed by the court. Mervyn Davies J held that the court should exercise its power to remove the trustees under its inherent jurisdiction. A number of factors influenced his decision to remove, including the trustees' refusal to obey orders of the court and that the transfer of the funds abroad rendered them unavailable for the purposes for which they were contributed by the membership of the union.[144]

9 Summary

Having considered the range of powers by which trustees may be appointed, it is possible to summarize how they may operate in practice. This is set out in Figure 24.1.

---

[139] *Re Wrightson* [1908] 1 Ch 789; *Re Henderson* [1940] Ch 764.   [140] (1884) 9 App Cas 371.
[141] (1884) 9 App Cas 371, at 386.
[142] *Re Chetwynd's Settlement* [1902] 1 Ch 692; *Re Wrightson* [1908] 1 Ch 789; *Re Henderson* [1940] Ch 764.
[143] [1985] ICR 606.
[144] The jurisdiction has also been used in *Bridge Trustees Ltd v Noel Penny Turbines* [2008] EWHC 2054 (Ch), to remove the donee of a fiduciary power against his will. The donee was not a trustee, and therefore fell outside the jurisdiction of the Trustee Act 1925, s 41.

25

Accountability of trustees

Throughout Part V it has been seen that trustees, by virtue of their legal ownership, enjoy powers of management and control over the trust property. They are under a duty to act in the best interests of the beneficiaries of the trust, but inevitably their position opens to them tremendous possibilities for abuse. There are some basic equitable duties and liabilities imposed on trustees to make them accountable to the beneficiaries, which are explored in this chapter.

1 Introduction

Part VII of this book considers the question of how the trustees of a trust are controlled and supervised, and in particular Chapter 26 details the general mechanisms by which such control is affected. It will be seen that the prime responsibility for supervising the activities of the trustees falls to the beneficiaries, who are able to complain to the court if they believe the trustees have committed, or are about to commit, a breach of trust. If the beneficiaries are able to apply to the court before the alleged breach has taken place they may obtain an injunction against the trustees to restrain them from committing the contemplated breach.[1] If the breach has already occurred, there are a number of other remedies which may be available to the beneficiaries.[2]

Trustees are also subject to a number of duties which enable the beneficiaries to keep a better check on their activities by entitling them to obtain information which will inform them of the trustees' actions and may enable the beneficiaries to detect breaches of trust. This chapter will consider those duties.

2 The duty to act unanimously

One safeguard to the proper conduct of a trust is the appointment of joint trustees. Where the trust property is held by a sole trustee, the opportunities for abuse will be

---

[1] See Chapter 6   [2] See Chapter 27.

greater, since a co-trustee cannot act alone without the concurrence of his fellow trustees. For this reason, in the context of land, overreaching, which defeats the interests of the beneficiaries of a trust of land, is only permitted by statute where any capital money is paid to or by the direction of at least two trustees.[3] The 'two-trustee' rule has been clarified and strengthened by the Trustee Delegation Act 1999 under which, if one of two trustees has delegated his powers relating to the sale of land to the other trustee, the sole trustee-cum-attorney cannot give a valid receipt without a second person being added as trustee.[4]

Except in the case of pension fund trusts[5] and charity trusts, co-trustees must generally act unanimously.[6] They cannot act on the basis of a majority decision.[7] The principle was stated by Jessel MR in *Luke v South Kensington Hotel Ltd*:

> There is no law that I am acquainted with which enables the majority of trustees to bind the minority. The only power to bind is the act of [them all].[8]

Illustrations of the application of the requirement of unanimity can be drawn from a number of areas. If one of several co-trustees enters into a contract to sell trust property to a third party, the duty to act unanimously means that the contract cannot be enforced against the trust.[9] Similarly, the trustees must act unanimously in the exercise of their discretions. In *Tempest v Lord Camoys*[10] one of two trustees wished to exercise their discretion to purchase land with the trust property, but the other trustee refused to concur in the purchase. The Court of Appeal held that, as the refusing trustee had properly exercised his discretion, the court could not interfere and the purchase could not take place as the trustees were not unanimous. However, in *Messeena v Carr*[11] Lord Romilly MR held that there was no breach of trust where a discretion was exercised by one of two trustees and the other 'approved and sanctioned what was done'. A receipt which is given for money by only one of two trustees will be ineffective to discharge the payor unless this is done by way of an express term in the trust instrument. Therefore, in *Lee v Sankey*[12] a firm of solicitors was held not to have been discharged when it paid over the proceeds of a testator's real estate and was given a receipt by one of the two trustees of the will, who misappropriated the money and died insolvent.

In some undefined but exceptional circumstances it seems that the duty to act unanimously will not apply. In *Nicholson v Smith*,[13] for example, it was held that notice of the intention to renew a lease by one of two trustees was sufficient.

---

[3] Law of Property Act 1925, ss 2 and 27. See also *State Bank of India v Sood* [1997] 1 All ER 169.

[4] Trustee Delegation Act 1999, s 7. The same is true where there are two or more trustees all of whom have delegated their powers to the same agent.

[5] S 32 Pensions Act 1995 provides that trustees of an occupational pension scheme may make decisions by a majority.

[6] The trust instrument may specify circumstances in which the trustees do not need to be unanimous.

[7] See *Leyton v Sneyd* (1818) 8 Taunt 532; *Tempest v Lord Camoys* (1882) 21 Ch D 571, CA; *Astbury v Astbury* [1898] 2 Ch 111; *Boardman v Phipps* [1967] 2 AC 46. HL.   [8] (1879) 11 Ch D 121, at 125.

[9] *Naylor v Goodall* (1877) 47 LJ Ch 53.   [10] (1882) 21 Ch D 571.   [11] (1870) LR 9 Eq 260.

[12] (1873) LR 15 Eq 204.   [13] (1882) 22 Ch D 640.

3 The duty to exercise discretions properly

(1) The duties of trustees relating to the exercise of discretion

Where trustees have discretion as to how the trust property should be managed or allocated, they must exercise their discretion properly. It is not for the courts to force the trustees to reach a particular conclusion in the exercise of their discretion, but they will intervene if the trustees exercise their discretion improperly or improperly fail to exercise it. In *Tempest v Lord Camoys*[14] Jessel MR said:

> It is settled law that when a [settlor] has given a pure discretion to trustees as to the exercise of a power, the court does not enforce the exercise of the power against the wish of the trustees, but it does prevent them from exercising it improperly.[15]

(2) The trustees' duty to consider exercising a discretion

Trustees are under a duty to consider whether they should exercise any discretion that they hold with regard to the trust property, even though the court cannot compel how the discretion should be exercised. These principles were applied in *Tempest v Lord Camoys*. Mr Fleming, one of the trustees, had properly considered the exercise of his discretion and had refused to invest the trust property in land or to raise money by way of a mortgage. As Brett LJ said:

> there was undoubtedly an absolute discretion in the trustees as to what land they should purchase. Mr Fleming has not refused to exercise the power at all, but has objected to purchase this particular property. It needs no authority to induce us to hold that if a discretion is given to trustees as to what property they should purchase the Court will not take it out of their hands.[16]

In *Turner v Turner*[17] the court set aside deeds of appointment which had been exercised by the trustees on the grounds that, although they appeared to be valid, the trustees had not even read them. In effect, there had been no real consideration whether or not the power should be exercised. In *Klug v Klug*,[18] a trustee had refused to concur in an advancement because the beneficiary (her daughter) had married without her consent. Neville J held that the court would intervene to direct the payment because the trustee 'has not exercised her discretion at all'.

(3) Relevance of the beneficiaries' wishes

Where the trustees of a trust hold discretionary powers it is they alone who must decide whether or not to exercise the discretion. Except in respect of a trust of land,[19] trustees

---

[14] (1882) 21 Ch D 571.   [15] (1882) 21 Ch D 571, at 578.   [16] (1882) 21 Ch D 571.
[17] [1984] Ch 100.   [18] [1918] 2 Ch 67.
[19] Trusts of Land and Appointment of Trustees Act 1996, s 11. Stevens and Pearce, *Land Law* (5th edn, 2013), Chapter 13.

are not subject to an obligation to consult their beneficiaries before they exercise their discretions, nor are they obliged to follow beneficiaries' wishes. In *Re Brockbank*[20] Vaisey J refused to compel a trustee to exercise his power to appoint new trustees under s 36 of the Trustee Act 1925[21] in the manner demanded by the beneficiaries and other trustees. He emphasized the discretionary nature of the power:

> The power of nominating a new trustee is a discretionary power, and, in my opinion is no longer exercisable and, indeed, can no longer exist if it has become one of which the exercise can be dictated by others.

This statement no longer holds completely true following the Trusts of Land and Appointment of Trustees Act 1996, which gives beneficiaries a limited authority to direct the appointment of new trustees.[22] However, the proposition set out remains accurate in respect of other trustee discretions, even in situations where the beneficiaries can call for the appointment of new trustees or bring the trust to an end under the rule in *Saunders v Vautier*.[23] The beneficiaries cannot dictate how the trustees should exercise their discretion.

(4) **Improper exercise of discretion**

(a) **General principles**

Given that the courts will intervene if trustees exercise, or threaten to exercise, their discretion improperly, the question naturally arises as to the circumstances in which an exercise will be regarded as improper. The difficulty, similar to that faced in the judicial review of administrative decisions, is that the court does not act as the judge of whether trustees make the 'right' decision. The court will only interfere in limited circumstances. This was explained by Lord Truro LC in *Re Beloved Wilkes' Charity*:

> it is to the discretion of the trustees that the execution of the trust is confided, that discretion being exercised with an entire absence of indirect motive, with honesty of intention, and with a fair consideration of the subject. The duty of supervision on the part of the court will thus be confined to the question of the honesty, integrity, and fairness with which the deliberation has been conducted, and will not be extended to the accuracy of the conclusion arrived at…[24]

However, it is clear that trustees do not enjoy an absolute discretion.

There are circumstances in which the court will be prepared to intervene.

(b) **Fraudulent exercise**

The court will clearly intervene if it can be shown that a discretion was exercised fraudulently.[25]

---

[20] [1948] Ch 206.   [21] See Chapter 24.
[22] See Chapter 24. Trusts of Land and Appointment of Trustees Act 1996, ss 19–21 enable the beneficiaries of a trust to direct the trustees to make appointments, or compel retirements, if they would otherwise be able to bring the trust to an end under the rule in *Saunders v Vautier*.   [23] (1841) 4 Beav 115.
[24] (1851) 3 Mac & G 440.   [25] *Cloutte v Storey* [1911] 1 Ch 18.

(c) Improper motives

The court will intervene if the trustee exercises or refuses to exercise the power for irrelevant and extraneous motives. For example, in *Klug v Klug*[26] the court intervened where one of two trustees refused to exercise her discretionary power of advancement[27] in favour of her daughter because she had married without her consent. In the Irish case of *Tomkin v Tomkin*[28] a valuable house and land near Dublin had been left under a family trust. The trustee, who was also a beneficiary, had a power to postpone sale. TC Smyth J held that the trustee 'by deliberate inaction, was content to let matters lie so that at a future date he could more conveniently acquire the trust property without having explored or realised its development potential'. He also allowed members of his family to occupy the property without payment of rent. It was held that the trustee was in breach of trust for acting as if he were the sole owner and for disregarding the interests of the other beneficiaries. The judge indicated that the property should be sold.

(d) Failure to take account of relevant matters

The ability of the court to intervene and impugn an exercise of the trustees' discretion was recognized by the House of Lords in *Dundee General Hospital Board of Management v Walker*,[29] where Lord Reid stated:

> If it can be shown that the trustees considered the wrong question, or that, although they purported to consider the right question they did not really apply their minds to it or perversely shut their eyes to the facts or that they did not act honestly or in good faith, then there was no true decision and the court will intervene.[30]

This statement raises the possibility that the courts might be prepared to intervene and annul a decision on which trustees were simply misdirected or in error, rather than acting fraudulently or improperly. A number of cases, establishing a doctrine known as the rule in *Re Hastings-Bass*,[31] took the view that decisions of trustees which were demonstrated to be erroneous could be annulled. The doctrine was reviewed by the Supreme Court in *Futter v Revenue and Customs*.[32] The case involved two conjoined appeals in which the court was asked to set aside decisions of trustees which had attracted unforeseen tax disadvantages. The Court of Appeal[33] had held that the law had taken a 'seriously wrong turn' and that the court should 'reverse that error

---

[26] [1918] 2 Ch 67. This is one possible explanation of the case. Another is that the discretion had not even been considered.   [27] See Chapter 15.

[28] 1998/6924P (8 July 2003).   [29] [1952] 1 All ER 896.

[30] [1952] 1 All ER 896, at 905. This formulation was cited with approval by Robert Walker J in *Scott v National Trust* [1998] 2 All ER 705, at 717–718.

[31] [1975] Ch 25. The view of the Supreme Court was that the doctrine actually originated in *Mettoy Pension Trustees Ltd v Evans* [1990] 1 WLR 1587.   [32] [2013] UKSC 26.

[33] [2011] EWCA Civ 197. This was a conjoined appeal from the earlier decisions in *Pitt v Holt* [2010] EWHC 45 (Ch) and *Futter v Futter* [2010] EWHC 449 (Ch).

and put the law back on the right course.'[34] The Supreme Court affirmed this ruling, but held that in one case the decision of the trustees could be reversed on the grounds of mistake.[35] The view of the Supreme Court (confirming the Court of Appeal decision) was that the circumstances in which a decision of trustees could be set aside was significantly narrower than the first instance decisions applying the rule in *Re Hastings-Bass* had suggested. A decision of trustees would be void where the trustees acted beyond their powers ('excessive execution').[36] On the other hand, where a decision was within the powers of the trustees, it could be set aside as improperly made (or held voidable for 'inadequate deliberation') only where there had been a breach of duty on the part of the trustees.[37] Where the trustees 'have been given, and have acted on, information or advice from an apparently trustworthy source, and what the trustees purport to do is within the scope of their power' the only remedies would be for mistake (if applicable) or an action in negligence against the provider of the advice. An intermediate situation was where a discretion had been exercised fraudulently (for an improper purpose), where there was problematic[38] Court of Appeal authority,[39] which might need to be revisited, that the exercise of the power was void rather than merely voidable.

The rule in *Re Hastings-Bass* appeared to have become what some had described as a 'get out of jail free' card, in which, where a decision had been made that proved with hindsight to be disadvantageous (often because of the tax liabilities which it generated), the trustees and the beneficiaries could collude together to reverse the decision. The decision in *Futter v Revenue Commissioners* significantly limits the rule, and exposes trustees to greater jeopardy for incorrect decisions.[40]

(e) Excessive execution

Examples of excessive execution which will deprive an act of trustees of any effect would include a failure by trustees to act unanimously, or the use of the wrong instrument to make a purported transfer. Similarly, going beyond the scope of a discretion or power (which should logically include an administrative power—as Bean J appeared to indicate in *Dalriada Trustees v Faulds*[41]), for instance by making an appointment to a person who is not within the class of beneficiaries, will also be cases of excessive execution. Since a power of advancement can be used only to benefit an eligible beneficiary, a purported advance which fails to do so will also be an instance of excessive execution and so void.[42]

---

[34] [2011] EWCA Civ 197, per Longmore LJ, at [227]. By contrast Deputy Bailiff Birt, in the Jersey case of *In the Matter of the Green GLG Trust* [2002] JLR 571, at [25] to [28], considered that the rule in *Re Hastings-Bass* was 'entirely consistent with precedent and principle'.

[35] This aspect of the decision is considered in Chapter 4.

[36] [2013] UKSC 26 at [60], [80], and [93].   [37] [2013] UKSC 26 at [41], [73], and [93].

[38] [2013] UKSC 26, at [62].   [39] *Cloutte v Storey* [1911] 1 Ch 18.

[40] Given that what is alleged is a breach of trust, it is for a beneficiary to 'grasp the nettle' at ([2011] EWCA Civ 197, per Lloyd LJ at [130]) and bring the action for breach of fiduciary duty. It would be rare for trustees to bring such actions.   [41] [2012] 2 All ER 734, at [58].

[42] Lloyd LJ in the Court of Appeal [2011] EWCA Civ 197, at [66]; *Roadchef (Employee Benefits Trustees) Limited v Hill* [2014] EWHC 109 (Ch), at [110]–[123].

(f) Inadequate deliberation

According to Lloyd LJ in the Court of Appeal in *Futter v Revenue Commissioners,* the breach of duty required to make a decision voidable needs to be a breach of a fiduciary duty. This was confirmed by the Supreme Court. Fiduciary duty in this context must mean more than the breach of a duty of loyalty, and extend to a failure to take account of a material factor (such as the criteria for the exercise of a power,[43] or the fiscal consequences of a decision), or to consider an irrelevant matter.[44] Failing to consider a matter which was unlikely to have had an impact on a decision will be insufficient to justify the court's intervention.[45] Where trustees have with due care sought and acted upon professional advice from a competent adviser, they will not be in breach of fiduciary duty if the advice turns out to be incorrect. The remedy of the beneficiaries would then be a claim for breach of duty against the advisers. Lloyd LJ accepted:

> that this distinction makes potentially vulnerable an act done by trustees who fail to take any advice, whereas the same act done in the same circumstances by trustees who take advice which proves to be incorrect is not vulnerable.[46]

The Supreme Court did not require, as a condition of relief by the courts, that it must be shown that the trustees would have acted differently had they been properly informed.[47] It was felt that a more flexible approach might be required.[48] Whether to afford relief is subject to the discretion of the court, a discretion which can be subject to terms,[49] and which is unlikely to be exercised if prejudice would thereby be caused to third parties.

(g) Capriciousness

Re Manisty's Settlement[50] suggests that the court will intervene if trustees exercise a discretion capriciously. Templeman J stated that:

> The court may also be persuaded to intervene if the trustees act 'capriciously', that is to say, act for reasons which I apprehend could be said to be irrational, perverse or irrelevant to any sensible expectation of the settlor; for example, if they chose a beneficiary by height or complexion or by the irrelevant fact that he was a resident of Greater London.

(h) Unreasonableness

There have been some cases in which the courts appear to have been willing to interfere with the exercise of a discretion by trustees merely on the grounds that it can be considered as unreasonable. For example in *Re Roper's Trust*[51] Fry J considered that

---

[43] *Roadchef (Employee Benefits Trustees) Limited v Hill* [2014] EWHC 109 (Ch), at [107].

[44] This was the interpretation adopted by Proudman J in *Roadchef (Employee Benefits Trustees) Limited v Hill* [2014] EWHC 109 (Ch), at [105].

[45] *Re Prudential Staff Pension Scheme* [2011] EWHC 960 (Ch).

[46] [2011] EWCA Civ 197, at [128].

[47] See *Sieff v Fox* [2005] 1 WLR 3811, at [119] (a decision of Lloyd LJ before *Futter v Revenue and Customs*).

[48] [2013] UKSC 26, at [91]–[92].   [49] [2013] UKSC 26, at [91]–[92].   [50] [1974] Ch 17.

[51] (1879) 11 Ch D 272.

the court could intervene if the trustees had 'not exercised a sound discretion'.[52] In contrast, cases from the mid-twentieth century favour the view that the court will not intervene merely on the grounds that the exercise was unreasonable if it was made in good faith.[53] In the Scottish case of *Dundee General Hospitals v Walker*[54] the trustees had accepted that the test for the exercise of their discretion was whether it was reasonable, but the House of Lords doubted that this was appropriate. Lord Normand concluded:

> I desire to reserve the question whether the trustee's decision was open to question on any other grounds save that it was dishonest, or that it involved a trespass beyond the limits of what was committed to them by the [settlor]. [I]t is one thing to say that the trustees must honestly discharge their trust and keep within the bounds of the powers and duties entrusted to them, and quite another to say that they must not fall into errors which other persons, including a court of law, might consider unreasonable.[55]

The possible breadth of the revised *Hastings-Bass* principle, as explained by the Supreme Court in *Futter v Revenue and Customs,* would permit intervention in some cases where trustees have acted unreasonably, but a level of unreasonableness amounting to perversity is likely to be required. In *Edge v Pensions Ombudsman* Scott V-C, in speaking of the basis on which a court would review pension trustees' decisions, said:

> The judge may disagree with the manner in which the trustees have exercised their discretion, but unless they can be seen to have taken into account irrelevant, improper or irrational factors, or unless their decision can be said to be one that no reasonable body of trustees properly directing themselves could have reached, the judge cannot intervene.[56]

The judge indicated that 'Their exercise of the discretionary power cannot be set aside simply because a judge... thinks it was not fair'.[57]

(i) Compelling action

According to Park J in *Breadner v Granville-Grossman,*[58] there is a substantial distinction 'between on the one hand, the courts declaring something which the trustees have done to be void, and, on the other hand, the courts holding that a trust takes effect as if the trustees had done something which they never did at all'. He considered that he had no jurisdiction to treat as effective the purported exercise of a power outside the time limits for its exercise where the trustees had made a mistake about the last date for its exercise. The power in that instance was a mere power, which in his view lapsed when the time limit expired. Fiduciary powers may be treated differently by the courts. It was recognized in *McPhail v Doulton*[59] that there were various ways in which the courts could secure the performance of discretionary trusts, and those methods may be equally applicable to fiduciary powers. They include directing the trustees to

---

[52] See also *Re Hodges* (1878) 7 Ch D 754; *Re Lofthouse* (1885) 29 Ch D 921, CA.
[53] See *Re Steed's Will Trusts* [1960] Ch 407, at 418.   [54] [1952] 1 All ER 896.
[55] [1952] 1 All ER 896, at 901. See also *Re Gulbenkian's Settlement Trusts* [1970] AC 508.
[56] [1998] Ch 512, at 534.   [57] [1998] Ch 512, at 535.   [58] [2000] 4 All ER 705, at 723.
[59] [1971] AC 424.

act in a particular way. For instance in *Klug v Klug*[60] the court ordered a payment to be made to a beneficiary despite the improper refusal of one trustee to concur in the decision; and in *Mettoy Pension Trustees Ltd v Evans*[61] Warner J was prepared to exercise a fiduciary power himself where there was no other person able to do so by reason of a conflict of interest. Also, in *Bridge Trustees Ltd v Noel Penny Turbines*[62] Purle QC felt able to invoke the court's inherent jurisdiction to replace an ex-trustee[63] of a pension trust for failure to exercise a fiduciary power to distribute surplus assets vested in him under the terms of the pension scheme.

(5) **Are trustees required to give reasons for their decisions?**

(a) No duty to give reasons

The basic rule was stated by Harman LJ in *Re Londonderry's Settlement*:[64]

> trustees exercising a discretionary power are not bound to disclose to their beneficiaries the reasons actuating them in coming to a decision.

This statement accords with a long line of authorities establishing that trustees, who have decided either to exercise or not to exercise their discretion, are under no duty to provide the beneficiaries with reasons for their decision. [65] The absence of a requirement to give reasons for a decision is well illustrated in *Re Beloved Wilkes' Charity*.[66] The case concerned a trust to provide for the education of a boy from one of three named parishes, or, if there was no suitable candidate from those parishes, a boy from any parish. The trustees decided to use the funds to support a boy, Charles Joyce, who was outside of the parish. Their exercise of the discretion was challenged on the grounds that there was a suitable boy, William Gale, from within the parishes. Lord Truro LC held that the trustees were under no duty to disclose the 'particulars' of why they had exercised the discretion in that way, and that there was no ground for imputing bad motives to the trustees from the affidavits.

(b) Justification for the rule

The main justification for the non-disclosure principle is that it is considered to be in the best interests of the decision-making process that it should be confidential.[67] In *Re Londonderry's Settlement*[68] Salmon LJ provided an explanation:

> So long as the trustees exercise [the power] bona fide with no improper motive, their exercise of the power cannot be challenged in the courts—and their reasons for acting as they did are, accordingly, immaterial. This is one of the grounds for the rule that trustees

---

[60] [1918] 2 Ch 67.   [61] [1990] 1 WLR 1587.   [62] [2008] EWHC 2054 (Ch).
[63] If the donee had remained a trustee, the court would have been able to use the power to remove trustees under Trustee Act 1925, s 41.   [64] [1965] Ch 918, at 928.
[65] *Re Gresham Life Assurance Society, ex p Penney* (1872) 8 Ch App 446; *Breakspear v Ackland* [2008] EWHC 220 (Ch); *Edge v Pensions Ombudsman* [1998] Ch 512, at 534. See also *Wilson v Law Debenture Trust Corpn* [1995] 2 All ER 337.   [66] (1851) 3 Mac & G 440.
[67] *Breakspear v Ackland* [2008] EWHC 220 (Ch).   [68] [1965] Ch 918, CA.

are not obliged to disclose to beneficiaries their reasons for exercising a discretionary power. Another ground for this rule is that it would not be for the good of the beneficiaries as a whole, and yet another that it might make the lives of trustees intolerable should an obligation rest upon them. Nothing would be more likely to embitter family feelings and the relationship between the trustees and members of the family, were the trustees obliged to state their reasons for the exercise of the powers entrusted to them. It might indeed well be difficult to persuade any persons to act as trustees were a duty to disclose their reasons, with all the embarrassment, arguments and quarrels that might ensue, added to their present not inconsiderable burdens.[69]

Similar sentiments have been expressed by Briggs J in *Breakspear v Ackland*.[70] The judge held that a beneficiary under a discretionary family settlement should not be provided with disclosure of a 'wish letter' in which the settlor had given non-binding guidance to the trustees. Briggs J conducted an extensive overview of authorities (including the Australian and Jersey decisions) and academic commentary relating to the *Londonderry* principle and concluded:

> Such confidentiality serves the due administration of family trusts both because it tends to reduce the scope for litigation about the rationality of the exercise by trustees of their discretions, and because it is likely to encourage suitable trustees to accept office, undeterred by a perception that their discretionary deliberations will be subjected to scrutiny by disappointed or hostile beneficiaries, and to potentially expensive litigation in the courts.[71]

The letter of wishes supported an inherently confidential process and should therefore, itself be confidential.[72]

(c) Trustees voluntarily provide reasons

Although there is no obligation on the trustees to give reasons for decisions regarding the exercise of their discretion, if they do choose to give reasons this may reveal grounds for the court to intervene. As Lord Truro LC said in *Re Beloved Wilkes' Charity*:

> If, however, as stated by Lord Ellenborough in *R v Archbishop of Canterbury*,[73] trustees think fit to state a reason and the reason is one which does not justify their conclusion, then the Court may say that they have acted by mistake and in error, and that it will correct their decision; but if, without entering into details, they simply state, as in many cases it would be most prudent and judicious for them to do, that they have met and considered and come to a conclusion, the Court has then no means of saying that they have failed in their duty, or to consider the accuracy of their conclusion.[74]

---

[69] [1965] Ch 918, CA, at 936–937.
[70] [2009] Ch 32. See Griffiths 'An Inevitable Tension? The Disclosure of Letters of Wishes' [2008] Conv 322; Fox 'Disclosure of a Settlor's Wish Letter in a Discretionary Trust' (2008) 67 CLJ 252.
[71] [2009] Ch 32, at 51 [54].
[72] [2009] Ch 32, at 52 [58]. The same conclusion was reached in Australia (*Hartigan Nominees Ltd v Rydge* (1992) 29 NSWLR 405) and Jersey (*Re Rabaiotti's 1989 Settlement* [2001] WTLR 953).
[73] (1812) 15 East 117.   [74] (1851) 3 Mac & G 440.

(d) **Where beneficiary has a legitimate expectation**

While there has been no general relaxation of the rule that beneficiaries are not entitled to be informed by trustees of their reason for a decision, in *Scott v National Trust*[75] Robert Walker J suggested that where the beneficiaries of a trust enjoy a legitimate expectation that a discretion will be exercised in their favour, they may be entitled to be given the reasons for a change of policy. He stated:

> If (for instance) trustees (whether of a charity, or a pension fund, or a private family trust) have for the last ten years paid £1,000 per quarter to an elderly, impoverished beneficiary of the trust it seems at least arguable that no reasonable body of trustees would discontinue the payment, without any warning, and without giving the beneficiary the opportunity of trying to persuade the trustees to continue the payment, at least temporarily. The beneficiary has no legal or equitable right to continued payment, but he or she has an expectation. So I am inclined to think that legitimate expectation may have some part to play in trust law as well as in judicial review cases.[76]

It has yet to be seen how far such a principle may be taken in the context of private trusts. However, it might perhaps have led to a different result in *Wilson v Law Debenture Trust Corpn plc*,[77] where it was held that pension trustees were not required to disclose their reasons for reversing a policy that they had pursued in the preceding years concerning the transfer of a fund surplus.

(6) **Access to information about the trust**

Although it has long been held that trustees cannot be obliged to disclose their reasons for making a discretionary decision, it has always been the case that they have been obliged to provide information to the beneficiaries such as the trust accounts showing how the trust funds are invested and how they have been distributed.

(i) *A beneficial right to disclosure of trust documents?*

The beneficiaries of a trust were historically regarded as enjoying the entitlement to access to trust documents on the basis of their proprietary right in the trust property. In *O'Rourke v Darbishire*[78] Lord Wrenbury explained:

> The beneficiary is entitled to see all trust documents because they are trust documents and because he is a beneficiary. They are in this sense his own. The proprietary right is a right to access to documents which are your own.[79]

(ii) *Supervisory jurisdiction*

The traditional rationale for the disclosure of trust information has at least two problems: it can at times conflict with the rule that trustees cannot be obliged to disclose reasons for discretionary decisions; and it does not explain what information

---

[75] [1998] 2 All ER 705.   [76] [1998] 2 All ER 705, at 718.   [77] [1995] 2 All ER 337.
[78] [1920] AC 581.   [79] [1920] AC 581, at 626–627.

should be provided to the objects of discretionary trusts. The first problem led the Court of Appeal in *Re Londonderry's Settlement* to a circular reasoning in attempting to explain why some documents held by trustees were not 'trust documents'.[80] The second problem is that the objects of a discretionary trust become beneficiaries only if a distributive decision is made in their favour; until that point they can therefore have no proprietary interest in the trust documents. The Privy Council in *Schmidt v Rosewood Trust Ltd*[81] addressed these issues. The case concerned an appeal from the Isle of Man by the object of a power of appointment under a trust who sought access to the trust documents. The Privy Council rejected the contention that an object of a power of appointment could not obtain disclosure of trusts documents because he did not have a proprietary interest under the trust. Instead the court took as the starting point that trusts are subject to the supervision of the courts, and to make that supervision effective, the beneficiaries or potential beneficiaries must have access to sufficient information. The right to seek disclosure of trust documents was an aspect of the inherent jurisdiction of the court to supervise the administration of trusts. On this basis a beneficiary will not enjoy an absolute right to disclosure of trust documents, as the court may exercise its inherent jurisdiction so as to limit disclosure. Lord Walker stated:

> no beneficiary (and least of all a discretionary object) has any entitlement as of right to disclosure of anything which can plausibly be described as a trust document. Especially when there are issues as to personal or commercial confidentiality, the court may have to balance the competing interests of different beneficiaries, the trustees' themselves and third parties. Disclosure may have to be limited and safeguards may have to be put in place. Evaluation of the claims of a beneficiary (and especially of a discretionary object) may be an important part of the balancing exercise which the court has to perform on the materials placed before it.[82]

The case did not require the Privy Council to decide whether the object of the power of appointment in question should be entitled to the disclosure sought, as this was remitted to the High Court of the Isle of Man for further consideration. The Privy Council did not provide comprehensive guidance as to the circumstances in which a request for disclosure might be denied. However, it did suggest that limits and safeguards may have to be put in place where there are issues of personal confidentiality and a need to balance the competing interests of different beneficiaries, the trustees, and third parties.[83]

---

[80] [1965] Ch 918, at 938. Salmon LJ appears to suggest that a document is a trust document because the trustee is entitled to see it, but that he is entitled to see it because it is a trust document in which he has a proprietary right.

[81] [2003] 2 AC 709; Davies 'Integrity of Trusteeship' (2004) 120 LQR 1. Hayton argues that the courts should take a lead from this decision and regard it as appropriate to insist on pension trustees providing reasons for their decisions: 'Pension Trusts and Traditional Trusts: Drastically Different Species of Trusts' [2005] Conv 229.   [82] [2003] 2 AC 709, at 734 [67].

[83] See also *Foreman v Kingstone* [2004] 1 NZLR 841 for further examination of the circumstances in which the court may refuse to limit disclosure of trust documents to beneficiaries.

Schmidt v Rosewood Trust Ltd[84] was followed and applied by Briggs J in *Breakspear v Ackland*.[85] The rationale allows the court to decline to order disclosure of documents such as an expression of wishes, or the minutes of trustees' meetings, even if those documents can properly be described as trust documents.[86]

(iii) Voluntary disclosure

Even in cases where the trustees cannot be compelled to provide information to beneficiaries, they may be permitted to do so if they consider that it is in the best interests of the trust.[87]

(iv) Ban on disclosure

Is it possible for a settlor to restrict the information which the trustees can provide to beneficiaries? Briggs J thought in *Breakspear v Ackland*[88] that such a fetter would not be lawful. The Supreme Court of Bermuda addressed the question in *Re Application for Information about a Trust*,[89] an appeal from Bermuda. There was an express provision in a trust deed that the trustees could provide information to the beneficiaries only with the consent of the protector, who was the principal beneficiary. There was a family feud between the protector and another beneficiary, who was entitled to around one third of the trust fund. The protector had instructed the trustees to release no information at all. The court held that a ban on providing information which purported to exclude the court's supervisory jurisdiction would be void because it would impact upon the accountability of trustees for the irreducible core obligations inherent in a trust. Otherwise, the court would have regard to the restriction of providing information when exercising its supervisory jurisdiction. In this case the family dispute meant that the mechanism was not working as the settlor must have intended, and disclosure of key information, subject to appropriate safeguards, was ordered.

(v) Disclosable information

Although the *Schmidt* case adopts a flexible approach in which there is no category of trust document which all beneficiaries have an absolute right to see, it does recognize that trustees have a duty to provide information enabling beneficiaries to ascertain their rights. Subject to the caveat that other considerations may operate, some of the older cases on disclosure provide a guide to the information which trustees can normally be expected to disclose. These hold that beneficiaries, unless there are special considerations, will be entitled to copies of the governing instruments, and to be told who the trustees are and

---

[84] [2003] 2 AC 709; Davies 'Integrity of Trusteeship' (2004) 120 LQR 1. Hayton argues that the courts should take a lead from this decision and regard it as appropriate to insist on pension trustees providing reasons for their decisions: 'Pension Trusts and Traditional Trusts: Drastically Different Species of Trusts' [2005] Conv 229.   [85] [2009] Ch 32.

[86] This result is consistent with the view of Harman LJ in *Re Londonderry's Settlement* [1965] Ch 918, at 933 and was also the conclusion reached by Potter J in *Foreman v Kingstone* [2004] 1 NZLR 841, at [89] applying the *Schmidt* rationale.   [87] *Breakspear v Ackland* [2009] Ch 32, at [67].

[88] [2009] Ch 32.   [89] (2013) 16 ITELR 85.

given their addresses.[90] In addition, most beneficiaries, including the objects of a discretionary trust,[91] will be entitled (at their own expense[92]) to see the trust accounts. In *Low v Bouverie*,[93] Lindley LJ said the trustees must: 'give all his cestui que trust, on demand, information with respect to the mode in which the trust fund has been dealt with, and where it is'. If the trustee fails to deliver accounts without good cause he will be liable to pay the costs of any application to the court to enforce the performance of his duty.[94]

Even before *Schmidt* it was recognized that the right to information was not unconditional. In *Low v Bouverie* a beneficiary who was entitled to a life interest sought information about any incumbrances on his interest as a prelude to obtaining a loan secured on his life interest. Lindley LJ said[95] that trustees were not required to provide this information. His reason was that: 'It is no part of the duty of a trustee to assist his cestui que trust in selling or mortgaging his beneficial interest and in squandering or anticipating his fortune.' In modern parlance it would be said that the information which the beneficiary was seeking was not required as part of making the trustees accountable.

(vi) Advice

The duty of the trustees is simply to provide the beneficiaries with information, not to provide them with advice. As Megarry V-C said in *Tito v Waddell (No 2)*:

> trustees...are under a duty to answer inquiries by the beneficiaries about the trust property...But that is a far remove from saying that trustees have a duty to proffer information and advice to their beneficiaries; and I think the courts should be very slow to advance along the road of imposing such a duty. I say nothing about what may be kindly or helpful; I deal only with a duty for the breach of which the trustees may be held liable in equity.[96]

(vii) Relevant considerations

Potter J in the New Zealand case of *Foreman v Kingstone* [97] summarized the factors which she thought could be derived from the from the judgment of the Board in *Schmidt* as matters that may be taken into account by the court in the exercise of its supervisory jurisdiction:

(a) Whether there are issues of personal or commercial confidentiality;

(b) the nature of the interests held by the beneficiaries seeking access;

(c) the impact on the trustees, other beneficiaries and third parties;

(d) whether some or all of the documents can be withheld in full or redacted form;

(e) whether safeguards can be imposed on the use of the trust documentation (for example, undertakings, professional inspection etc) to limit any use of the documentation beyond that which is legitimate; and

---

[90] *Re Murphy's Settlements* [1998] 3 All ER 1, a case where the settlor was required to provide this information to the objects of a discretionary trust.
[91] *Chaine-Nickson v Bank of Ireland* [1976] IR 393.
[92] See *Ottley v Gilby* (1845) 8 Beav 602; *Kemp v Burn* (1863) 4 Giff 348; *Re Watson* (1904) 49 Sol Jo 54.
[93] [1891] 3 Ch 82, at 99.   [94] *Re Skinner* [1904] 1 Ch 289.   [95] [1891] 3 Ch 82, at 99.
[96] [1977] Ch 106, at 242–243.   [97] [2004] 1 NZLR 841, at [90].

(f) whether (in the case of a family trust) disclosure would be likely to embitter family feelings and the relationship between the trustees and beneficiaries to the detriment of the beneficiaries as a whole.

Taking just one example, in a trust in favour of 'any charity in New Zealand', the trustees could be expected to react more positively to a request for information from a charity which had already received a distribution than another charity making a random request.

(7) **Reform required?**

The rule that trustees are not obliged to provide reasons for their decisions may mean that it is almost impossible for the beneficiaries to challenge a decision because they do not have sufficient evidence to sustain a claim that the trustees acted dishonestly, took irrelevant matters into consideration, or failed to take account of all relevant factors. For example, in *Re Beloved Wilkes' Charity*[98] one suggestion was that the trustees had chosen Charles Joyce rather than William Gale because Joyce was the brother of a clergyman who had been in contact with one of the trustees, who was also a clergyman. Without a comprehensive statement of the trustees' deliberations and reasons it was impossible to demonstrate that the discretion had been improperly exercised. In the contrasting case of *Klug v Klug*,[99] a daughter was able to show that her mother had acted improperly because she had letters where she had made clear that she would not exercise the discretion because of her daughter marrying contrary to her wishes.

Thus, the present law creates an inherent inconsistency. While equity seeks to prevent trustees acting improperly, it also fails to provide the beneficiaries with the right to know how decisions were reached so as to enable them to be subjected to proper scrutiny. This inconsistency runs deeper than this. Where a beneficiary takes legal action to challenge the exercise of a discretion, it is likely that he will be able to force the trustees to disclose their reasons. As Robert Walker J observed in *Scott v National Trust*:

> If a decision taken by trustees is directly attacked in legal proceedings, the trustees may be compelled either legally (through discovery or subpoena) or practically (in order to avoid adverse inferences being drawn) to disclose the substance of the reasons for their decision.[100]

However, it is submitted that the real need for reasons arises before any question relating to an exercise of discretion is brought to court. At present, the beneficiary is required to decide whether there are sufficient grounds to mount a legal challenge to an exercise of discretion—and to provide evidence to support this claim—while remaining in the dark as to the real reasons for it. In some circumstances the facts

---

[98] (1851) 3 Mac & G 440.   [99] [1918] 2 Ch 67.   [100] [1998] 2 All ER 705, at 719.

themselves may prima facie indicate that the discretion was wrongly exercised, but in many cases there may be no such external indications. In such circumstances the presumption that, in the absence of evidence to the contrary, a trustee has exercised his discretion properly, operates so as to present an insurmountable obstacle to effective scrutiny of the trustees' decision-making. The problems facing beneficiaries were well captured in a submission of counsel for the plaintiffs in *Wilson v Law Debenture Trust Corpn plc*,[101] where he argued that the trustee of a pension scheme was:

> in fact bound to give reasons for the exercise of discretions conferred upon the trustee by the relevant trust instrument because e eca it would be unreasonable that members of the scheme who had bought their interests should not be able to see that the trustee has exercised its discretion properly—which they cannot see in the absence of reasons given for the trustee's actual exercise of its discretion.[102]

In contrast to the reluctance of equity to oblige trustees to provide reasons for their decisions the law relating to the scrutiny of decision-making by public bodies has developed rapidly over the past fifty years, including the emergence of a duty to give reasons for decisions.[103] There is a strong case for a similar principle to apply to at least some trusts, such as pension schemes, where the beneficiaries have helped to generate the trust funds, even if the case is less compelling for family trusts.

This distinction is certainly inherent in *Breakspear v Ackland*,[104] where Briggs J deliberately left open the question of whether the principle of immunity applied outside the family trusts context.[105]

4 The duty to keep accounts and records

(1) Accounts and their availability to beneficiaries

Trustees are under a duty to keep a copy of the trust instrument, other essential trust documents, and accounts of the trust funds. This was so held in *Pearse v Green*,[106] where Plumer MR said that: 'It is the first duty of an accounting party, whether an agent, trustee, a receiver or executor to be constantly ready with his accounts.'[107]

(2) Audit

There is no general duty on trustees to have the trust accounts audited. However, a number of statutory provisions permit either the trustees or the beneficiaries to obtain an audit of the accounts. Audits may also be required by the trust instrument.

---

[101] [1995] 2 All ER 337.   [102] [1995] 2 All ER 337, at 348, summarized by Rattee J.
[103] See *Padfield v Minister of Agriculture, Fisheries and Food* [1968] AC 997; *R v Secretary of State for the Home Department, ex p Doody* [1994] 1 AC 531; *R v Secretary of State for the Home Department, ex p Fayed* [1997] 1 All ER 228.   [104] [2009] Ch 32.
[105] [2009] Ch 32, at 52 [58].   [106] (1819) 1 Jac & W 135.
[107] See also *Clarke v Lord Ormonde* (1821) Jac 108; *Springett v Dashwood* (1860) 2 Giff 521.

(a) The Trustee Act 1925, s 22(4)

This section enables the trustees in their absolute discretion to have the trust account audited once every three years, or more frequently if the nature of the trust or any dealings make it reasonable.

The costs of such an audit may be met from the capital and income of the trust property.

(b) The Public Trustee Act 1906, s 13(1)

This section enables any trustee or beneficiary to apply for an audit of the trust accounts provided (unless the court gives leave) that no other audit has taken place in the previous twelve months.

This section has been described as an 'exceedingly drastic enactment'[108] as it establishes the right to an audit. However, if an improper application is made, the applicant may be ordered to bear the costs of the audit.[109]

(c) Pensions

The Pensions Act 2004 imposes special requirements for periodic actuarial valuations.[110]

(d) Charities

Charities are under special duties to provide audit information to the Charity Commission under the Charities Act 2011. These are detailed in Chapter 26.

---

[108] *Re Oddy* [1911] 1 Ch 532, per Parker J.
[109] *Re Oddy* [1911] 1 Ch 532; *Re Utley* (1912) 106 LT 858.   [110] S 224.

PART VII

Checks, Controls, and Remedies

26

Control of trusts and trustees

In Parts IV and V it has been seen how the mechanisms developed by equity, primarily the trust and the power, enable the separation of the management and the ownership of property. This chapter looks at the means by which trustees can be prevented from abusing their position.

1 The need for control

(1) The potential for abuse

It is obvious that whenever one person has the effective control of property but is required to act for the benefit of another there is a possibility that he will misuse the powers that he holds. For example, a trustee may be tempted to apply the trust property for his own benefit rather than for the benefit of the beneficiaries, or the donee of a special power of appointment may attempt to appoint to someone outside of the class. The exact limits that circumscribe the actions of a person enjoying the responsibility to manage and allocate property are determined by the nature of the relationship that has been created. He will have a range of rights and duties, some of which are imposed by the general principles of equity, and others of which may have been imposed expressly when the mechanism was created. The question arises as to how to ensure that the holder of the management responsibility carries out his duties properly.

(2) The reality of abuse

Human nature being what it is, the reports are littered with cases where trustees enjoying the responsibility to manage trust property have abused their position and failed to carry out their duties. For example, in *Lipkin Gorman v Karpnale Ltd*[1] a solicitor misappropriated money from his firm's client account to finance his gambling habit. *Bishopsgate Investment Management Ltd v Maxwell (No 2)*[2] concerned the infamous Maxwell pension fraud. Ian and Kevin Maxwell were directors of a company that held assets on trust for the pension schemes of companies owned by Robert Maxwell. To

---

[1] [1987] 1 WLR 987.   [2] [1994] 1 All ER 261.

support other private companies that Robert Maxwell owned, property was misappropriated from the trust fund. Kevin and Ian, as directors, were responsible for signing transfer forms authorizing the misappropriations. This was a classic case where those who held the management power over the property by virtue of their position as directors and trustees abused their position and were able to apply the property for improper purposes, rather than for the benefit of the pensioners.

(3) **Preventing abuse**

It is often impossible to prevent those who are dishonest from taking advantage of the opportunities for abuse that their position brings, and the crucial question is generally whether an adequate remedy is available when an abuse has taken place. However, the legal system possesses some mechanisms by which to attempt to prevent abuses occurring.

(a) **Supervision and regulation**

The law could introduce methods requiring the ongoing supervision of trustees, by the court or by independent regulators, so that their dealings are closely scrutinized and the potential for abuse is greatly reduced. It might be possible to establish regulatory bodies with the responsibility of ensuring that trustees do their duty, although in practice this would prove impossible because of the number and range of trusts that exist. However, in the case of charitable trusts a sophisticated scheme of regulation is in place through the Charity Commission.[3] Regulatory regimes have been introduced in specific contexts where trust relationships may play an important part, for example to oversee the financial services industry and especially pension fund managers. The Pensions Act 1995 introduced the Occupational Pensions Regulatory Authority with the object of reducing the opportunities for fraud.

Generally, abuse occurs because of the dishonesty of an individual trustee or trustees. The choice of trustee is therefore of the utmost importance. At present, there is no general provision disqualifying certain individuals from holding office as trustees, although the Charities Act 2011 does disqualify certain persons from serving as charity trustees. Following the recommendations of the Pension Law Review Committee, which sat under the chairmanship of Professor Roy Goode after the Maxwell scandal, s 29(1) of the Pensions Act 1995 provides that a person is disqualified from being a trustee of any pension trust scheme if he has been convicted of any offence involving dishonesty or deception, is an undischarged bankrupt, or is disqualified to act as a company director.[4] A company cannot serve as trustee of a pension fund if any of its directors are disqualified from acting as trustee under the section.

---

[3] The efficacy of this regulation, and the Charity Commission itself, has been called into question recently, not least following the National Audit Office's investigation into the 'Cup Trust' scandal (a tax avoidance scheme). The Commission's handling of this affair has attracted media and extra-judicial criticism. This is considered later in the chapter.

[4] Under the Company Directors' Disqualification Act 1986.

Obviously, the greatest dangers of abuse arise where the trust property is held and managed by a sole trustee. Where there are multiple trustees the general rule that all decisions must be unanimous provides a measure of protection for the beneficiaries.

(b) Deterrence and remedies

Rather than supervising trustees so as to prevent abuse occurring, equity has put in place powerful remedies that are available when an abuse occurs, which therefore act to deter those who might consider abusing their position. If the remedies available to the beneficiaries of a trust operate to deprive a trustee of any gain made through abuse of his position, this will act as a disincentive to abuse in the first place. Some abuses, particularly the misappropriation of trust property, also constitute criminal offences, in which case the possibility of criminal conviction will also act as a deterrent.

2 The means of control

(1) Criminal sanctions

Some measure of control over the conduct of trustees is provided by the general criminal law. In particular, if a trustee misappropriates trust property he will be guilty of theft. The Theft Act 1968 defines theft in s 1(1):

> A person is guilty of theft if he dishonestly appropriates property belonging to another with the intention of permanently depriving the other of it.

'Property belonging to another' is defined in s 5(2) to include property held on trust so that 'where property is subject to a trust, the persons to whom it belongs shall be regarded as including any person having a right to enforce the trust, and an intention to defeat the trust shall be regarded accordingly as an intention to deprive of the property any person having that right'. Thus, the trustee, or anyone else who misappropriates the trust property, will be guilty of theft.[5] However, although the prospect of a conviction for theft may serve as a deterrent to abuse, it does not restore the trust property to the beneficiaries, which is often their prime concern.

(2) Supervision by the court

Every trust is technically under the jurisdiction and the supervision of the court. However, in practice the court does not exercise a day-to-day function of supervising the activities of trustees, ensuring that they do not abuse their powers and that

---

[5] See *Re A-G's Reference (No 1 of 1985)* [1986] QB 491; (1986) 102 LQR 486; (1986) 45 CLJ 367 (Gearty); (1986) 136 NLJ 913 (Smart); [1987] Conv 209 (Martin).

they carry out their duties properly. The court is dependent on the beneficiaries of the trust to bring complaints regarding the trustees' conduct to their attention. If the beneficiaries approach the court before a trustee acts improperly, it will be able to issue an injunction to restrain the proposed breach of trust. Where a breach has already occurred, the beneficiaries will be awarded an appropriate remedy.

Even though it does not act as a day-to-day watchdog over trustees, the court serves the very important function of setting the standard of probity that trustees are required to observe in their dealings, by which their conduct will be tested if a claim is made against them by the beneficiaries. The higher the standard of care that is required, the greater the probability that the trustee will not be able to gain by abusing his position, and the greater the deterrent effect. Traditionally, the courts have set extremely high standards for the conduct of trustees, and the remedies available border on the draconian.

(a) The fiduciary position of the trustee

Trustees stand in a fiduciary position to the beneficiaries of the trust. This means that they are always expected to act in the interests of the beneficiaries, with the implication that they are not permitted to take advantage of their position for their own benefit. As such, they owe a duty of exclusive loyalty to the beneficiaries. Trustees are not the only persons deemed fiduciaries in equity. Those occupying positions of trust and responsibility for the affairs of others, such as company directors, agents, and partners, are also regarded as fiduciaries. Equity imposes a rigid rule that a fiduciary must not benefit by virtue of his position, which thus acts as a safeguard to ensure that there is no possibility that he is abusing it. A fiduciary will be forced to disgorge any profits that he may have made in breach of his fiduciary duty by making restitution of them to the persons to whom the duty was owed. The standard of probity expected of a fiduciary is extremely high, as was confirmed in *Boardman v Phipps*,[6] where the majority of the House of Lords held that a fiduciary was liable to make restitution of profits he had made if there had been a mere possibility of a conflict between his duty and his personal interests.

(b) The standard of care expected of trustees

Equity imposes an objective standard of care on the way that trustees carry out their duties. They are expected to act with the standard of care of an ordinary prudent man of business who is acting on behalf of someone else.[7] If the trustee fails to exercise the requisite standard of care, or fails to carry out his duties, or acts outside of his powers or the terms of the trust, he will have committed a breach of trust and will be liable to compensate the beneficiaries for any loss caused by his breach.

---

[6] [1967] 2 AC 46.

[7] *Speight v Gaunt* (1883) 9 App Cas 1, HL; *Bartlett v Barclay's Bank Trust Co Ltd* [1980] Ch 515.

(3) **Supervision by the beneficiaries**

As the court cannot supervise the activities of every trustee, the prime responsibility for such supervision falls to the beneficiaries of the trust. They are expected to monitor the trustee's activities, and to complain to the court if there is any breach of fiduciary duty or breach of trust. It is entirely appropriate that this burden should fall to them, as they are the very people who are most interested in the proper performance of the trust. It is they who will be most anxious to ensure that the trustee carries out his duties properly, that trust property is not misapplied, and that the trustee does not use his position to his own advantage at their expense. A number of principles, which have been examined earlier in this book, confirm that the beneficiaries are the persons primarily responsible for the supervision of the trustees.

(a) **Beneficiary principle**

The beneficiary principle examined in Chapter 14 is predicated on the understanding that the beneficiaries are primarily responsible for supervising the trustees. The very reason equity requires a trust to have identifiable legal persons as beneficiaries is that in the absence of such a beneficiary no one possesses the necessary locus standi to apply to the court in the event of a breach by the trustees, and there is no one in whose favour the court can decree specific performance of the trust.[8] If the trust is created in favour of a pure purpose, who can enforce the trust? In the case of charitable trusts this problem has been overcome, as they are enforced by the Attorney-General, acting on behalf of the Crown, or by the Charity Commission. It is notable that the limited anomalous exceptions to the beneficiary principle give rise to valid but unenforceable trusts.

(b) **Beneficiaries' entitlement to information**

As was seen in Chapter 25, although the beneficiaries of a trust cannot require the trustees to provide reasons for the exercise, or non-exercise, of their discretions,[9] they are entitled to receive information detailing how the trust assets are held.[10] The fact that the beneficiaries are entitled to obtain such information enables them to supervise to some measure the activities of the trustees. The court will intervene if a trustee can be shown to have exercised his discretion wrongly.[11] The general effect-iveness of the beneficiaries' supervision of the trustees' exercise of their discretion is limited by the fact that they are not entitled to reasons from the trustees for their decisions. This means that, although a beneficiary may suspect that a discretion has been exercised wrongly, he is unable to gain the evidence necessary to make out his case.

---

[8] *Morice v Bishop of Durham* (1804) 9 Ves 399; *Bowman v Secular Society Ltd* [1917] AC 406; *Re Astor's Settlement* [1952] Ch 534; *Re Shaw* [1957] 1 WLR 729.

[9] *Re Beloved Wilkes' Charity* (1851) 3 Mac & G 440; *Re Londonderry's Settlement* [1965] Ch 918, CA; *Wilson v Law Debenture Trust Corpn* [1995] 2 All ER 337.

[10] *Low v Bouverie* [1891] 3 Ch 82, at 99.   [11] *Klug v Klug* [1918] 2 Ch 67.

(c) Beneficiaries may approve breaches of trust

Whilst it might be expected that trustees are subject to an absolute obligation to carry out the terms of a trust as specified by the original settlor, this is not in fact the case. If the beneficiaries consent to the trustees acting otherwise than in accordance with the terms of the trust, then they will not attract liability for their breach. Trustees may vary the terms of the trust with the consent of the beneficiaries, or even bring the trust to an end.[12] The courts have no jurisdiction to step in and prevent a breach of trust which is made with the full consent of all the beneficiaries, even if this defeats the intentions of the settlor.

(d) Beneficiaries entitled to seek remedies

Where a trustee has abused his powers or position the trustees may come to the court to seek a remedy. There are a variety of remedies that may be available to them, each of which will be examined in detail in the following chapters.

(i) Compensation for breach of trust

Where trustees have committed a breach of trust, the beneficiaries are prima facie entitled to recover compensation from them for any loss the trust has sustained as a result of the breach. The remedy of damages for breach of trust is purely personal against the trustee, and will therefore be ineffective if the trustee is insolvent. The nature and scope of the remedy for breach of trust is considered in Chapter 27.

(ii) Account of profits for breach of fiduciary duty

If the trustee has made an unauthorized profit for himself by allowing his duty and his personal interest to conflict, he will be in breach of his fiduciary duty and the beneficiaries will be able to recover from him any profit that he has made. The duty to account for profits made is a purely personal duty, although the beneficiaries may have a proprietary claim to receipt of profits that involves a clear misuse of the beneficiary's assets (such as misappropriating the principal's property) or taking advantage of opportunities that were properly those of the principal.[13] The nature and scope of the equitable duty to account for profits received in breach of fiduciary duty is considered in Chapter 28.

(iii) Proprietary remedies

If the trustee who has committed a breach of trust or made an unauthorized profit is insolvent, any personal remedies of the beneficiaries will be rendered largely ineffective. They will merely rank amongst the trustee's general creditors. However, if they can show that the trustee has property amongst his assets which was trust property, or if he has assets which can be shown to be the product of trust property by application of the rules of tracing, the beneficiaries will be able to claim those assets as belonging

---

[12] *Saunders v Vautier* (1841) Cr & Ph 240; see also Chapter 18.
[13] See *Sinclair Investments (UK) Ltd v Versailles Trade Finance* [2012] Ch 453.

to the trust. They will not fall to be considered as comprising part of his general assets, and in effect the trust will gain priority over the interests of the general creditors. The availability of proprietary remedies, and the rules used to identify trust property, are considered in Chapter 30.

(iv) Remedies against strangers to the trust

Where a breach of trust involves third parties who are strangers to the trust, the beneficiaries may have both personal and proprietary remedies against them. If such a stranger has received and retained property that was misappropriated from the trust, the beneficiaries will be able to assert their equitable entitlement to it unless he had acquired it as a bona fide purchaser for value without notice of the existence of the trust. This is also the case if he can be shown to have property amongst his assets which is the product of trust property he received by the rules of tracing. If, however, he received property from the trust but has subsequently dissipated it, or its proceeds, he may yet be liable to account to the trust for the value of the property he received. The obligation to account for the value of such property is a restitutionary remedy and at present only in circumstances where the court would consider it unconscionable for a recipient to retain the value of the property, as for example where he acted dishonestly, will he be obliged to make restitution. There are increasing calls by academics for the adoption of a strict liability to make restitution against the recipients of trust property.

A stranger who has not himself received trust property, but who has assisted the trustees in a misappropriation of trust property, may also be liable to compensate the trust for the value of the misappropriated property. This liability is analogous to the tort of conversion. Such an assistor will only attract liability if he acted dishonestly. The remedies available to the beneficiaries against strangers to a trust are considered in Chapter 29.

(4) Evaluating the effectiveness of supervision by the beneficiaries

It is obvious that the beneficiaries of a trust have a strong vested interest in ensuring that it is properly carried out according to its terms, and that the trustees do not abuse their position. However, the effectiveness of their supervision depends upon the nature of the trust. In the case of a small family trust, where the trustees and the terms of the trust are well known to the beneficiaries, such scrutiny is likely to be close and effective. In the case of large modern trust funds, with many thousands of beneficiaries and millions of pounds of assets, the beneficiaries are not in a position to scrutinize the day-to-day conduct of the trustees, both because of the enormity of the task, and the complexity of the situations involved. In such circumstances it is not realistic to expect the beneficiaries effectively to supervise the trustees' performance of their duties. To take the Maxwell pension fraud as an example: could the employees entitled to pensions realistically be expected to scrutinize the dealings of the directors of the companies holding the assets on trust so as to prevent the wrongful transfer of trust assets to the Maxwell private companies? Another limitation is that the trustees' misconduct often only comes to light after the event, when it is too late to prevent it, and when the beneficiaries' remedies may be all but ineffective because of the trustees' insolvency and because the trust property has been dissipated. Both these problems demonstrate the limitation of the effectiveness of supervision by the beneficiaries, and emphasize the importance of appointing appropriate persons to act in that capacity.

3 Controlling and supervising charitable trusts

Just as the trustees of a private trust have the potential to breach their duty and act in their own interests rather than in the interests of their beneficiaries, the trustees of charitable trusts have the opportunity to defraud both the charity for which they act as trustee and the public at large who make donations. It is essential to protect against spurious charities, and to ensure that the funds of genuine charities are properly applied. In 2009, the Commission reported on the Children's Welfare Foundation (CWF), a registered charity which, following an investigation into concerns, was removed from the register of charities. CWF was set up in March 2006. Its only fundraising came from selling unwanted clothing and similar items acquired through door-to-door collections. Over two years it raised £36,519 but spent £35,303—or 97 per cent—on 'expenses' and the only welfare activity claimed (but never substantiated) was taking a boy in a wheelchair for a day out in Blackpool.[14] The damage that can be done to the credibility of the sector, and to the reputation of the Commission as an effective regulator, by serious misconduct by a charity is sharply illustrated by the 'Cup Trust' saga. The 'Cup Trust' was established on 10 March 2009, and registered by the Commission on 7 April 2009. The trust was run by a sole corporate trustee, Mountstar (PTC) Limited, which was registered in the British Virgin Islands. The trust was established as a general grant-making charity with the intention of giving grants to small or start-up charities that aim to improve the lives of children and young adults. This purpose was, however, a cover for an elaborate tax avoidance scheme,[15] and the Cup Trust submitted claims for £46m Gift Aid on more than £176m in private donations, but it gave just £152,292 to charitable causes over two years. HMRC did not pay the Gift Aid claims. The Commission eventually opened an inquiry in April 2013, acting on evidence from HMRC and its own concerns about the charity, but has been subject to considerable criticism from both the National Audit Office[16] and the Public Accounts Committee.[17] Sir Stuart Etherington, chief executive of the National Council for Voluntary Organisations, said that the Commission's handling of the affair 'has brought damage and disrepute to the sector as a whole, putting [it] at serious

[14] A holiday resort on the north-west coast of England.
[15] For details of the operation of the scheme, see HC 814 National Audit Office, 'Charity Commission: The Cup Trust' (4 December 2013), paras 1.5–1.7.
[16] HC 814 National Audit Office, 'Charity Commission: The Cup Trust' (4 December 2013), paras 1.5–1.7.
[17] HC 792, 'The Charity Commission: Forty-second Report of Session 2013–14' (29 January 2014).

risk of losing the trust and confidence of the public'.[18] The impacts of this sorry tale are discussed later in the chapter.

In the case of private trusts the primary task of supervising the trustees and ensuring that they do not abuse their position falls to the beneficiaries. Charitable trusts do not have beneficiaries as such since, by their very nature, they are purpose trusts[19] and an exception to the beneficiary principle, although there may obviously be persons who are interested in seeing that assets held on trust for charity are properly applied, for example, donors. Historically, charities were supervised and controlled by the Attorney-General acting on behalf of the Crown. However, his function has largely been replaced by a regulatory system with a statutory footing. The law was revised by the Charities Acts 1993 and 2006, and is further revised by the consolidating Charities Act 2011.

(1) **Features of the regulatory system**

The main feature of the regulatory mechanism for charities is the role of the Charity Commission, which is now a body corporate.[20] The Charity Commission has the task of overseeing charities in general and investigating abuses. It is obliged to maintain a register of charities. The legislation provides, as we have seen, that some persons (for instance undischarged bankrupts) are disqualified from holding office as trustees and requires charity trustees to maintain accounts and to submit an annual report of the charity's activities and an annual statement of accounts to the Commission. The report and accounting requirements enable the Commission to supervise the conduct of charities, and they are also open to public inspection. Some charities which used to be exempt charities,[21] such as universities, are now regulated by the Higher Education Funding Council for England as principal regulator.[22]

The Charities Act 2011, incorporating changes made by the Charities Act 2006, extended the role of the Charity Commission in the regulation of charities, conferring on it extended powers to suspend or remove trustees,[23] to give specific directions for the protection of charity,[24] and to direct the application of charity property.[25] The Commission is given the power, on issue of a search warrant, to enter premises.[26] There is, however, an obligation on the Charity Commission to have regard to the principles of best regulatory practice, 'including the principles under which regulatory activities should be proportionate, accountable, consistent, transparent and targeted only at cases in which action is needed'.[27] The role of the Charity Commission is considered in detail later.

---

[18] See www.thirdsector.co.uk/charity-commission-brought-sector-disrepute-says-ncvo-chief/governance/article/1181487.   [19] See Chapter 19.

[20] Charities Act 2011, Pt 2, s 13. While the functions of the Commission are to be exercised on behalf of the Crown, s 13(4) makes clear that it shall not be subject to control by a government department or any Minister of the Crown.   [21] Charities Act 2011, s 22 and Sch 3.

[22] Charities Act 2011, Pt 3, ss 25–28 describe the duties and powers of the principal regulator. Universities in Wales are no longer exempt.   [23] Charities Act 2011, s 83.

[24] Charities Act 2011, s 84.   [25] Charities Act 2011, s 85.   [26] Charities Act 2011, s 48.

[27] Charities Act 2011, s 16(4).

(2) **The Crown**

The Crown is *parens patriae* of charity,[28] and therefore protector of charity in general.[29] However, this function is exercised on behalf of the Crown by the Attorney-General.

(3) **The Attorney-General**

Historically, the main mechanism for the supervision and control of charitable trusts was the Attorney-General, acting on behalf of the Crown. As Hoffmann J stated in *Bradshaw v University College of Wales, Aberystwyth*: 'So far as the enforcement of the trust is a matter of public interest, the guardian of that interest is the Attorney-General.'[30]

Prior to the Charities Act 1993 the Attorney-General was generally a necessary party to charity proceedings[31] because he represented the beneficial interest,[32] in other words, the charitable purposes of the trust. As Lord Simmonds observed in *National Anti-Vivisection Society v IRC*,[33] it is the right and duty of the Attorney-General to inform the courts if the trustees of a charity fall short of their duty,[34] and to help the court formulate schemes for the execution of charitable trusts.[35]

Hence, only the Attorney-General was entitled to bring an action to determine whether a trust was charitable. However, what is now s 144 of the Charities Act 2011[36] grants the Charity Commission the same powers as the Attorney-General to take legal proceedings with reference to charities, or the property affairs of charities, and to compromise claims to avoid or end proceedings. This emphasizes that the primary responsibility for controlling and enforcing charitable trusts falls today to the Commission.

(4) **The court**

(a) **The jurisdiction of the court**

The court possesses a general inherent jurisdiction[37] over charitable trusts. It has the power to draw up schemes for the administration of a charity,[38] particularly where there is a need to administer a fund cy-près,[39] and it remedies breaches of trust by charity trustees. This jurisdiction derives from the court's general jurisdiction over trusts. If a gift has been made to charity in general, or simply to one of the heads of

---

[28] *Wallis v Solicitor-General for New Zealand* [1903] AC 173, at 181–182.

[29] *A-G v Glegg* (1738) 1 Atk 356; *Moggridge v Thackwell* (1803) 7 Ves 36; *Incorporated Society v Richards* (1841) 1 Dr & War 258; *A-G v Compton* (1842) 1 Y & C Ch Cas 417; *National Anti-Vivisection Society v IRC* [1948] AC 31, HL; *Re Belling* [1967] Ch 425; *Hauxwell v Barton-upon-Humber UDC* [1974] Ch 432.

[30] [1987] 3 All ER 200, at 203.

[31] See *Wellbeloved v Jones* (1822) 1 Sim & St 40; *National Anti-Vivisection Society v IRC* [1948] AC 31, HL; *Hauxwell v Barton-upon-Humber UDC* [1974] Ch 432.

[32] *Ware v Cumberlege* (1855) 20 Beav 503; *Re King* [1917] 2 Ch 420.   [33] [1948] AC 31, at 62.

[34] *A-G v Brown* (1818) 1 Swan 265; *National Anti-Vivisection Society v IRC* [1948] AC 31.

[35] *National Anti-Vivisection Society v IRC* [1948] AC 31; *Re Harpur's Will Trusts* [1962] Ch 78, CA.

[36] Originally Charities Act 1993, s 32.

[37] *Mills v Farmer* (1815) 1 Mer 55; *A-G v Sherborne Grammar Schools Governors* (1854) 18 Beav 256.

[38] See *A-G v Coopers' Co* (1812) 19 Ves 187; *A-G v St Olave's Grammar School* (1837) Coop Pr Cas 267; *A-G v Dedham School* (1857) 23 Beav 350.   [39] See Chapter 18.

charity, for example 'the poor', the court has the jurisdiction to draw up a scheme for the application of the property if a trust was intended, but if no trust was intended the Crown applies the property under the sign manual.[40] The court has no jurisdiction in the case of a charity founded by Royal Charter[41] or over a charity completely regulated by statute.[42] However, the court does have jurisdiction to ensure that the terms of the charter or statute are properly kept. The court retains an inherent jurisdiction over corporate charities, even though, in the strict sense, a company required to apply its assets for charitable purposes does not hold those assets on trust.[43]

An example of the exercise of the court's supervisory jurisdiction over charitable trusts is provided by *Royal Society for the Prevention of Cruelty to Animals v A-G*.[44] The Society sought to exclude members and applicants for membership who had joined for the ulterior purpose of changing its anti-hunting policy. Members and applicants who fell within defined categories would be treated as conclusively proved deserving of exclusion, without the need to consider the merits of their individual cases. Lightman J held that whilst the policy of exclusion did not contravene the Human Rights Act, the Society should not operate its chosen method of implementing its membership policy. He considered that it was 'arbitrary and unattractive' and that it was not necessary to exclude from membership persons to whom no conceivable objection could be taken if the full facts were allowed to be taken into account. Given that emergency action was not required, the 'plight of the innocent' needed to be given greater weight. He also considered that the 'public image and reputation' of the Society had not been sufficiently taken into account in adopting such a draconian policy.

(b) Concurrent jurisdiction of the Charity Commission

The primacy of the role of the Charity Commission in the supervision and control of charitable trusts is also evident, in that the Commission enjoys concurrent jurisdiction alongside that of the court. It is thus able to exercise many of the functions formerly the exclusive preserve of the court. By s 69(1) and (2) of the Charities Act 2011, the Charity Commission enjoys the same jurisdiction and powers that are exercisable by the High Court in charity proceedings for the purposes of:

(a) establishing a scheme for the administration of a charity;

(b) appointing, discharging, or removing a charity trustee or trustee for a charity, or removing an officer or employee;

(c) vesting or transferring property, or requiring or entitling any person to call for or make any transfer of property or any payment.

---

[40] *Moggridge v Thackwell* (1803) 7 Ves 36; *Paice v Archbishop of Canterbury* (1807) 14 Ves 364; *Spiller v Maude* (1881) 32 Ch D 158n; *Re Slevin* [1891] 2 Ch 236, CA; *Re White* [1893] 2 Ch 41, CA; *Re Bennett* [1960] Ch 18.

[41] *A-G v Smart* (1748) 1 Ves Sen 72; *A-G v Middleton* (1751) 2 Ves Sen 327; *A-G v Governors of the Foundling Hospital* (1793) 2 Ves 42. If the charity was granted a Royal Charter subsequent to its foundation to provide an incorporated trustee, the court retains its inherent jurisdiction: *A-G v Dedham School* (1857) 23 Beav 350.   [42] *Re Shrewsbury Grammar School* (1849) 1 Mac & G 324.

[43] *Liverpool and District Hospital for Diseases of the Heart v A-G* [1981] 1 All ER 994.

[44] [2001] 3 All ER 530.

(c) Charity proceedings

The effectiveness of the supervision of charitable trusts by the court depends on those who might have some interest being able to start an action. Other than the Attorney-General and the Charity Commission, s 115(1) of the Charities Act 2011 provides that:

> Charity proceedings may be taken with reference to a charity either by—
>
> (a) the charity,
>
> (b) any of the charity trustees,
>
> (c) any person interested in the charity, or
>
> (d) if it is a local charity, any two more inhabitants of the area of the charity,
>
> but not by any other person.

(i) Any person interested in the charity

The definition of this phrase has been considered in a number of cases. *Re Hampton Fuel Allotment Charity*[45] concerned a charity relieving hardship and distress amongst residents of Hampton. The charity sought to sell land that it owned to a supermarket for £8m. A minority of the trustees felt that the sale was at a gross undervalue, and that the real value was some £14m. They started an action seeking orders concerning the administration of the charity along with Richmond Council, which had the power to appoint three of the trustees and in whose borough the charity operated. At first instance the council was struck out as not being a person 'interested in the charity'. However, the Court of Appeal held that it did enjoy sufficient interest to maintain an action. It was unwilling to attempt a comprehensive definition of 'any person interested in the charity' but stated that:

> If a person has an interest in securing the due administration of a trust materially greater than, or different from, that possessed by ordinary members of the public...that interest may, depending on the circumstances, qualify him as a 'person interested'...[46]

The council had an interest greater than that of the ordinary public because it had a functional role with regard to the charity, in that it appointed three of the eleven trustees, and it was the local authority of the area benefited by the carrying out of the purposes. The Court of Appeal referred to *Haslemere Estates Ltd v Baker*,[47] where Megarry V-C had held that enjoyment of an adverse interest against a charity did not necessarily equate with having a good reason for seeking to enforce the trust. Thus, he suggested that not even tenants of charity land, or those with easements, profits, mortgages, or restrictive covenants, or those who had contracted to repair or decorate charity houses or had agreed to buy or sell goods to the charity, would have sufficient interest. It seems that a donor to a charity may have sufficient interest,[48] but not the executors of a donor.[49]

---

[45] [1989] Ch 484.   [46] [1989] Ch 484, at 494.   [47] [1982] 1 WLR 1109.

[48] *Brooks v Richardson* [1986] 1 WLR 385.

[49] *Bradshaw v University College of Wales, Aberystwyth* [1988] 1 WLR 190.

Haslemere Estates Ltd v Baker, which concerned a claim by a property developer against the trustees of Dulwich College, was distinguished by Robert Walker J in *Scott v National Trust*[50] on the grounds that it concerned a wholly commercial dispute which had no real connection with the internal or functional administration of charitable trusts.[51] In contrast, he held that the hunts and tenant farmers which were affected by a decision of the National Trust not to allow the hunting of deer with hounds on its land in Devon and Somerset were sufficiently interested in the charity to bring proceedings. He pointed out that they had been hunting there since long before the land had belonged to the Trust, and that they had been partners with the National Trust in the management of its land.[52]

The ambit of s 115(1) was most recently considered in *Royal Society for the Prevention of Cruelty to Animals v A-G*.[53] The RSPCA sought to change its membership rules so as to exclude members who had been campaigning to persuade the Society to change its anti-hunting stance and prevent applicants becoming members who shared this objective. Lightman J held that an existing member of the Society did have sufficient interest in the charity to commence charity proceedings challenging the propriety of the Society's actions, but that a mere applicant for membership did not:

> But I do not think that a disappointed applicant for membership has any such sufficient interest. Any member of the public is free to apply for membership; the exercise of that liberty cannot elevate the status of a non-member into that of a person interested. To extend the right of suit to any such applicant would be to cast the net too wide.[54]

(ii) Consent of the Charity Commission

Section 115(2) provides that no proceedings shall be taken in any court without the authorisation of the Charity Commission. The Commission is not to authorize proceedings if the case could be dealt with under their own powers.[55] The reason for these limitations is to prevent pointless actions which would simply waste the charity's money.

(5) The Charity Commission

The Charity Commissioners were first appointed under the Charitable Trusts Act 1853. Their position was modernized by the Charities Act 1960, which implemented the recommendations of the Nathan Committee Report.[56] It was enshrined in the Charities Act 1993, which followed the Woodfield Report,[57] was further amended by the Charities Act 2006, and is now consolidated in the Charities Act 2011.[58] The

---

[50] [1998] 2 All ER 705. Note, the section was then the Charities Act 1993, s 33(1).

[51] [1998] 2 All ER 705, at 715.   [52] [1998] 2 All ER 705.   [53] [2001] 3 All ER 530.

[54] [2001] 3 All ER 530, at [21].   [55] S 115(3).

[56] The Committee on the Law and Practice relating to Charitable Trusts, Cmnd 8710 of 1952.

[57] Efficiency Scrutiny of the Supervision of Charities, 1987; National Audit Office Report, House of Commons Paper 380, 1986–87; Annual Report 1987.

[58] This consolidating Act came into force on 14 March 2012, and replaces the Charities Act 1992, 1993, 2006 and the Recreational Charities Act 1958.

Charity Commission is a body corporate with a membership and structure specified in Schedule 1 to the Charities Act 2011, and with specified objectives:[59]

(1) The public confidence objective is to increase public trust and confidence in charities.

(2) The public benefit objective is to promote awareness and understanding of the operation of the public benefit requirement.

(3) The compliance objective is to promote compliance by charity trustees with their legal obligations in exercising control and management of the administration of their charities

(4) The charitable resources objective is to promote the effective use of charitable resources.

(5) The accountability objective is to enhance the accountability of charities to donors, beneficiaries and the general public.

The functions of the Charity Commission underline the importance of the Charity Commission in applying charity law, regulating charities, disseminating information, and providing information and advice.

The Charity Commission has undertaken a Strategic Review of its activities[60] and engaged in a process of consultation with key members of the charity sector and its advisors. This process resulted in the publication of its Strategic Plan 2012–2015[61] which indicates that the Commission's priorities will be developing the compliance and accountability of the sector and developing the self-reliance of the sector. The plan states:

> Over the three years of this plan most of our attention will be concentrated on our objectives relating to accountability and compliance. The public benefit objective will be addressed with rigour at registration and through public benefit reporting. Our charity resources objective will be met by the provision of web based advice to promote good governance. It is our achievement of the whole that will determine our success in meeting the public confidence objective.

The clear implication of this is that the Charity Commission will concentrate on its role as independent regulator of the sector, rather than champion of the sector, leaving other charitable organizations (such as the National Council for Voluntary Organisations) to fill the gap on highlighting and sharing good practice and providing individual advice.[62] This is welcome, as there is a tension between acting as champion of the sector and the Commission's statutory objectives as regulator. However, as

---

[59] Charities Act 2011, s 14.
[60] The review was prompted by a 33 per cent cut to funding over four years as a result of the public spending squeeze: see http://charitycommissionreview.blogspot.com for details.
[61] See www.charity-commission.gov.uk/Library/about_us/strategic_plan_2015.pdf.
[62] General guidance on the operation of the law would, it is suggested, continue, as part of the regulatory role would require the Commission to issue guidance to help compliance with pertinent legal issues, and the Commission is under a statutory duty in relation to its role in registration, compliance and, in particular, issuing guidance on the assessment of public benefit for all charities.

mentioned earlier in relation to the Cup Trust saga, there are very real concerns about the Commission's ability to be an effective regulator. The Public Accounts Committee was scathing of the approach of the Commission to the Cup Trust, suggesting that it that it had not regulated the charity sector effectively, had a lack of direction and clear leadership problems, and concluding that the Committee 'had little confidence in the Commission's ability to put right its problems and failings'.[63]

(a) Annual report

The Commission has the duty under Sch 1 para 11 of the Charities Act 2011 to make an annual report, which must be laid before Parliament. These reports provide a review of the administration of charities and bring attention to any particular problems. The Commission also provides precedents for purposes that it has registered as charitable, and any changes in their requirements.

(b) Power to institute inquiries

By s 46(1) the Commission has the power to 'institute inquiries with regard to charities, or a particular charity or class of charities'.[64] In connection with this power it has wide-ranging ancillary powers to obtain relevant information. It may order any person to furnish accounts and statements and to return answers in writing to any questions or inquiries,[65] to furnish copies of documents under his control[66] and to give evidence,[67] which may be taken under oath.[68] By s 60 of the Act it is a criminal offence knowingly or recklessly to provide the Commission with false or misleading information, or to willfully alter, suppress, conceal, or destroy any document required to be produced to the Commission. As has been noted earlier, the Commission may obtain a warrant to search premises.

The Charity Commission had been increasingly adopting a risk-based approach in order to concentrate its engagement with charities where it was most needed and which takes account of the risk involved to the charity and its beneficiaries, and the capacity of the charity to comply. For example, in the year ending March 2009, only twenty-one statutory inquiries were completed and reports published, which concerned the most serious cases.[69] The Commission completed 167 regulatory compliance cases that did not require the use of their statutory powers to resolve. This was symptomatic of a move towards resolving most compliance issues through guidance and supervision, on the basis that '[p]revention is invariably better than cure'.[70] However, in the wake of the Cup Trust affair, this approach is not sustainable. The Public Accounts Committee review felt that the Commission was not using its resources well to deal with potentially serious abuse of charitable status:

---

[63] HC 792, 'The Charity Commission: Forty-second Report of Session 2013-14' (29 January 2014), p 6.

[64] This power did not extend to exempt charities, but this was modified by the Charities Act 2006 meaning that the Commission can investigate at the request of the principal regulator of the exempt charity (s 46(2). [65] S 47(2)(a).

[66] S 47(2)(b).   [67] S 47(3)(b).   [68] S 47(3)(a).   [69] *Annual Report 2008–2009*, p 21.

[70] *Annual Report 2008–2009*, p 2.

In the last 3 years, the Commission has not removed any trustees, it has only suspended a trustee twice and it has only restricted charities from entering into specific transactions 17 times when it is responsible for overseeing 165,000 charities... and, when faced with clear cases of abuse, it has failed to act promptly and robustly, or use the full range of powers to intervene that it has available.[71]

The current Chairman of the Charity Commission responded to this criticism, suggesting that the Commission was 'making rapid, visible progress'[72] towards improving regulation on the basis of the (markedly less critical) National Audit Report recommendations.[73] It has opened forty-eight inquiries between 1 April 2013 and 5 February 2014; as opposed to just fifteen inquiries in the financial year April 2012–2013, and since 1 April 2013 has used its legal enforcement powers in inquires or operational compliance cases six hundred and fifty-seven times, as opposed to two hundred and sixteen times in the previous financial year. It is clear that the Commission is seeking to become more effective, and, therefore, more demonstrably interventionist in regulatory matters. Another challenge the Commission faces is the threat of misuse of the charity sector for terrorist financing.[74] The Commission has published a strategy to safeguard the sector, based on four key strands: awareness, oversight and supervision, cooperation and intervention.[75]

(c) Power to act for the protection of charities

Section 76 grants the Commission wide-ranging powers to take action where it has instituted an inquiry under s 46 and is satisfied:

(a) that there is or has been any misconduct or mismanagement in the administration of the charity; or

(b) that it is necessary or desirable to act for the purpose of—

   (i) protecting the property of the charity or,

   (ii) securing a proper application for the purposes of the charity of that property or of property coming to the charity.[76]

The action the Commission may take includes: the suspension of any trustee pending consideration of his removal;[77] appointing additional trustees;[78] vesting the property of the charity in the Official Custodian;[79] restraining persons who hold property on behalf of the charity from parting with it without their approval;[80] restricting the

[71] HC 792, 'The Charity Commission: Forty-second Report of Session 2013-2014' (29 January 2014), p 5.

[72] See www.charitycommission.gov.uk/news/charity-commission-rebuts-pac-criticism/.

[73] HC 814 National Audit Office, 'Charity Commission: The Cup Trust' (4 December 2013), paras 1.5–1.7.

[74] Money laundering is another serious concern. In June 2013, acting on advice of the Serious Organised Crime Agency, the Commission issued guidance to charities to be alert to suspicious donations which were made using fraudulently obtained credit cards. These would usually have a condition attached that part of the money be sent to another charity in another country, therefore unwittingly involving the charities in a money laundering scam. See www.charitycommission.gov.uk/our-regulatory-work/how-we-regulate-charities/alerts-and-warnings/be-aware-of-suspect-donations---advice-for-charities/.

[75] Charity Commission, *Charity Commission's Counter-Terrorism Strategy* (April 2012).

[76] S 76(1).   [77] S 76(3)(a).   [78] S 76(3)(b).   [79] S 76(3)(c).   [80] S 76(3)(d).

transactions and payments that may be entered or made without approval;[81] and appointing a receiver and manager.[82] In addition, where the Commission is satisfied that both criteria (a) and (b) above are met, it has the power to: (i) remove any trustee, charity trustee, officer, agent, or employee of the charity who has been responsible for or privy to the misconduct or mismanagement or has by his conduct contributed to it or facilitated it; (ii) by order establish a scheme for the administration of the charity.[83] Additional powers were conferred on the Charity Commission by the Charities Act 2006, including the power to give specific directions for the protection of charity and to direct the application of charity property.[84]

(d) Duty to maintain a register of charities

Section 29 of the Charities Act 2011 requires the Charity Commission to maintain a register of all charities. The scope and purpose of this register is considered later.

(e) Duty to inform the Charity Commission of the desirability of bringing legal proceedings

Section 115(2) place the trustees under a duty to inform the Charity Commission if it is desirable to take legal proceedings with reference to any charity. The Charity Commission will inform the Attorney-General if it feels legal proceedings are desirable under s 115(7).

(f) Power to give advice to charity trustees

Section 110 empowers the Commission to give its opinion or advice to a charity trustee on any matter affecting the performance of his duties as such or the proper administration of the trust. A charity trustee who acts in accordance with such advice is deemed 'to have acted in accordance with his trust',[85] unless he knew or had reasonable cause to suspect that the advice had been given in ignorance of material facts,[86] or a decision of the First Tier-Tribunal (Charity) is pending or has been obtained on the matter in question.[87]

(g) The Official Custodian

By s 21(3) of the Charities Act 2011 the Charity Commission is required to designate a person to act as the Official Custodian for charitable trusts, so that charity trustees can vest charity property in him as custodian trustee, thereby obviating the need for property (and, in particular, land) to be transferred to the new trustees every time the trustees of a charity change.[88]

(h) Cost

We have already seen that the operating budget of charities is due to sharply decline. The Commission estimates that this will be worth 48 per cent in real terms, dropping

---

[81] S 76(3)(e).   [82] S76(3)(g).   [83] S 79.   [84] See now Charities Act 2011, ss 84 and 85.
[85] S 110(2).   [86] S 110(3)(a).   [87] S 110(3)(b).
[88] Provisions relating to the powers and duties of the Official Custodian are contained in Sch 2 of the Act.

from £32.6m in 2007–2008 to £20.4m by 2015–2016.[89] Its operating budget for 2013-2014 was £22.7m. In response, the Commission is conducting yet another thorough review of its regulatory and business delivery model in preparation for the next spending review. We have already seen that it is pushing its regulatory function to the fore, and seeking other methods (such as the removal of a dedicated, personalized advice service to charities and its replacement with internet advice publications)[90] to address its other statutorily required functions. It will be interesting to see what the eventual shape of the regulator will be, and how effectively it can manage a greatly reduced resource to carry out its functions under increasing pressure from bodies such as the Public Accounts Committee and the National Audit Office.

(6) The Charities Register

A scheme of general registration of charities was first introduced by the Charities Act 1960. It is now the duty of the Commission to maintain the register, which by s 29(2) of the Charities Act 2011 shall contain the name of the charity and such other particulars or any other information the Commission thinks fit. Some charities are not required to register, namely: the 'exempt' charities;[91] charities which are excepted by order or regulations and which have a gross income of less than £100,000 per annum;[92] charities with a low income (less than £5,000 gross per annum).[93] All other charities are required to register[94] and are required to provide a copy of their trusts when they apply for registration.[95] The register, including the copies of the charities' trust instruments, is open to public inspection at all reasonable times.[96] The register can be inspected online.

It was formerly the case that exempt charities were exempt not only from the requirement to register, but also from many of the regulatory provisions contained in the Charities Acts. This was because they were drawn from sectors which had alternative forms of regulation. The Charities Act 2006, which has now been consolidated within the 2011 Act, significantly altered that position. It made some changes (now s 22 and Sch 3 of the 2011 Act) to the categories of institution with exempt charity status. The law now requires a 'principal regulator' to be appointed for all exempt charities.[97] The principal regulator is charged to 'promote compliance by the charity trustees with their legal obligations in exercising control and management of the administration of the charity'.[98] The Charities Act 2011 gives the Charity Commission, inter alia, the power to institute inquiries. This was an increase in regulation first introduced by the

[89] See www.charitycommission.gov.uk/about-the-commission/our-status/strategic-plan-2012-2015/.

[90] The negative impact of this change of advice function, against the backdrop of changes to advice for charities (and those helped by charities) by the removal of funding by the Legal Aid, Sentencing and Punishment of Offenders Act 2012, is considered in Morris & Barr 'The impact of cuts on legal aid funding in charities' (2013) 35 JSWFL 79.

[91] S30(2). The definition of exempt charities is contained in s 22 and Sch 3.

[92] S 30(2)(b) (orders); s 30(2)(c) (regulations).   [93] S 30(2)(d).   [94] S 30(1).

[95] Ss 35(1) and (2).   [96] S 38(1).   [97] S 25.   [98] S 26(1).

Charities Act 2006. This power to institute an inquiry can only be exercised at the request of the principal regulator.[99]

Universities are exempt charities, and as such are not required to register with the Charity Commission. Universities were already subject to detailed scrutiny by the Higher Education Funding Councils in England and Wales, and in England (but not in Wales) the Funding Council is now the principal regulator for this group of exempt charities. Universities in Wales will be regulated directly by the Charity Commission in regard to charity matters.

(7) **The First-Tier Tribunal (Charity)**

The Charities Act 2006 established a new body, the Charity Tribunal.[100] On 1 September 2009, the Charity Tribunal was abolished and its jurisdiction passed to the First-Tier Tribunal (Charity), following the Transfer of Functions of the Charity Tribunal Order 2009/1834. The First-Tier Tribunal (Charity) is administered by the unified Tribunals Service, an executive agency of the Ministry of Justice.[101] Before the establishment of any tribunal service for charity appeals, a person who was unhappy with a decision of the Charity Commission, for instance because of a refusal to register a body or a trust as a charity, could ask the Commission to review the decision using its own internal review processes and, if still unhappy, could appeal to the High Court. There is now in many cases a right of appeal to the First-Tier Tribunal (Charity) following a final decision, direction, or order of the Charity Commission.[102]

There is then a further right of appeal to the Upper-Tier Tribunal and then the High Court, but only on points of law. The Upper-Tier Tribunal, established under the wholesale reform of the Tribunal system under the Tribunals, Courts and Enforcement Act 2007, is established as a court of superior record with the power to bind itself and the Lower-Tier Tribunals on matters within its remit.[103] The Attorney-General has the right to refer certain matters to the Tribunal,[104] and is given the power to intervene in proceedings before the Tribunal, to which he is not a party.[105]

The sorts of matter over which the First-Tier Tribunal (Charity) has jurisdiction are appeals against decisions to register or to refuse to register an institution as a charity, to institute an inquiry with regard to a particular institution or group of institutions, a decision to appoint or remove a charity trustee, and many other decisions listed in Sch 6 of the 2011 Act. It was anticipated that the flexible Tribunal procedure would allow matters of law to be 'fast-tracked' directly to the Upper-Tier Tribunal, and, if

[99] S.46(2).   [100] See now Charities Act 2011, Pt 17, ss 315–330 and Sch 6.
[101] The First-Tier Tribunal is regulated by the Tribunal Procedure (First-Tier Tribunal) (General Regulatory Chamber) Rules 2009 (UK) SI 2009/1976 (as amended). The Upper-Tier Tribunal is regulated by the Tribunal Procedure (Upper Tribunal) Rules 2008 (UK), SI 2008/2698.
[102] S 319 and Sch 6, col 1.
[103] Indeed, under s 25 of the Tribunals, Courts and Enforcement Act 2007 it has the same powers as the High Court for matters within its remit. See further McKenna 'Transforming Tribunals: The Reform of the Charity Tribunal by the Tribunals, Courts and Enforcement Act 1997' (2009) 11 *Charity Law and Practice Review* 1.   [104] S 326.
[105] S 318.

necessary, remitted to the First-Tier Tribunal. This would promote a particular saving in terms of cost to charities. This was certainly the wish of the then President[106] of the original Charity Tribunal[107] (now principal judge of the First-Tier Tribunal (Charity)). It is fair to say that the operation of the Tribunal is not without its critics.[108]

Before the introduction of the Tribunal system for charities, disputed decisions made by the Charity Commission did not get any further than the internal review process, due to the high expense of an appeal action in the High Court. The Tribunal system was intended to offer a cheaper and speedier alternative, which should increase the number of Charity Commission decisions that are appealed. Despite the introduction of the original Charity Tribunal, there was still major criticism of the way in which the service operated. Namely, it was considered that the legal costs of accessing the Charity Tribunal were too high for most charities, the lack of formal rules led to lengthy procedural arguments, and a combination of an adversarial atmosphere and a feeling that it was an uneven playing field for the parties weakened the effectiveness of the system.[109] Despite 'bedding in' to the wider Tribunal structure, there is still concern. The difference in quality of the legal advice that a charity might call upon compared to the Commission helps produce a perception of unfairness.[110] Some of the decisions reached by the First-Tier Tribunal, and the Upper Tribunal have also provoked robust, critical comment.[111] Principal Judge McKenna, writing extra-judicially on the operation of the First-Tier Tribunal (Charity),[112] noted that approximately three to six cases a year receive a full hearing at the Tribunal, which was too few to influence procedure of the Tribunal service more generally.

Suggestions for reform to the operation of the Tribunal service came from Lord Hogdson's review of the Charity Act 2006, which was published in July 2012,[113] which included streamlining the procedure and reducing the cost and time of action. The government responded positively to most of this report, and the Law Commission is to publish a consultation paper as part of its work on reform of charity law, including the operation of the tribunal service, by the end of 2014.

It is important that an effective and efficient service is available to charities, In particular, the powers and remit of the Upper-Tier Tribunal are likely to mean that, where

---

[106] This person now serves as a judge of the First-Tier Tribunal and as a Deputy Judge of the Upper Tribunal—The Transfer of Functions of the Charity Tribunal Order 2009/1834, art 3.

[107] McKenna 'Transforming Tribunals: The Reform of the Charity Tribunal by the Tribunals, Courts and Enforcement Act 1997' (2009) 11 *Charity Law and Practice Review* 1, at p 10.

[108] See, for example, Morris 'The First-tier Tribunal (Charity): Enhanced Access to Justice for Charities or a Case of David versus Goliath?' (2010) 29 CJQ 89.

[109] Third Sector, 'Teething Problems for the Charity Tribunal' (23 June 2008).

[110] Morris 'The First-tier Tribunal (Charity): Enhanced Access to Justice for Charities or a Case of David versus Goliath?' (2010) 29 CJQ 89.

[111] See, for example, Luxton 'Opening Pandora's box: the Upper Tribunal's decision on public benefit and independent schools' (2012) CLPR 15.

[112] McKenna 'Should the Charity Tribunal Be Reformed?' (2012) CLPR 1.

[113] 'Trusted and Independent: Giving Charity back to charities', Review of the Charities Act 2006 (TSO, 2012). This was carried out pursuant to s 73 of the Charities Act 2006, which required the review to take place. See also the current government's response—Cmnd 8700 (TSO, September 2013).

a point of law is involved, fewer cases will be dealt with by the courts. The role of the Tribunals in the development and interpretation of charity law, and in particular the recognition of charitable purposes, is therefore likely to be considerable. The Law Commission consultation paper is therefore awaited with considerable interest.

(8) Control of charity trustees

The legislative framework recognizes the importance of the role of the trustees of charities, and that they enjoy major opportunities for abuse. Some persons are disqualified from serving as charity trustees, whilst those who can occupy such positions are subject to onerous duties.

(a) Disqualification

We have already seen in Chapter 24 that the Charities Act 2011 disqualifies certain individuals from acting as charity trustees. The main circumstances in which a person will be so disqualified are:[114] (i) previous conviction of any offence involving dishonesty or deception; (ii) undischarged bankruptcy; (iii) previous removal from the office of a charity trustee by an order of the Commission; (iv) previous disqualification from serving as a company director under the Company Directors' Disqualification Act 1986. Any person who serves as a charity trustee while disqualified commits a criminal offence.[115] The Charity Commission now has a power, in limited circumstances, to waive the disqualification.[116]

(b) Duties of charity trustees

The trustees of most charities are under a duty to keep proper financial records and to provide an annual report to the Charity Commission. Under the Charities (Accounts and Reports) Regulations 1995[117] a new framework was introduced for charity accounting requiring charities to produce annual accounts and a trustee report, the Statement of Recommended Practice (SORP).[118] The presentation of this information is required to be uniform, thus allowing people to see more clearly how charities are spending their money and to compare different charities. A system of thresholds seeks to ensure that the heaviest burden falls to the larger charities, where a stricter regime of external scrutiny will apply. Smaller charities are subject to less demanding requirements.[119] The reporting requirements for charities are now consolidated in Pt 8 of the Charities Act 2011.[120] The annual report and charity accounts are open to public inspection.[121] The trustees of exempt charities are merely under a duty to keep

---

[114] S 178(1). There are two other cases listed in the statute.   [115] S 183.   [116] S 181.

[117] SI 1995/2724.

[118] The SORP has undergone many revisions since its inception. The most current detailed regulations are Charities (Accounts and Reports) Regulations 2011 and Charity Commission CC15b, 'Charity reporting and accounting: the essentials' (January 2013).   [119] Charities Act 2011, s 133.

[120] Ss 130–175. This is split into five chapters, with Chapters 1 and 2 dealing with individual and group accounts, Chapter 3 with audit requirements and the remaining Chapters with annual reports and powers to set financial thresholds.   [121] S 170.

proper books of account that must be preserved for six years.[122] Where the charity is a company the trustees are exempt from the accounting requirements of the Charities Act 2011,[123] but must comply with the company law provisions relating to accounts.[124]

(i) Duty to apply for registration

Under s 35(1)of the Charities Act 2011, the trustees of a charity which is not registered and is not exempted or excepted from the requirement to be registered are under a duty to apply for it to be registered.

(ii) Duty to keep accounts

Charity trustees are under a duty to keep accounting records that are sufficient to show and explain all the charity's transactions, and which must be retained for at least six years.[125]

(iii) Duty to prepare annual accounts

They are also under a duty to prepare an annual statement of accounts in accordance with the regulations made by the Secretary of State.[126]

(iv) Duty to have an annual audit

If the annual income of the charity exceeds a specified limit the accounts must be audited, but if it does not exceed that amount they can be examined by an independent examiner. If an audit is not carried out the Commission may order an audit at the expense of the charity or the charity trustees.[127]

(v) Duty to prepare an annual report

The trustees of a charity are under a duty to prepare an annual report for each financial year containing a report on the activities of the charity during the past year and other information, as may be prescribed by regulation.[128] The annual report must be transmitted to the Charity Commission and have attached the statement of accounts[129] and, where appropriate, the auditor or independent examiner's report.[130] The annual report is to be kept open to public inspection by the Commission.[131]

(9) **Local authorities and local charities**

Although the Charity Commission operates a national scheme for the registration and supervision of charities, the Charities Act 2011 also makes provision for localized schemes. Under s 294 county and district councils, London borough councils, and the Common Council of the City of London may maintain an index of local charities,

---

[122] S 136.   [123] S 135.   [124] Companies Act 2006, Pt 15.
[125] Ss 130 (accounts) and 131 (preservation).
[126] S 132. These statements must also be retained for the next six years.   [127] S 146.
[128] S 162.   [129] With the exception of charities which are companies: s 164(3).
[130] S 164(1).   [131] S 170.

from which they may publish information, summaries, or extracts, and which is to be open to public inspection. They are entitled to receive from the Commission copies of entries on the register which are relevant for the index.

(10) **Judicial review of decisions taken by charities**

In *Scott v National Trust*,[132] Robert Walker J considered the question whether a decision of the National Trust to ban deer hunting with hounds on its land was amenable to judicial review. He noted that charitable trusts involved a public element and that the charity enjoyed powers and discretions which might affect different sections of the public directly or indirectly. Whilst he was unwilling to consider whether any charity, or even any charity specially established by statute is subject to judicial review, he stated his opinion that the National Trust would be susceptible:

> the National Trust is a charity of exceptional importance to the nation, regulated by its own special Acts of Parliament. Its purposes and functions are of high public importance, as is reflected by the special statutory provisions (in the fields of taxation and compulsory acquisition) to which I have already referred. It seems to me to have all the characteristics of a public body which is, prima facie, amenable to judicial review, and to have been exercising its statutory public functions in making the decision which is challenged.[133]

However, he held that the availability of judicial monitoring through charity proceedings in the Chancery Division meant that judicial review would not be appropriate in all but the most exceptional cases, which he suggested might include where a local authority held land on charitable trusts and questions about its dealings with that land were caught up with other questions about its dealings with land which it owned beneficially.[134]

In contrast, in *Royal Society for the Prevention of Cruelty to Animals v A-G*[135] Lightman J held that disappointed applicants for membership of the Society were not entitled to seek judicial review. He held that, whilst the Society was a very important charity and its activities were of great value to society, it could be distinguished from the National Trust on the grounds that it had no statutory or public law role. Thus, although it is the largest non-governmental law enforcement agency in England and Wales, in carrying out these activities it is in no different position from that of any citizen or other organization.

More recently, the Court of Appeal in *R (Weaver) v London and Quadrant Housing*[136] held that a registered social landlord was a 'public body' for the purposes of judicial review in carrying out allocation or management of housing stock. The claimant, an assured tenant, contended that the trust was in breach of a legitimate expectation in failing to pursue all reasonable alternatives before resorting to a mandatory ground

---

[132] [1998] 2 All ER 705.   [133] [1998] 2 All ER 705, at 716.
[134] [1998] 2 All ER 705, at 717–718.   [135] [2001] 3 All ER 530.
[136] [2009] EWCA Civ 587. See Alderson 'R (Weaver) v London and Quadrant Housing Trust' (2013) 16 CLPR 129.

for possession and that the decision was in breach of, inter alia, art 8 of the European Convention on Human Rights, guaranteeing respect for home life. Although the claim was dismissed, Richards LJ held that the functions a social landlord carried out were of a public nature. The nature and level of public subsidy and state control of such bodies were essential factors in finding that a social landlord was a public authority. The fact that eviction may be considered a private act was not sufficient to withdraw the public character of the action.

This has since been applied in *R (McIntyre) v Gentoo Group Ltd.*[137] Judicial review was not approved on the facts, as the tenants had other options open to them, where it was confirmed that the decision in *R v London and Quadrant Housing* extended beyond acts relating to termination of a tenancy, and would allow for review of other management functions of a social landlord in relation to stock—the case concerned a mutual exchange of tenancies.

The impact of the decision in *R v London and Quadrant Housing* for other charities has yet to be felt, but it suggests that a restrictive approach is no longer tenable.

(11) **Human Rights Act**

Those charities which are public authorities are subject to the provisions of the Human Rights Act 1998. The Charity Commission is a public authority, and thus subject to the provisions of the Act. Most charities, however, as *RSPCA v A-G*[138] shows, will not be considered to be public authorities. It is now clear that registered social landlords in discharging at least some of their functions will be classified as 'public authorities' for the purposes of s 6(3)(b) of the Human Rights Act 1998, and decisions relating to management and allocation of stock must adhere to human rights principles or can be challenged in court. This is likely to be a fertile source of litigation over the coming years.

---

[137] [2010] EWHC 5.   [138] [2001] 3 All ER 530.

27

Remedies against the trustee for breach of trust

The duties and obligations imposed on trustees are enforceable by the beneficiaries against the trustees. The nature of such liability for breach of trust is, as we shall see, personal, so that trustees are liable to make good any losses to the trust property from their own pockets. In addition to the remedies against a trustee for breach of trust, trustees are also subject to fiduciary duties that limit their ability to act in conflict with the trust (considered in the next chapter). There are also situations in which personal remedies will be available against third parties who have assisted a breach of trust or come into contact with trust property (considered in Chapter 29) and proprietary remedies against both trustees and third parties to reclaim the trust property itself (explored in Chapter 30).

1 Meaning of breach of trust

(1) General definition

It is difficult to provide a simple definition of a breach of trust. Sir Robert Megarry V-C was unwilling to attempt any 'comprehensive definition of a breach of trust' in *Tito v Waddell (No 2)*,[1] but referred to two American definitions that had found approval in the courts. First, Pomeroy's *Equity Jurisprudence*[2] states that 'every omission or violation by a trustee of a duty which equity lays on him tates is a breach of trust'. Second, Professor Scott states that a trustee 'commits a breach of trust if he violates any duty which he owes as trustee to the beneficiaries'.[3] These two definitions demonstrate that the essence of a breach of trust is the failure of the trustees properly to carry out the duties expected of them. Their duties may either be expressly required of them by the trust deed creating the trust, or imposed by the general principles of equity. Trustees can be liable for breach of trust for both their acts and their omissions. Part of the difficulty in defining a breach of trust is that

---

[1] [1977] 3 All ER 129. He regarded such an attempt as a 'perilous task' (at 247).
[2] As adopted by Corpus Juris Secundum (1955) vol 90, pp 225 and 228, para 247.
[3] *Scott on Trusts* (3rd edn, 1967), vol 3, p 1605, para 201.

there are three kinds of breach of trust: acting inconsistently with the terms of the trust; failing to discharge a duty of care; and acting inconsistently with fiduciary obligations.

(a) Acting inconsistently with the trust (ultra vires)

Trustees do not have power or authority to do anything that they wish. Their powers and authority are limited. If they exceed the boundaries of their powers and authority, then their actions will constitute a breach of trust.[4] The concept is essentially the same as the public law and company law concept of ultra vires, although there are very few cases where that term has been used in relation to breaches of trust.[5] Other cases[6] have used the expression excessive execution, but that is a very much more limited concept, since it is normally associated only with the exercise of powers of appointment. Where a trustee acts ultra vires, by exceeding his powers or by acting inconsistently with the general law, there will be a breach of trust.[7] As Lord Walker said in *Futter v Revenue and Customs*: 'That can be seen as a form of strict liability in that it is imposed regardless of personal fault.'[8]

So, for example, a trustee will commit a breach of trust if he sells property when he has no power of sale.[9] Similarly, if the trustees of a discretionary trust allocate the trust property to a person outside the class of potential beneficiaries, they will also be acting in breach of trust.[10] In *Lloyds TSB Bank Plc v Markandan & Uddin (A Firm)*,[11] a firm of solicitors held mortgage loan funds on trust from a bank 'until completion.' They were duped into paying out the money to a fictitious firm acting for a fictitious buyer as part of a fraudulent scheme. It was held that this was a breach of trust because the purported sale was a nullity and 'completion' as defined in the terms of the trust had not therefore taken place.

It may seem hard on trustees who are duped like this that they are in breach of trust for acting inconsistently with the terms of the trust. They are liable for the breach notwithstanding that they have acted with reasonable care, or even that they have taken, and acted upon, apparently competent professional advice.[12] This apparently draconian liability may be tempered by Trustee Act 1925, s 61 (considered later in this

---

[4] *Pye v Gorges* (1710) Prec Ch 308; *Mansell v Mansell* (1732) 2 P Wms 678; *Charitable Corpn v Sutton* (1742) 9 Mod Rep 349; *Clough v Bond* (1838) 3 My & Cr 490; *Harrison v Randall* (1851) 9 Hare 397; *Reid v Thompson and M'Namara* (1851) 2 I Ch R 26; *Dance v Goldingham* (1873) 8 Ch App 902.

[5] See *Pitt v Holt* [2011] EWCA Civ 197, at [72], [161], and [231]; *Edge v Pension Ombudsman* [1999] EWCA Civ 2013; *Breadner v Granville-Grossman* [2000] EWHC Ch 224, at [91].

[6] See *Futter v Revenue and Customs* [2013] UKSC 26, at [60]. This was an appeal from the Court of Appeal decision in *Pitt v Holt*.

[7] *Adair v Shaw* (1803) 1 Sch & Lef 243; *Collier v M'Bean* (1865) 34 Beav 426.

[8] See *Futter v Revenue and Customs* [2013] UKSC 26, at [80].

[9] *Perrins v Bellamy* [1899] 1 Ch 797. Both this and the next example were given by Lord Walker in *Futter v Revenue and Customs* [2013] UKSC 26, at [79].

[10] *National Trustees Co of Australasia Ltd v General Finance Co of Australasia Ltd* [1905] AC 373.

[11] [2012] EWCA Civ 65.

[12] *Futter v Revenue and Customs* [2013] UKSC 26, at [80]; *National Trustees Co of Australasia Ltd v General Finance Co of Australasia Ltd* [1905] AC 373.

chapter) which allows a court to grant relief where trustees have acted with reasonable care.[13]

(b) Duties of care

In relation to some of their responsibilities, trustees are not strictly liable, but are required to act with reasonable care or prudence. If they fail to fulfil their duties to the trust through neglect or omission, they will commit a breach of trust.[14] Historically, the standard of care required of trustees was the objective standard of the 'ordinary prudent man of business', a description contained in the leading case of *Speight v Gaunt*.[15] As Brightman J said in *Bartlett v Barclays Bank Trust Co Ltd*:[16]

> The cases establish that it is the duty of a trustee to conduct the business of the trust with the same care as an ordinary prudent man of business would extend towards his own affairs.[17]

It is suggested that this formulation of the duty of a trustee is simply an expression, using the language of the Victorian era, of a duty to take reasonable care.[18] This interpretation is reinforced by observations which suggest that the standard of the 'ordinary prudent man of business' can vary according to the context. Thus it has been said that a higher standard of care is demanded of professional trustees,[19] such as a trust corporation because of 'the special care and skill which it professes to have'.[20]

The duty of care demanded of trustees in respect of the performance of some of their duties has now been placed on a statutory footing. Section 1(1) of the Trustee Act 2000 provides that:

---

[13] See *Lloyds TSB Bank Plc v Markandan & Uddin (A Firm)* [2012] EWCA Civ 65, at [52].and [61] (duped solicitors did not act with reasonable care); another almost identical decision to the same effect is *Santander UK v RA Legal Solicitors* [2014] EWCA Civ 183. Compare *Nationwide Building Society v Davisons Solicitors* [2012] EWCA Civ 1626 (solicitors acted reasonably).

[14] *Charitable Corpn v Sutton* (1742) 9 Mod Rep 349; *Lord Montfort v Lord Cadogan* (1810) 17 Ves 485; *Moyle v Moyle* (1831) 2 Russ & M 710; *Taylor v Tabrum* (1833) 6 Sim 281; *Clough v Bond* (1838) 3 My & Cr 490; *Fenwick v Greenwell* (1847) 10 Beav 412; *Dix v Burford* (1854) 19 Beav 409; *Stone v Stone* (1869) 5 Ch App 74; *Jefferys v Marshall* (1870) 19 WR 94; *Re Brogden* (1888) 38 Ch D 546, CA; *Evans v London Co-operative Society* (1976) *The Times*, 6 July; *Bartlett v Barclays Bank Trust Co Ltd* [1980] Ch 515.

[15] (1883) 9 App Cas 1.   [16] [1980] Ch 515, at 531.

[17] *Re Speight* (1883) 22 Ch D 727; affd sum nom *Speight v Gaunt* (1883) 9 App Cas 1; *Learoyd v Whiteley* (1887) 12 App Cas 727, HL; *Re Godfrey* (1883) 23 Ch D 483; *Re Chapman* [1896] 2 Ch 763, CA; *Re Lucking's Will Trusts* [1967] 3 All ER 726, [1968] 1 WLR 866.

[18] However, even in 2014, there have been judicial references to duties based on prudence and diligence: see *Richards v Wood* (27 February 2014, unreported), CA (Civil Division); *AIB Group (UK) plc v Mark Redler & Co Solicitors* [2013] EWCA Civ 45, at [12] (referring to a duty to be prudent, but including within this duty the trustees' duties in relation to investment which are subject to the statutory duty to take reasonable care); compare *Englewood Properties Ltd v Patel* [2005] 3 All ER 307 (vendor of land under duty as constructive trustee to take reasonable care of the land).

[19] *Nestle v National Westminster Bank* [1992] EWCA Civ 12 applying the view of the Radcliffe Committee on the Powers and Duties of Trustees (Cmnd 8733), para 2.15.

[20] *Bartlett v Barclays Bank Trust Co Ltd* [1980] Ch 515, at 531, per Brightman J. See also *Re Waterman's Will Trusts* [1952] 2 All ER 1054.

Whenever the duty under this subsection applies to a trustee, he must exercise such care and skill as is reasonable in the circumstances, having regard in particular—

(a) to any special knowledge or experience that he has or holds himself out as having, and

(b) if he acts as trustee in the course of a business or profession, to any special knowledge or experience that it is reasonable to expect of a person acting in the course of that kind of business or profession.[21]

This statutory duty of care applies to certain specific situations which are outlined in Sch 1 to the Trustee Act 2000. These include the exercise of the power of investment, review of the trust investments, obtaining advice about trust investments, the exercise of powers in relation to land (including the power to acquire land), and the appointment of agents, custodians, or nominees. The statutory duty adds little if anything to the concept of the 'prudent' trustee. Most of a trustee's functions are governed by a duty to act prudently or with reasonable care.

If a trustee has failed to exercise the required standard of care, and loss is caused to the trust, he will be liable for breach of trust. For example, in *Re Lucking's Will Trusts*[22] a trustee was held liable for his failure adequately to supervise the management of a company in which the trust held a controlling interest. Similarly, in *Bartlett v Barclays Bank Trust Co Ltd (No 2)*[23] a bank was held liable for its failure to supervise two land development projects undertaken by a company of which the bank held 99.8 per cent of the shares as trustee for the Bartlett Trust.[24] The investment proved imprudent and hazardous and wholly unsuitable for a trust. It may not always be easy to determine whether a trustee's breach was one of commission or omission, as was seen in *Bishopsgate Investment Management Ltd v Maxwell (No 2)*,[25] but the distinction may be important, especially as to the issue of causation.

(c) Fiduciary duties

Trustees are fiduciaries, and as such owe duties of loyalty to their beneficiaries. The duties include not acting in ways which put personal interest above the interests of the beneficiaries (such as making a personal profit), keeping confidences entrusted to them, and maintaining a fair balance between the interests of different classes of beneficiary. Just because a trustee is a fiduciary does not mean that all a trustee's duties are fiduciary, and it is possible for people who are not trustees (such as agents) to be fiduciaries. Unfortunately, the limits of fiduciary duties are not clearly defined, which can lead to a lack of clarity about the boundary between fiduciary duties and duties of

---

[21] Detailed statutory duties have also been imposed on company directors under Pt 2, Ch 10 of the Companies Act 2006, including a duty to exercise due care, skill, and diligence under s 174, which are of relevance where the directors act as trustees. This largely replicates the same duty as that applicable to trustees, with the realization that higher standards may be required of trustee directors than lay trustees. Hence, s 174(2)(a) holds that the duty is one of a reasonably diligent person with the 'the general knowledge, skill and experience that may reasonably be expected of a person carrying out the functions carried out by the director in relation to the company'. See further, in relation to fiduciary duties of directors, Chapter 28.

[22] [1967] 3 All ER 726; [1968] 1 WLR 866.   [23] [1980] Ch 515.

[24] See also *Armitage v Nurse* [1997] 2 All ER 705, at 716.   [25] [1994] 1 All ER 261.

care.[26] Fiduciary duties are so important that they are considered in a separate chapter (Chapter 28).

(d) Exemption clauses

(i) Exemption clauses are in principle permissible

While trustees are subject to the general duty to act with reasonable care or the prudence of an ordinary man of business, the trust instrument may specifically exclude their liability for conduct that was not dishonest.[27] Even the new statutory duty of care introduced by s 1 of the Trustee Act 2000 may be expressly excluded by the trust instrument.[28] In *Armitage v Nurse*[29] the Court of Appeal considered the efficacy of a clause in a trust instrument which provided that:

> No trustee shall be liable for any loss or damage which may happen to Paula's fund or any part thereof or the income thereof at any time or from any cause whatsoever unless such loss or damage shall be caused by his own actual fraud o trus

The Court of Appeal held that, in principle, exemption clauses could be valid, but that there was a limit to their validity.

(ii) Irreducible core values

The limit which Millett LJ applied to exemption clauses was that there was an irreducible minimum core set of values attached to trusteeship, and no exemption clause could go so far as to cut into this core. This core included an obligation to act without fraud. However, he held that the irreducible core did not include the obligation to act without negligence:

> But I do not accept the further submission that these core obligations include the duties of skill and care, prudence and diligence. The duty of the trustee to perform the trusts honestly and in good faith for the benefit of the beneficiaries is the minimum necessary to give substance to the trusts, but in my opinion it is sufficient.[30]

He therefore held that a clause, like the one he was considering, restricting liability to actual fraud, was effective to exclude a trustee from liability for loss or damage to the trust property 'no matter how indolent, imprudent, lacking in diligence, negligent or wilful he may have been, so long as he has not acted dishonestly'.[31]

Subsequent cases support the view taken in *Armitage v Nurse*.

---

[26] See *Futter v Revenue and Customs* [2013] UKSC 26 where the Supreme Court said that a breach of fiduciary duty is required to enable a trustee's decision to be avoided for inadequate deliberation, despite the fact that an obligation to consider a decision is a duty of care.

[27] Some groups of trustees, such as pension trustees, may not exclude their liability for a breach of trust in this way—Pensions Act 1995, s 33. This includes trustees of unit trusts (Financial Services and Markets Act 2000, s 253) and trustees of debenture trusts (Companies Act 2006, s 750).   [28] Sch 1, para 7.

[29] [1998] Ch 241; Pollard and Walsh 'Exclusion Clause in Trust Deed Validly Excludes Liability for Gross Negligence' (1997) 11 TLI 52; McBride 'Trustee Exemption Clauses' [1998] CLJ 33.

[30] [1998] Ch 421, at 253–254.

[31] [1998] Ch 421, at 251. Trustees of pension funds cannot exclude liability for breach of the duty of skill and care in the performance of investment functions: Pensions Act 1995, s 33.

(iii) Liability for fraud

Common precedents for exclusion or exoneration clauses exempt trustees for all liability except their actual fraud.[32] The question therefore arises of what constitutes fraud in this context. Millett LJ suggested that if a trustee acted in a way which he did not honestly believe was in the interests of the beneficiaries, he would be acting fraudulently. Further elucidation has been given by the Court of Appeal in *Walker v Stones*.[33] The central issue concerned the application of an exclusion clause which purported to protect trustees from liability arising other than through 'wilful fraud or dishonesty'. The Court of Appeal held that the test for dishonesty could not be limited to an inquiry into the subjective state of mind of the trustee, but included an irreducible objective standard.[34] How the standard was to be applied would vary from case to case and could take into account whether a trustee was acting in a professional capacity, and whether the trustee had put his own interests above those of the beneficiaries.[35] Giving the judgment of the court, Sir Christopher Slade held that the exclusion clause must be interpreted so as to 'take account of the case where the trustee's so-called "honest belief", though actually held, is so unreasonable that, by any objective standard, no reasonable solicitor trustee could have thought that what he did or agreed to was for the benefit of the beneficiaries'.[36] Summarizing the result of the case, Lewison J in *Fattal v Walbrook Trustees (Jersey) Ltd*[37] put forward a number of propositions. A trustee will not be considered to have acted dishonestly simply because he has committed a deliberate breach of trust. This could be done without dishonesty. What is required to show dishonesty in the case of a professional trustee is that he is a trustee who has committed a deliberate breach of trust, and:

(a) Who knows that the deliberate breach is contrary to the interests of the beneficiaries; or

(b) Who is recklessly indifferent whether the deliberate breach is contrary to their interests or not; or

(c) Whose belief that the deliberate breach is not contrary to the interests of the beneficiaries is so unreasonable that, by any objective standard, no reasonable professional trustee could have thought that what he did or agreed to do was for the benefit of the beneficiaries.[38]

Lewison J considered that the test for dishonesty derived from *Walker v Stones* had not been changed by cases considering the meaning of dishonesty in the context of dishonest assistance in breach of trust.[39]

---

[32] See *Fattal v Walbrook Trustees (Jersey) Ltd* [2010] EWHC 2767 (Ch), at [73].

[33] [2001] QB 902.

[34] Applying the test of dishonesty adopted by the House of Lords in *Royal Brunei Airlines Sdn Bhd v Tan* [1995] 3 All ER 97 and by the Court of Appeal in *Twinsectra Ltd v Yardley* [1999] Lloyd's Rep Bank 438.

[35] [2001] QB 902, at 939 and *Fattal v Walbrook Trustees (Jersey) Ltd* [2010] EWHC 2767 (Ch), at [82].

[36] [2001] QB 902, at 939.

[37] *Fattal v Walbrook Trustees (Jersey) Ltd* [2010] EWHC 2767 (Ch). See also *Newgate Stud Company v Penfold* [2004] EWHC 2993 (Ch).

[38] *Fattal v Walbrook Trustees (Jersey) Ltd* [2010] EWHC 2767 (Ch), at [81].

[39] *Fattal v Walbrook Trustees (Jersey) Ltd* [2010] EWHC 2767 (Ch). See Chapter 29.

(iv) Gross negligence

Millett LJ addressed the argument in *Armitage v Nurse* that it was not possible to exempt a trustee from liability for gross negligence.[40] He considered that the argument was without foundation, even though such a distinction was made in Scotland. In English law, in his view, 'we regard the difference between negligence and gross negligence as merely one of degree'. His view that it is possible to exclude liability for gross negligence has been followed by Behrens J in *Re Clapham (Decd)*,[41] and in *Spread Trustee Company Ltd v Hutcheson*[42] the Privy Council held by a majority that English law (and therefore also, in the view of the majority, Guernsey law until amended by statute on this point) permits an exemption clause to exclude liability for gross negligence. The view that there is no distinction between ordinary negligence and gross negligence apart from a vituperative epithet[43] is not, however, universally held. Gross negligence (in the slightly different context of defining the term when used in a contract) has been defined by a Supreme Court judge in Ireland as 'something flagrantly and conspicuously wrong, and conduct undertaken with actual appreciation of the risks involved, or in serious disregard of, or with indifference to an obvious risk, akin to recklessness'.[44] If gross negligence should properly be defined in this or a similar way, it casts doubt on the reasoning of the Court of Appeal in *Armitage v Nurse* that it would be irrational to distinguish between liability for negligence and liability for gross negligence.

(v) Reform

Millett LJ in *Armitage v Nurse*[45] expressed the opinion that trusts exemption clauses had gone too far, with the result that professional trustees were able to exclude liability even for gross negligence despite charging for their services and in circumstances where they would not dream of excluding liability for ordinary professional negligence. However, he thought that it was for Parliament to deny them effect, even though it may be noted that a minority of the Privy Council in *Spread Trustee Company Ltd v Hutcheson*[46] thought that before *Armitage v Nurse* it was not clear that an exemption clause could have applied to gross negligence.[47] In *Re Clapham (Decd)*,[48] Behrens J also observed that this was an area of law 'ripe for reform'.

The Law Commission conducted a review of the operation of trustee exemption clauses[49] and issued a final report in 2006.[50] The Law Commission found that it was relatively common to find express provision for exclusion of liability in modern trust

---

[40] An argument made in Matthews [1989] Conv 42.   [41] [2005] EWHC 3387 (Ch).

[42] [2011] UKPC 13. See Shearman and Pearce 'Exempting a trustee for gross negligence' [2011] Denning LJ 181–191.   [43] *Grill v General Iron Screw Collier Company* (1866) LR 1 CP 600, at 612 (Willes J).

[44] O'Donnell J in *ICDL GCC Foundation FZ-LLC v European Computer Driving Licence Foundation Ltd* [2012] IESC 55, at [16]. The majority of the court adopted a slightly different formulation requiring proof that the defendant has 'to a significant extent, been negligent': see Fennelly J at [142].

[45] [1998] Ch 241, at 256.   [46] [2011] UKPC 13.

[47] See also Hayton, 'The Irreducible Core Content of Trusteeship' in Oakley, *Trends in Contemporary Trust Law* (1996); McCormack 'The Liability of Trustees for Gross Negligence' [1998] Conv 100.

[48] [2005] EWHC 3387 (Ch), at [89].   [49] *Trustee Exemption Clauses*, Law Com No 171 (2003).

[50] *Trustee Exemption Clauses*, Law Com No 301 (2006).

instruments and that professional trustees have come to rely on them as a means of affording protection from liability for breach of trusts. Thus, it rejected an absolute prohibition on all trustee exemption clauses on the grounds that denying settlers all power to modify or restrict the extent of the obligations and liabilities of trustees would undermine the flexibility and adaptability of the trust relationship. However, while many professional trustees considered such clauses to be a necessary component of modern trust practice, and the inclusion of an exclusion clause is likely to lead to lower liability insurance premiums, the Law Commission had originally considered that there was a very strong case for some regulation of trustee exemption clauses. More particularly, it proposed that professional trustees should not be able to rely on clauses which exclude their liability for breach of trust arising from negligence, and that in so far as professional trustees may not exclude liability for breach of trust, that they should not be permitted to claim indemnity from the trust fund. There was little support for this approach in the consultation exercise, and the Law Commission abandoned proposing legislative intervention.[51] Instead, it proposed that trustee exemption clauses should be regulated by rules of good practice agreed by the professional and regulatory bodies,[52] and that, where an exemption clause seeks to limit liability for negligence for paid trustees, such steps must be taken as are reasonable to inform the settlor of the meaning and effect of the clause.[53] Breach of any of the rules would not lead to damages for breach of trust, but breach of discipline. It is striking that Guernsey and Jersey have both legislated to prevent exemption clauses applying to trustee liability for gross negligence,[54] and this strongly suggests that the Law Commission may have been too timid in its approach.[55]

(e) Breach of trust in the context of constructive and resulting trusts

Whereas the trustees of an express trust are liable for breach of trust, the position of a trustee of a resulting or constructive trust is more complex. The essential difference relates to the nature of the duties of such trustees, since in many cases they will not be expected to perform the ordinary functions of express trustee such as the investment of the trust fund. As Millett LJ observed in *Lonrho plc v Al-Fayed (No 2)*:

> It is a mistake to suppose that in every situation in which a constructive trust arises the legal owner is necessarily subject to all the fiduciary obligations and disabilities of an express trustee.[56]

---

[51] It appears other legislative enactments regulating the use of exemption clauses are inapplicable in the trust context—see *Baker v J E Clark Co (Transport) UK Ltd* [2006] EWCA Civ 464, at [21], where Tuckey LJ held that the Unfair Contract Terms Act 1977 did not apply to trustee exemption clauses.

[52] *Trustee Exemption Clauses*, Law Com No 301 (2006), at para 7.2.

[53] *Trustee Exemption Clauses*, Law Com No 301 (2006), at para 6.65.

[54] See *Spread Trustee Company Ltd v Hutcheson* [2011] UKPC 13.

[55] See Kenny 'Conveyancer's Notebook: The Good, the Bad and the Law Commission' [2007] Conv 103, at 103–108. See also Delaney 'Trustee Exemption Clauses—Proposals for Regulation in Ireland' (2009) Tru LI 89, at 99, where she concluded that there 'is a strong case for some form of statutory regulation, and the Law Commission's earlier assertion that the current legal position is too deferential to professional trustees in particular is one that has commanded support from both academics and members of the judiciary'.

[56] [1992] 1 WLR 1, at 12.

The primary duty of a constructive trustee is often simply to preserve the trust property for the benefit of the beneficiaries, and to ensure that it is not dissipated. If the trust property is dissipated by the trustee he may be liable to compensate the beneficiaries for their loss, ie the value of the trust property. A person held liable as a constructive trustee for knowingly receiving trust property will be under the same custodial duties as if the trust had been a voluntarily assumed express trust.[57] However, it appears that a constructive trustee will only be personally liable in this way if, at the relevant time that the property, he was consciously aware of his obligations as a trustee, or of the factors that gave rise to the imposition of a trust. In *Westdeutsche Landesbank Girozentrale v Islington London Borough Council*, Lord Browne-Wilkinson stated:

> Since the equitable jurisdiction to enforce trusts depends upon the conscience of the holder of the legal interest being affected, he cannot be a trustee of the property if and so long as he is ignorant of the facts alleged to affect his conscience, i.e. until he is aware that he is intended to hold the property for the benefit of others in the case of an express trust, or, in the case of a constructive trust, of the factors which are alleged to affect his conscience.[58]

While the precise import of this analysis is somewhat obscure, the best interpretation is probably that although someone may become a trustee unknowingly, he cannot be held personally liable for any breach of trust, or breach of fiduciary duty, if he was unaware of the fact that he was such a trustee, or of the circumstances making him a trustee. Thus, a third party who is improperly given trust property becomes a constructive trustee of it (subject to the defence of being a bona fide purchaser), and the beneficial interest of the beneficiaries is preserved. However, the fact that he is a trustee does not mean that he will attract personal liability for breach of trust if he dissipates the property in circumstances where he was unaware of the constructive trust. In *Bristol and West Building Society v Mothew*, Millett LJ adopted this analysis as a summary of the practical outworking of Lord Browne-Wilkinson's comments:

> In *Westdeutsche Landesbank Girozentrale v Islington London Borough Council* Lord Browne-Wilkinson expressly rejected the possibility that a recipient of trust money could be personally liable, regardless of fault, for any subsequent payment away of the moneys to third parties even though, at the date of such payment, he was ignorant of the existence of any trust.[59]

(2) Nature of liability for breach of trust

(a) Trustees are personally liable

The liability of a trustee for a breach of trust is a personal liability, and any remedy is available only against the trustee as an individual, and not against any specific assets.

---

[57] *Arthur v Attorney General of the Turks and Caicos Islands* [2012] UKPC 30, at [34]–[37].
[58] [1996] AC 669.
[59] [1996] 4 All ER 698, at 716. See also *Statek Corp v Alford* [2008] EWHC 32, discussed in Chapter 29.

If the trustee in breach has died, his personal liability continues against his estate.[60] There may be separate remedies in relation to any assets retained by the trustee or in the hands of a third party, and different remedies are also available for breach of fiduciary duty. These other remedies are considered in Chapters 28, 29, and 30.

(b) Trustees are liable only for their own breaches of trust

Trustees are only liable for their own breaches of trust and not for the breaches of their co-trustees.[61] However, where several trustees are liable for a breach of trust they are jointly and severally liable. Thus, in *Bishopsgate Investment Management Ltd v Maxwell (No 2)*[62] Kevin and Ian Maxwell, who had both signed transfers misappropriating assets held on trust for the pensions of the employees of Maxwell-owned companies, were jointly and severally liable for their breaches. Joint and several liability means that the beneficiary can recover the entire loss to the trust from any one of the trustees alone.[63] Even where the beneficiary has obtained a judgment against all the trustees he may choose to execute it against any one.[64] As Leach MR stated in *Wilson v Moore*:[65] 'all parties to a breach of trust are equally liable; there is between them no primary liability'.

Although the beneficiaries may be able to recover the entire loss suffered by the trust from just one of the trustees in breach, that trustee may be able to recover a contribution to the damages he has had to pay from his fellow trustees.[66]

(c) Breaches before appointment

A trustee is not liable for breaches of trust which were committed before his appointment.[67] On appointment he is obliged to make reasonable inquiries to ensure that the trust affairs are in order,[68] but, except in so far as a discrepancy appears, he 'is entitled to assume that everything has been duly attended to up to the time of his becoming trustee'.[69] However, if he does discover such a breach he should take proceedings against the former trustees responsible.

(d) Liability after retirement

Retirement does not save a trustee from liability for breaches of trust committed while he was a trustee. He will also be liable if he retired to enable a breach of trust to take place. The principle was stated by Kekewich J in *Head v Gould*:

> in order to make a retiring trustee liable for a breach of trust committed by his successor you must shew, and shew clearly, that the very breach of trust which was in fact committed

---

[60] See *Fry v Fry* (1859) 27 Beav 144.   [61] *Townley v Sherborn* (1634) J Bridg 35.
[62] [1994] 1 All ER 261, CA.
[63] *Walker v Symonds* (1818) 3 Swan 1; *Re Harrison* [1891] 2 Ch 349; *McCheane v Gyles (No 2)* [1902] 1 Ch 911.   [64] *A-G v Wilson* (1840) Cr & Ph 1; *Fletcher v Green* (1864) 33 Beav 426.
[65] (1833) 1 My & K 126, at 146.   [66] Discussed later in the chapter.
[67] *Re Strahan* (1856) 8 De GM & G 291.
[68] *Harvey v Oliver* (1887) 57 LT 239; *Re Lucking's Will Trusts* [1968] 1 WLR 866.
[69] *Re Strahan* (1856) 8 De GM & G 291, at 309, per Turner LJ.

was not merely the outcome of the retirement and new appointment, but was contemplated by the former trustee when such retirement and appointment took place.[70]

The key factor which renders a retired trustee liable is the fact that he was fully aware of, and connived in, the subsequent breach of trust.

(e) Trustees not vicariously liable for each other

The Trustee Act 2000 repealed a contentious provision in the Trustee Act 1925 (s 30(1)), which addressed the issue of when trustees would be liable for the acts of other trustees. It did not replace it, with the effect that trustees will be liable for losses caused by other trustees only when they themselves are in breach of trust, for instance by concurring in an ultra vires decision, or by wrongly failing to act to prevent another trustee committing a breach of trust.

(f) Election between compensatory and restitutionary remedies

It will be seen that in some circumstances beneficiaries may have more than one remedy. For instance where a trustee has improperly used trust property for his own purposes and made a profit, the beneficiary may be able to pursue both an action for the loss caused to the trust by the breach (equitable compensation), and also an action to deprive the trustee of the profit (a claim for restitution based on unjust enrichment). These remedies are not cumulative. In *Tang Man Sit (Decd) v Capacious Investments Ltd*[71] the Privy Council held that the remedies of compensation for breach of trust and restitution where a trustee has breached his fiduciary duty are alternative, and that the beneficiaries must elect between them to prevent double recovery. The case concerned a planned joint venture for the development of land. The defendant provided land for the development, which was funded by the plaintiff company. It was agreed that the defendant would assign legal title to sixteen of the houses built to the plaintiffs. It was held that this created a trust of the houses for the plaintiff, but in breach of trust the title was never assigned by the defendants. Over a period of years the defendant let the houses to tenants and received a profit of some HK$2m in the form of rent. The plaintiffs claimed that they were entitled to an equitable account of these profits on the grounds that they were unauthorized remuneration received by the defendant trustee in breach of its fiduciary duty, and also damages for breach of trust for the rent that they could have obtained from the houses if they had been assigned at the appropriate time, a sum which was assessed at HK$17m. The defendant had paid HK$1.8m to the plaintiffs by way of account of the profit received, and the plaintiffs subsequently sought the damages due. The defendant argued that by accepting the account of profits the plaintiffs had made an irrevocable election between the restitutionary and compensatory remedies. The Privy Council held that in the circumstances no election

---

[70] [1898] 2 Ch 250, at 273–274.
[71] [1996] AC 514. See Stevens 'Election between Alternative Remedies' [1996] RLR 117; Birks 'Inconsistency between Compensation and Restitution' (1996) 112 LQR 375.

had been made, so that the plaintiffs were entitled to recover full damages, less the HK$1.8m they had already received. The Privy Council stated that:

> Faced with alternative and inconsistent remedies a plaintiff must choose, or elect, between them. He cannot have both.[72]

2 Compensation for breach of trust

(1) General principles

(a) A compensatory remedy

The remedy for breach of trust is essentially compensatory.[73] When a breach has been committed the trustee responsible is liable to compensate the trust (rather than an individual beneficiary[74]) for all the loss flowing directly or indirectly from the breach.[75] As Street J said in *Re Dawson*:

> the trustee is liable to place the trust estate in the same position it would have been in if no breach had been committed.[76]

In some cases, for example *Target Holdings Ltd v Redferns*[77] this compensation has been described as 'restitution' of the trust estate.[78] However, this usage is likely to cause confusion. As a legal term of art, restitution is the response which consists in a defendant giving up to the claimant any unjust gain, known as an enrichment, which he has received at the claimant's expense without legal justification.[79] A trustee in breach of trust may not have received any personal gain, in which case it is impossible to regard him as 'enriched'. The trustee is required to compensate the trust for the loss it has sustained in consequence of his conduct, not to return an enrichment he has received. As Lord Browne-Wilkinson observed in *Target Holdings Ltd v Redferns*:

> in the case of a breach of such a trust involving the wrongful paying away of trust assets, the liability of the trustee is to restore to the trust fund, often called the trust estate, what ought to have been there.[80]

---

[72] [1996] 1 All ER 193, at 197 (Lord Nicholls).

[73] See Oakley, 'The Liberalising Nature of Remedies for Breach of Trust' in Oakley, *Trends in Contemporary Trust Law* (1996), pp 219–230; Capper 'Compensation for Breach of Trust' [1997] Conv 14; Sealy 'Mortgagees and Receivers—A Duty of Care Resurrected and Extended' (2000) 59 CLJ 31; P Birks and F Rose (eds), *Restitution and Equity, Vol 1: Resulting Trusts and Equitable Compensation* (2000).

[74] *Re X Trust* [2013] WTLR 731 (Royal Court of Jersey).

[75] *Bateman v Davis* (1818) 3 Madd 98; *Lander v Weston* (1855) 3 Drew 389; *Knott v Cottee* (1852) 16 Beav 77; *Re Miller's Deed Trusts* [1978] LS Gaz R 454; *Bartlett v Barclays Trust Co Ltd* [1980] Ch 515. See also Baxter 'Trustees' Personal Liability and the Role of Liability Insurance' [1996] Conv 186.

[76] [1966] 2 NSWLR 211, at 215.   [77] [1996] 1 AC 421.

[78] [1996] 1 AC 421, at 434, per Lord Browne-Wilkinson. See also Hanbury and Martin, *Modern Equity* (18th edn, 2009), which describes the liability as 'restitutionary' (at p 685).

[79] Birks, *Introduction to the Law of Restitution* (1985), pp 9–27.

[80] [1996] 1 AC 421, at 434.

(b) **Causation**

A trustee who has acted in breach is only liable to compensate the trust for loss which was caused by his breach. If there is no causal link between the breach and the loss, the trustee will not be liable. This is clear from the decision of the Court of Appeal in *Bishopsgate Investment Management Ltd v Maxwell (No 2).*[81] This case arose out of the infamous Robert Maxwell pension fraud. Robert Maxwell had conducted a fraud on a massive scale which included misappropriating pension funds held by the plaintiff company of which Ian Maxwell was a director. Ian Maxwell, as a director, had signed transfers to Robert Maxwell's private companies beneath the signature of his brother, Kevin, and had also signed blank transfers. He had made no inquiry about the transactions and had signed the transfers because his brother had done so. The plaintiff obtained summary judgment against him. Ian Maxwell appealed on the basis that the plaintiff had not shown that his inactivity had caused the loss. The Court of Appeal made it clear that where a fiduciary has committed a breach of duty by omission, the plaintiff claiming damages must prove that the omission caused the loss, in the sense that compliance would have prevented the damage.[82] However, the court held that this was not a case where the breach was in the nature of an omission, but that the breach was simply the improper transfer of the shares to Robert Maxwell Group plc. Causation was thus clearly established and the summary judgment was upheld.

The requirement of causation was considered at length by the House of Lords in *Target Holdings Ltd v Redferns.*[83] The case concerned a complex mortgage fraud. Mirage Properties Ltd agreed to sell properties in Birmingham to Crowngate Developments Ltd, a company companies owned by Mr Kohli and Mr Musafir, for £775,000. To execute the fraud, Kholi and Musafir arranged for the purchase to be made through two intermediary companies they owned (first Panther Ltd and then Kholi & Co), so that it appeared that the sale to Crowngate was for a consideration of £2m. Crowngate applied to Target Holdings for a loan of £1.7m, and employed Redferns as their solicitors. The loan application was supported by a £2m valuation of the properties made by a firm of estate agents. The loan was paid into Redferns' client account on 28 June 1989, without any express instructions as to the release of the funds. On 29 June £1.25m was transferred to the account of Panther in Jersey, although at this stage the contract for the purchase of the properties had not yet been entered, and it was not until July that the contracts and mortgages in favour of Target were executed. Subsequently, the value of the properties dropped sharply and Target sought to recover their loss.

Any action against the estate agents, who had carried out the valuation, was of little value because they were in liquidation. Target therefore sought to recover its loss (allowing for the amount recovered from the sale of the property) from Redferns. Target applied for summary judgment. There was no doubt that the transfer of funds

---

[81] [1994] 1 All ER 261.
[82] [1994] 1 All ER 261, at 264, per Hoffmann LJ.
[83] [1996] 1 AC 421, (1996) 112 LQR 27 (Rickett); [1996] LMCLQ 161 (Nolan); [1997] Conv 14 (Capper); (1995) 9 TLI 86 (Ulph). See also (1998) 114 LQR 214 (Sir Peter Millett).

before the contracts for sale and the mortgages had been entered had constituted a breach of trust. The only question for the court was whether Redferns had any defence. Warner J at first instance held that Redferns had an arguable defence. The Court of Appeal, by a majority, disagreed. It held that once a breach of trust was established, the trustee was obliged to make good the deficiency in the trust fund, and the rules about remoteness of damage applicable to contract claims had no application.[84] Ralph Gibson LJ delivered a powerful dissenting judgment, in which he held that Warner J had been correct to refuse to give Target final judgment. He took the view that there was an arguable defence that the breach had not caused the loss. Although he felt that Target was likely to succeed, he held that it was arguable that it would have gone ahead with the transaction in any event, relying on the valuation of the properties by the estate agents, and that in such circumstances the breach of trust by Redferns would not have been the cause of the loss.

Redferns appealed to the House of Lords, which, agreeing with Ralph Gibson LJ, held that Target was not entitled to final judgment. Lord Browne-Wilkinson stated the underlying principle as follows:

> there does have to be some causal connection between the breach of trust and the loss to the trust estate for which compensation is recoverable, viz the fact that the loss would not have occurred but for the breach.[85]

He went on to conclude that, on the assumption that the transaction would have gone ahead irrespective of the breach of trust, the breach had not been the cause of the loss suffered:

> Target has not demonstrated that it is entitled to any compensation for breach of trust.... Target obtained exactly what it would have obtained had no breach occurred, ie a valid security for the sum advanced.[86]

In the course of his judgment he rejected Target's argument that Redferns were under an immediate duty to restore the trust fund, holding that in a commercial conveyancing context a client has no right to have the solicitor's client account reconstituted after the transaction is completed.[87] He also rejected the argument that the quantum of compensation was to be fixed at the date that the alleged breach occurred. Instead he held:

> The quantum is fixed at the date of judgment, at which date, according to the circumstances then pertaining, the compensation is assessed as the figure then necessary to put the trust estate or the beneficiary back into the position it would have been in had there been no breach.[88]

---

[84] Referring to *Clough v Bond* (1838) 3 My & Cr 490; *Re Dawson* [1966] 2 NSWLR 211; *Alliance and Leicester Building Society v Edgestop Ltd* [1994] 2 All ER 38; *Bishopsgate Investment Management Ltd v Maxwell (No 2)* [1994] 1 All ER 261, CA.

[85] [1996] 1 AC 421, at 434. See also *Re Miller's Deed Trusts* [1978] LS Gaz 454; *Nestlé v National Westminster Bank plc* [1994] 1 All ER 118.   [86] [1996] 1 AC 421, at 440.

[87] [1996] 1 AC 421, at 436.   [88] [1996] 1 AC 421, at 437.

Despite concluding that Target had not proved causation, the House of Lords was doubtful whether Redferns would ultimately be able to show that their breach had not caused the loss. Lord Browne-Wilkinson summarized:

> There must be a high probability that, at trial, it will emerge that the use of Target's money to pay for the purchase from Mirage and the other intermediate transactions was a vital feature of this transaction...If the moneys made available by Redfern's breach of trust were essential to enable the transaction to go through, but for Redfern's breach of trust Target would not have advanced any money. In that case the loss suffered by Target by reason of the breach of trust will be the total sum advanced to Crowngate less the proceeds of the security.[89]

In conclusion, the decision of the House of Lords in *Target Holdings Ltd v Redferns* requires a claimant seeking compensation when trust property has been transferred contrary to the terms of the trust (or in the case of a bare trust, contrary to the instructions of the beneficiary) to demonstrate that, but for the alleged breach of trust, he would not have suffered the loss sustained. Conversely, the defendant can escape liability by demonstrating that the loss would have been sustained even if the breach had not occurred.

By way of qualification to this general proposition, there may be circumstances in which the burden of proof shifts to the defendant. In *Bristol and West Building Society v May, May & Merrimans (No 1)*[90] Chadwick J held that where a solicitor had made a warranty or misrepresentation to a mortgagee which the solicitor knew[91] to be misleading there was no need for the claimant to answer the 'what if' question:

> It would, as it seems to me, be a strange principle of equity which allowed a solicitor who, in breach of the duty of good faith owed to his client, had given a warranty which he knew to be false with the intention that the client should act upon it, to say, in answer to a claim for compensation in respect of loss which had resulted from the client relying on the warranty and acting as he intended, that the client must establish that he would not have so acted if he had been told the true facts. After all, a common reason for giving a warranty which the warrantor knows to be false is the fear that, without the false warranty, the lender will refuse to proceed. If it were not for that fear the warrantor would have no reason to withhold the truth. [W]here a fiduciary has failed to disclose material facts, he cannot be heard to say, in answer to a claim for equitable compensation, that disclosure would not have altered the decision to proceed with the transaction.[92]

He held that this approach was supported by the earlier decision of the Privy Council in *Brickenden v London Loan & Savings Co*,[93] which he considered had not been overruled by the House of Lords in *Target Holdings Ltd v Redferns*.

---

[89] [1996] 1 AC 421, at 440–441.
[90] [1996] 2 All ER 801; Alcock 'Limiting Contractual and Tortious Damages' [1997] LMCLQ 26.
[91] Or must be taken to have known.   [92] [1996] 2 All ER 801, at 825–826.
[93] [1934] 3 DLR 465.

(c) Liability only for loss caused by the breach

The cases dealing with the liability of a solicitor for releasing mortgage funds without authority show that the liability extends only to the loss caused by the breach and does not include other losses arising from entering into the mortgage.[94] There is no reason to think that the rule is not of general application to other breaches of trust. Where the transaction was induced by fraud, and would not have been made but for the fraud, then compensation will be based on the direct losses caused by the transaction,[95] but this is simply a case of applying the ordinary rules about causation.[96]

(d) Remoteness and foreseeability of loss

Although *Target Holdings Ltd v Redferns (a firm)*[97] demonstrates a need to establish causation in order to render a trustee liable to compensate for breach of trust, the further question arises whether, where such causation is established, a trustee is liable for all the loss which flows from his breach, directly or indirectly, or whether some principle of remoteness operates to limit his liability to such losses as were reasonably foreseeable as a result of the breach. Traditionally it has been held that the trustee's liability is not mitigated by such principles as remoteness of damage.[98] Indeed, in *Target Holdings Ltd v Redferns* itself,[99] the House of Lords held that the common law principle of remoteness of damage has no application to liability where trust property was wrongly transferred by the trustee in breach of the terms of the trust. Lord Browne-Wilkinson stated:

> If specific restitution of the trust property is not possible, then the liability of the trustee is to pay sufficient compensation to the trust estate to put it back to what it would have been had the breach not been committed. Even if the immediate cause of the loss is the dishonesty or failure of a third party the trustee is liable to make good that loss to the trust estate if, but for the breach, such loss would not have occurred. Thus the common law rules of remoteness of damage and causation do not apply.[100]

However, where a trustee has acted without due care, thus causing a loss to the trust, it is possible that the principles of remoteness may apply. In *Bristol and West Building Society v Mothew*[101] the Court of Appeal considered the nature of the equitable liability of a fiduciary in breach of his duty to act with due skill and care. Millett LJ stated:

> Although the remedy which equity makes available for breach of the equitable duty of skill and care is equitable compensation rather than damages, this is merely the product of history and in this context is in my opinion a distinction without a difference. Equitable

---

[94] *Swindle v Harrison* [1997] 4 All ER 705.
[95] *Swindle v Harrison* [1997] 4 All ER 705; Elliott 'Restitutionary Compensatory Damages for Breach of Fiduciary Duty?' [1998] RLR 135.   [96] *Collins v Brebner*, 26 January 2000 (CA), at [57]–[64].
[97] [1996] AC 421.
[98] Underhill and Hayton, *Law Relating to Trusts and Trustees* (16th edn, 2003), p 855.
[99] [1996] 1 AC 421.
[100] [1996] 1 AC 421, at 434. For criticism of this position, see: *Bank of New Zealand v New Zealand Guardian Trust Co Ltd* [1999] 1 NZLR 213; affd [1999] 1 NZLR 664; *Collins v Brebner* [2000] Lloyd's Rep PN 587; Elliott 'Remoteness Criteria in Equity' (2002) 65 MLR 588.   [101] [1998] Ch 1.

compensation for breach of the duty of skill and care resembles common law damages in that it is awarded by way of compensation to the plaintiff of his loss. There is no reason in principle why the common law rules of causation, remoteness of damage and measure of damages should not be applied by analogy in such a case.[102]

(e) Accounting for tax liability

The rule that tax liability is to be taken into account when calculating damages for personal injury in tort[103] is not applied, and in *Re Bell's Indenture*[104] it was held that a trustee should restore the value of misappropriated property to the trust without allowance for the tax that would have had to be paid on it by the trust if it had not been misappropriated.

(2) Investment

Trustees now have much wider powers of investment than used to be the case, so it will now be rare for a trust to hold or to make an unauthorized investment. However, where a trustee does purchase an unauthorized investment, he will be liable for any loss resulting from the purchase which will be the amount by which those investments have fallen in value[105] or for the difference between the value of the investments actually made and those which should have been purchased or retained.[106] In the same way, if a trustee retains unauthorized investments he will be liable to the beneficiaries for any loss that the trust suffers as a result. The measure of loss will be the amount that the investments could have realized if they had been sold at the proper time, less the value that they actually realized.[107]

Even where trust funds have been invested in permitted investments, under Trustee Act 2000, s 5 a trustee is under duty to review the investments of the trust and to obtain and consider proper advice about whether they should be varied. If he fails to fulfil this duty, or fails to exercise the requisite duty of reasonable care, he will be liable to compensate the trust for the resulting loss. The Trustee Act 1925, ss 8 and 9 contain some special rules relating to investments made by lending on the security of a mortgage (a common form of trustee investment in the Victorian era, but now very rare).

(3) Assessing compensation

(a) Date for assessing compensation

In *Target Holdings Ltd v Redferns*[108] it was held that the quantum of equitable compensation payable in respect of a breach of trust is to be assessed not at the date that the

---

[102] [1998] Ch 1, at 17.
[103] *British Transport Commission v Gourley* [1956] AC 185, HL.   [104] [1980] 1 WLR 1217.
[105] *Knott v Cottee* (1852) 16 Beav 77.   [106] *Re Massingberd's Settlement* (1890) 63 LT 296.
[107] *Fry v Fry* (1859) 27 Beav 144. See also *Jaffray v Marshall* [1994] 1 All ER 143.
[108] [1996] 1 AC 401.

breach occurred, but at the date of judgment. The House of Lords overruled the decision in *Jaffray v Marshall*,[109] where it had been held that a trustee who committed an ongoing breach of trust by failing to restore trust property to the trust fund was required to compensate the beneficiaries on the basis of the property's value at the date on which the action was brought.

(b) Subsequent events

Since the purpose of equitable compensation is to restore any loss caused by the breach, if as a result of events subsequent to the breach the loss is mitigated or reversed, those events will be taken into account. Thus in *Target Holdings,* it was relevant that the mortgage security had been obtained, albeit later than should have been the case. Equally, in *Hulbert v Avens*,[110] where trustees incurred a penalty by not paying tax on time, but made a profit by favourably investing the money that should have been used for tax, the profit was to be set against the penalty, and the trustees could be held liable only for the difference. Again, in *AIB Group (UK) Plc v Mark Redler & Co Solicitors*[111] a firm of solicitors carelessly failed to discharge a prior loan on a remortgage. In consequence, the lending bank obtained only a second charge. This was a breach of trust since the solicitors had not complied with the terms of their authority. The borrower defaulted and the bank was unable to recover its loan in full. The Court of Appeal held that the solicitors were only liable for the extent to which the bank would have recovered more if it had received the first charge; most of their loss was attributable to the property being worth less than it had expected.

(c) Offsetting losses and gains

(i) The general rule

It is a basic principle that each breach of trust is to be treated independently of the trustee's other activities. A loss suffered by the trust as a result of a breach in one transaction cannot be offset against a gain achieved for the trust in another. The trustee remains liable for the loss caused by his breach, irrespective of the gain. This principle was accepted in *Bartlett v Barclays Bank Trust Co Ltd (No 2)*,[112] where Brightman J stated:

> The general rule…is that where a trustee is liable in respect of distinct breaches of trust, one of which resulted in a loss and the other in a gain, he is not entitled to set the gain against the loss, unless they arise in the same transaction.[113]

This rule was applied in *Dimes v Scott*,[114] where the trustees of a settlement created on the death of Captain Piercey in 1802 failed to sell an investment in the East India Company which they had been directed to convert into money by the Captain's will.

---

[109] [1994] 1 All ER 143.   [110] [2003] EWHC 76 (Ch).   [111] [2013] EWCA Civ 45.
[112] [1980] Ch 515; [1980] Conv 155 (Shindler); [1983] Conv 127 (Pearce and Samuels).
[113] [1980] Ch 515, at 538. See also *Adye v Feuilleteau* (1783) 3 Swan 84n; *Robinson v Robinson* (1848) 11 Beav 371; *Wiles v Gresham* (1854) 2 Drew 258.   [114] (1828) 4 Russ 195.

The trustees paid the full income received (10 per cent per annum) to the life beneficiary. Under the (now abolished) rule in *Howe v Dartmouth*[115] the life tenant was only
entitled to a 4 per cent return on the value of the investment as income. When the
unauthorized investment was realized in 1813 the proceeds were used to purchase
Consols. As the price of the Consols had fallen since the date of the testator's death,
they were able to purchase more than they would have been able to at that time. It was
held that the gain to the beneficiaries of the extra Consols could not be offset against
the trustees' liability for excessive payments made to the life tenant while the unauthorized investment was retained.

(ii) Distinct breaches of trust

The rule preventing any set-off between losses and gains only applies if there are distinct, independent breaches of trust. If the breaches occur in the course of one indivisible transaction then any gain will be taken into account. This provides an adequate
explanation for *Fletcher v Green*.[116] Here the trustee of a settlement committed a breach
of trust by lending money on a mortgage which proved insufficient security. When the
security was realized the money was invested in Consols, which rose in value, producing a gain of £251. The court held that this gain must be set off against the trustee's
liability for the failure of the security.

(iii) Set-off in exceptional circumstances

In *Bartlett v Barclays Bank Trust Co Ltd (No 2)*[117] the general principle that there should
be no set-off between gains and losses flowing from a breach of trust was reaffirmed,
although without enthusiasm. However, on the specific facts Brightman J did permit the defendant bank to set off the gain that had been made in one investment in
breach of trust against a loss made in another. A company owned by the trust made
two investments in property development schemes which were wholly inappropriate,
and the bank was liable for having failed adequately to supervise the operations of the
company. On one project, the 'Old Bailey Project', the company lost £580,000 capital
and a great deal of income. On another project, the 'Guildford Development', which
was entered under exactly the same policy of investment, the company made a profit of
some £271,000. Brightman J held that this profit could be offset against the liability of
the bank for the loss incurred by the 'Old Bailey Project'. However he failed to provide
an adequate explanation of why the set-off was permitted. Having stated the general
principle, he continued:

> the relevant cases are he relnot altogether easy to reconcile. All are centenarians and
> none is quite like the present. The Guildford development stemmed from exactly the
> same policy and (to a lesser degree because it proceeded less far) exemplified the same
> folly as the Old Bailey project. Part of the profit was in fact used to finance the Old Bailey
> disaster. By sheer luck the gamble paid off handsomely, on capital account. I think it
> would be unjust to deprive the bank of this element of salvage in the course of assessing

---

[115] (1802) 7 Ves 137.   [116] (1864) 33 Beav 426.   [117] [1980] Ch 515.

the cost of the shipwreck. My order will therefore reflect the bank's right to an appropriate set-off.[118]

Despite the fact that the developments took place under the same policy, it cannot be said that they were effectively part of the same transaction so as not to be 'distinct' breaches of trust.

(iv) A new approach?

It is hard to reconcile the decision in *Bartlett v Barclays Bank Trust Co Ltd (No 2)* with *Dimes v Scott,* and indeed, the facts of the latter case seem a better illustration of connected losses and gains than the former. Brightman J showed no enthusiasm for the general rule, and was astute to find a basis for distinguishing his own decision in order to achieve justice between the parties. The approach to the assessment of compensation adopted by the House of Lords in *Target Holdings* is consistent with this. Lord Browne-Wilkinson emphasized that beneficiaries should only be able to recover what they had actually lost:

> Equitable compensation for breach of trust is designed to achieve exactly what the word compensation suggests: to make good a loss in fact suffered by the beneficiaries and which, using hindsight and common sense, can be seen to have been caused by the breach.[119]

It may be that if the Supreme Court has the opportunity to review the decision in *Dimes v Scott* it will conclude that common sense requires that a realistic, rather than a purist, approach should be taken to balancing profits and losses made by trustees in breach.

(4) **Interest**

Where a trustee is liable to compensate the trust for loss caused by his misapplication of trust property, the trust is also entitled to recover interest on the sum misapplied. The rationale for this was explained by Buckley LJ in *Wallersteiner v Moir (No 2)*:

> It is well established in equity that a trustee who in breach of trust misapplies trust funds will be liable not only to replace the misapplied principal fund but to do so with interest from the date of the misapplication. This is on the notional ground that the money so applied was in fact the trustee's own money and that he has retained the misapplied trust money in his own hands and used it for his own purposes.[120]

The court assumes that the trustee has retained the misapplied property and has therefore had the opportunity to earn interest on it. A number of cases have considered the rate of interest which should be payable. Ultimately, the determination of the appropriate rate of interest is a matter for the discretion of the court, and decisions have taken account of factors such as the Bank of England base rate,[121] other relevant

---

[118] [1980] Ch 515, at 538.   [119] [1996] AC 421, at 163.   [120] [1975] QB 373, at 397.
[121] *Wallersteiner v Moir (No 2)* [1975] QB 373, 508n; *Belmont Finance Corpn Ltd v Williams Furniture Ltd (No 2)* [1980] 1 All ER 393, CA; *O'Sullivan v Management Agency and Music Ltd* [1985] QB 428, CA.

interest rates,[122] and the character,[123] conduct or fault of the trustee.[124] Compound interest can be charged in an appropriate case, for instance where the trustee has been fraudulent or made personal use of the money.[125] It may even be that there is now a general principle that compound interest should be paid truly to reflect the beneficiaries' loss.[126]

3 Defences to liability for breach of trust

Even if a trustee has committed a breach of trust which has caused loss to the trust, it is not inevitable that he will be required to pay equitable compensation to the trust. A number of defences are available to trustees which may wholly or partially protect them from liability.

(1) Beneficiaries' consent or concurrence

(a) General principles

A beneficiary cannot complain of a breach of trust by a trustee to which he consented, or in which he actively concurred or passively acquiesced.[127] As Wilmer LJ stated in the context of an advance of trust property made by a trustee bank to the beneficiaries in breach of trust in *Re Pauling's Settlement Trusts*:

> if the bank can establish a valid request or consent by the advanced beneficiary to the advance in question, that is a good defence on the part of the bank to the beneficiary's claim, even though it can be plain that the advance was made in breach of trust.[128]

The case concerned a marriage settlement created in 1919 on the marriage of Violet Pauling and Commander Younghusband. The trustees were the bank Coutts & Co. By an express provision of the trust deed the trustees had the power to advance up to one-half of the beneficiaries' presumptive share under the trust for their advancement or absolute use. The family consistently lived beyond its means, and Violet's current account with the trustees was often overdrawn. Between 1948 and 1954 a number of advancements were made to the children of the marriage, Francis, George, Anne, and

---

[122] *Guardian Ocean Cargoes Ltd v Banco do Brasil (No 3)* [1992] 2 Lloyd's Rep 193; *Bartlett v Barclays Bank Trust Co Ltd (No 2)* [1980] Ch 515, at 547.

[123] *Re Evans (Decd)*, [1999] 2 All ER 777 (non-professional administrator of a small estate charged interest at the lower end of the possible range).

[124] *A-G v Alford* (1855) 4 De GM & G 843 (fraudulent trustee expected to pay a higher rate of interest).

[125] *Wallersteiner v Moir (No 2)* [1975] QB 373; *Piety v Stace* (1799) 4 Ves 620; *Heathcote v Hulme* (1819) 1 Jac & W 122; *Brown v Sansome* (1825) M'Cle & Yo 427; *Jones v Foxall* (1852) 15 Beav 388; *Penny v Avison* (1856) 3 Jur NS 62; *Re Davis* [1902] 2 Ch 314.

[126] *Wallersteiner v Moir (No 2)* [1975] QB 373, at 388.

[127] *Walker v Symonds* (1818) 3 Swan 1; *Stafford v Stafford* (1857) 1 De G & J 193; *Chillingworth v Chambers* [1896] 1 Ch 685, CA. [128] [1964] Ch 303, at 335.

Anthony, who were all of age by 1951, ostensibly for such purposes as improvements to their homes and the purchase of furniture. The money advanced was generally paid into Violet's overdrawn current account. The children subsequently complained that the bank had acted in breach of trust in making these advancements.

In respect of a number of advances the Court of Appeal held that the bank was not liable because the beneficiaries had validly consented to the advances being made, with full knowledge that the money would be applied to reduce their mother's overdraft.

If a trustee wishes to avoid liability completely he must have gained the consent of all the beneficiaries of the trust. If only some had consented, the remainder will retain the right to maintain an action against him for his breach (but only for their share of the loss).

(b) Requirements for relief from liability

(i) The beneficiary must be of age

A beneficiary must have reached the age of majority for his consent to a breach of trust to be effective to protect the trustee from liability. The consent of a minor is ineffective.[129] However, a minor who fraudulently misrepresents his age to persuade trustees to pay trust money over to him will not be permitted to deny that his consent was effective because of his age.[130]

(ii) The beneficiary must not have consented while under any other incapacity

If the beneficiary is under any incapacity that would invalidate his consent a trustee remains liable.[131] Therefore, a beneficiary who is of age but under a mental incapacity cannot give an effective consent to a breach of trust. In *Re Pauling's Settlement Trusts*[132] one son, Francis, was a schizophrenic, but it was held that his mental condition was not sufficiently serious to render his consent invalid.[133]

(iii) The beneficiary must have freely given consent

Only the freely given consent of a beneficiary will be sufficient to protect a trustee from liability. In *Re Pauling's Settlement Trusts*[134] it was held that the trustees could not rely on the beneficiaries' consent where it was given while the children were acting under the undue influence of their parents. It was only when they were 'emancipated' from parental control that their consent was effective. However, in such circumstances a trustee will only be liable 'if he knew, or ought to have known that the beneficiary was acting under the undue influence of another'.[135]

---

[129] *Adye v Feuilleteau* (1783) 3 Swan 84n; *Lord Montfort v Lord Cadogan* (1816) 19 Ves 635; *Wilkinson v Parry* (1828) 4 Russ 272; *March v Russell* (1837) 3 My & Cr 31.

[130] *Overton v Banister* (1844) 3 Hare 503; *Wright v Snowe* (1848) 2 De G & Sm 321.

[131] *Crosby v Church* (1841) 3 Beav 485; *Mara v Manning* (1845) 2 Jo & Lat 311; *Fletcher v Green* (1864) 33 Beav 426.   [132] [1961] 3 All ER 713, at 731–732; on appeal [1964] Ch 303, at 347–348.

[133] See now Mental Capacity Act 2005, which provides a presumption of capacity in relation to a transaction, unless it can be proved otherwise.   [134] [1964] Ch 303.

[135] [1964] Ch 303, at 338, per Willmer LJ.

(iv) The beneficiary must have given an informed consent

A trustee will only be protected if the beneficiary's consent to the breach of trust was an informed consent.[136] The principle was stated by Wilberforce J, at first instance, in *Re Pauling's Settlement Trusts*:

> the court has to consider all the circumstances in which the concurrence of the cestui que trust was given with a view to seeing whether it is fair and equitable that, having given his concurrence, he should afterwards turn round and sue the trustees: that subject to this, it is not necessary that he should know that what he is concurring in is a breach of trust, provided that he fully understands what he is concurring in...[137]

This principle was also adopted by Harman J in *Holder v Holder*[138] and Goff LJ in *Re Freeston's Charity*.[139]

(v) The beneficiary need not have benefited from the breach of trust

In *Fletcher v Collis*[140] it was held that a trustee will be protected from liability where a beneficiary has consented to the breach even if he did not obtain any personal benefit from that breach.[141]

(2) Breach subsequently condoned by the beneficiaries

A trustee is similarly protected from liability if, after a breach has been committed, the beneficiaries condone it, release him from liability, or indemnify him. This principle is subject to the same qualifications as apply to the rule that a trustee is not liable to a beneficiary who has consented to a breach of trust: ie the condoning or releasing beneficiary must be of age;[142] the condoning or releasing beneficiary must not be under any other incapacity; the beneficiary must freely condone the breach or release the trustee from liability;[143] the beneficiary must have known what he was condoning or from what he was releasing the trustee. Condonation obtained through undue influence will be of no effect. As Westbury LC stated in *Farrant v Blanchford*:[144]

> Where a breach of trust has been committed from which a trustee alleges that he has been released, it is incumbent on him to show that such release was given by the cestui que trust deliberately and advisedly, with full knowledge of all the circumstances, and of his own rights and claims against the trustee...[145]

---

[136] There must be a full and frank disclosure by the trustee. See *Phipps v Boardman* [1964] 2 All ER 187.

[137] [1961] 3 All ER 713, at 730.   [138] [1968] Ch 353.   [139] [1979] 1 All ER 51.

[140] [1905] 2 Ch 24.

[141] See also *Re Pauling's Settlement Trusts* [1961] 3 All ER 713, at 730; *Allen v Rea Brothers Trustees Ltd* [2002] WTLR 625.   [142] *Wade v Cox* (1835) 4 LJ Ch 105; *Parker v Bloxam* (1855) 20 Beav 295.

[143] Westbury LC stated in *Farrant v Blanchford* that a trustee must be able to show that the beneficiary 'gave the release freely and without pressure or undue influence or any description'. See also *Lloyd v Attwood* (1859) 3 De G & J 614; *Reade v Reade* (1881) 9 LR Ir 409.   [144] (1863) 1 De GJ & Sm 107, at 119.

[145] See also *Ramsden v Hylton* (1751) 2 Ves Sen 304; *Hore v Becher* (1842) 12 Sim 465; *Pritt v Clay* (1843) 6 Beav 503; *Thomson v Eastwood* (1877) 2 App Cas 215, HL; *Re Garnett* (1885) 31 Ch D 1, CA.

(3) **The discretion of the court to grant relief from liability**

(a) **Trustee Act 1925, s 61**

Trustee Act 1925, s 61[146] confers upon the court a general discretion to grant a trustee relief from liability for breach of trust. The section provides:

> If it appears to the court that a trustee, whether appointed by the court or otherwise, is or may be personally liable for any breach of trust f it abut has acted honestly and reasonably, and ought fairly to be excused for the breach of trust and for omitting to obtain the direction of the court in the matter in which he committed such breach, then the court may relieve him either wholly or in part from personal liability for the same.

This section clearly grants a wide discretion to the court, both as to whether a trustee should be relieved at all and, if so, the extent to which he should be relieved. This enables the court to take account of the circumstances in which the breach occurred and to assess the culpability of the trustee in the light of them. However, the starting point of the law is that a trustee is prima facie liable even for honest technical breaches of trust, and the burden falls to the trustee to demonstrate that he should be granted relief.[147]

(b) **Preconditions for the grant of relief under s 61**

The courts have emphasized that the discretion conferred by s 61 is not to be exercised on the basis of strict and narrow interpretations. As Byrne J observed in *Re Turner*:[148]

> It would be impossible to lay down any general rules or principles to be acted on in carrying out the provisions of the section, and I think that each case must depend on its own circumstances.[149]

However, for the court even to consider relief the trustee must show that he had acted 'honestly and reasonably', and that he 'ought fairly to be excused'. Although there is little authority, some consideration has been given to the meaning of these requirements.

(i) *'Honesty'*

It is clear that a trustee cannot be granted relief from liability if he has acted dishonestly. However, as Kekewich J observed in *Perrins v Bellamy*,[150] in a large majority of cases where a breach of trust has been committed the trustee will not have

---

[146] Trustee Act 1925, s 61 re-enacts s 3 of the Judicial Trustees Act 1896, and many of the cases discussed here consider the effect of s 3.

[147] *Re Stuart* [1897] 2 Ch 583; *Santander UK v RA Legal Solicitors* [2014] EWCA Civ 183.

[148] [1897] 1 Ch 536, at 542.

[149] See also *Re Pauling's Settlement Trusts* [1964] Ch 303, at 359, per Upjohn LJ: 's 61 is purely discretionary, and its application necessarily depends on the particular facts of each case'.

[150] [1898] 2 Ch 521. See, however, *Re Clapham* [2005] EWHC 3387 (Ch), where, in the case of a wrongful payment out of the trust funds by the trustee, it was confirmed that the section does not apply where the mistaken actions of the trustee have been grossly negligent.

acted dishonestly and the real question will concern whether the trustee had acted 'reasonably':

> The legislature has made the absence of all dishonesty a condition precedent to the relief of the trustee from all liability. But that is not the grit of the section. The grit is in the words 'reasonably, and ought fairly to be excused for the breach of trust' …[151]

(ii) 'Reasonably'

A trustee will only be granted relief from liability if he had acted reasonably. As Kekewich J pointed out in *Perrins v Bellamy*[152] this means that the trustees must have 'acted reasonably in their breach of trust'. It will therefore be very hard for a trustee to gain relief if the very basis of his breach of trust was that he had failed to observe the appropriate standard of care expected of a trustee.[153] For example, in *Bartlett v Barclays Bank Trust Co Ltd (No 2)*[154] the bank was liable because they had failed adequately to supervise the management of the company owned by the trust. Since the very grounds of their liability was their negligence they could not be said to be entitled to relief under s 61 as they had not acted 'reasonably'. Gross J in *The Mortgage Business plc v Conifer & Pines Solicitors & Essex Solicitors*[155] said:

> those much better versed in this area than me do take the view that even under Section 61 a person found liable for a breach of trust which involves lack of reasonable care can nonetheless satisfy a court that he acted reasonably. It may seem odd, but there it is.

It would be very odd indeed, and oxymoronic, if a person who had failed to exercise reasonable care could still be said to have acted reasonably.[156] However, the context was that Gross J was dealing in that case with solicitors who had admitted to negligence by paying out mortgage funds before completion. That kind of breach of trust, of course, is a breach of an absolute duty to act within the limits of the authority to disperse funds, and a breach can therefore occur without negligence. In these kinds of case it is quite possible for a breach of trust to have been committed even where a trustee has acted reasonably.[157] However, the Court of Appeal has said very clearly in *Santander UK v RA Legal Solicitors*[158] that where a breach of trust is based on negligence, it is highly unlikely that the trustee could be considered to have acted reasonably. A trustee will not be considered to have acted reasonably if he did not follow usual accepted practice without good reason. For instance in *Re Stuart*[159] a trustee who had invested money on a mortgage did not follow the procedure set out in what is now s 8 of the Trustee Act 1925.[160] Although Stirling J held that this 'was not necessarily

---

[151] [1898] 2 Ch 521, at 527–528.   [152] [1898] 2 Ch 521, at 529.

[153] The appropriate standard of care will either be the new statutory duty of care under s 1 of the Trustee Act 2000 or, if this does not apply, the common law standard of the 'ordinary prudent man of business'.

[154] [1980] Ch 515.   [155] [2009] EWHC 1808 (Comm).

[156] Although just this possibility is anticipated by Companies Act 2006, s 1157(1).

[157] See *Re Turner* [1897] 1 Ch 536; *Re Stuart* [1897] 2 Ch 583; *Re Dive* [1909] 1 Ch 328; *Shaw v Cates* [1909] 1 Ch 389; *Re Mackay* [1911] 1 Ch 300.   [158] [2014] EWCA Civ 183, at [31]–[32]

[159] [1897] 2 Ch 583.   [160] Then s 4 of the Trustee Act 1888 and s 8 of the Trustee Act 1893.

fatal' to the application of s 61, the legislature had laid down a standard by which the trustee was to be judged. He concluded that, if the trustee had been dealing with his own money, he would not have advanced the mortgage without further precautions.[161]

Cases where solicitors have been caught up by a mortgage fraud and have paid out mortgage funds without authority provide useful illustrations. In some of the cases, the solicitors have ignored warning signs, or failed to carry out normal checks.[162] They cannot then be said to be acting reasonably. By contrast, the careful, conscientious and thorough solicitor, who conducts the transaction by the book and acts honestly and reasonably in relation to it in all respects but still does not discover the fraud, may still be held to have been in breach of trust for innocently parting with the loan money to a fraudster. He is, however, likely to be treated mercifully by the court on his section 61 application.[163]

Solicitors who have complied with best practice in most respects, even if there may be some immaterial minor respects in which they have lapsed, are much more likely to be held to have acted reasonably[164]—'the requisite standard is that of reasonableness not of perfection.'[165] In *Santander UK v RA Legal Solicitors*[166] the Court of Appeal held that whilst it was wrong to apply a rigid or mechanistic approach, there were a number of factors relevant to deciding whether a solicitor had acted reasonably: the extent to which recognized best or usual conveyancing practice had been adopted; the materiality or relevance of any lapses, having regard particularly to their causative connection with the loss; and the seriousness of any departure from good practice (regardless of its causative impact). In that case the number and seriousness of the solicitors' failings meant that they could not be considered to have acted reasonably, in the view of Briggs LJ, even if the sophistication of the fraud to which they were subject was such that it would have been committed even if they had taken all reasonable care.[167] Etherton LC agreed, but placed more weight on the materiality of the breaches by the solicitors. He was prepared to contemplate that even despite unreasonable conduct a trustee could convince the court that his or her unreasonable conduct did not materially contribute to the opportunity for the loss or did not materially increase the risk of such loss,[168] in which case the court could consider exercising a discretion to exculpate the trustee under s 61.

The Trustee Act 1925, s 61 applies to professional as well as non-professional trustees.[169] However, in the case of a 'professional trustee', or a paid trustee[170] the courts

[161] [1897] 2 Ch 583, at 591–592.
[162] As in *Lloyds TSB Bank Plc v Markandan & Uddin (A Firm)* [2012] EWCA Civ 65, [2012] 2 All ER 884 for reasons given at [60].   [163] [2012] EWCA Civ 65, at [61].
[164] As in *Nationwide Building Society v Davisons Solicitors* [2012] EWCA Civ 1626.
[165] [2012] EWCA Civ 1626, at [48].   [166] [2014] EWCA Civ 183, at [20]–[32].
[167] [2014] EWCA Civ 183, at [96]–[102].   [168] [2014] EWCA Civ 183, at [110].
[169] In *Re Pauling's Settlement Trusts* [1964] Ch 303, at 338 the Court of Appeal said that 'it would be a misconstruction of the section to say that it does not apply to professional trustees'; and (at 356) Wilmer LJ said that 'all of us are agreed that in the very special circumstances of this case the bank should be accorded some relief notwithstanding the fact that they were professional trustees paid for their services'.
[170] *Santander UK plc v RA Legal Solicitors* [2014] EWCA Civ 183, at [30].

have held that a higher standard of care is expected,[171] and they are more reluctant to grant relief under s 61. As the Court of Appeal said in *Re Pauling's Settlement Trusts*:

> Where a banker undertakes to act as a paid trustee of a settlement created by a customer, and so deliberately places itself in a position where its duty as trustee conflicts with its interest as a banker, we think that the court should be very slow to relieve such a trustee under [s 61].[172]

Conversely, the courts have shown greater sympathy to lay trustees. In *Iles v Iles*[173] a lay trustee, who was also a beneficiary, did not realize that she should have been paying some of the income from the rent on trust property to her daughter. Briggs J held that (at least initially) she had acted reasonably. He took into account:[174]

> her complete lack of business experience...and the absence of any indication to a lay person with that degree of inexperience from reading the 1992 Declaration of Trust (without its Schedule) that she was accountable to her daughter for rent from a defined part of the Forge between 2000 and 2004.

Another relevant factor is whether the trustee sought and acted on professional advice. In *Ward-Smith v Jebb*[175] a lay trustee was held to have acted unreasonably for failing to seek legal advice on a technical question about the eligibility of a potential beneficiary; in contrast in *Re Evans*[176] it was a factor in holding a lay trustee had acted reasonably that she had taken advice from her solicitors.

(iii) 'Ought fairly to be excused'

Most cases dealing with s 61 focus on the question of reasonable conduct and often assume that if this is established, relief should follow almost as of course. As Kekewich J observed in *Perrins v Bellamy*:

> I venture ventuto think that, in general and in the absence of special circumstances, a trustee who has acted 'reasonably' ought to be relieved, and that it is not incumbent on the Court to consider whether he ought 'fairly' to be excused, unless there is evidence of a special character showing that the provisions of the section ought not to be applied in his favour.[177]

However, he recognized in a later case (*Davis v Hutchings*,[178]) that there might be circumstances where a trustee who had acted both honesty and reasonably ought not to be relieved from liability. This was a case where the trustees gave a share of the trust fund to their solicitor, who claimed that he was the assignee of the share. They failed to investigate his title, which would have revealed that the assignment was subject to the plaintiff's charge over the share. Kekewich J held that there was no justification

---

[171] *National Trustees Co of Australasia Ltd v General Finance Co of Australasia Ltd* [1905] AC 373; *Bartlett v Barclays Bank Trust Co Ltd* [1980] Ch 515.   [172] [1964] Ch 303, at 339.
[173] [2012] EWHC 919 (Ch).   [174] [2012] EWHC 919 (Ch), at [49].
[175] *Ward-Smith v Jebb* (1964) 108 Sol Jo 919.   [176] *Re Evans* [1999] 2 All ER 777.
[177] [1898] 2 Ch 521, at 529.
[178] [1907] 1 Ch 356. But see *Re Allsop* [1914] 1 Ch 1, where the Court of Appeal, while accepting that *Davis v Hutchings* may have been right on its facts, rejected the wider dicta of Kekewich J.

for the trustees being 'let off'.[179] This appears to be an exercise of discretion, but the case can perhaps be better explained on the grounds that the trustees' conduct was unreasonable because of the failure to investigate title, an obvious precaution. It is undoubtedly the case that the court has a discretion as to whether to grant relief. As Evershed MR said in *Marsden v Regan*, having found that the trustee had acted honestly and reasonably:

> There still remains the question: Ought she fairly to be excused? That is the most difficult point of all. But it is essentially a matter within the discretion of the judge…[180]

The best judicial guidance on the exercise of the discretion is given by Briggs LJ in *Santander UK plc v RA Legal Solicitors*.[181] He pointed out that granting relief impacted upon the beneficiary of the trust. The primary cause of a loss in the case of mortgage fraud were the actions of the fraudsters, but the affected beneficiary might either be an institutional lender with deep pockets or insurance against the risk, or an individual purchaser whose life savings were on the line.

> Relief under section 61 is often described as an exercise of mercy by the court. In my judgment the requirement to balance fairness to the trustee with a proper appreciation of the consequences of the exercise of the discretion for the beneficiaries means that this old-fashioned description of the nature of the section 61 jurisdiction should be abandoned. In this context mercy lies not in the free gift of the court. It comes at a price.[182]

(c) The extent of relief

If the court finds that the conditions for granting relief are met, the extent to which the trustee may be relieved is a matter for the discretion of the court. Section 61 provides that the trustee may be relieved 'wholly or in part'. In *Re Pauling's Settlement Trusts*[183] one breach of trust by the bank involved the advance of £2,600 to Francis and George to pay off a debt owed by their mother secured on her life interest, known as the 'Hodson Loan'. In return, the mother assigned to them life policies with a surrender value of £650, on which she promised to continue to pay the premiums, and which would pay £3,000 on her death. There was a division between the members of the Court of Appeal as to the extent to which the bank should be relieved of liability in respect of this transaction. The majority found that, in the circumstances, the bank had acted honestly and reasonably, but that it should only be relieved to the extent of the surrender value of the policies which had been assigned to them. Willmer J, dissenting, held that they should be relieved from all liability:

> whereas my brethren think that the bank should be relieved only in part, I take the view that if relief is to be accorded to all, it should be accorded in full. I can see no logical reason for stopping short of relief in full.[184]

---

179 [1907] 1 Ch 356, at 365.
180 [1954] 1 WLR 423, at 435. See also *Re Wightwick's Will Trusts* [1950] Ch 260.
181 [2014] EWCA Civ 183.   182 [2014] EWCA Civ 183, at [34].
183 [1964] Ch 303.   184 [1964] Ch 303, at 356.

In *Re Evans (Decd)*[185] the lay trustee, after taking advice from her solicitor, had taken out insurance cover for a potential claim for a beneficiary she had not been in contact with for years and who she thought was probably dead. When the beneficiary later turned up, the insurance policy was insufficient to cover the interest due on his share. The judge granted partial relief against liability to pay interest.

(4) Limitation

The current limitation rules[186] have been described by the Law Commission as 'unfair, complex, uncertain and outdated'.[187] The rules are contained in the Limitation Act 1980, but there are gaps which the courts have had to grapple with. The Supreme Court looked at the limitation rules in Court of Appeal in *Williams v Central Bank of Nigeria*[188] and this case must be taken as the starting point for any analysis. What that case shows is that, as explained there and in earlier decisions of the Court of Appeal, the position is less complex than the Law Commission suggested. However, the reasoning which reaches 'a simple and logical interpretation' of the statutory provisions is itself complex and contentious. This account summarizes the outcome without exploring all of that reasoning.

(a) General principle

The general principle contained in the Limitation Act 1980 is that most claims are subject to a six-year limitation period. The same limitation period applies to most claims for breach of trust,[189] but there are two important exceptions. It is now taken as the starting-point (although this was not always so) that all claims are subject to a limitation period of six years unless there is some other statutory provision.[190]

(b) Two exceptions

(i) Trustee was party to fraud

The Limitation Act 1980, s 21(1)(a) provides that there is no limitation period to an action by the beneficiary 'in respect of any fraud or fraudulent breach of trust to which the trustee was a party or privy'.[191] Fraud in this context almost certainly means dishonesty[192] rather than simply a conscious breach of trust.[193] The exception will only apply if

---

[185] [1999] 2 All ER 777.
[186] See Birks and Pretto (eds), *Breach of Trust* (2002), Chs 11 and 12.
[187] *Limitation of Actions*, Law Com No 270 (2001), para 1.5.
[188] *Williams v Central Bank of Nigeria* [2014] UKSC 10.   [189] Limitation Act 1980, s 21(3).
[190] *Gwembe Valley Development Company Ltd v Koshy* [2003] EWCA Civ 1048.
[191] This used to be the general rule for all actions for breach of trust. See *North American Land and Timber Co Ltd v Watkins* [1904] 1 Ch 242; affd [1904] 2 Ch 233, CA.
[192] See Millett LJ in *Armitage v Nurse* [1998] Ch 241.
[193] The meaning attributed to the provision included deliberate but not dishonest breach of trust in *Re Sale Hotel and Botanical Gardens Co* (1897) 77 LT 681. See also *Vane v Vane* (1873) 8 Ch App 383; *North American Land and Timber Co Ltd v Watkins* [1904] 2 Ch 233, CA.

the trustee himself was involved in the fraud.[194] In *Thorne v Heard*[195] the trustees allowed a solicitor who was acting for them to retain the proceeds of sale of trust property, which he then fraudulently applied to his own use. The Court of Appeal held that the plaintiff's action was barred by the Statute of Limitations and that the case did not fall within the exception because the fraud was the fraud of the solicitor and not of the trustees, who were therefore neither party nor privy to the fraud.

(ii) Trustee who retains trust property in his hands

Section 21(1)(b) provides that there is no limitation period to an action by the benefi-ciary 'to recover from the trustee trust property or the proceeds of trust property in the possession of the trustee, or previously received by the trustee and converted to his use'. There is no requirement here that the trustee be guilty of fraud. The action lies due to the mere fact that the trustee still holds trust property, or its proceeds, in his hands. The exception was applied in *Re Howlett*,[196] where a trustee occupied trust property without paying any occupational rents to the beneficiary. Danckwerts J held that the benefi-ciary could recover occupation rent from the trustee even after the limitation period had expired because the situation fell within the exception. The trustee should have obtained a rent from the property, and since he had not done so he 'must be considered as having it in his own pocket at the material date'.[197] If the trust property has been dissipated by the trustee, for example if it has been lost,[198] spent on the maintenance of an infant beneficiary,[199] or applied in the discharge of a debt,[200] the exception will not apply.

(c) Constructive trusts

The two exceptions to the six-year limitation period apply to actions for breach of trust. The 1980 Act defines the terms trusts and trustees by reference to the defini-tion found in the Trustee Act 1925 and therefore includes express trustees, personal representatives, and trustees holding property on implied or constructive trusts.[201] Millett LJ in a much praised analysis in *Paragon Finance plc v DB Thackerar & Co*[202] thought that it was relevant in this context to divide constructive trustees into two categories: the first where the trust relationship arose prior to the breach through a voluntary assumption of fiduciary responsibilities; the second where the construc-tive trust was imposed 'as a direct consequence of the unlawful transaction which is

---

[194] *Williams v Central Bank of Nigeria* [2014] UKSC 10; *Madoff Securities International Ltd v Raven* [2013] EWHC 3147 (Comm), at [384].   [195] [1894] 1 Ch 599.

[196] [1949] Ch 767. See also *James v Williams* [2000] Ch 1.   [197] [1949] Ch 767, at 778.

[198] *Re Tufnell* (1902) 18 TLR 705; *Re Fountaine* [1909] 2 Ch 382.

[199] *Re Page* [1893] 1 Ch 304; *Re Timmis* [1902] 1 Ch 176.

[200] Even when the trustee was a partner in the bank to which the debt was owed. See *Re Gurney* [1893] 1 Ch 590.

[201] Trustee Act 1925, s 68(17). It has also been held to include fiduciary agents: *Burdick v Garrick* (1870) 5 Ch App 233; company directors: *Re Lands Allotment Co* [1894] 1 Ch 616, CA; a mortgagee in respect of the proceeds of sale: *Thorne v Heard* [1895] AC 495; but not a trustee in bankruptcy: *Re Cornish* [1896] 1 QB 99; nor the liquidator of a company in voluntary liquidation: *Re Windsor Steam Coal Co (1901) Ltd* [1928] Ch 609.   [202] [1999] 1 All ER 400.

impeached by the plaintiff'. These two situations have been described as Class 1 and Class 2 constructive trusts respectively. That distinction was affirmed by the Supreme Court in *Williams v Central Bank of Nigeria*[203] which confined Class 2 constructive trusts to the two types of accessory liability, knowing receipt of trust property, and dishonest assistance in breach of trust. Class 1 constructive trusts (examples would include *Quistclose* trusts, trusteeship *de son tort,* or the position of a company director[204]) are subject to the same limitation regime as express trusts. Class 2 constructive trusts (ie accessory liability) are not, so even where dishonesty is involved, the normal six-year limitation period applies.[205]

(d) Breach of fiduciary duty

There has been some uncertainty about the limitation periods (if any) applicable to claims for breach of a fiduciary duty since such claims are not expressly mentioned in the Limitation Act 1980.[206] However, applying the principle that all actions are subject to a six-year limitation period unless there is an express provision to the contrary,[207] it has now become clear that actions based on breach of fiduciary duty must normally be brought within six years of the breach.[208] In *Coulthard v Disco Mix Club Ltd*[209] this conclusion was reached by analogy with the limitation period applying to a common law action for damages.[210] Where the claim against the fiduciary is for a liability which falls within the description of a Class 1 constructive trustee, the exceptions for fraud and the retention of trust property will apply. [211]

(e) Postponing the start of the limitation period

(i) 'The date on which the right of action accrued'

Section 21(3) (setting out the general limitation period for breaches of trust) provides that 'for the purposes of this subsection, the right of action shall not be treated as having accrued to any beneficiary entitled to a future interest in the trust property until the interest fell into possession'. This means that time does not begin to run against a remainderman, or beneficiary with a reversionary interest, until his interest has fallen into possession.

(ii) Fraud

Section 32(1) provides that the date from which the Limitation Act shall run may be postponed to a date later than the date of the cause of action where either:

    (a) the action is based upon the fraud of the defendant; or

---

[203] *Williams v Central Bank of Nigeria* [2014] UKSC 10.

[204] *Yong v Panweld Trading Pte Ltd* [2012] SGCA 59; 15 ITELR 445 (Singapore Court of Appeal).

[205] For the reasons for this, see *Williams v Central Bank of Nigeria* [2014] UKSC 10.

[206] *A-G v Cocke* [1988] Ch 414; *Nelson v Rye* [1996] 2 All ER 186; Stevens 'Too Late to Face the Music? Limitation and Laches as Defences to an Action for Breach of Fiduciary Duty' [1997] Conv 225.

[207] *Gwembe Valley Development Company Ltd. v Koshy* [2003] EWCA Civ 1048.

[208] *Seaton v Seddon* [2012] EWHC 735 (Ch); *Page v Hewetts Solicitors* [2013] EWHC 2845 (Ch).

[209] [2000] 1 WLR 707.   [210] *Paragon Finance v DB Thakerar & Co* [1999] 1 All ER 400.

[211] *Seaton v Seddon* [2012] EWHC 735 (Ch); *Kleanthous v Paphitis* [2011] EWHC 2287 (Ch).

(b) any fact relevant to the plaintiff's right of action has been deliberately concealed from him by the defendant; or

(c) the action is for relief from the consequences of a mistake.

In these three cases the period of limitation does not begin to run 'until the plaintiff has discovered the fraud, concealment or mistake (as the case may be) or could with reasonable diligence have discovered it.' It has been held that this section applies to actions against trustees.[212] Section 32(2) extends the postponement of the running of time to include cases of deliberate breach 'in circumstances in which it is unlikely to be discovered for some time'. The breach will not be deliberate unless the defendant knows that what he is doing amounts to a breach of trust.[213]

(f) Claims to the personal estate of a deceased person

Limitation Act 1980 s 22(1)(a) provides that:

> No action in respect of any claim to the personal estate of a deceased person or to any share or interest in any such estate (whether under a will or on intestacy) shall be brought after the expiration of twelve years from the date on which the right to receive the share or interest accrued.

Since a personal representative may also be a trustee, the question has arisen whether in such circumstances the six-year limitation period in s 21(3), or the twelve-year period in s 22(1)(a), should apply. Under the preceding legislation,[214] it was essential to determine whether the personal representative had become a trustee. If he had, then the six-year period would displace the twelve-year period.[215] The prevailing view seems to be that under the Limitation Act 1980 the period of twelve years will apply to all actions concerning the personal estate of a deceased person, whether or not the personal representative became a trustee.[216]

(g) Actions for account

Limitation Act 1980, s 23 prescribes that the time limit for actions for an account are the same as the time limits applicable to the claim which is the basis of the duty to account. This can include breach of trust or breach of fiduciary duty, for both of which the normal limitation period is six years.

---

[212] *Beaman v ARTS Ltd* [1949] 1 KB 550, CA; *Kitchen v Royal Air Forces Association* [1958] 1 WLR 563; *Phillips-Higgins v Harper* [1954] 1 QB 411; *Bartlett v Barclays Bank Trust Co Ltd* [1980] Ch 515. See also footnote to *Halton International v Guernroy* [2006] EWCA Civ 801.

[213] *Cave v Robinson Jarvis & Rolf* [2003] 1 AC 384.

[214] Real Property Limitation Act 1874, s 8; Trustee Act 1888, s 8.

[215] See *Re Swain* [1891] 3 Ch 233; *Re Timmis* [1902] 1 Ch 176; *Re Richardson* [1920] 1 Ch 423, CA; *Re Oliver* [1927] 2 Ch 323; *Re Diplock* [1948] Ch 465, CA; affd sub nom *Ministry of Health v Simpson* [1951] AC 251, HL.

[216] See, in support of this view, *Re Loftus* [2007] 1 WLR 591; Preston and Newsom, *Limitation of Actions* (4th edn, 1989), p 51.

(h) **Reform of limitation**

The Law Commission has recommended sweeping reform of the limitation period applicable to claims for a remedy for a wrong in its Report, *Limitation of Actions*,[217] which, if implemented, would simplify and radically alter the limitation period applicable to actions for breach of trust. The Law Commission proposes the introduction of a single core limitation regime applicable to all claims. This would consist of a primary limitation period of three years starting from the date on which the claimant knows, or ought reasonably to know (a) the facts which give rise to the cause of action; (b) the identity of the defendant; and (c) if the claimant has suffered injury, loss, or damage or the defendant has received a benefit, that the injury, loss, damage, or benefit was significant. This primary limitation period would be supplemented by a long-stop limitation period of ten years, starting from the date of the accrual of the cause of action, or from the date of the act or omission which gives rise to the cause of action. It is proposed that this core regime should apply to all claims for breach of trust and claims to recover trust property,[218] and to claims for breach of fiduciary duty.[219] No distinction would be made between fraudulent and non-fraudulent breaches of trust,[220] nor would a special limitation period operate where the claimant was bringing a claim to recover property against his or her trustee.[221] A special rule would operate in the case of a claim for the recovery of property held on a bare trust so that the cause of action shall not accrue unless and until the trustee acts in breach of trust.[222]

(5) **Laches**

Actions for breach of trust were not originally subject to any period of limitation, for reasons explained in *Williams v Central Bank of Nigeria*.[223] However, if a claimant delayed bringing his action, the court might have considered that it was inequitable for him to succeed, and would therefore protect the defendant from liability. The doctrine was explained by the Privy Council in *Lindsay Petroleum Co v Hurd*:

> the doctrine of laches[224] in courts of equity is not an arbitrary or a technical doctrine. Where it would be practically unjust to give a remedy, either because the party has, by his conduct, done that which might fairly be regarded as equivalent to waiver of it, or where by his conduct and neglect he has, though perhaps not waiving that remedy, yet put the other party in a situation in which it would not be reasonable to place him if the remedy were afterwards to be asserted, in either of these cases, lapse of time and delay are most material.[225]

---

[217] Law Com No 270 (2001).   [218] Law Com No 270 (2001), para 4.94.
[219] Law Com No 270 (2001), para 4.95.   [220] Law Com No 270 (2001), paras 4.97–4.101.
[221] Law Com No 270 (2001), paras 4.102–4.106.   [222] Law Com No 270 (2001), para 4.105.
[223] [2014] UKSC 10.   [224] This is pronounced as 'lay cheese'.
[225] (1874) LR 5 PC 221, at 239–240.

(a) Relation to statutory limitation periods

In *Re Pauling's Settlement Trusts*[226] Wilberforce J held that there was no room for the operation of the equitable doctrine of laches because 'there was an express statutory provision providing a period of limitation'.[227] The Court of Appeal in *Re Loftus*[228] took the view that the remark applied only to instances where there was a statutory limitation period, and that in cases where no limitation period applied (trustees guilty of fraud or retaining trust property), the doctrine of laches was preserved by Limitation Act 1980, s 36.[229] This position is confirmed by the Supreme Court decision in *Adamson v Paddico (267) Ltd*.[230]

(b) How the doctrine operates

Although it was not a direct decision on the doctrine, the Supreme Court said in *Adamson v Paddico (267) Ltd*[231] about laches that it 'generally requires (a) knowledge of the facts [by the claimant], and (b) acquiescence, or (c) detriment or prejudice [to the defendant]'. In *Patel v Shah*[232] the Court of Appeal said that:

> The inquiry should require a broad approach, directed to ascertaining whether it would in all the circumstances be unconscionable for a party to be permitted to assert his beneficial right.

Laddie J was somewhat more forthcoming about relevant considerations in *Nelson v Rye*.[233] He stated that there were no defined hurdles over each of which a litigant must struggle before the defence is made out,[234] and instead identified a number of main factors which should be taken in to account by the court:

> The courts have indicated over the years some of the factors which must be taken into consideration in deciding whether the defence runs. Those factors include the period of the delay, the extent to which the defendant's position has been prejudiced by the delay, and the extent to which the prejudice was caused by the actions of the plaintiff.[235]

(c) Knowledge of the right of action

It is unlikely that the doctrine of laches will prevent a claimant from bringing and action unless the claimant had knowledge of the rights he failed to pursue. In *Lindsay Petroleum Co v Hurd*[236] the Privy Council stated that 'in order that the remedy should be lost by laches or delay, it is . . . necessary that there should be sufficient knowledge of the facts constituting the title to relief'.

---

[226] [1961] 3 All ER 713.
[227] [1961] 3 All ER 713, at 735. Affirmed by the Court of Appeal [1964] Ch 303.
[228] [2007] 1 WLR 591, at [41], per Chadwick LJ.
[229] See also *Patel v Shah* [2005] EWCA Civ 157, at [22].   [230] [2014] UKSC 7, at [30]–[32].
[231] [2014] UKSC 7, at [34].   [232] [2005] EWCA Civ 157.
[233] [1996] 2 All ER 186; Stevens 'Too Late to Face the Music? Limitation and Laches as Defences to an Action for Breach of Fiduciary Duty' [1997] Conv 225.   [234] [1996] 2 All ER 186, at 200.
[235] [1996] 2 All ER 186, at 201.   [236] (1874) LR 5 PC 221, at 241.

(d) Length of delay

There is no set length of time that will cause the court to apply the doctrine of laches. Instead the court must determine whether, given the circumstances, it would be inequitable to allow the claim to succeed. Very short periods, if not accompanied by acts of acquiescence by the claimant, will not be sufficient. In *Lindsay Petroleum Co v Hurd*[237] the Privy Council held that a delay of fifteen months was insufficient, as was a delay of two-and-a-quarter years in *Re Sharpe*.[238] In *Weld v Petre*,[239] in the context of the redemption of a mortgage, the Court of Appeal suggested a period of twenty years, therefore holding that a delay of eighteen years and four months was 'not of itself sufficient to disentitle the plaintiffs to relief'.[240]

(e) Prejudice to the defendant

The doctrine of laches operates very closely with the principle of acquiescence. As the Privy Council noted in *Lindsay Petroleum Co v Hurd*,[241] equity will grant relief where to allow the claimant his remedy would be practically unjust because he has 'by his conduct, done that which might fairly be regarded as equivalent to a waiver'.

While the authorities recognize that the defence may apply where the only action (or rather, inaction) on the part of the claimant has been a prolonged period of silence or inactivity,[242] the mere fact of a delay in commencing proceedings is not usually sufficient to give rise to the defence of laches. As Laddie J observed in *Nelson v Rye*:

> I accept that mere delay alone will almost never suffice, but the court has to look at all the circumstances accepand then decide whether the balance of justice or injustice is in favour of granting the remedy or withholding it. If substantial prejudice will be suffered by the defendant, it is not necessary to prove that it was caused by the delay. On the other hand, the plaintiff's knowledge that the delay will cause such prejudice is a factor to be taken into account.[243]

In *Fisher v Brooker*[244] (in which one of the composers of Procol Harum's *A Whiter Shade of Pale* sought to enforce his authorship after a delay of over thirty years), Lord Neuberger said:

> Although I would not suggest that it is an immutable requirement, some sort of detrimental reliance is usually an essential ingredient of laches, in my opinion.[245]

The House of Lords in that case did not think that the delay, in itself, was a bar to equitable relief. There were no evidential problems and any prejudice on the part of

---

[237] (1874) LR 5 PC 221.

[238] [1892] 1 Ch 154. In *Bunn v BBC* [1998] 3 All ER 552; Lightman J refused to grant an injunction preventing a television broadcast because it had been delayed until the last minute. This would not, however, have affected any remedy in damages for the alleged breach of confidence.

[239] [1929] 1 Ch 33, at 54–55.   [240] [1929] 1 Ch 33, at 55, per Lawrence LJ.

[241] (1874) LR 5 PC 221, at 239–240.

[242] *Lindsay Petroleum Co v Hurd* (1874) LR 5 PC 221; *Erlanger v New Sombrero Phosphate Co* (1878) 3 App Cas 1218; *Brooks v Muckleston* [1909] 2 Ch 519.   [243] [1996] 2 All ER 186, at 201.

[244] [2009] 1 WLR 1764.   [245] [2009] 1 WLR 1764, at [64].

the defendants was balanced by the fact that they had not had to account for royalties to the composer until he indicated that he intended to enforce his rights.

4 Contribution and indemnity where a trustee is liable

Although a trustee may be liable to the beneficiaries for breach of trust without any defence, in some circumstances he may be entitled to a contribution or indemnity from his co-trustees, or from the beneficiaries of the trust, which will have the practical effect of partially or completely alleviating his obligation to provide equitable compensation.

(1) Indemnity from co-trustees

As was noted earlier, trustees who together commit a breach of trust are jointly and severally liable for that breach. However, in some circumstances a trustee may be entitled to receive a full indemnity from liability for his breach from his fellow trustees.

(a) Co-trustee acted fraudulently

Where one of several trustees acts fraudulently, the others are entitled to a complete indemnity from liability. In *Re Smith*[246] two trustees invested in debentures. One, who was also the tenant for life of the settlement, invested because he believed that this would increase his income from the trust, while the other invested because he had received a bribe to do so. Kekewich J held that, because of his dishonesty, the bribed trustee alone was liable.

(b) Co-trustee is a professional

A trustee may be entitled to an indemnity if his co-trustee was a professional whose advice he could reasonably be expected to rely on. This has most often been the case where a co-trustee was a solicitor.[247] In *Re Partington*[248] the two trustees of a settlement invested in a mortgage which was an improper investment for the trust. Stirling J held that Mr Allen, who was a solicitor, was liable to indemnify his co-trustee, Mrs Partington, because she had 'been misled by her co-trustee by reason of his not giving her full information as to the nature of the investments which he was asking her to advance the money upon'. For an indemnity the trustee must have acted purely on the basis of reliance on the solicitor trustee. In *Head v Gould*[249] Kekewich J said that there was no right to an indemnity merely because a co-trustee is a solicitor when the trustee 'was an active participator in the breach of trust complained of, and is not

---

[246] [1896] 1 Ch 71.
[247] See *Lockhart v Reilly* (1856) 25 LJ Ch 697; *Bahin v Hughes* (1886) 31 Ch D 390, CA.
[248] (1887) 57 LT 654.   [249] [1898] 2 Ch 250.

proved to have participated merely in consequence of the advice and control of the solicitor'.[250]

(c) Co-trustee has personally benefited from the breach of trust

The general principle was considered by the Court of Appeal in *Bahin v Hughes*.[251] Cotton LJ said that a trustee is entitled to an indemnity from his co-trustee either when they are both liable to the beneficiary because the co-trustee got trust money into his own hands and made use of it,[252] or 'against a trustee who has himself got the benefit of the breach of trust'.[253] Where the trustee is also a beneficiary, and has benefited by the breach of trust, he is liable to indemnify his co-trustees to the extent of his beneficial interest. The principle was stated by Kay J in *Chillingworth v Chambers*:

> the weight of authority is in favour of the holding that a trustee who, being also a [beneficiary], has received, as between himself and his co-trustee, an exclusive benefit by the breach of trust, must indemnify his co-trustee to the extent of his interest in the trust fund, and not merely to the extent of the benefit which he has received.[254]

The trustees of a will invested in mortgages which proved to provide insufficient security. Chillingworth had also become a beneficiary, and the purposes of the investment had been to produce a higher rate of interest from the trust property, which was for his benefit. The court held that the deficit of £1,580 was to be made good from Chillingworth's beneficial interest, and that Chambers was indemnified from liability. If the trustee-beneficiary's interest is insufficient to cover the total loss, the trustees will be equally liable for the remaining loss.

(2) Contribution from co-trustees

The Civil Liability (Contribution) Act 1978 gives the court a wide discretion to apportion liability between trustees who are jointly and severally liable for breach of trust.[255] Section 1(1) states the general principle of contribution:

> any person liable in respect of any damage suffered by another person may recover contribution from any other person liable in respect of the same damage (whether jointly with him or otherwise).

The general discretion of the court is found in s 2(1):

> in any proceedings for contribution under s 1 n any the amount of the contribution recoverable from any person shall be such as may be found by the court to be just and equitable having regard to the extent of that person's responsibility for the damage in question.

---

[250] [1898] 2 Ch 250, at 265.   [251] (1886) 31 Ch D 390.
[252] See *Thompson v Finch* (1856) 25 LJ Ch 681.   [253] (1886) 31 Ch D 390, at 396.
[254] [1896] 1 Ch 685, at 707.
[255] S 6(1) makes clear that the statute applies to damage caused by breach of trust. *Friends' Provident Life Office v Hillier Parker May & Rowden (a firm)* [1997] QB 85; *Dubai Aluminium Co Ltd v Salaam* [2003] 2 AC 366; *Charter plc v City Index Ltd* [2008] Ch 313; Virgo 'Contribution Revisited' (2008) 67 CLJ 254.

The court can therefore reflect the respective blameworthiness of co-trustees in the extent to which they permit contribution. Under s 2(2) the court has the power to find that a trustee is exempt from making contributions to his co-trustee, or that a trustee is entitled to a complete indemnity from his co-trustee.

(3) Indemnity from a beneficiary

As has already been noted, a trustee will not incur any liability for a breach of trust to a beneficiary who consented to it, or subsequently concurred in it. The trustee remains liable to any beneficiaries who did not so consent or concur. However, the trustee may be entitled to be indemnified from the beneficial interest of any beneficiary who requested, or consented to the breach.

(a) The court's inherent jurisdiction

If a trustee commits a breach of trust at the instigation or the request of a beneficiary the court has the power, under its inherent jurisdiction, to impound the beneficiary's beneficial interest to indemnify the trustee for any liability he might incur.[256] There is no need for the request or instigation to be made in writing.[257] However, the trustee will not be entitled to an indemnity unless the beneficiary knew the facts of what was happening. Where the beneficiary has not requested or instigated the breach of trust but merely consented to it, the trustee may still be entitled to an indemnity from his beneficial interest. This will only be the case if the consent was given in writing and the beneficiary gained a personal benefit from the breach.[258] The indemnity will only extend to the amount of that benefit.[259]

(b) Trustee Act 1925, s 62

This section grants the court a wide discretion to impound the beneficial interest of a beneficiary who has instigated, requested, or consented in writing to a breach of trust.

In *Re Pauling's Settlement Trusts (No 2)*[260] Wilberforce J stated that the purpose of the section was to extend the courts' inherent jurisdiction, and in *Bolton v Curre*[261] Romer J said that the forerunner to s 62[262] 'was intended to enlarge the power of the court as to indemnifying trustees, and to give greater relief to trustees, and was not intended and did not operate to curtail the previously existing rights and remedies of trustees, or to alter the law except by giving greater power to the court'. It has been held that the requirement of writing applies only to a beneficiary's consent,[263] and the court may impound the beneficiary's interest under s 62 where there has been instigation

---

[256] *Booth v Booth* (1838) 1 Beav 125; *Lincoln v Wright* (1841) 4 Beav 427; *Raby v Ridehalgh* (1855) 7 De GM & G 104; *Bentley v Robinson* (1859) 9 I Ch R 479; *Sawyer v Sawyer* (1885) 28 Ch D 595, CA; *Ricketts v Ricketts* (1891) 64 LT 263; *Chillingworth v Chambers* [1896] 1 Ch 685.

[257] *Griffiths v Hughes* [1892] 3 Ch 105; *Mara v Browne* [1895] 2 Ch 69.

[258] *Booth v Booth* (1838) 1 Beav 125; *Chillingworth v Chambers* [1896] 1 Ch 685.

[259] *Raby v Ridehaigh* (1855) 7 De GM & G 104.   [260] [1963] Ch 576.

[261] [1895] 1 Ch 544, at 549.   [262] Trustee Act 1888, s 6; repeated by the Trustee Act 1893, s 45.

[263] *Griffiths v Hughes* [1892] 3 Ch 105; *Re Somerset* [1894] 1 Ch 231.

or a request irrespective of the absence of writing. The court will only impound the beneficiary's interest if he had sufficient knowledge. In *Re Somerset* Smith LJ stated:

> upon the true reading of this section, a trustee in order to obtain the benefit conferred thereby, must establish that the beneficiary knew the facts which rendered what he was instigating, requesting or consenting to in writing a breach of trust.[264]

It is not necessary that he actually know that those facts amount to a breach of trust. In *Re Pauling's Settlement Trusts (No 2)*[265] Wilberforce J held that the protection of the section was not only available to existing trustees of the trust, but also to former trustees who had since retired from the trust or been replaced. The only requirement is that the person seeking the indemnity was a trustee at the time of the breach.

(c) Contributory negligence

It was held at first instance in *Lloyds TSB Bank v Markandan & Uddin*[266] that the Law Reform (Contributory Negligence) Act 1945 is not applicable, either directly or by analogy, to reduce a claim against a trustee to reflect the extent to which the claimant's own fault has directly or directly contributed to the loss.[267] The judge (Roger Wyand QC) said:

> Section 61 of the Trustee Act gives limited relief to trustees where the trustees have acted reasonably and honestly. It could have provided for the conduct of the beneficiary to be taken into account as the Defendant here wishes. It did not and it is not for the Court to extend the law in a way that was not done by the legislature.

---

[264] [1894] 1 Ch 231.   [265] [1963] Ch 576.   [266] [2010 EWHC 2517.
[267] No appeal was made against this part of the decision: see [2012] 2 All ER 884, at [55].

28

Fiduciary position of trustees

In the previous chapter it was seen that a trustee will be liable to pay equitable compensation for any loss suffered in consequence of a breach of trust. Such a breach will occur if he acts in a manner inconsistent with the express terms of the trust, or if he fails to act as required with insufficient care. However, the duties of a trustee are not confined solely to his obligation not to act in breach of trust. A further essential aspect of the multifaceted nature of trusteeship is that a trustee stands in a fiduciary relationship to the beneficiaries of the trust. This means that he must not allow any conflict between his own interests and the interests of the beneficiary, and that he must not make any unauthorized profit for himself from his position as trustee. Other parties acting alongside the trust, such as solicitor advisors, may also owe fiduciary duties to the beneficiaries of the trust. The nature and extent of fiduciary duties are explored in this chapter.

1 Fiduciary relationships

(1) The trustee as a fiduciary

The fiduciary[1] position of a trustee[2] subjects him to onerous negative obligations in equity, which are designed to prevent him from abusing his position by acting in his own interests at the expense of the interests of his beneficiaries. The division between legal and equitable ownership under a trust separates the control and management of property from the entitlement to its ultimate enjoyment and this separation provides both great flexibility and opportunity for abuse. The trustee who controls the property can use it for his own advantage, for example by selling himself the trust property at an undervalue. To prevent the trustee gaining personal advantages at the expense of the beneficiaries' equity characterizes the relationship as a 'fiduciary', which entitles the beneficiaries to a remedy if the trustee makes unauthorized personal gains by virtue of his position. A trustee in breach of his fiduciary duty will be required to make

---

[1] See Goff and Jones, *The Law of Unjust Enrichment* (8th edn, 2011), Ch 38; Oakley, *Constructive Trusts* (3rd edn, 1997), Ch 3; Finn, *Fiduciary Obligations* (1977); Shepherd 'Towards a Unified Concept of Fiduciary Relationships' (1981) 97 LQR 51.
[2] *Keech v Sandford* (1726) Sel Cas Ch 61; *Price v Blakemore* (1843) 6 Beav 507.

restitution to the beneficiaries of any unauthorized profits he has received through the abuse of his position.

(2) Fiduciary relationships

(a) Types of fiduciary relationship

The fiduciary relationship has been described as 'one of the most ill-defined, if not altogether misleading terms in our law'.[3] It has also been said that 'there are few legal concepts more frequently invoked but less conceptually certain than that of the fiduciary relationship'.[4] As Frankfurter J said in the American case *SEC v Chenery Corpn*:[5]

> To say that a man is a fiduciary only begins analysis; it gives direction to further inquiry. To whom is he a fiduciary? What obligations does he owe as a fiduciary? In what respect has he failed to discharge these obligations? And what are the consequences of his deviation from duty?[6]

It is important to recognize that a fiduciary relationship may arise in a number of ways. In *LAC Minerals Ltd v International Corona Resources Ltd*,[7] a decision of the Canadian Supreme Court, Wilson J distinguished between relationships which in their very nature are fiduciary, and those which take on a fiduciary character because of the particular relationship between the parties:

> It is...my view of the law that there are certain relationships which are almost per se fiduciary, such as trustee and beneficiary, guardian and ward, principal and agent, and that where such relationships subsist they give rise to fiduciary duties. On the other hand, there are relationships which are not in their essence fiduciary, such as the relationship brought into being by the parties in the present case by virtue of their arm's length negotiations towards a joint venture agreement, but this does not preclude a fiduciary duty from arising out of specific conduct engaged in them or either of them within the confines of the relationship.[8]

(b) Relationships fiduciary per se

English law has never provided a comprehensive definition of fiduciary relationships. Instead, certain relationships, because of their very nature, have come to be regarded as fiduciary. This obviously allows for flexibility as circumstances and commercial practice change. As Finn has stated, a fiduciary 'is, simply, someone who undertakes to act for or on behalf of another in some particular matter or matters'.[9] In the unusual case of *Reading v A-G*[10] the House of Lords held that an army sergeant who had used his uniform to enable lorries smuggling spirits and drugs to pass through army

---

[3] Finn, *Fiduciary Obligations* (1977), p 1.
[4] *LAC Minerals Ltd v International Corona Resources Ltd* (1989) 61 DLR (4th) 14, at 26, per La Forest J.
[5] 518 US 80 (1943), at 85–86.
[6] Cited by the Privy Council in *Re Goldcorp Exchanges Ltd* [1994] 2 All ER 806.
[7] (1989) 61 DLR (4th) 14.   [8] (1989) 61 DLR (4th), at 16.
[9] Finn, *Fiduciary Obligations* (1977), p 201.   [10] [1951] AC 507.

checkpoints was a fiduciary, and therefore he was obliged to account to the Crown for the money he had received from the smugglers for his services. In the Court of Appeal Asquith LJ had attempted a summary of the characteristics of a fiduciary relationship:

> a fiduciary relationship exists (a) whenever the plaintiff entrusts to the defendant property... and relies on the defendant to deal with such property for the benefit of the plaintiff or purposes authorised by him, and not otherwise, and (b) whenever the plaintiff entrusts to the defendant a job to be performed and relies on the defendant to procure for the plaintiff the best terms available...[11]

The relationship of trustee and beneficiary is not the only one that is characterized as fiduciary by equity. Other recognized fiduciary relationships include: mortgagee and mortgagor;[12] principal and agent;[13] solicitor and client;[14] partners and co-partners;[15] company directors and the company;[16] senior management and their employer company;[17] confidential employees and their employers;[18] government employees and the Crown;[19] and pawnbroker and pawnor.[20] The essence of all these relationships is that one person occupies a position in which he has a duty to act on behalf of another,

[11] [1949] 2 KB 232, at 236.   [12] *Farrars v Farrars Ltd* (1888) 40 Ch D 395, CA.

[13] *De Bussche v Alt* (1878) 8 Ch D 286; *Kirkham v Peel* (1880) 43 LT 171; *Lamb v Evans* [1893] 1 Ch 218, CA; *New Zealand Netherlands Society Oranje Inc v Kuys* [1973] 1 WLR 1126, PC; *Imageview Management Ltd v Jack* [2009] EWCA Civ 63; *FHR European Ventures LLP v Mankarious* [2011] EWHC 2308 (Ch); [2014] UKSC 45.

[14] *Re Hallett's Estate* (1880) 13 Ch D 696, CA; *McMaster v Byrne* [1952] 1 All ER 1362; *Brown v IRC* [1965] AC 244, HL; *Oswald Hickson Collier Co v Carter-Ruck* [1984] AC 720n; *Swindle v Harrison* [1997] 4 All ER 705; *Logstaff v Birtles* [2002] 1 WLR 470. In *Conway v Ratiu* [2006] 1 All ER 571, the Court of Appeal said, contra Lord Millett in *Prince Jefri Bolkiah v KPMG (a firm)* [1999] 2 AC 222, that the fiduciary relationship of a solicitor to his client is distinct from the contractual obligations arising under his retainer. As such the fiduciary duty is not necessarily to be found or confined to the terms of the contractual retainer, so that the fiduciary relationship may outlive the contractual solicitor/client relationship. See also *Hilton v Barker Booth and Eastwood (a firm)* [2005] 1 All ER 651, at [28]–[29], per Lord Walker; *Cobbetts LLP v Hodge* [2009] EWHC 786.

[15] *Bentley v Craven* (1853) 18 Beav 75; *Aas v Benham* [1891] 2 Ch 244; *Thompson's Trustee in Bankruptcy v Heaton* [1974] 1 WLR 605. See also *Holiday Inns Inc v Yorkstone Properties (Harlington)* (1974) 232 *Estates Gazette* 951.

[16] *Sinclair v Brougham* [1914] AC 398; *Regal (Hastings) v Gulliver* [1967] 2 AC 134n; *Selangor United Rubber Estates Ltd v Craddock (No 3)* [1968] 1 WLR 1555; *Industrial Development Consultants Ltd v Cooley* [1972] 1 WLR 443; *Cowan de Groot Properties Ltd v Eagle Trust plc* [1992] 4 All ER 700; *Item Software (UK) Ltd v Fassihi* [2004] EWCA 1244; *O'Donnell v Shanahan* [2009]\ EWC Civ 751. See Berg 'Fiduciary Duties: A Director's Duty to Disclose His Own Misconduct' (2005) 121 LQR 213. See Koh 'Once a Director, Always a Fiduciary?' [2003] 62 CLJ 403 for a consideration whether a director continue to be a fiduciary even after he ceases to be a director of the company.

[17] *Sybron Corpn v Rochem Ltd* [1984] Ch 112; *Canadian Aero-Services v O'Malley* (1973) 40 DLR (3d) 371; *Agip (Africa) Ltd v Jackson* [1990] Ch 265.

[18] *Triplex Safety Glass Co Ltd v Scorah* [1938] Ch 211; *British Celanese Ltd v Montcrieff* [1948] Ch 564; *British Syphon Co v Homewood* [1956] 1 WLR 1190; *A-G v Guardian Newspapers Ltd (No 2)* [1990] 1 AC 109, HL; *A-G v Blake* [1998] 1 All ER 833.

[19] *Reading v A-G* [1951] AC 507; *A-G v Guardian Newspapers Ltd (No 2)* [1990] 1 AC 109; *A-G for Hong Kong v Reid* [1994] 1 All ER 1, PC; *A-G v Blake* [1998] 1 All ER 833.

[20] *Mathew v TM Sutton Ltd* [1994] 4 All ER 793; *Hurstanger v Wilson* [2007] EWCA Civ 299.

thereby enjoying the potential to abuse his position by acting for his own interests. They are relationships in which there is an inherent element of 'trust and confidence'[21] between the parties. The duties of directors have been codified in the Companies Act 2006.

In Canada it has been held that the relationship between doctor and patient[22] and between child-abuser and victim[23] are also fiduciary, and it has been suggested that the relationship between priest and parishioner should likewise be fiduciary.[24] English law has not yet adopted these relationships as fiduciary per se, although individual relationships of this type could be found to be fiduciary if the circumstances suggested that there was a sufficient degree of reliance between the parties.

In *Independent Trustee v GP Noble Trustees*[25] Lloyd LJ raised the interesting possibility that a trustee might sometimes not be characterised as a fiduciary, despite the normal view that trustees are fiduciaries automatically by virtue of their position. The situation which he was concerned with was where a husband used pension trust funds to pay financial provision to his divorced wife under a court order which was later revoked. Since, on the finding of the Court of Appeal, this was to be treated as a transfer without consideration, the wife was accountable to the pension fund for any sums which she retained. Differing from a view expressed by Lord Browne-Wilkinson in *Westdeutsche Landesbank Girozentrale v Islington London Borough Council*[26] (that in such a case there was no trust even though legal and equitable titles were severed) Lloyd LJ considered that it would be appropriate to describe the wife as a constructive trustee holding the funds on trust for the beneficiaries under the pension fund trusts, although 'she would have been under no relevant duty as regards the money until she had notice of the interest of the beneficiaries.'[27] The concept of a trust in which the trustee owes no duties is a novel one, and as Lloyd LJ recognized,[28] needs to be qualified lest the categorization leads to inappropriate conclusions. The warning, as we have seen in Chapter 9, that the term 'constructive trustee' comprises a range of different situations must also be borne in mind.

(c) Fiduciary duties arising within relationships not fiduciary per se

The majority of commercial relationships cannot be characterized as fiduciary per se,[29] as the parties simply bargain with each other at arm's length. However, the specific nature of a particular relationship may bring about a fiduciary relationship between the parties. This was the case in *LAC Minerals Ltd v International Corona Resources Ltd*,[30] where two companies were negotiating at arm's length about the possibility of a joint venture of exploit minerals from land over which the plaintiff company (LAC)

---

[21] *Conway v Raitu* [2006] 1 All ER 571, at [71], per Auld LJ.

[22] *Norberg v Wynrib* (1992) 92 DLR (4th) 449.

[23] *M (K) v M (H)* (1992) 96 DLR (4th) 289.

[24] Frankel, *Equity, Fiduciaries and Trusts*, ed Waters (1993).   [25] [2012] EWCA Civ 195.

[26] [1996] AC 669, at 707.   [27] [2012] EWCA Civ 195, at [81].

[28] [2012] EWCA Civ 195, at [79].

[29] See Oakley, 'The Liberalising Nature of Remedies for Breach of Trust' in Oakley, *Trends in Contemporary Trust Law* (1996), pp 230–233.   [30] (1989) 61 DLR (4th) 14.

owned mining rights. In the course of these negotiations it was clear to the defendants from results of the plaintiffs' drilling that adjacent land was also likely to include
mineral deposits. The defendants then purchased the adjacent land, defeating a competing bid from the plaintiffs, and developed a mine alone. Although the relationship
between the defendants and the plaintiffs was not fiduciary per se, the Supreme Court
held that fiduciary duties were owed because the defendants had received confidential
information from the plaintiffs in the course of the negotiations. In *A-G v Blake*[31] Lord
Woolf MR similarly suggested that a fiduciary relationship arises whenever information is imparted by one person to another in confidence,[32] although he noted that in
the majority of cases such information will be imparted in the context of a relationship
which is already fiduciary, for example where the recipient of the information was an
employee.

In contrast, in *Re Goldcorp Exchange Ltd (In Receivership)*[33] the Privy Council held
that a relationship had remained exclusively commercial so that it had not become
fiduciary. The case concerned a company in New Zealand that dealt in gold bullion
and other precious metals. Customers purchased what was described as 'non-allocated
metal' that would be held for them by the company free of charge. They were entitled to
take physical delivery of the metal by giving seven days' notice, at which point it would
be appropriated from the metal that the company held in bulk. It was argued that the
company stood in a fiduciary relationship to the customers, but the Privy Council held
that their relationship was purely contractual. As Lord Mustill explained:

> No doubt the fact that one person is placed in a particular position vis-à-vis another
> through the medium of a contract does not necessarily mean that he does not also owe
> fiduciary duties to that other by virtue of being in that position. But the essence of a fidu-
> ciary relationship is that it creates obligations of a different character from those deriv-
> ing from the contract itself. Their Lordships have not heard in argument any submission
> which went beyond suggesting that by virtue of being a fiduciary the company was obliged
> honestly and conscientiously to do what it had by contract promised to do...It is possible,
> without misuse of language to say that the customers put faith in the company, and that
> their trust has not been repaid. But the vocabulary is misleading; high expectations do not
> necessarily lead to equitable remedies.[34]

The case of *Sinclair Investment Holdings SA v Versailles Trade Finance Ltd*[35] provides
an example of a commercial relationship giving rise to a fiduciary status, and of the
core content of a fiduciary relationship. The facts as alleged were that Mr Cushnie was
a director and had a substantial interest in companies within the Versailles Group. The
Versailles Group inflated its turnover through dishonest dealings, and as a result Mr
Cushnie was able to sell his shareholding at a profit, repay a mortgage on a property
he owned, and sell it for £8.6m. One of the Group's victims was Sinclair, which was

---

[31] [1998] 1 All ER 833.   [32] [1998] 1 All ER 833, at 842.
[33] [1994] 2 All ER 806. See also *Khodai v Tamimi* [2009] EWCA Civ 1109 (relationship between lender
and borrower).   [34] [1994] 2 All ER 806, at 821–822.
[35] [2005] EWCA Civ 722. See Panesar 'The Nature of Fiduciary Liability in English Law' [2007] Conv 2,
11–12.

seeking to recover from Mr Cushnie the money that had been misappropriated. It was argued that he stood in a fiduciary position in relation to the claimants. A company director is not normally a fiduciary for people dealing with the company, even where he makes personal representations,[36] but the Court of Appeal held that the pleadings in the case contained an arguable case that Mr Cushnie had undertaken a duty of loyalty to Sinclair so as to make him a fiduciary. According to Arden LJ:

> if it is alleged that a person who does not fall within the usual categories of a fiduciary relationship, such as trustee and director, made manifest his intention to enter into a fiduciary relationship—that is, to undertake to the other a duty of loyalty—there would be a sufficient pleading of fiduciary relationship.[37]

The fiduciary did not need to receive the claimant's property, but in her view:

> In a case such as this, it seems to me to be necessary that the fiduciary relationship should be with respect to an item of property, and that requirement explains why a fiduciary relationship may be specific and govern only part of a party's relationship with another.[38]

That condition would have been satisfied in this case because there was an express term that Sinclair's funds were to be held on trust if they were not used for trading.

(3) **The function of fiduciary relationships in English law**

It has been seen that it is difficult to define fiduciary relationships with comprehensive accuracy.[39] This difficulty is compounded by the varied functions that they perform in English law at present. They operate so as to impose duties that restrict the fiduciary's ability to act in his own interests, and also as a trigger that may lead to the creation of an equitable trust interest in property by way of a constructive trust.

(a) **Fiduciary duties**

A person who stands in a fiduciary relationship may owe a range of duties to his principal.[40] Not all of these duties can properly be characterized as fiduciary in nature. For example a trustee, who is by definition also a fiduciary, will owe duties of care regarding his conduct of the trust business to the beneficiaries alongside his fiduciaries duties. In *Bristol and West Building Society v Mothew*[41] Millett LJ commented:

> The expression fiduciary duty is properly confined to those duties which are peculiar to fiduciaries and the breach of which attracts legal consequences differing from those consequent upon the breach of other duties. Unless the expression is so limited it is lacking in

---

[36] See *Hageman v Holmes* [2009] EWHC 50 (Ch), where a fiduciary obligation was not imposed on a director in relation to a deed of covenant, on the basis that the rights between the relevant parties were contractual only.   [37] [2005] EWCA Civ 722, at [20].

[38] [2005] EWCA Civ 722, at [21].

[39] See Conaglen 'The Nature and Function of Fiduciary Loyalty' (2005) 121 LQR 452; Hilliard 'The Flexibility of Fiduciary Doctrine in Trust Law: How Far Does It Stretch in Practice?' (2009) TLI 119.

[40] See Austin, 'Moulding the Content of Fiduciary Duties' in Oakley, *Trends in Contemporary Trust Law* (1996).

[41] [1996] 4 All ER 698; Nolan 'Multiple Duties and Multiple Employment' [1997] CLJ 39.

practical utility. In this sense it is obvious that not every breach of duty by a fiduciary is a breach of fiduciary duty.[42]

He therefore held that it was inappropriate to apply the expression fiduciary to the obligation of a trustee to use proper skill and care in the discharge of his duties. In *A-G v Blake*[43] the Court of Appeal similarly held that an employee in the security services who had published an unauthorized autobiography had acted in breach of contract but not in breach of fiduciary duty. In *Swindle v Harrison*[44] the Court of Appeal considered that the duties imposed by equity upon a fiduciary go beyond the common law duties of skill and care.[45]

Given that not every duty owed by a fiduciary to his principal can be characterized as fiduciary in nature, the question arises as to the content of his specifically fiduciary duties. In *Bristol and West Building Society v Mothew*[46] Millett LJ identified the core content of the fiduciary duty:

> A fiduciary is someone who has undertaken to act for or on behalf of another in a particular matter in circumstances which give rise to a relationship of trust and confidence. The distinguishing obligation of a fiduciary is the obligation of loyalty. The principal is entitled to the single-minded loyalty of his fiduciary. This core liability has several facets: a fiduciary must act in good faith; he must not make a profit out of his trust; he must not place himself in a position where his duty and his interest may conflict; he may not act for his own benefit or the benefit of a third person without the informed consent of his principal. This is not intended to be an exhaustive list, but it is sufficient to indicate the nature of fiduciary obligations.[47]

While the core content of a fiduciary duty can be identified as an obligation of exclusive loyalty, the precise content of specific fiduciary relationships will vary. As Lord Browne-Wilkinson observed in *Henderson v Merrett Syndicates Ltd*,[48] the phrase 'fiduciary duties' is a dangerous one, giving rise to a mistaken assumption that all fiduciaries owe the same duties in all circumstances. In *A-G v Blake* Lord Woolf MR stated:

> There is more than one category of fiduciary relationship, and the different categories possess different characteristics and attract different kinds of fiduciary obligations.[49]

The duration of the core fiduciary duty of loyalty is also determined by the context of the relationship in which the fiduciary duty arose. The mere fact that a person once occupied a fiduciary position does not necessarily mean that they will be subject to a lifelong duty of loyalty. *A-G v Blake* concerned the nature of the fiduciary duties of a former secret service agent. George Blake had served as a member of the security services from 1944 until 1960. In 1951 he had become an agent for the Soviet Union. He was arrested and imprisoned, but escaped to live in Moscow. He subsequently wrote

---

[42] [1996] 4 All ER 698, at 710.   [43] [1998] 1 All ER 833.   [44] [1997] 4 All ER 705.
[45] [1997] 4 All ER 705, at 716, per Evans LJ.   [46] [1998] Ch 1.
[47] [1998] Ch 1, at 18. See also *A-G v Blake* [1998] 1 All ER 833, at 842, per Lord Woolf MR.
[48] [1995] 2 AC 145, at 206.   [49] [1998] 1 All ER 833, at 842.

an autobiography entitled *No Other Choice*, which was published in England. The Crown sought to recover the profits derived from the book on the grounds that the publication was in breach of fiduciary duty. The Court of Appeal held that, although Blake's employment had rendered him subject to a fiduciary duty, his fiduciary duties did not endure beyond the termination of his employment. Lord Woolf MR explained:

> We do not recognise the concept of a fiduciary obligation which continues notwithstanding the determination of the particular relationship which gives rise to it. Equity does not demand a duty of undivided loyalty from a former employee to his former employer...A former employee owes no duty of loyalty to his former employer. It is trite law that an employer who wishes to prevent his employee from damaging his legitimate commercial interests after he has left his employment must obtain contractual undertakings from his employee to this effect. He cannot achieve his object by invoking the fiduciary relationship which formerly subsisted between them.[50]

Whether Blake was a fiduciary or not was not an issue that arose in the subsequent appeal to the House of Lords.[51] However, Lord Nicholls[52] and Lord Steyn[53] were both at pains to stress that the position he occupied was at least very closely akin to a fiduciary relationship, suggesting that this might have been a fruitful avenue for appeal.

(b) Remedies for breach of fiduciary duties

Where a fiduciary acts in breach of his duty he will have committed an equitable wrong against his principal. As such, his principal will be able to recover either equitable compensation or restitution from his fiduciary.

(i) *Equitable compensation for loss sustained*

If a fiduciary commits a breach of duty his principal will be entitled to recover equitable damages to compensate him for any loss he has suffered.[54] Where the fiduciary was a trustee his breach will probably have constituted a breach of trust, entitling the beneficiaries to receive compensation. A right to receive equitable compensation for breach of fiduciary duty will arise where the fiduciary was not also a trustee. The principal will be entitled to recover such compensation as would put him in the position he would have been in if the wrong had not been committed. To establish the right to compensation, the principal must demonstrate that the alleged breach of fiduciary duty caused the loss sustained. In *Swindle v Harrison*[55] Mrs Harrison mortgaged her house in order to enable her son to purchase and restore a hotel. Further finance was required to complete the transaction that it was expected would be provided by way of a loan from a brewery. At the date of completion the loan had not been forthcoming and the plaintiff solicitors therefore offered her a bridging loan to complete the hotel

---

[50] [1998] 1 All ER 833, at 841–842.   [51] [2000] 4 All ER 385.   [52] [2000] 4 All ER 385, at 400.
[53] [2000] 4 All ER 385, at 404.
[54] See Conaglen 'Equitable Compensation for Breach of Fiduciary Dealing Rules' (2003) 119 LQR 246.
[55] [1997] 4 All ER 705; Tjio and Yeo 'Limited Liability for Breach of Fiduciary Duty' (1998) 114 LQR 181; Elliott 'Restitutionary Compensatory Damages for Breach of Fiduciary Duty?' [1998] RLR 135. See also Sir Peter Millett 'Equity's Place in the Law of Commerce' (1998) 114 LQR 214.

purchase. She wished to go ahead with the transaction because she felt the purchase would be advantageous to her and her son. However, the solicitors failed to disclose to her that they would be making a profit for themselves from the bridging loan, and that her son's bank was unlikely to provide him with the references needed to obtain the brewery loan. The hotel business was unsuccessful and the solicitors sought possession. Mrs Harrison counterclaimed that she was entitled to receive equitable compensation for the equity she had lost in her home on the grounds that the solicitors has committed a breach of their fiduciary duty. The Court of Appeal held that the solicitors had breached their duty by failing to make full disclosure of the circumstances and that they were therefore liable to compensate her for any loss suffered. However, the essential issue was whether her loss had been caused by the breach. Mrs Harrison submitted that she was not required to prove that she would not have completed the purchase in any event,[56] and that she should be compensated merely because the bridging loan had enabled her to complete the purchase. The Court of Appeal rejected this submission and held that, unless the breach could properly be regarded as the equivalent of fraud,[57] she was required to demonstrate causation. In the circumstances it concluded that she would have completed the transaction anyway. Evans LJ explained that she had failed to establish causation:

> The failure to disclose cannot be said to have led to the making of the loan, even on a 'but for' basis, precisely because disclosure of the true facts would not have affected her decision to accept it. Since she would have accepted the loan and completed the purchase, even if full disclosure had been made to her, she would have lost the value of the equity in her home in any event. She cannot recover damages or compensation for that loss, in my judgement, except on proof *either* that the plaintiffs acted fraudulently *or* in a manner equivalent to fraud or that she would not have completed the purchase if full disclosure had been made, i.e. if the breach of duty had not occurred.[58]

The obligation to pay equitable compensation for breach of fiduciary duty is a purely personal remedy.

(ii) Restitution of the unauthorized profit

Where a fiduciary breaches his duty of exclusive loyalty and receives an unauthorized profit he will be liable to make restitution[59] to his principal by way of an equitable duty to account for the profit received. He is obliged to pay over to his principal a sum of money equivalent to the amount of profit received, though not necessarily the actual money (or its proceeds) which comprised the profit. It is sometimes said that the fiduciary is required to disgorge his unauthorized profit. The obligation to account operates as a personal remedy.

---

[56] Cf *Target Holdings v Redferns* [1996] AC 421.   [57] [1997] 4 All ER 705, at 717 per Evans LJ.
[58] [1997] 4 All ER 705, at 718 (emphasis in original).
[59] See Goff and Jones, *The Law of Unjust Enrichment* (8th edn, 2011), Ch 6; Birks, *Introduction to the Law of Restitution* (1985), pp 313–357; Burrows, *The Law of Restitution* (2nd edn, 2002), pp 493–508; (1989) CLJ 302 (Jackman).

(iii) Constructive trust of the unauthorized profit

An area of considerable debate in English law has been when a fiduciary who is under a personal obligation in equity to account for the profit received will also be subject to a constructive trust of the specific property comprising the profit. The ability to establish such a constructive trust would prove especially significant if the fiduciary is insolvent, since otherwise the principal will merely rank as a general creditor of the fiduciary, in which case the personal duty to account is unlikely to provide an adequate remedy. If the actual profit, or its proceeds,[60] can be identified as the principal's, his principal will be entitled to it in equity, and will be able to claim priority ahead of any other general creditors. A constructive trust of an unauthorized profit obtained in breach of fiduciary duty was held to have arisen in *A-G for Hong Kong v Reid*.[61] Reid, the acting Director of Public Prosecutions for Hong Kong, had accepted bribes in the course of his duties. The Privy Council held that three houses that Reid had purchased in New Zealand with the bribe money were held on trust for the Crown. However, in *Paragon Finance v DB Thakerar & Co*[62] Millett LJ held that no constructive trust would arise if the fiduciary was an agent who received payments on behalf of his principal which he was entitled to pay into his own account and mix with his own money. Such an agent would not have been subject to a duty to keep the receipts separate from his own and to apply them exclusively to the benefit of his principal. Thus a manager of a musician who had received royalty payments on behalf of his client, which had been paid into his own account, mixed with his own money, and from which his commission had been deducted, would be liable to account to his client for any underpayments, but no constructive trust would arise.[63]

The decision in *Reid* was widely criticized,[64] and the Court of Appeal held in *Sinclair Investments (UK) Ltd v Versailles Trade Finance Ltd (in Administration)*[65] that it did not accurately state the position of English law. According to Lord Neuberger MR, a constructive trust will arise only where the fiduciary was acting as an agent of the principal, expressly appointed (or perhaps impliedly appointed) for the purpose of acquiring the property concerned, or where the property acquired by the fiduciary is the proceeds of property (or an opportunity) already beneficially owned by the principal. Bribes, such as those in *Reid*, gave rise to a personal remedy only.

The Supreme Court in *FHR European Ventures LLP v Cedar Capital Partners LLC*[66] has, in a very clear and forthright decision, overruled the *Sinclair Investment* case. The rule which was approved by the Supreme Court was that all unauthorised benefits (including bribes and secret profits) received by a fiduciary are held on constructive trust. In *FHR European Ventures LLP v Cedar Capital Partners LLC* FHR acquired

---

[60] Whether the fiduciary retain in his hands any property that is or represents the profit received will depend on the laws of tracing. See Chapter 30. [61] [1994] 1 All ER 1.

[62] [1999] 1 All ER 400.

[63] Thus rejecting the earlier decision of Laddie J in *Nelson v Rye* [[1996] 2 All ER 186.

[64] See Crilley 'A Case of Proprietary Overkill' [1994] RLR 57; Tang 'Confidence and the Constructive Trust' (2003) 23 LS 135.

[65] [2011] EWCA Civ 34.   [66] [2014] UKSC 45.

the shares in the company which owned the Monte Carlo Gand Hotel. Cedar, a company established to provide hotel industry consultancy services, acted as its agent in the purchase, and was paid a commission. Cedar had also entered into an exclusive brokerage agreement with the sellers to procure the sale of the hotel, in return for which Cedar would receive €10m. Cedar failed to disclose to FHR the €10m commission which was duly paid on the sale. FHR sought a proprietary remedy. The Court of Appeal, purporting to apply *Sinclair Investments,* upheld this claim on the basis that Cedar was a fiduciary, it had breached its duty of full disclosure, and it had diverted an opportunity to purchase at the lowest possible price.[67] In doing so, it would seem that 'the Court made the facts fit the law, rather than applying the law to the facts'.[68]

The Supreme Court upheld the outcome, but for different reasons. Lord Neuberger, delivering the judgment of the court, said that 'it is not possible to identify any plainly right or plainly wrong answer to the issue of the extent of the Rule, as a matter of pure legal authority'.[69] The rule adopted by the Supreme Court (that any benefit acquired by an agent as a result of his agency and in breach of his fiduciary duty is held on trust for the principal[70]) was supported by a number of policy considerations. It had the merit of simplicity, as opposed to the contrary view, which was more likely to result in uncertainty.[71] It meant that there were particularly stringent rules relating to bribes and secret commissions, which undermined trust in the business world.[72] It also made it possible to trace or follow into other assets or other recipients.[73] It was acknowledged that unsecured creditors might be affected, but they lost only the right to claim assets which the agent should never have received, and 'at any rate in many cases, the bribe or commission will very often have reduced the benefit from the relevant transaction which the principal will have obtained, and therefore can fairly be said to be his property.'[74]

The arguments for and against imposing a constructive trust on all unauthorized benefits could both draw upon supporting caselaw. However, the majority of the earlier cases supported the general rule adopted by the Supreme Court. The contrary view could be traced to three decisions, *Tyrrell v Bank of London,*[75] *Metropolitan Bank v Heiron,*[76] and *Lister & Co v Stubbs,*[77] all of which could be criticized.[78] Those cases and any other cases applying them should therefore be treated as overruled.

Because of the context, the focus of the Supreme Court was on the treatment of bribes and secret commissions by expressly appointed agents, but it can reasonably be assumed that their decision applies to all unauthorized profits made in breach of

---

[67] [2013] EWCA Civ 17, at [24] and [116]. See Hedlund 'Secret commissions and constructive trusts: yet again!' (2013) JBL 747; Chambers 'Constructive trusts and breach of fiduciary duty' [2013] Conv 241.

[68] Hedlund 'Secret commissions and constructive trusts: yet again!' (2013) JBL 747, at 755.

[69] [2014] UKSC 45, at [32].   [70] [2014] UKSC 45, at [35].   [71] [2014] UKSC 45, at [35].

[72] [2014] UKSC 45, at [42].

[73] [2014] UKSC 45, at [44]. Although Lord Neuberger spoke of following into the hands of knowing recipients, the right to follow applies more generally subject to the defence of bona fide purchase without knowledge. Knowing recipients might also have personal liability.   [74] [2014] UKSC 45, at [43].

[75] (1862) 10 HL Cas 26.   [76] (1880) 5 Ex D 319.   [77] (1890) 45 Ch D 1.

[78] [2014] UKSC 45, at [47]–[49].

fiduciary duty whether or not the fiduciary is an agent. However, this does not resolve all potential problems. One such is how the rule will apply in cases like *Paragon Finance* where an agent is permitted to mix funds with his own property (which is inconsistent with the assertion of an express trust). Another will be identifying an unauthorized gain: for instance, in the *Sinclair* case, part of the property to which the claimant asserted proprietary rights represented the proceeds of selling shares at a value which had been enhanced by fictitious trading using funds derived from the claimant. There could be significant issues involved in identifying such indirect gains where mixed funds have been used or other factors have influenced the achievement of the gains.

The impact and extent of the *FHR* decision, and the continuing debate over whether a personal or proprietary claim arises over unauthorized profits by a fiduciary, are considered further later in the chapter.

(c) Fiduciary relationships and equitable property rights

Property which is misappropriated by a fiduciary from his principal will also be subject to a constructive trust, irrespective of whether the property was received by the fiduciary or a third party. For example, in *Agip (Africa) Ltd v Jackson*[79] a company was defrauded by its chief accountant, Zdiri, who altered the name of the payees of genuine payment orders so that they were payable to dummy companies he had created. Millett J held that as the accountant was a fiduciary of the company by virtue of his senior position and responsibility, the misappropriated money was held on constructive trust by the recipient dummy companies and Agip was enabled to trace it. The money paid to such companies was not previously subject to a trust but had been the absolute property of the company. Similarly, in *Brinks Ltd v Abu-Saleh (No 3)*[80] Rimmer J held that gold bullion that had been stolen was subject to a constructive trust in favour of its corporate owners because the robbery had been carried out with the assistance of a security guard who stood in a fiduciary relationship.

Some cases have held that the mere fact that a transaction was subject to a vitiating factor entitling the transferor to restitution from the transferee will establish a fiduciary relationship between them, so that the transferee holds the property received subject to a constructive trust in favour of the transferor. In *Chase Manhattan Bank NA v Israel-British Bank (London) Ltd*[81] the plaintiff bank paid $1m to the defendant bank by mistake, having forgotten that they had previously made an identical payment. Goulding J held that as a consequence of the mistaken payment the defendant bank had become a fiduciary of the plaintiff bank, so that the $1m was held on constructive trust for them. By means of this reasoning, the plaintiff could maintain a proprietary claim to $1m in the assets of the defendant, which was insolvent, thus negating the value of any personal right to restitution at common law on the grounds of mistake.

---

[79] [1990] Ch 265; [1992] 4 All ER 385; (1989) 105 LQR 528 (Birks); (1991) 107 LQR 71 (Sir Peter Millett); [1991] Ch 547; [1992] 4 All ER 451; (1991) 50 CLJ 409 (Harpum); [1992] Conv 367 (Goulding); All ER Rev 1992, 258–265 (Swadling).

[80] (1995) *The Times*, 23 October; Stevens 'Delimiting the Scope of Accessory Liability' [1996] Conv 447.

[81] [1981] Ch 105.

However, it is far from clear that this approach is correct. In *Westdeutsche Landesbank Girozentrale v Islington London Borough Council*[82] Lord Browne-Wilkinson considered that, while the decision in *Chase Manhattan* could be regarded as rightly decided, the reasoning of Goulding J was erroneous. He considered that a constructive trust was constituted not by the mere receipt of the mistaken payment, but by the fact that the bank to whom the payment had been made knew of the mistake within two days of their receipt of the money:

> Although the mere receipt of the moneys, in ignorance of the mistake, gives rise to no trust, the retention of the moneys after the recipient bank learned of the mistake may well have given rise to a constructive trust.[83]

However, it is submitted that even this reasoning does not adequately explain the creation of an equitable proprietary interest in the money mistakenly paid. The central question should focus rather on the proprietary effects of the mistaken payment. If the mistake was sufficient to prevent property in the money passing to the payee, then the payee will hold it subject to an immediate constructive trust from the moment that it was received. He may not become a fiduciary for the payor until he becomes aware that the mistake had been made and he was conscious of the circumstances giving rise to the constructive trust. The mere fact that he becomes aware of a mistake rendering him subject to a personal obligation to make restitution should neither make him a fiduciary of the payor nor subject the money in his hands to a constructive trust.

(d) The artificial use of fiduciary relationships

The power of a fiduciary relationship to generate proprietary rights and remedies has provided a major incentive for the encroachment of such relationships into the commercial arena. For example, increasingly, the employment relationship has come to be characterized as fiduciary and not merely contractual. The lack of a clear definition has enabled the courts to manipulate fiduciary relationships as a means of achieving remedial justice, so that the use of the term 'fiduciary' has often seemed artificial. It has already been argued that the finding of a fiduciary relationship in *Chase Manhattan Bank NA v Israel-British Bank (London) Ltd*[84] was artificial, and the reason for it was to ensure that the mistaken payor bank was entitled to a proprietary remedy so as to gain priority over the payee's general creditors. This artificiality was recognized by the Supreme Court of Canada in *LAC Minerals Ltd v International Corona Resources Ltd,*[85] where La Forest J said that there was a third category of the usage of 'fiduciary':

> [the] third usage of 'fiduciary' stems, it seems, from a perception of remedial inflexibility in equity. Courts have resorted to fiduciary language because of the view that certain remedies, deemed appropriate in the circumstances, would not be available unless a fiduciary relationship was present. In this sense, the label fiduciary imposes no obligations, but is rather merely instrumental or facilitative in achieving what appears to be the appropriate result.

---

[82] [1996] AC 669.   [83] [1996] AC 669, at 715.   [84] [1981] Ch 105.   [85] (1989) 61 DLR (4th) 14.

He regarded the use of 'fiduciary' in *Chase Manhattan* as an example of this 'third usage'. It was not that the relationship between the banks was genuinely 'fiduciary', as they were simply businesses operating at arm's length. Rather, the characterization of the relationship as fiduciary was an essential prerequisite to the availability of tracing in equity, and the relationship was so characterized merely to facilitate the availability of such tracing as the foundation of a proprietary claim. The requirement of a fiduciary relationship with regard to tracing will be fully discussed in Chapter 30.

(e) Directors of trustee companies and 'dog's leg' claims

The directors of corporate trustees will not be liable to beneficiaries for a breach of trust or breach of directors' duty of care owed to the trustee company. Such claims, referred to as 'dog's leg claims', arise where the trustee company has no assets to meet a claim, but the directors do, and a beneficiary of a trust seeks to make the directors liable for breach of a duty of care owed to the company, which as it comprises trust property, makes them liable to the beneficiary. This arose in *Gregson v HAE Trustees Ltd*,[86] where Ms Gregson argued that the trust company, HAE Trustees Ltd, was in breach of the duty to diversify investments of the trust settlement. The trust investments had become worthless and the trust company had no other assets. Mrs Gregson therefore sued the directors. She argued that the duties of the directors were directed to avoid losses to the trust, and, by analogy to advisers such as solicitors, claims against the directors formed part of the trust property itself. In rejecting Ms Gregson's claim, Deputy Judge Robert Miles QC held that the fiduciary duties owed by directors were owed to the company, not to the beneficiaries.[87] Moreover, he held that to allow such a claim 'would for all practical purposes, circumvent the clear and established principle that no direct duty is owed by the directors to the beneficiaries'.[88] However, as *Sinclair Investment Holdings SA v Versailles Trade Finance Ltd*[89] shows, a direct duty can arise in the very rare situation where a director represents directly to a beneficiary that he is undertaking a personal duty of loyalty to that beneficiary.

(4) **Abuse of position**

(a) **Fiduciaries owe a duty of exclusive loyalty to their principals**

As Millett LJ indicated in *Bristol and West Building Society v Mothew*,[90] a fiduciary owes a duty of exclusive loyalty to his principal. This duty of loyalty applies to prevent the fiduciary abusing his position. It operates to deter fiduciaries from acting in

---

[86] [2008] EWHC 1006 (Ch); Court '*Gregson v HAE Trustees Ltd*: It's a Dog's Life' [2008] PCB 298; Nolan 'Shopping for Defendants: Worthless Trust Companies and Their Directors' (2008) 67 CLJ 472.

[87] [2008] EWHC 1006 (Ch), at [58]. The fiduciary duties of directors have been codified under the Companies Act 2006, and operate according to existing legal principles—s 170(3). The statutory duty on directors to exercise reasonable care, skill, and diligence is found in s 174.

[88] [2008] EWHC 1006 (Ch), at [46].

[89] [2005] EWCA Civ 722. See Panesar 'The Nature of Fiduciary Liability in English Law' [2007] Conv 2, 11–12.   [90] [1998] Ch 1.

breach and to provide restitution for the principal if a breach is committed. Where the fiduciary is a trustee the potential for abuse of position arises because the trustee may use his powers of management over the trust property for his own benefit rather than in the best interest of the beneficiaries. This danger was recognized in early cases. In *Keech v Sandford*[91] a trustee held the lease of a market on trust for an infant. When the lease came to an end the lessor refused to renew it to the trust and the trustee took it personally. King LC held that the trustee could not take the lease for himself and noted the danger of the trustee abusing his position at the expense of the interests of the beneficiary:

> I very well see, if a trustee, on the refusal to renew, might have a lease for himself, few trust estates would be renewed to the [beneficiary].

Similarly, if the trustee wishes to sell part of the trust property he may be tempted to sell it to himself at an undervalue. In his capacity as trustee his duty would be to gain the best possible price for the beneficiaries, but as an individual he would obviously wish to obtain the lowest price to enjoy the best bargain for himself. As trustee he would be both the purchaser, who offers a price, and the seller, who agrees to the price. It would be easy for him to abuse his position so that he benefits at the expense of the beneficiaries by selling to himself at an undervalue.[92]

In *Item Software (UK) Ltd v Fassihi*[93] the Court of Appeal held that a fiduciary was under a duty to disclose his own misconduct to his principal, even though he had not obtained any unauthorized profit. However, this decision has been criticized,[94] and it remains unclear whether such an extension of the fiduciary duty is consistent with earlier authorities.[95]

(b) The difficulty of weighing motives

If a trustee does act in circumstances where it could be suggested that he had abused his position to gain a personal benefit, it may be impossible to weigh his true motives: ie whether he was in fact allowing his own interests to prevail over those of the beneficiaries. As Lord Eldon LC observed in *Ex p James*,[96] 'no court is equal to the examination and ascertainment' of these facts. Indeed, because of the practical impossibility of discovering a fiduciary's true motives, equity has taken the very strict view that a fiduciary is liable to account for any profits he makes whenever there was an objective possibility of a conflict between his interests and his duty.[97] There is no need to demonstrate that the fiduciary acted with the subjective intention of benefiting himself at

---

[91] (1726) Sel Cas Ch 61.
[92] See *Holder v Holder* [1968] Ch 353; *Re Thompson's Settlement* [1986] Ch 99; *O'Donnell v Shanahan* [2009] EWCA Civ 751.
[93] [2004] EWCA 1244; Conaglen 'Directorial Disclosure' [2005] *64* CLJ 48.
[94] See Berg 'Fiduciary Duties: A Director's Duty to Disclose His Own Misconduct' (2005) 121 LQR 213.
[95] See *Horcal Ltd v Gatland* [1984] BCLC 549, at 554, per Robert Goff LJ.
[96] (1803) 8 Ves 337, at 345.
[97] See *Regal (Hastings) Ltd v Gulliver* [1967] 2 AC 134n; [1942] 1 All ER 378, HL; *Boardman v Phipps* [1967] 2 AC 46, HL.

the expense of the beneficiaries. This is a blunt instrument applied in the beneficiaries' favour. As Lord Herschell stated in *Bray v Ford*:

> It is an inflexible rule of a Court of Equity that a person in a fiduciary position...is not, unless otherwise expressly provided, entitled to make a profit; he is not allowed to put himself in a position where his interest and duty conflict.[98]

The duty of exclusive loyalty imposed by a fiduciary duty is not absolute. The fiduciary is not prevented from ever acting in his own interests and receiving a benefit by virtue of his position. He is only prevented from retaining unauthorized profits for himself. A fiduciary will not be liable to make restitution if he breaches his duty with the full informed consent of his principal.

2 Unauthorized remuneration

(1) General principle

As a general rule a trustee is not entitled to receive remuneration for his work[99] unless authorized by the trust deed appointing him, or by statute.[100] The rationale for this principle was stated by Lord Normand in *Dale v IRC*:

> it is not that reward for services is repugnant to the fiduciary duty, but that he who has the duty shall not take any secret remuneration or any financial benefit not authorised by the law...or by the trust deed under which he acts...[101]

This statement makes clear that the bar on remuneration is not absolute, so that properly authorized remuneration may be retained by the trustee. In the modern commercial world, where the majority of trusts are administered by professional trustees, the general principle still stands, but it has been recognized that there are other competing objectives. As Fox LJ observed in *Re Duke of Norfolk's Settlement Trusts*:

> the court has to balance two influences which are to some extent in conflict. The first is that the office of trustee is, as such, gratuitous; the court will accordingly be careful to protect the interests of the beneficiaries against claims by the trustees. The second is that it is of great importance to the trust that the trust should be well administered.[102]

To balance these objectives the courts have a wide inherent jurisdiction to permit trustees to receive remuneration.

---

[98] [1896] AC 44.

[99] Bishop and Prentice 'Some Legal and Economic Aspects of Fiduciary Remuneration' (1983) 46 MLR 289.

[100] *How v Godfrey and White* (1678) Cas temp Finch 361; *Bonithon v Hockmore* (1685) 1 Vern 316; *Robinson v Pett* (1734) 3 P Wms 249; *Re Ormsby* (1809) 1 Ball & B 189; *Taylor v Taylor* (1843) 4 Dr & War 124; *Re Barber* (1886) 34 Ch D 77; *Re Bedingfield* (1887) 57 LT 332; *Barrett v Hartley* (1866) LR 2 Eq 789; *Re Accles Ltd* [1902] WN 164.　　　　　　　　　　　　　　　　　　　　　　[101] [1954] AC 11, at 27.

[102] [1982] Ch 61, at 79.

(2) **Reimbursement of trustee's expenses**

Although a trustee is not prima facie entitled to receive remuneration, he is entitled to the reimbursement of any expenses incurred by him in the work of the trust.[103] Section 31(1)(a) of the Trustee Act 2000 provides that a trustee is entitled to be reimbursed from the trust funds for 'expenses properly incurred by him when acting on behalf of the trust'.

(3) **Authorized remuneration**

A trustee is perfectly entitled to retain remuneration that he was authorized to receive, and he is therefore not liable to make restitution of it to the trust.

(a) **Trust instrument**

A trustee is not accountable for remuneration he is entitled to receive under the trust instrument.[104] Such provisions are extremely common, and professional trustees will only act if the trust deed contains such a provision. Section 28 of the Trustee Act 2000 provides that a trustee who is acting in a professional capacity is entitled to receive payment for his services on behalf of the trust even if those services are capable of being provided by a lay trustee.

(b) **Statute**

Section 29 of the Trustee Act 2000 provides that, in the absence of an express entitlement in the trust instrument, a trust corporation, or a professional trustee who is not a sole trustee,[105] is entitled to receive reasonable remuneration for any services provided on behalf of the trust. Such a professional trustee will only be entitled to reasonable remuneration if 'each other trustee has agreed in writing that he may be remunerated for the services'. It should be noted that different rules apply to the remuneration of the trustees of a charitable trust.[106]

　　Other statutory provisions govern the remuneration of certain specialized trustees. Trustees of charitable purpose trusts may be remunerated if the four sets of conditions set out in s 185 of the Charities Act 2011 are met, one of which is that remuneration is clearly in the interests of the charity.[107] The Public Trustee may charge fees fixed by the Treasury,[108] as may anybody appointed a custodian trustee.[109] The court may grant

---

[103] *Stott v Milne* (1884) 25 Ch D 710; *Re Chapman* (1894) 72 LT 66, CA; *Hardoon v Belilios* [1901] AC 118; *Holding and Management Ltd v Property Holding and Investment Trust plc* [1990] 1 All ER 938, CA; see also *Boardman v Phipps* [1967] 2 AC 46, HL, where the fiduciary received payment 'on a liberal scale' for his work and skill in obtaining a profit for himself and the trust.

[104] *Webb v Earl of Shaftesbury* (1802) 7 Ves 480; *Willis v Kibble* (1839) 1 Beav 559; *Public Trustee v IRC* [1960] AC 398, HL; *Space Investments Ltd v Canadian Imperial Bank of Commerce Trust Co (Bahamas) Ltd* [1986] 1 WLR 1072, PC.   [105] S 29(1),(2).

[106] Ss 28(3), 29(1), (2), and 30 of the Trustee Act 2000.

[107] Guidance on the use of these powers may be found in Charity Comm, CC11 *Trustee expenses and payments* (March 2012).   [108] *Re Masters* [1953] 1 WLR 81.

[109] Public Trustee Act 1906, s 9, as amended by the Public Trustee (Fees) Act 1957 and subsequent orders.

remuneration to a person appointed a judicial trustee.[110] If the court appoints a corporation to be a trustee, then it may authorize the corporation to receive remuneration for its services.[111]

(c) Court's inherent jurisdiction

The court enjoys an inherent jurisdiction to authorize a trustee to receive remuneration, both in respect of work already done and for future work.[112] However, as Lord Goff recognized in *Guinness plc v Saunders*,[113] this jurisdiction is irreconcilable with the rule that a trustee is not entitled to remuneration for services rendered by him to the trust except as expressly provided in the trust deed. He therefore held that the exercise of the jurisdiction should be 'restricted to those cases where it cannot have the effect of encouraging the trustees in any way to put themselves in a position where their interests conflict with their duties as trustees'.

The scope of the inherent jurisdiction was examined in *Re Duke of Norfolk's Settlement Trusts*.[114] The Court of Appeal accepted 'without doubt' that the court possesses an inherent jurisdiction to authorize the payment of remuneration to trustees, both in the case of prospective trustees for future services and in the case of an unpaid trustee who has already accepted office and has embarked on his fiduciary duties on a voluntary basis. It also held that the court had the jurisdiction to increase the level of remuneration to which a trustee was entitled under the trust instrument. Fox LJ indicated the factors that the court should take into account in exercising this jurisdiction:

> If therefore the court concludes, having regard to the nature of the trust, the experience and skill of a particular trustee and to the amounts which he seeks to charge when compared with what other trustees might require to be paid for their services and to all the other circumstances of the case, that it would be in the interests of the beneficiaries to increase the remuneration, then the court may properly do so.[115]

(d) Solicitor-trustees

A solicitor-trustee who acts in legal proceedings on behalf of the trust, himself, and his co-trustees, or himself and his beneficiaries, is entitled to receive the usual costs under the rule in *Cradock v Piper*.[116] In *Re Worthington*,[117] Upjohn J said that this rule was 'exceptional, anomalous and not to be extended'.[118]

---

[110] Public Trustee Act 1906, s 4(3).   [111] Judicial Trustees Act 1896, s 1(5).

[112] *Brown v Litton* (1711) 1 P Wms 140; *Re Masters* [1953] 1 All ER 19; *Re Worthington* [1954] 1 WLR 526; *Re Jarvis* [1958] 2 All ER 336; *Boardman v Phipps* [1967] 2 AC 46, HL; *Re Duke of Norfolk's Settlement Trusts* [1982] Ch 61, CA; *O'Sullivan v Management Agency and Music Ltd* [1985] QB 428, CA.

[113] [1990] 1 All ER 652, at 667.

[114] [1982] Ch 61; (1981) 40 CLJ 243 (Ockleton); (1982) 45 MLR 211 (Green); (1982) 98 LQR 181 (PVB); [1982] Conv 231 (Hodkinson); (1982) 126 Sol Jo 195 (Fox).   [115] [1982] Ch 61, at 79.

[116] (1850) 1 Mac & G 664; *Lincoln v Windsor* (1851) 9 Hare 158; *Broughton v Broughton* (1855) 5 De GM & G 160; *Whitney v Smith* (1869) 4 Ch App 513; *Pince v Beattie* (1863) 9 Jur NS 1119; *Re Corsellis* (1887) 34 Ch D 675; *Re Worthington* [1954] 1 All ER 677.   [117] [1954] 1 WLR 526.

[118] [1954] 1 WLR 526, at 529.

3 Purchase of trust property by trustees

The court is keen to ensure that fiduciaries do not gain any advantage by exploiting their position at the expense of those for whose benefit they are supposed to be acting. One of the most obvious dangers is that the trustee, who has control over the trust property, will sell it to himself at an undervalue. A similar difficulty is that the trustee may use the advantages of his position to purchase the beneficial interest from the beneficiaries at an undervalue. Equity has applied two rules, or presumptions, which are designed to prevent the trustee abusing his position. They were summarized by Megarry V-C in *Tito v Waddell (No 2)*:

> there are two separate rules. The self-dealing rule is that if a trustee sells the trust prop-
> erty to himself the sale is voidable by any beneficiary ex debito justitiae, however fair the
> transaction. The fair-dealing rule is that if a trustee purchases the beneficial interest of
> any of his beneficiaries, the transaction is not voidable ex debito justitiae, but can be set
> aside by the beneficiary unless the trustee can show that he has taken no advantage of his
> position and has made full disclosure to the beneficiary, and that the transaction is fair
> and honest.[119]

These two rules therefore differ in their sphere of operation and standard of liability.

(1) The self-dealing rule

(a) Application of the self-dealing rule

The self-dealing rule[120] applies when a trustee[121] purchases property from the trust. As Arden MR stated in *Campbell v Walker*:

> Any trustee purchasing the trust property is liable to have the purchase set aside, if in any
> reasonable time the [beneficiary] trust chooses to say, he is not satisfied with it.[122]

The self-dealing rule also applies against a trustee who has retired from the trust with the object of buying trust property[123] and a trustee who has recently retired.[124] However, in *Re Boles and British Land Co's Contract*[125] it was held that it did not apply where a trustee had retired for twelve years. It will have no application against trustees with no active duties to perform[126] or who have disclaimed the trust.[127] The rule will not catch a transaction completed by a trustee if the contract was entered before he became a fiduciary.[128]

---

[119] [1977] Ch 106.

[120] See McPherson J, 'Self-dealing Trustees' in Oakley, *Trends in Contemporary Trust Law* (1996).

[121] The rule cannot apply in the absence of a trust relationship over the property concerned—see *Hollis v Rolfe* [2008] EWHC 1747 (Ch), where it was held there was no breach of the rule against self-dealing by a trustee joining with her co-trustees in transferring the property to her ex-husband, who had no relationship either with the trustee or the trust property.   [122] (1800) 5 Ves 678, at 680.

[123] *Spring v Pride* (1864) 4 De GJ & Sm 395; *Re Mulholland's Will Trusts* [1949] 1 All ER 460.

[124] *Wright v Morgan* [1926] AC 788.   [125] [1902] 1 Ch 244.

[126] *Parkes v White* (1805) 11 Ves 209.   [127] *Stacey v Elph* (1833) 1 My & K 195.

[128] *Vyse v Foster* [1874] LR 7 HL 318; *Re Mulholland's Will Trusts* [1949] 1 All ER 460.

The leading authority concerning the application of the self-dealing rule is *Holder v Holder*.[129] Frank Holder died, leaving an estate that included two farms. He appointed as his executors his wife, one of his daughters, and one of his sons, Victor. Victor was the tenant of one of the two farms, 'Lower Farm'. He renounced his executorship to enable him to buy the farm, although beforehand he had performed some minor acts in the administration of the estate, including signing a few cheques for trivial sums and endorsing a few insurance policies. He subsequently purchased the farm at public auction. His brother sought to have the sale set aside on the basis that he had, as executor, purchased trust property. The Court of Appeal held that although the purported renunciation of his executorship was technically ineffective he had never assumed the duties of an executor and had not interfered in any way with the administration of the estate. He had not therefore been in the position of both vendor and purchaser of the farm and the sale was not set aside.[130]

The self-dealing rule was also applied in *Kane v Radley-Kane*.[131] The defendant was the administrator of her husband's estate and stepmother to his three sons. He had died intestate, leaving amongst his assets shares in a software company that were valued at £50,000 at the date of his death. Since the entire estate was worth only £93,000, and the defendant was entitled by statute to a legacy of £125,000, she transferred the shares into her own name. Some three years later she sold them for £1,131,438. The plaintiff, one of her stepsons, sought a declaration that the transaction by which the defendant had appropriated the shares to herself was rendered void by the self-dealing rule. Sir Richard Scott V-C held that the self-dealing rule applied to the transaction. He explained that it had involved a conflict of interest:

> It was her duty as a personal representative owed to the other beneficiaries in the intestate estate, that is to say, to the three sons, to realise the assets of the estate as advantageously as she properly could, and not to apply a greater part of those assets towards payment or discharge of any liability or charge payable out of the estate than was necessary for that purpose. If she had been a creditor of the estate and, as I understand it, she may well be, and had purported to take some asset of the estate in satisfaction of her debt, that would have been a transaction in which her duty and interest would have conflicted. Similarly, in taking the Shiredean shares in satisfaction of her £125,000 statutory legacy she was entering into a transaction in which her duty and interest conflicted.[132]

As the transaction was not expressly or impliedly authorized by statute, and the beneficiaries had not consented to it, it was held to be void. The proceeds of sale were therefore to be treated as part of the assets of the state and the defendant entitled merely to the legacy of £125,000.

---

[129] [1968] Ch 353.

[130] This explanation of the case was preferred by Vinelott J in *Re Thompson's Settlement* [1986] Ch 99. See also *In Plus Group Ltd v Pyke* [2002] 2 BCLC 201; [2003] 62 CLJ 42 (Koh), where the Court of Appeal held that a company director was not in breach of his fiduciary duties by competing with the company in circumstances where he had been wholly excluded from the management of the company such that his position was entirely nominal.   [131] [1999] Ch 274.

[132] [1998] 3 All ER 753, at 757.

(b) **Standard required by the self-dealing rule**

From the earliest cases the self-dealing rule has been applied strictly, and the courts have been unwilling to enter into any consideration of whether the trustee in fact abused his position. An affected transaction is liable to be set aside whenever a trustee has purchased trust property, no matter whether the purchase was to all intents and purposes fair. As Lord Eldon LC stated in *Ex p James*:

> This doctrine as to purchase by trustees, assignees, and persons having a confidential character, stands more upon general principle than upon the circumstances of any individual case. It rests upon this: that the purchase is not permitted in any case, however honest the circumstances; the general interests of justice requiring it to be destroyed in every instance.[133]

The law has adopted a strict objective approach that whenever a trustee is both vendor and purchaser the transaction may be set aside. Thus, even a purchase by a trustee at public auction can be set aside by the beneficiaries.[134] In *Wright v Morgan*[135] the Privy Council held that a sale of land to the trustee at a price fixed by independent valuers must be set aside.

Some doubt was cast upon this strict application of the self-dealing rule by the Court of Appeal in *Holder v Holder*.[136] Sachs LJ took the view that there was no longer any need for the court to be shackled by a rigid rule of an irrebuttable presumption 'which stems from the alleged inability of a court to ascertain the state of mind of a trustee',[137] and that it should be treated merely as a rule of practice. Danckwerts LJ seemed, similarly, to take the view that the rule was a matter for the discretion of the judge. However, in *Re Thompson's Settlement*[138] Vinelott J seemed to prefer to view the decision in *Holder v Holder* as turning on the fact that the brother had never acted as executor in a way which could be taken to amount to acceptance of a duty to act in the interests of the beneficiaries under the will. He affirmed the more traditional approach:

> The principle is applied stringently in cases where a trustee concurs in a transaction which cannot be carried into effect without his concurrence and who also has an interest or owes a fiduciary duty to another in relation to the same transaction. The transaction cannot stand if challenged by a beneficiary because in the absence of an express provision in the trust instrument the beneficiaries are entitled to require that the trustees act unanimously and that each brings to bear a mind unclouded by any contrary interest or duty in deciding whether it is in the interests of the beneficiaries that the trustees concur in it.[139]

The application of a strict approach was also supported by Sir Richard Scott V-C in *Kane v Radley-Kane*, where he stated that it was 'a general and highly salutary principle

---

[133] (1803) 8 Ves 337, at 344.
[134] *Whichcote v Lawrence* (1798) 3 Ves 740; *Campbell v Walker* (1800) 5 Ves 678; *Dyson v Lum* (1866) 14 LT 588.   [135] [1926] AC 788.
[136] [1968] Ch 353.   [137] [1968] Ch 353, at 402.   [138] [1986] Ch 99.   [139] [1986] Ch 99, at 115.

of law that a trustee cannot validly contract with himself and cannot exercise his trust powers to his own advantage'.[140]

(c) Exceptions to the self-dealing rule

The self-dealing rule will not apply if the trust instrument authorizes the trustee to purchase trust property.[141] Similarly, if the beneficiaries consent to the purchase, they cannot subsequently have it set aside. The court also possesses the discretion to permit a purchase.[142] Where land is subject to a strict settlement,[143] s 68 of the Settled Land Act 1925 provides that the tenant for life of settled land may purchase the property.

(d) Remedies of the beneficiary

Where trust property has been acquired by a trustee in contravention of the self-dealing rule, the transaction is voidable at the option of the beneficiaries. If the trustee has resold the property, he will be required to make restitution to the trust of any profits he made.[144] If he has retained the property, the beneficiary may insist that it is re-conveyed to the trust, or a new sale may be ordered.

(2) The fair-dealing rule

The fair-dealing rule applies where a trustee purchases the beneficial interest from one or more of the beneficiaries. Since such a transaction is the result of negotiation between the trustee and the beneficiary, there is less risk that the trustee will exploit his position. Equity therefore adopts a less strict approach than under the self-dealing rule. Transactions entered in violation of the fair-dealing rule are voidable by the beneficiary unless the trustee can show that he has not taken any advantage by virtue of his position.[145] The rule was stated by Lord Eldon in *Coles v Trecothick*:

> a trustee may buy from the [beneficiary], provided that there is a distinct and clear contract, ascertained to be such after a jealous and scrupulous examination of all the circumstances, proving that the [beneficiary of the] trust intended the trustee should buy; there is no fraud, no concealment, no advantage taken, by the trustee of information acquired by him in the character of trustee.[146]

In *Thomson v Eastwood*[147] Lord Cairns stated that a court of equity would examine such a transaction and 'ascertain that value paid by the trustee, and will throw upon the trustee the onus of proving that he gave full value, and that all information was laid before the [beneficiary] when it was sold'.

---

[140] [1998] 3 All ER 753, at 757.   [141] *Sargeant v National Westminster Bank plc* (1990) 61 P & CR 518.
[142] *Farmer v Dean* (1863) 32 Beav 327.
[143] Following the introduction of the trust of land in the Trusts of Land and Appointment of Trustees Act 1996, no new strict settlements can be created, but existing settlements will continue.
[144] *Hall v Hallet* (1784) 1 Cox Eq Cas 134; *ex p James* (1803) 8 Ves 337.
[145] *Clarke v Swaile* (1762) 2 Eden 134; *Coles v Trecothick* (1804) 9 Ves 234; *Randall v Errington* (1805) 10 Ves 423; *Morse v Royal* (1806) 12 Ves 355; *Sanderson v Walker* (1807) 13 Ves 601; *Dover v Buck* (1865) 5 Giff 57.   [146] (1804) 9 Ves 234.
[147] (1877) 2 App Cas 215.

4 Incidental profits

As a trustee stands in a fiduciary relationship to the beneficiaries of the trust, he will not be permitted to retain unauthorized profits that he receives as a result of holding his position.[148] He must not permit his interests and his duties to conflict. The rationale for this rule was clearly expressed by Lord Herschell in *Bray v Ford*:

> It is an inflexible rule of a court of equity that a person in a fiduciary position, such as the respondent, is not, unless otherwise expressly provided, entitled to make a profit; he is not allowed to put himself in a position where his interest and his duty conflict. It does not appear to me that this rule is as has been said, founded upon principles of morality. I regard it rather as based on the consideration that, human nature being what it is, there is danger, in such circumstances, of the person holding a fiduciary position being swayed by interest rather than by duty, and thus prejudicing those whom he was bound to protect. It has, therefore, been deemed expedient to lay down this positive rule.[149]

The concept of conflict of interest, which the rule aims to prevent, was explained by Lord Cranworth LC in *Aberdeen Rly Bros v Blaikie*:[150]

> And it is a rule of universal application, that no one, having such duties to discharge, shall be allowed to enter into engagements in which he has, or can have, a personal interest conflicting, or which possibly may conflict, with the interests of those whom he is bound to protect.[151]

It is necessary to consider first the circumstances in which the courts have held trustees liable to account for incidental profits which they have made as a result of their conflict of interest, and, second the standard of liability required by the rule.

(1) Renewal of a lease

A trustee who renews for himself a lease which was previously held on trust for the beneficiaries will hold the lease on trust for them. This rule was applied in *Keech v Sandford*.[152] The trustee held the profits of Romford market on trust for a minor. When the lease expired, the landlord refused to renew the lease to the trust. Instead, he renewed the lease to the trustee personally. King LC held that the lease should be assigned by the trustee to the infant and that he should account for the profits he had made. He recognized that it 'may seem hard that the trustee is the only person of all

---

[148] A vendor of land who holds the property on constructive trust for the purchaser as a result of the specifically enforceable contract for sale is not required to account for benefits received from the trust property in the absence of agreement to the contrary: *Englewood Properties v Patel* [2005] 3 All ER 307.

[149] [1896] AC 44, at 51.   [150] (1854) 2 Eq Rep 1281.

[151] See also *Richardson v Chapman* (1760) 7 Bro Parl Cas 318, HL; *Phayre v Peree* (1815) 3 Dow 116, HL; *Shallcross v Oldham* (1862) 2 John & H 609; *Bennett v Gas Light and Coke Co* (1882) 52 LJ Ch 98; *Lagunas Nitrate Co v Lagunas Syndicate* [1899] 2 Ch 392; *Costa Rica Rly Co v Forwood* [1901] 1 Ch 746; *Re Thomson* [1930] 1 Ch 203.   [152] (1726) Sel Cas Ch 61.

mankind who might not have the lease', but justified the result in the light of general policy considerations:

> it is very proper that the rule should be strictly pursued, and not in the least relaxed; for it is very obvious what would be the consequences of letting trustees have the lease, on refusal to renew to [the beneficiary].[153]

The principle of *Keech v Sandford* applies only where a lease owned by a trust is renewed to a fiduciary. In *Re Biss*[154] a man rented premises for his business. When he died his widow, who was the administratrix of his estate, continued the business with the help of their adult son. The landlord refused to renew the lease to the widow but granted it to the adult son. It was held that the son did not hold the lease on trust for the estate because he did not stand in a fiduciary relationship with the estate. He was therefore under no personal incapacity to take the benefit, the renewal was not an accretion to the original term, and it had not been renewed to him until there had been an absolute refusal by the landlord to renew to the administratrix for the estate.

In *Don King Productions Inc v Warren*[155] the principle of *Keech v Sandford* was applied by analogy to the renewal of a contract held on trust for a partnership to one of the partners in a personal capacity. The case concerned a partnership established between boxing promoters Don King and Frank Warren in 1994. The partnership was subsequently dissolved in 1997. On the basis that partners stand in a fiduciary relationship, the Court of Appeal held that the entire benefit of any management or promotion agreements concluded by a partner after the date of the dissolution but before the conclusion of the winding up of the partnership affairs with a boxer with whom he already has such an agreement would be held on trust for the partnership.

(2) **Purchase of a freehold reversion**

The principle of *Keech v Sandford* has been extended to include the purchase by a trustee of the freehold reversion of land leased to the trust. Until recently there were doubts whether the rule operated in the same absolute manner. In *Protheroe v Protheroe*[156] the rule was applied strictly to a husband who purchased the freehold reversion of a house he held on trust jointly with his wife, but earlier cases suggested that the rule would only apply if the lease was renewable to the trust by law or custom.[157] However, it was applied without any such qualification in *Thompson's Trustee in Bankruptcy v Heaton*,[158] where a partner had purchased the freehold reversion of a farm that was a partnership asset. Following *Protheroe v Protheroe*,[159] Pennycuick V-C held that:

---

[153] (1726) Sel Cas Ch 61, at 62.   [154] [1903] 2 Ch 40.   [155] [2000] Ch 291.
[156] [1968] 1 WLR 519; (1968) 32 Conv 220 (Crane); (1968) 31 MLR 707 (Jackson); (1968) 84 LQR 309 (Megarry).
[157] *Re Lord Ranelagh's Will* (1884) 26 Ch D 590; *Phillips v Phillips* (1885) 29 Ch D 673, CA; *Longton v Wilsby* (1897) 76 LT 770; *Bevan v Webb* [1905] 1 Ch 620; *Phipps v Boardman* [1964] 1 WLR 993, at 1009; (1969) Conv (NS) 161 (Cretney).   [158] [1974] 1 WLR 605.
[159] [1968] 1 WLR 519.

it is also well established that where someone holding a leasehold interest in a fiduciary capacity acquires the freehold reversion, he must hold that reversion as part of the trust estate.[160]

Thompson's Trustee in Bankruptcy v Heaton was cited with approval by the Court of Appeal in *Don King Productions Inc v Warren*,[161] suggesting that the rule will be applied equally strictly where a trustee acquires the freehold reversion.

(3) **Remuneration received as a director**

Where the trust assets include company shares, the trustees control the associated voting rights at company meetings. If the trustees exploit this power to appoint themselves as directors of the company they will be liable to account for any remuneration they thereby receive. The position was considered in *Re Macadam*,[162] where the trustees of a will were granted the power to appoint two directors of a company. They duly appointed themselves and received remuneration for their services. Cohen J held that they were accountable to the trust for the remuneration they had received, and stated the general principles that apply:

> I think the root of the matter really is: did [the trustee] acquire the position in respect of which he drew the remuneration by virtue of his position as trustee? In the present case there can be no doubt that the only way in which the plaintiffs became directors was by the exercise of the powers vested in the trustees of the will although the remuneration was remuneration for services as director of the company, the opportunity to receive that remuneration was gained as a result of the exercise of a discretion vested in the trustees, and they had put themselves in a position where their interest and duty conflicted.[163]

It follows from this that a trustee will not be accountable for any remuneration he received from a directorship if he did not in fact use his position to obtain it.[164] Thus, in *Re Dover Coalfield Extension Ltd*[165] it was held that a trustee would be able to retain remuneration received from a directorship to which he had been appointed before becoming a trustee, as it would not have been obtained by use of his position. In *Re Gee*[166] it was held that a trustee who is elected to a directorship would be entitled to retain any remuneration he received if he would still have been elected a director even if the trust shares he controlled had been voted against him, since he would not then have obtained his position through the use of the trust share. However, he would not be protected from liability merely because he abstained from using the trust shares.

Trustees will not be liable to make restitution if the trust instrument permits them to appoint themselves directors and receive remuneration.[167] The court also possesses an inherent jurisdiction to permit trustees to retain remuneration they receive

---

[160] [1968] 1 WLR 519, at 521.   [161] [2000] Ch 291, at 340.
[162] [1946] Ch 73. See also *Re Francis* (1905) 74 LJ Ch 198; *Re Orwell's Will Trusts* [1982] 1 WLR 1337.
[163] [1946] Ch 73, at 82.   [164] *Re Lewis* (1910) 103 LT 495.   [165] [1907] 2 Ch 76.
[166] [1948] Ch 284.   [167] *Re Llewellin's Will Trusts* [1949] Ch 225.

as directors on a similar basis to the inherent jurisdiction accepted in *Re Duke of Norfolk's Settlement Trusts*.[168] Goulding J considered that the court would permit a trustee 'to retain reasonable remuneration for effort and skill applied by him in performing the duties of the directorship over and above the effort and skill ordinarily required of a director appointed to represent the interests of a substantial shareholder'.[169]

(4) **Commission earned**

A trustee who receives a commission for introducing trust business will be liable to account for the commission he has received as unauthorized profit. In *Williams v Barton*[170] a trustee was employed as a clerk at a firm of stockbrokers. The firm was employed to value the trust securities and the trustee received a commission for introducing the business. Russell J held that the commission received was to be treated as part of the trust estate.

(5) **Competition**

If the trust assets include a business the trustee must not set up in competition. In *Re Thomson*[171] Clauson J held that it would be a breach of fiduciary duty for a trustee of a yacht broking business to set up independently as a yacht broker because he would have been 'entering into an engagement in which he would have a personal interest conflicting or which possibly might conflict with the interests of those he was bound to protect'.[172] The rationale for this decision may be the relatively specialized nature of the yacht broking business, where it was inevitable that brokers would be in competition with each other. In *Aas v Benham*[173] it was held that there was no breach of fiduciary duty where a member of a partnership of shipbrokers formed a company to build ships. The two operations would not be in competition. In *In Plus Group Ltd v Pyke*[174] Sedley LJ considered that a director of a company could not simply become involved with a competing third party without the consent of the company because of his fiduciary duty,[175] although on the facts of the case he held that the fiduciary duty had not been breached.

(6) **Bribes**

A trustee or other fiduciary who receives a bribe by virtue of his position will not be entitled to retain it. He will be required to make restitution to the trust, or his principal, by way of an equitable liability to account. His liability to make personal

---

[168] [1979] Ch 37.   [169] [1979] Ch 37, at 162–163.   [170] [1927] 2 Ch 9.   [171] [1930] 1 Ch 203.
[172] [1930] 1 Ch 203, at 216.   [173] [1891] 2 Ch 244; *Moore v M'Glynn* [1894] 1 IR 74.
[174] [2002] 2 BCLC 201; Grantham 'Can Directors Compete with the Company?' (2003) 66 MLR 109.
[175] Rejecting dicta to the opposite effect in *London and Marshonaland Exploration Co Ltd v New Mashonaland Exploration Co Ltd* [1891] WN 165.

restitution in this way is uncontroversial. However, in *A-G for Hong Kong v Reid*[176] the Privy Council held that a fiduciary also holds such a bribe on constructive trust for the principal. This decision has been confirmed by the Supreme Court in *FHR European Ventures LLP v Cedar Capital Partners LLC*[177] which has clarified that any unauthorized profit made by a fiduciary will be held upon constructive trust.

(7) **Opportunities**

A fiduciary is liable to make restitution to his principal if he obtains a profit by exploiting an opportunity that rightfully belonged to his principal. A fiduciary who exploits such an opportunity for his own benefit without the authorization of his principal will be liable to account even where the principal could not have taken advantage of the opportunity himself.[178]

(a) **Company directors**

One of the most common situations in which fiduciaries exploit opportunities belonging to their principals is that of company directors who take up opportunities properly belonging to their company, to which they stand in a fiduciary relationship. In *Cook v Deeks*[179] three of the four directors of a company who were negotiating for a contract to construct a railway took the contract for themselves in their private capacity so as to exclude the fourth director. The Privy Council held that this amounted to a breach of their fiduciary duty, and that they were liable to account to the company for the profits they made from the transaction. In the leading case, *Regal (Hastings) Ltd v Gulliver*,[180] a company that owned cinemas, wanted to acquire two other cinemas in Hastings. To enable the company to achieve this objective it formed a subsidiary with 5,000 shares. The company was financially only able to take up 2,000 of the shares in the subsidiary. Since the owner of the cinemas refused to sell them unless the share capital was completely taken up, the directors of the company purchased the remaining 3,000 shares and the deal went ahead. The company was subsequently sold and the directors made a profit of £2 16s 1d on each of the shares they had taken up. The House of Lords held that the directors were accountable to the purchasers of the company for the profit they had made on the shares because they had obtained it by reason of their fiduciary position. As Lord Russell of Killowen concluded:

> The directors standing in a fiduciary relationship to Regal... and having obtained these shares by reason and only by reason of the fact that they were directors of Regal and in the course of the execution of that office, are accountable for the profits which they have made out of them.[181]

---

[176] [1994] 1 All ER 1. See Pearce 'Personal and Proprietary Claims Against Bribees' [1994] LMCLQ 189.
[177] [2014] UKSC 45.
[178] See *Regal (Hastings) Ltd v Gulliver* [1967] 2 AC 134n; [1942] 1 All ER 378; *Industrial Development Consultants Ltd v Cooley* [1972] 1 WLR 443; *Boardman v Phipps* [1967] 2 AC 46, HL; *O'Donnell v Shanahan* [2009] EWCA Civ 751.   [179] [1916] 1 AC 554.
[180] [1967] 2 AC 134n; [1942] 1 All ER 378.   [181] [1942] 1 All ER 378, at 389.

It made no difference that the company could not have taken up the opportunity itself for lack of finance, nor that the directors had acted bona fides without fraud.[182]

In *Industrial Development Consultants Ltd v Cooley*[183] Neville Cooley was the managing director of Industrial Development Consultants Ltd, a company that provided construction consultancy services. He entered into negotiations on behalf of the company with the Eastern Gas Board for a contract to build new depots. The Board refused to enter into a contract with the company because of their policy of not employing development companies, but they offered a contract to Cooley in his personal capacity, which he accepted. He then gained release from his position as managing director by representing that he was suffering from a serious illness. Roskill J held that Cooley was liable to account for the profit he had gained from the contract because in entering it he had allowed his duty and his interests to conflict.

In *O'Donnell v Shanahan*[184] a company had, though it was not part of its normal business, agreed to procure finance and advise a particular investor who was interested in purchasing a development company. The company would earn both fees and a commission for their services. The deal did not proceed beyond valuation reports, but the defendant directors, who ran a property development partnership on the side, procured the property deal for themselves and a third party and did not pay the company commission. The claimant director was, however, paid a sum, representing her lost commission but she later brought a claim that the investment in the development company was an unauthorized profit. Rimer LJ held that the directors had exploited an opportunity that they obtained only through the company. It did not matter that property development was not in the company's normal course of business; the opportunity should have been disclosed so that the company could decide where or not to exploit it itself. He stated:

> I would regard it as correct to characterise the nature of a director's fiduciary duties as being so unlimited and as akin to a 'general trusteeship'…the scope of the company's business was in no manner relevantly circumscribed by its constitution: it was fully open to it to engage in property investment if the directors so chose.[185]

Although directors are prima facie liable to make restitution of any profit they receive by appropriating an opportunity belonging to their company, they will be protected from liability if they were authorized to take up the opportunity. This seems to be the correct analysis of the decision of the Privy Council in *Queensland Mines Ltd v Hudson*.[186] Hudson was the managing director of Queensland Mines, a company that was investigating the possibility of mining iron ore in Tasmania. Two licences were obtained from the Tasmanian government, but the company was not able to start

---

[182] For a review of the authorities in this area, see *Ultraframe (UK) Ltd v Fielding* [2005] EWHC 1638 (Ch), where Lewison J preferred the dissenting opinion of Lord Upjohn in *Boardman v Phipps* [1967] 2 AC 46, at 124 that there must be a realistic possibility of conflict of duty and interest for the duty to be breached.
[183] [1972] 1 WLR 443.   [184] [2009] EWCA Civ 751.   [185] [2009] EWCA Civ 751, at [68]–[69].
[186] (1978) 18 ALR 1; Sullivan 'Going it Alone—*Queensland Mines v Hudson*' (1979) 42 MLR 711. See also *Island Export Finance Ltd v Umunna* [1986] BCLC 460; *In Plus Group Lyd v Pyke* [2002] 2 BCLC 201.

mining operations because of lack of finance. Instead, Hudson resigned as managing director and exploited the licences himself, eventually selling them to an American company from which he received royalties on the ore mined. The company argued that he should account for the profits he had made, but the Privy Council held that he was not liable. As Lord Scarman observed, the difficulty of the case lay 'not in the formulation of the law but in the analysis of the facts'.[187] On the facts the Privy Council concluded that by 1962 the board of directors, 'fully informed as to all the relevant facts, had reached a firm decision to renounce all interest in the exploitation of the licence and had assented to Mr Hudson taking over the venture for his own account'. The basis of the decision thus seems to be that the directors had decided that the company would not take up the opportunity, and that Hudson was therefore free to take it up himself. Although this reasoning is attractive, it is open to the objection that the board of directors is not the appropriate organ of the company to reject such an opportunity and permit a director to take it up for himself. The only organ of the company competent to grant such authorization is the shareholders' meeting.[188]

The equitable duties of directors have been codified in the Companies Act 2006.[189] Hence, by s 175(1):

> A director of a company must avoid a situation in which he has, or can have, a direct or indirect conflict of interest that conflicts, or possibly may conflict, with the interests of the company.

The director must also not exploit any property, information, or opportunity, and it is immaterial whether the company could take advantage of it.[190] In distinction to the authorities explored earlier relating to the strict nature of liability, it is clear that the duty is not infringed if the situation complained of cannot reasonably be regarded as likely to give rise to a conflict of interest.[191] The Act also codifies that there will be no conflict of duty and interest if the matter in question has been authorized by the directors.[192]

(b) Trustees

Since a trustee is a fiduciary vis-à-vis the beneficiaries of the trust he will similarly act in breach of duty if he takes personal advantage of opportunities that properly belong to the trust. For example, if a trust includes shares amongst its assets, and a rights issue is proposed, the trustees cannot purchase the shares offered under the rights issue for themselves unless authorized to do so by the beneficiaries. If they do

---

[187] (1978) 18 ALR 1, at 3.

[188] Sullivan 'Going it Alone—*Queensland Mines v Hudson*' (1979) MLR 711. See also *Prudential Assurance Co v Newman Industries (No 2)* [1980] 2 All ER 841, at 862; *Shaker v Al-Bedrawi* [2002] 4 All ER 835.

[189] This followed from recommendation of the Law Commission in *Company Directors: Regulating Conflicts of Interest and Formulating a Statement of Duties* Law Com No 261.

[190] Companies Act 2006, s 175(2).   [191] Companies Act 2006, s 175(4)(a).

[192] Companies Act 2006, s 175(4)(b). The conditions for the exercise of effective authorization are contained in ss 175(5) and (6), and 180.

purchase the shares without authorization they will be held on constructive trust for the beneficiaries.

(c) Other fiduciaries

Fiduciaries other than company directors and trustees will also be held liable to account for any unauthorized profits they receive through exploiting an opportunity belonging to their principal. This can be seen from the leading case of *Boardman v Phipps*.[193] A trust had been established by Charles Phipps on behalf of his wife for life, and after her death for his four children. The trustees were his widow, daughter, and a professional trustee. One asset of the trust was a 27 per cent holding in a private company, Lester & Harris Ltd. Thomas Boardman was the solicitor to the trust and the Phipps family. Boardman and one of the beneficiaries, Thomas Phipps, were unhappy with the way that the company was being run and decided that the only way to protect the trust asset was to acquire a controlling interest in the company. Boardman suggested this to the managing trustee, who made it clear that he was against the trustees buying such a controlling interest and that, without applying to the court, they had no power to do so. Boardman and Phipps, having informed two of the trustees but not the third, who was the testator's elderly widow, subsequently purchased a controlling interest in the company. They then capitalized some of the company's assets, making a profit of some £47,000 for the trust and £75,000 for themselves. One of the other beneficiaries, John Phipps, claimed that they should account for this profit to the trust. By a bare majority the House of Lords held that Boardman was liable to account. He had stood in a fiduciary relationship to the trust and, although he had acted honestly throughout, in exploiting the opportunity there had been a possibility of a conflict between his duty and his interest.

(8) Use of confidential information

A fiduciary who makes use of confidential information[194] belonging to his principal will be liable for any profit that he makes.[195] In *A-G v Guardian Newspapers Ltd (No 2)*[196] the House of Lords held that the *Sunday Times* was liable to account for the profits made by its publication of extracts of *Spycatcher*, a book written by a former member of the British security services, who stood in a fiduciary relationship to the Crown, and which contained confidential information.[197] In *Peter Pan Manufacturing Corpn v Corsets Silhouette Ltd*[198] the defendant company's designer was shown a sample copy of the design of a new brassiere in confidence by the plaintiff company. When the defendants subsequently manufactured it Pennycuick J ordered that they account for their profits. Liability on the basis of the exploitation of confidential information

---

[193] [1967] 2 AC 46, HL.

[194] See Glover 'Is Breach of Confidence a Fiduciary Wrong?' (2001) 21 LS 595.

[195] *York and North Midland Rly Co v Hudson* (1853) 16 Beav 485; *Kirkham v Peel* (1881) 44 LT 195.

[196] [1990] 1 AC 109.   [197] See Jones 'Breach of Confidence after *Spycatcher*' [1989] CLP 49.

[198] [1964] 1 WLR 96.

was also established in the Canadian case of *LAC Minerals Ltd v International Corona Resources Ltd.*[199] LAC received confidential information from Corona during the course of negotiations with a view to establishing a joint venture to exploit minerals from land owned by Corona, which indicated that adjacent land was also likely to contain mineral deposits. LAC subsequently purchased the adjacent land in their own right, and exploited the minerals themselves. The Supreme Court held that there was a fiduciary relationship between the parties, and that LAC should hold the land on constructive trust for Corona because of their breach of confidence.[200]

The exploitation of confidential information provides a further possible explanation for the decision in *Boardman v Phipps.*[201] In the course of negotiations for the purchase of the majority shareholding in the company Boardman, while purporting to act as the trust solicitor on the business of the trust, received essential information about the value of the company's assets and the prices at which shares had recently changed hands. This information enabled him to put forward his offer for the majority shareholding. Lord Hodson and Lord Guest held that Boardman was accountable for the profit he made because he had acquired the shares using this confidential information, which they considered to be trust property. However, Lord Cohen took the view that the information that had been obtained was not 'property in the strict sense'[202] and decided the case on the basis of the rule in *Regal (Hastings) Ltd v Gulliver,*[203] and Lord Upjohn rejected the argument that the information was to be regarded as part of the trust assets.[204]

However, it is clear that the duty not to profit from confidential information only subsists for so long as the information received retains its confidential status. Once it has entered the public sphere, the obligation of confidentiality no longer subsists. Thus, in *A-G v Blake*[205] the Court of Appeal held that a former spy was not in breach of any fiduciary duty when he had published an autobiography that contained information concerning his work which had entered the public sphere prior to publication. Lord Woolf MR commented:

> The duty to respect confidence is also a fiduciary duty, but it subsists only as long as the information remains confidential.[206]

This was subsequently confirmed by the House of Lords.[207] It has also been held that a third party who receives confidential information disclosed by a fiduciary in breach of his duty is not automatically liable to account for any profits resulting from his

---

[199] (1989) 61 DLR (4th) 14.
[200] Tang argues that there was no justification for a constructive trust in *LAC Minerals v International Corona Resources*: 'Confidence and the Constructive Trust' (2003) 23 LS 135.
[201] [1967] 2 AC 46, HL.
[202] [1967] 2 AC 46, at 103. Note that in *Crown Dilmun plc v Sutton* [2004] 1 BCLC 468 it was accepted that confidential information was not property. However, it may have a market value, and can, indeed, be sold on the market—see *Douglas v Hello! Ltd (No 3)* [2008] 1 AC 1. The potential development of the concept of the law of privacy was considered in Chapter 6.   [203] [1967] 2 AC 134n; [1942] 1 All ER 378.
[204] [1967] 2 AC 46, at 127–128.
[205] [1998] 1 All ER 833, at 842.   [206] [1998] 1 All ER 833, at 842.   [207] [2000] 4 All ER 385.

exploitation of that information. In *Satnam Ltd v Dunlop Heywood & Co Ltd*[208] a development company owned an option to purchase a site that was determinable by the site owners if it went into receivership. The company of surveyors acting for the development company subsequently told a rival developer that their client had been placed into receivership and that the local authority was favourable towards development. On the basis of this information the rival developers purchased the site. While the surveyors had clearly breached their fiduciary duty in revealing this confidential information, the Court of Appeal held that the rival developers did not hold the land acquired on constructive trust for the original developers, nor were they liable to account for their profits. Nourse LJ, giving the judgment of the court, explained that mere knowledge of a breach of fiduciary duty was insufficient to render a person who was not himself a fiduciary a constructive trustee. He held that the third party would only have been liable to make an account of profits if it had acted dishonestly.

5 Liability for breach of fiduciary duty

Having examined the circumstances in which a fiduciary will be held to have acted in breach of his duty, it is possible to extrapolate from the cases the standard of liability required to trigger a remedy. It appears that the courts have adopted a strict test of liability that does not require the principal to demonstrate that the fiduciary in fact permitted his duty and his interest to conflict. Instead, a fiduciary will be liable to account if there was a mere possibility that his duty and his interests would conflict. The adoption of such a strict approach has attracted criticism. While in the majority of cases a fiduciary who has profited from his position will have acted dishonestly and without regard for the interest of his principle, in some cases a fiduciary who received a profit may have been entirely innocent of any wrongdoing or fraudulent conduct, especially if he exploited an opportunity which his principal could not have exploited, or where the danger of a conflict of interest had been so remote that there was no realistic possibility that such a conflict had occurred. In such cases it may seem questionable whether the fiduciary should be liable to make restitution of his profits. Such difficulties were evident in *Boardman v Phipps*,[209] the facts of which were discussed earlier The House of Lords consistently emphasized that Boardman and his colleague had been entirely innocent of any misconduct. Lord Cohen, for example, said that their integrity was 'not in doubt' and that they had acted 'with complete honesty throughout'.[210] However, it nevertheless held that Boardman was required to make restitution of the profits he had received. Given the success of the defendants' venture, which it must be remembered also resulted in a considerable profit for the trust, the plaintiff was, as Lord Cohen observed, a 'fortunate man in that the rigour of equity enables him to participate in the profits'.[211]

---

[208] [1999] 3 All ER 652.   [209] [1967] 2 AC 46.   [210] [1967] 2 AC 46, at 104.
[211] [1967] 2 AC 46, at 104.

(1) **Strict liability**

Despite the potential for unfairness in some cases, English law has adopted a strict principle that a fiduciary is liable to account for any unauthorized profits obtained in circumstances where there was a mere possibility that his duty and his interest had conflicted. In *Bray v Ford*[212] Lord Herschell described this as 'an inflexible rule of equity'. In *Regal (Hastings) Ltd v Gulliver*[213] Lord Russell of Killowen stressed that the fiduciary was required to give up the profit he had made irrespective of his honesty:

> The rule of equity, which insists on those, who by use of a fiduciary position make a profit, being liable to account for that profit, in no way depends on fraud, or absence of bona fides; or upon such questions or considerations as whether the profit would or should otherwise have gone to the plaintiff, or whether the profiteer was under a duty to obtain the source of the profit for the plaintiff, or whether he took a risk or acted as he did for the benefit of the plaintiff, or whether the plaintiff has in fact been damaged or benefited by his action. The liability arises from the mere fact of a profit having, in the stated circumstances, been made. The profiteer, however honest and well intentioned, cannot escape the risk of being called upon to account.[214]

In reaching this conclusion he drew upon the language of Lord King LC in *Keech v Sandford*,[215] and of Lord Eldon LC in *Ex p James*,[216] who had said that the self-dealing rule 'rests upon this: that the purchase is not permitted in any case however honest the circumstances'. In *Guinness plc v Saunders*[217] the House of Lords held that a company director who had received an unauthorized payment of £5.2m was liable to account to his company because he had allowed his duty and his interest to conflict, even though he had acted in complete good faith throughout.[218]

A divergence of views was apparent in the House of Lord in *Boardman v Phipps*[219] as to the degree of likelihood of a real conflict of interest required to render a fiduciary liability to account. It was alleged that Boardman had allowed his duty and his interest to conflict by purchasing a controlling interest in a company partially owned by the trust while there was a possibility that, as the trust solicitor, he could be called upon by the trustees to advise whether it would be wise for them to seek to acquire the power to pursue a similar investment. Lord Upjohn, dissenting, took the view that a fiduciary should only be required to disgorge his profits where there had been a 'real sensible possibility' of a conflict of interest. In the circumstances, he considered that the possibility of a conflict was simply too remote to render Boardman liable:

> The relevant rule for the decision of this case is the fundamental rule of equity that a person in a fiduciary capacity must not make a profit out of his trust which is a part of the wider rule that a trustee must not place himself in a position where his duty and his interest may conflict. It is perhaps most highly against trustees or directors in the celebrated speech of Lord Cranworth LC in *Aberdeen Rly Bros v Blaikie Bros*, where he said: 'And it is a rule of universal application, that no one, having such duties to discharge, shall be

---

[212] [1896] AC 44, at 51.   [213] [1942] 1 All ER 378.   [214] [1942] 1 All ER 378, at 386.
[215] (1726) Sel Cas Ch 61.   [216] (1803) 8 Ves 337.   [217] [1990] 2 AC 663.
[218] [1990] 2 AC 663, at 710, per Lord Goff.   [219] [1967] 2 AC 46.

allowed to enter into engagements in which he has, or can have, a personal interest conflicting, or which possibly may conflict, with the interests of those whom he is bound to
protect.' The phrase 'possibly may conflict' requires consideration. In my view it means
that the reasonable man looking at the relevant facts and circumstances of the particular
case would think that there was a real sensible possibility of conflict; not that you could
imagine some situation arising which might, in some conceivable possibility in events not
contemplated as real sensible possibilities by any reasonable person, result in a conflict.[220]

He therefore concluded that Boardman had not acted in breach of his duty because
there had been no 'real sensible possibility' of a conflict of interest, and that he should
not be required to disgorge his profits.

In contrast, the majority of the House of Lords held that the remoteness of the possibility of a genuine conflict of interest was irrelevant to the liability of a fiduciary. Lord
Cohen,[221] Lord Hodson, and Lord Guest cited with approval the statement of principle
of Lord Russell in *Regal (Hastings) Ltd v Gulliver*.[222] As Lord Hodson observed:

No doubt it was but a remote possibility that Mr Boardman would ever be asked by the
trustees to advise on the desirability of an application to the court in order that the trustees might avail themselves of the information obtained. Nevertheless, even if the possibility of conflict is present between personal interest and the fiduciary position the rule
of equity must be applied.[223]

In consequence of the decision of the majority in *Boardman v Phipps*, English law
imposes a very strict liability for breach of fiduciary duty so that a fiduciary is liable to
account for profits he has received whenever there was a mere possibility, no matter
how remote, that his duty and his interest might conflict.

A number of arguments can be put forward in defence of the strict liability of
fiduciaries. First, it should be remembered that a fiduciary is only required to make
restitution of *unauthorized* profits. He is able to protect himself from liability by full
disclosure of his proposed activities to his principal, which in the case of a trust will
mean the beneficiaries. If the principal consents or acquiesces in the conduct disclosed the fiduciary will not be held accountable for any profits he receives thereby.
However, where a fiduciary fails to fully disclose his intended course of action to
his principal it is not unfair to presume that he was acting in a manner that he did
not expect would be condoned. Second, it has already been noted that it is impossible to conduct an inquiry into the subjective motives that influenced a fiduciary's
conduct to determine whether a genuine conflict of interest occurred.[224] The court
can only look to the objective reality of external appearances, and the mere possibility of such a conflict triggers a remedial response in favour of the principal. This
ensures that a situation can never arise where the fiduciary does in fact profit from
a breach of his duty. Third, it has to be remembered that the rule has implications

---

[220] [1967] 2 AC 46, at 124.
[221] Who had read the speeches to be delivered by Lord Hodson and Lord Guest and agreed in substance
with them.   [222] [1967] 2 AC 134n; [1942] 1 All ER 378.
[223] [1967] 2 AC 46, at 111.   [224] *Ex p James* (1803) 8 Ves 337.

beyond any immediate case in point. It operates to deter fiduciaries who may consider abusing their position. This has been described as the prophylactic function of the rule: equity does not wait to see whether the principal has suffered any detriment as a result of the fiduciary's conduct but imposes a duty which will hold the fiduciary accountable if he might have been tempted to sacrifice the interests of the beneficiary.[225] This prophylactic approach appeared to be to the fore in the reasoning of the House of Lords in *Guinness plc v Saunders*,[226] where Lord Goff emphasized that the court must not act in a manner that would provide any encouragement to trustees to put themselves in a position where their duty would conflict with their personal interests.

(2) **Amelioration of the consequences of strict liability**

While the adoption of a strict liability to make restitution of unauthorized profits may sometimes be perceived to operate unfairly against an honest fiduciary, such unfairness may partially be alleviated at the remedial stage. Whereas, prima facie, a fiduciary in breach will be required to disgorge the entirety of the profit he received, in some circumstances the courts have held that a fiduciary may be permitted to retain a proportion thereof for himself.[227] The exercise of such relief is akin to the inherent jurisdiction to authorize a trustee to retain past remuneration, and to recoup his expenses from the trust. For example, in *Boardman v Phipps*[228] the majority of the House of Lords held that although Boardman was liable to account for the profits he had received, he should enjoy an allowance to represent his work and skill, which had contributed substantially to the making of the profit. This allowance was to be calculated 'on a liberal scale'.

It remains unclear, however, whether the allowance granted in *Boardman v Phipps* included any share of the profits made, or whether it was intended solely to reflect the expenses he had incurred. In *O'Sullivan v Management Agency and Music Ltd*[229] the court expressly permitted a fiduciary to retain a share of the profit it had received. An exclusive management contract between a musician and a management company was set aside on the grounds of undue influence. The Court of Appeal held that while the company was required to account for the profits that it had received under contract, it should be permitted to retain an allowance of reasonable remuneration for their skill and labour. This allowance explicitly included a small share of the profits made. The principle was stated by Fox LJ:

---

[225] P Birks, *Introduction to the Law of Restitution* (1985), pp 332–333, 339–343.

[226] [1990] 2 AC 663.

[227] In *Warman International v Dwyer* (1995) 128 ALR 201, the High Court suggested that where a fiduciary had acted in breach of his duty in the context of a business rather than through the receipt of a specific asset it may well be inappropriate and inequitable to compel the errant fiduciary to account for the whole of the profit of his conduct of the business or exploitation of the principal's goodwill over an indefinite period of time. In such a case it might therefore be appropriate to allow the fiduciary a proportion of the profits, depending upon the particular circumstances.   [228] [1967] 2 AC 46.

[229] [1985] QB 428.

> Once it is accepted that the court can make an appropriate allowance to a fiduciary for his skill and labour I do not see why, in principle, it should not be able to give him some part of the profit of the venture if it was thought that justice as between the parties demanded that.[230]

The allowance is therefore entirely within the court's discretion, and on the facts it was held that a profit element should be included to recognize the contribution that the company had made to the singer's success, but that this would be less than the profit they might have made if the contract had been properly negotiated in the first place to reflect disapprobation of their conduct in obtaining the contract through undue influence.[231]

The stated objective was to 'achieve substantial justice between the parties'.[232] It might be thought that this would provide a way of adjusting the harsh consequences of the strict approach taken in *Boardman v Phipps*.[233] However, *Guinness plc v Saunders*[234] suggests that the courts will be unlikely to award a share of the profits to directors or trustees who allow their duty and their interests to conflict. The case concerned a director, Mr Ward, who received £5.2m under a contract he had entered into to provide his services to help with a takeover bid. He was held liable to account for this money because he had acted in breach of fiduciary duty and had not disclosed his interest to the company board. The question arose whether he should receive any allowance for the services he had performed. The House of Lords held that he should not. Lord Goff analysed the rationale for the award of an allowance on a liberal scale in *Boardman v Phipps*[235] and concluded:

> The decision has to be reconciled with the fundamental principle that a trustee is not entitled to remuneration for services rendered by him to the trust except as expressly provided in the trust deed. Strictly speaking, it is irreconcilable with the rule so stated. It seems to me therefore that it can only be reconciled with it to the extent that the exercise of the equitable jurisdiction does not conflict with the policy underlying the rule. As I see it, such a conflict will only be avoided if the exercise of the jurisdiction is restricted to those cases where it cannot have the effect of encouraging trustees in any way to put themselves in a position where their interests conflict with their duties as trustees.[236]

The allowance in *Boardman v Phipps* was therefore justified because of the 'equity underlying Mr Boardman's claim', and as such it would not provide any encouragement to trustees to put themselves in a position where their duties as trustees conflicted with their interests. In the case of Mr Ward, remuneration would be inappropriate because he had agreed to provide his services in return for a substantial fee and 'was most plainly putting himself in a position in which his interests were in stark contrast with his duty as a director'.[237]

---

[230] [1985] QB 428, at 468.
[231] [1985] QB 428, at 469, per Fox LJ: 'the defendants must suffer…because of the circumstances in which the contracts were procured'.   [232] [1985] QB 428, at 469, per Fox LJ.
[233] [1967] 2 AC 46.   [234] [1990] 2 AC 663, HL.   [235] [1967] 2 AC 46.
[236] [1990] 2 AC 663, at 701.   [237] [1990] 2 AC 663, at 702.

(3) **A higher threshold before a fiduciary is liable for breach of duty?**

There are now indications that the English courts wish to move away from the strict liability advocated in *Boardman v Phipps*,[238] but are unable to do so, given the strength of authority.[239] In *Murad v Al-Saraji*,[240] for example, Clarke, Arden, and Jonathan Parker LJJ all expressed a desire to soften the position of the law on fiduciary liability where a fiduciary had acted without concealment, but felt unable to do so.[241] The decision of the Supreme Court in *FHR European Ventures LLP v Cedar Capital Partners LLC*[242] is not inconsistent with this sentiment since no consideration was given to when a gain will be unauthorized.[243] Academic opinion remains divided on the subject, with some commentators welcoming a potential relaxation of strict liability,[244] while others feel that the strictness of the rules serves a useful purpose.[245]

(4) **Conclusion**

It might be thought that in practice there is very little difference between the two standards of liability propounded by the House of Lords in *Boardman v Phipps*.[246] Lord Upjohn's 'real sensible possibility' of a conflict of interest test will exclude only those cases where it seems there is absolutely no danger of the beneficiaries in fact being prejudiced by the fiduciary's conduct. It is an objective test and therefore there is still no need to inquire into actual motives, and it is sufficiently harsh to serve as an adequate deterrent to trustees who might contemplate abusing their position. However, although Lord Upjohn's test has much to commend it, and it has found

---

[238] [1967] 2 AC 46.

[239] *Guinness v Saunders* [1990] 2 AC 663. Note, however, the dicta of Sedley LJ in *In Plus Group Ltd v Pyke* [2002] 2 BCLC 201 that a company director would not commit a breach of fiduciary duty by serving a competing company without consent if he had been treated unfairly. Grantham argues that this is inconsistent with the strict duty imposed on fiduciaries: (2003) 66 MLR 109.

[240] [2005] EWCA Civ 959, CA; McInnes 'Account of Profits for Breach of Fiduciary Duty' (2006) LQR 11; *Ultraframe (UK) Ltd v Fielding* [2005] EWHC 1638 (Ch) (where Lewison J expressed his support for an approach based on a realistic possibility of conflict of interest, in preference to the strict approach).

[241] See also the dicta of Sedley LJ in *In Plus Group Ltd v Pyke* [2002] 2 BCLC 201 that a company director would not commit a breach of fiduciary duty by serving a competing company without consent if he had been treated unfairly. Grantham argues that this is inconsistent with the strict duty imposed on fiduciaries: (2003) 66 MLR 109.   [242] [2014] UKSC 45.

[243] This was considered in the Court of Appeal but was no longer an issue by the time of the Supreme Court hearing.

[244] See, for example, Panesar 'The Nature of Fiduciary Liability in English Law' [2007] Conv 2, 11–19: 'whilst the strict liability rule was justified in the context of some of the nineteenth century cases where evidential issues prevented the court from ascertaining the intention of the fiduciary, in modern cases it is questionable whether such an approach is justified. There is much to be said for recent judicial calls for recognition that it is not appropriate to apply laws decided in a wholly different context to a different kind of situation.'

[245] See, for example, Samet 'Guarding the Fiduciary's Conscience—A Justification of a Stringent Profit-Stripping Rule' (2008) OJLS 763, arguing that allowing the fiduciary to argue that he acted as an honest person would therefore be more than a mere decrease in its overall deterrent effect. The strict no-profit rule prevents manipulation.   [246] [1967] 2 AC 46.

favour with academic commentators,[247] the strict approach that a fiduciary will be liable to account whenever there was a mere possibility of a conflict of interest, no matter how remote or unlikely the circumstances, represents the present position of English law. This, in the context of company law, has been said to raise 'the fiduciary "no-conflict" rule from pragmatic prophylaxis to something far more draconian'.[248] The only way that the fiduciary can avoid liability, no matter how honest he may have been, is by ensuring that his profit-making activities are authorized by his principal following full disclosure.

6 Remedies where a fiduciary makes an unauthorized profit

A fiduciary who has made an unauthorized profit will be required to make restitution thereof to his principal. Such restitution or disgorgement can be effected either by a personal or a proprietary remedy. It has often proved difficult to determine whether a personal or proprietary remedy is available, and in many cases the courts have not clearly identified the remedy awarded. The problem was stated clearly in the Australian High Court by Gibbs J in *Consul Development Pty Ltd v DPC Estates Pty Ltd*:

> The question whether the remedy which the person to whom the duty is owed may obtain against the person who has violated the duty is proprietary or personal may sometimes be one of some difficulty. In some cases the fiduciary has been declared a trustee of the property which he has gained by his breach; in others he has been called upon to account for his profits and sometimes the distinction between the two remedies has not...been kept clearly in mind.[249]

In many cases it will not be necessary to determine whether the principal is entitled to a proprietary remedy, as a personal remedy will suffice. However, the availability of a proprietary remedy will be of crucial importance if the fiduciary is insolvent,[250] or if he has invested the profit received in assets that have appreciated in value. In the case of insolvency a principal will gain priority over the general creditors of the fiduciary if he can demonstrate a proprietary entitlement to any assets that represent the profit received. In the case of asset appreciation the principal will only be able to claim entitlement to the increased value by means of a proprietary right.

---

[247] Jones 'Unjust Enrichment and the Fiduciary's Duty of Loyalty' (1968) *84* LQR 472; Finn, *Fiduciary Obligations* (1997), pp 130–168. It is also arguably the basis of the rule relating to directors duties in s 175(4)(a) of the Companies Act 2006.

[248] Gower and Davies, *Principles of Modern Company Law* (9th edn, 2012) at p 601. They argue that the operation of the rules essentially gives companies a right of first refusal on opportunities seen by directors as worth pursuing. Looking to the facts of *O'Donnell v Shanahan* [2009] EWCA Civ 751, this could happen even where the business opportunity was incidental to the company's main business.

[249] (1975) 5 ALR 231, at 249.

[250] See Oakley 'Proprietary Claims and their Priority in Insolvency' [1995] CLJ 377.

It should be noted that if a trustee has received a profit in breach of fiduciary duty his conduct may also constitute a breach of trust. If so, his obligations to make restitution of his profit gained in breach of fiduciary duty and to compensate the trust for any loss suffered in consequence of his breach are alternative remedies. The beneficiaries are required to elect between them and cannot recover both, otherwise they would gain double recovery. The need to elect was identified by the Privy Council in *Tang Man Sit (Decd) v Capacious Investments*,[251] which was discussed in detail in Chapter 27.

(1) Personal remedies

Whenever a fiduciary receives an unauthorized profit in breach of his fiduciary duty he is subject to a personal obligation to make restitution of the amount of the profit received to his principal. This personal restitutionary obligation is effected through the equitable duty to account. The personal remedy of account will be adequate to effect restitution where the fiduciary remains solvent and able to pay his principal an amount of money equivalent to the profit he received. Such a personal remedy appeared to have been awarded in *Boardman v Phipps*.[252] In many cases where an equitable account of profits was ordered there was no need to determine whether a proprietary remedy by way of a constructive trust was also available because the personal remedy provided adequate satisfaction of the principal's right to receive restitution. As Professor Birks notes,[253] 'the vital fact is that [Boardman] was not insolvent. It was not necessary, therefore, for the plaintiff to claim any right in rem.'[254] A personal remedy will also be preferred to a proprietary claim if the fiduciary is solvent but the assets remaining in his hands representing the profit he received have fallen in value. As Lord Templeman stated in *A-G for Hong Kong v Reid*:

> If the property representing the [profit[255]] decreases in value the fiduciary must pay the difference between that value and the initial amount of the [profit]…[256]

The relevant date for the assessment of the quantum of the personal remedy is the date that the profit was received. The principal will only be entitled to recover the actual or net profit that was received by the fiduciary.[257]

(2) Proprietary remedies

(a) A constructive trust of unauthorized profits

It has always been clear that in some circumstances a proprietary constructive trust is imposed when a fiduciary receives an unauthorized profit in breach of his duty.

---

[251] [1996] AC 514. See Stevens 'Election between Alternative Remedies' [1995] RLR 117; Birks 'Inconsistency between Compensation and Restitution' (1996) 112 LQR 375.

[252] [1967] 2 AC 46.   [253] Birks, *An Introduction to the Law of Restitution* (Oxford, 1985).

[254] Birks, An Introduction to the Law of Restitution, p 388.

[255] In fact, Lord Templeman used the term 'bribe', since this was what the fiduciary had in fact received, but the principle remains the same irrespective of the source of the profit received.

[256] [1994] 1 All ER 1.   [257] *Patel v London Borough of Brent* [2003] EWHC 3081.

This is evident in *Keech v Sandford*,[258] where the court held that a lease that had been renewed to a trustee in his personal capacity, rather than on behalf of the trust, should be assigned to the infant beneficiary. This suggests that the infant enjoyed an equitable entitlement to the lease from the moment that the trustee had acquired it. The trustee was also obliged to account for the profits he had received in the meantime. This account of profits is also explicable on the basis that the lease was always the property of the trust. In *Cook v Deeks*[259] the Privy Council similarly held that a contract entered by directors personally, in breach of their fiduciary duty, was held 'on behalf of the company',[260] such that 'it belonged in equity to the company and ought to have been dealt with as an asset of the company'.[261] In *Williams v Barton*[262] the court held that a commission received by a trustee in breach of fiduciary duty was to be treated as part of the estate of which he was executor, as he held it on constructive trust. In *Boardman v Phipps*[263] the House of Lords seems to have come to the conclusion that the majority shareholding that had been acquired in breach of fiduciary duty was held on constructive trust for the beneficiaries of the trust,[264] now confirmed by the Court of Appeal in *FHR European Ventures LLP v Mankarious*.[265] Likewise, in *Guinness plc v Saunders*[266] the House of Lords held that a £5.2m fee received by a director in breach of fiduciary duty was held on constructive trust for the company. He was therefore required to 'restore that money'[267] to the company.[268]

Although these cases established that a fiduciary may sometimes hold any unauthorized profits he has received on constructive trust, it remained unclear whether such a trust would arise in all such circumstances. This has now been resolved by the holding of the Supreme Court in *FHR European Ventures LLP v Cedar Capital Partners LL*[269] that a constructive trust attaches to all unauthorized gains make by an agent (or other fiduciary) in breach of fiduciary duty.

(b) Constructive trust of a bribe received by a fiduciary

Historically, a bribed fiduciary did not hold the bribe received on constructive trust, and the principal was confined to a personal remedy of account.[270] In *Lister & Co v Stubbs*[271] Stubbs, the foreman dyer of Lister & Co, received £5,500 in bribes from another company with whom he placed business while acting as agent for Lister. The Court of Appeal held that the money he received was not held on constructive trust, and that Lister & Co therefore had had no proprietary claim to it. Stubbs was under a

---

[258] (1726) Sel Cas Ch 61.   [259] [1916] 1 AC 554.   [260] [1916] 1 AC 554, at 563.
[261] [1916] 1 AC 554, at 564.   [262] [1927] 2 Ch 9.   [263] [1967] 2 AC 46.
[264] 1967] 2 AC 46, at 117, per Lord Guest: 'I have no hesitation in coming to the conclusion that the appellants hold the Lester & Harris shares as constructive trustees...' This understanding of the claim in *Boardman v Phipps* was also expressed by the Privy Council in *A-G for Hong Kong v Reid* [1994] 1 All ER 1, at 11.
[265] [2013] EWCA Civ 17, at [91], per Etherton C. The point was confirmed by the Supreme Court on Appeal: *FHR European Ventures LLP v Cedar Capital Partners LLC* [2014] UKSC 45, at [14].
[266] [1990] 2 AC 663.   [267] [1990] 2 AC 663, at 702, per Lord Goff.
[268] See also *Neptune (Vehicle Washing Equipment) Ltd v Fitzgerald* [1996] Ch 274; *CMS Dolphin Ltd v Simonet* [2001] BCLC 704.   [269] [2014] UKSC 45.
[270] *Metropolitan Bank v Heiron* (1880) 5 Ex D 319, CA.   [271] (1890) 45 Ch D 1.

personal duty to account for the money he had received, and the relationship between Stubbs and the company was simply one of debtor and creditor.

Lister & Co v Stubbs was followed in *A-G's Reference (No 1 of 1985)*.[272] A pub land-lord was contractually obliged to sell only goods supplied by a brewery. He moved barrels of his own beer into the pub at night. He was charged under s 25(1) of the Theft Act 1968 with going equipped for theft. The trial judge ruled that there was no case to answer, and it was referred to the Court of Appeal by the Attorney General. The central issue was whether the landlord would have been a constructive trustee of any money paid to him by customers for beer sold in breach of his contract. The Court of Appeal held that this did not fall within the ambit of s 5 of the Theft Act because 'a person in a fiduciary position who uses that position to make a secret profit erson is not a trustee'.[273] Lord Lane CJ concluded that:

> A trustee is not permitted to make a profit from his trust. Therefore if he uses trust prop-erty to make a profit from the trust, he is accountable for that profit. If and when such a profit is identified as a separate piece of property, he may be a constructive trustee of it. However, until the profit is identifiable as a separate piece of property, it is not trust prop-erty and his obligation is to account only.[274]

However, it is contended that little weight should be placed upon this decision. It is clearly correct that a proprietary remedy cannot subsist when specific property cannot be identified as representing the profit received, but it does not follow that no such pro-prietary entitlement exists at the moment that such a profit is received. The property is specifically identifiable when the customer pays over the price of the beer, although if mixed with other money it may then prove impossible to identify it subsequently in the assets of the recipient.

Although the rule in *Lister & Co v Stubbs*[275] was supported by some academic com-mentators,[276] it was subjected to heavy criticism by others.[277] In *A-G for Hong Kong v Reid*[278] the Privy Council considered that it should no longer be followed. Reid received bribes exceeding NZ$2.5m in the course of his work as a public prosecutor in Hong Kong. Part of this money was used to purchase three freehold properties in New Zealand. The Privy Council considered that, since Reid had acted in breach of

---

[272] [1986] QB 491; (1986) 102 LQR 486; (1986) 45 CLJ (Gearty); (1986) 136 NLJ 913 (Smart); [1987] Conv 209 (Martin). See also *Powell and Thomas v Evans Jones & Co* [1905] 1 KB 11, CA; *A-G's Reference (No 1 of 1985)* [1986] QB 491; *Logicrose Ltd v Southend United Football Club Ltd* [1988] 1 WLR 1256; *A-G for Hong Kong v Reid* [1992] 2 NZLR 385. For those who supported the decision in *Lister v Stubbs*, see Birks, *An Introduction to the Law of Restitution* (1985), p 388; (1987) 103 LQR 433 (Goode).

[273] [1986] QB 491, at 503, citing *Reading v A-G* [1951] AC 507, HL; *Re Sharpe* [1980] 1 WLR 219; *R v Governor of Pentonville Prison, ex p Tarling* (1978) 70 Cr App Rep 77; *Lister & Co v Stubbs* (1890) 45 Ch D 1.

[274] [1986] QB 491, at 506.   [275] (1890) 45 Ch D 1.

[276] Goode 'Ownership and Obligation in Commercial Transactions' (1987) 103 LQR 433.

[277] Underhill and Hayton, *Law Relating to Trust and Trustees* (15th edn, 1995), p 877; Oakley, *Constructive Trusts* (2nd edn, 1997), p 56; Meagher, Gummow, and Lehane, *Equity Doctrines and Remedies* (3rd edn, 1992), para 1323; Sir Anthony Mason, *Essays in Equity* (1985), p 246; Finn, *Fiduciary Obligations* (1977), para 513; Jacobs, *Law of Trusts in Australia* (5th edn), p 297; (1979) 95 LQR 536 (Needham); [1980] Conv 200 (Braithwaite); [1993] RLR 7 (Sir Peter Millett).

[278] [1994] 1 All ER 1; Allen 'Bribes and Constructive Trusts: *A-G of Hong Kong v Reid*' (1995) 58 MLR 87.

his fiduciary duty, he held the money he received on constructive trust for the Crown. Since the houses were the traceable proceeds of the bribes received, they were also held on trust for the Crown. Lord Templeman, delivering the advice of the Board, explained the rationale for the decision:

> The decision in *Lister & Co v Stubbs* is not consistent with the principles that a fiduciary must not be allowed to benefit from his own breach of duty, that the fiduciary should account for the bribe as soon as he receives it and that equity regards as done that which ought to be done. From these principles it would appear to follow that the bribe and the property from time to time representing the bribe are held on a constructive trust for the person injured.[279]

This rejection of *Lister & Co v Stubbs* eliminated an apparent anomaly in the law. As can be seen from *Boardman v Phipps*,[280] an 'honest' fiduciary will be held to be a constructive trustee of any unauthorized profit received if there was the mere possibility of a conflict between his interest and his duty. It seemed unacceptable that a proprietary remedy was available against an honest fiduciary but not against a 'dishonest' fiduciary who had accepted a bribe.

The exact status of the Privy Council decision in *A-G for Hong Kong v Reid* was often debated and some cases suggested that *Lister & Co v Stubbs* continued to be binding on English courts.[281] However in *Daraydan Holdings Ltd v Solland International Ltd*,[282] which concerned a defendant who had received a secret commission of £1.8m from the claimants on contracts for the luxurious refurbishment of properties in London and Qatar, Lawrence Collins J held that *A-G for Hong Kong v Reid* ought to be applied:

> The system of precedent would be shown in a most unfavourable light if a litigant in such a case were forced by the doctrine of binding precedent to go to the House of Lords in order to have the decision of the Privy Council affirmed. That would be particularly so where the decision of the Privy Council is recent, where it was a decision on the English common law, where the Board consisted mainly of serving Law Lords, and where the decision had been made after full argument on the correctness of the earlier decision.[283]

The uncertainty has been resolved by the finding in *FHR European Ventures LLP v Cedar Capital Partners LLC*[284] that all unauthorized gains made by a fiduciary in breach of fiduciary duty are held on constructive trust.

(c) Constructive trust of unauthorized profits in all circumstances

In *Sinclair Investments (UK) Ltd v Versailles Trade Finance Ltd (In Administration)*,[285] the Court of Appeal indicated that *AG for Hong Kong v Reid* was inconsistent with

---

[279] [1994] 1 All ER 1, at 9. See also *Sumitomo Bank Ltd v Kartika Rathna Thahir* (1993) 1 SLR 735.
[280] [1967] 2 AC 46, HL.
[281] *A-G v Blake* [1997] Ch 84; *Halifax Building Society v Thomas* [1996] Ch 217. See, however, *Ocular Sciences Ltd v Aspect Vision Care Ltd* [1997] RPC 289 and *Fyffes Group Ltd v Templeman* [2000] Lloyd's Rep 643, where *A-G for Hong Kong v Reid* was applied and *Hurstanger v Wilson* [2007] 1 WLR 2351.
[282] [2005] 4 All ER 73.   [283] [2005] 4 All ER 73, at [85]–[86].   [284] [2014] UKSC 45.
[285] [2011] EWCA Civ 347.

other decisions of the English courts, both in the Court of Appeal and in the House of Lords, and that it should not therefore be followed. At first instance[286] Lewison J, after an extensive review of the authorities,[287] distinguished between 'real' trusts and a secondary class of trusts, which were no more than a method of expressing a liability to account in equity.[288] In the former, proprietary remedies would be available against the trust property, in the latter the claimant was only entitled to a personal remedy. The key to distinguishing between the two concepts was whether the fiduciary concerned had assumed pre-existing fiduciary duties towards the property, in which case a proprietary remedy was available.[289] On the facts, the director had not made his unauthorized profits before the transaction complained of, so his fiduciary obligations only took place in relation to the transaction leading to his unauthorized profits, hence the principal's only connection to the profits was that they had been acquired by breach of the fiduciary obligation. It followed that only a personal remedy was available against the director, which could not be traced into proceeds of property he had purchased with these profits.

In the Court of Appeal, Lord Neuberger MR sought to clarify the law on the availability of proprietary remedies for unauthorized profits. Following similar reasoning to Lewison J, his Lordship stated that there could be no proprietary claim to unauthorized profits where there was no proprietary base on which to impose it, and the property remedy was the personal remedy to account 'unless the asset or money is or has been beneficially the property of the beneficiary or the trustee acquired the asset or money by taking advantage of an opportunity or right which was properly that of the beneficiary.'[290]

In the subsequent Court of Appeal decision, *FHR European Ventures LLP v Mankarious*,[291] Etherton C cast doubt on whether *Sinclair Investments* was correctly decided, but felt bound to follow it on the rules of precedent. The Supreme Court agreed that the *Sinclair* case was wrongly decided, and in a judgment which is a model of clarity, rejected the decision on the basis that, although the caselaw was not entirely consistent, the weight of authority favoured the view that an agent would always hold unauthorised gains on constructive trust. This view was supported both by considerations of policy (simplicity and certainty, and treating bribery harshly) and by the fact that the rule adopted by the Supreme Court was consistent with the view in other Commonwealth legal jurisdictions.[292]

---

[286] [2010] EWHC 1614 (Ch).

[287] Lewison J felt bound to follow the decision in *Lister v Stubbs* (1890) 45 Ch D 1. Lewison J was influenced in this decision by making comparison to the cases concerning the Limitation Act 1980, particularly *Gwembe Valley Development Co Ltd v Koshy (No 3)* [2003] EWCA Civ 1048—for a sharp summary of Lewison J's reasoning see Hicks 'Constructive trusts of fiduciary gain: *Lister* revived? [2011] 75 Conv 62, at 64–66.   [288] [2010] EWHC 1614 (Ch), at [80].

[289] [2010] EWHC 1614 (Ch), at [80].   [290] [2011] EWCA Civ 347, at [88].

[291] [2013] EWCA Civ 17.

[292] *FHR European Ventures LLP v Cedar Capital Partners LLC* [2014] UKSC 45.

The rule adopted by the Supreme Court explains cases like *Keech v Sandford*[293] and *Boardman v Phipps*,[294] but it also required overruling a number of inconsistent decisions, including *Sinclair*.[295]

(d) Agent not required to apply money exclusively for principal's benefit

The issue here is whether a constructive trust will arise where an agent has failed to account to his principal for money received on his behalf if he was not subject to a duty to keep the money received separate from his own, and to apply it exclusively for the benefit of his principal. In *Nelson v Rye*[296] the manager of a musician had agreed to receive all the income arising from his client's activities, and to account annually to him for the income received, less his agreed commission and expenses. Laddie J held that in these circumstances the manager was a constructive trustee of any income he had failed to pay to his client in accordance with their agreement, citing with approval an academic article authored by Sir Peter Millett.[297] Somewhat ironically, in *Paragon Finance plc v Thakerar & Co*[298] Millett LJ suggested that *Nelson v Rye* had been wrongly decided, and that the income wrongly retained could not have been held on constructive trust for the client. Millett LJ explained that, in his opinion, the nature of the agency agreement had rendered it impossible to establish a constructive trust:

> Unless I have misunderstood the facts or they were very unusual it would appear that the defendant was entitled to pay receipts into his own account, mix them with his own money, use them for his own cash flow, deduct his own commission, and account for the balance to the plaintiff only at the end of the year. It is fundamental to the existence of a trust that the trustee is bound to keep the trust property separate from his own and apply it exclusively for the benefit of the beneficiary. Any right on the part of the defendant to mix the money which he received with his own and use it for his own cash flow would be inconsistent with the existence of a trust.[299]

The reasoning in *Paragon Finance plc v Thakerar & Co*, which was followed by Jules Sher QC in *Coulthard v Disco Mix Club Ltd*, will only apply in a very narrow range of circumstances. This has been largely superseded by the developments in *Sinclair Investments* and *Mankarious*.

(e) Identifying assets subject to a constructive trust

Where a constructive trust does arise, as in most cases, a proprietary right can only subsist in respect of specific property. A principal will therefore only be able to assert his equitable ownership against assets in the hands of his fiduciary (or a third party) which he can identify as representing the profit received, or the proceeds of the profit received. Whether such identification is possible will be determined by the equitable

---

[293] (1726) Sel Cas Ch 61.   [294] [1967] 2 AC 46.
[295] The Supreme Court overruled *Tyrrell v Bank of London* (1862) 10 HL Cas 26, *Metropolitan Bank v Heiron* (1880) 5 Ex D 319 and *Lister & Co v Stubbs* (1890) 45 Ch D 1 and other cases in which these decisions were applied.   [296] [1996] 2 All ER 186.
[297] 'Bribes and Secret Commissions' [1993] RLR 7.   [298] [1999] 1 All ER 400.
[299] [1999] 1 All ER 400, at 416.

rules of tracing. In some cases it will be relatively straightforward to identify assets representing the profit received. If it is not possible to identify any traceable proceeds of the profit received, the principal will be confined to seeking a personal remedy by way of an equitable account. The rules of tracing will be examined in Chapter 30.

(3) Constructive trust or personal liability to account: critiques and criticism

It is now clear that in English law, in consequence of the decision in *FHR European Ventures LLP v Cedar Capital Partners LLC*[300] a constructive trust will normally arise whenever a fiduciary receives an unauthorized profit in breach of fiduciary duty. This confirms the position in *A-G for Hong Kong v Reid*. which similarly held that a constructive trust arose in all circumstances where a fiduciary made an authorized profit. As the Supreme Court acknowledged in *FHR*, the issue had attracted debate 'revealing "passions of a force uncommon in the legal world"'.[301]

(a) Support for the non-imposition of a constructive trust for all unauthorized profits

A-G of Hong Kong v Reid[302] was the subject of vociferous criticism.[303] The imposition of a constructive trust in *Reid* was clearly motivated by policy considerations. As Lord Templeman observed:

> Bribery is an evil practice which threatens the foundation of any civilised society. In particular, bribery of policemen and prosecutors brings the administration of justice into disrepute. Where bribes are accepted by a trustee, servant, agent or other fiduciary, loss and damage are caused to the beneficiaries, master or principal whose interests have been betrayed. The amount of loss or damage resulting from the acceptance of a bribe may or may not be quantifiable.[304]

Lord Neuberger MR in *Sinclair Investments (UK) Ltd v Versailles Trade Finance Ltd (In Administration)*[305] was unimpressed by this argument, stating:

> Why, it may be asked, should the fact that a fiduciary is able to make a profit as a result of the breach of his duties to a beneficiary, without more, give the beneficiary a proprietary interest in the profit? After all, a proprietary claim is based on property law, and it is not entirely easy to see conceptually how the property rights of the beneficiary in the misused funds should follow into the profit made on the sale of the shares.[306]

This illustrates the central criticism of the constructive trust analysis adopted in *Reid*, namely, that there is insufficient nexus between the principal and the bribe

---

[300] [2014] UKSC 45.   [301] [2014] UKSC 45, at [29] quoting Pill LJ [2014] Ch 1, at [61].
[302] [1994] 1 All ER 1.
[303] See Crilley 'A Case of Proprietary Overkill' [1994] RLR 57; Tang 'Confidence and the Constructive Trust' (2003) 23 LS 135; Penner 'The difficult doctrinal basis for the fiduciary's proprietary liability to account for bribes' (2012) 18 T&T 1000; Virgo 'Profits obtained in breach of fiduciary duty: personal or proprietary claim?' (2011) 70 CLJ 502.   [304] [1994] 1 All ER 1, at 4.
[305] [2011] EWCA Civ 347.   [306] [2011] EWCA Civ 347, at [52].

received by the fiduciary to justify the imposition of a proprietary right, irrespective of the fact that the relationship between the fiduciary and his principal justifies a personal obligation to make restitution. The imposition of liability post-*Sinclair Investments* depended, as we have seen, on a 'proprietary base' to the claims or to agency. This was supported by Professor Birks, who argued that a proprietary remedy should only be available where there was a sufficient 'proprietary base' connecting the profit and the principal.[307] Hanbury and Martin[308] argued that a constructive trust should only arise where a profit has been made by the fiduciary's use of trust property, and that in all other circumstances there should only be a personal duty to account. The need for a proprietary nexus between the profit and the principal meant that the proceeds of a bribe could not be subject to a constructive trust as the principal had no prior connection with the property constituting the bribe, and the bribe was not received by the fiduciary as a product of property belonging to the principal.[309]

Another strong argument against the imposition of a constructive trust for unauthorized profits concerns the perceived danger of unfairness to other creditors of the fiduciary if he is insolvent and assets representing the bribe received are subject to a constructive trust, thus gaining the principal priority. This danger did not in fact arise in *Reid* because he was not insolvent. Lord Templeman considered that the right of the principal should prevail over the entitlements of other general creditors:

> it is said that if the false fiduciary holds property representing the bribe in trust for the person injured, and if the false fiduciary is or becomes insolvent, the unsecured creditors of the false fiduciary will be deprived of their right to share in the proceeds of that property. But the unsecured creditors cannot be in a better position than their debtor. The authorities show that property acquired by a trustee innocently but in breach of trust and the property from time to time representing the same belong in equity to the cestui que trust and not to the trustee personally, whether he is solvent or insolvent. Property acquired by a trustee as a result of a criminal breach of trust and the property from time to time representing the same must also belong in equity to the cestui que trust and not to the trustee whether he is solvent or insolvent.

(b) Arguments supporting the imposition of a constructive trust wherever an unauthorized profit is made

It is somewhat ironic that *Lister & Co v Stubbs*,[310] which was approved in *Sinclair Investments (UK) Ltd v Versailles Trade Finance Ltd (In Administration)*,[311] had itself been subjected to strong criticism, as we have seen. It was, for example, argued that it was unacceptable that an honest fiduciary might hold an unauthorized profit on constructive trust, such as Boardman in *Boardman v Phipps*, but a blatantly dishonest

---

[307] *An Introduction to the Law of Restitution* (1985), pp 378–393.
[308] *Modern Equity* (14th edn, 1993), p 598. See now (18th edn, 2009), pp 656–659.
[309] See also Tang 'Confidence and the Constructive Trust' (2003) 23 LS 135.
[310] (1890) 45 Ch D 1.   [311] [2011] EWCA Civ 347.

fiduciary who had accepted a bribe or secret commission would not. The remedy if it was harsh in one, should be harsh in the other, as the limits of the fiduciary concept itself were breached.[312]

The imposition of a constructive trust in all cases of unauthorized profits also sends a clear policy message, that fiduciary duties are not to be taken lightly. Lawrence Collins J was strongly of this opinion in *Daraydan Holdings Ltd v Solland International Ltd*:

> There are powerful policy reasons for ensuring that a fiduciary does not retain gains acquired in violation of fiduciary duty, and I do not consider that it should make any difference whether the fiduciary is insolvent. There is no injustice to the creditors in their not sharing in an asset for which the fiduciary has not given value, and which the fiduciary should not have had.[313]

The alleged 'special treatment' that the finding of a constructive trust in all circumstances for unauthorized profits gives over other unsecured creditors, is, as Hayton argues, part of the integrity of the fiduciary concept, and the approach in *Sinclair Investments* was in danger of undermining it.[314] This may feel uncomfortable in commercial settings, where parties are used to dealing at arm's length, but there is a difference between duties that are fiduciary in character and are protected by equity, and those which the parties impose on themselves by negotiation. Perhaps the concerns of the commercial world could be addressed if the extension of the concept of 'fiduciary relationship' into commercial relationships was addressed, rather than complaining when the horse has already bolted the stable and that the remedies imposed by that special, protected status are too draconian in character.[315] It may be that the solution proposed in *Sinclair Investments* to the baggage associated with the imposition of constructive trust liability for unauthorized profits by a fiduciary addressed the wrong side of the debate; the law should not seek to control the impact of the fiduciary status but instead address itself more clearly as to when such a status arises.

Perhaps most damning of all is the assertion of Etherton C in *Mankarious*, effectively endorsed by the Supreme Court, that the categorization of the imposition of a constructive trust following *Sinclair Investments* is fact dependent, rather than dependent on clear, bright line principles of law.[316]

---

[312] See Hayton 'No Proprietary Liability for Bribes and other Secret Profits?' (2011) TLI 1; Hayton 'Proprietary Liability for Secret Profits' (2011) 127 LQR 487; Millett 'Bribes and Secret Commissions Again' (2012) CLJ 583.

[313] [2004] EWHC 622, at [86]. See also Goff and Jones, *The Law of Restitution* (6th edn, 2002), who argue at p 739 that *A-G for Hong Kong v Reid* should be followed.

[314] Hayton 'No Proprietary Liability for Bribes and other Secret Profits?' (2011) TLI 1.

[315] See *Customer Systems Plc v Ranson* [2012] EWCA Civ 841, where the Court of Appeal drew a distinction between a fiduciary duty of loyalty owed to the company and an employee's duty of fidelity to carry out employment. Employees were not necessarily fiduciaries, and whether they had such obligations would depend upon the interpretation of their contract of employment in the first instance.

[316] See Hedlund 'Secret commissions and constructive trusts: yet again!' (2013) JBL 747.

(4) **Conclusion**

It is clear that the debate over the correctness of the current position in English law will run and run, and it is difficult to consider which is the 'correct' side. Both the approach in *Reid*, now definitively endorsed in *FHR European Ventures LLP v Cedar Capital Partners LLC*, and the approach in *Sinclair Investments*, have their merits. It is, however, worth noting that if the position of the Privy Council in *Reid* had not been followed, English law would have set itself against the position in many other parts of the common law world.[317] This is not unique, as we have seen in relation to the English position on remedial constructive trusts in Chapter 9. Despite criticism and alternatives, it must now be taken as settled that a fiduciary who receives an unauthorized profit will hold it on constructive trust for his principal whenever the profit is sufficiently identifiable to be the subject of a proprietary claim. There will also be a personal liability to account which can be pursued as an alternative, or which will be available for breach of fiduciary duty if a proprietary claim is not possible (for instance where the assets subject to a proprietary claim have been dissipated).

7 Defences to an action for breach of fiduciary duty

(1) **Conduct authorized by principal**

A fiduciary is not subject to an absolute duty of self-denial preventing him from retaining any benefits for himself. He will only be required to make restitution of unauthorized profits that were obtained without the consent or acquiescence of his principal. He will only be entitled to rely on such consent or acquiescence if he made full disclosure of the course he intended to pursue. In *Boardman v Phipps*[318] the House of Lords accepted that if Boardman had acted with the consent of the trustees and beneficiaries he would not have been in breach of fiduciary duty and would not therefore have been liable to account for the profits he had received.[319] However, he had failed to obtain the consent of one of the trustees,[320] and had not sought the approval of the plaintiff beneficiary. By contrast, in *Queensland Mines Ltd v Hudson*[321] a company director who had taken up an opportunity initially offered to the company was not held liable to account for his profits because he had acted after full disclosure to the other directors.

(2) **Limitation**

The defence of limitation in regard to an action for compensation for breach of trust was examined in the previous chapter. It has proved more difficult to apply the

---

[317] See, for example, *ICBC v Lo* 278 DLR (4th) 148, *Grimaldi v Chameleon Mining NL (No 2)* [2012] FCAFC 6.   [318] [1967] 2 AC 46.

[319] [1967] 2 AC 46, at 93, per Viscount Dilhorne.

[320] Who was, incidentally, suffering from senile dementia.

[321] (1978) 18 ALR 1; Sullivan 'Going it Alone—*Queensland Mines v Hudson*' (1979) 42 MLR 711.

provisions of the Limitation Act 1980 to actions against fiduciaries who have received an unauthorized profit, because the legislation does not make any express provision for such claims. Instead, provisions designed primarily with express trusts in mind have had to be interpreted so as to provide a limitation period for actions for breach of fiduciary duty and the concomitant constructive trusts of unauthorized profits which arise from them. The relevant principles have been considered and clarified by a number of decisions.[322]

The major turning point came in *Gwembe Valley Development Company Ltd v Koshy*, where Mummery LJ confirmed that all actions are subject to a six-year limitation period unless there is express provision to the contrary:

> [I]t is possible to simplify the court's task when considering the application of the 1980 Act to claims against fiduciaries. The starting assumption should be that a six-year limitation period will apply—under one or other provision of the Act, applied directly or by analogy—unless it is specifically excluded by the Act or established case-law. Personal claims against fiduciaries will normally be subject to limits by analogy with claims in tort or contract...By contrast, claims for breach of fiduciary duty, in the special sense explained in Mothew, will normally be covered by section 21. The six-year time limit under section 21(3) will apply, directly or by analogy, unless excluded by subsection 21(1)(a) (fraud) or (b).[323]

The case concerned a company director who had received undisclosed profits from a contract with the company. The court held that his position meant that he had had 'trustee-like responsibilities' in the exercise of his powers of management of the property of the company and in dealing with the application of its property, and that therefore the claim for an account was within the scope of s 21. Since he had acted dishonestly in breaching his fiduciary duty, s 21(1)(a) applied to exclude the six-year limitation period and he was not entitled to any defence of limitation. This has been followed in two decisions at first instance, and must now be considered to represent the position of the law.[324]

The equitable doctrine of laches will be available where a claim to an account is not subject to a statutory limitation period, in which case it may protect a fiduciary from unduly delayed proceedings if it would be inequitable to allow them to proceed, for example because he would suffer substantial prejudice or detriment. However, there is debate as to whether the defence of laches will be available where s 21(1) of the Limitation Act 1980 applies. In *Gwembe Valley Development Co Ltd v Koshy* the Court of Appeal held that the defence of laches was not available as a defence to the action for dishonest breach of fiduciary duty, as the defence of laches was not available where

---

[322] *Bristol and West Building Society v Mothew* [1998] Ch 1; *Paragon Finance plc v DB Thackerar* [1999] 1 All ER 400; *Cia De Seguros Imperio v Heath (REBX) Ltd* [2001] 1 WLR 112; *JJ Harrison (Properties) Ltd v Harrison* [2002] BCLC 162; *Gwembe Valley Development Company Ltd (In Receivership) v Koshy* [2003] EWCA Civ 1048; *Re Loftus* [2007] 1 WLR 591; *Seaton v Seddon* [2012] EWHC 735 (Ch); *Page v Hewitts Solicitors* [2013] EWHC 2845 (Ch).

[323] [2003] EWCA Civ 1048, at [111].

[324] *Seaton v Seddon* [2012] EWHC 735 (Ch); *Page v Hewetts Solicitors* [2013] EWHC 2845 (Ch).

s 21(1) applies.[325] This has since been doubted in *Re Loftus*,[326] where it was suggested that the equitable doctrine was not excluded under cases coming within s 21(1) of the Limitation Act 1980. Chadwick LJ, on reprising earlier authorities, concluded:

> If the court were saying, in the *Gwembe Valley* case, that there is no scope for a defence of laches or acquiescence in a case where the 1980 Act prescribes no period of limitation, I would respectfully disagree; although, of course, if that proposition were binding upon me I would have no choice but to apply it. But the court did not say that in terms; and, because I think the proposition obviously wrong, I am not persuaded that the court intended to be understood as endorsing it.[327]

It would appear that Chadwick LJ's position is the better view. The operation of the doctrine of laches was examined in detail in the previous chapter in the context of actions for breach of trust.

[325] [2003] EWCA Civ 1048, at [140].   [326] [2007] 1 WLR 591, at [41], per Chadwick LJ.
[327] [2007] 1 WLR 591, at [40].

29

Remedies against strangers to the trust

In some circumstances beneficiaries will be able to bring claims not only against the trustees, but also against third parties who have assisted in the breach of a trust, who have received trust property in breach of trust, or who have assumed the mantle of trusteeship by acting as a trustee in relation to the trust property. This is a complex and challenging area. Such problems occur because of the highly complex factual situations in which an action against a third party may be sought, and the difficulty of defining an appropriate legal test for liability so as to balance the rights of beneficiaries and third parties.

This chapter seeks to explain the nature of the remedies against third parties in context, demonstrating how they fit with remedies against the trustees explored in previous chapters and the proprietary process of tracing (explored in Chapter 30). The practical and legal difficulties of finding an assistant or a recipient liable to the beneficiaries of a trust will be explored separately to enhance understanding. This chapter ends by suggesting a structure to help navigate through the difficult issues presented by application of the equitable principles.

1 Introduction

This is an area that causes considerable difficulties in practice and for students. Third parties are liable, not because they are trustees of the trust, but because they have come into contact with the trust property, either through dealing with it or receiving it outright, or because they have been instrumental in contributing to a loss suffered by the trust. The factual circumstances are often highly complex instances of commercial fraud. The concepts of liability can be complex, and are not aided by a lack of clarity and confusion over the tests to be applied in the case law, or, more accurately, how the tests should be applied to any given set of facts.

(1) Relationship to remedies against trustees

The previous two chapters have examined the remedies that beneficiaries may pursue against a trustee who acts in breach of trust, or in breach of his fiduciary duty.

However, if a trustee commits a breach of trust which involves a third party who was a stranger to the trust, either as a participant in the breach or as the recipient of trust property transferred to him in breach of trust, the beneficiaries of the trust may be entitled to pursue remedies against the stranger. The third party is termed a 'stranger to the trust' because he was not a trustee and therefore was not subject to any obligations prior to his involvement in the breach. It includes those parties who have normal business transactions with trusts, such as banks, and accountants.

Remedies against third parties may prove more attractive to the beneficiaries than their remedies against the trustee in breach. The availability of remedies against a stranger to the trust will be especially important if the trustee is insolvent, thus rendering direct remedies against him ineffective. While a stranger to a trust may be liable at common law in tort, for example if he provides the trustee with negligent advice,[1] beneficiaries may enjoy equitable remedies against a stranger who has wrongfully received trust property or wrongfully involved himself in the administration of the trust.

(2) Personal and proprietary remedies against strangers to the trust

Where a stranger is liable in equity to the beneficiaries of a trust, the beneficiaries may enjoy either personal or proprietary remedies. It is important to distinguish between them, as proprietary remedies relate to the property itself in the hands of the stranger and cannot survive the dissipation of the property, whereas personal remedies are against the stranger personally for their participation in receiving trust property or becoming involved in the administration of the trust (see Figure 29.1).

(a) Proprietary remedies

It is a basic axiom of the law of property that a third party who receives property subject to a subsisting equitable interest cannot take free from that interest unless he is a bona fide purchaser for value without prior notice of the interest. Since the beneficiaries of a trust enjoy the equitable ownership of the trust property, it follows that, if the trustee transfers trust property to a stranger in breach of trust, the stranger will acquire the legal title subject to the beneficiaries' equitable pre-existing interests, unless he was a bona fide purchaser for value without notice thereof.[2] The beneficiaries' equitable interests in the trust property will be preserved and they will be able to claim the property in the stranger's hands as their own in equity. If the stranger has subsequently dealt with the trust property he received, for example by exchanging it for different property or mixing it with other property (whether his own or also

---

[1] See *Royal Brunei Airlines v Tan* [1995] 3 All ER 97, at 108.
[2] In the context of the equitable doctrine of notice, 'valuable consideration' means money or money's worth, and includes marriage consideration. The consideration need not be adequate and may be nominal. See *Midland Bank Trust Co Ltd v Green* [1981] AC 513, HL, where sale of land at a gross undervalue nevertheless would have been valuable consideration.

(i) The personal duty to account

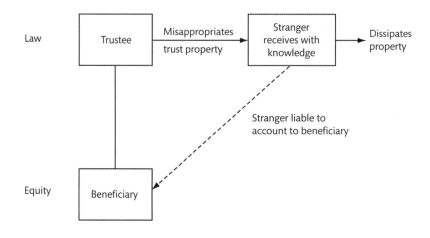

(ii) Holding the property on constructive trust

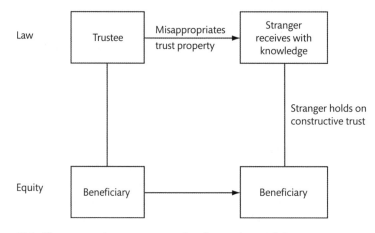

Figure 29.1 The contrast between personal and proprietary claims

belonging to a third party), the beneficiaries will be entitled to assert their equitable interest against any assets in his hands which can be shown to represent the trust property originally received. Equity has developed a complex set of rules to enable it to determine whether any such property can be identified in the hands of the stranger, known as the rules of tracing. An example can be provided here. In *Re Diplock*[3] the executors of Caleb Diplock had wrongfully distributed his residuary estate among

---

[3] [1948] Ch 465, CA.

various charities.[4] Since the charities were innocent volunteers, who had not provided valuable consideration, they received the money subject to the pre-existing equitable interests of the beneficiaries to whom it should have been allocated. His next of kin were therefore able to claim from the charities any assets that could be shown to represent the trust property by the rules of tracing.

If the stranger who receives trust property in breach of trust has disposed of it, so that no assets remain in his hands that can be said to represent the trust property, the property is said to have been dissipated. Once the trust property has been dissipated it is no longer possible for the beneficiaries to maintain any proprietary claim against the stranger who had received it. However, the stranger may still be subject to a personal liability to make restitution of the value of the property he had received in breach of trust.

(b) Personal remedies

Where a stranger has participated in the commission of a breach of trust, but has not received any trust property into his hands, it will not be possible for the beneficiaries to seek a proprietary remedy against him. Similarly, if a stranger did receive trust property, but it has been dissipated so that no traceable proceeds remain in his hands, the beneficiaries cannot enjoy any proprietary remedy. They will be confined to a personal action for restitution. If the stranger has only partially dissipated the trust property he received, or it is traceable into assets that have fallen in value, a personal action may also be preferred, as the stranger will be liable to restore the value of the trust property. The personal liability of the stranger who has assisted in the commission of a breach of trust or who has received trust property is by way of an equitable action of account. He is often said to be 'liable to account as a constructive trustee'. In effect, the stranger is held liable to account to the trust just as if he had been a properly appointed trustee, even though in fact he was not. In *Polly Peck International plc v Nadir (Asil) (No 2)*[5] Scott LJ described this remedy as 'the *in personam* constructive trust claim'. The personal nature of the claim can also be seen from cases such as *Re Montagu*[6] and *Lipkin Gorman v Karpnale Ltd*,[7] which are considered later in the chapter. The equitable liability to account as a constructive trustee is essentially fault-based, so that a stranger will only be required to account if he acted with the requisite degree of fault.

(3) Circumstances in which a stranger will be liable as a constructive trustee

The circumstances in which a stranger may be held liable as a 'constructive trustee' were identified by Lord Selbourne LC in *Barnes v Addy*:

---

[4] The executors acted under the mistaken belief that their power under the will to distribute the residuary estate amongst 'such charitable institutions or other charitable or benevolent object or objects in England' was valid. The court held that it was void, as it was not exclusively charitable.

[5] [1992] 4 All ER 769, at 781.   [6] [1987] Ch 264; [1992] 4 All ER 308.

[7] [1992] 4 All ER 331; [1987] 1 WLR 987.

those who create a trust clothe the trustee with a legal power and control over the trust property, imposing on him a corresponding responsibility. That responsibility may no doubt be extended in equity to others who are not properly trustees, if they are found either making themselves trustees de son tort, or actually participating in any fraudulent conduct of the trustee to the injury of the [beneficiary]. But, on the other hand, strangers are not to be made constructive trustees merely because they act as agents of trustees in transactions within their legal powers, transactions, perhaps of which the Court of Equity may disapprove, unless those agents receive and become chargeable with some part of the trust property, or unless they assist with knowledge in a dishonest and fraudulent design on the part of the trustees...[8]

More modern terminology is now used to describe the three circumstances in which a stranger will be held liable.

(a) Trustee de son tort

Where a stranger who had not been appointed as a trustee takes it upon himself to act as a trustee, and deals with the trust property accordingly, he will be held liable for any breach of trust that was committed just as if he were in fact a properly appointed trustee.

(b) Dishonest assistance in a breach of trust

Where a stranger dishonestly participates in a breach of trust committed by the trustees he will be liable to account personally as a constructive trustee for any loss suffered by the trust.

(c) Knowing receipt of trust property

Where a stranger receives trust property, knowing that it is trust property, he will be liable to account as a constructive trustee to the trust for the value of the property received.

(4) Implications of making a stranger to a trust liable

Lord Selbourne LC, in outlining the situations when a stranger would be liable as a constructive trustee in *Barnes v Addy*,[9] was principally concerned to stress the practical importance of setting limits to the scope of the remedies. The category of strangers is so wide that it would be inappropriate to impose liability without some element of fault on the stranger's part. Solicitors or bankers may temporarily be in possession of trust property as part of the normal process of trust management and delegation, but this does not necessarily mean that if their conduct is inconsistent with the terms of the trust they should be liable as constructive trustees, as where they honestly follow instructions from the trustees. Similarly, commercial companies may come into contact with trustees and trust funds as part of everyday commerce. They may make attractive defendants to beneficiaries in a breach of trust action, as they have deep pockets from

---

[8] (1874) 9 Ch App 244, at 251–252.   [9] (1874) 9 Ch App 244.

which to meet a personal liability to account as a constructive trustee. If all of these parties were liable for breaches of trust irrespective of knowledge or fault, they would be over-exposed to liability, which could deter them from dealing with trust funds and inhibit the normal operations of trade or business. The protection of beneficiaries needs to be balanced by safeguards that do not hinder ordinary business transactions.

(5) **The nomenclature of personal remedies**

While the liability of a stranger to a trust has historically been termed 'liability to account as a constructive trustee' the language of constructive trusteeship has been subjected to criticism on the grounds of artificiality. In *Paragon Finance plc v Thakerar & Co*, Millett LJ considered that it had been unfortunate that such liability was described in this way:

> In such a case the expressions 'constructive trust' and 'constructive trustee' are mis-leading, for there is no trust and usually no possibility of a proprietary remedy; they are 'nothing more than a formula for equitable relief': *Selangor United Rubber Estates Ltd v Craddock (No 3)*[10] per Ungoed Thomas J.[11]

While this is certainly true in respect of the liability of a stranger who has dishonestly assisted in a breach of trust, it is questionable whether the criticism applies equally forcefully to the liability of strangers who have dealt with the trust property as a trustee de son tort, or who have knowingly received and misapplied trust property. In such cases the stranger is liable to account because of his conscious misdealing with the trust property. It is not artificial to regard him as a 'constructive trustee', and the language of constructive trusteeship is not operating as a mere formula for equitable relief.[12] Nevertheless, caution needs to be exercised when encountering the phrase 'constructive trustee'. In *Dubai Aluminium Co Ltd v Salaam*[13] Lord Millett suggested that the terminology 'accountable in equity' should replace the terminology 'accountable as a constructive trustee'.[14] This has not been adopted in subsequent decisions. It is to be remembered, whatever the phrasing, that the remedy is a personal liability to account by the stranger.[15] It is also important to note what type of constructive trust the court is employing. The matter came before the Supreme Court in *Williams v Central Bank of Nigeria*,[16] under the guise of which limitation period applied to trustees de son tort, dishonest assistors, and those in knowing receipt of trust property. A trustee de son tort, as someone whose trust relationship arose prior to a breach through a voluntary assumption of responsibilities (a Category 1[17] constructive trust) was very different to

---

[10] [1999] 1 All ER 400, at 409.   [11] [1968] 2 All ER 1073, at 1097.
[12] See Martin 'Recipient Liability after *Westdeutsche*' [1998] Conv 13.   [13] [2003] 2 AC 366.
[14] [2003] 2 AC 366, at 404 [142].
[15] The liability to account was discussed in relation to receipt of unauthorized profits by a fiduciary in Chapter 28. It is now clear that such an authorized profit gives rise instead to a constructive trust.
[16] [2014] UKSC 10.
[17] This distinction was first stated by Millett LJ in in *Paragon Finance plc v DB Thackerar & Co* [1999] 1 All ER 400.

knowing receipt of trust property or dishonest assistance in breach of trust. In those cases, the constructive trust arose as a direct consequence of an unlawful transaction (a Category 2 constructive trust). Hence, a trustee de son tort was subject to the same limitation period as an express trust, but for the other two categories, the normal six-year limitation period applies.

(6) **A multiplicity of remedies**

One of the difficulties in approaching stranger liability is placing the actions in context with the other remedies available to beneficiaries where there has been a breach of trust and trust property has been misapplied. The key to understanding is to recognize that this is not an action against the trustee for their breach of trust in dealing with the trust property improperly, but an action which seeks to make a person liable who is not the trustee, but who nonetheless has come into contact with and misapplied the trust property. Similarly, beneficiaries may have an action against the trust property itself, to have the property or its substitute value returned. This involves the process of tracing the property into the hands of someone other than the trustee. Any remedy as a result of the tracing process is directed against the property itself, rather than the person who currently holds it. This might be useful where the property is of unique value, such as an original Picasso painting or a bespoke Vivienne Westwood smock, so that a remedy against either the trustee for breach of trust or against a stranger would not provide adequate compensation.

2 Stranger who takes it upon himself to act as a trustee

(1) **Definition**

A person who has not been appointed a trustee but intermeddles in the administration of a trust by taking it upon himself to act as if he were a trustee, will be held liable as if he were in fact a properly appointed trustee. He is known as a trustee de son tort. The principle was explained by Smith LJ in *Mara v Browne*:

> if one, not being a trustee and not having authority from a trustee, takes upon himself to intermeddle with trust matters or to do acts characteristic of the office of trustee, he may thereby make himself what is called in law a trustee of his own wrong—i.e. a trustee de son tort, or, as it is also termed a constructive trustee.[18]

The same essential characteristics were identified by Ungoed-Thomas J in the later case of *Selangor United Rubber Estates Ltd v Cradock (No 3)*:

> Those who, though not appointed trustees, take on themselves to act as such and to possess and administer trust property for the beneficiaries, become trustees de son tort.

---

[18] [1896] 1 Ch 199, at 209.

Distinguishing features...are (a) they do not claim to act in their own right but for the beneficiaries, and (b) their assumption to act is not itself a ground of liability...and so their status as trustees precedes the occurrence which may be the subject of a claim against them.[19]

The principle that an intermeddling stranger may become a trustee de son tort is an application to the law of trusts of the principle that anyone who takes it upon himself to act in a fiduciary capacity will be treated and held accountable as if he in fact held the fiduciary position he assumed. Thus, a person who takes it upon himself to act as an agent for another will be held liable to account to his principal just as if he had been properly appointed.[20] The principle was applied in *Blyth v Fladgate*,[21] where a firm of solicitors, Fladgates, held Exchequer bills that were assets of a marriage settlement. After all three trustees of the settlement had died, the moneys were advanced by the firm on a mortgage at the instigation of the husband. The securities proved to be insufficient and it was held that the partners of the firm were liable to make good the shortfall. The rationale for this was that when the Exchequer bills were sold, the firm (meaning each and every partner) became a constructive trustee of the money. They could not possibly be seen as acting as the agents of the trustees[22] because at that stage there were no trustees. By their actions they had assumed upon themselves the position of trustees and it was their duty to see that the moneys were properly applied. They were therefore liable.[23]

One limitation to the principle seems to be that a person will only be held liable as a trustee de son tort if he had the trust property vested in him or had the right to call for its transfer. This was made clear in *Re Barney*,[24] where Kekewich J held that it was essential to the character of a trustee that 'he should have trust property actually vested in him, or so far under his control that he has nothing to do but require that...it should be vested in him', and that 'if that is true of a trustee properly appointed, why is it not also true of a trustee de son tort'.[25] However, it should be noted that he may be using the concept of a trustee de son tort in the wider sense of a constructive trustee, rather than the more limited modern usage of an intermeddling stranger.

---

[19] [1968] 2 All ER 1073, at 1095.

[20] See *Lyell v Kennedy* (1889) 14 App Cas 437, HL; *English v Dedham Vale Properties Ltd* [1978] 1 WLR 93.

[21] [1891] 1 Ch 337.

[22] A person who receives and deals with trust property as an agent of the trustees will not be held liable as a trustee de son tort when he deals with the property. In *Williams-Ashman v Price and Williams* [1942] Ch 219, Bennett J held that *Mara v Browne* [1896] 1 Ch 199, CA, was authority that 'an agent in possession of money which he knows to be trust money, so long as he acts honestly, is not accountable to the beneficiaries interested in the trust money unless he intermeddles in the trust by doing acts characteristic of a trustee and outside the duties of an agent'. Any liability will be governed by the principles concerning delegation: see Chapter 23.

[23] Following the explanation of the case by Vinelott J in *Re Bell's Indenture* [1980] 3 All ER 425, at 433–435.   [24] [1892] 2 Ch 265.

[25] [1892] 2 Ch 265, at 272–273.

(2) **Remedies**

In *Soar v Ashwell* Lord Esher MR took the view that an intermeddling stranger must be treated, and therefore held liable, as if he were a properly appointed trustee:

> Where a person has assumed, either with or without consent, to act as a trustee of money or other property...a Court of Equity will impose upon him all the liabilities of an express trustee...[26]

The prime liability of the express trustee is not to act in breach of trust, and the trustee de son tort will likewise be held personally liable to account for any such breach. In particular, if he has wrongfully transferred or dissipated trust property he will have to account for it to the trust. As already illustrated in *Blyth v Fladgate*,[27] the partners of a firm of solicitors who had become trustees de son tort were held liable to the trust for the loss caused by an investment in a mortgage. If the trustee de son tort has trust property, or property which can be shown to represent the original trust property, in his hands the trust will be able to claim that property as its own. This will be particularly important if the trustee de son tort is insolvent.

3 **Strangers who assist a breach of trust**

(1) **Definition**

Where a trustee commits a breach of trust he will be personally liable to compensate the trust for any loss suffered in consequence of his breach.[28] His liability is a primary liability, as he was subject to the trust obligations. However, equity will also hold liable a stranger who participates in a breach of trust by assisting a trustee in action that constitutes a breach. The liability of such an assisting stranger is a secondary liability. The stranger is liable as an accessory to the breach of trust. Such accessory liability may provide the only effective remedy for the beneficiaries if the trustee is insolvent. Equity will hold a stranger who assisted a breach of trust liable to account as a constructive trustee. This was recognized in *Barnes v Addy*,[29] where Lord Selbourne stated that the responsibilities and liabilities of a trustee may be 'extended to those who are not properly trustees, if they are found...actually participating in any fraudulent conduct of the trustees to the injury of the [beneficiary] trust'. The rationale for the imposition of accessory liability against strangers to a trust was examined by the Privy Council in *Royal Brunei Airlines Sdn Bhd v Tan*,[30] where Lord Nicholls stated:

---

[26] [1893] 2 QB 390, at 394.   [27] [1891] 1 Ch 337.

[28] See (1996) 112 LQR 56 (Gardner); A J Oakley, 'The Liberalising Nature of Remedies for Breach of Trust' in Oakley, *Trends in Contemporary Trust Law* (1996), pp 239–247; Elliott and Mitchell 'Remedies for Dishonest Assistance' (2004) 67 MLR 16.   [29] (1874) 9 Ch App 244, at 251–252.

[30] [1995] 2 AC 378; [1995] 3 All ER 97; (1995) 111 LQR 545 (Harpum); [1995] Conv 339 (Halliwell); (1995) 54 CLJ 505 (Nolan); [1995] RLR 105 (Stevens); [1996] LMCLQ 1 (Birks); (1996) 112 LQR 56 (Gardner); (1997) 60 MLR 443 (Berg).

Beneficiaries are entitled to expect that those who become trustees will fulfil their obligations. They are also entitled to expect, and this is only a short step further, that those who
become trustees will be permitted to fulfil their obligations without deliberate intervention from third parties. They are entitled to expect that third parties will refrain from
intentionally intruding in the trustee–beneficiary relationship and thereby hindering
a beneficiary from receiving his entitlement in accordance with the terms of the trust
instrument. There is here a close analogy with breach of contract. A person who knowingly procures a breach of contract, or knowingly interferes with the due performance of
a contract, is liable to the innocent party. The underlying rationale [of accessory liability]
is the same.[31]

The accessory liability may prove particularly important if a misappropriation of
trust property was perpetrated by a trustee in breach of trust and a financial institution, such as a bank, was involved in the transaction. For example in *Lipkin Gorman v
Karpnale Ltd*[32] Cass, a partner in a firm of solicitors, had used money from the firm's
client account to finance his gambling habit. As well as seeking a remedy against the
club in which the money had been spent, the firm claimed that the bank at which the
client account was held was liable as an accessory to the partner's breach of trust. The
manager of the bank, which also held Cass's personal account, had been aware that
Cass had been cashing cheques at the casino and had warned him that his gambling
was not controlled. At first instance it was held that the bank had sufficient knowledge
of Cass's misuse of funds to render them liable to account for the money that had been
misappropriated. The claim against the bank was, however, subsequently dismissed
by the Court of Appeal[33] on the grounds that the bank had not been sufficiently aware
that a breach of trust was being committed. Thus, there is a clear element of fault
required on the part of the third party before constructive trusteeship is imposed, and
it is in determining the degree of fault required that most of the difficulties have arisen
in the case law.

(2) **A personal remedy**

A stranger who acts as an accessory to a breach of trust will generally only be subject
to a personal liability to account to the trust for the loss suffered in consequence of the
breach. Ordinarily he will not have received any trust property, and consequently the
beneficiaries will be unable to identify any assets in his hands that could be the subject
of a proprietary claim.[34] As has been noted earlier, it is highly artificial to describe
the liability of a stranger who has assisted a breach of trust as 'liability to account as a

---

[31] [1995] 3 All ER 97, at 103–104.   [32] [1992] 4 All ER 331; [1987] 1 WLR 987.
[33] [1992] 4 All ER 409: on the grounds that the bank could not be liable to account as a constructive trustee unless it was also liable for breach of contract to its customer and that there had been wholly inadequate
material on which to base a finding of fraud or dishonesty on the part of the bank manager.
[34] However, many of the cases concern banks or other financial organizations where the trust property has passed through their hands. See *Baden Delvaux and Lecuit v Société Générale pour Favoriser le
Développement du Commerce et de l'Industrie en France SA* [1983] BCLC 325; *Lipkin Gorman v Karpnale
Ltd* [1987] 1 WLR 987; *Agip (Africa) Ltd v Jackson* [1990] Ch 265.

constructive trustee'. Nor can his liability be characterized as genuinely restitutionary. Since he did not receive any trust property he was not enriched at the expense of the beneficiaries by his assistance. By definition, restitution is only available to reverse an unjust enrichment. This was recognized by the Privy Council in *Royal Brunei Airlines Sdn Bhd v Tan*:

> Liability as an accessory is not dependent upon receipt of trust property, It arises even though no trust property has reached the hands of the accessory. It is a form of secondary liability in the sense that it only arises where there has been a breach of trust.[35]

The extent of liability of the accessory is considered to be joint and several with that of the trustee for any loss caused to the trust.[36] However, where a profit has arisen from the breach, the stranger is only liable for his own share of the profit, not that of the trustee.[37]

(3) Requirements of accessory liability

A stranger will only be held liable as an accessory to a breach of trust if four requirements are satisfied. These requirements were identified by Peter Gibson J in *Baden Delvaux v Société Générale*[38] and subjected to significant revision by the Privy Council in *Royal Brunei Airlines Sdn Bhd v Tan*.

(a) The existence of a trust

A stranger can only be held liable as an accessory to a breach of trust if there was in fact a trust in existence. This requirement is generally uncontroversial, although some cases have extended the principle to other fiduciary relationships. *Royal Brunei Airlines v Tan* is a case involving a trust. The plaintiffs were an airline that employed a firm to act as their agents for the sale of tickets. Under the contract between the parties, the firm agreed to hold any money received from the sale of tickets on trust for the airline until it was paid over. The defendant was the founder and principal shareholder of the firm. In breach of the terms of the contract the firm, authorized by the defendant, used money received from ticket sales for its own purposes. On the insolvency of the firm the airline claimed that the defendant was liable to account as an accessory to the breach of trust that had been committed by the firm. In these circumstances there was clearly an express trust, thus opening the possibility of accessory liability. Cases which have extended accessory liability to other fiduciary relationships include *Selangor United Rubber Estates v Craddock (No 3)*.[39] The directors of the company were treated as having sufficient control of the company's property for an action as an

---

[35] [1995] 3 All ER 97, at 99–100. This is considered further later in the chapter under knowing receipt.
[36] *Ultraframe (UK) Ltd v Fielding* [2007] WTLR 835; *Novoship (UK) Ltd v Mikhaylyuk* [2012] EWHC 3586, at [98], per Christopher Clarke J.
[37] See Ridge 'Justifying the Remedies for Dishonest Assistance' (2008) 124 LQR 445.
[38] *Baden, Delvaux and Lecuit v Société Générale pour Favoriser le Développement du Commerce et de l'Industrie en France SA* [1983] BCLC 325.
[39] [1968] 2 All ER 1073; see also *FHR European Ventures LLP v Cedar Capital Partners LLC* [2014] UKSC 45 (secret profits of a fiduciary).

accessory to be run against them. There may even be no need for there to be property. In *JD Wetherspoon Plc v Van de Berg & Co Ltd*[40] an action was brought in respect of allegations of breach of fiduciary duty by a company engaged to find new pubs for the Wetherspoon chain. The claims included allegations of accessory liability. Peter Smith J stated:[41]

> In my view in a case for accessory liability there is no requirement for there to be trust property. Such a requirement wrongly associates accessory liability with trust concepts... Accessory liability does not involve a trust. It involves providing dishonest assistance to somebody else who in a fiduciary capacity has committed a breach of his fiduciary duties.

In the event that he was wrong about this point, he was willing to find that confidential information could be treated as property for the purpose of the claim.

(b) A breach of trust

A stranger will almost certainly[42] only be liable as an accessory if a breach of trust was committed by a trustee or the fiduciary has broken his fiduciary duties. In *Baden Delvaux v Société Générale*,[43] Peter Gibson J had held that a stranger would only be liable if the trustee had assisted in a dishonest and fraudulent design of the trustees.[44] In *Royal Brunei Airlines v Tan*[45] the defendant therefore claimed that he should not be liable as an accessory because the firm, which had misused money held on trust, had not acted fraudulently or dishonestly.[46] A trustee may commit a breach of trust innocently or negligently. The Privy Council rejected the defendant's argument and held that there was no need to demonstrate that the trustee had acted dishonestly or fraudulently.[47] All that was required was a breach of trust, irrespective of whether it had been committed honestly or dishonestly. A stranger will therefore be liable as an accessory if he acted with a sufficient degree of personal fault, irrespective of the degree of fault of the trustee in breach:

> what matters is the state of mind of the third party sought to be made liable, not the state of mind of the trustee. The trustee will be liable in any event for the breach of trust, even if he acted innocently, unless excused by an exemption clause in the trust instrument or

---

[40] [2009] EWHC 639.   [41] [2009] EWHC 639, at 518.

[42] The cases so far indicate that there must be a breach of trust but, by analogy with the tort of interference with contract, there is no reason why a dishonest assistor could not be liable even if a trustee is protected by a valid trust provision excluding liability.

[43] *Baden, Delvaux and Lecuit v Société Générale pour Favoriser le* Développement *du Commerce et de l'Industrie en France SA* [1983] BCLC 325.

[44] This position was also supported in *Barnes v Addy* (1874) 9 Ch App 244 and *Belmont Finance Corpn Ltd v Williams Furniture Ltd* [1979] Ch 250.   [45] [1995] 3 All ER 97.

[46] The Privy Council held that, in fact, the company had acted dishonestly since the state of mind of the defendant could be imputed to it: [1995] 3 All ER 97, at 109.

[47] The Privy Council relied on earlier authorities to reach this conclusion: *Fyler v Fyler* (1841) 3 Beav 550; *A-G v Leicester Corpn* (1844) 7 Beav 176; *Eaves v Hickson* (1861) 30 Beav 136. In Canada it has been held that a fraudulent and dishonest breach must have been committed by the trustee: *Air Canada v M & C Travel Ltd* (1993) 108 DLR (4th) 592; *Gold v Rosenberg* (1995) 25 OR (3d) 601.

relieved by the court. But *his* state of mind is essentially irrelevant to the question whether the *third party* should be made liable to the beneficiaries for the breach of trust. If the liability of the third party is fault-based, what matters is the nature of his fault, not that of the trustee. In this regard dishonesty on the part of the third party would seem to be a sufficient basis for his liability, irrespective of the state of mind of the trustee who is in breach. It is difficult to see why, if the third party dishonestly assisted in a breach, there should be a further prerequisite to his liability, namely that the trustee also must have been acting dishonestly. The alternative view would mean that a dishonest third party is liable if the trustee is dishonest, but if the trustee did not act dishonestly that of itself would excuse a dishonest third party from liability. That would make no sense.[48]

Similarly, there is no requirement that the original breach of trust (or fiduciary duty) to itself cause loss for a dishonest third party to be held liable.[49] There is no need for the defendant to have known of the existence of the trust or to be aware what the concept of a trust in English law means.[50]

(c) Assistance in the breach of trust

A stranger will only be liable as an accessory if he in fact assisted the commission of a breach of trust or breach of fiduciary duty. Peter Smith J in *JD Wetherspoon plc v Van de Berg & Co Ltd*[51] observed that 'in most cases the breach can only occur as a result of the activities of the assistor'. In *Royal Brunei Airlines Sdn Bhd v Tan*[52] the defendant had authorized the use of trust money by the firm for its ordinary business purposes, including the paying of salaries and expenses and keeping its bank overdraft down. He had clearly assisted in the commission of the breach. However, where it cannot be shown that the stranger has assisted the breach of trust, there will be no grounds for any accessory liability. In *Brinks Ltd v Abu-Saleh (No 3)*[53] the defendant's husband had couriered some of the proceeds of the Brinks-Matt gold robbery to Switzerland. It was claimed that the defendant had knowingly assisted in a breach of trust by accompanying her husband on his trips so as to give the impression that they were enjoying a family holiday, thus cloaking the illegal nature of his activities and making it easier for him to cross borders. Rimer J held that she had not in fact assisted the breach of trust, and that she was not therefore liable to account for the £3m her husband had couriered. He held that she had not participated in the breach because she was not party to the couriering agreements entered into by her husband, and he had carried out all elements of the couriering exercise. Her only role had been to provide him with company on the long and tiring drives. In essence, Rimer J seems to have held that a stranger will only be liable as an accessory if he participates in the breach by performing positive acts of

---

[48] [1995] 3 All ER 97, at 102 (emphasis added).

[49] See *Madoff Securities International Ltd (In Liquidation) v Raven* [2013] EWHC 3147, at [340], per Popplewell J, where a defendant tried to escape potential liability for dishonest assistance on the basis that the original breach of trust had caused no loss.

[50] See *Barlow Clowes v Eurotrust* [2006] 1 All ER 333.   [51] [2009] EWHC 639, at [518].

[52] [1995] 3 All ER 97.

[53] (1995) *The Times*, 23 October; Stevens 'Delimiting the Scope of Accessory Liability' [1996] Conv 447; Oakley 'Is Knowledge Still a Prerequisite of the Imposition of "Accessory Liability"'? (1996) 10 TLI 53.

assistance. Mere passive acquiescence in the activity alleged to constitute a breach of trust will accordingly be insufficient to establish liability. It is submitted that this reasoning is unduly narrow, and that a person should be liable as an accessory whenever his or her conduct passively encourages the commission of a breach of trust, provided that it was dishonest.

(d) Dishonesty

We have already seen that the equitable liability of a stranger as an accessory to a breach of trust is fault-based.[54] It operates as a species of equitable wrong, similar to a common law tort. Much of the debate over the years has concerned the degree of fault that must be demonstrated before an assistor will be held liable as an accessory. Prior to *Royal Brunei Airlines Sdn Bhd v Tan*,[55] this debate was couched in the language of 'knowledge'. In some cases it had been held that a stranger would be liable as a knowing assistor if he had participated in a breach of trust without any actual knowledge but in circumstances where he had been negligent in not realizing, or discovering, that he was assisting a breach of trust.[56] However, increasingly it came to be held that a higher standard of fault than mere negligence was required to establish accessory liability. In *Agip (Africa) Ltd v Jackson*[57] Millett J held a firm of accountants liable to account to the plaintiff company because they had knowingly participated in the laundering of money defrauded by its chief accountant.[58] He warned against over-refinement of the shades of knowledge required to establish accessory liability and suggested instead that the assistor must have acted with 'dishonesty'.[59] This higher threshold for liability was adopted by the Court of Appeal in *Lipkin Gorman v Karpnale Ltd*[60] and *Polly Peck International plc v Nadir (Asil) (No 2)*.[61] In *Royal Brunei Airlines Sdn Bhd v Tan*[62] the Privy Council held that accessory liability was founded upon the dishonesty of the assistor.[63] Lord Nicholls explained why the requirement of dishonesty was to be preferred to that of knowledge:

---

[54] *Twinsectra v Yardley* [2002] 2 All ER 377, at [107], per Lord Millett.   [55] [1995] 3 All ER 97.

[56] *Selangor United Rubber Estates Ltd v Cradock (No 3)* [1968] 1 WLR 1555; *Karak Rubber Co Ltd v Burden (No 2)* [1972] 1 WLR 602; *Rowlandson v National Westminster Bank Ltd* [1978] 1 WLR 798; *Baden, Delvaux and Lecuit v Société Générale pour Favoriser le Développement du Commerce et de l'Industrie en France SA* [1983] BCLC 325.

[57] [1990] Ch 265; [1992] 4 All ER 385; Sir Peter Millett 'Tracing the Proceeds of Fraud' (1991) 107 LQR 71; affd [1991] Ch 547; [1992] 4 All ER 451; Harpum 'Equitable Liability for Money Laundering' (1991) 50 CLJ 40; Goulding 'Equity and the Money Launderers' [1992] Conv 367; Nolan 'Knowing Assistance—A Plea for Help' (1992) 12 LS 332.

[58] While the Court of Appeal held that the lower negligence threshold was applicable, subsequent cases demonstrate that the approach of Millett J has prevailed. See also *Eagle Trust plc v SBC Securities Ltd* [1992] 4 All ER 488; *Cowan de Groot Properties Ltd v Eagle Trust plc* [1992] 4 All ER 700, at 754.

[59] Birks 'Misdirected funds again' (1989) 105 LQR 528.

[60] [1992] 4 All ER 409; [1989] 1 WLR 1340.   [61] [1992] 4 All ER 769, at 777, per Scott LJ.

[62] [1995] 3 All ER 97.

[63] *Royal Brunei Airlines v Tan* was followed by the Court of Appeal in *Satnam Ltd v Dunlop Hetwood Ltd* [1999] 3 All ER 652 and applied in *Cigna Life Insurance New Zealand Ltd v Westpac Securities Ltd* [1996] 1 NZLR 80.

To inquire...whether a person dishonestly assisted in what is later held to be a breach of trust is to ask a meaningful question, which is capable of being given a meaningful answer. That is not always so if the question is posed in terms of knowingly assisted. Framing the question in the latter form all too often leads one into tortious convolutions about the sort of knowledge required, when the truth is that knowingly is inapt as a criterion when applied to the gradually darkening spectrum where the differences are of degree and not kind.[64]

In *Twinsectra Ltd v Yardley*[65] the House of Lords confirmed that dishonesty was the necessary condition for the imposition of accessory liability, thus affirming the decision in *Royal Brunei Airlines Sdn Bhd v Tan*.

(4) The test for 'dishonesty'

While it is easy to specify that the dishonesty of the assistor is the requisite degree of fault to establish accessory liability, it is more difficult to identify precisely what conduct will be characterized as dishonest, and whether the test is objective or subjective. In *Royal Brunei Airlines Sdn Bhd v Tan* the Privy Council gave some indications as to how the concept should be applied. The courts have struggled with this concept ever since, and the applicable test has been thoroughly examined by the House of Lords in *Twinsectra Ltd v Yardley,* then re-examined by the Privy Council in *Barlow Clowes International Ltd (in liquidation) v Eurotrust*.[66] Now, following a series of cases, the approach has been settled by the Court of Appeal in *Starglade Properties Ltd v Nash*,[67] which confirmed the test as (re-)stated in *Barlow Clowes*. There are still some technical issues which are being addressed by the lower courts, but the position of the law is now confirmed, unless and until the Supreme Court says otherwise.[68]

(a) Dishonesty an objective criterion for liability

There has been much debate in the years since the decision in *Royal Brunei Airlines Sdn Bhd v Tan* as to the precise meaning of dishonesty, and especially whether it is objective or subjective in nature, and therefore whether the defendant must have been consciously aware that he was acting wrongly. In *Royal Brunei Airlines v Tan* Lord Nicholls was at pains to explain that dishonesty provided an objective criterion for assessment of the defendant's conduct:

Whatever may be the position in some criminal or other contexts...in the context of the accessory liability principle acting dishonestly, or with a lack of probity, which is synonymous, means simply not acting as an honest person would in the circumstances. This is an

---

[64] [1995] 3 All ER 97, at 107.

[65] [2002] 2 AC 164; [2002] 10 RLR 112 (Rickett); [2002] Con 303 (Kenny) and 387 (Thompson); (2002) 16 TLI 165 (Penner); [2003] Con 398 (Andrews); (2004) 120 LQR 208 (Yeo). See also *Barlow Clowes v Eurotrust* [2006] 1 All ER 333.   [66] [2006] 1 All ER 333.

[67] [2010] EWCA Civ 1314.

[68] The Supreme Court decision in *Williams v Central Bank of Nigeria* [2014] UKSC 10, which concerns limitation periods, is unhelpful in the application of the test of dishonesty, but does nothing to unsettle the position established in *Starglade v Nash*.

objective standard. At first sight this might seem surprising. Honesty has a connotation of subjectivity, as distinct from the objectivity of negligence. Honesty, indeed, does have a strong subjective element in that it is a description of a type of conduct assessed in the light of what a person actually knew at the time, as distinct from what a reasonable person would have known or appreciated. Further, honesty and its counterpart dishonesty are mostly concerned with adverting conduct, not inadvertent conduct. Carelessness is not dishonesty. Thus for the most part dishonesty is to be equated with conscious impropriety.[69]

He held that these inherently subjective characteristics of dishonesty did not mean that individuals were free to set their own standards. Honesty is not an optional scale, with higher and lower values according to the moral standards of each individual. Therefore, a person who knowingly appropriates a person's property will not escape a finding of dishonesty simply because he sees nothing wrong in such behaviour.[70] He considered that in the majority of circumstances there would be little difficulty identifying how an honest person would behave. For example, he stated:

> Unless there is a very good and compelling reason, an honest person does not participate in a transaction if he knows it involves a misapplication of trust assets to the detriment of the beneficiaries. Nor does an honest person in such a case deliberately close his eyes and ears, or deliberately not ask questions, lest he learn something he would rather not know, and then proceed regardless.[71]

He also indicated that any assessment of dishonesty would have to be contextual, taking account of the circumstances of the transaction which constituted a breach of trust and the personal attributes of the assistor, including his experience and intelligence,[72] and that strangers should not generally be liable as assistors if they had acted negligently.[73] Strangers who owe a duty of care to the trust (for example, advisers, consultants, bankers, and agents) are liable in tort if they fail to exercise reasonable skill and care, and there is no compelling reason to impose any additional liability in equity.

(b) Dishonesty a subjective criterion for liability?

In *Twinsectra Ltd v Yardley*, the House of Lords subjected the comments of Lord Nicholls to careful scrutiny in order to identify the essential elements of dishonesty, and made comments that appeared to require a subjective awareness of wrongdoing on the part of the defendant. Lord Hutton identified three ways in which the standard of dishonesty may be applied, varying by whether the concept is viewed subjectively or objectively. First, dishonesty may operate as a purely subjective standard, 'whereby a person is only dishonest if he transgresses his own standard of honesty, even if that standard is contrary to that of reasonable and honest people'.[74] This purely subjective standard has been rejected by the courts; for example; in *Walker v Stones*, Sir Christopher Slade LJ considered that a solicitor-trustee would have acted dishonestly even though he held an 'honest belief' that his actions were in the best interests of his beneficiaries if his belief was 'so unreasonable that, by any objective standard, no

---

[69] [1995] 3 All ER 97, at 106.　　[70] [1995] 3 All ER 97, at 106　　[71] [1995] 3 All ER 97, at 106.
[72] [1995] 3 All ER 97, at 107.　　[73] [1995] 3 All ER 97, at 108.　　[74] [2002] 2 AC 164, at [27].

reasonable solicitor-trustee could have thought that what he did or agreed to do was for the benefit of the beneficiaries'.[75] Second, dishonesty may operate as a purely object-ive standard, 'whereby a person acts dishonestly if his conduct is dishonest by the ordinary standards of reasonable and honest people'.[76] Finally, dishonesty may oper-ate in a manner that combines elements of objectivity and subjectivity. Lord Hutton explained:

> Thirdly, there is a standard which combines an objective and a subjective test, and which requires that before there can be a finding of dishonesty it must be established that the defendant's conduct was dishonest by the standards of reasonable and honest people and that he himself realised that by those standards his conduct was dishonest. I will term this 'the combined test'.[77]

A similar approach had previously been adopted by Nourse LJ in *Heinl v Jyske Bank*,[78] where it was suggested that the defendant actually had to appreciate that funds prob-ably had been procured in breach of trust, not whether he ought to have appreciated that they had been so procured. The majority of the House of Lords held that the com-bined test explained by Lord Hutton should be adopted as the standard of dishonesty necessary for the imposition of accessory liability. Lord Millett dissented in favour of the adoption of a purely objective test which does not require the defendant to have realized that he was acting dishonestly. In Lord Millett's view, the only subjective ele-ments were findings of fact as to the defendant's experience, intelligence, and actual state of knowledge of the breach of trust. The subjective parts of the test were thus an evidential aid to deciding objectively whether a defendant had been dishonest.

(c) Understanding the difficulties of the subjective criterion

It is clear from Lord Hutton's speech that the impact of a finding that a professional per-son had acted dishonestly weighed heavily in reaching his decision, and his Lordship drew assistance from the test used to determine the *mens rea* of theft in *R v Ghosh*[79] in formulating a subjective conception of dishonesty which required the defendant to appreciate that what he was doing would be regarded as dishonest by honest people:

> Notwithstanding that the issue arises in equity law and not in a criminal context. I think that it would be less than just for the law to permit a finding that a defendant had been 'dishonest' in assisting in a breach of trust where he knew of facts which created the trust and its breach but had not been aware that what he was doing would be regarded by honest men as being dishonest…[80]

Lord Hutton was thus equating civil liability with a need for guilt, which it is sug-gested is too high a standard on which to make the stranger liable.[81] If Lord Millett's

---

[75] [2001] QB 902, at 939. See Hunter 'The Honest Truth about Dishonesty' (2002) PCB 390.
[76] [2002] 2 AC 164, at [27].   [77] [2002] 2 AC 164, at [27].   [78] [1999] Lloyd's Rep Bank 511.
[79] [1982] QB 901.   [80] [2002] 2 AC 164, at [35].
[81] See Thompson 'Criminal Law and Property Law: An Unhappy Combination' [2002] Con 387. See also Lord Millett in *Twinsectra v Yardley* [2002] 2 AC 164, who said that: 'Consciousness of wrongdoing is an aspect of mens rea and an appropriate condition of criminal liability; it is not an appropriate condition of civil liability' (at [127]).

dissenting view of the test had been applied, then it would 'not be necessary that the defendant realized that his conduct was dishonest; it should be sufficient that it constituted intentional wrongdoing'.[82]

(d) The meaning of dishonesty clarified as a primarily objective criterion for liability

The test adopted by the majority in *Twinsectra Ltd v Yardley* was thus ambiguous, and open to a possible interpretation whereby a defendant would not be regarded as dishonest if he had acted dishonestly according to the objective standards of honest men, but had personally set himself a different standard of honesty such that he was not consciously aware that his conduct would be regarded as dishonest by ordinary standards.[83] In the light of this ambiguity and uncertainty the exact meaning and application of the test of dishonesty suggested by the House of Lords in *Twinsectra Ltd v Yardley* was clarified by the Privy Council in *Barlow Clowes International Ltd v Eurotrust International Ltd*.[84] The central issue in this case was whether liability on the basis of dishonesty required the court to conduct an inquiry into the defendant's views as to what the ordinary standards of honesty would be, so as to then determine whether he had consciously reflected that he was transgressing them. Lord Hoffmann stated that, although some of the comments made in *Twinsectra Ltd v Yardley* might have contained an 'element of ambiguity', they had not intended to be different from the principles stated in *Royal Brunei Airlines Sdn Bhd v Tan*.[85] Lord Hoffmann therefore explained that Lord Hutton, who had stated in *Twinsectra v Yardley* that a defendant should not escape liability 'because he sets his own standards of honesty and does not regard as dishonest what he knows would offend the normally accepted standards of honest conduct',[86] had not intended to impose a requirement that the defendant must have had reflections about what the normally accepted standards were. He further indicated that his own comments in *Twinsectra Ltd v Yardley* that a dishonest state of mind meant 'consciousness that one is transgressing ordinary standards of honest behaviour'[87] were only intended 'to require consciousness of those elements of the transaction which make participation transgress ordinary standards of honest behaviour'.[88] They did not, therefore, 'also require him to have thought about what those standards were'.[89] The Privy Council therefore accepted the following statement of the trial judge as a correct statement of the law:

> liability for dishonest assistance requires a dishonest state of mind on the part of the person who assists in a breach of trust. Such a state of mind may consist in knowledge that the

---

[82] [2002] 2 AC 164, at [127]. Lord Millett's reasoning is explored later in the chapter.

[83] The Court of Appeal of New Zealand expressed obiter reservations about the subjective element of the combined test in *US International Marketing Ltd v National Bank of New Zealand Ltd*, 28 October 2003; Yeo 'Twinsectra: New Zealand's "Reasonable Banker" Response' (2004) 120 LQR 208. Note, however, that in *Harvey v The Law Society* [2003] EWHC 535, Patton J, while purporting to apply the majority test in *Twinsectra*, instead seemed to apply a more objective version of the test by asking whether an honest person in the defendant's position would act as he did, knowing what the defendant knew.

[84] [2006] 1 All ER 333.   [85] [1995] 2 AC 378.   [86] [2002] 2 AC 164, at [36].

[87] [2002] 2 AC 164, at [20].   [88] [2006] 1 All ER 339, at [16].   [89] [2006] 1 All ER 339, at [16].

transaction is one in which he cannot honestly participate (for example, a misappropriation of other people's money), or it may consist in suspicion combined with a conscious decision not to make inquiries which might result in knowledge[90]...Although a dishonest state of mind is a subjective mental state, the standard by which the law determines whether it is dishonest is objective. If by ordinary standards a defendant's mental state would be characterized as dishonest, it is irrelevant that the defendant judges by different standards.[91]

Their Lordships made no mention of Lord Millett's dissenting opinion in *Twinsectra*, though it is difficult to see any real variance other than in language between Lord Millett's statement of an objective test of dishonesty and that adopted by the Privy Council.

(e) The application of the criterion of dishonesty

In *Barlow Clowes v Eurotrust*[92] the defendant, Mr Henwood, had been one of the principal directors of an Isle of Man company providing offshore financial services, which paid away money that had been misappropriated from investors by Peter Clowes and one of his associates, a Mr Cramer. The Privy Council held that there was sufficient evidence to conclude that Mr Henwood had acted dishonestly. The evidence indicated that he had been made fully aware of the Barlow Clowes business, such that it must have come home to him that there was a real possibility that the large amount of money being put through the company could well be the investors' money. He also knew of previous dishonesty by Mr Cramer, and told lies in evidence, denying that he had any knowledge of the Barlow Clowes business and the money laundering transactions which passed through the company. In contrast, in *Twinsectra Ltd v Yardley* the defendant solicitor was held not to have acted dishonestly. The claimant lenders had advanced £1m to a firm of solicitors subject to an undertaking that the money would be retained until it was applied in the acquisition of property by the borrower, Yardley. In breach of this undertaking the firm of solicitors subsequently paid the money to Leach, another solicitor who was acting for Yardley in respect of the transaction. Leach then failed to ensure that the money was utilized solely for the acquisition of property in accordance with the undertaking, and Yardley used £358,000 for other purposes. At first instance Carnwath J held that the money had not been held on trust, and that Leach had not acted dishonestly, although he had been 'misguided'. While he had been aware of all the facts he had 'simply shut his eyes to the problems' and had considered it a matter for the other solicitors whether he could release the money to his client. The Court of Appeal reversed these findings, holding that Leach had acted dishonestly because he had shut his eyes to the rights of *Twinsectra*. The House of Lords held by a majority that Leach had not acted dishonestly. Lords Hutton and Hoffmann considered it unfortunate that Carnwath J had referred to Leach as having shut his eyes to the obvious, but considered that this alone did not render him

---

[90] Citing *Manifest Shipping Co Ltd v Uni-Polaris Insurance Co Ltd* [2001] 1 All ER 743; [2003] 1 AC 469.
[91] [2006] 1 All ER 333, at [10].
[92] [2006] 1 All ER 33; Ryan '*Royal Brunei* Dishonesty: Clarity at Last?' [2006] Conv 188.

dishonest. Instead, the crucial question was whether 'Leach realized that his action was dishonest by the standards of responsible and honest solicitors'.[93] The majority held that Carnwath J had not applied an incorrect test, and there was no justification for taking the exceptional step of reversing a finding by the trial judge on a question of fact, as he had had the advantage of seeing the party give evidence in the witness box. In *Barlow Clowes v Eurotrust*[94] the Privy Council affirmed the decision in *Twinsectra Ltd v Yardley*, but seemed to do so for very different reasons from those that had been given in the judgments. Lord Hoffmann explained:

> On the facts of the *Twinsectra* case, neither the judge who acquitted Mr Leach of dishonesty nor the House undertook any inquiry into the views of the defendant solicitor Mr Leach about ordinary standards of honest behaviour. He had received on behalf of his client a payment from another solicitor who he knew had given an undertaking to pay it to Mr Leach's client only for a particular use. But the other solicitor had paid the money to Mr Leach without requiring any undertaking. The judge found that he was not dishonest because he honestly believed that the undertaking did not, so to speak, run with the money and that, as between him and his client, he held it for his client unconditionally. He was therefore bound to pay it upon his client's instructions without restriction on its use. The majority of the House of Lords considered that a solicitor who held this view of the law, even though he knew all the facts, was not by normal standards dishonest.[95]

It is hard to avoid the conclusion that this is a (welcome) re-rationalization of the decision.[96] The Privy Council appears to claim that the House of Lords held that Leach was honest because his conduct would not have been regarded as dishonest by the objective criteria of 'normal standards' for solicitors. In fact, the House of Lords repeatedly stressed that he was not dishonest because he had not subjectively realized that his conduct was dishonest by normal standards. Indeed, applying the test as stated by the Privy Council to the facts of *Twinsectra*, it is hard to escape the conclusion that Mr Leach would have been held dishonest.[97] Since the rationale given for the decision in *Twinsectra* is dubious, it appears that the Privy Council in *Barlow Clowes v Eurotrust* has changed the test for dishonesty without admitting that the House of Lords had been mistaken in the earlier case.

(f) Embedding the approach in *Barlow Clowes*

The *Barlow Clowes* decision does not represent the final word. The courts continued to grapple with the test for dishonesty. Two examples will suffice.[98] The reinterpretation of the dishonesty standard by the Privy Council in *Barlow Clowes* was applied in

---

[93] [2002] 2 AC 164, at [49], per Lord Hutton. See also at [20], per Lord Hoffmann.
[94] [2006] 1 All ER 333.   [95] [2006] 1 All ER 333, at [17].
[96] This has not gone unremarked—see, for example, Conaglen and Goymour 'Dishonesty in the Context of Assistance—Again' (2006) 65 CLJ 18, who suggest this is judicial 'sleight of hand'. See also Yeo 'Dishonest Assistance: Restatement from the Privy Council' [2006] LQR 171; Ryan '*Royal Brunei* Dishonesty: Clarity at Last?' [2006] Con 188.
[97] Mr Leach would also have been unlikely to escape liability under the old formulation of the test preceding *Royal Brunei v Tan*, as he clearly had actual knowledge of the terms of the undertaking.
[98] See also *Statek Corp v Alford* [2008] EWHC 32 (Ch).

Abou-Rahmah v Abacha,[99] in which Arden LJ confirmed that all that was required to impose liability was the defendant's knowledge of facts and that he acted contrary to normal standards of honest conduct.[100] Lady Justice Arden, in considering the apparent contradiction between the *Twinsectra* and *Barlow Clowes* approaches to dishonesty, noted that in fact:

> the *Barlow Clowes* case gives guidance as to the proper interpretation to be placed on it as a matter of English law. It shows how the *Royal Brunei* case and the *Twinsectra* case can be read together to form a consistent corpus of law.[101]

The test for dishonesty was comprehensively reviewed by Peter Smith J in *AG of Zambia v Meer Care & Desai,*[102] a case concerning a complex international fraud involving the corrupt spending of huge sums by the former President of Zambia and the actions of a solicitor in handling various tainted transactions through his client account. The judge thought that the issue was not as complicated as it had been made to appear:

> In my view when the cases are analysed the question of subjective/objective test is an over elaboration. All of the cases when analysed in my view actually determine that the test for dishonesty is essentially a question of fact whereby the state of mind of the Defendant had to be judged in the light of his subjective knowledge but by reference to an objective standard of honesty.[103]

Having considered the authorities, the judge concluded, following a formulation by Lord Clarke MR, writing extra-judicially:[104]

> the test for dishonest assistance is 'an objective one, but an objective one which takes account of the individuals in questions characteristics... It is a test which requires the Court to assess the individual's conduct according to an objective standard of dishonesty. In doing so the Court has to take into account as to what the individual knew; his experience, intelligence and reasons for acting as he did. Whether the individual was aware that his conduct fell below the objective standard is not part of the test.[105]

(g) Clarification of the test for dishonesty

Welcome clarity on the application of the test for dishonesty in accessory liability cases can be found in the Court of Appeal decision in *Starglade Properties Ltd v Nash.*[106] Sir Andrew Morritt, delivering the leading speech, confirmed that the approach of the Privy Council in *Barlow Clowes International v Eurotrust International Ltd,*[107] as applied in *Abou-Rahmah v Abacha*[108] is correct:[109]

---

[99] [2006] EWCA Civ 1492. See Lee 'Dishonesty and Bad Faith after *Barlow Clowes: Abou-Rahmah v Abacha*' [2007] JBL 209; Ruan '*Royal Brunei* Dishonesty: A Clear Welcome for *Barlow Clowes*' [2007] Conv 168.   [100] See also *Statek Corporation v Alford* [2008] EWHC 32 (Ch).
[101] [2006] EWCA Civ 1492, at [68].   [102] [2007] EWHC 952.   [103] [2007] EWHC 952, at [334].
[104] 'Claims Against Professionals: Negligence, Dishonesty and Fraud' [2006] 22 *Professional Negligence* 70/85.   [105] [2007] EWHC 952, at [357].
[106] [2010] EWCA Civ 1314.   [107] [2006] 1 All ER 333.   [108] [2006] EWCA Civ 1492.
[109] At first instance ([2009] EWHC 148), Strauss J had emphasized the subjective element of dishonesty and held that a defendant would not be dishonest where a different view as to whether the conduct was

There is a single standard of honesty objectively determined by the court. That standard is applied to specific conduct of a specific individual possessing the knowledge and qualities he actually enjoyed…The relevant standard…is the ordinary standard of honest behaviour. Just as the subjective understanding of the person concerned as to whether his conduct is dishonest is irrelevant so also it is irrelevant that here may be a body of opinion which regards the ordinary standard of honest behaviour as being set too high. Ultimately, in civil proceedings, it is for the court to determine what the standard is and to apply it to the facts of the case.[110]

Hence, on the facts of *Starglade*, the deliberate removal of the assets of an insolvent company in order to defeat the legitimate claims of creditors was 'not in accordance with the ordinary standards of honest commercial behaviour' and the director was therefore dishonest.[111] Some doubt might be cast on how the court determines these standards, but it is submitted that the Chancellor was simply suggesting, as in previous cases, that the requirement of dishonesty is an objective standard and is transgressed when that standard is not met.

(h) **Further developments**

In *Halliwells LLP v Nes Solicitors*,[112] Judge McCahill QC considered that a firm of solicitors had acted dishonestly when giving an undertaking to another firm of solicitors to secure a bridging loan of £1.5m to purchase property and shares when the funds had not cleared in their client account. The solicitors argued that, as they trusted the client and thought he would 'come good' on the undertaking, they were not dishonest. The judge nevertheless held that they had transgressed the 'ordinary standards of normal commercial behaviour' as set out in *Starglade*. They had lied at the prospect of commercial gain, and had transgressed the 'solemn and important nature of a solicitor's undertaking' as they were aware money would be advanced on the loan as a consequence of the undertaking.[113] The spectre of Mr Leach, and what his subjective appreciation of whether his actions had been dishonest in *Twinsectra v Yardley*[114] might be thought to finally be put to rest, as the court was here willing to find professional solicitors dishonest on an objective basis.

The issue arose again in *Secretary of State for Justice v Topland Group plc*,[115] in relation to pleadings of evidence to establish a claim of dishonest assistance against a property investment company. Here, King J emphasized the subjective elements of the dishonesty test once again. The company had agreed to pay a secret commission to agents employed by the then Secretary of State, Jack Straw, to manage a property transaction in their favour. On the facts, neither the property investment company nor the agents denied that the commission had been paid, but instead alleged that the commission was a standard introduction fee, and it was general market practice

---

dishonest could reasonably be held, demonstrating the propensity of some of the judiciary to continue to be confused by the requirements for accessory liability.

[110] [2010] EWCA Civ 1314, at [32].   [111] [2010] EWCA Civ 1314, at [39].
[112] [2011] EWHC 947 (QB); [2011] All ER (D) 243.   [113] [2011] EWHC 947 (QB), at [119].
[114] [2002] 2 AC 164.   [115] [2011] EWHC 983 (QB).

to both charge such a fee and not to require the consent of the incumbent lessee (the Secretary of State) to such a payment.

King J held that the views on general market practice could be admissible in deciding the question of dishonesty, as the objective test had to be applied in the light of the subjective state of mind of the defendant,[116] and, more significantly, following *Starglade*, the court had to determine whether the conduct had been 'commercially unacceptable conduct.'[117] However, he did not make clear that there was a difference in allowing evidence in pleading and actually proving that such conduct was not dishonest:

> Whether even if such commercial practice is shown to exist, the court at trial will accept this attitude of the Defendants as being 'commercially acceptable conduct' in accordance with honest standards of commercial behaviour as objectively determined by the court, will of course be a matter for the court…[118]

In *Novoship (UK) Ltd v Mikhaylyuk*,[119] the claim before the court was that Mr Mikhaylyuk, in breach of his fiduciary duties and receiving bribes to do so, had with Mr Ruperti's dishonest assistance, arranged for a sub-chartering arrangement to benefit some other co-defendants at the expense of his employer, Novoship. Christopher Clarke J found no difficulty in applying the dishonesty test as set out in *Barlow Clowes* and *Starglade*, holding that both Mr Mikhaylyuk and Mr Ruperti knew that 'bribery and the secret sub-chartering arrangements were (a) dishonest and (b) involved Mr Mikhaylyuk in a breach of his contractual and fiduciary obligations'.[120] Mr Ruperti had therefore dishonestly assisted Mr Mikhaylyuk in that breach by arranging payments and putting into effect the sub-chartering arrangements.

The issue of dishonesty was also simply resolved in *Vivendi SA v Richards*.[121] One of the questions before the court was whether Mr Richards had assisted in breaches of duty by the company director, Mr Block, who had procured nine payments totalling £10m from the company, which had gone into insolvency. Newey J, in finding that Mr Richards had dishonestly assisted in a breach of trust:

> On the basis…they acted in ways that they did not believe were in the interests of the [company]…or those of its creditors…Mr Richards and Mr Bloch sought to extract money from the company before it failed and to the thwart the landlord's claims: they caused the company to enter into transactions with a view to removing money before…and regardless of any failure of the company. There is an analogy with *Starglade Properties v Nash* [about deliberate removal of assets from an insolvent company]…Mr Richard's and Mr Bloch's conduct was, it seems to me, also contrary to normally acceptable standards of honest behaviour.'[122]

It is apparent that the courts are far from finished with their deliberations over the requirements of dishonesty, but the test would appear to be very well settled.

---

[116] [2011] EWHC 983 (QB), at [99].   [117] [2011] EWHC 983 (QB), at [101].
[118] [2011] EWHC 983 (QB), at [102].   [119] [2012] EWHC 3586 (Comm).
[120] [2012] EWHC 3586 (Comm), at [407].   [121] [2013] EWHC 3006 (Ch).
[122] [2013] EWHC 3006 (Ch), at [192].

(5) **Alternatives to dishonesty as the criteria for accessory liability**

While dishonesty has been firmly established as the touchstone for accessory liability in English law, other approaches have been advocated in the past.[123]

(a) Unconscionability

In *Royal Brunei Airlines Sdn Bhd v Tan*[124] the Privy Council considered the viability of unconscionability as a touchstone for liability but felt that it was either synonymous with dishonesty, or if not, that it was too vague:

> unconscionable is not a word in everyday use by non-lawyers. If it is to be used in this context, and if it is to be the touchstone for liability as an accessory, it is essential to be clear on what, *in this context*, unconscionable *means*. If unconscionable means no more than dishonesty, then dishonesty is the preferable label. If unconscionable means something different, it must be said that it is not clear what that something different is. Either way, therefore, the term is better avoided in this context.[125]

(b) Knowing assistance

Lord Millett delivered a dissenting opinion in *Twinsectra Ltd v Yardley*,[126] rejecting the 'combined test' for dishonesty adopted by the majority in favour of a purely objective test. He gave three reasons for preferring such an objective approach:

> (1) consciousness of wrongdoing is an aspect of mens rea and an appropriate condition of criminal liability: it is not an appropriate condition of civil liability. This generally results from negligent or intentional conduct. For the purpose of civil liability, it should not be necessary that the defendant realised that his conduct was dishonest; it should be sufficient that it constituted intentional wrongdoing. (2) The objective test is in accordance with Lord Selbourne LC's statement in *Barnes v Addy* and traditional doctrine. This taught that a person who knowingly participates in the misdirection of money is liable to compensate the injured party. While negligence is not sufficient condition of liability, intentional wrongdoing is. Such conduct is culpable and falls below the standards of honesty adopted by ordinary people. (3) The claim for 'knowing assistance' is the equitable counterpart of the economic torts. They are intentional torts; negligence is not sufficient and dishonesty is not necessary. Liability depends on knowledge. A requirement of subjective dishonesty introduces an unnecessary and unjustified distinction between the elements of the equitable claim and those of the tort of wrongful interference with the performance of a contract.[127]

In his opinion the adoption of such an objective standard for liability should lead to a return to the traditional nomenclature of the equitable claim as liability for 'knowing assistance':

---

[123] See also Andrews 'The Redundancy of Dishonest Assistance' [2003] Conv 398.
[124] [1995] 3 All ER 97.   [125] [1995] 3 All ER 97, at 108.   [126] [2002] 2 AC 164.
[127] [2002] 2 AC 164, at [127].

For my own part, I have no difficulty in equating the knowing mishandling of money with dishonest conduct. But the introduction of dishonesty is an unnecessary distraction, and conducive to error. Many judges would be reluctant to brand a professional man as dishonest where he was unaware that honest people would consider his conduct to be so. If the condition of liability is intentional wrongdoing and not conscious dishonesty as understood in the criminal courts, I think we should return to the traditional description of this head of equitable liability as arising from 'knowing assistance'.[128]

It seems somewhat ironic that Lord Millett, who had begun the task of cutting the Gordian knot of 'knowledge' and replacing it with 'dishonesty' in *Agip (Africa) Ltd v Jackson*,[129] should now seek a return to the earlier terminology. It also appears to be self-contradictory to advocate abandonment of the language of dishonesty to avoiding slurring the reputations of professionals who have committed intentional wrongdoing, while at the same time stating that such intentional wrongdoing is 'culpable and falls below the objective standards of honesty adopted by ordinary people'. It is perhaps explicable on the wider impact of holding a person 'dishonest', which could have an influence on their general business beyond their dealings on a particular set of facts. It is also clear that this aspect of his Lordship's reasoning has not been followed in any of the subsequent cases.

4 Proprietary remedies for receipt in breach of trust

The prime obligation of trustees is to allocate the trust property to those entitled to it under the terms of the trust. If they misappropriate the trust property and transfer it to third party strangers to the trust they will clearly have acted in breach. However, if the trustees are insolvent, any remedy that the beneficiaries might be able to maintain against them for breach of trust will be useless as a means of restoring the trust fund. In such circumstances the beneficiaries may instead seek a remedy against the stranger who received the trust property. A stranger who has received trust property may be liable as a constructive trustee, and the beneficiaries may be able to pursue either proprietary or personal remedies against him. This section briefly considers the proprietary remedies available to recover the property in the recipient's hands.

(1) Proprietary remedies against a stranger who has received trust property

Where property is subject to a pre-existing trust, the beneficiaries are already entitled to the equitable ownership of the trust property. They enjoy a proprietary interest in the trust fund that is capable of enduring through changes in the legal ownership thereof. While the trustees are able to transfer the legal title to the trust property, mere

---

[128] [2002] 2 AC 164, at [134].   [129] [1990] Ch 265.

transfer of the legal title does not defeat the interests of the beneficiaries. Thus, if trust property is transferred by trustees to a stranger in breach of trust, the beneficiaries may be able to assert a proprietary interest in such of the property (or its traceable proceeds) as remains in the hands of the stranger. If the stranger is insolvent, any assets identifiable in his hands as representing the trust property will continue to belong to the trust in equity, and they will not therefore be available to satisfy the claims of his creditors.

(2) Applying the proprietary remedies

A stranger who receives trust property transferred in breach of trust will not gain priority over the equitable interests of the beneficiaries unless he was a bona fide purchaser for value without notice. The interests of the beneficiaries will therefore be preserved if the stranger was a volunteer who had provided no consideration in return for receipt of the trust property, irrespective of whether he was aware of the existence of the trust or not. If the stranger had provided valuable consideration, the interests of the beneficiaries will only be preserved if he purchased the property with notice that it was subject to a trust. In essence, the burden falls to the recipient of trust property to demonstrate that his conscience was not affected so as to require him to observe the trust. He will only be able to do this if he can satisfy all the elements of the equitable doctrine of notice.

(a) Stranger was a volunteer

A stranger who receives trust property as an innocent volunteer will hold it subject to the beneficiaries' pre-existing equitable interest, irrespective of whether he had knowledge that it was trust property. The beneficiaries will be able to demand that he returns it or its traceable proceeds. As Lord Browne-Wilkinson observed in *Westdeutsche Landesbank Girozentrale Bank v Islington London Borough Council*:

> Even if the [third party recipient] is not aware that what he has received is trust property [the beneficiary] is entitled to assert his title in that property.[130]

The preservation of the beneficiaries' proprietary rights to the trust property is not therefore determined by the fault of the recipient, and it provides extremely important protection of their interests. In *Re Diplock*[131] the executors of a will transferred a testator's residuary estate to charities in the belief that valid charitable bequests had been made. As the recipient charities were innocent volunteers, who had provided no consideration in return for the gifts received, the Court of Appeal held that beneficiaries under the will were entitled to recover any trust property, or its traceable proceeds, remaining in their hands. Where the recipient of trust property was an innocent volunteer, the beneficiaries' proprietary interests therein will be preserved in any asset identifiable in his hands by the rules of tracing, but he will not be subject to

---

[130] [1996] AC 669, at 707.   [131] [1948] Ch 465, CA.

a personal liability to account as a constructive trustee. As Megarry V-C explained in *Re Montagu's Settlement Trusts*:

> Suppose…a trustee transfers trust property to a person who takes it in all innocence, believing that he is entitled to it as a beneficiary…He cannot claim to be a purchaser for value without notice, for he is a mere volunteer. If when the truth emerges he still has the property he must restore it, whereas if he no longer has either the property or its traceable proceeds, he is under no liability, unless he has become a constructive trustee.[132]

As will be seen later, liability as a constructive trustee is imposed only if the stranger had received the trust property with the requisite degree of fault. The position of an innocent volunteer who has received trust property without fault therefore clearly highlights the dichotomy between the proprietary and personal remedies which may be available against a stranger who receives trust property.[133]

(b) Stranger provided valuable consideration

A stranger who acquires trust property for valuable consideration will still hold it subject to the pre-existing equitable interest of the beneficiaries if, at the time he acquired it, he had sufficient knowledge that it was trust property to affect his conscience. He is not protected by the equitable doctrine of notice and must yield priority to the beneficiaries. If he still possesses the property received (or its traceable proceeds) he will hold it on constructive trust for the beneficiaries. The beneficiaries' equitable interests will be preserved if the purchaser acquired the trust property with actual, implied, or constructive notice of the existence of the trust. Such constructive notice includes notice of everything that he would have known about the property if he had made all the inspections and investigations expected of a reasonably prudent man of business.[134] As Millett J stated in *Macmillan Inc v Bishopsgate Investment Trust plc*:

> In English law notice…includes not only actual notice (including wilful blindness or contrived ignorance, where the purchaser deliberately abstains from an inquiry in order to avoid learning the truth) but also constructive notice, that is to say notice of such facts as he would have discovered if he had taken proper measures to investigate them.[135]

This amounts to a negligence standard, so that a purchaser will be affixed with constructive notice if he negligently failed to realize that the property was trust property. It is important to note that, while this negligence standard of constructive notice is sufficient to prevent a purchaser acquiring trust property free from the equitable interest of the beneficiaries, it seems that it is insufficient to fix the purchaser with a liability to account as a constructive trustee for the property he received. As Megarry V-C observed in *Re Montagu's Settlement Trusts*:

---

[132] [1987] Ch 264, at 271.

[133] See Birks, *Introduction to the law of Restitution* (1985), pp 411–412 and 439–447.

[134] See types (iv) and (v) of knowledge categorized by Peter Gibson J in *Baden Delvaux and Lecuit v Société Générale pour Favoriser le Développement du Commerce et de l'Industrie en France SA* [1983] BCLC 325. See also *Northern Bank Ltd v Henry* [1981] IR 1.   [135] [1995] 3 All ER 747, at 769.

one has to be very careful to distinguish the notice that is relevant in the doctrine of purchase without notice from the knowledge that suffices for the imposition of a constructive trust.[136]

Although the doctrine of constructive notice might seem to place a very heavy burden upon a purchaser of property to satisfy himself that it was not subject to a trust, in reality the extent of inquiries necessary to discharge that burden will vary with the nature of the property concerned and the circumstances of the transaction. While a purchaser of land is required to make comprehensive investigations into the title of the vendor, there has been a reluctance to carry a similarly onerous requirement into commercial transactions, where the speed of transfer does not permit such extensive pre-acquisition inquiries.[137] In *Macmillan Inc v Bishopsgate Investment Trust plc*[138] Millett J was reluctant to impose an onerous duty to investigate title to shares offered for sale when commercial custom and practice did not require close investigation of the transferor's title. He therefore held that banks which had acquired shares which were held on trust for the plaintiff, having been wrongly transferred as part of the attempt to support the ailing Maxwell business empire, were not affixed with constructive notice because they had not acted with actual knowledge or suspicion that the transferee was not the beneficial owner.[139] In *El Ajou v Dollar Land Holdings plc (No 1)*[140] he had cautioned that a commercial party was not expected to be unduly suspicious.[141]

(c) Stranger was a bona fide purchaser

Where trust property is received by a stranger to the trust who was a bona fide purchaser for value without knowledge of the existence of the trust (whether actual or constructive), the stranger will acquire the property free from any interests of the beneficiaries. They will no longer be able to maintain any proprietary claim to the erstwhile trust property (or its proceeds) in the stranger's hands, as equitable title has validly passed to the purchaser free from their interest. This does not affect the possibility of pursuing personal remedies.

5 Personal remedies for receipt in breach of trust

(1) Accounting as a constructive trustee for receipt in breach of trust

If a stranger receives trust property in breach of trust and subsequently dissipates it so that there are no traceable proceeds in his hands, the beneficiaries of the trust

---

[136] [1987] Ch 264; [1992] 4 All ER 308, at 324–325, citing the Court of Appeal in *Re Diplock* [1948] Ch 465, at 478–479.

[137] See *Manchester Trust v Furness* [1895] 2 QB 539; *Greer v Downs Supply Co* [1927] 2 KB 28.

[138] [1995] 3 All ER 747.

[139] [1995] 3 All ER 747, at 780–781. See N Gegal, 'Cross-Border Security Enforcement, Restitution and Priorities', Ch 7 in Rose (ed), *Restitution and Banking Law* (1998), pp 112–119.

[140] [1993] 3 All ER 717.   [141] [1993] 3 All ER 717, at 739.

will not be able to pursue a proprietary claim against him. They may, however, be entitled to seek a personal remedy requiring him to return to the trust the value of the property he received. This remedy is restitutionary, in that it requires him to restore the enrichment he received at the expense of the beneficiaries, who were entitled to the property under the trust.[142] The stranger who received the trust property in breach of trust was thereby unjustly enriched, and is required to make restitution to the trust of the value of his enrichment, ie the value of the trust property he received.

If the trust property has been partially dissipated the beneficiaries may likewise seek a personal remedy in respect of the value of the property that has been dissipated. The remedy by which such restitution is effected is the imposition of an equitable duty to account as a constructive trustee. Equity requires a stranger who has received trust property to restore equivalent value to the trust fund if he has wrongfully dissipated it. His liability is fault-based and rooted in equitable notions of conscience. Unless the stranger was aware that the property he received was subject to a trust, he was entitled to treat it as his own, for example by disposing of it, consuming it on services which leave no traceable end product, or transferring it to others. His conscience will only be affected if he knew that the property was subject to a trust, in which case he will have become subject to an obligation to preserve it for the beneficiaries. As Lord Browne-Wilkinson stated in *Westdeutsche Landesbank Girozentrale v Islington London Borough Council*:

> Since the equitable jurisdiction to enforce trusts depends upon the conscience of the holder of the legal interest being affected, he cannot be a trustee of the property if and so long as he is ignorant of the facts alleged to affect his conscience, i.e. until he is aware that he is intended to hold the property for the benefit of others in the case of an express or implied trust, or, in the case of a constructive trust, of the factors which are alleged to affect his conscience.[143]

This seems to mean that a recipient of trust property will not be subject to a duty to preserve the trust fund unless and until he knew that it was subject to a trust. If he dissipates the property after becoming aware that it was trust property he acts in breach of his duty to preserve the trust fund, which is imposed by equity because he is a constructive trustee. He will therefore be liable to account to the beneficiaries. As was noted earlier, the language of liability to account as a constructive trustee has been criticized on the grounds of artificiality. While this criticism is admittedly accurate in the case of the liability of strangers who have assisted in a breach of trust, it is less justified in the case of the liability of strangers who receive trust property. Their liability derives from the fact that they held the property on trust for the beneficiaries and failed to carry out their duties as trustee.

---

[142] This was made clear by Megarry V-C in *Re Montagu's Settlement Trusts*, where he described the imposition of liability to account as a constructive trustee as imposing 'a personal obligation on a man' in contrast to the equitable doctrine of notice, which determines 'the burdens on property': [1987] Ch 264, at 272–273.   [143] [1996] AC 669, at 705.

(2) **Factual requirement of receipt**

It goes almost without saying that liability for knowing receipt requires the person charged to have in fact received the trust property, unlike the liability of a dishonest accessory, where receipt of property is not a requirement. What constitutes receipt in this context is not entirely clear. Some situations will be clear-cut. Where a casino owed money for a gambling debt is paid money which the gambler has embezzled from a trust fund, it would undoubtedly be considered a recipient for the purposes of liability if the other conditions are met. A 'fence' engaged in a money laundering activity by paying misappropriated cheques through his bank account would similarly be considered a recipient.[144] It would also be a sufficient basis for liability (if the other conditions are met) if the property could have been traced to the hands of the stranger if they had retained it.[145] A vesting of legal or equitable title in the recipient is not necessary, since having control over the property appears to be sufficient.[146]

In some of the case law, it is suggested that property must be retained by the recipient for his own use and benefit, so that an agent would not be liable under recipient liability.[147] Indeed, Millett J (as he then was) in *Agip v Jackson* suggested that a bank would normally not be liable under receipt, as they would be acting de facto as the agents of their customers.[148] The application of *Agip v Jackson* was doubted by Lord Justice Moore-Bick in *Uzinterimpex JSC v Standard Bank plc*,[149] but on the facts there was sufficient receipt, as the account in question the bank had set up was a transaction account to allow the recipient bank to claim fees and expenses, and was clearly for the benefit of the bank, not a customer. If receipt as an agent cannot give rise to liability, but receipt on one's own account can, there would be a difference between an auctioneer selling antique furniture held on trust and a second-hand dealer who buys and resells. The exoneration of agents from liability may unduly limit the operation of personal liability for knowing receipt, but in many cases there will be an alternative claim for knowing assistance.

The receipt of trust property does not have to arise from a breach of trust, as with liability as a dishonest assistor. The circumstances in which the action may arise were summarized by Brightman J in *Karak Rubber Co Ltd v Burden (No 2)* as follows:

cases where a person:

(1) knowingly receives trust property in breach of trust, or

(2) receives trust property without notice of the trust, and subsequently deal with it in a manner inconsistent with trust of which she has become aware, or

---

[144] See *Statek Corporation v McNeill Alford & Anor* [2008] EWHC 32.

[145] *El Ajou v Dollar Land Holdings plc (No.2)* [1995] 2 All ER 213.

[146] See, for example, *Karak Rubber Co Ltd v Burden (No 2)* [1972] 1 WLR 602.

[147] See *Williams-Ashman v Price & Williams* [1942] 1 Ch. 219, and, in support, *Twinsectra v Yardley* [2002] 2 AC 164, at [105], per Lord Millett.

[148] [1990] Ch 265. In fact, Millett J suggested that it was only where a bank reduced an overdraft that this was seen as them acting for their own benefit so that they could be liable for receipt.

[149] [2008] EWCA Civ 819, at [39]–[40].

(3) receives trust property knowing it to be such but without breach of trust, and sub-
     sequently deals with it in a manner inconsistent with the trusts.[150]

(3) **Examples**

The operation of the personal liability to account can be illustrated by four important
cases. In *Re Montagu's Settlement Trusts*[151] the beneficiaries of a trust sought to render
a stranger liable to account for the value of trust property he had received and subsequently dissipated. In 1923 the tenth Duke of Manchester promised to create a trust
of the chattels to which he would become entitled on the death of the ninth Duke. The
trustees were supposed to draw up an inventory of such chattels, but failed to do so.
After the death of the ninth Duke in 1947 they released all the chattels to the tenth
Duke, who disposed of a number of them during his lifetime. On the death of the tenth
Duke in 1977, the eleventh Duke claimed that his estate was liable to account for the
value of the items that had been sold. As the tenth Duke had received the chattels as
a volunteer, he had received them subject to the trust because he was not a bona fide
purchaser. His estate was therefore required to return any remaining chattels or their
traceable proceeds. However, his estate was only liable to account for the value of the
chattels that had been sold if the tenth Duke had sold them with knowledge that they
were subject to the 1923 settlement. Megarry V-C held that, in the circumstances, the
Duke had not known that the chattels were subject to the trust when he had disposed
of them. In *Lipkin Gorman v Karpnale Ltd*,[152] Norman Cass was a partner in a firm of
solicitors who used some £223,000 from the firm's client account to finance his gambling at the Playboy Club. The firm subsequently sought to recover the money that had
been paid to the club. It alleged that the club was liable to account as a constructive
trustee for the money received, which was no longer identifiable by the rules of tracing
because it had become mixed with its other receipts. It was held that the club had not
received the money with sufficient knowledge that it was subject to a trust to render it
liable to account as a constructive trustee. In *Eagle Trust plc v SBC Securities Ltd*[153] the
defendants had received some £13.5m from the plaintiff company through the fraud of
its chief executive as part of the underwriting of a rights issue or cash alternative in the
course of a takeover. It claimed that the defendants were liable to account for what they
had received in equity because they had received it knowing that it had been misappropriated. It was held that the defendants had not received the property with sufficient knowledge to render them liable as constructive trustees. In *BCCI (Overseas) Ltd v Akindele*[154]
the liquidators of BCCI claimed that an investor was liable to account as a constructive
trustee for over $16m, which he had received in performance of an investment agreement
he had entered with a company controlled by the BCCI group, purportedly to buy and sell
shares in BCCI, which was alleged to have been a sham. Although the agreement was not
found to have been a sham, the payments were held to have been procured in consequence

---

[150] [1972] 1 WLR 602, at 632.   [151] [1987] Ch 264.
[152] [1992] 4 All ER 331; [1987] 1 WLR 987.   [153] [1992] 4 All ER 488.   [154] [2001] Ch 437.

of a fraudulent breach of fiduciary duty by directors of BCCI, and they were therefore impressed with a constructive trust. As such the investor had received trust property. The Court of Appeal held, however, that he was not personally liable to account for the trust money he had received because he had not acted 'unconscionably'. He had not been aware of the internal arrangements within BCCI that had rendered the payment a breach of fiduciary duty. These four cases clearly illustrate that the duty to account as a constructive trustee is a personal remedy, available against a person who has received property that he knew was trust property, with which he has subsequently dealt in a manner inconsistent with his duty to observe the trust.

(4) **Fault required to render a recipient of trust property liable to account**

There has been a great deal of debate, which engendered inevitable uncertainty, regarding the requirements which must be satisfied before a recipient of trust property will be held personally liable to account for the value of what he received. In his dissenting opinion in *Twinsectra Ltd v Yardley*, Lord Millett asserted that the personal liability of a recipient was not founded upon fault:

> Liability for 'knowing receipt' is receipt-based. It does not depend on fault. The cause of action is restitutionary and is available only where the defendant received or applied the money in breach of trust for his own use and benefit. There is no basis for requiring actual knowledge of the breach of trust, let alone dishonesty, as a condition of liability. Constructive notice is sufficient, and may not even be necessary. There is powerful academic support for the proposition that the liability of the recipient is the same as in other cases of restitution, that is to say strict but subject to a change of position defence.[155]

If this view were correct, then in order to avoid injustice, a narrow view would have to be taken of the circumstances in which a person is considered to be a recipient. However, these obiter comments are inconsistent with the tenor of the leading judgments of the House of Lords and Court of Appeal, which have consistently held that the equitable obligation to account as a constructive trustee for the value of property received in breach of trust is founded upon the fault of the recipient, and in only one exceptional situation have the courts found that liability should be strict.[156] As Lord Browne-Wilkinson stated in *Westdeutsche Landesbank Girozentrale v Islington London Borough Council*:

> unless [the recipient of trust property] has the requisite degree of knowledge he is not personally liable to account as trustee.[157]

---

[155] [2002] 2 AC 164, at [105].

[156] Lord Millett has argued extra-judicially that recipient liability should be strict—see, for example, his comments in a book review 'Landmark Cases in the Law of Restitution' (2007) 123 LQR 159, at 164–165.

[157] [1996] AC 669, at 707. In support of this proposition he cited *Re Diplock* [1948] Ch 465 and *Re Montagu's Settlement Trusts* [1987] Ch 264.

In the four cases discussed earlier, this crucial element was found to be lacking, demonstrating how difficult it can be to establish entitlement to a personal remedy.

The most controversial issue in relation to the personal liability to account has concerned the degree of fault required to establish liability. It is clear that the level of fault sufficient to found a personal liability to account as a constructive trustee is not synonymous with the element of notice that will determine whether a recipient of property acquired it free from pre-existing equitable rights. As Megarry V-C observed in *Re Montagu's Settlement Trusts*:

> It should be remembered that the doctrine of purchaser without notice and constructive trust are concerned with matters which differ in important respects. The former is concerned with the question whether a person takes property subject to or free from some equity. The latter is concerned with whether or not a person is to have imposed upon him the personal burdens and obligations of trusteeship.[158]

A stranger may therefore receive property subject to a trust because he is affixed with notice thereof, yet not attract any personal liability if he dissipates the trust property. It is clear that the law now appears to favour 'unconscionability' as stated by the Court of Appeal in *Akindele* as the test to describe the fault necessary to impose liability on a recipient of trust property. However, to understand the full implications of this approach, it is necessary to consider the varying methods used over the years to find this elusive element of fault.

(a) Degrees of knowledge

While some cases had indicated that liability can be founded upon the mere negligence of the recipient, or in very narrow circumstances that liability may even be strict, the majority of cases have required a higher threshold of fault, which is consistent with the developments in the context of accessory liability examined earlier, where the Privy Council has stated that an assisting stranger will only be liable if he acted dishonestly. Many cases have addressed the requirement of fault in terms of the knowledge of the stranger who received trust property, and this terminology was utilized by Lord Browne-Wilkinson in *Westdeutsche Landesbank Girozentrale v Islington London Borough Council*.[159] A scale of the knowledge that a recipient might have possessed was provided by Peter Gibson J in *Baden Delvaux v Société Général*.[160] Having considered all the previous decisions, and drawing heavily from the doctrine of notice operating in the context of land conveyancing, including the definition of constructive notice provided in s 199 of the Law of Property Act 1925, he identified five classes of knowledge:[161] (i) actual knowledge; (ii) wilfully shutting one's eyes to the obvious; (iii) wilfully and recklessly failing to make such inquiries as an honest and reasonable man would make; (iv) knowledge of circumstances which would indicate the facts to

---

[158] [1987] Ch 264, at 272–273; [1994] 4 All ER 308, at 320.   [159] [1996] AC 669, at 707.
[160] *Baden, Delvaux and Lecuit v Société Général pour Favoriser le Développement du Commerce et de l'Industrie en France SA* [1983] BCLC 325.
[161] [1983] BCLC 325, at 407, considered at 408–421.

an honest and reasonable man; (v) knowledge of circumstances which would put an honest and reasonable man on inquiry.

Although there is some correlation between knowledge and fault, equating the two is both confusing and misleading. Peter Gibson J's analysis shows that the concept of knowledge for these purposes includes not only facts that the recipient of trust property actually knew, but also facts that he could and should have known. In other words, someone would have knowledge if they failed to make such inquiries as an honest and reasonable person would make. Subsequent cases have sought to distinguish between knowledge of types (i)–(iii) and knowledge of types (iv) and (v). Whereas knowledge of types (i)–(iii) are rooted in some degree of conscious moral culpability on the part of the recipient, knowledge of types (iv) and (v) derive from his negligence or inadvertence. The question then becomes one of the degree of culpability required, rather than the extent of knowledge, although the link between the two remains. The majority of recent cases suggest that mere negligence on the part of the recipient should not be sufficient to give rise to liability to account as a constructive trustee, and that deliberate wrongdoing is needed. Putting this in the language of knowledge, the recipient will not be liable because of facts about which he ought to have made inquiries, but only for what he knows, pretends not to know, or refuses to know. Each of the degrees of fault that have been proposed as the touchstone for liability will be examined.

(b) Strict liability

It was noted earlier that there was one exceptional case in which strict liability was applied as the basis for recipient liability. In *Re Diplock*[162] the Court of Appeal held that charities which had mistakenly received money from an estate, because the executors had erroneously believed that a valid charitable bequest had been made, were personally liable to account to the estate for the property they had received, irrespective of the fact that they had acted entirely innocently. Liability of the charities was affirmed by the House of Lords.[163] The decision amounts to the imposition of a strict liability to account as a constructive trustee, and it has not found favour in subsequent decisions. Such strict liability has been confined to claims involving the administration of estates, or analogous circumstances. In *Ministry of Health v Simpson*,[164] Lord Simonds was careful to limit the principle to the administration of an estate. He started his judgment with a warning that it was 'important in the discussion of this question to remember that the particular branch of the jurisdiction of the Court of Chancery with which we are concerned relates to the administration of assets of a deceased person'.[165] He based his judgment on the principle stated by Lord Davey in *Harrison v Kirk*:

> The Court of Chancery in order to do justice and to avoid the evil of allowing one man to retain what is really and legally applicable to the payment of another man devised a remedy by which where the estate had been distributed without regard to the rights of a

---

[162] [1948] Ch 465.   [163] *Ministry of Health v Simpson* [1951] AC 251.
[164] [1951] AC 251.   [165] [1951] AC 251, at 265.

creditor, it has allowed the creditor to recover back what has been paid to the beneficiaries or the next of kin who derive title from the deceased testator or intestate.[166]

He then extended this principle to the facts of *Re Diplock*:[167]

> It would be strange if a court of equity, whose self-sought duty it was to see that the assets of a deceased person were duly administered and came into the right hands and not into the wrong hands, devised a remedy for the protection of the unpaid creditor but left the unpaid legatee or next of kin unprotected.[168]

Subsequent cases have extended the personal liability imposed in *Re Diplock*[169] to circumstances analogous to the administration of estates.[170] In *Butler v Broadhead*[171] and *Re J Leslie Engineers Co Ltd (in liquidation)*[172] it was held that there was sufficient analogy between the position of the executor of an estate and the liquidator of a company to entitle a creditor to recover from overpaid contributories in a winding-up. However, the claim did not succeed in either case,[173] and there has been no general extension of the principle to all trust situations.

The strict liability of the recipients in *Re Diplock* was also ameliorated by a requirement that the claimants first exhaust their personal remedies against the executors who had wrongly paid the charities. The Court of Appeal stated:

> Since the original wrong payment was attributable to the blunder of the personal representatives, the right of the unpaid beneficiary is in the first instance against the wrongdoing executor or administrator; and the beneficiary's direct claim in equity against those overpaid or wrongly paid should be limited to the amount which he cannot recover from the party responsible.[174]

As the court observed, this may mean that in some circumstances the whole amount will have to be recovered from the innocent volunteers, for example if the executors are insolvent, have acted under a court order, or are protected by s 27 of the Trustee Act 1925.[175] The strict liability imposed in *Re Diplock* has left the law in a state of confusion. The scope of the liability appears extremely limited if other remedies against the blundering executor must be exhausted first. It is submitted that the imposition of a strict liability to account as a constructive trustee is inconsistent with the equitable nature of the remedy. In *Westdeutsche Landesbank Girozentrale v Islington London Borough Council* Lord Browne-Wilkinson stressed that equity operates on the conscience of the owner of the legal interest,[176] but in *Re Diplock* the entirely innocent recipients of property, who had committed no wrong by disposing of it because they honestly believed that they were entitled to it, were required to account.

---

[166] [1904] AC 1.   [167] [1948] Ch 465.   [168] [1951] AC 251, at 266.   [169] [1948] Ch 465.

[170] See also Smith 'Unjust Enrichment, Property and the Structure of Trusts' (2000) 116 LQR 412.

[171] [1975] Ch 97.   [172] [1976] 1 WLR 292.

[173] In *Butler v Broadhead* the claim was barred by the Companies Act, and in *Re J Leslie Engineers Co Ltd* the creditors exhausted their claim against the liquidators.   [174] [1948] Ch 465, at 503.

[175] Trustee Act 1925, s 23 provides that the personal representatives may gain protection where they advertise their intention to distribute in the *Gazette* and a newspaper.

[176] [1996] AC 669, at 705.

In reality the award of an equitable account in *Re Diplock* was a consequence of an inadequacy in the availability of common law restitution at the time that the case was decided. Until the decision of the House of Lords in *Kleinwort Benson Ltd v Lincoln City Council*[177] a plaintiff was only entitled to recover restitution from the payee of money paid under a mistake of fact,[178] but not of money paid under a mistake of law.[179] The executors in *Re Diplock* had paid money to persons they believed were legally entitled to receive because of their misconstruction of the relevant law, and would not therefore have been entitled to recover restitution on the grounds of mistake. However, now that the barrier preventing recovery of money paid under a mistake of law has been removed,[180] such beneficiaries would be entitled to receive restitution from the wrongly paid charities, but the charities would also be entitled to claim the defence of change of position.[181] Provided that the charities had acted in good faith, it is unlikely that they would have to make restitution of the money they had dissipated, since such dissipation would constitute a change of position. They would therefore only be liable to make restitution in full if they had not acted in good faith, which is tantamount to the introduction of a species of fault-based liability.

While the general attitude of the courts towards *Re Diplock* has been hostile,[182] so that it has been characterized as exceptional and its scope has not been extended, some academics have suggested that it should provide the paradigm for the availability of personal restitutionary remedies against a stranger who received trust property.[183]

(c) Negligence of the recipient

Some English cases[184] have held that a stranger should be liable to account as a constructive trustee if he received trust property with knowledge of any of the five types identified in *Baden Delvaux*,[185] including mere negligence. In *El Ajou v Dollar Land*

---

[177] [1999] 2 AC 349; [1998] 4 All ER 513.

[178] See *Barclays Bank v W J Simms* [1980] QB 677; *Rover International Ltd v Cannon Film Sales Ltd (No 3)* [1989] 1 WLR 912, CA; *Lipkin Gorman v Karpnale Ltd* [1991] 2 AC 548, HL.

[179] See *Bilbie v Lumley* (1802) 2 East 469; *Brisbane v Dacres* (1813) 5 Taunt 143; *William Whiteley v R* (1909) 101 LT 741; *Sawyer and Vincent v Window Brace Ltd* [1943] 1 KB 32; *Avon County Council v Howlett* [1983] 1 All ER 1073, CA; *R v Tower Hamlets London Borough Council, ex p Chetnik Developments Ltd* [1988] AC 858; *Woolwich Building Society v IRC* [1993] AC 70, CA.

[180] The decision of the House of Lords to abrogate the distinction between mistakes of fact and law in *Kleinwort Benson v Lincoln City Council* [1999] 2 AC 349, [1998] 4 All ER 513 had been presaged in other jurisdictions. See Judicature Amendment Act 1958, s 2 (New Zealand); *Air Canada v British Columbia* (1989) 59 DLR (4th) 161 (Canada); *David Securities Pty Ltd v Commonwealth Bank of Australia* (1992) 109 ALR 57 (Australia); *Morgan Guaranty Trust Co of New York v Lothian Regional Council* 1995 SLT 299 (Scotland).   [181] *Lipkin Gorman v Karpnale Ltd* [1991] 2 AC 548.

[182] See the comments of Nourse LJ in *BCCI Ltd v Akindele* [2000] 4 All ER 221, at 236.

[183] Restitution is a technical term describing the remedy by which a defendant is required to return to a claimant the amount of an enrichment he unjustly received at the claimant's expense, For a good treatment of this law of restitution (now referred to as the law of 'unjust enrichment'), see Goff and Jones, *The Law of Unjust Enrichment* (8th edn, 2011).

[184] *Selangor United Rubber Estates v Cradock (No 3)* [1968] 1 WLR 1555; *Karak Rubber Co Ltd v Burden (No 2)* [1972] 1 All ER 1210; *Rowlandson v National Westminster Bank Ltd* [1978] 3 All ER 370; *Belmont Finance Corpn v Williams Furniture Ltd* [1979] 1 All ER 118, CA.   [185] [1983] BCLC 325.

Holdings plc[186] Millett J suggested, albeit obiter, that liability could be founded upon something less than dishonesty:

> I am content to assume, without deciding, that dishonesty or want of probity involving actual knowledge (whether proved or inferred) is not a precondition of liability; but that a recipient is not expected to be unduly suspicious and is not to be held liable unless he went ahead without further inquiry in circumstances in which an honest and reasonable man would have realised that the money was probably trust money and was being misapplied.[187]

In New Zealand the courts have held that knowledge of all five types identified in *Baden Delvaux*, therefore including negligence, are sufficient to give rise to liability.[188] Until the judgment of the Court of Appeal in *BCCI (Overseas) Ltd v Akindele*[189] it was generally thought that the criteria of negligence had been rejected in favour of a requirement of conscious wrongdoing. However, Nourse LJ, while rejecting the formulation of a test of liability in terms of 'knowledge' in favour of a generalized requirement of 'unconscionability', held that dishonesty was not a 'necessary ingredient of liability in knowing receipt'.[190] He approved those English and New Zealand authorities favouring liability on the basis of the lower threshold of 'constructive knowledge', which thus favours the adoption of a negligence standard.

It would almost certainly be wrong to interpret these English cases as accepting that 'mere' negligence will be sufficient to ground liability. The language of Millett J in *El Ajou* falls short of accepting that mere negligence would be sufficient. At the least he would have required that the recipient *ought* because of the circumstances to have been made suspicious. Similarly, it is submitted that, despite the suggestions in more recent cases, Nourse LJ in *BCCI (Overseas) v Akindele* did not suggest that mere negligence should be enough for liability; he cited with approval the statements of Megarry VC in *Re Montagu's Settlement Trusts* requiring conscious impropriety and did consider that an element of fault was necessary. Indeed, on the facts it was held that the decision of an investor to enter into an agreement with a commercial bank was to be treated as an 'arm's length business transaction'. The investor was not therefore put on notice that some fraud or breach of trust was being perpetrated merely because the agreement was artificial in nature and offered a high rate of interest.[191] Moreover, this view is consistent with other authorities in which negligence was held to be insufficient, which have not been overruled.[192] This accords with the view that commercial parties in particular should not be burdened by the imposition of personal liability for receipt of trust property unless they are at fault. Indeed, in *Cowan de Groot Properties*

---

[186] [1993] 3 All ER 717.   [187] [1993] 3 All ER 717, at 739.
[188] *Westpac Banking Corpn v Savin* [1985] 2 NZLR 41; *Powell v Thompson* [1991] 1 NZLR 597; *Equiticorp Industries Group v Hawkins* [1991] 3 NZLR 700; *Lankshear v ANZ Banking Group* [1993] 1 NZLR 481; *Nimmo v Westpac Banking Corpn* [1993] 3 NZLR 218; *Springfield Acres (in liquidation) v Abacus (Hong Kong)* [1994] 3 NZLR 502.   [189] [2000] 4 All ER 221.
[190] [2000] 4 All ER 221, at 231.   [191] [2000] 4 All ER 221, at 237.
[192] See the cases under headings (d)–(e) in the treatment earlier.

v Eagle Trust[193] Knox J pointed out that the duty of the directors of a purchasing company is to buy as cheaply as they can.[194] This, after all, fits the philosophy of profit: buy cheap and sell dear. In the view of Knox J, it would be unduly onerous to impose upon directors of a company a positive duty to inquire into the reasons for a sale to them at a bargain price. His view is supported by *Eagle Trust plc v SBC Securities Ltd*,[195] where Vinelott J emphasized that the doctrines of constructive notice had developed 'in the field of property transactions' and that the courts had been particularly reluctant to extend the doctrine of constructive notice to cases where moneys are paid in the ordinary course of business to the defendant in discharge of a liability.[196]

There is therefore no real authority if favour of the proposition that 'mere negligence' is sufficient for liability. The lowest test suggested is that the circumstances should have been such that a reasonable and honest recipient would have made further enquiries.

(d) Conscious wrongdoing

The requisite degree of fault for the imposition of liability to account as a constructive trustee was examined by Megarry V-C in *Re Montagu's Settlement Trusts*,[197] the facts of which were considered earlier. He held that the tenth Duke of Manchester should only be held liable to account for the value of the chattels sold in breach of trust if he had acted with 'want of probity'.[198] He considered that knowledge stemming from negligence would not establish sufficient fault to justify liability:

> knowledge is not confined to actual knowledge, but includes at least knowledge of types (ii) and (iii) in the *Baden* case... for in such cases there is a want of probity which justifies imposing a constructive trust... Whether knowledge of the *Baden* types (iv) and (v) suffices for this purpose is at best doubtful; in my view it does not, for I cannot see that the carelessness involved will normally amount to a want of probity.[199]

He referred to authorities decided prior to *Baden Delvaux*, where it had been held that negligence was insufficient to give rise to a constructive trust,[200] and emphasized that the requirement of 'knowledge' was essentially different from the concept of 'notice' used to determine whether equitable property rights had been defeated. Subsequent cases followed the approach of Megarry V-C. In *Lipkin Gorman v Karpnale Ltd*[201] Alliott J held that 'want of probity is the key aspect in the approach the court should

---

[193] [1992] 4 All ER 700, at 761.   [194] [1992] 4 All ER 700, at 761.   [195] [1992] 4 All ER 488.
[196] [1992] 4 All ER 488, at 507.
[197] [1987] Ch 264; [1992] 4 All ER 308; (1986) 102 LQR 267 and (1987) 50 MLR 217 (C Harpum); [1987] CLJ 385 (Hayton).
[198] This picks up the language of Sachs LJ in *Carl-Zeiss-Stifung v Herbert Smith & Co (No 2)* [1969] 2 All ER 367, at 379 that there must be an 'element... of dishonesty or of consciously acting improperly, as opposed to an innocent failure to make what a court may later decide to have been proper enquiry', and Edmund Davies LJ, who spoke of 'want of probity'.
[199] [1987] Ch 264, at 285. See earlier in the chapter for a description of the types of knowledge identified in *Baden*.
[200] *Carl-Zeiss-Stifung v Herbert Smith & Co (No 2)* [1969] 2 Ch 276; *Competitive Insurance Co Ltd v Davies Investments Ltd* [1975] 1 WLR 1240.   [201] [1992] 4 All ER 331; [1987] 1 WLR 987.

take'.[202] This was affirmed by the Court of Appeal.[203] In *Eagle Trust plc v SBC Securities Ltd*[204] Vinelott J reiterated that in the context of a commercial transaction:

> to make a defendant liable as a constructive trustee, it must be shown that he knew, in one of the senses set out in categories (i) (ii) and (iii) of Peter Gibson J's analysis in *Baden*, that the moneys were misapplied.[205]

In *Cowan de Groot Properties v Eagle Trust*[206] Knox J similarly held that it was essential for a plaintiff to demonstrate that the recipient of trust property had knowledge within categories (i), (ii), and (iii).[207] *Re Montagu* was also endorsed by Lord Browne-Wilkinson in *Westdeutsche Landesbank Girozentrale v Islington London Borough Council*[208] and by Knox J in *Hillsdown Holdings plc v Pensions Ombudsman*.[209]

(e) Dishonesty

While *Re Montagu* held that liability to account as a constructive trustee would only be imposed against a conscious wrongdoer, the standard of liability could also be expressed as a requirement of dishonesty. In *Agip (Africa) Ltd v Jackson*[210] Millett J warned against an 'over refinement or a too ready assumption that categories (iv) and (v) are necessarily cases of constructive notice only' and suggested that the 'true distinction is between honesty and dishonesty', which is essentially a jury question.[211] As was discussed above, in the context of liability of a stranger as an accessory to a breach of trust, the Privy Council has adopted dishonesty as the touchstone of liability in preference to knowledge.[212] In the context of the liability of a recipient of trust property, it is arguable that dishonesty is synonymous with the want of probity identified in *Re Montagu*. Both terms were used by the Court of Appeal in *Carl-Zeiss-Stiftung v Herbert Smith & Co (No 2)*.[213] More recently, the requirement of dishonesty was applied by the Court of Appeal in *Twinsectra Ltd v Yardley*.[214] As was noted earlier, the requirement of dishonesty was rejected by the Court of Appeal in *BCCI (Overseas) v Akindele* in favour of a requirement of 'unconscionability' which might encompass elements of constructive notice. Although Nourse LJ rejected the language of dishonesty, he did accept that at least some degree of fault would be required to render it unconscionable for the defendant to retain the benefit he had received, and it is very difficult to determine where this line is to be drawn. At all events, it is clear that no personal liability to account can be maintained against an innocent recipient who has received trust property, except in the anomalous situations where *Re Diplock* may still apply.

---

[202] [1992] 4 All ER 331, at 349.

[203] [1992] 4 All ER 409, at 420, per May LJ; Jones 'The Gambling Fiduciary, the Casino and the Bank' [1990] CLJ 17.   [204] [1992] 4 All ER 488; [1991] BCLC 438.

[205] [1991] BCLC 438, at 509.   [206] [1992] 4 All ER 700.

[207] [1992] 4 All ER 700, at 760. He also held that if it was necessary to have regard to knowledge of types (iv) and (v) that there still was no knowledge on the facts.

[208] [1996] AC 669, at 707. See also *Hillsdown Holdings plc v Pensions Ombudsman* [1997] 1 All ER 862.

[209] [1997] 1 All ER 862, at 902–903.   [210] [1990] Ch 265; [1992] 4 All ER 385, at 405.

[211] See also *Metall und Rohstoff AG v Donaldson Lufkin & Jenrette Inc* [1990] 1 QB 391, at 474; *Polly Peck International plc v Nadir (No 2)* [1992] 4 All ER 769, at 781–782.

[212] *Royal Brunei Airlines v Tan* [1995] 3 All ER 97; *Barlow Clowes v Eurotrust* [2006] 1 All ER 333.

[213] [1969] 2 All ER 367.   [214] [1999] Lloyd's Rep Bank 438; (2000) 59 CLJ 444 (D Fox).

(f) Unconscionability

The determination of an appropriate standard of personal liability applicable to a stranger who has received trust property has been bedevilled by terminological debates. In *BCCI (Overseas) v Akindele*[215] the Court of Appeal sought to cut through this Gordian knot by means of the introduction of a new test of 'unconscionability'.[216] Nourse LJ rejected previous attempts to provide a categorization of different types of knowledge or notice and proposed a new generalized test of liability:

> I have come to the view that, just as there is now a single test of dishonesty for knowing assistance, so ought there to be a single test of knowledge for knowing receipt. The recipient's state of knowledge must be such as to make it unconscionable for him to retain the benefit of the receipt.[217]

However, it must be questioned whether this new approach provides a more comprehensible means of determining liability. The use of the test of unconscionability has been eschewed in other areas because of its vague and uncertain meaning. It fails to resolve the significant question whether 'conscious wrongdoing', as understood by Megarry VC in *Re Montagu's Settlement Trusts*,[218] is required for a successful action, or whether some species of negligence is sufficient to found a claim. The adoption of unconscionability as the test indeed reopens the possibility that something akin to negligence on behalf of the recipient may well be sufficient to impose liability. To put it in other language, there may be times when it is unconscionable for the recipient to receive the trust property, not because of what he knew or ought to have known, but because of what could have been discovered had the transaction been conducted differently and a different range of information had been disclosed. The test could even conceivably make liability appropriate in other circumstances where there is no kind of knowledge whatsoever, but where the recipient can be considered, for instance, to have been unfairly enriched.

Nourse LJ himself noted that the test of unconscionability would not avoid 'difficulties of application', although he felt that it would 'avoid those difficulties of definition and allocation to which the previous categorizations have led'.[219] While Nourse LJ appears to acknowledge the difficulties associated with the adoption of 'knowledge' as a criterion for liability, he reintroduces them by requiring the court to determine if the recipient's 'state of knowledge' would render it unconscionable to retain the benefit. Moreover, it is difficult to see how the test of unconscionability differs from that of dishonesty in practice, particularly as Nourse LJ found on the facts that the investor had not acted 'unconscionably' on the basis that he had not acted dishonestly.[220] If it is different in a substantive sense, as Nourse LJ clearly intended by dismissing dishonesty as an essential ingredient of recipient liability as we have seen earlier in

---

[215] [2000] 4 All ER 221; Stevens 'No New Landmark—An Unconscionable Mess in Knowing Receipt' [2001] RLR 99.

[216] See Barkehall '"Goodbye" Knowing Receipt. "Hello" Unconscientious Receipt' (2001) 21(2) OJLS 239.

[217] [2000] 4 All ER 221, at 235.   [218] [1987] Ch 264.   [219] [2000] 4 All ER 221, at 236.

[220] [2000] 4 All ER 221, at 236, at 238.

the discussion of negligence, Nourse LJ gives no guidance as to what that difference is. This gives considerable weight to Lord Nicholls' assertion in *Royal Brunei Airlines v Tan* that 'if unconscionable means something different, it must be said that it is not clear what that something different is'.[221] At best, what this seems to create is a value judgement for the court, based upon individual facts, because the vague concept of 'unconscionability' is so malleable. If it involves concepts of dishonesty, it is submitted it would be better to use a test of dishonesty and have a single measure of liability for both categories of the personal liability of strangers to the trust. There would also be clear limits, understandable by both the courts and recipients, as to when personal liability may be imposed for improper receipt of trust property.

(g) Unconscionability confirmed but not explained

The application of 'unconscionability' to provide the requisite fault for imposing liability has been followed in subsequent cases, though they have done little to help define the boundaries of how the test will operate in practice. In *City Index Ltd v Gawler*, Carnwarth and Mummery LJJ were of the view that:

> In this court also it is accepted that *Akindele* represents the present law. Accordingly liability for 'knowing receipt' depends on the defendant having sufficient knowledge of the circumstances of the payment to make it 'unconscionable' for him to retain the benefit or pay it away for his own purposes.[222]

Since the recipient in this case, City Index Ltd, was on the assumed facts aware that that the monies it received had been procured in breach of trust or fiduciary duty by an employee of the claimant, there was no need for the limits of the test to be explored.[223]

A transfer of land owned by a charity, alleged to have been made in breach of trust to the recipient was the issue that came before Evans-Lombe J in *Hollis v Rolfe*.[224] In finding that the transfer of the property had not been in breach of trust, it followed that 'Mr Rolfe could not have received title to the Property in circumstances where it was unconscionable for him to retain it.'[225]

In *Independent Trustee Services Ltd v GP Noble Trustees Ltd & Ors*,[226] a freezing order had been made to protect pension funds which had been improperly invested, a contributing factor being the alleged dishonesty of two directors. Lewison J had to deal with an application to vary the order on the application of a defendant company that had received some of the funds and wanted a relaxation to enable it to pay for its legal defence. Without stating what the test was, Lewison J expressed his view that there was an arguable case that the defendant had been dishonest, but added that: 'It is

---

[221] [1995] 3 All ER 97, at 108.
[222] [2008] Ch 313 (CA). Mummery LJ did not give a separate opinion, but agreed with Carnwarth LJ. Arden LJ seemed to consider the case to be one of unjust enrichment.
[223] Leave was given to appeal to the then House of Lords, but no decision has been forthcoming. It was strongly hoped this would give some clarity to the boundaries and nature of unconscionability and knowing receipt—Gardner 'Moment of Truth for Knowing Receipt' (2009) LQR 20.
[224] [2008] EWHC 1747 (Ch).   [225] [2008] EWHC 1747 (Ch), at [174].
[226] [2009] EWHC 161 (Ch).

also clear from *BCCI v Akindele* that a lower threshold than dishonesty will suffice to impose liability for knowing receipt'.[227] He considered that the recipient could well be liable for failing to make further enquiries on the constraints on the investment powers, as that 'may well amount to notice'.[228] The recipient should also have been alerted to issues over the terms of the bonds which made them questionable investments, and should not have relied solely on the assertions of the trustee. It was suggested that such manifestly bad investments 'may themselves amount to notice of a breach of trust'.[229] This is an interesting application of the requirements of fault, and does suggest that negligence will be sufficient to impose liability on the recipient. It is also noteworthy that the language used throughout the judgment of Lewison J is couched in terms of 'notice'; a return to the language used in the cases before *Re Montagu's Settlement Trusts*. It is not clear how this adds to any suggestion of how unconscionability works as a separate concept of liability. On appeal, the issue did not come up for assessment by their Lordships.[230]

A simple application of the unconscionability test again arose in *Horler v Rubin*,[231] where a claim for knowing receipt was made out against a trustee in bankruptcy. A transfer had been made to creditors, with knowledge that the assets transferred were part of a disputed claim that the bankrupt had been in a partnership. Since the creditors were not members of the partnership, it was held that the trustee in bankruptcy had acted unconscionably in transferring the assets in advance of a determination of the partnership claim.

The latest statement on the application of unconscionability is an obiter dictum of Popplewell J in *Madoff Securities International Ltd (In Liquidation) v Raven*,[232] who had to deal with the fallout from the failure of a Ponzi scheme,[233] leaving some $17 billion dollars owing at its collapse. The claim was against a Mrs Kohn, who had received over $27m in the course of fifteen years for research conducted by her on behalf of the investment company and for personal introductions to clients and others. Having found that the payments had been properly made, and that there was no breach of fiduciary duty by the directors in making them, any claim to knowing receipt necessarily failed for want of a breach of trust or fiduciary duty. However, Popplewell J opined that: 'Mrs Kohn's knowledge was not such as to render receipt and retention of the payments unconscionable. They were no more than reasonable remuneration for services legitimately provided by her and she acted honestly in relation to them in all material respects.'[234]

---

[227] [2009] EWHC 161 (Ch), at [16].   [228] [2009] EWHC 161 (Ch).

[229] [2009] EWHC 161 (Ch), at [17].

[230] *Independent Trustee Services Ltd v GP Noble Trustees Ltd* [2012] EWCA Civ 195.

[231] [2011] EWHC 453 (Ch).   [232] [2013] EWHC 3147 (Comm).

[233] This is fraudulent investment scheme in which high returns are promised on investments, but the returns are paid for using funds provided by new investors. This was the same sort of scheme that came before the courts in *Sinclair Investments (UK) Ltd v Versailles Trade Finance Ltd (in Administration)* [2011] EWCA Civ 347, discussed in Chapter 28.   [234] [2011] EWCA Civ 347, at [373].

(g) Personal attributes

In *Re Clasper Group Services Ltd*[235] it was held that in determining whether a defendant had the requisite knowledge to justify the imposition of liability to account as a constructive trustee the court must take his personal 'attributes'[236] into account. Whereas a mature and experienced person might be held to have had sufficient knowledge, an innocent and inexperienced person might not. The case concerned a boy employed by his father's company who was given a cheque for £2,000 by his father a month before the company went into voluntary liquidation. He paid it into his bank account and then lent £3,000 from the account to another company that his father had acquired. Warner J held that, bearing in mind the youth of the boy,[237] the fact that his only experience was his work in a lowly position for a group of companies owned by his father, and the fact that he was not particularly intelligent, he did not have sufficient knowledge affecting his conscience to justify the imposition of a constructive trust. In *Royal Brunei Airlines Sdn Bhd v Tan*[238] the Privy Council likewise held that in determining whether a person had acted dishonestly the court should have regard to the personal attributes of the person concerned, including his experience and intelligence.

(h) Commercial transactions

In *Eagle Trust plc v SBC Securities Ltd*,[239] Vinelott J held that the level of enquiry that purchasers of land are expected to make should not be transposed to other types of business deal. He applied instead the criterion of whether there was commercially unacceptable conduct in the particular context involved, an approach approved in *Royal Brunei Airlines v Tan*.[240]

(i) Time of knowledge or fault

A recipient of trust property will only be held liable to account as a constructive trustee if he had the requisite level of knowledge or fault when he received it or disposed of it. A recipient of trust property will not therefore be liable to account if he had been aware of the existence of the trust before he received the property, but had honestly forgotten that it was subject to a trust at the time that it was received. Thus, in *Re Montagu's Settlement Trusts*[241] Megarry V-C held that the tenth Duke of Manchester was not liable to account for the value of the trust chattels he had received because he had not been aware of the existence of the trust at the date that he had received them. He explained:

> If a person once has clear and distinct knowledge of some fact, is he treated as knowing that fact for the rest of his life, even after he has genuinely forgotten all about it?... it seems to me that a person should not be said to have knowledge of a fact that he once knew if at the time in question he has genuinely forgotten all about it, so that it could not be said to operate on his mind any longer.[242]

---

[235] [1989] BCLC 143.
[236] Following Lawson J in *International Sales and Agencies Ltd v Marcus* [1982] 3 All ER 551, at 558.
[237] Who was 17 years old.   [238] [1995] 3 All ER 97, at 107.   [239] [1992] 4 All ER 488.
[240] [1995] 3 All ER 97, at 107.   [241] [1987] Ch 264.   [242] [1987] Ch 264, at 284.

He suggested a cautious approach, stating that the court should be slow to conclude that what was once known had been forgotten. Conversely, a stranger who received property without any awareness that it was subject to the trust, but without having given value for it, will still be held liable to account as a constructive trustee if he subsequently disposed of it after having become aware that it was trust property.[243] This follows from the comment of Lord Browne-Wilkinson in *Westdeutsche Landesbank Girozentrale v Islington London Borough Council*[244] that a person is liable as a trustee from such time as he becomes aware that it was intended to be held on trust.[245] He will not be liable to account for any part of such property dissipated before he became aware of the trust, as his conduct would not, to that extent, have been dishonest. Nor will he be liable, despite subsequent knowledge if, at the time of acquiring the property, he was a bona fide purchaser for value without notice.[246]

(j) Conclusion

It cannot easily be said that the test for liability for 'knowing receipt' is clear. There remains much confusion between knowledge, notice, and fault, none of which is resolved by the use of the inherently vague notion of unconscionability. There does appear to be a need for some level of fault, which at the very least is a failure to enquire further when the circumstances reasonably give cause to be suspicious. There may even be a need for conscious wrongdoing. The courts have, however, been hampered by two considerations: a desire not to hinder trade or business by setting too low a threshold of what should make a recipient suspicious; and a desire not to taint professionals with the badge of having acted fraudulently. These two considerations point in opposite directions and the courts have as yet been unable to find a way of expressing intelligibly where the middle ground is to be found. The task is complicated further by an occasional difficulty in determining the boundaries between knowing receipt, dishonest assistance, and restitutionary claims.[247] It is clear that unconscionability is the preferred test, but not what that actually encompasses, and, as we have seen earlier, subsequent cases have done little to answer any questions. In fact, it can be said that the authorities provide no elaboration whatsoever on what is meant by 'unconscionable' in this context. What is needed, it is suggested, is an authoritative review of the existing case law in the Supreme Court, and the establishment of a clear and coherent set of boundaries on unconscionability or a replacement test for it which provides that required clarity. Until then, this remains a difficult area on which to advise clients, which is an issue that needs to be resolved.

---

[243] See *Karak Rubber Co Ltd v Burden (No 2)* [1972] 1 WLR 602, at 632, per Brightman J.

[244] [1996] AC 669, at 705.

[245] See *Sheridan v Joyce* (1844) 1 Jo & Lat 401, where a trustee loaned trust money in breach of trust. The recipient, Fair, did not initially know that the money was trust money, but later discovered. The Court of Chancery of Ireland held that he had become a constructive trustee of the money as soon as he had become aware of the facts.   [246] See earlier.

[247] See *Criterion Properties plc v Stratford UK Properties LLC* [2004] 1 WLR 1846; [2004] LMCLQ 421, where it was held that the Court of Appeal had fallen into error by considering 'knowing receipt' in a claim to recover benefits conferred under a contract which is set aside since this does not involve any trust property, and hence is a matter for the common law of restitution, where the personal liability is strict, subject to the defence of change of position.

6 Mapping a way through personal stranger claims

What follows in Figures 29.2 and 29.3 is a tabular synopsis of how to apply the tests for personal liability for dishonest assistors and knowing recipients of trust property. It is intended as an aid only, and the relevant law has already been discussed in the rest of this chapter in detail.

(1) Stranger who assists in a breach of trust

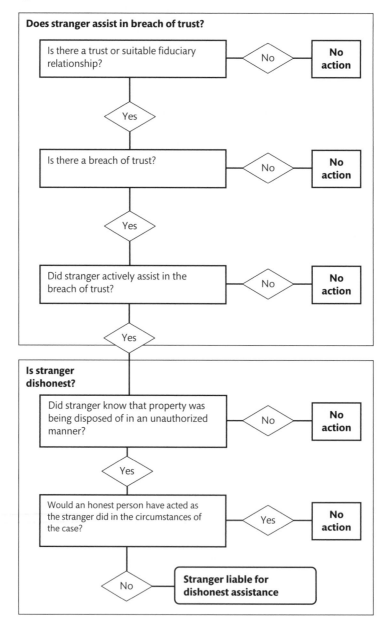

Figure 29.2 Dishonest assistance

(2) **Stranger who receives trust property in breach of trust**

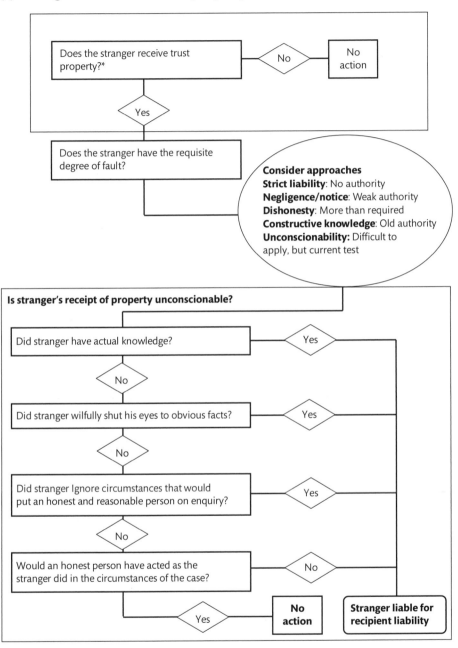

*Receipt needs control (and benefit) of the property.

Figure 29.3 Recipient liability

30

Tracing

The previous chapters have considered the remedies available against trustees and other fiduciaries for breach of their duties, and remedies against third parties who become involved with the trust property (strangers to the trust). This chapter considers the process of tracing, in other words the ways in which a person who is entitled to property can continue to assert a claim to the property even if it is now in the hands of someone else, or even if it has been mixed with other property.

1 What is tracing?

(1) Tracing is a process by which property is identified

(a) Following the original property

Tracing describes the process by which the law allows the original owner of property to identify and claim as his assets in the hands of a third party.[1] For instance if a trustee (Tim) holds 1,000 Royal Mail shares on trust for Billy, and in breach of trust transfers them to his daughter Dolly as an eighteenth birthday gift, tracing is the process by which Billy can assert his rights against Dolly. That form of tracing is known as 'following' because the asset is in its original form.

(b) Tracing substitute property

If Tim, instead of giving the shares directly to Dolly, had sold them and given the cash proceeds to Dolly as a gift, tracing could still apply. Billy will be unable to claim the shares back (unless the buyer was aware that they were held on trust), but he could claim the money as representing the shares. He could also have used tracing against Tim himself if Tim had sold the shares and bought a car with the proceeds. In *Foskett v McKeown*, one of the leading modern cases on tracing, Lord Millett distinguished between 'following' and 'tracing' as follows:

---

[1] For extensive considerations of tracing see Birks (ed), *Laundering and Tracing* (1995); Smith, *The Law of Tracing* (1997).

Following is the process of following the same asset as it moves from hand to hand. Tracing is the process of identifying a new asset as the substitute for the old.[2]

Where the property concerned is intangible property, it may not always be easy to discern the difference between the original property changing hands and new property being created in substitution for the old.[3] Fortunately, the distinction is rarely important. For convenience, the word 'tracing' is often used in this chapter to describe both following and tracing.

(c) There must be property to follow or trace

Since tracing and following are proprietary concepts, they can only be used if there was initially and there remains (in its original or any substituted form) an asset or property to which claim can be made. As Christopher Clarke J said in *Yugraneft v Abramovich*:[4]

> In order to be able successfully to trace property it is necessary for the claimant, firstly, to identify property of his, which has been unlawfully taken from him ('a proprietary base'); secondly, that that property has been used to acquire some other new identifiable property. The new property may then have been used to acquire another identifiable asset ('a series of transactional links'). Thirdly, the chain of substitutes must be unbroken.

The property need not be physical property; it could be intangible. In *Armstrong v Winnington*[5] Deputy High Court Judge Stephen Morris QC held that European Union Allowances (EUAs)—carbon trading units of account—had the necessary characteristics set out in *National Provincial Bank v Ainsworth*[6] to be recognized as intangible property. The same would be true of other legally constructed, but transferable rights such a milk quotas or possibly taxi licences, although in the latter case the need to satisfy requirements of suitability may introduce too great a personal element.

(d) Mixing

Tracing is possible in the simple situations described earlier. It can also be used in more complex situations, where property held on trust for one beneficiary has been mixed up with property held on trust for other beneficiaries (for instance with an investment fraud), or where a trustee has mixed trust funds with his own.

(e) Breach of trust

It is easy to forget that in most, if not all, cases of tracing or following, the trustee will have acted in breach of trust and will personally be liable. Tim should not give trust

---

[2] [2001] 1 AC 102, at 127; Stevens 'Vindicating the Proprietary Nature of Tracing' [2001] Conv 94; Grantham and Rickett 'Tracing and Property Rights: The Categorical Truth' [2000] 63 MLR 905; Berg 'Permitting A Trustee To Retain A Profit' (2001) 117 LQR 366; Sir Robert Walker 'Tracing after *Foskett v McKeown*' [2000] RLR 573; Jaffey 'Tracing, Property and Unjust Enrichment' (2000) 14 Tru LI 194.

[3] *Armstrong DLW GmbH v Winnington Networks Ltd* [2012] 3 All ER 425, at [67].

[4] [2008] EWHC 2613 (QBD), at [349].

[5] *Armstrong DLW GmbH v Winnington Networks Ltd* [2012] 3 All ER 425.

[6] [1965] AC 1175, at 1247–1248.

property to his daughter (unless she is entitled as a beneficiary) and will personally be liable to Billy for the loss this causes.

(2) Why use tracing?

Tracing is resorted to most frequently when the trustee is insolvent, so that a personal claim is of limited value.[7] It can also be used where a profit has been made using funds or property which originally belonged to the trust so that a claim to the property itself would be more valuable than a personal claim for damages.[8]

(3) Tracing at common law and in equity

Despite the extent to which legal and equitable rules have been harmonized, a distinction continues (at least at present) to be made between the legal and equitable rules governing tracing. While the common law rules have little application beyond the most simple of dealings with property, the equitable rules are considerably more generous and facilitate tracing through more complex transactions. The rules in equity have developed particularly to trace property through mixed funds. The equitable rules also have a moral dimension, operating more harshly against a wrongdoer who misappropriates property than an innocent party.

(4) Tracing and claiming

Tracing is merely a process that enables an owner of property to identify assets as representing his original property. As such, the process of tracing does not itself determine the rights that the original owner may assert in any assets identified by the rules of tracing. Tracing is not therefore a remedy but a mechanism. However, tracing provides a foundation for the assertion of a right or a remedy. The original owner may seek to assert a proprietary right to any assets identified through tracing. Alternatively, he may seek a purely personal remedy requiring that the holder of the identified assets make restitution of the value of the property he has received. The assertion of an appropriate remedy in respect of assets identified through rules of tracing has been termed 'claiming'.[9] This purpose and nature of tracing was explained by Lord Millett in *Foskett v McKeown*:

> Tracing is thus neither a claim nor a remedy. It is merely the process by which a claimant demonstrates what has happened to his property, identifies its proceeds and the persons who have handled or received them, and justifies his claim that the proceeds can properly be regarded as representing his property.[10]

---

[7] See Oakley 'Proprietary Claims and Their Priority in Insolvency' [1995] CLJ 377.

[8] *Re Tilley's Will Trust* [1967] Ch 1179; *Jones (FC) & Sons v Jones* [1996] 4 All ER 721; *Foskett v McKeown* [2001] 1 AC 102.   [9] See Smith, *The Law of Tracing* (1997), pp 284–369.

[10] [2001] 1 AC 102, at 128.

Whether an original owner will be able to assert a proprietary claim to any assets identified by the tracing process as representing his property will depend upon a number of factors, including the nature of his interest in the original asset, and whether any intervening defences negate his ability to claim. Where he can assert a proprietary claim his right of ownership is, in effect, preserved into the exchange product of his original property.

This chapter will examine in turn the rules of tracing at common law and in equity, and then the ensuing claiming rights of an original owner who has been able to identify assets which represent his original property.

(5) The nature of the tracing process

(a) Tracing and restitution

There has been a great deal of debate as to the conceptual nature[11] of tracing.[12] Traditionally, tracing was understood to form part of the law of property, and to operate by preserving title to property through substitutions and mixtures. However, some academics have argued that the tracing process should be understood as part of the law of restitution.

Restitution is the response which consists of a defendant giving up to a claimant an unjust enrichment that he has received at the claimant's expense. Generally, restitution will be effected by means of a personal remedy, so that the defendant will be ordered to pay to the claimant a sum of money equivalent to the enrichment he has received. In his seminal work *Introduction to the Law of Restitution*, Professor Birks classified this remedy as 'restitution in the first measure', and the measure of the restitution is the 'value received', ie the extent to which the defendant was unjustly enriched. However, he has argued that restitution will sometimes be effected by means of a proprietary remedy, so that the defendant is forced to give up to the claimant any property in his hands which represents the enrichment he received. This is termed 'restitution in the second measure', and the measure of restitution is the 'value surviving' in the defendant's hands.[13] Tracing is regarded merely as a process by which 'value surviving' is identified. This is not a matter of mere semantics as this analysis has important consequences for understanding of the tracing process.

This restitutionary analysis cuts to the very heart of the nature of tracing. Traditionally, tracing has been understood to operate by descent of title, or 'vested interest'. A claimant is entitled to trace because he initially had title to property, which title he is able to follow into mixtures and exchange products because it was never lost. This analysis is rejected by Birks because of the perceived danger of a 'geometric

---

[11] See Birks 'Mixing and Tracing: Property and Restitution' (1992) 45 CLP 69; Moriarty, 'Tracing, Mixing and Laundering' in Birks (ed), *Laundering and Tracing* (1995), pp 73–94; Smith, *The Law of Tracing* (1997); Birks 'On Taking Seriously the Difference Between Tracing and Claiming' (1997) 11 TLI 2; Smith 'Unjust Enrichment, Property and the Structure of Trusts' (2000) 116 LQR 412; Burrows 'Proprietary Restitution: Unmasking Unjust Enrichment' (2001) 117 LQR 412.

[12] Including in the courts. See *Armstrong DLW GmbH v Winnington Networks Ltd* [2012] 3 All ER 425, at [62]–[98].   [13] Birks, *Introduction to the Law of Restitution* (1985), pp 75–98 and 358–401.

multiplication'[14] in the claimant's wealth as he gains interests in all the exchange products for his property as well. For example, if a trustee takes £5,000 from the trust and purchases a diamond ring, which he sells for £10,000 and then purchases a car with the money, the beneficiary could have equitable title to the ring, the car, and the £10,000 in the hands of the seller of the car, all at the same time (although he will be required to elect between these rights to prevent double recovery). As an alternative to this 'vested interest' approach, Professor Birks has argued that the original owner of property has only a 'power in rem which he can bring down on assets that by the rules of tracing are identified as the surviving enrichment'.[15] The original owner has no proprietary rights to any mixed fund or to assets purchased out of a mixed fund, but only a 'power to crystallise such a right'.[16]

In his later work Professor Burrows has also argued that tracing operates to prevent unjust enrichment. He asserts that the tracing of rights into substitute assets cannot be explained on a proprietary basis:

> Ownership of a pig can explain ownership of the piglets but does not explain why P can be said to own the horse that D has obtained in substitution for the pig stolen from P. To reason from one to the other is to apply a very tempting but, in truth, fictional notion of property.[17]

In his view, where a substitution occurs the owner of the original property is given a new title to reverse the unjust enrichment of the third party who has substituted it. Unmasking the underlying principle of unjust enrichment thus opens the door to consideration whether the act of substitution should automatically entitle an original owner to obtain title to the new asset. However, it can be countered that it is well established in English law that an original owner has an automatic right to claim entitlement to assets which are substituted for his property. Given that 'unjust enrichment' and 'property' are both legal constructs it is just as legitimate for a legal system to characterize such an automatic entitlement as an aspect of property as it would be to characterize it as unjust enrichment. The same goes for the conventions by which one determines the ownership of piglets produced by a pig.

In his final work before his untimely death, Professor Birks reiterated his long-held view that tracing is merely a power on the part of an owner to vest a currently traceable substitute in himself, not a right, although he acknowledged that this view is not uncontroversial.[18]

---

[14] Birks, *Introduction to the Law of Restitution* (1985), p 394. See also Burrows, *The Law of Restitution* (2nd edn, 2002), p 92.

[15] See Birks 'Mixing and Tracing: Property and Restitution' (1992) 45(2) CLP 69, at 89–95.

[16] Birks, *Introduction to the Law of Restitution* (1985), p 393. See also *Re J Leslie Engineers Co Ltd* [1976] 1 WLR 292.

[17] 'Proprietary Restitution: Unmasking Unjust Enrichment' (2002) 117 LQR 412, at 418. See also Craig Rotherham 'The Metaphysics of Tracing: Substituted Title and Property Rhetoric' (1996) 34 Osgoode Hall LJ 321.

[18] Birks, *Unjust Enrichment* (2nd edn, 2005), p 198. See also Hedley and Halliwell (eds), *The Law of Restitution* (2002), p 58.

(b) Tracing as a proprietary process

It is submitted that the relegation of tracing to a mere process without proprietary implications is unduly reductionist and at odds with both authority and principle.[19] While tracing is sometimes used only as a basis for making a personal claim, the process of tracing is intrinsically proprietary in nature. Stephen Morris QC in *Armstrong v Winnington*[20] considered that some claims could be treated as 'proprietary restitutionary claims', because they had a proprietary base, but this confusingly and unnecessarily elides the distinct concepts of descent of title with the principles of unjust enrichment.[21] The leading cases concerning the right to trace at common law and in equity support the view that tracing operates by 'descent of title', or by way of charge, another proprietary concept.[22] This is illustrated by *Lipkin Gorman v Karpnale Ltd*, the leading case concerning common law tracing, where money had been wrongly taken from the client account of a firm of solicitors. Lord Goff held that the implication of the firm tracing the money was that it remained 'their property at common law'.[23] In *Jones (FC) & Sons (a firm) v Jones*[24] the Court of Appeal similarly held that money was traceable at common law because the recipient had not obtained title to it. In *Foskett v McKeown*, which concerned the tracing of trust property in equity, the House of Lords clearly stated that the tracing process was to be viewed as part of the law of property, rather than restitution. Lord Millett explained:

> The transmission of a claimant's property rights from one asset to its traceable proceeds is part of our law of property, not of the law of unjust enrichment. There is no 'unjust factor' to justify restitution (unless 'want of title' be one, which makes the point). The claimant succeeds if at all by virtue of his own title, not to reverse unjust enrichment. Property rights are to be determined by fixed rules and settled principles, they are not discretionary. They do not depend upon ideas of what is 'fair, just or reasonable'. Such concepts, which in reality mask decisions of legal policy, have no place in the law of property. A beneficiary of a trust is entitled to a continuing beneficial interest not merely in the trust property but in its traceable proceeds also, and his interest binds every one

[19] See *Westdeutsche Landesbank Girozentrale v Islington London Borough Council* [1996] AC 669 at 709, where Lord Browne-Wilkinson stated in respect of Professor Birks' argument that unjust enrichment would give rise to an automatic resulting trust: 'First, the argument elides rights in property (which is the only proper subject matter of a trust) into rights in "the value transferred". A trust can only arise where there is defined property: it is therefore not consistent with trust principles to say that a person is a trustee of property which cannot be defined. The same argument applies to the right to trace in equity. It can only subsist in respect of identified property which is held on trust for the person tracing and not in respect of some abstract concept of value.'
[20] *Armstrong DLW GmbH v Winnington Networks Ltd* [2012] 3 All ER 425, at [88]–[92]. See Smith 'The vindication of an owner's rights to intangible property' (2013) 7 JIBFL 412
[21] The term proprietary restitutionary claim is normally used where the proprietary right is created (for instance by way of a constructive trust) to reverse unjust enrichment, but did not exist prior to the claim.
[22] See *Re Hallett's Estate* (1880) 13 Ch D 696 and the judgment of Robert Walker J in *El Ajou v Dollar Land Holdings plc (No 2)* [1995] 2 All ER 213, who suggested (at 223) that: 'tracing claims depend not on equitable ownership as such but on the concept of an equitable charge'.
[23] [1992] 4 All ER 512, at 529.   [24] [1997] Ch 159.

who takes the property or its traceable proceeds except a bona fide purchaser for value without notice.[25]

Professor Burrows[26] considers this affirmation of the proprietary nature of tracing to have been unfortunate. He argues that it is a fiction to say that a claimant is given ownership of traced property because his or her ownership of the original property continues through the substitute property, and he argues that the truth is that the claimant may be given a new title to the traced property to reverse the defendant's unjust enrichment at the claimant's expense.[27] However, the rules of tracing, which will be examined later, have evolved specifically to identify property. Their one object is to identify specific assets in which the claimant has a continuing proprietary interest. This is evident from rules such as the 'lowest intermediate balance', which prevents tracing into money added later to an account which has been depleted, because that additional money is not in equity the property of the claimant. Similarly, the limitation that property will not be traced into the hands of a bona fide purchaser for value without notice demonstrates that the basis is descent of title. Tracing is impossible in such circumstances, because the proprietary chain is broken at the point where the equitable interest is defeated. The right of a claimant to take advantage of any increase in value of assets identified by the rules of tracing also points to the proprietary nature of the tracing process.[28]

It is questionable whether the supposed fear of 'geometric multiplication' of the claimant's property is justified in practice. The danger is only apparent at common law in consequence of the principle *nemo dat quod non habet*.[29] The well-established limitation that the common law cannot trace into a mixed fund itself prevents such 'geometric progression'. In equity, 'geometric multiplication' is curtailed by the principle that the right to trace is lost as against a bona fide purchaser for value. Geometric multiplication is also inhibited by the principle that a claimant cannot recover twice for the same loss. Geometric multiplication provides a claimant with a choice of trails of ownership from among which he can choose. It is therefore no more of a problem than other situations in which a claimant has a choice of remedies, as for example where the purchaser of a defective product can choose to sue either the manufacturer in tort or the retailer for breach of contract.

---

[25] [2001] 1 AC 102, at 127. Similar sentiments were also expressed by Lord Browne-Wilkinson, at 109. Earlier cases supporting the proprietary nature of tracing in equity include: *Sinclair v Brougham* [1914] AC 398; *Re Diplock* [1948] Ch 465; *Chase Manhattan Bank NA v Israeli-British Bank (London) Ltd* [1981] Ch 105; *Agip v Jackson* [1992] 4 All ER 451. For criticism of such a proprietary understanding of the tracing process see Burrows 'Proprietary Restitution: Unmasking Unjust Enrichment' (2001) 117 LQR 412.

[26] Burrows, *The Law of Restitution* (2nd edn, 2002), p 81. See also Burrows 'Proprietary Restitution: Unmasking Unjust Enrichment' (2001) 117 LQR 412 and Birks 'Property, Unjust Enrichment, And Tracing' (2001) 54 CLP 231.

[27] See also Rotherham 'Tracing Misconceptions in *Foskett v McKeown*' [2003] RLR 57.

[28] See also the arguments of Grantham and Rickett 'Property Rights as a Legally Significant Event' (2003) 62 CLJ 717.

[29] On a literal translation, 'no one gives what he does not have', this is interpreted to mean that no person may give a better title to property than he enjoys himself.

2 Tracing and claiming at common law

(1) Common law tracing through clean substitutions

It is well established that the common law rules of tracing are capable of following the ownership of property through a clean substitution, in other words through an exchange which did not involve any mixing of the original property being traced with other property.[30] This was established in the leading early case, *Taylor v Plumer*.[31] Sir Thomas Plumer had entrusted a stockbroker, Walsh, with money for investment in Exchequer bills. Walsh instead misappropriated the money and used it to purchase bullion and American bonds. He was apprehended and surrendered the property. The central issue was whether the bullion and bonds were rightly the property of Sir Thomas or of Walsh's trustee in bankruptcy. Lord Ellenborough held that the money which Sir Thomas had given to Walsh could be traced into the bullion and securities, and that they were properly the property of Sir Thomas. He stated the principle:

> It makes no difference in reason or law into what other form, different from the original, the change may have been made... for the product or the substitute for the original thing still follows the nature of the thing itself...

(2) Common law tracing of tangible property into a mixed bulk

Alongside tracing property through clean substitutions, the common law is also able to trace tangible property which is mixed with identical property so as to create a bulk. Where such mixing occurs the owners of the goods which have been mixed become tenants in common of the whole in the proportions which they have contributed to it.[32] In *Indian Oil Corpn Ltd v Greenstone Shipping Co SA (Panama) (The Ypatianna)*[33] an owner's crude oil was mixed with other crude oil belonging to a shipowner, which was already on board a vessel. Staughton J held that the owner was entitled to trace his oil into the bulk. In *Glencore International AG v Metro Trading International Inc (No 2)*,[34] Moore-Bick J extended this principle to a situation where oil was blended with oil of a different grade or specification, with the result that a new product was produced. The original owner was held able to trace his oil into the mixture, identifying a proportion in the new blend which takes account of both the quantity and the value of the oil contributed to the new bulk. However, the right to trace will be lost where tangible

---

[30] See Worthington, *Proprietary Interests in Commercial Transactions* (1996), pp 133–144; Smith, *The Law of Tracing* (1997), pp 162–174; Matthews, 'The Legal and Moral Limits of Common Law Tracing', in Birks (ed), *Laundering and Tracing* (1995), pp 23–72; Burrows, *The Law of Restitution* (2nd edn, 2002), pp 83–93; (1966) 7 WALR 463 (Scott); (1976) 92 LQR 360 (Goode); (1976) 40 Conv (NS) 277 (Pearce); (1979) 95 LQR 78 (Khurshid and Matthews); [1997] LMCLQ 65 (Band).

[31] (1815) 3 M & S 562. It has been argued that this case has been fundamentally misinterpreted.

[32] *Spence v Union Marine Insurance Co* (1868) LR 3 CP 427.   [33] [1988] QB 345.

[34] [2001] 1 Lloyd's Rep 284.

property is not merely mixed to form a bulk but is consumed in the manufacture of an entirely new product so as to lose its identity altogether. Thus, in *Borden (UK) Ltd v Scottish Timber Products Ltd*[35] it was not possible to trace resin which was, with the authority of the owner, mixed with other materials so as to manufacture chipboard. The result might have been different if the mixing had not been by consent.[36] Where tangible property is mixed so as to form a bulk, the rights of the original owner will vary depending upon whether the mixing was wrongful or innocent, and whether the property can be divided between the parties.

(3) Common law tracing of money through mixed funds

While *Taylor v Plumer*[37] demonstrates that the common law can trace property through clean substitutions, it also established the limitation that the common law is incapable of tracing money through a mixed fund. Lord Ellenborough stated that it was only possible to follow assets where they are able to be 'ascertained' to represent the original property, and that such ascertainment becomes impossible 'when the subject is turned into money, and mixed and confounded in a general mass of the same description'.

Subsequent cases have thus held that the common law cannot trace money through a mixed fund.[38] Say, for example, that an agent holds shares on behalf of his principal. If the agent sells the shares and uses the proceeds to purchase a diamond ring, the common law can trace his property into the ring. However, if the agent sells the shares and then mixes the proceeds with money of his own to create a mixed fund (for instance by paying it into his personal bank account), and then uses money from the fund to purchase the ring, the common law can no longer trace because of the mixing which has taken place. The rationale for this limitation was said by Lord Ellenborough to be a difficulty of fact, not law. Money has no ear-mark and therefore cannot be distinguished within a mixed fund, whereas 'money in a bag, or otherwise kept apart from other money' is ear-marked and so outside of the limitation.

The limitation was accepted by the Court of Appeal in *Banque Belge Pour l'Etranger v Hambrouck*.[39] The case concerned a man who obtained cheques by fraud from his employers, which were paid into his bank account. He then passed the money to his mistress, Mlle Spanoghe, who paid it into her bank account. The Court of Appeal held that it was possible to trace the money at common law into Mlle Spanoghe's account. Previously it had been thought that the common law would not trace money into a bank account at all, but the court held that, following the equity case *Re Hallett's Estate*,[40]

---

[35] [1981] Ch 25.

[36] See Smith (2013) 7 JIBFL 412, who distinguishes between specification, (mixtures which create a new thing, like the chipboard in *Borden*), accession (adding a minor component to a dominant asset, like painting a car) and true mixtures which are capable of separation.   [37] (1815) 3 M & S 562.

[38] See *Re Diplock* [1948] Ch 465, at 519–520; *Agip (Africa) Ltd v Jackson* [1990] Ch 265; *El Ajou v Dollar Land Holdings plc* [1993] BCLC 735; *Bank Tejarat v Hong Kong and Shanghai Banking Corpn* [1995] 1 Lloyd's Rep 239; *Jones (FC) & Sons v Jones* [1997] Ch 159.   [39] [1921] 1 KB 321.

[40] (1880) 13 Ch D 696.

there was nothing to prevent the court examining the details of a bank account.[41] The mere fact that the money had been paid into a bank account did not itself cause a failure of the means of ascertainment.[42] However, in granting the claim, the court stressed that there had been no mixing of the money in the bank accounts concerned. If there had been mixing, then it seems that common law tracing, unlike equitable tracing, would not have been available.[43] Similarly, in *Lipkin Gorman v Karpnale Ltd*[44] common law tracing was only possible because the defendants had conceded that there had been no mixing of the misappropriated money.

It is important to note that while the common law is incapable of tracing money *through* a mixed fund, it is capable of tracing money *into* a mixed fund so as to establish that the recipient is subject to a personal remedy based on the receipt of that property.

(4) **Common law tracing of money through the banking system**

While the common law is prima facie capable of tracing money through a bank account, provided that it remains unmixed, later cases have found that tracing is not possible at common law where money has been transferred between bank accounts and the means of exchange has inevitably involved some element of mixing.[45] In *Agip (Africa) Ltd v Jackson*[46] the claimant firm was defrauded by its chief accountant, Zdiri. He altered the names of the payee on genuine payment orders in favour of dummy companies he had created. One payment of $518,000 was made to a dummy company, Baker Oil Services Ltd, who held an account at a branch of Lloyds Bank in London. On receiving the payment order Agip's bankers telegraphed instructions to Lloyds Bank Overseas Division to credit the account of Baker Oil at their London Branch with a corresponding amount. At the same time, their correspondent bank in New York debited their account and credited Lloyds Bank's correspondent bank in New York. The next day the money was transferred from the Baker Oil account to the account of the defendants, who were a firm of accountants in the Isle of Man. All but $45,000 was then paid out. There had been no mixing of the money in the Baker Oil account. At first instance Millett J held that Agip could not trace the money at common law. One reason for this denial focused on the nature of the transfer. He held that:

> The money was transmitted by telegraphic transfer. There was no cheque or any equiva-
> lent. The payment order was not a cheque or its equivalent...Nothing passed between
> Tunisia and London but a stream of electrons. It is not possible to treat the money as

---

[41] See *Jones (FC) & Sons v Jones* [1997] Ch 159, where money was traced at common law into a bank account.

[42] As Atkin LJ graphically said: 'But if in 1815 the common law halted outside the banker's door, by 1879 equity had the courage to lift the latch, walk in and examine the books...I see no reason why the means of ascertainment so provided should not now be available both for common law and equity proceedings.'

[43] [1921] 1 KB 321, at 336, per Atkin LJ; at 330, per Scrutton LJ.   [44] [1991] 2 AC 548.

[45] See Smith, *The Law of Tracing* (1997), pp 249–262.

[46] [1990] Ch 265; [1992] 4 All ER 385; Birks 'Misdirected Funds Again' (1989) 105 LQR 528; Sir Peter Millett 'Tracing the Proceeds of Fraud' (1991) 107 LQR 71; [1991] Ch 547; [1992] 4 All ER 451; Harpum 'Equitable Liability For Money Laundering' (1991) 50 CLJ 409; Goulding 'Equity and the Money Launderers' [1992] Conv 367; Swadling 'The Law of Restitution' All ER Rev 1992, 258–265.

received by Lloyds Bank of London, or its correspondent bank in New York, as representing the proceeds of the payment order or of any other physical asset previously in its
hands...[47]

This argument was rejected by the Court of Appeal, where Fox LJ took the view that
it did not matter that the transfer had been by order rather than cheque.[48] More significantly, however, Millett J had held that the claimants were not entitled to trace at
common law because the money must have been mixed with other money when the
transfer took place through the New York clearing system between Agip and Lloyds'
correspondent banks. This reasoning was supported by the Court of Appeal,[49] and
tracing at common law was thus prevented.

Similar reasoning was employed in *Bank Tejarat v Hong Kong and Shanghai
Banking Corpn (CI) Ltd*,[50] where the claimant had paid the defendants DM3.4m via the
Frankfurt clearing system. Tuckey J applied the principle identified in *Agip (Africa)
Ltd v Jackson* and held that, as the claimant's money would inevitably have become
mixed with other money through the Frankfurt deutschmark clearing system, it was
impossible to trace the money at common law into the hands of the defendants.[51] The
claimant's claim to personal restitution at common law by way of an action for money
had and received therefore failed.

In both cases the inadequacy of the common law rules of tracing required the
claimants to turn instead to equity, asserting that the misappropriated money was subject to a trust and that the respective defendants were liable on the grounds of knowing
assistance.[52] It is submitted that the refusal to allow common law tracing on the
grounds of inevitable mixing during the process of transfer of funds involves an
unduly literalistic analysis of the tracing process. Whenever transfers occur between
banks, whether by virtue of an electronic transfer or a cheque which is presented
through the clearing system, it is not as if the specific money held in the account from
which the funds are drawn is transferred to the bank holding the account into which
it is to be paid. Where money is held in a bank account, the nature of the relationship
between the bank and its customer is one of debtor and creditor, so that there is no real
connection between the balance in an account and any specific money as such. Where
money is debited from one account and credited to another, there should simply be
an evidential presumption that the money represented thereby has passed from one
account to the other. The means of transfer operative between the banks holding the
accounts should not prevent that inference.

Unless such an inference is operative there is no reason why the common law should
ever be able to trace into or through a bank account. The mere transfer of money
between accounts held at different domestic banks is effected through the clearing

---

[47] [1990] Ch 265, at 399.   [48] [1992] 4 All ER 451, at 465.
[49] [1992] 4 All ER 451, at 465, per Fox LJ.
[50] [1995] 1 Lloyd's Rep 239; Birks 'Tracing Misused *Bank Tejarat v Hong Kong and Shanghai Banking
Corp*' (1995) 9 TLI 91 and 'Persistent Problems in Misdirected Money' [1996] LMCLQ 1.
[51] [1995] 1 Lloyd's Rep 239, at 245.
[52] Now dishonest assistance: *Royal Brunei Airlines v Tan* [1995] 2 AC 378.

system and yet this does not seem to have prevented common law tracing. In *Jones (FC) & Sons (a firm) v Jones*[53] the partner of the claimant firm drew cheques totalling £11,700 on a joint account at the Midland Bank, which were paid into an account opened in the name of his wife with a firm of commodity brokers. She then received cheques for £50,760 from the commodity brokers, which she paid into a deposit account. The Court of Appeal held that the firm's trustee in bankruptcy should be entitled to trace at common law and that it was not necessary to take account of the reality of the clearing system which lay behind the transaction. Millett LJ stated that:

> Accordingly, the trustee can follow the money in the joint account at Midland Bank, which had been vested by statute in him, into the proceeds of the three cheques which Mrs Jones received from her husband. The trustee does not need to follow money from one recipient to another or follow it through the clearing system; he can follow the cheques as they pass from hand to hand. It is sufficient for him to be able to trace the money into the cheques and the cheques into their proceeds.[54]

If this reasoning is correct (and it is suggested that it is, since it reflects the reality of banking practice), there is equally no reason why the court should have been concerned with the means of transfer through the clearing system in *Agip (Africa) Ltd v Jackson* and *Bank Tejarat v Hong Kong and Shanghai Banking Corpn (CI) Ltd*. Surely it is enough to identify a debit from one account echoed by a corresponding receipt by another. This is as much a swap of one chose in action for another as if a cheque had physically changed hands. Millett LJ seems to lay great stress upon the presence of a physical cheque, which would suggest a return to his argument in *Agip (Africa) Ltd v Jackson*[55] that the common law cannot trace through an electronic transfer, which was rejected by the Court of Appeal.[56]

The nature of a bank account is also a cause for difficulty in relation to common law tracing. As has been noted, the relationship between banker and customer is one of debtor and creditor. In *R v Preddy*,[57] a criminal case concerning mortgage fraud, the House of Lords held that where money was debited from one account and paid into another account, the second account holder had not obtained the property of the first account holder so as to render him liable to conviction for theft under s 15(1) of the Theft Act 1968.[58] Lord Goff explained:

> The question remains…whether the debiting of the lending institution's bank account, and the corresponding crediting of the bank account of the defendant or his solicitor, constitutes obtaining of that property. The difficulty in the way of that conclusion is simply that, when the bank account of the defendant (or his solicitor) is credited, he does not obtain the lending institutionom one account and paid into another account, the second account holder had not obtainedtanto, and a chose in action is brought into existence

---

[53] [1997] Ch 159.   [54] [1997] Ch 159, at 169.   [55] [1990] Ch 265; [1992] 4 All ER 385.

[56] In *SmithKline Beecham v Apotex Europe Ltd* [2007] Ch 71, Jacobs LJ considered that the *Jones* case was a clear example of constructive trusteeship and therefore equitable tracing would have been available. If true, this would, of course, solve the issue, as will be demonstrated later in the chapter.

[57] [1996] AC 815; Fox 'Property Rights and Electronic Funds Transfers' [1996] LMCLQ 456.

[58] Obtaining property by deception.

representing a debt in an equivalent sum owed by a different bank to the defendant or his solicitor. In these circumstances it is difficult to see how the defendant thereby obtained property belonging to another, ie to the lending institution.

Professor Sir John Smith has suggested that 'Effectively, the victim's property has been changed into another form and now belongs to the defendant. There is the gain and equivalent loss which is characteristic of, and perhaps the substance of, obtaining'.[59] But even if this were right, I do not for myself see how this can properly be described as obtaining property belonging to another. In truth the property which the defendant has obtained is the new chose in action constituted by the debt now owed to him by his bank, and represented by the credit entry in his own bank account.[60]

If this analysis is correct, it appears to remove any ability of the common law to trace money through bank accounts. If the increased balance in the credited account cannot be identified with the corresponding reduction in the balance of the debited account, then it is untraceable into that account. This is fundamentally inconsistent with the decision of the Court of Appeal in *Jones (FC) & Sons (a firm) v Jones*,[61] where it was held that the money credited to Mrs Jones' account belonged at law to the firm from whose account it had been debited. It is equally inconsistent with *Banque Belge Pour l'Etranger v Hambrouck*.[62] Even though the claimants were seeking a personal remedy, their right to restitution was dependent upon establishing that the defendant had received their money into her bank account. It is also submitted that it is inconsistent with the judgment of the House of Lords in *Lipkin Gorman v Karpnale Ltd*,[63] where Lord Goff held that the claimant firm of solicitors was entitled to trace money misappropriated from their client account:

> There is in my opinion no reason why the solicitors should not be able to trace their property at common law in that chose in action, or in any part of it, into its products, ie cash drawn by Cass from their client account at the bank. Such a claim is consistent with their assertion that the money so obtained by Cass was their property at common law.[64]

It would be utterly illogical if the firm were permitted to trace if Cass withdrew cash from their client account, and presumably also if he subsequently paid the cash into his own bank account, but not if he arranged for a direct transfer of money from their client account to his own bank account. Yet this would seem to be the implication of the decision in *R v Preddy*.[65] The ramifications of this case for the ability to trace through bank accounts at common law have yet to be fully considered by the courts.[66] However, the decision prompted statutory reform of the law of theft to ensure that defendants who received mortgage funds by fraud would be guilty of an offence.[67]

---

[59] [1995] Crim LR 564, 565–566.   [60] [1996] AC 815, at 834.   [61] [1997] AC 159.
[62] [1921] 1 KB 321.   [63] [1991] 2 AC 548.   [64] [1991] 2 AC 548, at 574.
[65] [1996] AC 815.
[66] Master Bowles in *Metrogem Limited v Paul Corrett* (Ch D, 22 May 2001) considered that the case did not prevent an instruction to a bank to make a transfer from operating as an assignment in equity, and a less precious interpretation of entitlement to the proceeds of a cheque was adopted in *R v Adams* [2003] EWCA Crim 3620. For comment on the implications of *R v Preddy* in the context of tracing, see Fox 'Property Rights and Electronic Funds Transfers' [1996] LMCLQ 456.   [67] Theft (Amendment) Act 1996.

(5) **Criticism of the common law rules of tracing**

While the authorities have consistently held that the common law is incapable of tracing property through a mixed fund, this limitation has been subject to much criticism. The very origins of this limitation have been challenged by Lionel Smith, who has argued that in *Taylor v Plumer*[68] the common law court was in fact considering the equitable rules of tracing, with the implication that there was therefore no reason for the common law to consider itself limited in subsequent cases.[69] While this misunderstanding was acknowledged by Millett LJ in *Jones (FC) & Sons (a firm) v Jones*,[70] he made clear that this alone did not permit the overthrow of the settled common law principle which had emerged despite the misunderstanding.[71]

Even though the limitation cannot be eliminated merely because of historical misunderstanding of *Taylor v Plumer*,[72] it is open to objections on its own terms. It appears to be rooted in the perception that the common law cannot identify property in a mixed fund but, as commentators have pointed out,[73] there is no reason why the common law cannot recognize joint title to a mixed fund through a tenancy-in-common. This possibility was recognized in *Spence v Union Marine Insurance Co Ltd*,[74] where bales of wool were mixed and it was not possible to identify their owners, because the identifying marks had been lost in a shipwreck. The court held that there was a tenancy-in-common.

There appears to be no rational justification for treating money differently. The consequence has been to force claims to mixed funds to be made in equity. To enable equitable tracing claims to succeed where there is no express trust, the courts may have been tempted to expand the circumstances in which constructive trusts will be found. It is questionable whether the expansion of equitable rights and interests in the commercial field is appropriate.[75] The common law rules of tracing have also restricted the availability of common law restitution through the action for money had and received, since it cannot be demonstrated that a defendant was enriched by the receipt of the claimant's property where it has passed through a mixed fund. Thus, in *Bank Tejarat v Hong Kong and Shanghai Banking Corpn (CI) Ltd*[76] the claimant's claim for common law restitution on the grounds of mistake failed because it was not able to trace its money into the hands of the defendants because it had become mixed in the Frankfurt clearing system. At present it is impossible to utilize the equitable rules of tracing to found a common law claim to restitution.[77]

It is therefore submitted that there is no basis in principle, or in practice, for emasculating the common law rules by prohibiting tracing through a mixed fund. If the common law rules were to develop so as to enable such tracing, there would be less

---

[68] (1815) 3 M & S 562.
[69] Smith 'Tracing in *Taylor v Plumer*: Equity in the Court of King's Bench' (1995) LMCLQ 240.
[70] [1997] AC 159.   [71] [1997] AC 159, at 169.   [72] (1815) 3 M & S 562.
[73] Pearce 'A Tracing Paper' (1976) Conv (NS) 277.   [74] (1868) LR 3 CP 427.
[75] Eg *Re Goldcorp Exchange* [1995] 1 AC 74; *Westdeutsche Landesbank Girozentrale v Islington London Borough Council* [1996] AC 669.   [76] [1995] 1 Lloyd's Rep 239; (1995) 9 TLI 91 (Birks).
[77] See *Jones (FC) & Sons v Jones* [1997] AC 159, at 169–170, per Millett LJ.

need for an inappropriate expansion of equity and fiduciary relationships into the commercial sphere. In *Jones (FC) & Sons (a firm) v Jones*[78] Millett LJ expressed dissatisfaction with the present position:

> There is no merit in having distinct and different tracing rules at law and in equity, given that tracing is neither a right nor a remedy but merely the process by which the plaintiff establishes what has happened to his property and makes good his claim that the assets which he claims can properly be regarded as representing his property. The fact that there are different tracing rules at law and in equity is unfortunate through probably inevitable, but unnecessary differences should not be created where they are not required by the different nature of legal and equitable doctrines and remedies. There is, in my view, even less merit in the present rule which precludes the invocation of the equitable tracing rules to support a common law claim; until that rule is swept away unnecessary obstacles to the development of a rational and coherent law of restitution will remain.[79]

In *Foskett v McKeown* he reiterated his dissatisfaction with the current position in the House of Lords, and stated:

> Given its nature, there is nothing inherently legal or equitable about the tracing exercise. There is thus no sense in maintaining different rules for tracing at law and in equity. One set of tracing rules is enough... There is certainly no logical justification for allowing any distinctions between them to produce capricious results in cases of mixed substitutions by insisting on the existence of a fiduciary relationship as a precondition for applying equity's tracing rules. The existence of such a relationship may be relevant to the nature of the claim which the plaintiff can maintain, whether personal or proprietary, but that is a different matter.[80]

However, given that the case involved a straightforward situation where a trustee had misappropriated trust property, and that the equitable tracing rules were therefore undoubtedly available, he concluded that it was not the occasion to explore the relationship between equitable and common law tracing rules further. His comments are therefore strictly obiter, and the traditional dichotomy between the rules of tracing in equity and at common law remains intact, albeit on notice of impending demise.[81]

(6) Claiming at common law

It has been seen that the common law enables legal owners to trace their property though clean substitutions, and to trace tangible property into a mixed bulk. Once the tracing process has identified assets which represent the original property, the original owner may be able to assert a claim thereto. The original owner may be entitled to assert a proprietary right, or he may be entitled to claim restitution, which is a personal remedy.

---

[78] [1997] Ch 159.   [79] [1997] Ch 159, at 169–170.   [80] [2001] 1 AC 102, at 128.
[81] See, however, *Shalson v Russo* [2005] Ch 281, at 314 [104], where Rimer J opined that the distinction between common law and equitable tracing remained, despite obiter comments to the contrary by Lord Millett in *Foskett v McKeown* [2001] 1 AC 102 (at 129).

(a) Claiming assets which are the product of a clean substitution

Common law tracing through clean substitutions operates on the basis of the preservation of the claimant's title to the property being traced. The claimant had legal title before any clean substitutions took place, and such substitutions are not able to deprive him of his title. Except in the case of currency (banknotes and coins), to which special rules apply,[82] even a bona fide purchaser will not take free from the claimant's original title because his legal title is good against the world and cannot be defeated. This seems to have been the rationale of *Taylor v Plumer*,[83] where Lord Ellenborough said that Sir Thomas had simply 'repossessed himself of that, of which said the had never ceased to be the lawful proprietor'. In *Lipkin Gorman v Karpnale Ltd*, where a solicitor had taken money for gambling from the client account of his firm, Lord Goff held that the firm could trace at common law:

> There is in my opinion no reason why the solicitors should not be able to trace their property at common law in that chose in action [the client account], in any part of it, into its product, ie cash drawn by Cass from their client account at the bank. Such a claim is consistent with their assertion that the money so obtained by Cass was their property at common law.[84]

Historically, except for land, the common law did not possess adequate remedies to enable the claimant to vindicate his proprietary entitlement to assets identified as representing his original property. As Professor Goode[85] has pointed out, until changed by statute,[86] the common law was only ever able to offer a personal remedy in damages for detinue or conversion. However, in some older cases the owner was able to recover his property through self-help[87] and more recent cases have now established beyond doubt that an original owner may claim legal title to any assets identified by the rules of tracing.[88]

Where a legal owner can identify assets in the hands of a third party as representing his original property, he will be entitled to claim them as his own.[89] In *Lipkin Gorman v Karpnale Ltd*,[90] Lord Goff stated that the legal owner of property was entitled to trace or follow his property into its product. This principle was applied by the Court of Appeal in *Jones (FC) & Sons (a firm) v Jones*,[91] where the defendant had received money

---

[82] See Fox 'Bona Fide Purchase and the Currency of Money' [1996] CLJ 547; Fox 'The Transfer of Legal Title to Money' [1996] RLR 60.　　　　　　　　　　　　　　　　　　[83] (1815) 3 M & S 562.

[84] [1991] 2 AC 548; at 529, [1992] 4 All ER 512; (1991) Lloyd's MCLQ 473 (Birks); (1991) 107 LQR 521 (Watts); [1992] Conv 124 (Halliwell); (1992) 55 MLR 377 (McKendrick); (1992) 45(2) CLP 69 (Birks).

[85] Goode 'The Right to Trace and its Impact in Commercial Transactions' (1976) LQR 360.

[86] Torts (Interference with Goods) Act 1977 s 3, replacing the Common Law Procedure Act 1854 s 78, entitles the court to order the delivery of goods.　　　　　[87] As in *Taylor v Plumer* (1815) 3 M & S 562.

[88] See *Jones (FC) & Sons v Jones* [1997] AC 159.

[89] *Armstrong DLW GmbH v Winnington Networks Ltd* [2012] 3 All ER 425, at [88]–[92]. Stephen Morris QC considered this to be a proprietary restitutionary claim, although this confuses the historic distinction between proprietary claims and restitutionary claims.　　　　　　　　[90] [1991] 2 AC 548, at 573.

[91] [1997] Ch 159; Andrews and Beatson 'Common Law Tracing: Springboard or Swan Song?'; Fox 'Common Law Claims to Substituted Assets' [1997] CLJ 30. See also Davern 'Common Law Tracing, Profits and the Doctrine of Relation Back' [1997] RLR 92–96.

drawn from the bank account of a firm which had committed an act of bankruptcy before it had been adjudicated bankrupt. The money was invested in an account held by a firm of commodity brokers which dealt in potato futures. The investment was highly successful and the account contained almost five times as much money as had been initially invested. The Court of Appeal held that, as the firm could trace the money at common law into the account with the brokers, its trustee in bankruptcy was entitled to the money in the account (which had been paid into court). Beldam LJ stated:

> There is now ample authority for the proposition that a person who can trace his property into its product, provided the product is identifiable as the product of his property, may lay legal claim to that property.[92]

Where an owner is entitled to claim specific assets at common law he will be entitled to take advantage of any appreciation in value which they have experienced.

(b) Claiming assets where tangible property has been mixed to form a bulk

The common law permits the tracing of tangible property into a mixed bulk. Where a mixed bulk has been created, the rights of an original owner will vary depending upon whether the bulk can be separated into proportionate shares representing the assets of the contributors.

(i) Claiming where the bulk can be divided into proportionate shares

Where the bulk is capable of division, a contributor will be entitled to claim the proportionate share which represents his original property, and of which he is a tenant-in-common. Such division will usually be possible if the property is fungible in nature, such as when it consists of grain, oil, or wine.[93] The principle was stated by Staughton J in *Indian Oil Corpn Ltd v Greenstone Shipping Co SA (Panama) (The Ypatianna)*:

> where B wrongfully mixes the goods of A with goods of his own, which are substantially of the same nature and quality, and they cannot in practice be separated, the mixture is held in common and A is entitled to receive out of it a quantity equal to that of his goods which went into the mixture, any doubt as to that quantity being resolved in favour of A.[94]

(ii) Claiming where the bulk cannot be divided into proportionate shares

In contrast, where property was wrongfully mixed to form a bulk that cannot be divided into the proportionate shares of the contributors, the original owner will be entitled to claim the entire bulk. The right to claim the entire bulk in such circumstances was recognized by the House of Lords in *Foskett v McKeown*,[95] on the grounds that the wrongdoer is entitled to claim only what he can prove is his own. Such circumstances are admittedly likely to be rare, but Lord Millett referred to the Canadian case of *Jones v De Marchant*[96] by way of example. In that case, a husband had wrongfully used eighteen beaver skins belonging to his wife, together with four skins of his

---

[92] [1997] Ch 159, at 171.   [93] *Foskett v McKeown* [2001]1 AC 102, at 133, per Lord Millett.
[94] [1988] QB 345, 371.   [95] [2001] 1 AC 102.   [96] (1916) 28 DLR 561.

own, to have a fur coat made up, which he gave to his mistress. Since the skins could no longer be separated it was held that the wife was entitled to ownership of the entire coat. If the amalgamation of two products to make a new one had been carried out with consent, then any claim to the original materials or to the new product would be lost.[97]

(c) Claiming personal restitution at common law

The process of tracing may also provide a foundation for a personal claim to restitution. Where property is misappropriated or misdirected, a recipient will be treated as having been unjustly enriched. The extent of his enrichment is the value of the property that he had received. If he has received, but subsequently dissipated, misappropriated property, then a proprietary claim will not be available because there is no longer any specifically identifiable asset. As Lord Lane CJ observed in *A-G's Reference (No 1 of 1985)*,[98] there can be no proprietary remedy unless there is an asset which can be 'identified as a separate piece of property'. The original owners may, however, be entitled to claim personal restitution from the recipient: a claim that because the recipient had been enriched by the receipt of the property, he must compensate the original owner to that extent. A personal restitutionary claim may also be more advantageous to an original owner than a proprietary claim, even where the property has not been dissipated, if the assets which represent his property have subsequently fallen in value, since the measure of restitution will be determined by the value of the property at the point of receipt. However, such a personal remedy will only be more advantageous in practice if the recipient is solvent and able to discharge the obligation to make restitution.

The liability of a person who has received property belonging to another to make restitution at common law is strict, subject to the availability of the defence of change of position. The role of common law tracing as a foundation for a personal liability to make restitution is evident in *Lipkin Gorman v Karpnale Ltd*,[99] where a solicitor had misappropriated money from his firm's client account in order to finance his gambling at the Playboy Club. His firm sought to recover restitution from the club of the misappropriated money it had received. The firm could not make a proprietary claim to any assets in the club's hands as none could be identified which were the product of the money received. The common law rules would not permit tracing once the money had become mixed with other money of the club. However, the rules of common law tracing did establish that the club had received money which belonged to the firm, and thus entitled the firm to maintain the common law action for money had and received. As Lord Goff explained:

> It is well established that a legal owner is entitled to trace his property into its product, provided that the latter is indeed identifiable as the product of his property... Before Cass drew upon the solicitor's client account at the bank, there was of course no question of

---

[97] *Borden (UK) Ltd v Scottish Timber Products Ltd* [1981] Ch 25.   [98] [1986] QB 491, at 506.
[99] [1991] 2 AC 548.

the solicitor's having any legal property in any cash lying at the bank. The relationship of the bank with the solicitors was essentially that of debtor and creditor; and since the client account was at all material times in credit, the bank was the debtor and the solicitors were its creditors. Such a debt constitutes a chose in action, which is a species of property; and since the debt was enforceable at common law, the chose in action was legal property belonging to the solicitors at common law. There is in my opinion no reason why the solicitors should not be able to trace their property at common law in that chose in action, or in any part of it, into its product, ie cash drawn by Cass from their client account at the bank. Such a claim is consistent with their assertion that the money obtained by Cass was their property at common law...it further follows, from the concession made by the respondents,[100] that the solicitors can follow their property into the hands of the respondents when it was paid to them at the club.[101]

Thus, the firm's ability to trace the money drawn from the client account into the hands of the club, via the activities of the misappropriating solicitor, was vital to the establishment of their entitlement to restitution by way of an action for money had and received. Lord Goff stressed that the firm's claim was not proprietary, although it was founded upon the receipt of property.[102]

3 Tracing and claiming in equity

(1) The scope of equitable tracing

Whereas the common law rules of tracing have remained restricted, equity developed rules which are much more flexible. There is no barrier preventing the tracing of equitable proprietary interests through a mixed fund. The rules, which originated in the context of the misappropriation of property subject to an express trust, are derived from evidential presumptions which enable the court to determine whether property has survived through mixing, and whether any assets purchased with money from a mixed fund can be said to represent property contributed to the mixture. The equitable rules are particularly designed to deal with mixing of funds in a bank account. By necessity they are rough and ready and not overly sophisticated. The presumptions on which they are founded also take account of the moral blameworthiness of the parties whose funds have been mixed. If a mixed fund consists of misappropriated trust property and the property of the wrongdoing trustee, the rules operate harshly against the wrongdoer. In contrast, if the mixture is comprised of misappropriated trust property and that of an innocent volunteer, they seek to achieve a fair balance between the two innocent parties.

---

[100] The respondents had conceded that if it could be shown that the firm enjoyed legal title to the money from the client account in the hands of the solicitor, then that title was not defeated by mixing of that money with other money in his hands.   [101] [1991] 2 AC 548, at 572–573.
[102] [1991] 2 AC 548, at 572.

(2) **The right to trace in equity**

Equitable tracing is not available in every situation in which property has been misappropriated or misapplied. Historically, equity has taken the view that tracing is only possible where there was an initial fiduciary relationship. While the language of a fiduciary relationship in this context is somewhat imprecise and opaque,[103] what is really required is that the property sought to be traced was subject to a trust and thus belonged to the claimant in equity.

(a) **The requirement of a fiduciary relationship**

The present position of the English cases is that an initial fiduciary relationship is a prerequisite of the right to trace in equity. This was reaffirmed in *Westdeutsche Landesbank Girozentrale v Islington London Borough Council*.[104] While the House of Lords overruled the earlier decision of *Sinclair v Brougham*,[105] Lord Browne-Wilkinson was at pains to stress that this did not amount to a rejection of the requirement of a fiduciary relationship, since the House of Lords was not wishing to cast any doubt on the principles of tracing established in the later case of *Re Diplock*.

In *Re Diplock*[106] charities had wrongly received payments of £203,000 under a will. The next of kin were held entitled to trace the money in equity into the charities' hands, because the executors clearly stood in a fiduciary relationship to the estate. The Court of Appeal had examined the judgments of the House of Lords in *Sinclair v Brougham*[107] and concluded that a fiduciary relationship was a prerequisite to tracing in equity. Lord Greene MR stated:

> Lord Parker and Lord Haldane both predicate the existence of a right of property recognised by equity which depends upon there having existed at some stage a fiduciary relationship of some kind (though not necessarily a positive duty of trusteeship) sufficient to give rise to the equitable right to trace property. Exactly what relationships are sufficient to bring such an equitable right into existence for the purposes of the rule which we are considering is a matter which has not been precisely laid down. Certain relationships are clearly included; eg trustee (actual or constructive) and cestui que trust; and 'fiduciary' relationships such as that of principal and agent...[108]

In *Sinclair v Brougham* a building society had operated an ultra vires banking business. The case concerned the rights of the depositors who had invested their money with the bank when the building society had become insolvent. The House of Lords held that they were not entitled to claim restitution at common law through the action for money had and received, which would have meant that they would have stood as creditors in the insolvency and they would have ranked pari passu with the other general creditors of the society. At that time the right to restitution was said to be founded upon

---

[103] See Chapter 28.
[104] [1996] AC 669. In *Dublin Corpn v Building and Allied Trade Union* [1996] 1 IR 468 the Irish Supreme Court doubted that *Sinclair v Brougham* was authority for the proposition that a fiduciary relationship was a prerequisite of equitable tracing. [105] [1914] AC 398.
[106] [1948] Ch 465.   [107] [1914] AC 398.   [108] [1948] Ch 465, at 540.

an implied contract to repay money had and received. The House of Lords held that, since the building society had acted ultra vires in conducting the banking business, any contract to repay the depositors would also have been ultra vires and was therefore void and unenforceable. Since this would have the consequence that the depositors would have no entitlement to claim as creditors in the insolvency, the House of Lords held that the building society had received their deposits as a fiduciary and that they were entitled to trace their money in equity into its remaining assets. In subsequent cases, the implied contract theory was rejected as artificial, and the right to restitution is now available through the autonomous cause of action in unjust enrichment. In *Westdeutsche Landesbank Girozentrale v Islington London Borough Council*[109] the House of Lords therefore held that, if the same facts had arisen for decision today, the depositors would have been entitled to personal restitution on the grounds that the building society had been unjustly enriched by the receipt of their deposits when there had been a total failure of consideration because their promise to repay was ultra vires and void. There would therefore be no need to trace in equity and, in as far as the House of Lords had found that the deposits were held on trust for the depositors by the building society so as to be traceable in equity, it was overruled.

Other cases also support the view that a fiduciary relationship is an essential prerequisite for equitable tracing.[110] While in *Foskett v McKeown*[111] Lord Millett considered that there was no logical justification for insisting upon the existence of a fiduciary relationship as a precondition for applying equity's tracing rules, the requirement was not overruled because the case concerned a straightforward case of the misappropriation of trust money.

Where trust property has been misappropriated or misdirected, the essential requirement of a fiduciary relationship will be satisfied. The trustee stood in a fiduciary relationship vis-à-vis the beneficiary who is seeking to trace in equity. However, the fiduciary relationship need not have existed prior to the misappropriation or misdirection of the property concerned, since the circumstances of the misappropriation or misdirection may themselves give rise to a fiduciary relationship entitling the original owner to trace in equity. In *Chase Manhattan Bank NA v Israeli-British Bank (London) Ltd*[112] Chase Manhattan paid the Israeli-British Bank $1m. Due to a clerical error the same amount was paid again later the same day. The Israeli-British bank became insolvent and Chase Manhattan sought to trace the second mistaken payment money into its assets. Although they would clearly have had a personal action for restitution of the sum paid by mistake, it was essential that they could maintain a proprietary claim, because they would otherwise merely rank among the general creditors. However, the banks were two commercial organizations, dealing with each other at arm's length, and as such they did not stand in a fiduciary relationship, nor was the money paid subject to a pre-existing trust. Despite this, Goulding J held that

---

[109] [1996] AC 669.
[110] *Agip (Africa) Ltd v Jackson* [1992] 4 All ER 451, at 466 (Foxx LJ); *Boscawen v Bajwa* [1995] 4 All ER 769, at 777 (Millett LJ).   [111] [2001] 1 AC 102, at 128–129.
[112] [1981] Ch 105.

the very fact that the payment had been made by mistake brought about a fiduciary relationship that entitled Chase Manhattan to trace. He stated his rationale:

> a person who pays money to another under a factual mistake retains an equitable property in it and the conscience of that other is subjected to a fiduciary duty to respect his proprietary right.[113]

However, this decision was subjected to criticism by the House of Lords in *Westdeutsche Landesbank Girozentrale v Islington London Borough Council*,[114] where Lord Browne-Wilkinson stated that he could not agree that the mere fact that the payment had been made by mistake meant that the payor retained the equitable interest in the money paid when it had not previously been subject to a trust.[115] Although the judge's reasoning was doubted, Lord Browne-Wilkinson felt that the case may have been rightly decided:

> The defendant bank knew of the mistake made by the paying bank within two days of the receipt of the moneys. The judge treated this fact as irrelevant but in my judgement it may well provide a proper foundation for the decision. Although the mere receipt of the moneys, in ignorance of the mistake, gives rise to no trust, the retention of the moneys after the recipient bank learned of the mistake may well have given rise to a constructive trust.[116]

It is submitted, however, that this reasoning is spurious. If the mistaken payment effected a transfer of the ownership of the money to the payee when it was received, there is no reason why a trust should have been imposed when the bank discovered that a mistake had occurred. The bank was clearly subject to an obligation to make restitution at common law, but the mere fact that it should have to make restitution does not generate a constructive trust. While the equitable obligation to account has been held to give rise to a constructive trust because of the operation of the maxim that equity treats as done that which ought to be done, there is no equivalent principle at common law. It is submitted that the crucial question should focus on the proprietary consequences of the mistaken payment at the moment it was made, in other words, whether the mistake prevented title in the money passing to the payee. Lord Goff indicated that a fundamental mistake might prevent the beneficial interest in property passing to a payee.[117]

The requirement of an initial fiduciary relationship has been subject to heavy criticism, both on the grounds that it is not supported in authority and that it is not justified in principle.[118] The major criticism is that the requirement is artificial, the courts being willing to find, or 'discover',[119] a fiduciary relationship whenever they feel that tracing is justified, as in *Chase Manhattan Bank NA v Israeli-British Bank*

---

[113] [1981] Ch 105, at 119.   [114] [1996] AC 669.   [115] [1996] AC 669, at 714.

[116] [1996] AC 669, at 715.   [117] [1996] AC 669, at 690.

[118] See Goff and Jones, *The Law of Restitution* (6th edn, 2002), pp 104–106; Birks, *Introduction to the Law of Restitution* (1985), pp 377–385; Pearce 'A Tracing Paper' (1976) 40 Conv 277. It is argued that *Sinclair v Brougham* [1914] AC 398 did not require an initial fiduciary relationship and that the case was misunderstood by the Court of Appeal in *Re Diplock* [1948] Ch 465.

[119] Goff and Jones, *The Law of Restitution* (6th edn, 2002), p 105.

(London) Ltd.[120] For this reason, Goff and Jones suggested in an earlier edition of their seminal text that whether tracing (which they call a 'restitutionary proprietary claim') should be available should 'depend on whether it is just, in the particular circumstances of the case, to impose a constructive trust on, or an equitable lien over, particular assets...'.[121] However, this proposal is equally unsuitable because of its arbitrary nature and it has not been maintained in subsequent editions, where it is regretted that the courts have not taken opportunities which have been presented to overrule the requirement.[122]

In practice, it seems that the requirement of a 'fiduciary relationship' is less of a limitation than some critics have suggested. It is the commercial situations which have generated the most difficulty. However, even in the commercial context the require-ment is easily circumvented. As Millett J observed in *Agip (Africa) Ltd v Jackson*[123] it is 'readily satisfied in most cases of commercial fraud, since the embezzlement of a company's funds almost invariably involves a breach of fiduciary duty on the part of one of the company's employees or agents'.[124] Although he noted the criticism, he felt that it was not for a court of first instance to reconsider the requirement, and as has been seen the Court of Appeal merely reasserted it.[125]

(b) Equitable ownership of the property traced

While it is true that the requirement of a fiduciary relationship has not prevented tra-cing in practice, the language is confusing because it conceals the true basis of equitable tracing. Equity is not concerned with the presence of a fiduciary relationship per se, but rather with the identification of a trust. A person will only be entitled to trace property in equity of which he was the equitable owner. Where trust property was misappro-priated or misdirected, the beneficiaries are entitled to trace the trust property which belongs to them in equity. Where the property of an absolute owner is misappropri-ated or misdirected, he will only be entitled to trace if the circumstances of the misap-propriation or misdirection gave rise to a trust in his favour.[126] An alternative analysis of tracing was propounded by Pearce, who argued that equitable tracing should be available whenever there is a 'continuing right of property recognised in equity', which would recognize the possibility of using equity to trace beneficial ownership.[127] If the circumstances do not disclose a transfer of equitable beneficial ownership, the recipi-ent should be obliged to give effect to the owner's continuing proprietary interest. Professor Birks has adopted the argument that equitable tracing should be available whenever there is a sufficient 'proprietary base'. By this he means that:

---

[120] [1981] Ch 105.   [121] Goff and Jones, *The Law of Restitution* (3rd edn, 1987), p 79.
[122] Goff and Jones, *The Law of Restitution* (6th edn, 2002), pp 104–106. In this edition, Goff and Jones argue that the comments of the House of Lords in *Foskett v McKeown* [2001] 1 AC 102 that 'there is no sense in maintaining different rules for tracing at law and in equity' lead to the conclusion that the courts should no longer insist on a fiduciary relationship before a claimant can trace in equity.
[123] [1992] 4 All ER 385.   [124] [1992] 4 All ER 385, at 402.   [125] [1992] 4 All ER 451.
[126] See *Westdeutsche Landesbank Girozentrale v Islington London Borough Council* [1996] AC 669, at 706, per Lord Browne-Wilkinson.   [127] (1976) 40 Conv 275.

the circumstances of the original receipt by the defendant must be such that, either at law or in equity, the plaintiff retained or obtained the property in the matter received by the defendant, and then continued to retain it until the moment at which the substitution or intermixture took place.[128]

The trust analysis of the right to trace in equity was supported by the Privy Council in *Re Goldcorp Exchange Ltd (in receivership)*.[129] The customers who had purchased 'non-allocated metal' were not entitled to trace their purchase money into the bulk of metal held by the company because they could not be shown to have any equitable proprietary interest in it arising through the contract of sale.[130]

It is submitted that there is a strong argument for permitting equitable tracing to be employed wherever property has changed hands in circumstances where there has been no transfer of the equitable beneficial interest. However, such a development would not lead to any significant practical change in the operation of equitable tracing, since there is such a close connection between equitable ownership and a fiduciary relationship that the two terms could almost be seen to be synonymous. This much is admitted by Birks:

> the requirement of a fiduciary relationship is, in this context one and the same as the requirement of an undestroyed proprietary base...a plaintiff who wants to assert an equitable proprietary interest in the surviving enrichment must show facts such that the property in the original receipt did not pass at law and in equity to the recipient. If he can show such facts, so that, at least in equity, he retained the property in the res, he will, after identifying the surviving enrichment, be able to raise an equitable proprietary interest in those different assets. Where such facts are shown, the relationship between him and the recipient can, rightly, be described as 'fiduciary' in that it will resemble the relationship between cestui que trust and trustee.[131]

While the continuing proprietary interest analysis may be little more than an alternative label for the present search for a 'fiduciary relationship', it has the definite merit of de-mythologizing the process because it is a more accurate and precise description of what the court is looking for. That said, the mere fact that a different label is used does not answer the difficult questions as to the circumstances in which a trust will arise so as to justify tracing in equity.

(c) Circumstances in which it will be possible to trace in equity

(i) Misappropriation of trust property by a trustee

Equitable tracing will always be available against a trustee who has wrongfully misappropriated trust property, because the beneficiary retains his equitable title to the trust property. Thus equitable tracing was permitted in *Foskett v McKeown*,[132] where

---

[128] Birks, *Introduction to the Law of Restitution* (1985), p 378.   [129] [1994] 2 All ER 806.

[130] See Birks 'Establishing a Proprietary Base' [1995] RLR 83. Compare *El Ajou v Dollar Land Holdings plc (No 2)* [1995] 2 All ER 213, where Robert Walker J suggested that tracing depends on the concept of an equitable charge and not equitable ownership.

[131] Birks, *Introduction to the Law of Restitution* (1985), p 381.   [132] [2001] 1 AC 102.

a trustee had wrongfully used trust money to pay the premiums due under his insurance policy.

(ii) Receipt of trust property by a stranger to a trust

Where property subject to a trust is transferred to a stranger in breach of trust, the beneficiary will be entitled to trace the trust property into the hands of the stranger unless he was a bona fide purchaser for value without notice, in which case the beneficiary's equitable title will be defeated.

(iii) Profits received by a fiduciary in breach of duty

It now appears clear that unauthorized profits received by a fiduciary are held on constructive trust for his principal, so that the principal will be entitled to trace them in equity.[133]

(iv) Stolen or misappropriated property

In *Lipkin Gorman v Karpnale Ltd*[134] Lord Templeman approved Australian authorities which hold that a thief does not gain title to his property, but holds it on trust. He cited with approval O'Connor J in *Black v S Freedman & Co*:

> Where money has been stolen, it is trust money in the hands of the thief and he cannot divest it of that character. If he pays it over to another person, then it may be followed into that person's hands. If, of course, that other person shows that it has come to him bona fides for valuable consideration, and without notice, it then may lose its character as trust money and cannot be recovered…[135]

In *Westdeutsche Landesbank Girozentrale v Islington London Borough Council*[136] Lord Browne-Wilkinson also held that theft would generate a constructive trust sufficient to give rise to the right to trace in equity. He considered whether a resulting trust would arise when a thief stole a bag of coins:

> I agree that the stolen moneys are traceable in equity. But the proprietary interest which equity is enforcing in such circumstances arises under a constructive, not a resulting, trust. Although it is difficult to find clear authority for the proposition, when property is obtained by fraud equity imposes a constructive trust on the fraudulent recipient; the property is recoverable and traceable in equity… Money stolen from a bank account can be traced in equity.[137]

---

[133] See FHR European Ventures LLP v Cedar Capital Partners LLC [2014] UKSC 45, and the discussion of this issue in Chapter 28.

[134] [1991] 2 AC 548; [1992] 4 All ER 512.   [135] (1910) 12 CLR 105.   [136] [1996] AC 669.

[137] [1996] AC 669, at 716. The following cases were cited in favour of this proposition: *Stocks v Wilson* [1913] 2 KB 235; *R Leslie Ltd v Sheill* [1914] 3 KB 607; *Bankers Trust Co v Shapira* [1980] 1 WLR 1274; *McCormick v Grogan* (1869) LR 4 HL 82. The proposition has been doubted in a number of subsequent authorities, including *Halifax Building Society v Thomas* [1996] Ch 217; *Paragon Finance v DB Thakerar* [1999] 1 All ER 400; *Shalson v Russo* [2003] WTLR 1165; *Sinclair Investment Holding SA v Versailles Trade Finance Ltd* [2005] EWCA Civ 722.

This principle would have been sufficient to justify tracing in equity in *Agip (Africa) Ltd v Jackson*[138] without having to find that the accountant, Zdiri, was a fiduciary. He was simply a thief who never gained title to the money he misappropriated, so it was possible to follow it into Baker Oil's account and beyond. The principle that a constructive trust arises from the fraudulent receipt of property was applied to establish a right to trace by Lawrence Collins J in *Commerzbank Aktiengesellschaft v IMB Morgan plc*,[139] where a stockbroker in Nigeria had received money into its accounts which had been obtained as a result of fraud.

It may be noted that, although the authorities now support the view that the thief holds on trust, it is an unusual kind of trust since, so far as the property originally stolen is concerned, the thief does not normally have legal title. This is always the case where tangible property is stolen, and may even be the case in relation to certain intangible property, such as money.[140] Because of this unusual characteristic, there is much to be said for the view that the right to trace exists because of the continuing equitable proprietary rights of the true owner, rather than because of the existence of a trust in the conventional sense.

(v) Payments made under a void contract

An area of controversy is whether a payment made under a contract void ab initio is traceable in equity.[141] It had been argued that such a payment would give rise to a resulting trust in favour of the payor, thus entitling him to trace the payment into the assets of the payee. However, this analysis was comprehensively rejected by the House of Lords in *Westdeutsche Landesbank Girozentrale v Islington London Borough Council*,[142] where it was held that money paid under a void interest rate swap agreement was not subject to a resulting trust. Lord Goff stated:

> there is no general rule that the property in money paid under a void contract does not pass to the payee; and it is difficult to escape the conclusion that, as a general rule, the beneficial interest in the money likewise passes to the payee.[143]

The House of Lords reversed the decision of the Court of Appeal[144] that a resulting trust had arisen, and overruled *Sinclair v Brougham*.[145] It therefore seems that it will generally be impossible to trace money paid under a void contract in equity and that the payor will be confined to seeking restitution at common law. However, Lord Browne-Wilkinson did seem to suggest that a trust would be imposed if the recipient

---

[138] [1990] Ch 265; affd [1992] 4 All ER 451. [139] [2004] EWHC 2771.

[140] Where intangible property is obtained by fraud, legal title may pass to the thief, as for instance if shares or registered land are registered in his name.

[141] See Worthington, *Proprietary Interests in Commercial Transactions* (1996), pp 148–161.

[142] [1996] AC 669. [143] [1996] AC 669, at 690.

[144] [1994] 1 WLR 938; [1994] RLR 73 (Swadling). Dillon LJ had adopted the following conclusion: 'Since, contrary to the expectation of the parties, the swap transaction and contract are, and were from the outset, ultra vires and void, the purpose for which the £2.5 million was paid by the bank to the council has wholly failed, and the £2.5 million has, from the time the council received it, been held on a resulting trust for the bank.' [145] [1914] AC 398.

of the payment was aware of the invalidity of the contract so as to affect his conscience and justify the imposition of a constructive trust, and that such a trust could arise even after receipt if the payee became aware of the invalidity while the payment was still identifiable in his hands.

(vi) Payments made under a voidable contract

In *El Ajou v Dollar Land Holdings plc (No 1)*[146] Millett J held that a resulting trust arose when a payment had been made under a voidable contract. The case concerned a fraudulent share-selling scheme operated by three Canadians. The claimants' money was invested in the scheme after their agent was bribed to invest in it. The proceeds were eventually invested in a property development project carried on with the defendants, Dollar Land Holdings. The claimants sought to recover their money from the defendants. Millett J held that although they could not trace at common law, because the money had been mixed, they could trace in equity because there was a fiduciary relationship between them and their agent, who was bribed. However, Millett J went on to consider the position of other victims of the fraud who had not invested through a fiduciary and concluded that they too would be entitled to trace:

> Other victims, however, were less fortunate. They employed no fiduciary. They were simply swindled. No breach of any fiduciary obligation was involved. It would, of course, be an intolerable reproach to our system of jurisprudence if the plaintiff were the only victim who could trace and recover his money. Neither party before me suggested that this is the case; and I agree with them. But if the other victims of the fraud can trace their money in equity it must be because, having been induced to purchase the shares by false and fraudulent misrepresentations, they are entitled to rescind the transaction and revest the equitable title to the purchase money in themselves, at least to the extent necessary to support an equitable tracing claim…[147]

While this neatly emphasizes that the essence of the right to trace is not a fiduciary relationship per se but the need to demonstrate an equitable proprietary interest, the judgment of the Privy Council in *Re Goldcorp Exchange Ltd (in receivership)*[148] casts doubt upon the proposition. The purchasers of 'non-allocated metal' argued that they were entitled to rescind the contract on the grounds of misrepresentation. Although they had not in fact rescinded their contracts, the Privy Council suggested that even if they had they would not have been entitled to an equitable proprietary right. As Lord Mustill explained:

> even if this fatal objection could be overcome, the argument would, in their Lordships' opinion, be bound to fail. While it is convenient to speak of the customers 'getting their money back' this expression is misleading. Upon payment by the customers the purchase moneys became, and rescission or no rescission remained, the unencumbered property of

---

[146] [1993] BCLC 735; revsd [1994] BCLC 464, CA. See also *Daly v Sydney Stock Exchange* (1986) 160 CLR 371; *Lonrho plc v Fayed (No 2)* [1992] 1 WLR 1; *Halifax Building Society v Thomas* [1996] Ch 217. See Worthington, *Proprietary Interests in Commercial Transactions* (1996), pp 161–168.
[147] [1993] BCLC 735, at 753.   [148] [1994] 2 All ER 806.

the company. What the customers would recover on rescission would not be 'their' money, but an equivalent sum...[149]

In the light of *Westdeutsche Landesbank Girozentrale v Islington London Borough Council*,[150] it seems that the mere fact that a contract is avoided will not give rise to a trust entitling a payor to trace in equity.[151]

(vii) *Payments made by mistake*

As has already been seen in *Chase Manhattan Bank NA v Israeli-British Bank (London) Ltd*,[152] it was held that a payor was entitled to trace in equity a payment caused by his mistake of fact. However, it remains unclear why equitable tracing was permitted. In *Westdeutsche Landesbank Girozentrale v Islington London Borough Council*[153] Lord Browne-Wilkinson doubted that the payor could be said to have retained the equitable title to his money when it was not subject to a trust prior to the payment, and the payee had not known at the moment that the payment was made that the payor was acting under a mistake. He seemed to suggest that a trust only arose because the payee became aware of the mistake two days later, thus affecting his conscience and leading to the imposition of a trust. This analysis has been subject to criticism[154] and, as was noted earlier, the true question should be whether the payee received good title to the money paid at the moment that it was transferred to him. If so, no trust arises and, while the recipient may be required to make restitution of the amount of the payment, the payor should not be entitled to trace. Tracing should only be possible if the money was paid under a mistake of fact so fundamental as to prevent property passing. The real difficulty is in identifying mistakes sufficiently fundamental to prevent property passing. As Robert Goff J said in *Barclays Bank Ltd v W J Simms*[155] in the majority of cases property will pass in payments made under a mistake of fact.[156] In *Re Goldcorp Exchange Ltd*[157] the Privy Council emphasized that the mistake in *Chase Manhattan* was a mistake whereby one party mistakenly made the same payment twice.[158] In *Westdeutsche* Lord Goff suggested that only a fundamental mistake of fact might prevent the equitable interest in money passing to a payee.[159]

(3) **Equitable tracing through clean substitutions**

Where trust property has been exchanged for other property, the beneficiaries are entitled to trace into the exchange product. Thus, if a trustee uses £5,000 of trust money to purchase a diamond ring for that price, the beneficiaries will be able to trace their equitable ownership into the ring.

---

[149] [1994] 2 All ER 806, at 825–826.   [150] [1996] AC 669.
[151] See also *Criterion Properties plc v Stratford UK Properties LLC* [2004] 1 WLR 1846.
[152] [1981] Ch 105.   [153] [1996] AC 669.
[154] Birks 'Trusts Raised to Avoid Unjust Enrichment: The *Westdeutche* Case' [1996] RLR 3, 21–23.
[155] [1980] QB 677.   [156] See Swadling 'Restitution for No Consideration' [1994] RLR 73.
[157] [1994] 2 All ER 806.   [158] [1994] 2 All ER 806, at 826.   [159] [1996] AC 669, at 690.

(4) **Equitable tracing of tangible property into a mixed bulk**

If the trust property consists of tangible property, for example if it is a quantity of crude oil, it is possible that the trustee may wrongfully allow the trust property to be mixed with other property so as to form a bulk. In such circumstances, by analogy with the common law rules, the beneficiaries would be entitled to trace the trust property into the bulk, and they would be entitled to a share of the equitable ownership proportionate to their contribution.[160]

(5) **Equitable tracing of money through a mixed fund**

More difficult problems present themselves if misappropriated trust property is mixed with other property so that it can no longer be identified as such. Assets purchased from the mixed fund cannot then be regarded as solely the product of the trust property. Unlike the rules of tracing at common law, the equitable rules of tracing permit the trust property to be traced through a mixed fund of money and into assets acquired from it. *Foskett v McKeown*[161] involved just such a situation. The case concerned a Mr Murphy, who in 1986 had taken out a unit-linked life insurance policy, which provided for the payment of a death benefit of £1m. The proceeds of the life insurance policy were written in trust for the benefit of his children. The initial annual premiums due under this policy were paid by Mr Murphy using his own money. However, the premiums due in 1989 and 1990 were paid using money from a bank account which he held on trust for the customers of a company he controlled which had contracted to buy land on their behalf in Portugal. In 1991 Mr Murphy committed suicide, and the death benefit was paid. The question at issue was whether the beneficiaries were entitled to trace their misappropriated money into the proceeds of the policy. The House of Lords held, by a bare majority, that the beneficiaries were entitled to a share of the proceeds proportionate to the contribution of the trust money to the payment of the premiums. Lord Millett explained that the beneficiaries were able to trace their trust money into the insurance policy itself, and thence into the proceeds of the policy:

> It is, however, of critical importance in the present case to appreciate that the purchasers do not trace the premiums directly into the insurance money. They trace them first into the policy and thence into the proceeds of the policy. It is essential not to elide the two steps. In this context, of course, the word 'policy' does not mean the contract of insurance. You do not trace the payment of a premium into the insurance contract any more than you trace a payment into a bank account in to the banking contract. The word 'policy' is here used to describe the bundle of rights to which the policyholder is entitled in return for the premiums. These rights, which may be very complex, together constitute a chose in action, viz the right to payment of a debt payable on a future event and contingent upon the continued payment of further premiums until the happening of the event. That chose in action represents the traceable proceeds of the premiums; its current value fluctuates from time to time. When the property matures, the insurance money represents the

---

[160] *Foskett v McKeown* [2001] 1 AC 102, at 141.   [161] [2001] 1 AC 102.

traceable proceeds of the policy and hence indirectly of the premiums. It follows that, if a claimant can show that premiums were paid with his money, he can claim a proportionate share of the policy.[162]

Foskett v McKeown involved a somewhat unusual mixture of funds in the form of the payment of premiums of an insurance policy. More commonly, misappropriated funds will become mixed in a bank account. Equity has developed special rules to determine whether trust property can be traced through a mixture of funds in a bank account.

(6) **Equitable tracing of money through the banking system**

While equity is capable of tracing property through a mixed fund, the process of identification can be extremely complex where money has become mixed with funds in a bank account. Where trust property was paid into a bank account, it may be essential to determine whether the remaining balance, or assets purchased from it, can be seen as representing the original trust property. Of necessity, this inquiry is often conducted ex post facto, only after the misappropriation of the trust property has been discovered and the transactions have taken place. The rules that have evolved are simply rough and ready presumptions which operate to determine whether any remaining balance, or property purchased, can be identified as the product of the trust money. They operate differently depending upon whether the mixture consisted of trust money and the money of the wrongdoing trustee, or the money of the trust and of another innocent party, for example money misappropriated from another trust. The rules emerged in the last century, and they are only really appropriate for simple bank accounts.

(a) **Mixture of the trust property and the trustee's own property**

Where a wrongdoing trustee has mixed trust property with his own property in a bank account, the rules operate harshly against him. If the mixed fund has been partially dissipated, any remaining balance, or assets acquired from the account, are presumed to belong to the trust. The burden is on the wrongdoer to show that the asset or balance represents his own money.[163] In *Sinclair Investments v Versailles Trade Finance*[164] part of the defence to a tracing claim was that the money claimed had become irretrievably mixed with the defendant's own funds. Lord Neuberger MR dismissed this bluntly:[165]

> I do not see why...a proprietary claim should be lost simply because the defaulting fiduciary, while still holding much of the money, has acted particularly dishonestly or cunningly by creating a maelstrom. Where he has mixed the funds held on trust with his own funds, the onus should be on the fiduciary to establish that part, and what part, of the mixed fund is his property.

Where the account balance has been reduced by withdrawals which have been dissipated, the court will presume that the remaining balance represents the trust property

---

[162] [2001] 1 AC 102, at 134.   [163] *Lupton v White* (1808) 15 Ves 432.
[164] [2011] 4 All ER 335.   [165] At [138].

and that the wrongdoer's own money has been dissipated. The wrongdoer will not be permitted to assert that it represents his own money and that the money he has spent and dissipated was the trust money. As Millett LJ stated in *Boscawen v Bajwa*:

> A trustee will not be allowed to defeat the claim of his beneficiaries by saying that he has resorted to trust money when he could have made use of his own.[166]

This presumption was applied in *Re Hallett's Estate*. A solicitor, who was a trustee of his own marriage settlement, was entrusted with money by a client for investment. He paid money from the trust and his client's money into his bank account, which also contained some of his own money. He made various payments out, which had been dissipated. On his death, the account contained enough money to satisfy the claims of the trust and the client, but not his other creditors. The central question was whether the money in the account could be said to be the property of the trust and client, in which case they would gain priority over the general creditors. The Court of Appeal held that the trustee must be presumed to have spent his own money first, and to have preserved the trust monies. Lord Walker in *Re Lehman Bros International (Europe)*[167] evocatively described the process this way:

> Client money held temporarily in a house account does not, in the eyes of trust law, 'swill around', but sinks to the bottom in the sense that when the firm is using money for its own purposes it is treated as withdrawing its own money from a mixed fund before it touches trust money.

If the presumption adopted in *Re Hallett's Estate* were absolute, it would produce an anomalous result if the wrongdoing trustee purchased assets from the account and then dissipated the remaining balance. The trustee would be able to claim that the assets had been acquired with his own money, since he was deemed to spend this first. In consequence, the presumption that the trustee withdraws and spends his own money first is not absolute but a specific application of the general maxim that 'everything is presumed against a wrongdoer'. Whatever the circumstances and the order of events, the wrongdoer is presumed to have acted so as to preserve the trust money. Thus, assets acquired before the remaining balance of the account was dissipated may be claimed to represent the trust property. As Millett LJ stated in *Boscawen v Bajwa*:

> if the beneficiary asserts that the trustee has made use of the trust money there is no reason why he should not be allowed to prove it.[168]

Hence in *Re Oatway*,[169] where application of the presumption in *Re Hallett's Estate* would have worked an injustice, exactly the opposite presumption was applied, namely that the trustee had spent the trust money first. Lewis Oatway was a solicitor and the trustee of a will. He misappropriated £3,000 from the trust and paid this into a bank account where it was mixed with his own money. He purchased Oceana shares for £2,137 using money from the account. At the time that he purchased them there

---

[166] [1995] 4 All ER 769, at 778.   [167] [2012] 3 All ER 1, at [65].
[168] [1995] 4 All ER 769, at 778.   [169] [1903] 2 Ch 356.

would have been enough of his own money in the account to purchase the shares. After the purchase, he dissipated the balance of the account and died insolvent, leaving the shares, now valued at £2,474. If the rule in *Re Hallett* were applied, the shares would have been purchased with his money, and therefore form part of his general assets. However, Joyce J held that the shares were to be regarded as the product of the trust money. Having examined the rule in *Re Hallett's Estate* he concluded:

> It is, in my opinion, equally clear that when any of the money drawn out has been invested, and that investment remains in the name or under the control of the trustee, the rest of the balance having been afterwards dissipated by him, he cannot maintain that the investment which remains represents his own money alone, and that what has been spent and can no longer be traced and recovered was the money belonging to the trust.[170]

The contrasting decisions in *Re Hallett's Estate*[171] and *Re Oatway*[172] are not in conflict with each other, but are applications of a general principle that the trustee is estopped from asserting that he has preserved his own money at the expense of trust funds. It has been described as 'cherry picking' since the beneficiaries are allowed to choose the most beneficial construction of what has happened.[173] This rule works to the advantage of the beneficiaries of the trust, but it must be remembered that it acts to the detriment of the general creditors, who will inevitably receive a lower dividend from the insolvency. It is questionable whether this priority is always just.

In most cases where tracing is argued the claimant is trying to salvage a small part of what they have lost as a result of a trustee's wrongdoing. What would happen where a trustee mixes his own money with trust funds and then makes a profitable purchase, but leaves enough money in the mixed account to satisfy the claims of beneficiaries? It has been argued that in such a case both beneficiary and trustee should share the profits.[174] This was addressed in *Turner v Jacob*.[175] Mrs Turner put money to which her daughter (Mrs Jacob) was entitled into a deposit account. A number of withdrawals were made which reduced the balance to around £10,000. The balance in the account never subsequently fell below this level, but there were a significant number of deposits and withdrawals, including withdrawals to support the purchase of two houses. Patten J considered that Mrs Jacob could not claim that the money to which she had a claim had been used to purchase either of the houses:

> It seems to me that in a case (such as the present) where the trustee maintains in the account an amount equal to the remaining trust fund, the beneficiary's right to trace is limited to that fund. It is not open to the beneficiary to assert a lien against an investment made using monies out of the mixed account unless the sum expended is of such a size that it must have included trust monies or the balance remaining in the account after the investment is then expended so as to become untraceable.[176]

---

[170] [1903] 2 Ch 356, at 360.   [171] (1880) 13 Ch D 696.   [172] [1903] 2 Ch 356.

[173] *Dyson Technology Ltd v Curtis* [2010] EWHC 3289 (Ch) (20 September 2010), at [20].

[174] Birks, *Introduction to the Law of Restitution* (1985), p 370.   [175] [2006] EWHC 1317 (Ch).

[176] [2006] EWHC 1317 (Ch), at [102]. Mrs Jacob was the residuary beneficiary under her mother's will. A personal claim by Mrs Jacob against her mother would have reduced the value of the residuary estate, which also included the proceeds of selling the first house to be purchased. Mrs Jacob claimed to be entitled

(b) **Property of trusts or innocent volunteers mixed**

The harsh presumptions which operate against a wrongdoer who has mixed trust property with his own are not applied where trust property has been mixed with that of other trusts or other innocent volunteers. In such a case, the rules reflect the moral blamelessness of the parties whose money has been mixed, and they aim to do substantive justice between them. For over a century the preferred method of distribution has been what is called 'pari passu' distribution, or, in colloquial English, 'share and share alike'.

(i) Ponzi schemes

A very common type of investment fraud is known as a Ponzi scheme, named after the Italian crook who ran such a scam. An example is described in *Madoff Securities International Ltd v Raven*.[177] For over twenty years before his confession, Bernard Madoff took billions of dollars from 'investors' through his New York company, Bernard L. Madoff Investment Securities LLC. He purported to run the investment advisory business as a legitimate and highly successful business with impressive returns. Flaux J said:

> the reality was that the investment advisory business made no material investments at all. Clients' money was pooled in a single account at JP Morgan and treated by Mr Madoff and his associates as his own. He would pay 'profits' or 'redemptions' to clients ostensibly by way of return on their investment, but in reality this consisted of other clients' money, the Ponzi scheme being funded by a constant influx of funds. However, in December 2008, requests for redemptions by customers nervous at the financial crisis and the collapse of Lehman Brothers exceeded the amount of funds deposited by new customers and the scheme collapsed. The customers of the investment advisory business had between them lost about US$ 19.5 billion.

In cases such as this, the remaining funds are able to meet only a fraction of the sums due to investors. How should they be returned?

(ii) Individually identifiable assets

Where assets can specifically be linked to an individual investor, then the investor can lay claim to that specific asset. For instance in *Russell-Cooke Trust Co v Prentis*[178] a solicitor ran a secured investment scheme in which some investors' payments were linked to specific mortgage loans. Lindsay J held that where this link was established, the investor was entitled to that specific asset.

(iii) Assets not capable of individual allocation

It will often be the case that it is not possible to identify a link to a specific asset, or where there are several claims to a single asset. This would be so if a dishonest solicitor

---

to a proportion of the value of the second house to be purchased, which her mother had left in her will to her husband.

[177] [2011] EWHC 3102 (Comm).

[178] [2003] 2 All ER 478. See also *Re Diplock* [1948] Ch 465, where some of the funds were specifically identifiable.

has put clients' money into his client account, but has improperly withdrawn money for his own purposes, or where there are some unallocated assets acquired with the deposits made by investors in a Ponzi scheme. Three ways of allocating the assets have been identified.

(iv) Pari passu allocation

Pari passu allocation works by identifying the proportion which each individual contribution has made to the total value of the valid claims, and then distributing the available assets in the same proportions. So, if £50,000 of Joey's money was paid by a Ponzi scheme fraudster into an empty 'investment account' in July, the next month £100,000 of Melanie's money was paid in, and in September the fraudster withdrew £90,000 for his own use, the remaining £60,000 would be shared as to one-third by Joey and two-thirds by Melanie. If in October, and before the fraud was discovered, the fraudster paid in another £100,000 from Nikita, and in November took another £80,000 from the account, the remaining £80,000 would be shared as to one-fifth by Joey (since that is the proportion he contributed to the total of £250,000 originally invested), two-fifths by Melanie (since that is the share she contributed) and two-fifths by Nikita. The shares would therefore be worth £16,000, £32,000, and £32,000 respectively: see Figure 30.1.

(v) Rolling charge allocation

Pari passu allocation divides assets using a global calculation—that is, it looks only at the total invested and the total available for distribution. A more sophisticated method known as the rolling charge or North American method recalculates shares every time a transaction occurs. So if the facts were as described earlier, in July the whole fund would belong to Joey. After Melanie's money was deposited, the fund would belong one-third to Joey and two-thirds to Melanie. In September the withdrawal would make those shares of a reduced pot of £60,000, so the addition of Nikita's money would reduce Joey's share to £20,000 of the £160,000 total, or one-eighth, Melanie would have a share of two-eighths (one-quarter) and Nikita's share would be five-eighths. The fraudster's withdrawal in November would leave those shares worth £10,000, £20,000, and £50,000, respectively. It can be seen that the system is complicated and requires detailed records: see Figure 30.2.

(vi) 'First in, first out' allocation

The final type of allocation applies the tag, 'first in, first out.' It was the method adopted in *Clayton's case*[179] and hence has been named the rule in *Clayton's case*. Under this rule it is presumed that money is paid out of a current account in the same order in which it had been paid in. If this rule is applied to the Ponzi scheme fraudster's investment account described earlier (and there are good reasons why it would *not* be applied in this situation), the effect would be that of the £170,000 withdrawn and dissipated by the fraudster, the first £50,000 would be treated as having been taken from

---

[179] (1816) 1 Mer 572.

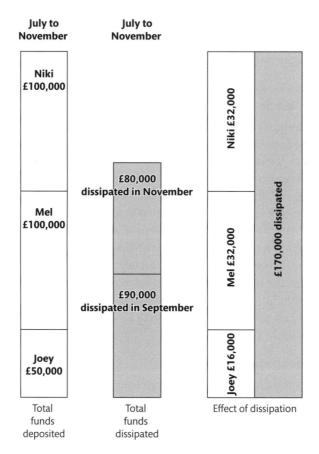

Figure 30.1 Pari passu allocation

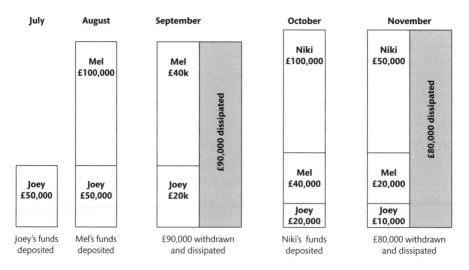

Figure 30.2 Rolling charge allocation

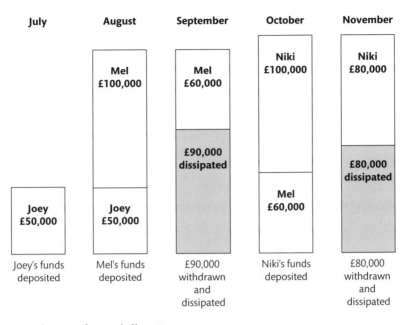

Figure 30.3 'First in, first out' allocation

Joey, the next £100,000 from Melanie, and the last £20,000 from Nikita. As a consequence only Nikita would receive anything, and Nikita's share would be the whole remaining £80,000 with neither Joey nor Melanie receiving anything: see Figure 30.3.

(vii) Which method of application to use?

The rule in *Clayton's case* was applied in a number of cases in the nineteenth century.[180] However, the case has been so rarely applied since to innocent beneficiaries of a breach of trust, possibly the only reported example being *Re Diplock* in 1948,[181] that one judge has said that 'it might be more accurate to refer to the exception that is, rather than the rule in, *Clayton's case*'.[182] The main reason why the rule is applied so rarely is that it is not perceived as operating fairly between innocent beneficiaries. Leggatt LJ in *Barlow Clowes International Ltd (in liquidation) v Vaughan*[183] described the rule as 'capricious, arbitrary and inapposite'. The judicial approach has not been directly to challenge the rule, but to find ways of avoiding its application.

In *Barlow Clowes International Ltd v Vaughan*, the Court of Appeal was faced with the consequences of the collapse of the Barlow Clowes investment company in Gibraltar. Depositors had paid into investment plans, but the money had been

---

[180] See *Re Hallett's Estate* (1880) 13 Ch D 696 (Fry J); *Hancock v Smith* (1889) 41 Ch D 456; *Re Stenning* [1895] 2 Ch 433; *Mutton v Peat* [1899] 2 Ch 556.   [181] *Re Diplock* [1948] Ch 465, CA.

[182] Lindsay J in *Russell-Cooke Trust Co v Prentis* [2003] 2 All ER 478, at [55].

[183] *Barlow Clowes International Ltd (in liquidation) v Vaughan* [1992] 4 All ER 22, at 46. See Fox 'Legal Title as a Ground of Restitutionary Liability' [2000] RLT 465.

misapplied and the company was left owing some £115m to investors, with assets far less than that amount. Some investors argued that the rule in *Clayton's case* should be applied, with the consequence that the late investors would recover virtually all their money, leaving the early investors with nothing. After a wide-ranging examination of the authorities, the court held that the rule was well established and that it was not open to the Court of Appeal to overrule it. As Dillon LJ observed:

> the decisions of this court he decestablish and recognise a general rule of practice that *Clayton's case* is to be applied when several beneficiaries' moneys have been blended in one bank account and there is a deficiency. It is not...for this court to reject that long established general practice.[184]

There are four ways in which the courts have avoided applying the rule In *Clayton's case*. First, the rule was originally devised to regulate the banker–client relationship, so that a line could be drawn under old ledger entries. That was a purpose far removed from the relationship between innocent beneficiaries. The rule has been held applicable only to active running bank accounts (like a current account, where there are regular deposits and withdrawals), and not to other types of account like deposit accounts,[185] or to disentangling transactions involving other property.[186] Secondly, the application of *Clayton's case* is not possible if the state of records is such that it would be impossible or impracticable to apply.[187] Thirdly, it has been said that the rule will give way to even the slightest contra-indication.[188] Finally, the courts have declined to apply the rule where it would result in injustice. This last reason is the principal reason why the Court of Appeal in *Barlow Clowes* felt free to depart from applying the rule. The principles governing the application of the rule were summarized by Woolf LJ:

> The rule need only be applied when it is convenient to do so and when its application can be said to do broad justice having regard to the nature of the competing claims...It is not applied if this is the intention or presumed intention of the beneficiaries. The rule is sensibly not applied when the cost of applying it is likely to exhaust the fund available for the beneficiaries.[189]

On the facts, it was held that the rule would not be applied because the investment fund was regarded by the investors as a common pool, and that they should share pari passu in what remained because they had experienced a common misfortune. It would have been wholly inequitable to apply the rule in *Clayton's case*, which would have meant some investors recovering everything to the exclusion of the rest, who would recover nothing. Subsequent cases have continued to reject the application of the rule.[190]

---

[184] [1992] 4 All ER 22, at 33.
[185] *Sinclair v Brougham* [1914] AC 398; *Re Diplock* [1948] Ch 465, CA.
[186] *Re Goldcorp Exchange Ltd* [1995] 1 AC 74.
[187] *Re Eastern Capital Futures Ltd* [1989] BCLC 371.
[188] *Barlow Clowes International Ltd (in liquidation) v Vaughan* [1992] 4 All ER 22.
[189] [1992] 4 All ER 22, at 39.
[190] See also the discussion of the rule in *Re French Caledonia Travel* (2004) 22 ACLC 498; [2003] NSWSC 1008; Conaglen 'Contests between Rival Beneficiaries' [2005] 64 CLJ 45.

In *Russell-Cooke Trust Co v Prentis*,[191] Lindsay J declined to apply the rule to victims of a common misfortune because it would operate unfairly. Lawrence Collins J also refused to apply the rule in *Commerbank Aktiengesellschaft v IMB Morgan plc*,[192] where money obtained by fraud had been paid into the account of a firm of stockbrokers, where it had become mixed so that it was not possible to identify any part of the funds as belonging to a particular client. He held that the rule would be 'impracticable and unjust' to apply, and held that the balance in the account should be divided in proportion among the clients (pari passu).

The rolling charge or North American method of allocation 'appears never to have been applied in England'[193] and has been expressly rejected twice. In the *Barlow Clowes* case, Woolf LJ accepted that the solution could have advantages over a distribution pari passu, but considered that the complications made it impracticable to apply in the circumstances of that case.[194] In *Russell-Cooke Trust Co v Prentis*,[195] Lindsay J noted this rejection and added that the method was inappropriate because it was 'complicated and may be expensive to apply'. The consequence is that the pari passu method of allocation is universally, or almost universally, the method of distribution adopted.

(c) The lowest intermediate balance

Whether a fund consists of a mixture of trust money with the wrongdoer's own, or the money of an innocent volunteer, if money has been dissipated from the account and then further money is paid into the account, the trust has no claim to any of that other money. The trust is limited to what is known as the lowest intermediate balance, because it is impossible that anything in the account above that figure represents trust property. The operation of this rule is seen in *Roscoe v Winder*.[196] A wrongdoer misappropriated some £455, which he paid into his own bank account. After a few days the balance was reduced to £25, though by his death it had risen to £358. It was held that a charge could only extend over the £25. Sargant J explained this on the basis that the principle of *Re Hallett's Estate*[197] could only apply to money which came from the trust fund: any increase in the balance above the lowest intermediate balance must have come from other sources. If the subsequent payments in had been specifically intended to replenish the trust funds, then the trust would be entitled to a charge over them because this would be expressly imposing upon the later payment a trust equivalent to the trust which rested on the previous balance.[198] The rule preventing

---

[191] *Russell-Cooke Trust Co v Prentis* [2003] 2 All ER 478, Conaglen 'Contests between Rival Beneficiaries' [2005] 64 CLJ 45.   [192] [2004] EWHC 2771.

[193] *Steele v Steele* [2001] All ER (D) (Ferris J). This was a family case involving a question of ownership of funds in a joint account. The judge applied the presumption in such cases that the funds are owned jointly.

[194] [1992] 4 All ER 22, at 39.   [195] *Russell-Cooke Trust Co v Prentis* [2003] 2 All ER 478 [57].

[196] [1915] 1 Ch 62.   [197] (1880) 13 Ch D 696.

[198] Sargant J took the view that if the account was a separate trust account then, the mere fact of a payment in would be sufficient indication of an intention to substitute the additional moneys (see eg *Re Hughes* [1970] IR 237), but there was no such intention in the case of a payment into a general trading account.

tracing beyond the lowest intermediate balance was reaffirmed by the Court of Appeal in *Bishopsgate Investment Management v Homan*.[199]

(d) Bank trustee depositing trust money with itself

The situations described earlier have all involved cases where a trustee has mixed trust money with either his own or that of innocent volunteers in bank accounts. However, given that banks may themselves act as trustees, they may deposit trust money with themselves. If they then become insolvent, the question may arise as to whether the beneficiaries can trace the money in the hands of the bank. This issue was considered by the Privy Council in *Space Investments Ltd v Canadian Imperial Bank of Commerce Trust Co (Bahamas) Ltd*.[200] The case concerned a bank, the Mercantile Bank Trust Co Ltd, which was the trustee of various settlements. The trust instruments contained clauses permitting the trustee to open and maintain savings accounts with any bank, including itself. The bank deposited trust money with itself, and then became insolvent. The question was whether the beneficiaries were entitled to trace the trust money into the bank accounts and therefore gain priority over the other unsecured creditors of the bank. The Privy Council held that they were not entitled to do so because the deposit was entirely lawful and not in breach of trust. The beneficiaries were to be treated like all the other depositors of the bank, who were restricted to proving in the liquidation as unsecured creditors for the amount that ought to have been credited to their accounts at the date of liquidation. However, the Privy Council considered that the position would have been different if the bank trustee had misappropriated the trust money and had acted in breach of trust by depositing the trust property with itself. In such circumstances the beneficiaries would be entitled to an equitable charge over all the assets of the bank. Lord Templeman explained the Board's reasoning:

> A bank in fact uses all deposit moneys for the general purposes of the bank…in these circumstances it is impossible for the beneficiaries interested in trust money misappropriated from their trust to trace their money to any particular asset belonging to the trustee bank. But equity allows the beneficiaries, or a new trustee appointed in place of an insolvent bank trustee to protect the interests of the beneficiaries, to trace the trust money to all the assets of the bank and to recover the trust money by the exercise of an equitable charge over all the assets of the bank.[201]

This accorded the beneficiaries priority over all the unsecured creditors of the bank. This was justified by the Board on the grounds that the settlor and beneficiaries of the trust had never accepted the risks involved in the possible insolvency of the bank, whereas the unsecured other creditors had voluntarily accepted that risk. In conclusion, the distinction between the beneficiaries' position where the deposit was authorized and where it was not was justified on the basis that:

---

[199] [1995] 1 All ER 347; Smith 'Tracing, "Swollen Assets" and the Lowest Intermediate Balance: *Bishopsgate Investment Management Ltd v Homan*' (1994) 8 TLI 102. See also *British Columbia v National Bank of Canada* (1994) 119 DLR (4th) 669.   [200] [1986] 1 WLR 1072.
[201] [1986] 1 WLR 1072, at 1974.

Equity…protects beneficiaries against breaches of trust. But equity does not protect beneficiaries against the consequences of the exercise in good faith of powers conferred by the trust instrument.[202]

This decision has been criticized, since in effect it enables the beneficiaries to maintain a security interest over assets that could not possibly be the product of the trust property.[203] In *Re Goldcorp Exchange Ltd*[204] the Privy Council referred to *Space Investments* and the criticisms which had been levelled at the judgment, but concluded that:

In the present case it is not necessary or appropriate to consider the scope and ambit of the observations in *Space Investments* or their application to trustees other than bank trustees…

The exact scope and application of the principle therefore awaits further judicial clarification.

(7) Tracing into assets acquired prior to misappropriation

The question has arisen whether misappropriated money can be traced in equity into an asset acquired before the trust property was received.[205] Such a process has been described as 'backward tracing'. In *Bishopsgate Investment Management v Homan*[206] Dillon LJ was willing to accept that in some circumstances trust money could be traced into a pre-acquired asset. The first instance judge had suggested that tracing would be possible if property had been acquired with borrowed money, either by way of loan or overdraft, and there was an inference that when the borrowing was incurred it was the intention that it should be repaid[207] with the misappropriated money. He considered that the beneficiary would be entitled to a charge over the asset acquired provided that the connection between the misappropriation and the asset was sufficiently proved. In contrast, Leggatt LJ entirely dismissed the possibility of such backward tracing:

there can be no equitable remedy against an asset acquired *before* misappropriation of money takes place, since ex hypothesi it cannot be followed into something which existed and so had been acquired before the money was received and therefore without its aid.[208]

In *Foskett v McKeown*[209] in the Court of Appeal, Scott V-C expressed the opinion that it should be possible to trace into assets acquired with borrowed money if the trust money was used to repay the borrowing and it had always been the intention that the trust money would be used to acquire the asset.

---

[202] [1986] 1 WLR 1072.
[203] Goode 'Ownership and Obligation in Commercial Transactions' (1987) 103 LQR 433.
[204] [1994] 2 All ER 806.
[205] Sir Peter Millett 'Law of Restitution (Publication Review)' (1995) 111 LQR 517; Oliver 'The Extent of Equitable Tracing' (1995) 9 TLI 78; Oakley 'Propriety Claims and Their Priority in Insolvency' (1995) 54 CLJ 377. [206] [1995] 1 All ER 347.
[207] [1995] 1 All ER 347, at 351. [208] [1995] 1 All ER 347, at 355. [209] [1997] 3 All ER 392, at 409.

(8) **The limits of equitable tracing**

While the right to trace in equity is not lost merely because the property becomes mixed with other property, there are circumstances in which it will no longer be possible to identify assets as representing the original property.

(a) **Bona fide purchaser**

It is not possible to trace trust property into the hands of a bona fide purchaser for value without notice. In such circumstances the equitable ownership of the property is entirely defeated and the purchaser receives the absolute ownership thereof.[210] The beneficiaries may, however, be able to trace into the consideration provided by the purchaser, since this will represent the proceeds of the property. There are two components to the defence.

(i) *For value*

An interesting question fell to be determined by the Court of Appeal in *Independent Trustee v GP Noble Trustees*.[211] A wife (Mrs Morris) had obtained an order for financial provision in divorce proceedings. This required her husband to pay her more than £1m. Unbeknown to Mrs Morris, her (by now ex-) husband made this payment using funds which he had misappropriated from pension trusts. If this was where matters had rested Mrs Morris would have been able to defend any claim for the recovery of these funds by the pension fund trustee by asserting her position as a bona fide purchaser for value without notice. She was unaware of the illegitimate source of the funds, and the satisfaction of the court order meant that she provided value. However, matters did not rest in this way. Still ignorant of her ex-husband's fraud, Mrs Morris discovered from her children that Mr Morris was enjoying a standard of living inconsistent with the assets which he had disclosed to the divorce court. Mrs Morris therefore successfully applied to have the financial provision order set aside so that she could make a claim for a higher sum. Before the new hearing could take place, Mr Morris was found guilty of dishonest assistance in breach of trust and knowing receipt of trust funds. Could Mrs Morris retain the sums which she had already been paid? The Court of Appeal held that she could not. By having the financial provision order set aside, she had provided no value in return for the funds she had received and could no longer claim to be a bona fide purchaser for value, regardless of any lack of knowledge on her part. She was therefore accountable to the pension fund for any sums she still had in her hands, and for the traceable proceeds of any money of which she had disposed.

(ii) *Without notice*

The question of what amounts to notice defeating a claim to be a bona fide purchaser in relation to the knowing receipt of trust property was considered in *Sinclair*

---

[210] It was suggested in *Armstrong GmbH v Winnington Networks Ltd* [2012] 3 All ER 425, at [101] that the defence might also operate to 'clear' a legal claim, but this is contrary to a well-established principle. It may be that the defence to a restitutionary claim based on change of position could operate in the same way.
[211] [2012] 3 All ER 210.

Investments v Versailles Trade Finance.[212] Banks had been repaid loans with money which had been derived from a complex fraud. The issue was whether the banks had notice of the illegitimate source of the funds. Part of the problem in many cases like this is that there can be growing suspicions of wrongdoing: at what point do those suspicions amount to notice? The starting point in commercial transactions is that parties are entitled to proceed on the assumption that they are dealing with honest men.[213] The first hint of a suspicion does not amount to notice,[214] nor does knowledge of a claim connote notice of a right.[215] Knowing the facts does not automatically equate to knowledge of the legal consequences. A person should only be treated as appreciating the legal consequences where he actually knew them, or ought reasonably to have known them.[216] It is essentially a question for the judge at what point 'a reasonable and honest person in the position of the banks, with all their experience and available sources of advice, should have known, done, and appreciated, as well as what they actually knew, did, and appreciated'.[217] What amounts to constructive notice might vary in different situations[218] and will not be established until it is shown that 'the facts known to the defendant made it imperative for him to seek an explanation, because in the absence of an explanation it was obvious that the transaction was probably improper.'[219]

(b) Dissipation

Once property and its proceeds have been dissipated, or used up, tracing is impossible because there is clearly no asset that represents the original property. The principle was stated by the Court of Appeal in *Re Diplock*:

> The equitable remedies presuppose the continued existence of the money either as a separate fund or as part of a mixed fund or as latent in property acquired by means of such a fund. If, on the facts of any individual case, such continued existence is not established, equity is as helpless as the common law itself.[220]

Therefore, beneficiaries would be unable to trace if a trustee used trust property to pay for a meal which he consumed, or a foreign holiday which he has taken, as no asset would remain. Similarly, if the property has been used to discharge a debt, nothing would be left that could be said to represent the trust property.[221] A debt is a chose in action and once it has been paid it ceases to exist. There is no longer a relationship of debtor and creditor. In *Re Diplock*,[222] the Court of Appeal held that it was not possible to trace trust money wrongfully transferred to two charities which had used it to discharge debts.

---

[212] [2011] 4 All ER 335.
[213] See *Macmillan Inc v Bishopsgate Investment Trust plc (no 3)* [1995] 3 All ER 747, at 782–783, per Millett J.   [214] [2011] 4 All ER 335, at [101].
[215] [2011] 4 All ER 335, at [108].   [216] [2011] 4 All ER 335, at [104].
[217] [2011] 4 All ER 335, at [101].   [218] At [106]–[107].
[219] At [108] adopting a statement by Millett J in *Macmillan Inc v Bishopsgate Investment Trust plc (no 3)* [1995] 3 All ER 747, at 782–783.   [220] [1948] Ch 465, at 521.
[221] For an alternative view, see Smith 'Tracing into the Payment of a Debt' [1995] 54 CLJ 290.
[222] [1948] Ch 465.

In *Re Tilley's Will Trusts*[223] it was held that it was not possible to trace money paid into an overdrawn bank account, because such payment only goes to reduce the amount of the overdraft, which is simply a debt owed by the customer to the bank. The inability to trace money paid into an overdrawn account was also accepted by the Court of Appeal in *Bishopsgate Investment Management Ltd v Homan*[224] and by the Privy Council in *Re Goldcorp Exchange.*[225] This was also the position in *Moriarty v Atkinson.*[226] A yacht brokering company received client funds to finance the purchase of new boats. Some of these funds were paid into the client account and were found to be held subject to a trust. Most, however, was paid into the company's current account that was always in debit. The Court of Appeal held that there was no trust in respect of these sums as the purchase money 'was effectively used to reduce the company's liability with the bank and it effectively disappeared so that there was never any fund on which a proprietary claim could operate'.[227] The court did not accept that the undertaking of the company to pay the money into the client account was sufficient to impose a trust on a different account from the one into which the money had been paid.[228]

Nevertheless, where a beneficiary's money is used in breach of trust to discharge a *secured* debt the beneficiary will be entitled to be subrogated to the position of the secured creditor and therefore able to recover the amount of the discharged loan from the debtor. This was considered in *Boscawen v Bajwa.*[229] Money was held on trust by a solicitor for the Abbey National, which had advanced it intending that it be used to complete the purchase of a house owned by Mr Bajwa which was subject to a charge in favour of the Halifax. In breach of trust, the money was used to redeem the charge but the purchase fell through. The Court of Appeal held that the Abbey National's money could be traced into the discharge of the debt and that they should be subrogated to the position of the Halifax, which had been the creditor of the legal charge. Millett LJ explained that the Abbey National was entitled to subrogation because they had intended to retain the beneficial interest in its money unless and until that interest was replaced by a first legal mortgage on the property[230] and that in the circumstances Mr Bajwa could not claim that the charge had been redeemed for his benefit as this would be unconscionable.[231] While subrogation may provide some answer to the problem of dissipation where money has been used to discharge a debt, it will only operate to the claimant's advantage if the debt was secured. Despite these authorities supporting the view that it is impossible to trace into an overdrawn bank account, in *Foskett v*

---

[223] [1967] Ch 1179.

[224] [1995] Ch 211; Gullifer 'Recovery of Misappropriated Assets: Orthodoxy Re-established?' [1995] LMCLQ 446.

[225] [1995] 1 AC 74. See also *Boscawen v Bajwa* [1995] 4 All ER 769, at 775; *PMPA v PMPS* (27 June 1994, unreported) [1995] RLR 217, HC of Ireland.   [226] [2008] EWCA Civ 1604.

[227] [2008] EWCA Civ 1604, at [15], per Lord Neuberger.

[228] [2008] EWCA Civ 1604, at [16]–[21].

[229] [1995] 4 All ER 769; Birks 'Tracing, Subrogation and Change of Position' (1995) 9 TLI 124; Mitchell 'Subrogation, Tracing and the *Quistclose* Principle' [1995] LMCLQ 451; Andrews 'Tracing and Subrogation' (1996) 55 CLJ 199; Oakley 'The Availability of Proprietary Remedies' [1997] Conv 1.

[230] [1995] 4 All ER 769, at 782.   [231] [1995] 4 All ER 769, at 784.

McKeown[232] Scott V-C considered that it remained an open question whether it was possible to trace into assets acquired from an overdrawn bank account:

> The availability of equitable remedies ought, in my view, to depend upon the substance of the transaction in question and not upon the strict order in which associated events happen…I would wish, for my part, to make it clear that I regard the point as still open and, in particular, that I do not regard the fact that an asset is paid for out of borrowed money with the borrowing subsequently repaid out of trust money as being necessarily fatal to an equitable tracing claim by the trust beneficiaries. If, in such a case, it can be shown that it was always the intention to use the trust money to acquire the asset, I do not see why the order in which the events happen should be regarded as critical to the claim.[233]

In *Re Diplock*[234] the Court of Appeal suggested that the use of trust property to improve a house where the improvement added no value to the house, or even caused a loss in value, would amount to a dissipation preventing tracing. In such circumstances there is nothing to trace, because 'the money will have disappeared leaving no monetary trace behind'. If the property has been dissipated, the only possible remedy will be a personal remedy against the trustee for breach of trust, or if it was received by a stranger who is liable to account for its value as a constructive trustee because he acted dishonestly.

(c) Unascertained goods

It is not usually possible to trace in equity into unascertained goods, because the purchaser does not gain title to those goods under the contract of sale until they have been separated from the bulk. This was so held in *Re London Wine Co (Shippers) Ltd*[235] and by the Privy Council in *Re Goldcorp Exchange Ltd*.[236] In the latter case, a company dealing in precious metals sold customers 'non-allocated metal' which the company stored as a bulk on their behalf. The customers were entitled to physical delivery of the metal on seven days' notice. The company became insolvent and, after the payment of the secured creditors, there would be nothing left for the customers who had bought 'non-allocated metal'. The customers claim to a proprietary right to the gold failed. One reason was that the customers had purchased unascertained goods and that title, including equitable title, would not pass until the goods were ascertained by the seller from the bulk. Clearly, there could be a declaration of trust on behalf of the purchaser of unascertained goods by the seller, but on the facts the Privy Council held that was not the intention of the company:

> The company cannot have intended to create an interest in its general stock of gold which would have inhibited any dealings with it otherwise than for the purpose of delivery under the non-allocated sale contracts.[237]

---

[232] [1997] 3 All ER 392.

[233] [1997] 3 All ER 392, at 409. In support of this proposition he cited *Agricultural Credit Corpn of Saskatchewan v Pettyjohn* (1991) 79 DLR (4th) 22 and Smith 'Tracing into the Payment of a Debt' (1995) 54 CLJ 290.   [234] [1948] Ch 465, at 547.

[235] (1975) 126 NLJ 977.   [236] [1994] 2 All ER 806.   [237] [1994] 2 All ER 806, at 815.

It follows that if trust property is used to purchase unascertained goods, there will be no possibility of tracing into the bulk unless the relationship is such that it can be shown that there was a trust in favour of the purchaser.[238]

(d) Inequitable to trace

In *Re Diplock*[239] the Court of Appeal considered that there should be no tracing if an innocent volunteer has used trust property to improve land. To impose a charge over the land for the increase in value in such circumstances would not, in the court's view, produce an equitable result.[240] The reason for this is that a charge is enforceable by sale, and the result is that the innocent volunteer could be compelled to sell his land. This limitation may perhaps be seen as an example of the general defence of change of position, which was recognized by the House of Lords in *Lipkin Gorman Ltd v Karpnale*.[241] Whether it will be inequitable to trace will depend on the circumstances of each case. *Re Diplock*[242] concerned charities who were innocent volunteers. As Goff and Jones suggest,[243] the result might have been different if the innocent volunteer had been a rich banker who had used trust money wisely to increase the value of his country house, and he has ample liquid assets to discharge any charge over the house without having to sell it. It may now be the case that the Trusts of Land and Appointment of Trustees Act 1996 contains sufficient safeguards to protect the innocent volunteer against the unfair pursuit of a claim to an interest in land through the rules of tracing.

(9) Claiming in equity

Once the equitable tracing process has identified assets which represent the original trust property, the beneficiaries may be able to assert a claim thereto. The potential claims available to beneficiaries in equity are wider than at common law. Depending upon the precise circumstances, the beneficiaries may either be able to assert a proprietary claim to the assets identified, an equitable lien to restore the trust fund, or a personal claim to restitution.

(a) Claiming assets identified as representing the original trust property

Where assets have been identified as representing the original trust property, the beneficiaries may wish to claim a proprietary entitlement to them by asserting their equitable ownership. The ability to make such a claim will be especially important if the person who possesses the assets is insolvent, since this will gain the beneficiaries priority over their other creditors. Beneficiaries may also wish to assert a proprietary claim

---

[238] See *Hunter v Moss* [1994] 3 All ER 215.   [239] [1948] Ch 465.

[240] [1948] Ch 465, at 546–548. The inability to trace where money has been expended on maintaining or improving land was accepted by Lord Browne-Wilkinson in *Foskett v McKeown* [2001] 1 AC 102, at 109. Where property is used for such purposes, he considered that it would 'at most' give rise to a proprietary lien to recover the money expended.   [241] [1991] 2 AC 548.

[242] [1948] Ch 465.   [243] Goff and Jones, *The Law of Restitution* (6th edn, 2002), p 111.

in order to take advantage of any rise in value of the assets identified.[244] A proprietary claim may therefore enable them to gain a windfall benefit. In *Foskett v McKeown*[245] Lord Millett considered that if A misappropriates B's money and uses it to buy a winning ticket in the lottery, B is entitled to claim the winnings.

(i) Claiming assets that were cleanly substituted for the trust property

It has long been established that where trust property has been misappropriated the beneficiaries will be entitled to claim any assets which can be identified as the product of a clean substitution.[246] Lord Millett explained as follows:

> The simplest case is where a trustee wrongfully misappropriates trust property and uses it exclusively to acquire other property for his benefit. In such a case the beneficiary is entitled *at his option* either to assert his beneficial ownership of the proceeds or to bring a personal claim against the trustees for breach of trust and enforce an equitable lien or charge on the proceeds to secure restoration of the trust fund. He will normally be able to exercise the option in the way most advantageous to himself.[247]

(ii) Claiming assets that were acquired from a mixed fund

Prior to *Foskett v McKeown* a distinction appears to have been drawn between the rights of beneficiaries where assets were acquired from a mixed fund consisting of the trust property and the property of another innocent party, and where they had been acquired from a mixed fund consisting of the trust property and the property of the wrongdoing trustee. Where the mixed fund had consisted of the trust property and the property of another innocent party, for example another trust or an innocent volunteer, the assets acquired would be shared pari passu and the beneficiaries would be entitled to claim a share of the equitable ownership proportionate to their contribution. However, where the mixed fund consisted of the misappropriated trust property and the property of the wrongdoing trustee it was thought that the beneficiaries were not able to claim a proportionate share of any assets acquired. Instead, they were limited to claiming an equitable lien over the property to secure the restoration of the trust fund. This distinction originated with the judgment of Jessel MR in *Re Hallett's Estate*,[248] and was applied by Scott V-C in the Court of Appeal in *Foskett v McKeown*.[249] However, in the House of Lords, Lord Millett held that no such distinction was to be drawn between the right of beneficiaries to claim a proportionate share of assets acquired from a mixed fund:

> In my view the time has come to state unequivocally that English law has no such rule. It conflicts with the rule that a trustee must not benefit from his trust. I agree with Burrows

---

[244] Some earlier cases, such as the decision of the House of Lords in *Sinclair v Brougham* [1914] AC 398, suggested that a beneficiary was not able to assert a proprietary claim so as to take advantage of an increase in the value of the property. However, this was questioned in *Re Tilley's Will Trusts* [1967] 1 Ch 1179, and in *Foskett v McKeown* [2001] 1 AC 102 the House of Lords finally held definitively that beneficiaries are entitled to gain the advantage of an increase in value of assets acquired from the trust property.

[245] [2001] 1 AC 102.   [246] *Re Hallett's Estate* (1880) 13 Ch D 696.

[247] [2001] 1 AC 102, at 130.   [248] (1880) 13 Ch D 696.   [249] [1998] Ch 265.

that the beneficiary's right to elect to have a proportionate share of a mixed substitution necessarily follows once one accepts, as English law does (i) that a claimant can trace in equity into a mixed fund and (ii) that he can trace unmixed money into its proceeds and assert ownership of the proceeds.

Accordingly, I would state the basic rule as follows. Where a trustee wrongfully uses trust money to provide part of the cost of acquiring an asset, the beneficiary is entitled at his option either to claim a proportionate share of the asset or to enforce a lien upon it to secure his personal claim against the trustee for the amount of the misapplied money.[250]

(iii) Claiming assets where tangible property has been mixed to form a bulk

If the trust property consists of tangible property that has been mixed so as to form a physical bulk, the beneficiary will be entitled to claim a share of the equitable ownership of the bulk proportionate to his contribution. In the event that pro rata division is impossible, the beneficiary will be entitled to take the whole bulk.[251] However, given the greater ability of equity to facilitate the co-ownership of property through the medium of a trust, it is much less likely that such a situation will arise than at common law.

(b) Enforcing an equitable lien

Beneficiaries are able to claim a proportionate share of assets acquired from a mixed fund that included the trust property. In many cases, this proprietary claim will prove most advantageous to the beneficiaries, since it will enable them to gain priority over other general creditors in the event of an insolvency, or to take advantage of any increase in value of the assets. Such a proprietary claim will not, however, be advantageous if the assets acquired from the mixed fund have fallen in value, since a proprietary claim will force the beneficiaries to bear a rateable share of the loss. In order to protect the beneficiaries in such circumstances, they are entitled to choose to claim to enforce an equitable lien against the mixed fund to secure their personal claim against the trustee to have the trust fund restored. The availability of such a lien was recognized in *Re Hallett's Estate*.[252] In *Foskett v McKeown*, the House of Lords asserted a general rule that a beneficiary has the right to elect between claiming a proportionate share of an asset acquired from a mixed fund and enforcing an equitable lien. However, Lord Millett explained that a lien will only be available where the mixed fund consisted of the trust property and the wrongdoing trustee's own property, and not where the mixed fund consisted of the property of equally innocent parties:

> Innocent contributors, however, must be treated equally inter se. Where the beneficiary's claim is in competition with the claims of other innocent contributors, there is no basis upon which any of the claims can be subordinated to any of the others. Where the fund is

---

[250] [2001] 1 AC 102, at 131.   [251] *Foskett v McKeown* [2001] 1 AC 102, at 132, per Lord Millett.
[252] (1880) 13 Ch D 696.

deficient, the beneficiary is not entitled to enforce a lien for his contribution; all must share rateably in the fund. The primary rule in regard to a mixed fund, therefore, is that gains and losses are borne by the contributors rateably. The beneficiary's right to elect instead to enforce a lien to obtain repayment is an exception to the primary rule, exercisable where the fund is deficient and the claim is made against the wrongdoer and those claiming through him.[253]

Thus if a trustee misappropriates £5,000 from a trust fund and mixes it with £5,000 of his own money and purchases shares for £10,000, the beneficiaries will either be able to claim half of the equitable interest in the shares or enforce a lien for £5,000 against the shares. If the shares have risen in value to £12,000 the assertion of a proportionate proprietary interest will be more advantageous. If they have fallen in value to £8,000 the enforcement of a lien will ensure that the trust fund is fully restored, and that the beneficiaries do not have to bear the consequences of the wrongdoer's poor investment.

(c) Claiming personal restitution in equity

Where trust property has been misapplied and dissipated so that there are no longer any assets remaining which can be identified as its traceable proceeds, the beneficiaries will not be able to assert a proprietary claim. However, they may be able to claim personal restitution from a stranger who received the trust property. In this context the rules of tracing operate as a process by which it can be established that a stranger had in fact received trust property. This was recognized by Millett LJ in *Boscawen v Bajwa*:

> Tracing properly so-called…is neither a claim nor a remedy but a process. Moreover, it is not confined to the case where the plaintiff seeks a proprietary remedy; it is equally necessary where he seeks a personal remedy against the knowing recipient or knowing assistant.[254]

The personal liability of a stranger who has received trust property to make restitution was considered in the previous chapter. As was seen, unlike at common law the mere fact of receipt alone is presently insufficient to generate a personal liability to make restitution in equity. The equitable liability to account as a knowing recipient of trust property requires that the recipient has such a state of knowledge that it would be 'unconscionable' for the benefit of receipt to be retained.

(d) Choice of remedy

The Supreme Court confirmed in *Test Claimants in the Franked Investment Income Group Litigation v Revenue and Customs Commissioners*[255] that where more than one remedy is available to a claimant, the claimant is 'free to choose the remedy that best suits his case.'[256] This is a general principle of English law.[257]

---

[253] [2001] 1 AC 102, at 132.   [254] [1995] 4 All ER 769, at 776.   [255] [2012] 3 All ER 909.
[256] Lord Hope, at [21].
[257] See Lord Walker, at [41] and *Deutsche Morgan Grenfell Group v IRC* [2006] UKHL 49.

Index

PREFACE

Why produce yet another A-level Maths textbook?

Now that GCSE courses have been introduced it can no longer be
assumed that all students enter an A-level course with the algebraic
skills and geometric knowledge that used to be expected. Many more
students now move in to sixth-form colleges to do A-levels and hence
come from a variety of backgrounds, including those who wish to
embark on an A-level course from intermediate level GCSE.

In much the same way as multiplication tables are the tools needed to
build a mathematics course from 11 to 16, skill in algebraic techniques
are the tools necessary for building a body of mathematical knowledge
beyond the 16+ level. This book starts with work designed to help
those students acquire a facility in using algebra. To interest those
students who already have these skills, new work is included in all
chapters. Chapter 2 for example, includes an introduction to simple
partial fractions.

All too many students regard A-level mathematics as being intrinsically
difficult – an opinion with which we strongly disagree. Part of the
reason for this myth may be that students, at an early stage in their
course, tackle problems that are too sophisticated. The exercises in
this book are designed to overcome this problem, all starting with
straightforward questions. The more sophisticated A-level type
questions are given in consolidation sections which appear at regular
intervals throughout the book. These are intended for use at a later
date to give practice in examination type questions when confidence
and sophistication have been developed. The consolidation sections
also include a summary of the work in preceeding chapters and a set
of multiple choice questions, which are very useful for self-testing even
if they do not form part of the examination to be taken.

There are many computer programs that aid in the understanding of
mathematics. In particular, a good graph drawing package is
invaluable for investigating graphical aspects of functions. In a few
places we have indicated a program that we think is relevant. This is
either *Super Graph* or a program from *132 Short Programs for the
Mathematics Classroom*.

Super Graph by David Tall is a flexible graph drawing package and is available from Abco Design Ltd., Unit 11, Stirling Industrial Centre, Stirling, Boreham Wood, Herts WD6 2BT. Tel: 081 953 9292.
132 Short Programs for the Mathematics Classroom is published in book form by Stanley Thornes (Publishers) Ltd.

We are grateful to the following Examination Boards for permission to reproduce questions from their past examination papers (part questions are indicated by the suffix p):

University of London (U of L)
Joint Matriculation Board (JMB)
University of Cambridge Local Examinations Syndicate (C)
The Associated Examining Board (C)

L. Bostock
1990   S. Chandler

CONTENTS

ix

skew lines. The scalar product. Resolved parts of a vector. The vector equation of a plane; cartesian and parametric equations of a plane. The angle between two planes and between a line and a plane.

NOTES ON USE OF THE BOOK

Notation

$=$	is equal to	$:$	is such that
$\equiv$	is identical to	$\mathbb{N}$	the natural numbers
$\approx$	is approximately equal to*	$\mathbb{Z}$	the integers
$>$	is greater than	$\mathbb{Q}$	the rational numbers
$\geqslant$	is greater than or equal to	$\mathbb{R}$	the real numbers
$<$	is less than	$\mathbb{R}^+$	the positive real numbers
$\leqslant$	is less than or equal to		excluding zero
∞	infinity; infinitely large	$\mathbb{C}$	the complex numbers
$\Rightarrow$	implies	$[a, b]$	the interval $\{x : a \leqslant x \leqslant b\}$
$\Leftarrow$	is implied by	$(a, b]$	the interval $\{x : a < x \leqslant b\}$
$\Leftrightarrow$	implies and is implied by	(a, b)	the interval $\{x : a < x < b\}$
$\in$	is a member of		

A stroke through a symbol negates it, e.g. $\neq$ means 'is not equal to'

Abbreviations

$\parallel$	is parallel to	w.r.t.	with respect to
+ve	positive	exp	exponential, e.g. $\exp x$ means e^x
$-$ve	negative		

Useful Formulae

For a cone with base radius r, height h and slant height l

$\qquad$ volume $= \frac{1}{3}\pi r^2 h \qquad$ curved surface area $= \pi r l$

For a sphere of radius r

$\qquad$ volume $= \frac{4}{3}\pi r^3 \qquad$ surface area $= 4\pi r^2$

For any pyramid with height h and base area a

$\qquad$ volume $= \frac{1}{3}ah$

*Practical problems rarely have exact answers. Where numerical answers are given they are correct to two or three decimal places depending on their context, e.g. π is 3.142 correct to 3 d.p. and although we write $\pi = 3.142$ it is understood that this is not an exact value. We reserve the symbol $\approx$ for those cases where the approximation being made is part of the method used.

Computer Program References

Marginal symbols indicate a computer program which is helpful, programs being identified in the following manner,

Program No. 47 from *132 Short Programs for the Mathematics Classroom*

Super Graph

Instructions for Answering Multiple Choice Exercises

These exercises are included in each consolidation section. The questions are set in groups, each group representing one of the variations that may arise in examination papers. The answering techniques are different for each group and are classified as follows:

TYPE I
These questions consist of a problem followed by several alternative answers, only *one* of which is correct.

Write down the letter corresponding to the correct answer.

TYPE II
In this type of question some information is given and is followed by a number of responses. *One or more* of these follow(s) directly and necessarily from the information given.

Write down the letter(s) corresponding to the correct response(s).
e.g. PQR is a triangle

 A $\angle P + \angle Q + \angle R = 180°$
 B   PQ + QR is less than PR
 C   if $\angle P$ is obtuse, $\angle Q$ and $\angle R$ must both be acute.
 D $\angle P = 90°$, $\angle Q = 45°$, $\angle R = 45°$

The correct responses are **A** and **C**.
B is definitely incorrect and **D** may or may not be true of triangle PQR, i.e. it does not follow directly and necessarily from the information given. Responses of this kind should not be regarded as correct.

TYPE III
A single statement is made. Write T if it is true and F if it is false.

ALGEBRA 1

The ability to manipulate algebraic expressions is an essential base for any mathematics course beyond GCSE. Applying the processes involved needs to be almost as instinctive as the ability to manipulate simple numbers. This and the next two chapters present the facts and provide practice necessary for the development of these skills.

MULTIPLICATION OF ALGEBRAIC EXPRESSIONS

The multiplication sign is usually omitted, so that, for example,

$$2q \text{ means } 2 \times q$$

and $\qquad x \times y$ can be simplified to xy

Remember also that if a string of numbers and letters are multiplied, the multiplication can be done in any order, for example

$$2p \times 3q = 2 \times p \times 3 \times q$$

$$= 6pq$$

Powers can be used to simplify expressions such as $x \times x$,

i.e. $\qquad x \times x = x^2$

and $\qquad x \times x^2 = x \times x \times x = x^3$

But remember that a power refers only to the number or letter it is written above, for example

$$2x^2 \text{ means that } x \text{ is squared, but 2 is not.}$$

1

Example 1a _____

Simplify   (a) $(4pq)^2 \times 5$ (b) $\dfrac{ax^2}{y} \div \dfrac{x}{ay^2}$

(a) $(4pq)^2 \times 5 = 4pq \times 4pq \times 5$

$= 80p^2q^2$

(b) $\dfrac{ax^2}{y} \div \dfrac{x}{ay^2} = \dfrac{ax^{\cancel{2}}}{\cancel{y}} \times \dfrac{ay^{\cancel{2}}}{\cancel{x}}$

$= a^2xy$

EXERCISE 1a

Simplify

1. $3 \times 5x$ 2. $x \times 2x$ 3. $(2x)^2$

4. $5p \times 2q$ 5. $4x \times 2x$ 6. $2pq \times 5pr$

7. $(3a)^2$ 8. $7a \times 9b$ 9. $8t \times 3st$

10. $2a^2 \times 4a$ 11. $25x^2 \div 15x$ 12. $12m^2 \div 6m$

13. $b^2 \times 4ab$ 14. $25x^2y \div 5x$ 15. $(7pq)^2 \times (2p)^2$

16. $\dfrac{22ab}{11b}$ 17. $\dfrac{18ax^2}{3x}$ 18. $\dfrac{36xy}{18y}$

19. $\dfrac{72ab^2}{40a^2b}$ 20. $\dfrac{2}{5} \div \dfrac{1}{x}$ 21. $\dfrac{x^2}{y} \div \dfrac{y}{x}$

ADDITION AND SUBTRACTION OF EXPRESSIONS

The *terms* in an algebraic expression are the parts separated by a plus or minus sign.

Like terms contain the same combination of letters; like terms can be added or subtracted.

For example, $2ab$ and $5ab$ are like terms and can be added,

i.e. $2ab + 5ab = 7ab$

Unlike terms contain different algebraic expressions; they cannot be added or subtracted. For example, ab and ac are unlike terms and $ab + ac$ cannot be simplified.

Example 1b

Simplify $5x - 3(4 - x)$

$$5x - 3(4 - x) = 5x - 12 + 3x$$
$$= 8x - 12$$

Note that $-3(4 - x)$ means 'take away 3 times everything inside the bracket': remember that $(-3) \times (-x) = +3x$

EXERCISE 1b

Simplify

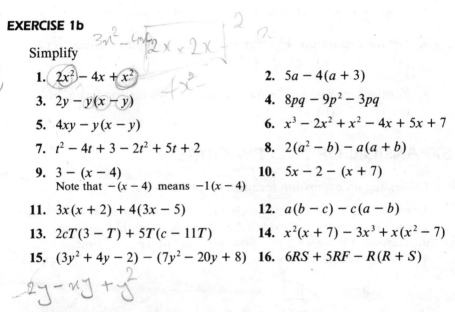

1. $2x^2 - 4x + x^2$

2. $5a - 4(a + 3)$

3. $2y - y(x - y)$

4. $8pq - 9p^2 - 3pq$

5. $4xy - y(x - y)$

6. $x^3 - 2x^2 + x^2 - 4x + 5x + 7$

7. $t^2 - 4t + 3 - 2t^2 + 5t + 2$

8. $2(a^2 - b) - a(a + b)$

9. $3 - (x - 4)$
   Note that $-(x - 4)$ means $-1(x - 4)$

10. $5x - 2 - (x + 7)$

11. $3x(x + 2) + 4(3x - 5)$

12. $a(b - c) - c(a - b)$

13. $2cT(3 - T) + 5T(c - 11T)$

14. $x^2(x + 7) - 3x^3 + x(x^2 - 7)$

15. $(3y^2 + 4y - 2) - (7y^2 - 20y + 8)$

16. $6RS + 5RF - R(R + S)$

COEFFICIENTS

We can identify a particular term in an expression by using the letter, or combination of letters, involved, for example

$2x^2$ is 'the term in x^2'

$3xy$ is 'the term in xy'

The number in front of the letters is called the *coefficient*, for example

in the term $2x^2$, 2 is the coefficient of x^2

in the term $3xy$, 3 is the coefficient of xy

If no number is written in front of a term, the coefficient is 1 or -1, depending on the sign of the term.

Consider the expression $x^3 + 5x^2y - y^3$

the coefficient of x^3 is 1

the coefficient of x^2y is 5

the coefficient of y^3 is -1

There is no term in x^2, so the coefficient of x^2 is zero.

EXERCISE 1c

1. Write down the coefficient of x in $x^2 - 7x + 4$

2. What is the coefficient of xy^2 in the expression $y^3 + 2xy^2 - 7xy$?

3. For the expression $x^2 - 5xy - y^2$ write down the coefficient of
   (a) x^2 (b) xy (c) y^2

4. For the expression $x^3 - 3x + 7$ write down the coefficient of
   (a) x^3 (b) x^2 (c) x

EXPANSION OF TWO BRACKETS

Expanding an expression means multiplying it out.

To expand $(2x + 4)(x - 3)$ each term in the first bracket is multiplied by each term in the second bracket. To make sure that nothing is missed out, it is sensible to follow the same order every time.
The order used in this book is:

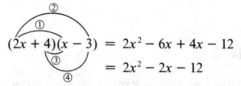

$$(2x + 4)(x - 3) = 2x^2 - 6x + 4x - 12$$
$$= 2x^2 - 2x - 12$$

Use the next exercise to practice expanding and to develop the confidence to go straight to the simplified form.

EXERCISE 1d

Expand and simplify

1. $(x + 2)(x + 4)$ 2. $(x + 5)(x + 3)$

3. $(a + 6)(a + 7)$ 4. $(t + 8)(t + 7)$

5. $(s + 6)(s + 11)$ 6. $(2x + 1)(x + 5)$

7. $(5y + 3)(y + 5)$ 8. $(2a + 3)(3a + 4)$

9. $(7t + 6)(5t + 8)$ 10. $(11s + 3)(9s + 2)$

11. $(x - 3)(x - 2)$ 12. $(y - 4)(y - 1)$

13. $(a - 3)(a - 8)$ 14. $(b - 8)(b - 9)$

15. $(p - 3)(p - 12)$ 16. $(2y - 3)(y - 5)$

17. $(x - 4)(3x - 1)$ 18. $(2r - 7)(3r - 2)$

19. $(4x - 3)(5x - 1)$ 20. $(2a - b)(3a - 2b)$

21. $(x - 3)(x + 2)$ 22. $(a - 7)(a + 8)$

23. $(y + 9)(y - 7)$ 24. $(s - 5)(s + 6)$

25. $(q - 5)(q + 13)$ 26. $(2t - 5)(t + 4)$

27. $(x + 3)(4x - 1)$ 28. $(2q + 3)(3q - 5)$

29. $(x + y)(x - 2y)$ 30. $(s + 2t)(2s - 3t)$

Difference of Two Squares

Consider the expansion of $(x - 4)(x + 4)$,

$$(x - 4)(x + 4) = x^2 - 4x + 4x - 16$$
$$= x^2 - 16$$

EXERCISE 1e

Expand and simplify

1. $(x - 2)(x + 2)$ 2. $(5 - x)(5 + x)$

3. $(x + 3)(x - 3)$ 4. $(2x - 1)(2x + 1)$

5. $(x + 8)(x - 8)$ 6. $(x - a)(x + a)$

From Questions 1 to 6 it is clear that an expansion of the form $(ax + b)(ax - b)$ can be written down directly,

i.e. $(ax + b)(ax - b) = a^2x^2 - b^2$

Use this result to expand the following brackets.

7. $(x - 1)(x + 1)$ 8. $(3b + 4)(3b - 4)$

9. $(2y - 3)(2y + 3)$ 10. $(ab + 6)(ab - 6)$

11. $(5x + 1)(5x - 1)$ 12. $(xy + 4)(xy - 4)$

Squares

$(2x + 3)^2$ means $(2x + 3)(2x + 3)$

$\therefore$ $(2x + 3)^2 = (2x + 3)(2x + 3)$

$$= (2x)^2 + (2)(2x)(3) + (3)^2$$

$$= 4x^2 + 12x + 9$$

In general, $(ax + b)^2 = a^2x^2 + (2)(ax)(b) + b^2$

$$= a^2x^2 + 2abx + b^2$$

and $(ax - b)^2 = a^2x^2 - 2abx + b^2$

EXERCISE 1f

Use the results above to expand

1. $(x + 4)^2$	**2.** $(x + 2)^2$	**3.** $(2x + 1)^2$
4. $(3x + 5)^2$	**5.** $(2x + 7)^2$	**6.** $(x - 1)^2$
7. $(x - 3)^2$	**8.** $(2x - 1)^2$	**9.** $(4x - 3)^2$
10. $(5x - 2)^2$	**11.** $(3t - 7)^2$	**12.** $(x + y)^2$
13. $(2p + 9)^2$	**14.** $(3q - 11)^2$	**15.** $(2x - 5y)^2$

Important Expansions

The results from the last two sections should be memorised. They are summarised here.

$$(ax + b)^2 = a^2x^2 + 2abx + b^2$$
$$(ax - b)^2 = a^2x^2 - 2abx + b^2$$
$$(ax + b)(ax - b) = a^2x^2 - b^2$$

The next exercise contains a variety of expansions including some of the forms given above.

Example 1g

Expand $(4p + 5)(3 - 2p)$

$$(4p + 5)(3 - 2p) = (5 + 4p)(3 - 2p)$$
$$= 15 + 2p - 8p^2$$

EXERCISE 1g

Expand

1. $(2x - 3)(4 - x)$ 2. $(x - 7)(x + 7)$

3. $(6 - x)(1 - 4x)$ 4. $(7p + 2)(2p - 1)$

5. $(3p - 1)^2$ 6. $(5t + 2)(3t - 1)$

7. $(4 - p)^2$ 8. $(4t - 1)(3 - 2t)$

9. $(x + 2y)^2$ 10. $(4x - 3)(4x + 3)$

11. $(3x + 7)^2$ 12. $(R + 3)(5 - 2R)$

13. $(a - 3b)^2$ 14. $(2x - 5)^2$

15. $(7a + 2b)(7a - 2b)$ 16. $(3a + 5b)^2$

17. Write down the coefficients of x^2 and x in the expansion of
    (a) $(2x - 4)(3x - 5)$ (b) $(5x + 2)(3x + 5)$
    (c) $(2x - 3)(7x - 5)$ (d) $(9x + 1)^2$

FACTORISING QUADRATIC EXPRESSIONS

In the last four exercises, each bracket contained a *linear expression*, i.e. an expression that contained an x term and a number term.

An expression of the form $ax + b$, where a and b are numbers, is called a linear expression in x

When two linear expressions in x are multiplied, the result usually contains three terms: a term in x^2, a term in x and a number.

Expressions of this form, i.e. $ax^2 + bx + c$ where a, b and c are numbers and $a \neq 0$, are called *quadratic expressions in x*

Since the product of two linear brackets is quadratic, we might expect to be able to reverse this process. For instance, given a quadratic such as $x^2 - 5x + 6$, we could try to find two linear expressions in x whose product is $x^2 - 5x + 6$. To be able to do this we need to appreciate the relationship between what is inside the brackets and the resulting quadratic.

Consider the examples

$$(2x + 1)(x + 5) = 2x^2 + 11x + 5 \qquad [1]$$

$$(3x - 2)(x - 4) = 3x^2 - 14x + 8 \qquad [2]$$

$$(x - 5)(4x + 2) = 4x^2 - 18x - 10 \qquad [3]$$

The first thing to notice about the quadratic in each example is that

the coefficient of x^2 is the product of the coefficients of x in the two brackets,

the number is the product of the numbers in the two brackets,

the coefficient of x is the sum of the coefficients formed by multiplying the x term in one bracket by the number term in the other bracket.

The next thing to notice is the relationship between the signs.

Positive signs throughout the quadratic come from positive signs in both brackets, as in [1].

A positive number term and a negative coefficient of x in the quadratic come from a negative sign in each bracket, as in [2].

A negative number term in the quadratic comes from a negative sign in one bracket and a positive sign in the other, as in [3].

Examples 1h _____

1. Factorise $x^2 - 5x + 6$

The x term in each bracket is x as x^2 can only be $x \times x$
The sign in each bracket is $-$, so $x^2 - 5x + 6 = (x - \;)(x - \;)$
The numbers in the brackets could be   6 and 1   or   2 and 3
Checking the middle term tells us that the numbers must be 2 and 3

$$x^2 - 5x + 6 = (x - 2)(x - 3)$$

Mentally expanding the brackets checks that they are correct.

_____

2. Factorise $x^2 - 3x - 10$

The x term in each bracket is x $\Rightarrow$ $x^2 - 3x - 10 = (x - \;)(x + \;)$
The numbers could be   10 and 1   or   5 and 2
Checking the middle term shows that they are 5 and 2

$$x^2 - 3x - 10 = (x - 5)(x + 2)$$

Mentally expanding the brackets confirms that they are correct.

EXERCISE 1h

Factorise

1. $x^2 + 8x + 15$	**2.** $x^2 + 11x + 28$	**3.** $x^2 + 7x + 6$
4. $x^2 + 7x + 12$	**5.** $x^2 - 10x + 9$	**6.** $x^2 - 6x + 9$
7. $x^2 + 8x + 12$	**8.** $x^2 - 9x + 8$	**9.** $x^2 + 5x - 14$
10. $x^2 + x - 12$	**11.** $x^2 - 4x - 5$	**12.** $x^2 - 10x - 24$
13. $x^2 + 9x + 14$	**14.** $x^2 - 2x + 1$	**15.** $x^2 - 9$
16. $x^2 + 5x - 24$	**17.** $x^2 + 4x + 4$	**18.** $x^2 - 1$
19. $x^2 - 3x - 18$	**20.** $x^2 + 10x + 25$	**21.** $x^2 - 16$
22. $4 + 5x + x^2$	**23.** $2x^2 - 3x + 1$	**24.** $3x^2 + 4x + 1$
25. $9x^2 - 6x + 1$	**26.** $6x^2 - x - 1$	**27.** $9 + 6x + x^2$
28. $4x^2 - 9$	**29.** $x^2 + 2ax + a^2$	**30.** $x^2y^2 - 2xy + 1$

Harder Factorising

When the number of possible combinations of terms for the brackets increases, common sense considerations can help to reduce the possibilities.

For example, if the coefficient of x in the quadratic is odd, then there must be an even number and an odd number in the brackets.

Example 1i _____

Factorise $12 - x - 6x^2$

The x terms in the brackets could be $6x$ and x, or $3x$ and $2x$, one positive and the other negative.

The number terms could be   12 and 1   or   3 and 4   (not 6 and 2 because the coefficient of x in the quadratic is odd).

Now we try various combinations until we find the correct one.

$$12 - x - 6x^2 = (3 + 2x)(4 - 3x)$$

EXERCISE 1i

Factorise

1. $6x^2 + x - 12$ 2. $4x^2 - 11x + 6$ 3. $4x^2 + 3x - 1$

4. $3x^2 - 17x + 10$ 5. $4x^2 - 12x + 9$ 6. $3 - 5x - 2x^2$

7. $25x^2 - 16$ 8. $3 - 2x - x^2$ 9. $5x^2 - 61x + 12$

10. $9x^2 + 30x + 25$ 11. $3 + 2x - x^2$ 12. $12 + 7x - 12x^2$

13. $1 - x^2$ 14. $9x^2 + 12x + 4$ 15. $x^2 + 2xy + y^2$

16. $1 - 4x^2$ 17. $4x^2 - 4xy + y^2$ 18. $9 - 4x^2$

19. $36 + 12x + x^2$ 20. $40x^2 - 17x - 12$ 21. $7x^2 - 5x - 150$

22. $36 - 25x^2$ 23. $x^2 - y^2$ 24. $81x^2 - 36xy + 4y^2$

25. $49 - 84x + 36x^2$ 26. $25x^2 - 4y^2$ 27. $36x^2 + 60xy + 25y^2$

28. $4x^2 - 4xy - 3y^2$ 29. $6x^2 + 11xy + 4y^2$ 30. $49p^2q^2 - 28pq + 4$

Common Factors

Consider $4x^2 + 8x + 4$

$$4x^2 + 8x + 4 = 4(x^2 + 2x + 1)$$

The quadratic inside the bracket now has smaller coefficients and can be factorised more easily:

$$4x^2 + 8x + 4 = 4(x + 1)(x + 1)$$
$$= 4(x + 1)^2$$

Not all quadratics factorise.

Consider $3x^2 - x + 5$

The options we can try are $(3x - 5)(x - 1)$ [1]

$(3x - 1)(x - 5)$ [2]

From [1], $(3x - 5)(x - 1) = 3x^2 - 8x + 5$

From [2], $(3x - 1)(x - 5) = 3x^2 - 16x + 5$

As neither of the possible pairs of brackets expand to give $3x^2 - x + 5$, we conclude that $3x^2 - x + 5$ has no factors of the form $ax + b$ where a and b are integers.

Example 1j _____

Factorise $2x^2 - 8x + 16$

$$2x^2 - 8x + 16 = 2(x^2 - 4x + 8)$$

The possible brackets are $(x - 1)(x - 8)$ and $(x - 2)(x - 4)$
Neither pair expands to $x^2 - 4x + 8$, so there are no further factors.

_____

EXERCISE 1j

Factorise where possible

1. $x^2 + x + 1$ **2.** $2x^2 + 4x + 2$ **3.** $x^2 + 3x + 2$

4. $3x^2 + 12x - 15$ **5.** $x^2 + 4$ **6.** $x^2 - 4x - 6$

7. $x^2 + 3x + 1$ **8.** $2x^2 - 8x + 8$ **9.** $3x^2 - 3x - 6$

10. $2x^2 - 6x + 8$ **11.** $3x^2 - 6x - 24$ **12.** $x^2 - 4x - 12$

13. $x^2 + 1$ **14.** $4x^2 - 100$ **15.** $5x^2 - 25$

16. $7x^2 + x + 4$ **17.** $10x^2 - 39x - 36$ **18.** $x^2 + xy + y^2$

HARDER EXPANSIONS

Consider the product $(x - 2)(x^2 - x + 5)$

This expansion should be done in a systematic way.

First multiply each term of the quadratic by x, writing down the separate results as they are found. Then multiply each term of the quadratic by -2. Do not attempt to simplify at this stage.

$$(x - 2)(x^2 - x + 5)$$
$$= x^3 - x^2 + 5x - 2x^2 + 2x - 10$$

Now simplify

$$= x^3 - 3x^2 + 7x - 10$$

Example 1k _____

Expand $(x + 2)(2x - 1)(x + 4)$

First we expand the last two brackets.

$$
\begin{aligned}
(x + 2)(2x - 1)(x + 4) &= (x + 2)(2x^2 + 7x - 4) \\
&= 2x^3 + 7x^2 - 4x + 4x^2 + 14x - 8 \\
&= 2x^3 + 11x^2 + 10x - 8
\end{aligned}
$$

EXERCISE 1k

Expand and simplify

1. $(x - 2)(x^2 + x + 1)$

2. $(3x - 2)(x^2 - x - 1)$

3. $(2x - 1)(2x^2 - 3x + 5)$

4. $(x - 1)(x^2 - x - 1)$

5. $(2x + 3)(x^2 - 6x - 3)$

6. $(x + 1)(x + 2)(x + 3)$

7. $(x + 4)(x - 1)(x + 1)$

8. $(x - 2)(x - 3)(x + 1)$

9. $(x + 1)(2x + 1)(x + 2)$

10. $(x + 2)(x + 1)^2$

11. $(2x - 1)^2(x + 2)$

12. $(3x - 1)^3$

13. $(4x + 3)(x + 1)(x - 4)$

14. $(x - 1)(2x - 1)(2x + 1)$

15. $(2x + 1)(x + 2)(3x - 1)$

16. $(x + 1)^3$

17. $(x - 2)(x + 2)(x + 1)$

18. $(x + 3)(2x + 3)(x - 1)$

19. $(3x - 2)(2x + 5)(4x - 1)$

20. $2(x - 7)(2x + 3)(x - 5)$

21. Expand and simplify $(x - 2)^2(3x - 4)$. Write down the coefficients of x^2 and x.

22. Find the coefficients of x^3 and x^2 in the expansion of $(x - 4)(2x + 3)(3x - 1)$

23. Expand and simplify $(x + y)^3$

24. Expand and simplify $(x + y)^4$

PASCAL'S TRIANGLE

58

It is sometimes necessary to expand expressions such as $(x + y)^4$ but the multiplication is tedious when the power is three or more.
We now describe a far quicker way of obtaining such expansions.

Consider the following expansions,

$$(x + y)^1 = x + y$$
$$(x + y)^2 = x^2 + 2xy + y^2$$
$$(x + y)^3 = x^3 + 3x^2y + 3xy^2 + y^3$$
$$(x + y)^4 = x^4 + 4x^3y + 6x^2y^2 + 4xy^3 + y^4$$

The first thing to notice is that the powers of x and y in the terms of each expansion form a pattern. Looking at the expansion of $(x + y)^4$ we see that the first term is x^4 and then the power of x decreases by 1 in each succeeding term while the power of y increases by 1. For all the terms, the sum of the powers of x and y is 4 and the expansion ends with y^4. There is a similar pattern in the other expansions.

Now consider just the coefficients of the terms. Writing these as a triangular array gives

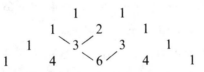

This array is called *Pascal's Triangle* and clearly it has a pattern.
Each row starts and ends with 1 and each other number is the sum of the two numbers in the row above it, as shown. When the pattern is known, Pascal's triangle can be written down to as many rows as needed. Using Pascal's triangle to expand $(x + y)^6$, for example, we go as far as row 6:

```
            1       1
        1       2       1
    1       3       3       1
  1     4       6       4     1
1     5      10      10     5     1
1    6     15     20     15    6     1
```

We then use our knowledge of the pattern of the powers, together with row 6 of the array, to fill in the coefficients,

i.e. $(x + y)^6 = x^6 + 6x^5y + 15x^4y^2 + 20x^3y^3 + 15x^2y^4 + 6xy^5 + y^6$

The following worked examples show how expansions of other brackets can be found.

Examples 1l _____

1. Expand $(x + 5)^3$

From Pascal's triangle $(x + y)^3 = x^3 + 3x^2y + 3xy^2 + y^3$

Replacing y by 5 gives $(x + 5)^3 = x^3 + 3x^2(5) + 3x(5)^2 + (5)^3$

$$= x^3 + 15x^2 + 75x + 125$$

2. Expand $(2x - 3)^4$

From Pascal's triangle, $(x + y)^4 = x^4 + 4x^3y + 6x^2y^2 + 4xy^3 + y^4$

Replacing x by $2x$ and y by -3 gives

$$(2x - 3)^4 = (2x)^4 + 4(2x)^3(-3) + 6(2x)^2(-3)^2 + 4(2x)(-3)^3 + (-3)^4$$
$$= 16x^4 - 96x^3 + 216x^2 - 216x + 81$$

EXERCISE 1l

Expand

1. $(x + 3)^3$	**2.** $(x - 2)^4$	**3.** $(x + 1)^4$
4. $(2x + 1)^3$	**5.** $(x - 3)^5$	**6.** $(p - q)^4$
7. $(2x + 3)^3$	**8.** $(x - 4)^5$	**9.** $(3x - 1)^4$
10. $(1 + 5a)^4$	**11.** $(2a - b)^6$	**12.** $(2x - 5)^3$

MIXED EXERCISE 1

1. Find the coefficient of x in the expansion of $(3x - 7)(5x + 4)$

2. Expand $5(3x - 2)(3 - 7x)$

3. Write down the coefficient of y^2 in the expansion of $(2y + 9)^3$

4. Factorise $3x^2 - 9x + 6$

5. Write down the coefficient of x^3 in the expansion of $(x - 5)^5$

6. Factorise $4x^2 - 36$

7. Expand $x(2x - 1)^2$

8. Find the factors of $25 + x^2 - 10x$

9. Find the coefficient of x in the expansion of $(x - 4)(3 - x)$

CHAPTER 2

FRACTIONS

SIMPLIFICATION OF FRACTIONS

The value of a fraction is unaltered if *numerator* and *denominator* are multiplied or divided by the same number,

e.g. $$\frac{3}{6} = \frac{1}{2} = \frac{2}{4} = \frac{7}{14} = \ldots$$

and $$\frac{ax}{ay} = \frac{x}{y} = \frac{3x}{3y} = \frac{x(a+b)}{y(a+b)} = \ldots$$

A fraction can be simplified by multiplying or dividing *top* and *bottom* by a factor which is common to both.

When simplifying fractions, it is sensible first to get rid of any fractions in the numerator and/or denominator. Then factorise the numerator and denominator and look for any common factors.

Examples 2a

1. Simplify $\dfrac{2a^2 - 2ab}{6ab - 6b^2}$

$$\frac{2a^2 - 2ab}{6ab - 6b^2} = \frac{\cancel{2}a(a - b)}{\cancel{6}b(a - b)}_{3}$$

$$= \frac{a}{3b}$$

16

2. Simplify $\dfrac{\frac{1}{2}x^2 - 2}{\frac{1}{4}y^2 + 3}$

$$\frac{\frac{1}{2}x^2 - 2}{\frac{1}{4}y^2 + 3} = \frac{2x^2 - 8}{y^2 + 12} \qquad \text{Multiplying top and bottom by 4}$$

$$= \frac{2(x^2 - 4)}{y^2 + 12}$$

$$= \frac{2(x - 2)(x + 2)}{y^2 + 12}$$

EXERCISE 2a

Simplify where possible.

1. $\dfrac{x - 2}{4x - 8}$

2. $\dfrac{2x + 4}{3x - 6}$

3. $\dfrac{2a + 8}{3a + 12}$

4. $\dfrac{3p - 3q}{5p - 5q}$

5. $\dfrac{x^2 + xy}{xy + y^2}$

6. $\dfrac{x - 3p}{2x + p}$

7. $\dfrac{a - 4}{a - 2}$

8. $\dfrac{x^2y + xy^2}{y^2 + \frac{2}{5}xy}$

9. $\dfrac{\frac{1}{3}a - b}{a + \frac{1}{6}b}$

10. $\dfrac{2x(b - 4)}{6x^2(b + 4)}$

11. $\dfrac{(x - 4)(x - 3)}{x^2 - 16}$

12. $\dfrac{4y^2 + 3}{y^2 - 9}$

13. $\dfrac{\frac{1}{3}(x - 3)}{x^2 - 9}$

14. $\dfrac{x^2 - x - 6}{2x^2 - 5x - 3}$

15. $\dfrac{(x - 2)(x + 2)}{x^2 + x - 2}$

16. $\dfrac{\frac{1}{2}(a + 5)}{a^2 - 25}$

17. $\dfrac{3p + 9q}{p^2 + 6pq + 9q^2}$

18. $\dfrac{a^2 + 2a + 4}{a^2 + 7a + 10}$

19. $\dfrac{x^2 + 2x + 1}{3x^2 + 12x + 9}$

20. $\dfrac{4(x - 3)^2}{(x + 1)(x^2 - 2x - 3)}$

MULTIPLICATION AND DIVISION

Fractions are multiplied by taking the product of the numerators and the product of the denominators,

e.g.

$$\frac{x}{a} \times \frac{y}{b} = \frac{x \times y}{a \times b} = \frac{xy}{ab}$$

To divide by a fraction, we multiply by the reciprocal of that fraction, for example

$$\frac{x}{a} \div \frac{y}{b} = \frac{x}{a} \times \frac{b}{y} = \frac{xb}{ay}$$

Example 2b

Simplify $\dfrac{2\pi x^2}{7y^2} \div 4\pi x$

$$\frac{2\pi x^2}{7y^2} \div 4\pi x = \frac{\cancel{2\pi x^2}}{7y^2} \times \frac{1}{\cancel{4\pi x}_2}$$

$$= \frac{x}{14y^2}$$

EXERCISE 2b

Simplify

1. $\dfrac{4x}{y} \times \dfrac{x}{6y}$

2. $2st \times \dfrac{3t}{s^2}$

3. $\dfrac{4uv}{3} \div \dfrac{u}{2v}$

4. $\dfrac{4\pi r^2}{3} \div 2\pi r$

5. $x(2-x) \div \dfrac{2-x}{3}$

6. $\dfrac{3x^2}{2y} \Big/ \dfrac{6xy}{9}$

7. $\dfrac{\pi x^3}{3} \div 8\pi x$

8. $\dfrac{1}{a^2 + ab} \Big/ \dfrac{1}{2}$

9. $\dfrac{1}{x^2 - 1} \div \dfrac{1}{x - 1}$

10. $\left(\dfrac{1}{a}\right)^2 \times \tfrac{1}{2}a$

11. $(x + 1) \times \dfrac{1}{x^2 - 1}$

12. $\dfrac{x - 4}{x + 3} \div \dfrac{2(x - 4)}{3}$

13. $\dfrac{a^2}{3} \times \left(\dfrac{a}{3}\right)^2$

14. $\dfrac{x^2}{6} \Big/ \left(\dfrac{x}{2}\right)^2$

15. $\dfrac{2r^3}{3} \times \left(\dfrac{1}{rs}\right)^2$

16. $\dfrac{3x^2}{2y} \times \dfrac{y}{y - 2}$

17. $\dfrac{ab}{c} \div \dfrac{ac}{b}$

18. $\dfrac{x^2 + 4x + 3}{5} \times \dfrac{10}{x + 1}$

19. $\dfrac{x^2 + x - 12}{3} \Big/ (x + 4)$

20. $\dfrac{4x^2 - 9}{(x - 1)^2} \div \dfrac{2x + 3}{x(x - 1)}$

ADDITION AND SUBTRACTION OF FRACTIONS

Before fractions can be added or subtracted, they must be expressed with the same denominator, i.e. we have to find a common denominator. Then the numerators can be added or subtracted,

e.g.
$$\frac{2}{p} + \frac{3}{q} = \frac{2q}{pq} + \frac{3p}{pq} = \frac{2q + 3p}{pq}$$

Example 2c _____

Simplify $x - \dfrac{1}{x}$

$$x - \frac{1}{x} = \frac{x}{1} - \frac{1}{x} = \frac{x^2}{x} - \frac{1}{x} = \frac{x^2 - 1}{x}$$

$$= \frac{(x - 1)(x + 1)}{x}$$

EXERCISE 2c

Simplify

1. $\dfrac{1}{a} - \dfrac{1}{b}$

2. $\dfrac{1}{3x} + \dfrac{1}{5x}$

3. $\dfrac{1}{p} - \dfrac{1}{q}$

4. $\dfrac{1}{2x} + \dfrac{3}{5x}$

5. $x + \dfrac{1}{x}$

6. $\dfrac{x}{y} - \dfrac{y}{x}$

7. $2p - \dfrac{1}{p}$

8. $\dfrac{x}{3} + \dfrac{x+1}{4}$

9. $\frac{1}{2}(x-1) + \frac{1}{3}(x+1)$

10. $\dfrac{x+2}{5} - \dfrac{2x-1}{3}$

11. $\dfrac{1}{\sin A} + \dfrac{1}{\sin B}$

12. $\dfrac{1}{\cos A} + \dfrac{1}{\sin A}$

13. $3x + \dfrac{1}{4x}$

14. $x - \dfrac{2}{2x+1}$

15. $x + 1 + \dfrac{1}{x+1}$

16. $1 + \dfrac{1}{x} + \dfrac{1}{2x}$

17. $1 - x + \dfrac{1}{x}$

18. $\dfrac{1}{n} + \dfrac{1}{n^2}$

19. $\dfrac{x}{a^2} + \dfrac{x}{b^2}$

20. $1 + \dfrac{1}{a} + \dfrac{1}{a+1}$

Example 2d

Simplify $\dfrac{2}{x+2} - \dfrac{x-4}{2x^2+x-6}$

$$\dfrac{2}{x+2} - \dfrac{x-4}{2x^2+x-6} = \dfrac{2}{x+2} - \dfrac{x-4}{(x+2)(2x-3)}$$

$$= \dfrac{2(2x-3)}{(x+2)(2x-3)} - \dfrac{x-4}{(x+2)(2x-3)}$$

$$= \dfrac{2(2x-3) - (x-4)}{(x+2)(2x-3)}$$

$$= \dfrac{4x-6-x+4}{(x+2)(2x-3)}$$

$$= \dfrac{3x-2}{(x+2)(2x-3)}$$

EXERCISE 2d

Simplify

1. $\dfrac{1}{x+1} + \dfrac{1}{x-1}$

2. $\dfrac{1}{x+1} + \dfrac{1}{x-2}$

3. $\dfrac{4}{x+2} + \dfrac{3}{x+3}$

4. $\dfrac{1}{x^2-1} + \dfrac{1}{x+1}$

5. $\dfrac{2}{a^2-1} - \dfrac{3}{a-1}$

6. $\dfrac{1}{x^2+2x+1} + \dfrac{1}{x+1}$

7. $\dfrac{3}{4x^2+4x+1} - \dfrac{2}{2x+1}$

8. $\dfrac{2}{x^2+5x+4} - \dfrac{3}{x+1}$

9. $\dfrac{4}{(x+1)^2} + \dfrac{2}{x+1}$

10. $\dfrac{3}{(x+2)^2} - \dfrac{1}{x+4}$

11. $\dfrac{1}{2(x-1)} + \dfrac{2}{3(x+4)}$

12. $\dfrac{7}{5(x+2)} - \dfrac{2}{x+4}$

13. $\dfrac{4}{3(x+2)} - \dfrac{3}{2(3x-5)}$

14. $\dfrac{3}{x+1} - \dfrac{2}{x-2} + \dfrac{4}{x+3}$

15. $\dfrac{1}{x+1} - \dfrac{2}{x+2} + \dfrac{3}{x+3}$

16. $\dfrac{x+2}{(x+1)^2} - \dfrac{1}{x}$

17. $\dfrac{4t}{t^2+2t+1} + \dfrac{3}{t+1}$

18. $\dfrac{2t}{t^2+1} - \dfrac{t^2+1}{t^2-1}$

19. $\dfrac{1}{y^2-x^2} + \dfrac{3}{y+x}$

20. $1 + \dfrac{1}{n} + \dfrac{1}{n+1} + \dfrac{1}{n+2}$

PARTIAL FRACTIONS

In the last two exercises you were asked to express two separate fractions as a single fraction with a common denominator. Later on in the course it is necessary to take an expression such as

$\dfrac{x-2}{(x+3)(x-4)}$ and express it as the sum of two separate fractions.

This process is called splitting up, or decomposing, into *partial fractions*.

Consider again $\dfrac{x-2}{(x+3)(x-4)}$

This fraction is a *proper fraction* because the highest power of x in the numerator (1 in this case) is less than the highest power of x in the denominator (2 in this case when the brackets are expanded).

Therefore its separate (or partial) fractions also will be proper,

i.e. $\dfrac{x-2}{(x+3)(x-4)}$ can be expressed as $\dfrac{A}{x+3} + \dfrac{B}{x-4}$

where A and B are numbers. The worked example which follows shows how the values of A and B can be found.

Example 2e _____

Express $\dfrac{x-2}{(x+3)(x-4)}$ in partial fractions.

$$\frac{x-2}{(x+3)(x-4)} = \frac{A}{x+3} + \frac{B}{x-4}$$

Expressing the separate fractions on the RHS as a single fraction over a common denominator gives

$$\frac{x-2}{(x+3)(x-4)} = \frac{A(x-4)+B(x+3)}{(x+3)(x-4)}$$

This is not an equation because the RHS is just another way of expressing the LHS. It follows that, as the denominators are identical the numerators also are identical.

i.e. $\qquad\qquad x-2 = A(x-4)+B(x+3)$

Remembering that this is *not* an equation but two ways of writing the same expression, it follows that LHS = RHS for any value that we choose to give to x.

Choosing to substitute 4 for x (to eliminate A) gives

$$2 = A(0) + B(7)$$

$\Rightarrow\qquad\qquad\qquad B = \dfrac{2}{7}$

Choosing to substitute -3 for x (to eliminate B) gives

$$-5 = A(-7) + B(0)$$

$\Rightarrow\qquad\qquad\qquad A = \dfrac{5}{7}$

Therefore $\qquad \dfrac{x-2}{(x+3)(x-4)} = \dfrac{5/7}{x+3} + \dfrac{2/7}{x-4}$

$$= \dfrac{5}{7(x+3)} + \dfrac{2}{7(x-4)}$$

EXERCISE 2e

Express the following fractions in partial fractions.

1. $\dfrac{x-2}{(x+1)(x-1)}$

2. $\dfrac{x+4}{(x+3)(x-5)}$

3. $\dfrac{2x-1}{(x-1)(x-7)}$

4. $\dfrac{3x+1}{(2x-1)(x-1)}$

5. $\dfrac{4}{(x+3)(x-2)}$

6. $\dfrac{2x-3}{(x-2)(4x-3)}$

7. $\dfrac{7x}{(2x-1)(x+4)}$

8. $\dfrac{3-x}{(x+1)(2x-1)}$

9. $\dfrac{2}{x(x-2)}$

10. $\dfrac{3}{x(2x+1)}$

11. $\dfrac{2x-1}{x^2-3x+2}$

12. $\dfrac{4}{x^2-7x-8}$

13. $\dfrac{3}{x^2-9}$

14. $\dfrac{4x}{4x^2-9}$

15. $\dfrac{6x+7}{3x(x+1)}$

16. $\dfrac{4x-2}{x^2+2x}$

17. $\dfrac{9}{2x^2+x}$

18. $\dfrac{3x}{2x^2-2x-4}$

19. $\dfrac{x+1}{3x^2-x-2}$

20. $\dfrac{3x+2}{2x^2-4x}$

MIXED EXERCISE 2

1. Simplify (a) $\dfrac{x^2-9}{2x-6}$ (b) $\dfrac{1}{x^2-9} \div \dfrac{1}{x+3}$

2. Simplify (a) $\left(\dfrac{2p}{r}\right)^2 \times \dfrac{ar}{p^3}$ (b) $\dfrac{2p}{r} - \dfrac{3}{p}$

3. Simplify (a) $\dfrac{2n - 4}{3} \div (n^2 - 4)$ (b) $\dfrac{1}{x + 1} + \dfrac{1}{2x - 1} + \dfrac{1}{x}$

4. Express $\dfrac{3}{x^2 - 1}$ in partial fractions.

5. Express $\dfrac{4}{(2x + 1)(x - 3)}$ in partial fractions.

6. Express $\dfrac{5}{x^2 - x}$ in partial fractions.

7. Simplify (a) $\dfrac{4x^2 - 25}{4x^2 + 20x + 25}$ (b) $\dfrac{2t}{t^2 + 1} \div \dfrac{t^2 - 1}{t^2 + 1}$

8. Simplify (a) $\left(\dfrac{x - 1}{x + 1}\right)^2 \times (x^2 - 1)$ (b) $\dfrac{1}{a} + \dfrac{1}{b} + \dfrac{1}{c}$

9. Express $\dfrac{3x - 2}{(x + 1)(4x - 3)}$ in partial fractions.

10. Express $\dfrac{2t}{t^2 - 1}$ in partial fractions.

CHAPTER 3

SURDS AND INDICES

SQUARE ROOTS

When we express a number as the product of two equal factors, that factor is called the *square root* of the number, for example

$$4 = 2 \times 2 \implies 2 \text{ is the square root of } 4$$

This is written $\qquad 2 = \sqrt{4}$

Now -2 is also a square root of 4, as $4 = -2 \times -2$ but we do *not* write $\sqrt{4} = -2$

The symbol $\sqrt{}$ is used *only for the positive square root.*

So, although $x^2 = 4 \implies x = \pm 2$, the only value of $\sqrt{4}$ is 2

The negative square root of 4 would be written as $-\sqrt{4}$ and, when both square roots are wanted, we write $\pm\sqrt{4}$

CUBE ROOTS

When a number can be expressed as the product of three equal factors, that factor is called the *cube root* of the number,

e.g. $\qquad 27 = 3 \times 3 \times 3 \qquad$ so 3 is the cube root of 27

This is written $\sqrt[3]{27} = 3$

OTHER ROOTS

The notation used for square and cube roots can be extended to represent fourth roots, fifth roots, etc,

e.g. $\qquad 16 = 2 \times 2 \times 2 \times 2 \implies \sqrt[4]{16} = 2$

and $\qquad 243 = 3 \times 3 \times 3 \times 3 \times 3 \implies \sqrt[5]{243} = 3$

In general, if a number, n, can be expressed as the product of p equal factors then each factor is called the pth root of n and is written $\sqrt[p]{n}$

RATIONAL NUMBERS

A number which is either an integer, or a fraction whose numerator and denominator are both integers, is called a *rational number*.

The square roots of certain numbers are rational,

e.g. $\qquad\qquad \sqrt{9} = 3, \ \sqrt{25} = 5, \ \sqrt{\frac{4}{49}} = \frac{2}{7}$

This is not true of all square roots however, e.g. $\sqrt{2}, \ \sqrt{5}, \ \sqrt{11}$ are not rational numbers. Such square roots can be given to as many decimal places as are required, for example

$$\sqrt{3} = 1.73 \qquad \text{correct to 2 d.p.}$$

$$\sqrt{3} = 1.732\,05 \quad \text{correct to 5 d.p.}$$

but they can never be expressed exactly as a decimal. They are called *irrational numbers*.

The only way to give an exact answer when such irrational numbers are involved is to leave them in the form $\sqrt{2}, \ \sqrt{7}$ etc; in this form they are called *surds*. At this level of mathematics *answers should always be given exactly unless an approximate answer is asked for*, e.g. give your answer correct to 3 s.f.

Surds arise in many topics and the reader will find it necessary to be able to manipulate them.

Simplifying Surds

Consider $\sqrt{18}$

One of the factors of 18 is 9, and 9 has an exact square root,

i.e. $\qquad\qquad \sqrt{18} = \sqrt{(9 \times 2)} = \sqrt{9} \times \sqrt{2}$

But $\sqrt{9} = 3$, therefore $\sqrt{18} = 3\sqrt{2}$

$3\sqrt{2}$ is the simplest possible surd form for $\sqrt{18}$

Similarly $\sqrt{\dfrac{2}{25}} = \dfrac{\sqrt{2}}{\sqrt{25}} = \dfrac{\sqrt{2}}{5}$

EXERCISE 3a

Express in terms of the simplest possible surd.

1. $\sqrt{12}$	**2.** $\sqrt{32}$	**3.** $\sqrt{27}$	**4.** $\sqrt{50}$
5. $\sqrt{200}$	**6.** $\sqrt{72}$	**7.** $\sqrt{162}$	**8.** $\sqrt{288}$
9. $\sqrt{75}$	**10.** $\sqrt{48}$	**11.** $\sqrt{500}$	**12.** $\sqrt{20}$

Multiplying Surds

Consider $(4 - \sqrt{5})(3 + \sqrt{2})$

The multiplication is carried out in the same way and order as when multiplying two linear brackets,

i.e.
$$(4 - \sqrt{5})(3 + \sqrt{2}) = (4)(3) + (4)(\sqrt{2}) - (3)(\sqrt{5}) - (\sqrt{5})(\sqrt{2})$$
$$= 12 + 4\sqrt{2} - 3\sqrt{5} - \sqrt{5}\sqrt{2}$$
$$= 12 + 4\sqrt{2} - 3\sqrt{5} - \sqrt{10}$$

In this example there are no like terms to collect but if the same surd occurs in each bracket the expansion can be simplified.

Examples 3b

1. Expand and simplify $(2 + 2\sqrt{7})(5 - \sqrt{7})$

$$(2 + 2\sqrt{7})(5 - \sqrt{7}) = (2)(5) - (2)(\sqrt{7}) + (5)(2\sqrt{7}) - (2\sqrt{7})(\sqrt{7})$$
$$= 10 - 2\sqrt{7} + 10\sqrt{7} - 14$$
$$= 8\sqrt{7} - 4$$

2. Expand and simplify $(4 - \sqrt{3})(4 + \sqrt{3})$

$$(4 - \sqrt{3})(4 + \sqrt{3}) = 16 + 4\sqrt{3} - 4\sqrt{3} - (\sqrt{3})(\sqrt{3})$$
$$= 16 - 3$$
$$= 13$$

Example 3b number 2 is a special case because the result is a single rational number. The reader will notice that the two given brackets were of the form $(x - a)(x + a)$, i.e. the factors of $a^2 - x^2$.

The product of any two brackets of the type $(p - \sqrt{q})(p + \sqrt{q})$ is, similarly, $p^2 - (\sqrt{q})^2 = p^2 - q$, which is always rational.

This property has an important application in a later section of this chapter.

EXERCISE 3b

Expand and simplify where this is possible.

1. $\sqrt{3}(2 - \sqrt{3})$ 2. $\sqrt{2}(5 + 4\sqrt{2})$
3. $\sqrt{5}(2 + \sqrt{75})$ 4. $\sqrt{2}(\sqrt{32} - \sqrt{8})$
5. $(\sqrt{3} + 1)(\sqrt{2} - 1)$ 6. $(\sqrt{3} + 2)(\sqrt{3} + 5)$
7. $(\sqrt{5} - 1)(\sqrt{5} + 1)$ 8. $(2\sqrt{2} - 1)(\sqrt{2} - 1)$
9. $(\sqrt{5} - 3)(2\sqrt{5} - 4)$ 10. $(4 + \sqrt{7})(4 - \sqrt{7})$
11. $(\sqrt{6} - 2)^2$ 12. $(2 + 3\sqrt{3})^2$

Multiply by a bracket which will make the product rational.

13. $(4 - \sqrt{5})$ 14. $(\sqrt{11} + 3)$
15. $(2\sqrt{3} - 4)$ 16. $(\sqrt{6} - \sqrt{5})$
17. $(3 - 2\sqrt{3})$ 18. $(2\sqrt{5} - \sqrt{2})$

Rationalising a Denominator

A fraction whose denominator contains a surd is more awkward to deal with than one where a surd occurs only in the numerator.

There is a technique for transferring the surd expression from the denominator to the numerator; it is called *rationalising the denominator* (i.e. making the denominator into a rational number).

Examples 3c _____

1. Rationalise the denominator of $\dfrac{2}{\sqrt{3}}$

The square root in the denominator can be removed if we multiply it by another $\sqrt{3}$. If this is done we must, of course, multiply the numerator also by $\sqrt{3}$, otherwise the value of the fraction is changed.

$$\frac{2}{\sqrt{3}} = \frac{2\sqrt{3}}{(\sqrt{3})(\sqrt{3})} = \frac{2\sqrt{3}}{3}$$

2. Rationalise the denominator and simplify $\dfrac{3\sqrt{2}}{5 - \sqrt{2}}$

We saw in Example 3b number 2, that a product of the type $(a - \sqrt{b})(a + \sqrt{b})$ is wholly rational so in this question we multiply numerator and denominator by $5 + \sqrt{2}$

$$\frac{3\sqrt{2}}{5 - \sqrt{2}} = \frac{3\sqrt{2}(5 + \sqrt{2})}{(5 - \sqrt{2})(5 + \sqrt{2})}$$

$$= \frac{15\sqrt{2} + 3(\sqrt{2})(\sqrt{2})}{25 - (\sqrt{2})(\sqrt{2})}$$

$$= \frac{15\sqrt{2} + 6}{23}$$

EXERCISE 3c

Rationalise the denominator, simplifying where possible.

1. $\dfrac{3}{\sqrt{2}}$ **2.** $\dfrac{1}{\sqrt{7}}$ **3.** $\dfrac{2}{\sqrt{11}}$

4. $\dfrac{3\sqrt{2}}{\sqrt{5}}$ **5.** $\dfrac{1}{\sqrt{27}}$ **6.** $\dfrac{\sqrt{5}}{\sqrt{10}}$

7. $\dfrac{1}{\sqrt{2} - 1}$ **8.** $\dfrac{3\sqrt{2}}{5 + \sqrt{2}}$ **9.** $\dfrac{2}{2\sqrt{3} - 3}$

10. $\dfrac{5}{2 - \sqrt{5}}$ **11.** $\dfrac{1}{\sqrt{7} - \sqrt{3}}$ **12.** $\dfrac{4\sqrt{3}}{2\sqrt{3} - 3}$

13. $\dfrac{3 - \sqrt{5}}{\sqrt{5} + 1}$ **14.** $\dfrac{2\sqrt{3} - 1}{4 - \sqrt{3}}$ **15.** $\dfrac{\sqrt{5} - 1}{\sqrt{5} - 2}$

16. $\dfrac{3}{\sqrt{3} - \sqrt{2}}$ **17.** $\dfrac{3\sqrt{5}}{2\sqrt{5} + 1}$ **18.** $\dfrac{\sqrt{2} + 1}{\sqrt{2} - 1}$

19. $\dfrac{2\sqrt{7}}{\sqrt{7} + 2}$ **20.** $\dfrac{\sqrt{5} - 1}{3 - \sqrt{5}}$ **21.** $\dfrac{1}{\sqrt{11} - \sqrt{7}}$

22. $\dfrac{4 - \sqrt{3}}{3 - \sqrt{3}}$ **23.** $\dfrac{1 - 3\sqrt{2}}{3\sqrt{2} + 2}$ **24.** $\dfrac{1}{3\sqrt{2} - 2\sqrt{3}}$

25. $\dfrac{\sqrt{3}}{\sqrt{2}(\sqrt{6} - \sqrt{3})}$ **26.** $\dfrac{1}{\sqrt{3}(\sqrt{21} + \sqrt{7})}$ **27.** $\dfrac{\sqrt{2}}{\sqrt{3}(\sqrt{5} - \sqrt{2})}$

INDICES

Base and Index

In an expression such as 3^4, the *base* is 3 and the 4 is called the *power* or *index* (the plural is *indices*).

Working with indices involves using some properties which apply to any base, so we express these rules in terms of a general base a (i.e. a stands for any number).

Rule 1

Because a^3 means $a \times a \times a$ and a^2 means $a \times a$ it follows that

$$a^3 \times a^2 = (a \times a \times a) \times (a \times a) = a^5$$

i.e. $a^3 \times a^2 = a^{3+2}$

Similar examples with different powers all indicate the general rule that

$$a^p \times a^q = a^{p+q}$$

Rule 2

Now dealing with division we have

$$a^7 \div a^4 = \frac{\cancel{a} \times \cancel{a} \times \cancel{a} \times \cancel{a} \times a \times a \times a}{\cancel{a} \times \cancel{a} \times \cancel{a} \times \cancel{a}} = a^3$$

i.e. $a^7 \div a^4 = a^{7-4}$

Again this is just one example of the general rule

$$a^p \div a^q = a^{p-q}$$

When this rule is applied to certain fractions some interesting cases arise.

Consider $a^3 \div a^5$

$$\frac{a^3}{a^5} = \frac{\cancel{a} \times \cancel{a} \times \cancel{a}}{\cancel{a} \times \cancel{a} \times \cancel{a} \times a \times a} = \frac{1}{a^2}$$

But from Rule 2 we have

$$a^3 \div a^5 = a^{3-5} = a^{-2}$$

Therefore a^{-2} means $\dfrac{1}{a^2}$

In general
$$a^{-p} = \frac{1}{a^p}$$

i.e.
a^{-p} means 'the reciprocal of a^p'

Now consider $a^4 \div a^4$

$$\frac{a^4}{a^4} = \frac{\cancel{a} \times \cancel{a} \times \cancel{a} \times \cancel{a}}{\cancel{a} \times \cancel{a} \times \cancel{a} \times \cancel{a}} = 1$$

From Rule 2,
$$\frac{a^4}{a^4} = a^{4-4} = a^0$$

Therefore
$$a^0 = 1$$

i.e.
any base to the power zero is equal to 1

Rule 3

$$(a^2)^3 = (a \times a)^3$$
$$= (a \times a) \times (a \times a) \times (a \times a)$$
$$= a^6$$

i.e. $(a^2)^3 = a^{2 \times 3}$

In general
$$(a^p)^q = a^{pq}$$

Rule 4
This rule explains the meaning of a fractional index.

From the first rule we have
$$a^{1/2} \times a^{1/2} = a^{1/2 + 1/2} = a^1 = a$$

i.e.
$$a = a^{1/2} \times a^{1/2}$$

But
$$a = \sqrt{a} \times \sqrt{a}$$

Therefore $a^{1/2}$ means $\sqrt{a}$, i.e. the positive square root of a

Similarly $a^{1/3} \times a^{1/3} \times a^{1/3} = a^{1/3 + 1/3 + 1/3} = a^1 = a$

But $\sqrt[3]{a} \times \sqrt[3]{a} \times \sqrt[3]{a} = a$

Therefore $a^{1/3}$ means $\sqrt[3]{a}$, i.e. the cube root of a

In general
$$a^{1/p} = \sqrt[p]{a}, \text{ i.e. the } p\text{th root of } a$$

For a more general fractional index, $\frac{p}{q}$, the third rule shows that

$$a^{p/q} = (a^p)^{1/q} \quad \text{or} \quad (a^{1/q})^p$$

For example

$$a^{3/4} = (a^3)^{1/4} \quad \text{or} \quad (a^{1/4})^3$$
$$= \sqrt[4]{a^3} \quad \text{or} \quad (\sqrt[4]{a})^3$$

i.e. $a^{3/4}$ represents either 'the fourth root of a^3'
$\qquad\qquad\qquad\qquad$ or 'the cube of the fourth root of a'

All the general rules can be applied to simplify a wide range of expressions containing indices *provided that the terms all have the same base.*

Examples 3d _____

1. Simplify (a) $\dfrac{2^3 \times 2^7}{4^3}$ (b) $(x^2)^7 \times x^{-3}$ (c) $\sqrt[3]{(a^4 b^5)} \times b^{1/3}/a$

(a) First we express all the terms to a base 2

$$\frac{2^3 \times 2^7}{4^3} = \frac{2^3 \times 2^7}{(2^2)^3}$$
$$= \frac{2^{3+7}}{2^{2 \times 3}}$$
$$= \frac{2^{10}}{2^6} = 2^4$$

(b) $\qquad\qquad (x^2)^7 \times x^{-3} = x^{2 \times 7} \times \dfrac{1}{x^3}$

$$= x^{14} \times \frac{1}{x^3} = x^{11}$$

(c) $\qquad \sqrt[3]{(a^4 b^5)} \times b^{1/3}/a = (a^{4/3})(b^{5/3})(b^{1/3})(a^{-1})$

$$= (a^{4/3 - 1})(b^{5/3 + 1/3})$$
$$= a^{1/3} b^2$$

2. Evaluate (a) $(64)^{-1/3}$ (b) $\left(\dfrac{25}{9}\right)^{-3/2}$

(a) $\qquad\qquad (64)^{-1/3} = \dfrac{1}{(64)^{1/3}} = \dfrac{1}{\sqrt[3]{64}} = \dfrac{1}{4}$

(b) $\left(\dfrac{25}{9}\right)^{-3/2} = \left(\dfrac{9}{25}\right)^{3/2} = \left(\sqrt{\dfrac{9}{25}}\right)^3 = \left(\dfrac{3}{5}\right)^3 = \dfrac{27}{125}$

Note that $\left(\dfrac{9}{25}\right)^{3/2}$ could have been expressed as $\sqrt{\left(\dfrac{9}{25}\right)^3}$ but this form involves *much* bigger numbers.

EXERCISE 3d

Simplify

1. $\dfrac{2^4}{2^2 \times 4^3}$

2. $4^{1/2} \times 2^{-3}$

3. $(3^3)^{1/2} \times 9^{1/4}$

4. $\dfrac{x^{1/3} \times x^{4/3}}{x^{-1/3}}$

5. $\dfrac{p^{1/2} \times p^{-3/4}}{p^{-1/4}}$

6. $(\sqrt{t})^3 \times (\sqrt{t^5})$

7. $(y^2)^{3/2} \times y^{-3}$

8. $(16)^{5/4} \div 8^{4/3}$

9. $\dfrac{y^{1/2}}{y^{-3/4}} \times \sqrt{(y^{1/2})}$

10. $x^2 \times x^{5/2} \div x^{-1/2}$

11. $\dfrac{y^{1/6} \times y^{-2/3}}{y^{1/4}}$

12. $(p^{1/3})^2 \times (p^2)^{1/3} \div \sqrt[3]{p}$

Evaluate

13. $\left(\dfrac{1}{3}\right)^{-1}$

14. $\left(\dfrac{1}{4}\right)^{5/2}$

15. $(8)^{-1/3}$

16. $\dfrac{1}{(16)^{-1/4}}$

17. $\left(\dfrac{1}{9}\right)^{-3/2}$

18. $\left(\dfrac{27}{8}\right)^{2/3}$

19. $\left(\dfrac{100}{9}\right)^{0}$

20. $\dfrac{1}{4^{-2}}$

21. $(0.64)^{-1/2}$

22. $\left(-\dfrac{1}{5}\right)^{-1}$

23. $(121)^{3/2}$

24. $\left(\dfrac{125}{27}\right)^{-1/3}$

25. $18^{1/2} \times 2^{1/2}$ **26.** $3^{-3} \times 2^0 \times 4^2$

27. $\dfrac{8^{1/2} \times 32^{1/2}}{(16)^{1/4}}$ **28.** $5^{1/3} \times 25^0 \times 25^{1/3}$

29. $27^{1/4} \times 3^{1/4} \times (\sqrt{3})^{-2}$ **30.** $\dfrac{9^{1/3} \times 27^{-1/2}}{3^{-1/6} \times 3^{-2/3}}$

LOGARITHMS

Consider the statement $10^2 = 100$

If this is expressed in words we have

the base 10   raised to the power 2   gives 100

Now this relationship can be rearranged to give the same information, but with a different emphasis, i.e.

the power to which the base 10 must be raised   to give 100   is 2

> In this form the power is called a logarithm (log)

The whole relationship can then be abbreviated to read

the logarithm to the base 10   of 100   is 2

or $\log_{10} 100 = 2$

In the same way, $2^3 = 8$ $\Rightarrow$ $\log_2 8 = 3$

and $3^4 = 81$ $\Rightarrow$ $\log_3 81 = 4$

Similarly $\log_5 25 = 2$ $\Rightarrow$ $5^2 = 25$

and $\log_9 3 = \tfrac{1}{2}$ $\Rightarrow$ $9^{1/2} = 3$

Although we have so far used only 10, 2 and 3, the base of a logarithm can be any positive number, or even an unspecified number represented by a letter, for example

$$b = a^c \quad \Leftrightarrow \quad \log_a b = c$$

Note that the symbol $\Leftrightarrow$ means that each of these facts implies the other.

Example 3e

(a) Write $\log_2 64 = 6$ in index form.
(b) Write $5^3 = 125$ in logarithmic form.
(c) Complete the statement $2^{-3} = ?$ and then write it in logarithmic form.

(a) If $\log_2 64 = 6$ then the base is 2, the number is 64 and the power (i.e. the log) is 6

$$\log_2 64 = 6 \quad \Rightarrow \quad 2^6 = 64$$

(b) If $5^3 = 125$ then the base is 5, the log (i.e. the power) is 3 and the number is 125

$$5^3 = 125 \quad \Rightarrow \quad \log_5 125 = 3$$

(c) $2^{-3} = \frac{1}{8}$

The base is 2, the power (log) is -3 and the number is $\frac{1}{8}$

$$2^{-3} = \frac{1}{8} \quad \Rightarrow \quad \log_2\left(\frac{1}{8}\right) = -3$$

EXERCISE 3e

Convert each of the following facts to logarithmic form.

1. $10^3 = 1000$ 2. $2^4 = 16$ 3. $10^4 = 10\,000$
4. $3^2 = 9$ 5. $4^2 = 16$ 6. $5^2 = 25$
7. $10^{-2} = 0.01$ 8. $9^{1/2} = 3$ 9. $5^0 = 1$
10. $4^{1/2} = 2$ 11. $12^0 = 1$ 12. $8^{1/3} = 2$
13. $p = q^2$ 14. $x^y = 2$ 15. $p^q = r$

Convert each of the following facts to index form.

16. $\log_{10} 100\,000 = 5$ 17. $\log_4 64 = 3$ 18. $\log_{10} 10 = 1$
19. $\log_2 4 = 2$ 20. $\log_2 32 = 5$ 21. $\log_{10} 1000 = 3$
22. $\log_5 1 = 0$ 23. $\log_3 9 = 2$ 24. $\log_4 16 = 2$
25. $\log_3 27 = 3$ 26. $\log_{36} 6 = \frac{1}{2}$ 27. $\log_a 1 = 0$
28. $\log_x y = z$ 29. $\log_a 5 = b$ 30. $\log_p q = r$

Evaluating Logarithms

It is generally easier to solve a simple equation in index form than in log form so we often use an index equation in order to evaluate a logarithm. For example to evaluate $\log_{49} 7$ we can say

if $x = \log_{49} 7$ then $49^x = 7$ $\Rightarrow$ $x = \frac{1}{2}$

therefore $\log_{49} 7 = \frac{1}{2}$

In particular, for any base b,

if $x = \log_b 1$ then $b^x = 1$ $\Rightarrow$ $x = 0$

i.e.   the logarithm to any base of 1 is zero.

EXERCISE 3f

Evaluate

1. $\log_2 4$	**2.** $\log_{10} 1\,000\,000$	**3.** $\log_2 64$	**4.** $\log_3 81$
5. $\log_8 64$	**6.** $\log_4 64$	**7.** $\log_9 3$	**8.** $\log_{1/2} 4$
9. $\log_{10} 0.1$	**10.** $\log_{121} 11$	**11.** $\log_5 1$	**12.** $\log_2 2$
13. $\log_{64} 4$	**14.** $\log_{99} 1$	**15.** $\log_{27} 3$	**16.** $\log_a a^3$

THE LAWS OF LOGARITHMS

When working with indices earlier in this chapter we found certain rules that powers obey in the multiplication and division of numbers. Because logarithm is just another word for index or power, it is to be expected that logarithms too obey certain laws and these we are now going to investigate.

Consider $x = \log_a b$ and $y = \log_a c$

$\Rightarrow$ $a^x = b$ and $a^y = c$

Now $bc = (a^x)(a^y)$

$\Rightarrow$ $bc = a^{x+y}$

Therefore $\log_a bc = x + y$

i.e. $\log_a bc = \log_a b + \log_a c$

This is the first law of logarithms and, as a can represent *any* base, this law applies to the log of *any* product *provided that the same base is used for all the logarithms in the formula.*

Using x and y again, a law for the log of a fraction can be found.

$$\frac{b}{c} = \frac{a^x}{a^y} \quad \Rightarrow \quad \frac{b}{c} = a^{x-y}$$

Therefore $\qquad\qquad$ $\log_a (b/c) = x - y$

i.e. $\qquad\qquad$ $\log_a (b/c) = \log_a b - \log_a c$

A third law allows us to deal with an expression of the type $\log_a b^n$

Using $\qquad\qquad$ $x = \log_a b^n \quad \Rightarrow \quad a^x = b^n$

i.e. $\qquad\qquad\qquad\qquad\qquad$ $a^{x/n} = b$

Therefore $\qquad\qquad$ $x/n = \log_a b \quad \Rightarrow \quad x = n \log_a b$

i.e. $\qquad\qquad\qquad$ $\log_a b^n = n \log_a b$

So we now have the three most important laws of logarithms. Because they are true for *any* base it is unnecessary to include a base in the formula but

in each of these laws every logarithm must be to the same base

$$\log bc = \log b + \log c$$
$$\log b/c = \log b - \log c$$
$$\log b^n = n \log b$$

Examples 3g

1. Express $\log pq^2\sqrt{r}$ in terms of $\log p$, $\log q$ and $\log r$

$$\log pq^2\sqrt{r} = \log p + \log q^2 + \log \sqrt{r}$$
$$= \log p + 2 \log q + \tfrac{1}{2} \log r$$

2. Simplify $3 \log p + n \log q - 4 \log r$

$$3 \log p + n \log q - 4 \log r = \log p^3 + \log q^n - \log r^4$$
$$= \log \frac{p^3 q^n}{r^4}$$

EXERCISE 3g

Express in terms of $\log p$, $\log q$, and $\log r$

1. $\log pq$ 2. $\log pqr$ 3. $\log p/q$ 4. $\log pq/r$

5. $\log p/qr$ 6. $\log p^2q$ 7. $\log q/r^2$ 8. $\log p\sqrt{q}$

9. $\log p^2q^3/r$ 10. $\log \sqrt{(q/r)}$ 11. $\log q^n$ 12. $\log p^nq^m$

Simplify

13. $\log p + \log q$ 14. $2 \log p + \log q$

15. $\log q - \log r$ 16. $3 \log q + 4 \log p$

17. $n \log p - \log q$ 18. $\log p + 2 \log q - 3 \log r$

MIXED EXERCISE 3

1. Simplify (a) $\sqrt{84}$ (b) $\sqrt{300}$ (c) $\sqrt{45}$

2. Expand and simplify (a) $(3 + \sqrt{2})(4 - 2\sqrt{2})$ (b) $(\sqrt{5} - \sqrt{2})^2$

3. Multiply by a bracket that will make the product rational

    (a) $(7 - \sqrt{3})$ (b) $(2\sqrt{2} + 1)$ (c) $(\sqrt{7} - \sqrt{5})$

4. Rationalise the denominator and simplify where possible

    (a) $\dfrac{5}{\sqrt{7}}$ (b) $\dfrac{3}{\sqrt{13} - 2}$ (c) $\dfrac{4}{\sqrt{3} - \sqrt{2}}$ (d) $\dfrac{\sqrt{3} - 1}{\sqrt{3} + 1}$

5. Simplify (a) $\dfrac{2^3 \times 4^{-2}}{2^{-1}}$ (b) $(x^3)^{-2} \times (x^2)^3$

6. Evaluate (a) $(64)^{-1/3}$ (b) $\left(\dfrac{49}{16}\right)^{-1/2}$ (c) $\left(\dfrac{8}{27}\right)^{3/2}$

7. Simplify (a) $8^{1/6} \times 2^0 \times 2^{-1/2}$ (b) $(\sqrt{5})^{-2} \times 75^{1/2} \times 25^{-1/4}$

8. Evaluate (a) $\log_2 128$ (b) $\log_{25} 5$ (c) $\log_{12} 1$

9. Express in terms of $\log a$, $\log b$ and $\log c$

    (a) $\log a^3/(bc^2)$ (b) $\log a^n/b$ (c) $\log ab/c$

10. Simplify (a) $3 \log a - \log b$ (b) $\log 1/a + \log 1$

CHAPTER 4

QUADRATIC EQUATIONS AND SIMULTANEOUS EQUATIONS

QUADRATIC EQUATIONS

When a quadratic expression has a particular value we have a quadratic equation, for example

$$2x^2 - 5x + 1 = 0$$

Using a, b and c to stand for any numbers, any quadratic equation can be written in the general form

$$ax^2 + bx + c = 0$$

(x_2) w

Solution by Factorising

Consider the quadratic equation $x^2 - 3x + 2 = 0$

The quadratic expression on the left-hand side can be factorised,

i.e. $x^2 - 3x + 2 = (x - 2)(x - 1)$

Therefore the given equation becomes

$$(x - 2)(x - 1) = 0 \qquad\qquad [1]$$

Now if the product of two quantities is zero then one, or both, of those quantities must be zero.

Applying this fact to equation [1] gives

$$x - 2 = 0 \quad \text{or} \quad x - 1 = 0$$

i.e. $x = 2 \quad \text{or} \quad x = 1$

This is the solution of the given equation.
The values 2 and 1 are called the *roots* of that equation.

This method of solution can be used for any quadratic equation in which the quadratic expression factorises.

Example 4a

Find the roots of the equation $x^2 + 6x - 7 = 0$

$$x^2 + 6x - 7 = 0$$
$$\Rightarrow \qquad (x - 1)(x + 7) = 0$$
$$\therefore \qquad x - 1 = 0 \quad \text{or} \quad x + 7 = 0$$
$$\therefore \qquad x = 1 \quad \text{or} \quad x = -7$$

The roots of the equation are 1 and −7

EXERCISE 4a

Solve the equations.

1. $x^2 + 5x + 6 = 0$

2. $x^2 + x - 6 = 0$

3. $x^2 - x - 6 = 0$

4. $x^2 + 6x + 8 = 0$

5. $x^2 - 4x + 3 = 0$

6. $x^2 + 2x - 3 = 0$

7. $2x^2 + 3x + 1 = 0$

8. $4x^2 - 9x + 2 = 0$

9. $x^2 + 4x - 5 = 0$

10. $x^2 + x - 72 = 0$

Find the roots of the equations.

11. $x^2 - 2x - 3 = 0$

12. $x^2 + 5x + 4 = 0$

13. $x^2 - 6x + 5 = 0$

14. $x^2 + 3x - 10 = 0$

15. $x^2 - 5x - 14 = 0$

16. $x^2 - 9x + 14 = 0$

Rearranging the Equation

The terms in a quadratic equation are not always given in the order $ax^2 + bx + c = 0$. When they are given in a different order they should be rearranged into the standard form.

For example

$$x^2 - x = 4 \qquad \text{becomes} \qquad x^2 - x - 4 = 0$$
$$3x^2 - 1 = 2x \qquad \text{becomes} \qquad 3x^2 - 2x - 1 = 0$$
$$x(x - 1) = 2 \qquad \text{becomes} \qquad x^2 - x = 2 \quad \Rightarrow \quad x^2 - x - 2 = 0$$

It is usually best to collect the terms on the side where the x^2 term is positive, for example

$$2 - x^2 = 5x \quad \text{becomes} \quad 0 = x^2 + 5x - 2$$

i.e. $$x^2 + 5x - 2 = 0$$

Losing a Solution

Quadratic equations sometimes have a common factor containing the unknown quantity. It is very tempting in such cases to divide by the common factor, but doing this results in the loss of part of the solution, as the following example shows.

First solution

$$x^2 - 5x = 0$$
$$x(x - 5) = 0$$
$$\therefore \quad x = 0 \quad \text{or} \quad x - 5 = 0$$
$$\Rightarrow x = 0 \text{ or } 5$$

Second solution

$$x^2 - 5x = 0$$
$$x - 5 = 0 \quad \text{(Dividing by } x\text{)}$$
$$\therefore \quad x = 5$$

The solution $x = 0$ has been lost.

Although dividing an equation by a numerical common factor is correct and sensible, dividing by a common factor containing the unknown quantity results in the loss of a solution.

Examples 4b

1. Solve the equation $4x - x^2 = 3$

$$4x - x^2 = 3$$
$$\Rightarrow \qquad 0 = x^2 - 4x + 3$$
$$\Rightarrow \qquad x^2 - 4x + 3 = 0$$
$$\Rightarrow \qquad (x - 3)(x - 1) = 0$$
$$\Rightarrow \qquad x - 3 = 0 \quad \text{or} \quad x - 1 = 0$$
$$\Rightarrow \qquad x = 3 \quad \text{or} \quad x = 1$$

2. Find the roots of the equation $x^2 = 3x$

$$x^2 = 3x$$

$\Rightarrow$
$$x^2 - 3x = 0$$

$\Rightarrow$
$$x(x - 3) = 0$$

$\Rightarrow$
$$x = 0 \quad \text{or} \quad x - 3 = 0$$

$\Rightarrow$
$$x = 0 \quad \text{or} \quad x = 3$$

Therefore the roots are 0 and 3

EXERCISE 4b

Solve the equations.

1. $x^2 + 10 - 7x = 0$ **2.** $15 - x^2 - 2x = 0$

3. $x^2 - 3x = 4$ **4.** $12 - 7x + x^2 = 0$

5. $2x - 1 + 3x^2 = 0$ **6.** $x(x + 7) + 6 = 0$

7. $2x^2 - 4x = 0$ **8.** $x(4x + 5) = -1$

9. $2 - x = 3x^2$ **10.** $6x^2 + 3x = 0$

11. $x^2 + 6x = 0$ **12.** $x^2 = 10x$

13. $x(4x + 1) = 3x$ **14.** $20 + x(1 - x) = 0$

15. $x(3x - 2) = 8$ **16.** $x^2 - x(2x - 1) + 2 = 0$

17. $x(x + 1) = 2x$ **18.** $4 + x^2 = 2(x + 2)$

19. $x(x - 2) = 3$ **20.** $1 - x^2 = x(1 + x)$

Solution by Completing the Square

When there are no obvious factors, another method is needed to solve the equation. One such method involves adding a constant to the x^2 term and the x term, to make a perfect square. This technique is called *completing the square*.

Consider $\qquad\qquad\qquad\qquad x^2 - 2x$

Adding 1 gives $\qquad\qquad\qquad x^2 - 2x + 1$

Now $x^2 - 2x + 1 = (x - 1)^2$ which is a perfect square.

Adding the number 1 was not a guess, it was found by using the fact that

$$x^2 + 2ax + \boxed{a^2} = (x + a)^2$$

We see from this that the number to be added is always
$$\text{(half the coefficient of } x)^2$$

Hence $x^2 + 6x$ requires 3^2 to be added to make a perfect square,

i.e. $\qquad\qquad\qquad x^2 + 6x + 9 = (x + 3)^2$

To complete the square when the coefficient of x^2 is not 1, we first take out the coefficient of x^2 as a factor,

e.g. $\qquad\qquad\qquad 2x^2 + x = 2(x^2 + \tfrac{1}{2}x)$

Now we add $(\tfrac{1}{2} \times \tfrac{1}{2})^2$ inside the bracket, giving

$$2(x^2 + \tfrac{1}{2}x + \tfrac{1}{16}) = 2(x + \tfrac{1}{4})^2$$

Take extra care when the coefficient of x^2 is negative

e.g. $\qquad\qquad\qquad -x^2 + 4x = -(x^2 - 4x)$

Then $\qquad\qquad\qquad -(x^2 - 4x + 4) = -(x - 2)^2$

$\therefore \qquad\qquad\qquad -x^2 + 4x - 4 = -(x - 2)^2$

Examples 4c

1. Solve the equation $x^2 - 4x - 2 = 0$, giving the solution in surd form.

$$x^2 - 4x - 2 = 0$$

No factors can be found so we isolate the two terms with x in,

i.e. $\qquad\qquad\qquad x^2 - 4x = 2$

Add $\{\tfrac{1}{2} \times (-4)\}^2$ to *both* sides

i.e. $\qquad\qquad\qquad x^2 - 4x + 4 = 2 + 4$

$\Rightarrow \qquad\qquad\qquad (x - 2)^2 = 6$

$\therefore \qquad\qquad\qquad x - 2 = \pm\sqrt{6}$

$\therefore \qquad\qquad\qquad x = 2 + \sqrt{6} \quad \text{or} \quad x = 2 - \sqrt{6}$

2. Find in surd form the roots of the equation $2x^2 - 3x - 3 = 0$

$$2x^2 - 3x - 3 = 0$$
$$2x^2 - 3x = 3$$
$$2(x^2 - \tfrac{3}{2}x) = 3$$
$$x^2 - \tfrac{3}{2}x = \tfrac{3}{2}$$
$$x^2 - \tfrac{3}{2}x + \tfrac{9}{16} = \tfrac{3}{2} + \tfrac{9}{16}$$
$$(x - \tfrac{3}{4})^2 = \tfrac{33}{16}$$

$\therefore \qquad x - \tfrac{3}{4} = \pm\sqrt{\tfrac{33}{16}} = \pm\tfrac{1}{4}\sqrt{33}$

$\therefore \qquad x = \tfrac{3}{4} \pm \tfrac{1}{4}\sqrt{33}$

The roots of the equation are $\tfrac{1}{4}(3 + \sqrt{33})$ and $\tfrac{1}{4}(3 - \sqrt{33})$

EXERCISE 4c

Add a number to each expression so that the result contains a perfect square as a factor.

1. $x^2 - 4x$ **2.** $x^2 + 2x$ **3.** $x^2 - 6x$

4. $x^2 + 10x$ **5.** $2x^2 - 4x$ **6.** $x^2 + 5x$

7. $3x^2 - 48x$ **8.** $x^2 + 18x$ **9.** $2x^2 - 40x$

10. $x^2 + x$ **11.** $3x^2 - 2x$ **12.** $2x^2 + 3x$

Solve the equations by completing the square, giving the solutions in surd form.

13. $x^2 + 8x = 1$ **14.** $x^2 - 2x - 2 = 0$ **15.** $x^2 + x - 1 = 0$

16. $2x^2 + 2x = 1$ **17.** $x^2 + 3x + 1 = 0$ **18.** $2x^2 - x - 2 = 0$

19. $x^2 + 4x = 2$ **20.** $3x^2 + x - 1 = 0$ **21.** $2x^2 + 4x = 7$

22. $x^2 - x = 3$ **23.** $4x^2 + x - 1 = 0$ **24.** $2x^2 - 3x - 4 = 0$

The Formula for Solving a Quadratic Equation

Solving a quadratic equation by completing the square is rather tedious. If the method is applied to a general quadratic equation, a formula can be derived which can then be used to solve any particular equation.

Using a, b and c to represent any numbers we have the general quadratic equation

$$ax^2 + bx + c = 0$$

Using the method of completing the square for this equation gives

$$ax^2 + bx = -c$$

i.e.

$$a\left(x^2 + \frac{b}{a}x\right) = -c$$

$\Rightarrow$

$$x^2 + \frac{b}{a}x = -\frac{c}{a}$$

$\therefore$

$$x^2 + \frac{b}{a}x + \left(\frac{b}{2a}\right)^2 = \left(\frac{b}{2a}\right)^2 - \frac{c}{a}$$

$\therefore$

$$\left(x + \frac{b}{2a}\right)^2 = \frac{b^2}{4a^2} - \frac{c}{a} = \frac{b^2 - 4ac}{4a^2}$$

$\Rightarrow$

$$x + \frac{b}{2a} = \pm\sqrt{\frac{(b^2 - 4ac)}{4a^2}}$$

$\Rightarrow$

$$x = -\frac{b}{2a} \pm \frac{\sqrt{(b^2 - 4ac)}}{2a}$$

i.e.

$$x = \frac{-b \pm \sqrt{(b^2 - 4ac)}}{2a}$$

Example 4d

Find, by using the formula, the roots of the equation
$2x^2 - 7x - 1 = 0$ giving them correct to 3 decimal places.

$$2x^2 - 7x - 1 = 0$$

Comparing with $ax^2 + bx + c = 0$ gives $a = 2$, $b = -7$, $c = -1$

$$x = \frac{-b \pm \sqrt{(b^2 - 4ac)}}{2a}$$

$$= \frac{7 \pm \sqrt{\{49 - 4(2)(-1)\}}}{4}$$

Therefore, in surd form,
$$x = \frac{7 \pm \sqrt{57}}{4}$$

Correct to 3 d.p. the roots are 3.637 and -0.137

EXERCISE 4d

Solve the equations by using the formula. Give the solutions in surd form.

1. $x^2 + 4x + 2 = 0$ 2. $2x^2 + x - 2 = 0$

3. $x^2 + 5x + 1 = 0$ 4. $2x^2 - x - 4 = 0$

5. $x^2 + 1 = 4x$ 6. $2x^2 - x = 5$

7. $1 + x - 3x^2 = 0$ 8. $3x^2 = 1 - x$

Find, correct to 3 d.p., the roots of the equations.

9. $5x^2 + 9x + 2 = 0$ 10. $2x^2 - 7x + 4 = 0$

11. $4x^2 - 7x - 1 = 0$ 12. $3x = 5 - 4x^2$

13. $4x^2 + 3x = 5$ 14. $1 = 5x - 5x^2$

15. $8x - x^2 = 1$ 16. $x^2 - 3x = 1$

SIMULTANEOUS EQUATIONS

When only one unknown quantity has to be found, only one equation is needed to provide a solution.

If two unknown quantities are involved in a problem we need two equations connecting them. Then, between the two equations we can eliminate one of the unknowns, producing just one equation containing just one unknown. This is then ready for solution.

SOLUTION OF THREE LINEAR EQUATIONS

63

For three unknown quantities we need three connections, i.e. three equations. Then one unknown at a time can be eliminated. One way to eliminate an unknown quantity is to add or subtract two of the equations and then go on to eliminate the second unknown in a similar way.

Examples 4e _____

1. Solve the equations $\begin{cases} x + y - z = 4 \\ 2x + z = 7 \\ 3x - 2y = 5 \end{cases}$

$$x + y - z = 4 \qquad [1]$$
$$2x + z = 7 \qquad [2]$$
$$3x - 2y = 5 \qquad [3]$$

As z appears only in equations [1] and [2] we can eliminate z from these two equations – in this case by adding.

[1] + [2] gives $\qquad\qquad 3x + y = 11 \qquad\qquad$ [4]

Now bring in [3] $\qquad\qquad 3x - 2y = 5 \qquad\qquad$ [3]

[4] − [3] gives $\qquad\qquad 3y = 6$

$\Rightarrow \qquad\qquad\qquad\qquad\qquad y = 2$

Using $y = 2$ in [3] gives $\qquad\qquad 3x - 4 = 5$

$\Rightarrow \qquad\qquad\qquad\qquad\qquad 3x = 9$

$\Rightarrow \qquad\qquad\qquad\qquad\qquad x = 3$

Now using $x = 3$ in [2] gives $6 + z = 7$

Therefore the solution of the three simultaneous equations is
$$x = 3, \ y = 2, \ z = 1$$

It is not always as easy to eliminate the first of the unknown quantities. If all three unknowns occur in all three equations it is necessary to eliminate the same unknown from each of two different pairs of equations.

---

2. Solve the equations
$$\begin{cases} x - y + 2z = 6 \\ 2x + y + z = 3 \\ 3x - y + z = 6 \end{cases}$$

$$x - y + 2z = 6 \qquad [1]$$
$$2x + y + z = 3 \qquad [2]$$
$$3x - y + z = 6 \qquad [3]$$

The easiest letter to eliminate from two pairs of equations is y

[1] + [2] gives $3x + 3z = 9$

Dividing by 3 gives $x + z = 3$ [4]

[2] + [3] gives $5x + 2z = 9$ [5]

Now we eliminate either x or z from [4] and [5]

$5 \times$ [4] − [5] gives $3z = 6$

$\Rightarrow$ $z = 2$

Using $z = 2$ in [4] gives $x + 2 = 3$

$\Rightarrow$ $x = 1$

Then using $x = 1$ and $z = 2$ in [2] gives

$2 + y + 2 = 3$

$\Rightarrow$ $y = -1$

Therefore the solution is $x = 1, \; y = -1, \; z = 2$

This topic is needed later on in the course and will be revised and developed at that stage. For the present, a short exercise of simple sets of equations is provided.

EXERCISE 4e

Solve the following sets of equations.

Remember first to look for a letter which occurs in only two equations because it can be eliminated completely in one step.

1. $x + 2y = 4$

$x + 3z = 5$

$2y - z = 1$

2. $\quad y - z = 3$

$x - 2y + z = -4$

$x + 2y = 11$

3. $x + y + 3z = 6$

$2x - y = 3$

$4x - z = 2$

4. $2x - y - z = 5$

$4y + 3z = 5$

$x + 2y = 7$

5. $x + y + 4z = 15$

$x - y + z = 2$

$x + 2y - 3z = -4$

6. $2x - 3y + z = 13$

$x + y - 2z = -1$

$3x - y + 2z = 17$

SOLUTION OF ONE LINEAR AND ONE QUADRATIC EQUATION

Another way to eliminate an unknown quantity from two equations is by substitution. From the linear equation we can express one unknown in terms of the other, and then substitute in the quadratic equation.

Example 4f

Solve the equations $x - y = 2$

$$2x^2 - 3y^2 = 15$$

$$x - y = 2 \qquad\qquad [1]$$
$$2x^2 - 3y^2 = 15 \qquad\qquad [2]$$

Equation 1 is linear so we use it for the substitution, i.e. $x = y + 2$

Substituting $y + 2$ for x in [2] gives

$$2(y + 2)^2 - 3y^2 = 15$$

$\Rightarrow \qquad\qquad 2(y^2 + 4y + 4) - 3y^2 = 15$

$\Rightarrow \qquad\qquad 2y^2 + 8y + 8 - 3y^2 = 15$

Collecting terms on the side where y^2 is positive gives

$$0 = y^2 - 8y + 7$$

$\Rightarrow \qquad\qquad 0 = (y - 7)(y - 1)$

$\therefore \qquad\qquad y = 7 \quad \text{or} \quad 1$

Now we use $x = y + 2$ to find corresponding values of x

y	7	1
x	9	3

$\therefore$ either $x = 9$ and $y = 7$

or $x = 3$ and $y = 1$

Note that the values of x and y must be given in *corresponding pairs*.

It is incorrect to write the answer as $y = 7$ or 1 and $x = 9$ or 3

because $\begin{cases} y = 7 & \text{with} \quad x = 3 \\ y = 1 & \text{with} \quad x = 9 \end{cases}$ are *not* solutions

EXERCISE 4f

Solve the following pairs of equations.

1. $x^2 + y^2 = 5$
$y - x = 1$

2. $y^2 - x^2 = 8$
$x + y = 2$

3. $3x^2 - y^2 = 3$
$2x - y = 1$

4. $y = 4x^2$
$y + 2x = 2$

5. $y^2 + xy = 3$
$2x + y = 1$

6. $x^2 - xy = 14$
$y = 3 - x$

7. $xy = 2$
$x + y - 3 = 0$

8. $2x - y = 2$
$x^2 - y = 5$

9. $y - x = 4$
$y^2 - 5x^2 = 20$

10. $x + y^2 = 10$
$x - 2y = 2$

11. $4x + y = 1$
$4x^2 + y = 0$

12. $3xy - x = 0$
$x + 3y = 2$

13. $x^2 + 4y^2 = 2$
$2y + x + 2 = 0$

14. $x + 3y = 0$
$2x + 3xy = 1$

15. $3x - 4y = 1$
$6xy = 1$

16. $x^2 + 4y^2 = 2$
$x + 2y = 2$

17. $xy = 9$
$x - 2y = 3$

18. $4x + y = 2$
$4x + y^2 = 8$

19. $1 + 3xy = 0$
$x + 6y = 1$

20. $x^2 - xy = 0$
$x + y = 1$

21. $xy + y^2 = 2$
$2x + y = 3$

22. $xy + x = -3$
$2x + 5y = 8$

PROPERTIES OF THE ROOTS OF A QUADRATIC EQUATION

A number of interesting facts can be observed by examining the formula used for solving a quadratic equation, especially when it is written in the form

$$x = -\frac{b}{2a} \pm \frac{\sqrt{(b^2 - 4ac)}}{2a}$$

The Sum of the Roots

The separate roots are

$$-\frac{b}{2a} + \frac{\sqrt{(b^2 - 4ac)}}{2a} \quad \text{and} \quad -\frac{b}{2a} - \frac{\sqrt{(b^2 - 4ac)}}{2a}$$

When the roots are added, the terms containing the square root disappear giving

$$\text{sum of roots} = -\frac{b}{a}$$

This fact is very useful as a check on the accuracy of roots that have been calculated.

The Nature of the Roots

In the formula there are two terms. The first of these, $-\dfrac{b}{2a}$, can always be found for any values of a and b.

The second term however, i.e. $\dfrac{\sqrt{(b^2 - 4ac)}}{2a}$, is not so straightforward as there are three different cases to consider.

1) If $b^2 - 4ac$ is positive, its square root can be found and, whether it is a whole number, a fraction or a decimal, it is a number of the type we are familiar with – it is called a *real* number.

The two square roots, i.e. $\pm \sqrt{(b^2 - 4ac)}$ have different (or distinct) values giving two different real values of x
So the equation has *two different real roots*.

2) If $b^2 - 4ac$ is zero then its square root also is zero and

$$x = -\frac{b}{2a} - \frac{\sqrt{(b^2 - 4ac)}}{2a} \quad \text{gives}$$

$$x = -\frac{b}{2a} + 0 \quad \text{and} \quad x = -\frac{b}{2a} - 0$$

i.e. there is just one value of x that satisfies the equation.

An example of this case is $x^2 - 2x + 1 = 0$

From the formula we get $x = -\dfrac{(-2)}{2} \pm 0$

i.e. $\qquad\qquad\qquad\qquad x = 1 \text{ or } 1$

By factorising we can see that there are two equal roots,

i.e. $\qquad\qquad\qquad (x - 1)(x - 1) = 0$

$\Rightarrow \qquad\qquad\qquad x = 1 \quad \text{or} \quad x = 1$

This type of equation can be said to have a *repeated root*.

3) If $b^2 - 4ac$ is negative we cannot find its square root because there is no real number whose square is negative. In this case the equation has *no real roots*.

From these three considerations we see that the roots of a quadratic equation can be

either   real and different
or   real and equal
or   not real

and that it is the value of $b^2 - 4ac$ which determines the nature of the roots, i.e.

Condition	Nature of Roots
$b^2 - 4ac > 0$	Real and different
$b^2 - 4ac = 0$	Real and equal
$b^2 - 4ac < 0$	Not real

Sometimes it matters only that the roots are real, in which case the first two conditions can be combined to give

if $b^2 - 4ac \geqslant 0$, the roots are real.

Examples 4g

1. Determine the nature of the roots of the equation $x^2 - 6x + 1 = 0$

$$x^2 - 6x + 1 = 0$$

$a = 1, \ b = -6, \ c = 1$

$$b^2 - 4ac = (-6)^2 - 4(1)(1) = 32$$

$b^2 - 4ac > 0$ so the roots are real and different.

---

2. If the roots of the equation $2x^2 - px + 8 = 0$ are equal, find the value of p.

$$2x^2 - px + 8 = 0$$

$a = 2, \ b = -p, \ c = 8$

The roots are equal so $b^2 - 4ac = 0,$

i.e. $$(-p)^2 - 4(2)(8) = 0$$

$\Rightarrow$ $$p^2 - 64 = 0$$

$\Rightarrow$ $$p^2 = 64$$

$\therefore$ $$p = \pm 8$$

---

3. Prove that the equation $(k - 2)x^2 + 2x - k = 0$ has real roots whatever the value of k

$$(k - 2)x^2 + 2x - k = 0$$

$a = k - 2, \ b = 2, \ c = -k$

$$b^2 - 4ac = 4 - 4(k - 2)(-k)$$
$$= 4 + 4k^2 - 8k$$
$$= 4k^2 - 8k + 4$$
$$= 4(k^2 - 2k + 1) = 4(k - 1)^2$$

Now $(k - 1)^2$ cannot be negative whatever the value of k, so $b^2 - 4ac$ cannot be negative. Therefore the roots are always real.

EXERCISE 4g

Without solving the equation, write down the sum of its roots.

1. $x^2 - 4x - 7 = 0$ **2.** $3x^2 + 5x + 1 = 0$

3. $2 + x - x^2 = 0$ **4.** $3x^2 - 4x - 2 = 0$

5. $x^2 + 3x + 1 = 0$ **6.** $7 + 2x - 5x^2 = 0$

Without solving the equation, determine the nature of its roots.

7. $x^2 - 6x + 4 = 0$ **8.** $3x^2 + 4x + 2 = 0$

9. $2x^2 - 5x + 3 = 0$ **10.** $x^2 - 6x + 9 = 0$

11. $4x^2 - 12x - 9 = 0$ **12.** $4x^2 + 12x + 9 = 0$

13. $x^2 + 4x - 8 = 0$ **14.** $x^2 + ax + a^2 = 0$

15. $x^2 - ax - a^2 = 0$ **16.** $x^2 + 2ax + a^2 = 0$

17. If the roots of $3x^2 + kx + 12 = 0$ are equal, find k

18. If $x^2 - 3x + a = 0$ has equal roots, find a

19. The roots of $x^2 + px + (p - 1) = 0$ are equal. Find p

20. Prove that the roots of the equation $kx^2 + (2k + 4)x + 8 = 0$ are real for all values of k

21. Show that the equation $ax^2 + (a + b)x + b = 0$ has real roots for all values of a and b

22. Find the relationship between p and q if the roots of the equation $px^2 + qx + 1 = 0$ are equal.

Summary

Methods for solving quadratic equations.

1) Collect the terms in the order $ax^2 + bx + c = 0$, then factorise the left-hand side.

2) Arrange in the form $ax^2 + bx = -c$, then complete the square on the left-hand side, adding the appropriate number to *both* sides.

3) Use the formula $x = \dfrac{-b \pm \sqrt{(b^2 - 4ac)}}{2a}$

Note. Roots that are not rational should be given in surd form (i.e. the exact form) unless an approximate form (such as correct to 3 s.f.) is specifically asked for.

Properties of Roots

$$b^2 - 4ac > 0 \quad \Rightarrow \quad \text{real different roots}$$

$$b^2 - 4ac = 0 \quad \Rightarrow \quad \text{real equal roots}$$

$$b^2 - 4ac \geqslant 0 \quad \Rightarrow \quad \text{real roots}$$

$$b^2 - 4ac < 0 \quad \Rightarrow \quad \text{no real roots}$$

$$\text{Sum of roots} = -\frac{b}{a}$$

LOSING SOLUTIONS

It has already been shown that a solution is lost if an equation is divided by a *common factor containing the unknown quantity*.

There is another situation where a valid solution *may* be overlooked.

The Infinite Solution

Consider the equation $\quad t(t - 1) = t^2 + 2$
This gives $\quad t^2 - t = t^2 + 2$
and $\quad t = -2 \quad$ appears to be the only solution.

Suppose, however, that the value of t can be very large indeed, so large that t approaches infinity (we write, $t \to \infty$). Then, in the equation $t(t - 1) = t^2 + 2$, we see that

$\quad$ 1 is so small compared with the value of t
$\quad$ that $t(t - 1)$ is very nearly equal to t^2

also $\quad$ 2 is so small compared with the value of t^2
$\quad$ that $t^2 + 2$ is very nearly equal to t^2

That is, for very large values of t, $t(t - 1)$ is nearly equal to $t^2 + 2$ and, the larger t becomes the more nearly is the equation satisfied. Therefore, in an equation where the squared terms cancel, we must always *consider* a solution of the type $\quad t \to \infty$

In real problems the unknown quantity usually represents something specific and in most cases it could not possibly have an infinitely large value.

There are cases, however, when the infinite solution is meaningful. The reader will meet some of these later on and will probably have met one already, i.e. if the unknown quantity, t, represents the tangent of an angle, then $t \to \infty$ gives an angle of $90°$

MIXED EXERCISE 4

In each Question from 1 to 10

(a) write down the value of $-b/a$

(b) use any suitable method to find the roots of the equation, giving any irrational roots in surd form.

(c) find the sum of the roots and check that it is equal to the answer to (a).

1. $x^2 - 5x - 6 = 0$ **2.** $x^2 - 6x - 5 = 0$

3. $2x^2 + 3x = 1$ **4.** $5 - 3x^2 = 4x$

5. $x(2 - x) = 1$ **6.** $4x^2 - 3 = 11x$

7. $(x - 1)(x + 2) = 1$ **8.** $x^2 + 4x + 4 = 16$

9. $x^2 + 2x = 2$ **10.** $2(x^2 + 2) = x(x - 4)$

In Questions 11 to 16, solve the equations giving *all possible* solutions.

11. $x(x - 2) = 0$ **12.** $x(x + 3) = 4$

13. $x^2 + x + 8 = x(x + 5)$ **14.** $x^2 + 5x + 2 = 2(2x + 1)$

15. $x(x - 5) = 2(x + 5)$ **16.** $2x(x + 3) = x(2x - 1) + 7$

17. Determine the nature of the roots of the equations

(a) $x^2 + 3x + 7 = 0$ (b) $3x^2 - x - 5 = 0$

(c) $ax^2 + 2ax + a = 0$ (d) $2 + 9x - x^2 = 0$

18. For what values of p does the equation $px^2 + 4x + (p - 3) = 0$ have equal roots?

19. Show that the equation $2x^2 + 2(p + 1)x + p = 0$ always has real roots.

20. The equation $x^2 + kx + k = 1$ has equal roots. Find k

In Questions 21 and 22 solve the set of equations. (Choose your substitution carefully, to keep the amount of squaring to a minimum.)

21. $2x^2 - y^2 = 7$ **22.** $2x = y - 1$

     $x + y = 9$ $x^2 - 3y + 11 = 0$

23. Use the formula to solve the equation $3x^2 - 17x + 10 = 0$

(a) Are the roots of the equation rational or irrational?

(b) What does your answer to (a) tell you about the LHS of the equation?

CONSOLIDATION A

SUMMARY

TERMS AND COEFFICIENTS

In an algebraic expression, terms are separated by plus or minus signs. An individual term is identified by the combination of letters involved. The coefficient of a term is the number in the term, e.g.  $②\,x^2y$

EXPANSION OF BRACKETS

Important results are

$$(ax + b)^2 = a^2x^2 + 2abx + b^2$$
$$(ax - b)^2 = a^2x^2 - 2abx + b^2$$
$$(ax + b)(ax - b) = a^2x^2 - b^2$$

PASCAL'S TRIANGLE

$$
\begin{array}{ccccccccc}
 & & & & 1 & & 1 & & \\
 & & & 1 & & 2 & & 1 & \\
 & & 1 & & 3 & & 3 & & 1 \\
 & 1 & & 4 & & 6 & & 4 & & 1
\end{array}
$$

The 1st, 2nd, 3rd, ... rows in this array give the coefficients in the expansion of $(1 + x)^1$, $(1 + x)^2$, $(1 + x)^3$, ...

PARTIAL FRACTIONS

A fraction like $\dfrac{3}{(x + 3)(2x - 1)}$ can be expressed as $\dfrac{A}{x + 3} + \dfrac{B}{2x - 1}$

INDICES

$$a^n \times a^m = a^{n + m}$$
$$a^n \div a^m = a^{n - m}$$
$$(a^n)^m = a^{nm}$$
$$\sqrt[n]{a} = a^{1/n}$$
$$a^0 = 1$$

LOGARITHMS

$$\log_a b = c \quad \Longleftrightarrow \quad a^c = b$$
$$\log_a b + \log_a c = \log_a bc$$
$$\log_a b - \log_a c = \log_a b/c$$
$$\log_a b^n = n \log_a b$$

QUADRATIC EQUATIONS

The general quadratic equation is $ax^2 + bx + c = 0$

The roots of this equation can be found by
factorising when this is possible,

or completing the square,

or by using the formula $x = \dfrac{-b \pm \sqrt{(b^2 - 4ac)}}{2a}$

When $b^2 - 4ac > 0$, the roots are real and different.

When $b^2 - 4ac = 0$, the roots are real and equal.

When $b^2 - 4ac < 0$, the roots are not real.

MULTIPLE CHOICE EXERCISE A

TYPE I

1. The roots of the equation $x^2 - 3x + 2 = 0$ are

   A 2, 1   C $-3, 2$ E not real
   B $-2, -1$ D $0, \frac{2}{3}$

2. The coefficient of xy in the expansion of $(x - 3y)(2x + y)$ is

   A 1   B 6   C 5   D 0   E -5

3. The value of $\log_5 0.04$ is

   A 4   B 5   C $\frac{1}{2}$ D -2 E 0.25

4. $\dfrac{1 - \sqrt{2}}{1 + \sqrt{2}}$ is equal to

   A 1   C $3 - \sqrt{2}$ E $2\sqrt{2} - 3$
   B -1 D $1 - \frac{2}{3}\sqrt{2}$

5. Expanding $(1 + \sqrt{2})^3$ gives

A $3 + 3\sqrt{2}$ C $1 + 3\sqrt{2}$ E $1 + 2\sqrt{2}$
B $7 + 5\sqrt{2}$ D $3 + \sqrt{6}$

6. The fraction $\dfrac{1}{(x + 1)(x - 1)}$ can be expressed as

A $\dfrac{1}{2(x - 1)} - \dfrac{1}{2(x + 1)}$ D $\dfrac{1}{x^2} - \dfrac{1}{1}$

B $\dfrac{1}{x + 1} + \dfrac{1}{x - 1}$ E $\dfrac{1}{x + 1} - \dfrac{1}{x - 1}$

C $\dfrac{2}{x + 1} - \dfrac{2}{x - 1}$

7. If $\dfrac{x + p}{(x - 1)(x - 3)} \equiv \dfrac{q}{x - 1} + \dfrac{2}{x - 3}$, the values of p and q are

A $p = -2, q = 1$ D $p = 1, \quad q = 1$
B $p = 2, q = 1$ E $p = 1, q = -1$
C $p = 1, q = -2$

8. If $x^2 + px + 6 = 0$ has equal roots and $p > 0$, p is

A $\sqrt{48}$ B 0 C $\sqrt{6}$ D 3 E $\sqrt{24}$

9. If $x^2 + 4x + p \equiv (x + q)^2 + 1$, the values of p and q are

A $p = 5, q = 2$ D $p = -1, q = 5$
B $p = 1, q = 2$ E $p = 0, q = -1$
C $p = 2, q = 5$

10. $\dfrac{p^{-1/2} \times p^{3/4}}{p^{-1/4}}$ simplifies to

A 1 B $p^{-1/2}$ C $p^{3/4}$ D p E $p^{1/2}$

11. In the expansion of $(a - 2b)^3$ the coefficient of b^2 is

A $-2a^2$ C $12a$ E -12
B $-8a$ D $-4a$

12. If $\log_x y = 2$ then

A $x = 2y$ C $x^2 = y$ E $y = \sqrt{x}$
B $x = y^2$ D $y = 2x$

13. $\dfrac{2}{(x + 1)(x - 1)} \equiv \dfrac{A}{x + 1} + \dfrac{B}{x - 1}$ corresponds to

    A $A = 1, B = 1$ **D** $A = 0, B = 2$

    B $A = -1, B = 1$ **E** $A = x - 1, B = x + 1$

    C $A = x, B = 1$

14. $\log 5 - 2 \log 2 + \tfrac{3}{2} \log 16$ is equal to

    A $\log 80$ **C** 0 **E** 1

    B 10 **D** $2 \log 12$

TYPE II

15. When $(3 - 5x)^4$ is expanded

    A   the coefficient of x^4 is 1

    B   the coefficient of x is -540

    C   there are four terms after all simplification.

16. $f(x) = \dfrac{2}{(x + 1)(x - 1)}$

    A $f(x) = 0$ has two real roots

    B $f(x) = \dfrac{1}{x - 1} - \dfrac{1}{x + 1}$

    C $f(x) = \dfrac{1}{x^2}$

17. $f(x) = x^2 - 2x + 2$

    A $f(x) = (x - 1)^2 + 1$

    B $f(1) = 0$

    C $f(x) = 0$ has equal roots.

18. $\tfrac{1}{2} \log 16 - 1$

    A   can be expressed as a single logarithm

    B   has an exact decimal value

    C   is equal to $\log 7$

19. $f(x) = 2x^2 + 3x - 2$

    A $f(x)$ can be expressed as the sum of two partial fractions

    B   the equation $f(x) = 0$ has two real distinct roots

    C $x + 2$ is a factor of $f(x)$

20. $\dfrac{2\sqrt{3}-2}{2\sqrt{3}+2}$

    A can be expressed as a fraction with a rational denominator
    B is an irrational number
    C is equal to -1

TYPE III

21. If $x - a$ is a factor of $x^2 + px + q$, the equation $x^2 + px + q = 0$ has a root equal to a

22. $3\log x + 1 = \log 10x^3$ is an equation.

23. In the expansion of $(1 + x)^6$ the coefficient of x is 6

24. Values of A and B can be found such that
$$\frac{x}{(x-2)(x+1)} \equiv \frac{A}{x-2} + \frac{B}{x+1}$$

MISCELLANEOUS EXERCISE A

1. Express $3x^2 + 6x - 4$ in the form $a[(x + b)^2 + c]$

2. Find the coefficient of x^3 in the expansion of $(3 - 2x)^4$

3. Find the values of A and B for which
$$\frac{x-2}{(x+3)(2x-1)} = \frac{A}{x+3} + \frac{B}{2x-1}$$

4. Find the value of a) $\log_3 3\sqrt{3}$ b) $\log_{25} 125\sqrt{5}$

5. Find the value of a for which $x - 1$ is a factor of $2x^2 - 3x + a$

6. Find the value of k for which the equation $x^2 - 9x + k$ has equal roots.

7. Find the values of p and q for which
$$x^2 - 4x + p \equiv (x - q)^2 + 4$$

8. Given that k is a real constant such that $0 < k < 1$, show that the roots of the equation
$$kx^2 + 2x + (1 - k) = 0$$
are (a) always real
      (b) always negative.   (U of L 88)

9. Given that $\log(2x - 4) + \log 3 = 3 \log y$ find an expression for x in terms of y

10. Express $\dfrac{3}{x(x + 1)}$ in partial fractions.

11. Find the values of p and q for which
$$2x^2 + px + 3 = 2[(x - 1)^2 + q]$$
Hence show that there are no real values of x for which $2[(x - 1)^2 + q] = 0$

12. Find the values of a and b for which
$$(2x - a)^3 = 8x^3 + bx^2 + 6a^2x - 27$$

13. Find the values of x and y which satisfy the equations
$$2 \log x = \log y + \log 3$$
$$x + y = 1$$

14. Find the value of c for which $x = 2$ is a root of the equation $3x^2 - 4x + c = 0$

STRAIGHT LINE GEOMETRY

PROOF

This chapter contains some geometric facts and definitions that will be needed later in this course.

Up to now, many rules have been based on investigating a few particular cases. For example the reader may have accepted that the sum of the interior angles in any triangle is 180°, only because the measured angles in some specific triangles had this property.
This fact may be reinforced by our not being able to find a triangle whose angles have a different sum but that does not rule out the possibility that such a triangle exists.

It is no longer satisfactory to assume that a fact is *always* true without *proving that it is*, because as a mathematics course progresses, one fact is often used to produce another. Hence it is very important to distinguish between a 'fact' that is assumed from a few particular cases and one that has been *proved* to be true, as results deduced from an assumption cannot be reliable.

A proof deals with a general case, e.g. a triangle in which the sides and angles are not specified. The formal statement of a proved result is called a *theorem*.

63

PROOF THAT THE ANGLES OF A TRIANGLE ADD UP TO 180°

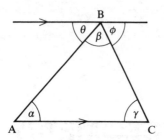 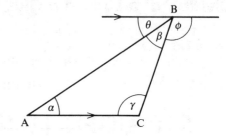

Let ABC be any triangle.

Draw a straight line through B parallel to AC.

Using the notation on the diagram, and the fact that alternate angles are equal, we have

$$\alpha = \theta \quad \text{and} \quad \gamma = \phi$$

At B, $\qquad\qquad \theta + \beta + \phi = 180°$ $\qquad$ (angles on a straight line)

$\therefore \qquad\qquad\quad \alpha + \beta + \gamma = 180°$

We have proved the general case and hence can now be certain that, for *all* triangles *the angles of a triangle add up to 180°*

Proof that in any triangle, an exterior angle is equal to the sum of the two interior opposite angles

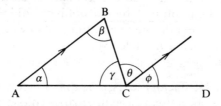

Let ABC be any triangle, with AC produced to D.

Draw a line through C parallel to AB.

Using the notation on the diagram,

$$\theta = \beta \ \text{(alternate } \angle\text{s)} \quad \text{and} \quad \phi = \alpha \ \text{(corresponding } \angle\text{s)}$$

$\therefore \qquad\qquad\qquad\qquad \theta + \phi = \beta + \alpha$

i.e. $\angle BCD = \angle BAC + \angle CBA$

DEFINITIONS

Division of a Line in a Given Ratio

A point P is said to divide a line AB *internally* if P is between A and B.

Further, if P divides AB internally in the ratio $p:q$, then

$$AP:PB = p:q$$

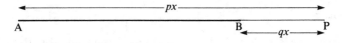

If a point P is on AB produced, or on BA produced, then P is said to divide a line AB *externally*.

Further, if P divides AB externally in the ratio $p:q$ then
$AP:PB = p:q$

Examples 5a _____

1. A line AB of length 15 cm is divided internally by P in the ratio 2:3. Find the length of PB.

As P divides AB internally in the ratio 2:3, P is between A and B and is nearer to A than to B.

AB is divided into 5 portions of which PB is 3 portions. If one portion is x cm, then

$$AB = 5x = 15$$

$\Rightarrow$ $\qquad\qquad\qquad\qquad x = 3$

$\therefore$ $\qquad\qquad\qquad PB = 3x = 9$

i.e. PB is 9 cm long.

_____

2. A line AB of length 15 cm is divided externally by P in the ratio 2:3. Find the length of PB.

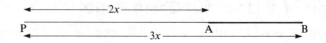

As AP:PB = 2:3, P is nearer to A than to B, so P is on BA produced.

$$AB = 3x - 2x = 15$$

$$\Rightarrow \qquad\qquad\qquad x = 15$$

$$\therefore \qquad\qquad PB = 3x = 45$$

i.e. PB is 45 cm long.

EXERCISE 5a

1. A line AB of length 12 cm is divided internally by P in the ratio 1:5. Find the length of AP.

2. A line AB of length 18 cm is divided externally by P in the ratio 5:6. Find the length of AP.

3. The point D divides a line PQ internally in the ratio 3:4. If PQ is of length 35 cm, find the length of DQ.

4. A line LM is divided externally by a point T in the ratio 5:7 Find the length of MT if (a) LM = 24 cm (b) LM = 2x cm.

5. P is a point on a line AB of length 12 cm and AP = 5 cm. Find the ratio in which P divides AB.

6. AB is a line of length 16 cm and M is a point on AB produced such that AM = 24 cm. Find the ratio in which M divides AB.

7. AB is a line of length x units and P is a point on AB such that AP is of length y units. Find, in terms of x and y, the ratio in which P divides AB.

8. PQ is a line of length a units. It is divided externally in the ratio n:m by a point L, where n > m. Find, in terms of a, n and m, the length of QL.

9. ST is a line of length a units and L is a point on ST produced such that TL is of length b units. Find, in terms of a and b, the ratio in which L divides ST.

THE INTERCEPT THEOREM

> A straight line drawn parallel to one side of a triangle divides the other two sides in the same ratio.

i.e.

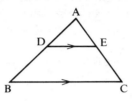

if DE is parallel to BC then AD/DB = AE/EC

Proof

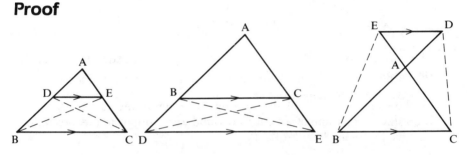

Triangle ABC is any triangle and DE is parallel to BC.

Three different positions for DE must be considered, as shown in the diagrams. The proof that follows applies to all three cases. This proof uses the fact that the area of a triangle can be found by multiplying half the base by the height.

Area $\triangle DEC$ = area $\triangle DEB$

($\triangle$s have same base DE and equal heights)

$\therefore$ area$\triangle AED$: area$\triangle DEB$ = area$\triangle AED$: area$\triangle DEC$

Now   area$\triangle AED$: area$\triangle DEB$ = AD : DB

($\triangle$s have the same heights)

and   area$\triangle AED$: area$\triangle DEC$ = AE : EC

($\triangle$s have the same heights)

Therefore AD : DB = AE : EC

The converse of this theorem is also true, i.e. if a line divides two sides of a triangle in the same ratio, then it is parallel to the third side of the triangle.

PYTHAGORAS' THEOREM AND ITS CONVERSE

Pythagoras' theorem is familiar and very useful. Here is a reminder.

> In any right-angled triangle, the square on the hypotenuse is equal to the sum of the squares on the other two sides.

i.e.

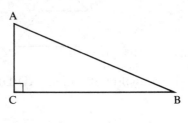

$$AB^2 = AC^2 + BC^2$$

The converse of this theorem is less well known, but equally useful. It states that

> if the square on one side of a triangle is equal to the sum of the squares on the other two sides, then the angle opposite the first side is a right-angle.

EXERCISE 5b

1. In triangle ABC, DE is parallel to BC.
   If AD = 2 cm, DB = 3 cm and AE = 2.5 cm, find EC.

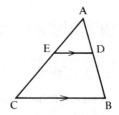

2. In triangle LMN, ST is parallel to MN.
   If LM = 9 cm, LS = 4 cm and LT = 2 cm, find
   (a) TN   (b) LN.

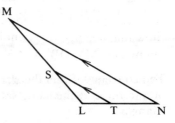

3. In the diagram, ED is parallel
   to AB.
   AC = 3 cm, CE = 1.5 cm
   and CD = 2 cm. Find BC.

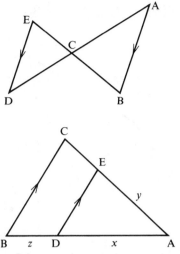

4. Using the measurements given in
   the diagram find the length of
   CE in terms of x, y and z

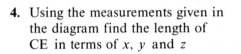

5. ABC is a triangle and a line PQ is drawn parallel to BC, but on
   the opposite side of A from BC. PQ cuts BA produced at P and
   cuts CA produced at Q.
   AC = 2.5 cm, AQ = 1 cm and AP = 0.5 cm. Find
   (a) the length of AB   (b) the ratio in which P divides AB.

6. Determine whether or not a triangle is right-angled if the lengths of
   its sides are

   (a) 3, 5, 4   (b) 2, 1, $\sqrt{3}$ (c) 2, 2, $\sqrt{8}$
   (d) $5x$, $12x$, $13x$ (e) 7, 5, 12   (f) $\sqrt{2}$, $\sqrt{3}$, 1

SIMILAR TRIANGLES

If one triangle is an enlargement of another triangle, then the two
triangles are *similar*.

This means that the three angles of one triangle are equal to the three
angles of the other triangle *and* that the corresponding sides of the two
triangles are in the same ratio.

However, to prove that triangles are similar it is necessary only to
show that *one* of these conditions is satisfied because the other one
follows, i.e.

if two triangles contain the same angles then their corresponding
sides are in the same ratio.

Proof

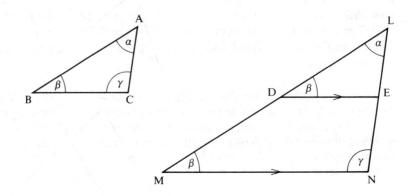

The angles of triangle ABC are equal to the angles of triangle LMN.

It follows that we can find a point D on LM such that LD = AB and a point E on LN such that LE = AC.

Joining DE, it is clear that △LDE and △ABC are identical, i.e. congruent.

∴ ∠ABC = ∠LDE

These are corresponding angles with respect to DE and MN.

∴ DE is parallel to MN

The intercept theorem then tells us that DE divides LM and LN in the same ratio, i.e.

$$LD:LM = LE:LN$$

⇒ $$AB:LM = AC:LN$$

The converse of this theorem is also true, i.e.

> if two triangles are such that their corresponding sides are in the same ratio, then corresponding pairs of angles are equal.

It is left to the reader to prove this in Question 11 in the next exercise.

SIMILAR FIGURES

Two figures are similar if one figure is an enlargement of the other. This means that their corresponding sides are in the same ratio and that the angles in one figure are equal to the corresponding angles in the other figure.

To show that figures other than triangles are similar, both the side and the angle property have to be proved. In the case of triangles, we have seen that it is necessary only to show that one of these conditions is satisfied to prove the triangles similar, because the other condition follows, i.e.

> two triangles are similar if we can show
>   either that the angles of the triangles are equal
>   or that the corresponding sides of the triangles are in the same ratio

THE ANGLE BISECTOR THEOREM

Another useful fact concerning triangles and ratios is

> the line bisecting an angle of a triangle divides the side opposite to that angle in the ratio of the sides containing the angle.

e.g. if AD bisects $\angle A$, then $BD:DC = AB:AC$

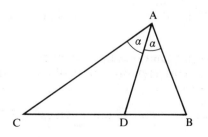

Proof

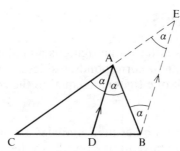

In △ABC, AD bisects the angle at A.

Drawing BE parallel to DA to cut CA produced at E, we have

$$\angle BEA = \angle DAC \quad \text{(corresponding angles)}$$

and $\qquad \angle EBA = \angle BAD \quad$ (alternate angles)

∴ △BEA is isosceles   ⇒   EA = AB

In △BCE the intercept theorem gives

$$BD:DC = EA:AC$$

⇒ $\qquad\qquad\qquad BD:DC = AB:AC$

ALTITUDES AND MEDIANS

We end this chapter with a couple of definitions.
The line drawn from a vertex of a triangle, perpendicular to the opposite side, is called an *altitude*, for example

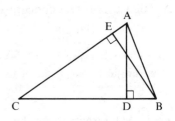

AD is the altitude through A,
and   BE is the altitude through B.

A *median* of a triangle is the line joining a vertex to the midpoint of the opposite side, for example

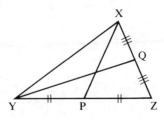

XP is the median through X,
and   YQ is the median through Y.

Example 5c _____

In △ABC, AB = 4 cm, AC = 3 cm and ∠A = 90°. The bisector of ∠A cuts BC at D. Find the length of BD.

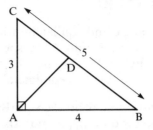

From Pythagoras' theorem, BC = 5 cm.

From the angle bisector theorem, BD:DC = AB:AC = 4:3

∴   BD:BC = 4:7

⇒   BD = $\frac{4}{7}$ × 5

                                           = $2\frac{6}{7}$

∴ BD is $2\frac{6}{7}$ cm long.

_____

EXERCISE 5c

1. XYZ is a triangle with a right angle at X, XW is the altitude from X. Show that triangles XYZ, XWZ and XYW are all similar.

2. In △ABC, AB = 6 cm, AC = 5 cm and BC = 7 cm. BD is the median from B to AC and BE is the bisector of ∠B to AC. Find the length of DE.

3. Triangles PQR and XYZ are such that ∠P = ∠X and ∠Q = ∠Z. XY = 3 cm, YZ = 4 cm, PQ = 7 cm and PR = 12 cm. Find the lengths of XZ and QR.

4.
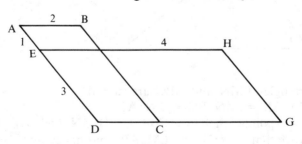

ABCD and EDGH are parallelograms. Prove that they are similar.

5. PQR is a triangle in which PQ = 4 cm, PR = 3 cm and QR = 6 cm. T is a point outside the triangle on the side of QR, and ∠RQT = ∠PRQ and ∠QRT = ∠QPR. Find the lengths of QT and RT.

6. ABC is any triangle and equilateral triangles ABD and ACE are drawn on the sides AB and AC respectively. The bisector of ∠BAC meets BC at F such that BF:FC = 3:2. Find the ratio of the areas of the two equilateral triangles.

7. D and E are two points on the side BC of △ABC such that AD is the bisector of ∠BAC and AE is an altitude of the triangle. If ∠ACB = 40° and ∠ABC = 60° find ∠DAE.

8. In triangle ABC, AB = 24 cm, BC = 7 cm and AC = 25 cm. Show that △ABC is right-angled. The bisector of ∠BAC meets BC at D. Find the lengths of BD, DC and AD.

9. AB and CD are two lines that intersect at E. AC and DB are parallel. Show that triangles ACE and EDB are similar.

10. Triangle ABC has a right-angle at B and BE is an altitude of the triangle. BC = 5 cm and BE = 4 cm. Calculate the length of EC and of AC.

11. (Proof that if the corresponding sides of two triangles are in the same ratio, then the triangles contain the same angles.)

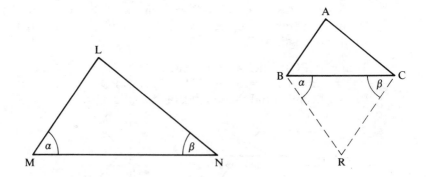

Triangles LMN and ABC are such that
LM:AB = MN:BC = LN:AC.
R is a point such that ∠CBR = ∠LMN and ∠BCR = ∠LNM.
Prove that LM:BR = LM:AB and hence that BR = AB.
Similarly show that CR = AC. *Hence* show that △LMN and △ABC have equal angles.

CHAPTER 6

COORDINATE GEOMETRY

LOCATION OF A POINT IN A PLANE

Graphical methods lend themselves particularly well to the investigation of the geometrical properties of many curves and surfaces. At this stage we will restrict ourselves to rectilinear plane figures (i.e. two dimensional figures bounded by straight lines). To begin, we need a simple and unambiguous way of describing the position of a point on a graph.

Consider the problem of describing the location of a city, London say.

There are many ways in which this can be done, but they all require reference to at least one known place and known directions. This is called a *system* or *frame of reference*. Within this frame of reference, two measurements are needed to locate the city precisely. These measurements are called coordinates.

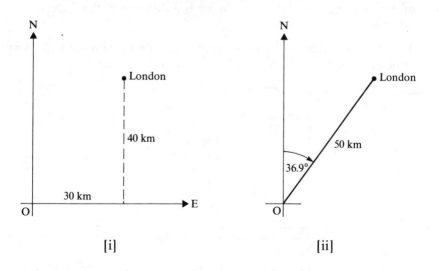

[i]   [ii]

The position of London is described in two alternative ways in the diagrams above.

In [i] the frame of reference comprises a fixed point O and the directions due east and due north from O. The coordinates of London are 30 km east of O and 40 km north of O.

In [ii] the frame of reference comprises a fixed point O and the direction due north from O. The coordinates of London are 50 km from O and a bearing of 036.9°

The system used at this level for graphical work is based on the first of the two practical systems described above.

CARTESIAN COORDINATES

This system of reference uses a fixed point O, called *the origin*, and a pair of perpendicular lines through O. One of these lines is drawn horizontally and is called the *x*-axis. The other line is drawn vertically and is called the *y*-axis.

The coordinates of a point P are the directed distances of P from O parallel to the axes.

A positive coordinate is a distance measured in the positive direction of the axis and a negative coordinate is a distance in the opposite direction.

The coordinates are given as an ordered pair (a, b) with the x-*coordinate* or *abscissa* first and the y-*coordinate* or *ordinate* second.

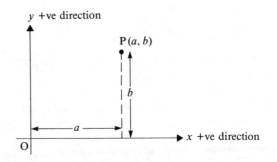

The diagram opposite represents the points whose Cartesian coordinates are $(7, 4)$ and $(-3, -1)$

These points are referred to in future simply as the points $(7, 4)$ and $(-3, -1)$

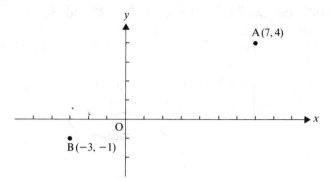

EXERCISE 6a

1. Represent on a diagram the points whose coordinates are

   (a) $(1, 6)$ (b) $(0, 5)$ (c) $(-4, 0)$ (d) $(-3, -2)$ (e) $(3, -4)$

2. Two adjacent corners of a square are the points $(3, 5)$ and $(3, -1)$. What could the coordinates of the other two corners be?

3. The two opposite corners of a square are $(-2, -3)$ and $(3, 2)$. Write down the coordinates of the other two corners.

COORDINATE GEOMETRY

Coordinate geometry is the name given to the graphical analysis of geometric properties. For this analysis we need to refer to three types of points:

1) fixed points whose coordinates are known, e.g. the point $(1, 2)$

2) fixed points whose coordinates are not known numerically. These points are referred to as (x_1, y_1), (x_2, y_2), ... etc. or (a, b), etc.

3) points which are not fixed. We call these general points and we refer to them as (x, y), (X, Y), etc.

It is conventional to use the letters A, B, C, ... for fixed points and the letters P, Q, R, ... for general points.

It is also conventional to graduate the axes using identical scales. This avoids distorting the shape of figures.

THE LENGTH OF A LINE JOINING TWO POINTS

Consider the line joining the points A(1, 2) and B(3, 4)

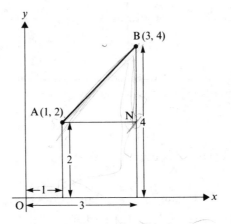

The length of the line joining A and B can be found by using Pythagoras' theorem, i.e.

$$AB^2 = AN^2 + BN^2$$
$$= (3 - 1)^2 + (4 - 2)^2$$
$$= 8$$

Therefore $AB = \sqrt{8} = 2\sqrt{2}$

In the same way the length of the line joining any two points $A(x_1, y_1)$ and $B(x_2, y_2)$ can be found.

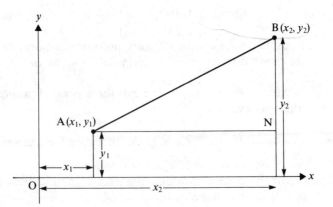

From the diagram, $AB^2 = AN^2 + BN^2$

$$= (x_2 - x_1)^2 + (y_2 - y_1)^2$$

$\Rightarrow \qquad AB = \sqrt{[(x_2 - x_1)^2 + (y_2 - y_1)^2]}$

i.e.   the length of the line joining $A(x_1, y_1)$ to $B(x_2, y_2)$ is given by

$$AB = \sqrt{[(x_2 - x_1)^2 + (y_2 - y_1)^2]}$$

This formula still holds when some, or all, of the coordinates are negative. This is illustrated in the next worked example.

Examples 6b

1. Find the length of the line joining $A(-2, 2)$ to $B(3, -1)$

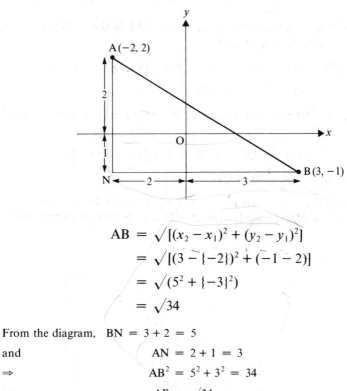

$$\begin{aligned}
AB &= \sqrt{[(x_2 - x_1)^2 + (y_2 - y_1)^2]} \\
&= \sqrt{[(3 - \{-2\})^2 + (-1 - 2)]} \\
&= \sqrt{(5^2 + \{-3\}^2)} \\
&= \sqrt{34}
\end{aligned}$$

From the diagram, $BN = 3 + 2 = 5$

and $AN = 2 + 1 = 3$

$\Rightarrow \qquad\qquad\qquad AB^2 = 5^2 + 3^2 = 34$

$\Rightarrow \qquad\qquad\qquad AB = \sqrt{34}$

This confirms that the formula used above is valid when some of the coordinates are negative.

THE MIDPOINT OF THE LINE JOINING TWO GIVEN POINTS

Consider the line joining the points $A(1, 1)$ and $B(3, 5)$

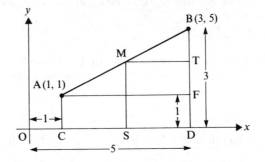

Using the intercept theorem, we see that if M is the midpoint of AB then S is the midpoint of CD.

Therefore the x-coordinate of M is given by OS, where

$$OS = OC + \tfrac{1}{2}CD = 1 + \tfrac{1}{2}(5 - 1) = 3$$

Similarly, T is the midpoint of BF, so the y-coordinate of M is given by SM ($= $ DT), where

$$DT = DF + \tfrac{1}{2}FB = 1 + \tfrac{1}{2}(3 - 1) = 2$$

Therefore M is the point $(3, 2)$

In general, if $A(x_1, y_1)$ and $B(x_2, y_2)$ are two points, then the coordinates of M, the midpoint of AB, can be found in the same way.

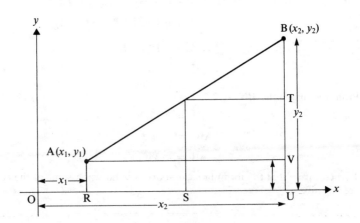

At M, $\qquad x = \text{OS} = \text{OR} + \tfrac{1}{2}\text{RU}$

$$= x_1 + \tfrac{1}{2}(x_2 - x_1) = \tfrac{1}{2}(x_1 + x_2)$$

and $\qquad\qquad y = \text{SM} = \text{UT} = \text{UV} + \tfrac{1}{2}\text{BV}$

$$= y_1 + \tfrac{1}{2}(y_2 - y_1) = \tfrac{1}{2}(y_1 + y_2)$$

Note that the coordinates of M are the average of the coordinates of A and B. Hence

the coordinates of the midpoint of the line joining $A(x_1, y_1)$ and $B(x_2, y_2)$ are $[\tfrac{1}{2}(x_1 + x_2), \tfrac{1}{2}(y_1 + y_2)]$

The next worked example shows that this formula holds when some of the coordinates are negative.

Examples 6b (continued) _____

2. Find the coordinates of the midpoint of the line joining $A(-3, -2)$ and $B(1, 3)$.

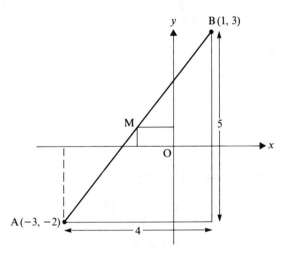

The coordinates of M are $[\tfrac{1}{2}(x_1 + x_2), \tfrac{1}{2}(y_1 + y_2)]$

$$= [\tfrac{1}{2}(-3 + 1), \tfrac{1}{2}(-2 + 3)] = (-1, \tfrac{1}{2})$$

Alternatively, from the diagram, M is half-way from A to B horizontally and vertically, i.e.

at M $\qquad x = -3 + \tfrac{1}{2}(4) = -1 \quad$ and $\quad y = -2 + \tfrac{1}{2}(5) = \tfrac{1}{2}$

This confirms that the formula works when some of the coordinates are negative.

EXERCISE 6b

1. Find the length of the line joining
   (a) A(1, 2) and B(4, 6)   (b) C(3, 1) and D(2, 0)
   (c) J(4, 2) and K(2, 5)

2. Find the coordinates of the midpoints of the lines joining the points in Question 1.

3. Find (i) the length, (ii) the coordinates of the midpoint of the line, joining
   (a) A(−1, −4), B(2, 6)   (b) S(0, 0), T(−1, −2)
   (c) E(−1, −4), F(−3, −2)

4. Find the distance from the origin to the point (7, 4)

5. Find the length of the line joining the point (−3, 2) to the origin.

6. Find the coordinates of the midpoint of the line from the point (4, −8) to the origin.

7. Show, by using Pythagoras' Theorem, that the lines joining A(1, 6), B(−1, 4) and C(2, 1) form a right-angled triangle.

8. A, B and C are the points (7, 3), (−4, 1) and (−3, −2) respectively.
   (a) Show that △ABC is isosceles.
   (b) Find the midpoint of BC.
   (c) Find the area of △ABC.

9. The vertices of a triangle are A(0, 2), B(1, 5) and C(−1, 4) Find
   (a) the perimeter of the triangle
   (b) the coordinates of D such that AD is a median of △ABC
   (c) the length of AD.

10. Show that the lines OA and OB are perpendicular where A and B are the points (4, 3) and (3, −4) respectively.

11. M is the midpoint of the line joining A to B. The coordinates of A and M are (5, 7) and (0, 2) respectively. Find the coordinates of B.

GRADIENT

The gradient of a straight line is a measure of its slope with respect to the x-axis. Gradient is defined as

the increase in y divided by the increase in x between one point and another point on the line.

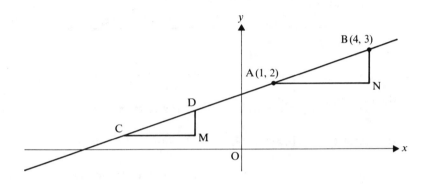

Consider the line passing through $A(1, 2)$ and $B(4, 3)$.

From A to B,
the increase in y is 1
the increase in x is 3

Therefore the gradient of AB is $\frac{1}{3}$.

Now NB measures the increase in the y-coordinate and AN measures the increase in the x-coordinate, so the gradient can be written as $\dfrac{NB}{AN}$.

If C and D are any other two points on the line then $\triangle ABN$ and $\triangle CDM$ are similar, so

$$\frac{NB}{AN} = \frac{MD}{CM} = \frac{1}{3}$$

i.e.

the gradient of a line may be found from *any* two points on the line.

Now consider the line through the points A(2, 3) and B(6, 1)

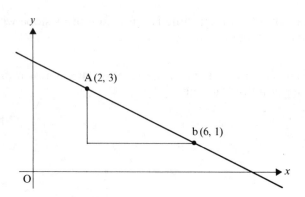

Moving from A to B $\dfrac{\text{increase in } y}{\text{increase in } x} = \dfrac{-2}{4} = -\dfrac{1}{2}$

Alternatively, moving from B to A $\dfrac{\text{increase in } y}{\text{increase in } x} = \dfrac{2}{-4} = -\dfrac{1}{2}$

This shows that it does not matter in which order the two points are considered, provided that they are considered in the *same* order when calculating the increases in x and in y.

From these two examples we see that the gradient of a line may be positive or negative.

A positive gradient indicates an 'uphill' slope with respect to the positive direction of the x-axis, i.e. the line makes an acute angle with the positive sense of the x-axis.

A negative gradient indicates a 'downhill' slope with respect to the positive direction of the x-axis, i.e. the line makes an obtuse angle with the positive sense of the x-axis.

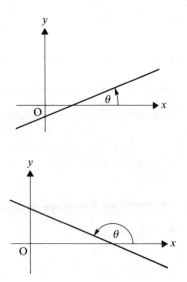

In general,

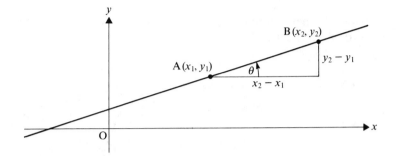

the gradient of the line passing through $A(x_1, y_1)$ and $B(x_2, y_2)$ is

$$\frac{\text{the increase in } y}{\text{the increase in } x} = \frac{y_2 - y_1}{x_2 - x_1}$$

As the gradient of a straight line is the increase in y divided by the increase in x from one point on the line to another,

gradient measures the increase in y per unit increase in x, i.e. the rate of increase of y with respect to x.

PARALLEL LINES

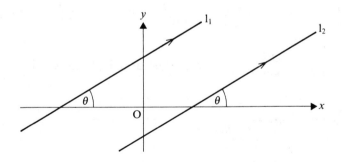

If l_1 and l_2 are parallel lines, they are equally inclined to the positive direction of the x-axis, i.e.

parallel lines have equal gradients.

PERPENDICULAR LINES

Consider the perpendicular lines AB and CD whose gradients are m_1 and m_2 respectively.

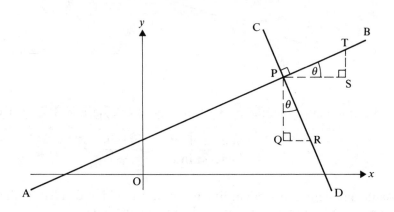

If AB makes an angle θ with the x-axis then CD makes an angle θ with the y-axis. Therefore triangles PQR and PST are similar.

Now the gradient of AB is $\dfrac{ST}{PS} = m_1$

and the gradient of CD is $\dfrac{-PQ}{QR} = m_2$, i.e. $\dfrac{PQ}{QR} = -m_2$

But $\dfrac{ST}{PS} = \dfrac{QR}{PQ}$ ($\triangle$s PQR and PST are similar)

therefore $m_1 = -\dfrac{1}{m_2}$ or $m_1 m_2 = -1$

i.e.

> the product of the gradients of perpendicular lines is -1, or, if one line has gradient m, any line perpendicular to it has gradient $-\dfrac{1}{m}$

Example 6c

Determine, by comparing gradients, whether the following three points are collinear (i.e. lie on the same straight line).

$$A(\tfrac{2}{3}, 1), \ B(1, \tfrac{1}{2}), \ C(4, -4)$$

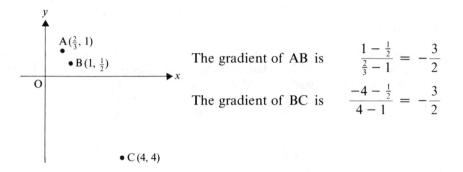

The gradient of AB is $\quad \dfrac{1 - \tfrac{1}{2}}{\tfrac{2}{3} - 1} = -\dfrac{3}{2}$

The gradient of BC is $\quad \dfrac{-4 - \tfrac{1}{2}}{4 - 1} = -\dfrac{3}{2}$

As the gradients of AB and BC are the same, A, B and C are collinear.

The diagram, although not strictly necessary, gives a check that the answer is reasonable.

EXERCISE 6c

1. Find the gradient of the line through the pair of points.
   (a) $(0, 0)$, $(1, 3)$ (b) $(1, 4)$, $(3, 7)$ (c) $(5, 4)$, $(2, 3)$
   (d) $(-1, 4)$, $(3, 7)$ (e) $(-1, -3)$, $(-2, 1)$ (f) $(-1, -6)$, $(0, 0)$
   (g) $(-2, 5)$, $(1, -2)$ (h) $(3, -2)$, $(-1, 4)$ (i) (h, k), $(0, 0)$

2. Determine whether the given points are collinear.
   (a) $(0, -1)$, $(1, 1)$, $(2, 3)$ (b) $(0, 2)$, $(2, 5)$, $(3, 7)$
   (c) $(-1, 4)$, $(2, 1)$, $(-2, 5)$ (d) $(0, -3)$, $(1, -4)$, $(-\tfrac{1}{2}, -\tfrac{5}{2})$

3. Determine whether AB and CD are parallel, perpendicular or neither.
   (a) $A(0, -1)$, $B(1, 1)$, $C(1, 5)$, $D(-1, 1)$
   (b) $A(1, 1)$, $B(3, 2)$, $C(-1, 1)$, $D(0, -1)$
   (c) $A(3, 3)$, $B(-3, 1)$, $C(-1, -1)$, $D(1, -7)$
   (d) $A(2, -5)$, $B(0, 1)$, $C(-2, 2)$, $D(3, -7)$
   (e) $A(2, 6)$, $B(-1, -9)$, $C(2, 11)$, $D(0, 1)$

PROBLEMS IN COORDINATE GEOMETRY

This chapter ends with a miscellaneous selection of problems on coordinate geometry. A clear and reasonably accurate diagram showing all the given information will often suggest the most direct method for solving a particular problem.

Example 6d _____

The vertices of a triangle are the points $A(2, 4)$, $B(1, -2)$ and $C(-2, 3)$ respectively. The point $H(a, b)$ lies on the altitude through A. Find a relationship between a and b

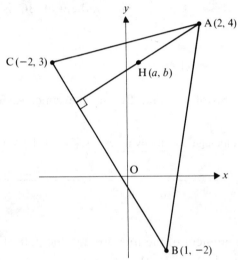

As H is on the altitude through A,   AH is perpendicular to BC.

The gradient of AH is $\dfrac{4 - b}{2 - a}$,

the gradient of BC is $\dfrac{3 - (-2)}{-2 - 1} = -\dfrac{5}{3}$

The product of the gradients of perpendicular lines is -1

Therefore $\left[\dfrac{4 - b}{2 - a} \right]\left[-\dfrac{5}{3} \right] = -1$

$\Rightarrow$ $\dfrac{-20 + 5b}{6 - 3a} = -1$

$\Rightarrow$ $5b = 3a + 14$

EXERCISE 6d

1. A$(1, 3)$, B$(5, 7)$, C$(4, 8)$, D(a, b) form a rectangle ABCD. Find a and b

2. The triangle ABC has its vertices at the points A$(1, 5)$, B$(4, -1)$ and C$(-2, -4)$

    (a) Show that $\triangle$ABC is right-angled.

    (b) Find the area of $\triangle$ABC.

3. Show that the point $(-\frac{32}{3}, 0)$ is on the altitude through A of the triangle whose vertices are A$(1, 5)$, B$(1, -2)$ and C$(-2, 5)$

4. Show that the triangle whose vertices are $(1, 1)$, $(3, 2)$, $(2, -1)$ is isosceles.

5. Find, in terms of a and b, the length of the line joining (a, b) and $(2a, 3b)$

6. The point $(1, 1)$ is the centre of a circle whose radius is 2. Show that the point $(1, 3)$ is on the circumference of this circle.

7. A circle, radius 2 and centre the origin, cuts the x-axis at A and B and cuts the positive y-axis at C. *Prove* that $\angle$ACB $= 90°$

8. Find in terms of p and q, the coordinates of the midpoint of the line joining C(p, q) and D(q, p). Hence show that the origin is on the perpendicular bisector of the line CD.

9. The point (a, b) is on the circumference of the circle of radius 3 whose centre is at the point $(2, 1)$. Find a relationship between a and b

10. ABCD is a quadrilateral where A, B, C and D are the points $(3, -1)$, $(6, 0)$, $(7, 3)$ and $(4, 2)$. Prove that the diagonals bisect each other at right angles and hence find the area of ABCD.

11. The vertices of a triangle are at the points A$(a, 0)$, B$(0, b)$ and C(c, d) and $\angle$B $= 90°$. Find a relationship between a, b, c and d

12. A point P(a, b) is equidistant from the y-axis and from the point $(4, 0)$. Find a relationship between a and b

CHAPTER 7

OBTUSE ANGLES, SINE AND COSINE FORMULAE

TRIGONOMETRIC RATIOS OF ACUTE ANGLES

The sine, cosine and tangent of an acute angle in a right-angled triangle are defined in terms of the sides of the triangle as follows

$$\cos A = \frac{\text{adjacent}}{\text{hypotenuse}}$$

$$\sin A = \frac{\text{opposite}}{\text{hypotenuse}}$$

$$\tan A = \frac{\text{opposite}}{\text{adjacent}}$$

If any of these trig ratios is given as a fraction, the lengths of two of the sides of the right-angled triangle can be marked. Then the third side can be calculated by using Pythagoras' theorem.

Example 7a _____

Given that $\sin A = \frac{3}{5}$ find $\cos A$ and $\tan A$

Because $\sin A = \dfrac{\text{opp}}{\text{hyp}}$, we can draw a right-angled triangle with the side opposite to angle A of length 3 units and a hypotenuse of length 5 units.

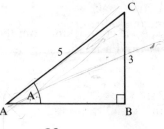

90

Applying Pythagoras' theorem to $\triangle ABC$ gives

$$(AB)^2 + (BC)^2 = (AC)^2$$

i.e. $\qquad\qquad (AB)^2 + 3^2 = 5^2$

$\Rightarrow \qquad\qquad (AB)^2 = 25 - 9 = 16$

$\Rightarrow \qquad\qquad AB = 4$

Then $\qquad\qquad \cos A = \dfrac{\text{adj}}{\text{hyp}} = \dfrac{4}{5}$

and $\qquad\qquad \tan A = \dfrac{\text{opp}}{\text{adj}} = \dfrac{3}{4}$

EXERCISE 7a

If any of the square roots in this exercise are not integers, leave them in surd form.

1. If $\tan A = \frac{12}{5}$ find $\sin A$ and $\cos A$

2. Given that $\cos X = \frac{4}{5}$ find $\tan X$ and $\sin X$

3. If $\sin P = \frac{40}{41}$ find $\cos P$ and $\tan P$

4. Tan $A = 1$ Find $\sin A$ and $\cos A$

5. If $\cos Y = \frac{2}{3}$ find $\sin Y$ and $\tan Y$

6. Given that $\sin A = \frac{1}{2}$ what is $\cos A$? Use your calculator to find the size of angle A

7. If $\sin X = \frac{?}{25}$ and $\tan X = \frac{7}{?}$ find $\cos X$

In each question from 8 to 12, use $\sin X = \frac{3}{5}$.

8. Find $\cos X$ and hence calculate $\cos^2 X - \sin^2 X$. Use a calculator to determine the value of angle X and hence find $\cos 2X$ correct to 2 s.f. What conclusion can you draw?

9. Find $\cos^2 X + \sin^2 X$

10. Evaluate $2 \sin X \cos X$ as a decimal. Find correct to 2 s.f. the value of $\sin 2X$ and draw any conclusion that you can.

11. Work out the value of $\dfrac{2\tan X}{1 - \tan^2 X}$. Compare this with the value you found in Question 10 for $\sin 2X$

12. Work out the value of $\dfrac{1 - \tan^2 X}{1 + \tan^2 X}$. How does this quantity compare with the value of $\cos 2X$ found in Question 8?

TRIGONOMETRIC RATIOS OF OBTUSE ANGLES

The Cosine of an Obtuse Angle

Clearly the definition in the preceeding paragraph is restricted to acute angles, so if we want to work with the cosine of an obtuse angle we need a broader definition.

First however we will examine the values given by a calculator for the cosines of angles from 0 to 180°

θ	0	30°	45°	60°	90°	120°	135°	150°	180°
$\cos\theta$ (to 2 d.p.)	1	0.87	0.71	0.50	0	−0.50	−0.71	−0.87	−1

Plotting these figures on graph paper gives a shape which is called a cosine curve. Note that θ, the symbol used for the angle, is the most commonly used symbol for a varying angle.

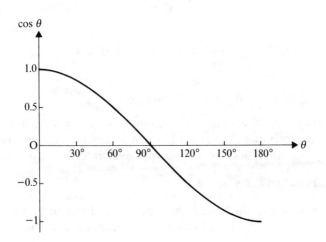

From the graph or the table it can be seen that

$$\cos 60° = 0.5$$

and $$\cos 120° = -0.5$$

i.e. $$\cos 120° = -\cos 60° \qquad (120° + 60° = 180°)$$

also $$\cos 45° = 0.71$$

and $$\cos 135° = -0.71$$

i.e. $$\cos 135° = -\cos 45° \qquad (135° + 45° = 180°)$$

The reader can find many more pairs of angles where the relationship is

$$\cos \theta = -\cos (180° - \theta)$$

This property is confirmed by looking again at the graph.

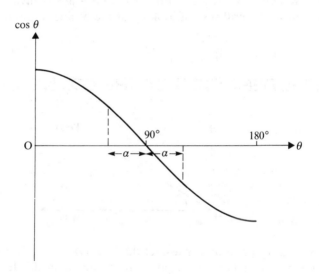

It appears that the curve has rotational symmetry about the point $(90°, 0)$, suggesting that

$$\cos (90° - \alpha) = -\cos (90° + \alpha)$$

But $\theta = 90° - \alpha$,   so $\cos \theta = -\cos (180° - \theta)$

So far, it just *looks as though* this relationship is true and, at this level of study, we should now look for a more general explanation of this relationship. To do this we first consider a broader concept of what an angle is.

GENERAL DEFINITION OF AN ANGLE

Consider a line which can rotate
from its initial position OP_0
about the point O to any other
position OP.

The amount of rotation is indicated by the angle between OP_0 and
OP, i.e.

> an angle is a measure of the rotation of a line about a fixed point.

The anticlockwise sense of rotation is taken as positive and clockwise
rotation is negative. It follows that an angle formed by the
anticlockwise rotation of OP is a positive angle.

When we define an angle in this way no triangle is involved, so we
need a more general way of looking at the cosine of an angle.

GENERAL DEFINITION OF THE COSINE RATIO

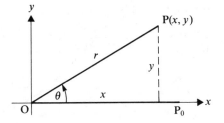

Using standard x and y axes, let the line OP_0 be drawn on the x-axis
as shown and let OP be the position reached after this line has rotated
through an angle θ. The coordinates of P are (x, y) and we shall
refer to the length of OP as r. Using these symbols, the cosine of θ is
defined by

$$\cos \theta = \frac{x}{r}$$

Note that this is consistent with the earlier definition, i.e.

$$\cos \theta = \frac{\text{adjacent}}{\text{hypotenuse}}$$

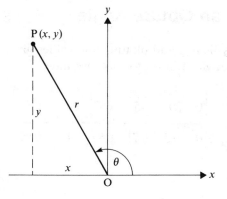

The definition $\cos \theta = \dfrac{x}{r}$ continues to be used when OP has rotated through an obtuse angle, but now it can be seen that the x-coordinate of P is negative. The value of r is always positive, because $r = \sqrt{(x^2 + y^2)}$, so it follows that $\dfrac{x}{r}$ is negative, i.e.

the cosine of an obtuse angle is negative.

This explains the *signs* of the values given in a calculator for the cosines of obtuse angles.

Further, if OP′ is the reflection in the y-axis of OP, then OP′ represents a rotation of $(180° - \theta)$

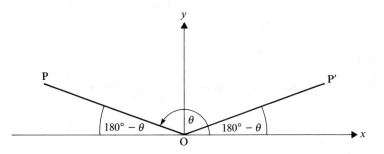

Both r and x have the same numerical values for OP′ and OP therefore the *numerical values* of $\cos \theta$ and $\cos (180° - \theta)$ are equal.

We have now proved, from the general definition, that

$$\cos (180° - \theta) = -\cos \theta$$

The Sine of an Obtuse Angle

If we start by listing, and plotting, the values given by a calculator for the sines of angles from 0 to 180°, we have

θ	0	30°	45°	60°	90°	120°	135°	150°	180°
$\sin \theta$ (to 2 d.p.)	0	0.5	0.71	0.87	1	0.87	0.71	0.5	0

and

This graph is called a sine curve; notice that it looks symmetrical about a vertical line through 90°

Again relationships can be observed between the sines of pairs of angles, for example

$$\sin 30° = 0.5$$

and $\qquad \sin 150° = 0.5$

i.e. $\qquad \sin 150° = \sin 30° \qquad (150° + 30° = 180°)$

also $\qquad \sin 60° = 0.87$

and $\qquad \sin 120° = 0.87$

i.e. $\qquad \sin 120° = \sin 60° \qquad (120° + 60° = 180°)$

This time it looks as if $\sin \theta = \sin(180° - \theta)$ and we shall now check this relationship from a definition similar to that used for the cosine of a general angle.

GENERAL DEFINITION OF THE SINE RATIO

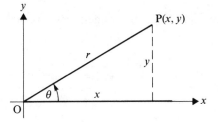

Using the same axes and symbols as we used when defining the cosine ratio, the sine ratio is defined by

$$\sin \theta = \frac{y}{r}$$

$$\left(\text{Again this is consistent with the concept } \sin \theta = \frac{\text{opposite}}{\text{hypotenuse}} \right)$$

When θ is obtuse, both r and y are positive, so the sine ratio of an obtuse angle is positive.

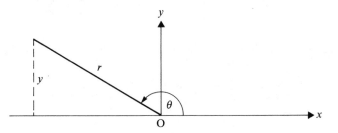

Also, the line OP', which represents a rotation of $(180° - \theta)$, is the reflection of OP in the y-axis. Therefore the values of y at P and P' are equal, i.e. y/r has the same value at P and at P'.

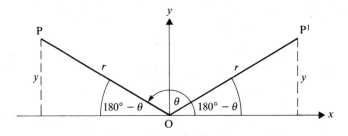

This proves that, in general,

$$\sin (180° - \theta) = \sin \theta$$

GENERAL DEFINITION OF THE TANGENT RATIO

Using the same notation, the tangent ratio is defined by $\tan \theta = \dfrac{y}{x}$

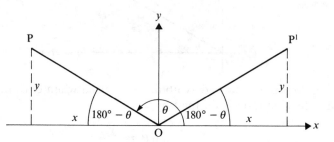

Reasoning similar to that used when considering $\sin \theta$ and $\cos \theta$ shows that

$$\tan(180° - \theta) = -\tan \theta$$

Examples 7b _____

1. If $\sin \theta = \frac{1}{5}$ find two possible values for θ

As given by a calculator, the angle with a sine of 0.2 is 11.5°

But $\sin \theta = \sin(180° - \theta)$ so $\sin 11.5° = \sin(180° - 11.5°)$
if $\sin \theta = \frac{1}{5}$, two values of θ are 11.5° and 168.5°

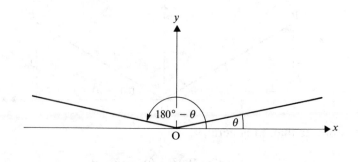

2. Use the information in the diagram to find $\cos\theta$ and $\tan\theta$

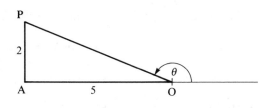

In $\triangle OPA$ $\qquad\qquad OP^2 = 4 + 25 = 29$ (Pythagoras)

and $\qquad\qquad\qquad\qquad A\widehat{O}P = (180° - \theta)$

$$\cos(180° - \theta) = \frac{OA}{OP} = \frac{5}{\sqrt{29}}$$

$$\cos\theta = -\cos(180° - \theta) = -\frac{5}{\sqrt{29}}$$

$$\tan\theta = -\tan(180° - \theta) = -\frac{AP}{OA} = -\tfrac{2}{5}$$

EXERCISE 7b

In each question from 1 to 4, find $\sin\theta$, $\cos\theta$ and $\tan\theta$, giving unknown lengths in surd form when necessary.

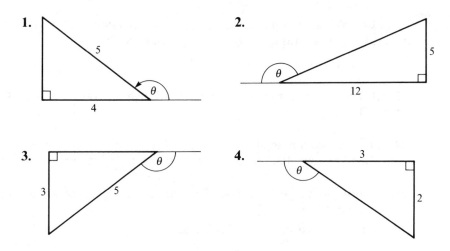

1.

5

4

θ

2.

5

12

θ

3.

3

5

θ

4.

3

2

θ

In each question from 5 to 16, find X where X is an angle from 0 to 180°

5. $\sin X = \sin 80°$ 6. $\tan X = -\tan 120°$

7. $\cos X = -\cos 75°$ 8. $\sin X = \sin 128°$

9. $\tan 45° = -\tan X$ 10. $\cos 30° = -\cos X$

11. $\sin X = \sin 81°$ 12. $-\cos 123 = \cos X$

13. $\sin 90° = \sin X$ 14. $\tan X = -\tan 100°$

15. $\cos 91° = -\cos X$ 16. $\cos 0 = -\cos X$

The unknown angles in questions 17 to 23 are in the range 0 to 180°

17. If $\sin A = \frac{3}{5}$ find two possible values of $\cos(180° - A)$

18. If $\cos X = -\frac{12}{13}$ find $\sin X$

19. If $\sin\theta = \frac{4}{5}$ find, to the nearest degree, two possible values of θ

20. Given that $\sin A = 0.5$ and $\cos A = -0.8660$, find $\angle A$

21. Find the angle P if $\cos P = -0.7071$ and $\sin P = 0.7071$

22. Is there an angle X for which
     (a) $\cos X = 0$ and $\sin X = 1$
     (b) $\sin X = 0$ and $\cos X = 1$
     (c) $\cos X = 0$ and $\sin X = -1$
     (d) $\tan X = 0$ and $\sin X = 0$?

23. If $\cos A = -\cos B$, what is the relationship between $\angle A$ and $\angle B$

24. Draw a diagram to show the angle T for which $\tan T = \frac{3}{4}$.
     Draw on your diagram an angle with a tangent of $-\frac{3}{4}$.

25. Within the range $0 < \theta < 180°$, are there angles for which $\sin\theta$ and $\cos\theta$ are
     (a) both positive   (b) both negative?

FINDING UNKNOWN SIDES AND ANGLES IN A TRIANGLE

Triangles are involved in many practical measurements (e.g. surveying) so it is important to be able to make calculations from limited data about a triangle.

Although a triangle has three sides and three angles, it is not necessary to know all of these in order to define a particular triangle. If enough information about a triangle is known, the remaining sides and angles can be calculated. This is called *solving* the triangle and it requires the use of one of a number of formulae.

The two relationships that are used most frequently are the sine rule and the cosine rule.

When working with a triangle ABC the side opposite to $\angle$A is denoted by a, the side opposite to $\angle$B by b and so on.

THE SINE RULE

In a triangle ABC, $$\frac{a}{\sin A} = \frac{b}{\sin B} = \frac{c}{\sin C}$$

Proof

Consider a triangle ABC in which there is no right angle.

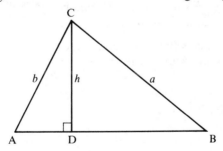

A line drawn from C, perpendicular to AB, divides triangle ABC into two right-angled triangles, CDA and CDB.

In $\triangle$CDA $\sin A = h/b \;\Rightarrow\; h = b \sin A$

In $\triangle$CDB $\sin B = h/a \;\Rightarrow\; h = a \sin B$

Therefore $a \sin B = b \sin A$

i.e. $$\frac{a}{\sin A} = \frac{b}{\sin B}$$

We could equally well have divided $\triangle ABC$ into two right-angled triangles by drawing the perpendicular from A to BC (or from B to AC). This would have led to a similar result,

i.e. $$\frac{b}{\sin B} = \frac{c}{\sin C}$$

By combining the two results we produce the sine rule,

$$\frac{a}{\sin A} = \frac{b}{\sin B} = \frac{c}{\sin C}$$

Note that this proof is equally valid when $\triangle ABC$ contains an obtuse angle.

Suppose that $\angle A$ is obtuse.

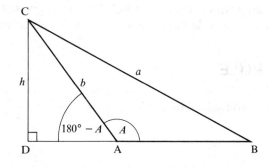

This time $h = b \sin(180° - A)$ but, as $\sin(180° - A) = \sin A$, we see that once again $h = b \sin A$

In all other respects the proof given above is unaltered, showing that the sine rule applies to any triangle.

Using the Sine Rule

$$\frac{a}{\sin A} = \frac{b}{\sin B} = \frac{c}{\sin C}$$

This rule is made up of three separate fractions, only two of which can be used at a time. We select the two which contain three known quantities and only one unknown.

Note that, when the sine rule is being used to find an unknown angle, it is more conveniently written in the form

$$\frac{\sin A}{a} = \frac{\sin B}{b} = \frac{\sin C}{c}$$

Examples 7c _____

1. In $\triangle ABC$, $BC = 5\,\text{cm}$, $A = 43°$ and $B = 61°$. Find the length of AC.

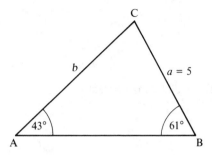

$\angle A$, $\angle B$ and b are known and b is required, so the two fractions we select from the sine rule are

$$\frac{a}{\sin A} = \frac{b}{\sin B}$$

i.e.
$$\frac{5}{\sin 43°} = \frac{b}{\sin 61°}$$

$\Rightarrow$
$$b = \frac{5 \sin 61°}{\sin 43°} = 6.412$$

Therefore $AC = 6.41\,\text{cm}$ correct to 3 s.f.

_____

2. In ABC, $AC = 17\,\text{cm}$, $\angle A = 105°$ and $\angle B = 33°$. Find AB.

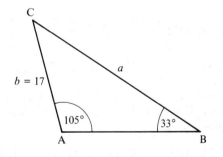

The two sides involved are b and c, so before the sine rule can be used we must find C.

$$\angle A + \angle B + \angle C = 180° \qquad \Rightarrow \qquad \angle C = 42°$$

Now from the sine rule we can use

$$\frac{b}{\sin B} = \frac{c}{\sin C}$$

$\Rightarrow$ $$\frac{17}{\sin 33°} = \frac{c}{\sin 42°}$$

i.e. $$c = \frac{17 \times 0.6691}{0.5446} = 20.88$$

Therefore AB = 20.9 cm correct to 3 s.f.

C, b = 17, 105°, 33°, A, B

EXERCISE 7c

1. In $\triangle ABC$, AB = 9 cm, $\angle A = 51°$ and $\angle C = 39°$
   Find BC.

2. In $\triangle XYZ$, $\angle X = 27°$, YZ = 6.5 cm and $\angle Y = 73°$
   Find ZX.

3. In $\triangle PQR$, $\angle R = 52°$, $\angle Q = 79°$ and PR = 12.7 cm.
   Find PQ.

4. In $\triangle ABC$, AC = 9.1 cm, $\angle A = 59°$ and $\angle B = 62°$
   Find BC.

5. In $\triangle DEF$, DE = 174 cm, $\angle D = 48°$ and $\angle F = 56°$
   Find EF.

6. In $\triangle XYZ$, $\angle X = 130°$, $\angle Y = 21°$ and XZ = 53 cm.
   Find YZ.

7. In $\triangle PQR$, $\angle Q = 37°$, $\angle R = 101°$ and PR = 4.3 cm.
   Find PQ.

8. In $\triangle ABC$, BC = 73 cm, $\angle A = 54°$ and $\angle C = 99°$
   Find AB.

9. In $\triangle LMN$, LN = 637 cm, $\angle M = 128°$ and $\angle N = 46°$
   Find LM.

10. In $\triangle XYZ$, XY = 92 cm, $\angle X = 59°$ and $\angle Y = 81°$
    Find XZ.

11. In $\triangle$PQR, $\angle Q = 64°$, $\angle R = 38°$ and PR $= 15$ cm.
Find QR.

12. In $\triangle$ABC, AB $= 24$ cm, $\angle A = 132°$ and $\angle C = 22°$
Find AC.

13. In $\triangle$XYZ, $\angle X = 49°$, XY $= 98$ cm and $\angle Z = 100°$
Find XZ.

14. In $\triangle$ABC, AB $= 10$ cm, BC $= 9.1$ cm and AC $= 17$ cm.
Can you use the sine rule to find $\angle A$? If you answer YES, write
down the two parts of the sine rule that you would use. If you
answer NO, give your reason.

The Ambiguous Case

Consider a triangle specified by two sides and one angle.

If the angle is between the two sides there is only one possible triangle,
e.g.

If, however, the angle is not between the two given sides it is sometimes
possible to draw two triangles from the given data.

Consider, for example, a triangle ABC in which $\angle A = 20°$,
$b = 10$ and $a = 8$

The two triangles with this specification are shown in the diagram; in
one of them B is an acute angle, while in the other one, B is obtuse.

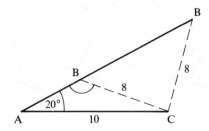

Therefore, when two sides and an angle of a triangle are given,

it is essential to check whether the obtuse angle is possible.

The following worked examples illustrate this special case.

Examples 7d

1. In the triangle ABC, find C given that AB = 5 cm, BC = 3 cm and A = 35°

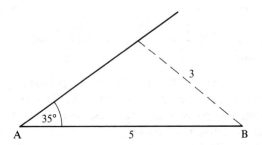

We know a, c and $\angle A$ so the sine rule can be used to find $\angle C$.

As we are looking for an angle, the form we use is

$$\frac{\sin A}{a} = \frac{\sin C}{c} \quad \Rightarrow \quad \frac{\sin 35°}{3} = \frac{\sin C}{5}$$

Hence
$$\sin C = \frac{5 \times 0.5736}{3} = 0.9560$$

One angle whose sine is 0.9560 is 73° but there is also an obtuse angle with the same sine, i.e. 107°

If C = 107, then A + C ≑ 107 + 35 = 142
⇒ B = 180 − 142 = 38

So in this case ∠C = 107° *is* an acceptable solution and we have two possible triangles.

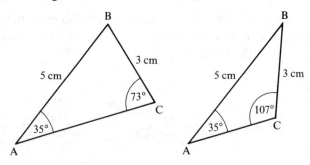

Therefore ∠C is either 73° or 107°

The reader should *not* assume that there are *always* two possible angles when the sine rule is used to find a second angle in a triangle. The next example shows that this is not so.

Examples 7d (continued) _____

2. In the triangle XYZ, $\angle Y = 41°$, $XZ = 11$ cm and $YZ = 8$ cm.
Find $\angle X$.

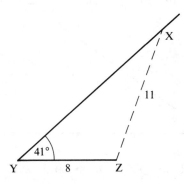

Using the part of the sine rule that involves x, y, $\angle X$ and $\angle Y$ we have

$$\frac{\sin X}{x} = \frac{\sin Y}{y} \quad \Rightarrow \quad \frac{\sin X}{8} = \frac{\sin 41°}{11}$$

Hence
$$\sin X = \frac{8 \times 0.6561}{11} = 0.4771$$

The two angles with a sine of 0.4771 are $28°$ and $152°$

Checking to see whether $152°$ is a possible value for $\angle X$ we see that

$$\angle X + \angle Y = 152° + 41° = 193°$$

This is greater than $180°$, so it is not possible for the angle X to have
the value $152°$.

In this case then, there is only one possible triangle containing the
given data, i.e. the triangle in which $\angle X = 28°$

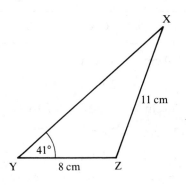

It is interesting to notice how the two different situations that arose in Examples 1 and 2 above can be illustrated by the construction of the triangles with the given data.

When AB = 5 cm, BC = 3 cm and ∠A = 35° we have

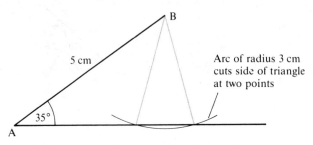

Arc of radius 3 cm cuts side of triangle at two points

When XZ = 11 cm, YZ = 8 cm and ∠Y = 41° we have

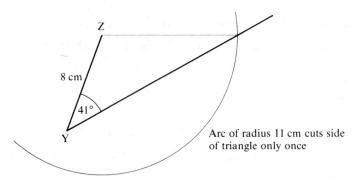

Arc of radius 11 cm cuts side of triangle only once

EXERCISE 7d

In each of the following questions, find the angle indicated by the question mark, giving two values in those cases where there are two possible triangles. Illustrate your solution to each question.

	AB	BC	CA	∠A	∠B	∠C
1.		2.9 cm	6.1 cm	?	40°	
2.	5.7 cm		2.3 cm		20°	?
3.	21 cm	36 cm		29.5°		?
4.		2.7 cm	3.8 cm	?	54°	
5.	4.6 cm		7.1 cm		?	33°
6.	9 cm	7 cm		?		40°

THE COSINE RULE

When solving a triangle, the sine rule cannot be used unless the data given includes one side and the angle opposite to that side. If, for example, a, b and C are given then in the sine rule we have

$$\frac{\boxed{a}}{\sin A} = \frac{\boxed{b}}{\sin B} = \frac{c}{\sin \boxed{C}}$$

and it is clear that no pair of fractions contains only one unknown quantity.

Some other method is therefore needed in such circumstances and the one we use is called the *cosine rule*. This rule states that

$$a^2 = b^2 + c^2 - 2bc \cos A$$

Proof

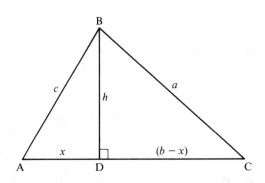

Let ABC be a non-right-angled triangle in which BD is drawn perpendicular to AC. Taking x as the length of AD, the length of CD is $(b - x)$. Then, using h as the length of BD, we can use Pythagoras' theorem to find h in each of the right-angled triangles BDA and BDC, i.e.

$$h^2 = c^2 - x^2 \quad \text{and} \quad h^2 = a^2 - (b - x)^2$$

Therefore $\qquad c^2 - x^2 = a^2 - (b - x)^2$

$\Rightarrow \qquad c^2 - x^2 = a^2 - b^2 + 2bx - x^2$

$\Rightarrow \qquad a^2 = b^2 + c^2 - 2bx$

But $x = c \cos A$

Therefore $\qquad a^2 = b^2 + c^2 - 2bc \cos A$

The proof is equally valid for an obtuse-angled triangle, as is shown overleaf.

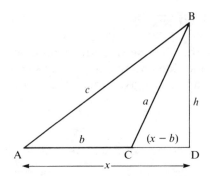

In this case the length of CD is $(x - b)$, so in $\triangle BCD$ we have

$$h^2 = a^2 - (x - b)^2 = a^2 - x^2 + 2bx - b^2$$

This is identical to the expression found for h^2 above.

The remainder of the proof above is unchanged so we have now proved that, in *any* triangle,

$$a^2 = b^2 + c^2 - 2bc \cos A$$

When the altitude is drawn from A or from C similar expressions for the other sides of a triangle are obtained, i.e.

$$b^2 = c^2 + a^2 - 2ca \cos B$$

and $\qquad\qquad c^2 = a^2 + b^2 - 2ab \cos C$

Examples 7e

1. In $\triangle ABC$, $BC = 7\,cm$, $AC = 9\,cm$ and $C = 61°$. Find AB.

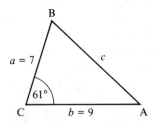

Using the cosine rule, starting with c^2, we have

$$c^2 = a^2 + b^2 - 2ab \cos C$$

$\Rightarrow \qquad\qquad c^2 = 7^2 + 9^2 - (2)(7)(9)(0.4848)$

$\Rightarrow \qquad\qquad c = 8.302$

Hence $AB = 8.30\,cm$ correct to 3 s.f.

2. XYZ is a triangle in which $\angle Y = 121°$, $XY = 14$ cm and $YZ = 26.9$ cm. Find XZ

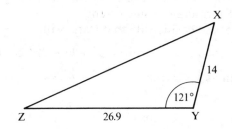

Using $y^2 = z^2 + x^2 - 2zx \cos Y$ gives

$$y^2 = (14)^2 + (26.9)^2 - (2)(14)(26.9)(-0.5150)$$

Note that, because Y is an obtuse angle, it has a negative cosine. Extra care therefore has to be taken with the sign of the term $-2zx \cos Y$. The best way to avoid mistakes is to enclose the cosine in brackets as shown.

Hence $y^2 = 1307.51 \implies y = 36.16$

Therefore XZ $= 36.2$ cm correct to 3 s.f.

EXERCISE 7e

In each question use the data given for $\triangle PQR$ to find the length of the third side.

	PQ	QR	RP	P	Q	R
1.		8 cm	4.6 cm			39°
2.	11.7 cm		9.2 cm	75°		
3.	29 cm	37 cm			109°	
4.		2.1 cm	3.2 cm			97°
5.	135 cm		98 cm	48°		
6.	4.7 cm	8.1 cm			138°	
7.		44 cm	62 cm			72°
8.	19.4 cm		12.6 cm	167°		

Using the Cosine Rule to Find an Angle

So far the cosine rule has been used only to find an unknown side of a triangle. When we want to find an unknown angle, it is advisable to rearrange the formula to some extent.

The version of the cosine rule that starts with c^2,

i.e. $$c^2 = a^2 + b^2 - 2ab \cos C$$

can be written as $\quad 2ab \cos C = a^2 + b^2 - c^2$

and further as $$\cos C = \frac{a^2 + b^2 - c^2}{2ab}$$

The reader should find this last form quite easy to remember if it is noted that the side opposite to the angle being found, c^2 in this case, appears only once as the last term in the formula. Some readers however may prefer to work from the basic cosine formula for all calculations, carrying out any necessary manipulation in each problem as it arises.

Examples 7f

1. If, in $\triangle ABC$, $a = 9$, $b = 16$ and $c = 11$, find, to the nearest degree, the largest angle in the triangle.

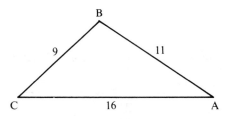

The largest angle in a triangle is opposite to the longest side, so in this question we are looking for angle B and we use

$$\cos B = \frac{c^2 + a^2 - b^2}{2ca}$$

$$= \frac{121 + 81 - 256}{(2)(11)(9)}$$

$$= -0.2727$$

The negative sign shows that $\angle B$ is obtuse.

Hence $B = 106°$ and this is the largest angle in $\triangle ABC$.

2. The sides a, b, c of a triangle ABC are in the ratio $3:6:5$ Find the smallest angle in the triangle.

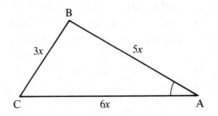

The actual lengths of the sides are not necessarily 3, 6 and 5 units so we represent them by $3x$, $6x$ and $5x$. The smallest angle is A (opposite to the smallest side).

$$\cos A = \frac{b^2 + c^2 - a^2}{2bc}$$

$$= \frac{36x^2 + 25x^2 - 9x^2}{60x^2}$$

$$= \frac{52}{60}$$

$$= 0.8667$$

Therefore the smallest angle in $\triangle$ABC is $30°$

EXERCISE 7f

1. In $\triangle$XYZ, XY $= 34$ cm, YZ $= 29$ cm and ZX $= 21$ cm. Find the smallest angle in the triangle.

2. In $\triangle$PQR, PQ $= 1.3$ cm, QR $= 1.8$ cm and RP $= 1.5$ cm. Find $\angle$Q.

3. In $\triangle$ABC, AB $= 51$ cm, BC $= 37$ cm and CA $= 44$ cm. Find $\angle$A.

4. Find the largest angle in $\triangle$XYZ given that $x = 91$, $y = 77$ and $z = 43$

5. What is the size of (a) the smallest, (b) the largest angle in $\triangle$ABC if $a = 13$, $b = 18$ and $c = 7$?

6. In △PQR the sides PQ, QR and RP are in the ratio 2:1:2 Find ∠P.

7. ABCD is a quadrilateral in which AB = 5 cm, BC = 8 cm, CD = 11 cm, DA = 9 cm and angle ABC = 120° Find the length of AC and the size of the angle ADC.

GENERAL TRIANGLE CALCULATIONS

If three independent facts are given about the sides and/or angles of a triangle and further facts are required, a choice must be made between using the sine rule or the cosine rule for the first step.

As the sine rule is easier to work out, it is preferred to the cosine rule whenever the given facts make this possible, i.e. whenever an angle and the opposite side are known. (Remember that if two angles are given, then the third angle is also known.)

The cosine rule is used only when the sine rule is not suitable and it is never necessary to use it more than once in solving a triangle.

Suppose, for example, that the triangle PQR given below is to be solved.

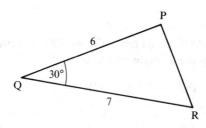

Only one angle is known and the side opposite to it is not given. We must therefore use the cosine rule first to find the length of PR.

Once we know q as well as ∠Q, the sine rule can be used to find either of the remaining angles, the third angle then following from the sum of the angles in the triangle.

EXERCISE 7g

Each of the following questions refers to a triangle ABC. Fill in the blank spaces in the table.

	$\angle$A	$\angle$B	$\angle$C	a	b	c
1.		80°	50°			68 cm
2.			112°	15.7 cm	13 cm	
3.	41°	69°		12.3 cm		
4.	58°				131 cm	87 cm
5.		49°	94°		206 cm	
6.	115°		31°			21 cm
7.	59°	78°		17 cm		
8.		48°	80°		31.3 cm	
9.	77°				19 cm	24 cm
10.		125°		14 cm		20 cm

11. A tower stands on level ground. From a point P on the ground, the angle of elevation of the top of the tower is 26° Another point Q is 3 m vertically above P and from this point the angle of elevation of the top of the tower is 21° Find the height of the tower.

12. A survey of a triangular field, bounded by straight fences, found the three sides to be of lengths 100 m, 80 m and 65 m. Find the angles between the boundary fences.

MIXED EXERCISE 7

1. Find the value, between 0° and 180°, of $\angle$A if
   (a) $\cos A = -\cos 64°$ (b) $\sin 94° = \sin A$

2. If $\angle$X is acute and $\sin X = \frac{7}{25}$, find $\cos(180° - X)$

3. Given that $\sin A = \frac{5}{8}$, find $\tan A$ in surd form if
   (a) $\angle$A is acute   (b) $\angle$A is obtuse

4. Find, in surd form, $\sin \theta$ and $\cos \theta$, given

(a)   (b)

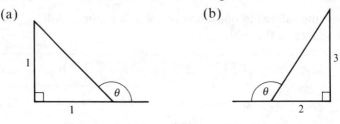

5. Given that $\sin X = \frac{12}{13}$ and X is obtuse, find $\cos X$.

6. In $\triangle ABC$, BC = 11 cm, $\angle B = 53°$ and $\angle A = 76°$, find AC.

7. In $\triangle PQR$, $p = 3$, $q = 5$ and R = 69°, find r

8. In $\triangle XYZ$, XY = 8 cm, YZ = 7 cm and ZX = 10 cm, find $\angle Y$.

9. In $\triangle ABC$, AB = 7 cm, BC = 6 cm and $\angle A = 44°$, find all possible values of $\angle ACB$.

10. Find the angles of a triangle whose sides are in the ratio $2:4:5$

11. Use the cosine formula, $\cos A = \dfrac{b^2 + c^2 - a^2}{2bc}$, to show that

(a) $\angle A$ is acute if $a^2 < b^2 + c^2$
(b) $\angle A$ is obtuse if $a^2 > b^2 + c^2$

CHAPTER 8

TRIANGLES

THE AREA OF A TRIANGLE

The simplest way to find the area of a triangle is to use the formula

Area $= \frac{1}{2}$ base $\times$ perpendicular height

Clearly this is of immediate use only when the perpendicular height is known. It can be adapted, however, to cover other cases.

Consider the triangle shown below, in which b, c, and A are known

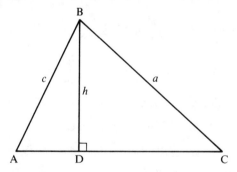

The line BD, drawn from B perpendicular to AC, is the height, h, of the triangle, so the area of the triangle is $\frac{1}{2}bh$

In the triangle ADB, $\qquad \sin A = \dfrac{h}{c} \;\Rightarrow\; h = c \sin A$

Therefore the area of triangle ABC is

$$\tfrac{1}{2}bc \sin A$$

Drawing the perpendicular heights from A to C give similar expressions, i.e.

Area of triangle ABC $= \frac{1}{2}ab \sin C = \frac{1}{2}ac \sin B$

Each of these formulae can be expressed in the 'easy to remember' form

Area $= \frac{1}{2}$ product of two sides $\times$ sine of included angle

Example 8a

Find the area of triangle PQR, given that P = 65°, Q = 79° and PQ = 30 cm.

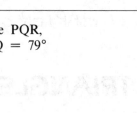

The given facts do not include two sides and the included angle so we must first find another side. To do this the sine rule can be used and we need angle R.

$$\angle R = 180° - 65° - 79° = 36°$$

From the sine rule, $\dfrac{p}{\sin P} = \dfrac{r}{\sin R}$

$\Rightarrow$ $p = \dfrac{30 \times \sin 65°}{\sin 36°} = 46.26$

i.e. QR = 46.3 cm (correct to 3 s.f.).

Now we can use   area PQR $= \frac{1}{2}pr \sin Q$

$$\tfrac{1}{2}pr \sin Q = \tfrac{1}{2} \times 46.26 \times 30 \times \sin 79 = 681.2$$

So the area of triangle PQR is 681 cm^2 (corr to 3 s.f.).

EXERCISE 8a

Find the area of each triangle given in Questions 1 to 5.

1. $\triangle$XYZ; XY = 180 cm, YZ = 145 cm, $\angle$Y = 70°

2. $\triangle$ABC; AB = 75 cm, AC = 66 cm, $\angle$A = 62°

3. $\triangle$PQR; QR = 69 cm, PR = 49 cm, $\angle$R = 85°

4. $\triangle$XYZ; x = 30, y = 40, $\angle$Z = 49°

5. $\triangle$PQR; p = 9, r = 11, $\angle$Q = 120°

6. In triangle ABC, AB = 6 cm, BC = 7 cm and CA = 9 cm. Find $\angle$A and the area of the triangle.

7. △PQR is such that ∠P = 60°, ∠R = 50° and QR = 12 cm. Find PQ and the area of the triangle.

8. In △XYZ, XY = 150 cm, YZ = 185 cm and the area is 11 000 cm². Find ∠Y and XZ.

9. The area of triangle ABC is 36.4 cm². Given that AC = 14 cm and ∠A = 98°, find AB.

PROBLEMS

Many practical problems which involve distances and angles can be illustrated by a diagram. Often, however, this diagram contains too many lines, dimensions, etc. to be clear enough to work from. In these cases we can draw a second figure by extracting a triangle (or triangles) in which three facts about sides and/or angles are known. The various methods given in Chapter 7 can then be used to analyse this triangle and so to solve the problem.

Examples 8b

1. Two boats, P and Q, are 300 m apart. The base, A, of a lighthouse is in line with PQ. From the top, B, of the lighthouse the angles of depression of P and Q are found to be 35° and 48°. Write down the values of the angles BQA, PBQ and BPQ and find, correct to the nearest metre, the height of the lighthouse.

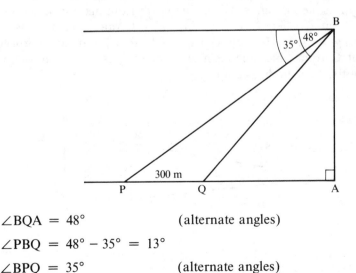

∠BQA = 48°   (alternate angles)

∠PBQ = 48° − 35° = 13°

∠BPQ = 35°   (alternate angles)

Now we can extract △PBQ, knowing two angles and a side.

From the sine rule,

$$\frac{p}{\sin P} = \frac{b}{\sin B}$$

∴ $$p = \frac{(300)(\sin 35°)}{\sin 13°}$$

$$= 764.9$$

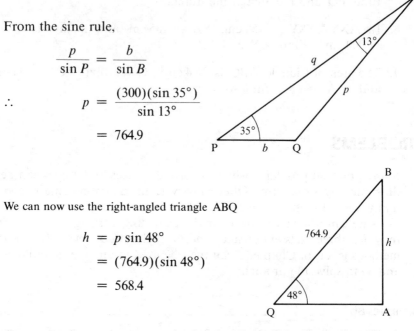

We can now use the right-angled triangle ABQ

$$h = p \sin 48°$$

$$= (764.9)(\sin 48°)$$

$$= 568.4$$

Correct to the nearest metre the height of the light-house is 568 m

2. A traveller pitches camp in a desert. He knows that there is an oasis in the distance, but cannot see it. Wishing to know how far away it is, he measures 250 m due north from his starting point, A, to a point B where he can see the oasis, O, and finds that its bearing is 276°. He then measures a further 250 m due north to point C from which the bearing of the oasis is 260°. Find how far from the oasis he has camped.

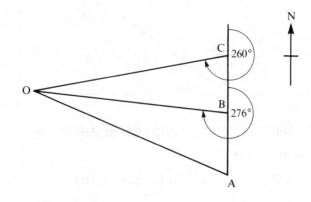

$\angle OCB = 260° - 180° = 80°$ and $\angle OBC = 360° - 276° = 84°$

As two angles and a side are known, $\triangle OBC$ can be used.

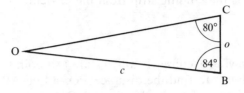

$\angle BOC = 180° - 80° - 84° = 16°$

From the sine rule, $\dfrac{c}{\sin C} = \dfrac{o}{\sin O}$

$\Rightarrow$ $\qquad\qquad\qquad c = \dfrac{250 \times \sin 80°}{\sin 16°} = 893.2$

Now in $\triangle ABO$, $\angle ABO = 276° - 180° = 96°$ and we also know OB and AB. As two sides and the included angle are known, it is the cosine rule that must be used.

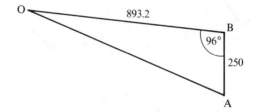

$$OA^2 = OB^2 + AB^2 - 2 \times OB \times AB \times \cos ABO$$

$$= (893.2)^2 + (250)^2 - 2 \times 893.2 \times 250 \times \cos 96°$$

$$= 906\,989$$

$\Rightarrow$ $\qquad OA = 952.4$

To the nearest metre the initial distance from the oasis was 952 m

---

EXERCISE 8b

1. In a quadrilateral PQRS, PQ = 6 cm, QR = 7 cm, RS = 9 cm, $\angle PQR = 115°$ and $\angle PRS = 80°$. Find the length of PR. Considering it as split into two separate triangles, find the area of the quadrilateral PQRS.

2. A light aircraft flies from an airfield, A, a distance of 50 km on a bearing of 049° to a town, B. The pilot then changes course and flies on a bearing of 172° to a landing strip, C, 68 km from B. How far is the landing strip from the airfield?

3. In a surveying exercise, P and Q are two points on land which is inaccessible. To find the distance PQ, a line AB of length 300 metres is marked out so that P and Q are on opposite sides of AB. The directions of P and Q relative to the line AB are then measured and are shown in the diagram. Calculate the length of PQ. (Hint. Find AP and AQ.)

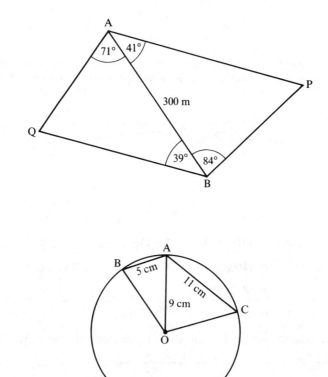

4.

AB, of length 5 cm, and AC, of length 11 cm, are two chords of a circle with centre O and radius 9 cm. Find each of the angles BAO and CAO and hence calculate the area of the triangle ABC.

5.

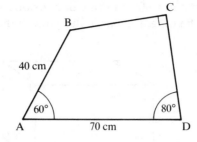

The diagram shows the cross section of a beam of length 2 m.
Calculate

(a) the length of BD
(b) the angle ADB
(c) the length of CD
(d) the area of the cross section
(e) the volume of the beam.

THREE-DIMENSIONAL PROBLEMS

One of the difficulties which many people experience with this topic,
arises when attempting to illustrate a three-dimensional situation on a
two-dimensional diagram. The following hints may help in producing
a clear representation of the 3-D problem from which appropriate
calculations can be made.

1) Vertical lines should be drawn vertically on the page.

2) Lines in the East–West direction should be drawn horizontally on
the page. North–South lines are shown as inclined at an acute angle
to the East direction.

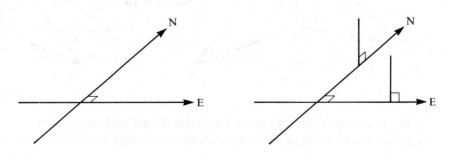

3) All angles that are 90° in three dimensions should be marked as right angles on the diagram, particularly those that do not *appear* to be 90°

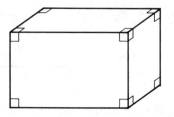

4) Perspective drawing is rarely used, so parallel lines are drawn parallel in the diagram.

5) When viewing a 3-D object, some of its sides are usually not visible. It is helpful to indicate these by broken lines.

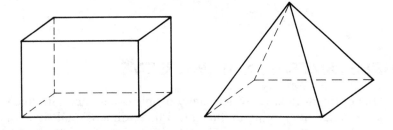

6) In a situation involving two points in the foreground and an object in the background it is usually clearer to draw the object *between* the two points.

e.g.

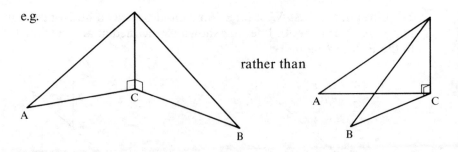

rather than

7) It is often helpful to draw a separate diagram showing each individual triangle in which calculations are needed.

The following facts and definitions should also be known.

1) Two non-parallel planes meet in a line called the common line.

2) A line that is perpendicular to a plane is also perpendicular to every line in that plane

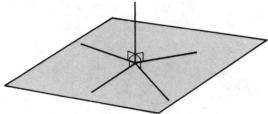

and if a line is perpendicular to two non-parallel lines in a plane, then it is perpendicular to the plane.

3) The angle between a line and a plane is defined as the angle between that line and its projection on the plane. (Its projection can be thought of as the shadow of the line cast on the plane by a beam of light shining at right-angles to the plane.)

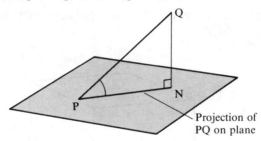

4) The angle between two planes is defined as follows. From any point A, on the common line of two planes P_1 and P_2, lines AB and AC are drawn, one in each plane, perpendicular to the common line. Then angle BAC is the angle between the two planes.

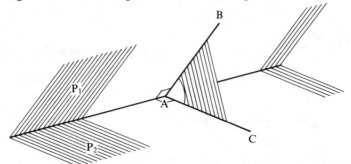

5) If, in fact 4, one of the planes, P_2 say, is horizontal, then AB is called *a line of greatest slope* of the plane P_1

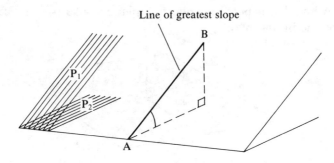

Line of greatest slope

Examples 8c _____

1. The diagram shows a cube of side 6 cm. M is the midpoint of AB. Find

   (a) the length of MC   (b) the length of MR

   (c) to the nearest degree, the angle between MR and the plane ABCD.

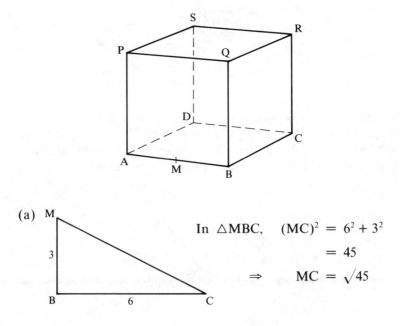

(a)

In △MBC, $(MC)^2 = 6^2 + 3^2$

$= 45$

$\Rightarrow \quad MC = \sqrt{45}$

Therefore the length of MC is 6.71 cm (correct to 3.s.f).

(b)

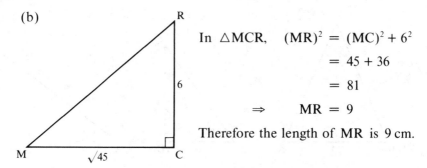

In $\triangle MCR$, $(MR)^2 = (MC)^2 + 6^2$

$= 45 + 36$

$= 81$

$\Rightarrow \quad MR = 9$

Therefore the length of MR is 9 cm.

To find the angle between RM and the plane ABCD, we need the projection of RM on the plane. As RC is perpendicular to ABCD, it follows that CM is the projection of RM on that plane. So the angle we are looking for is RMC.

(c)

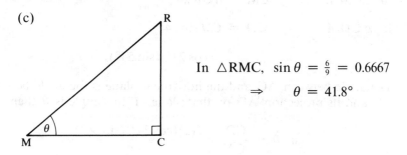

In $\triangle RMC$, $\sin\theta = \frac{6}{9} = 0.6667$

$\Rightarrow \quad \theta = 41.8°$

Therefore, to the nearest degree, the angle between RM and the plane ABCD is 42°

---

2. The base AB of an isosceles triangle ABC is horizontal. The plane containing the triangle is inclined to the horizontal at 54° If the angle ACB is 48°, find the angle between AC and the horizontal plane.

AB is the line common to the horizontal plane and the plane of the triangle and M is its midpoint. Because the triangle is isosceles, CM is perpendicular to AB. So CM is a line of greatest slope and therefore makes an angle of 54° with its projection, MD, on the horizontal plane.

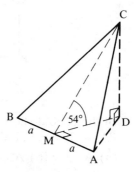

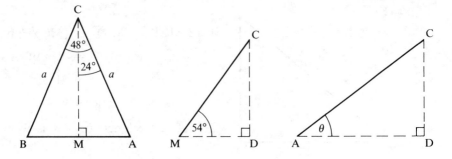

Let the length of AC and BC be *a*

In △CMA,   CM = *a* cos 24°

In △CDM,   CD = *CM* sin 54°

                        = (*a* cos 24°)(sin 54°)

The angle between AC and the horizontal plane is the angle between
AC and its projection AD on that plane. If this angle is θ then

$$\sin \theta = \frac{CD}{CA} = \frac{(a)(\cos 24°)(\sin 54°)}{a}$$

⇒ $\theta = 47.7°$

EXERCISE 8c

1.

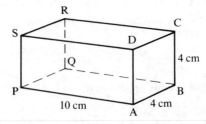

In the cuboid shown above, ABCD is a square of side 4 cm and
PA = 10 cm. Find the length of
(a) AC   (b) AS   (c) AQ   (d) a diagonal of the cuboid.

2.

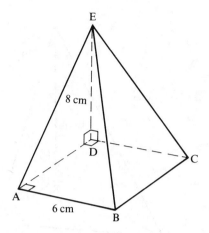

The pyramid ABCDE has a square base of side 6 cm. E is 8 cm vertically above D. Calculate

(a) the lengths of AD, BD and BE

(b) the angle between AE and the plane ABCD

(c) the angle between BE and the plane ABCD

(d) the angle between the planes EBC and ABCD.

3.

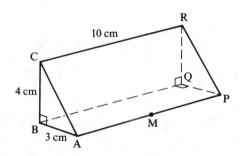

Given the triangular prism in the diagram, in which M is the midpoint of AP, find the following lengths and angles.

(a) RM   (b) RA   (c) QA

(d) the angle between RA and the plane ABQP

(e) the angle between RM and the plane ABQP.

4. Given a regular tetrahedron (i.e. a pyramid where each face is an equilateral triangle), find the cosine of the angle between two of the faces.

5.

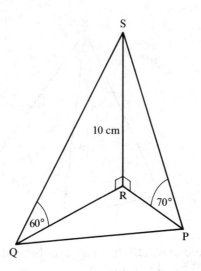

Three points, P, Q and R lie in a plane. The line RS is perpendicular to the plane and is of length 10 cm. If angle SPR = 70°, angle SQR = 60° and PQ = 7 cm, calculate each of the angles in triangle PQR.

6. Find the angle between two diagonals of a cube.

7.

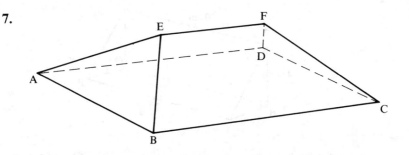

The diagram shows a roof whose base is a rectangle of length 15 m and width 9 m. Each end face is an isosceles triangle inclined to the horizontal at an angle, α, and each long face is a trapezium inclined to the horizontal at an angle β
If $\tan \alpha = 2$ and $\tan \beta = \frac{4}{3}$, calculate

(a) the height of the ridge (EF) above the base

(b) the length of the ridge

(c) the angle between AE and the horizontal

(d) the total surface area of the roof.

8.

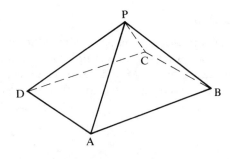

The diagram shows a solid figure in which ABCD is a horizontal
rectangle. AB = 13 cm, BC = 8 cm, AP = DP = 9 cm and
BP = CP = 7 cm. Calculate

(a) the length of AC

(b) the height of P above the plane ABCD

(c) the angle between AP and the horizontal

(d) the angle between the faces APB and ABCD.

9. An aircraft is noted simultaneously by three observers, A, B and
C, stationed in a horizontal straight line. AB and BC are each
200 m and the noted angles of elevation of the aircraft from A
and C are 25° and 40° respectively. What is the height of the
aircraft? Find also the angle of elevation of the aircraft from B.

10.

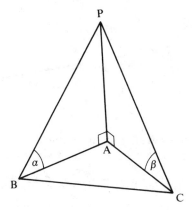

ABC is a horizontal triangle in which BC = 10 m. P is a point
12 m vertically above A. The angles of elevation of P from B
and C are α and β, where $\tan \alpha = 1$ and $\tan \beta = \frac{6}{7}$. Find
the angle between the planes PBC and ABC.

Harder Problems

Certain problems in three dimensions are rather more demanding than those seen up to now. An example of such a problem is given below and, in the following Mixed Exercise, Questions 8 to 10 are also a little harder. It is recommended that they be used at a later date for revision.

Example 8d _____

A, B and C are points on a horizontal line such that AB = 60 m and BC = 30 m. The angles of elevation, from A, B and C respectively, of the top of a clock tower are α, β, and γ, where $\tan\alpha = \frac{1}{13}$, $\tan\beta = \frac{1}{15}$ and $\tan\gamma = \frac{1}{20}$. The foot of the tower is at the same level as A, B and C. Find the height of the tower.

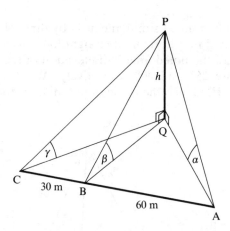

If the height of the tower, PQ, is h then

$$h = QA \tan\alpha = QB \tan\beta = QC \tan\gamma$$

i.e. $$h = \frac{QA}{13} = \frac{QB}{15} = \frac{QC}{20}$$

$\Rightarrow$ QA = 13h,   QB = 15h,   QC = 20h

Now considering the base triangle ABCQ, we have

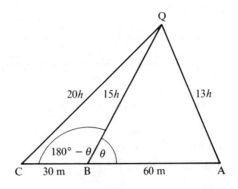

Using the cosine rule in $\triangle ABQ$ gives

$$\cos\theta = \frac{(60)^2 + (15h)^2 - (13h)^2}{2(60)(15h)}$$

and using the cosine rule in $\triangle CBQ$ gives

$$\cos(180° - \theta) = -\cos\theta = \frac{(30)^2 + (15h)^2 - (20h)^2}{2(30)(15h)}$$

$\therefore$ $$\frac{(60)^2 + (15h)^2 - (13h)^2}{2(60)(15h)} = \frac{(20h)^2 - (30)^2 - (15h)^2}{2(30)(15h)}$$

$\Rightarrow$ $$3600 + 56h^2 = 2(175h^2 - 900)$$

$\Rightarrow$ $$5400 = 294h^2$$

Hence $$h = 4.285$$

The height of the clock tower is 4.29 m (correct to 3 s.f.).

MIXED EXERCISE 8

1. In $\triangle PQR$, $PQ = 11\,cm$, $PR = 14\,cm$ and $QPR = 100°$. Find the area of the triangle.

2. The area of ABC is $9\,cm^2$. If $AB = AC = 6\,cm$, find $\sin A$. Are there two possible triangles? Give a reason for your answer.

3.

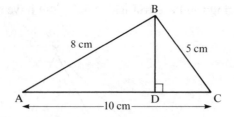

Given the information in the diagram,

(a) find ∠ABC

(b) find the area of △ABC

(c) *hence* find the length of BD.

4. Triangle PQR, in which PRQ = 120°, lies in a horizontal plane and X is a point 6 cm vertically above R. If XQR = 45° and XPR = 60°, find the lengths of the sides of △PQR. Find also the area of this triangle.

5.

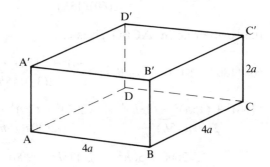

Given the cuboid shown in the diagram, find

(a) the angle between AC and the plane ABB′A′

(b) the angle between the planes ACD′ and ABCD.

6. Two rectangular panels, ABCD and ABEF, each measure 1.5 m by 2 m. They are hinged along the edge AB which is 2 m long. If the angle between their planes is 60°, find the angle between the diagonals AC and AE.

7. A river running due east has straight parallel banks. A vertical post stands with its base, P, on the north bank of the river. On the south bank are two surveyors, A who is to the east, and B who is to the west of the post. A and B are at a distance $\frac{2}{7}a$ apart and the angle APB is 150° The angles of elevation from A and B of the top, Q, of the post are 45° and 30° Find, in terms of a, the width of the river and the height of the post.

The remaining questions are a little more demanding.

8. ABCD is a tetrahedron whose horizontal base ABC is an equilateral triangle. The angle between each pair of slant edges is θ where $\tan \theta = \frac{5}{12}$ and the length of these edges is a. Find the height of D above ABC.

9. Two lamp standards are each of height h m. They are d m apart on level ground where a man of height t m is also standing. Each light casts a shadow of the man on the ground. Prove that, no matter where the man stands, the distance between the ends of his two shadows is $\dfrac{dt}{h-t}$ m. (Hint. Look for similar triangles.)

10. The roof of a south-facing house slopes down at an angle α to the horizontal. A gulley at the end of the roof is in the direction θ east of north. If the gulley is inclined to the horizontal at an angle β, show that $\tan \beta = \tan \alpha \cos \theta$

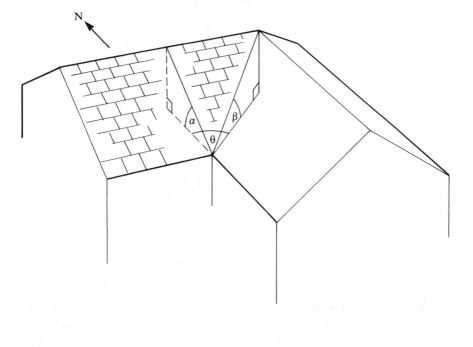

STRAIGHT LINES 1

THE MEANING OF EQUATIONS

The Cartesian frame of reference provides a means of defining the position of any point in a plane. This plane is called the xy-plane.

In general x and y are independent variables. This means that they can each take any value independently of the value of the other unless some restriction is placed on them.

Consider the case when the value of x is restricted to 2

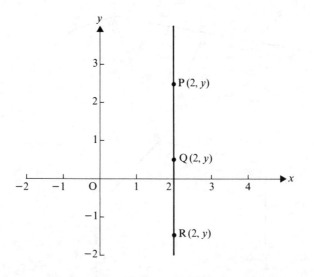

As the value of y is not restricted, the condition above gives a set of points which form a straight line parallel to the y-axis and passing through P, Q and R as shown. Therefore the condition that x is equal to 2, i.e. $x = 2$, defines the line through P, Q and R, i.e.

in the context of the xy-plane, the equation $x = 2$ defines the line shown in the diagram. Further, $x = 2$ is called *the equation of this line* and we can refer briefly to *the line* $x = 2$

Now consider the set of points for which the condition is $x > 2$

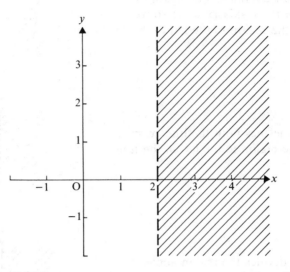

All the points to the right of the line $x = 2$ have an x-coordinate that is greater than 2

So the inequality $x > 2$ defines the shaded region of the xy-plane shown above.
Similarly, the inequality $x < 2$ defines the region left unshaded in the diagram.

✶ Note that the region defined by $x > 2$ does not include the line $x = 2$

> When a region does not include a boundary line this is drawn as a broken line. When the points on a boundary *are* included in a region, this boundary is drawn as a solid line.

Example 9a _____

Draw a sketch of the region of the xy-plane defined by the inequalities $0 \leqslant x \leqslant 2$ and $0 < y < 4$

The relationship $0 \leqslant x \leqslant 2$ contains two inequalities which must be considered separately, i.e. $x \geqslant 0$ and $x \leqslant 2$. Similarly, $0 < y < 4$ contains two relationships, i.e. $y > 0$ and $y < 4$. The required region is found by considering each inequality in turn and shading the unwanted region. This leaves the required region clear.

$x \geqslant 0$ defines both the line $x = 0$ (i.e. the y-axis) and the region to the right of the y-axis ($x > 0$) so we shade the region to the left of the y-axis.

$x \leqslant 2$ defines both the line $x = 2$ and the region to the left of the line.

$y > 0$ defines the region above the x-axis, but does not include the x-axis.

$y < 4$ defines the region below the line $y = 4$ but does not include the line $y = 4$

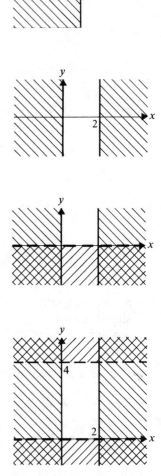

Therefore the unshaded region in the bottom figure, including the solid boundary lines but not the broken ones, is the set of points that satisfy all the given inequalities.

Note that in this book, we use the convention of shading unwanted regions when dealing with more than one inequality in a plane. This convention is not universal and some problems ask for such a diagram to be drawn with the required region shaded. In this case we recommend that the reader follows the procedure used in the worked example and then redraws the diagram to shade the required region.

EXERCISE 9a

1. Draw a sketch showing the lines defined by the equations $x = 5$, $x = -3$, $y = 0$, $y = 6$

2. Draw a sketch showing the lines defined by the equations $y = -3$, $y = -10$, $x = 7$, $x = -5$

Draw a sketch showing the region of the xy-plane defined by the following inequalities.

3. $x > 3$ 4. $y \leqslant 2$ 5. $x \geqslant -8$

6. $0 < x < 5$ 7. $-1 < y < 4$ 8. $-2 \leqslant x < 2$

9. $0 \leqslant x \leqslant 5, -1 \leqslant y \leqslant 3$ 10. $x \leqslant -3, x \geqslant 4, y < -2$

THE EQUATION OF A STRAIGHT LINE

A straight line may be defined in many ways; for example, a line passes through the origin and has a gradient of $\frac{1}{2}$.

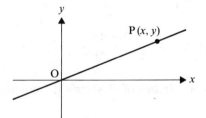

The point $P(x, y)$ is on this line if and only if the gradient of OP is $\frac{1}{2}$

In terms of x and y, the gradient of OP is $\dfrac{y}{x}$, so the statement above can be written in the form

$P(x, y)$ is on the line if and only if $\quad \dfrac{y}{x} = \dfrac{1}{2}$, i.e. $2y = x$

Therefore the coordinates of points on the line satisfy the relationship $2y = x$, and the coordinates of points that are not on the line do not satisfy this relationship.

$2y = x$ is called the equation of the line.

The equation of a line (straight or curved) is a relationship between the x and y coordinates of all points on the line and which is not satisfied by any other point in the plane.

Examples 9b _____

1. Find the equation of the line through the points (1, −2) and (−2, 4).

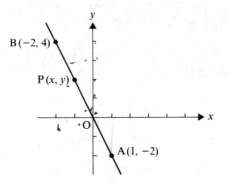

$P(x, y)$ is on the line if and only if the gradient of PA is equal to the gradient of AB (or PB).

The gradient of PA is $\dfrac{y - (-2)}{x - 1} = \dfrac{y + 2}{x - 1}$

The gradient of AB is $\dfrac{-2 - 4}{1 - (-2)} = -2$

Therefore the coordinates of P satisfy the equation $\dfrac{y + 2}{x - 1} = -2$

i.e. $\qquad\qquad\qquad\qquad y + 2x = 0$

Consider the more general case of the line whose gradient is m and which cuts the y-axis at a directed distance c from the origin. Note that c is called the *intercept* on the y-axis.

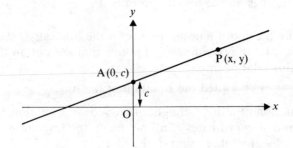

Now $P(x, y)$ is on this line if and only if the gradient of AP is m

Therefore the coordinates of P satisfy the equation $\dfrac{y - c}{x - 0} = m$

i.e. $\qquad\qquad\qquad\qquad y = mx + c$

This is the *standard form* for the equation of a straight line.

An equation of the form $y = mx + c$ represents a straight line with gradient m and intercept c on the y-axis.

Because the value of m and/or c may be fractional, this equation can be rearranged and expressed as $ax + by + c = 0$, i.e.

$$ax + by + c = 0$$

where a, b and c are constants, is the equation of a straight line.

Note that in this form c is *not* the intercept.

Examples 9b (continued)

2. Write down the gradient of the line $3x - 4y + 2 = 0$ and find the equation of the line through the origin which is perpendicular to the given line.

Rearranging $3x - 4y + 2 = 0$ in the standard form gives

$$y = \tfrac{3}{4}x + \tfrac{1}{2}$$

Comparing with $y = mx + c$ we see that the gradient (m) of the line is $\tfrac{3}{4}$ (and the intercept on the y-axis is $\tfrac{1}{2}$).

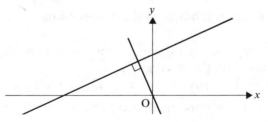

The gradient of the perpendicular line is given by $-\dfrac{1}{m} = -\dfrac{4}{3}$

and it passes through the origin so the intercept on the y-axis is 0

Therefore its equation is $\qquad y = -\tfrac{4}{3}x + 0$

$\Rightarrow \qquad\qquad\qquad\qquad 4y + 3x = 0$

3. Sketch the line $x - 2y + 3 = 0$

This line can be located accurately in the xy-plane when we know two points on the line. We will use the intercepts on the axes as these can be found easily (i.e. $x = 0 \Rightarrow y = \frac{3}{2}$ and $y = 0 \Rightarrow x = -3$).

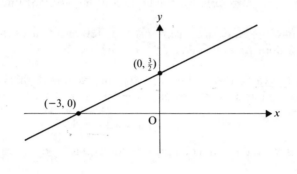

Notice that the diagrams in the worked examples are sketches, not accurate plots, but they show reasonably accurately the position of the lines in the plane.

EXERCISE 9b

1. Write down the equation of the line through the origin and with gradient

(a) 2   (b) -1 (c) $\frac{1}{3}$ (d) $-\frac{1}{4}$ (e) 0   (f) ∞

Draw a sketch showing all these lines on the same set of axes.

2. Write down the equation of the line passing through the given point and with the given gradient.

(a) $(0, 1), \frac{1}{2}$ (b) $(0, 0), -\frac{2}{3}$ (c) $(-1, -4), 4$

Draw a sketch showing all these lines on the same set of axes.

3. Write down the equation of the line passing through the points

(a) $(0, 0), (2, 1)$ (b) $(1, 4), (3, 0)$ (c) $(-1, 3), (-4, -3)$

4. Write down the equation of the line passing through the origin and perpendicular to

(a) $y = 2x + 3$ (b) $3x + 2y - 4 = 0$ (c) $x - 2y + 3 = 0$

5. Write down the equation of the line passing through $(2, 1)$ and perpendicular to

   (a) $3x + y - 2 = 0$ (b) $2x - 4y - 1 = 0$

   Draw a sketch showing all four lines on the same set of axes.

6. Write down the equation of the line passing through $(3, -2)$ and parallel to

   (a) $5x - y + 3 = 0$ (b) $x + 7y - 5 = 0$

7. $A(1, 5)$ and $B(4, 9)$ are two adjacent vertices of a square. Find the equation of the line on which the side BC of the square lies. How long are the sides of this square?

Formulae for Finding the Equation of a Line

Straight lines play a major role in graphical analysis and it is important to be able to find their equations easily. This section gives two formulae derived from the commonest ways in which a straight line is defined.

The appropriate formula can then be used to write down the equation of a particular line.

The equation of a line with gradient m and passing through the point (x_1, y_1)

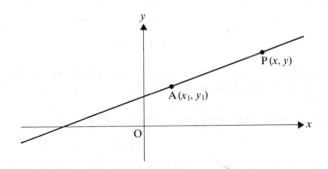

$P(x, y)$ is a point on the line if and only if the gradient of AP is m

i.e.
$$\frac{y - y_1}{x - x_1} = m$$

$\Rightarrow$
$$y - y_1 = m(x - x_1) \qquad [1]$$

The equation of the line passing through (x_1, y_1) and (x_2, y_2)

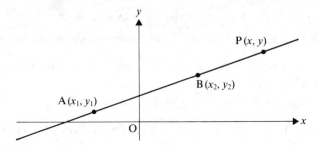

The gradient of AB is $\dfrac{y_2 - y_1}{x_2 - x_1}$

so the formula given in [1] becomes

$$y - y_1 = \left[\frac{y_2 - y_1}{x_2 - x_1}\right](x - x_1) \tag{2}$$

Examples 9c

1. Find the equation of the line with gradient $-\frac{1}{3}$ and passing through $(2, -1)$

Using [1] with $m = -\frac{1}{3}$, $x_1 = 2$ and $y_1 = -1$ gives

$$y - (-1) = -\tfrac{1}{3}(x - 2)$$

$$\Rightarrow \qquad x + 3y + 1 = 0$$

Alternatively the equation of this line can be found from the standard form of the equation of a straight line, i.e. $y = mx + c$

Using $y = mx + c$ and $m = -\frac{1}{3}$ we have

$$y = -\tfrac{1}{3}x + c$$

The point $(2, -1)$ lies on this line so its coordinates satisfy the equation, i.e.

$$-1 = -\tfrac{1}{3}(2) + c \quad \Rightarrow \quad c = -\tfrac{1}{3}$$

Therefore $$y = -\tfrac{1}{3}x - \tfrac{1}{3}$$

$$\Rightarrow \qquad x + 3y + 1 = 0$$

2. Find the equation of the line through the points $(1, -2)$, $(3, 5)$

Using formula [2] with $x_1 = 1$, $y_1 = -2$, $x_2 = 3$ and $y_2 = 5$
gives

$$y - (-2) = \frac{-2 - 5}{1 - 3}(x - 1)$$

$\Rightarrow \qquad \qquad 7x - 2y - 11 = 0$

The worked examples in this book necessarily contain a lot of explanation but this should not mislead readers into thinking that their solutions must be equally long. The temptation to 'overwork' a problem should be avoided, particularly in the case of coordinate geometry problems which are basically simple. With practice, any of the methods illustrated above enable the equation of a straight line to be written down directly.

---

3. Find the equation of the line through $(1, 2)$ which is perpendicular to the line $3x - 7y + 2 = 0$

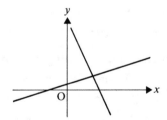

Expressing $3x - 7y + 2 = 0$ in standard form gives $y = \frac{3}{7}x + \frac{2}{7}$

Hence the given line has gradient $\frac{3}{7}$.

So the required line has a gradient of $-\frac{7}{3}$ and it passes through $(1, 2)$

Using $y - y_1 = m(x - x_1)$ gives its equation as

$$y - 2 = -\tfrac{7}{3}(x - 1) \qquad \Rightarrow \qquad 7x + 3y - 13 = 0$$

In the last example note that the line perpendicular to

$$3x - 7y + 2 = 0$$

has equation $7x + 3y - 13 = 0$

i.e. the coefficients of x and y have been transposed and the sign between the x and y terms has changed. This is a particular example of the general fact that

> given a line with equation $ax + by + c = 0$ then the equation of any perpendicular line is $bx - ay + k = 0$

This property of perpendicular lines can be used to shorten the working of problems,
e.g. to find the equation of the line passing through $(2, -6)$ which is perpendicular to the line $5x - y + 3 = 0$, we can say that the required line has an equation of the form $y + 5x + k = 0$ and then use the fact that the coordinates $(2, -6)$ satisfy this equation to find the value of k.

EXERCISE 9c

1. Find the equation of the line with the given gradient and passing through the given point.
   (a) 3, $(4, 9)$ (b) -5, $(2, -4)$ (c) $\frac{1}{4}$, $(4, 0)$
   (d) 0, $(-1, 5)$ (e) $-\frac{2}{5}$, $(\frac{1}{2}, 4)$ (f) $-\frac{3}{8}$, $(\frac{22}{5}, -\frac{5}{2})$

2. Find the equation of the line passing through the points
   (a) $(0, 1)$, $(2, 4)$ (b) $(-1, 2)$, $(1, 5)$ (c) $(3, -1)$, $(3, 2)$

3. Determine which of the following pairs of lines are perpendicular.
   (a) $x - 2y + 4 = 0$ and $2x + y - 3 = 0$
   (b) $x + 3y - 6 = 0$ and $3x + y + 2 = 0$
   (c) $x + 3y - 2 = 0$ and $y = 3x + 2$
   (d) $y + 2x + 1 = 0$ and $x = 2y - 4$

4. Find the equation of the line through the point $(5, 2)$ and perpendicular to the line $x - y + 2 = 0$

5. Find the equation of the perpendicular bisector of the line joining
   (a) $(0, 0)$, $(2, 4)$ (b) $(3, -1)$, $(-5, 2)$ (c) $(5, -1)$, $(0, 7)$

6. Find the equation of the line through the origin which is parallel to the line $4x + 2y - 5 = 0$

7. The line $4x - 5y + 20 = 0$ cuts the x-axis at A and the y-axis at B. Find the equation of the median through O of $\triangle$OAB.

8. Find the equation of the altitude through O of the triangle OAB defined in Question 7.

9. Find the equation of the perpendicular from $(5, 3)$ to the line $2x - y + 4 = 0$

10. The points $A(1, 4)$ and $B(5, 7)$ are two adjacent vertices of a parallelogram ABCD. The point $C(7, 10)$ is another vertex of the parallelogram. Find the equation of the side CD.

INTERSECTION

The point where two lines (or curves) cut is called a point of intersection.

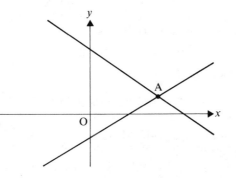

If A is the point of intersection of the lines $y - 3x + 1 = 0$ [1]

and $y + x - 2 = 0$ [2]

then the coordinates of A satisfy both of these equations. A can be found by solving [1] and [2] simultaneously, i.e.

$[2] - [1]$ $\Rightarrow$ $4x - 3 = 0$ $\Rightarrow$ $x = \frac{3}{4}$ and $y = \frac{5}{4}$

Therefore $(\frac{3}{4}, \frac{5}{4})$ is the point of intersection.

Note that the coordinates of A can also be found using a graphics calculator or a graph drawing package on a computer.

Example 9d _____

A circle has radius 4 and its centre is the point C(5, 3).

(a) Show that the points A(5, −1) and B(1, 3) are on the circumference of the circle.

(b) Prove that the perpendicular bisector of AB goes through the centre of the circle.

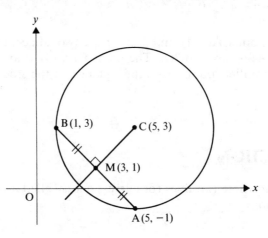

(a) From the diagram, BC = 4

∴ B is on the circumference.

Similarly AC = 4,

∴ A is on the circumference.

(b) The midpoint, M, of AB is $\left[\dfrac{5+1}{2}, \dfrac{-1+3}{2}\right]$ i.e. (3, 1)

The gradient of AB is $\dfrac{-1-3}{5-1} = -1$

If l is the perpendicular bisector of AB, its gradient is 1 and it goes through (3, 1).

∴ the equation of l is

$$y - 1 = 1(x - 3) \qquad \Rightarrow \qquad y = x - 2 \qquad\qquad [1]$$

In equation [1], when $x = 5$, $y = 3$

∴ the point (5, 3) is on l,

i.e. the perpendicular bisector of AB goes through C.

MIXED EXERCISE 9

1. Show that the triangle whose vertices are $(1, 1)$, $(3, 2)$ and $(2, -1)$ is isosceles.

2. Find the area of the triangular region enclosed by the x and y axes and the line $2x - y - 1 = 0$

3. Find the coordinates of the triangular region enclosed by the lines $y = 0$, $y = x + 5$ and $x + 2y - 6 = 0$

4. Write down the equation of the perpendicular bisector of the line joining the points $(2, -3)$ and $(-\frac{1}{2}, 3\frac{1}{2})$

5. Find the equation of the line through $A(5, 2)$ which is perpendicular to the line $y = 3x - 5$. Hence find the coordinates of the foot of the perpendicular from A to the line.

6. Find, in terms of a and b, the coordinates of the foot of the perpendicular from the point (a, b) to the line $x + 2y - 4 = 0$

7. The coordinates of a point P are $(t + 1, 2t - 1)$. Sketch the position of P when $t = -1, 0, 1$ and 2 Show that these points are collinear and write down the equation of the line on which they lie.

8. Write down the equation of the line which goes through $(7, 3)$ and which is inclined at $45°$ to the positive direction of the x-axis.

9. Find the equation of the perpendicular bisector of the line joining the points (a, b) and $(2a, -3b)$

10. The centre of a circle is at the point $C(3, 7)$ and the point $A(5, 3)$ is on the circumference of the circle. Find

    (a) the radius of the circle,

    (b) the equation of the line through A that is perpendicular to AC.

11. The equations of two sides of a square are $y = 3x - 1$ and $x + 3y - 6 = 0$. If $(0, -1)$ is one vertex of the square find the coordinates of the other vertices.

12. The lines $y = 2x$, $2x + y - 12 = 0$ and $y = 2$ enclose a triangular region of the xy-plane. Find

    (a) the coordinates of the vertices of this region,

    (b) the area of this region.

CHAPTER 10

CIRCLE GEOMETRY

PARTS OF A CIRCLE

We start this chapter with a reminder of the language used to describe parts of a circle.

Part of the circumference is called an *arc*.
If the arc is less than half the circumference it is called a *minor arc*; if it is greater than half the circumference it is called a *major arc*.

A straight line which cuts a circle in two distinct points is called a *secant*. The part of the line inside the circle is called a *chord*.

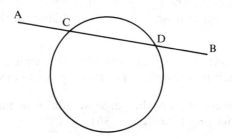

AB is a secant,
CD is a chord.

The area enclosed by two radii and an arc is called a *sector*.

The area enclosed by a chord and an arc is called a *segment*. If the segment is less than half a circle it is called a *minor segment*; if it is greater than half a circle it is called a *major segment*.

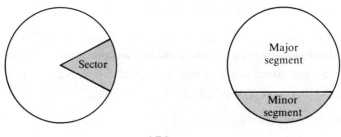

150

THE ANGLE SUBTENDED BY AN ARC

Consider the points A, B and C
on the circumference of a circle
whose centre is O.

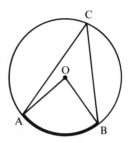

We say that $\angle ACB$ stands on the minor arc AB.

The minor arc AB is said to *subtend* the angle ACB at the
circumference (and the angle is *subtended* by the arc).

In the same way, the arc AB is said to subtend the angle AOB at the
centre of the circle.

Example 10a _____

A circle of radius 2 units which has its centre at the origin, cuts the
x-axis at the points A and B and cuts the y-axis at the point C.
Prove that $\angle ACB = 90°$

All the information given in the
question, and gleaned from the known
properties of the figure, can be marked
in the diagram as shown. The diagram
can then be referred to as justification
for steps taken in the solution.

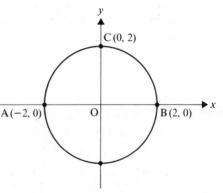

From the diagram, the gradient of AC is $\dfrac{2-0}{0-(-2)} = 1$

and the gradient of BC is $\dfrac{2-0}{0-2} = -1$

$\therefore$ (gradient of AC) $\times$ (gradient of BC) $= -1$

i.e. AC is perpendicular to BC $\Rightarrow$ $\angle ACB = 90°$

EXERCISE 10a

1.

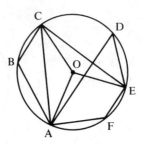

Name the angles subtended
(a) at the circumference by the minor arc AE
(b) at the circumference by the major arc AE
(c) at the centre by the minor arc AC
(d) at the circumference by the major arc AC
(e) at the centre by the minor arc CE
(f) at the circumference by the minor arc CD
(g) at the circumference by the minor arc BC.

2. AB is a chord of a circle, centre O, and M is its midpoint. The radius from O is drawn through M. Prove that OM is perpendicular to AB.

3. C(5, 3) is the centre of a circle of radius 5 units.
    (a) Show that this circle cuts the x-axis at A(1, 0) and B(9, 0)
    (b) Prove that the radius that is perpendicular to AB goes through the midpoint of AB.
    (c) Find the angle subtended at C by the minor arc AB.
    (d) The point D is on the major arc AB and DC is perpendicular to AB. Find the coordinates of D and hence find the angle subtended at D by the minor arc AB.

4. A and B are two points on the circumference of a circle centre O. C is a point on the major arc AB. Draw the lines AC, BC, AO, BO and CO, extending the last line to a point D inside the sector AOB. Prove that ∠AOD is twice ∠ACO and that ∠BOD is twice angle ∠BCO. Hence show that the angle subtended by the minor arc AB at the centre of the circle is twice the angle that it subtends at the circumference of the circle.

ANGLES IN A CIRCLE

The solutions to questions in the last exercise illustrate two important results.

1)   The perpendicular bisector of a chord of a circle goes through the centre of the circle.

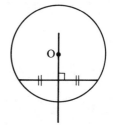

2)   The angle subtended by an arc at the centre of a circle is twice the angle subtended at the circumference by the same arc.

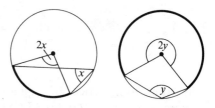

Further important results follow from the last fact.

3)

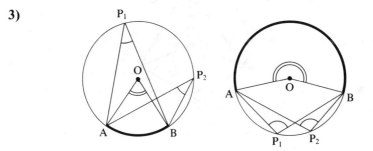

In both diagrams, $\angle AOB = 2\angle P_1 = 2\angle P_2$

So it follows that $\angle P_1 = \angle P_2$

i.e.

> all angles subtended at the circumference by the same arc are equal.

4)   A semicircle subtends an angle of 180° at the centre of the circle; therefore it subtends an angle half that size, i.e. 90°, at any point on the circumference. This angle is called the angle in a semicircle.

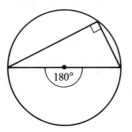

Hence   the angle in a semicircle is 90°

5)   If all four vertices of a quadrilateral ABCD lie on the circumference of a circle, ABCD is called a *cyclic quadrilateral*.

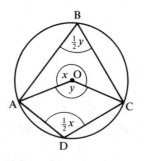

In the diagram, O is the centre of the circle.

∴ $\angle ADC = \frac{1}{2}x$ and $\angle ABC = \frac{1}{2}y$

But $x + y = 360°$, therefore $\angle ADC + \angle ABC = 180°$

i.e.   the opposite angles of a cyclic quadrilateral are supplementary

Example 10b

A circle circumscribes a triangle whose vertices are at the points A(0, 4), B(2, 3) and C(−2, −1). Find the centre of the circle.

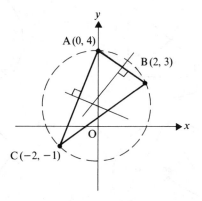

When a circle circumscribes a figure, the vertices of the figure lie on the circumference of the circle. The centre of the circle can be found by locating the point of intersection of the perpendicular bisectors of two chords.

The gradient of AC is $\dfrac{4 - (-1)}{0 - (-2)} = \dfrac{5}{2}$

and its midpoint is $\left[\dfrac{0 - 2}{2}, \dfrac{4 - 1}{2}\right] \quad \Rightarrow \quad (-1, \tfrac{3}{2})$,

∴ the gradient of the perpendicular bisector of AC is $-\tfrac{2}{5}$ and its equation is

$$y = -\tfrac{2}{5}x + \tfrac{11}{10} \quad \Rightarrow \quad 4x + 10y - 11 = 0 \qquad [1]$$

Similarly the gradient of AB is $-\tfrac{1}{2}$ and its midpoint is $(1, \tfrac{7}{2})$

∴ the gradient of the perpendicular bisector of AB is 2 and its equation is

$$y = 2x + \tfrac{3}{2} \quad \Rightarrow \quad 4x - 2y + 3 = 0 \qquad [2]$$

Solving equations [1] and [2] simultaneously gives

$$12y - 14 = 0 \quad \Rightarrow \quad y = \tfrac{7}{6} \text{ and } x = -\tfrac{1}{6}$$

Therefore the centre of the circle is the point $(-\tfrac{1}{6}, \tfrac{7}{6})$.

EXERCISE 10b

1. Find the size of each marked angle.

(a)   (b)

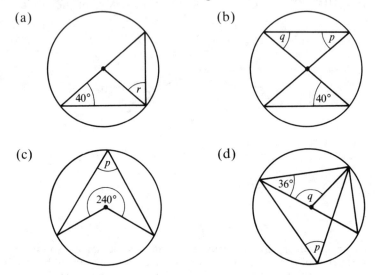

(c)   (d)

2. AB is a diameter of a circle centre O. C is a point on the circumference. D is a point on AC such that OD bisects ∠AOC. Prove that OD is parallel to BC.

3. A triangle has its vertices at the points A(1, 3), B(5, 1) and C(7, 5). Prove that △ABC is right-angled and hence find the coordinates of the centre of the circumcircle of △ABC.

4. Find the size of the angle marked *e* in the diagram.

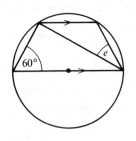

5. AB and CD are two chords of a circle that cut at E. (E is not the centre of the circle.) Show that △s ACE and BDE are similar.

6. A circle with centre O circumscribes an equilateral triangle ABC. The radius drawn through O and the midpoint of AB meets the circumference at D. Prove that △ADO is equilateral.

7. The line joining $A(5, 3)$ and $B(4, -2)$ is a diameter of a circle. If $P(a, b)$ is a point on the circumference find a relationship between a and b

8. ABCD is a cyclic quadrilateral. The side CD is produced to a point E outside the circle. Show that $\angle ABC = \angle ADE$.

9. A triangle has its vertices at the points $A(1, 3)$, $B(-2, 5)$ and $C(4, -2)$. Find the coordinates of the centre, and correct to 3 s.f., the radius of the circle that circumscribes $\triangle ABC$.

10. In the diagram, O is the centre of the circle and CD is perpendicular to AB. If $\angle CAB = 30°$ find the size of each marked angle.

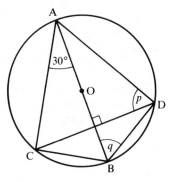

TANGENTS TO CIRCLES

If a line and a circle are drawn on a plane then there are three possibilities for the position of the line in relation to the circle. The line can miss the circle, or it can cut the circle in two distinct points, or it can touch the circle at one point. In the last case the line is called a *tangent* and the point at which it touches the circle is called the *point of contact.*

The length of a tangent drawn from a point to a circle is the distance from that point to the point of contact.

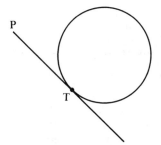

T is the point of contact.

PT is the length of the tangent from P.

Properties of Tangents to Circles

There are two important and useful properties of tangents to circles.

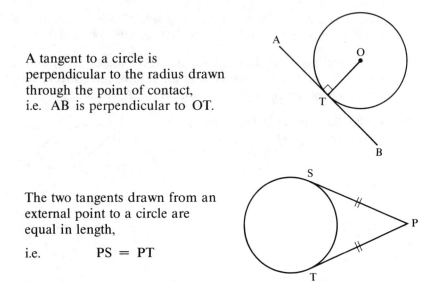

A tangent to a circle is
perpendicular to the radius drawn
through the point of contact,
i.e. AB is perpendicular to OT.

The two tangents drawn from an
external point to a circle are
equal in length,

i.e.   PS = PT

The second property is proved in the following worked example.

Examples 10c _____

1. PS and PT are two tangents drawn from a point P to a circle
   whose centre is O. Prove that PT = PS.

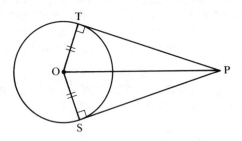

In △s OTP, OSP   ∠T = ∠S = 90°

                      OS = OT (radii)

                      and OP is common

∴ △s OTP, OSP are congruent.

Hence PT = PS.

Another useful property follows from the last example, namely

when two tangents are drawn from a point to a circle, the line joining that point to the centre of the circle bisects the angle between the tangents.

---

2. A circle of radius 10 units is circumscribed by a right-angled isosceles triangle. Find the lengths of the sides of the triangle.

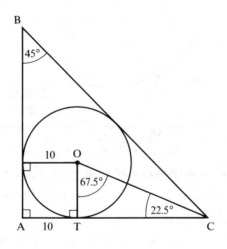

A circle is *circumscribed* by a figure when all the sides of the figure touch the circle. Note also that the circle is inscribed in the figure.

From the diagram

in $\triangle OTC$,	$TC = 10 \tan 67.5°$
	$= 24.14$
	$AT = 10$
$\therefore$	$AC = 34.14 = AB$
in $\triangle ABC$,	$BC = \sqrt{(34.14^2 + 34.14^2)}$ (Pythagoras)
	$= 48.28$

$\therefore$ correct to 3 s.f. the lengths of the sides of the triangle are
34.1 units, 34.1 units and 48.3 units.

---

3. The centre of a circle of radius 3 units is the point C(2, 5). The equation of a line, l, is $x + y - 2 = 0$

(a) Find the equation of the line through C, perpendicular to l

(b) Find the distance of C from l and hence determine whether l is a tangent to the circle.

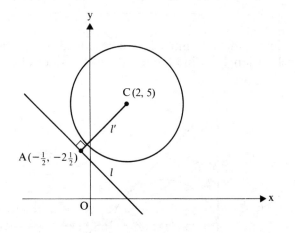

(a) The line l' is perpendicular to $x + y - 2 = 0$

so its equation is $\qquad\qquad x - y + k = 0$

The point $(2, 5)$ lies on l'

$\therefore \qquad\qquad\qquad 2 - 5 + k = 0 \quad\Rightarrow\quad k = 3$

$\therefore$ the equation of l' is $\qquad x - y + 3 = 0$

(b) To find the distance of C from l we need the coordinates of A, the point of intersection of l and l'.

Adding the equations of l and l' gives $2x + 1 = 0$

$\Rightarrow \qquad\qquad\qquad x = -\tfrac{1}{2}$ and $y = \tfrac{5}{2}$

so A is the point $(-\tfrac{1}{2}, \tfrac{5}{2})$

$\therefore$ CA $= \sqrt{[\{2 - (-\tfrac{1}{2})\}^2 + \{5 - \tfrac{5}{2}\}^2]} = 3.54$ to 3 s.f.

For the line to be a tangent, CA would have to be 3 units exactly (i.e. equal to the radius).

CA > 3, therefore l is not a tangent.

EXERCISE 10c

1. The two tangents from a point to a circle of radius 12 units are each of length 20 units. Find the angle between the tangents.

2. Two circles with centres C and O have radii 6 units and 3 units respectively and the distance between O and C is less than 9 units. AB is a tangent to both circles, touching the larger circle at A and the smaller circle at B, where AB is of length 4 units. Find the length of OC.

3. The two tangents from a point A to a circle touch the circle at S and at T. Find the angle between one of the tangents and the chord ST given that the radius of the circle is 5 units and that A is 13 units from the centre of the circle.

4. An equilateral triangle of side 25 cm circumscribes a circle. Find the radius of the circle.

5. AB is a diameter of the circle and C is a point on the circumference. The tangent to the circle at A makes an angle of 30° with the chord AC. Find the angles in △ABC.

6. The centre of a circle is at the point C(4, 8) and its radius is 3 units. Find the length of the tangents from the origin to the circle.

7. A circle touches the y-axis at the origin and goes through the point A(8, 0). The point C is on the circumference. Find the greatest possible area of △OAC.

8. A triangular frame is made to enclose six identical spheres as shown. Each sphere has a radius of 2 cm. Find the lengths of the sides of the frame.

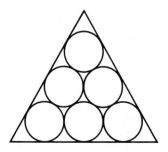

9. The line $y = 3x - 4$ is a tangent to the circle whose centre is the point $(5, 2)$. Find the radius of the circle.

10. A circle of radius 6 units has its centre at the point $(9, 0)$. If the two tangents from the origin to the circle are inclined to the x-axis at angles α and β, find $\tan \alpha$ and $\tan \beta$

11. A, B and C are three points on the circumference of a circle. The tangent to the circle at A makes an angle α with the chord AB. The diameter through A cuts the circle again at D and D is joined to B. Prove that $\angle ACB = \alpha$

12. The equations of the sides of a triangle are $y = 3x$, $y + 3x = 0$ and $3y - x + 12 = 0$ Find the coordinates of the circumcircle of this triangle.

13. The line $x - 2y + 4 = 0$ is a tangent to the circle whose centre is the point $C(-1, 2)$.
    (a) Find the equation of the line through C that is perpendicular to the line $x - 2y + 4 = 0$
    (b) Hence find the coordinates of the point of contact of the tangent and the circle.

14. The point $A(6, 8)$ is on the circumference of a circle whose centre is the point $C(3, 5)$. Find the equation of the tangent that touches the circle at A.

CHAPTER 11

RADIANS, ARCS AND SECTORS

ANGLE UNITS

An angle is a measure of rotation and the units which have been used up to now are the revolution and the degree. It is interesting to note why the number of degrees in a revolution was taken as 360. The ancient Babylonian mathematicians, in the belief that the length of the solar year was 360 days, divided a complete revolution into 360 parts, one for each day as they thought. We now know they did not have the length of the year quite right but the number they used, 360, remains as the number of degrees in one revolution.

Part of an angle smaller than a degree is usually given as a decimal part but until recently the common practice was to divide a degree into 60 minutes (60′) and each minute into 60 seconds (60″). Limited use is still made of this system.

Now we consider a different unit of rotation which is of great importance in much of the mathematics that follows.

THE RADIAN

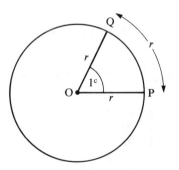

If O is the centre of a circle and an arc PQ is drawn so that its length is equal to the radius of the circle then the angle POQ is called a *radian* (one radian is written 1 rad or 1ᶜ), i.e.

> An arc equal in length to the radius of a circle subtends an angle of 1 radian at the centre.

163

It follows that the number of radians in a complete revolution is the number of times the radius divides into the circumference.

Now the circumference of a circle is of length $2\pi r$

Therefore the number of radians in a revolution is

$$\frac{2\pi r}{r} = 2\pi$$

i.e. 2π radians $= 360°$

Further π radians $= 180°$

and $\frac{1}{2}\pi$ radians $= 90°$

When an angle is given in terms of π it is usual to omit the radian symbol, i.e. we would write $180° = \pi$ (not $180° = \pi^c$)

If an angle is a simple fraction of $180°$, it is easily expressed in terms of π

e.g. $60° = \frac{1}{3}$ of $180° = \frac{1}{3}\pi$

and $135° = \frac{3}{4}$ of $180° = \frac{3}{4}\pi$ '

Conversely, $\frac{7}{6}\pi = \frac{7}{6}$ of $180° = 210°$

and $\frac{2}{3}\pi = \frac{2}{3}$ of $180° = 120°$

Angles that are not simple fractions of $180°$, or of π, can be converted by using the relationship $\pi = 180°$ and the value of π from a calculator,

e.g. $73° = \frac{73}{180} \times \pi = 1.27^c$ (correct to 3 s.f.)

and $2.36^c = \frac{2.36}{\pi} \times 180° = 135°$ (correct to the nearest degree)

It helps in visualising the size of a radian to remember that 1 radian is just a little less than $60°$.
($180° = \pi$ rad $= 3.142$ rad $\Rightarrow$ 1 rad $= 180°/3.142 \approx 57°$)

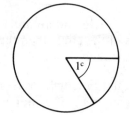

EXERCISE 11a

1. Express each of the following angles in radians as a fraction of π.
   45°, 150°, 30°, 270°, 225°, 22.5°, 240°, 300°, 315°

2. Without using a calculator express each of the following angles in degrees.
   $\frac{1}{6}\pi$, π, $\frac{1}{10}\pi$, $\frac{1}{4}\pi$, $\frac{5}{6}\pi$, $\frac{1}{12}\pi$, $\frac{1}{8}\pi$, $\frac{4}{3}\pi$, $\frac{1}{9}\pi$, $\frac{3}{2}\pi$, $\frac{4}{9}\pi$

3. Use a calculator to express each of the following angles in radians.
   35°, 47.2°, 93°, 233°, 14.1°, 117°, 370°

4. Use a calculator to express each of the following angles in degrees.
   1.7 rad, 3.32 rad, 1 rad, 2.09 rad, 5 rad, 6.283 19 rad

MENSURATION OF A CIRCLE

The reader will already be familiar with the formulae for the circumference and the area of a circle, i.e.

$$\text{Circumference} = 2\pi r \quad \text{and} \quad \text{Area} = \pi r^2$$

Now that we have defined a radian, these formulae can be used to derive other results.

The Length of an Arc

Consider an arc which subtends an angle θ at the centre of a circle, *where θ is measured in radians*

From the definition of a radian, the arc which subtends an angle of 1 radian at the centre of the circle is of length r. Therefore an arc which subtends an angle of θ radians at the centre is of length $r\theta$

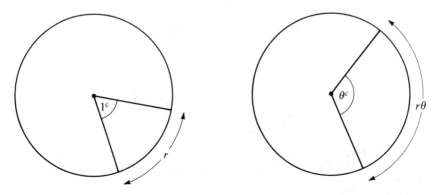

The Area of a Sector

The area of a sector can be thought of as a fraction of the area of the whole circle.

Consider a sector containing an angle of θ radians at the centre of the circle.

The complete angle at the centre of the circle is 2π, hence

$$\frac{\text{Area of sector}}{\text{Area of circle}} = \frac{\theta}{2\pi}$$

$\Rightarrow \qquad$ Area of sector $= \dfrac{\theta}{2\pi} \times \pi r^2$

$\qquad\qquad\qquad\qquad = \frac{1}{2}r^2\theta$

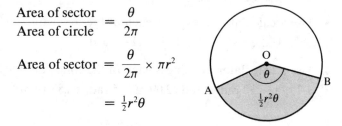

We now have two important facts about a circle in which an arc AB subtends an angle θ at the centre of the circle

The length of arc $AB = r\theta$

The area of sector $AOB = \frac{1}{2}r^2\theta$

When solving problems involving arcs and sectors, answers are usually given in terms of π. If a numerical answer is required it will be asked for specifically.

Examples 11b _____

1. An elastic belt is placed round the rim of a pulley of radius 5 cm. One point on the belt is pulled directly away from the centre, P, of the pulley, until it is at A, 10 cm from P. Find the length of the belt that is in contact with the rim of the pulley.

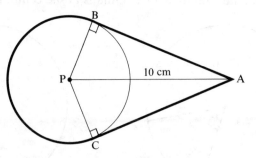

The belt leaves the pulley at B and at C. At these two points the belt is a tangent to the rim, so AB is perpendicular to the radius BP. Similarly, AC and PC are perpendicular.

In $\triangle ABP$ $BP = 5\,cm$, $AP = 10\,cm$ and $\angle ABP = 90°$

Therefore $\cos APB = \frac{5}{10} = \frac{1}{2}$

$\Rightarrow$ $\angle APB = 60° = \frac{1}{3}\pi$

Similarly $\angle APC = \frac{1}{3}\pi$

The angle subtended at P by the major arc BC is given by

$$2\pi - \angle BPA - \angle CPA = 2\pi - \tfrac{1}{3}\pi - \tfrac{1}{3}\pi = \tfrac{4}{3}\pi$$

The length of an arc is given by $r\theta$, therefore

the length of the major arc BC is $5 \times \frac{4}{3}\pi = \frac{20}{3}\pi$

i.e. the length of belt in contact with the pulley is $\frac{20}{3}\pi$ cm.

-----

2. AB is a chord of a circle with centre O and radius 4 cm. AB is of length 4 cm and divides the circle into two segments. Find, correct to two decimal places, the area of the minor segment.

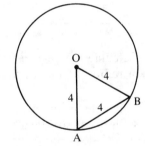

Each side of $\triangle ABC$ is 4 cm,
∴ ABC is an equilateral triangle
∴ each angle is 60°,

Area of sector $AOB = \frac{1}{2}r^2\theta$

$= \frac{1}{2}(4^2)(\frac{1}{3}\pi)$

$= \frac{8}{3}\pi$

Area of minor segment $=$ area of sector AOB $-$ area of $\triangle AOB$

$= \frac{8}{3}\pi - \frac{1}{2}(4)(4)(\sin 60°)$

$= 8.378 - 6.928$

$= 1.450$

The area of the minor segment is 1.45 cm^2 correct to 2 d.p.

EXERCISE 11b

In questions 1 to 10, s is the length of an arc subtending an angle θ at the centre of a circle of radius r, and a is the area of the corresponding sector. Complete the table.

	s (cm)	θ	r (cm)	a (cm^2)
1.		$30°$	4	
2.		$\frac{5}{6}\pi$	10	
3.	15	π		
4.	20	$\frac{4}{5}\pi$		
5.		$135°$	8	
6.			2	π
7.			5	12
8.		$\frac{1}{6}\pi$		3π
9.	5π			20π

10. Calculate, in degrees, the angle subtended at the centre of a circle of radius 2.7 cm by an arc of length 6.9 cm.

11. Calculate, in radians, the angle at the centre of a circle of radius 83 mm contained in a sector of area 974 mm^2.

12. The diameter of the moon is about 3445 km and the distance between the moon and earth is about 382 100 km. Find the angle subtended at a point on the earth's surface by the moon (give your answer as a decimal part of a degree to 2 d.p.).

13. In a circle with centre O and radius 5 cm, AB is a chord of length 8 cm. Find
    (a) the area of triangle AOB
    (b) the area of the sector AOB (in square centimetres, correct to 3 s.f.).

14. A chord of length 10 mm divides a circle of radius 7 mm into two segments. Find the area of each segment.

15. A chord PQ, of length 12.6 cm, subtends an angle of $\frac{2}{3}\pi$ at the centre of a circle. Find

    (a) the length of the arc PQ

    (b) the area of the minor segment cut off by the chord PQ.

16. A curve in the track of a railway line is a circular arc of length 400 m and radius 1200 m. Through what angle does the direction of the track turn?

17. Two discs, of radii 5 cm and 12 cm, are placed, partly overlapping, on a table. If their centres are 13 cm apart find the perimeter of the 'figure-eight' shape.

18. Two circles, each of radius 14 cm, are drawn with their centres 20 cm apart. Find the length of their common chord. Find also the area common to the two circles.

The next three questions are a little more demanding.

19. A chord of a circle subtends an angle of θ radians at the centre of the circle. The area of the minor segment cut off by the chord is one eighth of the area of the circle.
Prove that $4\theta = \pi + 4\sin\theta$

20. A chord PQ of length $6a$ is drawn in a circle of radius $10a$. The tangents to the circle at P and Q meet at R. Find the area enclosed by PR, QR and the minor arc PQ.

21. Two discs are placed, in contact with each other, on a table. Their radii are 4 cm and 9 cm. An elastic band is stretched round the pair of discs. Calculate

    (a) the angle subtended at the centre of the smaller disc by the arc that is in contact with the elastic band.

    (b) the length of the part of the band that is in contact with the smaller disc.

    (c) the length of the part of the band that is in contact with the larger disc.

    (d) the total length of the stretched band.

(*Hint*. The straight parts of the stretched band are common tangents to the two circles.)

CONSOLIDATION B

SUMMARY

PLANE GEOMETRY

Intercept Theorem

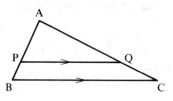

$$PQ \parallel BC \iff AP:BP = AQ:QC$$

Pythagoras' Theorem

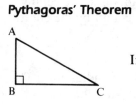

$$\text{In } \triangle ABC, \ \angle B = 90° \iff AC^2 = AB^2 + BC^2$$

Similar Triangles

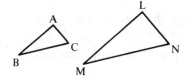

$$\angle A = \angle L, \ \angle B = \angle M, \ \angle C = \angle N$$
$$\iff AB:LM = BC:MN = AC:LN$$

Angle Bisector Theorem

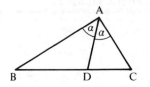

$$AD \text{ bisects } \angle A \iff BD:DC = AB:AC$$

170

Circle Theorems

The perpendicular bisector of any chord goes through O, and conversely.

$\angle O = 2\angle P$

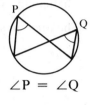

$\angle P = \angle Q$

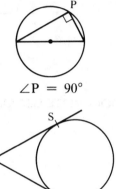

$\angle P = 90°$

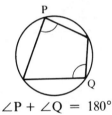

$\angle P + \angle Q = 180°$

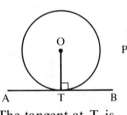

The tangent at T is
perpendicular to OT

$PS = PT$

TRIGONOMETRY

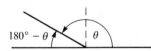

$\sin\theta = \sin(180° - \theta)$
$\cos\theta = -\cos(180° - \theta)$
$\tan\theta = -\tan(180° - \theta)$

In any triangle ABC,

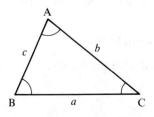

$$\frac{a}{\sin A} = \frac{b}{\sin B} = \frac{c}{\sin C} \qquad \text{(sine rule)}$$

$a^2 = b^2 + c^2 - 2bc\cos A$

$b^2 = a^2 + c^2 - 2ac\cos B \qquad \text{(cosine rule)}$

$c^2 = a^2 + b^2 - 2ab\cos C$

The area of $\triangle ABC$ is $\frac{1}{2}ab\sin C$, or $\frac{1}{2}bc\sin A$, or $\frac{1}{2}ac\sin B$

CIRCULAR MEASURE

One radian (1^c) is the size of the angle
subtended at the centre of a circle by an arc
equal in length to the radius of the circle.

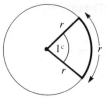

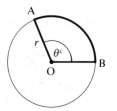

The length of arc AB is $r\theta$

The area of sector AOB is $\frac{1}{2}r^2\theta$

COORDINATE GEOMETRY

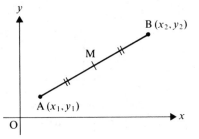

Length of AB is $\sqrt{[(x_2 - x_1)^2 + (y_2 - y_1)^2]}$

Midpoint, M of AB is $[\frac{1}{2}(x_1 + x_2), \frac{1}{2}(y_1 + y_2)]$

Gradient of AB is $\dfrac{y_2 - y_1}{x_2 - x_1}$

Parallel lines have equal gradients.

When two lines are perpendicular, the product of their gradients is -1

The standard equation of a straight line is $y = mx + c$, where m is its
gradient and c its intercept on the y-axis.

Any equation of the form $ax + by + c = 0$ is a straight line.

The equation of a line passing through (x_1, y_1) and with gradient m is

$$y - y_1 = m(x - x_1)$$

Given a line with equation $ax + by + c = 0$,
then any perpendicular line has equation $bx - ay + k = 0$

MULTIPLE CHOICE EXERCISE B

TYPE I

1. A line AB is 10 cm long. P divides AB externally in the ratio 9 : 4. The length of PB is

   A   18 cm   C   8 cm   E   4 cm
   B $\frac{40}{13}$ cm   D   40 cm

2. In △ABC, $a = 3$ cm, $b = 4$ cm and $c = 5$ cm,

   A   A = 90°   C   B = 45°   E   C = 90°
   B   C = 60°   D   B = 90°

3.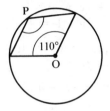

   In the diagram, O is the centre
   of the circle. Angle P is

   A   110°   B   90°   C   125°   D   55°   E   220°

4. If angle θ is 120° then $\cos\theta$ is

   A $\frac{1}{2}$ B $\frac{\sqrt{2}}{2}$ C $\frac{\sqrt{3}}{2}$ D $-\frac{\sqrt{3}}{2}$ E $-\frac{1}{2}$

5.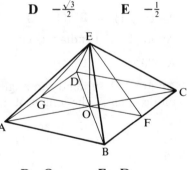

   ABCDE is a right square-based
   pyramid (i.e. E is vertically
   above the centre of the base).
   The angle between the face
   BEC and the base ABCD is

   A   F   B   B   C   C   D   O   E   D

6. The length of the line joining $(3, -4)$ to $(-7, 2)$ is

   A $2\sqrt{13}$ C $2\sqrt{34}$ E   6
   B   16   D $2\sqrt{5}$

7. The midpoint of the line joining $(-1, -3)$ to $(3, -5)$ is

   A $(1, 1)$ C $(2, -8)$ E $(1, -1)$
   B $(0, 0)$ D $(1, -4)$

8. The gradient of the line joining $(1, 4)$ and $(-2, 5)$ is

    A $\frac{1}{3}$ **B** $-\frac{1}{3}$ **C** 3   **D** -3 **E** 1.3

9. The gradient of the line perpendicular to the join of $(-1, 5)$ and $(2, -3)$ is

    A $\frac{3}{8}$ **B** $-2\frac{2}{3}$ **C** $\frac{1}{2}$ **D** 2   **E** $2\frac{2}{3}$

10. The line joining $(1, 3)$ to (a, b) has unit gradient.

    A $b - a = 2$ **C** $a + b = 2$ **E** $a - b = 4$
    B $a - b = 2$ **D** $b - a = 4$

11. The equation of the line through the origin and perpendicular to $3x - 2y + 4 = 0$ is

    A $3x + 2y = 0$ **C** $2x + 3y = 0$ **E** $3x - 2y = 0$
    B $2x + 3y + 1 = 0$ **D** $2x - 3y - 1 = 0$

12. The equation of the line with gradient 1 and passing through the point (h, k) is

    A $y = x + k - h$ **C** $y = x + h - k$ **E** $y + x = k - h$
    B $y = \dfrac{k}{h}x + 1$ **D** $ky = hx - 1$

13. The two lines $x + y = 0$ and $2x - y + 3 = 0$ intersect at the point

    A $(-\frac{1}{3}, \frac{1}{3})$ **B** $(1, -1)$ **C** $(-3, 3)$ **D** $(-1, 1)$ **E** $(3, -3)$

14. An angle of 1 radian is equivalent to:

    A $90°$ **B** $60°$ **C** $67.3°$ **D** $57.3°$ **E** $45°$

15. An arc PQ subtends an angle of $60°$ at the centre of a circle of radius 1 cm. The length of the arc PQ is

    A 60 cm   **B** 30 cm   **C** $\frac{1}{6}\pi$ cm   **D** $\frac{1}{3}\pi$ cm   **E** $\frac{1}{18}\pi^2$ cm

TYPE II

16. In triangle ABC

    A $\dfrac{a}{\sin A} = \dfrac{b}{\sin \alpha}$

    B $b^2 = a^2 + c^2 + 2ac \cos \alpha$
    C $a^2 = b^2 + c^2 + 2bc \cos A$

17. π can represent

    A   the ratio of the circumference to the radius of a circle
    B   half a revolution
    C   half the circumference of a circle.

18. In triangle ABC, AD bisects angle A

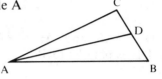

    A   BD = DC
    B   AB:AC = BD:DC
    C $DC^2 = AD^2 + AC^2 - 2(AD)(AC)\cos\frac{1}{2}A$

19. A and B are two points with coordinates $(3,4),\ (-1,6)$

    A   Gradient of AB is $-\frac{1}{2}$
    B   Midpoint of AB is the point $(2,5)$
    C   Length of AB is $2\sqrt{5}$

20. A, B and C are the points $(5,0),\ (-5,0),\ (2,3)$

    A   AB and BC are perpendicular.
    B   Area of triangle ABC is 15 square units.
    C   A, B and C are collinear.

21. A, B, C are the points $(0,13),\ (0,-13),\ (5,-12)$.

    A   A, B, C lie on the circumference of a circle, centre the origin.
    B   The equation of AC is $5x + y - 13 = 0$
    C   The midpoint of BC is the origin.

22. The equation of a line l is $y = 2x - 1$

    A   The line through the origin perpendicular to l is $y + 2x = 0$
    B   The line through $(1,2)$ parallel to l is $y = 2x - 3$
    C l passes through $(1,1)$.

23. The equation of a line l is $7x - 2y + 4 = 0$

    A l has a gradient of $3\frac{1}{2}$
    B l is parallel to $7x + 2y - 3 = 0$
    C l is perpendicular to $2x + 7y - 5 = 0$

TYPE III

24. If an arc of a circle of radius $0.5\,\text{cm}$ subtends an angle of $60°$ at the centre of the circle, then the length of the arc is $30\,\text{cm}$.

25. If in triangle ABC, angle A is $30°$ then $\sin B = b/2a$

26.

If $AD = \frac{1}{3}AB$ and $AE = \frac{1}{3}AC$
then DE is parallel to BC.

27.

If $BD = DC$
then AD bisects angle A.

28. The line joining $(0,0)$ and $(1,3)$ is equal in length to the line joining $(0,1)$ and $(3,0)$

29. If a line has gradient m and intercept d on the x-axis, its equation is $y = mx - md$

30. The line passing through $(3,1)$ and $(-2,5)$ is perpendicular to the line $4y = 5x - 3$

31. π radians $= 360°$

MISCELLANEOUS EXERCISE B

1. A circle, centre O and radius a, has AB as a diameter and C is a point on AB produced such that $BC = a$. Points P and Q lie on the circle and $PC = QC$. Given that angle $POC = \theta$, show that L, the perimeter of the area enclosed by the lines CP, CQ and the arc PAQ, is given by

$$L = 2a\pi - 2a\theta + 2a(5 - 4\cos\theta)^{1/2}$$ (U of L 86)$_p$

2. A chord divides a circle, centre O, into two regions whose areas are in the ratio $2:1$. Prove that the angle θ, subtended by this chord at O, satisfies the equation $f(\theta) = 0$, where

$$f(\theta) = \theta - \sin\theta - 2\pi/3$$ (U of L 87)$_p$

3. Show that the volume V of a right circular cone of slant height l and semi-vertical angle θ, where $0 < \theta < \pi/2$, is given by

$$V = \tfrac{1}{3}\pi l^3 \sin^2 \theta \cos \theta \qquad\qquad \text{(U of L 87)}_p$$

4. A is the point $(0, 6)$ and B is the point $(4, 0)$. Calculate the coordinates of the centre of the circle which passes through A, B and the origin O. Hence find the radius of this circle.

5. A vertical wall, 2.7 m high, runs parallel to the wall of a house and is at a horizontal distance of 6.4 m from the house. An extending ladder is placed to rest on the top B of the wall with one end C against the house and the other end A resting on horizontal ground, as shown in the figure.

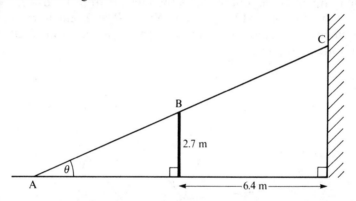

The points A, B and C are in a vertical plane at right angles to the wall and the ladder makes an angle θ, where $0 < \theta < \pi/2$, with the horizontal. Show that the length, y metres, of the ladder is given by

$$y = \frac{2.7}{\sin \theta} + \frac{6.4}{\cos \theta} \qquad\qquad \text{(U of L 87)}_p$$

6. In the triangle ABC, the point D is the foot of the perpendicular from A to BC. Show that

$$AD = \frac{BC \sin B \sin C}{\sin A}$$

The triangle ABC lies in a horizontal plane. A vertical pole FT stands with its foot F on AD and between A and D. The top T of the pole is at a height 3 m above the plane, and the angle of elevation of T from D is $65°$. Given that $BC = 7$ m, $\angle B = 62°$ and $\angle C = 34°$, calculate AF correct to two decimal places.

Find, to the nearest degree, the angle between the planes ATC and ABC. (JMB 86)

7. A circular sector, of area A cm^2, has bounding radii, each of length x cm, and the angle between these radii is θ radians.
   Given that the perimeter of the sector is 12 cm,

   (a) express θ in terms of x

   (b) show that $A = 6x - x^2$ (AEB 86)$_p$

8. The diagram shows a plane *PQRS* inclined at 30° to the horizontal. The line *AB* is 60 cm long and runs down a line of greatest slope. The point C is on the inclined plane; the length of *AC* is 48 cm and the angle *CAB* is 73°. Find

   (a) the length of *BC*, to the nearest centimetre

   (b) the angle *ABC*, to the nearest degree.

   The point *D* is the foot of the perpendicular from *C* to *AB*. Show that the vertical height of *D* above *B* is 23 cm to the nearest centimetre. Find, to the nearest degree, the angle between *BC* and the horizontal plane.

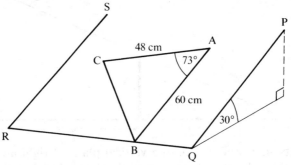

(JMB 88)

9. The figure shows three circular discs with centres A, B and C and radii 3 cm, 2 cm and 1 cm respectively touching each other externally.

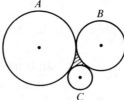

   Show that the tangent of angle *BAC* is $\frac{3}{4}$

   Find the area of the shaded region enclosed by the three discs, giving your answer in cm^2 to 3 significant figures.   (AEB 87)

10. In the triangle ABC, AB = 8, BC = 7, $\angle A = 60°$. Given that AC < 4, find AC.   (C 87)

11. A pyramid *VABCD* has a horizontal square base *ABCD*, of side $6a$. The vertex *V* of the pyramid is at a height $4a$, vertically above the centre of the base. Calculate, in degrees, to one decimal place, the acute angle between

   (a) the edge *VA* and the horizontal

   (b) the plane *VAB* and the horizontal

   (c) the planes *VBA* and *VBC*   (AEB 88)

12. The rectangle *ABCD* is the horizontal base of a pyramid, and the vertex *V* of the pyramid is vertically above the centre of the base. The length of *AB* is 6 cm, the length of *BC* is 12 cm and the length of *VA* is 20 cm. The points *X* on *VB* and *Y* on *BC* are such that *AX* and *YX* are both perpendicular to *VB*.

   (a) Show that the length of *BX* is 0.9 cm, and calculate the length of *BY*.

   (b) Calculate, to the nearest degree, the angle between the planes *VAB* and *VBC*.   (C 87)

13.

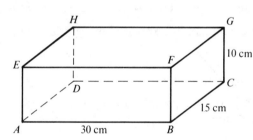

   The diagram shows a rectangular solid *ABCDEFGH*, with $AB = 30$ cm, $BC = 15$ cm and $CG = 10$ cm. Calculate

   (a) the angle between *DG* and *BG*, giving your answer correct to the nearest $0.1°$

   (b) the perpendicular distance of *C* from *BD*, giving your answer correct to three significant figures

   (c) the angle between the planes *DGB* and *DCB*, giving your answer correct to the nearest $0.1°$ (C 88)

14. The coordinates of a point P are $(t + 1, 2t - 1)$. Draw a sketch showing the positions of P when $t = -1, 0, 1, 2$. Show that these four points are collinear and find the equation of the line on which they lie.

15. The equations of two adjacent sides of a rhombus are $y = 2x + 4$, $y = -\frac{1}{3}x + 4$. If $(12, 0)$ is one vertex and all vertices have positive coordinates, find the coordinates of the other three vertices.

CHAPTER 12

FUNCTIONS

MAPPINGS

If, on a calculator, the number 2 is entered and then the x^2 button is pressed, the display shows the number 4

We say that 2 is mapped to 2^2 or $2 \to 2^2$

Under the same rule, i.e. squaring the input number,
$3 \to 9$, $25 \to 625$, $0.5 \to 0.25$, $-4 \to 16$ and in fact,

(any real number) $\to$ (the square of that number)

The last statement can be expressed more briefly as

$$x \to x^2$$

where x is any real number.

This mapping can be represented graphically by plotting values of x^2 against values of x

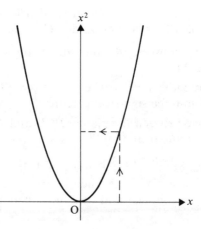

The graph, and knowledge of what happens when we square a number, show that one input number gives just one output number.

180

Now consider the mapping which maps a number to its square roots; the rule by which, for example, $4 \to +2$ and -2

This rule gives a real output only if the input number is greater than zero (negative numbers do not have real square roots). This mapping can now be written in general terms as

$$x \to \pm\sqrt{x} \text{ for } x \geqslant 0$$

The graphical representation of this mapping is shown below.

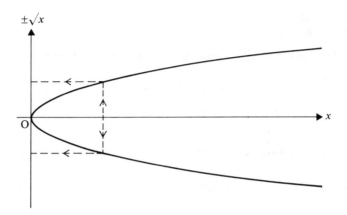

This time we notice that one input value gives two output values.

From these two examples, we can see that a mapping is a rule for changing a number to another number or numbers.

FUNCTIONS

Under the first mapping, $x \to x^2$, one input number gives one output number. However, for the second mapping, $x \to \pm\sqrt{x}$, one input number gives two output numbers.

We use the word *function* for any rule that gives the same kind of result as the first mapping, i.e. one input value gives one output value.

A function is a rule which maps a single number to another single number.

The second mapping does not satisfy this condition so we cannot call it a function.

Consider again what we can now call the function for which $x \rightarrow x^2$
Using f for 'function' and the symbol : to mean 'such that',
we can write $f : x \rightarrow x^2$

We use the notation $f(x)$ to represent the output values of the
function.

e.g.

$$\text{for } f : x \rightarrow x^2, \text{ we have } f(x) = x^2$$

Examples 12a

1. Determine whether these mappings are functions,

(a) $x \rightarrow \dfrac{1}{x}$ (b) $x \rightarrow y$ where $y^2 - x = 0$

(a) For any value of x, except $x = 0$, $\dfrac{1}{x}$ has a single value,

therefore $x \rightarrow \dfrac{1}{x}$ is a function provided that $x = 0$ is excluded.

Note that $\dfrac{1}{0}$ is meaningless, so to make this mapping a function we have to

exclude 0 as an input value. The function can be described by $f(x) = \dfrac{1}{x}$, $x \neq 0$

(b) If, for example, we input $x = 4$, then the output is the value
of y when

$$y^2 - 4 = 0 \Rightarrow y = 2 \text{ and } y = -2$$

therefore an input gives more than one value for the output,
so $x \rightarrow y$ where $y^2 - x = 0$ is not a function.

2. If $f(x) = 2x^2 - 5$, find $f(3)$ and $f(-1)$

As $f(x)$ is the output of the mapping, $f(3)$ is the output when 3 is the input,
i.e. $f(3)$ is the value of $2x^2 - 5$ when $x = 3$

$$f(3) = 2(3)^2 - 5 = 13$$
$$f(-1) = 2(-1)^2 - 5 = -3$$

EXERCISE 12a

1. Determine which of these mappings are functions.

   (a) $x \rightarrow 2x - 1$ (b) $x \rightarrow x^3 + 3$ (c) $x \rightarrow \dfrac{1}{x - 1}$

   (d) $x \rightarrow k$ where $k^2 = x$ (e) $x \rightarrow \sqrt{x}$

   (f) $x \rightarrow$ the length of the line from the origin to $(0, x)$

   (g) $x \rightarrow$ the greatest integer less than or equal to x

   (h) $x \rightarrow$ the height of a triangle whose area is x

2. If $f(x) = 5x - 4$ find $f(0)$, $f(-4)$

3. If $f(x) = 3x^2 + 25$ find $f(0)$, $f(8)$

4. If $f(x) =$ the value of x correct to the nearest integer, find $f(1.25)$, $f(-3.5)$, $f(12.49)$

5. If $f(x) = \sin x$, find $f(\tfrac{1}{2}\pi)$, $f(\tfrac{2}{3}\pi)$

DOMAIN AND RANGE

We have assumed that we can use any real number as an input for a function unless some particular numbers have to be excluded because they do not give real numbers as output.

The set of inputs for a function is called the *domain* of the function.

The domain does not have to contain all possible inputs; it can be as wide, or as restricted, as we choose to make it. Hence to define a function fully, the domain must be stated.

If the domain is not stated, we assume that it is the set of all real numbers (ℝ).

Consider the mapping $x \rightarrow x^2 + 3$

We can define a function f for this mapping over any domain we choose. Some examples, together with their graphs are given overleaf.

1) $f(x) = x^2 + 3$ for $x \in \mathbb{R}$

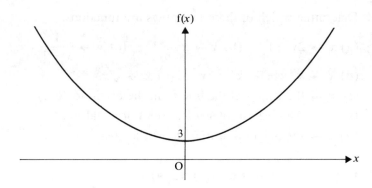

2) $f(x) = x^2 + 3$ for $x \geqslant 0$

Note that the point on the curve where $x = 0$ is included and we denote this on the curve by a solid circle.

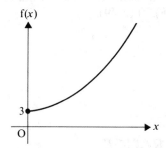

If the domain were $x > 0$,   then the point would not be part of the curve and we indicate this fact by using an open circle.

3) $f(x) = x^2 + 3$ for $x \in \{1, 2, 3, 4, 5\}$

This time the graphical representation consists of just five discrete (i.e. separate) points.

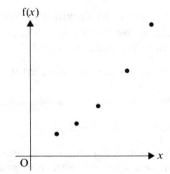

For each domain, there is a corresponding set of output numbers.

> The set of output numbers is called the *range* or *image-set* of the function.

Thus for the function defined in **(1)** above, the range is $f(x) \geqslant 3$ and for the function given in **(2)**, the range is also $f(x) \geqslant 3$ For the function defined in **(3)**, the range is the set $\{4, 7, 12, 19, 28\}$.

Sometimes a function can be made up from more than one mapping, where each mapping is defined for a different domain. This is illustrated in the next worked example.

Example 12b _____

The function, f, is defined by $f(x) = x^2$ for $x \leqslant 0$
and $f(x) = x$ for $x > 0$

(a) Find $f(4)$ and $f(-4)$ (b) Sketch the graph of f
(c) Give the range of f

(a) For $x > 0$, $f(x) = x$, $\therefore \quad f(4) = 4$

For $x \leqslant 0$, $f(x) = x^2$, $\therefore \quad f(-4) = (-4)^2 = 16$

(b) To sketch the graph of a function, we can apply our knowledge of lines and curves in the xy-plane to the equation $y = f(x)$. In this way we can interpret $f(x) = x$ for $x > 0$, as that part of the line $y = x$ which corresponds to positive values of x

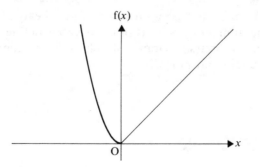

(c) The range of f is $f(x) \geqslant 0$

EXERCISE 12b

1. Find the range of each of the following functions.
   (a) $f(x) = 2x - 3$ for $x \geqslant 0$
   (b) $f(x) = x^2 - 5$ for $x \leqslant 0$
   (c) $f(x) = 1 - x$ for $x \leqslant 1$
   (d) $f(x) = 1/x$ for $x \geqslant 2$

2. Draw a sketch graph of each function given in Question 1.

3. The function f is such that $f(x) = -x$ for $x < 0$
   and $f(x) = x$ for $x \geqslant 0$
   (a) Find the value of $f(5)$, $f(-4)$, $f(-2)$ and $f(0)$
   (b) Sketch the graph of the function.

4. The function f is such that $f(x) = x$ for $0 \leqslant x \leqslant 5$
   and $f(x) = 5$ for $x > 5$
   (a) Find the value of $f(0)$, $f(2)$, $f(4)$, $f(5)$ and $f(7)$
   (b) Sketch the graph of the function.
   (c) Give the range of the function.

5. In Utopia, the tax on earned income is calculated as follows. The first £20 000 is tax free and remaining income is taxed at 20%.
   (a) Find the tax payable on an earned income of £15 000 and of £45 000
   (b) Taking x as the number of pounds of earned income and y as the number of pounds of tax payable, define a function f such that $y = f(x)$. Draw a sketch of the function and state the domain and range.

CURVE SKETCHING

When functions have similar definitions they usually have common properties and graphs of the same form. If the common characteristics of a group of functions are known, the graph of any one particular member of the group can be sketched without having to plot points.

Quadratic Functions

> The general form of a quadratic function is
>
> $$f(x) = ax^2 + bx + c \quad \text{for} \quad x \in \mathbb{R}$$
>
> where a, b and c are constants and $a \neq 0$

When a graphics calculator, or a computer, is used to draw the graphs of quadratic functions for a variety of values of a, b and c, the basic shape of the curve is always the same. This shape is called a *parabola*.

Every parabola has an axis of symmetry which goes through the vertex, i.e. the point where the curve turns back upon itself.

If the coefficient of x^2 is positive, i.e. $a > 0$,
then $f(x)$ has a least value,
and the parabola looks like this.

If the coefficient of x^2 is negative, i.e. $a < 0$,
then $f(x)$ has a greatest value
and the curve is this way up.

These properties of the graph of a quadratic function can be proved algebraically.

For $f(x) = ax^2 + bx + c$, 'completing the square' on the RHS and simplifying, gives

$$f(x) = \left[\frac{4ac - b^2}{4a} \right] + a \left[x + \frac{b}{2a} \right]^2 \qquad [1]$$

Now the first bracket is constant and, as the second bracket is squared, its value is zero when $x = -\dfrac{b}{2a}$ and greater than zero for all other values of x.

Hence

> when a is positive,
>
> $$f(x) = ax^2 + bx + c \quad \text{has a least value when} \quad x = -\frac{b}{2a}$$
>
> and when a is negative,
>
> $$f(x) = ax^2 + bx + c \quad \text{has a greatest value when} \quad x = -\frac{b}{2a}$$

Further, taking values of x that are symmetrical about $x = -\dfrac{b}{2a}$,
e.g. $x = \pm k - \dfrac{b}{2a}$, we see from [1] that

$$f\left(k - \frac{b}{2a}\right) = f\left(-k - \frac{b}{2a}\right) = \left[\frac{4ac - b^2}{4a}\right] + ak^2$$

i.e.   the value of $f(x)$ is symmetrical about $x = -\dfrac{b}{2a}$

These properties can now be used to draw *sketches* of the graphs of quadratic functions.

Examples 12c _____

1. Find the greatest or least value of the function given by $f(x) = 2x^2 - 7x - 4$ and hence sketch the graph of $f(x)$.

$$f(x) = 2x^2 - 7x - 4 \quad \Rightarrow \quad a = 2, \ b = -7 \ \text{and} \ c = -4$$

As $a > 0$, $f(x)$ has a least value

and this occurs when $x = -\dfrac{b}{2a} = \dfrac{7}{4}$

$\therefore$ the least value of $f(x)$ is $f(\tfrac{7}{4}) = 2(\tfrac{7}{4})^2 - 7(\tfrac{7}{4}) - 4$

$$= -\tfrac{81}{8}$$

We now have one point on the graph of $f(x)$ and we know that the curve is symmetrical about this value of x. However, to locate the curve more accurately we need another point; we use $f(0)$ as it is easy to find.

$f(0) = -4$

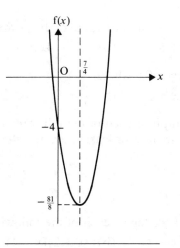

2. Draw a quick sketch of the graph of $f(x) = (1 - 2x)(x + 3)$

The coefficient of x^2 is negative, so $f(x)$ has a greatest value.
The curve cuts the x-axis when $f(x) = 0$

When $f(x) = 0$, $\qquad (1 - 2x)(x + 3) = 0$

$\Rightarrow \qquad\qquad\qquad x = \tfrac{1}{2}$ or -3

The average of these values is $-\tfrac{5}{4}$, so the curve is symmetrical
about $x = -\tfrac{5}{4}$

We now have enough information to draw a quick sketch, but note that this
method is suitable only when the quadratic function factorises.

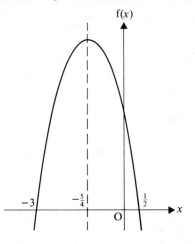

EXERCISE 12c

1. Find the greatest or least value of $f(x)$ where $f(x)$ is
    (a) $x^2 - 3x + 5$ (b) $2x^2 - 4x + 5$ (c) $3 - 2x - x^2$

2. Find the range of f where $f(x)$ is
    (a) $7 + x - x^2$ (b) $x^2 - 2$ (c) $2x - x^2$

3. Sketch the graph of each of the following quadratic functions, showing the greatest or least value and the value of x at which it occurs.
    (a) $x^2 - 2x + 5$ (b) $x^2 + 4x - 8$ (c) $2x^2 - 6x + 3$
    (d) $4 - 7x - x^2$ (e) $x^2 - 10$ (f) $2 - 5x - 3x^2$

4. Draw a quick sketch of each of the following functions.
    (a) $(x - 1)(x - 3)$ (b) $(x + 2)(x - 4)$ (c) $(2x - 1)(x - 3)$
    (d) $(1 + x)(2 - x)$ (e) $x^2 - 9$ (f) $3x^2$

CUBIC FUNCTIONS

The general form of a cubic function is

$$f(x) = ax^3 + bx^2 + cx + d$$

where a, b, c and d, are constants and $a \neq 0$

Investigating the curve $y = ax^3 + bx^2 + cx + d$ for a variety of values of a, b, c and d shows that the shape of the curve is

   and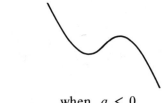

when $a > 0$ when $a < 0$

Sometimes there are no turning points and the curve looks like this

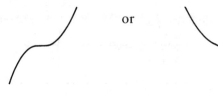   or

POLYNOMIAL FUNCTIONS

The general form of a polynomial function is

$$f(x) = a_n x^n + a_{n-1} x^{n-1} + \ldots + a_2 x^2 + a_1 x + a_0$$

where $a_n, a_{n-1}, \ldots, a_0$ are constants, n is a positive integer and $a_n \neq 0$

Examples of polynomials are

$$f(x) = 3x^4 - 2x^3 + 5, \quad f(x) = x^5 - 2x^3 + x, \quad f(x) = x^2$$

The *order* of a polynomial is the highest power of x in the function. Thus, the order of $x^4 - 7$ is 4, and the order of $2x - 1$ is 1

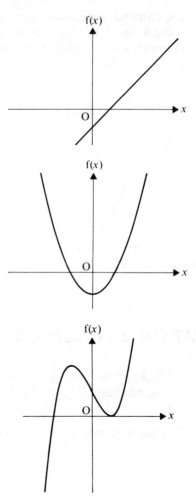

We have already investigated the graphs of polynomials of order 1,

e.g. $f(x) = 2x - 1$

which gives a straight line,

and of order 2,

e.g. $f(x) = x^2 - 4$

which gives a parabola,

and of order 3,

e.g. $f(x) = x^3 - 2x + 1$

which gives a cubic curve.

The shape of the curve
$f(x) = x^4 - 3x^3 + 2x^2 + 1$
looks like this.

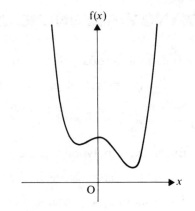

Experimenting with the curves of other polynomial functions of order 4 shows that, in general, the curve has three turning points although some or all of these may merge,
e.g.

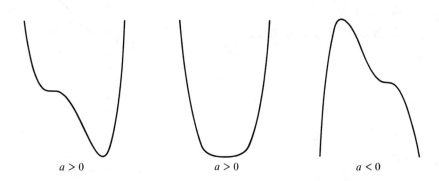

$a > 0$ $a > 0$ $a < 0$

RATIONAL FUNCTIONS

A rational function is one in which both numerator and denominator are polynomial.

Examples of rational functions of x are

$$\frac{1}{x}, \qquad \frac{x}{x^2 - 1}, \qquad \frac{3x^2 + 2x}{x - 1}$$

Now consider the familiar function $f(x) = 1/x$ and its graph. From its form we can infer various properties of $f(x)$

1) As the value of x increases, the value of $f(x)$ gets closer to zero, e.g. when $x = 100$, $f(x) = 1/100$
and when $x = 1000$, $f(x) = 1/1000$
We write this as $x \to \infty$, $f(x) \to 0$

Similarly as the value of x decreases, i.e. as $x \to -\infty$, the value of $f(x)$ again gets closer to zero, i.e. $f(x) \to 0$

2) $f(x)$ does not exist when $x = 0$, so this value of x must be excluded from the domain of f
x can get as close as we like to zero however, and can approach zero in two ways.

If $x \to 0$ from above (i.e. from positive values, $- -\overset{!}{\underset{0}{\vphantom{|}}}\!\longleftarrow - - \,$)
then $f(x) \to \infty$

If $x \to 0$ from below (i.e. from negative values, $- - \longrightarrow \underset{0}{\overset{!}{\vphantom{|}}} - - \,$)
then $f(x) \to -\infty$

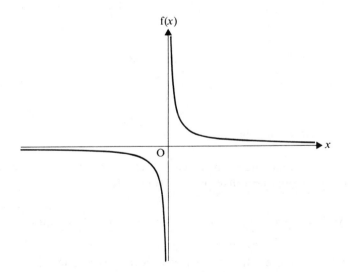

Notice that, as $x \to \pm\infty$, the curve gets closer to the x-axis but does not cross it. Also, as $x \to 0$, the curve approaches the y-axis but again does not cross it.
We say that the x-axis and the y-axis are *asymptotes* to the curve.

EXPONENTIAL FUNCTIONS

Exponent is another word for index or power.

An exponential function is one where the variable is in the index.

For example, 2^x, 3^{-x}, 10^{x+1} are exponential functions of x

Consider the function $f(x) = 2^x$ for which a table of corresponding values of x and $f(x)$ and a graph are given below.

x	$-\infty \leftarrow \dots$	-10	-1	$-\frac{1}{10}$	0	$\frac{1}{10}$	1	10	$\dots \rightarrow \infty$
$f(x)$	$0 \leftarrow \dots$	$\frac{1}{1024}$	$\frac{1}{2}$	0.93	1	1.07	2	1024	$\dots \rightarrow \infty$

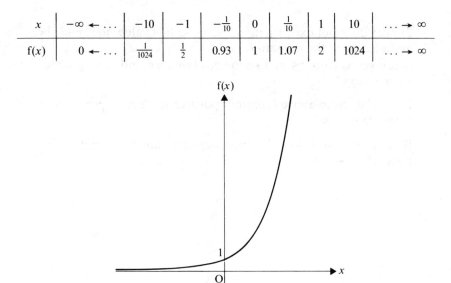

From these we see that

1) 2^x has a real value for all real values of x and 2^x is positive for all values of x, i.e. the range of f is $f(x) > 0$

2) As $x \rightarrow -\infty$, $f(x) \rightarrow 0$, i.e. the x-axis is an asymptote.

3) As x increases, $f(x)$ increases at a rapidly accelerating rate.

Note also that the curve crosses the y-axis at $(0, 1)$, i.e. $f(0) = 1$. In fact for any function of the form $f(x) = a^x$, where a is a constant and greater than 1, $f(0) = 1$, and the curve representing it is similar in shape to that for 2^x

Example 12d _____

Sketch the graph of the function given by $f(x) = \dfrac{1}{2-x}$

$f(x) = \dfrac{1}{2-x}$ does not exist when $x = 2$, so the curve $y = f(x)$ does not cross the line $x = 2$

As $x \to 2$ from above, $2 - x$ is negative and approaches zero,

$$\text{so} \qquad \frac{1}{2-x} \to -\infty$$

As $x \to 2$ from below, $2 - x$ is positive and approaches zero,

$$\text{so} \qquad \frac{1}{2-x} \to \infty$$

Therefore the line $x = 2$ is an asymptote.

As $x \to \infty$, $\dfrac{1}{2-x} \to 0$ from below

and as $x \to -\infty$, $\dfrac{1}{2-x} \to 0$ from above

$\left. \rule{0pt}{40pt} \right\}$ $\therefore$ the x-axis is an asymptote.

As this is similar to $f(x) = \dfrac{1}{x}$, we now have enough information to sketch the graph.

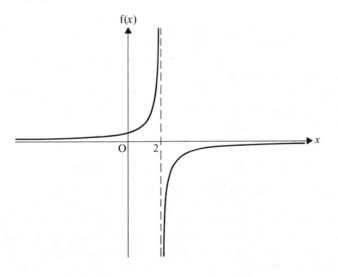

EXERCISE 12d

1. Draw sketch graphs of the following functions.

    (a) 3^x (b) $\dfrac{1}{2x}$ (c) 4^{2x} (d) $\dfrac{1}{x-3}$

2. Write down the values of $f(x) = (\frac{1}{2})^x$ corresponding to $x = -4$, $-3, -2, -1, 0, 1, 2, 3$ and 4 From these values deduce the behaviour of $f(x)$ as $x \to \pm\infty$ and hence sketch the graph of the function.

3. What value of x must be excluded from the domain of
   $f(x) = \dfrac{1}{x+2}$? Describe the behaviour of $f(x)$ as x approaches
   this value from above and from below. Describe also the behaviour of $f(x)$ as $x \to \pm\infty$. Use this information to sketch the graph of $f(x)$

4. By following a procedure similar to that given in Question 3 draw sketch graphs of the following functions.

    (a) $-\dfrac{1}{x}$ (b) $\dfrac{1}{1-2x}$ (c) $\dfrac{2}{x+1}$ (d) $1+\dfrac{1}{x}$

5. Find the values of x where the curve $y = f(x)$ cuts the x-axis and sketch the curve when

    (a) $f(x) = x(x-1)(x+1)$ (b) $f(x) = x(x-1)(x+1)(x-2)$

    (c) $f(x) = (x^2-1)(2-x)$ (d) $f(x) = (x^2-1)(4-x^2)$

SIMPLE TRANSFORMATION OF CURVES

Transformations of curves are best appreciated if they can be 'seen', so this section starts with an investigative approach using a graphics calculator or a computer with a graph-drawing package. This exercise is not essential and all the necessary conclusions are drawn analytically in the next part of the text.

EXERCISE 12e

You will need a graphics calculator or computer for this exercise.

1. (a) On the screen, draw the graph of $y = 2^x$. Superimpose the graphs of $y = 2^x + 2$ and $y = 2^x - 1$ Clear the screen and again draw the graph of $y = 2^x$. This time superimpose the graph of $y = 2^x + c$ for a variety of values of c
   (b) Describe the transformation that maps the graph of $f(x) = 2^x$ to the graph of $g(x) = 2^x + c$
   (c) Repeat (a) and (b) for other simple functions, e.g., x^2, x^3, $1/x$

2. Use a procedure similar to that described in Question 1 to investigate the relationship between the graphs of $f(x)$ and $f(x + c)$

3. Investigate the relationship between the graphs of
   (a) $f(x)$ and $-f(x)$ (b) $f(x)$ and $f(-x)$

TRANSLATIONS

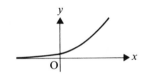

Consider the function f where $f(x) = 2^x$
The graph of this function is the curve $y = 2^x$

1) Now consider the function g where $g(x) = f(x) + 2$

Comparing $f(x) = 2^x$ with $g(x) = 2^x + 2$ we can see that for a particular value of x, the value of $g(x)$ is 2 units greater than the corresponding value of $f(x)$. Therefore, for equal values of x, points on the curve $y = g(x)$ are two units above points on the curve $y = f(x)$, i.e. the curve $y = 2^x + 2$ is a translation of the curve $y = 2^x$ by two units in the positive direction of the y-axis.

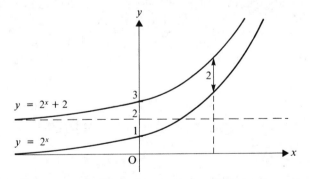

In general, for any function f, the curve $y = f(x) + c$ is the translation of the curve $y = f(x)$ by c units parallel to the y-axis.

2) Consider the function $g(x) = 2^{x-2}$

Comparing $f(x) = 2^x$ with $g(x) = 2^{x-2}$ we can see that the values of $f(x)$ and $g(x)$ are the same when the input value to $g(x)$ is 2 units greater than the input value for $f(x)$, i.e. $f(a) = g(a + 2)$

Therefore, for equal values of y, points on the curve $y = 2^{x-2}$ are 2 units to the *right* of points on the curve $y = 2^x$, i.e. the curve $y = 2^{x-2}$ is a translation of the curve $y = 2^x$ by 2 units in the positive direction of the x-axis.

Similarly, considering $h(x) = 2^{x+5}$, the values of $f(x)$ and $h(x)$ are the same when the input to $h(x)$ is five units less than the input to $f(x)$. Thus for equal values of y, points on the curve $y = 2^{x+5}$ are 5 units to the *left* of points on the curve $y = 2^x$

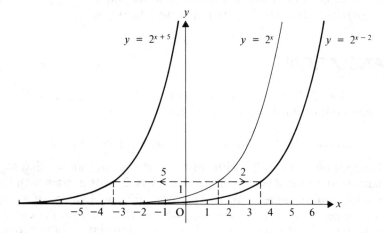

In general, the curve $y = f(x + c)$ is a translation of the curve $y = f(x)$ by c units parallel to the x-axis.

If $c > 0$, the translation is in the negative direction of the x-axis and if $c < 0$, the translation is in the positive direction of the x-axis.

REFLECTIONS

1) Consider the function $g(x) = -f(x)$

For a given value of x, $g(x)$ is equal to $-f(x)$. Therefore for equal values of x, points on the curve $y = -2^x$ are the reflection in the

x-axis of points on the curve $y = 2^x$, i.e. the curve $y = -f(x)$ is the reflection in the x-axis of the curve $y = f(x)$

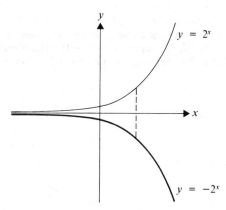

In general, the curve $y = -f(x)$ is the reflection of the curve $y = f(x)$ in the x-axis.

2) Consider the function $g(x) = 2^{-x}$

Comparing $f(x) = 2^x$ with $g(x) = 2^{-x}$ we see that $f(x)$ and $g(x)$ have the same value when the inputs to $g(x)$ and $f(x)$ are equal in value but opposite in sign, i.e. $g(a) = f(-a)$

Therefore points with the same y-coordinates on the curves $y = 2^{-x}$ and $y = 2^x$, are symmetrical about $x = 0$, i.e. the curve $y = 2^{-x}$ is the reflection of the curve $y = 2^x$ in the y-axis.

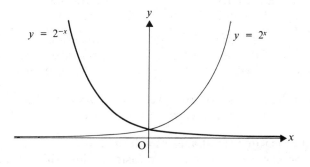

In general, the curve $y = f(-x)$ is the reflection of the curve $y = f(x)$ in the y-axis.

Example 12f _____

Sketch the curve $y = (x - 1)^3$.

The shape and position of the curve $y = x^3$ is known. If $f(x) = x^3$, then $(x - 1)^3 = f(x - 1)$, so the curve $y = (x - 1)^3$ is a translation of the first curve by one unit in the positive direction of the x-axis.

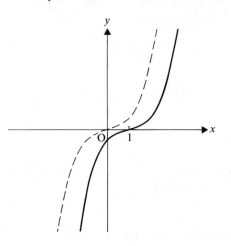

_____

EXERCISE 12f

Sketch each of the following curves.

1. $y = -x^2$ 2. $y = -\dfrac{1}{x}$ 3. $y = -3^x$

4. $y = 1 + \dfrac{1}{x}$ 5. $y = 2^x - 3$ 6. $y = \dfrac{1}{x} - 2$

7. $y = (x - 4)^4$ 8. $y = x^2 - 9$ 9. $y = \dfrac{1}{x - 2}$

10. On the same set of axes sketch the graphs of $f(x) = x^3$, $f(x) = (x + 1)^3$, $f(x) = -(x + 1)^3$ and $f(x) = 2 - (x + 1)^3$

11. On the same set of axes sketch the lines $y = 2x - 1$ and $y = \frac{1}{2}(x + 1)$. Describe a transformation which maps the first line to the second line.

12. Repeat Question 11 for the curves $y = 1 + \dfrac{1}{x}$ and $y = \dfrac{1}{x - 1}$

13. Find the coordinates of the reflection of the point $(2, 5)$ in the line $y = x$

14. P′ is the reflection of the point $P(a, b)$ in the line $y = x$. Find the coordinates of P′ in terms of a and b

INVERSE FUNCTIONS

Consider the function f where $f(x) = 2x$ for $x \in \{2, 3, 4\}$

Under this function, the domain $\{2, 3, 4\}$ maps to the image-set $\{4, 6, 8\}$ and this is illustrated by the arrow diagram.

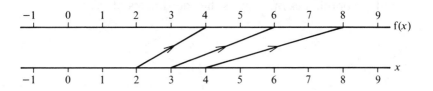

It is possible to reverse this mapping, i.e. we can map each member of the image-set back to the corresponding member of the domain by halving each member of the image-set.

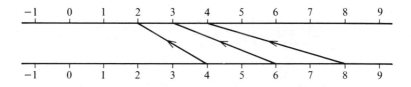

This procedure can be expressed algebraically, i.e.
for $x \in \{4, 6, 8\}$, $x \to \frac{1}{2}x$ maps 4 to 2, 6 to 3 and 8 to 4

This reverse mapping is a function in its own right and it is called the *inverse* function of f where $f(x) = 2x$

Denoting this inverse function by f^{-1} we can write $f^{-1}(x) = \frac{1}{2}x$
In fact, $f(x) = 2x$ can be reversed for all real values of x and the procedure for doing this is a function.

Therefore, for $f(x) = 2x$, $f^{-1}(x) = \frac{1}{2}x$ is such that f^{-1} reverses f for all real values of x, i.e. f^{-1} maps the output of f to the input of f.

In general, for any function f,

> if there exists a function, g, that maps the output of f back to its input, i.e. $g: f(x) \rightarrow x$, then this function is called the inverse of f and it is denoted by f^{-1}.

THE GRAPH OF A FUNCTION AND ITS INVERSE

Consider the curve that is obtained by reflecting $y = f(x)$ in the line $y = x$. The reflection of a point $A(a, b)$ on the curve $y = f(x)$, is the point A' whose coordinates are (b, a), i.e. interchanging the x and y coordinates of A gives the coordinates of A'.

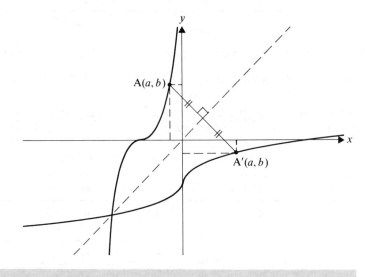

> We can therefore obtain the equation of the reflected curve by interchanging x and y in the equation $y = f(x)$

Now the coordinates of A on $y = f(x)$ can be written as $[a, f(a)]$. Therefore the coordinates of A' on the reflected curve are $[f(a), a]$, i.e. the equation of the reflected curve is such that the output of f is mapped to the input of f.

> Hence if the equation of the reflected curve can be written in the form $y = g(x)$, then g is the inverse of f, i.e. $g = f^{-1}$.

To illustrate these properties, consider the curve $y = 2^x$ and its reflection in the line $y = x$

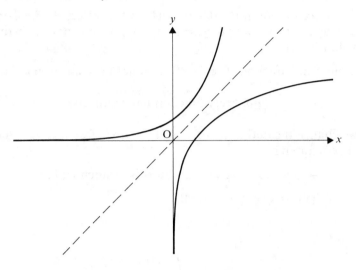

The equation of the reflected curve is given by $x = 2^y$

Using the 'log' notation introduced in Chapter 3, we can write this equation in the form $y = \log_2 x$

Therefore for the function $f(x) = 2^x$ the inverse function is given by $f^{-1}(x) = \log_2 x$

Any curve whose equation can be written in the form $y = f(x)$ can be reflected in the line $y = x$. However this reflected curve may not have an equation that can be written in the form $y = f^{-1}(x)$

Consider the curve $y = x^2$ and its reflection in the line $y = x$

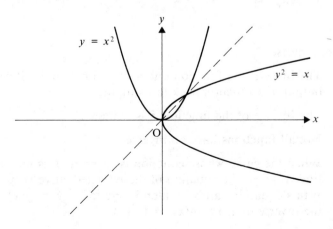

The equation of the image curve is $x = y^2 \Rightarrow y = \pm\sqrt{x}$ and $x \rightarrow \pm\sqrt{x}$ is not a function.

(We can see this from the diagram as, on the reflected curve, one value of x maps to two values of y. So in this case y cannot be written as a function of x.)

Therefore the function $f : x \rightarrow x^2$ does not have an inverse, i.e.

> not every function has an inverse.

If we change the definition of f to $f : x \rightarrow x^2$ for $x \in \mathbb{R}^+$ then the inverse mapping

is $x \rightarrow \sqrt{x}$ for $x \in \mathbb{R}^+$ and this is a function, i.e.

$$f^{-1}(x) = \sqrt{x} \text{ for } x \in \mathbb{R}^+$$

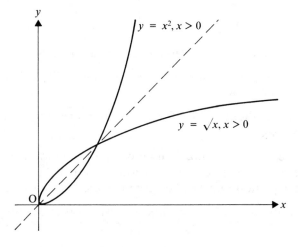

To summarise:

> The inverse of a function undoes the function, i.e. it maps the output of a function back to its input.
>
> The inverse of the function f is written f^{-1}
>
> Not all functions have an inverse.
>
> When the curve whose equation is $y = f(x)$ is reflected in the line $y = x$, the equation of the reflected curve is $x = f(y)$
> If this equation can be written in the form $y = g(x)$ then g is the inverse of f, i.e. $g(x) = f^{-1}(x)$

Examples 12g _____

1. Determine whether there is an inverse of the function f given by

    $$f(x) = 2 + \frac{1}{x}$$

    If f^{-1} exists, express it as a function of x

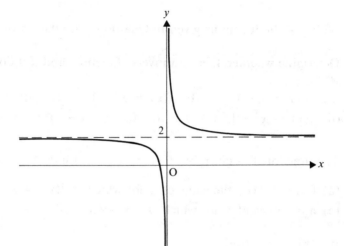

    From the sketch of $f(x) = 2 + \frac{1}{x}$, we see that one value of $f(x)$
    maps to one value of x, therefore the reverse mapping is a function.
    The equation of the reflection of $y = 2 + \frac{1}{x}$ can be written as

    $$x = 2 + \frac{1}{y} \ \Rightarrow \ y = \frac{1}{x-2}$$

    $\therefore$ when $f(x) = 2 + \frac{1}{x}$, $f^{-1}(x) = \frac{1}{x-2}$

    _____

2. Find $f^{-1}(4)$ when $f(x) = 5x - 1$

    _____

    If $y = f(x)$, i.e. $y = 5x - 1$,

    then $x = 5y - 1$ $\Rightarrow$ $y = \frac{1}{5}(x + 1)$

    i.e. $f^{-1}(x) = \frac{1}{5}(x + 1)$

    $\therefore$ $f^{-1}(4) = \frac{1}{5}(4 + 1) = 1$

    _____

EXERCISE 12g

1. Sketch the graphs of $f(x)$ and $f^{-1}(x)$ on the same axes.
   (a) $f(x) = 3x - 1$ (b) $f(x) = 2^{-x}$ (c) $f(x) = (x - 1)^3$
   (d) $f(x) = 2 - x$ (e) $f(x) = \dfrac{1}{x - 3}$ (f) $f(x) = \dfrac{1}{x}$

2. Which of the functions given in Question 1 are their own inverses?

3. Determine whether f has an inverse function, and if it does, find it when
   (a) $f(x) = x + 1$ (b) $f(x) = x^2 + 1$ (c) $f(x) = x^3 + 1$
   (d) $f(x) = x^2 - 4, \ x \geqslant 0$ (e) $f(x) = (x + 1)^4, \ x \geqslant -1$

4. The function f is given by $f(x) = 1 - \dfrac{1}{x}$. Find
   (a) $f^{-1}(4)$ (b) the value of x for which $f^{-1}(x) = 2$
   (c) any values of x for which $f^{-1}(x) = x$

5. If $f(x) = 3^x$, find
   (a) $f(2)$ (b) $f^{-1}(9)$ (c) $f^{-1}(\tfrac{1}{3})$

COMPOUND FUNCTIONS

Consider the two functions f and g given by

$$f(x) = x^2 \quad \text{and} \quad g(x) = \frac{1}{x}$$

These two functions can be combined in several ways.

1) They can be added or subtracted,

i.e. $f(x) + g(x) = x^2 + \dfrac{1}{x} \quad$ and $\quad f(x) - g(x) = x^2 - \dfrac{1}{x}$

2) They can be multiplied or divided,

i.e. $f(x)g(x) = (x^2)\left(\dfrac{1}{x}\right) = x \quad$ and $\quad \dfrac{f(x)}{g(x)} = \dfrac{x^2}{1/x} = x^3$

3) The output of f can be made the input of g,

i.e. $x \xrightarrow{\;f\;} x^2 \xrightarrow{\;g\;} \dfrac{1}{x^2}$ or $g[f(x)] = g(x^2) = \dfrac{1}{x^2}$

Therefore the function $x \rightarrow 1/x^2$ is obtained by taking the function g of the function f.

FUNCTION OF A FUNCTION

A compound function formed in the way described in **(3)** above is known as a *function of a function* and it is denoted by gf

For example, if $f(x) = 3^x$ and $g(x) = 1 - x$ then gf(x) means the function g of the function $f(x)$,

i.e. $gf(x) = g(3^x) = 1 - 3^x$

Similarly $fg(x) = f(1 - x) = 3^{(1-x)}$

Note that gf(x) is *not* the same as fg(x)

EXERCISE 12h

1. If f, g and h are functions defined by $f(x) = x^2$, $g(x) = 1/x$, $h(x) = 1 - x$ find as a function of x
   (a) fg   (b) fh   (c) hg   (d) hf   (e) gf

2. If $f(x) = 2x - 1$ and $g(x) = x^3$ find the value of
   (a) gf(3)   (b) fg(2)   (c) fg(0)   (d) gf(0)

3. Given that $f(x) = 2x$, $g(x) = 1 + x$ and $h(x) = x^2$, find as a function of x
   (a) hg   (b) fhg   (c) ghf

4. The function $f(x) = (2 - x)^2$ can be expressed as a function of a function. Find g and h as functions of x such that gh$(x) = f(x)$

5. Repeat Question 4 when $f(x) = (x + 1)^4$

6. Express the function $f(x)$ as a combination of functions $g(x)$ and $h(x)$, and define $g(x)$ and $h(x)$, where $f(x)$ is
   (a) $10^{(x+1)}$ (b) $1/(3x - 2)^2$ (c) $2^x + x^2$
   (d) $(2x + 1)/x$ (e) $(5x - 6)^4$ (f) $(x - 1)(x^2 - 2)$

MIXED EXERCISE 12

1. A function f is defined by $f(x) = 1/(1 - x)$, $x \neq 1$
   (a) Why is 1 excluded from the domain of f?
   (b) Find the value of $f(-3)$
   (c) Sketch the curve $y = f(x)$
   (d) Find $f^{-1}(x)$ in terms of x and give the domain of f^{-1}

2. Find the greatest or least value of each of the following functions, stating the value of x at which they occur.
   (a) $f(x) = x^2 - 3x + 5$ (b) $f(x) = 2x^2 - 7x + 1$
   (c) $f(x) = (x - 1)(x + 5)$

3. If $f(x) = 10^x$, sketch the following curves on the same set of axes.
   (a) $y = f(x)$ (b) $y = f(x + 3)$ (c) $y = f^{-1}(x)$

4. Given that $f(x) = 10^x$, $g(x) = x^2$ and $h(x) = 1/x$,
   (a) find fg(2), hg(3) and gf(-1)
   (b) find, in terms of x, hfg(x) and gfh(x)
   (c) if they exist, find $f^{-1}(x)$, $g^{-1}(x)$ and $h^{-1}(x)$
   (d) the value(s) of x for which $gh(x) = 9$
   (e) does the function $(gh)^{-1}$ exist?

5. Draw sketches of the following curves, showing any asymptotes.
   (a) $(x - 2)(x - 3)(x - 4)$ (b) $y = \dfrac{1}{3 - x}$ (c) $y = 2^{4 - x}$

6. The function f is given by $f(x) = 2^{(3x - 2)}$
   (a) find $g(x)$ and $h(x)$ such that $f = gh$
   (b) evaluate ff(2) and $f^{-1}(2)$

7. The functions f, g and h are defined by $f(x) = 2x$, $g(x) = 3x^2$ and $h(x) = x - 1$
   (a) Sketch the curves $y = g(x - 3)$ and $y = gf^{-1}(x)$
   (b) Find the value(s) of x for which $f^{-1}(x) = g(x)$

CHAPTER 13

INEQUALITIES

MANIPULATING INEQUALITIES

An inequality compares two unequal quantities.

Consider, for example, the two real numbers 3 and 8 for which

$$8 > 3$$

The inequality remains true, i.e. the inequality sign is unchanged, when the same term is added or subtracted on both sides, e.g.

$$8 + 2 > 3 + 2 \quad \Rightarrow \quad 10 > 5$$

and
$$8 - 1 > 3 - 1 \quad \Rightarrow \quad 7 > 2$$

The inequality sign is unchanged also when both sides are multiplied or divided by a positive quantity, e.g.

$$8 \times 4 > 3 \times 4 \quad \Rightarrow \quad 32 > 12$$

and
$$8 \div 2 > 3 \div 2 \quad \Rightarrow \quad 4 > 1\tfrac{1}{2}$$

If, however, both sides are multiplied or divided by a *negative* quantity the inequality is no longer true. For example, if we multiply by -1, the LHS becomes -8 and the RHS becomes -3 so the correct inequality is now LHS < RHS, i.e.

$$8 \times -1 < 3 \times -1 \quad \Rightarrow \quad -8 < -3$$

Similarly, dividing by -2 gives $-4 < -1\tfrac{1}{2}$

These examples are illustrations of the following general rules.

Adding or subtracting a term, or multiplying or dividing both sides by a positive number, does not alter the inequality sign.

Multiplying or dividing both sides by a *negative* number reverses the inequality sign.

i.e. if a, b and k are real numbers, and $a > b$ then,

$a + k > b + k$ for *all* values of k

$ak > bk$ for *positive* values of k

$ak < bk$ for *negative* values of k

SOLVING LINEAR INEQUALITIES

SG

When an inequality contains an unknown quantity, the rules given above can be used to 'solve' it. Whereas the solution of an equation is a value, or values, of the variable, the solution of an inequality is a range, or ranges of values, of the variable.

If the unknown quantity appears only in linear form, we have a *linear inequality* and the solution range has only *one boundary*.

Example 13a _____

Find the set of values of x that satisfy the inequality $x - 5 < 2x + 1$

$$x - 5 < 2x + 1$$

$\Rightarrow$ $x < 2x + 6$ adding 5 to each side

$\Rightarrow$ $-x < 6$ subtracting $2x$ from each side

$\Rightarrow$ $x > -6$ multiplying both sides by -1

Therefore the set of values of x satisfying the given inequality is

$$x > -6$$

_____

EXERCISE 13a

Solve the following inequalities.

1. $x - 4 < 3 - x$ **2.** $x + 3 < 3x - 5$ **3.** $x < 4x + 9$

4. $7 - 3x < 13$ **5.** $x > 5x - 2$ **6.** $2x - 1 < x - 4$

7. $1 - 7x > x + 3$ **8.** $2(3x - 5) > 6$ **9.** $3(3 - 2x) < 2(3 + x)$

SOLVING QUADRATIC INEQUALITIES

A quadratic inequality is one in which the variable appears to the power 2, e.g. $x^2 - 3 > 2x$

The solution is a range or ranges of values of the variable with *two boundaries*.

If the terms in the inequality can be collected and factorised, a graphical solution is easy to find.

Example 13b _____

Find the range(s) of values of x that satisfy the inequality
$x^2 - 3 > 2x$

$$x^2 - 3 > 2x$$

$$\Rightarrow \qquad x^2 - 2x - 3 > 0$$

$$\Rightarrow \qquad (x - 3)(x + 1) > 0$$

or $\qquad$ $f(x) > 0$ where $f(x) = (x - 3)(x + 1)$

If we sketch the graph of $f(x)$ then $f(x) > 0$ where the graph is above the x-axis.
The values of x corresponding to these portions of the graph satisfy $f(x) > 0$
The points where $f(x) = 0$, i.e. where $x = 3$ and -1 are not part of this
solution and this is indicated on the sketch by open circles.

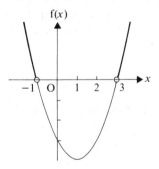

From the graph we see that the ranges of values of x which satisfy the given inequality are

$$x < -1 \quad \text{and} \quad x > 3$$

_____

Note that the solution in the above example was two separate ranges each with its own boundary. If however we consider the inequality $(x - 3)(x + 1) < 0$ the part of the graph of $f(x)$ for which $f(x) < 0$ is below the x-axis and the corresponding values of x are $-3 < x < 1$
This time there is only one range, but it still has two boundaries.

EXERCISE 13b

Find the ranges of values of x that satisfy the following inequalities.

1. $(x - 2)(x - 1) > 0$ 2. $(x + 3)(x - 5) \geqslant 0$

3. $(x - 2)(x + 4) < 0$ 4. $(2x - 1)(x + 1) \geqslant 0$

5. $x^2 - 4x > 3$ 6. $4x^2 < 1$

7. $(2 - x)(x + 4) \geqslant 0$ 8. $5x^2 > 3x + 2$

9. $(3 - 2x)(x + 5) \leqslant 0$ 10. $(x - 1)^2 > 9$

11. $(x + 1)(x + 2) \leqslant 4$ 12. $(1 - x)(4 - x) > x + 11$

RATIONAL FRACTIONS IN INEQUALITIES

Consider the inequality $\dfrac{x - 2}{x + 5} < 3$

The initial problem here is that we do not know whether $x + 5$ is positive or negative. This prevents the apparently obvious step of multiplying both sides by $x + 5$. A number of different ways of solving inequalities of this type are demonstrated in the worked examples that follow. No one method is ideal in all cases and the reader is advised to consider a variety of approaches before deciding how to solve a particular example.

Examples 13c _____

1. Find the range of values of x for which $\dfrac{x - 2}{x - 5} > 3$

Although we cannot multiply both sides by $x - 5$ because its sign is not known, we *can* multiply both sides by $(x - 5)^2$ which cannot be negative.

$$\frac{x - 2}{x - 5} > 3$$

$\therefore \qquad\qquad\qquad (x - 2)(x - 5) > 3(x - 5)^2$

$\Rightarrow \qquad\qquad (x - 5)\{(x - 2) - 3(x - 5)\} > 0$

Note that $(x - 5)$ must not be cancelled because we do not know its sign.

$\Rightarrow \qquad\qquad\qquad (x - 5)(13 - 2x) > 0$

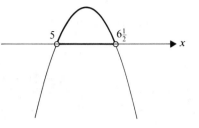

∴ the required range is $5 < x < 6\frac{1}{2}$

---

2. Find the possible values of x for which $\dfrac{(x-2)(x+3)(x-4)}{x-1} < 0$

$$f(x) = \frac{(x-2)(x+3)(x-4)}{x-1} < 0$$

The critical values of x in this inequality are -3, 1, 2 and 4 so we construct a table in which the columns are separated by these values, i.e.

	$x < -3$	$-3 < x < 1$	$1 < x < 2$	$2 < x < 4$	$x > 4$
$x + 3$	$-$	$+$	$+$	$+$	$+$
$x - 1$	$-$	$-$	$+$	$+$	$+$
$x - 2$	$-$	$-$	$-$	$+$	$+$
$x - 4$	$-$	$-$	$-$	$-$	$+$
$f(x)$	$+$	$-$	$+$	$-$	$+$

Therefore $\dfrac{(x-2)(x+3)(x-4)}{x-1} < 0$ if $-3 < x < 1$ or $2 < x < 4$

3. What values of x satisfy the inequality $\dfrac{(x-2)^2-8}{5-4x} > 1$?

$$\frac{(x-2)^2-8}{5-4x} > 1 \quad \Rightarrow \quad \frac{(x-2)^2-8}{5-4x} - 1 > 0$$

$$\Rightarrow \quad \frac{(x-2)^2-8-(5-4x)}{(5-4x)} > 0$$

$$\Rightarrow \quad \frac{x^2-9}{5-4x} > 0$$

$$\Rightarrow \quad \frac{(x-3)(x+3)}{5-4x} > 0$$

i.e. $\dfrac{f(x)}{g(x)} > 0$ where $f(x) = (x-3)(x+3)$
                     and $g(x) = 5-4x$

This fraction is positive if $f(x)$ and $g(x)$ have the same sign.

     $f(x) > 0$ if $x < -3$ or $x > 3$ and $g(x) > 0$ if $x < 1\frac{1}{4}$

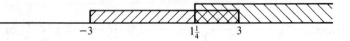

$\therefore$ $f(x)$ and $g(x)$ are *both* positive if $x < -3$

Similarly,

         $f(x) < 0$ if $-3 < x < 3$ and $g(x) < 0$ if $x > 1\frac{1}{4}$

$\therefore$ $f(x)$ and $g(x)$ are *both* negative if $1\frac{1}{4} < x < 3$

$\therefore \quad \dfrac{x^2 - 9}{5 - 4x}$ is positive, i.e. $\dfrac{(x - 2)^2}{5 - 4x} > 1$

for values of x in *both* of the ranges found above,

i.e. for $\qquad\qquad\qquad 1\frac{1}{4} < x < 3 \ \textit{and} \ x < -3$

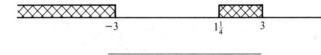

4. Find the range of values of x for which $\ 3x + 4 < x^2 - 6 < 9 - 2x$

$3x + 4 < x^2 - 6 < 9 - 2x$ is called a *double inequality* because it contains two inequalities, i.e. $3x + 4 < x^2 - 6$ and $x^2 - 6 < 9 - 2x$

We are looking for the set of values of x for which *both* inequalities are satisfied so we first solve each of them separately.

$$3x + 4 < x^2 - 6 \qquad\qquad\qquad\qquad x^2 - 6 < 9 - 2x$$

$\Rightarrow \quad 3x - x^2 + 10 < 0 \qquad\qquad\qquad \Rightarrow \quad x^2 + 2x - 15 < 0$

$\Rightarrow \quad x^2 - 3x - 10 > 0 \qquad\qquad\qquad \Rightarrow \quad (x + 5)(x - 3) < 0$

$\Rightarrow (x - 5)(x + 2) > 0$

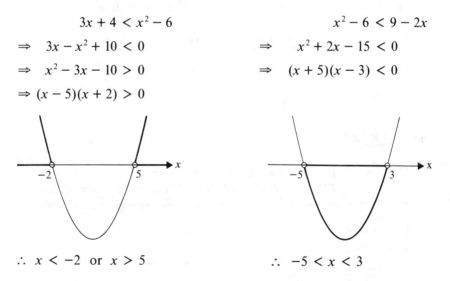

$\therefore \ x < -2 \ \text{or} \ x > 5 \qquad\qquad\qquad \therefore \ -5 < x < 3$

The required set of values of x must satisfy *both* of these conditions,

i.e.

$\therefore$ the solution set is $\ -5 < x < -2$

EXERCISE 13c

For what range(s) of values of x are the following inequalities valid?

1. $\dfrac{x-1}{2+x} < 1$

2. $\dfrac{x-1}{2+x} > 1$

3. $\dfrac{3}{x-1} > 2$

4. $\dfrac{x}{2x-8} > 3$

5. $\dfrac{12}{x-3} < x+1$

6. $\dfrac{x}{x-2} < \dfrac{x}{x-1}$

7. $\dfrac{(x-2)}{(x-1)(x-3)} > 0$

8. $\dfrac{2x}{(x-4)^2} > 1$

9. $\dfrac{(x-1)(x-2)}{(x+1)(x-3)} < 0$

10. $(3x-2)(2x+1) < 6x-3$

11. $(x+1)(x+3)(x+5) > 0$

12. $2-x > 2x+4 > x$

13. $x-1 < 3x+1 < x+5$

14. $2x-1 < x^2-4 < 12$

15. $x-4 < x(x-4) < 5$

16. $x-3 > x^2-9 > -5$

PROBLEMS

The types of problem which involve inequalities are very varied. Their solutions depend not only on all the methods used so far in this chapter but also on other facts known to the reader, for example:

1) a perfect square can never be negative.

2) the nature of the roots of a quadratic equation $ax^2 + bx + c = 0$ depends upon whether $b^2 - 4ac = 0$ or $b^2 - 4ac > 0$ or $b^2 - 4ac < 0$. As two of the above conditions are inequalities, many problems about the roots of a quadratic equation require the solution or interpretation, of inequalities.

The worked examples that follow are intended to give the reader some ideas to use in problem solving and make no claim to cover every situation.

Examples 13d _____

1. Find the range(s) of values of k for which the roots of the equation $kx^2 + kx - 2 = 0$ are real.

$$kx^2 + kx - 2 = 0$$

For real roots '$b^2 - 4ac$' $\geqslant 0$

i.e. $\qquad k^2 - 4(k)(-2) \geqslant 0$

$\Rightarrow \qquad\qquad k(k + 8) \geqslant 0$

From the sketch we see that
$k(k + 8) \geqslant 0$ for
$k \leqslant -8$ and $k \geqslant 0$

$f(k) = k(k + 8)$

Therefore the equation $kx^2 + kx - 2 = 0$ has real roots if the value of k lies in either of the ranges $k \leqslant -8$ or $k \geqslant 0$

_____

Note. This type of question is sometimes expressed in another, less obvious, way, i.e. 'If x is real and $kx^2 + kx - 2 = 0$, find the values that k can take'. Once the reader appreciates that, because x is real the roots of the equation are real, the solution is identical to that above.

_____

2. Prove that $x^2 + 2xy + 2y^2$ cannot be negative.

Knowing that a perfect square cannot be negative, we rearrange the given expression in the form of perfect squares.

$$x^2 + 2xy + 2y^2 = x^2 + 2xy + y^2 + y^2$$
$$= (x + y)^2 + y^2$$

Each of the two terms on the RHS is a square and so cannot be negative.

Therefore $x^2 + 2xy + 2y^2$ cannot be negative.

_____

3. Find the values of p for which $x^2 - 2px + p + 6$ is positive for all real values of x

$x^2 - 2px + p + 6$ is positive for all values of x

Therefore the graph of f(x), where f(x) $= x^2 - 2px + p + 6$, is entirely above the x-axis, i.e.

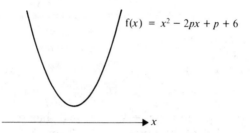

f(x) $= x^2 - 2px + p + 6$

The graph never crosses the x-axis so there are no values of x for which f(x) $= 0$, i.e. $x^2 - 2px + p + 6 = 0$ has no real roots.

$\therefore$ '$b^2 - 4ac$' < 0 $\Rightarrow$ $(-2p)^2 - 4(1)(p + 6) < 0$

$\Rightarrow$ $4p^2 - 4p - 24 < 0$

$\Rightarrow$ $p^2 - p - 6 < 0$

$\Rightarrow$ $(p + 2)(p - 3) < 0$

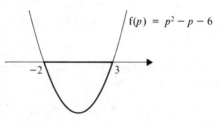

f(p) $= p^2 - p - 6$

From the graph of f(p) $= p^2 - p - 6$ we see that f(p) < 0 for values of p between -2 and 3

Therefore $x^2 - 2px + p + 6$ is positive for all real values of x provided that $-2 < p < 3$

4. If x is real find the set of possible values of the function $\dfrac{x^2}{x+1}$

If we use $y = \dfrac{x^2}{x+1}$ we are looking for the range of values of y

To make use of the fact that x is real we need a quadratic equation in x

$$y = \frac{x^2}{x+1} \;\Rightarrow\; x^2 - yx - y = 0$$

Since x is real, the roots of this equation are real, so '$b^2 - 4ac$' $\geqslant 0$

i.e. $(-y)^2 - 4(1)(-y) \geqslant 0 \;\Rightarrow\; y(y+4) \geqslant 0$

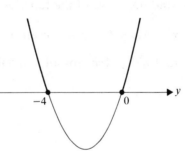

$\therefore\; y \leqslant -4$ or $y \geqslant 0$

Therefore, for real values of x,

$$\frac{x^2}{x+1} \leqslant -4 \quad\text{or}\quad \frac{x^2}{x+1} \geqslant 0$$

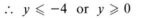

EXERCISE 13d

1. Find the values of p for which the given equation has real roots.
   (a) $x^2 + (p+3)x + 4p = 0$ (b) $x^2 + 3x + 1 = px$

2. Find the range of values of a for which the equation
   $x^2 - ax + (a+3) = 0$ has no real roots.

3. What is the set of values of p for which $p(x^2 + 2) < 2x^2 + 6x + 1$
   for all real values of x?

In Questions 4 to 9 find the set of possible values of the given function.

4. $\dfrac{x+1}{2x^2+x+1}$ **5.** $\dfrac{1+x^2}{x}$ **6.** $\dfrac{x-2}{(x+2)(x-3)}$

7. $\dfrac{x}{1+x^2}$ **8.** $\dfrac{x-1}{x(x+1)}$ **9.** $x+1+\dfrac{1}{x+1}$

10. Find the set of values of k for which $x^2+3kx+k$ is positive for all real values of x

11. Show that, if x is real, the function $\dfrac{2-x}{x^2-4x+1}$ can take any real value.

12. If x is real, find the range of the function $\dfrac{(2x+1)}{(x^2+2)}$

13. Show that $x^2-4xy+5y^2 \geqslant 0$ for all real values of x and y

14. Prove that $(a+b)^2 \geqslant 4ab$ for all real values of a and b

MIXED EXERCISE 13

Solve each of the inequalities given in Questions 1 to 10.

1. $2x+1 < 4-x$ **2.** $x-5 > 1-3x$

3. $6x-5 > 1+2x$ **4.** $(x-3)(x+2) > 0$

5. $(2x-3)(3x+2) < 0$ **6.** $x^2-3 < 10$

7. $(x-3)^2 > 2$ **8.** $(3-x)(2-x) < 20$

9. $x(4x+3) > 2x-1$ **10.** $(x-6)(x+1) > 2x-12$

In Questions 11 to 16 find the set of values of x for which:

11. $-3 < 5-2x < 3$ **12.** $x^2+x+1 < x+2 < x^2-6x+12$

13. $\dfrac{2x-4}{x-1} < 1$ **14.** $\dfrac{x-1}{x+1} \leqslant x$

15. $2 \geqslant \dfrac{x-1}{x+1} \geqslant 0$ **16.** $\dfrac{(x-1)(x+1)}{(x+2)(x-2)} \leqslant 0$

17. Prove that $x^2 + y^2 - 10y + 25 \geqslant 0$ for all real values of x and y

18. For what values of k does the equation $4x^2 + 8x - 8 = k(4x - 3)$ have real roots?

19. If x is real find the set of possible values of the function
$$\frac{x^2 + 1}{x^2 + x + 1}$$

20. Provided that x is real, prove that the function $\dfrac{2(3x + 1)}{3(x^2 - 9)}$ can take all real values.

CHAPTER 14

DIFFERENTIATION — BASIC

CHORDS, TANGENTS AND NORMALS

Consider any two points, A and B, on any curve.

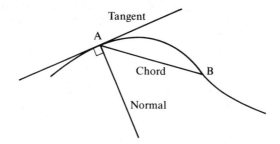

The line joining A and B is called a chord.

The line that touches the curve at A is called the tangent at A.

Note that the word *touch* has a precise mathematical meaning, i.e. a line that meets a curve at a point and carries on without crossing to the other side of the curve at that point, is said to *touch* the curve at the *point of contact*.

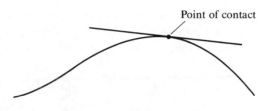

The line perpendicular to the tangent at A is called the normal at A.

THE GRADIENT OF A CURVE

107

108

Gradient, or slope, defines the direction of a line (lines can be straight or curved).

If we imagine walking along a straight line, we walk in the same direction all the time, i.e. the gradient of a straight line is constant.

If, however, we imagine walking along a curve, our direction is continually changing. It follows that the gradient of a curve is not constant but has different values at different points on the curve.

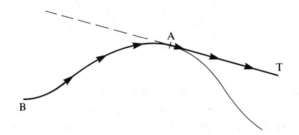

Suppose that we move from B to A along the curve in the diagram above, then our direction is changing all the time. Now if at A we continued to move, but without any further change in direction, we would go along the straight line AT, i.e. along the tangent to the curve at A, so

> the gradient of the curve at A is the same as the gradient of the tangent to the curve at A.

Before a numerical value can be given to a gradient, the line or curve must be drawn on a pair of x and y axes. Then, as the reader will already know, the gradient is the rate at which y increases with respect to x.

For a straight line this is found by taking the coordinates of two points and working out

$$\frac{\text{increase in } y}{\text{increase in } x}$$

This can be used to find the gradient of a tangent to a curve but, if the tangent is just drawn by eye, the value obtained can only be an approximation.

A more precise method is needed for determining the gradient of a curve whose equation is known, so that further analysis can be made of the properties of such a curve.

Let us consider the problem of finding the gradient of the tangent at a point A on a curve.

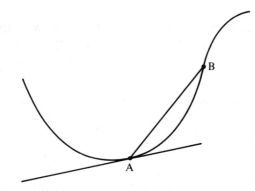

If B is another point on the curve, fairly close to A, then the gradient of the chord AB gives an *approximate* value for the gradient of the tangent at A. As B gets nearer to A, the chord AB gets closer to the tangent at A, so the approximation becomes more accurate.

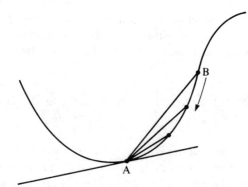

So, as B gets closer and closer to A, we can say,

as   B → A

the gradient of chord AB → the gradient of the tangent at A

This fact can also be expressed in the form

$$\underset{\text{as } B \to A}{\text{limit}} \ (\text{gradient of chord AB}) = \text{gradient of tangent at A}$$

This definition can be applied to a particular point on a particular curve. Suppose, for instance, that we want the gradient of the curve $y = x^2$ at the point where $x = 1$

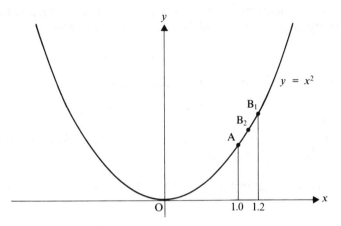

A is the point $(1, 1)$ and we need a succession of points, B_1, B_2, ... getting closer and closer to A. Let us take the points where $x = 1.2, 1.1, 1.05, 1.01, 1.001$, then calculate the corresponding y coordinates, find the increases in x and y between A and B and hence find the gradient of AB.

x	1.2	1.1	1.05	1.01	1.001
$y \quad (= x^2)$	1.44	1.21	1.1025	1.0201	1.002 001
Increase in y	0.44	0.21	0.1025	0.0201	0.002 001
Increase in x	0.2	0.1	0.05	0.01	0.001
Gradient of chord AB	2.2	2.1	2.05	2.01	2.001

From the numbers in the last row of the table it is clear that, as B gets nearer to A, the gradient of the chord gets nearer to 2, i.e.

$$\underset{\text{as } B \to A}{\text{limit}} \ (\text{gradient of chord AB}) = 2$$

It is equally clear that it is much too tedious to go through this process each time we want the gradient at just one point on just one curve and that we need a more general method. For this we use a general point $A(x, y)$ and a variable small change in the value of x between A and B.

A new symbol, δ, is used to denote this small change.

When δ appears as a prefix to any letter representing a variable quantity, it denotes a small increase in that quantity,

e.g. δx means a small increase in x

                          δy means a small increase in y

                          δt means a small increase in t

Note that δ is only a prefix. It does not have an independent value and cannot be treated as a factor.

Now consider again the gradient of the curve with equation $y = x^2$

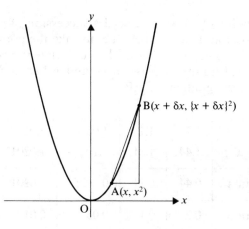

This time we will look for the gradient at *any* point $A(x, y)$ on the curve and use a point B where the x-coordinate of B is $x + \delta x$.

For any point on the curve, $y = x^2$

So, at B, the y-coordinate is $(x + \delta x)^2 = x^2 + 2x\delta x + (\delta x)^2$

Therefore the gradient of chord AB, which is given by $\dfrac{\text{increase in } y}{\text{increase in } x}$,
is

$$\frac{(x + \delta x)^2 - x^2}{(x + \delta x) - x} = \frac{2x\delta x + (\delta x)^2}{\delta x}$$

$$= 2x + \delta x$$

Now as B → A, δx → 0, therefore

$$\text{gradient of curve at } A = \lim_{\text{as B → A}} (\text{gradient of chord AB})$$

$$= \lim_{\text{as } \delta x \to 0} (\text{gradient of chord AB})$$

$$= \lim_{\text{as } \delta x \to 0} (2x + \delta x)$$

$$= 2x$$

This result can now be used to give the gradient at any point on the curve with equation $y = x^2$, where the x-coordinate is given, e.g.

at the point where $x = 3$, the gradient is $2(3) = 6$
and at the point (4, 16), the gradient is $2(4) = 8$

Looking back at the longer method we used on page 225 to find the gradient at the point where $x = 1$, we see that the value obtained there is confirmed by using the general result,
i.e. gradient $= 2x = 2(1) = 2$

DIFFERENTIATION

The process of finding a general expression for the gradient of a curve at any point is known as differentiation.

The general gradient expression for a curve $y = f(x)$ is itself a function so it is called the *gradient function*. For the curve $y = x^2$ for example, the gradient function is $2x$.

Because the gradient function is derived from the given function, it is more often called the *derived function* or the *derivative*.

The method used above, in which the limit of the gradient of a chord was used to find the derived function, is known as *differentiating from first principles*. It is the fundamental way in which the gradient of each new type of function is found and, although many short cuts can be developed, it is important to understand this basic method.

Example 14a _____

By differentiating from first principles, find the gradient function of the expression $x^3 + 5$. Find also the gradient at the point $(2, 13)$ on the curve $y = x^3 + 5$

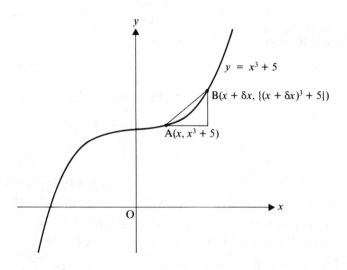

Let A and B be two neighbouring points on the curve, where A is the point (x, y) and the x-coordinate of B is $x + \delta x$

Therefore at A $\qquad\qquad y = x^3 + 5$

and $\qquad$ at B $\qquad\qquad y = (x + \delta x)^3 + 5$

The gradient of chord AB is $\qquad \dfrac{\{(x + \delta x)^3 + 5\} - \{x^3 + 5\}}{\{x + \delta x\} - x}$

which simplifies to $\qquad 3x^2 + 3x\delta x + (\delta x)^2$

The gradient of the curve at A $= \underset{\text{as } \delta x \to 0}{\text{limit}} \ \{3x^2 + 3x\delta x + (\delta x)^2\}$

$\qquad\qquad\qquad\qquad\qquad = 3x^2$

Therefore the gradient function of $x^3 + 5$ is $3x^2$

At the point $(2, 13)$, $x = 2$, so the gradient is $3(2)^2 = 12$

_____

EXERCISE 14a

Find, by differentiating from first principles, the derivative (i.e. the gradient function) of each of the following expressions. Hence find the gradient of the curve $y = f(x)$ at the given point.

1. $4x$; $(1, 4)$ **2.** $x - 1$; $(3, 2)$

3. x^3; $(1, 1)$ **4.** $x^2 + 2$; $(2, 6)$

5. $x^2 - x$; $(1, 0)$ **6.** x^4; $(2, 16)$
                                              (Pascal's triangle will help)

NOTATION

We have seen that differentiating x^2 gives $2x$

One way to write this fact, based on the equation of the curve, is

for the curve $y = x^2$, $\dfrac{dy}{dx} = 2x$ (we say dy by dx)

Each of the results obtained in Exercise 14a can be written using this notation, e.g.

for $y = x^2 - x$, $\dfrac{dy}{dx} = 2x - 1$ and   for $y = x^4$, $\dfrac{dy}{dx} = 4x^3$

Note carefully that d has no independent meaning and must never be regarded as a factor.

The complete symbol $\dfrac{d}{dx}$ means 'the derivative with respect to x of'

So, $\dfrac{dy}{dx}$ means 'the derivative with respect to x of y'

and $\dfrac{d}{dx}(x^2 - x)$ means 'the derivative with respect to x of $(x^2 - x)$'

An alternative notation concentrates on the function of x rather than the equation of the curve. An example is

for $f(x) = x^2$, $f'(x) = 2x$

In this form, f' means 'the gradient function' or 'the derived function'.

Again we can illustrate this notation using results from Exercise 14a, e.g.

for $f(x) = x^3$, $f'(x) = 3x^2$ and for $f(x) = x^4$, $f'(x) = 4x^3$

Either of these notations can be used for variables other than x, e.g.

if $y = z^3$ then we differentiate y with respect to z

and write $\dfrac{dy}{dz} = 3z^2$

Similarly, if $s = t^2 - t$, we differentiate s with respect to t

and write $\dfrac{ds}{dt} = 2t - 1$

(Because the phrase 'with respect to' is used very frequently, it is often abbreviated to w.r.t.)

THE GENERAL GRADIENT FUNCTION

Consider any curve with equation $y = f(x)$

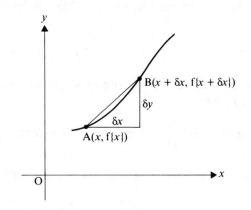

Taking two points on the curve, $A(x, y)$ and $B(x + \delta x, y + \delta y)$ we have,

at A $\qquad y = f(x)$ $\qquad$ and at B $\qquad y + \delta y = f(x + \delta x)$

Therefore the gradient of AB is given by

$$\frac{\delta y}{\delta x} = \frac{f(x + \delta x) - f(x)}{\delta x}$$

Now as $\delta x \to 0$, $\dfrac{\delta y}{\delta x} \to \dfrac{dy}{dx}$ therefore, in general

$$\frac{dy}{dx} = f'(x) = \lim_{\text{as } \delta x \to 0} \frac{f(x + \delta x) - f(x)}{\delta x}$$

Example 14b

Find the derivative of the function $1/x$

$$f(x) = \frac{1}{x} \Rightarrow f(x + \delta x) = \frac{1}{x + \delta x}$$

$$f(x + \delta x) - f(x) = \frac{1}{x + \delta x} - \frac{1}{x} = \frac{x - (x + \delta x)}{x(x + \delta x)}$$

$$= \frac{-\delta x}{x(x + \delta x)}$$

$$\frac{f(x + \delta x) - f(x)}{\delta x} = \frac{-\delta x}{x(x + \delta x)(\delta x)} = \frac{-1}{x(x + \delta x)}$$

Hence

$$f'(x) = \lim_{\text{as } \delta x \to 0} \frac{f(x + \delta x) - f(x)}{\delta x}$$

$$= \lim_{\text{as } \delta x \to 0} \frac{-1}{x(x + \delta x)}$$

$$= \frac{-1}{x^2}$$

i.e. the derivative of $1/x$ is $-1/x^2$

EXERCISE 14b

Use the general formula for the derivative of $f(x)$ to differentiate

1. $1/x^2$ 2. $1/x$ 3. $2/x$

DIFFERENTIATING x^n WITH RESPECT TO x

Some of the results that have been produced so far can now be collected and tabulated.

y	x^2	x^3	x^4	x^{-1}
$\dfrac{dy}{dx}$	$2x$	$3x^2$	$4x^3$	$-x^{-2}$ (or $-1/x^2$)

From this table it *appears* that when we differentiate a power of x we multiply by the power and then reduce the power by 1, i.e. it looks as though

$$\text{if } y = x^n, \quad \text{then} \quad \frac{dy}{dx} = nx^{n-1}$$

This result, although deduced from just a few examples, is in fact valid for all powers, including those that are fractional or negative. It is not possible to give a proof at this stage and this is one example of a 'rule' which, for the moment, we must just take on trust. It is easy to apply and makes the task of differentiating a power of x very much simpler, e.g.

$$\frac{d}{dx}(x^7) = 7x^6 \qquad \frac{d}{dx}(x^3) = 3x^2$$

$$\frac{d}{dx}(x^{-2}) = -2x^{-3} \qquad \frac{d}{dx}(x^{3/2}) = (3/2)x^{1/2}$$

Example 14c _____

Differentiate with respect to x

(a) $x^{-1/3}$ (b) $\sqrt[4]{(x^3)}$

(a) Using $\dfrac{d}{dx}(x^n) = nx^{n-1}$, where $n = -1/3$, we have

$$\frac{dy}{dx} = -\tfrac{1}{3}x^{-1/3-1} = -\tfrac{1}{3}x^{-4/3} \quad \text{or} \quad -\frac{1}{3x^{4/3}}$$

(b) $\sqrt[4]{(x^3)}$ can be written $x^{3/4}$, i.e. $n = 3/4$

Therefore $\dfrac{d}{dx}(x^{3/4}) = \tfrac{3}{4}x^{3/4-1} = \tfrac{3}{4}x^{-1/4} \quad \text{or} \quad \dfrac{3}{4\sqrt[4]{x}}$

EXERCISE 14c

Differentiate with respect to x.

1. x^5	**2.** x^{-3}	**3.** $x^{4/3}$	**4.** $1/x$
5. x^{10}	**6.** $1/x^2$	**7.** $\sqrt{x^3}$	**8.** $x^{-1/2}$
9. $1/x^4$	**10.** $x^{1/3}$	**11.** $x^{-1/4}$	**12.** x
13. $\sqrt{x^7}$	**14.** $1/x^7$	**15.** $x^{1/7}$	**16.** $\sqrt{(x^2)^3}$

Differentiating a Constant

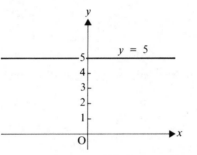

Consider the equation $y = 5$. Graphically this is a horizontal straight line and its gradient is zero, i.e. $\dfrac{dy}{dx} = 0$

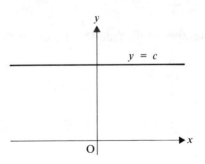

This argument applies to any equation of the form $y = c$ where c is a constant,

i.e.
$$\text{if } y = c \text{ then } \frac{dy}{dx} = 0$$

Differentiating a Linear Function of *x*

The graph of the equation $y = kx$, where k is a constant, is a straight line with gradient k.

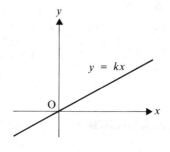

Hence
$$\frac{\mathrm{d}}{\mathrm{d}x}(kx) = k$$

Now if we apply the general rule for differentiating x^n to $y = x$, i.e. to $y = x^1$

$$\frac{\mathrm{d}}{\mathrm{d}x}(x^1) = 1x^0 = 1$$

Combining these two facts shows that

$$\frac{\mathrm{d}}{\mathrm{d}x}(kx) = k \times \frac{\mathrm{d}}{\mathrm{d}x}(x)$$

This conclusion applies, in fact, to a constant multiple of *any* function of x, e.g.

$$\text{if } y = 3x^5, \quad \frac{\mathrm{d}y}{\mathrm{d}x} = 3 \times 5x^4 = 15x^4$$

$$\text{and if } y = 4x^{-2}, \quad \frac{\mathrm{d}y}{\mathrm{d}x} = 4 \times -2x^{-3} = -8x^{-3}$$

In general then, if a is a constant,

$$\frac{\mathrm{d}}{\mathrm{d}x}ax^n = anx^{n-1}$$

This rule, although not proved for the general case, can be used freely.

Another very useful property is

> a function of x which contains a number of different terms can be differentiated term by term, applying the basic rule to each in turn.

For example

$$\text{if } y = x^4 + \frac{1}{x} - 6x \quad \text{then} \quad \frac{dy}{dx} = \frac{d}{dx}(x^4) + \frac{d}{dx}(x^{-1}) - \frac{d}{dx}(6x)$$

$$= 4x^3 - \frac{1}{x^2} - 6$$

(This property is justified, though not proved, by Question 5 in Exercise 14a.)

EXERCISE 14d

Differentiate each of the following functions w.r.t. x

1. $x^3 - x^2 + 5x - 6$ 2. $3x^2 + 7 - 4/x$

3. $\sqrt{x} + 1/\sqrt{x}$ 4. $2x^4 - 4x^2$

5. $x^3 - 2x^2 - 8x$ 6. $x^2 + 5\sqrt{x}$

7. $x^{-3/4} - x^{3/4} + x$ 8. $3x^3 - 4x^2 + 9x - 10$

9. $x^{3/2} - x^{1/2} + x^{-1/2}$ 10. $\sqrt{x} + \sqrt{x^3}$

11. $\dfrac{1}{x^2} - \dfrac{1}{x^3}$ 12. $\dfrac{1}{\sqrt{x}} - \dfrac{2}{x}$

13. $x^{-1/2} + 3x^{3/2}$ 14. $x^{1/4} - x^{1/5}$

15. $\dfrac{4}{x^3} + \dfrac{x^3}{4}$ 16. $\dfrac{4}{x} + \dfrac{5}{x^2} - \dfrac{6}{x^3}$

17. $3\sqrt{x} - 3x$ 18. $x - 2x^{-1} - 3x^{-3}$

19. $x\sqrt{x} - x^2\sqrt{x}$ 20. $\dfrac{\sqrt{x}}{x^2} + \dfrac{x^2}{\sqrt{x}}$

Differentiating Products and Fractions

All the rules given above can be applied to the differentiation of expressions containing products or quotients provided that, at this stage, they are multiplied out or divided into separate terms.

Examples 14e _____

1. If $y = (x - 3)(x^2 + 7x - 1)$, find $\dfrac{dy}{dx}$

$$y = (x - 3)(x^2 + 7x - 1) = x^3 + 4x^2 - 22x + 3$$

$\Rightarrow$
$$\frac{dy}{dx} = 3x^2 + 8x - 22$$

_____

2. Find $\dfrac{dt}{dz}$ given that $t = \dfrac{6z^2 + z - 4}{2z}$

$$t = \frac{6z^2 + z - 4}{2z} = \frac{6z^2}{2z} + \frac{z}{2z} - \frac{4}{2z}$$

$$= 3z + \tfrac{1}{2} - 2/z$$

$\Rightarrow$
$$\frac{dt}{dz} = 3 + 0 - 2(-z^{-2})$$

$$= 3 + \frac{2}{z^2}$$

_____

EXERCISE 14e

Differentiate each of the following expressions with respect to the variable concerned.

1. $y = (x + 1)^2$

2. $z = x^{-2}(2 - x)$

3. $y = (3x - 4)(x + 5)$

4. $y = (4 - z)^2$

5. $s = \dfrac{t^{-1} + 3t^2}{2t^2}$

6. $s = \dfrac{t^2 + t}{2t}$

7. $y = \left(\dfrac{1}{x}\right)(x^2 + 1)$

8. $y = \dfrac{z^3 - z}{\sqrt{z}}$

9. $y = 2x(3x^2 - 4)$

10. $s = (t + 2)(t - 2)$

11. $s = \dfrac{t^3 - 2t^2 + 7t}{t^2}$

12. $y = \dfrac{\sqrt{x} + 7}{x^2}$

GRADIENTS OF TANGENTS AND NORMALS

If the equation of a curve is known, and the gradient function can be found, then the gradient, m say, at a particular point A on that curve can be calculated. This is also the gradient of the tangent to the curve at A.

The normal at A is perpendicular to the tangent at A, therefore its gradient is $-1/m$

Examples 14f _____

1. The equation of a curve is $s = 6 - 3t - 4t^2 - t^3$. Find the gradient of the tangent and of the normal to the curve at the point $(-2, 4)$.

$$s = 6 - 3t - 4t^2 - t^3 \quad \Rightarrow \quad \frac{ds}{dt} = 0 - 3 - 8t - 3t^2$$

At the point $(-2, 4)$, $\dfrac{ds}{dt} = -3 - 8(-2) - 3(-2)^2 = 1$

Therefore the gradient of the tangent at $(-2, 4)$ is 1 and the gradient of the normal is $-1/1$, i.e. -1

_____

2. Find the coordinates of the points on the curve $y = 2x^3 - 3x^2 - 8x + 7$ where the gradient is 4

$$y = 2x^3 - 3x^2 - 8x + 7 \quad \Rightarrow \quad \frac{dy}{dx} = 6x^2 - 6x - 8$$

If the gradient is 4 then $\dfrac{dy}{dx} = 4$

i.e. $6x^2 - 6x - 8 = 4 \quad \Rightarrow \quad 6x^2 - 6x - 12 = 0$

$\Rightarrow \quad x^2 - x - 2 = 0$

$\therefore \qquad (x - 2)(x + 1) = 0 \quad \Rightarrow \quad x = 2 \text{ or } -1$

When $x = 2$, $y = 16 - 12 - 16 + 7 = -5$

when $x = -1$, $y = -2 - 3 + 8 + 7 = 10$

Therefore the gradient is 4 at the points $(2, -5)$ and $(-1, 10)$

_____

EXERCISE 14f

Find the gradient of the tangent and the gradient of the normal at the given point on the given curve.

1. $y = x^2 + 4$ where $x = 1$

2. $y = 3/x$ where $x = -3$

3. $y = \sqrt{z}$ where $z = 4$

4. $s = 2t^3$ where $t = -1$

5. $v = 2 - 1/u$ where $u = 1$

6. $y = (x + 3)(x - 4)$ where $x = 3$

7. $y = z^3 - z$ where $z = 2$

8. $s = t + 3t^2$ where $t = -2$

9. $z = x^2 - 2/x$ where $x = 1$

10. $y = \sqrt{x} + 1/\sqrt{x}$ where $x = 9$

11. $s = \sqrt{t}(1 + \sqrt{t})$ where $t = 4$

12. $y = \dfrac{x^2 - 4}{x}$ where $x = -2$

Find the coordinates of the point(s) on the given curve where the gradient has the value specified.

13. $y = 3 - 2/x; \frac{1}{2}$ 14. $z = x^2 - x^3; -1$

15. $s = t^3 - 12t + 9; 15$ 16. $v = u + 1/u; 0$

17. $s = (t + 3)(t - 5); 0$ 18. $y = 1/x^2; \frac{1}{4}$

19. $y = (2x - 5)(x + 1); -3$ 20. $y = z^3 - 3z; 0$

MIXED EXERCISE 14

1. Differentiate $3x^2 + x$ with respect to x from first principles.

2. Find the derivative of
   (a) $x^{-3} - x^3 + 7$ (b) $x^{1/2} - x^{-1/2}$ (c) $1/x^2 + 2/x^3$

3. Differentiate w.r.t. x.
   (a) $y = x^{3/2} - x^{2/3} + x^{-1/3}$ (b) $y = \sqrt{x} - 1/x + 1/x^3$
   (c) $1/x^{3/4} - 1/x^{1/4}$

4. Find the gradient of the curve $y = 2x^3 - 3x^2 + 5x - 1$ at the point

   (a) $(0, -1)$ (b) $(1, 3)$ (c) $(-1, -11)$

5. Find the gradient of the given curve at the given point.

   (a) $y = x^2 + x - 9$; $x = 2$ (b) $y = x(x - 4)$; $x = 5$

6. The equation of a curve is $y = (x - 3)(x + 4)$. Find the gradient of the curve

   (a) at the point where the curve crosses the y-axis

   (b) at each of the points where the curve crosses the x-axis

7. If the equation of a curve is $y = 2x^2 - 3x - 2$ find

   (a) the gradient at the point where $x = 0$

   (b) the coordinates of the points where the curve crosses the x-axis

   (c) the gradient at each of the points found in (b).

8. Find the coordinates of the point(s) on the curve $y = 3x^3 - x + 8$ at which the gradient is

   (a) 8   (b) 0

9. Find $\dfrac{dy}{dx}$ if

   (a) $y = x^4 - x^2$ (b) $y = (3x + 4)^2$ (c) $y = \dfrac{x - 3}{\sqrt{x}}$

10. Find the gradient of the tangent at the point where $x = 2$ on the curve $y = (2 - \sqrt{x})^2$

11. Find the coordinates of the point on the curve $y = x^2$ where the gradient of the normal is $\frac{1}{4}$.

12. The equation of a curve is $s = 4t^2 + 5t$. Find the gradient of the normal at each of the points where the curve crosses the t-axis.

13. Find the coordinates of the points on the curve $y = x^3 - 6x^2 + 12x + 2$ at which the tangent is parallel to the line $y = 3x$

14. The curve $y = (x - 2)(x - 3)(x - 4)$ cuts the x-axis at the points $P(2, 0)$, $Q(3, 0)$ and $R(4, 0)$. Prove that the tangents at P and R are parallel and find the gradient of the normal at Q.

15. For a certain equation, $\dfrac{dy}{dx} = 2x + 1$ Which of the following could be the given equation

(a) $y = 2x^2 + x$ (b) $y = x^2 + x - 1$ (c) $y = x^2 + 1$

(d) $y = x^2 + x$

TANGENTS, NORMALS AND STATIONARY POINTS

THE EQUATIONS OF TANGENTS AND NORMALS

We have seen how to find the gradient of a tangent at a particular point, A, on a curve. We also know that the tangent passes through the point A. Therefore the tangent is a line passing through a known point and having a known gradient and its equation can be found using

$$y - y_1 = m(x - x_1)$$

The equation of a normal can be found in the same way.

Examples 15a _____

1. Find the equation of the normal to the curve $y = \dfrac{4}{x}$ at the point where $x = 1$

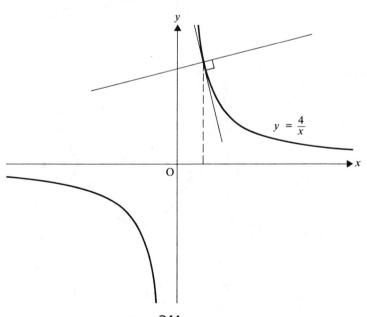

$$y = \frac{4}{x} \quad \Rightarrow \quad \frac{dy}{dx} = -\frac{4}{x^2}$$

When $x = 1$, $y = 4$ and $\dfrac{dy}{dx} = -4$

The gradient of the tangent at $(1, 4)$ is -4, therefore the gradient of the normal at $(1, 4)$ is $-\frac{1}{-4}$ i.e. $\frac{1}{4}$

The equation of the normal is given by $y - y_1 = m(x - x_1)$

i.e. $$y - 4 = \tfrac{1}{4}(x - 1)$$

$\Rightarrow$ $$4y = x + 15$$

---

2. Find the equation of the tangent to the curve $y = x^2 - 6x + 5$ at each of the points where the curve crosses the x-axis. Find also the coordinates of the point where these tangents meet.

The curve crosses the x-axis where $y = 0$,

i.e. where $x^2 - 6x + 5 = 0 \quad \Rightarrow \quad (x - 5)(x - 1) = 0$

$\Rightarrow \qquad x = 5$ and $x = 1$

Therefore the curve crosses the x-axis at $(5, 0)$ and $(1, 0)$

$$y = x^2 - 6x + 5 \quad \Rightarrow \quad \frac{dy}{dx} = 2x - 6$$

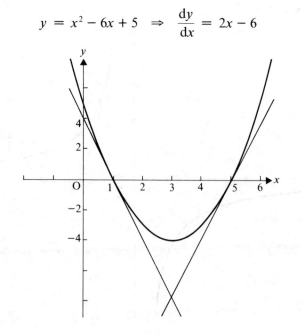

At $(5, 0)$, the gradient of the tangent is given by

$$\frac{dy}{dx} = 10 - 6 = 4$$

therefore the equation of this tangent is

$$y - 0 = 4(x - 5) \quad \Rightarrow \quad y = 4x - 20$$

At $(1, 0)$ the gradient of the tangent is given by

$$\frac{dy}{dx} = 2 - 6 = -4$$

Therefore the equation of the tangent is

$$y - 0 = -4(x - 1) \quad \Rightarrow \quad y + 4x = 4$$

If the two tangents meet at **P** then, at **P**,

$$y + 4x = 4 \qquad\qquad\qquad\qquad\qquad [1]$$

and $\qquad\qquad\qquad\qquad y - 4x = -20 \qquad\qquad\qquad\qquad [2]$

$[1] + [2]$ gives $\qquad 2y = -16 \quad \Rightarrow \quad y = -8$

Using $y = -8$ in $[1]$ gives $\quad -8 + 4x = 4 \quad \Rightarrow \quad x = 3$

Therefore the tangents meet at $(3, -8)$

EXERCISE 15a

In each question from 1 to 6 find, at the given point,
(a) the equation of the tangent
(b) the equation of the normal.

1. $y = x^2 - 4$ $\qquad\qquad$ where $x = 1$

2. $y = x^2 + 4x - 2$ $\qquad$ where $x = 0$

3. $y = 1/x$ $\qquad\qquad\quad$ where $x = -1$

4. $y = x^2 + 5$ $\qquad\qquad$ where $x = 0$

5. $y = x^2 - 5x + 7$ $\qquad$ where $x = 2$

6. $y = (x - 2)(x^2 - 1)$ $\quad$ where $x = -2$

7. Find the equation of the normal to the curve $y = x^2 + 4x - 3$ at the point where the curve cuts the y-axis.

8. Find the equation of the tangent to the curve $y = x^2 - 3x - 4$ at the point where this curve cuts the line $x = 5$

9. Find the equation of the tangent to the curve $y = (2x - 3)(x - 1)$ at each of the points where this curve cuts the x-axis. Find the point of intersection of these tangents.

10. Find the equation of the normal to the curve $y = x^2 - 6x + 5$ at each of the points where the curve cuts the x-axis.

11. Find the equation of the tangent to the curve $y = 3x^2 + 5x - 1$ at each of the points of intersection of the curve and the line $y = x - 1$

12. Find the equations of the tangent to the curve $y = x^2 + 5x - 3$ at the points where the line $y = x + 2$ crosses the curve.

13. Find the coordinates of the point on the curve $y = 2x^2$ at which the gradient is 8 Hence find the equation of the tangent to $y = 2x^2$ whose gradient is 8

14. Find the coordinates of the point on the curve $y = 3x^2 - 1$ at which the gradient is 3

15. Find the equation of the tangent to the curve $y = 4x^2 + 3x$ which has a gradient of -1

16. Find the equation of the normal to the curve $y = 2x^2 - 2x + 1$ which has a gradient of $\frac{1}{2}$

17. Find the value of k for which $y = 2x + k$ is a tangent to the curve $y = 2x^2 - 3$

18. Find the equation of the tangent to the curve $y = (x - 5)(2x + 1)$ which is parallel to the x-axis.

19. Find the coordinates of the point(s) on the curve $y = x^2 - 5x + 3$ where the gradient of the normal is $\frac{1}{3}$

20. A curve has the equation $y = x^3 - px + q$. The tangent to this curve at the point $(2, -8)$ is parallel to the x-axis. Find the values of p and q.
Find also the coordinates of the other point where the tangent is parallel to the x-axis.

STATIONARY VALUES

110

Consider a function $f(x)$. The derived function, $f'(x)$, expresses the rate at which $f(x)$ increases with respect to x

If, at a particular point, $f'(x)$ is positive then $f(x)$ is increasing as x increases, whereas if $f'(x)$ is negative then $f(x)$ is decreasing as x increases.

Now there may be points where $f'(x)$ is zero, i.e. $f(x)$ is momentarily neither increasing nor decreasing with respect to x

The value of $f(x)$ at such a point is called a *stationary value* of $f(x)$

i.e. $f'(x) = 0$ $\Rightarrow$ $f(x)$ has a stationary value.

To look at this situation graphically we consider the curve with equation $y = f(x)$.

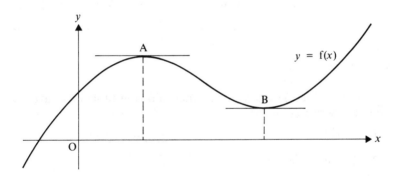

At A and B, $f(x)$, and therefore y, is neither increasing nor decreasing with respect to x. So the values of y at A and B are stationary values.

i.e. $\dfrac{dy}{dx} = 0$ $\Rightarrow$ y has a stationary value.

The point on a curve where y has a stationary value is called a *stationary point* and we see that, at any stationary point, the gradient of the tangent to the curve is zero, i.e. the tangent is parallel to the x-axis.

To sum up:

at a stationary point $\begin{cases} y \quad \text{[or } f(x)] \quad \text{has a stationary value} \\ dy/dx \quad \text{[or } f'(x)] \quad \text{is zero} \\ \text{the tangent is parallel to the } x\text{-axis.} \end{cases}$

Example 15b

Find the stationary values of the function $x^3 - 4x^2 + 7$.

If $\qquad$ $f(x) = x^3 - 4x^2 + 7$

then $\qquad$ $f'(x) = 3x^2 - 8x$

At stationary points, $f'(x) = 0$, i.e. $3x^2 - 8x = 0$

$\Rightarrow \qquad x(3x - 8) = 0 \qquad \Rightarrow \qquad x = 0$ and $x = \frac{8}{3}$

Therefore there are stationary points where $x = 0$ and $x = \frac{8}{3}$

When $x = 0$, $\qquad f(x) = 0 - 0 + 7 = 7$

When $x = \frac{8}{3}$, $\qquad f(x) = (\frac{8}{3})^3 - 4(\frac{8}{3})^2 + 7 = -2\frac{13}{27}$

Therefore the stationary values of $x^3 - 4x^2 - 5$ are 7 and $-2\frac{13}{27}$

EXERCISE 15b

Find the value(s) of x at which the following functions have stationary values.

1. $x^2 + 7$

2. $2x^2 - 3x - 2$

3. $x^3 - 4x^2 + 6$

4. $4x^3 - 3x - 9$

5. $x^3 - 2x^2 + 11$

6. $x^3 - 3x - 5$

Find the value(s) of x for which y has a stationary value.

7. $y = x^2 - 8x + 1$

8. $y = x + 9/x$

9. $y = 2x^3 + x^2 - 8x + 1$

10. $y = 9x^3 - 25x$

11. $y = 2x^3 + 9x^2 - 24x + 7$

12. $y = 3x^3 - 12x + 19$

Find the coordinates of the stationary points on the following curves.

13. $y = \dfrac{x^2 + 9}{2x}$

14. $y = x^3 - 2x^2 + x - 7$

15. $y = (x - 3)(x + 2)$

16. $y = x^{3/2} - x^{1/2}$

17. $y = \sqrt{x} + \dfrac{1}{\sqrt{x}}$

18. $y = 8 + \dfrac{x}{4} + \dfrac{4}{x}$

TURNING POINTS

In the immediate neighbourhood of a stationary point a curve can have any one of the shapes shown in the following diagram.

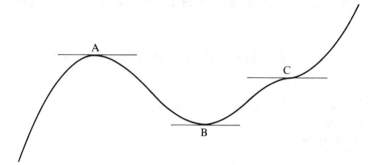

Moving through A from left to right we see that the curve is rising, then turns at A and begins to fall, i.e. the gradient changes from positive to zero at A and then becomes negative.

At A there is a *turning point*.

The value of y at A is called a *maximum value* and A is called a *maximum point*.

Moving through B from left to right the curve is falling, then turns at B and begins to rise, i.e. the gradient changes from negative to zero at B and then becomes positive.

At B there is a *turning point*.

The value of y at B is called a *minimum value* and B is called a *minimum point*.

The tangent is always horizontal at a turning point.

Note that a maximum value of y is *not necessarily the greatest value of* y *overall*. The terms maximum and minimum apply only to the behaviour of the curve in the neighbourhood of a stationary point.

At C the curve does not turn. The gradient goes from positive, to zero at C and then becomes positive again, i.e. the gradient does not change sign at C.

C is not a turning point but, because there is a change in the sense in which the curve is turning (from clockwise to anti-clockwise), C is called a *point of inflexion*.

Any point on a curve where the sense of turning changes, is a point of inflexion. In the diagram there are two points of inflexion other than C; one is between A and B and the other is between B and C. We see from these points that

the tangent is not necessarily horizontal at a point of inflexion.

INVESTIGATING THE NATURE OF STATIONARY POINTS

We already know how to locate stationary points on a curve and now examine several ways of distinguishing between the different types of stationary point.

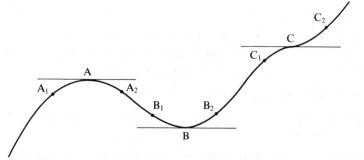

METHOD (i)

This method compares the value of y at the stationary point with values of y at points on either side of, and near to, the stationary point.

For a maximum value, e.g. at A

$$y \text{ at } A_1 < y \text{ at } A$$

$$y \text{ at } A_2 < y \text{ at } A$$

For a minimum point, e.g. at B

$$y \text{ at } B_1 > y \text{ at } B$$

$$y \text{ at } B_2 > y \text{ at } B$$

For a point of inflexion, e.g. at C

$$y \text{ at } C_1 < y \text{ at } C$$

$$y \text{ at } C_2 > y \text{ at } C$$

Collecting these conclusions we have:

	Maximum	Minimum	Inflexion
y values on each side of the stationary point	both smaller	both larger	one larger and one smaller

Note that the points chosen on either side of the stationary point must be such that no *other* stationary point, nor any discontinuity on the graph, lies between them.

METHOD (ii)

110

SG

This method examines the sign of the gradient, again at points close to, and on either side of, the stationary point where the gradient is zero.

For a maximum point, A

$$\frac{dy}{dx} \text{ at } A_1 \text{ is +ve}$$

$$\frac{dy}{dx} \text{ at } A_2 \text{ is } -ve$$

For a minimum point, B

$$\frac{dy}{dx} \text{ at } B_1 \text{ is } -ve$$

$$\frac{dy}{dx} \text{ at } B_2 \text{ is +ve}$$

For a point of inflexion, C

$$\frac{dy}{dx} \text{ at } C_1 \text{ is +ve}$$

$$\frac{dy}{dx} \text{ at } C_2 \text{ is +ve}$$

Collecting these conclusions we have:

Sign of $\dfrac{dy}{dx}$	Passing through maximum + 0 −	Passing through minimum − 0 +	Passing through point of inflexion + 0 + or − 0 −
Gradient of tangent	╱ ‾ ╲	╲ _ ╱	╱ ‾ ╱ or ╲ _ ╲

METHOD (iii)

In this method we observe how dy/dx changes with respect to x as we pass through a stationary point. Now the rate at which dy/dx increases with respect to x could be written $\dfrac{d}{dx}\left(\dfrac{dy}{dx}\right)$ but, because this notation is clumsy, it is condensed to $\dfrac{d^2y}{dx^2}$ (we say d 2 y by dx squared).

For example, using this notation the fact that $\dfrac{dy}{dx}$ is increasing as x increases can be expressed as $\dfrac{d^2y}{dx^2}$ is +ve.

$\left(\dfrac{d^2y}{dx^2}\text{ is the }second\ derivative\text{ with respect to }x,\text{ of }y\right)$

Now we can examine the behaviour of $\dfrac{dy}{dx}$ at each stationary point.

For the maximum point A,

at A_1 $\dfrac{dy}{dx}$ is +ve   and   at A_2 $\dfrac{dy}{dx}$ is −ve

so, passing through A, $\dfrac{dy}{dx}$ goes from + to −,   i.e. $\dfrac{dy}{dx}$ decreases

$\Rightarrow$ at A, $\dfrac{d^2y}{dx^2}$ is negative.

For the minimum point B,

at B_1 $\dfrac{dy}{dx}$ is −ve   and   at B_2 $\dfrac{dy}{dx}$ is +ve

so, passing through B, $\dfrac{dy}{dx}$ goes from − to +,   i.e. $\dfrac{dy}{dx}$ increases

$\Rightarrow$ at B, $\dfrac{d^2y}{dx^2}$ is positive.

Points of inflexion are not so easily dealt with by this method because, although $\dfrac{d^2y}{dx^2}$ is zero at a point of inflexion it is also possible for $\dfrac{d^2y}{dx^2}$ to be zero at a turning point. So, for any stationary point where $\dfrac{d^2y}{dx^2} = 0$, this method fails and one of the other two approaches must be used.

Summing up method (iii) we have:

	Maximum	Minimum
Sign of $\dfrac{d^2y}{dx^2}$	negative (or zero)	positive (or zero)

Note that, if $\dfrac{d^2y}{dx^2}$ is zero one of the other two methods must be used to determine the nature of a stationary point.

Examples 15c

1. Locate the stationary points on the curve $y = 4x^3 + 3x^2 - 6x - 1$ and determine the nature of each one.

$$y = 4x^3 + 3x^2 - 6x - 1 \quad \Rightarrow \quad \frac{dy}{dx} = 12x^2 + 6x - 6$$

At stationary points, $\dfrac{dy}{dx} = 0$

i.e. $\qquad 12x^2 + 6x - 6 = 0 \quad \Rightarrow \quad 6(2x - 1)(x + 1) = 0$

$\therefore$ there are stationary points where $x = \frac{1}{2}$ and $x = -1$

When $x = \frac{1}{2}$, $y = -2\frac{3}{4}$ and when $x = -1$, $y = 4$

i.e. the stationary points are $(\frac{1}{2}, -2\frac{3}{4})$ and $(-1, 4)$

Differentiating $\dfrac{dy}{dx}$ w.r.t. x gives

$$\frac{d^2y}{dx^2} = 24x + 6$$

When $x = \frac{1}{2}$, $\dfrac{d^2y}{dx^2} = 12 + 6$ which is positive

$\Rightarrow \qquad\qquad (\frac{1}{2}, -2\frac{3}{4})$ is a minimum point.

When $x = -1$, $\dfrac{d^2y}{dx^2} = -24 + 6$ which is negative

$\Rightarrow \qquad\qquad (-1, 4)$ is a maximum point.

2. Find the stationary values of the function $3x^4 - 8x^3 + 6x^2 - 3$ and investigate their nature.

$f(x) = 3x^4 - 8x^3 + 6x^2 - 3 \quad \Rightarrow \quad f'(x) = 12x^3 - 24x^2 + 12x$

At stationary values $f'(x) = 0$

i.e. $\quad 12x^3 - 24x^2 + 12x = 0 \quad \Rightarrow \quad 12x(x^2 - 2x + 1) = 0$

$\qquad\qquad\qquad\qquad\qquad\quad \Rightarrow \quad 12x(x-1)(x-1) = 0$

there are stationary values when $x = 0$ and $x = 1$

$\qquad x = 0 \quad \Rightarrow \quad f(x) = -3$

$\qquad x = 1 \quad \Rightarrow \quad f(x) = 3 - 8 + 6 - 3 = -2$

i.e. the stationary values of $f(x)$ are -2 and -3

Differentiating $f'(x)$ w.r.t. x [the notation for $f'\{f'(x)\}$ is $f''(x)$] gives

$\qquad f''(x) = 36x^2 - 48x + 12 = 12(3x^2 - 4x + 1)$

When $x = 0$, $f''(x) = 12$ which is positive

$\Rightarrow \qquad\qquad f(x) = -3$ is a minimum value

when $x = 1$, $f''(x) = 12(3 - 4 + 1)$ which is zero.

This is inconclusive so we will look at the signs of $f'(x)$ on either side of $x = 1$

x	$\frac{1}{2}$	1	$1\frac{1}{2}$
$f'(x)$	+	0	+
Gradient	/	−	/

From this table we see that the stationary value at $x = 1$, i.e. -2, is an inflexion.

EXERCISE 15c

Find the stationary points on the following curves and distinguish between them.

1. $y = 2x - x^2$

2. $y = 3x - x^3$

3. $y = 9/x + x$

4. $y = x^2(x - 5)$

5. $y = x^2$ **6.** $y = x + 1/2x^2$

7. $y = 2x^2 - x^4$ **8.** $y = x^4$

9. $y = (2x + 1)(x - 3)$ **10.** $y = x^5 - 5x$

11. $y = x^2(x^2 - 8)$ **12.** $y = x^2 + 16/x^2$

Find the stationary value(s) of each of the following functions and determine their character.

13. $x + 1/x$ **14.** $3 - x + x^2$ **15.** $4x^3 - x^4$

16. $8 - x^3$ **17.** $x^3 + 7$ **18.** $x^2(3x^2 - 2x - 3)$

PROBLEMS

Examples 15d _____

1. An open box is made from a square sheet of cardboard, with sides half a metre long, by cutting out a square from each corner, folding up the sides and joining the cut edges. Find the maximum capacity of the box.

The capacity of the box depends upon the unknown length of the side of the square cut from each corner so we denote this by x metres. The side of the cardboard sheet is $\frac{1}{2}$ m, so we know that $0 < x < \frac{1}{4}$

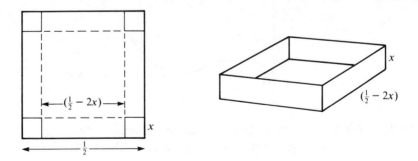

Using metres throughout,

the base of the box is a square of side $(\frac{1}{2} - 2x)$ and the height of the box is x

∴   the capacity, C, of the box is given by

$$C = x(\tfrac{1}{2} - 2x)^2 = \tfrac{1}{4}x - 2x^2 + 4x^3 \quad \text{for} \quad 0 < x < \tfrac{1}{4}$$

⇒ $$\frac{dC}{dx} = \tfrac{1}{4} - 4x + 12x^2$$

At a stationary value of C, $\dfrac{dC}{dx} = 0$

i.e. $12x^2 - 4x + \tfrac{1}{4} = 0 \quad \Rightarrow \quad 48x^2 - 16x + 1 = 0$

$(4x - 1)(12x - 1) = 0 \quad \Rightarrow \quad x = \tfrac{1}{4} \text{ or } x = \tfrac{1}{12}$

there are stationary values of C when $x = \tfrac{1}{4}$ and when $x = \tfrac{1}{12}$

It is obvious that it is not possible to make a box if $x = \tfrac{1}{4}$ so we need only check that $x = \tfrac{1}{12}$ gives a maximum capacity.

$$\frac{d^2C}{dx^2} = -4 + 24x \quad \text{which is negative when} \quad x = \tfrac{1}{12}$$

Therefore C has a maximum value of $\tfrac{1}{12}(\tfrac{1}{2} - \tfrac{1}{6})^2$, i.e. $\tfrac{1}{108}$

i.e. the maximum capacity of the box is $\tfrac{1}{108}$ m^3

or, correct to 3 s.f., 9260 cm^3

Alternatively the nature of the stationary point where $x = \tfrac{1}{12}$ can be investigated by using the sketch given by a graphics calculator for the curve $C = \tfrac{1}{4}x - 2x^2 + 4x^3$ and looking at the section for which $0 < x < \tfrac{1}{4}$, i.e.

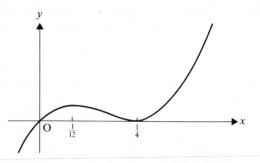

The sketch shows that there is a maximum point between $x = 0$ and $x = \tfrac{1}{4}$ so $x = \tfrac{1}{12}$ must give the maximum value of C.

The sketch also shows that there is a minimum point *on the curve* where $x = \tfrac{1}{4}$ but this is *not* a minimum value of the *capacity*, as a box cannot be made if $x = \tfrac{1}{4}$

2. The function $ax^2 + bx + c$ has a gradient function $4x + 2$ and a stationary value of 1. Find the values of a, b and c

$$f(x) = ax^2 + bx + c \quad \Rightarrow \quad f'(x) = 2ax + b$$

But we know that $f'(x) = 4x + 2$

$\therefore$ $2ax + b$ is identical to $4x + 2$

i.e. $a = 2$ and $b = 2$

The stationary value of $f(x)$ occurs when $f'(x) = 0$

i.e. when $4x + 2 = 0 \quad \Rightarrow \quad x = -\tfrac{1}{2}$

the stationary value of $f(x)$ is $2(-\tfrac{1}{2})^2 + 2(-\tfrac{1}{2}) + c = -\tfrac{1}{2} + c$

But the stationary value of $f(x)$ is also 1

$\therefore$ $-\tfrac{1}{2} + c = 1 \quad \Rightarrow \quad c = \tfrac{3}{2}$

---

3. A cylinder has a radius r metres and a height h metres. The sum of the radius and height is 2 m. Find an expression for the volume, V cubic metres, of the cylinder in terms of r only. Hence find the maximum volume.

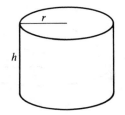

$$V = \pi r^2 h \quad \text{and} \quad r + h = 2$$

$\therefore$ $V = \pi r^2 (2 - r) = \pi(2r^2 - r^3)$

Now for maximum volume, $\dfrac{dV}{dr} = 0,$

i.e. $\pi(4r - 3r^2) = 0 \quad \Rightarrow \quad \pi r(4 - 3r) = 0$

Therefore there are stationary values of V when $r = 0$ and $r = \tfrac{4}{3}$

It is obvious that, when $r = 0$, $V = 0$ and no cylinder exists, so we check the sign of $\dfrac{d^2V}{dr^2}$ only for $r = \tfrac{4}{3}$

$$\frac{d^2V}{dr^2} = \pi(4 - 6r) \quad \text{which is negative when} \quad r = \tfrac{4}{3}$$

Therefore the maximum value of V occurs when $r = \tfrac{4}{3}$ and is $\pi(\tfrac{4}{3})^2(2 - \tfrac{4}{3})$

i.e. the maximum volume is $\dfrac{32\pi}{27} \text{ m}^3$

Note that the solution of this problem depends fundamentally on having an expression for V in terms of only one other variable. This is true of *all* problems on stationary points so, if three or more variables are involved initially, some of them must be replaced so that we have a basic relationship containing only two variables.

EXERCISE 15d

1. A farmer has an 80 m length of fencing. He wants to use it to form three sides of a rectangular enclosure against an existing fence which provides the fourth side. Find the maximum area that he can enclose and give its dimensions.

2. A large number of open cardboard boxes are to be made and each box must have a square base and a capacity of 4000 cm³. Find the dimensions of the box which contains the minimum area of cardboard.

3.

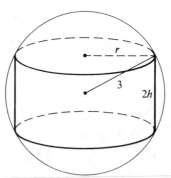

The diagram shows a cylinder cut from a solid sphere of radius 3 cm. Given that the cylinder has a height of $2h$, find its radius in terms of h. Hence show that the volume, V cubic metres, of the cylinder is given by

$$V = 2\pi h(9 - h^2)$$

Find the maximum volume of the cylinder as h varies.

4. A variable rectangle has a constant perimeter of 20 cm. Find the lengths of the sides when the area is maximum.

5. A variable rectangle has a constant area of 35 cm². Find the lengths of the sides when the perimeter is minimum.

6. The curve $y = ax^2 + bx + c$ crosses the y-axis at the point $(0, 3)$ and has a stationary point at $(1, 2)$. Find the values of a, b and c

7. The gradient of the tangent to the curve $y = px^2 - qx - r$ at the point $(1, -2)$ is 1 If the curve crosses the x-axis where $x = 2$, find the values of p, q and r. Find the other point of intersection with the x-axis and sketch the curve.

8. y is a quadratic function of x. The line $y = 2x$ is a tangent to the curve at the point $(3, 6)$. The turning point on the curve occurs where $x = -2$ Find the equation of the curve.

MIXED EXERCISE 15

1. Find the gradient of the curve with equation $y = 6x^2 - x$ at the point where $x = 1$ Find the equation of the tangent at this point. Where does this tangent meet the line $y = 2x$?

2. Find the equation of the normal to the curve $y = 1 - x^2$ at the point where the curve crosses the positive x-axis. Find also the coordinates of the point where the normal meets the curve again.

3. Find the coordinates of the points on the curve $y = x^3 + 3x$ where the gradient is 15

4. Find the equations of the tangents to the curve $y = x^3 - 6x^2 + 12x + 2$ which are parallel to the line $y = 3x$

5. Find the equation of the normal to the curve $y = x^2 - 6$ which is parallel to the line $x + 2y - 1 = 0$

6. Locate the turning points on the curve $y = x(x^2 - 12)$, determine their nature and draw a rough sketch of the curve.

7. Find the stationary values of the function $x + 1/x$ and sketch the function.

8. If the perimeter of a rectangle is fixed in length, show that the area of the rectangle is greatest when it is square.

9. A door is in the shape of a rectangle surmounted by a semicircle whose diameter is equal to the width of the rectangle. If the perimeter of the door is 7 m, and the radius of the semicircle is r metres, express the height of the rectangle in terms of r. Show that the area of the door has a maximum value when the width is $7/(4 + \pi)$.

10. An open tank is constructed, with a square base and vertical sides, to hold 32 cubic metres of water. Find the dimensions of the tank if the area of sheet metal used to make it is to have a minimum value.

11. Triangle ABC has a right angle at C. The shape of the triangle can vary but the sides BC and CA have a fixed total length of 10 cm. Find the maximum area of the triangle.

CHAPTER 16

TRIGONOMETRIC FUNCTIONS

THE TRIG RATIOS OF 30°, 45°, 60°

The sine, cosine and tangent of 30°, 45°, and 60°, can be expressed exactly in surd form and are worth remembering.

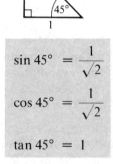

This triangle shows that

$$\sin 45° = \frac{1}{\sqrt{2}}$$

$$\cos 45° = \frac{1}{\sqrt{2}}$$

$$\tan 45° = 1$$

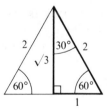

And this triangle gives

$$\sin 60° = \frac{\sqrt{3}}{2}, \quad \sin 30° = \frac{1}{2}$$

$$\cos 60° = \frac{1}{2}, \quad \cos 30° = \frac{\sqrt{3}}{2}$$

$$\tan 60° = \sqrt{3}, \quad \tan 30° = \frac{1}{\sqrt{3}}$$

THE TRIGONOMETRIC FUNCTIONS

In Chapter 7, we gave the general definition of an angle as a measure
of the rotation of a line OP about a fixed point O. Taking Ox as the
initial direction of OP, anticlockwise rotation describes a positive
angle and clockwise rotation describes a negative angle. The rotation
of OP is not limited to one revolution, so an angle can be as big as we
choose to make it.

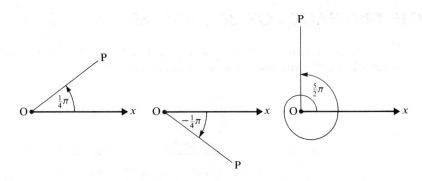

If θ is any angle, then θ can be measured
    either in degrees (one revolution $= 360°$)
    or   in radians (one revolution $= 2\pi$ radians)
and in either case we see that θ can take all real values.

Chapter 7 also contained the general definition of the sine, cosine and
tangent of θ, but used those definitions only for values of θ in the
range $0 \leqslant \theta \leqslant 180°$. They are valid for all values of θ however and,
as a reminder, we repeat them here.

If OP is drawn on x and y axes as shown and if, for all values of θ,
the length of OP is r and the coordinates of P are (x, y), then the
sine, cosine and tangent functions are defined as follows.

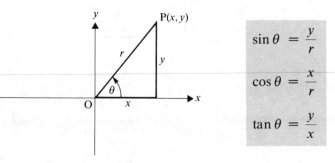

$$\sin \theta = \frac{y}{r}$$

$$\cos \theta = \frac{x}{r}$$

$$\tan \theta = \frac{y}{x}$$

We will now look at each of these functions in turn.

THE SINE FUNCTION

From the definition $f(\theta) = \sin\theta$, and measuring θ in radians, we can see that

for $0 \leqslant \theta \leqslant \frac{1}{2}\pi$, OP is in the first quadrant; y is positive and increases in value from 0 to r as θ increases from 0 to $\frac{1}{2}\pi$. Now r is always positive, so $\sin\theta$ increases from 0 to 1

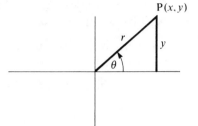

for $\frac{1}{2}\pi \leqslant \theta \leqslant \pi$, OP is in the second quadrant; again y is positive but decreases in value from r to 0, so $\sin\theta$ decreases from 1 to 0

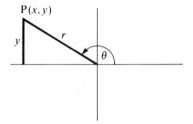

for $\pi \leqslant \theta \leqslant \frac{3}{2}\pi$, OP is in the third quadrant; y is negative and decreases from 0 to $-r$, so $\sin\theta$ decreases from 0 to -1

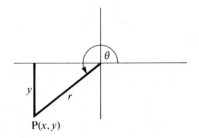
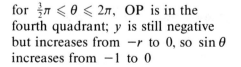

for $\frac{3}{2}\pi \leqslant \theta \leqslant 2\pi$, OP is in the fourth quadrant; y is still negative but increases from $-r$ to 0, so $\sin\theta$ increases from -1 to 0

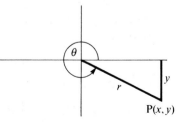

For $\theta \geqslant 2\pi$, the cycle repeats itself as OP travels round the quadrants again. For negative values of θ, OP rotates clockwise round the quadrants in the order 4th, 3rd, 2nd, 1st, etc. So $\sin \theta$ decreases from 0 to -1, then increases to 0 and on to 1 before decreasing to zero and repeating the pattern.

From this analysis we see that $\sin \theta$ is positive for $0 < \theta < \pi$ and negative when $\pi < \theta < 2\pi$

Further, $\sin \theta$ varies in value between -1 and 1 and the pattern repeats itself every revolution.

A plot of the graph of $f(\theta) = \sin \theta$ confirms these observations.

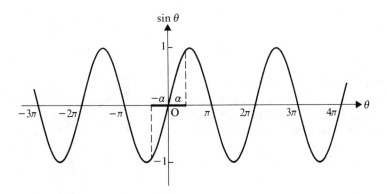

A graph of this shape is called, for obvious reasons, a *sine wave* and shows clearly the following characteristics of the sine function.

The curve is continuous (i.e. it has no breaks).

$$-1 \leqslant \sin \theta \leqslant 1$$

The shape of the curve from $\theta = 0$ to $\theta = 2\pi$ is repeated for each complete revolution. Any function with a repetitive pattern is called *periodic* or *cyclic*. The width of the repeating pattern, as measured on the horizontal scale, is called the *period*.

The period of the sine function is 2π

Other properties of the sine function shown by the graph are as follows.

$$\sin \theta = 0 \quad \text{when} \quad \theta = n\pi \quad \text{where } n \text{ is an integer.}$$

The curve has rotational symmetry about the origin so, for any angle α

$$\sin(-\alpha) = -\sin \alpha, \quad \text{e.g.} \quad \sin(-30°) = -\sin 30° = -\tfrac{1}{2}$$

Taking an enlarged section of the graph for $0 \leqslant \theta \leqslant 2\pi$, we find further relationships.

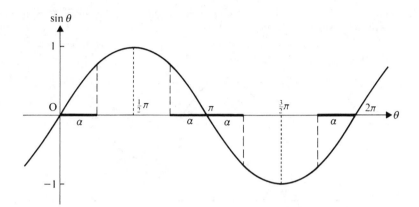

The curve is symmetrical about the line $\theta = \frac{1}{2}\pi$, so

$$\sin(\pi - \alpha) = \sin \alpha, \quad \text{e.g.} \quad \sin 130° = \sin(180° - 130°) = \sin 50°$$

The curve has rotational symmetry about $\theta = \pi$, so

$$\sin(\pi + \alpha) = -\sin \alpha \quad \text{and} \quad \sin(2\pi - \alpha) = -\sin \alpha$$

Examples 16a _____

1. Find the exact value of $\sin \frac{4}{3}\pi$.

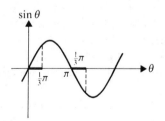

$$\sin \tfrac{4}{3}\pi = \sin(\pi + \tfrac{1}{3}\pi) = -\sin \tfrac{1}{3}\pi = -\frac{\sqrt{3}}{2}$$

2. Sketch the graph of $y = \sin(\theta - \frac{1}{4}\pi)$ for values of θ between 0 and 2π

Remember that the curve $y = f(x - a)$ is a translation of the curve $y = f(x)$ by a units in the positive direction of the x-axis.

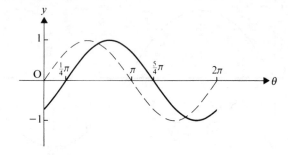

EXERCISE 16a

Find the exact value of

1. $\sin 120°$ 2. $\sin -2\pi$ 3. $\sin 300°$ 4. $\sin -210°$

5. Write down all the values of θ between 0 and 6π for which $\sin\theta = 1$

6. Write down all the values of θ between 0 and -4π for which $\sin\theta = -1$

Express in terms of the sine of an acute angle

7. $\sin 125°$ 8. $\sin 290°$ 9. $\sin -120°$ 10. $\sin\frac{7}{6}\pi$

Sketch each of the following curves for values of θ in the range $0 \leqslant \theta \leqslant 3\pi$

11. $y = \sin(\theta + \frac{1}{3}\pi)$ 12. $y = -\sin\theta$ 13. $y = \sin(-\theta)$

14. $y = 1 - \sin\theta$ 15. $y = \sin(\pi - \theta)$ 16. $y = \sin(\frac{1}{2}\pi - \theta)$

Use a graphics calculator or computer for Questions 17 to 19 and set the range for θ as -2π to 4π.

17. On the same set of axes draw the graphs of $y = \sin\theta$, $y = 2\sin\theta$, and $y = 3\sin\theta$. What can you deduce about the relationship between the curves $y = \sin\theta$ and $y = a\sin\theta$?

18. On the same set of axes draw the curves $y = \sin \theta$ and $y = \sin 2\theta$

19. On the same set of axes draw the curves $y = \sin \theta$ and $y = \sin 3\theta$
What can you deduce about the relationship between the two curves?

20. *Sketch* the curves (a) $y = \sin 4\theta$ (b) $y = 4 \sin \theta$

One-way Stretches

Questions 17 to 20 in the last exercise show examples of one-way stretches. For example, the curve $y = 2 \sin \theta$ is seen to be a one-way stretch of the curve $y = \sin \theta$ by a factor 2 parallel to the y-axis.

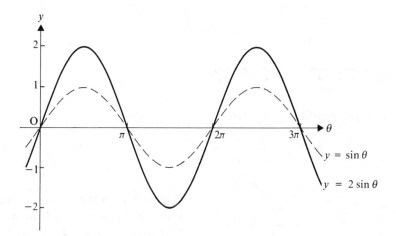

In general, if we compare points on the curves $y = f(x)$ and $y = af(x)$ with the same x-coordinate, then the y-coordinate of the point on $y = af(x)$ is a times the y-coordinate of the point on $y = f(x)$. Therefore

> the curve $y = af(x)$ is a one-way stretch of the curve $y = f(x)$
> by a factor a parallel to the y-axis.

Also, the curve $y = \sin 2\theta$ was seen to be a one-way stretch of the curve $y = \sin \theta$ by a factor $\frac{1}{2}$ parallel to the x-axis (or a one-way shrinkage by a factor 2).

Now consider points on the curves $y = f(x)$ and $y = f(ax)$ with the same y-coordinate. The x-coordinate on $y = f(ax)$ must be $\frac{1}{a}$ times the x-coordinate on $y = f(x)$. Therefore, in general,

the curve $y = f(ax)$ is a one-way stretch of the curve $y = f(x)$ by a factor $\frac{1}{a}$ parallel to the x-axis.

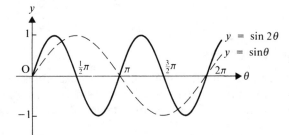

THE COSINE FUNCTION

For any position of P, $\cos \theta = \dfrac{x}{r}$

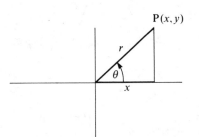

When P is in the first quadrant, x decreases from r to 0 as θ increases, so $\cos \theta$ decreases from 1 to 0

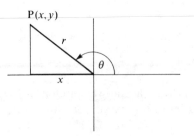

When P is in the second quadrant, x decreases from 0 to $-r$, so $\cos \theta$ decreases from 0 to -1

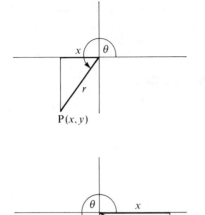

Similarly, when P is in the third quadrant, $\cos \theta$ increases from -1 to 0,

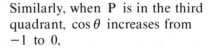

and when P is in the fourth quadrant, $\cos \theta$ increases from 0 to 1

The cycle then repeats itself, and we get this graph of $f(\theta) = \cos \theta$

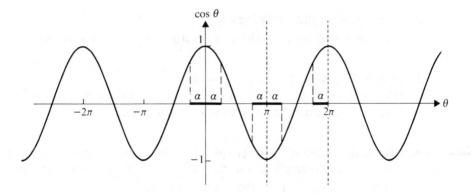

The characteristics of this graph are as follows.

> The curve is continuous
>
> $$-1 \leqslant \cos \theta \leqslant 1$$
>
> It is periodic with a period of 2π

It is the same shape as the sine wave but is translated a distance $\frac{1}{2}\pi$ to the left. Such a translation of a sine wave is called a *phase shift*.

$$\cos \theta = 0 \quad \text{when} \quad \theta = \ldots -\tfrac{1}{2}\pi, \tfrac{1}{2}\pi, \tfrac{3}{2}\pi, \tfrac{5}{2}\pi, \ldots$$

The curve is symmetric about $\theta = 0$, so $\cos{-\alpha} = \cos\alpha$

The curve has rotational symmetry about $\theta = \frac{1}{2}\pi$, so
$$\cos(\pi - \alpha) = -\cos\alpha$$
Further considerations of symmetry show that
$$\cos(\pi + \alpha) = -\cos\alpha \quad \text{and} \quad \cos(2\pi - \alpha) = \cos\alpha$$

EXERCISE 16b

1. Write in terms of the cosine of an acute angle
   (a) $\cos 123°$ (b) $\cos 250°$ (c) $\cos(-20°)$ (d) $\cos(-154°)$

2. Find the exact value of
   (a) $\cos 150°$ (b) $\cos\frac{3}{2}\pi$ (c) $\cos\frac{5}{4}\pi$ (d) $\cos 6\pi$

3. *Sketch* each of the following curves.
   (a) $y = \cos(\theta + \pi)$ (b) $y = \cos(\theta - \frac{1}{3}\pi)$ (c) $y = \cos(-\theta)$

4. Sketch the graph of $y = \cos(\theta - \frac{1}{2}\pi)$
   What relationship does this suggest between $\sin\theta$ and $\cos(\theta - \frac{1}{2}\pi)$?
   Is there a similar relationship between $\cos\theta$ and $\sin(\theta - \frac{1}{2}\pi)$?

5. Sketch the graph of $y = \cos(\theta - \frac{1}{4}\pi)$ for values of θ between $-\pi$
   and π. Use the graph to find the values of θ in this range for which
   (a) $\cos(\theta - \frac{1}{4}\pi) = 1$ (b) $\cos(\theta - \frac{1}{4}\pi) = -1$
   (c) $\cos(\theta - \frac{1}{4}\pi) = 0$

6. On the same set of axes, sketch the graphs $y = \cos\theta$ and
   $y = 3\cos\theta$

7. On the same set of axes, sketch the graphs $y = \cos\theta$ and
   $y = \cos 3\theta$

8. Sketch the graph of $f(\theta) = \cos 4\theta$ for $0 \leqslant \theta \leqslant \pi$
   Hence find the values of θ in this range for which $f(\theta) = 0$

THE TANGENT FUNCTION

For any position of P, $\tan \theta = \dfrac{y}{x}$

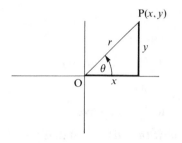

As OP rotates through the first quadrant, x decreases from r to 0 while y increases from 0 to r. This means that the fraction y/x increases from 0 to very large values indeed. In fact, as $\theta \to \frac{1}{2}\pi$, $\tan \theta \to \infty$

Similar analysis of the behaviour of y/x in the other quadrants shows that in the second quadrant, $\tan \theta$ is negative and increases from $-\infty$ to 0, in the third quadrant, $\tan \theta$ is positive and increases from 0 to ∞, and in the fourth quadrant, $\tan \theta$ is negative and increases from $-\infty$ to 0. The cycle then repeats itself and we can draw the graph of $f(\theta) = \tan \theta$

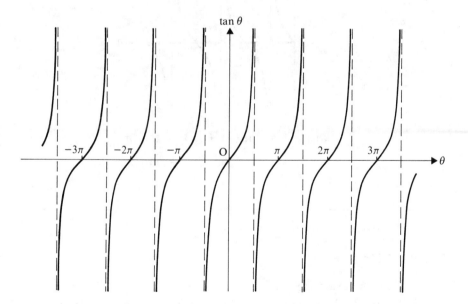

From the graph we can see that the characteristics of the tangent function are different from those of the sine and cosine functions in several respects.

It is not continuous, being *undefined* when $\theta = \ldots -\frac{1}{2}\pi, \frac{1}{2}\pi, \frac{2}{3}\pi, \ldots$

The range of values of $\tan\theta$ is unlimited.

It is periodic with a period of π (not 2π as in the other cases).

The graph has rotational symmetry about $\theta = 0$, so

$$\tan(-\alpha) = -\tan\alpha$$

The graph has rotational symmetry about $\theta = \frac{1}{2}\pi$, giving

$$\tan(\pi - \alpha) = -\tan\alpha$$

As the cycle repeats itself from $\theta = \pi$ to 2π, we have

$$\tan(\pi + \alpha) = \tan\alpha \quad \text{and} \quad \tan(2\pi - \alpha) = -\tan\alpha$$

Example 16c _____

Express $\tan\frac{11}{4}\pi$ as the tangent of an acute angle.

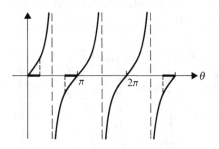

$$\tan(\tfrac{11}{4}\pi) = \tan(2\pi + \tfrac{3}{4}\pi) = \tan\tfrac{3}{4}\pi$$
$$= \tan(\pi - \tfrac{1}{4}\pi)$$
$$= -\tan\tfrac{1}{4}\pi$$

_____

EXERCISE 16c

1. Find the exact value of
   (a) $\tan\frac{9}{4}\pi$ (b) $\tan 120°$ (c) $\tan -\frac{2}{3}\pi$ (d) $\tan\frac{7}{4}\pi$

2. Write in terms of the tangent of an acute angle
   (a) $\tan 220°$ (b) $\tan\frac{12}{7}\pi$ (c) $\tan 310°$ (d) $\tan -\frac{7}{5}\pi$

3. Sketch the graph of $y = \tan \theta$ for values of θ in the range 0 to 2π. From this sketch find the values of θ in this range for which

(a) $\tan \theta = 1$ (b) $\tan \theta = -1$ (c) $\tan \theta = 0$ (d) $\tan \theta = \infty$

4. Using the basic definitions of $\sin \theta$, $\cos \theta$ and $\tan \theta$, show that

$$\tan \theta = \frac{\sin \theta}{\cos \theta}$$

for all values of θ

RELATIONSHIPS BETWEEN SIN θ, COS θ AND TAN θ

Because each trig ratio is a ratio of two of the three quantities x, y and r, we would expect to find several relationships between $\sin \theta$, $\cos \theta$ and $\tan \theta$. Most of these relationships will be investigated in later chapters, but here is a summary of the results from the various exercises so far.

If the graph of $\cos \theta$ is shifted by $\frac{1}{2}\pi$ to the right we get the graph of $\sin \theta$. So $\cos (\theta - \frac{1}{2}\pi) = \sin \theta$

But $\cos (\theta - \frac{1}{2}\pi) = \cos (\frac{1}{2}\pi - \theta)$

Therefore $\cos (\frac{1}{2}\pi - \theta) = \sin \theta$

Two angles which add up to $\frac{1}{2}\pi$ (90°) are called *complementary* angles.

i.e.   the sine of an angle is equal to
            the cosine of the complementary angle and vice-versa.

Now $\sin \theta = \dfrac{y}{r}$, $\cos \theta = \dfrac{x}{r}$ and $\tan \theta = \dfrac{y}{x}$

$\therefore$ $\dfrac{\sin \theta}{\cos \theta} = \dfrac{y/r}{x/r} = \dfrac{y}{x} = \tan \theta$

i.e. for all values of θ, $\tan \theta = \dfrac{\sin \theta}{\cos \theta}$

We have also seen that the sign of each trig ratio depends on the size of the angle, i.e. the quadrant in which P is. So we can summarise the sign of each ratio in a quadrant diagram:

sin +ve	All +ve
tan +ve	cos +ve

Examples 16d _____

   1. Give all the values of x between 0 and 360° for which
      $\sin x = -0.3$

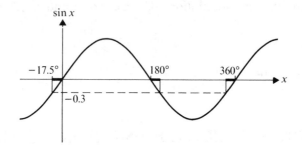

The value given for x by a calculator is $-17.5°$

From the graph, we see that, when $\sin x = -0.3$, the values of x in the specified range are $180° + 17.5°$ and $360° - 17.5°$

When $\sin x = -0.3$, $x = 197.5°$ and $342.5°$

(Note that when the range of values is given in degrees, the answer should also be given in degrees and the same applies for radians.)

_____

   2. Find the smallest positive value of θ for which $\cos\theta = 0.7$ and $\tan\theta$ is negative.

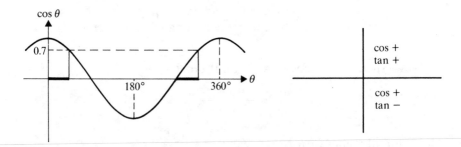

If $\cos\theta = 0.7$, the possible values of θ are $45.6°$, $314.4°, \ldots$
Now $\tan\theta$ is positive if θ is in the first quadrant and negative if θ is in the fourth quadrant.

Therefore the required value of θ is $314.4°$

_____

EXERCISE 16d

1. Within the range $-2\pi \leqslant \theta \leqslant 2\pi$, give all the values of θ for which
   (a) $\sin \theta = 0.4$ (b) $\cos \theta = -0.5$ (c) $\tan \theta = 1.2$

2. Within the range $0 \leqslant \theta \leqslant 720°$, give all the values of θ for which
   (a) $\tan \theta = -0.8$ (b) $\sin \theta = -0.2$ (c) $\cos \theta = 0.1$

3. Find the smallest angle (positive or negative) for which
   (a) $\cos \theta = 0.8$ and $\sin \theta \geqslant 0$
   (b) $\sin \theta = -0.6$ and $\tan \theta \leqslant 0$
   (c) $\tan \theta = \sin \frac{1}{6}\pi$

4. Using $\tan \theta = \dfrac{\sin \theta}{\cos \theta}$, show that the equation $\tan \theta = \sin \theta$ can be written as $\sin \theta(\cos \theta - 1) = 0$, provided that $\cos \theta \neq 0$. Hence find the values of θ between 0 and 2π for which $\tan \theta = \sin \theta$.

5. Sketch the graph of $y = \sin 2\theta$. Use your sketch to help find the values of θ in the range $0 \leqslant \theta \leqslant 360°$ for which $\sin 2\theta = 0.4$

6. Sketch the graph of $y = \cos 3\theta$. Hence find the values of θ in the range $0 \leqslant \theta \leqslant 2\pi$ for which $\cos 3\theta = -1$

THE RECIPROCAL TRIGONOMETRIC FUNCTIONS

The reciprocals of the three main trig functions have their own names and are sometimes referred to as the *minor* trig ratios.

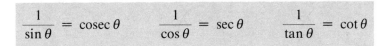

$$\frac{1}{\sin \theta} = \operatorname{cosec} \theta \qquad \frac{1}{\cos \theta} = \sec \theta \qquad \frac{1}{\tan \theta} = \cot \theta$$

The names given above are abbreviations of cosecant, secant and cotangent respectively.

The graph of $f(\theta) = \operatorname{cosec} \theta$ is given below.

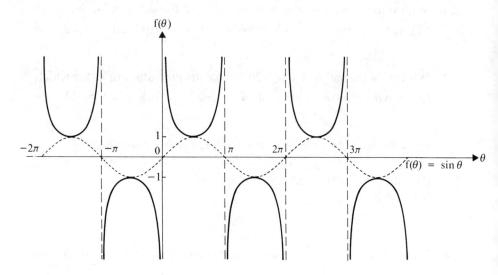

From this graph we can see that

the cosec function is not continuous, being undefined when θ is any integral multiple of π (we would expect this because these are values of θ where $\sin \theta = 0$ and the reciprocal of 0 is $\pm\infty$).

The pattern of the graph of $f(\theta) = \sec \theta$ is similar to that of the cosec graph, as would be expected.

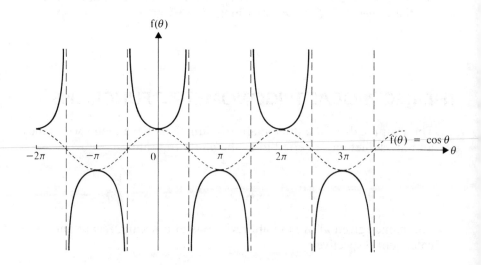

The graph of $f(\theta) = \cot\theta$ is given below.

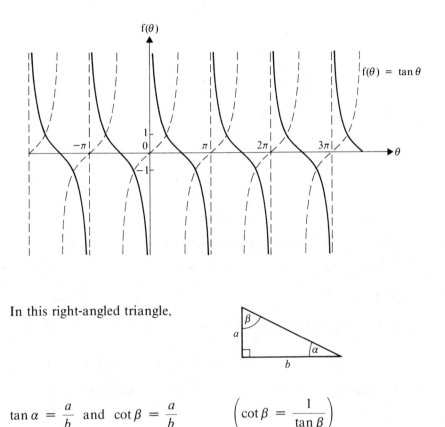

In this right-angled triangle,

$$\tan\alpha = \frac{a}{b} \quad \text{and} \quad \cot\beta = \frac{a}{b} \qquad \left(\cot\beta = \frac{1}{\tan\beta}\right)$$

Now $\alpha + \beta = 90°$, i.e. α and β are complementary angles.

Hence

the cotangent of an angle is equal to the tangent of its complement.

In fact, for *any* angle θ, $\cot\theta = \tan(\tfrac{1}{2}\pi - \theta)$

This can be seen from the graph.

Reflecting the curve $y = \tan\theta$ in the vertical axis gives $y = \tan(-\theta)$

Then translating this curve $\tfrac{1}{2}\pi$ to the left gives $y = \tan(\tfrac{1}{2}\pi - \theta)$, which is the curve $y = \cot\theta$

Example 16e

For $0 \leqslant \theta \leqslant 360°$, find the values of θ for which $\operatorname{cosec} \theta = -8$

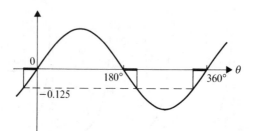

$$\sin \theta = \frac{1}{\operatorname{cosec} \theta} = -\frac{1}{8} = -0.125$$

∴ from a calculator $\theta = -7.2°$

From the sketch, the required values of θ are 187.2° and 352.8°

EXERCISE 16e

1. Find, for values of θ in the range $0 \leqslant \theta \leqslant 360°$, the values of θ for which
   (a) $\sec \theta = 2$　　　(b) $\cot \theta = 0.6$　　　(c) $\operatorname{cosec} \theta = 1.5$

2. Within the range $-180° \leqslant \theta \leqslant 180°$ find the values of θ for which
   (a) $\cot \theta = 1.2$　　　(b) $\sec \theta = -1.5$　　　(c) $\operatorname{cosec} \theta = -2$

3. Given that $\tan \theta = \dfrac{\sin \theta}{\cos \theta}$, write $\cot \theta$ in terms of $\sin \theta$ and $\cos \theta$. Hence show that $\cot \theta - \cos \theta = 0$ can be written in the form $\cos \theta (1 - \sin \theta) = 0$, provided that $\sin \theta \neq 0$
   Thus find the values in the range $-\pi \leqslant \theta \leqslant \pi$ for which $\cot \theta - \cos \theta = 0$

4. Find, in surd form, the values of
   (a) $\cot \frac{1}{4}\pi$　　　(b) $\sec \frac{5}{4}\pi$　　　(c) $\operatorname{cosec} \frac{11}{6}\pi$

5. Sketch the graph of $f(\theta) = \sec(\theta - \frac{1}{4}\pi)$ for $0 \leqslant \theta \leqslant 2\pi$ and give the values of θ for which $f(\theta) = 1$

6. Sketch the graph of $f(\theta) = \cot(\theta + \frac{1}{3}\pi)$ for $-\pi \leqslant \theta \leqslant \pi$. Hence give the values of θ in this range for which $f(\theta) = 1$

GRAPHICAL SOLUTIONS OF TRIG EQUATIONS

If you have worked through all the exercises in this chapter, you will
already have solved several trig equations with the help of sketch
graphs. In this section we are going to look at more complicated
equations which require accurate plots of the graphs to solve them.

Consider the equation $\theta = 3 \sin \theta$

The values of θ for which $\theta = 3 \sin \theta$ can be found by plotting the
graphs of $y = \theta$ and $y = 3 \sin \theta$ on the same axes and hence
finding the values of θ at points of intersection.

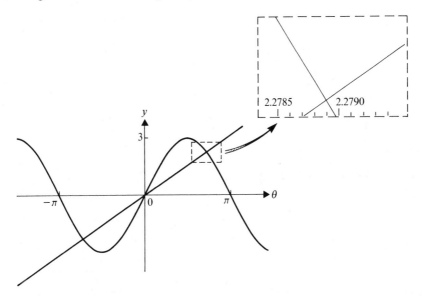

From the enlarged section of the graph $\theta = 2.2789$ rad

Therefore the three points of intersection occur where

$$\theta = -2.2789 \text{ rad}, \quad 0, \quad 2.2789 \text{ rad} \quad \text{correct to } 4 \text{ d.p.}$$

If these graphs are produced on a graphics calculator or on a
computer using suitable software, then it is possible to zoom in on the
points of intersection and get very accurate values for θ. If the graphs
are hand drawn, the accuracy of the results will depend on the
patience and accuracy of the drawer! Plotting accurate graphs
manually is tedious, so if you do not have either of the tools
mentioned above, try just Question 1 in the following exercise and do
not attempt to get answers correct to more than 2 s.f.

EXERCISE 16f

1. Plot the graphs of $y = \theta$ and $y = 2\cos\theta$ for values of θ in the range $-\pi \leqslant \theta \leqslant \pi$. Hence find the values of θ for which
   $\theta = 2\cos\theta$

   Repeat this question using *sketch* graphs and measuring θ in degrees. If this was plotted accurately, would it give the same solutions as when the angle is measured in radians?

2. Measuring the angle in radians throughout, find graphically the values of θ for which

   (a) $2\theta = 4\sin\theta$ (b) $\sin\theta = \theta^2$ (c) $\cos\theta = \theta - 1$

TRIGONOMETRIC IDENTITIES AND EQUATIONS

IDENTITIES

At this stage it is important to know the difference between identities and equations.

This is an equation: $(x - 1)^2 = 4$
The equality is true only when $x = 3$ or when $x = -1$
In any equation, the equality is valid only for a restricted set of values.

This is an identity: $(x - 1)^2 = x^2 - 2x + 1$
The RHS is a different way of expressing the LHS, and the equality is true for all values of x.

In an identity, the equality is true for *any* value of the variable, and we use the symbol $\equiv$ to mean 'is identical to',

i.e. we would write $(x - 1)^2 \equiv x^2 - 2x + 1$

In this chapter we concentrate on some trigonometric identities and some of their uses.

One such identity was introduced in Chapter 16, namely

$$\tan \theta \equiv \frac{\sin \theta}{\cos \theta}$$

THE PYTHAGOREAN IDENTITIES

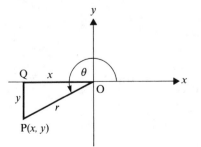

For any angle θ,

$$\sin \theta = \frac{y}{r}, \quad \cos \theta = \frac{x}{r} \quad \text{and}$$

$$\tan \theta = \frac{y}{x}$$

Also, in right-angled triangle OPQ,

$$x^2 + y^2 = r^2 \qquad \text{(Pythagoras)}$$

279

Therefore, $(\cos\theta)^2 + (\sin\theta)^2 = \left(\dfrac{x}{r}\right)^2 + \left(\dfrac{y}{r}\right)^2 = \dfrac{x^2+y^2}{r^2} = 1$

Using the notation $\cos^2\theta$ to mean $(\cos\theta)^2$, etc., we have

$$\cos^2\theta + \sin^2\theta \equiv 1 \qquad\qquad [1]$$

Using the identity $\tan\theta \equiv \dfrac{\sin\theta}{\cos\theta}$ we can write [1] in two other forms.

$[1] \div \cos^2\theta \Rightarrow$ $1 + \dfrac{\sin^2\theta}{\cos^2\theta} \equiv \dfrac{1}{\cos^2\theta}$

$\Rightarrow$ $1 + \tan^2\theta \equiv \sec^2\theta$

$[1] \div \sin^2\theta \Rightarrow$ $\dfrac{\cos^2\theta}{\sin^2\theta} + 1 \equiv \dfrac{1}{\sin^2\theta}$

$\Rightarrow$ $\cot^2\theta + 1 \equiv \mathrm{cosec}^2\theta$

These identities can be used to

> simplify trig expressions,
> eliminate trig terms from pairs of equations,
> derive a variety of further trig relationships,
> calculate other trig ratios of any angle for which one trig ratio is known.

These identities are also very useful in the solution of certain types of trig equations and we will look at this application later in this chapter.

Examples 17a _____

1. Simplify $\dfrac{\sin\theta}{1 + \cot^2\theta}$

$$\dfrac{\sin\theta}{1 + \cot^2\theta} \equiv \dfrac{\sin\theta}{\mathrm{cosec}^2\theta} \equiv \sin^3\theta$$

Using $1 + \cot^2\theta \equiv \mathrm{cosec}^2\theta$ and $\mathrm{cosec}\,\theta \equiv \dfrac{1}{\sin\theta}$

_____

2. Eliminate θ from the equations $x = 2\cos\theta$ and $y = 3\sin\theta$

$$\cos\theta = \tfrac{1}{2}x \quad \text{and} \quad \sin\theta = \tfrac{1}{3}y$$

Using $\cos^2\theta + \sin^2\theta \equiv 1$ gives

$$\left(\frac{x}{2}\right)^2 + \left(\frac{y}{3}\right)^2 = 1$$

$$\Rightarrow \qquad\qquad 9x^2 + 4y^2 = 36$$

In Example 2, both x and y initially depend on θ, a variable angle. Used in this way, θ is called a *parameter*, and is a type of variable that plays an important part in the analysis of curves and functions.

3. If $\sin A = -\tfrac{1}{3}$ and A is in the third quadrant, find $\cos A$ without using a calculator.

There are two ways of doing this problem.   The first method involves drawing a quadrant diagram and working out the remaining side of the triangle, using Pythagoras theorem.

From the diagram, $x = -2\sqrt{2}$

$$\therefore \qquad \cos A = \frac{x}{r} = -\frac{2\sqrt{2}}{3}$$

The second method uses the identity $\cos^2 A + \sin^2 A \equiv 1$ giving

$$\cos^2 A + \frac{1}{3} = 1 \quad \Rightarrow \quad \cos A = \pm\sqrt{\frac{8}{3}} = \pm\frac{2\sqrt{2}}{3}$$

As A is between π and $\tfrac{3}{2}\pi$, $\cos A$ is negative, i.e.

$$\cos A = -\frac{2\sqrt{2}}{3}$$

4. Prove that $(1 - \cos A)(1 + \sec A) \equiv \sin A \tan A$

Because the relationship has yet to be proved, we must not assume its truth by using the complete identity in our working. The left and right hand sides must be isolated throughout the proof, preferably by working on only one of these sides.

Consider the LHS:

$$(1 - \cos A)(1 + \sec A) \equiv 1 + \sec A - \cos A - \cos A \sec A$$

$$\equiv 1 + \sec A - \cos A - \cos A \left(\frac{1}{\cos A} \right)$$

$$\equiv \sec A - \cos A$$

$$\equiv \frac{1 - \cos^2 A}{\cos A}$$

$$\equiv \frac{\sin^2 A}{\cos A} \qquad (\cos^2 A + \sin^2 A \equiv 1)$$

$$\equiv \sin A \left[\frac{\sin A}{\cos A} \right]$$

$$\equiv \sin A \tan A \equiv \text{RHS}$$

5. Prove that $(\operatorname{cosec} A - \sin A)(\sec A - \cos A) \equiv \dfrac{1}{\tan A + \cot A}$

LHS is $(\operatorname{cosec} A - \sin A)(\sec A - \cos A)$

$$\equiv \left(\frac{1}{\sin A} - \sin A \right)\left(\frac{1}{\cos A} - \cos A \right)$$

$$\equiv \left(\frac{1 - \sin^2 A}{\sin A} \right)\left(\frac{1 - \cos^2 A}{\cos A} \right)$$

$$\equiv \left(\frac{\cos^2 A}{\sin A} \right)\left(\frac{\sin^2 A}{\cos A} \right)$$

$$\equiv \cos A \sin A$$

Now this is already a very simple form but as it is not yet in the form of the given RHS, we begin working independently on the RHS.

$$\text{RHS is } \frac{1}{\tan A + \cot A} \equiv 1 \div \left(\frac{\sin A}{\cos A} + \frac{\cos A}{\sin A} \right)$$

$$\equiv 1 \div \left(\frac{\sin^2 A + \cos^2 A}{\cos A \sin A} \right)$$

$$\equiv \cos A \sin A$$

Since both LHS and RHS reduce to $\cos A \sin A$ they are identical.

EXERCISE 17a

1. Without using a calculator, complete the following table.

	$\sin \theta$	$\cos \theta$	$\tan \theta$	type of angle
(a)		$-\frac{5}{13}$		reflex
(b)	$\frac{3}{5}$			obtuse
(c)			$\frac{7}{24}$	acute
(d)				straight line

Simplify the following expressions.

2. $\dfrac{1 - \sec^2 A}{1 - \operatorname{cosec}^2 A}$

3. $\dfrac{\sin \theta}{\sqrt{(1 - \cos^2 \theta)}}$

4. $\dfrac{\sin \theta}{\cos \theta} + \dfrac{\cos \theta}{\sin \theta}$

5. $\dfrac{\sqrt{(1 + \tan^2 \theta)}}{\sqrt{(1 - \sin^2 \theta)}}$

6. $\dfrac{1}{\cos \theta \sqrt{(1 + \cot^2 \theta)}}$

7. $\dfrac{\sin \theta}{1 + \cot^2 \theta}$

Eliminate θ from the following pairs of equations.

8. $x = 4 \sec \theta$
$y = 4 \tan \theta$

9. $x = a \operatorname{cosec} \theta$
$y = b \cot \theta$

10. $x = 2 \tan \theta$
$y = 3 \cos \theta$

11. $x = 1 - \sin \theta$
$y = 1 + \cos \theta$

12. $x = 2 + \tan \theta$
$y = 2 \cos \theta$

13. $x = a \sec \theta$
$y = b \sin \theta$

Prove the following identities.

14. $\cot\theta + \tan\theta \equiv \sec\theta\,\mathrm{cosec}\,\theta$

15. $\dfrac{\cos A}{1 - \tan A} + \dfrac{\sin A}{1 - \cot A} \equiv \sin A + \cos A$

16. $\tan^2\theta + \cot^2\theta \equiv \sec^2\theta + \mathrm{cosec}^2\theta - 2$

17. $\dfrac{\sin A}{1 + \cos A} \equiv \dfrac{1 - \cos A}{\sin A}$ (Hint. Multiply top and bottom of LHS by $(1 - \cos A)$.)

18. $(\sec^2\theta + \tan^2\theta)(\mathrm{cosec}^2\theta + \cot^2\theta) \equiv 1 + 2\sec^2\theta\,\mathrm{cosec}^2\theta$

19. $\dfrac{\sin A}{1 + \cos A} + \dfrac{1 + \cos A}{\sin A} \equiv \dfrac{2}{\sin A}$

20. $\sec^2 A \equiv \dfrac{\mathrm{cosec}\,A}{\mathrm{cosec}\,A - \sin A}$

21. $(1 + \sin A + \cos A)^2 \equiv 2(1 + \sin A)(1 + \cos A)$

22. $\dfrac{\tan^2 A + \cos^2 A}{\sin A + \sec A} \equiv \sec A - \sin A$

SOLVING EQUATIONS

We have already solved some simple trig equations in Chapter 16. We can now solve slightly more complicated equations using the Pythagorean identities.

Examples 17b _____

1. Solve the equation $2\cos^2\theta - \sin\theta = 1$ for values of θ in the range 0 to 2π

The given equation is quadratic, but it involves the sine and the cosine of θ, so we use $\cos^2\theta + \sin^2\theta \equiv 1$ to express the equation in terms of $\sin\theta$ only.

$$2\cos^2\theta - \sin\theta = 1$$

$\Rightarrow \qquad\qquad 2(1 - \sin^2\theta) - \sin\theta = 1$

$\Rightarrow \qquad\qquad 2\sin^2\theta + \sin\theta - 1 = 0$

$\Rightarrow \qquad (2\sin\theta - 1)(\sin\theta + 1) = 0 \qquad \Rightarrow \qquad \sin\theta = \tfrac{1}{2} \text{ or } -1$

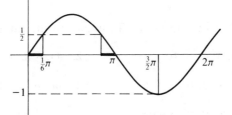

If $\sin\theta = \frac{1}{2}$, $\theta = \frac{1}{6}\pi, \frac{5}{6}\pi$

If $\sin\theta = -1$, $\theta = \frac{3}{2}\pi$

Therefore the solution of the equation is $\theta = \frac{1}{6}\pi, \frac{5}{6}\pi, \frac{3}{2}\pi$

---

2. Solve the equation $\cot x = \sin x$ for values of x from 0 to 360°

Using $\cot x \equiv \dfrac{\cos x}{\sin x}$ gives

$$\frac{\cos x}{\sin x} = \sin x$$

We can now multiply the equation by $\sin x$ provided that $\sin x \neq 0$ Thus we must exclude any values of x for which $\sin x = 0$ from the solution set.

$\Rightarrow \qquad\qquad\qquad\qquad \cos x = \sin^2 x$

$\Rightarrow \qquad\qquad\qquad \cos^2 x + \cos x - 1 = 0$

This equation does not factorise, so we use the formula, giving

$$\cos x = \tfrac{1}{2}(-1 \pm \sqrt{5})$$

$\therefore \quad \cos x = -1.618$ and there is no value of x for which this is true.

or $\cos x = 0.618$

$\Rightarrow \qquad x = 51.8°$ or $308.2°$

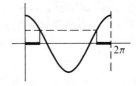

EXERCISE 17b

Solve the following equations for angles in the range $0 \leqslant \theta \leqslant 360°$

1. $\sec^2 \theta + \tan^2 \theta = 6$ **2.** $4 \cos^2 \theta + 5 \sin \theta = 3$

3. $\cot^2 \theta = \operatorname{cosec} \theta$ **4.** $\tan \theta + \cot \theta = 2 \sec \theta$

5. $\tan \theta + 3 \cot \theta = 5 \sec \theta$ **6.** $\sec \theta = 1 - 2 \tan^2 \theta$

Solve the following equations for angles in the range $-\pi \leqslant \theta \leqslant \pi$

7. $5 \cos \theta - 4 \sin^2 \theta = 2$ **8.** $4 \cot^2 \theta + 12 \operatorname{cosec} \theta + 1 = 0$

9. $4 \sec^2 \theta - 3 \tan \theta = 5$ **10.** $2 \cos \theta - 4 \sin^2 \theta + 2 = 0$

GENERAL SOLUTIONS OF TRIG EQUATIONS

Consider the equation $\sin \theta = 1$

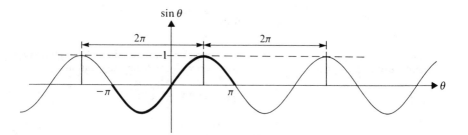

We see that, in the range $-\pi \leqslant \theta \leqslant \pi$, there is one solution, $\theta = \tfrac{1}{2}\pi$
We can also see that there are many more values of θ that satisfy
$\sin \theta = 1$

> The general solution is an expression which represents all angles
> which satisfy the given equation. From the graph we can see that
> the general solution is an infinite set of angles.

In looking for a general solution, use can be made of the graphs of trig
functions and their periodic nature.

Now consider the equation $\sin \theta = \frac{1}{2}$

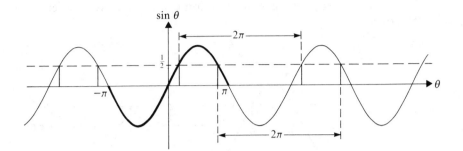

The period of the sine function is covered by the interval $[-\pi, \pi]$ and repeats every 2π

In the interval $[-\pi, \pi]$, $\theta = \frac{1}{6}\pi$ and $\theta = \frac{5}{6}\pi$ and we can get further solutions by adding (or subtracting) any multiple of 2π to $\frac{1}{6}\pi$ or to $\frac{5}{6}\pi$

Therefore the general solution of $\sin \theta = \frac{1}{2}$ can be expressed as

$$\theta = \begin{cases} \frac{1}{6}\pi + 2n\pi \\ \frac{5}{6}\pi + 2n\pi \end{cases} \quad \text{where} \quad n \in \mathbf{Z}$$

The same argument can be applied to any equation $\sin \theta = s$, where $-1 \leqslant s \leqslant 1$, which usually has two solutions in the interval $[-\pi, \pi]$, showing that

the general solution of $\sin \theta = s$, where $-1 \leqslant s \leqslant 1$, is

$$\theta = \begin{cases} \theta_1 + 2n\pi \\ \theta_2 + 2n\pi \end{cases} \quad \text{or} \quad \theta = \begin{cases} \theta_1 + 360n° \\ \theta_2 + 360n° \end{cases}$$

where $n \in \mathbf{Z}$, and θ_1 and θ_2 are the solutions in the range $-\pi \leqslant \theta \leqslant \pi$

A similar situation occurs when the equation $\cos \theta = c$ is considered. The cosine function is periodic with a period of 2π, and one period is covered by the interval $[-\pi, \pi]$

Within this interval there are usually two solutions, θ_1 and θ_2, and adding or subtracting any multiple of 2π gives another angle with the same cosine ratio. But, because the graph is symmetrical about $\theta = 0$, $\theta_2 = -\theta_1$, the general solution can be expressed in terms of θ_1 alone.

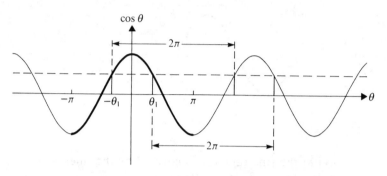

The general solution of the equation $\cos\theta = c$, where $-1 \leqslant c \leqslant 1$ is

$$\theta = \pm\theta_1 + 2n\pi$$

where $n \in \mathbb{Z}$ and θ_1 is a solution in the range $-\pi \leqslant \theta \leqslant \pi$

The situation with the equation $\tan\theta = t$ is different because the tangent function has a period of π which is covered by the interval $[-\frac{1}{2}\pi, \frac{1}{2}\pi]$. Within this interval there is only one solution of the equation $\tan\theta = t$ and adding or subtracting any multiple of π gives another angle with the same tangent ratio.

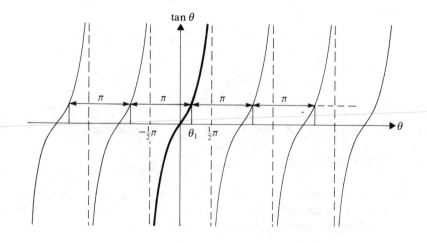

> The general solution of the equation $\tan \theta = t$ is
>
> $$\theta = \theta_1 + n\pi$$
>
> where $n \in \mathbf{Z}$ and θ_1 is the solution in the range $-\frac{1}{2}\pi \leqslant \theta \leqslant \frac{1}{2}\pi$

Examples 17c

1. Find the general solution of the equation $\tan \theta = -\sqrt{3}$

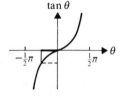

In the interval $[-\frac{1}{2}\pi, \frac{1}{2}\pi]$ the solution
of $\tan \theta = -\sqrt{3}$ is $\theta = -\frac{1}{3}\pi$

Therefore the general solution is
$\theta = -\frac{1}{3}\pi + n\pi$ where $n \in \mathbf{Z}$

2. Find the general solution of the equation $\cos \theta = \dfrac{1}{\sqrt{2}}$

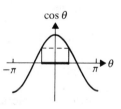

In the interval $[-\pi, \pi]$, the solutions
of $\cos \theta = \dfrac{1}{\sqrt{2}}$ are $\pm \frac{1}{4}\pi$

So the general solution is
$\theta = \pm\frac{1}{4}\pi + 2n\pi$ where $n \in \mathbf{Z}$

3. Find the general solution of the equation $\sin \theta = -\frac{1}{2}$

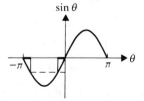

In the interval $[-\pi, \pi]$, the solutions
are $\theta = -\frac{1}{6}\pi$ and $\theta = -\frac{5}{6}\pi$

So the general solution is

$\left. \begin{array}{l} \theta = -\frac{1}{6}\pi + 2n\pi \\ \text{and } \theta = -\frac{5}{6}\pi + 2n\pi \end{array} \right\}$ where $n \in \mathbf{Z}$

4. Find the general solution of the equation $3 \sec^2 \theta - 5 \tan \theta - 4 = 0$ giving answers in degrees correct to 1 d.p.

Using $1 + \tan^2 \theta \equiv \sec^2 \theta$ we have

$$3(1 + \tan^2 \theta) - 5 \tan \theta - 4 = 0$$

$\Rightarrow \qquad\qquad\qquad 3 \tan^2 \theta - 5 \tan \theta - 1 = 0$

This equation does not have any simple factors so we solve it by the formula.

$\Rightarrow \qquad\qquad \tan \theta = \dfrac{5 \pm \sqrt{(25 + 12)}}{6}$

$$= 1.8471 \text{ or } -0.1805$$

In the interval $[-90°, 90°]$

$\tan \theta = 1.8471 \quad \Rightarrow \quad \theta = 61.6°$

$\tan \theta = -0.1805 \quad \Rightarrow \quad \theta = -10.2°$

The general solution is therefore $\theta = \begin{cases} 61.6° + 180n° \\ -10.2° + 180n° \end{cases}$ where $n \in \mathbb{Z}$

EXERCISE 17c

Find the general solutions of each of the following equations.
Give answers in radians when they are exact; otherwise give answers in degrees to 1 d.p.

1. $\sin \theta = \frac{\sqrt{3}}{2}$ **2.** $\cos \theta = 0$ **3.** $\tan \theta = -\sqrt{3}$

4. $\sin \theta = -\frac{1}{4}$ **5.** $\cos \theta = -\frac{1}{2}$ **6.** $\tan \theta = 1$

7. $\sec \theta = 1$ **8.** $\operatorname{cosec} \theta = 2$ **9.** $\sin^2 \theta = \frac{1}{4}$

10. $5 \cos \theta - 4 \sin^2 \theta = 2$ **11.** $4 \cot^2 \theta + 12 \operatorname{cosec} \theta + 1 = 0$

12. $4 \sec^2 \theta - 3 \tan \theta = 5$ **13.** $2 \cos \theta - 4 \sin^2 \theta + 2 = 0$

14. $2 \sin \theta \cos \theta + \sin \theta = 0$ **15.** $4 \cos \theta = \cos \theta \operatorname{cosec} \theta$

16. $\sqrt{3} \tan \theta = 2 \sin \theta$ **17.** $\cot \theta = \sin \theta$

EQUATIONS INVOLVING MULTIPLE ANGLES

Many trig equations involve ratios of a multiple of θ, for example

$$\cos 2\theta = \tfrac{1}{2} \qquad \tan 3\theta = -2$$

Simple equations of this type can be solved by finding first the values of the multiple angle and then, by division, the corresponding values of θ

Examples 17d _____

1. Find the general solution of the equation $\cos 2\theta = \tfrac{1}{2}$

Using $2\theta = \phi$ gives $\cos \phi = \tfrac{1}{2}$

In the interval $[-\pi, \pi]$, the solutions

of $\cos \phi = \tfrac{1}{2}$ are $\phi = \pm \tfrac{1}{3}\pi$

So the general solution for ϕ is $\qquad \phi = \pm \tfrac{1}{3}\pi + 2n\pi$

but $\phi = 2\theta$, therefore $\qquad 2\theta = \pm \tfrac{1}{3}\pi + 2n\pi$

Hence $\qquad\qquad\qquad\qquad\qquad \theta = \pm \tfrac{1}{6}\pi + n\pi$

_____

2. Find the general solution of the equation $\cot(\tfrac{1}{3}\theta - 90°) = 1$, giving the answer in degrees.

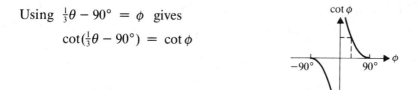

Using $\tfrac{1}{3}\theta - 90° = \phi$ gives

$$\cot(\tfrac{1}{3}\theta - 90°) = \cot \phi$$

The general solution of the equation $\cot \phi = 1$ is

$$\phi = 45° + 180n°$$

But $\phi = \tfrac{1}{3}\theta - 90°$, so $\qquad \tfrac{1}{3}\theta - 90° = 45° + 180n°$

$\Rightarrow \qquad\qquad\qquad\qquad\qquad \theta = 135° + 270° + 540n°$

i.e. $\qquad\qquad\qquad\qquad\qquad\quad \theta = 405° + 540n°$

_____

EXERCISE 17d

Find the general solutions of the following equations, giving your answers in degrees.

1. $\tan 2\theta = 1$ 2. $\cos 3\theta = -0.5$

3. $\sin \frac{1}{2}\theta = -\frac{\sqrt{2}}{2}$ 4. $\sec 5\theta = 2$

5. $\cot \frac{1}{3}\theta = -4$ 6. $\cos 2\theta = 0.63$

7. $\cos(2\theta - 45°) = 0$ 8. $\sin(\frac{1}{4}\theta + 30°) = -1$

9. $\tan(\theta - 60°) = 0$

Find the general solutions of the following equations, giving your answers in radians.

10. $\cos(\theta + \frac{1}{4}\pi) = \frac{1}{2}$ 11. $\tan(2\theta - \frac{1}{3}\pi) = -1$

12. $\sin(2\theta + \frac{1}{6}\pi) = \frac{1}{2}$

Sometimes an equation involving multiple angles requires a solution in a specified range and this can be found from the general solution.

Example 17e _____

Find the angles in the interval $[-180°, 180°]$ which satisfy the equation $\tan 3\theta = -2$

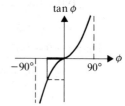

Using $\phi = 3\theta$ gives $\tan \phi = -2$

In the interval $[-90°, 90°]$, $\phi = -63.4°$

∴ the general solution is $3\theta = -63.4° + 180n°$

$\Rightarrow$ $\theta = -21.1° + 60n°$

Now to get values of θ from $-180°$ to $180°$, we see that we need values of n from -2 to 3

When $n = -2, -1, 0, 1, 2, 3$

$\theta = -141.1°, -81.1°, -21.1°, 38.9°, 98.9°, 158.9°$

_____

Note that   when a multiple angle is involved, it is the general solution of the multiple angle that must be found.

EXERCISE 17e

Solve the equations for values of θ in the range $-180° \leqslant \theta \leqslant 180°$

1. $\tan 2\theta = 1.8$ **2.** $\sin 3\theta = 0.7$ **3.** $\cos \frac{1}{2}\theta = 0.85$

Solve the equations for values of θ in the range $0 \leqslant \theta \leqslant 2\pi$

4. $\tan 4\theta = -\sqrt{3}$ **5.** $\sec 5\theta = 2$ **6.** $\cot \frac{1}{2}\theta = -1$

MIXED EXERCISE 17

1. Eliminate α from the equations $x = \cos\alpha, \ y = \operatorname{cosec}\alpha$

2. If $\cos\beta = 0.5$, find possible values for $\sin\beta$ and $\tan\beta$, giving your answers in exact form.

3. Simplify the expression $\dfrac{1}{1 + \cos\theta} + \dfrac{1}{1 - \cos\theta}$. Hence solve the equation $\dfrac{1}{1 + \cos\theta} + \dfrac{1}{1 - \cos\theta} = 4$ for values of θ in the range $0 \leqslant \theta \leqslant 2\pi$

4. Find the general solution of the equation $\sec\theta + \tan^2\theta = 5$ Give the answer in degrees.

5. Prove that $(\cot\theta + \operatorname{cosec}\theta)^2 \equiv \dfrac{1 + \cos\theta}{1 - \cos\theta}$

6. Find the values of θ for which $\tan(3\theta - \frac{1}{3}\pi) = 1$ in the interval $[-\pi, \pi]$

7. Eliminate θ from the equations
(a) $x - 2 = \sin\theta, \ y + 1 = \cos\theta$
(b) $x = \sec\theta - 3, \ y = 2 - \tan\theta$

8. Find the general solution of the equation $\tan 2\alpha = \cot 2\alpha$

9. Prove that $(\cos A + \sin A)^2 + (\cos A - \sin A)^2 \equiv 2$

10. Simplify $(1 + \cos A)(1 - \cos A)$

11. Find in degrees the general solution of the equation $\tan\theta = 3\sin\theta$

12. Simplify $\sec^4\theta - \sec^2\theta$

COMPOUND ANGLE IDENTITIES

COMPOUND ANGLES

It is often useful to be able to express a trig ratio of an angle $A + B$ in terms of trig ratios of A and of B.

It is dangerously easy to think, for instance, that $\sin(A + B)$ is $\sin A + \sin B$. However, this is *false* as can be seen by considering

$$\sin(45° + 45°) = \sin 90° \qquad = 1$$

whereas $\qquad \sin 45° + \sin 45° = \tfrac{1}{2}\sqrt{2} + \tfrac{1}{2}\sqrt{2} \neq 1$

Thus the sine function is *not distributive* and neither are the other trig functions.

The correct identity is $\sin(A + B) = \sin A \cos B + \cos A \sin B$.

This is proved geometrically when A and B are both acute, from the diagram below.

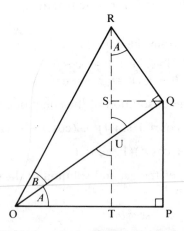

The right-angled triangles OPQ and OQR contain angles A and B as shown.

From the diagram, $\angle URQ = A$

$$\sin (A + B) = \frac{TR}{OR} = \frac{TS + SR}{OR} = \frac{PQ + SR}{OR}$$

$$= \frac{PQ}{OQ} \times \frac{OQ}{OR} + \frac{SR}{QR} \times \frac{QR}{OR}$$

$\therefore$ $\quad\quad\quad\quad \sin(A + B) \equiv \sin A \cos B + \cos A \sin B$

This identity is in fact valid for all angles and it can be adapted to give the full set of compound angle formulae. The reader is left to do this in the following exercise.

EXERCISE 18a

1. In the identity $\sin (A + B) \equiv \sin A \cos B + \cos A \sin B$, replace B by $-B$ to show that $\sin (A - B) \equiv \sin A \cos B - \cos A \sin B$

2. In the identity $\sin (A - B) \equiv \sin A \cos B - \cos A \sin B$, replace A by $(\frac{1}{2}\pi - A)$ to show that $\cos (A + B) \equiv \cos A \cos B - \sin A \sin B$

3. In the identity $\cos (A + B) \equiv \cos A \cos B - \sin A \sin B$, replace B by $-B$ to show that $\cos (A - B) \equiv \cos A \cos B + \sin A \sin B$

4. Use $\dfrac{\sin (A + B)}{\cos (A + B)}$ to show that $\tan (A + B) \equiv \dfrac{\tan A + \tan B}{1 - \tan A \tan B}$

5. Replace B by $-B$ in the formula for $\tan (A + B)$ to show that

$$\tan (A - B) \equiv \frac{\tan A - \tan B}{1 + \tan A \tan B}$$

Collecting these results we have:

$$\sin (A + B) \equiv \sin A \cos B + \cos A \sin B$$
$$\sin (A - B) \equiv \sin A \cos B - \cos A \sin B$$

$$\cos (A + B) \equiv \cos A \cos B - \sin A \sin B$$
$$\cos (A - B) \equiv \cos A \cos B + \sin A \sin B$$

$$\tan (A + B) \equiv \frac{\tan A + \tan B}{1 - \tan A \tan B}$$

$$\tan (A - B) \equiv \frac{\tan A - \tan B}{1 + \tan A \tan B}$$

Examples 18b _____

1. Find exact values for (a) sin 75°   (b) cos 105°

To find exact values, we need to express the given angle in terms of angles whose trig ratios are known as exact values, e.g. 30°, 60°, 45°, 90°, 120°, ...
Now 75° = 45° + 30° (or 120° − 45° or other alternative compound angles).

(a) $\sin 75° = \sin(45° + 30°) = \sin 45° \cos 30° + \cos 45° \sin 30°$

$$= \left(\frac{\sqrt{2}}{2}\right)\left(\frac{\sqrt{3}}{2}\right) + \left(\frac{\sqrt{2}}{2}\right)\left(\frac{1}{2}\right)$$

$$= \frac{\sqrt{2}}{4}(\sqrt{3} + 1)$$

(b) $\cos 105° = \cos(60° + 45°) = \cos 60° \cos 45° - \sin 60° \sin 45°$

$$= \left(\frac{1}{2}\right)\left(\frac{\sqrt{2}}{2}\right) - \left(\frac{\sqrt{3}}{2}\right)\left(\frac{\sqrt{2}}{2}\right)$$

$$= \frac{\sqrt{2}}{4}(1 - \sqrt{3})$$

_____

2. A is obtuse and $\sin A = \frac{3}{5}$, B is acute and $\sin B = \frac{12}{13}$. Find the exact value of $\cos(A + B)$.

$\cos(A + B) \equiv \cos A \cos B - \sin A \sin B$

In order to use this formula, we need values for cos A and cos B.   These can be found using Pythagoras' theorem in the appropriate right-angled triangle.

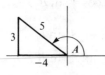

$$\cos A = -\tfrac{4}{5} \qquad\qquad \cos B = \tfrac{5}{13}$$

$$\therefore \qquad \cos(A + B) = \left(-\frac{4}{5}\right)\left(\frac{5}{13}\right) - \left(\frac{3}{5}\right)\left(\frac{12}{13}\right) = -\frac{56}{65}$$

_____

3. Simplify $\sin\theta\cos\frac{1}{3}\pi - \cos\theta\sin\frac{1}{3}\pi$ and hence find the smallest positive value of θ for which the expression has a minimum value.

$\sin\theta\cos\frac{1}{3}\pi - \cos\theta\sin\frac{1}{3}\pi$ is the expansion of $\sin(A - B)$ with $A = \theta$ and $B = \frac{1}{3}\pi$

$$\sin\theta\cos\tfrac{1}{3}\pi - \cos\theta\sin\tfrac{1}{3}\pi = \sin(\theta - \tfrac{1}{3}\pi)$$

Let $f(\theta) = \sin(\theta - \frac{1}{3}\pi)$

Now the graph $f(\theta)$ is a sine wave, but translated $\frac{1}{3}\pi$ in the direction of the positive θ-axis.

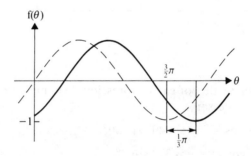

Therefore $f(\theta)$ has a minimum value of -1 and the smallest $+$ve value of θ at which this occurs is $\frac{3}{2}\pi + \frac{1}{3}\pi = \frac{11}{6}\pi$

---

4. Prove that $\dfrac{\sin(A - B)}{\cos A \cos B} + \dfrac{\sin(B - C)}{\cos B \cos C} \equiv \tan A - \tan C$

Expanding each of the numerators, the LHS becomes

$$\frac{\sin A \cos B - \cos A \sin B}{\cos A \cos B} + \frac{\sin B \cos C - \cos B \sin C}{\cos B \cos C}$$

$$\equiv \frac{\sin A \cos B}{\cos A \cos B} - \frac{\cos A \sin B}{\cos A \cos B} + \frac{\sin B \cos C}{\cos B \cos C} - \frac{\cos B \sin C}{\cos B \cos C}$$

$$\equiv \tan A - \tan B + \tan B - \tan C$$

$$\equiv \tan A - \tan C \equiv \text{RHS}$$

---

5. Find the general solution of the equation $2 \cos \theta = \sin (\theta + \frac{1}{6}\pi)$

$$2 \cos \theta = \sin (\theta + \frac{1}{6}\pi)$$
$$= \sin \theta \cos \frac{1}{6}\pi + \cos \theta \sin \frac{1}{6}\pi = \frac{\sqrt{3}}{2} \sin \theta + \frac{1}{2} \cos \theta$$

$\therefore \quad \frac{3}{2} \cos \theta = \frac{\sqrt{3}}{2} \sin \theta$

$\Rightarrow \quad \dfrac{3}{\sqrt{3}} = \dfrac{\sin \theta}{\cos \theta} \quad \Rightarrow \quad \tan \theta = \sqrt{3}$

$\tan \frac{1}{3}\pi = \sqrt{3}$

Therefore the general solution is $\theta = \frac{1}{3}\pi + n\pi$

EXERCISE 18b

Find the exact value of each expression, leaving your answer in surd form where necessary.

1. $\cos 40° \cos 50° - \sin 40° \sin 50°$

2. $\sin 37° \cos 7° - \cos 37° \sin 7°$

3. $\cos 75°$ **4.** $\tan 105°$

5. $\sin 165°$ **6.** $\cos 15°$

Simplify each of the following expressions.

7. $\sin \theta \cos 2\theta + \cos \theta \sin 2\theta$

8. $\cos \alpha \cos (90° - \alpha) - \sin \alpha \sin (90° - \alpha)$

9. $\dfrac{\tan A + \tan 2A}{1 - \tan A \tan 2A}$ **10.** $\dfrac{\tan 3\beta - \tan 2\beta}{1 + \tan 3\beta \tan 2\beta}$

11. A is acute and $\sin A = \frac{7}{25}$, B is obtuse and $\sin B = \frac{4}{5}$. Find an exact expression for
    (a) $\sin (A + B)$ (b) $\cos (A + B)$ (c) $\tan (A + B)$

12. Find the greatest value of each expression and the value of θ between 0 and 360° at which it occurs.
    (a) $\sin \theta \cos 25° - \cos \theta \sin 25°$ (b) $\sin \theta \sin 30° + \cos \theta \cos 30°$
    (c) $\cos \theta \cos 50° - \sin \theta \sin 50°$ (d) $\sin 60° \cos \theta - \cos 60° \sin \theta$

Prove the following identities.

13. $\cot (A + B) \equiv \dfrac{\cot A \cot B - 1}{\cot A + \cot B}$

14. $(\sin A + \cos A)(\sin B + \cos B) \equiv \sin (A + B) + \cos (A - B)$

15. $\sin (A + B) + \sin (A - B) \equiv 2 \sin A \cos B$

16. $\sin (\frac{1}{4}\pi + A) + \sin (\frac{1}{4}\pi - A) \equiv \sqrt{2} \cos A$

17. $\cos (A + B) + \cos (A - B) \equiv 2 \cos A \cos B$

18. $\dfrac{\sin (A + B)}{\cos A \cos B} \equiv \tan A + \tan B$

19. $\sin (\theta + 60°) \equiv \sin (120° - \theta)$

20. $\tan (x + y) - \tan x \equiv \dfrac{\sin y}{\cos x \cos (x + y)}$

Solve the following equations for values of θ in the range $0 \leqslant \theta \leqslant 360°$

21. $\cos (45° - \theta) = \sin \theta$

22. $3 \sin \theta = \cos (\theta + 60°)$

23. $\tan (A - \theta) = \frac{2}{3}$ and $\tan A = 3$

24. $\sin (\theta + 60°) = \cos \theta$

Find the general solution of the following equations.

25. $\sin (x + \frac{1}{3}\pi) = \cos x$ **26.** $\sin x = \cos (x - \frac{2}{3}\pi)$

THE DOUBLE ANGLE IDENTITIES

The compound angle formulae deal with any two angles A and B and can therefore be used for two equal angles, i.e. when B = A

Replacing B by A in the trig identities for (A + B) gives the following set of double angle identities.

$$\sin 2A \equiv 2 \sin A \cos A$$

$$\cos 2A \equiv \cos^2 A - \sin^2 A$$

$$\tan 2A \equiv \dfrac{2 \tan A}{1 - \tan^2 A}$$

The second of these identities can be expressed in several forms because

$$\cos^2 A - \sin^2 A \equiv \begin{cases} (1 - \sin^2 A) - \sin^2 A \equiv 1 - 2\sin^2 A \\ \cos^2 A - (1 - \cos^2 A) \equiv 2\cos^2 A - 1 \end{cases}$$

i.e.

$$\cos 2A \equiv \begin{cases} \cos^2 A - \sin^2 A \\ 1 - 2\sin^2 A \\ 2\cos^2 A - 1 \end{cases}$$

Examples 18c

1. If $\tan \theta = \frac{3}{4}$, find the values of $\tan 2\theta$ and $\tan 4\theta$

Using $\tan 2A \equiv \dfrac{2\tan A}{1 - \tan^2 A}$ with $A = \theta$ and $\tan\theta = \frac{3}{4}$ gives

$$\tan 2\theta = \frac{2(\frac{3}{4})}{1 - (\frac{3}{4})^2} = \frac{24}{7}$$

Using the identity for $\tan 2A$ again, but this time with $A = 2\theta$, gives

$$\tan 4\theta = \frac{2\tan 2\theta}{1 - \tan^2 2\theta} = \frac{2(\frac{24}{7})}{1 - (\frac{24}{7})^2} = -\frac{336}{527}$$

2. Eliminate θ from the equations $x = \cos 2\theta$, $y = \sec\theta$

Using $\cos 2\theta \equiv 2\cos^2\theta - 1$ gives

$$x = 2\cos^2\theta - 1 \quad \text{and} \quad y = \frac{1}{\cos\theta}$$

$$\therefore \qquad x = 2\left(\frac{1}{y}\right)^2 - 1$$

$$\Rightarrow \qquad (x + 1)y^2 = 2$$

Note that this is a Cartesian equation which has been obtained by *eliminating the parameter* θ from a *pair of parametric equations.*

3. Prove that $\sin 3A \equiv 3 \sin A - 4 \sin^3 A$

$$\sin 3A \equiv \sin (2A + A)$$

$$\equiv \sin 2A \cos A + \cos 2A \sin A$$

$$\equiv (2 \sin A \cos A)\cos A + (1 - 2 \sin^2 A)\sin A$$

$$\equiv 2 \sin A \cos^2 A + \sin A - 2 \sin^3 A$$

$$\equiv 2 \sin A(1 - \sin^2 A) + \sin A - 2 \sin^3 A$$

$$\equiv 3 \sin A - 4 \sin^3 A$$

---

4. Find the general solution of the equation $\cos 2x + 3 \sin x = 2$

When a trig equation involves different multiples of an angle, it is usually sensible to express the equation in a form where the trig ratios are all of the same angle and, when possible, only one trig ratio is included.

Using $\cos 2x \equiv 1 - 2 \sin^2 x$ gives

$$1 - 2 \sin^2 x + 3 \sin x = 2$$

$$\Rightarrow \qquad 2 \sin^2 x - 3 \sin x + 1 = 0$$

$$\Rightarrow \qquad (2 \sin x - 1)(\sin x - 1) = 0$$

$$\therefore \qquad \sin x = \tfrac{1}{2} \quad \text{or} \quad \sin x = 1$$

When $\quad \sin x = \tfrac{1}{2}$,

$$x = \begin{cases} \tfrac{1}{6}\pi + 2n\pi \\ \tfrac{5}{6}\pi + 2n\pi \end{cases}$$

When $\quad \sin x = 1$,

$$x = \tfrac{1}{2}\pi + 2n\pi$$

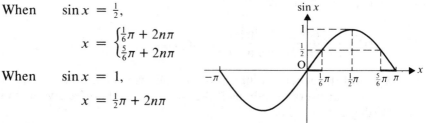

The general solution is therefore $x = \tfrac{1}{6}\pi + 2n\pi, \ \tfrac{5}{6}\pi + 2n\pi, \ \tfrac{1}{2}\pi + 2n\pi$

EXERCISE 18c

Simplify, giving an exact value where this is possible.

1. $2 \sin 15° \cos 15°$

2. $\cos^2 \frac{1}{8}\pi - \sin^2 \frac{1}{8}\pi$

3. $\sin \theta \cos \theta$

4. $1 - 2 \sin^2 4\theta$

5. $\dfrac{2 \tan 75°}{1 - \tan^2 75°}$

6. $\dfrac{2 \tan 3\theta}{1 - \tan^2 3\theta}$

7. $\sqrt{(1 + \cos 6\theta)}$

8. $2 \cos^2 \frac{3}{8}\pi - 1$

9. $\dfrac{1 + \tan x}{1 - \tan x}$ (Hint. $\tan 45° = 1$) **10.** $1 - 2 \sin^2 \frac{1}{8}\pi$

11. Find the value of $\cos 2\theta$ and $\sin 2\theta$ when θ is acute and when
(a) $\cos \theta = \frac{3}{5}$ (b) $\sin \theta = \frac{7}{25}$ (c) $\tan \theta = \frac{12}{5}$

12. If $\tan \theta = -\frac{7}{24}$ and θ is obtuse, find
(a) $\tan 2\theta$ (b) $\cos 2\theta$ (c) $\sin 2\theta$ (d) $\cos 4\theta$

13. Eliminate θ from the following pairs of equations.
(a) $x = \tan 2\theta,\ y = \tan \theta$ (b) $x = \cos 2\theta,\ y = \cos \theta$
(c) $x = \cos 2\theta,\ y = \operatorname{cosec} \theta$ (d) $x = \sin 2\theta,\ y = \sec 4\theta$

14. Prove the following identities.

(a) $\dfrac{1 - \cos 2A}{\sin 2A} \equiv \tan A$

(b) $\sec 2A + \tan 2A \equiv \dfrac{\cos A + \sin A}{\cos A - \sin A}$

(c) $\tan \theta + \cot \theta \equiv 2 \operatorname{cosec} 2\theta$

(d) $\cos 4A \equiv 8 \cos^4 A - 8 \cos^2 A + 1$

(e) $\sin 2\theta = \dfrac{2 \tan \theta}{1 + \tan^2 \theta}$

(f) $\dfrac{1 - \cos 2A + \sin 2A}{1 + \cos 2A + \sin 2A} \equiv \tan A$

15. Find the general solutions of the following equations.
Give answers in radians if they are exact: otherwise give them in degrees to 1 d.p.
(a) $\cos 2x = \sin x$ (b) $\sin 2x + \cos x = 0$
(c) $4 - 5 \cos \theta = 2 \sin^2 \theta$ (d) $\tan 2\theta \tan \theta = 2$
(e) $\sin 2\theta - 1 = \cos 2\theta$ (f) $5 \cos x \sin 2x + 4 \sin^2 x = 4$

THE HALF-ANGLE IDENTITIES

If we replace A by $\frac{1}{2}\theta$ in the double angle formula for $\tan 2A$, we get

$$\tan \theta \equiv \frac{2 \tan \frac{1}{2}\theta}{1 - \tan^2 \frac{1}{2}\theta} \qquad [1]$$

If we now make the substitution $t = \tan \frac{1}{2}\theta$, [1] becomes

$$\tan \theta \equiv \frac{2t}{1 - t^2}$$

From the diagram, and using Pythagoras' theorem,

$$r = 1 + t^2$$

Hence we can express $\sin \theta$, $\cos \theta$ and $\tan \theta$ in terms of t, i.e.

$$\sin \theta = \frac{2t}{1 + t^2}$$

$$\cos \theta = \frac{1 - t^2}{1 + t^2} \qquad \text{where} \quad t = \tan \frac{1}{2}\theta$$

$$\tan \theta = \frac{2t}{1 - t^2}$$

These identities allow all the trig ratios of any one angle to be expressed in terms of a common variable t. This group can be helpful in problems where it is not possible to apply any of the identities used previously.

There is one other group of identities that can be useful, and these are derived from the different forms of the cosine double angle formulae.

Starting with $\cos 2A \equiv 2\cos^2 A - 1$ we have

$$\cos^2 A \equiv \tfrac{1}{2}(1 + \cos 2A)$$

Similarly starting with $\cos 2A \equiv 1 - 2\sin^2 A$, we get

$$\sin^2 A \equiv \tfrac{1}{2}(1 - \cos 2A)$$

Examples 18d _____

1. Express $\sin \theta + 2 \cos \theta$ in terms of t, where $t = \tan \frac{1}{2}\theta$. Hence solve the equation $\sin \theta + 2 \cos \theta = 1$ for values of θ in the range $0 \leqslant \theta \leqslant 360°$

$$\sin \theta + 2 \cos \theta \equiv \frac{2t}{1 + t^2} + 2\left(\frac{1 - t^2}{1 + t^2}\right) \equiv \frac{2 + 2t - 2t^2}{1 + t^2}$$

Hence $\qquad \sin \theta + 2 \cos \theta = 1 \qquad \Rightarrow \qquad \dfrac{2 + 2t - 2t^2}{1 + t^2} = 1$

$$\Rightarrow \qquad 3t^2 - 2t - 1 = 0$$

$$\Rightarrow \qquad (3t + 1)(t - 1) = 0$$

$\therefore \qquad\qquad\qquad\qquad t = -\frac{1}{3} \quad \text{or} \quad t = 1$

i.e. $\tan \frac{1}{2}\theta = -\frac{1}{3}$ or 1

The general solution is $\frac{1}{2}\theta = -18.43° + 180n°$ or $\frac{1}{2}\theta = 45° + 180n°$

$$\theta = -36.9° + 360n° \quad \text{or} \quad \theta = 90° + 360n°$$

$\therefore$ in the specified range, $\theta = 90°, 323.1°$

_____

The next worked example deals with a very similar equation and it illustrates that extra care is needed when using this method to solve equations.

_____

2. Find the general solution of the equation $\sin \theta - \cos \theta = 1$

Using $t = \tan \frac{1}{2}\theta$, $\sin \theta - \cos \theta = 1$

$$\Rightarrow \qquad \frac{2t}{1 + t^2} - \frac{1 - t^2}{1 + t^2} = 1$$

$$\Rightarrow \qquad 2t - 1 + t^2 = 1 + t^2$$

It was seen on page 55 that if we can cancel the two t^2 terms, the solution $t = \infty$ is lost. In this problem we cannot ignore this solution as $t = \infty$ corresponds to a real value of θ. So we proceed as follows.

$\Rightarrow$ $\qquad\qquad\qquad t = \infty \quad$ or $\quad t = 1$

$\therefore$ $\qquad\qquad\qquad \tan\frac{1}{2}\theta = \infty \quad$ or $\quad \tan\frac{1}{2}\theta = 1$

$\Rightarrow$ $\qquad\qquad \frac{1}{2}\theta = \frac{1}{2}\pi + n\pi \quad$ or $\quad \frac{1}{2}\theta = \frac{1}{4}\pi + n\pi$

$\Rightarrow$ $\qquad\qquad \theta = \begin{cases} \frac{1}{2}\pi + 2n\pi \\ (2n+1)\pi \end{cases}$

---

3. If $\tan\theta = \frac{3}{4}$, find the possible values of

(a) $\tan\frac{1}{2}\theta$ $\qquad$ (b) $\cos 2\theta$

(a) Using $\tan\frac{1}{2}\theta = t$ gives $\qquad \dfrac{3}{4} = \dfrac{2t}{1-t^2}$

$\Rightarrow$ $\qquad\qquad 3t^2 + 8t - 3 = 0$

$\Rightarrow$ $\qquad\qquad (3t - 1)(t + 3) = 0$

$\Rightarrow$ $\qquad\qquad t = \frac{1}{3}$ or -3

i.e. $\tan\frac{1}{2}\theta = \frac{1}{3}$ or $\tan\frac{1}{2}\theta = -3$

(b) The half-angle formulae are valid for any angle where t is the tan of half the given angle. In this case the given angle is 2θ so $\quad t = \tan\theta$

Using $\qquad\qquad \cos 2\theta = \dfrac{1-t^2}{1+t^2} \qquad$ with $\quad t = \tan\theta$

$\Rightarrow$ $\qquad\qquad \cos 2\theta = \dfrac{1-(\frac{3}{4})^2}{1+(\frac{3}{4})^2} = \dfrac{7}{25}$

---

4. Express $\sqrt{\left(\dfrac{1-\sin 2\theta}{1+\sin 2\theta}\right)}$ in terms of $\tan\theta$

If we double the angle in the formula for $\sin\theta$ in terms of t, we get

$\sin 2\theta = \dfrac{2t}{1+t^2} \qquad$ where $\quad t = \tan\theta$

$\therefore$ $\qquad 1 - \sin 2\theta = 1 - \dfrac{2t}{1+t^2} = \dfrac{1+t^2-2t}{1+t^2} = \dfrac{(1-t)^2}{1+t^2}$

and $\qquad 1 + \sin 2\theta = 1 + \dfrac{2t}{1+t^2} = \dfrac{1+t^2+2t}{1+t^2} = \dfrac{(1+t)^2}{1+t^2}$

Hence $\qquad \dfrac{1 - \sin 2\theta}{1 + \sin 2\theta} = \dfrac{(1-t)^2}{1+t^2} \bigg/ \dfrac{(1+t)^2}{1+t^2} = \left(\dfrac{1-t}{1+t}\right)^2$

$\therefore \qquad \sqrt{\left(\dfrac{1 - \sin 2\theta}{1 + \sin 2\theta}\right)} = \dfrac{1-t}{1+t} = \dfrac{1 - \tan\theta}{1 + \tan\theta}$

EXERCISE 18d

1. If $\tan\theta = \frac{4}{3}$, find the possible values of
   (a) $\sin 2\theta$ (b) $\cot 2\theta$ (c) $\tan\frac{1}{2}\theta$ (d) $\cos\frac{1}{2}\theta$

Expressing the following in terms of t where $t = \tan\frac{1}{2}\theta$

2. $\dfrac{1 - \cos\theta}{1 + \cos\theta}$

3. $\dfrac{\sin\theta}{1 - \cos\theta}$

4. $\cot\theta \cot\frac{1}{2}\theta$

5. $\dfrac{\cos^2(\frac{1}{2}\theta)}{3\sin\theta + 4\cos\theta - 1}$

6. Prove that $\operatorname{cosec} A + \cot A \equiv \cot\frac{1}{2}A$

7. If $\sec\theta - \tan\theta = x$ prove that $\tan\frac{1}{2}\theta = \dfrac{1-x}{1+x}$

Using $t = \tan\frac{1}{2}\theta$, solve the following equations for values of θ in the interval $[-180°, 180°]$.

8. $3\cos\theta + 2\sin\theta = 3$ 9. $5\cos\theta - \sin\theta + 4 = 0$

10. $\cos\theta + 7\sin\theta = 5$ 11. $2\cos\theta - \sin\theta = 1$

MIXED EXERCISE 18

1. Eliminate θ from the equations $x = \sin\theta$ and $y = \cos 2\theta$

2. Prove the identity $\dfrac{\sin 2\theta}{1 + \cos 2\theta} \equiv \tan\theta$

3. Prove that $\tan(\theta + \frac{1}{4}\pi)\tan(\frac{1}{4}\pi - \theta) \equiv -1$

4. If $\cos A = \frac{4}{5}$ and $\cos B = \frac{5}{13}$ find the possible values of $\cos(A + B)$

5. Eliminate θ from the equations $x = \cos 2\theta$ and $y = \cos^2\theta$

6. Solve the equation $8 \sin \theta \cos \theta = 3$ for values of θ from $-180°$ to $180°$

7. Find the general solution of the equation $\cos^2\theta - \sin^2\theta = 1$

8. Prove the identity $\cos^4 \theta - \sin^4 \theta \equiv \cos 2\theta$

9. Simplify the expression $\dfrac{1 + \cos 2x}{1 - \cos 2x}$

10. Find the values of A between 0 and $360°$ for which $\sin(60° - A) + \sin(120° - A) = 0$

CONSOLIDATION C

SUMMARY

INEQUALITIES

If $a > b$ then $a + k > b + k$ for all values of k

$ak > bk$ for all positive values of k

$ak < bk$ for all negative values of k

FUNCTIONS

A function f is a rule that maps a number x to another single number $f(x)$. The domain of a function is the set of input numbers, i.e. the set of values of x.

The range of a function is the set of output values, i.e. the set of values of $f(x)$.

The general form of a quadratic function is $f(x) = ax^2 + bx + c$ where $a \neq 0$
If $a > 0$, $f(x)$ has a minimum value where $x = -b/2a$
If $a < 0$, $f(x)$ has a maximum value where $x = -b/2a$

The general form of a polynomial function is
$f(x) = a_n x^n + a_{n-1} x^{n-1} + \ldots + a_0$ where n is a positive integer and $a_n, a_{n-1}, \ldots$ are constants.

The general form of a rational function is $f(x)/g(x)$ where $f(x)$ and $g(x)$ are polynomials.

The function that maps the output of f to its input is called the inverse function of f, and is denoted by f^{-1}, i.e. $f^{-1} : f(x) \rightarrow x$
Note that while it is always possible to reverse a mapping, the rule that does this may not be a function, so not all functions have an inverse.

When a function f operates on a function g we have a function of a function, or a composite function, which is denoted by fg, or $f \circ g$

TRANSFORMATIONS OF CURVES

$y = f(x) + c$ is a translation of $y = f(x)$ by c units in the direction Oy

$y = f(x + c)$ is a translation of $y = f(x)$ by c units in the direction xO

308

$y = -f(x)$ is the reflection of $y = f(x)$ in the x-axis

$y = f(-x)$ is the reflection of $y = f(x)$ in the y-axis

$y = af(x)$ is a one-way stretch of $y = f(x)$ by a factor, a, parallel to Oy

$y = f(ax)$ is a one-way stretch of $y = f(x)$ by a factor, $1/a$, parallel to Ox

CURVES

A chord is a straight line joining two points on a curve.

A tangent to a curve is a line that touches the curve at one point, called the point of contact.

A normal to a curve is the line perpendicular to a tangent and through its point of contact.

The gradient of a curve at a point on the curve is the gradient of the tangent at that point.

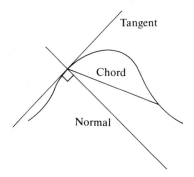

DIFFERENTIATION

Differentiation is the process of finding a general expression for the gradient of a curve at any point on the curve.
This general expression is called the gradient function, or the derived function or the derivative.

The derivative is denoted by $\dfrac{dy}{dx}$ or by $f'(x)$ where

$$\frac{dy}{dx} = \lim_{\delta x \to 0} \left[\frac{f(x + \delta x) - f(x)}{\delta x} \right]$$

When $y = x^n$, $\dfrac{dy}{dx} = nx^{n-1}$

When $y = ax^n$, $\dfrac{dy}{dx} = anx^{n-1}$

When $y = c$, $\dfrac{dy}{dx} = 0$

Stationary Values

A stationary value of $f(x)$ is its value where $f'(x) = 0$

The point on the curve $y = f(x)$ where $f(x)$ has a stationary value is called a stationary point.

At all stationary points, the tangents to the curve $y = f(x)$ are parallel to the x-axis.

Turning Points

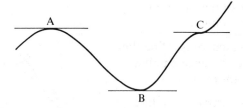

A, B and C are stationary points on the curve $y = f(x)$
The points A and B are called turning points.
The point C is called a point of inflexion.

At A, $f(x)$ has a maximum value and A is called a maximum point.
At B, $f(x)$ has a minimum value and B is called a minimum point.

There are three methods for distinguishing stationary points:

		Max	Min	Inflexion
1.	Find value of y on each side of stationary value	Both smaller	Both larger	One smaller One larger
2.	Find sign of $\dfrac{dy}{dx}$ on each side of stationary value	$+\ 0\ -$	$-\ 0\ +$	$+\ 0\ +$ or $-\ 0\ -$
	Gradient	╱⌢╲	╲⌣╱	╱─╱ or ╲─╲
3.	Find sign of $\dfrac{d^2y}{dx^2}$ at stationary value	$-$ve (or 0)	$+$ve (or 0)	

Method 3 is often the easiest to apply but it fails if $\dfrac{d^2y}{dx^2}$ is zero.
In this case use one of the other methods.

TRIGONOMETRIC FUNCTIONS

The sine function, $f(x) = \sin x$,

is defined for all values of x

is periodic with a period 2π

has a maximum value of 1 when $x = (2n + \frac{1}{2})\pi$

and a minimum value of -1 when $x = (2n + \frac{3}{2})\pi$

is zero when $x = n\pi$

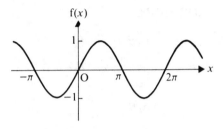

The cosine function, $f(x) = \cos x$,

is defined for all values of x

is periodic with a period 2π

has a maximum value of 1 when $x = 2n\pi$

and a minimum value of -1 when $x = (2n - 1)\pi$

is zero when $x = \frac{1}{2}(2n + 1)\pi$

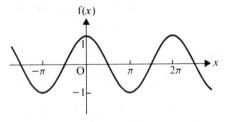

The tangent function, $y = \tan x$,

is undefined for some values of x

these values being all odd multiples of $\frac{1}{2}\pi$

is periodic with period π

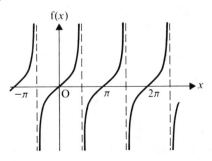

The reciprocal trig functions are

$$\sec x \left(= \frac{1}{\cos x}\right) \quad \operatorname{cosec} x \left(= \frac{1}{\sin x}\right) \quad \cot x \left(= \frac{1}{\tan x}\right)$$

TRIGONOMETRIC IDENTITIES

$$\sin \theta \equiv \cos \left(\tfrac{1}{2}\pi - \theta\right)$$

$$\cos \theta \equiv \cos \left(\tfrac{1}{2}\pi - \theta\right)$$

$$\tan \theta \equiv \frac{\sin \theta}{\cos \theta}$$

Pythagorean Identities

$$\cos^2\theta + \sin^2\theta \equiv 1$$

$$1 + \tan^2\theta \equiv \sec^2\theta$$

$$\cot^2\theta + 1 \equiv \operatorname{cosec}^2\theta$$

Compound Angle Identities

$$\sin (A \pm B) \equiv \sin A \cos B \pm \cos A \sin B$$

$$\cos (A \pm B) \equiv \cos A \cos B \mp \sin A \sin B$$

$$\tan (A \pm B) \equiv \frac{\tan A \pm \tan B}{1 \mp \tan A \tan B}$$

Double Angle Identities

$$\sin 2A \equiv 2 \sin A \cos A$$

$$\cos 2A \equiv \begin{cases} \cos^2 A - \sin^2 A \\ 2\cos^2 A - 1 \\ 1 - 2\sin^2 A \end{cases} \quad \text{and} \quad \begin{cases} \cos^2 A \equiv \tfrac{1}{2}(1 + \cos 2A) \\ \sin^2 A \equiv \tfrac{1}{2}(1 - \cos 2A) \end{cases}$$

$$\tan 2A \equiv \frac{2 \tan A}{1 - \tan^2 A}$$

'Little t' Identities

$$\left. \begin{array}{l} \tan \theta \equiv \dfrac{2t}{1 - t^2} \\[2mm] \sin \theta \equiv \dfrac{2t}{1 + t^2} \\[2mm] \cos \theta \equiv \dfrac{1 - t^2}{1 + t^2} \end{array} \right\} \quad \text{where} \ \ t = \tan \tfrac{1}{2}\theta$$

GENERAL SOLUTIONS OF TRIGONOMETRIC EQUATIONS

If $\sin \theta = c$ has solutions $\theta = \theta_1$ and $\theta = \theta_2$ in the interval $[-\pi, \pi]$

the general solution is $\theta = \begin{cases} \theta_1 + 2n\pi \\ \theta_2 + 2n\pi \end{cases}$

If $\cos \theta = c$ has a solution $\theta = \theta_1$ in the interval $[0, \pi]$
the general solution is $\theta = \pm\theta_1 + 2n\pi$

If $\tan \theta = t$ has a solution $\theta = \theta_1$ in the interval $[-\tfrac{1}{2}\pi, \tfrac{1}{2}\pi]$
the general solution is $\theta = \theta_1 + n\pi$

MULTIPLE CHOICE EXERCISE C

TYPE I

1. The minimum value of $(x - 1)(x - 3)$ is when x equals

    A 1   **B** 3   **C** 2   **D** 0   **E** −2

2. If $f(x) = 2x - 1$ then $f^{-1}(x)$ is

    A $1 - 2x$ **C** $2y - 1$ **E** $2x + 1$
    B $\tfrac{1}{2}(x + 1)$ **D** $\tfrac{1}{2}x - 1$

3. The values of x for which $(x - 1)(x - 5) < 0$ are

    A $x < 3$ **C** $x < 0$ **E** $1 \leqslant x \leqslant 5$
    B $x < 1, x > 5$ **D** $1 < x < 5$

4. The curve $y = f(x)$ is

The curve $y = f(-x)$ could be

A 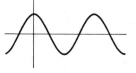   C   E

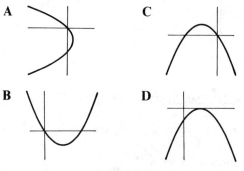

B   D

5. The curve $y = \sin(x - 30°)$ could be

A   C   E

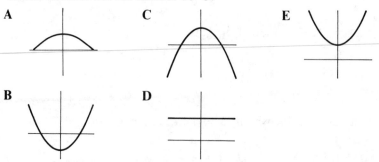

B   D

6. The equation of a curve C is $y = ax^2 + 1$, where a is a constant. Which of these curves cannot be C?

A   C   E

B   D

7. One of these is not an identity. Which one is it?

   A $\cos^2\theta = 1 - \sin^2\theta$ **D** $1 + \tan^2\theta = \sec^2\theta$

   B $\cos 2\theta = 2\cos^2\theta + 1$ **E** $\tan 2\theta = \dfrac{2\tan\theta}{1 - \tan^2\theta}$

   C $\cos^2\theta = \frac{1}{2}(\cos 2\theta + 1)$

8. The function $x^3 - 12x + 5$ has a stationary value when

   A $x = \sqrt{6}$ **C** $x = 0$ **E** $x = 1$
   B $x = -2$ **D** $x = 4$

9. When $x = 1$ the function $x^3 - 3x^2 + 7$ is

   A stationary   **C** maximum   **E** minimum
   B increasing   **D** decreasing

10. The rate of increase w.r.t. x of the function $x^2 - \dfrac{1}{x^2}$ is

   A $2x + \dfrac{2}{x^3}$ **C** $2x - \dfrac{2}{x^3}$ **E** $2x + \dfrac{1}{2x}$

   B $2x - \dfrac{2}{2x}$ **D** $2x + \dfrac{3}{x^3}$

11. The gradient function of $y = (x - 3)(x^2 + 2)$ is

   A $2x$ **C** $3x^2 - 6x + 2$ **E** $x^3 - 3x^2 + 2x - 6$
   B $2x - 3$ **D** $-3(2x + 2)$

12. If $\cos\theta = \frac{1}{2}$, the general solution is

   A $\theta = 2n\pi \pm \frac{1}{6}\pi$ **C** $\theta = 2n\pi + \frac{1}{3}\pi$ **E** $\theta = n\pi \pm \frac{1}{6}\pi$
   B $\theta = n\pi + \frac{1}{3}\pi$ **D** $\theta = 2n\pi \pm \frac{1}{3}\pi$

13. The graph of the function $f(\theta) \equiv \cos(2\theta - \frac{1}{2}\pi)$ has a period

   A 2π **C** $\frac{1}{2}\pi$ **E** none of these
   B π **D** $-\frac{1}{2}\pi$

14. Using $t \equiv \tan\frac{1}{2}\theta$ converts the equation $2\cos\theta + 3\sin\theta + 4 = 0$ into

   A $2t^2 + 3t + 6 = 0$ **D** $t^2 + 6t + 5 = 0$
   B $3 + 3t + t^2 = 0$ **E** $3t^2 + 3t + 1 = 0$
   C $6 + 6t - 2t^2 = 0$

15. One of the following expressions is not identical to any of the others. Which one is it?

A $\dfrac{2\tan\theta}{1+\tan^2\theta}$ C $1-\sin^2\theta$ E $\sin 2\theta$

B $2\cos^2\frac{1}{2}\theta$ D $\dfrac{1}{1+\tan^2\theta}$

TYPE II

16. If $\dfrac{x-2}{x-3} < 1$ then

A $x-2 < x-3$
B $(x-2)(x-3) < (x-3)^2$
C $-2 < -3$

17. If $f(x) = x^2$ then

A $f(x+a)$ has a minimum value when $x = 0$
B $f^{-1}(x) = \pm\sqrt{x}$
C $f(ax)$ goes through the origin.

18. When $\tan\theta = 1$

A $\cos\theta = \sqrt{2}$
B $\theta = \frac{1}{4}\pi + n\pi$
C θ lies in quadrants 1 and 2

19. $f(x) = x + \dfrac{1}{x}$

A $f(x)$ is stationary when $x = -1$
B $\dfrac{d}{dx}f(x) = 1 - \dfrac{1}{x^2}$
C $y = f(x)$ has no turning points.

20. $y = x^3 - 4x + 5$

A $\dfrac{d^2y}{dx^2} = 9x$
B The curve has two turning points.
C y is increasing when $x = 2$

21. $y = x^4$

   A y is decreasing when $x = 1$
   B x^4 has only one stationary value
   C $\dfrac{dy}{dx} = 4x^3$

22. An angle θ is such that $\tan\theta = 1$ and $\cos\theta$ is negative.

   A $\sin\theta$ is positive   B $\cos\theta = -\frac{1}{2}\sqrt{2}$ C $\cot\theta = -1$

23. $f(\theta) = \cos\theta$

   A   For $-\frac{1}{2}\pi < \theta < \frac{1}{2}\pi$, $f(\theta) > 0$
   B $f(\theta)$ is undefined when $\theta = (2n+1)\frac{1}{2}\pi$
   C $-1 \leqslant f(\theta) \leqslant 1$

24. The graph of $f(\theta) = \cos\theta$ compared with the graph of $f(\theta) = \sin\theta$ is

   A   inverted   B   90° to the left   C   90° to the right

25. The general solution of the equation $\cos 2\theta = \frac{1}{2}$ is the same as the solution of the equation

   A $\tan 2\theta = \sqrt{3}$ B $\cos(-2\theta) = \frac{1}{2}$ C $4\cos^2\theta = 3$

26. If $x = 1 - \tan\theta$ and $y = \sec\theta$ the Cartesian equation given by eliminating θ is

   A $x^2 - y^2 = 2x$
   B $x^2 - y^2 + 2 = 2x$
   C $(1-x)^2 = (y-1)(y+1)$

27. $\sin(\theta - \frac{1}{2}\pi)$ is identical to

   A $\cos(\theta + \frac{1}{2}\pi)$ B $\sin(\frac{1}{2}\pi - \theta)$ C $\sin(\theta + \frac{3}{2}\pi)$

TYPE III

28. The function $f(\theta) = \cos\theta$ is such that $|\theta| \leqslant 1$

29. $\sin\theta = 0$ when $\theta = n\pi$

30. The function $f(\theta) = \sec\theta$ is undefined when $\theta = \frac{1}{2}(2n+1)\pi$

31. The general solution of the equation $\cos\theta = -1$ is $\theta = (2n+1)\pi$

32. $\sin 2\theta \equiv \dfrac{2t}{1+t^2}$ where $t \equiv \tan \frac{1}{2}\theta$

33. $\cos 4\theta = \sin 3\theta \implies \cos 4\theta = \sin(3\theta - \frac{1}{2}\pi)$

34. $y = \dfrac{1}{x^2} \implies \dfrac{dy}{dx} = -\dfrac{1}{2x}$

35. If $\dfrac{1}{x} < 2$ then $\dfrac{1}{2} < x$

MISCELLANEOUS EXERCISE C

Most questions in this exercise are from the short question sections of examination papers.

1. Show that

$$\frac{\sin \theta}{\cos \theta} + \frac{\cos \theta}{\sin \theta} \equiv 2 \operatorname{cosec} 2\theta$$

for $0 < \theta < \frac{1}{2}\pi$ (U of L 88)

2. Given that $x \neq 2$, find the complete set of values of x for which

$$\frac{3x + 1}{x - 2} > 2$$ (U of L 88)

3. The function f is defined by

$$f : x \to \frac{3x + 1}{x - 2}, \quad x \in \mathbb{R}, \quad x \neq 2$$

Find, in a similar form, the functions
(a) ff   (b) f^{-1} (U of L 88)

4. Given that $f(x) = x^4$ and $g(x) = x + 2$, simplify

$$fg(x) - gf(x)$$ (JMB 87)

5. Find, in terms of π, the general solution of the equation

$$\tan^4 x - 4\tan^2 x + 3 = 0$$ (AEB 88)

6. A quadratic function f, defined by $f : x \to x^2 + bx + c$, $x \in \mathbb{R}$, has the following properties:

$$f(3) = -17$$
$$f'(3) = 0$$

Find the value of b and the value of c and state the range of f. Sketch the graph of f.

A second quadratic function g has the same rule as f and has domain all real $x \geqslant 3$. Find the inverse function g^{-1} of g in the form $g^{-1}:x \to g^{-1}(x)$, stating clearly $g^{-1}(x)$ in terms of x *and* stating the domain of this inverse function.

Sketch in the same diagram the graphs of g and g^{-1} and by observing the symmetry of your graphs, or otherwise, calculate the value of x for which

$$g(x) = g^{-1}(x) \qquad \text{(AEB 88)}$$

7. Given that $f(x) \equiv x^3 + 2x^2 - 5x - 6$, find
   (a) $f(2)$
   (b) the complete set of values of x for which $f(x) < 0$

   (U of L 89)

8. The functions f and g are defined by
$$f:x \to x - 2, \quad x > 2$$
$$g:x \to e^x, \quad x > 0$$
   Given that the function h is defined by
$$h = gf, \quad x > 2$$
   state
   (a) the range of h,
   (b) the domain and range of h^{-1}
   Sketch the curves with equations
   (c) $y = h(x)$ (d) $y = h^{-1}(x)$

   (U of L 89)

9. Sketch the curve C given by the equation
$$xy = 1$$
   A line of gradient m, where $m \neq 0$, passes through the point $A(3,0)$ and meets C at the points P and Q. Show that the x-coordinates of P and Q are the roots of the equation
$$mx^2 - 3mx - 1 = 0$$
   (a) Find the set of values of m for which this equation has real unequal roots. Find also the (non-zero) value of m for which the roots are equal, and hence, or otherwise, find the equation of the tangent to C from the point A.
   (b) Show that the mid-point M of PQ lies on the line $x = \frac{3}{2}$. Show on your diagram of C the line $x = \frac{3}{2}$ and the possible positions of M on this line. Indicate that part of the line which corresponds to positive values of m.   (JMB 88)

10. The figure shows a sketch of the part of the graph of $y = f(x)$ for $0 \leqslant x \leqslant 2a$

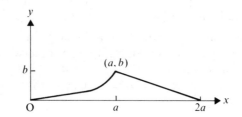

The line $x = 2a$ is a line of symmetry of the graph.

Sketch on separate axes the graphs of

(a) $y = f(x)$ for $0 \leqslant x \leqslant 4a$

(b) $y = -f(2x)$ for $0 \leqslant x \leqslant a$

(c) $y = 3f(\frac{1}{2}x)$ for $0 \leqslant x \leqslant 2a$

(d) $y = f(x - a)$ for $2a \leqslant x \leqslant 4a$ (AEB 87)

11. Prove the identity

$$\cot 2\theta + \tan \theta = \csc 2\theta$$

Hence find the values of θ, in the interval $0° < \theta < 180°$, for which

$$3(\cot 2\theta + \tan \theta)^2 = 4 \qquad \text{(AEB 87)}$$

12. Given that $f(x) = 2x^3 - 5x^2 - 4x + 3$, find the stationary values of $f(x)$. Show that $f(x) = (x + 1)(2x - 1)(x - 3)$

Hence sketch the curve with equation $y = f(x)$, marking on your sketch the coordinates of the points where the curve crosses the coordinate axes.

(a) Solve the inequalities
   (i) $2x^3 - 5x^2 - 4x + 3 > 0$
   (ii) $2e^{3x} - 5e^{2x} - 4e^x + 3 > 0$

(b) Express $\cos 2x$ and $\cos 3x$ in terms of $\cos x$ only, and hence find the general solution in radians, in terms of π, of the equation

$$1 + \cos 3x = 5(\cos 2x + \cos x) \qquad \text{(AEB 87)}$$

13. Sketch the graph of the curve with equation $y = x(1 - x)$.
Determine the greatest and least values of y when $-1 \leqslant x \leqslant 1$.
         (C 87)

14. Find all values of θ, such that $0° \leqslant \theta \leqslant 180°$, which satisfy the equation $2 \sin 2\theta = \tan \theta$ (C 87)

15. A function f is defined by

$$f:x \to 1 - \frac{1}{x}, \quad x \in \mathbb{R}, \quad x \neq 0, \quad x \neq 1$$

Find (a) ff(x)   (b) fff(x)   (c) $f^{-1}(x)$ (U of L 86)

16. Find, in radians, the general solution of the equation
$$\cos x \,(2\cos x + 1) = 1 \qquad\qquad \text{(U of L 87)}$$

17. Find, in degrees to one decimal place, the values of x for which $0 \leqslant x < 360°$ and

$$\sin x = 2\sin(60° - x) \qquad\qquad \text{(U of L 87)}$$

18. The function f is defined by
$$f:x \to 4 - x^2, \quad x \in \mathbb{R}$$

(a) State the range of f.
(b) Determine the values of x for which
$$ff(x) = 0 \qquad\qquad \text{(U of L 87)}$$

19. Find all the solutions in the interval $-\pi \leqslant \theta \leqslant \pi$ of the equation
$$2\sin^2\theta + 5\cos\theta + 1 = 0$$
giving each solution in terms of π.
State the general solution of the equation.   (JMB 85)

20. Solve the inequality

$$\frac{x+2}{x-1} < 3 \qquad\qquad \text{(JMB 84)}$$

21. Express $2x^2 - 12x + 9$ in the form
$$a[(x-r)^2 + s]$$
where a, r and s are constants.
The graph of $y = 2x^2 - 12x + 9$ may be obtained from the graph of $y = x^2$ by means of appropriate translations and scalings (stretches). Describe suitable transformations in detail and in the order in which they are to be used.
The function f is defined for the domain $x \geqslant 3$ by
$$f(x) = 2x^2 - 12x + 9$$
Sketch the graph of $y = f(x)$
State the domain and range of f^{-1} and determine $f^{-1}(x)$ (JMB 85)

22. The functions f and g are defined by

$$f: x \rightarrow x^2 - 3, \quad x \in \mathbb{R}$$
$$g: x \rightarrow 2x + 5, \quad x \in \mathbb{R}$$

Find in a similar form the composite function f ∘ g

Sketch on separate axes the graphs of f and f ∘ g

Hence, or otherwise, show that the range of f corresponding to the domain $-4 \leqslant x \leqslant 4$ is $-3 \leqslant f(x) \leqslant 13$, and find the range of f ∘ g corresponding to this domain.   (AEB 86)

23. A circular sector, of area A cm^2, has bounding radii, each of length x cm, and the angle between these radii is θ radians. Given that the perimeter of the sector is 12 cm,

(a) express θ in terms of x

(b) show that $A = 6x - x^2$

(c) find the greatest value of A as x varies.   (AEB 86)

24. Find the equation of the normal to the curve $y = -3x^3 + 5$ at the point $(-1, 8)$.   (C 86)

25. (a) Given that

$$\cos(\theta - \alpha) = 3 \cos(\theta + \alpha)$$

show that

$$\tan \theta = \tfrac{1}{2} \cot \alpha$$

Hence, or otherwise, find, correct to 0.1 of a degree, the general solution of the equation

$$\cos(\theta - 60°) = 3 \cos(\theta + 60°)$$

(b) Find, correct to 0.1 of a degree, the general solution of the equation

$$\csc x = \sqrt{3} \sec^2 x$$ (C 87)

26. Find all the values of x for which $0 \leqslant x \leqslant 2\pi$ and
$\cos 2x = 1 + \sin x$ (U of L 84)

27. Find, in radians, the general solution of the equation

$$\cos 2x - 3 \cos x + 2 = 0$$ (U of L 85)

28. Find the set of values of x for which

$$\frac{2}{x - 2} < \frac{1}{x + 1}$$ (U of L 85)

29. Given that $f(x) \equiv a - 2x - x^2$, where a is a constant, find

(a) the value of a for which the roots of the equation $f(x) = 0$ differ by 3

(b) the set of values of a for which $f(x) < 0$ for all values of x.
(U of L 85)

30.

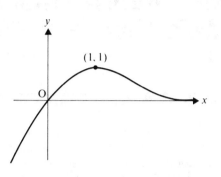

The diagram shows the graph of $y = f(x)$. The curve passes through the origin, and has a maximum point at $(1, 1)$. Sketch, on separate diagrams, the graphs of

(a) $y = f(x) + 2$ (b) $y = f(x + 2)$ (c) $y = f(2x)$

giving the coordinates of the maximum point in each case.   (C 88)

31. (a) Starting from the identity
$\cos(A + B) \equiv \cos A \cos B - \sin A \sin B$, prove the identity
$\cos 2\theta \equiv 2\cos^2\theta - 1$

(b) Find the general solution of the equation
$\sin \theta + \tan \theta \cos 2\theta = 0$, giving your answer in radians in terms of π.

(c) Prove the identity $2\cos^2\theta - 2\cos^2 2\theta \equiv \cos 2\theta - \cos 4\theta$

(d) By substituting $\theta = \pi/5$ in the identity in (c), prove that

$$\cos\left(\frac{\pi}{5}\right) - \cos\left(\frac{2\pi}{5}\right) = \frac{1}{2}$$

(e) Hence find the value of $\cos \pi/5$ in the form $a + b\sqrt{5}$, stating the values of a and b.   (AEB 87)

32. Given that

$$2\sin(\theta - 60°) = \cos(\theta + 60°)$$

show that $\tan \theta = a\sqrt{3} + b$, where a and b are integers. (JMB 86)

CHAPTER 19

DIFFERENTIATION OF COMPOUND FUNCTIONS

DIFFERENTIATING A FUNCTION OF A FUNCTION

Suppose that we want to differentiate $(2x - 1)^3$. We could expand the bracket and differentiate term by term, but this is tedious and, for powers higher than three, very long and not easy. We obviously need a more direct method for differentiating an expression of this kind.

Now $(2x - 1)^3$ is a cubic function of the linear function $(2x - 1)$, i.e. it is a *function of a function*.

A function of this type is of the form $gf(x)$, i.e. $g\{f(x)\}$

For example

$(x^2 - 3)^3$ is a cubic function, g, of a quadratic function, f
$\sqrt{(1 + x^4)}$ is a square root function, g, of a quartic function, f

Consider any equation of the form $y = gf(x)$
If we make the substitution $u = f(x)$ then $y = gf(x)$ can be expressed in two simple parts, i.e.

$$u = f(x) \quad \text{and} \quad y = g(u)$$

A small increase of δx in the value of x causes a corresponding small increase of δu in the value of u.
Then if $\delta x \to 0$, it follows that $\delta u \to 0$

Hence $$\frac{dy}{dx} = \lim_{\delta x \to 0}\left(\frac{\delta y}{\delta x}\right) = \lim_{\delta x \to 0}\left(\frac{\delta y}{\delta u}\right)\left(\frac{\delta u}{\delta x}\right)$$

$\Rightarrow$ $$\frac{dy}{dx} = \left(\lim_{\delta u \to 0}\frac{\delta y}{\delta u}\right) \times \left(\lim_{\delta x \to 0}\frac{\delta u}{\delta x}\right)$$

i.e. $$\frac{dy}{dx} = \frac{dy}{du} \times \frac{du}{dx}$$

This is known as *the chain rule*.

Examples 19a _____

1. Find $\dfrac{dy}{dx}$ if $y = (2x - 4)^4$

If $u = 2x - 4$ then $y = u^4$

Then $\dfrac{dy}{dx} = \dfrac{dy}{du} \times \dfrac{du}{dx}$ gives

$$\dfrac{dy}{dx} = (4u^3)(2) = 8u^3$$

But $u = 2x - 4$

$\therefore$ $$\dfrac{dy}{dx} = 8(2x - 4)^3$$

_____

Example 1 is a particular case of the equation $y = (ax + b)^n$. Similar working shows that, in general,

if $y = (ax + b)^n$ then $\dfrac{dy}{dx} = an(ax + b)^{n-1}$

This fact is needed very often and is quotable.

_____

2. Given $y = (x^3 + 1)^4$ find $\dfrac{dy}{dx}$

If $u = x^3 + 1$ then $y = u^4$

Using $\dfrac{dy}{dx} = \dfrac{dy}{du} \times \dfrac{du}{dx}$ gives

$$\dfrac{dy}{dx} = (4u^3)(3x^2) = 12x^2u^3$$

Replacing u by $x^3 + 1$ we have

$$\dfrac{dy}{dx} = 12x^2(x^3 + 1)^3$$

_____

3. Differentiate w.r.t. x the function $\dfrac{1}{(1-x^2)^5}$

$$y = (1-x^2)^{-5} \quad \Rightarrow \quad y = u^{-5} \text{ where } u = 1-x^2$$

Now
$$\frac{dy}{dx} = \frac{dy}{du} \times \frac{du}{dx}$$

$\therefore \qquad \dfrac{d}{dx}\left[\dfrac{1}{(1-x^2)^5}\right] = (-5u^{-6})(-2x) = 10x(u^{-6})$

$$= \frac{10x}{(1-x^2)^6}$$

After some time the reader will find that in most cases the necessary substitution can be done mentally and the answer written down directly, e.g. to differentiate $(x^3 - x)^{3/2}$ we mentally use the substitutions $u = x^3 - x$ and $y = u^{3/2}$ giving

$$\frac{d}{dx}(x^3 - x)^{3/2} = [\tfrac{3}{2}(x^3 - x)^{1/2}](3x^2 - 1)$$

This skill is important and well worth the practice required for its achievement.

EXERCISE 19a

Use a substitute to differentiate each function with respect to x

1. $(3x + 1)^2$ **2.** $(3 - x)^4$ **3.** $(4x - 5)^5$

4. $(x^2 + 1)^3$ **5.** $(2 + 3x)^7$ **6.** $(2 - 6x)^3$

7. $(2x^4 - 5)^{1/2}$ **8.** $(x^2 + 3)^{-1}$ **9.** $\sqrt{(3x^3 - 4)}$

10. $\dfrac{1}{(\sqrt{x} + 3x)}$ **11.** $\dfrac{3}{\sqrt{(4 - x^2)}}$ **12.** $\dfrac{7}{(x^3 + 3x)^{1/3}}$

Differentiate each function directly.

13. $(4 - 2x)^5$ **14.** $(x^2 + 3)^2$ **15.** $(3x - 4)^7$

16. $(x^2 + 4)^2$ **17.** $(1 - 2x^2)$ **18.** $(2 - x^3)^4$

19. $(2 + x^2)^{3/4}$ **20.** $\sqrt[3]{(x^2 - x)}$ **21.** $(2 - 3x^2)^{-1}$

22. $(4 - x^2)^{-2}$ **23.** $(x^5 - 3)^{-1/2}$ **24.** $\sqrt[4]{(6 - \sqrt{x})}$

DIFFERENTIATING A PRODUCT

Suppose that $y = uv$ where u and v are both functions of x, e.g. $y = x^2(x^4 - 1)$

It is dangerously tempting to think that $\dfrac{dy}{dx}$ is given by $\left(\dfrac{du}{dx}\right)\left(\dfrac{dv}{dx}\right)$

But this is *not so* as is clearly shown by a simple example such as $y = (x^2)(x^3)$ where, because $y = x^5$, we know that $\dfrac{dy}{dx} = 5x^4$ which is *not* equal to $(2x)(3x^2)$.

i.e.   differentiation is *not* distributive across a product.

Returning to $y = uv$ where $u = f(x)$ and $v = g(x)$, we see that if x increases by a small amount δx then there are corresponding small increases of δu, δv and δy in the values of u, v and y

$\therefore$ $\qquad\qquad y + \delta y = (u + \delta u)(v + \delta v)$

$\qquad\qquad\qquad\quad = uv + u\delta v + v\delta u + \delta u\delta v$

But $y = uv$

$\therefore$ $\qquad\qquad \delta y = u\delta v + v\delta u + \delta u\delta v$

$\Rightarrow$ $\qquad\qquad \dfrac{\delta y}{\delta x} = u\dfrac{\delta v}{\delta x} + v\dfrac{\delta u}{\delta x} + \delta u\dfrac{\delta v}{\delta x}$

Now as $\delta x \to 0$, $\dfrac{\delta v}{\delta x} \to \dfrac{dv}{dx}$, $\dfrac{\delta u}{\delta x} \to \dfrac{du}{dx}$ and $\delta u \to 0$

Therefore $\qquad \dfrac{dy}{dx} = \lim_{\delta x \to 0}\dfrac{\delta y}{\delta x} = u\dfrac{dv}{dx} + v\dfrac{du}{dx} + 0$

i.e. $\qquad\qquad\qquad \dfrac{d}{dx}(uv) = v\dfrac{du}{dx} + u\dfrac{dv}{dx}$

This formula is verified by the simple example we considered above, i.e. $y = (x^2)(x^3)$.

Using $u = x^2$ and $v = x^3$ gives $\dfrac{dy}{dx} = (x^3)(2x) + (x^2)(3x^2) = 5x^4$ which is correct.

Example 19b _____

Differentiate with respect to x

(a) $(x + 1)^3(2x - 5)^2$ (b) $\dfrac{(x - 1)^2}{(x + 2)}$

(a) If $\qquad\qquad u = (x + 1)^3, \quad \dfrac{du}{dx} = 3(x + 1)^2$

and if $\qquad\qquad v = (2x - 5)^2, \quad \dfrac{dv}{dx} = 2(2x - 5)$

$\dfrac{d}{dx}(uv) = v\dfrac{du}{dx} + u\dfrac{dv}{dx}$ gives

$\dfrac{d}{dx}(x + 1)^3(2x - 5)^2 = \{(2x - 5)^2\}\{3(x + 1)^2\} + \{(x + 1)^3\}\{2(2)(2x - 5)\}$

$\qquad\qquad\qquad = (2x - 5)(x + 1)^2\{3(2x - 5) + 4(x + 1)\}$

$\qquad\qquad\qquad = (2x - 5)(x + 1)^2(10x - 11)$

(b) If we write $\dfrac{(x - 1)^2}{(x + 2)}$ as $(x - 1)^2(x + 2)^{-1}$

then $\qquad\qquad u = (x - 1)^2$ gives $\dfrac{du}{dx} = 2(x - 1)$

and $\qquad\qquad v = (x + 2)^{-1}$ gives $\dfrac{dv}{dx} = -(x + 2)^{-2}$

Using $\dfrac{d}{dx}(uv) = v\dfrac{du}{dx} + u\dfrac{dv}{dx}$ we have

$\dfrac{d}{dx}\left[\dfrac{(x - 1)^2}{(x + 2)}\right] = (x + 2)^{-1}\{2(x - 1)\} + (x - 1)^2\{-(x + 2)^{-2}\}$

$\qquad\qquad = \dfrac{(x - 1)}{(x + 2)^2}\{2(x + 2) - (x - 1)\}$

$\qquad\qquad = \dfrac{(x - 1)(x + 5)}{(x + 2)^2}$

EXERCISE 19b

Differentiate each function with respect to x

1. $x^2(x - 3)^2$ 2. $x\sqrt{(x - 6)}$ 3. $(x + 2)(x - 2)^5$

4. $x(2x + 3)^3$ 5. $(x + 1)^2(x - 1)^4$ 6. $\sqrt{x}(x - 3)^3$

7. $\dfrac{(x + 5)^4}{(x - 3)}$ 8. $\dfrac{x}{(3x + 2)^2}$ 9. $\dfrac{(2x - 7)^2}{\sqrt{x}}$

10. $x^3\sqrt{(x - 1)}$ 11. $x(x + 3)^{-1}$ 12. $x^2(2x - 3)^2$

DIFFERENTIATING A QUOTIENT

To differentiate a function of the form u/v, where u and v are both functions of x, it is sometimes convenient to rewrite the function as uv^{-1} and differentiate it as a product. This method was used in part (b) of the previous worked example but it is not always the neatest way to differentiate a quotient. The alternative is to apply the formula derived below.

When a function is of the form u/v, where u and v are both functions of x, a small increase of δx in the value of x causes corresponding small increases of δu and δv in the values of u and v. Then, as $\delta x \to 0$, δu and δv also tend to zero.

If $y = \dfrac{u}{v}$ then $y + \delta y = \dfrac{(u + \delta u)}{(v + \delta v)}$

$\therefore$ $\qquad \delta y = \dfrac{u + \delta u}{v + \delta v} - \dfrac{u}{v} = \dfrac{v\delta u - u\delta v}{v(v + \delta v)}$

$\therefore$ $\qquad \dfrac{\delta y}{\delta x} = \left(v\dfrac{\delta u}{\delta x} - u\dfrac{\delta v}{\delta x}\right)\Big/v(v + \delta v)$

$\Rightarrow$ $\qquad \dfrac{dy}{dx} = \lim_{\delta x \to 0}\dfrac{\delta y}{\delta x} = \left(v\dfrac{du}{dx} - u\dfrac{dv}{dx}\right)\Big/v^2$

i.e. $\qquad \dfrac{dy}{dx} = \dfrac{v\dfrac{du}{dx} - u\dfrac{dv}{dx}}{v^2}$

Example 19c

If $y = \dfrac{(4x - 3)^6}{(x + 2)}$ find $\dfrac{dy}{dx}$

Using $\qquad u = (4x - 3)^6$ gives $\dfrac{du}{dx} = 24(4x - 3)^5$

and $\qquad v = x + 2$ gives $\dfrac{dv}{dx} = 1$

Then $\qquad \dfrac{dy}{dx} = \left(v\dfrac{du}{dx} - u\dfrac{dv}{dx}\right)\Big/v^2$

$$= \dfrac{(x + 2)\{24(4x - 3)^5\} - (4x - 3)^6}{(x + 2)^2}$$

$$= \dfrac{(4x - 3)^5(20x + 51)}{(x + 2)^2}$$

EXERCISE 19c

Use the quotient formula to differentiate each of the following functions with respect to x

1. $\dfrac{(x - 3)^2}{x}$

2. $\dfrac{x^2}{(x + 3)}$

3. $\dfrac{(4 - x)}{x^2}$

4. $\dfrac{(x + 1)^2}{x^3}$

5. $\dfrac{4x}{(1 - x)^3}$

6. $\dfrac{2x^2}{(x - 2)}$

7. $\dfrac{x^{5/3}}{(3x - 2)}$

8. $\dfrac{(1 - 2x)^3}{x^3}$

9. $\dfrac{\sqrt{(x + 1)^5}}{x}$

IDENTIFYING THE CATEGORY OF A FUNCTION

Before any of the techniques explained earlier can be used to differentiate a given function, it is important to recognise the category to which the function belongs, i.e. is it a product or a function of a function or, if it is a fraction, is it one which would better be expressed as a product.

A product comprises two parts, each of which is an *independent* function of x, whereas *if one operation is carried out on another function of x* we have a function of a function.

MIXED EXERCISE 19

This exercise contains a mixture of compound functions. In each case first identify the type of function and then use the appropriate method to find its derivative.

1. $x\sqrt{(x + 1)}$

2. $(x^2 - 8)^3$

3. $x/(x^2 + 1)$

4. $\sqrt[3]{(2 - x^4)}$

5. $(x^2 + 1)/(x^2 + 2)$

6. $x^2(\sqrt{x} - 2)$

7. $(x^2 - 2)^3$

8. $\sqrt{(x - x^2)}$

9. $x/(\sqrt{x} + 1)$

10. $x^2\sqrt{(x - 2)}$

11. $\sqrt{(x + 1)}/x^2$

12. $(x^4 + x^2)^3$

13. $\sqrt{(x^2 - 8)}$

14. $x^3(x^2 - 6)$

15. $(x^2 - 6)^3$

16. $x/(x^2 - 6)$

17. $(x^4 + 3)^{-2}$

18. $\sqrt{x}(2 - x)^3$

19. $\sqrt{x}/(2 - x)^3$

20. $(x - 1)(x - 2)^2$

21. $(2x^3 + 4)^5$

CHAPTER 20

THE EXPONENTIAL AND LOGARITHMIC FUNCTIONS

THE EXPONENTIAL FUNCTION

SG

The general shape of an exponential curve was seen in Chapter 12. The next diagram shows a few more members of the exponential family.

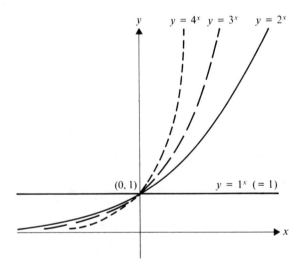

Note that these curves and, in fact, *all* exponential curves, pass through the point (0, 1).

This is because, for any positive base a,

$$\text{when } x \text{ is } 0, \quad y = a^x = a^0 = 1$$

Each exponential curve has a unique property which the reader can discover experimentally by using an accurate plot of the curve $y = 2^x$. Choose three or four points on the curve and, at each one, draw the tangent as accurately as possible and determine its gradient. Then complete the following table.

Point	Gradient of tangent, i.e. $\dfrac{dy}{dx}$	y-coordinate	$\dfrac{dy}{dx} \div y$
1			
2			
3			
4			

An accurate drawing should result in numbers in the last column that are all reasonably close to 0.7

When this experiment is carried out for 3^x and 4^x we find again that $\dfrac{dy}{dx} \div y$ has a constant value; for 3^x the constant is about 1.1 and for 4^x it is about 1.4 So we have

Base	2	3	4
$\dfrac{dy}{dx} \div y$	0.7	1.1	1.4

⇒

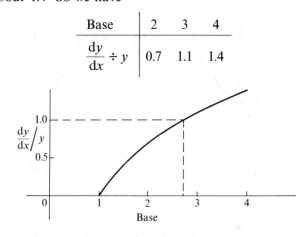

From this graph it can be seen that there is a base, somewhere between 2 and 3, for which $\dfrac{dy}{dx} \div y = 1$, i.e. $\dfrac{dy}{dx} = y$

Calling this base e we have

$$\text{if } y = e^x \text{ then } \frac{dy}{dx} = e^x$$

The function e^x is the only function which is unchanged when differentiated.

In the early eighteenth century, a number of mathematicians, working along different lines of investigation, all discovered the number e at about the same time.

The number e is irrational, i.e. like π, $\sqrt{2}$, etc., it cannot be given an exact decimal value but, to 4 significant figures, e = 2.718 The value of various powers of e, such as e^2, e^3, e^4, can be obtained from a calculator.

Summing up:

> for any value of a $(a > 0)$, a^x is *an* exponential function
>
> for the base e (e $\approx$ 2.718), e^x is *the* exponential function
>
> $$\frac{d}{dx}(e^x) = e^x$$

The following diagrams show sketches of $y = e^x$ and of some simple variations.

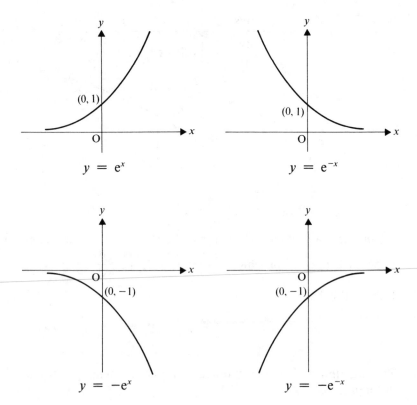

$y = e^x$

$y = e^{-x}$

$y = -e^x$

$y = -e^{-x}$

Example 20a

Find the coordinates of the stationary point on the curve $y = e^x - x$, and determine its type. Sketch the curve showing the stationary point clearly.

$$y = e^x - x \qquad \Rightarrow \qquad \frac{dy}{dx} = e^x - 1$$

At a stationary point, $\dfrac{dy}{dx} = 0$ therefore $e^x - 1 = 0$

i.e. $\qquad\qquad\qquad e^x = 1 \qquad \Rightarrow \qquad x = 0$

When $x = 0$, $y = e^0 - 0 = 1$

Therefore $(0, 1)$ is a stationary point.

$$\frac{d^2y}{dx^2} = e^x \quad \text{and this is positive when } x = 0$$

Therefore $(0, 1)$ is a minimum point.

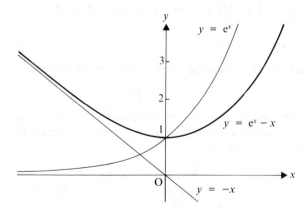

This curve is made up from separate sketches of $y = e^x$ and $y = -x$ by adding their ordinates.

EXERCISE 20a

1. Evaluate, correct to 3 s.f.
   (a) e^2 (b) e^{-1} (c) $e^{1.5}$ (d) $e^{-0.3}$

2. Write down the derivative of
   (a) $2e^x \cdot$ (b) $x^2 - e^x$ (c) e^x

In questions 3 to 5 find the gradient of each curve at the specified value of x

3. $y = e^x - 2x$ where $x = 2$
4. $y = x^2 + 2e^x$ where $x = 1$
5. $y = e^x - 3x^3$ where $x = 0$

6. Find the value of x at which the function $e^x - x$ has a stationary value.

7. Sketch each given curve.
   (a) $y = 1 - e^x$ (b) $y = e^x + 1$ (c) $y = x - e^x$
   (d) $y = 1 - e^{-x}$ (e) $y = 1 + e^{-x}$ (f) $y = x^2 + e^x$

NATURAL (NAPERIAN) LOGARITHMS

Suppose that the equation $e^x = 0.59$ has to be solved.

We know that this equation can be written in logarithmic form

i.e. $$x = \log_e 0.59$$

Logarithms to the base e are called *natural* or *Naperian* logarithms. To avoid having to insert the base e in every natural logarithm, the notation ln is used, i.e.

$$\log_e a \quad \text{is written} \quad \ln a$$

i.e. $$\ln a = b \quad \Longleftrightarrow \quad a = e^b$$

Values of natural logs can be found by using a scientific calculator.

Returning to the equation $e^x = 0.59$ we now have

$$e^x = 0.59 \quad \Rightarrow \quad x = \ln 0.59 = -0.528 \quad \text{to 3 s.f.}$$

Logarithms to the base 10 are called *common logarithms* and are denoted by log or lg. They used to be an important tool for calculations but calculators have eliminated their usefulness in that respect.

The laws used for working with logarithms to a general base, given in Chapter 3, apply equally well to natural logarithms, i.e.

$$\ln a + \ln b = \ln ab$$
$$\ln a - \ln b = \ln a/b$$
$$\ln a^n = n \ln a$$

One further rule can be added to this list. It is needed when we want to change the base of a logarithm.

Changing the Base of a Logarithm

Suppose that $x = \log_a c$ and that we wish to express x as a logarithm to the base b

$$\log_a c = x \quad \Rightarrow \quad c = a^x$$

Now taking logs to the base b gives

$$\log_b c = x \log_b a \quad \Rightarrow \quad x = \frac{\log_b c}{\log_b a}$$

i.e.
$$\log_a c = \frac{\log_b c}{\log_b a}$$

In the special case when $c = b$, i.e. when $\log_b c = 1$, this relationship becomes

$$\log_a b = \frac{1}{\log_b a}$$

When the change of base rule is used to convert a logarithm into a natural logarithm, i.e. to change the base of a log to e, we have

$$\log_a c = \frac{\ln c}{\ln a}$$

The base of an exponential function can be changed in a similar way. Suppose that we wish to express 3^x as a power of e.

Using $\qquad\qquad 3^x = e^p \quad$ gives $\quad x \ln 3 = p$

$\therefore \qquad\qquad\qquad\qquad 3^x = e^{x \ln 3}$

In general $\qquad\qquad\quad a^x = e^{x \ln a}$

Examples 20b

1. Separate $\ln(\tan x)$ into two terms.

$$\ln(\tan x) = \ln\left(\frac{\sin x}{\cos x}\right)$$

$$= \ln \sin x - \ln \cos x$$

2. Express $4 \ln(x + 1) - \frac{1}{2} \ln x$ as a single logarithm.

$$4 \ln(x + 1) - \frac{1}{2} \ln x = \ln(x + 1)^4 - \ln \sqrt{x}$$

$$= \ln\left(\frac{(x + 1)^4}{\sqrt{x}}\right)$$

EXERCISE 20b

1. Evaluate
   (a) $\ln 3.451$ (b) $\ln 1.201$ (c) $\ln 17.3$

2. Express as a sum or difference of logarithms or as a product
   (a) $\ln \dfrac{x}{x - 1}$ (b) $\ln(5x^2)$ (c) $\ln(x^2 - 4)$
   (d) $\ln \tan x$ (e) $\ln(\sin^2 x)$ (f) $\ln \sqrt{\left(\dfrac{x + 1}{x - 1}\right)}$

3. Express as a single logarithm
   (a) $\ln x - 2 \ln(1 - x)$ (b) $1 - \ln x$
   (c) $\ln \sin x + \ln \cos x$ (d) $2 \ln x + \frac{1}{2} \ln(x - 1)$

4. Given that $\ln a = 3$
   (a) express $\log_a x^2$ as a simple natural logarithm
   (b) express as a single logarithm $\ln x^3 + 6 \log_a x$

5. Solve the following equations for x
   (a) $e^x = 8.2$ (b) $e^{2x} + e^x - 2 = 0$ (Hint. Use $e^{2x} = (e^x)^2$)
   (c) $e^{2x-1} = 3$ (d) $e^{4x} - e^x = 0$

6. Given that $\ln a = 2$ solve the following equations for x
   (a) $a^x = e^2$ (b) $a^x = e^6$ (c) $a^x = 1$

THE LOGARITHMIC FUNCTION

Consider the curve with equation $y = f(x)$ where $f(x) = \ln x$

If $y = \ln x$ then $x = e^y$,

i.e. the logarithmic function is the inverse of the exponential function.

It follows that the curve $y = \ln x$ is the reflection of the curve
$y = e^x$ in the line $y = x$

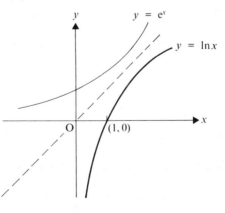

There is no part of the curve $y = \ln x$ in the second and third
quadrants. This is because, if $x = e^y$ (i.e. if $y = \ln x$), x is positive
for all real values of y. Therefore

$\ln x$ does not exist for negative values of x

THE DERIVATIVE OF ln x

We know that $y = \ln x \iff x = e^y$ and we also know how to differentiate the exponential function. So a relationship between $\dfrac{d}{dx}(y)$ and $\dfrac{d}{dy}(x)$ would help in finding the derivative of $\ln x$

Consider the equation $y = f(x)$ where $f(x)$ is any function of x

$$\frac{dy}{dx} = \lim_{\delta x \to 0} \frac{\delta y}{\delta x} = \lim_{\delta x \to 0} \left(1 \bigg/ \frac{\delta x}{\delta y} \right)$$

Now $\delta y \to 0$ as $\delta x \to 0$

$\therefore$
$$\frac{dy}{dx} = \lim_{\delta y \to 0} \left(1 \bigg/ \frac{\delta x}{\delta y} \right)$$

i.e.
$$\frac{dy}{dx} = 1 \bigg/ \frac{dx}{dy}$$

This relationship can be used to find the derivative of *any* function if the derivative of its inverse is known. We will now apply it to differentiate $\ln x$.

$$y = \ln x \iff x = e^y$$

Differentiating e^y w.r.t. y gives

$$\frac{dx}{dy} = e^y = x$$

Therefore $\dfrac{dy}{dx} = 1 \bigg/ \dfrac{dx}{dy} = \dfrac{1}{x}$

i.e.
$$\frac{d}{dx} \ln x = \frac{1}{x}$$

This result can be used to differentiate many log functions if they are first simplified by applying the laws given on page 337.

Examples 20c _____

1. Find the derivative of (a) $\ln(1/x^3)$ (b) $\ln(4\sqrt{x})$

(a) $f(x) = \ln(1/x^3) = \ln(x^{-3}) = -3\ln x$

$$\frac{d}{dx}\{f(x)\} = \frac{d}{dx}\{-3\ln x\} = \frac{-3}{x}$$

(b) $f(x) = \ln(4\sqrt{x}) = \ln 4 + \ln(\sqrt{x}) = \ln 4 + \frac{1}{2}\ln x$

$$\frac{d}{dx}\{f(x)\} = \frac{d}{dx}(\ln 4) + \frac{d}{dx}(\tfrac{1}{2}\ln x)$$

$$= 0 + \frac{\frac{1}{2}}{x} = \frac{1}{2x}$$

_____

2. Find $\dfrac{dy}{dx}$ if $y = \log_a x^2$

We only know how to differentiate natural logs, so first we must change the base from a to e.

$$y = \log_a x^2 = \frac{\ln x^2}{\ln a} = \frac{2\ln x}{\ln a}$$

$$\therefore \qquad \frac{dy}{dx} = \frac{2}{x\ln a}$$

_____

EXERCISE 20c

1. Write down the derivative of each of the following functions.
   (a) $\ln x^3$ (b) $\ln(3x)$ (c) $\ln(x^{-2})$ (d) $\ln(3/\sqrt{x})$
   (e) $\ln(1/x^5)$ (f) $\ln(2x^{1/2})$ (g) $\ln(x^{-3/2})$ (h) $\ln(x^3/\sqrt{x})$

2. Locate the stationary points on each curve.
   (a) $y = \ln x - x$ (b) $y = x^3 - 2\ln x^3$ (c) $y = \ln x - \sqrt{x}$

3. Sketch each of the following curves.
   (a) $y = -\ln x$ (b) $y = \ln(-x)$ (c) $y = 2 + \ln x$
   (d) $y = \ln x^2$

FURTHER DIFFERENTIATION OF EXPONENTIAL AND LOG FUNCTIONS

Methods were introduced in Chapter 19 for differentiating a product, a quotient and a function of a function, i.e.

if $\qquad y = uv$ then $\quad \dfrac{dy}{dx} = v\dfrac{du}{dx} + u\dfrac{dv}{dx}$

if $\qquad y = \dfrac{u}{v}$ then $\quad \dfrac{dy}{dx} = \left(v\dfrac{du}{dx} - u\dfrac{dv}{dx}\right)\bigg/v^2$

if $\quad y = g(u)$ and $u = f(x)$ then $\quad \dfrac{dy}{dx} = \dfrac{dy}{du} \times \dfrac{du}{dx}$

(Remember that the substitution can often be done mentally.)

These techniques can now be applied when exponential and log functions are involved.

The function of a function result is particularly useful as many derivatives of this type can be written down directly and easily.

To Differentiate e^u where $u = f(x)$

If $y = e^u$ then $\quad \dfrac{dy}{dx} = \dfrac{dy}{du} \times \dfrac{du}{dx}$ gives

$$\dfrac{dy}{dx} = e^u \times \dfrac{du}{dx}$$

This can also be expressed in the form

$$\dfrac{d}{dx}e^{f(x)} = e^{f(x)}f'(x)$$

i.e. $$\dfrac{d}{dx}e^{f(x)} = f'(x)e^{f(x)}$$

e.g. $\qquad$ if $y = e^{(x^2 + 1)}$ then $\quad \dfrac{dy}{dx} = 2xe^{(x^2 + 1)}$

The case when u is a linear function of x is particularly useful,

i.e. $\qquad\qquad y = e^{(ax + b)} \quad \Rightarrow \quad \dfrac{dy}{dx} = ae^{(ax + b)}$

To Differentiate ln u where $u = f(x)$

If $y = \ln u$ then $\dfrac{dy}{dx} = \dfrac{dy}{du} \times \dfrac{du}{dx}$ gives

$$\dfrac{dy}{dx} = \dfrac{1}{u} \times \dfrac{du}{dx}$$

This can also be expressed in the form

$$\dfrac{d}{dx}\{\ln f(x)\} = \dfrac{1}{f(x)} \times f'(x) = \dfrac{f'(x)}{f(x)}$$

e.g.   if $y = \ln(2 + x^3)$ then $\dfrac{dy}{dx} = \dfrac{3x^2}{2 + x^3}$

Again the case when u is $ax + b$ occurs frequently and is worth noting,

i.e. $y = \ln(ax + b) \quad \Rightarrow \quad \dfrac{dy}{dx} = \dfrac{a}{ax + b}$

Compound Exponential and Logarithmic Functions

For any given function the first step is to identify its category, e.g. $x^2 e^x$ and $(1 + x)\ln x$ are both products. Whereas e^{x^2} and $\ln(1 - x^2)$ are both functions of a function.

EXERCISE 20d

In Questions 1 to 9

(a) identify the type of function

(b) express the function in terms of u and/or v, stating clearly the substitutions that have been made.

1. $e^x(x^2 + 1)$ 2. $e^{(x^2 + 1)}$ 3. $x \ln x$

4. $\sqrt{\{e^{(x + 1)}\}}$ 5. $e^x \ln x$ 6. $\ln(3 - x^2)$

7. $(\ln x)^2$ 8. e^{-2x} 9. $1/\ln x$

10. If f and g are the functions defined by $f : x \rightarrow x^2$ and $g : x \rightarrow e^x$ write down the functions fg(x) and gf(x)

11. The functions f, g and h are defined as follows

$$f:x \to x^2 \qquad g:x \to 1/x \qquad h:x \to \ln x$$

Write down the functions

(a) fg(x)   (b) hf(x)   (c) hg(x)

(d) fh(x)   (e) hfg(x)   (f) fg⁻¹(x)

Examples 20e

1. Find the derivative of $x^3 e^x$

$y = x^3 e^x$ becomes $y = uv$ if $u = x^3$ and $v = e^x$

$\Rightarrow$
$$\frac{du}{dx} = 3x^2 \quad \text{and} \quad \frac{dv}{dx} = e^x$$

$\therefore$
$$\frac{dy}{dx} = v\frac{du}{dx} + u\frac{dv}{dx} = e^x(3x^2) + x^3(e^x)$$

i.e.
$$\frac{dy}{dx} = x^2(3+x)e^x$$

2. Differentiate $\ln(x\sqrt{\{x^2-4\}})$, w.r.t. x

First we simplify the log expression by changing it into a sum.

$$\ln(x\sqrt{\{x^2-4\}}) = \ln x + \ln\sqrt{(x^2-4)} = \ln x + \tfrac{1}{2}\ln(x^2-4)$$

$\therefore$
$$\frac{d}{dx}\ln\{x\sqrt{(x^2-4)}\} = \frac{d}{dx}\ln x + \frac{d}{dx}\{\tfrac{1}{2}\ln(x^2-4)\}$$

$$= \frac{1}{x} + \frac{1}{2}\left(\frac{2x}{x^2-4}\right)$$

$$= \frac{1}{x} + \frac{x}{x^2-4}$$

Simplifying the given function at the start, made the differentiation in this problem much easier. *Before differentiating any function, all possible simplification should be done*, particularly when complicated log expressions are involved.

EXERCISE 20e

Differentiate the following functions with respect to x

1. xe^x

2. $x^2 \ln x$

3. $e^x(x^3 - 2)$

4. $x^2 \ln (x - 2)^6$

5. $(x - 1)e^x$

6. $(x^2 + 4) \ln \sqrt{x}$

7. $x\sqrt{(2 + x)}$

8. $x \ln \sqrt{(x - 5)}$

9. $(x^2 - 2)e^x$

10. $\dfrac{x}{e^x}$

11. $\dfrac{e^x}{x^2}$

12. $\dfrac{(\ln x)}{x^3}$

13. $\dfrac{\sqrt{(x + 1)}}{\ln x}$

14. $\dfrac{e^x}{x^2 - 1}$

15. $\dfrac{e^x}{e^x - e^{-x}}$

16. e^{4x}

17. $\ln (x^2 - 1)$

18. e^{x^2}

19. $6e^{(1 - x)}$

20. $e^{(x^2 + 1)}$

21. $\ln \sqrt{(x + 2)}$

22. $(\ln x)^2$

23. $1/(\ln x)$

24. $\sqrt{(e^x)}$

MIXED EXERCISE 20

In this exercise a variety of functions are to be differentiated. In each case identify the type of function and then use the appropriate method to find the derivative. Some of the given functions can be differentiated by using one of the basic rules so do not assume that special techniques are always needed.

In Questions 1 to 18 differentiate the given function with respect to x

1. $x \ln x$

2. $(4x - 1)^{2/3}$

3. $\dfrac{e^x}{x - 1}$

4. $\dfrac{\sqrt{(1 + x^3)}}{x^2}$

5. $\dfrac{\ln x}{\ln (x - 1)}$

6. 10^{3x}

7. $\dfrac{(1 + 2x^2)}{1 + x^2}$

8. $e^{-2/x}$

9. $\ln (1 - e^x)$

10. $e^{3x}x^3$

11. $\dfrac{2x}{(2x - 1)(x - 3)}$

12. $\dfrac{e^{x/2}}{x^5}$

13. $\ln\left[\dfrac{x^2}{(x+3)(x^2-1)}\right]$ **14.** $\ln 4x^3(x+3)^2$ **15.** $(\ln x)^4$

16. $\dfrac{(x+3)^3}{x^2+2}$ **17.** $\sqrt{(e^x-x)}$ **18.** $4\ln(x^2+1)$

Find and simplify $\dfrac{dy}{dx}$ and hence find $\dfrac{d^2y}{dx^2}$ if

19. $y = \dfrac{(1+2x)}{(1-2x)}$ **20.** $y = \ln\dfrac{x}{x+1}$ **21.** $y = \dfrac{e^x}{e^x-4}$

CHAPTER 21

FURTHER TRIGONOMETRIC IDENTITIES

THE FACTOR FORMULAE

The last set of identities considered in this book are called the factor formulae. They convert expressions such as $\sin A + \sin B$ into a product, so *factorising* the expression.

Consider the compound angle identities

$$\sin A \cos B + \cos A \sin B \equiv \sin (A + B)$$

$$\sin A \cos B - \cos A \sin B \equiv \sin (A - B)$$

Adding these gives $2 \sin A \cos B \equiv \sin (A + B) + \sin (A - B)$ [1]

Subtracting gives $2 \cos A \sin B \equiv \sin (A + B) - \sin (A - B)$ [2]

Working similarly with the compound angle identities for $\cos (A + B)$ and $\cos (A - B)$ gives

$$2 \cos A \cos B \equiv \cos (A + B) + \cos (A - B) \qquad [3]$$

and $-2 \sin A \sin B \equiv \cos (A + B) - \cos (A - B) \qquad [4]$

Identities [1] to [4] can be used when a product has to be expressed as a sum or difference. For example, to express $2 \cos 7\theta \cos 2\theta$ as a sum we would use [3] to give

$$2 \cos 7\theta \cos 2\theta \equiv \cos(7\theta + 2\theta) + \cos(7\theta - 2\theta) \equiv \cos 9\theta + \cos 5\theta$$

However, when a sum or difference has to be expressed as a product, these identities are more easily remembered when they are expressed in an alternative form as follows.

Using $A + B = P$
and $A - B = Q$ gives $A = \frac{1}{2}(P + Q)$ and $B = \frac{1}{2}(P - Q)$

Then equations [1] to [4] become

$$\sin P + \sin Q \equiv 2 \sin \tfrac{1}{2}(P + Q) \cos \tfrac{1}{2}(P - Q) \qquad [5]$$

$$\sin P - \sin Q \equiv 2 \cos \tfrac{1}{2}(P + Q) \sin \tfrac{1}{2}(P - Q) \qquad [6]$$

$$\cos P + \cos Q \equiv 2 \cos \tfrac{1}{2}(P + Q) \cos \tfrac{1}{2}(P - Q) \qquad [7]$$

$$\cos P - \cos Q \equiv -2 \sin \tfrac{1}{2}(P + Q) \sin \tfrac{1}{2}(P - Q) \qquad [8]$$

For example, to express $\sin 6\theta - \sin 4\theta$ as a product, we would use [6], to give

$$\sin 6\theta - \sin 4\theta \equiv 2 \cos \tfrac{1}{2}(6\theta + 4\theta) \sin \tfrac{1}{2}(6\theta - 4\theta) \equiv 2 \cos 5\theta \sin \theta$$

Many people find that these identities are more easily remembered in words than in symbols, for example [5] can be remembered as

sum of two sines $\equiv$ twice sin (half sum) cos (half difference)

However, remembering every one of these identities in detail is not necessary but it is *important* to know that they exist and that they provide a powerful tool for dealing with trig functions. Formulae books provide details when it is known what is being looked for.

This group of identities can now be used to solve equations, simplify expressions, prove further identities and so on.

Examples 21a _____

1. Find the general solution of the equation $\sin 5x - \sin 3x = 0$

Using identity [6], the LHS of the equation can be expressed as a product.

$$\sin 5x - \sin 3x = 0$$
$$\Rightarrow \qquad 2\cos \tfrac{1}{2}(5x + 3x)\sin \tfrac{1}{2}(5x - 3x) = 0$$
$$\Rightarrow \qquad \cos 4x \sin x = 0$$
$$\Rightarrow \qquad \cos 4x = 0 \qquad \text{or} \qquad \sin x = 0$$

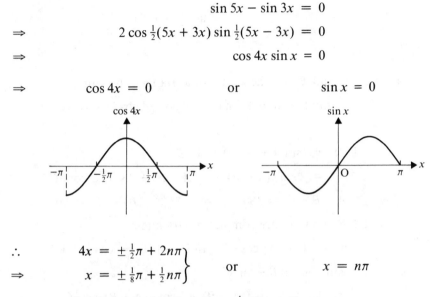

$$\therefore \qquad 4x = \pm\tfrac{1}{2}\pi + 2n\pi \left.\right\}$$
$$\Rightarrow \qquad x = \pm\tfrac{1}{8}\pi + \tfrac{1}{2}n\pi \left.\right\} \qquad \text{or} \qquad x = n\pi$$

The general solution is therefore $x = \tfrac{1}{8}\pi(4n \pm 1),\ n\pi$

_____

2. Factorise $\cos\theta - \cos 3\theta - \cos 5\theta + \cos 7\theta$

As a first step, we take two terms and factorise them, and then take the remaining two terms and factorise them. With a bit of forethought, we can arrange the pairs of terms so that both pairs are in the form $(\cos + \cos)$. In any case, the terms should be rearranged so that this first factorisation results in a common factor.

$$(\cos 7\theta + \cos\theta) - (\cos 5\theta + \cos 3\theta)$$
$$\equiv 2\cos 4\theta \cos 3\theta - 2\cos 4\theta \cos\theta$$
$$\equiv 2\cos 4\theta(\cos 3\theta - \cos\theta)$$
$$\equiv 2\cos 4\theta(-2\sin 2\theta \sin\theta) \equiv -4\cos 4\theta \sin 2\theta \sin\theta$$

_____

3. Prove that $\dfrac{\sin A + \sin B}{\cos A + \cos B} \equiv \tan \dfrac{A+B}{2}$

$$\text{LHS} \equiv \frac{\sin A + \sin B}{\cos A + \cos B} \equiv \frac{2 \sin \frac{1}{2}(A+B) \cos \frac{1}{2}(A-B)}{2 \cos \frac{1}{2}(A+B) \cos \frac{1}{2}(A-B)}$$

$$\equiv \tan \tfrac{1}{2}(A+B)$$

---

4. If A, B and C are the angles of a triangle, show that

$$\sin A + \sin B + \sin C = 4 \cos \tfrac{1}{2}A \cos \tfrac{1}{2}B \cos \tfrac{1}{2}C$$

$$\text{LHS} = (\sin A + \sin B) + \sin C$$

$$= 2 \sin \tfrac{1}{2}(A+B) \cos \tfrac{1}{2}(A-B) + 2 \sin \tfrac{1}{2}C \cos \tfrac{1}{2}C$$

Now $\quad A + B + C = 180° \quad \Rightarrow \quad \tfrac{1}{2}(A+B) + \tfrac{1}{2}C = 90°$

i.e. $\tfrac{1}{2}(A+B)$ and $\tfrac{1}{2}C$ are complementary angles

$\Rightarrow \qquad \sin \tfrac{1}{2}(A+B) = \cos \tfrac{1}{2}C \quad$ and $\quad \sin \tfrac{1}{2}C = \cos \tfrac{1}{2}(A+B)$

$\therefore \qquad \sin A + \sin B + \sin C$

$$= 2 \cos \tfrac{1}{2}C \cos \tfrac{1}{2}(A-B) + 2 \cos \tfrac{1}{2}(A+B) \cos \tfrac{1}{2}C$$

$$= 2 \cos \tfrac{1}{2}C \left\{ \cos \tfrac{1}{2}(A-B) + \cos \tfrac{1}{2}(A+B) \right\}$$

$$= 2 \cos \tfrac{1}{2}C \left\{ 2 \cos \tfrac{1}{2}A \cos \left(-\tfrac{1}{2}B\right) \right\}$$

$$= 4 \cos \tfrac{1}{2}A \cos \tfrac{1}{2}B \cos \tfrac{1}{2}C \qquad (\cos -\theta = \cos \theta)$$

EXERCISE 21a

1. Express as a product of two trig functions

    (a) $\sin 3\theta + \sin \theta$ (b) $\cos 5\theta + \cos 3\theta$ (c) $\sin 4\theta - \sin 2\theta$

    (d) $\cos 7\theta - \cos \theta$ (e) $\sin 3A - \sin 5A$ (f) $\cos A - \cos 5A$

    (g) $\sin 2A + \sin 20°$ (h) $\sin 2\theta + 1$ (*Hint.* $\sin 90° = 1$)

2. Express as a sum or difference of two trig functions

    (a) $2 \sin 2\theta \cos \theta$ (b) $2 \cos 3\theta \cos 2\theta$ (c) $2 \cos \theta \sin 4\theta$

    (d) $-2 \sin 3\theta \sin \theta$ (e) $2 \sin 4\theta \sin 2\theta$ (f) $\cos \theta \cos 4\theta$

3. Simplify

   (a) $\cos(\theta - 60°) + \cos(\theta + 60°)$ (b) $\sin(x - 45°) - \sin(x + 45°)$

   (c) $\sqrt{3}\cos\theta - \sin(\theta + 60°) - \sin(\theta + 120°)$

4. Evaluate, leaving your answers in surd form,

   (a) $\sin 105° + \sin 15°$ (b) $\cos 15° + \cos 75°$

5. Find the general solutions of the following equations.

   (a) $\cos 2x + \cos 4x = 0$ (b) $\sin 3x - \sin x = 0$

   (c) $\cos x - \cos 3x = 0$ (d) $\sin 4\theta + \sin 2\theta = 0$

6. Factorise the expression $\cos\theta + \cos 3\theta + \cos 2\theta$. Hence find the general solution of the equation $\cos\theta + \cos 3\theta + \cos 2\theta = 0$

7. Factorise the expression $\sin 3\theta - \sin\theta + \sin 7\theta - \sin 5\theta$. Hence find the general solution of the equation $\sin 3\theta - \sin\theta = \sin 5\theta - \sin 7\theta$.

8. Solve the following equations for angles from 0 to 180°

   (a) $\cos x = \cos 2x + \cos 4x$

   (b) $\cos x + \cos 3x = \sin x + \sin 3x$

   (c) $\sin 3\theta + \sin 6\theta + \sin 9\theta = 0$

   (d) $\sin 3\theta - \sin\theta = \cos 2\theta$

   (e) $\cos 5\theta - \cos\theta = \sin 3\theta$

   (f) $\cos 2x = \cos(30° - x)$

9. Prove the following identities.

   (a) $\dfrac{\sin 2A + \sin 2B}{\sin 2A - \sin 2B} \equiv \dfrac{\tan(A + B)}{\tan(A - B)}$

   (b) $\dfrac{\cos 2A + \cos 2B}{\cos 2B - \cos 2A} \equiv \cot(A + B)\cot(A - B)$

   (c) $\dfrac{\sin A \sin 2A + \sin 3A \sin 6A}{\sin A \cos 2A + \sin 3A \cos 6A} \equiv \tan 5A$

   (d) $\dfrac{\sin 3x + \sin 5x}{\sin 4x + \sin 6x} \equiv \dfrac{\sin 4x}{\sin 5x}$

   (e) $\sin\theta + \sin 2\theta + \sin 3\theta \equiv (1 + \cos 2\theta)\sin 2\theta$

   (f) $1 + 2\cos 2\alpha + \cos 4\alpha \equiv 4\cos^2\alpha \cos 2\alpha$

10. If A, B and C are the angles of a triangle, prove that
   (a) $\cos(B + C) = -\cos A$ (b) $\sin C = \sin(A + B)$
   (c) $\sin\frac{1}{2}(A + B) = \cos\frac{1}{2}C$ (d) $\sin\frac{1}{2}B = \cos\frac{1}{2}(A + C)$
   (e) $\sin B + \sin(A - C) = 2\sin A \cos C$
   (f) $\cos(A - B) - \cos C = 2\cos A \cos B$
   (g) $\sin(A + B) + \sin(B + C) = 2\cos\frac{1}{2}B\cos\frac{1}{2}(A - C)$
   (h) $\cos A + \cos B + \cos C = 1 + 4\sin\frac{1}{2}A\sin\frac{1}{2}B\sin\frac{1}{2}C$

The next exercise contains questions that may require any of the identities from Chapters 17 and 18 as well as those from this one.

MIXED EXERCISE 21

1. If A is acute and $\sin A = \frac{1}{2}$ and if B is obtuse and $\sin B = \frac{1}{3}$, find in surd form the value of
   (a) $\tan(A + B)$ (b) $\cos(A - B)$

2. Find the values of θ in the range $-90° \leqslant \theta \leqslant 90°$ for which $\tan^2\theta + \sec\theta = 11$

3. Find the general solution of the equation $\sin 3x - \sin x = \cos 2x$

4. By writing $\frac{3}{10}\pi$ as $\frac{1}{2}\pi - \frac{1}{5}\pi$, show that $\cos\frac{3}{10}\pi = \sin\frac{1}{5}\pi$

5. Find the general solution of the equation $\tan 2\theta + 2\sin\theta = 0$

6. Prove that if $\sec\alpha = \cos\beta + \sin\beta$ then $\tan^2\alpha = \sin 2\beta$

7. Find the values of θ from 0 to 180° for which $\sin 5\theta - \sin\theta = \cos 3\theta$

8. Prove the identity $\dfrac{1}{\sin x} + \dfrac{1}{\tan x} \equiv \cot\frac{1}{2}x$ and hence find in surd form the value of $\tan\frac{1}{8}\pi$

9. Find the Cartesian equation of the curve whose parametric equations are $x = \cos 2\theta$ and $y = \sin\theta$

10. Solve the simultaneous equations $\cos x - \cos y = 1$ and $\sin^2 x - \sin^2 y = 0$ for values of x and of y from 0 to 360°

11. Prove the identity $\cos 3\theta \equiv 4\cos^3\theta - 3\cos\theta$

12. Find the general solution of the equation $\tan x \sec x = \sqrt{2}$

13. Use the substitution $t \equiv \tan \frac{1}{2}x$ to find the values of x from 0 to $360°$ for which $4\cos x - 6\sin x = 5$

14. Find the Cartesian equation of the curve whose parametric equations are $x = 2\sin(\theta + \frac{1}{3}\pi)$ and $y = \cos(\theta - \frac{1}{6}\pi)$

15. Find the values of θ from 0 to $360°$ for which $\sin 2\theta = \sin 3\theta$

16. Find the Cartesian equation of the curve given parametrically by $x = a\cos 2t$ and $y = a\sin t$

17. Find the values of θ from 0 to $360°$ for which $\cos \theta = 2\sin(\theta - 30°)$

18. Use the substitution $t = \tan \theta$ to show that

$$\frac{1}{3 + 5\sin 2\theta} = \frac{1 + t^2}{(3t + 1)(t + 3)}$$

19. Find the general solution of the equation $\sin 2x - \sin 4x = 0$

20. Express $\sin \theta$ in the form $\cos \alpha$ giving α in terms of θ. Hence solve the equation $\cos 3\theta = \sin \theta$ for values of θ between 0 and $360°$

CHAPTER 22

FURTHER TRIGONOMETRIC FUNCTIONS

$f(\theta) = a\cos\theta + b\sin\theta$

SG The diagrams below show the graphs of $f(\theta) = a\cos\theta + b\sin\theta$ for a variety of values of a and b.

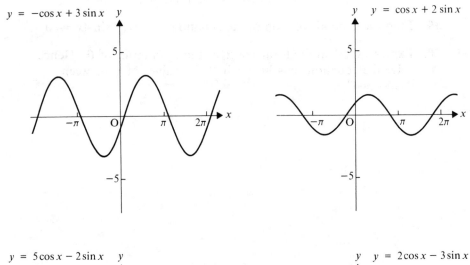

$y = -\cos x + 3\sin x$

$y = \cos x + 2\sin x$

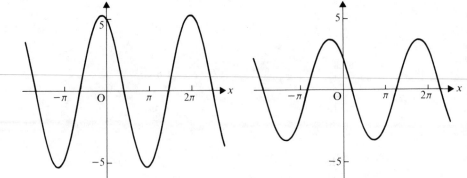

$y = 5\cos x - 2\sin x$

$y = 2\cos x - 3\sin x$

If the reader has access to the appropriate technology, we suggest that the graph of $f(\theta)$ is drawn for some other values of a and b. Each of these graphs is a sine wave, although with differing amplitude and phase shift.

These diagrams suggest that it is possible to express $a \cos \theta + b \sin \theta$ as $r \sin (\theta + \alpha)$ where the values of r and α depend on the values of a and b. This is possible provided that we can find values of r and α such that

$$r \sin (\theta + \alpha) \equiv a \cos \theta + b \sin \theta$$

i.e. $$r \sin \theta \cos \alpha + r \cos \theta \sin \alpha \equiv a \cos \theta + b \sin \theta$$

Since this is an identity we can compare coefficients of $\sin \theta$ and of $\cos \theta$

$$\Rightarrow \qquad\qquad\qquad r \sin \alpha = a \qquad\qquad\qquad [1]$$

and $$r \cos \alpha = b \qquad\qquad\qquad [2]$$

Equations [1] and [2] can now be solved to give r and α in terms of a and b.

Squaring and adding equations [1] and [2] gives

$$r^2(\sin^2\alpha + \cos^2\alpha) = a^2 + b^2 \qquad \Rightarrow \qquad r = \sqrt{(a^2 + b^2)}$$

Dividing equation [1] by equation [2] gives

$$\frac{r \sin \alpha}{r \cos \alpha} = \frac{a}{b} \qquad \Rightarrow \qquad \tan \alpha = \frac{a}{b}$$

Therefore

$$r \sin (\theta + \alpha) \equiv a \cos \theta + b \sin \theta$$

$$\text{where} \quad r = \sqrt{(a^2 + b^2)} \quad \text{and} \quad \tan \alpha = \frac{a}{b}$$

It is also possible to express $a \cos \theta + b \sin \theta$ as $r \sin (\theta - \alpha)$ or as $r \cos (\theta \pm \alpha)$, using a similar method.

Examples 22a

1. Express $3 \sin \theta - 2 \cos \theta$ as $r \sin (\theta - \alpha)$

$$3 \sin \theta - 2 \cos \theta \equiv r \sin (\theta - \alpha)$$

$\Rightarrow \qquad 3 \underline{\sin \theta} - 2 \underline{\cos \theta} \equiv r \underline{\sin \theta} \cos \alpha - r \underline{\cos \theta} \sin \alpha$

Comparing coefficients of $\sin \theta$ and of $\cos \theta$ gives

$$\left. \begin{array}{l} 3 = r \cos \alpha \\ 2 = r \sin \alpha \end{array} \right\} \quad \Rightarrow \quad \left\{ \begin{array}{l} 13 = r^2 \\ \tan \alpha = \frac{2}{3} \end{array} \right. \quad \begin{array}{l} \Rightarrow \quad r = \sqrt{13} \\ \Rightarrow \quad \alpha = 33.7° \end{array}$$

$\therefore \qquad\qquad 3 \sin \theta - 2 \cos \theta = \sqrt{13} \sin (\theta - 33.7°)$

---

2. Find the maximum value of $f(x) = 3 \cos x + 4 \sin x$ and the smallest positive value of x at which it occurs.

Expressing $f(x)$ in the form $r \sin (x + \alpha)$ enables us to 'read' its maximum value, and the values of x at which they occur, from the resulting sine wave. Note also that in this question there is a choice of form in which to express $f(x)$: in this case it is sensible to choose $r \cos (x - \alpha)$ as this fits $f(x)$ better than $r \sin (x + \alpha)$

$$3 \underline{\cos x} + 4 \underline{\sin x} \equiv r \cos (x - \alpha) \equiv r \underline{\cos x} \cos \alpha + r \underline{\sin x} \sin \alpha$$

Hence $\left. \begin{array}{l} r \cos \alpha = 3 \\ r \sin \alpha = 4 \end{array} \right\} \quad \Rightarrow \quad \left\{ \begin{array}{l} r^2 = 25 \\ \tan \alpha = \frac{4}{3} \end{array} \right. \quad \begin{array}{l} \Rightarrow \quad r = 5 \\ \Rightarrow \quad \alpha = 53.1° \end{array}$

$\therefore \qquad\qquad f(x) \equiv 5 \cos (x - 53.1°)$

The graph of $f(x)$ is a cosine wave with amplitude 5 and phase shift $53.1°$

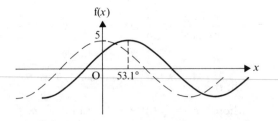

$\therefore$ $f(x)$ has a maximum value of 5 and, from the sketch, the smallest positive value of x at which it occurs is $53.1°$

---

3. Find the greatest and least values of $\dfrac{2}{\sin x - \cos x}$

We first express $\sin x - \cos x$ in the form $r \sin (x - \alpha)$ then the given function can be expressed as a cosec function and we can sketch its graph. Note that values of x are not required so we do not need the value of α. Note also that the greatest and least values of a function are not necessarily the same as the maximum and minimum value of that function.

If $\ f(x) \equiv \underline{\sin x} - \underline{\underline{\cos x}} \equiv r \sin (x - \alpha) \equiv r \underline{\sin x} \cos \alpha - r \underline{\underline{\cos x}} \sin \alpha$

then $\qquad \left.\begin{array}{l} r \cos \alpha = 1 \\ r \sin \alpha = 1 \end{array}\right\} \quad \Rightarrow \quad r^2 = 2, \ \text{i.e.} \ r = \sqrt{2}$

$\therefore \qquad\qquad\qquad \sin x - \cos x \equiv \sqrt{2} \sin (x - \alpha)$

Hence $\qquad \dfrac{2}{f(x)} \equiv \dfrac{2}{\sqrt{2} \sin (x - \alpha)} \equiv \sqrt{2} \cosec (x - \alpha)$

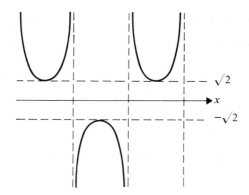

From the sketch, the greatest value of $\dfrac{2}{\sin x - \cos x}$ is ∞ and the least value is $-\infty$

Note that $\dfrac{2}{f(x)}$ has a maximum value of $-\sqrt{2}$ and a minimum value of $\sqrt{2}$

THE EQUATION $a \cos x + b \sin x = c$

One way of solving an equation of this type was covered in Chapter 18; it uses the half angle formulae involving t where $t = \tan \frac{1}{2}x$. An alternative method is to express the LHS of the equation in the form $r \cos(x + \alpha)$. This method, which has the advantage that solutions are not easily lost, is illustrated in the next example.

Examples 22a (continued) _____

4. Find, in radians, the general solution of the equation
$$\sqrt{3} \cos x + \sin x = 1$$

If $\underline{\sqrt{3} \cos x} + \underline{\sin x} \equiv r \cos(x - \alpha) \equiv r \underline{\cos x} \cos \alpha + r \underline{\sin x} \sin \alpha$

then $\quad \begin{cases} r \cos \alpha = \sqrt{3} \\ r \sin \alpha = 1 \end{cases} \Rightarrow \quad \begin{cases} r^2 = 4 \\ \tan \alpha = \frac{1}{\sqrt{3}} \end{cases} \Rightarrow \quad \begin{aligned} r &= 2 \\ \alpha &= \tfrac{1}{6}\pi \end{aligned}$

i.e. $\sqrt{3} \cos x + \sin x \equiv 2 \cos(x - \tfrac{1}{6}\pi)$

$\therefore$ the equation becomes

$$2 \cos(x - \tfrac{1}{6}\pi) = 1$$

$\Rightarrow \qquad \cos(x - \tfrac{1}{6}\pi) = \tfrac{1}{2}$

$\Rightarrow \qquad x - \tfrac{1}{6}\pi = \pm\tfrac{1}{3}\pi + 2n\pi$

$\therefore \qquad x = \tfrac{1}{2}\pi + 2n\pi, \; -\tfrac{1}{6}\pi + 2n\pi$

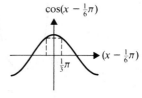

_____

EXERCISE 22a

_____

1. Find the values of r and α for which
   (a) $\sqrt{3} \cos \theta - \sin \theta \equiv r \cos(\theta + \alpha)$
   (b) $\cos \theta + 3 \sin \theta \equiv r \cos(\theta - \alpha)$
   (c) $4 \sin \theta - 3 \cos \theta \equiv r \sin(\theta - \alpha)$

2. Express $\cos 2\theta - \sin 2\theta$ in the form $r \cos(2\theta + \alpha)$

3. Express $2 \cos 3\theta + 5 \sin 3\theta$ in the form $r \sin (3\theta + \alpha)$

4. Express $\cos \theta - \sqrt{3} \sin \theta$ in the form $r \sin (\theta - \alpha)$. Hence sketch the graph of $f(\theta) = \cos \theta - \sqrt{3} \sin \theta$. Give the maximum and minimum values of $f(\theta)$ and the values of θ between 0 and 360° at which they occur.

5. Express $7 \cos \theta - 24 \sin \theta$ in the form $r \cos (\theta + \alpha)$. Hence sketch the graph of $f(\theta) = 7 \cos \theta - 24 \sin \theta + 3$ and give the maximum and minimum values of $f(\theta)$ and the values of θ between 0 and 360° at which they occur.

6. Find the greatest and least values of $\cos x + \sin x$. Hence find the maximum and minimum values of $\dfrac{1}{\cos x + \sin x}$

7. Find the maximum and minimum values of $\dfrac{\sqrt{2}}{\cos \theta - \sqrt{2} \sin \theta}$

8. Find the general solution of the following equations.
   (a) $\cos x + \sin x = \sqrt{2}$ (b) $7 \cos x + 6 \sin x = 2$
   (c) $\cos x - 3 \sin x = 1$ (d) $2 \cos x - \sin x = 2$

THE EQUATION $\cos A = \cos B$

An equation such as $\cos 2x = \cos x$ can be solved by using a factor formula, but there is another very simple method of solution, based on consideration of the graph of $\cos x$

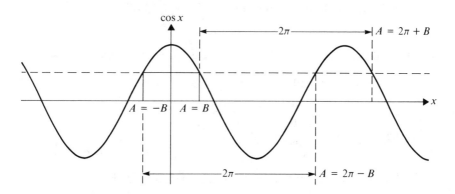

If $$\cos A = \cos B$$

then, from the graph, we see that $$A = 2n\pi \pm B$$

i.e. $$\cos A = \cos B \quad \Rightarrow \quad A = 2n\pi \pm B$$

A similar conclusion is reached from the graphs of $\tan x$ and of $\sin x$

$$\tan A = \tan B \quad \Rightarrow \quad A = B + n\pi$$

$$\sin A = \sin B \quad \Rightarrow \quad A = \begin{cases} 2n\pi + B \\ (2n+1)\pi - B \end{cases}$$

This method can also be used for equations of the form $\cos A = \sin B$, and this is illustrated in Examples 22b, number 2.

Examples 22b

1. Find the general solution of the equation $\cos 4\theta = \cos \theta$

Using only the conclusion to the argument above, we can write

$$4\theta = 2n\pi \pm \theta$$

hence $$5\theta = 2n\pi$$
or $$3\theta = 2n\pi$$ $\Rightarrow \quad \theta = \tfrac{2}{5}n\pi, \tfrac{2}{3}n\pi$

2. Find the general solution of the equation $\cos 3x = \sin x$

We know that $\sin x = \cos(\tfrac{1}{2}\pi - x)$, so the equation can be written

$$\cos 3x = \cos(\tfrac{1}{2}\pi - x)$$

$\therefore$ $$3x = 2n\pi \pm (\tfrac{1}{2}\pi - x)$$

Hence $$4x = 2n\pi + \tfrac{1}{2}\pi$$
or $$2x = 2n\pi - \tfrac{1}{2}\pi$$ $\Rightarrow \quad x = \tfrac{1}{2}n\pi + \tfrac{1}{8}\pi, \; n\pi - \tfrac{1}{4}\pi$

3. Find the values of θ between 0 and $360°$ for which
$\tan(3\theta - 40°) = \tan\theta$

The general solution is $\qquad 3\theta - 40° = 180n° + \theta$

$\Rightarrow \qquad\qquad\qquad\qquad\qquad \theta = 90n° + 20°$

For $0 \leqslant \theta \leqslant 360°$, $\quad n = 0, 1, 2$ and 3

$\Rightarrow \qquad\qquad\qquad\qquad \theta = 20°, 110°, 200°, 290°$

EXERCISE 22b

Find the general solution of the following equations.

1. $\cos 4\theta = \cos 3\theta$ 2. $\tan 7\theta = \tan 2\theta$ 3. $\cos 3\theta = \sin 2\theta$

4. $\cot 4\theta = \tan 5\theta$ 5. $\sin 4\theta = \sin 3\theta$ 6. $\cos 5\theta \sec\theta = 1$

7. $\cos\left(\theta - \dfrac{\pi}{4}\right) = \cos\left(4\theta + \dfrac{\pi}{4}\right)$ 8. $\tan 2\theta = \cot\theta$

Find the solutions, from 0 to π inclusive, of the following equations.

9. $\cos 3\theta = \cos 7\theta$ 10. $\tan 3\theta = \cot 2\theta$

11. $\sin 7\theta = \sin 2\theta$ 12. $\sec 6\theta = \sec 5\theta$

Solve the following equations giving values from $-180°$ to $+180°$.

13. $\cos(2\theta + 60°) = \cos\theta$ 14. $\tan 3\theta = \tan(\theta - 50°)$

15. $\sin\theta = \cos(2\theta + 60°)$ 16. $\cos(30° - \theta) = \cos 2\theta$

17. $\tan(2\theta + 60°) = \tan 4\theta$ 18. $\sin 3\theta = \sin(\theta + 80°)$

THE INVERSE TRIGONOMETRIC FUNCTIONS

Consider the function given by $f:x \rightarrow \sin x$ for $x \in \mathbb{R}$

The inverse mapping is given by $\sin x \rightarrow x$ but this is not a function because one value of $\sin x$ maps to many values of x, i.e. $f(x) = \sin x$ does not have an inverse function for the domain $x \in \mathbb{R}$

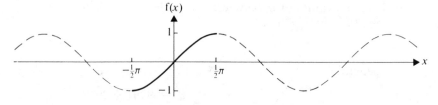

However, if we now consider the function $f: x \rightarrow \sin x$ for $-\frac{1}{2}\pi \leqslant x \leqslant \frac{1}{2}\pi$ then the reverse mapping, $\sin x \rightarrow x$, is such that one value of $\sin x$ maps to only one value of x

Therefore $f: x \rightarrow \sin x$ for $-\frac{1}{2}\pi \leqslant x \leqslant \frac{1}{2}\pi$ does have an inverse, i.e. f^{-1} exists.

Now the equation of the graph of f is $y = \sin x$ for $-\frac{1}{2}\pi \leqslant x \leqslant \frac{1}{2}\pi$ and the curve $y = f^{-1}(x)$ is obtained by reflecting $y = \sin x$ in the line $y = x$

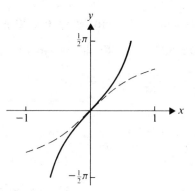

Therefore interchanging x and y gives the equation of this curve, i.e. $\sin y = x$, so $y =$ the angle between $-\frac{1}{2}\pi$ and $\frac{1}{2}\pi$ whose sine is x

Using *arcsin* to mean 'the angle between $-\frac{1}{2}\pi$ and $\frac{1}{2}\pi$ whose sine is', we have $y = \arcsin x$

Thus   if $f: x \rightarrow \sin x$ $-\frac{1}{2}\pi \leqslant x \leqslant \frac{1}{2}\pi$

               then $f^{-1}: x \rightarrow \arcsin x$ $-1 \leqslant x \leqslant 1$

It is important to realise that $\arcsin x$ is an angle, and further that this angle is in the interval $[-\frac{1}{2}\pi, \frac{1}{2}\pi]$

Thus, for example, $\arcsin 0.5$ is the angle between $-\frac{1}{2}\pi$ and $\frac{1}{2}\pi$ whose sine is 0.5, i.e. $\arcsin 0.5 = \frac{1}{6}\pi$

Note that the alternative notation $\sin^{-1}$ is sometimes used to mean 'the angle whose sine is', and if this notation is adopted, care is needed not to confuse it with $1/\sin x$

Now consider the function given by $f:x \to \cos x, \ 0 \leqslant x \leqslant \pi$

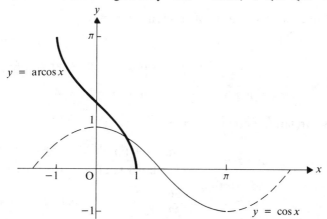

From the diagram, we see that f^{-1} exists and it is denoted by arccos where $\arccos x$ means 'the angle between 0 and π whose cosine is x'

Thus   if $f:x \to \cos x$ $0 \leqslant x \leqslant \pi$

           then $f^{-1}:x \to \arccos x$ $-1 \leqslant x \leqslant 1$

Note that $\arccos x$ is an angle in the range $0 \leqslant x \leqslant \pi$

Thus, for example, $\arccos -0.5 = x$ $\Rightarrow$ $x = \frac{2}{3}\pi$

Similarly, if $f:x \to \tan x$ for $-\frac{1}{2}\pi \leqslant x \leqslant \frac{1}{2}\pi$, then f^{-1} exists and is written *arctan* where $\arctan x$ means 'the angle between $-\frac{1}{2}\pi$ and $\frac{1}{2}\pi$ whose tangent is x'

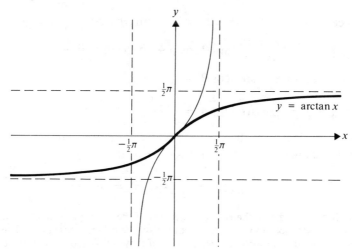

Examples 22c _____

1. Find the exact value of $\arctan \frac{3}{4} + \arctan \frac{5}{12}$

If $\qquad\qquad\qquad \alpha = \arctan \frac{3}{4} \quad$ and $\qquad \beta = \arctan \frac{5}{12}$

then $\qquad\qquad\qquad \tan \alpha = \frac{3}{4} \qquad\qquad$ and $\quad \tan \beta = \frac{5}{12}$

Now $\arctan \frac{3}{4} + \arctan \frac{5}{12} = \alpha + \beta$

and $\qquad\qquad \tan (\alpha + \beta) = \dfrac{\tan \alpha + \tan \beta}{1 - \tan \alpha \tan \beta} = \dfrac{(\frac{3}{4}) + (\frac{5}{12})}{1 - (\frac{3}{4})(\frac{5}{12})}$

$$= \frac{56}{33}$$

$\therefore \qquad\qquad\qquad (\alpha + \beta) = \arctan \dfrac{56}{33}$

i.e. $\arctan \frac{3}{4} + \arctan \frac{5}{12} = \arctan \frac{56}{33}$

_____

2. Solve the equation $\arcsin x + \arccos \frac{1}{2}x = \frac{5}{6}\pi$

If $\qquad\qquad\qquad \arcsin x = \theta \qquad$ and $\quad \arccos \frac{1}{2}x = \phi$

then $\qquad\qquad\qquad\qquad x = \sin \theta \quad$ and $\qquad\qquad \frac{1}{2}x = \cos \phi$

Therefore the given equation becomes $\quad \theta + \phi = \frac{5}{6}\pi$

Hence $\qquad\qquad\qquad\qquad\qquad\qquad \sin (\theta + \phi) = \frac{1}{2}$

$\Rightarrow \qquad\qquad\qquad\qquad \sin \theta \cos \phi + \cos \theta \sin \phi = \frac{1}{2} \qquad\qquad\qquad$ [1]

Now $\sin \theta = x \quad$ so $\quad \cos \theta = \sqrt{(1 - x^2)}$

and $\cos \phi = \frac{1}{2}x \quad$ so $\quad \sin \phi = \dfrac{\sqrt{(4 - x^2)}}{2}$

$\therefore$ [1] becomes $\qquad x \left(\dfrac{1}{2}x \right) + \sqrt{(1 - x^2)} \left(\dfrac{\sqrt{(4 - x^2)}}{2} \right) = \dfrac{1}{2}$

$\Rightarrow \qquad\qquad\qquad \sqrt{(1 - x^2)}\sqrt{(4 - x^2)} = 1 - x^2$

Squaring both sides of the equation gets rid of the square roots, but it can introduce extra solutions which do not satisfy the original equation. It is therefore _essential_ that all solutions are tested to see if they satisfy the original equation.

$$\therefore \qquad\qquad (1 - x^2)(4 - x^2) = (1 - x^2)^2$$

$$\Rightarrow \qquad\qquad (1 - x^2)(4 - x^2 - 1 + x^2) = 0$$

$$\Rightarrow \qquad\qquad (1 - x^2) = 0 \quad \text{or} \quad (4 - x^2 - 1 + x^2) = 0$$

$$\therefore \qquad\qquad x = \pm 1 \quad \text{or} \qquad\qquad x = \infty$$

Now $x = \sin\theta$, $\therefore$ $x = \infty$ is not a possible solution.

Substituting $x = 1$ into the LHS of the original equation gives

$$\arcsin 1 + \arccos \tfrac{1}{2} = \tfrac{1}{2}\pi + \tfrac{1}{3}\pi = \tfrac{5}{6}\pi = \text{RHS}$$

$$\therefore \; x = 1 \; \text{is a solution.}$$

Substituting $x = -1$ into the LHS of the original equation gives

$$\arcsin -1 + \arccos -\tfrac{1}{2} = -\tfrac{1}{2}\pi + \tfrac{2}{3}\pi \neq \text{RHS}$$

$$\therefore \; x = -1 \; \text{is not a solution.}$$

So the only solution is $x = 1$

---

3. Prove that $\arctan x + \arctan\left(\dfrac{1-x}{1+x}\right) \equiv \dfrac{1}{4}\pi$

First we will simplify the LHS of the identity.

If $\qquad\qquad \alpha = \arctan x \qquad\qquad$ then $\qquad\qquad x = \tan\alpha$

and if $\qquad \beta = \arctan\left(\dfrac{1-x}{1+x}\right) \qquad$ then $\qquad \dfrac{1-x}{1+x} = \tan\beta$

Now $\arctan x + \arctan\left(\dfrac{1-x}{1+x}\right) = \alpha + \beta$

and $\qquad \tan(\alpha + \beta) \equiv \dfrac{\tan\alpha + \tan\beta}{1 - \tan\alpha\tan\beta} = \dfrac{x + \left(\dfrac{1-x}{1+x}\right)}{1 - x\left(\dfrac{1-x}{1+x}\right)}$

$$= \dfrac{x^2 + 1}{1 + x^2} = 1$$

Hence $\alpha + \beta = \arctan 1 = \tfrac{1}{4}\pi$, i.e. $\arctan x + \arctan\left(\dfrac{1-x}{1+x}\right) \equiv \dfrac{1}{4}\pi$

EXERCISE 22c

1. Find the value of the following in terms of π
   (a) $\arctan \sqrt{3}$ (b) $\arcsin -1$ (c) $\arccos 0$
   (d) $\arcsin -\frac{\sqrt{3}}{2}$ (e) $\arccos -\frac{1}{2}$ (f) $\arctan -1$

2. Find the value of the following in terms of π
   (a) $\arctan \frac{1}{3} + \arctan \frac{1}{2}$ (b) $\arcsin \frac{1}{2} + \arccos \frac{1}{2}$

3. Simplify
   (a) $\arcsin x + \arccos x$ (b) $\sin (2 \arctan x)$
   (c) $\arctan x + \arctan \frac{1}{x}$ (d) $\tan (\arctan \frac{1}{3} + \arctan \frac{1}{4})$

4. Prove that
   (a) $\cos (2 \arcsin x) \equiv 1 - 2x^2$ (b) $\sin (\arccos x) \equiv \sqrt{(1 - x^2)}$

5. Solve the following equations.
   (a) $\tan^{-1} 2 = \tan^{-1} 4 - \tan^{-1} x$
   (b) $\sin^{-1}\left(\dfrac{x}{x - 1}\right) + 2 \tan^{-1}\left(\dfrac{1}{x + 1}\right) = \dfrac{\pi}{2}$
   (c) $\arctan (1 + x) + \arctan (1 - x) = \arctan 2$

SMALL ANGLES

Using a calculator to find the sine and tangent of small angles measured in radians, we find that $\sin \theta$ and $\tan \theta$ are approximately equal to θ. For example, correct to three significant figures
$\sin 0.1 = 0.100$ and $\tan 0.1 = 0.100$

This can be proved as follows.
In the diagram a small angle, θ radians, is subtended by the arc AB at the centre O of a circle of radius r. AB is a chord of the circle and AC is the tangent to the circle at A, cutting OB produced at C.

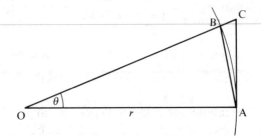

Now area $\triangle OAB$ < area sector OAB < area $\triangle OAC$

i.e. $\frac{1}{2}r^2 \sin\theta < \frac{1}{2}r^2\theta < \frac{1}{2}r^2 \tan\theta$

Dividing by $\frac{1}{2}r^2$, which is positive, gives

$$\sin\theta < \theta < \tan\theta \qquad [1]$$

Dividing by $\sin\theta$, which is positive as θ is a small positive angle, gives

$$1 < \frac{\theta}{\sin\theta} < \sec\theta$$

Now as $\theta \to 0$, $\sec\theta \to 1$ so $\dfrac{\theta}{\sin\theta}$ lies between 1 and a number that approaches 1 as θ gets smaller,

i.e. $$\lim_{\theta \to 0}\left(\frac{\theta}{\sin\theta}\right) = 1$$

Similarly, dividing [1] by $\tan\theta$, we can show that

$$\lim_{\theta \to 0}\left(\frac{\theta}{\tan\theta}\right) = 1$$

These limiting values verify that, for small positive values of θ,

$$\sin\theta \approx \theta \quad \text{and} \quad \tan\theta \approx \theta$$

To find an approximate value for $\cos\theta$ when θ is small, we use the identity

$$\cos\theta \equiv 1 - 2\sin^2\tfrac{1}{2}\theta$$

But if $\frac{1}{2}\theta$ is small, $\sin\frac{1}{2}\theta \approx \frac{1}{2}\theta$, so $\cos\theta \approx 1 - 2(\frac{1}{2}\theta)^2$

i.e. $$\cos\theta \approx 1 - \tfrac{1}{2}\theta^2$$

Collecting these results, we have

when θ is small and measured in radians,

$\sin\theta \approx \theta$, $\tan\theta \approx \theta$ and $\cos\theta \approx 1 - \tfrac{1}{2}\theta^2$

These approximations are correct to 3 s.f. for angles in the range -0.105 rad $< \theta < 0.105$ rad, i.e. $-6° < \theta < 6°$

Example 22d _____

Find, as a rational function of θ, an approximation for the expression
$\dfrac{\sin 3\theta}{1 + \cos 2\theta}$ when 3θ is small.

When 3θ is small, $\sin 3\theta \approx 3\theta$

and 2θ is also small, so $\cos 2\theta \approx 1 - \dfrac{(2\theta)^2}{2}$

$\therefore$ $\qquad\qquad\qquad \dfrac{\sin 3\theta}{1 + \cos 2\theta} \approx \dfrac{3\theta}{2(1 - \theta^2)}$

_____

EXERCISE 22d

1. If θ is small enough to regard 4θ as small, find approximations for the following expressions.

   (a) $\dfrac{2\theta}{\sin 4\theta}$ (b) $\dfrac{\theta \sin \theta}{\cos 2\theta}$ (c) $\sin \tfrac{1}{2}\theta \sec \theta$

   (d) $\dfrac{\theta \tan \theta}{1 - \cos \theta}$ (e) $\dfrac{2 \sin \tfrac{1}{2}\theta}{\theta}$ (f) $\dfrac{\sin \theta \tan \theta}{\theta^2}$

2. If θ is small enough for θ^2 to be neglected (i.e. $\theta^2 \approx 0$), show that

   (a) $2 \cos \left(\tfrac{1}{3}\pi + \theta\right) \approx 1 - \theta\sqrt{3}$ (b) $4 \sin \left(\tfrac{1}{4}\pi - \theta\right) \approx 2\sqrt{2}(1 - \theta)$

3. Find the limiting value as $\theta \rightarrow 0$ of the following expressions.

   (a) $\dfrac{\sin \theta}{2\theta}$ (b) $\dfrac{\tan 2\theta}{\sin 3\theta}$

   (c) $\sin \left(\tfrac{1}{3}\pi + \theta\right)$ (d) $\tan \left(\tfrac{1}{4}\pi + \theta\right)$

MIXED EXERCISE 22

1. Express $4 \sin \theta - 3 \cos \theta$ in the form $r \sin (\theta - \alpha)$. Hence find the maximum and minimum values of $\dfrac{7}{4 \sin \theta - 3 \cos \theta + 2}$
   State the greatest and least values.

2. If $\alpha = \arctan \tfrac{1}{2} - \arctan \tfrac{1}{4}$, find the value, in surd form, of
   (a) $\tan \alpha$ (b) $\cos \alpha$ (c) $\sin \alpha$

3. Express $\sin 2\theta - \cos 2\theta$ in the form $r\sin(2\theta - \alpha)$. Hence find the smallest positive value of θ for which $\sin 2\theta - \cos 2\theta$ has a maximum value.

4. If $\arctan x + \arctan y = \frac{1}{4}\pi$, show that $x + y = 1 - xy$

5. Find the limiting value as $\theta \to 0$ of $\dfrac{\frac{1}{2}(1 - \sin\theta - \cos\theta)}{2\theta}$

6. Express $\cos x + \sin x$ in the form $r\cos(x - \alpha)$. Hence find the smallest positive value of x for which $\dfrac{1}{(\cos x + \sin x)}$ has a minimum value.

7. Find all the values of x in the range $0 \leqslant x \leqslant 2\pi$ for which $\cos 3x = \cos 2x$

8. Find all the values of x between 0 and $180°$ for which $\sin(x - 30°) = \cos 4x$

9. Show that $x = \frac{1}{14}\pi$ is a solution of the equation $\sin 3x = \cos 4x$

10. Find the general solution of the equation $\tan 5\theta = \cot 2\theta$

11. Express $3\cos x - 4\sin x$ in the form $r\cos(x + \alpha)$. Hence express $4 + \dfrac{10}{3\cos x - 4\sin x}$ in the form $4 + k\sec(x + \alpha)$ and sketch the graph of $4 + \dfrac{10}{3\cos x - 4\sin x}$

CHAPTER 23

DIFFERENTIATION OF TRIGONOMETRIC FUNCTIONS

THE DERIVATIVE OF $\sin x$

110

The derivative of any new function, $f(x)$, can be found by differentiating from first principles. This involves finding the limit of the gradient of the chord joining any two neighbouring points on the curve $y = f(x)$

Consider the curve $y = \sin x$

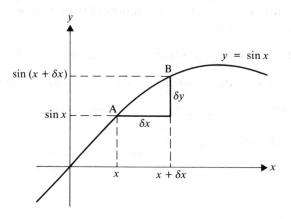

A is any point (x, y) on the curve $y = \sin x$ and at the nearby point B the x-coordinate is $x + \delta x$

At A, $y = \sin x$ and at B, $y = \sin(x + \delta x)$

Now
$$\frac{\delta y}{\delta x} = \frac{\sin(x + \delta x) - \sin x}{\delta x}$$

$$= \frac{2 \cos(x + \tfrac{1}{2}\delta x) \sin(\tfrac{1}{2}\delta x)}{\delta x} \qquad \text{(using a factor formula)}$$

$$= \frac{\cos(x + \tfrac{1}{2}\delta x) \sin(\tfrac{1}{2}\delta x)}{\tfrac{1}{2}\delta x}$$

370

Then, *provided that x is measured in radians,*

$$\text{as} \quad \delta x \rightarrow 0, \quad \cos(x + \tfrac{1}{2}\delta x) \rightarrow \cos x \quad \text{and} \quad \frac{\sin\left(\tfrac{1}{2}\delta x\right)}{\tfrac{1}{2}\delta x} \rightarrow 1$$

$$\therefore \qquad \frac{dy}{dx} = \lim_{\delta x \to 0} \frac{\delta y}{\delta x} = \lim_{\delta x \to 0} \frac{\cos(x + \tfrac{1}{2}\delta x)\sin\left(\tfrac{1}{2}\delta x\right)}{\tfrac{1}{2}\delta x} = \cos x$$

i.e.

$$\text{if} \quad y = \sin x \quad \text{then} \quad \frac{dy}{dx} = \cos x$$

In a similar way it can be shown that

$$\text{if} \quad y = \cos x \quad \text{then} \quad \frac{dy}{dx} = -\sin x$$

These two results can be quoted whenever they are needed.

It is important to realise that they are valid only when x is measured in radians.

Throughout all subsequent work on the calculus of trig functions in this book, the angle is measured in radians unless it is stated otherwise.

Examples 23a

1. Find the smallest positive value of x for which there is a stationary value of the function $x + 2\cos x$

$$f(x) = x + 2\cos x \qquad \Rightarrow \qquad f'(x) = 1 - 2\sin x$$
$$\text{where} \quad f'(x) = \frac{d}{dx}f(x)$$

For stationary values $f'(x) = 0$

i.e. $\qquad\qquad 1 - 2\sin x = 0 \qquad \Rightarrow \qquad \sin x = \tfrac{1}{2}$

The smallest positive angle with a sine of $\tfrac{1}{2}$ is $\tfrac{1}{6}\pi$

NOTE that the answer *must* be given in radians because the rule used to differentiate $\cos x$ is valid only for an angle in radians.

2. Find the smallest positive value of θ for which the curve
$y = 2\theta - 3 \sin \theta$ has a gradient of $\frac{1}{2}$

$$y = 2\theta - 3 \sin \theta \quad \text{gives} \quad \frac{dy}{d\theta} = 2 - 3 \cos \theta$$

when $\dfrac{dy}{d\theta} = \frac{1}{2}$ $\qquad 2 - 3 \cos \theta = \frac{1}{2}$

$$3 \cos \theta = \frac{3}{2}$$

$$\cos \theta = \frac{1}{2}$$

The smallest positive value of θ for which $\cos \theta = \frac{1}{2}$, is $\frac{1}{3}\pi$

EXERCISE 23a

1. By differentiating from first principles, show that
$$\frac{d}{dx}(\cos x) = -\sin x$$

2. Write down the derivative of each of the following expressions.
   (a) $\sin x - \cos x$ (b) $\sin \theta + 4$ (c) $3 \cos \theta$
   (d) $5 \sin \theta - 6$ (e) $2 \cos \theta + 3 \sin \theta$ (f) $4 \sin x - 5 - 6 \cos x$

3. Find the gradient of each curve at the point whose x-coordinate is given.
   (a) $y = \cos x$; $\frac{1}{2}\pi$ (b) $y = \sin x$; 0
   (c) $y = \cos x + \sin x$; π (d) $y = x - \sin x$; $\frac{1}{2}\pi$
   (e) $y = 2 \sin x - x^2$; $-\pi$ (f) $y = -4 \cos x$; $\frac{1}{2}\pi$

4. For each of the following curves find the smallest positive value of θ at which the gradient of the curve has the given value.
   (a) $y = 2 \cos \theta$; -1 (b) $y = \theta + \cos \theta$; $\frac{1}{2}$
   (c) $y = \sin \theta + \cos \theta$; 0 (d) $y = \sin \theta + 2\theta$; 1

5. Considering only positive values of x, locate the first two turning points on each of the following curves and determine whether they are maximum or minimum points.
   (a) $2 \sin x - x$ (b) $x + 2 \cos x$
   In each case illustrate your solution by a sketch.

6. Find the equation of the tangent to the curve $y = \cos\theta + 3\sin\theta$ at the point where $\theta = \frac{1}{2}\pi$

7. Find the equation of the normal to the curve $y = x^2 + \cos x$ at the point where $x = \pi$

8. Find the coordinates of a point on the curve $y = \sin x + \cos x$ at which the tangent is parallel to the line $y = x$

COMPOUND FUNCTIONS

The variety of functions which can be handled when they occur in products, quotients and functions of a function, now includes the sine and cosine ratios.

Differentiation of $\sin f(x)$

If $y = \sin f(x)$ then using $u = f(x)$ gives $y = \sin u$

Then $\qquad \dfrac{dy}{dx} = \dfrac{dy}{du} \times \dfrac{du}{dx} \qquad \Rightarrow \qquad \dfrac{dy}{dx} = \cos u \, \dfrac{du}{dx}$

i.e. $\qquad \dfrac{d}{dx}\{\sin f(x)\} = f'(x)\cos f(x)$

Similarly $\qquad \dfrac{d}{dx}\{\cos f(x)\} = -f'(x)\sin f(x)$

e.g. $\qquad \dfrac{d}{dx}\sin e^x = e^x \cos e^x \quad$ and $\quad \dfrac{d}{dx}\cos \ln x = -\dfrac{1}{x}\sin \ln x$

In particular $\qquad \dfrac{d}{dx}(\sin ax) = a\cos ax$

and $\qquad \dfrac{d}{dx}(\cos ax) = -a\sin ax$

These results are quotable.

Examples 23b

1. Differentiate $\cos\left(\frac{1}{6}\pi - 3x\right)$ with respect to x

$$\frac{d}{dx}\left\{\cos\left(\tfrac{1}{6}\pi - 3x\right)\right\} = -(-3)\sin\left(\tfrac{1}{6}\pi - 3x\right)$$

$$= 3\sin\left(\tfrac{1}{6}\pi - 3x\right)$$

2. Find the derivative of $\dfrac{e^x}{\sin x}$

$$y = \frac{e^x}{\sin x} = \frac{u}{v}$$

where $u = e^x$ and $v = \sin x$

$$\Rightarrow \qquad \frac{du}{dx} = e^x \quad \text{and} \quad \frac{dv}{dx} = \cos x$$

$$\frac{dy}{dx} = \left(v\frac{du}{dx} - u\frac{dv}{dx}\right)\Big/v^2 = \frac{e^x\sin x - e^x\cos x}{\sin^2 x}$$

$$\therefore \qquad \frac{d}{dx}\left(\frac{e^x}{\sin x}\right) = \frac{e^x}{\sin^2 x}(\sin x - \cos x)$$

3. Find $\dfrac{dy}{d\theta}$ if $y = \cos^3\theta$

$$y = \cos^3\theta = [\cos\theta]^3$$

$$\therefore \qquad y = u^3 \quad \text{where} \quad u = \cos\theta$$

$$\frac{dy}{d\theta} = \frac{dy}{du}\frac{du}{d\theta} = (3u^2)(-\sin\theta) = 3(\cos\theta)^2(-\sin\theta)$$

$$\therefore \qquad y = \cos^3\theta \qquad \Rightarrow \qquad \frac{dy}{d\theta} = -3\cos^2\theta\sin\theta$$

This is one example of a general rule, i.e.

and

$$\text{if } y = \cos^n x \quad \text{then} \quad \frac{dy}{dx} = -n \cos^{n-1} x \sin x$$

$$\text{if } y = \sin^n x \quad \text{then} \quad \frac{dy}{dx} = n \sin^{n-1} x \cos x$$

EXERCISE 23b

Differentiate each of the following functions with respect to x

1. $\sin 4x$

2. $\cos(\pi - 2x)$

3. $\sin(\frac{1}{2}x + \pi)$

4. $\dfrac{\sin x}{x}$

5. $\dfrac{\cos x}{e^x}$

6. $\sqrt{\sin x}$

7. $\sin^2 x$

8. $\sin x \cos x$

9. $e^{\sin x}$

10. $\ln(\cos x)$

11. $e^x \cos x$

12. $x^2 \sin x$

13. $\sin x^2$

14. $e^{\cos x}$

15. $\ln \sin^3 x$

16. $\sec x$, i.e. $\dfrac{1}{\cos x}$

17. $\tan x$, i.e. $\dfrac{\sin x}{\cos x}$

18. $\operatorname{cosec} x$

19. $\cot x$

Using the answers to Questions 9 to 12, we can now make a complete list of the derivatives of the basic trig functions:

function	derivative
$\sin x$	$\cos x$
$\cos x$	$-\sin x$
$\tan x$	$\sec^2 x$
$\cot x$	$-\operatorname{cosec}^2 x$
$\sec x$	$\sec x \tan x$
$\operatorname{cosec} x$	$-\operatorname{cosec} x \cot x$

DIFFERENTIATING INVERSE TRIG FUNCTIONS

In the previous section the derivative of a log function was found, without differentiating from first principles, by treating it as the inverse of an exponential function. A similar approach is used to find the derivative of each of the inverse trig functions.

Differentiation of arcsin x

If $y = \arcsin x$, the inverse relationship is $x = \sin y$ and this can be differentiated.

We can also use the property proved on page 340

that
$$\frac{dy}{dx} = 1 \bigg/ \frac{dx}{dy}$$

Hence if $\quad x = \sin y \quad$ then $\quad \dfrac{dx}{dy} = \cos y \quad \Rightarrow \quad \dfrac{dy}{dx} = \dfrac{1}{\cos y}$

Now $\cos^2 y = 1 - \sin^2 y = 1 - x^2$

Therefore
$$\frac{dy}{dx} = \frac{1}{\sqrt{(1 - x^2)}}$$

i.e.
$$\frac{d}{dx}(\arcsin x) = \frac{1}{\sqrt{(1 - x^2)}}$$

Remember that $y = \arcsin x$ exists only within the range $-\frac{1}{2}\pi \leqslant y \leqslant \frac{1}{2}\pi$. For these values of y, $\cos y \geqslant 0$, therefore $\cos y = \sqrt{(1 - x^2)}$ and not $-\sqrt{(1 - x^2)}$

Similarly
$$\frac{d}{dx}(\arccos x) = -\frac{1}{\sqrt{(1 - x^2)}}$$

and
$$\frac{d}{dx}(\arctan x) = \frac{1}{1 + x^2}$$

It is left to the reader to prove these results in the next exercise.

Example 23c _____

Differentiate with respect to x

(a) $\arcsin e^x$ (b) $x \arctan x$

(a) $\arcsin e^x$ is an inverse trig function of an exponential function so the chain rule can be used.

$$\frac{d}{dx}(\arcsin e^x) = \frac{1}{\sqrt{\{1 - (e^x)^2\}}} e^x$$

$$= \frac{e^x}{\sqrt{(1 - e^{2x})}}$$

(b) $\dfrac{d}{dx}(x \arctan x) = \arctan x + x \dfrac{d}{dx} \arctan x$

$$= \arctan x + \frac{x}{1 + x^2}$$

_____

EXERCISE 23c

1. Show that $\dfrac{d}{dx}(\arccos x) = -\dfrac{1}{\sqrt{(1 - x^2)}}$

2. Show that $\dfrac{d}{dx}(\arctan x) = \dfrac{1}{1 + x^2}$

Differentiate each function with respect to x

3. $x^2 \arcsin x$ 4. $(\arctan x)^2$ 5. $\arcsin 3x$

6. $e^{\arctan x}$ 7. $\ln(\arcsin x)$ 8. $\arccos x^3$

EXTENDING THE CHAIN RULE

We have already seen that the chain rule can be used to write down directly the derivative of $y = fg(x)$ where $u = g(x)$

i.e. $\dfrac{dy}{dx} = \dfrac{dy}{du} \dfrac{du}{dx} = f'(u)g'(x)$

e.g. $\dfrac{d}{dx} \ln(\tan x) = \dfrac{1}{\tan x}(\sec^2 x)$

This direct differentiation of a succession of functions of x can be extended to deal quickly and easily with $y = \text{fgh}(x)$ where $y = \text{f}(u)$, $u = \text{g}(v)$ and $v = \text{h}(x)$,

i.e.
$$\frac{d}{dx}\{\text{fgh}(x)\} = \frac{dy}{du}\frac{du}{dv}\frac{dv}{dx} = \text{f}'(u)\text{g}'(v)\text{h}'(x)$$

e.g.
$$\frac{d}{dx}\left(e^{\sin x^2}\right) = \left(e^{\sin x^2}\right)(\cos x^2)(2x)$$

and
$$\frac{d}{dx}\{\ln(\cos x)\}^3 = 3\{\ln(\cos x)\}^2\left(\frac{1}{\cos x}\right)(-\sin x)$$

This extended use of the chain rule allows quite complex functions to be differentiated without *writing down* detailed substitutions.
The reader will find it helpful to express the given function in words before applying the chain rule as this automatically places the operators in the correct order for differentiation.

Consider, for example, the function $\ln(\sin e^x)$, which is

a log function of a sine function of an exponential function.

Using the chain rule to write down the derivative, we apply in succession,

the rule for differentiating a log function
the rule for differentiating a sine function
the rule for differentiating an exponential function

i.e.
$$\frac{d}{dx}\{\ln(\sin e^x)\} = \left(\frac{1}{\sin e^x}\right)(\cos e^x)(e^x)$$

The reader has already had practice in using the chain rule to differentiate simple expressions of the type $\text{gf}(x)$. The real benefit of the chain rule is that the derivatives of apparently complicated functions, $\text{fgh}(x)$ or even $\text{fghj}(x)$, can be written down just as easily as for simpler ones.

EXERCISE 23d

Questions 1 to 4 are simple expressions. The reader is advised to revise the use of the chain rule on these easy examples before going on to the rest of the exercise. Some of the remaining questions look more complicated than would be found in most A-level examination papers but they are fun to try and surprisingly easy.

Using the chain rule to differentiate each function

1. $\sqrt{(1 + \ln x)}$

2. $\cos(x^2 + 3)$

3. $e^{(x^3 - x)}$

4. $\sin(\ln x)$

5. $\ln(\cos x^2)$

6. $\left(1 + e^{x^2}\right)^2$

7. $\sqrt{(3 - \sin^2 x)}$

8. $\{\ln(\tan x)\}^2$

9. $e^{\sqrt{(2 - x^2)}}$

10. $\cos^2(x^2 + 1)$

Compound Functions of More Than One Type

Example 23e

Differentiate $e^{x^2}\sin x$ with respect to x

If $y = e^{x^2}\sin x$ then, using $u = e^{x^2}$ and $v = \sin x$ gives $y = uv$

Now u is a function of a function which can be differentiated mentally giving $\dfrac{du}{dx} = 2xe^{x^2}$. Then the product formula can be used.

$$\frac{dy}{dx} = v\frac{du}{dx} + u\frac{dv}{dx} = \{\sin x\}\{2xe^{x^2}\} + e^{x^2}\cos x$$

EXERCISE 23e

Differentiate each function with respect to x

1. $e^{x^2}\sin x$

2. $\dfrac{\cos^2 x}{x}$

3. $x(\ln \sin x)$

4. $\dfrac{x^2 - 1}{\ln x}$

5. $e^x\sqrt{(x^2 + 2)}$

6. $\dfrac{\ln x}{\sqrt{\cos x}}$

7. $(x + 1)e^{\sin x}$

8. $\dfrac{x^2}{\sin^2 x}$

9. $e^{x^2}\ln x$

MIXED EXERCISE 23

This exercise contains a variety of functions of all the types covered in Chapters 19, 20 and 23. Consider carefully what method to use in each case and do not forget to check first whether a given function has a standard derivative.

Find the derivative of each function in Questions 1 to 26.

1. (a) $-\sin 4\theta$ (b) $\theta - \cos \theta$ (c) $\sin^3 \theta + \sin 3\theta$

2. (a) $x^3 + e^x$ (b) $e^{(2x+3)}$ (c) $e^x \sin x$

3. (a) $\ln \frac{1}{3} x^{-3}$ (b) $\ln 2/x^2$ (c) $\ln \sqrt{x}/4$

4. (a) $3 \sin x - e^{-x}$ (b) $\ln x^{1/2} - \frac{1}{2} \cos x$
    (c) $x^4 + 4e^x - \ln 4x$ (d) $\frac{1}{2} e^{-x} + x^{-1/2} - \ln \frac{1}{2} x$

5. $(x+1)\ln x$ **6.** $\sin^2 3x$ **7.** $(4x-1)^{2/3}$

8. $(3\sqrt{x} - 2x)^2$ **9.** $\dfrac{(x^4 - 1)}{(x+1)^3}$ **10.** $\dfrac{\ln x}{\ln(x-1)}$

11. $\ln \cot x$ **12.** $x^2 \sin x$ **13.** $\dfrac{e^x}{x-1}$

14. $\dfrac{1 + \sin x}{1 - \sin x}$ **15.** $x^2 \sqrt{(x-1)}$ **16.** $(1-x^2)(1-x)^2$

17. $\ln \sqrt{\dfrac{(x+3)^3}{(x^2+2)}}$ **18.** $\dfrac{e^x \cos x}{x^5}$ **19.** $\sin x \cos^3 x$

20. $e^{\cos^2 x}$ **21.** $e^{\arcsin x}$ **22.** $(\arccos x)^3$

23. $\arctan e^x$ **24.** xa^x **25.** $\log_a(x^2 + 1)$

26. Find the value(s) of x for which the following functions have stationary values.
    (a) $3x - e^x$ (b) $x^2 - 2\ln x$ (c) $\ln 1/x + 4x$

In each Question from 27 to 30, find
(a) the gradient of the curve at the given point,
(b) the equation of the tangent to the curve at that point,
(c) the equation of the normal to the curve at that point.

27. $y = \sin x - \cos x$; $x = \frac{1}{2}\pi$ **28.** $y = x + e^x$; $x = 1$

29. $y = 1 + x + \sin x$; $x = 0$ **30.** $y = 3 - x^2 + \ln x$; $x = 1$

31. Considering only positive values of θ, locate the first two turning points, if there are two, on each of the following curves and determine whether they are maximum or minimum points.

    (a) $y = 1 - \sin x$ (b) $y = \frac{1}{2}x + \cos x$ (c) $y = e^x - 3x$

32. Find the coordinates of a point on the curve where the tangent is parallel to the given line.

    (a) $y = 3x - 2\cos x$; $y = 4x$ (b) $y = 2\ln x - x$; $y = x$

CHAPTER 24

DIFFERENTIATING IMPLICIT AND PARAMETRIC FUNCTIONS

IMPLICIT FUNCTIONS

All the differentiation carried out so far has involved equations that could be expressed in the form $y = f(x)$

However the equations of some curves, for example $x^2 - y^2 + y = 1$, cannot easily be written in this way, as it is too difficult to isolate y

A relationship of this type, where y is not given explicitly as a function of x, is called an *implicit function*, i.e. it is *implied* in the equation that $y = f(x)$

TO DIFFERENTIATE AN IMPLICIT FUNCTION

The method we use is to differentiate, term by term, with respect to x, but first we need to know how to differentiate terms like y^2 with respect to x

If $\qquad g(y) = y^2$ and $y = f(x)$

then $\qquad g(y) = \{f(x)\}^2$ which is a function of a function

Using the mental substitution $u = f(x)$ we have

$$\frac{d}{dx}\{f(x)\}^2 = 2\{f(x)\}\left(\frac{d}{dx}f(x)\right) = 2y\left(\frac{dy}{dx}\right) = \left(\frac{d}{dy}g(y)\right)\left(\frac{dy}{dx}\right)$$

In general, $\qquad\qquad \dfrac{d}{dx}g(y) = \left(\dfrac{d}{dy}g(y)\right)\left(\dfrac{dy}{dx}\right)$

e.g. $\dfrac{d}{dx}y^3 = 3y^2\dfrac{dy}{dx}$ and $\dfrac{d}{dx}e^y = e^y\dfrac{dy}{dx}$

We can now differentiate, term by term with respect to x, the example considered above, i.e.

if
$$x^2 - y^2 + y = 1$$

then
$$\frac{d}{dx}(x^2) - \frac{d}{dx}(y^2) + \frac{dy}{dx} = \frac{d}{dx}(1)$$

$\Rightarrow$
$$2x - 2y\frac{dy}{dx} + \frac{dy}{dx} = 0$$

Hence
$$2x = \frac{dy}{dx}(2y - 1) \qquad \Rightarrow \qquad \frac{dy}{dx} = \frac{2x}{(2y - 1)}$$

Examples 24a

1. Differentiate each equation with respect to x and hence find $\dfrac{dy}{dx}$ in terms of x and y.

(a) $x^3 + xy^2 - y^3 = 5$ (b) $y = xe^y$

(a) If $x^3 + xy^2 - y^3 = 5$ then, differentiating term by term,

$$\frac{d}{dx}(x^3) + \frac{d}{dx}(xy^2) - \frac{d}{dx}(y^3) = \frac{d}{dx}(5)$$

The term xy^2 is a product so we differentiate it using the product rule, i.e.

$$\frac{d}{dx}(xy^2) = y^2\frac{d}{dx}(x) + x\frac{d}{dx}(y^2) = y^2 + (x)(2y)\frac{dy}{dx}$$

$\therefore$
$$3x^2 + y^2 + 2xy\frac{dy}{dx} - 3y^2\frac{dy}{dx} = 0$$

Hence
$$\frac{dy}{dx} = \frac{(3x^2 + y^2)}{y(3y - 2x)}$$

(b) If $y = xe^y$ then
$$\frac{dy}{dx} = \frac{d}{dx}(xe^y)$$

$$= e^y\frac{d}{dx}(x) + x\frac{d}{dx}(e^y)$$

$\Rightarrow$
$$\frac{dy}{dx} = e^y + xe^y\frac{dy}{dx}$$

Hence
$$\frac{dy}{dx} = \frac{e^y}{1 - xe^y}$$

2. If $e^x y = \sin x$ show that $\dfrac{d^2 y}{dx^2} + 2\dfrac{dy}{dx} + 2y = 0$

In a problem of this type it is tempting to express $e^x y = \sin x$ in the form $y = e^{-x}\sin x$, find $\dfrac{dy}{dx}$ and $\dfrac{d^2 y}{dx^2}$ and show that they satisfy the given equation, which is called a *differential equation*. However it is much more direct to differentiate the implicit equation as given.

Differentiating $e^x y = \sin x$ w.r.t. x gives

$$e^x y + e^x \frac{dy}{dx} = \cos x$$

Differentiating again w.r.t. x gives

$$\left(e^x y + e^x \frac{dy}{dx} \right) + \left(e^x \frac{dy}{dx} + e^x \frac{d^2 y}{dx^2} \right) = -\sin x = -e^x y$$

Hence $\quad e^x \dfrac{d^2 y}{dx^2} + 2e^x \dfrac{dy}{dx} + 2e^x y = 0$

There is no finite value of x for which $e^x = 0$ so we can divide the equation by e^x

i.e. $\quad \dfrac{d^2 y}{dx^2} + 2\dfrac{dy}{dx} + 2y = 0$

---

3. Find the equation of the tangent at the point (x_1, y_1) to the curve with equation $x^2 - 2y^2 - 6y = 0$

To find the equation of the tangent we need the gradient of the curve and in this case it must be found by implicit differentiation.

$$x^2 - 2y^2 - 6y = 0 \quad \Rightarrow \quad 2x - 2\left(2y\frac{dy}{dx} \right) - 6\frac{dy}{dx} = 0$$

$$\Rightarrow \quad \frac{dy}{dx} = \frac{x}{(3 + 2y)}$$

$\therefore$ the gradient of the tangent at the point (x_1, y_1) is $\dfrac{x_1}{(3 + 2y_1)}$ and the

equation of the tangent is $y - y_1 = \dfrac{x_1}{(3 + 2y_1)}(x - x_1)$ which

simplifies to $xx_1 - 2yy_1 - 3(y + y_1) = x_1^2 - 2y_1^2 - 6y_1$

Because (x_1, y_1) is on the given curve, $x_1^2 - 2y_1^2 - 6y_1 = 0$, so the equation of the tangent becomes

$$xx_1 - 2yy_1 - 3(y + y_1) = 0$$

Note that in the last example the equation of the curve can be converted into the equation of the tangent by changing x^2 into xx_1, y^2 into yy_1 and y into $\frac{1}{2}(y + y_1)$.

In fact, for any curve whose equation is of degree two, the equation of the tangent at (x_1, y_1) can be written down directly by making the replacements listed above, together with two more, i.e.

$$x \;\rightarrow\; \tfrac{1}{2}(x + x_1) \quad \text{and} \quad xy \;\rightarrow\; \tfrac{1}{2}(xy_1 + x_1 y)$$

This property can be applied to advantage when the numerical values of the coordinates of the point of contact are known,

e.g. the equation of the tangent at the point $(1, -1)$ to the curve

$$3x^2 - 7y^2 + 4xy - 8x = 0$$

can be written down as

$$3x(1) - 7y(-1) + 2\{x(-1) + (1)y\} - 4(x + 1) = 0$$

i.e. $9y - 3x = 4$

Question 18 in the following exercise gives the reader the opportunity to justify using these mechanical replacements in the equation of a curve, to give the equation of a tangent.

Note that, although this method allows the equation of a tangent to be *written down*, its use is not suitable when the *derivation* of the equation is required.

EXERCISE 24a

Differentiate the following equations with respect to x

1. $x^2 + y^2 = 4$

2. $x^2 + xy + y^2 = 0$

3. $x(x + y) = y^2$

4. $\dfrac{1}{x} + \dfrac{1}{y} = e^y$

5. $\dfrac{1}{x^2} + \dfrac{1}{y^2} = \dfrac{1}{4}$

6. $\dfrac{x^2}{4} - \dfrac{y^2}{9} = 1$

7. $\sin x + \sin y = 1$

8. $\sin x \cos y = 2$

9. $xe^y = x + 1$

10. $\sqrt{\{(1 + y)(1 + x)\}} = x$

11. Find $\dfrac{dy}{dx}$ as a function of x if $y^2 = 2x + 1$

12. Find $\dfrac{d^2y}{dx^2}$ as a function of x if $\sin y + \cos y = x$

13. Find the gradient of $x^2 + y^2 = 9$ at the points where $x = 1$

14. If $y \cos x = e^x$ show that $\dfrac{d^2y}{dx^2} - 2 \tan x \dfrac{dy}{dx} - 2y = 0$

15. Write down the equation of the tangent to
    (a) $x^2 - 3y^2 = 4y$ (b) $x^2 + xy + y^2 = 3$
    at the point (x_1, y_1).

16. Show that the equation of the tangent to $x^2 + xy + y = 0$ at the point (x_1, y_1) is
$$x(2x_1 + y_1) + y(x_1 + 1) + y_1 = 0$$

17. Write down the equation of the tangent at $(1, \tfrac{1}{3})$ to the curve whose equation is
$$2x^2 + 3y^2 - 3x + 2y = 0$$

18. Show that the equation of the tangent at (x_1, y_1) to the curve $ax^2 + by^2 + cxy + dx = 0$ is
$$axx_1 + byy_1 + \tfrac{1}{2}c(xy_1 + yx_1) + \tfrac{1}{2}d(x + x_1) = 0$$

19. Given that $\sin y = 2 \sin x$ show that $\left(\dfrac{dy}{dx}\right)^2 = 1 + 3 \sec^2 y$. By differentiating this equation with respect to x show that

$$\frac{d^2 y}{dx^2} = 3 \sec^2 y \tan y$$

and hence that $\cot y \dfrac{d^2 y}{dx^2} - \left(\dfrac{dy}{dx}\right)^2 + 1 = 0$

LOGARITHMIC DIFFERENTIATION

The advantage of simplifying a logarithmic expression before attempting to differentiate it has already been noted.

We are now going to examine some equations which are awkward to differentiate as they stand but which are much easier to deal with if we first take logs of both sides of the equation. The types of equation where this method is particularly important are

1) those in which the variable is an index

2) complicated functions involving fractions, roots, products, etc.

The process used is called *logarithmic differentiation*.

Examples 24b

1. Differentiate x^x with respect to x

$$y = x^x$$

$$\ln y = x \ln x$$

thus

$$\frac{1}{y} \frac{dy}{dx} = x \frac{1}{x} + \ln x$$

$\Rightarrow$

$$\frac{dy}{dx} = y(1 + \ln x)$$

Therefore

$$\frac{d}{dx}(x^x) = x^x(1 + \ln x)$$

2. If $y = \dfrac{x\sqrt{(x^2-1)}}{x+2}$ find $\dfrac{dy}{dx}$

$y = \dfrac{x\sqrt{(x^2-1)}}{x+2}$ $\Rightarrow$ $\ln y = \ln x + \tfrac{1}{2}\ln(x^2-1) - \ln(x+2)$

$\therefore$ $\dfrac{1}{y}\dfrac{dy}{dx} = \dfrac{1}{x} + \dfrac{1}{2}\left(\dfrac{2x}{x^2-1}\right) - \dfrac{1}{x+2}$

$\Rightarrow$ $\dfrac{dy}{dx} = (y)\left(\dfrac{x^3+4x^2-2}{x(x^2-1)(x+2)}\right)$

$= \left(\dfrac{x\sqrt{(x^2-1)}}{x+2}\right)\left(\dfrac{x^3+4x^2-2}{x(x^2-1)(x+2)}\right)$

i.e. $\dfrac{dy}{dx} = \dfrac{x^3+4x^2-2}{(x+2)^2\sqrt{(x^2-1)}}$

---

3. Differentiate the equation $x = y^x$ with respect to x

$x = y^x$ $\Rightarrow$ $\ln x = x \ln y$

$\therefore$ $\dfrac{1}{x} = \ln y + (x)\left(\dfrac{1}{y}\dfrac{dy}{dx}\right)$

i.e. $x^2\dfrac{dy}{dx} + xy \ln y = y$

Note that in the third example it is not easy to express $\dfrac{dy}{dx}$ as a function of x, because it is difficult in the first place to find y in terms of x. So although the usual practice is to give a derived function in terms of x it is not always possible, or sensible, to do so.

Differentiation of a^x where a is a Constant

The basic rule for differentiating an exponential function applies when the base is e but not for any other base. So for a^x, where we need another approach, we use logarithmic differentiation.

Using $\qquad y = a^x$ gives $\ln y = x \ln a$

Differentiating w.r.t. x gives $\qquad \dfrac{1}{y} \dfrac{dy}{dx} = \ln a$

Hence $\qquad \dfrac{dy}{dx} = y \ln a = a^x \ln a$

i.e. $\qquad \dfrac{d}{dx} a^x = a^x \ln a$

This result is quotable.

EXERCISE 24b

Differentiate each equation with respect to x

1. $x^y = e^x$ $\qquad$ **2.** $x^y = (y + 1)$ $\qquad$ **3.** $y = (x + x^2)^x$

Find $\dfrac{dy}{dx}$ if

4. $y = \dfrac{x}{(x + 2)(x - 4)}$ $\qquad$ **5.** $y = \dfrac{x^2}{(x - 1)(x - 3)}$

6. $y = (1 - x)^5 (x^2 + 2)$ $\qquad$ **7.** $y = \sqrt{\{(x + 1)(x - 3)^3\}}$

8. $y = \dfrac{x}{(x + 2)^2 (x^2 - 1)}$ $\qquad$ **9.** $y = \dfrac{1}{\sqrt{\{(x^2 + 4)(3x - 2)\}}}$

PARAMETRIC EQUATIONS

Sometimes a direct relationship between x and y is awkward to analyse; in such cases it is often easier to express x and y each in terms of a third variable, called a *parameter*.

Consider, for example, the equations

$$x = t^3$$

$$y = t^2 - t$$

The direct relationship between x and y can be found by eliminating t from these two *parametric equations*. It is $y = x^{2/3} - x^{1/3}$

While the gradient and general shape of the curve, as well as the equation of a tangent or a normal, can be obtained from the cartesian equation, they are often more simply derived from the parametric equations.

Sketching a Curve Given in Parametric Form

To get an idea of the shape of the curve whose parametric equations are

$$x = t^3 \quad \text{and} \quad y = t^2 - t$$

we can

1) *plot* a small number of points by calculating the values of x and y that correspond to certain chosen values of t,

t	-2	-1	0	1	2
x	-8	-1	0	1	8
y	6	2	0	0	2

2) examine the behaviour of the curve as $t \to \pm\infty$,

as $t \to \infty$, $\quad x \to \infty \quad$ and $\quad y \to \infty$

as $t \to -\infty$, $\quad x \to -\infty \quad$ and $\quad y \to \infty$

There is no finite value of t for which either x or y is undefined so it is reasonable to assume that the curve is continuous.

Based on all this information, a sketch of the curve can now be made.

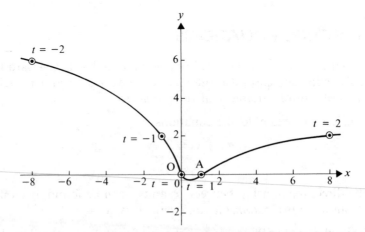

The location of turning points is a further aid to curve sketching. To use this we need to be able to find the gradient of a curve given parametrically.

FINDING THE GRADIENT FUNCTION USING PARAMETRIC EQUATIONS

If both x and y are given as functions of t then a small increase of δt in the value of t results in corresponding small increases of δx and δy in the values of x and y

As $\delta t \to 0$, δx and δy also approach zero, therefore

$$\frac{dy}{dx} = \frac{dy}{dt} \times \frac{dt}{dx}$$

But $\dfrac{dt}{dx} = 1 \Big/ \dfrac{dx}{dt}$

Therefore

$$\frac{dy}{dx} = \frac{dy}{dt} \Big/ \frac{dx}{dt}$$

Hence, for the parametric equations considered above, i.e. $x = t^3$ and $y = t^2 - t$, we have

$$\frac{dy}{dx} = \frac{(2t - 1)}{3t^2}$$

Each point on the curve is defined by a value of t which also gives the value of $\dfrac{dy}{dx}$ at that point. Similarly, the value(s) of t where $\dfrac{dy}{dx}$ has a special value lead to the coordinates of the relevant point(s) on the curve.

At turning point(s) $\dfrac{dy}{dx} = 0$ $\Rightarrow$ $2t - 1 = 0$ $\Rightarrow$ $t = \frac{1}{2}$

$t = \frac{1}{2}$ $\Rightarrow$ $x = \frac{1}{8}$ and $y = -\frac{1}{4}$ therefore $(\frac{1}{8}, -\frac{1}{4})$ is a turning point.

In this case the curve sketched before the turning point was known is now only marginally improved, showing that it is not always necessary to carry out this investigation. Some curves, on the other hand, would be difficult to draw without finding their turning points.

Examples 24c

1. Find the cartesian equation of the curve whose parametric equations are

    (a) $x = t^2$ (b) $x = \cos\theta$ (c) $x = 2t$

          $y = 2t$ $y = \sin\theta$ $y = 2/t$

(a) $y = 2t \quad \Rightarrow \quad t = \frac{1}{2}y$

$\therefore \quad\quad x = t^2 \quad \Rightarrow \quad x = (\frac{1}{2}y)^2 = \frac{1}{4}y^2 \quad \Rightarrow \quad y^2 = 4x$

(b) Using $\cos^2\theta + \sin^2\theta = 1$ where $\cos\theta = x$ and $\sin\theta = y$ gives

$$x^2 + y^2 = 1$$

(c) $y = 2/t \quad \Rightarrow \quad t = 2/y$

$\therefore \quad\quad\quad x = 2t \quad \Rightarrow \quad x = 4/y \quad \Rightarrow \quad xy = 4$

---

2. Find the stationary point on the curve whose parametric equations are $x = t^3$, $y = (t + 1)^2$ and determine its nature. Sketch the curve, showing the stationary point and the behaviour of the curve as $x \to \pm\infty$

$$\frac{dy}{dx} = \frac{dy}{dt} \Big/ \frac{dx}{dt} = \frac{2(t + 1)}{3t^2}$$

At stationary points $\dfrac{dy}{dx} = 0$ i.e. $t = -1$

When $t = -1$, $x = -1$ and $y = 0$

Therefore the stationary point is $(-1, 0)$

To determine the nature of the stationary point we examine the sign of $\dfrac{dy}{dx}$ in the neighbourhood of the point by first choosing appropriate values for x and then finding the corresponding values of t

The equations $x = t^3$ and $y = (t + 1)^2$ show that there is no finite value of t for which either x or y is not defined, so the curve is continuous. Also there is no other stationary point.

Value of t	$-\sqrt[3]{2}$	-1	0
Sign of $\dfrac{dy}{dx}$	$-$ $\searrow$	0 $-$	$+$ $\nearrow$

Hence $(-1, 0)$ is a minimum point.

Also

t	-3	-2	1	2	3
x	-27	-8	1	8	27
y	4	1	4	9	16

The equations $x = t^3$ and $y = (t + 1)^2$ show that there is no finite value of t for which either x or y is undefined, so the curve is continuous.

Also we see that,

$$\text{as } t \to \infty, \quad x \to \infty \quad \text{and } y \to \infty$$

and $\qquad$ $$\text{as } t \to -\infty, \quad x \to -\infty \quad \text{and } y \to \infty$$

The curve can now be sketched.

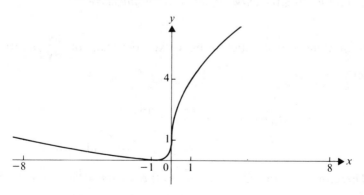

3. The parametric equations of a curve are

$$x = \sin^2\theta, \quad y = 1 + 2\sin\theta$$

Show that the equation of the tangent to the curve at the point $P(\sin^2\theta, 1 + 2\sin\theta)$ is $y = x + \sin\theta + \sin^2\theta$ and find the point(s) where the tangent is parallel to the y-axis.

$$y = 1 + 2\sin\theta \quad \text{and} \quad x = \sin^2\theta$$

$\Rightarrow \qquad\qquad \dfrac{dy}{d\theta} = 2\cos\theta \qquad \text{and} \qquad \dfrac{dx}{d\theta} = 2\sin\theta\cos\theta$

$\therefore \qquad \dfrac{dy}{dx} = \dfrac{dy}{d\theta} \div \dfrac{dx}{d\theta} = \dfrac{2\cos\theta}{2\sin\theta\cos\theta}$

$$= \dfrac{1}{\sin\theta} \qquad\qquad (\text{provided that } \cos\theta \neq 0)$$

The equation of the tangent is given by $y - y_1 = m(x - x_1)$, i.e.

$$y - (1 + 2\sin\theta) = \dfrac{1}{\sin\theta}(x - \sin^2\theta)$$

$\Rightarrow \qquad\qquad\qquad y\sin\theta = x - \sin^2\theta + \sin\theta + 2\sin^2\theta$

i.e. $\qquad\qquad\qquad y\sin\theta = x + \sin\theta + \sin^2\theta$

*This is the **general** equation of the tangent because it is the equation of the tangent to the given curve at **any** point on the curve.*

If the tangent is parallel to the y-axis, the value of $\dfrac{dy}{dx}$ is infinitely large,

i.e. $\qquad\qquad \dfrac{1}{\sin\theta} \to \infty \qquad \Rightarrow \qquad \sin\theta = 0$

$$\Rightarrow \qquad x = 0 \quad \text{and} \quad y = 1$$

Therefore the tangent is parallel to the y-axis at the point $(0, 1)$

4. Find the equation of the normal to the curve $x = t^2$, $y = t + 2/t$, at the point where $t = 1$. Show, without sketching the curve, that this normal does not cross the curve again.

$$x = t^2 \quad \text{and} \quad y = t + \frac{2}{t} \qquad \text{give} \qquad \frac{dy}{dt} = 1 - \frac{2}{t^2} \quad \text{and} \quad \frac{dx}{dt} = 2t$$

$$\therefore \qquad \frac{dy}{dx} = \frac{dy}{dt} \div \frac{dx}{dt} = \frac{1 - 2/t^2}{2t} = \frac{t^2 - 2}{2t^3}$$

When $t = 1$; $x = 1$, $y = 3$ and $\dfrac{dy}{dx} = -\dfrac{1}{2}$

Therefore the gradient of the normal at $P(1, 3)$ is $\dfrac{-1}{-\frac{1}{2}} = 2$

The equation of this normal is $\qquad\qquad y - 3 = 2(x - 1)$
i.e. $\qquad\qquad\qquad\qquad\qquad\qquad\qquad y = 2x + 1$

All points for which $x = t^2$ and $y = t + 2/t$ are on the given curve, therefore, for any point that is on both the curve and the normal, these coordinates also satisfy the equation of the normal,
i.e., at points common to the curve and the normal,

$$t + \frac{2}{t} = 2t^2 + 1 \qquad \Rightarrow \qquad 2t^3 - t^2 + t - 2 = 0 \qquad\qquad [1]$$

If a cubic equation can be factorised, each factor equated to zero gives a root of the equation, just as in the case of a quadratic equation.

Now we know that one point where the curve and normal meet is the point where $t = 1$, so $t = 1$ is a root of [1] and $(t - 1)$ is a factor of the LHS,

i.e. $\qquad\qquad\qquad (t - 1)(2t^2 + t + 2) = 0$

Therefore, at any other point where the normal meets the curve, the value of t is a root of the equation $2t^2 + t + 2 = 0$

Checking the value of $b^2 - 4ac$ shows that this equation has no real roots so there are no more points where the normal meets the curve.

EXERCISE 24c

1. Find the gradient function of each of the following curves in terms of the parameter.

   (a) $x = 2t^2$, $y = t$ (b) $x = \sin\theta$, $y = \cos\theta$

   (c) $x = t$, $y = 4/t$

2. If $x = \dfrac{t}{1-t}$ and $y = \dfrac{t^2}{1-t}$, find $\dfrac{dy}{dx}$ in terms of t. What is the value of $\dfrac{dy}{dx}$ at the point where $x = 1$?

3. (a) If $x = t^2$ and $y = t^3$, find $\dfrac{dy}{dx}$ in terms of t

   (b) If $y = x^{3/2}$, find $\dfrac{dy}{dx}$

   (c) Explain the connection between these two results.

4. Find the cartesian equation of each of the curves given in Question 1 and hence find $\dfrac{dy}{dx}$. Show in each case that $\dfrac{dy}{dx}$ agrees with the gradient function found in Question 1.

5. Find the turning points of the curve whose parametric equations are $x = t$, $y = t^3 - t$, and distinguish between them.

6. A curve has parametric equations $x = \theta - \cos\theta$, $y = \sin\theta$ Find the coordinates of the points at which the gradient of this curve is zero.

7. Find the equation of the tangent to the curve $x = t^2$, $y = 4t$ at the point where $t = -1$

8. Find the equation of the general normal to the curve $x = t$, $y = 1/t$

9. Find the equation of the general tangent to the curve $x = t^2$, $y = 4t$

10. Find the equation of the normal to the curve $x = \cos\theta$, $y = \sin\theta$ at the point where $\theta = \frac{1}{4}\pi$. Find the coordinates of the point where this normal cuts the curve again.

11. The parametric equations of a curve are $x = e^t$ and $y = \sin t$.

   (a) Find the gradient function in terms of t

   (b) Find the equation of the curve in the form $y = f(x)$

   (c) Find $\dfrac{dy}{dx}$

   (d) Eliminate x from the result obtained in part (c) and compare with the answer to part (a).

12. The parametric equations of a curve are $x = t$ and $y = 1/t$
Find the general equation of the tangent to this curve (i.e. the equation at the point $(t, 1/t)$).
Find, in terms of t, the coordinates of the points at which the tangent cuts the x and y axes. Hence show that the area enclosed by this tangent and the coordinate axes is constant.

13. A curve has parametric equations $x = t^2$, $y = 4t$. Find the equation of the normal to this curve at the point $(t^2, 4t)$.
Find the coordinates of the point where this normal cuts the coordinate axes. Hence find, in terms of t, the area of the triangle enclosed by the normal and the axes.

MIXED EXERCISE 24

1. Differentiate with respect to x

   (a) y^4 (b) xy^2 (c) $1/y$ (d) $x \ln y$

   (e) $\sin y$ (f) e^y (g) $y \cos x$ (h) $y \cos y$

In each Question from 2 to 13, find $\dfrac{dy}{dx}$

2. $x^2 - 2y^2 = 4$ **3.** $1/x + 1/y = 2$

4. $x^2y^3 = 9$ **5.** $y = \dfrac{x^4(2 - x^2)}{(1 + x)^3}$

6. $yx^5 = \dfrac{(x - 1)^4}{(x + 3)}$ **7.** $x^2y^2 = \dfrac{(y + 1)}{(x + 1)}$

8. $x = t^2$, $y = t^3$ **9.** $x = (t + 1)^2$, $y = t^2 - 1$

10. $x = \sin^2\theta$, $y = \cos^3\theta$ **11.** $x = 4t$, $y = 4/t$

12. $y^2 - 2xy + 3y = 7x$ **13.** $x = \dfrac{t}{1-t}, \; y = \dfrac{t^2}{1-t}$

14. If $x = \sin t$ and $y = \cos 2t$, find $\dfrac{dy}{dx}$ in terms of x and prove that $\dfrac{d^2y}{dx^2} + 4 = 0$

15. If $x = e^t - t$ and $y = e^{2t} - 2t$, show that $\dfrac{dy}{dx} = 2(e^t + 1)$

CHAPTER 25

APPLICATIONS OF DIFFERENTIATION

RATE OF INCREASE

When the variation of y depends upon another variable x, then

$\dfrac{dy}{dx}$ gives the rate at which y increases compared with x

This fact forms the basis of methods which can be used to analyse practical situations in which two variables are related.

SMALL INCREMENTS

Consider two variables, x and y, related by the equation $y = f(x)$

If x increases by a small increment δx

then y increases by a corresponding small amount δy

Now $$\lim_{\delta x \to 0} \frac{\delta y}{\delta x} = \frac{dy}{dx}$$

so,

provided that δx is small, $\dfrac{\delta y}{\delta x} \approx \dfrac{dy}{dx} \quad \Rightarrow \quad \delta y \approx \dfrac{dy}{dx}(\delta x)$

or, alternatively, $\qquad \delta\{f(x)\} \approx f'(x)\,\delta x$

This approximation can be used to estimate the value of a function close to a known value, i.e. $y + \delta y$ can be estimated if y is known at a particular value of x

For example, knowing that $\ln 1 = 0,$ an approximate value for $\ln 1.1$ can be found from $y = \ln x$ as follows

$$y = \ln x \quad \longrightarrow \quad \frac{dy}{dx} = \frac{1}{x}$$

so

$$\delta y \approx \frac{dy}{dx}(\delta x) = \frac{1}{x}(\delta x)$$

Now x increases from 1 to 1.1, i.e. $\delta x = 0.1$

$\therefore$

$$\delta y \approx \tfrac{1}{1}(0.1)$$

Hence

$$\ln 1.1 = y + \delta y \approx (\ln 1) + 0.1$$

but $\ln 1 = 0$

$\therefore$

$$\ln 1.1 \approx 0.1$$

Examples 25a _____

1. Using $y = \sqrt{x},$ estimate the value of $\sqrt{101}$

$$y = \sqrt{x} \quad \Rightarrow \quad \frac{dy}{dx} = \tfrac{1}{2}x^{-1/2}$$

$$\delta y \approx \frac{dy}{dx}\delta x \quad \text{gives} \quad \delta y \approx \frac{1}{2\sqrt{x}}\delta x$$

So that the value of y can be written down, the value we take for x must be a number with a known square root.

Taking $x = 100,$ $y = \sqrt{100}$ and $\delta x = 1$ gives

$$\delta y \approx \frac{1}{2\sqrt{100}}(1) = \frac{1}{20}$$

Then

$$\sqrt{101} = y + \delta y \approx \sqrt{100} + \tfrac{1}{20}$$

i.e. $\sqrt{101} \approx 10.05$

_____

2. Given that $1° = 0.0175$ rad and that $\cos 30° = 0.8660$, use $f(\theta) = \sin \theta$ to find an approximate value for

(a) $\sin 31°$ (b) $\sin 29°$

Using $\delta\{f(\theta)\} \approx f'(\theta)\,\delta\theta$ gives $\delta(\sin \theta) \approx (\cos \theta)\,\delta\theta$

(a) Taking $\theta = \frac{1}{6}\pi$, $\sin \theta = \frac{1}{2}$ and $\delta\theta = 0.0175$ gives

$$\delta(\sin \theta) \approx (\cos \tfrac{1}{6}\pi)(0.0175) \quad \text{and} \quad \sin 31° \approx \sin 30° + \delta(\sin \theta)$$

Hence $\qquad\qquad\qquad \sin 31° \approx 0.5 + (0.8660)(0.0175)$

i.e. $\qquad\qquad\qquad\quad \sin 31° \approx 0.515$

(b) Again $\theta = \frac{1}{6}\pi$ and $\sin \theta = \frac{1}{2}$, but this time, because the angle *decreases* from $30°$ to $29°$, $\delta\theta = -0.0175$

$$\delta(\sin \theta) \approx (\cos \tfrac{1}{6}\pi)(-0.0175)$$

Hence $\quad \sin 29° \approx \sin 30° + \delta(\sin \theta) = 0.5 + (0.8660)(-0.0175)$

i.e. $\quad \sin 29° \approx 0.485$

Small Percentage Increases

In order to adapt the method used above to estimate the percentage change in a dependent variable caused by a small change in the independent variable we use the additional fact that

$$\text{if } x \text{ increases by } r\% \text{ then } \delta x = \frac{r}{100}(x)$$

and the corresponding percentage increase in y is $\dfrac{\delta y}{y} \times 100$

Examples 25a (continued)

3. The period, T, of a simple pendulum is calculated from the formula $T = 2\pi\sqrt{(l/g)}$, where l is the length of the pendulum and g is the constant gravitational acceleration. Find the percentage change in the period caused by lengthening the pendulum by 2 per cent.

$$T = 2\pi\sqrt{\left(\frac{l}{g}\right)} \quad \Rightarrow \quad \frac{dT}{dl} = \left(\frac{2\pi}{\sqrt{g}}\right)(\tfrac{1}{2}l^{-1/2}) = \frac{\pi}{\sqrt{(lg)}}$$

The length *increases* so the small increment in the length is positive and is given by

$$\delta l = (\tfrac{2}{100})(l) = \tfrac{1}{50}l$$

Using $\delta T \approx \dfrac{dT}{dl}\delta l$ gives

$$\delta T \approx (\tfrac{1}{50}l)\{\pi/\sqrt{(lg)}\} = (\tfrac{1}{50})\pi\sqrt{(l/g)}$$

The percentage change in the period is given by $\dfrac{\delta T}{T} \times 100$

i.e. $\tfrac{1}{50}\{\pi\sqrt{(l/g)}\} \div \{2\pi\sqrt{(l/g)}\} \times 100\% = 1\%$

This is a positive change, so we see that the period *increases* by 1%

EXERCISE 25a

1. Using $y = \sqrt[3]{x}$, find, *without using a calculator*, an approximate value for
   (a) $\sqrt[3]{1001}$ (b) $\sqrt[3]{9}$ (c) $\sqrt[3]{63}$
   Work to 6 d.p.
   Now use a calculator to find the accuracy of each approximation.

2. Given that $1° = 0.0175$ rad, $\sin 60° = 0.8660$ and $\sin 45° = 0.7071$, use $f(\theta) = \cos\theta$ to find an approximate value for
   (a) $\cos 31°$ (b) $\cos 59°$ (c) $\cos 44°$

3. If $f(x) = x \ln(1 + x)$ find an approximation for the increase in $f(x)$ when x increases by δx
Hence estimate the value of $\ln(2.1)$ given that $\ln 2 = 0.6931$

4. If $y = \tan x$ find an approximation for δy when x is increased by δx and use it to estimate, in terms of π, the value of $\tan \frac{9}{32}\pi$

5. Use $f(x) = \sqrt[5]{x}$ to find the approximate value of $\sqrt[5]{33}$

6. Given that $y = \sqrt{\left(\dfrac{x-2}{x-1}\right)}$ determine the value of $\dfrac{dy}{dx}$ when
$x = 3$ Deduce the approximate increase in the value of y when x increases from 3 to $3 + \alpha$ where α is small.

COMPARATIVE RATES OF CHANGE

Some problems involving the rate of change of one variable compared with another do not provide a direct relationship between these two variables. Instead, each of them is related to a third variable.

The identity $\dfrac{dy}{dx} = \dfrac{dy}{dt} \times \dfrac{dt}{dx}$ is useful in solving problems of this type.

Suppose, for instance, that the radius, r, of a circle is increasing at a rate of 1 mm per second. This means that $\dfrac{dr}{dt} = 1$. The rate at which the area, A, of the circle is increasing is $\dfrac{dA}{dt}$

We do not know A as a function of t but we do know that $A = \pi r^2$ and that

$$\frac{dA}{dt} = \frac{dA}{dr} \times \frac{dr}{dt}$$

Then $\dfrac{dA}{dt}$ can be calculated, as $\dfrac{dr}{dt}$ is given and $\dfrac{dA}{dr}$ can be found from $A = \pi r^2$

In some cases, more than three variables may be involved but the same approach is used with a relationship of the form

$$\frac{dy}{dx} = \frac{dy}{dp} \times \frac{dp}{dq} \times \frac{dq}{dx}$$

Examples 25b

1. A spherical balloon is being blown up so that its volume increases at a constant rate of 1.5 cm³/s. Find the rate of increase of the radius when the volume of the balloon is 56 cm³.

If, at time t, the radius of the balloon is r and the volume is V then

$$V = \tfrac{4}{3}\pi r^3 \quad \Rightarrow \quad \frac{dV}{dr} = 4\pi r^2$$

We are looking for $\dfrac{dr}{dt}$ and we are given $\dfrac{dV}{dt} = 1.5$ so we use

$$\frac{dr}{dt} = \frac{dr}{dV} \times \frac{dV}{dt} = \frac{dV}{dt} \div \frac{dV}{dr} \quad \Rightarrow \quad \frac{dr}{dt} = \frac{1.5}{4\pi r^2} = \frac{3}{8\pi r^2}$$

Now substituting $V = 56$ in $V = \tfrac{4}{3}\pi r^3$ gives $r = 2.373$ to 4 s.f.

Therefore, when $V = 56$, $\qquad \dfrac{dr}{dt} = \dfrac{3}{8\pi(2.373)^2} = 0.021\,20$

i.e. the radius is increasing at a rate of 0.0212 cm/s (correct to 3 s.f.)

---

2. A vessel containing liquid is in the form of an inverted hollow cone with a semi-vertical angle of 30°. The liquid is running out of a small hole at the vertex of the cone, at a constant rate of 3 cm³/s. Find the rate at which the surface area which is in contact with the liquid is changing, at the instant when the volume of liquid left in the vessel is 81π cm³.

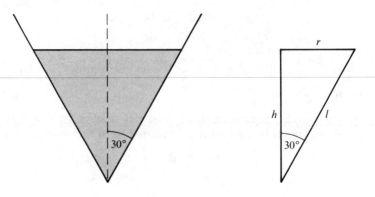

At any time, t, the volume, V, of liquid in the vessel is given by

$$V = \tfrac{1}{3}\pi r^2 h$$

In this equation, V, r and h are all variables so it cannot yet be differentiated.

Using $r = l \sin 30° = \tfrac{1}{2}l$ and $h = l \cos 30° = \tfrac{1}{2}\sqrt{3}l$ gives

$$V = \tfrac{1}{24}\pi l^3 \sqrt{3} \quad \Rightarrow \quad \frac{dV}{dl} = \tfrac{1}{8}\pi l^2 \sqrt{3}$$

The surface area, S, in contact with the liquid at any time is given by

$$S = \pi r l = \tfrac{1}{2}\pi l^2 \quad \Rightarrow \quad \frac{dS}{dl} = \pi l$$

Now $\dfrac{dS}{dt}$ is required and $\dfrac{dV}{dt}$ is given as -3 (negative because the volume is decreasing). There is no equation from which $\dfrac{dS}{dV}$ can be obtained so this time we use a three-step link,

i.e. $$\frac{dS}{dt} = \frac{dS}{dl} \times \frac{dl}{dV} \times \frac{dV}{dt} = \frac{dS}{dl} \div \frac{dV}{dl} \times \frac{dV}{dt}$$

$$= (\pi l)\left(\frac{8}{\pi l^2 \sqrt{3}}\right)(-3) = \frac{-8\sqrt{3}}{l}$$

At the instant that the value of $\dfrac{dS}{dt}$ is required, $V = 81\pi$

i.e. $$\tfrac{1}{24}\pi l^3 \sqrt{3} = 81\pi \quad \Rightarrow \quad l = 6\sqrt{3}$$

At this instant, $$\frac{dS}{dt} = \frac{-8\sqrt{3}}{6\sqrt{3}} = -\frac{4}{3}$$

i.e. the wet surface area is decreasing at $1\tfrac{1}{3}$ cm^2/s.

EXERCISE 25b

1. Ink is dropped on to blotting paper forming a circular stain which increases in area at a rate of 2.5 cm^2/s. Find the rate at which the radius is changing when the area of the stain is 16π cm^2.

2. The surface area of a cube is increasing at a rate of 10 cm^2/s. Find the rate of increase of the volume of the cube when the edge is of length 12 cm.

3. The circumference of a circular patch of oil on the surface of a pond is increasing at 2 m/s. When the radius is 4 m, at what rate is the area of the oil changing?

4. A container in the form of a right circular cone of height 16 cm and base radius 4 cm is held vertex downward and filled with liquid. If the liquid leaks out from the vertex at a rate of 4 cm³/s, find the rate of change of the depth of the liquid in the cone when half of the liquid has leaked out.

5. A right circular cone has a constant volume. The height h and the base radius r can both vary. Find the rate at which h is changing with respect to r at the instant when r and h are equal.

6. The radius of a hemispherical bowl is a cm. The bowl is being filled with water at a steady rate of $3\pi a^3$ cm³ per minute. Find, in terms of a, the rate at which the water is rising when the depth of water in the bowl is $\frac{1}{2}a$ cm.

   (The volume of the shaded part of this hemisphere is $\frac{1}{3}\pi h^2(3a - h)$)

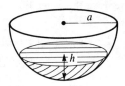

CONSOLIDATION D

SUMMARY

Throughout this summary, a and b represent constant quantities.

TRIGONOMETRY

General Solutions

If $\cos\theta = \cos\alpha$ then $\theta = 2n\pi \pm \alpha$

If $\tan\theta = \tan\alpha$ then $\theta = n\pi + \alpha$

If $\sin\theta = \sin\alpha$ then $\theta = 2n\pi + \alpha$ or $(2n-1)\pi - \alpha$

Factor Formulae

Before using these formulae it is wise to ensure that $A > B$, rearranging the given expression if necessary.

In the form for converting a sum or difference into a product,

$$\sin A + \sin B = 2\sin\tfrac{1}{2}(A+B)\cos\tfrac{1}{2}(A-B)$$

$$\sin A - \sin B = 2\cos\tfrac{1}{2}(A+B)\sin\tfrac{1}{2}(A-B)$$

$$\cos A + \cos B = 2\cos\tfrac{1}{2}(A+B)\cos\tfrac{1}{2}(A-B)$$

$$\cos A - \cos B = -2\sin\tfrac{1}{2}(A+B)\sin\tfrac{1}{2}(A-B)$$

In the form for converting a product into a sum or difference,

$$2\sin A\cos B = \sin(A+B) + \sin(A-B)$$

$$2\cos A\sin B = \sin(A+B) - \sin(A-B)$$

$$2\cos A\cos B = \cos(A+B) + \cos(A-B)$$

$$-2\sin A\sin B = \cos(A+B) - \cos(A-B)$$

Expressing $a\cos\theta \pm b\sin\theta$ as a Single Term

For various values of a and b, $a\cos\theta \pm b\sin\theta$ can be expressed as

$$r\cos(\theta \pm \alpha) \quad \text{or} \quad r\sin(\theta \pm \alpha)$$

where $r = \sqrt{(a^2 + b^2)}$ and $\tan\alpha$ is either a/b or b/a

Small Angles

When θ is a small angle measured in radians, then

$$\sin\theta \approx \theta \qquad \tan\theta \approx \theta \qquad \cos\theta \approx 1 - \tfrac{1}{2}\theta^2$$

and $\displaystyle\lim_{\theta\to0}\left[\frac{\sin\theta}{\theta}\right] = 1$

LOGARITHMS

For any positive numbers a and b the formula for changing the base of a logarithm is

$$\log_a x = \frac{\log_b x}{\log_b a}$$

Natural logarithms obey the standard laws of logarithms.

$$\ln a + \ln b = \ln(ab)$$

$$\ln a - \ln b = \ln(a/b)$$

$$\ln a^p = p\ln a$$

$$\log_p a = \frac{\ln a}{\ln p}$$

FUNCTIONS

Exponential functions:

$f:x \to a^x$ is an exponential function

$f:x \to e^x$ is *the* exponential function: $e = 2.71828\ldots$

Logarithmic functions:

$f:x \to \log_n x$, is a logarithmic function

$f:x \to \log_e x = \ln x$ is the natural logarithmic function

Inverse trigonometric functions:

The inverse trig functions are $\arcsin x$, $\arccos x$, $\arctan x$

$\arcsin x$ means 'the angle in the range $-\tfrac{1}{2}\pi \leqslant \theta \leqslant \tfrac{1}{2}\pi$ whose sine is x'

$\arccos x$ means 'the angle in the range $0 \leqslant \theta \leqslant \pi$ whose cosine is x'

$\arctan x$ means 'the angle in the range $0 \leqslant \theta \leqslant \tfrac{1}{2}\pi$ whose tangent is x'

DIFFERENTIATION

Standard Results

$f(x)$	$\dfrac{d}{dx}f(x)$	$f(x)$	$\dfrac{d}{dx}f(x)$
x^n	nx^{n-1}	e^x	e^x
		$\ln x$	$1/x$
$\sin x$	$\cos x$	a^x	$a^x \ln a$
$\cos x$	$-\sin x$		
$\tan x$	$\sec^2 x$	$\arcsin x$	$\dfrac{1}{\sqrt{(1-x^2)}}$
$\sec x$	$\sec x \tan x$		
$\operatorname{cosec} x$	$-\operatorname{cosec} x \cot x$	$\arccos x$	$-\dfrac{1}{\sqrt{(1-x^2)}}$
$\cot x$	$-\operatorname{cosec}^2 x$	$\arctan x$	$\dfrac{1}{(1+x^2)}$

Further Quotable Results

$f(x)$	$\dfrac{d}{dx}f(x)$
$\sin ax$	$a \cos ax$
e^{ax}	$a e^{ax}$
$\ln(ax)$	$1/x$ (*not* a/x)
$\arcsin \dfrac{x}{a}$	$\dfrac{1}{\sqrt{(a^2-x^2)}}$
$\arctan \dfrac{x}{a}$	$\dfrac{a}{(a^2+x^2)}$

COMPOUND FUNCTIONS

If u and v are both functions of x then

$$y = uv \quad \Rightarrow \quad \frac{dy}{dx} = v\frac{du}{dx} + u\frac{dv}{dx}$$

$$y = \frac{u}{v} \quad \Rightarrow \quad \frac{dy}{dx} = \left(v\frac{du}{dx} - u\frac{dv}{dx}\right)\Big/ v^2$$

If $y = f(u)$ and $u = g(x)$ then $\dfrac{dy}{dx} = \dfrac{dy}{du} \times \dfrac{du}{dx}$

This process, known as the Chain Rule, can be extended, e.g. if
$y = f(u)$, $u = g(v)$, $v = h(x)$ then $\dfrac{dy}{dx} = \dfrac{dy}{du} \times \dfrac{du}{dv} \times \dfrac{dv}{dx}$

IMPLICIT DIFFERENTIATION

When y cannot be isolated, each term can be differentiated with respect to x,

e.g. $\dfrac{d}{dx}(y^2) = (2y)\left(\dfrac{dy}{dx}\right)$ and $\dfrac{d}{dx}(xy) = y + (x)\left(\dfrac{dy}{dx}\right)$ (by product rule)

LOGARITHMIC DIFFERENTIATION

Sometimes it is easier to differentiate $y = f(x)$ with respect to x if we first take logs of both sides.
When doing this remember that $\dfrac{d}{dx}(\ln y) = \dfrac{1}{y}\dfrac{dy}{dx}$

This process is called logarithmic differentiation. It is *essential* when differentiating functions such as x^x

Parametric Differentiation

If $y = f(t)$ and $x = g(t)$ then $\dfrac{dy}{dx} = \dfrac{dy}{dt} \div \dfrac{dx}{dt}$

Small Increments

If $y = f(x)$ and x increases by a small amount, δx, then

$$\delta y \approx \left(\dfrac{dy}{dx}\right)(\delta x)$$

Comparative Rates of Change

If a quantity p depends on a quantity q and the rate at which q increases with time t is known, then

$$\dfrac{dp}{dt} = \dfrac{dp}{dq} \times \dfrac{dq}{dt}$$

MULTIPLE CHOICE EXERCISE D

TYPE I

1. $\cos(A + B) + \cos(A - B) \equiv$

   A $2 \cos A \sin B$ C $2 \cos A \cos B$
   B $-2 \sin A \cos B$ D $-2 \sin A \sin B$

2. If $x^2 + y^2 = 4$ then $\dfrac{dy}{dx}$ is

   A $2x + 2y$ B $4 - x^2$ C $-\dfrac{x}{y}$ D $\dfrac{y}{x}$

3. The approximate value, when θ is small, of the expression $\dfrac{2\theta - \sin\theta}{\sin 2\theta - \theta}$ is

   A 1 B 2 C -1 D -2

4. $\dfrac{d}{dx}\left(\dfrac{1}{1 + x}\right)$ is

   A $\dfrac{-1}{(1 + x)^2}$ C $\ln(1 + x)$

   B $\dfrac{1}{1 - x}$ D $\dfrac{-1}{1 + x^2}$

5. $\dfrac{d}{dx}\ln\left(\dfrac{x + 1}{2x}\right)$ is

   A $\dfrac{1}{2}$ C $\dfrac{2x}{x + 1}$

   B $\dfrac{1}{x + 1} - \dfrac{1}{2x}$ D $\dfrac{1}{x + 1} - \dfrac{1}{x}$

6. $\dfrac{d}{dx}a^x$ is

   A xa^{x-1} B a^x C $x \ln a$ D $a^x \ln a$

7. If $x = \cos\theta$ and $y = \cos\theta + \sin\theta$, $\dfrac{dy}{dx}$ is

   A $1 - \cot\theta$ C $\cot\theta - 1$
   B $1 - \tan\theta$ D $\cot\theta + 1$

8. The greatest value of $5 \cos \theta - 4 \sin \theta$ is

    A 3   **B** 1   **C** $\sqrt{41}$ **D** ± 5

TYPE II

9. $3 \cos \theta - 4 \sin \theta \equiv$

    A $5 \cos (\theta + \alpha)$ where $\tan \alpha = \frac{3}{4}$
    B $5 \sin (\alpha - \theta)$ where $\tan \alpha = \frac{3}{4}$
    C $5 \cos (\theta + \alpha)$ where $\tan \alpha = \frac{4}{3}$
    D $-5 \cos (\theta - \alpha)$ where $\tan \alpha = \frac{4}{3}$

10. Given that α is a very small angle measured in radians,

    A $\sin (2\pi + \alpha) = \sin \alpha$ **C** $\sin (2\pi + \alpha) \approx 2\pi + \alpha$
    B $\sin \alpha \approx \alpha$ **D** $\cos \alpha \approx \alpha$

11. Given that $y = \arccos x$,

    A $\cos y = x$ **C** $y = \sec x$
    B $0 \leqslant x \leqslant \pi$ **D** $0 \leqslant y \leqslant \pi$

12. If $y = \ln (\ln x)$ and $x > 1$ then

    A $\dfrac{dy}{dx} = \dfrac{1}{\ln x}$ **C** $\dfrac{dy}{dx} = \dfrac{1}{x \ln x}$

    B $e^y = \ln x$ **D** $y = \ln x^2$

13. Given that $x = \cos^2 \theta$ and $y = \sin^2 \theta$,

    A $x^2 + y^2 = 1$ **C** $0 \leqslant y \leqslant 1$

    B $\dfrac{dy}{dx} = \tan \theta$ **D** $y = x - \frac{1}{2}\pi$

TYPE III

14. $\sin 3\theta = \cos 4\theta \quad \Rightarrow \quad \frac{1}{2}\pi - 3\theta = 2n\pi \pm 4\theta$

15. $\dfrac{d}{dx}(uv) = \dfrac{du}{dx} \times \dfrac{dv}{dx}$

16. $\dfrac{d}{dx}(x^2 y^2) = 2xy^2 + 2x^2 y$

17. Given that $y = \ln x^2$ and x increases by δx

then $\delta y \approx \left(\dfrac{1}{x^2}\right)(\delta x)$

18. When $y = \cos 2\theta$ and $x = \sin \theta$, $\dfrac{dy}{dx} = -4x\sqrt{(1 - x^2)}$

19. If $y = f(t)$ and $x = g(t)$ then $\dfrac{dy}{dx} = \dfrac{dy}{dt} \div \dfrac{dx}{dt}$

20. If $y = \ln\left(\dfrac{x}{1 + x}\right)$ then $\dfrac{dy}{dx} = \dfrac{d}{dx}\{\ln x\} - \dfrac{d}{dx}\{\ln(1 + x)\}$

MISCELLANEOUS EXERCISE D

1. Differentiate with respect to x

   (a) $\dfrac{x}{2x + 1}$ (b) $\arcsin(x^2)$ (C 86)

2. Find all the values of θ, such that $0 \leqslant \theta \leqslant 180°$, satisfying the
   equation $\cos \theta + \cos 3\theta = 0$ (C 88)

3. Differentiate with respect to x
   (a) $\sin(2x^2)$ (b) 2^x (U of L 88)

4. Find the values of x, in the interval $0 \leqslant x \leqslant 2\pi$, which satisfy the
   equation
$$\sin 3x + \sin x = \sin 2x$$
   giving your answers in terms of π (AEB 85)$_p$

5. Find $\dfrac{dy}{dx}$ when

   (a) $y = \dfrac{1 + \sin x}{1 + \cos x}$ (b) $y = \ln\sqrt{\left(\dfrac{1 + x}{1 - x}\right)}$, $|x| < 1$

   and simplify your answers as far as possible.   (U of L 85)

6. A curve has parametric equations
$$x = 2t + \sin 2t \quad y = \cos 2t, \quad 0 < t < \tfrac{1}{2}\pi$$
   Show that, at the point with parameter t, the gradient of the curve
   is $-\tan t$ (C 87)

7. Show that, when x is small,
$$(1 - \sin^2 3x) \cos 2x \approx 1 - 11x^2$$

8. Evaluate $\dfrac{dy}{dx}$ when $y = 1$, given that

   (a) $y(x + y) = 3$ (b) $x = \dfrac{1}{(4 - t)^2}$, $y = \dfrac{t}{4 - t}$, $0 < t < 4$

   (U of L 85)

9. Prove the identity
$$\sqrt{3} \cos \theta + \sin \theta \equiv 2 \cos (\theta - \tfrac{1}{6}\pi)$$
   Find, in terms of π, the general solution of the equation
$$\sqrt{3} \cos \theta + \sin \theta = 1$$ (AEB 86)

10. For a given mass of gas, the volume, $V\,\text{cm}^3$, and pressure, p cm of mercury, are related by $p = kV^n$ where k and n are constants.

    (a) Prove that $\dfrac{dp}{dV} = \dfrac{np}{V}$

    (b) For a particular mass of gas $n = -1.4$. At the instant when the volume is 20 cm^3, the pressure is 150 cm of mercury and the volume is decreasing at a rate of 0.5 cm^{3}s^{-1}. Calculate the rate of change of pressure at this instant, in cm of mercury per second.

    (AEB 87)

11. Differentiate with respect to x
    (a) $(4x - 1)^{20}$ (b) $\arctan (\sqrt{x})$

12. The parametric equations of a curve are $x = 5a \sec \theta$ and $y = 3a \tan \theta$ where $-\tfrac{1}{2}\pi < \theta < \tfrac{1}{2}\pi$ and a is a positive constant. Find the coordinates of the point on the curve where the gradient is -1

13. Given that $y = e^x \ln (1 + \sin 2x)$, $-\tfrac{1}{2}\pi \leqslant x \leqslant \tfrac{1}{2}\pi$, find $\dfrac{dy}{dx}$ in terms of x.   (U of L 88)

14. A curve is given by the equation
$$y = \sin x + \tfrac{1}{2} \sin 2x \quad 0 \leqslant x \leqslant 2\pi$$
    Find the values of x for which y is zero.
    Find the exact coordinates of the stationary points on the curve and sketch the curve.   (JMB 84)

15. Find all the values of θ for which $0 \leqslant \theta \leqslant \tfrac{1}{2}\pi$ and $\sin 8\theta = \sin 2\theta$
    (U of L 88)

16. The parametric equations of a curve are

$$x = \cos 2\theta + 2 \cos \theta \quad y = \sin 2\theta - 2 \sin \theta$$

Show that $\dfrac{dy}{dx} = \tan \tfrac{1}{2}\theta$

Find the equation of the normal to the curve at the point where $\theta = \tfrac{1}{2}\pi$ (AEB 85)

17. Given that $3 \cos \theta + 4 \sin \theta \equiv R \cos (\theta - \alpha)$, where $R > 0$ and $0 \leqslant \alpha \leqslant \pi/2$, state the value of R and the value of $\tan \alpha$.

For each of the following equations, solve for θ in the interval $0 \leqslant \theta \leqslant 2\pi$ and give your answers in radians correct to one decimal place.

(a) $3 \cos \theta + 4 \sin \theta = 2$

(b) $3 \cos 2\theta + 4 \sin 2\theta = 5 \cos \theta$

The curve with equation $y = \dfrac{10}{3 \cos x + 4 \sin x + 7}$, between

$x = -\pi$ and $x = \pi$, cuts the y-axis at A, has a maximum point at B and a minimum point at C. Find the coordinates of A, B and C.   (AEB 88)

18. A curve has parametric equations

$$x = 2t - \ln (2t) \quad y = t^2 - \ln (t^2)$$

where $t > 0$

Find the value of t at the point on the curve at which the gradient is 2   (C 86)

19. Write down $\sin x + \sin 3x$ as a product of factors.

Find, in terms of π, the solutions of the equation

$$\sin x + \sin 3x = \sin 2x$$

which lie in the interval $-\pi < x \leqslant \pi$.

Find also the general solution of the equation.   (JMB 87)

20. A curve has parametric equations

$$x = 1 + \sqrt{(32)} \cos \theta \quad y = 5 + \sqrt{(32)} \sin \theta \quad 0 \leqslant \theta \leqslant 2\pi$$

Show that the tangent to the curve at the point with parameter θ is given by

$$(y - 5) \sin \theta + (x - 1) \cos \theta = \sqrt{(32)}$$

Find the two values of θ such that this tangent passes through the point $A(1, -3)$. Hence, or otherwise, find the equations of the two tangents to the curve from the point A.   (U of L 88)

21. The equation of a curve is
$$3x^2 + y^2 = 2xy + 8x - 2$$
Find an equation connecting x, y and $\dfrac{dy}{dx}$ at all points on the curve.
Hence show that the coordinates of all points on the curve at which $\dfrac{dy}{dx} = 2$ satisfy the equation
$$x + y = 4$$
Deduce the coordinates of these points.   (JMB 85)

22. A curve is defined by the parametric equations $x = \cos^3 t$, $y = \sin^3 t$, $0 \leqslant t \leqslant \frac{1}{4}\pi$.
Show that the equation of the normal to the curve at the point $P(\cos^3 t, \sin^3 t)$ is
$$x \cos t - y \sin t = \cos^4 t - \sin^4 t \qquad \text{(JMB 87)}$$

23. Given that $y = \sqrt{\left(\dfrac{2+x}{3+x}\right)}$, find the value of $\dfrac{dy}{dx}$ when $x = 1$.
Hence find the approximate increase in the value of y when x increases from 1 to $1 + \alpha$, where α is small.

24. Find approximations, when θ is very small, for the following expressions

(a) $\cos \theta + \sin \theta$

(b) $\dfrac{2 \tan \theta - \theta}{\sin 2\theta}$

(c) $\cot \theta (1 - \cos \theta)$

(d) $\dfrac{\sqrt{2} - \sin \theta}{\cos \theta}$

25. The radius of a sphere is increasing at a rate of 4 cm/s. Obtain, as a multiple of π, the rate of increase of the volume of the sphere when the radius is 10 cm.   (C Spec Paper)

26. A straight metal bar, of square cross-section, is expanding due to heating. After t seconds the bar has dimensions x cm by x cm by $10x$ cm. Given that the area of the cross-section is increasing at $0.024 \text{ cm}^2 \text{ s}^{-1}$ when $x = 6$, find the rate of increase of the side of the cross-section at this instant. Find also the rate of increase of the volume when $x = 6$ (JMB 86)

27. Given that x is so small that terms in x^3 and higher powers of x may be neglected, show that
$$11 \sin x - 6 \cos x + 5 = A + Bx + Cx^2$$
and state the values of the constants A, B, C.   (U of L 89)

CHAPTER 26

STRAIGHT LINES 2

COORDINATE GEOMETRY AND STRAIGHT LINES

In any graphical work, particularly that of a geometric nature, frequent use is made of straight lines. In Chapter 6 and in Chapter 9 a variety of methods and results involving points and straight lines are obtained using Cartesian coordinates. This chapter extends that work and before proceeding the reader should revise those earlier results.

THE COORDINATES OF A POINT DIVIDING A LINE IN A GIVEN RATIO

$A(x_1, y_1)$ and $B(x_2, y_2)$ are two fixed points and the point $P(X, Y)$ divides the line joining AB in the ratio $\lambda : \mu$

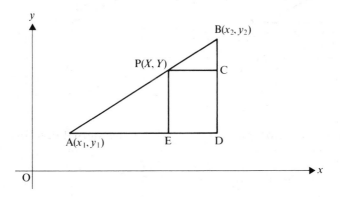

From the diagram, $\triangle APE$ and $\triangle PBC$ are similar,

$$\therefore \qquad \frac{AE}{PC} = \frac{AP}{PB} = \frac{\lambda}{\mu}$$

But $AE = X - x_1$, $PC = x_2 - X$ $\qquad \therefore \quad X = \dfrac{\lambda x_2 + \mu x_1}{\lambda + \mu}$

417

A similar result can be found for Y, so

> if the point P divides the line joining $A(x_1, y_1)$ to $B(x_2, y_2)$ in the ratio $\lambda : \mu$, then the coordinates of P are
>
> $$\left(\frac{\lambda x_2 + \mu x_1}{\lambda + \mu}, \frac{\lambda y_2 + \mu y_1}{\lambda + \mu} \right)$$

These formulae, which are quotable, apply to both internal and external division. Their use is not always necessary however. When the coordinates of A and B are known numbers, a diagram, together with simple mental arithmetic, is often adequate.

Examples 26a

1. Find the coordinates of the points P and Q which divide the line joining $A(-2, 5)$ and $B(4, 2)$ in the ratio $2:1$
   (a) internally   (b) externally.

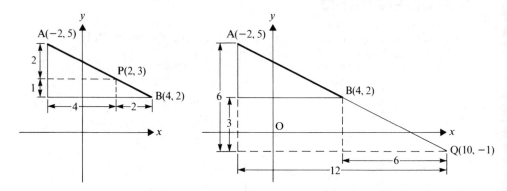

(a) Internal division   (b) External division

(a) From the diagram, P is the point $(2, 3)$

Alternatively, the formula can be used as follows.

P divides AB internally in the ratio $2:1$ so $\lambda = 2$ and $\mu = 1$

$$\Rightarrow \quad x = \frac{2(4) + 1(-2)}{2 + 1} = 2 \quad \text{and} \quad y = \frac{2(2) + 1(5)}{2 + 1} = 3$$

(b) The diagram shows that Q is the point $(10, -1)$

Or, using the formula,

Q divides AB externally in the ratio $2:1$, so $\lambda = 2$ and $\mu = -1$

$\Rightarrow \qquad x = \dfrac{2(4) - 1(-2)}{2 - 1} = 10 \quad \text{and} \quad y = \dfrac{2(2) - 1(5)}{2 - 1} = -1$

Note that in the external division, the sign of μ is opposite to the sign of λ because the direction of the line segment QB is opposite that of the line segment AQ. For this reason, external division is sometimes denoted by a negative ratio, e.g. $2:-1$.

THE EQUATION OF A STRAIGHT LINE

The equation of any straight line can be written in the form $ax + by + c = 0$ where a, b and c are constants.

When the equation is written in standard form, i.e. $y = mx + c$, then m is the gradient of the line and c is its intercept on the y-axis.

(Note that the c in the general form of the equation and the c in the standard form are not usually the same number.)

When m is positive, the line makes an acute angle with the positive direction of the x-axis, and when m is negative, the line makes an obtuse angle with the positive direction of the x-axis.

When θ is acute

gradient of $AB = \dfrac{BN}{AN} = \tan\theta$

When θ is obtuse

gradient of $AB = \dfrac{-AN}{BN}$

$= -\tan\alpha = \tan\theta$

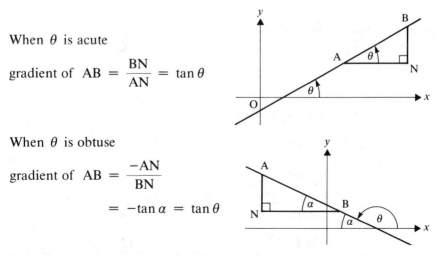

In both cases the gradient of $AB = \tan\theta$

Therefore the gradient of a line is equal to the tangent of the angle between the line and the positive direction of the x-axis.

i.e.
$$m = \tan\theta$$

THE ANGLE BETWEEN TWO LINES

Consider two lines with gradients m_1 and m_2, where $m_1 = \tan\theta_1$ and $m_2 = \tan\theta_2$

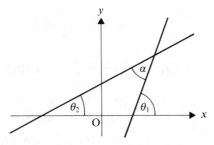

The angle, α, between the lines is given by $\alpha = \theta_1 - \theta_2$

Therefore $\tan\alpha = \tan(\theta_1 - \theta_2) = \dfrac{\tan\theta_1 - \tan\theta_2}{1 + \tan\theta_1\tan\theta_2}$

i.e.
$$\tan\alpha = \frac{m_1 - m_2}{1 + m_1 m_2}$$

Examples 26a (continued)

2. Find the tangent of the angle between the lines $3x - 2y = 5$ and $4x + 5y = 1$

If m_1 is the gradient of $3x - 2y = 5$, then $m_1 = \frac{3}{2}$

If m_2 is the gradient of $4x + 5y = 1$, then $m_2 = -\frac{4}{5}$

Then the angle, α, between these lines is given by

$$\tan\alpha = \frac{\frac{3}{2} - (-\frac{4}{5})}{1 + (\frac{3}{2})(-\frac{4}{5})} = \left(\frac{23}{10}\right)\Big/\left(\frac{-2}{10}\right) = -\frac{23}{2}$$

As $\tan\alpha$ is negative, α is the obtuse angle between the lines. The acute angle between them is arctan 23/2

THE DISTANCE OF A POINT FROM A STRAIGHT LINE

The 'distance of a point from a line' is understood to mean the perpendicular distance.

Consider the line with equation $ax + by + c = 0$ and any point $A(p, q)$ distant d from the line.

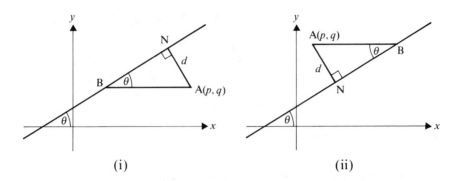

(i)   (ii)

In both diagrams, $d = AN = AB \sin \theta$

and AB is horizontal so, at B, $y = q$ and $x = -(bq + c)/a$

Hence in diagram (i) $\quad AB = p - \left(\dfrac{-(bq + c)}{a} \right) = \dfrac{ap + bq + c}{a}$

and in diagram (ii) $\quad AB = \left(\dfrac{-(bq + c)}{a} \right) - p = -\dfrac{ap + bq + c}{a}$

i.e. for any point A, $\quad AB = \pm \dfrac{ap + bq + c}{a}$

The gradient of the line, $\tan \theta$, is $-\dfrac{a}{b} \quad \Rightarrow \quad \sin \theta = \dfrac{a}{\pm \sqrt{(a^2 + b^2)}}$

Now $AN = AB \sin \theta$

hence $AN = \pm \left(\dfrac{ap + bq + c}{a} \right) \left(\dfrac{a}{\sqrt{(a^2 + b^2)}} \right) = \pm \left(\dfrac{ap + bq + c}{\sqrt{(a^2 + b^2)}} \right)$

The two signs ($\pm$) in this formula arise from points that are on opposite sides of the line. If only the *length*, d, of AN is required, we take the positive value of this formula, i.e.

$$d = \left| \frac{ap + bq + c}{\sqrt{(a^2 + b^2)}} \right|$$

Examples 26a (continued)

3. The vertices of a triangle are the points A(1, 2), B(3, 1), C(−1, −2). Find the length of the altitude through A and hence find the area of the triangle.

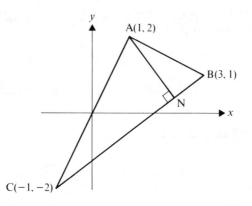

The equation of the line BC is $y = \frac{3}{4}x - \frac{5}{4}$

Writing this equation in the form $3x - 4y - 5 = 0$, then the length of the altitude AN through A(1, 2) is given by

$$d = \left| \frac{3(1) - 4(2) - 5}{\sqrt{(3^2 + \{-4\}^2)}} \right| = \left| -\frac{10}{5} \right| = 2$$

The length of BC is $\sqrt{\{(3)^2 + (4)^2\}} = 5$

Therefore the area of △ABC is $\frac{1}{2}$(CB)(AN) = 5 sq. units.

---

4. Determine, without the aid of a diagram, whether the points A(−3, 4) and B(−2, 3) are on the same side of the line $y + 3x + 4 = 0$. Find the acute angle between this line and AB, giving your answer in degrees correct to three significant figures.

We need to find the *sign* of the expression used to give the distance of each point from the line.

Writing the equation of the given line as $3x + y + 4 = 0$, and using the formula $\dfrac{ap + bq + c}{\sqrt{(a^2 + b^2)}}$ gives

for A, $\dfrac{3(-3) + 4 + 1}{\sqrt{(9 + 1)}} < 0$ and for B, $\dfrac{3(-2) + 3 + 4}{\sqrt{(9 + 1)}} > 0$

The signs are opposite so A and B are on opposite sides of the line.

The gradient of the given line is -3, and the gradient of AB is -1.
If α is an angle between the given line and AB then

$$\tan \alpha = \frac{m_1 - m_2}{1 + m_1 m_2} = \frac{-3 + 1}{1 + 3} = -\frac{1}{2}$$

Therefore the acute angle between the lines is $\arctan \frac{1}{2}$
which is $26.6°$ to 3 s.f.

---

5. Find the reflection of the point $A(-1, 5)$ in the line $2y = x + 1$

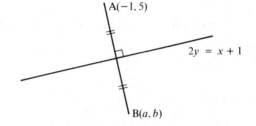

If $B(a, b)$ is the reflection of A in the given line, l, then

> AB is bisected by l and AB is at right angles to l

Let $C(x, y)$ be the point where AB and l cut.

As we have two facts about AB, we can use these to give two relationships between a and b. These can then be solved simultaneously to find a and b. First we can use the fact that l bisects AB.

$C(x, y)$ is the midpoint of AB, so $x = \frac{1}{2}(a - 1)$ and $y = \frac{1}{2}(b + 5)$
but $C(x, y)$ is on the line $2y = x + 1$, i.e.

$$b + 5 = \frac{1}{2}(a - 1) + 1 \quad \Rightarrow \quad a - 2b = 9 \qquad [1]$$

Then we can use the fact that AB and l are perpendicular, so the product of their gradients is -1

AB and l are perpendicular, so

$$\left(\frac{b - 5}{a + 1}\right)\left(\frac{1}{2}\right) = -1 \quad \Rightarrow \quad 2a + b = 3 \qquad [2]$$

Solving equations [1] and [2] simultaneously gives

$$a = 3 \quad \text{and} \quad b = -3$$

EXERCISE 26a

1. Find the coordinates of the point that divides AB in the given ratio in each of the following cases.
   (a) $A(2,4)$, $B(-3,9)$ $1:4$ internally
   (b) $A(-3,-4)$, $B(3,5)$ $3:1$ externally
   (c) $A(1,5)$, $B(8,-2)$ $4:3$
   (d) $A(-1,6)$, $B(3,-2)$ $3:-2$

2. A is the midpoint of BC. If A is (X, Y) and B is (x_1, y_1) show that C has coordinates $(2X - x_1, 2Y - y_1)$.

3. Find the distance from A to the given line in each of the following cases.
   (a) $A(3,4)$; $2x - y = 3$
   (b) $A(-1,-2)$; $3y = 4x - 1$
   (c) $A(a,b)$; $y = mx + c$
   (d) $A(4,-1)$; $x + y = 6$
   (e) $A(x,y)$; $ax + by + c = 0$
   (f) $A(0,0)$; $ax + by + c = 0$

4. Determine whether A and B are on the same or opposite sides of the given line in each of the following cases.
   (a) $A(1,2)$, $B(4,-3)$; $3x + y = 7$
   (b) $A(0,3)$, $B(7,6)$; $x - 4y + 1 = 0$
   (c) $A(-5,1)$, $B(-2,3)$; $7x + y - 6 = 0$

5. Find the tangents of the acute angles between the following pairs of lines.
   (a) $2x + 3y = 7$, $x - 6y = 5$
   (b) $x + 4y - 1 = 0$, $3x + 7y = 2$
   (c) $a_1 x + b_1 y + c_1 = 0$, $a_2 x + b_2 y + c_2 = 0$

6. $A(0,1)$, $B(3,7)$ and $C(-4,-4)$ are the vertices of a triangle. Find the tangent of each of the three angles in the triangle and the length of each altitude.

7. Find the equations of the two lines through the origin which are inclined at $45°$ to the line $2x + 3y - 4 = 0$

8. Find the image of the point $(5, 6)$ in the line
   (a) $3x - y + 1 = 0$
   (b) $y = 4x + 20$
   (c) $2x + 5y + 18 = 0$

9. A point $P(X, Y)$ is equidistant from the line $x + 2y = 3$ and from the point $(2, 0)$. Find an equation relating X and Y.

10. Show that $A(4, 1)$ and $B(2, -3)$ are equidistant from the line $2x + 5y = 1$. Is A the reflection of B in this line?

11. Write down the distance of the point $P(X, Y)$ from each of the lines $5x - 12y + 3 = 0$ and $3x + 4y - 6 = 0$. By equating these distances find the equations of two lines that bisect the angles between the two given lines [i.e. the equations of the set of points $P(X, Y)$].

12. $A(4, 4)$ and $B(7, 0)$ are two vertices of a triangle OAB. Find the equation of the line that bisects the angle OBA. If this line meets OA at C show that C divides OA in the ratio OB : BA.

REDUCTION OF A RELATIONSHIP TO A LINEAR LAW

In this part of the chapter we look at a practical application of the equation $y = mx + c$

Linear Relationships

If it is thought that a certain relationship exists between two variable quantities, this hypothesis can be tested by experiment, i.e. by giving one variable certain values and measuring the corresponding values of the other variable. The experimental data collected can then be displayed graphically. If the graph shows points that lie approximately on a straight line (allowing for experimental error) then a linear relationship between the variables (i.e. a relationship of the form $Y = mX + c$) is indicated. Further, the gradient of the line (m) and the vertical axis intercept (c) provide the values of the constants.

Examples 26b

1. An elastic string is fixed at one end and a variable weight is hung on the other end. It is believed that the length of the string is related to the weight by a linear law. Use the following experimental data to confirm this belief and find the particular relationship between the length of the string and the weight.

Weight (W) in newtons	1	2	3	4	5	6	7	8
Length (l) in metres	0.33	0.37	0.4	0.45	0.5	0.53	0.56	0.6

If l and W are related by a linear law then, allowing for experimental error, we expect that the points will lie on a straight line. Plotting l against W gives the following graph.

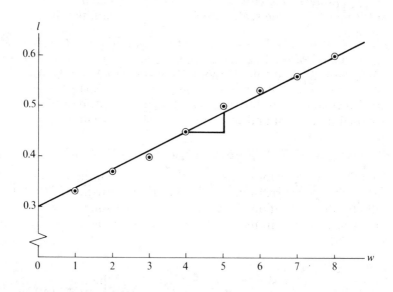

These points do lie fairly close to a straight line.

From the graph, l and W are connected by a linear relationship, i.e. a relationship of the form $l = aW + b$

Now we draw the line of 'closest fit'. This is the line that has the points distributed above and below it as evenly as possible; it is not necessarily the line which goes through the most points.

By measurement from the graph

$$\text{the gradient} = 0.04$$

$$\text{the intercept on the vertical axis} = 0.3$$

So comparing $\left.\begin{matrix} l = aW + b \\ Y = mX + c \end{matrix}\right\}$ we have $a = 0.04, \quad b = 0.3$
with

i.e. within the limits of experimental accuracy

$$l = 0.04W + 0.3$$

When the gradient of a line is found from a graph, the increase in a quantity is measured from the *scale used for that quantity* and it is worth noting that the scales used for the two quantities are *not* usually the same.

The values of the constants found from calculating the gradient and intercept from a drawn graph are approximate. Apart from experimental error in the data, selecting the line of best fit is a personal judgement and so is subject to slight variations which affect the values obtained.

There are methods for calculating the equation of the line of best fit; these are called regression lines and computer programmes exist which will give these equations from the data. Using such a programme, the values of a and b in the last example are given as $a = 0.039$ and $b = 0.291$

Now if the relationship is not of a linear form, the points on the graph will lie on a section of a curve. It is very difficult to identify the equation of a curve from a section of it, so the form of a non-linear relationship can rarely be verified in this way.

Non-linear relationships, however, can often be reduced to a linear form. The following examples illustrate some of the relationships which can be verified by plotting experimental data in a form which gives a straight line.

Relationships of the Form $y = ax^n$

A relationship of the form $y = ax^n$ where a is a constant can be reduced to a linear relationship by taking logarithms, since

$$y = ax^n \quad \Longleftrightarrow \quad \ln y = n \ln x + \ln a$$

(Although any base can be used, it is sensible to use either e or 10 as these are built into most calculators.)

Comparing $\qquad\qquad\qquad \ln y = n \ln x + \ln a$

with $\qquad\qquad\qquad\qquad Y = mX + c$

we see that plotting values of $\ln y$ against values of $\ln x$ gives a straight line whose gradient is m and whose intercept on the vertical axis is $\ln a$

Examples 26b (continued)

2. The following data, collected from an experiment is believed to obey a law of the form $p = aq^n$. Verify this graphically and find the values of a and n.

q	1	2	3	4	5	6
p	0.5	0.63	0.72	0.8	0.85	0.9

If the relationship $p = aq^n$ is correct, then $\qquad \ln p = n \ln q + \ln a$

comparing with $\qquad\qquad\qquad\qquad\qquad\qquad y = mx + c$

we see that $\ln p$ and $\ln q$ are related by a linear law.

First a table of values of $\ln p$ and $\ln q$ is needed.

$\ln q$	0	0.69	1.10	1.39	1.61	1.79
$\ln p$	−0.69	−0.46	−0.33	−0.22	−1.16	−0.11

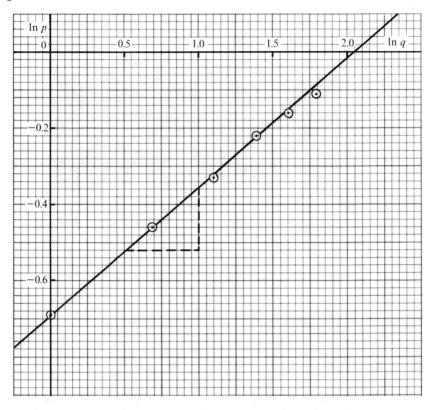

The points lie on a straight line confirming that there is a linear relationship between $\ln q$ and $\ln p$.

From the graph, the gradient of the line is 0.33, $\Rightarrow$ $n = 0.33$ and the intercept on the vertical axis is -0.69, so

$$\ln a = -0.69 \quad \Rightarrow \quad a = 0.5$$

Therefore the data does obey a law of the form $p = aq^n$, where $a \approx 0.5$ and $n \approx 0.33$

(Using the tabulated values of $\ln q$ and $\ln p$ and a computer programme, gives $n = 0.327$ and $\ln a = -0.687$)

An alternative method for investigating relationships of this form uses log–log graph paper, i.e. graph paper where the grids and the scales marked on them are adjusted to represent the logarithms of the numbers being plotted. So to plot $\log S$ against $\log T$ say, values of S and T can be plotted directly.

The diagram illustrates the use of log–log graph paper using the data given in the previous example.

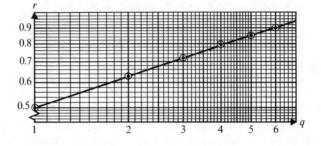

This straight line verifies that the relationship is of the form $p = aq^n$
When $q = 1$, $p = a$. So *from the graph* we see that $a = 0.5$

Reading another pair of values from the graph, (*not* from the table) and substituting these into the relationships gives $q = 2.5$ and $p = 0.68$,

then $\qquad\qquad 0.68 = (0.5)(2.5)^n \qquad \Rightarrow \qquad n = 0.335$

Relationships of the Form $y = ab^x$

A relationship of the form $y = ab^x$ where a and b are constant can be reduced to a linear relationship by taking logs, since

$$y = ab^x \qquad \Longleftrightarrow \qquad \log y = x \log b + \log a$$

Comparing $\qquad\qquad \log y = x \log b + \log a$

with $\qquad\qquad\qquad Y = mX + c$

we see that plotting values of $\log y$ against corresponding values of x gives a straight line whose gradient is $\log b$ and whose intercept on the vertical axis is $\log a$.

Relationships of the Form $\dfrac{1}{y} + \dfrac{1}{x} = \dfrac{1}{a}$

If a is a constant, $\dfrac{1}{y} + \dfrac{1}{x} = \dfrac{1}{a}$ is a linear relationship between $(1/y)$ and $(1/x)$

i.e. if values of $(1/y)$ are plotted against corresponding values of $(1/x)$, a straight line will result.

By comparing $\qquad$ $(1/y) = -(1/x) + (1/a)$

with $\qquad\qquad\qquad$ $Y = mX + c$

it can be seen that the gradient of the graph should be -1 and the intercept on the $(1/y)$ axis gives the value of $1/a$

Note that in all graphical work the scales should be chosen to give the greatest possible accuracy, i.e. the range of values given in the table should have as much spread as possible. This sometimes means that the horizontal scale does not include zero and the value of c cannot then be read from the graph. In these circumstances, which arise in the next example, we find c by using the equation $Y = mX + c$ together with the measured value of m and the coordinates of any point P on the graph (*not* a pair of values from the table).

Examples 26b (continued)

3. In an experiment, values of a variable y were measured for selected values of a variable x

   The results are shown in the table below. It is believed that x and y are related by a law of the form $2y + 10 = ab^{(x-3)}$. Confirm this graphically and find approximate values for a and b

x	10	12	15	20	21
y	37.5	90	320	2440	3700

If $2y + 10 = ab^{(x-3)}$, taking logs of both sides gives

$$\log(2y + 10) = (x - 3)\log b + \log a$$

which is of the form $\qquad\qquad$ $Y = mX + c$

where $Y = \log(2y + 10)$, $X = x - 3$ and $m = \log b$, $c = \log a$
i.e. $[\log(2y + 10)]$ and $[x - 3]$ obey a linear law.

So we need to tabulate corresponding values of $(x - 3)$ and $\log(2y + 10)$ from the given values of x and y

$x - 3$	7	9	12	17	18
$\log(2y + 10)$	1.9	2.3	2.8	3.7	3.9

Then plotting $\log(2y + 10)$ against $x - 3$ gives the graph below.

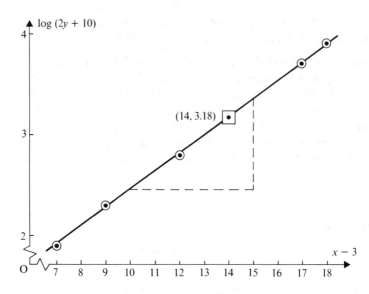

The straight line shows that there is a linear relationship between $\log(2y + 10)$ and $x - 3$, confirming that $2y + 10 = ab^{x-3}$

From the graph, the gradient is 0.175

$\therefore$ $\log b \approx 0.175 \quad \Rightarrow \quad b \approx 1.49$

Using the point $P(14, 3.18)$ and $m = 0.175$ then $Y = mX + c$ gives

$$3.18 = (0.175)(14) + c \quad \Rightarrow \quad c = 0.73$$

i.e. $\log a \approx 0.73 \quad \Rightarrow \quad a \approx 5.37$

When attempting to reduce a relationship between two variables to a form from which a straight line graph can be drawn, the given equation must be expressed in the form

$$Y = mX + c$$

where X and Y are variable terms, values for which must be calculable from the given data, i.e. X and Y must not contain unknown constants. On the other hand m and c must be constants, but may be unknown.

Now X and Y may be functions of one or both variables, as for example

$$f(xy) = m\, g(xy) + c$$

is a linear relationship between $f(xy)$ and $g(xy)$

So to reduce a non-linear relationship to a linear form we:

1) try to express it in a form containing three terms,

2) make one of those terms constant,

3) remove unknown constants from the coefficient of one of the variable terms.

These objectives will now be applied in the next worked example.

Examples 26b (continued) _____

4. It is known that two variables x and y are related by the law

(a) $ae^y = x^2 - bx$ (b) $y = \dfrac{1}{(x-a)(x-b)}$

In each case state how you would reduce the law to a linear form so that a straight line graph could be drawn from experimental data.

(a) $ae^y = x^2 - bx$

This equation has three terms, one of which becomes constant when we divide by x, giving $a\dfrac{e^y}{x} = x - b$

We also have a variable term (x) whose coefficient is a known constant. This equation may now be written as

$$x = a\frac{e^y}{x} + b$$

Comparing with $Y = mX + c$

we see that if values of x are plotted against corresponding values of e^y/x, a straight line will result whose gradient is a and whose intercept on the vertical axis is b

Note that the original equation can be arranged in linear form in a variety of ways

e.g. $\left(\dfrac{e^y}{x^2}\right) = -\dfrac{b}{a}\left(\dfrac{1}{x}\right) + \dfrac{1}{a}$ or $\left(\dfrac{x^2}{e^y}\right) = b\left(\dfrac{x}{e^y}\right) + a$

(b) $y = \dfrac{1}{(x-a)(x-b)}$

Although this form suggests the use of partial fractions, this approach increases the number of times the unknown constants appear. It is better to invert the equation giving

$$\frac{1}{y} = (x-a)(x-b)$$

$\Rightarrow$
$$\frac{1}{y} = x^2 - x(a+b) + ab$$

$\Rightarrow$
$$x^2 - \frac{1}{y} = (a+b)x - ab$$

We can now compare this form with $Y = mX + c$

Thus plotting values of $(x^2 - 1/y)$ against corresponding values of x will give a straight line whose gradient is $a+b$ and whose intercept on the vertical axis is $-ab$

EXERCISE 26b

1. Reduce each of the given relationships to the form $Y = mX + c$. In each case give the functions equivalent to X and Y and the constants equivalent to m and c

   (a) $\dfrac{1}{y} = ax + b$ (b) $y(y-b) = x - a$

   (c) $ae^x = y(y-b)$ (d) $x = y^2 + y - k$

   (e) $y = ax^{n+2}$ (f) $y^a = e^{x+k}$

In Questions 2–7, the table gives sets of values for the related variables and the law which relates the variables. By drawing a straight line graph find approximate values for a and b

2. $y = ax + ab$

x	3	5	7	10
y	-2	2	6	12

3. $s = ab^{-t}$

t	1	2	3	4
s	1.5	0.4	0.1	0.02

4. $r^2 = a\theta - b$

θ	1	4	10	25	40
r	1.6	2	2.6	3.8	4.7

5. $ay = b^x$

x	5	6	7	8
y	1.07	2.13	4.27	8.53

6. $\dfrac{a}{V} + \dfrac{b}{L} = 1$

V	2.5	3	5.5	7	12
L	2.5	1.5	0.79	0.7	0.6

7. $y = (x - a)(x - b)$

x	1	2	3	4	5	6
y	-6	-4	0	6	14	24

8. The variables x and y are believed to satisfy a relationship of the form $y = k(x + 1)^n$. Show that the experimental values shown in the table do satisfy the relationship. Find approximate values for k and n

x	4	8	15	19	24
y	4.45	4.60	4.80	4.89	5.00

9. Two variables s and t are related by a law of the form $s = ke^{-nt}$ The values in the table were obtained from an experiment. Show graphically that these values do verify the relationship and use the graph to find approximate values of k and n

t	1	1.5	2	2.5	3
s	1230	590	260	140	60

10. Two variables x and t are related by a law of the form $x = \cos(at + \varepsilon)$. The table shows the values of x obtained experimentally for some different values of t. Show graphically that these values do NOT satisfy this relationship unless two of the values of x are assumed to be incorrect.
Estimate the correct values of x

t	0.5	1	1.5	1.75	2	2.25
x	−0.26	−0.90	−0.40	−0.90	−0.71	−0.49

CHAPTER 27

COORDINATE GEOMETRY AND CURVES

LOCI

In general, within a plane a point P can be anywhere and, further, if (x, y) are the coordinates of P, then x and y can take any values independently of each other.

However, when the possible positions of P are restricted by some condition to a line (curved or straight), the set of points satisfying this condition is called the *locus* of P

Further, the relationship between x and y which applies only to the locus of P defines that locus and is called the *Cartesian equation* of P

Examples 27a

1. A point, P, is restricted so that it is equidistant from the points A(1, 2) and B(−2, −1). Find the Cartesian equation of P

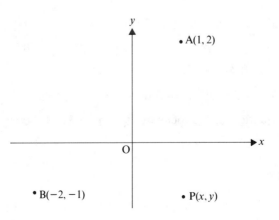

P is restricted to those positions where PA = PB

Translating this condition into a relationship between x and y gives the equation of the locus of P

$$PA^2 = (x - 1)^2 + (y - 2)^2 \quad \text{and} \quad PB^2 = (x + 2)^2 + (y + 1)^2$$

If PA = PB then $PA^2 = PB^2$

Using the given condition in this form avoids introducing square roots.

$$\therefore \quad PA = PB \quad \Rightarrow \quad (x - 1)^2 + (y - 2)^2 = (x + 2)^2 + (y + 1)^2$$

$$\Rightarrow \quad 0 = 6x + 6y$$

Therefore $x + y = 0$ is the equation of the locus of P

Note that the line $x + y = 0$ is the perpendicular bisector of AB

---

2. A point $P(x, y)$ is twice as far from the point $A(3, 0)$ as it is from the line $x = 5$. Find the equation of the locus of P.

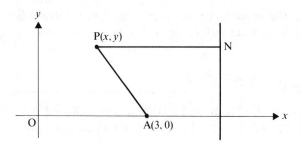

The restriction on P is that PA = 2PN

Now $\qquad\qquad$ PA = 2PN $\quad \Rightarrow \quad$ $PA^2 = 4PN^2$

But $\qquad$ $PA^2 = y^2 + (x - 3)^2$ and $PN^2 = (5 - x)^2$

$\therefore$ P satisfies the given condition $\quad \Longleftrightarrow \quad y^2 + (x - 3)^2 = 4(5 - x)^2$

i.e. the equation of the locus of P is $y^2 - 3x^2 + 34x = 91$

EXERCISE 27a

Find the Cartesian equation of the locus of the set of points P in each of the following cases.

1. P is equidistant from the point $(4, 1)$ and the line $x = -2$

2. P is equidistant from $(3, 5)$ and $(-1, 1)$

3. P is three times as far from the line $x = 8$ as from the point $(2, 0)$

4. P is equidistant from the lines $3x + 4y + 5 = 0$ and $12x - 5y + 13 = 0$

5. P is at a constant distance of two units from the point $(3, 5)$

6. P is at a constant distance of five units from the line $4x - 3y = 1$

7. A is the point $(-1, 0)$, B is the point $(1, 0)$ and angle APB is a right angle.

CIRCLES

If a point P is at a constant distance, r, from a fixed point C then the locus of P is a circle whose centre is C and whose radius is r. In this section we look at a variety of methods for dealing with coordinate geometry problems involving circles.

The Equation of a Circle

A point $P(x, y)$ is at a constant distance, r, from the point $C(a, b)$

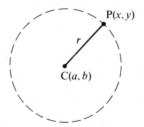

P is on the circle if and only if $CP = r$, i.e. $CP^2 = r^2$

Now $$CP^2 = (x - a)^2 + (y - b)^2$$

∴ $P(x, y)$ is on the circle $\iff$ $(x - a)^2 + (y - b)^2 = r^2$

$$(x - a)^2 + (y - b)^2 = r^2$$

is the equation of a circle with centre (a, b) and radius r

For example, the equation of a circle with centre $(-2, 3)$ and radius 1 is

$$[x - (-2)]^2 + [y - 3]^2 = 1$$

$\Rightarrow \qquad x^2 + y^2 + 4x - 6y + 12 = 0$

As well as being able to write down the equation of a circle given its centre and radius, it is equally important to be able to recognise an equation as that of a circle. Expanding and simplifying the equation of a circle with centre (a, b) and radius r gives

$$x^2 + y^2 - 2ax - 2ay + (a^2 + b^2 - r^2) = 0$$

which can be expressed as

$$x^2 + y^2 + 2gx + 2fy + c = 0$$

where g, f and c are constants.

Comparing coefficients gives

$$g = -a, \quad f = -b, \quad c = a^2 + b^2 - r^2 \quad \Rightarrow \quad r^2 = f^2 + g^2 - c$$

So

$x^2 + y^2 + 2gx + 2fy + c = 0$ is the general equation of a circle provided that $g^2 + f^2 - c > 0$

The centre of the circle is $(-g, -f)$ and the radius is $\sqrt{(g^2 + f^2 - c)}$

Note that the coefficients of x^2 and y^2 are equal and that no xy term is present.

Examples 27b _____

1. Find the centre and radius of the circle whose equation is

$$x^2 + y^2 + 8x - 2y + 13 = 0$$

There are two ways of finding the centre and radius of this circle. The first method involves forming perfect squares so that we can compare the given equation with $(x - a)^2 + (y - b)^2 = r^2$

$$x^2 + 8x + 16 + y^2 - 2y + 1 = 16 + 1 - 13$$

$\Rightarrow \qquad (x + 4)^2 + (y - 1)^2 = 4$

∴ the centre is $(-4, 1)$ and the radius is 2

Alternatively we can compare the given equation with the general equation of a circle giving

$$2g = 8 \Rightarrow g = 4, \quad 2f = -2 \Rightarrow f = -1 \quad \text{and} \quad c = 13$$

The centre, $(-g, -f)$, is $(-4, 1)$ and the radius, $\sqrt{(g^2 + f^2 - c)}$, is 2

---

2. Show that $2x^2 + 2y^2 - 6x + 10y = 1$ is the equation of a circle and find its centre and radius.

Before we can compare this equation with the general form for the equation of a circle, we must divide the given equation by 2

$$2x^2 + 2y^2 - 6x + 10y - 1 = 0 \quad \Rightarrow \quad x^2 + y^2 - 3x + 5y - \tfrac{1}{2} = 0$$

Comparing with $\qquad\qquad\qquad\qquad\qquad x^2 + y^2 + 2gx + 2fy + c = 0$

shows that $2g = -3, \; 2f = 5, \; c = -\tfrac{1}{2}$

$\Rightarrow \; (g^2 + f^2 - c) = 9$ which is greater than 0

Therefore the equation does represent a circle.

The centre is $(-\tfrac{3}{2}, \tfrac{5}{2})$ and the radius is 3

EXERCISE 27b

1. Write down the equation of the circle with
    (a) centre $(1, 2)$, radius 3   (b) centre $(0, 4)$, radius 1
    (c) centre $(-3, -7)$, radius 2   (d) centre $(4, 5)$, radius 3

2. Find the centre and radius of the circle whose equation is
    (a) $x^2 + y^2 + 8x - 2y - 8 = 0$
    (b) $x^2 + y^2 + x + 3y - 2 = 0$
    (c) $x^2 + y^2 + 6x - 5 = 0$
    (d) $2x^2 + 2y^2 - 3x + 2y + 1 = 0$
    (e) $x^2 + y^2 = 4$
    (f) $(x - 2)^2 + (y + 3)^2 = 9$
    (g) $2x + 6y - x^2 - y^2 = 1$
    (h) $3x^2 + 3y^2 + 6x - 3y - 2 = 0$

3. Determine which of the following equations represent circles.
    (a) $x^2 + y^2 = 8$ (b) $2x^2 + y^2 + 3x - 4 = 0$
    (c) $x^2 - y^2 = 8$ (d) $x^2 + y^2 + 4x - 2y + 20 = 0$
    (e) $x^2 + y^2 + 8 = 0$ (f) $x^2 + y^2 + 4x - 2y - 20 = 0$

Tangents to Circles and Other Problems

The following worked examples illustrate how a variety of problems concerning circles can be solved easily with the aid of a diagram and the use of the simple geometric properties of a circle.

It is unnecessary to use calculus methods to find the equation of a tangent to a circle.

Examples 27c _____

1. Find the equation of the tangent at the point $(3, 1)$ on the circle $x^2 + y^2 - 4x + 10y - 8 = 0$. What is the angle between this tangent and the positive direction of the x-axis?

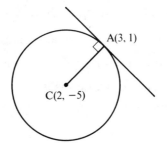

The centre of the circle is $C(2, -5)$

The tangent at A is perpendicular to the radius CA

The gradient of CA is $\dfrac{1 - (-5)}{3 - 2} = 6$

Therefore the gradient of the tangent at A is $-\frac{1}{6}$ and the tangent goes through $A(3, 1)$

So its equation is $\qquad\qquad y - 1 = -\frac{1}{6}(x - 3)$

i.e. $\qquad\qquad\qquad 6y + x = 9$

If α is the angle between the tangent and the positive direction of the x-axis,

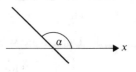

then $\qquad \tan \alpha = -\frac{1}{6}$

$\Rightarrow \qquad\qquad \alpha = 170.5°$

2. Determine whether the lines $5y = 12x - 33$ and $3x + 4y = 9$ are tangents to the circle $x^2 + y^2 + 2x - 8y = 8$

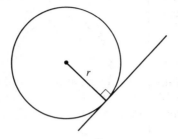

A line is a tangent to a circle if and only if the distance from the centre of the circle to the line is equal to the radius.

Writing the equation of the circle as

$$(x + 1)^2 + (y - 4)^2 = 8 + 1 + 16 = 25$$

shows that $C(-1, 4)$ is the centre and the radius is 5

For the line $5y = 12x - 33$, i.e. $12x - 5y - 33 = 0$, the distance d_1 from the centre $(-1, 4)$ is given by

$$d_1 = \left| \frac{12(-1) - 5(4) - 33}{\sqrt{[12^2 + (-5)^2]}} \right| = \left| -\frac{65}{13} \right| = 5$$

i.e. $d_1 = r$. Thus $12x - 5y - 33 = 0$ *is* a tangent.

For the line $3x + 4y = 9$, i.e. $3x + 4y - 9 = 0$, the distance d_2 from $(-1, 4)$ is given by

$$d_2 = \left| \frac{3(-1) + 4(4) - 9}{\sqrt{[3^2 + 4^2]}} \right| = \frac{4}{5}$$

i.e. $d_2 \neq 5$. Thus $3x + 4y - 9 = 0$ *is not* a tangent.

---

3. Find the equations of the tangents from the origin to the circle
$x^2 + y^2 - 5x - 5y + 10 = 0$

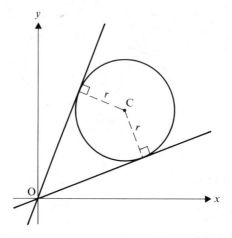

The given circle has centre $(\frac{5}{2}, \frac{5}{2})$

and radius $\sqrt{\left[\left(\frac{5}{2}\right)^2 + \left(\frac{5}{2}\right)^2 - 10\right]} = \frac{\sqrt{10}}{2}$

Any line through the origin has equation $y = mx$, i.e. $mx - y = 0$

If the line is a tangent to the circle, the distance from the centre, $(\frac{5}{2}, \frac{5}{2})$, to the line is equal to the radius

i.e. $\left|\dfrac{m(\frac{5}{2}) - (\frac{5}{2})}{\sqrt{[(m)^2 + (-1)^2]}}\right| = \dfrac{\sqrt{10}}{2}$

$\Rightarrow$ $\left(\dfrac{5}{2}m - \dfrac{5}{2}\right)^2 = \dfrac{10}{4}(m^2 + 1)$

$\Rightarrow$ $3m^2 - 10m + 3 = 0$

$\Rightarrow$ $(3m - 1)(m - 3) = 0$

$\Rightarrow$ $m = \frac{1}{3}$ or 3

So the two tangents from the origin to the given circle are

$$y = 3x \quad \text{and} \quad 3y = x$$

4. Find the equation of the circle whose diameter is the line joining the points $A(1, 5)$ and $B(-2, 3)$

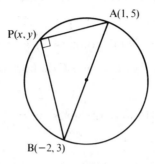

We can use the fact that the angle in a semicircle is $90°$

$P(x, y)$ is a point on the circle if and only if

$$\text{(gradient } AP) \times \text{(gradient } BP) = -1$$

The gradient of AP is $\dfrac{y - 5}{x - 1}$ and the gradient of PB is $\dfrac{y - 3}{x + 2}$

$\therefore$ $P(x, y)$ is on the circle $\Longleftrightarrow$ $\left(\dfrac{y - 5}{x - 1}\right)\left(\dfrac{y - 3}{x + 2}\right) = -1$

$\therefore$ the equation of the circle is $x^2 + y^2 + x - 8y + 13 = 0$

---

5. Find the equation of the circle that goes through the points $A(0, 1)$, $B(4, 7)$ and $C(4, -1)$

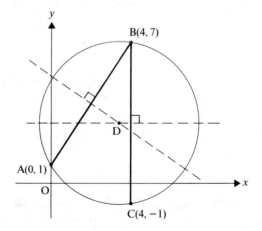

We can use the fact that the centre of a circle lies on the perpendicular bisector of a chord.

The midpoint of AB is the point $(2, 4)$ and the gradient of AB is $\frac{3}{2}$

∴ the perpendicular bisector of AB is the line

$$2x + 3y = 16 \qquad\qquad [1]$$

The midpoint of BC is the point $(4, 3)$ and BC is vertical

∴ the perpendicular bisector of BC is horizontal and its equation is

$$y = 3 \qquad\qquad [2]$$

Solving equations [1] and [2] gives $x = \frac{7}{2}$ and $y = 3$

∴   D is the point $(\frac{7}{2}, 3)$

The radius, r, is the length of DA (or DC or DB), i.e.

$$r^2 = (3 - 1)^2 + (\tfrac{7}{2} - 0)^2 = \tfrac{65}{4}$$

Therefore the equation of the circle is

$$(x - \tfrac{7}{2})^2 + (y - 3)^2 = \tfrac{65}{4} \;\Rightarrow\; x^2 + y^2 - 7x - 6y + 5 = 0$$

---

6. The lines $3y = 4x$, $4x + 3y = 0$ and $y = 8$ are tangents to a circle. Find the equation of the circle.

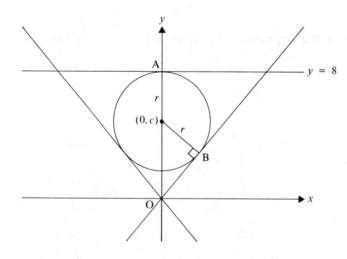

The centre, C, of the circle is on the line that bisects the angle between the tangents $3y = 4x$ and $4x + 3y = 0$. These two tangents are equally inclined to the y-axis so, from symmetry, C lies on the y-axis and its x-coordinate is 0

There is no information from which the y-coordinate of C can be found directly, so we will call it c. We can then use the fact that the distance from C to each tangent is equal to the radius, r, to form an equation in c.

$$r = \text{CA} = |8 - c| \quad \text{and} \quad r = \text{CB} = \pm(0 - 3c)/5$$

$$\therefore \quad 5(8 - c) = \pm(-3c) \quad \Rightarrow \quad c = 20 \quad \text{or} \quad c = 5$$

Therefore there are two circles that satisfy the given conditions.

From $r = |8 - c|$, the corresponding values of the radii are 12 and 3

The equation of the circle is either

$$x^2 + (y - 20)^2 = 144 \quad \text{or} \quad x^2 + (y - 5)^2 = 9$$

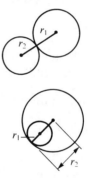

Touching Circles

If two circles touch externally then the distance between their centres is equal to the sum of their radii.

If the circles touch internally then the distance between their centres is equal to the difference of their radii.

---

7. Show that the circles $(x - 8)^2 + (y - 6)^2 = 25$ and $(5x - 16)^2 + (5y - 12)^2 = 25$ touch each other.

The circle $(x - 8)^2 + (y - 6)^2 = 25$ has centre $(8, 6)$ and radius 5

The equation $(5x - 16)^2 + (5y - 12)^2 = 25$ can be divided by 25, giving

$(x - \frac{16}{5})^2 + (y - \frac{12}{5})^2 = 1$ so the centre is $(\frac{16}{5}, \frac{12}{5})$ and the radius is 1

The distance between the centres is $\sqrt{[(8 - \frac{16}{5})^2 + (6 - \frac{12}{5})^2]} = 6$

The sum of the radii of the circles is $5 + 1 = 6$

Therefore the circles touch externally.

EXERCISE 27c

1. Determine whether the given line is a tangent to the given circle in each of the following cases.
   (a) $3x - 4y + 14 = 0$; $x^2 + y^2 + 4x + 6y - 3 = 0$
   (b) $5x + 12y = 4$; $x^2 + y^2 - 2x - 2y + 1 = 0$
   (c) $x + 2y + 6 = 0$; $x^2 + y^2 - 6x - 4y + 8 = 0$
   (d) $x + 2y + 6 = 0$; $x^2 + y^2 - 6x + 4y + 8 = 0$

2. Write down the equation of the tangent to the given circle at the given point.
   (a) $x^2 + y^2 - 2x + 4y - 20 = 0$; $(5, 1)$
   (b) $x^2 + y^2 - 10x - 22y + 129 = 0$; $(6, 7)$
   (c) $x^2 + y^2 - 8y + 3 = 0$; $(-2, 7)$

Find the equations of the following circles (in some cases more than one circle is possible).

3. A circle passes through the points $(1, 4)$, $(7, 5)$ and $(1, 8)$

4. A circle has its centre on the line $x + y = 1$ and passes through the origin and the point $(4, 2)$

5. The line joining $(2, 1)$ to $(6, 5)$ is a diameter of a circle.

6. A circle with centre $(2, 7)$ passes through the point $(-3, -5)$

7. A circle intersects the y-axis at the origin and at the point $(0, 6)$ and also touches the x-axis.

8. A circle touches the negative x and y axes and also the line $7x + 24y + 12 = 0$

Find the equations of the tangents specified in Questions 9 to 11.

9. Tangents *from* the origin to the circle $x^2 + y^2 - 10x - 6y + 25 = 0$

10. The tangent *at* the origin to the circle $x^2 + y^2 + 2x + 4y = 0$

11. Tangents to the circle $x^2 + y^2 - 4x + 6y - 7 = 0$ which are parallel to the line $2x + y = 3$

12. Show that if the point P is twice as far from the point $(4, -2)$ as it is from the origin then P lies on a circle. Find the centre and radius of this circle.

13. Determine which of the following pairs of circles touch.
    (a) $x^2 + y^2 + 2x - 4y + 1 = 0$; $x^2 + y^2 - 6x - 10y + 25 = 0$
    (b) $x^2 + y^2 + 8x + 2y - 8 = 0$; $x^2 + y^2 - 16x - 8y = 64$
    (c) $x^2 + y^2 + 6x = 0$; $x^2 + y^2 + 6x - 4y + 12 = 0$
    (d) $x^2 + y^2 + 2x - 8y + 1 = 0$; $x^2 + y^2 - 6y = 0$
    (e) $x^2 + y^2 + 2x = 3$; $x^2 + y^2 - 6x - 3 = 0$

14. If $y = 2x + c$ is a tangent to the circle
    $x^2 + y^2 + 4x - 10y - 7 = 0$ find the value(s) of c

15. Find the condition that m and c satisfy if the line $y = mx + c$
    touches the circle $x^2 + y^2 - 2ax = 0$

THREE MORE CLASSIC CURVES

The geometry of the circle, together with that of three more curves, the parabola, the ellipse and the hyperbola, has been part of mathematical investigation since classical times.

These curves were first defined and studied by Apollonius of Perga (c.250–200 BC). He defined them as curves traced out on the surface of a cone when it is cut by a plane; hence these curves are also known as conic sections.

Each of these curves can also be defined as a locus and its properties analysed using coordinate geometry.

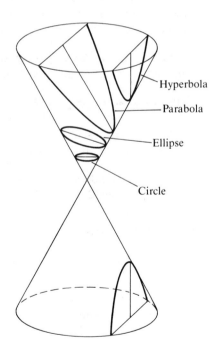

The general form of the Cartesian equation of the circle is now known, and in this section we will look briefly at the equations of the other curves.

The Parabola

If a point, P, is constrained so that its distance from a fixed line is equal to its distance from a fixed point, then the locus of P is a parabola. The curve given by this definition can be seen by plotting some of the possible positions of P.

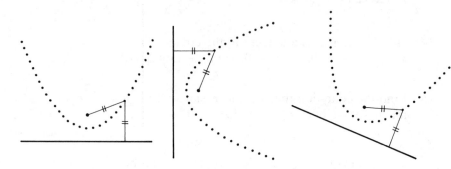

This is a familiar curve; it has an axis of symmetry and, in Chapter 12, we saw that when the axis of symmetry is parallel to Oy, the Cartesian equation of a parabola has the form $y = ax^2 + bx + c$

Similarly, when the axis of symmetry is parallel to Ox, the equation has the form $x = ay^2 + by + c$

The simplest forms of these equations are

$$y = x^2 \qquad\qquad x = y^2, \text{ (i.e. } y^2 = x)$$

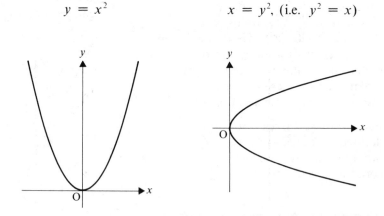

The classical position of the parabola for Cartesian analysis is with its axis parallel to Ox

The Ellipse

The locus of a point, P, is an ellipse when P moves so that its distance from a fixed point and its distance from a fixed line are in a constant ratio which is less than 1. This can be verified by plotting some positions of P for a value of the constant, say $\frac{1}{2}$

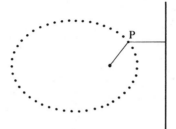

The Cartesian equation of a particular ellipse can be found from the locus definition using the method adopted earlier in this chapter.

The standard equation of an ellipse is $\dfrac{x^2}{a^2} + \dfrac{y^2}{b^2} = 1$

The Hyperbola

The locus definition of a hyperbola is very similar to that of the ellipse. A hyperbola is the locus of P when the ratio of the distance of P from a fixed point to the distance of P from a fixed line is constant and greater than 1. The shape of the hyperbola can be seen when some positions of P are plotted.

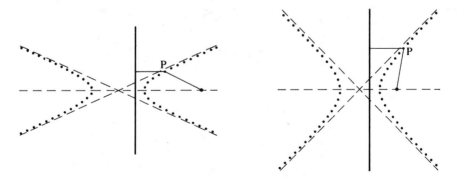

The standard equation of a hyperbola in this position is $\dfrac{x^2}{a^2} - \dfrac{y^2}{b^2} = 1$

All hyperbolas have a line of symmetry and a pair of asymptotes. When these asymptotes are perpendicular, the curve has a familiar shape; it is called a rectangular hyperbola. Further, when the asymptotes are the x and y axes, the equation of the curve has the form $y = c^2/x$ or $xy = c^2$

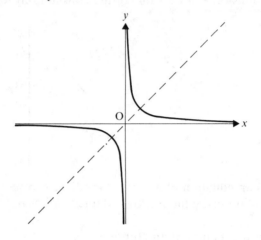

Example 27d _____

$P(x, y)$ is constrained so that the ratio of its distance from $(1, 0)$ to its distance from the line $x = 4$ is equal to $\frac{1}{2}$. Find the equation of the locus of P.

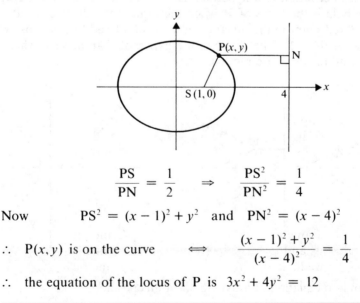

$$\frac{\text{PS}}{\text{PN}} = \frac{1}{2} \quad \Rightarrow \quad \frac{\text{PS}^2}{\text{PN}^2} = \frac{1}{4}$$

Now $\qquad \text{PS}^2 = (x - 1)^2 + y^2 \quad$ and $\quad \text{PN}^2 = (x - 4)^2$

$\therefore$ P(x, y) is on the curve $\qquad \Longleftrightarrow \qquad \dfrac{(x - 1)^2 + y^2}{(x - 4)^2} = \dfrac{1}{4}$

$\therefore$ the equation of the locus of P is $3x^2 + 4y^2 = 12$

EXERCISE 27d

Find the equation of the locus of P and name the curve in each of the following cases.

1. P is twice as far from the point $(2, 0)$ as it is from the line $x = 8$

2. P is equidistant from the point $(0, 4)$ and the line $y = -4$

3. P is half as far from the point $(2, 0)$ as it is from the line $x = 8$

4. Without plotting them, name each of the following curves.
   (a) $y = x^2 - 3$ (b) $y^2 + x^2 = 9$ (c) $xy = 1$
   (d) $x^2 - 3y^2 = 9$ (e) $y^2 = x + 2$ (f) $4x^2 + y^2 = 16$

5. The equation of a curve is $\dfrac{x^2}{9} + \dfrac{y^2}{4} = 1$. Find the coordinates of the points where the curve cuts the x and y axes. Sketch the curve.

6. Sketch the curve whose equation is $\dfrac{x^2}{a^2} + \dfrac{y^2}{b^2} = 1$

7. On the same set of axes sketch the curves
$$\frac{x^2}{16} + \frac{y^2}{4} = 1 \text{ and } \frac{x^2}{16} - \frac{y^2}{4} = 1$$
   (a) Give the coordinates of the points where curves cross the coordinate axes.
   (b) At how many points do the curves intersect?

PARAMETERS

The relationship between the x and y coordinates of a point on any standard conic involves at least one term of order 2 (i.e. x^2, y^2, xy). This relationship can often be expressed more simply in the form of two equations, i.e.

$$\left. \begin{array}{l} x = f(t) \\ y = g(t) \end{array} \right\} \text{ where } t \text{ is a parameter}$$

The use of parametric equations to plot curves, find gradients and hence tangents and normals to curves is covered in Chapter 23. In this chapter we look at other ways in which parametric equations can be used, and in particular at the parametric equations for conic sections.

Parametric Equations for a Circle

Consider the circle whose centre is the origin and whose radius is a.

The Cartesian equation of this circle is $\boxed{x^2 + y^2 = a^2}$ [1]

The parametric equations of this circle are $\boxed{\begin{cases} x = a\cos\theta \\ y = a\sin\theta \end{cases}}$ [2]

(Using the identity $\cos^2\theta + \sin^2\theta \equiv 1$ to eliminate θ from the parametric equations verifies that equations [2] are equivalent to equation [1].) The parameter, θ, has graphical significance in this case, as can be seen in the diagram below.

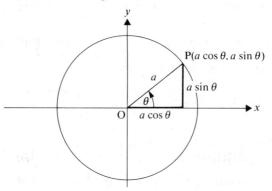

Parametric Equations for a Parabola

Consider the parabola whose vertex is the origin and whose axis is Ox.

If the Cartesian equation of this parabola is $\boxed{y^2 = 4ax}$ then

the parametric equations are $\boxed{\begin{cases} x = at^2 \\ y = 2at \end{cases}}$

In this case t has no geometrical meaning.

Parametric Equations for an Ellipse

The standard equation of the ellipse is $\dfrac{x^2}{a^2} + \dfrac{y^2}{b^2} = 1$

The parametric equations of this ellipse are $\begin{cases} x = a \cos \theta \\ y = b \sin \theta \end{cases}$

There is no *obvious* geometrical significance of θ in this case.

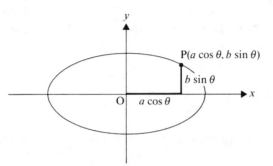

Parametric Equations for a Rectangular Hyperbola

The Cartesian equation of the rectangular hyperbola is $xy = c^2$

The parametric equations of this curve are $\begin{cases} x = ct \\ y = c/t \end{cases}$

Again, t has no *obvious* significance.

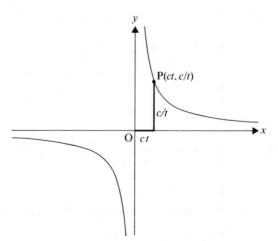

CURVE SKETCHING

Algebraic analysis is usually easier when the parametric equations of a curve are used. However sketching curves, particularly circles, is easier using Cartesian equations which show clearly the important features.

Examples 27e _____

1. On the same set of axes, sketch the curves

$$\begin{cases} x = 2\cos\theta + 1 \\ y = 2\sin\theta \end{cases} \quad \text{and} \quad \begin{cases} x = t^2 \\ y = 4t \end{cases}$$

Hence determine the number of points in which the curves cut.

The first pair of equations can be converted to a Cartesian equation by finding $\cos\theta$ in terms of x and $\sin\theta$ in terms of y and then using the identity $\cos^2\theta + \sin^2\theta \equiv 1$

$$\left.\begin{array}{l} x = 2\cos\theta + 1 \\ y = 2\sin\theta \end{array}\right\} \quad \Rightarrow \quad (x-1)^2 + y^2 = 4$$

This is a circle, centre $(1,0)$ radius 2

$$\left.\begin{array}{l} x = t^2 \\ y = 4t \end{array}\right\} \quad \Rightarrow \quad y^2 = 16x$$

This is a parabola, vertex $(0,0)$ and axis Ox.

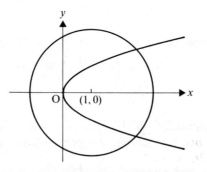

The sketch shows that there are two points of intersection.

_____

2. Find the coordinates of the points where the line $y = 3x - 1$ cuts the curve whose parametric equations are $x = t$, $y = 2t^2$

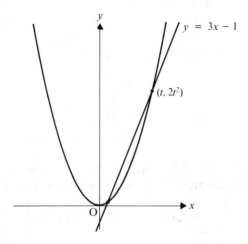

The coordinates of any point on the curve are $(t, 2t^2)$

The line cuts the curve where the coordinates of a point on the curve satisfy the equation of the line, i.e. where

$$2t^2 = 3t - 1$$

$$\Rightarrow \qquad 2t^2 - 3t + 1 = 0 \qquad \Rightarrow \qquad (t - 1)(2t - 1) = 0$$

This is a quadratic equation in t, giving two values of t and therefore giving two distinct points on the curve. This is expected from the sketch which indicates that there are two points of intersection.

So $\qquad\qquad\qquad\qquad\qquad t = 1 \text{ or } \frac{1}{2}$

Therefore the points of intersection are $(1, 2)$ and $(\frac{1}{2}, \frac{1}{2})$

---

3. Form an equation which gives the values of t at points where the line $y = mx + c$ crosses the curve whose parametric equations are $x = 2t$, $y = 2/t$

Find the condition that must be satisfied by m and c if

(a) the line cuts the curve in two places

(b) the line is a tangent to the curve.

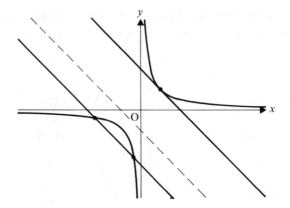

The point $(2t, 2/t)$ is any point on the curve, and the line $y = mx + c$ cuts the curve where $(2t, 2/t)$ is also a point on the line, i.e. where

$$\frac{2}{t} = m(2t) + c \quad \Rightarrow \quad 2mt^2 + ct - 2 = 0 \qquad [1]$$

This equation is quadratic in t, so it can have either two distinct real roots, a repeated root or no real roots.

(a) $y = mx + c$ cuts the curve in two places if equation [1] has real distinct roots,

i.e. if $\qquad$ '$b^2 - 4ac > 0$' $\quad \Rightarrow \quad c^2 - 4(2m)(-2) > 0$

$\qquad\qquad\qquad\qquad\qquad\qquad \Rightarrow \qquad c^2 + 16m > 0$

(b) $y = mx + c$ is a tangent to the curve if equation [1] has a repeated root,

i.e. if $\qquad$ '$b^2 - 4ac = 0$' $\quad \Rightarrow \quad c^2 + 16m = 0$

(If equation [1] has no real roots then the line $y = mx + c$ does not meet the curve.)

EXERCISE 27e

1. Sketch the curves given parametrically by

(a) $x = t^2, y = 2t$ $\qquad\qquad$ (b) $x = 3\cos\theta, y = 3\sin\theta$

(c) $x = t^2 + 1, y = t$ $\qquad\qquad$ (d) $x = 3t, y = 3/t$

(e) $x = 4t, y = t^2$ $\qquad\qquad$ (f) $x = 3\cos\theta, y = 4\sin\theta$

(g) $x = 3t + 2, y = t^2 - 1$ $\qquad\qquad$ (h) $x = \cos\theta + 2, y = \sin\theta - 1$

2. On the same set of axes sketch the curves defined parametrically by
   (a) $x = t^2, y = t$ and $x = \cos\theta, y = \sin\theta$
   (b) $x = 2/t, y = 2t$ and $x = 4\cos\theta, y = 6\sin\theta$
   (c) $x = t, y = 3t - 1$ and $x = 4t^2, y = 2t$

3. On the same set of axes sketch the curves given by
   $x = 2t, y = t^2$ and $x = 4\cos\theta, y = 4\sin\theta$
   Find the coordinates of the points of intersection of these two curves.

4. Determine whether the line $y = 2x + 1$ cuts, touches or misses
   each of the following curves.
   (a) $x = t^2, y = 4t$ (b) $x = t^2, y = t$
   (c) $x = 2t^2, y = 4t$ (d) $x = \cos\theta, y = \sin\theta + 1$

5. A curve has parametric equations $x = 2t^2, y = 4t$. Find
   (a) the Cartesian equation of the curve,
   (b) the equation of the tangent at the point where $y = 8$,
   (c) the equation of the chord joining the points on the curve
        where $t = p$ and $t = q$,
   (d) the coordinates of the points where $y = x - 6$ cuts the curve,
   (e) the value of k for which $y = x + k$ is a tangent to the
        curve,
   (f) the coordinates of the point(s) of intersection of the curve and
        the circle $x^2 + y^2 - 2x = 16$
   (g) the coordinates of the point(s) of intersection of the curve and
        the curve given parametrically by $x = 8s, y = 8/s$

CHAPTER 28

BASIC INTEGRATION

DIFFERENTIATION REVERSED

When x^2 is differentiated with respect to x the derivative is $2x$

Conversely, if the derivative of an unknown function is $2x$ then it is clear that the unknown function could be x^2

This process of finding a function from its derivative, which reverses the operation of differentiating, is called *integration*.

The Constant of Integration

As seen above, $2x$ is the derivative of x^2,
but it is also the derivative of $x^2 + 3$, $x^2 - 9$, and, in fact, the derivative of $x^2 +$ any constant.

Therefore the result of integrating $2x$, which is called *the integral of $2x$*, is not a unique function but is of the form

$$x^2 + K \quad \text{where } K \text{ is any constant}$$

K is called *the constant of integration*.

This is written

$$\int 2x \, dx = x^2 + K$$

where $\int \ldots dx$ means the integral of $\ldots$ w.r.t. x

Integrating *any* function reverses the process of differentiating so, for any function $f(x)$ we have

$$\int \frac{d}{dx} f(x) \, dx = f(x) + K$$

460

e.g. because differentiating x^3 w.r.t. x gives $3x^2$ we have

$$\int 3x^2 \, dx = x^3 + K$$

and it follows that $\qquad\qquad \int x^2 \, dx = \tfrac{1}{3}x^3 + K$

Note that it is not necessary to write $\tfrac{1}{3}K$ in the second form, as K represents *any* constant in either expression.

In general, the derivative of x^{n+1} is $(n+1)x^n$ so

$$\int x^n \, dx = \frac{1}{(n+1)}x^{n+1} + K$$

i.e. to integrate a power of x,

increase the power by 1 and *divide* by the new power.

This rule can be used to integrate any power of x *except -1, which is considered later.*

Integrating a Sum or Difference of Functions

We saw in Chapter 22 that a function can be differentiated term by term. Therefore, as integration reverses differentiation, integration also can be done term by term.

Example 28a _____

Find the integral of $x^7 + \dfrac{1}{x^2} - \sqrt{x}$

$$\int \left(x^7 + \frac{1}{x^2} - \sqrt{x} \right) dx = \int (x^7 + x^{-2} - x^{1/2}) \, dx$$

$$= \int x^7 \, dx + \int x^{-2} \, dx - \int x^{1/2} \, dx$$

$$= \frac{1}{8}x^8 + \frac{1}{-1}x^{-1} - \frac{1}{\tfrac{3}{2}}x^{3/2} + K$$

$$= \frac{1}{8}x^8 - \frac{1}{x} - \frac{2}{3}x^{3/2} + K$$

EXERCISE 28a

Integrate with respect to x,

1. x^5 **2.** $\dfrac{1}{x^5}$ **3.** $\sqrt[4]{x}$ **4.** x^{-3}

5. $\dfrac{1}{x^{5/2}}$ **6.** $x^{-1/2}$ **7.** x^1 **8.** $\dfrac{1}{\sqrt[3]{x}}$

Integrating $(ax + b)^n$

First consider the function $f(x) = (2x + 3)^4$

To differentiate $f(x)$ we make a substitution

i.e. $u = 2x + 3$ $\Rightarrow$ $f(x) = u^4$

giving $\dfrac{d}{dx}(2x + 3)^4 = (4)(2)(2x + 3)^3$

Hence $\displaystyle\int (4)(2)(2x + 3)^3 \, dx = (2x + 3)^4 + K$

or $\displaystyle\int (2x + 3)^3 \, dx = \dfrac{1}{(2)(4)}(2x + 3)^4 + K$

Considering $f(x) = (ax + b)^{n+1}$ in a similar way gives the general result

$$\int (ax + b)^n \, dx = \frac{1}{(a)(n + 1)}(ax + b)^{n+1} + K$$

USING INTEGRATION TO FIND AN AREA

The area shown in the diagram is bounded by the curve $y = f(x)$, the x-axis and the lines $x = a$ and $x = b$

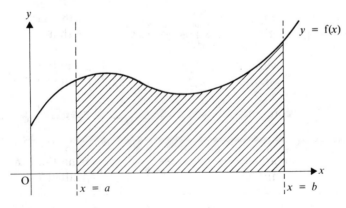

118

There are several elementary ways in which this area can be estimated, e.g. by counting squares on graph paper. A better method is to divide the area into thin vertical strips and treat each strip, or *element*, as being approximately rectangular.

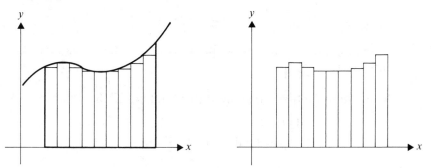

The sum of the areas of the rectangular strips then gives an approximate value for the required area. The thinner the strips are, the better is the approximation.

Note that every strip has one end on the x-axis, one end on the curve and two vertical sides, i.e., they all have the same type of boundaries.

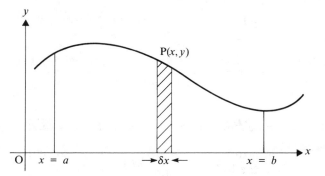

Now, considering a typical element bounded on the left by the ordinate through a general point $P(x, y)$, we see that

> the width of the element represents a small increase
> in the value of x and so can be called δx

Also, if A represents the part of the area up to the ordinate through P, then

> the area of the element represents a small increase
> in the value of A and so can be called δA

The shape of a typical strip is approximately a rectangle of height y and width δx

Therefore, for any element

$$\delta A \approx y\delta x \qquad [1]$$

The required area can now be found by adding the areas of all the strips from $x = a$ to $x = b$

The notation for a summation of this kind is $\sum\limits_{x=a}^{x=b} \delta A$

so, $\qquad$ total area $= \sum\limits_{x=a}^{x=b} \delta A$

$\Rightarrow \qquad$ total area $\approx \sum\limits_{x=a}^{x=b} y\,\delta x$

As δx gets smaller the accuracy of the results increases until, in the limiting case,

$$\text{total area} = \lim_{\delta x \to 0} \sum_{x=a}^{x=b} y\,\delta x$$

Equation [1] above can also be written in the alternative form

$$\frac{\delta A}{\delta x} \approx y$$

This form too becomes more accurate as δx gets smaller giving, in the limiting case,

$$\lim_{\delta x \to 0} \frac{\delta A}{\delta x} = y$$

But $\qquad \lim\limits_{\delta x \to 0} \dfrac{\delta A}{\delta x}$ is $\dfrac{dA}{dx}$ so $\dfrac{dA}{dx} = y$

Hence $\qquad A = \int y\,dx$

The boundary values of x defining the total area are $x = a$ and $x = b$ and we indicate this by writing

$$\text{total area} = \int_a^b y\,dx$$

The total area can therefore be found in two ways, either as the limit of a sum or by integration

i.e.
$$\lim_{\delta x \to 0} \sum_{x=a}^{x=b} y \, \delta x = \int_a^b y \, dx$$

and we conclude that   integration is a process of summation.

The application of integration to problems involving summation continues in Chapter 33. In this chapter we will use integration only to find areas bounded by straight lines and a curve, but first we must investigate the meaning of $\int_a^b y \, dx$

DEFINITE INTEGRATION

Suppose that we wish to find the area bounded by the x-axis, the lines $x = a$ and $x = b$ and the curve $y = 3x^2$

Using the method above we find that $A = \int 3x^2 \, dx$

i.e. $A = x^3 + K$

From this area function we can find the value of A corresponding to a particular value of x.

Hence using $x = a$ gives $A_a = a^3 + K$

and   using $x = b$ gives $A_b = b^3 + K$

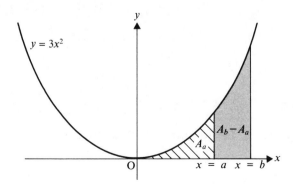

Then the area between $x = a$ and $x = b$ is given by $A_b - A_a$ where $A_b - A_a = (b^3 + K) - (a^3 + K) = b^3 - a^3$

Now $A_b - A_a$ is referred to as

the definite integral from a to b of $3x^2$

and is denoted by $\displaystyle\int_a^b 3x^2\,dx$

i.e. $\displaystyle\int_a^b 3x^2\,dx = (x^3)_{x=b} - (x^3)_{x=a}$

The RHS of this equation is usually written in the form $\left[x^3\right]_a^b$ where a and b are called the *boundary values* or *limits of integration*; b is the *upper limit* and a is the *lower limit*.

Whenever a definite integral is calculated, the constant of integration disappears.

Note. A definite integral can be found in this way only if the function to be integrated is defined for every value of x from a to b, e.g. $\displaystyle\int_{-1}^1 \frac{1}{x^2}\,dx$ cannot be found directly as $\dfrac{1}{x^2}$ is undefined when $x = 0$

Example 28b _____

Evaluate $\displaystyle\int_1^4 \frac{1}{(x+3)^2}\,dx$

$$\int_1^4 \frac{1}{(x+3)^2}\,dx \equiv \int_1^4 (x+3)^{-2}\,dx$$

$$= \left[-(x+3)^{-1}\right]_1^4$$

$$= \{-(4+3)^{-1}\} - \{-(1+3)^{-1}\}$$

$$= -\tfrac{1}{7} + \tfrac{1}{4} = \tfrac{3}{28}$$

EXERCISE 28b

Evaluate each of the following definite integrals.

1. $\displaystyle\int_0^2 x^3\,dx$ 2. $\displaystyle\int_1^2 \sqrt{x^5}\,dx$

3. $\displaystyle\int_2^4 (x^2 + 4)\,dx$ 4. $\displaystyle\int_3^8 \sqrt{(1+x)}\,dx$

5. $\displaystyle\int_0^3 (x^2 + 2x - 1)\, dx$ **6.** $\displaystyle\int_0^2 (x^3 - 3x)\, dx$

7. $\displaystyle\int_{-1}^0 \frac{1}{(1 - x)^2}\, dx$ **8.** $\displaystyle\int_{-1}^2 \frac{3}{\sqrt{(x + 2)}}\, dx$

9. $\displaystyle\int_{-1}^0 (2 + 3x)^6\, dx$ **10.** $\displaystyle\int_{1/2}^7 (4x - 1)^{1/3}\, dx$

FINDING AREA BY DEFINITE INTEGRATION

119

120

As we have seen, the area bounded by a curve $y = f(x)$, the lines $x = a$, $x = b$, and the x-axis, can be found from the definite integral

$$\int_a^b f(x)\, dx$$

It is recommended, however, that this is not regarded as a *formula* but that the required area is first considered as the summation of the areas of elements, a typical element being shown in a diagram.

Example 28c _____

Find the area in the first quadrant bounded by the x and y axes and the curve $y = 1 - x^2$

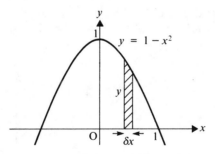

The required area starts at the y-axis, i.e. at $x = 0$ and ends where the curve crosses the x-axis, i.e. where $x = 1$. So it is given by

$$\lim_{\delta x \to 0} \sum_{x=0}^{x=1} y\, \delta x = \int_0^1 (1 - x^2)\, dx = \left[x - \frac{x^3}{3} \right]_0^1$$

$$= (1 - \tfrac{1}{3}) - (0 - 0) = \tfrac{2}{3}$$

The required area is $\tfrac{2}{3}$ of a square unit.

EXERCISE 28c

In each question find the area with the given boundaries.

1. The x-axis, the curve $y = x^2 + 3$ and the lines $x = 1$, $x = 2$

2. The curve $y = \sqrt{x}$, the x-axis and the lines $x = 4$, $x = 9$

3. The x-axis, the lines $x = -1$, $x = 1$, and the curve $x^2 + 1$

4. The curve $y = x^2 + x$, the x-axis and the line $x = 3$

5. The positive x and y axes and the curve $y = 4 - x^2$

6. The lines $x = 2$, $x = 4$, the x-axis and the curve $y = x^3$

7. The curve $y = 4 - x^2$, the positive y-axis and the negative x-axis.

8. The x-axis, the lines $x = 1$ and $x = 2$, and the curve
$y = \frac{1}{2}x^3 + 2x$

9. The x-axis and the lines $x = 1$, $x = 5$, and $y = 2x$
Check the result by sketching the required area and finding it by
mensuration

The Meaning of a Negative Result

Consider the area bounded by $y = 4x^3$ and the x-axis if the other
boundaries are the lines
(a) $x = -2$ and $x = -1$ (b) $x = 1$ and $x = 2$

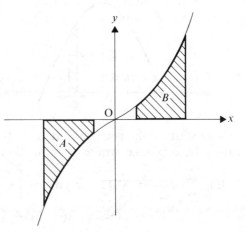

This curve is symmetrical about the origin so the two shaded areas are
equal.

(a) Considering A

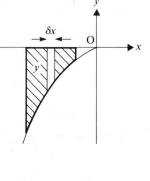

$$\lim_{\delta x \to 0} \sum_{x = -2}^{x = -1} y\, \delta x = \int_{-2}^{-1} y\, dx$$

$$= \int_{-2}^{-1} 4x^3\, dx$$

$$= \left[x^4 \right]_{-2}^{-1}$$

$$= 1 - 16 = -15$$

(b) Considering B

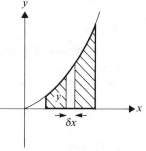

$$\lim_{\delta x \to 0} \sum_{x = 1}^{x = 2} y\, \delta x = \int_{1}^{2} y\, dx$$

$$= \int_{1}^{2} 4x^3\, dx$$

$$= \left[x^4 \right]_{1}^{2}$$

$$= 16 - 1 = 15$$

So we see that, while the magnitudes of the two areas are equal, the result for the area of A, which is below the x-axis, is negative. This is explained by the fact that the length of a strip in A was taken as y, which is negative for the part of the curve bounding A.

Note. Care must be taken with problems involving a curve that crosses the x-axis between the boundary values.

Example 28d _____

Find the area enclosed between the curve $y = x(x - 1)(x - 2)$ and the x-axis.

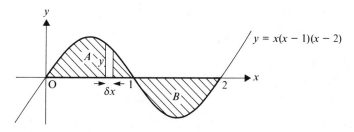

The area enclosed between the curve and the x-axis is the sum of the areas A and B.

For A we use
$$\int_0^1 y\,dx = \int_0^1 (x^3 - 3x^2 + 2x)\,dx$$

$$= \left[\frac{x^4}{4} - x^3 + x^2\right]_0^1$$

$$= \tfrac{1}{4}$$

For B we use
$$\int_1^2 (x^3 - 3x^2 + 2x)\,dx = \left[\frac{x^4}{4} - x^3 + x^2\right]_1^2$$

$$= (4 - 8 + 4) - (\tfrac{1}{4} - 1 + 1)$$

$$= -\tfrac{1}{4}$$

The minus sign refers only to the *position* of area B relative to the x-axis.
The actual area is $\tfrac{1}{4}$ of a square unit.
So the total shaded area is $\tfrac{1}{4} + \tfrac{1}{4} = \tfrac{1}{2}$ of a square unit.

EXERCISE 28d

In each Question from 1 to 5 find the specified area.

1. The area below the x-axis and above the curve $y = x^2 - 1$

2. The area bounded by the curve $y = 1 - x^3$, the x-axis and the lines $x = 2$, $x = 3$

3. The area between the x and y axes and the curve $y = (x - 1)^2$

4. Sketch the curve $y = x(x^2 - 1)$, showing where it crosses the x-axis. Find
   (a) the area enclosed above the x-axis and below the curve
   (b) the area enclosed below the x-axis and above the curve
   (c) the total area between the curve and the x-axis

5. Repeat Question 4 for the curve $y = x(4 - x^2)$

6. Evaluate

   (a) $\displaystyle\int_0^2 (x - 2)\,dx$ (b) $\displaystyle\int_2^4 (x - 2)\,dx$ (c) $\displaystyle\int_0^4 (x - 2)\,dx$

   Interpret your results by means of a sketch.

USING HORIZONTAL ELEMENTS

Suppose that area between the curve $x = y(4 - y)$ and the y-axis is required.

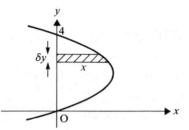

The curve crosses the y-axis where $y = 0$ and $y = 4$ as shown.

A vertical element is not suitable in this case because it has *both ends on the curve* and its length is therefore not easily found.

However it is easy to find the approximate area of a *horizontal* strip, by treating it as a rectangle with length x and width δy

i.e. area of element $\approx x \, \delta y$ and the required area is therefore given by

$$\lim_{\delta y \to 0} \sum_{y = 0}^{y = 4} x \, \delta y = \int_0^4 x \, dy = \int_0^4 y(y - 4) \, dy$$

EXERCISE 28e

1. Evaluate

   (a) $\int_3^6 (y^2 - y) \, dy$ (b) $\int_2^{10} \dfrac{1}{\sqrt{(2y + 5)}} \, dy$ (c) $\int_{-4}^3 (4 - y)^{-2/3} \, dy$

In Questions 2 to 5 find the area specified by the given boundaries.

2. The y-axis and the curve $x = 9 - y^2$

3. The curve $x = y^2$, the y-axis and the lines $y = 1$, $y = 2$

4. The y-axis, the curve $x = \sqrt{y}$ and the line $y = 4$

5. The y-axis and the curve $x = (y - 2)(y + 1)$

6. Find the area in the first quadrant bounded by the x and y axes and the curve $y = 16 - x^2$
   (a) by using vertical elements
   (b) by using horizontal elements and the equation of the curve in the form $x = \sqrt{(16 - y)}$

7. If $y = x^2$, show by means of sketch graphs and *not* by evaluating the integrals, that $\displaystyle\int_0^1 y \, dx = 1 - \int_0^1 x \, dy$

THE APPROXIMATE VALUE OF A DEFINITE INTEGRAL

We know that the definite integral $\displaystyle\int_a^b f(x) \, dx$ can be used to evaluate the area between the curve $y = f(x)$, the x-axis and the ordinates at $x = a$ and $x = b$. It is not always possible, however, to find a function whose derivative is $f(x)$. In such cases the definite integral, and hence the exact value of the specified area, cannot be found.

If, on the other hand, we divide the area into a *finite* number of strips then the sum of their areas gives an approximate value for the required area and hence an approximate value of the definite integral. When using this approach it is convenient to choose strips whose widths are all the same.

The Trapezium Rule

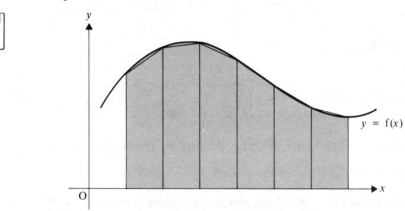

When the area shown in the diagram is divided into vertical strips, each strip is approximately a trapezium.

If the width of the strip and its two vertical sides are known, the area of the strip can be found using the formula

$$\text{area} = \tfrac{1}{2}(\text{sum of } \| \text{ sides}) \times \text{width}$$

The sum of the areas of all the strips then gives an approximate value for the area under the curve.

Now suppose that there are n strips, *all with the same width, d* say, and that the vertical edges of the strips (i.e. the ordinates) are labelled

$$y_0, y_1, y_2, \ldots, y_{n-1}, y_n$$

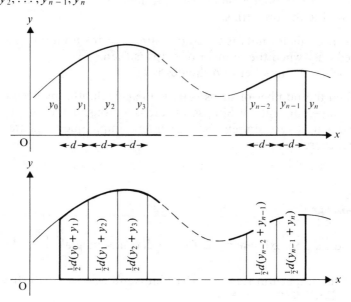

The sum of the areas of all the strips can be written down as follows:

$$\tfrac{1}{2}(y_0 + y_1)(d) + \tfrac{1}{2}(y_1 + y_2)(d) + \tfrac{1}{2}(y_2 + y_3)(d) + \ldots$$

$$\ldots + \tfrac{1}{2}(y_{n-2} + y_{n-1})(d) + \tfrac{1}{2}(y_{n-1} + y_n)(d)$$

Therefore the area, A, under the curve is given approximately by

$$A \approx \tfrac{1}{2}(d)\left[y_0 + 2y_1 + 2y_2 + \ldots + 2y_{n-1} + y_n \right]$$

This formula is known as the *Trapezium Rule*

An easy way to remember the formula in terms of ordinates is

half width of strip × (first + last + twice all the others)

Simpson's Rule

A formula which gives a better approximation than that obtained from the trapezium rule is known as *Simpson's Rule*.
Using the same notation as before it states that

$$A \approx \tfrac{1}{3}(d)\left[y_0 + 4y_1 + 2y_2 + 4y_3 + 2y_4 + \ldots 2y_{n-2} + 4y_{n-1} + y_n \right]$$

i.e. $A \approx \tfrac{1}{3}d\left[\{y_0 + y_n\} + 4\{y_1 + y_3 + \ldots\} + 2\{y_2 + y_4 + \ldots\} \right]$

This formula, given here without proof, is based on dividing the required area into equal width strips and, for each *pair* of strips, finding a parabola which passes through the top of the three ordinates bounding the two strips.

Because this formula is based on pairs of strips it follows that it can be used only when the number of strips is even, i.e. when the number of ordinates is odd.

When the number of strips is large the calculation involved in either the trapezium rule or Simpson's rule is tedious, but a computer can deal with it very simply. So only a few simple questions are set in the next exercise.

Example 28f _____

Find an approximate value for the definite integral $\displaystyle\int_1^5 x^3 \, dx$ using

(a) the trapezium rule   (b) Simpson's rule   with five ordinates.

The given definite integral represents the area bounded by the x-axis, the lines $x = 1$ and $x = 5$, and the curve $y = x^3$

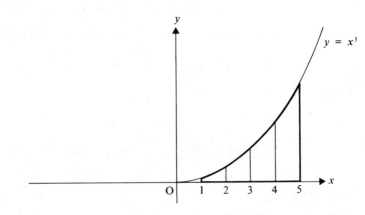

When five ordinates are used there are four strips and their widths must all be the same. From $x = 1$ to $x = 5$ there are four units so the width of each strip must be 1 unit. Hence the five ordinates are where $x = 1$, $x = 2$, $x = 3$, $x = 4$ and $x = 5$

$\therefore \quad y_0 = 1^3 = 1, \ y_1 = 2^3 = 8, \ y_2 = 3^3 = 27, \ y_3 = 64, \ y_4 = 125$

(a) Using the trapezium rule, the required area, A, is given by

$$A \approx \tfrac{1}{2}(1)\big[\,1 + 125 + 2\{8 + 27 + 64\}\,\big] = 162$$

The required area is approximately 162 square units.

(b) There is an odd number of ordinates so Simpson's rule can be used.
A is given by

$$A \approx \tfrac{1}{3}(1)\big[\,\{1 + 125\} + 4\{8 + 64\} + 2\{27\}\,\big] = 156$$

The required area is approximately 156 square units.

The degree of accuracy of an answer given by either of these rules clearly depends upon the number of strips into which the required area is divided, because the narrower the strip, (a) the nearer its shape becomes to a trapezium, (b) the more nearly does the top of two strips fit a parabola.

EXERCISE 28f

In Questions 1 to 6 estimate the value of each definite integral, using
(a) the trapezium rule   (b) Simpson's rule
each with   (i) 3 ordinates   (ii) 5 ordinates.

1. $\displaystyle\int_0^4 x^2 \, dx$ 2. $\displaystyle\int_1^3 \frac{1}{x^2} \, dx$

3. $\displaystyle\int_0^{2\pi/3} \sqrt{\sin x} \, dx$ 4. $\displaystyle\int_1^3 \ln x \, dx$

5. Find the true value of the definite integrals given in Questions 1 and 2 Complete the table below and note the comparative accuracy of the results given by the two rules.

Value using	$\displaystyle\int_0^4 x^2\,dx$	$\displaystyle\int_1^3 \frac{1}{x^2}\,dx$
Trapezium rule with 5 ordinates		
Simpson's rule with 5 ordinates		
Definite integration		

MIXED EXERCISE 28

Integrate with respect to x

1. $x^2 - 1/x^2$ 2. $\sqrt{(3x + 7)}$ 3. $\sqrt{x} + 1/\sqrt{x}$

4. $\dfrac{1}{(4x - 3)}$ 5. $x^3 - \dfrac{1}{(1 - x)^3}$ 6. $\dfrac{x^2 - 1}{\sqrt{x}}$

Evaluate

7. $\displaystyle\int_5^6 (6 - x)^4 \, dx$ 8. $\displaystyle\int_{-1}^{12} \dfrac{3}{\sqrt[3]{(2y + 3)}} \, dy$ 9. $\displaystyle\int_1^{32} \left(\sqrt[5]{x} - \dfrac{1}{\sqrt[5]{x}} \right) dx$

Find the areas specified in Questions 10 to 12

10. Bounded by the x and y axes and the curve $y = 1 - x^3$

11. Bounded by the curve $x = y^2 - 4$ and the y-axis.

12. The *total* area between the curve $y = (x - 1)(x - 2)(x - 3)$ and the x-axis.

13. (a) Find an approximate value for the area between the x-axis and the curve $y = (x - 1)(x - 4)$, using the trapezium rule with 4 ordinates.

   (b) Evaluate $\displaystyle\int_1^4 (x - 1)(x - 4) \, dx$

14. (a) Use the trapezium rule with 3 ordinates to estimate the value of $\displaystyle\int_0^5 (3 + x) \, dx$

   (b) Find the value of $\displaystyle\int_0^5 (3 + x) \, dx$

   (c) Explain the connection between the results of (a) and (b).

FURTHER INTEGRATION 1

STANDARD INTEGRALS

Whenever a function $f(x)$ is *recognised* as the derivative of a function $f(x)$ then

$$\frac{d}{dx} f(x) = f'(x) \quad \Rightarrow \quad \int f'(x)\, dx = f(x) + K$$

Thus any function whose derivative is known can be established as a standard integral.

INTEGRATING EXPONENTIAL FUNCTIONS

It is already known that $\dfrac{d}{dx} e^x = e^x$

hence

$$\int e^x\, dx = e^x + K$$

Further, we have

$$\frac{d}{dx}(ce^x) = ce^x$$

and

$$\frac{d}{dx} e^{(ax+b)} = ae^{(ax+b)}$$

Hence

$$\int ce^x\, dx = ce^x + K$$

and

$$\int e^{(ax+b)} = \frac{1}{a} e^{(ax+b)} + K$$

e.g. $\displaystyle\int 2e^x\, dx = 2e^x + K \quad$ and $\quad \displaystyle\int 4e^{(1-3x)}\, dx = (4)(-\tfrac{1}{3})e^{(1-3x)} + K$

To integrate an exponential function where the given base is not e but is some other constant, a say, the base must first be changed to e as follows.

Using $a^x = e^z$ and taking logs to the base e we have

$$x \ln a = z$$

Hence $a^x = e^{x \ln a}$ $\Rightarrow$ $\displaystyle\int a^x \, dx = \int e^{x \ln a} \, dx$

$$\Rightarrow \quad \int a^x \, dx = \frac{1}{\ln a} e^{x \ln a} + K$$

i.e. $$\int a^x \, dx = \frac{1}{\ln a} a^x + K$$

Alternatively, this result can be obtained directly if it is remembered that

$$\frac{d}{dx}(a^x) = (\ln a)a^x$$

Example 29a

Write down the integral of e^{3x} w.r.t. x and hence evaluate $\displaystyle\int_0^1 e^{3x} \, dx$

$$\int e^{3x} \, dx = \tfrac{1}{3}e^{3x} + K$$

The constant of integration disappears when a definite integral is calculated, hence

$$\int_0^1 e^{3x} \, dx = \left[\tfrac{1}{3}e^{3x}\right]_0^1 = \tfrac{1}{3}e^3 - \tfrac{1}{3}e^0$$

i.e. $$\int_0^1 e^{3x} \, dx = \tfrac{1}{3}(e^3 - 1)$$

EXERCISE 29a

Integrate each function w.r.t. x

1. e^{4x}
2. $4e^{-x}$
3. $e^{(3x-2)}$
4. $2e^{(1-5x)}$

5. $6e^{-2x}$
6. $5e^{(x-3)}$
7. $e^{(2+x/2)}$
8. 2^x

9. $4^{(2+x)}$
10. $e^{2x} + \dfrac{1}{e^{2x}}$
11. $a^{(1-2x)}$
12. $2^x + x^2$

Evaluate the following definite integrals.

13. $\displaystyle\int_0^2 e^{2x}\,dx$

14. $\displaystyle\int_{-1}^1 2e^{(x+1)}\,dx$

15. $\displaystyle\int_2^3 e^{(2-x)}\,dx$

16. $\displaystyle\int_0^2 -e^x\,dx$

FUNCTIONS WHOSE INTEGRALS ARE LOGARITHMIC

To Integrate $\dfrac{1}{x}$

At first sight it looks as though we can write $\dfrac{1}{x} = x^{-1}$ and integrate

by using the rule $\displaystyle\int x^n\,dx = \dfrac{1}{n+1}x^{(n+1)} + K$

However, this method fails when $n = -1$ because the resulting integral is meaningless.

Taking a second look at $\dfrac{1}{x}$ it can be *recognised* as the derivative of $\ln x$.

It must be remembered, however, that $\ln x$ is defined only when $x > 0$. Hence, provided that $x > 0$ we have

$$\frac{d}{dx}(\ln x) = \frac{1}{x} \quad \Longleftrightarrow \quad \int\frac{1}{x}\,dx = \ln x + K$$

Now if $x < 0$ the statement $\displaystyle\int\frac{1}{x}\,dx = \ln x$ is not valid because the log of a negative number does not exist.

However, $\dfrac{1}{x}$ exists for negative values of x, as the graph of $y = \dfrac{1}{x}$ shows.

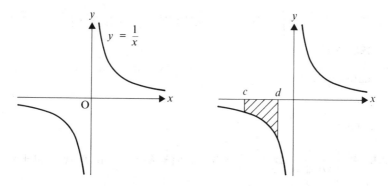

Also, the definite integral $\displaystyle\int_c^d \frac{1}{x}\,dx$, which is represented by the shaded

area, clearly exists. It must, therefore, be possible to integrate $\dfrac{1}{x}$ when

x is negative and we see below how to deal with the problem.

If $x < 0$ then $-x > 0$

i.e. $$\int \frac{1}{x}\,dx = \int \frac{-1}{(-x)}\,dx = \ln(-x) + K$$

Thus, when $x > 0$, $\displaystyle\int \frac{1}{x}\,dx = \ln x + K$

and   when $x < 0$, $\displaystyle\int \frac{1}{x}\,dx = \ln(-x) + K$

These two results can be combined so that, for both positive and
negative values of x, we have

$$\int \frac{1}{x}\,dx = \ln|x| + K$$

where $|x|$ denotes the numerical value of x regardless of sign

e.g. $|-1| = 1$ and $|-4| = 4$

The expression $\ln|x| + K$ can be simplified if K is replaced by $\ln A$,
where A is a positive constant, giving

$$\int \frac{1}{x}\,dx = \ln|x| + \ln A = \ln A|x|$$

Further $\dfrac{d}{dx}(\ln x^c) = \dfrac{d}{dx}(c\ln x) = \dfrac{c}{x}$

$\therefore$ $$\int \frac{c}{x}\,dx = c\ln|x| + K \quad\text{or}\quad c\ln A|x|$$

e.g. $$\int \frac{4}{x}\,dx = 4\ln|x| + K \quad\text{or}\quad 4\ln A|x|$$

Also $\dfrac{d}{dx}\ln(ax + b) = \dfrac{a}{ax + b}$

$\therefore$ $$\int \frac{1}{ax + b}\,dx = \frac{1}{a}\ln|ax + b| + K = \frac{1}{a}\ln A|ax + b|$$

e.g. $\displaystyle\int \frac{1}{2x+5}\,dx = \frac{1}{2}\ln|2x+5|$ or $\dfrac{1}{2}\ln A\,|2x+5|$

and $\displaystyle\int \frac{1}{4-3x}\,dx = -\frac{1}{3}\ln|4-3x|+K$ or $-\dfrac{1}{3}\ln A\,|4-3x|$

$$= \frac{1}{3}\ln\frac{A}{|4-3x|}$$

EXERCISE 29b

Integrate w.r.t. x giving each answer in a form which
(a) uses K (b) uses $\ln A$ and is simplified.

1. $\dfrac{1}{2x}$ 2. $\dfrac{4}{x}$ 3. $\dfrac{1}{3x+1}$ 4. $\dfrac{3}{1-2x}$

5. $\dfrac{6}{2+3x}$ 6. $\dfrac{3}{4-2x}$ 7. $\dfrac{4}{1-x}$ 8. $\dfrac{5}{6-7x}$

Evaluate

9. $\displaystyle\int_{1}^{2}\frac{3}{x}\,dx$ 10. $\displaystyle\int_{1}^{2}\frac{1}{2x}\,dx$ 11. $\displaystyle\int_{4}^{5}\frac{2}{x-3}\,dx$ 12. $\displaystyle\int_{0}^{1}\frac{1}{2-x}\,dx$

INTEGRATING TRIGONOMETRIC FUNCTIONS

Knowing the derivatives of the six trig functions, we can recognise the following integrals.

$\dfrac{d}{dx}(\sin x) = \cos x$ $\Longleftrightarrow$ $\displaystyle\int \cos x\,dx = \sin x + K$

$\dfrac{d}{dx}(\cos x) = -\sin x$ $\Longleftrightarrow$ $\displaystyle\int \sin x\,dx = -\cos x + K$

$\dfrac{d}{dx}(\tan x) = \sec^2 x$ $\Longleftrightarrow$ $\displaystyle\int \sec^2 x\,dx = \tan x + K$

$\dfrac{d}{dx}(\sec x) = \sec x\tan x$ $\Longleftrightarrow$ $\displaystyle\int \sec x\tan x\,dx = \sec x + K$

$\dfrac{d}{dx}(\operatorname{cosec} x) = -\operatorname{cosec} x\cot x$ $\Longleftrightarrow$ $\displaystyle\int \operatorname{cosec} x\cot x\,dx = -\operatorname{cosec} x + K$

$\dfrac{d}{dx}(\cot x) = -\operatorname{cosec}^2 x$ $\Longleftrightarrow$ $\displaystyle\int \operatorname{cosec}^2 x\,dx = -\cot x + K$

Remembering the derivatives of some variations of the basic trig functions we also have

$$\int c \cos x \, dx = c \sin x + K$$

and

$$\int \cos(ax + b) \, dx = \frac{1}{a} \sin(ax + b) + K$$

with similar results for the remaining trig integrals,

e.g.

$$\int 3 \sec^2 x \, dx = 3 \tan x + K$$

$$\int \sin 4\theta \, d\theta = -\tfrac{1}{4} \cos 4\theta + K$$

$$\int \csc^2(2x + \tfrac{3}{4}\pi) \, dx = -\tfrac{1}{2} \cot(2x + \tfrac{3}{4}\pi) + K$$

$$\int \csc 5\theta \cot 5\theta \, d\theta = -\tfrac{1}{5} \csc 5\theta + K$$

$$\int \sec(\tfrac{1}{2}\pi - 6x)\tan(\tfrac{1}{2}\pi - 6x) \, dx = -\tfrac{1}{6} \sec(\tfrac{1}{2}\pi - 6x) + K$$

Note that there is no need to *learn* these standard integrals. Knowledge of the standard derivatives is sufficient.

EXERCISE 29c

Integrate each function w.r.t. x

1. $\sin 2x$
2. $\cos 7x$
3. $\sec^2 4x$
4. $\sin(\tfrac{1}{4}\pi + x)$
5. $3 \cos(4x - \tfrac{1}{2}\pi)$
6. $\sec^2(\tfrac{1}{3}\pi + 2x)$
7. $\csc^2 4x$
8. $2 \sin(3x - a)$
9. $5 \cos(a - \tfrac{1}{2}x)$
10. $5 \sec 4x \tan 4x$
11. $\cos 3x - \cos x$
12. $\sec^2 2x - \csc^2 4x$

Evaluate

13. $\displaystyle\int_0^{\pi/6} \sin 3x \, dx$
14. $\displaystyle\int_{\pi/4}^{\pi/6} \cos(2x - \tfrac{1}{2}\pi) \, dx$

15. $\displaystyle\int_0^{\pi/2} 2 \sin(2x - \tfrac{1}{2}\pi) \, dx$
16. $\displaystyle\int_0^{\pi/8} \sec^2 2x \, dx$

FUNCTIONS WHOSE INTEGRALS ARE INVERSE TRIG FUNCTIONS

We know that $\qquad y = \arcsin x \qquad \Rightarrow \qquad \dfrac{dy}{dx} = \dfrac{1}{\sqrt{(1-x^2)}}$

Therefore

$$\int \frac{1}{\sqrt{(1-x^2)}}\,dx = \arcsin x + K$$

Similarly it can be seen that

$$\int \frac{1}{1+x^2}\,dx = \arctan x + K$$

Now consider $\qquad y = \arcsin \dfrac{x}{a} \qquad \Rightarrow \qquad x = a \sin y$

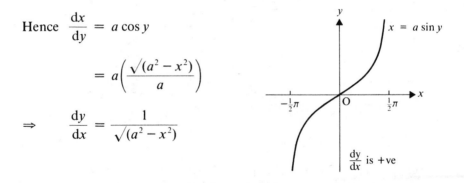

Hence $\quad \dfrac{dx}{dy} = a \cos y$

$$= a\left(\frac{\sqrt{(a^2-x^2)}}{a}\right)$$

$\Rightarrow \qquad \dfrac{dy}{dx} = \dfrac{1}{\sqrt{(a^2-x^2)}}$

$x = a \sin y$

$\dfrac{dy}{dx}$ is +ve

Therefore

$$\int \frac{1}{\sqrt{(a^2-x^2)}}\,dx = \arcsin \frac{x}{a} + K$$

Similar working shows that if $\quad y = \arctan \dfrac{x}{a} \qquad \Rightarrow \qquad x = a \tan y$

then

$$\frac{dx}{dy} = a \sec^2 y = a\left(\frac{\sqrt{(a^2-x^2)}}{a}\right)^2$$

Therefore

$$\int \frac{a}{a^2+x^2}\,dx = \arctan \frac{x}{a} + K$$

EXERCISE 29d

Write down the integral w.r.t. x of each function.

1. $\dfrac{1}{\sqrt{(1-x^2)}}$ 2. $\dfrac{2}{x^2+4}$ 3. $\dfrac{1}{\sqrt{(4-x^2)}}$ 4. $\dfrac{3}{1+x^2}$

5. $\dfrac{5}{x^2+9}$ 6. $\dfrac{1}{\sqrt{(9-x^2)}}$ 7. $\dfrac{1}{16+x^2}$ 8. $\dfrac{5}{\sqrt{(2-x^2)}}$

EXERCISE 29e

This exercise contains a variety of functions, including those dealt with in Chapter 28.
The reader is advised always to check that an integral is correct by differentiating it mentally.

Integrate w.r.t. x

1. $\sin(\tfrac{1}{2}\pi - 2x)$ 2. $e^{(4x-1)}$ 3. $\sec^2 7x$

4. $\dfrac{1}{2x-3}$ 5. $\dfrac{1}{\sqrt{(2x-3)}}$ 6. $\dfrac{1}{(3x-2)^2}$

7. 5^x 8. $\operatorname{cosec} \tfrac{1}{2}x \cot \tfrac{1}{2}x$ 9. $(3x-5)^2$

10. $e^{(4x-5)}$ 11. $\sqrt{(4x-5)}$ 12. $\operatorname{cosec}^2 3x$

13. $\dfrac{3}{2(1-x)}$ 14. $10^{(x+1)}$ 15. $\cos(3x - \tfrac{1}{3}\pi)$

Evaluate

16. $\displaystyle\int_{-1/2}^{1/2} \sqrt{(1-2x)}\,dx$ 17. $\displaystyle\int_{0}^{2} e^{(x/2+1)}\,dx$ 18. $\displaystyle\int_{\pi/4}^{\pi/2} \sin 4x\,dx$

THE RECOGNITION ASPECT OF INTEGRATION

We have already seen the importance of the recognition aspect of integration in compiling a set of standard integrals.
Recognition is equally important when it is used to avoid serious errors in integration.

Consider, for instance, the derivative of the product $x^2 \sin x$
Using the product formula gives

$$\frac{d}{dx}(x^2 \sin x) = 2x \sin x + x^2 \cos x$$

Clearly the derivative is not a simple product, therefore

> the integral of a product is not itself a product

i.e.   integration is not distributive when applied to a product

On the other hand, when we differentiate the function of a function $(1 + x^2)^3$ we get

$$\frac{d}{dx}(1 + x^2)^3 = 6x(1 + x^2)^2$$

This time the derivative *is* a product so clearly the integral of a product *may* be a function of a function.

INTEGRATING PRODUCTS

First consider the function e^u where u is a function of x. Differentiating as a function of a function gives

$$\frac{d}{dx}(e^u) = \left(\frac{du}{dx}\right)(e^u)$$

Thus any product of the form $\left(\dfrac{du}{dx}\right)e^u$ can be integrated by recognition, since

$$\int \left(\frac{du}{dx}\right)e^u \, dx = e^u + K$$

e.g.

$$\int 2x \, e^{x^2} \, dx = e^{x^2} + K \quad (u = x^2)$$

$$\int \cos x \, e^{\sin x} \, dx = e^{\sin x} + K \quad (u = \sin x)$$

$$\int x^2 \, e^{x^3} \, dx = \tfrac{1}{3} \int 3x^2 \, e^{x^3} \, dx = \tfrac{1}{3} e^{x^3} + K \quad (u = x^3)$$

In these simple cases the substitution of u for $f(x)$ is done mentally. All the results can be checked by differentiating them mentally.

Similar, but slightly less simple functions, can also be integrated by changing the variable but for these the substitution is written down.

Changing the Variable

Consider a general function $g(u)$ where u is a function of x

$$\frac{d}{dx}g(u) = \frac{du}{dx}g'(u) \quad \text{or} \quad g'(u)\frac{du}{dx}$$

Therefore $\qquad\qquad\qquad \int g'(u)\frac{du}{dx}dx = g(u) + K \qquad\qquad [1]$

We also know that $\qquad\quad \int g'(u)\,du = g(u) + K \qquad\qquad\qquad [2]$

Comparing [1] and [2] gives

$$\int g'(u)\frac{du}{dx}dx = \int g'(u)\,du$$

Replacing $g'(u)$ by $f(u)$ gives

$$\int f(u)\frac{du}{dx}dx = \int f(u)\,du$$

i.e. $\qquad\qquad\qquad\qquad \ldots\, \frac{du}{dx}dx \equiv \ldots\, du \qquad\qquad\qquad [3]$

Thus integrating (a function of u) $\dfrac{du}{dx}$ w.r.t. x is *equivalent to* integrating (the same function of u) w.r.t. u

i.e. the relationship in [3] is neither an equation nor an identity but is a pair of equivalent operations.

Suppose, for example, that we want to find $\displaystyle\int 2x(x^2 + 1)^5\,dx$

Writing the integral in the form $\displaystyle\int (x^2 + 1)^5\,2x\,dx$ and making the substitution $u = x^2 + 1$ gives

$$\int (x^2 + 1)^5\,2x\,dx = \int u^5(2x)\,dx$$

But $\qquad\qquad \dfrac{du}{dx} = 2x$ and $\ldots\,\dfrac{du}{dx}dx \equiv \ldots\,du$

Therefore $\qquad\qquad\qquad\qquad\qquad\qquad \ldots\,2x\,dx \equiv \ldots\,du$

i.e. $$\int (x^2 + 1)^5 2x \, dx = \int u^5 \, du$$

$$= \tfrac{1}{6}u^6 + K = \tfrac{1}{6}(x^2 + 1)^6 + K$$

In practice we can go direct from $\dfrac{du}{dx} = 2x$ to the equivalent

operators $\ldots 2x \, dx \equiv \ldots du$ by 'separating the variables'.

Products which can be integrated by this method are those in which one factor is basically the derivative of the function in the other factor.

Examples 29f

1. Integrate $x^2\sqrt{(x^3 + 5)}$ w.r.t. x

In this product x^2 is basically the derivative of $x^3 + 5$ so we choose the substitution $u = x^3 + 5$

If $u = x^3 + 5$ then $\dfrac{du}{dx} = 3x^2$

$\Rightarrow$ $\ldots du \equiv \ldots 3x^2 \, dx$

Hence $\displaystyle\int x^2\sqrt{(x^3 + 5)} \, dx = \tfrac{1}{3}\int (x^3 + 5)^{1/2}(3x^2 \, dx) = \tfrac{1}{3}\int u^{1/2} \, du$

$$= (\tfrac{1}{3})(\tfrac{2}{3})u^{3/2} + K$$

i.e. $\displaystyle\int x^2\sqrt{(x^3 + 5)} \, dx = \tfrac{2}{9}(x^3 + 5)^{3/2} + K$

2. Find $\displaystyle\int \cos x \sin^3 x \, dx$

Writing the given integral in the form $\cos x (\sin x)^3$ shows that a suitable substitution is $u = \sin x$

If $u = \sin x$ then $\ldots du \equiv \ldots \cos x \, dx$

$\therefore$ $\displaystyle\int \cos x \sin^3 x \, dx = \int (\sin x)^3 \cos x \, dx = \int u^3 \, du$

$$= \tfrac{1}{4}u^4 + K$$

i.e. $\displaystyle\int \cos x \sin^3 x \, dx = \tfrac{1}{4}\sin^4 x + K$

Applied generally, the method used above shows that

$$\int \cos x \sin^n x \, dx = \frac{1}{n+1} \sin^{(n+1)} x + K$$

and similarly that

$$\int \sin x \cos^n x \, dx = \frac{-1}{n+1} \cos^{(n+1)} x + K$$

---

3. Find $\int \dfrac{\ln x}{x} \, dx$

Initially this looks like a fraction but once it is recognised as the product of $\dfrac{1}{x}$ and $\ln x$, it is clear that $\dfrac{1}{x} = \dfrac{d}{dx}(\ln x)$ and that we can make the substitution $u = \ln x$

If $u = \ln x$ then $\ldots du \equiv \ldots \dfrac{1}{x} \, dx$

Hence $\int \dfrac{1}{x} \ln x \, dx = \int u \, du = \frac{1}{2}u^2 + K$

i.e. $\int \dfrac{\ln x}{x} \, dx = \frac{1}{2}(\ln x)^2 + K$

Note that $(\ln x)^2$ is *not* the same as $\ln x^2$

EXERCISE 29f

Integrate the following expressions w.r.t. x

1. $4x^3 e^{x^4}$

2. $\sin x \, e^{\cos x}$

3. $\sec^2 x \, e^{\tan x}$

4. $(2x + 1)e^{(x^2 + x)}$

5. $\csc^2 x \, e^{(1 - \cot x)}$

6. $(1 + \cos x) \, e^{(x + \sin x)}$

7. $2x \, e^{(1 + x^2)}$

8. $(3x^2 - 2) \, e^{(x^3 - 2x)}$

Find the following integrals by making the substitution suggested.

9. $\int x(x^2 - 3)^4 \, dx$ $\qquad\qquad u = x^2 - 3$

10. $\int x\sqrt{(1 - x^2)} \, dx$ $\qquad\qquad u = 1 - x^2$

11. $\int \cos 2x (\sin 2x + 3)^2 \, dx \quad u = \sin 2x + 3$

12. $\int x^2 (1 - x^3) \, dx$ $\qquad\qquad u = 1 - x^3$

13. $\int e^x \sqrt{(1 + e^x)} \, dx$ $\qquad\qquad u = 1 + e^x$

14. $\int \cos x \sin^4 x \, dx$ $\qquad\qquad u = \sin x$

15. $\int \sec^2 x \tan^3 x \, dx$ $\qquad\qquad u = \tan x$

16. $\int x^n (1 + x^{n+1})^2 \, dx$ $\qquad\qquad u = 1 + x^{n+1}$

17. $\int \text{cosec}^2 x \cot^2 x \, dx$ $\qquad\qquad u = \cot x$

18. $\int \sqrt{x} \sqrt{(1 + x^{3/2})} \, dx$ $\qquad\qquad u = 1 + x^{3/2}$

By using a suitable substitution, or by integrating at sight, find

19. $\int x^3 (x^4 + 4)^2 \, dx$ $\qquad\qquad$ 20. $\int e^x (1 - e^x)^3 \, dx$

21. $\int \sin \theta \sqrt{(1 - \cos \theta)} \, d\theta$ $\qquad\qquad$ 22. $\int (x + 1)\sqrt{(x^2 + 2x + 3)} \, dx$

23. $\int x \, e^{x^2 + 1} \, dx$ $\qquad\qquad$ 24. $\int \sec^2 x \, (1 + \tan x) \, dx$

DEFINITE INTEGRATION WITH A CHANGE OF VARIABLE

A definite integral can be evaluated only after the appropriate integration has been performed. Should this require a change of variable, e.g. from x to u, it is usually most convenient to change the limits of integration also from x values to u values.

Example 29g _____

By using the substitution $u = x^3 + 1$, evaluate $\displaystyle\int_0^1 x^2\sqrt{(x^3 + 1)}\, dx$

If $u = x^3 + 1$ then $\ldots du \equiv \ldots 3x^2\, dx$

$$\text{and} \quad \begin{cases} x = 0 \;\Rightarrow\; u = 1 \\ x = 1 \;\Rightarrow\; u = 2 \end{cases}$$

Hence $\displaystyle\int_0^1 x^2\sqrt{(x^3 + 1)}\, dx = \tfrac{1}{3}\int_1^2 \sqrt{u}\, du$

$$= \tfrac{1}{3}\left[\tfrac{2}{3}u^{3/2}\right]_1^2$$

$$= \tfrac{2}{9}(2\sqrt{2} - 1)$$

_____

EXERCISE 29g

Evaluate

1. $\displaystyle\int_0^1 x\, e^{x^2}\, dx$

2. $\displaystyle\int_0^{\pi/2} \cos x \, \sin^4 x \, dx$

3. $\displaystyle\int_1^2 \frac{1}{x}\ln x\, dx$

4. $\displaystyle\int_1^2 x^2(x^3 - 1)^4\, dx$

5. $\displaystyle\int_0^{\pi/4} \sec^2 x\, e^{\tan x}\, dx$

6. $\displaystyle\int_1^2 x(1 + 2x^2)\, dx$

7. $\displaystyle\int_2^3 (x - 1)e^{(x^2 - 2x)}\, dx$

8. $\displaystyle\int_0^{\pi/6} \cos x(1 + \sin^2 x)\, dx$

9. $\displaystyle\int_1^3 \frac{1}{x}(\ln x)^2\, dx$

10. $\displaystyle\int_0^{\sqrt{3}} x\sqrt{(1 + x^2)}\, dx$

INTEGRATION BY PARTS

It is not always possible to express a product in the form $f(u)\dfrac{du}{dx}$ so an alternative approach is needed.

Looking again at the differentiation of a product uv where u and v are both functions of x we have

$$\frac{d}{dx}(uv) = v\frac{du}{dx} + u\frac{dv}{dx} \quad \Rightarrow \quad v\frac{du}{dx} = \frac{d}{dx}(uv) - u\frac{dv}{dx}$$

Now $v\dfrac{du}{dx}$ can be taken to represent a product which is to be integrated w.r.t. x

Thus $$\int v\frac{du}{dx}\,dx = \int \frac{d}{dx}(uv)\,dx - \int u\frac{dv}{dx}\,dx$$

i.e. $$\int v\frac{du}{dx}\,dx = uv - \int u\frac{dv}{dx}\,dx$$

At this stage it may appear that the RHS is more complicated than the original product on the LHS.

However, by careful choice of the factor to be replaced by v we can ensure that $u\dfrac{dv}{dx}$ is easier to integrate than $v\dfrac{du}{dx}$

The factor chosen to be replaced by v is usually the one whose derivative is a simpler function. It must also be remembered, however, that the other factor is replaced by $\dfrac{du}{dx}$ and therefore it must be possible to integrate it.

This method for integrating a product is called *integrating by parts*.

Examples 29h

1. Integrate $x\,e^x$ w.r.t. x

Taking $$v = x \quad \text{and} \quad \frac{du}{dx} = e^x$$

gives $$\frac{dv}{dx} = 1 \quad \text{and} \quad u = e^x$$

Then
$$\int v \frac{du}{dx} dx = uv - \int u \frac{dv}{dx} dx$$

gives
$$\int x\, e^x\, dx = (e^x)(x) - \int (e^x)(1)\, dx$$
$$= x\, e^x - e^x + K$$

---

2. Find $\int x^2 \sin x\, dx$

Taking
$$v = x^2 \quad \text{and} \quad \frac{du}{dx} = \sin x$$

gives
$$\frac{dv}{dx} = 2x \quad \text{and} \quad u = -\cos x$$

Then
$$\int v \frac{du}{dx} dx = uv - \int u \frac{dv}{dx} dx$$

gives
$$\int x^2 \sin x\, dx = (-\cos x)(x^2) - \int (-\cos x)(2x)\, dx$$
$$= -x^2 \cos x + 2 \int x \cos x\, dx \qquad \text{[1]}$$

At this stage the integral on the RHS cannot be found without *repeating* the process of integrating by parts on the term $\int x \cos x\, dx$ as follows.

Taking
$$v = x \quad \text{and} \quad \frac{du}{dx} = \cos x$$

gives
$$\frac{dv}{dx} = 1 \quad \text{and} \quad u = \sin x$$

Then
$$\int x \cos x\, dx = (\sin x)(x) - \int (\sin x)(1)\, dx$$
$$= x \sin x + \cos x + K$$

Hence equation [1] becomes
$$\int x^2 \sin x\, dx = -x^2 \cos x + 2x \sin x + 2 \cos x + K$$

---

3. Find $\int x^4 \ln x \, dx$

Because $\ln x$ can be differentiated but *not integrated*, we must use $v = \ln x$

Taking $$v = \ln x \quad \text{and} \quad \frac{du}{dx} = x^4$$

gives $$\frac{dv}{dx} = \frac{1}{x} \quad \text{and} \quad u = \tfrac{1}{5}x^5$$

The formula for integrating by parts then gives

$$\int x^4 \ln x \, dx = (\tfrac{1}{5}x^5)(\ln x) - \int (\tfrac{1}{5}x^5)\left(\frac{1}{x}\right) dx$$

$$= \tfrac{1}{5}x^5 \ln x - \tfrac{1}{5} \int x^4 \, dx$$

$\Rightarrow \qquad \int x^4 \ln x \, dx = \tfrac{1}{5}x^5 \ln x - \tfrac{1}{25}x^5 + K$

Special Cases of Integration by Parts

An interesting situation arises when an attempt is made to integrate $e^x \cos x$ or $e^x \sin x$

---

4. Find $\int e^x \cos x \, dx$

Taking $$v = e^x \quad \text{and} \quad \frac{du}{dx} = \cos x$$

gives $$\frac{dv}{dx} = e^x \quad \text{and} \quad u = \sin x$$

Hence $$\int e^x \cos x \, dx = e^x \sin x - \int e^x \sin x \, dx \qquad\qquad [1]$$

But since $\int e^x \sin x \, dx$ is very similar to $\int e^x \cos x \, dx$ it seems that we have made no progress. However, if we now apply integration by parts to $\int e^x \sin x \, dx$ an interesting situation emerges.

Taking $\qquad\qquad v = e^x \quad\text{and}\quad \dfrac{du}{dx} = \sin x$

gives $\qquad\qquad \dfrac{dv}{dx} = e^x \quad\text{and}\quad u = -\cos x$

so that $\qquad \displaystyle\int e^x \sin x \, dx = -e^x \cos x + \int e^x \cos x \, dx$

or $\qquad\qquad \displaystyle\int e^x \cos x \, dx = e^x \cos x + \int e^x \sin x \, dx \qquad\qquad [2]$

Adding [1] and [2] gives

$$2\int e^x \cos x \, dx = e^x(\sin x + \cos x) + K$$

Clearly the same two equations can be used to give

$$2\int e^x \sin x \, dx = e^x(\sin x - \cos x) + K$$

Note that neither of the equations [1] and [2] contains a completed integration process, so the constant of integration is introduced only when these two equations have been combined.

Note also that the same choice of function for v must be made in both applications of integration by parts, i.e. we chose $v = e^x$ each time.

Integration of ln x

So far we have found no way to integrate $\ln x$. Now, however, if $\ln x$ is regarded as the product of 1 and $\ln x$ we can apply integration by parts as follows.

Examples 29h (continued) _____

5. Find $\displaystyle\int \ln x \, dx$

Taking $\qquad\qquad v = \ln x \quad\text{and}\quad \dfrac{du}{dx} = 1$

gives $\qquad\qquad \dfrac{dv}{dx} = \dfrac{1}{x} \quad\text{and}\quad u = x$

Then
$$\int v \frac{du}{dx} dx = uv - \int u \frac{dv}{dx} dx$$

becomes
$$\int \ln x \, dx = x \ln x - \int x \left(\frac{1}{x} \right) dx$$
$$= x \ln x - x + K$$

i.e.
$$\int \ln x \, dx = x(\ln x - 1) + K$$

This 'trick' of multiplying by 1 to create a product can also be used to integrate $\arcsin x$ and other inverse trig functions as will be shown in Examples 29i.

EXERCISE 29h

Integrate the following functions w.r.t. x

1. $x \cos x$
2. $x^2 e^x$
3. $x^3 \ln 3x$
4. $x e^{-x}$
5. $3x \sin x$
6. $e^x \sin 2x$
7. $e^{2x} \cos x$
8. $x^2 e^{4x}$
9. $e^{-x} \sin x$
10. $\ln 2x$
11. $e^x(x + 1)$
12. $x(1 + x)^7$
13. $x \sin (x + \frac{1}{6}\pi)$
14. $x \cos nx$
15. $x^n \ln x$
16. $3x \cos 2x$
17. $2e^x \sin x \cos x$
18. $x^2 \sin x$
19. $e^{ax} \sin bx$
20. By writing $\cos^3 \theta$ as $(\cos^2 \theta)(\cos \theta)$ use integration by parts to find $\int \cos^3 \theta \, d\theta$.

Each of the following products can be integrated either:
 (a) by immediate recognition, or
 (b) by a suitable change of variable, or
 (c) by parts.

Choose the best method in each case and hence integrate each function.

21. $(x - 1)e^{x^2 - 2x + 4}$
22. $(x + 1)^2 e^x$
23. $\sin x(4 + \cos x)^3$

24. $\cos x \, e^{\sin x}$ **25.** $x^4\sqrt{(1+x^5)}$ **26.** $e^x(e^x+2)^4$

27. $x \, e^{2x-1}$ **28.** $x(1-x^2)^9$ **29.** $\cos x \sin^5 x$

DEFINITE INTEGRATION BY PARTS

When using the formula

$$\int v \frac{du}{dx} dx = uv - \int u \frac{dv}{dx} dx$$

it must be appreciated that the term uv on the RHS is fully integrated. Consequently in a definite integration, uv must be *evaluated between the appropriate boundaries*

i.e.

$$\int_a^b v \frac{du}{dx} dx = \left[uv\right]_a^b - \int_a^b u \frac{dv}{dx} dx$$

Examples 29i

1. Evaluate $\displaystyle\int_0^1 x \, e^x \, dx$

$$\int x \, e^x \, dx = \int v \frac{du}{dx} dx$$

where

$$v = x \quad \text{and} \quad \frac{du}{dx} = e^x$$

Hence

$$\int_0^1 x \, e^x \, dx = \left[xe^x\right]_0^1 - \int_0^1 e^x \, dx$$

$$= \left[xe^x\right]_0^1 - \left[e^x\right]_0^1$$

$$= (e^1 - 0) - (e^1 - e^0)$$

$$= e - e + 1$$

i.e.

$$\int_0^1 x \, e^x \, dx = 1$$

2. Find the value of $\displaystyle\int_0^{1/2} \arccos x \, dx$

We regard $\arccos x$ as a product, i.e. $(1)(\arccos x)$ and integrate by parts. As $\arccos x$ cannot yet be integrated, it must be replaced by v

Taking $\qquad\qquad v = \arccos x \qquad$ and $\qquad \dfrac{du}{dx} = 1$

gives $\qquad\qquad \dfrac{dv}{dx} = \dfrac{-1}{\sqrt{(1-x^2)}} \qquad$ and $\qquad u = x$

Then $\displaystyle\int_0^{1/2} (1)(\arccos x)\, dx = \left[x\arccos x \right]_0^{1/2} - \int_0^{1/2} \dfrac{-x}{\sqrt{(1-x^2)}}\, dx$

$$= \{(\tfrac{1}{2})(\tfrac{1}{3}\pi) - 0\} + \int_0^{1/2} \dfrac{x}{\sqrt{(1-x^2)}}\, dx$$

Now $\displaystyle\int_0^{1/2} \dfrac{x}{\sqrt{(1-x^2)}}\, dx = \int_1^{3/4} \dfrac{1}{\sqrt{u}}(-\tfrac{1}{2}\,dt)$

where $t = 1 - x^2$ and

x	0	$\frac{1}{2}$
t	1	$\frac{3}{4}$

$$= \left[-\sqrt{t} \right]_1^{3/4}$$

$$= -\tfrac{1}{2}\sqrt{3} + 1$$

$\therefore \qquad \displaystyle\int \arccos x \, dx = \tfrac{1}{6}\pi - \tfrac{1}{2}\sqrt{3} + 1$

EXERCISE 29i

Evaluate

1. $\displaystyle\int_0^{\pi/2} x\sin x \, dx$
 2. $\displaystyle\int_1^{2} x^5 \ln x \, dx$
 3. $\displaystyle\int_0^{1} (x+1)\, e^x \, dx$

4. $\displaystyle\int_0^{\pi} e^x \cos x \, dx$
 5. $\displaystyle\int_1^{2} x\sqrt{(x-1)} \, dx$
 6. $\displaystyle\int_0^{\pi/2} x^2 \cos x \, dx$

7. $\displaystyle\int_0^{1} \arcsin x \, dx$
 8. $\displaystyle\int_0^{1} x^2 e^x \, dx$
 9. $\displaystyle\int_1^{\sqrt 3} \arctan x \, dx$

MIXED EXERCISE 29

Integrate the following functions, taking care to choose the best method in each case.

1. $x^2 e^{2x}$

2. $2x \exp(x^2)$

3. $\sec^2 x (3 \tan x - 4)$

4. $(x + 1)\ln(x + 1)$

5. $\sec^2 x \tan^3 x$

6. $x^2 \cos x$

7. $\sin x \, e^{\cos x}$

8. $x(2x + 3)^7$

9. $(1 - x)\exp(1 - x)^2$

10. $x e^{(2x - 1)}$

11. $\cos x \sin^5 x$

12. $\sin x (4 + \cos x)^3$

13. $(x - 1)e^{(x^2 - 2x + 3)}$

14. $x^2 (1 - x^3)^9$

Evaluate each definite integral.

15. $\displaystyle\int_1^3 e^{3x} \, dx$

16. $\displaystyle\int_0^{\pi/8} \cos 4x \, dx$

17. $\displaystyle\int_0^1 \frac{1}{x - 2} \, dx$

18. $\displaystyle\int_{\pi/4}^{\pi/2} \operatorname{cosec}^2 x \, dx$

19. $\displaystyle\int_0^1 x^2 e^{3x^3} \, dx$

20. $\displaystyle\int_0^{\pi/4} x \cos 2x \, dx$

21. $\displaystyle\int_0^1 \frac{1}{2 - x} \ln(2 - x) \, dx$

22. $\displaystyle\int_1^2 x^2 \ln x \, dx$

CHAPTER 30

ALGEBRA 2

RELATIONSHIPS BETWEEN ROOTS AND COEFFICIENTS OF A QUADRATIC EQUATION

The general quadratic equation $ax^2 + bx + c = 0$ can be written

$$x^2 + \frac{b}{a}x + \frac{c}{a} = 0 \qquad [1]$$

If the roots of the equation are α and β then the equation can also be written in the form

$$(x - \alpha)(x - \beta) = 0$$

$$\Rightarrow \qquad x^2 - (\alpha + \beta)x + \alpha\beta = 0 \qquad [2]$$

Comparing the terms in equations [1] and [2] shows that

$$\alpha + \beta = -\frac{b}{a} \text{ and } \alpha\beta = \frac{c}{a}$$

e.g. if the equation $2x^2 - 3x + 6 = 0$ has roots α and β, then

the sum of its roots, i.e. $\alpha + \beta$, is $-(-\frac{3}{2}) = \frac{3}{2}$

and the product of its roots, i.e. $\alpha\beta$, is $\frac{6}{2} = 3$

It also follows from the relationships above that any quadratic equation can be expressed in the form

$$x^2 - (\text{sum of roots})x + (\text{product of roots}) = 0$$

e.g. the quadratic equation with roots whose sum is 7 and whose product is 10, is $x^2 - 7x + 10 = 0$

Examples 30a _____

1. The roots of the equation $2x^2 - 7x + 4 = 0$ are α and β

   Find the values of $\dfrac{1}{\alpha} + \dfrac{1}{\beta}$ and $\dfrac{1}{\alpha\beta}$ and hence write down the

   equation whose roots are $\dfrac{1}{\alpha}$ and $\dfrac{1}{\beta}$

From $2x^2 - 7x + 4 = 0$ we have

$$\alpha + \beta = -(-\tfrac{7}{2}) = \tfrac{7}{2} \quad \text{and} \quad \alpha\beta = \tfrac{4}{2} = 2$$

To evaluate $\dfrac{1}{\alpha} + \dfrac{1}{\beta}$ we must first express it in terms of $\alpha + \beta$ and $\alpha\beta$ as these have known values.

Expressing $\dfrac{1}{\alpha} + \dfrac{1}{\beta}$ as a single fraction gives

$$\frac{1}{\alpha} + \frac{1}{\beta} = \frac{\alpha + \beta}{\alpha\beta} = \frac{\tfrac{7}{2}}{2} = \frac{7}{4}$$

and

$$\frac{1}{\alpha\beta} = \frac{1}{2}$$

The required equation has roots $\dfrac{1}{\alpha}$ and $\dfrac{1}{\beta}$ therefore

the sum of its roots is $\left(\dfrac{1}{\alpha} + \dfrac{1}{\beta}\right) = \dfrac{7}{4}$

and the product of its roots is $\alpha\beta = \tfrac{1}{2}$

Hence the required equation is $\quad x^2 - \tfrac{7}{4}x + \tfrac{1}{2} = 0$

i.e. $\qquad\qquad\qquad\qquad\qquad 4x^2 - 7x + 2 = 0$

Alternatively the following method can be used.

   For the given equation, $2x^2 - 7x + 4 = 0$, $\quad x = \alpha$ and β

and for the required equation, $aX^2 + bX + c = 0$, $\quad X = \dfrac{1}{\alpha}$ and $\dfrac{1}{\beta}$

Therefore $\qquad\qquad\qquad X = \dfrac{1}{x} \quad \Rightarrow \quad x = \dfrac{1}{X}$

Substituting $\dfrac{1}{X}$ for x in the given equation we get

$$2\left(\frac{1}{X}\right)^2 - 7\left(\frac{1}{X}\right) + 4 = 0$$

i.e. $4X^2 - 7X + 2 = 0$

and this is the required equation.

The alternative method can be used only if each new root depends in the same way on each original root. For example, if the given equation has roots α, β and the required equation has roots α^2, β^2 it can be used, but if the required equation has roots $\alpha + \beta$, $\alpha - \beta$ it cannot.

---

2. If α and β are the roots of $x^2 + 3x - 2 = 0$ find the values of $\alpha^3 + \beta^3$ and $\alpha^3\beta^3$. Write down the equation whose roots are α^3 and β^3

From $x^2 + 3x - 2 = 0$ we see that $\alpha + \beta = -3$

and $\alpha\beta = -2$

To express $\alpha^3 + \beta^3$ in terms of $\alpha + \beta$ and $\alpha\beta$ we can use

$$(\alpha + \beta)^3 \equiv \alpha^3 + 3\alpha^2\beta + 3\alpha\beta^2 + \beta^3$$

$$\equiv \alpha^3 + \beta^3 + 3\alpha\beta(\alpha + \beta)$$

therefore $\alpha^3 + \beta^3 \equiv (\alpha + \beta)^3 - 3\alpha\beta(\alpha + \beta)$

$$= (-3)^3 - 3(-2)(-3)$$

$$= -45$$

$$\alpha^3\beta^3 \equiv (\alpha\beta)^3 = (-2)^3 = -8$$

As the required equation has roots α^3 and β^3, the sum of its roots is $\alpha^3 + \beta^3 = -45$ and the product of its roots is $\alpha^3\beta^3 = -8$

Therefore the required equation is $x^2 - (-45)x + (-8) = 0$

i.e. $x^2 + 45x - 8 = 0$

Note that, although the alternative method could be used in this example, as $X = x^3$, it is not recommended because the resulting equation $(\sqrt[3]{X})^2 + 3(\sqrt[3]{X}) + 4 = 0$ is not easy to simplify.

---

3. Find the range of values of k for which the roots of the equation $x^2 - 2x - k = 0$ are real. If the roots of this equation differ by 1, find the value of k

If $x^2 - 2x - k = 0$ has real roots then $b^2 - 4ac \geqslant 0$

i.e. $\qquad\qquad\qquad (-2)^2 - 4(1)(-k) \geqslant 0$

$\Rightarrow \qquad\qquad\qquad\qquad 4 + 4k \geqslant 0$

$\therefore \qquad\qquad\qquad\qquad\quad k \geqslant -1$

If one root of the equation is α, then the other is $\alpha + 1$

The sum of the roots is $\qquad\qquad 2\alpha + 1 = -(-2)$

$\Rightarrow \qquad\qquad\qquad\qquad\quad 2\alpha = 1$

$\therefore \qquad\qquad\qquad\qquad\quad\ \alpha = \frac{1}{2}$

The product of the roots is $\qquad \alpha(\alpha + 1) = -k$

Therefore $\qquad\qquad\qquad\qquad k = -\frac{3}{4}$

EXERCISE 30a

1. Write down the sums and products of the roots of the following equations.

   (a) $x^2 - 3x + 2 = 0$ $\qquad\qquad$ (b) $4x^2 + 7x - 3 = 0$

   (c) $x(x - 3) = x + 4$ $\qquad\qquad$ (d) $\dfrac{x - 1}{2} = \dfrac{3}{x + 2}$

   (e) $x^2 - kx + k^2 = 0$ $\qquad\qquad$ (f) $ax^2 - x(a + 2) - a = 0$

2. Write down the equation, the sum and product of whose roots are

   (a) $3, 4$ $\qquad$ (b) $-2, \frac{1}{2}$ $\qquad$ (c) $\frac{1}{3}, -\frac{2}{5}$ $\qquad$ (d) $-\frac{1}{4}, 0$

   (e) a, a^2 $\qquad$ (f) $-(k + 1), k^2 - 3$ $\qquad\qquad$ (g) $\dfrac{b}{a}, \dfrac{c^2}{b}$

3. The roots of the equation $2x^2 - 4x + 5 = 0$ are α and β. Find the value of

   (a) $\dfrac{1}{\alpha} + \dfrac{1}{\beta}$ $\qquad$ (b) $(\alpha + 1)(\beta + 1)$ $\qquad$ (c) $\alpha^2 + \beta^2$

   (d) $\alpha^2\beta + \alpha\beta^2$ $\qquad$ (e) $(\alpha - \beta)^2$ $\qquad\qquad$ (f) $\dfrac{\alpha}{\beta} + \dfrac{\beta}{\alpha}$

4. The roots of $x^2 - 2x + 3 = 0$ are α and β. Find the equation whose roots are

(a) $\alpha + 2,\ \beta + 2$ (b) $\dfrac{1}{\alpha},\ \dfrac{1}{\beta}$ (c) $\alpha^2,\ \beta^2$ (d) $\dfrac{\alpha}{\beta},\ \dfrac{\beta}{\alpha}$

DIVISION OF ONE POLYNOMIAL BY ANOTHER POLYNOMIAL

Long division can be used to divide say $x^3 + 4x^2 - 7$ by $x^2 - 3$ ($x^3 + 4x^2 - 7$ is called the *dividend* and $x^2 - 3$ is called the *divisor*.)

$$
\begin{array}{r}
x + 4 \\
x^2 - 3 \overline{)x^3 + 4x^2 - 7} \\
\underline{x^3 - 3x} \\
4x^2 + 3x - 7 \\
\underline{4x^2 - 12} \\
+ 3x + 5
\end{array}
$$

Divide x^3 by x^2: it goes in x times.
Multiply the divisor by x and then subtract it
from the dividend.
The result is the new dividend; repeat the
process until the dividend is not divisible by x^2

The number over the division line is the *quotient*, and what is left is called the *remainder*.

The relationship between the divisor, the dividend, the quotient and the remainder can be expressed as

$$x^3 + 4x^2 - 7 \equiv (x + 4)(x^2 - 3) + 3x + 5$$

IMPROPER FRACTIONS

When the highest power of x in the numerator of a fraction is greater than or *equal* to the highest power of x in the denominator, the fraction is called *improper*.

For example, $\dfrac{x^3 + 4x^2 - 7}{x^2 - 3}$ and $\dfrac{x^2 + 7}{x^2 - 2}$ are improper fractions.

Improper fractions can be expressed in a form in which any fractions are proper, by dividing the numerator by the denominator,

i.e. $\dfrac{x^3 + 4x^2 - 7}{x^2 - 3}$ can be written as $x + 4 + \dfrac{3x + 5}{x^2 - 3}$

Long division is not always necessary; it is often simpler to rearrange the numerator by adding and subtracting appropriate terms. This is illustrated in the following worked example.

Example 30b _____

Express $\dfrac{x^3 + 5x^2 - 3x}{x^3 + 1}$ in a form without an improper fraction.

$$\frac{x^3 + 5x^2 - 3x}{x^3 + 1} \equiv \frac{x^3 + 1 + 5x^2 - 3x - 1}{x^3 + 1} \equiv \frac{x^3 + 1}{x^3 + 1} + \frac{5x^2 - 3x - 1}{x^3 + 1}$$

$$\equiv 1 + \frac{5x^2 - 3x - 1}{x^3 + 1}$$

Notice that we add 1 to x^3 so that the expression can be split into two fractions, one of which divides out exactly. It is important to realise that, having added 1 to the numerator we also have to subtract 1 so that the value of the numerator is not altered.

After some practice, it is possible to do the intermediate steps mentally.

_____

EXERCISE 30b

1. Find the quotient and the remainder for each of the following divisions.
   (a) $(x^3 + x^2 - 3x + 6) \div (x^2 + 3)$
   (b) $(x^4 - 5x^2 + 2) \div (x + 1)$
   (c) $(2x^3 - 4x^2 + 3x - 1) \div (x^2 - 1)$
   (d) $(3x^3 - 5) \div (x - 2)$
   (e) $(x^5 - 5x^2 + 1) \div (x^3 + 1)$

2. Express the following fractions as the sum of a polynomial and a proper fraction.

   (a) $\dfrac{x + 4}{x + 1}$ (b) $\dfrac{2x}{x - 2}$ (c) $\dfrac{x^2 + 3}{x^2 - 1}$

   (d) $\dfrac{x^2}{x - 2}$ (e) $\dfrac{x^2 + 3x}{x - 4}$ (f) $\dfrac{x^2 - 4}{x(x + 1)}$

PARTIAL FRACTIONS

It was seen in Chapter 2 that we can express a proper fraction whose denominator consists of linear factors as a number of separate fractions,

e.g. $\dfrac{x + 1}{(x - 2)(x + 2)}$ can be expressed as $\dfrac{3}{4(x - 2)} + \dfrac{1}{4(x + 2)}$

One method for finding the numerators of the separate fractions is given in Chapter 2 but there is a quicker way which we will now look at.

The Cover-up Method

Consider $f(x) = \dfrac{x}{(x-2)(x-3)} = \dfrac{A}{x-2} + \dfrac{B}{x-3}$

$$= \frac{A(x-3)+B(x-2)}{(x-2)(x-3)}$$

$\Rightarrow \qquad\qquad x \equiv A(x-3)+B(x-2)$

When $x = 2$, $A = \dfrac{2}{2-3} = -2$,

which is the value of $\dfrac{x}{(x-3)}$ when $x = 2$

i.e. $\quad A = f(2)$ with the factor $(x-2)$ 'covered up'.

Similarly when $x = 3$, $B = \dfrac{3}{3-2} = 3$

which is the value of $\dfrac{x}{(x-2)}$ when $x = 3$

i.e. $\quad B = f(3)$ with the factor $(x-3)$ covered up.

Hence $\qquad \dfrac{x}{(x-2)(x-3)} \equiv \dfrac{-2}{x-2} + \dfrac{3}{x-3}$

Note that this method can be used only for linear factors.

Examples 30c

1. Express $\dfrac{1}{(2x-1)(x+3)}$ in partial fractions.

$$\frac{1}{(2x-1)(x+3)} = \frac{f(\frac{1}{2}) \text{ with } (2x-1) \text{ covered up}}{(2x-1)} + \frac{f(-3) \text{ with } (x+3) \text{ covered up}}{(x+3)}$$

$$= \frac{2}{7(2x-1)} - \frac{1}{7(x+3)}$$

Note that the intermediate step does not need to be written down.

Quadratic Factors in the Denominator

It is also possible to decompose fractions with quadratic or higher degree factors.

Consider $\dfrac{x^2 + 1}{(x^2 + 2)(x - 1)}$

This is a proper fraction, so its partial fractions are also proper, i.e.

$\dfrac{x^2 + 1}{(x^2 + 2)(x - 1)}$ can be expressed in the form $\dfrac{Ax + B}{x^2 + 2} + \dfrac{C}{x - 1}$

Using the cover-up method gives $C = \frac{2}{3}$, but to find A and B the partial fraction form must be expressed as a single fraction giving

$$x^2 + 1 \equiv (Ax + B)(x - 1) + \tfrac{2}{3}(x^2 + 2)$$

The values of A and B can then be found by substituting any suitable values for x

We will choose $x = 0$ and $x = -1$ as these are simple values to handle. (We do not choose $x = 1$ as it eliminates A and B and it was used to find C.)

$x = 0$ gives $\qquad 1 = B(-1) + \tfrac{2}{3}(2) \qquad\qquad \Rightarrow \qquad B = \tfrac{1}{3}$

$x = -1$ gives $\qquad 2 = (-A + \tfrac{1}{3})(-2) + \tfrac{2}{3}(3) \qquad \Rightarrow \qquad A = \tfrac{1}{3}$

$\therefore \qquad\qquad \dfrac{x^2 + 1}{(x^2 + 2)(x - 1)} \equiv \dfrac{x + 1}{3(x^2 + 2)} + \dfrac{2}{3(x - 1)}$

A Repeated Factor in the Denominator

Consider the fraction $\dfrac{2x - 1}{(x - 2)^2}$

This is a proper fraction, and it is possible to express this as two fractions with numerical numerators as we can see if we adjust numerator,

i.e. $\qquad \dfrac{2x - 1}{(x - 2)^2} \equiv \dfrac{2(x - 2) - 1 + 4}{(x - 2)^2} \equiv \dfrac{2}{x - 2} + \dfrac{3}{(x - 2)^2}$

Any fraction whose denominator is a repeated linear factor can be expressed as separate fractions with numerical numerators, for example,

$$\frac{2x^2 - 3x + 4}{(x-1)^3} \quad \text{can be expressed as} \quad \frac{A}{x-1} + \frac{B}{(x-1)^2} + \frac{C}{(x-1)^3}$$

In the general case the values of the numerators can be found using the method in the next worked example.

To summarise, a proper fraction can be decomposed into partial fractions and the form of the partial fractions depends on the form of the factors in the denominator where

a linear factor gives a partial fraction of the form $\dfrac{A}{ax+b}$

a quadratic factor gives a partial fraction of the form $\dfrac{Ax+B}{ax^2+bx+c}$

a repeated factor gives two partial fractions of the form

$$\frac{A}{ax+b} + \frac{B}{(ax+b)^2}$$

Examples 30c (continued) _____

2. Express $\dfrac{x-1}{(x+1)(x-2)^2}$ in partial fractions.

$$\frac{x-1}{(x+1)(x-2)^2} \equiv \frac{-\frac{2}{9}}{x+1} + \frac{B}{(x-2)} + \frac{C}{(x-2)^2}$$

$$\Rightarrow \qquad x-1 \equiv (-\tfrac{2}{9})(x-2)^2 + B(x+1)(x-2) + C(x+1)$$

$x = 2$ gives $C = \tfrac{1}{3}$

Comparing coefficients of x^2 gives $0 = -\tfrac{2}{9} + B \Rightarrow B = \tfrac{2}{9}$

$$\therefore \qquad \frac{x-1}{(x+1)(x-2)^2} \equiv -\frac{2}{9(x+1)} + \frac{2}{9(x-2)} + \frac{1}{3(x-2)^2}$$

Note that C can be found by the cover-up method, but B cannot.

_____

3. Express $\dfrac{x^3}{(x+1)(x-3)}$ in partial fractions.

This fraction is improper and it must be divided out to obtain a mixed fraction before it can be expressed in partial fractions.

$$
\begin{array}{r}
x + 2 \\
x^2 - 2x - 3 \overline{\smash{)}x^3} \\
\underline{x^3 - 2x^2 - 3x} \\
2x^2 + 3x \\
\underline{2x^2 - 4x - 6} \\
7x + 6
\end{array}
$$

$$
\therefore \quad \frac{x^3}{(x+1)(x-3)} \equiv x + 2 + \frac{7x+6}{(x+1)(x-3)}
$$

$$
\equiv x + 2 + \frac{1}{4(x+1)} + \frac{27}{4(x-3)}
$$

EXERCISE 30c

1. Use the cover-up method to express in partial fractions,

   (a) $\dfrac{2}{(x+1)(x-1)}$ (b) $\dfrac{3}{(x-2)(x+1)}$ (c) $\dfrac{1}{x(x-3)}$

   (d) $\dfrac{4}{(x-1)(x+3)}$ (e) $\dfrac{1}{(x^2-1)}$ (f) $\dfrac{2}{(2x+1)(2x-1)}$

2. Express in partial fractions,

   (a) $\dfrac{2}{(x-1)(x^2+1)}$ (b) $\dfrac{x^2+1}{x(2x^2+1)}$

   (c) $\dfrac{x^2+3}{x(x^2+2)}$ (d) $\dfrac{2x^2+x+1}{(x-3)(2x^2+1)}$

   (e) $\dfrac{x^3-1}{(x+2)(2x+1)(x^2+1)}$ (f) $\dfrac{x^2+1}{x(2x^2-1)(x-1)}$

   (g) $\dfrac{x}{(x-1)(x-2)^2}$ (h) $\dfrac{x^2-1}{x^2(2x+1)}$

(i) $\dfrac{3}{x(3x-1)^2}$

(j) $\dfrac{x^2}{(x+1)(x-1)}$

(k) $\dfrac{x^2-2}{(x+3)(x-1)}$

(l) $\dfrac{x^3+3}{(x-1)(x+1)}$

THE REMAINDER THEOREM

When $f(x) = x^3 - 7x^2 + 6x - 2$ is divided by $x - 2$, we get a quotient and a remainder. The relationship between these quantities can be written as

$$f(x) = x^3 - 7x^2 + 6x - 2 \equiv (\text{quotient})(x-2) + \text{remainder}$$

Now substituting 2 for x eliminates the term containing the quotient, giving

$$f(2) = \text{remainder}$$

This is a particular illustration of the more general case, namely if a polynomial $f(x)$, is divided by $(x - a)$ then

$$f(x) \equiv (\text{quotient})(x-a) + \text{remainder}$$
$$\Rightarrow \qquad f(a) = \text{remainder}$$

This result is called the *remainder theorem* and can be summarised as

when a polynomial $f(x)$ is divided by $(x - a)$, the remainder is $f(a)$

Examples 30d

1. Find the remainder when
   (a) $x^3 - 2x^2 + 6$ is divided by $x + 3$
   (b) $6x^2 - 7x + 2$ is divided by $2x - 1$

   (a) When $f(x) = x^3 - 2x^2 + 6$ is divided by $x + 3$, the remainder is
   $$f(-3) = (-3)^3 - 2(-3)^2 + 6 = -39$$

   (b) If $f(x) = 6x^2 - 7x + 2$, then
   $$f(x) = (2x - 1)(\text{quotient}) + \text{remainder}$$
   $$\Rightarrow \qquad \text{remainder} = f(\tfrac{1}{2}) = 0$$

Note that as the remainder is zero, $2x - 1$ is a factor of $f(x)$

The Factor Theorem

This is a special case of the remainder theorem because if $x - a$ is a factor of a polynomial $f(x)$ then there is no remainder when $f(x)$ is divided by $x - a$,

i.e. $f(a) = 0$

This result, which is called the factor theorem, states that

> if, for a polynomial $f(x)$, $f(a) = 0$
> then $x - a$ is a factor of $f(x)$

The factor theorem is very helpful when factorising cubics or higher degree polynomials.

Examples 30d (continued) _____

2. Factorise $x^4 - 3x^3 + 4x^2 - 8$

$$f(x) \equiv x^4 - 3x^3 + 4x^2 - 8$$

We will test for factors of the form $x - a$ by finding $f(a)$ for various values of a. Note that, as the factors of 8 are 1, 2, 4 and 8, the values we choose for a must belong to the set $\{\pm 1, \pm 2, \pm 4, \pm 8\}$

$f(1) = 1 - 3 + 4 - 8 \neq 0$, so $x - 1$ is not a factor of $f(x)$

$f(-1) = 1 + 3 + 4 - 8 = 0$, therefore $x + 1$ is a factor of $f(x)$

Now that a factor has been found, it should be taken out; this can be done by inspection or by long division.

$$x^4 - 3x^3 + 4x^2 - 8 \equiv (x + 1)(x^3 - 4x^2 + 8x - 8)$$

If $g(x) = x^3 - 4x^2 + 8x - 8$,

then $g(-1) = -1 - 4 - 8 - 8 \neq 0$ so $x + 1$ is not a factor of $g(x)$

Note that, having taken $x - 1$ out of $f(x)$, we tried it again as a possible factor of $g(x)$. This should always be done as repeated factors are common.

$g(2) = 8 - 16 + 16 - 8 = 0$, therefore $x - 2$ is a factor of $g(x)$

By inspection, $x^3 - 4x^2 + 8x - 8 \equiv (x - 2)(x^2 - 2x + 4)$ and $x^2 - 2x + 4$ has no linear factors.

Therefore $x^4 - 3x^3 + 4x^2 - 8 \equiv (x + 1)(x - 2)(x^2 - 2x + 4)$

The Factors of $a^3 - b^3$ and $a^3 + b^3$

$a^3 - b^3 = 0$ when $a = b$, hence $a - b$ is a factor of $a^3 - b^3$

Therefore $a^3 - b^3 \equiv (a - b)(a^2 + ab + b^2)$

in particular $x^3 - 1 \equiv (x - 1)(x^2 + x + 1)$

Also, $a^3 + b^3 = 0$ when $a = -b$, so $a + b$ is a factor of $a^3 + b^3$

Therefore $a^3 + b^3 \equiv (a + b)(a^2 - ab + b^2)$

in particular $x^3 + 1 \equiv (x + 1)(x^2 - x + 1)$

EXERCISE 30d

1. Find the remainder when the following functions are divided by the linear factors indicated.

   (a) $x^3 - 2x + 4$, $x - 1$ (b) $x^3 + 3x^2 - 6x + 2$, $x + 2$

   (c) $2x^3 - x^2 + 2$, $x - 3$ (d) $x^4 - 3x^3 + 5x$, $2x - 1$

   (e) $9x^5 - 5x^2$, $3x + 1$ (f) $x^3 - 2x^2 + 6$, $x - a$

   (g) $x^2 + ax + b$, $x + c$ (h) $x^4 - 2x + 1$, $ax - 1$

2. Determine whether the following linear functions are factors of the given polynomials.

   (a) $x^3 - 7x + 6$, $x - 1$ (b) $2x^2 + 3x - 4$, $x + 1$

   (c) $x^3 - 6x^2 + 6x - 2$, $x - 2$ (d) $x^3 - 27$, $x - 3$

   (e) $2x^4 - x^3 - 1$, $2x - 1$ (f) $x^3 + ax^2 - a^2x - a^3$, $x + a$

3. Factorise the following functions as far as possible.

   (a) $x^3 + 2x^2 - x - 2$ (b) $x^3 - x^2 - x - 2$

   (c) $x^4 - 1$ (d) $x^4 + x^3 - 3x^2 - 4x - 4$

   (e) $2x^3 - x^2 + 2x - 1$ (f) $27x^3 - 1$

   (g) $x^3 + a^3$ (h) $x^3 - y^3$

4. If $x^2 - 7x + a$ has a remainder 1 when divided by $x + 1$, find a

5. If $x - 2$ is a factor of $ax^2 - 12x + 4$ find a

6. One solution of the equation $x^2 + ax + 2 = 0$ is $x = 1$, find a

7. One root of the equation $x^2 - 3x + a = 0$ is 2. Find the other root.

SOLUTION OF POLYNOMIAL EQUATIONS AND INEQUALITIES

The factor theorem is very useful when solving cubic or higher degree equations or inequalities.

Examples 30e

1. Find the values of x for which $x^3 - 2x^2 - x + 2 < 0$

Problems involving inequalities are often easier to solve if dealt with graphically.

Consider the curve $y = x^3 - 2x^2 - x + 2$

This is a cubic curve and it crosses the x-axis where $x^3 - 2x^2 - x + 2 = 0$ so we will try to factorise $x^3 - 2x^2 - x + 2$ using the factor theorem.

$$f(x) = x^3 - 2x^2 - x + 2$$

$f(1) = 0$, $\therefore$ $x - 1$ is a factor of $f(x)$

$\Rightarrow$ $x^3 - 2x^2 - x + 2 \equiv (x - 1)(x^2 - x - 2) \equiv (x - 1)(x + 1)(x - 2)$

$\therefore$ $y = f(x)$ cuts the x-axis at $x = -1, 1, 2$ $\Rightarrow$

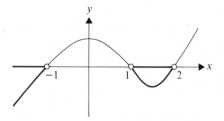

From the sketch,

$x^3 - 2x^2 - x + 2 < 0$ when $x < -1$ and $1 < x < 2$

2. The equation $f(x) = 0$ has a repeated root, where
$f(x) = 4x^2 + px + q$ When $f(x)$ is divided by $x + 1$ the
remainder is 1. Find the values of p and q.

$$f(-1) = 4 - p + q = 1 \quad \Rightarrow \quad p = q + 3 \qquad [1]$$

If $4x^2 + px + q = 0$ has a repeated root then '$b^2 - 4ac$' $= 0$

i.e. $$p^2 - 16q = 0 \qquad [2]$$

Solving equations [1] and [2] simultaneously gives

$$(q + 3)^2 - 16q = 0 \quad \Rightarrow \quad q^2 - 10q + 9 = 0$$
$$\Rightarrow \quad (q - 9)(q - 1) = 0$$

$\therefore$ either $q = 9$ and $p = 12$ or $q = 1$ and $p = 4$

EXERCISE 30e

1. Factorise $2x^3 - x^2 - 2x + 1$. Hence find the values of x for which
$2x^3 - x^2 - 2x + 1 > 0$

2. Given that $f(x) = x^3 - x^2 - x - 2$ show that $y = f(x)$ cuts the
x-axis once only. Find the values of x for which $x^3 - x^2 - x < 2$

3. Find the value of p for which $x = \frac{1}{2}$ is a solution of the equation
$4x^2 - px + 3 = 0$

4. Show that the x coordinates of the points of intersection of the
curves $$y = \frac{1}{x} \text{ and } x^2 + 4y^2 = 5$$
satisfy the equation $x^4 - 5x^2 + 4 = 0$
Solve this equation.

5. Factorise $x^4 - 5x^3 + 5x^2 + 5x - 6$. Hence sketch the curve
$y = x^4 - 5x^3 + 5x^2 + 5x - 6$

6. A function f is defined by
$$f(x) = 5x^3 - px^2 + x - q$$
When $f(x)$ is divided by $x - 2$, the remainder is 3. Given that
$(x - 1)$ is a factor of $f(x)$
(a) find p and q
(b) find the number of real roots of the equation
$$5x^3 - px^2 + x - q = 0$$

INTERSECTION OF CURVES

The points of intersection of any two curves (and/or lines) can be found by solving their equations simultaneously. Each real root then gives a point of intersection. Some roots may be repeated and we will now look at the significance of this situation.

If there are two equal roots
the curves meet twice at
the same point P,
i.e. they touch at P and
have a common tangent
at P.

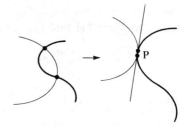

In particular, when a line
and a curve meet twice
at the same point P, the
line is a tangent to the
curve at P.

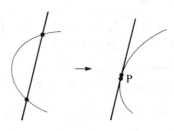

If there are three equal roots
the curves meet three times
at the same point Q.
The curves have a common
tangent at Q but this time
each curve crosses, at Q,
to the opposite side of the
common tangent.

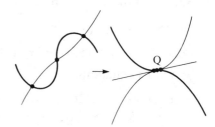

In particular, when a
line and a curve meet
at three coincident
points Q, the line is a
tangent to the curve at
Q and the curve has a
point of inflexion at Q.

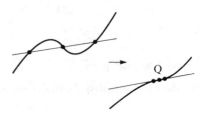

Taking this argument further it becomes clear that,

(a) when the number of coincident points of intersection of a line and a curve is even, the curve touches the line and remains on the same side of the line;

4 coincident points

(b) when the number of coincident points of intersection is odd, the curve touches the line and crosses it. Thus the curve has a point of inflexion.

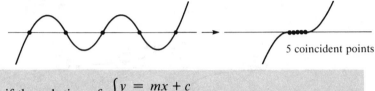

5 coincident points

so if the solution of $\begin{cases} y = mx + c \\ y = f(x) \end{cases}$

has $\begin{cases} \text{distinct roots, the curve crosses the line at distinct points.} \\ \text{repeated roots, the line touches the curve.} \end{cases}$

Examples 30f _____

1. Find the equations of the tangents with gradient 1 to the curve $x^2 + 2y^2 = 6$ and find the coordinates of their points of contact.

Any line with gradient 1 has equation $y = x + c$

This line meets the curve $x^2 + 2y^2 = 6$ where $x^2 + 2(x + c)^2 = 6$

i.e. where $\qquad\qquad 3x^2 + 4cx + (2c^2 - 6) = 0 \qquad\qquad$ [1]

For the line to touch the curve, this equation must have equal roots.

So $\qquad\qquad (4c)^2 - 12(2c^2 - 6) = 0 \qquad \Rightarrow \qquad c = \pm 3$

∴ the equations of the tangents are $y = x + 3$ and $y = x - 3$

To find the coordinates of the points of contact we have to go back to equation [1].

When $c = 3$, [1] becomes $x^2 + 4x + 4 = 0 \qquad \Rightarrow \qquad x = -2$

When $c = -3$, [1] becomes $x^2 - 4x + 4 = 0 \qquad \Rightarrow \qquad x = 2$

The corresponding values of y are found from the equations of the tangents.

The points of contact of the two tangents are $(2, -1)$ and $(-2, 1)$

2. Find the points of intersection of the curves $xy = 1$ and
$x^2 + y^2 + 2x + 2y - 6 = 0$

The curve $xy = 1$ is a rectangular hyperbola and the other curve is a circle.
Rearranging the equation of the circle as $(x + 1)^2 + (y + 1)^2 = 8$ tells us that its
centre is $(-1, -1)$ and its radius is $2\sqrt{2}$

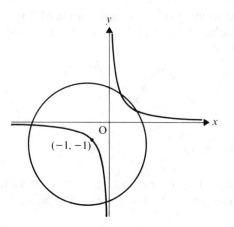

From the sketch, we expect 4 distinct points of intersection. However it is worth
noting that the points in the first quadrant appear to be close together, and as this
is only a sketch, it may be that these points are coincident or even do not exist.

Now points of intersection satisfy both equations simultaneously. Solving the
equations by eliminating y gives

$$x^2 + \left(\frac{1}{x}\right)^2 + 2x + 2\left(\frac{1}{x}\right)^2 - 6 = 0 \quad \Rightarrow \quad x^4 + 2x^3 - 6x^2 + 2x + 1 = 0$$

Using the factor theorem gives $(x - 1)(x - 1)(x^2 + 4x + 1) = 0$

Hence $x = 1$ (twice) and $x = -2 \pm \sqrt{3}$

i.e. there are two equal roots and two distinct roots.

Therefore (calculating the corresponding values of y from the equation $xy = 1$)

the curves *touch* at $(1, 1)$

and *cut* at $\left(-2 - \sqrt{3}, \dfrac{1}{-2 - \sqrt{3}}\right)$ and $\left(-2 + \sqrt{3}, \dfrac{1}{-2 + \sqrt{3}}\right)$

3. Find the points of intersection of the line $y = x + 2$ and the curve $y = x^4 - 2x^3 + 3x + 1$, showing that one of them is a point of inflexion on the curve.

The line and the curve meet at points whose x coordinates are given by

$$x^4 - 2x^3 + 3x + 1 = x + 2 \qquad \Rightarrow \qquad x^4 - 2x^3 + 2x - 1 = 0$$

Using the factor theorem gives $(x - 1)^3(x + 1) = 0$

Thus there are three coincident points where $x = 1$ and one point at $x = -1$

Therefore the line cuts the curve at a point of inflexion $(1, 3)$ and cuts it again at $(-1, 1)$

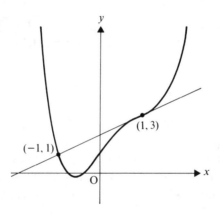

EXERCISE 30f

Investigate the possible intersection of the following lines and curves giving the coordinates of all common points. State clearly those cases where the line touches the curve.

1. $y = x + 1$; $y^2 = 4x$

2. $2y + x = 3$; $x^2 - y^2 - 3y + 3 = 0$

3. $y = x - 5$; $x^2 + 2y^2 = 7$

4. $2y - x = 4$; $x^2 + y^2 - 4x = 4$

5. $y = 0$; $y = x^2 - 3x + 2$

6. $y = 0; \quad y = x^3 + 5x^2 + 6x$

7. $y = 0; \quad y = (x - 1)^2(x - 2)^2$

8. $y = 0; \quad y = (x + 3)^3(x + 2)$

9. $x = 0; \quad x = y^4$

Find the value of k such that the given line shall touch the given curve.

10. $y = x + 2; \quad y^2 = kx$

11. $y = kx + 3; \quad xy + 9 = 0$

12. $y = 3x - k; \quad x^2 + 2y^2 = 8$

Find the points of intersection or points of contact (if any) of the following pairs of curves. Illustrate your results by drawing diagrams.

13. $y^2 = 8x; \quad xy = 1$

14. $x^2 + y^2 + 2x - 7 = 0; \quad y^2 = 4x$

15. $xy = 2; \quad 2x^2 + 2y^2 - 6x + 3y - 10 = 0$

16. $9x^2 = 2y; \quad y^2 = 6x$

17. Find the value(s) or ranges of values of λ for which the line $y = 2x + \lambda$
  (a) touches
  (b) cuts in real points
  (c) does not meet, the curve $y^2 + 2x^2 = 4$

18. Sketch the curves $y = 3x^4$, $y = 4(2 - x)^5$, $y = 2(x + 3)^7$ $y = -5x^6$

19. Find the equation(s) of the tangent(s):
  (i) from the point $(1, 0)$ (ii) with gradient $-\frac{1}{2}$
  to each of the following curves,
  (a) $y^2 + 4x = 0$ (b) $xy = 9$ (c) $x^2 = 6y$

CHAPTER 31

FURTHER INTEGRATION 2

INTEGRATING FRACTIONS

Some expressions have an integral that is a function but there are many others for which an exact integral cannot be found. In this book we are concerned mainly with expressions which *can* be integrated but even with this proviso the reader should be aware that, while the methods suggested usually work, they are not infallible.

There are several different methods for integrating fractions, the appropriate method in a particular case depending upon the form of the fraction. Consequently it is very important that each fraction be categorised carefully to avoid embarking on unnecessary and lengthy working.

Method 1 Using Recognition

Consider the function $\ln u$ where $u = f(x)$

Differentiating with respect to x gives

$$\frac{d}{dx}\ln u = \left(\frac{1}{u}\right)\left(\frac{du}{dx}\right) \quad \text{i.e.} \quad \frac{du/dx}{u}$$

i.e. $$\frac{d}{dx}\ln f(x) = \frac{f'(x)}{f(x)}$$

Hence $$\int \frac{f'(x)}{f(x)}\,dx = \ln|f(x)| + K$$

Thus all fractions of the form $f'(x)/f(x)$ can be integrated *immediately* by recognition, e.g.

$$\int \frac{\cos x}{1 + \sin x}\,dx = \ln|1 + \sin x| + K \quad \text{as} \quad \frac{d}{dx}(1 + \sin x) = \cos x$$

$$\int \frac{e^x}{e^x + 4}\,dx = \ln|e^x + 4| + K \quad \text{as} \quad \frac{d}{dx}(e^x + 4) = e^x$$

Note, however, that $\int \dfrac{x}{\sqrt{(1+x)}}\,dx$ is *not* equal to $\ln|\sqrt{(1+x)}| + K$

because $\qquad \dfrac{d}{dx}\sqrt{(1+x)}\qquad$ is not equal to x

Method 1 applies only to an integral whose numerator is basically the derivative of *the complete denominator*.

An integral whose numerator is the derivative, not of the complete denominator but of a function *within* the denominator, belongs to the next type.

Method 2   Using Substitution

Consider the integral $\int \dfrac{2x}{\sqrt{(x^2+1)}}\,dx$

Noting that $2x$ is the derivative of $x^2 + 1$ we make the substitution $u = x^2 + 1$, i.e.

$$\text{if}\quad u = x^2 + 1 \quad\text{then}\quad \ldots du \equiv \ldots 2x\,dx$$

By this change of variable the given integral is converted into the simple form $\int \dfrac{1}{\sqrt{u}}\,du$

Examples 31a

1. Find $\int \dfrac{x^2}{1+x^3}\,dx$

$$\int \frac{x^2}{1+x^3}\,dx = \frac{1}{3}\int \frac{3x^2}{1+x^3}\,dx$$

This integral is of the form $\int \dfrac{f'(x)}{f(x)}\,dx$ so we use recognition

$$= \tfrac{1}{3}\ln|1 + x^3| + K$$

---

2. By writing $\tan x$ as $\dfrac{\sin x}{\cos x}$ find $\int \tan x\,dx$

$$\int \tan x\,dx = \int \frac{\sin x}{\cos x}\,dx = -\int \frac{f'(x)}{f(x)}\,dx \quad\text{where}\quad f(x) = \cos x$$

so
$$\int \frac{\sin x}{\cos x}\,dx = -\ln|\cos x| + K$$

$\therefore$
$$\int \tan x\,dx = K - \ln|\cos x| \quad \text{or} \quad K + \ln|\sec x|$$

Note that, similarly, $\displaystyle\int \cot x\,dx = \ln|\sin x| + K$

These results are quotable.

---

3. Find $\displaystyle\int \frac{e^x}{(1-e^x)^2}\,dx$

e^x is basically the derivative of $1 - e^x$ but not of $(1 - e^x)^2$ so we make the substitution $u = 1 - e^x$

If $u = 1 - e^x$ then $\ldots du \equiv \ldots -e^x\,dx$

So
$$\int \frac{e^x}{(1-e^x)^2}\,dx = \int \frac{-1}{u^2}\,du = \frac{1}{u} + K$$

$\therefore$
$$\int \frac{e^x}{(1-e^x)^2}\,dx = \frac{1}{1-e^x} + K$$

---

4. Find $\displaystyle\int \frac{\sec^2 x}{\tan^3 x}\,dx$

$\sec^2 x$ is the derivative of $\tan x$ but not of $\tan^3 x$

Taking $u = \tan x$ gives $\ldots du \equiv \ldots \sec^2 x\,dx$

Then
$$\int \frac{\sec^2 x}{\tan^3 x}\,dx = \int \frac{1}{u^3}\,du = -\tfrac{1}{2}u^{-2} + K$$

i.e.
$$\int \frac{\sec^2 x}{\tan^3 x}\,dx = \frac{-1}{2\tan^2 x} + K$$

EXERCISE 31a

In Questions 1 to 18 integrate each function w.r.t. x

1. $\dfrac{\cos x}{4 + \sin x}$ **2.** $\dfrac{e^x}{3e^x - 1}$ **3.** $\dfrac{x}{(1 - x^2)^3}$

4. $\dfrac{\sin x}{\cos^3 x}$ **5.** $\dfrac{x^3}{1 + x^4}$ **6.** $\dfrac{2x + 3}{x^2 + 3x - 4}$

7. $\dfrac{x^2}{\sqrt{(2 + x^3)}}$ **8.** $\dfrac{\cos x}{(\sin x - 2)^2}$ **9.** $\dfrac{1}{x \ln x}$ i.e. $\dfrac{1/x}{\ln x}$

10. $\dfrac{\cos x}{\sin^6 x}$ **11.** $\dfrac{\csc^2 x}{\cot^4 x}$ **12.** $\dfrac{e^x}{\sqrt{(1 - e^x)}}$

13. $\dfrac{x - 1}{3x^2 - 6x + 1}$ **14.** $\dfrac{\cos x}{\sin^n x}$ **15.** $\dfrac{\sin x}{\cos^n x}$

16. $\dfrac{\sec x \tan x}{4 + \sec x}$ **17.** $\dfrac{\sec^2 x}{(1 - \tan x)^3}$ **18.** $\dfrac{\sin x}{(3 + \cos x)^2}$

19. By writing $\sec x$ as $\dfrac{\sec x (\sec x + \tan x)}{(\tan x + \sec x)}$ find $\displaystyle\int \sec x \, dx$

20. By writing $\operatorname{cosec} x$ as $\dfrac{\operatorname{cosec} x (\operatorname{cosec} x + \cot x)}{(\cot x + \operatorname{cosec} x)}$ find $\displaystyle\int \operatorname{cosec} x \, dx$

Evaluate

21. $\displaystyle\int_1^2 \dfrac{2x + 1}{x^2 + x} \, dx$ **22.** $\displaystyle\int_0^1 \dfrac{x}{x^2 + 1} \, dx$

23. $\displaystyle\int_2^3 \dfrac{2x}{(x^2 - 1)^3} \, dx$ **24.** $\displaystyle\int_0^1 \dfrac{e^x}{(1 + e^x)^2} \, dx$

25. $\displaystyle\int_{\pi/6}^{\pi/3} \dfrac{\sin 2x}{\cos(2x - \pi)} \, dx$ **26.** $\displaystyle\int_2^4 \dfrac{1}{x(\ln x)^2} \, dx$

Quotable Results

Some of the integrals found in Exercise 31a are important enough to be regarded as standard and are listed here

$$\int \tan x \, dx = \ln|\sec x| + K$$

$$\int \cot x \, dx = \ln|\sin x| + K$$

$$\int \sec x \, dx = \ln|\sec x + \tan x| + K$$

$$\int \csc x \, dx = -\ln|\csc x + \cot x| + K$$

USING PARTIAL FRACTIONS

If a fraction has not fallen into any of the previous categories, it may be that it is easy to integrate when expressed in partial fractions. Remember however that only proper fractions can be converted directly into partial fractions; an improper fraction must first be divided out until it comprises non-fractional terms and a proper fraction.

It is not very often that actual long division is needed. Usually a simple adjustment in the numerator is all that is required, as the following examples show. When such an adjustment is not obvious, however, long division can always be used.

Examples 31b

1. Integrate $\dfrac{2x - 3}{(x - 1)(x - 2)}$ w.r.t. x

Using the cover-up method gives

$$\frac{2x - 3}{(x - 1)(x - 2)} = \frac{1}{x - 1} + \frac{1}{x - 2}$$

$$\therefore \quad \int \frac{2x - 3}{(x - 1)(x - 2)} dx = \int \frac{1}{x - 1} dx + \int \frac{1}{x - 2} dx$$

$$= \ln|x - 1| + \ln|x - 2| + \ln A$$

$$= \ln A|(x - 1)(x - 2)|$$

2. Find $\displaystyle\int \frac{x^2 + 1}{x^2 - 1}\,dx$

This fraction is improper so, before we can factorise the denominator and use partial fractions we must adjust the given fraction as follows.

$$\frac{x^2 + 1}{x^2 - 1} = \frac{(x^2 - 1) + 2}{x^2 - 1} = 1 + \frac{2}{x^2 - 1} = 1 + \frac{2}{(x - 1)(x + 1)}$$

Then
$$\int \frac{x^2 + 1}{x^2 - 1}\,dx = \int 1\,dx + \int \frac{1}{x - 1}\,dx - \int \frac{1}{x + 1}\,dx$$

$$= x + \ln|x - 1| - \ln|x + 1| + \ln A$$

$$= x + \ln \frac{A|x - 1|}{|x + 1|}$$

Even when improper fractions do not need conversion into partial fractions, it is still essential to reduce to proper form before attempting to integrate, i.e.

$$\int \frac{2x + 4}{x + 1}\,dx = \int \frac{2(x + 1) + 2}{x + 1}\,dx = \int 2\,dx + \int \frac{2}{x + 1}\,dx$$

$$= 2x + 2\ln A|x + 1|$$

The reader should not fall into the trap of thinking that, whenever the denominator of a fraction factorises, integration will involve partial fractions.
Careful scrutiny is vital, as fractions requiring quite different integration techniques often *look* very similar. The following example shows this clearly.

Examples 31b (continued) _____

3. Integrate w.r.t. x,

(a) $\displaystyle\frac{x + 1}{x^2 + 2x - 8}$ (b) $\displaystyle\frac{x + 1}{(x^2 + 2x - 8)^2}$ (c) $\displaystyle\frac{x + 2}{x^2 + 2x - 8}$

(a) This fraction is basically of the form $f'(x)/f(x)$

$$\int \frac{x + 1}{x^2 + 2x - 8}\,dx = \frac{1}{2} \int \frac{2x + 2}{x^2 + 2x - 8}\,dx$$

$$= \tfrac{1}{2} \ln A|x^2 + 2x - 8|$$

(b) This time the numerator is basically the derivative of the function *within* the denominator so we use

$$u = x^2 + 2x - 8 \quad \Rightarrow \quad \ldots du \equiv \ldots (2x + 2)\, dx \equiv \ldots 2(x + 1)\, dx$$

$$\therefore \quad \int \frac{x + 1}{(x^2 + 2x - 8)^2}\, dx = \frac{1}{2} \int \frac{1}{u^2}\, du = -\frac{1}{2u} + K$$

$$= K - \frac{1}{2(x^2 + 2x - 8)}$$

(c) In this fraction the numerator is not related to the derivative of the denominator so, as the denominator factorises, we use partial fractions.

$$\int \frac{x + 2}{x^2 + 2x - 8}\, dx = \int \frac{\frac{1}{3}}{x + 4}\, dx + \int \frac{\frac{2}{3}}{x - 2}\, dx$$

$$= \tfrac{1}{3} \ln|x + 4| + \tfrac{2}{3} \ln|x - 2| + \ln A$$

$$= \ln A \,|(x + 4)^{1/3}(x - 2)^{2/3}|$$

EXERCISE 31b

Integrate each of the following functions w.r.t. x

1. $\dfrac{2}{x(x + 1)}$ **2.** $\dfrac{4}{(x - 2)(x + 2)}$ **3.** $\dfrac{x}{(x - 1)(x + 1)}$

4. $\dfrac{x - 1}{x(x + 2)}$ **5.** $\dfrac{x - 1}{(x - 2)(x - 3)}$ **6.** $\dfrac{1}{x(x - 1)(x + 1)}$

7. $\dfrac{x}{x + 1}$ **8.** $\dfrac{x + 4}{x}$ **9.** $\dfrac{x}{x + 4}$

10. $\dfrac{3x - 4}{x(1 - x)}$ **11.** $\dfrac{x^2 - 2}{x^2 - 1}$ **12.** $\dfrac{x^2}{(x + 1)(x + 2)}$

Choose the best method to integrate each function.

13. $\dfrac{x}{x^2 - 1}$ **14.** $\dfrac{2x}{(x^2 - 1)^2}$ **15.** $\dfrac{2}{x^2 - 1}$

16. $\dfrac{2x - 5}{x^2 - 5x + 6}$ **17.** $\dfrac{2x}{x^2 - 5x + 6}$ **18.** $\dfrac{2x - 3}{x^2 - 5x + 6}$

Evaluate

19. $\displaystyle\int_0^4 \frac{x+2}{x+1}\,dx$ **20.** $\displaystyle\int_{-1}^1 \frac{5}{x^2+x-6}\,dx$ **21.** $\displaystyle\int_1^2 \frac{x+2}{x(x+4)}\,dx$

22. $\displaystyle\int_0^1 \frac{2}{3+2x}\,dx$ **23.** $\displaystyle\int_{1/2}^3 \frac{2}{(3+2x)^2}\,dx$ **24.** $\displaystyle\int_1^2 \frac{2x}{3+2x}\,dx$

The Use of Partial Fractions in Differentiation

Rational functions with two or more factors in the denominator are often easier to differentiate if expressed in partial fractions. This method is an alternative to logarithmic differentiation which can also be used for functions of this type.

However, the use of partial fractions is of particular benefit when a second derivative is required.

Example 31c _____

Find the first and second derivatives of $\dfrac{x}{(x-1)(x+1)}$

Taking $y = \dfrac{x}{(x-1)(x+1)} = \dfrac{\frac{1}{2}}{(x-1)} + \dfrac{\frac{1}{2}}{(x+1)}$

$$= \tfrac{1}{2}(x-1)^{-1} + \tfrac{1}{2}(x+1)^{-1}$$

gives $\dfrac{dy}{dx} = -\tfrac{1}{2}(x-1)^{-2} - \tfrac{1}{2}(x+1)^{-2}$

$$= \frac{-1}{2(x-1)^2} - \frac{1}{2(x+1)^2}$$

and $\dfrac{d^2y}{dx^2} = (-2)(-\tfrac{1}{2})(x-1)^{-3} - (-2)(\tfrac{1}{2})(x+1)^{-3}$

$$= \frac{1}{(x-1)^3} + \frac{1}{(x+1)^3}$$

EXERCISE 31c

In each question express the given function in partial fractions and hence find its first and second derivatives.

1. $\dfrac{2}{(x-2)(x-1)}$ **2.** $\dfrac{3x}{(2x-1)(x-3)}$ **3.** $\dfrac{x}{(x+2)(x-4)}$

4. $\dfrac{5}{(x+2)(x-3)}$ **5.** $\dfrac{x}{(2x+3)(x+1)}$ **6.** $\dfrac{3}{(3x-1)(x-1)}$

SPECIAL TECHNIQUES FOR INTEGRATING SOME TRIGONOMETRIC FUNCTIONS

To Integrate a Function Containing an Odd Power of $\sin x$ or $\cos x$

When $\sin x$ or $\cos x$ appear to an odd power other than 1, the identity $\cos^2 x + \sin^2 x \equiv 1$ is often useful in converting the given function to an integrable form,

e.g. $\sin^3 x$ is converted to $(\sin^2 x)(\sin x)$ $\quad \Rightarrow \quad (1 - \cos^2 x)(\sin x)$

$\quad \Rightarrow \quad \sin x - \cos^2 x \sin x$

Examples 31d _____

1. Integrate w.r.t. x, (a) $\cos^5 x$ (b) $\sin^3 x \cos^2 x$

(a) $\qquad\qquad \cos^5 x = (\cos^2 x)^2 \cos x$

$\qquad\qquad\qquad = (1 - \sin^2 x)^2 \cos x$

$\qquad\qquad\qquad = (1 - 2\sin^2 x + \sin^4 x)\cos x$

$\therefore \quad \int \cos^5 x \, dx = \int \cos x \, dx - 2\int \sin^2 x \cos x \, dx + \int \sin^4 x \cos x \, dx$

For any value of n we know that $\int \sin^n x \cos x \, dx = \dfrac{1}{n+1}\sin^{n+1} x + K$

$\therefore \qquad\qquad \int \cos^5 x \, dx = \sin x - 2(\tfrac{1}{3})\sin^3 x + (\tfrac{1}{5})\sin^5 x + K$

$\qquad\qquad\qquad = \sin x - \tfrac{2}{3}\sin^3 x + \tfrac{1}{5}\sin^5 x + K$

(b) $\qquad\qquad \sin^3 x \cos^2 x = \sin x(1 - \cos^2 x)\cos^2 x$

$\qquad\qquad\qquad\qquad = \cos^2 x \sin x - \cos^4 x \sin x$

$\therefore \quad \int \sin^3 x \cos^2 x \, dx = \int \cos^2 x \sin x \, dx - \int \cos^4 x \sin x \, dx$

$\qquad\qquad\qquad\qquad = -\tfrac{1}{3}\cos^3 x + \tfrac{1}{5}\cos^5 x + K$

_____

To Integrate a Function Containing only Even Powers of $\sin x$ or $\cos x$

This time the double angle identities are useful,

e.g. $\cos^4 x$ becomes $(\cos^2 x)^2 = \{\frac{1}{2}(1 + \cos 2x)\}^2$

$$= \tfrac{1}{4}\{1 + 2\cos 2x + \cos^2 2x\}$$

then we can use a double angle identity again

$$= \tfrac{1}{4}(1 + 2\cos 2x) + \tfrac{1}{4}\{\tfrac{1}{2}(1 + \cos 4x)\}$$

$$= \tfrac{3}{8} + \tfrac{1}{2}\cos 2x + \tfrac{1}{4}\cos 4x$$

Now each of these terms can be integrated.

Examples 31d (continued)

2. Integrate w.r.t. x,   **(a)** $\sin^2 x$ **(b)** $16\sin^4 x \cos^2 x$

(a)
$$\int \sin^2 dx = \int \tfrac{1}{2}(1 - \cos 2x)\, dx$$

$$= \int \tfrac{1}{2}\, dx - \tfrac{1}{2}\int \cos 2x\, dx$$

$$= \tfrac{1}{2}x - \tfrac{1}{4}\sin 2x + K$$

(b) $16\displaystyle\int \sin^4 x \cos^2 x\, dx = 16\int \{\tfrac{1}{2}(1 - \cos 2x)\}^2 \{\tfrac{1}{2}(1 + \cos 2x)\}\, dx$

$$= 2\int (1 - \cos 2x - \cos^2 2x + \cos^3 2x)\, dx$$

$$= 2x - \sin 2x - 2\int \cos^2 2x\, dx + 2\int \cos^3 2x\, dx$$

Now $2\displaystyle\int \cos^2 2x\, dx = \int (1 + \cos 4x)\, dx = x + \tfrac{1}{4}\sin 4x$

and $2\displaystyle\int \cos^3 2x\, dx = 2\int \cos 2x(1 - \sin^2 2x)\, dx = \sin 2x - \tfrac{1}{3}\sin^3 2x$

$\therefore$ $16\displaystyle\int \sin^4 x \cos^2 x\, dx = x - \tfrac{1}{4}\sin 4x - \tfrac{1}{3}\sin^3 2x + K$

Note that for a product with an odd power in one term and an even power in the other, the method for an odd power is usually best (see Example 1(b) on page 527).

It is important to appreciate that the techniques used in these examples, although they are of most general use, are by no means exhaustive. Because there are so many trig identities there is always the possibility that a particular integral can be dealt with in several different ways,

e.g. to integrate $\sin^2x \cos^2x$ w.r.t. x the best conversion would use $2 \sin x \cos x \equiv \sin 2x,$ so that

$$\int \sin^2x \cos^2x \, dx = \int (\tfrac{1}{2} \sin 2x)^2 \, dx = \tfrac{1}{4} \int \tfrac{1}{2}(1 - \cos 4x) \, dx$$

So it is always advisable to look for the identity which will make the given function integrable as quickly and simply as possible.

Further, as mentioned earlier, it must be remembered that there are many expressions whose integrals cannot be found as a function at all. (In examination papers, of course, any integral asked for *can* be found!)

To Integrate any Power of $\tan x$

The identity $\tan^2x = \sec^2x - 1$ is useful here,

e.g. $\tan^3x$ becomes $\tan x(\sec^2x - 1) \Rightarrow \sec^2x \tan x - \tan x$

and we know that $\int \sec^2x \tan^nx \, dx = \dfrac{1}{n + 1} \tan^{n + 1}x + K$

Examples 31d (continued) _____

3. Integrate w.r.t. x, (a) $\tan^4x$ (b) $\tan^5x$

(a) $\int \tan^4x \, dx = \int \tan^2x(\sec^2x - 1) \, dx$

$$= \int \sec^2x \tan^2x \, dx - \int \tan^2x \, dx$$

$$= \tfrac{1}{3} \tan^3x - \int (\sec^2x - 1) \, dx$$

$$= \tfrac{1}{3} \tan^3x - \tan x + x + K$$

(b) $\displaystyle\int \tan^5 x\, dx = \int \tan^3 x(\sec^2 x - 1)\, dx$

$\displaystyle\qquad\qquad = \int \sec^2 x\, \tan^3 x - \int \tan x(\sec^2 x - 1)\, dx$

$\displaystyle\qquad\qquad = \int \sec^2 x\, \tan^3 x\, dx - \int \sec^2 x\, \tan x\, dx + \int \tan x\, dx$

$\displaystyle\qquad\qquad = \tfrac{1}{4}\tan^4 x - \tfrac{1}{2}\tan^2 x + \ln \sec x + K$

Note that, to integrate *any* power of tan x, the identity
$\tan^2 x = \sec^2 x - 1$ is used to convert *$\tan^2 x$ only, one step at a time*, i.e.
converting $\tan^4 x$ to $(1 - \sec^2 x)^2$ does not help.

Integrals Involving Multiple Angles

To integrate a product such as $\sin 5x \cos 3x$, the appropriate factor
formula can be used to express the product as a sum. In this case,

$$\int \sin 5x \cos 3x\, dx = \tfrac{1}{2}\int (\sin 8x + \sin 2x)\, dx$$

and the RHS consists of two standard integrals.

EXERCISE 31d

Integrate each function w.r.t. x

1. $\cos^2 x$ 2. $\cos^3 x$ 3. $\sin^5 x$ 4. $\tan^2 x$

5. $\sin^4 x$ 6. $\tan^3 x$ 7. $\cos^4 x$ 8. $\sin^3 x$

Find

9. $\displaystyle\int \sin^2\theta \cos^3\theta\, d\theta$ 10. $\displaystyle\int \sin^{10}\theta \cos^3\theta\, d\theta$

11. $\displaystyle\int \sin^n\theta \cos^3\theta\, d\theta$ 12. $\displaystyle\int \sin^2\theta \cos^2\theta\, d\theta$

13. $\displaystyle\int 4\sin^2\theta \cos 3\theta\, d\theta$ (*Hint.* Change $\sin^2\theta$ into the double angle.)

14. $\displaystyle\int \tan^2\theta \sec^4\theta\, d\theta$ (*Hint.* Change $\sec^2\theta$ into $\tan^2\theta + 1$.)

Integrate w.r.t. t

15. $2 \sin 4t \cos 3t$

16. $2 \cos 2t \cos 5t$

17. $\sin 2t \cos 6t$

18. $\sin t \sin 3t$

19. $2 \sin nt \cos mt$

20. $\cos nt \cos mt$

Evaluate

21. $\displaystyle\int_{0}^{\pi/2} \sin^{3}x \cos^{3}x \, dx$

22. $\displaystyle\int_{0}^{\pi/4} \tan^{6}x \, dx$

23. $\displaystyle\int_{\pi/6}^{\pi/3} 2 \sin 3x \cos 2x \, dx$

24. $\displaystyle\int_{0}^{\pi/3} \cos x \cos 3x \, dx$

CHAPTER 32

SYSTEMATIC INTEGRATION

At this stage it is possible to classify most of the integrals which the reader is likely to meet.

Once correctly classified, a given expression can be integrated using the method best suited to its category.

The simplest category comprises the quotable results listed below.

STANDARD INTEGRALS

Function	Integral	Function	Integral
x^n	$\dfrac{1}{n+1}x^{n+1}$ $(n \neq -1)$	$-\text{cosec}^2 x$	$\cot x$
		$\tan x$	$\ln|\sec x|$
e^x	e^x	$\sec x$	$\ln|\sec x + \tan x|$
$\dfrac{1}{x}$	$\ln|x|$	$\dfrac{1}{1+x^2}$	$\arctan x$
$\cos x$	$\sin x$		
$\sin x$	$-\cos x$	$\dfrac{1}{\sqrt{(1-x^2)}}$	$\arcsin x$
$\sec^2 x$	$\tan x$		

Each of these should be recognised equally readily when x is replaced by ax or $(ax + b)$, e.g.

for e^{ax+b} the standard integral is $\frac{1}{a}e^{ax+b}$ and for $\cos ax$ the standard integral is $\frac{1}{a}\sin ax$

CLASSIFICATION

When attempting to classify a particular function the following questions should be asked, *in order*, about the form of the integral.

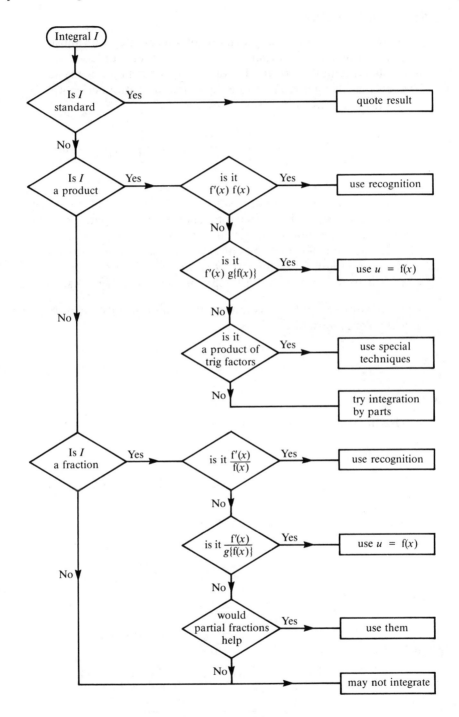

Other Techniques

Although this systematic approach deals successfully with most integrals at this level, inevitably the reader will encounter some integrals for which no method is obvious. A fraction, for instance may be such that its *numerator* can be separated, thus producing *two* (or more) fractions of different types, e.g.

$$\int \frac{x + 1}{\sqrt{(1 - x^2)}}\, dx = \int \frac{x}{\sqrt{(1 - x^2)}}\, dx + \int \frac{1}{\sqrt{(1 - x^2)}}\, dx$$

Further, many expressions other than products and fractions can be integrated by making a suitable substitution. Because at this stage the reader cannot always be expected to 'spot' an appropriate change of variable, a substitution is suggested in all but the simplest of cases. The resulting integral must be converted so that is is expressed in terms of the original variable *except in the case of a definite integral* when it is usually much easier to change the limits (See Chapter 29).

The following examples illustrate some of the integrals which respond to a change of variable.

Examples 32a

1. Use the substitution $u = 1 + 2x$ to find $\int x(1 + 2x)^{11}\, dx$

$$u = 1 + 2x \quad \Rightarrow \quad \ldots du \equiv 2\, dx \quad \Rightarrow \quad \tfrac{1}{2}\, du \equiv \ldots dx$$

Hence

$$\int x(1 + 2x)^{11}\, dx = \int \tfrac{1}{2}(u - 1)(u^{11})(\tfrac{1}{2}\, du)$$

$$= \tfrac{1}{4} \int (u^{12} - u^{11})\, du$$

$$= \tfrac{1}{4}(\tfrac{1}{13}u^{13} - \tfrac{1}{12}u^{12}) + K$$

$$= \tfrac{1}{624}u^{12}(12u - 13) + K$$

i.e.

$$\int x(1 + 2x)^{11}\, dx = \tfrac{1}{624}(1 + 2x)^{12}(24x - 1) + K$$

2. Integrate $\dfrac{1}{\sqrt{(9-16x^2)}}$ w.r.t. x by using $x = \frac{3}{4}\sin\theta$

$$x = \tfrac{3}{4}\sin\theta \quad \Rightarrow \quad \ldots dx \equiv \ldots \tfrac{3}{4}\cos\theta\, d\theta$$

Hence
$$\int \frac{1}{\sqrt{(9-16x^2)}}\, dx = \int \frac{1}{\sqrt{(9-9\sin^2\theta)}}\left(\tfrac{3}{4}\cos\theta\right) d\theta$$

$$= \frac{3}{4}\int \frac{\cos\theta}{3\sqrt{(1-\sin^2\theta)}}\, d\theta$$

$$= \frac{1}{4}\int \frac{\cos\theta}{\cos\theta}\, d\theta = \tfrac{1}{4}\theta + K$$

i.e.
$$\frac{1}{\sqrt{(9-16x^2)}}\, dx = \tfrac{1}{4}\arcsin\tfrac{4}{3}x + K$$

---

3. Complete the square in the denominator and then use $u = x+1$
to find (a) $\displaystyle\int_{-1}^{0} \frac{1}{x^2+2x+2}\, dx$ (b) $\displaystyle\int_{-1}^{0} \frac{1}{\sqrt{(3-2x-x^2)}}\, dx$

$$u = x+1 \quad \Rightarrow \quad \ldots du \equiv \ldots dx \quad \text{and} \quad \begin{cases} x & -1 & 0 \\ u & 0 & 1 \end{cases}$$

(a) First we deal with the denominator
$$x^2+2x+2 = (x+1)^2 + 1$$

Hence $\displaystyle\int_{-1}^{0} \frac{1}{x^2+2x+2}\, dx = \int_{-1}^{0} \frac{1}{(x+1)^2+1}\, dx = \int_{0}^{1} \frac{1}{u^2+1}\, du$

$$= \Big[\arctan u\Big]_0^1$$

i.e. $\displaystyle\int_{-1}^{0} \frac{1}{x^2+2x+2}\, dx = \tfrac{1}{4}\pi$

(b) $3-2x-x^2 = 4-(x+1)^2$

Hence $\displaystyle\int_{-1}^{0} \frac{1}{\sqrt{(3-2x-x^2)}}\, dx = \int_{0}^{1} \frac{1}{\sqrt{(4-u^2)}}\, du = \Big[\arcsin\frac{u}{2}\Big]_0^1$

$$= \tfrac{1}{6}\pi$$

---

4. Integrate $\sqrt{(1-x^2)}$ w.r.t. x, using the substitution $x = \sin\theta$

$$x = \sin\theta \quad \Rightarrow \quad \ldots dx \equiv \ldots \cos\theta \, d\theta$$

Hence $\quad \int \sqrt{(1-x^2)} \, dx = \int \sqrt{(1 - \sin^2\theta)} \cos\theta \, d\theta = \int \cos^2\theta \, d\theta$

$$= \int \tfrac{1}{2}(1 + \cos 2\theta) \, d\theta$$

$$= \tfrac{1}{2}(\theta + \tfrac{1}{2}\sin 2\theta) + K$$

This expression must now be given in terms of x, so we use $\theta = \arcsin x$ and $\sin 2\theta = 2\sin\theta\cos\theta = 2\sin\theta\sqrt{(1 - \sin^2\theta)} = 2x\sqrt{(1-x^2)}$

i.e. $\quad \int \sqrt{(1-x^2)} \, dx = \tfrac{1}{2}\{\arcsin x + x\sqrt{(1-x^2)}\} + K$

The fourth example has been included specifically to demonstrate how to convert a term like $\sin 2\theta$ back to the variable x. It is suggested that the reader now re-work this example for the *definite* integral

$$\int_0^1 \sqrt{(1-x^2)} \, dx$$

EXERCISE 32a

Find the following integrals using the suggested substitution.

1. $\displaystyle\int (x+1)(x+3)^5 \, dx; \quad x + 3 = u$

2. $\displaystyle\int \frac{1}{4+x^2} \, dx; \quad x = 2\tan\theta$

3. $\displaystyle\int \frac{x}{\sqrt{(3-x)}} \, dx; \quad 3 - x = u^2$

4. $\displaystyle\int x\sqrt{(x+1)} \, dx; \quad x + 1 = u^2$

5. $\displaystyle\int \frac{2x+1}{(x-3)^6} \, dx; \quad x - 3 = u$

6. $\int \dfrac{1}{\sqrt{(1 + x^2)}}\, dx;$ 　　　　$x = \tan\theta$

7. $\int 2x\sqrt{(3x - 4)}\, dx;$ 　　　　$3x - 4 = u^2$

8. $\int \dfrac{3}{25 + 4x^2}\, dx;$ 　　　　$2x = 5\tan\theta$

9. $\int \dfrac{1}{\sqrt{(x^2 + 4x + 3)}}\, dx;$ 　$x + 2 = \sec\theta,$ 　after 'completing the square' in the denominator.

Devise a suitable substitution and hence find:

10. $\int 2x(1 - x)^7\, dx$ 　　11. $\int \dfrac{1}{\sqrt{(1 - 4x^2)}}\, dx$ 　　12. $\int \dfrac{x + 3}{(4 - x)^5}\, dx$

EXERCISE 32b

Use the flow chart to classify each of the following integrals. Hence perform each integration using an appropriate method.

1. $\int e^{2x + 3}\, dx$ 　　　　　　　　2. $\int x\sqrt{(2x^2 - 5)}\, dx$

3. $\int \sin^2 3x\, dx$ 　　　　　　　　4. $\int x\, e^{-x^2}\, dx$

5. $\int \sin 3\theta \cos\theta\, d\theta$ 　　　　　6. $\int u(u + 7)^9\, du$

7. $\int \dfrac{x^2}{(x^3 + 9)^5}\, dx$ 　　　　　8. $\int \dfrac{\sin 2y}{1 - \cos 2y}\, dy$

9. $\int \dfrac{1}{2x + 7}\, dx$ 　　　　　　10. $\int \dfrac{1}{\sqrt{(1 - u^2)}}\, du$

11. $\int \sin 3x\sqrt{(1 + \cos 3x)}\, dx$ 　12. $\int x \sin 4x\, dx$

13. $\int \dfrac{x + 2}{x^2 + 4x - 5}\, dx$ 　　　14. $\int \dfrac{x + 1}{x^2 + 4x - 5}\, dx$

15. $\int \dfrac{x + 2}{(x^2 + 4x - 5)^3}\, dx$ 　　16. $\int 3y\sqrt{(9 - y^2)}\, dy$

17. $\int e^{2x} \cos 3x\, dx$ 　　　　　　18. $\int \ln 5x\, dx$

19. $\int \cos^3 2x \, dx$ **20.** $\int \text{cosec}^2 x \, e^{\cot x} \, dx$

21. $\int \dfrac{\sin y}{\sqrt{(7 + \cos y)}} \, dy$ **22.** $\int x^2 \, e^x \, dx$

23. $\int \dfrac{x}{x^2 - 4} \, dx$ **24.** $\int \dfrac{x^2}{x^2 - 4} \, dx$

25. $\int \dfrac{1}{x^2 - 4} \, dx$ **26.** $\int \cos 4x \cos x \, dx$

27. $\int \sin^5 2\theta \, d\theta$ **28.** $\int \cos^2 u \sin^3 u \, du$

29. $\int \tan^2 \theta \, d\theta$ **30.** $\int \dfrac{1 - 2x}{\sqrt{(1 - x^2)}} \, dx$

31. $\int y^2 \cos 3y \, dy$ **32.** $\int \dfrac{\sec^2 x}{1 - \tan x} \, dx$

33. $\int x\sqrt{(7 + x^2)} \, dx$ **34.** $\int \sin(5\theta - \pi/4) \, d\theta$

35. $\int \cos \theta \ln \sin \theta \, d\theta$ **36.** $\int \sec^2 u \, e^{\tan u} \, du$

DIFFERENTIAL EQUATIONS

An equation in which at least one term contains $\dfrac{dy}{dx}$, $\dfrac{d^2y}{dx^2}$ etc., is called a *differential equation*. If it contains only $\dfrac{dy}{dx}$ it is of the first order whereas if it contains $\dfrac{d^2y}{dx^2}$ it is of the second order, and so on.

For example, $x + 2\dfrac{dy}{dx} = 3y$ is a first order differential equation and $\dfrac{d^2y}{dx^2} - 5\dfrac{dy}{dx} + 4y = 0$ is a second order differential equation.

Each of these examples is a *linear* differential equation because none of the differential coefficients $\left(\text{i.e. } \dfrac{dy}{dx}, \dfrac{d^2y}{dx^2} \right)$ is raised to a power higher than 1.

A differential equation represents a relationship between two variables. The same relationship can often be expressed in a form which does not contain a differential coefficient,

e.g. $\dfrac{\mathrm{d}y}{\mathrm{d}x} = 2x$ and $y = x^2 + K$ express the same relationship

between x and y, but $\dfrac{\mathrm{d}y}{\mathrm{d}x} = 2x$ is a differential equation whereas

$y = x^2 + K$ is not.

Converting a differential equation into a direct one is called *solving the differential equation*. This clearly involves some form of integration. There are many different types of differential equation, each requiring a specific technique for its solution. At this stage however we are going to deal with only one simple type, i.e. linear differential equations of the first order.

FIRST ORDER DIFFERENTIAL EQUATIONS WITH SEPARABLE VARIABLES

Consider the differential equation $3y\dfrac{\mathrm{d}y}{\mathrm{d}x} = 5x^2$ 	[1]

Integrating both sides of the equation gives

$$\int 3y\frac{\mathrm{d}y}{\mathrm{d}x}\,\mathrm{d}x = \int 5x^2\,\mathrm{d}x$$

We saw in Chapter 29 that $\ldots \dfrac{\mathrm{d}y}{\mathrm{d}x}\,\mathrm{d}x \equiv \ldots \mathrm{d}y$

so 	$$\int 3y\,\mathrm{d}y = \int 5x^2\,\mathrm{d}x$$ 	[2]

Temporarily removing the integral signs from this equation gives

$$3y\,\mathrm{d}y = 5x^2\,\mathrm{d}x$$ 	[3]

This can be obtained direct from equation [1] by *separating the variables,* i.e. by *separating* $\mathrm{d}y$ *from* $\mathrm{d}x$ *and collecting on one side all the terms involving* y *together with* $\mathrm{d}y$, *while all the* x *terms are collected, along with* $\mathrm{d}x$ *on the other side.*

It is vital to appreciate that what is shown in [3] above does not, in itself, have any meaning, and it *should not be written down as a step in the solution.* It simply provides a way of making a quick mental conversion from the differential equation [1] to the form [2] which is ready for two separate integrations.

Now returning to equation [2] and integrating each side we have

$$\tfrac{3}{2}y^2 = \tfrac{5}{3}x^3 + A$$

Note that it is unnecessary to introduce a constant of integration on both sides. It is sufficient to have a constant on one side only.

When solving differential equations, the constant of integration is usually denoted by A, B, etc. and is called the *arbitrary constant.*

The solution of a differential equation including the arbitrary constant is called *the general solution*, or, very occasionally, *the complete primitive.* It represents a family of straight lines or curves, each member of the family corresponding to one value of A.

Example 32c _____

Find the general solution of the differential equation

$$\frac{1}{x}\frac{dy}{dx} = \frac{2y}{x^2 + 1}$$

$$\frac{1}{x}\frac{dy}{dx} = \frac{2y}{x^2 + 1} \quad\Rightarrow\quad \frac{1}{y}\frac{dy}{dx} = \frac{2x}{x^2 + 1}$$

So, after separating the variables we have,

$$\int \frac{1}{y}\,dy = \int \frac{2x}{x^2 + 1}\,dx$$

$\Rightarrow$
$$\ln|y| = \ln|x^2 + 1| + A$$

_____

Note that whenever we solve a differential equation some integration has to be done, so the systematic classification of each integral involved is an essential part of solving differential equations.

EXERCISE 32c

Find the general solution of each differential equation

1. $y\dfrac{dy}{dx} = \sin x$

2. $x^2\dfrac{dy}{dx} = y^2$

3. $\dfrac{1}{x}\dfrac{dy}{dx} = \dfrac{1}{y^2 - 2}$

4. $\tan y\,\dfrac{dy}{dx} = \dfrac{1}{x}$

5. $\dfrac{dy}{dx} = y^2$

6. $\dfrac{1}{x}\dfrac{dy}{dx} = \dfrac{1}{1-x^2}$

7. $(x-3)\dfrac{dy}{dx} = y$

8. $\tan y \dfrac{dx}{dy} = 4$

9. $u\dfrac{du}{dv} = v+2$

10. $\dfrac{y^2}{x^3}\dfrac{dy}{dx} = \ln x$

11. $e^x\dfrac{dy}{dx} = \dfrac{x}{y}$

12. $\sec x \dfrac{dy}{dx} = e^y$

13. $r\dfrac{dr}{d\theta} = \sin^2\theta$

14. $\dfrac{dv}{du} = \dfrac{v+1}{u+2}$

15. $xy\dfrac{dy}{dx} = \ln x$

16. $y(x+1) = (x^2+2x)\dfrac{dy}{dx}$

17. $v^2\dfrac{dv}{dt} = (2+t)^3$

18. $x\dfrac{dy}{dx} = \dfrac{1}{y}+y$

19. $r\dfrac{d\theta}{dr} = \cos^2\theta$

20. $y\sin^3 x \dfrac{dy}{dx} = \cos x$

21. $\dfrac{uv}{u-1} = \dfrac{du}{dv}$

22. $e^x\dfrac{dy}{dx} = e^{y-1}$

23. $\tan x \dfrac{dy}{dx} = 2y^2\sec^2 x$

24. $\dfrac{dy}{dx} = \dfrac{x(y^2-1)}{(x^2+1)}$

CALCULATION OF THE ARBITRARY CONSTANT

We saw on pp. 539–40 that

$$3y\dfrac{dy}{dx} = 5x^2 \quad \Longleftrightarrow \quad \tfrac{3}{2}y^2 = \tfrac{5}{3}x^3 + A$$

The equation $\tfrac{3}{2}y^2 = \tfrac{5}{3}x^3 + A$ represents a family of curves with similar characteristics. Each value of A gives one particular member of the family, i.e. a *particular solution*.

The value of A cannot be found from the differential equation alone; further information is needed.

Suppose that we require the equation of a curve which satisfies the differential equation $2\dfrac{dy}{dx} = \dfrac{\cos x}{y}$ and which passes through the point $(0, 2)$.

We want one member of the family of curves represented by the differential equation, i.e. the particular value of the arbitrary constant must be found.

The general solution has to be found first so, separating the variables, we have

$$\int 2y\, dy = \int \cos x\, dx \quad \Rightarrow \quad y^2 = A + \sin x$$

In order to find the required curve we need the value of A such that the general solution is satisfied by

$$x = 0 \quad \text{and} \quad y = 2$$

i.e. $\qquad\qquad 4 = A + 0 \quad \Rightarrow \quad A = 4$

Hence the equation of the specified curve is $y^2 = 4 + \sin x$

Examples 32d

1. Describe the family of curves represented by the differential equation $y = x\dfrac{dy}{dx}$ and sketch any three members of this family.

   Find the particular solution for which $y = 2$ when $x = 1$ and sketch this member of the family on the same axes as before.

By separating the variables,

$$y = x\frac{dy}{dx} \quad \Rightarrow \quad \int \frac{1}{y}\, dy = \int \frac{1}{x}\, dx$$

$$\Rightarrow \quad \ln|y| = \ln|x| + \ln A$$

i.e. the general solution is $y = Ax$

This equation represents a family of straight lines through the origin, each line having a gradient A, as shown in the following diagram.

If $y = 2$ when $x = 1$ then $A = 2$ and the corresponding member of the family is the line $y = 2x$

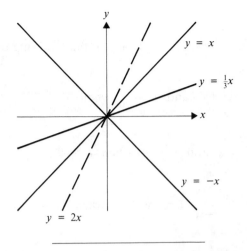

2. A curve is such that the gradient is proportional to the product of the x and y coordinates. If the curve passes through the points $(2, 1)$ and $(4, e^2)$, find its equation.

First find the general solution

$$\frac{\mathrm{d}y}{\mathrm{d}x} = kxy \text{ where } k \text{ is a constant of proportion.}$$

$$\therefore \qquad \int \frac{1}{y}\,\mathrm{d}y = \int kx\,\mathrm{d}x \quad \Rightarrow \quad \ln y = \tfrac{1}{2}kx^2 + A$$

There are *two* unknown constants this time so we need two extra pieces of information; these are

(i) $y = 1$ when $x = 2 \quad \Rightarrow \quad \ln 1 = 2k + A$

$\qquad\qquad\qquad\qquad\qquad\qquad \ln 1 = 0 \text{ so } A + 2k = 0$

(ii) $y = e^2$ when $x = 4 \quad \Rightarrow \quad \ln e^2 = 8k + A$

$\qquad\qquad\qquad\qquad\qquad\qquad \ln e^2 = 2 \text{ so } A + 8k = 2$

Solving these equations for A and k we get $k = \tfrac{1}{3}$ and $A = -\tfrac{2}{3}$

$\therefore$ the equation of the specified curve is $\ln y = \tfrac{1}{6}x^2 - \tfrac{2}{3}$

$$= \tfrac{1}{6}(x^2 - 4)$$

$$\text{or} \quad y^6 = e^{(x^2 - 4)}$$

EXERCISE 32d

Find the particular solution of each of the following differential equations.

1. $y^2 \dfrac{dy}{dx} = x^2 + 1$ and $y = 1$ when $x = 2$

2. $e^t \dfrac{ds}{dt} = \sqrt{s}$ and $s = 4$ when $t = 0$

3. $\dfrac{y}{x} \dfrac{dy}{dx} = \dfrac{y^2 - 1}{x^2 - 1}$ and $y = 3$ when $x = 2$

4. A curve passes through the origin and its gradient function is $2x - 1$. Find the equation of the curve and sketch it.

5. A curve for which $e^{-x} \dfrac{dy}{dx} = 1$, passes through the point $(0, -1)$
   Find the equation of the curve.

6. A curve passes through the points $(1, 2)$ and $(\frac{1}{5}, -10)$ and its gradient is inversely proportional to x^2. Find the equation of the curve.

7. If $y = 2$ when $x = 1$, find the coordinates of the point where the curve represented by $\dfrac{2y}{3} \dfrac{dy}{dx} = e^{-3x}$ crosses the y-axis.

8. Find the equation of the curve whose gradient function is $\dfrac{y + 1}{x^2 - 1}$ and which passes through the point $(-3, 1)$.

9. The gradient function of a curve is proportional to $x + 3$. If the curve passes through the origin and the point $(2, 8)$, find its equation.

10. Solve the differential equation $(1 + x^2) \dfrac{dy}{dx} - y(y + 1)x = 0$, given that $y = 1$ when $x = 0$

MIXED EXERCISE 32

Integrate w.r.t. x

1. $x(1 + x^2)^4$

2. xe^{-3x}

3. $\cos 2x \cos 3x$

4. $\dfrac{x + 3}{x + 2}$

5. $\dfrac{x^2}{(x^3 + 1)^2}$

6. $\dfrac{3}{(x - 4)(x - 1)}$

7. $\dfrac{(x + 1)}{x(2x + 1)}$

8. $\dfrac{x - 1}{(x^2 + 1)}$

9. $\dfrac{\sin x}{\sqrt{(\cos x)}}$

Evaluate

10. $\displaystyle\int_{\pi/2}^{\pi} (\sin \tfrac{1}{2}x + \cos 2x)\, dx$

11. $\displaystyle\int_{2}^{5} x\sqrt{(x - 1)}\, dx$

12. $\displaystyle\int_{0}^{\pi/4} \tan^3 x\, dx$

13. $\displaystyle\int_{1}^{2} x\sqrt{(5 - x^2)}\, dx$

14. $\displaystyle\int_{4}^{6} \dfrac{5}{x^2 - x - 6}\, dx$

15. $\displaystyle\int_{2}^{3} \dfrac{1}{x \ln x}\, dx$

16. $\displaystyle\int_{-2}^{-1} \dfrac{2 - x}{x(1 - x)}\, dx$

17. $\displaystyle\int_{0}^{1} \dfrac{x(1 - x)}{2 + x}\, dx$

18. Solve the differential equation $\dfrac{dy}{dx} = 3x^2 y^2$ given that $y = 1$ when $x = 0$

19. If $\dfrac{dy}{dx} = x(y^2 + 1)$ and $y = 0$ when $x = 2$ find the particular solution of the differential equation.

20. Find the equation of the curve which passes through the point $(\tfrac{1}{2}, 1)$ and is defined by the differential equation $ye^{y^2} \dfrac{dy}{dx} = e^{2x}$. Show that the curve also passes through the point $(2, 2)$ and sketch the curve.

CHAPTER 33

APPLICATIONS OF CALCULUS

GENERAL RATES OF INCREASE

We have already seen that

$$\frac{dy}{dx} \text{ represents the rate at which } y \text{ increases compared with } x$$

Whenever the variation in one quantity, p say, depends upon the changing value of another quantity, q, then the rate of increase of p compared with q can be expressed as $\frac{dp}{dq}$

There are many every-day situations where such relationships exist, e.g.

1) liquid expands when it is heated so, if V is the volume of a quantity of liquid and T is the temperature, then the rate at which the volume increases with temperature can be written $\frac{dV}{dT}$

2) if the profit, P, made by a company selling radios depends upon the number, n, of radios sold, then $\frac{dP}{dn}$ represents the rate of increase of profit compared with the increase in sales.

MOTION IN A STRAIGHT LINE

Consider a particle which moves in a straight line so that, at any time t, its displacement from a fixed point on that line is s, its velocity is v and its acceleration is a

Velocity is the rate at which the displacement is increasing with time,

i.e. $$v = \frac{ds}{dt} \text{ and hence } \int v \, dt = s$$

Acceleration is the rate at which the velocity is increasing with time,

i.e.
$$a = \frac{dv}{dt} \text{ and hence } \int a \, dt = v$$

Examples 33a _____

1. A particle, P, is moving along a straight line and Q is a fixed point on that line. The acceleration of P after t seconds is given by $3t^2 - 2$. When $t = 0$, P is at O, and has a velocity of 2 m/s. Find an expression for the velocity of P at any time t and find the velocity after 4 seconds.

$$a = 3t^2 - 2$$

$$v = \int a \, dt = \int (3t^2 - 2) \, dt$$

$$\therefore \qquad v = t^3 - 2t + K$$

When $t = 0$, $v = 2 \qquad \Rightarrow \qquad 2 = K$

$$\therefore \qquad v = t^3 - 2t + 2$$

Hence, after 4 seconds, i.e. when $t = 4$,

$$v = 4^3 - 2(4) + 2 = 58$$

The velocity after 4 seconds is 58 m/s.

_____

2. The velocity, at any time t, of a particle moving in a straight line is given by $v = 1 + e^{2t}$. Initially (i.e. when $t = 0$) the particle is at O, a fixed point on the line. Find

   (a) an expression for the acceleration of the particle at time t,

   (b) the displacement of the particle from O after 3 seconds.

$$v = 1 + e^{2t}$$

(a)
$$a = \frac{dv}{dt} = 2e^{2t}$$

i.e. at any time t, the acceleration is $2e^{2t}$

(b)
$$s = \int v \, dt = \int (1 + e^{2t}) \, dt$$

$$= t + \tfrac{1}{2}e^{2t} + K$$

When $t = 0$ the particle is at O, i.e. $s = 0$

$$\therefore \qquad 0 = 0 + \tfrac{1}{2}e^{0} + K \quad \Rightarrow \quad K = -\tfrac{1}{2}$$

$$\Rightarrow \qquad s = t + \tfrac{1}{2}e^{2t} - \tfrac{1}{2}$$

Hence, when $t = 3$, $s = 3 + \tfrac{1}{2}e^{6} - \tfrac{1}{2}$

i.e. after 3 seconds the displacement from O is $\tfrac{1}{2}(5 + e^{6})$

---

3. A particle starts from rest and travels in a straight line so that its acceleration is $(t + 3) \, \text{m/s}^2$ at any time t. Find the distance travelled in the interval of time from $t = 1$ to $t = 3$

$$a = t + 3$$

$$v = \int (t + 3) \, dt = \tfrac{1}{2}t^2 + 3t + K$$

The particle starts from rest so $v = 0$ when $t = 0$ $\quad \Rightarrow \quad K = 0$

$$\therefore \qquad v = \tfrac{1}{2}t^2 + 3t$$

$$s = \int (\tfrac{1}{2}t^2 + 3t) \, dt = \tfrac{1}{6}t^3 + \tfrac{3}{2}t^2 + K'$$

where s is the displacement at time t from a fixed point.

For positive values of t, s is always positive so the *distance* travelled in any time interval is given by the difference of the displacements at the beginning and end of that interval.

When $t = 1$, $\quad s_1 = \tfrac{1}{6} + \tfrac{3}{2} + K' = \tfrac{5}{3} + K'$

When $t = 3$, $\quad s_3 = \tfrac{1}{6}(27) + \tfrac{3}{2}(9) + K' = 18 + K'$

$$\therefore \quad s_3 - s_1 = (18 + K') - (\tfrac{5}{3} + K') = 16\tfrac{1}{3}$$

i.e. the distance travelled between $t = 1$ and $t = 3$ is $16\tfrac{1}{3}$ m.

EXERCISE 33a

1. A particle moving in a straight line starts from rest at a point O on the line, and, t seconds later, has an acceleration $(t - 6)$ m/s². Find expressions for the velocity and the displacement of the particle from O after t seconds. Find also the velocity and the displacement from O after 6 seconds.

2. A particle, P, moves in a straight line with acceleration $(3t - 1)$ m/s² where t is the time in seconds. If P has a velocity of 3 m/s when $t = 2$, find its velocity at time t and when $t = 5$

3. The velocity of a particle moving in a straight line is v m/s after t seconds where $v = 6t^2 + 1$. Find how far the particle travels in the interval from $t = 1$ to $t = 4$

4. A particle moves in a straight line with velocity v m/s where, after t seconds, $v = 2 + 1/(t + 1)^2$. Initially the particle is at a fixed point O on the line.
    (a) Find an expression for the displacement of the particle from after t seconds
    (b) Show that the velocity has a limiting value (i.e. v approaches a fixed value as t approaches infinity), and state this value.

5. The velocity of a particle moving in a straight line is $3t^2$ m/s at any time, t seconds. What is the acceleration of the particle at time t? If the particle passes through a fixed point A on the line, with velocity 12 m/s, find the displacement from A 6 seconds later.

NATURAL OCCURRENCE OF DIFFERENTIAL EQUATIONS

Differential equations often arise when a physical situation is interpreted mathematically (i.e. when a mathematical model is made of the physical situation).

Consider the following examples.

1) Suppose that a body falls from rest in a medium which causes the velocity to decrease at a rate proportional to the velocity.

Using v for velocity and t for time, the rate of *decrease* of velocity can be written as $-\dfrac{\mathrm{d}v}{\mathrm{d}t}$.

Thus the motion of the body satisfies the differential equation

$$-\frac{dv}{dt} = kv$$

2) During the initial stages of the growth of yeast cells in a culture, the number of cells present increases in proportion to the number already formed.

Thus n, the number of cells at a particular time t, can be found from the differential equation

$$\frac{dn}{dt} = kn$$

3) Suppose that a chemical mixture contains two substances A and B whose weights are W_A and W_B and whose combined weight remains constant. B is converted into A at a rate which is inversely proportional to the weight of B and proportional to the square of the weight of A in the mixture at any time t. The weight of B present at time t can be found using

$$\frac{d}{dt}(W_B) = \frac{k}{W_B} \times (W_A)^2$$

But $W_A + W_B$ is constant, W say

Hence
$$\frac{d}{dt}(W_B) = \frac{k(W - W_B)^2}{W_B}$$

This differential equation now relates W_B and t.

Note. In forming (and subsequently solving) differential equations from naturally occuring data, it is not actually necessary to understand the background of the situation or experiment.

EXERCISE 33b

In Questions 1 to 4 form, but *do not solve*, the differential equation representing the given data.

1. A body moves with a velocity v which is inversely proportional to its displacement s from a fixed point.

2. The rate at which the height h of a certain plant increases is proportional to the natural logarithm of the difference between its present height and its final height H.

3. The manufacturers of a certain brand of soap powder are concerned that the number, n, of people buying their product at any time t has remained constant for some months. They launch a major advertising programme which results in the number of customers increasing at a rate proportional to the square root of n. Express as differential equations the progress of sales.

(a) before advertising

(b) after advertising.

4. In an isolated community, the number, n, of people suffering from an infectious disease is N_1 at a particular time. The disease then becomes epidemic and spreads so that the number of sick people increases at a rate proportional to n, until the total number of sufferers is N_2. The rate of increase then becomes inversely proportional to n until N_3 people have the disease. After this, the total number of sick people decreases at a constant rate. Write down the differential equation governing the incidence of the disease.

(a) for $N_1 \leqslant N_2$

(b) for $N_2 \leqslant N_3$

(c) for $n \geqslant N_3$.

5. Two chemicals, P and Q, are involved in a reaction. The masses of P and Q present at any time t, are p and q respectively. The rate at which p is increasing at time t is k times the product of the two masses. If the masses of P and Q have a constant sum s, find a differential equation expressing $\dfrac{\mathrm{d}p}{\mathrm{d}t}$ in terms of p, s and k.

FINDING COMPOUND AREAS

In Chapter 28 we saw how integration can be used to calculate an area bounded by the x-axis, part of a known curve and two vertical lines. The method introduced there is based on the summation of the areas of vertical strips, or elements.

We also saw that an area bounded by two horizontal lines, the y-axis and part of a curve can be found in a similar way but in this case we use horizontal strips.

Only curves with algebraic equations were used in Chapter 28 but the methods apply to the graphs of other functions, as the following example shows.

Examples 33c

1. A plane region is defined by the line $y = 4$, the x and y axes and part of the curve $y = \ln x$. Find the area of the region.

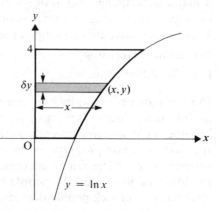

A vertical element is unsuitable in this case as the top and bottom are not always on the same boundaries, but a horizontal element is satisfactory.

The area, δA, of a typical horizontal element is given by $\delta A \approx x\, \delta y$. Because the width of our element is δy we will have to integrate w.r.t y, so we need the equation of the curve in the form $x = f(y)$

$$y = \ln x \quad \Rightarrow \quad x = e^y$$

$$\therefore \quad \delta A \approx e^y\, \delta y$$

$$\Rightarrow \qquad A = \lim_{\delta y \to 0} \sum_{y=0}^{y=4} e^y\, \delta y = \int_0^4 e^y\, dy$$

$$= \left[e^y \right]_0^4$$

$$= e^4 - e^0$$

The defined area is $(e^4 - 1)$ square units

Note that this area can also be found by subtracting the shaded region from the area of the rectangle OABC but this alternative is not always suitable.

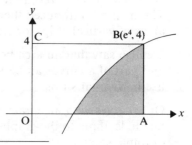

A similar approach can be made in a variety of circumstances provided that an element can be found

1) which has the same format throughout, i.e. the ends of all the elements are on the same boundaries;

2) whose length and width are measured parallel to the x and y axes.

---

2. Find the area between the curve $y = x^2$ and the line $y = 3x$

The line and curve meet where $x^2 = 3x$,
i.e. where $x = 0$ and $x = 3$

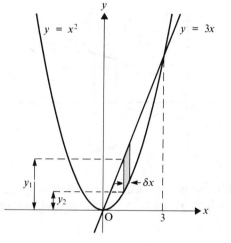

A vertical strip always has its top on the line and its foot on the curve so it is a suitable element. It is approximately a rectangle whose width is δx and whose height is the vertical distance between the line and the curve. The area of the element, δA, is given by

$$\delta A \approx (y_1 - y_2)\delta x = (3x - x^2)\delta x$$

$$\therefore \qquad A = \lim_{\delta x \to 0} \sum_{x=0}^{x=3} (3x - x^2)\delta x = \int_0^3 (3x - x^2)\,dx$$

$$= \left[\tfrac{3}{2}x^2 - \tfrac{1}{3}x^3 \right]_0^3$$

$$= 4\tfrac{1}{2}$$

The required area is $4\tfrac{1}{2}$ square units.

The area bounded partly by a curve whose equation is given parametrically can also be found by summing the areas of suitable elements.

---

3. Find the area bounded in the first quadrant by the x-axis, the line $x = 2$ and part of the curve with parametric equations $x = 2t^2$, $y = 2t$

The sketch of this curve need not be an accurate shape but it is important to realise that it goes through the origin because when $t = 0$, both x and y are zero.

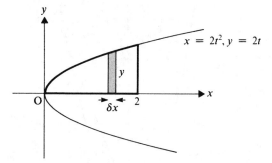

A suitable element is a vertical strip which is approximately a rectangle of height, y, width δx and area δA where $\delta A \approx y\,\delta x$

Considering $x = 2t^2$ gives

$$\delta x \approx \left(\frac{\mathrm{d}x}{\mathrm{d}t}\right)(\delta t) = 4t\delta t \qquad \text{and} \qquad \delta t \to 0 \quad \text{when} \quad \delta x \to 0$$

it also shows that, when $x = 2$, $t = 1$

$t \neq -1$, as it gives $y = -2$ which is not in the first quadrant.

$\therefore$ $$\delta A \approx (2t)(4t\delta t)$$

Then $$A = \lim_{\delta x \to 0} \sum_{x=0}^{x=2} 8t^2\delta t = \lim_{\delta t \to 0} \sum_{t=0}^{t=1} 8t^2\delta t$$

$\Rightarrow$ $$A = \int_0^1 8t^2\,\mathrm{d}t = \left[\tfrac{8}{3}t^3\right]_0^1 = \tfrac{8}{3}$$

The required area is $\tfrac{8}{3}$ square units.

EXERCISE 33c

1. Calculate the area bounded by the curve $y = \sqrt{x}$, the y-axis and the line $y = 3$

2. Find, by integration, the area bounded by
   (a) the x-axis, the line $x = 2$ and the curve $y = x^2$
   (b) the y-axis, the line $y = 4$ and the curve $y = x^2$
   Sketch these two areas on the same diagram and hence check the sum of the answers to (a) and (b).

3. Calculate the area in the first quadrant between the curve $y^2 = x$ and the line $x = 9$

4. Find the area between the y-axis and the curve $y^2 = 1 - x$

5. Find the area of the region whose boundaries are the y-axis, the line $y = \frac{1}{2}\pi$ and the curve $y = \arcsin x$

6. A region in the xy plane is bounded by the lines $y = 1$ and $x = 1$, and the curve $y = e^x$. Find its area.

7. Find the area bounded by the inequalities $y \leqslant 1 - x^2$ and $y \geqslant 1 - x$

8. Calculate the area bounded by the curve $y = \sin x$ and the lines $y = \frac{1}{2}$ and $x = \frac{1}{2}\pi$

9. Find the area of the region of the xy plane defined by
   (a) $y \geqslant e^x$, $x \geqslant 0$, $y \leqslant e$ (b) $1 \geqslant y \geqslant 1/(x + 1)$, $x \leqslant 2$

10. The equations of a curve are $x = 2t$, $y = 2/t$. Find the area bounded by this curve, the x-axis and the ordinates at $x = 1$, $x = 4$

The next two questions are a little harder.

11. Evaluate the area between the line $y = x - 1$ and the curve
    (a) $y = x(1 - x)$ (b) $y = (2x + 1)(x - 1)$

12. Calculate the area of the region of the xy plane defined by the inequalities $y \geqslant (x + 1)(x - 2)$ and $y \leqslant x$

VOLUME OF REVOLUTION

If an area is rotated about a straight line, the three-dimensional object so formed is called a *solid of revolution*, and its volume is a *volume of revolution*.

The line about which rotation takes place is always an axis of symmetry for the solid of revolution. Also, any cross-section of the solid which is perpendicular to the axis of rotation, is circular.

Consider the solid of revolution formed when the area shown in the diagram is rotated about the *x*-axis.

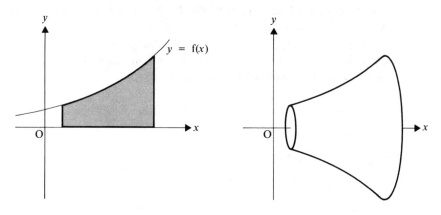

To calculate the volume of this solid we can divide it into 'slices' by making cuts perpendicular to the axis of rotation.

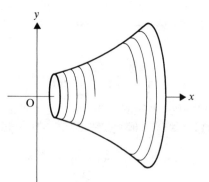

If the cuts are reasonably close together, each slice is approximately cylindrical and the approximate volume of the solid can be found by summing the volumes of these cylinders.

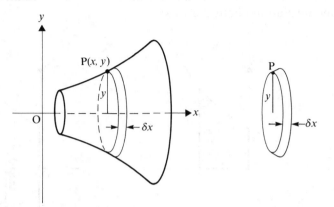

Consider an element formed by one cut through the point $P(x,y)$ and the other cut distant δx from the first.

The volume, δV, of this element is approximately that of a cylinder of radius y and 'height' δx

i.e. $$\delta V \approx \pi y^2 \, \delta x$$

Then the total volume of the solid is V, where

$$V \approx \sum \pi y^2 \, \delta x$$

The smaller δx is, the closer is this approximation to V,

i.e. $$V = \lim_{\delta x \to 0} \sum \pi y^2 \, \delta x = \int \pi y^2 \, dx$$

Now if the equation of the rotated curve is given, this integral ca evaluated and the volume of the solid of revolution found,

e.g. to find the volume generated when the area between part of curve $y = e^x$ and the x-axis is rotated about the x-axis, we use

$$\int \pi (e^x)^2 \, dx = \pi \int e^{2x} \, dx$$

When an area rotates about the y-axis we can use a similar method based on slices perpendicular to the y-axis, giving

$$V = \int \pi x^2 \, dy$$

Examples 33d _____

1. Find the volume generated when the area bounded by the x and
   y axes, the line $x = 1$ and the curve $y = e^x$ is rotated through
   one revolution about the x-axis.

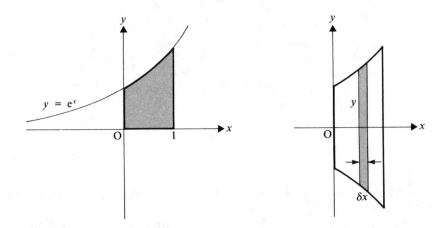

The volume, δV, of the element shown is approximately that of a
cylinder of radius y and thickness δx, therefore

$$\delta V \approx \pi y^2 \, \delta x$$

$\therefore$ the total volume is V, where $\displaystyle V \approx \sum_{x=0}^{x=1} \pi y^2 \, \delta x$

$\Rightarrow$
$$V = \lim_{\delta x \to 0} \sum_{x=0}^{x=1} \pi y^2 \, \delta x = \int_0^1 \pi y^2 \, dx$$

$$= \pi \int_0^1 (e^x)^2 \, dx$$

$$= \pi \int_0^1 e^{2x} \, dx$$

$$= \pi \left[\tfrac{1}{2} e^{2x} \right]_0^1$$

$$= \tfrac{1}{2}\pi(e^2 - e^0)$$

i.e. the specified volume of revolution is $\tfrac{1}{2}\pi(e^2 - 1)$ cubic units.

_____

2. The area defined by the inequalities $y \geqslant x^2 + 1$, $x \geqslant 0$, $y \leqslant 2$, is rotated completely about the y-axis. Find the volume of the solid generated.

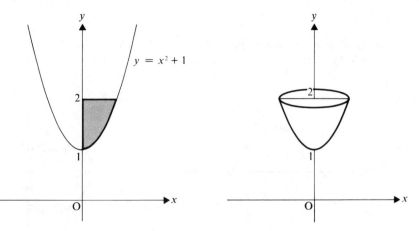

Rotating the shaded area about the y-axis gives the solid shown.

This time we use horizontal cuts to form elements which are approximately cylinders with radius x and thickness δy

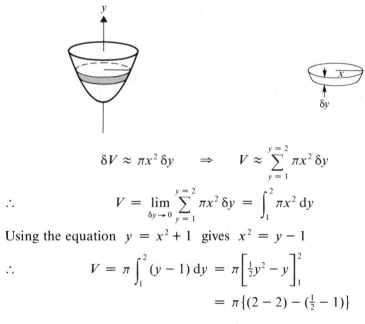

$$\delta V \approx \pi x^2 \, \delta y \qquad \Rightarrow \qquad V \approx \sum_{y=1}^{y=2} \pi x^2 \, \delta y$$

$$\therefore \qquad V = \lim_{\delta y \to 0} \sum_{y=1}^{y=2} \pi x^2 \, \delta y = \int_1^2 \pi x^2 \, dy$$

Using the equation $y = x^2 + 1$ gives $x^2 = y - 1$

$$\therefore \qquad V = \pi \int_1^2 (y - 1) \, dy = \pi \left[\tfrac{1}{2} y^2 - y \right]_1^2$$

$$= \pi \{ (2 - 2) - (\tfrac{1}{2} - 1) \}$$

i.e. the volume of the specified solid is $\tfrac{1}{2}\pi$ cubic units.

3. The area enclosed by the curve $y = 4x - x^2$ and the line $y = 3$ is rotated about the line $y = 3$. Find the volume of the solid generated.

The line $y = 3$ meets the curve $y = 4x - x^2$ at the points $(1, 3)$ and $(3, 3)$, therefore the volume generated is as shown in the diagram.

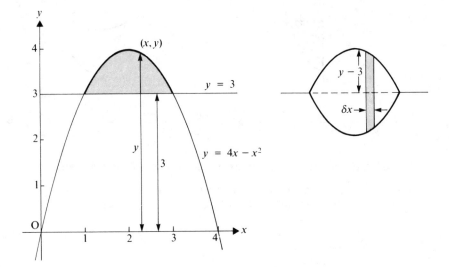

The element shown is approximately a cylinder with radius $(y - 3)$ and thickness δx, so its volume, δV, is given by $\delta V \approx \pi (y - 3)^2 \delta x$

i.e.
$$V = \lim_{\delta x \to 0} \sum_{x=1}^{x=3} \pi (y - 3)^2 \delta x = \pi \int_1^3 (y - 3)^2 \, dx$$

$\Rightarrow$
$$V = \pi \int_1^3 (4x - x^2 - 3)^2 \, dx$$

$$= \pi \int_1^3 (9 - 24x + 22x^2 - 8x^3 + x^4) \, dx$$

$$= \pi \left[9x - 12x^2 + \tfrac{22}{3}x^3 - 2x^4 + \tfrac{1}{5}x^5 \right]_1^3$$

$$= \tfrac{16}{15}\pi$$

$\therefore$ the required volume is $\tfrac{16}{15}\pi$ cubic units.

4. Find the volume generated when the area between the curve $y^2 = x$ and the line $y = x$ is rotated completely about the x-axis.

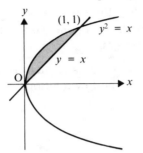

The defined area is shown in the diagram.

When this area rotates about Ox, the solid generated is bowl-shaped on the outside, with a conical hole inside.
The cross-section this time is not a simple circle but is an annulus, i.e. the area between two concentric circles.

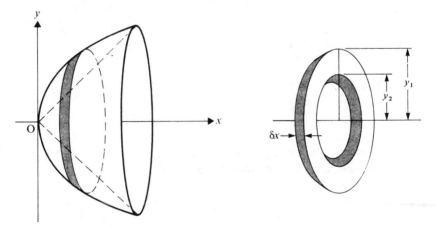

For a typical element the area of cross-section is $\pi y_1^2 - \pi y_2^2$

Therefore the volume of an element is given by $\delta V \approx \pi\{y_1^2 - y_2^2\}\delta x$

$$\therefore \qquad V \approx \sum_{x=0}^{x=1} \pi\{y_1^2 - y_2^2\}\delta x = \pi \int_0^1 (y_1^2 - y_2^2)\, dx$$

Now $y_1 = \sqrt{x}$ and $y_2 = x$

$$\therefore \qquad V = \pi \int_0^1 (x - x^2)\, dx = \pi\left[\tfrac{1}{2}x^2 - \tfrac{1}{3}x^3\right]_0^1 = \tfrac{1}{6}\pi$$

The volume generated is $\tfrac{1}{6}\pi$ cubic units.

Note that the volume specified in Example 4 could be found by calculating separately

1) the volume given when the curve $y^2 = x$ rotates about the x-axis;

2) the volume, by formula, of a cone with base radius 1 and height 1 and subtracting **(1)** from **(2)**.

The method in which an annulus element is used, however, applies whatever the shape of the hollow interior.

EXERCISE 33d

In each of the following questions, find the volume generated when the area defined by the following sets of inequalities is rotated completely about the x-axis.

1. $0 \leqslant y \leqslant x(4 - x)$

2. $0 \leqslant y \leqslant e^x, \qquad 0 \leqslant x \leqslant 3$

3. $0 \leqslant y \leqslant \dfrac{1}{x}, \qquad 1 \leqslant x \leqslant 2$

4. $0 \leqslant y \leqslant x^2, \qquad -2 \leqslant x \leqslant 2$

5. $y^2 \leqslant x, \qquad x \leqslant 2$

In each of the following questions, the area bounded by the curve and line(s) given is rotated about the y-axis to form a solid. Find the volume generated.

6. $y = x^2, \ y = 4$

7. $y = 4 - x^2, \ y = 0$

8. $y = x^3, \ y = 1, \ y = 2,$ for $x \geqslant 0$

9. $y = \ln x, \ x = 0, \ y = 0, \ y = 1$

10. Find the volume generated when the area enclosed between $y^2 = x$ and $x = 1$ is rotated about the line $x = 1$

11. The area defined by the inequalities

$$y \geqslant x^2 - 2x + 4, \ y \leqslant 4$$

is rotated about the line $y = 4$. Find the volume generated.

12. The area enclosed by $y = \sin x$ and the x-axis for $0 \leqslant x \leqslant \pi$ is rotated about the x-axis. Find the volume generated.

13. An area is bounded by the line $y = 1$, the x-axis and parts of the curve $y = 3 - x^2$. Find the volume generated when this area rotates completely about the y-axis.

14. The area enclosed between the curves $y = x^2$ and $y^2 = x$ is rotated about the x-axis. Find the volume generated.

CENTROID OF AREA

The centroid of an area is the *point* about which the area is evenly distributed.

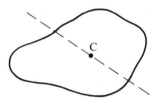

It follows that

the centroid lies on any line of symmetry.

Hence, the centroid of a rectangle is the point of intersection of the diagonals, the centroid of a circle is the centre and the centroid of a triangle is the point of intersection of the medians.

If we have a lamina (i.e. a thin flat plate) whose mass per unit area is constant, the centroid of the area of the lamina is also the *centre of mass of the lamina*, i.e. the point at which the lamina could be supported in perfect balance.

The same point *may* also be the *centre of gravity* of the lamina but only if, in addition to constant mass per unit area, gravitational attraction is constant over the whole area. This is really a problem of mechanics and outside the scope of this book.

First Moment of Area

If the point C is the centroid of an area A then the first moment of A about a particular axis is defined as

$$A \times (\text{distance of C from that axis})$$

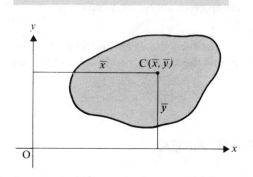

For an area A in the xy plane, the coordinates of the centroid are usually denoted by $(\bar{x}, \bar{y})$. So for the area A shaded in the diagram

$$\begin{cases} \text{the first moment of } A \text{ about } Ox \text{ is } A\bar{y} \\ \text{the first moment of } A \text{ about } Oy \text{ is } A\bar{x} \end{cases}$$

TO FIND THE COORDINATES OF THE CENTROID OF AN AREA

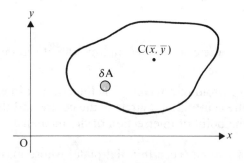

If $C(\bar{x}, \bar{y})$ is the centroid of the area A and if δA is a small element of that area, then the first moment of A about a given axis is given by

$$\Sigma(\text{first moment of } \delta A \text{ about that axis})$$

Hence $A\bar{x} = \Sigma(\text{first moment of } \delta A \text{ about } Oy)$

and $A\bar{y} = \Sigma(\text{first moment of } \delta A \text{ about } Ox)$

Examples 33e _____

1. For the area between the x-axis and the curve $y = x(2 - x)$, find
   (a) the first moment about Ox
   (b) the coordinates of the centroid.

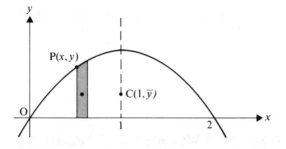

If we take as our element of area the vertical strip through $P(x, y)$ shown in the diagram, then

the area of the element, δA, is given by $\delta A \approx y \, \delta x$
and the distance of the centroid of the element from $Ox \approx \frac{1}{2}y$

$\therefore$ the first moment of the element about Ox is approximately $(y\delta x)(\frac{1}{2}y)$

(a) The first moment of the whole area A about Ox is $A\bar{y}$, where

$$A\bar{y} \approx \sum \frac{1}{2}y^2 \, \delta x$$

$$\Rightarrow \qquad A\bar{y} = \lim_{\delta x \to 0} \sum_{x=0}^{x=2} \frac{1}{2}y^2 \, \delta x = \frac{1}{2}\int_0^2 y^2 \, dx = \frac{1}{2}\int_0^2 x^2(2-x)^2 \, dx$$

$$= \frac{1}{2}\left[\frac{4}{3}x^3 - x^4 + \frac{1}{5}x^5\right]_0^2 = \frac{8}{15}$$

(b) From symmetry, $\bar{x} = 1$ and $\bar{y}$ is given by $A\bar{y} = \frac{8}{15}$

Now $$A = \int_0^2 y \, dx$$

$\therefore$ $$\bar{y} \int_0^2 y \, dx = \frac{8}{15}$$

i.e. $$\bar{y} \int_0^2 x(2 - x) \, dx = \bar{y}\left[x^2 - \frac{1}{3}x^3\right]_0^2 = \frac{8}{15}$$

$$\Rightarrow \qquad \frac{4}{3}\bar{y} = \frac{8}{15} \qquad \Rightarrow \qquad \bar{y} = \frac{2}{5}$$

i.e. the centroid of the area is the point $(1, \frac{2}{5})$ and the first moment of the area about Ox is $\frac{8}{15}$

_____

CENTROID OF VOLUME OF REVOLUTION

The centroid of a volume is the *point* about which the volume is evenly distributed.
Hence *the centroid of a volume of revolution lies on the axis of rotation.*

For a solid whose mass per unit volume is constant, the centroid is also the centre of mass.

First Moment of a Volume of Revolution

If the point C is the centroid of a volume V the first moment of V about a particular axis is defined as

$$V \times \text{(distance of C from that axis)}$$

If a volume V is formed by rotating an area about the x-axis, then the centroid of V must lie on the x-axis, i.e. C is the point $(\bar{x}, 0)$

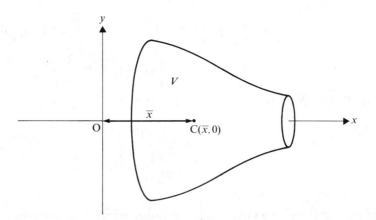

So, for the volume V, shown in the diagram,

$$\begin{cases} \text{the first moment about O}x \text{ is zero} \\ \text{the first moment about O}y \text{ is } V\bar{x} \end{cases}$$

TO FIND THE POSITION OF THE CENTROID OF A VOLUME OF REVOLUTION

If $C(\bar{x}, 0)$ is the centroid of the volume V shown on p. 566 and if δV is a small element of that volume, then the first moment of V about a specified axis can be found from

$$\Sigma(\text{first moment of } \delta V \text{ about that axis})$$

But, by definition, $V\bar{x} = \Sigma(\text{first moment of } \delta V \text{ about } Oy)$

Hence, by calculating V, $\bar{x}$ can be found.

Examples 33e (continued) _____

2. For the volume generated when the area bounded by the x-axis, the line $x = 4$ and the curve $y^2 = x$ is rotated completely about the x-axis find

    (a) the first moment about the y-axis

    (b) the coordinates of the centroid.

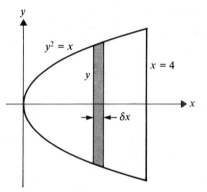

If we take as our element the slice shown, which is approximately a cylinder of radius y and thickness δx then,

the volume of the element, δV, is given by $\delta V \approx \pi y^2 \delta x$
and the approximate distance of its centroid from Oy is x

so the first moment of the element about Oy is approximately $(\pi y^2 \delta x)x$

(a) The first moment of the whole volume V about Ox is $V\bar{x}$ where

$$V\bar{x} \approx \sum_{x=0}^{x=4} \pi y^2 x\, \delta x$$

$\Rightarrow$
$$V\bar{x} = \lim \sum_{x=0}^{x=4} \pi y^2 x\, \delta x = \pi \int_0^4 y^2 x\, dx$$

$$= \pi \int_0^4 x^2\, dx$$

$$= \pi \left[\tfrac{1}{3} x^3 \right]_0^4$$

$$= \tfrac{64}{3} \pi$$

(b) Now $V = \displaystyle\int_0^4 \pi y^2\, dx = \pi \int_0^4 x\, dx = \left[\tfrac{1}{2}\pi x^2 \right]_0^4 = 8\pi$

$\therefore$
$$8\pi\bar{x} = \tfrac{64}{3}\pi$$

$\Rightarrow$
$$\bar{x} = \tfrac{8}{3}$$

The centroid is on the axis of rotation, i.e. $\bar{y} = 0$

Therefore the centroid is the point $(\tfrac{8}{3}, 0)$
and the first moment of volume about Oy is $\tfrac{64}{3}\pi$

EXERCISE 33e

1. The boundaries of a region of the xy plane are the x-axis, the lines $x = 3$ and $x = -3$ and the curve $y = x^2 + 1$. Find
   (a) the area of the region
   (b) the first moment of the area about the x-axis
   (c) the y-coordinate of the centroid of the region.

2. A region in the xy plane is defined by the inequalities $x \leqslant 4$, $0 \leqslant y \leqslant x$. Sketch the region and write down its area.
   Find the first moment of the area about (a) the x-axis (b) the y-axis.
   Determine the coordinates of the centroid of the region.

3. A region of the xy plane is defined by the inequalities

$$0 \leqslant y \leqslant \sin x, \ 0 \leqslant x \leqslant \pi$$

Find (a) the area of the region

(b) the first moment of this area about the x-axis

(c) the coordinates of the centroid of this area.

Find also

(d) the volume obtained when this area is rotated completely about the x-axis

(e) the first moment of this volume about the y-axis

(f) the centroid of this volume.

4. Repeat Question 1 for the region of the xy plane defined by the inequalities $0 \geqslant y \geqslant x(x - 1)$

5. A region of the xy plane is bounded by the curve $y = x^2$ and the line $y = 4$

Find: (a) the area of this region

(b) the first moment of this area about the x-axis

(c) the y coordinate of the centroid of the area.

Find also:

(d) the volume obtained when this area is rotated about the y-axis

(e) the first moment of the volume about the x-axis

(f) the centroid of this volume.

6. Repeat Question 5 for the area bounded by $y = \ln x, \ x = 0,$ $y = 0$ and $y = 1$

7. (a) Find the x coordinate of the centroid of the area bounded by

$$y = e^x, \ y = 0, \ x = 0, \ x = 2$$

(b) This area is rotated about the x-axis to give a volume of revolution.

Find (i) the volume generated

(ii) the coordinates of the centroid of this volume.

THE MEAN VALUE OF A FUNCTION

Consider the curve $y = f(x)$ for values of x in the interval $[a, b]$. The mean value of y in this interval is the arithmetic average value of y and is denoted by y_m or $\{f(x)\}_m$

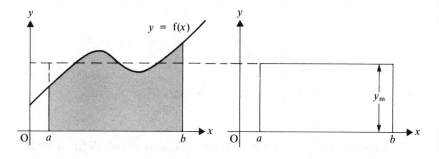

On the curve $y = f(x)$, some of the ordinates are above the line $y = y_m$ and some ordinates are below this line. As y_m is the *average* ordinate, it follows that these two cancel, i.e. the area between the line and the curve that is above $y = y_m$ is equal to the area between the line and the curve that is below the line.

Hence, the area of the rectangle in the diagram on the right is equal to the shaded area in the left-hand diagram.

i.e.

$$(b - a)y_m = \int_a^b y \, dx$$

Therefore

$$y_m = \frac{1}{b - a} \int f(x) \, dx$$

Examples 33f

1. Find the mean value of $\sin \theta$ within the interval $0 \leqslant \theta \leqslant \pi$

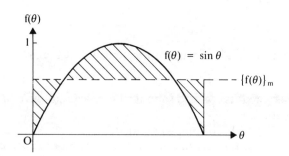

In general the mean value of $f(x)$ is given by $\dfrac{1}{b-a} \displaystyle\int_a^b f(x)\, dx$

So, for $f(\theta) = \sin\theta$ in the interval $0 \leqslant \theta \leqslant \pi$,

$$\{f(\theta)\}_m = \frac{1}{\pi - 0} \int_0^\pi \sin\theta\, d\theta$$

$$= \frac{1}{\pi}\Big[-\cos\theta\Big]_0^\pi$$

$$= \frac{2}{\pi}$$

Note that, to 2 s.f., $\dfrac{2}{\pi} = 0.64$ and that, on the graph, the line $f(\theta) = 0.64$ looks a reasonable average ordinate.

---

2. If $-1 \leqslant x \leqslant 1$, find the mean value of y given that
   $y = 4x(x-1)(x-2)$

Using $y_m = \dfrac{1}{b-a} \displaystyle\int_a^b y\, dx$ for $y = 4x(x-1)(x-2)$ in the interval $[-1, 1]$ gives

$$y_m = \frac{1}{1-(-1)} \int_{-1}^1 4x(x-1)(x-2)\, dx$$

$$= \tfrac{1}{2} \int_{-1}^1 (4x^3 - 12x^2 + 8x)\, dx$$

i.e. $y_m = \tfrac{1}{2}\Big[x^4 - 4x^3 + 4x^2\Big]_{-1}^1 = \tfrac{1}{2}(1 - 9) = -4$

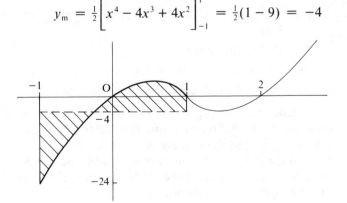

MIXED EXERCISE 33

1. The acceleration at any time, t, of a particle moving in a straight line, is $(4t - 3)$ m/s². Initially the particle is at a fixed point O on the line and has a velocity of 1 m/s. Find the times when the velocity of the particle is zero. Find also the displacement of the particle from O when $t = 3$

2. A particle, P, moves in a straight line with an acceleration of $1/t^3$ m/s² after t seconds. When $t = 1$, P is at rest at a point O on the line of motion. Find expressions for its velocity and its displacement from O at time t and when $t = 2$

3. The velocity at time, t, of a particle P travelling in a straight line, is v m/s where $v = 2 + 1/t^2$. What is the acceleration of P when $t = 1$? Find the distance travelled by P during the time interval between $t = 2$ and $t = 6$

4. Find the area between the curves $y = x^2$ and $y^2 = x$

5. A region of the xy plane is defined by the inequalities $0 \leqslant x \leqslant 4$ and $0 \leqslant y \leqslant e^x$. Find
   (a) the area of the region
   (b) the first moment of the region about Ox
   (c) the y-coordinate of the centroid of the region.

6. Find the mean value of $2x \exp(x^2)$ for the interval $[0, 2]$.

7. Find the area of the region in the first quadrant bounded by the y-axis, the line $y = 6$ and the curve $y = x^2 + 2$
   If this area is rotated completely about Oy to form a solid, find
   (a) the volume of the solid
   (b) the coordinates of the centre of mass of the solid.

8. A plane region is bounded by the curve $y = 6 - x^2$ and the line $y = 2$. Find
   (a) the area of the region
   (b) the first moment of the region about the x-axis
   (c) the coordinates of the centroid of the region.

9. If the part of the area given in Question 8 which is in the first quadrant is rotated through one revolution about the line $y = 2$ find the volume generated.
   Find also the first moment of this volume about the y-axis.
   State the y-coordinate of the centre of mass of the solid and find the corresponding x-coordinate.

10. Find the mean value of the function $x \cos x$ for $0 \leqslant x \leqslant \frac{1}{3}\pi$

CONSOLIDATION E

SUMMARY

COORDINATE GEOMETRY

Straight Lines

For two points, $A(x_1, y_1)$ and $B(x_2, y_2)$, the point which divides AB in the ratio $\lambda : \mu$ has coordinates

$$\left(\frac{\lambda x_2 + \mu x_1}{\lambda + \mu}, \frac{\lambda y_2 + \mu y_1}{\lambda + \mu} \right)$$

For internal division, λ and μ are both positive while, for external division, the smaller of λ and μ is negative, i.e. the ratio is negative.

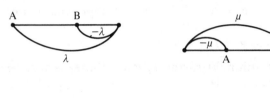

When a line with gradient m makes an angle θ with the positive x-axis, then $m = \tan \theta$

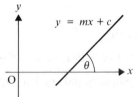

The acute angle α between two lines with gradients m_1 and m_2 is given by $\tan \alpha = \left| \dfrac{m_1 - m_2}{1 + m_1 m_2} \right|$

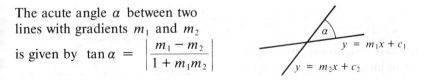

The distance from the point (p, q) to the line with equation $ax + by + c = 0$ is given by $\left| \dfrac{ap + bq + c}{\sqrt{(a^2 + b^2)}} \right|$

Reduction of Relationships to Linear Form

When a non-linear law, containing two unknown constants, connects two variables, the relationship can often be reduced to linear form. The aim is to produce an equation in which one term is constant and another term does not contain a constant. The law can then be expressed in the form
$$Y = mX + C$$

Some common conversions are

$p = a\sqrt{q} + b$; use $Y = p$ and $X = \sqrt{q}$

$p = aq^b$; take logs: $\ln p = \ln a + b \ln q$; use $Y = \ln p$ and $X = \ln q$

$\dfrac{a}{p} + \dfrac{b}{q} = c$; $\Rightarrow \dfrac{1}{p} = \dfrac{c}{a} - \dfrac{b}{a}\dfrac{1}{q}$; use $Y = \dfrac{1}{p}$ and $X = \dfrac{1}{q}$

Circles

The equation of a circle with centre (a, b) and radius r is
$$(x - a)^2 + (y - b)^2 = r^2$$

The equation $x^2 + y^2 + 2gx + 2fy + c = 0$ represents a circle
with centre $(-g, -f)$ and radius $\sqrt{(g^2 + f^2 - c)}$
provided that $g^2 + f^2 - c > 0$

Two circles with radii r_1 and r_2 touch if the distance between their centres is equal to $|r_1 \pm r_2|$

Conic Sections

The cartesian equation of this parabola is $y^2 = 4ax$

The corresponding parametric equations are
$x = at^2$, $y = 2at$

The cartesian equation of an ellipse with its centre at O is
$$\frac{x^2}{a^2} + \frac{y^2}{b^2} = 1$$

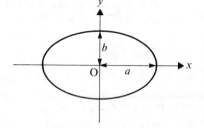

The corresponding parametric equations are $x = a\cos\theta$, $y = b\sin\theta$

The cartesian equation of this rectangular hyperbola is $xy = c^2$

The parametric equations are $x = ct,\ y = c/t$

ALGEBRA

Quadratic Equations

If the roots of the quadratic equation $ax^2 + bx + c = 0$ are α and β then $\alpha + \beta = -\dfrac{b}{a}$ and $\alpha\beta = \dfrac{c}{a}$

Any quadratic equation is of the form

$$x^2 - (\text{sum of roots})x + (\text{product of roots}) = 0$$

Partial Fractions

A proper fraction with a denominator which factorises can be expressed in partial fractions as follows:

The numerators which can be found by the cover-up method are screened.

$$\frac{f(x)}{(x-a)(x-b)} = \frac{A}{(x-a)} + \frac{B}{(x-b)}$$

$$\frac{f(x)}{(x-a)(x-b)^2} = \frac{A}{(x-a)} + \frac{B}{(x-b)} + \frac{C}{(x-b)^2}$$

$$\frac{f(x)}{(x-a)(x^2+b)} = \frac{A}{(x-a)} + \frac{Bx+C}{(x^2+b)}$$

The Remainder Theorem

When a polynomial, $f(x)$, is divided by $(x-a)$ the remainder is equal to $f(a)$

The Factor Theorem

If $f(a) = 0$ then $(x-a)$ is a factor of $f(x)$

INTEGRATION

Standard Integrals

Function	Integral
x^n	$\dfrac{1}{n+1}x^{n+1}$ $(n \neq -1)$
e^x	e^x
$\dfrac{1}{x}$	$\ln|x|$
$\cos x$	$\sin x$
$\sin x$	$-\cos x$
$\sec^2 x$	$\tan x$
$\operatorname{cosec}^2 x$	$-\cot x$
$\tan x$	$\ln|\sec x|$
$\cot x$	$\ln|\sin x|$
$\dfrac{1}{\sqrt{(1-x^2)}}$	$\arcsin x$
$\dfrac{1}{1+x^2}$	$\arctan x$

The following methods are general guide lines; alternative approaches can be better in individual cases.

Integrating products can be done by

a) recognition:

in particular $\displaystyle\int f'(x)\,e^{f(x)}\,dx = e^{f(x)} + K$

$$\int \sin^p x \cos x \, dx = \frac{1}{p+1}\sin^{p+1}x + K \qquad (p \neq -1)$$

$$\int \cos^p x \sin x \, dx = -\frac{1}{p+1}\cos^{p+1}x + K \qquad (p \neq -1)$$

$$\int \tan^p x \sec^2 x \, dx = \frac{1}{p+1}\tan^{p+1}x + K \qquad (p \neq -1)$$

b) change of variable: suitable for the type $f'(x)g\{f(x)\}$

c) by parts: $\displaystyle\int v\frac{du}{dx}\,dx = uv - \int u\frac{dv}{dx}\,dx$

Integration by parts can be used also to integrate $\ln x$ and inverse trig functions.

Integrating fractions can be done by

a) recognition: in particular $\int \dfrac{f'(x)}{f(x)}\,dx \;=\; \ln f(x) + K$

b) change of variable: suitable for the type $\dfrac{f'(x)}{g\{f(x)\}}$

c) using partial fractions.

Integration as a Process of Summation

$$\lim_{\delta x \to 0} \sum_{x=a}^{x=b} f(x)\,\delta x \;=\; \int_a^b f(x)\,dx$$

DIFFERENTIAL EQUATIONS

A first order linear differential equation is a relationship between x, y and dy/dx. It can be solved by collecting all the x terms, along with dx, on one side, with all y terms and dy on the other side. Then each side is integrated with respect to its own variable. A constant of integration called an arbitrary constant is introduced on one side only to give a general solution which is a family of lines or curves.
If extra information provides the value of this constant we have a particular solution, i.e. one member of the family.

PRACTICAL APPLICATIONS OF INTEGRATION

Area

The area bounded by the x-axis, the two lines $x = a$ and $x = b$, and part of the curve $y = f(x)$ can be found by summing the areas of vertical strips of width δx and using

(i)

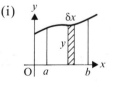

$$\text{Area} \;=\; \lim_{\delta x \to 0} \sum_{x=a}^{x=b} y\,\delta x \;=\; \int_a^b y\,dx$$

Similarly, for horizontal strips.

(ii)

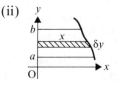

$$\text{Area} \;=\; \lim_{\delta y \to 0} \sum_{y=a}^{y=b} x\,\delta y \;=\; \int_a^b x\,dy$$

For compound areas the length of a strip is usually a difference of two quantities.

(iii)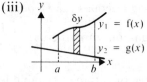

The area shown is given by

$$\text{Area} = \lim_{\delta x \to 0} \sum_{x=a}^{x=b} (y_1 - y_2)\,\delta x = \int_a^b (y_1 - y_2)\,dx$$

An approximate value for the area shown in diagram (i) above can be found by taking strips of equal width, d, and using:

a) the Trapezium Rule

$$\int_a^b f(x)\,dx \approx \tfrac{1}{2}d[y_0 + 2y_1 + \ldots + 2y_{n-2} + y_{n-1}]$$

b) Simpson's Rule (in this case there must be an even number of strips)

$$\int_a^b f(x)\,dx \approx \tfrac{1}{3}d[(1\text{st} + \text{last}) + 4(2\text{nd} + 4\text{th} + \ldots) + 2(3\text{rd} + 5\text{th} + \ldots)]$$

Volume

When the area bounded by the x-axis, the ordinates at a and b, and part of the curve $y = f(x)$ rotates completely about the x-axis, the volume generated is given by

$$\text{Volume} = \lim_{\delta x \to 0} \sum_{x=a}^{x=b} \pi y^2\,\delta x = \int_a^b \pi y^2\,dx$$

For rotation about the y-axis, $\text{volume} = \lim_{\delta y \to 0} \sum_{y=a}^{y=b} \pi x^2\,\delta y = \int_a^b \pi x^2\,dy$

Mean Value

The mean value, y_m, of a function $f(x)$ from $x = a$ to $x = b$ is given by

$$y_m = \frac{1}{(b-a)} \int_a^b f(x)\,dx$$

MULTIPLE CHOICE EXERCISE E

TYPE I

1. The equation of the line through the origin and perpendicular to $3x - 2y + 4 = 0$ is

    A $3x + 2y = 0$ **C** $2x + 3y = 0$ **E** $3x - 2y = 0$
    B $2x + 3y + 1 = 0$ **D** $2x - 3y - 1 = 0$

2. A point P moves so that is equidistant from A and B. The locus of the set of points P is

A a circle on AB as diameter

B a line parallel to AB

C the perpendicular bisector of AB

D a parabola

3. The point dividing $A(1, 2)$ and $B(7, -4)$ in the ratio $1:2$ has coordinates

A $(3, -2)$ **C** $(\frac{8}{3}, -\frac{4}{3})$ **E** $(13, -10)$

B $(5, -2)$ **D** $(3, 0)$

4.

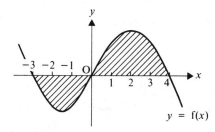

$y = f(x)$

The shaded area in the diagram is given by

A $\displaystyle\int_{-3}^{4} f(x)\,dx$ **C** $\displaystyle\int_{-3}^{1} f(x)\,dx + \int_{1}^{4} f(x)\,dx$

B $\displaystyle\int_{-3}^{0} f(x)\,dx + \int_{0}^{4} f(x)\,dx$ **D** none of these

5. e^{x^2} could be the integral w.r.t. x of

A e^{2x} **C** $\dfrac{e^{x^2}}{2x}$ **E** none of these

B $2xe^{x^2}$ **D** $x^2 e^{x^2} - 1$

6. If $\displaystyle\int_{1}^{5} \frac{dx}{2x - 1} = \ln K$, the value of K is

A 9   **B** 3   **C** undefined   **D** 81   **E** 8

7. $I = \displaystyle\int_1^2 x\sqrt{(x^2 - 1)}\, dx$ is found as follows. Where does an error first occur?

    A   Let $u \equiv x^2 - 1$ **C** $I = \frac{1}{2} \displaystyle\int_1^2 u^{1/2}\, du$

    B $\ldots du \equiv \ldots 2x\, dx$ **D** $I = \frac{3}{4}\left[u^{3/2}\right]_1^2$

8. $\displaystyle\int_0^{\pi/6} \sin^n x \cos x\, dx = \frac{1}{64};$ n is

    A   6   **B**   5   **C**   4   **D**   3   **E**   none of these

9. The differential equation of a curve is $\dfrac{x}{y}\dfrac{dy}{dx} = 1$. The sketch of the curve could be

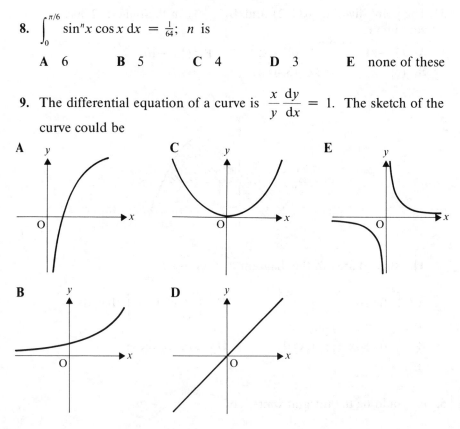

10. The value of $\displaystyle\int_0^2 2e^{2x}\, dx$ is

    A e^4 **B** $e^4 - 1$ **C** ∞ **D** $4e^4$ **E** $\frac{1}{2}e^4$

11. $x^3 - 3x^2 + 2x - 6$ has a factor

    A $x - 3$ **C** $x - 4$ **E** $x + 2$
    B $x - 2$ **D** $x + 3$

12. $x^3 - 3x^2 + 6x - 2$ has remainder 2 when divided by

    A $x - 1$ **C** x **E** $2x - 1$

    B $x + 1$ **D** $x + 2$

13.

x	1	2	3
y	0	3	6

Given the information in the table, using the trapezium rule with 3 ordinates to find $\int_1^3 y\,dx$ gives

    A   12   **B**   9/2   **C**   9   **D**   6   **E**   8

14. The value of k for which $x - 1$ a factor of $4x^3 - 3x^2 - kx + 2$ is

    A -1 **B**   0   **C**   1   **D**   2   **E**   3

TYPE II

15. Which of the following relationships gives a straight line when $\ln y$ is plotted against $\ln x$, assuming that a and b are constants.

    A $ay^3 = bx^2$ **C** $y = ax^b$

    B $y = a + b^x$ **D** $y^a = b^x$

16. If the equation $ax^2 + by^2 + 2gx + 2fy + c = 0$ represents a circle through the origin,

    A $g = 0$ and $f = 0$ **C** $a = b$

    B $c = 0$ **D** $a = -b$

17. $f(x) \equiv (3 - 5x)^4$

    A $f(x)$ has a remainder 16 when divided by $x - 1$

    B   the expansion of $f(x)$ contains four terms

    C   the equation $f(x) = 0$ is satisfied by only one value of x

18. $f(x) \equiv 2x^2 + 3x - 2$

    A $f(x)$ can be expressed as the sum of two partial fractions,

    B   the equation $f(x) = 0$ has two real distinct roots

    C $x + 2$ is a factor of $f(x)$.

19. Using $x = \sin\theta$ transforms $\displaystyle\int \frac{x^2}{\sqrt{(1-x^2)}}\,dx$ into

A $\displaystyle\int \frac{\sin^2\theta}{\cos\theta}\,d\theta$ C $-\displaystyle\int \sin^2\theta\,d\theta$

B $\dfrac{1}{2}\displaystyle\int (1-\cos 2\theta)\,d\theta$ D $\dfrac{1}{2}\displaystyle\int (1+\cos 2\theta)\,d\theta$

20. Integration by parts can be used to find

A $\displaystyle\int x^2 e^x\,dx$ C $\displaystyle\int \ln x\,dx$

B $\displaystyle\int e^x \ln x\,dx$ D $\displaystyle\int (\ln x)(\sin x)\,dx$

21. Which of the following definite integrals can be evaluated?

A $\displaystyle\int_0^1 \frac{1}{x-1}\,dx$ C $\displaystyle\int_1^2 \sqrt{(1-x^2)}\,dx$

B $\displaystyle\int_0^{\pi/2} \sin x\,dx$ D $\displaystyle\int_{-2}^1 \ln x\,dx$

22. Which of the following differential equations can be solved by separating the variables?

A $\displaystyle x\frac{dy}{dx} = y + x$ C $\displaystyle e^{x+y} = y\frac{dy}{dx}$

B $\displaystyle xy\frac{dy}{dx} = x + 1$ D $\displaystyle x + \frac{dy}{dx} = \ln y$

23. $\displaystyle\int_1^2 x e^x\,dx$

A   is a definite integral   C   is equal to $\left[\frac{1}{2}e^{x^2}\right]_1^2$

B   is equal to $x e^x - e^x$ D   can be integrated by parts.

24. The centroid of this volume of revolution is

A   on the x-axis
B   on the y-axis
C   at the point $(1, 0)$
D   right of the point $(1, 0)$

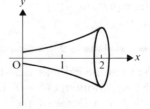

TYPE III

25. $\displaystyle\sum_{x=a}^{x=b} y\,\delta x = \int_a^b y\,dx$

26. If $x - a$ is a factor of $x^2 + px + q$, the equation $x^2 + px + q = 0$ has a root equal to a

27. $\displaystyle\int \tan x\,dx = \sec^2 x + K$

28. $\displaystyle\int_0^a f(y)\,dy = \lim_{\delta y \to 0} \sum_{y=0}^{y=a} f(y)\,\delta y$

29. $\displaystyle\left[f(x) \right]_0^a = f(a) - 0$

30. A differential equation must contain $\dfrac{dy}{dx}$

31. $x^2 + y^2 - 2x - 4y + 6 = 0$ is the equation of a circle.

32. The area between the curve $y = 1 - x^2$ and the x-axis is given by $\displaystyle\int_{-1}^1 y\,dx$

MISCELLANEOUS EXERCISE E

1. Given that $(x + 2)$ is a factor of $x^4 + kx^2 + 4x + 1$, find the value of k.

2. Express $\dfrac{13x + 16}{(x - 3)(3x + 2)}$ in partial fractions.

   Hence find the value of $\dfrac{d}{dx}\left[\dfrac{13x + 16}{(x - 3)(3x + 2)} \right]$ when $x = 2$

   (AEB 86)

3. Given that $f(x)$, where $f(x) \equiv x^2 + ax + 3$ and a is a constant, is such that the remainder on dividing $f(x)$ by $x - 1$ is three times the remainder on dividing $f(x)$ by $x + 1$, find the value of a (AEB 86)p

4. Given that $f(x) \equiv x^2 + px + q$ determine the values of the constants p and q so that both

  (a) $f(x)$ has a turning point when $x = -3$ and

  (b) the remainder when $f(x)$ is divided by $x + 2$ is 2

Show that, with these values of p and q, $f(x) \geqslant 1$ (U of L 88)

5. (a) Write down the coordinates of the mid-point M of the line joining $A(0, 1)$ and $B(6, 5)$.

  (b) Show that the line $3x + 2y - 15 = 0$ passes through M and is perpendicular to AB.

  (c) Calculate the coordinates of the centre of the circle which passes through A, B and the origin O.   (U of L 87)

6. Given that
$$y = \frac{3x - 14}{(x - 2)(x + 6)}$$

express y as a sum of partial fractions. Hence find $\dfrac{dy}{dx}$ and $\dfrac{d^2y}{dx^2}$.

Show that $\dfrac{dy}{dx} = 0$ for $x = 10$ and for one other value of x

Find the maximum and minimum values of y, distinguishing between them.   (JMB 86)

7. The function
$$f:x \rightarrow 2x^3 + ax^2 + bx + 36 \quad x \in \mathbb{R}$$

is such that $f(3) = 0$ and the remainder when $f(x)$ is divided by $(x + 2)$ is -30. Find the values of a and b and express $f(x)$ as the product of three linear factors.   (AEB 86)

8. A circle S is given by the equation
$$x^2 + y^2 - 4x + 6y - 12 = 0$$

Find the radius of S and the coordinates of the centre of S.

Calculate the length of the perpendicular from the centre of S to the line L whose equation is
$$3x + 4y = k$$

where k is a constant. Deduce the values of k for which L is a tangent to S.   (JMB 87)

9. The circle with equation $(x - 5)^2 + (y - 7)^2 = 25$ has centre C. The point P(2, 3) lies on the circle. Determine the gradient of PC and hence, or otherwise, obtain the equation of the tangent to the circle at P.

Find also the equation of the straight line which passes through the point C and the point Q(−1, 4). The tangent and the line CQ intersect at R.

Determine the size of angle PRC, to the nearest 0.1°   (AEB 87)

10. The straight lines $3x + 4y = 14$ and $x - 7y = 13$ intersect at the point A, and the line $4x - 3y + 23 = 0$ cuts the other two lines at the points B and C respectively.

   (a) Show that the length of BC is 10 units.

   (b) Calculate the value of the acute angle BAC.

   (c) Find the coordinates of A and calculate the perpendicular distance from A to BC. Hence find the equation of the circle with centre A for which BC is a tangent.   (AEB 86)

11. The following measurements of the volume, $V\,\mathrm{cm}^3$, and the pressure, p cm of mercury, of a given mass of gas were taken.

V	10	50	110	170	230
p	1412.5	151.4	50.3	27.4	18.6

By plotting values of $\log_{10} p$ against $\log_{10} V$, verify graphically the relationship $p = kV^n$ where k and n are constants.

Use your graph to find approximate values for k and n, giving your answers to two significant figures.   (AEB 1987)$_p$

12.

x	2.1	2.8	4.7	6.2	7.3
y	13	32	316	2000	7080

The above table shows corresponding values of variables x and y obtained experimentally. By drawing a suitable graph, show that these values support the hypothesis that x and y are connected by a relationship of the form $y = a^x$, where a is a constant. Use your graph to estimate the value of a to 2 significant figures.   (U of L 85)

13. The variables x and y are known to satisfy an equation of the form $y = ab^x$, where a and b are constants. For five different values of x, corresponding approximate values of y were obtained experimentally. The results are given in the following table.

x	2.0	2.5	3.0	3.5	4.0
y	11.3	18.0	27.1	44.5	70.4

By drawing a suitable linear graph, estimate the values of a and b, giving both answers to one decimal place.   (JMB 87)

14. (a) Find $\int (3x + 4)\, e^{2x}\, dx$

    (b) By using the substitution $x = 2\tan\theta$, evaluate

    $$\int_0^2 \frac{1}{(4 + x^2)^2}$$ (U of L 85)

15. Given that α and β are the costs of the equation $x^2 - px + 2 = 0$, express $\alpha^2 + \beta^2$ in terms of p

    Without solving the given equation, find a quadratic equation whose roots are

    $$\alpha^2 + \frac{\alpha}{\beta} \quad \text{and} \quad \beta^2 + \frac{\beta}{\alpha}$$

    giving the coefficients in a simplified form not involving α and β.
                                                                  (JMB 84)

16. Find the following integrals

    (a) $\int \cos^2(3x)\, dx$

    (b) $\int \dfrac{1}{e^x + 4e^{-x}}\, dx$, by means of the substitution $u = e^x$, or otherwise

    (c) $\int x e^{2x}\, dx$ (C 86)

17. Given that $\dfrac{x}{(1 + x)^2} = \dfrac{A}{(1 + x)^2} + \dfrac{B}{1 + x}$, find the values of the constants A and B.

    Hence, or otherwise, evaluate

    $$\int_0^1 \frac{x}{(1 + x)^2}\, dx$$ (U of L 85)

18. By means of the substitution $u = e^x$, or otherwise, evaluate

$$\int_0^1 \frac{e^x}{1 + e^{2x}} \, dx$$

giving the answer correct to two decimal places.   (JMB 87)

19. By using a substitution, or otherwise, find the exact value of

$$\int_0^{\pi/2} \frac{\cos x}{(4 + \sin x)^2}$$ (JMB 84)

20. Given that $\dfrac{7x - x^2}{(2 - x)(x^2 + 1)} \equiv \dfrac{A}{(2 - x)} + \dfrac{Bx + C}{(x^2 + 1)}$, determine the values of A, B and C.

A curve has equation $y = \dfrac{7x - x^2}{(2 - x)(x^2 + 1)}$.

Determine the equation of the normal to the curve at the point $(1, 3)$.
Prove that the area of the region bounded by the curve, the x-axis and
the line $x = 1$ is $\dfrac{7}{2} \ln 2 - \dfrac{\pi}{4}$.   (AEB 87)

21. Using the same axes, sketch the curves with equations
$$y^2 = 4x \quad \text{and} \quad x^2 = 4y$$
Verify that the curves intersect at the two points $(0, 0)$ and $(4, 4)$.
Hence find the area of the finite region enclosed by the curves.
                    (U of L 88)

22. (a) The finite region bounded by the x-axis, the curve $y = e^{-x}$ and
the lines $x = \pm a$ is denoted by R Find, in terms of a, the
volume of the solid generated when R is rotated through one
revolution about the x-axis.

(b) (i) By using a suitable substitution, or otherwise, evaluate

$$\int_0^1 x(1 - x)^9 \, dx$$

(ii) Find $\displaystyle\int 2x \tan^{-1} x \, dx$ (C 87)

23. Given that $x < 4$, find

$$\int \frac{8}{(4 - x)(8 - x)} \, dx$$

A chemical reaction takes place in a solution containing a substance S. At noon there are two grams of S in the solution and t hours later there are x grams of S. The rate of the reaction is such that x satisfies the differential equation

$$8 \frac{dx}{dt} = (4 - x)(8 - x)$$

Solve this equation, giving t in terms of x.

Find, to the nearest minute, the time at which there are three grams of S present.   (JMB 87)

24. Express $\dfrac{1}{(1 + x)(3 + x)}$ in partial fractions.

Hence find the solution of the differential equation

$$\frac{dy}{dx} = \frac{y}{(1 + x)(3 + x)} \quad x > -1$$

given that $y = 2$ when $x = 1$.

Express your answer in the form $y = f(x)$.   (U of L 88)

25. Find the solution of the differential equation

$$(x^2 - 5)^{1/2} \frac{dy}{dx} = 2xy^{1/2}, \quad x^2 > 5$$

for which $y = 4$ when $x = 3$, expressing y in terms of x
(JMB 84)

26.

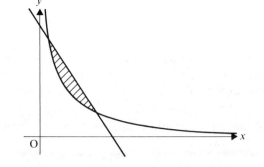

The diagram shows a sketch of the curve $xy = 6$ and part of the line $y = 9 - 3x$. Use integration to find the area of the shaded region.   (C 86)

27. The quadratic function $q(x)$ is given by
$$q(x) = x^2 + 2kx + k + 2, \quad x \in \mathbb{R}$$
where k is a constant. Given that the roots of the equation $q(x) = 0$ are α and β, show that
$$(\alpha - \beta)^2 = 4(k^2 - k - 2).$$

(a) Find the values of k for which the roots of the equation $q(x) = 0$ differ by 4.

(b) Given that $k \neq -2$, form a quadratic equation, with coefficients in terms of k, whose roots are
$$(1 + \alpha/\beta) \quad \text{and} \quad (1 + \beta/\alpha) \hspace{2cm} \text{(U of L 87)}$$

28. In a model to estimate the depreciation of the value of a car, it is assumed that the value, £V, at age t months, decreases at a rate which is proportional to V. Using this model, write down a differential equation relating V and t. Given that the car has an initial value of £6000, solve the differential equation and show that
$$V = 6000e^{-kt} \text{ where } k \text{ is a positive constant.}$$

The value of the car is expected to decrease to £3000 after 36 months. Calculate

(a) the value, to the nearest pound, of the car when it is 15 months old

(b) the age of the car, to the nearest month, when its value is £2000
$$\hspace{10cm} \text{(JMB 86)}$$

29. The gradient of a curve at any point (x, y) on the curve is directly proportional to the product of x and y. The curve passes through the point $(1, 1)$ and at this point the gradient of the curve is 4. Form a differential equation in x and y and solve this equation to express y in terms of x. $\hspace{3cm}$ (U of L 85)

30. Use the trapezium rule, with ordinates at $x = 1$, $x = 2$ and $x = 3$, to estimate the value of
$$\int_1^3 \sqrt{(40 - x^3)} \, dx \hspace{3cm} \text{(C 87)}$$

31. By using a substitution, or otherwise, find the exact value of
$$\int_0^{1/\sqrt{2}} \frac{x}{\sqrt{(1 - x^4)}} \, dx.$$

State the mean value of $\dfrac{x}{\sqrt{(1 - x^4)}}$ as x varies from 0 to $\dfrac{1}{\sqrt{2}}$.
$$\hspace{10cm} \text{(JMB 86)}$$

32. Shade on a sketch the finite region R in the first quadrant bounded by the x-axis, the curve $y = \ln x$ and the line $x = 5$
By means of integration, calculate the area of R.

The region R is rotated completely about the x-axis to form a solid of revolution S.

x	1	2	3	4	5
$(\ln x)^2$	0	0.480	1.207	1.922	2.590

Use the given table of values and apply the trapezium rule to find an estimate of the volume of S, giving your answer to one decimal place.
(AEB 87)

33. Show that

(a) $\displaystyle\int_0^{\pi/2} \cos^2 x \, dx = \frac{\pi}{4}$

(b) $\displaystyle\int_0^{\pi/2} x \cos x \, dx = \frac{\pi}{2} - 1$

Sketch and label the region R defined by

$$x \geqslant 0 \quad y \geqslant 0 \quad y \leqslant \cos x \quad x \leqslant \frac{\pi}{2}$$

Find in terms of π,

(c) the x-coordinate of the centroid of the region R

(d) the y-coordinate of the centroid of the region R

Find also, in terms of π, the volume obtained when the region R is revolved through 2π about the x-axis.

34. (a) Find $\displaystyle\int x \ln x \, dx$.

(b) By means of the substitution $t = \tan x$, or otherwise, find

$$\int \frac{1}{1 + \cos^2 x} \, dx$$

(c) The region bounded by the curve $y = (1 + \cos x)^{-1/2}$, the x-axis, and the lines $x = 0$ and $x = \frac{1}{2}\pi$, is denoted by R. Use the trapezium rule with ordinates at $x = 0$, $x = \frac{1}{4}\pi$ and $x = \frac{1}{2}\pi$ to estimate the area of R, giving two significant figures in your answer.
(C 88)

35. The roots of the equation $x^2 - 2px + q = 0$ are α and β.
(a) Find, in terms of p and q, an expression for $\alpha^2 + \beta^2$.
(b) Show that $\alpha^3 - 2p\alpha^2 + q\alpha = 0$ and $\beta^3 - 2p\beta^2 + q\beta = 0$.
(c) *Hence* show that $\alpha^3 + \beta^3 = 8p^3 - 6pq$.

CHAPTER 34

NUMBER SERIES

SEQUENCES

Consider the following sets of numbers,

$$2, 4, 6, 8, 10, \ldots$$
$$1, 2, 4, 8, 16, \ldots$$
$$4, 9, 16, 25, 36, \ldots$$

Each set of numbers, in the order given, has a pattern and there is an obvious rule for obtaining the next number and as many subsequent numbers as we wish to find.

Such sets are called *sequences* and each member of the set is a term of the sequence.

SERIES

When the terms of a sequence are added, a series is formed,
e.g., $1 + 2 + 4 + 8 + 16 + \ldots$ is a series.

If the series stops after a finite number of terms it is called a finite series,
e.g., $1 + 2 + 4 + 8 + 16 + 32 + 64$ is a finite series of seven terms.

If the series continues indefinitely it is called an infinite series,
e.g., $1 + \frac{1}{2} + \frac{1}{4} + \frac{1}{8} + \frac{1}{16} + \frac{1}{32} + \ldots + \frac{1}{1024} + \ldots$ is an infinite series.

Consider again the series $1 + 2 + 4 + 8 + 16 + 32 + 64$

As each term is a power of 2 we can write this series in the form

$$2^0 + 2^1 + 2^2 + 2^3 + 2^4 + 2^5 + 2^6$$

All the terms of this series are of the form 2^r, so 2^r is a general term. We can then define the series as the sum of terms of the form 2^r where r takes all integral values in order from 0 to 6 inclusive.

591

Using Σ as a symbol for 'the sum of terms such as' we can redefine our series more concisely as $\Sigma 2^r$, r taking all integral values from 0 to 6 inclusive, or, even more briefly,

$$\sum_{r=0}^{6} 2^r$$

Placing the lowest and highest value that r takes below and above the sigma symbol respectively, indicates that r takes all integral values between these extreme values.

Thus $\sum_{r=2}^{10} r^3$ means 'the sum of all terms of the form r^3 where r takes all integral values from 2 to 10 inclusive',

i.e. $$\sum_{r=2}^{10} r^3 = 2^3 + 3^3 + 4^3 + 5^3 + 6^3 + 7^3 + 8^3 + 9^3 + 10^3$$

Note that a finite series, when written out, should always end with the last term even if intermediate terms are omitted, e.g. $3 + 6 + 9 + \ldots + 99$

The infinite series $1 + \frac{1}{2} + \frac{1}{4} + \frac{1}{8} + \frac{1}{16} + \ldots$

may also be written in the sigma notation. The continuing dots after the last written term indicate that the series is infinite, i.e. there is *no* last term. Each term of this series is a power of $\frac{1}{2}$ so a general term can be written $(\frac{1}{2})^r$. The first term is 1 or $(\frac{1}{2})^0$, so the first value that r takes is zero. There is no last term of this series, so there is no upper limit for the value of r.

Therefore $1 + \frac{1}{2} + \frac{1}{4} + \frac{1}{8} + \frac{1}{16} + \ldots$ may be written as $\sum_{r=0}^{\infty} (\frac{1}{2})^r$

Note that when a given series is rewritten in the sigma notation it is as well to check that the first few values of r give the correct first few terms of the series.

Writing a series in the sigma notation, apart from the obvious advantage of brevity, allows us to select a particular term of a series without having to write down all the earlier terms.

For example, in the series $\sum_{r=3}^{10} (2r + 5)$,

the first term is the value of $2r + 5$ when $r = 3$, i.e. $2 \times 3 + 5 = 11$
the last term is the value of $2r + 5$ when $r = 10$, i.e. 25
the fourth term is the value of $2r + 5$ when r takes its fourth value in order from $r = 3$, i.e. when $r = 6$

Thus the fourth term of $\sum_{r=3}^{10} (2r + 5)$ is $2 \times 6 + 5 = 17$

Example 34a _____

Write the following series in the sigma notation,
(a) $1 - x + x^2 - x^3 + \ldots$ (b) $2 - 4 + 8 - 16 + \ldots + 128$

(a) A general term of this series is $\pm x^r$, having a positive sign when r is even and a negative sign when r is odd.
Because $(-1)^r$ is positive when r is even and negative when r is odd, the general term can be written $(-1)^r x^r$

The first term of this series is 1, or x^0

Hence $1 - x + x^2 - x^3 + \ldots = \sum_{r=0}^{\infty} (-1)^r x^r$

(b) $2 - 4 + 8 - 16 + \ldots + 128 = 2 - (2)^2 + (2)^3 - (2)^4 + \ldots + (2)^7$

So a general term is of the form $\pm 2^r$, being positive when r is odd and negative when r is even,
i.e. the general term is $(-1)^{r+1} 2^r$

Hence $2 - 4 + 8 - 16 + \ldots + 128 = \sum_{r=1}^{7} (-1)^{r+1} 2^r$

EXERCISE 34a

1. Write the following series in the sigma notation:
   (a) $1 + 8 + 27 + 64 + 125$
   (b) $2 + 4 + 6 + 8 + \ldots + 20$
   (c) $\frac{1}{2} + \frac{1}{3} + \frac{1}{4} + \frac{1}{5} + \ldots + \frac{1}{50}$
   (d) $1 + \frac{1}{3} + \frac{1}{9} + \frac{1}{27} + \ldots$
   (e) $-4 - 1 + 2 + 5 \ldots + 17$
   (f) $8 + 4 + 2 + 1 + \frac{1}{2} + \ldots$

2. Write down the first three terms and, where there is one, the last term of each of the following series:

(a) $\displaystyle\sum_{r=1}^{\infty} \frac{1}{r}$

(b) $\displaystyle\sum_{r=0}^{5} r(r+1)$

(c) $\displaystyle\sum_{r=0}^{20} \frac{r+2}{(r+1)(2r+1)}$

(d) $\displaystyle\sum_{r=0}^{\infty} \frac{1}{(r^2+1)}$

(e) $\displaystyle\sum_{r=-1}^{8} r(r+1)(r+2)$

(f) $\displaystyle\sum_{r=0}^{\infty} a^r(-1)^{r+1}$

3. For the following series, write down the term indicated, and the number of terms in the series.

(a) $\displaystyle\sum_{r=1}^{9} 2^r$,   3rd term

(b) $\displaystyle\sum_{r=-1}^{8} (2r+3)$,   5th term

(c) $\displaystyle\sum_{r=-6}^{-1} \frac{1}{(2r+1)}$,   last term

(d) $\displaystyle\sum_{r=0}^{\infty} \frac{1}{(r+1)(r+2)}$,   20th term

(e) $\displaystyle\sum_{r=1}^{\infty} \left(\frac{1}{2}\right)^r$, nth term

(f) $8 + 4 + 0 - 4 - 8 - 12 \ldots - 80$ 15th term

(g) $\frac{1}{16} + \frac{1}{8} + \frac{1}{4} + \frac{1}{2} + \ldots + 32$,   7th term

ARITHMETIC PROGRESSION

Consider the sequence 5, 8, 11, 14, 17, ..., 29
Each term of this sequence exceeds the previous term by 3, so the sequence can be written in the form

   5, $(5+3)$, $(5+2 \times 3)$, $(5+3 \times 3)$, $(5+4 \times 3)$, ..., $(5+8 \times 3)$

This sequence is an example of an arithmetic progression (AP) which is a sequence where any term differs from the preceding term by a constant, called the *common difference*.
The common difference may be positive or negative. For example, the first six terms of an AP whose first term is 8 and whose common difference is -3, are 8, 5, 2, -1, -4, -7

In general, if an AP has a first term a, and a common difference d, the first four terms are a, $(a + d)$, $(a + 2d)$, $(a + 3d)$, and the nth term, u_n, is $a + (n - 1)d$

Thus   an AP with n terms can be written as

a, $(a + d)$, $(a + 2d)$, $\ldots$, $[a + (n - 1)d]$

Examples 34b _____

1. The 8th term of an AP is 11 and the 15th term is 21. Find the common difference, the first term of the series, and the nth term.

If the first term of the series is a and the common difference is d, then the 8th term is $a + 7d$,

∴ $a + 7d = 11$ [1]

and the 15th term is $a + 14d$,

∴ $a + 14d = 21$ [2]

$[2] - [1]$ gives $7d = 10$ $\Rightarrow$ $d = \frac{10}{7}$

and $a = 1$

so the first term is 1 and the common difference is $\frac{10}{7}$

Hence the nth term is $a + (n - 1)d = 1 + (n - 1)\frac{10}{7} = \frac{1}{7}(10n - 3)$

_____

2. The nth term of an AP is $12 - 4n$. Find the first term and the common difference.

If the nth term is $12 - 4n$, the first term $(n = 1)$ is 8
The second term $(n = 2)$ is 4

Therefore the common difference is -4

_____

The Sum of an Arithmetic Progression

Consider the sum of the first ten even numbers, which is an AP.

Writing it first in normal, then in reverse, order we have

$$S = 2 + 4 + 6 + 8 + \ldots + 18 + 20$$
$$S = 20 + 18 + 16 + 14 + \ldots + 4 + 2$$

Adding gives $\quad 2S = 22 + 22 + 22 + 22 + \ldots + 22 + 22$

As there are ten terms in this series, we have

$$2S = 10 \times 22 \quad \Rightarrow \quad S = 110$$

This process is known as finding the sum from first principles. Applying it to a general AP gives formulae for the sum, which may be quoted and used.

If S_n is the sum of the first n terms of an AP with last term l,

then $\qquad S_n = a + (a + d) + (a + 2d) + \ldots + (l - d) + l$

reversing $\quad S_n = l + (l - d) + (l - 2d) + \ldots + (a + d) + a$

adding $\quad 2S_n = (a + l) + (a + l) + (a + l) + \ldots + (a + l) + (a + l)$

as there are n terms we have $\qquad 2S_n = n(a + l)$

$\Rightarrow \quad S_n = \frac{1}{2}n(a + l) \qquad$ i.e. $S_n = $ (number of terms) × (average term)

Also, because the nth term, l, is equal to $a + (n - 1)d$, we have

$$S_n = \frac{1}{2}n[a + a + (n - 1)d]$$

i.e. $\qquad\qquad S_n = \frac{1}{2}n[2a + (n - 1)d]$

Either of these formulae can now be used to find the sum of the first n terms of an AP.

Examples 34b (continued) _____

3. Find the sum of the following series,

(a) an AP of eleven terms whose first term is 1 and whose last term is 6

(b) $\displaystyle\sum_{r=1}^{8}\left(2 - \frac{2r}{3}\right)$

(a) We know the first and last terms, and the number of terms so we use
$S_n = \frac{1}{2}n(a + l)$

$\Rightarrow$ $\qquad\qquad\qquad\qquad S_{11} = \frac{11}{2}(1 + 6) = \frac{77}{2}$

(b) $\displaystyle\sum_{r=1}^{8}\left(2 - \frac{2r}{3}\right) = \frac{4}{3} + \frac{2}{3} + 0 - \frac{2}{3} - \ldots - \frac{10}{3}$

This is an AP with 8 terms where $a = \frac{4}{3}$, $d = -\frac{2}{3}$

Using $S_n = \frac{1}{2}n[2a + (n - 1)d]$ gives
$$S_8 = 4\left[\frac{8}{3} + 7\left(-\frac{2}{3}\right)\right] = -8$$

_____

4. In an AP the sum of the first ten terms is 50 and the 5th term is three times the 2nd term. Find the first term and the sum of the first 20 terms.

If a is the first term and d is the common difference, and there are n terms, using $S_n = \frac{1}{2}n[2a + (n - 1)d]$ gives
$$S_{10} = 50 = 5(2a + 9d) \qquad\qquad [1]$$

Now using $u_n = a + (n - 1)d$ gives
$$u_5 = a + 4d \text{ and } u_2 = a + d$$

Therefore $\qquad\qquad a + 4d = 3(a + d) \qquad\qquad [2]$

From [1] and [2] we get $d = 1$ and $a = \frac{1}{2}$
so the first term is $\frac{1}{2}$ and the sum of the first 20 terms is S_{20} where
$$S_{20} = 10(1 + 19 \times 1) = 200$$

_____

5. Show that the terms of $\displaystyle\sum_{r=1}^{n} \ln 2^r$ are in arithmetic progression.

Find the sum of the first 10 terms of this series.

By taking $r = 1, 2, 3 \ldots$ we have

$$\sum_{r=1}^{n} \ln 2^r = \ln 2 + \ln 2^2 + \ln 2^3 + \ldots + \ln 2^n$$

$$= \ln 2 + 2 \ln 2 + 3 \ln 2 + \ldots + n \ln 2$$

We now see that there is a common difference of $\ln 2$ between successive terms, so the terms of this series are in arithmetic progression.

Hence $\qquad \displaystyle\sum_{r=1}^{10} \ln 2^r = \ln 2 + 2 \ln 2 + 3 \ln 2 + \ldots + 10 \ln 2$

$$= (1 + 2 + 3 + \ldots + 10) \ln 2$$

$$= \tfrac{10}{2}(1 + 10) \ln 2 = 55 \ln 2$$

Note that the sum of the first n natural numbers.

i.e. $\qquad\qquad\qquad 1 + 2 + 3 + \ldots + n$

is an **AP** in which $a = 1$ and $d = 1$ so

$$\sum_{r=1}^{n} r = \tfrac{1}{2}n(n + 1)$$

This is a result that may be quoted, unless a proof is specifically asked for.

---

6. The sum of the first n terms of a series is given by $S_n = n(n + 3)$
Find the fourth term of the series and show that the terms are in arithmetic progression.

If the terms of the series are $a_1, a_2, a_3, \ldots a_n$

then $\qquad\qquad S_n = a_1 + a_2 + \ldots + a_n = n(n+3)$

So $\qquad\qquad S_4 = a_1 + a_2 + a_3 + a_4 = 28$

and $\qquad\qquad S_3 = a_1 + a_2 + a_3 \qquad\;\; = 18$

Hence the fourth term of the series, a_4, is 10

Now $\qquad\qquad S_n = a_1 + a_2 + \ldots + a_{n-1} + a_n = n(n+3)$

and $\qquad S_{n-1} = a_1 + a_2 + \ldots + a_{n-1} \qquad = (n-1)(n+2)$

Hence the nth term of the series, a_n, is given by

$$a_n = n(n+3) - (n-1)(n+2) = 2n+2$$

Replacing n by $n-1$ gives the $(n-1)$th term

i.e. $\qquad\qquad\qquad a_{n-1} = 2(n-1) + 2 = 2n$

Then $\qquad\qquad a_n - a_{n-1} = (2n+2) - 2n = 2$

i.e. there is a common difference of 2 between successive terms, showing that the series is an AP.

EXERCISE 34b

1. Write down the fifth term and the nth term of the following APs.

(a) $\displaystyle\sum_{r=1}^{n} (2r-1)$ (b) $\displaystyle\sum_{r=1}^{n} 4(r-1)$ (c) $\displaystyle\sum_{r=0}^{n} (3r+3)$

(d) first term 5, common difference 3

(e) first term 6, common difference -2

(f) first term p, common difference q

(g) first term 10, last term 30, 11 terms

(h) 1, 5, $\ldots$ (i) 2, $1\frac{1}{2}, \ldots$ (j) $-4, -1, \ldots$

2. Find the sum of the first ten terms of each of the series given in Question (1).

3. The 9th term of an AP is 8 and the 4th term is 20. Find the first term and the common difference.

4. The 6th term of an AP is twice the 3rd term and the first term is 3. Find the common difference and the 10th term.

5. The nth term of an AP is $\frac{1}{2}(3 - n)$. Write down the first three terms and the 20th term.

6. Find the sum, to the number of terms indicated, of each of the following APs.
   (a) $1 + 2\frac{1}{2} + \ldots$, 6 terms
   (b) $3 + 5 + \ldots$, 8 terms
   (c) the first twenty odd integers
   (d) $a_1 + a_2 + a_3 + \ldots + a_8$ where $a_n = 2n + 1$
   (e) $4 + 6 + 8 + \ldots + 20$
   (f) $\sum_{r=1}^{3n} (3 - 4r)$
   (g) $S_n = n^2 - 3n$, 8 terms
   (h) $S_n = 2n(n + 3)$, m terms

7. The sum of the first n terms of an AP is S_n where $S_n = n^2 - 3n$. Write down the fourth term and the nth term.

8. The sum of the first n terms of a series is given by S_n where $S_n = n(3n - 4)$. Show that the terms of the series are in arithmetic progression.

9. In an arithmetic progression, the 8th term is twice the 4th term and the 20th term is 40. Find the common difference and the sum of the terms from the 8th to the 20th inclusive.

10. How many terms of the AP, $1 + 3 + 5 + \ldots$ are required to make a sum of 1521?

11. Find the least number of terms of the AP, $1 + 3 + 5 + \ldots$ that are required to make a sum exceeding 4000.

12. If the sum of the first n terms of a series is S_n where $S_n = 2n^2 - n$,
    (a) prove that the series is an AP, stating the first term and the common difference,
    (b) find the sum of the terms from the 3rd to the 12th inclusive.

13. In an AP the 6th term is half the 4th term and the 3rd term is 15.
    (a) Find the first term and the common difference.
    (b) How many terms are needed to give a sum that is less than 65?

GEOMETRIC PROGRESSIONS

Consider the sequence

$$12, \ 6, \ 3, \ 1.5, \ 0.75, \ 0.375, \ \ldots$$

Each term of this sequence is half the preceeding term so the sequence may be written

$$12, \ 12(\tfrac{1}{2}), \ 12(\tfrac{1}{2})^2, \ 12(\tfrac{1}{2})^3, \ 12(\tfrac{1}{2})^4, \ 12(\tfrac{1}{2})^5, \ \ldots$$

Such a sequence is called a geometric progression (GP) which is a sequence where each term is a constant multiple of the preceding term. This constant multiplying factor is called the common ratio, and it may have any real value.

Hence, if a GP has a first term of 3 and a common ratio of -2 the first four terms are

$$3, \ 3(-2), \ 3(-2)^2, \ 3(-2)^3$$

or

$$3, \ -6, \ 12, \ -24$$

In general if a GP has a first term a, and a common ratio r, the first four terms are

$$a, \ ar, \ ar^2, \ ar^3$$

and the nth term, u_n, is ar^{n-1}, thus

a GP with n terms can be written $a, \ ar, \ ar^2, \ \ldots, \ ar^{n-1}$

The Sum of a Geometric Progression

Consider the sum of the first eight terms, S_8, of the GP with first term 1 and common ratio 3

i.e.
$$S_8 = 1 + 1(3) + 1(3)^2 + 1(3)^3 + \ldots + 1(3)^7$$

$\Rightarrow$
$$3S_8 = \qquad 3 + 3^2 + 3^3 + \ldots + 3^7 + 3^8$$

Hence
$$S_8 - 3S_8 = 1 + 0 + 0 + 0 + \ldots + 0 - 3^8$$

So
$$S_8(1 - 3) = 1 - 3^8$$

$\Rightarrow$
$$S_8 = \frac{1 - 3^8}{1 - 3} = \frac{3^8 - 1}{2}$$

This process can be applied to a general GP.

Consider the sum, S_n, of the first n terms of a GP with first term a and common ratio r,

i.e. $$S_n = a + ar + \ldots + ar^{n-2} + ar^{n-1}$$

Multiplying by r gives

$$rS_n = \quad ar + ar^2 + \ldots \quad + ar^{n-1} + ar^n$$

Hence $$S_n - rS_n = a - ar^n$$

$\Rightarrow$ $$S_n(1 - r) = a(1 - r^n)$$

$\Rightarrow$ $$S_n = \frac{a(1 - r^n)}{1 - r}$$

If $r > 1$ the formula may be written $\dfrac{a(r^n - 1)}{r - 1}$

Examples 34c

1. The 5th term of a GP is 8, the third term is 4, and the sum of the first ten terms is positive. Find the first term, the common ratio, and the sum of the first ten terms.

For a first term a and common ratio r, the nth term is ar^{n-1}

Thus we have $\qquad ar^4 = 8 \qquad\qquad\qquad (n = 5)$

and $\qquad\qquad\quad ar^2 = 4 \qquad\qquad\qquad (n = 3)$

dividing gives $\qquad\quad r^2 = 2$

$\Rightarrow \quad r = \pm\sqrt{2}$ and $a = 2$

Using the formula $\qquad S_n = \dfrac{a(r^n - 1)}{r - 1} \qquad$ gives,

when $r = \sqrt{2}$, $\qquad S_{10} = \dfrac{2[(\sqrt{2})^{10} - 1]}{\sqrt{2} - 1} = \dfrac{62}{\sqrt{2} - 1}$

when $r = -\sqrt{2}$, $\qquad S_{10} = \dfrac{2[(-\sqrt{2})^{10} - 1]}{-\sqrt{2} - 1} = \dfrac{-62}{\sqrt{2} + 1}$

But we are told that $S_{10} > 0$, so we deduce that

$r = \sqrt{2}$ and $S_{10} = \dfrac{62}{\sqrt{2} - 1} = 62(\sqrt{2} + 1)$

2. A prize fund is set up with a single investment of £2000 to provide an annual prize of £150. The fund accrues interest at 5% p.a. paid yearly. If the first prize is awarded one year after the investment, find the number of years for which the full prize can be awarded.

After one year the value of the fund is the initial investment of £2000, plus 5% interest, less one £150 prize, i.e. $£\{(1.05)(2000) - 150\}$

If $£P_n$ is the value of the fund after n years then

$$P_1 = 2000(1.05) - 150$$

$$P_2 = 1.05P_1 - 150 = 2000(1.05)^2 - 150(1.05) - 150$$

$$P_3 = 1.05P_2 - 150 = 2000(1.05)^3 - 150(1.05)^2 - 150(1.05) - 150$$

- - - - - - - - - - - - - - -

$$P_n = 2000(1.05)^n - 150(1.05)^{n-1} - 150(1.05)^{n-2} - \ldots - 150$$

$$= 2000(1.05)^n - 150\{1 + 1.05 + \ldots + (1.05)^{n-1}\}$$

The expression in square brackets is a **GP** of n terms with $a = 1$ and $r = 1.05$ and hence

$$P_n = 2000(1.05)^n - 150\left[\frac{(1.05)^n - 1}{1.05 - 1}\right]$$

$$= 3000 - 1000(1.05)^n$$

The fund can award the full prize as long as there is money left in the fund at the end of a year, i.e. as long as $P_n \geqslant 0$

$\Rightarrow$ $\qquad\qquad 3000 - 1000(1.05)^n \geqslant 0$

$\Rightarrow$ $\qquad\qquad\qquad 1.05^n \leqslant 3$

$\Rightarrow$ $\qquad\qquad\quad n \ln 1.05 \leqslant 3$

$\Rightarrow$ $\qquad\qquad n \leqslant \ln 3 \div \ln 1.05 = 22.5$

Dividing by $\ln 1.05$ does not alter the inequality as $\ln 1.05$ is positive.

Therefore the prize fund contains some money after 22 years but would not after 23 years, so the full prize can be awarded for 22 years.

-----

3. The sum of the first n terms of a series is 3^{n-1}. Show that the terms of this series are in geometric progression and find the first term, the common ratio and the sum of the second n terms of this series.

If the series is $a_1 + a_2 + \ldots + a_n$

then $S_n = a_1 + a_2 + \ldots + a_{n-1} + a_n = 3^n - 1$

and $S_{n-1} = a_1 + a_2 + \ldots + a_{n-1} \qquad = 3^{n-1} - 1$

therefore $a_n = 3^n - 1 - (3^{n-1} - 1)$

i.e. the nth term is $3^n - 3^{n-1} = 3^{n-1}(3 - 1) = (2)3^{n-1}$

Similarly $a_{n-1} = (2)3^{n-2}$ so $a_n \div a_{n-1} = 3$

showing that successive terms in the series have a constant ratio of 3
Hence this series is a GP with first term 2 and common ratio 3

The sum of the second n terms is

(the sum of the first $2n$ terms) $-$ (the sum of the first n terms)

$$= S_{2n} - S_n$$
$$= (3^{2n} - 1) - (3^n - 1)$$
$$= 3^n(3^n - 1)$$

EXERCISE 34c

1. Write down the fifth term and the nth term of the following GPs:
   (a) 2, 4, 8, ...   (b) 2, 1, $\frac{1}{2}$, ...   (c) 3, -6, 12, ...
   (d) first term 8, common ratio $-\frac{1}{2}$
   (e) first term 3, last term $\frac{1}{81}$, 6 terms

2. Find the sum, to the number of terms given, of the following GPs.
   (a) $3 + 6 + \ldots$, 6 terms   (b) $3 - 6 + \ldots$, 8 terms
   (c) $1 + \frac{1}{2} + \frac{1}{4} + \ldots$, 20 terms
   (d) first term 5, common ratio $\frac{1}{5}$, 5 terms
   (e) first term $\frac{1}{2}$, common ratio $-\frac{1}{2}$, 10 terms
   (f) first term 1, common ratio -1, 2001 terms.

3. The 6th term of a GP is 16 and the 3rd term is 2. Find the first term and the common ratio.

4. Find the common ratio, given that it is negative, of a GP whose first term is 8 and whose 5th term is $\frac{1}{2}$

5. The nth term of a GP is $(-\frac{1}{2})^n$. Write down the first term and the 10th term.

6. Evaluate $\displaystyle\sum_{r=1}^{10} (1.05)^r$

7. Find the sum to n terms of the following series.

(a) $x + x^2 + x^3 + \ldots$ (b) $x + 1 + \dfrac{1}{x} + \ldots$ (c) $1 - y + y^2 - \ldots$

(d) $x + \dfrac{x^2}{2} + \dfrac{x^3}{4} + \dfrac{x^4}{8} + \ldots$ (e) $1 - 2x + 4x^2 - 8x^3 + \ldots$

8. Find the sum of the first n terms of the GP $2 + \frac{1}{2} + \frac{1}{8} + \ldots$ and find the least value of n for which this sum exceeds 2.65

9. The sum of the first 3 terms of a GP is 14. If the first term is 2, find the possible values of the sum of the first 5 terms.

10. Evaluate $\displaystyle\sum_{r=1}^{10} 3(3/4)^r$

11. A mortgage is taken out for £10 000 and is repaid by annual instalments of £2000. Interest is charged on the outstanding debt at 10%, calculated annually. If the first repayment is made one year after the mortgage is taken out find the number of years it takes for the mortgage to be repaid.

12. A bank loan of £500 is arranged to be repaid in two years by equal monthly instalments. Interest, *calculated monthly*, is charged at 11% p.a. on the remaining debt. Calculate the monthly repayment if the first repayment is to be made one month after the loan is granted.

CONVERGENCE OF SERIES

If a piece of string, of length l, is cut up by first cutting it in half and keeping one piece, then cutting the remainder in half and keeping one piece, then cutting the remainder in half and keeping one piece, and so on, the sum of the lengths retained is

$$\frac{l}{2} + \frac{l}{4} + \frac{l}{8} + \frac{l}{16} + \ldots$$

As this process can (in theory) be carried on indefinitely, the series formed above is infinite.

After several cuts have been made the remaining part of the string will be very small indeed, so the sum of the cut lengths will be very nearly equal to the total length, l, of the original piece of string. The more cuts that are made the closer to l this sum becomes, i.e. if after n cuts, the sum of the cut lengths is

$$\frac{l}{2} + \frac{l}{2^2} + \frac{l}{2^3} + \ldots + \frac{l}{2^n}$$

then, as $n \to \infty$, $\dfrac{l}{2} + \dfrac{l}{2^2} + \ldots + \dfrac{l}{2^n} \to l$

or $\displaystyle\lim_{n \to \infty} \left[\frac{l}{2} + \frac{l}{2^2} + \ldots + \frac{l}{2^n} \right] = l$

l is called the sum to infinity of this series.

In general, if S_n is the sum of the first n terms of any series and if $\displaystyle\lim_{n \to \infty} [S_n]$ exists and is finite, the series is said to be *convergent*.

In this case the sum to infinity, S_∞, is given by

$$S_\infty = \lim_{n \to \infty} [S_n]$$

The series $l/2 + l/2^2 + l/2^3 + \ldots$, for example, is convergent as its sum to infinity is l.

However, for the series $1 + 2 + 3 + \ldots + n$, we have $S_n = \frac{1}{2}n(n + 1)$ As $n \to \infty$, $S_n \to \infty$ so this series does not converge and is said to be divergent.

For any AP, $S_n = \frac{1}{2}n[2a + (n - 1)d]$, which always approaches infinity as $n \to \infty$. Therefore any AP is divergent.

THE SUM TO INFINITY OF A GP

Consider the general GP $a + ar + ar^2 + \ldots$

Now
$$S_n = \frac{a(1 - r^n)}{1 - r}$$

and if $|r| < 1$, then $\lim_{n \to \infty} r^n = 0$

So
$$\lim_{n \to \infty} S_n = \lim_{n \to \infty} \left[\frac{a(1 - r^n)}{1 - r} \right] = \frac{a}{1 - r}$$

If $|r| > 1$, $\lim_{n \to \infty} r^n = \infty$ and the series does not converge.

Therefore, provided that $|r| < 1$, a GP converges to a sum of $\dfrac{a}{1 - r}$

i.e.

for a GP $\quad S_\infty = \dfrac{a}{1 - r}$

provided that $|r| < 1$

Arithmetic Mean

If three numbers, p_1, p_2, p_3, are in arithmetic progression then p_2 is called the *arithmetic mean* of p_1 and p_3

If $p_1 = a$, we may write p_2, p_3 as $a + d$, $a + 2d$ respectively,

hence $\quad p_1 + p_3 = 2a + 2d = 2(a + d) = 2p_2$

$\therefore \quad p_2 = \frac{1}{2}(p_1 + p_3)$

i.e.   the arithmetic mean of two numbers m and n is $\frac{1}{2}(m + n)$

Geometric Mean

If p_1, p_2, p_3 are in geometric progression, p_2 is called the *geometric mean* of p_1 and p_3

If $p_1 = a$, then we may write $p_2 = ar$, $p_3 = ar^2$

thus $\quad p_1 p_3 = a^2 r^2 = p_2^2 \quad \Rightarrow \quad p_2 = \sqrt{(p_1 p_3)}$

i.e.   the geometric mean of two numbers m and n is $\sqrt{(mn)}$

Examples 34d

1. Determine whether each series converges. If it does, give its sum to infinity.

   (a) $3 + 5 + 7 + \ldots$ (b) $1 - \frac{1}{4} + \frac{1}{16} - \frac{1}{64} + \ldots$ (c) $3 + \frac{9}{2} + \frac{27}{4} + \ldots$

(a) $3 + 5 + 7 + \ldots$ is an AP ($d = 2$) and so does not converge.

(b) $1 - \frac{1}{4} + \frac{1}{16} - \frac{1}{64} + \ldots = 1 + (-\frac{1}{4}) + (-\frac{1}{4})^2 + (-\frac{1}{4})^3 + \ldots$

which is a GP where $r = -\frac{1}{4}$, i.e. $|r| < 1$

So this series converges and $S_\infty = \dfrac{a}{1 - r} = \dfrac{1}{1 - (-\frac{1}{4})} = \dfrac{4}{5}$

(c) $3 + \frac{9}{2} + \frac{27}{4} + \ldots = 3 + 3(\frac{3}{2}) + 3(\frac{9}{4}) + \ldots = 3 + 3(\frac{3}{2}) + 3(\frac{3}{2})^2 + \ldots$

This series is a GP where $r = \frac{3}{2}$ and, as $|r| > 1$, the series does not converge.

---

2. Find the condition satisfied by x so that $\displaystyle\sum_{r=0}^{\infty} \frac{(x-1)^r}{2^r}$ converges.

   Evaluate this expression when $x = 1.5$

$$\sum_{r=0}^{\infty} \frac{(x-1)^r}{2^r} = 1 + \frac{x-1}{2} + \left(\frac{x-1}{2}\right)^2 + \ldots$$

This series is a GP with common ratio $\left|\dfrac{x-1}{2}\right|$ and so converges

if $\dfrac{x-1}{2} < 1$

i.e. if $-1 < \dfrac{x-1}{2} < 1$

$\Rightarrow$ $-1 < x < 3$

When $x = 1.5$, the series converges

and $\displaystyle\sum_{r=0}^{\infty} \frac{(x-1)^r}{2^r} = \sum_{r=0}^{\infty} (\tfrac{1}{4})^r = 1 + \tfrac{1}{4} + (\tfrac{1}{4})^2 + \ldots$

using $S_\infty = \dfrac{a}{1-r}$ where $r = \frac{1}{4}$ and $a = 1$ gives

$$S_\infty = \frac{1}{1 - \frac{1}{4}} = \frac{4}{3}$$

---

3. Express the recurring decimal $0.1\overset{...}{5}7\overset{...}{6}$ as a fraction in its lowest terms.

$$0.1\overset{...}{5}7\overset{...}{6} = 0.1\overbrace{57}\,\overbrace{657}\,\overbrace{657}\,\overbrace{657}\,6\ldots$$

$$= 0.1 + 0.0576 + 0.000\,0576 + 0.000\,000\,0576 + \ldots$$

$$= \frac{1}{10} + \frac{576}{10^4} + \frac{576}{10^7} + \frac{576}{10^{10}} + \ldots$$

$$= \frac{1}{10} + \frac{576}{10^4}\left[1 + \frac{1}{10^3} + \frac{1}{10^6} + \ldots\right]$$

$$= \frac{1}{10} + \frac{576}{10^4}\left[1 + \frac{1}{10^3} + \left(\frac{1}{10^3}\right)^2 + \ldots\right]$$

Now the series in the square bracket is a GP whose first term is 1, and whose common ratio is $\dfrac{1}{10^3}$.

Hence it has a sum to infinity of $\dfrac{1}{1 - 10^{-3}} = \dfrac{10^3}{999}$

$$\Rightarrow \quad 0.1\overset{...}{5}7\overset{...}{6} = \frac{1}{10} + \frac{576}{10^4} \times \frac{10^3}{999} = \frac{1}{10} + \frac{576}{9990} = \frac{1575}{9990} = \frac{35}{222}$$

---

4. The 3rd term of a convergent GP is the arithmetic mean of the 1st and 2nd terms.
Find the common ratio and, if the first term is 1, find, the sum to infinity.

If the series is $a + ar + ar^2 + ar^3 + \ldots$

then $\qquad\qquad\qquad\qquad ar^2 = \tfrac{1}{2}(a + ar)$

$a \neq 0$, so $\qquad\qquad 2r^2 - r - 1 = 0$

$\Rightarrow \qquad\qquad\qquad (2r + 1)(r - 1) = 0$

i.e. $\qquad\qquad\qquad\qquad r = -\tfrac{1}{2} \text{ or } 1$

As the series is convergent, the common ratio is $-\tfrac{1}{2}$

When $r = -\tfrac{1}{2}$ and $a = 1$,

$$S_\infty = \frac{1}{1 + \frac{1}{2}} = \tfrac{2}{3}$$

EXERCISE 34d

1. Determine whether each of the series given below converge.

    (a) $4 + \dfrac{4}{3} + \dfrac{4}{3^2} + \ldots$

    (b) $9 + 7 + 5 + 3 + \ldots$

    (c) $20 - 10 + 5 - 2.5 + \ldots$

    (d) $\dfrac{5}{10} + \dfrac{5}{100} + \dfrac{5}{1000} + \ldots$

    (e) $p + 2p + 3p + \ldots$

    (f) $3 - 1 + \dfrac{1}{3} - \dfrac{1}{9} + \ldots$

2. Find the range of values of x for which the following series converge.

    (a) $1 + x + x^2 + x^3 + \ldots$

    (b) $x + 1 + \dfrac{1}{x} + \dfrac{1}{x^2} + \ldots$

    (c) $1 + 2x + 4x^2 + 8x^3 + \ldots$

    (d) $1 - (1 - x) + (1 - x)^2 - (1 - x)^3 + \ldots$

    (e) $(a + x) + (a + x)^2 + (a + x)^3 + \ldots$

    (f) $(a + x) - 1 + \dfrac{1}{a + x} + \dfrac{1}{(a + x)^2} + \ldots$

3. Find the sum to infinity of those series in Question 1 that are convergent.

4. Express the following recurring decimals as fractions

    (a) $0.16\dot{2}$ (b) $0.\dot{3}\dot{4}$ (c) $0.0\dot{2}\dot{1}$

5. The sum to infinity of a GP is twice the first term. Find the common ratio.

6. If $\ln y$ is the arithmetic mean of $\ln x$ and $\ln z$ show that y is the geometric mean of x and z

7. The sum to infinity of a GP is 16 and the sum of the first 4 terms is 15. Find the first four terms.

8. If a, b and c are the first three terms of a GP, prove that $\sqrt{a}$, $\sqrt{b}$ and $\sqrt{c}$ form another GP.

FINDING THE SUMS OF SOME OTHER NUMBER SERIES

15

It is sometimes possible to find the sum of a series which is neither an AP nor a GP.

Consider the series $\displaystyle\sum_{r=1}^{n} \frac{1}{r(r+1)}$

The general term can be expressed as two terms using partial fractions,

i.e. $\dfrac{1}{r(r+1)} \equiv \dfrac{1}{r} - \dfrac{1}{r+1}$ (using the cover-up method)

Hence $\displaystyle\sum_{r=1}^{n} \frac{1}{r(r+1)} \equiv \sum_{r=1}^{n} \left(\frac{1}{r} - \frac{1}{r+1}\right)$

$$= \left(1 - \tfrac{1}{2}\right) + \left(\tfrac{1}{2} - \tfrac{1}{3}\right) + \left(\tfrac{1}{3} - \tfrac{1}{4}\right) + \ldots + \left(\tfrac{1}{n-1} - \tfrac{1}{n}\right) + \left(\tfrac{1}{n} - \tfrac{1}{n-1}\right)$$

All the terms cancel except for the first and last terms,

therefore $\displaystyle\sum_{r=1}^{n} \frac{1}{r(r+1)} = 1 - \frac{1}{n+1} = \frac{n}{n+1}$

The summation of this series was possible because we were able to express the general term of the given series as the *difference* of two consecutive terms of another series. This is known as the *method of differences* which can be summarised as follows.

If the general term, u_r, of a series can be expressed as $f(r) - f(r+1)$

then

$$\sum_{r=1}^{n} u_r = \sum_{r=1}^{n} [f(r) - f(r+1)]$$

$$= [f(1) - f(2)] + [f(2) - f(3)] + \ldots$$

$$+ [f(n-1) - f(n)] + [f(n) - f(n+1)]$$

$$= f(1) - f(n+1)$$

Example 34e

Show that $(r + 1)^3 - r^3 \equiv 3r^2 + 3r + 1$. Hence find $\displaystyle\sum_{r=1}^{n} (3r^2 + 3r + 1)$

and deduce that $\displaystyle\sum_{r=1}^{n} r^2 = \tfrac{1}{6}n(n + 1)(2n + 1)$

LHS $= (r + 1)^3 - r^3 \equiv r^3 + 3r^2 + 3r + 1 - r^3 \equiv 3r^2 + 3r + 1 =$ RHS

i.e. $\quad (r + 1)^3 - r^3 \equiv 3r^2 + 3r + 1$

$\therefore \quad \displaystyle\sum_{r=1}^{n} (3r^2 + 3r + 1) = \sum_{r=1}^{n} \{(r + 1)^3 - r^3\}$

$$= (2^3 - 1^3) + (3^3 - 2^3) + \ldots + \{(n + 1)^3 - n^3\}$$

$$= (n + 1)^3 - 1$$

Now $\quad \displaystyle\sum_{r=1}^{n} (3r^2 + 3r + 1) = \sum_{r=1}^{n} 3r^2 + \sum_{r=1}^{n} 3r + \sum_{r=1}^{n} 1$

$\therefore \quad \displaystyle\sum_{r=1}^{n} 3r^2 + \sum_{r=1}^{n} 3r + \sum_{r=1}^{n} 1 = (n + 1)^3 - 1$ [1]

But $\displaystyle\sum_{r=1}^{n} 3r$ is an AP $(a = 3, \ d = 3)$ so using $S_n = \tfrac{1}{2}n(a + l)$

gives $\displaystyle\sum_{r=1}^{n} 3r = \tfrac{3}{2}n(n + 1)$ and $\displaystyle\sum_{r=1}^{n} 1 = 1 + 1 + \ldots + 1 = n$

Hence [1] becomes $\displaystyle\sum_{r=1}^{n} 3r^2 + \tfrac{3}{2}n(n + 1) + n = (n + 1)^3 - 1$

$\Rightarrow \quad \displaystyle\sum_{r=1}^{n} 3r^2 = (n + 1)^3 - (1 + n) - \tfrac{3}{2}n(n + 1)$

$$= (n + 1)[(n + 1)^2 - 1 - \tfrac{3}{2}n]$$

$$= (n + 1)[\tfrac{1}{2}n(2n + 1)]$$

Now $\displaystyle\sum_{r=1}^{n} 3r^2 = 3 \sum_{r=1}^{n} r^2$,

$\therefore \quad \displaystyle\sum_{r=1}^{n} r^2 = \tfrac{1}{6}n(n + 1)(2n + 1)$

EXERCISE 34e

In Questions 1 to 4 express the general term in partial fractions and hence find the sum of the series.

1. $\displaystyle\sum_{r=1}^{n} \frac{1}{r(r+2)}$

2. $\displaystyle\sum_{r=3}^{n} \frac{1}{(r+1)(r+2)}$

3. $\displaystyle\sum_{r=n}^{2n} \frac{1}{r(r+1)}$

4. $\displaystyle\sum_{r=1}^{n} \frac{r}{(2r-1)(2r+1)(2r+3)}$

5. Verify that $4r^3 + r \equiv (r+\frac{1}{2})^4 - (r-\frac{1}{2})^4$. Hence find $\displaystyle\sum_{r=1}^{n} (4r^3 + r)$

Deduce that $\displaystyle\sum_{r=1}^{n} r^3 = \frac{1}{4}n^2(n+1)^2$

6. If $f(r) \equiv \dfrac{1}{r(r+1)}$, simplify $f(r+1) - f(r)$

Hence find $\displaystyle\sum_{r=1}^{n} \frac{1}{r(r+1)(r+2)}$

7. If $f(r) \equiv \dfrac{1}{r^2}$, simplify $f(r) - f(r+1)$

Hence find the sum of the first n terms of the series
$$\frac{3}{(1^2)(2^2)} + \frac{5}{(2^2)(3^2)} + \frac{7}{(3^2)(4^2)} + \ldots$$

8. Given that $\displaystyle\sum_{r=1}^{n} r^2 = \frac{1}{6}n(n+1)(2n+1)$, use the identity
$$r^4 - (r-1)^4 \equiv 4r^3 - 6r^2 + 4r - 1$$
to find the sum of the cubes of the first n natural numbers,
i.e. $\displaystyle\sum_{r=1}^{n} r^3$

9. If $f(r) \equiv \cos 2r\theta$, simplify $f(r) - f(r+1)$
Use you result to find the sum of the first n terms of the series
$$\sin 3\theta + \sin 5\theta + \sin 7\theta + \ldots$$

NATURAL NUMBER SERIES

The natural numbers are the positive integers, i.e. 1, 2, 3, ...

The series $1 + 2 + 3 + \ldots + n$ is the sum of the first n natural numbers and can be written $\displaystyle\sum_{r=1}^{n} r$

This series is an AP with $a = 1$ and $d = 1$, so using $S_n = \frac{1}{2}n(a+1)$

gives
$$\sum_{r=1}^{n} r = \tfrac{1}{2}n(n+1)$$

Now consider the series $1^2 + 2^2 + 3^2 + \ldots + n^2$ which is the sum of the squares of the first n natural numbers.

This series is written $\displaystyle\sum_{r=1}^{n} r^2$ and its sum was found in Example 34e,

i.e.
$$\sum_{r=1}^{n} r^2 = \tfrac{1}{6}n(n+1)(2n+1)$$

The series $1^3 + 2^3 + 3^3 + \ldots + n^3$ is called the sum of the cubes of the first n natural numbers and we saw in Exercise 34e that

$$\sum_{r=1}^{n} r^3 = \tfrac{1}{4}n^2(n+1)^2 = \left[\tfrac{1}{2}n(n+1)\right]^2 = \left[\sum_{r=1}^{n} r\right]^2$$

The results are quotable and can be used to sum other series.

Examples 34f

1. Find $\displaystyle\sum_{r=1}^{n} r(r+1)(r+2)$

$$r(r+1)(r+2) \equiv r^3 + 3r^2 + 2r$$

$$\therefore \quad \sum_{r=1}^{n} r(r+1)(r+2) = \sum_{r=1}^{n} r^3 + 3\sum_{r=1}^{n} r^2 + 2\sum_{r=1}^{n} r$$

$$= \tfrac{1}{4}n^2(n+1)^2 + 3\left[\tfrac{1}{6}n(n+1)(2n+1)\right]$$
$$+ 2\left[\tfrac{1}{2}n(n+1)\right]$$

$$= \tfrac{1}{4}n(n+1)(n+2)(n+3)$$

2. Find $\displaystyle\sum_{r=5}^{10} r^2$

$$\sum_{r=5}^{10} r^2 = \sum_{r=1}^{10} r^2 - \sum_{r=1}^{4} r^2 = \tfrac{10}{6}(10+1)(20+1) - \tfrac{4}{6}(4+1)(8+1)$$

$$= 355$$

---

3. Find the sum of the squares of the first n odd numbers.

The odd numbers can be represented by $2r-1$ where $r = 1, 2, 3, \ldots$

So we want $\displaystyle\sum_{r=1}^{n} (2r-1)^2$

Now $(2r-1)^2 = 4r^2 - 4r + 1$

$$\therefore \quad \sum_{r=1}^{n} (2r-1)^2 = 4\sum_{r=1}^{n} r^2 - 4\sum_{r=1}^{n} r + \sum_{r=1}^{n} 1$$

$$= 4\left[\tfrac{1}{6}n(n+1)(2n+1)\right] - 4\left[\tfrac{1}{2}n(n+1)\right] + n$$

$$= \tfrac{1}{3}n(4n^2 - 1)$$

EXERCISE 34f

Find the sum of the series.

1. $\displaystyle\sum_{r=1}^{n} r(r+1)$

2. $\displaystyle\sum_{r=1}^{n} r(r+1)(r+2)$

3. $\displaystyle\sum_{r=n}^{2n} r^2(1+r)$

4. $\displaystyle\sum_{r=10}^{20} r^3$

5. $(1)(3) + (2)(4) + (3)(5) + \ldots + (n-1)(n+1)$

6. $1^2 - 2^2 + 3^2 - 4^2 + 5^2 - 6^2 + \ldots - (2n)^2$

(*Hint.* Consider two series, the sum of the squares of even numbers and sum of the squares of odd numbers.)

7. $(1)(3) + (3)(5) + (5)(7) + \ldots + (2n-1)(2n+1)$

GENERAL METHODS FOR SUMMING A NUMBER SERIES

The basic method for summing a number series relies on recognition, and a systematic approach is helpful, i.e.

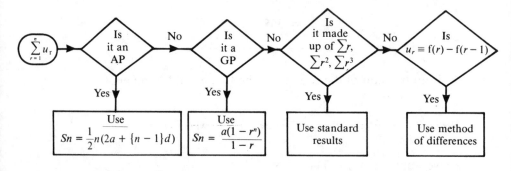

For example, $\displaystyle\sum_{r=n}^{\infty} (\tfrac{1}{3})^r(\tfrac{1}{2})^{r-2}$ can be recognised as a **GP** with first

term $(\tfrac{1}{3})^n(\tfrac{1}{2})^{n-2}$ and common ratio $(\tfrac{1}{3})(\tfrac{1}{2})$

Similarly, $\displaystyle\sum_{r=1}^{2n} (1+2n)(1-n)$ can be written as $\displaystyle\sum_{r=1}^{2n} (1+n-2n^2)$

when it can be recognised as being made up of natural number series.

THE SUM TO INFINITY OF A NUMBER SERIES

We saw on p. 606 that if S_n is the sum of the first n terms of a series and if $\lim_{n\to\infty} S_n$ exists, then the series is convergent with a sum to infinity, S, where

$$S = \lim_{n\to\infty} S_n$$

Note that when evaluating $\lim_{n\to\infty} S_n$ certain assumptions may be made, i.e. as $n \to \infty$, then $\tfrac{1}{n} \to 0$, $a^n \to 0$ if $0 < a < 1$, and $a^n \to \infty$ if $a > 1$

If $S_n \to \dfrac{\infty}{\infty}$ or $\dfrac{0}{0}$, both of which are indeterminate, it may be possible to evaluate $\lim_{n\to\infty} S_n$ by expressing S_n as a proper fraction, e.g. if $S_n = \dfrac{n-1}{n+1}$ then $\lim\limits_{n \to \infty} \dfrac{n-1}{n+1}$ is indeterminate,

but $\dfrac{n-1}{n+1} = 1 - \dfrac{2}{n+1}$ so $\lim\limits_{n \to \infty} S_n = \lim\limits_{n \to \infty} \left[1 - \dfrac{1}{n+1} \right] = 1$

Example 34g _____

Find the sum to infinity of the series $\dfrac{1}{(1)(3)} + \dfrac{1}{(3)(5)} + \dfrac{1}{(5)(7)} + \ldots$

The general term of this series is $\dfrac{1}{(2r-1)(2r+1)}$, and using partial

fractions, this becomes $\dfrac{1}{2(2r-1)} - \dfrac{1}{2(2r+1)}$

Therefore the sum of the first n terms of the given series is S_n where

$$S_n = \sum_{r=1}^{\infty} \left[\dfrac{1}{2(2r-1)} - \dfrac{1}{2(2r+1)} \right]$$

$$= \tfrac{1}{2}\left[(\tfrac{1}{1} - \tfrac{1}{3}) + (\tfrac{1}{3} - \tfrac{1}{5}) + \ldots + \left(\dfrac{1}{2n-1} - \dfrac{1}{2n+1} \right) \right]$$

$$\Rightarrow S_n = \tfrac{1}{2}\left(1 - \dfrac{1}{2n+1} \right)$$

Now as $n \to \infty$, $\dfrac{1}{2n+1} \to 0$ so $S_n \to \tfrac{1}{2}$

Therefore the sum to infinity of this series is $\tfrac{1}{2}$

_____

MIXED EXERCISE 34

Find the sum of each of the following series.

1. $1 - \tfrac{1}{2} + \tfrac{1}{4} - \tfrac{1}{8} + \ldots$

2. $2 - (2)(3) + (2)(3)^2 - (2)(3)^3 + \ldots + (2)(3)^{10}$

3. $\displaystyle\sum_{r=2}^{n} ab^{2r}$

4. $1 + 4 + 9 + 16 + \ldots + 144$

5. $\displaystyle\sum_{r=5}^{n} 4r$

6. $\displaystyle\sum_{r=1}^{n} r(r^2 + 1)$

7. $\displaystyle\sum_{r=2}^{n} \frac{1}{(r-1)(r+1)}$

8. $\ln 3 + \ln 3^2 + \ln 3^3 + \ldots + \ln 3^{20}$

9. $e + e^2 + e^3 + \ldots + e^n$

10. $\displaystyle\sum_{r=1}^{n} r(2r+1)(r+2)$

11. $\displaystyle\sum_{r=n}^{2n} \frac{1}{(r+1)(r+2)}$

12. $\displaystyle\sum_{r=1}^{\infty} \frac{1}{2^r}$

13. The sum of the squares of the first n even numbers.

14. $\displaystyle\sum_{r=2}^{n} \ln\left(1 - \frac{1}{r}\right)$

15. The sum of the first n terms of a series is n^3. Write down the first four terms and the nth term of the series.

16. The fourth term of an AP is 8 and the sum of the first ten terms is 40. Find the first term and the tenth term.

17. The second, fourth and eighth terms of an AP are the first three terms of a GP. Find the common ratio of the GP.

18. Find the value of x for which the numbers $x + 1$, $x + 3$, $x + 7$, are in geometric progression.

19. The second term of a GP is $\frac{1}{2}$ and the sum to infinity of the series is 4. Find the first term and the common ratio of the series.

CHAPTER 35

PERMUTATIONS AND COMBINATIONS

ARRANGEMENTS

Suppose that three different pictures, A, B and C are to be hung, in line, on a wall. The pictures can be hung in various orders,
e.g.   A B C, A C B, B A C and others.

Each of these orders is a particular arrangement of the pictures and is called a *permutation*.

> A permutation is an ordered arrangement of the items in a set.

CHOICES

Now we look at a different situation. Suppose that, from a set of seven pictures, A, B, C, D, E, F and G, three pictures are to be chosen for display.

Choosing the group of three pictures does *not* involve the order in which they will be hung.
If, say, B, D and F are chosen then, although they can be hung in six different orders, the subset B, D and F comprises *only one choice*, which is called a *combination*.

i.e.   B D F ⎫
         B F D ⎪
         D B F ⎬ are six different permutations
         D F B ⎪ but only one combination
         F B D ⎪
         F D B ⎭

> A combination is an unordered group chosen from the items in a set.

Once a combination has been selected, its members can be arranged in different orders forming permutations should this be required.

For example, a news vendor stocks ten weekly magazines but the display stand at his kiosk has room for only five. As he cannot display all ten of his magazines he must *choose* a group of five. The order in which he picks up the five is irrelevant; the set of five is *only one combination*. However, once he has made his choice he can display them in different orders on the stand. He is now *arranging* them and each arrangement is a permutation.

EXERCISE 35a

Each question asks either for a number of combinations or for a number of permutations. Without attempting to find that number, decide whether you are looking for combinations or permutations.

1. How many arrangements of the letters X, Y and Z are there?

2. A team of four is to be chosen from nine players. How many different teams can be selected?

3. If eight records can be taken to a desert island, from a collection of one hundred records, how many different sets can be chosen?

4. Five hundred raffle tickets are sold. When the first, second and third prizes are draw, in how many different ways can the prizes be won?

5. A museum lists its exhibits by code numbers of seven digits. How many code numbers are available?

6. A door is to be painted in two shades of green paint. If six suitable shades are available, in how many ways can the two shades be selected?

7. In how many ways can fifteen books be placed on a shelf?

PERMUTATIONS

Suppose that we wish to calculate the number of permutations of the three letters, A, B and C.

Arranging them from left to right, the first letter can be

$$A \quad \text{or} \quad B \quad \text{or} \quad C$$

i.e. there are 3 ways of choosing the first letter.

When we come to place the second letter there are only two left to choose from,
e.g. if the first letter were B then only A or C can be in second place.

A   B   C
B or C   A or C   A or B

For *each* of the 3 ways of selecting the first letter, there are 2 ways of selecting the second letter, i.e. there are 3×2 ways of selecting the first two letters.

Once the first two are in place there is only one letter left for third place

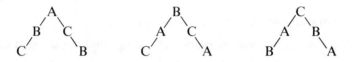

So there are $3 \times 2 \times 1$ ways of arranging three letters in order.

This argument can be applied equally well to any number of objects (although the 'choice tree' is cumbersome for a large number).

Considering, say, the number of permutations of eight different books, we see that

first place can be filled by any one of the 8 books (leaving seven books)
second place can be filled by any one of the remaining 7 books
third place can be filled by any one of 6 books
... and so on

Hence there are $8 \times 7 \times 6 \times 5 \times 4 \times 3 \times 2 \times 1$ permutations of eight items.

Because this product, and others like it, is clumsy to write out in full, a special notation is used to express it more neatly.

Factorial Notation

To represent $8 \times 7 \times 6 \times 5 \times 4 \times 3 \times 2 \times 1$ we write 8! and say 'eight factorial'. Similarly 5! means $5 \times 4 \times 3 \times 2 \times 1$

In general, the product of all the whole numbers from any number, n, down to 1 is called n *factorial* and written as $n!$

PERMUTATION PROBLEMS

The simplest problems are those in which the n items in a set are (a) all different, (b) all to be used, (c) each used only once.

In such cases, as we have already seen, there are $n!$ permutations.

There are many other situations, however, and all but the simplest problems should be worked from first principles.

Suppose, for instance, that there are eight different objects available, but that there is room for only five of those objects, then

first place can be filled in 8 ways
second place can be filled in 7 ways

- - - - - - - - - - - - - -

fifth place can be filled in 4 ways

and, as there are no more places left to be filled, we see that there are

$$8 \times 7 \times 6 \times 5 \times 4 \quad \text{permutations}$$

Now this product cannot be written as 8! because it stops short at 4 and $3 \times 2 \times 1$ are missing. It *can* be abbreviated however because

$$8 \times 7 \times 6 \times 5 \times 4 = \frac{8 \times 7 \times 6 \times 5 \times 4 \times 3 \times 2 \times 1}{3 \times 2 \times 1} = \frac{8!}{3!} = \frac{8!}{(8-5)!}$$

The number of arrangements of 5 objects when 8 different objects are available is denoted by $^8P_5$

Therefore
$$^8P_5 = \frac{8!}{(8-5)!}$$

In general, if n different objects are available but only r of them are arranged, then the number of arrangements is ^nP_r where

$$^nP_r = \frac{n!}{(n-r)!}$$

So far we have considered only those arrangements of different objects in which each object is available for use only once. Certain items can be placed in an arrangement more than once, however; using the digits 0 to 9 to form telephone numbers is a good example of this situation.

Using the digits 3, 4 and 5 to form as many three-digit numbers as possible we see that the first digit can be any one of the three available.

Any one of the three digits can also be used in second place and again in third place so there are $3 \times 3 \times 3$, i.e. 27, possible numbers.

There are many other variations that arise in problems about arrangements. Some of these are illustrated in the following examples but no attempt is made to cover all possibilities. The essence of these problems is to treat each one as an individual puzzle to be thought out.

Examples 35b _____

1. How many arrangements of the letters in the word GROUP start with a vowel?

If the first letter is to be a vowel there are only 2 possibilities, O or U. When the first letter has been chosen, any of the remaining 4 letters (including the vowel not in first place) can be used in second place, so there are 2×4 ways of arranging the first two letters. Then there are three letters available for third place, and so on.

	1st	2nd	3rd	4th	5th
No. of ways of selecting the letter	2	4	3	2	1

The number of arrangements starting with a vowel is

$$2 \times 4 \times 3 \times 2 \times 1 = 2(4!) = 48$$

2. Four girls and two boys are to sit in a row. The two boys, Alan and Tim, insist on sitting together. In how many different ways can the six children be arranged?

As Alan and Tim must be together we first treat them as one unit, i.e. we have only five items to arrange, four girls and 'a pair of boys'.

Five different objects can be arranged in 5! ways.

In any one of these arrangements, the boys can be seated in one of two ways, i.e.   Tim Alan   or   Alan Tim.

So the total number of arrangements is $2 \times 5!$

Note that if the two boys *refused* to sit together we would first find the number of arrangements in which they *are* next to each other (as above) and subtract this value from the total number of arrangements without any restriction, i.e. $6! - 2 \times 5!$

3. How many odd numbers between 2000 and 3000 can be formed from the digits 1, 2, 3, 4, 5 and 6?

Because the number is between 2000 and 3000, it has only four digits and the first digit can only be 2. The number is odd so the last digit must be taken from 1, 3 or 5. Once the first and last digit are placed there are four digits available for second place and three for third place

	1st	4th	2nd	3rd
Number of ways of selecting digit	1	3	4	3

∴ there are $1 \times 3 \times 4 \times 3$, i.e. 36 numbers.

---

4. In how many different ways can four people stand in a circle?

No one place is special and there is no first or last place in a circle. What matters here is the order in which each person stands relative to the others.

Starting at a particular place with any one of the four people, the person standing next on the left (say) can be any one of the remaining three, and so on,
i.e. there are 4! arrangements starting from that particular place.

However, if the places are numbered 1 to 4 and the people denoted by A to D, we see that some of the arrangements accounted for above are not, in fact, different *relative* orders.
e.g. if all four people move one place clockwise they are still in the *same relative order* but so far this has been counted as a different permutation. This can be repeated giving four positions which are not different permutations

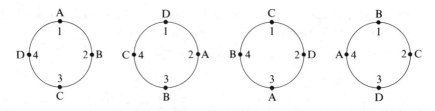

i.e. the total of 4! arrangements is 4 times too big.

So the number of different arrangements is 4!/4, i.e. 3!

In general, n objects can be arranged in a circle in $(n - 1)!$ ways.

Considering four beads on a circular wire we see that the number of different orders in which they can be threaded is reduced even further because the wire can be turned over. In this way the two arrangements shown below are actually identical. So we see that the number of arrangements on a reversible ring is half the number of arrangements obtained for a circle that cannot be turned over.

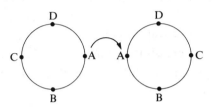

So the number of different ways of threading four beads on a circular wire is $\dfrac{4!}{4 \times 2}$

Again we have a similar general result for arranging n different objects on a circular wire, i.e. there are $\dfrac{n!}{n \times 2}$ arrangements.

EXERCISE 35b

1. In how many ways can seven different trophies be arranged on a shelf?

2. How many three-digit numbers can be formed from the set $\{2, 3, 4, 5, 6\}$ if the three digits are
    (a) all different   (b) all the same?

3. In how many ways can six different books be placed in a rack?

4. How many numbers greater than 4000 can be formed from the integers 1, 3, 5, 7, using each of them only once in each number?

5. Stevenage telephone numbers have six digits the first of which may not be zero. What is the greatest possible number of separate lines in Stevenage?

6. How many arrangements can be made from the letters of the word PRINCE if
    (a) the first letter must be a consonant
    (b) the last letter must be a vowel
    (c) the P and R must not be separated?

7. Given three red cubes, three blue cubes and three green cubes, in how many ways can three cubes be placed in a row if they are
   (a) of different colours   (b) all the same colour?

8. In how many different ways can ten people be seated at a round table?

9. How many five-digit numbers can be formed from the set $\{1, 2, 3, 4, 5, 6, 7, 8, 9\}$ if
   (a) the digits are all different
   (b) the digits are all the same
   (c) the digits are all different and the number is greater than 60 000?

10. In how many orders can twelve cows be placed in a circular milking parlour?

11. Two different maths books and three other books are to be placed on a shelf. How many different arrangements are possible if
    (a) the two maths books are together
    (b) the two maths books are separated?

12. In how many ways can five beads of different colours be arranged on a wire ring?

13. Using the digits 2, 4, 6, 8, find how many whole numbers between 3000 and 7000 can be found in which the digits are all different.

14. Twelve children stand in a row. In how many different ways can they be arranged if
    (a) one particular child has to stand at one end
    (b) two particular children must be separated?

15. How many whole numbers between 100 and 1000 can be formed from the digits 3, 5, 7, 8 if
    (a) the digits in each number are all different
    (b) each digit can be repeated as often as required?

16. How many of the numbers in 15(a) are even?

COMBINATIONS

Consider again the situation where three pictures have to be *chosen*, but not ordered, from seven available different pictures.
We are now going to investigate the number of different sets, or combinations, of three pictures.

First we will not only select three pictures but also arrange them in order as we do so.

This can be done in $7 \times 6 \times 5$ ways, i.e. in $\dfrac{7!}{4!}$ ways.

This number includes, as separate arrangements, the number of permutations of the pictures represented by B, D and F (see p. 619), i.e. 3! permutations.
These permutations comprise only one set, or choice. The same is true for each group of three pictures, so the *number of different sets* of three pictures that can be taken from the seven available is given by

$$\frac{\text{total number of permutations}}{\text{number of permutations of each set}}$$

The number of combinations of three objects chosen from seven different objects is denoted by $^7C_3$,

i.e. $$^7C_3 \;=\; \frac{7!}{4!\,3!} \;=\; \frac{7!}{3!(7-3)!}$$

In general, if a set of r objects is chosen from n different objects then the number of combinations is denoted by ^nC_r where

$$^nC_r \;=\; \frac{n!}{r!(n-r)!}$$

i.e. $$^nC_r \;=\; \frac{(\text{total number available})!}{(\text{number chosen})!\,(\text{number not chosen})!}$$

Now if we have to choose $(n - r)$ from n different objects, the number of objects not chosen is r so

$$^nC_{n-r} \;=\; \frac{n!}{(n-r)!\,r!} \;=\; \frac{n!}{r!(n-r)!} \;=\; {}^nC_r$$

i.e. $$^nC_{n-r} \;=\; {}^nC_r$$

The Meaning of 0!

There is clearly only one way of choosing n objects from n available objects. As this is represented by ^nC_n we have,

$$^nC_n = 1$$

Using the definition $^nC_r = \dfrac{n!}{r!(n-r)!}$ in the case when $r = n$

gives

$$^nC_n = \dfrac{n!}{n!\,0!}$$

This is equal to unity only if we define 0! as having the value 1

i.e.

$$0! = 1$$

PROBLEMS ON COMBINATIONS

As was the case with permutations, problems involving combinations are very varied. Each one is a puzzle and should be carefully thought through. Some of the many variations are illustrated in the following examples.

Examples 35c _____

1. In how many different ways can eight cards can be dealt from a pack of fifty-two playing cards?

    The fifty-two cards in the pack are all different so this question is straightforward, with no complications, and we can use ^nC_r

    A set of eight cards can be chosen from fifty-two in $^{52}C_8$ ways

    i.e. the number of different hands is $\dfrac{52!}{8!(52-8)!} = \dfrac{52!}{8!\,44!}$

    _____

    Note. Unless a numerical answer is specifically asked for, answers to this type of problem are usually given in factorial notation.

    _____

2. In how many ways can five boys be chosen from a class of twenty boys if the class prefect must be included?

One particular boy has to be chosen and the group is then completed by choosing four boys from the remaining nineteen.

Four boys can be chosen from nineteen boys in $^{19}C_4$ ways, i.e. in

$$\frac{19!}{4!(19-4)!} \text{ ways}$$

$\therefore$ the number of groups of five boys including the prefect is $\dfrac{19!}{4!\,15!}$

---

3. In how many ways can a party of ten children be divided into two groups of

    (a) six children and four children   (b) five children each?

(a) Each time a group of six children is chosen, those not chosen automatically form a group of four. So we need consider only forming groups of six.

Six children can be chosen from ten in $^{10}C_6$, i.e. $\dfrac{10!}{6!(10-6)!}$ ways.

$\therefore$ the number of ways in which the children can be divided into groups of four and six is $\dfrac{10!}{6!\,4!}$

(b) Again we begin by considering the choice of one group of five children.

The number of ways of choosing a set of five children is

$$\frac{10!}{5!(10-5)!} = \frac{10!}{5!\,5!}$$

Each time a group of five is selected, a group is formed of the other five, i.e. each *pair* of groups is chosen twice. For example, if the children are denoted by the letters A to J then one chosen could be ABCDE leaving FGHIJ for the corresponding second group. Now the first group chosen could be FGHIJ for which the corresponding second group is ABCDE.

But dividing the children into ABCDE/FGHIJ and FGHIJ/ABCDE gives the same *pair* of groups in both cases, i.e. the number of ways of choosing a group of five children, found above, is twice the number of different pairs of groups.

$\therefore$ the number of ways of dividing the children into two groups each of five is $\left(\dfrac{1}{2}\right)\left(\dfrac{10!}{5!\,5!}\right)$

EXERCISE 35c

1. Write in factorial notation
   (a) the number of permutations of six objects if eleven different objects are available
   (b) the number of combinations of six objects chosen from eleven different objects
   (c) the number of combinations of three objects chosen from twenty different objects.

2. Describe in words a situation which could be represented by
   (a) $\dfrac{8!}{4!}$ (b) $\dfrac{14!}{5!\,9!}$ (c) $\dfrac{7!}{5!\,2!}$

3. How many different combinations of six letters can be chosen from the letters A, B, C, D, E, F, G, H if each letter may be chosen only once?

4. In how many ways can the eight letters given in Question 3 be divided into two groups containing six and two letters respectively?

5. To compete in a quiz contest a team of four is to be selected from a class of twenty children. How many different teams can be chosen if
   (a) the oldest member of the class must be included as team leader
   (b) there is a completely free choice?

6. A shop stocks nine different varieties of tinned meat. In how many ways can a shopper buy three tins if
   (a) three different varieties are chosen
   (b) there are two tins of the same variety?

7. The nine members of a committee comprise: one married couple, three more men and four more women. In how many ways can a working party of five people be selected?
   How many of these working parties are such that
   (a) at least one man and at least one woman must be chosen
   (b) the husband *or* the wife but not both, may be included
   (c) it is formed entirely of women?

8. How many different hands of five cards can be dealt from a suit of thirteen cards?

9. How many of the hands dealt in Question 8 contain the ace?

10. From a large bowl of apples, pears, oranges and bananas, three pieces of fruit are chosen. How many different selections can be made if
    (a) the three chosen are all different but must include a banana
    (b) two are the same kind and the third is different but no pears are chosen?

11. A large box packet contains nine different kinds of biscuit. In how many ways can four biscuits be chosen if
    (a) four different varieties are taken
    (b) two each of two varieties are selected
    (c) three are the same and the fourth is different
    (d) all four are the same?

USING THE FACTORIAL NOTATION

The factorial notation has proved to be very useful in permutation and combination problems, whenever we need to write the product of all the whole numbers from a given number n down to 1. There are other topics which require the use and manipulation of factorial expressions so we will now examine the ways in which factorials can be simplified or evaluated.

One of the forms in which factorials occur very frequently is, for example, $\dfrac{9!}{6!}$

Written in full, $\dfrac{9!}{6!} = \dfrac{9 \times 8 \times 7 \times 6 \times 5 \times 4 \times 3 \times 2 \times 1}{6 \times 5 \times 4 \times 3 \times 2 \times 1} = 9 \times 8 \times 7$

i.e. dividing the top and bottom by 6! leaves the product of numbers from 9 to 7

i.e. $\dfrac{9!}{6!}$ = the product of integers from 9 to (6 + 1)

In general $\dfrac{n!}{r!}$ is the product of the integers from n down to $(r + 1)$

Examples 35d _____

1. Without using a calculator, evaluate   (a) $\dfrac{10!}{8!}$ (b) $\dfrac{19!}{2!\,17!}$

(a) $\dfrac{10!}{8!} = 10 \times 9 = 90$

(b) $\dfrac{19!}{2!\,17!} = \dfrac{19 \times 18}{2 \times 1} = 19 \times 9 = 171$

_____

2. Express $\dfrac{9 \times 8 \times 7 \times 6}{4 \times 3 \times 2 \times 1}$ in factorial notation.

$$9 \times 8 \times 7 \times 6 = \frac{9!}{5!}$$

$\therefore$
$$\frac{9 \times 8 \times 7 \times 6}{4 \times 3 \times 2 \times 1} = \frac{9!}{5!\,4!}$$

_____

3. Factorise $8! - 5(7!)$

$$8! = 8 \times 7!$$

$\therefore$
$$8! - 5(7!) = 8(7!) - 5(7!)$$
$$= 7!(8 - 5) = 3(7!)$$

_____

4. Factorise $(n + 1)! + n^2(n - 1)!$

$$(n + 1)! = (n + 1) \times n!$$

and
$$n^2(n - 1)! = n\{n \times (n - 1)!\} = n\{n!\}$$

$\therefore$
$$(n + 1)! + n^2(n - 1)! = (n + 1)\{n!\} + n\{n!\}$$
$$= \{n!\}(n + 1 + n)$$
$$= (2n + 1)n!$$

_____

5. Show that the number of groups of r objects that can be chosen from n different objects is $\dfrac{n(n-1)(n-2)\ldots(n-r+1)}{r!}$

The number of possible groups is given by

$$^nC_r = \frac{n!}{r!(n-r)!} = \frac{n!}{(n-r)!} \div r!$$

Now when $(n-r)!$ is cancelled from $n!$ the last number left in the numerator is one greater than $(n-r)$, i.e. $(n-r+1)$

$\therefore$ the number of groups is $\dfrac{n(n-1)(n-2)\ldots(n-r+1)}{r!}$

EXERCISE 35d

Do not use a calculator in this exercise.

Evaluate

1. $3!$ **2.** $4!$ **3.** $5!$ **4.** $6!$

5. $\dfrac{6!}{4!}$ **6.** $\dfrac{12!}{10!}$ **7.** $\dfrac{7!}{3!}$ **8.** $\dfrac{5!}{2!}$

9. $\dfrac{8!}{6!\,2!}$ **10.** $\dfrac{9!}{2!\,3!\,4!}$ **11.** $\dfrac{8!}{(4!)^2}$ **12.** $\dfrac{(3!)^2}{2!\,4!}$

Write in factorial form.

13. $5 \times 4 \times 3$ **14.** 11×10

15. $(n+1)n(n-1)$ **16.** $(n+2)(n+1)$

17. $\dfrac{20 \times 19 \times 18}{3 \times 2 \times 1}$ **18.** $\dfrac{8 \times 7 \times 6}{6 \times 5 \times 4}$

19. $\dfrac{5 \times 4 \times 3}{3 \times 2 \times 1}$ **20.** $\dfrac{40 \times 39}{2 \times 1}$

21. $\dfrac{n(n-1)(n-2)}{3 \times 2 \times 1}$ **22.** $\dfrac{(n-1)(n-2)(n-3)(n-4)}{4 \times 3 \times 2 \times 1}$

Factorise

23. $8! + 9!$ **24.** $7! - 2(5!)$ **25.** $n! + (n-1)!$ **26.** $(n+1)! - n!$

27. Show that the number of ways in which $(r-1)$ objects can be chosen from $(n+1)$ different objects is
$$\frac{(n+1)(n)(n-1)\ldots(n-r+3)}{(r-1)!}$$

28. Find an expression similar to that given in Question 27 for the number of combinations of

(a) r objects chosen from $2n$ different objects

(b) n objects chosen from $2n$ different objects

FURTHER PROBLEMS ON PERMUTATIONS AND COMBINATIONS

Permutations Involving some Identical Objects

Consider the number of possible arrangements of the letters of the word DIGIT.

This word contains two Is which are identical, but which can be distinguished by adding suffixes, i.e. D I_1 G I_2 T.

Then the number of permutations of the letters D I_1 G I_2 T is 5!

But this number includes separately the two permutations

$$\text{D } I_1 \text{ G } I_2 \text{ T} \quad \text{and} \quad \text{D } I_2 \text{ G } I_1 \text{ T}$$

so the arrangement DIGIT is counted twice. Because I_1 and I_2 can be arranged in 2! ways, every distinct arrangement of the letters DIGIT is included 2! times in the permutations of D I_1 G I_2 T.

Hence there are $\dfrac{5!}{2!}$ arrangements of the letters D I G I T

Now consider the number of permutations of the letters

$$\text{D E F E A T E D}$$

There are three Es and two Ds.

The number of permutations of D_1 E_1 F E_2 A T E_3 D_2 is 8!

But E_1, E_2, E_3 can be arranged in 3! ways, and D_1, D_2 can be arranged in 2! ways,

so the number of arrangements of D_1 E_1 F E_2 A T E_3 D_2 is $3! \times 2!$ times the number of arrangements of D E F E A T E D.

Therefore there are $\dfrac{8!}{3!\,2!}$ permutations of D E F E A T E D

Using a similar argument in a more general case we have,

> there are $\dfrac{n!}{r!}$ permutations of n objects, r of which are identical.

and, for n objects, p of which are alike and q of which are alike (but different from the set of p objects), the number of permutations is $\dfrac{n!}{p!\,q!}$

Examples 35e _____

1. In how many of the possible permutations of the letters of the word ADDING are the two Ds (a) together (b) separated?

(a) The number of permutations in which the Ds are together can be found easily by bracketing the Ds and treating them as one item in the arrangements of A, (DD), I, N, G. There are now five different items which can be arranged in 5! ways.

(b) As the Ds are either together or separated,

(number of permutations without restriction)

$-$ (number of arrangements with Ds together)

$=$ (number of arrangements with Ds separated)

Now the number of arrangements without restriction is $\dfrac{6!}{2!}$

Hence the number of arrangements in which the Ds are separated is

$$\frac{6!}{2!} - 5! = 240$$

_____

Note. The number of permutations in which G and A are next to each other is found in a similar way to (a) above, but these two letters can be written (GA) or (AG). Therefore there are twice as many arrangements of A, D, D, I, N, G in which A and G are adjacent than when the two Ds are adjacent.

Independent Permutations and Combinations

A security firm wishes to use a code for each of its clients, all codes are to be made up of three different letters followed by two different digits excluding zero.

The number of different codes which the firm can use is given by considering the number of permutations of three letters from the alphabet and the number of permutations of two digits from the nine digits available.

These two sets of permutations are independent of each other as the order of the letters has no effect upon the order of the digits.

There are $^{26}P_3$ ways of arranging the letters and $^9P_2$ ways of arranging the digits in the code.

Each of the $^{26}P_3$ permutations of letters can be followed by *any* of the $^9P_2$ permutations of digits.

Therefore the number of possible codes is $^{26}P_3 \times {}^9P_2$

Using a similar argument for a general case we see that

> when the number of permutations, P_1, of objects from one set, is followed by the number of permutations, P_2, of objects from an *independent* set, then the total number of permutations is $P_1 \times P_2$

This result applies also when combinations of objects from independent sets are combined and can be extended to cover more than two sets.

Examples 35e (continued)

2. A cellar contains thirty different bottles of wine, fifteen different cans of beer and ten different fruit juices. Six bottles of wine, ten cans of beer and three fruit juices are chosen for a party. How many different selections of drinks are possible?

The six bottles of wine can be chosen in $^{30}C_6$ ways.
The ten cans of beer can be chosen in $^{15}C_{10}$ ways.
The three fruit juices can be chosen in $^5C_3$ ways.

The choice of each type of drink is independent of the others,

∴ there are $^{30}C_6 \times {}^{15}C_{10} \times {}^5C_3$ different selections of drinks.

Mutually Exclusive Permutations or Combinations

Consider in how many ways a number greater than 20 can be made from the integers 2, 3 and 4, no integer being repeated.

The number may contain *either* two digits *or* three digits. These permutations are mutually exclusive since the number obviously cannot contain *both* two digits *and* three digits.

We can make a two-digit number in $^3P_2$ ways and a three-digit number in $^3P_3$ ways and these two cases cover all possible permutations. So there are $^3P_2 + ^3P_3$ numbers greater than 20

Extending this argument to a general case we see that

> when the number of permutations, P_1, of one set of objects is combined with the number of permutations, P_2, of a mutually exclusive set, then the total number of permutations is $P_1 + P_2$

This result applies equally well to combinations and also to more than two mutually exclusive sets.

When appraising a situation, care is needed to distinguish between the types of problem which involve

1) *both* one set of objects *and* another set of objects

2) *either* one set of objects *or* another set of objects.

Examples 35e (continued)

3. How many groups of six children can be chosen from a class of twenty, if the class contains one set of twins who will not be separated.

In choosing the six children we have to consider two cases, i.e.
either   six children including the twins
or   six children excluding the twins

These two cases are mutually exclusive as clearly the group cannot both include *and* exclude the twins.

If the twins are included, four more children must be chosen from the remaining eighteen. This can be done in $^{18}C_4$ ways.
If the twins are excluded, all six children must be chosen from the other eighteen. This can be done in $^{18}C_6$ ways.

There are no more possible combinations so the number of different groups of six children is $^{18}C_4 + ^{18}C_6$

These examples continue with assorted problems which illustrate some of the varied situations in which permutations or combinations arise.

Examples 35e (continued) _____

4. If the three Es must be separated, how many permutations of the letters in the word DEFEATED are there?

The most direct approach is first to remove all the Es and find the number of permutations of the letters D F A T D, i.e. of five letters, two of which are the same, so there are $\dfrac{5!}{2!}$ permutations.

In any one of these 60 arrangements there are six spaces into which the three Es can be inserted,

i.e. $\uparrow D \uparrow F \uparrow A \uparrow T \uparrow D \uparrow$

The three positions for the Es can be chosen in $^6C_3$ ways, i.e. 20 ways, so there are 20 different positions of the Es in *each* of the 60 arrangements of the other letters.

Therefore there are 60×20 permutations of the given letters in which the Es are separated

Note that the arrangements of DFATD and the choices of position for the Es are independent.

---

5. A box of counters for a board game contains three red counters, two black ones, a white one and a green one. In how many ways can three counters be chosen?

There are three mutually exclusive cases here,

    (a) three counters of the same colour

    (b) two of the same colour and one different

    (c) all three of different colours.

For case (a), i.e. all the red counters, there is only 1 choice

For case (b) we can choose *either* two red counters *or* two black counters and for each of these the third counter must be one of the other three colours. So for case (b) there are 2×3, i.e. 6 choices.

In case (c) there are four different colours to choose from so the number of combinations is $^4C_3$, i.e. 4

Hence the total number of ways of choosing three counters is
$$1 + 6 + 4 = 11$$

6. A bookshelf holds six paperbacks and twelve hardbacks. If four books are taken from the shelf, how many combinations contain at least one paperback?

The books chosen could include *either* one paperback *or* two paperbacks *or* three paperbacks *or* four paperbacks. The number of combinations in each of these mutually exclusive cases could be found and then added to give the total required. However, realising that the only combination *not* wanted is one which *does not contain a paperback*, we see that there is a much more direct approach to this problem (and to many others of the 'containing at least ...' type).

The number of ways of choosing *any* four books is $^{18}C_4$ [1]

The number of ways of choosing four hardbacks is $^{12}C_4$ [2]

The only combinations that do not contain a paperback are those in [2] so the number of combinations containing at least one paperback is given by subtracting the number in [2] from the number in [1],

i.e. $^{18}C_4 - {}^{12}C_4 = \dfrac{18!}{4!\,14!} - \dfrac{12!}{4!\,8!} = 2565$

EXERCISE 35e

1. Find how many numbers between 10 and 300 can be made from the digits 1, 2, 3, if
   (a) each digit may be used only once
   (b) each digit may be used more than once?

2. How many combinations of three letters taken from the letters A, A, B, B, C, C, D are there?

3. A mixed team of ten players is chosen from a class of thirty, eighteen of whom are boys and twelve of whom are girls. In how many ways can this be done if the team has five boys and five girls?

4. Find the number of permutations of the letters of the word

   MATHEMATICS

5. Find the number of permutations of four letters from the word

   MATHEMATICS

6. How many of the permutations in Question 5 contain two pairs of letters that are the same?

7. In how many of the permutations in Question 4 do all the consonants come together?

8. A team of two pairs, each consisting of a man and a woman, is chosen to represent a club at a tennis match. If these pairs are chosen from five men and four women, in how many ways can the team be selected?

9. Two sets of books contain five novels and three reference books respectively. In how many ways can the books be arranged on a shelf

   (a) if the novels and reference books are not mixed

   (b) the three reference books are all separated?

10. In a multiple choice test there is one correct answer and four wrong answers to each question. For two such questions, in how many ways is it possible to select the wrong answer to both questions?

11. How many even numbers less than 500 can be made from the integers 1, 2, 3, 4, 5, each integer being used only once?

12. Four boxes each contain a large number of identical balls, those in one box are red, those in a second box are blue, those in a third box are yellow and those in the remaining box are green. In how many ways can five balls be chosen if

   (a) there is no restriction   (b) at least one ball is red?

13. In how many ways can three letters from the word GREEN be arranged in a row if at least one of the letters is E?

MIXED EXERCISE 35

1. Find the number of ways in which a committee of four can be chosen from six men and six women if

   (a) it must contain two men and two women

   (b) it must contain at least one man

   (c) either the youngest man or the youngest woman, but not both, must be included?

2. The home team's results in four hockey matches are to be forecast. Each result can be a win, a draw or a loss. Find the number of different possible forecasts and show how this number is divided into forecasts containing 0, 1, 2, 3 and 4 errors respectively.

3. Find the number of ways in which twelve trees can be planted in a row so that no two of three particular trees are planted next to each other. Give the answer in factorial notation.

4. How many numbers, greater than 6000 and divisible by 3, can be made from the digits 1, 3, 5, 6 and 7 if each digit can be used only once in each number?

5. A badminton club has to select a team of three mixed pairs for a match. If eight men and seven women are eligible for selection, in how many ways can the three pairs be chosen?

6. In how many ways can twelve children be divided into two groups of seven and five respectively? In how many ways can this be done if the two oldest children must be

   (a) in the same group

   (b) not in the same group?

7. Find how many numbers between 20 000 and 50 000 can be made from the digits 1, 2, 3, 4 and 5 if each digit can be used

   (a) only once   (b) more than once in each number.

8. In how many ways can the letters of the word COMMITTEE be arranged?

   In how many of these arrangements are

   (a) the two Es adjacent

   (b) the C and the O adjacent

   (c) all the consonants together?

CHAPTER 36

THE BINOMIAL THEOREM AND OTHER POWER SERIES

POWER SERIES

A series such as $x + x^2 + x^3 + \ldots$ is called a power series because the terms involve powers of a variable quantity. Series, such as those considered in Chapter 34, each of whose terms has a fixed numerical value, are called number series.

THE BINOMIAL THEOREM

We saw in Chapter 1 that when an expression such as $(1 + x)^4$ is expanded, the coefficients of the terms in the expansion can be obtained from Pascal's Triangle. Now $(1 + x)^{20}$ could be expanded in the same way but, as the construction of the triangular array would be tedious we need a more general method to expand powers of $(1 + x)$.

Consider $(1 + x)^6 \equiv (1 + x)(1 + x)(1 + x)(1 + x)(1 + x)(1 + x)$

When the six brackets are expanded, each term is obtained by multiplying together either x or 1 from each of the six brackets and then collecting like terms.

Taking 1 from each bracket we get 1 as a term in the expansion.

Taking x from only one bracket and 1 from the other five, we get $1 \times x$. But this can be done six times because we can choose to take x from each of the six brackets in turn, (i.e. in $^6C_1$ ways). So the x term in the expansion is $6x$

Taking x from any two brackets and 1 from all the remaining brackets we get $1 \times x^2$. But this can be done $^6C_2$ times, as the number of ways in which two brackets can be selected from six brackets is $^6C_2$. So the x^2 term in the expansion is $^6C_2 x^2$

Similarly we see that the coefficients of x^3, x^4 ... are $^6C_3$, $^6C_4$ ...

Thus, arranging the expansion of $(1 + x)^6$ as a series of ascending powers of x,

$$(1 + x)^6 \equiv 1 + {}^6C_1x + {}^6C_2x^2 + {}^6C_3x^3 + {}^6C_4x^4 + {}^6C_5x^5 + {}^6C_6x^6$$

$$= 1 + 6x + 15x^2 + 20x^3 + 15x^4 + 6x^5 + x^6$$

The RHS of this identity is called the *series expansion* of $(1 + x)^6$

Notice that the expansion has 7 terms, i.e. (6 + 1) terms.

This argument can be generalised as follows.

If n is any positive integer, $(1 + x)^n$ can be expanded to give a series of terms in ascending powers of x where the term containing x^r is obtained by multiplying together xs from r brackets and 1s from the remaining brackets. There are ${}^nC_r$ ways in which r brackets can be chosen from n brackets, so the coefficient of x^r is ${}^nC_r$

$$\therefore \quad (1 + x)^n = 1 + {}^nC_1x + {}^nC_2x^2 + \ldots + {}^nC_rx^r + \ldots + {}^nC_nx^n$$

This result is known as the Binomial Theorem.

The coefficients of the powers of x are called binomial coefficients.

Now the binomial coefficient of x^r is ${}^nC_r$

and

$${}^nC_r = \frac{n(n-1)\ldots(n-r+1)}{r!}$$

An alternative notation for the binomial coefficient of x^r is $\binom{n}{r}$

i.e.

$$\binom{n}{r} = \frac{n(n-1)\ldots(n-r+1)}{r!}$$

Hence the binomial theorem states that, if n is a positive integer,

$$(1 + x)^n = 1 + \binom{n}{1}x + \binom{n}{2}x^2 + \ldots + \binom{n}{r}x^r + \ldots + \binom{n}{n}x^n \qquad [1]$$

$$= 1 + nx + \frac{n(n-6)}{2!}x^2 + \ldots + \frac{n(n-1)\ldots(n-r+1)}{r!}x^r + \ldots + x^n \qquad [2]$$

Note that [1] can be written in the form $\sum\limits_{r=0}^{n} \binom{n}{r}x^r$

Notice that

1) the expansion of $(1 + x)^n$ is a finite series with $n + 1$ terms,

2) the coefficient of x^r, i.e. $\dfrac{n(n - 1)(n - 2)\ldots(n - r + 1)}{r!}$,

has r factors in the numerator,

3) the term containing x^2 is the third term, the term in x^3 is the fourth term, and *the term in x^r is the $(r + 1)$th term,*

so the rth term is $\left(\begin{array}{c} n \\ r - 1 \end{array} \right) x^{r-1}$,

4) the form of the expansion given in [1] is useful when the coefficient of a large power of x is required, or when the general term is required. The form of the expansion given in [2] is useful when the first few terms of an expansion are required.

Now consider $(a + x)^n$, where n is a positive integer.

$$(a + x)^n \equiv a^n \left(1 + \frac{x}{a} \right)^n$$

Replacing x by $\dfrac{x}{a}$ in the binomial series gives

$$(a + x)^n = a^n \left[1 + \binom{n}{1}\left(\frac{x}{a}\right) + \binom{n}{2}\left(\frac{x}{a}\right)^2 + \ldots + \binom{n}{r}\left(\frac{x}{a}\right)^r + \ldots + \binom{n}{n}\left(\frac{x}{a}\right)^n \right]$$

$$= a^n + \binom{n}{1}a^{n-1}x + \binom{n}{2}a^{n-2}x^2 + \ldots + \binom{n}{r}a^{n-r}x^r + \ldots + \binom{n}{n}x^n$$

$$= a^n + na^{n-1}x + \frac{n(n-1)}{2!}a^{n-2}x^2 + \ldots + x^n$$

i.e.   if n is a positive integer

$$(a + x)^n = \sum_{r=0}^{n} \binom{n}{r}a^{n-r}x^r$$

Note that this last form need not be memorised.
The expansion of any expression in the form $(a + x)^n$ can be obtained directly from $a^n \left(1 + \dfrac{x}{a} \right)^n$

Examples 36a

1. Write down the first three terms in the expansion in ascending powers of x of

   (a) $\left(1 - \dfrac{x}{2}\right)^{10}$ (b) $(3 - 2x)^8$

(a) Using the result [2] above and replacing x by $-\dfrac{x}{2}$ and n by 10 we have

$$\left(1 - \frac{x}{2}\right)^{10} = 1 + (10)\left(-\frac{x}{2}\right) + \frac{10 \times 9}{2!}\left(-\frac{x}{2}\right)^2 + \ldots$$

$$= 1 - 5x + \tfrac{45}{4}x^2 + \ldots$$

(b) Using the result for $(a + x)^n$ and replacing a by 3, x by $-2x$ and n by 8 gives

$$(3 - 2x)^8 = \sum_{r=0}^{8} \binom{8}{r}(3)^{8-r}(-2x)^r$$

Therefore the first three terms of this series $(r = 0, 1, 2)$ are

$$3^8 + 8 \times (3)^7(-2x) + \frac{8 \times 7}{2}(3)^6(-2x)^2$$

i.e. $3^8 - 16 \times 3^7 x + 112 \times 3^6 x^2$

---

2. Find the fourth term in the expansion of $(a - 2b)^{20}$ as a series in ascending powers of b

$$(a - 2b)^{20} = \sum_{r=0}^{20} \binom{20}{r}(a)^{20-r}(-2b)^r$$

As the first term in the series is the one for which $r = 0$, the fourth term is that for which $r = 3$,

i.e. the fourth term is $\binom{20}{3}(a)^{17}(-2b)^3 = \dfrac{(20)(19)(18)}{3!}(a^{17})(8b^3)$

$$= 9120a^{17}b^3$$

---

3. Write down the first three terms in the binomial expansion of

$$(1 - 2x)(1 + \tfrac{1}{2}x)^{10}$$

The third term in the binomial expansion is the term containing x^2, so start by expanding $(1 + \tfrac{1}{2}x)^{10}$ as far as the term in x^2

$$(1 + \tfrac{1}{2}x)^{10} = 1 + (10)(\tfrac{1}{2}x) + \frac{(10)(9)}{2!}(\tfrac{1}{2}x)^2 + \ldots$$

$$= 1 + 5x + \tfrac{45}{4}x^2 + \ldots$$

$$\therefore \quad (1 - 2x)(1 + \tfrac{1}{2}x)^{10} = (1 - 2x)(1 + 5x + \tfrac{45}{4}x^2 + \ldots)$$

$$= 1 + 5x + \tfrac{45}{4}x^2 + \ldots - 2x - 10x^2 + \ldots$$

$$= 1 + 3x + \tfrac{5}{4}x^2 + \ldots$$

Notice that we do not write down the product of $-2x$ and $\tfrac{45}{4}x^2$, as terms in x^3 are not required.

EXERCISE 36a

1. Write down the first four terms in the binomial expansion of:

   (a) $(1 + 3x)^{12}$ (b) $(1 - 2x)^9$ (c) $(2 + x)^{10}$

   (d) $\left(1 - \dfrac{x}{3}\right)^{20}$ (e) $\left(2 - \dfrac{3}{2}x\right)^7$ (f) $\left(\dfrac{3}{2} + 2x\right)^9$

2. Write down the term indicated in the binomial expansion of each of the following functions.

   (a) $(1 - 4x)^7$, 3rd term   (b) $\left(1 - \dfrac{x}{2}\right)^{20}$, 2nd term

   (c) $(2 - x)^{15}$, 12th term   (d) $(p - 2q)^{10}$, 5th term

   (e) $(3a + 2b)^8$, 2nd term   (f) $(1 - 2x)^{12}$, the term in x^4

   (g) $\left(2 + \dfrac{x}{2}\right)^9$, the term in x^5 (h) $(a + b)^8$, the term in a^3

3. Write down the binomial expansion of each function as a series of ascending powers of x as far as, and including, the term in x^2.

   (a) $(1 + x)(1 - x)^9$ (b) $(1 - x)(1 + 2x)^{10}$

   (c) $(2 + x)\left(1 - \dfrac{x}{2}\right)^{20}$ (d) $(1 + x)^2(1 - 5x)^{14}$

USING SERIES TO FIND APPROXIMATIONS

Consider $(1 + x)^{20}$ and its binomial expansion,

$$(1 + x)^{20} = 1 + 20x + \frac{(20)(19)}{2!}x^2 + \frac{(20)(19)(18)}{3!}x^3 + \ldots + x^{20}$$

This is valid for all values of x so if, for example, $x = 0.01$ we have

$$(1.01)^{20} = 1 + 20(0.01) + \frac{(20)(19)}{2!}(0.01)^2 + \frac{(20)(19)(18)}{3!}(0.01)^3 + \ldots + (0.01)^{20}$$

i.e. $(1.01)^{20} = 1 + 0.2 + 0.019 + 0.001\ 14 + 0.000\ 048\ 45 + \ldots + 10^{-40}$

Because the value of x (i.e. 0.01) is small, we see that adding successive terms of the series makes progressively smaller contributions to the accuracy of $(1.01)^{20}$.
In fact, taking only the first four terms gives $(1.01)^{20} \approx 1.22014$

This approximation is correct to three decimal places as the fifth and succeeding terms do not add anything to the first four decimal places.

In general, if x is small so that successive powers of x quickly become negligible in value, then the sum of the first few terms in the expansion of $(1 + x)^n$ gives an approximate value for $(1 + x)^n$

The number of terms required to obtain a good approximation depends on two considerations

1) the value of x (the smaller x is, the fewer are the terms needed to obtain a good approximation).

2) the accuracy required (an answer correct to 3 s.f. needs fewer terms than an answer correct to 6 s.f.)

When finding an approximation, the binomial expansion of $(1 + x)^n$ and *not* $(a + x)^n$ should be used, e.g. to find the approximate value of $(3.006)^5$ we use $3^5(1 + 0.002)^5$

Examples 36b

1. By substituting 0.001 for x in the expansion of $(1 - x)^7$ find the value of $(1.998)^7$ correct to five significant figures.

Now $(1.998)^7 = (2 - 0.002)^7 = 2^7(1 - 0.001)^7$

$\qquad\qquad\qquad\qquad\qquad = 2^7(1 - x)^7$ when $x = 0.001$

Hence

$$(1.998)^7 = 2^7 \left[1 - 7(0.001) + \frac{(7)(6)}{2!}(0.001)^2 - \frac{(7)(6)(5)}{3!}(0.001)^3 + \ldots \right]$$

To give an answer correct to 5 s.f. we will work to 7 s.f. so only the first three terms need be considered.

$$\therefore \qquad (1.998)^7 = 128(1 - 0.007 + 0.000\ 021\ 0) \quad \text{to } 7 \text{ s.f.}$$

$$= 127.11 \quad \text{correct to } 5 \text{ s.f.}$$

In the example above, a calculator will give the value of $(1.998)^7$ to about 8 s.f. (depending on the particular calculator). If, however, the value is required to, say, 15 s.f., the method used in the worked example will give the extra accuracy.

The next worked example illustrates how a series expansion enables us to find a simple function which can be used as an approximation to a given function when x has values that are close to zero.

---

2. If x is so small that x^2 and higher powers can be neglected show that

$$(1 - x)^5 \left(2 + \frac{x}{2} \right)^{10} \approx 2^9(2 - 5x)$$

Using the binomial expansion of $(1 - x)^5$ and neglecting terms containing x^2 and higher powers of x we have

$$(1 - x)^5 \approx 1 - 5x$$

Similarly

$$\left(2 + \frac{x}{2} \right)^{10} \equiv 2^{10} \left(1 + \frac{x}{4} \right)^{10}$$

$$\approx 2^{10} \left[1 + 10 \left(\frac{x}{4} \right) \right]$$

Therefore

$$(1 - x)^5 \left(2 + \frac{x}{2} \right)^{10} \approx 2^{10}(1 - 5x) \left(1 + \frac{5x}{2} \right)$$

$$= 2^9(1 - 5x)(2 + 5x)$$

$$\approx 2^9(2 - 5x)$$

again neglecting the term in x^2

The graphical significance of the approximation in the last example is interesting.

If
$$y = (1 - x)^5\left(2 + \frac{x}{2}\right)^{10}$$

then, for values of x close to zero, $y \approx 2^9(2 - 5x)$ which is the equation of a straight line,

i.e. $y = 2^9(2 - 5x)$ is the tangent to $y = (1 - x)^5\left(2 + \frac{x}{2}\right)^{10}$ at the point where $x = 0$

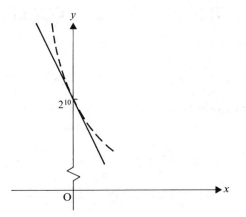

Note that the function $2^9(2 - 5x)$ is called a *linear approximation* for the function $(1 - x)^5\left(2 + \frac{x}{2}\right)^{10}$ in the region where $x \approx 0$

EXERCISE 36b

1. By substituting 0.01 for x in the binomial expansion of $(1 - 2x)^{10}$, find the value of $(0.98)^{10}$ correct to four decimal places.

2. By substituting 0.05 for x in the binomial expansion of $\left(1 + \frac{x}{5}\right)^6$, find the value of $(1.01)^6$ correct to four significant figures.

3. By using the binomial expansion of $(2 + x)^7$, show that, correct to 3 d.p., $(2.08)^7 = 168.439$

4. Show that, if x is small enough for x^2 and higher powers of x to be neglected, the function $(x - 2)(1 + 3x)^8$ has a linear approximation of $-2 - 47x$

5. If x is so small that x^3 and higher powers of x are negligible, show that $(2x + 3)(1 - 2x)^{10} \approx 3 - 58x + 500x^2$

6. By neglecting x^2 and higher powers of x find linear approximations for the following functions in the immediate neighbourhood of $x = 0$

(a) $(1 - 5x)^{10}$ (b) $(2 - x)^8$ (c) $(1 + x)(1 - x)^{20}$

EXTENDING THE BINOMIAL THEOREM

We have shown that, when n is a positive integer,

$$(1 + x)^n = 1 + nx + \binom{n}{2}x^2 + \ldots + x^n$$

Although it cannot be proved at this stage, a very similar expansion of $(1 + x)^n$ exists for *any* real value of n, i.e.

$$(1 + x)^n \equiv 1 + nx + \binom{n}{2}x^2 + \binom{n}{3}x^3 + \ldots \quad \text{for any real value of } n$$

$$\text{provided that } -1 < x < 1$$

Notice that when n is not a positive integer, the binomial expansion of $(1 + x)^n$ does not terminate but carries on to infinity.

Notice also that the expansion is valid only if x is in the range $-1 < x < 1$ and this *range must always be stated*.

Finally it should be noted that the expansion is *not* valid for $(a + x)^n$.

To expand $(a + x)^n$ it must first be written in the form $a^n\left(1 + \dfrac{x}{a}\right)^n$

and this expansion is valid only for $-1 < \dfrac{x}{a} < 1$

Although we cannot prove the binomial expansion of $(1 + x)^n$, it can be verified when $n = -1$, as follows.

Consider the series $1 - x + x^2 - x^3 + x^4 - \ldots$

This is an infinite GP whose common ratio is $-x$
Therefore, provided that $|x| < 1$, the series converges

and the sum to infinity is $\dfrac{1}{1 - (-x)} = (1 + x)^{-1}$

Now consider the binomial expansion of $(1 + x)^{-1}$

$$(1+x)^{-1} = 1 + (-1)(x) + \frac{(-1)(-2)}{2!}x^2 + \frac{(-1)(-2)(-3)}{3!}x^3 + \frac{(-1)(-2)(-3)(-4)}{4!}x^4 + \ldots$$

$$= 1 - x + x^2 - x^3 + x^4 - \ldots$$

and we have shown that the sum to infinity of this series is $(1 + x)^{-1}$

This series occurs frequently and is worth memorising. So also is the series obtained by replacing x by $-x$, i.e.

$$(1 - x)^{-1} = 1 + x + x^2 + x^3 + \ldots$$

Examples 36c

1. Expand each of the following functions as a series of ascending powers of x up to and including the term in x^3 stating the set of values of x for which each expansion is valid.

   (a) $(1 + x)^{1/2}$ (b) $(1 - 2x)^{-3}$ (c) $(2 - x)^{-2}$

For $|x| < 1$

$$(1 + x)^n = 1 + nx + \frac{n(n-1)}{2!}x^2 + \frac{n(n-1)(n-2)}{3!}x^3 + \ldots \qquad [1]$$

(a) Replacing n by $\frac{1}{2}$ in [1] gives

$$(1 + x)^{1/2} = 1 + \tfrac{1}{2}x + \frac{\frac{1}{2}(\frac{1}{2} - 1)}{2!}x^2 + \frac{\frac{1}{2}(\frac{1}{2} - 1)(\frac{1}{2} - 2)}{3!}x^3 + \ldots$$

$$= 1 + \tfrac{1}{2}x + \frac{\frac{1}{2}(-\frac{1}{2})}{2!}x^2 + \frac{\frac{1}{2}(-\frac{1}{2})(-\frac{3}{2})}{3!}x^3 + \ldots$$

$$= 1 + \frac{x}{2} - \frac{x^2}{8} + \frac{x^3}{16} - \ldots \quad \text{for } |x| < 1$$

(b) Replacing n by -3 and x by $-2x$ in [1] gives

$$(1 - 2x)^{-3} = 1 + (-3)(-2x) + \frac{(-3)(-4)}{2!}(-2x)^2 + \frac{(-3)(-4)(-5)}{3!}(-2x)^3 + \ldots$$

$$= 1 + 6x + 24x^2 + 80x^3 + \ldots$$

provided that $-1 < -2x < 1$, i.e. $\frac{1}{2} > x > -\frac{1}{2}$

(c) $(2 - x)^{-2} = 2^{-2}(1 - \frac{1}{2}x)^{-2}$

Replacing n by -2 and x by $-\frac{1}{2}x$ in [1] gives

$$(2 - x)^{-2} = \frac{1}{4}\left[1 + (-2)(-\frac{1}{2}x) + \frac{(-2)(-3)}{2!}(-\frac{1}{2}x)^2 + \frac{(-2)(-3)(-4)}{3!}(-\frac{1}{2}x)^3 + \ldots\right]$$

$$= \frac{1}{4}(1 + x + \frac{3}{4}x^2 + \frac{1}{2}x^3 + \ldots)$$

$$= \frac{1}{4} + \frac{1}{4}x + \frac{3}{16}x^2 + \frac{1}{8}x^3 + \ldots$$

The expansion of $(1 - \frac{1}{2}x)^{-2}$ is valid for $-1 < -\frac{1}{2}x < 1$, i.e. for $2 > x > -2$

Therefore the expansion of $(2 - x)^{-2}$ also is valid for $2 > x > -2$

---

2. Expand $\dfrac{5}{(1 + 3x)(1 - 2x)}$ as a series of ascending powers of x giving the first four terms and the range of values of x for which the expansion is valid.

Expressing $\dfrac{5}{(1 + 3x)(1 - 2x)}$ in partial fractions gives

$$\frac{5}{(1 + 3x)(1 - 2x)} = \frac{3}{(1 + 3x)} + \frac{2}{(1 - 2x)} = 3(1 + 3x)^{-1} + 2(1 - 2x)^{-1}$$

Now $(1 + x)^{-1} = 1 - x + x^2 - x^3 + \ldots$ for $-1 < x < 1$

Replacing x by $3x$ gives

$$(1 + 3x)^{-1} = 1 - 3x + (3x)^2 - (3x)^3 + \ldots$$

$$= 1 - 3x + 9x^2 - 27x^3 + \ldots \quad \text{for } -1 < 3x < 1$$

Also $(1 - x)^{-1} = 1 + x + x^2 + \ldots$ and replacing x by $2x$ gives

$$(1 - 2x)^{-1} = 1 + (2x) + (2x)^2 + (2x)^3 + \ldots$$

$$= 1 + 2x + 4x^2 + 8x^3 + \ldots \quad \text{for } -1 < -2x < 1$$

Hence $\dfrac{5}{(1 + 3x)(1 - 2x)} = 3(1 + 3x)^{-1} + 2(1 - 2x)^{-1}$

$$= (3 + 2) + (-9 + 4)x + (27 + 8)x^2 + (-81 + 16)x^3 + \ldots$$

provided that $-\frac{1}{3} < x < \frac{1}{3}$ and $-\frac{1}{2} < x < \frac{1}{2}$

Therefore the first four terms of the series are $5 - 5x + 35x^2 - 65x^3$

The expansion is valid for the range of values of x satisfying both $-\frac{1}{3} < x < \frac{1}{3}$ and $-\frac{1}{2} < x < \frac{1}{2}$

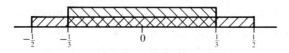

i.e. for $-\frac{1}{3} < x < \frac{1}{3}$

_____

3. Expand $\sqrt{\left(\dfrac{1+x}{1-2x}\right)}$ as a series of ascending powers of x up to and including the term containing x^2

$$\sqrt{\left(\frac{1+x}{1-2x}\right)} \equiv (1+x)^{1/2}(1-2x)^{-1/2}$$

Now $\quad (1+x)^{1/2} = \left[1 + \tfrac{1}{2}x + \dfrac{(\tfrac{1}{2})(-\tfrac{1}{2})}{2!}x^2 + \ldots\right] \quad$ for $-1 < x < 1$

and $\quad (1-2x)^{-1/2} = \left[1 + (-\tfrac{1}{2})(-2x) + \dfrac{(-\tfrac{1}{2})(-\tfrac{3}{2})}{2!}(-2x)^2 + \ldots\right]$

$\qquad\qquad\qquad\qquad\qquad\qquad\qquad$ for $-1 < 2x < 1$

Hence $\quad \sqrt{\left(\dfrac{1+x}{1-2x}\right)} \equiv (1+x)^{1/2}(1-2x)^{-1/2}$

$$= (1 + \tfrac{1}{2}x - \tfrac{1}{8}x^2 + \ldots)(1 + x + \tfrac{3}{2}x^2 + \ldots)$$

$$= 1 + (\tfrac{1}{2}x + x) + (\tfrac{1}{2}x^2 - \tfrac{1}{8}x^2 + \tfrac{3}{2}x^2) + \ldots$$

$$= 1 + \tfrac{3}{2}x + \tfrac{15}{8}x^2 + \ldots$$

provided that $-1 < x < 1$ and $-\frac{1}{2} < x < \frac{1}{2}$,

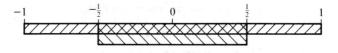

i.e. $-\frac{1}{2} < x < \frac{1}{2}$

_____

It is interesting to compare the methods used in the last two examples.

In Example 2, the function is expressed as the sum of two binomials and the series is obtained by adding two binomial expansions.

In Example 3 the function is expressed as a product of two binomials and the series is obtained by multiplying two binomial expansions.

The first method has the advantage that it is very much easier to add the terms of two series than it is to multiply them.

Therefore, *whenever possible, a compound function should be expressed as a sum of simpler functions before it is expanded as a series* and, when this is not possible, a compound function should be expressed as a product of simpler functions.

Further Approximations

17

We have seen how a series can be used to find an approximate value of a rational number without having to calculate its exact value. The next example illustrates how a series can be used to find the decimal value, to any required degree of accuracy, of an irrational quantity.

---

4. Use the expansion of $(1 - x)^{1/2}$ with $x = 0.02$ to find the decimal value of $\sqrt{2}$ correct to nine decimal places.

$$(1 - x)^{1/2} = 1 - \tfrac{1}{2}x + \frac{(\tfrac{1}{2})(-\tfrac{1}{2})}{2!}(-x)^2 + \frac{(\tfrac{1}{2})(-\tfrac{1}{2})(-\tfrac{3}{2})}{3!}(-x)^3$$

$$+ \frac{(\tfrac{1}{2})(-\tfrac{1}{2})(-\tfrac{3}{2})(-\tfrac{5}{2})}{4!}(-x)^4 + \ldots$$

$$= 1 - \tfrac{1}{2}x - \tfrac{1}{8}x^2 - \tfrac{1}{16}x^3 - \tfrac{5}{128}x^4 - \tfrac{7}{256}x^5 - \ldots$$

This is valid for $-1 < 1$ and so is valid when $x = 0.02$
Replacing x by 0.02 gives

$(0.98)^{1/2} = 1 - 0.01 - 0.000\,05 - 0.000\,000\,5 - 0.000\,000\,006\,25 - 0.000\,000\,000\,087\,5 - \ldots$

The next term in the series is 1.3125×10^{-12} and as this does not contribute to the first ten decimal places we do not need it, or any further terms.

i.e. $\sqrt{\tfrac{98}{100}} = 0.989\,949\,493\,7$ to 10 d.p.

$\Rightarrow$ $\tfrac{7}{10}\sqrt{2} = 0.989\,949\,493\,7$ to 10 d.p.

$\therefore$ $\sqrt{2} = 1.414\,213\,562$ correct to 9 d.p.

EXERCISE 36c

Expand the following functions as series of ascending powers of x up to and including the term in x^3. In each case give the range of values of x for which the expansion is valid.

1. $(1 - 2x)^{1/2}$ **2.** $(3 + x)^{-1}$ **3.** $\left(1 + \dfrac{x}{2}\right)^{-1/2}$

4. $\dfrac{1}{(1 - x)^2}$ **5.** $\sqrt{\left(\dfrac{1}{1 + x}\right)}$ **6.** $(1 + x)\sqrt{(1 - x)}$

7. $\dfrac{x + 2}{x - 1}$ **8.** $\dfrac{2 - x}{\sqrt{(1 - 3x)}}$ **9.** $\dfrac{1}{(2 - x)(1 + 2x)}$

10. $\sqrt{\left(\dfrac{1 + x}{1 - x}\right)}$ **11.** $\left(1 + \dfrac{x^2}{9}\right)^{-1}$

12. $\left(1 + \dfrac{1}{x}\right)^{-1}$ $\left[\text{Hint. } \left(1 + \dfrac{1}{x}\right)^{-1} \equiv \left(\dfrac{x + 1}{x}\right)^{-1} \equiv \dfrac{x}{1 + x}\right]$

13. Expand $\left(1 + \dfrac{1}{p}\right)^{-3}$ as a series of descending powers of p, as far as and including the term containing p^{-4}. State the range of values of p for which the expansion is valid.
(*Hint.* Replace x by $\frac{1}{p}$ in $(1 + x)^{-3}$)

14. By substituting 0.08 for x in $(1 + x)^{1/2}$ and its expansion find $\sqrt{3}$ correct to four significant figures.

15. By substituting $\frac{1}{10}$ for x in $(1 - x)^{-1/2}$ and its expansion find $\sqrt{10}$ correct to six significant figures.

16. Expand $\sqrt{\left(\dfrac{1 + 2x}{1 - 2x}\right)}$ as a series of ascending powers of x up to and including the term in x^2

17. If x is so small that x^2 and higher powers of x may be neglected show that $\dfrac{1}{(x - 1)(x + 2)} \approx -\frac{1}{2} - \frac{1}{4}x$

18. By neglecting x^3 and higher powers of x, find a quadratic function that approximates to the function $\dfrac{1 - 2x}{\sqrt{(1 + 2x)}}$ in the region close to $x = 0$

19. Find a quadratic function that approximates to

$$f(x) = \frac{1}{\sqrt[3]{(1 - 3x)^2}}$$

for values of x close to zero.

20. Use partial fractions and the binomial series to find a linear approximation for

$$\frac{3}{(1 - 2x)(2 - x)}$$

21. If terms containing x^4 and higher powers of x can be neglected, show that

$$\frac{2}{(x + 1)(x^2 + 1)} \approx 2(1 - x)$$

22. Show that

$$\frac{12}{(3 + x)(1 - x)^2} \approx 4 + \tfrac{20}{3}x + \tfrac{88}{9}x^2$$

provided that x is small enough to neglect powers higher than 2

23. If x is very small, find a cubic approximation for

$$\frac{1}{(3 - x)^3}$$

SERIES EXPANSIONS OF EXPONENTIAL FUNCTIONS

We have shown that functions such as $(1 + x)^n$ can be expressed as infinite series of ascending powers of x and there are many other functions that can be expressed as power series.

In this section we give, without proof, the series expansion of e^x

$$e^x = 1 + x + \frac{x^2}{2!} + \frac{x^3}{3!} + \frac{x^4}{4!} + \ldots + \frac{x^r}{r!} + \ldots \quad \text{for } all \text{ real values of } x$$

Note that this series is infinite and valid for any value of x

The following worked examples show how the series for e^x can be used to find the series expansion of compound exponential functions. The principles governing the expansion of compound binomial functions apply to any series expansion, i.e. whenever possible a compound function should be expressed as a *sum* of simpler functions and, when this is not possible, it should be expressed as a product of simpler functions.

Examples 36d _____

1. Expand each of the following functions as a series of ascending ,
   powers of x up to and including the term in x^3

   (a) e^{3x} (b) $\dfrac{e^x - 1}{e^x}$ (c) e^{x-2} (d) $(1 + x)e^x$

(a) Replacing x by $3x$ in the expansion of e^x gives

$$e^{3x} = 1 + (3x) + \frac{(3x)^2}{2!} + \frac{(3x)^3}{3!} + \dots$$

$$= 1 + 3x + \tfrac{9}{2}x^2 + \tfrac{9}{2}x^3 + \dots$$

(b) $\dfrac{e^x - 1}{e^x} = \dfrac{e^x}{e^x} - \dfrac{1}{e^x} = 1 - e^{-x}$

Replacing x by $-x$ in the series for e^x gives

$$\frac{e^x - 1}{e^x} = 1 - \left(1 - x + \frac{1}{2!}x^2 - \frac{1}{3!}x^3 + \dots\right)$$

$$= x - \tfrac{1}{2}x^2 + \tfrac{1}{6}x^3 - \dots$$

(c) $e^{x-2} = \dfrac{e^x}{e^2} = e^{-2}e^x = e^{-2}\left(1 + x + \dfrac{1}{2!}x^2 + \dfrac{1}{3!}x^3 + \dots\right)$

$$= e^{-2} + e^{-2}x + \tfrac{1}{2}e^{-2}x^2 + \tfrac{1}{6}e^{-2}x^3 + \dots$$

(d) $(1 + x)e^x = e^x + xe^x$

$$= 1 + x + \frac{x^2}{2!} + \frac{x^3}{3!} + \dots$$

$$+ \qquad x + x^2 + \frac{x^3}{2!} + \dots$$

$$= 1 + 2x + \tfrac{3}{2}x^2 + \tfrac{2}{3}x^3 + \dots$$

_____

2. Show that, if x is small enough for x^2 and higher powers of x to be ignored, $e^x + e^{2x} \approx 2 + 3x$

$$e^x + e^{2x} = \left[1 + x + \frac{x^2}{2!} + \ldots \right] + \left[1 + 2x + \frac{(2x)^2}{2!} + \ldots \right]$$

$$= 2 + 3x + \ldots$$

$$\approx 2 + 3x \quad \text{when } x \text{ is small.}$$

Note that $2 + 3x$ is a linear approximation to $e^x + e^{2x}$ and further, the line $y = 2 + 3x$ is the tangent to the curve $y = e^x + e^{2x}$ at the point where $x = 0$

EXERCISE 36d

Find the first three terms of the series expansion of each of the following functions.

1. e^{2x} **2.** e^{-2x} **3.** $e^{x/2}$ **4.** $\sqrt{(e^{3x})}$

5. $\dfrac{e^x - e^{2x}}{e^x}$ **6.** $\dfrac{1 - e^{2x}}{1 - e^x}$ **7.** $\dfrac{x - e^x}{e^x}$ **8.** $\dfrac{e^x}{1 + x}$

9. Using the series expansion of e^x with $x = \frac{1}{2}$, find the value of $\sqrt{e}$ correct to five decimal places.

SERIES EXPANSIONS OF LOGARITHMIC FUNCTIONS

The function given by $\ln(1 + x)$ can be expanded as a series of ascending powers of x, and again we quote this expansion without proof.

$$\ln(1 + x) = x - \frac{x^2}{2} + \frac{x^3}{3} - \frac{x^4}{4} + \ldots \qquad \text{provided that } -1 < x \leqslant 1$$

Replacing x by $-x$ gives

$$\ln(1 - x) = -x - \frac{x^2}{2} - \frac{x^3}{3} - \frac{x^4}{4} - \ldots \qquad \text{provided that } -1 \leqslant x < 1$$

Notice that both series are infinite and that they are valid for different ranges of values of x

Example 36e

Find the first four terms in the expansion of $\ln \dfrac{1-2x}{(1+2x)^2}$ as a series of ascending powers of x

$$\ln \frac{1-2x}{(1+2x)^2} = \ln(1-2x) - \ln(1+2x)^2 = \ln(1-2x) - 2\ln(1+2x)$$

Using the expansion of $\ln(1-x)$ and replacing x by $2x$ gives

$$\ln(1-2x) = -(2x) - \frac{(2x)^2}{2} - \frac{(2x)^3}{3} - \frac{(2x)^4}{4} - \ldots$$

$$\text{for} \quad -1 \leqslant 2x < 1$$

Similarly

$$\ln(1+2x) = (2x) - \frac{(2x)^2}{2} + \frac{(2x)^3}{3} - \frac{(2x)^4}{4} + \ldots$$

$$\text{for} \quad -1 < 2x \leqslant 1$$

Hence

$$\ln \frac{1-2x}{(1+2x)^2} = \left[-(2x) - \frac{(2x)^2}{2} - \frac{(2x)^3}{3} - \frac{(2x)^4}{4} - \ldots \right]$$

$$- 2\left[(2x) - \frac{(2x)^2}{2} + \frac{(2x)^3}{3} - \frac{(2x)^4}{4} + \ldots \right]$$

$$= -6x + 2x^2 - 8x^3 + 4x^4 + \ldots$$

provided that $-\frac{1}{2} < x \leqslant \frac{1}{2}$ and $-\frac{1}{2} \leqslant x < \frac{1}{2}$

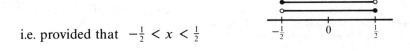

i.e. provided that $-\frac{1}{2} < x < \frac{1}{2}$

EXERCISE 36e

For each function find the first three terms in the expansion as a series of ascending powers of x, stating the range of values of x for which it is valid.

1. $\ln(1+3x)$ 2. $\ln(1+x)^2$ 3. $\ln(1-\frac{1}{2}x)$

4. $\ln(1-x^2)$ 5. $\ln\sqrt{(1-2x)}$ 6. $x\ln(1+x)$

7. $(1+x)\ln(1+x)$ 8. $\ln\sqrt{\left(\dfrac{1-x}{1+x}\right)}$ 9. $\ln(1+x)e^x$

MIXED EXERCISE 36

1. Find the first three terms and the last term in the expansion of $(1 + 2x)^9$ as a series of ascending powers of x. For what values of x is this expansion valid?

2. Expand $\dfrac{1}{1 + 2x}$ as a series of ascending powers of x, giving the first three terms and the range of values of x for which the expansion is valid.

3. Find the first three terms in the expansion of $\dfrac{x}{1 - x}$ as a series of ascending powers of x giving the range of values of x for which the expansion is valid.

4. Express $f(x) = \dfrac{1 + x}{1 - 2x}$ as a series of ascending powers of x, as far as the term in x^2, giving the values of x for which the series converges to $f(x)$.

5. Express $f(x) = \dfrac{1}{(1 + x)(1 - 2x)}$ in partial fractions. Hence find a quadratic function which is approximately equal to $f(x)$ when x is small enough for powers of x greater than x^2 to be ignored.

6. Find the coefficient of x^2 when $\left(\dfrac{1 + x}{1 - x}\right)^2$ is expanded as a series of ascending powers of x

7. Show that $\dfrac{e^{2x} - 1}{e^x} \approx 2x$ if x is small enough for x^2 and higher powers of x to be ignored.

8. Find the first two terms in the expansion of $e^x + \ln(1 - x)$ as a series of ascending powers of x

9. Show that $2^x = e^{x \ln 2}$. Hence find the first three terms in the expansion of 2^x as a series of ascending powers of x. Use your series with $x = \frac{1}{3}$ to find an approximate value for $\sqrt[3]{2}$

10. (a) Expand $\dfrac{1}{\sqrt{(1 - 3x)}}$ as a series of ascending powers of x, giving the first three terms and the range of values of x for which the series converges.

    (b) Use the expansion in (a) to find an approximate value for $\sqrt{2}$

11. When $\dfrac{1}{(1-ax)^2} - \dfrac{1}{\sqrt{(1-4x)}}$ is expanded as a series of ascending powers of x, the first term is $-3x^2$

(a) Find the value of a

(b) Find the second term of the series.

CHAPTER 37

CURVE SKETCHING

In this chapter we start by looking at some methods for sketching curves without recourse to a graphics calculator.

TRANSFORMATIONS

The graphs of many functions can be obtained from transformations of the curves representing basic functions. These transformations are introduced in Chapters 12 and 16. We revise them briefly here.

$y = f(x) + c$ is a translation of $y = f(x)$
by c units in the direction Oy

$y = f(x + c)$ is a translation of $y = f(x)$
by $-c$ units in the direction Ox

$y = -f(x)$ is the reflection of $y = f(x)$
in the x-axis.

$y = f(-x)$ is the reflection of $y = f(x)$
in the y-axis.

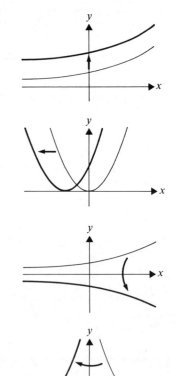

$y = af(x)$ is a one-way stretch of
$y = f(x)$ by a factor a parallel to the
y-axis.

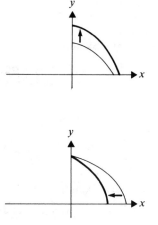

$y = f(ax)$ is a one-way stretch of
$y = f(x)$ by a factor $\frac{1}{a}$ parallel to the
x-axis.

Now consider the curve $y = \dfrac{x}{x+1}$

It looks as if $\dfrac{x}{x+1}$ is related to $f(x) = \dfrac{1}{x}$ and we see that we can

write $y = \dfrac{x}{x+1} = 1 - \dfrac{1}{x+1}$, i.e. $y = 1 - f(x+1)$

We can now build up a picture of the curve $y = \dfrac{x}{x+1}$ in stages,
with rough sketches.

1) Sketch $f(x) = \dfrac{1}{x}$

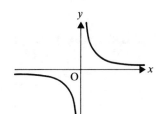

2) Sketch $g(x) = \dfrac{1}{x+1} = f(x+1)$
($f(x)$ moved one unit to the left.)

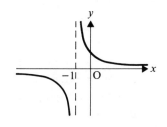

3) Sketch $h(x) = -\dfrac{1}{x+1} = -g(x)$

($g(x)$ reflected in the x-axis.)

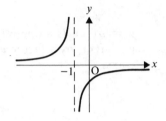

4) Sketch $y = 1 - \dfrac{1}{x+1} = 1 + h(x)$

($h(x)$ moved up one unit.)

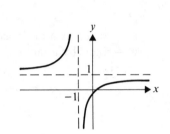

From the last sketch, we see that the asymptotes to the curve are $y = 1$ and $x = -1$

From the equation of the curve, $y = 0$ when $x = 0$, so the curve goes through the origin and there are no other intercepts on the axes. We can now draw a more accurate sketch.

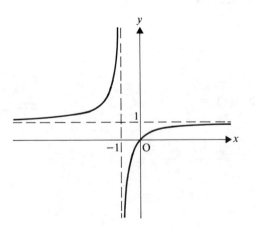

In general, a sketch graph should clearly show the following features of a curve: asymptotes, intercepts on the axes and turning points when they exist.

EXERCISE 37a

1. Find the values of a and b such that $x^2 - 4x + 1 \equiv (x - a)^2 + b$. On the same set of axes sketch the curves $y = x^2$ and $y = x^2 - 4x + 1$

2. For $-2\pi < x < 2\pi$ and on the same set of axes sketch the graphs of
   (a) $y = \cos x$ and $y = 3\cos x$
   (b) $y = \sin x$ and $y = \sin 2x$
   (c) $y = \cos x$ and $y = \cos(x - \frac{1}{6}\pi)$
   (d) $y = \sin x$ and $y = 2\sin(\frac{1}{6}\pi - x)$

3. On the same set of axes sketch the graphs of $y = 1/x$, $y = 3/x$ and $y = 1/3x$

4. Show that $\dfrac{x - 2}{x - 3} \equiv 1 + \dfrac{1}{x - 3}$. Sketch the curve $y = \dfrac{x - 2}{x - 3}$ clearly showing the asymptotes and the intercepts on the axes.

Sketch the following curves clearly showing any asymptotes, turning points and intercepts on the axes.

5. $y = \dfrac{1}{x - 1}$

6. $y = 1 - 2\sin x$

7. $y = 1 - (x - 2)^2$

8. $y = \dfrac{1}{1 - x}$

9. $y = \dfrac{1 - x}{x}$

10. $y = 1 - x^3$

11. $y = \dfrac{2x + 1}{x}$

12. $y = \dfrac{x + 1}{x - 1}$

13. $y = 3 - (x - 2)^2$

14. $y = 2\sin(x - \frac{1}{3}\pi)$

15. $y = 3\cos(x + \frac{1}{6}\pi)$

16. $y = \dfrac{1 + 2x}{1 - x}$

17. $y = 3x^3 - 4$ **18.** $y = 3 - 2x^4$

19. $y = 3 - (x + 2)^3$ **20.** $y = (x - 1)^4$

RECIPROCAL CURVES

Consider the curve $y = \dfrac{1}{f(x)}$ when the graph of f(x) is known.

The following simple properties of reciprocals enable the graph of $1/f(x)$ to be deduced from the graph of f(x).

1) For a given value of x, f(x) and $1/f(x)$ both have the same sign.

2) When the value of f(x) is increasing the value of $1/f(x)$ is decreasing, i.e. when $\dfrac{d}{dx} f(x)$ is positive, $\dfrac{d}{dx}\left(\dfrac{1}{f(x)}\right)$ is negative and conversely.

3) If f(x) = 1 then $\dfrac{1}{f(x)} = 1$ also.

Similarly when f(x) = −1, $\dfrac{1}{f(x)} = -1$

4) If f(x) → ∞ then $\dfrac{1}{f(x)} \to 0$ from above,

and if f(x) → −∞ then $\dfrac{1}{f(x)} \to 0$ from below.

5) If f(x) → 0 from above then $\dfrac{1}{f(x)} \to \infty$,

and if f(x) → 0 from below then $\dfrac{1}{f(x)} \to -\infty$

6) If f(x) has a maximum value then $\dfrac{1}{f(x)}$ has a minimum value, and conversely.

Examples 37b _____

1. Use the curve $y = x^2$ to sketch the curve whose equation is $y = 1/x^2$

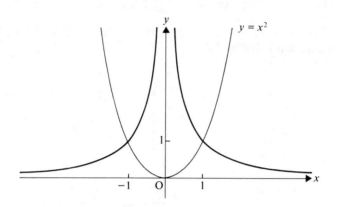

From the sketch of $y = x^2$ we see that

(a) $x^2 > 0$ for all values of x, so $1/x^2 > 0$ for all values of x;

(b) when $x > 0$, x^2 is increasing so $1/x^2$ is decreasing, and when $x < 0$, x^2 is decreasing so $1/x^2$ is increasing;

(c) when $x \to \pm\infty$, $x^2 \to \infty$ so $1/x^2 \to 0$
and when $x \to 0$, $x^2 \to 0$ so $1/x^2 \to \infty$

Notice that when $x = 0$, $1/x^2$ is undefined so the fact that $f(x) = x^2$ has a minimum value when $x = 0$ has no relevance in this case.

From this information the graph of $y = 1/x^2$ can be drawn.

_____

2. Sketch the curve $y = \dfrac{1}{x^2 + 2}$

Sketching the graph of $f(x) = x^2 + 2$ and then making the following observations enables the curve $y = \dfrac{1}{f(x)}$ to be drawn.

(a) $f(x) > 0$ for all values of x, therefore so is $1/f(x)$;

(b) for $x < 0$, $f'(x)$ is negative so the gradient of $1/f(x)$ is positive;
   for $x > 0$, $f'(x)$ is positive so the gradient of $1/f(x)$ is negative;

(c) when $x \rightarrow \pm\infty$, $f(x) \rightarrow \infty$ so $1/f(x) \rightarrow 0$;

(d) when $x = 0$, $f(x)$ has a minimum value of 2 so $1/f(x)$ has a
   maximum value of $\frac{1}{2}$

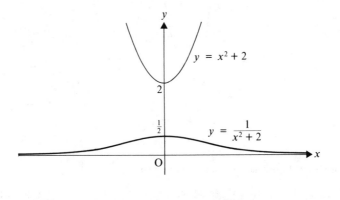

3. Sketch the curve $y = \dfrac{1}{(1+x)(4-x)}$ clearly showing asymptotes
   and any turning points.

First we sketch the graph of $f(x) = (1+x)(4-x)$

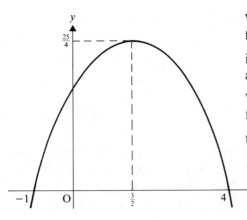

When $x = -1$ and 4,
$f(x) = 0 \Rightarrow 1/f(x) \rightarrow \infty$

i.e. $x = -1$ and $x = 4$ are
asymptotes to $y = 1/f(x)$

Where $x = \frac{3}{2}$,
$f(x)$ has a maximum value of $\frac{25}{4}$

therefore

$1/f(x)$ has a minimum value of $\frac{4}{25}$

Remembering that when $f(x)$ is +ve, $1/f(x)$ is positive also and conversely, and noting that as $x \to \pm\infty$, $f(x) \to -\infty$, so $1/f(x) \to 0$ from below, we can now sketch the curve $y = \dfrac{1}{(1+x)(4-x)}$

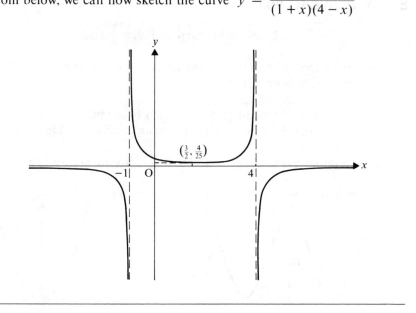

EXERCISE 37b

Sketch each curve, clearly showing any asymptotes, turning points and intercepts on the axes.

1. $y = \dfrac{1}{x^2 - 3x + 2}$

2. $y = \dfrac{1}{x^2 - 4}$

3. $y = \dfrac{1}{\sin x}$

4. $y = \dfrac{1}{1 - x^2}$

5. $y = \dfrac{1}{\ln x}$

6. $y = \dfrac{1}{x^3}$

7. $y = \dfrac{1}{x^3 - 1}$

8. $y = \dfrac{1}{x(x-1)(x-2)}$

9. $y = 1 - \dfrac{1}{x^2}$

10. $y = \dfrac{x^2}{x^2 - 1}$

11. $y = \dfrac{1}{e^x - 1}$

12. $y = 1 - \dfrac{1}{x^3 + 5}$

Next we look at some functions with interesting properties.

EVEN FUNCTIONS

A function is even if $f(x) = f(-x)$

Since the curve $y = f(-x)$ is the reflection of the curve $y = f(x)$ in the y-axis, it follows that

when $f(x)$ is an even function,
the curve $y = f(x)$ is symmetrical about Oy

Some familiar even functions and their graphs are shown below.

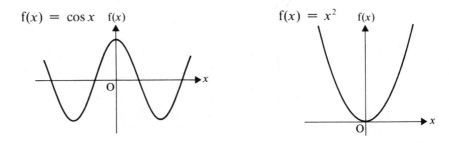

$f(x) = \cos x$ f(x) $f(x) = x^2$ f(x)

ODD FUNCTIONS

A function is odd if $f(x) = -f(-x)$

As the curve $y = -f(-x)$ is a reflection of the curve $y = f(x)$ in Oy followed by a reflection in Ox, it follows that

when $f(x) = -f(-x)$ the curve $y = f(x)$ has rotational symmetry
of order 2 about the origin.

Some familiar odd functions and their graphs are shown below.

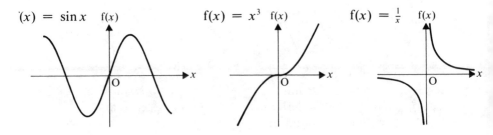

$(x) = \sin x$ f(x) $f(x) = x^3$ f(x) $f(x) = \frac{1}{x}$ f(x)

PERIODIC FUNCTIONS

A function whose graph consists of a basic pattern which repeats at regular intervals is called a *periodic* function. The width of the basic pattern is the *period* of the function.

$f(x) = \sin x$, for example, is periodic and its period is 2π

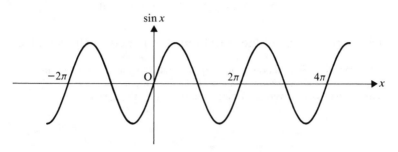

If $f(x)$ is periodic with period a, then it follows that

$$f(x + a) = f(x) \text{ for all values of } x$$

Therefore the definition of $f(x)$ within one period (e.g. for $0 < x \leqslant a$) together with the definition $f(x + a) = f(x)$ for $x \in \mathbb{R}$, defines a periodic function.

For example, if $\begin{cases} f(x) = 2x - 1 \text{ for } 0 < x \leqslant 1 \\ f(x + 1) = f(x) \text{ for all values of } x \end{cases}$

then we know that the function is periodic with a period of 1

The graph of this function can be sketched by drawing $f(x) = 2x - 1$ for $0 < x \leqslant 1$ and repeating the pattern at unit intervals in either direction.

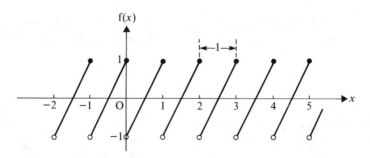

The basic pattern in the graph of a periodic function can be made up of two or more different definitions. The next worked example illustrates such a compound periodic function.

Example 37c _____

Sketch the graph of the function f defined by

$$f(x) = x \qquad \text{for} \ \ 0 \leqslant x < 1$$

$$f(x) = 4 - x^2 \quad \text{for} \ \ 1 \leqslant x < 2$$

$$f(x + 2) = f(x) \qquad \text{for all real values of } x$$

From the last line of the definition, f is periodic with period 2

The graph of this function is built up by first drawing $f(x) = x$ in the interval $0 \leqslant x < 1$, then drawing $f(x) = 4 - x^2$ in the interval $1 \leqslant x < 2$
This pattern is then repeated every 2 units along the x-axis.

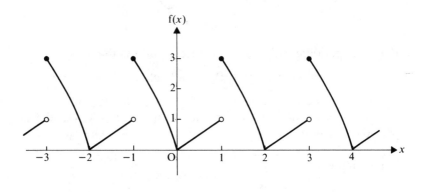

CONTINUOUS FUNCTIONS

A function f is continuous at $x = a$ if $f(a)$ is defined
and if $f(x) \to f(a)$ as $x \to a$ from above and from below.

For example, $f(x) = x^2$ is
continuous at $x = 1$ because
$f(1)$ is defined and is equal to 1
and $f(x) \to f(1)$ as $x \to 1$
from above and below.

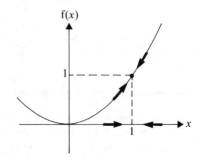

Now consider the function f
defined by

$$f(x) = x \quad \text{for } 0 \leqslant x < 1$$

and $f(x) = \tfrac{1}{2}x \quad \text{for } 1 \leqslant x < 2$

When $x = 1$, $f(1)$ is defined
and is equal to $\tfrac{1}{2}$

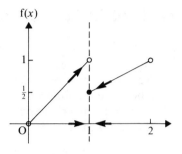

but

as $x \to 1$ from below, $f(x) \to 1$
as $x \to 1$ from above, $f(x) \to \tfrac{1}{2}$ $\bigg\}$ so $f(x)$ is not continuous at $x = 1$

> A *continuous function* satisfies the conditions for continuity
> at all values of x in its domain.

EXERCISE 37c

1. Sketch each function and state whether it is even, odd and/or
   periodic.
   (a) $\cos x$ (b) $\tan x$ (c) e^{-x} (d) $\ln(1 + x)$
   (e) $\cot x$ (f) $(x - 1)^2$ (g) $x - 1$ (h) $1/x$

2. Sketch the graph of $f(x)$ within the interval $-4 < x \leqslant 6$ if
   $$f(x) = 4 - x^2 \quad \text{for } 0 < x \leqslant 2$$
   and $\qquad f(x) = f(x - 2) \quad \text{for all values of } x$

3. If $\qquad\qquad f(\theta) = \sin\theta \quad \text{for } 0 < x \leqslant \tfrac{1}{2}\pi$
   $$f(\theta) = \cos\theta \quad \text{for } \tfrac{1}{2}\pi < x \leqslant \pi$$
   and $\qquad\qquad f(\theta + \pi) = f(\theta) \quad \text{for all values of } \theta$
   sketch the function $f(\theta)$ for the range $-2\pi < \theta \leqslant 2\pi$

4. A function $f(x)$ is periodic with a period of 4. Sketch the graph of
   the function for $-6 \leqslant x \leqslant 6$, given that
   $$f(x) = -x \qquad \text{for } 0 < x \leqslant 3$$
   $$f(x) = 3x - 12 \quad \text{for } 3 < x \leqslant 4$$

THE MODULUS OF A FUNCTION

When $f(x) = x$, $f(x)$ is negative when x is negative.
But if $g(x) = |x|$, g takes the *positive* numerical value of x,
e.g. when $x = -3$, $|x| = 3$, so $g(x)$ is always positive.
Therefore the graph of $g(x) = |x|$ can be obtained from the graph of
$f(x) = x$ by changing, to the equivalent positive values, the part of
the graph of $f(x) = x$ for which $f(x)$ is negative.

Thus for negative values of $f(x)$, the graph of $g(x) = |x|$ is the
reflection of $f(x) = x$ in the y-axis.

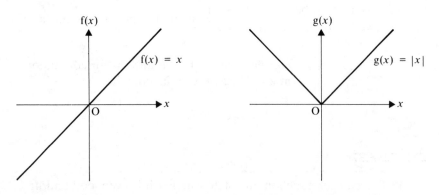

In general, the curve C_1 whose equation is $y = |f(x)|$ is obtained
from the curve C_2 with equation $y = f(x)$, by reflecting in the x-axis
the parts of C_2 for which $f(x)$ is negative. The remaining sections of
C_1 are not changed.

For example, to sketch $y = |(x - 1)(x - 2)|$ we start by sketching the
curve $y = (x - 1)(x - 2)$. We then reflect in the x-axis the part of
this curve which is below the x-axis.

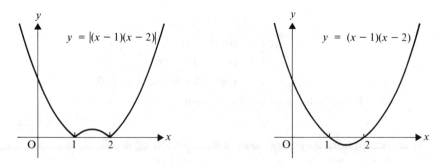

Note that for any function f, the mapping $x \rightarrow |f(x)|$ is also a
function.

Example 37d _____

Sketch the graph of $y = 3 - |1 - 2x|$ -

We can use transformations to build up the picture in stages.

1. Draw $f(x) = 1 - 2x$

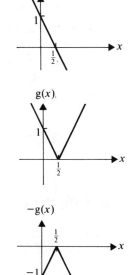

2. Draw $g(x) = |1 - 2x|$

3. Draw $-|1 - 2x|$
   ($-g(x)$ is the reflection of $g(x)$ in Ox.)

4. $y = 3 - |1 - 2x|$ is the graph of $-g(x)$ translated 3 units upwards.

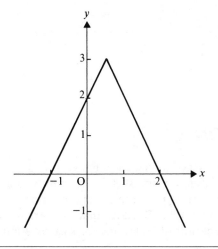

EXERCISE 37d

Sketch the following graphs.

1. $y = |2x - 1|$ 2. $y = |x(x - 1)(x - 2)|$

3. $y = |x^2 - 1|$ 4. $y = |x^2 + 1|$

5. $y = |\sin x|$ 6. $y = |\ln x|$

7. $y = |\cos x|$ 8. $y = 3 + |x + 1|$

9. $y = |2x + 5| - 4$ 10. $y = |x^2 - x - 20|$

11. $y = 1 + |2 - x^2|$ 12. $y = |\tan x|$

The Effect of a Modulus Sign on a Cartesian Equation

When a section of the curve $y = f(x)$ is reflected in Oy, the equation of that part of the curve becomes $y = -f(x)$,

e.g., if $y = |x|$ for $x \in \mathbb{R}$
we can write this equation as

$$\begin{cases} y = x & \text{for } x \geqslant 0 \\ y = -x & \text{for } x < 0 \end{cases}$$

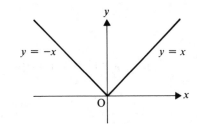

INTERSECTION

To find the points of intersection between two graphs whose equations involve a modulus, we first sketch the graphs to locate the points roughly. Then we identify the equations in non-modulus form for each part of the graph. If these equations are written on the sketch then the correct pair of equations for solving simultaneously can be identified.

For example, the points common to $y = x - 1$ and $y = |x^2 - 3|$ can be seen from the sketch.

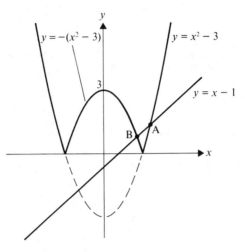

We can also see from the sketch that

the coordinates of A satisfy the equations

$$y = x - 1 \quad \text{and} \quad y = x^2 - 3 \qquad\qquad [1]$$

and the coordinates of B satisfy the equations

$$y = x - 1 \quad \text{and} \quad y = 3 - x^2 \qquad\qquad [2]$$

Solving equations [1] gives $x^2 - x - 2 = 0 \quad \Rightarrow \quad x = -1 \text{ or } 2$

It is clear from the diagram that $x \neq 1$, so A is the point $(2, 1)$

Similarly, solving equations [2] gives $x^2 + x - 4 = 0$

$$\Rightarrow \qquad\qquad x = -\tfrac{1}{2}(1 \pm \sqrt{17})$$

Again from the diagram, it is clear that the x-coordinate of B is positive, so at B, $x = -\tfrac{1}{2}(1 - \sqrt{17})$
Then using $y = x - 1$ gives $y = \tfrac{1}{2}(-3 + \sqrt{17})$

This example illustrates the importance of checking solutions to see if they are relevant to the given problem.

Example 37e

Find the coordinates of the points of intersection of the graphs

$$y = 2 - |x - 1| \quad \text{and} \quad y = |x + 2| - 3$$

The sequence of diagrams show how the graphs and the non-modulus forms of the equations are built up from transformations.

For $y = 2 - |x - 1|$

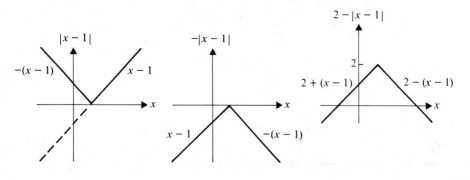

For $y = |x + 2| - 3$

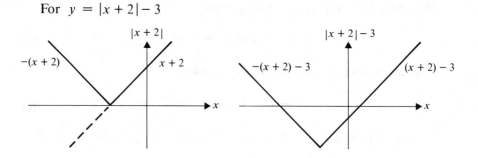

Both graphs are then drawn on the same set of axes.

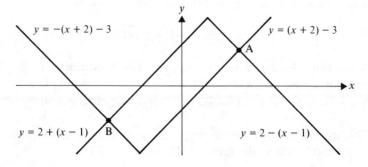

From this graph we can see that the coordinates of A satisfy the equations

$$y = (x + 2) - 3 \quad \text{and} \quad y = 2 - (x - 1) \quad \Rightarrow \quad x = 2 \quad \text{and} \quad y = 1$$

and the coordinates of B satisfy the equations

$$y = 2 + (x - 1) \quad \text{and} \quad y = -(x + 2) - 3 \quad \Rightarrow \quad x = -3 \quad \text{and} \quad y = -2$$

Therefore the points of intersection are $(2, 1)$ and $(-3, -2)$

EXERCISE 37e

Find the points of intersection of the graphs.

1. $y = |x|$ and $y = 1 - |x|$

2. $y = x$ and $y = |x^2 - 2x|$

3. $y = 2|x|$ and $y = 3 + 2x - x^2$

4. $y = |1/x|$ and $y = |x|$

5. $y = |x^2 - 4|$ and $y = 2x + 1$

Solve the following equations.

6. $|x^2 - 1| - 1 = 3x - 2$ **7.** $2 - |x + 1| = |4x - 3|$

8. $2|1 - x| = x$ **9.** $|2 - x^2| + 2x + 1 = 0$

INEQUALITIES

Many inequalities can be solved easily with the aid of sketch graphs. The following worked examples illustrate how to use graphs to solve a variety of inequality problems. In some cases they provide an alternative method, though not always as direct an approach, for solving the similar problems discussed in Chapter 13.

Examples 37f

1. Find the set of values of x for which $|x - 3| < 5 - |x|$

We start by drawing on the same set of axes the graphs $y = |x - 3|$ and $y = 5 - |x|$

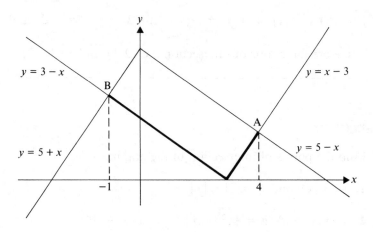

At A $x - 3 = 5 - x$ $\Rightarrow$ $x = 4$

and at B $3 - x = 5 + x$ $\Rightarrow$ $x = -1$

From the graph we see that $|3 - x| < 5 - |x|$ for $-1 < x < 4$

---

2. Find the set of values of x for which $\dfrac{(x - 1)^2}{x + 5} < 1$

Dividing out $\dfrac{(x - 1)^2}{x + 5}$ so that it contains only proper fractions gives

$$\frac{(x - 1)^2}{x + 5} = x - 7 + \frac{36}{x + 5}$$

The inequality then becomes $x - 7 + \dfrac{36}{x + 5} < 1$

$\Rightarrow$ $\dfrac{36}{x + 5} < 8 - x$

On the same set of axes we now draw sketches of $y = 8 - x$ and $y = \dfrac{36}{x + 5}$

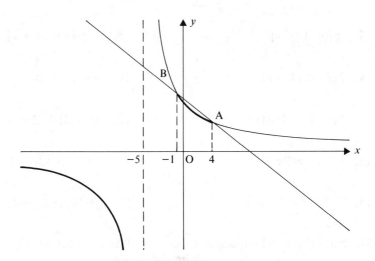

The x coordinates of A and B are the solutions of the equation

$$\frac{36}{x + 5} = 8 - x \quad \Rightarrow \quad x^2 - 3x - 4 = 0 \quad \Rightarrow \quad x = -1 \text{ and } 4$$

$\dfrac{36}{x + 5} < 8 - x$ where the curve is below the line.

From the graph we see that this is

$$\text{when } x < -5 \text{ and when } -1 < x < 4$$

Notice that we adjusted the inequality so that each side was an expression whose graph was easily recognised.

EXERCISE 37f

Solve the following inequalities.

1. $\dfrac{1}{x - 1} < x$

2. $\dfrac{1}{x} > x^2$

3. $\dfrac{x}{x - 1} < 0$

4. $\dfrac{x + 1}{x} < 0$

5. $\dfrac{x+1}{x+2} < 0$

6. $\dfrac{1+x^2}{x} > 0$

7. $|x| < 1 - |x|$

8. $|x - 1| < |x + 2|$

9. $2|x| < |1 - x|$

10. $|x + 1| < 2x$

11. $3x - 1 < 1 + |x|$

12. $|3x + 2| > 2 - |x + 1|$

13. $1 + x^2 > 2x + 1$

14. $1 + x^2 > |2x + 1|$

15. $|1 - x^2| < 2x + 1$

16. $1 - |x| > x^2 - 1$

17. Find the set of values of x between 0 and 2π for which
$$|\sin x| < |\cos x|$$

18. On the same set of axes, sketch the curves whose equations are
$$y = (x - 2)(x - 4) \quad \text{and} \quad y = \dfrac{1}{(x - 2)(x - 4)}$$
clearly showing any asymptotes and turning points.
Hence find the range of f where $\;f : x \to \dfrac{1}{(x - 2)(x - 4)}$

19. On the same set of axes sketch the curves whose equations are
$$y = x \quad \text{and} \quad y = \dfrac{1}{x}$$
Deduce the shape of the curve whose equation is $y = x + \dfrac{1}{x}$
and the range of $\;f : x \to x + \dfrac{1}{x}$

20. Use any method to find the range of the function, f, where

(a) $f(x) = \dfrac{1}{1 - x}$

(b) $f(x) = \dfrac{1}{(x - 2)(x - 6)}$

(c) $f(x) = \dfrac{x}{(1 - x)^2}$

(d) $f(x) = \dfrac{4}{(x - 1)(x - 3)}$

MIXED EXERCISE 37

1. Sketch the curve whose equation is $y = 1 - \dfrac{1}{x-3}$

   Give the equations of the asymptotes and the coordinates of the intercepts on the axes.

2. The function f is defined by

   $$f(x) = \sin x \quad \text{for} \quad 0 \leqslant x < \tfrac{1}{2}\pi$$
   $$f(x) = \pi - x \quad \text{for} \quad \tfrac{1}{2}\pi \leqslant x < \pi$$
   $$f(x) = f(x + \pi) \quad \text{for} \quad x \in \mathbb{R}$$

   Sketch the graph of $f(x)$ for $0 \leqslant x < 4\pi$

3. Draw a sketch of the curve whose equation is $y = x^2 - 1$.
   Hence superimpose a sketch of the curve whose equation is

   $$y = \frac{1}{(x^2 - 1)}$$

4. Sketch the graph of $g(x) = \dfrac{x+2}{x+1}$.

   On the same set of axes sketch the graph of the function g^{-1} and hence state the range of g^{-1}

5. Find the set of values of x for which $|x - 1| > 1 + |1 + x|$

6. Find the range of values of x for which $\dfrac{x^2 - 2}{x} > 1$

7. The function f is periodic with period 2 and

   $$f(x) = x^2 \quad \text{for} \quad 0 \leqslant x < 1$$
   $$f(x) = 3 - 2x \quad \text{for} \quad 1 \leqslant x < 2$$

   Sketch the graph of f for $-2 \leqslant x \leqslant 4$
   For which values of x in this range is $f(x)$ not continuous?

8. State whether $f(x)$ is odd, even, periodic (in which case give the period) or none of these.

   (a) $f(x) = \tan x$ (b) $f(x) = (x + 1)(x)(x - 1)$
   (c) $f(x) = x^4$ (d) $f(x) = \sin(x - \tfrac{1}{2}\pi)$

9. Sketch the graph of $y = |\sin x|$

   Which of the following statements apply to $f(x) = |\sin x|$?

   (a) $f(x)$ is even   (b) $f(x)$ is odd   (c) $f(x)$ is periodic.

10. Find the minimum value of $f(x)$ and the values of x for which $f(x) = 0$ where $f(x) = 2x^2 + x - 6$

   On the same set of axes sketch the curves $y = f(x)$ and $y = 1/f(x)$. Use your sketch to deduce the number of distinct roots of the equation $[f(x)]^2 = 1$

CONSOLIDATION F

SUMMARY

FACTORIALS

$n!$ is the product of all the integers from n to 1 inclusive,

e.g. $4! = (4)(3)(2)(1)$

$0!$ is defined as 1, i.e. $0! \equiv 1$

PERMUTATIONS

A permutation is an ordered arrangement of items.

The number of permutations of n different items is $n!$

The number of permutations of n items, p of which are identical, is $\dfrac{n!}{p!}$

The number of permutations in a circle of n different objects is $(n - 1)!$

The number of permutations of r items taken from n different items is ^nP_r

where $$^nP_r = \frac{n!}{(n - r)!}$$

COMBINATIONS

A combination is an unordered choice of items from a set.

The number of combinations of r items chosen from n different items is ^nC_r

where $$^nC_r = \frac{n!}{r!(n - r)!} \quad \text{and} \quad ^nC_r = {}^nC_{n-r}$$

Independent Permutations and Combinations

If P_1 is the number of permutations of items from one set and if P_2 is the number of permutations of items from another independent set, then the total number of permutations of items from the first set followed by the items from the second set is $P_1 \times P_2$

This result applies also to combinations.

685

Mutually Exclusive Permutations and Combinations

Two sets of items are mutually exclusive if no item can be in both sets.

If P_1 is the number of permutations of items from one set and if P_2 is the number of permutations of items from another mutually exclusive set, then the number of permutations of items either from the first set or from the second set is $P_1 + P_2$.
This result is true also for combinations.

The **arithmetic mean** of two numbers, a and b, is $\frac{1}{2}(a + b)$

The **geometric mean** of two numbers, a and b, is $\sqrt{(ab)}$

NUMBER SERIES

Each term in a number series has a fixed numerical value.

A finite series has a finite number of terms,

e.g. $a_1 + a_2 + a_3 + \ldots + a_{10}$ is a finite series with ten terms.

The sum of the first n terms of a series is denoted by S_n, i.e.

$$S_n = a_1 + a_2 + a_3 + \ldots + a_n$$

An infinite series has no last term.

If, as $n \to \infty$, S_n tends to a finite value, S, then the series converges and S is called its sum to infinity.

If $S_n \to \infty$ as $n \to \infty$ then the series is divergent.

ARITHMETIC PROGRESSIONS

In an arithmetic progression, each term differs from the preceeding term by a constant (called the common difference).

An AP with first term a, common difference d and n terms, is

$$a, a + d, a + 2d, \ldots \{a + (n - 1)d\}$$

The sum of the first n terms of an AP is given by

$$S_n = \frac{1}{2}n(a + l) \qquad \text{where } l \text{ is the last term,}$$
$$= \frac{1}{2}n\{2a + (n - 1)d\}$$

GEOMETRIC PROGRESSIONS

In a geometric progression each term is a constant multiple of the preceeding term. This multiple is called the common ratio.

A GP with first term a, common ratio r and n terms is

$$a, \ ar, \ ar^2, \ \dots \ ar^{n-1}$$

The sum of the first n terms is given by $S_n = \dfrac{a(1 - r^n)}{1 - r}$

The sum to infinity is given by $S = \dfrac{a}{1 - r}$ provided that $|r| < 1$

The Natural Number Series

The natural numbers are the positive integers, 1, 2, 3, ...

The sum of the first n natural numbers is $\displaystyle\sum_{r=1}^{n} r = \tfrac{1}{2}n(n + 1)$

The sum of their squares is $\displaystyle\sum_{r=1}^{n} r^2 = \tfrac{1}{6}n(n + 1)(2n + 1)$

The sum of their cubes is $\displaystyle\sum_{r=1}^{n} r^3 = \tfrac{1}{4}n^2(n + 1)^2 = \left\{ \sum_{r=1}^{n} r \right\}^2$

POWER SERIES

The terms of a power series involve powers of a variable, e.g.

$$1 + x + x^2 + x^3 + \dots$$

THE BINOMIAL THEOREM

If n is a positive integer then $(1 + x)^n$ can be expanded as a finite series,

where $\qquad (1 + x)^n = 1 + nx + \dbinom{n}{2}x^2 + \dbinom{n}{3}x^3 + \dots + x^n$

and where $\qquad \dbinom{n}{r} = \dfrac{n(n - 1)(n - 2)\dots(n - r + 1)}{r!}$

Further, $(a + x)^n = a^n + na^{n-1}x + \dbinom{n}{2}a^{n-2}x^2 + \dbinom{n}{3}a^{n-3}x^3 + \dots + x^n$

For any real value of n other than the positive integers, $(1 + x)^n$ can be expanded as the infinite series

$$1 + nx + \dbinom{n}{2}x^2 + \dbinom{n}{3}x^3 + \dbinom{n}{4}x^4 + \dots \quad \text{provided that } |x| < 1$$

This result can be used to expand $(a + x)^n$ provided that it is expressed in the form $a^n \left(1 + \dfrac{x}{a} \right)^n$

Exponential functions and some logarithmic functions can also be expanded as infinite series of ascending powers of x. The basic series are

$$e^x = 1 + x + \frac{x^2}{2!} + \frac{x^3}{3!} + \frac{x^4}{4!} + \dots \quad \text{for all values of } x$$

$$\ln(1 + x) = x - \frac{x^2}{2} + \frac{x^3}{3} - \frac{x^4}{4} + \dots \qquad \text{for } -1 < x \leqslant 1$$

$$\ln(1 - x) = -x - \frac{x^2}{2} - \frac{x^3}{3} - \frac{x^4}{4} - \dots \qquad \text{for } -1 \leqslant x < 1$$

FUNCTIONS

A function is *even* if $f(x) = f(-x)$
Even functions are symmetrical about the y-axis

A function is *odd* if $f(x) = -f(-x)$
Odd functions have rotational symmetry about the origin.

A *periodic* function has a basic pattern which repeats at regular intervals. The width of the interval is called the period.

The *modulus* function, $f(x) = |x|$ is such that $|x|$ is the positive numerical value of x, e.g. when $x = -3$, $|x| = 3$
The curve $y = |f(x)|$ is obtained from the curve $y = f(x)$ by reflecting in the x-axis the parts of the curve for which $f(x)$ is negative. The sections for which $f(x)$ is positive remain unchanged.

MULTIPLE CHOICE EXERCISE F

TYPE I

1. The graph of $f(x) = 1 - |x|$ could be

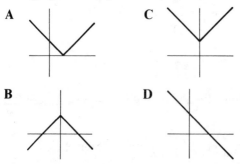

2. The number of permutations of the letters in the word EGGS is

A 4! **B** 3! **C** 4!/2! **D** $2 \times 4!$ **E** 3

3. The period of the function given by $\begin{cases} f(x) = x & 0 \leqslant x < 1 \\ f(x) = 1 & 1 \leqslant x < 2 \\ f(x) = f(x+2) \end{cases}$ is

A 2 **B** 1 **C** 4 **D** $\frac{1}{2}$ **E** -2

4. The number of security codes that can be made from two letters followed by a two digit number (including 00) is

A 26! 10! **C** 26! + 10! **E** $(26^2)(10^2)$
B 26!/24! × 10!/8! **D** $(26 \times 25) + (10 \times 9)$

5. If $|x| = |2 - x|$ then x is

A 0 **B** 2 **C** 1 and -1 **D** -1 **E** 1

6. The curve $y = \dfrac{x}{x+1}$ has an asymptote with equation

A $y = 0$ **C** $y = 1$ **E** $x = 0$
B $y = -1$ **D** $y = \frac{1}{2}$

7. Numbers less than 50 are made from the digits 1, 4 and 5. The number of them is

A 9 **B** 18 **C** 12 **D** 6 **E** 7

8. The sum of the series $1 + 5 + 9 + 13 + 17 + 21 + 25 + 29$ is

A 30 **B** 240 **C** 120 **D** 112 **E** 28

9. The sum to infinity of the series $1 + 2x + 4x^2 + 8x^3 + \ldots$, for $-\frac{1}{2} < x < \frac{1}{2}$ is

A $\dfrac{2x}{1 - 2x}$ **C** $\dfrac{1}{1 + 2x}$ **E** $1 - 2x$

B $\dfrac{1}{1 - 2x}$ **D** $\dfrac{2}{1 - x}$

10. The first three terms of the series $\sum\limits_{r=0}^{\infty} (-1)^{r+1} 2^r x^{-r}$ are

A $\quad -1 + \dfrac{2}{x} - \dfrac{4}{x^2}$ $\qquad$ C $\quad 1 + 2x - 4x^2$ $\qquad$ E $\quad$ none of these

B $\quad 1 + \dfrac{2}{x} - \dfrac{4}{x^2}$ $\qquad$ D $\quad \dfrac{2}{x} - \dfrac{4}{x^2} + \dfrac{8}{x^3}$

11. 3 is the geometric mean of a and b. Possible values of a and b are

A $\quad 5, 4$ $\qquad$ B $\quad 0, 9$ $\qquad$ C $\quad 3, 1$ $\qquad$ D $\quad 4, 2$ $\qquad$ E $\quad 9, 1$

12. The series $1 - x + 2x^2 - 3x^3 + 4x^4 + \dots$ may be written more briefly as

A $\quad \sum\limits_{r=0}^{\infty} (-1)^r rx^r$ $\qquad\qquad$ D $\quad 1 - \sum\limits_{r=0}^{\infty} (-1)^r rx^r$

B $\quad 1 + \sum\limits_{r=0}^{\infty} (-1)^r rx^r$ $\qquad\qquad$ E $\quad \sum\limits_{r=1}^{\infty} (-1)^{r+1} rx^r$

C $\quad \sum\limits_{r=1}^{\infty} rx^r$

13. The coefficient of x^3 in the binomial expansion of $(2 - x)^8$ is

A $\quad 1792$ $\qquad$ C $\quad -1792$ $\qquad$ E $\quad -448$

B $\quad 56$ $\qquad$ D $\quad -2000$

14. The series $1 - 3x + 9x^2 - 27x^3 + \dots$ converges to the value

A $\quad \frac{1}{10}$ when $x = 3$ $\qquad$ D $\quad \frac{3}{2}$ when $x = \frac{1}{9}$

B $\quad \frac{1}{2}$ when $x = \frac{1}{3}$ $\qquad$ E $\quad \frac{1}{4}$ when $x = 1$

C $\quad \frac{2}{3}$ when $x = \frac{1}{6}$

15. The first two terms in the expansion of $e^x + e^{2x}$ are

A $\quad 1 + 3x$ $\qquad$ C $\quad 3 + 3x$ $\qquad$ E $\quad 1 + 2x^2$

B $\quad 1 + x$ $\qquad$ D $\quad 2 + 3x$

16. A linear approximation for $\ln(2 + x)$ in the region where $x \approx 0$ is

A $\quad x$ $\qquad$ C $\quad 2 + \frac{1}{2}x$ $\qquad$ E $\quad \ln 2 + \frac{1}{2}x$

B $\quad 2 + x$ $\qquad$ D $\quad \ln 2 - \frac{1}{2}x$

TYPE II

17. $|\sin x|$ is

A $\quad$ periodic $\qquad$ B $\quad$ even $\qquad$ C $\quad$ odd

18. If $f(x) = x^2 - 1$ then the curve $y = \dfrac{1}{f(x)}$ has

    A   a maximum point at $(0, -1)$
    B   rotational symmetry about the origin
    C   an asymptote $x = -1$

19. $f(x) = \sin^2 x$

    A $f(x) = f(-x)$
    B $f(x)$ is periodic with period 2π
    C $f(x)$ has a minimum value of zero.

20. In the interval $0 < x < 1$

    A $|x + 1| > 0$ **B** $|x - 1| < 0$ **C** $|x + 1| = |x| + 1$

21. The sum of the first n terms, S_n, of a given series is given by
$$S_n = \frac{2n^2}{n^2 + 1}$$

    A   The first two terms of the series are $1, \frac{8}{5}$
    B   The sum of the third and fourth terms is $\frac{24}{85}$
    C   The series converges.

22. $\displaystyle\sum_{r=2}^{12} \frac{2^r}{r}$

    A   The series has eleven terms
    B   The series is a G.P.
    C   The third term of the series is $\dfrac{2^3}{3}$

23. $(1 + x)^3(1 - x)^{20}$ is expanded as a series of ascending powers of x

    A   The series is finite
    B   The first two terms of the series are $1 - 17x$
    C   The last term of the series is x^{20}

24. In the expansion of $\dfrac{1}{(1 - x)(1 + x)}$ as a series of ascending powers of x

    A   there are only even powers of x
    B   the first three terms are $\frac{1}{2} + \frac{1}{2}x^2 + \frac{1}{2}x^4$
    C   the expansion is valid for $1 \leqslant x \leqslant 1$

TYPE III

25. $f(x) = \cos x$ is such that $f(x) = f(x + \pi)$

26. The function f where $f(x) = \dfrac{1}{2x^2 - 6x + 1}$ has a maximum value of $-2/7$

27. The third term in the binomial expansion of $(2 - 3x)^{10}$ is $(45)(2^7)(3^3)(x^3)$

28. If $2^n - 1$ is the sum of the first n terms of a series, $4^n - 1$ is the sum of the first $2n$ terms.

29. 3 is the arithmetic mean of 4 and 1

30. The fourth term of the series $\displaystyle\sum_{r=0}^{n} (-1)^{(r+1)}2^r$ is 16

31. The geometric mean of $3x$ and $12x$ is $6x$

MISCELLANEOUS EXERCISE F

Most of the questions in this exercise come from the short question sections of examination papers.

1. Show that

$$\sum_{r=1}^{n} \frac{1}{(2r-1)(2r+1)} = \frac{n}{2n+1}$$

Find $\displaystyle\lim_{n \to \infty} \dfrac{n}{2n+1}$ (U of L 85)

2. The registration number of a car consists of 3 letters of the alphabet followed by an integer between 1 and 999 inclusive followed by a letter of the alphabet, e.g. *ABC* 123 *D*, *XYZ* 78 *A*, *PQR* 5 *S*. Given that *all* 26 letters of the alphabet may be used and that any letter or digit may be repeated, find the total number of different registration numbers which could be formed.

Find also in how many of these registration numbers the letters and digits are all different.

(Answers may be left in factor form.)   (U of L 85)

3. An arithmetic progression has first term a and common difference -1. The sum of the first n terms is equal to the sum of the first $3n$ terms. Express a in terms of n.   (C 88)

4. Expand $(1 - 4x)^{1/2}$ as a series of ascending powers of x, where $|x| < \frac{1}{4}$, up to and including the term in x^3, expressing the coefficients in their simplest form.   (C 88)

5. A student must answer exactly 7 out of 10 questions in an examination. Given that she must answer *at least* 3 of the first 5 questions, determine the number of ways in which she may select the 7 questions.   (U of L 84)

6. Find the positive constants a and b such that 0.25, a, 9 are in geometric progression and 0.25, a, $9 - b$ are in arithmetic progression.   (U of L 84)

7. Find the set of values of x for which
$$x > |3x - 8|$$ (U of L 84)

8. The first term of an arithmetic series is 2 and the terms of the series are not all equal. The first, third and eleventh terms of this series are also the first, second, and third terms, respectively, of a geometric series. Find the common difference of the arithmetic series. (JMB 84)

9. Find the first four terms in the expansion in ascending powers of x of
$$\frac{1}{(1 + 3x)^{1/3}}$$
State the values of x for which the expansion converges.   (JMB 85)

10. Find the set of values of x for which
$$|3x - 2| < 1 - 4x$$ (U of L 87)

11. From a class of eight students it is decided to send a party of either three or four or five students to a meeting.
    (a) Calculate the total number of different parties which could be formed.
    (b) Find the number of these parties in which two specific students are always members.   (U of L 87)

12. A geometric series has first term $\sin \theta$ and common ratio $\cos \theta$, where $0 < \theta < \pi/2$.
    (a) Show that the sum to infinity of this series is $\cot(\theta/2)$.
    (b) Given that $\theta = \pi/3$, find the sum of the first seven terms of this series to two decimal places.   (U of L 87)

13. Given that $\sum_{r=1}^{n} 2^{r+1} = 1020$, find the value of n.   (U of L 87)

14. A bag contains nine discs of which exactly three are white and the other six are each of different colour. Seven discs are selected together from the bag. Find the number of different selections that can be made. (U of L 87)

15. Show that $\displaystyle\sum_{r=1}^{2n} (2r-1)^2 = \frac{2}{3}n(16n^2 - 1)$. (U of L 86)

16. A geometric progression has first term a and common ratio $1/\sqrt{2}$. Show that the sum to infinity of the progression is $a(2 + \sqrt{2})$. (C 87)

17. Find the first three terms in the expansion in ascending powers of x of $(1 - 2x)^{1/3}$, and state the set of values of x for which the expansion is valid. (C 87)

18. Sketch the graph of $y = |x + 2|$ and hence, or otherwise, solve the inequality
$$|x + 2| > 2x + 1 \quad x \in \mathbb{R}$$ (C 87)

19. The first term of an arithmetic progression is -13 and the last term is 99. The sum of the progression is 1419. Find the number of terms and the common difference.

Find also the sum of all the positive terms of the progression. (AEB 87)

20. In the expansion of
$$\frac{1}{\sqrt{(1 + ax)}} - \frac{1}{1 + 2x}$$
in ascending powers of x, the first non-zero term is the term in x^2. Find the value of the constant a and hence find the terms in x^2 and x^3. (JMB 88)

21. Find the number of different arrangements that can be made using all eight letters of the word ROTATION.

Find the number of these arrangements in which the letters T are not consecutive. (U of L 89)

22. The first four terms of an arithmetic progression are 2, $a - b$, $2a + b + 7$ and $a - 3b$ respectively, where a and b are constants. Find a and b and hence determine the sum of the first 30 terms of the progression. (U of L 89)

23. Find the complete solution set of each of the inequalities
(a) $|3x - 2| < 4$
(b) $y^3 + 7y^2 - y - 7 \geqslant 0$ (AEB 88)

24. Sketch on the same diagram the graphs of
$$y = 2|x| \quad \text{and} \quad y = |x - 3|$$
Solve the inequality
$$2|x| \leqslant |x - 3| \qquad\qquad\qquad \text{(JMB 87)}$$

25. Sketch the curve $y = (2x - 1)^2(x + 1)$, showing the coordinates of
(a) the points where it meets the axes
(b) the turning points
(c) the point of inflexion.
By using your sketch, or otherwise, sketch the graph of
$$y = \frac{1}{(2x - 1)^2(x + 1)}$$
Show clearly the coordinates of any turning points.   (U of L 88)

26. Given that
$$f(x) \equiv 2 - \frac{3}{x^2 - 2x + 4}$$
show that $f(x)$ is always positive.
Sketch the graph of the curve $y = f(x)$, stating the equations of any asymptotes and the coordinates of any points of intersection with the coordinate axes.   (U of L 84)

27. Evaluate in terms of $\ln 2$
(a) $\ln 2 + \ln (2^2) + \ldots + \ln (2^n) + \ldots + \ln (2^{100})$
(b) $\displaystyle\sum_{r=1}^{\infty} (\ln 2)^n$ (JMB 86)

28. Obtain the first three non-zero terms in the expansion of $(1 + y)^{1/2}$, where $|y| < 1$, as a series of ascending powers of y.
Given that $\qquad\qquad f(x) \equiv (1 + x^{1/2})^{1/2}$
write down the coefficients a_0, a_1, a_2 in the expansion
$$a_0 + a_1 x^{1/2} + a_2 x + \ldots$$
of $f(x)$ as a series of ascending powers of $x^{1/2}$.
Using this expansion, or otherwise, estimate the value of
$$\int_0^{0.01} f(x) \, dx$$
giving your answer to 4 decimal places.   (U of L 84)

29. Using the same axes, sketch the curves

$$y = \frac{1}{x} \quad \text{and} \quad y = \frac{x}{x + 2}$$

State the equations of any asymptotes, the coordinates of any points of intersection with the axes and the coordinates of any points of intersection of the two curves.

Hence, or otherwise, find the set of values of x for which

$$\frac{1}{x} > \frac{x}{x + 2} \qquad \qquad \text{(U of L 86)}$$

30. Use the binomial expansion to express $x^4(1 - x)^4$ as a polynomial in x.

Hence, or otherwise, verify that

$$x^4(1 - x)^4 \equiv (1 + x^2)(x^6 - 4x^5 + 5x^4 - 4x^2 + 4) - 4$$

Use this result to evaluate

$$\int_0^1 \frac{x^4(1 - x)^4}{1 + x^2} \, dx$$

and deduce that $\pi < 22/7$. (U of L 86)

31. Given that $y = \dfrac{1 + 3x}{(1 - 2x)^4}$ and $|x| < \frac{1}{3}$, find in simplified form the first three non-zero terms in ascending powers of x of the series expansions of

(a) y

(b) $\ln y$ (AEB 86)

32. Find, in ascending powers of x, as far as the term in x^2, series expansions for e^{-px} and $(1 + 2x)^{-q}$.

Given that the first non-zero term in the series expansion of

$$e^{-px} - (1 + 2x)^{-q}$$

in ascending powers of x is $-4x^2$, find the value of p and the value of q. (AEB 88)

33. Write down and simplify the first three terms in the series expansion of $\left(1 + \dfrac{x}{3}\right)^{-1/2}$ in ascending powers of x.

State the set of values of x for which the series is valid.

Given that x is so small that terms in x^3 and higher powers of x may be neglected, show that

$$e^{-x}\left(1 + \frac{x}{3}\right)^{-1/2} = 1 - \frac{7}{6}x + \frac{17}{24}x^2 \qquad \qquad \text{(AEB 87)}$$

CHAPTER 38

SOLUTION OF EQUATIONS

Equations of various forms have appeared at intervals throughout this book, usually when some new mathematics has provided the means to solve a different form of equation. In these situations, the method of solution was usually obvious. However, equations often arise from mathematical models of practical situations and may not be connected obviously to the mathematical knowledge needed to solve them.

This chapter starts by bringing together some categories of equation which have exact solutions and, by looking at the form of the equation, suggesting possible ways of solving them. It must be remembered though, that it is not always possible to find exact solutions even when they exist, so this chapter ends with some methods for finding approximate solutions.

TRIGONOMETRIC EQUATIONS

Successful solutions of trig equations depend on three factors; recognising and knowing the trig identities, correctly classifying the equation so that the first attempt at solution is likely to be successful and, finally, experience.

There are two general approaches to trig equations. First see whether the equation can be factorised, either in its given form or by applying an appropriate identity. If this is not possible (and often it is not) try to reduce the equation to a form which involves only one variable, i.e. one trig ratio of one angle.

In this section we give most of the common categories of trig equation followed by an appropriate method of solution. This list is neither exhaustive nor infallible, but it covers most forms of equation met at this level.

A. Equations Containing One Angle Only

Form of Equation	Method
1. $a\cos\theta + b\sin\theta = 0$	Divide by $\cos\theta$, provided that $\cos\theta \neq 0$
2. $a\cos\theta + b\sin\theta = c$	Write LHS as $R\cos(\theta + \alpha)$ or use the 'little t' identities.
3. $a\cos^2\theta + b\sin\theta = c$ $a\sin^2\theta + b\cos\theta = c$ $a\tan^2\theta + b\sec\theta = c$	Use the Pythagorean identities to express in terms of one ratio only.
4. $a\cos\theta + b\tan\theta = 0$ $a\sin\theta + b\tan\theta = 0$	Multiply by $\cos\theta$

Note that any of the equations in Section A can be solved by using the 'little t' identities. However this is often not the simplest method and sometimes leads to a polynomial in t whose roots are far from obvious.

B. Equations Containing Multiples of One Angle

Form of Equation	Method
1. $a\cos\theta + b\cos 2\theta = c$ $a\sin\theta + b\cos 2\theta = c$	Use the double angle formulae to reduce to Section A type.
2. $\cos\theta = \sin a\theta$	Express $\sin a\theta$ as $\cos(\tfrac{1}{2}\pi - a\theta)$ and use $\cos A = \cos B$
3. $\cos a\theta + \cos b\theta + \cos c\theta = 0$ $\sin a\theta + \sin b\theta$ $\qquad + \sin c\theta + \sin d\theta = 0$	Use the factor formulae on a pair(s) of terms to give a common factor.

C. Equations Containing Different Angles

Form of Equation	Method
1. $\cos\theta + \sin(\theta - \alpha) = 0$ etc.	Reduce to $\cos A = \cos B$ or to $\tan A = \tan B$ and quote solution, or use factor formulae to factorise.
2. $\cos\theta \sin(\theta - \alpha) = c$	Use compound angle formulae to reduce to a section A type equation

Note that equations of the form given in B and C can often be reduced to equations involving one angle only, by using double and compound angle formulae. However this rarely leads to an easy solution so should only be tried as a last resort.

It is important to realise that a method given in this list does not represent the only way of solving a particular equation, nor does it always lead to the quickest solution. Sometimes an equation can be simplified quickly when part of it is recognised as part of a trig identity. Sometimes it may be necessary to classify each side of an equation independently. This is illustrated in the next worked example.

Example 38a _____

Find the general solution of the equation
$$\cos 2\theta \sin \theta + \sin 2\theta \cos \theta = \cos 4\theta$$

$$\cos 2\theta \sin \theta + \sin 2\theta \cos \theta = \cos 4\theta$$

The LHS is recognised as the expansion of $\sin(2\theta + \theta)$, i.e. $\sin 3\theta$, giving

$$\sin 3\theta = \cos 4\theta$$

$\sin 3\theta$ may be expressed as $\cos\left(\frac{1}{2}\pi - 3\theta\right)$, giving

$$\cos\left(\tfrac{1}{2}\pi - 3\theta\right) = \cos 4\theta$$

Using the solution to $\cos A = \cos B$ gives

$$\tfrac{1}{2}\pi - 3\theta = 2n\pi \pm 4\theta$$

$$\therefore \quad \theta = \tfrac{1}{14}\pi(1 - 4n) \quad \text{or} \quad \tfrac{1}{2}\pi(4n - 1)$$

_____

The equation in the worked example illustrates that one approach does not always lead directly to the solution. The situation should be reappraised at each step.

EXERCISE 38a

Find the general solution in radians of each equation.

1. $\sin 2x \cos x + \cos 2x \sin x = 1$ 2. $\cos 3x = \sin x$

3. $2 \sin^2 x + \cos x = 1$ 4. $5 \cos x + 12 \sin x = 13$

5. $2 \sin x + \sin 2x = 0$ 6. $\cos x + \cos 2x + \cos 3x = 0$

7. $\cos^2 x + 2 \sin^2 x = 2$ 8. $4 \sin x - 5 = 3 \cos x$

9. $\sin^2 x = 2 \cos x + 1$ 10. $\cos x = 2 \tan x$

Solve each equation for $0 \leqslant x < 360°$ giving answers correct to 1 d.p. where necessary.

11. $\cos 2x + \sin x = 1$ 12. $2 \sin x - \cos x = 1$

13. $\sin x + \tan x = 0$ 14. $\cos 2x + 2 \sin x = 0$

15. $\tan x + 2 \sec^2 x = 3$ 16. $2 \cos x + \cos 2x = 2$

17. $\cos (x + 30°) + \sin x = 0$

18. $\sin x + \sin 2x + \sin 3x + \sin 4x = 0$

19. $\cos x \cos 2x - \sin x \sin 2x = \frac{1}{2}$

EXPONENTIAL AND LOGARITHMIC EQUATIONS

When the unknown quantity forms part of an index, taking logs will often transform the index into a factor.

For example, if $5^x = 10$ then taking logs of both sides gives

$$x \ln 5 = \ln 10 \quad \Rightarrow \quad x = \frac{\ln 10}{\ln 5}$$

Taking logs can work when the terms containing a power involving x can be expressed as a single term, but this is not always possible. Consider for example the equation

$$2^{2x} + 3(2^x) - 4 = 0$$

Now $2^{2x} + 3(2^x)$ cannot be simplified into a single term. However recognising that 2^{2x} is $(2^x)^2$, the substitution $y = 2^x$ can be made,

i.e. $y^2 + 3y - 4 = 0$

This is a quadratic equation which can now be solved.

When an equation contains logarithms involving the unknown, first make sure that all logs are to the same base, then check to see if a simple substitution will reduce the equation to a recognisable form. Sometimes the best policy is to remove the logarithms. Equations of each of these types are considered in the following worked examples.

Examples 38b _____

1. Solve the equation $\log_3 x - 4 \log_x 3 + 3 = 0$

The two log terms have different bases so we begin by changing the base of the log in the second term to 3. The given equation then becomes

$$\log_3 x - \frac{4}{\log_3 x} + 3 = 0$$

$\Rightarrow$ $\qquad\qquad (\log_3 x)^2 - 4 + 3 \log_3 x = 0$

Substituting y for $\log_3 x$ gives $y^2 - 4 + 3y = 0 \Rightarrow y^2 + 3y - 4 = 0$

$\therefore \qquad\qquad\qquad (y + 4)(y - 1) = 0 \Rightarrow y = 1 \text{ or } -4$

i.e. $\log_3 x = 1$ or $\log_3 x = -4 \Rightarrow x = 3$ or $x = 3^{-4} = \frac{1}{81}$

_____

2. Solve for x and y the equations

$$yx = 16 \text{ and } \log_2 x - 2 \log_2 y = 1$$

$$yx = 16 \qquad\qquad\qquad [1]$$

$$\log_2 x - 2 \log_2 y = 1 \qquad\qquad [2]$$

Using the laws of logs, equation [2] can be written as

$$\log_2 \frac{x}{y^2} = 1 \quad \Rightarrow \quad \frac{x}{y^2} = 2, \text{ i.e. } x = 2y^2$$

Substituting $2y^2$ for x in equation [1] gives

$$2y^3 = 16 \quad \Rightarrow \quad y^3 = 8$$

$\therefore \ y = 2$ and, from [1], $x = 8$

_____

EXERCISE 38b

Solve the equations.

1. $3^x = 6$

2. $5^x = 4$

3. $2^{2x} = 5$

4. $3^{x-1} = 7$

5. $4^{2x+1} = 3$

6. $5^x(5^{x-1}) = 10$

7. $2(2^{2x}) - 5(2^x) + 2 = 0$

8. $3^{2x+1} - 26(3^x) - 9 = 0$

9. $4^x - 6(2^x) - 16 = 0$

10. $\log_2 x + \log_x 2 = 2$

11. $\log_2 x = \log_4(x + 6)$

12. $4\log_3 x = \log_x 3$

Solve the equations simultaneously.

13. $2\ln y = \ln 2 + \ln x$ and $2^y = 4^x$

14. $\log_x y = 2$ and $xy = 8$

15. $\log_3 x = y = \log_9(2x - 1)$

16. $\lg(x + y) = 0$ and $2\lg x = \lg(y + 1)$ (lg means $\log_{10}$)

POLYNOMIAL EQUATIONS

If a quadratic equation has real roots then these roots can always be found either by factorisation or by using the formula. If the equation is of higher degree, real roots can *sometimes* be found using the factor theorem but only if these roots are integers or simple rational numbers. When the factor theorem fails to find *exact* solutions, they can be found by other methods in some special cases, one of which we look at now.

Equations with a Repeated Root

If the equation $f(x) = 0$ has a repeated root, a, then $(x - a)^2$ is a factor of $f(x) = 0$. This means that the curve $y = f(x)$ *touches* the x-axis at $x = a$

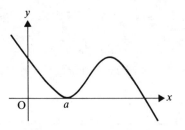

As $y = f(x)$ has a turning point at $x = a$, $f'(x) = 0$ when $x = a$, i.e. $f'(a) = 0$, therefore

$$f(a) = 0 \;\; and \;\; f'(a) = 0 \quad \Longleftrightarrow \quad f(x) \text{ has a repeated factor.}$$

Examples 38c

1. Solve the equation $18x^3 - 111x^2 + 224x - 147 = 0$ given that it has two equal roots.

The repeated root of the given equation

$$f(x) = 18x^3 - 111x^2 + 224x - 147 = 0 \qquad [1]$$

also satisfies the equation

$$f'(x) = 54x^2 - 222x + 224 = 0$$

$$\Rightarrow \qquad\qquad\qquad 27x^2 - 111x + 112 = 0$$

$$\Rightarrow \qquad\qquad\qquad (9x - 16)(3x - 7) = 0$$

So *either* $x = \frac{16}{9}$ *or* $x = \frac{7}{3}$ is a solution of the given equation.

To check which of these values is the repeated root of the given equation, each is substituted in turn into equation [1].
We find that $f(\frac{16}{9}) \neq 0$ and that $f(\frac{7}{3}) = 0$

Hence $f(x)$ and $f'(x)$ are both zero when $x = \frac{7}{3}$

So $x = \frac{7}{3}$ is the repeated root of the given equation.

Hence $\qquad 18x^3 - 111x^2 + 224x - 147 = (3x - 7)^2(ax + b)$

Comparing coefficients of x^3 gives $18 = 9a \;\Rightarrow\; a = 2$

Comparing constants gives $-147 = 49b \;\Rightarrow\; b = -3$

Therefore $\quad 18x^3 - 111x^2 + 224x - 147 = (3x - 7)^2(2x - 3)$

So $\qquad\qquad\qquad (3x - 7)^2(2x - 3) = 0$

$$\Rightarrow \qquad\qquad\qquad x = \tfrac{7}{3} \text{ or } \tfrac{3}{2}$$

Equations Involving Square Roots

When an equation contains square roots involving the unknown, we must eliminate those square roots. However when both sides of an equation are squared, an extra equation, and hence extra solutions, is introduced

For example if $x = 2$ then squaring gives $x^2 = 4$
But $x^2 = 4$ includes both $x = 2$ and $x = -2$, therefore

it is essential that whenever a solution involves squaring, all roots must be checked in the original equation.

Examples 38c (continued) _____

2. Solve the equation $\sqrt{(x + 8)} - \sqrt{(x + 3)} = \sqrt{(2x - 1)}$

Squaring both sides of the equation gives

$$x + 8 - 2\sqrt{(x + 8)}\sqrt{(x + 3)} + x + 3 = 2x - 1$$

$\Rightarrow \qquad\qquad\qquad\qquad 6 = \sqrt{(x + 8)}\sqrt{(x + 3)}$

Squaring again gives $\qquad 36 = (x + 8)(x + 3)$

$\Rightarrow \qquad\qquad\qquad x^2 + 11x - 12 = 0$

$\Rightarrow \qquad\qquad\qquad\quad x = 1 \text{ or } -12$

Checking these values of x in the original equation shows that
when $x = 1$, LHS $= \sqrt{9} - \sqrt{4} = 1$ and RHS $= \sqrt{1} = 1$
so $x = 1$ is a solution of the given equation,

when $x = -12$, RHS $= \sqrt{(-25)}$ which is not real
so $x = -12$ is not a solution of the given equation.

Therefore, $x = 1$ is the only solution.

_____

Note that we have looked at a very small sample of the possible types of equation which have exact solutions. Although there are rules for solving a few particular forms of equation, in most cases such rules do not exist. The solution of equations is an art; experience will suggest a likely form of attack but there is never any guarantee that the method will produce a solution and other methods have to be tried. In the following exercise, all the equations have exact solutions and most of them are of a type that has been discussed either in this chapter or earlier in the book. Just a few may be unfamiliar.

EXERCISE 38c

1. Find the values of x that satisfy the equation
$80x^3 + 88x^2 - 3x - 18 = 0$ given that it has a repeated root.

2. Show that $x = 0$ is not a root of the equation
$$5x^4 - 16x^3 - 42x^2 - 16x + 5 = 0$$
Divide the equation by x^2, then use $y = x + 1/x$ to show that
$$5(y^2 - 2) - 16y - 42 = 0$$
Hence solve the given equation.

3. The equation $20x^3 - 52x^2 + 21x + 18 = 0$ has a repeated root.
Solve the equation

Solve the given equations using any suitable methods.

4. $x^3 - 6x^2 + 11x - 6 = 0$

5. $1 + \sqrt{x} = \sqrt{(3x - 3)}$

6. $\sqrt{(2x - 5)} - \sqrt{(x - 2)} = 1$

7. $x^2 - 3x = 8$

8. $1 - \sqrt{x} + \sqrt{(x - 3)} = 0$

9. $\sqrt{(3x + 1)} + \sqrt{(x - 1)} = \sqrt{(7x + 1)}$

10. $x^4 - 12x^2 + 27 = 0$

11. $x^{4/3} - 5x^{2/3} + 4 = 0$

12. $|x| = 3 - |1 - x|$

13. $2x^3 - x^2 + 20 = 0$

14. $\dfrac{x^2}{4} + y^2 = 1$ and $xy = 1$

15. $x^2 + y^2 + 4x - 6y = 3$ and $y = x + 1$

16. $x^2 + y^2 + 8x - 4y + 15 = 0$ and $x^2 + y^2 + 6x + 2y - 15 = 0$

17. $x^4 - x^3 - 12x^2 - 4x + 16 = 0$ (*Hint*. Use $y = x + 4/x$)

APPROXIMATE SOLUTIONS

When the roots of an equation cannot be found exactly, we can find approximate solutions. The first step is to locate the roots roughly and this can be done graphically.

Consider, for example, the equation $e^x = 4x$

The roots of this equation are the values of x where the curve $y = e^x$ and the line $y = 4x$ intersect.

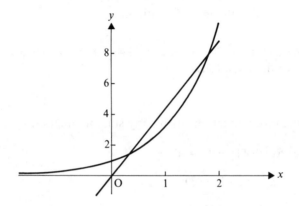

From the sketch we can see that there is one root between 0 and 0.5 and another root somewhere near 2

We now need a way to locate the roots more accurately.

Locating the Roots of an Equation

Suppose that we have very roughly located the roots of an equation $f(x) = 0$
Now consider the curve $y = f(x)$
The roots of the equation $f(x) = 0$ are the values of x where this curve crosses the x-axis, e.g.

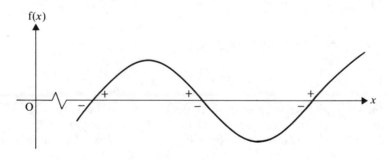

Each time that the curve crosses the x-axis, the sign of y changes. So

> if one root only of the equation $f(x) = 0$ lies between x_1 and x_2, and if the curve $y = f(x)$ is unbroken between the points where $x = x_1$ and $x = x_2$, then $f(x_1)$ and $f(x_2)$ are opposite in sign.

The condition that the curve $y = f(x)$ must be unbroken between x_1 and x_2 is essential as we can see from the curve below.

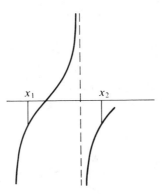

This curve crosses the x-axis between x_1 and x_2 but $f(x_1)$ and $f(x_2)$ have the same sign because the curve is broken between these values.

Returning to the equation $e^x = 4x$, we will now locate the larger root a little more precisely.

First we write the equation in the form $f(x) = 0$, i.e. $f(x) = e^x - 4x$, then we find where there is a change in the sign of $f(x)$

We know that there is a root in region of $x = 2$, so we will see if it lies between 1.8 and 2.2

Using $f(x) = e^x - 4x$, gives $f(1.8) = e^{1.8} - 4(1.8) = -1.1 \ldots$

and $f(2.2) = e^{2.2} - 4(2.2) = 0.2 \quad \ldots$

Therefore the larger root of the equation lies between 1.8 and 2.2 (and is likely to be nearer to 2.2 as $f(2.2)$ is nearer to zero then $f(1.8)$ is).

Example 38d

Find the turning points on the curve $y = x^3 - 2x^2 + x + 1$. Hence sketch the curve and use the sketch to show that the equation $x^3 - 2x^2 + x + 1 = 0$ has only one real root. Find two consecutive integers between which this root lies.

At turning points $\dfrac{dy}{dx} = 0$, i.e. $3x^2 - 4x + 1 = 0$

$$\Rightarrow \quad (3x - 1)(x - 1) = 0 \quad \text{so} \quad x = \tfrac{1}{3} \text{ and } 1$$

When $x = \tfrac{1}{3}$, $y = \tfrac{31}{27}$ and when $x = 1$, $y = 1$

As the curve is a cubic, and as $y \to \infty$ as $x \to \infty$, we deduce that the curve has a maximum point at $(\tfrac{1}{3}, \tfrac{31}{27})$ and a minimum point at $(1, 1)$

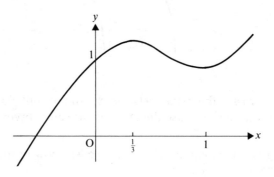

From the sketch, we see that the curve $y = x^3 - 2x^2 + x + 1$ crosses the x-axis at one point only, therefore

the equation $x^3 - 2x^2 + x + 1 = 0$ has only one real root.

Also from the sketch it appears that this root lies between $x = -1$ and $x = 0$

Using $f(x) = x^3 - 2x^2 + x + 1$ gives $f(-1) = -3$ and $f(0) = 1$

As $f(-1)$ and $f(0)$ are opposite in sign, the one real root of $x^3 - 2x^2 + x + 1 = 0$ lies between $x = -1$ and $x = 0$

EXERCISE 38d

1. Use sketch graphs to determine the number of real roots of each equation. (Some may have an infinite set of roots.)

    (a) $\sin x = \dfrac{1}{x}$ (b) $\cos x = x^2 - 1$ (c) $2^x = \tan x$

    (d) $2^x \sin x = 1$ (e) $(x^2 - 4) = \dfrac{1}{x}$ (f) $x2^x = 1$

    (g) $x \ln x = 1$ (h) $\sin x = x^2$ (i) $\ln x + 2^x = 0$

2. For each equation in Question 1 with a finite number of roots, locate the root, or the larger root where there is more than one, within an interval of half a unit.

3. Find the turning points on the curve whose equation is $y = x^3 - 3x^2 + 1$. Hence sketch the curve and use your sketch to find the number of real roots of the equation $x^3 - 3x^2 + 1 = 0$

4. Using a method similar to that given in Question 3, or otherwise, determine the number of real roots of each equation.

    (a) $x^4 - 3x^3 + 1 = 0$ (b) $x^3 - 24x + 1 = 0$ (c) $x^5 - 5x^2 + 4 = 0$

5. Show that the equation $3^{-x} = x^2 + 2$ has just one root and find this root to the nearest integer.

6. Find the successive integers between which the smallest root of the equation $2^x = \frac{1}{2}(x + 3)$ lies.

ITERATIVE APPROXIMATIONS

113

There are many ways in which successive numerical approximations can be used to find a root of an equation to any degree of accuracy required. The two given below are both common iterative methods.

Whatever iterative procedure is used we must first find an interval in which the required root lies. This can be done using the methods described in the last section.

Method 1 $x = g(x)$

115

This method can often be used to find a root of an equation
$f(x) = 0$ which can be written in the form $x = g(x)$.
The roots of the equation $x = g(x)$ are the values of x at the points
of intersection of the line $y = x$ and the curve $y = g(x)$.

Taking x_1 as a first approximation to a root α then in the diagram,
    A is the point on the *curve* where $x = x_1$, $y = g(x_1)$
    B is the point where $x = \alpha$, $y = g(x_1)$
    C is the point on the *line* where $x = x_2$, $y = g(x_1)$

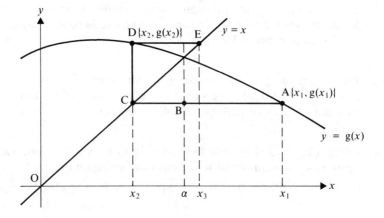

If, in the region of α, the slope of $y = g(x)$ is less steep than that of
the line $y = x$, i.e. provided that $|g'(x)| < 1$

then $\qquad\qquad\qquad\qquad$ CB < BA

so x_2 is closer to α than is x_1 and x_2 is a better approximation to α

But C is on the line $y = x$

therefore $\qquad\qquad\qquad\qquad x_2 = g(x_1)$

Now taking the point D on the curve where $x = x_2$, $y = g(x_2)$ and
repeating the argument above we find that x_3 is a better approximation
to α than is x_2

where $\qquad\qquad\qquad\qquad x_3 = g(x_2)$

This process can be repeated as often as necessary to achieve the
required degree of accuracy.
The rate at which these approximations converge to α depends on the
value of $|g'(x)|$ near α. The smaller $|g'(x)|$ is, the more rapid is the
convergence.

It should be noted that this method fails if $|g'(x)| > 1$ near α
The following diagrams illustrate some of the factors which determine
the success, or otherwise, of this method.

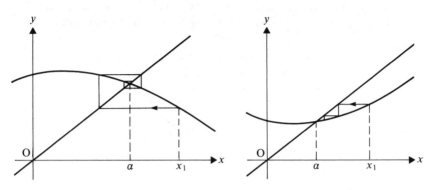

Rapid rate of convergence ($|g'(x)|$ small).

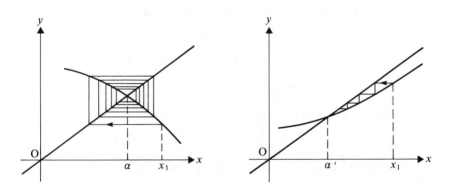

Slow rate of convergence ($|g'(x)| < 1$ but close to 1)

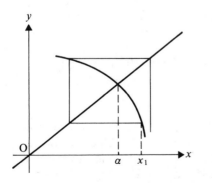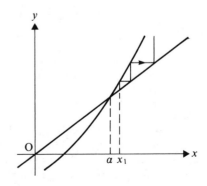

Divergence, i.e. failure, ($|g'(x)| > 1$)

As an example consider the equation

$$x^3 + 2x^2 + 5x - 1 = 0$$

The equation can be written $x^3 = 1 - 5x - 2x^2$ so that a sketch of $y = x^3$ and $y = 1 - 5x - 2x^2$ shows the number of roots.

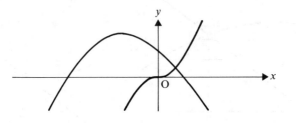

From the sketch we see that there is only one root and it is near the origin.

The given equation can be written in the form

$$x = g(x)$$

where $\qquad\qquad g(x) = -\tfrac{1}{5}(x^3 + 2x^2 - 1)$

We will take $x_1 = 0$ as our first approximation.

A better approximation, x_2, is found from

$$x_2 = g(x_1) = -\tfrac{1}{5}[0^3 + 2(0)^2 - 1] = 0.2$$

Further improvements are obtained by repeating this step,

i.e. $\qquad\quad x_3 = g(x_2) = -\tfrac{1}{5}[(0.2)^3 + 2(0.2)^2 - 1]$
$$= 0.1824$$

$$x_4 = g(x_3) = -\tfrac{1}{5}[(0.1824)^3 + 2(0.1824)^2 - 1]$$
$$= 0.1855 \quad \text{(to 4 d.p.)}$$

$$x_5 = g(x_4) = -\tfrac{1}{5}[(0.1855)^3 + 2(0.1855)^2 - 1]$$
$$= 0.1850 \quad \text{(to 4 d.p.)}$$

and so on.

The degree of accuracy at any stage can be checked by determining the sign of $f(x)$ on either side of the value so far obtained for the root, e.g., taking $x \approx 0.1850$ we find that $f(0.1846)$ is negative and $f(0.1854)$ is positive, so $x = 0.185$ correct to 3 d.p.

Note. This does *not* show that $x = 0.1850$ to 4 d.p.

Method 2   The Newton–Raphson or Newton's Method

This method is based on determining a linear approximation for a function. Suppose that the equation $f(x) = 0$ has a root α and that a is an approximation for α

The curve $y = f(x)$ cuts the x-axis where $x = \alpha$. If we consider the tangent to $y = f(x)$ at the point where $x = a$ then the point B where this tangent cuts the x-axis will, in most circumstances, be nearer to the point $x = \alpha$

i.e.

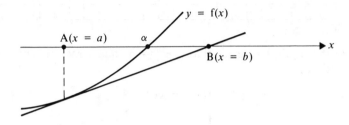

So if this tangent cuts the x-axis at B where $x = b$, then b is a better approximation to α than a is.

The gradient of $y = f(x)$ at the point A is $f'(a)$.
The coordinates of A are $(a, f(a))$.

So the equation of the tangent at A is

$$y - f(a) = f'(a)(x - a)$$

This line cuts the x-axis where $y = 0$, i.e. where $x = a - \dfrac{f(a)}{f'(a)}$

So if a is an approximation for a root of the equation $f(x) = 0$,
then $b = a - \dfrac{f(a)}{f'(a)}$ is a better approximation.

As an example we will use Newton's Method to find the root of $xe^x = 3$ correct to three decimal places.

A first approximation to the root is found by drawing the graphs of
$y = \dfrac{3}{x}$ and $y = e^x$

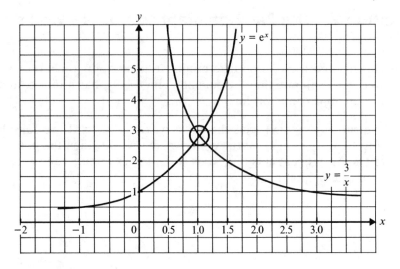

From these graphs we see that $xe^x = 3$ has a root α which is approximately 1

Now $f(x) = xe^x - 3$

$\Rightarrow$ $f'(x) = (x + 1)e^x$

Using $b = a - \dfrac{f(a)}{f'(a)}$, and taking $a = 1$ as our first approximation to α, the second approximation is

$$1 - \frac{e - 3}{2e} = 1.0518 \quad \text{(to 4 d.p.)}$$

Taking $a = 1.0518$ and repeating the procedure, the third approximation is

$$1.0518 - \frac{(1.0518)e^{1.0518} - 3}{(2.0518)e^{1.0518}} = 1.0499 \quad \text{(to 4 d.p.)}$$

So, to three decimal places, the root is likely to be 1.050 and we can check this by calculating $f(1.0495)$ and $f(1.0504)$
Now $f(1.0495)$ is negative and $f(1.0504)$ is positive. Thus the root lies between these values and, correct to 3 d.p., is 1.050

The rate of convergence using Newton's Method depends on the crudeness, or otherwise, of the first approximation and on the shape of the curve in the neighbourhood of the root. In extreme cases these factors may lead to failure. Some of these cases are illustrated by the following graphs.

In the following diagrams, α is a root of $f(x) = 0$; a is the first approximation for α and b is the second approximation for α given by Newton's Method.

(a) $f'(a)$ is too small.

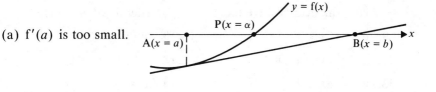

(b) $f'(x)$ increases too rapidly.

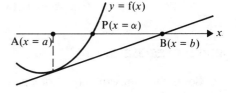

(c) A is too far from P.

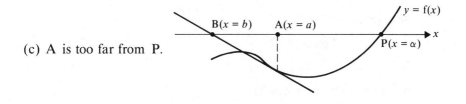

EXERCISE 38e

Show that each of the following equations has a root between $x = 0$ and $x = 1$. Using $x = g(x)$ find this root correct to 2 decimal places.

1. $x^3 - x^2 + 10x - 2 = 0$　　　　　**2.** $3x^3 - 2x^2 - 9x + 2 = 0$

3. $2x^3 + x^2 + 6x - 1 = 0$　　　　　**4.** $x^2 + 8x - 8 = 0$

Use the change of sign of $f(x)$ to find, correct to 2 significant figures, the smallest root of each of the following equations.

5. $4 + 5x^2 - x^3 = 0$　　　　　　　**6.** $x^4 - 4x^3 - x^2 + 4x - 10 = 0$

Use a graphical method to find a first approximation to the root(s) of each equation. Then apply two stages of Newton's Method to give a better approximation. State the accuracy of each of your results.

7. $\tan x = 2x$

(the smallest positive root)

8. $x^3 - 6x + 3 = 0$

(the negative root)

9. $e^x = 2x + 1$

10. $\sin x = 1 - x$

11. $x^2 = \ln(x + 1)$

12. $e^x(1 + x) = 2$

13. $e^x = 3x + 1$

14. $x = 1 + \ln x$

15. $3 + x - 2x^2 = e^x$

16. $x^3 - 3x^2 - 1 = 0$

17. $e^x = 2\cos x$ (the roots between $-\frac{1}{2}\pi$ and $\frac{1}{2}\pi$)

MIXED EXERCISE 38

Solve the following equations giving exact roots.

1. $3^{2x} = 10$

2. $4^x + 2^x - 6 = 0$

3. $2\log_2 x = \log_x 2$

4. $3\sin x - 4\cos x = 2$

5. $x^2 + y^2 = 4$ and $x + y = 1$

6. $\sin x - \sin 3x = \cos 2x$

7. $x^3 - 3x^2 + 3x - 1 = 0$

8. $|x| = 1 - 2|x|$

9. $\cos 2x + \cos x = 2$

10. $2x^4 - 15x^3 + 38x^2 - 39x + 18 = 0$ given that it has a repeated root.

11. Show that the equation $x^3 - 2x^2 - 1 = 0$ has a root between 2 and 3. Taking 2 as a first approximation to this root, use the Newton–Raphson method twice to obtain a better approximation.

12. Show that the equation $e^x = x^2 + 2$ has only one root and find this root correct to two significant figures.

13. Show that the equation $x^4 + x^2 - x = 0$ has two roots. By writing the equation in the form $x = \dfrac{x}{x^3 + x}$ find the larger root correct to one significant figure.

CHAPTER 39

WORKING IN THREE DIMENSIONS

VECTORS

Although we usually assume that two and two make four, this is not always the case.

If, for example, a point B is 2 cm from a point A and C is 2 cm from B then, in general, C is *not* 4 cm from A.

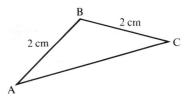

AB, BC and AC are displacements. Each of them has a magnitude and is related to a definite direction in space and so is called a *vector*.

> A vector is a quantity which has both magnitude and a specific direction in space.

A scalar quantity is one that is fully defined by magnitude alone. Length, for example, is a scalar quantity as the length of a piece of string does not depend on its direction when it is measured.

Vector Representation

A vector can be represented by a section of a straight line, whose length represents the magnitude of the vector and whose direction, indicated by an arrow, represents the direction of the vector.
Such vectors can be denoted by a letter in bold type, e.g. **a** or, when hand-written, by a̲.

Alternatively we can represent a vector by the magnitude and direction of a line joining A to B. When we denote the vector by $\overrightarrow{AB}$ or **AB**, the vector in the opposite direction, i.e. from B to A, is written $\overrightarrow{BA}$ or **BA**.

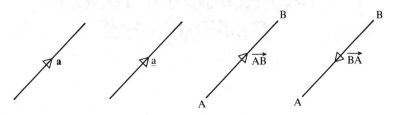

Equivalent Displacements

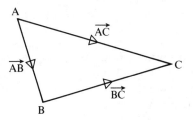

The displacement from A to B, followed by the displacement from B to C, is equivalent to the displacement from A to C.

This is written as the vector equation

$$\overrightarrow{AB} + \overrightarrow{BC} = \overrightarrow{AC}$$

Note that, in vector equations like the one above,
+ means 'together with'   and   = means 'is equivalent to'

Many quantities other than displacements behave in the same way and all of them are vectors.

PROPERTIES OF VECTORS

The Modulus of a Vector

The *modulus* of a vector **a** is its magnitude and is written $|\mathbf{a}|$ or a
i.e. $|\mathbf{a}|$ is the length of the line representing **a**

Equal Vectors

Two vectors with the same magnitude and the same direction are equal.

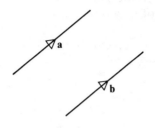

i.e. $\mathbf{a} = \mathbf{b}$ $\Longleftrightarrow$ $\begin{cases} |\mathbf{a}| = |\mathbf{b}| \qquad \text{and} \\ \text{the directions of } \mathbf{a} \text{ and } \mathbf{b} \text{ are the same.} \end{cases}$

It follows that a vector can be represented by *any* line of the right length and direction, regardless of position, i.e. each of the lines in the diagram below represents the vector **a**

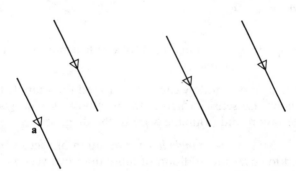

Negative Vectors

If two vectors, **a** and **b**, have the same magnitude but opposite directions we say that

$$\mathbf{b} = -\mathbf{a}$$

i.e. $-\mathbf{a}$ is a vector of magnitude $|\mathbf{a}|$ and in the direction opposite to that of **a**

We also say that **a** and **b** are *equal and opposite* vectors.

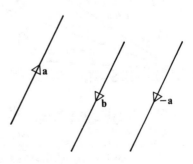

Multiplication of a Vector by a Scalar

If λ is a positive real number,
then $\lambda\mathbf{a}$ is a vector in the same
direction as $\mathbf{a}$ and of magnitude
$\lambda|\mathbf{a}|$
It follows that $-\lambda\mathbf{a}$ is a vector in
the opposite direction, with
magnitude $\lambda|\mathbf{a}|$

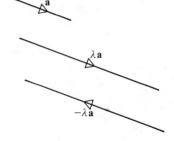

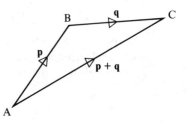

Addition of Vectors

If the sides AB and BC of a
triangle ABC represent the vectors
$\mathbf{p}$ and $\mathbf{q}$ then the third side AC
represents the vector sum, or
resultant, of $\mathbf{p}$ and $\mathbf{q}$, which is
denoted by $\mathbf{p} + \mathbf{q}$

(This property was demonstrated for displacement vectors at the
beginning of the chapter.)

Note that $\mathbf{p}$ and $\mathbf{q}$ follow each other round the triangle (in this case
in the clockwise sense), whereas the resultant, $\mathbf{p} + \mathbf{q}$, goes the
opposite way round (anticlockwise in the diagram).

This is known as *the triangle law* for addition of vectors. It can be
extended to cover the addition of more than two vectors.
Let $\overrightarrow{AB}$, $\overrightarrow{BC}$, $\overrightarrow{CD}$ and $\overrightarrow{DE}$ represent the vectors $\mathbf{a}$, $\mathbf{b}$, $\mathbf{c}$ and $\mathbf{d}$
respectively.

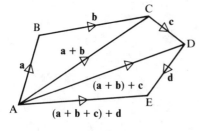

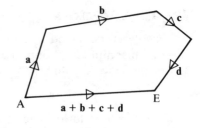

The triangle law gives $\qquad \overrightarrow{AB} + \overrightarrow{BC} = \mathbf{a} + \mathbf{b} = \overrightarrow{AC}$

then $\qquad\qquad\qquad\quad \overrightarrow{AC} + \overrightarrow{CD} = (\mathbf{a} + \mathbf{b}) + \mathbf{c} = \overrightarrow{AD}$

and $\qquad\qquad\qquad\quad \overrightarrow{AD} + \overrightarrow{DE} = (\mathbf{a} + \mathbf{b} + \mathbf{c}) + \mathbf{d} = \overrightarrow{AE}$

Now AE completes the polygon of which AB, BC, CD and DE are four sides taken in order, (i.e. they follow each other round the polygon in the *same sense*). Note that, again, the side representing the resultant closes the polygon in the *opposite* sense.

Note that the vectors **a**, **b**, **c** and **d** are not necessarily coplanar so the polygon may not be a plane figure.

The order in which the addition is performed does not matter as we can see by considering a parallelogram ABCD

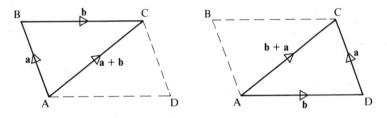

Because the opposite sides of a parallelogram are equal and parallel,
$\overrightarrow{AB}$ and $\overrightarrow{DC}$ both represent **a**   and $\overrightarrow{BC}$ and $\overrightarrow{AD}$ both represent **b**
In $\triangle ABC$ $\overrightarrow{AC} = \mathbf{a} + \mathbf{b}$ and in $\triangle ADC$ $\overrightarrow{AC} = \mathbf{b} + \mathbf{a}$

Therefore $\mathbf{a} + \mathbf{b} = \mathbf{b} + \mathbf{a}$

The Angle between Two Vectors

There are two angles between two lines
i.e. α and $180° - \alpha$

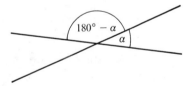

The angle between two vectors, however, is defined uniquely. It is the angle between their directions when the lines representing them *both converge* or *both diverge* (see diagrams i and ii).

In some cases one of the lines may have to be produced in order to mark the correct angle (see diagram iii).

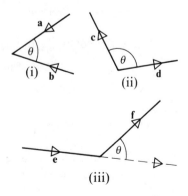

Examples 39a

1. Two vectors, **a** and **b**, are such that $|\mathbf{a}| = 3$, $|\mathbf{b}| = 5$ and the angle between **a** and **b** is $\frac{1}{3}\pi$. If the line OP represents the vector $3\mathbf{a} - 2\mathbf{b}$, find, correct to 1 d.p., the angle between $\overrightarrow{OP}$ and **a**

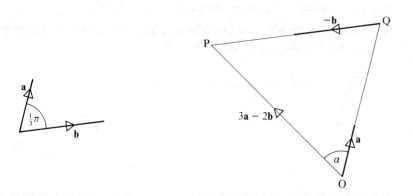

The line OP is found by drawing OQ parallel to **a** such that $\overrightarrow{OQ} = 3\mathbf{a}$, followed by QP parallel to **b** such that $\overrightarrow{QP} = -2\mathbf{b}$

Thus $\overrightarrow{OP} = 3\mathbf{a} - 2\mathbf{b}$

Now $OQ = 3|\mathbf{a}| = 9$

and $QP = 2|\mathbf{b}| = 10$

The angle between $\overrightarrow{OP}$ and **a** is α where

$$\frac{\sin \alpha}{10} = \frac{\sin \frac{1}{3}\pi}{OP}$$

So first we must find OP

Using the cosine formula in OPQ gives

$$OP^2 = 81 + 100 - (2)(9)(10)\cos \tfrac{1}{3}\pi = 91$$

$\Rightarrow$ $\qquad OP = \sqrt{91}$

Then $\dfrac{\sin \alpha}{10} = \dfrac{\sin \frac{1}{3}\pi}{\sqrt{91}}$ $\qquad \Rightarrow \qquad \sin \alpha = 0.9078$

$\therefore$ OP is inclined at 65.2° to **a**

2. In a triangle ABC, $\overrightarrow{AB}$ represents **a** and $\overrightarrow{BC}$ represents **b**. If D is the midpoint of AB express in terms of **a** and **b** the vectors $\overrightarrow{CA}$ and $\overrightarrow{DC}$.

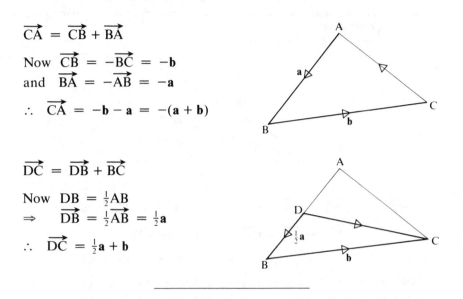

$\overrightarrow{CA} = \overrightarrow{CB} + \overrightarrow{BA}$

Now $\overrightarrow{CB} = -\overrightarrow{BC} = -\mathbf{b}$

and $\overrightarrow{BA} = -\overrightarrow{AB} = -\mathbf{a}$

$\therefore\ \overrightarrow{CA} = -\mathbf{b} - \mathbf{a} = -(\mathbf{a} + \mathbf{b})$

$\overrightarrow{DC} = \overrightarrow{DB} + \overrightarrow{BC}$

Now $DB = \frac{1}{2}AB$

$\Rightarrow\quad \overrightarrow{DB} = \frac{1}{2}\overrightarrow{AB} = \frac{1}{2}\mathbf{a}$

$\therefore\ \overrightarrow{DC} = \frac{1}{2}\mathbf{a} + \mathbf{b}$

---

3. If D is the midpoint of the side BC of a triangle ABC, show that $\overrightarrow{AB} + \overrightarrow{AC} = 2\overrightarrow{AD}$

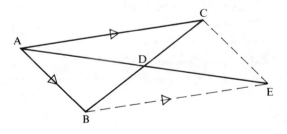

Completing the parallelogram ABEC we see that $\overrightarrow{BE} = \overrightarrow{AC}$

Therefore $\overrightarrow{AB} + \overrightarrow{AC} = \overrightarrow{AB} + \overrightarrow{BE} = \overrightarrow{AE}$

The diagonals of a parallelogram bisect each other.

Therefore $\overrightarrow{AE} = 2\overrightarrow{AD}$

$\Rightarrow\qquad \overrightarrow{AB} + \overrightarrow{AC} = 2\overrightarrow{AD}$

---

4. Four points O, A, B and C are such that $\overrightarrow{OA} = 10\mathbf{a}$, $\overrightarrow{OB} = 5\mathbf{b}$ and $\overrightarrow{OC} = 4\mathbf{a} + 3\mathbf{b}$. Show that A, B and C are collinear.

If A, B and C are collinear then AB and BC have the same direction so this is what we must show.

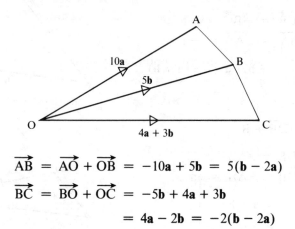

$$\overrightarrow{AB} = \overrightarrow{AO} + \overrightarrow{OB} = -10\mathbf{a} + 5\mathbf{b} = 5(\mathbf{b} - 2\mathbf{a})$$

$$\overrightarrow{BC} = \overrightarrow{BO} + \overrightarrow{OC} = -5\mathbf{b} + 4\mathbf{a} + 3\mathbf{b}$$

$$= 4\mathbf{a} - 2\mathbf{b} = -2(\mathbf{b} - 2\mathbf{a})$$

AB and BC both have a direction given by $\lambda(\mathbf{b} - 2\mathbf{a})$ so they are parallel. Hence, since C is a common point, A, B and C are collinear.

Note that $\overrightarrow{BC} = -\frac{2}{5}\overrightarrow{AB}$ so, although $\overrightarrow{AB}$ and $\overrightarrow{BC}$ are parallel, they are in opposite directions, showing that the diagram really looks like this.

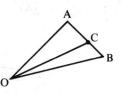

EXERCISE 39a

1. ABCD is a quadrilateral. Find the single vector which is equivalent to

(a) $\overrightarrow{AB} + \overrightarrow{BC}$ (b) $\overrightarrow{BC} + \overrightarrow{CD}$

(c) $\overrightarrow{AB} + \overrightarrow{BC} + \overrightarrow{CD}$ (d) $\overrightarrow{AB} + \overrightarrow{DA}$

2. ABCDEF is a regular hexagon in which $\overrightarrow{BC}$ represents $\mathbf{b}$ and $\overrightarrow{FC}$ represents $2\mathbf{a}$.

Express the vectors $\overrightarrow{AB}$, $\overrightarrow{CD}$ and $\overrightarrow{BE}$ in terms of $\mathbf{a}$ and $\mathbf{b}$

3. Draw diagrams representing the following vector equations.

(a) $\overrightarrow{AB} - \overrightarrow{CB} = \overrightarrow{AC}$ (b) $\overrightarrow{AB} = 2\overrightarrow{PQ}$

(c) $\overrightarrow{AB} + \overrightarrow{BC} = 3\overrightarrow{AD}$ (d) $2\overrightarrow{AB} + \overrightarrow{PQ} = 0$

4. If A, B, C, D are four points such that $\overrightarrow{AB} = \overrightarrow{DC}$ and $\overrightarrow{BC} + \overrightarrow{DA} = 0$ prove that ABCD is a parallelogram.

5. O, A, B, C, D are five points such that $\overrightarrow{OA} = $ **a**, $\overrightarrow{OB} = $ **b**, $\overrightarrow{OC} = $ **a** + 2**b**, $\overrightarrow{OD} = $ 2**a** − **b**
Express $\overrightarrow{AB}$, $\overrightarrow{BC}$, $\overrightarrow{CD}$, $\overrightarrow{AC}$, $\overrightarrow{BD}$ in terms of **a** and **b**

6.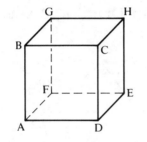

If **a**, **b**, **c** are represented by the edges $\overrightarrow{AB}$, $\overrightarrow{AD}$, $\overrightarrow{AF}$ of the cube in the diagram, find, in terms of **a**, **b** and **c**, the vectors represented by the remaining edges.

7. If O, A, B, C are four points such that $\overrightarrow{OA} = $ **a**, $\overrightarrow{OB} = $ 2**a** − **b**, $\overrightarrow{OC} = $ **b** show that A, B and C are collinear.

8.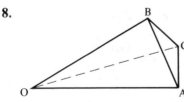

If OABC is a tetrahedron and $\overrightarrow{OA} = $ **a**, $\overrightarrow{OB} = $ **b**, $\overrightarrow{OC} = $ **c**, find $\overrightarrow{AC}$, $\overrightarrow{AB}$, $\overrightarrow{CB}$ in terms of **a**, **b**, **c**

9. For the cube defined in Question 6, find, in terms of **a, b** and **c,** the vectors $\overrightarrow{BE}$, $\overrightarrow{GD}$, $\overrightarrow{AH}$, $\overrightarrow{FC}$.

10. If **a** and **b** are vectors such that $|\mathbf{a}| = 2$, $|\mathbf{b}| = 4$ and the angle between **a** and **b** is $\frac{1}{3}\pi$, find the angle between

(a) **a** and **a** − **b**   (b) **b** and **a** + **b**   (c) 3**a** − **b** and **b**

POSITION VECTORS

In general a vector has no specific location in space and is called a *free vector*. Some vectors, however, are constrained to a specific position, e.g. the vector $\overrightarrow{OA}$ where O is a fixed origin.

$\overrightarrow{OA}$ is called the position vector of A relative to O.

This displacement is unique and *cannot* be represented by any other line of equal length and direction.

Vectors such as $\overrightarrow{OA}$, representing quantities that have a specific location, are called *position* vectors or *tied* vectors.

The Position Vector of a Point Dividing a Given Line in a Given Ratio

Consider a line AB
where the position vectors
relative to O of A and B
are **a** and **b** respectively.

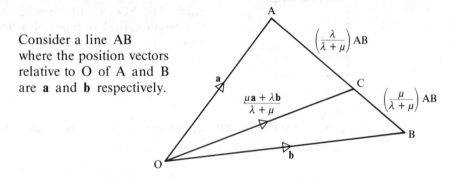

If C divides AB in the ratio $\lambda : \mu$ then

$$\overrightarrow{AC} = \frac{\lambda}{\lambda + \mu}\overrightarrow{AB} = \frac{\lambda}{\lambda + \mu}(\overrightarrow{OB} - \overrightarrow{OA})$$

i.e. $$\overrightarrow{AC} = \frac{\lambda}{\lambda + \mu}(\mathbf{b} - \mathbf{a})$$

Now $$\overrightarrow{OC} = \overrightarrow{OA} + \overrightarrow{AC} = \mathbf{a} + \frac{\lambda}{\lambda + \mu}(\mathbf{b} - \mathbf{a})$$

i.e.   if A and B are points with position vectors **a** and **b**,
         and C divides AB in the ratio $\lambda : \mu$,

         then   the position vector of C is $\dfrac{\mu\mathbf{a} + \lambda\mathbf{b}}{\lambda + \mu}$

A special case of this quotable
result arises when $\lambda = \mu$
i.e. when C is the midpoint of AB.

Then the position vector of C is

$$\tfrac{1}{2}(\mathbf{a} + \mathbf{b})$$

Examples 39b

1. In a triangle ABC, P is the midpoint of AB and Q divides BC in
   the ratio $2:1$. Given that $\overrightarrow{OA} = \mathbf{a}$, $\overrightarrow{OB} = \mathbf{b}$ and $\overrightarrow{OC} = \mathbf{c}$,
   find in terms of $\mathbf{a}$, $\mathbf{b}$ and $\mathbf{c}$, the position vectors of P, Q and the
   midpoint of PQ.

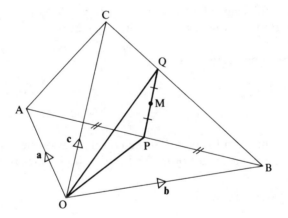

AP : PB $= 1:1$

$\therefore$ the position vector of P is $\tfrac{1}{2}(\mathbf{a} + \mathbf{b})$

BQ : QC $= 2:1$

$\therefore$ the position vector of Q is $\dfrac{(1)(\mathbf{b}) + (2)(\mathbf{c})}{2 + 1} = \tfrac{1}{3}(\mathbf{b} + 2\mathbf{c})$

If M is the midpoint of PQ then the position vector of M is

$$\tfrac{1}{2}(\overrightarrow{OP} + \overrightarrow{OQ}) = \tfrac{1}{2}\{\tfrac{1}{2}(\mathbf{a} + \mathbf{b}) + \tfrac{1}{3}(\mathbf{b} + 2\mathbf{c})\}$$
$$= \tfrac{1}{4}\mathbf{a} + \tfrac{5}{12}\mathbf{b} + \tfrac{1}{3}\mathbf{c}$$

2. Given that the centroid of a triangle divides each median in the ratio $2:1$ from vertex to opposite side, find the position vector of the centroid of $\triangle ABC$ where the position vectors of A, B and C are **a**, **b** and **c** respectively

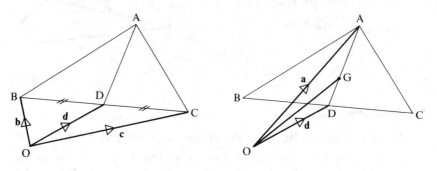

Considering the median AD we first find the position vector of D, the midpoint of BC.

The position vector of D is **d** where $\mathbf{d} = \frac{1}{2}(\mathbf{b} + \mathbf{c})$
The centroid, G, divides AD in the ratio $2:1$

So the position vector of G is $\dfrac{(1)(\mathbf{a}) + (2)(\mathbf{d})}{2 + 1} = \dfrac{\mathbf{a} + 2\{\frac{1}{2}(\mathbf{b} + \mathbf{c})\}}{3}$

$$= \tfrac{1}{3}(\mathbf{a} + \mathbf{b} + \mathbf{c})$$

Note that this result shows that the coordinates of the centroid of a triangle are the averages of the respective coordinates of the three vertices.

EXERCISE 39b

In this exercise the position vectors, relative to O, of A, B, C and D are **a**, **b**, **c** and **d** respectively. P, Q and R are the midpoints of AB, BC and CD respectively.

In Questions 1 to 4 find the position vector of each given point.

1. (a) The midpoint of AC   (b) The midpoint of BD.

2. The point L which divides AD in the ratio $1:3$

3. The point M which divides BC in the ratio $4:3$

4. (a) The midpoint of PQ   (b) The midpoint of QR.

5. Show that PQ is parallel to AC

6. Find the vector represented by LD

7. Find the vector represented by AR

8. Find the position vector of the point which
   (a) divides CP in the ratio 2:1   (b) divides AQ in the ratio 2:1
   Say what you notice about your answers to (a) and (b) and explain
   this relationship.

THE LOCATION OF A POINT IN SPACE

We saw in Chapter 5 that any point P in a plane can be located by
giving its distances from a fixed point O, in each of two perpendicular
directions. These distances are the cartesian coordinates of the point.

Now we consider locating a point in three-dimensional space.

If we have a fixed point, O, then any other point can be located by
giving its distances from O in each of *three* mutually perpendicular
directions, i.e. we need *three* coordinates to locate a point in space. So
we use the familiar x and y axes, together with a third axis Oz. Then
any point has coordinates (x, y, z) relative to the origin O.

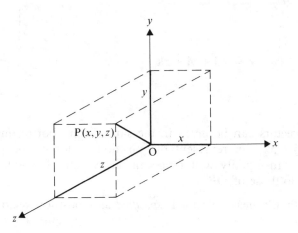

Cartesian Unit Vectors

> A unit vector is a vector whose magnitude is one unit.

Now if

i is a unit vector in the direction of Ox
j is a unit vector in the direction of Oy
k is a unit vector in the direction of Oz

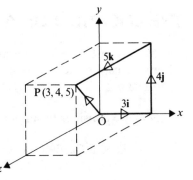

then the position vector, relative to O, of any point P can be given in terms of **i**, **j** and **k**.

e.g. the point distant
   3 units from O in the direction Ox
   4 units from O in the direction Oy
   5 units from O in the direction Oz

has coordinates $(3, 4, 5)$

and $\overrightarrow{OP} = 3\mathbf{i} + 4\mathbf{j} + 5\mathbf{k}$

In general, if P is a point, (x, y, z) and $\overrightarrow{OP} = \mathbf{r}$, then

$$\mathbf{r} = x\mathbf{i} + y\mathbf{j} + z\mathbf{k}$$

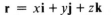

Free vectors can be given in the same form. For example, the vector $3\mathbf{i} + 4\mathbf{j} + 5\mathbf{k}$ *can* represent the position vector of the point P(3, 4, 5) but it can equally well represent *any* vector of length and direction equal to those of OP.

Note that, unless a vector is *specified* as a position vector it is taken to be free.

OPERATIONS ON CARTESIAN VECTORS

Addition and Subtraction

To add or subtract vectors given in $\mathbf{i}\,\mathbf{j}\,\mathbf{k}$ form, the coefficients of $\mathbf{i}$, $\mathbf{j}$ and $\mathbf{k}$ are collected separately,

e.g.   if $\mathbf{v}_1 = 3\mathbf{i} + 2\mathbf{j} + 2\mathbf{k}$ and $\mathbf{v}_2 = \mathbf{i} + 2\mathbf{j} - 3\mathbf{k}$

then
$$\mathbf{v}_1 + \mathbf{v}_2 = (3\mathbf{i} + 2\mathbf{j} + 2\mathbf{k}) + (\mathbf{i} + 2\mathbf{j} - 3\mathbf{k})$$
$$= (3 + 1)\mathbf{i} + (2 + 2)\mathbf{j} + (2 - 3)\mathbf{k}$$
$$= 4\mathbf{i} + 4\mathbf{j} - \mathbf{k}$$

and
$$\mathbf{v}_1 - \mathbf{v}_2 = (3 - 1)\mathbf{i} + (2 - 2)\mathbf{j} + (2 - \{-3\})\mathbf{k}$$
$$= 2\mathbf{i} + 5\mathbf{k}$$

Modulus

The modulus of $\mathbf{v}$, where $\mathbf{v} = 12\mathbf{i} - 3\mathbf{j} + 4\mathbf{k}$, is the length of OP where P is the point $(12, -3, 4)$.

Using Pythagoras twice we have

$OB^2 = OA^2 + AB^2 = 12^2 + 4^2$

$OP^2 = OB^2 + BP^2 = (12^2 + 4^2) + (-3)^2$

$\therefore \quad OP = \sqrt{(12^2 + 4^2 + 3^2)} = 13$

In general, if $\mathbf{v} = a\mathbf{i} + b\mathbf{j} + c\mathbf{k}$.

$$|\mathbf{v}| = \sqrt{(a^2 + b^2 + c^2)}$$

Parallel Vectors

Two vectors $\mathbf{v}_1$ and $\mathbf{v}_2$ are parallel if $\mathbf{v}_1 = \lambda\mathbf{v}_2$

e.g. $2\mathbf{i} - 3\mathbf{j} - \mathbf{k}$ is parallel to $4\mathbf{i} - 6\mathbf{j} - 2\mathbf{k}$ ($\lambda = 2$)
and $\mathbf{i} + \mathbf{j} + \mathbf{k}$ is parallel to $-3\mathbf{i} - 3\mathbf{j} - 3\mathbf{k}$ ($\lambda = -3$)

Equal Vectors

If two vectors $\mathbf{v}_1 = a_1\mathbf{i} + b_1\mathbf{j} + c_1\mathbf{k}$ and $\mathbf{v}_2 = a_2\mathbf{i} + b_2\mathbf{j} + c_2\mathbf{k}$ are equal then

$$a_1 = a_2 \text{ and } b_1 = b_2 \text{ and } c_1 = c_2$$

Examples 39c

1. Given the vector **v** where **v** = 5**i** − 2**j** + 4**k**, state whether each of the following vectors is parallel to **v**, equal to **v** or neither.

    (a) 10**i** − 4**j** + 8**k**   (b) $-\frac{1}{2}(-10\mathbf{i} + 4\mathbf{j} - 8\mathbf{k})$

    (c) −5**i** + 2**j** − 4**k**   (d) 4**i** − 2**j** + 5**k**

(a) 10**i** − 4**j** + 8**k** = 2(5**i** − 2**j** + 4**k**)   (λ = 2)

    ∴ 10**i** − 4**j** + 8**k** is parallel to **v**

(b) $-\frac{1}{2}(-10\mathbf{i} + 4\mathbf{j} - 8\mathbf{k})$ = 5**i** − 2**j** + 4**k**

    ∴ $-\frac{1}{2}(-10\mathbf{i} + 4\mathbf{j} - 8\mathbf{k})$ is equal to **v**

(c) −5**i** + 2**j** − 4**k** = −(5**i** − 2**j** + 4**k**)   (λ = −1)

    ∴ −5**i** + 2**j** − 4**k** is parallel to **v**

(d) 4**i** − 2**j** + 5**k** is not a multiple of 5**i** − 2**j** + 4**k**

    ∴ 4**i** − 2**j** + 5**k** is not parallel to **v**

2. A triangle ABC has its vertices at the points A(2, −1, 4), B(3, −2, 5) and C(−1, 6, 2). Find, in the form $a\mathbf{i} + b\mathbf{j} + c\mathbf{k}$, the vectors $\overrightarrow{AB}$, $\overrightarrow{BC}$ and $\overrightarrow{CA}$ and hence find the lengths of the sides of the triangle.

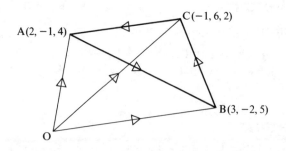

The coordinate axes are not drawn in this diagram as they tend to cause confusion when two or more points are illustrated. The origin should always be included however as it provides a reference point.

$$\vec{AB} = \vec{OB} - \vec{OA}$$

$$= (3i - 2j + 5k) - (2i - j + 4k)$$

$$= i - j + k$$

$$\vec{BC} = \vec{OC} - \vec{OB}$$

$$= (-i + 6j + 2k) - (3i - 2j + 5k)$$

$$= -4i + 8j - 3k$$

$$\vec{CA} = \vec{OA} - \vec{OC}$$

$$= (2i - j + 4k) - (-i + 6j + 2k)$$

$$= 3i - 7j + 2k$$

Hence $AB = |\vec{AB}| = \sqrt{\{(1)^2 + (-1)^2 + (1)^2\}} = \sqrt{3}$

$BC = |\vec{BC}| = \sqrt{\{(-4)^2 + (8)^2 + (-3)^2\}} = \sqrt{89}$

$CA = |\vec{CA}| = \sqrt{\{(3)^2 + (-7)^2 + (2)^2\}} = \sqrt{62}$

Two-dimensional problems can be solved by using the same principles as for three-dimensional cases but the working tends to be easier because it involves fewer terms.

---

3. Given that $\mathbf{p} = i + 3j$, $\mathbf{q} = 4i - 2j$, $\mathbf{OA} = 2\mathbf{p}$ and $\mathbf{OB} = 3\mathbf{q}$, find   (a) $|\mathbf{OA}|$ (b) $|\mathbf{OB}|$ (c) $|\mathbf{AB}|$

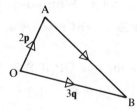

(a) $|\mathbf{OA}| = 2|i + 3j| = 2\sqrt{(1^2 + 3^2)} = 2\sqrt{10}$

(b) $|\mathbf{OB}| = 3|4i - 2j| = 3\sqrt{\{4^2 + (-2)^2\}} = 6\sqrt{5}$

(c) $\mathbf{AB} = \mathbf{OB} - \mathbf{OA} = 3(4i - 2j) - 2(i + 3j) = 10i - 12k$

$|\mathbf{AB}| = \sqrt{(10^2 + 12^2)} = 2\sqrt{61}$

---

4. If P is a point with position vector $(\cos\theta)\mathbf{i} + (\sin\theta)\mathbf{j}$, find the cartesian equation of the curve on which P lies.

If P is the point (x, y) and $\mathbf{OP} = (\cos\theta)\mathbf{i} + (\sin\theta)\mathbf{j}$ then

$$x = \cos\theta \quad \text{and} \quad y = \sin\theta$$

These are the parametric equations of the locus of P. We can find the cartesian equation by eliminating θ between them.

Using $\cos^2\theta + \sin^2\theta = 1$

gives $x^2 + y^2 = 1$

Therefore P lies on the curve $x^2 + y^2 = 1$ which can be recognised as a circle with radius 1 and centre at O.

EXERCISE 39c

1. Write down, in the form $a\mathbf{i} + b\mathbf{j} + c\mathbf{k}$, the vector represented by $\overrightarrow{OP}$ if P is a point with coordinates

    (a) $(3, 6, 4)$ (b) $(1, -2, -7)$ (c) $(1, 0, -3)$

2. $\overrightarrow{OP}$ represents a vector $\mathbf{r}$. Write down the coordinates of P if

    (a) $\mathbf{r} = 5\mathbf{i} - 7\mathbf{j} + 2\mathbf{k}$ (b) $\mathbf{r} = \mathbf{i} + 4\mathbf{j}$ (c) $\mathbf{r} = \mathbf{j} - \mathbf{k}$

3. Find the length of the line OP if P is the point

    (a) $(2, -1, 4)$ (b) $(3, 0, 4)$ (c) $(-2, -2, 1)$

4. Find the modulus of the vector $\mathbf{V}$ if

    (a) $\mathbf{V} = 2\mathbf{i} - 4\mathbf{j} + 4\mathbf{k}$ (b) $\mathbf{V} = 6\mathbf{i} + 2\mathbf{j} - 3\mathbf{k}$

    (c) $\mathbf{V} = 11\mathbf{i} - 7\mathbf{j} - 6\mathbf{k}$

5. If $\mathbf{a} = \mathbf{i} + \mathbf{j} + \mathbf{k}$, $\mathbf{b} = 2\mathbf{i} - \mathbf{j} + 3\mathbf{k}$, $\mathbf{c} = -\mathbf{i} + 3\mathbf{j} - \mathbf{k}$ find

    (a) $\mathbf{a} + \mathbf{b}$ (b) $\mathbf{a} - \mathbf{c}$ (c) $\mathbf{a} + \mathbf{b} + \mathbf{c}$ (d) $\mathbf{a} - 2\mathbf{b} + 3\mathbf{c}$

In Questions 6 to 8, $\overrightarrow{OA} = \mathbf{a} = 4\mathbf{i} - 12\mathbf{j}$ and $\overrightarrow{OB} = \mathbf{b} = \mathbf{i} + 6\mathbf{j}$.

6. Which of the following vectors are parallel to $\mathbf{a}$?

   (a) $\mathbf{i} + 3\mathbf{j}$ (b) $-\mathbf{i} + 3\mathbf{j}$ (c) $12\mathbf{i} - 4\mathbf{j}$ (d) $-4\mathbf{i} + 12\mathbf{j}$ (e) $\mathbf{i} - 3\mathbf{j}$

7. Which of the following vectors are equal to $\mathbf{b}$?

   (a) $2\mathbf{i} + 12\mathbf{j}$ (b) $-\mathbf{i} - 6\mathbf{j}$ (c) $\overrightarrow{AE}$ if E is $(5, -6)$

   (d) $\overrightarrow{AF}$ if F is $(6, 0)$

8. If $\overrightarrow{OD} = \lambda \overrightarrow{OA}$, find the value of λ for which $\overrightarrow{OD} + \overrightarrow{OB}$ is parallel to the x-axis

9. Which of the following vectors are parallel to $3\mathbf{i} - \mathbf{j} - 2\mathbf{k}$?

   (a) $6\mathbf{i} - 3\mathbf{j} - 4\mathbf{k}$ (b) $-9\mathbf{i} + 3\mathbf{j} + 6\mathbf{k}$ (c) $-3\mathbf{i} - \mathbf{j} - 2\mathbf{k}$
   (d) $-2(3\mathbf{i} + \mathbf{j} + 2\mathbf{k})$ (e) $\frac{3}{2}\mathbf{i} - \frac{1}{2}\mathbf{j} - \mathbf{k}$ (f) $-\mathbf{i} + \frac{1}{3}\mathbf{j} + \frac{2}{3}\mathbf{k}$

10. Given that $\mathbf{a} = 4\mathbf{i} + \mathbf{j} - 6\mathbf{k}$, state whether each of the following vectors is parallel or equal to $\mathbf{a}$ or neither.

    (a) $8\mathbf{i} + 2\mathbf{j} - 10\mathbf{k}$ (b) $-4\mathbf{i} - \mathbf{j} + 6\mathbf{k}$ (c) $2(2\mathbf{i} + \frac{1}{2}\mathbf{j} - 3\mathbf{k})$

11. The triangle ABC has its vertices at the points $A(-1, 3, 0)$, $B(-3, 0, 7)$, $C(-1, 2, 3)$,. Find in the form $a\mathbf{i} + b\mathbf{j} + c\mathbf{k}$ the vectors representing

    (a) $\overrightarrow{AB}$ (b) $\overrightarrow{AC}$ (c) $\overrightarrow{CB}$

12. Find the lengths of the sides of the triangle described in Question 11.

13. Find $|\mathbf{a} - \mathbf{b}|$ where $\mathbf{a} = \mathbf{i} - \mathbf{j} + 2\mathbf{k}$, $\mathbf{b} = 2\mathbf{i} - \mathbf{j}$

14. A, B, C and D are the points $(0, 0, 2)$, $(-1, 3, 2)$, $(1, 0, 4)$ and $(-1, 2, -2)$ respectively. Find the vectors representing $\overrightarrow{AB}$, $\overrightarrow{BD}$, $\overrightarrow{CD}$, $\overrightarrow{AD}$

15. If the position vector of P is $t^2\mathbf{i} + 2t\mathbf{j}$, find the cartesian equation of the locus of P and name this curve.

16. Show that, for all values of t, the point whose equation vector is $\mathbf{r} = t\mathbf{i} + (2t - 1)\mathbf{j}$ lies on the line $y = 2x - 1$

DIRECTION RATIOS

The vector $\mathbf{v} = a\mathbf{i} + b\mathbf{j} + c\mathbf{k}$ can be represented by $\overrightarrow{OP}$ where P is the point (a, b, c)

The coordinates of P determine the direction of OP relative to the axes and

> the ratios $a:b:c$ are called the direction ratios of $\mathbf{v}$

We often use the abbreviation d.r.s for direction ratios

e.g. the d.r.s of $5\mathbf{i} - 3\mathbf{j} + 7\mathbf{k}$ are $5:-3:7$

It follows that *the direction ratios of parallel vectors are equal,*

e.g. $\mathbf{i} - 2\mathbf{j} + 3\mathbf{k}$ has d.r.s $1:-2:3$ and is parallel to any vector whose d.r.s are $t:-2t:3t$, for instance $3:-6:9 = 1:-2:3$ and $-2:4:-6 = 1:-2:3$

FINDING A UNIT VECTOR

Consider the vector $\mathbf{v} = 6\mathbf{i} + 2\mathbf{j} + 3\mathbf{k}$, represented by $\overrightarrow{OP}$ where P is the point $(6, 2, 3)$

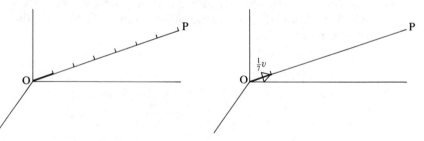

Now $|\mathbf{v}|$ is $\sqrt{(6^2 + 2^2 + 3^2)}$, i.e. OP is 7 units long.
Therefore $\frac{1}{7}\mathbf{v}$ is a vector of unit magnitude and is denoted by $\widehat{\mathbf{v}}$

i.e. $$\widehat{\mathbf{v}} = \frac{\mathbf{v}}{|\mathbf{v}|} \qquad \text{or} \qquad \mathbf{v} = |\mathbf{v}|\,\widehat{\mathbf{v}}$$

In general　　any vector $\mathbf{v}$ is the product of its magnitude and a unit vector in the same direction

and　　　　a unit vector in the direction of $\mathbf{v}$ is given by $\dfrac{\mathbf{v}}{|\mathbf{v}|}$

Using Direction Vectors

A vector which is used to specify the direction of another vector can be called a *direction* vector.

e.g. if we are told that a vector **v**, of magnitude 14 units, is parallel to the vector $3\mathbf{i} + 6\mathbf{j} + 2\mathbf{k}$, then $3\mathbf{i} + 6\mathbf{j} + 2\mathbf{k}$ is a direction vector for **v**

Therefore the unit vector in the direction of **v** is $\dfrac{3\mathbf{i} + 6\mathbf{j} + 2\mathbf{k}}{\sqrt{(3^2 + 6^2 + 2^2)}}$

i.e. $\quad \hat{\mathbf{v}} = \frac{1}{7}(3\mathbf{i} + 6\mathbf{j} + 2\mathbf{k})$

Then $\quad \mathbf{v} = |\mathbf{v}|(\hat{\mathbf{v}}) = (14)\{\frac{1}{7}(3\mathbf{i} + 6\mathbf{j} + 2\mathbf{k})\} = 6\mathbf{i} + 12\mathbf{j} + 4\mathbf{k}$

Examples 39d

1. Find the coordinates of P if OP is of length 5 units and is parallel to the vector $2\mathbf{i} - \mathbf{j} + 4\mathbf{k}$

A vector parallel to $2\mathbf{i} - \mathbf{j} + 4\mathbf{k}$ can be in either of the directions given by $\pm(2\mathbf{i} - \mathbf{j} + 4\mathbf{k})$

$\therefore \quad$ the direction vector for **OP** is $\pm(2\mathbf{i} - \mathbf{j} + 4\mathbf{k})$

$$|2\mathbf{i} - \mathbf{j} + 4\mathbf{k}| = \sqrt{(2^2 + \{-1\}^2 + 4^2)} = \sqrt{21}$$

$\therefore \quad$ the unit direction vector in the direction of **OP** is

$$\frac{\pm(2\mathbf{i} - \mathbf{j} + 4\mathbf{k})}{\sqrt{21}}$$

Now $\quad \mathbf{OP} = |\mathbf{OP}|(\widehat{\mathbf{OP}})$

therefore

$$\mathbf{OP} = (5)\left\{\frac{\pm(2\mathbf{i} - \mathbf{j} + 4\mathbf{k})}{\sqrt{21}}\right\} = \pm\left(\frac{10}{\sqrt{21}}\mathbf{i} - \frac{5}{\sqrt{21}}\mathbf{j} + \frac{20}{\sqrt{21}}\mathbf{k}\right)$$

The coordinates of P are

either $\left(\dfrac{10}{\sqrt{21}}, \dfrac{-5}{\sqrt{21}}, \dfrac{20}{\sqrt{21}}\right)$ or $\left(\dfrac{-10}{\sqrt{21}}, \dfrac{5}{\sqrt{21}}, \dfrac{-20}{\sqrt{21}}\right)$

2. **(a)** Write down the direction ratios of the vectors
   (i) $\mathbf{i} + 4\mathbf{j} - 7\mathbf{k}$ (ii) $2\mathbf{i} - 9\mathbf{k}$

   (b) Find a unit vector in the direction of the vector $2\mathbf{i} - \mathbf{j} - 2\mathbf{k}$

(a) (i) The d.r.s of $\mathbf{i} + 4\mathbf{j} - 7\mathbf{k}$ are $1:4:-7$
     (ii) $2\mathbf{i} - 9\mathbf{k} = 2\mathbf{i} + 0\mathbf{j} - 9\mathbf{k}$ so the d.r.s are $2:0:-9$

(b) If $\mathbf{v} = 2\mathbf{i} - \mathbf{j} - 2\mathbf{k}$ then $|\mathbf{v}| = \sqrt{\{2^2 + (-1)^2 + (-2)^2\}} = 3$

$$\therefore \quad \hat{\mathbf{v}} = \frac{\mathbf{v}}{|\mathbf{v}|} = \frac{2\mathbf{i} - \mathbf{j} - 2\mathbf{k}}{3} = \tfrac{2}{3}\mathbf{i} - \tfrac{1}{3}\mathbf{j} - \tfrac{2}{3}\mathbf{k}$$

EXERCISE 39d

1. Write down the direction ratios of the vectors
   (a) $2\mathbf{i} + 2\mathbf{j} - \mathbf{k}$ (b) $6\mathbf{i} - 2\mathbf{j} - 3\mathbf{k}$ (c) $3\mathbf{i} + 4\mathbf{k}$ (d) $\mathbf{i} + 8\mathbf{j} + 4\mathbf{k}$

2. Find a unit vector in the direction of each of the vectors in Qu. 1.

3. Find the coordinates of Q if $|\mathbf{OQ}| = 1$ and $\mathbf{OQ}$ is in the
   direction of
   (a) $\mathbf{i} + 2\mathbf{j} - 2\mathbf{k}$ (b) $3\mathbf{i} + 2\mathbf{j} + 6\mathbf{k}$ (c) $8\mathbf{i} - \mathbf{j} - 4\mathbf{k}$ (d) $\mathbf{i} - \mathbf{j} - \mathbf{k}$

4. Find the coordinates of P if
   (a) $|\mathbf{OP}| = 6$ and $\mathbf{OP}$ is in the direction of $2\mathbf{i} - 3\mathbf{j} + 6\mathbf{k}$
   (b) $|\mathbf{OP}| = 2$ and $\mathbf{OP}$ is in the direction of $8\mathbf{i} + 4\mathbf{j} - \mathbf{k}$

5. Find the vector $\mathbf{V}$ if
   (a) $\mathbf{V} = \mathbf{OP}$ where P is the point $(0, 4, 5)$
   (b) $|\mathbf{V}| = 24$ units and $\hat{\mathbf{V}} = \tfrac{2}{3}\mathbf{i} - \tfrac{2}{3}\mathbf{j} - \tfrac{1}{3}\mathbf{k}$
   (c) $\mathbf{V}$ is parallel to the vector $8\mathbf{i} + \mathbf{j} + 4\mathbf{k}$ and equal in magnitude
   to the vector $\mathbf{i} - 2\mathbf{j} + 2\mathbf{k}$

6. Find $\hat{\mathbf{r}}$ in the form $a\mathbf{i} + b\mathbf{j} + c\mathbf{k}$ if
   (a) $\mathbf{r} = \mathbf{i} - \mathbf{j} + \mathbf{k}$ (b) $\mathbf{r} = 5\mathbf{j} - 12\mathbf{k}$ (c) $\mathbf{r} = \mathbf{i}$

7. If $\mathbf{r}_1 = 2\mathbf{i} - \mathbf{j} + \mathbf{k}$ and $\mathbf{r}_2 = \mathbf{i} + 3\mathbf{j} + 2\mathbf{k}$, find the modulus and
   direction ratios of $\mathbf{r}_1 + \mathbf{r}_2$ and $\mathbf{r}_1 - \mathbf{r}_2$

8. If $\overrightarrow{\mathbf{OA}} = 3\mathbf{i} + \mathbf{j} - \mathbf{k}$ and $\overrightarrow{\mathbf{OB}} = \mathbf{i} - 3\mathbf{j} + 5\mathbf{k}$ show that $\overrightarrow{\mathbf{AB}}$ is
   parallel to the vector with d.r.s $1:2:-3$

PROPERTIES OF A LINE JOINING TWO POINTS

Consider the line joining the points $A(x_1, y_1, z_1)$ and $B(x_2, y_2, z_2)$

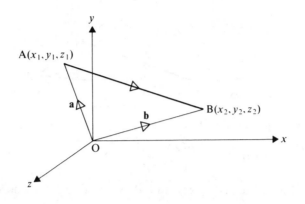

$$\overrightarrow{OA} = x_1\mathbf{i} + y_1\mathbf{j} + z_1\mathbf{k} \quad \text{and} \quad \overrightarrow{OB} = x_2\mathbf{i} + y_2\mathbf{j} + z_2\mathbf{k}$$

and $\quad \overrightarrow{AB} = \overrightarrow{AO} + \overrightarrow{OB} = \overrightarrow{OB} - \overrightarrow{OA}$

hence $\quad \overrightarrow{AB} = (x_2 - x_1)\mathbf{i} + (y_2 - y_1)\mathbf{j} + (z_2 - z_1)\mathbf{k}$

The Length of AB

$$AB = |(x_2 - x_1)\mathbf{i} + (y_2 - y_1)\mathbf{j} + (z_2 - z_1)\mathbf{k}|$$

so the length of the line joining (x_1, y_1, z_1) and (x_2, y_2, z_2) is

$$\sqrt{[(x_2 - x_1)^2 + (y_2 - y_1)^2 + (z_2 - z_1)^2]}$$

The Direction of AB

$$\overrightarrow{AB} = (x_2 - x_1)\mathbf{i} + (y_2 - y_1)\mathbf{j} + (z_2 - z_1)\mathbf{k}$$

so the direction ratios of $\overrightarrow{AB}$ are $(x_2 - x_1):(y_2 - y_1):(z_2 - z_1)$

The Position Vector of a Point Dividing AB in the Ratio $\lambda : \mu$

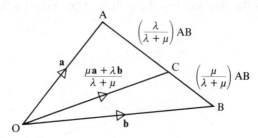

We saw on p. 726 that if C divides AB in the ratio $\lambda : \mu$ then the

position vector of C is $\dfrac{\mu \overrightarrow{OA} + \lambda \overrightarrow{OB}}{\lambda + \mu}$

If A is the point (x_1, y_1, z_1) and B is (x_2, y_2, z_2) the coordinates of C are

$$\frac{\mu x_1 + \lambda x_2}{\lambda + \mu}, \quad \frac{\mu y_1 + \lambda y_2}{\lambda + \mu}, \quad \frac{\mu z_1 + \lambda z_2}{\lambda + \mu}$$

In particular, if $\lambda = \mu$ so that C bisects AB we see that the coordinates of the midpoint of AB are

$$\tfrac{1}{2}(x_1 + x_2), \tfrac{1}{2}(y_1 + y_2), \tfrac{1}{2}(z_1 + z_2)$$

i.e.   the coordinates of the midpoint are the averages of
            the respective coordinates of the end points

Examples 39e

1. Find the length of the median through O of the triangle OAB, where A is the point $(2, 7, -1)$ and B is the point $(4, 1, 2)$

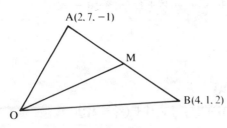

The coordinates of M, the midpoint of AB, are

$$\left(\tfrac{1}{2} \{ 2 + 4 \}, \tfrac{1}{2} \{ 7 + 1 \}, \tfrac{1}{2} \{ -1 + 2 \} \right)$$

i.e. $(3, 4, \tfrac{1}{2})$

So the length of OM is $\sqrt{(3^2 + 4^2 + \tfrac{1}{2}^2)} = \tfrac{1}{2}\sqrt{101}$

2. The points A, B and C have coordinates $(3, -1, 5)$, $(7, 1, 3)$ and $(-5, 9, -1)$ respectively. If L is the midpoint of AB and M is the midpoint of BC, find the length and direction ratios of LM.

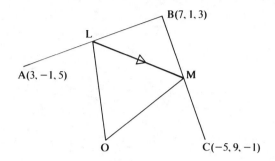

L is the point $\left(\frac{1}{2}\{3 + 7\}, \frac{1}{2}\{-1 + 1\}, \frac{1}{2}\{5 + 3\}\right)$, i.e. $(5, 0, 4)$

M is the point $\left(\frac{1}{2}\{7 - 5\}, \frac{1}{2}\{1 + 9\}, \frac{1}{2}\{3 - 1\}\right)$, i.e. $(1, 5, 1)$

$\therefore \quad$ LM $= \sqrt{(\{1 - 5\}^2 + \{5 - 0\}^2 + \{1 - 4\}^2)} = 5\sqrt{2}$

Now $\overrightarrow{LM} = (1 - 5)\mathbf{i} + (5 - 0)\mathbf{j} + (1 - 4)\mathbf{k}$

$\therefore \quad$ the d.r.s of LM are $-4 : 5 : -3$

---

3. A and B are two points with position vectors $3\mathbf{i} + \mathbf{j} - 2\mathbf{k}$ and $\mathbf{i} - 3\mathbf{j} - \mathbf{k}$ respectively. Find the position vectors of the points P and Q if

(a) P divides AB internally in the ratio $3 : 1$
(b) Q divides AB externally in the ratio $3 : 1$

(a) AP : PB $= 3 : 1$

$\therefore \quad \overrightarrow{OP} = \dfrac{1(3\mathbf{i} + \mathbf{j} - 2\mathbf{k}) + 3(\mathbf{i} - 3\mathbf{j} - \mathbf{k})}{3 + 1}$

$\qquad = \frac{3}{2}\mathbf{i} - 2\mathbf{j} - \frac{5}{4}\mathbf{k}$

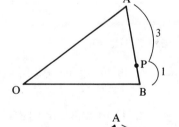

(b) AQ : QB $= 3 : -1$

$\therefore \quad \overrightarrow{OQ} = \dfrac{-1(3\mathbf{i} + \mathbf{j} - 2\mathbf{k}) + 3(\mathbf{i} - 3\mathbf{j} - \mathbf{k})}{3 - 1}$

$\qquad = -5\mathbf{j} - \frac{1}{2}\mathbf{k}$

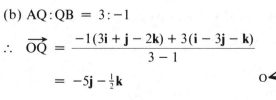

---

4. A, B and C are the points with position vectors $2\mathbf{i} - \mathbf{j} + 5\mathbf{k}$, $\mathbf{i} - 2\mathbf{j} + \mathbf{k}$ and $3\mathbf{i} + \mathbf{j} - 2\mathbf{k}$ respectively. If D and E are the respective midpoints of BC and AC, show that DE is parallel to AB.

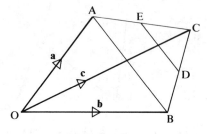

Using $\mathbf{a} = 2\mathbf{i} - \mathbf{j} + 5\mathbf{k}$, $\mathbf{b} = \mathbf{i} - 2\mathbf{j} + \mathbf{k}$ and $\mathbf{c} = 3\mathbf{i} + \mathbf{j} - 2\mathbf{k}$ we have

$$\overrightarrow{OD} = \tfrac{1}{2}(\mathbf{b} + \mathbf{c}) = \tfrac{1}{2}(4\mathbf{i} - \mathbf{j} - \mathbf{k})$$

and

$$\overrightarrow{OE} = \tfrac{1}{2}(\mathbf{a} + \mathbf{c}) = \tfrac{1}{2}(5\mathbf{i} + 3\mathbf{k})$$

∴

$$\overrightarrow{DE} = \overrightarrow{OE} - \overrightarrow{OD} = \tfrac{1}{2}(\mathbf{i} + \mathbf{j} + 4\mathbf{k})$$

Also

$$\overrightarrow{AB} = \mathbf{b} - \mathbf{a} = -\mathbf{i} - \mathbf{j} - 4\mathbf{k}$$

The d.r.s of $\overrightarrow{DE}$ are $1:1:4$

and the d.r.s of $\overrightarrow{AB}$ are $-1:-1:-4 = 1:1:4$

∴   AB and DE are parallel.

EXERCISE 39e

In this exercise A, B, C and D are the points with position vectors $\mathbf{i} + \mathbf{j} - \mathbf{k}$, $\mathbf{i} - \mathbf{j} + 2\mathbf{k}$, $\mathbf{j} + \mathbf{k}$ and $2\mathbf{i} + \mathbf{j}$ respectively.

1. Find $|\mathbf{AB}|$ and $|\mathbf{BD}|$.

2. Find the direction ratios of $\mathbf{CD}$ and $\mathbf{AC}$.

3. If P divides BD in the ratio $1:2$, find the position vector of P.

4. Find the position vector of the point which
   (a) divides BC internally in the ratio $3:2$
   (b) divides AC externally in the ratio $3:2$

5. Determine whether any of the following pairs of lines are parallel.
   (a) AB and CD   (b) AC and BD   (c) AD and BC.

6. If L and M are the position vectors of the midpoints of AD and BD respectively, show that $\overrightarrow{LM}$ is parallel to $\overrightarrow{AB}$.

7. If H and K are the midpoints of AC and CD respectively show that $\overrightarrow{HK} = \frac{1}{2}\overrightarrow{AD}$.

8. If L, M, N and P are the midpoints of AD, BD, BC and AC respectively, show that $\overrightarrow{LM}$ is parallel to $\overrightarrow{NP}$.

THE EQUATION OF A STRAIGHT LINE

A straight line is located uniquely in space if
either it passes through a known fixed point and has a known direction,
or it passes through two known fixed points.

In each of these cases we can find equations which describe the set of points on the line.

A Line with Known Direction and Passing through a Known Fixed Point

Consider a line for which **d** is a direction vector and which passes through a fixed point A with position vector **a**

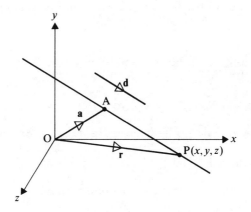

$\overrightarrow{OA} = \mathbf{a}$ and $\overrightarrow{AP} = \lambda\mathbf{d}$ where λ is a scalar

If $P(x, y, z)$ is *any* point on the line and **r** is the position vector of P

then $\qquad \overrightarrow{OP} = \overrightarrow{OA} + \overrightarrow{AP} \qquad \Rightarrow \qquad \mathbf{r} = \mathbf{a} + \lambda \mathbf{d}$

For example, the vector equation of the line which passes through the point $(5, -2, 4)$ and is parallel to the vector $2\mathbf{i} - \mathbf{j} + 3\mathbf{k}$, is

$$\mathbf{r} = 5\mathbf{i} - 2\mathbf{j} + 4\mathbf{k} + \lambda(2\mathbf{i} - \mathbf{j} + 3\mathbf{k}) \qquad [1]$$

> $\mathbf{r} = \mathbf{a} + \lambda \mathbf{d}$ is called the *vector equation* of the line.

Each value of the parameter λ gives the position vector of one point on the line, e.g. taking $\lambda = 1$ in equation [1] above gives the position vector $7\mathbf{i} - 3\mathbf{j} + 7\mathbf{k}$, so $(7, -3, 7)$ is a point on the given line.

Now replacing **r** by $x\mathbf{i} + y\mathbf{j} + z\mathbf{k}$ in equation [1] gives

$$x\mathbf{i} + y\mathbf{j} + z\mathbf{k} = (5 + 2\lambda)\mathbf{i} + (-2 - \lambda)\mathbf{j} + (4 + 3\lambda)\mathbf{k}$$

Hence $\qquad x = 5 + 2\lambda, \quad y = -2 - \lambda, \quad z = 4 + 3\lambda \qquad [2]$

These three equations also define the set of points on the given line, and are called the *parametric equations* of the line.

If we now isolate λ in each of the parametric equations in [2] we get

$$\frac{x - 5}{2} = \frac{y + 2}{-1} = \frac{z - 4}{3} \quad (= \lambda) \qquad [3]$$

These are the *cartesian equations* of the line.

Note that, as the direction of the line is given by $2\mathbf{i} - \mathbf{j} + 3\mathbf{k}$, the direction ratios of the line are $2 : -1 : 3$ and *these appear in the equation(s) of the line in all three forms.*

> In general, the equation(s) of a line parallel to $a\mathbf{i} + b\mathbf{j} + c\mathbf{k}$ and passing through $A(x_1, y_1, z_1)$ can be written
>
> $\qquad \mathbf{r} = x_1\mathbf{i} + y_1\mathbf{j} + z_1\mathbf{k} + \lambda(a\mathbf{i} + b\mathbf{j} + c\mathbf{k})$ $\qquad$ in vector form
>
> or $\quad x = x_1 + \lambda a, \quad y = y_1 + \lambda b, \quad z = z_1 + \lambda c$ $\quad$ in parametric form
>
> or $\qquad \dfrac{x - x_1}{a} = \dfrac{y - y_1}{b} = \dfrac{z - z_1}{c}$ $\qquad$ in cartesian form

Note that the point (x_1, y_1, z_1) is only one of an infinite set of fixed points on the line, so the equations above are *not* unique.

A Line Passing through Two Fixed Points

If a line passes through the points $A(x_1, y_1, z_1)$ and $B(x_2, y_2, z_2)$ then the direction vector for the line is $\mathbf{d}$ where

$$\mathbf{d} = (x_2 - x_1)\mathbf{i} + (y_2 - y_1)\mathbf{j} + (z_2 - z_1)\mathbf{k}$$

and the direction ratios of the line are

$$(x_2 - x_1):(y_2 - y_1):(z_2 - z_1)$$

These facts, together with either A or B as a fixed point on the line, allow the equations of the line to be written down in any of the three forms given above.

Examples 39f

1. A line passes through the point with position vector $2\mathbf{i} - \mathbf{j} + 4\mathbf{k}$ and is in the direction of $\mathbf{i} + \mathbf{j} - 2\mathbf{k}$. Find equations for the line in vector and in cartesian form.

The equation of the line in vector form is

$$\mathbf{r} = 2\mathbf{i} - \mathbf{j} + 4\mathbf{k} + \lambda(\mathbf{i} + \mathbf{j} - 2\mathbf{k})$$

This shows that the coordinates of any point P on the line are

$$(\{2 + \lambda\}, \{-1 + \lambda\}, \{4 - 2\lambda\})$$

Hence the cartesian equations are

$$x - 2 = y + 1 = \frac{z - 4}{-2} \qquad (= \lambda)$$

2. Find a vector equation for the line through the points $A(3, 4, -7)$ and $B(1, -1, 6)$.

$$\overrightarrow{OA} = \mathbf{a} = 3\mathbf{i} + 4\mathbf{j} - 7\mathbf{k}$$
$$\overrightarrow{OB} = \mathbf{b} = \mathbf{i} - \mathbf{j} + 6\mathbf{k}$$

For any point P on the line, $\overrightarrow{OP} = \mathbf{r}$

so
$$\mathbf{r} = \mathbf{a} + \lambda(\mathbf{b} - \mathbf{a})$$
$$= 3\mathbf{i} + 4\mathbf{j} - 7\mathbf{k} + \lambda(-2\mathbf{i} - 5\mathbf{j} + 13\mathbf{k})$$

3. Show that the line through the points $\mathbf{i} + \mathbf{j} - 3\mathbf{k}$ and $4\mathbf{i} + 7\mathbf{j} + \mathbf{k}$ is parallel to the line $\mathbf{r} = \mathbf{i} - \mathbf{k} + \lambda(\frac{3}{2}\mathbf{i} + 3\mathbf{j} + 2\mathbf{k})$.

The line through the two given points has direction ratios

$$(1 - 4):(1 - 7):(-3 - 1) = 3:6:4$$

The given line has direction ratios $\frac{3}{2}:3:2 = 3:6:4$

Hence the two lines are parallel.

---

4. (a) Find a vector equation for the line whose cartesian equations are

$$\frac{x - 5}{3} = \frac{y + 4}{7} = \frac{z - 6}{2}$$

(b) The vector equation of a line is $\mathbf{r} = \mathbf{i} - 3\mathbf{j} + 2\mathbf{k} + \lambda(5\mathbf{i} + 2\mathbf{j} - \mathbf{k})$. Express the equation of this line in parametric form and hence find the coordinates of the points where the line crosses the xy plane.

(a) Comparing $\dfrac{x - 5}{3} = \dfrac{y + 4}{7} = \dfrac{z - 6}{2}$ with

$$\frac{x - x_1}{a} = \frac{y - y_1}{b} = \frac{z - z_1}{c}$$

shows that one point on the line has coordinates $(5, -4, 6)$ and its position vector is therefore $5\mathbf{i} - 4\mathbf{j} + 6\mathbf{k}$

We also see that the d.r.s of the line are $3:7:2$ so its direction vector is $3\mathbf{i} + 7\mathbf{j} + 2\mathbf{k}$

Hence a vector equation for the line is

$$\mathbf{r} = 5\mathbf{i} - 4\mathbf{j} + 6\mathbf{k} + \lambda(3\mathbf{i} + 7\mathbf{j} + 2\mathbf{k})$$

(b) $\quad\quad\quad\quad \mathbf{r} = \mathbf{i} - 3\mathbf{j} + 2\mathbf{k} + \lambda(5\mathbf{i} + 2\mathbf{j} - \mathbf{k})$

gives $\quad\quad\quad\quad \mathbf{r} = (1 + 5\lambda)\mathbf{i} + (-3 + 2\lambda)\mathbf{j} + (2 - \lambda)\mathbf{k}$

So, for any point on the line, the coordinates are given by

$$x = 1 + 5\lambda, \quad y = -3 + 2\lambda, \quad z = 2 - \lambda$$

These are the parametric equations of the line.

At the point where the line crosses the xy plane, $z = 0$

i.e. $\qquad\qquad\qquad 2 - \lambda = 0 \quad\Rightarrow\quad \lambda = 2$

When $\qquad\qquad \lambda = 2, \ x = 11 \ \text{ and } \ y = 1$

Therefore the line crosses the xy plane at the point $(11, 1, 0)$

EXERCISE 39f

1. Convert the following vector equations to cartesian form.
   (a) $\mathbf{r} = 2\mathbf{i} + 3\mathbf{j} - \mathbf{k} + \lambda(\mathbf{i} + \mathbf{j} + \mathbf{k})$
   (b) $\mathbf{r} = 4\mathbf{j} + \lambda(3\mathbf{i} + 5\mathbf{k})$
   (c) $\mathbf{r} = \lambda(2\mathbf{i} + 3\mathbf{j} + 4\mathbf{k})$

2. Convert to vector form, the following equations,
   (a) $\dfrac{x - 3}{4} = \dfrac{y - 1}{2} = \dfrac{z - 7}{6}$
   (b) $x = 3\lambda + 2, \ y = \lambda - 5, \ z = 4\lambda + 1$
   (c) $\dfrac{1 - x}{3} = \dfrac{y}{5} = z$

3. Write down equations, in vector and in cartesian form, for the line through a point A with position vector $\mathbf{a}$ and with a direction vector $\mathbf{b}$ if
   (a) $\mathbf{a} = \mathbf{i} - 3\mathbf{j} + 2\mathbf{k} \qquad \mathbf{b} = 5\mathbf{i} + 4\mathbf{j} - \mathbf{k}$
   (b) $\mathbf{a} = 2\mathbf{i} + \mathbf{j} \qquad\qquad \mathbf{b} = 3\mathbf{j} - \mathbf{k}$
   (c) A is the origin $\qquad\quad \mathbf{b} = \mathbf{i} - \mathbf{j} - \mathbf{k}$

4. State whether or not the following pairs of lines are parallel.
   (a) $\mathbf{r} = \mathbf{i} + \mathbf{j} - \mathbf{k} + \lambda(2\mathbf{i} - 3\mathbf{j} + \mathbf{k}) \qquad$ and
   $\mathbf{r} = 2\mathbf{i} - 4\mathbf{j} + 5\mathbf{k} + \lambda(\mathbf{i} + \mathbf{j} - \mathbf{k})$
   (b) $\dfrac{x - 1}{2} = \dfrac{y - 4}{3} = \dfrac{z + 1}{-4} \quad$ and $\quad \dfrac{x}{4} = \dfrac{y + 5}{6} = \dfrac{3 - z}{8}$
   (c) $\mathbf{r} = 2\mathbf{i} - \mathbf{j} + 4\mathbf{k} + \lambda(\mathbf{i} + \mathbf{j} + 3\mathbf{k}) \quad$ and $\quad x - 4 = y + 7 = \dfrac{z}{3}$
   (d) $\mathbf{r} = \lambda(3\mathbf{i} - 3\mathbf{j} + 6\mathbf{k}) \quad$ and $\quad \mathbf{r} = 4\mathbf{j} + \lambda(-\mathbf{i} + \mathbf{j} - 2\mathbf{k})$
   (e) $\mathbf{r} = 3\mathbf{i} + \mathbf{k} + \lambda(\mathbf{i} - \mathbf{j} - 2\mathbf{k}) \quad$ and $\quad \dfrac{x - 3}{1} = \dfrac{y}{1} = \dfrac{z - 1}{2}$

5. The points $A(4, 5, 10)$, $B(2, 3, 4)$ and $C(1, 2, -1)$ are three vertices of a parallelogram ABCD. Find vector and cartesian equations for the sides AB and BC and find the coordinates of D.

6. Write down a vector equation for the line through A and B if

   (a) $\overrightarrow{OA}$ is $3\mathbf{i} + \mathbf{j} - 4\mathbf{k}$ and $\overrightarrow{OB}$ is $\mathbf{i} + 7\mathbf{j} + 8\mathbf{k}$

   (b) A and B have coordinates $(1, 1, 7)$ and $(3, 4, 1)$.

   Find, in each case, the coordinates of the points where the line crosses the xy plane, the yz plane and the zx plane.

7. A line has cartesian equations $\dfrac{x - 1}{3} = \dfrac{y + 2}{4} = \dfrac{z - 4}{5}$

   Find a vector equation for a parallel line passing through the point with position vector $5\mathbf{i} - 2\mathbf{j} - 4\mathbf{k}$ and find the coordinates of the point on this line where $y = 0$

8. The cartesian equations of a line are $x - 2 = 2y + 1 = 3z - 2$
   Find the direction ratios of the line and write down the vector equation of the line through $(2, -1, -1)$ which is parallel to the given line.

9. Given four points, $A(1, 2, 4)$, $B(2, 4, 2)$, $C(6, 7, 1)$ and $D(-3, 4, -2)$, find

   (a) parametric equations for the line, L, through A and B,

   (b) the coordinates of the point P where L cuts the xy plane.

   Show that P divides CD in the ratio $1 : 2$

PAIRS OF LINES

The location of two lines in space may be such that the lines

either   are parallel
or   are not parallel and intersect
or   are not parallel and do not intersect (such lines are *skew*).

Parallel Lines

We have already seen that parallel lines have equal direction ratios. So if two lines are parallel, this property can be observed from their equations.

Non-parallel Lines

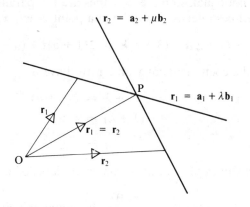

Consider two lines whose vector equations are

$$\mathbf{r}_1 = \mathbf{a}_1 + \lambda\mathbf{b}_1 \quad \text{and} \quad \mathbf{r}_2 = \mathbf{a}_2 + \mu\mathbf{b}_2$$

If these lines intersect it will be at a point where $\mathbf{r}_1 = \mathbf{r}_2$

This is possible only if there are unique values for λ and μ for which

$$\mathbf{a}_1 + \lambda\mathbf{b}_1 = \mathbf{a}_2 + \mu\mathbf{b}_2$$

If no such values can be found the lines do not intersect.

Example 39g

Find out whether the following pairs of lines are parallel, non-parallel and intersecting, or non-parallel and non-intersecting:

(a) $\mathbf{r}_1 = \mathbf{i} + \mathbf{j} + 2\mathbf{k} + \lambda(3\mathbf{i} - 2\mathbf{j} + 4\mathbf{k})$
    $\mathbf{r}_2 = 2\mathbf{i} - \mathbf{j} + 3\mathbf{k} + \mu(-6\mathbf{i} + 4\mathbf{j} - 8\mathbf{k})$,

(b) $\mathbf{r}_1 = \mathbf{i} - \mathbf{j} + 3\mathbf{k} + \lambda(\mathbf{i} - \mathbf{j} + \mathbf{k})$
    $\mathbf{r}_2 = 2\mathbf{i} + 4\mathbf{j} + 6\mathbf{k} + \mu(2\mathbf{i} + \mathbf{j} + 3\mathbf{k})$,

(c) $\mathbf{r}_1 = \mathbf{i} + \mathbf{k} + \lambda(\mathbf{i} + 3\mathbf{j} + 4\mathbf{k})$
    $\mathbf{r}_2 = 2\mathbf{i} + 3\mathbf{j} + \mu(4\mathbf{i} - \mathbf{j} + \mathbf{k})$.

(a) Checking first whether the lines are parallel we compare the direction ratios of the two lines.

The first line has direction ratios $\quad 3:-2:4$
The second line has direction ratios $\quad -6:4:-8 = 3:-2:4$

Therefore these two lines are parallel.

(b) In this case the two sets of direction ratios are $1:-1:1$ and $2:1:3$
These are not equal, so these two lines are not parallel.
Now if the lines intersect it will be at a point where $\mathbf{r}_1 = \mathbf{r}_2$, i.e. where

$$(1+\lambda)\mathbf{i} - (1+\lambda)\mathbf{j} + (3+\lambda)\mathbf{k} = 2(1+\mu)\mathbf{i} + (4+\mu)\mathbf{j} + (6+3\mu)\mathbf{k}$$

Equating the coefficients of $\mathbf{i}$ and $\mathbf{j}$, we have

$$1 + \lambda = 2(1+\mu)$$

and $\qquad\qquad\qquad -(1+\lambda) = 4 + \mu$

Hence $\qquad\qquad\qquad\qquad \mu = -2, \ \lambda = -3$

With these values for λ and μ, the coefficients of $\mathbf{k}$ become

first line $\qquad\qquad\qquad 3 + \lambda = 0$
second line $\qquad\qquad\quad\ 6 + 3\mu = 0$ $\quad$ i.e. equal values.

So $\ \mathbf{r}_1 = \mathbf{r}_2$ when $\lambda = -3$ and $\mu = -2$

Therefore the lines *do* intersect at the point with position vector

$$(1-3)\mathbf{i} - (1-3)\mathbf{j} + (3-3)\mathbf{k} \qquad (\lambda = -3 \ \text{in} \ \mathbf{r}_1)$$

i.e. $\qquad\qquad\qquad\qquad\qquad -2\mathbf{i} + 2\mathbf{j}$

(c) The direction ratios of these two lines are not equal so the lines
are not parallel.
If the lines intersect it will be where $\mathbf{r}_1 = \mathbf{r}_2$, i.e. where

$$(1+\lambda)\mathbf{i} + 3\lambda\mathbf{j} + (1+4\lambda)\mathbf{k} = (2+4\mu)\mathbf{i} + (3-\mu)\mathbf{j} + \mu\mathbf{k}$$

Equating the coefficients of $\mathbf{i}$ and $\mathbf{j}$ we have

$$1 + \lambda = 2 + 4\mu$$

and $\qquad\qquad\qquad\qquad 3\lambda = 3 - \mu$

Hence $\qquad\qquad\qquad\qquad \mu = 0, \ \lambda = 1$

With these values of λ and μ, the coefficients of $\mathbf{k}$ become

for the first line $\qquad\qquad 1 + 4\lambda = 5$
for the second line $\qquad\qquad\quad \mu = 0$

As these are unequal there are no values of λ and μ for which $\mathbf{r}_1 = \mathbf{r}_2$

Therefore these two lines do not intersect and are skew.

EXERCISE 39g

In Questions 1 to 3 find whether the given two lines are parallel, intersecting or skew. If they intersect, state the position vector of the common point.

1. $r_1 = i - j + k + \lambda(3i - 4j + k)$ and $r_2 = \mu(-9i + 12j - 3k)$

2. $\dfrac{x - 4}{1} = \dfrac{y - 8}{2} = \dfrac{z - 3}{1}$ and $\dfrac{x - 7}{6} = \dfrac{y - 6}{4} = \dfrac{z - 5}{5}$

3. $r_1 = i + 3k + \lambda(2i + j + k)$ and $r_2 = 2i - j + k + \mu(i - 2j)$

4. Two lines have equations $r_1 = 2i + 9j + 13k + \lambda(i + 2j + 3k)$ and $r_2 = ai + 7j - 2k + \mu(-i + 2j - 3k)$.
   Given that they intersect, find the value of a and the position vector of the point of intersection.

5. If the line $r_1 = 5j + tk + \lambda(-i + 3j + 4k)$ intersects the line $r_2 = -4i + j + k + \mu(5i + j + k)$, find the value of t and the coordinates of the point of intersection.

6. A line L has equation $r_1 = -3i + j + 4k + \lambda(4i + pj - 3k)$
   Find the value of p if
   (a) the line $r_2 = 5i - j - 2k + \mu(4i - 2j - 3k)$ is parallel to L,
   (b) the line $r_3 = -i + 3j - 3k + \mu(i - j + 2k)$ intersects L.

7. The equations of two lines are $r_1 = 2i - j + k + \lambda(i - 2j + 2k)$ and $r_2 = i - 3j + 4k + \mu(2i + 3j - 6k)$. Show that these lines are skew.
   $\overrightarrow{OQ}$ is the unit vector in the direction of the first line and $\overrightarrow{OR}$ is the unit vector in the direction of the second line. Write down the coordinates of Q and R .
   By using the cosine formula in triangle OQR find the angle between $\overrightarrow{OQ}$ and $\overrightarrow{OR}$ and hence the angle between the given lines.

8. If $\overrightarrow{OA}$ is the unit vector $l_1i + m_1j + n_1k$ and $\overrightarrow{OB}$ is the unit vector $l_2i + m_2j + n_2k$, use the cosine formula in triangle OAB to show that θ, the angle between $\overrightarrow{OA}$ and $\overrightarrow{OB}$, is given by $\cos \theta = l_1l_2 + m_1m_2 + n_1n_2$

THE SCALAR PRODUCT

We are now going to look at an operation involving two vectors and the angle between them. This operation is called a product but, because it involves vectors, it is in no way related to the product of real numbers.

The Definition of the Scalar Product

The scalar product of two vectors **a** and **b** is denoted by **a.b** and defined as $ab \cos \theta$ where θ is the angle between **a** and **b**

i.e. $\mathbf{a.b} = ab \cos \theta$

PROPERTIES OF THE SCALAR PRODUCT

Parallel Vectors

If **a** and **b** are parallel then

either $\mathbf{a.b} = ab \cos 0$ or $\mathbf{a.b} = ab \cos \pi$

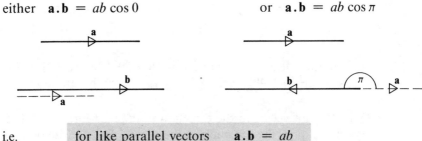

i.e.   for like parallel vectors $\mathbf{a.b} = ab$

and   for unlike parallel vectors $\mathbf{a.b} = -ab$

In the special case when $\mathbf{a} = \mathbf{b}$

$\mathbf{a.b} = \mathbf{a.a} = a^2$ (sometimes $\mathbf{a.a}$ is written $\mathbf{a}^2$)

In particular, for the cartesian unit vectors **i**, **j** and **k**

$$\mathbf{i.i} = \mathbf{j.j} = \mathbf{k.k} = 1$$

Perpendicular Vectors

If **a** and **b** are perpendicular then $\theta = \frac{1}{2}\pi$, $\Rightarrow$ **a.b** $= ab \cos \frac{1}{2}\pi = 0$

i.e.   for perpendicular vectors **a.b** $= 0$

For the unit vectors **i, j** and **k** we have

$$\mathbf{i.j} = \mathbf{j.k} = \mathbf{k.i} = 0$$

The Scalar Product is Commutative

This means that **a.b** $=$ **b.a** and this property is easy to prove as follows.

From the definition we have **a.b** $= ab \cos \theta$ and **b.a** $= ba \cos \theta$

Now $ab \cos \theta = ba \cos \theta$ therefore **a.b** $=$ **b.a**

The Scalar Product is Distributive for Addition

This means that **a.(b + c)** $=$ **a.b** $+$ **a.c**

It is not necessary to be able to prove this property but a proof is given below for readers who would like to see it.

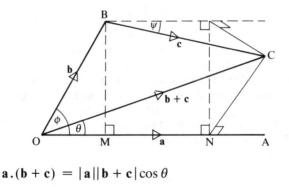

$$\begin{aligned}
\mathbf{a.(b + c)} &= |\mathbf{a}||\mathbf{b + c}| \cos \theta \\
&= (OA)(OC) \cos \theta \\
&= (OA)(ON) \\
&= (OA)(OM + MN) \\
&= (OA)(OB \cos \phi) + (OA)(BC \cos \psi) \\
&= \mathbf{a.b} + \mathbf{a.c}
\end{aligned}$$

CALCULATING **a.b** IN CARTESIAN FORM

If $\mathbf{a} = x_1\mathbf{i} + y_1\mathbf{j} + z_1\mathbf{k}$ and $\mathbf{b} = x_2\mathbf{i} + y_2\mathbf{j} + z_2\mathbf{k}$ then we can find **a.b** by using the properties given above.

$$\mathbf{a}.\mathbf{b} = (x_1\mathbf{i} + y_1\mathbf{j} + z_1\mathbf{k}).(x_2\mathbf{i} + y_2\mathbf{j} + z_2\mathbf{k})$$

$$= (x_1x_2\mathbf{i}.\mathbf{i} + y_1y_2\mathbf{j}.\mathbf{j} + z_1z_2\mathbf{k}.\mathbf{k})$$

$$+ (x_1y_2\mathbf{i}.\mathbf{j} + y_1z_2\mathbf{j}.\mathbf{k} + z_1x_2\mathbf{k}.\mathbf{i})$$

$$+ (y_1x_2\mathbf{j}.\mathbf{i} + z_1y_2\mathbf{k}.\mathbf{j} + x_1z_2\mathbf{i}.\mathbf{k})$$

$$= (x_1x_2 + y_1y_2 + z_1z_2) + (0) + (0),$$

i.e. $\boxed{(x_1\mathbf{i} + y_1\mathbf{j} + z_1\mathbf{k}).(x_2\mathbf{i} + y_2\mathbf{j} + z_2\mathbf{k}) = x_1x_2 + y_1y_2 + z_1z_2}$

For example,

$$(2\mathbf{i} - 3\mathbf{j} + 4\mathbf{k}).(\mathbf{i} + 3\mathbf{j} - 2\mathbf{k}) = (2)(1) + (-3)(3) + (4)(-2) = -15$$

Using the Scalar Product to Find the Angle Between Two Lines

The lines with equations $\mathbf{r}_1 = \mathbf{a}_1 + \lambda\mathbf{d}_1$ and $\mathbf{r}_2 = \mathbf{a}_2 + \mu\mathbf{d}_2$ are in the directions of $\mathbf{d}_1$ and $\mathbf{d}_2$ respectively.

The angle between two lines is defined as the angle between their direction vectors and does not depend upon their positions. It does not even depend on whether the lines intersect, so we are looking for the angle between the vectors $\mathbf{d}_1$ and $\mathbf{d}_2$ in any convenient position.

Drawing $\mathbf{d}_1$ and $\mathbf{d}_2$ from a common point, the angle θ between them is given by $\mathbf{d}_1.\mathbf{d}_2 = d_1d_2\cos\theta$

$$\therefore \quad \cos\theta = \frac{\mathbf{d}_1.\mathbf{d}_2}{d_1d_2}$$

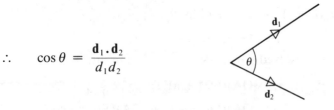

This confirms that, for perpendicular lines, $\mathbf{d}_1.\mathbf{d}_2 = 0$

Resolved Parts

We have seen that the resultant of
two vectors can be found by the
triangle law of addition.
i.e. $\mathbf{p} + \mathbf{q} = \mathbf{r}$

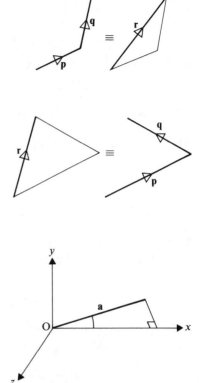

Conversely, a single vector $\mathbf{r}$ can
be replaced by two other vectors
which, together with $\mathbf{r}$, form a
closed triangle,
i.e. $\mathbf{r}$ is equivalent to $\mathbf{p} + \mathbf{q}$

The magnitudes of $\mathbf{p}$ and $\mathbf{q}$ are
called the *resolved parts* or
components of $\mathbf{r}$

Replacing a vector by its
components is of particular
importance when those
components are at right angles
to each other
In the diagram for example,
the resolved part of $\mathbf{a}$ in the
direction of Ox is $|\mathbf{a}|\cos\alpha$

Now suppose that we have two vectors $\mathbf{a}$ and $\mathbf{b}$ which enclose an
angle θ. The component of $\mathbf{a}$ in the direction of $\mathbf{b}$ is $|\mathbf{a}|\cos\theta$

But $\qquad\qquad\qquad |\mathbf{a}||\mathbf{b}|\cos\theta = \mathbf{a}.\mathbf{b}$

Therefore

$$|\mathbf{a}|\cos\theta = \frac{\mathbf{a}.\mathbf{b}}{|\mathbf{b}|} \quad \text{or} \quad \mathbf{a}.\widehat{\mathbf{b}}$$

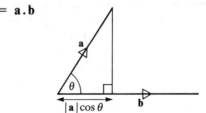

In this way the resolved part of any vector in the direction of another
vector can be found,
e.g. the component of $2\mathbf{i} + 3\mathbf{j} - \mathbf{k}$ in the direction of $\mathbf{i} - 5\mathbf{k}$ is

$$(2\mathbf{i} + 3\mathbf{j} - \mathbf{k}).\frac{(\mathbf{i} - 5\mathbf{k})}{\sqrt{26}} = \frac{7}{\sqrt{26}}$$

Examples 39h

1. Simplify $(\mathbf{a} - \mathbf{b}).(\mathbf{a} + \mathbf{b})$ and $(\mathbf{a} + \mathbf{b}).\mathbf{c} - (\mathbf{a} + \mathbf{c}).\mathbf{b}$

$$(\mathbf{a} - \mathbf{b}).(\mathbf{a} + \mathbf{b}) = \mathbf{a}.\mathbf{a} - \mathbf{b}.\mathbf{a} + \mathbf{a}.\mathbf{b} - \mathbf{b}.\mathbf{b}$$

but $\qquad \mathbf{a}.\mathbf{b} = \mathbf{b}.\mathbf{a}$ hence $\mathbf{a}.\mathbf{b} - \mathbf{b}.\mathbf{a} = 0$

also $\qquad \mathbf{a}.\mathbf{a} = a^2$ and $\mathbf{b}.\mathbf{b} = b^2$

Therefore $\qquad (\mathbf{a} - \mathbf{b}).(\mathbf{a} + \mathbf{b}) = a^2 - b^2$

Also $\qquad (\mathbf{a} + \mathbf{b}).\mathbf{c} - (\mathbf{a} + \mathbf{c}).\mathbf{b} = \mathbf{a}.\mathbf{c} + \mathbf{b}.\mathbf{c} - \mathbf{a}.\mathbf{b} - \mathbf{c}.\mathbf{b}$

$$= \mathbf{a}.\mathbf{c} - \mathbf{a}.\mathbf{b}$$

$$= \mathbf{a}.(\mathbf{c} - \mathbf{b})$$

2. Find the scalar product of $\mathbf{a} = 2\mathbf{i} - 3\mathbf{j} + 5\mathbf{k}$ and $\mathbf{b} = \mathbf{i} - 3\mathbf{j} + \mathbf{k}$ and hence find the cosine of the angle between $\mathbf{a}$ and $\mathbf{b}$.

$$\mathbf{a}.\mathbf{b} = (2)(1) + (-3)(-3) + (5)(1) = 16$$

But $\qquad \mathbf{a}.\mathbf{b} = |\mathbf{a}||\mathbf{b}|\cos\theta$

$$|\mathbf{a}| = \sqrt{(4 + 9 + 25)} = \sqrt{38}$$

$$|\mathbf{b}| = \sqrt{(1 + 9 + 1)} = \sqrt{11}$$

Hence $\qquad \cos\theta = \dfrac{\mathbf{a}.\mathbf{b}}{|\mathbf{a}||\mathbf{b}|} = \dfrac{16}{\sqrt{11}\sqrt{38}} = \dfrac{16}{\sqrt{418}}$

3. If $\mathbf{a} = 10\mathbf{i} - 3\mathbf{j} + 5\mathbf{k}$, $\mathbf{b} = 2\mathbf{i} + 6\mathbf{j} - 3\mathbf{k}$ and $\mathbf{c} = \mathbf{i} + 10\mathbf{j} - 2\mathbf{k}$, verify that $\mathbf{a}.\mathbf{b} + \mathbf{a}.\mathbf{c} = \mathbf{a}.(\mathbf{b} + \mathbf{c})$

$$\mathbf{a}.\mathbf{b} = (10)(2) + (-3)(6) + (5)(-3) = -13$$

$$\mathbf{a}.\mathbf{c} = (10)(1) + (-3)(10) + (5)(-2) = -30$$

$$\mathbf{b} + \mathbf{c} = 3\mathbf{i} + 16\mathbf{j} - 5\mathbf{k}$$

Hence $\qquad \mathbf{a}.(\mathbf{b} + \mathbf{c}) = (10)(3) + (-3)(16) + (5)(-5) = -43$

But $\qquad \mathbf{a}.\mathbf{b} + \mathbf{a}.\mathbf{c} = -13 - 30 = -43$

Therefore $\qquad \mathbf{a}.\mathbf{b} + \mathbf{a}.\mathbf{c} = \mathbf{a}.(\mathbf{b} + \mathbf{c})$

4. Find the resolved part of the vector $3\mathbf{i} - \mathbf{j} + 7\mathbf{k}$ in the direction of
(a) the vector $\mathbf{i} - 2\mathbf{j} - 2\mathbf{k}$ (b) the x-axis.

(a) If $\mathbf{a} = 3\mathbf{i} - \mathbf{j} + 7\mathbf{k}$ and $\mathbf{b} = \mathbf{i} - 2\mathbf{j} - 2\mathbf{k}$ then the resolved part
of $\mathbf{a}$ in the direction of $\mathbf{b}$ is given by $\mathbf{a} \cdot \hat{\mathbf{b}}$

i.e. $(3\mathbf{i} - \mathbf{j} + 7\mathbf{k}) \cdot \dfrac{(\mathbf{i} - 2\mathbf{j} - 2\mathbf{k})}{3} = -3$

(b) The direction vector of the x-axis is $\mathbf{i}$ which is a unit vector.
Therefore the resolved part of $\mathbf{a}$ in the direction of the x-axis is

$$\mathbf{a} \cdot \mathbf{i} = (3\mathbf{i} - \mathbf{j} + 7\mathbf{k}) \cdot \mathbf{i} = 3$$

---

5. Find the angle between the lines

$$\mathbf{r}_1 = \mathbf{i} - 2\mathbf{j} + 3\mathbf{k} + \lambda(2\mathbf{i} - 3\mathbf{j} + 6\mathbf{k}) \qquad [1]$$
$$\mathbf{r}_2 = 2\mathbf{i} - 7\mathbf{j} + 10\mathbf{k} + \mu(\mathbf{i} + 2\mathbf{j} + 2\mathbf{k}) \qquad [2]$$

The angle between the lines depends only upon their directions.
Line [1] has a direction vector $\mathbf{d}_1 = 2\mathbf{i} - 3\mathbf{j} + 6\mathbf{k}$
Line [2] has a direction vector $\mathbf{d}_2 = \mathbf{i} + 2\mathbf{j} + 2\mathbf{k}$
The angle θ between the lines is given by

$$\cos\theta = \frac{\mathbf{d}_1 \cdot \mathbf{d}_2}{d_1 d_2} = \frac{2 - 6 + 12}{(7)(3)}$$

$\Rightarrow$ $\theta = \arccos\frac{8}{21}$

---

6. Find a unit vector which is perpendicular to AB and AC if
$\overrightarrow{AB} = \mathbf{i} + 2\mathbf{j} + 3\mathbf{k}$ and $\overrightarrow{AC} = 4\mathbf{i} - \mathbf{j} + 2\mathbf{k}$

Let $a\mathbf{i} + b\mathbf{j} + c\mathbf{k}$ be a vector perpendicular to both AB and AC.
It is perpendicular to AB   so $(a\mathbf{i} + b\mathbf{j} + c\mathbf{k}) \cdot (\mathbf{i} + 2\mathbf{j} + 3\mathbf{k}) = 0$
It is perpendicular to AC   so $(a\mathbf{i} + b\mathbf{j} + c\mathbf{k}) \cdot (4\mathbf{i} - \mathbf{j} + 2\mathbf{k}) = 0$

Therefore $\begin{cases} a + 2b + 3c = 0 \\ 4a - b + 2c = 0 \end{cases}$

Eliminating b gives $\qquad a = -\frac{7}{9}c$

Eliminating a gives $\qquad b = -\frac{10}{9}c$

Hence $\qquad a\mathbf{i} + b\mathbf{j} + c\mathbf{k} = -\frac{7}{9}c\mathbf{i} - \frac{10}{9}c\mathbf{j} + c\mathbf{k}$

$$= \tfrac{1}{9}c(-7\mathbf{i} - 10\mathbf{j} + 9\mathbf{k})$$

Thus $-7\mathbf{i} - 10\mathbf{j} + 9\mathbf{k}$ is perpendicular to both AB and AC.

A unit vector perpendicular to AB and AC is therefore

$$(-7\mathbf{i} - 10\mathbf{j} + 9\mathbf{k})/\sqrt{230}$$

EXERCISE 39h

1. Calculate $\mathbf{a}.\mathbf{b}$ if
   (a) $\mathbf{a} = 2\mathbf{i} - 4\mathbf{j} + 5\mathbf{k}, \quad \mathbf{b} = \mathbf{i} + 3\mathbf{j} + 8\mathbf{k}$
   (b) $\mathbf{a} = 3\mathbf{i} - 7\mathbf{j} + 2\mathbf{k}, \quad \mathbf{b} = 5\mathbf{i} + \mathbf{j} - 4\mathbf{k}$
   (c) $\mathbf{a} = 2\mathbf{i} - 3\mathbf{j} + 6\mathbf{k}, \quad \mathbf{b} = \mathbf{i} + \mathbf{j}$
   What conclusion can you draw in (b)?

2. Find $\mathbf{p}.\mathbf{q}$ and the cosine of the angle between $\mathbf{p}$ and $\mathbf{q}$ if
   (a) $\mathbf{p} = 2\mathbf{i} + 4\mathbf{j} + \mathbf{k}, \quad \mathbf{q} = \mathbf{i} + \mathbf{j} + \mathbf{k}$
   (b) $\mathbf{p} = -\mathbf{i} + 3\mathbf{j} - 2\mathbf{k}, \quad \mathbf{q} = \mathbf{i} + \mathbf{j} - 6\mathbf{k}$
   (c) $\mathbf{p} = -2\mathbf{i} + 5\mathbf{j}, \quad \mathbf{q} = \mathbf{i} + \mathbf{j}$
   (d) $\mathbf{p} = 2\mathbf{i} + \mathbf{j}, \quad \mathbf{q} = \mathbf{j} - 2\mathbf{k}$

3. Simplify
   (a) $(\mathbf{a} - \mathbf{b}).\mathbf{a}$ $\qquad\qquad$ (b) $(\mathbf{a} - \mathbf{b}).(\mathbf{a} - \mathbf{b})$
   (c) $(\mathbf{a} + \mathbf{b}).\mathbf{b} - (\mathbf{a} + \mathbf{b}).\mathbf{a}$ $\qquad$ (d) $(\mathbf{a} + \mathbf{b}).\mathbf{c} - (\mathbf{a} - \mathbf{b}).\mathbf{c}$

4. Given that $\mathbf{a}$ and $\mathbf{b}$ are perpendicular, simplify
   (a) $\mathbf{a}.\mathbf{b}$ $\quad$ (b) $(\mathbf{a} - \mathbf{b}).\mathbf{b}$ $\quad$ (c) $(\mathbf{a} + \mathbf{b}).\mathbf{a}$ $\quad$ (d) $(\mathbf{a} - \mathbf{b}).(2\mathbf{a} + \mathbf{b})$

5. The angle between two vectors $\mathbf{v}_1$ and $\mathbf{v}_2$ is $\arccos \frac{4}{21}$
   If $\mathbf{v}_1 = 6\mathbf{i} + 3\mathbf{j} - 2\mathbf{k}$ and $\mathbf{v}_2 = -2\mathbf{i} + \lambda\mathbf{j} - 4\mathbf{k}$, find the positive value of λ

6. If $\mathbf{a} = 3\mathbf{i} + 4\mathbf{j} - \mathbf{k}, \ \mathbf{b} = \mathbf{i} - \mathbf{j} + 3\mathbf{k}$ and $\mathbf{c} = 2\mathbf{i} + \mathbf{j} - 5\mathbf{k}$, find
   (a) $\mathbf{a}.\mathbf{b}$ $\quad$ (b) $\mathbf{a}.\mathbf{c}$ $\quad$ (c) $\mathbf{a}.(\mathbf{b} + \mathbf{c})$ $\quad$ (d) $(2\mathbf{a} + 3\mathbf{b}).\mathbf{c}$ $\quad$ (e) $(\mathbf{a} - \mathbf{b}).\mathbf{c}$

7. In a triangle ABC, $\overrightarrow{AB} = i + 2j + 3k$ and $\overrightarrow{BC} = -i + 4j$.
   Find the cosine of angle ABC.
   Find the vector $\overrightarrow{AC}$ and use it to calculate the angle BAC.

8. A, B and C are points with position vectors a, b and c
   respectively, relative to the origin O. AB is perpendicular to OC
   and BC is perpendicular to OA.
   Show that AC is perpendicular to OB.

9. Given two vectors a and b ($a \neq 0$, $b \neq 0$), show that
   (a) if $a + b$ and $a - b$ are perpendicular then $|a| = |b|$,
   (b) if $|a + b| = |a - b|$ then a and b are perpendicular.

10. Three vectors a, b and c are such that $a \neq b \neq c \neq 0$.
    (a) If $a.(b + c) = b.(a - c)$ prove that $c.(a + b) = 0$
    (b) If $(a.b)c = (b.c)a$ show that c and a are parallel.

11. Find the angle between each of the following pairs of lines.
    (a) $r_1 = 3i + 2j - 4k + \lambda(i + 2j + 2k)$ and
        $r_2 = 5j - 2k - \mu(3i + 2j + 6k)$
    (b) A line with direction ratios $2:2:1$ and a line joining the
        points $(3, 1, 4)$ and $(7, 2, 12)$.
    (c) $\dfrac{x + 4}{3} = \dfrac{y - 1}{5} = \dfrac{z + 3}{4}$ and $\dfrac{x + 1}{1} = \dfrac{y - 4}{1} = \dfrac{z - 5}{2}$

12. Find the angle between the following pairs of lines.
    (a) $\dfrac{x - 2}{3} = \dfrac{y + 1}{-2}$, $z = 2$ and $\dfrac{x - 1}{1} = \dfrac{2y + 3}{3} = \dfrac{z + 5}{2}$
    (b) $r = 4i - j + \lambda(i + 2j - 2k)$ and
        $r = i - j + 2k - \mu(2i + 4j - 4k)$

13. Show that $i + 7j + 3k$ is perpendicular to both $i - j + 2k$ and
    $2i + j - 3k$

14. Show that $13i + 23j + 7k$ is perpendicular to both $2i + j - 7k$
    and $3i - 2j + k$

15. Find the resolved part of the vector $2i + 3j + 4k$ in the direction
    of
    (a) $i - 2j + 2k$ (b) i (c) $3j - 4k$

PLANES

There are a number of ways in which a plane can be specified.
For example, one and only one plane can be drawn

1) through three non-collinear points.

2) to contain two concurrent lines.

3) perpendicular to a specified direction and at a given distance from a fixed origin.

4) perpendicular to a given direction and through a fixed point.

The specifications described in (3) and (4) provide particularly simple methods for deriving the equation of a plane.

THE EQUATION OF A PLANE

The Vector Equation of a Plane

Consider a plane distant d from the origin O and perpendicular to a vector **n**, where $\overrightarrow{ON} = \mathbf{n}$

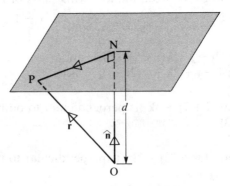

For any point P on the plane, $\overrightarrow{NP}$ is perpendicular to $\overrightarrow{ON}$ so

$$\overrightarrow{NP}.\overrightarrow{ON} = 0$$

Now if **r** is the position vector of P. $\overrightarrow{NP} = \overrightarrow{NO} + \overrightarrow{OP} = \mathbf{r} - \mathbf{n}$

Therefore $(\mathbf{r} - \mathbf{n}).\mathbf{n} = 0 \quad \Rightarrow \quad \mathbf{r}.\mathbf{n} - \mathbf{n}.\mathbf{n} = 0$

Now using $\mathbf{n} = d\,\hat{\mathbf{n}}$ and $\mathbf{n}.\mathbf{n} = d^2$ we have

$\mathbf{r}.\mathbf{n} - \mathbf{n}.\mathbf{n} = 0 \quad \Rightarrow \quad d\mathbf{r}.\hat{\mathbf{n}} - d^2 = 0 \quad \Rightarrow \quad \mathbf{r}.\hat{\mathbf{n}} - d = 0$

i.e.
$$\mathbf{r}.\hat{\mathbf{n}} = d$$

This is the equation, in *standard form*, of a plane distant d from the origin and perpendicular to **n**

This equation can be multiplied by any scalar quantity so, multiplying by $|\mathbf{n}|$, we have $\mathbf{r}.\mathbf{n} = D$, where $D = d|\mathbf{n}|$, i.e.

any equation of the form $\mathbf{r}.\mathbf{n} = D$ represents a plane perpendicular to **n** and distant $\dfrac{D}{|\mathbf{n}|}$ from the origin.

Now consider a plane which is perpendicular to a vector **n** and which passes through a fixed point A with position vector **a**

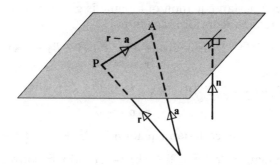

If **r** is the position vector of any point in the plane then

$\overrightarrow{AP} = \mathbf{r} - \mathbf{a}$ and $\overrightarrow{AP}$ is perpendicular to **n** $\Rightarrow \overrightarrow{AP}.\mathbf{n} = 0$

Therefore $(\mathbf{r} - \mathbf{a}).\mathbf{n} = 0$ or $\mathbf{r}.\mathbf{n} = \mathbf{r}.\mathbf{a}$

i.e. $(\mathbf{r} - \mathbf{a}).\mathbf{n} = 0$ is the vector equation of a plane which is perpendicular to **n** and contains the point with position vector **a**

The Cartesian Equation of a Plane

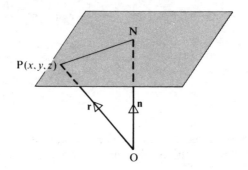

Consider again a plane distant d from the origin O and perpendicular to the vector $\mathbf{n}$, where $\mathbf{n} = A\mathbf{i} + B\mathbf{j} + C\mathbf{k}$

The vector equation of this plane can be given as $\mathbf{r.n} = D$

Now for any point $P(x, y, z)$ on the plane, $\mathbf{r} = (x\mathbf{i} + y\mathbf{j} + z\mathbf{k})$

i.e. $\qquad (x\mathbf{i} + y\mathbf{j} + z\mathbf{k}).(A\mathbf{i} + B\mathbf{j} + C\mathbf{k}) = D$

$\Rightarrow$
$$Ax + By + Cz = D$$

which is the cartesian form for the equation of the plane.

When the cartesian equation of a plane is given it is easy to convert it to the standard vector form as follows.

$Ax + By + Cz = D$ is equivalent to $\mathbf{r}.(A\mathbf{i} + B\mathbf{j} + C\mathbf{k}) = D$
or $\qquad\qquad\qquad\qquad\qquad \mathbf{r.n} = D$

Therefore dividing by $|\mathbf{n}| = \sqrt{(A^2 + B^2 + C^2)}$ gives

$$\mathbf{r}.\widehat{\mathbf{n}} = d$$

e.g. a plane whose cartesian equation is $2x + 3y + 6z = 21$ has

a vector equation $\mathbf{r}.(2\mathbf{i} + 3\mathbf{j} + 6\mathbf{k}) = 21$ which, converted to

standard form is $\mathbf{r}.(\frac{2}{7}\mathbf{i} + \frac{3}{7}\mathbf{j} + \frac{6}{7}\mathbf{k}) = 3$

From the last equation we see that the plane is 3 units from the origin and is perpendicular to a vector with direction ratios $2:3:6$.

Note that *a plane itself does not have direction ratios.*

When finding the equation of a plane, the given data sometimes suggests aiming at a vector equation but in other cases the cartesian equation is easier to find. Because these two forms are quickly interconvertible the choice of method can be based solely on convenience.

The Parametric Form for the Vector Equation of a Plane

A plane is defined uniquely if it contains two non-parallel direction vectors and a fixed point.

Suppose that the position vector of the fixed point is $\mathbf{a}$ and the two direction vectors are $\mathbf{d}_1$ and $\mathbf{d}_2$

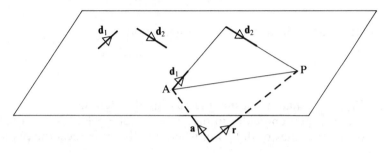

Any vector $\overrightarrow{AP}$ in the plane can be expressed in the form $\lambda\mathbf{d}_1 + \mu\mathbf{d}_2$ where λ and μ are scalar parameters. So if $\mathbf{r}$ is the position vector of any point in the plane we have

$$\mathbf{r} = \overrightarrow{OP} = \overrightarrow{OA} + \overrightarrow{AP} = \mathbf{a} + \lambda\mathbf{d}_1 + \mu\mathbf{d}_2$$

i.e.
$$\mathbf{r} = \mathbf{a} + \lambda\mathbf{d}_1 + \mu\mathbf{d}_2$$

This is the parametric form for the vector equation of a plane.

Examples 39i _____

1. (a) Find the vector equation, in standard form, of the plane whose cartesian equation is $x - 2y + 2z = 9$

   (b) Find the cartesian equation of the plane $\mathbf{r}.(3\mathbf{i} - 2\mathbf{j} - 6\mathbf{k}) = 8$

   In each case state the distance of the plane from the origin.

(a) The direction ratios of the normal to the plane $x - 2y + 2z = 9$ are $1:-2:2$
Hence a vector equation of the plane is $\mathbf{r}.(\mathbf{i} - 2\mathbf{j} + 2\mathbf{k}) = 9$

To express this equation in standard form we convert $\mathbf{i} - 2\mathbf{j} + 2\mathbf{k}$ to a unit vector, i.e. we divide by $|\mathbf{i} - 2\mathbf{j} + 2\mathbf{k}|$

giving
$$\mathbf{r}.(\tfrac{1}{3}\mathbf{i} - \tfrac{2}{3}\mathbf{j} + \tfrac{2}{3}\mathbf{k}) = 3$$

This plane is distant 3 units from the origin.

(b) The cartesian equation of the plane $\mathbf{r}.(3\mathbf{i} - 2\mathbf{j} - 6\mathbf{k}) = 8$ is

$$3x - 2y - 6z = 8$$

To express the vector equation in standard form we divide by the modulus of $3\mathbf{i} - 2\mathbf{j} - 6\mathbf{k}$ giving

$$\mathbf{r}.(\tfrac{3}{7}\mathbf{i} - \tfrac{2}{7}\mathbf{j} - \tfrac{6}{7}\mathbf{k}) = \tfrac{8}{7}$$

so the plane is distant $1\tfrac{1}{7}$ units from the origin.

---

2. Find the equation of the line passing through the point $(3, 1, 2)$ which is perpendicular to the plane $\mathbf{r}.(2\mathbf{i} - \mathbf{j} + \mathbf{k}) = 4$. Find also the coordinates of the point where the line intersects the plane.

As the line is perpendicular to the plane it is parallel to the normal to the plane, i.e. the line is parallel to the vector $2\mathbf{i} - \mathbf{j} + \mathbf{k}$

The equation of the line through $3\mathbf{i} + \mathbf{j} + 2\mathbf{k}$ and in the direction $2\mathbf{i} - \mathbf{j} + \mathbf{k}$ is

$$\mathbf{r} = (3\mathbf{i} + \mathbf{j} + 2\mathbf{k}) + \lambda(2\mathbf{i} - \mathbf{j} + \mathbf{k})$$

To deal with a point of intersection we must find separate expressions for the coordinates of a point on the line, i.e. the parametric coordinates.

At a general point on the line $x = 3 + 2\lambda$, $y = 1 - \lambda$, $z = 2 + \lambda$

At the point of intersection of line and plane these coordinates also satisfy the equation of the plane

i.e. $(\{3 + 2\lambda\}\mathbf{i} + \{1 - \lambda\}\mathbf{j} + \{2 + \lambda\}\mathbf{k}).(2\mathbf{i} - \mathbf{j} + \mathbf{k}) = 4$

$\Rightarrow$ $2(3 + 2\lambda) - (1 - \lambda) + (2 + \lambda) = 4$

$\Rightarrow$ $\lambda = -\tfrac{1}{2}$

$\Rightarrow$ $x = 2$, $y = \tfrac{3}{2}$ and $z = \tfrac{3}{2}$

$\therefore$ the line intersects the plane at the point $(2, \tfrac{3}{2}, \tfrac{3}{2})$

---

3. Show that the plane whose vector equation is $\mathbf{r}.(\mathbf{i} + 2\mathbf{j} - \mathbf{k}) = 3$
   contains the line with vector equation $\mathbf{r} = \mathbf{i} + \mathbf{j} + \lambda(2\mathbf{i} + \mathbf{j} + 4\mathbf{k})$

A line is contained in a plane if any two points on the line are also in the plane. In the equation of the line, each value of λ gives one point on the line.

Taking $\lambda = 0$ and $\lambda = 1$ we see that $\mathbf{i} + \mathbf{j}$ and $3\mathbf{i} + 2\mathbf{j} + 4\mathbf{k}$ are the position vectors of two points on the given line.

If $\mathbf{r} = \mathbf{i} + \mathbf{j}$ then $\mathbf{r}.(\mathbf{i} + 2\mathbf{j} - \mathbf{k}) = (\mathbf{i} + \mathbf{j}).(\mathbf{i} + 2\mathbf{j} - \mathbf{k})$

$$= 1 + 2 + 0 = 3$$

$\therefore$ $\mathbf{i} + \mathbf{j}$ is a point on the given plane.

If $\mathbf{r} = 3\mathbf{i} + 2\mathbf{j} + 4\mathbf{k}$ then $\mathbf{r}.(\mathbf{i} + 2\mathbf{j} - \mathbf{k}) = (3\mathbf{i} + 2\mathbf{j} + 4\mathbf{k}).(\mathbf{i} + 2\mathbf{j} - \mathbf{k})$

$$= 3 + 4 - 4 = 3$$

$\therefore$ $3\mathbf{i} + 2\mathbf{j} + 4\mathbf{k}$ is also a point on the given plane.

Two points on the line are also in the plane so the line is contained in the plane.

---

4. Find a vector equation of the plane through the origin and the points $(1, 2, 0)$ and $(-3, 0, 5)$

The plane passes through the origin so its distance from the O is zero.

The cartesian equation of the plane is

$$Ax + By + Cz = 0 \qquad\qquad [1]$$

$(1, 2, 0)$ and $(-3, 0, 5)$ are both on the plane

so $A(1) + B(2) + C(0) = 0$ and $A(-3) + B(0) + C(5) = 0$

$\Rightarrow$ $A + 2B = 0$ and $-3A + 5C = 0$

Hence $B = -\frac{1}{2}A$ and $C = \frac{3}{5}A$

Substituting these values in equation [1] gives

$$Ax - \tfrac{1}{2}Ay + \tfrac{3}{5}Az = 0 \quad \Rightarrow \quad 10x - 5y + 6z = 0$$

This is the cartesian equation of the required plane and the corresponding vector equation is

$$\mathbf{r}.(10\mathbf{i} - 5\mathbf{j} + 6\mathbf{k}) = 0$$

---

5. Find, in parametric form, the equation of the plane which contains the line $\mathbf{r} = \mathbf{i} + \mathbf{j} - \mathbf{k} + \lambda(3\mathbf{i} + 5\mathbf{j} - 2\mathbf{k}) = 6$ and the point $A(4, 3, 2)$. Show that the point $(8, 9, -1)$ is on the plane.

To find the parametric equation of the plane we need a fixed point, i.e. A and *two* direction vectors, one of which is $(3\mathbf{i} + 5\mathbf{j} - 2\mathbf{k})$. The second direction vector can be obtained by taking a point on the given line and finding the direction of the vector joining it to A.

One point on the given line is $\mathbf{i} + \mathbf{j} - \mathbf{k}$ and the direction of the line joining this point to A is $(4\mathbf{i} + 3\mathbf{j} + 2\mathbf{k}) - (\mathbf{i} + \mathbf{j} - \mathbf{k}) = 3\mathbf{i} + 2\mathbf{j} + 3\mathbf{k}$

The required plane contains the direction vectors $3\mathbf{i} + 5\mathbf{j} - 2\mathbf{k}$ and $3\mathbf{i} + 2\mathbf{j} + 3\mathbf{k}$ and passes through $4\mathbf{i} + 3\mathbf{j} + 2\mathbf{k}$

Therefore its parametric equation is

$$\mathbf{r} = 4\mathbf{i} + 3\mathbf{j} + 2\mathbf{k} + \lambda(3\mathbf{i} + 5\mathbf{j} - 2\mathbf{k}) + \mu(\mathbf{i} + \mathbf{j} - \mathbf{k})$$

Any pair of values for λ and μ give one point on the plane and we can see that when $\lambda = 1$ and $\mu = 1$ we get $\mathbf{r} = 8\mathbf{i} + 9\mathbf{j} - \mathbf{k}$

Therefore the point $(8, 9, -1)$ is on the plane.

---

6. L is a line whose vector equation is $\mathbf{r} = 2\mathbf{i} - 2\mathbf{j} + 3\mathbf{k} + \lambda(\mathbf{i} - \mathbf{j} + 4\mathbf{k})$. Π is a plane with vector equation $\mathbf{r}.(\mathbf{i} + 5\mathbf{j} + \mathbf{k}) = 5$
Show that L is parallel to Π and find the distance between them.

L is parallel to $\mathbf{i} - \mathbf{j} + 4\mathbf{k}$ and Π is perpendicular to $\mathbf{i} + 5\mathbf{j} + \mathbf{k}$

If L is parallel to Π, it must be perpendicular to the normal to Π

Now $\qquad (\mathbf{i} - \mathbf{j} + 4\mathbf{k}).(\mathbf{i} + 5\mathbf{j} + \mathbf{k}) = 1 - 5 + 4 = 0$

$\therefore \qquad \mathbf{i} - \mathbf{j} + 4\mathbf{k}$ and $\mathbf{i} + 5\mathbf{j} + \mathbf{k}$ are perpendicular

i.e. L is perpendicular to the normal to Π

$\therefore$ L is parallel to Π

If we find the equation of a plane containing L and parallel to Π we can find the distance from the origin to this plane, and to the plane Π, and hence the distance between them.

As $2\mathbf{i} - 2\mathbf{j} + 3\mathbf{k}$ is a point on L, the equation of a plane containing L must contain this point.

The equation of the plane Π_1, parallel to Π and containing L, can now be obtained in the form $\mathbf{r.n} = \mathbf{a.n}$

i.e. $\mathbf{r}.(\mathbf{i} + 5\mathbf{j} + \mathbf{k}) = (2\mathbf{i} - 2\mathbf{j} + 3\mathbf{k}).(\mathbf{i} + 5\mathbf{j} + \mathbf{k}) = -5$

Now if d is the distance from the origin to Π then

$$d = \frac{5}{\sqrt{(1^2 + 5^2 + 1^2)}} = \frac{5}{\sqrt{27}}$$

and if d_1 is the distance from the origin to Π_1 then

$$d_1 = \frac{-5}{\sqrt{(1^2 + 5^2 + 1^2)}} = \frac{-5}{\sqrt{27}}$$

The opposite signs obtained for d and d_1 indicate that Π and Π_1 are on opposite sides of the origin.

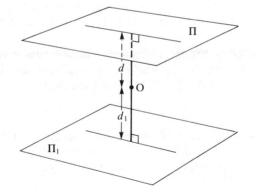

Therefore the distance between L and Π is $\dfrac{5}{\sqrt{27}} + \dfrac{5}{\sqrt{27}} = \dfrac{10}{\sqrt{27}}$

EXERCISE 39i

1. Write down the cartesian equation of the plane whose vector equation is

    (a) $\mathbf{r}.(\mathbf{i} - \mathbf{j} - \mathbf{k}) = 2$ (b) $\mathbf{r}.(2\mathbf{i} + 3\mathbf{j} - 4\mathbf{k}) = 0$

2. Find a vector equation for the plane whose cartesian equation is

    (a) $3x - 4y + 5x = 6$ (b) $x - 7y - z = 5$

3. Find the cartesian equations of the following planes.

    (a) $\mathbf{r}.(\mathbf{i} + \mathbf{j} - \mathbf{k}) = 2$ (b) $\mathbf{r}.(2\mathbf{i} + 3\mathbf{j} - 4\mathbf{k}) = 1$

4. Find the equation of the plane containing the points, A, B and C, in cartesian form and in scalar product form.

    (a) A, B and C are the points $(0, 0, -1)$, $(1, 3, 0)$, $(0, 2, 1)$ respectively.

    (b) The position vectors of A, B and C are $\mathbf{i} + \mathbf{j}$, $\mathbf{i} + \mathbf{k}$ and $\mathbf{j} - 3\mathbf{k}$

5. A plane goes through the three points whose position vectors are $\mathbf{a}$, $\mathbf{b}$ and $\mathbf{c}$ where,

$$\mathbf{a} = \mathbf{i} + \mathbf{j} + 2\mathbf{k}$$
$$\mathbf{b} = 2\mathbf{i} - \mathbf{j} + 3\mathbf{k}$$

   and $\mathbf{c} = -\mathbf{i} + 2\mathbf{j} - 2\mathbf{k}$

   Find the vector equation of this plane in scalar product form and hence find the distance of the plane from the origin.

6. A plane goes through the points whose position vectors are $\mathbf{i} - 2\mathbf{j} + \mathbf{k}$ and $2\mathbf{i} - \mathbf{j} - \mathbf{k}$ and is parallel to the line with equation $\mathbf{r} = \mathbf{i} - \mathbf{j} + \lambda(3\mathbf{i} + \mathbf{j} - 2\mathbf{k})$. Find the distance of this plane from the origin.

7. Two planes Π_1 and Π_2 have vector equations $\mathbf{r}.(2\mathbf{i} + \mathbf{j} - 2\mathbf{k}) = 3$ and $\mathbf{r}.(2\mathbf{i} + \mathbf{j} - 2\mathbf{k}) = 9$. Explain why Π_1 and Π_2 are parallel and hence find the distance between them.

8. Find the vector equation of the line through the origin which is perpendicular to the plane $\mathbf{r}.(\mathbf{i} - 2\mathbf{j} + \mathbf{k}) = 3$

9. Find the vector equation of the line through the point $(2, 1, 1)$ which is perpendicular to the plane $\mathbf{r}.(\mathbf{i} + 2\mathbf{j} - 3\mathbf{k}) = 6$

10. Find the vector equation of the plane which goes through the point $(0, 1, 6)$ and is parallel to the plane $\mathbf{r}.(\mathbf{i} - 2\mathbf{j}) = 3$

11. Find the vector equation of the plane which goes through the origin and which contains the line $\mathbf{r} = 2\mathbf{i} + \lambda(\mathbf{j} + \mathbf{k})$

12. Find the point of intersection of the line with equation $\mathbf{r} = (\mathbf{i} + \mathbf{j} - 2\mathbf{k}) + \lambda(\mathbf{i} - \mathbf{j} + \mathbf{k})$ and the plane $\mathbf{r}.(\mathbf{i} + 2\mathbf{j} - \mathbf{k}) = 2$

13. Find the point of intersection of the line $x - 2 = 2y + 1 = 3 - z$ and the plane $x + 2y + z = 3$

14. Show that the line $x + 1 = y = \frac{1}{2}(z - 3)$ is parallel to the plane $\mathbf{r}.(\mathbf{i} + \mathbf{j} - \mathbf{k}) = 3$ and find the distance between them.

15. Find the vector equation of the following planes in scalar product form.

    (a) $\mathbf{r} = \mathbf{i} - \mathbf{j} + \lambda(\mathbf{i} + \mathbf{j} + \mathbf{k}) + \mu(\mathbf{i} - 2\mathbf{j} + 3\mathbf{k})$

    (b) $\mathbf{r} = 2\mathbf{i} - \mathbf{k} + \lambda(\mathbf{i}) + \mu(\mathbf{i} - 2\mathbf{j} - \mathbf{k})$

    (c) $\mathbf{r} = (1 + s - t)\mathbf{i} + (2 - s)\mathbf{j} + (3 - 2s + 2t)\mathbf{k}$

16. Find the vector equation in parametric form of the plane that contains the lines

$$\mathbf{r} = -3\mathbf{i} - 2\mathbf{j} + t(\mathbf{i} - 2\mathbf{j} + \mathbf{k})$$
$$\mathbf{r} = \mathbf{i} - 11\mathbf{j} + 4\mathbf{k} + s(2\mathbf{i} - \mathbf{j} + 2\mathbf{k})$$

17. Find the vector equation in parametric form of the plane that goes through the point with position vector $\mathbf{i} + \mathbf{j}$ and which is parallel to the lines
$\mathbf{r}_1 = 2\mathbf{i} - \mathbf{j} + \lambda(\mathbf{i} + \mathbf{k})$ and $\mathbf{r}_2 = 2\mathbf{j} - \mathbf{k} + \mu(\mathbf{i} - \mathbf{j} + \mathbf{k})$.
Is either of these lines contained in the plane?

18. Determine whether the given lines are parallel to, contained in, or intersect the plane $\mathbf{r}.(2\mathbf{i} + \mathbf{j} - 3\mathbf{k}) = 5$

    (a) $\mathbf{r} = 3\mathbf{i} - \mathbf{j} + \mathbf{k} + \lambda(-2\mathbf{i} + \mathbf{j} - 3\mathbf{k})$

    (b) $\mathbf{r} = \mathbf{i} - \mathbf{j} + \mu(2\mathbf{i} + \mathbf{j} - 3\mathbf{k})$

    (c) $x = y = z$

    (d) $\mathbf{r} = (2\mathbf{i} + \mathbf{j}) + s(3\mathbf{i} + 2\mathbf{k})$

THE ANGLE BETWEEN TWO PLANES

Consider two planes Π_1 and Π_2 whose equations are

$$\mathbf{r}.\mathbf{n}_1 = d_1 \quad \text{and} \quad \mathbf{r}.\mathbf{n}_2 = d_2$$

i.e. $\mathbf{n}_1$ and $\mathbf{n}_2$ are perpendicular to Π_1 and Π_2 respectively.

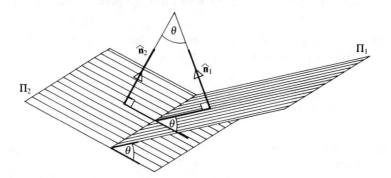

The angle between the planes is equal to the angle between their normals. Therefore

the angle θ between Π_1 and Π_2 is given by

$$\cos \theta = \widehat{\mathbf{n}}_1 . \widehat{\mathbf{n}}_2$$

e.g. the angle between the planes whose equations are

$\mathbf{r}.(\mathbf{i} + \mathbf{j} - 2\mathbf{k}) = 3$ and $\mathbf{r}.(2\mathbf{i} - 2\mathbf{j} + \mathbf{k}) = 2$ is given by

$$\cos \theta = \frac{(\mathbf{i} + \mathbf{j} - 2\mathbf{k})}{\sqrt{6}} \cdot \frac{(2\mathbf{i} - 2\mathbf{j} + \mathbf{k})}{3} = -\frac{\sqrt{6}}{9}$$

The negative sign shows that we have found the obtuse angle between the planes. The acute angle between them is $\arccos \frac{\sqrt{6}}{9}$

There are two special cases, i.e.

if $\widehat{\mathbf{n}}_1 . \widehat{\mathbf{n}}_2 = 0$ the two planes are perpendicular

and   if $\widehat{\mathbf{n}}_1 = \pm \widehat{\mathbf{n}}_2$ the two planes are parallel

THE ANGLE BETWEEN A LINE AND A PLANE

Consider the line $\mathbf{r} = \mathbf{a} + \lambda\mathbf{b}$ and the plane $\mathbf{r}.\mathbf{n} = D$

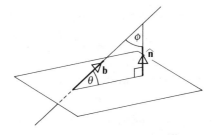

If ϕ is the angle between the line and the normal to the plane and θ is the angle between the line and the plane then

$$\theta = \tfrac{1}{2}\pi - \phi \quad \Rightarrow \quad \sin\theta = \cos\phi$$

Now $\cos\phi = \widehat{\mathbf{b}}.\widehat{\mathbf{n}} = \dfrac{\mathbf{b}.\mathbf{n}}{bn}$ therefore

> the angle between the line $\mathbf{r} = \mathbf{a} + \lambda\mathbf{b}$ and the plane $\mathbf{r}.\mathbf{n} = D$
>
> is given by $\sin\theta = \dfrac{\mathbf{b}.\mathbf{n}}{bn}$

e.g. the angle between the line $\mathbf{r} = (\mathbf{i} + 2\mathbf{j} - \mathbf{k}) + \lambda(\mathbf{i} - \mathbf{j} + \mathbf{k})$ and the plane $\mathbf{r}.(2\mathbf{i} - \mathbf{j} + \mathbf{k}) = 4$ is given by

$$\sin\theta = \frac{(\mathbf{i} - \mathbf{j} + \mathbf{k})}{\sqrt{3}}.\frac{(2\mathbf{i} - \mathbf{j} + \mathbf{k})}{\sqrt{6}} = \frac{2\sqrt{2}}{3}$$

If the exact value of $\cos\theta$ should be required, it can be found by using $\cos^2\theta + \sin^2\theta = 1$

EXERCISE 39j

In Questions 1 to 4 find the cosine of the angle between the two given planes.

1. The planes whose equations are
   $\mathbf{r}.(\mathbf{i} - \mathbf{j} + 3\mathbf{k}) = 3$ and $\mathbf{r}.(2\mathbf{i} - \mathbf{j} + 2\mathbf{k}) = 5$

2. The cartesian equations of the two planes are
   $2x + 2y - 3z = 3$ and $x + 3y - 4z = 6$

3. One plane passes through the points $(1, 0, 0)$, $(0, 1, 0)$ and $(0, 0, 1)$ and the other plane is perpendicular to the line with equation
$$\mathbf{r} = -2\mathbf{j} + 5\mathbf{k} + t(2\mathbf{i} + 3\mathbf{j} - 4\mathbf{k})$$

4. One plane has equations
$$\frac{x - 3}{2} = \frac{y + 1}{3} = \frac{z - 4}{6}$$
and the other is parallel to the xy plane.

In Questions 5 to 7 find the sine of the angle between the line and the plane whose equations are given.

5. $\mathbf{r} = \mathbf{i} - \mathbf{j} + \lambda(\mathbf{i} + \mathbf{j} + \mathbf{k})$ and $\mathbf{r}.(\mathbf{i} - 2\mathbf{j} + 2\mathbf{k}) = 4$

6. $(x - 2) = \frac{1}{2}(y + 1) = \frac{1}{2}(z + 3)$ and $2x - y - 2z = 4$

7. The equation of a plane is $\mathbf{r}.(\mathbf{i} + \mathbf{j}) = 7$ and the equation of a line is $\mathbf{r} = 3\mathbf{i} - \mathbf{k} + \lambda(a\mathbf{i} + \mathbf{j} - \mathbf{k})$ where a is a constant.
Find the value of a if the angle between the line and the plane is
(a) $30°$ (b) $45°$

8. Show that the angle between the line $\frac{1}{2}(x - 2) = \frac{1}{2}(y + 2) = z - 5$ and the plane $3x + 2y - 6z = 8$ is $\arccos \dfrac{5\sqrt{17}}{21}$

9. $\mathbf{r} = \mathbf{i} - 2\mathbf{j} + \mathbf{k} + \mu(2\mathbf{i} - \mathbf{j})$ and $\mathbf{r} = \mathbf{i} - \mathbf{j} + s(\mathbf{i} + \mathbf{k}) + t(\mathbf{j} - \mathbf{k})$

CHAPTER 40

COMPLEX NUMBERS

IMAGINARY NUMBERS

The numbers we have worked with up to now have been such that, when squared, the result is either positive or zero, i.e. for a number k, $k^2 \geqslant 0$

Such numbers are *real* numbers.

However, the roots of an equation such as $x^2 = -1$ are clearly not real since they give -1 when squared.
If we are to work with equations of this type we need another category of numbers, i.e. the set of numbers whose squares are negative real numbers.

Members of this set are called *imaginary* numbers and some examples are

$$\sqrt{-1}, \quad \sqrt{-7}, \quad \sqrt{-20}$$

In general any imaginary number can be represented by $\sqrt{(-n^2)}$ where n is real.

Now $\qquad \sqrt{(-n^2)} = \sqrt{[(n^2)(-1)]} = \sqrt{(n^2)} \times \sqrt{(-1)}$

i.e. $\qquad \sqrt{(-n^2)} = n\mathrm{i} \quad \text{where} \quad \mathrm{i} = \sqrt{(-1)}$

So any imaginary number can be written $n\mathrm{i}$ where n is real and

$$\mathrm{i} = \sqrt{(-1)}$$

e.g. $\qquad \sqrt{-16} = 4\mathrm{i} \quad \text{and} \quad \sqrt{-3} = \mathrm{i}\sqrt{3}$

Usually the real number is placed before i but we write $\mathrm{i}\sqrt{3}$ rather than $\sqrt{3}\mathrm{i}$ in order to avoid ambiguity.
Note that j is sometimes used instead of i for $\sqrt{-1}$ but in this book we use i.

Imaginary numbers can be added to, or subtracted from, each other.

For example $3i + 9i = 12i$ and $i\sqrt{7} - 2i = (\sqrt{7} - 2)i$

The product of two imaginary numbers is always real.

For example $2i \times 5i = 10i^2 = 10(\sqrt{-1})^2 = 10(-1)$

i.e. $2i \times 5i = -10$

The quotient of two imaginary numbers is always real.

For example $\dfrac{3i}{7i} = \dfrac{3}{7}$

Powers of i can be simplified.

For example $i^3 = (i^2)(i) = -i$ $i^4 = (i^2)^2 = (-1)^2 = 1$

$\qquad\qquad\quad i^5 = (i^4)(i) = i$ $i^{-1} = i/i^2 = i/-1 = -i$

COMPLEX NUMBERS

When a real number and an imaginary number are added or subtracted, the expression which is obtained cannot be simplified and is called a *complex number*,
e.g. $2 + 3i$, $4 - 7i$, and $-1 + 4i$ are complex numbers.

A general complex number can be represented by $a + bi$ where a and b can have any real value including zero.

If $a = 0$ we have numbers of the form bi, i.e. imaginary numbers.
If $b = 0$ we have numbers of the form a, i.e. real numbers.

Therefore

> the set of complex numbers includes all real numbers and all imaginary numbers.

OPERATIONS ON COMPLEX NUMBERS

Addition and Subtraction

Real terms and imaginary terms are collected separately in two groups,

e.g. $(2 + 3i) + (4 - i) = (2 + 4) + (3i - i) = 6 + 2i$

and $(4 - 2i) - (3 + 5i) = (4 - 3) - (2i + 5i) = 1 - 7i$

Multiplication

The distributive law of multiplication applied to two complex numbers gives their product,

e.g.
$$i(5 - 2i) = 5i - 2i^2$$
$$= 5i - 2(-1)$$
$$= 2 + 5i$$

and
$$(2 + 3i)(4 - i) = 8 - 2i + 12i - 3i^2$$
$$= 8 + 10i - 3(-1)$$
$$= 11 + 10i$$

and
$$(2 + 3i)(2 - 3i) = 4 - 6i + 6i - 9i^2$$
$$= 4 + 9$$
$$= 13$$

Conjugate Complex Numbers

Notice that the product in the last example above is a real number. This is because of the special form of the given complex numbers, $2 \pm 3i$, which are the factors of a 'difference of two squares'

Any pair of complex numbers of the form $a \pm bi$ have a product which is real, since

$$(a + bi)(a - bi) = a^2 - abi + abi - b^2i^2$$
$$= a^2 + b^2$$

Such complex numbers are said to be *conjugate* and each is the conjugate of the other. Thus $4 + 5i$ and $4 - 5i$ are conjugate complex numbers and $4 + 5i$ is the conjugate of $4 - 5i$

If $a + bi$ is denoted by z then its conjugate, $a - bi$, is denoted by $\bar{z}$ or z^*

Division

Division by a complex number cannot be carried out directly because the denominator is made up of two independent terms. This problem can be overcome by making the denominator real, a process called 'realising the denominator'. This is done by using the property that the product of conjugate complex numbers is real.

e.g. if we wish to divide $2 + 9i$ by $5 - 2i$ we multiply both numerator and denominator by the conjugate of the denominator, which is $5 + 2i$ in this case, giving

$$\frac{2 + 9i}{5 - 2i} = \frac{(2 + 9i)(5 + 2i)}{(5 - 2i)(5 + 2i)}$$

$$= \frac{10 + 49i + 18i^2}{25 - 4i^2}$$

$$= \frac{-8 + 49i}{29} = -\frac{8}{29} + \frac{49}{29}i$$

Note that the real term is given first, even when it is negative.

THE ZERO COMPLEX NUMBER

A complex number is zero if, and only if, the real term and the imaginary term are each zero.

i.e. $a + bi = 0 \iff a = 0 \text{ and } b = 0$

EQUAL COMPLEX NUMBERS

If $a + bi = c + di$ then $(a + bi) - (c + di) = 0$

$\Rightarrow$ $(a - c) + (b - d)i = 0$

Hence $a - c = 0$ and $b - d = 0$

$\Rightarrow$ $a = c$ and $b = d$

i.e. two complex numbers are equal if, and only if, the real terms are equal and the imaginary terms are equal.

Denoting the real part of $a + bi$ by $\text{Re}(a + bi)$ and the imaginary part by $\text{Im}(a + bi)$ we have

$$a + bi = c + di \iff \begin{cases} \text{Re}(a + bi) = \text{Re}(c + di) \\ \text{Im}(a + bi) = \text{Im}(c + di) \end{cases}$$

A complex equation is therefore equivalent to two separate equations.

This property provides an alternative (but not better) method for division by a complex number.

e.g. to divide $3 - 2i$ by $5 + i$ we can represent the quotient by $p + qi$, where p and q are real,

i.e.
$$\frac{3 - 2i}{5 + i} = p + qi$$

Hence
$$3 - 2i = (p + qi)(5 + i)$$
$$= 5p + pi + 5qi + qi^2$$
$$= (5p - q) + (p + 5q)i$$

Equating real and imaginary parts gives

$$3 = 5p - q \quad \text{and} \quad -2 = p + 5q$$

Solving these two equations gives $p = \frac{1}{2}$ and $q = -\frac{1}{2}$

∴
$$(3 - 2i) \div (5 + i) = \tfrac{1}{2} - \tfrac{1}{2}i$$

FINDING THE SQUARE ROOTS OF A COMPLEX NUMBER

Equating the real parts and the imaginary parts of a complex equation provides one method for determining the square roots of a complex number.

For example, if we assume that a square root of a complex number is itself a complex number then, using $\sqrt{(15 + 8i)}$ as an example we can say

$$\sqrt{(15 + 8i)} = a + bi \qquad \text{where } a \text{ and } b \text{ are real}$$

⇒
$$15 + 8i = (a + bi)^2$$
$$= a^2 - b^2 + 2abi$$

Equating real and imaginary parts gives

$$a^2 - b^2 = 15 \qquad\qquad [1]$$

and
$$2ab = 8 \qquad\qquad [2]$$

Using $b = \dfrac{4}{a}$ in [1] gives $\quad a^2 - \dfrac{16}{a^2} = 15$

$\Rightarrow \qquad\qquad\qquad\qquad a^4 - 15a^2 - 16 = 0$

$\Rightarrow \qquad\qquad\qquad\qquad (a^2 - 16)(a^2 + 1) = 0$

Thus $\qquad\qquad\qquad a^2 - 16 = 0 \quad$ or $\quad a^2 + 1 = 0$

Now a is real, so $a^2 + 1 = 0$ gives no suitable values

therefore the only values for a are $a = \pm 4$

Then from equation [2] we have

$$a = 4 \quad\Rightarrow\quad b = 1$$

and $\qquad\qquad\qquad a = -4 \;\Rightarrow\; b = -1$

Note. It is not correct to say $a = \pm 4$ therefore $b = \pm 1$ as this offers four different pairs of values for a and b (i.e. 4, 1; 4, -1; -4, 1; -4, -1) two of which are invalid.

Hence $\qquad\qquad \sqrt{(15 + 8i)} = 4 + i \quad$ or $\quad -4 - i$

$$= \pm(4 + i)$$

This result justifies our original assumption that the square root of a complex number is another complex number.

Sometimes it is possible to find the square roots of a complex number simply by observation.

In the example above, equation [2] shows that the product of a and b is half the coefficient of i in the given complex number.

Suitable integral values for a and b can then be checked quite quickly, e.g. to find $\sqrt{(8 - 6i)}$ we note that $ab = -3$ so possible values for a and b are: 1, -3; 3, -1

Checking: $\qquad (1 - 3i)^2 = -8 - 6i \quad$ which is not correct

$\qquad\qquad\qquad (3 - i)^2 = 8 - 6i \qquad$ which is correct

Hence one square root of $8 - 6i$ is $3 - i$ and the other is $-(3 - i)$

i.e. $\qquad\qquad\qquad \sqrt{(8 - 6i)} = \pm(3 - i)$

Note. Unless a and b are integers, this method is unlikely to be useful.

EXERCISE 40a

1. Simplify: i^7, i^{-3}, i^9, i^{-5}, i^{4n}, i^{4n+1}

2. Add the following pairs of complex numbers.
   (a) $3 + 5i$ and $7 - i$ (b) $4 - i$ and $3 + 3i$
   (c) $2 + 7i$ and $4 - 9i$ (d) $a + bi$ and $c + di$

3. Subtract the second number from the first in each part of Question 2.

4. Simplify
   (a) $(2 + i)(3 - 4i)$ (b) $(5 + 4i)(7 - i)$ (c) $(3 - i)(4 - i)$
   (d) $(3 + 4i)(3 - 4i)$ (e) $(2 - i)^2$ (f) $(1 + i)^3$
   (g) $i(3 + 4i)$ (h) $(x + yi)(x - yi)$ (i) $i(1 + i)(2 + i)$
   (j) $(a + bi)^2$

5. Realise the denominator of each of the following fractions and hence express each in the form $a + bi$
   (a) $\dfrac{2}{1 - i}$ (b) $\dfrac{3 + i}{4 - 3i}$ (c) $\dfrac{4i}{4 + i}$ (d) $\dfrac{1 + i}{1 - i}$
   (e) $\dfrac{7 - i}{1 + 7i}$ (f) $\dfrac{x + yi}{x - yi}$ (g) $\dfrac{3 + i}{i}$ (h) $\dfrac{-2 + 3i}{-i}$

6. Solve the following equations for x and y
   (a) $x + yi = (3 + i)(2 - 3i)$ (b) $\dfrac{2 + 5i}{1 - i} = x + yi$
   (c) $3 + 4i = (x + yi)(1 + i)$ (d) $x + yi = 2$
   (e) $x + yi = (3 + 2i)(3 - 2i)$ (f) $x + yi = (4 + i)^2$
   (g) $\dfrac{x + yi}{2 + i} = 5 - i$ (h) $(x + yi)^2 = 3 + 4i$

7. Find the real and imaginary parts of
   (a) $(2 - i)(3 + i)$ (b) $(1 - i)^3$ (c) $(3 + 4i)(3 - 4i)$
   (d) $\dfrac{3 + 2i}{4 - i}$ (e) $\dfrac{2}{3 + i} + \dfrac{3}{2 + i}$ (f) $\dfrac{1}{x + yi} - \dfrac{1}{x - yi}$

8. Find the square roots of
   (a) $3 - 4i$ (b) $21 - 20i$ (c) $2i$ $15 + 8i$ (e) $-24 + 10i$

COMPLEX ROOTS OF QUADRATIC EQUATIONS

Consider the quadratic equation $x^2 + 2x + 2 = 0$

The formula $x = \dfrac{-b \pm \sqrt{(b^2 - 4ac)}}{2a}$ gives $x = \dfrac{-2 \pm \sqrt{-4}}{2}$

Previously we dismissed solutions of this type, in which $b^2 - 4ac < 0$, as not being real. But now, because $\sqrt{-4} = 2i$, we see that the roots of this equation are the complex numbers $-1 + i$ and $-1 - i$.

Further, the roots are conjugate complex numbers.

We can show that if $b^2 - 4ac < 0$, the roots of the general quadratic equation $ax^2 + bx + c = 0$ are *always* conjugate complex numbers.

If $\qquad ax^2 + bx + c = 0$ and $b^2 - 4ac < 0$

then $\qquad x = \dfrac{-b \pm \sqrt{(b^2 - 4ac)}}{2a} = \dfrac{-b}{2a} \pm \dfrac{i\sqrt{(4ac - b^2)}}{2a}$

$\therefore\ x = p \pm qi$ where $p = -b/2a$ and $q = \sqrt{(4ac - b^2)}/2a$

i.e. when $b^2 - 4ac < 0$, the roots of the equation $ax^2 + bx + c = 0$ are

$$p + qi \quad \text{and} \quad p - qi$$

and these are conjugate complex numbers.

> So, if one root of a quadratic equation with real coefficients is known to be complex, the other root must also be complex and the conjugate of the first.

When the quadratic equation $ax^2 + bx + c = 0$ has real roots α and β we know that

$$\alpha + \beta = \frac{-b}{a} \quad \text{and} \quad \alpha\beta = \frac{c}{a}$$

We now show that these relationships are valid also when the roots are complex.

If $\alpha = p + qi$ and $\beta = p - qi$ then

$$\alpha + \beta = 2p = 2\left(\frac{-b}{2a}\right) = \frac{-b}{a}$$

and $\quad \alpha\beta = (p + qi)(p - qi) = p^2 + q^2 = \dfrac{b^2}{4a^2} + \dfrac{(4ac - b^2)}{4a^2} = \dfrac{c}{a}$

Hence, for *any* quadratic equation $ax^2 + bx + c = 0$, the roots α and β satisfy the relationships

$$\alpha + \beta = -b/a \quad \text{and} \quad \alpha\beta = c/a$$

Examples 40b

1. One root of the equation $x^2 + px + q = 0$ is $2 - 3i$. Find the values of p and q

If one root is $2 - 3i$ the other must be $2 + 3i$

Then $\alpha + \beta = 4$ and $\alpha\beta = (2 - 3i)(2 + 3i) = 13$

Now any quadratic equation can be written in the form

$$x^2 - (\text{sum of roots})x + (\text{product of roots}) = 0$$

So the equation with roots $2 \pm 3i$ is

$$x^2 - 4x + 13 = 0$$

Therefore $p = -4$ and $q = 13$

2. Find the complex roots of the equation $2x^2 + 3x + 5 = 0$. If these roots are α and β, confirm the relationships

$$\alpha + \beta = -\frac{b}{a} \quad \text{and} \quad \alpha\beta = \frac{c}{a}$$

If $2x^2 + 3x + 5 = 0$

then $x = \dfrac{-3 \pm \sqrt{(9 - 40)}}{4}$

$\Rightarrow$ $\alpha = -\dfrac{3}{4} + \dfrac{\sqrt{31}}{4}i \qquad \beta = -\dfrac{3}{4} - \dfrac{\sqrt{31}}{4}i$

Hence $\alpha + \beta = \left(-\dfrac{3}{4} + \dfrac{\sqrt{31}}{4}i\right) + \left(-\dfrac{3}{4} - \dfrac{\sqrt{31}}{4}i\right)$

$$= -\frac{3}{2} = -\frac{b}{a}$$

and $$\alpha\beta = \left(-\frac{3}{4} + \frac{\sqrt{31}}{4}i\right)\left(-\frac{3}{4} - \frac{\sqrt{31}}{4}i\right)$$

$$= \frac{9}{16} - \frac{31}{16}i^2$$

$$= \frac{40}{16} = \frac{5}{2} = \frac{c}{a}$$

EXERCISE 40b

1. Solve the following equations.
   (a) $x^2 + x + 1 = 0$ (b) $2x^2 + 7x + 1 = 0$
   (c) $x^2 + 9 = 0$ (d) $x^2 + x + 3 = 0$
   (e) $x^4 - 1 = 0$ (f) $3x^2 + x + 3 = 0$

2. Form the equation whose roots are
   (a) $i, -i$ (b) $2 + i, 2 - i$
   (c) $1 - 3i, 1 + 3i$ (d) $1 + i, 1 - i, 2$

3. Without calculating a, b and c, evaluate $-b/a$ and c/a if one root of the equation $ax^2 + bx + c = 0$ is
   (a) $2 + i$ (b) $3 - 4i$ (c) i (d) $5i - 12$

4. Find the equation, one of whose roots is
   (a) $-1 - i$ (b) $-5 + i$ (c) $1 - 3i$ (d) $4 + i$
   Explain why this question cannot be answered if the given root is 2

THE ARGAND DIAGRAM

In the complex number $a + bi$, a and b are both real numbers so $a + bi$ can be represented by the ordered pair $\begin{pmatrix} a \\ b \end{pmatrix}$.

This suggests that a and b could be used as the coordinates of a point $A(a, b)$ in the xy plane.

Then the vector $\overrightarrow{OA}$ provides a visual representation of the complex number.

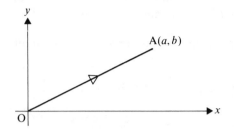

This idea was introduced by a French mathematician and his name, Argand, is given to the diagram which illustrates a complex number in this way. On an Argand diagram, the real part of a complex number is taken as the x-coordinate, and the coefficient of i is the y-coordinate. For this reason the x and y axes are often called the real and imaginary axes. It must be remembered however that the y-coordinate is the *real* number b.

A general complex number $x + y$i is represented by the vector $\overrightarrow{OP}$ where P is the point (x, y)

In an Argand diagram, the magnitude and direction of a line are used to represent a complex number in the same way that a section of line can be used to represent a vector quantity. The techniques and operations used in vector analysis can therefore be applied equally well to complex number analysis.

A COMPLEX NUMBER AS A VECTOR

On an Argand diagram a complex number such as $5 + 3$i can be represented by the vector $\overrightarrow{OA}$ where A is the point $(5, 3)$. However it can equally well be represented by any other vector with the same length and direction as $\overrightarrow{OA}$, e.g. by $\overrightarrow{BC}$ or $\overrightarrow{DE}$ in the diagram below.

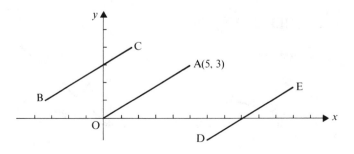

A complex number can be treated in this way only when it behaves as a *free* vector. If, on the other hand, $5 + 3i$ is regarded as a *position* vector, then *only* the vector $\overrightarrow{OA}$ represents $5 + 3i$. In this case the *actual point* $A(5, 3)$ is sometimes taken to represent $5 + 3i$

A vector representing a complex number is usually denoted by the symbol z, so

for a general complex number we have

$$z = x + y\mathrm{i}$$

and for unique complex numbers we use z_1, z_2, etc.,

e.g. $z_1 = 5 + 3\mathrm{i}, \quad z_2 = 7 - 4\mathrm{i}$

When z is used on an Argand diagram, an arrow is needed to indicate the direction of the line representing the complex number.

For example, in the diagram below the line BC without an arrow could represent *either* $4 - 2i$ *or* $-4 + 2i$
Whereas the arrow shows that this line represents the complex number $4 - 2i$ only

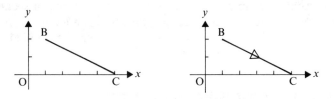

Graphical Addition and Subtraction of Complex Numbers

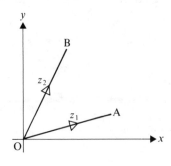
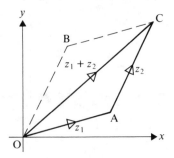

Consider two complex numbers, z_1 and z_2, represented on an Argand diagram by $\overrightarrow{OA}$ and $\overrightarrow{OB}$.

We know that the sum of the two *vectors* $\overrightarrow{OA}$ and $\overrightarrow{OB}$ is $\overrightarrow{OC}$ where AC is equal and parallel to OB. Therefore, as z_1 and z_2 behave as vectors, we have

$z_1 + z_2$ is represented by the diagonal $\overrightarrow{OC}$ of the parallelogram OACB.

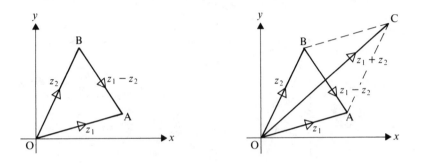

Now considering the vector triangle OAB we see that

$$\overrightarrow{BA} = \overrightarrow{BO} + \overrightarrow{OA}$$

But $\overrightarrow{OA}$ represents z_1 and $\overrightarrow{BO} = -\overrightarrow{OB}$ represents $-z_2$ therefore

$z_1 - z_2$ is represented by the diagonal joining B to A in parallelogram OACB.

Note carefully the direction of the vector represented by this diagonal.

Hence the two diagonals of the parallelogram OACB represent the sum and the difference of z_1 and z_2

If $z_1 = x_1 + y_1 i$ and $z_2 = x_2 + y_2 i$ then

$$z_1 + z_2 = (x_1 + x_2) + (y_1 + y_2)i$$

Therefore C is the point $(\{x_1 + x_2\}, \{y_1 + y_2\})$,

e.g. if $z_1 = 3 + 5i$ and $z_2 = 7 - 2i$ then $z_1 + z_2$ can be represented on the Argand diagram by $\overrightarrow{OC}$ where C is the point $(10, 3)$

Example 40c _____

If $z_1 = 5 - i$ and $z_2 = 3 + 4i$, represent on one Argand diagram the complex numbers z_1, z_2, $z_1 + z_2$, $z_1 - z_2$

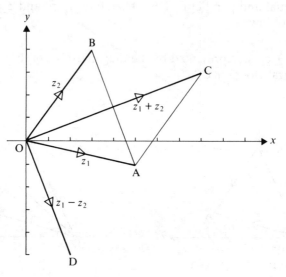

$\overrightarrow{OA}$ represents z_1 and $\overrightarrow{OB}$ represents z_2

$\overrightarrow{OC}$, the diagonal of the parallelogram OACB, represents $z_1 + z_2$

$z_1 - z_2$ is represented by the diagonal $\overrightarrow{BA}$ and also by $\overrightarrow{OD}$ which is equal and parallel to BA

_____

EXERCISE 40c

1. Represent each complex number on an Argand diagram.

   (a) $5 + i$ (b) $-2 + 6i$ (c) $3 - 5i$ (d) $-4 - 4i$

   (e) $4 + 4i$ (f) -3 (g) $3i$ (h) $-7i$

2. If $z_1 = 3 - i$, $z_2 = 1 + 4i$, $z_3 = -4 + i$, $z_4 = -2 - 5i$, represent the following by lines on Argand diagrams, showing the direction of each line by an arrow.

   (a) $z_1 + z_2$ (b) $z_2 - z_3$ (c) $z_1 - z_3$ (d) $z_2 + z_4$

   (e) $z_4 - z_1$ (f) $z_3 - z_4$ (g) z_1

   (h) z_4 (i) $z_2 - z_1$ (j) $z_1 + z_3$

3. If $z_1 = x_1 + y_1 i$ and $z_2 = x_2 + y_2 i$ show on an Argand diagram the position of the points representing $\frac{1}{2}(z_1 + z_2)$ and $\frac{1}{3}(2z_1 + z_2)$

MODULUS AND ARGUMENT

Consider the point $A(a, b)$, representing the complex number $a + bi$

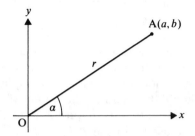

The length of the line OA is called the *modulus* of $a + bi$ and is denoted by r,

i.e.
$$|a + bi| = r = \sqrt{(a^2 + b^2)}$$

The angle between the positive x-axis and the line OA is called the *argument* or *amplitude* of $a + bi$ and is denoted by α, where α is within the range $-\pi < \alpha \leqslant \pi$

i.e.
$$\arg(a + bi) = \alpha = \arctan b/a$$

Even within this range there are usually two angles with the same tangent so, when giving the argument of a complex number in the form $\arctan b/a$, it is often necessary to include a diagram. Consider, for example, the complex numbers

$$4 + 3i, \quad -4 - 3i, \quad -4 + 3i \quad \text{and} \quad 4 - 3i$$

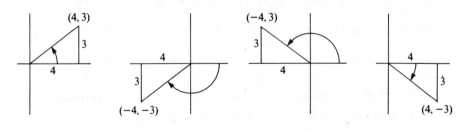

For $4 + 3i$, $\alpha = \arctan \frac{3}{4}$ and is positive and acute

$\Rightarrow \qquad \alpha = 0.644$ rad

For $-4 - 3i$, $\alpha = \arctan \frac{3}{4}$ and is negative and obtuse

$\Rightarrow \qquad \alpha = -2.498$ rad

For $-4 + 3i$, $\alpha = \arctan -\tfrac{3}{4}$ and is positive and obtuse

$\Rightarrow \qquad\qquad \alpha = 2.498$ rad

For $4 - 3i$, $\alpha = \arctan -\tfrac{3}{4}$ and is negative and acute

$\Rightarrow \qquad\qquad \alpha = -0.644$ rad

We see that the argument of each of the first two complex numbers is given by $\arctan\tfrac{3}{4}$ but the values of α are not the same: a similar observation can be made for the last two complex numbers.

This example shows that stating the value of $\arctan\alpha$ is ambiguous and that more information is required to define α uniquely, e.g. a diagram of the type used on page 787.

THE MODULUS/ARGUMENT FORM FOR A COMPLEX NUMBER

Consider a general complex number $x + yi$ represented on an Argand diagram by $\overrightarrow{OP}$ where P is the point (x, y) and OP is inclined at an angle θ to Ox.

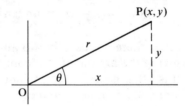

From the diagram we see that $x = r\cos\theta$ and $y = r\sin\theta$

Therefore $x + yi = r\cos\theta + ir\sin\theta = r(\cos\theta + i\sin\theta)$

Hence a complex number can be changed from the form $x + yi$ into the form $r(\cos\theta + i\sin\theta)$ by finding the modulus, r, and the argument, θ

To convert the complex number $1 - i$, for example, we have

$r = |1 - i| = \sqrt{(1^2 + \{-1\}^2)} = \sqrt{2}$

$\theta = \arg(1 - i) = \arctan(-1) = -\tfrac{1}{4}\pi$

Hence, in modulus/argument form,

$1 - i = \sqrt{2}(\cos\{-\tfrac{1}{4}\pi\} + i\sin\{-\tfrac{1}{4}\pi\})$

Conversely, a complex number given in modulus/argument form can be changed directly into cartesian form,

e.g. $4(\cos \frac{2}{3}\pi + i \sin \frac{2}{3}\pi) = 4(\{-\frac{1}{2}\} + i\{\frac{1}{2}\sqrt{3}\}) = -2 + 2i\sqrt{3}$

Note that the position where i is written varies according to the form of the complex term; the aim is always to make the term clear and unambiguous,
e.g. we write $6i$, $i \sin \theta$, $2i\sqrt{3}$, $3i \cos \frac{1}{2}\pi$,   etc.

Examples 40d

1. Express in the form $r(\cos \theta + i \sin \theta)$
   (a) $\sqrt{3} - i$ (b) -2 (c) $-5i$ (d) $-2 + 2i$

(a) For $\sqrt{3} - i$

$$r = \sqrt{(\{\sqrt{3}\}^2 + \{-1\}^2)} = 2$$

$$\tan \theta = -1/\sqrt{3} \quad \Rightarrow \quad \theta = -\frac{1}{6}\pi$$

$$\therefore \quad \sqrt{3} - i = 2(\cos \{-\frac{1}{6}\pi\} + \sin \{-\frac{1}{6}\pi\})$$

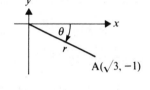

(b) For -2, $r = 2$ and $\theta = \pi$

$$(\theta \neq -\pi \text{ as } -\pi < \theta < \pi)$$

$$\therefore \qquad -2 = 2(\cos \pi + i \sin \pi)$$

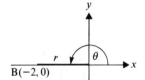

(c) For $-5i$, $r = 5$ and $\theta = -\frac{1}{2}\pi$

$$\therefore \qquad -5i = 5(\cos \{-\frac{1}{2}\pi\} + i \sin \{-\frac{1}{2}\pi\})$$

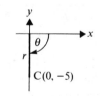

(d) For $-2 + 2i$

$$r = \sqrt{(\{-2\}^2 + 2^2)} = 2\sqrt{2}$$

$$\tan \theta = 2/-2 = -1 \quad \Rightarrow \quad \theta = \frac{3}{4}\pi$$

$$\therefore \quad -2 + 2i = 2\sqrt{2}(\cos \frac{3}{4}\pi + i \sin \frac{3}{4}\pi)$$

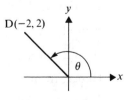

2. Find the modulus and argument of $\dfrac{7-i}{3-4i}$

First we express $\dfrac{7-i}{3-4i}$ in the form $a+bi$

$$\frac{7-i}{3-4i} = \frac{(7-i)(3+4i)}{(3-4i)(3+4i)} = \frac{25+25i}{25} = 1+i$$

Then $|1+i| = \sqrt{2}$

and $\arg(1+i)$ is the positive acute angle $\arctan 1$, i.e. $\frac{1}{4}\pi$

$\therefore$ the modulus and argument of $\dfrac{7-i}{3-4i}$ are $\sqrt{2}$ and $\frac{1}{4}\pi$

EXERCISE 40d

1. Represent each of the following complex numbers by a line on an Argand diagram. Find the modulus and argument of each complex number.

   (a) $3-2i$ (b) $-4+i$ (c) $-3-4i$ (d) $5+12i$

   (e) $1-i$ (f) $-1+i$ (g) 6 (h) $-4i$

   (i) $(1+i)^2$ (j) $i(1-i)$ (k) $i^2(1-i)$ (l) $(3+i)(4+i)$

   (m) $\cos\frac{3}{4}\pi + i\sin\frac{3}{4}\pi$ (n) $2(\cos\frac{2}{3}\pi + i\sin\frac{2}{3}\pi)$

   (p) $\cos(-\frac{5}{6}\pi) + i\sin(-\frac{5}{6}\pi)$ (q) $a+bi$

2. Express in the form $r(\cos\theta + i\sin\theta)$

   (a) $1+i$ (b) $\sqrt{3}-i$ (c) $-3-4i$ (d) $-5+12i$

   (e) $2-i$ (f) 6 (g) -3 (h) $4i$

   (i) $-3-i\sqrt{3}$ (j) $24+7i$

3. The modulus, r, and argument, θ, of a complex number are given. Express the complex number in the form $x+yi$ when r and θ are

   (a) $2, \frac{1}{6}\pi$ (b) $3, -\frac{1}{4}\pi$ (c) $1, \frac{2}{3}\pi$ (d) $3, 0$

   (e) $4, \pi$ (f) $1, -\frac{3}{4}\pi$ (g) $2, \frac{1}{2}\pi$ (h) $2, -\frac{1}{2}\pi$

PRODUCTS AND QUOTIENTS

The product and quotient of two complex numbers can already be found algebraically when the numbers are given in the form $a + bi$

Now we are going to investigate what happens when we multiply or divide complex numbers in the form $r(\cos\theta + i\sin\theta)$

Taking $z_1 = r_1(\cos\theta_1 + i\sin\theta_1)$ and $z_2 = r_2(\cos\theta_2 + i\sin\theta_2)$ we have

$$z_1 z_2 = r_1 r_2(\cos\theta_1 + i\sin\theta_1)(\cos\theta_2 + i\sin\theta_2)$$
$$= r_1 r_2[\cos\theta_1\cos\theta_2 + i\sin\theta_1\cos\theta_2 + i\sin\theta_2\cos\theta_1 + i^2\sin\theta_1\sin\theta_2]$$
$$= r_1 r_2[\cos\theta_1\cos\theta_2 - \sin\theta_1\sin\theta_2 + i(\sin\theta_1\cos\theta_2 + \cos\theta_1\sin\theta_2)]$$
$$= r_1 r_2[\cos(\theta_1 + \theta_2) + i\sin(\theta_1 + \theta_2)]$$

Hence

$z_1 z_2$ gives a complex number with modulus $r_1 r_2$ and argument $\theta_1 + \theta_2$

i.e.

$$|z_1 z_2| = r_1 r_2 \quad \text{and} \quad \arg(z_1 z_2) = \theta_1 + \theta_2$$

Similarly it can be shown that $\dfrac{z_1}{z_2} = \dfrac{r_1}{r_2}(\cos(\theta_1 - \theta_2) + i\sin(\theta_1 - \theta_2))$

i.e.

$$\left|\frac{z_1}{z_2}\right| = \frac{r_1}{r_2} \quad \text{and} \quad \arg\left(\frac{z_1}{z_2}\right) = (\theta_1 - \theta_2)$$

Note that when the argument of a product or a quotient is found in this way, the angle obtained may not lie between $-\pi$ and π. In such cases the corresponding argument within this range should be stated,

e.g. if $\theta_1 = \frac{2}{3}\pi$ and $\theta_2 = \frac{1}{2}\pi$

then $\qquad \theta_1 + \theta_2 = \frac{7}{6}\pi$

but $\qquad \arg(z_1 z_2) = -\frac{5}{6}\pi$

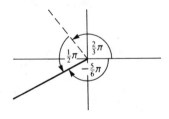

Example 40e _____

Write down the modulus and argument of $-\sqrt{3} + i$ and of $4 + 4i$. Hence express in the form $r(\cos\theta + i\sin\theta)$ the complex numbers

$(-\sqrt{3} + i)(4 + 4i)$ and $\dfrac{(-\sqrt{3} + i)}{4 + 4i}$

For $-\sqrt{3} + i$

$r_1 = 2$ and $\theta_1 = \frac{5}{6}\pi$

For $4 + 4i$

$r_2 = 4\sqrt{2}$ and $\theta_2 = \frac{1}{4}\pi$

If $(-\sqrt{3} + i)(4 + 4i) = r_3(\cos\theta_3 + i\sin\theta_3)$

then $r_3 = r_1r_2 = 8\sqrt{2}$ and $\theta_3 = \theta_1 + \theta_2 = \frac{13}{12}\pi$

As θ_3 is not between $-\pi$ and π
we refer to the diagram to find that
the required argument is $-\frac{11}{12}\pi$

$\therefore$ $(-\sqrt{3} + i)(4 + 4i) = 8\sqrt{2}(\cos\{-\frac{11}{12}\pi\} + i\sin\{-\frac{11}{12}\pi\})$

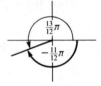

If $\dfrac{(-\sqrt{3} + i)}{(4 + 4i)} = r_4(\cos\theta_4 + i\sin\theta_4)$

then $r_4 = \dfrac{r_1}{r_2} = \dfrac{\sqrt{4}}{2}$ and $\theta_4{}^{\cdot} = \theta_1 - \theta_2 = \frac{7}{12}\pi$

this time θ_4 is between $-\pi$ and π so it is the required argument.

$\therefore$ $\dfrac{(-\sqrt{3} + i)}{(4 + 4i)} = \dfrac{\sqrt{2}}{4}(\cos\frac{7}{12}\pi + i\sin\frac{7}{12}\pi)$

EXERCISE 40e

In each Question from 1 to 4

(a) find the modulus and argument of the given complex number, without first expressing it in the form $a + bi$ and illustrate your result on an Argand diagram.

(b) express the given complex number in the form $a + bi$, find the modulus and argument and check the results against the answers to part (a).

1. $(3 - \sqrt{3}i)(1 - i)$ 2. $(1 + i)(1 - i)$

3. $\dfrac{(-2 - i\sqrt{3})}{(-2 + i\sqrt{3})}$ 4. $\dfrac{2}{(1 + i)}$

5. Illustrate on an Argand diagram lines representing z, $1/z$, z^2 and $z - z^2$ when z is

(a) $2 + i$ (b) $\frac{1}{2} - \frac{1}{2}i$ (c) $3 + 4i$ (d) $\frac{1}{2}\sqrt{3} + \frac{1}{2}i$ (e) $5 - 12i$

MIXED EXERCISE 40

1. Find, in the form $a + bi$,

(a) $\dfrac{1}{7 + 5i}$ (b) $(2 - i)(4 + 3i)$ (c) $\dfrac{2 - i}{3 + i}$ (d) $(2 + 5i)^2$

2. If $z = 3 - i$ express $z + 1/z$ in the form $a + bi$ where a and b are real.

3. Find the square roots of z where $z = 12 + 5i$. Illustrate z and its square roots on an Argand diagram.

4. Find the modulus and argument of each of the following complex numbers.

(a) $-1 + i$ (b) $3 + 4i$ (c) $(-1 + i)(3 + 4i)$

Represent each of these numbers by points on an Argand diagram and label these points A, B and C. Find the area of triangle ABC.

5. If $z_1 = 1 + i$ and $z_2 = 7 - i$, find the modulus of

(a) $z_1 - z_2$ (b) $z_1 z_2$ (c) $\dfrac{z_1}{z_2}$ (d) $\dfrac{z_1 - z_2}{z_1 z_2}$

6. Given that $(2 + 3i)\lambda - 2\mu = 3 + 6i$ find the values of λ and μ.

7. Two complex numbers z_1 and z_2 are such that $z_1 + z_2 = 1$. If $z_1 = \dfrac{a}{1+i}$ and $z_2 = \dfrac{b}{1+2i}$ find a and b

8. If $z = x + yi$ find the real and imaginary parts of $z - 1/z$

9. One root of the equation $x^2 - \lambda x - \mu = 0$ is $2 - i$. Find λ and μ.

10. Find the modulus and argument of each root of the equation $y^2 + 4y + 8 = 0$

11. If α and β are the roots of the equation $3x^2 + x + 2 = 0$, find the value of
    (a) $\alpha + \beta$ (b) $\alpha\beta$ (c) $3\alpha^2 + \alpha + 2$

12. Given that z^* is the conjugate of z and $z = a + bi$ where a and b are real, find the possible values of z if $zz^* - 2iz = 7 - 4i$

CONSOLIDATION G

SUMMARY

SOLUTION OF EQUATIONS

Trigonometric Equations

Listed below are some of the trig identities useful in solving equations.

$$\left. \begin{array}{l} \cos^2\theta + \sin^2\theta \equiv 1 \\ \tan^2\theta + 1 \equiv \sec^2\theta \\ \cot^2\theta + 1 \equiv \mathrm{cosec}^2\theta \end{array} \right\}$$
Use in an equation containing two ratios of one angle, at least one ratio being squared.

$$\left. \begin{array}{l} \cos 2\theta \equiv 2\cos^2\theta - 1 \\ \qquad\quad \equiv 1 - 2\sin^2\theta \end{array} \right\}$$
Use to express an equation in terms of trig ratios of θ only.

$$\sin A \pm \sin B$$
$$\equiv 2 \sin \tfrac{1}{2}(A \pm B) \cos \tfrac{1}{2}(A \mp B)$$
$$\cos A + \cos B$$
$$\equiv 2 \cos \tfrac{1}{2}(A + B) \cos \tfrac{1}{2}(A - B)$$
$$\cos A - \cos B$$
$$\equiv -2 \sin \tfrac{1}{2}(A + B) \sin \tfrac{1}{2}(A - B)$$

Use to factorise an expression, e.g.
$$\sin \theta + \sin 3\theta + \sin 5\theta + \sin 7\theta$$
$$= 2 \sin 2\theta \cos \theta + 2 \sin 6\theta \cos \theta$$
$$= 2 \cos \theta (\sin 2\theta + \sin 6\theta)$$

$$a \sin \theta + b \cos \theta \equiv r \sin (\theta + \alpha)$$
and variations of this form.

Use to reduce $a \sin \theta + b \cos \theta = c$ to $\sin (\theta + \alpha) = k$

$$\left. \begin{array}{l} \sin A \equiv \dfrac{2t}{1 + t^2} \\[2mm] \cos A \equiv \dfrac{1 - t^2}{1 + t^2} \\[2mm] \tan A \equiv \dfrac{2t}{1 - t^2} \end{array} \right\} \quad t = \tan \tfrac{1}{2}A$$

Use in equations, containing assorted trig ratios, which have not responded to other approaches.

$$\sin A \equiv \cos (\tfrac{1}{2}\pi - A)$$

Use for general solution of equations of the type $\sin 2\theta = \cos 5\theta$

795

Exponential Equations

If there is only one term on each side, take logs.

If a sum or difference of terms is involved, suspect a disguised quadratic equation, e.g.

$$e^{2x} - 2e^x - 3 = 0 \quad \Rightarrow \quad y^2 - 2y - 3 = 0 \quad \text{where } y = e^x$$

Logarithmic Equations

In general make all the bases the same and use the laws of logarithms.

Polynomial Equations

If $f(a) = 0$ and $f'(a) = 0$ then $y = f(x)$ has a repeated root $x = a$

Approximate Solutions

Using graphs
$f(x) = g(x)$ where the curves $y = f(x)$ and $y = g(x)$ cut.
$f(x) = 0$ between two points on the x-axis where $f(x) < 0$ and $f(x) > 0$

Newton–Raphson Method

If $x = a$ is an approximate solution of the equation $f(x) = 0$ then a better approximation is $x = b$ where $b = a - \dfrac{f(a)}{f'(a)}$

COMPLEX NUMBERS

A complex number is of the form $a + bi$ where a and b are real and

$$i = \sqrt{(-1)} \quad \text{and} \quad \sqrt{(-n^2)} = ni$$

$(a + bi) \pm (c + di) \equiv (a \pm c) + (b \pm d)i$

$(a + bi)(c + di) \equiv (ac - bd) + (ad + bc)i$

$\dfrac{(a + bi)}{(c + di)} \equiv \dfrac{(a + bi)(c - di)}{(c + di)(c - di)} \equiv \dfrac{(a + bi)(c - di)}{c^2 + d^2}$

$x + yi = q + bi \quad \Rightarrow \quad x = a \text{ and } y = b$

$x + yi = 0 \quad \Rightarrow \quad x = 0 \text{ and } y = 0$

$|a + bi| = \sqrt{(a^2 + b^2)}$

$\arg(a + bi) = \alpha$ where $\tan \alpha = \dfrac{b}{a}$ and $-\pi < \alpha \leqslant \pi$

$x + yi = r(\cos\theta + i\sin\theta)$ where $r = |x + yi|$ and $\theta = \arg(x + yi)$

If $z = a + bi$, $\bar{z} = a - bi$, where $\bar{z}$ and z are conjugate.

If a quadratic or cubic equation has any complex roots, they occur in conjugate pairs.

If $z_1 = r_1(\cos\theta_1 + i\sin\theta_1)$ and $z_2 = r_2(\cos\theta_2 + i\sin\theta_2)$

then $\quad |z_1 z_2| = r_1 r_2$ and $\arg z_1 z_2 = \theta_1 + \theta_2$

$$\left|\frac{z_1}{z_2}\right| = \frac{r_1}{r_2} \text{ and } \arg\frac{z_1}{z_2} = \theta_1 - \theta_2$$

VECTORS

A vector is a quantity with both magnitude and direction and can be represented by a line segment.

If lines representing several vectors are drawn 'head to tail' in order, then the line which completes a closed polygon represents the sum of the vectors (or the resultant vector).

A position vector has a fixed location in space.

The position vector of a point C which divides AB in the ratio $\lambda:\mu$ is given by $\dfrac{\lambda b + \mu a}{\lambda + \mu}$ where $\overrightarrow{OA} = a$ and $\overrightarrow{OB} = b$

Cartesian Unit Vectors

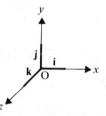

i, j and k are unit vectors in the directions of Ox, Oy and Oz respectively,

Any vector can be given in the form $a\mathbf{i} + b\mathbf{j} + c\mathbf{k}$

$(a_1\mathbf{i} + b_1\mathbf{j} + c_1\mathbf{k}) \pm (a_2\mathbf{i} + b_2\mathbf{j} + c_2\mathbf{k}) = (a_1 \pm a_2)\mathbf{i} + (b_1 \pm b_2)\mathbf{j} + (c_1 \pm c_2)\mathbf{k}$

$$|a\mathbf{i} + b\mathbf{j} + c\mathbf{k}| = \sqrt{(a^2 + b^2 + c^2)}$$

For two vectors $\mathbf{v}_1 = a_1\mathbf{i} + b_1\mathbf{j} + c_1\mathbf{k}$ and $\mathbf{v}_2 = a_2\mathbf{i} + b_2\mathbf{j} + c_2\mathbf{k}$

$\quad\mathbf{v}_1$ and $\mathbf{v}_2$ are parallel if $\mathbf{v}_1 = \lambda\mathbf{v}_2$,

$\qquad$ i.e. $a_1 = \lambda a_2$, $b_1 = \lambda b_2$, $c_1 = \lambda c_2$

$\quad\mathbf{v}_1$ and $\mathbf{v}_2$ are equal if $a_1 = a_2$, $b_1 = b_2$, $c_1 = c_2$

The direction ratios of $a\mathbf{i} + b\mathbf{j} + c\mathbf{k}$ are $a:b:c$

If $\mathbf{v} = a\mathbf{i} + b\mathbf{j} + c\mathbf{k}$ then the unit vector in the direction of $\mathbf{v}$ is $\hat{\mathbf{v}}$
where $\hat{\mathbf{v}} = \dfrac{\mathbf{v}}{|\mathbf{v}|}$

If a vector $\mathbf{v}$ is in the direction of a vector $\mathbf{d}$ then $\mathbf{v} = |\mathbf{v}|\hat{\mathbf{d}}$

Equations for a Line

For a line in the direction of the vector $\mathbf{d} = a\mathbf{i} + b\mathbf{j} + c\mathbf{k}$ and passing through a point with position vector $\mathbf{a} = x_1\mathbf{i} + y_1\mathbf{j} + z_1\mathbf{k}$.

    a vector equation in standard form is $\mathbf{r} = \mathbf{a} + \lambda\mathbf{d}$

    parametric equations are $x = x_1 + \lambda a, \ y = y_1 + \lambda b, \ z = z_1 + \lambda c$

    cartesian equations are $\dfrac{x - x_1}{a} = \dfrac{y - y_1}{b} = \dfrac{z - z_1}{c}$

Two lines with equations $\mathbf{r}_1 = \mathbf{a}_1 + \lambda\mathbf{d}_1$ and $\mathbf{r}_2 = \mathbf{a}_2 + \mu\mathbf{d}_2$

    are parallel if $\mathbf{d}_1$ is a multiple of $\mathbf{d}_2$

    intersect if there are values of λ and μ for which $\mathbf{r}_1 = \mathbf{r}_2$

    are skew in all other cases

The Scalar Product of Two Vectors

If θ is the angle between two vectors $\mathbf{a}$ and $\mathbf{b}$ then

$$\mathbf{a}.\mathbf{b} = |\mathbf{a}||\mathbf{b}|\cos\theta$$

$\mathbf{a}$ and $\mathbf{b}$ are perpendicular $\Rightarrow \mathbf{a}.\mathbf{b} = 0$

If $\mathbf{a} = x_1\mathbf{i} + y_1\mathbf{j} + z_1\mathbf{k}$ and $\mathbf{b} = x_2\mathbf{i} + y_2\mathbf{j} + z_2\mathbf{k}$ then
$$\mathbf{a}.\mathbf{b} = x_1x_2 + y_1y_2 + z_1z_2$$

Equations of a Plane

A plane perpendicular to a vector $\mathbf{n}$ has a vector equation in standard form of $\mathbf{r}.\mathbf{n} = D$ where D/n is the distance of the plane from O.

Taking $\mathbf{n} = A\mathbf{i} + B\mathbf{j} + C\mathbf{k}$ gives the cartesian equation for the plane

i.e. $Ax + By + Cz = D$

A plane perpendicular to $\mathbf{n}$ and containing the point with position vector $\mathbf{a}$ has the equation $(\mathbf{r} - \mathbf{a}).\mathbf{n} = 0$

A plane containing two direction vectors, $\mathbf{d}_1$ and $\mathbf{d}_2$, and a point with position vector $\mathbf{a}$, has a vector equation in parametric form

$$\mathbf{r} = \mathbf{a} + \lambda\mathbf{d}_1 + \mu\mathbf{d}_2$$

The acute angle θ between the two planes $\mathbf{r}_1 . \mathbf{n}_1 = d_1$ and $\mathbf{r}_2 . \mathbf{n}_2 = d_2$ is equal to the acute angle between the two normals.

i.e.
$$\cos \theta = \frac{\mathbf{n}_1 . \mathbf{n}_2}{n_1 n_2}$$

The acute angle ϕ between the plane $\mathbf{r} . \mathbf{n} = D$ and the line $\mathbf{r} = \mathbf{a} + \lambda \mathbf{d}$ is given by $\sin \phi = \dfrac{\mathbf{d} . \mathbf{n}}{dn}$

MULTIPLE CHOICE EXERCISE G

TYPE I

1. The modulus of the vector $6\mathbf{i} - 2\mathbf{j} - 3\mathbf{k}$ is

   A $\sqrt{23}$ B 7   C 1   D 49   E $\sqrt{11}$

2. $\overrightarrow{OP} = 2\mathbf{i} - 6\mathbf{j}$ and $\overrightarrow{OQ} = 4\mathbf{i} - 3\mathbf{k}$. The vector of magnitude 7 in the direction of $\overrightarrow{PQ}$ is

   A $2\mathbf{i} + 6\mathbf{j} - 3\mathbf{k}$ D $7(2\mathbf{i} + 6\mathbf{j} - 3\mathbf{k})$
   B $7(-2\mathbf{i} - 6\mathbf{j} + 3\mathbf{k})$ E $7(6\mathbf{i} - 6\mathbf{j} - 3\mathbf{k})$
   C $-2\mathbf{i} - 6\mathbf{j} + 3\mathbf{k}$

3. If $\mathbf{a} = \mathbf{i} - \mathbf{j} + \mathbf{k}$ and $\mathbf{b} = \mathbf{i} + \mathbf{j} - \mathbf{k}$ then $\mathbf{a} . \mathbf{b}$ is

   A $2\mathbf{i}$ B -1 C $-2\mathbf{j} + 2\mathbf{k}$ D 2   E 3

4. The line with equation $\mathbf{r} = \mathbf{j} + \lambda(2\mathbf{i} - 3\mathbf{k})$ has direction ratios

   A $2 : 1 : -3$ C $2 : 3$ E $2 : 0 : -3$
   B $0 : 1 : 0$ D $2\lambda : 1 : -3\lambda$

5. The plane whose equation is $\mathbf{r} . (\mathbf{i} - \mathbf{j} + \mathbf{k}) = 2$ contains the point

   A $(1, -1, 1)$ C $(0, 1, 1)$ E $(x, -y, z)$
   B $(-1, 1, 0)$ D $(2, 0, 0)$

6. The angle between the lines whose equations are $\mathbf{r}_1 = \mathbf{a}_1 + \lambda \mathbf{b}_1$ and $\mathbf{r}_2 = \mathbf{a}_2 + \mu \mathbf{b}_2$ is

   A $\arccos \dfrac{\mathbf{b}_1 . \mathbf{b}_2}{b_1 b_2}$ C $\arccos \dfrac{\mathbf{a}_1 . \mathbf{a}_2}{a_1 a_2}$ E $\arccos \lambda . \mu$

   B $\mathbf{b}_1 . \mathbf{b}_2$ D $\mathbf{r}_1 . \mathbf{r}_2$

7. The equation of the plane normal to $4\mathbf{i} + 3\mathbf{j}$ and 5 units from 0 is

   A $\mathbf{r}.(4\mathbf{i} + 3\mathbf{j}) = 5$ **C** $\mathbf{r}.(4\mathbf{i} + 3\mathbf{j}) = 1$ **E** $\mathbf{r}.5\mathbf{k} = 0$
   B $\mathbf{r}.5\mathbf{k} = 5$ **D** $\mathbf{r}.(4\mathbf{i} + 3\mathbf{j}) = 25$

8. The points A, B and C are collinear and $\overrightarrow{OA} = \mathbf{i} + \mathbf{j}$,
   $\overrightarrow{OB} = 2\mathbf{i} - \mathbf{j} + \mathbf{k}$, $\overrightarrow{OC} = 3\mathbf{i} + a\mathbf{j} + b\mathbf{k}$

   A $a = -3, \; b = 2$ **D** $a = -1, \; b = 0$
   B $a = 3, \; b = -2$ **E** $a = 6, \; b = -1$
   C $a = 0, \; b = 1$

9. The modulus of $12 - 5\mathbf{i}$ is

   A 119   **B** 7   **C** 13   **D** $\sqrt{119}$ **E** $\sqrt{7}$

10. On an Argand diagram OP represents a complex number z. The conjugate of z is $\bar{z}$
    If P and Q are the points $(3, 5)$ and $(5, -3)$ then OQ represents

    A $-\bar{z}$ **B** $i\bar{z}$ **C** $-z$ **D** iz **E** $-iz$

11. $\dfrac{3 + 2i}{3 - 2i}$ is equal to

    A $\dfrac{5 + 12i}{13}$ **C** $\dfrac{5 + 6i}{13}$ **E** $\dfrac{13 + 12i}{5}$

    B $\dfrac{13 + 12i}{13}$ **D** $\dfrac{5 + 6i}{5}$

12. When $\sqrt{3} - i$ is divided by $-1 - i$ the modulus and argument of the quotient are respectively

    A $2\sqrt{2}, \frac{7}{12}\pi$ **C** $\sqrt{2}, \frac{7}{12}\pi$ **E** $\sqrt{2}, \frac{11}{12}\pi$
    B $\sqrt{2}, -\frac{11}{12}\pi$ **D** $2\sqrt{2}, -\frac{11}{12}\pi$

13. The equation $x^2 + 3x + 1 = 0$ has

    A no roots   **D** two real roots
    B one real and one complex root   **E** two complex roots
    C two imaginary roots

14. $\arg\left(\dfrac{1 - i}{1 + i}\right) =$

    A $\frac{1}{2}\pi$ **B** 0   **C** $-\frac{1}{4}\pi$ **D** $-\frac{1}{2}\pi$ **E** π

15. The general solution of the equation $\tan 2x = 1$ is

A $x = n\pi + \frac{1}{4}\pi$ **C** $x = \frac{1}{2}n\pi + \frac{1}{8}\pi$ **E** $x = \frac{1}{8}\pi \pm 2n\pi$

B $x = n\pi \pm \frac{1}{4}\pi$ **D** $x = n\pi + \frac{1}{8}\pi$

16.

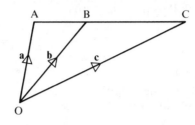

Given that $\overrightarrow{BC} = 2\overrightarrow{AB}$ then

A $\mathbf{a} - 3\mathbf{b} + 2\mathbf{c} = 0$ **D** $2\mathbf{a} + 3\mathbf{b} - \mathbf{c} = 0$

B $\mathbf{a} + 3\mathbf{b} - 2\mathbf{c} = 0$ **E** $2\mathbf{a} - 3\mathbf{b} + \mathbf{c} = 0$

C $\mathbf{a} + \mathbf{b} - 2\mathbf{c} = 0$

17. Given that $z_1 = 5 - 2i$ and $z_2 = 2 - i$, then if $\theta = \arg\left(\dfrac{z_1}{z_2}\right)$

A $\tan\theta = \frac{3}{4}$ **C** $\tan\theta = -\frac{3}{4}$ **E** $\tan\theta = -\frac{1}{12}$

B $\tan\theta = \frac{1}{12}$ **D** $\tan\theta = \frac{1}{8}$

18. A line has equation $\mathbf{r} = \mathbf{i} + 2\mathbf{j} + 3\mathbf{k} + \lambda(4\mathbf{i} - \mathbf{j} + 7\mathbf{k})$

A   The line has direction ratios $4 : -1 : 7$

B   The length of the line is $\sqrt{14}$

C   The line is parallel to the line $\mathbf{r} = \mu(\mathbf{i} + 2\mathbf{j} + 3\mathbf{k})$

19. Given that $e^{2x} + e^x = 2$,

A $2x + x = \ln 2$

B $e^{3x} = 2$

C $e^x = 1$ satisfies the equation

20. $\ln x + 3\ln y = 4$

A $\ln xy^3 = 4$

B $3xy = e^4$

C $y = 1$ when $x = 1$

TYPE II

21. The point P represents the complex number z on an Argand diagram and $|z - 1| = 4$

    A   The locus of P is a circle
    B   The locus of P is a straight line
    C $z = 3$

22. $\mathbf{V} = 3\mathbf{i} + 3\mathbf{j} + 3\mathbf{k}$

    A $\hat{\mathbf{V}} = \mathbf{i} + \mathbf{j} + \mathbf{k}$
    B $\mathbf{V}$ makes equal angles with $\mathbf{i}$, $\mathbf{j}$ and $\mathbf{k}$
    C $\mathbf{V}$ is perpendiculoar to $2\mathbf{i} + \mathbf{j} - 3\mathbf{k}$

23. $-\frac{3}{4}\pi$ is an argument of

    A $1 - i$ **B** $\cos\frac{3}{4}\pi - i\sin\frac{3}{4}\pi$ **C** $-1 - i$

24. The plane $x + 2y + 3z = 4$

    A   is 4 units from the origin
    B   has a vector equation $\mathbf{r}.(\mathbf{i} + 2\mathbf{j} + 3\mathbf{k}) = 4$
    C   passes through the point $(-1, 1, 1)$

25.

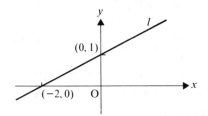

The line l

    A   is perpendicular to the vector $-\mathbf{i} + 2\mathbf{j}$
    B   passes through the point with position vector $2\mathbf{i} + \mathbf{j}$
    C   is parallel to the vector $\mathbf{i} + 2\mathbf{j}$

26. Given that $z_1 = 2 + 3i$ and $z_2 = 3 - 2i$,

    A $|z_2| = \sqrt{5}$
    B $|z_1| = \sqrt{13}$
    C z_1 and z_2 are conjugate complex numbers

27. If $f(x) = x^3 + 2x - 4$,

    A   the roots of $f(x) = 0$ are the values of x where $y = 2x$ cuts $y = x^3 - 4$
    B $f(x) = 0$ has a root between 1 and 2
    C $f(x)$ has no maximum or minimum values

TYPE III

28. If two lines do not intersect they are parallel.

29. $\mathbf{a.b} = 0 \quad \Rightarrow \quad \mathbf{a} = 0 \text{ or } \mathbf{b} = 0$

30. Any complex number whose modulus is unity can be expressed as $\cos\theta + i\sin\theta$

31. A complex number $a + bi$ is zero if $a = -b$

32. If the equation $f(x) = 0$ has a root near to $x = a$ then a better approximation to that root is $x = a - \dfrac{f'(a)}{f(a)}$

MISCELLANEOUS EXERCISE G

1. Find all values of θ, such that $0° \leqslant \theta \leqslant 180°$, which satisfy the equation $2\sin 2\theta = \tan\theta$ (C 87)

2. (a) Find, in radians, the general solution of the equation $4\sin\theta = \sec\theta$
   (b) If $\sin\theta + \sin 2\theta + \sin 3\theta + \sin 4\theta = 0$, show that θ is either a multiple of $\frac{1}{2}\pi$ or a multiple of $\frac{2}{5}\pi$

3. (a) Find the values of x, for angles between $0°$ and $360°$ inclusive, for which $3\sin 2x = 2\tan x$
   (b) Solve the equation $\sec\theta\tan\theta = 2$, giving solutions for $0° \leqslant \theta < 360°$

4. (a) Find, in radians, the general solution of the equation $2\sin\theta = \sqrt{3}\tan\theta$
   (b) Solve the equation $2\cos\theta\cos 2\theta + \sin 2\theta = 2(3\cos^3\theta - \cos\theta)$ for values of θ within the range $0 < \theta < 2\pi$

5. Solve the equation
$$2\log_3 x = 1 + \log_3(18 - x)$$ (AEB 86)

6. Solve the equation $3^{2x} = 4^{2-x}$, giving your answer to three significant figures.   (C 87)

7. Given that $\log_9 xy = 6$, prove that $\log_3 x + \log_3 y = 12$
   Hence solve for x and y the simultaneous equations
   $$\log_9 xy = 6$$
   $$(\log_3 x)(\log_3 y) = 20$$

8. (a) Find the values of x which satisfy the equation
   $$\log_4 x = 9 \log_x 4$$
   (b) By taking $\log_{10} 5 \approx 0.7$, obtain an estimate of the root of the equation
   $$10^{y-5} = 5^{y+2}$$
   giving your answer to the nearest integer.

9. Given that $f(x) = x^3 - 12x + 16$ show that $f(2) = f'(2) = 0$
   Hence factorise $f(x)$ completely.
   Sketch the graph of the curve
   $$y = x^3 - 12x + 16$$
   showing clearly the coordinates of the points where the curve cuts the coordinate axes.

10. Show that the equation $e^x \cos 2x - 1 = 0$ has a root between 0.4 and 0.45
    Taking 0.45 as a first approximation to this root, apply the Newton–Raphson process once to obtain a second approximation, giving your answer to 3 significant figures.   (U of L 85)

11. Show that $x^4 + 2x^2 - 100 = 0$ has a root near $x = 3$
    Taking $x = 3$ as the first approximation, use Newton's Method twice to obtain a better approximation.

12. By using sketch graphs, or otherwise, show that the equation
    $$x = 2 \sin x$$
    where the angle is measured in radians, has only one positive root.
    Verify, with the use of a calculator that this root lies between 1.8 and 1.9
    Determine the root correct to two places of decimals.

13. Show that the equation $\sin x - \ln x = 0$ has a root lying between $x = 2$ and $x = 3$
    Given that this root lies between $a/10$ and $(a + 1)/10$, where a is an integer, find the value of a
    Estimate the value of the root to 3 significant figures.   (U of L 85)

14. Given that $f(x) \equiv 3 + 4x - x^4$, show that the equation $f(x) = 0$ has a root $x = a$, where a is in the interval $1 \leqslant a \leqslant 2$

   It may be assumed that if x_n is an approximation to a, then a better approximation is given by x_{n+1}, where

$$x_{n+1} = (3 + 4x_n)^{1/4}$$

   Starting with $x_0 = 1.75$, use this result twice to obtain the value of a to 2 decimal places.   (U of L 88)

15. By investigating the turning values of

$$f(x) = x^3 + 3x^2 + 6x - 14$$

   or otherwise, show that the equation $f(x) = 0$ has only one real root.

   If this root lies between n and $n + 1$, find the value of the integer n.

   Taking n as a first approximation to the root, calculate two further successive approximations, giving your answers correct to 3 s.f.

16. Given that $z = 2 + 2i$, express z in the form $r(\cos \theta + i \sin \theta)$, where r is a positive real number and $-\pi < \theta \leqslant \pi$

   On the same Argand diagram, display and label clearly the numbers

$$z, \ z^2 \ \text{and} \ 4/z$$

   Find the values of $|z + z^2|$ and $\arg(z + 4/z)$ (AEB 86)

17. (a) Find all possible values of the real numbers a and b which satisfy

$$2 + ai = \frac{6 - 2i}{b + i}$$

   (b) Given that $w = -\frac{1}{2} + \frac{1}{2}i$, find the modulus and the argument of $\dfrac{1}{1 + w}$, giving the argument in radians between $-\pi$ and π

                                                                          (AEB 88)

18. Given that $z = 1 + i$, show that $z^3 = -2 + 2i$. For this value of z, the real numbers p and q are such that

$$\frac{p}{1 + z} + \frac{q}{1 + z^3} = 2i$$

   Find the values of p and q (JMB 84)

19. Given that $z_1 = -1 + i\sqrt{3}$ and $z_2 = \sqrt{3} + i$, find $\arg z_1$ and $\arg z_2$

Express z_1/z_2 in the form $a + ib$, where a and b are real, and hence find $\arg(z_1/z_2)$

Verify that $\arg(z_1/z_2) = \arg z_1 - \arg z_2$ (U of L 88)

20. Find the values of the real numbers a and b so that
$$(a + bi)^2 = 16 - 30i$$
Write down the two square roots of $16 - 30i$ (AEB 87)

21. Find the roots, z_1 and z_2, of the equation
$$z^2 - 5 + 12i = 0$$
in the form $a + bi$, where a and b area real, and give the value of $z_1 z_2$

Draw, on graph paper, an Argand diagram to illustrate the points representing (a) $z_1 z_2$ (b) $\dfrac{1}{z_1 z_2}$ (c) $z_1^* z_2^*$ where z^* denotes the conjugate of z.   (U of L 85)

22. Find, in terms of π, the argument of the complex number

(a) $(1 + i)^2$

(b) $\dfrac{3 + i}{1 + 2i}$

(c) $(\cos \frac{1}{3}\pi + i \sin \frac{1}{3}\pi)(\cos \frac{1}{4}\pi - i \sin \frac{1}{4}\pi)$ (AEB 86)

23. Given that the real and imaginary parts of the complex number $z = x + iy$ satisfy the equation
$$(2 - i)x - (1 + 3i)y - 7 = 0$$
find x and y

State the values of

(a) $|z|$ (b) $\arg z$ (U of L 88)

24. Given that p and q are real and that $1 + 2i$ is a root of the equation
$$z^2 + (p + 5i)z + q(2 - i) = 0$$
determine (a) the values of p and q

(b) the other root of the equation.   (AEB 87)

25. The complex number z satisfies the equation
$$2zz^* - 4z = 3 - 6i$$
where z^* is the complex conjugate of z. Find, in the form $x + iy$, the two possible values of z (JMB 86)

26. Given that $z_1 = 1 + i\sqrt{3}$ and $z_2 = 4 + 3i$, calculate the moduli and arguments of $z_1 z_2$ and z_2/z_1, giving the arguments in degrees to one decimal place.

Illustrate in one Argand diagram

(a) $z_1 - z_2$ (b) $z_1 z_2$ (c) z_2/z_1 (U of L 85)

27. The points A and B have coordinates $(2, 3, -1)$ and $(5, -2, 2)$ respectively. Calculate the acute angle between AB and the line with equation

$$r = \begin{pmatrix} 2 \\ 3 \\ -1 \end{pmatrix} + t \begin{pmatrix} 1 \\ -2 \\ -2 \end{pmatrix}$$

giving your answer correct to the nearest degree.

$[r = 2\mathbf{i} + 3\mathbf{j} - \mathbf{k} + t(\mathbf{i} - 2\mathbf{j} - 2\mathbf{k})]$ (C 87)

28. The magnitudes of the vectors $\mathbf{a}$ and $\mathbf{b}$ are 8 and 3, respectively, and the angle between the vectors is $60°$. Sketch a diagram showing these vectors and the vector $\mathbf{a} - \mathbf{b}$. Calculate

(a) the magnitude $\mathbf{a} - \mathbf{b}$

(b) the resolved part of $\mathbf{a}$ in the direction of $\mathbf{b}$ (JMB 84)

29. With respect to a fixed origin O, the straight lines l_1 and l_2 are given by

$$l_1 : \mathbf{r} = \mathbf{i} - \mathbf{j} + \lambda(2\mathbf{i} + \mathbf{j} - 2\mathbf{k})$$
$$l_2 : \mathbf{r} = \mathbf{i} + 2\mathbf{j} + 2\mathbf{k} + \mu(-3\mathbf{i} + 4\mathbf{k})$$

where λ and μ are scalar parameters.

(a) Show that the lines intersect.

(b) Find the position vector of their point of intersection.

(c) Find the cosine of the acute angle contained between the lines.

(d) Find a vector equation of the plane containing the lines.

                    (U of L 88)

30. Relative to an origin O, the points A and B have position vectors $3\mathbf{i} - 2\mathbf{j} + 2\mathbf{k}$ and $2\mathbf{i} - 4\mathbf{j} - 2\mathbf{k}$ respectively. Find the position vector of the point C in AB such that OC is perpendicular to AB.

Given that $\overrightarrow{OQ} = \frac{3}{4}\overrightarrow{OC}$, find

(a) the position vector of the point P where AQ produced intersects OB

(b) the angle OPA

(c) a unit vector perpendicular to the plane OAB.   (AEB 87)

31. Referred to a fixed origin O, the lines l_1 and l_2 have equations
$$l_1 : \mathbf{r} = (\mathbf{i} + \mathbf{j} + \mathbf{k}) + \lambda(\mathbf{i} - 7\mathbf{j} + 2\mathbf{k})$$
$$l_2 : \mathbf{r} = (4\mathbf{i} - 4\mathbf{j} + 9\mathbf{k}) + \mu(\mathbf{i} + \mathbf{j} + 3\mathbf{k})$$
where λ and μ are scalar parameters.

Show that the lines l_1 and l_2 are perpendicular and that they intersect at the point P whose position vector is $2\mathbf{i} - 6\mathbf{j} + 3\mathbf{k}$

Determine, to the nearest half-degree, the acute angle between $\overrightarrow{OP}$ and l_2
(AEB 87)

32. The position vectors of the points A and B are given by
$$\overrightarrow{OA} = 3\mathbf{i} - 2\mathbf{j} + 2\mathbf{k} \quad \overrightarrow{OB} = -\mathbf{i} + \mathbf{j} + 3\mathbf{k}$$
where O is the origin. Find a vector equation of the straight line passing through A and B. Given that this line is perpendicular to the vector $\mathbf{i} + 2\mathbf{j} + p\mathbf{k}$, find the value of p
(C 86)

33. With respect to a fixed origin O, the points L and M have position vectors $6\mathbf{i} + 3\mathbf{j} + 2\mathbf{k}$ and $2\mathbf{i} + 2\mathbf{j} + \mathbf{k}$ respectively.

   (a) Form the scalar product $\overrightarrow{OL} . \overrightarrow{OM}$ and hence find the cosine of angle LOM.

   (b) The point N is on the line LM produced such that angle MON is $90°$. Find an equation for the line LM in the form $\mathbf{r} = \mathbf{a} + \mathbf{b}t$ and hence calculate the position vector of N.
(AEB 88)

34. The points A and B have position vectors $4\mathbf{i} + \mathbf{j} - 7\mathbf{k}$ and $2\mathbf{i} + 6\mathbf{j} + 2\mathbf{k}$ respectively relative to the origin O. Show that the angle AOB is a right angle.

Find a vector equation for the median AM of the triangle OAB.

Find also, in the form $\mathbf{r} . \mathbf{n} = p$, a vector equation of the plane OAB.
(U of L 85)

35. Relative to an origin O, the points P and Q have position vectors
$$\mathbf{p} = 4\mathbf{i} - 3\mathbf{j} + 4\mathbf{k}, \quad \mathbf{q} = 6\mathbf{i} + \mathbf{j} - 2\mathbf{k} \quad \text{respectively.}$$

   (a) Prove that triangle OPQ is isosceles.

   (b) Hence, or otherwise, find a unit vector in the plane OPQ which is perpendicular to the line PQ.

   (c) Evaluate $(\mathbf{q} - \mathbf{p}) . \mathbf{q}$ and deduce the value of angle PQO, to the nearest $0.1°$.
(AEB 86)

36. Shade in an Argand diagram the region in which *both* of the following inequalities are satisfied

$$|z - 2i| \leqslant 2$$
$$\tfrac{1}{6}\pi \leqslant \arg z \leqslant \tfrac{1}{2}\pi \qquad\qquad \text{(JMB 84)}$$

37. With respect to the origin O the points A, B, C have position vectors

$$a(5\mathbf{i} - \mathbf{j} - 3\mathbf{k}) \quad a(-4\mathbf{i} + 4\mathbf{j} - \mathbf{k}) \quad a(5\mathbf{i} - 2\mathbf{j} + 11\mathbf{k})$$

respectively, where a is a non-zero constant.

Find (a) a vector equation for the line BC

    (b) a vector equation for the plane OAB

    (c) the cosine of the acute angle between the lines OA and OB.

Obtain, in the form $\mathbf{r}.\mathbf{n} = p$, a vector equation for Π, the plane which passes through A and is perpendicular to BC.

Find cartesian equations for

    (d) the plane Π,

    (e) the line BC.   (U of L 85)

38. Relative to the origin O, the position vectors of the points A, B and C are $\mathbf{j} - 4\mathbf{k}$, $6\mathbf{i} - 5\mathbf{j} - \mathbf{k}$ and $4\mathbf{i} + 7\mathbf{j} - 9\mathbf{k}$ respectively, the unit of length being the metre.

    (a) Show that, for all values of the scalar parameter t, the point P with position vector $2t\mathbf{i} + (1 - 2t)\mathbf{j} + (t - 4)\mathbf{k}$ lies on the straight line passing through A and B.

    (b) Use the scalar product $\overrightarrow{AB}.\overrightarrow{CP}$ to determine the value of t for which CP is perpendicular to AB.

    (c) Hence find the shortest distance from C to AB.   (AEB 86)

ANSWERS

Answers to questions taken from past examination papers are the sole responsibility of the authors and have not been approved by the Examining Boards.

CHAPTER 1

Exercise 1a – p. 2
1. $15x$
2. $2x^2$
3. $4x^2$
4. $10pq$
5. $8x^2$
6. $10p^2qr$
7. $9a^2$
8. $63ab$
9. $24st^2$
10. $8a^3$
11. $\frac{5}{3}x$
12. $2m$
13. $4ab^3$
14. $5xy$
15. $196p^4q^2$
16. $2a$
17. $6ax$
18. $2x$
19. $9b/5a$
20. $\frac{2}{5}x$
21. x^3/y^2

Exercise 1b – p. 3
1. $3x^2 - 4x$
2. $a - 12$
3. $2y - xy + y^2$
4. $5pq - 9p^2$
5. $3xy + y^2$
6. $x^3 - x^2 + x + 7$
7. $5 + t - t^2$
8. $a^2 - ab - 2b$
9. $7 - x$
10. $4x - 9$
11. $3x^2 + 18x - 20$
12. $ab - 2ac + cb$
13. $11cT - 2cT^2 - 55T^2$
14. $-x^3 + 7x^2 - 7x$
15. $-4y^2 + 24y - 10$
16. $5RS + 5RF - R^2$

Exercise 1c – p. 4
1. -7
2. 2
3. (a) 1 (b) -5 (c) -1
4. (a) 1 (b) 0 (c) -3

Exercise 1d – p. 4
1. $x^2 + 6x + 8$
2. $x^2 + 8x + 15$
3. $a^2 + 13a + 42$
4. $t^2 + 15t + 56$
5. $s^2 + 17s + 66$
6. $2x^2 + 11x + 5$
7. $5y^2 + 28y + 15$
8. $6a^2 + 17a + 12$
9. $35t^2 + 86t + 48$
10. $99s^2 + 49s + 6$
11. $x^2 - 5x + 6$
12. $y^2 - 5y + 4$
13. $a^2 - 11a + 24$
14. $b^2 - 17b + 72$
15. $p^2 - 15p + 36$
16. $2y^2 - 13y + 15$
17. $3x^2 - 13x + 4$
18. $6r^2 - 25r + 14$
19. $20x^2 - 19x + 3$
20. $6a^2 - 7ab + 2b^2$
21. $x^2 - x - 6$
22. $a^2 + a - 56$
23. $y^2 + 2y - 63$
24. $s^2 + s - 30$
25. $q^2 + 8q - 65$
26. $2t^2 + 3t - 20$
27. $4x^2 + 11x - 3$

28. $6q^2 - q - 15$
29. $x^2 - xy - 2y^2$
30. $2s^2 + st - 6t^2$

Exercise 1e – p. 5
1. $x^2 - 4$
2. $25 - x^2$
3. $x^2 - 9$
4. $4x^2 - 1$
5. $x^2 - 64$
6. $x^2 - a^2$
7. $x^2 - 1$
8. $9b^2 - 16$
9. $4y^2 - 9$
10. $a^2b^2 - 36$
11. $25x^2 - 1$
12. $x^2y^2 - 16$

Exercise 1f – p. 6
1. $x^2 + 8x + 16$
2. $x^2 + 4x + 4$
3. $4x^2 + 4x + 1$
4. $9x^2 + 30x + 25$
5. $4x^2 + 28x + 49$
6. $x^2 - 2x + 1$
7. $x^2 - 6x + 9$
8. $4x^2 - 4x + 1$
9. $16x^2 - 24x + 9$
10. $25x^2 - 20x + 4$
11. $9t^2 - 42t + 49$
12. $x^2 + 2xy + y^2$
13. $4p^2 + 36p + 81$
14. $9q^2 - 66q + 121$
15. $4x^2 - 20xy + 25y^2$

Exercise 1g – p. 7
1. $11x - 2x^2 - 12$
2. $x^2 - 49$
3. $6 - 25x + 4x^2$
4. $14p^2 - 3p - 2$
5. $9p^2 - 6p + 1$
6. $15t^2 + t - 2$
7. $16 - 8p + p^2$
8. $14t - 3 - 8t^2$
9. $x^2 + 4xy + 4y^2$
10. $16x^2 - 9$
11. $9x^2 + 42x + 49$
12. $15 - R - 2R^2$
13. $a^2 - 6ab + 9b^2$
14. $4x^2 - 20x + 25$
15. $49a^2 - 4b^2$
16. $9a^2 + 30ab + 25b^2$
17. (a) $6, -22$ (b) $15, 31$
       (c) $14, -31$ (d) $81, 18$

Exercise 1h – p. 9
1. $(x + 5)(x + 3)$
2. $(x + 7)(x + 4)$
3. $(x + 6)(x + 1)$
4. $(x + 4)(x + 3)$
1. $(x - 1)(x - 9)$
6. $(x - 3)^2$
7. $(x + 6)(x + 2)$
8. $(x - 8)(x - 1)$
9. $(x + 7)(x - 2)$
10. $(x + 4)(x - 3)$
11. $(x - 5)(x + 1)$
12. $(x - 12)(x + 2)$
13. $(x + 7)(x + 2)$
14. $(x - 1)^2$
15. $(x - 3)(x + 3)$
16. $(x + 8)(x - 3)$
17. $(x + 2)^2$
18. $(x - 1)(x + 1)$
19. $(x - 6)(x + 3)$
20. $(x + 5)^2$
21. $(x - 4)(x + 4)$
22. $(4 + x)(1 + x)$
23. $(2x - 1)(x - 1)$
24. $(3x + 1)(x + 1)$
25. $(3x - 1)^2$
26. $(3x + 1)(2x - 1)$
27. $(3 + x)^2$
28. $(2x - 3)(2x + 3)$
29. $(x + a)^2$
30. $(xy - 1)^2$

Exercise 1i
1. $(3x - 4)(2x + 3)$
2. $(4x - 3)(x - 2)$
3. $(4x - 1)(x + 1)$
4. $(3x - 2)(x - 5)$
5. $(2x - 3)^2$
6. $(1 - 2x)(3 + x)$
7. $(5x - 4)(5x + 4)$
8. $(3 + x)(1 - x)$
9. $(5x - 1)(x - 12)$
10. $(3x + 5)^2$
11. $(3 - x)(1 + x)$
12. $(3 + 4x)(4 - 3x)$
13. $(1 + x)(1 - x)$
14. $(3x + 2)^2$
15. $(x + y)^2$
16. $(1 - 2x)(1 + 2x)$
17. $(2x - y)^2$
18. $(3 - 2x)(3 + 2x)$
19. $(6 + x)^2$
20. $(5x - 4)(8x + 3)$

21. $(7x + 30)(x - 5)$
22. $(6 - 5x)(6 + 5x)$
23. $(x - y)(x + y)$
24. $(9x - 2y)^2$
25. $(7 - 6x)^2$
26. $(5x - 2y)(5x + 2y)$
27. $(6x + 5y)^2$
28. $(2x - 3y)(2x + y)$
29. $(3x + 4y)(2x + y)$
30. $(7pq - 2)^2$

Exercise 1j – p. 11
1. not possible
2. $2(x + 1)^2$
3. $(x + 2)(x + 1)$
4. $3(x + 5)(x - 1)$
5. not possible
6. not possible
7. not possible
8. $2(x - 2)^2$
9. $3(x - 2)(x + 1)$
10. $2(x^2 - 3x + 4)$
11. $3(x - 4)(x + 2)$
12. $(x - 6)(x + 2)$
13. not possible
14. $4(x - 5)(x + 5)$
15. $5(x^2 - 5)$
16. not possible
17. not possible
18. not possible

Exercise 1k – p. 12
1. $x^3 - x^2 - x - 2$
2. $3x^3 - 5x^2 - x + 2$
3. $4x^3 - 8x^2 + 13x - 5$
4. $x^3 - 2x^2 + 1$
5. $2x^3 - 9x^2 - 24x - 9$
6. $x^3 + 6x^2 + 11x + 6$
7. $x^3 + 4x^2 - x - 4$
8. $x^3 - 4x^2 + x + 6$
9. $2x^3 + 7x^2 + 7x + 2$
10. $x^3 + 4x^2 + 5x + 2$
11. $4x^3 + 4x^2 - 7x + 2$
12. $27x^3 - 27x^2 + 9x - 1$
13. $4x^3 - 9x^2 - 25x - 12$
14. $4x^3 - 4x^2 - x + 1$
15. $6x^3 + 13x^2 + x - 2$
16. $x^3 + 3x^2 + 3x + 1$
17. $x^3 + x^2 - 4x - 4$
18. $2x^3 + 7x^2 - 9$
19. $24x^3 + 38x^2 - 51x + 10$
20. $4x^3 - 42x^2 + 68x + 210$
21. $3x^3 - 16x^2 + 28x - 16; -16, 28$

22. $6, -17$
23. $x^3 + 3x^2y + 3xy^2 + y^3$
24. $x^4 + 4x^3y + 6x^2y^2 + 4xy^3 + y^4$

Exercise 1l – p. 14
1. $x^3 + 9x^2 + 27x + 27$
2. $x^4 - 8x^3 + 24x^2 - 32x + 16$
3. $x^4 + 4x^3 + 6x^2 + 4x + 1$
4. $8x^3 + 12x^2 + 6x + 1$
5. $x^5 - 15x^4 + 90x^3 - 270x^2 + 405x - 243$
6. $p^4 - 4p^3q + 6p^2q^2 - 4pq^3 + q^4$
7. $8x^3 + 36x^2 + 54x + 27$
8. $x^5 - 20x^4 + 160x^3 - 640x^2 + 1280x$
$$- 1024$$
9. $81x^4 - 108x^3 + 54x^2 - 12x + 1$
10. $1 + 20a + 150a^2 + 500a^3 + 625a^4$
11. $64a^6 - 192a^5b + 240a^4b^2 - 160a^3b^3$
$$+ 60a^2b^4 - 12ab^5 + b^6$$
12. $8x^3 - 60x^2 + 150x - 125$

Mixed Exercise 1 – p. 15
1. -23
2. $115x - 105x^2 - 30$
3. 108
4. $3(x - 2)(x - 1)$
5. 250
6. $4(x - 3)(x + 3)$
7. $4x^3 - 4x^2 + x$
8. $(x - 5)^2$
9. 7

CHAPTER 2

Exercise 2a – p. 17
1. $\frac{1}{4}$
2. $\dfrac{2(x + 2)}{3(x - 2)}$
3. $\frac{2}{3}$
4. $\frac{3}{5}$
5. $\dfrac{x}{y}$
6. not possible
7. not possible
8. $\dfrac{5x(x + y)}{5y + 2x}$
9. $\dfrac{2a - 6b}{6a + b}$
10. $\dfrac{b - 4}{3x(b + 4)}$
11. $\dfrac{x - 3}{x + 4}$

12. $\dfrac{4y^2 + 3}{(y + 3)(y - 3)}$

13. $\dfrac{1}{3(x + 3)}$

14. $\dfrac{x + 2}{2x + 1}$

15. $\dfrac{x - 2}{x - 1}$

16. $\dfrac{1}{2(a - 5)}$

17. $\dfrac{3}{p + 3q}$

18. $\dfrac{a^2 + 2a + 4}{(a + 5)(a + 2)}$; not possible

19. $\dfrac{x + 1}{3(x + 3)}$

20. $\dfrac{4(x - 3)}{(x + 1)^2}$

16. $\dfrac{3x^2}{2(y - 2)}$

17. $\dfrac{b^2}{c^2}$

18. $2(x + 3)$

19. $\dfrac{x - 3}{3}$

20. $\dfrac{x(2x - 3)}{x - 1}$

Exercise 2c – p. 19

1. $\dfrac{b - a}{ab}$

2. $\dfrac{8}{15x}$

3. $\dfrac{q - p}{pq}$

4. $\dfrac{11}{10x}$

5. $\dfrac{x^2 + 1}{x}$

6. $\dfrac{x^2 - y^2}{xy}$

7. $\dfrac{2p^2 - 1}{p}$

8. $\dfrac{7x + 3}{12}$

9. $\dfrac{5x - 1}{6}$

10. $\dfrac{11 - 7x}{15}$

11. $\dfrac{\sin B + \sin A}{\sin A \, \sin B}$

12. $\dfrac{\sin A + \cos A}{\cos A \, \sin A}$

13. $\dfrac{12x^2 + 1}{4x}$

14. $\dfrac{2x^2 + x - 2}{2x + 1}$

15. $\dfrac{x^2 + 2x + 2}{x + 1}$

16. $\dfrac{2x + 3}{2x}$

17. $\dfrac{1 + x - x^2}{x}$

18. $\dfrac{n + 1}{n^2}$

Exercise 2b – p. 18

1. $\dfrac{2x^2}{3y^2}$

2. $\dfrac{6t^2}{s}$

3. $\dfrac{8v^2}{3}$

4. $\dfrac{2r}{3}$

5. $3x$

6. $\dfrac{9x}{4y^2}$

7. $\dfrac{x^2}{24}$

8. $\dfrac{2}{a(a + b)}$

9. $\dfrac{1}{x + 1}$

10. $\dfrac{1}{2a}$

11. $\dfrac{1}{x - 1}$

12. $\dfrac{3}{2(x + 3)}$

13. $\dfrac{a^4}{27}$

14. $\frac{2}{3}$

15. $\dfrac{2r}{3s^2}$

19. $\dfrac{x(b^2 + a^2)}{a^2 b^2}$

20. $\dfrac{a^2 + 3a + 1}{a + 1}$

Exercise 2d – p. 21

1. $\dfrac{2x}{(x + 1)(x - 1)}$

2. $\dfrac{2x - 1}{(x + 1)(x - 2)}$

3. $\dfrac{7x + 18}{(x + 2)(x + 3)}$

4. $\dfrac{x}{(x - 1)(x + 1)}$

5. $\dfrac{-1 - 3a}{(a - 1)(a + 1)} = \dfrac{1 + 3a}{(1 - a)(1 + a)}$

6. $\dfrac{x + 2}{(x + 1)^2}$

7. $\dfrac{1 - 4x}{(2x + 1)^2}$

8. $\dfrac{-3x - 10}{(x + 1)(x + 4)} = -\dfrac{3x + 10}{(x + 1)(x + 4)}$

9. $\dfrac{2x + 6}{(x + 1)^2}$

10. $\dfrac{8 - x - x^2}{(x + 2)^2(x + 4)}$

11. $\dfrac{7x + 8}{6(x - 1)(x + 4)}$

12. $\dfrac{8 - 3x}{5(x + 2)(x + 4)}$

13. $\dfrac{15x - 58}{6(x + 2)(3x - 5)}$

14. $\dfrac{5x^2 - 9x - 32}{(x + 1)(x - 2)(x + 3)}$

15. $\dfrac{2x^2 + 6x + 6}{(x + 1)(x + 2)(x + 3)}$
$= \dfrac{2(x^2 + 3x + 3)}{(x + 1)(x + 2)(x + 3)}$

16. $-\dfrac{1}{x(x + 1)^2}$

17. $\dfrac{7t + 3}{(t + 1)^2}$

18. $\dfrac{-t^4 + 2t^3 - 2t^2 - 2t - 1}{(t^2 + 1)(t^2 - 1)}$

19. $\dfrac{1 + 3y - 3x}{(y - x)(y + x)}$

20. $\dfrac{n^3 + 6n^2 + 8n + 2}{n(n + 1)(n + 2)}$

Exercise 2e – p. 23

1. $\dfrac{3}{2(x + 1)} - \dfrac{1}{2(x - 1)}$

2. $\dfrac{9}{8(x - 5)} - \dfrac{1}{8(x + 3)}$

3. $\dfrac{13}{6(x - 7)} - \dfrac{1}{6(x - 1)}$

4. $\dfrac{4}{(x - 1)} - \dfrac{5}{(2x - 1)}$

5. $\dfrac{4}{5(x - 2)} - \dfrac{4}{5(x + 3)}$

6. $\dfrac{1}{5(x - 2)} + \dfrac{6}{5(4x - 3)}$

7. $\dfrac{7}{9(2x - 1)} + \dfrac{28}{9(x + 4)}$

8. $\dfrac{5}{3(2x - 1)} - \dfrac{4}{3(x + 1)}$

9. $\dfrac{1}{x - 2} - \dfrac{1}{x}$

10. $\dfrac{3}{x} - \dfrac{6}{2x + 1}$

11. $\dfrac{3}{x - 2} - \dfrac{1}{x - 1}$

12. $\dfrac{4}{9(x - 8)} - \dfrac{4}{9(x + 1)}$

13. $\dfrac{1}{2(x - 3)} - \dfrac{1}{2(x + 3)}$

14. $\dfrac{1}{2x - 3} + \dfrac{1}{2x + 3}$

15. $\dfrac{7}{3x} - \dfrac{1}{3(x + 1)}$

16. $\dfrac{5}{x + 2} - \dfrac{1}{x}$

17. $\dfrac{9}{x} - \dfrac{18}{2x + 1}$

18. $\dfrac{1}{(x - 2)} + \dfrac{1}{2(x + 1)}$

19. $\dfrac{2}{5(x - 1)} - \dfrac{1}{5(3x + 2)}$

20. $\dfrac{2}{(x - 2)} - \dfrac{1}{2x}$

Mixed Exercise 2 – p. 23

1. (a) $\dfrac{x^2 - 9}{2(x - 3)} = \dfrac{x + 3}{2}$ (b) $\dfrac{1}{x - 3}$

2. (a) $\dfrac{4a}{rp}$ (b) $\dfrac{2p^2 - 3r}{pr}$

3. (a) $\dfrac{2}{3(n + 2)}$ (b) $\dfrac{5x^2 + x - 1}{x(x + 1)(2x - 1)}$

4. $\dfrac{3}{2(x-1)} - \dfrac{3}{2(x+1)}$

5. $\dfrac{4}{7(x-3)} - \dfrac{8}{7(2x+1)}$

6. $\dfrac{5}{x-1} - \dfrac{5}{x}$

7. (a) $\dfrac{2x-5}{2x+5}$ (b) $\dfrac{2t}{t^2-1}$

8. (a) $\dfrac{(x-1)^3}{x+1}$ (b) $\dfrac{ab+bc+ac}{abc}$

9. $\dfrac{5}{7(x+1)} + \dfrac{1}{7(4x-3)}$

10. $\dfrac{1}{t-1} + \dfrac{1}{t+1}$

CHAPTER 3

Exercise 3a – p. 26

1. $2\sqrt{3}$
2. $4\sqrt{2}$
3. $3\sqrt{3}$
4. $5\sqrt{2}$
5. $10\sqrt{2}$
6. $6\sqrt{2}$
7. $9\sqrt{2}$
8. $12\sqrt{2}$
9. $5\sqrt{3}$
10. $4\sqrt{3}$
11. $10\sqrt{5}$
12. $2\sqrt{5}$

Exercise 3b – p. 28

1. $2\sqrt{3} - 3$
2. $5\sqrt{2} + 8$
3. $2\sqrt{5} + 5\sqrt{15}$
4. 4
5. $\sqrt{6} + \sqrt{2} - \sqrt{3} - 1$
6. $13 + 7\sqrt{3}$
7. 4
8. $5 - 3\sqrt{2}$
9. $22 - 10\sqrt{5}$
10. 9
11. $10 - 4\sqrt{6}$
12. $31 + 12\sqrt{3}$
13. $(4 + \sqrt{5})$
14. $(\sqrt{11} - 3)$
15. $(2\sqrt{3} + 4)$
16. $(\sqrt{6} + \sqrt{5})$
17. $(3 + 2\sqrt{3})$
18. $(2\sqrt{5} + \sqrt{2})$

Exercise 3c – p. 29

1. $\frac{3}{2}\sqrt{2}$
2. $\frac{1}{7}\sqrt{7}$
3. $\frac{2}{11}\sqrt{11}$
4. $\frac{3}{5}\sqrt{10}$
5. $\frac{1}{9}\sqrt{3}$
6. $\frac{1}{2}\sqrt{2}$
7. $\sqrt{2} + 1$
8. $\frac{1}{23}(15\sqrt{2} - 6)$
9. $\frac{1}{3}(4\sqrt{3} + 6)$
10. $-5(2 + \sqrt{5})$
11. $\frac{1}{4}(\sqrt{7} + \sqrt{3})$
12. $4(2 + \sqrt{3})$
13. $\sqrt{5} - 2$
14. $\frac{1}{13}(7\sqrt{3} + 2)$
15. $3 + \sqrt{5}$
16. $3(\sqrt{3} + \sqrt{2})$
17. $\frac{3}{19}(10 - \sqrt{5})$
18. $3 + 2\sqrt{2}$
19. $\frac{2}{3}(7 - 2\sqrt{7})$
20. $\frac{1}{2}(1 + \sqrt{5})$
21. $\frac{1}{4}(\sqrt{11} + \sqrt{7})$
22. $\frac{1}{6}(9 + \sqrt{3})$
23. $\frac{1}{14}(9\sqrt{2} - 20)$
24. $\frac{1}{6}(3\sqrt{2} + 2\sqrt{3})$
25. $\frac{1}{2}(2 + \sqrt{2})$
26. $\frac{1}{42}(3\sqrt{7} - \sqrt{21})$
27. $\frac{1}{9}(\sqrt{30} + 2\sqrt{3})$

Exercise 3d – p. 33

1. $\dfrac{1}{2^4}$
2. $\dfrac{1}{2^2}$
3. 3^2
4. x^2
5. 1
6. t^4
7. 1
8. 2
9. $y^{3/2}$
10. x^5
11. $\dfrac{1}{y^{3/4}}$
12. p
13. 3
14. $\frac{1}{32}$
15. $\frac{1}{2}$

16. 2
17. 27
18. $\frac{9}{4}$
19. 1
20. 16
21. $\frac{5}{4}$
22. -5
23. 1331
24. $\frac{3}{5}$
25. 6
26. $\frac{16}{27}$
27. 8
28. 5
29. 1
30. 1

Exercise 3e – p. 35

1. $\log_{10} 1000 = 3$
2. $\log_2 16 = 4$
3. $\log_{10} 10\,000 = 4$
4. $\log_3 9 = 2$
5. $\log_4 16 = 2$
6. $\log_5 25 = 2$
7. $\log_{10} 0.01 = -2$
8. $\log_9 3 = \frac{1}{2}$
9. $\log_5 1 = 0$
10. $\log_4 2 = \frac{1}{2}$
11. $\log_{12} 1 = 0$
12. $\log_8 2 = \frac{1}{3}$
13. $\log_q p = 2$
14. $\log_x 2 = y$
15. $\log_p r = q$
16. $10^5 = 100\,000$
17. $4^3 = 64$
18. $10^1 = 10$
19. $2^2 = 4$
20. $2^5 = 32$
21. $10^3 = 1000$
22. $5^0 = 1$
23. $3^2 = 9$
24. $4^2 = 16$
25. $3^3 = 27$
26. $36^{1/2} = 6$
27. $a^0 = 1$
28. $x^z = y$
29. $a^b = 5$
30. $p^r = q$

Exercise 3f – p. 36

1. 2
2. 6
3. 6

4. 4
5. 2
6. 3
7. $\frac{1}{2}$
8. -2
9. -1
10. $\frac{1}{2}$
11. 0
12. 1
13. $\frac{1}{3}$
14. 0
15. $\frac{1}{3}$
16. 3

Exercise 3g – p. 38

1. $\log p + \log q$
2. $\log p + \log q + \log r$
3. $\log p - \log q$
4. $\log p + \log q - \log r$
5. $\log p - \log q - \log r$
6. $2 \log p + \log q$
7. $\log q - 2 \log r$
8. $\log p + \frac{1}{2} \log q$
9. $2 \log p + 3 \log q - \log r$
10. $\frac{1}{2} \log q - \frac{1}{2} \log r$
11. $n \log q$
12. $n \log p + m \log q$
13. $\log pq$
14. $\log p^2 q$
15. $\log q/r$
16. $\log q^3 p^4$
17. $\log p^n/q$
18. $\log pq^2/r^3$

Mixed Exercise 3 – p. 38

1. (a) $2\sqrt{21}$ (b) $10\sqrt{3}$ (c) $3\sqrt{5}$
2. (a) $8 - 2\sqrt{2}$ (b) $7 - 2\sqrt{10}$
3. (a) $(7 + \sqrt{3})(7 - \sqrt{3}) = 46$
   (b) $(2\sqrt{2} - 1)(2\sqrt{2} + 1) = 7$
   (c) $(\sqrt{7} + \sqrt{5})(\sqrt{7} - \sqrt{5}) = 2$
4. (a) $\frac{5}{7}\sqrt{7}$ (b) $\frac{1}{3}(\sqrt{13} + 2)$
   (c) $4(\sqrt{3} + \sqrt{2})$ (d) $2 - \sqrt{3}$
5. (a) 1   (b) 1
6. (a) $\frac{1}{4}$ (b) $\frac{4}{7}$ (c) $\frac{16}{243}\sqrt{6}$
7. (a) 1   (b) $\frac{1}{5}\sqrt{15}$
8. (a) 7   (b) $\frac{1}{2}$ (c) 0
9. (a) $3 \log a - \log b - 2 \log c$
   (b) $n \log a - \log b$
   (c) $\log a + \log b - \log c$
10. (a) $\log \dfrac{a^3}{b}$ (b) $-\log a$

CHAPTER 4

Exercise 4a – p. 40
1. $x = -2$ or $x = -3$
2. $x = 2$ or $x = -3$
3. $x = 3$ or $x = -2$
4. $x = -2$ or $x = -4$
5. $x = 1$ or $x = 3$
6. $x = 1$ or $x = -3$
7. $x = -1$ or $x = -\frac{1}{2}$
8. $x = 2$ or $x = \frac{1}{4}$
9. $x = 1$ or $x = -5$
10. $x = 8$ or $x = -9$
11. $-1, 3$
12. $-1, -4$
13. $1, 5$
14. $2, -5$
15. $-2, 7$
16. $2, 7$

Exercise 4b – p. 42
1. $x = 2$ or $x = 5$
2. $x = 3$ or $x = -5$
3. $x = 4$ or $x = -1$
4. $x = 3$ or $x = 4$
5. $x = \frac{1}{3}$ or $x = -1$
6. $x = -1$ or $x = -6$
7. $x = 0$ or $x = 2$
8. $x = -1$ or $x = -\frac{1}{4}$
9. $x = \frac{2}{3}$ or $x = -1$
10. $x = 0$ or $x = -\frac{1}{2}$
11. $x = 0$ or $x = -6$
12. $x = 0$ or $x = 10$
13. $x = 0$ or $x = \frac{1}{2}$
14. $x = 5$ or $x = -4$
15. $x = 2$ or $x = -\frac{4}{3}$
16. $x = 2$ or $x = -1$
17. $x = 0$ or $x = 1$
18. $x = 0$ or $x = 2$
19. $x = 3$ or $x = -1$
20. $x = -1$ or $x = \frac{1}{2}$

Exercise 4c – p. 44
1. 4
2. 1
3. 9
4. 25
5. 2
6. $\frac{25}{4}$
7. 192
8. 81
9. 200

10. $\frac{1}{4}$
11. $\frac{1}{3}$
12. $\frac{9}{8}$
13. $x = -4 \pm \sqrt{17}$
14. $x = 1 \pm \sqrt{3}$
15. $x = -\frac{1}{2}(1 \pm \sqrt{5})$
16. $x = -\frac{1}{2}(1 \pm \sqrt{3})$
17. $x = -\frac{1}{2}(3 \pm \sqrt{5})$
18. $x = \frac{1}{4}(1 \pm \sqrt{17})$
19. $x = -2 \pm \sqrt{6}$
20. $x = -\frac{1}{6}(1 \pm \sqrt{13})$
21. $x = \frac{1}{2}(-2 \pm 3\sqrt{2})$
22. $x = \frac{1}{2}(1 \pm \sqrt{13})$
23. $x = -\frac{1}{8}(1 \pm \sqrt{17})$
24. $x = \frac{1}{4}(3 \pm \sqrt{41})$

Exercise 4d – p. 46
1. $x = -2 \pm \sqrt{2}$
2. $x = \frac{1}{4}(-1 \pm \sqrt{17})$
3. $x = \frac{1}{2}(-5 \pm \sqrt{21})$
4. $x = \frac{1}{4}(1 \pm \sqrt{33})$
5. $x = 2 \pm \sqrt{3}$
6. $x = \frac{1}{4}(1 \pm \sqrt{41})$
7. $x = \frac{1}{6}(1 \pm \sqrt{13})$
8. $x = -\frac{1}{6}(1 \pm \sqrt{13})$
9. $x = -0.260$ or -1.540
10. $x = 2.781$ or 0.719
11. $x = 1.883$ or -0.133
12. $x = 0.804$ or -1.554
13. $x = 0.804$ or -1.554
14. $x = 0.724$ or 0.276
15. $x = 3.303$ or -0.303
16. $x = 7.873$ or 0.127

Exercise 4e – p. 48
1. $x = 2, y = 1, z = 1$
2. $x = 3, y = 4, z = 1$
3. $x = 1, y = -1, z = 2$
4. $x = 3, y = 2, z = -1$
5. $x = 1, y = 2, z = 3$
6. $x = 4, y = -1, z = 2$

Exercise 4f – p. 50
1.

x	-2	1
y	-1	2

2. $x = -1, y = 3$
3. $x = 2, y = 3$

4.

x	-1	$\frac{1}{2}$
y	4	1

5.

x	2	$-\frac{1}{2}$
y	-3	2

6.

x	$\frac{7}{2}$	-2
y	$-\frac{1}{2}$	5

7.

x	1	2
y	2	1

8.

x	-1	3
y	-4	4

9. $x = 1, y = 5$

10.

x	6	-6
y	2	-4

11. $x = \frac{1}{2}, y = -1$

12.

x	1	0
y	$\frac{1}{3}$	$\frac{2}{3}$

13. $x = -1, y = -\frac{1}{2}$

14. $x = 1, y = -\frac{1}{3}$

15.

x	$-\frac{1}{3}$	$\frac{2}{3}$
y	$-\frac{1}{2}$	$\frac{1}{4}$

16. $x = 1, y = \frac{1}{2}$

17.

x	-3	6
y	-3	$\frac{3}{2}$

18.

x	1	$-\frac{1}{4}$
y	-2	3

19.

x	-1	2
y	$\frac{1}{3}$	$-\frac{1}{6}$

20.

x	$\frac{1}{2}$	0
y	$\frac{1}{2}$	1

21.

x	1	$3\frac{1}{2}$
y	1	-4

22.

x	-1	$7\frac{1}{2}$
y	2	$-\frac{7}{5}$

Exercise 4g – p. 54
1. 4
2. $-\frac{5}{3}$
3. 1
4. $\frac{4}{3}$
5. -3
6. $\frac{2}{5}$
7. real and different
8. not real
9. real and different
10. real and equal
11. real and different
12. real and equal
13. real and different
14. not real
15. real and different
16. real and equal
17. $k = \pm 12$
18. $a = 2\frac{1}{4}$
19. $p = 2$
22. $q^2 = 4p$

Mixed Exercise 4 – p. 56
1. (a) 5   (b) $-1, 6$ (c) 5
2. (a) 6   (b) $3 \pm \sqrt{14}$ (c) 6
3. (a) $-\frac{3}{2}$ (b) $\frac{1}{4}(-3 \pm \sqrt{17})$ (c) $-\frac{3}{2}$
4. (a) $-\frac{4}{3}$ (b) $\frac{1}{3}(-2 \pm \sqrt{19})$ (c) $-\frac{4}{3}$
5. (a) 2   (b) $1, 1$ (c) 2
6. (a) $\frac{11}{4}$ (b) $-\frac{1}{4}, 3$ (c) $\frac{11}{4}$
7. (a) -1 (b) $\frac{1}{2}(-1 \pm \sqrt{13})$ (c) -1
8. (a) -4 (b) $-6, 2$ (c) -4
9. (a) -2 (b) $-1 \pm \sqrt{3}$ (c) -2
10. (a) -4 (b) $-2, -2$ (c) -4
11. $x = 0$ or 2
12. $x = -4$ or 1
13. $x = 2$ or $x \to \infty$
14. $x = 0$ or -1
15. $x = \frac{1}{2}(7 \pm \sqrt{89})$
16. $x = 1$ or $x \to \infty$
17. (a) not real   (b) real and different
    (c) real and equal
    (d) real and different
18. $4, -1$
20. 2
21.

x	4	-22
y	5	31

22.

x	2	4
y	5	9

23. $x = 5$ or $\frac{2}{3}$;   (a) rational
    (b) it factorises

CONSOLIDATION A

Multiple Choice Exercise A – p. 58

1. A
2. E
3. D
4. E
5. B
6. A
7. E
8. E
9. A
10. E
11. C
12. C
13. B
14. A
15. B
16. B
17. A
18. A
19. B, C
20. A, B
21. T
22. F
23. T
24. T

Miscellaneous Exercise A – p. 61

1. $3[(x + 1)^2 - \frac{7}{3}]$
2. -96
3. $A = \frac{5}{7}, B = -\frac{3}{7}$
4. (a) $\frac{3}{2}$ (b) $\frac{7}{4}$
5. 1
6. $\frac{81}{4}$
7. $p = 8, q = 2$
9. $x = \frac{1}{6}(y^3 + 12)$
10. $\dfrac{3}{x} - \dfrac{3}{x + 1}$
11. $p = -4, q = \frac{1}{2}$
12. $a = 3, b = -36$
13. $x = \frac{1}{2}(\sqrt{21} - 3), y = \frac{1}{2}(5 - \sqrt{21})$
14. -4

CHAPTER 5

Exercise 5a – p. 66

1. 2 cm
2. 90 cm
3. 20 cm
4. (a) 84 cm   (b) $7x$ cm
5. $5 : 7$

6. $3 : 1$
7. $y : (x - y)$
8. $\dfrac{ma}{n - m}$
9. $(a + b) : b$

Exercise 5b – p. 68

1. 3.75 cm
2. $TN = 2.5$ cm, $LN = 4.5$ cm
3. $BC = 2.25$ cm
4. $\dfrac{yz}{x}$
5. (a) 1.25 cm   (b) $2 : 7$ externally
6. (a) Y   (b) Y   (c) Y
    (d) Y   (e) N   (f) Y

Exercise 5c – p. 73

2. $\frac{5}{26}$ cm
3. $XZ = \frac{7}{4}$ cm, $QR = 16$ cm
5. $RT = 12$ cm, $AT = 8$ cm
6. $9 : 4$
7. $10°$
8. $BD = \frac{24}{7}$, $DC = \frac{25}{7}$, $AD = \frac{120}{7}\sqrt{2}$
10. $EC = 3$ cm, $AC = \frac{25}{3}$ cm

CHAPTER 6

Exercise 6a – p. 77

1.

2. $(9, 5)$ and $(9, 1)$ or $(-3, 5)$ and $(-3, -1)$
3. $(-2, 2), (3, -3)$

Exercise 6b – p. 82

1. (a) 5   (b) $\sqrt{2}$ (c) $\sqrt{13}$
2. (a) $(\frac{5}{2}, 4)$ (b) $(\frac{5}{2}, \frac{1}{2})$ (c) $(3, \frac{7}{2})$
3. (a) $\sqrt{109}, (\frac{1}{2}, 1)$ (b) $\sqrt{5}, (-\frac{1}{2}, -1)$
    (c) $2\sqrt{2}, (-2, -3)$
4. $\sqrt{65}$
5. $\sqrt{13}$
6. $(2, -4)$
8. (b) $(-3\frac{1}{2}, -\frac{1}{2})$ (c) $17\frac{1}{2}$ sq units
9. (a) $\sqrt{5}(2 + \sqrt{2})$ (b) $(0, 4\frac{1}{2})$
    (c) $2\frac{1}{2}$
11. $(-5, -3)$

Exercise 6c – p. 87

1. (a) 3 (b) $\frac{3}{2}$ (c) $\frac{1}{3}$ (d) $\frac{3}{4}$
   (e) -4 (f) 6 (g) $-\frac{7}{3}$
   (h) $-\frac{3}{2}$ (i) $\dfrac{k}{h}$

3. (a) yes (b) no (c) yes
   (d) yes

3. (a) parallel (b) perpendicular
   (c) perpendicular (d) neither
   (e) parallel

Exercise 6d – p. 89

1. $a = 0, b = 4$
2. (b) $22\frac{1}{2}$ square units
5. $\sqrt{(a^2 + 4b^2)}$
8. $\left(\dfrac{p + q}{2}, \dfrac{p + q}{2} \right)$
9. $(a - 2)^2 + (b - 1)^2 = 9$
10. 8
11. $b(d - b) = ac$
12. $b^2 = 8a - 16$

CHAPTER 7

Exercise 7a – p. 91

1. $\sin A = \frac{12}{13}, \cos A = \frac{5}{13}$
2. $\tan X = \frac{3}{4}, \sin X = \frac{3}{5}$
3. $\cos P = \frac{9}{41}, \tan P = \frac{40}{9}$
4. $\sin A = \dfrac{1}{\sqrt{2}} = \cos A$
5. $\sin Y = \frac{1}{3}\sqrt{5}, \tan Y = \frac{1}{2}\sqrt{5}$
6. $\cos A = \frac{1}{2}\sqrt{3}; 30°$
7. $\cos X = \frac{24}{25}$
8. $\cos X = \frac{4}{5};$
   $\cos^2 X - \sin^2 X = 0.28 = \cos 2X$
9. 1
10. $2 \sin X \cos X = 0.96, \sin 2X = 0.96,$
    $\sin 2X = 2 \sin X \cos X$
11. $\dfrac{2 \tan X}{1 + \tan^2 X} = 0.96 = \sin 2X$
12. $\dfrac{1 - \tan^2 X}{1 + \tan^2 X} = 0.28 = \cos 2X$

Exercise 7b – p. 99

1. $\frac{3}{5}, -\frac{4}{5}, -\frac{3}{4}$
2. $\frac{5}{13}, -\frac{12}{13}, -\frac{5}{12}$
3. $\frac{3}{5}, -\frac{4}{5}, -\frac{3}{4}$
4. $\dfrac{2}{\sqrt{13}}, \dfrac{-3}{\sqrt{13}}, -\dfrac{2}{3}$
5. $80°$ or $100°$
6. $60°$

7. $105°$
8. $52°$ or $128°$
9. $135°$
10. $150°$
11. $81°$ or $99°$
12. $57°$
13. $90°$
14. $80°$
15. $89°$
16. $180°$
17. $\pm \frac{4}{5}$
18. $\frac{5}{13}$
19. $53°$ or $127°$
20. $150°$
21. $135°$
22. (a) yes, $90°$
    (b) yes, 0
    (c) no
    (d) yes, 0 or $180°$
23. $A + B = 180°$
24.

25. (a) Yes (b) No

Exercise 7c – p. 104

Answers are correct to 3 s.f.
1. 11.1
2. 13.7
3. 10.2
4. 8.83
5. 156
6. 113
7. 7.01
8. 89.1
9. 581
10. 141
11. 16.3
12. 28.1
13. 51.3
14. no; an angle and the side opposite to it are not known

Exercise 7d – p. 108

Answers are correct to the nearest degree.
1. $18°$

2. 58° or 122°

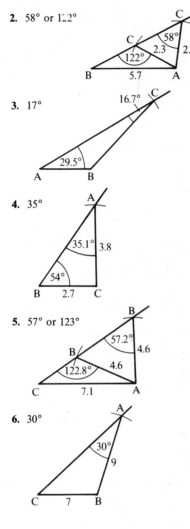

3. 17°

4. 35°

5. 57° or 123°

6. 30°

Exercise 7e – p. 111
1. 5.29
2. 12.9
3. 53.9
4. 4.04
5. 101
6. 12.0
7. 64.0
8. 31.8

Exercise 7f – p. 113
1. 38°
2. 55°
3. 45°

4. 94°
5. (a) 18°   (b) 126°
6. 29°
7. 11.4 cm, 68°

Exercise 7g – p. 115
1. 87.4 cm
2. 23.8 cm
3. 17.5 cm
4. $\angle B = 81°; a = 112$ cm
5. $a = 164$ cm; $c = 272$ cm
6. $\angle B = 34°; a = 37.0$ cm
7. $\angle C = 43°; b = 19.4$ cm; $c = 13.5$ cm
8. $\angle A = 52°; a = 33.2$ cm; $c = 41.5$ cm
9. $\angle B = 43°; \angle C = 60°; a = 27.1$ cm
10. $\angle A = 22°; \angle C = 33°; b = 30.3$ cm
11. 14.1 m
12. 40°, 53°, 87°

Mixed Exercise 7 – p. 115
1. (a) 116°   (b) 86°
2. $-\frac{24}{25}$
3. (a) $\dfrac{5}{\sqrt{39}}$ (b) $\dfrac{-5}{\sqrt{39}}$
4. (a) $\dfrac{1}{\sqrt{2}}, \dfrac{-1}{\sqrt{2}}$ (b) $\dfrac{3}{\sqrt{13}}, \dfrac{-2}{\sqrt{13}}$
5. $-\frac{5}{13}$
6. 9.05 cm
7. 4.82
8. 83°
9. 54° or 126°
10. 108°, 50°, 22°

CHAPTER 8

Exercise 8a – p. 118
1. 12 300 cm^2
2. 2190 cm^2
3. 1680 cm^2
4. 453 square units
5. 42.9 square units
6. 51°, 21.0 cm^2
7. 10.6 cm, 59.8 cm^2
8. 52°, 151 cm (or 150 cm)
9. 5.25 cm

Exercise 8b – p. 121
1. 11.0 cm, 67.7 cm^2 (or 67.8 cm^2)
2. 58.5 km
3. 477 m
4. $\angle BAO = 74°, \angle CAO = 52°; 22$ cm^2

5. (a) 60.8 cm   (b) 35°
   (c) 42.8 cm   (d) 2140 cm^2
   (e) 427 000 cm^3

Exercise 8c – p. 128

1. (a) $4\sqrt{2}$ cm   (b) $2\sqrt{29}$ cm
   (c) $2\sqrt{29}$ cm   (d) $2\sqrt{33}$ cm
2. (a) 6 cm, $6\sqrt{2}$ cm, $2\sqrt{34}$ cm
   (b) 53°   (c) 43°   (d) 53°
3. (a) $5\sqrt{2}$ cm   (b) $5\sqrt{5}$ cm
   (c) $\sqrt{109}$ cm   (d) 21°   (e) 34°
4. $\frac{1}{3}$
5. P = 55.4°, Q = 31.2°, R = 93.4°
6. 71°
7. (a) 6 m   (b) 9 m   (c) 48°
   (d) 240 m^2
8. (a) 15.3 m   (b) 2.29 cm
   (c) 15°   (d) 30°
9. 420 m; 31°
10. 46°

Mixed Exercise 8 – p. 133

1. 75.8 cm^2
2. $\frac{1}{2}$; yes, ∠A can be 30° or 150°
3. (a) 98°   (b) 19.8 cm^2
   (c) 3.96 cm
4. PQ = 8.29 cm, QR = 6 cm,
   RP = 3.46 cm; 9 cm^2
5. (a) 45°   (b) 35°
6. 35°
7. $\dfrac{a\sqrt{3}}{49}; \dfrac{2a}{7\sqrt{7}}$

8. $a\sqrt{\dfrac{37}{39}} = 0.974a$

CHAPTER 9

Exercise 9a – p. 139

1.
2.

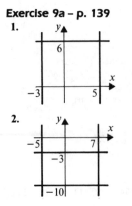

In questions 3–10, the unshaded region is the one required.

3.
4.
5.
6.
7.
8.
9.
10.

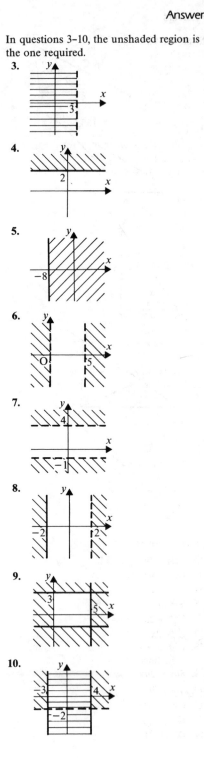

Exercise 9b – p. 142

1. (a) $y = 2x$ (b) $x + y = 0$
   (c) $3y = x$ (d) $4y + x = 0$
   (e) $y = 0$ (f) $x = 0$
2. (a) $2y = x + 2$ (b) $3y + 2x = 0$
   (c) $y = 4x$
3. (a) $2y = x$ (b) $y + 2x - 6 = 0$
   (c) $y = 2x + 5$
4. (a) $2y + x = 0$ (b) $2x - 3y = 0$
   (c) $2x + y = 0$
5. (a) $x - 3y + 1 = 0$
   (b) $2x + y - 5 = 0$
6. (a) $5x - y - 17 = 0$
   (b) $x + 7y + 11 = 0$
7. $3x + 4y - 48 = 0, 5$

Exercise 9c, p. 146

1. (a) $y = 3x - 3$
   (b) $5x + y - 6 = 0$
   (c) $x - 4y - 4 = 0$
   (d) $y = 5$
   (e) $2x + 5y - 21 = 0$
   (f) $15x + 40y + 34 = 0$
2. (a) $3x - 2y + 2 = 0$
   (b) $3x - 2y + 7 = 0$ (c) $x = 3$
3. (a), (c) and (d)
4. $x + y - 7 = 0$
5. (a) $x + 2y - 5 = 0$
   (b) $16x - 6y + 19 = 0$
   (c) $10x - 16y + 23 = 0$
6. $2x + y = 0$
7. $4x + 5y = 0$
8. $5x + 4y = 0$
9. $x + 2y - 11 = 0$
10. $3x - 4y + 19 = 0$

Mixed Exercise 9 – p. 149

2. $\frac{1}{4}$ sq. units
3. $(-\frac{4}{3}, \frac{11}{3}), (-5, 0), (6, 0)$
4. $10x - 26y - 1 = 0$
5. $x + 3y - 11 = 0, (\frac{13}{5}, \frac{14}{5})$
6. $[\frac{2}{5}(2 + 2a - b), \frac{1}{5}(4 - 2a + b)]$
7. $y = 2x - 3$
8. $y = x - 4$ (or $y + x = 10$ if line is inclined at $-45°$ to Ox)
9. $8by - 2ax + 8b^2 + 3a^2 = 0$
10. (a) $\sqrt{20}$ (b) $x - 2y + 1 = 0$
11. $(\frac{9}{10}, \frac{17}{10})$ and $(-\frac{18}{10}, \frac{26}{10}), (-\frac{27}{10}, -\frac{1}{10})$
    or $(\frac{36}{10}, \frac{8}{10}), (\frac{27}{10}, -\frac{19}{10})$
12. (a) $(1, 2), (5, 2), (3, 6)$ (b) 8

CHAPTER 10

Exercise 10a – p. 152

1. (a) $\angle ADE, \angle ACE$ (b) $\angle AFE$
   (c) $\angle AOC$ (d) $\angle ABC$
   (e) $\angle COE$ (f) $\angle CAD, \angle CED$
   (g) $\angle BAC, \ldots$
3. (c) $106.3°$ (d) $(5, 8), 53.1°$

Exercise 10b – p. 156

1. (a) $50°$ (b) $40°, 40°$ (c) $60°$
   (d) $54°, 108°$
3. $(4, 4)$
4. $30°$
7. $a^2 + b^2 - 9a - b + 14 = 0$
9. $(-\frac{115}{18}, -\frac{29}{6})$, 10.8 units to 3 s.f.
10. $60°, 60°$

Exercise 10c – p. 158

1. $61.9°$
2. 5 units
3. $67.4°$
4. 7.22 cm
5. $60°, 30°, 90°$
6. 8.43
7. 16 sq. units
8. 14.9 cm
9. 2.85
10. $\dfrac{2\sqrt{5}}{2}, -\dfrac{2\sqrt{5}}{5}$
12. $(-\frac{3}{4}, -\frac{9}{4})$
13. (a) $2x + y = 0$ (b) $(-\frac{4}{5}, \frac{8}{5})$
14. $x + y - 14 = 0$

CHAPTER 11

Exercise 11a – p. 165

1. $\frac{1}{4}\pi, \frac{5}{6}\pi, \frac{1}{6}\pi, \frac{3}{2}\pi, \frac{5}{4}\pi, \frac{1}{8}\pi, \frac{4}{3}\pi, \frac{5}{3}\pi, \frac{7}{4}\pi$
2. $30°, 180°, 18°, 45°, 150°, 15°, 22.5°,$
   $240°, 20°, 270°, 80°$
3. (Angles in radians, correct to 3 s.f.)
   0.611, 0.824, 1.62, 4.07, 0.246, 2.04, 6.46
4. (Angles to the nearest degree.)
   $97°, 190°, 57°, 120°, 286°, 360°$

Exercise 11b – p. 168

1. 2.09 cm, 4.19 cm^2
2. 26.2 cm, 131 cm^2
3. 4.77 cm, 35.8 cm^2
4. 7.96 cm, 79.6 cm^2
5. 18.8 cm, 75.4 cm^2
6. 3.14 cm, 1.57 rad
7. 4.8 cm, 0.96 rad

8. π cm, 6 rad
9. $\frac{5}{8}\pi$, 8 cm
10. $146°$
11. 0.283 rad
12. $0.52°$
13. (a) 12 cm^2 (b) 23.2 cm^2
14. 14.5 mm^2, 139 mm^2
15. (a) 15.2 cm   (b) 32.5 cm^2
16. $19.1°$
17. 85.6 cm
18. 19.6 cm, 108 cm^2
20. $0.979a^2$
21. (a) $135°$ (b) 9.41 cm
    (c) 35.4 cm   (d) 68.8 cm

CONSOLIDATION B

Multiple Choice Exercise B - p. 173

1. C
2. E
3. C
4. E
5. A
6. C
7. D
8. B
9. A
10. A
11. C
12. A
13. D
14. D
15. D
16. A, B
17. B
18. B, C
19. A, C
20. B
21. A, B
22. C
23. A, C
24. F
25. T
26. T
27. F
28. T
29. T
30. T
31. F

Miscellaneous Exercise B – p. 176

4. $(2, 3)$, $\sqrt{13}$
6. 2.08 m, $44.3°$
7. $(12 - 2x)/x$
8. (a) 65 cm   (b) $45°$; $21°$
9. 0.464 cm^2
10. 3
11. (a) $43.3°$ (b) $53.1°$ (c) $111.1°$
12. (a) 3 cm   (b) $96°$
13. (a) $79.9°$ (b) 13.4 cm   (c) $36.7°$
14. The points are $P_{-1}(0, -3)$, $P_0(1, -1)$,
    $P_1(2, 1)$ and $P_2(3, 3)$.
    Grad $P_{-1}P_0 =$ grad $P_{-1}P_1$
          $=$ grad $P_{-1}P_2 = 2$
    so the four points are collinear,
    $y = 2x - 3$
15. $(4\sqrt{2}, 8\sqrt{2} + 4)$, $(12 + 4\sqrt{2}, 8\sqrt{2})$,
    $(0, 4)$

CHAPTER 12

Exercise 12a – p. 183

1. (a) yes   (b) yes   (c) yes, $x \neq 1$
   (d) no   (e) yes, $x \geqslant 0$ (f) yes
   (g) yes   (h) no
2. $-4, -24$
3. $25, 217$
4. 1, not defined, 12
5. $1, \dfrac{\sqrt{3}}{2}$

Exercise 12b – p. 186

1. (a) $f(x) \geqslant -3$ (b) $f(x) \geqslant -5$
   (c) $f(x) \geqslant 0$ (d) $0 < f(x) \leqslant \frac{1}{2}$

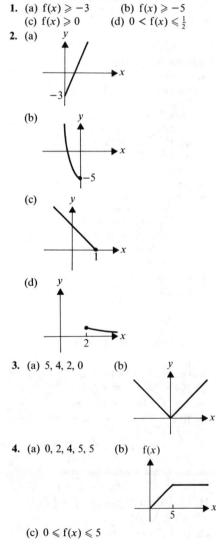

2. (a)

(b)

(c)

(d)

3. (a) $5, 4, 2, 0$ (b)

4. (a) $0, 2, 4, 5, 5$ (b) $f(x)$

(c) $0 \leqslant f(x) \leqslant 5$

5. (a) 0, £5000
(b) $f(x) = 0$ for $0 \leqslant x \leqslant 20\,000$
$f(x) = \frac{1}{5}(x - 20\,000)$ for $x > 20\,000$

domain $x \geqslant 0$ (but $x <$ GNP!)
range $f(x) \geqslant 0$

Exercise 12c – p. 190

1. (a) $\frac{11}{4}$ (b) 3   (c) 4
2. (a) $f(x) \leqslant \frac{29}{4}$ (b) $f(x) \geqslant -2$
   (c) $f(x) \leqslant 1$
3. (a)

(b)

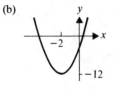

(c)

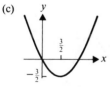

(d)

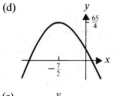

(e)

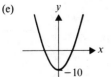

(f)

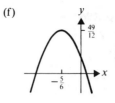

4. (a)

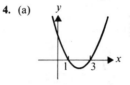

(b)

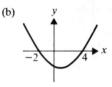

(c)

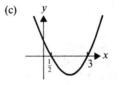

(d)

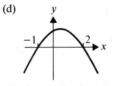

(e)

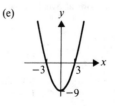

(f)

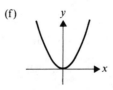

Exercise 12d – p. 196

1. (a)

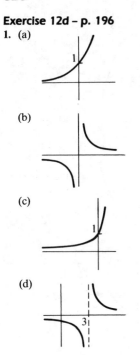

(b)

(c)

(d)

2. $16, 8, 4, 2, 1, \frac{1}{2}, \frac{1}{4}, \frac{1}{8}, \frac{1}{16}$
as $x \to \infty$, $f(x) \to 0$ and
as $x \to -\infty$, $f(x) \to \infty$

3. -2, as $x \to -2$ from below, $f(x) \to -\infty$
as $x \to -2$ from above, $f(x) \to \infty$

4. (a)

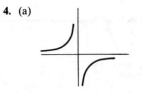

(b)

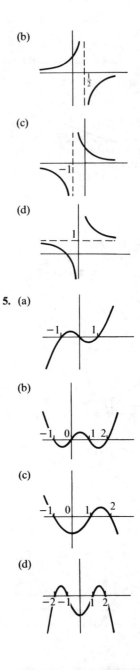

(c)

(d)

5. (a)

(b)

(c)

(d)

Exercise 12e – p. 197

1. (b) translation $\begin{pmatrix} 0 \\ c \end{pmatrix}$

2. translation $\begin{pmatrix} -c \\ 0 \end{pmatrix}$

3. (a) reflection Ox
   (b) reflection Oy

Exercise 12f – p. 200

11. Reflection in line $y = x$
   (there are several alternatives).
12. Reflection in line $y = x$
   (there are several alternatives).
13. (5, 2)
14. (b, a)

Exercise 12g – p. 206

1. (a)

(b)

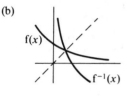

(c)

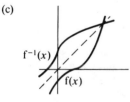

(d)

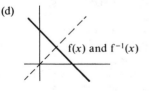

(e)

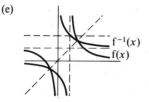

(f)

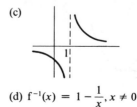

$f(x)$ and $f^{-1}(x)$

2. (d) and (f)
3. (a) $f^{-1} = (x - 1)$ (b) no
   (c) $f^{-1}(x) = \sqrt[3]{(x - 1)}$
   (d) $f^{-1}(x) = \sqrt{(x + 4)}, x \geqslant -4$
   (e) $f^{-1}(x) = \sqrt[4]{x} - 1, x \geqslant 0$
4. (a) $-\frac{1}{3}$ (b) $\frac{1}{2}$ (c) there isn't one
5. (a) 9   (b) 2   (c) -1

Exercise 12h – p. 207

1. (a) $\dfrac{1}{x^2}$ (b) $(1 - x)^2$ (c) $1 - \dfrac{1}{x}$
   (d) $1 - x^2$ (e) $\dfrac{1}{x^2}$
2. (a) 125   (b) 15   (c) -1
   (d) -1
3. (a) $(1 + x)^2$ (b) $2(1 + x)^2$
   (c) $1 + 4x^2$
4. $g(x) = x^2$, $h(x) = 2 - x$
5. $g(x) = x^4$, $h(x) = (x + 1)$
6. (a) $f(x) = gh(x), g(x) = 10^x,$
      $h(x) = x + 1$
   (b) $f(x) = gh(x), g(x) = \dfrac{1}{x^2}$
      $h(x) = 3x - 2$
   (c) $f(x) = g(x) + h(x), g(x) = 2^x,$
      $h(x) = x^2$
   (d) $f(x) = \dfrac{g(x)}{h(x)}, g(x) = 2x + 1,$
      $h(x) = x$
   (e) $f(x) = gh(x), g(x) = x^4,$
      $h(x) = 5x - 6$
   (f) $f(x) = g(x)h(x), g(x) = x - 1,$
      $h(x) = x^2 - 2$

Mixed Exercise 12 – p. 208

1. (a) $\frac{1}{0}$ is meaningless   (b) $\frac{1}{4}$
   (c)

   (d) $f^{-1}(x) = 1 - \dfrac{1}{x}, x \neq 0$

2. (a) $\frac{11}{4}$ when $x = \frac{3}{2}$
(b) $-\frac{41}{8}$ when $x = \frac{7}{4}$
(c) -9 when $x = -2$

3.
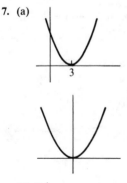

4. (a) $10\,000$, $\frac{1}{9}$, $\frac{1}{100}$
(b) 10^{-x^2}, $10^{2/x}$
(c) $\log x$, g^{-1} does not exist, $\dfrac{1}{x}$
(d) $\pm\frac{1}{3}$
(e) no for all x, yes for $x \geqslant 0$

5. (a)

(b)

(c)

6. (a) $g(x) = 2^x$, $h(x) = 3x - 2$
(b) 2^{16}, 1

7. (a)

(b) 0, $\frac{1}{6}$

CHAPTER 13

Exercise 13a – p. 210
1. $x < \frac{7}{2}$
2. $x > 4$
3. $x > -3$
4. $x > -2$
5. $x < \frac{1}{2}$
6. $x < -3$
7. $x < -\frac{1}{4}$
8. $x > \frac{8}{3}$
9. $x > \frac{3}{8}$

Exercise 13b – p. 212
1. $x > 2$ and $x < 1$
2. $x \geqslant 5$ and $x \leqslant -3$
3. $-4 < x < 2$
4. $x \geqslant \frac{1}{2}$ and $x \leqslant -1$
5. $x > 2 + \sqrt{7}$ and $x < 2 - \sqrt{7}$
6. $-\frac{1}{2} < x < \frac{1}{2}$
7. $-4 \leqslant x \leqslant 2$
8. $x > 1$ and $x < -\frac{2}{5}$
9. $x \geqslant \frac{3}{2}$ and $x \leqslant -5$
10. $x > 4$ and $x < -2$
11. $\frac{1}{2}(-3 - \sqrt{17}) \leqslant x \leqslant \frac{1}{2}(-3 + \sqrt{17})$
12. $x > 7$ and $x < -1$

Exercise 13c – p. 216
1. $x > -2$
2. $x < -2$
3. $1 < x < \frac{5}{2}$
4. $4 < x < \frac{24}{5}$
5. $-3 < x < 3$ and $x > 5$
6. $1 < x < 2$ and $x < 0$
7. $x > 3$ and $1 < x < 2$
8. $2 < x < 8$
9. $-1 < x < 1$ and $2 < x < 3$
10. $\frac{1}{6} < x < 1$
11. $x > -1$ and $-5 < x < -3$
12. $-4 < x < -\frac{2}{3}$
13. $-1 < x < 2$
14. $3 < x < 4$ and $-4 < x < -1$
15. $4 < x < 5$ and $-1 < x < 1$
16. $-2 < x < 3$

Exercise 13d – p. 219
1. (a) $p \geqslant 9$ and $p \leqslant 1$
   (b) $p \geqslant 5$ and $p \leqslant 1$
2. $-2 < a < 6$
3. $p < -1$

4. $-\frac{1}{7} \leqslant f(x) \leqslant 1$

5. $f(x) \geqslant 2$ and $f(x) \leqslant -2$

6. all values

7. $-\frac{1}{2} \leqslant f(x) \leqslant \frac{1}{2}$

8. $f(x) \geqslant 3 + \sqrt{8}$ and $f(x) \leqslant 3 - \sqrt{8}$

9. $f(x) \geqslant 2$ and $f(x) \leqslant -2$

10. $0 < k < \frac{4}{9}$

12. $-\frac{1}{2} \leqslant f(x) \leqslant 1$

Mixed Exercise 13 – p. 220

1. $x < 1$

2. $x > \frac{3}{2}$

3. $x > \frac{3}{2}$

4. $x > 3$, or $x < -2$

5. $-\frac{2}{3} < x < \frac{3}{2}$

6. $-\sqrt{13} < x < \sqrt{13}$

7. $x > 3 + \sqrt{2}$, or $x < 3 - \sqrt{2}$

8. $-2 < x < 7$

9. all values of x

10. $x > 6$, or $x < 1$

11. $1 < x < 4$

12. $-1 < x < 1$

13. $1 < x < 3$

14. $x > -1$

15. $x \geqslant 1$ and $x \leqslant -3$

16. $-2 < x \leqslant -1$ and $1 \leqslant x < 2$
   (Note: $x \neq 2$ or -2)

18. $k \leqslant 3$ and $k \geqslant 4$

19. $\frac{2}{3} \leqslant f(x) \leqslant 2$

CHAPTER 14

Exercise 14a – p. 229

1. $4; 4$

2. $1; 1$

3. $3x^2; 3$

4. $2x; 4$

5. $2x - 1; 1$

6. $4x^3; 32$

Exercise 14b – p. 231

1. $-\dfrac{2}{x^3}$

2. $-\dfrac{1}{x^2}$

3. $-\dfrac{2}{x^2}$

Exercise 14c – p. 233

1. $5x^4$

2. $-3x^{-4}$

3. $\frac{4}{3}x^{1/3}$

4. $-\dfrac{1}{x^2}$

5. $10x^9$

6. $-\dfrac{2}{x^3}$

7. $\frac{3}{2}\sqrt{x}$

8. $-\frac{1}{2}x^{-3/2}$

9. $-\dfrac{4}{x^5}$

10. $\frac{1}{3}x^{-2/3}$

11. $-\frac{1}{4}x^{-5/4}$

12. 1

13. $\frac{7}{2}\sqrt{x^5}$

14. $-\dfrac{7}{x^8}$

15. $\frac{1}{7}x^{-6/7}$

16. $3x^2$

Exercise 14d – p. 235

1. $3x^2 - 2x + 5$

2. $6x + \dfrac{4}{x^2}$

3. $\dfrac{1}{2\sqrt{x}} - \dfrac{1}{2x\sqrt{x}}$

4. $8x^3 - 8x$

5. $3x^2 - 4x - 8$

6. $2x + \dfrac{5}{2\sqrt{x}}$

7. $-\frac{3}{4}x^{-7/4} - \frac{3}{4}x^{-1/4} + 1$

8. $9x^2 - 8x + 9$

9. $\frac{3}{2}x^{1/2} - \frac{1}{2}x^{-1/2} - \frac{1}{2}x^{-3/2}$

10. $\dfrac{1}{2\sqrt{x}} + \dfrac{3\sqrt{x}}{2}$

11. $-\dfrac{2}{x^3} + \dfrac{3}{x^4}$

12. $\dfrac{-1}{2\sqrt{x^3}} + \dfrac{2}{x^2}$

13. $-\frac{1}{2}x^{-3/2} + \frac{9}{2}x^{1/2}$

14. $\frac{1}{4}x^{-3/4} - \frac{1}{5}x^{-4/5}$

15. $-\dfrac{12}{x^4} + \dfrac{3x^2}{4}$

16. $-\dfrac{4}{x^2} - \dfrac{10}{x^3} + \dfrac{18}{x^4}$

17. $\dfrac{3}{2\sqrt{x}} - 3$

18. $1 + 2x^{-2} + 9x^{-4}$

19. $\frac{3}{2}\sqrt{x} - \frac{5}{2}x\sqrt{x}$

20. $\dfrac{-3\sqrt{x}}{2x^3} + \dfrac{3x}{2\sqrt{x}}$

Exercise 14e – p. 236

1. $\dfrac{dy}{dx} = 2x + 2$

2. $\dfrac{dz}{dx} = -4x^{-3} + x^{-2}$

3. $\dfrac{dy}{dx} = 6x + 11$

4. $\dfrac{dy}{dz} = 2z - 8$

5. $\dfrac{ds}{dt} = -\dfrac{3}{2t^4}$

6. $\dfrac{ds}{dt} = \dfrac{1}{2}$

7. $\dfrac{dy}{dx} = 1 - \dfrac{1}{x^2}$

8. $\dfrac{dy}{dz} = \dfrac{5z^2 - 1}{2\sqrt{z}}$

9. $\dfrac{dy}{dx} = 18x^2 - 8$

10. $\dfrac{ds}{dt} = 2t$

11. $\dfrac{ds}{dt} = 1 - \dfrac{7}{t^2}$

12. $\dfrac{dy}{dx} = -\dfrac{3\sqrt{x} + 28}{2x^3}$

Exercise 14f – p. 238

1. $2; -\frac{1}{2}$
2. $-\frac{1}{3}; 3$
3. $\frac{1}{4}; -4$
4. $6; -\frac{1}{6}$
5. $1; -1$
6. $5; -\frac{1}{5}$
7. $11; -\frac{1}{11}$
8. $-11; \frac{1}{11}$
9. $4; -\frac{1}{4}$
10. $\frac{4}{27}; -\frac{27}{4}$
11. $\frac{5}{4}; -\frac{4}{5}$
12. $2; -\frac{1}{2}$
13. $(2, 2)$ and $(-2, 4)$
14. $(1, 0)$ and $(-\frac{1}{3}, \frac{4}{27})$
15. $(3, 0)$ and $(-3, 18)$
16. $(-1, -2)$ and $(1, 2)$
17. $(1, -16)$
18. $(-1, \frac{1}{4})$
19. $(0, -5)$
20. $(1, -2)$ and $(-1, 2)$

Mixed Exercise 14 – p. 238

1. $6x + 1$
2. (a) $-3x^{-4} - 3x^2$
   (b) $\frac{1}{2}x^{-1/2} + \frac{1}{2}x^{-3/2}$
   (c) $-\dfrac{2}{x^3} - \dfrac{6}{x^4}$
3. (a) $\dfrac{dy}{dx} = \frac{3}{2}x^{1/2} - \frac{2}{3}x^{-1/3} - \frac{1}{3}x^{-4/3}$
   (b) $\dfrac{dy}{dx} = \dfrac{1}{2\sqrt{x}} + \dfrac{1}{x^2} - \dfrac{3}{x^4}$
   (c) $-\dfrac{3}{4x^{7/4}} + \dfrac{1}{4x^{5/4}}$
4. (a) 5   (b) 5   (c) 17
5. (a) 5   (b) 6
6. (a) 1   (b) 7 and -7
7. (a) -3 (b) $(-\frac{1}{2}, 0)$ and $(2, 0)$
   (c) -5 and 5
8. (a) $(1, 10)$ and $(-1, 6)$
   (b) $(\frac{1}{3}, 7\frac{7}{9})$ and $(-\frac{1}{3}, 8\frac{2}{9})$
9. (a) $4x^3 - 2x$ (b) $6(3x + 4)$
   (c) $\dfrac{x + 3}{2x\sqrt{x}}$
10. $1 - \sqrt{2}$
11. $(-2, 4)$
12. $\frac{1}{5}$ and $-\frac{1}{5}$
13. $(1, 9)$ and $(3, 11)$
14. 1
15. (b), (d)

CHAPTER 15

Exercise 15a – p. 243

1. (a) $y = 2x - 5$
   (b) $2y + x + 5 = 0$
2. (a) $y = 4x - 2$
   (b) $4y + x + 8 = 0$
3. (a) $y + x + 2 = 0$ (b) $y = x$
4. (a) $y = 5$ (b) $x = 0$
5. (a) $y + x = 3$ (b) $y = x - 1$
6. (a) $y = 19x + 26$
   (b) $19y + x + 230 = 0$
7. $4y + x + 12 = 0$
8. $y = 7x - 29$
9. $y + x = 1, 2y = 2x - 3; (\frac{5}{4}, -\frac{1}{4})$
10. $4y - x + 1 = 0, 4y + x - 5 = 0$
11. $y = 5x - 1, 3y + 9x + 19 = 0$
12. $y = 7x - 4, y + 5x + 28 = 0$
13. $(2, 8), y = 8x - 8$
14. $(\frac{1}{2}, -\frac{1}{4})$
15. $y + x + 1 = 0$
16. $2y = x + 2$

17. $k = -\frac{7}{2}$
18. $8y + 121 = 0$
19. $(1, -1)$
20. $p = 12, q = 8; (-2, 24)$

Exercise 15b – p. 246
1. $x = 0$
2. $x = \frac{3}{4}$
3. $x = 0, x = \frac{8}{3}$
4. $x = \pm\frac{1}{2}$
5. $x = 0, x = \frac{4}{3}$
6. $x = \pm1$
7. $x = 4$
8. $x = \pm3$
9. $x = 1, x = -\frac{4}{3}$
10. $x = \pm\frac{5}{9}\sqrt{3}$
11. $x = 1, x = -4$
12. $x = \pm\frac{2}{3}\sqrt{3}$
13. $(3, 3), (-3, -3)$
14. $(1, -7), (\frac{1}{3}, -\frac{185}{27})$
15. $(\frac{1}{2}, -\frac{25}{4})$
16. $(\frac{1}{3}, \frac{-2}{9}\sqrt{3})$
17. $(1, 2)$
18. $(4, 10), (-4, 6)$

Exercise 15c – p. 252
1. $(1, 1)$
2. $(-1, -2)$ min; $(1, 2)$ max
3. $(3, 6)$ min; $(-3, -6)$ max
4. $(0, 0)$ max; $(\frac{10}{3}, -\frac{500}{27})$ min
5. $(0, 0)$ min
6. $(1, \frac{3}{2})$ min
7. $(-1, 1)$ max; $(0, 0)$ min; $(1, 1)$ max
8. $(0, 0)$ min
9. $(\frac{5}{4}, -\frac{49}{8})$ min
10. $(-1, 4)$ max; $(1, -4)$ min
11. $(-2, -16)$ min; $(0, 0)$ max; $(2, -16)$ min
12. $(-2, 8)$ min; $(2, 8)$ min
13. -2 max; 2 min
14. $2\frac{3}{4}$ min
15. 0 inflex; 27 max
16. 8 inflex
17. 7 inflex
18. $-\frac{5}{16}$ min, 0 max, -2 min

Exercise 15d – p. 256
1. 800 m^2; $20 \text{ m} \times 40 \text{ m}$
2. $20 \text{ cm} \times 20 \text{ cm} \times 10 \text{ cm}$
3. $r = \sqrt{(9 - h^2)}$; $12\pi\sqrt{3} \text{ cm}^3$
4. 5 cm square

5. $\sqrt{35} \text{ cm square}$
6. $a = 1, b = -2, c = 3$
7. $p = q = 1, r = 2; (-1, 0)$
8. $5y = x^2 + 4x + 9$

Mixed Exercise 15 – p. 257
1. 11; $y = 11x - 6$; $(\frac{2}{3}, \frac{4}{3})$
2. $2y = x - 1$; $(-\frac{3}{2}, -\frac{5}{4})$
3. $(2, 14), (-2, -14)$
4. $y = 3x + 6, y = 3x + 2$
5. $x + 2y + 9 = 0$
6. $(-2, 16)$ max, $(2, -16)$ min;

7. min 2, max -2;

9. $h = \frac{1}{2}(7 - 2r - \pi r)$
10. $4 \text{ m} \times 4 \text{ m} \times 2 \text{ m}$
11. 12.5 cm^2

CHAPTER 16

Exercise 16a – p. 264
1. $\frac{1}{2}\sqrt{3}$
2. 0
3. $-\frac{1}{2}\sqrt{3}$
4. $\frac{1}{2}$
5. $\frac{1}{2}\pi, \frac{5}{2}\pi, \frac{9}{2}\pi$
6. $-\frac{1}{2}\pi, -\frac{5}{2}\pi$
7. $\sin 55°$
8. $-\sin 70°$
9. $-\sin 60°$
10. $-\sin\frac{1}{6}\pi$
11.

832

Answers

12.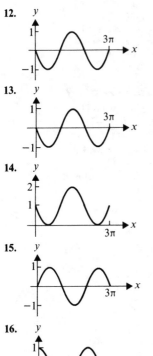

13.

14.

15.

16.

17. The curve $y = a\sin\theta$ is a one-way
stretch of the curve $y = \sin\theta$ by a
factor a parallel to the y-axis.

19. The curve $y = \sin 3\theta$ is a one-way
shrinkage of the curve $y = \sin\theta$ by a
factor $\frac{1}{3}$ parallel to the x-axis.

20. (a)

(b)

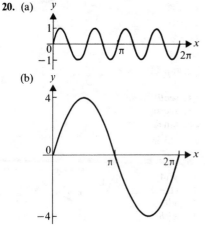

Exercise 16b – p. 268

1. (a) $-\cos 57°$ (b) $-\cos 70°$
   (c) $\cos 20°$ (d) $-\cos 26°$

2. (a) $-\dfrac{\sqrt{3}}{2}$ (b) 0 (c) $-\dfrac{1}{\sqrt{2}}$
   (d) 1

3. (a)

   (b)

   (c)

4.

$\sin\theta = \cos(\theta - \frac{1}{2}\pi)$
$\cos\theta = -\sin(\theta - \frac{1}{2}\pi)$

5.

(a) $\theta = \frac{1}{4}\pi$ (b) $\theta = -\frac{3}{4}\pi$
(c) $\theta = -\frac{1}{4}\pi$ and $\frac{3}{4}\pi$

6.

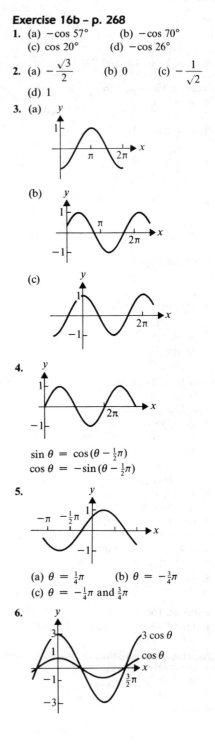

7.

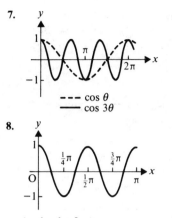

- - - cos θ
— cos 3θ

8.

y

$\frac{1}{8}\pi, \frac{3}{8}\pi, \frac{5}{8}\pi, \frac{7}{8}\pi$

Exercise 16c – p. 270

1. (a) 1   (b) $-\sqrt{3}$ (c) $\sqrt{3}$
   (d) -1
2. (a) tan 40°   (b) $-\tan \frac{2}{7}\pi$
   (c) $-\tan 50°$ (d) $\tan \frac{2}{5}\pi$
3. (a) $\frac{1}{4}\pi, \frac{5}{4}\pi$
   (b) $\frac{3}{4}\pi, \frac{7}{4}\pi$
   (c) $0, \pi, 2\pi$
   (d) $\frac{1}{2}\pi, \frac{3}{2}\pi$

Exercise 16d – p. 273

1. (a) 0.412 rad, 2.73 rad, -5.87 rad,
      -3.55 rad
   (b) $-\frac{4}{3}\pi, -\frac{2}{3}\pi, \frac{2}{3}\pi, \frac{4}{3}\pi$
   (c) 0.876 rad, 4.02 rad, -2.27 rad,
      -5.41 rad
2. (a) 141.3°, 321.3°, 501.3°, 681.3°
   (b) 191.5°, 348.5°, 551.5°, 708.5°
   (c) 84.3°, 275.7°, 444.3°, 635.7°
3. (a) 36.9°   (b) $-36.9°$ (c) 0.464 rad
4. $0, \pi, 2\pi$
5. 11.8°, 78.2°, 191.8°, 258.2°
6. $\frac{1}{3}\pi, \pi, \frac{5}{3}\pi$

Exercise 16e – p. 276

1. (a) 60°, 300°   (b) 59.0°, 239.0°
   (c) 41.8°, 138.2°
2. (a) $-140.2°$, 39.8°
   (b) $-131.8°$, 131.8°
   (c) $-150°$, $-30°$
3. $-\frac{1}{2}\pi, \frac{1}{2}\pi$
4. (a) 1   (b) $-\sqrt{2}$ (c) -2

5.

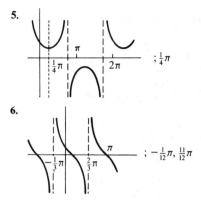

$; \frac{1}{4}\pi$

6.

$; -\frac{1}{12}\pi, \frac{11}{12}\pi$

Exercise 16f – p. 278

1.   1.0299 rad

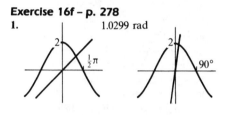

2. (a) $-1.89549, 0, 1.89549$
   (b) 0, 0.8767 rad   (c) 1.2834 rad

CHAPTER 17

Exercise 17a – p. 283

		sin θ	cos θ	tan θ
1.	(a)	$-\frac{12}{13}$	$-\frac{5}{13}$	$\frac{12}{5}$
	(b)	$\frac{3}{5}$	$-\frac{4}{5}$	$-\frac{3}{4}$
	(c)	$\frac{7}{25}$	$\frac{24}{25}$	$\frac{7}{24}$
	(d)	0	± 1	0

2. $\tan^4 A$
3. 1
4. $\sec\theta \operatorname{cosec}\theta$
5. $\sec^2\theta$
6. $\tan\theta$
7. $\sin^3\theta$
8. $x^2 - y^2 = 16$
9. $b^2x^2 - a^2y^2 = a^2b^2$
10. $y^2(4 + x^2) = 36$
11. $(1 - x)^2 + (y - 1)^2 = 1$
12. $y^2(x^2 - 4x + 5) = 4$
13. $x^2(b^2 - y^2) = a^2b^2$

Exercise 17b – p. 286

1. $57.7°, 122.3°, 237.7°, 302.3°$
2. $190.1°, 349.9°$
3. $38.2°, 141.8°$
4. $30°, 150°$
5. $30°, 150°$
6. $0°, 131.8°, 228.2°, 360°$
7. ± 0.723 rad
8. -0.314 rad, -2.83 rad
9. $-\frac{3}{4}\pi, -0.245$ rad, $\frac{1}{4}\pi, 2.90$ rad
10. $-\pi, -\frac{1}{3}\pi, \frac{1}{3}\pi, \pi$

Exercise 17c – p. 290

1. $\frac{1}{3}\pi + 2n\pi, \frac{2}{3}\pi + 2n\pi$
2. $\pm\frac{1}{2}\pi + 2n\pi \ (= \frac{1}{2}\pi + n\pi)$
3. $-\frac{1}{3}\pi + n\pi$
4. $-14.5° + 360n°, -165.5° + 360n°$
5. $\pm\frac{2}{3}\pi + 2n\pi$
6. $\frac{1}{4}\pi + n\pi$
7. $2n\pi$
8. $\frac{1}{6}\pi + 2n\pi, \frac{5}{6}\pi + 2n\pi$
9. $\pm\frac{1}{6}\pi + 2n\pi, \pm\frac{5}{6}\pi + 2n\pi$
10. $\pm 41.4° + 360n°$
11. $-18° + 360n°, -162° + 360n°$
12. $45° + 180n°, -14° + 180n°$
13. $\pm\frac{1}{3}\pi + 2n\pi, \pi + 2n\pi$
14. $n\pi, \pm\frac{1}{3}\pi + 2n\pi$
15. $\pm 90° + 360n°, 14.5° + 360n°,$
    $165.5° + 360n°$
16. $n\pi, \pm\frac{1}{6}\pi + 2n\pi$
17. $\pm 51.8° + 360n°$

Exercise 17d – p. 292

1. $22.5° + 90n°$
2. $\pm 40° + 120n°$
3. $-270° + 720n°, 630° + 720n°$
4. $\pm 12° + 72n°$
5. $-42.1° + 540n°$
6. $\pm 25.5° + 180n°$
7. $67.5° + 90n°$
8. $-480° + 1440n°$
9. $60° + 180n°$
10. $\frac{1}{12}\pi + 2n\pi, -\frac{7}{12}\pi + 2n\pi$
11. $\frac{1}{24}\pi + \frac{1}{2}n\pi$
12. $n\pi, \frac{1}{3}\pi + n\pi$

Exercise 17e – p. 293

1. $149.5°, 59.5°, 30.5°, 120.5°$
2. $-105.2°, 14.8°, 134.8°, -74.8°,$
    $45.2°, 165.2°$

3. $\pm 63.6°$
4. $\frac{1}{6}\pi, \frac{5}{12}\pi, \frac{2}{3}\pi, \frac{11}{12}\pi, \frac{7}{6}\pi, \frac{17}{12}\pi, \frac{5}{3}\pi, \frac{23}{24}\pi$
5. $\frac{1}{15}\pi, \frac{1}{3}\pi, \frac{7}{15}\pi, \frac{11}{15}\pi, \frac{13}{15}\pi, \frac{17}{15}\pi, \frac{19}{15}\pi, \frac{23}{15}\pi,$
    $\frac{5}{3}\pi, \frac{29}{15}\pi$
6. $\frac{3}{2}\pi$

Mixed Exercise 17 – p. 293

1. $x^2 + \dfrac{1}{y^2} = 1$

2. $\sin\beta = \pm\dfrac{\sqrt{3}}{2}, \tan\beta = \pm\sqrt{3}$

3. $\dfrac{2}{\sin^2\theta}; \frac{1}{4}\pi, \frac{3}{4}\pi, \frac{5}{4}\pi, \frac{7}{4}\pi$

4. $\pm 60° + 360n°, \pm 109.5° + 360n°$
6. $-\frac{29}{36}\pi, -\frac{17}{36}\pi, -\frac{5}{36}\pi, \frac{7}{36}\pi, \frac{19}{36}\pi, \frac{31}{36}\pi$
7. (a) $(x - 2)^2 + (y + 1)^2 = 1$
    (b) $(x + 3)^2 = 1 + (2 - y)^2$
8. $\pm\frac{1}{8}\pi + n\pi, \pm\frac{3}{8}\pi + n\pi \ (= \frac{1}{8}\pi + \frac{1}{4}n\pi)$
10. $\sin^2 A$
11. $180n°, \pm 70.5° + 360n°$
12. $\sec^2\theta \tan^2\theta$

CHAPTER 18

Exercise 18b – p. 298

1. 0
2. $\frac{1}{2}$
3. $\frac{1}{4}(\sqrt{6} - \sqrt{2})$
4. $-(2 + \sqrt{3})$
5. $\frac{1}{4}(\sqrt{6} - \sqrt{2})$
6. $\frac{1}{4}(\sqrt{6} + \sqrt{2})$
7. $\sin 3\theta$
8. 0
9. $\tan 3A$
10. $\tan\beta$
11. (a) $\frac{3}{5}$ (b) $-\frac{4}{5}$ (c) $-\frac{3}{4}$
12. (a) $1, 115°$ (b) $1, 30°$
    (c) $1, 310°$ (d) $1, 330°$
21. $67.5°, 247.5°$
22. $7.4°, 187.4°$
23. $37.9°, 217.9°$
24. $15°, 195°$
25. $\frac{1}{12}\pi + n\pi$
26. $\frac{7}{12}\pi + n\pi$

Exercise 18c – p. 302

1. $\frac{1}{2}$

2. $\dfrac{1}{\sqrt{2}}$

3. $\frac{1}{2}\sin 2\theta$

4. $\cos 8\theta$

5. $-\dfrac{1}{\sqrt{3}}$

6. $\tan 6\theta$

7. $\sqrt{2}\cos 3\theta$

8. $-\dfrac{1}{\sqrt{2}}$

9. $\tan(x + 45°)$

10. $\dfrac{1}{\sqrt{2}}$

11. (a) $\frac{24}{25}, -\frac{7}{25}$ (b) $\frac{336}{625}, \frac{527}{625}$
(c) $\frac{120}{169}, -\frac{119}{169}$

12. (a) $-\frac{336}{527}$ (b) $\frac{527}{625}$ (c) $-\frac{336}{625}$
(d) $\frac{164833}{390625}$

13. (a) $x(1 - y^2) = 2y$

(b) $x = 2y^2 - 1$ (c) $x = 1 - \dfrac{2}{y^2}$

(d) $2x^2y + 1 = y$

15. (a) $\frac{3}{2}\pi + 2n\pi, \frac{1}{6}\pi + 2n\pi, \frac{5}{6}\pi + 2n\pi$
(b) $\pm\frac{1}{2}\pi + 2n\pi, \frac{7}{6}\pi + 2n\pi, \frac{11}{6}\pi + 2n\pi$
(c) $\pm\frac{1}{3}\pi + 2n\pi$
(d) $\pm 35.3° + 180n°$
(e) $\frac{1}{2}\pi + n\pi, \frac{1}{4}\pi + n\pi$
(f) $90° + 180n°, 23.6° + 360n°,$
$156.4° + 360n°$

Exercise 18d – p. 306

1. (a) $\frac{24}{25}$ (b) $-\frac{7}{24}$ (c) $\frac{1}{2}, -2$
(d) $\pm\dfrac{2}{\sqrt{5}}, \pm\dfrac{1}{\sqrt{5}}$

2. t^2

3. $\dfrac{1}{t}$

4. $\dfrac{(1 - t^2)}{2t^2}$

5. $\dfrac{1}{(3 + 6t - 5t^2)}$

8. $0, 67.4°$

9. $-153°, 130.4°$

10. $36.9°, 126.9°$

11. $-90°, 36.8°$

Mixed Exercise 18 – p. 306

1. $y = 1 - 2x^2$

4. $\frac{56}{65}, -\frac{16}{65}$

5. $x = 2y - 1$

6. $-155.7°, 24.3°, -114.3°, 65.7°$

7. $n\pi$

9. $\cot^2 x$

10. $90°, 270°$

CONSOLIDATION C

Multiple Choice Exercise C - p. 313

1. C	**19.** A, B
2. B	**20.** B, C
3. D	**21.** B, C
4. C	**22.** B
5. E	**23.** A, C
6. B	**24.** B
7. B	**25.** B, C
8. B	**26.** B, C
9. D	**27.** C
10. A	**28.** F
11. C	**29.** T
12. D	**30.** T
13. B	**31.** T
14. B	**32.** T
15. B	**33.** F
16. B	**34.** F
17. C	**35.** F
18. B	

Miscellaneous Exercise C – p. 318

2. $x > 2$ and $x < -5$

3. (a) $(10x + 1)/(x + 5), x \neq -5$
(b) $f^{-1}: x \to (2x + 1)/(x - 3), x \neq 3$

4. $8x^3 + 24x^2 + 32x + 14$

5. $\pm\frac{1}{4}\pi + n\pi, \pm\frac{1}{3}\pi + n\pi$

6. $b = -6, c = -8; f(x) \geqslant -17;$
$g^{-1}(x) = 3 + \sqrt{(17 + x)}, x \geqslant -17; 8$

7. (a) 0 (b) $x < -3, -1 < x < 2$

8. (a) $h(x) > 1$
(b) $x > 1, h^{-1}(x) > 2$
(c)

(d)

9. (a) $m > 0$, $m < -\frac{4}{9}$; $m = -\frac{4}{9}$;

$9y + 4x - 12 = 0$

(b)

11. $30°$, $60°$, $120°$, $150°$

12. $(2, -9)$; $(-\frac{1}{3}, 3\frac{19}{27})$;

    (a) (i) $-1 < x < \frac{1}{2}$, $x > 3$

       (ii) $x < -\ln 2$, $x > \ln 3$

    (b) $(2n + 1)\pi$, $(2n \pm \frac{1}{3})\pi$

13. Least value is -2, greatest value is $\frac{1}{4}$

14. 0, $60°$, $120°$, $180°$

15. (a) $\dfrac{1}{1-x}$ (b) x (c) $\dfrac{1}{1-x}$

16. $2n\pi \pm \frac{1}{3}\pi$, $2n\pi + \pi$

17. $40.9°$, $220.9°$

18. (a) $f(x) \leqslant 4$ (b) $\pm\sqrt{2}$, $\pm\sqrt{6}$

19. $\pm\frac{2}{3}\pi$, $2n\pi \pm \frac{2}{3}\pi$

20. $x < 1$, $x > 2\frac{1}{2}$

21. The curve $y = x^2$ is translated 3 units in the direction Ox and translated $\frac{9}{2}$ units in the direction yO followed by a stretch of factor 2 parallel to Oy.

$f^{-1}(x) \geqslant 3$, $x \geqslant -\frac{9}{2}$;

$f^{-1}(x) = 3 + \sqrt{[\frac{1}{2}(x + 9)]}$

22. $f \circ g : x \rightarrow (2x + 5)^2 - 3$, $-3 \leqslant f \circ g \leqslant 166$

23. (a) $\dfrac{(12 - 2x)}{x}$ (c) 9

24. $x - 9y + 73 = 0$

25. (a) $16.1° + 180n°$

    (b) $27.2° + 360n°$, $152.8° + 360n°$

26. 0, π, $\frac{7}{6}\pi$, $\frac{11}{6}\pi$, 2π

27. $2n\pi$, $2n\pi \pm \frac{1}{3}\pi$

28. $x < -4$ and $-1 < x < 2$

29. (a) $a = \frac{5}{4}$ (b) $a < -1$

30. (a) $(1, 3)$ (b) $(-1, 1)$ (c) $(\frac{1}{2}, 1)$

31. (b) $2n\pi \pm \frac{1}{3}\pi$, $n\pi$ (e) $a = b = \frac{1}{4}$

32. $a = 3$, $b = -4$

CHAPTER 19

Exercise 19a – p. 326

1. $6(3x + 1)$

2. $-4(3 - x)^3$

3. $20(4x - 5)^4$

4. $6x(x^2 + 1)^2$

5. $21(2 + 3x)^6$

6. $-18(2 - 6x)^2$

7. $4x^3(2x^4 - 5)^{-1/2}$

8. $-2x(x^2 + 3)^{-2}$

9. $\dfrac{9x^2}{2\sqrt{(3x^3 - 4)}}$

10. $-\left(\dfrac{1}{2\sqrt{x}} + 3\right)\left(\sqrt{x} + 3x\right)^{-2}$

11. $\dfrac{3x}{(4 - x^2)^{3/2}}$

12. $\dfrac{-7(x^2 + 1)}{(x^3 + 3x)^{4/3}}$

13. $-10(4 - 2x)^4$

14. $4x(x^2 + 3)$

15. $21(3x - 4)^6$

16. $4x(x^2 + 4)$

17. $-4x$

18. $-12x^2(2 - x^3)^3$

19. $\frac{3}{2}x(2 + x^2)^{-1/4}$

20. $\frac{1}{3}(2x - 1)(x^2 - x)^{-2/3}$

21. $6x(2 - 3x^2)^{-2}$

22. $4x(4 - x^2)^{-3}$

23. $-\frac{5}{2}x^4(x^5 - 3)^{-3/2}$

24. $\dfrac{-1}{8\sqrt{x}(6 - \sqrt{x})^{3/4}}$

Exercise 19b – p. 329

1. $2x(x - 3)^2 + 2x^2(x - 3)$

    $= 2x(x - 3)(2x - 3)$

2. $\sqrt{(x - 6)} + \dfrac{x}{2\sqrt{(x - 6)}} = \dfrac{3(x - 4)}{2\sqrt{(x - 6)}}$

3. $(x - 2)^5 + 5(x + 2)(x - 2)^4$

    $= (x - 2)^4(6x + 8)$

4. $(2x + 3)^3 + 6x(2x + 3)^2$

    $= (2x + 3)^2(8x + 3)$

5. $4(x + 1)^2(x - 1)^3 + 2(x + 1)(x - 1)^4$

    $= 2(x + 1)(x - 1)^3(3x + 1)$

6. $3\sqrt{x}(x - 3)^2 + \dfrac{1}{2\sqrt{x}}(x - 3)^3$

    $= \dfrac{(x - 3)^2(7x - 3)}{2\sqrt{x}}$

7. $\dfrac{4(x - 3)(x + 5)^3 - (x + 5)^4}{(x - 3)^2}$

    $= \dfrac{(x + 5)^3(3x - 17)}{(x - 3)^2}$

8. $\dfrac{(3x + 2)^2 - 6x(3x + 2)}{(3x + 2)^4}$

    $= \dfrac{2 - 3x}{(3x + 2)^3}$

9. $\dfrac{4\sqrt{x}(2x-7) - (2x-7)^2\left(\dfrac{1}{2\sqrt{x}}\right)}{x}$

$= \dfrac{(2x-7)(6x+7)}{2x\sqrt{x}}$

10. $3x^2\sqrt{(x-1)} + \dfrac{x^3}{2\sqrt{(x-1)}}$

$= \dfrac{x^2(7x-6)}{2\sqrt{(x-1)}}$

11. $(x+3)^{-1} - x(x+3)^{-2} = 3(x+3)^{-2}$

12. $2x(2x-3)^2 + 4x^2(2x-3)$
$= 2x(2x-3)(4x-3)$

Exercise 19c – p. 330

1. $\dfrac{2x(x-3) - (x-3)^2}{x^2} = \dfrac{(x-3)(x+3)}{x^2}$

2. $\dfrac{(x+3)(2x) - x^2}{(x+3)^2} = \dfrac{x(x+6)}{(x+3)^2}$

3. $\dfrac{-x^2 - 2x(4-x)}{x^4} = \dfrac{x-8}{x^3}$

4. $\dfrac{2x^3(x+1) - (x+1)^2(3x^2)}{x^6}$

$= \dfrac{-(x+1)(x+3)}{x^4}$

5. $\dfrac{4(1-x)^3 + 12x(1-x)^2}{(1-x)^6} = \dfrac{4(1+2x)}{(1-x)^4}$

6. $\dfrac{(x-2)(4x) - 2x^2}{(x-2)^2} = \dfrac{2x(x-4)}{(x-2)^2}$

7. $\dfrac{\frac{5}{3}x^{2/3}(3x-2) - 3x^{5/3}}{(3x-2)^2} = \dfrac{2x^{2/3}(3x-5)}{3(3x-2)^2}$

8. $\dfrac{-3(1-2x)^2}{x^4}$

9. $\dfrac{(3x-2)(x+1)^{3/2}}{2x^2}$

Mixed Exercise 19 – p. 331

1. $\dfrac{3x+2}{2\sqrt{(x+1)}}$

2. $6x(x^2-8)^2$

3. $\dfrac{1-x^2}{(x^2+1)^2}$

4. $\dfrac{-4x^3}{3(2-x^4)^{2/3}}$

5. $\dfrac{2x}{(x^2+2)^2}$

6. $\frac{1}{2}x(5\sqrt{x}-8)$

7. $6x(x^2-2)^2$

8. $\dfrac{1-2x}{2\sqrt{(x-x^2)}}$

9. $\dfrac{\sqrt{x}+2}{2(\sqrt{x}+1)^2}$

10. $\dfrac{x(5x-8)}{2\sqrt{(x-2)}}$

11. $\dfrac{-(3x+4)}{2x^3\sqrt{(x+1)}}$

12. $6x^5(x^2+1)^2(2x^2+1)$

13. $\dfrac{x}{\sqrt{(x^2-8)}}$

14. $x^2(5x^2-18)$

15. $6x(x^2-6)^2$

16. $\dfrac{-(x^2+6)}{(x^2-6)^2}$

17. $-8x^3(x^4+3)^{-3}$

18. $\dfrac{(2-x)^2(2-7x)}{2\sqrt{x}}$

19. $\dfrac{2+5x}{2\sqrt{x}(2-x)^4}$

20. $(x-2)(3x-4)$

21. $30x^2(2x^3+4)^4$

CHAPTER 20

Exercise 20a – p. 336

1. (a) 7.39   (b) 0.368   (c) 4.48
   (d) 0.741

2. (a) $2e^x$ (b) $2x - e^x$ (c) e^x

3. $e^2 - 2$

4. $2 + 2e$

5. 1

6. 0

Exercise 20b – p. 338

1. (a) 1.24   (b) 0.183   (c) 2.85

2. (a) $\ln x - \ln(x-1)$
   (b) $\ln 5 + 2\ln x$
   (c) $\ln(x+2) + \ln(x-2)$
   (d) $\ln \sin x - \ln \cos x$
   (e) $2\ln \sin x$
   (f) $\frac{1}{2}\ln(x+1) - \frac{1}{2}\ln(x-1)$

3. (a) $\ln \dfrac{x}{(1-x)^2}$ (b) $\ln \dfrac{e}{x}$
   (c) $\ln(\sin x \cos x) = \ln(\frac{1}{2}\sin 2x)$
   (d) $\ln x^2\sqrt{(x-1)}$

4. (a) $\frac{2}{3}\ln x$ (b) $5\ln x$

5. (a) 2.10   (b) 0   (c) 1.05
    (d) 0

6. (a) $x = 1$ (b) $x = 3$
    (c) $x = 0$

Exercise 20c – p. 341

1. (a) $\dfrac{3}{x}$ (b) $\dfrac{1}{x}$ (c) $-\dfrac{2}{x}$

    (d) $-\dfrac{1}{2x}$ (e) $-\dfrac{5}{x}$ (f) $\dfrac{1}{2x}$

    (g) $-\dfrac{3}{2x}$ (h) $\dfrac{5}{2x}$

2. (a) $(1, -1)$ (b) $(2^{1/3}, \{2 - 2\ln 2\})$
    (c) $(4, \{\ln 4 - 2\})$

Exercise 20d – p. 343

(pr $\equiv$ product; f of f $\equiv$ function of a function)

1. (a) pr   (b) $u = e^x, v = x^2 + 1$
2. (a) f of f   (b) $u = x^2 + 1, y = e^u$
3. (a) pr   (b) $u = x, v = \ln x$
4. (a) f of f   (b) $u = x + 1, y = e^{u/2}$
5. (a) pr   (b) $u = e^x, v = \ln x$
6. (a) f of f   (b) $u = 3 - x^2, y = \ln u$
7. (a) f of f   (b) $u = \ln x, y = u^2$
8. (a) f of f   (b) $u = -2x, y = e^u$
9. (a) f of f   (b) $u = \ln x, y = \dfrac{1}{u}$

10. $fg(x) = e^{2x}; \, gf(x) = e^{x^2}$

11. (a) $\left(\dfrac{1}{x}\right)^2$ (b) $\ln x^2$

    (c) $\ln\left(\dfrac{1}{x}\right)$ (d) $(\ln x)^2$

    (e) $\ln\left(\dfrac{1}{x}\right)^2$ (f) $\left(\dfrac{1}{x}\right)^2$

Exercise 20e – p. 345

1. $e^x(x + 1)$
2. $x(2\ln x + 1)$
3. $e^x(x^3 + 3x^2 - 2)$
4. $12x \ln(x - 2) + \dfrac{6x^2}{(x - 2)}$
5. xe^x
6. $x\ln x + \dfrac{(x^2 + 4)}{2x}$
7. $\dfrac{4 + 3x}{2\sqrt{(2 + x)}}$
8. $\frac{1}{2}\ln(x - 5) + \dfrac{x}{2(x - 5)}$
9. $(x^2 + 2x - 2)e^x$

10. $\dfrac{1 - x}{e^x}$

11. $\dfrac{e^x(x - 2)}{x^3}$

12. $\dfrac{1 - 3\ln x}{x^4}$

13. $\dfrac{x\ln x - 2(x + 1)}{2x\sqrt{(x + 1)(\ln x)^2}}$

14. $\dfrac{e^x(x^2 - 2x - 1)}{(x^2 - 1)^2}$

15. $\dfrac{-2}{(e^x - e^{-x})^2}$

16. $4e^{4x}$

17. $\dfrac{2x}{x^2 - 1}$

18. $2xe^{x^2}$

19. $-6e^{(1-x)}$ or $-6e(e^{-x})$

20. $2xe^{(x^2 + 1)}$

21. $\dfrac{1}{2(x + 2)}$

22. $\dfrac{2\ln x}{x}$

23. $\dfrac{-1}{x(\ln x)^2}$

24. $\frac{1}{2}\sqrt{(e^x)}$

Mixed Exercise 20 – p. 345

1. $1 + \ln x$
2. $\frac{8}{3}(4x - 1)^{-1/3}$
3. $\dfrac{e^x(x - 2)}{(x - 1)^2}$
4. $\dfrac{-(x^3 + 4)}{2x^3\sqrt{(1 + x^3)}}$
5. $\dfrac{(x - 1)\ln(x - 1) - x\ln x}{x(x - 1)\{\ln(x - 1)\}^2}$
6. $3(\ln 10)10^{3x}$
7. $\dfrac{2x}{(1 + x^2)^2}$
8. $\dfrac{2}{x^2 e^{2/x}}$
9. $\dfrac{-e^x}{1 - e^x}$ or $\dfrac{e^x}{e^x - 1}$
10. $3x^2 e^{3x}(x + 1)$
11. $\dfrac{4}{5(2x - 1)^2} - \dfrac{6}{5(x - 3)^2}$
    $= \dfrac{2(3 - 2x^2)}{(2x - 1)^2(x - 3)^2}$

12. $\dfrac{e^{x/2}(x - 10)}{2x^6}$

13. $\dfrac{2}{x} - \dfrac{1}{x + 3} - \dfrac{2x}{x^2 - 1}$

14. $\dfrac{5x + 9}{x(x + 3)}$

15. $\dfrac{4}{x}(\ln x)^3$

16. $\dfrac{(x + 3)^2(x^2 - 6x + 6)}{(x^2 + 2)^2}$

17. $\dfrac{e^x - 1}{2\sqrt{(e^x - x)}}$

18. $\dfrac{8x}{x^2 + 1}$

19. $\dfrac{dy}{dx} = \dfrac{4}{(1 - 2x)^2}; \dfrac{d^2y}{dx^2} = \dfrac{16}{(1 - 2x)^3}$

20. $\dfrac{dy}{dx} = \dfrac{1}{x(x + 1)}; \dfrac{d^2y}{dx^2} = \dfrac{(2x + 1)}{x^2(x + 1)^2}$

21. $\dfrac{dy}{dx} = \dfrac{-4e^x}{(e^x - 4)^2}; \dfrac{d^2y}{dx^2} = \dfrac{4e^x(e^x + 4)}{(e^x - 4)^3}$

CHAPTER 21

Exercise 21a – p. 350

1. (a) $2 \sin 2\theta \cos \theta$
   (b) $2 \cos 4\theta \cos \theta$
   (c) $2 \cos 3\theta \sin \theta$
   (d) $-2 \sin 4\theta \sin 3\theta$
   (e) $2 \cos 4A \sin A$
   (f) $+2 \sin 3A \sin 2A$
   (g) $2 \sin (A + 10°) \cos (A - 10°)$
   (h) $2 \sin (\theta + 45°) \cos (\theta - 45°)$

2. (a) $\sin 3\theta + \sin \theta$
   (b) $\cos 5\theta + \cos \theta$
   (c) $\sin 5\theta + \sin 3\theta$
   (d) $\cos 4\theta - \cos 2\theta$
   (e) $\cos 2\theta - \cos 6\theta$
   (f) $\frac{1}{2} \cos 5\theta + \frac{1}{2} \cos 3\theta$

3. (a) $\cos \theta$ (b) $-\sqrt{2} \cos x$
   (c) 0

4. (a) $\frac{1}{2}\sqrt{6}$ (b) $\frac{1}{2}\sqrt{6}$

5. (a) $\pm\frac{1}{2}\pi + 2n\pi, \pm\frac{1}{6}\pi + \frac{2}{3}n\pi$
   (b) $\pm\frac{1}{4}\pi + n\pi, n\pi$
   (c) $\frac{1}{2}n\pi$ (d) $\frac{1}{3}n\pi, \frac{1}{2}\pi + n\pi$

6. $\cos 2\theta(2 \cos \theta + 1), \pm\frac{1}{4}\pi + n\pi,$
$\pm\frac{2}{3}\pi + 2n\pi$

7. $4 \cos \theta \sin 4\theta \cos 2\theta, \pm\frac{1}{8}\pi + \frac{1}{2}n\pi,$
$\pm\frac{1}{4}\pi + n\pi$

8. (a) $20°, 90°, 100°, 140°,$
   (b) $22\frac{1}{2}°, 90°, 112\frac{1}{2}°,$
   (c) $0°, 30°, 40°, 60°, 80°, 90°, 120°,$
     $150°, 160°, 180°,$
   (d) $30°, 45°, 135°, 150°,$
   (e) $0°, 60°, 105°, 120°, 165°, 180°,$
   (f) $10°, 130°$

Mixed Exercise 21 – p. 352

1. $\dfrac{3\sqrt{3} - 4\sqrt{2}}{2(3 + \sqrt{6})}$ (b) $\frac{1}{6}(1 - 2\sqrt{6})$

2. $\pm 70.5°$

3. $\pm\frac{1}{4}\pi + n\pi, \frac{1}{6}\pi + 2n\pi, \frac{5}{6}\pi + 2n\pi$

5. $n\pi, \pm\frac{1}{3}\pi + 2n\pi,$

7. $\pm\frac{1}{6}\pi + \frac{2}{3}n\pi, \frac{1}{12}\pi + n\pi, \frac{5}{12}\pi + n\pi$

8. $\sqrt{2} - 1$

9. $1 - 2y^2 = x$

10. $x = 60°, 300°, y = 120°, 240°$

12. $\frac{1}{4}\pi + 2n\pi, \frac{3}{4}\pi + 2n\pi$

13. $257.6°, 349.8°$

14. $y = \frac{1}{2}x, |x| \leqslant 2$

15. $0, 36°, 108°, 180°, 252°, 324°, 360°$

16. $ax = a^2 - 2y^2$

17. $49.1°, 229.1°$

19. $\pm\frac{1}{6}\pi + \frac{2}{3}n\pi, n\pi$

20. $\alpha = 90° - \theta; 135°, 315°, 22\frac{1}{2}°, 112\frac{1}{2}°,$
   $202\frac{1}{2}°, 292\frac{1}{2}°$

CHAPTER 22

Exercise 22a – p. 358

1. (a) $2, 30°$ (b) $\sqrt{10}, 71.6°$
   (c) $5, 36.9°$

2. $\sqrt{2} \cos (2\theta + \frac{1}{4}\pi)$

3. $\sqrt{29} \sin (3\theta + 21.8°)$

4. $-2 \sin (\theta - \frac{1}{6}\pi);$ max 2 at $\theta = 300°,$
   min -2 at $\theta = 120°$

5. $25 \cos (\theta + 73.7°);$ max 28 at
   $\theta = 286.3°,$ min -22 at $\theta = 106.3°$

6. $\sqrt{2}, -\sqrt{2}; -\frac{1}{\sqrt{2}}$ max, $\frac{1}{\sqrt{2}}$ min

7. $-\sqrt{\frac{2}{3}}$ max, $\sqrt{\frac{2}{3}}$ min

8. (a) $45° + 360n°$
   (b) $118.1° + 360n°, -36.9° + 360n°$
   (c) $360n°, 360n° - 143.2°$
   (d) $360n°, 360n° - 53.1°$

Exercise 22b – p. 361

1. $\frac{2}{7}n\pi$

2. $\frac{1}{5}n\pi$

3. $\frac{1}{2}(4n-1)\pi, \frac{1}{10}(4n+1)\pi$

4. $\frac{1}{18}(2n+1)\pi$

5. $2n\pi, \frac{1}{7}(2n+1)\pi$

6. $\frac{1}{2}n\pi, \frac{1}{3}n\pi$

7. $\frac{2}{3}n\pi - \frac{1}{6}\pi, \frac{2}{5}n\pi$

8. $\frac{1}{6}(2n+1)\pi$

9. $0, \frac{1}{5}\pi, \frac{2}{5}\pi, \frac{1}{2}\pi, \frac{3}{5}\pi, \frac{4}{5}\pi, \pi$

10. $\frac{1}{10}\pi, \frac{3}{10}\pi, \frac{1}{2}\pi, \frac{7}{10}\pi, \frac{9}{10}\pi$

11. $0, \frac{1}{9}\pi, \frac{2}{5}\pi, \frac{1}{3}\pi, \frac{5}{9}\pi, \frac{7}{9}\pi, \frac{4}{5}\pi, \pi$

12. $0, \frac{2}{11}\pi, \frac{4}{11}\pi, \frac{6}{11}\pi, \frac{8}{11}\pi, \frac{10}{11}\pi$

13. $-140°, -60°, -20°, 100°$

14. $-115°, -25°, 65°, 155°$

15. $-150°, -110°, 10°, 130°$

16. $-110°, -30°, 10°, 130°$

17. $-150°, -60°, 30°, 120°$

18. $-155°, -140°, -65°, 25°, 40°, 115°$

Exercise 22c – p. 366

1. (a) $\frac{1}{3}\pi$ (b) $-\frac{1}{2}\pi$ (c) $\frac{1}{2}\pi$
   (d) $-\frac{1}{3}\pi$ (e) $\frac{2}{3}\pi$ (f) $-\frac{1}{4}\pi$

2. (a) $\frac{1}{4}\pi$ (b) $\frac{1}{2}\pi$

3. (a) $\frac{1}{2}\pi$ (b) $\dfrac{2x}{x^2+1}$ (c) $\pm\frac{1}{2}\pi$
   (d) $\frac{7}{11}$

5. (a) $\frac{2}{9}$ (b) 0   (c) ± 1

Exercise 22d – p. 368

1. (a) $\frac{1}{2}$ (b) $\dfrac{\theta^2}{1-2\theta^2}$ (c) $\dfrac{\theta}{2-\theta^2}$
   (d) 2   (e) 1   (f) 1

3. (a) $\frac{1}{2}$ (b) $\frac{2}{3}$ (c) $\sqrt{\frac{3}{2}}$ (d) 1

Mixed Exercise 22 – p. 368

1. $5\sin(\theta-\alpha)$ where $\tan\alpha = \frac{3}{4}$;
   1 min, $-\frac{7}{3}$ max, $\pm\infty$

2. (a) $\frac{2}{9}$ (b) $\dfrac{9}{\sqrt{85}}$ (c) $\dfrac{2}{\sqrt{85}}$

3. $\sqrt{2}\sin(2\theta - \frac{1}{4}\pi); \frac{3}{8}\pi$

5. $-\frac{1}{4}$

6. $\sqrt{2}\cos(x - \frac{1}{4}\pi); \frac{1}{4}\pi$

7. $0, \frac{2}{5}\pi, \frac{4}{5}\pi, \frac{6}{5}\pi, \frac{8}{5}\pi, 2\pi$

8. $24°, 96°, 168°, 80°$

10. $\frac{1}{14}(1+2n)\pi$

11. $5\cos(x+\alpha)$ where $\tan\alpha = \frac{4}{3}$;
    $4 + 2\sec(x+\alpha)$

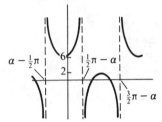

CHAPTER 23

Exercise 23a – p. 372

2. (a) $\cos x + \sin x$ (b) $\cos\theta$
   (c) $-3\sin\theta$ (d) $5\cos\theta$
   (e) $3\cos\theta - 2\sin\theta$
   (f) $4\cos x + 6\sin x$

3. (a) -1 (b) 1   (c) -1
   (d) 1   (e) $2(\pi-1)$ (f) 4

4. (a) $\frac{1}{6}\pi$ (b) $\frac{1}{6}\pi$ (c) $\frac{1}{4}\pi$
   (d) π

5. (a) $(\frac{1}{3}\pi, \sqrt{3} - \frac{1}{3}\pi)$, max;
   $(\frac{5}{3}\pi, -\sqrt{3} - \frac{5}{3}\pi)$, min
   (b) $(\frac{1}{6}\pi, \frac{1}{6}\pi + \sqrt{3})$, max;
   $(\frac{5}{6}\pi, \frac{5}{6}\pi - \sqrt{3})$, min

6. $y + \theta = 3 + \frac{1}{2}\pi$

7. $2\pi y + x = 2\pi^3 - \pi$

8. $(0, 1)$

Exercise 23b – p. 375

1. $4\cos 4x$

2. $2\sin(\pi - 2x)$ or $2\sin 2x$

3. $\frac{1}{2}\cos(\frac{1}{2}x + \pi)$ or $-\frac{1}{2}\cos\frac{1}{2}x$

4. $\dfrac{x\cos x - \sin x}{x^2}$

5. $-\dfrac{(\cos x + \sin x)}{e^x}$

6. $\dfrac{\cos x}{2\sqrt{(\sin x)}}$

7. $2\sin x \cos x$ or $\sin 2x$

8. $\cos^2 x - \sin^2 x$ or $\cos 2x$

9. $\cos x\, e^{\sin x}$

10. $-\tan x$

11. $e^x(\cos x - \sin x)$

12. $x^2\cos x + 2x\sin x$

13. $2x\cos x^2$

14. $-\sin x\, e^{\cos x}$

15. $3\cot x$

16. $\dfrac{\sin x}{\cos^2 x} = \sec x \tan x$

17. $\sec^2 x$

18. $\dfrac{-\cos x}{\sin^2 x} = -\csc x \cot x$

19. $\dfrac{-1}{\sin^2 x} = -\csc^2 x$

Exercise 23c – p. 377

3. $2x \arcsin x + \dfrac{x^2}{\sqrt{(1-x^2)}}$

4. $\dfrac{2 \arctan x}{1+x^2}$

5. $\dfrac{3}{\sqrt{(1-9x^2)}}$

6. $\dfrac{e^{\arctan x}}{1+x^2}$

7. $\dfrac{1}{(\arcsin x)\sqrt{(1-x^2)}}$

8. $\dfrac{-3x^2}{\sqrt{(1-x^6)}}$

Exercise 23d – p. 378

1. $\dfrac{1}{2x\sqrt{(1+\ln x)}}$

2. $-2x \sin (x^2 + 3)$

3. $(3x^2 - 1)\, e^{(x^3 - x)}$

4. $\dfrac{1}{x} \cos (\ln x)$

5. $-2x \tan (x^2)$

6. $4x\, e^{x^2}(1 + e^{x^2})$

7. $\dfrac{-\sin x \cos x}{\sqrt{(3 - \sin^2 x)}}$

8. $\dfrac{2 \sec^2 x \ln(\tan x)}{\tan x}$

9. $\dfrac{-x e^{\sqrt{(2-x^2)}}}{\sqrt{(2-x^2)}}$

10. $-4x \cos (x^2 + 1) \sin (x^2 + 1)$ or $-2x \sin \{2(x^2 + 1)\}$

Exercise 23e – p. 379

1. $e^{x^2}(\cos x + 2x \sin x)$

2. $-\left(\dfrac{x \sin 2x + \cos^2 x}{x^2}\right)$

3. $\ln \sin x + x \cot x$

4. $\dfrac{2x^2 \ln x - x^2 + 1}{x(\ln x)^2}$

5. $\dfrac{e^x(x^2 + x + 2)}{\sqrt{(x^2 + 2)}}$

6. $\dfrac{2 \cos x + x \sin x \ln x}{2x\sqrt{(\cos^3 x)}}$

7. $e^{\sin x}[1 + (x + 1) \cos x]$

8. $\dfrac{2x(\sin x - x \cos x)}{\sin^3 x}$

9. $\dfrac{e^{x^2}}{x}(1 + 2x^2 \ln x)$

Mixed Exercise 23 – p. 380

1. (a) $-4 \cos 4\theta$ (b) $1 + \sin \theta$ (c) $3 \sin^2 \theta \cos \theta + 3 \cos 3\theta$

2. (a) $3x^2 + e^x$ (b) $2e^{(2x + 3)}$ (c) $e^x(\sin x + \cos x)$

3. $-\dfrac{3}{x}$ (b) $-\dfrac{2}{x}$ (c) $\dfrac{1}{2x}$

4. (a) $3 \cos x + e^{-x}$ (b) $\dfrac{1}{2x} + \tfrac{1}{2} \sin x$ (c) $4x^3 + 4e^x - \dfrac{1}{x}$ (d) $-\tfrac{1}{2}(e^{-x} + x^{-3/2}) - \dfrac{1}{x}$

5. $1 + \dfrac{1}{x} + \ln x$

6. $3 \sin 6x$

7. $\tfrac{8}{3}(4x - 1)^{-1/3}$

8. $9 - 18\sqrt{x} + 8x$

9. $(x^4 + 4x^3 + 3)/(x + 1)^4$

10. $\dfrac{(x - 1)\ln(x - 1) - x \ln x}{x(x - 1)\{\ln(x - 1)\}^2}$

11. $-1/\sin x \cos x$ or $-2 \csc 2x$

12. $2x \sin x + x^2 \cos x$

13. $e^x(x - 2)/(x - 1)^2$

14. $2 \cos x/(1 - \sin x)^2$

15. $x(5x - 4)/2\sqrt{(x - 1)}$

16. $-2(1 - x)^2(2x + 1)$

17. $\dfrac{3}{2(x + 3)} - \dfrac{x}{x^2 + 2}$

18. $e^x\{(x - 5) \cos x - x \sin x\}/x^6$

19. $\cos^2 x (4 \cos^2 x - 3)$

20. $-\sin 2x\, e^{\cos^2 x}$

21. $e^{\arcsin x}/\sqrt{(1 - x^2)}$

22. $-3(\arccos x)^2/\sqrt{(1 - x^2)}$

23. $e^x/(1 + e^{2x})$

24. $a^x(1 + x \ln a)$

25. $2x/(x^2 + 1) \ln a$

26. (a) $x = \ln 3$ (b) $x = 1$ (not -1) (c) $x = \tfrac{1}{4}$

27. (a) 1   (b) $y - x = 1 - \frac{1}{2}\pi$
    (c) $y + x = 1 + \frac{1}{2}\pi$
28. (a) $1 + e$ (b) $y = x(1 + e)$
    (c) $y(1 + e) + x = (1 + e)^2 + 1$
29. (a) 2   (b) $y = 2x + 1$
    (c) $2y + x = 2$
30. (a) -1 (b) $x + y = 3$
    (c) $x - y + 1 = 0$
31. (a) $(\frac{1}{2}\pi, 0)$, min; $(\frac{3}{2}\pi, 2)$, max
    (b) $(\frac{1}{6}\pi, \{\frac{1}{12}\pi + \frac{1}{2}\sqrt{3}\})$, max;
       $(\frac{5}{6}\pi, \{\frac{5}{12}\pi - \frac{1}{2}\sqrt{3}\})$, min
    (c) $(\ln 3, \{3 - 3\ln 3\})$, min; only one
       turning point
32. (a) $(\frac{1}{6}\pi, \{\frac{1}{2}\pi - \sqrt{3}\})$ (b) $(1, -1)$

CHAPTER 24

Exercise 24a – p. 386

1. $2x + 2y \dfrac{dy}{dx} = 0$

2. $2x + y + (x + 2y) \dfrac{dy}{dx} = 0$

3. $2x + x \dfrac{dy}{dx} + y = 2y \dfrac{dy}{dx}$

4. $-\dfrac{1}{x^2} - \dfrac{1}{y^2} \dfrac{dy}{dx} = e^y \dfrac{dy}{dx}$

5. $-\dfrac{2}{x^3} - \dfrac{2}{y^3} \dfrac{dy}{dx} = 0$

6. $\dfrac{x}{2} - \dfrac{2y}{9} \dfrac{dy}{dx} = 0$

7. $\cos x + \cos y \dfrac{dy}{dx} = 0$

8. $\cos x \cos y - \sin x \sin y \dfrac{dy}{dx} = 0$

9. $e^y + xe^y \dfrac{dy}{dx} = 1$

10. $(1 + x) \dfrac{dy}{dx} = 2x - 1 - y$

11. $\dfrac{dy}{dx} = \pm \dfrac{1}{\sqrt{(2x + 1)}}$

12. $\dfrac{d^2 y}{dx^2} = \pm \dfrac{x}{\sqrt{(2 - x^2)^3}}$

13. $\pm \frac{1}{4}\sqrt{2}$
15. (a) $xx_1 - 3yy_1 = 2(y + y_1)$
    (b) $x(2x_1 + y_1) + y(2y_1 + x_1) = 6$
17. $3x + 12y - 7 = 0$

Exercise 24b – p. 389

1. $\dfrac{dy}{dx} = \dfrac{x - y}{x \ln x}$

2. $\dfrac{dy}{dx} \left(\dfrac{1}{y + 1} - \ln x \right) = \dfrac{y}{x}$

3. $\dfrac{1}{y} \dfrac{dy}{dx} = \ln(x + x^2) + \dfrac{1 + 2x}{1 + x}$

4. $\dfrac{-(x^2 + 8)}{(x + 2)^2 (x - 4)^2}$

5. $\dfrac{2x(3 - x)}{(x - 1)^2 (x - 3)^2}$

6. $-(1 - x)^4 (7x^2 - 2x + 10)$

7. $2x \sqrt{\dfrac{(x - 3)}{(x + 1)}}$

8. $\dfrac{x}{(x + 2)^2 (x^2 - 1)} \left\{ \dfrac{1}{x} - \dfrac{2}{x + 2} - \dfrac{2x}{x^2 - 1} \right\}$

   $= \dfrac{-(3x^3 + 2x^2 - x + 2)}{(x + 2)^3 (x^2 - 1)^2}$

9. $-\dfrac{y}{2} \left\{ \dfrac{9x^2 - 4x + 12}{(x^2 + 4)(3x - 2)} \right\}$

   $= \dfrac{-(9x^2 - 4x + 12)}{2\sqrt{(x^2 + 4)^3 (3x - 2)^3}}$

Exercise 24c – p. 396

1. (a) $\dfrac{1}{4t}$ (b) $-\tan\theta$ (c) $-\dfrac{4}{t^2}$

2. $\dfrac{dy}{dx} = 2t - t^2; \frac{3}{4}$

3. (a) $\frac{3}{2}t$ (b) $\frac{3}{2}\sqrt{x}$
   (c) $x = t^2 \Rightarrow t = \sqrt{x}$

4. (a) $x = 2y^2; \dfrac{dy}{dx} = \dfrac{1}{4y} = \dfrac{1}{4t}$

   (b) $x^2 + y^2 = 1; \dfrac{dy}{dx} = -\dfrac{x}{y} = -\tan\theta$

   (c) $xy = 4; \dfrac{dy}{dx} = -\dfrac{4}{x^2} = -\dfrac{4}{t^2}$

5. $(-\frac{1}{3}\sqrt{3}, \frac{2}{9}\sqrt{3})$, max; $(\frac{1}{3}\sqrt{3}, -\frac{2}{9}\sqrt{3})$, min
6. $(n\pi + \frac{1}{2}\pi, 1)$
7. $2x + y + 2 = 0$
8. $ty + t^4 = t^3 x + 1$
9. $ty = 2x + 2t^2$
10. $y = x; (-\frac{1}{2}\sqrt{2}, -\frac{1}{2}\sqrt{2})$

11. (a) $\dfrac{\cos t}{e^t}$ (b) $y = \sin(\ln x)$

    (c) $\dfrac{\cos(\ln x)}{x}$

12. $t^2y + x = 2t$; $(2t, 0)$, $\left(0, \dfrac{2}{t}\right)$; $A = 2$

13. $2y + tx = 8t + t^3$; $(8 + t^2, 0)$,
$(0, \frac{1}{2}t\{8 + t^2\})$; $A = |\frac{1}{4}t(8 + t^2)^2|$

Mixed Exercise 24 – p. 397

1. (a) $4y^3 \dfrac{dy}{dx}$ (b) $y^2 + 2xy \dfrac{dy}{dx}$

(c) $-\dfrac{1}{y^2} \dfrac{dy}{dx}$ (d) $\ln y + \dfrac{x}{y} \dfrac{dy}{dx}$

(e) $\cos y \dfrac{dy}{dx}$ (f) $e^y \dfrac{dy}{dx}$

(g) $\dfrac{dy}{dx} \cos x - y \sin x$

(h) $(\cos y - y \sin y) \dfrac{dy}{dx}$

2. $\dfrac{x}{2y}$

3. $-\dfrac{y^2}{x^2}$

4. $-\dfrac{2y}{3x}$

5. $-\dfrac{x^3(3x^3 + 6x^2 - 2x - 8)}{(1 + x)^4}$

6. $-\dfrac{(x - 1)^3(2x^2 - 3x - 15)}{x^6(x + 3)^2}$

7. $-\dfrac{y(y + 1)(3x + 2)}{x(x + 1)(y + 2)}$

8. $3t/2$

9. $\dfrac{t}{t + 1}$

10. $-\frac{3}{2} \cos \theta$

11. $-\dfrac{1}{t^2}$

12. $\dfrac{2y + 7}{2y - 2x + 3}$

13. $2t - t^2$

CHAPTER 25

Exercise 25a – p. 402

1. (a) $10.003\,333$; $10.003\,332$
(b) $2.083\,333$; $2.080\,084$
(c) $3.979\,167$; $3.979\,057$

2. (a) 0.857 (b) 0.515 (c) 0.719

3. $\left\{\dfrac{x}{1 + x} + \ln(1 + x)\right\}\delta x$; 0.75

4. $(\sec^2 x)\delta x$; $1 + \frac{1}{16}\pi$

5. 2.0125

6. $\frac{1}{8}\sqrt{2}$; $\frac{1}{8}a\sqrt{2}$

Exercise 25b – p. 405

1. 0.099 cm/s
2. 30 cm^3/s
3. 8 m^2/s
4. Decreasing at 0.126 cm/s
5. -2
6. $4a$ cm/minute

CONSOLIDATION D

Multiple Choice Exercise D - p. 411

1. C	**11.** A, D
2. C	**12.** B, C
3. A	**13.** C
4. A	**14.** T
5. D	**15.** F
6. D	**16.** F
7. A	**17.** F
8. C	**18.** T
9. B, C	**19.** T
10. A, B	**20.** T

Miscellaneous Exercise D – p. 413

1. (a) $\dfrac{1}{(2x + 1)^2}$ (b) $\dfrac{2x}{\sqrt{(1 - x^4)}}$

2. $45°, 90°, 135°$

3. (a) $4x \cos(2x^2)$ (b) $2^x \ln 2$

4. $0, \frac{1}{3}\pi, \frac{1}{2}\pi, \pi, \frac{3}{2}\pi, \frac{5}{3}\pi$

5. (a) $\dfrac{1 + \cos x + \sin x}{(1 + \cos x)^2}$

(b) $\dfrac{1}{1 - x^2}$

8. (a) $-\frac{1}{4}$ (b) 4

9. $2n\pi + \frac{1}{2}\pi$, $2n\pi - \frac{1}{6}\pi$

10. (b) 5.25 cm/s

11. (a) $80(4x - 1)^{19}$ (b) $\dfrac{1}{2\sqrt{x}(1 + x)}$

12. $(\frac{25}{4}a, -\frac{9}{4}a)$

13. $e^x\left\{\dfrac{2 \cos 2x}{1 + \sin 2x} + \ln(1 + \sin 2x)\right\}$

14. $x = 0, \pi, 2\pi$; $(\frac{1}{3}\pi, \frac{3}{4}\sqrt{3})$, $(\pi, 0)$,
$(\frac{5}{3}\pi, -\frac{3}{4}\sqrt{3})$

15. $\theta = 0, \frac{1}{10}\pi, \frac{3}{10}\pi, \frac{1}{3}\pi$

16. $x + y + 3 = 0$

17. $R = 5, \tan \alpha = \frac{4}{3}$
  (a) 2.1 rad, 2.9 rad
  (b) 0.3 rad, 0.9 rad, 2.4 rad, 4.5 rad
      A is $(0, 1)$; B is $(-2.2, 5)$;
      C is $(0.9, \frac{5}{6})$

18. 2

19. $2 \sin 2x \cos x$;
  $x = -\frac{1}{2}\pi, -\frac{1}{3}\pi, 0, \frac{1}{3}\pi, \frac{1}{2}\pi, \pi$;
  $x = \frac{1}{2}n\pi, 2n\pi \pm \frac{1}{3}\pi$

20. $\theta = -\frac{1}{4}\pi, \frac{5}{4}\pi$ (or $\frac{7}{4}\pi$ etc);
  $x + y + 2 = 0, x - y = 4$

21. $3x - y + (y - x)\dfrac{dy}{dx} = 4$; $(1, 3), (3, 1)$

23. $\dfrac{1}{48\sqrt{3}}; \frac{1}{48}a\sqrt{3}$

24. (a) $1 + \theta - \frac{1}{2}\theta^2$ (b) $\frac{1}{2}$
  (c) $\frac{1}{2}\theta$ (d) $\sqrt{2} - \theta$

25. 1600π cm^3/s

26. 0.002 cm/s; 2.16 cm^3/s

27. $A = -1, B = 11, C = 3$

CHAPTER 26

Exercise 26a – p. 424

1. (a) $(1, 5)$ (b) $(1.6, \frac{19}{2})$
  (c) $(5, 1)$ (d) $(11, -18)$

3. (a) $\dfrac{\sqrt{5}}{5}$ (b) $\frac{1}{5}$

  (c) $\dfrac{|ma - b + c|}{\sqrt{(m^2 + 1)}}$ (d) $\dfrac{3\sqrt{2}}{2}$

  (e) $\dfrac{|ax + by + c|}{\sqrt{(a^2 + b^2)}}$ (f) $\dfrac{|c|}{\sqrt{(a^2 + b^2)}}$

4. (a) opposite   (b) same
  (c) same

5. (a) $\frac{15}{16}$ (b) $\frac{5}{31}$
  (c) $\left|\dfrac{(a_1 b_2 - a_2 b_1)}{(a_1 a_2 + b_2 b_1)}\right|$

6. $\frac{3}{14}, \frac{9}{83}, \frac{3}{29}; \dfrac{9}{\sqrt{170}}, \dfrac{9}{\sqrt{41}}, \dfrac{3}{\sqrt{5}}$

7. $5y = x, 5x + y = 0$

8. (a) $(-1, 8)$ (b) $(-11, 10)$
  (c) $(-3, -14)$

9. $4X^2 + Y^2 - 14X + 12Y - 4XY + 11 = 0$

10. no

11. $\dfrac{|5X - 12Y + 3|}{13}, \dfrac{|3X + 4Y - 6|}{5}$;
  $14X + 112Y = 93$ and $64X - 8Y = 63$

12. $x + 2y = 7$

Exercise 26b – p. 434

1. (a) $\left(\dfrac{1}{y}\right) = a(x) + b$
  (b) $(y^2 - x) = b(y) - a$
  (c) $(y) = a(e^x/y) + b$
  (d) $(x) = (y^2 + y) - k; m = 1$
  (e) $(\ln y) = (n + 2)(\ln x) + \ln a$
  (f) $(x) = a(\ln y) - k$
  There are other alternatives.

2. $a = 2, b = -4$ (exactly)

3. $a = 6, b = 4$

4. $a = 0.5, b = -2$

5. $a = 30, b = 2$

6. $a = 2, b = \frac{1}{2}$

7. $a = 3, b = -2$ (or $a = -2, b = 3$)

8. $k = 4, n = 0.07$

9. $k = 5500, n = 1.5$

10. The 'incorrect' values are -0.26 and
  -0.40; the estimated correct values are
  -0.50 and -1.00

CHAPTER 27

Exercise 27a – p. 438

1. $y^2 = 2y + 12x - 13$

2. $x + y = 4$

3. $8x^2 + 9y^2 - 20x = 28$

4. $11y = 3x$ and $99x + 27y + 130 = 0$

5. $x^2 + y^2 - 6x - 10y + 30 = 0$

6. $4x - 3y = 26$ and $4x - 3y + 24 = 0$

7. $x^2 + y^2 = 1$

Exercise 27b – p. 441

1. (a) $x^2 + y^2 - 2x - 4y = 4$
  (b) $x^2 + y^2 - 8y + 15 = 0$
  (c) $x^2 + y^2 + 6x + 14y + 54 = 0$
  (d) $x^2 + y^2 - 8x - 10y + 32 = 0$

2. (a) $(-4, 1)$; 5
  (b) $(-\frac{1}{2}, -\frac{3}{2})$; $3\sqrt{2}/2$
  (c) $(-3, 0)$; $\sqrt{14}$
  (d) $(\frac{3}{4}, -\frac{1}{2})$; $\sqrt{5}/4$
  (e) $(0, 0)$; 2
  (f) $(2, -3)$; 3
  (g) $(1, 3)$; 3
  (h) $(-1, \frac{1}{2})$; $\sqrt{69}/6$

3. (a) and (f)

Exercise 27c – p. 448

1. (a) yes   (b) yes   (c) no
  (d) yes
2. (a) $3y + 4x = 23$
  (b) $4y = x + 22$
  (c) $3y = 2x + 25$
3. $2x^2 + 2y^2 - 15x - 24y + 77 = 0$
4. $x^2 + y^2 - 8x + 6y = 0$
5. $x^2 + y^2 - 8x - 6y + 17 = 0$
6. $x^2 + y^2 - 4x - 14y - 116 = 0$
7. $x^2 + y^2 - 6y = 0$
8. $x^2 + y^2 + 4x + 4y + 4 = 0$
  or $196(x^2 + y^2) + 84(x + y) + 9 = 0$
9. $y = 0, 8y = 15x$
10. $x + 2y = 0$
11. $2x + y - 11 = 0, 2x + y + 9 = 0$
12. $(-\frac{4}{3}, \frac{2}{3}); 4\sqrt{5}/3$
13. (a) and (c)
14. $9 \pm 6\sqrt{5}$
15. $2mac = a^2 - c^2$

Exercise 27d – p. 453

1. $3x^2 - y^2 - 60x + 252 = 0$; hyperbola
2. $16y = x^2$; parabola
3. $3x^2 + 4y^2 = 48$; ellipse
4. (a) parabola   (b) circle
  (c) rectangular hyperbola
  (d) hyperbola   (e) parabola
  (f) ellipse
5.

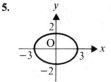

    $(3, 0), (-3, 0)$ and $(0, 2), (0, -2)$

6.

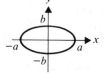

7. (a) $(\pm 4, 0), (0, \pm 2); (\pm 4, 0)$
  (b) they touch at $(\pm 4, 0)$

Exercise 27e – p. 458

1. (a)

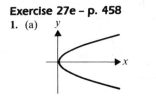

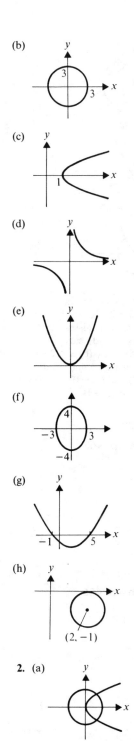

(b)

(c)

(d)

(e)

(f)

(g)

(h) $(2, -1)$

2. (a)

(b)

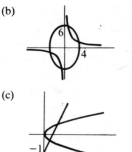

(c)

3.

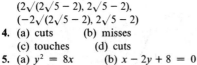

$(2\sqrt{(2\sqrt{5}-2)}, 2\sqrt{5}-2)$,
$(-2\sqrt{(2\sqrt{5}-2)}, 2\sqrt{5}-2)$
4. (a) cuts   (b) misses
     (c) touches   (d) cuts
5. (a) $y^2 = 8x$ (b) $x - 2y + 8 = 0$
     (c) $2x - y(p + q) + 4pq = 0$
     (d) (18, 12) and (2, −4)   (e) 2
     (f) (2, 4) and (2, −4)   (g) (8, 8)

CHAPTER 28

Exercise 28a – p. 462
1. $\frac{1}{6}x^6 + K$
2. $-\frac{1}{4}x^{-4} + K$
3. $\frac{4}{5}x^{5/4}$
4. $-\frac{1}{2}x^{-2}$
5. $-\frac{2}{3}x^{-3/2}$
6. $2x^{1/2}$
7. $\frac{1}{2}x^2$
8. $\frac{3}{2}x^{2/3}$

Exercise 28b – p. 466
1. 4
2. $\frac{2}{7}(8\sqrt{2}, -1)$
3. $26\frac{2}{3}$
4. $12\frac{2}{3}$
5. 15
6. −2
7. $\frac{1}{2}$
8. 6
9. $6\frac{1}{7}$
10. 15

Exercise 28c – p. 468
Answers in square units.
1. $5\frac{1}{3}$
2. $12\frac{2}{3}$
3. $2\frac{2}{3}$
4. $13\frac{1}{2}$
5. $5\frac{1}{3}$
6. 60
7. $5\frac{1}{3}$
8. $4\frac{7}{8}$
9. 24

Exercise 28d – p. 470
1. $\frac{4}{3}$
2. $15\frac{1}{4}$
3. $\frac{1}{3}$
4.

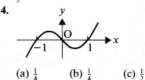

(a) $\frac{1}{4}$ (b) $\frac{1}{4}$ (c) $\frac{1}{2}$

5.

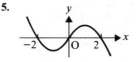

(a) 4   (b) 4   (c) 8
6. (a) −2   (b) 2   (c) 0

Exercise 28e – p. 471
1. (a) $49\frac{1}{2}$ (b) 2   (c) 3
2. 36
3. $2\frac{1}{3}$
4. $5\frac{1}{3}$
5. $4\frac{1}{2}$
6. (a) $42\frac{2}{3}$ (v) $42\frac{2}{3}$
7. $A = \int_0^1 x \, dy$ $B = \int_0^1 y \, dx$
    $A + B = 1$

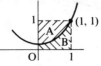

Exercise 28f – p. 475

1. (a) (i) 24 (ii) 22
   (b) (i) $21\frac{1}{3}$ (ii) $21\frac{1}{3}$
2. (a) (i) 0.806 (ii) 0.705
   (b) (i) 0.704 (ii) 0.671
3. (a) (i) 1.462 (ii) 1.625
   (b) (i) 1.625 (ii) 1.679
4. (a) (i) 1.243 (ii) 1.282
   (b) (i) 1.290 (ii) 1.295

5.

22	0.705
21.33	0.671
21.33	0.667

Simpson's rule is more accurate each time and is exact for x^2 because this is a parabola.

Mixed Exercise 28 – p. 476

1. $\frac{1}{3}x^3 + \frac{1}{x} + K$
2. $\frac{2}{9}(3x + 7)^{3/2} + K$
3. $\frac{2}{3}x^{3/2} + 2x^{1/2} + K = \frac{2}{3}\sqrt{x}(x + 3) + K$
4. $-\frac{1}{4(4x - 3)} + K$
5. $\frac{1}{4}x^4 - \frac{1}{2(1 - x)^2} + K$
6. $\frac{2}{5}\sqrt{x}(x^2 - 5) + K$
7. $\frac{1}{5}$
8. 18
9. $33\frac{3}{4}$
10. $\frac{3}{4}$
11. $10\frac{2}{3}$
12. $\frac{1}{2}$
13. (a) 4 square units
    (b) $-4\frac{1}{2}$
14. (a) $27\frac{1}{2}$
    (b) $27\frac{1}{2}$
    (c) (a) is exact because the area is that of a trapezium.

CHAPTER 29

All indefinite integrals in this chapter require the term $+K$.

Exercise 29a – p. 478

1. $\frac{1}{4}e^{4x}$
2. $-4e^{-x}$
3. $\frac{1}{3}e^{(3x - 2)}$
4. $-\frac{2}{5}e^{(1 - 5x)}$
5. $-3e^{-2x}$

6. $5e^{(x - 3)}$
7. $2e^{(x/2 + 2)}$
8. $\frac{2^x}{\ln 2}$
9. $\frac{4^{(2 + x)}}{\ln 4}$
10. $\frac{1}{2}e^{2x} - \frac{1}{2e^{2x}}$
11. $\frac{a^{(1 - 2x)}}{-2\ln a}$
12. $\frac{2^x}{\ln 2} + \frac{1}{3}x^3$
13. $\frac{1}{2}\{e^4 - 1\}$
14. $2\{e^2 - 1\}$
15. $1 - \frac{1}{e}$
16. $1 - e^2$

Exercise 29b – p. 481

Answers can be expressed in other forms also.

1. (a) $\frac{1}{2}\ln|x| + K$
   (b) $\frac{1}{2}\ln\{A|x|\}$
2. (a) $4\ln|x| + K$
   (b) $4\ln\{A|x|\}$ or $\ln(Ax^4)$
3. (a) $\frac{1}{3}\ln|3x + 1| + K$
   (b) $\frac{1}{3}\ln A|3x + 1|$ or $\ln A|\sqrt[3]{(3x + 1)}|$
4. (a) $-\frac{3}{2}\ln|1 - 2x| + K$
   (b) $-\frac{3}{2}\ln A|1 - 2x|$
   or $\ln A|(1 - 2x)^{-3/2}|$
5. (a) $2\ln|2 + 3x| + K$
   (b) $\ln A(2 + 3x)^2$
6. (a) $-\frac{3}{2}\ln|4 - 2x| + K$
   (b) $\ln A|(4 - 2x)^{-3/2}|$
   or $\ln\frac{A}{|(4x - 2x)^{3/2}|}$
   (or each of these results using $\ln|2 - x|$)
7. (a) $-4\ln|1 - x| + K$
   (b) $\ln\frac{A}{(1 - x)^4}$
8. (a) $-\frac{5}{7}\ln|6 - 7x| + K$
   (b) $\ln\frac{A}{|(6 - 7x)^{5/7}|}$
9. $3\ln 2$
10. $\frac{1}{2}\ln 2 = \ln\sqrt{2}$
11. $2\ln 2 = \ln 4$
12. $\ln 2$

Exercise 29c – p. 482

1. $-\frac{1}{2}\cos 2x$
2. $\frac{1}{7}\sin 7x$
3. $\frac{1}{4}\tan 4x$
4. $-\cos\left(\frac{1}{4}\pi + x\right)$
5. $\frac{3}{4}\sin\left(4x - \frac{1}{2}\pi\right)$
6. $\frac{1}{2}\tan\left(\frac{1}{3}\pi + 2x\right)$
7. $-\frac{1}{4}\cot 4x$
8. $-\frac{2}{3}\cos(3x - a)$
9. $-10\sin\left(a - \frac{1}{2}x\right)$
10. $\frac{5}{4}\sec 4x$
11. $\frac{1}{3}\sin 3x - \sin x$
12. $\frac{1}{2}\tan 2x + \frac{1}{4}\cot 4x$
13. $\frac{1}{3}$
14. $-\frac{1}{4}$
15. 0
16. $\frac{1}{2}$

Exercise 29d – p. 484

1. $\arcsin x$
2. $\arctan\left(\frac{1}{2}x\right)$
3. $\arcsin\left(\frac{1}{2}x\right)$
4. $3\arctan x$
5. $\frac{5}{3}\arctan\left(\frac{1}{3}x\right)$
6. $\arcsin\left(\frac{1}{3}x\right)$
7. $\frac{1}{4}\arctan\left(\frac{1}{4}x\right)$
8. $5\arcsin(x/\sqrt{2})$

Exercise 29e – p. 484

1. $\frac{1}{2}\cos\left(\frac{1}{2}\pi - 2x\right)$
2. $\frac{1}{4}e^{(4x-1)}$
3. $\frac{1}{7}\tan 7x$
4. $\frac{1}{2}\ln|2x - 3|$
5. $\sqrt{(2x - 3)}$
6. $-1/\{3(3x - 2)\}$
7. $5^x/\ln 5$
8. $-2\operatorname{cosec}\frac{1}{2}x$
9. $\frac{1}{9}(3x - 5)^3$
10. $\frac{1}{4}e^{(4x-5)}$
11. $\frac{1}{6}(4x - 5)^{3/2}$
12. $-\frac{1}{3}\cot 3x$
13. $-\frac{3}{2}\ln|1 - x|$
14. $10^{(x+1)}/\ln 10$
15. $\frac{1}{3}\sin\left(3x - \frac{1}{3}\pi\right)$
16. $\frac{2}{3}\sqrt{2}$
17. $2e(e - 1)$
18. $-\frac{1}{2}$

Exercise 29f – p. 488

1. e^{x^4}
2. $-e^{\cos x}$
3. $e^{\tan x}$
4. $e^{x^2 + x}$
5. $e^{(1 - \cot x)}$
6. $e^{(x + \sin x)}$
7. $e^{(1 + x^2)}$
8. $e^{(x^3 - 2)}$
9. $\frac{1}{10}(x^2 - 3)^5$
10. $-\frac{1}{3}(1 - x^2)^{3/2}$
11. $\frac{1}{6}(\sin 2x + 3)^3$
12. $-\frac{1}{6}(1 - x^3)^2$
13. $\frac{2}{3}(1 + e^x)^{3/2}$
14. $\frac{1}{5}\sin^5 x$
15. $\frac{1}{4}\tan^4 x$
16. $\dfrac{1}{3(n + 1)}(1 + x^{n+1})^3$
17. $-\frac{1}{3}\cot^3 x$
18. $\frac{4}{9}(1 + x^{3/2})^{3/2}$
19. $\frac{1}{12}(x^4 + 4)^3$
20. $-\frac{1}{4}(1 - e^x)^4$
21. $\frac{2}{3}(1 - \cos\theta)^{3/2}$
22. $\frac{1}{3}(x^2 + 2x + 3)^{3/2}$
23. $\frac{1}{2}e^{(x^2 + 1)}$
24. $\frac{1}{2}(1 + \tan x)^2$

Exercise 29g – p. 490

1. $\frac{1}{2}(e - 1)$
2. $\frac{1}{5}$
3. $\frac{1}{2}(\ln 2)^2$
4. $\dfrac{7^5}{15}$
5. $e - 1$
6. 9
7. $\frac{1}{2}(e^3 - 1)$
8. $\frac{13}{24}$
9. $\frac{1}{3}(\ln 3)^3$
10. $\frac{7}{3}$

Exercise 29h – p. 495

1. $x\sin x + \cos x$
2. $e^x(x^2 - 2x + 2)$
3. $\frac{1}{16}x^4(4\ln|3x| - 1)$
4. $-e^{-x}(x + 1)$
5. $3(\sin x - x\cos x)$
6. $\frac{1}{5}e^x(\sin 2x - 2\cos 2x)$
7. $\frac{1}{5}e^{2x}(\sin x + 2\cos x)$

8. $\frac{1}{32}e^{4x}(8x^2 - 4x + 1)$

9. $-\frac{1}{2}e^{-x}(\cos x + \sin x)$

10. $x(\ln|2x| - 1)$

11. $x\,e^x$

12. $\frac{1}{72}(8x - 1)(x + 1)^8$

13. $\sin(x + \frac{1}{6}\pi) - x\cos(x + \frac{1}{6}\pi)$

14. $\dfrac{1}{n^2}(\cos nx + nx\sin nx)$

15. $\dfrac{x^{n+1}}{(n+1)^2}[(n+1)\ln|x| - 1]$

16. $\frac{3}{4}(2x\sin 2x + \cos 2x)$

17. $\frac{1}{5}e^x(\sin 2x - 2\cos 2x)$

18. $(2 - x^2)\cos x + 2x\sin x$

19. $\dfrac{e^{ax}}{a^2 + b^2}(a\sin bx - b\cos bx)$

20. $\frac{1}{3}\sin\theta(3\cos^2\theta + 2\sin^2\theta)$

21. $\frac{1}{2}e^{x^2 - 2x + 4}$

22. $(x^2 + 1)e^x$

23. $-\frac{1}{4}(4 + \cos x)^4$

24. $e^{\sin x}$

25. $\frac{2}{15}\sqrt{(1 + x^5)^3}$

26. $\frac{1}{5}(e^x + 2)^5$

27. $\frac{1}{4}e^{2x-1}(2x - 1)$

28. $-\frac{1}{20}(1 - x^2)^{10}$

29. $\frac{1}{6}\sin^6 x$

Exercise 29i – p. 497

1. 1

2. $\frac{32}{3}\ln 2 - \frac{7}{4}$

3. e

4. $-\frac{1}{2}(e^\pi + 1)$

5. $\frac{16}{15}$

6. $\frac{1}{4}\pi^2 - 2$

7. $\frac{1}{2}\pi - 1$

8. $e - 2$

9. $\frac{1}{12}\pi(4\sqrt{3} - 3) - \ln\sqrt{2}$

Mixed Exercise 29 – p. 498

1. $\frac{1}{4}e^{2x}(2x^2 - 2x + 1)$

2. e^{x^2}

3. $\frac{1}{6}(3\tan x - 4)^2$

4. $\frac{1}{4}(x + 1)^2\{2\ln(x + 1) - 1\}$

5. $\frac{1}{4}\tan^4 x$

6. $(x^2 - 2)\sin x + 2x\cos x$

7. $-e^{\cos x}$

8. $\frac{1}{288}(2x + 3)^8(16x - 3)$

9. $-\frac{1}{2}e^{(1-x)^2}$

10. $\frac{1}{4}e^{(2x-1)}(2x - 1)$

11. $\frac{1}{6}\sin^6 x$

12. $-\frac{1}{4}(4 + \cos x)^4$

13. $\frac{1}{2}e^{(x^2 - 2x + 3)}$

14. $-\frac{1}{30}(1 - x^3)^{10}$

15. $\frac{1}{3}(e^9 - e^3)$

16. $\frac{1}{4}$

17. $\ln\frac{1}{2}$

18. 1

19. $\frac{1}{9}(e^3 - 1)$

20. $\frac{1}{8}(\pi - 2)$

21. $\frac{1}{2}(\ln 2)^2$

22. $\frac{1}{3}\ln 2^8 - \frac{7}{9}$

CHAPTER 30

Exercise 30a – p. 502

1. (a) 3, 2   (b) $-\frac{7}{4}, -\frac{3}{4}$
(c) 4, −4   (d) −1, −8
(e) k, k^2 (f) $(a + 2)/a, -1$

2. (a) $x^2 - 3x + 4 = 0$
(b) $2x^2 + 4x + 1 = 0$
(c) $15x^2 - 5x - 6 = 0$
(d) $4x^2 + x = 0$
(e) $x^2 - ax + a^2 = 0$
(f) $x^2 + (k + 1)x + k^2 - 3 = 0$
(g) $abx^2 - b^2x + ac^2 = 0$

3. (a) $\frac{4}{5}$ (b) $5\frac{1}{2}$ (c) −1
(d) 5   (e) −6   (f) $-\frac{2}{5}$

4. (a) $x^2 - 6x + 11 = 0$
(b) $3x^2 - 2x + 1 = 0$
(c) $x^2 + 2x + 9 = 0$
(d) $3x^2 + 2x + 3 = 0$

Exercise 30b – p. 504

1. (a) Q: $x + 1$, R: $-6x + 3$
(b) Q: $x^3 - x^2 - 4x + 4$, R: −2
(c) Q: $2x - 4$, R: $5x - 5$
(d) Q: $3x^2 + 6x + 12$, R: 19
(e) Q: x^2, R: $-6x^2 + 1$

2. (a) $1 + \dfrac{3}{x + 1}$

(b) $2 + \dfrac{4}{x - 2}$

(c) $1 + \dfrac{4}{x^2 - 1}$

(d) $x + 2 + \dfrac{4}{x - 2}$

(e) $x + 7 + \dfrac{28}{x - 4}$

(f) $1 - \dfrac{x + 4}{x(x + 1)}$

Exercise 30c – p. 508

1. (a) $\dfrac{1}{x - 1} - \dfrac{1}{x + 1}$

(b) $\dfrac{1}{x - 2} - \dfrac{1}{x + 1}$

(c) $\dfrac{1}{3(x - 3)} - \dfrac{1}{3x}$

(d) $\dfrac{1}{x - 1} - \dfrac{1}{x + 3}$

(e) $\dfrac{1}{2(x - 1)} - \dfrac{1}{2(x + 1)}$

(f) $\dfrac{1}{2x - 1} - \dfrac{1}{2x + 1}$

2. (a) $\dfrac{1}{x - 1} - \dfrac{x + 1}{x^2 + 1}$

(b) $\dfrac{1}{x} - \dfrac{x}{2x^2 + 1}$

(c) $\dfrac{3}{2x} - \dfrac{x}{2(x^2 + 2)}$

(d) $\dfrac{22}{19(x - 3)} + \dfrac{1 - 6x}{19(2x^2 + 1)}$

(e) $\dfrac{3}{5(x + 2)} - \dfrac{3}{5(2x + 1)} + \dfrac{x - 1}{5(x^2 + 1)}$

(f) $\dfrac{1}{x} - \dfrac{6x + 3}{2x^2 - 1} + \dfrac{2}{x - 1}$

(g) $\dfrac{1}{x - 1} - \dfrac{1}{x - 2} + \dfrac{2}{(x - 2)^2}$

(h) $\dfrac{2}{x} - \dfrac{1}{x^2} - \dfrac{3}{2x + 1}$

(i) $\dfrac{3}{x} - \dfrac{9}{3x - 1} + \dfrac{9}{(3x - 1)^2}$

(j) $1 + \dfrac{1}{2(x - 1)} - \dfrac{1}{2(x + 1)}$

(k) $1 - \dfrac{7}{4(x + 3)} - \dfrac{1}{4(x - 1)}$

(l) $x + \dfrac{2}{x - 1} - \dfrac{1}{x + 1}$

Exercise 30d – p. 511

1. (a) 3   (b) 18   (c) 47

(d) $\frac{35}{16}$ (e) $-\frac{16}{27}$

(f) $a^3 - 2a^2 + 6$ (g) $c^2 - ac + b$

(h) $\dfrac{1}{a^4} - \dfrac{2}{a} + 1$

2. (a) yes   (b) no   (c) no

(d) yes   (e) no   (f) yes

3. (a) $(x - 1)(x + 2)(x + 1)$

(b) $(x - 2)(x^2 + x + 1)$

(c) $(x - 1)(x + 1)(x^2 + 1)$

(d) $(x - 2)(x + 2)(x^2 + x + 1)$

(e) $(2x - 1)(x^2 + 1)$

(f) $(3x - 1)(9x^2 + 3x + 1)$

(g) $(x + a)(x^2 - ax + a^2)$

(h) $(x - y)(x^2 + xy + y^2)$

4. -7

5. 5

6. -3

7. 1

Exercise 30e – p. 513

1. $(x - 1)(2x - 1)(x + 1)$;

$-1 < x < \frac{1}{2}, x > 1$

2. $f(x) = (x - 2)(x^2 + x + 1) \Rightarrow f(x) = 0$

only when $x = 2$; $x < 2$

3. 8

4. $x = \pm 1, \pm 2$

5. $(x - 1)(x + 1)(x - 2)(x - 3)$

6. (a) $p = 11, q = -5$ (b) 3

Exercise 30f – p. 517

1. touch at $(1, 2)$

2. $(1, 1)$ and $(-5, 4)$

3. no intersection

4. $(0, 2)$ and $(\frac{8}{5}, \frac{14}{5})$

5. $(1, 0)$ and $(2, 0)$

6. $(0, 0)$, $(-3, 0)$ and $(-2, 0)$

7. touch at $(1, 0)$ and $(2, 0)$

8. touch and cross at $(-3, 0)$; $(-2, 0)$

9. touch at $(0, 0)$

10. $k = 8$

11. $k = \frac{1}{4}$

12. $k = \pm 2\sqrt{19}$

13. $(\frac{1}{2}, 0)$

14. $(1, 2)$ and $(1, -2)$

15. touch at $(-1, -2)$; cut at $(1, 2)$ and $(4, \frac{1}{2})$

16. $(0, 0)$ and $(\frac{2}{3}, 2)$

17. (a) $\pm 2\sqrt{3}$ (b) $-2\sqrt{3} < \lambda < 2\sqrt{3}$

(c) $\lambda < -2\sqrt{3}, \lambda > 2\sqrt{3}$

18.

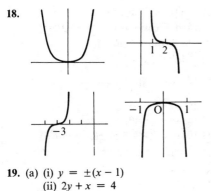

19. (a) (i) $y = \pm(x - 1)$
   (ii) $2y + x = 4$
   (b) (i) $y = 0, y = 36(1 - x)$
   (ii) $2y + x = \pm 6\sqrt{2}$
   (c) (i) $3y = 2(x - 1), y = 0$
   (ii) $8y + 4x + 3 = 0$

CHAPTER 31

All indefinite integrals in this chapter require the addition of a constant of integration.

Exercise 31a – p. 522

1. $\ln(4 + \sin x)$
2. $\frac{1}{3}\ln|3e^x - 1|$
3. $\dfrac{1}{4(1 - x^2)^2}$
4. $\dfrac{1}{2\cos^2 x}$
5. $\frac{1}{4}\ln(1 + x^4)$
6. $\ln|x^2 + 3x - 4|$
7. $\frac{2}{3}\sqrt{(2 + x^3)}$
8. $\dfrac{-1}{\sin x - 2}$
9. $\ln|\ln x|$
10. $\dfrac{-1}{5\sin^5 x}$
11. $\dfrac{1}{3\cot^3 x}$
12. $-2\sqrt{(1 - e^x)}$
13. $\frac{1}{6}\ln|3x^2 - 6x + 1|$
14. $\dfrac{-1}{(n - 1)\sin^{n-1}x}$ $(n \neq 1)$
15. $\dfrac{1}{(n - 1)\cos^{(n-1)}x}$ $(n \neq 1)$
16. $\ln|4 + \sec x|$

17. $\dfrac{1}{2(1 - \tan x)^2}$
18. $\dfrac{1}{(3 + \cos x)}$
19. $\ln|\sec x + \tan x|$
20. $-\ln|\cosec x + \cot x|$
21. $\ln 3$
22. $\ln\sqrt{2}$
23. $\frac{1}{18} - \frac{1}{128}$
24. $\dfrac{e - 1}{2(e + 1)}$
25. 0
26. $\dfrac{1}{\ln 4}$

Exercise 31b – p. 525

1. $2\ln\left|\dfrac{x}{x + 1}\right|$
2. $\ln\left|\dfrac{x - 2}{x + 2}\right|$
3. $\frac{1}{2}\ln|x^2 - 1|$
4. $\frac{1}{2}\ln\left|\dfrac{(x + 2)^3}{x}\right|$
5. $\ln\dfrac{(x - 3)^2}{|x - 2|}$
6. $\frac{1}{2}\ln\dfrac{|x^2 - 1|}{x^2}$
7. $x - \ln|x + 1|$
8. $x + 4\ln|x|$
9. $x - 4\ln|x + 4|$
10. $\ln\dfrac{|1 - x|}{x^4}$
11. $x - \frac{1}{2}\ln\left|\dfrac{x + 1}{x - 1}\right|$
12. $x + \ln\dfrac{|x + 1|}{(x + 2)^4}$
13. $\frac{1}{2}\ln|x^2 - 1|$
14. $\dfrac{-1}{x^2 - 1}$
15. $\ln\left|\dfrac{x - 1}{x + 1}\right|$
16. $\ln|x^2 - 5x + 6|$
17. $\ln\dfrac{(x - 3)^6}{(x - 2)^4}$
18. $\ln\left|\dfrac{(x - 3)^3}{x - 2}\right|$
19. $4 + \ln 5$

20. $\ln \frac{1}{6}$

21. $\frac{1}{2} \ln \frac{12}{5}$

22. $\ln \frac{5}{3}$

23. $\frac{5}{36}$

24. $1 - \frac{3}{2} \ln \frac{7}{5}$

Exercise 31c – p. 526

1. $\dfrac{2}{x-2} - \dfrac{2}{x-1}$; $\dfrac{-2}{(x-2)^2} + \dfrac{2}{(x-1)^2}$;

$\dfrac{4}{(x-2)^3} - \dfrac{4}{(x-1)^3}$;

2. $\dfrac{\frac{9}{5}}{x-3} - \dfrac{\frac{3}{5}}{2x-1}$;

$\dfrac{6}{5(2x-1)^2} - \dfrac{9}{5(x-3)^2}$;

$\dfrac{-24}{5(2x-1)^3} + \dfrac{18}{5(x-3)^3}$;

3. $\dfrac{\frac{2}{3}}{x-4} + \dfrac{\frac{1}{3}}{x+2}$;

$\dfrac{-1}{3(x+2)^2} - \dfrac{2}{3(x-4)^2}$;

$\dfrac{2}{3(x+2)^3} + \dfrac{4}{3(x-4)^3}$

4. $\dfrac{1}{x-3} - \dfrac{1}{x+2}$; $\dfrac{1}{(x+2)^2} - \dfrac{1}{(x-3)^2}$;

$\dfrac{-2}{(x+2)^3} + \dfrac{2}{(x-3)^3}$;

5. $\dfrac{3}{2x+3} - \dfrac{1}{x+1}$;

$\dfrac{-6}{(2x+3)^2} + \dfrac{1}{(x+1)^2}$;

$\dfrac{24}{(2x+3)^3} - \dfrac{2}{(x+1)^3}$

6. $\dfrac{\frac{3}{2}}{x-1} - \dfrac{\frac{9}{2}}{3x-1}$;

$\dfrac{27}{2(3x-1)^2} - \dfrac{3}{2(x-1)^2}$;

$\dfrac{-81}{(3x-1)^3} + \dfrac{3}{(x-1)^3}$

Exercise 31d – p. 530

1. $\frac{1}{4}(2x + \sin 2x)$

2. $\sin x - \frac{1}{3} \sin^3 x$

3. $-\frac{1}{15} \cos x (15 - 10 \cos^2 x + 3 \cos^4 x)$

4. $\tan x - x$

5. $\frac{1}{32}\{12x - 8 \sin 2x + \sin 4x\}$

6. $\frac{1}{2} \tan^2 x - \ln |\sec x|$

7. $\frac{1}{32}\{12x + 8 \sin 2x + \sin 4x\}$

8. $\frac{1}{3} \cos x (\cos^2 x - 3)$

9. $\frac{1}{15} \sin^3 \theta (5 - 3 \sin^2 \theta)$

10. $(\sin^{11} \theta)(\frac{1}{11} - \frac{1}{13} \sin^2 \theta)$

11. $(\sin^{(n+1)} \theta)\left(\dfrac{1}{n+1} - \dfrac{1}{n+3} \sin^2 \theta\right)$

$(n \neq -1 \text{ or } -3)$

12. $\frac{1}{32}(4\theta - \sin 4\theta)$

13. $\frac{1}{15}(10 \sin 3\theta - 3 \sin 5\theta - 15 \sin \theta)$

14. $\frac{1}{15} \tan^3 \theta (3 \tan^2 \theta + 5)$

15. $-\frac{1}{7}(\cos 7t + 7 \cos t)$

16. $\frac{1}{21}(3 \sin 7t + 7 \sin 3t)$

17. $\frac{1}{16}(2 \cos 4t - \cos 8t)$

18. $\frac{1}{8}(2 \sin 2t - \sin 4t)$

19. $\left(\dfrac{-1}{n+m}\right) \cos(n+m)t$

$- \left(\dfrac{1}{n-m}\right) \cos(n-m)t$

$(n^2 \neq m^2)$

20. $\dfrac{1}{2(n+m)} \sin(n+m)t$

$+ \dfrac{1}{2(n-m)} \sin(n-m)t$

$(n^2 \neq m^2)$

21. $\frac{1}{12}$

22. $\frac{13}{15} - \frac{1}{4}\pi$

23. $\frac{1}{5}(2\sqrt{3} - 3)$

24. $\frac{1}{16}\sqrt{3}$

CHAPTER 32

All indefinite integrals require the term $+K$.

Exercise 32a – p. 522

1. $\frac{1}{21}(x+3)^6(3x+2)$

2. $\frac{1}{2} \arctan \dfrac{x}{2}$

3. $-\frac{2}{3}(x+6)\sqrt{(3-x)}$

4. $\frac{2}{15}(3x-2)(x+1)^{3/2}$

5. $\dfrac{1-5x}{10(x-3)^5}$

6. $\ln |x + \sqrt{(1+x^2)}|$

7. $\frac{4}{135}(9x+8)(3x-4)^{3/2}$

8. $\frac{3}{10} \arctan \frac{2}{3}x$

9. $\ln |x + 2 + \sqrt{(x^2 + 4x + 3)}|$

10. $-\frac{1}{36}(8x + 1)(1 - x)^8$

11. $\frac{1}{2}\arcsin 2x$

12. $\dfrac{5 + 4x}{12(4 - x)^4}$

37. $\dfrac{2x - 1}{10(3 - x)^6}$

38. $\frac{1}{3}\tan^3 x$

Exercise 32b – p. 537

1. $\frac{1}{2}e^{2x + 3}$

2. $\frac{1}{6}(2x^2 - 5)^{3/2}$

3. $\frac{1}{12}(6x - \sin 6x)$

4. $-\frac{1}{2}e^{-x^2}$

5. $-\frac{1}{8}(\cos 4\theta + 2\cos 2\theta)$

6. $\frac{1}{110}(10u - 7)(u + 7)^{10}$

7. $\dfrac{1}{12(x^3 + 9)^4}$

8. $\frac{1}{2}\ln|1 - \cos 2y|$ $(y \neq n\pi)$

9. $\frac{1}{2}\ln|2x + 7|$

10. $\arcsin u$

11. $-\frac{2}{9}(1 + \cos 3x)^{3/2}$

12. $\frac{1}{16}(\sin 4x - 4x\cos 4x)$

13. $\frac{1}{2}\ln|x^2 + 4x - 5|$

14. $\frac{1}{2}\ln|x^2 + 4x + 5|$

15. $-\frac{1}{4}(x^2 + 4x - 5)^{-2}$

16. $-(9 - y^2)^{3/2}$

17. $\frac{1}{13}e^{2x}(2\cos 3x + 3\sin 3x)$

18. $x(\ln|5x| - 1)$

19. $\frac{1}{6}\sin 2x(3 - \sin^2 2x)$

20. $-e^{\cot x}$

21. $-2\sqrt{(7 + \cos y)}$

22. $e^x(x^2 - 2x + 2)$

23. $\frac{1}{2}\ln|x^2 - 4|$

24. $x + \ln\left|\dfrac{x - 2}{x + 2}\right|$

25. $\frac{1}{4}\ln\left|\dfrac{x - 2}{x + 2}\right|$

26. $\frac{1}{30}(3\sin 5x + 5\sin 3x)$

27. $-\frac{1}{30}\cos 2\theta(15 - 10\cos^2 2\theta + 3\cos^4 2\theta)$

28. $\frac{1}{15}\cos^3 u(3\cos^2 u - 5)$

29. $\tan\theta - \theta$

30. $\arcsin x + 2\sqrt{(1 - x^2)}$

31. $\frac{1}{27}(9y^2\sin 3y + 6y\cos 3y - 2\sin 3y)$

32. $-\ln|1 - \tan x|$

33. $\frac{1}{3}(7 + x^2)^{3/2}$

34. $-\frac{1}{5}\cos(5\theta - \frac{1}{4}\pi)$

35. $\sin\theta\{\ln|\sin\theta| - 1\}$

36. $e^{\tan u}$

Exercise 32c – p. 540

1. $y^2 = A - 2\cos x$

2. $\dfrac{1}{y} - \dfrac{1}{x} = A$

3. $2y^3 = 3(x^2 + 4y + A)$

4. $x = A\sec y$

5. $(A - x)y = 1$

6. $y = \ln\dfrac{A}{\sqrt{(1 - x^2)}}$

7. $y = A(x - 3)$

8. $x + A = 4\ln|\sin y|$

9. $u^2 = v^2 + 4v + A$

10. $16y^3 = 12x^4\ln|x| - 3x^4 + A$

11. $y^2 + 2(x + 1)e^{-x} = A$

12. $\sin x = A - e^{-y}$

13. $2r^2 = 2\theta - \sin 2\theta + A$

14. $u + 2 = A(v + 1)$

15. $y^2 = A + (\ln|x|)^2$

16. $y^2 = Ax(x + 2)$

17. $4v^3 = 3(2 + t)^4 + A$

18. $1 + y^2 = Ax^2$

19. $Ar = e^{\tan\theta}$

20. $y^2 = A - \operatorname{cosec}^2 x$

21. $v^2 + A = 2u - 2\ln|u|$

22. $e^{-x} = e^{1-y} + A$

23. $A - \dfrac{1}{y} = 2\ln|\tan x|$

24. $y - 1 = A(y + 1)(x^2 + 1)$

Exercise 32d – p. 544

1. $y^3 = x^3 + 3x - 13$

2. $e^t(5 - 2\sqrt{s}) = 1$

3. $3(y^2 - 1) = 8(x^2 - 1)$

4. $y = x^2 - x$

5. $y = e^x - 2$

6. $y = 5 - \dfrac{3}{x}$

7. $y = \pm\sqrt{(4 + e^{-3} - e)}$
   $= \pm 1.154$

8. $(y + 1)^2(x + 1) = 2(x - 1)$

9. $2y = x^2 + 6x$

10. $4y^2 = (y + 1)^2(x^2 + 1)$

Mixed Exercise 32 – p. 545

1. $\frac{1}{10}(1 + x^2)^5$

2. $-\frac{1}{9}e^{-3x}(3x + 1)$

3. $\frac{1}{10}(\sin 5x + 5\sin x)$

4. $x + \ln|x + 2|$

5. $\dfrac{-1}{3(x^3 + 1)}$

6. $\ln\left|\dfrac{x - 4}{x - 1}\right|$

7. $\ln\left|\dfrac{x}{2x + 1}\right|$

8. $\ln\sqrt{(x^2 + 1)} - \arctan x$

9. $-2\sqrt{(\cos x)}$

10. $\sqrt{2}$

11. $\frac{256}{15}$

12. $\frac{1}{2} - \ln\sqrt{2}$

13. $9 - \frac{16}{3}\sqrt{2}$

14. $\ln\frac{9}{4}$

15. $\ln\left\{\dfrac{\ln 3}{\ln 2}\right\}$

16. $\ln\frac{1}{6}$

17. $3\frac{1}{2} + 6\ln\frac{2}{3}$

18. $x^3 y = y - 1$

19. $y = \tan\{\frac{1}{2}(x^2 - 4)\}$

20. $y^2 = 2x$

CHAPTER 33

Exercise 33a – p. 549

1. $v = \frac{1}{2}t^2 - 6t; \; s = \frac{1}{6}t^3 - 3t^3$
$\quad v_6 = -18 \text{ m/s}; \; s_6 = -72 \text{ m}$

2. $v = \frac{3}{2}t^2 - t - 1; \; 31\frac{1}{2} \text{ m/s}$

3. 129 m

4. (a) $s = 2t - \dfrac{1}{t + 1} + 1$

   (b) $v \to 2$ as $t \to \infty$

5. $6t \text{ m/s}; \; 504 \text{ m} \quad (t = 2 \text{ at } A)$

Exercise 33b – p. 550

1. $s\dfrac{ds}{dt} = k$

2. $\dfrac{dh}{dt} = k\ln|H - h|$

3. (a) $\dfrac{dn}{dt} = 0$ \qquad (b) $\dfrac{dn}{dt} = k\sqrt{n}$

4. (a) $\dfrac{dn}{dt} = k_1 n$ \qquad (b) $\dfrac{dn}{dt} = \dfrac{k_2}{n}$

   (c) $\dfrac{dn}{dt} = -k_3$

5. (a) $\dfrac{dp}{dt} = kp(s - p)$

Exercise 33c – p. 555

1. 9

2. (a) $\frac{8}{3}$ \qquad (b) $\frac{16}{3}$

3. 18

4. $\frac{4}{3}$

5. 1

6. $e - 2$

7. $\frac{1}{6}$

8. $\frac{1}{2}\sqrt{3} - \frac{1}{6}\pi$

9. (a) 1 \qquad (b) $2 - \ln 3$

10. $8(\ln 2)$

11. (a) $\frac{4}{3}$ \qquad (b) $\frac{1}{3}$

12. $4\sqrt{3}$

Exercise 33d – p. 562

1. $\frac{512}{15}\pi$

2. $\frac{1}{2}\pi(e^6 - 1)$

3. $\frac{1}{2}\pi$

4. $\frac{64}{5}\pi$

5. 2π

6. 8π

7. 8π

8. $\frac{3}{5}\pi(\sqrt[3]{32} - 1)$

9. $\frac{1}{2}\pi(e^2 - 1)$

10. $\frac{16}{15}\pi$

11. $\frac{16}{15}\pi$

12. $\frac{1}{2}\pi^2$

13. $\frac{5}{2}\pi$

14. $\frac{3}{10}\pi$

Exercise 33e – p. 568

1. (a) 18 \qquad (b) $\frac{348}{10}$ \qquad (c) $\frac{58}{15}$

2. 8; (a) $\frac{64}{3}$ \quad (b) $\frac{32}{3}$; \quad $(\frac{8}{3}, \frac{4}{3})$

3. (a) 2 \qquad (b) $\frac{1}{4}\pi$ \qquad (c) $\frac{1}{2}\pi, \frac{1}{8}\pi)$
   (d) $\frac{1}{2}\pi^2$ \qquad (e) $\frac{1}{4}\pi^2$ \qquad (f) $(\frac{1}{2}\pi, 0)$

4. (a) $\frac{1}{6}$ \qquad (b) $\frac{1}{60}$ \qquad (c) $(\frac{1}{2}, -\frac{1}{10})$
   (d) $\frac{1}{30}\pi$ \qquad (e) $\frac{1}{60}\pi$ \qquad (f) $(\frac{1}{2}, 0)$

5. (a) $\frac{32}{3}$ \qquad $\frac{128}{5}$ \qquad $\frac{12}{5}$
   (d) 8π \qquad (e) $\frac{64}{3}\pi$ \qquad (f) $(0, \frac{8}{3})$

6. (a) $e - 1$ (b) 1 (c) $\dfrac{1}{e - 1}$

    (d) $\frac{1}{2}\pi(e^2 - 1)$ (e) $\frac{1}{4}\pi(e^2 + 1)$

    (f) $\left(0, \frac{1}{2}\left\{\dfrac{e^2 + 1}{e^2 - 1}\right\}\right)$

7. $\dfrac{e^2 + 1}{e^2 - 1}$

Mixed Exercise 33 – p. 572

1. $t = \frac{1}{2}$ or 1; 7.5 m

2. $v = \frac{1}{2} - \dfrac{1}{2t^2}$, $v_2 = \frac{3}{8}$ m/s

    $s = \dfrac{1}{2t^2} + \frac{1}{2}t - 1$, $s_2 = \frac{1}{4}$ m

3. -2 m/s^2; $8\frac{1}{3}$ m

4. $\frac{1}{3}$

5. (a) $e^4 - 1$ (b) $\frac{1}{4}(e^8 - 1)$

    (c) $\frac{1}{4}(e^4 + 1)$

6. $\frac{1}{2}(e^4 - 1)$

7. $\frac{16}{3}$ (a) 8π (b) $(0, \frac{14}{3})$

8. (a) $\frac{32}{3}$ (b) $\frac{192}{5}$ (c) $(0, \frac{18}{5})$

9. $\frac{256}{15}\pi$; $\frac{32}{3}\pi$; $\overline{y} = 2$, $\overline{x} = \frac{5}{8}$

10. $\frac{1}{2}\left(\sqrt{3} - \dfrac{3}{\pi}\right)$

CONSOLIDATION E

Multiple Choice Exercise E - p. 578

1. C	17. A, C
2. C	18. B, C
3. D	19. B
4. D	20. A, C
5. B	21. B
6. B	22. B, C
7. C	23. A, D
8. D	24. A, D
9. D	25. F
10. B	26. T
11. A	27. F
12. A	28. T
13. D	29. F
14. E	30. F
15. A, C	31. F
16. B, C	32. T

Miscellaneous Exercise E – p. 583

1. $-\frac{9}{4}$

2. $\dfrac{5}{x - 3} - \dfrac{2}{3x + 2}$; $-\dfrac{157}{32}$

3. 2

4. $p = 6, q = 10$

5. (a) $(3, 3)$ (c) $(\frac{14}{3}, \frac{1}{2})$

6. $\dfrac{-1}{x - 2} + \dfrac{4}{x + 6}$; $\dfrac{1}{(x - 2)^2} - \dfrac{4}{(x + 6)^2}$;

    $\dfrac{-2}{(x - 2)^3} + \dfrac{8}{(x + 6)^3}$; $x = -\frac{2}{3}$;

    $\frac{1}{8}$ max, $\frac{9}{8}$ min

7. $a = -11, b = 3$;

    $(x - 3)(x - 4)(2x + 3)$

8. Centre $(2, -3)$, radius 5;

    $\frac{1}{5}|6 + k|$; $k = 19$ or -31

9. $\frac{4}{3}$; $y - 3 = -\frac{3}{4}(x - 2)$; $2y = x + 9$;

    $63.4°$

10. (b) $45°$

    (c) $(6, -1)$; 10;

       $(x - 6)^2 + (y + 1)^2 = 100$

11. $33\,000$, -1.4

12. 3.3 to 3.5

13. 1.8, 2.5

14. (a) $\frac{1}{4}e^{2x}(6x + 5)$ (b) $\frac{1}{64}(\pi + 2)$

15. $p^2 - 4$; $2x^2 - 3(p^2 - 4)x + 18 = 0$

16. (a) $\frac{1}{12}(6x + \sin 6x) + K$

    (b) $\frac{1}{2}\arctan(\frac{1}{2}e^x) + K$

    (c) $\frac{1}{4}e^{2x}(2x - 1) + K$

17. $A = -1, B = 1$; $\ln 2 - \frac{1}{2}$

18. $\arctan e - \frac{1}{4}\pi = 0.43$ to 2 d.p.

19. $\frac{1}{20}$

20. $2, 3, -1$; $y - 3 = -\frac{2}{5}(x - 1)$

21. $5\frac{1}{3}$ sq. units

22. (a) $\dfrac{\pi(e^{4a} - 1)}{2e^{2a}}$

    (b) (i) $\frac{1}{110}$

       (ii) $(x^2 + 1)\arctan x - x + K$

23. $2\ln A\left|\dfrac{8 - x}{4 - x}\right|$; $t = 2\ln\left|\dfrac{8 - x}{3(4 - x)}\right|$;

    $2\ln\frac{5}{3}$ minutes, i.e. 61 minutes

24. $\dfrac{\frac{1}{2}}{x + 1} - \dfrac{\frac{1}{2}}{x + 3}$; $y^2(x + 3) = 8(x + 1)$

25. $y = x^2 - 5$

26. $\frac{9}{2} - 6\ln 2$

27. (a) $-2, 3$

    (b) $(k + 2)x^2 - 4k^2x + 4k^2 = 0$

28. $\dfrac{dV}{dt} = kV$ (a) £4495

    (b) 57 months

29. $y = \exp(2x^2 - 2)$

30. 10.6

31. $\frac{1}{12}\pi; \frac{1}{12}\pi\sqrt{2}$

32. $5\ln 5 - 4; 15.4$

33. (c) $\frac{1}{2}\pi - 1$ (d) $\frac{1}{8}\pi; \frac{1}{4}\pi^2$

34. (a) $\frac{1}{2}x^2\ln x - \frac{1}{4}x^2 + K$

  (b) $K + \arctan(\tan x)$

  (c) 1.3

35. (a) $4p^2 - 2q$

CHAPTER 34

Exercise 34a – p. 593

1. (a) $\sum_{r=1}^{5} r^3$ (b) $\sum_{r=1}^{10} 2r$

  (c) $\sum_{r=2}^{50} \frac{1}{r}$ (d) $\sum_{r=0}^{\infty} \frac{1}{3^r}$

  (e) $\sum_{r=0}^{7} (-4 + 3r)$

  (f) $\sum_{r=0}^{\infty} \left(\frac{8}{2^r}\right) = \sum_{r=0}^{\infty} \frac{1}{2^{r-3}}$

2. (a) $1 + \frac{1}{2} + \frac{1}{3} + \ldots$

  (b) $0 + 2 + 6 + 12 + \ldots + 30$

  (c) $2 + \frac{1}{2} + \frac{4}{15} + \ldots + \frac{22}{861}$

  (d) $1 + \frac{1}{2} + \frac{1}{5} + \ldots$

  (e) $0 + 0 + 6 + \ldots + 720$

  (f) $-1 + a - a^2 + \ldots$

3. (a) $8; 9$ (b) $9; 10$ (c) $-1; 6$

  (d) $\frac{1}{420}; \infty$ (e) $(\frac{1}{2})^n; \infty$

  (f) $-48; 23$ (g) $4; 10$

Exercise 34b – p. 599

1. (a) $9, 2n - 1$ (b) $16, 4(n - 1)$

  (c) $15, 3n$ (d) $17, 3n + 2$

  (e) $-2, 8 - 2n$

  (f) $p + 4q, p + (n - 1)q$

  (g) $18, 8 + 2n$ (h) $17, 4n - 3$

  (i) $0, \frac{1}{2}(5 - n)$ (j) $8, 3n - 7$

2. (a) 100   (b) 180   (c) 165

  (d) 185   (e) -30

  (f) $5(2p + 9q)$ (g) 190

  (h) 190   (i) $-\frac{5}{2}$ (j) 95

3. $a = 27.2, d = -2.4$

4. $d = 3; 30$

5. $1, \frac{1}{2}, 0; -8\frac{1}{2}$

6. (a) $28\frac{1}{2}$ (b) 80   (c) 400

  (d) 80   (e) 108   (f) $3n(1 - 6n)$

  (g) 40   (h) $2m(m + 3)$

7. $4, 2n - 4$

9. $2, 364$

10. 39

11. 64

12. (a) $1, 5$ (b) 270

13. (a) $a = 21, d = -3$

  (b) less than 4 or more than 11

Exercise 34c – p. 604

1. (a) $32, 2^n$ (b) $\frac{1}{8}, \frac{1}{2^{n-2}}$

  (c) $48, 3(-2)^{n-1}$

  (d) $\frac{1}{2}, (-1)^{n-1}(\frac{1}{2})^{n-4}$ (e) $\frac{1}{27}, (\frac{1}{3})^{n-2}$

2. (a) 189   (b) -255

  (c) $2 - (\frac{1}{2})^{19}$ (d) $781/125$

  (e) $341/1024$ (f) 1

3. $\frac{1}{2}, 2$

4. $-\frac{1}{2}$

5. $-\frac{1}{2}, 1/1024$

6. 13.21 to 4 s.f.

7. (a) $(x - x^{n+1})/(1 - x)$

  (b) $(x^n - 1)/x^{n-2}(x - 1)$

  (c) $(1 + (-1)^{n+1}y^n)/(1 + y)$

  (d) $x(2^n - x^n)/2^{n-1}(2 - x)$

  (e) $[1 - (-2)^n x^n]/(1 + 2x)$

8. $\frac{8}{3}(1 - (\frac{1}{4})^n), 4$

9. 62 or 122

10. 8.493 to 4 s.f.

11. 8 (last repayment is less than £2000)

12. £23.31

Exercise 34d – p. 610

1. (a) yes   (b) no   (c) yes

  (d) yes   (e) no   (f) yes

2. $-1 < x < 1$ (b) $x < -1, x > 1$

  (c) $-\frac{1}{2} < x < \frac{1}{2}$ (d) $0 < x < 2$

  (e) $-1 - a < x < 1 - a$

  (f) $x < -(1 + a), x > 1 - a$

3. (a) 6   (c) $13\frac{1}{3}$ (d) $\frac{5}{9}$ (f) $\frac{9}{4}$

4. (a) $161/990$ (b) $34/99$ (c) $7/330$

5. $\frac{1}{2}$

7. $8, 4, 2, 1$

Exercise 34e – p. 613

1. $\dfrac{1}{2r} - \dfrac{1}{2(r + 2)}; \dfrac{n(3n + 5)}{4(n + 1)(n + 2)}$

2. $\dfrac{1}{r + 1} - \dfrac{1}{r + 2}; \dfrac{n - 2}{4(n + 2)}$

3. $\dfrac{1}{r} - \dfrac{1}{r + 1}; \dfrac{n + 1}{n(2n + 1)}$

4. $\dfrac{1}{16(2r-1)} + \dfrac{1}{8(2r+1)} - \dfrac{3}{16(2r+3)}$;

$\dfrac{n(n+1)}{2(2n+1)(2n+3)}$

5. $\frac{1}{2}n(n+1)(2n^2+2n+1)$

6. $\dfrac{n(n+3)}{4(n+1)(n+2)}$

7. $\dfrac{n(n+2)}{(n+1)^2}$

8. $\frac{1}{4}n^2(n+1)^2$

9. $\dfrac{\cos 2\theta - \cos(2n+2)\theta}{2\sin\theta}$

Exercise 34f – p. 615

1. $\frac{1}{3}n(n+1)(n+2)$

2. $\dfrac{n}{4}(n+1)(n+2)(n+3)$

3. $\frac{1}{12}n(n+1)(45n^2+37n+2)$

4. $42\,075$

5. $\frac{1}{6}n(2n+5)(n-1)$

6. $-n(2n+1)$

7. $\frac{1}{3}n(4n^2+6n-1)$

Mixed Exercise 34 – p. 617

1. $\frac{2}{3}$

2. $\frac{1}{2}(1+3^{11}) = 88\,574$

3. $\dfrac{ab^4(1-b^{2(n-1)})}{1-b^2}$

4. 650

5. $2(n+5)(n-4)$

6. $\frac{1}{4}n(n+1)(n^2+n+2)$

7. $\dfrac{(n+4)(3n-1)}{4n(n+1)}$

8. $210\ln 3$

9. $\dfrac{e(1-e^n)}{1-e}$

10. $\frac{1}{6}n(n+1)(3n^2+13n+11)$

11. $\dfrac{1}{2(n+1)}$

12. 1

13. $\frac{2}{3}n(n+1)(2n+1)$

14. $-\ln n$

15. $1, 7, 19, 37; \; 3n^2 - 3n + 1$

16. $16, -8$

17. 2

18. 1

19. $a = 2 \pm \sqrt{2}, r = \frac{1}{4}(2 \pm \sqrt{2})$

CHAPTER 35

Exercise 35a – p. 620

1, 4 and **5** are permutations
2, 3 and **6** are combinations

Exercise 35b – p. 625

1. $7!$

2. (a) $\dfrac{5!}{2!}$ (b) 5

3. $6!$

4. $3!$

5. $9(10^5)$

6. (a) $4(5!)$ (b) $2(5!)$ (c) $2(5!)$

7. (a) $3!$ (b) 3

8. $9!$

9. (a) $\dfrac{9!}{4!}$ (b) 9 (c) $4\left(\dfrac{8!}{4!}\right)$

10. $11!$

11. (a) $2(4!)$ (b) $5! - 2(4!)$

12. $\frac{1}{2}(4!)$

13. 12

14. (a) $2(11!)$ (b) $12! - 2(11!)$

15. (a) $\dfrac{4!}{1!}$ (b) 4^3

16. $\dfrac{3!}{1!}$

Exercise 35c – p. 630

Answers are given in factorial form to facilitate method checks.

1. (a) $\dfrac{11!}{5!}$ (b) $\dfrac{11!}{6!5!}$ (c) $\dfrac{20!}{3!17!}$

2. (a) Arranging 4 out of 8 different objects.
   (b) Choosing a group of 5 (or a group of 9) from 14 different objects.
   (c) Choosing a group of 5 (or 2) from 7 different objects.

3. $\dfrac{8!}{6!2!}$

4. $\dfrac{8!}{6!2!}$

5. (a) $\dfrac{19!}{3!16!}$ (b) $\dfrac{20!}{4!16!}$

6. (a) $\dfrac{9!}{3!6!}$ (b) $\dfrac{9!}{2!7!} \times 2$

7. $\dfrac{9!}{5!4!}$;   (a) $\dfrac{9!}{4!5!} - 1$

   (b) $\dfrac{9!}{5!4!} - \dfrac{7!}{3!4!}$ (c) 1

8. $\dfrac{13!}{5!8!}$

9. $\dfrac{12!}{4!8!}$

10. (a) $\dfrac{3!}{2!1!}$ (b) $2\left(\dfrac{3!}{2!1!}\right)$

11. (a) $\dfrac{9!}{4!5!}$ (b) $\dfrac{9!}{2!7!}$

   (c) $2\left(\dfrac{9!}{2!7!}\right)$ (d) 9

Exercise 35d – p. 633

1. 6
2. 24
3. 120
4. 720
5. 30
6. 132
7. 840
8. 60
9. 28
10. 1260
11. 70
12. $\frac{3}{4}$
13. $\dfrac{5!}{2!}$
14. $\dfrac{11!}{9!}$
15. $\dfrac{(n+1)!}{(n-2)!}$
16. $\dfrac{(n+2)!}{n!}$
17. $\dfrac{20!}{3!17!}$
18. $\dfrac{8!3!}{6!5!}$
19. $\dfrac{5!}{3!2!}$
20. $\dfrac{40!}{38!2!}$
21. $\dfrac{n!}{3!(n-3)!}$
22. $\dfrac{(n-1)!}{4!(n-5)!}$
23. $8!(1+9)$
24. $5!(42-2)$
25. $(n-1)!(n+1)$
26. $n!(n+1-1)$

28. (a) $\dfrac{2n(2n-1)(2n-2)\dots(2n-r+1)}{r!}$

   (b) $\dfrac{2n(2n-1)(2n-2)\dots(n+1)}{n!}$

Exercise 35e – p. 639

1. (a) 10   (b) 27
2. 13
3. $\dfrac{18!}{13(5!)^2(7!)}$
4. $\dfrac{11!}{(2!)^3}$
5. 2454
6. 18
7. 75 600
8. 120
9. (a) $5! \times 3! \times 2$ (b) $5! \times \dfrac{6!}{3!}$
10. 16
11. 28
12. (a) 56   (b) 35
13. 27

Mixed Exercise 35 – p. 641

1. (a) 225   (b) 480   (c) 240
2. 81; 1, 8, 24, 32, 16
3. $9 \times 8 \times 10!$
4. 72
5. 11 760
6. $\dfrac{12!}{7!5!}$ (a) $\dfrac{10!}{5!5!} + \dfrac{10!}{3!7!}$

   (b) $2 \times \dfrac{10!}{6!4!}$

7. (a) $3 \times 4!$ (b) 3×5^4
8. $\dfrac{9!}{(2!)^3}$

   (a) $\dfrac{8!}{(2!)^2}$ (b) $2 \times \dfrac{8!}{(2!)^2}$

   (c) $\dfrac{(5!)^2}{(2!)^3}$

CHAPTER 36

Exercise 36a – p. 646

1. (a) $1 + 36x + 594x^2 + 5940x^3$
   (b) $1 - 18x + 144x^2 - 672x^3$
   (c) $1024 + 5120x + 11\,520x^2 + 15\,360x^3$
   (d) $1 - \frac{20}{3}x + \frac{190}{9}x^2 - \frac{380}{9}x^3$
   (e) $128 - 672x + 1512x^2 - 1890x^3$
   (f) $(\frac{3}{2})^9 + \dfrac{3^{10}}{2^7}x + \dfrac{3^9}{8}x^2 + \frac{7}{2}(3^7)x^3$

2. (a) $336x^2$ (b) $-10x$
(c) $-21\,840x^{11}$ (d) $3360p^6q^4$
(e) $16(3a)^7b$ (f) $7920x^4$
(g) $63x^5$ (h) $56a^3b^5$
3. (a) $1 - 8x + 27x^2$
(b) $1 + 19x + 160x^2$
(c) $2 - 19x + 85x^2$
(d) $1 - 68x + 2136x^2$

Exercise 36b – p. 649
1. 0.8171
2. 1.062
6. (a) $1 - 50x$ (b) $256 - 1024x$
(c) $1 - 19x$

Exercise 36c – p. 655
1. $1 - x - \dfrac{x^2}{2} - \dfrac{x^3}{3}, \; -\frac{1}{2} < x < \frac{1}{2}$

2. $\dfrac{1}{3} - \dfrac{x}{9} + \dfrac{x^2}{27} - \dfrac{x^3}{81}, \; -3 < x < 3$

3. $1 - \dfrac{x}{4} + \dfrac{3x^2}{32} - \dfrac{5x^3}{128}, \; -2 < x < 2$

4. $1 + 2x + 3x^2 + 4x^3, \; -1 < x < 1$
5. $1 - \frac{1}{2}x + \frac{3}{8}x^2 - \frac{5}{16}x^3, \; -1 < x < 1$
6. $1 + \frac{1}{2}x - \frac{5}{8}x^2 - \frac{3}{16}x^3, \; -1 < x < 1$
7. $-2 - 3x - 3x^2 - 3x^3, \; -1 < x < 1$
8. $2 + 2x + \frac{21}{4}x^2 + \frac{27}{8}x^3, \; -\frac{1}{3} < x < \frac{1}{3}$
9. $\frac{1}{2} - \frac{3}{4}x + \frac{13}{8}x^2 - \frac{51}{16}x^3, \; -\frac{1}{2} < x < \frac{1}{2}$
10. $1 + x + \frac{1}{2}x^2 + \frac{1}{2}x^3, \; -1 < x < 1$
11. $1 - \frac{1}{9}x^2, \; -3 < x < 3$
12. $x - x^2 + x^3, \; -1 < x < 1$
13. $1 - 3p^{-1} + 6p^{-2} - 10p^{-3} + 15p^{-4}, |p| < 1$
14. 1.732
15. 3.162 28
16. $1 + 2x + 2x^2$
18. $1 - 3x + \frac{7}{2}x^2$
19. $1 + 2x + 5x^2$
20. $\frac{3}{2} + \frac{15}{4}x$
23. $\frac{1}{729}[27 + 27x + 18x^2 + 10x^3]$

Exercise 36d – p. 658
1. $1 + 2x + 2x^2$
2. $1 - 2x + 2x^2$
3. $1 + \frac{1}{2}x + \frac{1}{8}x^2$
4. $1 + \frac{3}{2}x + \frac{9}{8}x^2$
5. $-x - \frac{1}{2}x^2 - \frac{1}{6}x^3$
6. $2 + x + \frac{1}{2}x^2$
7. $-1 + x - x^2$
8. $1 + \frac{1}{2}x^2 - \frac{1}{3}x^2$

9. $1 + 0.5 + 0.125 + 0.020\,833\,33$
    $+ \, 0.002\,606\,16 + 0.000\,260\,411$
    $+ \, 0.000\,021\,70 + 0.000\,001\,55$
    $+ \, 0.000\,000\,096 + \ldots$
    $= 1.648\,72$ correct to 5 d.p.

Exercise 36e – p. 659
1. $3x - \dfrac{9x^2}{2} + 9x^3, \; -\frac{1}{3} < x \leqslant \frac{1}{3}$

2. $2x - x^2 + \frac{2}{3}x^3, \; -1 < x \leqslant 1$
3. $-\frac{1}{2}x - \frac{1}{8}x^2 - \frac{1}{24}x^3, \; -2 \leqslant x < 2$
4. $-x^2 - \frac{1}{2}x^4 - \frac{1}{3}x^6, \; -1 < x < 1$
5. $-x - x^2 - \frac{4}{3}x^3, \; -\frac{1}{2} \leqslant x < \frac{1}{2}$
6. $x^2 - \frac{1}{2}x^3 + \frac{1}{3}x^4, \; -1 < x \leqslant 1$
7. $x + \frac{1}{2}x^2 - \frac{1}{6}x^3, \; -1 < x \leqslant 1$
8. $-x - \dfrac{x^3}{3} - \dfrac{x^5}{5}, \; -1 < x < 1$

9. $2x - \frac{1}{2}x^2 + \frac{1}{3}x^3$
    (note that $\ln e^x = x$), $- < x \leqslant 1$

Mixed Exercise 36 – p. 660
1. $1 + 18x + 144x^2 + \ldots + 2^9x^9$; all x
2. $1 - 2x + 4x^2 - \ldots; -\frac{1}{2} < x < \frac{1}{2}$
3. $x + x^2 + x^3 + \ldots; -1 < x < 1$
4. $1 + 3x + 6x^2 + \ldots; -\frac{1}{2} < x < \frac{1}{2}$
5. $\dfrac{1}{3(1 + x)} + \dfrac{2}{3(1 - 2x)}; 1 + x + 3x^2$
6. 8
8. $1 - \frac{1}{6}x^3$
9. $1 + x \ln 2 + \dfrac{x^2}{2}(\ln 2)^2; 1.2577 \ldots$
10. (a) $1 + \frac{3}{2}x + \frac{27}{8}x^2; |x| < \frac{1}{3}$
    (b) $1.343\,75$ with $x = \frac{1}{6}$
11. (a) 1   (b) $-16x^3$

CHAPTER 37

Exercise 37a – p. 665
1. $a = 2, b = -3$

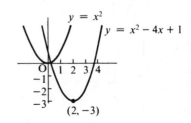

(2, −3)

2. (a)

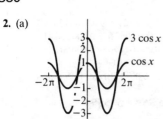

(b)

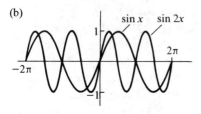

(c)

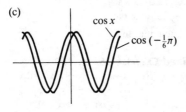

(d)

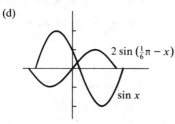

3.

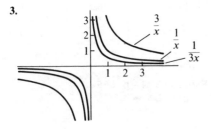

4.

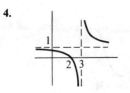

5.

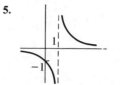

6.

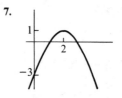

7.

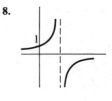

8.

9.

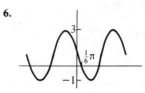

10.

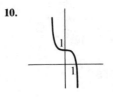

11.

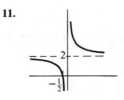

12.

13.

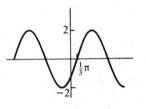

14.

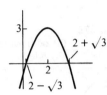

15.

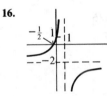

16.

17.

18.

19.

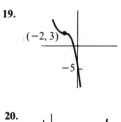

$(-2, 3)$

-5

20.

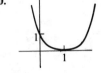

Exercise 37b – p. 669

1.

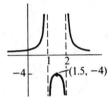

$(1.5, -4)$

2.

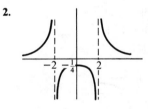

3.

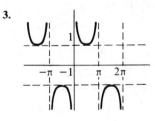

4.

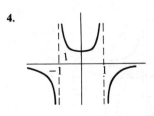

5.

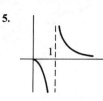

6.

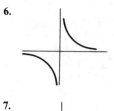

7.

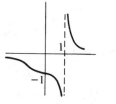

8.

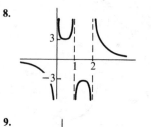

9.

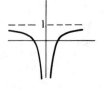

10.

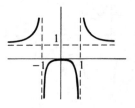

11.

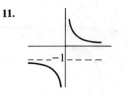

12.

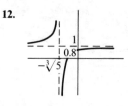

Exercise 37c – p. 673

1. (a) even, periodic   (b) odd, periodic
   (e) odd, periodic   (h) odd

2.

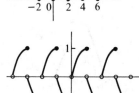

3.

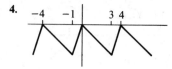

4.

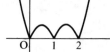

Exercise 37d – p. 676

1.

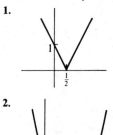

2.

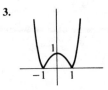

3.

4.

5.

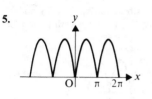

6.

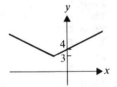

7.

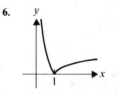

8.

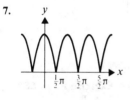

9.

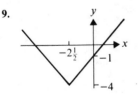

10.

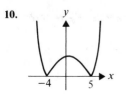

11.

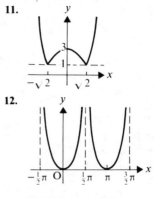

12.

Exercise 37e – p. 679

1. $(\frac{1}{2}, \frac{1}{2}), (-\frac{1}{2}, \frac{1}{2})$
2. $(0, 0), (1, 1)$
3. $(\sqrt{3}, 2\sqrt{3}), (2 - \sqrt{7}, 2\sqrt{7} - 4)$
4. $(1, 1), (-1, 1)$
5. $(1, 3), (1 + \sqrt{6}, 3 + 2\sqrt{6})$
6. 3 and $\frac{1}{2}(\sqrt{17} - 3)$
7. $\frac{4}{5}$ and $\frac{2}{3}$
8. $\frac{2}{3}$ and 2
9. $\sqrt{2} - 1$ and 3

Exercise 37f – p. 681

1. $\frac{1}{2}(1 - \sqrt{5}) < x < 0, x > \frac{1}{2}(1 + \sqrt{5})$
2. $0 < x < 1$
3. $0 < x < 1$
4. $-1 < x < 0$
5. $-2 < x < -1$
6. $x > 0$
7. $-\frac{1}{2} < x < \frac{1}{2}$
8. $x > -\frac{1}{2}$
9. $-1 < x < \frac{1}{3}$
10. $x > 1$
11. $x < 1$
12. $x < -\frac{5}{4}, x > -\frac{1}{4}$
13. $x < 0, x > 2$
14. $x < 0, x > 2$
15. $0 < x < 1 + \sqrt{3}$
16. $-1 < x < 1$
17. $0 < x < \frac{1}{4}\pi, \frac{3}{4}\pi < x < \frac{5}{4}\pi, \frac{7}{4}\pi < x < 2\pi$
18.

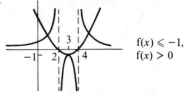

$f(x) \leqslant -1,$
$f(x) > 0$

19.

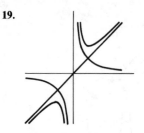

$f(x) \leqslant -2, f(x) \geqslant 2$

20. (a) $f(x) < 0, f(x) > 0$

(b) $f(x) \leqslant -\frac{1}{4}, f(x) > 0$

(c) $f(x) \geqslant -\frac{1}{4}$

(d) $f(x) \leqslant -4, f(x) > 0$

Mixed Exercise 37, p. 683

1.

$y = 1$ and $x = 3$; $(4, 0)$ and $(0, \frac{4}{3})$

2.

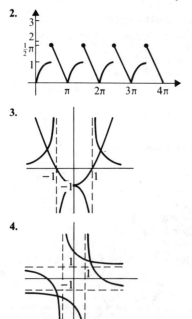

3.

4.

$g^{-1}(x) > 1, g^{-1}(x) < 1$

5. $x < -\frac{1}{2}$

6. $-1 < x < 0$ and $x > 2$

7.

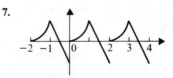

$x = -2, 0, 2, 4$

8. (a) odd with period π (b) odd

(c) even   (d) even with period 2π

9.

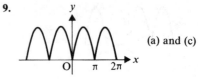

(a) and (c)

10. $-\frac{49}{8}$; $x = -2$ and $\frac{3}{2}$

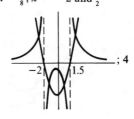

; 4

CONSOLIDATION F

Multiple Choice Exercise F - p. 688

1. B	**17. A, B**
2. C	**18. A, C**
3. A	**19. A, C**
4. E	**20. A, C**
5. E	**21. B, C**
6. C	**22. A**
7. A	**23. A, B**
8. C	**24. A**
9. B	**25. F**
10. A	**26. T**
11. E	**27. F**
12. B	**28. T**
13. C	**29. F**
14. C	**30. F**
15. D	**31. T**
16. E	

Miscellaneous Exercise F – p. 692

1. $\frac{1}{2}$

2. 999×26^4; $26 \times 25 \times 24 \times 23 \times 738$

3. $a = 2n - \frac{1}{2}$

4. $1 - 2x - 2x^2 - 4x^3$

5. 110

6. 1.5, 6.25

7. $2 < x < 4$

8. 3

9. $1 - x + 2x^2 - \frac{14}{3}x^3, -\frac{1}{3} < x < \frac{1}{3}$

10. $x < -1$

11. (a) 182   (b) 41

12. (b) 1.72

13. 8

14. 22

17. $1 - \frac{2}{3}x - \frac{4}{9}x^2, -\frac{1}{2} < x \frac{1}{2}$

18. $x < 1$

19. $33, 3\frac{1}{2}$; 1450

20. $4, 2x^2, -12x^3$

21. 10 080, 7560

22. $a = 2, b = -3$; 1365

23. (a) $-\frac{2}{3} < x < 2$

    (b) $-7 \leqslant y \leqslant -1, y \geqslant 1$

24. $-3 \leqslant x \leqslant 1$

25. (a)

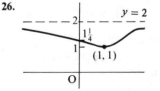

Inflexion

(b)

26.

27. (a) $5050 \ln 2$ (b) $\dfrac{\ln 2}{1 - \ln 2}$

28. $1 + \frac{1}{2}y - \frac{1}{8}y^2; a_0 = 1, a_1 = \frac{1}{2},$

    $a_2 = -\frac{1}{8}$; 0.0103

29. $x = 0, y = 0, x = -2, y = 1;$

    $(0, 0); (2, \frac{1}{2}), (-1, -1); 0 < x < 2,$

    $-2 < x < -1$

30. $x^8 - 4x^7 + 6x^6 - 4x^5 + x^4; \frac{22}{7} - \pi$

31. (a) $1 + 11x + 64x^2$

    (b) $11x + \frac{7}{2}x^2 + \frac{59}{3}x^3$

32. $1 - px + \dfrac{p^2x^2}{2}, 1 - 2qx + 2q(q + 1)x^2,$

    $p = 4, q = 2$

33. $1 - \frac{1}{6}x + \frac{1}{24}x^2, |x| < 3$

CHAPTER 38

Exercise 38a – p. 700

1. $\frac{1}{6}\pi(1 + 4n)$

2. $\frac{1}{8}\pi(1 + 4n), \frac{1}{4}\pi(n - 1)$

3. $2n\pi, \pm\frac{2}{3}\pi + 2n\pi$

4. $2n\pi + \tan^{-1}\frac{12}{5}$

5. $n\pi$

6. $\pm\frac{1}{4}\pi + n\pi, \pm\frac{2}{3}\pi + 2n\pi$

7. $\pm\frac{1}{2}\pi + 2n\pi$

8. $\tan^{-1}\frac{3}{4} + \frac{1}{2}\pi + 2n\pi$

9. $\pm\frac{1}{2}\pi + 2n\pi$

10. $2n\pi + \sin^{-1}(\sqrt{2} - 1),$

    $(2n + 1)\pi + \sin^{-1}(\sqrt{2} - 1)$

11. $0, 30°, 150°, 180°$

12. $53.1°, 180°$

13. $0, 180°$

14. $201.5°, 338.5°$

15. $26.6°, 135°, 206.6°, 315°$

16. $34.6°, 325.4°$

17. $120°, 300°$

18. $0, 72°, 90°, 144°, 180°, 216°, 270°, 288°$

19. $20°, 100°, 140°, 220°, 260°, 340°$

Exercise 38b – p. 702

1. 1.63

2. 0.861

3. 1.16

4. 2.77

5. -0.104

6. 1.22

7. $-1, 1$

8. 2

9. 3

10. 2

11. 3

12. $\sqrt{3}$ or $1/\sqrt{3}$

13. $x = \frac{1}{2}, y = 1$

14. $x = 2, y = 4$

15. $x = 1, y = 0$

16. $x = 1, y = 0$

Exercise 38c – p. 705

1. $-\frac{3}{4}, -\frac{3}{4}, \frac{2}{5}$
2. $-1, -1, \frac{1}{5}, 5$
3. $\frac{3}{2}, \frac{3}{2}, -\frac{2}{5}$
4. $1, 2, 3$
5. 4
6. $6 + 2\sqrt{3}$
7. $\frac{1}{2}(3 \pm \sqrt{41})$
8. 4
9. 5
10. $\pm 3, \pm\sqrt{3}$
11. $1, 8, -8$
12. $-1, 2$
13. -2
14. $x = \sqrt{2}, y = \frac{1}{2}\sqrt{2}$ and $x = -\sqrt{2}$, $y = -\frac{1}{2}\sqrt{2}$
15. $x = 2, y = 3$ and $x = -2, y = -1$
16. $x = -3, y = 4, x = -6, y = 3$
17. $-2, -2, 1, 4$

Exercise 38d – p. 709

1. (a) ∞ (b) 2   (c) ∞
   (d) ∞ and all $+$ve   (e) 3
   (f) 1   (g) 1   (h) 2   (i) 1
2. (b) $1 < x < 1.5$ (e) $2 < x < 2.5$
   (f) $0.5 < x < 1$ (g) $1.5 < x < 2$
   (h) $0.5 < x < 1$ (i) $0 < x < 0.5$
3. $(0, 1)$ max, $(2, -3)$ min, 3
4. (a) 2   (b) 3   (c) 3
5. -1 (exact)
6. $-3 < x < -2$

Exercise 38e – p. 715

1. 0.20
2. 0.22
3. 0.16
4. 0.90
5. 5.2
6. -1.5

In the remaining questions, the degree of accuracy depends upon the accuracy of the first approximation: these answers are correct to 5 significant figures.

7. 1.1656
8. -2.6691
9. 0 (exact), 1.2564
10. 0.51097
11. 0 (exact), 0.74685
12. 0.37482
13. 0 (exact), 1.9038
14. 1 (exact)

15. $-0.91735, 0.86366$
16. 3.1038
17. $-1.4537, 0.53979$

Mixed Exercise 38 – p. 716

1. $1/2\lg 3$
2. 1
3. $2^{\pm\sqrt{1/2}}$
4. $\pm\cos^{-1}\frac{2}{5} - \tan^{-1}\frac{4}{3} + 2n\pi$
5. $x = \frac{1}{2}(1 + \sqrt{7}), y = \frac{1}{2}(1 - \sqrt{7})$;
   $x = \frac{1}{2}(1 - \sqrt{7}), y = \frac{1}{2}(1 + \sqrt{7})$
6. $\pm\frac{1}{4}\pi + n\pi, \frac{7}{6}\pi + 2n\pi, \frac{11}{6}\pi + 2n\pi$
7. 1
8. $-\frac{1}{3}, \frac{1}{3}$
9. $2n\pi$
10. 3
11. 2.20707
12. 1.3
13. 0.7

CHAPTER 39

Exercise 39a – p. 724

1. (a) $\overrightarrow{AC}$ (b) $\overrightarrow{BD}$
   (c) $\overrightarrow{AD}$ (d) $\overrightarrow{DB}$
2. $\mathbf{a}, \mathbf{b} - \mathbf{a}, 2\mathbf{b} - 2\mathbf{a}$
5. $\mathbf{b} - \mathbf{a}, \mathbf{a} + \mathbf{b}, \mathbf{a} - 3\mathbf{b}, 2\mathbf{b}, 2\mathbf{a} - 2\mathbf{b}$
6. $\overrightarrow{DE} = \overrightarrow{CH} = \overrightarrow{BG} = \mathbf{c}$,
   $\overrightarrow{DC} = \overrightarrow{EH} = \overrightarrow{FG} = \mathbf{a}$,
   $\overrightarrow{FE} = \overrightarrow{GH} = \overrightarrow{BC} = \mathbf{b}$
8. $\mathbf{c} - \mathbf{a}, \mathbf{b} - \mathbf{a}, \mathbf{b} - \mathbf{c}$
9. $\mathbf{b} + \mathbf{c} - \mathbf{a}, \mathbf{b} - \mathbf{c} - \mathbf{a}, \mathbf{a} + \mathbf{b} + \mathbf{c}$,
   $\mathbf{a} + \mathbf{b} - \mathbf{c}$
10. (a) $90°$ (b) $19.1°$ (c) $40.9°$

Exercise 39b – p. 728

1. (a) $\frac{1}{2}(\mathbf{a} + \mathbf{c})$ (b) $\frac{1}{2}(\mathbf{b} + \mathbf{d})$
2. $\frac{1}{4}(3\mathbf{a} + \mathbf{d})$
3. $\frac{1}{7}(3\mathbf{b} + 4\mathbf{c})$
4. (a) $\frac{1}{4}(\mathbf{a} + 2\mathbf{b} + \mathbf{c})$ (b) $\frac{1}{4}(\mathbf{b} + 2\mathbf{c} + \mathbf{d})$
5. $\mathbf{PQ} = \frac{1}{2}(\mathbf{c} - \mathbf{a}), \mathbf{AC} = (\mathbf{c} - \mathbf{a}) = 2\mathbf{PQ}$
6. $\frac{3}{4}(\mathbf{d} - \mathbf{a})$
7. $\frac{1}{2}(\mathbf{c} + \mathbf{d} - 2\mathbf{a})$
8. (a) $\frac{1}{3}(\mathbf{a} + \mathbf{b} + \mathbf{c})$ (b) $\frac{1}{3}(\mathbf{a} + \mathbf{b} + \mathbf{c})$

Exercise 39c – p. 734

1. (a) $3\mathbf{i} + 6\mathbf{j} + 4\mathbf{k}$ (b) $\mathbf{i} - 2\mathbf{j} - 7\mathbf{k}$
   (c) $\mathbf{i} - 3\mathbf{k}$

2. (a) $(5, -7, 2)$ (b) $(1, 4, 0)$
    (c) $(0, 1, -1)$
3. (a) $\sqrt{21}$ (b) 5   (c) 3
4. (a) 6   (b) 7   (c) $\sqrt{206}$
5. (a) $3\mathbf{i} + 4\mathbf{k}$ (b) $2\mathbf{i} + 2\mathbf{j} + 2\mathbf{k}$
    (c) $2\mathbf{i} + 3\mathbf{j} + 3\mathbf{k}$ (d) $-6\mathbf{i} + 12\mathbf{j} - 8\mathbf{k}$
6. (b), (d) and (e)
7. (c)
8. $\lambda = \frac{1}{2}$
9. (b), (e) and (f)
10. (a) neither   (b) parallel
    (c) equal
11. (a) $-2\mathbf{i} - 3\mathbf{j} + 7\mathbf{k}$ (b) $-\mathbf{j} + 3\mathbf{k}$
    (c) $-2\mathbf{i} - 3\mathbf{j} + 4\mathbf{k}$
12. $\sqrt{62}, \sqrt{10}, 2\sqrt{6}$
13. $\sqrt{5}$
14. $\overrightarrow{AB} = -\mathbf{i} + 3\mathbf{j}, \overrightarrow{BD} = -\mathbf{j} - 4\mathbf{k}$
    $\overrightarrow{CD} = -2\mathbf{i} + 2\mathbf{j} - 6\mathbf{k},$
    $\overrightarrow{AD} = -\mathbf{i} + 2\mathbf{j} - 4\mathbf{k}$
15. $y^2 = 4x$; parabola

Exercise 39d – p. 738

1. (a) $2:2:-1$ (b) $6:-2:-3$
    (c) $3:0:4$ (d) $1:8:4$
2. (a) $\frac{2}{3}\mathbf{i} + \frac{2}{3}\mathbf{j} - \frac{1}{3}\mathbf{k}$ (b) $\frac{6}{7}\mathbf{i} + \frac{2}{7}\mathbf{j} - \frac{3}{7}\mathbf{k}$
    (c) $\frac{3}{5}\mathbf{i} + \frac{4}{5}\mathbf{k}$ (d) $\frac{1}{9}\mathbf{i} + \frac{8}{9}\mathbf{j} - \frac{4}{9}\mathbf{k}$
3. (a) $(\frac{1}{3}, \frac{2}{3}, -\frac{2}{3})$ $(\frac{3}{7}, \frac{2}{7}, \frac{6}{7})$
    (c) $(\frac{8}{9}, -\frac{1}{9}, -\frac{4}{9})$
    (d) $\left(\dfrac{1}{\sqrt{3}}, -\dfrac{1}{\sqrt{3}}, -\dfrac{1}{\sqrt{3}}\right)$
4. (a) $(\frac{12}{7}, -\frac{18}{7}, \frac{36}{7})$ (b) $(\frac{16}{9}, \frac{8}{9}, -\frac{2}{9})$
5. (a) $4\mathbf{j} + 5\mathbf{k}$ (b) $16\mathbf{i} - 16\mathbf{j} - 8\mathbf{k}$
    (c) $\pm(\frac{8}{3}\mathbf{i} + \frac{1}{3}\mathbf{j} + \frac{4}{3}\mathbf{k})$
6. (a) $\dfrac{1}{\sqrt{3}}\mathbf{i} - \dfrac{1}{\sqrt{3}}\mathbf{j} + \dfrac{1}{\sqrt{3}}\mathbf{k}$
    (b) $\frac{5}{13}\mathbf{j} - \frac{12}{13}\mathbf{k}$ (c) $\mathbf{i}$
7. $\sqrt{22}, \ 3:2:3; \ 3\sqrt{2}, \ 1:-4:-1$

Exercise 39e – p. 742

1. $\sqrt{13}; 3$
2. $2:0:-1; \ -1:0:2$
3. $\frac{1}{3}(4\mathbf{i} - \mathbf{j} + 4\mathbf{k})$
4. (a) $\frac{2}{5}\mathbf{i} + \frac{1}{5}\mathbf{j} + \frac{7}{5}\mathbf{k}$ (b) $-2\mathbf{i} + \mathbf{j} + 5\mathbf{k}$
5. (a) no   (b) no   (c) no

Exercise 39f – p. 747

1. (a) $x - 2 = y - 3 = z + 1$
    (b) $\dfrac{x}{3} = \dfrac{z}{5}$ and $y = 4$
    (c) $\dfrac{x}{2} = \dfrac{y}{3} = \dfrac{z}{4}$

2. (a) $\mathbf{r} = 3\mathbf{i} + \mathbf{j} + 7\mathbf{k} + \lambda(2\mathbf{i} + \mathbf{j} + 3\mathbf{k})$
    (b) $\mathbf{r} = 2\mathbf{i} - 5\mathbf{j} + \mathbf{k} + \lambda(3\mathbf{i} + \mathbf{j} + 4\mathbf{k})$
    (c) $\mathbf{r} = \mathbf{i} + \lambda(-3\mathbf{i} + 5\mathbf{j} + \mathbf{k})$
3. (a) $\mathbf{r} = \mathbf{i} - 3\mathbf{j} + 2\mathbf{k} + \lambda(5\mathbf{i} + 4\mathbf{j} - \mathbf{k})$;
    $$\frac{x - 1}{5} = \frac{y + 3}{4} = \frac{z - 2}{-1}$$
    (b) $\mathbf{r} = 2\mathbf{i} + \mathbf{j} + \lambda(3\mathbf{j} - \mathbf{k})$;
    $$x = 2, \frac{y - 1}{3} = \frac{z}{-1}$$
    (c) $\mathbf{r} = \lambda(\mathbf{i} - \mathbf{j} - \mathbf{k}); \ x = -y = -z$
4. (a) no   (b) yes   (c) yes
    (d) yes   (e) no
5. $\mathbf{r} = 4\mathbf{i} + 5\mathbf{j} + 10\mathbf{k} + \lambda(\mathbf{i} + \mathbf{j} + 3\mathbf{k})$,
    $$4 - x = 5 - y = \frac{10 - z}{3}$$
    $\mathbf{r} = 2\mathbf{i} + 3\mathbf{j} + 4\mathbf{k} + \lambda(\mathbf{i} + \mathbf{j} + 5\mathbf{k})$,
    $$2 - x = 3 - y = \frac{4 - z}{5}$$
6. (a) $\mathbf{r} = 3\mathbf{i} + \mathbf{j} - 4\mathbf{k} + \lambda(\mathbf{i} - 3\mathbf{j} - 6\mathbf{k})$;
    $(\frac{7}{3}, 3, 0); (0, 10, 14); (\frac{10}{3}, 0, -6)$
    (b) $\mathbf{r} = \mathbf{i} + \mathbf{j} + 7\mathbf{k} + \lambda(2\mathbf{i} + 3\mathbf{j} - 6\mathbf{k})$;
    $(\frac{10}{3}, \frac{9}{2}, 0); (0, -\frac{1}{2}, 10); (\frac{1}{3}, 0, 9)$
7. $\mathbf{r} = 5\mathbf{i} - 2\mathbf{j} - 4\mathbf{k} + \lambda(3\mathbf{i} + 4\mathbf{j} + 5\mathbf{k})$;
    $(\frac{13}{2}, 0, -\frac{3}{2})$
8. $6:3:2; \mathbf{r} = 2\mathbf{i} - \mathbf{j} - \mathbf{k} + \lambda(6\mathbf{i} + 3\mathbf{j} + 2\mathbf{k})$
9. (a) $x = 1 - \lambda, y = 2 - 2\lambda, z = 4 + 2\lambda$

Exercise 39g – p. 751

1. parallel
2. intersecting; $\mathbf{r} = \mathbf{i} + 2\mathbf{j}$
3. skew
4. $a = -3; \mathbf{r} = -\mathbf{i} + 3\mathbf{j} + 4\mathbf{k}$
5. $t = 6; (1, 2, 2)$
6. (a) $p = -2$ (b) $p = 0$
7. $(\frac{1}{3}, -\frac{2}{3}, \frac{2}{3}); (\frac{2}{7}, \frac{3}{7}, -\frac{6}{7}); \arccos -\frac{16}{21}$

Exercise 39h – p. 758

1. (a) 30
    (b) 0; $\mathbf{a}$ and $\mathbf{b}$ are perpendicular
    (c) -1
2. (a) $7, \frac{1}{3}\sqrt{7}$ (b) $14, \sqrt{(\frac{7}{19})}$
    (c) $3, \frac{3}{58}\sqrt{58}$ (d) $1, \frac{1}{5}$
3. (a) $a^2 - \mathbf{a} \cdot \mathbf{b}$ (b) $a^2 + b^2 - 2\mathbf{a} \cdot \mathbf{b}$
    (c) $b^2 - a^2$ (d) $2\mathbf{b} \cdot \mathbf{c}$
4. (a) 0   (b) $-b^2$ (c) a^2
    (d) $2a^2 - b^2$
5. 4
6. (a) -4 (b) 15   (c) 11
    (d) -12 (e) 29
7. $-\sqrt{\frac{7}{34}}; \arccos\sqrt{\frac{7}{10}}$

11. (a) $\arccos \frac{19}{21}$ (b) $\arccos \frac{2}{3}$
    (c) $\arccos \left(\frac{8}{15}\sqrt{3}\right)$
12. (a) $78.5°$ (b) 0, i.e. parallel lines
15. (a) $\frac{4}{3}$ (b) 2 (c) $-\frac{7}{5}$

Exercise 39i – p. 768

1. (a) $x - y - z = 2$
   (b) $2x + 3y - 4z = 0$
2. (a) $\mathbf{r}.(3\mathbf{i} - 4\mathbf{j} + 5\mathbf{k}) = 6$
   (b) $\mathbf{r}.(\mathbf{i} - 7\mathbf{j} - \mathbf{k}) = 5$
4. (a) $2x - y + z + 1 = 0$;
       $\mathbf{r}.(2\mathbf{i} - \mathbf{j} + \mathbf{k}) = -1$
   (b) $3x - y - z = 2$; $\mathbf{r}.(3\mathbf{i} - \mathbf{j} - \mathbf{k}) = 2$
5. $\mathbf{r}.(7\mathbf{i} + 2\mathbf{j} - 3\mathbf{k}) = 3$, $3/\sqrt{62}$
6. $3/\sqrt{5}$ 7. 2 8. $\mathbf{r} = \lambda(\mathbf{i} - 2\mathbf{j} + \mathbf{k})$
9. $\mathbf{r} = 2\mathbf{i} + \mathbf{j} + \mathbf{k} + \lambda(\mathbf{i} + 2\mathbf{j} - 3\mathbf{k})$
10. $\mathbf{r}.(\mathbf{i} - 2\mathbf{j}) = -2$
11. $\mathbf{r}.(\mathbf{j} - \mathbf{k}) = 0$
12. $(\frac{5}{2}, -\frac{1}{2}, -\frac{1}{2})$
13. $(1, -1, 4)$
14. $7\sqrt{3}/3$
15. (a) $\mathbf{r}.(5\mathbf{i} - 2\mathbf{j} - 3\mathbf{k}) = 7$
    (b) $\mathbf{r}.(-\mathbf{j} + 2\mathbf{k}) = -2$
    (c) $\mathbf{r}.(2\mathbf{i} + \mathbf{k}) = 5$
16. $\mathbf{r} = -3\mathbf{i} - 2\mathbf{j} + \lambda(\mathbf{i} - 2\mathbf{j} + \mathbf{k})$
        $+ \mu(2\mathbf{i} - \mathbf{j} + 2\mathbf{k})$
17. $\mathbf{r} = \mathbf{i} + \mathbf{j} + \lambda(\mathbf{i} + \mathbf{k}) + \mu(\mathbf{i} - \mathbf{j} + \mathbf{k})$;
    The second line is contained in the
    plane.
18. (a) intersecting   (b) intersecting
    (c) parallel
    (d) contained in the plane.

Exercise 39j – p. 771

1. $3/\sqrt{11}$
2. $20/\sqrt{442}$
3. $1/\sqrt{87}$
4. $\frac{6}{7}$
5. $\frac{1}{9}\sqrt{3}$
6. $\frac{4}{9}$
7. (a) $a = 2$ (b) $\frac{1}{2}$
9. $\frac{1}{5}\sqrt{15}$

CHAPTER 40

Exercise 40a – p. 779

1. $-i, i, i, -i, 1, i$
2. (a) $10 + 4i$ (b) $7 + 2i$
   (c) $6 - 2i$ (d) $(a + c) + (b + d)i$
3. (a) $-4 + 6i$ (b) $1 - 4i$
   (c) $-2 + 16i$ (d) $(a - c) + (b - d)i$

4. (a) $10 - 5i$ (b) $39 + 23i$
   (c) $11 - 7i$ (d) 25
   (e) $3 - 4i$ (f) $-2 + 2i$
   (g) $-4 + 3i$ (h) $x^2 + y^2$
   (i) $-3 + i$ (j) $(a^2 - b^2) + 2abi$
5. (a) $1 + i$ (b) $\frac{9}{25} + \frac{13}{25}i$
   (c) $\frac{4}{17} + \frac{16}{7}i$ (d) i (e) $-i$
   (f) $\dfrac{x^2 - y^2}{x^2 + y^2} + \dfrac{2xy}{x^2 + y^2}i$
   (g) $1 - 3i$ (h) $-3 - 2i$
6. (a) $x = 9, y = -7$
   (b) $x = -\frac{3}{2}, y = \frac{7}{2}$
   (c) $x = \frac{7}{2}, y = \frac{1}{2}$
   (d) $x = 2, y = 0$
   (e) $x = 13, y = 0$
   (f) $x = 15, y = 8$
   (g) $x = 11, y = 3$
   (h) $x = 2, y = 1$
       or $x = -2, y = -1$
7. (a) $7, -1$ (b) $-2, -2$
   (c) $25, 0$ (d) $\frac{10}{17}, \frac{11}{17}$
   (e) $\frac{9}{5}, -\frac{4}{5}$ (f) $0, \dfrac{-2y}{x^2 + y^2}$
8. (a) $\pm(2 - i)$ (b) $\pm(5 - 2i)$
   (c) $\pm(1 + i)$ (d) $\pm(4 + i)$
   (e) $\pm(1 + 5i)$

Exercise 40b – p. 782

1. (a) $-\frac{1}{2} \pm \frac{1}{2}i\sqrt{3}$ (b) $-\frac{7}{4} \pm \frac{1}{4}\sqrt{41}$
   (c) $\pm 3i$ (d) $-\frac{1}{2} \pm \frac{1}{2}i\sqrt{11}$
   (e) $\pm 1, \pm i$ (f) $-\frac{1}{6} \pm \frac{1}{6}i\sqrt{35}$
2. (a) $x^2 + 1 = 0$
   (b) $x^2 - 4x + 5 = 0$
   (c) $x^2 - 2x + 10 = 0$
   (d) $x^3 - 4x^2 + 6x - 4 = 0$
3. (a) $4, 5$ (b) $6, 25$ (c) $0, 1$
   (d) $-24, 169$
4. (a) $x^2 + 2x + 2 = 0$
   (b) $x^2 + 10x + 26 = 0$
   (c) $x^2 - 2x + 10 = 0$
   (d) $x^2 - 8x + 17 = 0$

When one root is real, so is the other and
there is no special relationship between
them.

Exercise 40d – p. 790

Arguments are given in terms of π when
exact and in degrees to 3 s.f. otherwise.
1. (a) $\sqrt{13}, -33.7°$ (b) $\sqrt{17}, 166°$
   (c) $5, -127°$ (d) $13, 67.4°$

(e) $\sqrt{2}, -\frac{1}{4}\pi$ (f) $\sqrt{2}, \frac{3}{4}\pi$

(g) $6, 0$ (h) $4, -\frac{1}{2}\pi$

(i) $2, \frac{1}{2}\pi$ (j) $\sqrt{2}, \frac{1}{4}\pi$

(h) $\sqrt{2}, \frac{3}{4}\pi$ (l) $\sqrt{170}, 32.5°$

(m) $1, \frac{3}{4}\pi$ (n) $2, \frac{2}{3}\pi$

(p) $1, -\frac{5}{6}\pi$

(q) $\sqrt{(a^2 + b^2)}$, $\arctan \dfrac{b}{a}$ (ambiguous until a and b are known)

2. (a) $\sqrt{2}(\cos\frac{1}{4}\pi + i \sin\frac{1}{4}\pi)$

(b) $2\{\cos(-\frac{1}{6}\pi) + i \sin(-\frac{1}{6}\pi)\}$

(c) $5\{\cos(-127°) + i \sin(-127°)\}$

(d) $13\{\cos(-113°) + i \sin(-113°)\}$

(e) $\sqrt{5}\{\cos(-26.6°) + i \sin(-26.6°)\}$

(f) $6\{\cos 0 + i \sin 0\}$

(g) $3\{\cos \pi + i \sin \pi\}$

(h) $4\{\cos\frac{1}{2}\pi + i \sin\frac{1}{2}\pi\}$

(i) $2\sqrt{3}\{\cos(-\frac{5}{6}\pi) + i \sin(-\frac{5}{6}\pi)\}$

(j) $25\{\cos(16.3°) + i \sin(16.3°)\}$

3. (a) $\sqrt{3} + i$ (b) $\frac{3}{2}\sqrt{2} - \frac{3}{2}i\sqrt{2}$

(c) $-\frac{1}{2} + \frac{1}{2}i\sqrt{3}$ (d) $3 + 0i$

(e) $-4 + 0i$ (f) $-\frac{1}{2}\sqrt{2} - \frac{1}{2}i\sqrt{2}$

(g) $0 + 2i$ (h) $0 - 2i$

Exercise 40e – p. 793

1. (a) $(2\sqrt{3})(\sqrt{2}) = 2\sqrt{6}$;
$-\frac{1}{6}\pi + (-\frac{1}{4}\pi) = -\frac{5}{12}\pi$

(b) $(3 - \sqrt{3}) - (3 + \sqrt{3})i$

2. (a) $(\sqrt{2})(\sqrt{2}) = 2; \frac{1}{4}\pi + (-\frac{1}{4}\pi) = 0$

(b) 2

3. (a) $(\sqrt{7}) \div (\sqrt{7}) = 1$;
$(-139°) - (139°) = -278° \Rightarrow 172°$

(b) $\frac{1}{7} + \frac{4}{7}i\sqrt{3}$

4. (a) $2 \div (\sqrt{2}) = \sqrt{2}; 0 - (\frac{1}{4}\pi) = -\frac{1}{4}\pi$

(b) $1 - i$

5. (a) $\dfrac{1}{z} = \dfrac{2 - i}{5}; z^2 = 3 + 4i$

(b) $\dfrac{1}{z} = 1 + i; z^2 = -\frac{1}{2}i$

(c) $\dfrac{1}{z} = \dfrac{3 - 4i}{25}; z^2 = -7 + 24i$

(d) $\dfrac{1}{z} = \frac{1}{2}\sqrt{3} - \frac{1}{2}i; z^2 = \frac{1}{2}(1 + i\sqrt{3})$

(e) $\dfrac{1}{z} = \dfrac{5 + 12i}{169}; z^2 = -119 - 120i$

Mixed Exercise 40 – p. 793

1. (a) $\dfrac{7 - 5i}{74}$ (b) $11 + 2i$

(c) $\frac{1}{2}(1 - i)$ (d) $-21 + 20i$

2. $\frac{3}{10}(11 - 3i)$

3. $\pm\frac{1}{2}\sqrt{2}(5 + i)$

4. (a) $\sqrt{2}, \frac{3}{4}\pi$ (b) $5, 53°$

(c) $5\sqrt{2}, -172°$, area $= 8.9$

5. (a) $2\sqrt{10}$ (b) 10 (c) 1

(d) $\frac{1}{5}\sqrt{10}$

6. $\lambda = 2, \mu = \frac{1}{2}$

7. $a = 4, b = -5$

8. $\dfrac{x(x^2 + y^2 - 1)}{x^2 + y^2}, \dfrac{y(x^2 + y^2 + 1)}{x^2 + y^2}$

9. $\lambda = 4, \mu = -5$

10. $2\sqrt{2}, \frac{3}{4}\pi; 2\sqrt{2}, -\frac{3}{4}\pi$

11. (a) $-\frac{1}{3}$ (b) $\frac{2}{3}$ (c) 0

12. $2 + i, 2 - 3i$

CONSOLIDATION G

Multiple Choice Exercise G - p. 799

1. B	17. B
2. A	18. A
3. B	19. C
4. E	20. A
5. D	21. A
6. A	22. B, C
7. D	23. B, C
8. A	24. B, C
9. C	25. A
10. E	26. B
11. A	27. B, C
12. C	28. F
13. D	29. F
14. D	30. T
15. C	31. F
16. E	32. F

Miscellaneous Exercise G – p. 803

1. $0, 60°, 120°, 180°, 90°$

2. (a) $n\pi + \frac{1}{12}\pi, n\pi + \frac{5}{12}\pi$

3. (a) $0, 180°, 360°, 54.7°, 125.3°, 234.7°, 305.3°$

(b) $51.3°, 128.7°$

4. (a) $n\pi, 2n\pi \pm\frac{1}{6}\pi$

(b) $\frac{1}{2}\pi, \frac{3}{2}\pi, 0.67$ rad, 2.48 rad

5. $x = 6$

6. 0.774

7. $x = 3^{10}, y = 3^2$ or $x = 3^2, y = 3^{10}$

8. (a) 64 or $\frac{1}{64}$ (b) 21

9. $(x - 2)^2(x + 4)$;

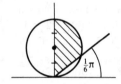

10. 0.433

11. 3.008

12. 1.90

13. $a = 22$; 2.22

14. 1.78

15. $n = 1$; 1.27, 1.24

16. $2\sqrt{2} (\cos \frac{1}{4}\pi + i \sin \frac{1}{4}\pi)$; $\sqrt{104}$;
     0.32 rad

17. (a)

a	-2	-4
b	2	1

(b) $\sqrt{2}$; $-\frac{1}{4}\pi$

18. $p = -2, q = -4$

19. ang $z_1 = \frac{2}{3}\pi$, ang $z_2 = \frac{1}{6}\pi$; i, $\frac{1}{2}\pi$

20. (a)

a	5	-5
b	-3	3

$\pm(5 - 3i)$

21. $\pm(3 - 2i)$; $-5 + 12i$

22. (a) $\frac{1}{2}\pi$ (b) $-\frac{1}{4}\pi$ (c) $\frac{1}{12}\pi$

23. $x = 3, y = -1$;
     (a) $\sqrt{10}$ (b) $-\arctan \frac{1}{3}$

24. (a) $-1, 7$ (b) $-7i$

25. $\frac{1}{2}(1 + 3i)$ or $\frac{3}{2}(1 + i)$

26. 10, 96.9°; $\frac{5}{2}$, $-23.1°$

27. 69°

28. (a) 7   (b) 4

29. (b) $(7, 2, -6)$ (c) $\frac{14}{15}$
     (d) $\mathbf{r} = \mathbf{i} - \mathbf{j} + \lambda(2\mathbf{i} + \mathbf{j} - 2\mathbf{k})$
        $+ \mu(-3\mathbf{i} + 4\mathbf{k})$
     or $\mathbf{r}.(4\mathbf{i} - 2\mathbf{j} + 3\mathbf{k}) = 6$

30. $\frac{2}{3}(4\mathbf{i} - 4\mathbf{j} + \mathbf{k})$
     (a) $\mathbf{i} - 2\mathbf{j} - \mathbf{k}$ (b) 83.5°
     (c) $(6\mathbf{i} + 5\mathbf{j} - 4\mathbf{k})/\sqrt{77}$

31. 77.5°

32. $\mathbf{r} = -\mathbf{i} + \mathbf{j} + 3\mathbf{k} + \lambda(4\mathbf{i} - 3\mathbf{j} - \mathbf{k})$; -2

33. (a) 20, $\frac{20}{21}$
     (b) $\mathbf{r} = (2\mathbf{i} + 2\mathbf{j} + \mathbf{k}) + t(4\mathbf{i} + \mathbf{j} + \mathbf{k})$;
        $-\frac{14}{11}\mathbf{i} + \frac{13}{11}\mathbf{j} + \frac{2}{11}\mathbf{k}$

34. $\mathbf{r} = \mathbf{i} + 3\mathbf{j} + \mathbf{k} + t(3\mathbf{i} - 2\mathbf{j} - 8\mathbf{k})$;
     $\mathbf{r}.(2\mathbf{i} - \mathbf{j} + \mathbf{k}) = 0$

35. (b) $\frac{1}{27}\sqrt{27}(5\mathbf{i} - \mathbf{j} + \mathbf{k})$
     (c) 28, 54.2°

36.

$\frac{1}{6}\pi$

37. (a) $\mathbf{r} = a(-4\mathbf{i} + 4\mathbf{j} - \mathbf{k})$
        $+ ta(9\mathbf{i} - 6\mathbf{j} + 12\mathbf{k})$
     (b) $\mathbf{r}.(13\mathbf{i} + 17\mathbf{j} + 16\mathbf{k}) = 0$
     (c) $\frac{1}{55}\sqrt{55}\sqrt{33}$; $\mathbf{r}.(9\mathbf{i} - 6\mathbf{j} + 12\mathbf{k}) = 15a$
     (d) $3x - 2y + 4z = 5a$
     (e) $\dfrac{x + 4a}{3} = \dfrac{y - 4a}{-2} = \dfrac{z + a}{4}$

38. (b) -1 (c) $\sqrt{68}$

INDEX